P9-DIF-721

The New
Cambridge Bibliography
of English Literature

in five volumes
Volume 4

The New Cambridge Bibliography of English Literature

Edited by

I. R. WILLISON

Volume 4
1900–1950

With the assistance of
R. J. ROBERTS   M. STATHAM
K. J. WORTH

CAMBRIDGE
AT THE UNIVERSITY PRESS
1972

Published by the Syndics of the Cambridge University Press
Bentley House, 200 Euston Road, London NW1 2DB
American Branch: 32 East 57th Street, New York, N.Y.10022

© Cambridge University Press 1972

Library of Congress Catalogue Card Number: 69-10199

ISBN: 0 521 08535 7

Printed in Great Britain
at the University Printing House, Cambridge
(Brooke Crutchley, University Printer)

CONTENTS

Editor's Preface   *page*   xi

List of contributors to volume 4   xvii

Abbreviations   xviii

1. INTRODUCTION

I. General works

(1) Bibliographies   *column*   1
(2) Literary histories, special studies and collections of essays   3
(3) Literary memoirs, reminiscences, journals and letters   15
(4) Relations with other literatures   25

II. Book production and distribution

(for detailed contents list see cols 33–6)

A   Literature, society and communication   35
B   Authorship   61
C   Production   73
D   Distribution   103
E   Reading   119

2. POETRY

I. General works

(1) Bibliographies   131
(2) Histories and studies   133
(3) Anthologies   149

II. Individual poets

Thomas Stearns Eliot   157
Robert Graves   201
Wystan Hugh Auden   207
Dylan Thomas   220

Acton, Allott, G. Barker, J. Bell, Berry, Betjeman, Blunden, Bottomley, Bottrall, Bowes-Lyon, Brooke, Bunting, Cameron, Campbell, W. Childe, Church, Clarke, Comfort, F. Cornford, J. Cornford, W. H. Davies, Day-Lewis, de la Mare, P. Dickinson, K. Douglas, Drinkwater, Durrell, Dyment, Empson, Flecker, Flint, G. S. Fraser, Freeman, Fuller, 'Robert Garioch', Gascoyne, 'John Gawsworth', Gibson, Gittings, Gogarty, Gould, W. S. Graham, Grenfell, Rostrevor Hamilton, Heath-Stubbs, Hendry, A. P. Herbert, Higgins, Hodgson, D. Jones, P. Kavanagh, Kendon, Keyes, Kirkup, E. V. Knox, Ledwidge, Lee, J. Lehmann, A. Lewis, MacCaig, 'Hugh MacDiarmid', T. MacDonagh, MacNeice, Madge, Masefield, Mew, Monro, N. Moore, Sturge Moore, E. Muir, R. Nichols, Nicholson, Noyes, 'Seumas O'Sullivan', Owen, H. E. Palmer, Parsons, Pitter, A. Porter, Prince, Raine, Reed, 'James Reeves', Ridler, 'Michael Roberts', Rodgers, Rosenberg, A. Ross, Ruddock, V. Sackville-West, Sassoon, Scovell, Seaman, Shanks, Shove, E. Sitwell, O. Sitwell, S. Sitwell, Goodsir Smith, S. Snaith, Sorley, Soutar, Spencer, Spender, Squire, Stephens, Swingler, J. Symons, Annand Taylor, Tessimond, E. Thomas, R. S. Thomas, Tiller, Todd, Treece, R. C. Trevelyan, Turner, Waley, Watkins, Wellesley, Whistler, 'Anna Wickham', Wingfield, Wolfe, A. Young   229

CONTENTS

3. THE NOVEL

I. General works

(1) Bibliographies   *column* 381
(2) Histories and studies   381

II. Individual novelists

Joseph Conrad   395
Herbert George Wells   417
Enoch Arnold Bennett   429
Edward Morgan Forster   437
James Joyce   444
Virginia Woolf   472
David Herbert Lawrence   481
Graham Greene   503

Aldington, W. Allen, Arlen, H. C. Bailey, Balchin, Baring, Baron, H. E. Bates, R. Bates, Beachcroft, A. Bell, 'Neil Bell', E. T. R. Benson, S. Benson, E. C. Bentley, P. Bentley, Beresford, 'Anthony Berkeley', Berners, 'George A. Birmingham', Blackwood, G. Blake, D. W. Bone, Bottome, E. Bowen, 'Marjorie Bowen', 'Ernest Bramah', J. Brophy, Buchan, Bullett, Burke, Butts, Calder-Marshall, G. Cannan, Carswell, Cary, Childers, Christie, Collier, Compton-Burnett, Coppard, Cronin, Rhys Davies, Deeping, 'E. M. Delafield', de Morgan, Dennis, H. de Selincourt, Diver, N. Douglas, D. du Maurier, Caradoc Evans, 'Margiad Evans', Firbank, Ford, Forester, E. T. Fowler, G. Frankau, R. Fraser, Galsworthy, D. Garnett, W. L. George, Gerhardie, 'Lewis Grassic Gibbon', Gibbons, Glyn, Godden, L. Golding, Grahame, F. L. Green, 'Henry Green', Gunn, Radclyffe Hall, 'John Hampson', Hanley, Hartley, 'Ian Hay', Hewlett, Hichens, Hilton, Holme, Holtby, Hoult, Household, 'Stephen Hudson', Hughes, V. Hunt, A. S. M. Hutchinson, R. C. Hutchinson, A. Huxley, 'Michael Innes', Irwin, Isherwood, Jacobs, M. R. James, Jameson, Jesse, Hansford Johnson, Kaye-Smith, Kennedy, Kitchin, Koestler, R. Lehmann, Leverson, P. Wyndham Lewis, D. Lindsay, J. Lindsay, Linklater, 'Richard Llewellyn', Locke, Belloc Lowndes, Lowry, Macaulay, Macdonnell, McFee, Machen, D. G. Mackail, McKenna, C. Mackenzie, F. Manning, O. Manning, 'Katherine Mansfield', 'Louis Marlow', A. E. W. Mason, Maugham, Maxwell, Mayne, V. Meynell, Middleton, Milne, Mitchison, Mitford, Monsarrat, Montague, Morgan, N. Morrison, Mottram, W. Muir, L. H. Myers, Newby, B. Nichols, Norris, 'Flann O'Brien', K. O'Brien, 'Frank O'Connor', O'Faoláin, O'Flaherty, 'Richard Oke', O'Kelly, E. M. Olivier, C. Oman, Onions, 'George Orwell', 'John Oxenham', Pain, Peake, Phillpotts, Plomer, Powell, J. C. Powys, T. F. Powys, Priestley, Pritchett, Pugh, Pym, Ransome, F. Reid, Reynolds, J. Rhys, Richardson, Ridge, C. E. M. Roberts, Rolfe, Royde-Smith, E. Sackville-West, 'Saki', Sansom, 'Sapper', Sayers, J. D. Scott, Seymour, Shiel, 'Nevil Shute', Sidgwick, M. Sinclair, J. C. Snaith, Snow, 'Somerville and Ross', Spring, Stapledon, Stead, Stern, Strong, Swinnerton, Thirkell, Thornton, Tolkien, Tomlinson, P. Toynbee, 'Robert Tressell', Upward, Vachell, Wallace, Walpole, R. Warner, Townsend Warner, A. Waugh, E. Waugh, M. Webb, Welch, A. West, 'Rebecca West', T. H. White, C. Williams, H. Williamson, A. Wilson, 'Romer Wilson', Wodehouse, 'Dornford Yates', E. H. Young, Brett Young   511

III. Children's books   783

4. DRAMA

I. General works

(1) Bibliographies   821
(2) Theatrical periodicals   823
(3) Collections of plays   827

CONTENTS

(4) Histories and studies   *column* 829

(5) The theatre outside London   845

(6) The theatre in Ireland   853

(7) Music hall, musical comedy, pantomime etc   853

(8) Radio and television drama and adaptations   861

(9) Actors and acting   863

(10) Producers and the art of production   867

(11) Theatre design and technical practice; Stage design and scenic method   869

(12) Economics and organisation of the theatre   871

(13) Theatre censorship   875

(14) Amateur drama; Drama and education   875

II. Individual dramatists

Sean O'Casey   879

Samuel Beckett   885

Ackerley, Ackland, 'Anthony Armstrong', 'Oscar Asche', Bagnold, Baker, Bax, R. Berkeley, Besier, Boland, 'John Brandane', 'James Bridie', Brighouse, W. Browne, Calderon, 'Denis Cannan', Carroll, Chapin, Corkery, Coward, 'Clemence Dane', Darlington, H. H. Davies, 'Gordon Daviot', Dean, Deevy, Delderfield, Douglas-Home, Dukes, Duncan, Fagan, H. Farjeon, C. Fry, Gielgud, Ginsbury, Gow, Granville-Barker, Greenwood, Guthrie, Hackett, P. Hamilton, Hankin, Harwood, Hassall, Hodge, Houghton, Hunter, Jennings, Johnston, King-Hall, Knoblock, Levy, 'Frederick Lonsdale', McCracken, D. MacDonagh, R. McDougall, McEvoy, R. Mackenzie, MacLiammóir, 'Brinsley Macnamara', Malleson, Millar, Monkhouse, 'C. K. Munro', Novello, Parker, du Garde Peach, Pertwee, Rattigan, Rubinstein, Savory, Shairp, Sherriff, Shiels, D. Smith, F. S. Smith, Sowerby, 'Lesley Storm', Strode, Sutro, Sylvaine, J. Temple, Travers, Ustinov, Van Druten, Vane, Vosper, E. Williams, H. R. Williamson, Winter, Wooll, P. Yates   905

5. PROSE

I. Critics and literary scholars, essayists and humourists

Abercrombie, Agate, P. Alexander, Barfield, Bateson, Beerbohm, C. Bell, Belloc, H. S. Bennett, Bodkin, Bowra, Bradbrook, Bradley, Brenan, I. Brown, Bullough, Burdett, 'Christopher Caudwell', Cecil, H. M. Chadwick, E. K. Chambers, R. W. Chambers, R. W. Chapman, Chesterton, K. Clark, Clutton-Brock, Connolly, F. M. Cornford, Craig, Craigie, Crowley, Daiches, E. de Selincourt, Dobrée, Ellis-Fermor, Elton, H. W. Fowler, R. Fry, Garrod, Gill, Greg, Grierson, Grigson, F. Harris, G. B. Harrison, J. E. Harrison, Hayward, House, Hulme, H. Jackson, D. G. James, Brimley Johnson, G. Keynes, 'Hugh Kingsmill', Wilson Knight, Knights, Lancaster, Laver, F. R. Leavis, Q. D. Leavis, Leishman, C. S. Lewis, D. B. Wyndham Lewis, Lubbock, E. V. Lucas, F. L. Lucas, R. Lynd, MacCarthy, J. W. Mackail, McKerrow, J. B. Morton, Murray, Murry, Newman, Nicoll, Ogden, Orage, Partridge, Pevsner, de Sola Pinto, A. W. Pollard, S. Potter, L. Powys, Quennell, H. Read, Richards, Sadleir, G. Scott, W. Dixon Scott, Nichol Smith, Pearsall Smith, Spurgeon, E. Starkie, Stokes, Summers, Sutherland, G. D. Thomson, G. Tillotson, Tillyard, Tovey, Waddell, Weekley, Wilenski, Willey, Dover Wilson, Wise, Wyld   995

II. Historians, autobiographers, writers on politics, society, economics etc

C. K. Allen, Angell, 'W. N. P. Barbellion', E. Barker, Berlin, Beveridge, Brailsford, Brogan, Bryant, Bury, Butterfield, Carr, V. G. Childe, Churchill, Clapham, G. N. Clark, Cole, Duff Cooper, Coulton, Dawson, Lowes Dickinson, Ensor, Evans-Pritchard, Feiling, Firth, Fisher, Gardiner, Gibbs, Gooch, Gorer, Guedalla, J. L. and B. Hammond, von Hayek, Hillary, Hobhouse, Hobson, Holdsworth, Jerrold, J. M. Keynes, Knowles, Laski, T. E. Lawrence, Leslie, Liddell Hart, Livingstone, Bruce Lockhart, Malinowski, Mannheim, Marett, Marriott, Masterman, Moorehead, Mowat, Namier, Neale, Nevinson, Nicolson, C. W. C. Oman, Pearson, Petrie, A. F. Pollard, Popper, Postgate, Power, Powicke, Radcliffe-Brown, Rashdall, L. Robbins, J. Robinson, Rowntree, Rowse, Runciman, J. A. Spender, Stamp, Storrs, J. Strachey, L. Strachey, St Loe Strachey, A. J. A. Symons, Tawney, A. J. P. Taylor, Temperley, Tout, A. Toynbee, G. M. Trevelyan, Trevor-Roper, Trotter, Vinogradoff, Wallas, B. Webb, S. Webb, C. K. Webster, Wedgwood, Westermarck, Wicksteed, Woodward, L. Woolf, Woolley, G. M. Young   *column* 1135

III. Philosophers, theologians, writers on natural science and on psychology

S. Alexander, Ayer, Baillie, Bernal, Bragg, Broad, Burt, Carritt, Collingwood, D'Arcy, Fraser Darling, Dodd, Dunne, Eddington, Gore, J. B. S. Haldane, J. S. Haldane, Hankey, G. H. Hardy, Heard, Henson, Dawes Hicks, Hogben, J. Huxley, Inge, E. O. James, Jeans, Joachim, Joad, W. E. Johnson, E. Jones, Joseph, Keith, R. Knox, W. McDougall, McTaggart, Martindale, Mascall, Matthews, Moffatt, G. E. Moore, Needham, J. Oman, Polanyi, H. H. Price, Prichard, Raven, Rivers, W. D. Ross, Russell, Ryle, Schiller, Sherrington, Singer, Kemp Smith, Spearman, Stebbing, Streeter, Sullivan, A. E. Taylor, W. Temple, Tennant, Wentworth Thompson, Underhill, Waddington, Whitehead, Cook Wilson, Wisdom, Wittgenstein, Woodger   1241

IV. Writers on travel, the countryside and sport

G. Bell, 'George Bourne', Byron, Cardus, Collis, Darwin, Fleming, Forbes, Gibbings, Cunninghame Graham, S. Graham, H. J. Massingham, H. V. Morton, Sheridan, Smythe, Stark, W. Starkie, Street, F. Thompson   1311

6. NEWSPAPERS AND MAGAZINES

A   Historical and general studies   1329
   (1) Histories and studies of the press   1329
   (2) Newspapers and their contents   1331
   (3) Magazines, general studies   1333
   (4) Little magazines   1335
   (5) University magazines   1335
   (6) Reminiscences and biographies   1335
B   Journalism   1337
   (1) Bibliographies   1337
   (2) General works   1337
   (3) The profession of journalism   1339
   (4) News agencies   1341
   (5) Advertising   1341
   (6) Periodicals relating to newspaper and magazine publishing   1343
C   Accounts and studies of individual newspapers and magazines   1343
D   Lists, indexes and directories   1347

CONTENTS

E   Individual newspapers and magazines   *column* 1349
   (1) Literary papers and magazines   1349
   (2) Amateur journals   1379
   (3) Romance, detective, thriller, western and science fiction
      magazines   1389
   (4) University and college magazines   1391
   (5) Newspapers and magazines not primarily devoted to
      literature   1399

Index   1409

EDITOR'S PREFACE

Volumes 1–3 of the *New Cambridge Bibliography of English Literature*, edited by George Watson and covering the periods 600–1660, 1660–1800 and 1800–1900, are based—as Mr Watson explains in his editorial prefaces—on the corresponding volumes of the *CBEL* (1940), edited by F. W. Bateson, and the *CBEL Supplement* of 1957. The present volume, however, constitutes a first treatment of its period. This preface therefore repeats the main points of Mr Watson's explanation of the *New CBEL* policy, but also notes variations made necessary by certain features characteristic of the period 1900–50.

SCOPE AND DESIGN

The volume aims to represent English studies relating to the earlier twentieth century as they stood at the end of 1969, though the attempt has been made to add subsequent information that helps to round off a section: for example, the date of an author's death.

The Introduction. CBEL is a bibliography of literature, not of publications in the wider sense; and although it is difficult to draw this distinction with any precision, it has not been thought suitable to include in the Introductions to the various volumes non-literary sections such as Political and Social Background, which were included in the original *CBEL*. However, in this volume, in view of the fact that the mass audience and the mass media played a direct and substantial role in literary life during the period, the section dealing with Book Production and Distribution has been enlarged to reflect this phenomenon. Even so, the items brought together for this purpose from the disciplines of sociology, psychology, education etc, are not intended to form specialist bibliographies of any of these subjects: instead, an attempt has been made to indicate some of the influences and pressures of which a student of the literature of the period might wish to be aware. The same policy of limitation has been adopted for those sections dealing with the more technical aspects of book production in the twentieth century, with the effect in this case of reducing the scale of the sections as compared with the earlier volumes.

Because of the substantial increase in the number of languages into which and from which translations were made in the period, it has been felt necessary in this volume to exclude translations from the section on Relations with Other Literatures, and the reader is referred to the various bibliographies of translations such as the UNESCO *Index Translationum*. For the same reason translations of individual authors' works have been excluded from the author sections.

The author sections. (a) *Selection of authors.* Like volumes 1–3, volume 4 of *New CBEL* is confined to literary authors, writing in English and native to or mainly resident in the British Isles, in this case those who were in some sense established after 1900 and before 1950 (or, where Irish authors are concerned, established after 1916—since the section on Anglo-Irish Literature in volume 3 extends approximately to this date). Consequently W. B. Yeats and George Bernard Shaw, for example, are not treated in this volume but in volume 3, and Ezra Pound is excluded from *New CBEL* altogether. In the absence of any authoritative, detailed literary history of the period to serve as a guide in the selection of authors, a consensus has been arrived at by collating the various surveys, dictionaries, encyclopedias and anthologies dealing with the period, bearing in mind that there are four categories of author where such a method is not, by itself, likely to be adequate. These categories are, first, 'cult' authors, i.e. ones whose names were spread, initially, more by word-of-mouth than print, and who are only now entering the mainstream of literary interest; next, novelists representative of the popular genres of the detective, historical, romantic, science-fiction and thriller novel, and dramatists representative of the genres of farce, musical comedy and revue—both categories of author having but recently become the object of serious study; finally, the scientists and other scholars whose prose is of literary interest—the question who these are having attracted almost no serious study at all. In the selection of authors in these four categories invaluable assistance has been received from many of the scholars and institutions listed in the Acknowledgements below.

(b) *Arrangement by genre*. The arrangement of authors by genre—Poetry, The Novel, Drama, Prose—is one of the most distinctive characteristics of *CBEL*; and despite the fact that a number, and not the least important, of the authors of the period worked for a substantial portion of their careers in more than one genre, the arrangement has been retained in the present volume. This means, for example, that many of the more important plays of the period, by Maugham, Priestley, Eliot and others, are to be found under The Novel or Poetry, with only a cross-reference under Drama.

(c) *Primary material*. Within each author section the canon of the author's work, the primary material, is usually given in a single chronological sequence, as the best way of demonstrating the pattern of his literary career; within the year the sequence continues to be chronological where a bibliography judged to be reliable has determined the order of publication; otherwise it is alphabetical by title. However, in view of the tendency of authors to work in more than one genre, we have thought it useful to separate out the dramatic work of certain poets and novelists, where it is of sufficient importance, into a sub-section: likewise, we have frequently separated a poet's verse from his other works. Where the single sequence has been retained, an explanatory endnote has been added to a title which does not belong to the genre under which the author is entered, unless the title is self-explanatory. Certain special categories such as letters and diaries, contributions to periodicals, contributions to or editions of books by other authors, unpublished plays, and translations by the author have also on occasion been allowed sub-sections of their own, or dealt with in footnotes. This applies especially to major authors, who are as a matter of principle treated in greater detail. Sections dealing with minor authors are confined to books written wholly by them.

In view of the multiplication of reprints which is characteristic of the period, the degressive principle has been applied to the listing of editions of a text with even greater severity than in earlier volumes. After the first British and American editions, only those editions of a work are listed that contain substantial revisions in text (or changes in illustration in the case of children's books), or have authorial and/or editorial introductions and apparatus substantial enough to justify inclusion. The number of copies in a privately printed or limited edition is normally given when it is under five hundred and when the number is ascertainable from the book itself or from a bibliography judged to be reliable. Translations of the work, as mentioned earlier, are not included, but if an author bibliography lists translations this fact is noted. The growing concern in drama studies with the drama as theatre gives a new importance to plays which have been performed but have not appeared in print. Accordingly, where a dramatist has been judged to be significant enough in this respect, details of his unpublished as well as published plays (including radio and television plays) have been given. The existence of screen plays and film adaptions has also been noted where possible.

The canon of primary material is preceded by sub-sections listing bibliographies and collections and selections, where such exist. By 'collections' and 'selections' are meant collections of and selections from material already published in book form. Collections or selections of material largely unpublished in book form are construed as part of the primary canon, typical examples being 'collected poems' or 'collected articles and papers'. Though authors' manuscripts have found their way into institutional archives to a greater extent than for earlier periods, the process is still under way, and it has been felt advisable to provide headnotes on the location of manuscripts only in cases where the archive is reasonably substantial and well publicized.

The married name of an author writing under her maiden name is added to the heading of her section only if books have been published under it.

(d) *Secondary material.* The list of secondary material is likewise arranged chronologically, with works by each individual scholar grouped together although under some major authors the sequence is divided for convenience into Books and Chapters in Books, and Articles in Periodicals. The aim is to provide a conspectus of what one might term the systematic discussion in print of an author, and therefore certain categories of material have normally been excluded: notably, unpublished dissertations and their published extracts, ephemeral journalism, encyclopedia articles, reviews of secondary works and brief notes of less than crucial interest to scholarship. Also excluded, for reasons of economy, are sections on an author in general works, such as literary histories or studies of a particular aspect of the genre as a whole; these are listed in their own sections at the head of each major division of the volume. However, compilers have been at liberty to include such references if there is little else of substance on the author or if, in the judgement of the compiler, the reference still occupied a significant place in the critical record at the end of 1969. It should be noted that editorial introductions to collections, selections or reprints of individual works are given in the sections appropriate to those publications and are not in general repeated in the list of secondary material.

In general, the degree of completeness of the information in this volume is inevitably influenced by the unevenness of the state of scholarship represented. Among the desiderata in this connection are indexes to the little magazines and to the theatrical yearbooks and magazines of the earlier part of the period; similarly, in many instances, adequate author bibliographies do not yet exist. (Consequently a number of privately printed items not in the British Museum or Library of Congress Catalogues may not be found under the authors.) Again, valuable supplementary information has been obtained from many of the scholars and institutions listed in the Acknowledgements below.

Newspapers and magazines. Because of the increasing specialization of tone and intention in the newspapers and magazines of the period it has been decided to restrict this section to periodicals judged to have been more particularly connected with the literary life of the time and to be of interest to the literary scholar.

The index. Since each volume of *New CBEL* has been designed to be used, if necessary, in isolation from the rest, a skeleton index has been provided by reproducing in alphabetical order the author and subject headings used in the volume. Greater detail—for example, titles of newspapers and magazines, changes of title and the names of editors—will be provided in the final index volume.

Design and conventions. The page, set in Monotype Ehrhardt (a compact fount with short descenders), has been designed to accommodate the maximum possible amount of text matter compatible with the degree of legibility necessary both for easy reference and for browsing.

Punctuation has been kept to the minimum: colons regularly precede subtitles, semicolons divide titles, and commas rather than semicolons ordinarily separate the dates of reprints. Capitalization has been reduced to the level of ordinary prose, and this has enabled titles within titles to be distinguished by a capital letter. Compilers' explanatory endnotes have been allowed to identify themselves simply by their position in the entry, without brackets. In the citation of periodical articles, monthlies and quarterlies are quoted by volume number where possible, and for this arabic numerals have been used in preference to roman.

Titles have been shortened to a certain degree. Thus, in the primary canon subtitles such as 'a play' or 'a novel' which virtually repeat the name of the genre under which the author is entered, are omitted, but more informative subtitles such as 'a play in three acts' or 'a romantic novel' are retained. In the list of secondary material, where a book is included of which only a section is relevant to the author concerned, the book's subtitle, if any, is omitted unless it adds useful information; the definite or indefinite article is omitted from its main title where it is felt that no obscurity results. Authors' Christian names (or initials) have been omitted from the titles of secondary material about them, except where the Christian name and surname alone constitute the whole title. Omissions are not indicated.

The number of volumes in the first edition of a work is specified if more than one and the place of publication given unless it is London. The number of volumes and place of publication indicated for the first edition is to be regarded as applying to all subsequent editions in the entry unless information is given to the contrary.

Where a compiler has been responsible for a group of two or more sections in succession his initials have been given only at the end of the sequence.

ACKNOWLEDGEMENTS

A draft of parts of this volume was prepared by Mr H. S. Harvey and Miss E. A. Boyd under the supervision of Mr F. W. Bateson. The Cambridge University Press asked the present Editor, through the then Director of the British Museum, Sir Frank Francis, to undertake the completion of the work, integrating it with the general revision of the *CBEL* under the *New CBEL* Advisory Committee of H. S. Bennett (Chairman), R. W. David, P. G. Burbidge, A. N. L. Munby and George Watson.

The volume is greatly indebted to the authorities of the British Museum Library on whose collections the work has been largely based. They have not only given active encouragement to the progress of the volume in general, but have made practical arrangements to meet various problems as they arose.

The Editor is indebted to Mr R. J. Roberts for his assistance in the crucial early phase of developing and converting the first draft; to Mr Michael Statham and to Dr Katharine Worth for their assistance in the management of the Prose and Drama sections respectively, and to Mr Statham for assistance in drawing up the contents list; to Mr Alan Spilman for the compilation of the index; to Mr P. N. Furbank and Mr Henry M. Rosenberg for informal counsel throughout the progress of the volume. Mr Statham and the Editor would like to thank Mr E. W. F. Tomlin for invaluable advice on the selection of authors for the Prose section. The Editor would like to thank Mr John Feather and Mr David McKitterick for help in last-minute checking.

To turn from the administration of the volume to its content, this volume owes a special debt to its contributors, many of whom have advised far beyond the borders of their own sections. The volume is also indebted to the advice and knowledge of the following: Dr R. C. Alston, Mr Ian Angus, Professor W. A. Armstrong, Mr Ken Blackwell, Mr F. W. Bateson, Mr B. C. Bloomfield, Miss Bridget Boland, Professor J. T. Boulton, Professor Fredson Bowers, Mr A. H. Bowyer, Mr Vincent Brome, Professor Harold Brooks, Professor J. R. Brown, Mr P. A. H. Brown, Mr R. Browne, Mr William Cagle, Professor Alan Cohn, Mr Maurice Cowling, the late Professor R. S. Crane, Professor David Daiches, Miss L. I. Edwards, Professor Richard Ellmann, Professor Norman Endicott, Professor John Fletcher, Mr G. S. Fraser, Mr K. B. Gardner, Professor W. H. Gardner, Mr Val Gielgud, Mr Stuart Hall, Professor Clive Hart, Dr James Hepburn, Professor Richard Hoggart, Miss Diana Howard, Professor Hugh Hunt, Dr Josef Jarab, Professor Michael Kirkham, Miss B. J. Kirkpatrick, Dr Paul Kirschner, Mr L. Kitchin, Dr J. S. Knowlson, Mr G. P. Lilly, Mr Ray Mackender, Dr

W. McKinnon, Dr R. Majumdar, Mr Peter Meade, Professor E. W. Mellown, Miss Robin Myers, Dr Joseph Needham, Professor Allardyce Nicoll, Mr Howard M. Nixon, Mr Eric Osborne, Mr George D. Painter, Mr Geoffrey Parrinder, Mr S. W. Parry, Mr Charles Peake, Professor I. Raknem, Miss Eiluned Rees, Professor J. M. Robson, Mrs Sheila Rosenberg, Miss Sybil Rosenfeld, Mr Anthony Rota, Professor G. S. Rousseau, Professor Edward Shils, Professor Irène Simon, Mr D. H. Simpson, Mr G .D. E. Soar, Mr B. C. Southam, Professor T. J. B. Spencer, Mr Hallam Tennyson, Mr Alan G. Thomas, Mr James W. Wells, Mr Jeremy Wilson, the late Professor A. S. P. Woodhouse, and Mr Cecil Woolf; the Centre for Contemporary Cultural Studies, University of Birmingham; the libraries of the British Broadcasting Corporation, the British Drama League, the British Film Institute, and the managements of the Abbey Theatre, Dublin, and the Citizens' Theatre, Glasgow. We are also grateful to Mr Nicholas Barker, Professor Malcolm Bradbury, Sir Julian Hall, Professor J. B. Harmer, Mr D. H. Merry, Mr C. D. Needham, Mr Oliver Stallybrass and Mr Watson for advice at the proof stage.

Finally, we are indebted to the many other members of the staff of the British Museum Library and scholars using the Library who helped us to minimize the inconsistencies and slips inevitable in a collaborative volume of this size; to Mrs Phyllis Parsons and Mr Spilman for help in assimilating our copy to the style of the *New CBEL*; and to the Cambridge University Library for allowing us the use of an office in which Mrs Parsons has typed the entire volume.

As the proofs were going through the press I learned of the death in California of Professor Carl Stratman, a personal friend as well as a valued contributor.

I. R. WILLISON

Department of Printed Books
British Museum
February 1972

CORRECTIONS

Corrections will be gratefully acknowledged. They should be sent to I. R. Willison, c/o Cambridge University Press, Trumpington Street, Cambridge CB2 1RP, England.

LIST OF CONTRIBUTORS
TO VOLUME 4

B.W.A.	Brian W. Alderson	A.H.M.	Alfred H. Marks
G.A.	Geoffrey Axworthy	E.M.	Edward Mendelson
R.A.	Ronald Ayling	L.O.	Leonee Ormond
P.G.B.	Peter G. Burbidge	M.P.	Michael Perkin
J.G.	Janet Garrod	J.M.P.	Jill M. Perry
P.C.	Pat Conoley	C.H.E.P.	C. H. E. Philpin
C.P.C.	C. P. Corney	R.J.R.	R. J. Roberts
P.D.	Peter Davison	H.M.R.	H. M. Rosenberg
E.D.	Eric Domville	N.J.S.	Nigel J. Seeley
R.P.D.	R. P. Draper	M.S.	Michael Statham
J.B.H.	J. B. Harmer	C.J.S.	Carl J. Stratman
A.P.H.	A. P. Howse	M.T.	Marjorie Thompson
N.H.	Nancy Hyde	K.W.	Keith Walker
D.K.	David Knott	W.W.	William White
D.J.M.	D. J. McKitterick	K.J.W.	Katharine J. Worth

ABBREVIATIONS

Acad	Academy	Inst	Institute
addn	addition	introd	introduction
Amer	American	JEGP	Journal of English and
anon	anonymous		Germanic Philology
Archiv	Archiv für das Studium der	JHI	Journal of the History of Ideas
	neueren Sprachen	Jnl	Journal
Assoc	Association	Lang	Language
b.	born	Lib	Library
Bibl	Bibliographical	Lit	Literature
bk	book	MÆ	Medium Ævum
BM	British Museum	Mag	Magazine
Br	British	ML	Muses' Library
Bull	Bulletin	MLN	Modern Language Notes
BNYPL	Bulletin of the New York Public	MLQ	Modern Language Quarterly
	Library	MLR	Modern Language Review
c.	circa	MP	Modern Philology
ch	chapter	ms	manuscript
CHEL	Cambridge History of English	Nat	National
	Literature	nd	no date
Chron	Chronicle	no	number
col	column	N & Q	Notes & Queries
CQ	Critical Quarterly	OHEL	Oxford History of English
d.	died		Literature
DNB	Dictionary of National	OSA	Oxford Standard Authors
	Biography	p.	page
ed	edited by	pbd	published
edn	edition	pbn	publication
E & S	Essays and Studies	PBSA	Publications of the Biblio-
et al	and others		graphical Society of America
EC	Essays in Criticism	PMLA	Publications of the Modern
EETS	Early English Text Society		Language Association of
EHR	English Historical Review		America
EL	Everyman's Library	PQ	Philological Quarterly
ELH	Journal of English Literary	priv	privately
	History	Proc	Proceedings
EML	English Men of Letters	pt	part
Eng	English	ptd	printed
E Studien	Englische Studien	Quart	Quarterly
E Studies	English Studies	REL	Review of English Literature
facs	facsimile	rev	revised by
HLQ	Huntington Library Quarterly	Rev	Review
illustr	illustrated by	RES	Review of English Studies

ABBREVIATIONS

rptd	reprinted	TLS	Times Literary Supplement
SB	Studies in Bibliography (University of Virginia)	tr	translated by
		trn	translation
SE	Studies in English (University of Texas)	Univ	University
		unpbd	unpublished
ser	series	UTQ	University of Toronto Quarterly
Soc	Society		
SP	Studies in Philology	vol	volume
Stud	Studies	WC	World's Classics
suppl	supplement		

1. INTRODUCTION

I. GENERAL WORKS

(1) BIBLIOGRAPHIES

This section lists bibliographies wholly or largely devoted to the twentieth century, as well as some general bibliographies of special use in studying the period. Non-period lists will be found in vol 1. See also the section on literature in A. J. Walford (ed), Guide to reference material (2nd edn), vol 3 1970. Further lists, dealing with special aspects of twentieth-century literature will be found in the sections on Relations with other Literatures, Book Production and Distribution, on Poetry, The Novel, Drama etc, and in sections on individual authors, below.

Critical studies in some European languages as well as in English are listed in the annual bibliographies pbd by the Modern Humanities Research Assoc, 1921 (for 1919–20) onwards, and in PMLA by the Modern Language Assoc, 1922 (for 1921) onwards. However, in both lists coverage of material in languages not using the Roman alphabet is limited, although the MHRA does mention some Russian items. Books and periodicals with trns and criticism of English literature, pbd outside the English-speaking world, may be located by using the various national bibliographies and periodical indices listed in L.-N. Malclès, Les sources du travail bibliographique, tome 1, Bibliographies générales, Geneva and Lille 1950, supplemented by R. L. Collison, Bibliographical services around the world 1950–9, Paris 1961 (suppl 1960–4 by P. Avicenne, Paris 1969) and in P. E. Vesenyi, European periodical literature in the social sciences and humanities, Metuchen NJ 1969. In particular, the USSR and Japan are the major centres of English studies inadequately covered by English or American bibliographies. For Soviet studies and trns see the notes in Kratkaia literaturnaia entsiklopediia, Moscow 1962 onwards and the serial biblio-graphy Literatura i iskusstvo narodov SSSR i zarubezhnykh stran, 1957 onwards. For Japanese items see T. Ueda, 1961, below; the Japanese periodical index, Zasshi kiji sakuin: jimbun kagaku hen, 1948 onwards; the section on Literature in Bibliography of the humanistic studies and social relations, 1955–63 (for 1952–61); and the bibliography of criticism and trns in each issue of the periodical Eigo Seinen (English title: The rising generation).

Bibliographies of modern authors. London Mercury Nov 1919–Sept 1921. Monthly 'skeleton lists'.

Danielson, H. Bibliographies of modern authors. 1921. On Beerbohm, Brooke, de la Mare, Drinkwater, Dunsany, Flecker, Letwidge, Mackenzie, Masefield, Walpole.

Manly, J. M. and E. Rickert. Contemporary British literature: bibliographies and study outlines. New York 1921, 1928 (rev), 1935 (rev F. B. Millett).

The nineteenth century and after. In The year's work in English studies, 1921 (for 1919–20) onwards. Separate ch for The twentieth century from vol 35 1956 (for 1954) onwards.

First Editions Club. A bibliographical catalogue of the first loan exhibition. 1922 (priv ptd). Includes lists of Chesterton, Huxley, Wells.

Stonehill, C. A. and H. W. Bibliographies of modern authors, ser 2. 1925. On Mansfield, Meynell.

Fabes, G. H. Modern first editions: points and values, ser 1–3. 1929–32.

Irish literature in English 1900–29. 1929. National Book Council book list no 96.

Cutler, B. D. and V. Stiles. Modern British authors: their first editions. New York 1930.

Checklists of twentieth-century authors, ser 1–3. Milwaukee 1931–3. Includes Bates, Davies, O'Flaherty, Sassoon, Joyce, Huxley, Armstrong, Aldington, Harris.

Muir, P. H., S. Nowell-Smith and A. Mitchell. Bibliographies of modern authors, ser 3. 1931. On Hewlett, Firbank.

'Gawsworth, John' (T. I. F. Armstrong). Ten contemporaries: notes toward their definitive bibliographies. 1932. On Abercrombie, Palmer, Egerton, Ross, S. Hudson, E. Sitwell, Gibson, Nichols, Davies, Shiel. Ser 2 1933, includes D. Richardson, F. Carter, O'Flaherty, S. Benson, Onions, Delafield, T. Burke, L. A. G. Strong, Collier, Bates.

Ulrich, K. Who wrote about whom: a bibliography of books on contemporary British authors. Berlin 1932.

Macleod, R. D. Modern Scottish literature: a popular guide-book catalogue. Glasgow 1933.

Author's and writer's who's who. 1934 etc.

Eppelsheimer, H. W. Handbuch der Weltliteratur. 2 vols Frankfurt 1935–7, 1947–9 (rev), 1 vol 1960 (rev). 1960 edn includes bibliographies of Conrad, Bennett, Galsworthy, Wells, Chesterton, Maugham, Forster, Joyce, Woolf, D. H. Lawrence, Eliot, T. E. Lawrence, Huxley, Mansfield, Morgan, Dylan Thomas.

Zabel, M. D. Recent works of American criticism; Collections of American criticism; American magazines publishing criticism. In his selection, Literary opinion in America, New York 1937, 1951 (rev, adds A supplementary list of essays in criticism: 1900–50; A note on contemporary English criticism), 2 vols 1962 (rev, adds American criticism since 1951). Includes many entries on twentieth-century English literature.

Batho, E. C. and B. Dobrée. In their The Victorians and after 1830–1914, 1938, 1950 (rev).

Muir, E. In his Present age from 1914, 1939.

Kunitz, S. J. and H. Haycraft. Twentieth-century authors: a biographical dictionary. New York 1942. Suppl by S. Kunitz, 1955. Includes brief bibliographies.

Northrup, C. S. and J. J. Parry. The Arthurian legends: modern retellings of the old stories: an annotated bibliography [1800–1944]. JEGP 43 1944.

Zhanteeva, D. G. and M. S. Morshchiner. Sovremennye angliiskie i amerikanskie pisateli. Moscow 1945. Bibliography of contemporary English and American writers.

Stallman, R. W. A selected bibliography of modern criticism 1920–48. In his selection, Critiques and essays in criticism 1920–48, New York 1949. Includes many entries on twentieth-century English literature.

Catalogue of an exhibition of 20th-century Scottish books at the Mitchell Library. Glasgow 1951.

Longaker, M. and E. C. Bolles. In their Contemporary English literature, New York 1953.

Current bibliography. In Twentieth-Century Lit 1 1955 onwards. Brief abstracts of critical articles.

English Fiction in Transition 1 1957 onwards (as English Lit in Transition from 6 1963). Contains occasional bibliographies of authors 1880–1920.

Browning, D. C. Everyman's dictionary of literary biography, English and American. 1958 (EL), 1960 (rev).

Daiches, D. In his Present age after 1920, 1958.

Watson, G. In his Concise Cambridge bibliography of English literature, Cambridge 1958, 1965 (rev).

Dizionario universale della letteratura contemporanea. 5 vols Verona 1959–63.

Juchhoff, R. and H. Föhl. Sammelkatalog der biographischen und literarkritischen Werke zu englischen Schriftstellern des 19. und 20. Jahrhunderts (1830–1958). Krefeld 1959.

Eastwood, W. and J. T. Good. Signposts: a guide to modern English literature. Cambridge 1960 (National Book League pamphlet).

Lexikon der Weltliteratur im 20. Jahrhundert. 2 vols Freiburg 1960–1. Tr and enlarged as Encyclopedia of world literature in the 20th century, ed W. B. Fleischmann, New York 1967–.

Samuel, J. [Bibliographical] Appendix. In Pelican guide to English literature vol 7, The modern age, ed B. Ford 1961, 1963 (rev).

Ueda, T. et al. Gendai ei-bei bungaku handobukku. Tokyo 1961. Bio-bibliographies of 90 modern English authors.

Contemporary authors. 1 1962 onwards. Bio-bibliographies. A selection was pbd as 200 contemporary authors, Detroit 1969.

English literature from the 16th century to the present: a select list of editions. 1962, 1965 (rev) (Br Council).

Sternfeld, W. Deutsche Exil-Literatur 1933–45. Heidelberg 1962. *See also* an exhibition catalogue, Exil-Literatur 1933–45, Frankfurt 1965. Includes literature written in England or in collaboration with English authors.

Stewart, J. I. M. In his Eight modern writers, Oxford 1963 (OHEL). On Conrad, Joyce, D. H. Lawrence.

Glen, D. In his Hugh MacDiarmid–C. M. Grieve–and the Scottish renaissance, Edinburgh 1964.

Bateson, F. W. In his Guide to English literature, New York 1965, 1968 (rev).

Connolly, C. The modern movement: 100 key books 1880–1950. 1966.

Cleeve, B. Dictionary of Irish writers. 2 vols Cork 1967–9.

Baxandall, L. Marxism and aesthetics: a selective annotated bibliography. New York 1968. Includes many entries on twentieth-century English literature.

Harmon, M. Modern Irish literature, 1800–1967: a reader's guide. Dublin 1968.

Phelps, R. and P. Deane. The literary life: a scrapbook almanac of the Anglo-American literary scene from 1900 to 1950. New York 1968.

Temple, R. Z. Twentieth-century British literature: a reference guide and bibliography. New York 1968.

Howard-Hill, T. H. Bibliography of British literary bibliographies. Oxford 1969. Includes lists of bibliographies of twentieth-century authors.

Richardson, K. (ed). Twentieth-century writing: a reader's guide to contemporary literature. 1969.

Schütze, S. Englische Literatur der Gegenwart: Prosa, Drama, Lyrik, Schauspiel: ein Auswahlverzeichnis. Dortmund 1969.

Jones, B. A bibliography of Anglo-Welsh literature 1900–65. [Glamorgan] 1970.

Myers, R. A dictionary of literature in the English language from Chaucer to 1940. 2 vols 1970.   E. M.

(2) LITERARY HISTORIES, SPECIAL STUDIES AND COLLECTIONS OF ESSAYS

See also the sections devoted to General Works under Poetry, The Novel etc, below.

Annual register: a review of public events at home and abroad for the year 1900 [etc]. 1901 onwards. Annual section on literature.

Nevinson, H. W. Books and personalities. 1905. Essays.

Ford, F. M. (formerly Hueffer). The critical attitude. 1911. Essays.

— Portraits from life: memories and criticisms. New York 1937, London 1938 (as Mightier than the sword). Essays. Conrad, Wells, Lawrence, Galsworthy.

— Critical writings of Ford Madox Ford. Ed F. MacShane, Lincoln Nebraska 1964.

Mair, G. English literature: modern. [1911], 1914 (expanded), 1944 (brought up to 1939 by A. C. Ward).

Fehr, B. Streifzüge durch die neueste englische Literatur. Strasburg 1912.

— Die englische Literatur des 19. und 20. Jahrhunderts. 16 pts Berlin 1923–5.

— Die englische Literatur der Gegenwart und die Kulturfragen unserer Zeit. Leipzig 1930.

— Das England von heute: Kulturprobleme, Denkformen, Schrifttum. Leipzig 1932.

Figgis, D. Studies and appreciations. 1912.

Scott-James, R. A. Personality in literature. 1913, 1931 (as Personality in literature 1913–31, with additional material).

— Fifty years of English literature 1900–50. 1951.

Boyd, E. Ireland's literary renaissance. New York 1916, 1922 (rev).

— Appreciations and depreciations: Irish literary studies. Dublin 1917.

Freeman, J. The moderns: essays in literary criticism. 1916.

— English portraits and essays. 1924.

Scott, D. Men of letters. 1916. Essays.

Bennett, A. Books and persons: being comments on a past epoch 1908–11. 1917.

Parker, W. Modern Scottish writers. Edinburgh 1917.

Sherman, S. P. On contemporary literature. New York 1917.

— Critical woodcuts: a collection of essays on modern authors. New York 1926.

— The main stream. New York 1927. Essays.

Pound, E. Pavannes and divisions. 1918.

Williams, H. Modern English writers: being a study of imaginative literature 1890–1914. 1918, 1920 (abridged, as Outlines of modern English literature 1890–1914).

Wright, H. Studies in contemporary literature. Bangor 1918.

Cunliffe, J. W. English literature during the last half century. New York 1919, 1923 (rev).

— English literature in the twentieth century. New York 1933.

Lynd, R. Old and new masters. 1919. Essays.

— Books and authors. [1922]. Essays.

— Books and writers. 1952. Essays.

Waugh, A. Tradition and change: studies in contemporary literature. 1919.

Goldring, D. Reputations: essays in criticism. 1920.

— The nineteen twenties: a general survey and some personal memories. 1945.

Mais, S. P. B. Books and their writers. 1920.

— Why we should read. 1921. Essays.

— Some modern authors: essays. 1923.

— In his Chronicle of English literature, 1936.

Murry, J. M. Aspects of literature. 1920.

— Katherine Mansfield and other literary portraits. 1949.

Squire, J. C. Life and letters: essays. [1920].

— Sunday mornings. 1930. Essays.

Hind, C. L. Authors and I. 1921. Essays.

— More authors and I. 1922. Essays.

Canby, H. S. Definitions: essays in contemporary criticism. 2 vols New York 1922–4.

— Seven years' harvest: notes on contemporary literature. New York 1936.

Garnett, E. Friday nights: literary criticisms and appreciations. 1922. Essays.

Muir, E. North and South. Freeman 15–19 Nov 1922.

— Transition: essays on contemporary literature. 1926.

— The present age, from 1914. 1939 (Introductions to English Literature 5).

Orage, A. R. Readers and writers 1917–21. 1922. Essays.

Schelling, F. E. Appraisements and asperities: as to some contemporary writers. Philadelphia 1922. Essays.

Schuster, G. In his The Catholic spirit in modern English literature, New York 1922.

Adcock, A. St J. Gods of modern Grub Street. 1923. Essays.
— The glory that was Grub Street. 1928. Essays.

Collins, J. The doctor looks at literature: psychological studies of life and letters. New York [1923].
— Taking the literary pulse: psychological studies of life and literature. New York 1924. Essays.

Drinkwater, J. (ed). The outline of literature. 2 vols [1923], 1940 (rev and extended by H. Pollock and C. Nairne), 1950 (rev and enlarged by H. Shipp), 1957 (rev H. Shipp).

Huxley, A. On the margin: notes and essays. 1923.
— Literature and science. 1963.

Shanks, E. First essays on literature. 1923.
— Second essays on literature. 1927.

Baring, M. Punch and Judy and other essays. 1924.

Dell, F. Looking at life. New York 1924. Essays.

O'Conor, N. J. Changing Ireland: literary backgrounds of the Irish Free State 1889-1922. Cambridge Mass 1924.

Overton, G. M. Authors of the day: studies in contemporary literature. New York 1924.

Priestley, J. B. Figures in modern literature. 1924. Essays.
— In his Literature and western man, 1960.

Douglas, N. Experiments. 1925. Essays.

Larbaud, V. Ce vice impuni, la lecture...domaine anglaise. Paris 1925. Wells, Conrad, Bennett.

Mason, E. Considered writers, old and new. 1925. Essays.

Van Doren, C. and M. American and British literature since 1890. New York 1925, 1940 (rev and enlarged).

Calverton, V. F. In his Sex expression in literature, New York 1926.

Cazamian, L. Modern times. In E. Legouis and L. Cazamian, A history of English literature, 1926, 1964 (rev by Cazamian and R. Las Vergnas).

Grieve, C. M. Contemporary Scottish studies. 1926.
— (as H. MacDiarmid). English ascendancy in British literature. Criterion 10 1931.
— (as H. MacDiarmid). Selected essays. Ed D. Glen 1969.

Lalou, R. Panorama de la littérature anglaise contemporaine. Paris 1926.
— La littérature anglaise des origines à nos jours. Paris 1951.

Law, H. Anglo-Irish literature. 1926. See ch 2, The last 25 years.

Lucas, F. L. Authors dead and living. 1926. Essays.

Coblentz, S. A. The literary revolution. New York 1927.

Cooper, A. P. Authors and others. Garden City NY 1927. Essays.

Gosse, E. Leaves and fruit. 1927. Essays.

Lewis, W. Time and western man. 1927, New York 1928.
— The diabolical principle and the dithyrambic spectator. 1931.
— Men without art. 1934.
— The writer and the absolute. 1952.

Vines, S. Movements in modern English poetry and prose. Tokyo 1927.
— 100 years of English literature. 1950. 1830 onwards.

Wells, H. W. The realms of literature. New York 1927.
— Judgment of literature. New York 1929.

Woolf, L. Essays on literature, history, politics etc. 1927.
— Hunting the highbrow. 1927.

MacCarthy, D. Literary taboos. Life & Letters 1 1928.
— The bubble reputation. Life & Letters 7 1931.
— Portraits. 1931. Essays.
— Criticism. 1932. Essays.
— Experience. 1935. Essays.

Read, H. English prose style. 1928, 1952 (rev).

Rickword, E. (ed). Scrutinies. 2 vols 1928-31. Essays.

Riding, L. Contemporaries and snobs. 1928.
— (ed). The world and ourselves. 1938.

Swinnerton, F. A London bookman. 1928. Essays.
— The Georgian scene: a literary panorama. New York 1934, London 1935 (as The Georgian literary scene), 1938 (rev), 1950 (rev), 1969 (rev).

Ward, A. C. Twentieth-century literature 1901-25. 1928, 1940 (enlarged to 1940), 1960 (enlarged to 1960).
— The nineteen-twenties: literature and ideas in the postwar decade. 1930.

'West, Rebecca' (C. I. Andrews). The strange necessity: essays and reviews. 1928.

Wild, F. Die englische Literatur der Gegenwart (seit 1870). Wiesbaden 1928.

Wolfe, H. Dialogues and monologues. 1928. Essays.

The Columbia University course in literature vol 15, Writers of modern England. New York 1929.

Dobrée, B. The lamp and the lute: studies in six modern authors. Oxford 1929, 1964 ('seven authors'). Forster, Lawrence, Eliot; adds Durrell in 1964.

Downey, J. E. Creative imagination: studies in the psychology of literature. 1929.

McNeill, K. The literature of the Highlanders. Stirling 1929. Ed with an additional ch by J. M. Campbell: Progress and the Gaelic Renaissance 1903-28. First pbd Inverness 1892.

Tradition and experiment in present-day literature: addresses delivered at the City Literary Institute. 1929. Blunden, E. Sitwell, A. J. A. Symons, O. Burdett, Eliot et al.

Wickham, H. The impuritans: a glimpse of the new world whose Pilgrim fathers are Weininger, Ellis, Cabell, Proust, Joyce, Mencken, Lawrence, Anderson et id genus omne. New York 1929.

Wilson, E. A preface to modern literature. New Republic 20 March 1929.
— Axel's castle: a study in the imaginative literature of 1870-1930. New York 1931.
— The triple thinkers: ten essays on literature. New York 1938, 1949 (rev).
— Europe without Baedeker: sketches among the ruins of Italy, Greece and England. New York 1947.

Gillett, E. Books and writers. Singapore 1930. Essays.
— In W. Entwistle and E. Gillett, The literature of England 500-1942, 1943, 1962 (rev to 1961).

Krutch, J. W. The modern temper. New York 1930.

Slosson, P. W. The great crusade and after 1914-28. New York 1930.

Eastman, M. The literary mind: its place in an age of science. New York 1931. Essays.

Kreemers, R. Engelsche oorlogsboeken en oorlogsschrijvers. Leuvensche Bijdragen 23 1931.
— Overzicht der Engelsche letteren. Dietsche Warande en Belfort 33 1934.

Nicolson, H. The new spirit in literature. [1931]. BBC talks. No 2 in a symposium, The changing world.

Sackville, Lady M. Some aspects of modern Scottish literature. Essays by Divers Hands 10 1931.

Thorndike, A. H. The outlook for literature. New York 1931.

Linati, C. Scrittori anglo-americani d'oggi. Milan 1932. Huxley, W. Lewis, L. O'Flaherty, Eliot, Craig, Forster, V. Woolf et al.

Shaw, G. B. Pen portraits and reviews. 1932.

Strachey, J. The decay of capitalist culture: literature. In his Coming struggle for power, 1932.

Vočadlo, O. Anglická literatura: xx. století 1901-1931. Prague 1932.

Charques, R. D. Contemporary literature and social revolution. [1933].

Mackenzie, C. Literature in my time. 1933. Essays.

Mégroz, R. L. Five novelist poets of to-day. 1933. Lawrence, de la Mare, O. Sitwell, M. Armstrong, L. A. G. Strong.

The Post-Victorians. 1933. By various authors.

Routh, H. V. In his Money, morals and manners as revealed in modern literature, 1933. On the Edwardian age.

—— Humanism: past, present and future. Essays by Divers Hands 20 1943.

—— English literature and ideas in the 20th century: an inquiry into present difficulties and future prospects. 1950.

Cowley, M. Exile's return: a narrative of ideas. New York 1934, 1951 (rev, with subtitle A literary odyssey of the 1920's).

—— The generation that wasn't lost. College Eng 5 1944.

—— Think back on us: a contemporary chronicle of the 1930's. Ed N. D. Piper, Carbondale 1967. Chiefly essays from New Republic. Spender et al.

Eliot, T. S. After strange gods: a primer of modern heresy. 1934.

Hoops, R. Der Einfluss der Psychoanalyse auf die englische Literatur. Heidelberg 1934.

Alexander, C. The Catholic literary revival: three phases in its development from 1845 to the present. Milwaukee 1935.

Day Lewis, C. Revolution in writing. 1935.

—— (ed). The mind in chains: socialism and the cultural revolution. 1937.

Drew, E. The enjoyment of literature. Cambridge 1935.

Grigson, G. (ed). The arts today. 1935.

Henderson, P. Literature and a changing civilization. 1935.

Hollingsworth, K. In the first person. Eng Jnl 24 1935.

Machen, A. Farewell to materialism. Atlantic Monthly 36 1935.

'Maurois, André' (E. S. W. Hertzog). Magiciens et logiciens. Paris 1935. Tr New York 1935 (as Prophets and poets), 1969 (with 2 additional essays, as Points of view: from Kipling to Greene).

Millett, F. B. Contemporary British literature: a critical survey and 232 author bibliographies. New York 1935. Based on J. M. Manly and E. Rickert, Contemporary British literature, New York [1921].

Mirsky, D. The intelligentsia of Great Britain. Tr A. Brown 1935.

Osgood, C. G. In his Voice of England: a history of English literature, New York 1935. Pt 8, With many voices, extends into the 30's.

Power, W. The modern revival: the literary 'idea' of Scotland. In his Literature and oatmeal: what literature has meant to Scotland, 1935.

Reade, A. R. Main currents in modern literature. 1935.

Spender, S. The destructive element: a study of modern writers' beliefs. 1935.

—— The new realism: a discussion. 1939.

—— The creative element: a study of vision, despair and orthodoxy among some modern writers. 1953.

—— The struggle of the modern. 1963.

—— Writers and politics. Partisan Rev 34 1967.

Chadwick, H. M. and N. K. The growth of literature, vol 2. Cambridge 1936.

Daiches, D. New literary values: studies in modern literature. Edinburgh 1936.

—— Literary essays. Edinburgh 1956.

—— The present age, after 1920. 1958, Bloomington 1958 (as The present age in British literature). (Introductions to English literature 5.)

—— In his Critical history of English literature, 2 vols New York 1960, 4 vols London 1968.

Forster, E. M. Abinger harvest. 1936. Essays.

—— The new disorder. Horizon 4 1941.

—— Two cheers for democracy. 1951. Essays.

Gwynn, S. Irish literature and drama in the English language. 1936.

Kelly, B. M. The well of English. New York 1936.

Lawrence, D. H. Phoenix: the posthumous papers of D. H. Lawrence. Ed E. McDonald, New York 1936.

—— Selected literary criticism. Ed A. Beal 1955.

Tweedsmuir, Lord (John Buchan). The clash of old and new in literature. Canadian Author March 1936.

'A.E.' (G. W. Russell). The living torch. Ed M. Gibbon 1937. Short essays and notes.

Norman, C. H. The revolutionary spirit in modern literature and drama and the class war in Europe 1918–36. 1937.

West, Alick. Crisis and criticism. 1937.

Batho, E. and B. Dobrée. The Victorians and after: 1830–1914. 1938 (Introductions to English Literature 4), 1950 (rev).

'Caudwell, Christopher' (C. St J. Sprigg). Studies in a dying culture. 1938.

—— Further studies in a dying culture. Ed E. Rickword 1949. Selections from this and the previous item included in his Concept of freedom, 1965.

Connolly, C. Enemies of promise. 1938, New York 1948 (rev), Garden City NY 1960 (as Enemies of promise and other essays: an autobiography of ideas).

—— The condemned playground: essays 1927–44. 1945.

—— Ideas and places. 1953. Rptd from Horizon.

—— Previous convictions. 1963. Essays. Section on The modern movement.

Cruse, A. In her After the Victorians, 1938. Books most widely read 1887–1914.

Dupee, F. W. The English literary left. Partisan Rev 5 1938.

Flores, A. (ed). Literature and Marxism: a controversy by Soviet critics. New York 1938.

Madle, H. Die Maschine und der technische Fortschritt in der englischen Literatur des 19. und 20. Jahrhunderts. Breslau 1938.

The Times Literary Supplement. 30 April 1938. Special number: Scottish literature to-day.

—— 5 August 1955. Special number: The Scottish literary revival.

Anderson, M. The essence of tragedy, and other footnotes and papers. Washington 1939.

Elwin, M. Old gods falling. 1939. On best-sellers.

Feibleman, J. In praise of comedy: a study in its theory and practice. 1939.

Kemp, H., L. Riding et al. The Left heresy in literature and life. 1939.

Lawrence, T. E. Men in print: essays in literary criticism. Ed A. W. Lawrence 1939.

Lehmann, J. New writing in England. New York 1939 (Critic's Group Pamphlets 12).

—— The open night. 1952. Essays.

—— (ed). The craft of letters in England: a symposium. 1956.

Blackmur, R. P. The expense of greatness. New York 1940. Essays.

Evans, B. I. In his A short history of English literature, 1940 (Pelican).

—— English literature between the wars. 1951.

'Orwell, George' (E. A. Blair). Inside the whale, and other essays. 1940.

—— Critical essays. 1946, New York 1946 (as Dickens, Dali and others: studies in popular culture).

—— Shooting an elephant and other essays. 1950.

—— Such, such were the joys. New York [1953]. Essays.

—— Collected essays, journalism and letters. Ed S. Orwell and I. Angus 4 vols 1968.

Speirs, J. The Scots literary tradition: an essay in criticism. 1940, 1962 (enlarged).

Spender, J. A. New lamps and ancient lights. 1940.

Brooks, V. W. On literature today. New York 1941.

—— Opinions of Oliver Allston. New York 1941.

—— Reflections on the avant-garde. New York Times Book Rev 30 Dec 1956.

Burke, K. The philosophy of literary form: studies in symbolic action. Baton Rouge 1941.

—— A rhetoric of motives. New York 1950.

—— Language as symbolic action: essays on life, literature and method. Berkeley 1966.

Sampson, G. The concise Cambridge history of English literature. 1941, 1961 (with ch by R. C. Churchill on The age of T. S. Eliot), 1970 (with Churchill's ch rev as The age of T. S. Eliot: the mid-twentieth century literature of the English-speaking world).

Tate, A. Reason in madness. New York 1942.
— The hovering fly and other essays. Cummington Mass 1949.
Barzun, J. Romanticism and the modern ego. Boston 1943.
Church, R. British authors: a twentieth century gallery. 1943.
Nicholson, N. Man and literature. 1943.
Coates, J. B. Ten modern prophets. 1944. Huxley, Lawrence, Wells et al.
Fontaine no 37–40 1944. Special number: Aspects de la littérature anglaise (1918–1940). Essays by Forster, C. Morgan, Spender, E. Bowen, D. W. Brogan, Orwell, M. Beerbohm, Muir et al.
Brown, S. J. and T. MacDermott. A survey of Catholic literature. Milwaukee [1945]. Section on Our own times.
Chase, R. The sense of the present. Kenyon Rev 7 1945.
— Myth as literature. New York 1948 (Eng Inst Essays 1947).
— Art, nature, politics. Kenyon Rev 12 1950.
— The fate of the avant-garde. Partisan Rev 24 1957.
— The democratic vista. 1958.
Hoffman, F. J. Freudianism and the literary mind. Baton Rouge 1945, 1957 (rev).
— The imagination's new beginning: theology and modern literature. Notre Dame 1961.
Slochower, H. No voice is wholly lost: writers and thinkers in war and peace. 1945, 1964 (as Literature and philosophy between two wars).
Baker, D. V. (ed). Writers of to-day. 2 vols 1946–8. Huxley, Greene, Joyce, E. Sitwell, Priestley, Sayers, Eliot, Forster et al.
Beerbohm, M. Mainly on the air. 1946, 1957 (enlarged).
Gordon, G. The discipline of letters. Oxford 1946.
Hospers, J. Meaning and truth in the arts. Chapel Hill 1946.
Lewis, E. Some aspects of Anglo-Welsh literature. Welsh Rev 5 1946.
Clarke, D. W. Modern English writers. 1947. Essays.
— Writers of today. 1956. Essays.
Neff, E. The poetry of history: the contribution of literature and literary theory to the writing of history since Voltaire. New York 1947.
Phelps, G. (ed). Living writers: being critical studies broadcast in the BBC Third Programme. 1947.
Tindall, W. Y. Forces in modern British literature 1885–1946. New York 1947.
— The literary symbol. New York 1955.
West, H. F. The mind on the wing: a book for readers and collectors. New York 1947. Essays on the literature of mountaineering, travel and exploration, nature writers, and the literature of war.
Beres, P. Cubism, futurism, dadaism, expressionism and the surrealist movement in literature and art. New York 1948.
Chew, S. The nineteenth century and after 1879–1939. In A literary history of England, ed A. Baugh, New York 1948, 4 vols 1967 (Chew's section rev R. Altick).
The importance of Scrutiny. Ed E. Bentley, New York 1948.
Schorer, M., J. Miles and G. McKenzie (ed). Criticism: the foundations of modern literary judgment. New York 1948.
Stauffer, D. The modern myth of the modern myth. New York 1948 (Eng Inst Essays 1947).
Woodcock, G. The writer and politics. 1948. Orwell, Greene et al,
Engel, C. E. Esquisses anglaises: C. Morgan, Greene, Eliot. Paris 1949.
Fiedler, L. Out of the whale. 1949. Essays.
— No! in thunder: essays on myth and literature. Boston [1960]. Essay on class war in British literature etc.
Gaunt, W. The march of the moderns. 1949.
Highet, G. In his The classical tradition: Greek and Roman influences in western literature, Oxford 1949. T. E. Lawrence, Joyce, Eliot.

— People, places and books. New York 1953. Rptd talks.
Rahv, P. Image and idea: twenty essays on literary themes. New York 1949, [1957] (rev and enlarged).
Shipley, J. T. Trends in literature. Syracuse NY 1949.
Stallman, R. W. (ed). Critiques and essays in criticism, 1920–1948: representing the achievement of modern British and American critics. New York [1949].
Tymms, R. Doubles in literary psychology. Cambridge 1949.
Wellek, R. and R. Warren. Theory of literature. New York 1949, 1966 (rev), London 1966 (Peregrine).
Beach, J. W. The literature of the nineteenth and early twentieth centuries: 1798 to the First World War. In A history of English literature, ed H. Craig, New York 1950.
Bowen, E. Collected impressions. 1950. Essays.
Ellis, H. H. From Marlowe to Shaw: the studies 1576–1936 in English literature of Ellis. Ed 'John Gawsworth' (T. I. F. Armstrong) 1950.
Hetherington, H. A. No profits for prophets. Meanjin 9 1950.
Hübner, W. Die Stimmen der Meister: eine Einführung in die Meisterwerke des englischen Dichtens und Denkens. Berlin 1950.
Jameson, S. The writer's situation and other essays. 1950.
Meissner, P. Englische Literaturgeschichte von den Anfängen bis zum ersten Weltkrieg. Heidelberg 1950.
Ross, A. The forties: a period piece. 1950.
Adams, J. D. Literary frontiers. New York 1951.
Brower, R. A. The fields of light: an experiment in critical reading. 1951, New York 1951. On V. Woolf, Forster, Yeats et al.
Collins, A. S. English literature of the twentieth century. 1951, 1960 (with a postscript on the 1950s by F. Whitehead).
Garlick, R. In Dock Leaves 2 1951. On twentieth-century Anglo-Welsh writing.
Getlein, R. The old reductio ad obscenum. Commentary 7 1951.
Greene, G. The lost childhood and other essays. 1951.
Isaacs, J. An assessment of twentieth-century literature. 1951.
Williams, T. G. English literature: a critical survey. New York 1951.
Ghiselin, B. (ed). The creative process: a symposium. Berkeley 1952.
Hopper, S. R. (ed). Spiritual problems in contemporary literature: a series of addresses and discussions. New York 1952.
Jones, H. M. The bright Medusa. Urbana 1952.
Leavis, F. R. The common pursuit. 1952. Essays.
— (ed). A selection from Scrutiny. 2 vols Cambridge 1968.
— English literature in our time and the university. 1969.
Levy, H. and H. Spalding. Literature for an age of science. 1952.
Morton, A. L. In his English Utopia, 1952. Last ch, Yesterday and tomorrow, up to 1984.
Norton, D. S. and P. Rushton. Classical myths in English literature. New York 1952. Introd by C. G. Osgood.
'O'Donnell, Donat' (C. C. O'Brien). In his Maria Cross: imaginative patterns in a group of modern Catholic authors. New York 1952.
O'Brien, C. C. Writers and politics. 1965.
Scott, N. A. jr. Rehearsals of discomposure: alienation and reconciliation in modern literature. New York 1952.
— Modern literature and the religious frontier. New York 1958.
— Negative capability: studies in the new literature and the religious situation. New Haven 1969.
Bell, H. I. The Welsh literary renascence of the twentieth century. Proc Br Acad 39 1953.
Fraser, G. S. The modern writer and his world. 1953, 1964 (rev) (Pelican).

Longaker, M. and E. Bolles. Contemporary English literature. New York [1953] (Appleton-Century Handbooks of Literature).

Nott, K. The emperor's clothes. 1953.

— A soul in the quad. 1969.

Rantavaara, I. Virginia Woolf and Bloomsbury. Helsinki 1953.

Spiel, H. Der Park und die Wildnis: zur Situation der neueren englischen Literatur. Munich 1953.

Strong, L. A. G. Personal remarks. 1953. Essays.

Brewster, D. East-West passage: a study in literary relationships. 1954. See ch 4, The pink decade, et passim.

Jarrett-Kerr, M. Studies in literature and belief. [1954].

Johnstone, J. K. The Bloomsbury group: a study of Forster, Strachey, Woolf and their circle. 1954.

Taylor, E. R. The modern Irish writers: cross currents of criticism. Lawrence Kansas 1954.

Bogan, L. Selected criticism: poetry and prose. New York 1955. Essays.

Friedman, M. Stream of consciousness. New Haven 1955.

Martin, P. W. Experiment in depth. 1955. Jung, Eliot, Toynbee.

Meyerhoff, H. Time in literature. Berkeley 1955.

Moore, M. Predilections. New York 1955. Essays.

Galinsky, H. Deutschland in der Sicht von D. H. Lawrence und T. S. Eliot: eine Studie zum anglo-amerikanischen Deutschlandbild des 20. Jahrhunderts. Wiesbaden 1956.

Melchiori, G. The tightrope walkers: studies of mannerism in modern English literature. 1956.

Roppen, G. Evolution and poetic belief: a study in some Victorian and modern writers. Oslo 1956.

Coveney, P. In his Poor monkey: the child in literature, 1957, 1967 (rev as The image of childhood).

Enright, D. J. The apothecary's shop: essays on literature. 1957.

— Conspirators and poets. 1966. Essays.

Frye, N. Anatomy of criticism. Princeton 1957.

Hoggart, R. The uses of literacy. 1957.

— Speaking to each other. 2 vols 1970. Essays on society and literature.

Holroyd, S. Emergence from chaos. 1957. Essays.

Jones, G. The first forty years: some notes on Anglo-Welsh literature: the W. D. Thomas memorial lecture. Cardiff 1957.

Levin, H. Contexts of criticism. Cambridge Mass 1957 (Harvard Studies in Comparative Literature no 22).

— On the dissemination of realism. Tri-Quarterly 11 1968.

West, A. Principles and persuasions. New York 1957. Essays.

Astaldi, M. L. Nuove letture inglesi. Florence 1958. Essays. D. Garnett, V. Woolf, Lawrence, Orwell, B. Russell, J. Huxley, A. Huxley, Eliot, E. Bowen.

Cary, J. Art and reality. Cambridge 1958.

Howarth, H. The Irish writers 1880–1940: literature under Parnell's star. [1958].

— Notes on some figures behind Eliot. 1965.

Kenner, H. Gnomon: essays on contemporary literature. New York 1958.

— Words in the dark. Essays by Divers Hands 29 1958.

Noon, W. Modern literature and the sense of time. Thought 33 1958.

Raymond, J. England's on the anvil! and other essays. 1958.

Tillyard, E. M. W. In his The muse unchained: an intimate account of the revolution in English studies at Cambridge. 1958.

Wilder, A. Theology and modern literature. Cambridge Mass 1958.

Williams, R. In his Culture and society 1780–1950. 1958.

— In his The long revolution. 1961.

Wittig, K. In his The Scottish tradition in literature. Edinburgh 1958.

Writers at work: the Paris Review interviews. Ser 1–3 New York 1958–67. Ed M. Cowley, A. Kazin.

Senior, J. The way down and out: the occult in English literature. Ithaca 1959.

Walsh, W. The use of imagination: educational thought and the literary mind. 1959.

Wood, N. Communism and British intellectuals. 1959.

Elliott, R. C. The power of satire: magic, ritual, art. Princeton 1960. On W. Lewis, Empson et al.

Ellmann, R. (ed). Edwardians and late Victorians. New York 1960 (Eng Inst Essays 1959).

— and C. Feidelson (ed). The modern tradition: backgrounds of modern literature. 1965.

Glicksberg, C. I. Literature and religion: a study in conflict. Dallas 1960.

— The self in modern literature. University Park Pa 1963.

Hough, G. Image and experience: studies in a literary revolution. 1960.

— The dream and the task: literature and morals in the culture of today. 1963.

Moorman, C. Arthurian triptych: mythic materials in Charles Williams, C. S. Lewis and Eliot. Berkeley 1960.

— The precincts of felicity: the Augustan city of the Oxford Christians. Gainesville 1966. C. Williams, C. S. Lewis, Tolkien, Eliot, D. L. Sayers.

Seward, B. The symbolic rose. New York 1960.

Symons, J. The thirties: a dream revolved. 1960.

— Critical occasions. 1966. Essays.

— A glimpse of thirties' sunlight. TLS 24 April 1969.

Approaches to the study of twentieth-century literature: Proceedings of the Conference on the Study of Twentieth-century Literature. East Lansing 1961–.

Dahlberg, E. and H. Read. Truth is more sacred: a critical exchange on modern literature. New York 1961. Joyce, Lawrence, Graves, Eliot.

Ford, B. (ed). The modern age. 1961 (Pelican guide to English literature vol 7).

Green, M. A mirror for Anglo-Saxons. 1961.

Mander, J. The writer and commitment. 1961.

Cecchi, E. Scrittori inglesi e americani. 2 vols Milan 1962–4. Conrad, Corvo, Wells, Douglas, Belloc, Beerbohm, Chesterton, 'Bloomsbury', Strachey, V. Woolf, Keynes, D. H. and T. E. Lawrence, Eliot et al.

Jarrell, R. A sad heart at the supermarket: essays and fables. New York 1962.

Kain, R. M. Dublin in the age of William Butler Yeats and James Joyce. Norman Oklahoma 1962.

Kermode, F. Puzzles and epiphanies: essays and reviews 1958–61. 1962.

— Continuities. 1968.

The Partisan Review Anthology. Ed W. Phillips and P. Rahv 1962.

Poggioli, R. Teoria dell'arte d'avan-guardia. Bologna 1962; tr Cambridge Mass 1968.

Putt, S. G. Scholars of the heart: essays in criticism. 1962.

Wilson, C. The strength to dream: literature and the imagination. 1962.

Frank, J. The widening gyre: crisis and mastery in modern literature. New Brunswick 1963.

Stewart, J. I. M. Eight modern authors. Oxford 1963 (OHEL). Includes Conrad, Joyce, Lawrence.

Wain, J. Essays on literature and ideas. 1963.

Andreach, R. Studies in structure: the stages of the spiritual life in four modern authors. New York 1964. Hopkins, Joyce, Eliot, H. Crane.

Browne, R. B. (ed). The Celtic cross: studies in Irish culture and literature. West Lafayette Indiana 1964.

Glen, D. Hugh MacDiairmid–C. M. Grieve–and the Scottish renaissance. Edinburgh 1964.

Holloway, J. The colours of clarity: essays on contemporary literature and education. 1964.

— English literature: 20th century. Encyclopaedia Britannica vol 8 Chicago 1969. See other edns as well.

Kostelanetz, R. (ed). On contemporary literature: an anthology of critical essays on the major movements and writers of contemporary literature. New York 1964.

Matthews, J. Surrealism and England. Comparative Lit Stud 1 1964.
——An introduction to surrealism. University Park Pa 1965.
Nojima, H. Exile's literature: a study of Joyce, D. H. Lawrence and Eliot. Tokyo 1964.
Nowell-Smith, S. (ed). Edwardian England 1901–14. Oxford 1964.
Review 11–12 1964. Special number: The thirties.
Rodway, A. Science and modern writing. 1964.
Weisinger, H. The agony and the triumph: papers on the use and abuse of myth. East Lansing 1964.
Will, F. (ed). Hereditas: seven essays on the modern experience of the classical. Austin 1964.
Writers on themselves. 1964. BBC talks. N. Nicholson, R. West, W. Sansom, V. Scannell et al.
Bergonzi, B. Heroes' twilight: a study of the literature of the Great War. 1965.
—— (ed). The twentieth century. 1970 (Sphere history of Lit in the Eng Lang vol 7).
Dyson, A. E. The crazy fabric: essays in irony. 1965. Strachey, Huxley, Waugh, Orwell.
Hutchins, P. Ezra Pound's Kensington. 1965.
Skelton, R. and D. R. Clark (ed). Irish renaissance: a gathering of essays, memoirs and letters from the Massachusetts Review. Dublin 1965.
Cronin, A. A question of modernity. 1966.
Fowler, R. (ed). Essays on style and language: linguistic and critical approaches to literary style. 1966.
Harris, H. The symbol of the frontier in the social allegory of the thirties. Zeitschrift für Anglistik und Amerikanistik 14 1966.
Harrison, J. The reactionaries: Yeats, Lewis, Pound, Eliot, Lawrence, a study of the anti-democratic intelligentsia. 1966.
Proceedings of the IVth Congress of the International Comparative Literature Association, Fribourg 1964. Ed F. Jost, 2 vols The Hague 1966.
Robson, W. Critical essays. 1966.
—— Modern English literature. 1970.
Samuels, S. The Left Book Club. Jnl of Contemporary History April 1966.
—— The left intelligentsia in England in the thirties. 1968.
—— English intellectuals and politics in the 1930's. In On intellectuals, ed P. Rieff, Garden City NY 1969.
Stansky, P. and W. Abrahams. Journey to the frontier: Julian Bell and John Cornford, their lives and the 1930s. 1966.
Tradition and innovation in contemporary literature: a round table discussion of the International PEN, Budapest 16–17 Oct 1964. Budapest 1966.
Vickery, J. (ed). Myth and literature: contemporary theory and practice. Lincoln Nebraska [1966].
West, P. The wine of absurdity: essays on literature and consolation. University Park Pa 1966. Yeats, Lawrence, Eliot, Greene.
Woolf, V. Collected essays. Ed L. Woolf 4 vols 1966–9.
Young, D. Whither the 'Scottish Renaissance'. Forum for Mod Lang Stud 2 1966.
Babbage, S. The mark of Cain: studies in literature and theology. Grand Rapids 1967 (for 1966).
Benson, F. Writers in arms: the literary impact of the Spanish Civil War. New York 1967.
Bronsged, M. The transformations of the concept of fate in literature. In Fatalistic beliefs in religion, folklore and literature: papers read at the Symposium of Fatalistic Beliefs held at Åbo on 7th–9th of September 1964. Stockholm 1967.
Cantrell, L. Marxism and literature: the beginning. Balcony 6 1967.
Hillegas, M. The future as nightmare: H. G. Wells and the anti-Utopians. New York 1967. Also Forster, Huxley, Orwell, C. S. Lewis.
—— (ed). Shadows of imagination: the fantasies of C. S. Lewis, J. R. R. Tolkien and Charles Williams. Carbondale 1969.

Lombardo, A. (ed). Studi e ricerche di letteratura inglese e americana. 2 vols Milan 1967.
Martin, W. The New Age under Orage. Manchester 1967.
—— The sources of imagist aesthetic. PMLA 85 1970.
Molnar, T. Utopia: the perennial heresy. New York 1967.
Raine, K. Defending ancient springs. 1967. Essays. Muir, Watkins, Gascoyne, Yeats et al.
Alvarez, A. Beyond all this fiddle: essays 1955–67. 1968.
Armytage, W. The disenchanted mecanophobes in 20th-century England. Extrapolation 9 1968.
Batts, M. Tristan and Isolde in modern literature: l'éternel retour. Seminar 5 1968.
Bell, Q. Bloomsbury. 1968.
Burgess, A. Urgent copy: literary studies. 1968.
Caligor, L. and R. May. Dreams and symbols: man's unconscious language. New York 1968.
Critical Quarterly: special tenth anniversary issue. CQ 10 1968.
Donoghue, D. The ordinary universe: soundings in modern literature. 1968.
Ehrmann, J. (ed). Game, play, literature. New Haven 1968. Rptd and new essays.
Fingestein, P. Symbolism and allegory. In Helen Adolf Festschrift, ed S. Buehne, J. Hodge and L. B. Pinto, New York 1968.
Goodheart, E. The cult of the ego: the self in modern literature. Chicago 1968.
Heilbrun, C. The Bloomsbury group. Midway 9 1968.
Hynes, S. The Edwardian turn of mind. Princeton 1968.
Jones, G. The dragon has two tongues: essays on Anglo-Welsh writers and writing. 1968.
Lawall, S. Critics of consciousness: the existential structure of literature. Cambridge Mass 1968.
Lester, J. A. Journey through despair 1880–1914: transformations in British literary culture. Princeton 1968.
Martin, M. Futurist art and theory 1910–15. Oxford 1968.
Matthews, H. The hard joinery: the myth of man's rebirth. New York 1968.
Rodman, B-S. War and aesthetic sensibility: an essay in cultural history. Soundings 1 1968.
Seerveld, C. A Christian critique of art and literature. Ontario 1968.
Stanford, W. The Ulysses theme: a study in adaptability of a traditional hero. Ann Arbor 1968.
Stromberg, R. Realism, naturalism and symbolism: modes of thought and expression in Europe 1848–1914. New York 1968.
Sypher, W. Literature and technology: the alien vision. New York 1968.
Greenberger, A. The British image of India: a study in the literature of imperialism 1880–1960. 1969.
Gross, J. The rise and fall of the man of letters: aspects of English literary life since 1800. 1969.
Grosshans, H. (ed). To find something new: studies in contemporary literature. Pullman Washington 1969.
Hampshire, S. Modern writers and other essays. 1969.
Hodgart, M. Satire. 1969.
Hoskins, K. Today the struggle: literature and politics in England during the Spanish Civil War. Austin 1969.
Lewis, C. S. Selected literary essays. Ed W. Hooper, Cambridge 1969.
Merivale, P. Pan the goat-god: his myth in modern times. Cambridge Mass 1969.
Ower, J. Manichaean metaphor: the Black African in modern literature. Mosaic 2 1969.
Rühle, J. Literature and revolution: a critical study of the writer and Communism in the twentieth century. Tr J. Steinberg, New York 1969.
Seymour-Smith, M. Fallen women: a skeptical enquiry into the treatment of prostitutes, their clients and their pimps, in literature. 1969.
Stanford, D. Thoughts on the 'forties. Poetry Rev 60 1969.
Chapple, J. Documentary and imaginative literature 1880–1920. 1970.   H. M. R.

(3) LITERARY MEMOIRS, REMINISCENCES, JOURNALS AND LETTERS

The standard biographies, collections of letters etc will be found in the sections devoted to individual writers. See also W. Matthews, British diaries: an annotated bibliography of British diaries written between 1442 and 1942, Berkeley and Los Angeles 1950, and his British autobiographies: an annotated bibliography of British autobiographies published or written before 1951, Berkeley and Los Angeles 1955.

Bennett, A. The truth about an author. 1903 (anon), New York [1911] (with preface), London 1914.
— Things that interested me: being leaves from a journal. 3 sers (ser 2, 3 as Things which have interested me) Burslem 1906–8. Priv ptd. Not rptd in The journals, below.
— Paris nights and other impressions of places and people. 1913. Includes life in England 1907–11.
— Books and persons: being comments on a past epoch 1908–11. 1917.
— Things that have interested me. 3 sers 1921–6. Different from Things that interested me 1906–8, above.
— Journal, 1929. 1930, Garden City NY 1930 (as Journal of things old and new).
— The journals of Arnold Bennett 1896–1928. Ed N. Flower 3 vols 1932–3, New York 1932–3 (rev, as The journal of Arnold Bennett). This and the preceding abridged by F. Swinnerton 1954 (Penguin).
Archer, W. Real conversations. 1904. Dialogues with Pinero, Hardy, Stephen Phillips, George Moore et al.
Benson, A. C. The house of quiet: an autobiography. 1904 (anon), 1907 (with preface and introd).
— Memories and friends. 1924.
— The diary of A. C. Benson. Ed P. Lubbock 1926.
— Rambles and reflections. 1926.
Davies, W. H. The autobiography of a super-tramp. 1908, 1920 (with author's note), 1923 (with foreword).
— Later days. 1925.
O'Connor, E. I myself. 1910.
Austin, A. Autobiography. 2 vols 1911.
Harrison, F. Autobiographic memoirs. 2 vols 1911.
Hueffer, F. H. M. (afterwards Ford). Ancient lights and certain new reflections. 1911, New York 1911 (as Memories and impressions: a study in atmospheres).
— Thus to revisit: some reminiscences. 1921.
— Joseph Conrad: a personal remembrance. 1924. As F. M. Ford.
— Return to yesterday (reminiscences 1894–1914). 1931. As F. M. Ford.
— It was the nightingale. Philadelphia 1933. As F. M. Ford.
— Portraits from life: memories and criticisms [of various authors]. New York 1937, London 1938 (as Mightier than the sword). Conrad, Wells, Lawrence, Galsworthy et al. As F. M. Ford
Moore, G. 'Hail and farewell!' 3 vols 1911–14, 2 vols 1925.
— Avowals. 1919 (priv ptd), 1921 (rev).
— Conversations in Ebury Street. 1924, 1930 (rev).
— A communication to my friends. 1933.
Colum, P. My Irish year. [1912].
— and M. M. Colum. Our friend James Joyce. Garden City NY 1958.
Conrad, J. Some reminiscences. 1912, 1916 (as A personal record).
Coburn, A. L. Men of mark. 1913.
— More men of mark. 1922.
— Alvin Langdon Coburn, photographer: an autobiography. Ed H. and A. Gernsheim 1966.
Gregory, A. Our Irish theatre: a chapter of autobiography. 1913.
— Journals 1916–30. Ed L. Robinson 1946.
Tynan, K. Twenty-five years: reminiscences. 1913.
— The middle years. 1916.
— The years of the shadow. 1919.
— The wandering years. 1922.

'Vere, Percy' (E. C. Jones). The confessions of a literary free-lance. Edinburgh 1913.
Ellis, H. Impressions and comments. 3 sers 1914–24, 1 vol Boston 1931 (as Fountain of life).
— My life. Boston 1939.
Harris, F. Contemporary portraits. 4 sers New York 1915–23.
— My life and loves. Vols 1–4 only, Paris 1922–7 (priv ptd); ed G. Richards 1947 (abridged as Frank Harris: his life and adventures); ed J. F. Gallagher, 5 vols New York 1963.
— Latest contemporary portraits. New York [1927].
— Confessional: a volume of intimate portraits, sketches and studies. New York [1930].
Carpenter, E. My days and dreams: being autobiographical notes. 1916.
Clodd, E. Memories. 1916.
Pound, E. Gaudier-Brzeska: a memoir, including the published writings of the sculptor and a selection from his letters. 1916.
— Letters 1907–41. Ed D. D. Paige, New York 1950.
— Pound/Joyce: the letters of Ezra Pound to James Joyce. Ed F. Read, New York 1967.
Morley, J. Recollections. 2 vols 1917.
Yeats, J. B. Passages from the letters of John Butler Yeats. Ed E. Pound, Churchtown, Dundrum 1917.
— J. B. Yeats: letters to his son W. B. Yeats and others, 1869–1922. Ed J. Hone 1944.
Blunt, W. S. My diaries: being a personal narrative of events, 1888–1914. 2 vols 1919–20.
'Cumberland, Gerald' (C. F. Kenyon). Set down in malice: a book of reminiscences. 1919.
— Written in friendship: a book of reminiscences. 1923.
Smyth, E. M. Impressions that remained: memoirs. 2 vols 1919, 1923 (rev).
— Streaks of life. 1921.
— As time went on —. 1936.
— What happened next. 1940.
Murry, J. M. The evolution of an intellectual. 1920.
— Son of woman: the story of D. H. Lawrence. 1931.
— Reminiscences of D. H. Lawrence. 1933.
— Between two worlds: an autobiography. 1935.
Colvin, S. Memories and notes of persons and places 1852–1912. 1921.
McKenna, S. While I remember. 1921.
Pearson, H. Modern men and mummers. 1921. On F. Harris, Strachey, Chesterton, Wells, Conrad et al.
— Hesketh Pearson by himself. 1965.
Salt, H. S. Seventy years among the savages. 1921.
— Company I have kept. 1930.
Ainslie, D. Adventures social and literary. 1922.
Baring, M. The puppet show of memory. 1922.
— Lost lectures: or, the fruits of experience. 1932.
Ervine, St J. G. Some impressions of my elders. New York 1922.
— Living and reading: first excursions into literature. Listener 19 May 1949.
— Bernard Shaw: his life, work and friends. 1956.
Hewlett, M. Beginnings: a literary study. Cornhill new ser 52 1922.
Jackson, H. Occasions. 1922.
Strachey, J. St L. The adventure of living. 1922.
Walpole, H. The crystal box: fragments of autobiography. Bookman (New York) 56, 57 1922–3.
— The apple trees: four reminiscences. Waltham St Lawrence 1932.

Kernahan, C. Celebrities: little stories about famous folk. New York 1923.

Nevinson, H. W. Changes and chances. 1923.
— More changes, more chances. 1925.
— Last changes, last chances. 1928. This and preceding abridged as Fire of life, 1935.

Ridge, W. P. A story teller: forty years in London. [1923].
— I like to remember. [1925].

Russell, J. F. S. (2nd Earl Russell). My life and adventures. 1923.

Sichel, W. The sands of time: recollections and reflections. 1923.

Vachell, H. A. Fellow-travellers. 1923.
— Distant fields: a writer's autobiography. 1937.

Waugh, A. R. Myself when young: confessions. 1923.
— Thirteen such years. 1932.
— The early years of Alec Waugh. 1962.
— My brother Evelyn and other profiles. 1967.

Bernstein, H. Celebrities of our time. New York 1924. Interviews.

Doyle, A. C. Memories and adventures. 1924.

Galsworthy, J. Memorable days. 1924 (priv ptd).

Guedalla, P. A gallery. 1924.

Tittle, W. Portraits in pencil and pen. Century 108 1924. On Bennett, Graham, Conrad, Locke, Walpole, Noyes et al.

Bax, C. Inland far: a book of thoughts and impressions. 1925.
— Ideas and people. 1936.
— Evenings in Albany. 1942.
— Rosemary for remembrance. 1948.
— Some I knew well. 1951.

Boyd, E. A. Portraits, real and imaginary: being memories and impressions of friends and contemporaries. 1925.

Powys, L. Skin for skin. New York 1925.

Symons, A. Notes on Joseph Conrad, with some unpublished letters. 1925.
— From Toulouse-Lautrec to Rodin, with some personal impressions. 1929.
— Mes souvenirs. Chapelle-Réanville 1931.

Conrad, Jessie. Joseph Conrad as I knew him. 1926.
— Joseph Conrad and his circle. 1935.

Frankau, G. My unsentimental journey. [1926].
— Self-portrait: a novel of his own life. New York 1940, London 1944 (rev).

Gwynn, S. Experiences of a literary man. 1926.

Haggard, H. R. The days of my life. 2 vols 1926.

Hind, C. L. Naphtali: being influences and adventures while earning a living. 1926.

Hunt, V. The flurried years. [1926], New York [1926] (as I have this to say).

Jerome, J. K. My life and times. 1926.

Reid, F. Apostate. 1926.
— Private road. 1940.
— Retrospective adventures. 1941.

Thomas, H. As it was. By 'H.T.' [i.e. H. Thomas]. 1926.
— World without end. 1931.

Wallace, E. People: a short autobiography. 1926, 1929 (as Edgar Wallace: a short autobiography).

Webb, B. My apprenticeship. 1926.
— Our partnership. Ed B. Drake and M. I. Cole 1948.
— Diaries 1912–24, 1924–32. Ed M. I. Cole 2 vols 1952–56.

Yeats, W. B. Autobiographies. 1926, New York 1938 (enlarged as The autobiography of Yeats), London 1955 (enlarged as Autobiographies).

'Hope, Anthony' (A. H. Hawkins). Memories and notes. [1927].

The journal of Katherine Mansfield. Ed J. M. Murry 1927, 1954 (with some addns).

Shorter, C. K. An autobiography. Ed J. M. Bullock 1927.

Spender, J. A. Life, journalism and politics. 2 vols 1927.

Beresford, J. D. Writing aloud. [1928].

Blanche, J-E. Mes modèles. Paris 1928.
— Portraits of a lifetime: the late Victorian era, the Edwardian pageant 1870–1914. Tr and ed W. Clement 1937.
— More portraits of a lifetime. Tr and ed W. Clement 1939.

Curle, R. The last twelve years of Joseph Conrad. 1928.
— Caravansary and conversation. 1937.

The memoirs of J. M. Dent 1849–1926. 1928, 1938 (rev, as The house of Dent, 1888–1938).

Garland, H. Back-trailers from the middle border. New York 1928.

Riding, L. Contemporaries and snobs. 1928.

'Crowley, Aleister' (E. A. Crowley). The spirit of solitude: an autohagiography subsequently re-antichristened The confessions of Aleister Crowley. Vol 1–2, 1929; ed J. Symonds and K. Grant 1 vol 1969 (as The Confessions of Aleister Crowley) (the complete text).

Douglas, A. Autobiography. 1929.
— Without apology. 1938.

Draper, M. Music at midnight. 1929.

Graves, R. Goodbye to all that. 1929, Garden City NY 1957 (rev).

MacManus, L. White light and flame: memories of the Irish literary revival and the Anglo-Irish war. Dublin 1929.

Meynell, V. Alice Meynell: a memoir. 1929.
— (ed). Friends of a lifetime: letters to Sydney Carlyle Cockerell. 1940.

Meynell, V. Francis Thompson and Wilfred Meynell: a memoir. 1952.

Anderson, M. My thirty years' war: an autobiography. New York 1930.
— The fiery fountains. New York 1951.

Dixon, E. H. 'As I knew them': sketches of people I have met on the way. 1930.

Golding, L. Adventures in living dangerously. 1930.

Hardy, F. E. The later years of Thomas Hardy, 1892–1928. 1930. Rptd in the Life of Thomas Hardy, 1840–1928, 1962. Mainly by Hardy.

Archer, C. William Archer: life, work and friendships. 1931.

Gerhardi, W. Memories of a polyglot. 1931.

MacCarthy, D. Portraits. 1931.
— Memories. 1953.

MacColl, D. S. Confessions of a keeper. 1931.

Rhys, E. Everyman remembers. 1931.
— Wales England wed: an autobiography. 1940.

Rothenstein, W. Men and memories: recollections (1872–1938). 3 vols 1931–9.

Scott Moncrieff, C. K. Memories and letters. Ed J. M. Scott Moncrieff and L. W. Lunn 1931.

Thirkell, A. Three houses. 1931.

Waugh, Arthur. One man's road: being a picture of life in a passing generation. 1931.

Whyte, F. A bachelor's London (1889–1914). 1931.

Atherton, G. F. Adventures of a novelist. New York 1932.

Benson, E. F. As we are. 1932.
— Final edition. 1940.

Del Re, A. Georgian reminiscences. Stud in Eng Lit (Tokyo) 12 1932, 14 1934.

Drinkwater, J. Discovery: being the second book of an autobiography 1897–1913. 1932.

Hamnett, N. Laughing torso: reminiscences. 1932.
— Is she a lady?: a problem in autobiography. 1955.

Lucas, E. V. Reading, writing and remembering: a literary record. 1932.

Newbolt, H. My world as in my time: memoirs 1862–1932. 1932.

'Roberts, Michael' (W. E. Roberts). Meetings with some men of letters. Queen's Quart 39 1932.

Brittain, V. Testament of youth: an autobiographical study of the years 1900–25. 1933.
— Testament of experience: an autobiographical story of the years 1925–50. 1957.

Compton-Rickett, A. I look back: memories of fifty years. 1933.

— Portraits and personalities. 1937.

Douglas, N. Looking back: an autobiographical excursion. 2 vols 1933.

— Late harvest. 1946.

Fausset, H. I'A. A modern prelude. 1933.

Hamilton, C. People worth talking about. New York 1933.

Jameson, M. S. No time like the present. 1933.

— Journey from the north: autobiography. 2 vols 1969, 70.

Luhan, M. D. Intimate memories. 4 vols New York [1933–7].

MacCarthy, L. Myself and my friends. 1933.

Mackenzie, C. Literature in my time. 1933.

— My life and times: octave 1–10. 1963–71.

Sharp, E. Unfinished adventure. 1933.

Stein, G. The autobiography of Alice B. Toklas. New York 1933.

Sutro, A. Celebrities and simple souls. 1933.

Campbell, R. Broken record: reminiscences. 1934.

— Light on a dark horse: an autobiography 1901–35. 1951.

Inge, W. R. Vale: autobiographical reflections. 1934.

Lawrence, F. 'Not I but the wind'. New York 1934, Berlin 1936 (German version, enlarged). An account of the author's life with D. H. Lawrence.

— The memoirs and correspondence. Ed E. W. Tedlock 1961.

Powys, J. C. Autobiography. 1934.

Richards, G. Author hunting by an old literary sportsman: memories of years spent mainly in publishing, 1897–1925. 1934, 1960 (rev).

Rittenhouse, J. B. My house of life: an autobiography. Boston 1934.

Wells, H. G. Experiment in autobiography: discoveries and conclusions of a very ordinary brain. 2 vols 1934.

Wharton, E. A backward glance. New York 1934.

Agate, J. Ego (Ego 2–9): the autobiography of Agate. 9 pts 1935–48.

Beginnings. 1935. Autobiographical essays by A. Alington and other writers of fiction. Ed L. A. G. Strong.

Blathwayt, R. Looking down the years. 1935.

'Eglinton, John' (W. K. Magee). Irish literary portraits. 1935.

— A memoir of A.E. [George William Russell]. 1937.

Fay, W. G. and C. Carswell. The Fays of the Abbey Theatre: an autobiographical record. 1935.

Goldring, D. Odd man out: the autobiography of a propaganda novelist. 1935.

— South lodge: reminiscences of Violet Hunt, Ford Madox Ford and the English Review circle. 1943.

— The nineteen-twenties: a general survey and some personal memories. 1945.

— Life interests. 1948.

Harrap, G. G. Some memories: 1901–1935. 1935.

Squire, J. C. Reflections and memories. 1935.

— The honeysuckle and the bee: autobiographical reminiscences. 1937.

Bloomfield, P. Half the battle: Harrow–Oxford–London. 1936.

Chesterton, G. K. Autobiography. 1936.

Sibley, C. Barrie and his contemporaries: cameo portraits of ten living authors. Webster Groves, Mo 1936.

Smith, L. P. Reperusals and re-collections. 1936.

— Unforgotten years. 1938.

— Tavistock Square. Orion 2 1945.

— A portrait of Logan Pearsall Smith: drawn from his letters and diaries by J. Russell. 1950.

Swinnerton, F. A. Swinnerton: an autobiography. Garden City NY 1936.

— Authors I never met. 1956. On Conrad, Norman Douglas, D. H. Lawrence et al.

— Background with chorus: a footnote to changes in English literary fashion between 1901 and 1917. 1956.

— Figures in the foreground: literary reminiscences 1917–40. 1963.

Van Doren, C. Three worlds. New York 1936.

Birrell, A. Things past redress. [1937].

Coward, N. Present indicative. 1937.

— Future indefinite. 1954.

Fletcher, J. G. Life is my song. New York 1937.

Glyn, E. Romantic adventure. 1937.

Gogarty, O. St J. As I was going down Sackville Street: a phantasy in fact. 1937.

— It isn't this time of year at all!: an unpremeditated autobiography. Garden City NY 1954.

Housman, L. The unexpected years. 1937.

Jepson, E. Memories of an Edwardian and neo-Georgian. 1937, 1938 (rev).

Jerrold, D. Georgian adventure. 1937.

Kaye-Smith, S. Three ways home. 1937.

— All the books of my life: a bibliobiography. 1956.

Kipling, R. Something of myself. 1937.

Lewis, W. Blasting and bombardiering. 1937, 1967 (with additional chs).

— Rude assignment: a narrative of my career up-to-date. 1950.

Mais, S. P. B. All the days of my life. 1937.

— Buffets and rewards: an autobiographical record 1937–51. 1952.

— The happiest days of my life. 1953.

More, P. E. Pages from an Oxford diary. Princeton 1937.

Nevinson, C. R. W. Paint and prejudice. 1937.

Priestley, J. B. Midnight on the desert: a chapter of autobiography. 1937.

— Rain upon Godshill: a further chapter of autobiography. 1939.

— Margin released: a writer's reminiscences and reflections. 1962.

John Cornford: a memoir. Ed P. Sloan 1938.

Dunsany, Lord. Patches of sunlight. 1938.

Hilton, J. To you, Mr Chips. 1938. Includes a ch of autobiography.

Isherwood, C. Lions and shadows: an education in the twenties. 1938.

Leslie, S. The film of memory. 1938.

— Long shadows: a book of reminiscences. 1966.

McAlmon, R. Being geniuses together: an autobiography. 1938, New York 1968 (rev with K. Boyle as Being geniuses together 1920–1930).

Maugham, W. S. The summing up. 1938.

— A writer's notebook. 1949. Rptd 1954, with The summing up, as The partial view.

Monroe, H. A poet's life: seventy years in a changing world. New York 1938.

Mottram, R. H. Autobiography with a difference. 1938.

Olivier, E. Without knowing Mr Walkley: personal memories. 1938.

Robinson, L. Three homes. 1938. With T. Robinson and N. Dorman.

— Curtain up: an autobiography. 1942.

Sassoon, S. The old century and seven more years. 1938.

— The weald of youth. 1942.

— Siegfried's journey 1916–1920. 1945.

Sitwell, O. Those were the days. 1938.

— Left hand, right hand!: an autobiography. 5 vols Boston 1944–50.

Van Druten, J. The way to the present: a personal record. 1938.

— Playwright at work. New York 1953.

— The widening circle. 1957.

Wolfe, H. The upward anguish. 1938.

'Bowen, Marjorie' (G. M. V. Campbell). The debate continues: being the autobiography of Marjorie Bowen. 1939.

Bridie, J. One way of living. 1939.

Collingwood, R. G. An autobiography. 1939.

Marsh, E. H. A number of people. 1939. *See also* C. Hassall, Edward Marsh, patron of the arts: a biography, 1959.

Milne, A. A. It's too late now: the autobiography of a writer. 1939.

Phelps, W. L. Autobiography, with letters. New York 1939.

Ricketts, C. Self-portrait. Ed C. Lewis 1939.

Shaw, G. B. Shaw gives himself away: an autobiographical miscellany. Newtown 1939.

— Sixteen self sketches. 1949.

Bain, J. S. A bookseller looks back. 1940.

Bentley, E. C. Those days: an autobiography. 1940.

Buchan, J. Memory hold-the-door. 1940, Boston 1940 (as Pilgrim's way).

Epstein, J. Let there be sculpture. 1940, 1955 (rev, as Epstein: an autobiography).

Gill, E. Autobiography. 1940.

'Green, Henry' (H. V. Yorke). Pack my bag: a self-portrait. 1940.

Muir, E. The story and the fable. 1940, 1954 (rev and enlarged as An autobiography).

Read, H. Annals of innocence and experience. 1940, 1946 (rev).

— The contrary experience: autobiographies. 1963.

Vulliamy, C. E. Calico pie: an autobiography. 1940.

Aldington, R. Life for life's sake: a book of reminiscences. New York 1941.

— Pinorman: personal recollections of Norman Douglas, Pino Orioli and Charles Prentice. 1954.

Bowen, S. Drawn from life: reminiscences. 1941.

Emmons, R. The life and opinions of Walter Richard Sickert. 1941.

Linklater, E. The man on my back: an autobiography. 1941.

— A year of space: a chapter in autobiography. 1953.

Nicholson, H. Half my days and nights: autobiography of a reporter. 1941.

Oppenheim, E. P. The pool of memory. 1941.

Retinger, J. H. Conrad and his contemporaries: souvenirs. 1941.

Starkie, E. A lady's child. 1941.

Mackail, D. G. Life with Topsy. 1942.

Spring, H. In the meantime. 1942.

Woodward, E. L. Short journey. 1942.

Coulton, G. G. Fourscore years: an autobiography. Cambridge 1943.

'MacDiarmid, Hugh' (C. M. Grieve). Lucky poet: a self-study in literature and political ideas, being the autobiography of H. MacDiarmid. 1943.

— The company I've kept. 1966.

Plomer, W. Double lives: an autobiography. 1943.

— At home: memoirs. 1958.

Welch, D. Maiden voyage. 1943.

— The Denton Welch journals. Ed J. Brooke 1952.

Hamilton, M. A. Remembering my good friends. 1944.

'Q' (A. Quiller-Couch). Memories and opinions: an unfinished autobiography. Ed S. C. Roberts, Cambridge 1944.

Sadleir, M. Things past. 1944.

Santayana, G. Persons and places. 3 vols New York 1944-53.

— The letters of Santayana, ed D. Cory, New York 1955.

Hutchinson, R. C. Interim. 1945.

Sackville-West, E. Sketches for an autobiography. Orion 3 1945, 4 1947.

Woolf, L. Memoirs of an elderly man. Orion 1 1945.

— Sowing, 1880-1904; Growing, 1904-11; Beginning again, 1911-18; Downhill all the way, 1919-39; The journey not the arrival matters, 1939-69, 5 vols 1960-9. Autobiography.

Young, E. Flowering dusk: things remembered accurately and inaccurately about Yeats, Mabel Dodge Luhan [et al]. New York 1945.

Burke, T. Son of London. 1946.

Gibbs, P. The pageant of the years. 1946.

— Crowded company. 1949.

Lowndes, M. A. B. The merry wives of Westminster. 1946.

— A passing world. 1948.

Cardus, N. Autobiography. 1947.

— Second innings. 1950.

Colum, M. M. Life and the dream. Garden City NY 1947.

Hichens, R. S. Yesterday. 1947.

Hirst, F. W. In the golden days. 1947.

Orczy, E. Links in the chain of life. 1947.

Putnam, S. Paris was our mistress: memoirs of a lost and found generation. New York 1947.

Acton, H. Memoirs of an aesthete. 1948.

— More memoirs of an aesthete. 1970.

Benn, E. Happier days: recollections and reflections. 1949.

Cole, M. I. Growing up into revolution. 1949.

Keynes, J. M. My early beliefs. In his Two memoirs, 1949.

Nichols, B. All I could never be: some recollections. 1949.

— Laughter on the stairs. 1953.

— The sweet and twenties. 1958.

Trevelyan, G. M. An autobiography and other essays. 1949.

Asquith, C. M. E. Haply I may remember. 1950.

— Remember and be glad. 1952.

— Diaries, 1915-18. Ed E. M. Hartley 1968.

Bolitho, H. A biographer's notebook. 1950.

Carswell, C. Lying awake: an unfinished autobiography with other posthumous papers. Ed J. Carswell 1950.

Grigson, G. The crest on the silver: an autobiography. 1950.

— A man of the thirties. World Rev Oct 1951.

Herbert, A. P. Independent member. 1950.

Joyce, S. Recollections of James Joyce. New York 1950.

— My brother's keeper. Ed R. Ellmann 1958.

Stein, L. Journey into the self: being the letters, journals and papers of Leo Stein. Ed E. Fuller, New York 1950.

Toklas, A. B. They who came to Paris to write. New York Times Book Rev 6 Aug 1950.

— What is remembered. 1963.

Clark, B. H. Intimate portraits. New York 1951. On Galsworthy et al.

Phillpotts, E. From the angle of 88. 1951.

Spender, S. World within world. 1951.

— It began at Oxford. New York Times Book Rev 13 March 1955.

Williams, W. C. Autobiography. New York 1951.

— Selected letters. Ed J. C. Thirlwall, New York 1957.

Aiken, C. Ushant: an essay. New York 1952.

Croft-Cooke, R. The life for me. 1952; and subsequent autobiographical volumes.

Cronin, A. J. Adventures in two worlds. 1952.

Gollancz, V. My dear Timothy: an autobiographical letter to his grandson. 1952.

— More for Timothy. 1953.

John, A. Chiaroscuro: fragments of autobiography. 1952.

— Finishing touches. Ed D. George 1964.

Koestler, A. Arrow in the blue; The invisible writing. 2 vols 1952-4. Autobiography.

Masefield, J. So long to learn: chapters of an autobiography. 1952.

— Grace before ploughing: fragments of autobiography. 1966.

Robert Ross, friend of friends: letters to Robert Ross, art critic and writer. Ed M. Ross 1952.

Cooper, D. Old men forget: the autobiography of Duff Cooper. 1953.

Crosby, C. The passionate years. New York 1953.

Faber, G. Forty years back: a fragment of autobiography. Bookseller 10, 17 Jan 1953.

Garnett, D. The golden echo; The flowers of the forest; The familiar faces. 3 vols 1953-62. Autobiography.

— Some writers I have known: Galsworthy, Forster, Moore and Wells. Texas Quart 4 1961.

Le Gallienne, E. With a quiet heart: an autobiography. New York 1953.

Maclaren-Ross, J. The weeping and the laughter: a chapter of autobiography. 1953.
— Memoirs of the forties. 1965.

'Marlow, Louis' (L. U. Wilkinson). Seven friends. 1953. Includes F. Harris, Crowley, the Powys brothers, Maugham.

Noyes, A. Two worlds for memory. 1953.

Robertson, G. Letters. Ed K. Preston 1953.

Stern, G. B. A name to conjure with. 1953.
— And did he stop and speak to you? 1957. On Beerbohm, Betjeman, S. Kaye-Smith, Sherriff, Maugham et al.

Tomlinson, H. M. A mingled yarn: autobiographical sketches. 1953.

Woolf, V. A writer's diary. Ed L. Woolf 1953.

Brooks, V. W. Scenes and portraits: memories of childhood and youth. New York 1954.
— Days of the Phoenix: the nineteen-twenties I remember. New York 1957.

Brown, I. The way of my world. 1954.

Meynell, E. Small talk in Sussex. 1954.

Murray, G. G. I remember. Listener 25 Feb, 4, 11 March 1954.
— Gilbert Murray: an unfinished autobiography. Ed J. Smith and A. Toynbee 1960.

'Shute, Nevil' (N. S. Norway). Slide rule: the autobiography of an engineer. 1954.

Toynbee, P. Friends apart: a memoir of Esmond Romilly and Jasper Ridley in the thirties. 1954.

'Bell, Neil' (S. Southwold). My writing life. 1955 [1956].

Church, R. Over the bridge; The golden sovereign. 2 vols 1955–7. Autobiography.
— The voyage home. 1964.

Lehmann, J. The whispering gallery; I am my brother; The ample proposition. 3 vols 1955–66. Autobiography.
— (ed). Coming to London. 1957. By William Plomer et al.

Lewis, C. S. Surprised by joy: the shape of my early life. 1955.

Abercrombie, C. Memories of a poet's wife. Listener 15 Nov 1956.

Bell, C. Old friends: personal recollections. 1956.

Cockburn, C. In time of trouble. 1956, New York 1956 (as A discord of trumpets).
— Crossing the line. 1958.

O'Casey, S. Mirror in my house: autobiographies. 2 vols New York 1956.

Powys, L. C. Still the joy of it. 1956.

Russell, B. Portraits from memory and other essays. 1956. On Wells, Conrad, Lawrence, Orwell et al.
— Autobiography. 3 vols 1967–9.

Simon, O. Printer and playground: an autobiography. 1956.

Wodehouse, P. G. America, I like you. New York 1956, London 1957 (as Over seventy: an autobiography with digressions).

Coppard, A. E. It's me, o Lord! 1957.

Craig, E. G. Index to the story of my days: some memoirs, 1872–1907. 1957.

Eberhart, R. Memory of meeting Yeats, AE, Gogarty, James Stephens. Literary Rev 1 1957.

Sieveking, L. The eye of the beholder. 1957.

Thomas, C. Leftover life to kill. 1957.

Travers, B. Vale of laughter: an autobiography. 1957.

Trevelyan, J. Indigo days. 1957.

Cooper, Diana. The rainbow comes and goes; The light of common day; Trumpets from the steep. 3 vols 1958–60.

Ferguson, R. We were amused. 1958.

O'Connor, P. Memoirs of a public baby. 1958.

Beach, S. Shakespeare and Company. New York 1959.

Dickson, L. The ante-room. 1959.

Selver, P. Orage and the 'New Age' circle: reminiscences and reflections. 1959.

Bartlett, V. And now, tomorrow. 1960.

Day Lewis C. The buried day. 1960.

Heppenstall, R. Four absentees. 1960. Dylan Thomas, Orwell, Gill, J. M. Murry.
— The intellectual part. 1963.

Newman, B. Speaking from memory. 1960.

Patmore, D. Private history: an autobiography. 1960.

Rees, G. A bundle of sensations: sketches in autobiography. 1960.

Unwin, S. The truth about a publisher. 1960.

Christiansen, A. Headlines all my life. 1961.

'O'Connor, Frank' (M. F. O'Donovan). An only child. 1961.

Strong, L. A. G. Green memory. 1961. Autobiography to 1924.

Bentley, P. O dreams, o destinations: an autobiography. 1962.

Bottome, P. The goal. 1962.

Brenan, G. A life of one's own: childhood and youth. 1962.

'Bryher' (A. W. Ellerman). The heart to Artemis: a writer's memoirs. 1963.

Durrell, L. and H. Miller. A private correspondence. Ed G. Wickes, New York 1963.

Green, R. L. Authors and places. 1963.

Ottoline: early memoirs of Lady Ottoline Morrell. Ed R. Gathorne-Hardy 1963.

Rees, R. A theory of my time. 1963.

Warner, S. T. Sketches from nature. Wells 1963.

Duncan, R. All men are islands: an autobiography. 1964.

Frost, R. Selected letters. Ed L. Thompson, New York 1964.

O'Faolain, S. Vive moi! an autobiography. Boston 1964.

Waugh, E. A little learning: the first volume of an autobiography. 1964.

Dickinson, P. The good minute: an autobiographical study. 1965.

Frewin, L. (ed). Parnassus near Piccadilly—an anthology: the Café Royal centenary book. 1965.

Hamilton, G. R. Rapids of time: sketches from the past. 1965.

Knight, L. The magic of a line: autobiography. 1965.

Liddell Hart, B. H. Memoirs. 2 vols 1965.

MacNeice, L. The strings are false: an unfinished autobiography. 1965.

Rothenstein, J. Summer's lease, 1901–38; Brave day, hideous night; Time's thievish progress. 3 vols 1965–70. Autobiography.

Sitwell, E. Taken care of: an autobiography. 1965.

Skelton, R. and D. R. Clark (ed). Irish renaissance: a gathering of essays, memoirs and letters from the Massachusetts Review. Dublin 1965.

Sparrow, J. Confessions of an eccentric. 1965.

Willey, B. Spots of time: a retrospect of the years 1897–1920; Cambridge and other memories, 1920–53. 2 vols 1965–8.

Du Maurier, A. Old maids remember. 1966.

Martin, K. Father figures, 1897–1931; Editor, 1931–45. 2 vols 1966–8. Autobiography.

Maugham, R. Somerset and all the Maughams. 1966.

Nicolson, H. Diaries and letters. Ed N. Nicolson 3 vols 1966–8.

Sewell, B. My dear time's waste. Aylesford 1966. On Gill, Chesterton, Belloc.

Steen, M. Looking glass: an autobiography. 1966.

Forester, C. S. Long before forty. 1967. Autobiography.

Greenwood, W. There was a time. 1967.

Roberts, C. E. M. The growing boy, 1892–1908; The years of promise, 1908–19; The bright twenties, 1920–9. 3 vols 1967–70. Autobiography.

Toynbee, A. Acquaintances. 1967.
— Experiences. 1969.

Clarke, A. A penny in the clouds: more memories of Ireland and England. 1968.

Fielding, D. W. L. Emerald and Nancy: Lady Cunard and her daughter. 1968.

Brian Howard: portrait of a failure. Ed M.-J. Lancaster 1968.

Lindsay, J. Meetings with poets: memories of Dylan Thomas, Edith Sitwell, Louis Aragon [et al]. 1968.

Patmore, B. My friends when young: memoirs. Ed D. Patmore 1968.

Bagnold, E. Autobiography. 1969.

Bates, H. E. The vanished world: an autobiography. 1969–.

Davies, R. Print of a hare's foot: an autobiographical beginning. 1969.

Pinto, V. de S. The city that shone: an autobiography. 1969.

Wall, B. Headlong into change: an autobiography and a memoir of ideas since the thirties. 1969.

J.B.H.

(4) RELATIONS WITH OTHER LITERATURES

See also the sections dealing with Literary Relations with the Continent in earlier vols, and the sections devoted to General Works under Poetry, The Novel, etc, below.

This section is confined to secondary material dealing explicitly with literary relations. (1) For discussions of 'intellectual' or 'background' influences emanating from abroad or shared with foreign literatures (e.g. F. J. Hoffman, Freudianism and the literary mind, 1945, or R. Ellmann's and C. Feidelson's anthology, The modern tradition: backgrounds of modern literature, 1965), see Literary Histories etc, above, and under Poetry, The Novel, etc, below. (2) Likewise for discussions of a foreign country as a theme in twentieth-century English literature, e.g. G. D. Killam, Africa in English fiction 1874–1939, 1968, see the same Literary Histories, Poetry etc. (3) The considerable mass of primary material in this period, such as trns of individual works, or anthologies, has been excluded from this volume of New CBEL and can be traced through the Encyclopedia of world literature in the 20th century, *ed W. B. Fleischmann, New York 1967– and* The literatures of the world in English translation, *New York 1967–; in the* Index translationum *nos 1–30, 1932–40, new ser 1948–; and in the various national bibliographies listed in L.-N. Malclès,* Les sources du travail bibliographique *tome 1, Geneva and Lille 1950, supplemented by R. L. Collison,* Bibliographical services around the world 1950–9, *Paris 1961 (suppl 1960–4 by P. Avicenne, Paris 1969); and in the specialized bibliographies listed below (anthologies can also be traced through the BM Subject Index). Discussions of the critical reception of certain widely influential authors' works in trn (e.g. H. Muchnic, Dostoevsky's English reputation 1881–1936, 1939) are, included.*

Discussions of the relations between individual English authors of the period and foreign literatures are normally excluded since they are to be found in the entry for the particular author in the main body of the volume.

For the few studies of relations with other literatures in general that have appeared to date, see W. P. Friederich, Realism-symbolism, in his Outline of comparative literature, *Chapel Hill 1954 (a brief sketch); J. M. Cohen, Poetry of this age 1908–1958, 1960, 1966 (rev to 1965); M. Hamburger, The truth of poetry: tensions in modern poetry from Baudelaire to the 1960's, [1969], and the pioneering works mentioned in the last, particularly C. M. Bowra, The heritage of symbolism, 1943 and The creative experiment, 1949, and E. Wilson, Axel's castle: a study in the imaginative literature of 1870–1930, New York 1931. See also the essays by H. Levin, What was modernism? and L. Trilling, The modern element in modern literature, noted in Ellmann and Feidelson, op cit, and ptd in* Varieties of literary experience, *ed S. Burnshaw, New York 1962.*

See also F. Baldensperger and W. P. Friederich, Bibliography of comparative literature, *Chapel Hill 1950, and the annual bibliographies in the* Yearbook of Comparative and General Literature *(Chapel Hill 1952–60; Bloomington 1961–) and in* PMLA.

European Literatures

French

Horn-Monval, M. Répertoire bibliographique des traductions et adaptations françaises du théâtre étranger du xve siècle à nos jours: tome 5, théâtre anglais, théâtre américain, Paris 1963.

Bizet, R. L'influence anglais sur la littérature contemporaine. Anglo-French Rev 4 1920.

Taupin, R. L'influence du symbolisme français. Paris 1929.

Holmes, U. T. The French novel in English translation. Chapel Hill 1930.

Hughes, G. The origins of imagism. In his Imagism and the imagists, Stanford 1931.

Peyre, H. The influence of contemporary French literature in the world. Sewanee Rev 48 1940.

Cazamian, L. Symbolisme et poésie: l'exemple anglais. Paris 1947.

Temple, R. Z. The critic's alchemy: a study of the introduction of French symbolism into England. New York 1953.

Starkie, E. From Gautier to Eliot: the influence of France on English literature 1851–1939. 1960.

Bédouin, J-L. Vingt ans de surréalisme 1939–1959. Paris 1961.

Albérès, R-M. Aux sources du 'nouveau roman': l'impressionisme anglais. Revue de Paris 69 1962.

Matthews, J. H. Surrealism and England. Comparative Lit Stud 1 1964.

Campos, C. The view of France from Arnold to Bloomsbury. 1965.

Turquet-Milnes, G. The influence of Baudelaire in France and England. 1913.

Starkie, E. Baudelaire et l'Angleterre. Table Ronde no 232 1967.

Engstrom, A. G. The changing accent in English and American criticism of Baudelaire. South Atlantic Bull 33 1968.

Taupin, R. The example of Rémy de Gourmont. Criterion 10 1931.

Burne, G. S. Rémy de Gourmont: his ideas and influence in England and America. Carbondale 1963.

German

Morgan, B. Q. A bibliography of German literature in translation. Madison 1922, Stanford 1938 (rev, with suppl 1928–35); suppl 1928–55, New York 1965.

Anglo-German literary bibliography 1933–. Annually in JEGP 1935–.

Schloesser, A. Die englische Literatur in Deutschland von 1895 bis 1934; mit einer vollständigen Bibliographie der deutschen Übersetzungen und der im deutschen Sprachgebiet erschienenen englischen Ausgaben. 1937.

Mönnig, R. Amerika und England im deutschen, österreichischen und schweizerischen Schrifttum der Jahre 1945–9: eine Bibliographie. Stuttgart 1951.

Price, L. M. In his English literature in Germany, below.

Sternfeld, W. Deutsche Exil-Literatur 1933–45. Heidelberg 1962. See also an exhibition catalogue, Exil-Literatur 1933–45, Frankfurt 1965. Includes literature written in England or in collaboration with English authors.

Galinsky, H. Deutsches Schrifttum der Gegenwart in der englischen Kritik der Nachkriegszeit 1919–35. Munich 1938.

Price, L. M. In his English literature in Germany, Berkeley 1953, Berne and Munich 1961 (enlarged and tr, as Die Aufnahme englischer Literatur in Deutschland 1500–1960).

Forster, L. England und die deutsche Literatur. Deutsche Akademie für Sprache und Dichtung, Jahrbuch 1958/59, 1959.

Höllerer, W. Deutsche Lyrik in der Mitte des 20. Jahrhunderts und einige Verbindungslinien zur französischen und englischen Lyrik. In Comparative literature: proceedings of the Second Congress of the Comparative Literature Association vol 2, ed W. P. Friederich, Chapel Hill 1959.

Oppel, H. Der Einfluss der englischen Literatur auf die deutsche. In Deutsche Philologie im Aufriss vol 3, ed W. Stammler, Berlin 1962 (rev).

Gray, R. D. English resistance to German literature from Coleridge to D. H. Lawrence. In his German tradition in literature 1871–1945, Cambridge 1965.

Haines, G. Professionalization of the humanistic studies. In his Essays on German influence upon English education and science 1850–1919, New London Conn 1969.

Neumeyer, P. F. Kafka and England. German Quart 40 1967.

Italian

Bianchi, R. In his La poetica dell'imagismo, Milan 1965. Brief discussion of the relations between Imagism and Marinetti's Futurism.

Ferretti, L. Carducci e la letteratura inglese. Milano 1927.

Scalia, S. E. Carducci et la critique Anglo-Saxonne. Revue de Littérature Comparée 15 1935.

— Carducci: his critics and translators in England and America 1881–1932. New York 1937.

Fucilla, J. G. and J. M. Carrière. D'Annunzio abroad: a bibliographical essay. 2 vols New York 1935–7.

Illiano, A. Pirandello in England and the United States: a chronological list of criticism. BNYPL 71 1967.

Guidi, A. Pirandello in Inghilterra e negli Stati Uniti. Lettere Italiane 20 1968.

Frampton, M. The Anglo-American critical reception of Svevo's fiction. In Essays on Italo Svevo, ed T. F. Staley, Tulsa 1969.

Scandinavian

Allen, R. B. Bibliography of translations and summaries; General bibliography of Icelandic studies; Bibliography of novels. In his Old Icelandic sources in the English novel, Philadelphia 1933.

Øksnevad, R. Nittende og tyvende århundre. In his Det Britiske samvelde og Eire i norsk litteratur: en bibliografi, Oslo 1949.

Bredsdorff, E. Danish literature in English translation. Copenhagen 1950.

Fæhn, I. and H. Haave. Norwegian literature in English translation since 1742. In E. Grönland, Norway in English, Oslo 1961.

Haltsonen, S. Suomalaista kaunokirjallisuutta vierailla kielillä. Helsinki 1961.

Gustafson, E. A list of translations of Swedish literature into English. Stockholm 1962.

Franc, M. A. Ibsen in England. Boston 1919.

Burchardt, C. Ibsen in England. Norwegian Life & Lit 1920.

Qvamme, N. Ibsen og det engelske teater. Edda 42 1942.

Wright, H. G. Icelandic themes in recent literature; Strindberg and England. In his Studies in Anglo-Scandinavian literary relations, Bangor 1919.

— Strindberg in England. TLS 30 Jan 1930.

Morgan, M. M. Strindberg and the English theatre. Modern Drama 7 1964–5.

Slavonic and East European

Zhanteeva, D. G. and M. S. Morshchiner. Sovremennye angliiskie i amerikanskie pisateli. Moscow 1945. Includes a brief list of trns and critical material in Russian.

Pǎduraru, O. Anglo-Roumanian and Roumanian-English bibliography. Bucharest 1946.

Lewanski, R. C. The Slavic literatures. New York 1967 (The literatures of the world in English translation: a bibliography, vol 2).

Maciuszko, J. The Polish short story in English: a guide and critical bibliography. Detroit 1968.

Czigány, M. Hungarian literature in English translation published in Great Britain 1830–1968: a bibliography. 1969.

Brewster, D. The Russian soul: an English literary pattern. Amer Scholar 17 1948.

— East-West passage: a study in literary relationships. 1954.

Phelps, G. Russian realism and English fiction. Cambridge Jnl 3 1950.

— The Russian novel in English fiction. 1956.

Orel, H. English critics and the Russian novel 1850–1917. Slavonic and East European Rev 33 1955.

Davie, D. (ed). Russian literature and modern English fiction: a collection of critical essays. Chicago 1965.

Heifetz, A. Chekhov in English: a list of works by and about him. New York 1949; suppl 1949–60 by R. Yachnin, 1960.

Meister, C. W. Chekhov's reception in England and America. Amer Slavic & East European Rev 12 1953.

Brewster, D. Chekhov in America and England. Masses & Mainstream 7 1954.

Sereševskaya, M. A. Angliyskiye pisateli i kritiki o Chekhove. In Literaturnoye nasledstvo 68, Moscow and Leningrad 1960.

Erlich, V. (ed). Chekhov and western European drama: a symposium. Yearbook of Comparative & General Lit 12 1963.

Subbotina, K. Tvorchestvo A. P. Chekhova v otsenke angliyskoy kritiki 1910–1920-kh godov. Russkaya Literatura no 2 1964.

Neuschaffer, W. Dostojewskijs Einfluss auf den englischen Roman. Heidelberg 1935.

Muchnic, H. Dostoevsky's English reputation 1881–1936. Northampton Mass 1939.

Colemann, M. M. Mickiewicz in English 1827–1955. Cambridge 1954.

Yassukovitch, A. Tolstoy in English 1878–1929. BNYPL 33 1929.

Zinner, E. P. Tolstoy i angliyskaya realisticheskaya drama kontsa xix nachala xx stoletiya. Uchonyye Zapiski Irkutskogo Pedagogicheskogo Instituta no 5 1940.

— Tvorchestvo Tolstogo i angliyskaya realisticheskaya literatura kontsa xix nachala xx stoletiya. Irkutsk 1961.

Gettmann, R. A. Turgenev in England and America. Urbana 1941. With list of trns and criticism.

Kain, R. M. The literary reputation of Turgenev in England and America 1867–1906. Madison Quart 2 1942.

Davie, D. Turgenev in England 1850–1950. In Studies in Russian and Polish literature in honour of Wacław Lednicki, Hague 1962.

Yachnin, R. and D. H. Stam. Turgenev in English: a checklist of works by and about him, New York 1962.

Brown, E. J. Zamjatin and English literature. In American contributions to the Fifth International Congress of Slavists, Hague 1963. E.D.

American Literature

Bruce, P. A. American feeling toward England. Westminster Rev 154 1900.

British men of letters through American glasses. Pall Mall Gazette 24 Sept 1902.

Mowbray, J. D. Has America outgrown Matthew Arnold? Critic 40 1902.

Rhodes, H. G. The American invasion of the London stage. Cosmopolitan 33 1902.

Smalley, G. W. American authors abroad. Munsey's Mag 26 1902.

Brett, G. P. What the American people are reading. Outlook 75 1903.

Canfield, J. H. What are college students reading? Outlook 74 1903.

Higginson, T. W. English and American cousins. Atlantic Monthly 93 1904.

Roberts, C. American books in England. World's Work 8 1904.

Austin, L. F. Points of view. 1906.

Maurice, A. B. The American invasion. Bookman (New York) 27 1908.

Atherton, G. The American novel in England. Bookman (New York) 30 1910.

Hobson, J. A. A modern outlook: studies of English and American tendencies. 1910.

Bourne, R. S. Our cultural humility. Atlantic Monthly 114 1914.

Nicholson, M. The open season for American novelists. Atlantic Monthly 116 1915.

Boyd, E. Ireland's literary renaissance. New York 1916, 1922 (rev).

— Literary internationalism. Virginia Quart Rev 3 1927.

Cunningham, W. English influence in the United States. New York 1916.

Grasty, C. H. British and American newspapers. Atlantic Monthly 124 1919.

O'Sullivan, V. America and English literary tradition. Living Age 303 1919.

Young English and American writers. Literary Digest 63 1919.

Murry, J. M. America and England: a literary comparison. New Republic 24 1920.

Gosse, E. An intellectual entente. Forum 65 1921.

Young American abroad. Literary Rev 22 1921.

English opinions of American poetry. Living Age 20 May 1922.

Gibbs, A. H. English critics and American books. TLS 12 Jan 1922.

Leacock, S. Exporting humor to England. Harper's Mag 4 1922.

Ratcliffe, S. K. The intellectual reaction in America. Contemporary Rev 122 1922.

— English lecturers in America. Fortnightly Rev 138 1935.

Arvin, N. American poetry since 1900. Freeman 8 1923.

Quinn, A. H. National ideals in the drama 1922–3. Scribner's Mag 74 1923.

A note on the modern American novel. Nation-Athenaeum 38 1925.

Woolf, V. American fiction. Saturday Rev of Lit 1 Aug 1925.

Beach, J. W. English speech and American masters. In his Outlook for American prose, Chicago 1926.

Priestley, J. B. Contemporary American fiction as an English critic sees it. Harper's Mag 152 1926.

Strachey, J. St L. American soundings. [1926].

Hall, R. American literature in England. Bookman (New York) 65 1927.

Shipp, H. Home products and foreign affairs. Eng Rev 44 1927.

Agate, J. Your theatre in our country: an English critic's cheerful criticism. Century Mag 117 1928.

Measuring our culture by Europe's. Literary Digest 107 1929.

Anderson, M. My thirty years' war. 1930.

Adams, J. T. Americans abroad. New York Times Mag 21 June 1931.

As others see us. Living Age 341 1931.

Hughes, G. Imagism and the Imagists: a study in modern poetry. Stanford 1931.

Warner, O. How American books strike an English reader. Publishers' Weekly 7 Jan 1933.

Blodgett, H. Walt Whitman in England. Ithaca 1934.

Speare, M. E. The political novel: its development in England and America. New York 1934.

Brussel, I. R. Anglo-American first editions. 2 vols New York 1935–6. Pt 1, East to West 1826–1900; pt 2, West to East 1786–1936.

Charpentier, J. Humour anglais et humour américain. Mercure de France 264 1935.

Cowley, M. Exile's return: a narrative of ideas. New York 1935. Rptd as Exile's return: a literary odyssey of the 1920's, New York 1951.

— American books abroad. In Literary history of the United States, ed R. E. Spiller et al, New York 1946.

— Think back on us: a contemporary chronicle of the 1930's, ed H. D. Piper, Carbondale 1967. Essays mainly from New Republic.

Stearns, H. A street I know. New York 1935.

Brown, I. Broadway in London. Theatre Arts Monthly 20 1936.

Weygandt, C. The time of Yeats: English poetry of today against an American background. New York 1937.

Brown, J. M. English and American tastes. In his Two on the aisle, New York 1938.

Dickson, L. The American novel in England. Publishers' Weekly 29 Oct 1938.

Monroe, H. A poet's life. New York 1938.

Connolly, C. London diary. New Statesman 23 Nov 1939. Compares English and American novelists.

— Comment. Horizon 80 1946.

— Introduction. Horizon 93–4 1947.

— On Englishmen who write American: the main forces in British literature today stem from U.S. life and letters. New York Times Book Rev 18 Dec 1949.

Lehmann-Haupt, H. The book in America. New York 1939, 1951 (rev).

Heindel, R. H. The American impact on Great Britain 1898–1914. Philadelphia 1940.

Cargill, O. Intellectual America: ideas on the march. New York 1941.

Hutcherson, D. R. Poe's reputation in England and America 1850–1909. Amer Lit 14 1942.

Fischer, W Anglo-amerikanische Kultur– und Literaturbeziehungen in neuerer Zeit. Archiv 184 1943.

Wells, H. W. The American way of poetry. New York 1943 (Columbia Studies in American Culture no 13).

Hoffman, F. J. Freudianism American and English. In his Freudianism and the literary mind, Baton Rouge 1945.

Brooks, J. G. American culture abroad. Comparative Lit News Letter 4 1946.

Gregory, H. and M. Zaturenska. A history of American poetry. New York 1946.

Marjasch, S. Der amerikanische Bestseller: sein Wesen und seine Verbreitung unter besonderer Berücksichtigung der Schweiz. Berne 1946. Contains a bibliography of books pbd in Great Britain.

Eugene O'Neill on the London stage. Queen's Quart 54 1947.

Rothman, N. L. Thomas Wolfe and James Joyce: a study in literary influence. In A southern vanguard, ed A. Tate, New York 1947.

Boyd, A. K. The interchange of plays between London and New York 1910–39. New York 1948.

Gröger, E. Der bürgerliche Atomwissenschaftler im englisch–amerikanischen Roman von 1945 bis zur Gegenwart. Zeitschrift für Anglistik und Amerikanistik 16 1948.

Koht, H. The American spirit in Europe: a study of trans-atlantic influences. Philadelphia 1949.

Muray, J. Regards sur les lettres anglo-américaines. Revue Française no 1 1949.

Spender, J. The situation of the American writer. Horizon 19 1949.

— Movements and influences in English literature 1927–52. Books Abroad 27 1953.

— On English and American poetry. Saturday Rev 23 April 1966.

Hart, J. D. The popular book: a history of America's literary taste. New York 1950.

Levin, H. Some European views of contemporary American literature. In The American writer and the European tradition, ed M. Drury and W. Gilman, Minneapolis 1950.

Pound, E. Letters 1907–41. Ed D. D. Paige, New York 1950.

— Letters of Pound to James Joyce. Ed F. Read, New York 1967.

Reynolds, G. F. British and American theater: a personal tour. Western Humanities Rev 4 1950.

Bogan, L. Achievement in American poetry 1900–50. Chicago 1951.

Coffman, S. K. Imagism: a chapter for the history of modern poetry. Norman Oklahoma 1951.

The American threat to British culture. Arena special issue June–July 1951.

Wagenknecht, E. C. Cavalcade of the American novel, from the birth of the nation to the middle of the twentieth century. New York 1952.

West, R. B. The short story in America. Chicago 1952.

Brewster, D. East-West passage: a study in literary relationships. 1954.

Brooks, V. W. Scenes and portraits. New York 1954.

Knoles, G. H. The jazz age revisited: British criticism of American civilization during the 1920's. Stanford 1955.

Peterson, T. Magazines in the twentieth century. Urbana 1956.

Raleigh, J. H. Matthew Arnold and American culture. Berkeley 1957.

Alvarez, A. The shaping spirit: studies in modern English and American poets. 1958. Pbd New York 1958 as Stewards of excellence: studies of modern English and American poets.

Duncan, J. E. The revival of metaphysical poetry: the history of a style, 1800 to the present. Minneapolis [1959].

May, H. F. The end of American innocence: the first years of our own time, 1912–17. New York 1959.

Mott, F. L. In his American journalism: a history 1690–1960. New York [1962].

Allen, W. Tradition and dream: the English and American novel from the twenties to our time. 1964, New York 1964 (as The modern novel in Britain and the United States).

Stock, N. Poet in exile: Ezra Pound. Manchester 1964.

Hobsbaum, P. The growth of English modernism. Wisconsin Stud in Contemporary Lit 6 1965.

Howarth, H. Notes on some figures behind T. S. Eliot. 1965.

— Frost in a period setting. Southern Rev 2 1966.

Hutchins, P. Ezra Pound's Kensington: an exploration 1885–1913. 1965.

Straumann, H. The early reputation of Faulkner's work in Europe: a tentative appraisal. In English Studies Today ser 4, ed I. Cellini and G. Melchiori, Rome 1965.

Wees, W. C. Ezra Pound as a vorticist. Wisconsin Stud in Contemporary Lit 6 1965; addenda by various authors 7 1966.

Goodwin, K. L. The influence of Ezra Pound. New York 1966.

Holder, A. Three voyagers in search of Europe: a study of Henry James, Ezra Pound and T. S. Eliot. Philadelphia 1966.

Long, R. E. The Great Gatsby and the tradition of Joseph Conrad. Texas Stud in Lang & Lit 8 1966.

Nagy, N. C. de. Ezra Pound's poetics and literary tradition: the critical decade. Berne 1966. (Cooper Monographs 11).

Robson, W. R. The achievement of Robert Frost. Southern Rev 2 1966.

Smith, D. E. The enormous room, The pilgrim's progress and the 'demonic Trinity'. In his John Bunyan in America, Bloomington 1966.

Thompson, L. Robert Frost: the early years 1874–1915. New York 1966.

Welland, D. S. R. Hemingway's English reputation. In The literary reputation of Hemingway in Europe, ed R. Asselineau, Paris 1966.

Galinsky, H. William Carlos Williams: eine vergleichende Studie zur Aufnahme seines Werkes in Deutschland, England und Italien (1912–19), Teil II: England und Italien. Jahrbuch für Amerikastudien 12 1967.

— The overseas writer and the literary language of the mother country: American and British English as viewed by American writers from Whitman through Wilder; Stylistic aspects of linguistic borrowing: a stylistic and comparative view of American elements in modern German and British English; The expatriate poet's style: Eliot's and Auden's use of American-British speech differentiations. In his Amerika und Europa, Berlin 1968.

Leavis, F. R. The Americanness of American literature. In his Anna Karenina, and other essays, 1967.

Earnest, E. Expatriates and patriots: American artists, scholars and writers in Europe. Durham 1968.

Goetsch, P. W. H. Auden und Amerika. Jahrbuch für Amerikastudien 13 1968.

Holman, C. H. Europe as a catalyst for Thomas Wolfe. In Essays in American and English literature presented to B. R. McElderry jr, ed M. Schultz etc, Athens Ohio 1968.

Mohrt, M. Lettres anglo-américaines. Nouvelles Littéraires 4 Jan 1968.

Phelps, R. and P. Deane. The literary life: a scrapbook almanac of the Anglo-American literary scene from 1900 to 1950. New York 1968.

Mead, R. O. Atlantic legacy: essay in American-European cultural history. New York 1969.

H. M. R.

Oriental Literatures

Journal of Asian Studies. Bibliography issue, 1966 onwards.

Stucki, C. W. American doctoral dissertations on Asia, 1933–June 1966. Ithaca 1968 (Cornell Univ Southeast Asia Program, Data paper 71).

Shulman, F. J. Japan and Korea: an annotated bibliography of doctoral dissertations on western languages 1877–1969. Chicago 1970.

Flint, F. S. In his History of Imagism, Egoist 2 1915.

Seaver, H. L. The Asian lyric and English literature. In Essays in memory of Barrett Wendell, Cambridge Mass 1926.

Hughes, G. In his Imagism and the Imagists, Stanford 1931.

Fletcher, J. G. The Orient and contemporary poetry. In The Asian legacy and American life, ed A. Christy, New York 1945.

Coffman, S. K. In his Imagism, Norman Oklahoma [1951].

Ceadel, E. B. (ed). Literatures of the East: an appreciation. 1953.

Indiana University Conference on Oriental-Western literary relations: Papers, ed H. Frenz and G. L. Anderson, Chapel Hill 1955.

Asia and the humanities: papers presented at the Second Conference on Oriental-Western Literary and Cultural relations held at Indiana University. Ed H. Frenz, Bloomington 1959.

Chakravarty, A. Form and imagery in modern lyrical poetry, East and West. Yearbook of Comparative & General Lit 11 1962.

Dietrich, M. The Far East: its reflection in and influence on the European theatre. Theatre Research 4 1962.

Holloway, J. In his Widening horizons in English verse, 1966.

Chinese

Teele, R. E. Through a glass darkly: a study of English translations of Chinese poetry. Ann Arbor 1949.

Průšek, J. A confrontation of traditional oriental literature with modern European literature in the context of the Chinese literary revolution. Archiv Orientální 32 1964.

Liu, Wu-chi. Contemporary experiments and achievements. In his Introduction to Chinese literature, Bloomington 1966.

Japanese

Gatenby, E. The influence of Japan on English language and literature. Japan Soc Trans & Proc 34 1936-7.

Miner, E. The Japanese tradition in British and American literature. Princeton 1958.

— The future of Japanese literary relations with the West. Amer Literary Rev no 34 1961.

García Prada, C. La poesía imaginista. Universidad Pontificia Bolivariana 24 1960.

Blyth, R. Haiku in English literature. Eigo Seinen Sept 1961.

Fukuda, R. Japanese elements in Western literature. Yearbook of Comparative & General Lit 11 1962.

Colegrove, C. Kabuki and the West. Hikaku Bunka (Tokyo Women's College) no 8 1962.

Ozaki, et al. Foreign influences on Japanese drama. Higeki Kigeki Oct 1963.

Otsuka, Y. Modern Japanese literature and Western literature. Fukuoka Daigaku Ronsō April 1964.

Chiba, S. Modern Japanese novels and the West. Ichi no 6 1966.

Cohen, A. Noh and Kyogen in Europe. In Asian drama: a collection of festival papers, ed H. W. Wells, Vermillion S Dakota 1966.

T. S. Eliot: a tribute from Japan. Ed M. Hirai and E. W. F. Tomlin, Tokyo 1966. Includes T. Ninomiya, Some Japanese responses; M. Hirai, Eliot and the idea of wisdom.

Yano, K. Introduction and influence of English and American literature in Japan. Eigo Kyoiku 15 1966.

— A note on modern Japanese poetry with special reference to English influence. Stud in Eng Lit no 42 1966.

Henig, S. Virginia Woolf and Lady Murasaki. Lit East & West 11 1967.

Uchino, T. Western influence on modern Japanese poetry. Texas Quart 11 1968.

Indian

Spencer, D. M. Indian fiction in English: an annotated bibliography. Philadelphia 1960.

Latif, S. A. The influence of English literature on Urdu literature. 1924. This and the next item include some remarks on the early years of the twentieth century.

Sen, P. Western influence in Bengali literature. Calcutta 1932.

Singh, B. A survey of Anglo-Indian fiction. 1934.

Iyengar, K. R. S. Indo-Anglian literature. Bombay 1943.

— The Indian contribution to English literature. Bombay 1945.

— Indian writing in English. 1962.

Wheelwright, P. Eliot's philosophical themes. In Focus three: T. S. Eliot: a study of his writings by several hands, ed B. Rajan 1947.

Bose, A. Eliot and Bengali poetry. In T. S. Eliot: a symposium, ed Tambimuttu and R. March 1948.

McCarthy, H. T. S. Eliot and Buddhism. Philosophy East & West 2 1952.

Saksena, U. Western influence on Premchand. Yearbook of Comparative & General Lit 11 1962.

Misra, B. Indian inspiration of James Joyce. Agra 1963.

Bose, B. Modern Bengali literature: a study in Indian-Western relations. Comparative Lit Stud 1 1964.

T. S. Eliot: homage from India. Ed P. Lal, Calcutta [1965].

Karanth, K. S. How deep is Western influence on Indian writers of fiction? Literary Criterion (Mysore) 7 1966.

Dasgupta, R. K. Western response to Indian literature. Indian Lit 10 1967.

Indian writing today. 1967 onwards.

McCutchion, D. Western and Indian approaches to literature. Mahfil 4 1967-8.

Hookens. W. Creative writing in India. Treveni 37 1968.

Spencer, M. Hinduism in E. M. Forster's A passage to India. Jnl of Asian Stud 27 1968.

A.H.M.

II. BOOK PRODUCTION AND DISTRIBUTION

A. LITERATURE, SOCIETY AND COMMUNICATION: *Introductory studies; Literature and society: Taste, mass culture and communication; Relations with other media (General works; The gramophone; Film; Broadcasting).*

B. AUTHORSHIP: *General works; Manuals, guides and handbooks (Preparation of manuscripts; Writing fiction and the novel; Writing detective and mystery fiction; Writing the romantic novel; Writing humour; Short story and article writing; Writing words for songs; Technical and educational writing; Writing for film; Writing for broadcasting – radio and television; Marketing authors' work; Ghosting); Translating; Patronage; The literary agent; Relations with publishers and editors; The author and politics; Literary conferences and festivals; Periodicals.*

C. PRODUCTION

Printing and binding (Bibliographies; History and general studies; Paper; Periodicals relating to paper; Ink; Composition; Proofing; Colour printing and silk-screen process; Binding; Business management for printers; Printing and allied trade organizations; Individual printers; Individual printing houses; Printing trade periodicals; Amateur printing periodicals);

Book design (General works, including lettering and type design; Legibility; Designers and typographers; Illustration and graphic processes; Book jackets);

Publishing (Bibliographies; Histories and studies; Publishing, book production and textual transmission; Unfinished and unpublished work; Individual publishers and publishers' memoirs; University publishing, general works; Individual university presses; Private publishing, general works; Individual private presses; Reprints; Paperback editions; National Book Council – National Book League; Specialized publishing methods; Periodicals devoted to publishing; The law and publishing: General works including defamation and taxation, Copyright, Censorship, obscenity and pornography).

D. DISTRIBUTION
 Reviewing;
 Bookselling (Bibliographies; General works; Bookshops and auctions; Net Book Agreement; Booksellers' organizations; Periodicals);
 Book Collecting (Bibliographies; General works; Book plates and book stamps, including periodicals; Book care; Deceptions: hoaxes and forgeries; Periodicals);
 Libraries and Librarianship (Bibliographies; Libraries, general works; National libraries, including the British Museum; University and College libraries; Public libraries; The public lending right; Special libraries; School libraries; Circulating libraries; Personal libraries; The practice of librarianship; Information retrieval; Periodicals);
 Periodicals relating to current and forthcoming books.

E. READING: *General works; How and what to read; Bibliotherapy; Content analysis; Literary prizes; The best-seller; Popular genres (Comics, strip cartoons and graffiti; Crime and detection; Historical fiction; Picture postcards; Popular song and ballad; Pulp novels; Romance and confession; Science fiction; War, adventure, thriller and ghost stories; Westerns).*

A. LITERATURE, SOCIETY AND COMMUNICATION

For exploratory essays surveying the subject and the state of its literature, see P. D. Hazard, The public arts and the private sensibility *and L. Grey,* Literary audience, *both in* Contemporary literary scholarship: a critical review, *ed L. Leary, New York 1958; R. Hoggart,* Contemporary cultural studies *and R. Meyersohn,* Sociology and cultural studies, *both Birmingham 1969; C. I. Harland,* Effects of the new media of communication [*with bibliography*], *in* Handbook of social psychology, *ed G. Lindzey, Cambridge Mass 1954 (rptd in* Mass media and communication, *ed C. S. Steinberg, New York 1966;* Handbook *itself in process of revision); H. D. Duncan,* Language and literature in society, *with a bibliographical guide to the sociology of literature, Chicago 1953; M. Bradbury,* The social context of Modern English literature, *Oxford 1971.*
 The first two sections below include various pioneering studies, together with studies in other fields which have influenced the understanding of the social context of literature. The sections are not intended as specialist bibliographies of any of these fields. Items are listed chronologically according to date of publication.

(1) INTRODUCTORY STUDIES

A London bibliography of the social sciences. 4 vols 1931–2. With supplementary vols 1934 onwards.

Dudley, F. A. et al (ed). The relations of literature and science: a selected bibliography 1930–49. Pullman 1950. Continued (usually annually) in Symposium from vol 5, 1951 onwards.

Kiell, N. Psychoanalysis, psychology and literature: a bibliography. Madison 1963.

Baxandall, L. (ed). Marxism and aesthetics: a selective annotated bibliography. New York 1968.

Sills, D. L. (ed). International encyclopaedia of the social sciences. 17 vols New York 1968.

See also bibliographies at head of subsection (2), Literature and society, below. A survey of literature of the social sciences is given by P. R. Lewis in The literature of the social sciences: an introductory survey and guide, *1960.*

Wilde, O. The soul of man under socialism. New York 1892, London 1912 (introd by R. Ross).

Le Bon, G. Psychologie des foules. Paris 1895; tr 1896 (as The crowd); New York 1969 (introd by 'Adam Smith').

Veblen, T. The theory of the leisure class: an economic study in the evolution of institutions. New York 1899.

Wells, H. G. Anticipation of the reaction of mechanical and scientific progress on human life and thought. 1902 (for 1901), 1914 (with new introd).

Bentley, A. F. The process of government: a study of social pressures. Chicago 1906.

Lukács, G. The sociology of modern drama. 1909. In Hungarian. Tr Tulane Drama Rev 28 1965; tr German, Archiv für Sozialwissenschaft und Sozialpolitik 38 1914.

Santayana, G. The intellectual temper of the age. In his Winds of doctrine: studies in contemporary opinion, New York 1913.

Gill, E. The control of industry. The Game no 1 1916.

Wohlgemuth, A. Pleasure – unpleasure. Cambridge 1919.

Marinetti, F. T. I manifesti del futurismo. 4 vols Milan 1920.

Maritain, J. Art et scolastique. Paris 1920. Tr J. O'Connor as The philosophy of art, Ditchling, 1923; rev edn tr J. F. Scanlan, New York 1930.

Tawney, R. H. The acquisitive society. 1921.

Cassirer, E. Philosophie der symbolischen Formen. Berlin 1923–9. Tr R. Manheim et al, New Haven, 1953–57.

Hulme, T. E. Speculations: essays on humanism and the philosophy of art. Ed H. Read 1924 [1923].

Lukács, G. Geschichte und Klassenbewusstein. Berlin 1923. Tr 1969 (as History and class consciousness).

Ogden, C. K. and I. A. Richards. The meaning of meaning: a study of the influence of language upon thought and of the science of symbolism. 1923 (with subsequent revisions).

Collingwood, R. G. Outlines of a philosophy of art. 1925.

Ortega y Gasset, J. La deshumanización del arte: ideas sobre la novela. Madrid 1925. Tr H. Weyl, Princeton 1948.

Whitehead, A. N. Science and the modern world. New York 1925.

Richards, I. A. Science and poetry. 1926, 1935 (rev).

Dabney, J. P. The relation between music and poetry. Musical Quart 13 1927.

Lewis, W. Time and western man. 1927.

Whitehead, A. N. Symbolism, its meaning and effect. New York 1927.

Bell, C. Civilization. 1928.

Wells, H. G. The open conspiracy: blue prints for a world revolution. 1928.

Gill, E. Art nonsense and other essays. 1929. *See* D. H. Lawrence, Book Collector's Quart 12 1933. A review, rptd in his Phoenix, New York 1936.

Mannheim, K. Ideologie und Utopie. Bonn 1929. Tr L. Wirth and E. Shils 1936 (in enlarged form, as Ideology and utopia: an introduction to the sociology of knowledge).

Whitehead, A. N. The aims of education. New York 1929. Especially ch 4, Technical education and its relation to science and literature.

Duhamel, G. Scènes de la vie future. Paris 1930.

Freud, S. Das Unbehagen in der Kultur. Vienna 1930. Tr J. Riviere 1930 (as Civilization and its discontents).

Lewis, W. The apes of god. 1930. A novel.

Maritain, J. Religion et culture. Paris 1930. Tr J. F. Scanlan 1931.

Ortega y Gasset, J. La rebelión de las masas. Madrid 1930. Tr 1932 (as Revolt of the masses).

Lewis, W. The diabolical principle and the dithyrambic spectator. 1931.

Woolf, L. After the deluge. 2 vols 1931–9.

Leavis, Q. D. Middleman of ideas. Scrutiny 1 1932. On the work of Stuart Chase as 'educational publicist' and its implications.

Whitehead, A. N. Adventures of ideas. Cambridge 1933.

Dewey, J. Art as experience. New York 1934.

Gill, E. Art and a changing civilization. 1934.

Ginsberg, M. Sociology. 1934.

Lewis, W. Men without art. 1934.

O'Malley, R. Culture and early environment. Scrutiny 3 1934.

Auden, W. H. Psychology and art today. In The arts today, ed G. Grigson 1935.

Gill, E. Work and leisure. 1935.

Maritain, J. Frontières de la poésie, et autres essais. Paris 1935. Last three chs tr as Art and poetry, by E. de P. Matthews, 1945.

Mirsky, D. S. The intelligentsia of Great Britain. Tr Alec Brown 1935.

Mueller, J. H. Is art the product of its age? Social Forces 13 1935.

National Book Council. The cheapest amusement. 1935.

Benjamin, W. L'œuvre d'art à l'époque de sa reproduction mecanisée. Zeitschrift für Sozialforschung 5 1936. Tr in his Illuminations, New York 1968.

Hodge, A. and L. Riding. Philosophy and poetry. Epilogue 2 1936.

Lawrence, D. H. Education of the people; Democracy. In his Phoenix, New York 1936.

Malraux, A. Our cultural heritage. Left Rev 2 1936. International Writers' Conference number.

Mann, T. Freud und die Zukunft. Vienna 1936. Tr in Freud, Goethe, Wagner, New York, 1937, by H. T. Lowe-Porter.

Wais, K. Symbiose der Künste. Stuttgart 1936.

'West, Rebecca' (C. I. Andrews). Mind and materialism. In The university of books, 1936.

Adler, M. Art and prudence. New York 1937.

Harding, D. W. The role of the onlooker. Scrutiny 6 1937.

Jennings, H. and C. Madge (ed). May the twelfth: mass-observation day surveys. 1937.

Leavis, F. R. Literary criticism and philosophy: a reply [to R. Wellek]. Scrutiny 6 1937.

Lynd, R. S. and H. M. Middletown in transition: a study in cultural conflicts. New York 1937. See D. W. Harding, Vitality in social surveys, Scrutiny 6 1937.

Madge, C. and T. Harrisson. Mass-observation. 1937.

Read, H. Art and society. 1937.

Sorokin, P. A. Social and cultural dynamics. 4 vols New York 1937–41.

'Caudwell, Christopher' (C. St J. Sprigg). Studies in a dying culture. 1938.

Collingwood, R. G. The principles of art. Oxford 1938.

Mumford, L. The culture of cities. New York 1938.

Pound, E. Guide to Kulchur. 1938.

Archibald, R. C. Mathematicians and poetry and drama. Science (New York) 13 and 20 Jan 1939. Relations between poetry and mathematics.

Church, R. et al. The claim of politics: a symposium. Scrutiny 7 1939.

Eliot, T. S. The idea of a Christian society. 1939.

Wyndham Lewis the artist: from Blast to Burlington House. 1939. Selection of his writings.

Muggeridge, M. The thirties: 1930–1940 in Great Britain. 1940.

Read, H. Annals of innocence and experience. 1940.

Znaniecki, F. The social role of the man of knowledge. New York 1940.

Graves, R. and A. Hodge. The long week-end. 1941.

Lewis, W. The vulgar streak. 1941.

Mack, E. C. Public schools and British opinion since 1860. New York 1941.

Sorokin, P. A. The crisis of our age: the social and cultural outlook. New York 1941.

Witte, W. The sociological approach to literature. MLR 36 1941.

Camus, A. Le mythe de Sisyphe. Paris 1942. Tr J. O'Brien 1955.

Fromm, E. The fear of freedom. 1942.

Gill, E. Last essays. 1942.

Leavis, F. R. Education and the university. 1943.

Muller, H. Science and criticism: the humanistic tradition in contemporary thought. New Haven 1943.

Rothenstein, M. Can we be educated up to art?: notes on lecturing to the army. Horizon 7 1943.

Shrodes, C. et al (ed). Psychology through literature: an anthology. New York 1943. With bibliography.

Gill, E. In a strange land. 1944.

Kluckhohn, C. and O. H. Mowrer. Culture and personality: a conceptual scheme. Amer Anthropologist 46 1944.

Trevelyan, G. M. English social history. 1944.

Popper, K. The open society and its enemies. 2 vols 1945.

Collingwood, R. G. The idea of history. 1946.

Hourticq, L. L'art et la littérature. Paris 1946.

Polanyi, M. Science, faith and society. 1946.

Sartre, J.-P. Existentialisme est un humanisme. Paris 1946. Tr P. Mairet 1947.

Bantock, G. H. The cultural implications of planning and popularization. Scrutiny 14 1947.

Malinowski, B. Freedom and civilization. 1947.

Notcutt, B. Some relations between psychology and literature. Peoria 1947.

'Orwell, George' (E. A. Blair). The English people. 1947. Version as originally written ptd in his Collected essays etc vol 3, 1968.

Polanyi, M. The foundation of academic freedom. Oxford 1947.

Sorokin, P. A. Society, culture and personality. 1947.

Souriau, E. La correspondance des arts. Paris 1947.

Trilling, L. Freud and literature. Horizon 16 1947; rptd in his Liberal imagination, 1951.

Arnheim, R. Psychological notes on the poetical process. In Poets at work, essays by R. Arnheim et al, New York [1948].

Bantock, G. H. Some cultural implications of freedom in education. Scrutiny 15 1948. Reply by B. Ford, ibid, and correspondence to 16 1949.

Conference on integration of the humanities and the social sciences, Southern Methodist University 1947. Dallas 1948.

Eliot, T. S. Notes towards the definition of culture. 1948.

Grene, M. Dreadful freedom: a critique of existentialism. Chicago 1948, 1959 (as Introduction to existentialism).

Livingstone, R. Some thoughts on university education. Cambridge 1948. National Book League annual lecture 1947.

Brown, C. Music and literature. Athens Georgia 1949.

'Caudwell, Christopher' (C. St J. Sprigg). Further studies in a dying culture. 1949.

Harap, L. Social roots of the arts. New York 1949.

Lewis, R. and A. Maude. The English middle classes. 1949.

McCurdy, H. G. Literature as a resource in personality study: theory and methods. Jnl of Aesthetics 8 1949.

Munro, T. The arts and their interrelations. New York 1949.

Shannon, C. E. and W. Weaver. The mathematical theory of communication. Urbana, 1949. The implications are discussed in non-mathematical terms.

Thompson, D. The importance of leisure. 1949.

Weber, M. Max Weber on the methodology of the social sciences. Tr and ed E. A. Shils and H. A. Finch, Glencoe Ill 1949. Three essays first pbd in Sozialwissenschaft und Sozialpolitik, 1904 and 1905, and Logos 1917.

Jnl of Social Issues 6 1950. Special issue: Values and the social scientist.

Morris, B. The arts and their cultural matrix. Western Humanities Rev 4 1950.

Sachs, C. The commonwealth of art. Washington 1950. Lecture.

UNESCO. Impact of science on society. Vol 1 no 1, Paris 1950 onwards.

Arena no 8 [1951]. Special issue: Britain's cultural heritage.

Arena no 9 [1951]. Special issue: The American threat to British culture.

Hauser, A. The social history of art. 2 vols 1951.

Parsons, T. The social system. Glencoe Ill 1951.

— and Shils, E. (ed). Toward a general theory of action. Cambridge Mass 1951.

Polanyi, M. The logic of liberty: reflections and rejoinders. 1951.

Rowntree, S. B. and G. R. Lavers. English life and leisure: a social study. 1951.

UNESCO. Freedom and culture. 1951.

Comfort, A. Social responsibility in science and art. 1952.

Hartley, E. L. and R. E. Fundamentals of social psychology. New York 1952. Especially: Communication: the basic social process, pp 15-195.

Mannheim, K. Essays on the sociology of knowledge. 1952.

Russell, B. Impact of science on society. 1952.

UNESCO. Basic facts and figures: illiteracy, education, libraries, museums, books, newspapers, newsprint, film and radio. Paris 1952 onwards.

Znaniecki, F. Cultural sciences: their origin and development. Urbana 1952.

Fishman, S. The disinherited of art. Berkeley 1953.

Riesman, D. Some observations on changes in leisure attitudes. Perspectives 5 1953.

Spender, S. The creative element: a study of vision, despair and orthodoxy among some modern writers. 1953.

Williams, R. The idea of culture. EC 3 1953.

Evans, B. I. Literature and science. 1954.

Lewis, W. The demon of progress in the arts. 1954.

Lazarsfeld, P. F. and M. Rosenberg (ed). The language of social research: a reader in the methodology of social research. Glencoe Ill 1955.

Linton, R. The tree of culture. New York 1955.

Marcuse, H. Eros and civilization: a philosophical inquiry into Freud. Boston 1955.

Pear, T. H. English social differences. 1955.

Mannheim, K. Towards the sociology of mind: an introduction; The problem of the intelligentsia: an inquiry into its past and present role; The democratization of culture. In his Essays on the sociology of culture, 1956.

Tawney, R. H. Social history and literature. Sydney 1956, Leicester 1958 (rev). Lecture.

White, D. L. (ed). The state of the social sciences. Chicago 1956. Especially B. Berelson, The study of public opinion.

Kroeber, A. L. Style and civilization. Ithaca 1957.

Lowenthal, L. Literature and the image of man. Boston 1957.

Merton, R. K. The sociology of knowledge. In his Social theory and social structure, Glencoe Ill 1957.

Nicolson, M. Science and imagination. Ithaca 1957.

A sense of direction. TLS 16 Aug 1957.

Hughes, H. S. Consciousness and society. New York 1958. Re-orientation of social thinking 1890-1930.

Larrabee, E. and R. Meyersohn (ed). Mass leisure. Glencoe Ill [1958]. Bibliography 1900-1958 compiled R. Meyersohn and M. Marc.

Marsh, D. C. The changing social structure in England and Wales, 1871-1961. 1958, 1965 (rev).

Riesman, D. et al. The lonely crowd. New Haven 1958.

Stark, W. The sociology of knowledge: an essay in aid of a deeper understanding of the history of ideas. 1958.

Williams, R. Culture and society 1780-1950. 1958, 1961 (rev).

Barnett, J. H. The sociology of art. In Sociology today, ed R. K. Merton et al, New York 1959.

Duverger, M. Méthodes de la science politique. Paris 1959. Tr from 2nd edn (Méthodes des sciences sociales) as An introduction to the social sciences, with special reference to their methods, by M. Anderson, New York 1964.

Fischer, E. Von der Notwendigkeit der Kunst. Dresden 1959. Tr A. Bostock 1963 (as The necessity of art: a Marxist approach).

Lewis, J. L. The lure of pseudo-science. Twentieth Century 165 1959.

Mills, C. W. The sociological imagination. New York 1959.

Tillich, P. Theology of culture. Ed R. C. Kimball, New York 1959.

Walsh, W. Autobiographical literature and educational thought. Leeds 1959. Lecture.

— The use of imagination: educational thought and the literary mind. 1959.

Glicksberg, C. I. Literature and religion. Dallas 1960.

Goodman, P. Growing up absurd: problems of youth in the organized system. New York 1960.

James, D. G. Literature and science. School Science Rev 41 1960.

McLuhan, M. Myth and mass media. In Myth and mythmaking, ed H. A. Murray, New York 1960.

Parsons, T. Structure and process in modern society. New York 1960.

Shapiro, H. L. Man, culture and society. New York 1960.

TLS 9 Sept 1960. Special issue: The British imagination. Rptd 1961.

Williams, R. The long revolution. 1960.

Halsey, A. H. et al (ed). Education, economy and society: a reader in the sociology of education. New York 1961.

Macrae, D. G. Ideology and society. 1961.

Matza, D. Subterranean traditions of youth. Annals of Amer Acad of Political & Social Science 338 1961.

Parsons, T. et al (ed). Theories of society. New York 1961.

Jackson, B. and D. Thompson. English in education. 1962.

Kuhn, T. S. The structure of scientific revolutions. In International encyclopaedia of unified science vol 2 no 2, Chicago 1962.

Sampson, A. The anatomy of Britain today. 1962.

Toulmin, S. and J. Goodfield. The architecture of matter. 1962.

Williams, D. C. (ed). The arts as communication. Toronto 1962.

Bantock, G. H. Education in an industrial society. 1963.

Coser, L. A. (ed). Sociology through literature: an introductory reader. Englewood Cliffs 1963.

Culture and environment: essays in honour of Sir Cyril Fox, ed I. L. Foster and L. Alcock 1963.

Koestler, A. (ed). Suicide of a nation? An enquiry into the state of Britain today. 1963.

Madge, J. The origins of scientific sociology. 1963.

Medawar, P. B. Hypothesis and imagination. TLS 25 Oct 1963. Expanded in his The art of the soluble, 1967.

TLS 26 July, 27 Sept 1963. Special issues: The critical moment and Critics abroad. Rptd 1964. The state of criticism.

Wicker, B. Culture and the liturgy. 1963.

Bourne, R. War and the intellectuals: essays 1915-19. New York 1964. Ed C. Resek.

Hymes, D. (ed). Language and culture in society: a reader in linguistics and anthropology. New York [1964].

Walsh, W. A human idiom: literature and humanity. 1964.

Wilson, R. N. (ed). The arts in society. Englewood Cliffs 1964. Especially E. Shils, The high culture of the age.

Woolf, H. (ed). Science as a cultural force. Baltimore 1964.

Hoggart, R. Higher education and cultural change. Newcastle-upon-Tyne 1965; rptd in his Speaking to each other, vol 1 1970.

Marcuse, H. Kultur und Gesellschaft. Frankfurt 1965. Partly tr in Negations: essays in critical theory, New York 1968.

Daedalus 94 1965. Special issue: Science and culture.

Structure and society. TLS 30 Sept 1965.

Wax, B. Newspaper collections and history. Library Trends 13 1964–5.

Berger, P. L. Invitation to sociology. 1966.

Bruyn, S. T. The human perspective in sociology: the methodology of participant observation. Englewood Cliffs 1966.

Emmett, B. P. The design of investigations into the effects of radio and television programmes and other mass communications. Jnl of Royal Statistical Soc 129 pt 1, 1966; rptd in Media sociology, ed J. Tunstall, 1970.

Fagen, R. R. Politics and communication. Boston 1966.

Parsons, T. Societies: evolutionary and comparative perspectives. Englewood Cliffs 1966.

Shuttleworth, A. Two working papers in cultural studies. Birmingham 1966.

Wicker, B. Culture and theology. 1966. See C. Buckley, The sacred and the whole, New Blackfriars 48 1967.

Yale French Stud 36–7 1966. Special issue: Structuralism. Especially V. L. Rippere, Towards an anthropology of literature.

Adorno, T. W. Cultural criticism and society. In his Prisms, tr S. and S. Weber 1967.

Bantock, G. H. Education, culture and the emotions. 1967.

Barbu, Z. The sociology of drama. New Society 2 Feb 1967.

Dumazedier, J. Toward a society of leisure. New York 1967.

Hall, S. Cultural analysis. Cambridge Rev 21 Jan 1967.

Krieghbaum, H. Science and the mass media. New York 1967.

Laing, R. D. The politics of experience and the bird of paradise. 1967. Analyses alienation.

Laqueur, W. Literature and the historian. Jnl of Contemporary History 2 1967.

Manis, J. G. and B. N. Meltzer. Symbolic interaction: a reader in social psychology. Boston 1967.

Miller, J. E. and P. D. Herring (ed). The arts and the public. Chicago 1967.

Nisbet, R. A. The sociological tradition. 1967.

Rickman, H. P. Understanding and the human studies. 1967.

TLS 27 July, 28 Sept 1967. Special issues: Crosscurrents 1 (England), 2 (Europe).

Albrecht, M. Art as an institution. Amer Sociological Rev 33 1968.

Bergonzi, B. (ed). Innovations – where is our culture going? 1968.

Broxis, P. F. Organizing the arts. 1968.

Fyvel, T. R. Intellectuals today. 1968.

Green, M. British Marxists and American Freudians. In Innovations, ed B. Bergonzi 1968.

Kantorowitsch, W. Soziologie und Literatur. Kunst und Literatur 16 1968.

McMullen, R. Art, affluence and alienation: the fine arts today. 1968.

Rosengren, K. E. Sociological aspects of the literary system. Stockholm 1968.

What is sociology? TLS 4 April 1968.

Wolheim, R. Art and its objects. New York 1968.

Daedalus 98 1969. Special issue: The future of the humanities.

Leavis, F. R. 'English' – unrest and continuity. TLS 29 May 1969; correspondence follows.

Meyersohn, R. Sociology and cultural studies: some problems. Birmingham 1969.

Moore, T. Claude Lévi-Strauss and the cultural scene. Birmingham 1969.

Robinson, P. A. The Freudian left. New York 1969.

Samuels, S. English intellectuals and politics in the 1930s. In On intellectuals, ed P. Rieff, New York 1969.

Wolff, R. et al. A critique of pure tolerance. 1969.

Egbert, D. D. Social radicalism and the arts: Western Europe. New York 1970.

Hoggart, R. Speaking to each other. 2 vols 1970. Vol 1, About society; vol 2, About literature.

(2) LITERATURE AND SOCIETY: TASTE, MASS CULTURE AND COMMUNICATION

The main headnote, cols 35–6 (above), should be consulted when using this subsection.

Lasswell, H. D. et al. Propaganda and promotional activities: an annotated bibliography. Minneapolis 1935.

Smith, B. L. et al. Propaganda, communication and public opinion: a comprehensive reference guide. Princeton 1946. Continuation of preceding. Itself continued, not as broadly in scope, by B. L. and C. M. Smith, International communication and political opinion: a guide to the literature, Princeton 1956.

Fearing, F. and G. Rogge. A selected and annotated bibliography in communications research. Quart of Film, Radio & Television 6 1951.

Marshall, T. F. et al. Literature and society 1950–5: a select bibliography. Coral Gables 1956. Suppl 1956–60, 1962.

Dumazedier, J. and C. Guinchat. La sociologie du loisir. Paris 1961. Unesco.

Blum, E. Reference books in the mass media. Urbana 1962.

Benzi, L. and M. Marchetti. Bibliografia classificata di sociologia della letteratura. Quarderni di Sociologia 18 1968.

Hansen, D. A. and J. H. Parsons. Mass communications: a research bibliography. Santa Barbara Calif. 1968.

Hardt, H. Paperbacks in mass communication: a comprehensive bibliography. Journalism Quart 45 1968.

See also serial bibliographies in Journalism Quart 7 1930– *and* Journal of Popular Culture 1967–.

Howells, W. D. Literature and life. New York 1902.

Wells, F. L. Statistical study of literary merit with remarks on some new phases of the method. Archives of Psychology no 7 1907.

Bennett, E. A. Literary taste and how to form it. 1909, 1912 (rev); ed F. Swinnerton 1937, 1938 (enlarged, Penguin).

The decadence of the novel. Author 19 1909.

Houghton, S. Mr Maugham's 'Smith'. Manchester Guardian 1909; rptd in Houghton's Works vol 3, ed H. Brighouse, 1914. The 'smart dramatist' and 'Society'.

Beyer, F. C. Die volkswirtschaftliche und sozialpolitische Bedeutung der Einführung der Setzmaschine im Buchdruckgewerbe. Karlsruhe 1910.

Brooke, R. Democracy and the arts. [1910]; pbd 1946.

Marinetti, F. T. The foundation of futurism. In E. Weber, Paths to the present, New York 1960. See also Initial manifesto of futurism, Sackville Gallery exhibition of works by Italian futurist painters, March 1912.

Mordell, A. The shifting of literary values. Philadelphia 1912.

Symons, J. D. The novel under commerce. Eng Rev 25 1917.

Rowntree, J. S. and E. E. Taylor. Extension through the printed word, libraries, literature, advertising. Harrogate 1918.

Goldring, D. English literature and the revolution. Coterie no 3 1919.

—— Post-Georgian poet in search of a master. Coterie no 4 1920.

Moult, T. The present position of the arts in England. Eng Rev 30 1920.

Page, B. F. Reading for the workers: an undelivered lecture. 1921.

Peck, H. W. The social criticism of literature. Sewanee Rev 29 1921.

Canby, H. S. Why popular novels are popular. Century 104 1922.

Lippmann, W. Public opinion. New York 1922.

Orage, A. R. Readers and writers, 1917–1921. New York 1922.

Proletcult. Youth no 7 1922.

Lawrence, D. H. The proper study. Adelphi 1 1923; rptd in his Phoenix, New York 1936.

Schücking, L. L. Die Soziologie der literarischen Geschmacksbildung. Munich 1923. Tr E. W. Dickes 1944 (as The sociology of literary taste).

Drinkwater, J. The public and literature: the direction of taste in Great Britain and America. Independent 6 Dec 1924.

Galsworthy, J. Time, tides and taste. Saturday Rev of Lit 5 Dec 1925.

Lawrence, D. H. Art and morality; Morality and the novel. Calendar of Modern Letters 2 1925; rptd in his Phoenix, New York 1936.

Lippmann, W. The phantom public. New York 1925.

Sitwell, O. Literarische Koterien in London. Die Literatur 27 1925.

Angell, N. The public mind: its disorders and exploitation. 1926.

Calverton, V. F. Sex expression in literature. New York 1926.

Benda, J. La trahison des clercs. Paris 1927. Tr R. Aldington 1928 (as The great betrayal).

Lasswell, H. D. Propaganda technique in the world war. New York 1927.

Lawrence, D. H. Review of T. Burrow, The social basis of consciousness, Amer Bookman 66 1927; rptd in his Phoenix, New York 1936. The individual and the mass.

Lewis, W. The enemy. Jan 1927. Editorial.

Lissitsky, L. M. The future of the book. Gutenberg-Jahrbuch, Mainz 1927; rptd in New Left Rev 41 1967.

Arnheim, R. Stimme von der Galerie: 25 Kleine Aufsätze zur Kultur der Zeit. Berlin 1928.

Belgion, M. British and American taste. Eng Jnl 17 1928.

Gill, E. Art and prudence. 1928.

Lawrence, D. H. John Galsworthy. In Scrutinies, ed E. Rickword 1928; rptd in his Phoenix, New York 1936.

Lynd, R. Why literature declines. Atlantic Monthly 142 1928.

Kellett, E. E. The whirligig of taste. 1929.

Speer, R. K. Measurement of appreciation in poetry, prose and art, and studies in appreciation. New York 1929.

Winterich, J. T. Books and the man. New York 1929.

Duffus, R. L. Books: their place in a democracy. Boston 1930.

Huxley, A. Vulgarity in literature. 1930.

Leavis, F. R. Mass civilization and minority culture. Cambridge 1930.

Powys, J. C. The meaning of culture. 1930.

Wilson, J. S. Whirligigs of time and taste. Virginia Quart Rev 6 1930.

Hofmann, W. Die Lektüre der Frau: Beiträge zur Leserkunde und zur Leserführung. Leipzig 1931. Leipziger Beiträge zur Grundlegung der praktischen Literaturpflege I. Hofmann was Director of the Leipziger Institut für Leser- und Schrifttumskunde.

Kellett, E. E. Fashion in literature: a study of changing taste. 1931.

Wembridge, E. Life among the lowbrows. Boston 1931.

Chambers, F. P. The history of taste: an account of the revolution of art criticism and theory in Europe. New York 1932.

Eastman, M. The literary mind. New York 1932.

Jackson, H. The fear of books. 1932.

Knights, L. C. and D. Culver. Scrutiny: a manifesto. Scrutiny 1 1932.

Leavis, Q. D. Fiction and the reading public. 1932.

Browne, W. The culture-brokers. London Mercury 28 1933. A critique of the aims of Scrutiny and those associated with it.

Carswell, D. and C. The crisis in criticism. Nineteenth Century & After 113 1933.

Krutch, J. W. Literature and propaganda. Eng Jnl 22 1933.

Leavis, F. R. and D. Thompson. Culture and environment. 1933.

Macaulay, R. The return of horridness in literature. Spectator 10 March 1933.

Annis, A. D. and N. C. Meier. The induction of opinion through suggestion by means of 'planted content'. Jnl of Social Psychology 5 1934.

Craig, A. Sex and revolution. 1934. Ethics and sex.

Devoe, A. Books by the roadside. Atlantic Monthly 153 1934. Contemporary reading taste.

Eliot, T. S. After strange gods. 1934.

Gould, G. The novel, its influence in propaganda. Aryan Path 5 1934.

Monroe, H. Art and propaganda. Poetry 44 1934.

Strachey, E. J. St L. Literature and dialectical materialism. New York 1934. Rev and enlarged version of lecture: Literature and fascism. Section on social problems in literature.

Thompson, D. Reading and discrimination. 1934.

Williamson, H. R. Last notes at random. Bookman (London) 87 1934 (Christmas Suppl).

Empson, W. Proletarian literature. Scrutiny 3 1935.

Grigson, G. (ed). The arts today. 1935.

Guérard, A. L. Literature and society. Boston 1935.

Harding, D. W. Propaganda and rationalisation in war. Scrutiny 4 1935.

Hunt, E. L. The social interpretation of literature. Eng Jnl 24 1935.

Leavis, Q. D. Lady novelists and the lower orders. Scrutiny 4 1935.

Marshall, A. C. Fiction today. In The arts today, ed G. Grigson, 1935.

Rea, B. (ed). Five on revolutionary art. 1935. H. Read, F. D. Klingender, E. Gill, A. L. Lloyd, A. West.

Arns, K. Literatur und Leser im heutigen England. Rheinisch-Westfälische Zeitung 52 1936.

Clark, A. F. B. Purity and propaganda in art. UTQ 5 1936. Includes literature.

Huxley, A. Training in realism. In The university of books, 1936. A reader's guide.

Lawrence, D. H. Why the novel matters. In his Phoenix, New York 1936.

Swinnerton, F. What novels can teach. In The university of books, 1936. A reader's guide.

Wells, H. G. The anatomy of frustration: a modern synthesis. 1936.

Fox, R. The novel and the people. 1937.

Hughes, H. M. Human interest stories and democracy. Public Opinion Quart 1 1937; rptd in Reader in public opinion and communication, ed B. Berelson and M. Janowitz, Glencoe Ill 1953.

Lehmann, J. et al (ed). Ralph Fox, a writer in arms. 1937. Selection of Fox's work.

Marshall, A. C. The changing scene: essays on contemporary English society. 1937.

Norman, C. H. The revolutionary spirit in modern literature and drama. 1937.

Punke, H. H. Cultural change and changes in popular literature. Social Forces 15 1937.

Young, G. M. The new Cortegiano. In his Daylight and champaign, 1937. Social desirability of unity of culture and a defence of 'middle-brow' culture.

Cole, M. Books and the people. 1938.

Cruse, A. After the Victorians. 1938. Books, readers, and intellectual life.

Daiches, D. Literature and society. 1938.

Durant, H. W. The problem of leisure. 1938.

Daiches, D. The novel and the modern world. Chicago 1939.

Greenberg, C. Avant-garde and Kitsch. Partisan Rev 6 1939 and Horizon 1 1940; rptd in Partisan reader, ed W. Phillips and P. Rahv, New York 1946.

Lasswell, H. D. and D. Blumenstock. World revolutionary propaganda. New York 1939.

Leavis, Q. D. The background of twentieth-century letters. Scrutiny 8 1939.

Wickenden, H. S. Of literary coteries. Dalhousie Rev 19 1939.

Bombs versus books. TLS 26 Oct 1940. Learning will survive bombing of libraries.

Daiches, D. Poetry and the modern world. Chicago 1940.

Harrisson, T. H. What is public opinion? Political Quart 11 1940.

Leavis, F. R. Retrospect of a decade. Scrutiny 9 1940. The thirties.

Rée, H. Kitsch, culture and adolescence. Horizon 2 1940.

Steed, H. W. The press and the fifth arm. 1940.

Cecil, D. The author in a suffering world: war's impact on our literature. TLS 11 Jan 1941.

Cromwell, P. The propaganda problem. Horizon 3 1941.

Horkheimer, M. Art and mass culture. Stud in Philosophy and Social Science no 9 1941.

Mass observation. Home propaganda. 1941.

Stud in Philosophy & Social Science 9 1941. Special issue on communications.

Witte, W. The sociological approach to literature. MLR 36 1941.

Caillois, R. Sociología de la novela. Buenos Aires 1942.

Unwin, S. The status of books. 1942.

Waples, D. (ed). Print, radio and film in a democracy. Chicago 1942.

Angell, N. Shall we writers fail again? Literature and literacy have increased but remain unequal to their biggest test. Saturday Rev of Lit 20 March 1943. Round table discussion of this article by M. Lerner, J. T. Adams, J. Chamberlain, A. Nevins, S. Strunsky and Angell, 3 April 1943.

Bethell, S. L. The literary outlook. 1943.

Bloch, H. A. Towards the development of a sociology of literary and art forms. Amer Sociological Rev 8 1943.

Leavis, F. R. Literature and society. Scrutiny 12 1943; rptd in his Common pursuit, 1952.

Leavis, Q. D. The discipline of letters: a sociological note. Scrutiny 12 1943.

Nicholson, N. Man and literature. 1943.

'Orwell, George' (E. A. Blair). Pamphlet literature. New Statesman 9 Jan 1943; rptd in his Collected essays vol 2, 1968.

Blackmur, R. P. et al. Mr Eliot and notions of culture: a discussion. Partisan Rev 11 1944.

Macdonald, D. A theory of popular culture. Politics 1 1944.

Bax, C. Style and fashion in literature. Essays by Divers Hands 21 1945.

Farrell, J. T. The league of frightened Philistines. In his League of frightened Philistines and other papers, New York 1945. On freedom and culture.

Housman, L. Fame versus fashion in literature. Essays by Divers Hands 21 1945.

Leavis, F. R. Sociology and literature. Scrutiny 13 1945; rptd in his Common pursuit, 1952.

'Orwell, George' (E. A. Blair). Funny but not vulgar. Leader 28 July 1945; rptd in his Collected essays vol 3, 1968.

Blumer, H. The mass, the public and public opinion. In New outlines of the principles of sociology, ed A. McC. Lee, New York 1946.

Katz, D. The interpretation of survey findings. Jnl of Social Issues 2 1946; rptd in Reader in public opinion and communication, ed B. Berelson and M. Janowitz, Glencoe Ill 1953.

Levin, H. Literature as an institution. Accent 6 1946.

'Orwell, George' (E. A. Blair). Critical essays. 1946, New York 1946 (as Dickens, Dali & others: studies in popular culture).

—— Riding down from Bangor. Tribune 22 Nov 1946; rptd in his Collected essays vol 4, 1968.

Rosenblatt, L. M. Toward a cultural approach to literature. College Eng 7 1946.

Cantril, H. Gauging public opinion. Princeton 1947.

Chafee, Z. Government and mass communications. Chicago 1947.

Cooper, E. and M. Jahoda. The evasion of propaganda: how prejudiced people respond to anti-prejudice propaganda. Jnl of Psychology 23 1947.

Finkelstein, S. Art and society. New York 1947.

Howell, W. S. Literature as an enterprise in communication. Quart Jnl of Speech 33 1947.

Jnl of Social Issues 3 1947. Special issue: Mass media—content, function and measurement.

Knights, L. C. Literature and the study of society. Sheffield 1947. Lecture.

Kornhauser, A. The problems of bias in opinion research. International Jnl of Opinion & Attitude Research 1 1947; rptd in Reader in public opinion and communication, ed B. Berelson and M. Janowitz, Glencoe Ill 1953.

Kris, E. and N. Leites. Trends in twentieth-century propaganda. In Psychoanalysis and the social sciences, ed G. Roheim, New York 1947; rptd in Reader in public opinion and communication, ed B. Berelson and M. Janowitz, Glencoe Ill 1953.

Laws, F. (ed). Made for millions: a critical study of the new media of information and entertainment. 1947.

Tomlinson, H. M. The power of books. Atlantic Monthly 179 1947.

Auden, W. H. In Poets at work: essays based on the Modern Poetry Collection at the Lockwood Memorial Library, University of Buffalo, New York 1948.

Bethell, S. L. Shakespeare and the popular dramatic tradition. 1948. Twentieth-century implications of mass media on drama of Shakespeare, T. S. Eliot etc.

Bryson, L. (ed). The communication of ideas. New York 1948. Especially P. Lazarsfeld and R. Merton, Mass communication, popular taste and organized social action.

Doob, L. W. Public opinion and propaganda. New York 1948.

Koppel, J. W. Book clubs and the evaluation of literature. Public Opinion Quart 12 1948.

Schramm, W. (ed). Communications in modern society. New York 1948.

Evans, B. I. and M. Glasgow. The arts in England. 1949.

Herz, M. F. Some psychological lessons from leaflet propaganda in World War II. Public Opinion Quart 13 1949.

Hovland, C. I. et al. Experiments on mass communication. Princeton 1949.

Katz, D. Psychological barriers to communication. In Mass communications, ed W. Schramm, Urbana 1949.

Klapper, J. T. The effects of mass media. New York 1949. Includes bibliography.

Lazarsfeld, P. and F. N. Stanton (ed). Communications research 1948-9. New York 1949.

Lynes, R. Highbrow, lowbrow, middlebrow. Harper's Mag 198 1949; rptd in his Taste-makers, New York 1959.

Merton, T. Elected silence. 1949. Introd E. Waugh. A Catholic, autobiographical, response to modern society.

Schramm, W. The effects of mass communications: a survey. Journalism Quart 26 1949.
— (ed). Mass communications: a book of readings selected for the Institute of Communications Research in the University of Illinois. Urbana 1949, 1960 (rev).
Votaw, A. The literature of extreme situations. Horizon 20 1949. The theme of pure violence in contemporary literature.
Berelson, B. and M. Janowitz. Reader in public opinion and communication. Glencoe Ill 1950, 1953 (rev).
Churchill, R. C. Disagreements: a polemic on culture in the English democracy. 1950.
Crossman, R. H. S. (ed). The god that failed: six studies in communism. 1950.
Fast, H. Literature and reality. New York 1950.
Fleming, R. Cultural anxiety and the romantic audience. Partisan Rev 17 1950.
Greenberg, L. H. Letters to the editor: teen-age tastes. Saturday Rev of Lit 1 April 1950.
Hart, J. D. The popular book: a history of America's literary taste. New York 1950.
Lowenthal, L. Historical perspectives of popular culture. Amer Jnl of Sociology 55 1950; rptd in his Literature, popular culture and society, Englewood Cliffs 1961.
Seldes, G. The great audience. New York 1950.
Stowell, F. S. Democratic writers versus the class weapon. Humanist 10 1950.
UNESCO. World communication, press, radio, television, film. Paris 1950. Frequent subsequent revisions.
Williams, R. Literature and society. In his Reading and criticism, 1950.
Arena no 8 [1951]. Britain's cultural heritage. Introd by G. Thomson.
Arena no 9 [1951]. The American threat to British culture. Introd by S. Aaronvitch.
Forster, E. M. Art for art's sake. In his Two cheers for democracy, 1951.
Jones, H. M. Patterns of writing and the middle class. Amer Lit 23 1951.
Leavis, F. R. Keynes, Spender and currency-values. Scrutiny 18 1951.
— Mr Pryce-Jones, the British Council and British culture. Scrutiny 18 1951.
Malraux, A. Les voix du silence. Paris 1951. Tr S. Gilbert 1953 (as The voices of silence).
Brembeck, W. L. and W. S. Howell. Persuasion. New York 1952.
Glicksberg, C. I. Literature and society. Arizona Quart 8 1952.
Heilman, R. B. Literature and the adult laity. Pacific Spectator 6 1952.
Raymond, J. The reading tastes of the under forties. TLS 29 Aug 1952; rptd in his England's on the anvil! and other essays, 1958.
Weibe, G. D. Mass communications. In E. L. and R. E. Hartley (ed), Fundamentals of social psychology, New York, 1952.
Bateson, F. W. The function of criticism at the present time. EC 3 1953. See also F. R. Leavis, The responsible critic, Scrutiny 19 1953 and ensuing correspondence.
Davie, D. The earnest and the smart: provincialism in letters. Twentieth Century 154 1953.
Duncan, H. D. Language and literature in society. Chicago 1953. With bibliographical guide to sociology of literature.
Fraser, G. S. The modern writer and his world. 1953, 1964 (rev).
Freidson, E. Communications research and the concept of the mass. Amer Sociological Rev 18 1953.
Gurko, L. Heroes, highbrows and the popular mind. Indianapolis 1953.
Hovland, C. I. et al. Communication and persuasion. New Haven 1953. Psychological studies of opinion change.
International Social Science Bull 5 1953. Special issue: Public opinion research. Introd by G. Gallup.
Jarrell, R. Poetry and the age. New York 1953.
Leavis, F. R. Valedictory. Scrutiny 19 1953.
Lewis, M. H. The importance of illiteracy. 1953.
UNESCO. Reports on the facilities of mass communications. Paris 1953–.
Albrecht, M. C. The relationship of literature to society. Amer Jnl of Sociology 59 1954.
Barton, J. The effect of a decrease in the value of money on taste and literature. Dalhousie Rev 33 1954.
Bentley, A. F. An inquiry into inquiries: essays in social theory. Boston 1954. An examination of basic problems in natural and social sciences and in the theory of knowing and the known.
Borinski, L. Die Funktion der Literatur in der englischen Gesellschaft. Die Neueren Sprachen 3 1954.
Brogan, D. W. The problem of high culture and mass culture. Diogenes no 5 1954.
Cauter, T. and J. S. Downham. The communication of ideas: a study of contemporary influences on urban life. 1954.
Davie, D. Is there a London literary racket? Twentieth Century 155 1954; replies ibid.
Fearing, F. Social impact of the mass media of communications. Nat Soc for the Study of Education Yearbook 53 1954.
Friedsam, H. J. Bureaucrats as heroes. Social Forces 32 1954. Bureaucrats as fictional heroes.
Herzog, H. Motivations and gratifications of daily serial listeners. In The process and effects of mass communications, ed W. Schramm, Urbana 1954.
Katz, D. et al (ed). Public opinion and propaganda: a book of readings. New York 1954.
McLuhan, M. Poetry and society. Poetry 84 1954.
Mass communication, power and influence. Nature 16 Oct 1954. Leading article.
Riesman, D. Culture: popular and unpopular. In his Individualism reconsidered, New York 1954.
Saunders, J. W. Poetry in the managerial age. EC 4 1954.
Schramm, W. (ed). The process and effects of mass communication. Urbana 1954. With annotated bibliography.
Wagner, G. The parade of pleasure. 1954.
Weaver, R. Economics of our literature. Queen's Quart 60 1954.
Katz, E. and P. Lazarsfeld. Personal influence: the part played by people in the flow of mass communication. Glencoe Ill [1955].
Schramm, W. Information theory and mass communications. Journalism Quart 32 1955.
Wright, C. R. Evaluating mass media campaigns. International Social Science Bull 7 1955.
Albrecht, M. C. Does literature reflect common values? Amer Sociological Rev 21 1956.
Daiches, D. Criticism and sociology; Criticism and the cultural context. In his Critical approaches to literature, Englewood Cliffs 1956.
Krieghbaum, H. Facts in perspective: the editorial page and news interpretation. Englewood Cliffs 1956.
Priestley, J. B. The writer in a changing society. 1956. Lecture.
Seldes, G. The public arts. New York 1956. Identifies the public arts and argues 'the people have valid rights' over such cultural institutions.
Snow, C. P. The two cultures. New Statesman 6 Oct 1956.
— The two cultures and the scientific revolution. Cambridge 1959. See F. R. Leavis, Two cultures?—the significance of C. P. Snow, 1962.
— Recent thoughts on the two cultures. [1962].
— The two cultures; and A second look: an expanded version of The two cultures and the scientific revolution, Cambridge 1964.
Bolton, C. D. Sociological relativism and one new freedom. Ethics 68 1957.
Chapin, R. E. Mass communications: a statistical analysis. Ann Arbor 1957.

Chase, R. The fate of the avant-garde. Partisan Rev 24 1957.

Fraser, L. M. Propaganda. 1957.

Haag, E. van den. Of happiness and of despair we have no measure. In Mass culture, ed B. Rosenberg and D. M. White, Glencoe Illinois 1957; rptd in E. van den Haag and R. Ross, The fabric of society: an introduction to the social sciences, New York 1957.

Hoggart, R. The uses of literacy. 1957.

— A matter of rhetoric? American writers and British readers. Nation 27 April 1957; rptd in his Speaking to each other vol 2, 1970.

Hovland, C. I. (ed). The order of presentation in persuasion. New Haven 1957.

Journal of Social Issues 13 1957. Special Issue: Brain washing.

Katz, E. The two-step flow of communication: an up-to-date report on an hypothesis. Public Opinion Quart 21 1957.

Klapper, J. T. What we know about the effects of mass communication: the brink of hope. Ibid.

Lang, K. Mass appeal and minority tastes. In Mass culture: the popular arts in America, 1957, below.

Lerner, M. Arts and popular culture. In his America as a civilization, New York 1957.

Rieser, M. The aesthetic theory of social realism. Jnl of Aesthetics & Art Criticism 16 1957.

Rosenberg, B. and D. M. White (ed). Mass culture: the popular arts in America. Glencoe Ill 1957.

Schramm, W. Responsibility in mass communication. New York 1957.

Scott, R. I. Modern themes of communication and types of literature. James Joyce Rev 1 1957.

Shils, E. Daydreams and nightmares: reflections on the criticism of mass culture. Sewanee Rev 65 1957.

De Fleur, M. L. and O. N. Larsen. The flow of information. New York 1958.

Escarpit, R. Sociologie de la littérature. Paris 1958. Tr E. Pick, vol 4, Lake Erie College Studies, Painesville Ohio 1965.

Fiedler, L. (ed). The art of the essay. New York 1958. Section 3: Essays on mass culture and high culture.

Gamberg, H. The modern literary ethos: a sociological interpretation. Social Forces 37 1958.

Hoffman, F. The knowledge of literature. Amer Quart 10 1958.

Knapp, R. H. Achievement and aesthetic preference. In Motives in fantasy, action and society: a method of assessment and study, ed J. W. Atkinson, Princeton 1958.

Lerner, D. Comfort and fun: morality in a nice society. Amer Scholar 1958.

Lukács, G. Zur Gegenwartsbedeutung des kritischen Realismus. Berlin 1958. Tr 1963 (as The meaning of contemporary realism. Introd G. Steiner).

Public Opinion Quart 21 1958. Special issue: Twenty years of public opinion research.

Steiner, G. Marxism and the literary critic. Encounter 11 1958.

Williams, R. Culture and society 1780–1950. 1958, 1961 (with postscript).

Winger, H. W. (ed). Iron curtains and scholarship: the exchange of knowledge in a divided world. Chicago 1958.

Bode, C. The anatomy of American popular culture 1840–1861. Berkeley 1959.

Buckley, V. Poetry and morality: studies in the criticism of Arnold, Eliot and Leavis. 1959.

Halsey, Van R. Fiction and the businessman. Amer Quart 11 1959.

Howe, I. Mass society and post-modern fiction. Partisan Rev 26 1959.

Knapp, R. H. et al. Educational level, class status and aesthetic preference. Jnl of Social Psychology 50 1959.

Kulischeck, C. How high is the English teacher's brow? Western Humanities Rev 9 1959.

McLuhan, M. Printing and social change. Renascence 11 1959.

Sussman, L. Mass political letter writing in America: the growth of an institution. Public Opinion Quart 23 1959.

Tannenbaum, P. H. and J. E. Noah. Sportuguese: a study of sports page communication. Journalism Quart 36 1959.

UNESCO. The provision of popular reading materials. Ed C. G. Richards, Paris 1959.

White, L. A. The concept of culture. Amer Anthropologist 61 1959.

Wright, C. Mass communication: a sociological perspective. New York 1959.

Betsky, S. Literature and general culture. Universities Quart 14 1960.

— Towards a new definition of culture. Chicago Rev 14 1960.

Carpenter, E. S. and M. McLuhan (ed). Explorations in communication. Boston 1960.

Daedalus 89 1960. Special no: Mass culture and mass media.

Davison, W. On the effects of communication. Public Opinion Quart 24 1960; rptd in People, society and mass communications, ed L. A. Dexter and D. M. White, New York 1964.

Dudek, L. Literature and the press: a history of printing, printed media and their relation to literature. Toronto 1960.

Emery, E. et al. Introduction to mass communications. New York 1960, 1968 (rev).

Glicksberg, C. I. Literature and religion. Dallas 1960.

Green, M. A mirror for Anglo-Saxons. 1960. A cultural evaluation of Britain from within and abroad.

Institut de Littérature et de Techniques Artistiques de Masse. Le réalisme. Bordeaux 1960.

Klapper, J. T. The effects of mass communication. Glencoe Ill [1960], 1965 (rev).

Kristol, I. High, low, modern: some thoughts on pop culture and pop government. Encounter 15 1960. Reply by J. G. Weightman.

Macdonald, D. Masscult and midcult. Partisan Rev 27 1960.

Popular culture and personal responsibility. 1960. N.U.T. conference report.

Rühle, J. Literatur und Revolution. Köln, Berlin 1960. Tr (in expanded form) by J. Steinberg, as Literature and revolution: a critical study of the writer and communism in the twentieth century, 1969. With bibliography.

Van Nostrand, A. The denatured novel. Indianapolis 1960. Effect of publishing pressures.

Weber, E. (ed). Paths to the present. New York 1960.

Berelson, B. The great debate on cultural democracy. Stud in Public Communication 1 1961.

Institut de Littérature et de Techniques Artistiques de Masse. L'originalité. Bordeaux 1961.

Jacobs, N. (ed). Culture for the millions?: mass media in modern society. Princeton 1961.

Lewis, C. S. Experiment in criticism. Cambridge 1961.

Lowenthal, L. Literature, popular culture and society. Englewood Cliffs 1961.

McLuhan, M. The humanities in the electronic age. Humanities Assoc Bull 34 1961.

Mander, J. The writer and commitment. 1961.

Reitlinger, G. The economics of taste: the rise and fall of picture prices 1760–1960. 1961. Plastic arts.

Twentieth Century 169 1961. Special issue on Comedy. Various forms, including literary and popular.

Bergonzi, B. Literary criticism and humanist morality. New Blackfriars 43 1962.

Escarpit, R. Le livre et le conscrit. Bordeaux 1962.

Habermas, J. Strukturwandel der Öffentlichkeit. Berlin 1962.

Jeffreys, M. V. C. Personal values in the modern world. 1962.

McLuhan, M. The Gutenberg galaxy: the making of typographic man. Toronto 1962.

Morin, E. L'esprit du temps: essai sur la culture de masse. Paris 1962.

Ong, W. J. Wired for sound: teaching, communications and technological culture; The barbarian within: outsiders inside society today. In his Barbarian within, New York 1962.

Peterson, T. From mass media to class media. Challenge 10 1962; rptd in People, society and mass communications, ed L. A. Dexter and D. M. White, New York 1964.

Robbe-Grillet, A. Pour un nouveau roman. Paris 1962. Tr B. Wright, with Instantanés, Paris 1963, as Snapshots and Towards a new novel, 1965.

Stanton, F. Mass media and mass culture. Hanover New Hampshire 1962.

Warshow, R. The immediate experience. New York 1962. Essays, especially on cinema, from point of view of culture and society.

Williams, R. Communications. 1962, 1966 (rev).

— The existing alternative in communication. 1962.

Brown, J. A. C. Techniques of persuasion: from propaganda to brainwashing. 1963.

Fryer, P. Mrs Grundy: studies in English prudery. 1963. Censorship and cultural attitudes.

Halloran, J. D. Control or consent? 1963. Development and effects of mass media.

Hartley, A. The cultural debate. In his A state of England, 1963.

Hoggart, R. Difficulties of democratic debate: the reception of the Pilkington Report on broadcasting. Teachers College Record 64 1963; CQ 5 1963; rptd in his Speaking to each other, 1970.

Institut de Littérature et de Techniques Artistiques de Masse. Littérature et sous-littérature. Bordeaux 1963.

Krieghbaum, H. Reporting science information through the mass media. Journalism Quart 40 1963.

Leavis, F. R. Scrutiny: a retrospect. Scrutiny 20 1963.

Nafziger, R. O. and D. M. White. Introduction to mass communications research. Baton Rouge 1963.

Read, H. To hell with culture. 1963.

Schramm, W. (ed). The science of human communication: new directions and new findings in communication research. New York 1963.

Berelson, B. In the presence of culture. Public Opinion Quart 28 1964.

Dexter, L. A. and D. M. White (ed). People, society and mass communications. New York 1964. With critical bibliography.

Goldmann, L. Pour une sociologie du roman. Paris 1964.

Green, M. Science and the shabby curate of poetry. 1964. The 'two cultures' etc.

Hall, S. and P. Whannel. The popular arts. 1964.

Hausdorff, D. Magazine humor and popular morality 1929–34. Journalism Quart 41 1964.

Is this us?—a symposium. Twentieth Century 173 1964. The face of Britain in TV, films, theatre, schools etc.

Knights, L. C. Literature and theology: a discussion [by various writers] with L. C. Knights. Life of the Spirit 18 1964.

Koestler, A. The act of creation. 1964. A study of the process of creativity.

McLuhan, M. New media and the arts. Arts in Society Mag 3 1964.

Mendelsohn, H. Sociological perspectives on the study of mass communications. In People, society and mass communications, ed L. A. Dexter and D. M. White, New York 1964.

Thompson, D. (ed). Discrimination and popular culture. 1964.

UNESCO. Mass media and national development, by W. Schramm. Paris 1964.

Watt, I. Literature and society. In The arts in society, ed R. N. Wilson, Englewood Cliffs 1964.

White, D. W. Mass-communications research: a view in perspective. In people, society and mass communications, ed L. A. Dexter and D. M. White, New York 1964.

Wilenski, H. L. High culture and mass culture. New Society 14 May 1964.

Bantock, G. H. The implications of literacy. Leicester 1965.

Bergonzi, B. Heroes' twilight. 1965. Literature and First World War.

Centre for Contemporary Cultural Studies, Birmingham. Annual reports, 1965–. Reports work in progress (literature and society, mass media) and approaches thereto.

Halloran, J. D. The effects of mass communications. Leicester 1965.

Levin, H. Towards a sociology of the novel. JHI 26 1965.

McLeod, J. et al. Alienation and uses of the mass media. Public Opinion Quart 29 1965.

Peterson, T. et al. The mass media and modern society. New York 1965.

Trilling, L. Beyond culture. New York 1965.

UNESCO. The book revolution, by R. Escarpit. Paris 1965; tr 1966.

Adler, M. Poetry and politics. Pittsburgh 1966.

Baumol, W. J. and W. G. Bowen (ed). Performing arts—the economic dilemma: a study of problems common to theatre, opera, music, drama. Boston 1966.

Crisis in criticism. TLS 23 June 1966.

De Fleur, M. L. Theories of mass communications. New York 1966.

— Mass communication and social change. Social Forces 44 1966.

DeMott, B. The anatomy of Playboy. In his You don't say, New York 1966.

Harrison, J. R. The anti-democratic intelligentsia. In his Reactionaries, 1966.

Hoggart, R. Literature and society. Amer Scholar 35 1966; rptd in his Speaking to each other, vol 2 1970.

Institut de Littérature et de Techniques Artistiques de Masse. La littérature à l'heure du livre de poche. Bordeaux 1966. By R. Escarpit et al.

Kavolis, V. Community dynamics and artistic creativity. Amer Sociological Rev 31 1966.

Mendelsohn, H. Mass entertainment. New Haven 1966.

Smith, A. G. (ed). Communications and culture: readings in the codes of human interaction. New York 1966.

Smith, H. A. The cult of the dull not-being. Alta 1 1966. Drama and society.

Spearman, D. The novel and society. 1966.

Steinberg, C. S. (ed). Mass media and communication. New York 1966.

Tucker, N. Understanding the mass media. Cambridge 1966.

Wilding, M. Literary critics and mass media culture. Dissent 18 1966.

Bear, A. Cultural criticism: the convergence of two traditions. Cambridge Rev 6 May 1967.

Gerson, W. M. and S. H. Lund. Playboy magazine: sophisticated smut or social revolution? Jnl of Popular Culture 1 1967.

Goldmann, L. The sociology of literature: status and problems of method. International Social Science Jnl 19 1967.

Halloran, J. D. Attitude formation and change. Leicester 1967. Television Research Committee working paper no 2.

L'Institut de Sociologie. Littérature et société: problèmes de méthodologie de la sociologie de la littérature. Brussels 1967. See also later pbns of the Institut.

Leenhardt, J. The sociology of literature: some stages in its history. International Social Science Jnl 19 1967.

MacIntyre, A. Sociology and the novel. TLS 27 July 1967.

Ong, W. J. In the human grain: further explorations in contemporary culture. New York 1967.

Pospelov, G. N. Literature and sociology. International Jnl of Social Science 19 1967.

Stearn, G. E. (ed). McLuhan hot and cool. New York 1967. Critiques of McLuhan's pronouncements.

Stein, W. Humanism and tragic redemption. New Blackfriars 48 1967.

—— Redemption and revolution. Ibid.

—— Redemption and tragic transcendence. Slant no 15 1967.

Stephenson, W. The play theory of mass communications. Chicago 1967.

Trenaman, J. M. Communication and comprehension. 1967.

Worsley, P. Libraries and mass culture. Library Assoc Record 69 1967.

Anderson, P. Components of the national culture. New Left Rev 50 1968; rptd in Student power, ed A. Cockburn and R. Blackburn 1969. See D. Martin, Encounter 24 1970 and C. Ricks, Listener 13 March 1969.

Briggs, A. Mass entertainment: the origins of a modern industry. Adelaide 1968.

Cantor, N. F. and M. S. Werthman (ed). The history of popular culture. New York 1968. A general reader from the ancient world to twentieth century.

Duncan, H. D. Symbolism in society. New York 1968.

Finkelstein, S. Sense and nonsense of McLuhan. New York 1968.

Halloran, J. D. Producer researcher co-operation in mass media research. 1968. European Broadcasting Union.

Hancock, A. Mass communication. 1968.

Hoggart, R. The literary imagination and the study of society. Birmingham 1968.

King, C. Industry and mass communication. 1968.

Larsen, O. N. (ed). Violence and the mass media. New York 1968.

'Orwell, George' (E. A. Blair). Collected essays, journalism and letters. Ed S. Orwell and I. Angus. 4 vols 1968. A number of the most relevant essays are listed separately above according to date of their first appearance.

UNESCO. New trends in the study of mass communications, by E. Morin. Paris 1968. Rptd Birmingham 1969 (Centre for Contemporary Cultural Studies, Occasional paper 7).

Wicker, B. and T. Eagleton. From culture to revolution. 1968. Includes T. Eagleton, The idea of a common culture; M. Green, Literary values and left politics: a liberal criticism; R. Williams, Culture and revolution: a response. See J. M. Cameron, New Blackfriars 50 1969.

Bergonzi, B. Character and liberalism I and II. New Blackfriars 50 1969.

Hall, S. The hippies: an American 'moment'. In Student power, ed J. Nagel 1969. General cultural implications.

McQuail, D. Towards a sociology of mass communications. 1969. With annotated bibliography.

Poole, R. C. Lévi-Strauss: myth's magician. New Blackfriars 50 1969.

—— Structuralism sidetracked. Ibid.

'West, Rebecca' (C. I. Andrews). McLuhan and the future of literature. Oxford 1969. Eng Assoc address.

Brown, R. L. Approaches to the historical development of mass media studies. In Media sociology, ed J. Tunstall 1970.

Chaney, D. The social organization of mass communications. 1970.

Hoggart, R. Speaking to each other. 2 vols 1970.

Roszak, T. The making of a counter culture. New York 1970. The technocratic society and its opposition.

Tunstall, J. (ed). Media sociology: a reader. 1970.

20th-Century Studies no 3 1970. Special Issue: Structuralism.

(3) RELATIONS WITH OTHER MEDIA

Includes introductory studies of the media (a number of titles being selected from different periods in the development of a medium when possible); those discussing the technical and aesthetic aspect of the media which might be helpful to the literary scholar; and studies which purport to relate a non-literary medium to literature. It has been thought useful to include a fairly wide range of the periodical literature devoted to these media. Reference should also be made to Authorship, cols 67–8, below, for titles concerned with writing for film and broadcasting. For the adaptation of plays for the film or for broadcasting, see under Drama, cols 861–4, below.

General Works

UNESCO. Report of the Commission on technical needs in press, radio, film. Paris 1947.

—— Press, film and radio in the world today. Paris 1949 onwards.

—— World communications, press, radio, television, film. Paris 1950. Frequent subsequent edns.

Gurko, L. Three arts that beat as one. In The art of the essay, ed L. Fiedler, New York 1950. Film, radio, television.

Literature and the lively arts. TLS 14 Nov 1952. Correspondence, including L. MacNeice and P. Dickinson, 21 Nov–19 Dec.

McLuhan, M. Media as art forms. Explorations 3 1954.

—— Sight, sound and the fury. Commonweal 60 1954. Relates reading to other media.

—— Media alchemy in art and society. Jnl of Communication 8 1958.

—— Understanding media: the extensions of man. New York 1964.

The Gramophone

For a checklist of recorded poetry and literature see Literary recordings, *Washington 1966 (Library of Congress).*

Faber, G. The exploitation of books by broadcasting and talking machine. Author 47 1936.

Batten, J. Joe Batten's book: the story of sound recording. 1956.

Gelatt, R. The fabulous phonograph. 1956.

Hughes, D. Recorded music. In Discrimination and popular culture, ed D. Thompson 1964.

Murrells, J. Daily Mail book of golden discs. 1966.

Gramophone Periodicals

Sound wave and talking machine record. Vol 1 no 1–vol 14 no 12, 1907–Dec 1920. Continued as Sound wave and gramophone journal, vol 15 no 1–vol 17 no 1, Jan 1921–Jan 1923. Continued as Sound wave: the gramophone journal and wireless times, vol 17 no 2–vol 19 no 2, Feb 1923–Feb 1925. Continued as Sound wave: the gramophone journal, vol 19 no 3–vol 25 no 9, March 1925–Sept 1931. Continued as Sound wave, the gramophone journal and wireless times, vol 25 no 10–vol 35 no 1, Oct 1931–Jan 1941. Continued as Sound wave illustrated, Jan/Feb 1943–Sept 1945; then Sound, Oct 1945–July 1950. Continued as Sound and vision, Sept 1950 onwards. Incorporated Phono trader and recorder, June 1904–Aug 1913.

The gramophone. April 1923 onwards.

The gramophone record. Title varies 1933–?

Film

Bibliographies of special interest include: A. G. S. Enser, Filmed books and plays: a list of books and plays from which films have been made 1928–49, 1951, with suppls;

R. B. Dimmitt, A title guide to the talkies, Oct 1927–Dec 1963, *New York 1965 (with details of sources); and* National film archive index 1933–68, *British Film Institute (on microfilm, giving film review references; films prior to 1933 are included). The catalogue,* Films for universities, *British Universities Film Council,* 1968, *should be consulted.*

Lescarboura, A. C. Behind the motion-picture screen: how the scenario writer, director, cameraman and others work. New York 1919.

Ramsaye, T. A million and one nights. New York 1926.

Pudovkin, V. I. On film technique. 1929. Tr and annotated by I. Montague 1930; 1933 (enlarged edn, as Film technique).

Rotha, P. The film till now. 1930, 1960 (rev).
—— The documentary film. 1939.

Arnheim, R. Film als Kunst. Berlin 1932; tr 1933 (as Film). Expanded as Film as art, Berkeley 1957.

Ervine, St J. G. The alleged art of the cinema. 1934.

Bardèche, M. and R. Brasillach. Histoire du cinéma. Paris 1935; tr New York 1938 (as The history of motion pictures).

Lye, L. and L. Riding. Film-making. Epilogue 1 1935.

Spottiswoode, R. A grammar of the film. 1935.

Barnes, W. Photoplay as a literary art. Newark NJ 1936.

Benjamin, W. L'œuvre d'art à l'époque de sa reproduction mecanisée. Zeitschrift für Sozialforschung 5 1936; tr in his Illuminations, New York 1968. The film as the art form which initiates a change in role of the work of art from ritual to politics.

Nicoll, A. Film and theatre. New York 1936.
—— Literature and the film. Eng Jnl 26 1937.

Perlman, W. J. (ed). The movies on trial. New York 1936.

Box, S. Film publicity: a handbook on the production and distribution of propaganda films. 1937.

Davy, C. (ed). Footnotes to the film. 1937.

League of Nations. R. Arnheim [et al], Le rôle intellectuel du cinéma, 1937.

Eisenstein, S. M. The film sense. [1938]. Tr J. Leyda 1942.
—— Film form. Tr J. Leyda 1949.

Jacobs, L. The rise of the American film: a critical history. New York 1939. With detailed bibliography.

Manvell, R. Film 1944, 1946 (rev).
—— The film and its public. 1955.
—— The living screen. 1961. Film and television.

Farrell, J. T. The language of Hollywood. In his League of frightened Philistines, New York 1945.

Mayer, J. P. Sociology of film. 1945.
—— British cinemas and their audiences. 1948.

Golding, L. Novel into film. Film Quart no 1 1946.

Grierson, J. Grierson on documentary. Ed F. Hardy 1946.

Kennedy, M. M. The mechanized muse. 1947. Films and writing.

Low, R. The history of the British film. Vol 1, 1896–1906. With R. Manvell 1948; vol 2, 1906–14, 1949; vol 3, 1914–18, 1950. Details of adaptations. Continuing.

Walker, F. Hollywood in fiction. Prairie Schooner 2 1948.

Warshow, R. The gangster as tragic hero. Partisan Rev 15 1948; rptd in his Immediate experience, New York 1962.
—— Movie chronicle: the western. Partisan Rev 21 1954; rptd in his Immediate experience, New York 1962.

Reisman, L. Cinema technique and mass culture. Amer Quart 1 1949.

Rippy, F. W. On tragedy, motion pictures and Greta Garbo. Arizona Quart 5 1949.

Handel, L. A. Hollywood looks at its audience. Urbana 1950.

Leites, N. and M. Wolfenstein. Movies: a psychological study. Glencoe Ill 1950.

Powdermaker, H. Hollywood: the dream factory: an anthropologist looks at the movie-makers. Boston 1950.

Asheim, L. From book to film: class appeal. Quart of Film, Radio & Television 6 1952; rptd in Reader in public opinion and communication, ed B. Berelson and M. Janowitz, Glencoe Ill 1953.

Political and Economic Planning. The British film industry. 1952.

Ross, L. Picture. New York 1952. Problems of creativity in practical film-making.

Balázs, B. Theory of the film: character and growth of a new art. New York 1953.

Montgomery, J. M. Comedy films 1894–1954. 1954.

Orrom, M. and R. Williams. Preface to the film. 1954.

Kael, P. Movies, the desperate art. Berkley Book of Modern Writing 3, ed W. Phillips and P. Rahv, New York 1956; rptd and rev, Film, an anthology, ed D. Talbot, Berkeley 1959. Inadequacies of Hollywood and avant-garde approaches.

Riesman, D. The oral tradition: the written word and the screen image. Yellow Springs 1956.

Bluestone, G. Novels into film. Baltimore 1957.

Novel into film and film into novel. Author 68 1957.

Knight, A. The liveliest art. 1959.

Hunt, A. The film. In Discrimination and popular culture, ed D. Thompson 1964.

Costello, D. P. The serpent's eye: Shaw and the cinema. Notre Dame Ind 1965. Introd by C. Lewis.

Hunco, G. A. The sociology of film art. New York 1965. Introd by L. Lowenthal.

Groves, P. D. (ed). Film in higher education and research. New York 1966.

Lahue, K. C. Continued next week. Norman Oklahoma 1966. On film serials.

Fielding, R. (ed). A technological history of motion pictures and television. Berkeley 1967.

Sontag, S. Theatre and film. In her Styles of radical will, New York 1969.

Tyler, P. Underground film: a critical history. New York 1969.

Baxter, J. Science fiction in the cinema. New York 1970.

Curran, J. The impact of television on the audience for national newspapers, 1945–68. In Media sociology, ed J. Tunstall 1970.

Film Periodicals

Optical lantern and kinematograph journal. Vol 1 no 1–vol 3 no 6, Nov 1904–April 1907. Continued as Kinematograph weekly no 658, 4 Dec 1919 onwards.

Cinematograph monthly. 1 only, Oct 1911.

Pictures. Nos 1–60, 21 Oct 1911–7 Dec 1912.

The Kinematograph Weekly monthly alphabetical film record. Nos 1–63, ? April 1912–July 1917. Continued as Monthly alphabetical film record, nos 64–74, Aug 1917–June 1918. Continued as Monthly film record nos 75–81, July 1918–Jan 1919. Continued as Kinematograph monthly record, nos 82–124, Feb 1919–Aug 1927.

Film censor. Nos 1–192, 26 June 1912–25 Feb 1916.

Moving picture offered list. Nos 1–207, 11 July 1913–15 March 1918. Continued as British kinema chronicle, nos 208–9, 15 April–16 May 1918.

Pathés [sic] cine journals. Nos 1–5, 4 Oct–1 Nov 1913. Continued as Pathé cinema journal, nos 6–64, 8 Nov 1913–30 July 1914.

Picturegoer. 11 Oct 1913 onwards. Title varies between 1914 and 1931, including Pictures and the picturegoer, Picturegoer and theatre monthly, Picturegoer weekly, Picturegoer and film weekly.

Pictures and pleasures. Manchester. Nos 1–52, 17 Nov 1913–9 Nov 1914. Continued as Film renter, nos 53–695, 16 Nov 1914–5 March 1937. Incorporated in Daily film renter.

Cinematograph exhibitor's mail. Vol 4 no 12, 25 March 1914–vol 5 no 22, 2 Sept 1914.

The screen. Woodchester. Vol 1 no 1–vol 10 no 7, June 1914–21 July 1917. Not found; only included because title indicates possibly a film jnl.

Pathé weekly bulletin. New ser nos 1–72, 20 Aug 1914–16 Dec 1915.

Cinegoer. Nos 1–8, 26 Feb–15 April 1916.

Photo playwright. Croydon. 1 only? Aug 1916.

Picture show. 3 May 1919–? Stories from film-plays.

British films. Registration issue, Dec 1919.

Motion picture studio. Nos 1–142, 11 June 1921–23 Feb 1924. Incorporated in Kinematograph weekly.

Film fiction. 1 only? Aug 1921.

Pictureland. Dec 1924–Dec 1939.

Daily film renter. 10 Jan 1927 onwards.

Ideal kinema. 17 Feb 1927 onwards.

Cinema world illustrated. Vol 1 no 1–vol 2 no 10, May 1927–Feb 1929.

Motion picture news. Vol 1 nos 1–4, June–Oct 1927; vol 1 nos 1–8, Dec 1927–July 1928. Continued as British motion picture news, vol 1 nos 10–13, 18 Aug–3 Nov 1928.

Close-up. Territet, Switzerland. Vol 1 no 1–vol 10 no 4 July 1927–Dec 1933.

Amateur film maker. 1 only, Jan 1928.

Cinematograph Exhibitors' Association of Great Britain and Ireland. Cinematograph times, Vol 1 nos 1–3, 10–24 Nov 1928 [registration issues]; nos 1–419, 8 Dec 1928–12 Aug 1939. Technical section vol 1 no 1–vol 15 no 391, 1928–15 April 1937 when incorporated in Era. Film report, 31 Jan 1938–29 Dec 1944. Annual reports 1920–3, 1926, 1930, 1950 onwards.

The British film journal. Nos 1–6, 1928–July 1929.

Who's who in filmland. 1928.

Cinema construction. Vol 1–vol 2 no 1, [1929]–March 1930. Continued as Cinema theatre and allied construction, vol 2, no 2–vol 3, no 2, April 1930–April 1931. Continued as Cinema theatre and general construction, vol 3 no 3–vol 6 no 10, May 1931–Dec 1934. Continued as Cinema and theatre construction, vol 6 no 11–vol 14 no 5, Jan 1935–Oct 1947. Continued as Cinema and theatre, vol 14 no 6–vol 16 no 1, Nov 1947–June 1948.

Experimental cinema. Philadelphia. Feb 1930–June 1934.

Film truth. Vol 1 nos 1–2 Nov–Dec 1930.

Weekly kinema guide. Nos 1–17. 1 Dec 1930–23/29 March 1931.

British film-studio mirror. Nos 1–3, Dec 1931–Feb/March 1932.

British kinematograph society. Proceedings 1–6, 1931–6. Journal, vol 1 no 1–vol 10 no 3, Dec 1937–June 1947. Continued as British kinematography, vol 11 onwards. Incorporated B.K.S. bulletin, vol 1 no 1–vol 2 no 4, 1940–1. Film production division. Proceedings 1945/46. Sub-standard division proceedings 1944/45. Theatre division proceedings 1944/45–1945/46.

Film pictorial. Nos 1–397, 27 Feb 1932–30 Sept 1939. Incorporated in Picture show.

Illustrated British film aspirant. Nos 1–2, Aug–Sept 1932.

Cinema quarterly. Edinburgh. Vol 1 no 1–vol 3 no 4, autumn 1932–summer 1935 [vol 3 no 2 dated winter 1935]. Continued as World film news and television progress, London, vol 1 no 1–vol 3 no 4, April 1936–Aug 1938. Continued as See: world film news, vol 3 no 5–vol 5 no 7, Sept–Nov 1938.

Films and fiction. Nos 1–24, Nov 1932–April 1933.

Cinema express. Nos 1–4, 16 Dec 1932–7 Jan 1933.

Film. No 1, spring 1933. Ed B. Braun Continued as Film art: review of advanceguard cinema, nos 1–10, summer 1933–spring 1937; nos 1–5 ed B. Braun; nos 6–10 ed Irene Nicholson and J. C. Moore, no 10 with R. Fairthorne.

Scenario: the film scenario magazine. Nos 1–4, March–June 1934.

Film picture stories. Vol 1 no 1–vol 2 no 30, 28 July 1934–16 Feb 1935.

British Film Institute. Annual report 1934 onwards. News letter, nos 1–3, Feb–Nov 1935. New index series 1950–?

The commercial film. Feb 1935–? Incorporated Commercial television and radio.

The film quarterly. Spring–summer 1935.

Cinegram. Vol 1 no 1–vol 4 no 79, 1937–9. Continued as Cinegram preview, vol 5 nos 1–23, 1939–40. Continued as March of time series nos 1–13, 1942–3. Continued as Cinegram review, 14–?, 1943.

Commercial film review. 1938–?

Documentary news letter. Vol 1 no 1–vol 6 no 10, Jan 1940–Nov/Dec 1947. Continued as Documentary film news, vol 7 no 61–vol 8 no 71, Jan 1948–Jan 1949.

British Film Producers' Association. Annual report 1942/43–?

Film review. 1944–? Ed F. Maurice Speed.

British film yearbook. 1946–?

Film quarterly. 1–4?, summer 1946–summer 1947. Ed P. Noble.

Sub-standard film. 23 May 1946–?

Film Book Club. News-letter. No 1, Dec 1946. Continued as Film Book Club news, no 2–? 1947–?

Mini-cinema. Dec 1946–?

The Penguin film review. Nos 1–9, 1946–9. Continued as The cinema, 1–?, 1950–2.

See hear: the radio & television pictorial. 1946–?

World film digest. Vol 1 no 1–vol 3 no 1, 1946–9. Annual suppls 1947–8.

The British film industry year book. 1947.

Film to-day books. ? 1947–?

Informational film year book. Edinburgh 1947–? With television from 1949/50.

R.A.F. Cinema Corporation. Ad astra: film news for the R.A.F. 1947–?

British film review. Nos 1–5, March–July 1948. Incorporated in Film monthly review.

Cinema studio. 31 March 1948–?

Broadcasting

See also H. L. Ewbank, A classified bibliography on radio speaking and writing, Quart Jnl of Speech 23 1937; British Broadcasting Corporation, British broadcasting: a bibliography, 1958; R. Fielding, Broadcast literature in motion picture periodicals: a bibliography, Whittier, Calif 1959 and J. Lohisse and N. Brichet, La télévision et l'enseignement, Louvain 1968 (an annotated world bibliography).

Milne, A. A. Authors and the BBC. Author 36 1926.

British Library of Political and Economic Science. (Coll. G. 406.) Collections of correspondence (a) on influence of British Broadcasting Corporation talks and reviews on the demand for books, 11 Sept 1932; and (b) from Times, 1931, on British Broadcasting Corporation literary criticism.

Cantril, H. and G. W. Allport. The psychology of radio. New York 1935. Compares radio and the printed page.

James, A. L. The broadcast word. 1935.

Arnheim, R. Radio. Tr M. Ludwig and H. Read 1936.

Faber, G. The exploitation of books by broadcasting and talking machines. Author 47 1936.

Mersand, J. Radio makes readers. Eng Jnl 27 1938.

Beville, H. M. Social stratification of the radio audience. Princeton 1939.

Reid, L. Broadcasting books. Saturday Rev of Lit 14 Jan 1939.

Cantril, H. The invasion from Mars. Princeton 1940. Analysis of panic resulting from broadcast by Orson Welles.

Lambert, R. S. Ariel and all his quality. 1940.

Lazarsfeld, P. F. Radio and the printed page. New York 1940.

Benn, E. J. P. The BBC monopoly. 1941.

Farquharson, M. G. et al. Glossary of broadcasting terms. 1941. For BBC staff.

Siepmann, C. A. Further thoughts on radio criticism. Public Opinion Quart 5 1941. By former employee of BBC.

'Orwell, George' (E. A. Blair). Poetry and the microphone. New Saxon Pamphlets 3 1945; rptd in his Collected essays vol 2, 1968.

Salmon, C. Broadcasting, speech and writing. Mint 1 1946.

British Broadcasting Corporation. The third programme: a symposium of opinions and plans. 1947.

Hughes, R. The second revolution: literature and radio. Virginia Quart Rev 23 1947.

—— The birth of radio drama. Atlantic Monthly 200 1957.

Sterner, A. P. Radio, motion pictures and reading interests: a study of high school pupils. New York 1947.

Warner, W. L. and W. E. Henry. The radio day-time serial: a symbolic analysis. Genetic Psychology Monograph no 37 1948; rptd in part in Reader in public opinion and communication, ed B. Berelson and M. Janowitz, Glencoe Ill 1953.

Wilson, F. C. The effectiveness of documentary broadcasts. Public Opinion Quart 12 1948.

McLuhan, M. Color-bar of BBC English. Canadian Forum 29 1949.

—— Project on understanding new media. 1960. Report to the National Association of Educational Broadcasters.

Cross, J. K. Broadcasting and the creative artist. Arts & Philosophy 1 1950.

O'Brien, M. Children's reactions to radio adaptations of juvenile books. New York 1950.

Kaiser, W. H. Television and reading. Lib Jnl 26 1951.

Report of the Broadcasting Committee, 1949. 1951. The Beveridge report.

Silvey, R. The intelligibility of broadcast talks. Public Opinion Quart 15 1951.

UNESCO. Television: a world survey. Paris 1953.

Bogart, L. Magazines since the rise of television. Journalism Quart 33 1956.

Paulu, B. Radio and television in the United Kingdom. Oxford 1956.

—— British broadcasting in transition. 1961.

Barnes, A. M. Research in radio and television news 1947–57. Journalism Quart 34 1957.

Hargreaves, J. The plight of the magazines. Author 67 1957. Effect of television.

Political and Economic Planning. Citizenship and television. 1957.

—— Television in Britain. 1958.

Himmelweit, H. T. et al. Television and the child. 1958.

Belson, W. A. Television and the family. 1959.

—— The impact of television. New York 1967.

McWhinnie, D. The art of radio. 1959.

Davis, D. The grammar of television production. 1960.

Briggs, A. The history of broadcasting in the United Kingdom. 1961 onwards.

Collison, R. L. Broadcasting in Britain. 1961.

Postman, N. The literature of television. In The committee on the study of television of the National Council of Teachers of English, Television and the teaching of English, New York 1961. Rptd in Mass media and communication, ed C. S. Steinberg, New York 1966.

Report of the Committee on broadcasting, 1960. 1962. The Pilkington Report. See H. Henry (ed), A Sunday Times enquiry [into public opinion and recommendations of the Pilkington Committee], 1962. Pamphlet.

Parker, E. B. The effects of television on public library circulation. Public Opinion Quart 27 1963.

Abrams, P. Radio and television. In Discrimination and popular culture, ed D. Thompson 1964.

Blumler, J. G. British television: the outlines of a research strategy. Br Jnl of Sociology 15 1964.

Skornia, H. J. Television and society. 1965.

Whitley, O. Broadcasting and the national culture. 1965.

Greene, H. What price culture? An examination of broadcasting finance. 1966.

Radio and the writer. Author 77 1966.

Hood, S. A survey of television. 1967.

Appia, H. and B. Cassen. Presse, radio et télévision en Grande-Bretagne. Paris 1969. Introd by A. Sampson.

Brown, R. L. Television and the arts. In The effects of television, ed J. Halloran. 1970.

Hoggart, R. Speaking to each other. 2 vols 1970. Includes The BBC and society; Difficulties of democratic debate (on the Pilkington report); Television as the archetype of mass communications: basic considerations; and The uses of television.

Broadcasting Periodicals

Sound wave and talking machine record. 1907 onwards. See col 54 above, for full details.

The broadcaster: the radiophone monthly for listeners-in. Vol 1 no 1–vol 28 no 387, Aug 1922–21 March 1936. Continued as Retailers' journal, wireless retailer and broadcaster. Issued Radio trade directory, nos 1–3, 1926–8, annual.

Radio times. 28 Sept 1923 onwards. Allied Expeditionary Force, British Expeditionary Force, Midland, North of England, Northern Ireland, Scottish, Welsh, West of England and television edns.

The broadcast listeners' year book. 1924.

Irish radio review. Dublin. Oct 1925–June 1926. Continued as Irish radio and musical review, July 1926–Feb 1927. Continued as Irish radio review March 1927–Feb 1928. Weekly suppl 6 March–12 June 1926.

The Elstree radio news. 1927.

Irish radio news. Dublin. No 1–? New ser no 1–? March 1928–?

Television (and short wave world). Vol 1 no 1–vol 12 no 139, March 1928–Sept 1939. Continued as Electronics and television, vol 12 no 140–vol 14 no 159, Oct 1939–May 1941. Continued as Electronic engineering, vol 14 no 160, June 1941 onwards.

BBC handbook. 1928–9. Continued as BBC yearbook, 1930–4. Continued as BBC annual, 1935–7. Continued as BBC handbook, 1938–42. Continued as BBC yearbook, 1943–52. Not pbd 1953–4. Continued as BBC handbook 1955 onwards.

The listener. 16 Jan 1929 onwards.

Television pictorial. Nos 1–2, 1–8 Dec 1933.

Who's who in broadcasting. 1933–?

Who's who on the wireless. 1934–?

Short wave. Vol 1 no 1–vol 2 no 4, Aug 1935–7.

BBC quarterly. Vol 1 no 1–vol 9 no 3, 1946–54.

The radio digest. 1946–? Monthly.

Television. Vols 1–4, 1946–9. Continued as Television and the viewers, vol 5–?, 1950.

The voice of the world: a quarterly selection of broadcasts of all nations. Vol 1 no 1–vol 2 no 2, 1947–8.

British television year book. 1947/48–?

Scan: the television journal. Vol 1 no 1–vol 3 no 8. May 1948–Dec 1950. Continued with Television news as Scan television news, vol 3 no 9–vol 4 no 2, Jan–June 1951. Continued as Television news vol 4 no 3–vol 6, July 1951–3.

Television news. Vol 1 no 1–vol 2 no 2, Nov 1948–Dec 1949. Incorporated in Scan.

B. AUTHORSHIP

(1) GENERAL WORKS

This section includes a number of autobiographies which touch upon the general problems of authorship. See also Literary Memoirs cols 15–26, above. The subsection, The author and politics, below, and some of the titles listed in Literature, Society and Communication, above, are also relevant.

The archives of The author, quarterly jnl of the Society of Authors, Playwrights and Composers, were transferred to the Manuscripts Department of the BM in April 1969. These are for the period 1884–1930 (but with certain extensions, e.g. for Shaw and Masefield). These archives are particularly strong in such matters as copyright, royalties and contracts. Some publishers are now depositing all but their most recent records with great libraries. Thus, after various vicissitudes (see W. E. Fredeman, The bibliographical significance of a publisher's archive: The Macmillan papers, SB 23 1970), much material from Macmillan's has found its way to BM, Reading University and New York Public Library (where the Macmillan Co of New York has deposited its correspondence files). Studies concerned with the situation of the author in America have been included where it is thought that these complement English studies or suggest approaches to the study of the situation in Britain.

Besant, W. Autobiography. 1902.

Bennett, E. A. The truth about an author. 1903 (anon).

Burnand, F. C. Records and reminiscences. 1904.

Freud, S. Der Dichter und das Phantasieren. Neue Revue 1 1908. Tr in Freud, Works vol 9, 1959 (Standard edn) (as Creative writers and day-dreaming).

Sheehan, P. A. Intellectuals: an experiment in Irish club life. New York 1911.

Flowerdew, H. The lost industry of novel-writing. Nineteenth Century & After 72 1912.

Green, A. S. Woman's place in the world of letters. 1913.

'Vere, Percy' (E. C. Jones). The confessions of a literary freelance. Edinburgh 1913.

Rollo, W. (ed). The writer's art by those who have practised it. Cambridge 1921.

Halliday, R. C. and A. van Rensselaer. The business of writing. New York 1922.

Adcock, A. St J. Gods of modern Grub street: impressions of contemporary authors. 1923.

Macdonald, W. The intellectual worker and his work. 1923.

Forster, E. M. Anonymity. Calendar of Modern Letters 2 1926. On signing one's work and the effect of anonymity.

Howe, M. A. de W. (ed). Later years of the Saturday Club 1870–1920. Boston 1927.

Paull, H. M. Literary ethics: a study in the growth of literary conscience. 1928.

Downey, J. E. The creative imagination: studies in the psychology of literature. 1929.

Sherwin, L. Literary thieves. Amer Bookman 68 1929.

Montague, C. E. A writer's notes on his trade. 1930.

Warren, D. On the working habits of authors. Amer Bookman 70 1930.

Ford, F. M. (formerly Hueffer). Return to yesterday. 1931.

Mottram, R. H. The faith of a writer in the twentieth century. Amer Bookman 74 1931.

Weeks, E. Method in their madness: sidelights in the writing habits of authors. New York 1932.

Brennecke, E. Manufacturing the writer. Commonweal 4 Jan 1933.

Brittain, V. Testament of youth. 1933.
— Thrice a stranger. 1938.
— On becoming a writer. 1947.

Horler, S. Excitement, an impudent autobiography. 1933.
— Strictly personal. 1934.
— More strictly personal. 1935.

Williamson, H. The difficulties of rural writing. Countryman 6 1933.

Jones, L. Psychoanalysis and creative literature. Eng Jnl 23 1934.

Hawkins, A. D. Fiction chronicle. Criterion Oct 1936.

Unemployed writers. Saturday Rev of Lit 6 June 1936.

Hart, H. (ed). The writer in a changing world. 1937. Papers from the Second Congress of American Writers.

Patrick, C. Creative thought in artists. Jnl of Psychology 4 1937.

The rights and wrongs of authors: publisher despotism and its decline. TLS 1 May 1937.

Uzzell, T. H. The literary impulse. Eng Jnl (College edn) 26 1937.

West, A. Crisis and criticism. 1937.

Maugham, W. S. The professional writer. Saturday Rev of Lit 29 June 1938.

Palmer, C. The truth about writing. 1938.

Royde-Smith, N. Attack and defence. Author 49 1938. The plight of the author.

Schullian, D. M. Latin in the schooling of British authors. Classical Jnl 35 1939. Refers to Howard Spring and A. A. Milne.

Straus, R. Authorship 1914–39. Author 50 1939.

Davis, E. Some aspects of the economics of authorship. New York 1940.

'Orwell, George' (E. A. Blair). The proletarian writer. Listener 19 Dec 1940; rptd in his Collected essays vol 2, 1968.

Bridgwater, W. Who writes on the campus? Saturday Rev of Lit 17 June 1944.

Marshall, A. C. The journalist in our midst. Author 54 1944. Journalists as authors.

Sitwell, O. What it feels like to be an author. Saturday Rev of Lit 19 Feb 1944.

Strong, L. A. G. Authorship. 1944.
— The writer's trade. 1953.

Spender, S. Modern writers in a world of necessity. Partisan Rev 12 1945.

Why I write. Gangrel nos 1–4, 1945. Series of articles by R. Heppenstall, G. Orwell, N. M. Gunn and A. Perlès. Article by G. Orwell rptd in his Collected essays, vol 1 1968.

The cost of letters. Horizon 14 1946.

Gelder, R. van. Writers and writing. New York 1946.

Morgan, C. The artist in the community. Yale Rev 35 1946.

Barrett, W. Writers and madness. Partisan Rev 14 1947.

Why do I write? an exchange of views between E. Bowen, G. Greene and V. S. Pritchett. 1948.

Bowen, E. English and American writing. Author 59 1949.

Hunt, C. A dictionary of word makers: pen pictures of the people behind our language. 1949.

Hull, H. R. (ed). The writer's book; presented by the Authors' Guild. New York 1950.

Jameson, M. S. The writer's situation. In her The writer's situation and other essays. 1950.
— The writer in contemporary society. Amer Scholar 35 1956.
— Parthian words. 1970. The state of the novel.

Smith, H. A. To the aid of the writer 1946–9. Birmingham 1950. Report of Atlantic Awards Scheme.

Casper, L. The writer as a calculated risk. Antioch Rev 11 1951.

Graves, R. Occupation: writer. 1951.

Brome, V. The writer's dilemma in Britain. Nation 174 1952.

Emmanuel, P. The vocation of the writer. Commonweal 27 June 1952.

Lehmann, J. On discovering authors. TLS 29 Aug 1952.

— (ed). The craft of letters in England. 1956.

Munson, G. The condition of the writer. Saturday Rev of Lit 16 Feb 1952.

Rice, E. The industrialization of the writer. Saturday Rev of Lit 12 April 1952.

Critical times for authors. Author 63 1953.

Wagner, G. The minority writer in England. Author 64 1953.

Godden, R. The writer must become a child. New York Times Book Rev 14 Nov 1954.

Priestley, J. B. Like it or lump it: come hell or high water, I am a writer. New York Times Book Rev 30 May 1954.

Smith, J. A. The poet's lot. Author 65 1954.

The status of the author. TLS 25 June 1954.

West, R. B. The modern writer. College Eng 15 1954.

Howarth, H. Writing in the welfare state. Commonweal 30 Sept 1955.

Brown, I. Fame that endures is for authors a sometime thing. New York Times Book Rev 11 March 1956.

Gordan, J. D. What is in a name? Authors and their pseudonyms. BNYPL 60 1956.

Six virtues for authors. Listener 22 Nov–27 Dec 1956. Includes articles by J. M. Murry, P. G. Wodehouse, L. C. Knights et al.

Snow, C. P. Writers in the welfare state. Commonweal 12 Oct 1956.

— Which side of the Atlantic? In Writing in America, ed J. Fisher and R. B. Silvers, New Brunswick 1960.

Cranston, M. et al. The writer in his age. London Mag 4 1957.

Guilford, J. P. Creative abilities in the arts. Psychological Rev 64 1957.

Quennell, P. Odi et amo: a note on the origins of the literary temperament. London Mag 4 1957.

Wedgwood, C. V. (ed). The author and the public: problems of communication. 1957.

Borden, M. Personal experience and the art of fiction. Essays by Divers Hands 29 1958.

Gunston, D. How long to write a book? Trace no 26 1958.

Pritchett, V. S. London literary letter: a report on writers and writing. New York Times Book Rev 11 May 1958.

Prospects for poets. Author 69 1959.

Limits of control. TLS 13 May–15 July 1960. An article each week with correspondence to 22nd July; rptd as The writers' dilemma, 1961. See C. P. Snow, TLS 9 June 1961.

Writers and the welfare state. Copenhagen 1960. Conference report. See particularly I. Murdoch, Against dryness; P. Rohde, Twenty theses about the writer and the welfare state.

Lord, W. J. How authors make a living: an analysis of free-lance writers' incomes 1953–7. Univ of Illinois dissertation 1961.

Lowenthal, L. The position of the writer in society. In his Literature, popular culture and society, New York 1961.

Altick, R. D. The sociology of authorship: social origins, education and occupations of 1,100 British writers 1800–1935. BNYPL 66 1962.

'Findlater, Richard' (B. Bain). What are writers worth? 1963. For Soc of Authors.

— The book writers: who are they? 1966. For Soc of Authors.

Jacobson, D. Jewish writing in England. Commentary 37 1964.

Kavolis, V. Economic conditions of artistic creativity. Amer Jnl of Sociology 70 1964.

— Artistic expression: a sociological analysis. Cornell 1968.

'O'Connor, Frank' (M. F. O'Donovan). The role of the Catholic novelist. Greyfriar 7 1964.

Saunders, J. W. In his Profession of English letters, 1964.

Campbell, C. The business of authorship. 1965. The New Writers' Guide series.

Church, R. How a novelist works. Essays by Divers Hands 33 1965.

Laski, M. The reader who matters. Guardian 25 Aug 1965. On amateur authors who plague established writers.

Institut de Littérature et de Techniques Artistiques de Masse. La solitude de l'écrivain. Bordeaux 1966.

Roberts, S. C. Adventures with authors. Cambridge 1966.

Sontag, S. The artist as exemplary sufferer. In her Against interpretation, New York 1966.

International Social Science Jnl 19 1967. Sociology of literary creativity.

The writer and the university. Alta no 7 winter 1968/9. Includes R. Hoggart, T. Stoppard, D. Lodge et al.

Astbury, R. The writer in the market place. 1969.

(2) MANUALS, GUIDES AND HANDBOOKS

For manuals etc on play writing, many of which were written for amateur playwrights, see The player's library: the catalogue of the library of the British Drama League, *1950 and suppls. A relatively small number of manuals and guides pbd in America has been included in order to give representation to the large number of such pbns circulated (and often reviewed) in Britain. Various levels and qualities of guidance are represented.* The Writers & Artists Year Book *gives guidance to authors on a variety of matters. See also* Guides for Journalists, *cols 1339–40, below, and the relevant sections of vol 3.*

Putnam, G. H. and G. P. Authors and publishers: a manual of suggestions for beginners in literature. New York 1883, 1900. Anon.

Miles, E. H. How to prepare essays, lectures, articles, books, speeches and letters. 1902.

Watson, E. H. L. Hints to young authors. 1902.

Bennett, E. A. How to become an author: a practical guide. 1903.

Heisch, C. E. The art and craft of the author: practical hints upon literary work. 1905.

Lorimer, A. The author's progress. Edinburgh 1906.

Booth, W. S. A practical guide to authors in their relations with publishers and printers. Boston 1907.

Good, A. Why your manuscripts return. [1907].

Sonnenschein, W. S. and J. A. Farquharson. A writer's manual. 1909.

Goodyear, R. A. H. Making money by the pen. Scarborough 1911.

Neal, R. W. Thought-building in composition: a training manual in the methods and mechanics of writing, with a supplementary division on journalistic writing as a means of practice. New York 1912.

'Fairfax, Larry'. How to earn money by writing. Pendlebury [1914].

Glyn, E. The Elinor Glyn system of writing. Auburn NY 4 vols 1922.

Uzzell, T. H. Narrative technique. New York 1923, 1934 (rev) (with W. C. Uzzell), 1959 (rev).

— Writing as a career: a handbook of literary vocational guidance. New York 1938.

Lawrence, C. E. The gentle art of authorship: a guide to literary practice. 1924.

Canby, H. S. Better writing. New York 1926.

Harrison, P. Free-lance fallacies. 1927.

—— Free-lance fiction. 1928.

Wilhelm, D. Writing for profit: with contributions by many editors and writers. New York 1930.

Straus, R. A whip for the women: being perhaps a little unexpectedly an impartial account of the present state of the novel market and intended to be a guide to all literary aspirants. 1931.

Horler, S. Writing for money. 1932.

Marriot, J. W. The art and craft of writing. 1933.

Hogarth, B. The technique of novel writing. 1934.

Weston, H. Form in literature: a theory of technique and construction. 1934. Introd J. Drinkwater.

The writer's desk book. 1934. By J. Brophy et al.

Freeman, W. Writing. 1935. Black's Writers' and Artists' Library no 1.

Weeks, E. This trade of writing. Boston 1935. With bibliography.

Houghton, S. G. and U. G. Olsen (ed). The writer's handbook. Boston 1936.

Hunt, C. Living by the pen. 1936, 1951 (rev).

—— Why editors regret. 1937.

—— How to write a book. 1952.

Peacocke, E. H. Writing for women. 1936.

What is a book? thoughts about writing [by various writers]. 1936.

Hepburn, A. G. Writers' guide to information. 1937. Black's Writers' and Artists' Library no 10.

Cherrington, E. Poems editors buy: a textbook of verse marketing. Pasadena 1939.

Graves, R. and A. Hodge. The reader over your shoulder: a handbook for writers of English prose. 1943.

Green, L. G. Author's post-war guide. 1947.

Flesch, R. and A. H. Lass. The way to write. New York 1948.

Brickell, H. Workouts for writers. Saturday Rev of Lit 2 April 1949.

Brooks, C. and R. P. Warren. Modern rhetoric. New York 1949. Rev as Fundamentals of good writing, a handbook of modern rhetoric, 1950.

Chamberlin, J. You too can write! Amer Mercury 69 1949.

Foster, R. E. and O. J. Anderson. Work in progress: practical aids to writing. Philadelphia [1949].

Michener, J. A. Reading before writing. Saturday Rev of Lit 30 April 1949.

Trilling, L. The lesson and the sequel. Horizon 14 1949. Short story about a 'Techniques for creative writing' group.

Meredith, S. Writing to sell. New York 1950.

Walter, M. The Martin Walter plot formula. Wendover nd [? 1950].

Writers at work. Author 60 1950. Methods of 11 authors.

Heaton, V. Writing for the American market. Kingswood Surrey 1953.

Strong, L. A. G. The writer's trade. 1953.

—— Instructions to young writers. 1958.

Dunbar, J. Writing for women's papers. 1954.

Dyson, A. E. The technique of debunking. Twentieth Century 157 1955. Refers particularly to Lytton Strachey but with wider implications.

Birmingham, F. A. et al. The writer's craft. 1958.

Farley, G. A. Income Tax for authors: an informed guide. 1960. New Writers' Guide.

Rice, K. The easy way to plot. nd [? 1960].

Campbell, C. The writers' reference book. 1963. New Writers' Guide.

Leed, J. (ed). The computer and literary style. Kent Ohio 1966.

Thomas, D. St J. Non-fiction: a guide to writing and publishing. Newton Abbot 1970.

Preparation of Manuscripts

Hart, H. Rules for compositors and readers at the University Press, Oxford. Oxford 1893 with frequent revisions; 37th edn 1967.

Collins, F. H. Author & printer: a guide for authors, editors, printers, correctors of the press, compositors and typists. 1905, 1909 (as Authors' & printers' dictionary).

Carey, G. V. Mind the stop: a brief guide to punctuation with a note on proof-correction. Cambridge 1939.

Crutchley, B. Preparation of manuscripts and correction of proofs. Cambridge 1951. Cambridge Authors' and Printers' Guides no 2. First edn: anon; frequently rev.

—— Making an index. Cambridge 1951. Cambridge Authors' and Printers' Guides no 3.

The MLA style sheet. Washington 1951, 1970 (rev).

Burbidge, P. G. Notes and references. Cambridge 1952. Cambridge Authors' and Printers' guides no 4.

—— Prelims and end-pages. Cambridge 1963. Cambridge Authors' and Printers' Guides no 7.

Spiker, S. Indexing your book: a practical guide for authors. Madison 1954.

British Federation of Master Printers. Authors' alterations cost money and cause delay. 1956.

British Standards Institution. Recommendations for proof correction and copy preparation. 1958.

—— Recommendations for the preparation of indexes for books, periodicals and other publications. 1964.

—— Recommendations for the abbreviation of titles of periodicals. 1967.

The indexer. 1958 onwards. Jnl of the Soc of Indexers.

Writing Fiction and the Novel

Hamilton, C. M. Materials and methods of fiction. New York. 1908, 1918 (rev and enlarged). Introd B. Matthews.

—— A manual of the art of fiction, New York 1918; rev as The art of fiction: a formulation of fundamental principles, with supplementary suggestions and laboratory notes by B. Johnson, New York 1939. Introds B. Tarkington and B. Matthews.

Joseph, M. How to write serial fiction. 1928. With M. Cumberland.

Uzzell, T. H. The technique of the novel: a handbook on the craft of the long narrative. New York 1947, 1959 (rev), 1964 (rev).

Neal, H. E. Writing and selling fact and fiction. New York 1949.

Van Nostrand, A. Making and marketing fiction. Arizona Quart 8 1956.

The book and the serial. Author 68 1958.

Writing Detective and Mystery Fiction

Hogarth, B. Writing thrillers for profit. 1936. Black's Writers' and Artists' Library no 6.

Morland, N. How to write detective novels. 1936.

Burack, A. S. Writing detective and mystery fiction. Boston 1945, 1967 (rev).

Highsmith, P. Plotting and writing suspense fiction. 1956.

Writing the Romantic Novel

Britton, A. and M. Collin. Romantic fiction. 1960. New Writers' Guide.

Ritchie, C. Writing the romantic novel. 1962.

Writing Humour

Thomson, A. A. Written humour. 1936. Black's Writers' and Artists' Library no 5.

Short Story and Article Writing

Knowlson, T. S. Money-making by short story writing. 1904.

Neal, R. W. Short stories in the making. New York 1914.

—— To-day's short stories analysed: an informal encyclopaedia of short story art as exemplified in contemporary magazine fiction, for writers and students. New York 1918.

Joseph, M. Short story writing for profit. 1923.

—— The magazine story: ten examples analysed. 1928.

Moseley, S. A. Short story writing and free-lance journalism. 1926.

The writer's market guide to 100 provincial newspapers; The writer's market guide to 100 selected magazines. 2 pts Cambridge [1931].

Maconochie, D. The craft of the short story. 1936.

'Campbell, W. S.' (S. Vestal). Writing magazine fiction. New York 1940.

Bird, G. L. Article writing and marketing. New York 1948.

Hunt, C. Short stories and how to write them. 1950.

Boland, B. J. Short-story writing. 1960. New Writers' Guide.

Heald, L. V. Encyclopaedia of article ideas. nd [1960?].

Wedlick, L. Writing modern articles and magazine fiction. Melbourne 1962.

Writing Words for Songs

See also periodicals devoted to song-writing, col 74, below.

Day, J. E. How to write words for songs. 1936.

Technical and Educational Writing

Brown, B. Trade and technical writing for profit. 1931.

Holroyd, G. H. Educational authorship. Author 49 1938.

Hill, W. L. Making known: the partnership of author, publisher and bookseller in the advancement of science and technology. 1954.

Parr, G. and J. W. Godfrey. The technical writer. 1959.

Writing for Film

The Writers & Artists Year Book *usually contains a section devoted to writing for the film and on marketing scenarios.*

Esenwein, J. B. and A. Leeds. Writing the photoplay. Springfield Mass 1913.

Talbot, F. A. A. Practical cinematography and its applications. 1913.

Dench, E. A. Playwriting for the cinema. 1914.

Farquharson, J. Picture plays and how to write them. 1916.

Weston, H. The art of photo-play writing. 1916.

Ball, E. H. Cinema plays: how to write them. 1917.

Palmer, F. Photoplay plot encyclopaedia. Los Angeles 1920.

—— Techniques of the photoplay. Hollywood 1924.

Bowen, M. Film from an author's point of view. Author 36 1926.

Fawcett, L'E. Writing for the film. 1932.

Strasser, A. Ideas for short films: simple scripts for amateurs. 1937.

Vale, E. Techniques of screenplay writing. Los Angeles 1944.

Clarke, T. E. B. Screenwriter and director. Author 57 1946.

White, M. and F. Stock. The right way to write for the films. Kingswood Surrey 1948.

Beranger, C. Writing for the screen. Dubuque 1950.

Wright, B. Film-making and screenwriting. Author 60 1950. Reply by M. Slater 61 1950.

Herman, L. H. Practical manual of screen playwriting for theatre and television films. Cleveland Ohio 1952, 1963 (rev).

Harrison, R. How to write film stories for amateur films. 1954.

Kazan, E. Writers and motion pictures. Atlantic Monthly 199 1957.

Writing for Broadcasting (Radio and Television)

The Writers & Artists Year Book *usually contains sections on writing for broadcasting.*

Whitaker-Wilson, C. Writing for broadcasting. 1935. Black's Writers' and Artists' Library no 2.

Wylie, M. Radio writing. New York 1939.

Cowgill, R. Fundamentals of writing for radio: drama, talks, continuities and non-dramatic features, with guidance in program planning, production and marketing. New York 1949.

Jonsson, J. Writing for broadcasting. 1949.

Campbell, L. R. et al. A guide to radio-TV writing. Ames 1950.

Yoakem, L. G. (ed). Television and screen writing. Berkeley 1958.

Douglass, S. et al. A first play for television. In The armchair theatre: how to write, design, direct, act, enjoy television plays, 1959.

Wood, D. et al. Make 'em laugh: on writing television comedy. 1964. Delysé recording.

British Broadcasting Corporation. Writing for the BBC. 1966.

Dunbar, J. Script-writing for television. 1966.

Hilliard, R. L. Writing for television and radio. 1967.

Willis, E. E. Writing television and radio programmes. 1968.

Andrews, V. How to write successful TV comedy. nd.

Green, P. Writing for television. nd.

Phillip, E. Writing for radio. nd.

Marketing Authors' Work

The Writers & Artists Year Book *devotes considerable space each year to the marketing of authors' work.*

Magazines and their contributors. Author 23 1913. Terms of contract.

Joseph, M. The commercial side of literature. 1925.

Cheap books and authors' royalties: a symposium. Author 41 1931.

Thring, G. H. The marketing of literary property: book and serial rights. 1933.

Bird, G. L. Article writing and marketing. New York 1948.

Van Nostrand, A. Making and marketing fiction. American Quart 8 1956.

Yass, M. What your book will cost. Author 77 1966.

Martin, H. R. The business side of writing. nd.

Ghosting

Should well-known writers 'farm out' fiction? Author 14 1903-4. Includes reply by W. S. Gilbert.

Nisbet, H. The author, the 'ghost' and the Society [of Authors]. 1904.

The ethics of ghosting. Author 28 1918.

Thorncroft, A. The ghosting business. Author 77 1966.

(3) TRANSLATING

Beerbohm, M. Advice to those about to translate plays. Saturday Rev 18 July 1903.

Burton, R. The difficulties of translation. In his Little essays in literature and life, New York 1914.

Harrison, F. The art of translation. Forum 65 1921.

Orage, A. R. When shall we translate? In his Readers and writers 1917–21, 1922.

Postgate, J. B. Translation and translations: theory and practice. 1922.

Granville-Barker, H. On translating plays. Essays by Divers Hands 5 1925.

Dukes, A. Play translation. Author 41 1930.

Smith, F. S. The classics in translation: an annotated guide to the best translations of the Greek and Latin classics into English. 1930.

Belloc, H. On translation. 1931.

Bates, E. S. Modern translation. 1936.

— Intertraffic: studies in translation. 1943.

Grierson, H. Verse translation. 1948.

Highet, G. The art of translation. In his People, places, books, New York 1953.

MT: mechanical translation. Cambridge Mass 1954 onwards.

Locke, W. N. and A. D. Booth. Machine translation of languages. New York 1955.

Institut de Littérature et de Techniques Artistiques de Masse. La traduction. Bordeaux 1956.

Knox, R. A. On English translation. Oxford 1957

Savory, T. H. The art of translation. 1957.

Brower, R. A. (ed). On translation. Cambridge Mass 1959.

Auden, W. H. Translating opera libretti. In his The dyer's hand, 1962. With C. Kallman.

(4) PATRONAGE

Wells, H. G. Thought in the modern state. In his Mankind in the making, 1903. Includes discussion of endowment of authors.

Drinkwater, J. Art and the state. Liverpool 1930.

The state and the arts. Author 54 1944.

Priestley, J. B. The arts under socialism. 1947.

Shaw, G. B. Art workers and the state. Atlantic Monthly 179 1947.

Smith, H. A. To the aid of the writer. Birmingham 1950. Report of Atlantic Awards Scheme 1946–8.

Leavis, F. R. Mr Pryce-Jones, the British Council and British culture. Scrutiny 18 1951.

Lynes, R. Government as a patron of the arts. Yale Rev 41 1952.

Evans, B. I. Prospects for a ministry of fine arts. [1959].

Gulbenkian Foundation. Help for the arts. 1959.

Higgins, J. Public patronage of the arts. 1965. PEP pamphlet.

Herbert, A. P. Literature and the state. Essays by Divers Hands 34 1966.

The panel game. TLS 20 Oct 1966 and following issues. On the Arts Council.

Widgery, D. The Arts Council: a counter plan. Univ and College Mag no 4 1966.

Eells, R. S. F. The corporation and the arts. New York 1967.

Hoggart, R. et al. Cultural policies in Britain: a report to Unesco. Birmingham 1967, 1968 (rev).

Hoggart, R. The arts and state support. In his Speaking to each other, 1970.

Harris, J. S. Government patronage of the arts in Great Britain. Chicago 1970.

(5) THE LITERARY AGENT

For a full bibliography of books, articles and references in reminiscences concerning the literary agent in Britain and America see J. G. Hepburn, The author's empty purse and the rise of the literary agent, 1968.

Watson, E. H. L. Hints to young authors. 1902.

The literary agent. Publisher & Bookseller 29 July 1905.

[Brown, C.] 'The commercialism of literature' and the literary agent. Fortnightly Rev 80 1906. Anon.

Brown, C. Contacts. 1935. Autobiography of a literary agent.

The literary agent in England. Bull of Authors' League of America 1 1914.

Literary agents who poach. Publishers' Circular 20 March 1920.

Swinnerton, F. In his Authors and the book trade, 1932.

Thring, G. H. The literary agent. In Who's who among authors and writers, 1934–5.

Allnutt, E. F. The dramatic agent: what should be his function? Author 48 1938.

Brooks, C. H. and A. Heath. The agent's point of view. In their Author's handbook, 1939.

Thomson, C. C. I am a literary agent: memories personal and professional. [1951].

Author, agent and publisher, by 'An author's agent'. In The book world today, ed J. Hampden 1957.

Colvert, J. B. Agent and author: Ellen Glasgow's letters to Paul Revere Reynolds. SB 14 1961.

Letters of Arnold Bennett, ed J. Hepburn. Vol 1: to J. B. Pinker, 1966.

Firth, J. James Pinker to James Joyce, 1915–20. SB 21 1968. Letters.

(6) RELATIONS WITH PUBLISHERS AND EDITORS

Booth, W. S. A practical guide to authors in their relations with publishers and printers. Boston 1907.

Hardy, H. Unauthorized alterations in a serial story. Author 18 1908. Report of a libel action.

Klickmann, F. What editors have to put up with. Everyone's no 1 1913.

On the ethics of advertising [an author's work]. Author 23 1913.

Are novels too cheap? Author 24 1914, 25 1915. In 3 issues.

[Sadleir, M.] Publishers' advertising: being the reactions of a practising publisher-advertiser to the exhortations of non-publisher theorists. 1930. Anon.

Sadleir, M. Authors and publishers. 1932.

Swinnerton, F. Authors and the book trade. 1932, 1933 (rev, with new preface).

— Authors and advertising. In G. Stevens, Best sellers: are they born or made?, 1939.

— The adventures of a manuscript: being the story of The ragged-trousered philanthropists [by 'Robert Tressell']. 1956.

Waugh, A. Authors, publishers and the public. Quart Rev 259 1932.

Read, H. The sweated author. London Mercury 31 1935; reply by G. Faber, Sailing through the air, ibid.

Authors and advertisement: a symposium. Author 56 1945.

Publishers' Association. Royalty agreements: a guide for the use of publishers. 1946.

Cherne, L. The writer and the entrepreneur. Saturday Rev of Lit 19 Jan 1952.

Slater, M. Robert Tressell's novel. TLS 11 April 1952.

Bowen, C. D. The editor: midwife or meddler? Saturday Rev of Lit 11 Oct 1958.

Scholes, R. Grant Richards to James Joyce. SB 16 1963. Letters.

Firth, J. Harriet Weaver's letters to James Joyce 1915–20. SB 20 1967.

The writer and the theatre. Author 78 1967.

(7) THE AUTHOR AND POLITICS

See also Literature, Society and Communication, cols 35–54, above.

Trotsky, L. Literature and revolution. [1924]. In Russian. Tr R. Strunsky, New York 1925.

'Ajax'. The writer's war. Left Rev 1 1934.

King, C. The author and politics. Author 44 1934.

Madge, C. Pens dipped in poison. Left Rev 1 1934. War and the writer.

MacLeish, A. The writer and revolution. Saturday Rev of Lit 26 Jan 1935.

Spender, S. Writers and manifestos. Left Rev 1 1935.

— War and politics. Partisan Rev 34 1967.

Allen, J. The socialist theatre. Left Rev 3 1937.

Lehmann, J. Should writers keep to their art? Left Rev 3 1937.

Marxism and literature. TLS 14 Aug 1937.

Phelan, G. B. The freedom of the artist. Liturgical Arts 5 1937.

Riding, L., R. Graves et al. Politics and poetry. Epilogue no 3 1937.

Writing in revolt. Fact no 4 1937.

Hicks, G. Literature and the war. College Eng 1 1939.

Salter, C. H. Poetry and politics. Poetry Rev 30 1939.

Authors and the war. Author 50 1940. 14 authors comment in the spring and summer issues.

'Orwell, George' (E. A. Blair). Literature and totalitarianism. Listener 19 June 1941; rptd in his Collected essays vol 2, 1968.

— Literature and the left. Tribune 4 June 1943; rptd in his Collected essays vol 2, 1968.

— In defence of P. G. Wodehouse. Windmill 2 1945; rptd in his Collected essays vol 3, 1968.

— Politics and the English language. Horizon 76 1946; rptd in Collected essays vol 4, 1968.

Leavis, F. R. Literary criticism and politics. Politics & Letters 1 1948.

Woodcock, G. The writer and politics. 1948.

Riesman, D. and R. Denney. Do mass media 'escape' from politics? In their Changing American character, New Haven 1950.

Stowell, F. S. Democratic writers versus the 'class weapon'. Humanist 10 1950.

Turnell, M. The writer and social strategy. Partisan Rev 18 1951.

Barzun, J. Artist against society: some articles of war. Partisan Rev 19 1952.

Blotner, J. L. The political novel. Garden City NY 1955.

O'Brien, C. C. Writers and politics. New York 1955.

Howe, I. Politics and the novel. New York 1957.

— A world more attractive. New York 1963.

Fiedler, L. A. Class war in British literature. Esquire 69 1958; rptd in On contemporary literature, ed R. Kostelanetz, New York 1964.

Stanford, D. and W. Esty. From engagement to indifference: politics and the writer. Commonweal 67 1958.

Aaron, D. Writers on the left. New York 1961.

Mander, J. The writer and commitment. 1961.

Craig, D. Socialism and contemporary poetry. New Left Rev 17 1962.

Symons, J. Politics and the novel. Twentieth Century 170 1962.

Read, H. The freedom of the artist. In his To hell with culture, 1963.

Ford, H. D. British poets and the Spanish Civil War. Philadelphia 1964.

Mitchell, S. Marxism and art. New Left Rev 23 1964.

Kavolis, V. Political dynamics and artistic creativity. Sociology & Social Research 49 1965.

Hargreaves, J. D. and A. Rutherford. War poets and peace ballots. In Papers presented to the Past and Present conference on literature and the historians, 1967.

(8) LITERARY CONFERENCES AND FESTIVALS

Humphries, R. On writers' conferences. Nation 6 May 1950.

Patterson, C. C. Why a writers' conference? Writer 65 1952.

Cross, W. How valuable is a writers' conference? Writer 70 1957.

Arts and festivals, recreation and leisure. In Essays in local government and enterprise, ed E. Hillman 1964.

Miller, K. Writers. New Statesman 21 Oct 1966; reply, 11 Nov. On literary festivals.

(9) PERIODICALS

The author: organ of the Incorporated Society of Authors. Vol 1 no 1–vol 36 no 4, May 1890–April 1919, monthly. Continued as quarterly July 1919–July 1926. Continued as Author, playwright and composer, vol 37 no 1–vol 59 no 2, Oct 1926–winter 1948. Continued as Author, vol 60, no 3, spring 1949 onwards. First ed Walter Besant.

The freelance. Nos 1–12 Sept 1900–Aug 1901.

The writer. Blackburn. Nos 1–3. Aug 1901–March 1902.

The writers' year book. Nos 1–3, 1902–4. Continued as Writers' and artists' year book 1, 1906 onwards.

The art and craft of letters. Nos 1–10, 1915–16.

The Louise Heilgers magazine. Richmond. Vol 1 nos 1–6, Sept 1920–Feb 1921. Continued as The writer, London, vols 1–20, no 9, March 1921–March 1939. New series,

vols 1–8, no 12, April 1939–March 1947. New series, vol 1, nos 1–9, April–Dec 1947. New series, vol 1, Jan 1948 onwards. From vol 14 pbd in Colchester.

Youth: the authors' magazine. Nos 1–3, 15 Feb–June 1922.

What editors and publishers want. Liverpool. 1924–30? Continuation of part of Literary year book, *see col 1354*, below.

The freelance. 1925–?

Free-lance weekly. 1926–?

The outside contributor and free-lance journalist. Nos 1–4, Jan–April 1927.

The writer's own magazine. Vol 1 no 1–vol 12 no 9, Jan 1928–Sept 1939. Incorporates Verse and song from vol 2 no 1, Jan 1929.

Popular writing. Cosham. Nos 1–8, July 1929–Feb 1930.

The author's annual. 1930.
Books and authors. Vol 1 no 1–vol 2 no 16. April 1931–
Dec 1932.
The freelance register. 1 only, 1931.
The writer's series. 1931–?
Amateur writers' annual guide. Nos 1–3, 1933–5.
The writer's monthly. Cambridge. Vol 1 no 1–vol 3 no 26,
Aug 1934–Sept 1936. Written and pbd by G. J. Matson.
The authors' playwrights' and composers' handbook for
1935 [etc]. 1935 onwards. Title varies.
Writing news. 1935–?
Free-lance weekly. Cambridge. ?Aug 1936–? Ed S. S.
Harris.
The freelance register. 1936–? Ed N. Morland.
The truth about writing. Hinckley. 1936–?
The writer's journal: a monthly magazine for the free-lance
writer. Nos 1–10, May 1937–Feb 1938.
International writers' digest and readers' review. 1 only?
March 1939. Ed C. Pasco.
Every writer's herald. Coventry. 1–7?, 1st Dec 1939–
Aug 1940.
The lesser-known markets guide: a handbook for fiction-
writers, journalists, verse-writers, artists and photo-
graphers. Axminster. 1939–?
Phoenix: a magazine for young writers. Ayton. Vol 1
no 1–vol 3 no 4, ?1939–autumn 1942.
Warner's world-guide writers' weekly. Hinckley. 1939–?
The writers' medley. 1 only? 1939.
Chats with writers. Nos 1–7, Dec 1944–Dec 1945. New
series, 1–6, Feb–Dec 1946.
Writers parade. Nos 1–3, 1945–6.

Freelance market news. Bristol. Vol 1 no 1–vol 6 no 4,
14 Sept 1946–June 1948.
Free-lance writer and photographer. St Ives, Hunts.
1946–?
Writer's gazette. Bristol. New series 1–3, autumn 1947–
spring 1948.
Writers' and photographers' reference guide. St Ives,
Hunts. 1947–?
Personality (for writers). Southport. 1948–?
The J. C. Walls authors' quarterly. Nos 1–4, winter 1949–
autumn 1950.
Writer's diary (an idea a day). Bristol. 1949, 1950.
Annual.
Press: press & free lance writer and photographer. South-
port. 1950–?
SONA [Society of New Authors]. 1950–?

Song-Writing Periodicals

Words for music: a journal for composers and lyric
writers. Nos 1–2, Oct 1909, March 1910. Ed W. B.
Baldry.
Verse and song. 1928. Incorporated in The writer's own
magazine, Jan 1929.
Words and music: bulletin of The British Song Society.
1928–?
The songwriter. 1 only? June 1937.
British songwriter and poet. 1940–?
Song Writers' Guild of Great Britain. Bulletin. ?1947/
48–?

C. PRODUCTION

(1) PRINTING AND BINDING

See also vol 3, cols 35–62, and Book Design, cols 83–90, below.

Bibliographies

Steele, R. R. The revival of printing: a bibliographical
catalogue of works issued by the chief modern English
presses. 1912.
Peddie, R. A. (ed). Catalogue of the technical reference
library, St Bride Foundation Institute. 1919.
Berry, W. T. A selected list of books on practical printing.
1921.
—The St Bride Typographical Library. 1932.
McMurtrie, D. C. A list of books on typographical style
and proofreading. Greenwich Conn 1922.
— Printing history, typography, the techniques of print-
ing. Chicago 1935.
Library of Congress. A selected list of references on
printing machinery and printing inks. Washington 1924.
Leicester Free Public Libraries. Catalogue of the books on
printing, bookbinding and papermaking and related
industries. Leicester 1927.
Typothetae: books on printing and related subjects.
Typothetae Educational Bull 5 1927.
Printing: a list of books in English. 1928 (National Book
Council Bibliography 3).
Tomkinson, G. S. A selected bibliography of the prin-
cipal modern presses, public and private, in Great
Britain and Ireland. 1928.
British Museum. Catalogue of an exhibition of books
illustrating British and foreign printing 1919–29. 1929.
Bristol Public Library. List of books on printing and the
allied trades. Bristol 1936.
Morison, S. Hand list of printing trade documents issued
by the London associations of master printers, book-
sellers, compositors, press-men and machine-men,
1795–1919. Cambridge 1936.
Thomerson, L. G. Classified list of text books, reference
books and periodicals. 1937. Pbd by Printing and
Allied Trades Research Association.

Winship, G. P. The literature of printing. In A history of
the printed book, ed L. C. Wroth, New York 1938
(Dolphin no 3).
Lehmann-Haupt, H. Seventy books about bookmaking:
a guide to the study and appreciation of printing. New
York 1941, 1949 (rev, as One hundred books about
bookmaking).
Kirk, A. One hundred technical books: a suggested
nucleus for a printing works library. 1948.
Thomson, M. C. and W. H. Hughes. Photo typesetting.
1957 (Library Assoc special subject list 14).
Public Library of South Australia. Colour printing.
Adelaide 1958.
Hancock, P. D. Books and printing. In his Bibliography of
works relating to Scotland 1916–50, Edinburgh 1959–60.
Newberry Library, Chicago. Dictionary catalogue of the
history of printing from the John M. Wing Foundation.
6 vols Boston 1961.
Manchester Public Libraries Reference Library Subject
Catalogue. Printing pt 2: type & typesetting, printing
processes, publishing & bookselling, copyright. Ed
G. E. Haslam, Manchester 1963.

History and General Studies

Fisher, T. The elements of letterpress printing, composing
and proof reading. Madras 1895–1906.
Southward, J. Modern printing: a handbook of the prin-
ciples and practice of typography and the auxiliary arts.
4 vols 1898–1900, 2 vols 1912.
List of some newspapers and other publications in Great
Britain set by Linotype. 1901. With about 400 fac-
similes.
Thomas, F. W. A concise manual of platen presswork.
Chicago 1903.
The Times. 10 Sept 1912; 13 Oct 1927; 15 Jan 1940;
4 July 1955. Special issues on printing.
The Times. 29 Oct 1929. Special issue on printing in the
twentieth century. Pbd separately 1930.

Catalogue of the British section of the International Exhibition of the Book Industry and Graphic Arts. Leipzig 1914. With essays by B. H. Newdigate et al.

Legros, L. A. and J. C. Grant. Typographical printing surfaces: the technology and mechanism of their production. 1916.

Farrell, F. J. Yarmouth printing and printers. Great Yarmouth 1917.

Bailey, J. The poor printer: being the letters of one master man to another for the benefit of printers in general. 1918.

Neves, G. History of the rotary press. 1920.

Bullen, H. L. Printing and civilisation. 1924.

Mason, J. H. Notes on printing considered as an industrial art. 1924.

Gibson, S. English printing 1700–1925. 1925. Designed by F. Meynell at the Pelican Press.

Holden, J. A. The bookman's glossary: a compendium of information relating to the production and distribution of books. New York 1925, 1932 (rev).

Morison, S. The art of the printer. 1925.

— The art of printing. 1938.

Sadleir, M. Servants of books. 1925.

Austen-Leigh, R. A. The romance of printing. 1926.

Knights, C. C. The businessman's guide to printing. 1927.

— Printing: reproductive means and materials. 1932.

Thorp, J. (ed). Design in modern printing. [1928]. Introd by L. Weaver.

Training schools number. Monotype Recorder 27 1928. With insets printed by five training schools.

Rogers, B. and A. W. Pollard. The trained printer and the amateur, and the pleasure of small books. 1929.

The printing industry today and tomorrow. Monotype Recorder 29 1930. Special number.

Isaacs, G. A. The story of the newspaper printing press. 1931.

Printing, paper, publicity. Manchester Guardian Commercial 18 June 1931.

Simon, H. and H. Carter. Printing explained. Leicester 1931.

Atkins, W. The art and practice of printing. 6 vols 1932.

Johnson, J. The printer, his customers and his men. 1933.

Thompson, L. Printing methods and publishing tactics. Publishers' Weekly 7 Jan 1933.

Pepler, H. D. C. The hand press: an essay written and printed by hand for the Society of Typographic Arts, Chicago. Ditchling Common, Sussex 1934.

Bendikson, L. Some photo-technical methods for the preservation and restoration of the contents of documents. Lib Jnl 60 1935.

Wroth, L. C. (ed). A history of the printed book. Dolphin 3 1938.

Taylor, A. and G. O. Arlt. Printing and progress: two lectures. Berkeley 1941.

Howe, E. 'The trade': passages from the literature of the printing craft, 1550–1935. 1943.

Polk, R. W. The practice of printing. Peoria Ill 1945.

Tarr, J. C. Printing to-day. 1945, 1949 (rev). Introd by F. Meynell.

Whetton, H. (ed). Practical printing and binding. 1946.

Gill, E. 500 years of printing. In his Last essays, 1947.

Milne, J. Printer's devil: or how books happen. 1948.

Hogben, L. T. From cave painting to comic strip. 1949.

Fishenden, R. B. Craftsmanship and the printer. Birmingham 1950.

Berry, W. T. The printed word. In A century of technology, 1851–1951, ed P. Dunsheath 1951.

— and H. E. Poole. Annals of printing: a chronological encyclopaedia to 1950. 1966. See also S. H. Steinberg, Library 5th ser 23 1968.

Mann, G. Print: a manual for librarians and students. 1952.

Gillespie, S. C. A hundred years of progress: the record

of the Scottish Typographical Association 1853 to 1952. Glasgow 1953.

Mackenzie, A. D. The Bank of England note: a history of its printing. Cambridge 1953.

Bissett, C. D. A short history of platen presses. Print in Britain 1 1954.

Musson, A. E. The Typographical Association: origins and history up to 1949. 1954.

Verry, H. R. Some methods of printing and reproduction: an outline guide. Paris 1954 (UNESCO, Education Studies and Documents no 11).

— Document copying and reproduction processes. 1958.

Johnson, E. D. Communication: a concise introduction to the history of the alphabet, printing, books and libraries. New Brunswick NJ 1955.

Ryder, J. Printing for pleasure: a practical guide for amateurs. 1955.

Steinberg, S. H. The nineteenth century and after. In his 500 years of printing, 1955, 1961 (rev).

Smith, G. Recent technical advances in printing. Author 66 1956.

National Library of Scotland. 450 years of Scottish printing. Edinburgh 1958.

Bundock, C. J. The story of the National Union of Printing, Bookbinding and Paper Workers. 1959.

McLuhan, M. Printing and social change. Renascence 11 1959.

— The Gutenberg galaxy: the making of typographic man. Toronto 1962.

Morgan, P. English provincial printing. Birmingham 1959.

Dudek, L. Literature and the press: a history of printing, printed media and their relation to literature. Toronto 1960.

Glaister, G. A. Glossary of the book: terms used in papermaking, printing. 1960. Includes private presses and printing societies.

Skipper, J. E. (ed). Photoduplication in libraries. Lib Trends 8 1960. With bibliography.

University of Reading Library. Reading printing 1736–1962. Reading 1962. Exhibition catalogue.

Arnold, E. C. Ink on paper: a handbook of the graphic arts. New York 1963.

Carter, J. and P. H. Muir (ed). Printing and the mind of man. 1963, 1967 (rev). International Printing Exhibition catalogue. See also M. McLuhan, TLS 19 June 1964.

Clowes, W. A guide to printing: an introduction for print buyers. 1963.

Kenneison, W. C. and A. J. B. Spilman. Dictionary of printing, papermaking and bookbinding. 1963.

New techniques in printing. Author 74 1963.

Clair, C. In his History of printing in Britain, 1965.

— A chronology of printing. 1969.

Delafons, A. The structure of the printing industry. 1965.

Moran, J. A condensed history of the relief printing press. Black Art 3 1965.

Coupe, R. R. Science of printing technology. 1966.

D., R. The print jungle. New Left Rev 40 1966.

Strauss, V. The printing industry. 1967.

Simon, H. Introduction to printing: the craft of letterpress. Illustr T. Hughes 1968.

Williams, F. B. Photo-facsimiles of STC books: a cautionary list. SB 21 1968. Problems posed by photo-facsimile reprinting. See also A sequel, SB 23 1970.

Hutchings, E. A. D. A survey of printing processes. 1970.

Rather, L. Women as printers. Oakland 1970.

Paper

Labarre, E. J. Dictionary and encyclopaedia of paper and papermaking. Oxford 1937, 1952 (rev).

Association of Special Libraries and Information Bureaux. The paper industry. 1948.

Overton, J. A bibliography of paper and paper-making. Cambridge 1955 (National Book League pamphlet).

Spicer, A. D. The paper trade. 1907.

A specimen book of pattern papers designed for and in use at the Curwen Press. 1928. Introd by P. Nash.

Library Association. The durability of paper. 1930.

Clapperton, R. H. Paper and its relationship to books. 1934.

—— Paper: an historical account of its making by hand from the earliest times down to the present day. Oxford 1934.

—— and W. Henderson. Modern paper-making. Oxford 1941.

Albert Spicer, 1847–1934: a man of his time, by one of his family. 1938. Spicers Ltd.

The dictionary of paper, including pulp, boards, paper properties and related papermaking terms. New York 1940.

Hunter, D. Papermaking: the history and technique of an ancient craft. New York 1943, 1947 (rev and enlarged).

Maddox, M. A. Paper: its history, sources and manufacture. 1945.

Economist Intelligence Unit. The problem of newsprint and other printing paper. Paris 1949 (Press, film and radio in the world today).

—— Paper for printing today and tomorrow. Paris 1952 (Press, film and radio in the world today).

Paper Makers' Association of Great Britain and Ireland. Paper making: a general account of its history, processes and applications. Kenley 1950.

Shears, W. S. William Nash of St Paul's Cray, paper-makers. 1950.

A brief history of British paper mills. Paper Making & Paper Selling 70 1951, 72 1953.

Sutermeister, E. The story of papermaking. Boston 1954.

Evans, J. The endless web: John Dickinson & Co Ltd 1804–1954. 1955.

Mais, S. P. B. Gateway House. [1956]. Wiggin Teape.

Mason, J. Paper-making as an artistic craft. 1959.

Higham, R. R. A. A handbook of papermaking. 1963.

Morris, H. Omnibus: instructions for amateur paper-makers with notes and observations on private presses, book printing and some people who are involved in these activities. North Hills Pa 1967.

Periodicals Relating to Paper

Paper Makers' Association of Great Britain and Ireland. Bibliography of periodical publications on papermaking and allied subjects. 1921 onwards.

Paper makers' monthly journal. Vol 1 no 1–vol 70 no 3. Jan 1863–15 March 1932.

The paper makers' circular and rag price current. Nos 1–433, 19 Jan 1874–March 1907.

The world's paper trade review (originally Paper trade review, 1879–91) vol 15 no 9, 8 May 1891 onwards. Supplements issued.

Paper making. Vol 1 no 1–vol 42 no 6, 1881–June 1923. Continued as Paper making and paper selling, vol 42 no 7–vol 55 no 6, July 1923–June 1936. Continued as Paper making and the printer, vol 55 no 7–vol 65 no 1, Sept 1936–winter 1945. Not pbd 1942–44. Continued as Paper making and paper selling, vol 65 no 2, 1946 onwards. Issues Paper trade directory.

Directory of paper makers of the United Kingdom. 1885 onwards; pocket edn also from 1915.

The paper-maker and British paper trade journal. 26 Jan 1891 onwards.

Stationery world and paper market. 29 Jan 1892–17 Dec 1927. Continued as Paper market, 17 Jan 1928 onwards.

Amalgamated Society of Paper Makers. Quarterly reports. Dartford 1893 onwards.

'Good copy': a paper for makers of papers. 1914–?

Paper and print. March 1928–?

Paper Makers' Association of Great Britain and Ireland. Interim report 1929. Second [etc] report, 1936 onwards.

British paper. March 1933–41; 1946 onwards.

Paper-maker. 15 April 1937 onwards.

Paper-making abstracts. Kenley. 1948–50. Pbd by Printing and Allied Trades Research Assoc.

The Bowater papers. Birmingham, London. 1–4? 1950–58?

Ink

Seymour, A. Modern printing inks. 1910.

Kriegel, H. G. Encyclopaedia of printing, lithographic inks and accessories. New York 1932.

B. Winstone and Sons. Ink in the making, 1849–1948. 1948.

The story of printing inks. Paper and Print 21–2 1948–9.

[L. G. Ridley]. Talking to an inkmaker. 1960.

Apps, E. A. Printing ink technology. 1961.

Bowles, R. F. (ed). Printing ink manual. 1961, 1969 (rev).

Composition

Reference should be made in particular to issues of The Monotype Recorder.

Hart, H. Rules for compositors and readers at the University Press, Oxford. Oxford 1893. Frequent revisions.

De Vinne, T. L. The practice of typography: modern methods of book composition. New York 1904.

—— Modern methods of book composition: a treatise on typesetting by hand and by machine and on the proper arrangement and imposition of pages. New York 1914.

Collins, F. M. Author & printer: a guide for authors, editors, printers, correctors of the press, compositors and typists. 1905, 1909 (as Authors' & printers' dictionary). With frequent revisions.

De la Mare, W. The printing of poetry. Cambridge 1931. Lecture to Double Crown Club 1927.

Galozzi, C. The Varityper. Lib Jnl 60 1935.

Pickering, C. L. Compositors' equipment. 1946, 1962 (rev).

Sherman, F. M. The genesis of machine typesetting. Chicago 1950.

Canford, R. J. Effects of the teletypesetter upon newspaper practices. Journalism Quart 29 1952.

Wilson, C. E. Impact of the teletypesetter on publishing media. Journalism Quart 30 1953.

Hitchings, S. H. The printing of poetry. Printing & Graphic Arts 2 Sept 1954.

Ashworth, J. Operation and mechanism of Linotype and Intertype. 1955.

Book composition by photography. TLS 11 April 1958.

Moran, J. Filmsetting: bibliographical implications. Library 5th ser 15 1960.

—— The composition of reading matter. 1965.

New techniques in printing. Author 74 1963. On film-setting.

Barnett, M. P. Computer typesetting: experiments and prospects. Cambridge Mass 1965.

Filmsetting in focus. Monotype Recorder 43 1965.

Copyfitting tables for Monotype and Monophoto faces. [c. 1966]. Monotype pbn.

Phillips, A. H. Computer peripherals and typesetting. 1968.

Proofing

Hart, H. Rules for compositors and readers at the University Press, Oxford. Oxford 1893. Frequent revisions.

Crutchley, B. Preparation of manuscripts and correction of proofs. Cambridge 1951 (Cambridge Authors' and Printers' Guides no 2). First edn anon; frequent revisions.

The MLA style sheet. Washington 1951, 1970 (rev).

Glover, A. S. B. Proof correction. TLS 22 Aug 1952. Correspondence.

Hewitt, R. A. Style for print and proof correcting. 1957.

British Standards Institution. Recommendations for proof correction and copy preparation. 1958.

Colour Printing and Silk-Screen Process

Burch, R. M. Colour printing and colour printers. 1910.

Martin, L. C. Colour and methods of colour reproduction. 1923.

Tritton, E. J. A survey of colour photography. 1939.

Hiett, H. L. Silk screen process production. Ed for Great Britain by W. Clemence et al [1947]; 1960 (rev, with H. K. Middleton).

Griffits, T. E. Colour printing. 1948.

Binding

Hobson, A. R. A. The literature of bookbinding. Cambridge 1954 (National Book League pamphlet).

St Bride Foundation. Library book lists: bookbinding and warehouse work, literature available to 1957. 1959.

Cockerell, D. Bookbinding and the care of books: a textbook for bookbinders and librarians. 1901. Frequent revisions.

The bookbinder. May 1902. Periodical; 1 only.

Loring, R. B. Marbled papers. Boston 1933.

— Decorated book papers: being an account of their design and fashions. Cambridge Mass 1942; ed P. Hofer 1952.

Harrison, T. What to look for in a modern binding. Book Collectors' Quart 13 1934.

— Fragments of bookbinding technique. 1950.

Symons, A. J. A. Post-war English bookbinding. Book Collectors' Quart 13 1934.

Leighton, D. Modern bookbinding: a survey and a prospect. 1935.

Thomas, H. Modern English bookbindings. Bookman Quart 9 1935, 13 1939.

Diehl, E. Bookbinding: its background and technique. 2 vols New York 1946.

Adams, J. The house of Kitcat: a story of bookbinding 1798–1948. 1948 (priv ptd).

Town, L. Bookbinding by hand, for students and craftsmen. 1951, 1963 (rev).

Lewis, A. W. Basic bookbinding. 1952.

[Hunter and Foulis]. A hundred years of publishers' bookbinding, 1857–1957. Edinburgh [1957].

Darley, L. S. Bookbinding then and now: a survey of the first 178 years of James Burn and Co. 1959.

— Introduction to bookbinding. 1965.

Harthan, J. P. Bookbindings. 1962.

Clements, J. Bookbinding. 1963.

Middleton, B. A history of English craft bookbinding technique. 1963.

Modern design in bookbinding: the work of Edgar Mansfield. 1966. Introd by H. M. Nixon.

Holt, P. and E. Thorpe. Gold and books. 1969. Use of gold in decorating books and bindings.

Business Management for Printers

Gotts, J. B. Estimating, book keeping system, for letterpress and lithographic printers. 1901.

British Federation of Master Printers. Profit for printers: or what is cost? 1904. Frequent revisions.

— Estimating for printers. 1916. Frequent revisions.

— Salesmanship for printers. 1934.

Naylor, T. E. How to start in business as a printer. 1905.

Hull, A. D. An introduction to the British Master Printers' Federation costing system for the smaller business. 1948.

Spector, C. Management in the printing industry. 1967.

Printing and Allied Trade Organizations

Scottish Typographical Association. Report. Glasgow 1920–?

Book Manufacturers' Association. Statement of policy. April 1934.

Temple, H. S. Printing trade organizations. 1938.

Howe, E. and H. E. Waite. The London Society of Compositors: a centenary history. 1948.

— The British Federation of Master Printers 1900–1950. 1950.

— and J. Child. The Society of London Bookbinders 1780–1951. 1952.

Gillespie, S. C. A hundred years of progress: the records of the Scottish Typographical Association. 1953.

Musson, A. E. The Typographical Association: origins and history up to 1949. 1954.

Burdock, C. J. The National Union of Printing, Bookbinding and Paper Workers. 1959.

Moran, J. NATSOPA: seventy-five years. 1964.

Child, J. Industrial relations in the British printing industry. 1967.

Individual Printers

See also Designers and Typographers and Individual Publishers, cols 87–8, 93–5, below. For private presses see cols 96–8, below.

'Beaujon, Paul' (B. Warde). Unjustified lines: a volume of verse about printers and their ancestry. Chiswick 1935.

S[imon], H. and F. Meynell. Harold Spedding Curwen: two appreciations. 1950.

Simon, O. Printer and playground: an autobiography. 1956.

Crutchley, B. A printer's Christmas books, 1930–58. Cambridge 1959. Christmas books produced at Cambridge since 1930.

Mosley, J. The press in the parlour: some notes on the amateur printer and his equipment. Black Art 2 1963.

Wallis, L. W. Leonard Jay: master printer-craftsman. 1963.

Gaskell, P. The bibliographical press movement. Printing Historical Soc Jnl 1 1965.

Carter, W. Portfolio one: specimen sheets of printing, type-design and letter-cutting…between 1959 and 1967. Cambridge 1967.

Tarling, A. Will Carter: printer. 1968.

Individual Printing Houses

David Allen

    Allen, W. E. D. David Allen's: the history of a family firm, 1857–1957. 1957.

Balding and Mansell

    Rosner, C. Printer's progress: a comparative study of the craft of printing, 1851–1951. 1951.

    Type: principles and application. nd.

Bemrose & Co

    Bemrose, H. H. The house of Bemrose 1826–1926. Derby 1926.

George Bradshaw & Co

    Katin, L. One hundred years of Bradshaw. Printing Rev 8 1939.

William Clowes & Sons

    Clowes, W. B. Family business 1803–1953. [1953].

Co-operative Printing Society

    Hall, F. The history of the Co-operative Printing Society, Manchester, 1869–1919. Manchester 1920.

W. S. Cowell Ltd

    Ireland, G. The press in the Butter Market. Ipswich 1960.

De La Rue Co Ltd

    The world of De La Rue, 1813–1963. 1963.

J. M. Dent & Sons Ltd

    Thornton, J. A tour of the Temple Press. 1935.

Harrison & Sons

    The house of Harrison: printers to the king. 1914.

    Harrison: a family imprint. 2 pts 1950.

Hazell, Watson & Viney Ltd

    Keefe, H. J. A century in print: the story of Hazell's, 1839–1939. 1939.

    Viney, E. (ed). Hazells in Aylesbury 1867–1967. Aylesbury 1968.

Jarrold & Sons

    History of Jarrold and Sons 1823–1948. Norwich 1948.

Neill & Co
History of the firm of Neill & Co Ltd, Printers. Edinburgh 1900.
The house of Neill 1749–1949. Edinburgh 1949.

Thomas Nelson & Sons
The story of a famous firm of printer-publishers. British & Colonial Printer, 2nd suppl 8 June 1951.

William Sessions, the Ebor Press
The story of a printing house, 1865–1965. York 1965.

Spottiswoode & Co
Austen-Leigh, R. A. The story of a printing house: being a short history of the Strahans and Spottiswoodes. 1911, 1912 (rev).

Straker Bros
The house of Straker 1800–1950. 1950.

Waterlow Brothers & Layton
Boon, J. Under six reigns: being some account of 114 years of progress and development of the house of Waterlow. 1925.

Witherby & Co
Leigh-Bennett, E. P. Points from the house of Witherby & Co from 1720–1925. 1925.

C. H. Wyman & Sons
Lawrence, A. The story of Wyman and Sons. 1907.

Yelf Bros
Daish, A. N. Printer's pride: the house of Yelf at Newport, Isle of Wight 1816–1966. Newport 1967.

Printing Trade Periodicals

Karch, R. R. (ed). Index to graphic arts periodical literature 1933–40. Evanston 1941.

Ulrich, C. F. and K. Küp. Books and printing: a selected list of periodicals 1800–1942. Woodstock Vermont 1943.

St Bride Foundation Institute. Catalogue of the periodicals relating to printing and allied subjects in the technical library. 1951.

Pritchard, A. A catalogue of journals relevant to printing held at Watford College of Technology. Watford 1963.

The Scottish typographical calendar. Edinburgh. Sept 1857–Dec 1908. Continued as Scottish typographical journal no 569, Jan 1909 onwards.

The printers' register. Gloucester etc. July 1863–1952. Incorporated Newspaper press.

London, provincial and colonial press news. 15 Jan 1866–12 Dec 1912.

The British and colonial printer and stationer. Dec 1878 onwards. Bookbinding suppl nos 16–28, 8 Feb 1912–20 Feb 1913.

The British printer. Leicester etc. 1888 onwards. Incorporated British lithographer and Bookbinder.

The printing world. Vols 1–19. New series, vols 1–18, 25 Jan 1891–Sept 1911.

Process work: Penrose's circular. 1893–1929.

Penrose's annual: the process work year book 1895. Continued as Process year book nos 2–7, 1896–1901. Continued as Penrose's pictorial annual nos 8–19, 1902–1913/14. Continued as Penrose's annual nos 20–37, 1915–16, 1920–35. Continued as The Penrose annual, no 38 onwards, 1936–40, 1949 onwards. Not pbd 1941–8.

Linotype Users' Association. Monthly circular. 1897–Nov 1904.

Linotype notes (and printing machine record). Vol 1 no 1–vol 11 no 132, 1898–Sept 1908. New series, vol 1 no 1–vol 6 no 70, Oct 1908–July 1914. Continued as Linotype (and printing machine) record, Oct 1921–Dec 1929.

The Caxtonian quarterly. Nos 1–22, Feb 1898–May 1904.

The printers' pocket guide. 1899–1914.

The printers' and stationers' year book and diary. 1900, 1904–5, 1912–17, 1919–20, 1924–6.

The Caxton magazine. Vols 1–2, April 1901–2. Incorporated with The press as Caxton magazine and the press, vol 3 onwards, Sept 1902–59. Incorporated with

Modern lithographer as Lithographer and offset printer, vol 55 no 5, 1959 onwards.

The printing machinery record. Vols 1–7, 1901–08. Incorporated in Linotype notes.

The Monotype recorder. Jan 1902–39; 1949 onwards. Not pbd 1940–8. Irregular.

The lithographic circular. Glasgow. Vols 1–4, 1902–16.

The lithographic gazette. Vol 1 no 1–vol 3 no 32, Jan 1903–Feb 1905.

The modern lithographer (and offset printer) (and offset press printer). Vol 1 no 1–vol 55 no 4, Jan 1905–1959. Subtitle varies. Incorporated with Caxton magazine as Lithographer and offset printer, vol 55 no 5, 1959 onwards.

Irish printer. Dublin. Vol 1 no 1–vol 35 no 6, Aug 1905–Jan 1940.

The master printer. Birmingham. Vols 1–3, Oct 1906–July 1909.

The lithographic artist and process worker's quarterly. Vol 1 no 1–vol 2 no 8, 1910–11.

The printing art. 1910–?

Imprint. Vol 1 no 1–vol 2 no 9, Jan–Aug, Nov 1913. Ed F. E. Jackson, J. H. Mason, E. Johnston and G. T. Meynell.

Dublin typographer. ? May 1913.

Type and talent: a magazinelet of suggestions for those interested in printing and its possibilities. Nos 1–4, 1915–16. Continued as Type: the house journal of the Morland Press, nos 5–9, 1917–23.

The managing printer. 1916–? Organ of the Printers', Managers' and Overseers' Assoc.

Printing world. Nos 1–1064, 15 March 1919–13 April 1940.

Master printers' annual and typographical year book. 1920 onwards.

The Linotype record. Vol 1 no 1–vol 4 no 1, Oct 1921–Jan 1925. Continued as Linotype and printing machine record, vol 4 no 2–vol 5, April 1925–Dec 1929.

A printer's miscellany. Nos 1–4, with Christmas inset, 1921–2. The Pelican Press.

The printers' watchword. 1921 onwards. Organ of the London Society of Compositors.

The fleuron: a journal of typography. Cambridge. Vols 1–7 1923–30. 1–4 ed O. Simon; 5–7 ed S. Morison.

Printing Federation bulletin. Vol 1 no 1–vol 8 no 10, 1923–Oct/Dec 1949. New series 1, Feb 1950 onwards.

The printer's pilot. Vol 1 no 1–vol 2 no 10, June 1926–March 1928.

Printing trades journal. Nos 1–58, ? June 1926–March 1931.

The Brideian: monthly journal of the St Bride Institute. Vol 1 no 1–vol 14 no 6, Sept 1926–Sept 1940. Continued as The Brideian: an occasional news sheet nos 1, 2, Feb, May 1941.

Linotype and machinery news. 1927 onwards.

Print and progress. Vol 1 no 1–vol 2 no 20, 1927–31. New series, 1939 onwards.

The Scottish printer and publisher. Motherwell. Nos 1–7, Jan–July 1927.

Scottish printing. Glasgow. Vol 1 nos 1–12, Oct 1927–Dec 1928. Continued as Printing, vol 2 no 1–vol 3 no 7, Jan 1929–Aug 1930.

The woodcut. Vols 1–4, 1927–30. Ed Robert Furst. Published by Fleuron.

Printing and Allied Trades Research Assoc. The budget exchange. New series no 40, Feb 1928–?

Activity: the organ of the Home Counties Master Printers' Alliance. 1929–?

Printing review. Summer 1931 onwards.

Monotype news letter. Redhill. No 1, May 1932 onwards. Suspended 1939–50.

Printing. Nos 2–81, Dec 1932–Aug 1939. Suppl to World's press news.

Leicester College of Arts and Crafts. Printing year book. ? 1932–?

Who's who in press, publicity, printing etc. 1932 onwards.

Typographica. Vol 1 nos 1–2, Dec 1933–April 1934. Continued as Bastien typographica, vol 1 no 3–4; nos 5–8 (no vol number) autumn 1935–1945/47.

Torch, 1933–? Birmingham School of Printing.

The book craftsman: a technical journal for printers and collectors of fine editions. Flansham. Vol 1 no 1, 1934. Ed J. Guthrie.

Impression. Vol 1 no 1, 1934. Continued as Printerest, vol 1 no 2–vol 2 no 20, Nov 1934–May 1936. Continued as Printing industry, vol 2 no 21–vol 6 no 67, June 1936–April 1940. Absorbed Printers' plant.

Print user's year book. 1–3, 1934–6.

Signature: a quadrimestrial of typographic and graphic arts. Nos 1–15, Nov 1935–Dec 1940. New series 1–18, 1946–54. Ed O. Simon.

The cornerstone: a magazine for progressive printers. Dunstable 1935–?

Typography: a quarterly. Nos 1–8, autumn 1936–summer 1939. Ed Robert Harling. Continued as Alphabet and image, nos 1–8, spring 1946–Dec 1948. Continued as Alphabet: an annual of typography [not pbd?]. Continued as Image: a quarterly of the visual arts, nos 1–8, summer 1949–summer 1952. A and I stop press: supplement to Alphabet and image, vol 1 nos 1–3, Sept 1947–Dec 1948. Postscript to Image: an occasional supplement, summer 1949–autumn 1952.

Printing Industry Research Association Journal. Vols 1–13, 1937–50. Continued as Patra news, no 1, Sept 1950 onwards.

Linotype matrix. Spring 1938–summer 1939; 1948 onwards.

Print. New Haven. 1940 onwards.

Graphis. 1944 onwards.

Printing theory and practice. 1946–?

Printing abstracts. Leatherhead. Vol 2 Jan 1947 onwards. Pbd by Printing and Allied Trades Research Assoc. Vol 1, Aug 1945–Dec 1946, issued as part of Patra Journal.

Inky way annual. Dec 1947 onwards.

Impromptu (typography). West Drayton. 1947–?

International printing. Norwich. Vols 1–2, 1947–51.

Printcraft (Printcraft and the magazine publisher). Twickenham. Nos 1–33, Feb 1948–spring 1956. Title varies.

Print. Dublin. 1948–?

The jobbing printer. 1949–?

Typographica. Nos 1–16, 1949–1960? New series 1, nos 1–16 June 1960–7.

The colophon: a monthly magazine for booklovers. Nos 1–11, 1950–1. Distinguish from New York journal of this name.

Amateur Printing Periodicals

See also Amateur journals, *cols 1379–88, below.*

Amateur printing. Woolwich Common. Nos 1–75? 1895–1914.

The torch: official organ of the Amateur Printing Association. New series nos 1–3, 1945. Continued as Hobby printer, nos 1–3, spring 1946–8? Ed W. R. Brace.

Side notes (for amateur printers). Dundee till 1950, then Edinburgh. Sept 1946–spring 1951. New series nos 1–2, summer–Christmas 1951. Overseas suppl Dec 1950, spring 1951. Incorporated in Collectors' items, summer 1953. Ed J. A. Birkbeck.

News letter of the International Small Printers' Association. Nos 1–29?, June 1947–June 1951.

Small printer's directory and year book. Newton Abbot. 1950.

Platen. Sutton Coldfield. 1950–3. Year book of International Small Printers' Assoc.

(2) BOOK DESIGN

See also Printing and binding: history and general studies, cols 74–6, above.

General Works, including Lettering and Type Design

Hart, H. Bibliotheca typographica: a list of books about books. New York 1933.

National Book Council Library. Books about books. 1933. Various subsequent edns.

Howe, E. Bibliotheca typographica. Signature new ser 10 1950.

Williamson, H. Book typography: a handlist for book designers. Cambridge 1955 (National Book League pamphlet).

De Vinne, T. L. The practice of typography: a treatise on title pages. New York 1901.

Linotype Co Ltd. Specimens of types, borders, etc. [1901].

Cobden-Sanderson, T. J. Ecce mundus: the book beautiful. 1902.

Hitchcock, F. H. (ed). Building of a book. New York 1906. Introd by T. L. De Vinne.

Wyse, H. T. Modern type display and the use of type ornament. 1911.

Currier, E. R. Type spacing. New York [1912].

'Maclaren, Ian' (J. Watson). Concerning books and bookmen. 1912.

Steele, R. The revival of printing. 1912. Aesthetics of printing.

Holme, C. (ed). Art of the book: a review of some recent European and American works on typography, page decoration and binding. 1914. Studio special no.

St Bride Foundation Printing School. The features of the printed book. 1915.

Stephen, G. A. Modern decorative title pages. 1915.

Aldis, H. G. The printed book. Cambridge 1916, 1941 (rev J. Carter and B. Crutchley).

Goudy, F. W. The alphabet: fifteen interpreted designs. New York 1918.

— Design and beauty in printing. New York 1934.

— Type revivals: an exposition regarding independent new designs. Lexington Va 1937.

— A half century of type design and typography. New York 1946.

—and B. M. Goudy. Elements of lettering. New York 1922.

McRae, J. F. Two centuries of typefounding. 1920. William Caslon.

Morison, S. The craft of printing. 1921.

— Four centuries of fine printing. 1924, 1949 (rev); 1960 (rev).

— Type designs of the past and present. 1926.

— Decorated types. Fleuron 6 1928.

— First principles of typography. Cambridge 1936, 1967 (with postscript).

— Business *is* business. Philobiblon (Vienna) 10 1938. On typography.

— The typographic arts. 1949. Contains The art of printing (1938) and The typographic arts (1944).

— Fifty years of type-cutting, 1900–50. Monotype Recorder 39 1950. Anon.

— Tact in typographical design. Cambridge 1962. Octavian type.

— and K. Day. The typographic book 1450–1935. 1963.

See also J. Carter, A handlist of the writings of Stanley Morison, 1950; and P. M. Handover, A second handlist, 1959.

Updike, D. B. Printing types, their history, forms and use: a study in survivals. 2 vols Cambridge Mass 1922, 1937 (rev).

Pelican Press. Typography: the written word and the printed word. 1923. By F. Meynell?

Stephenson, Blake and Co Ltd. Printing types, borders, initials, electros, brass rules, spacing material, ornaments. Sheffield 1924.

Orcutt, W. D. In quest of the perfect book. 1926.

—— Master makers of the book. 1929.

Dahl, S. Bogens historie. Copenhagen 1927. Tr New York 1968 (as History of the book).

Newdigate, B., W. Ransom et al. Modern book production. 1928.

——The art of the book. 1938. Studio special no.

Simon, O. and J. Rodenberg. Printing of to-day: an illustrated survey of post-war typography in Europe and the United States. 1928. Introd by A. Huxley.

The Studio. Modern book production. 1928.

Thireau, M. Modern typography. Paris 1928.

Thorp, J. Design in modern printing. 1928.

Warde, F. Printers' ornaments applied to the composition of decorative borders, panels and patterns. 1928.

Davenport, C. Beautiful books. 1929.

Meynell, F. The typography of newspaper advertisements. 1929.

Young, J. L. Books, from manuscript to the bookseller. 1929.

Johnston, P. Biblio-typographia: a survey of contemporary fine printing styles. New York 1930.

Gill, E. An essay in typography. 1931.

—— Printing and piety: an essay on life and work in the England of 1931 and particularly typography. 1931.

Jay, L. Of making books there is no end. Birmingham 1931.

Smith, P. Lettering: a plea. 1932.

Unwin, S. The book in the making. 1932.

McPharlin, P. Modern typography: sans-serif types. N & Q 8 April 1933.

Shaw, G. B. Typography. 1933.

Ehrlich, F. New typography and modern layouts. New York [1934].

Johnson, A. F. Type designs: their history and development. 1934, 1959 (rev), 1967 (rev).

Steer, V. Printing design and layout. 1934.

Symons, A. J. A. The art of the book in Great Britain. Studio 107 1934.

—— Book design in this year. Studio 110 1935.

Tschichold, J. Typographische Gestaltung. Basel 1935. Tr as Asymetric typography, Toronto 1967. See the review, Jnl of Printing Historical Society, no 4, 1968, on differences between original and translation.

—— Geschichte der Schrift in Bildern. Basel 1940. Tr 1946 (as An illustrated history of writing and lettering).

—— Designing books. New York 1951.

De la Mare, R. A publisher on book production. 1936.

—— Author to public: thoughts on the principles of book production. 1945. Trueman Wood lecture.

Pevsner, N. Pioneers of the modern movement 1936, New York 1949 (rev as Pioneers of Modern design).

Smith, P. J. Lettering: a handbook of modern alphabets. 1936.

Thomas, D. B. Type for print: or what the beginner should know about typography, letter design and type faces. 1936.

TLS. Special issue on A century of English letters. 1 May 1937. Includes Book Production: 'The comely and well-looking book'.

—— 10 Feb 1950. Special Book production section. British book design. 3 Sept 1954.

—— Special issue on book production. 26 April 1963.

Curwen, H. Typography and mass production. 1938. Royal Soc of Arts lecture.

Jones, H. Type in action. 1938.

Katin, L. Trends in British book typography. Publishers' Weekly 3 Sept 1938.

Mansbridge, F. R. British and American book-making. Publishers' Weekly 6 Aug 1938.

Tarr, J. C. How to plan print. 1938.

The Fanfare Press. A book of Fanfare ornaments [designed by B. L. Wolpe]. [1939]. Introd J. Laver.

Jackson, H. The dictatorship of the lay-out man. 1939.

—— Design and function in typography. Horizon 13 1946.

Harrison, F. A book about books. 1943.

Evans, B. A note on modern typography. In J. C. Tarr, Printing to-day 1945, 1949 (rev).

Newton, E. Lettering of books. TLS 10 March 1945. Correspondence, 10 March–19 May.

Simon, O. Introduction to typography. 1945, 1963 (rev and enlarged by D. Bland).

—— Mass production and the art of the book in England. Gutenberg-Jahrbuch 1951.

Thompson, T. How to render Roman letter forms: a pattern for understanding and drawing Roman letters and other styles of lettering and type faces related to them. 1946.

Craig, A. The design and spacing of lettering. 1948.

Diringer, D. The alphabet: a key to the history of mankind. New York 1948, 1968 (rev).

Beattie, W. The Scottish tradition in printed books. 1949.

Biggs, J. R. An approach to type. 1949, 1961 (rev).

——The use of type. 1954.

—— Basic typography. 1968.

Brinkley, J. Design for print: a handbook of design and reproductive processes. 1949.

Birkett, W. N. et al. Books are essential. 1951.

Chiswick Press. Ornaments. 1951.

Jennett, S. The making of books. 1951, 1967 (4th edn).

McLean, R. Modern book design: from William Morris to the present day. 1951.

—— Magazine design. 1969.

Ballinger, R. Lettering art in modern use. New York 1952.

Chapman, R. W. Capitals in verse. TLS 22 Aug 1952. Reply by T. Besterman, 5 Sept.

Lehner, E. Alphabets and ornaments. Cleveland Ohio 1952.

Mann, G. Print: a manual for librarians and students. 1952.

Spencer, H. Design in business printing. 1952.

Typographic transformations. Monotype Recorder 39 1952.

Berry, W. T. and A. F. Johnson. Encyclopaedia of type faces. 1953, 1962 (rev).

Eckerstrom, R. E. Contemporary book design. Urbana 1953.

Dowding, G. Finer points in the spacing and arrangement of type. 1954, 1957 (rev), 1966 (rev).

—— Factors in the choice of type faces. 1957.

—— An introduction to the history of printing types. 1962.

Freer, P. Bibliography and modern book production: notes and sources for student librarians, printers, booksellers, stationers, book-collectors. Johannesburg 1954.

Holme, R. and K. M. Frost. Modern lettering and calligraphy. New York 1954.

Tracy, W. A note on Eric Gill's Pilgrim type. Book Collector 2 1954.

Horn, F. A. Lettering at work: a reference book of modern lettering. 1955.

Howe, E. The typecasters. 1955 (priv ptd, for Monotype Casters' and Typefounders' Soc).

Warde, B. The crystal goblet: sixteen essays on typography. 1955. Ed H. Jacob.

Williamson, H. Methods of book design. 1956, 1966 (rev).

Krimpen, J. van. On designing and devising type. New York and Heemstede 1957.

Macrobert, T. M. Printed books: a short introduction to fine typography. 1957.

Benham's book of printing types. 1960.

Dunlap, J. R. The typographical Shaw: GBS and the revival of printing. BNYPL 64 1960.

Glaister, G. A. Glossary of the book. 1960.

A grammar of type ornament. Monotype Recorder 42 1960, 1963 (rptd).

Lewis, J. Printed ephemera: the changing uses of type and letterforms in English and American printing. 1962.

—— Typography: basic principles, influences and trends since the nineteenth century. 1963.

—— The twentieth-century book: its illustration and design. 1967.

Western Printing Services Ltd. The Western type book. 1962. Introd H. Schmoller.

Bell, Q. The schools of design. 1963.

Blumenthal, W. H. Eccentric typography and other diversions in the graphic arts. Worcester Mass 1963.

Downie, R. A. (ed). Languages of the world. Monotype Recorder 42 1963. Types for the different languages.

Rosen, B. Type and typography. 1963. Specimens of most founts in contemporary use.

Lambert, F. Letter forms: alphabets for designers. 1964.

Avis, F. C. Type face terminology. 1965.

Day, K. (ed). Book typography 1815–1965 in Europe and the United States of America. Nijmegen 1965 (in Dutch), London 1966.

Roberts, R. Typographic design. 1966.

Astbury, R. Bibliography and book production. 1967.

Davis, A. Package and print. 1967. Label design.

Archer, H. R. and W. Ritchie. Modern fine printing. Los Angeles 1968.

Harrop, D. Modern book production. 1968.

Design in the bookshop. TLS 29 May 1969. Concerned with book design, not bookshops.

Legibility

A study of legibility together with a bibliography is to be found in R. L. Pyke, The legibility of print, Medical Research Council special report ser no 110, 1926, and H. Spencer, The visible word, 1969

Huey, E. B. The psychology and pedagogy of reading. New York 1910.

'Typoclastes'. A plea for the reform of printing. Imprint 17 June 1913.

Burtt, H. E. and C. Basch. The legibility of Bodoni, Baskerville and Cheltenham type faces. Jnl of Applied Psychology 17 1923.

Ovink, G. W. Legibility, atmosphere value and forms of printing types. Leiden 1938.

Paterson, D. G. and M. A. Tinker. How to make type readable. New York 1940.

—— The effect of typography on the perceptual span in reading. Amer Jnl of Psychology 60 1947.

Carmichael, L. and W. F. Dearborn. Reading and visual fatigue. 1948.

Burt, C., W. F. Cooper and J. L. Martin. A psychological study of typography. Br Jnl of Statistical Psychology 8 1955; rptd with introd by S. Morison, Cambridge 1959.

Prince, J. H. Studies of visual acuity and reading in relation to letter and word design. Columbus Ohio 1961.

Tinker, M. A. The legibility of print. Ames Iowa 1963.

Designers and Typographers

Carter, W. Portfolio one: specimen sheets of printing, type-design and letter cutting between 1959 and 1967. Cambridge 1967.

Thorp, J. Eric Gill. 1929.

Gill, E. Autobiography. 1940.

Attwater, D. Eric Gill: workman. [1945].

Harling, R. The early alphabets of Eric Gill. Alphabet & Image 3 1946.

Gill, E. R. Bibliography of Eric Gill. 1953.

—— The inscriptional work of Eric Gill. 1964.

Tracy, W. A note on Eric Gill's Pilgrim type. Book Collector 2 1954.

Brady, E. M. Eric Gill: twentieth-century book designer. New York 1961.

Physick, J. F. The engraved work of Eric Gill. 1963.

Speaight, R. The life of Eric Gill. 1966.

The triumph of Edward Johnston. TLS 3 Nov 1945.

Johnston, P. Edward Johnston. 1959.

Dreyfus, J. The work of Jan van Krimpen. 1952. Introd by S. Morison.

—— Italic quartet. Cambridge 1966.

Ovink, G. W., S. H. de Roos en J. van Krimpen. Het Boek 33 1958.

Dreyfus, J. Mr Morison as 'typographer'. Signature new ser 3 1947.

Carter, J. W. (ed). Handlist of the writings of Stanley Morison. Cambridge 1950. With notes by S. Morison. A second handlist, P. M. Handover 1959.

Moran, J. Stanley Morison, 1889–1967. Monotype Recorder 43 1968.

Barker, N. and D. Cleverdon. Stanley Morison, 1889–1967: a radio portrait. Ipswich 1969.

Blackwell, B. Bernard Newdigate: typographer. 1945.

Thorp, J. B. H. Newdigate: scholar-printer, 1869–1944. Oxford 1950.

Avis, F. C. Edward Philip Prince: type punchcutter. 1967.

Pollard, A. W. Modern fine printing in England and Mr Bruce Rogers, with a list of books and other pieces of printing designed by Mr Rogers. Newark NJ 1916.

Warde, F. Bruce Rogers. Cambridge Mass 1925.

Illustration and Graphic Processes

For the illustration of children's books, see col 789 below.

Steeves, H. A. Index to graphic arts printing processes. New York 1943.

Engraving and the graphic arts: bibliography. Paper & Print 20 1947.

British Federation of Master Printers. A selected list of graphic arts literature: books and periodicals. 1948.

Hassall, J. Wood engraving. Cambridge 1949 (National Book League Readers' Guides).

Bland, D. A bibliography of book illustration. Cambridge 1955 (National Book League pamphlet).

Gill, E. M. Half-tone, line and colour plates. In The building of a book, ed F. H. Hitchcock 1906.

Boivin, L. and H. Lecène. Le livre illustré moderne. Paris 1917.

Beedham, R. J. Wood engraving. 1920. Introd and appendix by E. Gill.

Drinkwater, J. and A. Rutherston. Claud Lovat Fraser. 1923.

Macfall, C. H. C. The book of Lovat Claud Fraser. 1923.

Millard, C. The printed work of Claud Lovat Fraser. 1923.

Pilworth, E. S. Electrotyping in its relation to the graphic arts. New York 1923.

Furst, H. The modern woodcut: a study of the evolution of the craft, with a chapter on the practice of xylography by W. T. Smith. 1924.

Bliss, D. P. Blake and the modern English wood-engravers; Modern wood-engraving. In his History of wood-engraving, 1928.

Salaman, M. C. The new woodcut. 1930. Studio special no.

Strang, D. The printing of etchings and engravings. Introd M. Hardie, 1930.

Darton, F. J. H. Modern book illustration in Great Britain and America. 1931.

Leighton, C. Wood-engraving and woodcuts. 1932.

—— (ed). Wood engravings of the 1930s. 1936. Studio special no.

Poortenaar, J. The technique of prints and art reproduction processes. 1933.

—— The art of the book and its illustration. 1935.

Curwen, H. Processes of graphic reproduction in printing. 1934, 1967 (rev).

Sharpe, L. The artist in commerce. 1936 (Black's Writers' and Artists' Library no 8).

Bateman, H. M. H. M. Bateman. 1937.

Gossop, R. P. Book illustration: a view of the art as it is today. 1937.

Weitenkampf, F. The illustrated book. Cambridge Mass 1938.

Flader, L. and J. S. Mertle. Modern photoengraving. Chicago 1948.

Hayter, S. W. New ways of gravure. 1949, 1966 (rev).

Newhall, B. History of photography from 1839 to the present day. New York 1950.

Balston, T. English wood-engraving 1900–50. 1951.

Bland, D. The illustration of books. 1951, 1953 (rev), 1962 (rev).

— A history of book illustration. 1958, 1969 (rev).

Ellis, R. W. Book illustration: a survey of its history and development. Kingsport Tenn 1952.

Jeffreys, H. G. G. The story of the aquatint and its employment in book illustration. In Antiquarian Booksellers' Assoc Annual 1952.

Ivins, W. H. Prints and visual communication. Cambridge Mass 1953.

Man, F. H. 150 years of artists' lithographs, 1803–1953. 1953. With bibliography.

Wright, J. B. Etching and engraving: techniques and the modern trend. 1953.

Lewis, J. and J. Brinkley. Graphic design. 1954.

Griffits, T. E. The rudiments of lithography. 1956.

McLean, R. (introd). The wood engravings of Joan Hassall. 1960.

Trivick, H. H. Autolithography: the technique. 1960.

Garvey, E. M. (ed). The artist and the book, 1860–1960, in Western Europe and the United States. Boston 1961.

Brunner, F. A handbook of graphic reproduction processes. Teufen 1962.

Lamb, L. Drawing for illustration. 1962.

Cahoon, H. T. F. The author as illustrator. In Essays on book illustration, ed F. J. Brewer, Berlin 1963.

Cleaver, J. A history of graphic art. 1963.

Gill, B. and J. Lewis. Illustration: aspects and directions. 1964.

Weber, W. Saxa loquuntur. 2 pts Heidelberg 1961–4. Tr 1966 (as A history of lithography).

Graham, R. A note on the book illustrations of Paul Nash. Wymondham 1965.

Allen, P. Beresford Egan: an introduction. 1966.

Lewis, J. The twentieth-century book: its illustration and design. 1967.

— and E. Smith. The graphic reproduction and photography of works of art. 1969.

Easton, M. The books of Lovat. TLS 24 Oct 1968. Review of exhibition of work of Claud Lovat Fraser.

Neumann, E. Functional graphic design in the twenties. New York 1968.

Reid, A. A check-list of the book illustrations of John Buckland Wright, together with a personal memoir. Pinner 1968. Private libraries Assoc.

Holt, P. and E. Thorpe. Gold and books. 1969. Use of gold in decorating books and bindings.

Gross, A. Etching, engraving and intaglio printing. 1970.

Book Jackets

Lee-Elliott, T. The art of the book-jacket. Author 41 1930.

Englefield, W. A. D. Check list of Rex Whistler book-wrappers. Book Collectors' Quart 17 1935.

Blair, F. G. Jacket illustrations. TLS 29 March 1947. Correspondence, ibid 12 April–24 May.

Rosner, C. The art of the book jacket. 1949.

— The growth of the book-jacket. 1954.

Apple, R. W. Can you sell a book by its cover? New York Herald Tribune Book Review 28 July 1963.

Tanselle, G. T. Dust-jackets, blurbs and bibliography. Library 5th ser 26 1971. With checklist.

(3) PUBLISHING

Bibliographies

Peet, W. H. Bibliography. In F. A. Mumby, The romance of bookselling, 1910, 1930 (rev, as Publishing and bookselling). Frequent revisions.

Tomkinson, G. S. Bibliography of the principal modern presses, public and private. 1928.

Classified catalogue of a collection of works on publishing and bookselling in the British Library of Political and Economic Science. 1936, 1962 (rev).

A book trade bibliography. In British books in print, 1967 onwards.

Histories and Studies

Authors' and Booksellers' Co-operative Publishing Alliance. The plan: a new departure in publishing. 1901.

International Publishers' Congress. 1901. Report. Leipzig 1902.

The emoluments of publishing. Publisher & Bookseller 27 May 1905.

O & Y. The author as publisher: or why authors don't publish their books. 1912.

R., C. Letters from a publisher to his son. 2 pts [1913].

Yard, R. S. The publisher. Boston 1913.

Heinemann, W. Publishing simplified. Publishers' Circular 30 Nov 1918. Replies to 18 Jan 1919, and 6 Dec 1919.

Unwin, S. The price of books. 1925.

— The truth about publishing. 1926. Frequent revisions.

— The advertising of books. In G. Stevens, Best-sellers are they born or made? 1939.

— Publishing in peace and war. 1944.

— How governments treat books. 1950.

— Publishing from manuscript to bookshop. Cambridge 1955.

Raymond, H. Publishing and bookselling. New York 1928.

— Publishing and bookselling: a survey of post-war developments and present-day problems. 1938. 8th Dent Memorial Lecture.

Beevers, S. Publishers' accounts. 1929.

Young, J. L. Books: from the manuscript to the bookseller. 1929.

Sadleir, M. Publishers' advertising: being the reactions of a practising publisher-advertiser to the exhortations of non-publisher theorists. 1930. Based on articles first ptd in Constable's monthly list.

Booksellers' Association. A summary of publishers' terms. 1931. Not available to the public.

Blackwell, B. The world of books. 1932.

— A new order in the book trade? 1943.

Waugh, A. Authors, publishers and the public. Quart Rev 259 1932.

Blurbing. Saturday Rev of Literature 24 Nov 1934.

Dearmer, G. The blurb. Author 45 1935.

Hampden, J. (ed). The book world: a new survey. 1935.

— (ed). The book world today. 1957.

Schramm, J. R. Publication as a scientific problem. Proc of Amer Philosophical Soc 75 1935.

De la Mare, R. A publisher on book production. 1936.

Canfield, C. The book fair, the publisher and the reading public. New York Times Book Rev 31 Oct 1937.

Ford, F. M. (formerly Hueffer). The sad state of publishing. Forum 98 1937.

Gosse, P. Pirates and the books. Essays by Divers Hands 16 1937.

Hitchcock, C. N. The publisher's function in the contemporary world. New York Times Book Rev 7 Nov 1937.

Saunders, F. D. (ed). British book trade organization: a report on the work of the Joint Committee of the Publishers' Association and the Association of Booksellers. 1939. Introd by S. Unwin.

Walpole, H., J. B. Priestley et al. The book crisis. 1940.
Hamilton, H. Anglo-American publishing: a problem in mutual understanding. Saturday Rev of Lit 23 1941.
Read, H. Planning for publishing. TLS 3 Oct 1942. Correspondence, 24 Oct–26 Dec.
Strong, L. A. G. The state as publisher. Author 53 1943.
Jackson, H. Bookman's holiday. 1945.
Thrush, A. Representative majority: twenty-one years of the Book-Publishers' Representatives' Association. 1945.
Brophy, J. Britain needs books. 1947.
Hopkins, G. (ed). The battle of the books. 1947. John Hampden, Osbert Sitwell, Stanley Unwin et al.
MacGibbon, J. and B. Batsford. Book publishing in the British zone of Germany. 1947.
Marshall, A. C. The book front. 1947.
Joseph, M. The adventure of publishing. 1949.
Wilkinson, B. The art of the blurb. New York Times Book Rev 12 June 1949.
Horrocks, S. The state as publisher. 1952.
Macleod, R. D. The Scottish publishing houses. Glasgow 1953.
Publishers' Association. Report of the 1948 Book Trade Committee. 1954.
— Book distribution. 1961.
— Publishing problems and responsibilities. TLS 17 Sept 1954.
Lacy, D. Books and the future: a speculation. BNYPL 60 1956.
Political and Economic Planning. Publishing and bookselling. 1956.
Grannis, C. B. What happens in book publishing. New York 1957, 1967 (rev).
The publishing empires. Author 70 1960.
Dakers, A. Publishing. 1961.
Cut-price reading. Author 73 1962.
Shugg, R. W. The professors and their publishers. Daedalus 92 1963.
Olle, J. G. An introduction to British government publications. 1965.
TLS. 27 May 1965. Special series on Books in the balance.
Bingley, C. Book publishing practice. Hamden Conn 1966.
Madison, C. A. Book publishing in America. New York 1966. Accounts of American pbn of British authors.
Smith, M. T. The quiet revolution in publishing. Times 11 May 1967.
The publishing scene. Author 79 1968.
Becket, M. Who owns whom. Bookselling news 6 1970. Ownership and groupings of British book publishers.
Kingsford, R. J. L. The Publishers Association, 1896–1946. Cambridge 1970.
Lane, M. Books and their publishers. In Media sociology ed J. Tunstall 1970.
Tanselle, G. T. Dust-jackets, blurbs and bibliography. Library 5th ser, 26 1971. With checklist.

Publishing, Book Production and Textual Transmission

A selection of general statements together with some studies of particular texts which discuss problems posed by textual transmission in the twentieth century. The titles include those which deal with the application of twentieth-century techniques to earlier texts (e.g. the making of facsimiles of sixteenth-century books). A number of studies of the transmission of American texts is included where the techniques involved are not confined to American publishing practice.

See also A Selective check list of bibliographical scholarship in SB annually, and Bibliography in Britain: a classified list of books and articles published in the United Kingdom, ed J. S. G. Simmons, Oxford 1963 onwards. Reference should also be made to the frequently relevant studies of nineteenth-century problems in these lists. A selection of studies of the period, and a bibliography, are to be found in Bibliography and textual criticism: English and

American literature, 1700 to the present, ed O. M. Brack, Jr and W. Barnes, Chicago 1969.

Muir, P. H. Points 1874–1930: being extracts from a bibliographer's notebook. 1931 (Bibliographia no 5).
— Points, 2nd ser 1866–1934. 1934 (Bibliographia no 8).
Bowers, F. T. The nineteenth and twentieth centuries. In his Principles of bibliographical description, Princeton 1949.
— Bibliography, pure bibliography and literary studies. PBSA 46 1952.
— Textual and literary criticism. Cambridge 1959.
Wyllie, J. C. The forms of twentieth-century cancels. PBSA 47 1953.
Alspach, R. K. Some textual problems in Yeats. SB 9 1957.
Beare, R. L. Notes on the text of T. S. Eliot: variants from Russell Square. SB 9 1957.
Willoughby, E. E. The uses of bibliography to the students of literature and history. Hamden Conn 1957.
Bassi, S. Lezioni di bibliogia I: bibliogia tecnica. Turin nd. Lectures given in 1958.
Hayman, D. From Finnegans Wake: a sentence in progress. PMLA 63 1958.
Willison, I. R. Historical bibliography. In Five years' work in librarianship 1951–55, ed P. H. Sewell, 1958.
— Towards a general theory of historical bibliography. 1958 (North-Western Polytechnic, School of Librarianship, Occasional Papers 11).
Bruccoli, M. J. Twentieth-century books. Lib Trends 7 1959. On detecting plate damage, re-imposition, re-impression etc.
— A mirror for bibliographers: duplicate plates in modern printing. PBSA 54 1960.
— Hidden printings in Edith Wharton's The children. SB 15 1962.
— Some transatlantic texts: west to east. In Bibliography and textual criticism, ed O. M. Brack Jr and W. Barnes, 1969.
— and J. Katz. Scholarship and mere artefacts: the British and Empire publication of Stephen Crane. SB 22 1969.
Foxon, D. Modern aids to bibliographic research. Library Trends 7 1959.
Harkness, B. Bibliography and the novelistic fallacy. SB 12 1959. Dependence of much literary criticism on inaccurate texts.
Moran, J. Filmsetting: bibliographical implications. Library 5th ser 15 1960.
Cummings, L. Pitfalls of photocopy research. BNYPL 65 1961. Ways in which film and photostat can prove misleading.
Meriwether, J. B. et al. Bibliographical and textual studies of twentieth-century writers. In Approaches to the study of twentieth-century literature, East Lansing 1961.
Parrish, S. M. Problems in the making of computer concordances. SB 15 1962.
Scholes, R. E. Some observations on the text of Dubliners: The dead. SB 15 1962.
— Further observations on the text of Dubliners. SB 17 1964.
Adams, R. M. Light on Joyce's Exiles? SB 17 1964.
Woodward, D. H. Notes on the publishing history and text of The waste Land. PBSA 58 1964.
Jarvis, J. P. A textual comparison of the first British and American editions of D. H. Lawrence's Kangaroo. PBSA 59 1965.
Thorpe, J. The aesthetics of textual criticism. PMLA 80 1965.
Tanselle, G. T. A system of color identification for bibliographical description. SB 20 1967.
Bowden, E. T. The Thurber Carnival: bibliography and printing history. Texas Stud in Lit and Language 9 1968. Possibility of variation between original edn and photographically offset reprint.
Williams, F. B. Photo-facsimiles of STC books: a cautionary list. SB 21 1968. A sequel, SB 23 1970.

McKenzie, D. F. Printers of the mind: some notes on bibliographical theories and printing-house practices. SB 22 1969. Considers implications of certain bibliographic approaches. *See* P. Davison, SB 25 1972.

Padwick, E. W. Nineteenth and twentieth centuries. In his Bibliographical method, 1969.

Brooks, H. F. The editor and the literary text: requirements and opportunities. In Librarianship and literature: essays in honour of Jack Pafford, ed A. T. Milne, 1970.

Unfinished and Unpublished Work

Corns, A. R. and A. Sparke. A bibliography of unfinished books in the English language. 1915.

Walbridge, E. F. Unfinished novels, here and abroad. Publishers' Weekly 22 June 1929.

Wormser, R. S. Fabulous fiction. PBSA 47 1953. Literary hoaxes.

Krieg, M. O. (ed). Mehr nicht erschienen: ein Verzeichnis unvollendet gebliebener Druckwerke. 2 pts. Vienna 1954–8

McKie, D. The great unpublished grows. Guardian 17 Jan 1966.

Individual Publishers and Publishers' Memoirs

Arranged in chronological order. See also bibliographies listed under Publishing, col 89, above.

Lyons, A. N. Robert Blatchford: the sketch of a personality. 1910.

Thayer, J. A. Astir: a publishers's life-story. Boston 1910, London 1911 (as Getting on: the confessions of a publisher).

Friederichs, H. Life of Sir George Newnes. 1911.

Newbery, A. Le B. Records of the house of Newbery from 1274–1910. Derby 1911.

Rivington, S. The publishing family of Rivington. 1919.

The centenary volume of Charles Griffin and Co Ltd, publishers, 1820–1920. 1920.

Huxley, L. The house of Smith Elder. 1923.

The house of Jarrolds 1823–1923. Norwich 1924.

Benn, E. J. P. The confessions of a capitalist. 1925.

Cox, H. and J. E. Chandler. The house of Longman 1724–1924. 1925.

Methuen, A. 1856–1924: Sir Algernon Methuen, Baronet, a memoir. 1925.

Secker, M. A calendar of letters: extracts from the publications of Number five John Street, 1910–25. 1926.

Dent, J. M. Memoirs, 1849–1926. 1928.

Whyte, F. William Heinemann: a memoir. 1928.

Waugh, A. A hundred years of publishing: being the story of Chapman & Hall Ltd. 1930.

Rhys, E. Everyman remembers. 1931.

Waugh, A. One man's road. 1931. Chapman and Hall.

Pitman, A. Half a century of commercial education and publishing. 1932. Sir Isaac Pitman and Sons.

Pocklington, G. R. The story of W. H. Smith and Son. 1921, 1932 (rev F. E. K. Foat).

Faber, G. A publisher speaking. 1934.

Howe, Garfield (ed). Of the making of CXXV books— a publisher's bibliography: Gerald Howe, 1926–33. 1934.

Mumby, F. A. The house of Routledge 1834–1934. 1934.

Richards, G. Author hunting by an old literary sportsman: memoires of years spent mainly in publishing 1897–1925. 1934; 1960 with introd by A. Waugh and postscript by M. Secker.

Harrap, G. G. Some memories 1901–35: a publisher's contribution to the history of publishing. 1935.

Holmes, J. C. Self and partners: mostly self. 1936. Rivington & Co.

Brief notes on the origins of T. and A. Constable. 1937.

Dent, J. M. and H. R. Dent. The house of Dent 1888–1936. 1938.

Hadfield, J. An English publisher in New York. Saturday Rev of Lit 31 Dec 1938.

McAlmon, R. Being geniuses together: an autobiography. 1938, New York 1968 (rev with K. Boyle as Being geniuses together 1920–1930).

Kehane, J. Memoirs of a booklegger. 1939. Obelisk Press.

Faber, G. The house of Longman. N & Q 14 March 1942.

Joseph, M. The sword in the scabbard. 1942.

Williams, H. The house of Longman. N & Q 12 April 1942.

Bolitho, H. (ed). A Batsford century. 1943, 1944 (rev).

Morgan, C. The house of Macmillan, 1843–1943. 1943.

Armstrong, A. C. Bouverie Street to Bowling Green Lane: fifty years of specialized publishing, 1891–1946. 1946. Temple Press Ltd.

'Indiaman'. Three addresses (Longmans 1939–47): an essay in publishing ecology. 1947.

1698 and after: the story of the SPCK. 1947.

Gerald Duckworth & Co. Fifty years, 1898–1948. 1948.

Benn, E. Happier days: recollections and reflections. 1949.

Blagden, C. Fire more than water: notes for the story of a ship. 1949. Longmans, Green & Co.

Joseph, M. The adventure of publishing. 1949.

McLaren, M. (ed). The house of Neill, 1749–1949. 1949.

Whyte, A. G. The story of the R.P.A. 1899–1949. 1949. Rationalist Press Association.

Flower, N. Just as it happened. 1950. Cassell & Co.

Penguins: a retrospect. 1951.

Abbott, J. The story of Francis, Day & Hunter. 1952.

Keir, D. The house of Collins: the story of a Scottish family of publishers from 1789 to the present day. 1952.

Trewin, J. C. and E. M. King. Printer to the House: the story of Hansard. 1952.

Clowes, W. B. Family business, 1803–1953. 1953. William Clowes.

Faber, G. Forty years back: a fragment of autobiography. Bookseller 10, 17 Jan 1953.

Liveing, E. G. D. Adventure in publishing: the house of Ward, Lock, 1854–1954. 1954.

Tredrey, F. D. The house of Blackwood 1804–1954. Edinburgh 1954.

Lehmann, J. The whispering gallery: autobiography I. 1955.

— I am my brother: autobiography II. 1960.

— The ample proposition: autobiography III. 1966.

Low, D. M. A century of writers 1855–1955. 1955. Chatto & Windus.

Mumby, R. A. and F. H. S. Stallybrass. From Swan Sonnenschein to George Allen and Unwin Ltd. 1955.

Cumbers, F. The book room: the story of the Epworth Press and the Methodist publishing house. 1956.

Williams, W. E. The Penguin story 1935–1956. 1956.

Knoll, R. E. Robert McAlmon, expatriate publisher and writer. Lincoln, Nebraska 1957.

— (ed). McAlmon and the lost generation. Lincoln, Nebraska 1962.

N[ewth], J. D. Adam and Charles Black 1807–1957: some chapters in the history of a publishing house. 1957.

Nowell-Smith, S. The house of Cassell 1848–1958. 1958.

Blackie, A. A. C. Blackie & Son 1809–1959: a short history of the firm. 1959.

Dickson, L. The ante-room. 1959.

— The house of words. 1963.

Warburg, F. An occupation for gentlemen. 1959.

Flower, D. et al. Penguin's progress 1935–60. 1960.

Unwin, S. The truth about a publisher: an autobiographical record. 1960.

A century and a half in Soho: a short history of the firm of Novello, publishers and printers of music, 1811–1961, 1961.

Gross, G. (ed). Publishers on publishing. New York 1961, introd F. G. Melcher; London 1962, introd by F. Swinnerton.

Partners in progress: some recollections of the past quarter-century at 182 High Holborn. 1961. Harrap & Co Ltd.

Arnold, M. et al. A service to education: the story of E. J. Arnold & Son Ltd. [1963].

Arnold, R. C. M. Orange Street and Brickhole Lane. 1963. Constable & Co.

King, A. and A. F. Stuart. The house of Warne: one hundred years of publishing. 1965.

Grant, J. Harold Monro and the poetry bookshop. 1967.

Nowell-Smith, S. (ed). Letters to Macmillan. 1967.

Hiscock, E. Last boat to Folly Bridge. 1970.

University Publishing, General Works

A few of the many studies of university publishing in America have been selected for inclusion among general accounts of university publishing.

Day, G. P. The function and organising of university presses. New Haven 1915.

Mumby, F. A. The learned press. In his Publishing and bookselling, 1930. Frequent revisions.

Marshall, J. Publication of books and monographs by learned societies. Washington 1931.

Couch, W. T. What it takes to start a university press. Saturday Rev of Lit 9 June 1945.

— The university presses: their role varies with time and place. New York Herald Tribune 25 Sept 1949.

Kerr, C. Report on American university presses. New Haven 1949.

Silver, H. M. The conservative university press. Amer Scholar 18 1949.

Morison, S. On learned presses. Cambridge 1955.

Harman, E. (ed). The university as publisher. Toronto 1961.

Wells, J. M. The scholar printers. Chicago 1964.

Hawes, G. R. To advance knowledge: a handbook on American university press publishing. New York 1967.

Shugg, R. The two worlds of university publishing. Lawrence Kansas 1967.

Individual University Presses

Aberdeen
  Keith, A. Aberdeen University Press. 1963.
Cambridge
  Crutchley, B. A history and description of the Pitt Press. Cambridge 1938.
  Rogers, B. Report on the typography of the Cambridge University Press, prepared in 1917. Cambridge 1950.
  A brief history of the Cambridge University Press. Cambridge 1955.
  Roberts, S. C. The evolution of Cambridge publishing. Cambridge 1956.
  The University printing houses at Cambridge from the sixteenth to the twentieth century. Cambridge 1962.
Glasgow
  Maclehose, J. The Glasgow University Press 1638–1931. 1931.
Liverpool
  Droop, J. P. The University Press of Liverpool, 1899–1946. 1947.
Oxford
  Chapman, R. W. The press to-day. In his Some account of the Oxford University Press, 1468–1921, Oxford 1922, 1926 (as Some account of the Oxford University Press to 1926). Ptd with Fell types.
  Redman, B. R. The Oxford University Press, New York, 1896–1946. New York 1946.
  Batey, C. Horace Hart and the Oxford University Press, 1883–1915. Signature new ser 18 1954.
  — The printing and making of books. Oxford 1954.

Private Publishing, General Works

See also Individual Printing Houses cols 80–1 and Designers and Typographers, cols 87–8, above.

Ashbee, C. R. The private press: a study in idealism—to which is added a bibliography of the Essex House press. Broad Campden 1909.

Piper, A. C. Private printing presses in Sussex. 1914.

Tomkinson, G. S. A select bibliography of the principal modern presses, public and private in Great Britain and Ireland. 1928.

Ransom, W. Private presses and their books. New York 1929.

— Selective check list of press books: a compilation of all significant private presses, or press books which are collected. 12 pts New York 1945–50.

Williams, H. Book clubs and printing societies of Great Britain and Ireland. 1929.

Haas, I. A periodical bibliography of private presses. Bull of Bibliography & Dramatic Index 15 1934.

— A bibliography of private presses. Amer Book Collector 5 1934.

— A bibliography of material relating to private presses. Chicago 1937. Introd by W. Ransom.

Muir, P. H. Private presses and their background. [? 1950].

Turner, G. The private press: its achievement and influence. Birmingham 1953.

Binns, N. E. (ed). Union list of private press material in the East Midlands. Nottingham 1955.

Modern private presses: a catalogue of books in Johannesburg Public Library. Johannesburg 1955.

Rae, T. and G. Handley-Taylor (ed). The book of the private press. 1958.

Archer, H. R. Private presses and collectors' editions. Library Trends 7 1959.

Manchester Public Libraries. Reference Library Subject Catalogue. Section 094: private press books. Ed S. Horrocks 2 pts Manchester 1959–60.

Private Libraries Association. Private press books, 1959 [etc]. 1960 onwards. With annual checklist.

Times Bookshop. English private presses 1757–1961. 1961. Exhibition catalogue.

Skelton, R. Twentieth-century Irish literature and the private press tradition: Dun Emer, Cuala, and Dolmen Presses, 1902–1963. In Irish renaissance, ed R. Skelton and D. R. Clark, Dublin 1965.

Loughborough Technical College. The private press: handbook to an exhibition held in the School of Librarianship. Loughborough 1968.

Franklin, C. The private presses. 1969. Bibliography; selection of recent auction prices.

Cave, R. The private press. 1971.

Individual Private Presses

Reference should also be made to the check lists included in the preceding section:

Ashendene Press
  A handlist of the books printed at the Ashendene press, 1895–1925. 1925.
  A descriptive bibliography of the books printed at the Ashendene press 1895–1935. 1935. By C. H. St J. Hornby.
  Ward, S. The Ashendene press. Philobiblon (Vienna) 10 1938. With bibliography.
  C. H. St J. Hornby: an anthology of appreciations. 1946.
Beaumont Press
  Beaumont, C. W. The first score: an account of the foundation and development of the Beaumont press and its first twenty publications. 1927.
Black Sun Press
  Bell, M. The Black Sun press, 1927 to the present. Books at Brown 17 1955.

Brewhouse Press
  The private press today. 1967.
Corvinus Press
  A list of books printed at the Corvinus press.
  [? 1939].
Curwen Press
  Hilton, J. and J. Thorp (ed). Change: the beginning of
  a chapter, in twelve volumes. Plaistow 1919. 2 vols
  only pbd.
  Catalogue raisonné of books printed at the Curwen press
  1920–23. 1924. Introd by Holbrook Jackson.
  The Curwen press almanac. 1926.
  Catalogue of an exhibition of books printed at the
  Curwen press. 1927.
  Simon, O. The Curwen press: type specimen book.
  1928.
  —— (ed). The Curwen press miscellany. 1931.
  Printer and playground: an autobiography. 1956.
  Jackson, H. A cross-section of English printing: the
  Curwen press, 1918–34. 1935.
  Rodenburg, J. Oliver Simon und die Curwen Press in
  Plaistow. Gutenberg-Jahrbuch 1951.
Daniel Press
  The Daniel press: memorials of C. H. O. Daniel with
  a bibliography of the press. Oxford 1921. Addenda
  and corrigenda, by F. Madan, Oxford 1922.
Doves Press
  Catalogue raisonné of books printed and published at the
  Doves press, 1900–16. 1916.
  Cobden-Sanderson, T. J. Cosmic vision. 1922.
  Pollard, A. W. Cobden-Sanderson and the Doves press:
  the history of the press and the story of its type. San
  Francisco 1929.
  Avis, F. C. The Doves press 1900–17. Gutenberg-
  Jahrbuch 1951.
Dun Emer Press
  Miller, L. The Dun Emer press. Irish Book 2 1963.
Eragny Press
  Moore, T. S. A brief account of the origin of the Eragny
  press. 1903.
  Pissarro, L. Notes on the Eragny press and a letter to
  J. B. Manson. Ed A. Fern, Cambridge 1957.
Fanfrolico Press
  Fanfrolicana: being a statement of the aims of the press.
  1928.
  Lindsay, J. Fanfrolico and after. 1962. Third vol of
  autobiography.
Golden Cockerel Press
  Chanticleer: a bibliography of the Golden Cockerel
  press, April 1921–Aug 1936. 1937. Pertelote: a
  sequel, Oct 1936–April 1943, 1943. Cockalorum:
  a sequel, June 1943–Dec 1948, 1951.
Gregynog Press
  Jones, T. The Gregynog press. Oxford 1954.
High House Press
  Matthewmen, S. The High House press: a short history
  and appreciation. Shaftesbury 1930.
Hogarth Press
  Smith, L. P. Tavistock Square. Orion 2 1945.
  Lehmann, J. The whispering gallery: autobiography I.
  1955.
  —— I am my brother: autobiography II. 1960.
  —— The ample proposition: autobiography III. 1966.
  Woolf, L. In his Beginning again: an autobiography of
  the years 1911–18, 1964.
  —— In his Downhill all the way: an autobiography of the
  years 1919–39, 1967.
  —— In his The journey not the arrival matters: an auto-
  biography of the years 1939–1969, 1969.
Hours Press
  Cunard, N. The Hours press: retrospect, catalogue,
  commentary. Book Collector 13 1964.
  —— These were the hours: memories of my Hours press,
  Reanville and Paris, 1928–1931. Carbondale 1969.
  Ed H. Ford.

Keepsake Press
  Cave, R. The Keepsake press. Amer Book Collector 14
  1963.
Nonesuch Press
  Bibliography of the first ten years of the Nonesuch press.
  Book Collector's Quart nos 13–14 1934. Commentary
  by F. Meynell.
  The Nonesuch century. 1936. By A. J. A. Symons,
  D. Flower and F. Meynell. The first hundred books.
  Meynell, F. The Nonesuch press. TLS 15 Oct 1938.
Pelican press
  [Meynell, F.]. Type specimens prepared for the Pelican
  press. [1923].
Saint Dominic's Press
  Aylesford Rev 7 1965. Special issue on Hilary Pepler
  and the St Dominic's press, with check-list of writings
  of H. D. C. Pepler.
Scholartis Press
  Partridge, E. H. The first three years. 1930.
Seizin Press
  Moran, J. The Seizin press of Laura Riding and Robert
  Graves. Black Art 2 1963. See also M. L. Turner,
  The Seizin press: an additional note. Ibid.
Twyn Barlwm Press
  'Gawsworth, John' (T. I. F. Armstrong). The Twyn
  Barlwm press 1931–2. 1933.
Vale Press
  Ricketts, C. A bibliography of books printed between
  1896 and 1903 by Hacon and Ricketts. 1904.
Ye Sette of Odd Volumes
  Straus, R. An odd bibliography: being a list of all the
  publications of Ye Sette of Odd Volumes from 1878–
  1924. 1925.

Reprints

Alden, W. L. The vice of complete editions. Author 17 1907.
Adcock, A. St J. More about anthologies. Bookman (Lon-
  don) 78 1930.
Symons, A. J. A. Edition and impression. Book Collec-
  tor's Quart 5 1932.
Pritchett, V. S. The pocket edition. Author 45 1934.
Lewis, F. The distribution of reprint books: a survey of
  the market and the means of reaching it. Publishers'
  Weekly 30 March 1935.
Everybody's books: popular taste and clever enterprises.
  TLS 1 May 1937.
Breit, H. The anthologies: of remaking many books there
  is no end. New York Times Book Rev 22 Dec 1946.
Hutchens, J. K. The strange new world of reprints. New
  York Herald Tribune Book Rev 25 Sept 1949.
Schmoller, H. Reprints: Aldine and after. Penrose
  Annual 1953.
Altick, R. D. From Aldine to Everyman: cheap reprint
  series of the English classics, 1830–1906. SB 11 1958.
Towards a processed literature. TLS 27 May 1965.

Paperback Editions

Appel, B. The paperback revolution. Saturday Rev of Lit
  28 Nov 1953.
Lewis, F. The future of paper-bound books. BNYPL 57
  1953.
Enoch, K. The paper-bound book: a twentieth-century
  publishing phenomenon. Lib Quart 24 1954; rptd in
  Mass media and communication, ed C. S. Steinberg,
  New York 1966.
Hemley, C. The problem of the paper-backs. Common-
  weal 29 Oct 1954.
Krim, S. The success of the highbrow paper-backs. New
  Republic 20 Dec 1954 and 31 Jan 1955.
One thousand Penguins. TLS 30 July 1954.
Williams, W. E. The Penguin story 1935–1956. 1956.
Schick, F. L. The paperbound book in America. New
  York 1958.

Walker, C. L. Big boom in good books. Saturday Rev of Lit 41 1958.

Paperback books. Writer 71 1958.

Becher, R. A. The paperback revolution. Cambridge Rev 7 Nov 1959.

Blum, E. Paperback book publishing. Journalism Quart 36 1959.

Flower, D. The paper back: its past, present and future. 1959.

Bound-up paperbacks in the public library. Author 71 1960.

Morpurgo, J. E. Paper-backs across frontiers. nd [? 1960].

Rolph, C. H. The paperback 'revolution'. Author 70 1960.

Brown, W. P. The titles of paperback books. Br Jnl of Psychology 55 1964.

National Book Council
(National Book League)

Selected pbns of the Council and the League are included under appropriate headings (e.g. How and what to read, Binding etc).

Corp, W. G. The English National Book Council. Publishers' Weekly 12 March 1938.

Marston, M. The National Book Council: a survey of fourteen years' work. 1940.

National Book Council annual lectures. 1943 onwards.

National Book Council to National Book League. 1944.

Morpurgo, J. E. The National Book League. In The book world today, ed J. Hampden 1957.

Specialized Publishing Methods

Includes Book clubs, book tokens, gift coupon trading, subscription book publishing. Reference should also be made to the bibliography following D. E. Strout, Book club publishing, Lib Trends 7 1959. A collection of items on gift coupon trading, 1932–3, is contained in the British Library of Political and Economic Science; see also R. L. Kilgour, Reference and subscription book publishing, Lib Trends 7 1959.

Williams, H. H. Book clubs and printing societies of Great Britain and Ireland. First Edn Club 15 1929.

Leavis, F. R. Mass civilization and minority culture. 1930. Effect of book clubs on literary taste.

Leavis, Q. D. The Book Society recommends. Scrutiny 1 1932.

—— The middlemen. In her Fiction and the reading public, 1932.

Associated Booksellers of Great Britain and Ireland. Book tokens: first [etc] revenue account and balance sheet. 1933–.

Hockliffe, M. Book tokens. Author 44 1933.

Publishers' Association. Book tokens to-day: a report. 1934.

—— Book tokens: a statement. 1943.

The Book Society news. Jan 1936–Jan/Feb 1946. Continued as Bookman (annual) new ser 1–?, March 1946–?

Mason, H. A. Education by book club? Scrutiny 6 1937. Correspondence in following number.

Book clubs: annual report of the Joint Committee on Book Clubs appointed by the Publishers' Association and the Association of Booksellers. 1–3?, 1937–1939.

Hutchinson, K. The battle of the book clubs. Nation 30 April 1938.

Fisher, D. C. Book clubs. BNYPL 51 1947.

Folio: the Times Book Club review. 1948–?

Koppel, J. W. Book clubs and the evaluation of books. Public Opinion Quart 12 1948.

Kim, W. Buchklubs und Buchgemeinschaften des Auslandes und ihre Beziehungen zum Buchhandel. Zurich 1950.

Baker, J. Book clubs. In The book world today, ed J. Hampden 1957.

Symons, J. The Left Book Club. In his The thirties, 1960.

Folio 21: a bibliography of the Folio Society, 1947–67. 1968.

Lewis, J. The Left Book Club: an historical record. 1970.

Periodicals devoted to Publishing
Publishers' house journals are not listed.

The publishers' circular (etc). Vol 1–vol 173 no 4846, 2 Oct 1837–16 May 1959. Continued as British books vol 173 no 4847, 23 May 1959; incorporated in The publisher (28 Jan 1964–winter 1966) as vol 180, 1967 onwards.

The bookseller. Nos 1–1042, Jan 1858–1921. Continued as Bookseller and stationery trades journal, nos 1043–1167, 1922–March 1928 (but as Bookseller 23 Sept 1927–30 March 1928). Continued as Publisher and bookseller, nos 1168–1454, 6 April 1928–29 Sept 1933. Continued as Bookseller, no 1455, 6 Oct 1933 onwards. Incorporated Monthly literary adviser and, temporarily, Stationery trades journal.

The Aldine newsagents' trade journal. Nos 1–92, 1897–Dec 1904.

Book and news trade gazette. 1 Jan 1898–?

Book trade. Nos 1–32, Dec 1901–Nov 1904.

The publisher and bookseller. Vol 1 no 1–vol 7 no 142, 1 April 1905–14 Dec 1907.

Publishers' trade announcements. Nos 1–2, 1905.

The international publisher and stationer. 1909–?

Publishers' mail. 1915.

Publishing world. 1 only? Jan 1925.

The publisher's miscellany. 1931.

The British book trade directory. 1933.

The book trade handbook, 1937.

The Law and Publishing
General works, including defamation and taxation

Hardy, Y. H. Unauthorized alterations in a serial story. Author 18 1908. Report of libel action.

Bull, W. V. The law of libel as affecting newspapers and journalists. 1912.

Dawson, T. The law of the press. 1927.

McAllister, G. (ed). The book crisis. 1940. Speeches by Sir Hugh Walpole, J. B. Priestley, G. Faber et al, opposing proposed purchase tax on books.

National Book Council. The battle of the books. 1940. The campaign against purchase tax on books.

Rothenberg, I. Damages for newspaper libel in Great Britain. Journalism Quart 20 1943.

Terrou, F. and L. Solal. Legislation for press, film and radio. Paris 1951 (Press, film and radio in the world today.)

Spring, S. Risks & rights in publishing, television, radio, [etc]. 1952.

Herbert, A. P. No fine on fun: the comical history of the entertainments duty. 1957.

Abrahams, G. The law for writers and journalists. 1958.

O'Sullivan, R. and R. Brown. The law of defamation. 1958.

Lloyd, H. The legal limits of journalism. 1968.

Copyright
See headnote to Authorship, cols 61–62, above, regarding archives of The Author.

Copinger, W. A. The law of copyright in works of literature and art. 1870. Frequent revisions; ed J. M. Easton 1904; ed F. E. Skone James 1927 onwards.

Strong, A. A. The law of copyright for actor and composer. 1901.

Macgillivray, E. J. Treatise upon the law of copyright in the United Kingdom and the Dominions of the Crown and in the United States of America. 1902.

—— Copyright cases, 1901–4 (1905–10) [etc]. 1905–?

—— The copyright act 1911, annotated. 1912.

—— Guide to the copyright act 1911. 1912.

—— Fair use. Author 54 1944.

Hamlin, A. S. (ed). Copyright cases: a summary of leading American cases on the law of copyright and on literary property from 1891–1903, together with the text of the United States Copyright Statute and a selection of recent copyright decisions of Great Britain and Canada. New York 1904.

Report of the Committee on the Law of Copyright. 1909.

Imperial Copyright Conference. 1910. Memorandum of the proceedings. British Parliamentary Papers 65 1910.

Hurrell, H. Copyright law and the copyright act 1911. 1912.

Kerr, S. P. The copyright act 1911. 1912.

Strahan, J. A. and N. H. Oldham. The copyright act 1911. 1912.

U.S. Library of Congress. Copyright in England. Washington Bull 16 1912.

Weller, B. Stage copyright at home and abroad. 1912.

Société de Législation Comparée. Nouvelle législation anglaise sur le droit d'auteur. 1913.

Potu, E. La convention de Berne. Paris 1914.

International Convention for the Protection of Literary and Artistic Works, Rome 2 June 1928. Report. 1928.

Siebert, F. S. International protection of rights in news. Journalism Quart 9 1932.

Plant, A. The economic aspects of copyright in books. Economica May 1934.

Ladas, S. P. The international protection of literary and artistic property. New York 1938.

Copyright law symposium. New York. No 1 1939; suspended 1940–50; 2 onwards. American Society of Composers, Authors and Publishers.

Howard, G. W. and S. Unwin. International copyright. TLS 14 Nov 1942.

UNESCO copyright bulletin. 1948 onwards.

Evans, L. H. Copyright and the public interest. BNYPL 53 1949.

James, C. F. The story of the Performing Right Society. 1951.

Ewart, K. Copyright. Cambridge 1952 (Cambridge Authors' and Printers' Guides no 5).

Ransom, H. Ownership of literary titles. SE 31 1952.

Bulletin of the Copyright Society of the USA. 1953 onwards.

Durham, H. N. Copyright law. New Mexico Quart 24 1955.

UNESCO. Copyright laws and treaties of the world. Washington 1956. Suppl 1960.

Copyright Society of the United States of America. Studies on copyright. South Hackensack NJ 1963.

Manchester Public Libraries. Reference Library Subject Catalogue. Section 655: printing pt 2, type and typesetting, printing processes, publishing & bookselling, copyright. Ed G. E. Haslam, Manchester 1963.

Hattery, L. H. and G. P. Bush (ed). Reprography and copyright law. Washington 1964.

Hurst, W. E. and W. S. Hale. The U.S. master producers & British music scene book. Hollywood 1968. Vol 4 in Entertainments Industry Series. On contracts.

Censorship, Obscenity and Pornography

See also K. Young and R. D. Lawrence, Bibliography on censorship and propaganda, *Eugene 1928*.

'Officer'. Smith of the Shamrock Guards: or the 'ragged' lieutenant. 1903. Preface and introd discuss specific censorship case.

Stoker, B. The censorship of fiction. Nineteenth Century 64 1908.

Hurley, T. Legislation of the Catholic church on the production and distribution of literature. Dublin 1911.

Haynes, E. S. P. et al. The taboos of the British Museum Library. Eng Rev 16 1913.

Bell, E. P. The British censorship. 1916.

Harrison, A. Literature and the policeman. Eng Rev 38 1924.

International convention for the suppression of the circulation of and traffic in obscene publications. British Parliamentary Papers 30 1926.

The censorship of books: a symposium. Nineteenth Century 105 1929. By Havelock Ellis, E. M. Forster, Virginia Woolf et al.

Curling, J. Obscenity in modern art. Spectator 24 Aug 1929.

Herrick, R. What is dirt? Amer Bookman 70 1929.

Lawrence, D. H. Pornography and obscenity. This Quarter 2 July/Sept 1929. Also pbd as pamphlet; rptd in his Phoenix New York 1936.

Causton, B. and G. C. Young. Keeping it dark: or the censor's handbook. 1930.

Scott-James, R. A. Should reviewers be censors? Spectator 3 March 1933.

Haight, A. L. Banned books: informal notes on some books banned for various reasons at various times and various places. New York 1935.

Craig, A. The banned books of England. 1937.

— Above all liberties. 1942.

— The banned books of England and other countries: a study of the conception of literary obscenity. 1962, Cleveland [1963] (as Suppressed books).

Mackwood, J. Some reflections on obscenity. Horizon 53 1944.

'Orwell, George' (E. A. Blair). The prevention of literature. Atlantic Monthly 179 1947.

Penton, B. C. Censored! Sydney 1947.

Schary, D. Censorship and stereotypes. Saturday Rev of Lit 30 April 1949.

Censorship and controversy. National Council of Teachers of English, Committee on Censorship of Teaching Materials for Classroom and Library, Report. Chicago 1953.

Obscene publications. Chichester 1954; rptd from Justice of Peace and Local Government Rev.

Blanshard, P. The right to read. Boston 1955.

Allsop, K. I am a pornographer. Spectator 21 Oct 1960. Interview with Maurice Girodias of the Olympia press.

Radcliffe, C. J. Censors. Cambridge [1961]. Rede lecture.

Rolph, C. H. (ed). The trial of Lady Chatterley. 1961.

Widmer, K. and E. Literary censorship. Belmont 1961.

Sheed, W. Pornography and literary pleasure. Catholic World 194 1962.

Fryer, P. Mrs Grundy: studies in English prudery. 1963.

— Private case: public scandal. 1966.

Murphy, T. J. Censorship: government and obscenity. Baltimore and Dublin 1963.

Read, H. The problem of pornography. In his To hell with culture, 1963.

Censorship: a quarterly report on censorship of ideas and the arts. Nos 1–9 1964–7. Ed M. Midlin.

Ernst, M. L. and A. W. Schwartz. Censorship: the search for the obscene. 1964.

Hyde, H. M. History of pornography. 1964.

Reisner, R. G. Show me the good parts: the reader's guide to sex in literature. New York 1964.

Gallico, P. Writers should be heard but not obscene. Writer 78 1965.

Gillmor, D. M. The puzzle of pornography. Journalism Quart 42 1965.

Coyne, J. R. Pornography, literature and the library. Colorado Acad Lib 3 1966.

Jacobson, D. An end to pornography. Commentary 42 1966.

Freeman, G. The undergrowth of literature. 1967.

Wincor, R. Literary property. New York 1967.

Censorship and obscenity: a symposium. Author 79 1968.

Hynes, S. The organization of morality. In his Edwardian turn of mind, Princeton 1968.

Thomas, D. A long time burning: the history of literary censorship in England. 1969. With bibliography.

D. DISTRIBUTION

(1) REVIEWING

As many problems posed by reviewing are common to Britain and America, a number of American studies have been included.

Ascher, I. G. Unreviewed books. Author 23 1913.

McFee, W. A new and entertaining method of reviewing books highly recommended to the profession. Bookman (New York) 50 1920; rptd in his Harbours of memory, Garden City NY 1921.

Canby, H. S. The sins of book reviewers. Bookman (London) 54 1921.

Ferguson, C. W. The business of reviewing. Southwest Rev 13 1928.

The literary racket. Scrutiny 1 1932.

Strong, L. A. G. Criticism and reviewing. Spectator 20 Aug 1932.

Scott-James, R. A. Should reviewers be censors? Spectator 3 March 1933.

Zabel, M. D. Titans, tea-hounds, rasslers and reviewers. Poetry 41 1933.

Blurbing. Saturday Rev of Lit 24 Nov 1934. Three approaches to reviewing.

Thompson, K. S. Are reviewers critics? Nation 3 Jan 1934.

Review copies: a symposium. Author 44 1934.

Riding, L. On reviewing 'difficult' books. TLS 7 March 1936.

Gardner, F. M., H. Spring and R. A. Scott-James. Book reviewing: notes by a librarian, a reviewer and an editor. Library Assoc Record 40 1938.

Roberts, M. The critic and the public. Southern Rev 4 1938.

Spender, S. A plea for more anonymity: the future of reviewing. TLS 8 Oct 1938.

— Modern poets and reviewers. Horizon 5 1942.

Hawkins, D. English reviewing. Saturday Rev of Lit 1 April 1939.

Swinnerton, F. The reviewing and criticism of books. 1939.

Woolf, V. Reviewing. 1939.

Thompson, R. The popular review and the scholarly book. Eng Inst Annual 1940.

Reviewing reviewed: a symposium. Author 53 1943. By G. B. Shaw, H. G. Wells et al.

Drewry, J. E. Book reviewing. Boston 1945, 1966 (rev).

Rowland, J. Reviewing versus criticism. Wind & Rain 2 1945.

Rates for reviewing. Author 57 1947.

Brickell, H. Problems of the literary craftsman: book reviewing. Saturday Rev of Lit 23 April 1949.

Hansen, H. Reviewing as a democratic weapon. In Journalism in wartime, ed F. L. Mott, New York 1949.

Vivas, E. Criticism and the little mags. Western Rev 16 1951.

Hitchin, M. M. Reviewers' opinions. TLS 22 Aug 1952.

Mortimer, R. Reflections of a reviewer. Sunday Times 30 Dec 1955.

Potter, S. The art of reviewmanship. New York Times Book Rev 8 May 1955.

Steinbeck, J. Critics, from a writer's point of view. Saturday Rev of Lit 27 Aug 1955.

Organs of critical opinion. EC 6–7, 1956–7. F. W. Bateson: The Review of English Studies; R. Hayman: Reviewing in The New Statesman and The Spectator; M. Roberts: Reviewing in The London Magazine and some other monthlies; F. W. Bateson: The Times Literary Supplement.

Wagner, G. The decline of book reviewing. Amer Scholar 26 1957.

The critic's responsibility. Author 69 1959.

Hollander, J. Some animadversions on current reviewing. Daedalus 92 1963.

Peyre, H. What is wrong with American book-reviewing? Daedalus 92 1963.

Anonymous reviewing: a forum. Author 76 1965.

Ewart, G. Poetry reviewing: a protest. Author 78 1967.

(2) BOOKSELLING

Bibliographies

The international directory of second-hand booksellers and bibliophiles' manual (formerly Directory of second-hand booksellers, Rochdale, 1886–8, 1891). 1894, 1899, 1903, 1906, 1910, 1914. Continued as The librarian, including booksellers, publishers, binders, paper makers, printers, agents etc. Gravesend 1927. Ed A. J. Philip. Continued as Clegg's international directory new ser no 2, 1930/31 onwards.

Peet, W. H. Bibliography. In F. A. Mumby, The romance of bookselling, 1910, 1930 (as Publishing and bookselling). Frequent revisions.

Classified catalogue of a collection of works on publishing and bookselling in the British Library of Political and Economic Science. 1936, 1962 (rev).

General Works

What will it cost? A reference book for booksellers, stationers and printers. 1905.

The successful bookseller: a complete guide to success to all engaged in a retail bookselling, stationery and fancy goods business. 1906.

The art of bookselling: eight essays by managers of W. H. Smith & Son. 1907.

Report of a departmental committee of information upon the circulation of British books, periodicals, in foreign countries. 1918.

Raymond, H. Publishing and bookselling. New York 1928.

Wilson, J. G. The business of bookselling. 1930, 1945 (rev).

Associated Booksellers of Great Britain. Code of practice for booksellers. 1931.

Department of Overseas Trade. Memorandum on the sale of English books abroad. 1932.

Blackwell, B. Provincial bookselling. In The book world, ed J. Hampden 1935.

— The bookshop: yesterday, today and tomorrow. Author 53 1942.

— Of university bookshops. Author 77 1966.

Seligo, I. Vom englischen Buchmarkt. Frankfurter Zeitung 50 1935.

Vowinckel, E. Vom englischen Büchermarkt. Neuphilologische Monatsschrift 7 1936.

Plant, M. The English book trade: an economic history of the making and selling of books. 1939.

Langdon-Davies, B. N. The practice of bookselling: with some opinions on its nature, status and future. 1951.

Joy, T. Bookselling. 1953, 1964 (rev).

Carter, J. Bibliography and the rare book trade. PBSA 48 1954.

Political and Economic Planning. Publishing and bookselling. 1956.

Shatzkin, L. The book in search of a reader. Daedalus 92 1963.

Barnes, J. J. Free trade in books: a study of the London book trade since 1800. Oxford 1964.

Smith, F. S. Bibliography in the bookshop. 1964.
Booksellers Association of Great Britain. Better bookselling series, ed G. Bartlett. No 1, P. Stockham, University bookselling, 1965; no 2, G. Bartlett, Stock control in bookselling, 1965; no 3, G. Bartlett, Bookselling by mail, 1966; no 4, R. G. Peacham, Library and educational supply in bookselling, 1966; no 5, H. E. Bailey, The economics of bookselling, 1965; no 6, M. Fuchs, Accounting for booksellers, 1965.
Reavell, M. A. C. Bookselling in universities. Author 77 1966.
Heffer, E. W. Training of the bookseller. 1967.
Mann, P. H. Books, book readers and bookshops. In Media sociology, ed J. Tunstall 1970. Based on lecture to Annual conference of Booksellers' Association of Great Britain, 1968.

Bookshops and Auctions

One hundred years of book auctions 1807–1907, with notes on methods and advantages of book auctions. 1908. Hodgson & Co.
Shaylor, J. The fascination of books: with other papers on books and bookselling. 1912.
— Sixty years a bookman: with other recollections and reflections. 1923.
— The pleasures of bookland. nd.
Laurance, R. M. A century of bookselling. 1814–1914. Aberdeen 1914. David Wyllie & Son.
Hobson, G. D. Notes on the history of Sotheby's. 1917.
Vincent, W. Seen from the railway station: fifty years' reminiscences. 1919. W. H. Smith & Son.
Pocklington, G. R. The story of W. H. Smith & Son 1820–1920. 1921, 1932 (rev F. K. Foat).
McFee, W. The high seas bookshop. Cassell's Weekly 24 Oct 1923; rptd in his Swallowing the anchor, New York 1925. Operating a bookshop aboard ship.
Spencer, W. T. Forty years in my bookshop. Ed T. Moult 1923.
Rosenbach, A. S. W. Books and bidders: the adventures of a bibliophile. 1928.
Smith, G. and F. Benger. The oldest London bookshop: a history of 200 years. 1928. A history of the firm of Ellis.
Fabes, G. H. The romance of a bookshop 1904–1929. 1929. W. & G. Foyle Ltd.
Darling, W. Y. The private papers of a bankrupt bookseller. Edinburgh 1931, 1932 (rev).
— The bankrupt bookseller speaks again. Edinburgh 1938. Both anon, and both rptd as The bankrupt bookseller, Edinburgh 1947.
Block, A. A short history of the principal London booksellers and book auctioneers. 1933.
Stevens, A. A. The recollections of a bookman: a record of thirty-three years with three famous book houses and some account of noted books, their authors and others. 1933.
Milne, J. The memoirs of a bookman. 1934.
Blackwell, B. The book world. 1935.
Bain, J. S. A bookseller looks back. 1940.
Lewis's 1844–1944. 1945. H. K. Lewis.
B. Quaritch Ltd. One hundredth anniversary, 1847–1947. 1947.
Wrentmore, C. Q. A portrait study of Bernard Quaritch, by his daughter. [1947].
James Thin, 1848–1948. Edinburgh 1948.
Laver, J. Hatchards of Piccadilly, 1797–1947. 1948.
Clear, G. The story of W. H. Smith & Son. 1949. Privately circulated.
Bason, F. Fred Bason's diary. Ed N. Bentley 1950.
Adventures of an Irish bookman: a selection from the writings of M. J. Macmanus. Ed F. Macmanus, Dublin 1952.
Bell, R. F. Gordon & Gotch, London: the story of the G. & G century, 1853–1953. 1953.

Muir, P. H. Minding my own business. 1956.
Wolf, E. and J. F. Fleming. Rosenbach: a biography. Cleveland 1960.
The Menzies group. Edinburgh 1965.
Thomas, A. G. The country bookshop. TLS 17 June 1965.
— Fine books. 1967.
Ettinghausen, M. L. Rare books and royal collectors: memoirs of an antiquarian bookseller. New York 1966.

Net Book Agreement

The Times. The history of the book war. 1907.
Net Books Committee. Net books question. 1908.
MacMillan, F. The Net Book Agreement, 1899. Glasgow 1924.
— The Net Book Agreement 1899 and the book war 1906–8. 1926.
The net book system. 1931. A leaflet for the public issued by the Associated Booksellers of Great Britain and Ireland.
Blackwell, B. The nemesis of the Net Book Agreement: an address. 1933.
Barker, R. E. and G. R. Davies (ed). Books are different. 1966. Evidence submitted in defence of the Net Book Agreement to the Monopolies Commission.

Booksellers' Organizations

Bowes, R. Booksellers' associations past and present. 1905.
How the organization of the trade came about. Bookseller 25 June 1909.
Corp, W. G. Fifty years: a brief account of the Associated Booksellers of Great Britain and Ireland 1895–1945. Oxford 1946.
Blagden, C. The Stationers' Company. 1960.

Periodicals

The bookseller. Nos 1–1042, Jan 1858–1921. Continued as Bookseller and stationery trades journal, nos 1043–1167, 1922–March 1928 (but as Bookseller, 23 Sept 1927–30 March 1928). Continued as Publisher and bookseller, nos 1168–1454, 6 April 1928–29 Sept 1933. Continued as Bookseller, no 1455, 6 Oct 1933 onwards. Incorporated Monthly literary adviser and, temporarily, Stationery trades journal.
The international directory of second-hand booksellers and bibliophiles' manual (formerly Directory of second-hand booksellers, Rochdale 1886–88, 1891). 1894, 1899, 1903, 1906, 1910, 1914. Continued as The librarian, including booksellers, publishers, binders, paper makers, printers, agents etc, Gravesend 1927. Ed A. J. Philip. Continued as Clegg's international directory new ser no 2, 1930/31 onwards.
Book-prices current. Dec 1886–Nov 1887, 1888. Annually to 1957. Auction prices.
The clique: the antiquarian booksellers' medium. 1890 onwards.
The bookman. Vol 1 no 1–vol 87 no 519, Oct 1891–Dec 1934. Incorporated in London mercury.
What to read. 1 only Nov 1902.
Book-auction records (formerly Sale records). 3 June 1902–27 June 1903. Rev edn ed Frank Karslake pbd 1908 but dated 1903; vol 1 pt 2 pbd 1907, dated 1904. In progress.
The stationers' year book. 1912.
Newsboy: a quarterly for boys of W. H. Smith & Son. 1914–31. Continued as Junior staff journal, 1931–?
The bookmark. Nos 1–6, Aug 1918–July 1920.
The Scottish newsagent. Glasgow. Nov 1919–?
Bookpost: a weekly organ for booksellers, publishers and booklovers. Vol 1 no 1–vol 4 no 81, 4 June 1920–11 Aug 1922.
Retail newsagent. Bristol. Nos 1–199, July 1921–Oct 1939.

Melrose's book post. Nos 1–3, Nov 1922–Jan 1923.

British booksellers. Liverpool 1924. Continuation of section of Literary year book. *See col 1354, below.*

The bookseller and print dealers' weekly. Vol 1 no 1–vol 3 no 159, 30 Sept 1926–10 Oct 1929. Continued as Bookseller and collector, vol 4 no 160–vol 5 no 240, Oct 1929–Aug 1931. Incorporated in Plaindealer.

Foylibra: monthly record of a bookshop. Nos 1–? June 1927–? Foyles.

The book window. Vol 1 no 1–vol 6 no 5, July 1927–Christmas 1941; then 1952–7. W. H. Smith & Son.

Books of the month. New ser Nos 1–? June 1929–?

The bookmart: incorporating Antiquarian book trader gazette. Nos 1–22, May 1930–March 1931.

The book-dealers' weekly (and publisher's guide). Nos 1–542, 1 March 1932–1 Aug 1942. Incorporated in Clique.

The plaindealer. Nos 1–3, 1933. Incorporated Bookseller and collector.

The book trade journal and librarians' guide. Nos 1–206, 17 May 1935–21 April 1939. Incorporated in Book-dealers weekly.

Bookman circle. ? 1937.

Bookmen's broadsheet. 1944–? Assoc of Yorkshire bookmen.

The booksellers' handbook. 1944/45–?

W. H. Smith & Son trade circular. No 1208 = 4 Jan 1947.

The book exchange. 1948.

(3) BOOK COLLECTING

Bibliographies

Dobell, B. Catalogue of books printed for private circulation. 1906.

Williams, I. A. Books on book-collecting. Book Collector's Quart 5 1932.

Vail, R. W. G. The literature of book collecting. New York 1936.

Webber, W. L. Books about books. Boston 1937. For collectors.

Sadleir, M. Book-collecting: a reader's guide. 1947 (National Book League pamphlet).

General Works

See also articles in Book Collector *on individual collectors, and entries under Personal Libraries, col 115, below.*

Hazlitt, W. C. The book collector. 1904.

Slater, J. H. How to collect books. 1905.

Pollard, A. W. Books in the house. 1907.

In memoriam William Noble. Liverpool 1913. A catalogue of the books he collected and bequeathed to Liverpool University Library.

De Ricci, S. The book collector's guide. Philadelphia 1921.

—— English collectors of books and manuscripts 1530–1930. Cambridge 1930. The Sandars Lectures.

The First Edition Club. A bibliographical catalogue of the first loan exhibition of books and manuscripts held by the First Edition Club. 1922.

—— Catalogue of fifty books of the year. 1928–?

Gosse, P. My pirate library. [1926].

Orcutt, W. D. In quest of the perfect book: reminiscences & reflections of a bookman. Boston 1926.

Williams, I. A. The elements of book-collecting. 1927.

—— On collecting book-illustrations. Bookman (London) 82 1932.

Boutell, H. S. First editions and how to tell them, American, British and Irish. 1928, 1937 (rev), 1949 (rev); rev W. Underhill, Berkeley 1965.

Newton, A. E. This book-collecting game. New York 1930.

Currie, B. Fishers of books. Boston 1931.

Jackson, H. The anatomy of bibliomania. 2 vols 1931.

Block, A. The book collector's vade-mecum. 1932.

The First Edition Club. TLS 23 June 1932.

Fletcher, I. K. Sentimental collecting: or books on topography and local history. Book Collector's Quart no 8 1932.

Symons, A. J. A. On selecting the fifty books of the year. Ibid.

—— Modern English bindings at the First Edition Club reviewed. Book Collector's Quart no 13 1934.

Carter, J. (ed). New paths in book collecting: essays by various hands. 1934.

—— Taste and technique in book-collecting. Cambridge 1948. Sandars Lectures. 3rd edn, rev with epilogue, 1970.

—— ABC for book collectors. 1952. Frequent revisions.

—— Books and book collectors. 1956.

Jordan-Smith, P. For the love of books: the adventures of an impecunious collector. 1934.

Brussel, I. R. Anglo-American first editions: 1826–1900, east to west; west to east, 1786–1930. 2 pts 1935, 1936 (Bibliographia nos 9, 10).

Sadleir, M. Bibliomania: new style. TLS 10 Jan 1935.

Muir, P. H. Book collecting as a hobby: a series of letters to everyman. 1944, 1945 (rev).

—— Book-collecting: more letters to everyman. 1949.

—— (ed). Talks on book-collecting: delivered under the authority of the Antiquarian Booksellers' Association. 1952.

'Orwell, George' (E. A. Blair). Books v. cigarettes. Tribune 8 Feb 1946; rptd in his Collected essays vol 4, 1968.

Munby, A. N. L. Some caricatures of book-collectors: an essay. 1948.

Chapman, R. W. et al. Book collecting: four broadcast talks. Cambridge 1950.

Horrox, R. (ed). Book handbook: an illustrated guide to old and rare books. 1951.

Blegen, T. C. et al. Book collecting and scholarship. Minneapolis 1954.

Millert, A. T. Trends in modern first edition collecting since 1939. Book Collector 4 1955.

Collison, R. L. Book collecting. 1957.

Prance, C. A. Peppercorn papers: a miscellany on books and book-collecting. Cambridge 1964.

Folio 21: a bibliography of the Folio Society 1947–67. 1968. Introd by F. Meynell.

Book Plates and Book Stamps, including Periodicals

Arellanes, A. S. Bookplates: a selective annotated bibliography of the periodical literature. Detroit 1971. See The Library 27 1972.

The book of book-plates. London and Edinburgh. Vol 1 no 1–vol 3 no 4, April 1900–July 1903. Continued as Books and book-plates, Edinburgh, vols 4–5, Oct 1903–July 1904. Continued as Book-lover's magazine, vols 6–8 no 6, 1905–9. Ed J. W. Simpson.

Warren, J. B. L. A guide to the study of bookplates. Manchester 1900.

Nelson, H. Reproductions of twenty-five designs for book plates. Edinburgh 1910.

Davenport, C. Cameo book-stamps, figured and described. 1911.

Badeley, J. F. Bookplates 1927.

Vaughan, H. M. Catalogue, with notes, of the Aneurin Williams collection of bookplates. Aberystwyth 1938.

Severin, M. F. Making a bookplate. 1949.

Beddingham, P. Concerning bookplates. 1960.

—— et al. Concerning book labels. [1963].

Book Care

Blades, W. The enemies of books. 1880, 1882 (rev), 1902 (rev).

Clark, J. W. The care of books. Cambridge 1902.

Book of trade secrets: recipes and instructions for renovating, repairing, improving and preserving old books and prints. 1910.

Solechnik, N. Y. (ed). New methods for restoration and preservation of documents and books. Jerusalem 1964. Tr from Russian.

Thompson, L. S. The incurable mania. Berkeley Calif. 1966.

— Bibliogica comica: or humorous aspects of the caparisoning and conservation of books. Hamden Conn 1969.

Cunha, G. D. M. Conservation of library materials. Metuchen NJ 1967. With bibliography.

Deceptions: Hoaxes and Forgeries

See bibliography compiled by P. W. Filby in Crime and literati: fraud and forgery in literature, *Baltimore 1962. Catalogue of exhibition at Peabody Institute. See also T. J. Wise, cols 1131–4, below.*

Dickinson, A. D. Frauds, forgeries, fakes and facsimiles. Lib Jnl 60 1935.

Ehrlich, E. S. Photomicrography as a bibliographical tool [for detecting forgeries]. Harvard Lib Bull 4 1950.

Holstein, M. A five-foot shelf of literary forgeries. Colophon 2 1953.

Wormser, R. S. Fabulous fiction. PBSA 47 1953. Ptd pbns as hoaxes.

Collison, R. L. Book collecting: an introduction to modern methods of literary and bibliographical detection. 1957.

Arnau, F. [Heinrich Schmitt]. Kunst der Fälscher, Fälscher der Kunst. Düsseldorf 1959. Tr by J. M. Brownjohn as Three thousand years of deception in art and antiques, 1961. *See ch on Printing.*

Todd, W. B. (ed). T. J. Wise centenary studies. Austin Texas 1959. With T. J. Wise handlist.

Manchester Public Libraries. Wise after the event: a catalogue of books, pamphlets and letters relating to T. J. Wise. Ed G. E. Haslam, Manchester 1964.

Moran, J. Thomas J. Wise and his printers. Black Art 3 1964/5.

Katz, W. A. Machinery of detection [of forged books]. Amer Book Collector 16 1965.

Periodicals

There is a discussion of such periodicals in Magazines for book-collectors, TLS 26 April 1947. *For periodicals dealing with bookplates, see Book Plates, col 108, above.*

Book queries. Liverpool. Vol 5 no 182–vol 18 no 640 March 1894–25 Dec 1902. Ed C. Taylor. Originally (International) Book finder. Continued as Book finder, Derby, vol 19, 641–56, 7 Oct 1911–19 Jan 1912.

The book lover. Vol 1 no 1–vol 11 no 61, Jan 1898–Oct 1915. New ser vols 1–8, July 1924–April 1928.

The bibliophile. Vol 1 no 1–vol 4 no 1 (nos 1–19), March 1908–Sept 1909.

The book exchange. Folkestone. Nos 1–4, Aug–Nov 1909.

The Irish book lover. Vols 1–32, 1909–57. Not pb 1926–7.

The international bibliographer. 1–2, April, May 1910. Ed G. Eller.

The bookroom quarterly. 1–14. New ser 1–3, 1910–12.

The Aberdeen book-lover. Vols 1–7, May 1913–May 1934.

The bookman's journal and print collector. Vol 1 no 1–vol 4 no 94, 31 Oct 1919–12 Aug 1921. Ed W. Partington. New ser (subtitled: for connoisseurs of literature and art) vol 5 no 1–vol 14 no 59, Oct 1921–Sept/Oct 1926. Ed W. Partington. New ser vol 15 no 1–vol 18 no 16, 1927–31.

The first edition and book collector. 1924–?

The young booklover. Edinburgh 1926.

Modern first editions: points and values. Ser 1–3, 1929–32. Ed G. H. Fabes.

The book-collector's quarterly (Organ of the First Edition Club). Nos 1–17, Dec 1930–Dec 1934. Ed Desmond Flower and A. J. A. Symons.

First editions and their values. Nos ? 1–3 1932–3.

The Scottish bookman. Edinburgh. Nos 1–6, Sept 1935–Feb 1936. Ed D. C. Thomson.

The bookworm. 1939.

Irish bookman. Dublin. 1946–? Ed S. Campbell.

Book handbook. Bracknell (vol 2 London). Vol 1 no 1–vol 2 no 4. Feb 1947–March 1951. Ed Reginald Horrox. Continuing as Book collector, spring 1952 onwards.

International P.E.N. Bulletin of selected books. 1950–?

(4) LIBRARIES AND LIBRARIANSHIP

The Library Association publishes many books and lists for the benefit of librarians in addition to the few noted under the various subsections here.

Bibliographies

Guthrie, A. L. Library work, cumulated 1905–11: a bibliography and digest of library literature. Minneapolis 1912.

Cannons, H. G. T. Bibliography of library economy 1876–1920. Chicago 1927. Library of literature: a supplement to Cannons' bibliography of library economy, 1921–32, ed L. M. Morsch, New York 1934. Continued as Library literature 1933–5 [etc], New York 1936 onwards.

Association of Special Libraries and Information Bureaux. The Aslib directory: a guide to sources of information in Great Britain and Ireland, 1928, 1957 (rev), 1968 (rev).

The year's work in librarianship. Vols 1–17, 1928–50 (vol 12, 1939–45). Continued as Five years' work in librarianship 1951–5 [etc], 1958 onwards.

Burton, M. and M. E. Vosburgh (ed). A bibliography of librarianship. 1934.

Libraries, General Works

Rye, R. A. The students' guide to the libraries of London. 1908, 1927 (rev).

Brown, J. D. A British library itinerary. 1913.

Rowntree, J. S. and E. E. Taylor. Extensions through the printed word: libraries, literature and advertising. Harrogate 1918.

Hessel, A. Geschichte der Bibliotheken. Göttingen 1925. Tr with supplementary material by R. Peiss (as History of libraries), Washington 1950.

Baker, E. A. The uses of libraries. 1927.

Kenyon, F. G. Libraries and museums. 1930.

Standing Commission on Museums and Art Galleries. Reports, 1933 onwards.

— Brief guide to the national museums and galleries of London. 1935. Subsequent revisions.

Partridge, R. C. B. The history of the legal deposit of books throughout the British Empire. 1938.

Jast, L. S. The library and the community. 1939.

Predeek, A. A history of libraries in Great Britain and North America. Chicago 1947. Tr L. S. Thompson from article in Handbuch der Bibliothekswissenschaft vol 3, Leipzig 1940 ed F. Milkau.

Thompson, L. S. Notes on bibliokleptomania. New York. Pamphlet rptd from BNYPL 48 1944. Book thefts.

Laski, H. J. The library in the post-war world. Lib Jnl 70 1945.

McColvin, L. R. and J. Revie. British libraries. 1946, 1949 (rev) (British Life & Thought no 22).

Berelson, B. The library's public. New York 1949.

Irwin, R. (ed). The libraries of London. 1949.

Philip, A. J. Index to the special collections in libraries, museums and art galleries in Great Britain and Ireland. 1949.

Plant, M. et al. The supply of foreign books and periodicals to the libraries of the United Kingdom. 1949.

Library Association. Books without libraries: a symposium of papers on book supply to persons unable to use public libraries. 1950.

— Library resources in the Greater London area. 1953.

Photographs for the record. Times 27 July 1950. Microfilms in libraries.

Clift, D. H. (ed). Library associations in the United States and in the British Commonwealth. Lib Trends 3 1955.

Powell, L. C. Libraries and learning. Los Angeles 1956.

Landheer, B. Social functions of libraries. New York 1957.

Goldstein, H. (ed). Current trends in bookmobiles. Lib Trends 9 1961. With bibliography.

Ministry of Education. Inter-library cooperation in England and Wales. 1962.

Harrison, K. C. The library and the community. 1963.

— The library committee in the United Kingdom. In Library boards, ed J. A. Eggen, Lib Trends 11 1963.

Thompson, A. Library buildings of Britain and Europe. 1963.

Foskett, D. J. Science, humanism and libraries. 1964.

Chandler, G. Libraries and the modern world. 1965.

Johnson, E. D. History of libraries of the western world. New York 1965.

Linden, R. O. Books and libraries. 1965.

Munford, W. A. (ed). Annals of the Library Association 1877-1960. 1965.

Coyne, J. R. Pornography, literature and the library. Colorado Academic Lib 3 1966.

Shera, J. H. Libraries and the organization of knowledge. 1966.

Wilson, L. R. Education and libraries. Chicago 1966.

The writer and the library. Author 77 1966.

Smith, J. M. A chronology of librarianship. 1967.

Worsley, P. Libraries and mass culture. Lib Assoc Record 69 1967.

Astbury, R. (ed). Libraries and the book trade. 1968.

Smith, C. and R. S. Walker. Library resources in Scotland. Glasgow 1968.

Thompson, J. The librarian and English literature. 1968.

Jefferson, G. Libraries and society. Cambridge 1969 (Aspects of Librarianship).

Lewis, M. J. Libraries for the handicapped. 1969. Essay.

Benge, C. Libraries and cultural change. 1970.

Milne, A. T. (ed). Librarianship and literature: essays in honour of Jack Pafford. 1970.

National Libraries, including the British Museum

Rawlings. G. B. The British Museum library. 1916.

Barwick, G. F. The reading room of the British Museum. 1929.

Esdaile, A. J. K. (ed). The world's great libraries. Vol 1: National libraries, 1934, 1957 (rev F. J. Hill); vol 2: Famous libraries (by M. Burton), 1937.

— The British Museum library: a short history and survey. 1946.

Waples, D. and H. D. Lasswell. National libraries and scholarship. Chicago 1936.

Davies, W. L. The National Library of Wales: a survey of its history, its contents and its activities. 1937.

Irwin, R. The national library service. 1947. Inter-library loans, co-operation etc.

The National Library of Wales. TLS 10 July 1953.

Ehrman, J. The Friends of the National Libraries. Book Collector 2 1954.

The British Museum Library. TLS 17, 24 June 1955.

The National Library of Scotland. TLS 28 Aug 1953, 6 July 1956.

National libraries: their problems and prospects. Paris 1960 (UNESCO Manuals for Libraries).

National Libraries Committee. Report. 1969. The Dainton report.

Francis, F. The British Museum in recent times: some reflections. In Librarianship and literature: essays in honour of Jack Pafford, ed A. T. Milne, 1970.

University and College Libraries

Gibson, S. Some Oxford libraries. Oxford 1914.

Wilson, L. R. Essentials in the training of university librarians. Chicago 1939.

Woledge, G. and B. S. Page. A manual of university and college library practice. 1940.

Wilson, L. R. and M. F. Tauber. The university library: the organization, administration and function of academic libraries. Chicago 1945.

Library Association. University and research libraries in Great Britain: their post-war development. 1946.

Craster, E. History of the Bodleian Library 1845-1945. Oxford 1952.

Cambridge University Library. TLS 26 March 1954.

The Bodleian Library. TLS 24 Sept 1954.

Fussler, H. H. (ed). The future of the library in the modern college. Chicago 1954.

The library of Trinity College Dublin. TLS 16 March 1956.

Powell, L. C. Education for academic librarianship. In his A passion for books, Cleveland 1958.

Ellsworth, R. E. Planning the college and university library building. Colorado 1960.

Munby, A. N. L. Cambridge college libraries: aids for research students. Cambridge 1960, 1962 (rev).

Buck, P. Libraries and universities. Cambridge Mass 1964.

Clapp, V. W. The future of the research library. Urbana 1964.

MacKenna, R. O. Recent developments in university librarianship in Great Britain. In European university libraries: current status and developments, ed R. Vosper, Lib Trends 12 1964.

Metcalfe, K. D. Planning academic and research library buildings. New York 1965.

Bryan, H. A critical survey of university libraries and librarianship in Great Britain. Adelaide 1966.

Oxford University Committee on University Libraries. Report 1966. The Shackleton report.

Wright, G. H. The library in colleges of commerce and technology. 1966.

Association of Teachers in Colleges and Departments of Education, and the Library Association. College of education libraries: recommended standards for their development. 1967.

University Grants Committee. Report of the committee on libraries. 1967. The Parry report.

Saunders, W. L. (ed). University and research library studies. 1968.

Braden, I. A. The undergraduate library. Chicago 1969. (ACRL Monograph 31).

Hawgood, J. et al. Final report: prospect for evaluating the benefits from university libraries. Durham 1969.

Scott, J. W. The development of British university libraries. In Librarianship and literature: essays in honour of Jack Pafford, ed A. T. Milne, 1970.

Public Libraries

See also Lib Assoc Record.

Greenborough, W. H. The public libraries: a retrospect of 30 years, 1882-1912. Reading 1913.

Guppy, H. The work of the public library during and after the war. Aberdeen 1917.

— The John Rylands Library, 1899-1924. Manchester 1924.

Library Association. Public libraries: their development and future organization. 1918.
— Small municipal libraries: a manual of modern methods. Edinburgh 1931.
— Eight million books. 1946. On county libraries.
— A century of public library service: where do we stand today? 1949.
Macleod, R. D. County rural libraries. 1923.
Baker, E. A. The public library. 1924.
Board of Education. Report on public libraries in England and Wales. 1927. The Kenyon report.
Hewitt, A. R. The law relating to public libraries in England and Wales. 1930.
Minto, J. A history of the public library movement in Great Britain and Ireland. 1932.
Cooke, A. S. et al. County libraries manual. 1935.
Laski, H. J. Uses of the public library. Lib Jnl 60 1935.
Smith, G. A. The British benefactions of Andrew Carnegie. New York 1936.
Leyland, E. The public library: its history, organization and functions. 1937.
McColvin, L. R. A survey of libraries: reports on a survey made by the Library Association during 1936-7. 1938.
— The public library system of Great Britain: a report [to the Library Association] on its present condition with proposals for post-war reorganization. 1942.
— The chance to read: public libraries in the world today. 1956.
Sharp, M. A. Branch libraries: modern problems and administration. 1938.
Welland, J. H. The public library comes of age. 1940.
Munford, W. A. Penny rate: aspects of British public library service, 1850-1950. 1951.
— James Duff Brown 1862-1914: portrait of a library pioneer. 1968.
Vollans, R. F. Library co-operation in Great Britain. 1952.
Hawkes, R. P. The Luton mobile library service. Luton 1959.
Ministry of Education. Report of the Committee on the structure of the public library service in England and Wales. 1959. The Roberts report.
Snook, I. W. J. The Roberts report and county libraries: some anticipations. Exeter 1959.
Maurois, A. Public libraries and their mission. Paris 1961 (UNESCO pbn).
Jolliffe, H. Public library extension activities. 1962.
Notes on the history of the Birmingham public libraries, 1861-1961. Birmingham 1962.
Harrison, K. C. Public libraries today. 1963.
Conant, R. The public library and the city. Cambridge Mass 1965.
Berriman, S. G. and K. C. Harrison. British public library buildings. 1966.
Fry, W. G. and W. A. Munford. Louis Stanley Jast. 1966.
Jefferson, G. Library co-operation. 1966.
Parish, C. History of the Birmingham Library. 1966.
Wood, B. The public library service. 1966 (The L.S.E. Town Government in South East England Research Study no 3.)
Department of Education and Science. Public libraries and education. 1967.
Eastwood, C. R. Mobile libraries and other public library transport. 1967.
The Leeds Library, 1768-1968. Leeds 1968.
Stockham, K. A. British county libraries, 1919-1969. 1969.

The Public Lending Right
Discussion on the public lending right antecedes 1950 but the debate reached a peak after that date. The arguments are to be found conveniently in pbns issued later than 1950.

Herbert, A. P. Public lending right. Author 71 1960.
— Public lending right: authors, publishers and libraries. 1960.

Harris, R. (ed). Libraries: free for all? 1962. Includes A. P. Herbert's appeal, The rate for reading.
The Arts Council and the public lending right. 1968.

Special Libraries
Thornton, J. L. Cataloguing in special libraries: a survey of methods. 1938.
Treasury: Organization and Methods Division. Government libraries. 1950 (rev).
— A guide to government libraries. 1952.
Lewis, J. Newspaper libraries. 1952.
Collison, R. L. Recent developments in special libraries in Great Britain. In Current trends in special libraries, ed H. H. Henkle, Lib Trends 1 1953.
Grenfell, D. Periodicals and serials: their treatment in special libraries. 1953.
Ashworth, W. (ed). Handbook of special librarianship and information work. 1955.
Sharp, H. S. (ed). Readings in special librarianship. New York 1963.
Library Association. Scientific library services. 1968.
Johns, A. W. Special libraries: development of the concept, their organizations and their services. Metuchen NJ 1969.

School Libraries
The School Library Association issues a large number of books and lists, in addition to the few noted here.

The school library review. Vols 1-6 no 3, 1936-53 (irregular 1944-50). Incorporated in The School librarian (1937), March 1954.
Library Association. School libraries in post-war reconstruction. 1945, 1950 (as School libraries today).
Stott, C. A. School libraries. 1947.
— The school library movement in England and Wales. In Current trends in school libraries, ed A. Lohrer, Lib Trends 1 1953.
School Library Association. Suggestions for primary school libraries. 1953.
— The library in the primary school. 1958.
Culpan, N. Modern adult fiction for school and college libraries. 1955, 1960 (rev). Books pbd since 1918.
Douglas, M. P. The primary school library and its services. Paris 1961 (UNESCO Manuals for Libraries).
Roe, E. Teachers, libraries and children. 1965.
Swarthout, C. The school library as part of the instructional system. Metuchen NJ 1967.
Pollard, M. The library in the junior school. 1968.
Dyer, C. et al. School libraries: theory and practice. 1970.

Circulating Libraries
Shaylor, J. Fiction: its issue and classification. Publishers' Circular 14 May 1898; rptd in his Fascination of books, 1912.
Society of Bookmen. Report on the commercial circulating libraries. 1928.
Pollard, A. W. Commercial circulating libraries and the price of books. 1929.
Simpkin, Marshall Ltd. The lending library: how to run it for profit. 1930 (2nd edn).
Bostwick, A. E. (ed). Popular libraries of the world. Chicago 1933.
Milne, J. A library of to-day. Cornhill Mag 150 1934. Boots Book-lovers' Library.
— A great circulating library. Cornhill Mag 151 1935. W. H. Smith & Son.
Richardson, F. R. The circulating library. In The book world, ed J. Hampden 1935.
Joy, T. The right way to run a library business. 1949.

Personal Libraries
See also Book Collecting, cols 107-10, above and How and What to Read, cols 121-2, below.

Brown, J. D. The small library: a guide to the collection and care of books. 1907.

Nicoll, W. R. A library for five pounds. 1917.

Major, H. D. A. A library for everybody. In The university of books, 1936.

McColvin, L. R. The personal library. 1953.

The Practice of Librarianship

The following selection of titles gives only a very small number of the pbns on the practice of librarianship. The bibliographies listed in col 109, above, and entries under Libraries, general, Public Libraries and Special Libraries ought to be consulted. See also the pbns of the Library Assoc, only a few of which are included here.

Possibly the most obvious use of automation in connection with the book is in the process of binding. Since the first use of the word (in the American motor industry in 1936) automation has spread, at first slowly but recently increasing rapidly, from processes dealing with the physical aspects of books to their content. This development is reflected in the CBEL by the inclusion of a few discussions of automation as applied to librarianship (below) and by the inclusion of a very short section on information retrieval (col 116, below).

Brown, J. D. Manual of library economy. 1903. Frequent revisions.

Cataloguing rules: author and title entries, compiled by committees of the American Library Association and the British Library Association. 1908, 1967 (rev). *See* M. Gorman, A study of the rules for entry and heading in the Anglo-American cataloguing rules 1967 (British text), 1968.

Sayers, W. C. B. An introduction to library classification: theoretical, historical and practical. 1918. Frequent revisions.

Sharp, H. A. The approach to librarianship: a guide to the profession and to the elementary examination of the Library Association. 1934.

Bendikson, L. Some phototechnical methods for the preservation and restoration of the contents of documents. Lib Jnl 60 1935.

Wilson, L. R. Essentials in the training of university librarians. Chicago 1939.

Thornton, J. L. The chronology of librarianship. 1941.

— Selected readings in the history of librarianship. 2 pts 1948–57, 1966 (rev).

British Standards Institution. Guide to the universal decimal classification. Complete British edn and 4th International edn, 1943. Frequent revisions.

Irwin, R. Librarianship. 1949.

Harrison, K. C. First steps in librarianship. 1950, 1960 (rev), 1964 (rev).

Malclès, L-N. Sources du travail bibliographique. 3 vols in 4, Geneva 1950–8.

— Cours de bibliographie. Geneva 1954, Paris 1969 (rev).

Bryan, A. I. The public library: a report of the public library enquiry with a section on the education of librarians by R. D. Leigh. New York 1953.

Lemaître, H. Vocabularium bibliothecarii. Revised and enlarged by A. Thompson, Paris 1953, 1962 (by A. Thompson, further enlarged). Multilingual glossary of library terms. Pbd by UNESCO.

Grasberger, F. On the psychology of librarianship. Lib Quart 24 1954.

Mallaber, K. A. A primer of bibliography. 1954. Association of Assistant Librarians p bn.

Caldwell, W. An introduction to county library practice. 1956, 1964 (rev).

Landau, T. (ed). Encyclopaedia of librarianship. 1958, 1961 (rev), 1965 (rev).

Powell, L. C. A passion for books. Cleveland 1958. Essays on the art of librarianship.

Davinson, D. E. Periodicals: a manual of practice for librarians. 1960, 1964 (rev).

Jolley, L. The principles of cataloguing. 1960.

Brookes, B. C. Editorial practice in libraries. 1961.

Butler, P. An introduction to library science. Chicago 1961. Introd by L. Asheim.

Lock, R. N. Library administration. 1961.

Corbett, E. V. An introduction to librarianship. 1963.

Pipics, Z. (ed). Dictionarum bibliothecarii practicum: the librarian's practical dictionary in twenty languages. Budapest 1963, Munich 1969.

Sharp, H. S. (ed). Readings in special librarianship. New York 1963.

Verry, H. R. and G. H. Wright. Microcopying methods. 1964.

Horblitt, H. D. Bibliographical collation computer. 1965. Based on slide-rule principle.

Kent, A. (ed). Library planning for automation. Washington 1965.

Bowers, F. Bibliography and modern librarianship. Berkeley 1966.

Cox, N. S. M. et al. The computer and the library. 1966.

— and M. Grose (ed). Organization and handling of bibliographic records by computer. 1967.

Millard, P. (ed). Modern library equipment. 1966.

Cunha, G. D. M. Conservation of library materials. Metuchen NJ 1967.

Downs, R. B. and F. D. Jenkins (ed). Bibliography: current state and future trends. Urbana 1967; rptd from Lib Trends 15 1967.

Line, M. B. Library surveys. 1967.

Saunders, W. L. (ed). Librarianship in Britain today. 1967.

Smith, J. M. A chronology of librarianship. 1967.

Wasserman, P. and M. L. Bundy (ed). Reader in library administration. Washington 1968.

Hewitt, R. Library management case studies. 1969.

Padwick, E. W. Bibliographical method. Cambridge 1969. Aspects of librarianship.

Shaffer, D. E. Librarianship as a profession. New York 1969.

Stokes, R. The function of bibliography. 1969. With special reference to librarianship.

Irwin, R. The education of a librarian. In Librarianship and literature: essays in honour of Jack Pafford, ed A. T. Milne 1970.

Simsova, S. and M. Mackee. A handbook of comparative librarianship. 1970.

Information Retrieval

Perry, J. W. et al. Machine literature searching. 1956.

Mitchell, S. O. and L. Sears. An information retrieval system for modern language studies. PBSA 58 1960.

Fairthorne, R. A. Towards information retrieval. 1961, 1968 (rev).

Kent, A. Textbook on mechanized information retrieval. New York 1962, 1966 (rev).

Gross, B. M. Operation basic: the retrieval of wasted knowledge. Jnl of Communication 12 1962; rptd in People, society and mass communications, ed L. A. Dexter and D. M. White 1964.

Sharp, H. S. (ed). Readings in information retrieval. New York 1964.

Sharp, J. R. Some fundamentals of information retrieval. New York 1965.

Cox, N. S. M. and M. W. Grose (ed). Organization and handling of bibliographic records by computer. 1967.

Bakewell, K. G. B. (ed). Classification for information retrieval. 1968.

Houghton, B. (ed). Computer based information retrieval. 1968.

Vickery, B. C. Techniques of information retrieval. 1970.

Periodicals

This selection of periodicals excludes local library bulletins. For a fuller bibliography see M. A. Springman and B. M. Brown, The directory of library periodicals, Philadelphia 1967.

Library Association (year) (hand) book. 1891–3, 1895, 1899–1905, 1907, 1909, 1914, 1921–8, 1932 onwards. Title varies.

The library assistant. Vols 1–45, Jan 1898–1952. Continued as Assistant librarian, vol 46, 1953 onwards.

The library world (and book selector). July 1898–? Title varies.

The Library Association record. Vols 1–24. New ser vols 1–8 New ser vols 1–3. New ser vol 1, 1899 onwards. Incorporated Broadcast.

British library year book (formerly Greenwood's library year book, 1897) 1900–1. Continued as The libraries, museums and art galleries year book, 1910–11 onwards.

The librarian (and book world). 1910–.

The librarian series. No 1–9?, 1911–.

The librarian. Nos 1–4 March–June 1913.

Central Library for Students. Annual reports. Nos 1–14. 1916/17–1929/30. Continued as Annual report of the National Central Library, no 15, 1930/31 onwards.

The librarians' guide. Vols 1–8, 1923–32. Liverpool. Continuation of section of The literary year book, col 1354, below.

ASLIB conference on special libraries and information bureaux. 1–22, 1925–48. Continued with Proceedings of the British Society for International Bibliography as ASLIB proceedings, Jan 1949 onwards.

British Museum quarterly. Vols 1–14, May 1926–Dec 1940; vol 15 for 1941/50 pbd 1952; vol 16, 1951 onwards.

Librarianship magazine. Librarianship Students' Assoc, University College London. Vol 1 no 1–vol 2 no 6; [unnumbered]; new ser vol 1 nos 1–4, 1927–36.

Library review: a popular quarterly magazine on libraries and literature. Dunfermline. 1927–?

ASLIB information. Sept 1929–?

ASLIB offprint series. 1930–?

The link. No 1, 1930 onwards.

Library world pamphlets. Nos 1–? 1931–?

The lending library and book borrowers record. Vols 1–13, Nov 1933–Nov 1944.

The librarian: series of practical manuals. 1934–?

— professional text-books. Parts 1–4, 1938–44.

Book trolley: organ of the Guild of Hospital Librarians. April 1935–?

ASLIB. Classified list of annual and yearbooks. 1937.

Fiction for library readers. 1937–?

The 2d and no-deposit libraries monthly book guide and circular. Nos 1–9, 14 April 1938–Feb 1939.

ASLIB. War-time guides to British sources of specialized information. 1–5, 1940–3.

Irish library bulletin. Dublin. 1940–?

ASLIB Microfilm service. 1942. New ser 1943–?

— Memoranda, 1943–?

— Guides to sources of information in Great Britain, 1945 onwards.

— Journal of documentation, June 1945–?

— Year's work 1946/7, 1948 onwards.

Desiderata: a direct link between library and bookseller. 1948–.

Library Association pamphlets. No 1– 1950–.

Library Association. Library science abstracts. Vol 1, 1950 onwards.

Microdoc: journal of the Council on Microphotography and Document Reproduction [later, Microfilm Association of Great Britain]. Vols 1–4, 1962–5.

PLA quarterly. Vol 1 Jan 1957–March 1958. Continued as The private library, vols 2–8, July 1958–1967; new ser 1968–.

Progress in library science. 1965 onwards. Annual. Ed R. L. Collison.

Journal of librarianship. No 1, Jan 1969 onwards.

(5) PERIODICALS RELATING TO CURRENT AND FORTHCOMING BOOKS

Reference should also be made to Literary Papers and Magazines cols 1349–80, below. Periodicals issued by public libraries and publishers are not normally listed.

Gazette of current literature. 1858–1908. Continued as Current literature of the month. New ser no 1–? 1909–?

(The) books of to-day and the books of tomorrow. Title varies. April 1894–June 1933. Continued as Books of to-day, July 1933–Dec 1945. New ser vol 1 no 1–vol 5 no 4, Jan 1946–April 1950. New ser nos 1–12, May 1950–April 1951. New ser nos 1–8, June 1951–June 1952.

The bookman booklets (The bookman biographies). Title varies. Nos 1–8, 1902–3.

The book monthly. Vols 1–15, Oct 1903–June 1920.

M.A.B.: mainly about books. Autumn 1903. New ser vol 1 no 1–vol 17 no 3, March 1907–summer 1924.

Books and pictures: a quarterly record and review of books and pictures—mainly religious. Nos 1–5, June 1905–Nov 1906.

The bookshelf. Vol 1 no 1–vol 3 no 14, Dec 1905–April 1909.

The readers' review: a monthly guide to books and reading. Vol 1 no 1–vol 3 no 26, Feb 1908–March 1910.

The book review. 1 only 1908.

The book finder. 1911–?

Books, pictures and the arts of the church. 1919–27.

The easy chair: a gossipy guide to good books. Nos 1–5, Aug–Dec 1920.

The book index. Nos 1–74, Sept 1920–June 1922.

Monthly guide (book index). Title varies. No 1, March 1921. Continued as Monthly guide alphabetical, nos 2–8, April–Oct 1921. Continued as Monthly guide classified, nos 2–16, 1921–June 1922. Incorporated in Books of the month.

The clue (book index). Title varies. Nos 1–8, Nov 1921–June 1922.

The book-selector. Nos 1–12, Feb 1923–Jan 1924.

National Book Council. Book list. Nos 1–212?, 1926–43. New ser (pbd by National Book League) no 1, 1949 onwards.

Books illustrated. Vol 1, nos 1–5, 1927. Continued as Bookfinder illustrated, vol 1 no 6–, 1929–?

The book hour. Nos 1–3, Nov 1928–Feb 1929.

Books: an occasional paper for church people. Oxford. 1928–?

Book of the month. New ser nos 1–? June 1929–? Incorporated The book index, Monthly guide, and British books to come.

National Book Council. News sheet. Nos 1–182, Oct 1929–Nov 1944; then Books (pbd by National Book League) nos 183–? Dec 1944–?

The book guild. Nos 1–10? nd [c. 1930s].

The book tag. Vol 1 no 1–vol 4 no 85, 1931–4.

Books and authors. 1931–?

Books worth reading. Vol 1 no 1 1931. Continued as Norbury review, vol 1 no 2.

The British annual of literature. 1938–? Books of the year, 1947–? Includes reviews therefrom.

National Book Council. Selection of recent books. Nos 1–14, March 1940–April 1941. Continued as British book news, nos 15–? May 1941–?

The bookshelf. Vol 1 no 1–vol 2 no 17, Jan 1946–May 1947.

British books to come. Nos 1–79, Aug 1946–May 1951. Continued as Books to come, 80–95, June 1951–Sept 1952. Incorporated in Books of the month.

Books for the sixth-former. 1946-?
Future books. Vol 1 nos 1–4, 1946. Continued as Future: the magazine of industry etc, 1947–?
Periodicals and books. Worthing. 1948.

Books and authors: a review of modern literature. 1950 onwards.
The colophon: a monthly magazine for booklovers. Nos 1–11 1950–1. Distinguish from New York pbn of same name.

E. READING

(1) GENERAL WORKS

A number of studies concerned with continental and American literature have been included where it is thought that these may throw light on reading in Britain. A selection of studies of magazine and newspaper reading is included.

[Page, W. H.] Why 'bad' novels succeed and 'good' ones fail. In his A publisher's confession, New York 1905.
Jenkins, M. Reading public. Boston 1914.
Johnson, B. The alleged depravity of popular taste. Harper's Mag 142 1921.
Page, B. F. Reading for the workers: an undelivered lecture. 1921.
Dark, S. The new reading public. 1922.
Gray, W. S. and R. Munroe. The reading interests and habits of adults: a preliminary study. New York 1929. With bibliography.
Lowes, J. L. Of reading books: four essays. Boston 1929.
Stamp, J. C. The tyranny and liberty of books. Birmingham 1930.
Griffiths, D. C. The psychology of literary appreciation: a study in psychology and education. Melbourne 1932.
Jackson, H. A digression of women readers. Book Collector's Quart no 5 1932.
— The reading of books. 1946.
Leavis, Q. D. Fiction and the reading public. 1932.
Vernon, M. D. The experimental study of reading. Cambridge 1932.
Waples, D. The relation of subject interest to actual reading. Lib Quart 2 1932; rptd in part in Reader in public opinion and communication, ed B. Berelson and M. Janowitz, Glencoe Ill 1953.
— et al. What reading does to people. Chicago 1940.
Biaggini, E. G. English in Australia—taste and training in a modern community: a preliminary enquiry into the power of the adult to recognize good and logical English, with some references to common ways of thinking. Melbourne 1934. Foreword by F. R. Leavis.
Compton, C. H. Who reads what? Essays on the readers of Mark Twain, Hardy, Sandburg, Shaw, William James, the Greek classics. New York 1934.
Gallup Research Bureau. A study of reader interest in Sunday newspapers. Neenah Wisconsin 1935.
Holtby, W. What we read and why we read it. Left Rev 1 1935.
Kaufmann, F. W. and W. S. Taylor. Literature as adjustment. Jnl of Abnormal & Social Psychology 31 1936.
Miller, R. A. The relation of reading characteristics to social indexes. Amer Jnl of Sociology 41 1936.
Abramson, B. The influence of books on people who do not read. Saturday Rev of Lit 24 July 1937.
Harding, D. W. The role of the onlooker. Scrutiny 6 1937. On the nature of the response to reading.
— Experience into words. 1963.
Marshall, A. C. The audience is the thing. Fortnightly Rev 143 1938.
Twentieth-century verse. June/July 1939. Special issue on The poet and the public.
Jenkinson, A. J. What do boys and girls read? 1940.
Kellett, E. E. Ex libris: confessions of a constant reader. 1940.
Barrett, W. C. Reading and the liberal arts. Kenyon Rev 3 1941.
Muller, H. Two major approaches to the social psychology of reading. Library Quart 12 1942.

The utility-reader. TLS 18 Nov 1944.
Huse, H. R. Reading and understanding. In Studies in language and literature, ed G. R. Coffman, Chapel Hill 1945.
Link, H. C. and H. Hopf. People and books: a study of reading and book-buying habits. New York 1946.
Ogden, A. Readers and writers in London. New York Times Book Rev 28 April 1946.
Hulton readership survey. 1947–?
Savage, E. A. A librarian looks at readers. 1947.
Folland, H. F. Reading and being. Western Humanities Rev 3 1949.
Griffith, A. The magazines women read. Amer Mercury 68 1949.
Ludwig, M. C. Hard words and human interest: their effect on readership. Journalism Quart 26 1949.
Smith, H. Only half of us read books. Saturday Rev of Lit 5 Aug 1950.
Williams, R. Reading and criticism. 1950.
Berelson, B. Who read what books and why? Saturday Rev of Lit 12 May 1951; rptd in Mass culture, ed B. Rosenberg and D. M. White, Glencoe Ill 1957.
Kaiser, W. H. Television and reading. Lib Jnl 26 1951.
Munro, D. H. The argument of laughter. Melbourne 1951. Psychological approaches to laughter.
Trevelyan, G. M. English literature and its readers. 1951.
Reading habits in three London boroughs. 1952. London School of Economics Reprint Ser no 11.
Holliday, S. C. The reader and the bookish manner. 1953.
Jones, R. L. and L. A. Beldo. Methodological improvements in readership data gathering. Journalism Quart 30 1953.
Moos, S. et al. Newspaper reading by university students. Durham 1953.
Reed, E. O. (ed). The reader and his needs. Eastbourne 1953.
Wilson, E. H. Who reads a book any more? Colorado Quart 1 1953.
Barton, J. Effect of a decrease in the value of money on taste and literature. Dalhousie Rev 33 1954.
Carter, R. F. Writing controversial stories for comprehension. Journalism Quart 32 1955.
Levine, J. Responses to humor. Scientific Amer Feb 1956.
New statesmanship: a survey of the readership of the New Statesman and Nation. 1956.
Cecil, D. The fine art of reading. In his Fine art of reading and other literary essays, 1957.
Gomme, A. Criticism and the reading public. Cambridge Rev 78 1957.
Grey, L. The literary audience. In Contemporary literary scholarship: a critical review, ed L. Leary, New York 1958.
Asheim, L. Portrait of a book reader as depicted in current research. In Mass communications, ed. W. Schramm, Urbana Ill 1960.
Belson, W. A. Studies in readership. 1962.
Murphy, D. R. A record of experiments with readership 1938–61. Ames Iowa 1962.
Nutz, W. Der Trivialroman. Köln 1962.

Boussinesq, J. La lecture dans les bibliothèques d'entreprise de Bordeaux. Bordeaux 1963.

Brower, R. A. Book reading and the reading of books. Daedalus 92 1963.

Escarpit, R. and N. Robine. Atlas de la lecture à Bordeaux. Bordeaux 1963.

Brown, A. The great variety of readers. Shakespeare Survey 18 1965. Modern edns of Shakespeare for readers of different kinds.

Larrabee, E. Science and the common reader. Commentary 41 1966.

Ravar, R. and P. Anrieu. Le spectateur au théâtre. Brussels 1966. A study of audience response.

Johnson, P. H. On iniquity. 1967. Refers specifically to post-1950 but has general implications.

Lane, M. J. and K. A. Furness-Lane. Books girls read. 1967.

Alderson, C. Magazines teenagers read. 1968.

Mann, P. H. and J. L. Burgoyne. Books and reading. 1969.

(2) HOW AND WHAT TO READ

Sonnenschein, W. S. A reader's guide to contemporary literature. 1901.

Baker, E. A. A descriptive guide to the best fiction, British and American, including translations. London and New York 1903, 1913 (rev), 1932 (rev with J. Packman).

Macpherson, M. Books and how to read them. 1904.

Buckley, R. R. How and what to read: suggestions towards a home library. 1919.

Quiller-Couch, A. On the art of reading. Cambridge 1920.

Ogden, C. K. and I. A. Richards. The meaning of meaning. 1923 and subsequent revisions.

National Book Council. The reader's guides. 240 parts in 12 series. 1928–34. Ser 9, literature; ser 11, fiction; new ser (National Book League) 1947–?

Richards, I. A. Practical criticism. 1929.

— How to read a page. 1943.

Pound, E. How to read. 1931.

— A.B.C. of reading. 1934.

Sharp, R. F. The reader's guide to Everyman's Library; being a catalogue of the first 888 volumes, with an essay by E. Rhys. 1932, 1939 (rev, 950 vols).

Leavis, F. R. How to teach reading: a primer for Ezra Pound. Cambridge 1933; rptd in his Education and the university, 1943.

McColvin, L. R. How to use books and enjoy them. 1933.

The university of books 1936. By F. Swinnerton et al.

Thompson, D. Between the lines: how to read a newspaper. 1939.

Van Thal, H. Recipe for reading: a letter to my godsons. Denver 1948.

H. W. Wilson Co. How to use the reader's guide to periodical literature and other indexes. New York 1951.

Brown, W. N. On writing, reading and literary appreciation: a practical and cultural guide. Altrincham 1952.

Smith, F. S. What shall I read next? A personal selection of twentieth-century English books. Cambridge 1953. National Book League.

— Know-how books. 1956. Includes introductions to literature for the beginner and home student.

National Poetry Association of America. Speed reader course. New York 1958.

Williams, W. E. ed. The reader's guide. 1960.

Holbrook, D. English for maturity. Cambridge 1961.

— English for the rejected: training literacy in the lower streams of the secondary school. Cambridge 1964.

National Book League. Books, the teacher and the child. 1961.

Jackson, B. and D. Thompson. English in education: a selection of articles on the teaching of English at different levels from school to university. 1962. Selected from English in schools and The use of English.

Herrick, M. Q. The Collier quick and easy guide to effective reading. New York 1963. Typical of popularization of speed reading.

Segal, S. S. Help in reading: books for the teacher and the backward reader. 1964. National Book League.

Mathews, M. M. Teaching to read historically considered. Chicago 1966.

Marland, L. Following the news: a course in the effective reading of newspapers. 1967.

Mann, P. H. and J. L. Burgoyne. Books and reading. 1969.

(3) BIBLIOTHERAPY

Bryan, A. I. Can there be a science of bibliotherapy? Lib Jnl 64 1939.

Tews, R. M. (ed). Bibliotherapy. Lib Trends 11 1963. With bibliography

(4) CONTENT ANALYSIS

This selection is designed to introduce a number of methodological approaches, irrespective of the literature with which they are concerned. A content analysis of over 1,700 books, articles and theses concerned with content analysis and pbd between 1900 and 1958 has been prepared by F. E. Barcus and is available on microfilm from University Microfilms, Ann Arbor, Michigan. See also Budd, R. W. et al, Content analysis of communications, New York 1967.

McKenzie, V. Treatment of war themes in magazine fiction. Public Opinion Quart 5 1941.

Lasswell, H. D. Analyzing the content of mass communications: a brief introduction. Washington 1942.

Leites, N. C. and I. de S. Pool. On content analysis. Washington 1942.

Berelson, B. and P. Salter. Majority and minority Americans: an analysis of magazine fiction. Public Opinion Quart 10 1946.

Berelson, B. and P. Lazarsfeld. The analysis of communication content. Chicago 1948.

Johns-Heine, P. and H. H. Gerth. Values in mass periodical fiction, 1921–40. Public Opinion Quart 13 1949; rptd in Mass culture, ed B. Rosenberg and D. M. White Glencoe Ill 1957.

Berelson, B. Content analysis as a tool of communications research. Glencoe Ill [1952].

— Content analysis. In Handbook of social psychology, ed G. Lindzey, Cambridge Mass 1954.

Harvey, J. The content characteristics of best selling books. Public Opinion Quart 17 1953.

Ginglinger, G. Basic values in Reader's Digest, Selection and Constellation. Journalism Quart 32 1955.

Steinbeck, J. How to tell good guys from bad guys. Reporter 10 March 1955.

Gerbner, G. On content analysis and critical research in mass communication. Audio-visual Communication Rev 6 1958; rptd in People, society and mass communications, ed L. A. Dexter and D. M. White, New York 1964.

Pool, I. de S. (ed). Trends in content analysis. Urbana 1959. With selective bibliography.

Barcus, F. E. A content analysis of trends in Sunday comics 1900–59. Journalism Quart 38 1961.

Danielson, W. A. Content analysis. In Introduction to mass communications research, ed R. O. Nafziger and D. M. White, Baton Rouge 1963.

Winick, C. A content analysis of orally communicated humor. Amer Imago 1963.

(5) LITERARY PRIZES

The Writers & Artists Year Book usually contains a chapter on literary awards and prizes.

Graham, B. Famous literary prizes and the winners. New York 1935. Subsequent revisions by various editors.

Millett, F. B. Literary prizes. Eng Jnl 24 1935.

National Book Council. A list of the better known literary rewards. 1935, 1944 (3rd edn).

Clapp, J. International dictionary of literary awards. New York 1963.

Dempsey, D. The literary prize game. Horizon (New York) 5 1963.

(6) THE BEST-SELLER

A systematic study of the reviewing of best-sellers in America from 1944–53 is to be found in a Univ of Michigan thesis: M. T. Boaz, A qualitative analysis of the criticism of best sellers, 1955.

Bennett, E. A. Fame and fiction: an enquiry into certain popularities. 1901.

Tilby, A. W. The best-seller problem. Edinburgh Rev 236 1922.

Partridge, E. Best-sellers in fiction. Nineteenth Century & After 112 1932.

Flower, D. S. Century of best sellers 1830–1930. 1934.

Hicks, G. The mystery of the best seller. Eng Jnl 23 1934.

Russell, J. L. The scientific best seller. Scrutiny 2 1934; rptd in Determinations, ed F. R. Leavis 1934.

Leavis, Q. D. The case of Dorothy Sayers. Scrutiny 6 1937.

Stevens, G. Lincoln's doctor's dog and other famous best sellers. Philadelphia 1938, London 1939 (with S. Unwin, F. Swinnerton, as Best-sellers: are they born or made?).

Hackett, A. P. Fifty years of bestsellers 1895–1945. New York 1945, 1968 (as 70 years of bestsellers 1895–1965).

Mott, F. L. Golden multitudes: the story of best sellers in the United States. New York 1947.

Breit, H. Best sellers: how are they made? New York Times Book Rev 4 Jan 1948.

Krutch, J. W. On not being a best-seller. Nation 16 July 1949.

Keyes, F. P. The cost of a best-seller. Atlantic Monthly 186 1950.

Harvey, J. The content characteristics of best selling books. Public Opinion Quart 17 1953.

Usborne, R. Clubland heroes: a nostalgic study of some recurrent characters in romantic fiction of Yates, Buchan and 'Sapper' 1953. *See* J. G. Weightman, The hero as gentleman, Twentieth Century 155 1954.

Kaye-Smith, S. The mystery of the best seller. In her All the books of my life, 1956.

Schneider, L. and S. H. Dornbusch. Inspirational books in America. Chicago 1958. Religious best-sellers 1875–1955.

Furbank, P. N. The twentieth-century best-seller. In The Pelican Guide to English Literature vol 7, ed B. Ford 1961.

Benschoten, V. van. Changes in best sellers since World War One. Jnl of Popular Culture 1 1968.

(7) POPULAR GENRES

No clear line can be drawn between 'serious' and 'popular' genres, as will be apparent from many of the discussions in Literature, Society and Communication cols 35–54, above. The following genres have not been included here: political (see J. C. Blotner, The political novel, New York 1955); propaganda (see E. Bowman, The propaganda novel, Northwest Missouri State Teachers' College Stud 12 1948); university (see M. Proctor, The English university novel, 1957); and working-class life (see 'Oliver Edwards', Annals of the poor, The Times, 16 June 1955). W. W. Schumauch, Christmas literature through the centuries, Chicago 1938 might also be considered appropriate to the popular genre.

The line is most difficult to draw in connection with the historical novel. P. N. Furbank finds similarities between the 'historical romance' and the detective story in his Twentieth-century best-seller (*in the* Pelican guide to English literature *vol 7, ed B. Ford 1961). Thus a short list of treatments of the genre is included here, although certain authors of historical novels are treated individually in* The Novel, *below.*

Comics, Strip Cartoons and Graffiti

Many of the studies listed are American. This is in part because of the attention paid to the genres in America before they were much considered in Britain, and in part because the American primary material has often circulated widely in Britain.

Dyson, W. Kultur cartoons. 1915. Introd by H. G. Wells.

Seldes, G. The 'vulgar' comic strip. In his Seven lively arts, New York and London 1924.

— The great audience. New York 1950.

Murrell, W. A. A history of American graphic humor. New York 1933.

Kris, E. Ego development of the comics. International Jnl of Psychoanalysis 19 1938.

Brown, S. The coming of Superman. New Republic 2 Sept 1940.

'Orwell, George' (E. A. Blair). Boys' weeklies. Horizon 1 1940; reply by F. Richards [C. Hamilton], Horizon 1 1940; both rptd in Orwell, Collected essays vol 1, 1968.

Hill, G. E. The relation of children's interests in comic strips to the vocabulary of these comics. Jnl of Educational Psychology 34 1943.

— Word distortion in comic strips. Elementary School Jnl 43 1943. With bibliographical references.

Rosner, C. The writing on the wall, 1813–1943. 1943. Cartoons, prints and broadsheets.

Deming, B. The artlessness of Walt Disney. Partisan Rev 12 1945.

Gallacher, S. A. The ideal hero of antiquity and his counterpart in the comic strip of today. Southern Folklore Quart 11 1947.

Waugh, C. The comics. New York 1947.

Turner, E. S. Boys will be boys. 1948, 1957 (rev). Boys' papers.

Low, D. Years of wrath: a cartoon history 1932–45. 1949. Cartoons and introd.

Wolf, K. M. and M. Fiske. The children talk about comics. In Communications research 1948–9, ed P. L. Lazarsfeld and F. Stanton, New York 1949.

In The art of the essay, ed L. Fiedler, 1950.

Mott, F. L. American journalism. New York 1950.

Lewis, J. The comic strip. Arena 2 1951.

McLuhan, M. The mechanical bride: the folklore of industrial man. New York 1951.

— Comics and culture. In Our sense of identity: a book of Canadian essays, ed M. Ross, Toronto 1954.

Capp, A. It's hideously true. Life 13 March 1952. A cartoonist on comic strips.

Schwartz, D. Masterpieces as cartoons. Partisan Rev 19 1952.

Spiegelman, M. et al. The content of comic strips. Jnl of Social Psychology 35 1952.

The comic strip in American life. TLS 17 Sept 1954.

Wertham, F. Seduction of the innocent. New York 1954. See R. P. Warshow, The horror comics and Dr Wertham, Commentary 17 1954; rptd in his Immediate experience, New York 1962; and in Mass culture, ed B. Rosenberg and D. M. White, New York 1957.

Saenger, G. Male and female relations in the American comic strip. Public Opinion Quart 19 1955.

Wagner, G. Parade of pleasure: a study of popular iconography in the USA. New York 1955.

Enough of blood. TLS 4 Dec 1959. Comics and penny dreadfuls.

Klapper, J. T. The effects of mass communication. Glencoe Ill 1960, 1965 (rev).

Barcus, F. E. A content analysis of trends in Sunday comics 1900–59. Journalism Quart 38 1961.

MacInnes, C. The Express families. In his England, half English, 1961. Families featured in cartoons published by Daily Express.

Bagdikian, B. H. Stop laughing: it's the funnies. New Republic 8 Jan 1962.

Hall, S. and P. Whannel. The popular arts. 1964.

White, D. M. (ed). From Dogpatch to Slobbovia: the—gasp—world of L'il Abner. Boston 1964.

Hildick, E. W. A close look at magazines and comics. 1966.

Kluger, R. Sex and the superman. Partisan Rev 33 1966.

Adler, Bill. Graffiti. New York 1967.

Feiffer, J. The great comic book heroes. 1967.

Howe, R. W. From writer to stripper. Author 78 1967.

Perry, G. and A. Aldridge. The Penguin book of comics. 1967.

Reisner, R. Great wall writing and button graffiti. New York 1967.

Crime and Detection

See also O. A. Hagen, Who done it?—a guide to detective, mystery and suspense fiction, New York 1969 (especially for writings on the mystery novel); W. B. Stevenson, Detective fiction, Cambridge 1958, and D. T. Brett, Crime detection, Cambridge 1959 (both bibliographies pbd by National Book League); and 'Ellery Queen' (F. Dannay and M. B. Lee), The detective short story: a bibliography, Boston 1943.

Chesterton, G. K. A defence of detective stories. In his Defendant, 1901.

Wright, W. H. The detective novel. Scribner's Mag 80 1926.

Knox, R. Introduction. In The best detective stories of 1928, 1929.

Sayers, D. L. Introductions. In Great short stories of detection, 3 sers 1928–34.

— Introduction. In Tales of detection, 1936 (EL).

Messac, R. Le 'detective novel' et l'influence de la pensée scientifique. Paris 1929.

Riding L. Crime. Epilogue 2 1936.

Tomlin, M. Police in fiction. In his Police and public, 1936.

Carter, J. Collecting detective fiction. 1938.

Haycraft, H. Murder for pleasure: the life and times of the detective story. New York 1941.

Caillois, R. In his Sociología de la novela. Buenos Aires 1942.

Chandler, R. The simple art of murder. Atlantic Monthly 174 1944.

'Orwell, George' (E. A. Blair). Raffles and Miss Blandish. Horizon 10 1944; rptd in his Collected essays vol 3, 1968.

Auden, W. H. The guilty vicarage. Harper's Mag 196 1948. Rptd in his The dyer's hand, 1962.

Aydelotte, W. O. The detective story as a historical source. Yale Rev 39 1949.

Bazelon, D. Dashell Hammett's private eye. Commentary 7 1949.

Legman, G. Love and death. New York 1949.

Wilson, E. Who cares who killed Roger Ackroyd?; Why do people read detective stories? In his Classics and commercials: a literary chronicle of the forties, New York 1950. First essay rptd in Mass culture, ed B. Rosenberg and D. M. White, Glencoe Ill 1957.

'Queen, Ellery' (F. Dannay and M. B. Lee). Queen's quorum: a history of the detective-crime short story as revealed by the 106 most important books published in the field since 1845. Boston 1951, New York 1967 (rev).

Maugham, W. S. The decline and fall of the detective story. In his Vagrant mood, 1952.

Rolo, C. J. Simenon and Spillane: the metaphysics of murder for the millions. New World Writing no 1 1952; rptd in Mass culture, ed B. Rosenberg and D. M. White, New York 1957.

Publishing detective novels. TLS 25 Feb 1955.

Flanagan, T. The life and early death of the detective story. Columbia Univ Forum 1 1957.

Murch, A. E. The development of the detective novel. 1958.

White, J. D. The future of the crime novel. Author 68 1958.

Gilbert, M. (ed). Crime in good company. 1959.

Crime, detection and society. TLS 23 June 1961.

Radine, S. Quelques aspects du roman policier psychologique. Paris 1961.

Raymond Chandler speaking. Ed D. Gardiner and K. S. Walker, Boston Mass 1962.

Maclaren-Ross, J. Seventy years of Sexton Blake. London Mag 3 1963.

Symons, J. Bloody murder. 1972.

Historical Fiction

Nield, J. A guide to the best historical novels and tales. 1902, 1911 (rev), 1929 (rev).

Baker, E. A. History in fiction. 2 vols London and New York 1907. A guide to historical fiction, 1 vol 1914, developed therefrom.

Buckley, J. A. and W. T. Williams. A guide to British historical fiction. 1912.

Sheppard, A. T. The art and practice of historical fiction. 1930.

Williamson, H. R. History and the writer. Essays by Divers Hands 27 1955.

Duggan, A. Historical fiction. Cambridge 1957 (National Book League Reader's Guides).

Cam, H. M. Historical novels. 1961.

McGarry, D. D. and S. H. White. Historical fiction guide. New York 1963.

Picture Postcards

'Orwell, George' (E. A. Blair). The art of Donald McGill. Horizon 1 1941; rptd in his Collected essays vol 2, 1968.

Carline, R. Pictures in the post. Bedford 1959.

Calder-Marshall, A. Wish you were here: the art of Donald McGill. 1966.

Staff, F. The picture postcard and its origins. 1966.

Nørgaard, E. With love: the erotic postcard. 1969.

Popular Song and Ballad

Nettleingham, F. T. Tommy's tunes: a comprehensive collection of soldiers' songs, marching melodies, rude rhymes and popular parodies. 1917.

Henderson, A. C. Who writes folk-songs? Poetry 18 1921.

Brophy, J. and E. Partridge (ed). Songs and slang of the British soldier. 1930, 1930 (rev), 1931 (rev).

Pulling, C. They were singing. 1952.

Hayakawa, S. I. Popular songs versus the facts of life. ETC: a review of general semantics 12 1955; rptd in Mass culture, ed B. Rosenberg and D. M. White, Glencoe Ill 1957.

Shepard, L. The broadside ballad. 1962.

Ritchie, J. T. R. The singing street. Edinburgh 1964. Street songs and rhymes.

— Golden city. Edinburgh 1965. Continuation of Singing street.

Lloyd, A. L. Folksong in England. 1967. Much expanded and revised from his Singing Englishman, Workers' Music Association [1944]. With bibliography.

Cray, E. The erotic muse. New York 1968. With bibliography.

Lomax, A. Folk song style and culture. Washington 1968.

Mabey, R. The pop process. 1969. Development and significance of 'pop'.

Malone, B. C. Country music U.S.A. Austin, Texas 1969. Discusses its subject in social and commercial contexts. With bibliography and discography.

Davison, P. H. A Briton true? A short account of patriotic songs and verse as popular entertainment. Alta 10 1970.

— Songs of the British music-hall: a critical study. New York 1971. With bibliography and discography.

Pulp Novels

The pulp and dime novel is hardly a literary genre; it is rather a mode of publishing. Nevertheless the kind of literature so published has attracted attention in its own right and that published in America has frequently been issued in Britain also.

Robinson, H. M. The dime novel. Century Mag 116 1928.

Pearson, E. Dime novels. Boston 1929.

Admari, R. Bibliography of dime novels. Amer Book Collector 5 1934.

Hersey, H. B. Pulpwood editor: the fabulous world of the thriller magazine revealed by a veteran editor and publisher. New York 1937.

MacMullen, M. Pulps and confessions. Harper's Mag 175 1937.

Noel, M. Dime novels. Amer Heritage 7 1956.

Bronze shadows. Sylvania Ohio. No 1, 1966 onwards. Ed Fred Cook; devoted to pulp magazines of twenties and thirties. 6 a year.

Gruber, F. The pulp jungle. 1967.

Romance and Confession

Confessions of a confession story writer. Amer Bookman 72 1930.

Philip, A. J. Fifty glorious years of English romantic literature 1870-1920. Gravesend 1948.

Usborne, R. Clubland heroes: a nostalgic study of some recurrent characters in romantic fiction of Yates, Buchan and 'Sapper'. 1953.

Institut de Littérature et de Techniques Artistiques de Masse. Romanesque et romantiques. Bordeaux 1954.

—Sentiments et sensibilité. Bordeaux 1957.

Gerbner, G. The social role of the confession magazine. Social Problems 6 1958.

Happy endings. TLS 8 Dec 1961. On popular romances.

Henrey, M. G. The dream makers. 1961.

Hofstadter, B. Popular culture and the romantic heroine. Amer Scholar 30 1961.

Axthelm, P. M. The modern confessional novel. New Haven 1967.

Mann, P. The romantic novel: a survey of reading habits. 1969.

Science Fiction

Bleiler, E. F. (ed). Checklist of fantastic literature: a bibliography of fantasy, weird and science fiction books published in the English language. Chicago 1948.

Day, D. B. (ed). Index to the science-fiction magazines 1926-50. Portland Oregon 1952.

Derleth, A. Bibliography of representative science-fiction since 1940. Eng Jnl 41 1952.

Crawford, J. H. et al. 333: a bibliography of the science-fantasy novel. Providence RI 1953.

Roger, D. Fantastic novels: a check list. Perth 1957.

Massachusetts Institute of Technology. Index to science-fiction magazines 1951-65. 1966.

See also Extrapolation: news letter of the Conference on Science Fiction, Modern Language Assoc of America, *Wooster Ohio, 1959 onwards.*

Bailey, J. O. Pilgrims through space and time. New York 1947.

Bradbury, R. Day after tomorrow: why science fiction? Nation 2 May 1953. *See also* Poet of the pulps, Time 23 March 1953. About Ray Bradbury.

Bretnor, R. (ed). Modern science fiction. New York 1953.

De Camp, L. S. Science fiction handbook. 1953.

Finer, A. A profile of science fiction. Sociological Rev new ser 2 1954.

Knight, D. In search of wonder. Chicago 1956.

Green, R. L. Into other worlds: space-flight in fiction from Lucian to Lewis. 1957.

Moore, P. A. Science and fiction. 1957.

Plank, R. Lighter than air but heavy as hate. Partisan Rev 24 1957.

Hirsch, W. The image of the scientist in science fiction. Amer Jnl of Sociology 63 1958.

Davenport, B. (ed). The science action novel: imagination and social criticism. Chicago 1959, 1964 (rev).

Amis, K. New maps of hell. 1961.

Clarke, I. F. The tale of the future from the beginning to the present day published in the UK between 1644 and 1960. 1961.

Pauwels, L. and J. Bergier. Le matin des magiciens: introduction au réalisme fantastique. Paris 1961, London 1963 as The dawn of magic.

Hamilton, J. B. Notes toward a definition of science fiction. Extrapolation 4 1962.

Conquest, R. Science fiction and literature. CQ 5 1963.

Green, M. Science and sensibility. Kenyon Rev 25 1963; rptd in his Science and the shabby curate of poetry, 1964.

Moskowitz, S. Explorers of the infinite: shapers of science-fiction. Cleveland 1963.

— Seekers of tomorrow. Cleveland 1965.

— (ed). Science fiction by gaslight: a history and anthology, 1891-1911. Cleveland 1968.

Masterpieces of science fiction. Cleveland 1966. Introd by S. Moskowitz; companion vol to Explorers of the infinite, 1963.

Modern masterpieces of science fiction. Cleveland 1966. Introd by S. Moskowitz; companion vol to Seekers of tomorrow, 1965.

'Atheling, William, jr' (J. Blish). The issue at hand: studies in contemporary magazine science fiction. Chicago 1964.

Eshbach, L. A. (ed). Of worlds beyond—the science of science fiction. Chicago 1964.

Handlin, O. Science and technology in popular culture. Daedalus 94 1965.

Campbell, J. W. Selected editorials from Analog. Ed H. Harrison, New York 1966.

Evans, I. O. (ed). Science fiction through the ages. 1966.

Franklin, H. B. Future perfect. Oxford 1966.

Menzies, I. S. The changing dream. New Scientist 32 1966.

Lewis, C. S. Of other worlds. 1967.

Butor, M. Science fiction: the crisis of its growth. Partisan Rev 34 1967.

Hillegas, M. R. The future as nightmare: H. G. Wells and the anti-utopians. New York 1967.

Harbottle, P. The multi-man. Wallsend 1968. Bibliographic study of J. F. Fearn.

Pushkin, A. Heinlein in dimension. Chicago 1968.

Fremlin, J. H. A scientist looks at science fiction. Alta 9 1969.

Shippey, T. A. Breaking a culture: a theme in science fiction. Ibid.

War, Adventure, Thriller and Ghost Stories

Summers, M. The Gothic quest. 1938.

Sholl, A. McC. Goose flesh in literature. Catholic World 150 1939. On ghost stories.

Harrisson, T. War books. Horizon 1 1941.

Roelofs, H. D. Thrill as standard. Southern Rev 6 1941.

Altrocchi, R. Sleuthing in the stacks. Cambridge Mass 1944. Ancestors of Tarzan.

Remenyi, J. Psychology of war literature. Sewanee Rev 52 1944.

Bernstein, W. Soldiers and war books. Saturday Rev of Lit 7 July 1945.

Lovecraft, H. P. Supernatural horror in literature. New York 1945.

Institut de Littérature et de Techniques Artistiques de Masse. Le roman picaresque. Bordeaux 1952.

Penzoldt, P. The supernatural in fiction. 1952.

The ugliest trend. Author 62 1952. The search for horror.

Noel, M. Villains galore: the heyday of the popular story weekly. New York 1954.

Institut de Littérature et de Techniques Artistiques de Masse. Aventure et anticipation. Bordeaux 1955.

Out of the ordinary: the novel of pursuit and suspense. TLS 25 Feb 1955.

Bergonzi, B. The case of Mr Fleming. Twentieth Century 163 1958. On writer of thrillers.

Spindler, R. S. The military novel. Madison 1964.

Barzun, J. Meditations on the literature of spying. Amer Scholar 34 1965.

Freeman, G. The fladge market. London Mag 5 1965.

— The undergrowth of literature. 1967.

Richardson, M. It's all been done before: a cursory review of sadistic and violent trends in popular fiction from the nineteenth century to the present day. TLS 8 Dec 1966. Correspondence 15, 22 Dec.

Fenton, R. The big swingers. Englewood Cliffs NJ 1967. Edgar Rice Burroughs and Tarzan.

Harper, R. The world of the thriller. Cleveland Ohio 1969.

Moore, T. Notes towards the analysis of the Bond stories. In his Claude Lévi-Strauss and the cultural sciences, Birmingham 1969. Methodology of approach to genre.

Bear, A. Popular reading: the new 'sensation novel'. In Sphere history of literature in the English language, vol 7, ed B. Bergonzi, 1970.

Westerns

A select list. See also J. C. Bay, A handful of western books, *Cedar Rapids Iowa 1935*; Second handful *1936*; Third handful *1937*; *R. F. Adams*, Six-guns and saddle leather: a bibliography of books and pamphlets on western outlaws and gunmen, *Norman Oklahoma 1954. A convenient account of the reality behind the Western is to be found in D. Lavender*, The American heritage history of the Great West, *New York 1965, London 1969 (abridged*, as The Penguin book of the American West).

Branch, D. The cowboy and his interpreters illustrated. New York 1926.

Smith, H. N. The western hero in the dime novel. Southwest Rev 33 1948.

De Voto, B. Western fiction. Harper's Mag 209 1954.

Rieupeyrout, J. L. Le Western ou le cinéma américain par excellence. Paris 1954. Introd A. Bazin.

Warshow, R. The westerner. Partisan Rev 21 1954.

Paeschke, H. Zeitgeist und Zeitschriften des Westerns. Neue Deutsche Hefte 42 1958.

Brashers, H. C. The cowboy story from stereotype to art. Moderna Språk 56 1963.

Bellour, R. et al. Le Western: sources, thèmes, mythologies, auteurs, acteurs, filmographies. Paris 1966.

Folsom, J. K. The American western novel. New Haven 1966. With bibliography.

P.D.

2. POETRY

I. GENERAL WORKS

(1) BIBLIOGRAPHIES

Books containing the words Poems or Poetry in their titles are grouped together in the English catalogue of books, *1864–.
Single vols of poems pbd since 1950 are listed in the* British national bibliography 1950–, 1951– (*under English poetry since
1901: individual poets*), *and in the* Library of Congress catalog, books: subjects 1950–, Ann Arbor 1955– (*under English
poetry*).

Granger, E. An index to poetry and recitations [in anthologies]. Chicago 1904, 1918 (rev), 1940 (rev, as Granger's index to poetry, ed H. H. Bessey), New York 1953 (rev, ed R. J. Dixon), 1962 (rev, ed W. F. Bernhardt). Suppl (1960–5), ed W. F. Bernhardt and K. W. Sweeney, New York 1967. Title, author, first line and, later, subject indices.

Spaulding, F. B. Poets of to-day. New York 1915 (New York Public Lib).

Maynard, K. Twentieth-century poetry: a list of references to English and American poetry 1900 to 1915. New York 1916. Also in Bull of Bibliography 9 1916–17. A list of books of verse.

Library of Congress. List of English and American anthologies of poetry 1912–16. Washington 1917. A leaflet.
—— List of collections of poetry relating to the European war. Washington 1922.

Monroe, H. and A. C. Henderson. In their The new poetry, New York 1917, 1923 (enlarged), 1932 (enlarged). *See* Anthologies, col 151, below.

'Recorder' (A. Monro). A bibliography of modern poetry (1912–1920), with notes on some contemporary poets. Chapbook 2 1920.

Birmingham Public Libraries. Catalogue of the war poetry collection. Birmingham 1921 (priv ptd).

Danielson, H. Bibliographies of modern authors. 1921; ser 2, by C. A. and H. W. Stonehill, 1925. Includes Brooke, de la Mare, Drinkwater, Masefield et al.

Manly, J. M. and E. M. Rickert. In their Contemporary British literature, New York 1921, 1928 (rev), 1935 (rev F. B. Millett). *See* Introduction, col 1, above.

Omond, T. S. Bibliographical appendices. In his English metrists: being a sketch of English prosodical criticism from Elizabethan times to the present day, Oxford 1921.

Modern poetry: a selection [i.e. a list] of English verse published since 1900, compiled by I. A. Williams and approved by the National Home Reading Union. 1928 (National Book Council Bibliography 98). A leaflet.

Sanders, G. D. and J. H. Nelson. In their Chief modern poets of England and America, New York 1929, 1936 (rev), 1943 (rev), 1962 (rev, with M. L. Rosenthal), 1970 (rev). *See* Anthologies, col 152, below.

Cutler, B. D. and V. Stiles. Modern British authors: their first editions. New York 1930. Includes Brooke, de la Mare, Dowson, Drinkwater, Masefield et al.

'Gawsworth, John' (T. I. F. Armstrong). Ten contemporaries: notes towards their definitive bibliography. 1932; ser 2 1933. Includes Abercrombie, E. Sitwell, W. Gibson, R. Ross, H. E. Palmer, L. A. G. Strong et al.

Belknap, G. N. A guide to reading in aesthetics and theory of poetry. Univ Oregon Stud in College Teaching vol 1 bull 5 1934.

Readers' guide to modern poetry. 1937 (Lib Assoc, County Libraries Section [no 6]).

Zabel, M. D. Recent works of American criticism; Collections of contemporary American criticism; American magazines publishing criticism. In his selection, Literary opinion in America, New York 1937, [1951] (rev, adds A supplementary list of essays in criticism 1900–50; A note on contemporary English criticism), 2 vols 1962 (rev, adds American criticism since 1951). Lists many articles on Anglo-American poetics.

Muir, E. In his The present age from 1914, 1939. *See* Introduction, col 4 above.

Basler, R. P. et al. A checklist of explication (1944–). Explicator 3– 1945–. Included with the annual index to the magazine.

Hayward, J. In his English poetry: a catalogue of first and early editions, 1947, 1950 (rev, with facs).

Shapiro, K. A bibliography of modern prosody. Baltimore 1948.

Stallman, R. W. A selected bibliography of modern criticism 1920–48. In his selection Critiques and essays in criticism 1920–48, New York 1949. Lists many essays on Anglo-American poetics.

Arms, G. W. and J. M. Kuntz. Poetry explication: a checklist of interpretation since 1925 of British and American poems past and present. New York 1950, Denver 1962 (rev, by J. M. Kuntz only).

Ross, A. In his Poetry 1945–50, 1951 (Br Council pamphlet). *See* Histories etc, col 143, below.

Bloomfield, B. C. English poetry in the '30s: a short title list. 1958, 1960 (rev, as New verse in the '30s).

Blunden, E. In his War poets 1914–18, 1958, 1963 (rev) (Br Council pamphlet). *See* Histories etc, col 136, below.

Daiches, D. In his The present age after 1920, 1958. *See* Introduction, col 7, above.

Handley-Taylor, G. The international who's who in poetry. 2 vols 1958.

Currey, R. N. In his Poets of the 1939–45 war. 1960 (Br Council pamphlet). *See* Histories, etc, col 146, below.

Contemporary authors. Vol 1–, Detroit 1962–. Bio-bibliography.

Spender, S. and D. Hall (ed). The concise encyclopaedia of English and American poets and poetry. New York 1963. Bio-bibliography.

Glen, D. In his 'Hugh MacDiarmid'—Christopher Murray Grieve—and the Scottish renaissance, Edinburgh 1964. *See* Histories, etc, col 147, below.

Goetsch, P. and H. Kosok. Literatur zur modernen englischen Lyrik: eine ausgewählte Bibliographie. In Die moderne englische Lyrik: Interpretationen, ed H. Oppel, Berlin 1967. *See* Histories etc, col 150, below.

Poetry in the making: catalogue of an exhibition of poetry manuscripts in the British Museum. 1967.

Temple, R. Z. In her Twentieth-century British literature, New York 1968.

Press, J. In his A map of modern English verse, 1969. *See* Histories etc, col 145, below.

E. M.

(2) HISTORIES AND STUDIES

Archer, W. Poets of the younger generation. 1902.

Hueffer, F. H. M. (afterwards Ford). Modern poetry. In his The critical attitude, 1911.

— Preface to his Collected poems. 1914 (for 1913). Rptd with changes in his Collected poems, New York 1936.

— The poet's eye. New Freewoman 1, 15 Sept 1913.

Jack, A. A. Poetry and prose: being essays in modern English poetry. 1912.

Pound, E. Prolegomena. Poetry Rev 1 1912.

— A few dont's by an Imagiste. Poetry 1 1913. Both rptd as A retrospect, in Pavannes and divisions, New York 1918; and as A stray document in Make it new, 1934, below.

— The serious artist. New Freewoman 15 Oct, 1, 15 Nov 1913; rptd in Pavannes and divisions.

— In the vortex. In his Instigations, New York 1920. T. S. Eliot, The new poetry etc. Rptd from Egoist, Poetry, Little Rev, Future.

— Make it new: essays. 1934.

— Polite essays. 1937. Monro, Hueffer (Ford), Eliot etc. Much of this and the above rptd in Literary essays of Pound, ed Eliot 1954.

Flint, F. S. Imagisme. Poetry 1 1913.

— The history of imagism. Egoist 1 May 1915.

— Presentation: notes on the art of writing. Chapbook 2 1920.

Gosse, E. The future of English poetry. 1913 (Eng Assoc pamphlet 25). Rptd in his Some diversions of a man of letters, 1919.

— Some soldier poets. In his Some diversions of a man of letters, 1919.

Abercrombie, L. Poetry and contemporary speech. 1914 (Eng Assoc pamphlet 27).

Aldington, R. Modern poetry and the imagists. Egoist 1 June 1914.

— Free verse in England. Egoist 15 Sept 1914.

— A propos de la jeune poésie anglaise. Marges 15 June 1922.

Alvis, A. Some contemporary poets: a lecture. Colombo 1914.

Holmes, M. Futurist poetry. Irish Rev 4 1914.

Hulme, T. E. Lecture on modern poetry. [1914]. In M. Roberts, T. E. Hulme, 1938. Rptd in Hulme, Further speculations, ed S. Hynes, Minneapolis 1955.

Benson, A. C. New poets. Cornhill Mag 111 1915.

Holley, H. The new poetry. Forum 52 1915. On free verse etc.

Monro, H. The Imagists discussed. Egoist 1 May 1915.

— Some contemporary poets. 1920.

Poets of the insurrection. (MacDonagh, Pearse, Plunkett, MacEntee) Studies 5, 6 1916–17. Articles by various authors, rptd as pamphlet, Dublin 1918.

Sturgeon, M. C. Studies of contemporary poets. 1916, 1920 (enlarged).

Waugh, A. The new poetry. Quart Rev 226 1916.

Eliot, T. S. Reflections on 'vers libre'. New Statesman 3 March 1917. Rptd in his To criticize the critic, 1965.

— Reflections on contemporary poetry. Egoist 4 1917.

— Tradition and the individual talent. Egoist 6 1919. Rptd in his Sacred wood, 1920.

— A brief treatise on the criticism of poetry. Chapbook 2 1920.

— A note on poetry and belief. Enemy 1 1927.

— Poetry and propaganda. Bookman (London) 70 1930.

— The modern mind. In his The use of poetry and the use of criticism, 1933.

— In his After strange gods: a primer of modern heresy, 1934.

— In his On poetry and poets, 1957.

Martin, G. C. Poets of the democracy. 1917. On Masefield, Gibson et al.

Phelps, A. L. The new [English] poetry. Trans Royal Soc Canada 10 1917.

Adcock, A. St J. For remembrance: soldier poets who have fallen in the war. 1918, 1920 (rev).

Read, H. Definitions towards a modern theory of poetry. Arts & Letters 3 1918.

— Form in modern poetry. 1932, 1948 (with prefatory note).

— The modern long poem. Yale Rev 21 1932.

— The present state of poetry, 1: in England. Kenyon Rev 1 1939.

— Poetry in war time. Listener 18, 25 Jan 1945.

— In his The true voice of feeling: studies in English romantic poetry, 1953.

— The drift of modern poetry. Encounter 4 1955.

— The image in modern English poetry. In his The tenth muse, 1957.

— Poetry in my time. Texas Quart 1 1958.

Wright, H. G. Studies in contemporary literature. Bangor 1918. On Davies, E. Thomas, Drinkwater, soldier poets.

Aiken, C. Scepticisms: notes on contemporary poetry. New York 1919.

— In his A reviewer's ABC, New York 1958, 1968 (as Collected criticism, preface by I. A. Richards).

Boyd, E. A. The drift of Anglo-Irish literature. Irish Commonwealth 1919.

Hodgson, G. E. Criticism at a venture. 1919.

Lawrence, D. H. Poetry of the present. Playboy no 4–5 1919. Rptd as preface to his New poems, New York 1920, and in his Phoenix, New York 1936. On immediacy and free verse.

Lowes, J. L. Convention and revolt in poetry. Boston 1919, London 1930 (corrected).

Moore, T. S. Some soldier poets. 1919.

Phelps, W. L. The advance of English poetry in the twentieth century. New York 1919.

Squire, J. C. The future poet and our time. London Mercury 1 1919. Rptd in his Essays on poetry, below.

— Essays on poetry. [1923]. On Yeats's later verse, Blunden etc.

Cutler, F. W. Soldier-poets of England. Sewanee Rev 28 1920.

Huxley, A. The subject-matter of poetry. Chapbook 2 1920.

— The only way to write a modern poem about a nightingale. Harper's Mag 227 1963.

Tinker, C. B. British poetry under the stress of war. Yale Rev 9 1920.

Winchester, C. T. The new poetry. Methodist Rev 103 1920.

Delattre, F. La poésie anglaise d'aujourd'hui. Paris 1921.

— Les poètes anglais et la guerre. In his Deux essais sur la psychologie sociale de l'Angleterre, Paris 1931.

Fehr, B. Zur zeitgenössischen englischen Literatur: die Lyrik. Beiblatt zur Anglia 32 1921.

— Expressionismus in der neuesten englischen Lyrik. In Britannica: Max Förster zum 60. Geburtstag, Leipzig 1929.

Olivero, F. Tendenze nella lirica inglese contemporanea. Nuova Antologia (Rome) no 210 1921.

Perry, B. A study of poetry. 1921.

Sitwell, O. Who killed Cock Robin? 1921.

Symons, A. Some makers of modern verse. Forum 67 1921.

Van Doren, M. The progress of poetry: England. Nation (New York) 22 June 1921.

Atkins, E. The poet's poet: essays on the character and mission of the poet as interpreted in English verse of the last 150 years. Boston 1922.

Clark, A. M. The realist revolt in modern poetry. Oxford 1922.

Kernahan, C. Six famous living poets. 1922. On Kipling, Newbolt, Noyes, Drinkwater, Baring, Masefield.

—— Five more famous living poets. 1928. On Davies, de la Mare, Kaye-Smith, O. Seaman, W. Watson.

Maynard, T. Our best poets, English and American. New York 1922.

Strachan, R. H. The soul of modern poetry. 1922.

Williams-Ellis, A. Short studies of some modern poets. In his Anatomy of poetry, Oxford 1922.

Wright, C. The dance of the impotent. Double Dealer 4 1922. On dada, egoism etc in poetry.

Cammaerts, E. Contemporary French and English poetry. Fortnightly Rev new ser 114 1923.

Cecil, D. Character in modern poetry. Saturday Rev 2 June 1923.

Roy, J. A. Realism in modern poetry. Queen's Quart 30–31 1923.

Hoyt, A. S. The spiritual message of modern English poetry. 1924.

Leval, R. de. Cinq essais sur la poésie anglaise contemporaine. Paris 1924.

Collins, H. P. Modern poetry. 1925.

Graves, R. Contemporary techniques of poetry: a political analogy. 1925 (Hogarth Essays 8).

—— Another future of poetry. 1926. (Hogarth Essays 18). Rptd (rev) in Hogarth Essays, Garden City NY 1928. A reply to R. Trevelyan's Thamyris: or is there a future for poetry? 1925.

—— War poetry in this war. Listener 23 Oct 1941. Rptd in The common asphodel, below.

—— The common asphodel. 1949. Essays on 20th-century poets.

—— Working models for young poets? TLS 1 Oct 1954, and see letters 15 Oct–19 Nov 1954.

—— These be your gods, O Israel! In his The crowning privilege, 1955.

——In his On poetry: collected talks and essays. Garden City NY 1969. See also L. Riding, below.

Jones, L. First impressions: essays on poetry, criticism and prosody. New York 1925. On de la Mare, Yeats, Abercrombie, Sturge Moore et al.

Richards, I. A. A background for contemporary poetry. Criterion 3 1925.

—— In his Science and poetry, 1926, 1935 (rev).

—— In his Practical criticism, 1929.

Bain, R. Scottish poetry of to-day. Burns Chron ser 2 vol 1 1926, 2 1927, 8 1933, 14 1939.

Binyon, L. Tradition and reaction in modern poetry. 1926 (Eng Assoc pamphlet 63).

Davison, E. Some notes on modern English poetry. Eng Jnl 15 1926.

—— Some modern poets and other critical essays. New York 1928. On Masefield, de la Mare, J. Stephens, Noyes et al.

Graves, C. Scottish poetry of to-day. Scots Mag 3rd ser 5 1926.

—— Younger Scottish poets. Scotland 1 1947.

'MacDiarmid, Hugh' (C. M. Grieve). In his A drunk man looks at the thistle, Edinburgh 1926.

—— Contemporary Scottish poetry: another view. Nineteenth Century 106 1929.

—— Poetry in Scotland to-day. Poetry Scotland 1 1943.

—— Signposts in Scottish poetry to-day. Scots Independent nos 220–223 1944–5.

—— Scottish poetry 1923–53. Lines Rev nos 4–5 1954.

—— The future of Scots poetry. Burns Chron ser 3 vol 4 1955.

Mégroz, R. L. The clowning spirit in modern poetry. Nineteenth Century 99 1926.

—— Modern English poetry 1882–1932. 1933.

—— Five novelist poets of the day. 1933. On Lawrence, de la Mare, O. Sitwell, M. Armstrong, L. A. G. Strong.

Fairclough, H. R. The classics and our twentieth-century poetry. Stanford Univ Pbns in Lang & Lit 5 1927.

Riding, L. and R. Graves. A survey of modernist poetry. 1927.

Riding, L. Contemporaries and snobs. 1928.

—— and R. Graves. A pamphlet against anthologies. 1928.

Riding, L. Experts are puzzled. 1930.

—— et al. Politics and poetry. Epilogue 7 1937.

Vines, S. Movements in modern English poetry and prose. Tokyo 1927.

Williams, I. A. Poetry to-day. 1927.

Bridges, R. Humdrum and harum-scarum: a lecture on free verse. In his Collected essays vol 2, 1928.

Péron, A. R. La jeune poésie irlandaise. Revue Anglo-américaine 5–6 1928.

Sackville-West, V. Some tendencies in modern English poetry. Essays by Divers Hands 6 1928.

Thompson, E. Cock Robin's disease: an irregular inquest. 1928.

Blunden, E. Tradition in poetry. In Tradition and experiment in present-day literature, 1929.

—— War poets 1914–18. 1958, 1964 (rev) (Br Council pamphlet).

Buxton, C. R. Some modern poets. In his A politician plays truant, 1929.

Deutsch, B. Potable gold: some notes on poetry and this age. New York 1929.

—— This modern poetry. New York 1935.

—— Poetry at the mid-century. Virginia Quart Rev 26 1950.

—— Poetry in our time. New York 1952, 1963 (rev).

Elliott, G. R. The cycle of modern poetry. Princeton 1929. Mostly on 19th-century poetry.

Farnham, W. The lost innocence of poetry. Univ of Calif Pbns in Eng 1 1929.

Helsztyński, S. Liryka angielska 20 wieku. Warsaw 1929.

Morton, D. The renaissance of Irish poetry 1880–1930. New York 1929.

Sitwell, E. Experiment in poetry. In Tradition and experiment in present-day literature, 1929.

—— Aspects of modern poetry. 1934.

—— Three eras of modern poetry. In Trio, by O., E. and S. Sitwell, 1938.

—— Lecture on poetry since 1920. Life & Letters 39 1943.

——, N. Nicholson, L. MacNeice and G. Barker. [Essays on imagery]. Orpheus 2 1949.

Spence, L. Scots poetry of today. Nineteenth Century 106 1929.

—— Poets at loggerheads. Scotland's Mag 50 1954.

Spender, S. The problems of poet and public. Spectator 3 Aug 1929.

—— This age in poetry. Bookman (London) 83 1932.

—— Poetry and revolution. In New country, ed M. Roberts 1933.

—— In his Destructive element, 1935.

—— Poetry (writing in revolt). Fact no 4 1937.

—— Poetry and mass-observation. New Statesman 15 Oct 1938.

—— War poetry in this war. Listener 16 Oct 1941.

—— Life and the poet. 1942.

—— Poetry since 1939. 1946.

—— The present position of poetic writing in England. Cairo Stud in Eng 1961–2.

—— Are poets out of touch with life? Listener 20 Sept 1962.

—— For a wider view of poetry. Saturday Rev 19 May 1962.

—— In his Imagination in the modern world, Washington 1962.

—— The struggle of the modern. 1963.

——, P. Kavanagh, T. Kinsella and W. D. Snodgrass. Poetry since Yeats: an exchange of views. Tri-Quarterly 4 1965.

—— Un-common poetic language. TLS 5 Oct 1967.

Arns, K. Neue englische Lyrik. Die Neueren Sprachen 38 1930.

Braybrooke, P. Some celebrities in verse. 1930.

Brenner, R. Ten modern poets. New York 1930. On de la Mare, Masefield, Noyes et al.

—— Poets of our time. New York 1941. On Eliot, Auden, Spender, Yeats et al.

Flint, F. C. Metaphor in contemporary poetry. Symposium 1 1930.

—— New leaders in English poetry. Virginia Quart Rev 14 1938. On Auden et al.

Lehman, B. H. The most significant tendency in modern poetry. Scripps College Papers 2 1930.

Lowell, A. Poetry and poets: essays. Boston 1930. On Lawrence, Masefield et al.

Vinal, H. The new lyricism. Poetry Rev 21 1930.

Williams, C. Poetry at present. Oxford 1930.

Wright, G. H. Immortality in the poets of to-day. 1930.

Armitage, G. Remarks on the current view of the relation of poetry to society. In Scrutinies, ed E. Rickword vol 2, 1931.

Brede, A. Theories of poetic diction in Wordsworth and others and in contemporary poetry. Papers Michigan Acad 14 1931.

Davidson, D. Expectancy of doom. Virginia Quart Rev 7 1931.

Heller, E. The hazard of modern poetry. 1931.

Hughes, G. Imagism and the imagists: a study in modern poetry. Stanford 1931.

The poets of 1916. Dublin 1931.

Wild, F. Die englische Literatur der Gegenwart seit 1870: Versdichtungen. Leipzig 1931.

Wilson, E. In his Axel's castle: a study in the imaginative literature of 1870–1930, New York 1931.

Bunting, B. English poetry today. Poetry 39 1932.

Doorn, W. van. Theory and practice of English narrative verse since 1833: an inquiry. Amsterdam 1932.

Gibson, W. The 'Georgian poets': or twenty years after. Bookman (London) 82 1932.

—— Contemporary English poetry. UTQ 6 1936.

—— A letter from England. Poetry 49 1936. Reply by W. Empson, 49 1937.

—— On a present kind of poetry. Polemic no 7 1947. Mostly on Dylan Thomas.

Grigson, G. Notes on contemporary poetry. Bookman (London) 82 1932.

Kreemers, R. Studiebronnen voor de moderne engelsche dichtkunst. Leuvensche Bijdragen 29 1932.

Leavis, F. R. New bearings in English poetry. 1932, 1950 (with Retrospect 1950). On Eliot, Hopkins et al.

'Roberts, Michael' (W. E. Roberts). Introduction to New signatures, ed Roberts 1932.

—— Introduction to New country, ed Roberts 1933.

—— In his A critique of poetry, 1934.

—— Poetry and propaganda. London Mercury 31 1935.

—— Introduction to The Faber book of modern verse, ed Roberts 1936.

—— Aspects of English poetry 1932–7. Poetry 49 1937.

—— In his T. E. Hulme, 1938.

Stevenson, L. Darwin among the poets. 1932.

Walraf, E. Soziale Lyrik in England 1880–1914. Leipzig 1932.

Woolf, V. A letter to a young poet. 1932. Rptd in her The death of the moth, 1942.

—— The leaning tower. Folios of New Writing 2 1940. Replies by E. Upward, B. L. Coombes, L. MacNeice and J. Lehmann, 3 1941. On writers of the 1930's.

Alexander, W. H. English poetry of these twenty-five years. In These twenty-five years: a symposium, Toronto 1933.

Brown, L. Our contemporary poetry. Sewanee Rev 41 1933.

Gordon, I. A. Modern Scots poetry. In Edinburgh essays on Scots literature, Edinburgh 1933.

Housman, A. E. The name and nature of poetry. Cambridge 1933. A lecture.

Watts, N. 'Poiêsis' and the modern world. Dublin Rev 193 1933.

Wolfe, H. Romantic and unromantic poetry. Bristol 1933. A lecture.

Wood, C. Poetry's new tools. Eng Jnl 22 1933. On free verse.

Answers to an enquiry [on poetry]. New Verse no 11 1934. By Laura Riding, Graves, MacNeice, Wyndham Lewis, D. Thomas, A. J. M. Smith, H. Read, Gascoigne, Campbell, Cameron, Muir, Ewart, 'Hugh MacDiarmid', Barker et al.

Barkas, P. A critique of modern English prosody 1880–1930. Halle 1934.

Bullough, G. The trend of modern poetry. Edinburgh 1934, 1941 (rev), 1949 (rev).

—— The war-poetry of two wars. Cairo Stud in Eng 1959.

—— The mirror of minds: changing psychological beliefs in English poetry. 1962.

Day Lewis, C. A hope for poetry. Oxford 1934, New York 1935 (in his Collected poems 1929–33 and A hope for poetry), Oxford 1936 (new postscript).

—— Revolutionaries and poetry. Left Rev 1 1935.

—— Poetry today. Left Rev 2 1937.

—— The poetic image. 1947.

—— The poet's task. Oxford 1951. A lecture.

—— [Four talks on modern poetry]. Listener 22 Jan–12 Feb 1953.

—— The poet's way of knowledge. Cambridge 1957. A lecture.

—— A need for poetry? Hull 1968. A lecture.

Gore-Hickman, E. I. Reflections on war poetry. Army Quart 28 1934.

Muir, E. Contemporary Scottish poetry. Bookman (London) 86 1934.

—— The present language of poetry. London Mercury 31 1934.

—— In his The present age since 1914, 1939 (Introductions to English Literature 5).

—— The estate of poetry. 1962.

Phelps, W. Sensibility and modern poetry. Dynamo 1 1934.

Powell, D. Descent from Parnassus. 1934.

Sparrow, J. Sense and poetry. 1934. Anti-modern essays.

Strong, L. A. G. English poetry since Brooke. Nineteenth Century 116 1934; rptd in Amer Mercury 35 1935.

Swinnerton, F. In his Georgian scene: a literary panorama, New York 1934, London 1935 (as The Georgian literary scene 1910–35), 1935, 1938 (EL) (rev), 1950 (rev).

Wood, F. T. On three more modern poets. Poetry Rev 24 1934. On Alan Porter, Campbell, W. B. Nichols.

Brandl, A. Von der Auffassung des Todes bei neuenglischen Dichtern. Anglia 49 1935.

Brooks, C. Three revolutions in poetry. Southern Rev 1 1935–6.

—— The reading of modern poetry. Amer Rev 8 1937.

—— Modern poetry and the tradition. Chapel Hill 1939, New York 1965 (new introd).

—— Poetry since The waste land. Southern Rev new ser 1 1965.

Clarke, A. Irish poetry today. Dublin Mag 10 1935.

—— Poetry in modern Ireland. Dublin 1951, 1962 (rev).

Gilkes, M. H. Introduction to modern poetry. 1935.

—— A key to modern English poetry. 1937, 1945 (rev).

Gordon, G. S. Poetry and the moderns: an inaugural lecture. Oxford 1935.

Hütteman, G. Irische Dichter machen Geschichte. Germania no 23 1935.

Jakobitz, E. Der Ausdruck des poetischen Empfindens in der modernen englischen Poesie. Greifswald 1935.

Jeffrey, W. Poetry and the vernacular. Scottish Standard 1 1935.

MacNeice, L. Poetry. In The arts today, ed G. Grigson 1935.

—— Subject in modern poetry. E & S 22 1936.

—— Modern poetry: a personal essay. 1938, Oxford 1968 (introd by W. Allen).

—— English poetry today. Listener 2 Sept 1948.

—— Poetry, the public and the critic. New Statesman 8 Oct 1949.

O'Faoláin, S. Irish poetry since the war. London Mercury 31 1935.

Powell, S. W. Modern poetry. Poetry Rev 26 1935.

Ransom, J. C. Autumn of poetry. Southern Rev 1 1935.

— Poets without laurels. Yale Rev 24 1935.

— The poetry of 1900–50. ELH 18 1951. Rptd in Kenyon Rev 13 1951.

Vordtriede, F. Der Imagismus: sein Wesen und seine Bedeutung. Freiburg 1935.

Watson, F. Poets and politics. Nineteenth Century 117 1935.

Carter, B. B. Modern English poetry. Catholic World 143 1936.

Daiches, D. Dialect and the lyric poet. Outlook 1 1936. On Scottish poetry.

— Poetry and the modern world: a study of poetry in England between 1900 and 1939. Chicago 1940.

— Poetry in the first World War. Poetry 56 1940.

Grierson, H. J. C. The problems of the Scottish poet. E & S 21 1936.

'Kenmare, Dallas'. The future of poetry. 1936.

Lehmann, J. Some revolutionary trends in English poetry 1930–5. International Lit (Moscow) April 1936.

— In his New writing in England, New York 1939.

Shankwar, B. Studies in modern English poetry. Allahabad 1936.

Yeats, W. B. Modern poetry. 1936. Broadcast lecture; rptd in his Essays 1931 to 1936, Dublin 1937, and his Essays and introductions, 1961.

— Introduction to The Oxford book of modern verse, ed Yeats, Oxford 1936.

— Letters on poetry from Yeats to Dorothy Wellesley. 1940.

'Caudwell, Christopher' (C. St J. Sprigg). Illusion and reality: a study of the sources of poetry. 1937. A Marxist poetics.

Dubois, L.-P. La littérature irlandaise contemporaine. Revue des Deux Mondes 1 Sept 1937. On Yeats, Russell, Stephens.

Edgar, P. The changing aspects of poetry. Queen's Quart 44 1937.

Engle, P. Poetry in a machine age. Eng Jnl 26 1937.

— New English poets. Eng Jnl 27 1938.

— Why modern poetry? College Eng 15 1953.

Fraser, G. S. Poetry and civilization. London Mercury 36 1937.

— In his The modern writer and his world, 1953, 1964 (rev, Pelican).

— Vision and rhetoric: studies in modern poetry. 1959.

Glicksberg, C. I. Poetry and Marxism: three English poets take their stand. UTQ 6 1937. On Auden, Day Lewis, Spender.

— Poetry and social revolution. Dalhousie Rev 17 1938.

— Poetry and the second World War. South Atlantic Quart 44 1945.

— The malady of modern poetry. Prairie Schooner 21 1947.

— The poetry of doubt and despair. Humanist 7 1947.

— World war poetry. Welsh Rev 4 1947.

— The personal accent in modern poetry. South Atlantic Quart 47 1948.

— Poetry and the Freudian aesthetic. UTQ 17 1948.

— The religious problem in modern poetry. South Atlantic Quart 57 1958.

Hogan, J. L. Swinburne, the moderns and the tradition of English poetry. Studies 26 1937.

Jaspert, W. Die Dichtung Irlands. Geist der Zeit 15 1937.

M[adge], C. Poetic description and mass-observation. New Verse no 24 1937.

Madge, C. Some reflections on popular poetry. New Writing new ser 3 1939.

Mayer, E. Die Leistungen der modernen Technik in der Dichtung Englands und der Vereinigten Staaten. Endingen 1937.

Tate, A. Modern poets and convention. Amer Rev 8 1937; rptd in his Collected essays, Denver 1959, and Essays of four decades, Chicago 1968.

— Understanding modern poetry. College Eng 1 1940.

Walcott, J. C. English and American surrealists. Forum 97 1937.

Warren, R. P. and C. Brooks. The reading of modern poetry. Amer Rev 8 1937.

Weygandt, C. The time of Yeats: English poetry of to-day against an American background. New York 1937.

Chakravarty, A. The Dynasts and the post-war age in poetry: a study in modern ideas. 1938.

Connolly, C. In his Enemies of promise, 1938, 1949 (rev).

— The breakthrough in modern verse. London Mag new ser 1 1961.

Hort, G. M. The tendencies of modern poetry. English 2 1938.

Jameson, G. Irish poets of today and Blake. PMLA 53 1938.

Kelling, L. Contemporary poetry. Chapel Hill 1938; ser 2, 1945.

Palmer, H. E. Post-Victorian poetry. 1938.

— A brief history of the poetry of despair. English 3 1941.

Power, Sr M. J. Poets at prayer. New York 1938.

Thielke, K. Slang und Umgangssprache in der englischen Lyrik der Gegenwart. Zeitschrift für Neusprachlichen Unterricht 37 1938.

Turnell, M. Poetry and crisis. 1938.

Upton, W. T. Aspects of the modern art-song. Musical Quart 24 1938.

Bailey, R. A dialogue on modern poetry. Oxford 1939.

Berti, L. Avanguardia della poesia inglese d'oggi. L'Orto (Florence) 1939.

Deroisin, S. La poésie anglaise pendant la Grande Guerre. Revue Générale (Brussels) 142 1939.

Ford, W. Poetry and who cares anyway. Poetry & the People no 8 1939.

Häusermann, H. W. Left-wing poetry. E Studies 21 1939.

Hays, H. R. Surrealist influence in contemporary English and American poetry. Poetry 54 1939.

Hellmann, G. Ideen und Kräfte in der englischen Nachkriegsjugend, nach literarischen Selbstzeugnissen. Breslau 1939.

Henderson, P. The poet and society. 1939.

— The Georgians revisited. Orient/West 7 1962.

Sassoon, S. On poetry. Bristol 1939. A lecture.

Savage, D. S. Poetry politics in London. Poetry 53 1939. See correspondence, ibid, 54 1939.

— The personal principle: studies in modern poetry. 1944.

— The poet's perspectives. Poetry 64 1944.

— Form in modern poetry. Poetry 65 1945.

Treece, H. Some notes on poetry now. Voice of Soctland 2 1939.

— Some notes on the Apocalyptic movement. Northman 11 1941–2.

— How I see Apocalypse. 1946.

Trevanion, M. Modern poetry. TLS 5 Aug 1939.

Warner, R. Modern English poetry. International Lit (Moscow) July 1939.

Byrne, J. P. Sound in modern Irish poetry. Queen's Quart 47 1940.

Cahiers de Paris vol 8 no 32 1940. Special number on English poetry of the first World War.

Drew, E. and J. L. Sweeney. Directions in modern poetry. New York [1940].

— and G. Connor. Discovering modern poetry. New York 1961.

Gierasch, W. Reading modern poetry. College Eng 2 1940.

'Orwell, George' (E. A. Blair). Inside the whale. In his Inside the whale and other essays, 1940.

Southworth, J. G. Sowing the spring: studies in British poets from Hopkins to MacNeice. Oxford 1940.

Stryjewski, K. Reimform und Reimfunktion: Untersuchungen zum Problem des reinen und unreinen Reimes in der englischen Dichtung des 20. Jahrhunderts. Breslau 1940.

Waller, J. Oxford poetry and disillusionment. Poetry Rev 31 1940.

Wells, H. W. New poets from old: a study in literary genetics. New York 1940.

—— Where poetry stands now. Toronto 1948. A pamphlet.

Whittridge, A. English poetry and the Spanish war. Dalhousie Rev 19 1940.

Wilder, A. N. The spiritual aspects of the new poetry. New York 1940.

—— Modern poetry and the Christian tradition. New York 1952.

Barker, G. Therefore all poems are elegies. In New poems 1940, ed O. Williams, New York 1941.

Church, R. Eight for immortality. 1941. On Davies, de la Mare, Yeats, Blunden, Eliot, Graves et al.

Colville, K. N. New poetry and old readers. Queen's Quart 48 1941.

Muller, H. J. The New Criticism in poetry. Southern Rev 6 1941.

Rickword, E. Poetry and two wars. Our Time 1 1941.

Schwartz, D. The isolation of modern poetry. Kenyon Rev 3 1941.

—— The vocation of the poet in the modern world. Poetry 88 1951.

Wittig, K. Die Nachkriegsliteratur Irlands 2: Versdichtung. Archiv 178 1941.

Alspach, R. K. A consideration of the poets of the literary revival in Ireland 1889–1929. Philadelphia 1942.

Beck, W. Poetry between two wars. Virginia Quart Rev 18 1942.

Scarfe, F. Auden and after: the liberation of poetry 1930–41. 1942.

Williams, G. G. British poetry of two world wars. Rice Inst Pamphlet 29 1942.

Bowra, C. M. The heritage of symbolism. 1943.

—— The background of modern poetry. Oxford 1946. A lecture.

—— The creative experiment. 1949.

—— Poetry and the first World War. Oxford 1961. A lecture; rptd in his In general and particular, 1964.

—— Poetry and politics 1900–60. Cambridge 1966.

Comfort, A. English poetry and the war. Partisan Rev 10 1943.

—— On interpreting the war. Horizon 5 1944. Letter on the role of poets; reply by S. Spender, ibid.

De Vries, P. Poetry and the war. College Eng 5 1943.

Evans, G. E. An emergent national literature. Wales 2 1943.

Lindsay, M. Scottish poetry and the Scottish renaissance. Life & Letters Today 39 1943.

—— Poetry in Scotland today. Adam no 186 1948.

—— The Scottish renaissance. Edinburgh 1948.

—— Romanticism in Scottish poetry. In A new romantic anthology, ed S. Schimanski and H. Treece 1949.

McFadden, R. and G. Taylor. Poetry in Ireland: a discussion. Bell 6 1943.

McFadden, R. A trend in poetry. Dublin Mag 19 1944.

—— A note on contemporary Ulster writing. Northman 14 1946.

Rodman, S. Poetry between the wars. College Eng 5 1943.

[Taylor, G. and S. O'Faoláin]. Sense and nonsense in poetry. Bell 7 1943.

Ingalls, J. The classics and new poetry. Classical Jnl 40 1944.

Lindsay, J. Perspective for poetry. 1944.

—— The position of English poets. Meanjin 17 1958.

Mendonca, P. Modern English poetry. New Rev (Calcutta) 19 1944.

Pound, L. The future of poetry. College Eng 5 1944.

Devaney, J. Obscurantism. Meanjin Papers 4 1945. Replies by S. Musgrave and A. King, ibid.

—— Poetry in our time: a review of contemporary values. Melbourne 1952.

Frank, J. Spatial form in modern literature. Sewanee Rev 53 1945; rptd, rev, in his The widening gyre, New Brunswick 1963.

Koch, V. Poetry in World War II. Briarcliff Quart 2–3 1945–6.

MacDonagh, P. Poems marked urgent. Dublin Mag 20 1945.

Shapiro, K. Essay on rime. New York 1945. In verse. Comment by R. Richman, Sewanee Rev 54 1946.

—— English prosody and modern poetry. ELH 14 1947. Rptd separately Baltimore 1947.

—— Modern poetry as a religion. Amer Scholar 28 1959.

—— (ed). Prose keys to modern poetry. New York 1962.

Williams, O. (ed). Comments by the poets. In The war poets, ed Williams, New York 1945. Comments by Grigson, Watkins, Symons, Treece, A. Ross, Muir, Ewart, Pudney et al. See Anthologies, col 154, below.

Durkan, J. Background to the present impasse in poetry. Dublin Rev 218 1946.

Iremonger, V. Aspects of poetry today. Bell 12 1946.

Mayhall, J. Riddle and reason in modern poetry. Antioch Rev 6 1946.

Miles, J. In her Major adjectives in poetry: from Wyatt to Auden, Univ of Calif Pbns in Eng 12 1946.

—— The primary language of poetry in the 1940's. Berkeley 1951.

—— In her Eras and modes in English poetry, Berkeley 1957, 1964 (rev).

—— Renaissance, eighteenth-century and modern language in English poetry: a tabular view. Berkeley 1960.

O'Connor, W. V. Nature and the anti-poetic in modern poetry. Jnl of Aesthetics 5 1946.

—— The poet's private reality. Quart Rev of Lit 3 1946.

—— The influence of the metaphysicals on modern poetry. College Eng 9 1948.

—— Sense and sensibility in modern poetry. Chicago 1948, New York 1963 (new foreword). Mostly previously pbd essays.

O'Donnell, M. J. Feet on the ground: being an approach to modern verse. 1946.

Thomas, R. S. Some contemporary Scottish writing. Wales no 23 1946.

—— A Welsh view of the Scottish renaissance. Wales no 30 1948.

Caird, J. B. Some reflections on Scottish literature, 1: poetry. Scottish Periodical 1 1947.

Capetanakis, D. Notes on some contemporary writers. In his Capetanakis, a Greek poet in England, 1947, Philadelphia 1947 (as Shores of darkness).

Cattaui, G. Trois poètes: Hopkins, Yeats, Eliot. Paris 1947.

Cazamian, L. Symbolisme et poésie: l'exemple anglais. Neuchâtel 1947.

Enright, D. J. The significance of Poetry London. Poet & Critic 1 1947.

—— The literature of the first World War. In The modern age, Pelican guide to English literature vol 7, ed B. Ford 1961.

Farren, R. The course of Irish verse in English. New York 1947.

Fletcher, E. G. Imagism: some notes and documents. Univ of Texas Stud in Eng [26] 1947.

Gilbert, K. Recent poets on man and his place. Philosophical Rev 56 1947.

Greacen, R. Trends in Irish poetry. Irish Bookman 1 1947.

—— The way we write now. Irish Writing no 2 1947. On the new 'romanticism'.

MacLeod, J. Poet and people. Anvil 1 1947. On Scottish poetry.

Mallinson, V. English poetry. Revue des Langues Vivantes 13 1947.

Morrison, T. 'The fault, dear Brutus': poetic example and poetic doctrine today. Pacific Spectator 1 1947.

O'Lochlainn, C. Anglo-Irish songwriters since Moore. Dublin 1947.

Rajan, B. Georgian poetry: a retrospect. Critic 1 1947.

Stanford, D. The freedom of poetry: studies in contemporary verse. 1947.

— Movements in English poetry 1900–58. 1959. A pamphlet.

— Stephen Spender, Louis MacNeice, Cecil Day Lewis. Grand Rapids Mich 1969 (Contemporary Writers in Christian Perspective). A pamphlet.

— Thoughts on the 'forties. Poetry Rev 60 1969.

Stormon, E. J. Virgil and the modern poet. Meanjin 6 1947.

Winters, Y. In defense of reason. Denver 1947.

Fitzgerald, R. D. An attitude to modern poetry. Southerly 9 1948.

Hamilton, K. M. Present self-consciousness in poetry. Dalhousie Rev 28 1948.

Kavanagh, P. Poetry in Ireland today. Bell 16 1948.

Poets at work. Buffalo 1948. Essays on the poetic process by D. A. Stauffer, K. Shapiro, R. Arnheim and W. H. Auden.

Whalley, G. The metaphysical revival. Yale Rev 37 1948.

Every, G. Poetry and personal responsibility: an interim report on contemporary literature. 1949.

Frankenberg, L. Pleasure dome: on reading modern poetry. Boston 1949.

Hamilton, G. R. The tell-tale article: a critical approach to modern poetry. 1949.

Howarth, R. G. Notes on modern poetic technique: English and Australian. Sydney 1949.

McCallum, N. Lallans. New Statesman 26 Feb 1949.

Powys, L. Advice to a young poet. 1949.

Baker, J. V. The public versus the poet. Prairie Schooner 24 1950.

Bush, D. In his Science and English poetry, New York 1950.

Hewitt, J. Poetry and Ulster: a survey [1920–50]. Poetry Ireland no 8 1950.

Jameson, S. The writer's situation. 1950.

Keith, C. Modern Scots poetry. Britain Today no 165 1950.

Lombardo, A. La poesia inglese, dall'estetismo al simbolismo. Rome 1950.

Thomson, A. The poetry of the Scottish renaissance. Jabberwock 3 1950.

Woodcock, G. British poetry today: an address. Vancouver 1950.

Coffman, S. K. Imagism: a chapter for the history of modern poetry. Norman Oklahoma 1951.

Isaacs, J. The assessment of twentieth-century literature. 1951.

— The background of modern poetry. 1951.

Murphy, R. Why has narrative poetry failed? Listener 9 Aug 1951.

Pinto, V. de S. Crisis in English poetry 1880–1940. 1951, 1961 (rev).

Prys-Jones, A. G. Anglo-Welsh poetry. Dock Leaves 2 1951.

Ross, A. Poetry 1945–50. 1951 (Br Council pamphlet).

Sergeant, H. Tradition in the making of modern poetry. Vol 1 1951 (no more pbd).

— British poetry today. Canadian Poetry 16 1953.

— The effect of changing patterns of thought on modern poetry. Southerly 15 1954.

— Contemporary British poetry. Whetstone (Philadelphia) 2 1958.

— Music and modern poetry. Aylesford Rev 10 1964.

— Religion in modern British poetry. Aryan Path 37 1966.

Thomas, D. Poetic manifesto [1951]. Texas Quart 4 1961. Rptd in A garland for Dylan Thomas, ed G. J. Firmage, New York 1963.

Tschumi, R. Thought in twentieth-century English poetry. 1951.

Blackmur, R. P. In his Language as gesture: essays in poetry, New York 1952. A selection from this book was pbd as Form and value in modern poetry, New York 1957.

Durrell, L. Key to modern poetry. 1952, Norman Oklahoma 1952 (as A key to modern British poetry).

Georgian poetry. TLS 21 Nov 1952.

Hopper, S. R. (ed). Spiritual problems in contemporary literature. New York 1952. Includes essays on poetry by D. Daiches, A. N. Wilder et al.

Ikeda, M. The spirit of recent English and American poetry. Shiratama Feb 1952. In Japanese.

Macartney, F. T. B. The modern schism in poetry. Meanjin 11 1952.

Marcus, D. Contemporary Irish poetry (1939–52). Ibid.

Shinoda, K. The genealogy of modern poetry. Stud in Eng Lit (Tokyo) 28 1952. In Japanese.

Edwardian poets. TLS 20 March 1953.

Mulkerns, V. Ourselves surveyed. Irish Writing 24 1953.

Temple, R. Z. In her The critic's alchemy: a study of the introduction of French symbolism into England, New York 1953.

Wharton, G. Romanticism and exile. Irish Writing 24 1953.

Bell, H. I. The Welsh literary renaissance of the twentieth century. Proc Br Acad 39 1954.

Dobrée, B. English poets today: the younger generation. Sewanee Rev 52 1954.

Hyman, S. E. The language of Scottish poetry. Kenyon Rev 16 1954.

— Modern literature. In his Poetry and criticism: four revolutions in literary taste, New York 1961. On Eliot's revaluation of Milton.

Nishio, M. A special quality of British modernist poetry. Rev Kobe Univ in Humanities & Social Science no 2 1954. In Japanese.

Saunders, J. W. Poetry in the managerial age. EC 4 1954.

Auden, W. H. On writing poetry today. Listener 30 June 1955.

— Making, knowing and judging. Oxford 1956. Rptd in his The dyer's hand, New York 1962, below. A lecture.

— In his The dyer's hand. New York 1962.

— Today's poet. Mademoiselle 54 1962.

Baxter, J. K. The fire and the anvil: notes on modern poetry. Wellington 1955.

Davie, D. In his Articulate energy: an inquiry into the syntax of English poetry, 1955.

— The poet in the imaginary museum. Listener 11–18 July 1957.

Folk, B. N. Modern verse: not blank, but not free. Catholic World 181 1955.

Kitchin, G. The modern makars. In Scottish poetry: a critical survey, ed J. Kinsley 1955.

Knoll, R. E. The style of contemporary poetry. Prairie Schooner 29 1955.

Lectures on some modern poets. Carnegie Ser in Eng 2 1955. Includes essays on Auden and Isherwood by E. R. Steinberg, on Eliot by A. F. Sochatoff, on D. Thomas by D. W. Goodfellow etc.

Melchiori, G. Poesia inglese contemporanea. Spettatore Italiano 8 1955.

Quinn, Sr M. B. The metamorphic tradition in modern poetry. New Brunswick 1955. On Eliot, Yeats et al.

Sanesi, R. Esistenza e relazione nella poesia inglese contemporanea. Aut–Aut 27 1955.

Sasaki, T. The expression of modern English poetry. Tokyo 1955.

Smith, W. J. Modern poetry: texture and text. Shenandoah 6 1955.

Wilson, A. H. The categories of modern British poetry. Susquehanna Univ Stud 5 1955.

Geiger, D. Imagism: the new poetry forty years later. Prairie Schooner 30 1956.

Habart, M. Situation présente de la poésie anglaise. Age Nouveau no 96 1956.

Hubbell, L. W. Some characteristics of modern poetry. Jnl of Eng Lit & Philology (Doshisha Univ) no 19 1956.

Izzo, C. La poesia (L'Inghilterra oggi). Ulisse no 23 1956.

Mills, J. G. Some English poets in Japan. Japan Quart 3 1956.

Pack, R. The Georgians, Imagism and Ezra Pound. Arizona Quart 12 1956

Schlauch, M. Modern English and American poetry: techniques and ideologies. 1956.

Scott, T. Some poets of the Scottish renaissance. Poetry 88 1956.

Skelton, R. The poetic pattern. 1956.

Bayley, J. The romantic survival: a study in poetic evolution. 1957. Mostly on Yeats, Auden, D. Thomas.

Harper, E. Experimentation: poetry in the British Isles. Experiment (Seattle) 7 1957.

Kermode, F. Romantic image. 1957.

— Modern poetry and tradition. Yearbook of Comparative and General Lit 14 1965.

Keir, W. Post-war poetry in Scots. Saltire Rev 4 1957.

Langbaum, R. In his The poetry of experience: the dramatic monologue in modern literary tradition, New York 1957.

MacFarlane, J. W. The Tiresian vision. Durham Univ Jnl 18 1957.

Scott, A. F. The poet's craft: a course in the critical appreciation of poetry, based on the study of holograph manuscripts. Cambridge 1957. Includes E. Thomas, Brooke, Owen, Rosenberg.

Stallman, R. W. The position of poetry today. Eng Jnl 46 1957.

Takemori, O. A view of modern nature-myth in English poetry. Bull Univ of Osaka Prefecture 5 1957. In Japanese.

Thwaite, A. Essays on contemporary English poetry. Tokyo 1957, London 1959 (as Contemporary English poetry).

Vickery, J. B. 'The golden bough' and modern poetry. Jnl of Aesthetics 15 1957.

Wheelock, J. H. A view of contemporary poetry. Amer Scholar 26 1957.

Whittemore, R. The 'modern idiom' of poetry and all that. Yale Rev 46 1957.

Woods, W. G. La poesía inglesa del siglo XX. Revista Nacional de Cultura (Caracas) 18 1957.

Alvarez, A. The shaping spirit: studies in modern English and American poets. 1958, New York 1958 (as Stewards of excellence). On Yeats, Eliot, Empson, Auden, Lawrence et al.

— Introduction to The new poetry, ed Alvarez 1962 (Penguin), 1966 (rev).

Blaeser, R. New Scots renaissance. Düren 1958. In German.

Hewitt, J. Irish poets, learn your trade. Threshold 3 1958. On Yeats, F. R. Higgins, Clarke.

Macgregor-Hastie, R. Obscurity in modern poetry. European no 61 1958.

— Mid-century English poetry. Letterature Moderne 9 1959.

Moore, G. Poetry to-day. 1958 (Br Council pamphlet).

Parkinson, T. Intimate and personal: an aspect of modern poetics. Jnl of Aesthetics 16 1958.

Press, J. In his The chequer'd shade: reflections on obscurity in poetry, 1958.

— Rule and energy: trends in British poetry since the second World War. 1963.

— A map of modern English verse. 1969.

Scott, N. A. jr. In his Modern literature and the religious frontier, New York 1958.

— (ed). Four ways of modern poetry. Richmond Virginia 1965. Includes Scott on Auden and R. J. Mills on D. Thomas.

Scott, N. A. jr. In his The broken center, New Haven 1966.

— Poetry and prayer. Thought 41 1966.

Singer, B. The top ten. Twentieth Century 164 1958.

Warburg, J. Poetry and industrialism. MLR 53 1958.

Whigham, P. Poetry in the first half of the twentieth century. European no 68–9 1958.

Bhalla, M. M. Trends in modern poetry. Literary Criterion (Mysore) 4 1959.

Blackburn, T. and J. Mitchell. Argument of poetry. London Mag 6 1959. Two essays; reply by P. E. Dunn, ibid.

Blackburn, T. The price of an eye. 1961.

Block, H. M. Surrealism and modern poetry. Jnl of Aesthetics 18 1959.

Cohen, J. M. In his Poetry of this age 1908–58, 1959, 1966 (rev, as Poetry of this age 1908–65).

Conran, A. The English poet in Wales. Anglo-Welsh Rev 10 1959–60.

Cook, A. Modern verse: diffusion as a principle of composition. Kenyon Rev 21 1959.

Duncan, J. E. The revival of metaphysical poetry: the history of a style, 1800 to the present. Minneapolis 1959.

English poetry since 1945. London Mag 6 1959. A symposium by G. S. Fraser, J. Holloway, R. Fuller, G. MacBeth, E. Jennings and A. N. Jeffares.

Golffing, F. and B. Gibbs. The public voice: remarks on poetry today. Commentary 28 1959.

Guidacci, M. Poesia inglese del dopoguerra. Poesia Nuova 5 1959.

Schulte, E. Ritmi vecchi e nuovi nella poesia inglese moderna. Annali Istituto Universitario Orientale di Napoli (Sezione Germanica) 2 1959.

West, P. Symbol and equivalent: the poetry of industrialism. EC 9 1959.

— Poetic form today. English 13 1960.

Whittock, T. An essay on poetic diction. Pretoria 1959.

Beach, J. W. Obsessive images: symbolism in poetry of the 1930's and 1940's. Minneapolis 1960.

Burckhardt, S. and R. H. Pearce. Poetry, language and the condition of modern man. Centennial Rev 4 1960. Two essays.

Conquest, R. Mistah Eliot—he dead?. Audit 1 1960.

Currey, R. N. Poets of the 1939–45 war. 1960 (Br Council pamphlet).

Gerhard, M. Goodbye to all that: a child's guide to two decades. X: a Quart Rev 1 1960. On poets of 1940–60.

Grillo, G. Poesia inglese del dopoguerra. Idea 16 1960.

Hough, G. Image and experience: studies in a literary revolution. 1960. Partially pbd as Reflections on a literary revolution, Washington 1960. On Imagism.

Hrushovski, B. On free rhythms in modern poetry. In Style and language, ed T. A. Sebeok, Cambridge Mass 1960.

Manganelli, G. Poesia inglese contemporanea. Ulisse no 38 1960.

Miller, J. E. jr, K. Shapiro and B. Slote. Start with the sun: studies in cosmic poetry. Lincoln Nebraska 1960.

Narasimhaiah, C. D. Trends in modern English poetry. Literary Criterion (Mysore) 4 1960.

Poets on poetry. X: a Quart Rev 1 1960. Essays by 'Hugh MacDiarmid', Watkins, Kavanagh and S. Smith.

Rosenthal, M. L. The modern poets: an introduction. New York 1960.

— The new poets: American and British poetry since World War II. New York 1967.

Symons, J. In his The thirties, 1960.

Williams, C. The state of English poetry. Twentieth Century 168 1960.

Collie, M. The old pose and the new poetry. Dalhousie Rev 41 1961–2.

Hobsbaum, P. The road not taken. Listener 23 Nov 1961. On E. Thomas, Owen, Rosenberg.

— The growth of English modernism. Wisconsin Stud in Contemporary Lit 6 1965.

Jennings, E. Every changing shape. 1961. Includes essays on Hopkins, Muir, Eliot, Gascoyne et al.

Jones, A. R. Notes towards a history of Imagism. South Atlantic Quart 60 1961.

Joost, N. English poetic satire and the modern Christian temper. Delta Sigma Epsilon Bull (Alton Ill) 6 1961. On Auden, Campbell, Eliot.

Mander, J. The writer and commitment. 1961.

Matsuura, K. On the nuances of reality explored by modern English poetry. Essays and Stud, Tokyo Women's Christian College 11 1961. In Japanese.

Rodway, A. A note on contemporary English poetry. Texas Quart 4 1961.

Rattray, R. F. Poets in the flesh. Cambridge 1961. A pamphlet.

Smith, C. P. Semi-classical poetry and the great tradition. Massachusetts Rev 3 1961. On Eliot et al.

Stock, N. Modern poetry and the norm of language. Texas Quart 4 1961.

Tomlinson, C. Poetry today. In The modern age, Pelican guide to English literature vol 7, ed B. Ford 1961, 1963 (rev).

Villgradter, F. R. Über Grundzüge der Dichtungstheorie der Lyriker Wystan Hugh Auden, Cecil Day Lewis und Stephen Spender. Berlin 1962 (for 1961).

Benziger, J. G. Images of eternity: studies in the poetry of religious vision from Wordsworth to Eliot. Carbondale Ill 1962.

Berry, F. In his Poetry and the physical voice, 1962.

Burnshaw, S. The three revolutions in modern poetry. Sewanee Rev 70 1962.

Cambon, G. Revolution and tradition. Poetry 100 1962. On Imagism.

Craig, D. The new poetry of socialism. New Left Rev no 17 1962. On 'Hugh MacDiarmid' et al.

Davies, A. T. William Barnes, Gerard Manley Hopkins, Dylan Thomas: the influence of Welsh prosody on modern English poetry. Proc of the Third Congress of the International Comparative Lit Assoc (s'Gravenhage) 1962.

Dickinson, P. Poets of the first World War. Listener 8 Feb 1962.

Fairchild, H. N. Religious trends in English poetry, vol 5: 1880–1920, Gods of a changing poetry, New York 1962; vol 6: 1920–65, Valley of dry bones, 1968.

Fein, R. Modern war poetry. Southwest Rev 47 1962.

Holbrook, D. Llareggub revisited: Dylan Thomas and the state of modern poetry. 1962.

Kapoor, A. N. and N. Das Gupta. Modern English poetry. 2 vols Allahabad 1962–3.

MacBeth, G. Georgian poetry 1912–22. London Mag new ser 2 1962.

Morgan, K. E. Poets and the imagery of fire. English 14 1962.

— Christian themes in contemporary poets. 1965.

Pearson, G. Romanticism and contemporary poetry. New Left Rev no 16 1962.

Pratt, J. C. The meaning of modern poetry. New York 1962.

Shepard, L. The broadside ballad. 1962. Includes an account of 20th-century examples.

Steele, P. Time-death and the modern poet. Twentieth Century (Melbourne) 16 1962.

Cox, C. B. and A. E. Dyson. Modern poetry: studies in practical criticism. 1963.

Hamilton, I. The dragon trappers. Lines Rev no 20 1963. On Scottish poetry.

— The forties. London Mag new ser 4 1964–5.

— (ed). The modern poet: essays from The Review. 1968. On Empson et al.

Pilch, H. Die Ballade von Roger Casement. Germanisch-romanische Monatsschrift 13 1963.

Burns, G. L. The obscurity of modern poetry. Thought 39 1964.

Glen, D. 'Hugh MacDiarmid'—Christopher Murray Grieve—and the Scottish renaissance. Edinburgh 1964.

Gross, H. Sound and form in modern poetry: a study of prosody from Hardy to Robert Lowell. Ann Arbor 1964.

Holloway, J. The colours of clarity. 1964. Essays, mostly on modern poetry.

— The lion hunt. 1965. On the nature of poetry.

— In his Widening horizons in English verse, 1966.

Johnston, J. H. English poetry of the first World War: a study in the evolution of lyric and narrative form. Princeton 1964.

Loftus, R. J. Nationalism in modern Anglo-Irish poetry. Madison 1964.

— The poets of the Easter rising. Eire–Ireland 2 1967.

Lowbridge, P. The Spanish War. Review (Oxford) no 11–12 1964.

Moore, A. K. The case for poetic obscurity. Neophilologus 48 1964.

Replogle, J. The Auden group. Wisconsin Stud in Contemporary Lit 5 1964.

Stead, C. K. The new poetic: Yeats to Eliot. 1964.

Torchiana, D. T. Contemporary Irish poetry. Chicago Rev 17 1964.

Ashraf, S. A. Rural sentimentalism in English poetry during the inter-war period. In Essays presented to Amy G. Stock, ed R. K. Kaul, Jaipur 1965.

Bergonzi, B. Heroes' twilight: a study of the literature of the Great War. 1965. Mostly on poetry.

Bianchi, R. La poetica dell'imagismo. Milan 1965.

Clinton-Baddeley, V. C. The written and the spoken word. E & S new ser 18 1965. On recording modern poetry.

Dickins, A. Tambimuttu and Poetry London. London Mag new ser 5 1965.

Emma, J. E. The ethic of disintegration: a recent case in poetics. Wisconsin Stud in Contemporary Lit 6 1965.

Ford, H. D. A poets' war: English poets and the Spanish Civil War. Philadelphia 1965.

Grubb, F. Scowling at a cigarette: the 30's poets. Poetry Rev 56 1965.

— A vision of reality: a study of liberalism in twentieth-century verse. 1965.

Lawler, J. G. The Christian image. Pittsburgh 1965.

Middleton, C. Documents on Imagism from the papers of T. E. Hulme. Review (Oxford) no 15 1965.

Miller, J. H. Poets of reality: six twentieth-century writers. Cambridge Mass 1965. On Yeats, Eliot, D. Thomas et al.

Ross, R. H. The Georgian revolt 1910–22: rise and fall of a poetic ideal. Carbondale Ill 1965.

Scully, J. (ed). Modern poetics. New York 1965, London 1966 (as Modern poets on modern poetry).

Walsh, C. The postwar revolt in England against 'modern poetry'. Bucknell Rev 13 1965.

Woodhouse, A. S. P. In his The poet and his faith: religion and poetry in England from Spenser to Eliot and Auden, Chicago 1965.

Fauchereau, S. Irlande: vers une renaissance poétique? Lettres Nouvelles July–Sept 1966.

Friedman, A. B. The ballad revival. Chicago 1966. Includes a chapter on the ballad in modern poetry.

Harrison, J. R. The reactionaries. 1966. On Yeats, Eliot, Lawrence et al.

Martin, A. To make a right rose tree: reflections on the poetry of 1916. Studies 55 1966.

Meller, H. Wege der Gedichtinterpretation in England 1910–60. In Zeitgenössische englische Dichtung, ed H. Meller, Frankfurt 1966.

Moore, J. R. Now Yeats has gone: three Irish poets. Hollins Critic 3 1966. On Clarke, Kavanagh, Devlin.

Mortimer, A. Modern English poets: five introductory essays. Milan 1966, Toronto 1968 (enlarged). On Auden, Eliot, Thomas et al.

Muste, J. M. Say that we saw Spain die: literary consequences of the Spanish Civil War. Seattle 1966.

Nichols, W. Preface in retrospect. Poetry Rev 57 1966. On Georgian poetry.

Orr, P. (ed). The poet speaks: interviews with contemporary poets. 1966.

Parker, T. H. and F. J. Teskey. An approach to modern poetry. 1966.

Prince, F. T. Modern poetry in England. Theoria 26 1966.

Smith, A. J. M. The poet and the nuclear crisis. Eng Poetry in Quebec [no 47] 1966.

Tsvasheva, V. Sovremennaya angliiskaya poeziya. Voprosy Literatury 10 1966. Modern English poetry.

Walcutt, C. C. and J. Whitesell (ed). The Explicator cyclopaedia vol 1, modern poetry. Chicago 1966. Brief essays, rptd from Explicator.

Young, D. Whither the 'Scottish renaissance'? Forum for Modern Lang Stud 2 1966.

Arinshtein, L. M. Nekotorye nablyudeniya nad stilem sovremennoi angliiskoi poezii. Uchenye Zapiski: Kalininskii Gosudarstvennyi Pedagogicheskii Institut 47 1967. On the style of contemporary English poetry.

Baker, W. E. Syntax in English poetry 1870–1930. Berkeley 1967.

Binni, F. Poeti inglesi degli anni trenta: l'immagine impura. Ponte 23 1967.

Coblentz, S. A. The poetry circus. New York 1967.

Ellmann, R. Eminent domain: Yeats among Wilde, Joyce, Pound, Eliot and Auden. New York 1967, 1970 (corrected).

Fulton, R. Scottish writing today: poetry. English 16 1967.

Gordan, J. D. Letters to an editor [E. H. Marsh]: Georgian Poetry 1912–22. New York 1967 (New York Public Lib). Notes on contributors to Georgian Poetry.

Grant, J. Harold Monro and the Poetry Bookshop. 1967.

Hoffman, D. Barbarous knowledge: myth in the poetry of Yeats, Graves, Muir. New York 1967.

Ionkis, G. E. Angliiskaya poeziya pervoi poloviny 20 veka (English poetry of the first half of the twentieth century). Moscow 1967.

Jankowsky, K. R. Die Versauffassung bei Gerard Manley Hopkins, den Imagisten und T. S. Eliot: Renaissance altgermanischen Formgestaltens in der Dichtung des 20. Jahrhunderts. Munich 1967.

Noon, W. T. Poetry and prayer. New Brunswick 1967.

Oppel, H. Entwicklungsphasen der englischen Lyrik im 20. Jahrhundert. Die Neueren Sprachen 16 1967.

—— (ed). Die moderne englische Lyrik: Interpretationen. Berlin 1967.

Piper, H. W. (ed). The beginnings of modern poetry. Melbourne 1967.

Power, P. C. The story of Anglo-Irish poetry 1800–1922. Cork 1967.

Rackin, P. Hulme, Richards and the development of contextualistic poetic theory. Jnl of Aesthetics 25 1967.

Stephens, M. The second flowering. Poetry Wales 3 1967.

Thompson, W. I. In his Imagination of an insurrection—Dublin, Easter 1916: a study of an ideological movement, New York 1967.

Wees, W. C. England's avant-garde: the futurist-vorticist phase. Western Humanities Rev 21 1967.

Glen, H. Poetry and the shock of violence 1914–18. Critical Rev (Melbourne) 11 1968.

Hollander, J. (ed). Modern poetry: essays in criticism. New York 1968.

Smith, B. H. In her Poetic closure, Chicago 1968.

Tolley, A. T. The thirties poets at Oxford. UTQ 37 1968.

Barnes, T. R. Poetry appreciation: thirteen modern poems discussed. 1968 (for 1969).

Fuller, R. Poetry in my time. Essays by Divers Hands 35 1969.

Hamburger, M. The truth of poetry: tensions in modern poetry from Baudelaire to the 1960's. 1969.

Knight, G. W. Poetry and the arts. E & S 22 1969.

Maxwell, D. E. S. Poets of the thirties. 1969.

Simon, M. The Georgian poetic. In Poetic theory/Poetic practice, ed R. Scholes, Iowa City 1969.

E.M.

(3) ANTHOLOGIES

A selective list. Anthologies of verse written by amateur groups, or by schoolchildren, have in general been excluded.

'A.E.' (G. W. Russell). New songs: a lyric selection made by 'A.E.' from poems by P. Colum, E. Gore-Booth, T. Keohler, A. Milligan, S. Mitchell, S. O'Sullivan, G. Roberts and E. Young. Dublin 1904.

Leveson-Gower, M. F. S. Wayfarer's love: contributions from living poets. 1904.

Bowles, F. G. New songs: an anthology of contemporary verse. 1907.

Jerrold, W. The book of living poets. 1907.

The Poets' Club. For Christmas MDCCCCVIII. [1909].

—— The book (The second book; The third book) of the Poets' Club. 3 vols 1909–13.

Sackville, M. A book of verse by living women. 1910.

[Marsh, E. H.] Georgian poetry 1911–12 (1913–15, 1916–17, 1918–19, 1920–2). 5 pts [1912]–22. Prefatory notes signed 'E.M.'

The Vigo verse anthology: selections from some of the early volumes of the Vigo Cabinet series. 1912.

Oxford poetry. 1913–. Vol for 1910–13 pbd 1913, then annually 1914–32; vol for 1942–3 pbd 1943, then annually 1947–57.

Tillyard, A. Cambridge poets 1900–1913. Cambridge 1913.

[Kyle, G.] A cluster of grapes: a book of twentieth-century poetry. 1914.

Pound, E. Des imagistes: an anthology. New York 1914, London 1914.

—— Catholic anthology 1914–1915. 1915.

—— Profile: an anthology collected in MCMXXXI. Milan 1932.

—— Active anthology. 1933.

Songs & sonnets for England in war time: being a collection of lyrics by various authors inspired by the Great War. 1914.

Elliott, H. B. Lest we forget: a war anthology. 1915.

English Association. Poems of to-day. 5 ser 1915–63.

Some imagist poets. 3 vols 1915–17, Boston 1915–17 (New Poetry ser).

Colum, P. and E. J. O'Brien. Poems of the Irish revolutionary brotherhood. Boston 1916, 1916 (enlarged edn).

Cunliffe, J. W. Poems of the Great War: selected on behalf of the Belgian Scholarship Committee. New York 1916.

Holman, C. E. In the day of battle: poems of the Great War. Toronto 1916.

Richards, G. M. High tide: songs of joy and vision from the present-day poets of America and Great Britain. Boston 1916, London 1922.

—— The melody of earth: an anthology of garden and nature poems from present-day poets. Boston 1918.

—— Star-points: songs of joy, faith and promise from the present-day poets. Boston 1921.

Sitwell, E. Wheels: an anthology of verse. [First cycle] Oxford 1916, 1917 (2nd edn with preface); second cycle, 1917; third cycle, 1919; fourth cycle, 1919; fifth cycle London 1920; sixth cycle London 1921.

Soldier poets: songs of the fighting men. 1916.

More songs by the fighting men: soldier poets, second series. 1917.

Aftermath of Easter Week. Dublin 1917. Anon poems by Seumas O'Sullivan, Dora Sigerson, Oliver Gogarty et al. Names pencilled into BM copy.

An annual of new poetry. 1917.

Clarke, G. H. A treasury of war poetry: British and American poems of the World War 1914–1917. Boston 1917, 1919 (as A treasury...1914–1919), London [1919].
— A new treasury of war poetry. Boston 1943.

Macdonald, E. and G. S. Ford. A crown of amaranth: being a collection of poems to the memory of the brave and gallant gentlemen who have given their lives for Great & Greater Britain 1914–1917. 1917 (rev edn).

Monroe, H. and A. C. Henderson. The new poetry. New York 1917, 1923 (enlarged), 1932 (enlarged).

Osborn, E. B. The muse in arms: a collection of war poems, for the most part written in the field of action. 1917, New York [1918].

Prys-Jones, A. G. Welsh poets: a representative English selection from contemporary writers. 1917.

Wheeler, W. R. A book of verse of the Great War. New Haven 1917.

Andrews, C. E. From the front: trench poetry. New York 1918.

Beaumont, C. W. and M. T. H. Sadler. New paths: verse, prose, pictures 1917–18. 1918.

Foxcroft, F. War verse. New York [1918].

Jones, E. B. C. Songs for sale: an anthology of recent poetry. Oxford 1918.

Lloyd, B. Poems written during the Great War 1914–18. 1918.
— The paths of glory: a collection of poems written during the war 1914–19. 1919.

Secret springs of Dublin song. Dublin 1918.

Twelve poets: a miscellany of new verse. 1918.

Braithwaite, W. S. B. The book of modern British verse. Boston [1919].

Jenkinson, E. The Malory verse book: a collection of contemporary poetry for school and general use. 1919.

Seymour, W. K. A miscellany of poetry 1919. 1919, New York 1919 (as A miscellany of British poetry).
— A miscellany of poetry 1920–22. 1922.

Wetherell, J. E. The Great War in verse and prose. Toronto 1919.

American & British verse from the Yale Review: foreword by J. G. Fletcher. New Haven 1920.

Davison, E. Cambridge poets 1914–20. Cambridge 1920.

Grieve, C. M. Northern numbers: being representative selections from certain living Scottish poets. 3 ser Edinburgh, London 1920–2. Last ser pbd at Montrose.
— Living Scottish poets. [1931] (Augustan Books of Poetry).

Pocock, G. N. Modern poetry. 1920 (King's Treasuries of Literature).
— Later modern poetry. [1928] (King's Treasuries of Literature).

Trotter, J. Valour and vision: poems of the war 1914–18. 1920, 1923 (enlarged).

Untermeyer, L. Modern British poetry. New York 1920, [1925] (rev), [1930] (rev), [1936] (rev), [1942] (rev), [1950] (rev), [1962] (rev).
— Modern American and British poetry. New York [1922], 1923 (with suggestions for study by O. E. Hart), [1928] (rev and enlarged), [1930] (as A critical anthology: modern American poetry, modern British poetry) [1942] (as Modern American poetry, modern British poetry), [1950] (rev), [1962] (rev).
— Yesterday and today: a comparative anthology. New York 1926.

Walters, L. D'O. An anthology of recent poetry. 1920, 1920 (illustr, as The year's at the spring: an anthology of recent poetry), New York 1920 (as An anthology of recent poetry), London 1932 (enlarged), 1945 (again enlarged and rev by A. E. M. Bayliss).
— Irish poets of today. 1921.

Methuen, A. An anthology of modern verse. 1921, 1921 (4th edn enlarged), 1933 (27th edn with rev texts). Also numerous school edns with notes.

Squire, J. C. Selections from modern poets. 1921.

— Second selections from modern poets. 1924, 1927 (with Selections, above, as Selections from modern poets, complete edition).
— Younger poets of to-day. 1932, 1934 (as Third selections from modern poets).

Caldwell, T. The golden book of modern English poetry 1870–1920. 1922, 1923 (rev), 1930 (rev), 1935 (EL, ed P. Henderson).

Davies, W. H. Shorter lyrics of the twentieth century 1900–1922. 1922.

Fifty new poems for children: an anthology selected from books recently published by Basil Blackwell. Oxford [1922].

Guthrie, S. A little anthology of hitherto uncollected poems by modern writers. Flansham 1922.

Pertwee, E. G. The new spirit in verse: an anthology for readers and reciters. 1922.
— A miscellany of current verse. 1923.

Poems from Punch 1909–20. Introd by W. B. D. Henderson 1922.

Gordon, M. and M. B. King. Verse of our day: an anthology of modern American and British poetry. New York [1923].

Moult, T. The best poems of 1922(–1943). 22 pts 1923–44.
— Poems from books 1927. [1927] (Augustan Books of English Poetry).

Beauchamp, J. Poems of revolt: a twentieth-century anthology. 1924.

Binyon, L. The golden treasury of modern lyrics. 1924, New York 1924.

Strong, L. A. G. The best poems of 1923(–27). 5 pts Boston [1924–5], New York 1926–8.
— Eighty poems: an anthology. Oxford 1924.

Treble, H. A. A first (-third) book of modern poetry 1924–7. 3 pts.

Adcock, A. St J. The Bookman treasury of living poets. [1925], 1928 (enlarged), 1931 (rev and enlarged by H. Ross Williamson).

Edinburgh University English Literature Society Paumflet. Edinburgh 1925.

Robb, W. A book of twentieth-century Scots verse. 1925.

Smith, J. C. A book of modern verse. Oxford 1925.

Stevenson, B. E. The home book of modern verse: an extension of The home book of verse, being a selection from American and English poetry of the twentieth century. New York 1925. Frequently rptd, rev.

Ten singers: an anthology. 1925.

Parker, E. A. A book of longer modern verse. Oxford 1926.
— Longer poems of to-day. 1932.

Lucas, E. V. The joy of life: an anthology of lyrics drawn chiefly from the works of living poets. 1927.

Newbolt, H. New paths on Helicon. [1927].

University verses 1910–1927: being an anthology from the Glasgow University Magazine. Glasgow 1927.

Asquith, C. The treasure cave: a book of new prose and verse. [1928], New York [1928].

Robinson, L. A little anthology of modern Irish verse. Dublin 1928.

Hamilton, W. H. Holyrood: a garland of modern Scots poems. 1929.

Monro, H. Twentieth century poetry. 1929, 1946 (rev A. Monro).

Rodgers, A. Garnered: a collection of modern verse. 3 sections Hyde 1929.

Saltmarsh, C. et al. Cambridge poetry 1929. 1929 (Hogarth Living Poets 8).

Sanders, G. D. and J. H. Nelson. Chief modern poets of England and America. New York 1929, 1936 (rev), 1943 (rev), 1962 (rev, with M. L. Rosenthal), 1970 (rev).

'Brereton, F.' (F. T. Smith). An anthology of war poems. [1930].

Davenport, J. et al. Cambridge poetry 1930. 1930 (Hogarth Living Poets 13).

D'Oyley, E. Modern poetry. 1930.

Imagist anthology. 1930. 1930, New York [1930]. Forewords by Ford Madox Ford and G. Hughes.

Wellesley, D. A broadcast anthology of modern poetry. 1930 (Hogarth Living Poets 17).

Abercrombie, L. New English poems: a miscellany of contemporary verse never before published. 1931.

Arnell, C. J. A West Country new anthology of contemporary poets. 2 vols Exeter [1931–3].

Jones, I. M. and B. Sh. Saklatvala. The book of London verse: an anthology of verse recently produced in the University of London. 1931.

Leahy, M. An anthology of contemporary Catholic poetry. 1931.

The Mercury book of verse: being a selection of poems published in the London Mercury 1919–1930. Introd by H. Newbolt 1931.

One hundred and one ballades. 1931.

The second book of the Omar Khayyám Club 1910–29. 1931 (priv ptd).

Thomas, M. An anthology of Cambridge women's verse. 1931. (Hogarth Living Poets).

'Gawsworth, John' (T. I. F. Armstrong). Known signatures. 1932.

— Neo-Georgian poetry 1936–1937. [1937].

— Fifty years of modern verse. 1938. Greatly expanded from his Known signatures, 1932.

— The garland of Erica: poems by several kindly hands collected on the occasion of her birthday September 12, 1938, by J. G. [1938] (20 copies, priv ptd).

— Fifty modern poems by forty famous poets. Calcutta 1945. Abridgment of his Fifty years of modern verse.

Gillett, E. Poets of our time: poems by contemporary poets. 1932.

Roberts, M. New signatures. 1932.

— New country: prose and poetry by the authors of New signatures. 1933.

— The Faber book of modern verse. 1936, 1951 (with supplement chosen by A. Ridler), 1965 (rev with supplement chosen by D. Hall).

Vines, S. Whips & scorpions: specimens of modern satiric verse 1914–1931. 1932.

Møller, K. L. Poems of to-day. Copenhagen 1933.

Monro, A. Recent poetry 1923–1933. 1933.

Private business: a book of verse published by the English Literature Society of Edinburgh University. 1933.

The modern muse: poems of to-day, British and American. 1934.

Roberts, D. K. et al. The year's poetry: a selection. 5 pts 1934–8. Other joint editors include G. Gould and J. Lehmann (1934–5), J. Lehmann (1936), G. Grigson (1937–8).

Fitzhenry, E. C. Nineteen-sixteen: an anthology. Dublin 1935.

Moore, R. W. The threshold 1935(–37): an anthology of verse and prose contributed from the public and secondary schools of England. 3 pts 1935–7. Last 2 pts pbd at Oxford, and have sub-title, An anthology...from the schools of England.

Smith, J. A. Poems of to-morrow: anthology of contemporary verse, chosen from the Listener. 1935.

Wollman, M. Modern poetry 1922–1934: an anthology. 1935 (with notes, Scholar's Library).

— Poems of twenty years: an anthology 1918–1938. 1938 (also pbd with notes, Scholar's Library).

— Selections from modern poets: an anthology 1918–1938. 1939 (English Literature ser 139).

— Poems of the war years. 1948.

— Twentieth-century narrative poems. 1954 (for 1955) (Harrap's English Classics).

— Ten twentieth-century poets. 1957 (Harrap's English Classics).

— Ten contemporary poets. 1963 (Harrap's English Classics).

— Seven themes in modern verse. 1968.

— and K. B. Parker. The Harrap book of modern verse. 1958 (Harrap's Modern English ser).

— and D. M. Hurst. Harrap's junior book of modern verse. 1961.

Edwardian poetry. Bk 1, 1936.

Mégroz, R. L. A treasury of modern poetry: an anthology of the last forty years. 1936.

New Oxford poetry. 2 pts 1936–7.

Parsons, I. M. The progress of poetry: an anthology of verse from Hardy to the present day. 1936.

— Men who march away: poems of the first World War. 1965, New York [1965].

Poems of fifty years: 1886–1936. [1936].

Yeats, W. B. The Oxford book of modern verse 1892–1935. 1936.

Macleod, S. and V. B. Neuburg. The first Comment treasury. 1937.

Murphy, G. The modern poet. 1938.

Proems. 1938.

Rodman, S. A new anthology of modern poetry. New York 1938, 1947 (rev).

— 100 modern poems. New York 1949.

Russell, C. J. and J. F. Hendry. Albannach: a little anthology of 1938 Scots poetry. Dingwall 1938.

Grigson, G. New verse: an anthology. 1939.

— Poetry of the present: an anthology of the thirties and after. 1949.

Lynd, R. Modern poetry. 1939.

Noctes Binanianæ: certain voluntary and satyrical verses and compliments as were lately exchang'd between some of the choicest wits of the age. 1939 (priv ptd, 25 copies). By T. S. Eliot, G. C. Faber, F. V. Morley and John Hayward.

Poets of tomorrow. First (-third) selection 3 pts 1939–42.

Spender, S. and J. Lehmann. Poems for Spain. 1939.

Williams, M. Modern verse for young people. 1939 (Chameleon Books).

Fear no more: a book of poems for the present time by living English poets. Cambridge 1940.

Hardie, A. M. and K. Douglas. Augury: an Oxford miscellany of verse & prose. Oxford 1940.

Jones, P. M. Modern verse 1900–40. 1940, 1955 (enlarged, as Modern verse 1900–50) (WC).

The new apocalypse: an anthology of criticism, poems and stories, by Dorian Cooke, J. F. Hendry, Norman MacCaig, Robert Melville, Nicholas Moore, Philip O'Connor, Dylan Thomas, Henry Treece. Introd by Hendry [1940].

Escott, H. Minstrels of Christ: contemporary Christian verse. 1941 (Wayside Books).

Gardiner, W. This living stone: the Grey Walls anthology of new poems. Billericay 1941.

Hendry, J. F. and H. Treece. The white horseman: prose and verse of the new apocalypse. 1941.

— The crown and the sickle. [1945].

Lewis, C. D. and L. A. G. Strong. A new anthology of modern verse 1920–40. 1941.

— and J. Lehmann. The Chatto book of modern poetry 1915–55. 1956.

Meyer, M. and S. Keyes. Eight Oxford poets. 1941.

Rhys, K. Poems from the Forces. 1941.

— More poems from the Forces. 1943.

— Modern Welsh poetry. 1944.

Ridler, A. The little book of modern verse. 1941. Preface by T. S. Eliot.

Williams, O. New poems 1940 (1942–4): an anthology of British and American verse. 4 vols New York 1941–[4].

— The war poets: an anthology of the war poetry of the 20th century. New York [1945].

— A little treasury of modern poetry, English & American. New York 1946, London 1947, New York 1952 (rev).

— The pocket book of modern verse. New York 1954, 1958 (rev).

Bain, D. et al. Z: Oxford & Cambridge writing 1942. Cambridge 1942.

Bayliss, J. et al. The Fortune anthology: stories, criticism and poems. [1942].

Comfort, A. and R. Greacen. Lyra: an anthology of new lyric. Billericay 1942.

— and J. Bayliss. New road: new directions in European art and letters. 2 vols Billericay 1943-4.

Ledward, P. and C. Strang. Poems of this war by younger poets. Cambridge 1942, New York 1943, London 1947 (as Retrospect 1939-1942, ed C. Strang and P. Ledward).

Tambimuttu, M. J. Poetry in wartime. 1942.

Aistrop, J. and R. Moore. Bugle blast: an anthology from the Services. 4 ser 1943-7.

Baker, D. V. Little Reviews anthology. 5 vols 1943-9.

— Modern British writing. New York [1947].

Häusermann, H. W. Textbook of modern English poetry. Bern [1943] (Bibliotheca Anglicana 3).

Lowy, A. E. Poets now in the Services. 2 pts 1943.

Nichols, R. Anthology of war poetry 1914-18. 1943.

Schimanski, S. and H. Treece. Wartime harvest. 1943 (Modern Reading Library).

— A new romantic anthology. 1949.

Bebbington, W. G. Introducing modern poetry. 1944, 1957 (rev).

— Words in place: a selection of contemporary verse. 1961.

Cunard, N. Poems for France, written by British poets on France since the war. 1944.

Daiken, L. M. They go, the Irish: a miscellany of wartime writing. 1944.

Greacen, R. Northern harvest: anthology of Ulster writing. Belfast 1944.

— and V. Iremonger. Contemporary Irish poetry. 1949.

Lindsay, M. Sailing tomorrow's seas: an anthology of new poems. 1944.

— Modern Scottish poetry: an anthology of the Scottish Renaissance 1920-45. 1946, 1966 (rev).

MacDonagh, D. Poems from Ireland. Dublin 1944.

Martin, D. Rhyme and reason: 34 poems. 1944.

'O'Sullivan, Seumas' (J. S. Starkey). Editor's choice: a little anthology of poems selected from the Dublin Magazine. Dublin 1944.

Poems from the desert: verses by members of the Eighth Army. 1944.

Pudney, J. and H. Treece. Air force poetry. 1944.

Roscoe, T. and M. W. Were. Poems by contemporary women. [1944].

Taylor, G. Irish poems of today, chosen from the first seven volumes of the Bell. 1944.

Today's new poets: an anthology of contemporary verse. [1944].

Bell, W. Poetry from Oxford in wartime. 1945.

— More poetry from Oxford. [1947].

Carpenter, M. et al. New lyrical ballads. 1945.

Church, R. and M. M. Bozman. Poems of our time 1900-42. 1945, 1959 (as Poems...1900-60, modern supplement chosen by E. Sitwell) (EL).

Currey, R. N. and R. V. Gibson. Poems from India, by members of the Forces. [India] 1945, London 1946.

Fedden, R. et al. Personal landscape: an anthology of exile. 1945. Selected from the periodical Personal landscape pbd at Cairo.

Moore, N. and D. Newton. Atlantic anthology. 1945.

Poems from Italy: verses written by members of the Eighth Army in Sicily and Italy, July 1943-March 1944. 1945. Introd by S. Sassoon.

Moore, G. Poetry from Cambridge in wartime: a selection of verse by members of the University. 1946.

Poems from New Writing 1936-1946, with foreword by J. Lehmann 1946.

Sergeant, H. For those who are alive: an anthology of new verse. 1946.

— An anthology of contemporary Northern poetry. 1947.

— These years: an anthology of contemporary poetry. [1950].

Waller, J. and E. de Mauny. Middle East anthology. 1946.

Beckwith, E. G. C. Selections from The Quill: a collection of prose, verse and sketches by officers prisoners-of-war in Germany 1940-5. 1947.

Collins, A. S. Treasury of modern poetry. 1947.

Home is the soldier: an anthology of poems. 1947.

Arlott, J. First time in America: a selection of poems never before published in the USA. New York [1948].

Cambridge verse. 2 pts Cambridge [1948].

Garrity, D. A. New Irish poets: representative selections from the work of 37 contemporaries. New York 1948.

Holroyd, I. F. Scottish student verse 1937-47. Edinburgh 1948. Introd by E. Linklater.

Palmer, H. The Greenwood anthology of new verse. 1948.

Shand, W. and A. Girri. Poesía inglesa contemporánea: Contemporary English poetry. Buenos Aires 1948. With Spanish trns.

Evans, M. and K. C. Lawson. Contemporary verse. 1949 (Heritage of Literature ser).

Leeds University poetry 1949-. [Leeds] 1949-.

Mawdsley, N. Poetry from Oxford, Michaelmas 1946-Trinity 1948. 1949.

Poetry awards 1949(-52): a compilation of original poetry published in magazines of the English-speaking world. Philadelphia 1949-52. Continued as Borestone Mountain poetry awards 1953(-55), then as Best poems of 1955 onwards.

Rexroth, K. The new British poets. [Norfolk Conn 1949].

Allott, K. The Penguin book of contemporary verse. 1950, 1962 (rev, as The Penguin book of contemporary verse 1918-60).

Clay, N. L. This half-century: 50 poems from 1900 to 1949. 1950.

— The London Bridge book of verse: poems from 1900-60. 1962.

For your tomorrow: an anthology of poetry written by young men from eight public schools who fell in the World War 1939-45. 1950.

Izzo, C. Poesia inglese contemporanea da Thomas Hardy agli apocalittici. [Parma] 1950.

Linklater, E. The thistle and the pen: an anthology of modern Scottish writers. 1950.

Mack, M. et al. Modern poetry. New York [1950] (English Masterpieces 7), Englewood Cliffs NJ [1961] (rev).

Peschmann, H. The voice of poetry 1930-50. 1950, 1969 (rev).

Williamson, D. Poetry from Oxford, Michaelmas 1948 to Michaelmas 1949. 1950.

Friar, K. and J. M. Brinnin. Modern poetry, American and British. New York [1951].

Green, P. M. Poetry from Cambridge 1947-50: a selection of verse by members of the University and some others. 1951.

Concord of harps: an Irish PEN anthology of poetry. Dublin 1952.

Kreitman, N. The dove in flames: an anthology of modern verse. [1952].

Lehmann, J. Pleasures of New Writing: an anthology of poems, stories and other prose pieces from the pages of New Writing. 1952.

New poems 1952-: a PEN anthology. 1952. Continued annually.

New Scots poetry: a selection of short poems from the Festival of Britain Scots poetry competition. Edinburgh 1952 (for 1953).

Young, D. Scottish verse 1851-1951. 1952.

Heath-Stubbs, J. Images of tomorrow: an anthology of recent poetry. 1953.

— and D. Wright. The Faber book of twentieth-century verse: an anthology of verse in Britain 1900-50. 1953, 1965 (rev), 1967 (rev).

O'Donnell, M. J. An anthology of contemporary verse. 1953.

Rose, B. W. and R. S. Jones. Modern narrative poetry. 1953.
—— Modern lyrical verse. 1958.
Engle, P. and W. P. Carrier. Reading modern poetry: a critical anthology. Chicago 1955, 1968 (rev).
—— and P. Langland. Poet's choice. New York 1962. Poems with comments by the poets.
Fraser, G. S. Poetry now. 1956.
Causley, C. Peninsula: an anthology of verse from the west-country. 1957.
—— Modern folk ballads. 1966.
Holloway, J. Poems of the mid-century. 1957 (Harrap's English Classics).
Reeves, J. The modern poets' world. 1957 (Poetry Bookshelf).
—— Georgian poetry. 1962 (Penguin Poets).
Bonham-Carter, V. The Bryanston miscellany. Blandford [1958].
Cecil, D. and A. Tate. Modern verse in English. 1958, New York 1958.
Guinness book of poetry. 5 pts 1958–62.
Sanesi, R. Poesia inglese del dopoguerra. Milano [1958]. With Italian trns.
—— Poeti inglesi dell' 900. Milano [1960].
Ley, C. D. Twentieth-century English poetry. Madrid 1959.
MacCaig, N. Honour'd shade: an anthology of new Scottish poetry to mark the bicentenary of the birth of Robert Burns. Edinburgh 1959.
Pryce-Jones, A. Georgian poets. 1959 (Pocket Poets).
Blackburn, T. 45–60: an anthology of English poetry 1945–60. 1960.
—— Gift of tongues. 1967.
Hewett, S. This day and age: an anthology of modern poetry in English. 1960.
Jennings, E. An anthology of modern verse 1940–1960. 1961.
Boas, G. The school book of modern verse. 1962.
Pinion, F. B. Modern poetry for schools. 1962.
Skelton, R. Six Irish poets. 1962.
—— Poetry of the thirties. 1964 (Penguin Poets).
—— Poetry of the forties. 1968 (Penguin Poets).
Guterman, N. G. Antologiya novoi angliiskoi i amerikanskoi poezii. Leningrad 1963. In English.
Morgan, K. E. A book of modern prose and poetry. 1963.
Osgerby, J. R. Six modern poets: an anthology. [1963] (Queen's Classics).
Pratt, W. The imagist poem. New York 1963.
Wain, J. Anthology of modern poetry. 1963, 1967 (rev).
Gardner, B. Up the line to death: the war poets 1914–18. 1964.

—— The terrible rain: the war poets 1939–1945. 1966.
Graham, J. J. and T. A. Robertson. Nordern lichts: an anthology of Shetland verse and prose. Lerwick 1964.
Mansfield, R. Every man will shout: an anthology of modern verse, compiled by R. Mansfield, edited by I. Armstrong. 1964.
Shaw, R. Flash point: an anthology of modern poetry. Leeds [1964].
Trapp, J. Modern religious poems. 1964.
Walsh, C. Today's poets: American and British poetry since the 1930's. New York [1964].
Dudek, L. Poetry of our time. Toronto 1965.
Evans, A. A. Contemporary: an anthology of the poetry of our time 1940–1964. 1965 (London English Literature ser).
Finn, F. E. S. Poets of our time. [1965].
Gillam, C. W. Modern poems understood. 1965.
Hamilton, I. The poetry of war 1939–1945. 1965.
Miller, D. C. A choice of poems. Oxford 1965.
Moments of truth: nineteen short poems by living poets. 1965 (328 copies).
Sullivan, J. F. Poetry in English 1900–1930. 1965 (World of English).
Wright, D. The mid century: English poetry 1940–1960. 1965 (Penguin).
—— Longer contemporary poems. 1966 (Penguin).
Beaumont, T. Modern religious verse. 1966.
Black, E. L. Nine modern poets. 1966.
Charlton, J. M. Ten poets of our own time. 1966.
Hamblett, C. I burn for England: an anthology of the poetry of World War II. 1966.
Kirkman, A. J. Present-day English poetry. 1966.
Smith, J. Modern love poems. 1966.
Steiner, G. The Penguin book of modern verse translation. 1966.
Bolt, S. Poetry of the 1920s. 1967 (Longman's Eng ser).
Hughes, T. Poetry in the making. 1967.
Hussey, M. Poetry of the first World War. 1967 (Longman's Eng ser).
MacBeth, G. Poetry 1900 to 1965. [1967].
Rodway, A. Poetry of the 1930s. 1967 (Longman's Eng ser).
Rosenthal, M. L. The new modern poetry: British and American poetry since World War II. New York 1967.
—— One hundred modern poems: British and American. New York 1968.
Bruce, G. The Scottish literary revival: an anthology of twentieth-century poetry. 1968.
Cox, C. B. and A. E. Dyson. Poems of this century. 1968.
Hunter, J. Modern poets. 4 vols 1968.

R. J. R.

II. INDIVIDUAL POETS

THOMAS STEARNS ELIOT
1888–1965

There are significant collections of Eliot's mss in Houghton Library, Harvard (see note in Harvard Lib Bull 7 1953 and Houghton Lib Report of Accessions 1961–2); in Texas University Library, including an autograph fair copy of The waste land, made in 1960 (see exhibition catalogue, 1961, Bibliographies, below); in the John Hayward Bequest, King's College Cambridge; and in New York Public Library. This last holds the most important collection of Eliot's mss in a public institution. It originates from the collection of John B. Quinn, subsequently sold to the Berg Collection, was revealed as being there in 1968 and was described by D. Gallup, TLS 7 Nov 1968. It includes the ms and typescript of The waste land, with comments and deletions by Ezra Pound, a notebook containing Prufrock and other poems, and several sequences of loose sheets containing pbd and unpbd poems.

As an editor and later as a publisher Eliot corresponded with many writers; letters from him are thus to be found in various collections of authors' papers. For many deposits of these see the National Union Catalogue of Manuscripts; also M. A. F. Borrie, The Schiff papers, BMQuart 31 1966. The holograph and typescripts of Marina are in Bodley (see Beare, Bibliographies, below).

Bibliographies

Fry, V. Bibliography of the writings of Eliot. Hound & Horn 1 1928.
Gallup, D. A catalogue of English and American first editions of all the writings of Eliot exhibited at the Yale University Library 22 February to 20 March 1937. New Haven 1937.

—— A bibliographical check-list of the writings of Eliot. New Haven 1947.

—— Eliot: a bibliography, including contributions to periodicals and foreign translations. 1952, New York [1953], London 1969 (rev and extended). Also lists syllabuses, and recordings made by Eliot.

In Eliot: a selected critique, ed. L. Unger 1948.

Nelson, A. H. In his Critics and The waste land 1922–49, E Studies 36 1955.

Beare, R. L. Notes on the text of Eliot: variants from Russell Square. SB 9 1957.

Cattaui, G. T. S. Eliot. Paris [1957]. Includes a bibliography of French trns of Eliot.

Walmsley, D. M. Unrecorded article by Eliot. Book Collector 9 1960. Modern tendencies in poetry, from Shana'a: a magazine of art, literature and philosophy, 1 1920.

University of Texas, Humanities Research Center. An exhibition of the manuscripts and first editions of Eliot. Austin 1961.

Bloomfield, B. C. An unrecorded article by Eliot. Book Collector 11 1962. Religion, drama and the Church, from REP [the magazine of the Croydon and Westminster repertory theatres] 6 Oct 1934.

Woodward, D. H. John Quinn and Eliot's first book of criticism. PBSA 56 1962.

—— Notes on the publishing history and text of The waste land. PBSA 58 1964; rptd in Cox and Hinchliffe, 1968, below.

Bentz, H. W. Thomas Stearns Eliot in Übersetzungen. Frankfurt 1963 (Weltliteratur in Übersetzungen: Britische Autoren 1). Duplicated typescript.

Useful articles and books on Eliot by Indians and Pakistanis. In Eliot: homage from India, ed P. Lal, Calcutta [1965].

In Eliot: a tribute from Japan, ed M. Hirai and E. W. F. Tomlin, Tokyo 1966. Japanese trns and secondary material on Eliot, including chs in books (not listed below).

Malawsky, B. Y. Eliot: a check-list 1952–64. Bull of Bibliography 25 1967. Intended to supplement Gallup (above). Does not list works on Eliot.

Caretti, L. In her Eliot in Italia, Bari 1968.

Gunter, B. The Merrill checklist of Eliot. Columbus Ohio [1970]. Works by and on Eliot.

Collections

Complete poems and plays 1909–50. New York [1952].

Complete poems and plays. 1969.

§1

Poetry

For details of previous pbn of individual poems in magazines etc see Gallup, Bibliographies, above.

Prufrock and other observations. 1917.

Poems. Richmond 1919 (ptd by L. and V. Woolf). 7 poems, all rptd in next.

Ara vus prec. [1920] (264 copies: correct title Ara vos prec), New York 1920 (as Poems; with a different order of contents and one poem, Hysteria, substituted for Ode). For the text of Gerontion, here first pbd, see W. H. Marshall, The text of Eliot's Gerontion, SB 4 1951.

The waste land. New York 1922, Richmond 1923 (ptd by L. and V. Woolf), London 1961 (for 1962) (ptd at Verona by G. Mardersteig). First pbd in Criterion 1 1922, without notes, subsequently thus in Dial 73 1922. Eliot regarded the 1961 text as standard. *See* D. H. Woodward, Notes on the publishing history and text of The waste land, PBSA 58 1964. For preliminary discussion of the ms etc including some facsimiles, *see* D. Gallup TLS 7 Nov 1968.

Poems 1909–1925. 1925, New York [1932]. Collects contents of previous books.

Journey of the Magi. [1927] (Ariel Poems 8), New York 1927 (27 copies for copyright purposes). This and subsequent Ariel Poems were rptd in Collected poems, 1963, below.

A song for Simeon. [1928] (Ariel Poems 16).

Animula. 1929 (Ariel Poems 23).

Ash-Wednesday. 1930, New York 1930.

Anabasis: a poem by St J. Perse with a translation into English by Eliot. 1930, New York 1938 (rev), 1949 (rev and corrected), 1959 (with alterations by the author).

Marina. 1930 (Ariel Poems 29).

Triumphal march. 1931 (Ariel Poems 35).

Sweeney agonistes: fragments of an Aristophanic melodrama. 1932. A short concluding scene was pbd in H. Flanagan, Dynamo, New York [1943], and in C. H. Smith's Eliot's dramatic theory and practice, Princeton 1963, §2 below and elsewhere.

The builders: song from The rock. [1934]. Music by M. Shaw.

Words for music. [Bryn Mawr Pa] 1934 [for Feb 1935]. 2 poems, New Hampshire, Virginia, pbd in an edn of at least 20 copies by F. Prokosch; rptd in Collected poems, 1936, below.

Two poems. [Cambridge] 1935 (25 copies, ptd for F. Prokosch). 2 poems, Cape Anne, Usk, both rptd in next.

Collected poems 1909–1935. 1936, New York [1936].

Old Possum's book of practical cats. 1939, New York [1939], London 1940 (illustr N. Bentley), 1953 (with addition of Cat Morgan introduces himself).

The waste land and other poems. 1940, New York [1955]. Selection.

East Coker. 1940 (New Eng Weekly Easter no, suppl [an offprint]), 1940 (pbd Faber).

Burnt Norton. 1941. First pbd in Collected poems, 1936 above.

Later poems 1925–1935. 1941. Selection.

The Dry Salvages. 1941.

Little Gidding. 1942.

Four quartets. New York [1943], London 1944. Burnt Norton; East Coker; The Dry Salvages; Little Gidding.

A practical possum. Cambridge Mass 1947 (80 copies). Single poem, not rptd elsewhere.

Selected poems. 1948 (Penguin Poets), New York [1967] (Harbrace Paperback).

The undergraduate poems of Eliot, published when he was at college in The Harvard Advocate. Cambridge Mass [1949]. An unauthorized edn. These poems appear in the authorized Poems written in early youth, 1950 (below).

Poems written in early youth. Stockholm 1950 (priv ptd, 12 copies), London 1967, New York 1967 (trade edn, with note by Mrs Eliot). Compiled by John Hayward, includes 2 poems not previously pbd and corrected texts of poems in The undergraduate poems, [1949] (above).

Cat Morgan introduces himself. [1951]. Anon. Duplicated, with an issue of Faber Book News. Rptd as broadside, New Haven 1953 (30 copies) and in 1953 edn of Old Possum's book of practical cats, above.

The cultivation of Christmas trees. 1954 (Ariel Poems, new ser), New York [1956].

Collected poems 1909–1962. 1963, New York [1963].

Verse Plays

Sweeney agonistes. 1932. *See* Poems, above.

The rock: a pageant play written for performance at Sadler's Wells Theatre 28 May–9 June 1934. 1934, New York [1934].

Murder in the cathedral. (Festival of the Friends of Canterbury Cathedral May 1935, Mercury 1 Nov 1935). Canterbury 1935 (acting edn, altered and abbreviated for performance), London 1935, New York [1935], London 1936 (2nd edn with alterations), New York [1936], London 1937 (with further alterations), 1938 (4th edn, with further alterations), New York [1963] (with author's notes for first–fourth edns), 1965 (introd and notes by

N. Coghill). The text of the screen version appears in The film of Murder in the cathedral by Eliot and G. Hoellering, 1952, New York [1952]. For a study of textual differences between the various edns, *see* Beare, Bibliographies, above.

The family reunion: a play. (Westminster 21 March 1939). 1939, New York [1939].

The cocktail party: a comedy. (Edinburgh Festival 22 Aug 1949, New 3 May 1950). 1950, New York [1950]. For alterations to text made in 4th printing, 1950, for Faber, *see* Beare, Bibliographies, above.

The confidential clerk: a play. (Edinburgh Festival 25 Aug 1953, Lyric 16 Sept 1953). 1954, New York [1954].

The elder statesman. (Edinburgh Festival 25 Aug 1958, Cambridge 25 Sept 1958). 1959, New York 1959.

Collected plays. 1962. Excludes The rock.

Other Works

Ezra Pound, his metric and poetry. New York 1917. Anon. Rptd in To criticize the critic, 1965, below.

The sacred wood: essays on poetry and criticism. 1920, New York 1921, London 1928 (with preface by the author), New York 1930.

Homage to John Dryden: three essays on poetry of the seventeenth century. 1924 (Hogarth Essays 4).

Shakespeare and the stoicism of Seneca: an address read before the Shakespeare Association 18th March 1927. 1927.

For Lancelot Andrewes: essays on style and order. 1928, Garden City NY 1929.

Dante. 1929 (The Poets on the Poets 2).

Thoughts after Lambeth. 1931 (Criterion Miscellany 30).

Charles Whibley: a memoir. 1931 (Eng Assoc pamphlet 80).

Selected essays 1917–1932. 1932, New York [1932], London 1934 (with an additional essay), New York [1950] (with 4 essays additional to those in first edn), London 1951 (with these 4 essays added to contents of 1934 edn).

John Dryden the poet, the dramatist, the critic: three essays. New York 1932.

The use of poetry and the use of criticism: studies in the relation of criticism to poetry in England. 1933, Cambridge Mass 1933, London 1964 (with new preface).

After strange gods: a primer of modern heresy. 1934, New York [1934].

Elizabethan essays. 1934. Rptd from Selected essays, 1932, except for John Marston.

Essays ancient & modern. 1936, New York [1936].

The idea of a Christian society. 1939, New York [1940].

Points of view. 1941. Selection by J. Hayward of critical writings.

The classics and the man of letters: the presidential address delivered to the Classical Association on 15 April 1942. 1942. Rptd in To criticize the critic, 1965, below.

The music of poetry: the third W. P. Ker memorial lecture delivered in the University of Glasgow 24 February 1942. Glasgow 1942. Rptd in On poetry and poets, 1957, below.

Reunion by destruction: reflections on a scheme for Church union in South India. [1943]. (Council for the Defence of Church Principles pamphlet 7).

What is a classic? an address delivered before the Virgil Society on the 16th October 1944. 1945. Rptd in On poetry and poets, 1957, below.

Die Einheit der europäischen Kultur. Berlin 1946. Text in German and English; latter rptd as appendix to Notes towards the definition of culture, 1948, below.

On poetry: an address on the occasion of the twenty-fifth anniversary of Concord Academy. Concord 1947.

Milton. 1947 (Br Acad Annual Lecture on a Master Mind). Rptd in On poetry and poets, 1957, below.

A sermon preached in Magdalene College Chapel 7 March 1948. Cambridge 1948.

Notes towards the definition of culture. 1948, New York [1949], London 1962 (with minor alterations).

From Poe to Valéry. New York 1949 (priv ptd). Rptd in To criticize the critic, 1965, below.

The aims of poetic drama: the presidential address to the Poets' Theatre Guild. 1949.

Poetry and drama. Cambridge Mass 1951, London 1951. (Theodore Spencer Memorial Lecture). Rptd in On poetry and poets, 1957, below.

The value and use of cathedrals in England to-day: an address delivered to the Friends of Chichester Cathedral on June 16th, 1951. Chichester [1952].

An address to the members of the London Library, July 1952. 1952, Providence RI 1953.

Selected prose. Ed J. Hayward 1953 (Penguin).

American literature and the American language: an address delivered at Washington University on June 9 1953. St Louis [1953]. Rptd in To criticize the critic, 1965, below.

The three voices of poetry. 1953, New York 1954. Rptd in On poetry and poets, 1957, below.

Religious drama: mediaeval and modern. New York 1954. 'Delivered to the Friends of Rochester Cathedral in 1937'.

Gedenkschrift zur Verleihung des Hansischen Goethe-Preises 1954 der gemeinnützigen Stiftung F.V.S. zu Hamburg durch die Universität Hamburg an Thomas Stearns Eliot. [Hamburg 1955]. Consists mainly of Eliot's address Goethe as the sage, in English and German. Rptd in On poetry and poets, 1957, below.

The literature of politics: a lecture. 1955 (Conservative Political Centre pamphlet). Rptd in To criticize the critic, 1965, below.

Essays on Elizabethan drama. New York [1956], London 1963 (with preface, as Elizabethan dramatists). Selection from Selected essays, 1951 (3rd edn), above.

The frontiers of criticism: a lecture delivered at the University of Minnesota Williams Arena on April 30 1956. [Minneapolis 1956]. Rptd in next.

On poetry and poets. 1957, New York 1957. Consisting mainly of rptd lectures and introds; substantially unaltered, apart from Poetry and drama.

Christianity and culture. New York [1960]. Reprints The idea of a Christian society and Notes towards the definition of culture.

Geoffrey Faber 1889–1961. 1961 (priv ptd). A memorial address.

George Herbert. 1962 (Br Council pamphlet).

Knowledge and experience in the philosophy of F. H. Bradley. 1964, New York [1964]. Eliot's Harvard PhD thesis, with 2 articles on Leibniz rptd from the Monist. Some copies of a suppressed edn of 1963 survive.

To criticize the critic and other writings. 1965, New York [1965].

Contributions to Books

A few minor contributions have been omitted. Most of the contributions were rptd in Eliot's various collections of verse and prose above. For details see Gallup, Bibliographies, above.

Poetry

Harvard class day 1910. [Cambridge Mass 1910]. Contains The ode, by Eliot. Rptd in Poems written in early youth, 1950 above.

Pound, E. (ed). Catholic anthology 1914–1915. 1915. 5 poems.

Kreymborg, A. (ed). Others: an anthology of the new verse. New York 1916. Portrait of a lady.

The chapbook: a miscellany. No 39 1924. Doris's dream songs (3 poems).

Strong, L. A. G. (ed). The best poems of 1925. Boston 1925. The hollow men [pt 1].

Pound, E. (ed). Profile: an anthology collected in MCMXXXI. Milan 1932. Fragment of an agon, from Wanna go home, baby?

Moult, T. (ed). The best poems of 1934. [1934]. Words for music.

'Roberts, Michael' (ed). The Faber book of modern verse. 1936. 7 poems.

Noctes Binanianæ: certain voluntary and satyrical verses and compliments as were lately exchang'd between some of the choicest wits of the age. 1939 (priv ptd, 25 copies). 9 poems (anon).

The Queen's book of the Red Cross. [1939]. 2 poems.

Wheeler, M. Britain at war. New York [1941] (pbd Museum of Modern Art). Defense of the islands. Rptd in Collected poems 1909–1962. 1963.

Flanagan, H. Dynamo. New York [1943]. On a production of Sweeney Agonistes at Poughkeepsie; contains a letter to Mrs Flanagan and a short concluding scene for the drama.

Queen Mary's book for India. 1943. To the Indians who died in Africa.

Tribute to Walter de la Mare on his seventy-fifth birthday. 1948. To Walter de la Mare.

Castle, W. R. Fifty years. [Cambridge Mass] 1949 (priv ptd). Ballade of the Fox dinner.

Hall, D. (ed). The Harvard Advocate anthology. New York [1951]. 8 poems, all previously ptd in book form; and Gentlemen and seamen, in prose.

Betjeman, J. et al. Gala day London. 1953. 8 lines of verse.

Prose

Bagguley, W. H. (ed). Andrew Marvell 1621–1678: tercentenary tributes. 1922. Andrew Marvell.

Valéry, P. Le serpent. [1924]. Introd.

Eliot, C. Savonarola: a dramatic poem. [1926]. Introd.

Seneca. His tenne tragedies. 2 vols 1927 (Tudor Translations). Introd, rptd as Seneca in Elizabethan translation.

Collins, W. The moonstone. 1928 (WC). Introd; rptd as Wilkie Collins and Dickens.

Dryden, J. Of dramatick poesie, an essay, 1668; preceded by a dialogue on poetic drama by Eliot. 1928. Rptd as A dialogue on dramatic poetry.

Mowrer, E. A. This American world. 1928. Preface.

Pound, E. Selected poems. Ed Eliot 1928, 1948 [for 1949] (with postscript).

Tradition and experiment in present-day literature: addresses delivered at the City Literary Institute. 1929. Experiment in criticism.

Foerster, N. (ed). Humanism and America. New York [1930]. Religion without humanism.

Knight, G. W. The wheel of fire. 1930. Introd.

Baudelaire, C. Intimate journals. 1930. Introd; rptd as Baudelaire.

Johnson, S. London: a poem and The vanity of human wishes, with an introductory essay by Eliot. 1930.

De la Mare, W. (ed). The eighteen-eighties. Cambridge 1930. The place of Pater; rptd as Arnold and Pater.

Pascal's Pensées. [1931] (EL). Introd; rptd as The Pensées of Pascal.

Crosby, H. The transit of Venus: poems. Paris 1931. Preface.

Spencer, T. (ed). A garland for John Donne. Cambridge [Mass] 1931. Donne in our time.

Philippe, C.-L. Bubu of Montparnasse. Paris 1932, New York 1945. Preface.

The Cantos of Ezra Pound: some testimonies by Ernest Hemingway, Eliot [et al]. New York [1933].

Monro, H. The collected poems, with a critical note by Eliot. 1933.

Granville-Barker, H. and G. B. Harrison (ed). A companion to Shakespeare studies. Cambridge 1934. Shakespearian criticism. I. From Dryden to Coleridge.

Demant, V. A. (ed). Faith that illuminates. 1935. Religion and literature.

Moore, M. Selected poems. Ed Eliot, New York 1935, London 1935.

Poems of Tennyson. [1936]. Introd; rptd as In Memoriam.

Essays and studies by members of the English Association. Vol 21, Oxford 1936. A note on the verse of John Milton.

Conklin, G. (ed). The New Republic anthology 1915–1935. New York [1936]. The idealism of Julien Benda.

Church, community and state: synopses of [BBC] talks. [1936]. The Church's message to the world; rptd as an appendix to The idea of a Christian society, 1939.

Dobrée, B. (ed). From Anne to Victoria: essays by various hands. 1937. Byron (1788–1824).

Barnes, D. Nightwood. New York [1937], London 1950 (2nd edn, with preface and note by Eliot). Introd did not appear in first London edn.

Baillie, J. and H. Martin (ed). Revelation. 1937. Contributions by various authors, including Eliot.

Zabel, M. D. (ed). Literary opinion in America: essays. New York 1937. 3 essays, 2 previously pbd, and Poetry and propaganda.

Seventeenth-century studies presented to Sir Herbert Grierson. Oxford 1938. A note on two odes of Cowley.

Johnson, A. T. and A. Tate (ed). America through the essay: an anthology for English courses. New York 1938. Literature and the modern world.

G[angulee], N. The testament of immortality. 1940. Preface.

Manchester, F. and O. Shepard (ed). Irving Babbitt, man and teacher. New York 1941. Includes a memoir by Eliot.

Oldham, J. H. et al. The Church looks ahead: broadcast talks. 1941. Towards a Christian Britain.

A choice of Kipling's verse made by Eliot, with an essay on Kipling. 1941, New York 1943.

The life of the Church and the order of society: being the proceedings of the Archbishop of York's conference, (Malvern 1941). 1941. The Christian conception of education.

Ridler, A. (ed). The little book of modern verse. 1941 [Feb 1942]. Preface.

Introducing James Joyce: a selection of Joyce's prose by Eliot, with an introductory note. 1942.

Jameson, S. (ed). London calling. New York 1942. A note on war poetry.

Wilson, E. (ed). The shock of recognition: the development of literature in the United States. Garden City NY 1943. Henry James, 2 essays, also rptd as On Henry James in The question of Henry James, ed F. W. Dupee 1947.

Friendship, progress, civilisation: three war-time speeches to the Anglo-Swedish Society. [1943]. Civilisation: the nature of cultural relations.

Bethell, S. L. Shakespeare & the popular dramatic tradition. 1944, Durham NC 1945. Introd.

Reckitt, M. B. (ed). Prospect for Christendom. 1945. Cultural forces in the human order; rptd (rev) as ch 1 of Notes towards the definition of culture, 1948.

The dark side of the moon. 1946, New York 1 947 Preface.

Paul Valéry vivant. Marseilles 1946. Leçon de Valéry.

Givens, S. (ed). James Joyce: two decades of criticism. New York [1948]. Ulysses, order and myth, and A message to the fish.

Williams, C. All Hallows' Eve. New York [1948]. Introd.

En engelsk bog tilegnet Kai Friis Møller. København 1948. Introd.

Stallman, R. W. (ed). Critiques and essays in criticism 1920–1948. New York [1949]. The social function of poetry.

Eason, T. W. and R. Hamilton (ed). A portrait of Michael Roberts. 1949. Introd.

Hall, J. and M. Steinmann (ed). The permanence of Yeats: selected criticism. New York 1950. The poetry of W. B. Yeats.

Les prix Nobel en 1948. Stockholm 1949 [1950]. Speech.

Vivante, L. English poetry and its contribution to the knowledge of a creative principle. 1950. Preface.

Clemens, S. L. The adventures of Huckleberry Finn. 1950. Introd.

Russell, P. (ed). Ezra Pound: a collection of essays. 1950, Norfolk Conn 1950 (as An examination of Ezra Pound). Ezra Pound, rptd from Poetry 68 1946, with postscript, 1950.

'Tiverton, William' (M. Jarrett-Kerr). D. H. Lawrence and human existence. 1951. Foreword.

Gangulee, N. (ed). Thoughts for meditation: an anthology. 1951. Preface.

Festival of Britain 1951. London season of the arts. Official souvenir programme. 1951. The spoken word.

Pieper, J. Leisure the basis of culture. 1952. Introd.

Weil, S. The need for roots. 1952, New York 1952. Preface.

Chiari, J. Contemporary French poetry. 1952. Preface.

Fluchère, H. Shakespeare. 1953, New York 1956 (as Shakespeare and the Elizabethans). Foreword.

The unity of European culture: a series of broadcasts given over the BBC foreign service July to October 1953. Literature.

Pound, E. Literary essays. Ed with introd by Eliot 1954, Norfolk Conn 1954.

Ezra Pound at seventy. Norfolk Conn 1956. Statement.

Chiari, J. Symbolisme from Poe to Mallarmé. 1956. Foreword.

Joyce, S. My brother's keeper. New York 1958, London 1958. Preface.

Valéry, P. The art of poetry. New York [1958], London 1958. Introd.

At the memorial service for William Collin Brooks MC the following address was given by Eliot. [1959].

Murry, J. M. Katherine Mansfield, and other literary studies. 1959. Foreword.

Lewis, W. One-way song. 1960. Foreword.

John Davidson: a selection of his poems. 1961. Preface.

Hofmannsthal, H. von. Poems and verse plays. New York [1961], London 1961. Preface.

Jones, D. In parenthesis. 1961, New York [1962]. Introd.

Hofmannsthal, H. von. Selected plays and libretti. New York 1963, London 1964. A note on 'The tower'.

Sylvia Beach (1887–1962). [Paris 1963]. Miss Sylvia Beach.

Muir, E. Selected poems. 1965. Preface.

Huxley, J. (ed). Aldous Huxley 1894–1963: a memorial volume. 1965, New York 1966. Contribution.

Kershaw, A. and F.-J. Temple (ed). Richard Aldington: an intimate portrait. Carbondale [1965]. Contribution.

Gabrieli, V. (ed). Friendship's garland: essays presented to Mario Praz. 2 vols Rome 1966. A tribute to Mario Praz.

The Criterion 1922–1939. 18 vols 1967. Ed Eliot, this reprint also contains a preface.

Eliot was one of the editors of Harvard Advocate *1909–10, and assistant editor of* Egoist *1917–19. From 1922 to 1939 he was editor of* Criterion, *to which he frequently contributed* A commentary. *For Eliot and TLS, see T. S. Eliot, Bruce Lyttleton Richmond, TLS 13 Jan 1961.*

§2
Books and Chapters in Books

Lynd, R. Eliot as critic. In his Books and authors, [1922].

Aldington, R. The poetry of Eliot. In his Literary studies and reviews, 1924.

—— In his Life for life's sake: a book of reminiscences, New York 1941.

—— Ezra Pound & Eliot: a lecture. 1954.

Ransom, J. C. Waste lands. In Modern essays, ed C. Morley, New York 1925.

—— A cathedralist looks at murder. In his World's body, New York 1928.

—— Eliot: the historical critic. Norfolk Conn [1941].

Richards, I. A. On Mr Eliot's poetry. In his Principles of literary criticism, 1926 (2nd edn).

Dobrée, B. In his Lamp and the lute: studies in six modern authors, Oxford 1929.

Williamson, G. The talent of Eliot. Seattle 1929 (Univ of Washington Chapbooks 32).

—— A reader's guide to Eliot: a poem-by-poem analysis. New York 1953, 1955 (rev).

Burke, K. The allies of humanism abroad. In The critique of humanism, ed C. H. Grattan, New York 1930.

Roscoe, B. Pupils of Polonius. Ibid.

Williams, C. In his Poetry at present, 1930.

Brown, A. The lyric impulse in the poetry of Eliot. In Scrutinies vol 2, ed E. Rickword 1931.

Higgins, B. The critical method of Eliot. Ibid.

Jameson, R. D. Poetry and plain sense: a note on the poetic method of Eliot. Peiping 1931. Rptd from Tsing Hua Rev.

McGreevy, T. Thomas Stearns Eliot: a study. 1931.

Grudin, L. Mr Eliot among the nightingales. Paris 1932.

Leavis, F. R. In his New bearings in English poetry, 1932, 1950 (with Retrospect 1950).

—— (ed). A selection from Scrutiny vol 1, Cambridge 1968. Includes articles etc, on Eliot by various authors.

—— Eliot's classical standing. In F. R. and Q. D. Leavis, Lectures in America, 1969.

—— The present and the past: Eliot's demonstration; Eliot's 'axe to grind' and the nature of great criticism; Why Four quartets matters in a technological-Benthamite age; The necessary opposite, Lawrence: illustration —the opposed critics on Hamlet. In his English literature in our time and the university, 1969.

Oras, A. The critical ideas of Eliot. Tartu 1932 (Eesti Vabariigi Tartu Ülikooli toimetused).

Williamson, H. R. The poetry of Eliot. 1932.

Knight, G. W. The Christian renaissance: with interpretations of Dante, Shakespeare and Goethe, and a note on Eliot. Toronto 1933.

Lewis, W. In his Men without art, 1934.

Passmore, J. A. T. S. Eliot. Sydney 1934. Pamphlet.

Sitwell, E. In her Aspects of modern poetry, 1934.

Blackmur, R. P. The dangers of authorship. In his Double agent, New York [1935]. On After strange gods.

—— Eliot: from Ash Wednesday to Murder in the cathedral. Ibid.

—— 'It is later than he thinks'. In his Expense of greatness, New York 1940. On The idea of a Christian society.

Borowy, W. T. S. Eliot jako krytyk literacki i teoretyk tradycji. Warsaw [1935].

—— Wędrówka nowego Parsyfala: poezja T. S. Eliota. Warsaw [1935].

Matthiessen, F. O. The achievement of Eliot. Cambridge Mass 1935, 1947 (rev and enlarged), 1958 (rev and enlarged, with ch on Eliot's later work by C. L. Barber).

Spender, S. Eliot in his poetry; Eliot in his criticism. In his Destructive element, 1935.

Fukase, M. T. S. Eliot. Tokyo 1937. In Japanese.

—— Eliot's theory of art. Tokyo 1949, 1952 (as The poetics of Eliot). In Japanese.

—— Eliot's poetics. Tokyo 1952.

—— Eliot. Tokyo 1954. In Japanese.

—— (ed). Studies on Eliot. Tokyo 1955. In Japanese.

Partridge, A. C. T. S. Eliot. Pretoria 1937 (Pbns of Univ of Pretoria). Pamphlet.

Sato, K. Studies on the poetry of Eliot. Tokyo 1937. In Japanese.

Lewis, C. S. Shelley, Dryden and Mr Eliot. In his Rehabilitations, 1939.

Southworth, J. G. The poetry of Eliot. In Sowing the spring, ed Southworth, Oxford 1940.

Bodkin, M. The quest for salvation in an ancient and a modern play. 1941. On Aeschylus' Eumenides and The family reunion.

Brenner, R. In her Poets of our time, New York 1941.

Brooks, V. W. What is primary literature? In his Opinions of Oliver Allston, New York 1941; rptd in Unger, 1948, below.

Nuhn, F. Orpheus in hell: Eliot. In his The wind blew from the East, New York 1942.

Buck, P. M., jr. Faith of our fathers—Eliot. In Directions in contemporary literature, ed Buck, New York 1942.

Van Doren, M. Mr Eliot glances up. In his Private reader, New York 1942, and in Unger 1948, below. On Essays ancient and modern.

Mesterton, E. The waste land: some commentaries. Chicago 1943. Tr from introd to Eliot, Dikter, Stockholm 1942.

Stephenson, E. M. Eliot and the lay reader. 1944.

Basler, R. P. Psychological patterns in The love song of J. Alfred Prufrock. In Twentieth-century English, ed W. S. Knickerbocker, New York 1946.

Preston, R. Four quartets rehearsed: a commentary on Eliot's cycle of poems. New York 1946.

Tordeur, J. A la rencontre de Thomas Stearns Eliot: un classique vivant. Brussels [1946?].

Battenhouse, H. M. Poets of Christian thought: evaluations from Dante to Eliot. New York [1947].

Brooks, C. Eliot: discourse to the gentiles. In his Wellwrought urn: studies in the structure of poetry, New York 1947.

—— The hidden god: studies in Hemingway, Faulkner, Yeats, Eliot and Warren. New Haven 1963.

Cattaui, G. Trois poètes: Hopkins, Yeats, Eliot. Paris [1947].

—— T. S. Eliot. Paris [1957]; tr 1966.

Costello, Sr M. C. Between fixity and flux: a study of the concept of poetry in the criticism of Eliot. Washington 1947.

Rajan, B. (ed). Eliot: a study of his writings by several hands. 1947 (Focus 3). Includes C. Brooks, The waste land: an analysis; E. Duncan-Jones, Ash Wednesday; H. L. Gardner, Four quartets: a commentary; B. Rajan, The unity of the Quartets; P. Wheelwright, Eliot's philosophical themes; A. Ridler, A question of speech; M. C. Bradbrook, Eliot's critical method; W. Mankowitz, Notes on Gerontion.

Sansom, C. The poetry of Eliot. 1947. Pamphlet.

Barry, Sr M. M. An analysis of the prosodic structure of selected poems of Eliot. Washington 1948.

Hyman, S. E. Eliot and tradition in criticism. In his Armed vision, New York 1948, 1955 (rev).

—— In his Poetry and criticism: four revolutions in literary taste, New York 1961. On Eliot's revaluation of Milton.

March, R. and M. J. Tambimuttu (ed). Eliot: a symposium from C. Aiken, L. Anceschi, G. B. Angioletti, W. H. Auden, G. Barker, M. Belgion, C. Bell, J. Betjeman, Amalendu Bose, R. Bottrall, E. M. Browne, E. Cecchi, N. Coghill, E. R. Curtius, Bishnu Dey, A. Dukes, L. Durrell, W. Empson, G. Every, G. S. Fraser, H. Fluchère, M. Hamburger, D. Hawkins, J. Heath-Stubbs, P. J. Jouve, Wyndham Lewis, E. F. C. Ludowyk, L. MacNeice, C. E. Magny, R. March, E. Montale, M. Moore, N. Moore, F. V. Morley, E. Muir, N. Nicholson, H. G. Porteus, M. Praz, K. Raine, J. Reeves, A. Ridler, G. Seferis, E. Sitwell, S. Spender, Tambimuttu, R. Todd, V. Watkins. 1948.

Schaeder, G. and H. H. Ein Weg zu Eliot. Hameln 1948.

Unger, L. (ed). Eliot: a selected critique. New York [1948]. Mainly rptd; contributors include: C. Aiken, R. Aldington, E. M. Forster, E. Pound, M. van Doren, P. E. More, M. Cowley, G. Hicks, H. J. Laski, D. Schwartz, J. C. Ransom, Y. Winters, V. W. Brooks, F. Nuhn, D. S. Savage, K. Shapiro, T. H. Thompson, E. Wilson, F. R. Leavis, I. A. Richards, F. O. Matthiessen, R. P. Blackmur, S. Spender, W. B. Yeats, A. Tate, M. Praz, C. Brooks, L. Unger, J. J. Sweeney, C. L. Barber, L. L. Martz.

—— Fusion and experience; Ash Wednesday; Eliot's rose-garden; Laforgue, Conrad, and Eliot. In his The man in the name: essays on the experience of poetry, Minneapolis [1956].

—— T. S. Eliot. Minneapolis [1961] (Univ of Minnesota Pamphlets on American Writers).

—— Eliot: moments and patterns. Minneapolis 1966.

Vietta, E. Die Selbstbehauptung des Abendlandes im Werk von Eliot. Hamburg 1948.

Wilson, F. Six essays on the development of Eliot. 1948.

Bowra, C. M. Eliot: The waste land. In his Creative experiment, 1949.

Brombert, V. H. The criticism of Eliot: problems of an 'impersonal theory' of poetry. New Haven 1949.

Drew, E. Eliot: the design of his poetry. New York 1949.

Gardner, H. The art of Eliot. 1949.

—— T. S. Eliot and the English poetic tradition. Nottingham 1966 (Byron Foundation Lecture 1965).

Smidt, K. Poetry and belief in the work of Eliot. Oslo 1949, London 1961 (rev).

Bradbrook, M. C. T. S. Eliot. 1950, 1960 (rev) (Br Council pamphlet).

Wynn, D. The integrity of Eliot. In Writers of our years, ed A. M. I. Fiskin, Denver 1950.

Greene, E. J. H. T. S. Eliot et la France. Paris 1951.

Mordell, A. Eliot's deficiencies as a social critic: Eliot, special pleader as book reviewer and literary critic. Girard Kansas 1951. Pamphlet.

Robbins, R. H. The Eliot myth. New York [1951].

Maxwell, D. E. S. The poetry of Eliot. 1952.

Musgrove, S. Eliot and Walt Whitman. Wellington 1952.

Scott, N. A. Rehearsals of discomposure – alienation and reconciliation in modern literature: Kafka, Silone, D. H. Lawrence, Eliot. New York 1952.

—— In his Modern literature and the religious frontier, New York 1958.

—— (ed). The new Orpheus: essays towards a Christian poetic. New York 1964.

—— (ed). Man in the modern theatre. Richmond Va 1965.

Beer, E. T. S. Eliot und der Antiliberalismus des xx. Jahrhunderts. Vienna 1953 (Wiener Beiträge zur englischen Philologie 61).

Freddi, G. Idea di religione in Eliot. Brescia 1953.

Morris, D. The poetry of G. M. Hopkins and Eliot in the light of the Donne tradition. Berne 1953 (Swiss Stud in English 33).

Nott, K. Mr Eliot's liberal worries. In her Emperor's clothes, 1953.

On the Four quartets of Eliot. 1953. Anon; foreword by R. Campbell. Rptd New York 1965 as by C. Masirevich (i.e. C. McNab).

Ozu, J. Eliot's poetic drama. Tokyo 1953. In Japanese.

Read, H. A point of intensity: Eliot. In his True voice of feeling, 1953.

Gamberini, S. La poesia di Eliot. Genoa 1954.

Wheelwright, P. Pilgrim in the wasteland. In his Burning fountain, Bloomington 1954.

Christie, E. Mystikk og poesi i Four quartets. In his Tendenser og profiler, Oslo 1955.

Margolis, S. The love song of J. Alfred Prufrock. In Interpretations, ed J. Wain 1955.

Martin, P. W. Experiment in depth: a study of the work of Jung, Eliot and Toynbee. 1955.

Quinn, Sr M. B. Eliot and Crane: protean techniques. In her Metamorphic tradition in modern poetry, New Brunswick 1955.

Sochatoff, A. F. In Lectures on some modern poets, Carnegie Ser in Eng 2 1955.

Davidson, A. The Eliot enigma: a critical examination of The waste land. 1956. Pamphlet.

Esch, A. Eliot als Literaturkritiker. In Sprache und Literatur Englands und Amerikas, ed A. C. Weber, Tübingen 1956 (Lehrgangsvorträge der Akademie Comburg 2).

Fukase, K. A study of Eliot. Tokyo 1956.

Galinsky, H. Deutschland in der Sicht von D. H. Lawrence und Eliot: eine Studie zum anglo-amerikanischen Deutschlandbild des 20. Jahrhunderts. Wiesbaden 1956.

— The expatriate poet's style with reference to Eliot and Auden. In English Stud Today ser 3, ed G. I. Duthie, Edinburgh [1964].

Krieger, M. Eliot: expression and impersonality. In his New apologists for poetry, Minneapolis 1956.

Melchiori, G. In his Tightrope walkers: studies of mannerism in modern English literature, 1956.

Moore, M. Eliot: 'It is not forbidden to think': reticent candor. In her Predilections, 1956.

Murry, J. M. The plays of Eliot. In his Unprofessional essays, 1956.

Nishiwaki, J. T. S. Eliot. Tokyo 1956. In Japanese.

Smith, G. Eliot's poetry and plays: a study in sources and meaning. Chicago 1956, 1960 (rev, with ch on The elder statesman).

'Buttle, Myra' (V. Purcell). The Sweeniad. 1957 (priv ptd), 1958. Parody of Eliot.

Ferrara, F. Introduzione a Murder in the cathedral di Eliot. Rome 1957.

Holroyd, S. Eliot and the 'intellectual soul'. In his Emergence from chaos, 1957.

Kermode, J. F. 'Dissociation of sensibility': modern symbolist readings of literary history. In his Romantic image, 1957.

Lombardo, A. Dalla scuola di Eliot alla scuola di Auden. In his Realismo e simbolismo, Rome 1957.

Martin, P. M. Mastery and mercy: a study of two religious poems, The wreck of the Deutschland by Hopkins, and Ash Wednesday by Eliot. 1957.

Strömsdörfer, I. Der Begriff der Zeit bei T. S. Eliot. Munich 1957.

Wildi, M. Die Dramen von Eliot. Zürich 1957.

Bodelsen, C. A. Eliot's Four quartets: a commentary. Copenhagen 1958.

— T. S. Eliot. In Fremmede digtere i det 20. århundrede, ed S. M. Kristensen, vol 2 Copenhagen 1968.

Braybrooke, N. (ed). T. S. Eliot: a symposium for his seventieth birthday. 1958. By R. Macaulay, P. Mairet, E. Sewell, E. M. Browne, R. Speaight, W. F. J. Knight, V. Cronin, J. M. Cameron, I. Murdoch, R. Preston, S. Smith, M. Jarrett-Kerr, D. E. S. Maxwell, J. Betjeman, G. S. Fraser et al.

Braybrooke, N. Eliot: a critical essay. Grand Rapids Michigan 1967.

Kumashiro, S. Eliot and the problem of poetry. Tokyo 1958. In Japanese.

Bloom, H. Lawrence, Blackmur, Eliot and the tortoise. In A D. H. Lawrence miscellany, ed H. T. Moore, Carbondale 1959.

Buckley, V. Poetry and morality: studies on the criticism of M. Arnold, Eliot and F. R. Leavis. 1959.

Donoghue, D. In his Third voice: modern British and American verse drama, Princeton 1959; rptd, abridged, in Kenner 1962, below.

Fraser, G. S. The waste land revisited; A language by itself. In his Vision and rhetoric, 1959.

Kenner, H. The invisible poet: Eliot. New York 1959.

Kenner, H. (ed). Eliot: a collection of critical essays. Englewood Cliffs NJ [1962] (Twentieth-Century Views).

Raybould, E. The man with three staves in the structure of The waste land. In Anglistische Studien: Festschrift zum 70. Geburtstag von Friedrich Wild, ed K. Brunner et al, Vienna 1959.

Senior, J. The detail of the pattern: Eliot. In his Way down and out: the occult in symbolist literature, Ithaca NY 1959.

Bergsten, S. Time and eternity: a study in the structure and symbolism of Eliot's Four quartets. Stockholm 1960.

Brett, R. L. Reason and imagination: a study of form and meaning in four poems, 1960. Includes Four quartets.

Hough, G. In his Image and experience: studies in a literary revolution, 1960.

Izzo, C. Dall'Arnaldo da Brescia di G. B. Niccolini a The waste land di Eliot per il tramite di W. D. Howells. In Studi in onore di Lorenzo Bianchi, Bologna 1960.

Jones, D. E. The plays of Eliot. 1960.

Lucy, S. Eliot and the idea of tradition. 1960.

Moorman, C. Arthurian triptych: mythic materials in Charles Williams, C. S. Lewis and Eliot. Berkeley and Los Angeles 1960 (Perspectives in Criticism 5).

— The suburbs of the city: Eliot and Dorothy L. Sayers. In his Precincts of felicity: the Augustan city of the Oxford Christians, Gainesville 1966.

Rumble, T. C. Some Grail motifs in Eliot's Prufrock. In Studies in American literature, ed W. McNeir and L. B. Levy 1960.

Starkie, E. In her From Gautier to Eliot: the influence of France on English literature 1851–1939. 1960.

Wright, G. T. W. The poet in the poem: the personae of Eliot, Yeats and Pound. Berkeley and Los Angeles 1960 (Perspectives in Criticism 4).

Etienne, F. Thomas Stearns Eliot. Brussels [1961]. In Dutch. Pamphlet.

Hoskot, S. S. Eliot: his mind and personality. Bombay 1961.

Jennings, E. Articulate music: a study of the mystical content in the plays and Four quartets of Eliot. In her Every changing shape, 1961.

Metscher, T. Eliots Burnt Norton: eine Interpretation. In Kleine Beiträge zur amerikanischen Literaturgeschichte, ed H. Galinsky and H.-J. Lang, Heidelberg 1961.

Salingar, L. G. Eliot: poet and critic. In The modern age, Pelican guide to English literature vol 7, ed B. Ford 1961.

Aguilar, E. Eliot: el hombre, no el viejo gato. Santiago [1962].

Benziger, J. G. In his Images of eternity: studies in the poetry of religious vision from Wordsworth to Eliot. Carbondale 1962.

Chinol, E. Poesia e tradizione nel pensiero critico di Eliot. In Studi in onore di Vittorio Lugli e Diego Valeri, Venezia 1962.

Cornwell, E. F. The 'still point': theme and variations in the writings of Eliot, Coleridge, Yeats, Henry James, Virginia Woolf and D. H. Lawrence. New Brunswick 1962.

Freed, L. Eliot: aesthetics and history. La Salle [1962].

Rees, T. R. Eliot, Rémy de Gourmont and dissociation of sensibility. In Studies in comparative literature, ed W. F. McNeir, Baton Rouge 1962.

Schlüter, K. Der Mensch als Schauspieler: Studien zur Deutung von Eliots Gesellschaftsdramen. Bonn 1962.

Watson, G. In his Literary critics: a study of English descriptive criticism, 1962 (Pelican), 1964 (rev).

Bullough, G. Christopher Fry and the 'revolt' against Eliot. In Experimental drama, ed W. A. Armstrong 1963.

Emge, C. A. Die Frage nach einem neuen Kulturbegriff: Betrachtungen am Leitfaden der Auffassung von Eliot. Wiesbaden 1963.

Frye, N. T. S. Eliot. Edinburgh 1963 (Writers and Critics).

George, A. G. Eliot: his mind and art. Bombay [1963] (Literary Perspectives 1).

Germer, R. Eliot: The family reunion. In Das moderne englische Drama: Interpretationen, ed H. Oppel, Berlin 1963.

— T. S. Eliots Anfänge als Lyriker 1905–15. Heidelberg 1966 (Beihefte zum Jahrbuch für Amerikastudien 17).

— Eliot: Journey of the Magi. In Die moderne englische Lyrik: Interpretationen, ed H. Oppel, Berlin 1967.

Harding, D. W. In his Experience into words: essays on poetry, 1963.

Hathorn, R. Y. Eliot's Murder in the cathedral: myth and history. In his Tragedy, myth and mystery, Bloomington 1963.

Jones, P. M. Laforgue's 'vers libre' and the form of The waste land. In his Assaults on French literature and other essays, Manchester [1963].

Papajewski, H. Eliot: the elder statesman. In Das moderne englische Drama: Interpretationen, ed H. Oppel, Berlin 1963.

Sinha, K. N. On Four quartets of Eliot. Ilfracombe [1963].

Smith, C. H. Eliot's dramatic theory and practice, from Sweeney Agonistes to The elder statesman. Princeton 1963.

Terada, T. Eliot: the centre of the desert. Tokyo 1963. In Japanese.

Thompson, E. Eliot: the metaphysical perspective. Carbondale [1963].

Andreach, R. J. Studies in structure: the stages of the spiritual life of four modern authors. New York 1964. Hopkins, Joyce, Eliot, Hart Crane.

Dehaura, D. J. The place of the classics in Eliot's Christian humanism. In Hereditas, ed F. Will, Austin 1964.

Headings, P. R. T. S. Eliot. New York [1964] (Twayne's US Authors 57).

Howarth, H. Notes on some figures behind Eliot. Boston 1964.

Jones, G. Approach to the purpose: a study of the poetry of Eliot. 1964.

Kennedy, R. S. Working out salvation with diligence: the plays of Eliot. Wichita Kansas 1964.

Knoll, R. E. (ed). Storm over The waste land. Chicago 1964. Collection of critical essays.

Reiss, H. Tradition in modern poetry: Eliot and Rilke: a comparison. In Proc of 4th Congress of International Comparative Lit Assoc vol 2, Fribourg 1964.

Stead, C. K. In his New poetic, 1964.

Toppen, W. H. Enkele achtergronden van het werk van Eliot, vooral in verband met de ideeën van I. Babbitt en T. E. Hulme. Groningen 1964.

Bowers, J. L. Eliot's Murder in the cathedral. Cape Town 1965.

Congress for Cultural Freedom. T. S. Eliot. Bombay 1965. Proceedings of a seminar held at St Stephen's College, Delhi. Includes O. Paz, Inaugural address; M. M. Bhalla, Poetry as constructs of meaning; R. L. Bartholomew, The life theme and its treatment in Eliot's poetry; J. P. Guha, Eliot's theory of the poetic process; Vinod Sena, The poet as playwright; M. K. Haldar, Eliot's concept of culture; discussion etc.

Ferry, D. The diction of American poetry. In American poetry, ed J. R. Brown et al, 1965.

Gupta, N. D. Plato to Eliot: a literary criticism. Allahabad 1965.

Lal, P. (ed). Eliot: homage from India. Calcutta [1965].

Miller, J. H. In his Poets of reality: six twentieth-century writers, Cambridge Mass 1965.

Praz, M. Eliot e il simbolismo. In Il simbolismo nella letteratura Nord-Americana, ed M. Praz, Florence 1965.

— Joyce, T. S. Eliot: due maestri dei moderni. Turin 1967.

Rai, V. The waste land: a critical study. Varanasi 1965.

Sen, S. K. Metaphysical tradition and Eliot. Calcutta 1965.

Weiss, K. Das Bild des Weges: ein Schlüssel zum Verständnis des Zeitlichen und Überzeitlichen in Eliots Four quartets. Bonn 1965.

Woodhouse, A. S. P. In his Poet and his faith: religion and poetry in England from Spenser to Eliot and Auden, Chicago 1965.

Browne, E. M. The making of a play: Eliot's Cocktail party. Cambridge 1966 (Judith Wilson Lecture 1966).

— The making of Eliot's plays. 1969.

Dembo, L. S. Eliot: fac hominem. In his Conceptions of reality in modern American poetry, Berkeley 1966.

Glass, M. S. Eliot: Christian poetry through liturgical allusion. In The twenties, ed R. E. Langford and W. E. Taylor, De Land Florida 1966.

Goodwin, K. L. Pound and Eliot. In his Influence of Ezra Pound, New York 1966.

Harrison, J. R. The reactionaries: Yeats, Lewis, Pound, Eliot, Lawrence: a study of the anti-democratic intelligentsia. 1966.

Hirai, M. and E. W. F. Tomlin (ed). Eliot: a tribute from Japan. Tokyo 1966.

Hirai, M. (ed). T. S. Eliot. Tokyo 1967 (Guide to English and American literature 18). In Japanese.

Holder, A. Three voyagers in search of Europe: a study of James, Pound and Eliot. Philadelphia [1966].

Levi, A. W. Three. In The hidden harmony: essays in honor of P. Wheelwright, ed O. Johnson et al, New York 1966. On Wallace Stevens, Ezra Pound and Eliot.

Lu, Fei-pai. Eliot: the dialectical structure of his theory of poetry. Chicago 1966.

Mortimer, A. In his Modern English poets: five introductory essays, Milan 1966, Toronto 1968 (enlarged).

Nevo, R. The vanished mind: or The waste land revisited. In Studies in English language and literature, ed A. and A. A. Mendilow, Jerusalem 1966.

Tate, A. (ed). Eliot: the man and his work. New York 1966. Reprints contents of Eliot no of Sewanee Rev 74 1966, below.

Baker, W. E. Browning and Eliot. In his Syntax in English poetry 1870–1930, Berkeley 1967.

Bullaro, J. J. The Dante of Eliot. In A Dante profile, ed F. Schettino, Los Angeles 1967.

Cahill, A. F. T. S. Eliot and the human predicament. Pietermaritzburg 1967.

Ellmann, R. In his Eminent domain: Yeats among Wilde, Joyce, Pound, Eliot and Auden, New York 1967, 1970 (corrected).

Fabricius, J. The unconscious and Eliot: a study in expressionism. Copenhagen 1967.

Jankowsky, K. R. Die Versauffassung bei Hopkins, den Imagisten und Eliot: Renaissance altgermanischen Formgestaltens in der Dichtung des 20. Jahrhunderts. Munich 1967.

Pearce, T. S. T. S. Eliot. 1967.

Spanos, W. V. In his Christian tradition in modern British verse drama, New Brunswick 1967.

Baker, J. V. T. S. Eliot. In American winners of the Nobel Literary Prize, ed W. G. French and W. E. Kidd, Norman Oklahoma 1968.

Bedi, J. The love song of J. Alfred Prufrock: an explication. In Variations on American literature, ed D. S. Maini, New Delhi 1968.

Caretti, L. T. S. Eliot in Italia: saggio e bibliografia 1923–65. Bari 1968.

Cox, C. B. and A. P. Hinchliffe (ed). Eliot—The waste land: a casebook. [1968].

Knust, H. Wagner, the king and The waste land. University Park Pa 1968.

Martin, J. (ed). A collection of critical essays on The waste land. Englewood Cliffs NJ 1968 (Twentieth-Century Interpretations).

Sharma, M. The spiritual quest in the poetry of Eliot. In Variations on American literature, ed D. S. Maini, New Delhi 1968.

Williams, H. Eliot: The waste land. 1968.

Bergonzi, B. (ed). Eliot—Four quartets: a casebook. 1969.

Fryxell, D. R. Understanding The love song of J. Alfred Prufrock. In Robert Frost's Chicken feathers and other lectures from the Augustana College NDEA Eng Inst, ed A. R. Huseboe, Sioux Falls 1969.

Helmcke, H. Das wüste Land bei T. S. Eliot und Thomas Wolfe. In Literatur und Sprache der Vereinigten Staaten: Aufsätze zu Ehren von Hans Galinsky, ed H. Helmcke et al, Heidelberg 1969.

Iyengar, K. R. S. Understanding Four quartets. In Indian essays in American literature: papers in honour of Robert E. Spiller, Bombay 1969.

LeCroy, A. Murder in the cathedral: a question of structure. In Essays in memory of Christine Burleson, ed T. G. Burton, Johnson City 1969.

Link, F. H. Das christliche Schauspiel Eliots. In Literatur und Sprache der Vereinigten Staaten: Aufsätze zu Ehren von Hans Galinsky, ed H. Helmcke et al, Heidelberg 1969.

Ludwig, R. M. In Fifteen modern American authors: a survey of research and criticism, ed J. R. Bryer, Durham NC 1969.

Lynen, J. F. Selfhood and the reality of time: Eliot. In his Design of the present: essays on time and form in American literature, New Haven 1969.

Naik, M. K. The characters in Eliot's plays. In Indian essays in American literature: papers in honour of Robert E. Spiller, Bombay 1969.

Porter, T. E. In his Myth and modern American drama, Detroit 1969.

Articles in Periodicals

Aiken, C. Divers realists. Dial 63 1917; rptd in his Scepticisms, New York 1919 (as Varieties of realism: W. W. Gibson, W. A. Bradley, Eliot). On Prufrock.

—— The scientific critic. Freeman 2 1921; rptd in his A reviewer's ABC, New York 1958. On The sacred wood.

—— An anatomy of melancholy. New Republic 7 Feb 1923; rptd ibid. On The waste land.

—— The poetic dilemma. Dial 82 1927.

—— After Ash Wednesday. Poetry 45 1934; rptd ibid. On After strange gods, The rock. *See* A reviewer's ABC for other rptd reviews of Eliot's books.

Pound, E. Drunken helots and Eliot. Egoist 4 1917. Referring to Arthur Waugh's criticism of Catholic anthology in Quart Rev 226 1916.

—— T. S. Eliot. Poetry 10 1917. On Prufrock; rptd in his Instigations, New York 1920, Literary essays 1954 etc.

—— Eliot's solid merit. New Eng Weekly 12 July 1934; rptd in his Polite essays, 1937; and, abridged, in Kenner, 1962, above.

Sinclair, M. Prufrock and other observations: a criticism. Little Rev 4 1917.

Is this poetry? Athenaeum 20 June 1919. By Virginia Woolf: unsigned. Review of Poems 1919 and of The critic in judgement, by J. M. Murry.

Cummings, E. E. T. S. Eliot. Dial 68 1920. Review of Poems, New York 1920; rptd in E. E. Cummings: a miscellany, New York 1958.

Murry, J. M. The eternal footman. Athenaeum 20 Feb 1920. Review of Ara vos prec.

—— The 'classical' revival. Adelphi 3 1926. On Eliot and Virginia Woolf.

—— Eliot on Shakespeare and Seneca. New Adelphi 1 1928; rptd in his Poets, critics, mystics, 1970.

—— The return of the Mayflower. New Adelphi 2 1929.

—— Eliot at Lambeth. Adelphi 2 1931.

—— The treason of the clerks. Adelphi 8 1934. Accuses Eliot of *je m'en fichisme*.

—— Mr Eliot's Cocktail party. Fortnightly 168 1950. Partly rptd in his Unprofessional essays, 1956, above.

—— A note on The family reunion. EC 1 1951. Reply by S. Floersheimer, ibid.

Van Doren, M. England's critical compass. Nation 4 May 1921.

Aldington, R. The work of Eliot. Little Rev 6 1922.

Dial Award. Dial 73 1922. Given for The waste land.

Ely, C. B. Whitman and the radicals as poets of democracy. Open Court 36 1922. Deals briefly with Eliot, inter al.

Seldes, G. T. S. Eliot. Nation 6 Dec 1922. On The waste land; rptd in Cox and Hinchliffe, 1968, above.

Wilson, E. The poetry of drouth. Dial 73 1922. The waste land.

—— T. S. Eliot. New Republic 13 Nov 1929. This and the previous item rptd, rev, in his Axel's castle, New York 1931, and in Unger, 1948, above.

—— Eliot and the Church of England. New Republic 24 April 1929. On For Lancelot Andrewes; rptd in his Shores of light, New York 1952.

—— 'Miss Buttle' and Mr Eliot. New Yorker 24 May 1958.

Bell, C. T. S. Eliot. Nation-Athenaeum 22 Sept 1923. On The waste land.

Lucas, F. L. The waste land. New Statesman 3 Nov 1923; rptd in Cox and Hinchliffe, 1968, above.

Monroe, H. A contrast. Poetry 21 1923. On The waste land.

Munson, G. B. The esotericism of Eliot. 1924: a magazine of the arts no 1 1924. Reply by E. Pound.

Fernandez, R. Le classicisme de T. S. Eliot. Nouvelle Revue Française 24 1925. Tr in his Messages, 1927.

Muir, E. Contemporary writers: no 3—Eliot. Nation-Athenaeum 29 Aug 1925; rptd in his Transitions: essays on contemporary literature, 1926.

—— Past and present. Atlantic Monthly 140 1927.

—— Murder in the cathedral. London Mercury 32 1935. Review.

Rickword, E. The modern poet. Calendar of Modern Letters 2 1925; rptd in Towards standards of criticism, ed F. R. Leavis 1933. On Poems 1909–25.

Richards, I. A. T. S. Eliot. Living Age 10 April 1926; rptd in his Principles of literary criticism, 1926.

Tate, A. A poetry of ideas. New Republic 30 June 1926.

—— Critique of Ash Wednesday. Hound & Horn 4 1932; rptd in his Reactionary essays, New York 1936 and in Kenner, 1962, above.

—— The reading of modern poetry. Purpose 10 1938.

Van Doorn, W. How it strikes a contemporary: new series. 1, American poetry. E Studies 8 1926. Criticism of Emily Dickinson, E. Arlington Robinson and Eliot.

Collins, H. P. The poetry of Eliot. Adelphi 4 1927.

Fergusson, F. Eliot and his impersonal theory of art. Amer Caravan 1927.

—— Action as passion: Tristan and Murder in the cathedral. Kenyon Rev 9 1947.

—— Three allegorists: Brecht, Wilder and Eliot. Sewanee Rev 64 1956.

Williamson, G. The talent of Eliot. Sewanee Rev 35 1927; rptd with addns Seattle 1929 (Univ of Washington Chapbooks 32).

—— The structure of The waste land. MP 47 1950.

—— T. S. Eliot 1888–1965. Modern Age 9 1965.

Curtius, E. R. Eliot als Dichter. Neue Schweizer Rundschau 32–33 1927. Rptd in his Kritische Essays zur europäischen Literatur, Bern 1950.

—— Eliot als Kritiker. Die Literatur 32 1929.

—— T. S. Eliot. Merkur (Baden-Baden) 3 1949.

Blackmur, R. P. T. S. Eliot. Hound & Horn 1 1928.

—— Eliot in prose. Poetry 42 1933.

—— The whole poet. Poetry 50 1937. On Collected poems 1909–35.

——, C. Greenberg, W. Phillips and I. A. Richards. Mr Eliot and notions of culture: a discussion. Partisan Rev 11 1944.

Blackmur, R. P. Eliot on culture. Nation 23 April 1949. Review.

—— In the hope of straightening things out. Kenyon Rev 13 1951; rptd in his Lion and the honeycomb, 1955.

Moore, T. S. Eliot and Shelley's Skylark. TLS 13 Dec 1928.

Empson, W. Some notes on Eliot. Experiment 4 1929.

Forster, E. M. Some of our difficulties. New York Herald Tribune 12 May 1929; rptd in Life & Letters 2 1929 (as Eliot and his difficulties); and in his Abinger harvest, 1936 (as T. S. Eliot).

—— The three Eliots. Listener 20 Jan 1949. On Notes towards the definition of culture; this and the next rptd in his Two cheers for democracy, 1951.

—— Mr Eliot's 'comedy'. Listener 23 March 1950. On The cocktail party.

Frost, A. C. Donne and Eliot. Cambridge Rev 17 May 1929.

Leavis, F. R. Eliot: a reply to the condescending. Cambridge Rev 8 Feb 1929.
— Restatements for critics. Scrutiny 1 1933. On Scrutiny and Criterion.
— Mr Eliot, Mr Wyndham Lewis and Lawrence. Scrutiny 3 1934. Review of After strange gods; rptd in his Common pursuit, 1952.
— Mr Eliot and education. Scrutiny 5 1936. On Essays ancient & modern.
— East Coker. TLS 26 Sept 1940. Letter.
— Eliot's later poetry. Scrutiny 11 1942. On The Dry Salvages; rptd in his Education and the university, 1943, and in Kenner, 1962, above.
— Approaches to Eliot. Scrutiny 15 1947. On Eliot, a study of his writings, ed B. Rajan; rptd in his Common pursuit, 1952.
— Poet as executant. Scrutiny 15 1947. Review of Eliot's recording of Four quartets.
— Eliot and Milton. Sewanee Rev 57 1949; rptd in his Common pursuit, 1952.
— Eliot and Lawrence. Scrutiny 18 1951; rptd in his D. H. Lawrence: novelist, 1955.
— Eliot's stature as a critic: a revaluation. Commentary 26 1958; rptd in his Anna Karenina and other essays, 1967 (as Eliot as critic).
— Eliot and the life of English literature. Massachusetts Rev 10 1969.
Quennell, P. Mr T. S. Eliot. Life & Letters 2 1929.
— Mr T. S. Eliot. New Statesman 18 April 1936.
Rossiter, A. P. The poetry of Eliot. Stud in Eng Lit (Tokyo) 9 1929.
Brown, E. K. Eliot: poet and critic. Canadian Forum 10 1930.
— Eliot and some enemies. UTQ 8 1938.
Howard, B. Eliot's poetry. New Statesman 8 Nov 1930. On Ash Wednesday.
Mangan, S. A note: on the somewhat premature apotheosis of Thomas Stearns Eliot. Pagany 1 1930.
Morrow, F. The serpent's enemy. Symposium 1 1930.
Schappes, M. V. The irrational malady. Symposium 1 1930.
— Eliot moves right. Modern Monthly 7 1933.
Zabel, M. D. Eliot in mid-career. Poetry 36 1930. Ash Wednesday; Ariel poems; Dante.
— The still point. Poetry 41 1932. Triumphal march; Difficulties of a statesman.
— The use of the poet. Poetry 44 1934. The use of poetry and the use of criticism.
— Poetry for the theatre. Poetry 45 1934. The rock.
Arns, K. Kulturpessimismus und christliche Ethik in der neuen englischen Dichtung. Der Gral March 1931.
Baba, M. Eliot as a reactionary critic. Stud in Eng Lit (Tokyo) 11 1931.
Beachcroft, T. O. Mysticism as criticism. Symposium 2 1931.
Collin, W. E. T. S. Eliot. Sewanee Rev 39 1931.
— Eliot the critic. Ibid.
Hilton, C. The poetry of Eliot. Eng Jnl 20 1931.
Mégret, H. T. S. Eliot. Bulletin de l'Association des Elèves de Sèvres 1931.
Mirsky, D. S. Eliot et la fin de la poésie bourgeoise. Echanges no 5 1931.
Moore, M. A machinery of satisfaction. Poetry 39 1931.
Nimr, A. Introduction à la poésie de T. S. Eliot. Echanges no 4 1931.
Powell, D. The poetry of Eliot. Life & Letters 7 1931; rptd in her Descent from Parnassus, 1934.
Rice, P. B. A modern poet's technique. Symposium 2 1931.
— Out of the waste land. Symposium 3 1932.
— The critic as prophet. Poetry 50 1937.
Taupin, R. The example of R. de Gourmont. Criterion 10 1931.
— The classicism of Eliot. Symposium 3 1932.

Williamson, H. R. Eliot and his conception of poetry. Bookman (London) 79 1931.
— Commentary on Eliot's Waste land. Bookman (London) 82 1932.
Zukovsky, L. American poetry 1920–30. Symposium 2 1931.
Burgum, E. B. A garland for John Donne. Symposium 3 1932. Review.
Frank, W. The universe of Eliot. New Republic 26 Oct 1932; rptd in his In the American jungle, New York 1937.
More, P. E. The cleft Eliot. Saturday Rev of Lit 12 Nov 1932; rptd in Unger, 1948, above. On Selected essays.
Rahv, P. T. S. Eliot. Fantasy 2 1932.
'Roberts, Michael' (W. E. Roberts). T. S. Eliot. Poetry Rev 23 1932.
— The poetry of Eliot. London Mercury 34 1936.
— Eliot's new play. London Mercury 39 1939. On The family reunion.
Stonier, G. W. Eliot and the plain reader. Fortnightly Rev 138 1932; rptd in his Gog Magog, 1933.
Warren, C. H. Approach to Eliot. Sackbut 12 1932.
Arakawa, T. Eliot's interpretation of Arnold and Pater. Stud in Eng Lit (Tokyo) 13 1933. In Japanese.
Bates, E. S. Eliot: leisure class laureate. Modern Monthly 7 1933.
Benét, W. R. Eliot again. Saturday Rev of Lit 21 Jan 1933.
Boynton, G. R. Without a parable: an encounter with the poetry of Eliot. Windsor Quart 1 1933.
Brown, L. Our contemporary poetry. Sewanee Rev 41 1933.
Daniells, J. R. Eliot and his relation to T. E. Hulme. UTQ 2 1933.
Harding, D. W. Eliot at Harvard. Scrutiny 2 1933. On The use of poetry and the use of criticism; rptd in F. R. Leavis (ed), A selection from Scrutiny, 1968 above.
— The rock. Scrutiny 3 1934; rptd in his Experience into words, 1963.
— T. S. Eliot 1925–35. Scrutiny 5 1936. On Collected poems 1909–35; rptd ibid.
— Christian or Liberal? Scrutiny 8 1939. On The idea of a Christian society.
— 'We have not reached conclusion'. Scrutiny 11 1943. Review of Little Gidding; replies by R. N. Higginbotham, F. R. Leavis, ibid; rptd in his Experience into words, 1963. The whole exchange rptd in Bergonzi, 1969, above.
— Progression of theme in Eliot's modern plays. Kenyon Rev 18 1956; rptd in his Experience into words, 1963.
House, H. Eliot as critic. New Oxford Outlook 1 1933.
Knickerbocker, W. S. Bellwether: an exercise in dissimulatio. Sewanee Rev 41 1933. Review of Selected essays.
MacCarthy, D. The work of Eliot. Sunday Times 3 Nov 1933.
Palmer, H. E. The hoax and earnest of The waste land. Dublin Mag 8 1933.
Powys, L. Tutor-poet. Week-End Rev 20 May 1933.
Spencer, T. The poetry of Eliot. Atlantic Monthly 151 1933.
Strong, R. The critical attitude of Eliot. London Quart & Holborn Rev 158 1933.
Wheelwright, P. A contemporary classicist. Virginia Quart Rev 9 1933.
— The Burnt Norton trilogy. Chimera 1 1942.
Wellek, R. Thomas Stearns Eliot. Listy pro umění a kritiku 1 1933.
— The criticism of Eliot. Sewanee Rev 64 1956.
Calverton, V. F. Eliot: an inverted Marxian. Modern Monthly 8 1934.
Gillet, L. Eliot et les faux dieux. Revue des Deux Mondes 1 July 1934.
Irvine, L. Eliot among the critics. Monologue 1 1934.
Nicoll, A. Eliot and the revival of classicism. Eng Jnl (College edn) 23 1934.

Sengupta, S. K. A new force in English poetry. Calcutta Rev 50 1934.

Shiga, M. Reason and belief: an essay on Eliot. Stud in Eng Lit (Tokyo) 14 1934. In Japanese.

Thompson, T. H. The bloody wood. London Mercury 29 1934; rptd in Unger 1948, above.

Turnell, M. Tradition and Eliot. Colosseum 1 1934.

—— The poetry of Jules Laforgue. Scrutiny 5 1936.

—— Eliot's new play. Scrutiny 8 1939. Family reunion.

Wecter, D. The Harvard exiles. Virginia Quart Rev 10 1934.

Brown, W. C. Eliot and the demon of the ego. New Humanist 8 1935.

Good, T. Review of The rock. New Oxford Outlook 2 1935.

Hara, I. Poetry and belief: Richards versus Eliot. Stud in Eng Lit (Tokyo) 15 1935. In Japanese.

Häusermann, H. W. Eliots religiöse Entwicklung. E Studien 69 1935.

—— East Coker and The family reunion. Life & Letters Today 47 1945.

Jennings, H. Eliot and Auden and Shakespeare. New Verse no 18 1935. On Murder in the cathedral.

Kronenberger, L. Eliot as critic. Nation 17 April 1935.

Loring, M. L. S. Eliot on Matthew Arnold. Sewanee Rev 43 1935.

Oliphant, E. H. C. Tourneur and Eliot. SP 32 1935.

Scarfe, F. The achievement of Eliot. Cambridge Rev 15 Nov 1935.

Stone, G. Plays by Eliot and Auden. American Rev 6 1935. Review of Murder in the cathedral and The dog beneath the skin by Auden and Isherwood.

—— Morals and poetry. American Rev 9 1937.

Arvin, N. About Eliot. New Republic 15 Jan 1936.

Cowley, M. Afterthoughts on Eliot. New Republic 20 May 1936.

—— Eliot's ardent critics—and Eliot. New York Herald Tribune Book Rev 13 March 1949.

Downey, H. Eliot: poet as playwright. Virginia Quart Rev 12 1936. Review of The rock and Murder in the cathedral.

Elliott, G. R. Eliot and Irving Babbitt. Amer Rev 7 1936.

Hatcher, H. Drama in verse: Anderson, Eliot, Macleish. Eng Jnl 25 1936.

Hawkins, A. D. Fiction chronicle. Criterion 15 1936.

Hennecke, H. T. S. Eliot: der Dichter als Kritiker. Europäische Rev 12 1936.

Hicks, G. Eliot in our time. New Masses 11 Feb 1936.

Humphries, R. Eliot's poetry. New Masses 18 Aug 1936.

Krutch, J. W. Holy blissful martyr. Nation 8 April 1936.

Laboulle, M. J. J. Eliot and some French poets. Revue de Littérature Comparée 16 1936. Chiefly on Laforgue.

Otake, M. Eliot: the lyric prophet of chaos. Stud in Eng Lit (Tokyo) 16 1936. In Japanese.

Rees, G. A French influence on Eliot: Rémy de Gourmont. Revue de Littérature Comparée 16 1936.

Brooks, C. The waste land: an analysis. Southern Rev 3 1937; rptd (rev, as The waste land: critique of a myth) in his Modern poetry and the tradition, Chapel Hill 1939, New York 1965 (new introd). The waste land: an analysis rptd in Rajan, 1947, above. The waste land: critique of a myth rptd in Unger, 1948, above.

Burke, K. Acceptance and rejection. Southern Rev 2 1937.

Cattaui, G. Eliot: poète symboliste et chrétien. Vie Intellectuelle 10 Dec 1937.

—— Notes sur Eliot. Journal des Poètes 15 Nov 1951.

Davray, H. D. L'influence de Laforgue et de Péguy sur Eliot. Mercure de France 15 July 1937.

Praz, M. Eliot e Dante. Letteratura 1 1937; tr in Southern Rev 2 1937; rptd in Unger 1948, above, and in Praz, The flaming heart, Garden City NY 1958.

—— T. S. Eliot. L'Italia che scrive 39 1956.

—— Thomas Stearns Eliot. Terzo programma no 2 1965.

Brown, C. S., jr. Eliot and die Droste. Sewanee Rev 46 1938. Annette von Droste-Hülshoff's Durchwachte Nacht and Rhapsody on a windy night.

Harvard Advocate 125 1938. Homage to Eliot, by a number of writers.

Harvey-Jellie, W. Eliot among the prophets? Dalhousie Rev 18 1938.

Morrison, T. Ash Wednesday: a religious history. New England Quart 11 1938.

Van der Vat, D. G. The poetry of Eliot. E Studies 20 1938.

Bodkin, M. The Eumenides and present-day consciousness. Adelphi 15 1939. Review of The family reunion.

Deutsch, B. Eliot and the Laodiceans. Amer Scholar 9 1939.

Hawkins, D. Hamlet and Eliot. New Eng Weekly 20 July 1939.

Horton, P. Speculations on sin. Kenyon Rev 1 1939. Review of The family reunion.

Howarth, R. G. Eliot's literary reminiscences. N & Q 176 1939, 179 1940.

Ransom, J. C. Eliot as dramatist. Poetry 54 1939. Essay-review of The family reunion.

—— Eliot and the metaphysicals. Accent 1 1941.

—— The inorganic muses. Kenyon Rev 5 1943.

—— The poems of Eliot: a perspective. Nat Rev 127 1952.

—— Gerontion. Sewanee Rev 74 1966.

—— Eliot: a postscript. Southern Rev 4 1968.

Rousseaux, A. Mort d'une revue [The Criterion]: sur un texte de T. S. Eliot. Revue Universelle 76 1939.

—— La poésie de Eliot. Figaro Littéraire 27 Dec 1947.

Unger, L. Notes on Ash Wednesday. Southern Rev 4 1939; rptd in his Eliot: a selected critique, 1948, and in his Man in the name, 1956, above.

—— Eliot's rose garden: a persistent theme from the Vita nuova. Southern Rev 7 1942; rptd ibid.

Weidlé, W. Le renouveau du drama poétique en Angleterre et la Réunion de famille de T. S. Eliot. Le Mois 9 1939.

Yamamoto, T. Eliot as a literary critic. Stud in Eng Lit (Tokyo) 19 1939. In Japanese.

—— Eliot as a critic of culture. Stud in Eng Lit (Tokyo) 20 1940. In Japanese.

Barber, C. L. Eliot after strange gods. Southern Rev 6 1940; rptd in Unger, 1948, above, as Strange gods at Eliot's Family reunion.

Fluchère, H. Un grand poète anglais: Eliot. Cahiers du Sud 224 1940.

—— Le drame poétique de T. S. Eliot: The cocktail party. Etudes Anglaises 5 1952.

—— Un théâtre poétique intérieur. Cahiers du Sud 359 1961.

—— Eliot: ou l'intelligence faite homme. Nouvelles Littéraires 14 Jan 1965.

Kadoma, S. Arnold and Eliot. Stud in Eng Lit (Tokyo) 20 1940. In Japanese.

Porter, K. A. Notes on a criticism of Thomas Hardy. Southern Rev 6 1940.

—— On first meeting Eliot. Shenandoah 12 1961.

—— From the notebooks of Katherine Anne Porter: Yeats, Joyce, Eliot, Pound. Southern Rev new ser 1 1965.

Shapiro, L. The medievalism of Eliot. Poetry 56 1940.

Battles with words. TLS 22 Feb 1941. On East Coker.

Church, R. Eliot: a search for foundations. Fortnightly 169 1941; rptd in his Eight for immortality, 1941.

Cunningham, A. M. Eliot's poem East Coker. Downside Rev 59 1941.

Masters, C. Analysis of Burnt Norton. Amer Prefaces 6 1941.

Montgomerie, W. Harry, meet Mr Prufrock: Eliot's dilemma. Life & Letters Today 31 1941.

Sweeney, J. J. East Coker: a reading. Southern Rev 6 1941; rptd in Unger, 1948, and Bergonzi, 1969, above.

—— Little Gidding: introductory to a reading. Poetry 62 1943.

Winters, Y. T. S. Eliot: the illusion of reaction. Kenyon Rev 3 1941; reply by L. O. Coxe, ibid; rptd in his Anatomy of nonsense, Norfolk Conn 1943.

Bradbrook, M. C. The liturgical tradition in English verse: Herbert and Eliot. Theology 44 1942.
— The lyric and dramatic in the latest verse of Eliot. Ibid.
— Little Gidding. Theology 46 1943.
'Orwell, George' (E. A. Blair). T. S. Eliot. Poetry (London) 7 1942. On Burnt Norton, East Coker, Dry Salvages; rptd in his Collected essays vol 2, 1968.
Rowland, J. The spiritual background of Eliot. New Church Mag 61 1942.
Smith, D. F. Neither 'snow-bound' nor moribund. New Mexico Quart Rev 12 1942.
The Explicator 1943 etc. The following poems by Eliot have been explicated:
    Animula (T. A. Stroud 28 1969).
    Ash Wednesday (D. N. Dwyer 9 1950; E. M. Sickels 9 1950; V. Freimarck 9 1950).
    Burbank with a Baedeker (L. G. Locke 3 1945).
    Burnt Norton (A. O. Lewes 8 1949).
    The cocktail party (R. B. Shuman 17 1959).
    La figlia che piange (V. Hall, jr 5 1946).
    Four quartets (J. Beaver 11 1953).
    A game of chess (H. M. Schwalb 11 1953).
    Gerontion (W. R. Eshelman 4 1946; F. A. Pottle 4 1946; M. P. Pope 6 1948; G. Smith 7 1949; R. M. Brown and J. B. Yokelson 15 1957; T. Culbert 17 1958; E. F. Daniels 17 1959; G. Monteiro 18 1960; F. Dye 18 1960; R. B. Kaplan and R. J. Wall 19 1961; C. Griffith 21 1963).
    The hippopotamus (H. M. McLuhan 2 1944; F. Lee Utley 3 1944; C. Meyer 8 1949).
    The hollow men (R. S. Kinsman 8 1950).
    Journey of the Magi (J. H. Wills 12 1954; M. Church 18 1960; R. O. Kaplan 19 1960).
    The love song of J. Alfred Prufrock (D. N. Dwyer 9 1951; C. J. Fish 8 1950; J. Virtue 13 1954; L. H. Powers 14 1956; A. E. Waterman 17 1959; J. L. Jackson 18 1960; W. J. Stuckey 19 1961; R. White 20 1961; G. Smith 21 1962; I. S. Dunn 22 1963; J. Bracker 25 1966).
    Sunday Service (A. Shulenburger 10 1952).
    Sweeney among the nightingales (L. Kirschbaum and R. P. Basler 2 1943; C. C. Walcutt 2 1944; E. R. Homan 17 1959).
    The waste land (A. Cook 6 1947; E. M. Sickels 7 1948, 9 1950; L. Kemp 7 1949, 8 1950; L. A. Cotten 9 1950; L. Glazier 8 1950; R. Smith 9 1950; W. Weathers 9 1951; H. M. Schwalb 11 1953; J. R. Baker 14 1956; W. H. Marshall 17 1959; R. E. Fartin 21 1962, 21 1963; J. D. Merritt 23 1964; H. Knust 23 1965; D. Kramer 24 1966).
    Whispers of immortality (C. C. Walcutt 7 1948; Sr M. Cleophas 8 1949; V. Strandberg 17 1959).
Matthiessen, F. O. Eliot's Quartets. Kenyon Rev 5 1943; rptd in his Achievement of Eliot, 1947, above.
Price, F. The verse of Little Gidding. N & Q 184 1943.
Trilling, L. Eliot's Kipling. Nation 16 Oct 1943; rptd in his Liberal imagination 1941 (as Kipling).
Waggoner, H. H. Eliot and The hollow men. Amer Lit 15 1943.
Williams, C. A dialogue on Eliot's poem. Dublin Rev 212 1943. Four quartets.
Bradford, C. Footnotes to East Coker: a reading. Sewanee Rev 52 1944; rptd in Bergonzi 1969, above.
Campbell, H. M. An examination of modern critics: Eliot. Rocky Mountain Rev 8 1944.
Craig, A. The ideology of Eliot. Voices no 1 1944.
Jack, P. M. A review of reviews of Eliot's Four quartets. Amer Bookman 1 1944.
Marnau, F. Mr Eliot's music. Poetry Quart 6 1944.
Muir, K. A brief introduction to the method of Eliot. Durham Univ Jnl 5 1944.
— Kipling and Eliot. N & Q 199 1954.
Muraoka, I. Eliot's The waste land. Stud in Eng Lit (Tokyo) 24 1944-5. In Japanese.

Shand, J. Around Little Gidding. Nineteenth Century 136 1944.
Vivas, E. The objective correlative of Eliot. Amer Bookman 1 1944.
Battenhouse, R. W. Eliot's The family reunion as Christian prophecy. Christendom 10 1945.
Chase, R. The sense of the present. Kenyon Rev 7 1945.
— Eliot in Concord. Amer Scholar 16 1947.
Dupee, F. E. Difficulty as style. Amer Scholar 14 1945.
Foster, G. W. The archetypal imagery of Eliot. PMLA 60 1945.
Fowlie, W. Eliot and Tchelitchew. Accent 5 1945.
— Jorge Guillén, Marianne Moore, Eliot: some recollections. Poetry 90 1957.
Hackett, C. A. La poésie anglaise contemporaine. Confluences new ser 6 1945.
Hodin, J. P. Eliot on the condition of man today. Horizon 12 1945.
Peschmann, H. The later poetry of Eliot: the Four quartets and their relationship to his earlier work. Eng 5 1945.
— The significance of Eliot. Wind & Rain 6 1949.
— The cocktail party: some links between the poems and plays of Eliot. Wind & Rain 7 1950.
Pope, J. C. Prufrock and Raskolnikov. Amer Lit 17 1945.
— Prufrock and Raskolnikov again. Amer Lit 18 1947.
Schwartz, D. Eliot as the international hero. Partisan Rev 12 1945; rptd in Unger 1948, in Knoll 1964, and in Martin 1968, above.
— The literary dictatorship of Eliot. Partisan Rev 16 1949; rptd (rev) in Literary opinion in America, ed M. D. Zabel [1951].
— Eliot's voice and his voices. Poetry 85 1955.
Speaight, R. The later poetry of Eliot. Dublin Rev 216 1945.
— Sartre and Eliot. Drama new ser 17 1950.
— The plays of Eliot. Month 30 1963.
— Eliot: ou l'intelligence d'une sensibilité. Revue Générale Belge no 3 1965.
— T. S. Eliot, O. M.: a birthday tribute. Listener 25 Sept 1958.
Tindall, W. Y. Exiles: Rimbaud to Joyce. Amer Scholar 14 1945.
— Eliot in America: the recantation of Eliot. Amer Scholar 16 1947.
Vallette, J. Remarques sur le théâtre de T. S. Eliot. La Nef 2 June 1945.
— On parle de T. S. Eliot. Mercure de France no 1175 1961.
Blissett, W. The argument of Eliot's Four quartets. UTQ 15 1946.
— T. S. Eliot. Canadian Forum 28 1948.
Coats, R. H. An anchor for the soul: a study of Eliot's later verse. Hibbert Jnl 44 1946. On Four quartets.
Coomaraswamy, A. K. Primordial images. PMLA 61 1946; see also G. W. Foster, ibid.
Mason, H. A. Elucidating Eliot. Scrutiny 14 1946. On Four quartets.
Moloney, M. F. Eliot and critical tradition. Thought 21 1946.
— The critical faith of Eliot. Thought 22 1947.
Railing, P. Classicism in modern poetry. Poetry Rev Oct-Dec 1946.
Smith, F. J. A reading of East Coker. Thought 20 1946.
Smith, G. Observations on Eliot's Death by water. Accent 6 1946.
— Eliot and Sherlock Holmes. N & Q 193 1948.
— Eliot's Lady of the rocks. N & Q 194 1949.
— Charles-Louis Philippe and Eliot. Amer Lit 22 1950.
— Tourneur and Little Gidding; Corbière and East Coker. MLN 65 1950.
— The Fortuneteller in Eliot's Waste land. Amer Lit 25 1954.
Weiss, T. Eliot and the courtyard revolution. Sewanee Rev 54 1946.
Brown, W. C. Eliot without the nightingales. Univ of Kansas City Rev 14 1947.

Daiches, D. Some aspects of Eliot. College Eng 9 1947.
— T. S. Eliot. Yale Rev 38 1949.
Guidacci, M. I Quartetti di Eliot. Letteratura 9 1947.
Immagine Nov–Dec 1947. Special no on Eliot.
McCallum, H. R. The waste land after twenty-five years. Here & Now 1 1947.
Macri, O. Eliot e il classicismo europeo. Rassegna d'Italia 2 1947.
Martz, L. L. The wheel and the point: aspects of imagery and theme in Eliot's later poetry. Sewanee Rev 55 1947; rptd in his Poem and the mind, New York 1966.
Orsini, N. Nota in margine ad una poesia di Eliot. Letteratura 9 1947.
— Eliot e la teoria delle convenzioni drammatiche. Letterature Moderne 4 1953; tr in Trans of Wisconsin Acad 43 1954.
Smidt, K. Lyrikeren T. S. Eliot. Spektrum no 4 1947.
— Point of view in Eliot's poetry. Orbis Litterarum 14 1959.
— Eliot and W. B. Yeats. Revue des Langues Vivantes 31 1965.
— T. S. Eliot—tiden og teatret. Minerva's Kvartalsskrift 9 1965.
Smith, R. G. Eliot's Family reunion in the light of Buber's I and thou. Theology 50 1947.
Anér, K. Kipling and Eliot. Samtid och Framtid 5 1948.
Astre, G.-A. T. S. Eliot, poète spirituel. Critique 4 1948.
Bayley, J. Eliot: poet and portent. Nat Rev 131 1948. Review of Unger 1948, above.
Bischoff, D. Der Mord im Münster. Die Sammlung (Göttingen) 3 1948.
Brotman, D. B. Eliot: the music of ideas. UTQ 18 1948.
Clemen, W. T. S. Eliot. Deutsche Beiträge (Munich) 2 1948.
Dulęba, W. Poezja T. S. Eliota. Znak no 7 1948.
Fiera Letteraria 14 Nov 1948. Special no on Eliot.
Flint, R. W. The Four quartets reconsidered. Sewanee Rev 56 1948; rptd in Bergonzi 1969, above.
Fry, M. (ed). The poetic work of Eliot. Br Annual of Lit 1948.
Glicksberg, C. I. Eliot as critic. Arizona Quart 4 1948.
— The journey that must be taken: spiritual quest in Eliot's plays. Southwest Rev 40 1955.
— The spirit of irony in Eliot's plays. Prairie Schooner 29 1955.
Greene, E. J. H. Jules Laforgue et Eliot. Revue de Littérature Comparée 22 1948.
Hernigman, R. Two worlds and epiphany. Bard Rev 2 1948. Compares Eliot and Wallace Stevens.
Hesse, W. The waste land and the Duino elegies. Lingua (Univ of Cape Town) 1 1948.
Hirai, M. The problems of human nature in Eliot. Stud in Eng Lit (Tokyo) 25 1948. In Japanese.
Meyerhoff, H. Mr Eliot's evening service. Partisan Rev 15 1948.
Mortimer, R. Mr T. S. Eliot, O.M. Sunday Times 4 Jan 1948.
O'Connor, W. V. Gerontion and the Dream of Gerontius. Furioso 3 1948.
Pellegrini, A. Una conversazione londinese con T. S. Eliot e i Four quartets. Belfagor 3 1948. Tr in Sewanee Rev 57 1949.
Profile: T. S. Eliot, O.M. Observer 7 March 1948.
Rebora, P. Eliot e la poesia possibile. L'Ultima 3 1948.
Schoeck, R. J. Eliot, Mary, Queen of Scots, and Guillaume de Machaut. MLN 63 1948.
Traversi, D. A. The waste land revisited. Dublin Rev 221 1948.
— Los cuartetos de T. S. Eliot. Filología Moderna 1 1960.
Anceschi, L. Eliot, la poesia, l'Europa. Humanitas 4 1949.
— Eliot o le difficoltà del mondo. La Rassegna d'Italia 4 1949.

Bantock, G. H. Eliot and education. Scrutiny 17 1949.
Barker, G. A note for Eliot. New Eng Rev March 1949. An interpretation of Eliot's character.
Burney, S. M. H. The poetry of Eliot. Modern Rev (Calcutta) 85 1949.
Clark, J. A. Eliot and A. C. Benson's Fitzgerald. South Atlantic Quart 48 1949.
Danby, J. F. Intervals during rehearsals. Cambridge Jnl 2 1949.
Eliot, T. S. and I. Hamilton. Comments on Eliot's new play The cocktail party. World Rev new ser 9 1949. Interview with Eliot followed by Hamilton's Critic's view.
Johnson, M. The ghost of Swift in Four quartets. MLN 64 1949.
Kenner, H. Eliot's moral dialectic. Hudson Rev 2 1949.
— Prufrock of St Louis. Prairie Schooner 31 1957.
— Dante tra Pound ed Eliot. Verri no 18 1964.
— Eliot and the tradition of the anonymous. College Eng 28 1967.
Lehmann, T. Begegnung mit T. S. Eliot. Neuphilologische Zeitschrift 1 1949.
Levý, J. Ideový základ tvůrčí metody T. S. Eliota. (The foundation of the creative method of Eliot). Časopis pro moderní filologii 32 1949.
— Synthesis of antitheses in the poetry of Eliot. EC 2 1952.
— Rhythmical ambivalence in the poetry of Eliot. Anglia 77 1959.
Mende, G. Nobelpreis für einen Philister. Einheit (Leipzig) 4 1949.
Obertello, A. Eliot, premio Nobel 1948. Studium 45 1949.
Page, L. A. 'Cleansing affection from the temporal'— notes on Burnt Norton. Congregational Quart 27 1949.
Peter, J. The family reunion. Scrutiny 16 1949; rptd in A selection from Scrutiny, ed F. R. Leavis vol 1, 1968, above.
— Sin and soda. Scrutiny 17 1950–1. On The cocktail party; rptd ibid.
— A new interpretation of The waste land. EC 2 1952.
— Murder in the cathedral. Sewanee Rev 61 1953; rptd in Kenner 1962, above.
Pfeffer, F. Gespräch mit T. S. Eliot. Rheinischer Merkur (Koblenz) 4 1949.
Pierstorff, E. Eliot, the Swedish players and the Norwegian public. Norseman July–Aug 1949. Family reunion performed in Oslo.
Rago, H. Eliot on culture. Commonweal 50 1949.
Raine, K. The art of Eliot. Britain Today 164 1949.
Redman, B. R. Eliot: in sight of posterity. Saturday Rev of Lit 12 March 1949.
Reinsberg, M. A footnote to Four quartets. Amer Lit 21 1949.
Skórzewska, T. T. S. Eliot o kulturze. Zycie no 10 1949.
Stamm, R. The Orestes theme in three plays by O'Neill, Eliot and Sartre. E Studies 30 1949.
Suhrkamp, P. T. S. Eliot und das Modell des antiken Dramas: Einführung in Der Familientag. Thema (Hamburg) 4 1949.
Vinograd, S. S. The accidental: a clue to structure in Eliot's poetry. Accent 9 1949.
Viswanathan, K. Matthew Arnold and Eliot. New Rev (Calcutta) 29 1949.
Waldson, C. M. T. S. Eliot. Neuphilologische Zeitschrift 1 1949.
Ward, A. Speculations on Eliot's time world: an analysis of The family reunion in relation to Hulme and Bergson. Amer Lit 21 1949.
Wormhoudt, A. A psychoanalytic interpretation of The love song of J. Alfred Prufrock. Perspective 2 1949.

Worthington, J. The epigraphs to the poetry of Eliot. Amer Lit 21 1949.

Arrowsmith, W. English verse drama (2): The cocktail party. Hudson Rev 3 1950.

— Transfiguration in Eliot and Euripides. Sewanee Rev 63 1955.

— Eliot and Euripides. Arion 4 1965.

Bain, D. The cocktail party. Nine 2 1950. Review.

Barrett, W. Dry land, Dry Martini. Partisan Rev 17 1950. Review.

Bevan, I. T. S. Eliot est maintenant un auteur à succès. Le Figaro Littéraire 2 Sept 1950.

Bland, D. S. The tragic hero in modern literature. Cambridge Jnl 3 1950.

— Eliot on the Underground. MLN 68 1953.

— Eliot's case-book. MLN 75 1960. On The family reunion.

Carne-Ross, D. The position of The family reunion in the work of Eliot. Rivista di Letterature Moderne 1 1950.

Cleophas, Sr M. Notes on Four quartets. Renascence 2 1950.

— Ash Wednesday: the Purgatorio in a modern mode. Comparative Lit 11 1959.

The cocktail party. Wind & Rain 7 1950.

D., A. Some notes on The waste land. N & Q 195 1950.

— More notes on The waste land. N & Q 196 1951.

Fussell, P., jr. A note on The hollow men. MLN 65 1950.

Greenberg, C. Eliot: the criticism, the poetry. Nation 9 Dec 1950.

Hamalian, L. Mr Eliot's Saturday evening service. Accent 10 1950.

— Wishwood revisited. Renascence 12 1960. On The family reunion.

Heywood, R. Everybody's cocktail party. Renascence 3 1950.

Kramer, H. Eliot in New York. Western Rev 14 1950.

McLaughlin, J. J. A daring metaphysic: The cocktail party. Renascence 3 1950.

McLuhan, H. M. Eliot's historical decorum. Renascence 2 1950.

Maxwell, J. C. Reflections on Four quartets. Month new ser 4 1950.

— Flaubert in The waste land. E Studies 44 1963.

— Eliot and Husserl. N & Q 209 1964.

— The Dry Salvages: a possible echo of Graham Greene. N & Q 209 1964.

Morris, R. L. Eliot's Game of chess and Conrad's The return. MLN 65 1950.

Niedermayer, F. Eliot: der Dichter, Kritiker, Laientheologe. Stimmen der Zeit (Freiburg) 145 1950.

Pick, J. A note on The cocktail party. Renascence 3 1950.

Robbins, R. H. The Eliot myth. Science & Society 14 1950.

— A possible analogue for The cocktail party. E Studies 34 1953.

Russi, A. T. S. Eliot e il teatro. Lo Spettatore Italiano 3 1950.

Sen, M. K. The waste land: an attempt at a commentary. Modern Rev (Calcutta) 88 1950.

— Eliot's 'objective correlative'. Visvabharati Quart 22 1957.

— A psychological interpretation of The waste land. Literary Criterion (Mysore) 3 1957.

Shepherd, T. B. Four quartets re-examined. London Quart & Holborn Rev 185 1950.

Sherek, H. On giving a Cocktail party. Theatre Arts Monthly 34 1950.

Vincent, C. J. A modern pilgrim's progress. Queen's Quart 57 1950. On The cocktail party.

Wimsatt, W. K., jr. Eliot's comedy. Sewanee Rev 58 1950. On The cocktail party.

— Eliot's weary gestures of dismissal. Massachusetts Rev 7 1966.

Wool, S. Weston revisited. Accent 10 1950. On The cocktail party.

Adair, P. M. Eliot's Murder in the cathedral. Cambridge Jnl 4 1951.

Bateson, F. W. Dissociation of sensibility. EC 1 1951. See also later contributions by E. Thompson and F. W. Bateson, 1952, and I. A. Richards, A cooking egg: final scramble, EC 4 1954; F. W. Bateson, ibid.

— Burbank with a Baedeker, Eliot with a Laforgue. Review 4 1962.

— Eliot: the poetry of pseudo-learning. Jnl of General Education 20 1968.

— Eliot: 'impersonality' fifty years after. Southern Rev 5 1969.

Bergel, L. La fase più recente del pensiero critico di T. S. Eliot. Lo Spettatore Italiano 4 1951.

Bradbury, J. M. Four quartets: the structural symbolism. Sewanee Rev 59 1951.

Brett, R. L. Ambiguity and Mr Eliot. English 8 1951.

— Mysticism and incarnation in Four quartets. English 16 1966.

Child, R. C. The early critical work of Eliot: an assessment. College Eng 12 1951.

Emery, S. W. Saints and Eliot. Emory Univ Quart 7 1951.

Hollis, C. Saint of the cocktail bar? Listener 30 Aug 1951.

Knox, G. A. Quest for the word in Eliot's Four quartets. ELH 18 1951.

Melchiori, G. Echoes in The waste land. E Studies 32 1951; rptd in his Tight rope walkers: studies of mannerism in modern English literature, 1956.

— Eliot and the theatre. Eng Miscellany (Rome) 4 1953; rptd in his Tightrope walkers, 1956.

— La commedia degli equivoci. Lo Spettatore Italiano 7 1954. On The confidential clerk; rptd in pt in his Tightrope walkers, 1956.

— The lotus and the rose: D. H. Lawrence and Eliot's Four quartets. Eng Miscellany (Rome) 5 1954; rptd in his Tightrope walkers, 1956.

— The waste land and Ulysses. E Studies 35 1954; rptd in his Tightrope walkers, 1956.

— L'ultima commedia di Eliot. Studi Americani 5 1959. On The elder statesman.

— Eliot and Apollinaire. N & Q 209 1964.

Meyer, C. Some unnoted religious allusions in Eliot's The hippopotamus. MLN 66 1951.

Munz, P. The devil's dialectic. Hibbert Jnl 49 1951.

Politi, F. Due traduzioni delle poesie di Eliot. Belfagor 6 1951.

Reed, H. Towards The cocktail party. Listener 10–17 May 1951.

— If and perhaps and but. Listener 18 June 1953.

Squires, J. R. Literary intelligence: Harvard. Western Rev 15 1951.

Stepanchev, S. The origin of J. Alfred Prufrock. MLN 66 1951.

Symes, G. Eliot and old age. Fortnightly 169 1951.

Theall, D. F. Traditional satire in Eliot's 'Coriolan'. Accent 11 1951.

Thomas, R. Culture and Eliot. Modern Quart 6 1951.

Williamson, A. Poetry in the theatre: Eliot and Fry. Chrysalis 4 1951.

Yoklavich, J. M. Eliot's Cocktail party and Plato's Symposium. N & Q 196 1951.

Brooks, H. F. The family reunion and [Browning's] Colombe's birthday. TLS 12 Dec 1952.

— Between the waste land and the first Ariel poems: The hollow men. English 16 1966.

Castelli, A. Scrittori inglesi contemporanei di fronte al Cristianesimo. Humanitas 7 1952. On Eliot, Joyce, Lawrence.

Chinol, E. Teatro e poesia secondo Eliot. Comunità 6 1952.

— La poesia di Eliot. Studi Americani 3 1957.

Christie, E. Mystikk og poesi i Four quartets. Samtiden 61 1952.

Esch, A. Das dramatische Werk Eliots. Anglia 70 1952.

Freedman, M. Jazz rhythms and Eliot. South Atlantic Quart 51 1952.

— The meaning of Eliot's Jew. South Atlantic Quart 55 1956.

Frohock, W. M. The morals of Eliot. Southwest Rev 37 1952.

Lebel, M. Actualité d'Eschyle. Revue de l'Université Laval 7 1952.

Lebois, A. Eliot, les imagistes et Jean de Boschère. Revue de Littérature Comparée 26 1952.

Marshall, W. H. The text of Eliot's Gerontion. SB 4 1952.

— A note on Prufrock. N & Q 204 1959.

McCarthy, H. E. Eliot and Buddhism. Philosophy East & West (Univ of Hawaii) 2 1952.

Richman, R. The quiet conflict: the plays of Eliot. New Republic 8 Dec 1952.

Sleight, R. Mr Empson's complex words. EC 2 1952.

Thorlby, A. The poetry of Four quartets. Cambridge Jnl 5 1952.

Weisstein, U. The cocktail party: an attempt at an interpretation on mythological grounds. Western Rev 16 1952.

— Form as content in the drama of Eliot. Western Rev 23 1959.

Weitz, M. Eliot: time as a mode of salvation. Sewanee Rev 60 1952; rptd in Bergonzi, 1969, above.

Wood, F. Rilke and Eliot: tradition and poetry. Germanic Rev 27 1952.

Bates, R. Donner un sens plus pur aux mots de la tribu. N & Q 198 1953.

— A topic in The waste land: traditional rhetoric and Eliot's individual talent. Wisconsin Stud in Contemporary Lit 5 1964.

Beare, R. L. Eliot and Goethe. Germanic Rev 28 1953.

— Notes on the text of Eliot: variants from Russell Square. SB 9 1957.

Bodelsen, C. A. Two 'difficult' poems by Eliot. E Studies 34 1953.

Carter, P. J., jr. Who understands The cocktail party? Colorado Quart 12 1953.

D'Agostino, N. Gli anni di tirocinio di T. S. Eliot. Belfagor 8 1953.

Eliot as poet – The view of 1923; The waste land revisited [Thoughts and second thoughts]. TLS 28 Aug 1953.

Fowler, D. C. The waste land: Eliot's 'fragments'. College Eng 14 1953; pt rptd in Martin, 1968, above.

Gwynn, F. L. Eliot's Sweeney among the nightingales and The song of Solomon. MLN 68 1953.

— Sweeney among the epigraphs. MLN 69 1954.

— Correction to Sweeney among the epigraphs. MLN 70 1955.

Heilman, R. B. Alcestis and The cocktail party. Comparative Lit 5 1953.

Karlin, K. Critical notes. Chicago Rev 7 1953.

King, S. K. Eliot, Yeats and Shakespeare. Theoria 5 1953

Mackendrick, P. Eliot and the Alexandrians. Classical Jnl 49 1953.

Marx, L. Eliot, Mr Trilling and Huckleberry Finn. Amer Scholar 22 1953.

Moorman, C. Order and Eliot. South Atlantic Quart 52 1953.

— Myth and organic unity in The waste land. South Atlantic Quart 57 1958.

Morrissette, B. A. Eliot and Guillaume Apollinaire. Comparative Lit 5 1953.

Sastri, P. S. Eliot and the contemporary world. Modern Rev (Calcutta) 83 1953.

Schneider, K. T. S. Eliots poetische Technik. Germanisch-romanische Monatsschrift 34 1953.

Schwartz, E. Eliot's Cocktail party and the new humanism. PQ 32 1953.

Simon, I. Echoes in The waste land. E Studies 34 1953.

Spender. S. Rilke and the angels, Eliot and the shrines, Sewanee, Rev 61 1953.

— Remembering Eliot. Encounter 24 1965.

Stein, W. After the cocktails. EC 3 1953.

West, R. B., jr. Personal history and The four quartets. New Mexico Quart 23 1953.

Adams, R. M. Donne and Eliot: metaphysicals. Kenyon Rev 16 1954; rptd in his Strains of discord, Ithaca 1958.

Beach, J. W. Conrad Aiken and Eliot: echoes and overtones. PMLA 69 1954.

Berland, A. Some techniques of fiction in poetry. EC 4 1954. In Pope and Eliot especially.

Blau, H. A character study of drama. Jnl of Aesthetics 13 1954.

Bodelsen, M. and C. A. Eliot's jewelled unicorns. E Studies 35 1954.

Bolle, L. L'œuvre poétique de T. S. Eliot. La Gazette de Lausanne 5 June 1954.

Brooke, N. The confidential clerk: a theatrical review. Durham Univ Jnl new ser 15 1954.

Brown, S. Eliot's latest poetic drama. Commentary 17 1954.

Colby, R. A. The three worlds of The cocktail party. UTQ 24 1954.

— Orpheus in the counting house: The confidential clerk. PMLA 72 1957.

Dobrée, B. The confidential clerk. Sewanee Rev 62 1954.

Drew, A. P. Hints and guesses in Four quartets. Univ of Kansas City Rev 20 1954.

Evans, D. W. T. S. Eliot, Charles Williams and the sense of the occult. Accent 14 1954.

— The domesticity of Eliot. UTQ 23 1954.

— The case book of Eliot. MLN 71 1956.

— The penny world of Eliot. Renascence 10 1958.

Fitzgerald, R. Generations of leaves: the poet in the classical tradition. Perspectives USA 8 1954. Homer, Virgil, Dante, Hopkins, Eliot.

Hochwald, I. E. Eliot's Cocktail party and Goethe's Wahlverwandtschaften. Germanic Rev 29 1954.

Lawlor, J. The formal achievement of The cocktail party. Virginia Quart Rev 30 1954.

Lehmann, J. The other Eliot. Listener 28 Jan 1954.

— Conversazioni con Eliot. Veltro 9 1965.

Lübker, R. Vier Quartette von T. S. Eliot: Versuch zu einer Einführung. Die Neueren Sprachen 3 1954.

Matteucci, B. La Madonna in Eliot. Humanitas 9 1954.

Moakley, G. The Waite-Smith Tarot: a footnote to The waste land. BNYPL 58 1954.

Morris, G. L. K. 'Marie, Marie, hold on tight'. Partisan Rev 21 1954. Marie Larisch's My past, as a source for The waste land; rptd in Kenner 1962, and in Cox and Hinchliffe, 1968, above.

Musgrove, S. James Picot's use of T. S. Eliot. Meanjin 13 1954.

Noon, W. T. Four quartets: contemplatio ad amorem. Renascence 7 1954.

Sanesi, R. Con Eliot sui banchi di Terranova. Aut-Aut 4 1954.

— Gli alberi di Natale di Eliot. Aut–Aut 30 1955.

— Un' immagine di The waste land. Osservatore Politico Letterario 7 1961.

Seif, M. The impact of Eliot on Auden and Spender. South Atlantic Quart 53 1954.

Steiger, E. Gehalt und Gestalt des Dramas The cocktail party von T. S. Eliot. Die Neueren Sprachen 3 1954.

Stevenson, D. L. An objective correlative for Eliot's Hamlet. Jnl of Aesthetics 13 1954.

Wagner, R. D. The meaning of Eliot's rose-garden. PMLA 69 1954.

Webster, H. T. and H. W. Starr. Macavity: an attempt to unravel his mystery. Baker Street Jnl 4 1954.

Branford, W. R. G. Myth and theme in the plays of Eliot. Theoria 7 1955.

Breit, H. Tea. New York Times Book Rev 26 June 1955.

Holbrook, D. Eliot's Chinese wall. EC 5 1955.

Jayne, S. Mr Eliot's Agon. PQ 34 1955.

Male, R. R., jr. Toward The waste land: the theme of The Blithedale romance. College Eng 16 1955.

Merchant, W. M. The verse-drama of Eliot and Fry. Die Neueren Sprachen 4 1955.

Nelson, A. H. The critics and The waste land 1922–49. E Studies 36 1955.

Nicholas, C. The murders of Doyle and Eliot. MLN 70 1955.

Pallette, D. B. Eliot, Fry and Broadway. Arizona Quart 11 1955.

Plewka, K. The family reunion, a play by Eliot. Die Neueren Sprachen 4 1955.

Schanzer, E. Eliot's Sunday morning service. EC 5 1955.

Schöne, A. Berührungspunkte zwischen Nonsense-Dichtung und metaphysischem Humor in T. S. Eliots Scherzgedichten. Germanisch-romanische Monatsschrift 36 1955.

Shanahan, C. M. Irony in Laforgue, Corbière and Eliot. MP 53 1955.

Siegel, E. Eliot and W. C. Williams: a distinction. Univ of Kansas City Rev 22 1955.

Stanford, D. L. Two notes on Eliot. Twentieth-Century Lit 1 1955. Comments on The hollow men and Burbank with a Baedeker: Bleistein with a cigar.

— Mr Eliot's new play. Contemporary Rev no 1114 1958. On The elder statesman.

— Eliot's new play. Queen's Quart 65 1959. The elder statesman.

— Concealment and revelation in Eliot. Southwest Rev 50 1965.

Turner, W. A. The not so coy mistress of J. Alfred Prufrock. South Atlantic Quart 54 1955.

Weigand, E. Rilke and Eliot: the articulation of the mystic experience, a discussion centering on the Eighth Duino elegy and Burnt Norton. Germanic Rev 30 1955.

Adams, J. D. Speaking of books. New York Times Book Rev 16 Dec 1956.

Blumenberg, H. Rose und Feuer: Lyrik, Kritik und Drama T. S. Eliots. Hochland 49 1956.

Boulton, J. T. The use of original sources for the development of a theme: Eliot in Murder in the cathedral. English 11 1956.

Daus, H.-J. Eliot: The Boston Evening Transcript. Anglia 74 1956.

Davie, D. Eliot: the end of an era. Twentieth Century 159 1956; rptd in Kenner 1962 and in Bergonzi, 1969 above.

Hardenbrook, D. Eliot and the Great Grimpen Mire by Gaston Huret III. Baker Street Jnl 6 1956.

Heller, E. Glaube, Weisheit und Dichtung: zu Eliots Rede über Goethe. Merkur 10 1956.

— Eliot: die Tradition und das Moderne. Gestalt und Gedanke 11 1966.

Keeley, E. Eliot and the poetry of G. Seferis. Comparative Lit 8 1956.

— Seferis and the 'mythical method'. Ibid 6 1969.

Kühnelt, H. H. T. S. Eliot als Poe-Kritiker. Die Neueren Sprachen 5 1956.

Langslet, L. R. Tidsopplevelsen i Eliots Four quartets. Kirke og Kultur (Oslo) 61 1956.

Laurentia, Sr M. Structural balance and symbolism in Eliot's Portrait of a lady. Amer Lit 27 1956.

Lohner, E. Gottfried Benn und Eliot. Neue Deutsche Hefte 26 1956.

Lyman, D. B., jr. Aiken and Eliot. MLN 71 1956.

Mühlberger, J. Eliot als Lyriker. Welt und Wort 11 1956.

Musurillo, H. A note on The waste land (part iv). Classical Philology 51 1956. On the line Consider Phlebas...

Puhalo, D. Poezija T. S. Eliota. Savremenik 6 1956.

— Drame u stihu T. S. Eliota. Letopis Matice Srpske (Novi Sad) 1956.

— T. S. Eliot kao književni kritičar. Letopis Matice Srpske (Novi Sad) 1957.

Rizzardi, A. Eliot minore. Aut–Aut 33 1956.

Steinmann, M., jr. Coleridge, Eliot and organicism. MLN 71 1956.

Tello, J. El concepto del tiempo y del espacio en la poesía de Eliot. Revista Nacional de Cultura (Caracas) 18 1956.

Thompson, K. S. The lost lilac and the lost sea voices: old Essex in new writing. Essex Inst Historical Collections 92 1956.

Voisine, J. Le problème du drame poétique selon T. S. Eliot. Etudes Anglaises 9 1956.

Williams, R. Second thoughts: 1, Eliot on culture. EC 6 1956.

— Tragic resignation and sacrifice. CQ 5 1963. On Murder in the cathedral, The cocktail party and B. Pasternak's Dr Zhivago.

Young, P. Scott Fitzgerald's Waste land. Kansas Mag 23 1956.

Alvarez, A. Eliot and Yeats: orthodoxy and tradition. Twentieth Century 162 1957; rptd in his Shaping spirit, 1958, New York 1958 (as Stewards of excellence).

Beringause, A. F. Journey through The waste land. South Atlantic Quart 56 1957.

Blum, M. M. The 'fool' in The love song of J. Alfred Prufrock. MLN 72 1957.

Bollier, E. P. Eliot's Tradition and the individual talent reconsidered. Univ of Colorado Stud in Lang & Lit no 6 1957.

— Eliot and Milton: a problem in criticism. Tulane Stud in Eng 8 1958.

— Eliot and Donne: a problem in criticism. Tulane Stud in Eng 9 1959.

— Eliot and The sacred wood. Colorado Quart 8 1960.

— Eliot and F. H. Bradley: a question of influence. Tulane Stud in English 12 1963.

— From scepticism to poetry: a note on Conrad Aiken and Eliot. Tulane Stud in Eng 13 1963.

— A broken Coriolanus: a note on Eliot's Coriolan. Southern Rev 3 1967.

— Eliot's 'lost' ode of dejection. Bucknell Rev 16 1968.

Cargill, O. Mr Eliot regrets. Nation 23 Feb 1957.

Eleanor Mary, Mother. Eliot's Magi. Renascence 10 1957.

Falconieri, J. V. Il saggio di Eliot su Dante. Italica 34 1957.

Galinsky, H. G. B. Shaw als Gegenstand der Kritik und als Quelle dramatischer Anregnung für Eliot. Germanisch-romanische Monatsschrift 38 1957.

— Eliots Murder in the cathedral: Versuch einer Interpretation. Die Neueren Sprachen 7 1958.

Gregory, H. The authority of Eliot. Commonweal 8 Nov 1957.

Gross, S. L. Sterne and Eliot's Prufrock: an object lesson in explication. College Eng 19 1957.

Guidubaldi, E. Eliot e B. Croce: due opposti atteggiamenti critici di fronte a Dante. Aevum (Milan) 31 1957.

Hardy, J. E. An antic disposition. Sewanee Rev 65 1957. On The cocktail party.

Hart, J. P. Eliot: his use of Wycherley and Pope. N & Q 202 1957.

Holland, R. Miss Glasgow's Prufrock. Amer Quart 9 1957.

Holthusen, H. E. Das Schöne und das Wahre in der Poesie: zur Theorie des Dichterischen bei Eliot und Benn. Merkur 11 1957.

Howarth, H. Eliot, Beethoven and J. W. N. Sullivan. Comparative Lit 9 1957.

— Eliot's Criterion: the editor and his contributors. Comparative Lit 11 1959.

— Eliot: the expatriate as fugitive. Georgia Rev 13 1959.

— Eliot and Hofmannsthal. South Atlantic Quart 59 1960.

— Eliot and Milton: the American aspect. UTQ 30 1961.

— T. S. Eliot and the 'little preacher'. Amer Quart 13 1961.

Hyams, C. B. and K. H. Reichert. The month of April in English poetry, with special reference to Chaucer and

Eliot—a double lesson. Die Neueren Sprachen 6 1957.

Joseph, Brother, FSC. The concept of poetic sensibility in the criticism of Eliot. Fresco 8 1957.

McEldery, B. R., jr. Santayana and Eliot's objective correlative. Boston Univ Stud in Eng 3 1957. On Santayana's possible influence.

— Eliot's Shakespeherian rag. Amer Quart 9 1957; pt rptd in Martin 1968, above.

McFarlane, J. W. The Tiresian vision. Durham Univ Jnl 18 1957.

Marsh, T. N. The turning world: Eliot and the detective story. Eng Miscellany (Rome) 8 1957.

Marshall, R. Eliot et le Baudelaire de Swinburne. Bayou no 70 1957.

Mitchell, J. D. Applied psychoanalysis in the drama. Amer Imago 14 1957. With special examination of The confidential clerk.

Mizener, A. To meet Mr Eliot. Sewanee Rev 65 1957; rptd in Kenner 1962, above.

Osawa, M. Poetry, religion and science: K. Nott's criticism of Eliot. Stud in Eng Lit (Tokyo) 33 1957. In Japanese.

Shuman, R. B. Buddhistic overtones in Eliot's Cocktail party. MLN 72 1957.

Spector, R. D. Eliot, Pound and the conservative tradition. History of Ideas Newsletter 3 1957.

Takatari, T. The poetry of Eliot. Stud in Eng Lit (Tokyo) 33 1957. In Japanese.

Vickery, J. B. Eliot's poetry. Renascence 10 1957. The quest and the way.

— Gerontion: the nature of death and immortality. Arizona Quart 14 1958.

— Two sources of The burial of the dead. Lit & Psychology 10 1960. Freud's Totem and taboo; rptd in Martin 1968, above.

Vigée, C. Les artistes de la faim. Comparative Lit 9 1957. Baudelaire, Lautréamont, Flaubert, Mallarmé, Kafka, Eliot.

Walcutt, C. C. Eliot's Love song of J. Alfred Prufrock. College Eng 19 1957.

Webber, B. G. Lucasta angel. N & Q 202 1957.

Williamson, M. W. Eliot's Gerontion: a study in thematic repetition and development. Univ of Texas Stud in Eng 36 1957.

Wrenn, C. L. Eliot and the language of poetry. Thought 32 1957.

Arden, E. The echo of hell in Prufrock. N & Q 203 1958.

— The 'other' Lazarus in Prufrock. Univ of Kansas City Rev 26 1959.

Bacon, H. H. The sibyl in the bottle. Virginia Quart Rev 34 1958. The epigraph to The waste land.

Baldi, S. L'organizzazione espressiva della Terra desolata. Studi Americani 4 1958.

Bassi, E. Il teatro di T. S. Eliot. Annali Istituto Universitario Orientale, Napoli, Sezione Germanica 1 1958.

Beharriell, F. J. Freud and literature. Queen's Quart 65 1958. Review article discussing Lawrence, Joyce, Eliot, Kafka, T. Mann et al.

Braybrooke, N. Thomas Stearns Eliot. Critical Rev 194 1958.

— Eliot and children. Dalhousie Rev 39 1959.

— Eliot's search for a lost Eden. Catholic World 190 1959.

— Eliot's earliest writings. Twentieth Century (Australia) 19 1965.

Cauthen, I. B. jr. Another Webster allusion in The waste land. MLN 73 1958.

Chiereghin, S. Eliot e l'ultima opera del Pizzetti. Convivium 26 1958.

Cossu, N. Eliot e Dante. Fiera Letteraria no 23 1958.

— Dantismo politicoreligioso di Eliot. Nuova Antologia 495 1965.

Espey, J. J. The epigraph to Eliot's Burbank with a Baedeker: Bleistein with a cigar. Amer Lit 29 1958.

The family reunion. Theatre Arts Monthly 42 1958.

Ferrara, F. Aspetti e significati della Family reunion di Eliot. Studi Americani 4 1958.

Gardner, H. The 'aged eagle' spreads his wings: a 70th birthday talk with Eliot. Sunday Times 21 Sept 1958.

— The comedies of Eliot. Essays by Divers Hands 34 1966.

— The landscapes of Eliot's poetry. CQ 10 1969.

Germer, R. T. S. Eliot's Bedeutung als Dichter und Kritiker. Die Neueren Sprachen 7 1958.

— Schwierigkeiten bei der Interpretation von Eliots Waste land. Germanisch-romanische Monatsschrift 39 1958.

— Die Bedeutung Shakespeares für Eliot. Shakespeare Jahrbuch 95 1959.

— Eliot's Journey of the Magi. Jahrbuch für Amerikastudien 7 1962.

Graves, R. Sweeney among the nightingales. Texas Quart 1 1958.

Gross, H. Gerontion and the meaning of history. PMLA 73 1958.

— Music and the analogue of feeling: notes on Eliot and Beethoven. Centennial Rev of Arts & Sciences 3 1959.

Hewes, H. Eliot on Eliot: 'I feel younger than I did at 60'. Saturday Rev 13 Sept 1958.

— His new play: The elder statesman. Saturday Rev Ibid.

Iser, W. Eliot's Four quartets. Jahrbuch für Amerikastudien 3 1958.

— Pater und Eliot: der Übergang zur Modernität. Germanisch-romanische Monatsschrift 40 1959.

Iwasaki, S. Four quartets: a poem of unity. Stud in Eng Lit (Tokyo) 35 1958. In Japanese.

Jacobs, A. Murder in the cathedral as an opera. Listener 20 March 1958.

Kermode, F. Eliot on poetry. International Literary Annual 1 1958. Criticism of On poetry and poets.

Lelièvre, F. J. Parody in Juvenal and Eliot. Classical Philology 53 1958.

Levine, G. The cocktail party and Clara Hopgood. Graduate Student of English 1 1958.

Levy, W. T. The idea of the church in Eliot. Christian Scholar 41 1958.

Livesay, D. London notes. Canadian Forum 38 1958.

Mayo, E. L. The influence of ancient Hindu thought on Walt Whitman and Eliot. Aryan Path (Bombay) 29 1958.

Mickel, W. Die Chorpartien in Eliots Murder in the cathedral nach Gehalt, Stimmung und Stil. Die Neueren Sprachen 7 1958.

Miller, J. E. jr. Whitman and Eliot. The poetry of mysticism. Southwest Rev 43 1958.

Mudrick, M. The two voices of Mr Eliot. Hudson Rev 10 1958.

Mueller, W. R. Murder in the cathedral: an imitation of Christ. Religion in Life 27 1958.

Nathan, N. Eliot's incorrect note on C.i.f. London. N & Q 203 1958. The waste land 211.

Pagnini, M. La musicalità dei Four quartets di Eliot. Belfagor 13 1958.

Read, H. Poetry in my time. Texas Quart 1 1958. Pound, Eliot, Yeats et al.

Salmon, C. and L. Paul. Two views of Mr Eliot's new play. Listener 4 Sept 1958.

Standop, E. Bemerkungen zu einer neuen Verslehre mit Analyse von East Coker IV. Anglia 76 1958.

— Eliot's Journey of the Magi. Archiv 197 1960.

Steadman, J. M. Eliot and Husserl: the origin of the objective correlative. N & Q 203 1958.

Strothmann, F. W. and L. V. Ryan. Hope for Eliot's 'empty men'. PMLA 73 1958.

Virginia, Sr M. Some symbols of death and destiny in Four quartets. Renascence 10 1958.

Wain, J. A walk in the sacred wood. London Mag 5 1958.

— T. S. Eliot. Encounter 24 1965.

Weber, A. Ein Beitrag zur Chronologie und Genesis der Dichtung Eliots. Jahrbuch für Amerikastudien 3 1958.

West, A. The last Puritan: Edmund Wilson versus Eliot. Sunday Times 3 Aug 1958.

Whitfield, J. H. Pirandello and Eliot: an essay in counterpoint. Eng Miscellany (Rome) 9 1958.

—— Eliot's Four quartets and their Italian version. Eng Miscellany (Rome) 11 1960.

—— Pirandello e Eliot: identità e contrasti. Le Parole e le Idee 4 1962.

Wolff, E. Einheit und Kontinuität in Eliots Entwicklung als Lyriker. Germanisch-romanische Monatsschrift 39 1958.

Zizola, G. Assassinio nella cattedrale da Eliot a Pizzetti. Humanitas (Brescia) 13 1958.

—— Orgoglio e santità nel Tommaso Becket di Eliot. Studium 55 1959.

Zoltinek, H. The mythical method in the early poems of Eliot. In Anglistische Studien: Festschrift zum 70. Geburtstag von F. Wild, 1958.

Austin, A. Eliot's objective correlative. Univ of Kansas City Rev 25 1959.

—— Eliot's quandary. Univ of Kansas City Rev 26 1960.

—— Eliot's theory of dissociation. College Eng 23 1962.

—— Eliot's theory of personal expression. PMLA 81 1966.

Bæröe, P. R. Eliots eksistensielle holdning. Kirke og Kultur 64 1959.

Baumgartel, G. The concept of the pattern: conclusions from Eliot. Revue des Langues Vivantes 25 1959.

Benziger, J. The romantic tradition: Wordsworth and Eliot. Bucknell Rev 8 1959.

Bergsten, S. Illusive allusions: some reflections on the critical approach to the poetry of Eliot. Orbis Litterarum 14 1959.

Burne, G. S. T. S. Eliot and Rémy de Gourmont. Bucknell Rev 8 1959.

Cross, G. A note on The waste land. N & Q 204 1959.

Cruttwell, P. One reader's beginning. Orbis Litterarum 14 1959.

Dahlberg, E. and H. Read. Robert Graves and Eliot. Twentieth Century 166 1959. An exchange of letters; rptd in their Truth is more sacred, 1961.

Donoghue, D. Eliot in fair Colonus: The elder statesman. Studies (Dublin) 48 1959.

—— Eliot's Quartets: a new reading. Studies (Dublin) 54 1965; rptd in Bergonzi, 1969, above.

Erzgräber, W. Die Gartenszene in Eliots Burnt Norton. Archiv 196 1959.

Espmark, K. Ekelöf och Eliot: en studie kring Färjersång. Bonniers Litterära Magasin 28 1959.

Garçon, M. Compliment à T. S. Eliot. Mercure de France 335 1959.

Gerard, Sr M. Eliot of the Circle and John of the Cross. Thought 34 1959.

Good, T. T. S. Eliot et la tradition anglaise. Cahiers du Sud no 352 1959.

Grannove, R. J. Eliot's Portrait of a lady and Pound's Portrait d'une femme. Twentieth-Century Lit 5 1959.

Grigson, G. Leavis against Eliot. Encounter 12 1959.

Hovey, R. P. Psychiatrist and saint in The cocktail party. Lit & Psychology 9 1959.

Jarrett-Kerr, M. The poetic drama of Eliot. Eng Stud in Africa (Johannesburg) 2 1959.

Kahn, S. J. Eliot's polyphiloprogenitive: another Whitman link? Walt Whitman Rev 5 1959.

Kline, P. The spiritual center in Eliot's plays. Kenyon Rev 21 1959.

Kornbluth, M. L. A twentieth-century Everyman. College Eng 21 1959. On Murder in the cathedral.

Licht, M. What is the meaning of happening? Orbis Litterarum 14 1959.

Lo Schiavo, R. Poesie minori di T. S. Eliot. Studi Americani 5 1959.

MacGregor-Hastie, R. Waste land in Russell Square. Trace no 32 1959.

Major, J. M. Eliot's Gerontion and As you like it. MLN 74 1959.

Marsh, F. The ocean-desert: The ancient mariner and The waste land. EC 9 1959.

Preston, P. A note on Eliot and Sherlock Holmes. MLR 54 1959.

Rickman, M. P. Poetry and the ephemeral: Rilke's and Eliot's conceptions of the poet's task. German Life & Letters 12 1959.

Román, M. C. El pensamiento de Eliot a través de su teatro. Revista de Literatura 15 1959.

Schaar, C. Palimpsest technique in Little Gidding. Orbis Litterarum 14 1959.

Schmied, W. T. S. Eliot und Pound als Kritiker. Wort in der Zeit 5 1959.

Serpieri, S. Il significato di Gerontion nella poesia eliotiana. Studi Americani 5 1959.

—— La poesia di Eliot: dalla Terra desolata alla Terra promessa. Ponte 15 1959.

—— La fuga di Eliot dal tempo. Studi Americani 7 1961.

Sühnel, R. T. S. Eliot's Stellung zum Humanismus. Die Neueren Sprachen 8 1959.

Vergmann, F. Ash Wednesday: a poem of earthly and heavenly love. Orbis Litterarum 14 1959.

Amery, C. Der gelehrte Revolutionär. Frankfurter Hefte 15 1960.

Christian, H. Thematic development in Eliot's hysteria. Twentieth-Century Lit 6 1960.

Clowder, F. The bestiary of Eliot. Prairie Schooner 34 1960.

Conquest, R. Mistah Eliot—he dead? Audit 1 1960.

Craig, D. The defeatism of The waste land. CQ 2 1960; rptd in Knoll, 1964, and in Cox and Hinchliffe, 1968, above.

Cronin, A. A question of modernity. X: a Quart Rev 1 1960.

Dierickx, J. T. S. Eliot, dramaturge. Revue des Langues Vivantes 26 1960.

—— Eliot, de Griekse toneelschrijvers en Ibsen. Tijdschrift van de Vrije Universiteit van Brussel 5 1963.

Frattini, A. Eliot critico della poesia. Humanitas (Brescia) 15 1960.

Gerstenberger, D. The saint and the circle: the dramatic potential of an image. Criticism 2 1960.

Gillis, E. A., L. V. Ryan and F. W. Strothmann. Hope for Eliot's Hollow men? PMLA 75 1960.

Gillis, E. A. The spiritual status of Eliot's Hollow men. Texas Stud in Lit & Lang 2 1961.

—— Religion in a Sweeney world. Arizona Quart 20 1964.

Gleckner, R. F. Eliot's The hollow men and Shakespeare's Julius Caesar. MLN 75 1960.

Guidi, A. Il classicismo di T. S. Eliot. Veltro 4 1960; rptd in Studi in onore di Vittorio Lugli e Diego Valeri. Venezia 1962.

Haas, R. Der frühe T. S. Eliot. Die Neueren Sprachen 9 1960.

Hanzo, T. Eliot and Kierkegaard: the meaning of happening in The cocktail party. Modern Drama 3 1960.

Korg, J. Modern art techniques in The waste land. Jnl of Aesthetics & Art Criticism 18 1960; rptd in Martin, 1968, above.

Krajewska, W. Le théâtre de T. S. Eliot. Kwartalnik Neofilologiczny 7 1960.

Krause, S. J. Hollow men and false horses. Texas Stud in Lit & Lang 2 1960.

Lund, M. G. The androgynous moment: Woolf and Eliot. Renascence 12 1960.

—— Homesteading in the waste land: the populous legacy of Eliot. Southwest Rev 51 1966.

—— The social burden of Eliot. Discourse 9 1966.

—— Eliot's Book of happenings. Forum (Houston) 4 1967.

Mary Anthony, Mother. Verbal pattern in Burnt Norton I. Criticism 2 1960.

Nagano, Y. The stream of consciousness in The waste land by T. S. Eliot: its linguistic and technical problem. Stud in Eng Lit & Lang (Fukuoka) no 10 1960.

Oden, Thomas C. The Christology of Eliot: a study of the kerygma in Burnt Norton. Encounter (Indianapolis) 21 1960.

—— Meditation for Ash Wednesday. Cross Currents 15 1965.

Okumura, M. Eliot's The elder statesman. Stud in Eng Lit (Tokyo) 37 1960.

Peake, C. Sweeney erect and the Emersonian hero. Neophilologus 44 1960.

Ramamrutham, J. V. Eliot and Indian readers. Literary Half-Yearly no 1 1960.

Roos, A. Gunnar Björling, T. S. Eliot och litteraturhistorisk metodik. Samtid och Framtid 17 1960.

Schröder, F. R. Eliot und Harald der Strenge. Germanisch–romanische Monatsschrift 41 1960.

Shapiro, K. Eliot: the death of literary judgment. Saturday Rev of Lit 27 Feb 1960; rptd in his In defence of ignorance, New York 1960 and in Knoll, 1964, above.

—— The three hockey games of Eliot. Antioch Rev 22 1962.

Simister, O. E. The Four quartets—and other observations. Anglo–Irish Rev 10 1960.

Sinha, K. N. Imagery and diction in Eliot's later poetry. Indian Jnl of Eng Stud 1 1960.

—— The intimate and the unidentifiable: feeling in Eliot's Four quartets. Literary Criterion 5 1962.

Smith, G., Getting used to Eliot. Eng Jnl 49 1960.

—— The ghosts in Eliot's Elder statesman. N & Q 205 1960.

Spratt, P. Eliot and Freud. Literary Half-Yearly 1 1960.

Walmsley, D. M. Unrecorded article by Eliot. Book Collector 9 1960. Modern tendencies in poetry, from Shana'a: a magazine of art, literature and philosophy.

Wasser, H. A note on Eliot and Santayana. Boston Univ Stud in Eng 4 1960.

Allen, W. The time and place of Eliot. New York Times Book Rev 9 April 1961.

Boardman, G. R. Eliot and the mystery of Fanny Marlow. Modern Fiction Stud 7 1961. On various writings by 'F.M.' in Criterion, suggestive of Eliot.

—— Ash Wednesday: Eliot's Lenten Mass sequence. Renascence 15 1962.

Caffi, A. Stato, nazione e cultura: note su T. S. Eliot e Simone Weil. Tempo Presente 6 1961.

Chubb, M. D. The Heraclitean element in Eliot's Four quartets. PQ 40 1961.

Fleming, R. The elder statesman and Eliot's Programme for the métier of poetry. Wisconsin Stud in Contemporary Lit 2 1961.

Ghosh, P. C. Poetic drama and Murder in the cathedral. Bull of Dept of English, Univ of Calcutta 2 1961.

Gibson, W. M. Sonnets in Eliot's The waste land. Amer Lit 32 1961; rptd in Martin 1968, above.

Harvey, V. R. Eliot's Love song of J. Alfred Prufrock. Iowa Eng Yearbook 6 1961.

Hyman, S. E. Poetry and criticism: Eliot. Amer Scholar 30 1961.

Jolivet, P. Le personnage de Thomas Becket dans Der Heilige de C. F. Meyer, Murder in the Cathedral de T. S. Eliot et Becket ou l'honneur de Dieu de Jean Anouilh. Etudes Germaniques 16 1961.

Joost, N. English poetic satire and the modern Christian temper. Delta Epsilon Sigma Bull (Alton Illinois) 6 1961.

Joshi, B. N. Hopkins and Eliot—a study in linguistic innovation. Osmania Jnl of Eng Stud 1 1961.

Knieger, B. The dramatic achievement of Eliot. Modern Drama 3 1961.

Madhusudan, R. V. The concept of time in Eliot's Four quartets. Osmania Jnl of Eng Stud 1 1961.

Mahulkar, D. D. The language of Eliot's Burnt Norton. Jnl of the Univ of Baroda 10 1961.

Major, M. W. A St Louisan's view of Prufrock. CEA Critic 23 1961.

Marion, Sr T. Eliot's criticism of metaphysical poetry. Greyfriar 1961.

Moynihan, W. T. The goal of The waste land quest. Renascence 13 1961; pt rptd in Martin 1968, above.

Naik, M. K. Wit and humour in Eliot's verse. Jnl of Karnatak Univ 5 1961.

Rajasekharaiah, T. R. Pride and prejudice: a note on Eliot's criticism. Ibid.

Rawler, J. R. Eliot et Paul Valéry. Mercure de France 341 1961.

Reddy, V. M. The concept of time in the Four quartets. Osmania Jnl of Eng Stud 1 1961.

Smith, C. P. Semi-classical poetry and the great tradition. Massachusetts Rev 3 1961.

Stelzmann, Rainulf A. The theology of Eliot's dramas. Xavier Univ Stud 1 1961.

Sugiyama, Y. The waste land and contemporary Japanese poetry. Comparative Lit 13 1961.

Thomas, H. Le théâtre dans l'oeuvre de T. S. Eliot. Nouvelle Revue Française 9 1961.

Varie, T. Wallace Stevens and Eliot. Dartmouth College Lib Bull 4 1961.

Winter, J. Prufrockism in The cocktail party. MLQ 22 1961.

Wooton, C. The Mass: Ash Wednesday's objective correlative. Arizona Quart 17 1961.

Barth, J. R. Eliot's image of man: a thematic study of his drama. Renascence 14 1962.

Carey, Sr M. C. Baudelaire's influence on The waste land. Renascence 14 1962.

Gaskell, R. The family reunion. EC 12 1962.

Gowda, M. M. A. Four quartets: an aspect of Indian thought. Literary Half-Yearly 3 1962.

Inserillo, C. R. Wish and desire: two poles of the imagination in the drama of A. Miller and Eliot. Xavier Univ Stud 1 1962.

Kligerman, J. An interpretation of Eliot's East Coker. Arizona Quart 18 1962.

McConnell, D. J. The heart of darkness in Eliot's Hollow men. Texas Stud in Lit & Lang 4 1962.

Moffa, M. Ibsen e The elder statesman. Studi Americani 8 1962.

Ong, W. J. Burnt Norton in St Louis. Amer Lit 33 1962.

Palmer, R. E. Existentialism in Eliot's Family reunion. Modern Drama 5 1962.

Perkins, D. Rose garden to midwinter spring: achieved faith in the Four quartets. MLQ 23 1962; rptd in Bergonzi, 1969, above.

Review no 4 1962. Special no on Eliot. J. Bayley, The collected plays; M. Dodsworth, Gerontion and Christ; C. Falck, Hurry up, please, its time; J. Fuller, Five finger exercises; M. Hamburger, The unity of Eliot's poetry; G. R. Boardman, Restoring the hollow man; W. W. Robson, Eliot's later criticism.

Richardson, J. T. S. Eliot. Literary Half-Yearly 3 1962.

Rillie, J. A. M. Melodramatic device in Eliot. RES 13 1962.

Sen, S. C. Four quartets. Bull of Dept of Eng Univ of Calcutta 3 1962.

Wasserstrom, W. Eliot and the Dial. Sewanee Rev 70 1962.

Weatherhead, A. K. Four quartets: setting love in order. Wisconsin Stud in Contemporary Lit 3 1962.

—— Baudelaire in Eliot's Ash Wednesday IV. Eng Lang Notes 2 1965.

Adams, J. F. The fourth temptation in Murder in the cathedral. Modern Drama 5 1963.

Barnes, W. J. Eliot's Marina: image and symbol. Univ of Kansas City Rev 29 1963.

Basu, N. K. Eliot and literary criticism. Bull of Dept of Eng Univ of Calcutta 4 1963.

Carnell, C. S. Creation's lonely flesh: Eliot and Christopher Fry on the life of the senses. Modern Drama 6 1963.

Cecchin, G. Echi di Eliot nei romanzi di Evelyn Waugh. Eng Miscellany (Rome) 14 1963.

Greenhut, M. Sources of obscurity in modern poetry: the examples of Eliot, Stevens and Tate. Centennial Rev of Arts & Science 7 1963.

Hathaway, R. D. The waste land's benediction. Amer N & Q 2 1963.

Kosok, H. Gestaltung und Funktion der Rechtfertigungsszene in T. S. Eliots Murder in the cathedral. Die Neueren Sprachen 12 1963.

Kuna, F. M. Eliot's dissociation of sensibility and the critics of metaphysical poetry. EC 13 1963.

Lee, J. H. Alexander Pope in Eliot's East Coker. N & Q 208 1963.

Locke, F. W. Dante and Eliot's Prufrock. MLN 78 1963.

Nelson, C. E. Saint-John Perse and Eliot. Western Humanities Rev 17 1963.

Rehak, L. R. On the use of martyrs: Tennyson and Eliot on Thomas Becket. UTQ 33 1963.

Rickey, M. E. Christabel and Murder in the cathedral. N & Q 208 1963.

Scrimgeour, C. A. The family reunion. EC 13 1963. See also R. Gaskell, ibid.

Shankar, D. A. Eliot, I. A. Richards and the new critics. Literary Criterion 5 1963.

Spanos, W. V. Murder in the cathedral: the figura as mimetic principle. Drama Survey 3 1963.

—— Eliot's Family reunion: the strategy of sacramental transfiguration. Drama Survey 4 1965.

Stemmler, T. Eliot's Aunt Helen. Die Neueren Sprachen 12 1963.

Taranath, R. Coriolanus, The waste land and the Coriolan poems. Literary Criterion 6 1963.

Thompson, A. C. Eliot and the Journey of the Magi. Opinion (Adelaide) 7 1963.

Bardwell, H. Remembering Mr Eliot. Chicago Rev 17 1964.

Combecher, H. Zu Eliots Cultivation of Christmas trees. Die Neueren Sprachen 13 1964.

Dickerson, M. J. As I lay dying and The waste land: some relationships. Mississippi Quart 17 1964.

Dijkhuis, D. W. Nijhoff en Eliot/Eliot en Nijhoff. Merlyn 2 1964.

Dorris, G. E. Two allusions in the poetry of Eliot. Eng Lang Notes 2 1964.

Edmonds, D. Eliot: toward the still point. Ball State Teachers College Forum 5 1964.

French, A. L. Criticism and The waste land. Southern Rev (Adelaide) 1 1964. See also Critical exchange, ibid.

Holder, A. Eliot on Henry James. PMLA 79 1964.

Joselyn, Sr M. Twelfth Night quartet: four Magi poems. Renascence 16 1964.

Kaul, R. K. Rhyme and blank verse in drama: a note on Eliot. English 15 1964.

—— The poetry of Eliot. Banasthali Patrika 9 1967.

Koch, W. Ein Gespräch mit Eliot. Der Monat 16 1964.

Lees, F. N. T. S. Eliot and Nietzsche. N & Q 209 1964.

—— The dissociation of sensibility: Arthur Hallam and T. S. Eliot. N & Q 212 1967.

Lightfoot, M. J. Purgatory and The family reunion: in pursuit of prosodic description. Modern Drama 7 1964.

—— Charting Eliot's course in drama. Educational Theatre Jnl 20 1968.

—— The uncommon cocktail party. Modern Drama 11 1969.

Lorch, T. M. The relationship between Ulysses and The waste land. Texas Stud in Lit & Lang 6 1964.

Marks, E. R. Eliot and the ghost of S.T.C. Sewanee Rev 72 1964.

Mowat, J. Samuel Johnson and the critical heritage of Eliot. Studia Germanica Gandensia 6 1964.

Musacchio, G. L. A note on the fire-rose synthesis of Eliot's Four quartets. E Studies 45 1964.

Rabut, M. Le thème de Thomas Becket dans Becket de J. Anouilh et Murder in the cathedral de T. S. Eliot. Bull de l'Assoc Guillaume Budé no 4 1964.

Ramsey, W. The Oresteia since Hofmannsthal: images and emphases. Revue de Littérature Comparée 38 1964.

Randall, D. B. J. The 'seer' and 'seen' themes in Gatsby, and some of their parallels in Eliot and Wright. Twentieth-Century Lit 10 1964.

Rao, K. S. N. Eliot and the Bhagavad Gita. Amer Quart 15 1963; addenda, ibid 16 1964.

Reckford, K. J. Heracles and Eliot. Comparative Lit 16 1964.

Rubin, L. Eliot: a revaluation. Modern Age (Chicago) 8 1964.

Sperna, W. J. De vreemdeling bij Eliot. Wending 19 1964.

Stead, C. K. Classical authority and the dark embryo: a dichotomy in Eliot's criticism. Jnl of Australasian Univ Lang & Lit Assoc no 22 1964.

Toms, N. Eliot's The cocktail party: salvation and the common routine. Christian Scholar 47 1964.

Warren, A. Continuity in Eliot's criticism. East-West Rev 1 1964.

Watkins, F. C. Eliot's painter of the Umbrian school. Amer Lit 36 1964. On Mr Eliot's Sunday morning service.

Watson, C. B. Eliot and the interpretation of Shakespearean tragedy in our time. Etudes Anglaises 16 1964.

Wills, G. No habitation, no name. Modern Age (Chicago) 8 1964.

Yerbury, G. D. Of a city beside a river: Whitman, Eliot, Thomas, Miller. Walt Whitman Rev 10 1964.

Avery, H. P. The family reunion reconsidered. Educational Theatre Jnl 17 1965.

Chaturvedi, B. N. The Indian background of Eliot's poetry. English 15 1965.

Ciarletta, L. Cristianesimo nel teatro di Eliot. Approdo 11 1965.

Cohen, S. Jargon, Prufrock and the cop out. College Composition & Communication 16 1965.

Dallas, E. S. Canon Cancrizans and the Four quartets. Comparative Lit 17 1965.

Day, R. A. The 'city man' in The waste land: the geography of reminiscence. PMLA 80 1965.

DeLaura, D. J. Pater and Eliot: the origin of the 'objective correlative'. MLQ 26 1965.

—— Echoes of Butler, Browning, Conrad and Pater in the poetry of Eliot. Eng Lang Notes 3 1966.

Duparc, J. Eliot et le sens de réalité. La Nouvelle Critique no 168 1965.

Durrell, L. Tse-lio-t. Preuves no 170 1965.

Ellmann, R. Yeats and Eliot. Encounter 25 1965; rptd in his Eminent domain, New York 1967 (as Possum's conversion).

Foster, S. Relativity and The waste land: a postulate. Texas Stud in Lit & Lang 7 1965; pt rptd in Martin 1968, above.

Franck, J. Eliot: De la poésie et de quelques poètes. Revue Générale Belge no 2 1965.

Gallego, C. P. Notas a los Occasional verses de T. S. Eliot. Filología Moderna 4 1965.

Göller, K. H. Eliot, The waste land. Die Neueren Sprachen 14 1965.

Grobler, P. du P. In memoriam—Eliot. Theoria no 25 1965.

Gross, J. Eliot: from ritual to realism. Encounter 24 1965.

Halper, N. Joyce and Eliot. Wake Newslitter new ser 2 1965.

Hanshell, D. L'ascesa di Eliot. Letture 20 1965.

Harvey, C. J. D. Eliot: poet and critic. Standpunte 18 1965.

Hesse, E. Eliot: Schwierigkeiten beim Leben: Gerontion als Selbstinterpretation des Dichters. Merkur 19 1965.

Hewitt, E. K. Structure and meaning in Eliot's Ash Wednesday. Anglia 83 1965.

Hill, B. The literary criticism of Eliot: its source and tenets. Aylesford Rev 7 1965.

Hönnighausen, L. Die Verwendung der Dies Irae-Sequenz in Eliots Murder in the cathedral. Die Neueren Sprachen 14 1965.

Janoff, R. W. Eliot and Horace—aspects of the intrinsic classicist. Cithara 5 1965.

Le Breton, G. Eliot et la dialectique d' Héraclite. Mercure de France 353 1965.

Lindström, G. Eliot som dramatiker. Studiekamraten 47 1965.

McCord, H. The wryneck in The waste land. Classical Jnl 60 1965.

Morison, S. E. The Dry Salvages and the Thacher shipwreck. Amer Neptune 25 1965.

Nimkar, B. R. Eliot: the interpreter of the intellectual crisis. Modern Rev (Calcutta) 117 1965.

Nitchie, G. W. Eliot's borrowing: a note. Massachusetts Rev 6 1965.

Paul, L. A conversation with Eliot. Kenyon Rev 27 1965.

Peterson, S. Mr Eliot in The sacred wood. Greyfriar 8 1965.

Pons, C. T. S. Eliot, ou la critique moderne: critique et metacritique. Cahiers du Sud 52 1965.

Puhvel, M. Reminiscent bells in The waste land. Eng Lang Notes 2 1965. Echoes of Childe Roland.

Rayan, K. Rasa and the objective correlative. Br Jnl of Aesthetics 5 1965.

Rexine, J. E. Classical and Christian foundations of T. S. Eliot's Cocktail party. Books Abroad 39 1965.

Robson, W. W. Eliot as a critic of Dr Johnson. New Rambler 1965.

Roy, E. The Becket plays: Eliot, Fry and Anouilh. Modern Drama 8 1965.

Russel, F. Some non-encounters with Eliot. Horizon (New York) 7 1965.

Sealise, A. M. Eliot: due composizioni natalizie: La coltivazione degli alberi di Natale, Il viaggio dei Magi. Vita e Pensiero 48 1965.

Schmidt, G. Die asketische Regel: zum Verhältnis von Poesie und Drama bei Eliot. Die Neueren Sprachen 14 1965.

Sena. Ibsen and the latest Eliot. Literary Criterion 6 1965.

Servotte, H. Eliot 1888–1965: een inleiding. Dietsche Warande en Belfort 110 1965.

Shuttle, P. Eliot: an appreciation. Aylesford Rev 7 1965.

Siddiqui, M. N. The ambivalence of motives in Murder in the cathedral. Osmania Jnl of Eng Stud 5 1965.

Silverstein, N. Movie-going for lovers of The waste land and Ulysses. Salmagundi 1 1965.

Smith, J. A. Eliot and The Listener. Listener 21 Jan 1965. Rptd in Sewanee Rev 74 1966, Eliot special issue, below.

Sobreira, A. Eliot: um humanista. Brotéria 80 1965.

Spinucci, P. Eliot e Hart Crane. Studi Americani 11 1965.

Stormon, E. J. Some notes on Eliot and Jules Laforgue. Essays in French Lit no 2 1965.

Straumann, H. and C. Connolly. T. S. Eliot—der grosse Dichter der zeitgenössischen englischen Literatur. Universitas 20 1965.

Watson, G. The triumph of Eliot. CQ 7 1965. See also I. M. Parsons, ibid, and Watson's reply, ibid; rptd in Cox and Hinchliffe 1968, above. See also their joint Eliot's reputation, CQ 8 1966.

Wilson, R. The continuity of Eliot. Kano Stud no 1 1965.

Wright, K. Rhetorical repetition in Eliot's early verse. REL 6 1965.

— Word-repetition in Eliot's early verse. EC 16 1966.

Allen, A. Eliot's theory of personal expression. PMLA 81 1966.

Beery, J. A. The relevance of Baudelaire to Eliot's The waste land. Susquehanna Univ Stud 7 1966.

Broes, A. T. T. S. Eliot's Journey of the Magi: an explication. Xavier Univ Stud 5 1966.

Chalker, J. Aspects of rhythm and rhyme in Eliot's early poems. English 16 1966.

Clendenning, J. Time, doubt and vision: notes on Emerson and Eliot. Amer Scholar 36 1966.

Corrigan, M. The poet's intuition of prose fiction: Pound and Eliot on the novel. Univ of Windsor Rev 2 1966.

Davidson, C. Types of despair in Ash Wednesday. Renascence 18 1966.

Davidson, J. The end of Sweeney. College Eng 27 1966.

Dolan, P. J. Milton and Eliot: a common source. N & Q 211 1966. On a link between Paradise Lost and Marina.

— Ash Wednesday: a catechumenical poem. Renascence 19 1967.

Fleissner, R. F. Prufrock, Pater and Richard II: retracing a denial of princeship. Amer Lit 38 1966.

Headings, P. R. The question of exclusive art: Tolstoy and Eliot's The waste land. Revue des Langues Vivantes 32 1966.

Isaacs, J. I. Eliot the poet-playwright as seen in The family reunion. English 16 1966.

Jones, F. Eliot among the prophets. Amer Lit 38 1966.

Knust, H. Tristan and Sosostris. Revue de Littérature Comparée 40 1966.

— Sweeney among the birds and brutes. Arcadia 2 1967.

McCarron, W. E. An approach to the Four quartets. Poet & Critic 2 1966.

Maccoby, H. Z. Two notes on Ash Wednesday. N & Q 211 1966.

— Two notes on Murder in the cathedral. N & Q 212 1967.

— A commentary on Burnt Norton 1. N & Q 213 1968.

— Difficulties in the plot of The family reunion. Ibid.

— The family reunion and Kipling's The house surgeon. Ibid.

McCutchion, D. Yeats, Eliot and personality. Quest (Bombay) 50 1966.

Madeleine, Sr M. C. Eliot: poet as playwright. California Eng Jnl 2 1966.

Morton, A. L. Eliot: a personal view. Zeitschrift für Anglistik und Amerikanistik 14 1966.

Nowottny, W. The common privileges of poetry. Proc Br Acad 52 1966.

Sergeant, H. Religion in modern British poetry: the influence of Eliot. Aryan Path 37 1966.

Sewanee Review 74 1966. Eliot 1888–1965. Special issue, ed A. Tate; rptd as book, New York 1966. T. S. Eliot, American literature and the American language; I. A. Richards, On Eliot: notes for a talk at the Institute of Contemporary Arts, London, 29 June 1965; H. Read, Eliot—a memoir; S. Spender, Remembering Eliot; B. Dobrée, Eliot: a personal reminiscence; E. Pound, For Eliot; F. Morley, A few recollections of Eliot; C. Day Lewis, At East Coker (Poem); E. M. Browne, Eliot in the theatre: the director's memories; H. Gardner, The comedies of Eliot; R. Speaight, With Becket in Murder in the cathedral; C. Aiken, An anatomy of melancholy; L. Unger, Eliot's images of awareness; F. Kermode, A Babylonish dialect; R. Richman, The day of five signs: an elegy for Eliot (Poem); G. W. Knight, Eliot: some literary impressions; M. Praz, Eliot as a critic; A. Warren, Eliot's literary criticism; W. Fowlie, Baudelaire and Eliot: interpreters of their age; C. Brooks, Eliot: thinker and artist; J. A. Smith, Eliot and The Listener; R. Giroux, A personal memoir; F. N. Lees, Mr Eliot's Sunday morning Satura: Petronius and The waste land; H. S. Davies, Mistah Kurtz: he dead; B. Rajan, The overwhelming question; N. Braybrooke, Eliot in the south seas: a look at the poems that he wrote when he was sixteen in St Louis; A. Tate, Postscript.

Shulman, R. Myth, Eliot and the comic novel. Modern Fiction Stud 12 1966.

Verheul, K. Music, meaning and poetry in Four quartets. Lingua 16 1966.

Walz, R. Eliot: The love song of J. Alfred Prufrock behandelt an einer Prima. Die Neueren Sprachen 15 1966.

Webster, G. T. Eliot as critic: the man behind the masks. Criticism 8 1966.

Woodberry, P. Eliot's metropolitan world. Arizona Quart 22 1966.

Zulli, F. Eliot and Paul Bourget. N & Q 211 1966.

Adler, J. A source for Eliot in Shaw. N & Q 212 1967. Link between Murder in the cathedral and Saint Joan and between The cocktail party and Arms and the man.

Carey, J., OFM. T. S. Eliot's Wasteland. Cithara 7 1967.

Fasel, I. A 'conversation' between Faulkner and Eliot. Mississippi Quart 20 1967.

Fortenberry, G. Prufrock and the fool song. Ball State Univ Forum 8 1967.

Galvin, B. A note on Eliot's New Hampshire as a lyric poem. Massachusetts Stud in Eng 1 1967.

Geraldine, Sr M. The rhetoric of repetition in Murder in the cathedral. Renascence 19 1967.

Gil, K. J. 'You' in The love song of J. Alfred Prufrock. Phoenix 11 1967.

Grahn, H. Eliot: Journey of the Magi. Die Neueren Sprachen 16 1967.

Hirsch, D. H. Eliot and the vexation of time. Southern Rev 3 1967.

Holt, C. L. On structure and Sweeney Agonistes. Modern Drama 10 1967.

Jha, A. Eliot and Christopher Fry: a note on possible influence and counter-influence. Literary Criterion 8 1967.

LeBrun, P. Eliot and Henri Bergson. RES 18 1967.

Marcus, P. L. Eliot and Shakespeare. Criticism 9 1967.

Martin, B. K. Prufrock, Bleistein and company. N & Q 212 1967.

Martínez Menchén, A. Una lírica de la cultura (T. S. Eliot). Cuadernos Hispanoamericanos 71 1967.

Milward, P., SJ. 'In the end is my beginning': a study of Eliot's Elder statesman in comparison with The waste land. Stud in Eng Lit (Tokyo) 1967.

Montgomery, M. Wordsworth, Eliot and the 'personal heresy'. South Atlantic Bull 32 1967.

—— Eliot, Wordsworth and the problem of personal emotion in the poet. Southern Humanities Rev 2 1968.

O'Nan, M. Eliot's Le directeur. Symposium 21 1967.

Reeves, G. M. Eliot and Thomas Wolfe. South Atlantic Bull 32 1967.

Schmidt, G. Späte Fahrt ins Unbekannte: zur Interpretation von East Coker v 31–38. Die Neueren Sprachen 16 1967.

Seferis, G. T.S.E. (pages from a diary by Seferis). Quart Rev of Lit 15 1967.

Sena, V. Eliot's The family reunion: a study in disintegration. Southern Rev 3 1967.

Sheppard, R. W. Rilke's Duineser Elegien: a critical appreciation in the light of Eliot's Four quartets. Germanic Life & Letters 20 1967.

Stamm, R. Rebellion und Tradition im Werke Eliots. Universitas 22 1967.

Strickland, G. R. Flaubert, Pound and Eliot. Cambridge Quart 2 1967.

Tamplin, R. The tempest and The waste land. Amer Lit 39 1967.

Vaughn, F. H. Smog: the Old Possum's insidious cat. Lock Haven Rev 9 1967.

Ward, D. E. The cult of impersonality: Eliot, St Augustine and Flaubert. EC 17 1967.

Weatherby, H. L. Old-fashioned gods: Eliot on Lawrence and Hardy. Sewanee Rev 75 1967.

Weirick, M. C. Myth and water symbolism in Eliot's The waste land. Texas Quart 10 1967.

Whiteside, G. Eliot's dissertation. ELH 34 1967.

Atkins, A. Mr Eliot's Sunday morning parody. Renascence 21 1968.

Boyd, J. D., SJ. The Dry Salvages: topography as symbol. Renascence 20 1968.

—— Eliot as critic and rhetorician: the essay on Johnson. Criticism 11 1969.

Di Pasquale, P., jr. Coleridge's framework of objectivity and Eliot's objective correlative. Jnl of Aesthetics & Art Criticism 26 1968.

Faas, E. Formen der Bewusstseindarstellung in der dramatischen Lyrik Pounds und Eliots. Germanisch-romanische Monatsschrift 49 1968.

Franklin, R. F. The satisfactory journey of Eliot's Magus. E Studies 49 1968.

—— Death or the heat of life in the Handful of dust? Amer Lit 41 1969.

Halverson, J. Prufrock, Freud and others. Sewanee Rev 76 1968.

Holloway, J. The waste land. Encounter 31 1968.

Jain, N. K. An appreciation of Eliot's Marina. Banasthali Patrika 10 1968.

Kantra, R. A. A satiric theme and structure in Murder in the cathedral. Modern Drama 10 1968.

Kohli, D. Yeats and Eliot: the magnitude of contrast. Quest (Bombay) 58 1968.

Mendilow, A. A. Eliot's 'long unlovely street'. MLR 63 1968.

Milward, P., SJ. Sacramental symbolism in Hopkins and Eliot. Renascence 20 1968.

Oberg, A. K. The cocktail party and the illusion of autonomy. Modern Drama 11 1968.

Pickering, J. V. Form as agent: Eliot's Murder in the cathedral. Educational Theatre Jnl 20 1968.

Rahme, M. T. S. Eliot and the 'histrionic sensibility'. Criticism 10 1968.

Roche, P. Since Eliot: some notes towards a reassessment. Poetry Rev 59 1968; see reply by F. Grubb, ibid.

Sampley, A. M. The woman who wasn't there: Lacuna in Eliot. South Atlantic Quart 67 1968.

Sarang, V. A source for The hollow men. N & Q 213 1968.

Shorter, R. N. Becket as Job: Eliot's Murder in the cathedral. South Atlantic Quart 67 1968.

Slattery, Sr M. P. Structural unity in Eliot's Ash Wednesday. Renascence 20 1968.

Soldo, J. J. Knowledge and experience in the criticism of Eliot. ELH 35 1968.

Spangler, G. M. The Education of Henry Adams as a source for The love song of J. Alfred Prufrock. N & Q 213 1968.

Sutton, W. Mauberley, The waste land and the problem of unified form. Wisconsin Stud in Contemporary Lit 9 1968.

Thale, M. T. S. Eliot and Mrs Browning on the metaphysical poets. College Lang Assoc Jnl 11 1968.

Thrash, L. G. A source for the redemption theme in The cocktail party. Texas Stud in Lit & Lang 9 1968.

Vordtriede, W. Der junge Eliot. Neue Deutsche Hefte 120 1968.

Ward, D. Eliot, Murray, Homer and the idea of tradition: 'So I assumed a double part...'. EC 18 1968.

Wasson, R. The rhetoric of the theatre: the contemporaneity of T. S. Eliot. Drama Survey 6 1968.

—— Eliot's antihumanism and antipragmatism. Texas Stud in Lit & Lang 10 1968.

—— 'Like a burnished throne': Eliot and the demonism of technology. Centennial Rev 13 1969.

Yeomans, W. E. Eliot, ragtime and the blues. Univ Rev, Kansas 34 1968.

Andreach, R. J. Paradise lost and the Christian configuration of The waste land. Papers on Lang & Lit 5 1969.

Bell, V. M. A reading of Prufrock. E Studies 50 (Anglo-Amer Suppl) 1969.

Capellán Gonzalo, A. Dimensiones metafísicas del tiempo en Four quartets. Atlántida 7 1969.

Cargill, O. Death in a handful of dust. Criticism 11 1969.

Chancellor, P. The music of The waste land. Comparative Lit Stud 6 1969.

Dolan, P. J. Eliot's Marina: a reading. Renascence 21 1969.

Duffy, J. J. Eliot's objective correlative: a New England commonplace. New England Quart 42 1969.

Ellis, P. G. Eliot, F. H. Bradley and Four quartets. Research Stud 37 1969.

Hansen, E. A. Eliot's Landscapes. E Studies 50 1969.

Johnson, M. Eliot on satire, Swift and disgust. Papers on Lang & Lit 5 1969.

Keogh, J. G. Eliot's Hollow men as graveyard poetry. Renascence 21 1969.

Krieger, M. The critical legacy of Matthew Arnold: or the strange brotherhood of Eliot, I. A. Richards and North-rop Frye. Southern Rev 5 1969.

Lucas, J. and W. Myers. The waste land today. EC 19 1969; reply by J. McLauchlan, ibid.

Meckier, J. Eliot in 1920: the quatrain poems and The sacred wood. Forum for Modern Lang Stud 5 1969.

Miller, M. What the thunder meant. ELH 36 1969.

Monteiro, A. C. Teoria da impersonalidade: Fernando Pessoa e Eliot. O Tempo e o modo 68 1969.

Motola, G. The mountains of The waste land. EC 19 1969. On an allusion to Turgenev.

Mudford, P. G. Sweeney among the nightingales. EC 19 1969.

Peyre, H. T. S. Eliot et le classicisme. Revue d'Histoire Littéraire de France 69 1969.

Porter, M. G. Narrative stance in Four quartets: choreography and commentary. Univ Rev, Kansas 36 1969.

Pritchard, W. H. Reading The waste land today. EC 19 1969.

Rayan, K. Suggestiveness and suggestion. EC 19 1969.

Rees, T. R. The orchestration of meaning in Eliot's Four quartets. Jnl of Aesthetics & Art Criticism 28 1969.

Strandberg, V. Eliot's insomniacs. South Atlantic Quart 68 1969.

Waldoff, L. Prufrock's defenses and our responses. Amer Imago 26 1969.

Watts, H. H. The tragic hero in Eliot and Yeats. Centennial Rev 13 1969.

R.J.R.
D.J.M.

ROBERT VON RANKE GRAVES
b. 1895

The Lockwood Memorial Library (State Univ of New York, Buffalo), the Berg Collection (New York Public Library), the Humanities Research Center of the Univ of Texas (Austin), and the Univ of Southern Illinois (Carbondale) have collections of Graves mss. See F. H. Higginson, Bibliography, below.

Bibliographies

Boutell, H. S. Modern English first editions: Graves. Publishers Weekly 19 April 1930.

Moran, J. The Seizin Press of Laura Riding and Graves. Black Art 2 1963.

Turner, M. L. The Seizin Press—an additional note. Ibid.

Higginson, F. H. A bibliography of the works of Graves. 1966. Contains books and pamphlets, books containing contributions, contributions to press and periodicals by Graves, with notes on trns; miscellanea (mss, gramophone records, ephemera, radio broadcasts etc); selective list of works about Graves.

Collections and Selections

The crowning privilege: the Clark lectures 1954–1955, also various essays on poetry and sixteen new poems. 1955, Garden City NY 1956 (as The crowning privilege: collected essays on poetry; omits the poems and adds 9 essays), London 1959 (Penguin).

5 pens in hand. Garden City NY 1958. Lectures, essays, stories, 'historical anomalies' and poems.

Steps: stories, talks, essays, poems, studies in history.

1958. Much of the material is the same as in 5 pens in hand, above.

Food for centaurs: stories, talks, critical studies, poems. Garden City NY 1960.

Selected poetry and prose, chosen, introduced and annotated by J. Reeves 1961.

Poetry

Higginson (Bibliography, above) gives details of the frequent re-publication of individual poems, particularly in the series of major selections entitled Collected poems, but does not give details of Graves' constant revising of the texts.

Over the brazier. 1916, [1920] (with omissions).

Goliath and David. [1916] (priv ptd, 200 copies). Contents rptd in next.

Fairies and fusiliers. 1917, New York 1918.

Treasure box. [1919] (priv ptd, 200 copies). 10 poems, mostly rptd in The pier-glass, below.

Country sentiment. 1920, New York 1920.

The pier-glass. 1921, New York 1921.

Whipperginny. 1923, New York 1923.

The feather bed. Richmond Surrey 1923 (254 copies).

Mock Beggar Hall. 1924.

John Kemp's wager: a ballad opera. Oxford 1925, New York 1925.

Welchman's hose. 1925.

[Twenty-three poems.] [1925] (Augustan Books of Modern Poetry). Selection.

The marmosite's miscellany. [By] 'John Doyle'. 1925; rptd as by Graves in next.

Poems 1914–26. 1927, Garden City NY 1929.

Poems 1914–27. 1927 (115 copies). Poems 1914–26 with 9 additional poems.

Poems 1929. 1929 (Seizin 3, 225 copies).

Ten poems more. Paris 1930 (200 copies).

Poems 1926–1930. 1931.

To whom else? Deyá 1931 (Seizin 6, 200 copies).

Poems 1930–1933. 1933.

Collected poems. 1938, New York 1938.

No more ghosts: selected poems. 1940. Mainly from preceding.

Work in hand. [By] A. Hodge, N. Cameron, R. Graves. 1942. 18 poems by Graves.

[Thirty-one poems.] [1943] (Augustan Poets). Selection.

Poems 1938–1945. 1946, New York [1946].

Collected poems 1914–1947. 1948.

Poems and satires. 1951.

Poems 1953. 1953.

Collected poems 1955. Garden City NY 1955.

Poems selected by himself. 1957, 1961 (rev and enlarged), 1966 (rev and enlarged) (Penguin Poets).

The poems of Robert Graves chosen by himself. Garden City NY 1958.

Collected poems 1959. 1959.

The penny fiddle: poems for children. 1960, Garden City NY 1961.

More poems. 1961.

Collected poems. Garden City NY 1961.

The more deserving cases: eighteen old poems for reconsideration. [Marlborough] 1962 (400 copies). Pbd Marlborough College Press.

New poems. 1962, Garden City NY 1963.

Man does, woman is. 1964.

Ann at Highwood Hall: poems for children. 1964, Garden City NY 1966.

Love respelt. 1965 (250 copies) Garden City NY 1966. Most rptd in next.

Collected poems, 1965. 1965.

Collected poems, 1966. Garden City NY 1966.

Seventeen poems missing from Love respelt. 1966 (priv ptd, 330 copies).

Colophon to Love respelt. 1967 (priv ptd, 386 copies).

Poems 1965–1968. 1968, Garden City NY 1969.

Beyond giving. 1969 (priv ptd, 536 copies).

Fiction

My head! My head!: being the history of Elisha and the Shunamite woman; with the history of Moses as Elisha related it, and her questions put to him. 1925, New York 1925.

The shout. 1929.

No decency left, by 'Barbara Rich'. 1932. By Graves and Laura Riding.

The real David Copperfield. 1933, New York 1934 (with alterations, as David Copperfield by Dickens condensed).

I, Claudius: from the autobiography of Tiberius Claudius emperor of the Romans. 1934, New York 1934, 2 vols 1941 (Penguin), 1 vol New York 1965 (with introd).

Claudius the god and his wife Messalina. 1934, New York 1935.

'Antigua, penny, puce'. Deyá, London 1936, New York [1937] (as The Antigua stamp).

Count Belisarius. 1938, New York [1938].

Sergeant Lamb of the Ninth. 1940, New York [1940] (as Sergeant Lamb's America).

Proceed, Sergeant Lamb. 1941, New York [1941].

The story of Marie Powell, wife to Mr Milton. 1943, New York 1944 (as Wife to Mr Milton, the story of Marie Powell), London 1954 (Penguin).

The golden fleece. 1944, New York 1945 (as Hercules, my shipmate).

King Jesus. New York 1946, London 1946.

Watch the north wind rise. New York 1949, London 1949 (as Seven days in New Crete).

The islands of unwisdom. Garden City NY 1949, London 1950 (as The isles of unwisdom).

Homer's daughter. 1955, Garden City NY 1955.

¡Catacrok! Mostly stories, mostly funny. 1956.

The big green book. [New York] 1962. For children.

The siege and fall of Troy. 1962, Garden City NY 1963.

Collected short stories. Garden City NY 1964, London 1965.

Two wise children. New York [1966], London 1967.

The poor boy who followed his star and [3] children's poems. 1968.

Other Works

On English poetry: being an irregular approach to the psychology of this art, from evidence mainly subjective. New York 1922, London 1922.

The meaning of dreams. 1924.

Poetic unreason and other studies. 1925.

Contemporary techniques of poetry: a political analogy. 1925 (Hogarth Essays 8).

Another future of poetry. 1926. A reply to R. C. Trevelyan, Thamyris: or, is there a future for poetry, 1926.

The English ballad: a short critical survey. 1927, 1957 (rev, as English and Scottish ballads), New York 1957.

Lars Porsena: or the future of swearing and improper language. 1927, New York 1927, London 1936 (rev, as The future of swearing and improper language).

Impenetrability: or the proper habit of English. 1926 (for 1927) (Hogarth Essays 2nd ser 3).

John Skelton, laureate, 1460?–1529. [1927] (Augustan Books of English Poetry). Selection, modernisation of the poems, and editor's note by Graves.

Lawrence and the Arabs. 1927, Garden City NY 1928 (as Lawrence and the Arabian adventure), London 1934 ('concise' edn).

The less familiar nursery rhymes. [1927] (Augustan Books of English Poetry). Selection and foreword by Graves.

A survey of modernist poetry. 1927, Garden City NY 1928. With Laura Riding.

A pamphlet against anthologies. 1928, Garden City NY 1928. With Laura Riding.

Mrs Fisher: or the future of humour. 1928.

Goodbye to all that: an autobiography. 1929, New York [1930], Garden City NY 1957 (rev), London 1957. In most copies of the first edn pp. 289–90 and 341–4 are cancels, expurgating the text. The text was reset in this form in later impressions and in the American edn.

But it still goes on: an accumulation. 1930, New York [1931]. Sequel to Goodbye to all that, above. In most copies of the first edn pp. 157–8 are a cancel. In the second impression the text was reset.

Old soldiers never die, by Private Frank Richards [rewritten by Graves]. 1933, 1964 (with introd by Graves).

Old soldier sahib, by Private Frank Richards [rewritten by Graves]. 1936, New York [1936] (with introd by Graves), London 1965 (with new foreword by Graves).

T. E. Lawrence to his biographer, Robert Graves: information about himself, in the form of letters, notes and answers to questions edited with a critical commentary [by Graves]. New York 1938, London 1938 [1939], [1963] (as T. E. Lawrence to his biographers Robert Graves and Liddell Hart), Garden City NY 1963.

The long week-end: a social history of Great Britain 1918–1939. 1940, New York 1941. With Alan Hodge.

The reader over your shoulder: a handbook for writers of English prose. 1943, New York 1944, London 1947 (abridged). With Hodge.

The white goddess: a historical grammar of poetic myth. 1948, New York 1948, London 1952 (rev and enlarged), New York 1958, London 1961 (rev and enlarged).

The common asphodel: collected essays on poetry 1922–1949. 1949. With revisions.

Occupation: writer. New York 1950, London 1951. 'A collection of my short stories, plays and miscellaneous essays...revised'.

The Nazarene Gospel restored. 1953, Garden City NY 1954, London 1955 (pt 3, text of the Gospel, only). With Joshua Podro.

The Greek myths. 2 vols 1955, Baltimore 1955, 1 vol London 1958 (with rev introd) (Penguin).

Adam's rib and other anomalous elements in the Hebrew creation myth: a new view. 1955, New York 1958.

The crowning privilege. 1955. See Collections and selections, above.

Jesus in Rome: a historical conjecture. 1957. With Podro.

They hanged my saintly Billy. 1957, Garden City NY 1957 (as They hanged my saintly Billy: the life and death of Dr William Palmer).

5 pens in hand. 1958. See Collections and selections, above.

Steps. 1958. See Collections and selections, above.

Food for centaurs. 1960. See Collections and selections above.

Greek gods and heroes. Garden City NY 1960, London 1961 (as Myths of ancient Greece).

The comedies of Terence. Garden City NY 1962, London 1963. Echard's trn, ed with foreword by Graves.

Oxford addresses on poetry. 1962, Garden City NY 1962.

Oratio Creweiana MDCCCCLXII. [1962]. With English paraphrase.

Nine hundred iron chariots. Cambridge Mass 1963 (Arthur Dehon Little memorial lecture). Rptd in Mammon and the black goddess, 1965, below.

Mammon: oration delivered at the London School of Economics and Political Science 6 December 1963. 1964. Rptd in Mammon and the black goddess, 1965, below.

The Hebrew myths: the book of Genesis. Garden City NY 1964, London 1964. With Raphael Patai.

El fenomeno del turismo. Madrid 1964. English version pbd as Postscript 1965 in Majorca observed, below.

Oratio Creweiana MDCCCCLXIV. [1964]. With English paraphrase.

Mammon and the black goddess. 1965, Garden City NY 1965. Lectures and an essay.

Majorca observed. [1965], Garden City NY 1965. With Paul Hogarth.

Poetic craft and principle: lectures and talks. 1967.

The crane bag and other disputed subjects. 1969. Lectures, essays, reviews etc.

Translations

Schwarz, G. Almost forgotten Germany. 1936, Deyá, London 1936. With Laura Riding.

Lucius Apuleius. The transformation of Lucius, otherwise known as the golden ass. 1950 (Penguin Classics), New York 1951.

Galván, M. de J. 'Enriquillo': the cross and the sword. Bloomington [1954] (Unesco collection of representative works), London 1956 (as The cross and the sword).

Alarcón, P. A. de. The infant with the globe. Introd by Graves 1955, New York 1955.

'Sand, George'. Winter in Majorca, with José Quadrado's refutation of George Sand. 1956, Mallorca 1956.

Lucan. Pharsalia: dramatic episodes of the civil wars. 1956 (Penguin Classics), Baltimore 1957.

Gaius Suetonius Tranquillus. The twelve Caesars. 1957 (Penguin Classics).

Fable of the hawk and the nightingale, translated from Hesiod's Works and days. Lexington Kentucky 1959 (about 110 copies).

The anger of Achilles: Homer's Iliad translated. Garden City NY 1959, London 1960.

The Rubaiyat of Omar Khayaam: a new translation with critical commentaries by Graves and Omar Ali-Shah. 1967, Garden City NY 1968.

§2

Lucas, F. L. Critical unreason: or Dr Cottard's Saturday night. In his Authors dead and living, 1926. Review of Poetic unreason and other studies.

Muir, E. Robert Graves. In his Transition: essays on contemporary literature, 1926.

Graves, A. P. To return to all that: an autobiography. 1930. Includes ch on his son Robert.

Williams, C. Robert Graves. In his Poetry at present, Oxford 1930.

Algren, N. Sentiment with terror. Poetry (Chicago) 55 1939. Review of Collected poems, 1938.

Ball, D. Robert Graves. Cahiers de Paris 8 1940.

Church, R. Graves: a traveller in the desert. Fortnightly Rev 155 1941; rptd in his Eight for immortality, 1941.

Petter, E. C. The poetry of Graves. English 3 1941.

Fraser, G. S. The poetry of Graves. The Changing World 2 1947; rptd in his Vision and rhetoric, 1959.

Pick, J. B. The poet as cynic: a discussion of Graves' poetry. Outposts 14 1949.

Gregory, H. Graves: a parable for writers. Partisan Rev 20 1953.

Blissett, W. F. Robert Graves. Canadian Forum 34 1954.

Bogan, L. Satire and sentimentality. In her Selected criticism, New York 1955.

Hayman, R. Robert Graves. EC 5 1955.

Jarrell, R. Graves and The white goddess. Yale Rev 45 1956.

Schwartz, D. Graves in dock: the case for modern poetry. New Republic 19 March 1956.

Seymour-Smith, M. Robert Graves. 1956 (Br Council pamphlet).

Trilling, L. A ramble on Graves. In his A gathering of fugitives, Boston 1956.

Jones, R. G. The poetic creed of Graves. Dock Leaves 8 1957.

Swanson, R. A. Graves' Hercules at Nemea. Explicator 15 1957.
— In his Heart of reason, Minneapolis 1963.

West, A. The Greek myth. In his Principles and persuasions, New York 1957.

Dudek, L. Julian Huxley, Graves and the mythologies. Delta (Cambridge) 4 1958.
— The case of Graves. Canadian Forum 40 1960.

Fuller, R. Some vintages of Graves. London Mag 5 1958.

Vickery, J. B. Three modes and a myth. Western Humanities Rev 12 1958.

Creeley, R. Her service is perfect freedom. Poetry (Chicago) 93 1959.

Dahlberg, E. and H. Read. Graves and Eliot. Twentieth Century 166 1959.

Davie, D. The toneless voice of Graves. Listener 2 July 1959.

Hassall, C. In his Edward Marsh: patron of the arts, 1959.

Hoffman, D. G. The unquiet Graves. Sewanee Rev 67 1959.
— Significant wounds: the early poetry of Graves. Shenandoah 17 1966.
— Barbarous knowledge: myth in the poetry of Yeats, Graves and Muir. New York 1967.

Marković, C. Robert Grevs. Savremenik 5 1959.

A personal mythology. TLS 5 June 1959.

Cohen, J. M. Robert Graves. Edinburgh 1960 (Writers and Critics).

Simon, J. Nowhere is washing so well done. Mid-Century no 16 1960.

Steiner, G. The genius of Graves. Kenyon Rev 22 1960 and subsequent correspondence.

Enright, D. J. Graves and the decline of modernism. EC 11 1961. Pbd separately in Singapore [1960?].

Gaskell, R. The poetry of Graves. CQ 3 1961.

Dodsworth, M. The man in the iron mask. Review (Oxford) 2 1962.

Green, P. Graves as a historical novelist. Critic (Chicago) 20 1962.

Musgrove, S. The ancestry of The white goddess. Auckland NZ 1962.

Peschmann, H. Salute to Graves. English 14 1962.

Rosenberg, B. A. Graves' To Juan at the winter solstice. Explicator 21 1962.

Shenandoah 13 1962. Graves special no containing
  Auden, W. H. A poet of honor.
  Enright, D. J. The example of Graves.
  Fraser, G. S. The reputation of Graves.
  Gunn, T. In nobody's pantheon.
  Davie, D. Impersonal and emblematic.
  Sillitoe, A. I reminded him of Muggleton.
  Wilson, C. Some notes on Graves's prose.

Day, D. Swifter than reason: the poetry and criticism of Graves. Chapel Hill [1963].
— Graves, septuagenario: el viejo poeta en su mundo autoconstruido. Papeles de Son Armadans 39 1965.

Nemerov, H. The poetry of Graves. In his Poetry and fiction, New Brunswick NJ [1963].

Peeters, E. Apologie voor een fantast. Tijdschrift van de Vrije Universiteit van Brussel 5 1963.

Symons, J. An evening in Maida Vale: Laura Riding and Graves. London Mag new ser 3 1964.

Weisinger, H. A very curious and painstaking person—Graves as mythographer. In his The agony and the triumph, East Lansing [1964].

Bergonzi, B. In his Heroes' twilight: a study of the literature of the Great War, 1965.

Fauchereau, S. L'œuvre de Graves. Critique (Paris) 21 1965.

Hauge, I. Graves og hans plass i nyere engelsk lyrikk. Samtiden 74 1965.

Spears, M. K. The latest Graves: poet and private eye. Sewanee Rev 73 1965.

Kirkham, M. Incertitude and The white goddess. EC 16 1966.
— The poetic liberation of Graves. Minnesota Rev 6 1966.
— The poetry of Graves. 1969.

Stürzl, E. Der entthronte Apoll: zur Auffassung des Dichters bei Graves. Munich [1966] (Salzburger Universitätsreden Hft 9).

Stade, G. Robert Graves. New York 1967.

Stebner, G. Robert Graves: To Juan at the winter solstice.

In Die moderne englische Lyrik, ed H. Oppel, Berlin [1967].

Warmsley, N. Graves where is thy sting? Twentieth Century no 1033 1967.

Burgess, A. A note on Graves and Omar. Encounter 30 1968.

Bowley, C. C. Graves's Language of the seasons: a linguistic approach to poetic analysis. Te Reo 10/11 1967/8.

Sinclair, J. McH. A technique of stylistic description. Language & Style 1 1968. On The legs.

Hijmans, B. L. Graves, The white goddess and Vergil. Mosaic 2 1969.

R. J. R.

WYSTAN HUGH AUDEN
b. 1907

Bloomfield's Bibliography, *below, has a list of mss which 'cannot pretend to be complete; it merely records the existence of mss located during the completion of the bibliography'.*

Bibliographies

Writings by Auden [1924–37]. New Verse nos 26–7 1937. By R. Todd.

Clancy, J. P. A W. H. Auden bibliography. Thought 30 1955.

Beach, J. W. The making of the Auden canon. Minneapolis [1957]. 'A record of the facts in regard to W. H. Auden's procedure in making up the texts of the Collected Poetry (Random House, 1945) and the Collected Shorter Poems (Faber and Faber, 1950)'.

Callan, E. An annotated checklist of the works of Auden. Twentieth-Century Lit 4 1958; rptd (rev) Denver 1958. Continued, Twentieth-Century Lit 16 1970. Only lists separate vols of poetry, but attempts to list all essays and reviews.

Bloomfield, B. C. Notes and corrections on The making of the Auden canon by J. W. Beach. N & Q 204 1959.

— W. H. Auden's first book. Library 5th ser 17 1962.

— W. H. Auden: a bibliography; the early years through 1955. Charlottesville 1964. Contains books and pamphlets, works edited or having contributions, contributions to periodicals and miscellaneous poems by Auden, appendices of unpbd work, mss, anthologies, musical settings, bibliography, criticism and trns of Auden's work.

Tolley, A. T. The printing of Auden's Poems (1928) and Spender's Nine experiments. Library 5th ser 22 1967.

§I
Poetry

Poems. 1928 (priv ptd by Stephen Spender, c. 30 copies), Cincinnati [1964] (photo facs with preface by Spender). Some poems not rptd in later collections.

Poems. [1930] [1933] (with 7 substituted poems).

The orators: an English study. 1932, 1934 (with corrections and excisions), 1966 (further excisions and new preface), New York 1967 (further corrections). Verse and prose.

Poem. [New Haven] 1933 (priv ptd by F. Prokosch, c. 22 copies). Contains Hearing of harvest rotting in the valley; rptd in Look stranger!, 1936, below.

The witnesses. 1933. Single sheet; rptd from Listener, 20 copies.

Poems. New York [1934]. Contains Poems 1933, above, The orators and The dance of death (*see* Plays, below).

Two poems. [New Haven] 1934 (priv ptd by F. Prokosch, c. 22 copies). Contains Sleep on beside me though I wake for you, and The latest ferrule now has tapped the curb; rptd from New Verse 5 1933. The 2 poems also ptd separately in edns of c. 5 copies each.

Our hunting fathers. [Cambridge] 1935 (priv ptd for F. Prokosch, c. 22 copies); rptd in Look stranger!, 1936, below.

Sonnet. [Cambridge] 1935 (priv ptd for F. Prokosch, c. 22 copies). On the provincial lawn I watch you play; rptd from Rep 1 1934.

Look, stranger! 1936, New York [1937] (as On this island).

Spain. 1937, [Paris] 1937 (in Les poètes du monde défendent le peuple espagnol 5, priv ptd by Nancy Cunard).

Letters from Iceland. 1937, New York [1937], London 1967 (revisions and excisions), New York 1969. With L. MacNeice. Verse and prose.

Nightmail . [1938?]. Single sheet; rptd in Collected shorter poems 1927–1957, 1966 below.

Selected poems. 1938. Selected by the author.

Epithalamion commemorating the marriage of G. A. Borgese and E. Mann. [New York] 1939; rptd in Another time, 1940.

Journey to a war. 1939, New York [1939]. With C. Isherwood. Poems and commentary.

Another time. New York [1940], London 1940.

Some poems. 1940. Selected by the author.

The double man. New York [1941], London 1941 (as New Year letter).

Three songs for St Cecilia's Day. [New York] 1941 (priv ptd, 250 copies); rptd from Harper's Bazaar Dec 1941; rptd in The collected poetry of W. H. Auden, 1945, below.

For the time being. New York [1944], London 1945.

The collected poetry of W. H. Auden. New York [1945]. Selection from previous vols with some revision and some uncollected poems.

Litany and anthem for S. Matthew's Day, written for the Church of S. Matthew, Northampton. [Northampton 1946].

The age of anxiety: a baroque eclogue. New York [1947], London [1948].

Collected shorter poems 1930–1944. [1950]. Differs from the corresponding sections in The collected poetry [1945], above; there are omissions, changes of title and addns.

Nones. New York [1951], London 1952.

Mountains. 1954 (Ariel poem); rptd in next.

The shield of Achilles. New York [1955], London 1955.

The old man's road. New York 1956. Also separate limited edn, 50 copies.

Reflections in a forest. [Greencastle Ind] 1957. Single sheet; rptd in Homage to Clio, 1960.

Goodbye to the Mezzogiorno: poesia inedita e versione italiana di C. Izzo. Milan 1958; rptd in Homage to Clio, 1960.

W. H. Auden: a selection by the author. 1958 (Penguin Poets), New York 1959 (Modern Library, as The selected poetry of W. H. Auden). With revisions.

Homage to Clio. New York [1960], London 1960.

W. H. Auden: a selection with notes and a critical essay by R. Hoggart. 1961 (Hutchinson English Texts). Hoggart's essay rptd in Auden, ed M. K. Spears 1964, below.

The common life. Darmstadt 1964; rptd in About the house, 1965.

About the house. New York [1965], London 1966.

Half-way. Cambridge Mass 1965. Single sheet. 75 copies; rptd in Collected shorter poems 1927–1957, 1966.

The cave of making. Darmstadt 1965. Also in About the house, 1965, above.

Collected shorter poems 1927–1957. 1966, New York 1967.

But I can't. Cambridge Mass 1966. Single sheet. 12 copies, rptd from The collected poetry, 1945.

Marginalia. Cambridge Mass 1966. 150 copies.

Portraits. Northampton Mass 1966. 20 copies; poems rptd from The collected poetry, 1945.

River profile. Cambridge Mass 1967. c. 50 copies; rptd in City without walls, 1969, below.

Brussels in winter. [New Haven] 1967. Single sheet. 10 copies.

Collected longer poems. 1968, New York 1969. Contains Paid on both sides, Letter to Lord Byron, New Year letter, For the time being, The sea and the mirror, The age of anxiety. Some revisions.

Selected poems. 1968. With revisions.

Two songs. New York 1968. 126 copies; rptd in City without walls, 1969.

City without walls. 1969, New York 1970.

A New Year greeting. [New York 1969].

See also B. C. Bloomfield and E. Mendelson, A poem attributed to Auden [The Platonic blow]. Library 5th ser 25 1970.

Christopher Isherwood's Lions and shadows, 1938, in which Auden appears as 'Hugh Weston', contains some early poems by Auden. Auden has made a number of records of readings from his poetry. See Bloomfield, Bibliography, above, and Spears, The poetry of Auden, 1963, below.

Plays and Libretti

The dance of death. (Westminster 24 Oct 1934). 1933.

The dog beneath the skin: or, where is Francis?; a play in three acts. (Westminster 12 Jan 1936). 1935, New York 1935. With C. Isherwood.

The ascent of F6: a tragedy in two acts. (Mercury 26 Feb 1937). 1936, New York 1937 (rev), London 1937 (2nd edn again rev). With C. Isherwood, the verse being by Auden.

No more peace! By E. Toller, lyrics tr Auden. New York 1937, London 1937.

On the frontier: a melodrama in three acts. (Arts Theatre, Cambridge 14 Nov 1938). 1938, New York [1939]. With C. Isherwood.

The dark valley. (Columbia Workshop 2 June 1940). In Best broadcasts of 1939-40, New York [1940].

The rake's progress: opera in three acts. Music by I. Stravinsky, libretto by Auden and C. Kallman. (Venice, 11 Sept 1951). 1951, 1966 (rev).

The magic flute: an opera in two acts. Music by W. A. Mozart, English version after the libretto of Schikaneder and Giesecke by Auden and Kallman. (NBC Television 15 Jan 1956). New York [1956], London 1957.

Don Giovanni: opera in two acts. Music by W. A. Mozart, libretto by L. da Ponte. English version by Auden and Kallman. (NBC Television 10 April 1960). New York [1961].

Elegy for young lovers: opera in three acts by Auden and C. Kallman, music by H. W. Henze. (Stuttgart 20 May 1961). Mainz 1961.

The Bassarids: opera seria with intermezzo in one act based on The Bacchae by Euripides by Auden and C. Kallman. Music by H. W. Henze. (Salzburg 6 Aug 1966). Mainz [1966].

Auden also wrote the libretto for an operetta, Paul Bunyan, by Britten. It was performed at Columbia Univ in May 1941 but was later withdrawn by the composer. Another libretto by Auden and Kallman, Delia or a masque of night was pbd in Botteghe Oscure 12 1953. Auden collaborated with Brecht in adapting Webster's Duchess of Malfi in 1945-6, and translated, with Kallman, Brecht's Die sieben Todsünden (pbd Tulane Drama Rev 6 1961); with J. and T. Stern, Der kaukasische Kreidekreis (pbd in Brecht's Plays, vol 1 1960); and with Kallman, Mahagonny (1960, unpbd). He also translated Cocteau's Les chevaliers de la table ronde (pbd in Cocteau's Infernal machine and other plays, New York [1964]). He collaborated on the films Coal face, Night mail, The way to the sea and Londoners in 1935-9. See Bloomfield, Bibliography, above, and Spears, The poetry of Auden, 1963, below.

Other Works

Education today—and tomorrow. 1939 (Day to Day pamphlets 40). With T. C. Worsley

The enchafèd flood: or the romantic iconography of the sea. New York [1950], London 1951.

Making, knowing and judging: an inaugural lecture delivered before the University of Oxford. Oxford 1956; rptd in next.

The dyer's hand and other essays. New York [1962], London 1963. Selected critical pieces. 'I've reduced them, where possible, to sets of notes' (Foreword).

Louis MacNeice: a memorial address delivered at All Souls Langham Place. [1963] (priv ptd, 250 copies).

Selected essays. 1964. All from The dyer's hand. Two essays and Postscript rptd as Reading and Writing, Tokyo 1966.

Secondary worlds. 1968, New York [1969]. First Eliot lectures at University of Kent.

Worte und Noten. Salzburg 1968. An address.

Principal Works Edited or with Contributions by Auden

Public school verse, vol 4, 1923-4. 1924. Single poem by 'W. H. Arden'.

Oxford poetry 1926. Ed C. Plumb and Auden, Oxford 1926. 8 poems.

Oxford poetry 1927. Ed Auden and C. Day Lewis, Oxford 1927. One poem.

Oxford poetry 1928. Ed C. Parsons and 'B.B.', Oxford 1928. One poem.

New signatures: poems by several hands collected by M. Roberts. 1932. 3 poems.

An outline for boys and girls and their parents. Ed N. Mitchison 1932. Includes Writing: or the pattern between people.

New country: prose and poetry by the authors of New signatures. Ed M. Roberts 1933. 4 poems.

Oxford and the groups, ed R. H. S. Crossman, Oxford 1934. Contains The group movement and the middle classes.

The old school: essays by divers hands. Ed G. Greene 1934. Includes Honour.

The great Tudors. Ed K. Garvin 1935. Contains John Skelton.

The poet's tongue: an anthology chosen by Auden and J. Garrett. 2 vols 1935, 1 vol 1935 (with shortened introd).

The arts today. Ed G. Grigson 1935. Contains Psychology and art today.

Christianity and the social revolution. Ed J. Lewis et al 1935. Contains The good life.

Britten, B. Our hunting fathers. 1936, 1964. Symphonic cycle, devised [and with 2 poems] by Auden.

Selected poems by Robert Frost. 1936. Introductory essay by Auden.

From Anne to Victoria: essays by various hands. Ed B. Dobrée. 1937. Contains Pope, 1688-1744.

Authors take sides on the Spanish War. 1937.

The Oxford book of light verse, chosen by Auden. Oxford 1938.

Poems of freedom. Ed J. Mulgan, introd by Auden. 1938.

Poet venturers: a collection of poems written by Bristol school boys and girls. Foreword by Auden, Bristol 1938.

I believe: the personal philosophies of certain eminent men and women of our time. Ed C. Fadiman, New York 1939, London 1940.

Fifteen poets. Oxford 1941. Contains Byron.

The intent of the critic. Ed D. A. Stauffer, Princeton 1941. Contains Criticism in a mass society.

A selection from the poems of Alfred Lord Tennyson, selected and arranged with an introduction by Auden. Garden City NY 1944, London 1946 (as Tennyson: an introduction and a selection).

Cammaerts, E. The flower of grass. Foreword by Auden, New York 1945.

James, H. The American scene, together with three essays from Portraits of places. Ed with introd by Auden, New York 1946.

The Kafka problem. Ed A. Flores, New York [1946]. Contains K's quest.

The Yale series of younger poets. 1947-59. Auden was

editor of the series 1947–59 and contributed forewords to vols by the following: Joan Murray (1947), Robert Horan (1948), Rosalie Moore (1949), Adrienne Cecile Rich (1951), W. S. Merwin (1952), Edgar Bogardus (1953), Daniel G. Hoffman (1954), John Ashbery (1956), James Wright (1957), John Hollander (1958), William Dickey (1959).

Betjeman, J. Slick but not streamlined: poems and short pieces, selected and with an introd by Auden. Garden City NY 1947.

Baudelaire, C. Intimate journals; tr C. Isherwood, introd by Auden, Hollywood 1947, London 1949.

Poets at work: essays based on the Modern Poetry Collection at the Lockwood Memorial Library, University of Buffalo, by R. Arnheim, Auden, K. Shapiro, D. A. Stauffer. New York [1948].

The portable Greek reader. Ed and with an introd by Auden, New York 1948.

Yezierska, A. Red ribbon on a white horse. Introd by Auden, New York 1950.

Indian congress for cultural freedom 1951. Bombay 1951. Contains an address by Auden.

Poets of the English language. Ed Auden and N. H. Pearson, introd by Auden 5 vols New York 1950, London 1952.

Poe, selected prose and poetry. Ed with an introd by Auden. New York 1950, 1956 (rev).

The living thoughts of Kierkegaard, presented by Auden. New York [1952], London 1955 (as Kierkegaard, selected and introduced by Auden).

Tales of Grimm and Andersen. Introd by Auden, New York 1952.

New poems by American poets, edited by R. Humphries. New York 1953. 2 poems. Vol 2, 1957, contains 5 poems.

Rolfe, F. The desire and pursuit of the whole. Foreword by Auden 1953.

Riverside poetry 1953, selected by Auden, M. Moore, K. Shapiro. New York 1953.

Rudolf Kassner zum achtzigsten Geburtstag. Ed A. C. Kensik and D. Bodmer, Erlenbach-Zürich 1953. Includes an appreciation by Auden.

Macdonald, G. The visionary novels. Ed A. Fremantle with introd by Auden, New York 1954.

An Elizabethan song book: music ed Noah Greenberg, text ed Auden and C. Kallman. Garden City NY 1955, London 1956.

The Faber book of modern American verse. 1956, New York 1956 (as The Criterion book of modern American verse).

Modern Canterbury pilgrims: the story of twenty-three converts and why they chose the Anglican Communion. Ed J. A. Pike, New York 1956, London 1956.

Oratio Creweiana 1956 [1958, 1960]. 3 vols [Oxford 1956–60]. Latin texts by J. G. Griffith.

Selected writings of Sydney Smith. Ed with an introd by Auden. New York 1956, London 1957.

Williams, C. The descent of the Dove: a history of the Holy Spirit in the church. New York 1956. Introd.

Language: an enquiry into its meaning and function. Ed R. N. Anshen, New York 1957. Contains Squares and oblongs (different from essay with same title contained in Poets at work, 1948).

D'Ambra, N. Nullo vogliamo dal sogno. Milan 1957. Preface.

Goll, Y. Jean sans terre. New York 1958. Preface.

Shakespeare, W. Romeo and Juliet. Ed C. J. Sisson, New York 1958 (Laurel Shakespeare). Commentary by Auden.

The play of Daniel, edited by N. Greenberg. New York 1959, 1964. Narration by Auden.

Ibsen, H. Brand. Tr by M. Mayer with foreword by Auden, New York 1960.

McGinley, P. Times three: selected verse. New York 1960, London 1961. Foreword.

The complete poems of Cavafy. Tr Rae Dalven. New York 1961, London 1961. Introd.

'Perse, St-John' (A. St-Léger Léger). On poetry. Tr Auden, New York 1961, 1966 (in Two addresses).

Van Gogh: a self-portrait—letters revealing his life as a painter, selected by Auden. Greenwich Conn 1961, London 1961.

Goethe, J. W. Italian journey 1786–8. Tr Auden and E. Mayer 1962, New York 1962.

The seven deadly sins. 1962, New York 1962 (introd by I. Fleming). Contains Anger.

The Viking book of aphorisms: a personal selection by Auden and L. Kronenberger. New York 1962, London 1964 (as The Faber book of aphorisms).

A choice of De la Mare's verse, selected with an introd by Auden. 1963.

Jacobs, J. The Pied Piper and other fairy tales. New York 1963. Commentary by Auden.

The plough and the pen: writings from Hungary 1930–56, edited by I. Duczyńska and K. Polányi. Foreword by Auden 1963.

Fisher, M. F. K. The art of eating. 1963.

Bloomfield, B. C. W. H. Auden: a bibliography. Foreword by Auden, Charlottesville 1964.

Hammarskjöld, D. Markings. Tr L. Sjöberg and Auden, with a foreword by Auden, New York 1964, London 1964.

MacNeice, L. Selected poems, selected and introduced by Auden. 1964.

Shakespeare, W. The sonnets. Introd by Auden, New York 1964.

Stravinsky, I. Elegy for J.F.K. 1964. Setting of Auden poem.

Half-way to the moon: new writing from Russia. Ed P. Blake and M. Hayward. 1964. Contains 3 trns.

Immaculate, Sr M. (ed). The tree and the master. Preface by Auden, New York 1965.

New York Times. Hiroshima plus 20. New York 1965. Contains The bomb and man's consciousness.

Walton, W. The twelve. 1965. Setting of Auden poem.

Byron, G. G. Selected poetry and prose. Ed Auden, New York 1966.

Nineteenth century British minor poets. Ed Auden, New York 1966, London 1967 (as Nineteenth century minor poets).

To Nevill Coghill from friends. Collected by J. Lawlor and Auden, 1966. Includes a poem by Auden.

Tradition and innovation in contemporary literature. Budapest 1966. Contains A short defense of poetry.

Barfield, O. History in English words. Foreword by Auden, Grand Rapids 1967.

Woolf, C. and J. Bagguley (ed). Authors take sides on Vietnam. 1967, New York 1967.

Yanovsky, V. S. No man's time. Foreword by Auden 1967, New York 1967.

Handley-Taylor, G. and T. D'Arch-Smith. C. Day-Lewis, the poet laureate: a bibliography. 1968. Contains A letter of introduction.

Reinhold, H. A. H.A.R.: the autobiography of Father Reinhold. Foreword by Auden, New York 1968.

Völuspá: the song of the sybil. Tr P. B. Taylor and Auden. Iowa City 1968 (450 copies); rptd in The elder Edda, below.

Henze, H. W. Moralitäten. Mainz 1969. Setting of 3 scenic plays by Auden from fables by Aesop.

MacNeice, L. Persons from Porlock and other plays for radio. Introd by Auden 1969.

Rossiter, A. The pendulum. Foreword by Auden, New York 1969.

The elder Edda: a selection. Tr P. B. Taylor and Auden 1969, New York 1970.

With Jacques Barzun and L. Trilling, Auden edited Griffin, the magazine of the Reader's Subscription Book Club, *1951–8, and* Mid-Century, the magazine of the Mid-Century Book Soc, *1959–62, and contributed reviews to them.*

§2

Empson, W. A note on Auden's Paid on both sides. Experiment 7 1931.
— Early Auden. Review (Oxford) no 5 1963.
Grigson, G. Notes on contemporary poetry. Bookman (London) 82 1932.
Spender, S. Five notes on Auden's writing. Twentieth Century (Promethean Soc) 3 1932.
— In his Destructive element, 1935.
— The poetic dramas of Auden and Isherwood. New Writing new ser 1 1938.
— The importance of Auden. London Mercury 39 1939.
— Auden at Oxford. World Rev new ser 6 1949.
— Seriously unserious. Poetry (Chicago) 78 1951.
— In his World within world, 1951.
— Auden and his poetry. Atlantic Monthly 192 1953; rptd in Auden, ed M. K. Spears 1964.
— In his Creative element, 1953.
— Greatness of aim. TLS 6 Aug 1954. Review of Collected shorter poems and of Dylan Thomas, Collected poems.
— It began at Oxford. New York Times Book Rev 13 March 1955.
Burnham, J. Auden. Nation 8 Aug 1934.
Foxall, E. The politics of Auden. Bookman (London) 85 1934.
Leavis, F. R. Auden, Bottrall and others. Scrutiny 3 1934. Review of Poems (1933) and The dance of death.
Darlington, W. A. A theorist in the theatre. Discovery 16 1935.
Deutsch, B. In her This modern poetry, New York 1935.
— In her Poetry in our time, New York 1952.
Maynard, T. When the pie was opened. Commonweal 2 Aug 1935.
Stone, G. Plays by Eliot and Auden. Amer Rev 6 1935. Review of Murder in the Cathedral and of The dog beneath the skin.
Close, H. M. The development of Auden's poetry. Cambridge Rev 9 June 1937.
Glicksberg, C. Poetry and Marxism: three English poets take their stand. UTQ 6 1937. On Auden, Day Lewis, Spender.
— Poetry and social revolution. Dalhousie Rev 17 1938.
New Verse nos 26–7 1937. Auden double number containing: W. H. Auden, Dover [a poem]; C. Isherwood, Some notes on Auden's early poetry, rptd in Auden, ed M. K. Spears 1964; L. MacNeice, Letter to Auden; G. Grigson, Auden as a monster; K. Allott, Auden in the theatre; E. Rickword, Auden and politics; Sixteen comments on Auden [by various writers]; Writings by Auden [short bibliography].
Whistler, L. A note on the new Auden. Poetry Rev 28 1937. Review of Look, stranger!
Drummond, J. The mind of Mr Auden. Townsman 1 1938.
Isherwood, C. In his Lions and shadows: an education in the Twenties, 1938. With poems by Auden.
Flint, F. C. New leaders in English poetry. Virginia Quart Rev 14 1938.
— Auden's Our hunting fathers told the story. Explicator 2 1943.
MacNeice, L. In his Modern poetry, 1938.
Southworth, J. G. Auden. Sewanee Rev 46 1938; rptd in his Sowing the spring, Oxford 1940.
— In his More modern American poets, Oxford 1954.
Brooks, C. In his Modern poetry and the tradition, Chapel Hill 1939; excerpts rptd in Auden, ed M. K. Spears 1964.
— Auden as a critic. Kenyon Rev 26 1964.
— and R. P. Warren. As I walked out one evening. In their Understanding poetry, New York 1960 (3rd edn). An analysis of the poem.
Daiches, D. Auden: the search for a public. Poetry (Chicago) 54 1939.
— In his Poetry in the modern world, Chicago 1940.

Henderson, P. In his Poet and society, 1939.
Schwartz, D. The two Audens. Kenyon Rev 1 1939.
Symons, J. Auden and the poetic drama. Life & Letters Today 20 1939.
Brenner, R. In her Poets of our time, New York 1941.
Jarrell, R. Changes of attitude and rhetoric in Auden's poetry. Southern Rev 7 1941.
— Freud to Paul: the stages of Auden's ideology. Partisan Rev 12 1945; both essays rptd in his Third book of criticism, New York 1969.
Scarfe, F. Auden and after: the liberation of poetry 1930–41. 1942.
— Auden. Monaco 1949.
Savage, D. S. The strange case of Auden. In his Personal principle, 1944.
Brown, W. C. et al. Auden's Sir, no man's enemy, forgiving all. Explicator 3 1945.
Lechlitner, R. The Odyssey of Auden. Poetry (Chicago) 66 1945.
Lienhardt, R. G. Auden's inverted development. Scrutiny 13 1945.
Mizener, A. [Review of For the time being]. Accent 5 1945; rptd in Accent anthology, ed K. Quinn and C. Shattuck, New York 1946.
Philbrick, F. A. Auden's Have a good time. Explicator 4 1945.
— Auden's Crisis. Explicator 5 1947.
Morland, H. Auden's Crisis. Ibid.
Stauffer, D. A. Which side am I supposed to be on?: the search for beliefs in Auden's poetry. Virginia Quart Rev 22 1946.
Brooks, B. G. The poetry of Auden. Nineteenth Century 141 1947.
Griffin, H. The idiom of Auden. New Quart of Poetry 2 1947.
— Conversation on Cornelia Street: dialogue with Auden. Accent 10 1949.
— A dialogue with Auden. Hudson Rev 3 1951.
— Conversation on Cornelia Street, iv: a dialogue with Auden. Accent 12 1952.
— Conversation on Cornelia Street, v: a dialogue with Auden. Accent 13 1953.
— A dialogue with Auden. Partisan Rev 20 1953.
— Conversation on Cornelia Street: a dialogue with Auden. Poetry (Chicago) 83 1953.
Bloomfield, M. W. Doom is dark and deeper than any sea-dingle: Auden and Sawles warde. MLN 63 1948.
Bradbury, J. M. Auden and the tradition. Western Rev 12 1948.
Cleophas, Sr M. Auden's Family ghosts or The strings' excitement. Explicator 7 1948.
Greenberg, S. Auden: poet of anxiety. Masses & Mainstream 1 1948.
Kermode, F. The theme of Auden's poetry. Rivista di Letterature Moderne 3 1948.
— The poet in praise of limestone. Atlantic 225 1970.
Long, R. A. Auden's Ode to my pupils. Explicator 6 1948.
— Auden's Schoolchildren. Explicator 7 1949.
Mason, R. Auden. In Writers of today vol 2, ed D. V. Baker 1948.
Anderson, D. M. Aspects of Auden. Landfall 3 1949.
Beach, J. W. The poems of Auden and the prose diathesis. Virginia Quart Rev 25 1949.
— The making of the Auden canon. Minneapolis 1957.
Frankenberg, L. In his Pleasure dome, Boston 1949.
Hamilton, G. R. In his Tell-tale article, 1949.
Le Compte, C. B., jr. Which side am I supposed to be on? Explicator 8 1949.
McCoard, W. B. An interpretation of the times: a report of the oral interpretation of Auden's Age of anxiety. Quart Jnl of Speech 35 1949.
Fraser, G. S. Notes on the achievement of Auden. In his Post-war trends in English literature, Tokyo 1950.
— Auden as the young prophet; Auden in midstream; Auden's later manner. In his Vision and rhetoric, 1959;

excerpts rptd in Auden, ed M. K. Spears 1964 (as The career of Auden).

— Auden: the composite giant. Shenandoah 15 1964.

Vallette, J. Etat actuelle de l'œuvre de Auden. Mercure de France 310 1950.

— Auden: aspects d'une inquiétude. Langues Modernes 45 1951.

Carruth, H. Understanding Auden. Nation 22 Dec 1951.

Hoggart, R. Auden: an introductory essay. 1951.

— W. H. Auden. 1957, [1962] (rev), [1966] (rev) (Br Council pamphlet); rptd in his Speaking to each other vol 2, 1970.

Kavanagh, P. Auden and the creative mind. Envoy 5 1951.

Roth, R. The sophistication of Auden: a sketch in Longinian method. MP 48 1951.

Spears, M. K. Late Auden: the satirist as lunatic clergyman. Sewanee Rev 59 1951.

— The dominant symbols of Auden's poetry. Ibid.

— Auden in the fifties: rites of homage. Sewanee Rev 69 1961.

— The poetry of Auden: the disenchanted island. New York 1963, 1968 (rev).

— (ed). Auden: a collection of critical essays. Englewood Cliffs NJ 1964. All previously pbd.

Allen, W. Auden: the most exciting living poet. Listener 17 April 1952.

Enright, D. J. Reluctant admiration: a note on Auden and Rilke. EC 2 1952; rptd in his Apothecary's shop, 1957.

Farmer, A. J. Où va Auden? Etudes Anglaises 5 1952.

Frost, W. Auden's Fugal-chorus. Explicator 11 1952.

Mayhead, R. The latest Auden. Scrutiny 18 1952. Review of Nones.

Moore, G. Three who did not make a revolution. Amer Mercury 74 1952. On Auden, Spender and Isherwood.

— Luck in Auden. EC 7 1957.

Shepherd, T. B. For the time being: Auden's Christmas oratorio. London Quart & Holborn Rev 177 1952.

Wilder, A. N. Auden: towards a new Christian synthesis; Recovery of the tradition: Auden's Christmas oratorio. In his Modern poetry and the Christian tradition, New York 1952.

Christie, E. Auden og angstens tidsalder. Kirke og Kultur 58 1953; rptd in his Tendenser og profiler, Oslo 1955.

Pottle, F. A. Auden's Fugal-chorus. Explicator 11 1953.

Sanesi, R. Nota per la New Year letter di Auden. Aut-Aut 3 1953.

Braybrooke, N. Auden: the road from Marx. America 88 1954.

Duncan, C. The compassion of Auden. Canadian Forum 34 1954.

Gerevini, S. Note su Auden. Letterature Moderne 5 1954.

Mason, E. Auden's As I walked out one evening. Explicator 12 1954.

Seif, M. The impact of T. S. Eliot on Auden and Spender. South Atlantic Quart 53 1954.

Weisgerber, J. Auden as critic. Revue des Langues Vivantes 10 1954.

— Het dualisme in de poëzie van Auden. Kroniek van Kunst en Kultuur 14 1954.

Bartlett, P. and J. A. Pollard. Auden's September 1 1939, stanza 2. Explicator 14 1955.

Bogan, L. The quest of Auden. In her Selected criticism, New York 1955.

Hauge, I. Freud, Marx eller Kristus: en linje i Audens diktning. Samtiden 64 1955.

McFadden, G. The rake's progress: a note on the libretto. Hudson Rev 8 1955. Reply by A. Ansen 9 1956 apportioning libretto between Auden and Kallman.

Moore, M. Auden. In her Predilections, New York 1955; rptd in Auden, ed M. K. Spears, 1964.

Weales, G. A little faith, a little envy: a note on Santayana and Auden. Amer Scholar 24 1955.

Bennett, D. N. Auden's September 1 1939. Quart Jnl of Speech 42 1956.

The dog beneath the gown. New Statesman 9 June 1956; rptd in New Statesman profiles, 1957.

Kalow, G. Auden: der Christ und die Gesellschaft. In his Zwischen Christentum und Ideologie, Heidelberg 1956.

Maanen, W. van. Voorspel tot volmaaktheid. Gids 119 1956. On Auden's Shield of Achilles etc.

Rowan, M. et al. Auden's It's no use raising a shout. Explicator 15 1956.

Wilson, E. Auden in America. New Statesman 9 June 1956; rptd in Auden, ed M. K. Spears 1964, and in Wilson's Bit between my teeth, New York 1965.

Bayley, J. Auden. In his The romantic survival, 1957. Excerpts rptd in Auden, ed M. K. Spears, 1964.

— Our northern Manichee. Encounter 21 1963.

Hyams, C. B. and K. M. Reichert. A test lesson on Brueghel's Icarus and Auden's Musée des Beaux Arts. Die Neueren Sprachen 6 1957.

Kerman, J. Auden's Magic Flute. Hudson Rev 10 1957.

Lombardo, A. Dalla scuola di Eliot alla scuola di Auden. In his Realismo e simbolismo, Roma 1957.

McAleer, E. C. As Auden walked out. College Eng 18 1957. On As I walked out one evening.

Robson, W. W. Mr Auden's profession. Twentieth Century 161 1957; rptd in his Critical essays, 1966.

Whittemore, R. Auden on Americans. Sewanee Rev 65 1957. On Criterion book of modern American verse [1956].

Alvarez, A. Auden: poetry and journalism. In his The shaping spirit, 1958, New York 1958 (as Stewards of excellence).

Callan, E. The development of Auden's poetic theory since 1940. Twentieth Century Lit 4 1958.

— Auden on Christianity and criticism. Christian Scholar 46 1963.

— Auden's New year letter: a new style of architecture. Renascence 16 1963; rptd in Auden, ed M. K. Spears, 1964.

— Allegory in Auden's The age of anxiety. Twentieth Century Lit 10 1965.

— Auden and Kierkegaard: the artistic framework of For the time being. Christian Scholar 48 1965.

— Auden's ironic masquerade: criticism as morality play. UTQ 35 1966.

— Auden: the farming of a verse. Southern Rev 3 1967.

Power, W. Auden's Foxtrot from a play. Explicator 16 1958.

Rodway, A. E. and F. W. Cook. An altered Auden. EC 8 1958. Extended review of Beach's The making of the Auden canon, [1957] (see Bibliographies, above).

Clancy, J. P. Auden waiting for his city. Christian Scholar 42 1959.

Gorlier, C. Auden: protagonista e testimone. Questioni 7 1959.

Scott, N. A., jr. The poetry of Auden. Chicago Rev 13 1959; London Mag 8 1961; rptd (rev) in Four ways of modern poetry, ed N. A. Scott, jr, Richmond 1965.

Sunesen, B. All we are not stares back at what we are: a note on Auden. E Studies 40 1959.

Cook, F. W. The wise fool: Auden and the management. Twentieth Century 168 1960.

— Primordial Auden. EC 12 1962. On Paid on both sides.

Day Lewis, C. In his Buried day, 1960.

Highet, G. Auden on the baby: Kicking his mother. In his Powers of poetry, New York 1960.

Hough, I. Auden's Song for St Cecilia's day. Explicator 18 1960.

Larkin, P. What's become of Wystan? Spectator 15 July 1960.

Quinn, Sr M. Persons and places in Auden. Renascence 12 1960.

Replogle, J. Social philosophy in Auden's early poetry. Criticism 2 1960.
— The gang myth in Auden's early poetry. JEGP 61 1962.
— Auden's homage to Thalia. Bucknell Rev 11 1963.
— The Auden group. Wisconsin Stud in Contemporary Lit 5 1964.
— Auden's intellectual development 1950–60. Criticism 7 1965.
— Auden's Marxism. PMLA 80 1965.
— Auden's religious leap. Wisconsin Stud in Contemporary Lit 7 1966.
— Auden's poetry. Seattle 1969.
Ricks, C. O where are you going?: Auden and Christina Rossetti. N & Q 205 1960.
Rosenthal, M. L. Auden and the thirties. In his Modern poets, New York 1960.
Shapiro, K. J. The retreat of Auden. In his In defense of ignorance, New York 1960.
Stebner, G. Whitman—Liliencron—Auden: Betrachtung und Vergleich motivähnlicher Gedichte. Die Neueren Sprachen 9 1960.
— Auden, The ascent of F 6: Interpretation eines Dramas. Die Neueren Sprachen 10 1961; rptd in Das moderne englische Drama: Interpretationen, ed H. Oppel, Berlin 1963.
Blackburn, T. Auden. In his Price of an eye, 1961.
Bluestone, M. The iconographic sources of Auden's Musée des Beaux Arts. MLN 76 1961.
Cox, R. G. The poetry of Auden. In The modern age, ed B. Ford 1961 (Pelican guide to English literature).
Janet, Sr M. Auden: two poems in sequence. Renascence 13 1961.
Mander, J. Must we burn Auden? In his Writer and commitment, 1961.
Schrickx, W Auden, virtuoos en dichter van de vervreemding. De Vlaamse Gids 45 1961.
Ahern, E. M. There may be many answers. Eng Jnl 51 1962. On O what is that sound?
Gerstenberger, D. Poetry and politics: the verse dramas of Auden and Isherwood. Modern Drama 5 1962.
Haeffner, P. Auden and Ella Wheeler Wilcox. N & Q 207 1962. On O what is that sound?
Hagopian, J. V. Exploring Auden's limestone landscape. Die Neueren Sprachen 11 1962.
McDowell, F. P. W. The situation of our time: Auden in his American phase. In Aspects of American poetry, ed R. M. Ludwig, Columbus 1962; partly rptd in Auden, ed M. K. Spears 1964.
— Subtle, various, ornamental, clever: Auden in his recent poetry. Wisconsin Stud in Contemporary Lit 3 1962.
Wallace, C. C., Auden's New year letter and the fate of long poems. Melbourne Critical Rev 5 1962.
— Auden revisited. Dissent (Melbourne) 14 1965.
Brooke-Rose, C. Notes on the metre of Auden's The age of anxiety. EC 13 1963.
Chittick, V. L. O. Angry young poet of the thirties. Dalhousie Rev 43 1963.
Kinney, A. F. Auden, Bruegel and Musée des Beaux Arts. College Eng 24 1963.
Ohmann, R. M. Auden's sacred awe. Commonweal 78 1963; rptd in Auden, ed M. K. Spears 1964.
Rushmore, R. P. The criticism of Auden. Shenandoah 14 1963.
Satterwhite, J. N. Auden's A healthy spot. Explicator 21 1963.
Everett, B. Auden. Edinburgh 1964 (Writers and Critics).
Fuller, J. Early Auden: an allegory of love. Review (Oxford) nos 11–12 1964.
— A reader's guide to Auden. 1970.
Galinsky, H. The expatriate poet's style, with reference to T. S. Eliot and Auden. In English studies today ser 3, Edinburgh [1964]; rptd in his Amerika und Europa, Berlin 1968.

Hardy, B. The reticence of Auden. Review (Oxford) nos 11–12 1964.
— Auden's thirties to sixties: a face and a map. Southern Rev 5 1969.
Kleinstück, J. Paradies und Stadt in der Dichtung W. H. Audens. In his Mythos und Symbol in englischer Dichtung, Stuttgart 1964.
Kuna, F. M. Auden: der subtile 'Poeta doctus'. Die Neueren Sprachen 13 1964.
Ostroff, A. (ed). A symposium on Auden's A change of air, with essays by G. P. Elliott, K. Shapiro, S. Spender and Auden. Kenyon Rev 26 1964; rptd in The contemporary poet as artist and critic, ed A. Ostroff, Boston 1964.
Weatherhead, A. K. The good place in the latest poems of Auden. Twentieth-Century Lit 10 1964.
Bain, C. E. Auden. Emory Univ Quart 21 1965.
Binni, F. Definizione di poetica per Auden. Letteratura 29 1965.
— Auden: il dissenso della 'ragione'. Letteratura 31 1967.
— Saggio su Auden. Milan 1967.
— Su Auden critico. Letteratura 32 1968.
Blair, J. G. Auden: the poem as performance. Shenandoah 16 1965.
— The poetic art of Auden. Princeton 1965.
Dewsnap, T. The poetry of Auden. New York 1965.
Grubb, F. English Auden and the 30's ethos. In his A vision of reality, 1965.
Gustafson, R. The paragon style: Frost and Auden. Poet & Critic 2 1965.
Harris, H. The symbols and imagery of hawk and kestrel in the poetry of Auden and Day Lewis in the thirties. Zeitschrift für Anglistik und Amerikanistik 13 1965.
Mueller, H. Auden: paysage moralisé. Die Neueren Sprachen 14 1965.
Parkin, R. P. The facsimile of immediacy in Auden's In praise of limestone. Texas Stud in Lang & Lit 7 1965.
Rodway, A. Logicless grammar in Audenland. London Mag new ser 4 1965.
Stanley, F. R. Today the struggle: a critical commentary on Auden's sonnet sequence In time of war. Literary Half Yearly 6 1965.
Whitehead, J. Auden: an early poetical notebook. London Mag new ser 5 1965.
Williams, M. G. Auden's Petition: a synthesis of criticism. Personalist 46 1965.
Wright, G. T. A general view of Auden's poetry. Tennessee Stud in Lit 10 1965.
— Auden. New York 1969 (Twayne's US Authors).
Auden, us and them. TLS 6 Oct 1966. On The orators.
Bloom, R. Auden's bestiary of the human. Virginia Quart Rev 42 1966.
— The humanization of Auden's early style. PMLA 83 1968.
Falck, C. The exposed heart. Encounter 27 1966.
Friedman, S. Auden and Hardy. N & Q 211 1966.
Holthusen, H. E. Auden als Prosaist. Merkur 20 1966.
Mitchell, B. Auden and Isherwood: the 'German influence'. Oxford German Stud 1 1966.
Rosenheim, E. W. The elegiac act: Auden's In memory of W. B. Yeats. College Eng 27 1966.
Weimer, R. Rome sacked. In his City as metaphor, New York 1966.
Whitehead, L. M. Art as communion: Auden's Sea and the mirror. Perspective 14 1966.
Bruehl, W. J. Polus naufrangia: a key symbol in The ascent of F 6. Modern Drama 10 1967.
Ellmann, R. Gazebos and gashouses. In his Eminent domain, New York 1967.
Fitzgerald, D. Auden's city. Dublin Mag 6 1967.
Goetsch, P. Auden: Lay your sleeping head my love. In Die moderne englische Lyrik, ed H. Oppel, Berlin 1967.

— Auden und Amerika. Jahrbuch für Amerikastudien 13 1968.

Hollander, J. Auden at sixty. Atlantic 220 1967.

LeBreton, G. Auden. Preuves 17 1967.

Morse, D. E. For the time being: man's response to the incarnation. Renascence 19 1967.

— The nature of man in Auden's For the time being. Ibid.

— Meaning of time in Auden's For the time being. Renascence 22 1970.

Otten, K. Auden: In memory of W. B. Yeats. In Die moderne englische Lyrik, ed H. Oppel, Berlin 1967.

Platt, P. Auden. Amer Scholar 36 1967. Interview.

Sarang, V. Personal pronouns in the poetry of Auden. Literary Criterion (Mysore) 7 1967.

Sellers, W. H. New light on Auden's The orators. PMLA 82 1967.

Serpieri, A. Auden, lo specchio e il caos. Ponte 23 1967. Rptd in his Hopkins, Eliot, Auden, Bologna 1969.

Shenandoah 18 1967. A tribute to Auden on his sixtieth birthday, containing: R. Bloom, Auden's essays at man: some long views in the early poetry; E. Callan, Auden's goodly heritage; B. Dobrée, Auden; E. R. Dodds, Background to a poet: memories of Birmingham 1924–36; A. Fremantle, Anima naturaliter Christiana, rptd Month 37 1967 (as Auden and the Incarnation); C. Izzo, Good-bye to the Mezzogiorno; N. Mitchison, Young Auden; M. K. Spears, Auden and Dionysus; J. Symons, Early Auden.

Warren, R. Song for St Cecilia's Day. Belfast 1967.

Bauerle, R. H. Auden's Fish in the unruffled lakes. Explicator 26 1968.

Caswell, R. W. Auden's Lay your sleeping head my love. Ibid.

Fink, G. Auden: l'eccezione e la regola. Paragone 19 1968.

Greenberg, H. Quest for the necessary: Auden and the dilemma of divided consciousness. Cambridge Mass 1968. Preface by Spender.

Lewars, K. Auden's Swarthmore chart. Connecticut Rev 1 1968.

Mendelson, E. The coherence of Auden's The orators. ELH 35 1968.

Panaro, C. L'arte inclusiva di Auden. Convivium 36 1968.

Stead, C. K. Auden's Spain. London Mag new ser 7 1968.

Valgemae, M. Auden's collaboration with Isherwood on The dog beneath the skin. HLQ 31 1968.

Westlake, J. H. J. Auden's The shield of Achilles: an interpretation. Literatur in Wissenschaft und Unterricht 1 1968.

Woodberry, P. Redeeming the time: the theological argument of Auden's For the time being. Atlanta 1968.

Chatman, S. Auden's The questioner who sits so sly. Explicator 29 1969.

Grant, D. Tones of voice. CQ 11 1969.

Hampshire, S. Auden. In his Modern writers and other essays, 1969.

Hazard, F. E. The Father Christmas passage in Paid on both sides. Modern Drama 12 1969.

Holloway, J. The master as joker. Art International 13 1969.

Jäger, D. Das Haus als Raum des lyrischen Geschehens und als Gegenstand der lyrischen Meditation: das Thema der nächsten Umwelt des Menschen in Audens About the house und bei deutschen und angelsächsischen Zeitgenossen. Literatur in Wissenschaft und Unterricht 2 1969.

Mandle, W. F. Auden and the failure of the left. Australian National Univ Historical Jnl no 6 1969.

Maxwell, D. E. S. Auden: the island and the city. In his Poets of the thirties, 1969.

Nelson, G. Changes of heart: a study of the poetry of Auden. Berkeley 1969.

Thornburg, T. Auden's Mundus et infans, [lines] 46–56. Explicator 27 1969.

— Prospero, the magician-artist: Auden's The sea and the mirror. Muncie Indiana 1969.

R. J. R.

DYLAN MARLAIS THOMAS
1914–53

The Lockwood Memorial Library, Buffalo, has a collection of Thomas's letters and mss, including the four notebooks ed R. N. Maud as The notebooks of Thomas, *1967 (below, §1) and a prose notebook. Maud mentions other collections at the BM [Additional Ms 48217], in the Univ of Texas and in private hands. A copy of the script used for the final performance of* Under Milk Wood *during Thomas's lifetime is in Yale Univ Lib (see F. Manley, The text of Thomas' Under Milk Wood,* Emory Univ Quart 20 1964*). See also Maud, Thomas manuscripts in the Houghton Library [Harvard],* Audience 1 1955*; and L. Ash, Thomas mss at Ohio State University,* American N & Q 1 1963.

Bibliographies etc

Huff, W. H. Bibliography. In E. Olson, The poetry of Thomas, Chicago 1954. Includes reviews and other works about Thomas.

Rolph, J. A. Dylan Thomas: a bibliography. 1956. Includes trns, gramophone recordings by, and of works by, Thomas, and summaries of the textual histories of each of Thomas's pbd poems. *See* R. N. Maud, Thomas' Collected poems: chronology of composition, PMLA 76 1961, for the history of the poems in ms, and Appendix I to his Entrances to Thomas' poetry 1963, §2 below, for the history of certain of the miscellaneous prose writings. *See also* R. Sanesi, Dylan Thomas 1960, §2 below, for a more complete list of the Italian trns; W. B. Todd, The bibliography of Thomas, Book Collector 6 1957, for minor addns to Rolph; and W. White, Thomas, Mr Rolph and John O'London's Weekly, PBSA 60 1966, for the first printing of Ears in the turrets hear, not known to Rolph.

Brinnin, J. M. (ed). A casebook on Thomas. 1960, §2 below. Contains secondary sources, including reviews.

Slocombe, M. and P. Saul. Thomas discography. Recorded Sound 1 1961.

Fitzgibbon, C. The life of Thomas. 1965, §2 below. Contains appendices listing broadcasts, filmscripts, and lectures and readings in America by Thomas.

Williams, R. C. A concordance to the Collected poems of Thomas. Lincoln Nebraska 1967.

Theisen, Sr L. Thomas: a bibliography of secondary criticism. Bull Bibliography 26 1969.

Two Swansea poets: Thomas and Vernon Watkins, exhibition 3rd–12th July 1969. Swansea [1969] pbd Swansea Public Libraries.

Selections

Dylan Thomas: selected writings. Introd by J. L. Sweeney, New York [1946].

Dylan Thomas miscellany. 1963–. Selection.

§1
Poetry

18 poems. 1934. The edn pbd in 1942 was textually identical. *See* T. d'A. Smith, The second edition of Thomas's 18 poems, Book Collector 13 1964.

Twenty-five poems. 1936.

The map of love: verse and prose. 1939. *See* J. Campbell, Issues of Thomas's The map of love, Book Collector 6 1957.

The world I breathe. Norfolk Conn 1939. Selection of 40 poems, 11 stories.

From In memory of Ann Jones. Llanllechid [1942] (Caseg Broadsheet no 5). Shortened version of the poem in The map of love.

New poems. Norfolk Conn [1943] (Poets of the year).

Deaths and entrances: poems. 1946.

Twenty-six poems. 1950, Norfolk Conn 1950. 150 copies, ptd at Verona by G. Mardersteig. Selection.

In country sleep and other poems. New York [1952].

Collected poems 1934-1952. 1952, New York 1953 [with Elegy, reconstructed from drafts, with notes by Vernon Watkins], London 1966 (EL). R. C. Williams' Concordance (Bibliographies etc, above) gives minor textual differences between the English and American edns. Appendix 2 of R. N. Maud, Entrances to Thomas' poetry, 1963, §2 below, sets out some minor textual cruces.

The notebooks of Dylan Thomas. Ed R. N. Maud, Norfolk Conn 1967, London 1968 (as Poet in the making: the notebooks of Dylan Thomas). Contains text of poems in 4 notebooks used by Thomas 1930–33 now in Lockwood Memorial Library, Buffalo; together with 20 poems mainly from mss in BM.

The colour of saying: an anthology of verse spoken by Thomas, ed R. N. Maud and A. T. Davies, was pbd in 1963.

Other Works

Portrait of the artist as a young dog. 1940, Norfolk Conn [1940]. Stories.

The doctor and the devils. 1953, [Norfolk Conn] 1953. Film script based on a story by D. Taylor.

Under Milk Wood: a play for voices. Preface and musical settings by Daniel Jones. 1954, New York [1954], London [1958] (acting edn). First pbd in shorter version as Llareggub: a piece for radio perhaps, in Botteghe Oscure 9 1952. Final version during the author's lifetime first read publicly, under the sponsorship of the YM-YWHA Poetry Center, at the Kaufman Auditorium New York 24 Oct 1953; first broadcast, BBC Third Programme 25 Jan 1954. First stage production after a trial week at Newcastle-on-Tyne, at the Lyceum Theatre Edinburgh 21 Aug 1956 and at the New Theatre London 20 Sept 1956. For a tentative list of pbd and unpbd versions, see letter by D. Cleverdon, TLS 18 July 1968. For the revisions in the Yale Univ Lib copy of the YM-YWHA Poetry Center script, see F. Manley, Emory Univ Quart 20 1964. For textual variants, see D. Cleverdon, The growth of Milk Wood, 1969, §2 below.

Quite early one morning: broadcasts. 1954, New York [1954] (with addns, omissions and alterations).

Conversation about Christmas. [New York?] 1954 (priv ptd). First pbd in Picture Post 27 Dec 1947, rptd in A prospect of the sea, 1955, below.

Adventures in the skin trade and other stories. [New York, 1955]. Title story (unfinished by Thomas) and 20 others some previously uncollected. Title story pbd separately with introd by V. Watkins, London 1955.

A prospect of the sea and other stories and prose writings. Ed Daniel Jones 1955. 7 stories rptd from The map of love, 1939, the remainder uncollected.

A child's Christmas in Wales. Norfolk Conn [1955]. Rptd from American edn of Quite early one morning, 1954.

Return journey. In Durband, A. (ed), New directions: five one act plays, 1961. Broadcast 15 June 1947.

The beach of Falesá: based on a story by R. L. Stevenson. New York [1963], London 1964. Filmscript.

A film script of Twenty years a-growing, from the story by M. O'Sullivan. 1964.

Me and my bike. 1965, New York [1965], London 1968 (with next, as Two tales). Filmscript.

Rebecca's daughters. 1965. Filmscript.

The doctor and the devils and other scripts. [New York 1966]. Includes Twenty years a-growing, A dream of winter, The Londoner.

Letters

Letters to Vernon Watkins. Ed Watkins 1957, [New York] 1957.

W. White. The poet as critic: unpublished letters of Thomas. Orient/West (Tokyo) 7 1962.

Selected letters of Dylan Thomas. 1966, [New York 1967]. Ed C. Fitzgibbon.

Section D in Rolph's Bibliography, 1956, above, is a list of Thomas's contributions to books. These include a list of anthologies with first appearances of his writings or textually significant later versions. Notes on the art of poetry, by Thomas, was pbd in G. J. Firmage, A garland for Thomas, [1963], below. Thomas was invited to edit a regular column of book reviews in the Swansea & West Wales Guardian in 1936, but the column never materialized (see W. White, Presenting an unknown Thomas piece, Prairie Schooner 37 1963, with the text of Thomas's Introducing a review column).

§2

The bibliography in Brinnin 1960, below, includes the many short memoirs, reminiscences etc of Thomas, a selection of which have been rptd in Tedlock 1960, below.

Sitwell, E. Four new poets. London Mercury 33 1936. Empson, Bottrall, Thomas and Archibald MacLeish.

—— Comment on Thomas. The Critic: a Quart Rev of Criticism 1 1947. Rptd in Tedlock 1960, below.

—— Dylan Thomas. Atlantic Monthly 193 1954.

Cullis, M. F. Mr Thomas and Mr Auden. Purpose 9 1937.

Heseltine, N. Dylan Thomas. Wales 2 1937.

Treece, H. Thomas and the Surrealists. Seven no 3 1938.

—— Corkscrew or footrule? Some notes on the poetry of Thomas. Poetry (London) 1 1941.

—— Gerard Manley Hopkins and Thomas. In his How I see Apocalypse, 1946. Rptd in Brinnin 1960, below.

—— Dylan Thomas: 'dog among the fairies'. 1949; 1956 (rev). See R. G. Cox, The cult of Thomas, Scrutiny 16 1949.

Hays, H. R. Surrealist influence in contemporary English and American poetry. Poetry (Chicago) 54 1939.

Jones, G. Thomas. Welsh Rev 2 1939.

Berryman, J. The loud hill of Wales. Kenyon Rev 2 1940. Rptd in J. C. Ransom (ed), The Kenyon critics, New York 1951.

Scarfe, F. The poetry of Thomas. Horizon 2 1940; rptd in his Auden and after, 1942, and in Brinnin 1960 and Tedlock 1960, below.

Symons, J. Obscurity and Thomas. Kenyon Rev 2 1940.

The Explicator 3 1944/5-. The following poems by Thomas have been explicated:

Adventures in the skin trade (R. J. Stonesifer 17 1958-9).

After the funeral (M. W. Stearns 3 1944-5).

Altarwise by owl-light (R. N. Maud 14 1955-6; B. Knieger 15 1956-7; E. H. Essig 16 1957-8).

Among those killed in the dawn raid was a man aged a hundred (P. Bartlett 12 1953-4; E. L. Brooks ibid).

And death shall have no dominion (T. E. Connolly 14 1955-6).

Ballad of the long-legged bait (R. A. Condon 16 1957-8; A. R. and L. J. Neuville 23 1964-5).

The conversation of prayer (M. E. Rickey 16 1957-8; R. C. Jones 17 1958-9).

Death is all metaphors, shape in one history (B. Knieger 18 1959-60).

Especially when the October wind (L. Perrine 21 1962-3).

Fern Hill (M. Laurentia 14 1955-6).

First there was the lamb on knocking knees (B .Knieger 18 1959-60).

The force that through the green fuse drives the flower
(G. Giovannini 8 1949–50; S. F. Johnson 8 1949–50,
10 1951–2).

From love's first fever to her plague (S. Hynes 9 1950–1).

How soon the servant sun (M. Halperen 23 1964–5).

The hunchback in the park (S. F. Johnson 10 1951–2;
L. Perrine 20 1961–2).

If I were tickled by the rub of love (M. Halperen 21
1962–3).

In my craft or sullen art (D. R. Howard 12 1953–4;
P. M. Spacks 18 1959–60).

In the white giant's thigh (W. T. Moynihan 17 1958–9;
M. Chambers 19 1960–1).

Light breaks where no sun shines (B. Knieger 15 1956–7;
W. T. Moynihan 16 1957–8).

Love in the asylum (B. Knieger 20 1961–2).

O make me a mask (O. D. Harvill 26 1967–8).

On the marriage of a virgin (S. F. Johnson 10 1951–2;
B. Knieger 19 1960–1).

Poem in October (L. Perrine 27 1968–9).

A refusal to mourn the death, by fire, of a child in
London (J. A. Clair 17 1958–9).

To-day, this insect (B. Casey 17 1958–9; G. Montague
19 1960–1).

The tombstone told when she died (I. H. Hassan 15
1956–7).

Twenty-four years (B. Knieger 20 1961–2; D. Ormerod
22 1963–4).

When all my five and country senses see (J. Zigerell 19
1960–1).

Stearns, M. W. Unsex the skeleton: notes on the poetry of
Thomas. Sewanee Rev 52 1944; rptd in Tedlock 1960,
below.

Hoffman, F. J. In his Freudianism and the literary mind.
Baton Rouge 1945, 1957 (rev).

Horan, R. In defense of Thomas. Kenyon Rev 7 1945;
rptd in Tedlock 1960, below.

Mankowitz, W. Dylan Thomas. Scrutiny 14 1946.
Review of Deaths and entrances. See J. Parry, Scrutiny
and re-scrutiny, Polemic no 7 1947.

Savage, D. S. The poetry of Thomas. New Republic
29 April 1946. Rptd in D. V. Baker (ed) Little reviews
anthology 1947–8, 1948, and in Tedlock 1960, below.

Spender, S. Poetry for poetry's sake and poetry beyond
poetry. Horizon 13 1946.
— A romantic in revolt. Spectator 5 Dec 1952. Review
of Collected poems.

Stephens, P. J. Thomas: giant among moderns. New
Quart of Poetry 1 1946–7.

Empson, W. How to understand a modern poem. Strand
Mag 112 1947. A refusal to mourn the death, by fire, of
a child in London.
— Books in general. [Review of Collected poems and
Under Milk Wood]. New Statesman 15 May 1954; rptd
in Brinnin 1960 and Cox 1966, below.

Fiedler, L. The latest Dylan Thomas. Western Rev 11
1947.

Gibson, H. A comment. Critic: a Quart Rev of Criticism
1 1947. On A refusal to mourn, and We lying by sea-
sand; rptd in Tedlock 1960, below.

Gregory, H. Romantic heritage in the writings of Thomas.
Poetry (Chicago) 69 1947; rptd, rev, in Yale Literary
Mag 122 1954, and in Brinnin 1960, below.

Scott, H. From death to entrance. Outposts 7 1947.

Williams, M. Welsh voices in the short story. Welsh Rev 6
1947.

Astre, G.-A. Un jeune et grand poète anglais. Critique
(Paris) 4 1948.

Grigson, G. How much me now your acrobatics amaze. In
his The Harp of Aeolus, 1948; rptd in Brinnin 1960,
and in Tedlock 1960, below.
— Recollections of Thomas. London Mag 4 1957; rptd
in Brinnin 1960, below.

Huddlestone, L. An approach to Thomas. Penguin New
Writing no 35 1948.

Korg, J. The short stories of Thomas. Perspective 1 1948.
— Changed Dylan Thomas. Nation 24 April 1954.
— The sound of laughter. Nation 25 Dec 1954.
— Imagery and universe in Thomas' 18 Poems. Accent
17 1957.
— Dylan Thomas. New York 1965 (Twayne's English
Authors).

Lewis, E. G. Dylan Thomas. Welsh Rev 7 1948; rptd in
Tedlock 1960, below.

Moore, N. The poetry of Thomas. Poetry Quart 10 1948–
9.

Rhys, A. Thomas: a further estimate. Poetry Rev 39 1948.

Tindall, W. Y. The poetry of Thomas. Amer Scholar 17
1948.
— Burning and crested song. Amer Scholar 22 1953.
Review of Collected poems.
— A reader's guide to Thomas. New York 1962.

Frankenberg, L. In his Pleasure dome: on reading modern
poetry, Boston 1949.

Jones, N. A. Thomas as a pattern. Brit Annual of Lit 6
1949.

Rice, L. L. The poetry of Thomas. Amer Scholar 18 1949.

Aivaz, D. The poetry of Thomas. Hudson Rev 3 1950;
rptd in Tedlock 1960, below.

Werry, R. R. The poetry of Thomas. College Eng 11 1950.

Brinnin, J. M. Thomas in America. Vassar Alumnae Mag
37 1951.
— Cockles, brambles and Fern Hill: Thomas in Wales.
Atlantic Monthly 196 1955.
— Dylan Thomas in America: an intimate journal.
Boston 1955.
— (ed). A casebook on Thomas. New York [1960].
A collection of essays, with 10 of Thomas's poems and
a bibliography.

Deutsch, B. Orient wheat. Virginia Quart Rev 27 1951;
rptd as part of Alchemists of the word in her Poetry in
our time, New York 1952.

Hughes, R. Wales through the looking-glass. Listener 24
May 1951.

Mayhead, R. Dylan Thomas. Scrutiny 19 1952. Review
of Collected poems.

'Rothberg, Winterset' (T. Roethke). One ring-tailed
roarer to another. Poetry (Chicago) 81 1952. Review of
In country sleep; rptd in Tedlock 1960, below.

Adam no 238 1953. Dylan Thomas memorial no, containing poems, short memoirs (some rptd in Tedlock
1960, below) and notes, and:
M. Grindea, For Dylan;
R. S. Macleod, The Dylan I knew;
S. Roussillat, His work and background (rptd in Tedlock 1960, below);
W. S. Merwin, The religious poet (rptd in Brinnin 1960,
above, and in Tedlock 1960, below).

Cambon, G. After the first death, there is no other. Aut-
Aut 3 1953.
— The crazy boats: Thomas and Rimbaud. Eng Miscel-
lany (Rome) 7 1956. Ballad of the long-legged bait and
Bateau ivre.

Corman, C. Thomas: rhetorician in mid-career. Accent 13
1953; rptd in Tedlock 1960, below.

Davenport, J. Dylan Thomas. Twentieth Century 153
1953.

Halperen, M. Thomas: a soliloquy. Florida State Univ
Stud 11 1953.

Mr Dylan Thomas: innovation and tradition. Times 10
Nov 1953. A long obituary by Vernon Watkins.

Sanesi, R. Sesso, nascita e morte in Thomas. Aut-Aut 3
1953.
— Nella coscia del gigante bianco. Aut-Aut 4 1954.
— Nell' intricata immagine di Thomas. Inventario 8 1957.
— Dylan Thomas. Milano 1960. Includes a biblio-
graphy of Italian translations of Thomas's work.

Arrowsmith, W. The wisdom of poetry. Hudson Rev 6
1954. Joint review of Thomas' and Edwin Muir's collected poems; rptd in Tedlock 1960, below.

Asselineau, R. Dylan Thomas. Études Anglaises 7 1954.

Bollier, E. P. Love, death and the poet—Thomas. Colorado Quart 2 1954.

Daiches, D. The poetry of Thomas. Eng Jnl 43 1954; College Eng 16 1954. Rptd in his Literary essays, 1956; in his Two studies, 1958; and in Cox 1966, below.

Dock Leaves. 5 1954. A Dylan Thomas no, containing poems, short memoirs and notes by various authors.

Dylan Thomas: memories and appreciations [by] D. Jones, T. Roethke, L. MacNeice, M. Adix, G. Barker. Encounter 2 1954. Rptd in Tedlock 1960, below. (Jones, MacNeice and Adix also rptd in Brinnin 1960, above).

Garlick, R. The endless breviary: aspects of the work of Thomas. Month 11 1954.

Knauber, C. F. Imagery of light in Thomas. Renascence 6 1964.

Maud, R. N. Thomas's poetry. EC 4 1954.

—— A note on Dylan Thomas's serious poems. Audience 1 1955.

—— The 'Over Sir John's hill' worksheets. Explorations 6 1956.

—— Thomas' first published poem. MLN 74 1959. An early form of And death shall have no dominion.

—— Obsolete and dialect works as serious puns in Thomas. E Studies 41 1960.

—— Entrances to Thomas' poetry. Pittsburgh 1963.

—— A Clark Lecture revisited. EC 18 1968. On If my head hurt a hair's foot.

Ochshorn, M. The love song of Thomas. New Mexico Quart 24 1954.

Olson, E. The poetry of Thomas. Chicago 1954.

Rodgers, W. R. Dylan Thomas. Listener 27 May 1954.

Stanford, D. Dylan Thomas: a literary study. 1954.

—— Thomas' animal faith. Southwest Rev 42 1957.

—— Thomas: a literary post-mortem. Queen's Quart 71 1964.

Wells, H. W. Voice and verse in Thomas' play. College Eng 15 1954.

Williams, W. C. Dylan Thomas. In his Selected essays, New York [1954].

Woodcock, G. Thomas and the Welsh environment. Arizona Quart 10 1954.

Yale Literary Magazine 122 1954. A Dylan Thomas no. Communications by various authors, some rptd in Brinnin 1960, above, and Tedlock 1960, below.

Adams, R. M. Taste and bad taste in metaphysical poetry: Richard Crashaw and Thomas. Hudson Rev 8 1955; rptd as Crashaw and Thomas: devotional athletes, in his Strains of discord, Ithaca 1958; also rptd in Cox 1966, below.

Adix, M. Dylan Thomas. Explorations 4 1955.

Bogan, L. The later Thomas. In her Selected criticism, New York 1955. Review of In country sleep, first pbd New Yorker 2 Aug 1952.

Evans, O. The making of a poem: Thomas' Do not go gentle into that good night. Eng Miscellany (Rome) 6 1955.

—— The making of a poem II: Thomas' Lament. Eng Miscellany (Rome) 7 1956.

—— Thomas' birthday poems. In R. B. Davis and J. L. Lievsay (ed), Studies in honor of J. C. Hodges and A. Thaler, Knoxville 1961.

Graves, R. In his The crowning privilege, 1955; rptd in Brinnin 1960, above.

Lougée, D. The worlds of Thomas. Poetry (Chicago) 87 1955.

Moore, G. Dylan Thomas. Kenyon Rev 17 1955; rptd in Tedlock 1960, below.

Phelps, R. In country Dylan. Sewanee Rev 63 1955.

Poetry (Chicago) 87 1955. A Dylan Thomas no, including K. Shapiro, Dylan Thomas (rptd in his In defence of ignorance, New York [1960], and in Brinnin 1960, above, and Tedlock 1960 and Cox 1966, below), and R. Campbell, Memories of Thomas at the BBC (rptd in Tedlock 1960, below).

Blissett, W. Thomas: a reader in search of a poet. Queen's Quart 63 1956.

Hardwick, E. America and Thomas. Partisan Rev 23 1956; rptd in Brinnin 1960, above.

Melchiori, G. Thomas: the poetry of vision. In his The tightrope walkers, 1956.

Morgan, W. J. [Caradoc] Evans, Thomas and [Saunders] Lewis. Twentieth Century 160 1956.

Wilde, M. H. Thomas: the elemental poet. Transactions Wisconsin Acad 44 1956.

Amis, K. An evening with Thomas. Spectator 29 Nov 1957.

Bayley, J. In his The romantic survival, 1957; rptd in Cox 1966, below.

Durrell, L. The shades of Thomas. Encounter 9 Dec 1957; rptd in Tedlock 1960, below.

Fraser, G. S. Dylan Thomas. 1957 (Br Council pamphlet); rptd in his Vision and rhetoric, 1959.

Glick, B. S. A brief analysis of a short story by Thomas. American Imago 14 1957. On Followers.

Harding, J. Dylan Thomas and Edward Thomas. Contemporary Rev 192 1957.

Highet, G. Death of a poet. In his Talents and geniuses, New York 1957; rptd, with a new essay, The wild Welshman in his Powers of poetry, New York 1960.

Holroyd, S. Thomas and the religion of the instinctive life. In his Emergence from chaos, 1957; rptd in Brinnin 1960, above.

Julian, Sr M. Edith Sitwell and Thomas: neo-romantics. Renascence 9 1957.

Kazin, A. The posthumous life of Thomas. Atlantic Monthly 200 1957; rptd in his Contemporaries, New York 1962.

Lander, C. The macabre in Thomas. Canadian Forum 36 1957.

—— With Welsh and reverent look: the biblical element in Thomas. Queen's Quart 65 1958.

Peel, J. H. B. The echoes in the booming voice. New York Times Book Rev 20 Oct 1957. On Hopkins and Thomas.

Thomas, C. In her Leftover life to kill, 1957.

Wain, J. Thomas: a review of his Collected poems. In his Preliminary essays, 1957; rptd from Mandrake 2 1953; rptd in Brinnin 1960, above, and in Cox 1966, below.

Aiken, C. In his A reviewer's ABC, New York 1958; rptd reviews of The world I breathe (Poetry, Chicago, 56 1940) and New poems (New Republic 3 Jan 1944).

Carlson, H. The overwrought urn. Folio 23 1958.

Goñi, A. C. El poeta de Fern Hill: Thomas. Sur 253 1958.

Grenander, M. E. Sonnet V from Thomas' Altarwise by owl-light sequence. N & Q 203 1958.

John, A. Candid impressions—1. Thomas and company. Sunday Times 28 Sept 1958; rptd, rev, in Brinnin 1960, above.

Peters, R. L. The uneasy faith of Thomas: a study of the last poems. Fresco (Univ of Detroit) 9 1958.

Smith, A. J. The art of the intricate image. Letterature Moderne 8 1958. On Our eunuch dreams.

—— Ambiguity as a poetic shift. CQ 4 1962. On Our eunuch dreams.

Varney, H. L. and N. N. Kann. Glamorizing Thomas. American Mercury 86 1958.

Corin, F. En traduisant Dylan Thomas. Revue des Langues Vivantes 25 1959.

Cox, C. B. Thomas's Fern Hill. CQ 1 1959.

—— (ed). Dylan Thomas: a collection of critical essays. Englewood Cliffs NJ [1966]. Includes unpbd essay Thomas's prose, by A. Pratt.

Jenkins, D. C. Thomas and Wales Magazine. Trace no 30 1959.

Muecke, D. C. Come back! Come back! A theme in Thomas's prose. Meanjin 18 1959.

Williams, R. Thomas' play for voices. CQ 1 1959; rptd in Cox 1966, above.

Beardsley, M. C. and Hynes, S. Misunderstanding poetry:

notes on some readings of Thomas. College Eng 21 1960.

Bloom, E. A. Dylan Thomas' 'Naked vision'. Western Humanities Rev 14 1960.

Bloom, E. A. and L. D. Bloom. Thomas: his intimations of mortality. Boston Univ Stud in Eng 4 1960.

Conran, A. The English poet in Wales. II, The boys of summer in their ruin. Anglo-Welsh Rev 10 1960.

Hawkes, T. Thomas's Welsh. College Eng 21 1960.

— Some sources of Under Milk Wood. N & Q 210 1965.

Heppenstall, R. Four absentees. 1960. On Thomas, Orwell, Middleton Murry, Gill.

Logan, J. Thomas and the ark of art. Renascence 12 1960.

Miller, J. E. jr. et al. In their Start with the sun: studies in cosmic poetry, Lincoln Nebraska 1960. Whitman, Lawrence, Hart Crane, Thomas.

Mills, R. J., jr. Thomas: the endless monologue. Accent 20 1960.

Roditi, E. London reunion. Literary Rev 3 1960.

Tedlock, E. W. (ed). Dylan Thomas—the legend and the poet: a collection of biographical and critical essays. 1960. See E. Thomas, Burying a poet, Twentieth Century (Melbourne) 15 1961.

Emery, C. M. Two-gunned Gabriel in London. Carrell 2 1961.

— The world of Thomas. Miami 1962.

Holbrook, D. Metaphor and maturity: T. F. Powys and Thomas. In The modern age (vol 7, Pelican Guide to Eng Lit, ed B. Ford 1961).

— Llareggub revisited: Thomas and the state of modern poetry. Cambridge 1962, Carbondale [1964] (rev, as Dylan Thomas and poetic dissociation).

— R. D. Laing and the death circuit. Encounter 31 1968.

Jones, R. The Dylan Thomas country. Texas Quart 4 1961.

Leach, E. Dylan Thomas' Ballad of the long-legged bait. MLN 76 1961.

McCord, H. L. Thomas and Bhartrihari. N & Q 206 1961. A possible source of the Ballad of the long-legged bait.

Nist, J. Thomas: perfection of the work. Arizona Quart 17 1961.

Combecher, H. Interpretationen zu drei Gedichten von Thomas. Die Neueren Sprachen 11 1962. Twenty-four years; The conversation of prayer; Fern Hill.

— Tod und Transzendenz in zwei Gedichten von Thomas. Die Neueren Sprachen 12 1963. A refusal to mourn the death, by fire, of a child in London; When all my five and country senses see.

Davies, A. T. William Barnes, G. M. Hopkins, Thomas: the influence of Welsh prosody on modern English poetry. Proc of the Third Congress of the International Comparative Lit Assoc (The Hague) 1962.

— Dylan: druid of the broken body. 1964.

Dylan Thomas: présentation par H. Bokanowski et M. Alain. [Paris] 1962. (Poètes d'aujourd'hui).

Knieger, B. Thomas: the Christianity of the Altarwise by owl-light sequence. College Eng 23 1962.

Morton, R. Notes on the imagery of Thomas. E Studies 43 1962.

Nowottny, W. In her The language poets use, 1962; rptd in Cox 1966, above.

Sergeant, H. The religious development of Thomas. REL 3 1962.

Thomas, R. G. Bard on a raised hearth: Thomas and his craft. Anglo-Welsh Rev 12 1962.

— Thomas: a poet of Wales? English 14 1963.

Christensen, N. Thomas and the doublecross of death. Ball State Teachers College Forum 4 1963.

Connolly, C. Dylan Thomas. In his Previous convictions, 1963; rptd review of Tedlock, 1960, above.

Firmage, G. J. A garland for Dylan Thomas. New York [1963]. 84 poems by 78 poets.

Jones, T. H. Dylan Thomas. Edinburgh 1963 (Writers and Critics).

Kleinman, H. H. The religious sonnets of Thomas: a study in imagery and meaning. Berkeley, Los Angeles 1963 (Perspectives in Criticism 13).

Mackworth, C. Dylan Thomas et la double vision. Critique (Paris) 19 1963.

Meller, H. Zwischen Laugharne and Llaregyb: zur Entstehungsgeschichte von Thomas' Under Milk Wood. In D. Riesner and H. Gneuss (ed), Festschrift für Walter Hübner, Berlin [1964].

— Zum literarischen Hintergrund von Thomas' Under Milk Wood. Die Neueren Sprachen 15 1966.

Nemerov, H. The generation of violence. In his Poetry and fiction, [1963]. Review of Collected poems 1953, rptd from Kenyon Rev 15 1953.

Noel, J. Thomas and the state of modern poetry. Revue des Langues Vivantes 29 1963.

Tellier, A.-R. La poésie de Thomas: thèmes et formes. Paris 1963.

Tritschler, D. The metamorphic stop of time in A winter's tale. PMLA 78 1963.

Achar, K. R. H. Dylan Thomas. Jnl of Karnatak Univ 8 1964.

Ackerman, J. Thomas: his life and work. 1964.

Joselyn, Sr M. Green and dying: the drama of Fern Hill. Renascence 16 1964.

Maclaren-Ross, J. The polestar neighbour. London Mag 4 1964; rptd in his Memoirs of the forties, 1965.

Martin, J. H. Dylan Thomas. TLS 19 March 1964, and subsequent correspondence. Reminiscences.

Martin, R. For the love of man and in praise of God: an evaluation of Thomas' poem This bread I break. Die Neueren Sprachen 13 1964.

Phillips, R. S. Death and resurrection: tradition in Thomas' After the funeral. McNeese Rev 15 1964.

Rea, J. A topographical guide to Under Milk Wood. College Eng 25 1964.

Read, B. The days of Thomas. New York 1964.

Sachs, A. Sexual dialectic in the early poetry of Thomas. Southern Rev (Adelaide) 1 1964.

Yerbury, G. Of a city beside a river: Whitman, Eliot, Thomas, Miller. Walt Whitman Rev 10 1964.

Fitzgibbon, C. The life of Thomas. 1965.

Greif, L. K. Image and theme in Thomas' A winter's tale. Thoth 6 1965.

Leech, G. This bread I break—language and interpretation. REL 6 1965.

Miller, J. H. In his Poets of reality, Cambridge Mass 1965.

Ray, P. C. Thomas and the surrealists. N & Q 210 1965.

Robinson, T. R. Thomas's On the marriage of a virgin. Eng Stud in Africa 8 1965.

Thompson, K. An approach to the early poems of Thomas. Anglo-Welsh Rev 14 1965.

Broy, E. J. The enigma of Thomas. Dalhousie Rev 45 1966.

Gentili, V. Il mondo rappreso di Thomas. Paragone 202 1966.

Jenkins, J. L. How green is Fern Hill. Eng Jnl 55 1966.

Jones, M. R. The wellspring of Dylan. Eng Jnl 55 1966.

Lindsay, J. Memories of Thomas. Meanjin 25 1966; rptd in his Meetings with poets, 1968.

Moynihan, W. T. The craft and art of Thomas. Ithaca 1966.

Murdy, L. B. Sound and sense in Thomas's poetry. Hague 1966.

Saunders, T. Religious elements in the poetry of Thomas. Dalhousie Rev 45 1966.

Yeomans, W. E. Thomas: the literal vision. Bucknell Rev 14 1966.

Capone, G. Drammi per voci: Thomas, Samuel Beckett, Harold Pinter. Bologna 1967.

— Il sentimento del tempo nell' opera di Dylan Thomas. Convivium 35 1967.

French, W. Two portraits of the artist: James Joyce's Young man; Thomas's Young dog. University Rev (Kansas City) 33 1967.

Lewis, M. Laugharne and Thomas. 1967.

Trick, B. The young Thomas. Texas Quart 9 1967.

West, P. Thomas: the position in calamity. Southern Rev 3 1967.

Ayer, J. R. Thomas in the aural dimension. Computer Stud in the Humanities & Verbal Behavior 1 1968.

Cleverdon, D. Under Milk Wood. TLS 18 July 1968.

—— The growth of Milk Wood: with the textual variants of Under Milk Wood. 1969.

Davies, W. An allusion to Hardy's A broken appointment in Thomas's In country sleep. N & Q 213 1968.

—— Imitation and invention: the use of borrowed material in Thomas's prose. EC 18 1968.

D'Souza, F. 'The gay wild dog from Wales'. In Siddha 3, ed D'Souza and J. Shivpuri, Bombay 1968.

Happel, N. Thomas: The force that through the green fuse...Die Neueren Sprachen 17 1968.

Loesch, K. T. The shape of sound: configurational rime in the poetry of Thomas. Sammlung Metzler 35 1968.

Montague, G. Thomas and Nightwood. Sewanee Rev 76 1968.

Reddington, A. M. Thomas: a journey from darkness to light. New York 1968.

Shivpuri, J. Peter Pan: sticking the shadow. In Siddha 3, ed F. D'Souza and Shivpuri, Bombay 1968. On Portrait of the artist as a young dog.

Taig, T. Swansea between the wars. Anglo-Welsh Rev 17 1968. Thomas and Vernon Watkins.

Astley, R. Stations of the breath: end rhyme in the verse of Thomas. PMLA 84 1969.

Bremer, R. An analysis and interpretation of Over Sir John's Hill. Neophilologus 53 1969.

Davis, W. V. Several comments on A refusal to mourn the death, by fire, of a child in London. Concerning Poetry 6 1969.

Friedman, S. Whitman and Laugharne: Thomas's Poem in October. Anglo-Welsh Rev 18 1969.

Kelly, R. The lost vision of Thomas's One warm Saturday. Stud in Short Fiction 6 1969.

Mosher, H. F., jr. The structure of Thomas's The peaches. Stud in Short Fiction 6 1969.

Ormerod, D. The central image in Thomas's Over Sir John's Hill. Eng Stud 49 1969.

Wittreich, J. A., jr. Thomas's conception of poetry: a debt to Blake. Eng Lang Notes 6 1969.   R. J. R.

LASCELLES ABERCROMBIE
1881–1938
See cols 995–7, below.

HAROLD MARIO MITCHELL ACTON
b. 1904

§1
Poetry

Aquarium. 1923.
An Indian ass. 1925.
Five saints and an appendix. 1927.
This chaos. Paris 1930 (priv ptd, 150 copies).

Other Works

Cornelian: a fable. 1928. Short story.
Humdrum. 1928, New York [1929]. Novel.
The last of the Medici [an anon life of Gian Gastone de' Medici]. Tr Acton, introd by N. Douglas, Florence 1930 (priv ptd, 365 copies).
The last Medici. 1932, 1958 (rev), New York 1959. Biography.
Modern Chinese poetry. 1936. With Ch'ên Shih-hsiang.
Famous Chinese plays. Tr and ed L. C. Arlington and Acton, Peiping 1937, New York 1963.
Fêng Mêng-lung. Glue and lacquer: four cautionary tales. Tr Acton and Lee Yi-hsieh 1941 (350 copies), 1947 (as Four cautionary tales).
Peonies and ponies. 1941. Novel.
Memoirs of an aesthete. 1948. Autobiography.
Prince Isidore. 1950. Novel.
The Bourbons of Naples, 1734–1825. 1956, 1957 (rptd with corrections), New York 1958.
Art and ideas in eighteenth-century Italy: lectures given at the Italian Institute 1957–8. Rome 1960. With others.
Florence. [1961], New York 1961. With M. Hürlimann.
The last Bourbons of Naples, 1825–61. 1961, New York 1962.
Old lamps for new. 1965. Novel.
Ramage in South Italy, by C. T. Ramage. Abridged and ed E. Clay, introd by Acton 1965.
Acton, with P. Quennell, edited Oxford Poetry, 1924.

RICHARD ALDINGTON
1892–1962
See cols 511–14, below.

KENNETH ALLOTT
b. 1912

§1
Poetry

Poems. 1938.
The ventriloquist's doll. [1943].

Other Works

The rhubarb tree. 1937. Novel, with S. Tait.
Jules Verne. [1940], New York 1941. Biography.
The poems of William Habington. Ed with introd and commentary by Allott 1948 (Liverpool English Texts and Studies).
The Penguin book of contemporary verse. Ed with introd and notes by Allott 1950, 1962 (rev) (Penguin Poets).
The art of Graham Greene. 1951, New York 1963. With M. Farris.
A room with a view: a play adapted from the novel by E. M. Forster, by S. Tait and Allott. 1951.
Selected poems of W. M. Praed. Ed with introd and commentary by Allott 1953, Cambridge Mass 1953. (ML).
Five uncollected essays of Matthew Arnold. Ed Allott, [Liverpool] 1953, New York 1953 (Liverpool Reprints 9).
Matthew Arnold. 1955 (Br Council pamphlet), Lincoln Neb 1963.
The Pelican book of English prose. General editor: K. Allott. 5 vols 1956.
Browning, R. Selected poems, chosen and ed Allott 1967.
Allott has also edited Arnold's poems for Penguin Poets, *1954,* EL, *1965 and* Longman's Annotated English Poets, *1965.*

MAURICE BARING
1874–1945
See cols 517–19, below.

GEORGE GRANVILLE BARKER
b. 1913

§1
Poetry

Thirty preliminary poems. 1933.
Poems. 1935.
Calamiterror. 1937.
Elegy on Spain. Manchester 1939.
Lament and triumph. 1940.
Selected poems. New York 1941.
Sacred and secular elegies. Norfolk Conn 1943.
Eros in dogma. 1944.
Love poems. New York 1947.
News of the world. 1950.
The true confession of George Barker. 1950, New York 1964, London 1965 (enlarged).
A vision of beasts and gods. 1954.
Collected poems 1930–1955. 1957, New York 1958. Omits The true confession.
Penguin modern poets, 3: Barker, M. Bell, C. Causley. 1962. Selection, 15 poems.
The view from a blind I. 1962.
Collected poems 1930–1965. New York 1965.
Dreams of a summer night. 1966.
The golden chains. 1968.
At Thurgarton Church: a poem with drawings. 1969.
Runes and rhymes and tunes and chimes. 1969.

Other Works

Alanna autumnal. 1933. Novel.
Janus. 1935. Two tales: The documents of death and The Bacchant.
The dead seagull. 1950, New York 1951. Novel.
Two plays. 1958. The seraphina; In the shade of the old apple tree.
Alfred Tennyson. Idylls of the king and a selection of poems, with a foreword by Barker. New York 1961, London 1962.
Essays. 1970.

§2

Daiches, D. The lyricism of Barker. Poetry (Chicago) 69 1947.
Potts, P. The world of Barker. Poetry Quart 10 1948.
Cronin, A. Poetry and ideas: Barker. London Mag 3 1956.
Schwimmer, E. G. Barker: an exploration. Numbers 9 1959.
Swift, P. Prolegomenon to Barker. X, a Quarterly Rev 1 1960.
Farmer, A. J. Aspects de la poésie de Barker. Études Anglaises 14 1961.
Kleinstück, J. Barker: Battersea Park. In H. Oppel (ed), Die moderne englische Lyrik, Berlin 1967.
Fodaski, M. George Barker. New York 1969 (Twayne's English Authors).

JULIAN HEWARD BELL
1908–37

Collections

Essays, poems and letters. Ed Q. Bell 1938. Contributions by J. M. Keynes, D. Garnett, C. Mauron, C. Day Lewis and E. M. Forster.

§1
Poetry

Chaffinches. Cambridge 1929.
Winter movement and other poems. 1930.
Work for the winter and other poems. 1936.

Other Works

Cambridge poetry 1929–30. 2 vols 1929–30. 5 poems contributed by Bell.
New signatures. Ed M. Roberts 1932. 3 poems contributed by Bell.
We did not fight: 1914–18 experiences of war resisters. Ed J. Bell 1935.
Poems by Stéphane Mallarmé. Tr R. Fry; ed C. Mauron and J. Bell 1936. Rptd with additional material 1952.

§2

Evans, P. Julian Bell. Nineteenth Century 125 1939. Essay–review of Essays, poems and letters, above.
Lehmann, J. The whispering gallery. 1955. Reminiscences of Bell.
Grubb, F. In but not of: a study of Bell. CQ 2 1960; rptd (rev) in his A vision of reality, 1965.
Stansky, P. and W. Abrahams. Journey to the frontier: Bell and Cornford—their lives and the 1930's. 1966.
See also Essays, poems and letters, ed Q. Bell, above.

JOSEPH HILAIRE PIERRE RENÉ BELLOC
1870–1953

See cols 1004–10, below.

FRANCIS BERRY
b. 1915

§1

Gospel of fire. 1933.
Snake in the moon. 1936.
The iron Christ: a poem. 1938.
Fall of a tower and other poems. 1943.
Murdock and other poems. 1947.
The galloping centaur: poems 1933–1951. 1952, 1970 (adds Envoy—1968). Omits most of Gospel of fire, 1933.
Herbert Read. 1953, [1961] (rev) (Br Council pamphlet).
Poets' grammar: person, time and mood in poetry. 1958.
Morant Bay and other poems. 1961.
Poetry and the physical voice. 1962, New York 1962.
The Shakespeare inset: word and picture. 1965, New York 1966.
Ghosts of Greenland. 1966.
John Masefield: the narrative poet. 1968. Inaugural lecture, Univ of Sheffield.
Berry edited E & S 22 1969.

§2

Kenmare, D. The long pursuit, and search for synthesis: a review of the poetry of Berry and D. Gascoyne. Wind and the Rain 2 1945.
Knight, G. Wilson. In his Neglected powers, 1971.

SIR JOHN BETJEMAN
b. 1906

Bibliographies
Carter, J. Betjemaniana. Book Collector 9 1960.

§1
Poetry
Mount Zion: or, in touch with the infinite. [1931].
Continual dew: a little book of bourgeois verse. 1937.
Sir John Piers, by 'Epsilon' [i.e. Betjeman]. Mullingar
[1938]. 5 poems, rptd in next.
Old lights for new chancels: verses topographical and
amatory. 1940.
New bats in old belfries. 1945.
Slick, but not streamlined: poems and short pieces, selected
and with an introd by W. H. Auden, New York
1947.
Selected poems, chosen, with a preface, by J. Sparrow
1948.
A few late chrysanthemums. 1954.
Poems in the porch. 1954.
John Betjeman's collected poems, compiled and with an
introduction by the Earl of Birkenhead. 1958, Boston
1959, London 1962 (with addns).
[Thirty-one poems]. 1958 (Pocket Poets). Selection with
1 uncollected poem.
Summoned by bells. 1960, Boston 1960. Verse auto-
biography.
A ring of bells: poems of John Betjeman, introduced and
selected by I. Slade [1962], Boston 1963.
High and low. 1966.

Other Works
*Many minor contributions to books and anthologies have been
omitted.*
Ghastly good taste: or a depressing story of the rise and
fall of English architecture. 1933.
Cornwall illustrated in a series of views. Ed Betjeman
1934 (Shell Guides).
Devon. 1936, 1955 (rev by B. Watson) (Shell Guides).
An Oxford University chest: comprising a description of
the present state of the town and university of Oxford.
1938.
Antiquarian prejudice. 1939. Lecture on architecture.
Selected poems, by Sir Henry Newbolt, selected with an
introd by Betjeman 1940.
Vintage London. 1942.
English cities and small towns. 1943.
English, Scottish and Welsh landscape 1700–c. 1860:
[poems] chosen by Betjeman and G. Taylor 1944.
John Piper. 1944 (Penguin Modern painters).
The eighteen-nineties: a period anthology in prose and
verse, chosen by M. Secker with an introd by Betjeman
1948.
Murray's Buckinghamshire architectural guide. Ed Betje-
man and J. Piper 1948.
Murray's Berkshire architectural guide. Ed Betjeman and
J. Piper 1949.
Studies in the history of Swindon, by Betjeman [et al].
Swindon 1950.
The English scene: with a reading list compiled by L. R.
Muirhead. 1951 (National Book League Reader's
Guides). Essay.
Shropshire. 1951. By J. Piper and Betjeman (Shell
Guides).
First and last loves. 1952. Essays on architecture and
English towns.
R. S. Thomas. Song at the year's turning: poems 1942–
1954. 1955. Introd by Betjeman.
The English town in the last hundred years. Cambridge
1956. Lecture.

English love poems, chosen by Betjeman and G. Taylor.
1957.
Collins guide to English parish churches. Ed Betjeman
1958, New York 1959 (as An American's guide to
English parish churches), London 1968 (rev in 2 vols as
Collins Pocket guide [etc].).
Altar and pew: Church of England verses. 1959. Selection
by Betjeman.
Charles Tennyson Turner: a hundred sonnets, selected
and with an introd by Betjeman and C. Tennyson
1960.
Ground plan to skyline. [By] 'Richard M. Farran' [i.e.
Betjeman]. 1960.
A wealth of poetry, selected for the young in heart by
W. Hindley with the assistance of Betjeman. Oxford
[1963].
Cornwall: a Shell Guide. 1964. The work of 1934 com-
pletely rewritten.
English churches. 1964. With B. Clarke.
The City of London churches. [1965].
Victorian and Edwardian London from old photographs:
introd and commentaries by Betjeman 1969.
Betjeman was general editor of Shell Guides *first pbd in 1934.
He was also editor of* Watergate Children's Classics *from
1947. He contributed a weekly column,* City and suburban,
to Spectator *from 15 Oct 1954 to Jan 1958.*

§2
Bogan, L. [Review of Slick, but not streamlined, 1947]
New Yorker 13 Sept 1947. Rptd in her Selected criti-
cism, 1955.
A serious poet. TLS 12 Dec 1958.
Stanford, D. The poetry of Betjeman. Month new ser 19
1958.
— John Betjeman: a study. 1961. The ch, The poet:
ideological, appeared as Ideology and Mr Betjeman, in
Month new ser 23 1960, and also as Mr Betjeman's
satire, in Contemporary Rev 197 1960.
— John Betjeman: poet for export? Meanjin 20 1961.
Bergonzi, B. 'That's a Surrey sunset...': culture and Mr
Betjeman. Twentieth Century 165 1959.
Hollis, C. Mr Betjeman as thinker. Month new ser 21
1959.
Neame, A. Poet of Anglicanism. Commonweal 71 1960.
Interview.
Wain, J. A substitute for poetry. Observer 27 Nov 1960.
Review of Summoned by bells, 1960; rptd as John Betje-
man in his Essays on literature and ideas, 1963.
Kermode, F. Henry Miller and Betjeman. Encounter 16
1961. Review of Summoned by bells, 1960; rptd in his
Puzzles and epiphanies, 1962.
Brooke, J. Ronald Firbank and Betjeman. 1962 (Br
Council pamphlet).
Sieveking, L. Betjeman and Dorset. [Dorchester 1963].
Ullnaess, S. P. N. Betjeman—sjarmerende, betydelig
engelsk dikter. Samtiden 72 1963.
Wiehe, R. E. Summoned by nostalgia: Betjeman's poetry.
Arizona Quart 19 1963.
Singh, G. S. The poetry of Betjeman. In A. Lombardo
(ed), Studi e ricerche di letteratura inglese e americana,
Milan 1967.

EDMUND CHARLES BLUNDEN
b. 1896

Bibliographies
Muir, P. H. In his Points, ser 2 1934.
Saito, T. A Blunden bibliography. Today's Japan 5 1960.

Selections
Edmund Blunden: a selection of his poetry and prose made
by K. Hopkins. 1950, New York 1951.

§1

Poetry

Some single poems, many ptd in Japan and Hong Kong as greetings cards, have been omitted, as have some verse prologues written for student performances of plays by Shakespeare and others.

Poems, 1913 and 1914. Horsham 1914 (100 copies).

Poems translated from the French: July 1913–January 1914. Horsham 1914 (100 copies).

The barn, with certain other poems. Uckfield 1916 (priv ptd, 50 copies).

The harbingers: poems. Uckfield 1916 (priv ptd, 200 copies).

Pastorals: a book of verses. 1916.

Three poems. Uckfield 1916 (50 copies). Contains The silver bird of Herndyke Mill, Stane Street, The gods of the earth beneath.

The waggoner, and other poems. 1920 (400 copies), New York 1921 (100 copies).

Old homes: a poem. Clare 1922 (priv ptd, 100 copies).

The shepherd, and other poems of peace and war. 1922, New York 1922.

Dead letters. 1923 (50 copies).

To nature: new poems. 1923 (392 copies).

The birth, life and death of Scaramouch by Master Angelo Constantini. Tr C. W. Beaumont, together with Mezzetin's dedicatory poems and Loret's rhymed newsletters concerning Scaramouch now first rendered into English verse by Blunden. 1924 (390 copies).

English poems. Preface by Blunden 1925, New York 1926, London 1929 (rev). Most of poems 1921–5 with addns.

Masks of time: a new collection of poems, principally meditative. 1925 (390 copies).

[Twenty-one poems]. [1925] (Augustan Books of Modern Poetry). Selection.

Japanese garland. 1928 (390 copies).

Retreat: new sonnets and poems. 1928, Garden City NY 1928.

Winter nights: a reminiscence. [1928] (Ariel Poem).

Near and far: new poems. 1929, New York 1930.

The poems of Edmund Blunden. Preface by Blunden 1930, New York 1932.

A summer's fancy. 1930 (405 copies).

Constantia and Francis: an autumn evening. Edinburgh 1931 (priv ptd, 200 copies).

In summer: the rotunda of the Bishop of Derry. 1931 (priv ptd, 305 copies).

To Themis: poems on famous trials; with other pieces. 1931 (405 copies).

Halfway house: a miscellany of new poems. 1932, New York 1933.

Choice or chance: new poems. 1934.

Verses to HRH the Duke of Windsor. Oxford 1936 (100 copies).

An elegy, and other poems. 1937.

On several occasions, by 'A Fellow of Merton College'. 1939 (60 copies).

Poems 1930–1940. 1940 (for 1941), New York 1941.

Shells by a stream: new poems. 1944, New York 1945.

After the bombing, and other short poems. 1949, New York 1949.

Eastward: a selection of verses original and translated. Tokyo 1949 (250 copies).

Records of friendship: occasional and epistolary poems written during visits to Kyushu. Fukuoka 1950.

Poems of many years. Preface by Blunden 1957.

A Hong Kong house: poems, 1951–1961. 1962.

Eleven poems. Cambridge 1965.

A selection of the shorter poems. Long Melford [1966].

Poems on Japan, hitherto uncollected and mostly unprinted. Ed T. Saito, [Tokyo] 1967.

The midnight skaters: poems for young readers chosen and introduced by C. Day Lewis. 1968.

A selection from the poems. Long Melford [1969].

Other Works

Poems chiefly from manuscript by John Clare. Ed Blunden and A. Porter [1920] (200 copies), New York 1921.

The appreciation of literary prose: being one of the special courses of the art of life. [1921].

The Bonadventure: a random journal of an Atlantic holiday. 1922, New York 1923.

Christ's Hospital: a retrospect. [1923].

Madrigals and chronicles: being newly found poems by John Clare. Ed with a preface and commentary by Blunden 1924 (398 copies).

A song to David, with other poems, by Christopher Smart. Introd and notes by Blunden 1924.

Shelley and Keats as they struck their contemporaries: notes partly from manuscript sources. Ed Blunden 1925 (390 copies).

The actor: a poem by Robert Lloyd; to which is prefix'd an essay by Blunden. 1926 (270 copies).

Bret Harte: selected poems. Ed Blunden and B. Brady, Tokyo 1926.

Autobiography of Benjamin Robert Haydon. Introd by Blunden 1927 (WC).

A hundred English poems from the Elizabethan age to the Victorian. Ed Blunden, Tokyo 1927, 1949 (rev).

Lectures in English literature. Tokyo 1927, 1952 (enlarged).

On the poems of Henry Vaughan: characteristics and intimations; with his principal Latin poems carefully translated into English verse. 1927.

The autobiography of Leigh Hunt. Ed Blunden 1928 (WC).

Leigh Hunt's Examiner examined: comprising some account of that celebrated newspaper's contents etc 1808–25. 1928, New York 1931.

Undertones of war. 1928, New York 1929, London 1930 (rev), 1956 (WC) (with new preface), [1965] (with new introd).

Keats' view of poetry, by Takeshi Saito; to which is prefixed an essay on English literature in Japan by Blunden. 1929.

Last essays of Elia, by Charles Lamb. Ed Blunden 1929.

Nature in English literature. 1929, New York 1929 (Hogarth Lectures on Lit).

The poems of William Collins. Ed Blunden 1929, New York 1929.

Shakespeare's significances: a paper read before the Shakespeare Association. 1929, New York 1929.

An anthology of war poems, compiled by F. Brereton. Introd by Blunden 1930.

A book of narrative verse. Compiled by V. H. Collins, introd by Blunden 1930 (WC).

De bello Germanico: a fragment of trench history, written in 1918 by the author of Undertones of war. Hawstead 1930 (275 copies).

Great short stories of the war. Ed J. H. C. Minchin 1930. Introd by Blunden.

Leigh Hunt: a biography. 1930, New York 1930 (as Leigh Hunt and his circle).

The War, 1914–1918: a booklist. Compiled by Blunden and others [1930].

The poems of Wilfred Owen. 1931, New York 1931. With memoir by Blunden, also rptd in Owen's Collected poems, 1963.

The rime of the ancient mariner by Samuel Taylor Coleridge. Introd by Blunden New York 1931.

Sketches in the life of John Clare written by himself, now first published with an introduction, notes and additions by Blunden. 1931, New York 1931.

Tragical consequences, or a disaster at Deal: being an unpublished letter of William Godwin. Preface by Blunden 1931.

Votive tablets: studies chiefly appreciative of English authors and books. 1931 (60 copies), New York 1932. 39 essays rptd with some adjustment from TLS and Times.

The city of dreadful night, and other poems by James Thomson. Introd by Blunden 1932.

The face of England in a series of occasional sketches. 1932, New York 1932. Essays and 8 poems.

Fall in, ghosts: an essay on a battalion reunion. 1932 (50 copies).

Charles Lamb and his contemporaries. Cambridge 1933, New York 1933 (Clark Lectures).

We'll shift our ground: or two on a tour, almost a novel. 1933. With S. Norman.

Charles Lamb: his life recorded by his contemporaries. Compiled by Blunden 1934.

Coleridge: studies by several hands on the hundredth anniversary of his death. Ed Blunden and E. L. Griggs 1934.

The mind's eye: essays. 1934. Contains pt 1, Flanders; pt 2, Japan; pt 3, England; pt 4, The world of books.

Edward Gibbon and his age. Bristol [1935] (Arthur Skemp Memorial Lecture).

Keats's publisher: a memoir of John Taylor 1781–1864. 1936.

Shelley is expelled. In On Shelley, 1938.

English villages. 1941, New York 1941 (Britain in Pictures).

Thomas Hardy. 1941, New York 1942 (EML).

Poems of this war by younger poets. Ed P. Ledward and C. Strang, introd by Blunden, Cambridge 1942.

Romantic poetry and the fine arts. 1942 (Warton Lecture on English Poetry).

Return to husbandry: an annotated list of books dealing with the history, philosophy and craftsmanship of rural England, with four preliminary essays. Ed Blunden 1943.

Cricket country. 1944.

Poems, by C. W. Brodribb. Introd by Blunden 1946.

Shelley: a life story. 1946, New York 1947.

Hymns for the amusement of children by Christopher Smart. Ed Blunden, Oxford 1947 (Luttrell reprints 5).

The life of George Crabbe, by his son. Introd by Blunden 1947.

Shakespeare to Hardy: short studies of characteristic English authors. Tokyo 1948.

Shelley's Defence of poetry. Ed Blunden, Tokyo 1948.

Two lectures on English literature. Osaka 1948. Contains 4 poems.

Addresses on general subjects connected with English literature. Tokyo 1949.

Poetry and science, and other lectures. Osaka 1949.

Sons of light: a series of lectures on English writers. Hosei 1949.

Chaucer to 'B.V.'; with an additional paper on Herman Melville. Tokyo 1950.

Favourite studies in English literature. Tokyo 1950.

Hamlet and other studies. [Tokyo 1950].

Influential books: lectures given at Waseda University in 1948 and 1949. Tokyo 1950.

John Keats. 1950, 1954 (rev), 1966 (rev) (Br Council pamphlet).

Reprinted papers, partly concerning some English romantic poets. Tokyo 1950. Rptd from Stud in Eng Lit.

A wanderer in Japan: sketches and reflections in prose and verse. 1950, 1951 (without Japanese trn).

Sketches and reflections: with notes by S. Tomiyama, Tokyo [1951].

Essayists of the romantic period. Ed I. Nishizaki, Tokyo [1952].

Christ's Hospital book. Ed Blunden 1953.

The dede of pittie: dramatic scenes reflecting the history of Christ's Hospital and offered in celebration of the quatercentenary 1953. [1953]. In prose and verse.

Charles Lamb. 1954, 1964 (rev) (Br Council pamphlet).

Poems, by Ivor Gurney, principally selected from unpublished mss, with a memoir by Blunden. 1954.

Selected poems, by Shelley. Ed Blunden 1954.

Selected poems, by Keats. Ed Blunden 1955.

Thomson, J. The castle of indolence. Introd by Blunden, Hong Kong 1956.

Visick, M. The genesis of Wuthering Heights. Introd by Blunden, Hong Kong 1958.

War poets 1914–1918. 1958, 1964 (rev) (Br Council pamphlet).

Three young poets: critical sketches of Byron, Shelley and Keats. Tokyo 1959.

Selected poems of Tennyson. Ed Blunden 1960.

A Wessex worthy: Thomas Russell. Beaminster 1960 (100 copies).

English scientists as men of letters. Hong Kong 1961 (Jubilee Congress Lecture, University of Hong Kong).

Memoir of Thomas Bewick, written by himself 1822–1828. Introd by Blunden 1961.

Herrmanns, R. Lee Lan flies the dragon kite, English version by Blunden. 1962. Photographs with text.

A Corscombe inhabitant. Beaminster 1963.

Wayside poems of the seventeenth (early eighteenth) century: an anthology gathered by Blunden and B. Mellor, 2 vols Hong Kong 1963–4.

William Crowe 1745–1829. Beaminster 1963.

Guest of Thomas Hardy. Beaminster 1964.

A brief guide to the great Church of the Holy Trinity, Long Melford, Ipswich. 1965, 1966 (rev).

A few not quite forgotten writers? 1967. Eng Assoc Presidential Address.

Blunden also edited, with Neville Whymant, all 6 nos of Oriental Literary Times, *pbd by Japan Times, Tokyo, 1925.*

§2

Bridges, R. The dialectical words in Blunden's poems. Soc for Pure English Tract 5 1921.

Squire, J. C. In his Essays on poetry, [1923].

Twitchett, E. G. The poetry of Blunden. London Mercury 14 1926.

Dunn, W. H. Blunden and his poetry. London Quart Rev 150 1928.

Bliss, W. Blunden's poetry. London Mercury 23 1930.

Williams, C. In his Poetry at present, 1930.

Barker, F. E. The poetry of Blunden. Nineteenth Century 109 1931.

Bonnerot, L. La poésie d'Edmund Blunden. Revue Anglo-américaine 8 1931.

Wood, F. T. On the poetry of Blunden. Poetry Rev 23 1932.

Church, R. Edmund Blunden: agonist. Fortnightly Rev 148 1940; rptd in his Eight for immortality, 1941.

Aaronson, L. Edmund Blunden. Nineteenth Century 129 1941.

'Menander's Mirror' (Charles Morgan). Blunden's Thomasine. TLS 20 Jan 1945; rptd in Morgan's Reflections in a mirror ser 2, 1946.

Fausset, H. I'A. Blunden's later poetry. In his Poets and pundits, 1947.

House, H. Shelley II. In his All in due time, 1955. Review of Shelley: a life story.

Willy, M. The poetry of Blunden. English 11 1957.

Hardie, A. M. Edmund Blunden. 1958 (Br Council pamphlet).

Carr, I. Blunden and the 1914–18 war. Stand 4 1960.

Edmund Blunden, sixty-five. Hong Kong 1961. Tributes.

Amato, A. Introduzione alle poesie di guerra di Blunden. Le Lingue Straniere 12 1963.

Bergonzi, B. In his Heroes' twilight: a study of the literature of the Great War, 1965.

Fraser, G. S. Edmund Blunden. London Mag 6 1966.

Thorpe, M. The poetry of Blunden. E Studies 48 1967.

— Blunden's Joy poems. English 17 1968.

GORDON BOTTOMLEY
1874–1948
Collections

Poems and plays. Introd by C. C. Abbott 1953, New York 1953. Poems mainly from Poems of thirty years, 1925.

§1
Poetry and Verse Plays

Many of Bottomley's plays were produced by amateur companies. For details, see his A stage for poetry, *1948 below.*

The mickle drede and other verses. Kendal 1896 (150 copies).

Poems at white-nights: a book of verse. 1899.

The crier by night: a play in one act. 1902. First performed by the Portmanteau Theatre Co in Wyoming Sept 1916.

The gate of Smaragdus. 1904.

Midsummer eve. Flansham 1905 (120 copies). Play, first performed by the Arts League of Service, 1930.

Chambers of imagery. Ser 1, 1907; ser 2, 1912.

Laodice and Danaë: play in one act. (Lyric, Hammersmith 1930). 1909 (priv ptd; 150 copies), Boston 1916.

The riding to Lithend: a play in one act. (Festival Theatre, Cambridge 1928). Flansham 1909 (120 copies), Portland Maine 1910.

A vision of Giorgione: three variations on Venetian themes. Portland Maine 1910, London 1922 (rev with addns, as A vision of Giorgione: three variations on a Venetian theme). Extract from The gate of Smaragdus, 1904 above.

King Lear's wife: a play in one act. (Birmingham Repertory Theatre Sept 1915; His Majesty's 19 May 1916). New York 1916.

King Lear's wife; The crier by night; The riding to Lithend; Midsummer eve; Laodice and Danaë. 1920, Boston 1921, London 1922 (with a new poem), Boston 1924.

Gruach (Scottish National Theatre Soc, Glasgow March 1923; St Martin's Theatre 1924) and Britain's daughter (Old Vic 1922): two plays. 1921, Boston 1922.

Poems of thirty years. 1925. Selection, with uncollected poems.

Frescoes from buried temples, by J. Guthrie, with poems by G. Bottomley. Flansham 1927.

[Nineteen poems]. [1928] (Augustan Books of Verse). Selection.

A parting and The return. (Oxford Recitations 1928). New York 1928. Short duologues.

Scenes and plays. 1929, New York 1929. A parting; The return; The sisters; The widow; Towie Castle; Ardvorlich's wife; The singing sands.

Festival preludes. 1930 (110 copies).

The Viking's barrow at Littleholme. [Flansham] 1930 (20 copies).

Lyric plays. 1932, New York 1932. Marsaili's weeping; Culbin Sands; The Bower of Wandel; Suilven and the eagle; Kirkconnel Lea; The woman from the Voe.

The acts of Saint Peter: a cathedral festival play. (Exeter Cathedral 27 June 1933). 1933, Boston 1933.

The falconer's daughter. (Scottish Community Drama Festival, Edinburgh 1938). In Twenty-five modern one-act plays, ed J. Bourne 1938; rptd in Choric plays, 1939, as The falconer's lassie.

Choric plays and a comedy. 1939. Fire at Calbart; The falconer's lassie; Dunaverty.

Kate Kennedy: a comedy in three acts. (Pilgrim Players CEMA tour, Spring 1944). 1945.

Maids of Athens. [Dublin] 1945 (50 copies). Verse play.

Other Works

James Guthrie, his book of bookplates. Introd by Bottomley, Edinburgh 1907.

Poems by Isaac Rosenberg. Selected and ed G. Bottomley 1922.

Guenevere: two poems by William Morris. Foreword by Bottomley 1930.

The collected works of Isaac Rosenberg. Ed Bottomley and D. Harding 1937.

Deirdre: drama in four acts in Gaelic and English, adapted from A. Carmichael's Barra story and lay. Inverness 1944. Prose; with the additional passages tr into Gaelic by C. F. and D. Urquhart.

A note on poetry and the stage. [1944?] (Religious Drama pamphlet).

A stage for poetry: my purposes with my plays. Kendal 1948 (priv ptd).

The collected poems of Isaac Rosenberg. Ed Bottomley and D. Harding 1949, New York 1949.

Bottomley edited Essays by Divers Hands *1944.*

Letters

Poet and painter: being the correspondence between Bottomley and Paul Nash, 1910–46. Ed C. C. Abbott and A. Bertram 1955, New York 1955.

E. Farjeon, Edward Thomas: the last four years, *1958, contains extracts from 2 letters from Bottomley.*

§2

Bronner, M. Bottomley: a poet of three moods. Bookman (New York) 39 1914.

Benét, W. R. Bottomley's art. Literary Rev 19 Feb 1921.

Mégroz, R. L. Gordon Bottomley. Bookman (London) 64 1923.

Wild, F. Bottomleys Dramen. Die Neueren Sprachen 32 1924.

Lucas, F. L. In his Authors dead and living, 1926.

Robertson, D. A. Contemporary English poets: Bottomley. English Jnl 15 1926.

Carmer, C. Bottomley and poetic drama. Theatre Arts Monthly 14 1930.

Hood, A. Bottomley's cathedral festival play. Poetry Rev 24 1933. On The acts of Saint Peter.

Thouless, P. In her Modern poetic drama, 1934.

Weygandt, C. Doughty, Moore and Bottomley. In his Time of Yeats, New York [1937].

Farmer, A. J. Gordon Bottomley. Études Anglaises 9 1956.

Sitwell, E. Great writers rediscovered 5, Poets of delight: Bottomley and Ralph Hodgson. Sunday Times 5 May 1957.

Ross, R. H. In his The Georgian revolt, 1910–22: rise and fall of a poetic ideal, Carbondale 1965.

Spanos, W. V. The historical pageant: the rhetoric of action. In his The Christian tradition in modern British drama, New Brunswick NJ 1967.

Débax, J.-P. Gruach: fantaisie Shakespearienne. Caliban 6 1969.

FRANCIS JAMES RONALD BOTTRALL
b. 1906

§1
Poetry

The loosening and other poems. Cambridge 1931.

Festivals of fire. 1934.

The turning path. 1939.

Farewell and welcome. 1945.

Selected poems, with a preface by Edith Sitwell 1946.

The palisades of fear. 1949.

Adam unparadised. 1954.

Collected poems. Introd by C. Tomlinson [1961]. Selection, with 7 new poems.

Other Works

T. S. Eliot. Dikter. Samlade och utgivna av Bottrall och G. Ekelöf. Samt inledande av Bottrall och E. Mesterton. Stockholm [1942].

Collected English verse: an anthology chosen by Margaret and Ronald Bottrall. 1946.

Art centres of the world: Rome. 1968.

§2

Leavis, F. R. In his New bearings in English poetry, 1932.
Sitwell, E. Four new poets. London Mercury 33 1936.
  Empson, Bottrall, D. Thomas, Archibald MacLeish.
Winkler, R. O. C. Ronald Bottrall. Scrutiny 8 1939.
  Review of The turning path.
Mason, H. A. Room for doubt? Mr Bottrall's Selected
  poems. Scrutiny 14 1947. Review.
Lienhardt, P. The palisades of fear. Scrutiny 17 1950.
  Review.

LILIAN HELEN BOWES-LYON
1895-1949

§1

The buried stream. 1929. Novel.
The white hare and other poems. 1934.
Bright feather fading. 1936.
Tomorrow is a revealing. 1941.
Evening in Stepney and other poems. 1943.
A rough walk home and other poems. 1946.
Collected poems. Introd by C. Day Lewis 1948, New
  York 1948.

§2

Willy, M. The poetry of Lilian Bowes-Lyon. E & S new
  ser 5 1952.
Treneer, A. The poetry of Lilian Bowes-Lyon 1896 [sic]–
  1949. Poetry Rev 55 1964.

RUPERT CHAWNER BROOKE
1887-1915
*The principal collections of Brooke's mss are in the Temple
Library of Rugby School and in the Library of King's College
Cambridge (some as a deposit by the literary trustees). The
details are given in Keynes, Bibliographies, below.*

Bibliographies
Danielson, H. In his Bibliographies of modern authors,
  1921.
Potter, R. M. G. Rupert Brooke: a bibliographical note on
  his works published in book form 1911–1919. Hartford
  Conn 1923 (priv ptd; 52 copies).
Keynes, G. A bibliography of Brooke. 1954, 1959 (rev)
  (Soho Bibliographies). *See* D. A. Randall, The first
  American edition of 1914 and other poems, Book Collec-
  tor 13 1964, and Keynes' reply, ibid.

§1
Poetry
The Pyramids. Rugby 1904; rptd in Poetical works, 1946,
  below.
The Bastille: a prize poem recited in Rugby School 24
  June 1905. Rugby 1905 [c. 1920]; rptd in Poetical
  works, 1946, below.
Poems. 1911.
1914 and other poems. 1915, New York 1915 (as 1914 and
  other poems; limited to 87 copies for copyright purposes). Mostly rptd from periodicals, including many
  from New Numbers.
Collected poems. New York 1915. Introd by G. E. Woodberry and biographical note by M. Lavington; includes
  only Poems, 1911, and 1914 and other poems, 1915.
'1914': five sonnets. 1915. Rptd from New Numbers.
War poems. [1915]. According to Keynes 'an unknown
  number of copies were printed for Lady Desborough'.
  Contains 5 sonnets rptd from New Numbers Dec 1914
  and the fragment The feet that ran with mine have found
  their goal.

The Old Vicarage Grantchester. 1916. Single poem,
  which appeared in Basileon 1912, in Poetry Rev 1912,
  and in 1914 and other poems, 1915 above.
Poems. [c. 1916]. Thus dated by Keynes. 6 poems all
  previously pbd.
Selected poems. 1917. 37 poems.
Collected poems, with a memoir [by E. Marsh]. 1918,
  1928 (with 2 more poems, and order of poems made
  chronological), 1942 (with Marsh named as author of
  Memoir).
Fragments now first collected, some being hitherto un-
  published. Ed R. M. G. Potter, Hartford Conn 1925
  (99 copies).
[Twenty-two poems]. [1925] (Augustan Books of Modern
  Poetry). Selection.
Complete poems. 1932. Contents as in Collected poems
  1928, but without the Memoir.
Twenty poems. 1935. Selected by F. Sidgwick.
Two sonnets, with a memoir of W. S. Churchill. 1945.
  Secretly ptd by the Dutch Resistance; contains Safety,
  The soldier.
Poetical works. Ed G. Keynes 1946. Adds 26 poems to
  contents of Collected poems 1928.
Five poems: Tiare Tahiti, Clouds, The goddess in the
  wood, Mary and Gabriel, The Chilterns. 1948.
Poems. 1948 (Folio Soc). Illustr Buckland-Wright; con-
  tents as Collected poems, 1918.
Grantchester and The great lover. Christchurch New
  Zealand 1949.
Poems. Ed G. Keynes 1952. Adds 4 poems, in introd, to
  contents of Collected poems, 1928.
[Twenty-nine poems]. 1960 (Pocket Poets). Selection.

Other Works
Lithuania: a drama in one act. Chicago 1915, London
  1935.
John Webster and the Elizabethan drama. New York 1916,
  London 1916.
Letters from America. Preface by Henry James, New York
  1916, London 1916. Letters originally written to West-
  minster Gazette as articles.
A letter to the editor of the Poetry Review. Peekskill 1929
  (50 copies). 2 letters, first unpbd, 2nd rptd from Poetry
  Rev 1 1912.
Democracy and the arts. Preface by G. Keynes 1946 (for
  Feb 1947). Essay read in Cambridge 1910.
The prose of Rupert Brooke. Ed C. Hassall 1956. Selection from books, articles and unpbd mss.
*Brooke contributed a number of poems etc to the 'problems
page' of Westminster Gazette and Saturday Westminster.
He contributed poems and reviews to Cambridge Rev and
was one of the 4 poets whose work was pbd in New Numbers 1914. Poems by him (none of them new) appeared in
the first 2 vols of Georgian Poetry. An extract from a frag-
mentary novel, Death of John Rump, is ptd in Sir Edward
Marsh's autobiography, A number of people, 1939. This
work also contains letters from Brooke to Marsh (see §2,
below).*

Letters
The letters of Brooke. Chosen and ed G. Keynes. 1968,
  New York 1968.

§2

Lewis, W. Our contemporaries. Blast 2 1915. Satire on
  Brooke.
Drinkwater, J. Rupert Brooke: an essay. 1916; rptd in
  his Prose papers, 1917 (corrected).
—— Brooke on John Webster. In his Prose papers, 1917.
Mais, S. P. B. In his From Shakespeare to O. Henry,
  1917, 1923 (rev).
Perdriel-Vaissières, J. Rupert Brooke's death and burial,
  based on the log of the French hospital ship Duguay-
  Trouin. Tr V. O'Sullivan, New Haven 1917 (priv ptd).

De la Mare, W. Rupert Brooke and the intellectual imagination: a lecture. 1919.

Moore, T. S. In his Some soldier poets, 1919.

Waugh, A. Brooke and the war. In his Tradition and change, 1919.

Squire, J. C. Brooke in retrospect. In his Books in general, 2nd ser 1920.

Casson, S. Rupert Brooke and Skyros. 1921.

Hathaway, R. H. Rupert Brooke. Canadian Mag 56 1921.

Woodberry, G. E. In his Studies of a litterateur, 1921.

Sirin, V. Brooke: a Russian view. Living Age 313 1922.

Liljegren, S. B. Die Gedichte Brookes. Anglia Beiblatt 35 1924.

Browne, M. Recollections of Brooke. Chicago 1927. Letters from Brooke to Browne.

Block, E. A. Brooke and J. E. Flecker. Poetry Rev 20 1929.

Garrod, H. W. In his Profession of poetry, 1929.

Pye, S. Rupert Brooke. Life & Letters 2 1929.

Vanderborght, P. Hommage à Brooke 1887–1915. Bruxelles 1931. Includes French trns of some poems.

Grieg, N. De unge døde: Brooke-Sorley-Owen. Oslo 1932.

Douglas, N. Chapters from an autobiography: memories of D. H. Lawrence, Brooke, F. Harris. Bookman (New York) 76 1933.

Guibert, A. Rupert Brooke. Genoa 1933.

Heiseler, B. von. Bildnis Brookes. Münchener Neueste Nachricht no 309 1938.

Marsh, E. In his A number of people, 1939. Includes an extract from a novel by Brooke, Death of John Rump, and Marsh's original review of Brooke's Poems, Poetry Rev 1 1912.

Lemonnier, L. Rupert Brooke. Cahiers de Paris 8 1940.

Platnauer, M. Variants in the manuscripts of the poems of Brooke and A. E. Housman. RES 19 1943.

McCourt, E. A. Brooke: a reappraisal. Dalhousie Rev 24 1944.

Caldiero, F. A note on Wordsworth, Brooke and Masefield. N & Q 189 1945.

Williams, I. A. Brooke at Cambridge. TLS 5 April 1947.

Stringer, A. Red wine of youth: a life of Brooke. Indianapolis 1948. Contains portions of letters from Brooke.

Lehmann, J. But for Beaumont Hamel. In his The open night, 1952. On Brooke and W. Owen.

Srinwasan, R. Brooke: the thwarted genius. Indian Rev 55 1954.

Lennam, T. N. S. A nightingale amongst the china. Dalhousie Rev 36 1957. Debt of The great lover to Keats' Ode to a nightingale.

Moore, J. R. Dryden and Brooke. MLR 54 1959.

Matthews, G. Brooke and Owen. Stand 4 1960.

Hassall, C. Rupert Brooke: a biography. 1964.

Bergonzi, B. Brooke, Grenfell, Sorley. In his Heroes' twilight: a study of the literature of the Great War, 1965.

Hastings, M. The handsomest young man in England. 1967.

Iser, W. Rupert Brooke: The Old Vicarage, Grantchester. In H. Oppel (ed), Die moderne englische Lyrik, Berlin 1967.

Manning, O. An enemy in the mind. TLS 8 May 1969.

GERALD WILLIAM BULLETT
1893–1958

See cols 544–5, below.

BASIL BUNTING
b. 1900

§1

Redimiculum matellarum. Milan 1930.

Poems: 1950, prefaced by D. Flynn. Galveston Texas [1950].

Loquitur. [1965]. Mostly rptd from Poems: 1950, above, or from periodicals.

The spoils. Newcastle upon Tyne [1965]. First pbd in Poetry (Chicago) 79 1951.

Briggflatts. [1966] (500 copies), 1966 (trade edn).

First book of odes. [1966] (201 copies).

What the chairman told Tom. Cambridge Mass 1967 (226 copies). Single poem.

Collected poems. [1968].

Bunting contributed substantially to Active anthology, ed Ezra Pound, 1933.

§2

Read, H. Bunting: music or meaning? Agenda 4 1966.

Tomlinson, C. Experience into music: the poetry of Bunting. Ibid.

Creeley, R. A note on Bunting. Ibid.

Cox, K. The aesthetic of Bunting. Ibid.

JOHN NORMAN CAMERON
1905–53

The winter house and other poems. 1935.

Selected verse poems of Arthur Rimbaud. Tr Cameron 1942.

Work in hand: by A. Hodge, Cameron, R. Graves. 1942. 11 poems by Cameron.

Soupault, P. Ode to bombed London. Tr Cameron, Algiers 1944.

A season in hell; tr Cameron, with drawings by K. Vaughan and the original French text by Arthur Rimbaud 1949.

Forgive me, Sire [and other poems]. 1950.

Villon, F. Poems including The testament and other poems, tr to the original verse-forms by Cameron 1952.

Collected poems 1905–1953. Introd R. Graves 1957.

Cameron also tr works by Balzac, Baudelaire, Constant, Stendhal, Elsa Triolet, Voltaire and other writers, French and German. He revised Arnim Westerholt's novel Against the tide, 1943.

IGNATIUS ROY DUNNACHIE CAMPBELL
1901–57
Bibliographies

Eyre, C. J. Roy Campbell exhibition [at Durban Public Library]. South African Libraries 22 1954. Lists Campbell mss in some South African collections.

§1
Poetry

The flaming terrapin. 1924, New York 1924.

The wayzgoose: a South African satire. 1928.

Adamastor: poems. 1930, New York 1931, London 1941 (abridged, as Sons of the Mistral), Cape Town 1950 (with new preface).

The gum trees. 1930 (Ariel Poem).

Poems. Paris 1930 (priv ptd, 200 copies).

[Nineteen poems]. [1931] (Augustan Books of Poetry). Most of the poems previously pbd in Adamastor, 2 from Poems, 1930.

Choosing a mast. 1931 (Ariel Poem).

The Georgiad: a satirical fantasy in verse. 1931.

Pomegranates: a poem. 1932.

Flowering reeds: poems. 1933.

Mithraic emblems: poems. 1936.

Flowering rifle: a poem from the battlefield of Spain. 1939.

Sons of the Mistral. 1941. See Adamastor, 1930, above.

Talking bronco. 1946, Chicago 1956.

Collected poems. 3 vols 1949–60, Chicago 1959–60. Many poems rev, some previously uncollected. Vol 3,

Translations, is a selection, though some are previously unpbd.

Nativity. 1954 (Ariel Poem).

Poems of Roy Campbell, chosen and introduced by Uys Krige. Cape Town 1960.

Selected poetry. Ed J. M. Lalley 1968, Chicago 1968.

Other Works

Taurine Provence. 1932, New York 1932 (with subtitle, The philosophy, technique and religion of the bull-fighter).

Broken record: reminiscences. 1934.

Light on a dark horse: an autobiography 1901-1935. 1951, Chicago 1952, London 1969 (foreword by L. Lee).

Lorca: an appreciation of his poetry. Cambridge 1952, New Haven 1952.

Il Paradiso di Dante: an English version by T. W. Ramsey, with a foreword by Campbell. Aldington 1952.

The Mamba's precipice. 1953, New York 1954. For children.

Portugal. 1957, Chicago 1958.

Translations

Helge Krog. Three plays: The copy; Happily every after; The triad. 1934.

The poems of St John of the Cross. 1951.

Poems of Baudelaire: a translation of his Fleurs du mal. 1952, 1960 (as Baudelaire). Selection in Pocket Poets ser.

Eça de Queiroz. Cousin Bazilio. 1953.

Eça de Queiroz. The city and the mountains. 1955.

The classic theatre. Ed E. Bentley, vol 3, Garden City NY 1959. Contains Tirso de Molina's Trickster of Seville and his Guest of stone, and Calderón's Life is a dream, both tr Campbell.

Nostalgia: a collection of poems by J. Paço d'Arcos. Tr with introd by Campbell 1960.

Calderón de la Barca. The surgeon of his honour. Madison 1960.

With W. Plomer, Campbell founded and edited the magazine Voorslag (*Durban*) 1926-7 and, with R. Lyle, Catacomb 1949-52.

§2

Lucas, F. L. Turtle and mock terrapin. In his Authors dead and living, 1926; rptd from New Statesman.

Bonnerot, L. Campbell: un poète pêcheur d'images. Revue Anglo-américaine 10 1933.

Stone, G. Campbell: romantic paradox. Amer Rev 8 1936.

Weygandt, C. In his The time of Yeats, New York [1937].

Gillett, E. Two poets: Campbell and Auden. Nat & Eng Rev 135 1950.

Harvey, C. J. D. Poetry of Campbell. Standpunte 5 1950.

— Campbell and Les fleurs du mal. Ons Eie Boek 20 1954.

The poetry of statement. TLS 24 March 1950.

Russell, P. The poetry of Campbell. Nine no 3 1950.

Scott, T. Impressions of Campbell's poetry. Western Rev 14 1950.

Krige, U. Profiles. Trek 15 1951.

— Campbell as lyrical poet: some quieter aspects. Eng Stud in Africa 1 1958.

— First meeting with Campbell. Theoria 12 1959.

Gray, A. Genius of Campbell. African World 14 1952.

Eyre, C. J. Campbell exhibition. South African Libraries 22 1954.

Wagner, G. Campbell: triumphant torero. Catholic World 179 1954.

Abrahams, L. Campbell: conquistador-refugee. Theoria 8 1956.

Joost, N. The poetry of Campbell. Renascence 8 1956.

Rose, B. Campbell: a tribute. South African PEN Year Book 1956-7.

Guibert, A. Campbell: poète solaire. Jnl des Poètes 5 1957.

Paton, A. Campbell: poet and man. Theoria 9 1957.

Sergeant, H. Restive steer: a study of the poetry of Campbell. E & S 10 1957.

Seymour-Smith, M. Zero and the impossible: Campbell, W. Lewis, J. Cary, J. M. Murry. Encounter 9 1957.

Van den Bergh, T. Campbell: flaming Toreador. Poetry Rev 48 1957.

Gardner, W. H. Voltage of delight: an appraisal of Campbell. Month 19 1958.

John, A. Campbell: poet from South Africa. Sunday Times 12 Oct 1958.

Sitwell, E. Roy Campbell. Poetry 92 1958.

Temple, F.-J. [et al]. Hommage à Roy Campbell. Montpellier 1958.

Plomer, W. 'Voorslag' days. London Mag 6 1959.

Collins, H. R. Campbell: the talking bronco. Boston Univ Stud in Eng 4 1960.

Graves, R. It ended with a bang. In his Food for centaurs, Garden City NY 1960.

Rexroth, K. In his Assays, Norfolk Conn 1961.

Wright, D. Roy Campbell. 1961 (Br Council pamphlet).

Hamm, V. M. Campbell: satirist. Thought 37 1962.

Povey, J. F. A lyre of savage thunder: a study of the poetry of Campbell. Wisconsin Stud in Contemporary Lit 7 1966.

Paço d'Arcos, J. Roy Campbell: o homem e o poeta. Lisbon 1968.

GILBERT KEITH CHESTERTON
1874-1936

See cols 1021-8, below.

WILFRED ROWLAND MARY CHILDE
1890-1952

The little city. Oxford 1911.

The escaped princess and other poems. Oxford 1916, New York 1916.

Dream English: a fantastical romance. 1917, New York 1919. Fiction.

The hills of morning. Leeds [1921], 1923.

The Gothic rose and other poems. Oxford 1922, New York 1923.

The garland of armor: sixteen poems. Leeds 1923.

The ballad of Jak and Anne. Leeds 1925.

Ivory palaces. 1925 (for 1926), New York 1927.

The country of sweet bells. 1927.

The happy garden. [1927].

Blue distance. 1930. Brief sketches and fables. Pamphlet.

The golden thurible. 1931.

Fountains and forests. Bradford 1935.

Selected poems. 1936.

The blessèd pastures. Hull 1950.

RICHARD THOMAS CHURCH
1893-1972

§1
Poetry

The flood of life and other poems. 1917.

Hurricane and other poems. 1919.

Philip and other poems. Oxford 1923.

The portrait of the abbot: a story in verse. 1926.

The dream and other poems. [1927].

Mood without measure. 1927.

Theme with variations. [1928].

The glance backward: new poems. 1930.

News from the mountain. 1932.

Twelve noon. 1936.

The solitary man and other poems. 1941.
Twentieth-century psalter. 1943.
The lamp. 1946.
Collected poems. 1948.
Selected lyrical poems. 1951.
The prodigal: a play in verse. 1953.
The inheritors: poems 1948–1955. 1957.
[Forty-seven poems.] 1959 (Pocket Poets). Selection with 3 previously uncollected poems.
North of Rome. 1960.
The burning bush: poems 1958–1966. 1967.
Twenty-five lyrical poems from the hand of Richard Church. 1967. Selection.

Other Works
Mary Shelley. 1928, New York 1928.
Oliver's daughter: a tale. 1930.
High summer. 1931, New York 1932. Novel.
The prodigal father. 1933. Novel.
The apple of concord. 1935. Novel.
The porch. 1937, 1961 (with foreword). Pt 1 of trilogy of novels.
An essay in estimation of Dorothy Richardson's Pilgrimage. [1938].
Calling for a spade. 1939. Essays on country themes.
The stronghold. 1939. Pt 2 of trilogy.
Poems and prose, by A. C. Swinburne. Ed Church 1940 (EL).
The room within. 1940. Pt 3 of trilogy.
Eight for immortality. 1941. Essays on contemporary writers.
Plato's mistake. 1941. On the poet in society. Booklet.
A squirrel called Rufus. 1941, Philadelphia 1946. For children.
The sampler. 1942. Novel.
British authors: a twentieth century gallery. 1943, 1948 (rev).
Green tide. 1945. Essays, mainly on country themes.
Poems of our time 1900–42. Chosen by Church and M. M. Bozman 1945, 1959 (with supplement chosen by E. Sitwell) (EL).
John Keats: an introduction and a selection by Church 1948.
Kent. 1948. Topography.
Richard Jefferies centenary 1848–1948. Swindon [1948?]. Lecture.
Poems by P. B. Shelley. Ed Church 1949.
The cave. 1950, New York 1951 (as Five boys in a cave), London 1953 (rev). For children.
Poems for speaking: an anthology, with an essay on reading aloud. 1950.
The growth of the English novel. 1951.
A window on a hill. [1951]. Essays, mainly on country themes.
The nightingale. 1952. Novel.
Dog Toby: a frontier tale. [1953], New York 1958. For children.
A portrait of Canterbury. 1953, 1968 (rev).
Out of the dark: new poems by Phoebe Hesketh. Selected by Church 1954.
A selection of poems by Edmund Spenser. Introd by Church 1954.
Over the bridge: an essay in autobiography. 1955, New York 1956.
The spoken word: a selection from twenty-five years of the Listener. Ed Church 1955.
The dangerous years. 1956, New York 1958. Novel.
The royal parks of London. 1956. Guide book.
Down river. New York 1957, London 1958. For children.
The golden sovereign: a conclusion to Over the bridge. 1957, New York 1957. Autobiography.
Small moments. 1957, New York 1958. Essays.
A country window: a round of essays. 1958.
The crab-apple tree. 1959. Novel.

The bells of Rye. 1960, New York 1961. For children.
Calm October: essays. 1961.
Prince Albert. 1963. Novel.
Shorter works by Jane Austen. Introd by Church 1963.
The little kingdom: a Kentish collection. 1964. Anthology.
The voyage home. 1964, New York 1966. Autobiography.
A look at tradition. 1965 (Eng Assoc presidential address).
A stroll before dark: essays. 1965.
Speaking aloud. 1968.
The white doe. 1968. For children.
Little Miss Moffatt: a confession. 1969. Novel.

§2
Strong, L. A. G. Richard Church. In his Personal remarks, 1953.
Hardwick, M. An interview with Church. Texas Quart 10 1967.
Baker, D. An eternal patience: an essay on Church. Ibid.

AUSTIN CLARKE
b. 1896

Bibliographies
Miller, L. The books of Austin Clarke: a checklist. The Dubliner 6 1963; rev and rptd in A tribute to Austin Clarke, ed J. Montague and L. Miller 1966, §2, below.

§1
Poetry and Verse Plays
Most of Clarke's books of verse have been pbd in edns of less than 500 copies. See Miller, Bibliography, above.

The vengeance of Fionn. Dublin 1917.
The fires of Baäl. Dublin 1921.
The sword of the west. Dublin 1921.
The cattledrive in Connaught and other poems. 1925.
The son of learning: a poetic comedy in three acts. (Cambridge Festival Theatre Oct 1927; Abbey, Dublin June 1945). [1927].
Pilgrimage and other poems. 1929, New York 1930.
The flame: a play in one act. (School of Speech Training and Drama, Edinburgh June 1932; Dublin Verse-Speaking Soc, at the Peacock Theatre 1941). 1930.
Collected poems. Introd by P. Colum 1936.
Night and morning. Dublin 1938.
Sister Eucharia: a play in three scenes. (Gate, Dublin July 1939). Dublin and London 1939.
Black fast: a poetic farce in one act. (Abbey, Dublin Jan 1942). Dublin 1941.
As the crow flies: a lyric play for the air. (Dublin Verse-Speaking Soc, Radio Eireann 6 Feb 1942). Dublin and London 1943.
The straying student. Dublin 1944.
The viscount of Blarney and other plays. Dublin and London 1944. The kiss: a light comedy in one act after the French of T. de Banville (Dublin Verse-Speaking Soc, at the Peacock Theatre May 1942); The viscount of Blarney: a play for radio or stage in one act (Lyric Theatre Company at the Abbey, Dublin Dec 1944); The plot is ready: a play in four scenes (Dublin Verse-Speaking Soc, at the Peacock Theatre Oct 1943).
The second kiss: a light comedy. (Lyric Theatre Company at the Abbey, Dublin July 1946). Dublin and London 1946.
The plot succeeds: a poetic pantomime. (Lyric Theatre Company at the Abbey, Dublin Feb 1950). Dublin 1950.
The moment next to nothing: a play in three acts. (Players' Theatre, Trinity College, Dublin Jan 1958). Dublin 1953.
Ancient lights: poems and satires, first series. Templeogue 1955.

Too great a vine: poems and satires, second series. Templeogue 1957.

The horse-eaters: poems and satires, third series. Dublin 1960.

Later poems. Dublin 1961. Selection from works pbd 1929–60.

Forget-me-not. Dublin 1962.

Collected plays. Dublin 1963.

Flight to Africa and other poems. Dublin 1963.

Poems by Austin Clarke, Tony Connor and Charles Tomlinson. 1964. Selection.

Mnemosyne lay in dust. Dublin 1966.

Old-fashioned pilgrimage and other poems. Dublin 1967.

The echo at Coole and other poems. Dublin 1968.

Two interludes adapted from Cervantes: The student from Salamanca, La cueva de Salamanca; The silent lover, El viejo celoso. Dublin [1968]. The student from Salamanca produced at the Lantern Theatre, Dublin 29 Dec 1966.

Other Works

The bright temptation: a romance. 1932, New York 1932.

The singing-men at Cashel. 1936. Novel.

First visit to England and other memories. Dublin and London 1945.

Poetry in modern Ireland. Dublin 1951, 1962 (rev).

The sun dances at Easter: a romance. 1952.

Twice round the black church: early memories of Ireland and England. 1962.

The poems of Joseph Campbell, edited with an introduction by Clarke. Dublin 1963.

The plays of G. Fitzmaurice; dramatic fantasies. Dublin 1967. Introd by Clarke.

A penny in the clouds: more memories of Ireland and England. 1968.

The Celtic twilight and the nineties. Dublin 1969.

§2

Griffin, G. Austin Clarke. In his The wild geese, [1938].

Mercier, V. Clarke: the poet in the theatre. Life & Letters 53 1947.

Lane, T. Austin Clarke. Books Abroad 36 1962.

Sealy, D. Clarke: a survey of his work. The Dubliner 6 1963.

Harmon, M. The later poetry of Clarke. In The Celtic cross, ed R. B. Browne et al 1964.

Roscelli, W. J. The private pilgrimage of Clarke. Ibid.

Saul, G. B. The poetry of Clarke. Ibid.

Loftus, R. J. Clarke: Ireland of the black Church. In his Nationalism in modern Anglo-Irish poetry, Madison 1964.

Martin, A. The rediscovery of Clarke. Studies 54 1965.

Montague, J. and L. Miller (ed). A tribute to Clarke. Dublin 1966. Includes essays by Montague, S. Fauchereau, C. Ricks, D. Donoghue and checklist by Miller.

Moore, J. R. Now Yeats is gone: three Irish poets. Hollins Critic 3 1966. On Clarke, Kavanagh, D. Devlin.

Oppel, H. Austin Clarke: Three poems about children, III. In Die moderne englische Lyrik, ed Oppel, Berlin 1967.

Rosenthal, M. L. Contemporary Irish poetry: Clarke and D. Devlin. In his The new poets, Oxford 1967.

ALEXANDER COMFORT
b. 1920

§1
Poetry

France and other poems. [1941]. France rptd in A wreath for the living, 1942.

Three new poets: R. McFadden, Comfort, I. Serraillier. Billericay 1942. 8 poems by Comfort.

A wreath for the living. 1942.

Cities of the plain: a democratic melodrama. 1943. Prose and verse.

Elegies. 1944.

The song of Lazarus. Barnet 1945 (200 copies), New York 1945. Rptd in next.

The signal to engage. 1946.

And all but he departed. 1951.

Haste to the wedding. 1962.

Other Works

The silver river: being the diary of a schoolboy in the South Atlantic, 1936. 1938.

No such liberty. 1941. Novel.

The almond tree: a legend. 1942. Novel.

Into Egypt: a miracle play. Billericay 1942.

Lyra: an anthology of new lyric. Ed Comfort and R. Greacen, Billericay 1942.

Poetry folios. 10 nos. Ed Comfort and P. Wells 1942–6.

New road: new directions in European art and letters. Ed Comfort and J. Bayliss 2 vols Billericay 1943–4.

The power house. 1944, New York 1945. Novel.

Art and social responsibility: lectures on the ideology of romanticism. 1946.

C. F. Ramuz. The triumph of death. Tr A. R. Macdougall and Comfort 1946.

Peace and disobedience. [1946] (Peace News pamphlet).

Letters from an outpost. 1947. 12 stories.

Barbarism and sexual freedom: lectures on the sociology of sex from the standpoint of anarchism. 1948.

First-year physiological technique. 1948.

The novel & our time. 1948.

On this side nothing. 1949, New York 1949. Novel.

The pattern of the future. 1949. 4 broadcast talks.

The right thing to do: a broadcast talk, together with The wrong thing to do: a speech at a Peace Pledge Union meeting. 1949 (Peace News pamphlet).

Authority and delinquency in the modern state: a criminological approach to the problem of power. 1950.

Sexual behaviour in society. 1950, New York 1950, London 1963 (rev, as Sex in society).

Delinquency: a lecture delivered at the Anarchist summer school, London, August 1950. 1951.

A giant's strength. 1952. Novel.

Social responsibility in science and art. 1952 (Peace News pamphlet). Broadcast talk.

The biology of senescence. 1956, New York 1956, London 1964 (rev, as Ageing: the biology of senescence), New York 1964.

Come out to play. 1961. Novel.

Darwin and the naked body: discursive essays on biology and art. 1961, New York 1962.

The Koka Shastra: being the Ratirahasya of Kokkoka and other mediaeval writings on love, tr with an introd by Comfort [1964], New York 1965.

The process of ageing. New York 1964, London 1965.

Nature and human nature. 1966.

The anxiety makers: some curious preoccupations of the medical profession. 1967.

Comfort also contributed a section, Romanticism and English poetry, *to S. Schimanski and H. Treece,* A new romantic anthology, *1949. This contained a selection of his and other poets' work.*

§2

Stanford, D. Alex Comfort. In his The freedom of poetry, 1947.

Woodcock, G. The poetry of Comfort. Poetry Quart 9 1947.

Jarrell, R. A verse chronicle: Comfort. In his Poetry and the age, New York 1953.

FRANCES CROFTS CORNFORD
née DARWIN
1886–1960
A collection of mss is in BM.

§ I

Poems. Hampstead, Cambridge [1910].
Death and the princess: a morality. Cambridge 1912. Play in prose and verse.
Spring morning. 1915. Illustr G. Raverat.
Autumn midnight. 1923.
Different days. 1928.
Mountains & molehills. Cambridge 1934. Illustr G. Raverat.
Poems from the Russian. Chosen and tr F. Cornford and E. P. Salaman 1943.
Travelling home and other poems. 1948.
Le dur désir de durer, by Paul Eluard, with the translation in English verse by S. Spender and Frances Cornford. Philadelphia, London 1950.
Collected poems. 1954. Selection with some revision, with poems 1948–53 and occasional verses.
On a calm shore. 1960. Designs by C. Cornford.

§ 2

Stansky, P. and W. Abrahams. In their Journey to the frontier: Julian Bell & John Cornford, 1966.

RUPERT JOHN CORNFORD
1915–36

§ I

John Cornford: a memoir. Ed P. Sloan. 1938. Includes the text of his poems, extracts from his letters and other, mainly political, writings.

§ 2

Ford, H. D. A poets' war: British poets and the Spanish Civil War. Philadelphia 1965.
Stansky, P. and W. Abrahams. Journey to the frontier: Julian Bell and John Cornford, their lives and the 1930's. 1966.

WILLIAM HENRY DAVIES
1871–1940

Bibliographies

Murphy, G. Bibliographies of modern authors III: Davies. London Mercury 17 1928.
Looker, S. J. W. H. Davies: his later bibliography 1922–8. Bookman's Jnl 17 1930.

Selections

The essential W. H. Davies. Ed B. Waters 1951. Prose and verse.

§ I
Poetry

The soul's destroyer and other poems. [1905] (priv ptd, 40 poems), 1907 (abridged, 14 poems).
New poems. 1907, Boston [? 1916–17], London 1922 (rev).
Nature poems and others. 1908, Boston [? 1916–17].
Farewell to poesy and other pieces. 1910, Boston [? 1916–17].
Songs of joy and others. 1911, Boston [? 1916–17].
Foliage: various poems. 1913, Boston [? 1916–17], London 1922 (rev).
The bird of paradise and other poems. 1914.
Child lovers and other poems. 1916.

Collected poems. 1916, New York 1916. 111 selected poems. American edn has 12 additional poems.
Forty new poems. 1918. 42 poems.
Raptures: a book of poems. 1918 (272 copies). Contains 30 poems from Forty new poems.
The song of life and other poems. 1920.
The captive lion and other poems. New Haven 1921. Contains Forty new poems and The song of life.
The hour of magic and other poems. 1922, New York 1922.
Collected poems: second series. 1923, New York 1923. 112 poems selected from New poems, Foliage, Forty new poems, The song of life, The hour of magic.
Selected poems. 1923, New York 1925.
Secrets. 1924, New York 1924.
A poet's alphabet. 1925.
[Thirty poems]. [1925] (Augustan Books of Modern Poetry). Selection.
The song of love. 1926.
A poet's calendar. 1927, New York 1934.
Collected poems. 1928. 431 poems.
Forty-nine poems, selected and illustrated by Jacynth Parsons. 1928, New York 1929.
Moss and feather. [1928] (Ariel Poem).
Selected poems, arranged by E. Garnett, with a foreword by the author. Newtown 1928 (310 copies).
Ambition and other poems. 1929.
In winter. 1931 (priv ptd, 305 signed copies). Short poem.
Poems, 1930–31. 1932, New York 1932.
The lovers' song-book. Newtown 1933 (250 copies). Included in Love poems 1935, below.
The poems of W. H. Davies. 1934, New York 1935. 533 poems from Collected poems, 1928, Ambition, 1929, Poems 1930–31, and including poems from My birds and My garden (see below, Other works).
Love poems. 1935, New York 1935. Contains The lovers' song-book, with 20 additional poems.
The birth of song: poems 1935–36. 1936, New York 1936.
The loneliest mountain and other poems. 1939.
The poems of W. H. Davies, 1940. 1940, 1943 (as Collected poems, with introd by O. Sitwell), New York 1946. 636 poems from The poems of W. H. Davies 1934, Love poems, The birth of song, The loneliest mountain.
Common joys and other poems. 1941. Selection.
Complete poems, with an introd by O. Sitwell and a foreword by D. George 1963, Middletown Conn 1965. 749 poems. George was responsible for the addition of 113 poems omitted by Davies from 1943 collection.

Autobiographies

The autobiography of a super-tramp. 1908, New York 1917, London 1920 (with note by Davies and 5 poems from The soul's destroyer). Preface by G. B. Shaw.
Beggars. 1909.
The true traveller. 1912.
A poet's pilgrimage. 1918, New York 1929.
Later days. 1925, New York 1926.
The adventures of Johnny Walker, tramp. 1926. Material from Beggars and The true traveller, with additional material to form a continuous narrative.

Other Works

A weak woman. 1911. Novel.
Nature. 1914, New York 1914.
Shorter lyrics of the twentieth century, 1900–1922. Ed Davies 1922.
True travellers: a tramp's opera in three acts. 1923, New York 1923. Prose, with lyrics.
Introduction together with biographical note to the famous novel Moll Flanders. 1924. Rptd with the novel, [1925].
Burns' poetical works. Introd by Davies [1925?].
Dancing mad. 1927. Novel.

Jewels of song: an anthology of short poems. Ed Davies 1930, New York 1934, 1938 (as An anthology of short poems).

Maplet, J. A greene forest, reprinted from the edition of 1567. Introd by Davies 1930.

My birds. 1933, New York 1933. Nature studies, with some poems.

My garden. 1933, New York 1933. Nature studies, with some poems. Rptd with previous 1939.

Collins, W. J. T. The romance of the echoing wood. Newport 1937. Epilogue, Poetry in life and letters, by Davies.

§2

Armstrong, M. D. Recent English poetry. Fortnightly Rev 101 1914.

Pound, E. William H. Davies, poet. Poetry (Chicago) 11 1917.

Wright, H. G. In his Studies in contemporary literature, Bangor 1918.

Massingham, H. J. A modern lyrist. In his Letters to X, 1919.

Maynard, T. Davies: a case of dual personality. In his Our best poets, 1922.

Sitwell, E. In her Aspects of modern poetry, 1924.

Dillon, G. H. Davies' poetry. Poetry (Chicago) 27 1925.

Macleish, A. Four poets. Yale Rev new ser 14 1925.

Lucas, F. L. In his Authors dead and living, 1926.

Lock, D. R. The poetry of Davies. Holborn Rev 18 1927.

Kernahan, C. Five more famous living poets. 1928.

Looker, S. J. Man and super-tramp: Davies, his life and work. Bookman's Jnl 12 1928.

—The diamond ring. Amer N & Q 2 1943. On The trance.

Williams, C. In his Poetry at present, 1930.

Bonnerot, L. Davies, poète-vagabond. Revue Anglo-américaine 8 1931.

Duff, L. B. From a doss-house to Parnassus. Colophon 19 1934.

Moult, T. W. H. Davies. 1934.

Church, R. Davies: the man and his work. Fortnightly Rev 147 1940; rptd in his Eight for immortality, 1941.

Evans, C. W. H. Davies. Welsh Rev 3 1944.

Hockey, L. W. Davies and his family. Welsh Rev 5 1946.

— Edward Thomas and Davies. Welsh Rev 7 1948.

Stonesifer, R. J. Davies: a critical biography. 1963.

CECIL DAY-LEWIS
1904-72

Day-Lewis signed his books 'C. Day Lewis'.

Bibliographies

Handley-Taylor, G. and T. d'A. Smith C. Day-Lewis, the Poet Laureate: a bibliography, 1968.

§1

Poetry and Verse Translations

Beechen vigil and other poems. 1925.

Country comets. 1928.

Transitional poem. 1929.

From feathers to iron. 1931.

The magnetic mountain. 1933.

Collected poems 1929-1933. 1935, New York [1935] (as Collected poems, 1929-1933 & A hope for poetry).

A time to dance and other poems. 1935, New York [1936] (as A time to dance: Noah and the waters and other poems; with an essay, Revolution in writing).

Noah and the waters. 1936.

Overtures to death and other poems. 1938.

The georgics of Virgil. 1940. Verse trn.

Poems in wartime. 1940. Rptd in Word over all, 1943 below.

Selected poems. 1940.

[Seventeen poems.] [1943] (Augustan Poets). Selection.

Word over all. 1943.

Short is the time: poems 1936-43. New York 1945. Reprints contents of Overtures to death, and Word over all, above.

Valéry, P. The graveyard by the sea. 1946. Verse trn rptd in Poems 1943-1947, below.

Collected poems 1929-1936. 1948 (for March 1949). Omissions from A time to dance and Noah and the waters, above.

Poems 1943-1947. 1948, New York 1948.

Selected poems. 1951, 1969 (rev and expanded) (Penguin Poets). Preface by the author.

The Aeneid of Virgil. 1952, New York [1952]. Verse trn.

An Italian visit. 1953, New York [1953].

Collected poems. 1954. A complete collection from 1929, apart from omissions from A time to dance and Noah and the waters.

Christmas Eve. 1954 (Ariel Poem). Rptd in next.

Pegasus and other poems. 1957, New York 1958.

The newborn: D.M.B. 29th April 1957. [1957] (200 copies). Single poem.

The gate and other poems. 1962.

The eclogues of Virgil. 1963, Garden City NY 1964. Verse trn.

Requiem for the living. New York [1964]. Some poems previously pbd in The gate and other poems, 1962, others rptd in next.

The room and other poems. 1965.

The abbey that refused to die. Ballintubber Abbey, Co. Mayo. 1967. Single poem.

C. Day Lewis: selections from his poetry. Ed P. Dickinson 1967.

A number of Day-Lewis's poems, e.g. Lullaby, *1938, and* Madrigal, *1938, were issued by him as greetings cards. Both these were rptd from* A time to dance, *1935.*

Fiction

(a) as by C. Day Lewis

Dick Willoughby. Oxford [1933], New York 1938. For children.

The friendly tree. 1936, New York 1937.

Starting point. 1937, New York 1938.

Child of misfortune. 1939.

The Otterbury incident. 1948, New York 1949. For children.

(b) detective fiction as by 'Nicholas Blake'

A question of proof. [1935], New York 1935.

Thou shell of death. [1936], New York 1936 (as Shell of death).

There's trouble brewing. [1937], New York 1937.

The beast must die. [1938], New York 1938.

The smiler with the knife. 1939, New York 1939.

Malice in wonderland. 1940, New York [1940] (as The summer camp mystery).

The case of the abominable snowman. 1941, New York [1941] (as The corpse in the snowman).

Minute for murder. 1947, New York 1948.

Head of a traveller. 1949, New York 1949.

The dreadful hollow. 1953, New York 1953.

The whisper in the gloom. 1954, New York 1954.

A tangled web. 1956, New York 1956.

End of chapter. 1957, New York 1957.

A penknife in my heart. [1958], New York 1959.

The widow's cruise. [1959], New York 1959.

The worm of death. [1961], New York 1961.

The deadly joker. [1963].

The sad variety. [1964], New York 1964.

The morning after death. 1966.

The private wound. 1968.

As 'Nicholas Blake', Day-Lewis contributed an essay, The detective story—why? *to H. Haycraft (ed),* The art of the mystery story, *New York [1947]. He also contributed criticism of the genre to* Spectator.

Other Works

A hope for poetry. Oxford 1934, 1936 (with postscript).
Revolution in writing. 1935. Pamphlet.
Imagination and thinking. 1936. With L. S. Stebbing. 2 addresses.
We're not going to do nothing: a reply to Mr Aldous Huxley's pamphlet, 'What are you going to do about it?'. 1936.
Poetry for you: a book for boys and girls on the enjoyment of poetry. Oxford 1944, New York 1947.
The colloquial element in English poetry. Newcastle-upon-Tyne 1947. Lecture.
Enjoying poetry. 1947, 1951 (rev), 1956 (rev) (National Book League Reader's Guide).
The poetic image. 1947, New York 1947 (Clark lectures).
The poet's task: an inaugural lecture. Oxford 1951.
The grand manner. Nottingham [1952] (Byron Foundation lecture).
The lyrical poetry of Thomas Hardy. [1953] (Warton lecture on English poetry 1951).
Notable images of virtue: Emily Brontë, George Meredith, W. B. Yeats. Toronto 1954.
The poet's way of knowledge. Cambridge 1957. Lecture.
The buried day. 1960, New York 1960. Autobiography.
The lyric impulse. 1965, Cambridge Mass 1965 (Charles Eliot Norton lectures).
Thomas Hardy. 1965 (Br Council pamphlet). With R. A. Scott-James.
A need for poetry? Hull 1968. Lecture.

Principal works Edited or with Contributions by Day-Lewis

Ten singers: an anthology. 1925.
Oxford poetry 1927. Ed with W. H. Auden, Oxford 1927. Includes 1 poem by Day Lewis.
New signatures: poems by several hands, collected by M. Roberts 1932.
Frost, R. Selected poems, with introductory essays by W. H. Auden, Day Lewis, P. Engle and E. Muir 1936.
Lipton, J. Poems of strife. Introd by Day Lewis. [1936].
The echoing green: an anthology of verse. 3 vols Oxford 1937. For children.
The mind in chains: socialism and the cultural revolution. By various writers, ed with introd by Day Lewis 1937.
Ralph Fox: a writer in arms. Ed J. Lehmann, T. A. Jackson, Day Lewis 1937.
Anatomy of Oxford: an anthology compiled by Day Lewis and C. Fenby 1938.
Bell, J. Essays, poems and letters. Ed Q. Bell, contribution by Day Lewis 1938.
Scattering branches: tributes to the memory of W. B. Yeats. Ed S. Gwynn; A note on W. B. Yeats and the aristocratic tradition, by Day Lewis 1940.
A new anthology of modern verse, 1920–1940, introd by Day Lewis and L. A. G. Strong 1941.
Tolstoy, L. Anna Karenina. Introd by Day Lewis 1943.
Bowes-Lyon, L. Collected poems. Introd by Day Lewis 1948.
Meredith, G. Modern love. Introd by Day Lewis 1948.
The golden treasury, selected and arranged by F. T. Palgrave, with an introd and additional poems selected and arranged by Day Lewis 1954.
Frost, R. Selected poems. Introd by Day Lewis 1955 (Penguin Poets).
The Chatto book of modern poetry, 1915–1955. Ed Day Lewis and J. Lehmann 1956.
Hardy, T. Tess of the d'Urbervilles. Introd by Day Lewis 1958.
Hardy, T. Under the greenwood tree. Introd by Day Lewis 1958.
A book of English lyrics. Ed Day Lewis 1961, New York 1961 (as English lyric poems 1500–1900).
Owen, W. Collected poems. Ed with introd by Day Lewis 1963.

Blunden, E. The midnight skaters: poems for young readers, chosen and introduced by Day Lewis. 1968.
With Rosamund Lehmann, E. Muir and D. Kilham Roberts, Day-Lewis edited the periodical Orion *vols 1–3 1945–6.*

§2

Spender, S. The airman, politics and psychoanalysis. In his The destructive element, 1935.
—— World within world. 1951.
—— It began at Oxford. New York Times Book Rev 13 March 1955.
Gregory, H. The proletarian poet. Partisan Rev 3 1936. Review of A time to dance, rptd in Literary opinion in America, ed M. D. Zabel, New York 1937.
Glicksberg, C. Poetry and Marxism: three English poets take their stand. UTQ 6 1937. On Auden, Spender, Day Lewis.
Grigson, G. Day Lewis joins up. New Verse 25 1937. On Day Lewis's joining the Committee of the Book Society.
Southworth, J. G. Cecil Day Lewis. Sewanee Rev 45 1937; rptd in his Sowing the spring, 1940.
Daiches, D. Poetry in the 1930's: I, Cecil Day Lewis. In his Poetry and the modern world, 1940.
Stallman, R. Lewis's Come live with me and be my love. Explicator 2 1944.
Dupee, F. W. Lewis and MacNeice. Nation 13 Oct 1945.
Elton, W. Lewis' Rest from loving and be living. Explicator 6 1947 and 7 1948.
Gierasch, W. and D. C. Sheldon. Lewis' Rest from loving and be living. Explicator 6 1948.
Spark, M. Cecil Day Lewis. Poetry Quart 11 1949.
Saul, G. B. Yeats, Noyes and Day Lewis. N & Q 195 1950.
Tschumi, R. The philosophical element in Day Lewis's poetry. In his Thought in twentieth-century English poetry, 1951.
Strong, L. A. G. Cecil Day Lewis. In his Personal remarks, 1953.
Dyment, C. C. Day Lewis. 1955 (Br Council pamphlet).
Dodsworth, M. A poet nearly anonymous. Review (Oxford) 3 1962. Essay-review of The gate, 1962.
Replogle, J. M. The Auden group. Wisconsin Stud in Contemporary Lit 5 1964.
Cowley, M. A hope for poetry. In his Think back on us, Carbondale 1967.
Stanford, D. Stephen Spender, Louis MacNeice, Cecil Day Lewis: a critical essay. Grand Rapids Michigan 1969 (Contemporary Writers in Christian Perspective).

WALTER JOHN DE LA MARE
1873–1956

Bibliographies

Danielson, H. In his Bibliographies of modern authors, 1921.
Library of Congress. List of references on de la Mare. Washington 1923. Later references issued 1925.
Murphy, G. Bibliographies of modern authors. I, de la Mare. London Mercury 15, 16 1927.
Clark, L. A handlist of the writings in book form, 1902–1953, of de la Mare. SB 6 1954. Addendum, SB 8 1956.
—— Walter de la Mare: a checklist prepared on the occasion of an exhibition of his books and mss at the National Book League, 20th April to 19th May 1956. Cambridge 1956. Includes some contributions to books by others and some contributions to periodicals.
A list of de la Mare's contributions to the London Times Literary Supplement. Boston Univ Stud in Eng 1 1955.
See also the Bibliographical appendix to the Complete poems, *1969, below, which gives details of the contents of the previous collections of verse and, with the Editorial introduction, gives some information about de la Mare's revisions and his unpbd verse.*

Selections

Story and rhyme: a selection from the writings of de la Mare, chosen by the author. [1921].

Stories, essays and poems. Ed M. M. Bozman 1938 (EL). Introd (by de la Mare) was also priv ptd 1938 as An introduction to Everyman.

Walter de la Mare: a selection from his writings made by K. Hopkins. 1956.

§1

Poetry

For children's verse, see below. Some of de la Mare's novels and vols of short stories contain poems, many uncollected before Complete poems, *1969 (see Bibliographical appendix therein).*

Poems. 1906.

The listeners and other poems. 1912, New York 1916.

The old men. [1913]. Broadside. Poem rptd in Motley and other poems, 1918, below.

The sunken garden and other poems. 1917 (270 copies). All but one rptd in next.

Motley and other poems. 1918, New York 1918.

Flora: a book of drawings by P. Bianco, with 27 illustrative poems by de la Mare. [1919]. Copies exist with various matchings of poems and drawings.

Poems 1901 to 1918. 2 vols 1920.

The veil and other poems. 1921, New York 1922. Includes 7 poems from Flora, 1919, above.

Thus her tale. Edinburgh 1923. Poem; rptd in The fleeting and other poems, 1933, below.

A ballad of Christmas. [1924] (100 copies); rptd in The fleeting and other poems, 1933, below.

Before dawn. [1924] (100 copies). Rptd from The veil and other poems, 1921, above.

The hostage. [1925] (100 copies).

St Andrews: two poems specially contributed by Rudyard Kipling & de la Mare. 1926. A memory, by de la Mare, rptd in Poems 1919 to 1934, 1935, below.

[Twenty-nine poems]. [1926] (Augustan Books of Modern Poetry). Selection.

Alone. [1927], New York 1927 (Ariel Poem).

Selected poems. New York [1927].

Stuff and nonsense and so on. 1927, 1946 (with additional poems). Light verse.

The captive and other poems. New York 1928. Contents rptd in The fleeting and other poems, 1933, below.

Self to self. [1928] (Ariel Poem).

A snowdrop. 1929 (Ariel Poem).

News. 1930 (Ariel Poem).

To Lucy. 1931 (Ariel Poem).

The sunken garden and other verses. Birmingham 1931. Selection, with different contents from The sunken garden, 1917, above.

Two poems. 1931 (priv ptd, 100 copies). Contains Come! and The strange spirit.

The fleeting and other poems. 1933, New York 1933. Reprints all the Ariel Poems, 2 rev.

Poems 1919 to 1934. 1935, New York [1936]. Includes contents of The veil, The fleeting, most of Flora, selections from the children's books and 7 new poems.

Poems. 1937 (priv ptd, 40 copies). Contents all rptd in next.

Memory and other poems. 1938, New York [1938].

Two poems, by de la Mare and (but!) Arthur Rogers. Newcastle-upon-Tyne 1938 (priv ptd). In a library, by de la Mare, rptd in Collected poems, [1941].

Haunted. 1939. Broadside. Poem rptd in Inward companion, 1950, below.

Collected poems. New York [1941], London 1942. Contains almost all poems pbd to this year, except those intended primarily for children. 'Very few revisions'. New York edn has one poem more and is arranged differently from London edn.

Time passes and other poems. 1942. Selection by A. Ridler.

The burning-glass and other poems, including The travel-

ler. New York 1945, London 1945 (omits The traveller and Problems).

The traveller. 1946. Text differs from that pbd in New York edn of The burning glass, 1945.

Inward companion. 1950.

Winged chariot. 1951, New York 1951 (as Winged chariot and other poems). New York edn includes contents of preceding.

O lovely England and other poems. 1953.

The winnowing dream. 1954 (Ariel Poem, new ser).

Selected poems, chosen by R. N. Green-Armytage. 1954. Includes selection of children's verse.

The morrow. Bath 1955 (priv ptd, 50 copies). 2 unpbd poems, The morrow and The sun.

Walter de la Mare. Selected by J. Hadfield 1962 (Pocket Poets). Includes children's verse.

A choice of de la Mare's verse. Selected with an introd by W. H. Auden 1963.

Complete poems. 1969. 'Contains all the poems de la Mare published in book form during his lifetime; also all the uncollected poems that have been found and a selection of unpublished poems.' Intended as 'the definitive text'.

Children's Books in Poetry and Prose

Some of the collections and selections in the previous section contain children's verse.

Songs of childhood, by 'Walter Ramal'. 1902, 1916 (as by de la Mare, with revision), 1923 (enlarged with revision), 1935 (omitting 3 poems), 1942 (with poems as in 1916 edn, but with some poems in text of 1902 edn).

The three mulla-mulgars. 1910, 1935 (as The three royal monkeys).

A child's day: a book of rhymes to pictures by C. and W. Cadby. 1912, New York [1923].

Peacock pie: a book of rhymes. 1913, [1924] (with 10 additional poems).

Crossings: a fairy play, with music by C. A. Gibbs. 1921 (330 copies), New York 1923.

Down-adown-derry: a book of fairy poems. 1922. All but 5 poems previously collected.

Broomsticks & other tales. 1925, New York 1925.

Miss Jemima. Oxford [1925]. Story.

Readings: traditional tales. Oxford 1925-8. 6 bks.

Lucy. Oxford [1927]. Story.

Old Joe. Oxford [1927]. Story.

Told again: traditional tales. Oxford 1927, 1959 (as Tales told again).

Stories from the Bible. 1929. Stories of Joseph, Moses and Samuel and Saul rptd separately 1958-60.

Poems for children. [1930]. Selection from previously pbd vols, together with some poems rptd from periodicals and some previously unpbd.

Silver. Gaylordsville 1930 (priv ptd, 9 copies). Poem rptd from Peacock pie, 1913, above.

The Dutch cheese. New York 1931. Stories, rptd from Broomsticks, 1925, above.

Old rhymes and new, chosen for use in schools. 2 ser 1932. Selection.

The Lord Fish. [1933]. Stories.

Letters from Mr Walter de la Mare to Form Three. Blaydon 1936.

This year, next year. 1937. Poems.

Bells and grass: a book of rhymes. 1941, New York 1942.

Mr Bumps and his monkey. Philadelphia [1942]. Story, first pbd in The Lord Fish, [1933] (as The old lion).

The old lion and other stories. 1942. Selection.

The magic jacket and other stories. 1943. Selection.

Collected rhymes & verses. 1944, New York [1947] (with some changes and 60 more poems, as Rhymes and verses: collected poems for children).

The scarecrow and other stories. 1945. Selection.

The Dutch cheese and other stories. 1946. Apart from the title story, a different selection from that of 1931.

Collected stories for children. 1947.
Jack and the beanstalk. 1951, New York [1959]. This and
next 3 items are slightly adapted from the versions pbd
in Told again, 1927, above.
Dick Whittington. 1951.
Snow-White. 1952.
Cinderella. 1952.
Selected stories and verses. 1952 (Puffin).
A penny a day. New York 1960. Selection of stories.
Poems. Selected by E. Graham 1962 (Puffin).

Fiction

Henry Brocken: his travels and adventures in the rich,
strange, scarce-imaginable regions of romance. 1904,
[1924] (rev).
The return. 1910, 1922 (rev), 1945 (rev).
Memoirs of a midget. [1921], New York 1921, London
1933 (without introd).
Lispet, Lispett and Vaine. 1923 (200 copies); rptd in next.
The riddle and other stories. 1923.
Ding dong bell. 1924, New York 1924, London 1936
(with a fourth story).
Two tales: The green-room; The connoisseur. [1925]
(250 copies).
The connoisseur and other stories. [1926], New York 1926.
Seaton's aunt. 1927. Rptd from The riddle and other
stories, 1923, above.
At first sight: a novel. New York 1928; rptd in next.
On the edge: short stories. 1930.
Seven short stories. 1931. Selection.
The Walter de la Mare omnibus. [1933]. Contains Henry
Brocken, The return, Memoirs of a midget.
A froward child. 1934. Story.
The nap and other stories. [1936]. Selection.
The wind blows over. 1936. Stories.
The picnic and other stories. 1941. Selection.
Best stories of Walter de la Mare. 1942. Selection.
The almond tree. 1943. Rptd from The riddle and other
stories, 1923, above.
The orgy. 1943. Rptd from On the edge, 1930, above.
The collected tales of Walter de la Mare, chosen and with
an introduction by E. Wagenknecht. New York 1950.
A beginning and other stories. 1955.
Ghost stories. 1956.
Some stories. 1962. Selection.

Other Works

M. E. Coleridge: an appreciation. 1907 (about 200 copies).
Rupert Brooke and the intellectual imagination: a lecture.
1919.
Some thoughts on reading. [Bembridge] 1923 (priv ptd,
350 copies). Lecture.
The printing of poetry. Cambridge 1931 (90 copies).
Lecture.
Lewis Carroll. 1932. Essay, rptd from The eighteen
eighties, ed de la Mare 1930.
Poetry in prose. [1936]. Lecture.
Arthur Thompson: a memoir. [1938] (priv ptd).
Pleasures and speculations. 1940. Essays, lectures etc.
Private view. Introd by Lord D. Cecil 1953. Selected
reviews.

Works edited by de la Mare

*This list is confined mainly to anthologies. Clark's checklist
(Bibliographies, above) gives a number of books with forewords, introductions or other contributions.*

Come hither: a collection of rhymes and poems for the
young of all ages. 1923, New York [1923], London 1928
(rev and enlarged), New York [1928].
Desert islands and Robinson Crusoe. 1930, New York
1930, London 1932 (rev). Anthology, with commentary.
Christina Rossetti: poems chosen by de la Mare. Newtown
1930.

The eighteen-eighties: essays by Fellows of the Royal
Society of Literature. Cambridge 1930. Ed, with a
contribution, Lewis Carroll.
Tom Tiddler's ground. 3 vols [1932], 1 vol [1932], 1961
(with foreword by L. Clark). Verse anthology for
children.
Early one morning in the spring: chapters on children and
on childhood. 1935, New York 1935. Anthology with
commentary.
Animal stories: chosen, arranged and in some part rewritten by de la Mare. 1939, New York 1940.
Behold, this dreamer! 1939, New York 1939. Anthology
with commentary.
Love. 1943, New York 1946. Anthology with introd.

§2

Morley, C. Peacock pie. In his Shandygaff, Garden City
NY 1918.
Aiken, C. In his Scepticisms, New York 1919.
Gosse, E. Fairy in the garden. In his Books on the table,
1921.
Shanks, E. The poetry of de la Mare. London Mercury 3
1921. Review of Poems 1901 to 1918; rptd, rev, in his
First essays in literature, 1923.
— Mr de la Mare's prose. Saturday Rev 3 July 1926.
Fletcher, J. G. A poet of fancy. Freeman 9 Aug 1922.
Freeman, J. The work of de la Mare. Quart Rev 238 1922;
rptd in his English portraits and essays, 1924.
Jameson, S. Mr de la Mare and the grotesque. English
Rev 34 1922. On Memoirs of a midget.
Lothian, A. Walter de la Mare. North Amer Rev 216
1922.
Lucas, F. L. The poetry of de la Mare. New Statesman
23 Dec 1922; rptd in his Authors dead and living, 1926.
Maynard, T. de la Mare: the subtleties of simplicity. In
his Our best poets, New York 1922.
Squire, J. C. Mr de la Mare's romance. In his Books
reviewed, 1922. On Memoirs of a midget.
Jones, L. de la Mare: poet of Tishnar. Bookman (New
York) 57 1923; rptd in his First impressions, New York
1925.
Mégroz, R. L. The school days of a poet. Bookman (Lon-
don) 65 1923; rptd (rev) as A school magazine, in his
Thirty-one bedside essays, 1951. On the Choristers'
Journal of St Paul's Cathedral School, ed by de la Mare
as a schoolboy.
— de la Mare: a biographical and critical study. 1924.
— In his Five novelist poets of to-day, 1933.
Van Doorn, W. de la Mare: an appreciation. E Studies 5
1923.
Arns, K. Walter de la Mare. Zeitschrift für Französischen
und Englischen Unterricht 23 1924.
Collins, J. Psychology of the midget. In his Taking the
literary pulse, New York [1924]. On Memoirs of a
midget.
Priestley, J. B. Mr de la Mare's imagination. London
Mercury 10 1924; rptd in his Figures in modern litera-
ture, 1924.
King, H. Mr de la Mare. Adelphi 2 1925.
Macleish, A. Four poets. Yale Rev new ser 14 1925.
Davison, E. Walter de la Mare. Eng Jnl 15 1926.
— In his Some modern poets, New York 1928.
Sherman, S. P. Walter de la Mare. In his The main
stream, New York 1927.
Kernahan, C. In his Five more famous living poets, 1928.
Reid, F. de la Mare: a critical study. 1929.
Brenner, R. In her Ten modern poets, New York 1930.
Williams, C. de la Mare. In his Poetry at present, 1930.
Murry, J. M. The poetry of de la Mare. In his Countries
of the mind ser 1, 1931.
Chesterton, G. K. Walter de la Mare. Fortnightly Rev
new ser 132 1932; rptd in his The common man, 1950.
Wood, F. T. On the poetry of de la Mare. Poetry Rev 24
1933.

Hardy, T. J. The faerie way of writing. In his Books on the shelf, 1934.

Swinnerton, F. Pre-war poets. In his The Georgian Scene: a literary panorama, New York 1934, London 1935 (as The Georgian literary scene), 1938 (rev), 1950 (rev), 1969 (rev).

—— Three rogue poets. In his Figures in the foreground, 1963.

Roberts, W. W. de la Mare, the listener. Music & Letters 16 1935.

A poet of two worlds: the imagery of Mr de la Mare. TLS 1 Aug 1936.

Weygandt, C. The last romantics. In his The time of Yeats, New York 1937.

Church, R. In his Eight for immortality, 1941.

Wagenknecht, E. C. News of Tishnar. College Eng 3 1941; rptd (rev) in his Cavalcade of the English novel, New York [1943].

—— de la Mare's The riddle. College Eng 11 1949.

—— Winged chariot. In his Preface to literature, New York 1954.

—— de la Mare, book reviewer. Boston Univ Stud in Eng 1 1955.

Johnson, M. C. Fantasy and a real world in the poetry of de la Mare. In his Art and scientific thought, 1944.

Ferguson, De L. de la Mare's Listeners and Housman's On Wenlock Edge. Explicator 4 1945.

Purcell, J. M. de la Mare's Listeners. Explicator 3 1945; 4 1946.

Brown, E. K. The epilogue to Mr de la Mare's poetry. Poetry 68 1946.

Schneider, E. de la Mare's Maerchen. Explicator 4 1946.

Atkins, J. de la Mare: an exploration. 1947.

Fausset, H. I'A. The dreaming mind. In his Poets and pundits, 1947. On Behold, this dreamer!

Bishop, J. P. Poets in prose. In his Collected essays, New York 1948. On Memoirs of a midget.

Child, H. H. Mr de la Mare's world. In his Essays and reflections, 1948.

Tribute to Walter de la Mare on his 75th birthday. 1948. By various authors.

Duffin, H. C. de la Mare: a study of his poetry. 1949.

—— I knew de la Mare. Poetry Rev 48 1957.

Bianco, M. W. Walter de la Mare. In Writing and criticism: a book for M. Bianco, ed A. C. Moore and B. E. Miller, Boston 1951.

Greene, G. de la Mare's short stories. In his The lost childhood and other essays, 1951.

Gregory, H. The nocturnal traveller: de la Mare. Poetry 80 1952.

Hopkins, K. Walter de la Mare. 1953 (Br Council pamphlet).

Jarrell, R. A verse chronicle. In his Poetry and the age, New York 1953; rptd review of The burning glass.

Mr Walter de la Mare. TLS 24 April 1953.

Sackville-West, V. The personality of de la Mare. Listener 30 April 1953.

—— Walter de la Mare and The traveller. 1953 (Warton lecture on English poetry).

Ford, B. The rest was silence: de la Mare's last interview. Encounter 7 1956.

Howarth, R. G. de la Mare and Edith Sitwell. South African PEN Year Book 1956–7. 1957.

Noyes, A. The poetry of de la Mare. Contemporary Rev no 1088 1956.

Brain, R. Tea with de la Mare. 1957.

Cecil, D. The prose tales of de la Mare. In his The fine art of reading, [1957].

Endicott, N. J. de la Mare 1873–1956. UTQ 26 1957.

Peschmann, H. The poetry of de la Mare. English 11 1957.

Smith, W. J. Master of silences: de la Mare, 1873–1956. Poetry 91 1957.

Clark, L. Walter de la Mare. 1960, 1968 (rev, in Three Bodley Head monographs, ed K. Lines).

Dyson, A. E. de la Mare's Listeners. CQ 2 1960.

Coombes, H. Hardy, de la Mare and Edward Thomas. In Pelican Guide to English literature vol 7, The modern age, ed B. Ford 1961.

Spender, S. Non-recognizers. In his The struggle of the modern, 1963.

Pierson, R. M. The meter of The listeners. Eng Stud 45 1964.

Wills, J. H. Architecture of reality: the short stories of de la Mare. North Dakota Quart 32 1964.

McCrosson, D. R. Walter de la Mare. New York 1966 (Twayne's English Authors).

Deutsch, B. Thomas Hardy and de la Mare—who used to notice such things. Columbia Univ Forum 10 1967.

Stebner, G. de la Mare: The moth. In Die moderne englische Lyrik, ed H. Oppel, Berlin [1967].

Love, G. A. Frost's The census-taker and de la Mare's The listeners. Papers on Lang & Lit 4 1968.

Bonnerot, L. L'œuvre de de la Mare: une aventure spirituelle. Paris 1969.

Walter the rhymer: the poetic style of de la Mare. TLS 12 March 1970.

PATRIC THOMAS DICKINSON
b. 1914

§ 1
Poetry and Verse Plays and Translations

The seven days of Jericho. 1944.

Theseus and the Minotaur [a play] and poems. 1946.

Stone in the midst [a play] and poems. 1948.

The sailing race and other poems. 1952.

The scale of things. 1955.

Aristophanes against war: The Acharnians; The peace; Lysistrata. Tr Dickinson 1957.

The world I see. 1960.

Vergil—The Aeneid: a new translation. New York 1961.

A durable fire: a play. 1962.

This cold universe. 1964.

Selected poems. 1968.

Other Works

Soldiers' verse: verses chosen by Dickinson. 1945.

Byron: poems selected and introduced by Dickinson. 1949.

A round of golf courses: a selection of the best eighteen. 1951.

Poems to remember: a book for children. [1958]. Compiled with S. Shannon.

The good minute: an autobiographical study. 1965.

Cecil Day Lewis: selections from his poetry. Ed Dickinson 1967.

Poets' choice: an anthology of English poetry from Spenser to the present day. 1967. With S. Shannon.

Dickinson edited, with S. Shannon, the Personal portraits series, 1950–1.

KEITH CASTELLAIN DOUGLAS
1920–44
Most of Douglas's literary mss are in the BM.

§ 1
Poetry

Selected poems by J. Hall, K. Douglas, N. Nicholson. 1943.

Collected poems. Ed J. Waller and G. S. Fraser 1951, 1966 (in chronological order, with minor addns and introd by E. Blunden).

Selected poems, edited with introduction by T. Hughes. 1964, New York 1964.

Other Works

Augury: an Oxford miscellany of verse & prose. Ed A. M. Hardie and Douglas, Oxford 1940. Contains a short statement on the nature of poetry by Douglas, rptd in Collected poems, 1951, above.

Alamein to Zem Zem. 1946. War experiences, illustr Douglas; includes poems, rptd in Collected poems 1951, above.

§2

Tambimuttu, M. J. In memory of Douglas. Poetry London ten 1944.

Waller, J. The poetry of Douglas. Accent 8 1948.

Ross, A. The poetry of Douglas. TLS 6 Aug 1954.

Fraser, G. S. Douglas: a poet of the second world war. Proc Br Acad 42 1956.

Hughes, T. The poetry of Douglas. Listener 21 June 1962.

— The poetry of Douglas. CQ 5 1963.

JOHN DRINKWATER
1882–1937

Bibliographies

Danielson, H. In his Bibliographies of modern authors, 1921; rptd from Bookman's Journal with addns.

Cutler, B. D. and V. Stiles. In their Modern British authors, 1930. A checklist to 1928.

Times Bookshop. John Drinkwater 1882–1937: catalogue of an exhibition of books, manuscripts, paintings, drawings and associated items, to mark the twenty-fifth anniversary of his death. 1962. Includes a list of books with contributions by Drinkwater not exhibited.

§1
Poetry

Poems. Birmingham 1903.

The death of Leander and other poems. Birmingham 1906.

Lyrical and other poems. Cranleigh 1908.

Poems of men and hours. 1911.

Poems of love and earth. 1912.

Cromwell, and other poems. 1913.

Lines for the opening of the Birmingham Repertory Theatre. Birmingham 1913 (priv ptd).

Swords and ploughshares. 1915.

June dance. 1916 (priv ptd, 35 copies). Originally pbd in Lyrical and other poems, 1908. Here rev; rptd in Poems: 1908–1914, 1917, below.

Olton pools. 1916.

Poems 1908–1914. 1917, New York 1918.

Tides: a book of poems. 1917 (270 copies), 1917 (unlimited, with 15 additional poems).

Loyalties: a book of poems. 1918 (18 poems; 200 copies, illustr), 1919 (with 23 additional poems).

Poems 1908–1919. Boston 1919. Selection.

Persuasion: twelve sonnets. 1921 (priv ptd, 50 copies); rptd in next.

Seeds of time. 1921, Boston 1922.

Christmas 1922. [1922] (210 copies); rptd in From an unknown isle, 1924, below.

Preludes 1921–1922. 1922, Boston 1923.

Selected poems. 1922.

Collected poems. 3 vols 1923–37.

The atom of God. Sevenoaks 1924 (priv ptd) (Waterden broadsheets 2); rptd in next.

From an unknown isle. 1924.

From the German: verses written from the German poets. 1924.

Missolonghi April 19th 1824–1924. [Athens? 1924]. English poem with Greek trn. Also ptd in From an unknown isle, 1924, above.

Prayer: from the German of Eduard Mörike. 1924 (100 copies). Single poem, rptd from From the German, above.

At Pisa. Pisa [1925] (40 copies). Signed J.D.

New poems. Boston 1925. Contains From an unknown isle and From the German, above.

[Twenty-seven poems]. [1925] (Augustan Books of Modern Poetry). Selection.

An appeal for St George's Hospital in London. [1926] (priv ptd). Rptd from From an unknown isle, 1924, above.

A graduation song for the University of London. 1926.

Persephone. New York 1926. Single poem.

To be spoken with an appeal for funds for the rebuilding of the Shakespeare Memorial Theatre at Stratford-upon-Avon. [1926] (25 copies).

All about me: poems for a child. [1928], Boston 1928.

Poems: selected by the author for the Tauchnitz edition. Leipzig 1928.

Thomas Hardy, June 2nd 1925: his eighty-fifth birthday. 1928 (25 copies). Single poem, rptd from Sunday Times.

Uncle Wat. Roanoke [1928] (125 copies). Single poem; rptd in American vignettes, 1931, below.

More about me: poems for a child. [1929], Boston 1930.

Penelope's trees. Huntingdon 1930 (100 copies). Single poem; rptd in Summer harvest, 1933, below.

American vignettes, 1860–1865. Boston 1931. Rptd in Summer harvest, 1933, below.

Christmas poems. 1931.

Poems for a child: All about me—More about me. [1932].

P.A.D. aetat three, 26. vii. 32. Huntingdon 1932 (50 copies). Rptd in next.

Summer harvest: poems 1924–1933. 1933.

Plays

Cophetua: a play in one act. (Pilgrim Players 18 Nov 1911). 1911.

An English medley. Bournville 1911 (priv ptd). Performed at Bournville 1911. A masque.

Puss in boots: a play in five scenes. [1911].

The pied piper: a tale of Hamelin city. (Bournville 27 June 1912). 1912 (priv ptd). A masque.

The only legend: a masque of the scarlet pierrot. (Bournville 10 July 1913). 1913 (priv ptd).

Rebellion: a play in three acts. (Birmingham Repertory Theatre 2 May 1914). [1914].

Robin Hood and the pedlar. (Bournville 25 June 1914). [1914] (priv ptd). A masque.

The storm: a play in one act. (Birmingham Repertory Theatre 8 May 1915). [Birmingham] 1915.

The god of quiet: a play in one act. (Birmingham Repertory Theatre 7 Oct 1916). [Birmingham] 1916.

X = O: a night of the Trojan war. (Birmingham Repertory Theatre 14 April 1917). Birmingham 1917. Play in one act.

Pawns: three poetic plays. 1917. Contains The storm, The god of quiet, and X = O, with foreword. Pbd 1922 with Cophetua, as Pawns and Cophetua.

Abraham Lincoln. (Birmingham Repertory Theatre 12 Oct 1918). 1918, Boston 1919 (introd by A. Bennett).

Oliver Cromwell. (Theatre Royal, Brighton 19 Feb 1921; Haymarket 29 May 1921). 1921, Boston 1921.

Mary Stuart. (Everyman 25 Sept 1922). 1921, New York 1921, London 1922 (rev), Boston 1924.

Robert E. Lee. (Regent 20 June 1923). 1923, Boston 1923.

Collected plays. 2 vols 1925. All plays and masques etc except Puss in boots.

Robert Burns. 1925, Boston 1925.

Bird in hand: a play in three acts. (Birmingham Repertory Theatre 3 Sept 1927; Royalty 18 April 1928). 1927, 1927 (rev), [1930] (French's Acting edn).

John Bull calling: a political parable in one act. (Coliseum 12 Nov 1928). 1928.

Napoleon: the hundred days. (New 18 April 1932). A play by B. Mussolini and G. Forzano, adapted from the Italian for the English stage by Drinkwater.

Midsummer eve: a play primarily intended for wireless. (Broadcast Midsummer eve 1932). 1932.

Laying the devil: a play in three acts. (Playhouse, Liverpool 2 May 1933; Shaftesbury 2 July 1933). 1933.
A man's house: a play in three acts. (Malvern Festival 23 July 1934). 1934, [1935] (French's Acting edn).
Garibaldi: a chronicle play of Italian freedom in ten scenes. 1936.

Other Works

William Morris: a critical study. 1912.
Swinburne: an estimate. 1913, 1924 (with author's note).
The lyric. [1915] (Art and Craft of Letters).
Rupert Brooke: an essay. 1916 (115 copies). First pbd in Contemporary Rev; rptd in Prose papers, 1917, with corrections.
Politics and life. [Birmingham] 1917. Pbd by Birmingham Liberal Association.
Prose papers. 1917.
Lincoln: the world emancipator. Boston 1920.
Cotswold characters. New Haven 1921.
A tribute to the late C. Lovat Fraser. [1921] (priv ptd).
Some contributions to the English anthology, with special reference to the seventeenth century. [1922] (Warton Lecture on English Poetry).
The world and the artist. 1922 (156 copies); rptd in part in The muse in council, 1925.
Claud Lovat Fraser: a memoir. 1923. With A. Rutherston.
The poet and communication. 1923 (Conway Memorial Lecture, 1923).
Victorian poetry. 1923, New York 1924.
Patriotism in literature. 1924, New York [1924].
Robert Burns: an address. Edinburgh 1924; rptd in English edn of The muse in council.
The muse in council. 1925, Boston 1925 (omitting 5 essays in London edn, but adding 9, 5 rptd from Prose papers).
The pilgrim of eternity: Byron—a conflict. 1925, New York 1925.
A book for bookmen: being edited manuscripts & marginalia with essays on several occasions. 1926. Also issued (50 copies) with illustrations.
Mr Charles, king of England. 1926, New York 1926.
Cromwell: a character study. [1927], New York [1927] (as Oliver Cromwell: a character study).
The gentle art of theatre-going. 1927, Boston 1927 (as The art of theatre-going).
Charles James Fox. 1928, New York 1928.
'The other point of view...'. 1928. Oration delivered by Drinkwater at University College, London, Union Society.
The world's Lincoln. New York 1928.
Story-folk. [1929]. 4 booklets for children. With E. Terriss.
Art and the state. Liverpool 1930 (Roscoe Lecture, 1930).
Pepys: his life and character. 1930, Garden City NY 1930.
Inheritance: being the first book of an autobiography. 1931, New York [1931].
The life and adventures of Carl Laemmle. New York 1931, London 1931.
Poetry and dogma. Bristol [1931] (Arthur Skemp Memorial Lecture, 1931).
The stamps of the Confederate States of America 1861–5. [Leicester 1931] (priv ptd). Paper given at Eighteenth Philatelic Congress of Great Britain.
Discovery: being the second book of an autobiography, 1897–1913. 1932.
John Hampden's England. 1933.
Shakespeare. 1933.
This troubled world. New York 1933. 4 essays.
A pageant of England's life presented by her poets, with a running commentary by Drinkwater. 1934.
Speeches in commemoration of William Morris. Walthamstow 1934. By Drinkwater, H. Jackson and H. Laski.
The King's reign: a commentary in prose and picture. 1935. On the reign of George V.
Robinson of England. 1937, New York 1937. Novel.
English poetry: an unfinished history. 1938. Appendix reprints Poetry and dogma and Some contributions to the English anthology.

Books Edited or with Introductions by Drinkwater

The way of poetry. [1920], Boston 1922. Anthology for children.
The outline of literature. 26 pts [1923–4], New York 1923–4, 1 vol [1930], New York 1931, London 1940 (rev H. Pollock and C. Nairne), 1950 (rev H. Shipp), 1957 (rev).
An anthology of English verse. [1924], Boston 1924.
The way of prose. 4 bks [1924]. Anthology for children.
The eighteen-sixties: essays by Fellows of the Royal Society of Literature. Cambridge 1932. Ed Drinkwater, who also wrote the introd and an essay, Eneas Sweetland Dallas.
Drinkwater contributed introds to a great many works, particularly to collections of English verse by individual authors. He also edited Scallop Shell, the organ of the Pilgrim Players, 1911, contributed to the 4 parts of New Numbers, 1914, and to all the vols of Georgian Poetry, 1912–22. The Times Bookshop exhibition catalogue (see Bibliographies, above) lists a large number of works with introds by Drinkwater.

§2

Wright, H. G. In his Studies in contemporary literature, Bangor 1918.
Sherry, L. Drinkwater as poet and playwright. Poetry (Chicago) 19 1921.
Kernahan, C. In his Six famous living poets, 1922.
Wild, F. Drinkwater. E Studien 57 1923.
Morgan, A. E. In his Tendencies of modern English drama, 1924.
Sutton, G. In his Some contemporary dramatists, 1924.
Matthews, G. W. The poetry of Drinkwater. Liverpool 1925.
Arns, K. Drinkwater als Dramatiker. Die Neueren Sprachen 34 1926.
Röder, A. W. Drinkwater als Dramatiker. Giessen 1927.
Bergholz, H. Drinkwater als Dramatiker. E Studien 63 1929.
Mitchell, E. S. Negro speech in Drinkwater's Abraham Lincoln. Amer Speech 7 1931.
Weissgräber, K. Staat und Volk bei Drinkwater. Zeitschrift für Französischen und Englischen Unterricht 30 1931.
Clemens, C. Drinkwater. Sewanee Rev 40 1932.
Thoulous, P. Wilfred Wilson Gibson and Drinkwater. In her Modern poetic drama, 1934.
Barts, E. Der Führergedanke in Drinkwaters Drama 'Oliver Cromwell'. Neuphilologische Monatsschrift 6 1935.
Grosser, A. Das Bild eines Führers im englischen Unterricht: Drinkwaters Abraham Lincoln. Die Neueren Sprachen 44 1936.
Ghidelli, C. Drinkwater and his historical plays: Lincoln, Cromwell, Mary Stuart. Naples 1937.
Krause, G. Die Cromwell-Schau Drinkwaters. Zeitschrift für Neusprachlichen Unterricht 40 1941.
Papajewski, H. Drinkwater: Abraham Lincoln. Archiv für das Studium der Neueren Sprachen und Literaturen 195 1958.
Brundy, M. W. Drinkwater and The cats. Research Stud 33 1965. On The pilgrim of eternity.

LAWRENCE GEORGE DURRELL
b. 1912

Bibliographies

Thomas, A. G. and L. C. Powell. Some uncollected authors xxiii: Durrell. Recollections of a Durrell collector. Book Collector 9 1960.

Knerr, A. Regarding a checklist of Durrell. PBSA 55
1961. Addns etc to the above with a list of contributions
to periodicals.
Potter, R. A. and B. Whiting. Durrell: a checklist. Los
Angeles 1961. Chronological list of books and contribu-
tions to periodicals.
Beebe, M. Criticism of Durrell: a selected checklist.
Modern Fiction Stud 13 1967.
Thomas, A. G. In G. S. Fraser, Lawrence Durrell: a
study, 1968, §2 below.

§1
Poetry

Quaint fragment: poems written between the ages of
sixteen and nineteen. 1931 (priv ptd).
Ten poems. 1932.
A ballade of slow decay. [Bournemouth] 1932. Anon.
A Christmas card with a poem.
Transition: poems. 1934.
Mass for the old year. [Bournemouth] 1935. A New Year
card with a poem.
A private country. 1943.
Premature epitaphs and all. Alexandria 1944. Limited to
6 copies in typescript.
Cities, plains and people. 1946.
The Parthenon: for T. S. Eliot. [Rhodes 1945 or 1946]
(priv ptd). A Christmas card.
On seeming to presume. 1948.
A landmark gone. Los Angeles 1949. Limited to 125
copies for L. C. Powell (priv ptd).
Deus loci: a poem. Ischia 1950 (priv ptd, 200 copies).
Private drafts. Nicosia 1955 (priv ptd, 100 copies).
The tree of idleness and other poems. 1955.
Selected poems. 1956, New York 1956, London 1964 (as
Selected poems 1935–63). With additional poems.
Collected poems. 1960, New York 1960, London 1968
(rev).
Penguin modern poets, 1: Durrell, E. Jennings, R. S.
Thomas. 1962. Selection.
Poetry. New York 1962.
A Persian lady. [Edinburgh] 1963 (6 copies). Broadsheet.
The ikons and other poems. 1966.

Novels

Pied piper of lovers. 1935.
Panic spring: a romance by 'Charles Norden' (i.e.
Durrell). 1937, New York 1937.
The black book: an agon. Paris 1938 (Obelisk press, Villa
Saurat ser 1), Paris 1059 (Olympia press, with new
preface), New York 1960 (with introd by G. Sykes).
Extracts pbd in New Directions 4 1939 (as Gracie).
Preface to 1959 edn pbd in Two Cities 1 1959 (with
slight alterations).
Cefalû: a novel. 1947, 1958 (as The dark labyrinth; with
alterations), New York 1962.
Justine: a novel. 1957, New York 1957. 1st vol of
Alexandria quartet.
White eagles over Serbia. 1957, New York 1957, London
1961 (abridged by G. A. Verdin). For children.
Balthazar: a novel. 1958, New York 1958. 2nd vol of
Alexandria quartet.
Mountolive: a novel. 1958, New York 1959. 3rd vol of
Alexandria quartet.
Clea: a novel. 1960, New York 1960. 4th vol of Alexandria
quartet.
The Alexandria quartet: Justine, Balthazar, Mountolive,
Clea. 1962, New York 1962. Rev, with corrections
throughout, deletions from Balthazar and Mountolive,
addns to Clea and a new preface by the author.
Tunc. 1968, New York 1968.
Nunquam. 1970, New York 1970.

Other Works

Bromo Bombastes: a fragment from a laconic drama by
Gaffer Peeslake. 1933. Limited to 100 copies. A satire
on Shaw's Black girl in search of God.
Prospero's cell: a guide to the landscape and manners of
the island of Corcyra. 1945, New York 1960 (with
Reflections on a marine Venus, below).
Zero and Asylum in the snow. Rhodes 1946 (priv ptd),
Berkeley 1947 (as Two excursions into reality).
Sappho: a play in verse. 1950, New York [1958]. First
performed in German at Deutsches Schauspielhaus,
Hamburg, 2 Nov 1959; first performed in English,
Royal Lyceum Theatre, Edinburgh 28 Aug 1961.
Key to modern poetry. 1952, Norman Oklahoma 1952 (as
A key to modern British poetry).
Reflections on a marine Venus: a companion to the land-
scape of Rhodes. 1953, New York 1960 (with Prospero's
cell).
Bitter lemons. 1957, New York 1958. On Cyprus.
Esprit de corps: sketches from diplomatic life. 1957, New
York 1958 (with 2 additional sketches, La valise and
Cry wolf).
Stiff upper lip: life among the diplomats. 1958, New York
1959 (with an additional story, A smircher smirched, but
without the sketches, La valise and Cry wolf).
Art and outrage: a correspondence about Henry Miller
between A. Perlès and Durrell. 1959, New York 1961.
Briefwechsel über 'Actis'. Hamburg 1961. With G.
Gründgens.
Beccafico. Le becfigue. Montpellier 1963 (priv ptd).
Limited to 100 copies. With French trn by F.-J. Temple.
Essay.
An Irish Faustus: a morality in nine scenes. 1963, New
York 1964.
Lawrence Durrell and Henry Miller: a private correspon-
dence. Ed G. Wickes, New York 1963, London 1963.
La descente du Styx. Traduite de l'anglais par F.-J.
Temple et suivie du texte original. Montpellier 1964
(priv ptd). Limited to 250 copies.
Acte: a play. 1965, New York 1965. First performed in
German at Deutsches Schauspielhaus, Hamburg, Nov
1961.
Sauve qui peut. 1966, New York 1967. Sketches.
Spirit of place. 1969. Essays on travel, ed A. G. Thomas.

Works Translated or with Contributions by Durrell

*Books containing brief prefaces, and some contributions to
anthologies, have been omitted.*

Proems. 1938. Contains Unckebunck, Five soliloquies
upon the tomb, Themes heraldic.
Miller, H. The colossus of Maroussi. San Francisco 1941,
London 1942. Appendix contains letter from Durrell.
Tambimuttu, M. J. (ed). Poetry in wartime. 1942. 5 poems.
Moore, N. and D. Newton (ed). Atlantic anthology. 1945.
7 poems.
Personal landscape: an anthology of exile. Compiled by
by R. Fedden, T. Tiller, B. Spencer, L. Durrell 1945.
Selection from periodical Personal Landscape, Cairo
1942–5.
The happy rock: a book about Henry Miller. Berkeley
1945. First essay, The happy rock, by Durrell.
Waller, J. and E. de Mauny (ed). Middle East anthology.
1946. 3 poems.
Six poems from the Greek of Sekilianos (sic) and Seferis.
Rhodes 1946.
Stephanides, T. Climax in Crete. Foreword by Durrell
1946.
Seferis, G. The king of Asine and other poems. Tr from
the Greek by B. Spencer, N. Valaoritis, L. Durrell 1948.
Venezis, I. Aeolia. Preface by Durrell 1949.
Rexroth, K. (ed). The new British poets: an anthology.
[Norfolk Conn 1949]. 4 poems.

Royidis, E. Pope Joan: a romantic biography. Tr Durrell 1954, 1960 (rev), New York 1961. Originally planned for publication in 1948.

Temple, F.-J. [et al]. Hommage à Roy Campbell. Montpellier 1958. 2 contributions by Durrell.

Tremayne, P. Below the tide. Preface by Durrell 1958, Boston 1959. On Cyprus.

The Henry Miller reader. Ed Durrell New York 1959, London 1960 (as The best of Henry Miller).

Tedlock, E. W. (ed). Dylan Thomas: the legend and the poet. 1960. Essay, The shades of Dylan Thomas, by Durrell.

Groddeck, G. The book of the It. Introd by Durrell 1961. Rptd from Horizon 17 1948.

No clue to living. In The writer's dilemma, 1961.

New poems 1963. Ed Durrell 1963. A P.E.N. anthology of contemporary poetry.

Durrell edited, with others, the periodicals The Booster (*and its successor,* Delta) *Paris 1937-9*, Personal Landscape, *Cairo 1942-5, and the* Cyprus Review *1954-5. He also contributed a column to the* Egyptian Gazette *in 1941.*

§2

Stanford, D. Lawrence Durrell. In his The freedom of poetry, 1947; rptd in The world of Durrell, ed H. T. Moore 1962, below.

Waller, J. Durrell: a clever magician. Poetry Rev 38 1947.

Durrell, G. My family and other animals. 1956.

Kermode, F. Durrell and others. In his Puzzles and epiphanies, 1962. Partly rptd from London Mag 5 1958.

— Fourth dimension. REL 1 1960.

Flint, R. W. A major novelist. Commentary 28 1959.

Lund, M. G. Submerge for reality: the new novel form of Durrell. Southwest Rev 44 1959.

— The Alexandrian projection. Antioch Rev 21 1961.

— Soft focus on crime. Prairie Schooner 35 1961.

— Eight aspects of Melissa. Forum (Houston) 3 1962.

Two Cities 1 1959. Hommage à Durrell. Contributions by Henry Miller, A. Perlès, F.-J. Temple, R. Aldington, E. Mullins and Durrell. Those by Miller, Aldington and Durrell rptd in The world of Durrell, ed H. T. Moore 1962, below.

Young, K. A dialogue with Durrell. Encounter 13 1959.

Arban, D. Lawrence Durrell. Preuves no 109 1960.

Corke, H. Mr Durrell and Brother Criticus. Encounter 14 1960.

De Mott, B. Grading the Emanglons. Hudson Rev 13 1960. On the Alexandria quartet.

Engelborghs, M. Nieuwe Engelse romankunst: Durrell. Dietsche Warande en Belfort 105 1960.

Green, M. Durrell: a minority report. Yale Rev 49 1960. Rptd in The world of Durrell, ed H. T. Moore 1962, below.

Hamard, J.-P. L'espace et le temps dans les romans de Durrell. Critique (Paris) no 156 1960.

— Durrell: rénovateur assagi. Critique (Paris) no 163 1960.

Highet, G. The Alexandrians of Durrell. Horizon (New York) 2 1960.

Mackworth, C. Durrell and the new romanticism. Twentieth Century 167 1960; rptd in The world of Durrell, ed H. T. Moore 1962, below.

Michot, P. Durrell's Alexandria quartet. Revue des Langues Vivantes no 5 1960.

Mitchell, J. and G. Andrewski. The art of fiction xxiii: Durrell. Paris Rev 22 1960. An interview.

Steiner, G. Durrell: the baroque novel. Yale Rev 49 1960; rptd in The world of Durrell, ed H. T. Moore 1962, below.

Weyergans, F. Clea de Durrell. Revue Nouvelle July 1960

Baldanza, F. Durrell's word continuum. Critique (Minneapolis) 4 1961.

Becher, H. Durrells Tetralogie und die literarische Kritik. Stimmen der Zeit 168 1961.

Bode, C. Durrell's way to Alexandria. College Eng 22

1961; rptd in The world of Durrell, ed H. T. Moore 1962, below.

Cate, C. Durrell. Atlantic Monthly 208 1961.

Dobrée, B. Durrell's Alexandrian series. Sewanee Rev 69 1961; rptd in The world of Durrell, ed H. T. Moore 1962, below.

Enright, D. J. Alexandrian nights' entertainments: Durrell's Quartet. International Literary Annual 3 1961.

— In his Conspirators and poets. 1966.

O'Brien, R. A. Time, space and language in Durrell. Waterloo Rev 6 1961.

Perlès, A. My friend Durrell. Northwood Middx 1961.

Proser, M. N. Darley's dilemma: the problem of structure in Durrell's Alexandria quartet. Critique (Minneapolis) 4 1961.

Rexroth, K. Durrell. In his Assays, Norfolk Conn 1961.

Arthos, J. Durrell's gnosticism. Personalist 43 1962.

Crowder, R. Durrell, libido and Eros. Ball State Teachers College Forum 3 1962.

Eskin, S. G. Durrell's Themes in the Alexandria quartet. Texas Quart 5 1962.

Fricker, R. The Alexandria quartet. Gymnasium Helveticum 16 1962.

Gindin, J. J. Some current fads. In his Postwar British fiction, 1962. On C. P. Snow, Durrell and C. Wilson.

Gordon, A., jr. Time, space and Eros: the Alexandria quartet rehearsed. In Six contemporary novels, ed W. O. S. Sutherland, Austin 1962.

Hutchens, E. N. The heraldic universe in the Alexandria quartet. College Eng 24 1962.

Karl, F. R. Durrell: physical and metaphysical love. In his Contemporary English novel, New York 1962, London 1963 (as A reader's guide to the contemporary English novel).

Kihlman, C. Durrell och den moderna romanen. Nya Argus 55 1962.

Manzalaoui, M. Curate's egg: an Alexandrian opinion of Durrell's Quartet. Études Anglaises 15 1962.

Moore, H. T. (ed). The world of Durrell. Carbondale [1962]. 18 essays by various authors and 3 sections (2 interviews and some letters) by Durrell.

Silverstein, N. and A. L. Lewis. Durrell's Song for Zarathustra. Explicator 21 1962.

Bork, A. M. Durrell and relativity. Centennial Rev of Arts & Science 7 1963.

Glicksberg, C. I. The fictional world of Durrell. Bucknell Rev 11 1963.

Howarth, H. Durrell and some early masters. Books Abroad 37 1963.

— A segment of Durrell's Quartet. UTQ 32 1963.

Kelly, J. C. Durrell: the Alexandria quartet. Studies 52 1963.

— Durrell's style. Ibid.

Lemon, L. T. The Alexandria quartet: form and fiction. Wisconsin Stud in Contemporary Lit 4 1963.

Servotte, H. The Alexandria quartet. Dietsche Warande en Belfort 108 1963.

Sullivan, N. Durrell's epitaph for the novel. Personalist 44 1963.

Edel, L. A multiplicity of mirrors. In his The Modern psychological novel, New York 1964. On the Alexandria quartet.

Hagopian, J. V. The resolution of the Alexandria quartet. Critique (Minneapolis) 7 1964.

Scholes, R. Return to Alexandria: Durrell and the western narrative tradition. Virginia Quart Rev 40 1964.

— Durrell and the return to Alexandria. In his The fabulators, Oxford 1967.

Unterecker, J. Lawrence Durrell. New York and London 1964 (Columbia Essays on Modern Writers).

— The Protean world of Durrell. In On contemporary literature, ed R. Kostelanetz, New York 1964.

Weatherhead, A. K. Romantic anachronism in the Alexandria quartet. Modern Fiction Stud 10 1964.

Albérès, R.-M. Durrell ou le roman pentagonal. Revue de Paris 72 1965.

Dare, H. The quest for Durrell's Scobie. Modern Fiction Stud 10 1965.

Fraiberg, L. B. Durrell's dissonant quartet. In Contemporary British novelists, ed C. Shapiro 1965.

Fricker, R. Durrell: the Alexandria quartet. In Der moderne englische Roman, ed H. Oppel, Berlin 1965.

Littlejohn, D. The permanence of Durrell. Colorado Quart 14 1965.

Bosquet, A. Durrell ou l'azur ironique. Nouvelle Revue Française 14 1966.

Cole, D. Faust and anti-Faust in modern drama. Drama Survey 5 1966.

Gossman, A. Some characters in search of a mirror. Critique (Minneapolis) 8 1966.

Hagergård, S. Om medvetandets struktur. Horisont 13 1966. On the Alexandria quartet.

Howard, R. The plays of Durrell. Balcony no 5 1966.

Weigel, J. A. Lawrence Durrell. New York [1966] (Twayne's English Authors).

Friedman, A. W. A key to Durrell. Wisconsin Stud in Contemporary Lit 8 1967.

Kameyama, M. Lawrence Durrell: a sketch. In Collected essays by members of the faculty, Kyoritsu Women's Junior College no 11 1967.

Modern Fiction Studies 13 1967. Durrell no, containing: M. Beebe, Criticism of Durrell: a selected checklist; S. L. Brown, The Black Book: a search for method; J. C. Burns, Durrell's heraldic universe; A. Friedman, Place and Durrell's island books; W. L. Godshalk, Some sources of Durrell's Alexandria quartet; J. E. Kruppa, Durrell's Alexandria quartet and the implosion of the modern consciousness; M. P. Levitt, Art and correspondences: Durrell, Miller and the Alexandria quartet; M. L. Morcos, Elements of the autobiographical in the Alexandria quartet; P. L. Read, The illusion of personality: cyclical time in Durrell's Alexandria quartet.

Sertoli, G. Durrell e il Quartetto di Alessandria. Eng Miscellany (Rome) 18 1967.

Decancq, R. What lies beyond?: an analysis of Darley's quest in Durrell's Alexandria quartet. Revue des Langues Vivantes 34 1968.

Fraser, G. S. Durrell: a study with a bibliography by A. G. Thomas. 1968.

Hamard, J. Durrell: a European writer. Durham Univ Jnl 29 1968.

Goulianos, J. Durrell and Alexandria. Virginia Quart Rev 45 1969.

Katope, C. G. Cavafy and Durrell's Alexandria quartet. Comparative Lit 21 1969.

Lebas, G. Durrell's Alexandria quartet and the critics: a survey of published criticism. Caliban 6 1969.

CLIFFORD DYMENT
b. 1914

§1
Poetry

First day. 1935.
Straight or curly? 1937.
The axe in the wood. 1944.
Selected poems. 1945.
Poems 1935–1948. 1949. Selection with some revision and 16 uncollected poems.
Experiences and places: new poems. 1955.
Collected poems. 1970.

Other Works

Matthew Arnold: an introduction and a selection by Dyment 1948.
Poems by Thomas Hood, selected & introduced by Dyment 1948 [1949?].
Poems by Matthew Arnold, selected and introduced by Dyment 1949.

New poems 1952: a P.E.N. anthology. Ed Dyment [et al] 1952.
C. Day Lewis. 1955, 1963 (rev) (Br Council pamphlet).
The railway game: an early autobiography. 1962.

WILLIAM EMPSON
b. 1906

Bibliographies

Lowbridge, P. An Empson bibliography. Review (Oxford) 6–7 1963. Works by Empson. Includes selected correspondence but excludes contributions to Granta 1926–9.

§1
Poetry

Letter IV. Cambridge 1929.
Poems. [Tokyo?] 1934 (priv ptd). 14 poems.
Poems. 1935.
The gathering storm. 1940.
Collected poems. New York [1949].
Collected poems. 1955. Adds Chinese ballad and The birth of steel: a masque, to contents of Collected poems [1949].

Criticism

Seven types of ambiguity. 1930, 1947 (rev), 1953 (rev), New York 1955.
Some versions of pastoral. 1935, New York 1938 (as English pastoral poetry), London 1950 (with errata).
Shakespeare survey. [1937]. (Survey pamphlets no 2). With George Garrett. Includes The best policy and Timon's dog.
The structure of complex words. 1951, New York 1951.
Milton's God. 1961, Norfolk Conn 1962, London 1964 (rev, corrected, with notes and appendix).

Contributions to Books

Cambridge poetry. 1929. 6 poems by Empson.
Virginia Woolf. In Scrutinies, vol 2, ed E. Rickword 1931.
Science and well-being, by J. B. S. Haldane. Put into Basic by Empson. 1935 (Psyche miniatures 77).
The outlook of science, by J. B. S. Haldane. Put into Basic by Empson. 1935 (Psyche miniatures 80).
The style of the master. In T. S. Eliot: a symposium. Ed R. March and Tambimuttu 1948.
Emotions in poems. In The Kenyon critics, Cleveland 1951.
The symbolism of Dickens. In Dickens and the twentieth century, ed J. Gross and G. Pearson 1962.
Empson edited the first three numbers of Experiment (Nov 1928–May 1929), *and contributed to subsequent issues.*

§2

Bradbrook, M. C. The criticism of Empson. Scrutiny 2 1933–4.
Mason, H. A. Empson's criticism. Scrutiny 4 1935–6. Review of Some versions of pastoral.
Sitwell, E. Four new poets. London Mercury 33 1936. Empson, Bottrall, Dylan Thomas, Archibald MacLeish.
Ransom, J. C. Mr Empson's muddles. Southern Rev 4 1938.
—— I. A. Richards, the psychological critic, and William Empson, his pupil. In his The new criticism, Norfolk Conn [1941].
Richards, I. A. Note on Empson. Furioso 1940.
Burke, K. Exceptional improvisation, exceptional book. In his Philosophy of literary form, Baton Rouge 1941. Review of Some versions of pastoral.
—— Words anent logology. In J. Strelka (ed), Perspectives in literary symbolism, Philadelphia 1968.

Brooks, C. Empson's criticism. Accent 4 1944.

McLuhan, H. M. Poetic vs rhetorical exegesis: the case for Leavis against Richards and Empson. Sewanee Rev 52 1944.

Cox, R. G. Ambiguity revised. Scrutiny 15 1947–8.

Ford, N. F. Empson's and Ransom's mutilations of texts. PQ 29 1950.

Glicksberg, C. I. Empson: genius of ambiguity. Dalhousie Rev 29 1950.

Kenner, H. Son of spiders. Poetry (Chicago) 76 1950.

— Alice in Empsonland. Hudson Rev 5 1952; rptd in his Gnomon, New York 1958.

Olson, E. Empson, contemporary criticism and poetic diction. MP 47 1950; rptd in Critics and criticism, ed R. S. Crane, Chicago 1952.

Wain, J. Ambiguous gifts: notes on a twentieth-century poet. Penguin New Writing no 40 1950; rptd in his Preliminary essays, 1957

Burgum, E. B. The cult of the complex in poetry. Science & Society 15 1951.

Hyman, S. E. Empson and categorical criticism. In his The armed vision, New York 1952.

Sleight, R. Mr Empson's complex words. EC 2 1952.

Adams, R. N. Empson and Bentley: something about Milton too. Partisan Rev 21 1954.

Strickland, G. Empson's criticism. Mandrake 2 no 10 1954; reply by Empson and comment by Strickland 2 no 11 1955.

Fraser, G. S. On the interpretation of the difficult poem. In Interpretations, ed J. Wain 1955. Includes analysis of The teasers.

— 'Not wrongly moved...' (Empson). In his Vision and rhetoric, 1959.

Donoghue, D. Reading a poem: Empson's Arachne. Studies 45 1956.

Madge, C. Empson agonistes. Listen 2 1956. Review of Collected poems.

Alvarez, A. A style from despair: Empson. Twentieth Century 161 1957; rptd in his The shaping spirit, 1958.

Hedges, W. L. The Empson treatment. Accent 17 1957. Analysis of Four legs, three legs, two legs.

Wimsatt, W. K. and C. Brooks. The semantic principle. In their Literary criticism: a short history, New York 1957.

Pulos, C. E. William Empson. In his The new critics and the language of poetry, Lincoln Neb 1958.

Danby, J. F. William Empson. CQ 1 1959.

Morelli, A. La poesia di Empson. Catania 1959.

Spector, R. D. Form and content in Empson's Missing dates. MLN 74 1959.

Watson, G. William Empson. In his Literary critics, 1962, 1964 (rev).

Review (Oxford) 6–7 1963. Special no devoted to Empson. Contains: M. Dodsworth, Empson at Cambridge; C. Falck, This deep blankness: 1, Metaphysical and romantic; 2, The poetry of Empson; J. Fuller, Empson's tone; I. Hamilton, A girl can't go on laughing all the time; P. Hobsbaum, Empson as a critical practitioner; L. E. Sissman, Just a whack at Empson (Poem); S. Touster, Empson's legal fiction; Empson in conversation with Christopher Ricks.

Meller, H. Empsons Arachne: eine Interpretation. Archiv 201 1964.

Das, B. A note on the poetry of Empson. Literary Criterion 6 1965.

Jensen, J. The construction of Seven types of ambiguity. MLQ 27 1966.

— Some ambiguous preliminaries: Empson in The Granta. Criticism 8 1966.

Ormerod, D. Empson's Invitation to Juno. Explicator 25 1966.

Robson, W. W. More Empson than Milton. Oxford Rev no 1 1966.

Sale, R. The achievement of Empson. Hudson Rev 19 1966.

Gardner, P. Meaning in the poetry of Empson. Humanities Assoc Bull 18 1967.

Otten, K. William Empson: This last pain. In Die moderne englische Lyrik, ed H. Oppel, Berlin 1967.

Pinsker, S. Finite but unbounded: the poetic world of Empson. Univ of Windsor Rev 3 1967.

Maxwell–Mahon, W. D. The divided glancer: a comment on Empson. Eng Stud in Africa 11 1968.

Hawthorn, J. M. Commitment in the poetry of Empson. Trivium 4 1969.

Willis, J. H., jr. William Empson. New York 1969 (Columbia Essays on Modern Writers).

JAMES ELROY FLECKER
(b. HERMAN ELROY FLECKER)
1884–1915

The corrected typescript of Hassan *is in Bodley, and the ms of* Don Juan *is in Cheltenham Public Library (see* Friends of the National Libraries, Annual Report 1934–5*). There is other ms material in BM, Fitzwilliam Museum, Lockwood Memorial Library Buffalo, and British Embassy, Beirut.*

Bibliographies

Danielson, H. In his Bibliographies of modern authors, 1921.

Mercer, T. S. In his James Elroy Flecker: from school to Samarkand, Thames Ditton 1952, below.

§I
Poetry

The bridge of fire. 1907.

Thirty-six poems. 1910. 20 poems from previous, rev.

Forty-two poems. 1911. Contents of preceding with 6 new poems. Reissued 1924 with The Grecians.

The golden journey to Samarkand. 1913. Preface by author.

The burial in England. 1915 (20 copies). Ptd by Clement Shorter; rptd in Collected poems, 1916, below.

God save the King. 1915 (20 copies). Ptd by Shorter; rptd in Collected poems, 1916.

The old ships. [1915].

Collected poems. Ed with introd by J. C. Squire 1916, New York 1916, London 1935 (with additional introd), 1946 (with textual corrections).

Selected poems. 1918. Introductory note by J.C.S. [i.e. J. C. Squire].

14 poems. 1921. Ptd in Dijon, pbd Poetry Book Shop; 550 copies. Selection.

[Twenty-five poems]. [1931] (Augustan Books of Poetry). Selection.

Plays

Hassan: the story of Hassan of Bagdad and how he came to make the golden journey to Samarkand; a play in five acts. (His Majesty's 20 Sept 1923). 1922, New York 1922, London 1923 (introd by J. C. Squire), 1951 (acting edn with textual alterations, introd by B. Dean), 1966 (rev). The first performance was in the Hessische Landestheater, Darmstadt, 1 June 1923 in the German trn by Freissler.

Don Juan: a play in three acts. (Three Hundred Club, Court 25 April 1926). 1925, New York 1925. Preface by Hellé Flecker.

Other Works

The best man: Eights' Week, 1906. Oxford 1906. Anon. Miscellany.

The last generation: a story of the future. 1908.

The Grecians: a dialogue on education. 1910, New York 1910. Reissued 1924 with Forty-two poems, above.

The scholar's Italian book: an introduction to the study of the Latin origins of Italian. 1911.

The king of Alsander. 1914, New York 1914. Novel.

Collected prose. 1920. Contains Tales and sketches (9 pieces including The last generation), The Grecians, Critical studies (7 essays).

Letters

The letters of Flecker to F. Savery. Ed H. Flecker 1926 (590 copies).

Some letters from abroad, with a few reminiscences by H. Flecker and an introd by J. C. Squire 1930. Includes most of the letters to Savery.

§2

Roberts, C. M. James Elroy Flecker. Poetry Rev 6 1915.
—— Flecker: the last phase. Poetry Rev 8 1917.
Bronner, M. Flecker: English Parnassian. Bookman (New York) 43 1916.
Goldring, D. Flecker. Bookman (London) 51 1916; review of Collected poems.
—— Flecker: an appreciation and some personal memories. Dial 68 1920; rptd in his Reputations, 1920.
—— Flecker: an appreciation, with some biographical notes. 1922.
Hodgson, G. Concerning a poet's letter. Poetry Rev 8 1917.
—— Flecker and Paul Fort. Poetry Rev 12 1921.
—— The life of Flecker, from letters and material provided by his mother. Oxford 1925.
—— Roses in Flecker's The old ships. N & Q 155 1928.
—— A note on Flecker. Dublin Mag 12 1937.
Lynd, R. In his Old and new masters, 1919.
Massingham, H. J. A pilgrim who stopped half-way. In his Letters to X, 1919.
Phelps, W. L. In his Advance of English poetry in the twentieth century, 1919.
Waugh, A. In his Tradition and change, 1919; rptd review of Collected poems.
Arns, K. James Elroy Flecker. Die Neueren Sprachen 31 1923.
Joussaume, G. James Elroy Flecker. Les Langues Modernes 21 1923; review of Collected prose, 1920, and Hassan, 1922.
Palmer, H. E. Elroy Flecker: the ghost poet. Quest 14 1923.
—— Flecker: the poet of the sun. Bookman (London) 82 1932.
—— In his Post-Victorian poetry, 1938.
Shipp, H. The triumph of 'Hassan'. Eng Rev 37 1923.
Dukes, A. In his The youngest drama, 1924.
Macdonald, A. James Elroy Flecker. Fortnightly Rev 115 1924.
Mercer, T. S. Flecker: some early recollections. Bookman's Jnl 11 1925. Enlarged as James Elroy Flecker: from school to Samarkand, Thames Ditton 1952. With bibliography.
Lucas, F. L. 'Ah, did you once see Shelley plain?' In his Authors dead and living, 1926; rptd reviews of Hodgson's Life, Collected prose and Hassan.
Shanks, E. In his Second essays on literature, 1927.
Cunliffe, J. W. In his Modern English playwrights, New York 1927.
Block, E. A. Brooke and Flecker. Poetry Rev 20 1929.
Grigson, G. Creation of beauty: Flecker and the East. Bookman (London) 79 1931.
Wolfe, H. In his Portraits by inference, 1934.
Lawrence, T. E. An essay on Flecker. 1937 (30 copies), Garden City NY 1937.
Tillotson, G. Flecker and Byron. N & Q 183 1942.
Knight, G. W. The road to Samarkand: an essay on Flecker's Hassan. Wind & The Rain 2 1944.
—— In his The golden labyrinth, 1962.
Williams, C. In his Flecker of Dean Close, 1946.

Dunsany, Lord. James Elroy Flecker. Fortnightly Rev 159 1946.
Bullard, R. Flecker in Constantinople. Listener 15 Feb 1951.
Howarth, H. Flecker: the poet and his east. Commentary 11 1951.
Patmore, D. Flecker and Hassan. Month 5 1951.
Price, J. B. James Elroy Flecker. Contemporary Rev 191 1957.
Pozzi, L. L'opera poetica di Flecker. In Studi e ricerche di letteratura inglese e americana, ed A. Lombardo vol 1, Milan 1967.

FRANK STEWART FLINT
1885–1960

§1
Poetry

In the net of the stars. 1909.
Cadences. [1915].
The closed door by Jean de Bosschère, with a trn by Flint and an introd by M. Sinclair 1917.
Otherworld: cadences. Preface by Flint 1920.

Other Works

Some modern French poets: a commentary with specimens. 1919 (Monthly Chapbook 4).
The younger French poets. 1920 (Chapbook 17).
Economic equilibrium. [1940?]. Pamphlet.
Paying for war and peace. Southport [1941]. Pamphlet,
Flint's work appeared in the anthologies Des Imagistes, *1914.*
Some imagist poets, *1915–17 and* Imagist anthology, *1930. He translated numerous works of biography, history etc; and poems and a play,* Philip II, *by Emile Verhaeren. He was the regular contributor of a* French chronicle *to* Poetry & Drama, *1913–14.*

§2

Aldington, R. The poetry of Flint. Egoist 2 1915.
Sinclair, M. The poems of Flint. Eng Rev 32 1921.
Breunig, Le R. C. Flint: imagism's 'maître d'école'. Comparative Lit 4 1952.
Middleton, C. Documents on imagism from the papers of Flint. Review (Oxford) 15 1965.
Grant, J. In her Harold Monro and the Poetry Bookshop, 1967.

FORD MADOX FORD
formerly
JOSEPH LEOPOLD FORD
HERMANN MADOX HUEFFER
1873–1939

See cols 569–75, below.

GEORGE SUTHERLAND FRASER
b. 1915

§1
Poetry

Home town elegy. 1944.
The fatal landscape and other poems. [1948].
The traveller has regrets & other poems. 1948.
Leaves without a tree. [Tokyo?] 1953.
Conditions. [Nottingham] 1969.
Fraser also edited and contributed to Vaughan College Poems, *Leicester 1963.*

Other Works

The white horseman: prose and verse of the New Apocalypse. Ed J. F. Hendry and H. Treece; introd by Fraser 1941.
Vision of Scotland. 1948.
News from South America. 1949, New York 1952.
Post-war trends in English literature. [Tokyo? 1950?].
The collected poems of Keith Douglas. Ed J. Waller and Fraser 1951, 1966 (with J. C. Hall).
The modern writer and his world. 1953, New York 1953, London 1964 (rev), New York 1965.
Springtime: an anthology of young poets and writers. Ed Fraser and I. Fletcher 1953.
W. B. Yeats. 1954, 1962 (rev) (Br Council pamphlet).
Scotland: photographed by E. Smith, text by Fraser. 1955, New York 1955.
Poetry now: an anthology. Ed Fraser 1956.
Dylan Thomas. 1957 (Br Council pamphlet).
Vision and rhetoric: studies in modern poetry. 1959, New York 1960.
Ezra Pound. Edinburgh 1960 (Writers and Critics), New York [1961].
Selected poems of Robert Burns. Ed with introd by Fraser 1960.
Selections from the sacred writings of the Sikhs, translated by Trilochan Singh [et al], revised by Fraser. 1960 (Unesco Collection of Representative Works).
Lawrence Durrell: a study, with a bibliography by A. G. Thomas. 1968.
Fraser has also tr works from the French of Gabriel Marcel, Jean Mesnard, Serge Moreux and Patrice La Tour du Pin, and has contributed critical essays to a number of symposia.

§2

De Mauny, E. The poetry of G. S. Fraser. Poetry Quart 11 1949.

JOHN FREEMAN
1880–1929

§1
Poetry

Twenty poems. 1909.
Fifty poems. 1911.
Presage of victory and other poems of the time. 1916.
Stone trees and other poems. 1916.
Memories of childhood. 1918. Included in next.
Memories of childhood and other poems. 1919.
Out of the east. 1919. Duplicated for private circulation. Included in next.
Poems new and old. 1920.
Music: lyrical and narrative poems. 1921.
The red path: a narrative; and The wounded bird. Cambridge Mass 1921, London [1921] (425 copies).
The grove and other poems. 1924.
Prince Absalom. 1925. Verse play.
[Twenty poems.] [1925] (Augustan Books of Modern Poetry).
Solomon and Balkis. 1926.
Collected poems. 1928. Selection.
Last poems. Ed with an introd by J. C. Squire 1930.

Other Works

The moderns: essays in literary criticism. 1916.
Cobbett, W. A year's residence in America. Introd by Freeman [1922].
A portrait of George Moore in a study of his work. 1922 (priv ptd, 600 copies).
English portraits and essays. 1924.
Johnson, S. A journey to the western islands of Scotland. Introd by Freeman 1924, Boston 1925.
Herman Melville. 1926 (EML), New York 1926.

Letters

John Freeman's letters. Ed Gertrude Freeman and J. Squire 1936.

§2

Waugh, A. Mr John Freeman's criticism. In his Tradition and change, 1919.
Shanks, E. The poetry of Freeman. London Mercury 2 1920; rptd in his First essays on literature, 1923.
Bonnerot, L. La poésie de Freeman. Revue Anglo-américaine 6 1929.
Bliss, W. The poetry of Freeman. London Mercury 21 1930.

ROY BROADBENT FULLER
b. 1912

§1
Poetry

Poems. [1940].
The middle of a war. 1942.
A lost season. 1944.
Epitaphs and occasions. 1949.
Counterparts. 1954.
Brutus's orchard. 1957.
Collected poems 1936–1961. 1962, Philadelphia 1962. Selection, with unpbd poems.
Buff. 1965, Chester Springs Pa 1965.
New poems. 1968.
Roy Fuller and R. S. Thomas, selected by E. Owen 1968 (Pergamon Poets).
Offcourse. 1969 (250 copies).

Novels

Savage gold: a story of adventure. 1946. For children.
With my little eye: a mystery story for teenagers. 1948, New York 1957.
Fantasy and fugue. 1954, New York 1956.
The second curtain. 1954, New York 1956.
Image of a society. 1956, New York 1957.
The ruined boys. 1959, New York 1959 (as That distant afternoon).
The father's comedy. 1961.
The perfect fool. 1963.
My child, my sister. 1965.
Catspaw. 1966. For children.
Fuller has also edited several anthologies, a selection from Byron, and works on the law relating to building societies. He contributed an essay, Poetry: tradition and belief, to The craft of letters in England, ed J. Lehmann, 1956.

§2

Poet of the political animal. TLS 31 Aug 1962; review of Collected poems 1962.
McGuinness, F. The novels of Roy Fuller. London Mag new ser 3 1963.
Woodcock, G. Private images of public ills: the poetry of Fuller. Wascana Rev 4 1969.

'ROBERT GARIOCH',
ROBERT GARIOCH SUTHERLAND
b. 1909

17 poems for 6d, in Gaelic, Lowland Scots & English, by Somhairle MacGill-Eathain [Sorley Maclean] and Robert Garioch. Edinburgh 1940, 1940 (2nd edn with alterations). English and Scots poems by Garioch.
Chuckies on the cairn: poems in Scots & English. Hayes, Kent 1949.
The masque of Edinburgh. Edinburgh 1954.

DAVID EMERY GASCOYNE
b. 1916

Bibliographies

Atkinson, A. David Gascoyne: a check-list. Twentieth-Century Lit 6 1961. Also lists numerous anthologies containing Gascoyne's work, and some critical material.

§1
Poetry and Verse Translations

Roman balcony and other poems. 1932.
A bunch of carrots: twenty poems by B. Péret. Selected and tr by H. Jennings and Gascoyne 1936, 1936 (2nd edn rev, with 3 substituted poems, as Remove your hat).
Man's life is this meat. [1936].
Paul Eluard. Thorns of thunder: selected poems. Ed G. Reavey [1936]. 12 of the poems tr Gascoyne.
Hölderlin's madness. [1938]. Free adaptation, with introd, of poems by Hölderlin, linked with original poems.
Poems 1937–1942. 1943, 1948 (with minor alterations). Includes poems previously uncollected.
A vagrant and other poems. 1950.
Night thoughts. 1956, New York [1956].
Collected poems. Ed with an introd by R. Skelton 1965. Includes poems previously uncollected.

Other Works

Opening day. 1933. Novel.
Conquest of the irrational, by S. Dali. Tr Gascoyne, New York 1935.
A short survey of surrealism. 1935.
What is surrealism? by A. Breton. Tr Gascoyne 1936 (Criterion miscellany 43).
Outlaw of the lowest planet, [poems] by K. Patchen. Selected and introd by Gascoyne 1946.
Thomas Carlyle. 1952 (Br Council pamphlet).

§2

Lienhardt, R. G. The ultimate vision. Scrutiny 12 1944; review of Poems 1937–1942.
Kenmare, D. The long pursuit, and search for synthesis: a review of the poetry of F. Berry and Gascoyne. Wind and the Rain 2 1945.
Stanford, D. David Gascoyne. In his The freedom of poetry, 1947.
—— Gascoyne: poet of crisis. Poetry Quart 9 1947.
—— Gascoyne: a spiritual itinerary. Month 29 1963.
—— Gascoyne and the unacademics. Meanjin 23 1964.
—— Gascoyne in retrospect. Poetry Rev 56 1965.
Cronin, A. Poetry & ideas—ii: Gascoyne. London Mag 4 1957.
Jennings, E. The restoration of symbols: the poetry of Gascoyne. Twentieth Century 165 1959; rptd in her Every changing shape, 1961.
Raine, K. Gascoyne and the prophetic role. Sewanee Rev 75 1967.

'JOHN GAWSWORTH',
TERENCE IAN FYTTON
ARMSTRONG
1912–71

Bibliographies

Owen, J. H. R. John Gawsworth: some publications 1931–44. Italy 1944.
Bertram Rota, Catalogue no 25 1933, The personal library of John Gawsworth *includes 'a complete set, with some variant issues, of the writings'. It also lists some works ed Gawsworth anonymously which are omitted below.*

§1
Poetry

Confession: verses. 1931 (262 copies pbd by Twyn Barlwm Press).
Fifteen poems: three friends. 1931 (200 copies pbd by Twyn Barlwm Press).
Snowballs. [1931] (Blue Moon Booklets 9). By 'Orpheus Scrannel'.
An unterrestrial pity: being contributions towards a biography of the late Pinchbeck Lyre. Friern Barnet 1931 (250 copies, pbd by Blue Moon Press). By 'Orpheus Scrannel'.
Kingcup: suite sentimentale. 1932 (75 copies pbd by Twyn Barlwm Press), 1932 (rev as Lyrics to Kingcup) (Blue Moon Booklets 11).
Mishka and Madeleine: a poem sequence for Marcia. 1932 (225 copies, pbd by Twyn Barlwm Press).
Poems 1930–1932. 1933.
The flesh of Cypris. 1936 (500 copies).
Poems. 1938. Described as 4th edn of Poems 1930–1932.
New poems. 1939.
The mind of man. 1940.
Marlow Hill. 1941.
Legacy to love: selected poems 1931–1941. 1943. Described in The crimson thorn, 1945, below, as vol 1 of Poetical works.
Quatorze poèmes. [Séte, Algeria 1943] (7 copies). In English.
De Londres à Carthage: poèmes. Tunis [1944] (110 copies). In English.
Out of Africa: fourteen verses, November 1942–July 1943. Italy 1944.
Into Europe: ten verses, September–December 1943. Italy 1944.
The crimson thorn: poems for lovers 1931–1941 (Poetical works vol 2). Calcutta 1945.
In English fields: poems from books 1931–1941 (Poetical works vol 3). Calcutta 1945.
Snow and sand: poems from the Mediterranean 1942–1944 (Poetical works vol 5). Calcutta 1945.
Blow no bugles: poems from two wars 1942–1945 (Poetical works vol 6). Calcutta 1945.
The collected poems of John Gawsworth. 1948 [i.e. 1949]. Selection.
Vol 4 of the Poetical works *with the title* Farewell to youth: last poems 1931–1941 *was announced but apparently never pbd. Gawsworth also pbd single poems in limited edns. Pamphlets containing one or more poems by Gawsworth were pbd, with French or Italian trns by various authors, in Italy in 1944. See Owen, Bibliographies (above).*

Other Works and Works edited by Gawsworth

Above the river. 1931. Story.
Apes, japes and Hitlerism: a study and bibliography of Wyndham Lewis. 1932.
Backwaters—excursions in the shades: William Godwin; H. J. Pye; Lady Hester Stanhope; Leigh Hunt. 1932.
Known signatures: new poems. Ed with an introd by Gawsworth 1932 (80 copies), 1938 (with addns and substitutions, as Fifty years of modern verse: an anthology), Calcutta 1945 (abridged, as Fifty modern poems by forty famous poets).
Strange assembly: new stories. Ed and selected by Gawsworth 1932.
Ten contemporaries: notes towards their definitive bibliography. 1932.
Full score: 25 new stories, selected by Fytton Armstrong. 1933.
The pantomime man, by Richard Middleton. Ed with a foreword by Gawsworth 1933.
Ten contemporaries: notes towards their definitive bibliography, ser 2. 1933.

The Twyn Barlwm Press 1931–1932: a record of the venture and a list of publications. 1933 (50 copies).

Annotations on some minor writings of T. E. Lawrence. By 'G'. 1933.

The muse of monarchy: poems by kings and queens of England. Ed Gawsworth 1937.

Neo-Georgian poetry 1936–1937. Ed Gawsworth [1937].

The garland of Erica: poems by several kindly hands collected on the occasion of her birthday. By 'J.G.'. [1938] (20 copies, priv ptd).

The best short stories of M. P. Shiel. Selected by Gawsworth 1948.

The best stories of Thomas Burke. Selected by Gawsworth 1950.

From Marlowe to Shaw, by Havelock Ellis. Ed Gawsworth 1950.

The poetical works of Tennyson. Selected with an introd by Gawsworth. 1951.

Sex and marriage, by Havelock Ellis. Ed Gawsworth 1951, New York [1952].

The complete English poems of Milton. Ed with an introd by Gawsworth 1953.

Two poets 'J.G.' [John Gawsworth and John Gray]. In Frederick Rolfe and others, Aylesford 1961.

Gawsworth also edited several books by Wilfrid Ewart, the Eton, Harrow and Merchant Taylors' School vols in the Public Schools Poets series, most of the selections in Richards' Shilling Selections from Edwardian and Modern Poets, and other selections from 20th-century poets. He edited English Digest *from 1939,* Poetry Rev *1945–52,* Salamander *from 1947.*

§2

'Hugh MacDiarmid' (C. M. Grieve). When the rat-race is over: an essay in honour of the 50th birthday of John Gawsworth. 1962 (40 copies).

WILFRID WILSON GIBSON
1878–1962

Bibliographies

'Gawsworth, John' (T. I. F. Armstrong). In his Ten contemporaries: notes towards their definitive bibliographies. 1932. Includes brief essay by Gibson, Alms for oblivion.

§1

Urlyn the harper and other song. 1902.

Song. 1902. Broadsheet.

Mountain lovers. 1902. Broadsheet.

The queen's vigil and other song. 1902.

The golden helm and other verse. 1903.

The nets of love. 1905.

The stonefolds. Cranleigh 1907 (500 copies), 1916. 3 dramatic poems.

On the threshold. Cranleigh 1907 (500 copies). 3 dramatic poems.

The web of life: a book of poems. Cranleigh 1908 (300 copies).

Daily bread. 3 vols 1910, New York 1912, 1 vol London 1913, 1923 (rewritten), New York 1923. 17 dramatic poems.

Akra the slave. 1910.

Fires. 3 vols 1912, New York 1912, 1 vol London 1915.

Womenkind: a play in one act. (Pilgrim Players 24 Feb 1912). 1912, New York 1912. In verse. Rev as bk 1 of Krindlesyke 1922, below.

Borderlands. 1914, New York 1914 (with Thoroughfares, below, as Borderlands and thoroughfares).

Thoroughfares. 1914.

Battle. 1915, New York 1915.

Battle and other poems. New York 1916.

Friends. 1916.

Livelihood: dramatic reveries. 1917, New York 1917.

Poems 1904–1917. New York 1917. Selection.

Whin. [1918], New York 1918 (as Hill-tracks).

Twenty-three selected poems. [1919].

Home: a book of poems. 1920 (295 copies).

Neighbours. 1920, New York 1920.

Krindlesyke. 1922. Dramatic poem in 2 books. Early version of bk 1 pbd as Womenkind, 1912.

Yates, May. A Lancashire anthology, with introduction by Gibson. Liverpool 1923.

Kestrel edge and other plays. 1924. 5 dramatic poems.

I heard a sailor. 1925.

Sixty-three poems: selected for use in schools and colleges by E. A. Parker, with critical introduction. 1926.

Collected poems 1905–1925. 1926, New York 1931. Selection, all poems rev.

The early whistler. 1927 (Ariel Poem).

Between fairs: a comedy. 1928. Prose.

The golden room and other poems. 1928.

Hazards (poems 1928–1930). 1930.

[Thirty-two poems]. [1931]. (Augustan Books of Poetry). Selection.

Highland dawn. Bradford 1932 (250 copies).

Islands (poems 1930–1932). 1932.

Fuel. 1934. Poems and a dramatic poem.

A leaping flame—a sail! Derby 1935 (60 copies).

Coming and going. 1938.

The alert. 1941.

Challenge. 1942.

The searchlights. 1943.

The outpost. 1944.

Solway ford and other poems: a selection made by C. Williams. 1945.

Coldknuckles. 1947.

Within four walls. [1950]. 5 verse plays.

Gibson was one of the poets who contributed to New Numbers, *1914. He contributed also to the 5 vols of* Georgian Poetry, *1912–22.*

§2

Shafer, R. Two of the newest poets. Atlantic Monthly 111 1913. Gibson and Masefield.

Armstrong, M. D. Recent English poetry. Fortnightly Rev new ser 95 1914.

Bradley, W. A. Wilfrid Wilson Gibson. Dial 62 1917.

Dilla, G. P. The development of Gibson's poetic art. Sewanee Rev 30 1922.

— Wilfrid Gibson. South Atlantic Quart 26 1927.

Williams, C. In his Poetry at present, 1930.

Thouless, P. Gibson and Drinkwater. In her Modern poetic drama, 1934.

Digeon, A. Le dernier recueil poétique de Gibson. Revue Anglo-américaine 12 1934–5.

ROBERT WILLIAM VICTOR GITTINGS
b. 1911

§1

Poetry and Verse Plays

The Roman road and other poems. 1932.

The story of Psyche. Cambridge 1936. Single poem.

Wentworth Place. 1950.

The makers of violence: a play in two acts. 1951.

Through a glass, lightly. In Four one-act plays, 1952.

Famous meeting: poems narrative and lyric. 1953.

Man's estate: a play of St Richard of Chichester. In L. Lehman, Two saints' plays, 1954.

Out of this wood: a country sequence of five plays. 1955. Four in verse.

Love's a gamble: a ballad opera. [1961]. Libretto by Gittings.

This tower my prison and other poems. 1961.

Other Works

The peach blossom forest and other Chinese legends. 1951. With Jo Manton; for children.

John Keats: the living year, 21 September 1818 to 21 September 1819. 1954, Cambridge Mass 1954.

The mask of Keats: a study of problems. 1956, Cambridge Mass 1956.

Windows on history. 4 bks 1959–61. With J. G. Gittings; for children.

The living Shakespeare. Ed Gittings 1960, Greenwich Conn 1961.

Shakespeare's rival [Gervase Markham]: a study in three parts. 1960.

Some recollections, by Emma Hardy; together with some relevant poems by Thomas Hardy, with notes by Gittings. Ed Evelyn Hardy and Gittings 1961.

The story of John Keats. 1962, New York [1963]. With Jo Manton; for children.

The Keats inheritance. 1964, New York [1965]. On the estate left by John Jennings, Keats' grandfather.

Selected poems and letters of John Keats. Ed with an introd and commentary by Gittings 1966.

John Keats. 1968.

OLIVER ST JOHN GOGARTY
1878–1957
Bibliographies

Hewson, M. Gogarty's authorship of Blight. Irish Book 1 1959–60.

§1
Poetry

Cervantes: tercentenary of Don Quixote. Vice-chancellor's English verse prize, Trinity College, Dublin 1905. [Dublin, 1905?]

The ship and other poems. Dublin 1918.

An offering of swans. Dublin 1923 (300 copies).

Wild apples. Dublin 1928 (50 copies), New York [1929], Dublin 1930 (with addns and omissions and preface by W. B. Yeats) (250 copies).

Selected poems. Forewords by 'A. E.' and H. Reynolds, New York 1933.

Others to adorn. Preface by W. B. Yeats, forewords by 'A. E.' and H. Reynolds 1938.

Elbow room. Dublin 1939 (450 copies). New York 1942.

Perennial. Baltimore 1944, London 1946 [with slightly different contents].

The collected poems of Oliver St John Gogarty. 1951, New York 1954.

Unselected poems. Baltimore 1954.

Gogarty is said by O'Connor (below, §2) to have pbd a volume of verse, Hyperthuleana, in an edn of 5 copies in 1916.

Other Works

Blight: the tragedy of Dublin. An exposition in 3 acts, by Alpha and Omega. Dublin 1917. By Gogarty and Joseph O'Connor.

The enchanted trousers: a play in one act. (By 'Gideon Ouseley'.) [Dublin 1919].

A serious thing. By 'Gideon Ouseley'. [Dublin 1919.] Play.

As I was going down Sackville Street: a phantasy in fact. 1937, New York 1937. Reminiscences.

I follow Saint Patrick. 1938, New York [1938]. On the journeys of St Patrick.

Tumbling in the hay. 1939, New York [1939]. Novel.

Going native. New York 1940, London 1941. Sketches.

Mad grandeur. Philadelphia [1941], London 1943. Novel.

Mr Petunia. New York 1945, London 1946. Novel.

The fortunes and misfortunes of the famous Moll Flanders, by D. Defoe. Foreword by Gogarty 1948.

Mourning became Mrs Spendlove and other portraits, grave and gay. New York [1948].

James Augustine Joyce. Dallas 1949. Rptd from Times Herald (Dallas), 3 Apr 1949.

Intimations. New York [1950]. Essays.

Rolling down the lea. 1950. Essays.

It isn't this time of year at all! An unpremeditated autobiography. Garden City NY 1954, London 1954.

Start from somewhere else: an exposition of wit and humor, polite and perilous. Garden City NY 1955.

A week end in the middle of the week and other essays on the bias. Introductory essay by B. L. Burman, Garden City NY 1958.

William Butler Yeats: a memoir. Preface by M. Dillon, Dublin 1963.

§2

Griffin, G. Dr Oliver St John Gogarty. In his The wild geese, [1938].

Mercier, V. Oliver St John Gogarty. Poetry (Chicago) 93 1958.

Jeffares, A. N. Oliver St John Gogarty. 1961 (Chatterton lecture).

O'Connor, U. James Joyce and Oliver St John Gogarty: a famous friendship. Texas Quart 3 1960.

—— Oliver St John Gogarty: a poet and his times. 1964, New York 1964 (as The times I've seen: Oliver St John Gogarty).

Pritchett, V. S. Buck's biography. New Statesman 17 July 1964. Essay review of O'Connor's biography.

Angoff, C. In his The tone of the twenties and other essays, South Brunswick 1966.

GERALD GOULD
1885–1936

§1
Poetry

Lyrics. 1906.

Poems. 1911.

My lady's book. 1913.

Monogamy: a series of dramatic lyrics. 1918.

The happy tree and other poems. Oxford 1919.

The journey: odes and sonnets. [1920], New Haven 1921.

Beauty, the pilgrim: new poems. 1927, New York 1927.

[Thirty-three poems]. [1928] (Augustan Books of English Poetry). Selection.

Collected poems. 1929, New York 1929. Selection with 14 uncollected poems.

Other Works

An essay on the nature of lyric, illustrated from the history of English poetry. 1909 (Quain prize essay).

The helping hand: an essay in philosophy and religion for the unhappy. [1918], 1922 (with preface by Gould).

The coming revolution in Great Britain. Preface by G. Lansbury [1920].

Lady Adela. 1920. 11 satirical-political sketches.

The lesson of Black Friday [15 April 1921]: a note on trade union structure. 1921.

The English novel of to-day. 1924.

The return to the cabbage and other essays and sketches. 1926.

Democritus: or the future of laughter. 1929.

The musical glasses and other essays. 1929.

All about women: essays and parodies. 1931.

Isabel. 1932, New York 1932. Novel.

Refuge from nightmare. 1933. Essays.
The year's poetry 1934-5. Vols 1-2 1934-5. Compiled by D. K. Roberts, Gould, and J. Lehmann.
Falling angel: a play in three acts. 1936. With B. Burnham.
Gould was associate editor of Daily Herald *1919-22.*

§2

Garvin, V. G. Two Observer reviewers: Gould and Humbert Wolfe. English 5 1944.
Duffin, H. C. The poetry of Gould. English 8 1951.

WILLIAM SYDNEY GRAHAM
b. 1918

§1

Cage without grievance. Glasgow 1942.
The seven journeys. Glasgow 1944 (Poetry Scotland).
2nd poems. 1945.
The voyages of Alfred Wallis. New York 1948, London 1948 (200 copies). Single poem, rptd in next.
The white threshold. 1949, New York 1952.
The nightfishing. 1955, New York 1955.

§2

Koch, V. Graham: the technique of morality. Poetry Quart 9 1947-8.
Morgan, E. Graham's Threshold. Nine no 3 1950.
Short, R. W. S. Graham. Poetry Book Mag 4 1952.

JULIAN HENRY FRANCIS GRENFELL
1888-1915

§1

Into battle. Times 28 May 1915. Included in A crown of amaranth, 1915; The spirit of man, ed R. Bridges 1916, and in many other anthologies; also (with 4 other poems by Grenfell) in Soldier poets, 1916. Two copies ptd on single sheets by the Medici Soc 1915; one was presented to the poet's mother Lady Desborough, the other to the BM.

§2

Grenfell, E. A. P. (Lady Desborough). Pages from a family journal 1888-1915. [Eton] 1916 (priv ptd). Includes letters from Grenfell.
Meynell, V. Julian Grenfell. [1917]. Rptd from Dublin Rev 160 1917.
Moore, T. S. Soldier poets. 1: Grenfell. Eng Rev 26 1918; rptd in his Some soldier poets, 1919.
Johnston, J. H. In his English poetry of the first World War, Princeton 1964.
Bergonzi, B. Brooke, Grenfell, Sorley. In his Heroes' twilight: a study of the literature of the Great War, 1965.

GEOFFREY EDWARD HARVEY GRIGSON
b. 1905

See cols 1052-3, below.

SIR GEORGE ROSTREVOR HAMILTON
1888-1967

§1
Poetry

The search for loveliness and other verses. 1910.
Stars and fishes and other poems, by 'George Rostrevor'. London, New York 1917.
Escape and fantasy, by 'George Rostrevor'. 1918, New York 1919.
Pieces of eight, by 'George Rostrevor'. 1923.
The making. 1926.
Epigrams. 1928.
Light in 6 moods and other poems. 1930.
John Lord, satirist: a satire. 1934.
Unknown lovers and other poems. 1935.
Memoir 1887-1937 and other poems. 1938.
The sober war and other poems of 1939. 1940.
Apollyon and other poems of 1940. 1941.
The trumpeter of Saint George: an engraving by S. Gooden, with verses by G. Rostrevor Hamilton. 1941.
Death in April and other poems. Cambridge 1944, New York 1944.
Selected poems and epigrams. 1945. Includes a few previously uncollected poems.
Crazy Gaunt and other dramatic sketches. 1946. In verse.
The inner room. 1947.
The carved stone: small poems and epigrams. 1952.
The Russian sister and other poems. 1955.
Collected poems and epigrams. 1958. Selection, with some previously uncollected poems.
Landscape of the mind: late poems. 1963.

Other Works

Bergson and future philosophy: an essay on the scope of intelligence, by 'George Rostrevor'. 1921, New York 1921.
The soul of wit: a choice of English verse epigrams. Ed Hamilton 1924, New York 1926.
The Latin portrait: an anthology. Ed Hamilton 1929, New York 1929. Latin verse, with verse trns.
The Greek portrait: an anthology of English verse translations from the Greek poets, Homer to Meleager, with the corresponding Greek text. Ed Hamilton 1934, New York 1934 (425 copies).
Wit's looking-glass: French epigrams, madrigals, etc of all periods, chosen and reflected in English verse by Hamilton. 1934. Some rptd in Selected poems, 1945, above.
Poetry and contemplation: a new preface to poetics. Cambridge 1937, New York 1937.
The world to come. 1939 (I Believe ser).
Landmarks: a book of topographical verse for England and Wales. Ed Hamilton and J. Arlott, Cambridge 1943.
Hero or fool?: a study of Milton's Satan. 1944 (PEN Books).
James Hurnard, a Victorian character: being passages from The setting sun. Ed Hamilton, Cambridge 1946, New York 1946.
The tell-tale article: a critical approach to modern poetry. 1949, New York 1950.
Guides and marshals: an essay on words and imaginative order. 1956.
Walter Savage Landor. 1960 (Br Council pamphlet).
English verse epigram. 1965 (Br Council pamphlet).
Rapids of time: sketches from the past. 1965.
Hamilton edited E & S *1950 and 1956 and* Essays by Divers Hands *1955.*

JOHN FRANCIS ALEXANDER HEATH-STUBBS
b. 1918

§1
Poetry and Verse Translations

Wounded Thammuz. 1942.
Beauty and the beast. 1943.
The divided ways. 1946.
Poems from Giacomo Leopardi. Tr and introduced by Heath-Stubbs 1946.
The charity of the stars. New York [1949]. Contains some poems from Beauty and the beast, 1943, above, and some previously uncollected poems.
The swarming of the bees. 1950.
Aphrodite's garland: five ancient love poems translated by Heath-Stubbs. Saint Ives 1951.
Hafiz of Shiraz: thirty poems translated by P. Avery and Heath-Stubbs. 1952.
A charm against the toothache. 1954.
Helen in Egypt and other plays [The talking ass and The harrowing of hell]. 1958. Verse and prose.
The triumph of the muse and other poems. 1958.
The blue-fly in his head. 1962.
Selected poems. 1965. With introd. Includes previously uncollected poems.
Satires and epigrams. 1968.

Other Works

The darkling plain: a study of the later fortunes of romanticism in English poetry from George Darley to W. B. Yeats. 1950.
The forsaken garden: an anthology of poetry 1824–1909. Ed Heath-Stubbs and D. Wright 1950.
Mountains beneath the horizon [poems], by William Bell. Ed with an introd by Heath-Stubbs 1950.
Images of tomorrow: an anthology of recent poetry. Ed Heath-Stubbs 1953.
The Faber book of twentieth-century verse: an anthology of verse in Britain 1900–50. Ed Heath-Stubbs and D. Wright 1953, 1965 (rev), 1967 (rev).
Charles Williams. 1955 (Br Council pamphlet)
Collected plays by Charles Williams, with an introduction by Heath-Stubbs. 1963.
The ode. 1969.
The pastoral. 1969.
The verse satire. 1969.
Heath-Stubbs has also edited, for the Crown Classics ser, selections from the poetry of Swift, Shelley and Tennyson, and has also edited selections from Leopardi and Pope.

§2

Curtis, A. Heath-Stubbs: a symbolist poet. Poetry Quart 10 1948.
Kenner, H. The later discipline. Poetry (Chicago) 74 1949; review of The charity of the stars, 1949.
Megalli, C. H. A modern poet in Alexandria. Cairo Stud in English 1959. On Alexandria, ptd in The swarming of the bees, 1950.

JAMES FINDLAY HENDRY
b. 1912

§1
Poetry

The bombed happiness. 1942.
The orchestral mountain: a symphonic elegy. 1943.

Other Works

Albannach: a little anthology of 1938 Scots poetry. Collected by C. J. Russell and Hendry, Dingwall 1938.
The New Apocalypse: an anthology of criticism, poems and stories. Ed Hendry [1940].
The white horseman: prose and verse of the New Apocalypse. Ed Hendry and H. Treece 1941.
Scottish short stories. Ed T. and J. F. Hendry 1943. Includes Chrysalis by J. F. Hendry.
The blackbird of Ospo: stories of Jugoslavia. Glasgow 1945.
The crown and the sickle: an anthology, compiled by Hendry and H. Treece [1945].
Fernie brae: a Scottish childhood. Glasgow 1947. Novel.

SIR ALAN PATRICK HERBERT
1890–1971

Bibliographies

Fabes, G. H. The first editions of A. E. Coppard, Herbert and C. Morgan. 1933.

Selections

A. P. Herbert. 1933 (Methuen's Library of Humour). Verse and prose.

§1

Herbert was for many years a frequent contributor to Punch and many of the vols of poems and sketches etc below were rptd from it.

Poetry

Poor poems and rotten rhymes. Winchester 1910.
Play hours with Pegasus. Oxford 1912.
Half-hours at Helles. Oxford 1916.
The bomber gipsy and other poems. 1918, 1919 (rev and enlarged).
The wherefore and the why: some new rhymes for old children. 1921.
'Tinker, tailor...': a child's guide to the professions. [1922], Garden City NY 1923.
Laughing Ann and other poems. 1925, Garden City NY 1926.
She-shanties. 1926, Garden City NY 1927.
Plain Jane. 1927, Garden City NY 1927.
Ballads for broadbrows. 1930, Garden City NY 1931.
Wisdom for the wise: being 'Tinker, tailor...' and The wherefore and the why. 1930.
A book of ballads: being the collected light verse of A. P. Herbert. 1931, Garden City NY 1931 (as Ballads for broadbrows and others).
Siren song. 1940, New York 1941.
Let us be gay. 1941.
Let us be glum. 1941.
Bring back the bells. 1943.
A.T.I. 'There is no need for alarm'. 1944.
'Less nonsense'. 1944.
Light the lights. 1945.
Leave my old morale alone. Garden City NY 1948. Collects a number of earlier vols of verse.
'Full enjoyment' and other verses. 1952.
Silver stream: a beautiful tale of hare & hound for young and old. 1962.

Plays and Libretti

Double demon: an absurdity in one act. In Four one-act plays 1923; pbd separately Oxford 1926.
Riverside nights: an entertainment, written and arranged by Herbert and N. Playfair. (Lyric, Hammersmith 10 April 1926). 1926.
Two gentlemen of Soho. (Playhouse, Liverpool 3 Sept 1927). [1927] (French's Acting edn).

Fat King Melon and Princess Caraway: a drama in five scenes. [1927].

La vie Parisienne: a comic opera in three acts. (Lyric, Hammersmith 29 April 1929). 1929 (Contemporary British Dramatists). With A. Davies-Adams.

Tantivy Towers: a light opera in three acts. (Lyric, Hammersmith 16 Jan 1931). 1931, Garden City NY 1931.

Helen: a comic opera in three acts, based upon La belle Hélène by H. Meilhac and L. Halévy. English version by Herbert. (Adelphi 30 Jan 1932). 1932.

Derby day: a comic opera in three acts. (Lyric, Hammersmith 24 Feb 1932). 1931.

Big Ben: a light opera in two acts. (Adelphi 17 July 1946). 1946.

Bless the bride: a light opera in two acts. (Adelphi 26 April 1947). [1948] (French's Acting edn).

Come to the ball: or, Harlequin—a new libretto for the music of Die Fledermaus by Johann Strauss. 1951. With R. Arkell.

Other Works

Entries which are not annotated or self-explanatory consist of essays or sketches, mainly rptd from Punch.

The secret battle. 1919, New York 1920. Novel.
The house by the river. 1920, New York 1921.
Light articles only. 1921, New York 1921 (as Little rays of moonshine).
The man about town. 1923, Garden City NY 1923.
The old flame. 1925, Garden City NY 1925.
Misleading cases in the Common Law. 1927, New York 1930.
Honeybubble & Co. 1928.
The trials of Topsy. 1928.
Topsy, MP. 1929, Garden City NY 1930 (as Topsy).
More misleading cases. 1930.
The water gipsies. 1930, Garden City NY 1930. Novel.
'No boats on the river', with a technical essay by J. H. O. Bunge. 1932. On river transport for London.
Still more misleading cases. 1933.
Holy deadlock. 1934, Garden City NY 1934. Novel.
Mr Pewter: being the text of the broadcast series of talks entitled 'Mr Pewter works it out'. 1934. Dialogues on topical subjects.
Dolphin Square. [1935]. Advertising brochure.
Letter to the electors of Oxford University, General Election, November 1935. [1935].
Uncommon law: being sixty-six Misleading cases revised and collected in one volume, including ten cases not published before. 1935, New York 1936.
What a word! being an account of the principles and progress of 'The word war' conducted in Punch. 1935, Garden City NY 1936.
Mild and bitter. 1936, Garden City NY 1937.
The ayes have it: the story of the Marriage Bill. 1937, New York 1938.
Sip! Swallow! 1937, Garden City NY 1938.
General cargo. 1939, New York 1940.
Let there be liberty. 1940, New York 1940. Speech.
'Well, anyhow...': or, Little talks. 1942. Dialogues on topical subjects.
A better sky: or, Name this star. 1944. Astronomy.
The point of Parliament. 1946.
Topsy turvy. 1947.
Mr Gay's London: with extracts from the proceedings at the Sessions of the Peace, and Oyer and Terminer for the City of London and County of Middlesex in the years 1732 and 1733. 1948.
The Topsy omnibus: comprising The trials of Topsy, Topsy MP and Topsy turvy. 1949.
The English laugh. 1950. Eng Assoc presidential address 1950.
Independent member. 1950, Garden City NY 1951. Autobiography.

Number nine: or The mind-sweepers. 1951, Garden City NY 1952. Novel.
Codd's last case and other misleading cases. 1952, New York 1953.
Why Waterloo? 1952, Garden City NY 1953. Novel.
Pools pilot: or, Why not you? 1953. On football pools.
The right to marry. 1954. On divorce.
'No fine on fun': the comical history of the entertainments duty. 1957.
Made for man. 1958, Garden City NY 1958. Novel.
I object: letter to the electors of East Harrow. 1959.
Anything but action? a study of the uses and abuses of committees of inquiry. 1960.
Look back and laugh. 1960.
'Public lending right': authors, publishers & libraries—a preliminary memorandum. 1960 (priv ptd).
Libraries: free-for-all? some issues in political economy by R. Harris; The rate for the reading: an appeal to Parliament from authors and publishers prepared by Herbert. 1962.
Bardot MP? and other modern misleading cases. 1964, Garden City NY 1965.
Watch this space (six years of it): an anthology of space (fact) 4 October 1957–4 October 1963. 1964. Compiled and edited by Herbert; newspaper reports of objects in space.
The Thames. [1966].
Wigs at work. 1966 (Penguin). Selection from the vols of 'misleading cases'.
Sundials old and new: or, Fun with the sun. 1967.
The singing swan: a yachtsman's yarn. 1968. Novel.

§2

Price, R. G. G. A history of Punch. 1957.

MAURICE HENRY HEWLETT
1861–1923
See cols 600–2, below.

FREDERICK ROBERT HIGGINS
1896–1941
Bibliographies

MacManus, M. J. Bibliography of F. R. Higgins. Dublin Mag 21 1946.

§1

Salt air. Dublin 1923. Contents rptd in next.
Island blood. Foreword by AE. 1925.
The dark breed: a book of poems. 1927.
Arable holdings. Dublin 1933 (300 copies). Contents rptd in The gap of brightness, below.
Progress in Irish printing. Ed Higgins, Dublin 1936.
The gap of brightness: lyrical poems. 1940, New York 1940.
Higgins ed with W. B. Yeats the Cuala *Press broadsides new ser nos 1–12 1935 and contributed poems to the broadsides.*

§2

Loftus, R. J. Higgins: the gold and honey land. In his Nationalism in modern Anglo-Irish poetry, Madison 1964.
Clarke, A. Early memories of F. R. Higgins. Dublin Mag 6 1967.

RALPH HODGSON
1871–1962

Bibliographies
Westlake, N. M. Ralph Hodgson exhibition. Lib Chron Univ of Pennsylvania 30 1964.

§1

The last blackbird and other lines. 1907, New York 1917.
Eve and other poems. 1913 (priv ptd, At the Sign of Flying Fame). Included in Poems, 1917 below.
The bull. 1913 (priv ptd, At the Sign of Flying Fame). Included in Poems, 1917.
The song of honour. 1913 (priv ptd). Included in Poems, 1917.
The mystery and other poems. 1913 (priv ptd). Included in Poems, 1917.
Poems. 1917, New York 1917. 25 poems including 15 from previous Flying Fame pbns.
Hymn to Moloch. 1921; rptd in The skylark, 1958 below.
Silver wedding and other poems. Minerva Ohio 1941. Rptd in The skylark, 1958.
The muse and the mastiff. Pt 1, Minerva Ohio 1942 (priv ptd). Dramatic poem; rptd in The skylark, 1958.
The mystery. Bethesda Md 1956. Rptd from Poems, 1917, above.
The skylark and other poems. Ed C. Fenton 1958 (limited edn), 1959, New York 1960. Wood engravings by Reynolds Stone. Includes all poems pbd by Hodgson since Poems 1917, with several pbd before 1917 but not included in the collection of that year, and a note on date of composition and pbn of poems.
Collected poems. Ed C. Fenton 1961. Includes contents of The last blackbird, 1907, Poems, 1917, The skylark, 1958, and bibliographical note and a note on 2 uncollected poems.
The following poems were issued as broadsides, plain, coloured and on Japanese vellum (12 copies) for Flying Fame: A song, February, The beggar, The birdcatcher, The gipsy girl, The late, last rook, Playmates. Hodgson also issued, 1944–51, through Namleda & Co of Philadelphia, a series of broadsides entitled A flying scroll. They contain one or more short poems, all of which were rptd in The skylark, 1958.

§2

Lucas, E. V. The poetry of Hodgson. Nation 17 Sept 1914.
Fletcher, J. G. The poetry of Hodgson. Dial 63 1917.
Chesson, W. H. The poetry of Hodgson. Nineteenth Century 88 1920.
Maynard, T. Hodgson: the last blackbird becomes the phoenix. In his Our best poets, 1922.
Robertson, D. A. Contemporary English poets: Hodgson. Eng Jnl 15 1926.
Williams, C. In his Poetry at present, 1930.
Abel, D. How to teach students to read a poem. College Eng 16 1955. Hodgson's February.
Sitwell, Edith. Great writers rediscovered 5, Poets of delight: Bottomley and Hodgson. Sunday Times 5 May 1957.
Hodgson: a poet's journey in time. TLS 13 Feb 1959.
Takeshi, S. Hodgson in Japan. Japan Quart 9 1962.

THOMAS ERNEST HULME
1883–1917
See cols 1059–61, below.

DAVID MICHAEL JONES
b. 1895

Selections
Epoch and artist: selected writings. Ed H. Grisewood 1959, New York [1959].

§1

In parenthesis. 1937, 1961 (70 copies, with introd by T. S. Eliot), New York 1961 (unlimited edn, with the Eliot introd), London 1963.
David Jones. With introd by R. Ironside 1949 (Penguin Modern Painters).
The anathemata: fragments of an attempted writing. 1952, New York 1963.
Agenda 5 1967. David Jones special issue. Contains 6 poems, of which The wall, The dream of Private Clitus, The tutelar of the place, The hunt, together with the next 2 separately ptd items, constitute a 'work-in-progress'.
The fatigue, c. A.U.C. DCCLXXXIV, tantus labor non sit cassus. Cambridge 1965 (priv ptd, 298 copies).
The tribune's visitation. 1969.

§2

Gill, E. David Jones. Artwork 6 1930; rptd (rev) in his In a strange land, 1944. On Jones as artist.
Hague, R. Jones: a reconnaissance. Twentieth Century 168 1960; rptd in Agenda 5 1967 below.
Johnston, J. H. Jones: the heroic vision. Rev of Politics 24 1962.
Swank, E. R. Jones: In parenthesis. In Carnegie Inst of Technology (Pittsburgh) Lectures on modern novelists, 1963.
Bergonzi, B. Remythologizing: Jones's In parenthesis. In his Heroes' twilight, a study of the literature of the Great War, 1965.
Blamires, D. The ordered world: The anathemata of Jones. REL 7 1966; rptd (rev) in next.
Agenda 5 1967. David Jones special issue, with 15 articles on Jones.
Blissett, W. Jones: himself at the cave-mouth. UTQ 36 1967.

JAMES AUGUSTINE ALOYSIUS JOYCE
1882–1941
See cols 444–72, below.

PATRICK KAVANAGH
1905–1967

§1

Ploughman and other poems. 1936.
The green fool. 1938, New York 1939. Autobiography.
The great hunger. Dublin 1942 (250 copies), London 1966 [with minor changes]. Pt previously pbd as The old peasant in Horizon 5 1942. Single poem.
A soul for sale: poems. 1947.
Tarry Flynn. 1948, New York 1949. Novel.
Recent poems. New York 1958 (25 copies ptd on Peter Kavanagh's hand press).
Come dance with Kitty Stobling and other poems. 1960, Philadelphia 1964.
Collected poems. 1964, New York 1964.
Self portrait. Dublin 1964. Prose.
Collected prose. 1967.
He edited, and with his brother Peter wrote most of, Kavanagh's Weekly; a journal of literature and politics (Dublin), which ran for 13 nos in 1952.

§2

Cronin, A. Innocence and experience: the poetry of Kavanagh. Nimbus 3 1956.

Jordan, J. Mr Kavanagh's progress. Studies 49 1960.

Payne, B. The poetry of Kavanagh. Ibid.

Hewitt, J. The cobbler's son: a consideration of the work of Kavanagh. Threshold 5 1961.

Potts, P. Kavanagh, the poems and the poet. London Mag new ser 2 1963.

Warner, A. A poet of the countryside. REL 5 1964.

—— An angry foghorn: Kavanagh as critic. Dublin Mag 7 1968.

Sealy, D. The writings of Kavanagh. Dublin Mag 4 1965.

Moore, J. R. Now Yeats has gone: three Irish poets. Hollins Critic 3 1966. On A. Clarke, Kavanagh, D. Devlin.

Rosenthal, M. L. Contemporary Irish poetry: Kavanagh. In his The new poets, 1967.

Mahon, D. Patrick Kavanagh: a tribute in poetry and prose. Dublin Mag 7 1968.

Wright, D. Patrick Kavanagh 1905–1967. London Mag 8 1968.

Fahey, W. A. Patrick Kavanagh: a comment. Renascence 21 1969.

FRANK SAMUEL HERBERT KENDON
1893–1955

§1

Mural paintings in English churches during the middle ages: an introductory essay on folk influence in religious art. 1923.

Poems by four authors: J. R. Ackerley, A. Y. Campbell, E. Davison, F. Kendon. Cambridge 1923.

Poems and sonnets. 1924.

Arguments and emblems. 1925.

A life and death of Judas Iscariot. 1926.

The small years. Introd by W. de la Mare, Cambridge 1930, 1950 (with new ch, Christmas day). Autobiography.

The adventure of poetry. 1932.

Tristram. 1934.

The cherry minder. 1935.

The flawless stone: a poem on the theme proposed, 'Nature is the art of God'. Cambridge 1942. Seatonian Prize poem.

The time piece: a poem. Cambridge 1945.

Each silver fly: the Seatonian prize poem for 1945 upon the subject prescribed, 'A just balance and scales are the Lord's'. Cambridge 1946.

Cage & wing. Cambridge 1947. Seatonian Prize poem.

Jacob & Thomas: darkness. Cambridge 1950.

Martin Makesure. 1950. Novel.

Thirty-six Psalms: an English version. Cambridge 1963.

A long poem, The interrupter, was pbd in Fortnightly 147 1940 and not rptd.

§2

Davison, E. Kendon and analyzed rhyme. In his Some modern poets, New York 1928.

Warren, C. H. Frank Kendon. Bookman (London) 78 1930.

SIDNEY ARTHUR KILWORTH KEYES
1922–43

§1

Eight Oxford poets; selected by M. Meyer and Keyes. 1941. Contains 6 poems by Keyes.

The iron laurel. 1942.

The cruel solstice. 1943.

Collected poems. Ed with a memoir and notes by M. Meyer 1945, New York [1947] (with preface by H. Read).

Minos of Crete: plays and stories. Ed with selections from his notebook and letters and some early unpbd poems by M. Meyer 1948. Also containing The artist in society, rptd from P. Colson, The future of faith, [1942]. J. Guenther, Sidney Keyes, 1967 (§2 below), contains one unpbd poem. Keyes was joint-editor of Cherwell May to June 1941.

§2

Vallette, J. Trois poètes anglais morts à la guerre. Mercure de France 1 April 1947. Owen, Alun Lewis, and Keyes.

Guenther, J. Sidney Keyes: a biographical inquiry. 1967.

JAMES FALCONER KIRKUP
b. 1918

§1
Poetry and Verse Translations

The cosmic shape: an interpretation of myth and legend, with three poems, by R. Nichols and J. Kirkup. 1946. Includes The glass fable and The sleeper in the earth, poems by Kirkup.

The drowned sailor and other poems. 1947.

The creation. Hull 1951.

The submerged village and other poems. 1951.

A correct compassion and other poems. 1952.

The vision and other poems by Todja Tartschoff. Tr Kirkup and L. Sirombo 1953.

A spring journey and other poems of 1952–1953. 1954.

Upon this rock: a dramatic chronicle of Peterborough Cathedral. 1955.

The true mistery of the Nativity. Adapted and tr from the French medieval mystery cycle of A. and S. Gréban 1956.

The descent into the cave and other poems. 1957.

Five German plays. In The classic theatre, ed E. R. Bentley, vol 2, Garden City NY 1959. Contains Schiller's Don Carlos and Kleist's The prince of Homburg, both tr in verse by Kirkup.

Refusal to conform: last and first poems. 1963.

Paper windows: poems from Japan. 1968.

Other Works

The only child: an autobiography of infancy. 1957.

Sorrow, passions and alarms: an autobiography of childhood. 1959.

The love of others. 1962. Novel.

These horned islands: a journal of Japan. 1962, New York 1962.

Tropic temper: a memoir of Malaya. 1963.

Japan industrial: some impressions of Japanese industries. Osaka 1964.

Tokyo. 1966, South Brunswick NJ 1966.

Bangkok. 1968, South Brunswick NJ 1968.

Filipinescas: travels through the Philippine Islands. 1968.

One man's Russia. 1968.

Shepherding winds: an anthology of poetry from east and west. 1969.
Streets of Asia. 1969.
Kirkup also translated works, mainly novels, from French and German.

EDMUND GEORGE VALPY KNOX
1881–1971

Selections

E. V. Knox, 'Evoe'. 1934 (Methuen's Library of Humour), New York 1934 (as Bluebells). Prose and verse.

§1
Poetry

The brazen lyre. 1911.
A little loot. 1920. Verse, and sketches in prose.
'Parodies regained'. 1921.
These liberties. 1923. Parodies in verse and prose.
Poems of impudence. 1926, Garden City NY 1927.
A winter sports alphabet: pictures by Joyce Dennys, verses by Evoe. 1926.
I'll tell the world! A guide to the greatness of England, mainly intended for American use. 1927, Garden City NY 1928. Sketches and verse.
Blue feathers. 1929.
Folly calling. 1932.

Other Works

Fiction as she is wrote. 1923, New York 1924. Sketches.
An hour from Victoria and some other excursions. 1924. Sketches.
Fancy now. 1924. Sketches.
Quaint specimens. 1925. Sketches.
Gorgeous times. 1926. Essays and sketches.
It occurs to me. 1926. Sketches.
Awful occasions. 1927. Sketches.
Here's misery! A book of burlesques. 1928.
Wonderful outings. 1928. Sketches.
Mr Punch on the links. Ed Knox 1929, New York 1929.
This other Eden. 1929. Sketches.
Things that annoy me. 1930. Sketches.
Humorous verse: an anthology chosen by Knox. 1931.
Slight irritations. 1931. Sketches.
On running after one's hat and other whimsies, by G. K. Chesterton; selected by Knox. New York 1933.
The perfect salesman, by Stephen Leacock. Ed Knox, New York 1934.
The mechanism of satire: the Leslie Stephen lecture 10 May 1951. 1951.
Knox contributed to Punch *as 'Evoe', and the contents of most of his books were rptd from it. He edited* Punch *1932–49, and* Methuen's Library of humour *1933–35.*

§2

Price, R. G. G. A history of Punch. 1957.

DAVID HERBERT LAWRENCE
1885–1930

See cols 481–503, below.

FRANCIS LEDWIDGE
1891–1917

Bibliographies

Danielson, H. In his Bibliographies of modern authors, 1921.

Collections

Complete poems. 1919, New York 1919, London 1944 (with two corrections).

§1

Songs of the fields. 1916.
Songs of peace. 1917.
Last songs. 1918.
All the above have introds by Lord Dunsany.

§2

Chase, L. Francis Ledwidge. Century Mag 95 1917–18; rptd in Cornhill Mag new ser 48 1920. Includes long letter from Ledwidge.
Drinkwater, J. The poetry of Ledwidge. Edinburgh Rev 228 1918; rptd in his The muse in council, 1925.
The peasant poet of Meath. Irish Book Lover 9 1918.
Tynan, K. Francis Ledwidge. Eng Rev 26 1918; rptd with slight alterations in her The years of shadow, 1919.
Moore, T. S. Francis Ledwidge. In his Some soldier poets, 1919.
Aiken, C. Idiosyncrasy and tradition. Dial 68 1920. Essay-review of Complete poems.
Francis Ledwidge. Irish Book Lover 12 1920.
Zucker, L. C. The art of a minor poet. South Atlantic Quart 21 1922.
Dunsany, Lord. Francis Ledwidge. Fortnightly 158 1945.

LAURIE LEE
b. 1914

§1
Poetry and Verse Plays

The sun my monument. 1944, Garden City NY 1947.
The bloom of candles: verse from a poet's year. 1947.
The voyage of Magellan: a dramatic chronicle for radio. 1948.
Peasant's priest: a play. Canterbury [1952]. Pbd for the Festival of the Friends of Canterbury Cathedral.
My many-coated man. 1955, New York 1957.
[Thirty-nine poems]. 1960 (Pocket Poets). Selection.

Other Works

Land at war (The official story of British farming 1939–44). 1945. Anon. Ministry of Information pamphlet.
Vassos the goatherd: a story of Cyprus. 1947. An adaptation by J. Maddison of Lee's notes and script for the film Cyprus is an island.
We made a film in Cyprus. 1947. With R. Keene.
An obstinate exile. Los Angeles 1951 (priv ptd, 101 copies). Rptd from Listener 13 Sept 1951. Lee's reaction as a countryman to London.
A rose for winter: travels in Andalusia. 1955, New York [1956?].
Epstein: a camera study of the sculptor at work by G. Ireland. Introd by Lee 1958.
Cider with Rosie. 1959, New York 1960 (as The edge of day: a boyhood in the west of England).
Man must move: the story of transport. [1960], Garden City NY 1960, (as The wonderful world of transportation), London 1969 (rev and enlarged as The wonderful world of transport). With D. Lambert.
The firstborn. 1964. On his daughter.
As I walked out one midsummer morning. 1969. Autobiography.

RUDOLPH JOHN FREDERICK LEHMANN
b. 1907

Poetry
A garden revisited and other poems. 1931.
The noise of history. 1934.
Forty poems. 1942.
The sphere of glass and other poems. 1944.
The age of the dragon: poems 1930–1951. 1951, New York [1952]. Selection, with uncollected poems.
Collected poems 1930–1963. 1963. Selection, with uncollected poems.
Christ the hunter. 1965. Prose poems.

Other Works
Prometheus and the Bolsheviks. 1937, New York 1938. Travel.
Ralph Fox. A writer in arms. Ed Lehmann, T. A. Jackson, C. Day Lewis 1937. Introd to The imaginative writer by Lehmann.
Evil was abroad. 1938. Novel.
Down river: a Danubian study. 1939. Travel.
New writing in England. New York 1939 (Critics Group pamphlet).
Poems for Spain. Ed S. Spender and Lehmann 1939.
New writing in Europe. 1940 (Pelican), New York 1940.
Poems from New Writing, 1936–1946. 1946.
Demetrios Capetanakis: a Greek poet in England. 1947.
French stories from New Writing, selected by Lehmann. 1947, New York 1948 (as Modern French stories).
Shelley in Italy: an anthology. Selected with an introd by Lehmann 1947.
English stories from New Writing. Ed Lehmann 1951, New York 1951 (as Best stories from New Writing).
Edith Sitwell. 1952 (Br Council pamphlet).
The open night. 1952, New York 1952. Essays on literature.
Pleasures of New Writing: an anthology of poems, stories and other prose pieces from the pages of New Writing. Ed Lehmann 1952.
The whispering gallery: autobiography I. 1955, New York 1955.
The Chatto book of modern poetry, 1915–1955. Ed C. Day Lewis and Lehmann 1956.
The craft of letters in England: a symposium. Ed Lehmann 1956, Boston 1957.
Modern French stories. Ed Lehmann 1956.
Coming to London. Ed Lehmann 1957. Reminiscences by various writers.
Italian stories of today. Ed Lehmann 1959.
I am my brother: autobiography II. 1960, New York 1960.
Ancestors and friends. 1962. On the author's family, etc.
Selected poems of Edith Sitwell. Chosen with an introd by Lehmann 1965.
The ample proposition: autobiography III. 1966.
A nest of tigers: Edith, Osbert and Sacheverell Sitwell in their times. 1968.
In my own time: memoirs of a literary life. Boston 1969. Reissue in 1 vol of The whispering gallery, I am my brother, and The ample proposition.
Lehmann edited New Writing, *1936–9 (continued as* Folios of New Writing, *1940–1, and as* New Writing & Daylight, *1942–6);* Penguin New Writing, *1940–50;* Orpheus: a symposium of the arts, *1948–9;* London Mag, *1954–61. In or about 1928 he issued a set of 10 priv ptd single sheet poems, illustrated with his own wood engravings.*

§2
Jarka, H. Pre-war Austria as seen by Spender, Isherwood and Lehmann. Proc Pacific Northwest Conference on Foreign Languages 15 1964.

ALUN LEWIS
1915–44

Bibliographies
Williams, J. S. Alun Lewis: a select bibliography. Anglo-Welsh Rev 16 1967. With writings on Lewis, including reviews.

§1
Poetry
Two poems. Llanllechid [1941] (Caseg broadsheet). Contains Raiders' dawn and Song of innocence.
Raiders' dawn and other poems. 1942.
Ha! Ha! among the trumpets: poems in transit. Foreword by Robert Graves 1945.
Selected poetry and prose, with a biographical introduction by I. Hamilton. 1966. Includes previously uncollected poems.

Other Works
The last inspection. 1942, New York 1943. Short stories.
Letters from India, with a note by Mrs Alun Lewis and a preface by A. L. Rowse, Cardiff 1946. Included in In the green tree, below.
In the green tree, with a preface by A. L. Rowse. 1948 (for 1949). Postscript by Gwyn Jones. Contains Letters from India and 6 uncollected short stories.
Williams (Bibliography, above) lists printings of Lewis's letters. The same issue of Anglo-Welsh Rev *prints three letters from Lewis to Robert Graves. Some more letters were pbd as* One modern poet at war, TLS *12 July 1947.*

§2
Jones, G. Alun Lewis, 1915–1944. Welsh Rev 3 1944. This issue also contains a story and ten poems by Lewis, rptd in In the green tree, and Ha! Ha! among the trumpets, respectively.
Symes, G. Muse in India: an aspect of Alun Lewis. English 6 1947.
Vallette, J. Trois poètes anglais morts à la guerre. Mercure de France 1 April 1947. Owen, Lewis and Keyes.
Rowse, A. L. Alun Lewis: a foreword. In his The English past, 1951; rptd preface to Lewis's Letters from India, above.
Lehmann, J. A human standpoint. In his The open night, 1952.
Williams, J. S. The poetry of Alun Lewis. Anglo-Welsh Rev 14 1964.
— The short stories of Alun Lewis. Anglo-Welsh Rev 14 1964–5.

JACK LINDSAY
b. 1900
See cols 635–6, below.

NORMAN MACCAIG
b. 1910

§1
Far cry. 1943.
The inward eye. 1946.
Riding lights. 1955, New York 1956.
The Sinai sort. 1957, New York 1957.
Honour'd shade: an anthology of new Scottish poetry to mark the bicentenary of the birth of Robert Burns. Selected and ed MacCaig, Edinburgh 1959.
A common grace. 1960.
A round of applause. 1962.
Measures. 1965.

Surroundings. 1966.
Rings on a tree. 1968.
A man in my position. 1969.

§2

Smith, I. S. The poetry of MacCaig. Saltire Rev 6 1959.

'HUGH MACDIARMID', CHRISTOPHER MURRAY GRIEVE
b. 1892

Bibliographies

Aitken, W. R. C. M. Grieve/Hugh MacDiarmid. Bibliotheck 1 1958. Includes critical references; minor addns by D. M. Craig, 2 1959.
— A check list of books and periodicals—written, translated, edited, published or introduced by C. M. Grieve (Hugh MacDiarmid). In Hugh MacDiarmid: a festschrift, ed K. D. Duval and S. Goodsir Smith 1962, §2, below.
Buthlay, K. In his Hugh MacDiarmid, 1964, §2, below. Select bibliography includes criticism.
Glen, D. In his Hugh MacDiarmid and the Scottish renaissance, 1964, §2, below. Includes chronological bibliography, listing selection of uncollected prose contributions to periodicals, and periodicals to which MacDiarmid contributed.
— The literary masks of MacDiarmid. Glasgow 1964 (55 copies). On his pseudonymous writings.

§1
Poetry

Sangschaw. Edinburgh and London 1925.
Penny wheep. Edinburgh and London 1926.
A drunk man looks at the thistle. Edinburgh and London 1926, Glasgow 1953 (with introd by D. Daiches and note by the author), Edinburgh 1956 (rev).
The lucky bag. Edinburgh 1927 (Porpoise Press broadsheet).
To Circumjack Cencrastus: or, the curly snake. Edinburgh and London 1930.
First hymn to Lenin and other poems, with an introductory essay by 'AE' (George William Russell). 1931 (450 copies).
O wha's been here afore me, lass. 1931 (Blue Moon poem for Christmas) (100 copies). Rptd from A drunk man looks at the thistle, above.
Tarras. Edinburgh 1932 (20 copies); rptd in next.
Scots unbound and other poems. Stirling 1932 (350 copies).
Second hymn to Lenin. Thakeham Sussex [1932] (100 copies).
Stony limits and other poems. 1934.
Selected poems. 1934 (Macmillan's Contemporary poets).
Second hymn to Lenin and other poems. 1935.
Dìreadh. Dunfermline [1938] (20 copies).
Speaking for Scotland. 1939 (Lumphen Press broadsheet 3).
Cornish heroic song for Valda Trevlyn. Glasgow [1943]; rptd in A kist of whistles, 1947 below.
Selected poems. Ed R. C. Saunders, Glasgow [1944] (Poetry Scotland).
Poems of the east-west synthesis. 1946.
Speaking for Scotland: selected poems. Introd by Compton Mackenzie, Baltimore 1946 (Distinguished Poets ser). Similar to Selected poems 1934, omitting 2 and adding 3 poems.
A kist of whistles: new poems. Glasgow [1947] (Poetry Scotland).
Selected poems. Ed O. Brown, Glasgow 1954, 1955 (as Poems).
In memoriam James Joyce: from A vision of world language. Glasgow 1955.

Stony limits and Scots unbound and other poems. Edinburgh 1956. Includes poems suppressed in 1934 edn of Stony limits.
The battle continues. Edinburgh 1957.
Three hymns to Lenin. Edinburgh [1957].
The kind of poetry I want. Edinburgh 1961 (300 copies).
Bracken hills in autumn. 1962.
Collected poems. New York 1962, Edinburgh 1962, New York [1967] (with corrigenda and enlarged glossary). Selection, with previously uncollected poems.
Poetry like the hawthorn: from In memoriam James Joyce. Hemel Hempstead 1962.
Poems to paintings by William Johnstone, 1933. Edinburgh 1963. Most previously uncollected.
The ministry of water: two poems. Glasgow 1964 (125 copies).
Six vituperative verses. 1964 (priv ptd) (25 copies).
The terrible crystal: a vision of Scotland. Skelmarlie 1964 (55 copies).
The fire of the spirit: two poems. Glasgow 1965 (350 copies).
Whuchulls: a poem. Preston [1966] (100 copies); rptd in next.
A lap of honour. 1967.
On a raised beach: a poem. Preston 1967 (200 copies).
Early lyrics. Ed with an introd by J. K. Annand, Preston [1968] (350 copies).
A clyack-sheaf. 1969.

Other Works

A number of early pamphlets, mainly single articles, rptd from periodicals, have been omitted. No distinction has been made between items signed 'Hugh MacDiarmid' and those signed 'C. M. Grieve'.

Northern numbers: being representative selections from certain living Scottish poets. 3 sers Edinburgh and London 1920–2. Ed Grieve, and containing some of his poems. Ser 3 was pbd by him at Montrose.
Annals of the five senses. Montrose 1923, Edinburgh 1930. Poems and 'psychological sketches'.
Contemporary Scottish studies: first series. 1926.
Robert Burns 1759–1796. [1926] (Augustan Books of Poetry).
Albyn: or, Scotland and the future. 1927, New York 1927 (Today and Tomorrow ser).
Tenreiro, R. M. de. The handmaid of the Lord. 1930. Anon trn by MacDiarmid.
Living Scottish poets. Ed Grieve [1931] (Augustan Books of Poetry).
At the sign of the thistle: a collection of essays. [1934].
Five bits of Miller. 1934 (40 copies). Prose sketch.
Scottish scene: or, the intelligent man's guide to Albyn. 1934. With 'Lewis Grassic Gibbon' (J. L. Mitchell).
MacDonald, A. The Berlinn of Clanranald. Tr from the Scots Gaelic by MacDiarmid, St Andrews 1935 (100 copies).
Scottish eccentrics. 1936.
The islands of Scotland: Hebrides, Orkneys and Shetlands. 1939, New York 1939.
The golden treasury of Scottish poetry. Ed MacDiarmid 1940.
Auntran blads: an outwale o verse, by Douglas Young. Selected by MacDiarmid. Glasgow 1943.
Lucky poet: a self-study in literature and political ideas, being the autobiography of Hugh MacDiarmid (Christopher Murray Grieve). 1943. p. 172 is a cancel in most copies.
Collected poems, by William Soutar. Ed with an introd by MacDiarmid 1948.
Poems, by Robert Burns, selected and introduced by MacDiarmid 1949.
Cunninghame Graham: a centenary study. Glasgow [1952].

Selections from the poems of William Dunbar. Ed with an introd by MacDiarmid, Edinburgh 1952.

Francis George Scott: an essay on the occasion of his seventy-fifth birthday. Edinburgh 1955.

Selected poems of William Dunbar. Ed with an introd by MacDiarmid, Glasgow 1955.

Burns today and tomorrow. Edinburgh 1959.

David Hume, Scotland's greatest son: a transcript of the lecture given at Edinburgh University, April 1961. Edinburgh [1961?].

The man of—almost—independent mind. Edinburgh 1962. On David Hume.

Robert Burns. Love songs. Selected [with introd] by MacDiarmid 1962 (Pocket Poets).

The ugly birds without wings. Edinburgh 1962. Reply to attacks by I. H. Finlay et al.

When the rat-race is over: an essay in honour of the 50th birthday of John Gawsworth. 1962 (40 copies).

Martinson, H. Aniara. Adapted from the Swedish by MacDiarmid and E. M. Schubert. 1963.

Sydney Goodsir Smith. Edinburgh [1963] (135 copies). An address.

The company I've kept. 1966. Autobiography.

Scotland. In Celtic nationalism, 1968.

The uncanny Scot: a selection of prose by MacDiarmid, ed with an introd by K. Buthlay 1968.

Glen (Bibliographies, above) lists MacDiarmid's introds and other contributions to books, and the anthologies in which his work appeared. MacDiarmid edited the following periodicals: Scottish Chapbook 1922–3, Scottish Nation 1923, Northern Rev 1924, Voice of Scotland 1938–58, and the 5th no (PEN Congress no) of Scottish Art & Letters 1950. He was the 'guest editor' of the 4th and last no of Poetry Scotland 1949.

§2

Frost, A. C. M'Diarmid: Scotland's vortex-maker. Bookman (London) 86 1934.

Leavis, F. R. MacDiarmid. Scrutiny 4 1935. Review of Second hymn to Lenin.

Gregory, H. Contrast in satires. Poetry 49 1937. Review of Second hymn to Lenin.

Shepherd, N. The poetry of MacDiarmid. Aberdeen Univ Rev 26 1939.

Southworth, J. G. MacDiarmid. Sewanee Rev 48 1940; rptd in his Sowing the spring, 1940.

Saunders, R. C. The thistle in the lion's mouth: notes on the poetry of MacDiarmid. Life & Letters Today 44 1945.

Law, T. S. MacDiarmid—a new angle. New Scot 3 1947.

Scott, A. Scots since Sangschaw. Life & Letters 55 1947.

Daiches, D. MacDiarmid and Scottish poetry. Poetry 72 1948.

—— MacDiarmid's new poem. Lines Rev 9 1955. On In memoriam James Joyce.

Ramsay, M. P. Christopher Grieve: makar, fechter and J.P. New Scot 4 1948.

Aitken, M. B. The poetry of MacDiarmid. Scottish Art & Letters 4 1950.

Glicksberg, C. I. MacDiarmid: Marxist Messiah. Prairie Schooner 26 1952.

Leslie, A. The politics and poetry of MacDiarmid. Glasgow [1952]. Rptd from National Weekly.

—— Jerqueing every idioticon: some notes on Mac-Diarmid's Joyce poem. Voice of Scotland 6 1955.

Craig, D. MacDiarmid's poetry. Voice of Scotland 7 1956.

—— A rare poet. Cambridge Rev 78 1956–7. Review of Stony limits and Scots unbound.

Morgan, E. Jujitsu for the educated: reflections on the poem In memorian James Joyce. Twentieth Century 160 1956.

—— The case of MacDiarmid. Review (Oxford) no 3 1962. Essay-review of Collected poems.

—— MacDiarmid and Sherrington. N & Q 208 1963. A passage in In memoriam James Joyce.

Macmillan, A. MacDiarmid. Burns Chron 3rd ser 6 1957.

Singer, B. Scarlet eminence: a study of the poetry of MacDiarmid. Encounter 8 1957.

Blaeser, R. 'New Scots Renascence': literarische und linguistische Einführung in das Wesen der Dichtung MacDiarmids und seiner Schule. Düren 1958.

Summers, J. MacDiarmid and the Scottish renaissance. New Zealand Monthly Rev 15 1961.

Duval, K. D. and S. G. Smith (ed). Hugh MacDiarmid: a Festschrift. Edinburgh 1962.

Glen, D. MacDiarmid, rebel poet and prophet: a short note on the occasion of his seventieth birthday. Hemel Hempstead 1962 (55 copies).

—— Hugh MacDiarmid (Christopher Murray Grieve) and the Scottish renaissance. Edinburgh 1964.

Kocmanová, J. Art and revolution in the poetry of MacDiarmid. Philologica Pragensia 5 1962.

Milner, I. The poetic vision of MacDiarmid. Landfall 16 1962.

Buthlay, K. Hugh MacDiarmid (C. M. Grieve). Edinburgh 1964 (Writers & Critics).

Arundel, H. MacDiarmid and the Scottish tradition. In Essays in honour of William Gallacher, ed E. Lingner et al, Berlin 1966.

Keir, W. A. S. MacDiarmid and the Scottish renaissance. English (London) 16 1967.

Smith, I. C. The golden lyric: an essay on the poetry of MacDiarmid. Preston 1967.

Agenda 5–6 1967–8. MacDiarmid and Scottish poetry. Contains poems by MacDiarmid and T. Scott, Lament for the great music; J. Montague, The seamless garment and the muse; W. Cookson, Some notes on MacDiarmid; A. Scott, MacDiarmid and the Scots tradition; D. Glen, MacDiarmid: supporting roles; H. Moore, Nationalism to social revolution: MacDiarmid in politics; K. Cox, MacDiarmid's neoplatonism; M. P. MacDiarmid, Mac-Diarmid and the colloquial category.

Lundkvist, A. Rebell och utopist: MacDiarmid. Ord och Bild 77 1968.

THOMAS MACDONAGH
1878–1916

Most of MacDonagh's mss are in the National Library, Dublin. See also Parks, Bibliographies, below.

Bibliographies

Parks, E. W. and A. W. In their Thomas MacDonagh: the man, the patriot, the writer, Athens Georgia [1967], §2, below.

§1

April and May, with other verse. Dublin [1903].

Through the ivory gate. Dublin [1903].

The exodus: a sacred cantata. [1904]. Words by Mac-Donagh, music by B. Palmiers.

The golden joy. Dublin 1906.

When the dawn is come: a tragedy in three acts. Dublin 1908 (Abbey Theatre ser 10).

Songs of myself. Dublin 1910.

Lyrical poems. Dublin 1913.

Thomas Campion and the art of English poetry. Dublin 1913.

Literature in Ireland: studies, Irish and Anglo-Irish. Dublin 1916.

Poems of the Irish Revolutionary Brotherhood: Mac-Donagh, P. H. Pearse, J. M. Plunkett, Sir R. Casement. Ed P. Colum and E. J. O'Brien, Boston 1916.

The poetical works of Thomas MacDonagh. Ed James Stephens 1916, New York [1917?].

Pagans: a modern play in two conversations. Dublin and London 1920.

Poems, selected by his sister. Dublin [1925].

§2

Loftus, R. J. In his Nationalism in modern Anglo-Irish poetry, Madison 1964.

Colum, P. MacDonagh and his poetry. Dublin Mag 5 1966.

Parks, E. W. and A. W. Thomas MacDonagh: the man, the patriot, the writer. Athens Georgia [1967].

Thompson, W. I. In his Imagination of an insurrection—Dublin, Easter 1916: a study of an ideological movement, New York 1967.

FREDERICK LOUIS MACNEICE
1907–63

Some of MacNeice's mss were sold at Sotheby's on 12 Dec 1961. Many mss are now in the Library of the Univ of Texas. See F. G. Stoddard, The Louis MacNeice collection, *Lib Chron of the Univ of Texas 8 1968.*

Bibliographies

Press, J. In his Louis MacNeice, 1965, §2, below. (Br Council pamphlet). Select bibliography includes a list of important contributions to periodicals, notes on unpbd materials and some biographical and critical studies.

§1
Poetry and Verse Translations

Blind fireworks. 1929.

Poems. 1935, New York [1937].

The Agamemnon of Aeschylus. 1936, New York 1937. Verse trn.

Letters from Iceland. 1937, New York [1937]. Verse and prose. With W. H. Auden.

The earth compels. 1938.

I crossed the Minch. 1938. *See* Other works, below.

Autumn journal. 1939, New York [1939].

The last ditch. Dublin 1940.

Poems 1925–1940. New York [1940].

Selected poems. 1940.

Plant and phantom. 1941.

Springboard: poems 1941–1944. 1944, New York 1945.

Holes in the sky: poems 1944–1947. 1948, New York 1949.

Collected poems 1925–1948. 1949. Selection, with revision of late poems. Omits trns.

Goethe's Faust: parts 1 and 2; an abridged version translated by MacNeice. 1951, New York 1953.

Ten burnt offerings. 1952, New York 1953.

Autumn sequel: a rhetorical poem in xxvi cantos. 1954. Sequel to Autumn journal, 1939, above.

The other wing. 1954 (Ariel Poem); rptd in next.

Visitations. 1957, New York 1958.

Eighty-five poems. 1959, New York 1959. Selection.

Solstices. 1961, New York 1961.

The burning perch. 1963, New York 1963.

Selected poems: selected and introduced by W. H. Auden. 1964.

The collected poems of Louis MacNeice, edited by E. R. Dodds. 1966. Excludes juvenilia etc which were omitted from Collected poems, 1949; trns however are included. Omitted poems are listed in appendix.

Plays

The sale of some MacNeice mss at Sotheby's included duplicated scripts of unpbd radio and other plays. The BBC archives also hold copies of these.

Out of the picture: a play in two acts. (Group Theatre, at the Westminster 5 Dec 1937). 1937, New York 1938. Verse and prose.

Christopher Columbus: a radio play. (BBC Home Service 12 Oct 1942). 1944 (with introd on radio drama), 1963 (school edn with new introd).

The dark tower and other radio scripts. 1947, 1964 (containing The dark tower only). Includes further comments on radio drama; The dark tower: a radio parable play (BBC Home Service 1 Jan 1946); Sunbeams in his hat: a study of Tchehov as a man (BBC Home Service 16 July 1944); The nosebag: a Russian folk story (BBC Home Service 13 March 1944); The March Hare saga: 1, The March Hare resigns (BBC Home Service 29 March 1945), 2, Salute to All Fools (BBC Home Service 1 April 1946).

The mad islands (BBC Third Programme 4 April 1962); and The administrator (BBC Third Programme 10 March 1961): two radio plays. 1964.

One for the grave: a modern morality play. (Dublin Theatre Festival, at the Abbey Theatre 1966). 1968.

Persons from Porlock and other plays for radio. Introd by W. H. Auden. 1969. Enter Caesar: a study of the evolution and background of the first great dictator of the modern type (BBC Home Service 20 Sept 1946); East of the sun and west of the moon: a Norwegian folk tale (BBC Third Programme 25 July 1959); They met on Good Friday: a sceptical historical romance (BBC Third Programme 8 Dec 1959); Persons from Porlock: the story of a painter (BBC Third Programme 30 Aug 1963).

Other Works

Roundabout way. [By] 'Louis Malone'. 1932. Novel.

Grigson, G. (ed). The arts today. 1935. Contains Poetry, by MacNeice.

Verschoyle, D. (ed). The English novelists. 1936. Sir Thomas Malory, by MacNeice.

I crossed the Minch. 1938. Travel in the Hebrides. Prose, with verse.

Modern poetry: a personal essay. 1938, Oxford 1968 (introd by W. Allen).

Zoo. 1938. On the London Zoo.

The poetry of W. B. Yeats. 1941, 1967 (introd by R. Ellmann).

Meet the U.S. Army. 1943. Prepared for the Board of Education by the Ministry of Information.

Apuleius. The golden ass. Tr W. Adlington; introd by MacNeice 1946.

March, R. and Tambimuttu (ed). T. S. Eliot: a symposium. 1948. Contains Eliot and the adolescent, by MacNeice.

The penny that rolled away. New York 1954, London 1956 (as The sixpence that rolled away). For children.

Tedlock, E. (ed). Dylan Thomas: the legend and the poet. 1960. Contribution by MacNeice.

Astrology. 1964, Garden City NY 1964.

The strings are false: an unfinished autobiography. 1965, New York 1966.

Varieties of parable. Cambridge 1965 (Clark lectures 1963).

MacNeice edited, with S. Spender, Oxford poetry, 1929. *This includes 4 poems by him.*

§2

Bishop, J. P. The Hamlet of L. MacNeice. Nation 11 May 1940. Rptd in his Collected essays, 1948. Review of Autumn journal, 1939.

Southworth, J. G. Louis MacNeice. In his Sowing the spring, 1940.

Symons, J. Louis MacNeice: the artist as everyman. Poetry (Chicago) 56 1940.

Scarfe, F. MacNeice: poetry and commonsense. In his Auden and after, 1942.

Brown, S. G. Some poems of MacNeice. Sewanee Rev 51 1943.

Crowder, R. Mr MacNeice and Miss Sitwell. Poetry (Chicago) 63 1944.

Dupee, F. W. Lewis and MacNeice. Nation 13 Oct 1945.

Iremonger, V. MacNeice: a first study. The Bell 14 1947.

Greacen, R. The poetry of MacNeice. Poetry Quart 11 1949.

Matthiessen, F. O. Louis MacNeice. In his The responsibilities of the critic, New York 1952; rptd review of Poems, New York 1937.

Cragg, R. C. Snow, a philosophical poem: a study in critical procedure. EC 3 1953. Comments by various writers in EC 4 1954.

Bogan, L. Feats on the fjord. In her Selected criticism, 1955; rptd review of Letters from Iceland, 1937.

Barry, Sister M. M. MacNeice's Snow. Explicator 16 1957.

Borroff, M. What a poem is: for instance, Snow. EC 8 1958. Reply by P. A. W. Collins and R. P. Draper ibid and by Borroff EC 9 1959.

Fraser, G. S. Evasive honesty: the poetry of MacNeice. In his Vision and rhetoric, 1959.

Auden, W. H. Louis MacNeice: a memorial address delivered at All Souls Langham Place on 17 October 1963. [1963].

— Louis MacNeice. Encounter 21 1963.

Betjeman, J. MacNeice and Bernard Spencer. London Mag 3 1963-4.

Connolly, C. In his Previous convictions, 1963; rptd review of Solstices, 1961.

Elman, R. M. The legacy of MacNeice. New Republic 26 Oct 1963.

Hamilton, I. Louis MacNeice. London Mag 3 1963-4.

Curnow, A. Louis MacNeice. Landfall 18 1964.

Wall, S. Louis MacNeice and the line of least resistance. Review (Oxford) no 11-12 1964.

Pacey, D. The dance above the dazzling wave: the poetry of MacNeice. Proc & Trans of the Royal Soc of Canada new ser 3 1965.

Press, J. Louis MacNeice. 1965 (Br Council pamphlet).

Fauchereau, S. Louis MacNeice: un poète pendant les années 30: un poète de la radio. Critique (Paris) 22 1966.

Wain, J. MacNeice as critic. Encounter 27 1966.

Hough, G. MacNeice and Auden. CQ 9 1967.

Longley, M. A misrepresented poet. Dublin Mag 6 1967.

Smith, W. J. The black clock: the poetic achievement of MacNeice. Hollins Critic 4 1967.

Cope, J. I. MacNeice's Perseus. Explicator 26 1968.

Citizen, J. Louis MacNeice: the last decade. Twentieth-Century Lit 14 1968.

Allen, W. Louis MacNeice. Essays by Divers Hands 35 1969.

Brennan, M. A poet's revisions: a consideration of MacNeice's Blind fireworks. Western Humanities Rev 23 1969.

Stanford, D. Stephen Spender, Louis MacNeice, Cecil Day Lewis: a critical essay. Grand Rapids 1969 (Contemporary Writers in Christian Perspective).

CHARLES HENRY MADGE
b. 1912

§1
Poetry

The disappearing castle. 1937.
The father found. 1941.

Other Works

Mass-Observation. With T. Harrisson. Foreword by J. Huxley 1937 (Mass-Observation ser no 1).

May the twelfth: Mass-Observation day-surveys, 1937. 1937. By H. Jennings, Madge et al.

First year's work, 1937-38, by Mass-Observation. Ed Madge and T. Harrisson 1938.

Britain, by Mass-Observation, arranged and written by Madge and T. Harrisson. 1939, New York 1939.

War begins at home, by Mass Observation, ed and arranged by T. Harrisson [and] Madge. 1940.

Industry after the war: who is going to run it? 1943 (Target for Tomorrow ser). By Madge in consultation with D. Tyerman.

War-time pattern of saving and spending. Cambridge 1943, New York 1943 (National Inst of Economic and Social Research Occasional Papers 4).

Pilot guide to the general election. Ed Madge 1945.

Pilot papers: social essays and documents, vol 1. Ed Madge 1945. Continued as a quarterly jnl.

To start you talking: a collection of scripts with introductory sections by Madge and others. 1945.

Survey before development in Thai villages. [New York?] 1957. Pbd by United Nations.

Village meeting places: a pilot enquiry. [Delhi?] 1958. Pbd by Indian Ministry of Information.

Society in the mind: elements of social eidos. 1964, New York 1964 (Society Today and Tomorrow).

Madge edited the Target for Tomorrow ser 1943-5 and the periodical Pilot Papers 1946-7. For a discussion of Madge as a sociologist see Social science at Birmingham: Prof Charles Madge, Nature 166 1950.

JOHN EDWARD MASEFIELD
1878-1967

Bibliographies

Sherman, C. E. Masefield: a contribution toward a bibliography. Bull of Bibliography 8 1914-15. Includes articles on Masefield.

Bibliographies of modern authors: Masefield. London Mercury 2 1920.

Danielson, H. In his Bibliographies of modern authors, 1921.

Williams, I. A. Bibliographies of modern authors 2: Masefield. 1921. Based on bibliography in London Mercury, above.

Simmons, C. H. A bibliography of Masefield. New York 1930. Also lists works on Masefield. Errata and emendata, including Masefield's book reviews in Manchester Guardian, by F. B. Drew, PBSA 53 1959.

Nevinson, H. W. Masefield: an appreciation, together with a bibliography. 1931.

Handley-Taylor, G. Masefield, OM: a bibliography and eighty-first birthday tribute. [1960]. Includes notes on various Masefield collections.

Collections and Selections

Collected works: Wanderer edition. 5 vols 1935-7.
A book of both sorts: selections from the verse and prose of Masefield. 1947.
A book of prose selections. 1950, New York 1950.

§1
Poetry and Plays

Salt-water ballads. 1902, New York 1913.

Ballads. 1903.

The tragedy of Nan and other plays. 1909, New York 1909. Contains The tragedy of Nan (New Royalty 24 May 1908); The Campden wonder (Court Theatre 8 Jan 1907); Mrs Harrison. The tragedy of Nan rptd separately 1911, New York 1921, 1926. See G. T. Tanselle, Three unrecorded issues of Masefield's Tragedy of Nan. Library 5th ser 23 1968.

The tragedy of Pompey the great. (Aldwych 4 Dec 1910). 1910, Boston 1910, 1914 (rev), New York 1914.

Ballads and poems. 1910. Ballads, 1903, with addns including poems from Salt-water ballads 1902.

Ballads. 1911. Selection from Ballads, 1903, and Ballads and poems, 1910.

The everlasting mercy. 1911, Portland Maine 1911. Rptd from Eng Rev.

The everlasting mercy and The widow in the bye street. New York 1912. Both rptd from Eng Rev.

The widow in the bye street. 1912.

The story of a round-house and other poems. New York 1912, 1913 (rev). Selection, with 9 poems not previously pbd in book form, including Dauber.

The daffodil fields. New York 1913, London 1913.

Dauber: a poem. 1913.

Philip the King and other poems. 1914, New York 1914.

The faithful: a tragedy in three acts. (Birmingham Rep 4 Dec 1915). 1915, New York 1915.

Good Friday and other poems. New York 1916.

Good Friday. (Garrick 25 Feb 1917). Letchworth 1916, New York 1916 (as Good Friday: a dramatic poem). See also preceding.

Sonnets. New York 1916. 61 sonnets from Good Friday and other poems, 1916.

Sonnets and poems. Letchworth 1916 (200 copies) (46 sonnets from Good Friday and other poems, 1916, with one new sonnet), Lollingdon, Cholsey 1916 (slightly rev collection).

The locked chest; The sweeps of ninety-eight: two plays in prose. Letchworth 1916, New York 1916.

Salt-water poems and ballads. 1916.

The cold Cotswolds. Cambridge 1917. Rptd from Cambridge Mag.

Lollingdon Downs and other poems. New York 1917, London 1917 (as Lollingdon Downs and other poems, with Sonnets; includes poems from Good Friday and other poems, and Sonnets and poems).

Poems of John Masefield, selected by H. S. Canby and others. New York 1917.

Rosas. New York 1918.

The poems and plays of Masefield. 2 vols New York 1918.

A poem and two plays. 1919. Contains Rosas; The locked chest; The sweeps of ninety-eight.

Reynard the fox: or, the ghost heath run. New York 1919, London 1919, New York 1920 (illustr C. Moore Park, with introd by Masefield on 'Fox hunting' rptd in Recent prose, 1924, below), London 1921 (illustr G. D. Armour).

Animula. 1920 (priv ptd, 250 copies); rptd in next.

Enslaved and other poems. 1920, New York 1920.

Right Royal. New York 1920, London 1920.

King Cole. 1921, New York 1921.

Esther: a tragedy adapted and partially translated from the French of Jean Racine. 1922. In verse. For U.S. edn, see next.

Esther and Berenice: two plays. New York 1922. In verse.

Berenice: a tragedy translated from the French of Jean Racine. 1922. In verse. For U.S. edn, see preceding.

The dream. [1922], New York 1922 (illustr Judith Masefield).

Melloney Holtspur. 1922, New York 1922, 1923 (as Melloney Holtspur: or the pangs of love). Prose play.

Selected poems. 1922, 1922 (530 copies, containing the unpbd Nireus), New York 1923 (with 6 unpbd poems).

King Cole and other poems. 1923.

The dream and other poems. New York 1923. Same as King Cole and other poems, but omitting King Cole and The eye and the object.

A king's daughter: a tragedy in verse. 1923, New York 1923.

Collected poems. 1923.

The trial of Jesus. (RADA Theatre 28 March 1926). 1925, New York 1925.

Poems. 2 vols New York 1925. Collection.

Verse plays. New York 1925. Collection.

Prose plays. New York 1925. Collection.

Sonnets of good cheer to the Lena Ashwell Players from their well-wisher John Masefield. [1926] (priv ptd). 4 sonnets.

Tristan and Isolt: a play in verse. (Oxford Playhouse May 1923). 1927, New York 1927.

The coming of Christ. 1928, New York 1928. Play in verse.

Midsummer night and other tales in verse. 1928, New York 1928.

Oxford recitations. 1928.

Easter: a play for singers. 1929, New York 1929. In verse.

Poems, complete in one volume. New York 1929.

South and east. 1929, New York 1929. Rptd from Midsummer night, 1928, above.

The Wanderer of Liverpool. 1930, New York 1930. On the voyages of the 'Wanderer' in prose and verse, with A masque of Liverpool, and other poems.

Poems of The Wanderer: the ending. 1930 (priv ptd; 25 copies).

Minnie Maylow's story and other tales and scenes. 1931, New York 1931.

Collected poems. 1932. Enlarged edn of Collected poems, 1923, above.

A tale of Troy. 1932, New York 1932.

End and beginning. 1933, New York 1933. Verse play.

Poems: complete edition, with recent poems. New York 1935.

A letter from Pontus and other verse. 1936, New York 1936.

Lines spoken by Masefield at the Tercentenary of Harvard University. 1937 (150 copies), New York 1937 (150 copies) (as Lines on the tercentenary of Harvard University).

The country scene in poems by Masefield and pictures by E. Seago. [1937], New York [1938].

Selected poems. 1938, New York 1938. Rev edn of Selected poems, 1922, above.

Collected poems. 1938. Enlarged edn of Collected poems, 1932, above.

Tribute to ballet in poems by Masefield and pictures by E. Seago. [1938], New York 1938.

Some verses to some Germans. 1939, New York 1939.

Shopping in Oxford. 1941 (500 copies); rptd in next.

Gautama the enlightened and other verse. 1941, New York 1941.

Natalie Maisie and Pavilastukay: two tales in verse. 1942, New York 1942.

Land workers. 1942, New York 1943.

A generation risen. [1942], New York 1943. Illustr E. Seago.

Wonderings: between one and six years. 1943, New York 1943.

Reynard the fox: a tale in verse, with selected sonnets and lyrics. 1946.

Poems. 1946. Rev edn of Collected poems, 1938, above.

A play of St George. 1948, New York 1948. In verse.

On the hill. 1949, New York 1949.

Selected poems ('new edition'). 1950, New York 1950. A new selection.

In praise of nurses. [1950].

Poems: complete edition with recent poems. New York 1953.

Bluebells and other verse. 1961, New York 1961.

The western Hudson shore. [New York 1962?] (priv ptd).

Old Raiger and other verse. 1964, New York 1965.

Fiction and Other Works

Lyrists of the Restoration from Sir Edward Sherburne to William Congreve. Ed J. and C. Masefield 1905 (Chapbooks no 1).

A mainsail haul. 1905, 1913 (rev and enlarged), New York 1913, London 1954 (with 2 additional pieces), New York 1954. Stories.

Sea life in Nelson's time. 1905, New York 1925.

Essays moral and polite, 1660–1714. Ed J. and C. Masefield 1906 (Chapbooks no 2).

On the Spanish Main: or some English forays on the Isthmus of Darien; with a description of the buccaneers and a short account of old-time ships and sailors. 1906, New York 1906.

The poems of Robert Herrick. Ed with biographical introd by Masefield 1906 (Chapbooks no 5).

A sailor's garland. Selected and ed Masefield 1906, New York 1906.

Dampier's voyages. Ed Masefield 2 vols 1906, New York 1907.

Lyrics of Ben Jonson, Beaumont and Fletcher. Ed Masefield 1906 (Chapbooks no 4).

A tarpaulin muster. 1907, New York 1908. Stories.

An English prose miscellany. Ed Masefield 1907 (EL).

Hakluyt's voyages. Ed Masefield [1907] (EL).

Captain Margaret: a romance. 1908, Philadelphia 1908.

Defoe. Selections, ed Masefield 1909, New York 1909.

Multitude and solitude. 1909, New York 1910. Novel.

My faith in woman suffrage. [1910]. Speech.

Martin Hyde, the Duke's messenger. 1910, Boston 1910. Dramatized by Ruth P. Kimball, 1935, Boston 1935. For boys.

A book of discoveries. 1910, New York [1910]. For boys.

Lost endeavour. 1910, New York 1917. Story for boys.

Anson's voyage round the world. Introd by Masefield [1911] (EL).

The street of to-day. 1911, New York 1911. Novel.

William Shakespeare. [1911], New York 1911, London 1954 (rev), New York 1954.

Jim Davis. 1911, New York 1912, Boston 1918 (as The captive of the smugglers). Novel, for boys.

John M. Synge: a few personal recollections, with biographical notes. Churchtown, Dundrum 1915, New York 1915; rptd in The taking of Helen and other prose selections, 1924, below.

Gallipoli. 1916, New York 1916.

Anne Pedersdotter: a drama by H. Wiers-Jenssen. Tr Masefield, Boston 1917.

The old front line: or the beginning of the battle of the Somme. 1917, New York 1917 (as The old front line).

The war and the future. New York 1918, London 1919 (as St George and the dragon). Lectures.

The battle of the Somme. 1919 (268 copies).

John Ruskin. Bembridge 1920 (priv ptd, 150 copies).

A Foundation Day address [at Bembridge School]. Bembridge 1921, (priv ptd, 250 copies).

The taking of Helen. 1923, New York 1924 (750 copies). Novel.

The taking of Helen and other prose selections. New York 1924, London 1924 (as Recent prose), 1932 (rev and enlarged).

Shakespeare and spiritual life. Oxford 1924 (Romanes lecture).

Sard Harker. 1924, New York 1924. Novel.

With the living voice: an address given at the first general meeting of the Scottish Association for the Speaking of Verse. 1925, New York 1925.

Odtaa. 1926, New York 1926. Novel.

The midnight folk. 1927, New York 1927. Novel.

The hawbucks. 1929, New York 1929. Novel.

Speech after receiving the Freedom of the City of Hereford. 1930 (priv ptd).

Speech at a festival in honour of W. B. Yeats. 1930 (priv ptd).

Chaucer. Cambridge 1931, New York 1931 (Leslie Stephen lecture).

Poetry. 1931, New York 1932. Lecture.

The Conway from her foundation to the present day. 1933, New York 1933, London 1953 (rev), New York 1954. On the training ship 'Conway'.

The bird of dawning. 1933, New York 1933 (as The bird of dawning: or the fortunes of the sea). Novel.

The taking of the Gry. 1934, New York 1934. Novel.

The box of delights: or When the wolves were running. 1935, New York 1935. For children.

Victorious Troy: or The hurrying angel. 1935, New York 1935. Novel.

Eggs and Baker: or The days of trial. 1936, New York 1936. Novel.

The square peg: or The gun fella. 1937, New York 1937. Novel.

Dead Ned: the autobiography of a corpse. 1938, New York 1938. Novel.

Live and kicking Ned: a continuation of the tale of dead Ned. 1939, New York 1939.

Basilissa: a tale of the Empress Theodora. 1940, New York 1940.

Some memories of W. B. Yeats. Dublin 1940, New York 1940. Verse and prose.

The nine days wonder: the Operation Dynamo. 1941, New York 1941. On Dunkirk, 1940.

In the mill. 1941, New York 1941. Experiences in a factory.

Conquer: a tale of the Nika rebellion in Byzantium. 1941, New York 1941.

I want! I want! 1944, New York 1945. On books and reading; introd by G. Faber.

New chum. 1944, New York 1945. Experiences on the training ship 'Conway'.

A Macbeth production. 1945, New York 1946.

Thanks before going: notes on some of the original poems of D. G. Rossetti. 1946, New York 1947.

A reply to the toast of Honorary graduands at the University of Sheffield. [1946] (priv ptd).

Thanks before going, with other gratitude for old delights, including A Macbeth production and various papers not before printed. 1947.

Badon parchments. 1947. Novel.

My favourite English poems, gathered and introduced by Masefield. 1950, New York 1950.

The Ledbury scene as I have used it in my verse. Ledbury [1951] (priv ptd, 250 copies). Included in next.

St Katherine of Ledbury and other Ledbury papers. 1951.

So long to learn: chapters of an autobiography. 1952, New York 1952 (as So long to learn).

An Elizabethan theatre in London. 1954 (priv ptd).

Words spoken at the unveiling of the memorials to the poets Keats and Shelley. 1954 (priv ptd).

Words on the anniversary of the birthday of William Blake. 1957.

Grace before ploughing: fragments of autobiography. 1966, New York 1967.

§2

Montague, C. E. Masefield's tragedies. In his Dramatic values, 1911.

Buckley, R. R. Masefield: the realist in poetry. Poetry Rev 1 1912.

Shafer, R. Two of the newest poets. Atlantic Monthly 111 1913. Gibson and Masefield.

Armstrong, M. D. Recent English poetry. Fortnightly Rev new ser 95 1914.

Mais, S. P. B. The genius of Masefield. In his From Shakespeare to O. Henry, 1917, 1923 (rev).

Lynd, R. Masefield's secret. In his Old and new masters, 1919.

Fletcher, J. G. Masefield: a study. North Amer Rev 212 1920.

Murry, J. M. The nostalgia of Masefield. In his Aspects of literature, 1920.

Shanks, E. Masefield: some characteristics. London Mercury 2 1920.

Campbell, G. H. Masefield of the present day. Bookman (New York) 52 1921.

Kilmer, J. In his Circus and other essays, New York [1921].

Stidger, W. L. The hounds of hell. Methodist Rev 104 1921.

Garrett, R. M. Cargoes. Sewanee Rev 30 1922.

Hamilton, W. H. John Masefield: a critical study. 1922.

Hammond, J. The grave beauty of Masefield's verse. Personalist 3 1922.

Kernahan, C. In his Six famous living poets, 1922.

Macy, J. A. In his The critical game, [1922].

Maynard, T. Masefield: the mildness of murder. In his Our best poets, 1922.

Raven, A. A. A study in Masefield's vocabulary. MLN 37 1922.

Schelling, F. E. Masefield and the key poetic. In his Appraisements and asperities, Philadelphia 1922.

Clarke, G. H. Various Masefield. Sewanee Rev 31 1923.
— Masefield and Jezebel. Sewanee Rev 32 1924.
— Masefield's The everlasting mercy. Queen's Quart 33 1926.
— Masefield: poet-laureate. Dalhousie Rev 12 1932.

Dearmer, G. The strength and weakness of Masefield. Fortnightly Rev new ser 114 1923.

Biggane, C. Masefield: a study. Cambridge 1924.

Delattre, F. Le réalisme poétique de Masefield. Revue Anglo-américaine 1 1924.

Morgan, A. E. In his Tendencies of modern English drama, 1924.

Van Doorn, W. John Masefield, poet: some reflections. E Studies 6 1924.

Chase, S. P. Masefield: a biographical note. MLN 40 1925.
— The scene of The everlasting mercy. Southwest Rev 11 1926.

Drinkwater, J. Masefield's Reynard and Right royal. In his The Muse in council, 1925.

Fox, A. W. The collected poems of Masefield. Manchester Quart 51 1925.

Davison, E. The poetry of Masefield. Eng Jnl 15 1926; rptd in his Some modern poets, 1928.

Lucas, F. L. In his Authors dead and living, 1926.

Berkelman, R. G. Chaucer and Masefield. Eng Jnl 16 1927.

White, N. I. Masefield: an estimate. South Atlantic Quart 26 1927.

Edmonds, A. J. The sea pictures of Masefield. Holborn Rev new ser 19 1928.

Higgins, B. In Scrutinies, ed E. Rickword 1928.

Weygandt, C. The plays and poetry of Masefield. In his Tuesdays at ten, Philadelphia 1928.
— Masefield: apostle of beauty. In his Time of Yeats, [1937].

O'Faoláin, S. A note on Masefield. Dial 86 1929.

Scripture, E. W. Die Metrik in Masefields Sea fever. Die Neueren Sprachen 37 1929.

Stevenson, L. Masefield and the new universe. Sewanee Rev 37 1929.

Bookman (London) 79 1930. The poet laureate [leading articles]. The poetry of Masefield, by C. Davy; The prose of Masefield, by T. R. Henn; The plays of Masefield, by N. Marshall; Masefield and Crabbe: an affinity, by A. R. Boyden.

Brenner, R. In her Ten modern poets, 1930.

Du Bois, A. E. The cult of beauty: a study of Masefield. PMLA 45 1930.

Duffin, H. C. The new laureate: a lyric poet. Cornhill Mag 69 1930.

Lowell, A. In her Poetry and poets, 1930. Rptd reviews of Reynard the fox and King Cole.

Shepard, O. Masefield: poet laureate. Bookman (New York) 71 1930.

Shipp, H. John Masefield. Eng Rev 50 1930.

Williams, C. In his Poetry at present, 1930.

Aronstein, P. John Masefield. Neuphilologische Monatsschrift 2 1931.

Brégy, K. John Masefield. Catholic World 133 1931.

Eschenauer, W. John Masefield. Kreis von Halle 1 1931.

Nevinson, H. W. Masefield: an appreciation, together with a bibliography. 1931.

Woody, L. Masefield's use of dipodic meter. PQ 10 1931.

Beck, R. Lárviðarskáldið John Masefield. Eimreiðin 38 1932.

Gualtieri, F. M. John Masefield: il poeta laureato d'oggi. Venice 1932.

Cunliffe, J. W. Masefield and the new Georgian poets. In his English literature in the twentieth century, New York 1933.

Thomas, G. John Masefield. 1933.

Wood, F. T. The poetry of Masefield. Poetry Rev 24 1933.

Thouless, P. Laurence Binyon and Masefield. In her Modern poetic drama, 1934.

Hübner, W. Masefields Verserzählung The everlasting mercy. In Englische Kultur in sprachwissenschaftlicher Deutung: Max Deutschbein zum 60. Geburtstage, ed W. Schmidt, Leipzig 1936.

Woolf, S. J. Masefield ponders these prosy days. New York Times Mag 16 Feb 1936.

Palmer, H. Masefield: poet laureate. Cornhill Mag 156 1937.

Bishop, J. P. The poetry of Masefield. Poetry 53 1938; rptd in his Collected essays, New York 1948.

Mason, J. E. John Masefield. Exeter 1938.

Papajewski, H. Englands poeta laureatus. Deutsche Zukunft 6 1938.

Azzalino, W. Masefields Gedicht Cargoes als Kunstwerk. Zeitschrift für Neusprachlichen Unterricht 39 1940.

Price, C. Masefield talks on literature and war. New York Times Book Rev 17 March 1940.

Arms, G. Masefield's Cargoes. Explicator 1 1942.

Dickson, A. Blake's The clod and the pebble and Masefield's Cargoes. Explicator 2 1943.

McCutcheon, R. P. Masefield's Cargoes. Explicator 2 1944.

Caldiero, F. A note on Wordsworth, Brooke and Masefield. N & Q 189 1945.

Lloyd, F. V., jr. Masefield's Sea fever. Explicator 3 1945.

Gregory, H. Masefield: shock of rediscovery. Saturday Rev 20 May 1950.

Strong, L. A. G. John Masefield. 1952 (Br Council pamphlet).

Highet, G. Poetry and romance: Masefield. In his People, places and books, New York 1953.

Spark, M. John Masefield. 1953.

Couchman, G. W. Masefield's Dauber and Falconer's shipwreck. N & Q 199 1954.

Gierasch, W. Masefield's C.L.M. Explicator 13 1955.

Drew, F. Masefield's Dauber: autobiography or sailor's tale retold? MLN 72 1957.
— In New York with Masefield. Trace no 27 1958.
— Masefield and the Manchester Guardian. PQ 37 1958.
— Masefield in New Haven: the Sumner McKnight Crosby collection. Yale Lib Gazette 32 1958.
— Poetry and pugilism: Masefield fights. Canadian Forum 38 1958.
— The Irish allegiances of an English laureate: Masefield and Ireland. Eire-Ireland 3 1968.

Nault, C. A., jr. Masefield's Cargoes. Explicator 16 1958.

Stanford, D. Masefield at eighty. Contemporary Rev 194 1958.

Fisher, M. John Masefield. 1963 (Bodley Head monograph).

Gordan, J. D. The holograph of Salt-water ballads. In An anniversary exhibition: the Henry W. and Albert A. Berg collection, 1940–1965. BNYPL 69 1965.

Ross, R. H. In his The Georgian revolt, 1910–1922, Carbondale 1965.

Graves, R. Robert Graves on Masefield. TLS 22 June 1967.

Knight, G. W. Masefield and spiritualism. In Mansions of the spirit: essays in literature and religion, ed G. A. Panichas, New York 1967.

Spanos, W. V. The nativity: the humanization of the morality. In his The Christian tradition in modern British verse drama, New Brunswick NJ 1967.
Berry, F. Masefield: the narrative poet. Sheffield 1968. Lecture.
Gulston, C. Masefield: poet and storyteller. Contrast 18 1968.
Puccio, G. John Masefield. Nuova Antologia no 502 1968.
Lamont, C. A reminiscence of Masefield. Columbia Lib Columns 19 1969.

CHARLOTTE MARY MEW
1869-1928

§ 1

The farmer's bride. 1916, 1921 (with 11 new poems), New York 1921 (as Saturday market).
The rambling sailor. 1929.
Collected poems. 1953. With memoir by A. Monro.
8 letters from Charlotte Mew to Sir Sydney Cockerell are pbd in Friends of a lifetime, *ed V. Meynell 1940. Other unpbd letters are reproduced in* M. C. Davidow, Charlotte Mew: biography and criticism (see §2, below).

§ 2

Monro, H. Charlotte Mew. In his Some contemporary poets, 1920.
Robertson, D. A. Contemporary English poets: Charlotte Mew. Eng Jnl 15 1926.
Collard, L. K. Charlotte Mew. Contemporary Rev 137 1930.
Moore, V. Charlotte Mew. Yale Rev 22 1932-3.
— Charlotte Mew. In her Distinguished women writers, New York [1934].
Davidow, M. C. Charlotte Mew: biography and criticism. Dissertation Abstracts 24 1963.
Grant, J. In her Harold Monro and the Poetry Bookshop, 1967.

HAROLD EDWARD MONRO
1879-1932

The principal collections of Monro's mss are listed in Joy Grant, Harold Monro and the Poetry Bookshop, *1967 §2 below: they are in the Library of the University of California, Los Angeles, the Maurice Browne Collection, University of Michigan, and in the Edward Marsh Collection, New York Public Library.*

§ 1
Poetry

Poems. 1906.
Judas. Cranleigh 1907.
Before dawn: poems and impressions. 1911.
Children of love. 1914.
Trees. 1916. Rptd with alterations in next.
Strange meetings. 1917.
Real property. 1922.
[Sixteen poems.] [1927] (Augustan Books of English Poetry).
The earth for sale. 1928.
The winter solstice. 1928 (Ariel Poem). Drawings by D. Jones.
Elm angel. 1930 (Ariel Poem). Wood engravings by E. Ravilious.
Collected poems. Ed A. Monro, with biographical sketch by F. S. Flint and critical note by T. S. Eliot 1933.
The silent pool and other poems, chosen by A. Monro. 1942.

Other Works

Proposals for a voluntary nobility. Norwich 1907. Anon, with Maurice Browne.
The evolution of the soul. Norwich 1907.
The chronicle of a pilgrimage: Paris to Milan on foot. 1909.
Some contemporary poets: 1920. 1920.
One day awake: a morality. 1922 (Chapbook 32).
Twentieth century poetry: an anthology chosen by Monro. 1929, 1946 (rev and enlarged by A. Monro).
Monro edited Poetry Rev *during 1912,* Poetry & Drama *1913-14, and* Chapbook (*originally* Monthly chapbook) *1919-25. He founded the Poetry Bookshop in 1913 and directed it until his death, publishing among other books the five volumes of* Georgian Poetry. *He contributed poems to all of these.*

§ 2

Lowell, A. The Poetry Bookshop. Little Rev 2 1915.
Flint, F. S. Verse chronicle. Criterion 11 1932. Partly on Monro.
Pound, E. Harold Monro. Criterion 11 1932. Rptd in his Polite essays, 1937.
Savage, D. S. Monro: a study in integration. In his Personal principle, 1944; rptd from Poetry (Chicago) 60 1942.
Magalaner, M. Monro—literary midwife. Arizona Quart 5 1949.
Browne, M. Too late to lament: an autobiography. 1955.
Skelton, R. The creation of symbol: I [Trees, by Monro]. In his Poetic pattern, 1956.
Ross, R. H. Harold Monro. In his The Georgian revolt, 1910-22. Carbondale 1965.
Grant, J. Harold Monro and the Poetry Bookshop. 1967. Includes bibliography of works by and on Monro.

NICHOLAS MOORE
b. 1918

§ 1
Poetry

A book for Priscilla. Cambridge 1941.
Buzzing around with a bee and other poems. [1941].
The island and the cattle. [1941].
A wish in season. [1941].
The cabaret, the dancer, the gentlemen. [1942].
Acrobats in a red spotlight. In Three poems, by F. Marnau, W. Gardiner and N. Moore, 1944.
The glass tower. 1944. Includes some poems selected from previous vols.
Recollections of the gala: selected poems 1943-1948. 1950.
Identity. 1969 (140 copies).

Other Works

The Fortune anthology. Ed Moore et al [1942].
Henry Miller. Wigginton, Herts 1943.
Atlantic anthology: new voices. Ed Moore and D. Newton 1945.
The happy rock: a book about Henry Miller. Berkeley Cal 1945. Contains Henry Miller in England, by Moore.
New Poetry. Nos 1 & 2. Ed Moore [1945].
The PL book of modern American short stories. Ed Moore 1945.
Moore edited (*originally with John Goodland*) *the periodical* Seven, *1938-40, and also* Cambridge Front.

§ 2

Hendry, J. F. and H. Treece (ed). The white horseman: prose and verse of the New Apocalypse. 1941. Introd by G. S. Fraser discusses 3 poets, including Moore.

Scarfe, F. In his Auden and after, 1942.

Fraser, G. S. The poetry of Moore. Poetry Quart 9 1947.

Crosland, M. Nicholas Moore: a problem poet. Poetry Quart 14 1952.

THOMAS STURGE MOORE
1870–1944
Bibliographies

A bibliography of T. Sturge Moore. London Mercury 3 1920.

Gwynn, F. L. In his Sturge Moore and the life of art, 1951, §2 below. Includes a checklist with Moore's contributions to periodicals and reviews, criticism of Moore's work and a list of his ptd woodcuts.

§1
Poetry and Verse Plays

Two poems. 1893 (priv ptd). About hope and Mountain shadows.

The vinedresser and other poems. 1899.

Aphrodite against Artemis: a tragedy. 1901.

Absalom: a chronicle play in three acts. 1903.

Danaë: a poem. 1903, New York 1903. First pbd in Dial 1893, here rev, again rev 1920 (see below).

The centaur's booty. 1903. Dramatic poem.

The rout of the Amazons. 1903. Dramatic poem.

The gazelles and other poems. 1904.

Pan's prophecy. 1904. Dramatic poem.

To Leda and other odes. 1904.

Theseus, Medea, and lyrics. 1904.

The little school: a posy of rhymes. 1905, New York 1905, London 1917 (enlarged), New York 1920.

Poems. 1906. Reissue of The centaur's booty, The rout of the Amazons, The gazelles, To Leda, and Theseus, Medea and lyrics, in one vol.

Salome; A Florentine tragedy; Vera. By Oscar Wilde. Boston [1908] (vol 6 of Ross edn). Opening scene of A Florentine tragedy by Sturge Moore.

Mariamne. 1911. Play.

A Sicilian idyll; and Judith: a conflict. 1911. 2 plays.

The sea is kind. 1914, Boston 1914. Selection from The vinedresser and The little school, with 21 new poems.

Danaë, Aforetime, Blind Thamyris. 1920.

Tragic mothers: Medea, Niobe, Tyrfing. 1920. 3 plays.

Judas. 1923, Chicago 1924.

Roderigo of Bivar. New York 1925 (500 copies). Play, rptd in Poems, 1931–3, below.

Mystery and tragedy: two dramatic poems [Psyche in Hades, and Daimonassa]. 1930.

Nine poems. Maastricht 1930 (125 copies). Includes 3 previously unpbd poems.

The poems of T. Sturge Moore. 4 vols 1931–3. Collected edn. Includes poems previously pbd only in periodicals and some unpbd poems.

Selected poems. Ed M. Sturge Moore 1934.

The unknown known and a dozen odd poems. 1939.

Other Works

The passionate pilgrim and the songs in Shakespeare's plays. Ed Sturge Moore 1896.

The centaur; The bacchante, by M. de Guérin. Tr Sturge Moore 1899.

Shakespeare's sonnets, reprinted from the edition of 1609. (Seen through the press by Sturge Moore) 1899.

Altdorfer. 1900, New York 1901.

The Vale Shakespeare. Ed Sturge Moore 39 vols 1900–3.

Albrecht Altdorfer: a book of 71 woodcuts, with introduction by Sturge Moore, London, New York 1902.

Poems from Wordsworth chosen, edited and illustrated by Sturge Moore [1902].

A brief account of the origin of the Eragny Press & a note on the relation of the printed book as a work of art to life. 1903, New York 1904.

Albert Durer. 1905, New York 1905.

Correggio. London, New York 1906.

Art and life. 1910. Essays.

Hark to these three: talk about style. 1915.

Theory and practice: a paper read by Sturge Moore before the members of the Art Students' Union at the School of Art, Leicester, February 5 1916. Leicester 1916.

Some soldier poets. 1919, New York 1920. Essays, mainly rptd from Eng Rev.

The powers of the air. 1920. Prose and verse, rptd in Poems 1931–3 (see Poems, above).

A selection from the poems of Michael Field. Compiled by Sturge Moore 1923.

Ought art to be taught in schools? an address delivered at the Birmingham Central School of Arts & Crafts on 15th March 1923. Birmingham 1926.

Armour for Aphrodite. 1929. Aesthetics.

Watson, E. L. G. The common earth. Introd by Sturge Moore 1932.

Charles Ricketts, R. A.: sixty-five illustrations, introduced by Sturge Moore 1933.

Works and days, from the journal of Michael Field. Ed Sturge Moore and D. C. Sturge Moore 1933.

Poems of Wang Ching-wei, translated by Seyuan Shu. Foreword by Sturge Moore 1938.

Self-portrait, taken from the letters and journals of Charles Ricketts, R.A.; collected and compiled by Sturge Moore. Ed C. Lewis 1939.

Letters

W. B. Yeats and T. Sturge Moore: their correspondence 1901–1937. Ed Ursula Bridge 1953, New York 1953.

Moore was also known as a wood engraver and illustrator: his work decorates the covers of some of his books, and those of W. B. Yeats et al.

§2

Del Re, A. Sturge Moore: the idyllist. Poetry Rev 1 1912.

Bickley, F. The poetry of Sturge Moore. To-day 3 1918.

McDowall, A. The poetry of Sturge Moore. London Mercury 5 1922.

Jones, Ll. Sturge Moore: poet and critic. American Rev 1 1923. Rptd in his First impressions, New York 1925.

Wild, F. Sturge Moore und das 'Poetic Drama'. Anglia Beiblatt 34 1923.

Winters, Y. Sturge Moore. Hound & Horn 6 1933. Incorporated in his Primitivism and decadence, New York 1937.

—— The poetry of Moore. Southern Rev 2 1966.

Thouless, P. Sturge Moore. In her Modern poetic drama, 1934.

Valette, J. Regards sur la poésie de Sturge Moore. Études Anglaises 1 1937.

Weygandt, C. Doughty, Moore and Bottomley. In his Time of Yeats, New York [1937].

Shahani, R. G. Sturge Moore. In R. Moore (ed), Modern reading no 15 1947.

Gwynn, F. L. Moore's Love's faintness accepted. Explicator 7 1949; rptd in Explicator cyclopedia vol 1 1966.

—— Sturge Moore and the life of art. Lawrence Kansas 1951.

EDWIN MUIR
1887–1959

Some of Muir's mss materials have been deposited by Mrs Muir in the National Library of Scotland. BM Additional ms 52409 consists of a notebook of drafts, various separate drafts of poems, and heavily corrected ptd versions of Chorus of the newly dead, 1926 and A song ('I was haunted all that day by memories knocking').

Bibliographies

Mellown, E. W. Bibliography of the writings of Muir. University Alabama [1964], London 1966 (rev). Includes contributions to books, periodicals etc, trns by E. and Willa Muir, critical studies of Muir, including reviews. See also P. Hoy, A preliminary checklist of addenda to Mellown's Bibliography, Serif 6 1969.

— A checklist of critical writings about Muir. Bull of Bibliography 25 1968.

§1

Poetry

First poems. 1925, New York 1925.
Chorus of the newly dead. 1926.
Six poems. Warlingham 1932 (110 copies). Contents rptd, with changes, in Journeys and places, 1937, below.
Variations on a time theme. 1934.
Journeys and places. 1937.
The narrow place. 1943.
The voyage and other poems. 1946.
The labyrinth. 1949.
Collected poems 1921–1951. 1952, New York 1953. Selection, ed J. C. Hall.
Prometheus. 1954 (Ariel Poem, new ser).
One foot in Eden. 1956, New York 1956. Includes the new poems 1949–51 from Collected poems, 1952, above.
Collected poems 1921–1958. Ed Willa Muir and J. C. Hall 1960, 1963 (with alterations and an additional poem), New York 1965 (with preface by T. S. Eliot). Selection, but contains poems omitted from Collected poems 1921–1951, above.
Selected poems, with a preface by T. S. Eliot. 1965. Preface by Eliot to this and Collected poems 1921–1958, above, rptd from Listener 28 May 1964.

Essays and Criticism

We moderns: enigmas and guesses, by 'Edward Moore'. 1918, New York 1920 (by 'Edwin Muir', with minor alterations). Rptd from New Age.
Latitudes. [1924], New York 1924. 23 essays, mostly rptd from Freeman, New Statesman and Athenaeum.
Transition: essays on contemporary literature. 1926, New York 1926. 12 essays, rptd from Nation (NY) and Nation & Athenaeum.
The structure of the novel. 1928, New York 1929.
Scott and Scotland: the predicament of the Scottish writer. 1936, New York 1938.
The present age, from 1914. 1939, New York 1940 (Introductions to English Lit 5).
The politics of King Lear. Glasgow 1947 (W. P. Ker memorial lecture).
Essays on literature and society. 1949, 1965 (rev and enlarged; 6 new essays), Cambridge Mass 1965.
The estate of poetry. 1962, Cambridge Mass 1962 (Charles Eliot Norton lectures, 1955–6).

Other Works

The marionette. 1927, New York 1927. Novel.
John Knox: portrait of a Calvinist. 1929, New York 1929.
The three brothers. 1931, New York 1931. Novel.
Poor Tom. 1932. Novel.
Scottish journey. 1935.
Social credit and the Labour Party: an appeal. 1935 (Pamphlets on the New Economics 15).
Frost, R. Selected poems. 1936. Introductory essays by Muir et al.
A Franz Kafka miscellany. New York 1940. Contains Franz Kafka by Muir.
The story & the fable: an autobiography. 1940. See also An autobiography, 1954, below.
Żyw, A. Poles in uniform: sketches of the Polish army, navy and air force. 1943. Drawings with captions by Muir.

The Scots and their country. [1946].
Poznámka k Franzi Kafkovi. In Franz Kafka a Praha, Prague 1947. Rptd in English in Essays on literature and society, 1949, above.
Marsh, R. and M. J. Tambimuttu (ed). T. S. Eliot: a symposium. 1948. A tribute, by Muir.
Sir Walter Scott lectures 1940–8. Edinburgh 1950. Contains Walter Scott: the man, and Walter Scott: the writer, the lectures for 1944, by Muir. Also in Essays on literature and society, above.
An autobiography. 1954, New York 1954. First pbd as The story and the fable, 1940; here rev.
Brower, R. A. (ed). On translation. Cambridge Mass 1959. Translating from the German, by Muir.
New poets. Ed Muir 1959.
Muir (with Willa Muir) tr many works by contemporary German authors including Asch, Broch, Feuchtwanger, Hauptmann and Kafka (The castle, 1930, New York 1930; The Great Wall of China and other pieces, 1933; The trial, 1937, New York 1937; America, 1938, Norfolk Conn 1940; Parables in German and English, New York 1947; In the penal settlement, New York 1948, London 1949). With J. Lavrin, Muir edited European Quarterly, 1934–5. With Rosamund Lehmann, C. Day Lewis and D. Kilham Roberts, he edited the periodical Orion, vols 1–2 1945. A selection of Muir's letters to Stephen Hudson were pbd in Encounter 26 1966.

§2

Grieve, C. M. Edwin Muir. In his Contemporary Scottish studies 1st ser, 1926.
Spender, S. Edwin Muir. In his Poetry since 1939, 1946.
Hall, J. C. Muir: an introduction. Penguin New Writing 38 1949.
— Edwin Muir. 1956 (Br Council pamphlet).
Stanford, D. Absolute values in criticism: a study of the work of Muir. Month new ser 5 1951.
— Edwin Muir 1887–1959. Contemporary Rev no 1119 1959.
Tschumi, R. Thought in Muir's poetry. In his Thought in twentieth-century English poetry, 1951.
Cazamian, L. Muir et le temps. Études Anglaises 5 1952.
Dodderidge, M. The poetry of Muir. Letteratura Moderne 4 1953.
Grice, F. The poetry of Muir. EC 5 1955.
Carruth, H. To fashion the transitory. Poetry (Chicago) 88 1956.
— An appreciation of Muir. Prairie Schooner 32 1958.
Glicksberg, C. I. Muir: Zarathustra in Scotch dress. Arizona Quart 12 1956.
Blackmur, R. P. Muir: between the tiger's paws. Kenyon Rev 21 1959.
Bruce, G. Edwin Muir: poet. Saltire Rev 6 1959.
Galler, D. Edwin Muir. Poetry (Chicago) 94 1959.
Hassan, I. H. Of time and emblematic reconciliation: notes on the poetry of Muir. South Atlantic Quart 58 1959.
Mills, R. J. jr. Muir: a speech from darkness grown. Accent 19 1959.
— Eden's gate: the later poetry of Muir. Personalist 44 1963.
— Muir's poetry: an introductory note. Newberry Lib Bull 6 1963.
Peschmann, H. Muir: a return to radical innocence. English 12 1959.
Read, H. Edwin Muir. Encounter 12 1959.
Sawasaki, J. Muir: his vision. Stud in Eng Lit (Tokyo) 36 1959.
Hamburger, M. Edwin Muir. Encounter 15 1960.
Holloway, J. The poetry of Muir. Hudson Rev 13 1960–1.
Jennings, E. Muir as poet and allegorist. London Mag 7 1960. Rptd, rev, in her Every changing shape, 1961.
Marcel, G. Edwin Muir. Études Anglaises 13 1960.
Scholten, M. The humanism of Muir. College Eng 21 1960.

Gardner, H. Edwin Muir. Cardiff 1961 (W. D. Thomas memorial lecture).
Raine, K. Muir: an appreciation. Texas Quart 4 1961.
Summers, J. H. The achievement of Muir. Massachusetts Rev 2 1961.
Butter, P. H. Edwin Muir. Edinburgh 1962 (Writers & Critics).
—— Edwin Muir: man and poet. Edinburgh 1966.
—— Muir: The journey back. English 16 1967.
Cox, C. B. Muir's The horses. Critical Survey 1 1962.
Joselyn, Sr M. Herbert and Muir: pilgrims of their age. Renascence 15 1963.
Morgan, E. Edwin Muir. Review (Oxford) 5 1963.
Mellown, E. W. The development of a criticism: Muir and Kafka. Comparative Lit 16 1964.
—— Autobiographical themes in the novels of Muir. Wisconsin Stud in Contemporary Lit 6 1965.
Gross, H. S. Modern poetry in the metrical tradition. In his Sound and form in modern poetry, 1964.
Watson, J. R. Muir and the problem of evil. CQ 6 1964.
Garber, F. Muir's heraldic mode. Twentieth-Century Lit 12 1966.
Helmick, E. T. Muir's poetry: a new evolution toward permanent value. Carrell 7 1966.
Hoffman, D. Muir: the story and the fable. Yale Rev 55 1966.
—— Barbarous knowledge: myth in the poetry of Yeats, Graves and Muir. New York 1967.
Scott-Craig, T. S. K. Muir's Toy horse. Explicator 24 1966.
Jack, I. Edwin Muir. Filología Moderna 6 1967.
MacLeish, A. A memoir of Muir. In his A continuing journey, 1968.
Muir, Willa. Belonging: a memoir. 1968.

ROBERT MALISE BOWYER NICHOLS
1893–1944

Bibliographies
'Gawsworth, John' (T. I. F. Armstrong). In his Ten contemporaries: notes toward their definitive bibliography, 1932.

§ I
Poetry
Invocation: war poems and others. 1915.
Ardours and endurances, also A faun's holiday and poems and phantasies. 1917, New York 1918.
The assault and other war poems from Ardours and endurances. 1918. Selection, with new introd.
The budded branch. 1918 (200 copies).
Invocation and peace celebration hymn for the British peoples. 1919 (about 60 copies).
Aurelia and other poems. 1920 (110 copies), 1920 (trade edn).
Winter berries. Hollywood 1924 (priv ptd, 60 copies).
[Eleven poems]. [1932] (Augustan Books of Poetry). Selection.
Fisbo: or the looking-glass loaned. 1934.
A Spanish triptych: three poems of compassion. 1936 (116 copies).
Such was my singing: being a selection from poems written between the years 1915 and 1940. Introd by Nichols 1942. Contains extracts from unpbd work.
Frankel, B. The aftermath, op. 17: song cycle for tenor voice. [1949]. Words by Nichols.

Other Works
General William Booth enters into heaven, and other poems by Nicholas Vachel Lindsay. Introd by Nichols 1919.

The smile of the sphinx. 1920 (295 copies). Short stories.
A year's grain. Tokyo 1921 (priv ptd, 100 copies). Apophthegms.
Guilty souls: a drama in four acts. 1922, New York 1922.
Fantastica: being The smile of the sphinx and other tales of imagination. (Romances of idea, volume one). 1923, New York 1923.
Masterpieces of Chikamatsu. Tr Asataro Miyamori, revised by Nichols 1926.
Twenty below: being a drama of the road. 1927. With J. Tully.
Under the yew: or, the gambler transformed. [1928], New York 1928. Short novel.
Wings over Europe: a dramatic extravaganza on a passing theme. New York 1929, London 1932. With M. Browne.
Hamlet and Don Quixote: an essay by Turgenev. Tr Nichols 1930.
Peter Warlock: a memoir of Philip Heseltine by C. Gray, with contributions by Sir R. Terry and Nichols. 1934.
The birth of a poem [his Sunset poem]. In R. E. M. Harding, An anatomy of inspiration, 2nd edn Cambridge 1942, 1948 (rev).
Anthology of war poetry 1914–1918. Ed Nichols 1943.
William Nicholson. Introd by Nichols 1948 (Penguin Modern Painters).

§ 2
Moore, T. S. A half Pleiade. In his Some soldier poets, 1919.
Mais, S. P. B. In his Books and their writers, 1920.
Morgan, C. In his Reflections in a mirror, ser 2, 1946; rptd from TLS 30 Dec 1944.
Johnston, J. H. In his English poetry of the first world war, Princeton 1964.

NORMAN CORNTHWAITE NICHOLSON
b. 1914

§ I
Poetry and Verse Plays
Selected poems: by J. Hall, K. Douglas, N. Nicholson. 1943.
Five rivers. 1944, New York 1945.
The old man of the mountains: a play in three acts. (Mercury 13 Sept 1945). 1946, 1950 (rev), New York 1950.
Rock face. 1948.
Prophesy to the wind: a play in four scenes and a prologue. (Watergate 7 Aug 1951). 1950.
The pot geranium. 1954.
A match for the devil. (St Mary's Hall, Edinburgh 27 Aug 1953). 1955. Play.
Birth by drowning. (Quarry, Mirfield 9 July 1959). 1960. Play in verse and prose.
Selected poems. 1966.

Other Works
An anthology of religious verse, designed for the times. Ed Nicholson 1942 (Pelican books).
Man & literature: an enquiry into the assumptions as to the nature and purpose of man which underlie much of modern writing. 1943.
The fire of the Lord. 1944, New York 1946. Novel.
The green shore. 1947. Novel.
Cumberland and Westmorland. 1949, New York 1949.
Wordsworth: an introduction and a selection. 1949.
H. G. Wells. 1950, Denver 1950.
Poems by William Cowper, selected and introduced by Nicholson. 1951.
William Cowper. 1951.

The Lakers: the adventures of the first tourists. 1955.

Provincial pleasures. 1959. On life in a small industrial town.

William Cowper. 1960 (Br Council pamphlet).

Portrait of the Lakes. 1963.

Enjoying it all. 1964. Radio talks in ser 'Lift up your hearts'.

The second chance. In Writers on themselves, 1964.

Greater Lakeland. 1969.

§2

Fausset, H. I'A. What is man? In his Poets and pundits, 1947; rptd review of Man & literature.

Wilder, A. N. Nature in apocalypse: Nicholson. In his Modern poetry and the Christian tradition, New York 1952.

Melchiori, G. Nicholson ed altri poeti inglesi. Lo Spettatore Italiano 8 1955.

Spender, S. Duncan's Death of Satan and Nicholson's Match for the devil. London Mag 2 1955.

Morgan, K. Some Christian themes in the poetry of Nicholson. REL 5 1964; rptd in pt in The word in creation: poetry of Nicholson, in her Christian themes in contemporary poetry, 1965.

Gardner, P. The provincial poetry of Nicholson. UTQ 36 1967.

Spanos, W. V. The Mercury theatre poets. In his The Christian tradition in modern British verse drama, New Brunswick NJ 1967.

ALFRED NOYES
1880–1958

Bibliographies

Neale, C. M. Contemporary Catholic authors: Alfred Noyes, litterateur, with a list of his publications and material about him. Catholic Lib World 13 1941.

Tobin, J. E. Alfred Noyes: corrected bibliography. Catholic Lib World 15 1944.

§1
Poetry

The loom of years. 1902.

The flower of Old Japan: a dim strange tale for all ages. 1903, New York 1907 (as The flower of Old Japan and other poems).

Poems. Edinburgh 1904.

The forest of wild thyme: a tale for children under ninety. Edinburgh 1905, 1911 (with alterations).

Drake: an English epic. 2 vols Edinburgh 1906–8, 1 vol New York [1909].

Poems. Introd by H. W. Mabie, New York 1906.

Forty singing seamen and other poems. Edinburgh 1907, New York [1930].

The Golden Hynde and other poems. New York 1908.

The enchanted island and other poems. Edinburgh 1909, New York 1910.

In memory of Swinburne. Cleveland Ohio 1909 (priv ptd, 36 copies).

Collected poems. Vols 1 and 2, Edinburgh 1910, New York 1913 (with different contents), Edinburgh 1928–9 (rev with omissions, and additions including Robin Hood, below). For vols 3 and 4 see 1920, 1927 below.

The prayer for peace. Cleveland Ohio 1911 (priv ptd, 100 copies).

Sherwood: or Robin Hood and the three kings: a play. New York 1911, Edinburgh 1926 (with alterations, as Robin Hood).

Tales of the Mermaid Tavern. Edinburgh 1913, New York 1913.

The carol of the fir tree. [1913].

Two Christmas poems. Cleveland Ohio 1913 (priv ptd).

The wine-press: a tale of war. Edinburgh 1913, New York [1913].

The searchlights. [1914]. Single poem.

A tale of Old Japan. Edinburgh 1914. Rptd from Collected poems vol 2 (as The two painters).

The lord of misrule and other poems. New York 1915.

A salute from the fleet and other poems. 1915.

Songs of the trawlers. [1916] (priv ptd, 25 copies).

The avenue of the allies, and Victory. New York 1918.

The new morning. New York [1918].

The elfin artist and other poems. Edinburgh 1920, New York [1920].

Collected poems. Vol 3, Edinburgh 1920, New York 1920 [with different contents].

Selected verse including A victory dance and other poems, old and new. Edinburgh 1921.

The torch-bearers (The watchers of the sky; The book of the earth; The last voyage). 3 vols Edinburgh 1922–30, New York 1922–30, 1 vol London 1937.

Songs of Shadow-of-a-leaf and other poems. Edinburgh 1924.

Princeton, May 1917; The call of the spring. Dansville NY [1925]. With outline, study and explanatory notes by F. R. Signor.

Robin Hood: a play. 1926. See Sherwood, 1911 above.

Dick Turpin's ride and other poems. New York 1927.

Collected poems. Vol 4, Edinburgh 1927.

Ballads and poems. Edinburgh 1928. Selection.

The strong city. [1928].

[Twelve poems]. [1931] (Augustan Books of Poetry). Selection.

Poems: the author's own selection for schools. [1935].

Orchard's Bay. 1939. Contains poems previously unpbd in book form. See Other works, below.

If judgment comes: a poem. New York 1941.

Shadows on the down and other poems. New York [1941], London [1945].

Poems of the new world. Introd by Viscount Halifax, Philadelphia 1942.

Collected poems. Philadelphia 1947, London 1950, 1963 (adding a selection from A letter to Lucian, and four other poems), Port Washington NY 1966 (with 13 additional poems). Selection, excluding The torch-bearers.

Daddy fell into the pond and other poems for children. New York 1952.

A letter to Lucian and other poems. 1956, Philadelphia 1957.

Some single poems were ptd in small edns by E. H. Blakeney at his private press at Winchester. They include The cormorant, *1936,* Youth and memory [*verse only*], *1937,* Wizards, *1938,* The Assumption: an answer, *1950 and* A Roehampton School song, *1950. Not all were rptd in* Collected poems, *above.*

Other Works

The magic casement: an anthology of fairy poetry. Ed with introd by Noyes [1908], New York 1909.

The minstrelsy of the Scottish border, by Sir Walter Scott. Ed with introd by Noyes. 1908, New York 1913.

William Morris. [1908] (EML).

The temple of beauty: an anthology. Ed Noyes 1910, New York [1911] (as A poet's anthology of poems).

Lamszus, W. The human slaughterhouse. Introd by Noyes, New York 1913.

Rada: a drama of war in one act. New York 1914, London 1915 (as Rada: a Belgian Christmas Eve), New York [1915] (as A Belgian Christmas Eve: being Rada re-written and enlarged as an Episode of the Great War). In prose and verse.

A book of Princeton verse, 1916. Ed Noyes, Princeton 1916, London 1916.

Mystery ships: trapping 'U'-boats. 1916.

What is England doing? 1916.

Open boats. Edinburgh 1917, New York [1917]. On war at sea.

Walking shadows. 1918, New York 1918 (as Walking shadows: sea tales and others).

Beyond the desert: a tale of Death valley. New York [1920].

The hidden player. [1924], New York 1924. Tales.

Some aspects of modern poetry. [1924], New York 1924.

New essays and American impressions. New York [1927].

The opalescent parrot. 1929, New York 1929. Essays on literary and miscellaneous subjects.

The return of the scare-crow. 1929, New York 1929 (as The sun cure). Novel.

Tennyson. Edinburgh 1932.

The unknown god. 1934, New York 1934, London 1949 (with an epilogue).

Happiness and success, by S. Baldwin, A. Noyes [et al]. 1936.

Voltaire. 1936, New York 1936, London 1939 (with new preface). *See* M. Ryan, Noyes on Voltaire, Dublin [1938].

Youth and memory: spoken at the Empire Youth Rally, 18 May 1937. [1937]. In prose and verse.

Orchard's Bay. 1939, New York 1939, London 1955 (as The incompleat gardener). Essays, with 40 poems unpbd in book form.

The last man. 1940, New York 1940 (as No other man). Novel.

Pageant of letters. New York 1940. Literary essays.

The edge of the abyss. Sackville, New Brunswick [1942], London 1944 (with new preface). Lectures.

The secret of Pooduck Island. New York 1943, London [1946]. For children.

The golden book of Catholic poetry. Ed Noyes, Philadelphia 1946.

Portrait of Horace. 1947, New York 1947 (as Horace: a portrait).

Two worlds for memory. 1953, Philadelphia 1953. Autobiography.

The devil takes a holiday. 1955. Novel.

The accusing ghost: or justice for Casement. 1957, New York 1957 (as The accusing ghost of Roger Casement).

Noyes edited the Helicon poetry series, *4 vols 1925, and contributed a general introd to the series and introds to the individual poets Wordsworth, Tennyson, Longfellow, Keats.*

§2

Kernahan, C. Alfred Noyes. In his Six famous living poets, 1922.

Davison, E. The poetry of Noyes. Eng Jnl 15 1926.

Brenner, R. In her Ten modern poets, New York 1930.

Jerrold, W. Alfred Noyes. 1930.

Braybrooke, P. Noyes: poet and romantic. In his Some Victorian and Georgian Catholics, 1932.

Larg, D. G. Alfred Noyes. Toronto 1936.

Weygandt, C. Alfred Noyes. In his Time of Yeats, [1937].

Saul, G. B. Yeats, Noyes and Day Lewis. N & Q 195 1950.

Stanford, D. The poetic achievement of Noyes. English 12 1958.

'SEUMAS O'SULLIVAN', JAMES SULLIVAN STARKEY
1879–1958

Bibliographies

MacManus, M. J. Bibliographies of Irish authors 3: Seumas O'Sullivan. Dublin Mag 5 1930. Only lists books.

§1
Poetry

The twilight people. Dublin, London 1905.

Verses sacred and profane. Dublin 1908.

The earth lover and other verses. Dublin 1909.

Lyrics. Portland Maine 1910 (Bibelot 16 no 11).

Poems. Dublin 1912. Selection.

An epilogue to the praise of Angus and other poems. Dublin, London 1914.

Requiem and other poems. Dublin 1917 (priv ptd, 100 copies). Rptd in next.

The Rosses and other poems. Dublin, London 1918.

The poems of Seumas O'Sullivan. Introd by P. Colum, Boston 1923.

Common adventures: a book of prose and verse; Nicolas Flamel: a play in four acts from the French of G. de Nerval. Dublin 1926 (200 copies).

The lamplighter and other poems. Dublin 1929.

Twenty-five lyrics. Introd by 'A.E.' Flansham 1933 (150 copies). Selection.

At Christmas: verses. Dublin 1934 (priv ptd, 50 copies). Rptd in Collected poems, 1940, below.

Personal talk: a book of verses. Dublin 1936 (priv ptd, 100 copies). Mostly rptd in Collected poems, 1940, below.

Poems 1930–1938. Dublin 1938 (300 copies). Includes most of At Christmas and Personal talk.

Collected poems. Dublin 1940.

Dublin poems. Foreword by P. Colum, New York 1946.

Translations and transcriptions. Belfast 1950. Translations adaptations and imitations collected from earlier works.

Other Works

Impressions: a selection from the note-books of the late J. H. Orwell. Foreword by O'Sullivan, Dublin 1910.

Mud and purple: pages from the diary of a Dublin man. Dublin, London 1917.

Facetiae et curiosa: being a selection from the note books of the late J. H. Orwell, made by his friend Seumas O'Sullivan. Dublin 1937 (100 copies).

Poems by William Starkey, M.D. Selected with a preface by his son James Sullivan Starkey—Seumas O'Sullivan. Dublin 1938 (priv ptd).

Editor's choice: a little anthology of poems selected from the Dublin Magazine by O'Sullivan. Dublin 1944.

Essays and recollections. Dublin, Cork 1944.

The rose and the bottle and other essays. Dublin 1946.

O'Sullivan founded and edited the Dublin Mag *1923–58. He also edited the first two sers of Tower Press booklets 1906–8 and the third ser 1938–9 with Austin Clarke.*

§2

'A.E.' (G. W. Russell). A note on Seumas O'Sullivan. In his Imaginations and reveries, 1915.

—— A bibliophile. In his The living torch, 1937.

Colum, P. Seumas O'Sullivan's Dublin. In his The road round Ireland, 1926.

Strong, L. A. G. Three Irish poets. Commonweal 7 June 1935.

—— Seumas O'Sullivan. In his Personal remarks, 1953.

Höpfl, H. Seumas O'Sullivan. Neuphilologische Monatsschrift 8 1937.

WILFRED EDWARD SALTER OWEN
1893–1918

Most of Owen's mss other than letters and juvenilia are in the BM. See articles by Milne and Brown, below (Bibliographies).

Bibliographies

Milne, H. J. M. The poems of Wilfred Owen. BM Quart 9 1935. Description of Additional mss 43720 and 43721.

Welland, D. S. R. Wilfred Owen's manuscripts. TLS 15, 22 June 1956, and subsequent correspondence.

Brown, T. J. English literary autographs xlviii: Wilfred Owen 1893–1918. Book Collector 12 1963.

White, W. Wilfred Owen 1893–1918: a bibliography. Kent Ohio 1967. Rptd from Serif 2 1965. Includes critical material and reviews.

§1

Poems. With introd by S. Sassoon 1920, New York 1921, London 1931 (as The poems of Wilfred Owen: a new edition, including many pieces now first published and notices of his life and work by E. Blunden), New York 1931.

Thirteen poems. Northampton Mass 1956 (400 copies). Illustr B. Shahn. Selection.

The collected poems of Wilfred Owen. Ed with introd and notes by C. Day Lewis and with a memoir by E. Blunden 1963, New York 1964. Blunden's memoir rptd from Poems 1931, above.

Letters

Collected letters, edited by J. Bell and H. Owen 1967.

§2

Fletcher, I. K. Wilfred Owen. Welsh Outlook 15 1928.

Parsons, I. M. The poems of Owen, 1893–1918. New Criterion 10 1931.

Grieg, N. De unge døde: Brooke-Sorley-Owen. Oslo 1932.

Spender, S. Poetry and pity. In his The destructive element, 1935.

Daiches, D. The poetry of Owen. In his New literary values, 1936.

Loiseau, J. A reading of Owen's poems. E Studies 21 1939.

Ball, D. Wilfred Owen. Cahiers de Paris 8 1940.

Ledward, P. The poetry of Owen. Poetry Rev 32 1941.

Dickinson, P. Poetry of Owen. Fortnightly 162 1944.

Bushnell, A. Wilfred Owen. Poetry Rev 37 1946.

Vallette, J. Trois poètes anglais morts à la guerre. Mercure de France 1 April 1947. Owen, Alun Lewis and Keyes.

Cejp, L. Wilfred Owen. Profil válečného básníka. Slovesná Věda 2 1949.

—— Několik rysů básnického díla Wilfreda Owena. Časopis pro moderní filologii 32 1949.

—— Podivné setkání. Glossy k básni Wilfreda Owena. Sborník Vysoké školy pedagogické v Olomouci 4 1957.

Savage, D. S. Two prophetic poems [by Owen and Yeats]. Western Rev 13 1949.

Sitwell, O. Wilfred Owen. In his Noble essences, 1950.

Welland, D. S. R. Half-rhyme in Owen: its derivation and use. RES new ser 1 1950.

—— Wilfred Owen: poetry, pity, philosophy. Northern Rev (Montreal) 6 1953.

—— Owen: a critical study. 1960.

Lehmann, J. But for Beaumont Hamel. In his Open night, 1952. On R. Brooke and Owen.

Owen against the background of two wars. TLS 28 Aug 1953.

Sergeant, H. The importance of Owen. English 10 1954.

Thomas, D. In his Quite early one morning, 1954.

Cohen, J. The Owen war poetry collection. Lib Chron Univ of Texas 5 1955.

—— Owen's Greater love. Tulane Stud in Eng 6 1956.

—— Owen's The show. Explicator 16 1957.

—— In memory of W. B. Yeats—and Owen. JEGP 58 1959 and 59 1960.

—— The war poet as archetypal spokesman. Stand 4 1960.

—— Owen: fresher fields than Flanders. Eng Lit in Transition 7 1964.

—— Owen agonistes. Eng Lit in Transition 8 1965.

Masson, D. I. Owen's free phonetic patterns: their style and function. Jnl of Aesthetics & Art Criticism 13 1955.

Spear, H. D. Owen and poetic truth. Univ of Kansas City Rev 25 1958.

Hazo, S. J. The passion of Owen. Renascence 11 1959.

Matthews, G. Brooke and Owen. Stand 4 1960.

Gose, E. B., jr. Digging in: an interpretation of Owen's Strange meeting. College Eng 22 1961.

Hardin, G. La passion de Wilfred Owen. Esprit 29 1961.

Hobsbaum, P. The road not taken: three poets who died in the first world war. Listener 23 Nov 1961. E. Thomas, Owen, Rosenberg.

Freeman, R. Parody as a literary form: George Herbert and Owen. EC 13 1963.

—— Owen's Greater love. EC 16 1966.

Hill, J. J., jr. The text of Owen's Purple. N & Q 208 1963.

—— Owen's Greater love. EC 15 1965.

Owen, H. Journey from obscurity: Owen 1893–1918: i, Childhood; ii, Youth; iii, War. 3 vols 1963–5.

Wulfsberg, F. Han som kastet medaljen på sjön. Samtiden 72 1963.

Davie, D. In the pity. New Statesman 28 Aug 1964.

Fletcher, J. Owen re-edited. Études Anglaises 17 1964.

Fowler, A. The pity is in the music: Benjamin Britten's War requiem. Approach no 50 1964.

Walsh, T. J. (ed). A tribute to Owen. [1964]. Contributors include S. Sassoon, F. Berry and K. Muir.

Bergonzi, B. Rosenberg and Owen. In his Heroes' twilight: a study of the literature of the Great War, 1965.

Bouyssou, R. Le messianisme de Wilfred Owen. In Hommage à Paul Dottin, 1966.

Hackl, L. C. 'In search of a ram'—a study of a man in conflict. Eng Jnl 55 1966.

Combecher, H. Owen: Exposure. In Die moderne englische Lyrik, ed H. Oppel, Berlin 1967.

Varet, E. Les lettres de Wilfred Owen. Études Anglaises 21 1968.

White, G. M. Critic's key: poem or personality. Eng Lit in Transition 11 1968.

—— Wilfred Owen. New York [1969] (Twayne's English Authors).

Landon, G. M. The quantification of metaphoric language in the verse of Owen. In Statistics and style, ed L. Doležel and R. W. Baily, New York 1969.

'JOHN OXENHAM',
WILLIAM ARTHUR DUNKERLEY
1852–1941

See cols 696–7, below.

HERBERT EDWARD PALMER
1880–1961

Bibliographies

'Gawsworth, John' (T. I. F. Armstrong). In his Ten contemporaries: notes toward their definitive bibliography, 1932.

§1
Poetry

Two fishers and other poems. 1918.

Two foemen and other poems. 1920.

Two minstrels: The wolf knight, his book; The wolf minstrel, Cædmon's book. 1921.

The unknown warrior and other poems. 1924.

Songs of salvation, sin and satire. [1925] (300 copies).

Christmas miniature. St Albans 1928 (priv ptd). Poem issued as Christmas card.

The armed muse. 1930.

Jonah comes to Nineveh: a ballad. Stanford Dingley 1930 (125 copies). Rptd in Collected poems, 1933, below.

[Thirty poems]. [1931] (Augustan Books of Poetry). Selection, with two new poems.

Cinder Thursday. 1931. Parody and satire.

In autumn. 1931 (priv ptd, 260 copies). Single poem rptd in Summit and chasm, 1934.

Collected poems. 1933. Selection with some revisions.

Summit and chasm: a book of poems and rimes. 1934.

The vampire and other poems and rimes of a pilgrim's progress. 1936.

The gallows-cross: a book of songs and verses for the times. 1940.

Christmas signs: St Albans 1941. St Albans [1942?]. Single poem rptd in A sword in the desert, 1946, below.

Season and festival. 1943. Selection.

A sword in the desert: a book of poems and verses for the present times. 1946.

The old knight: a poem sequence for the present times. 1949.

The ride from hell: a poem-sequence of the times for three voices. 1958.

Other Works

The judgment of François Villon: a pageant-episode play in five acts. 1927 (400 copies).

Susanne Trautwein. The lady of laws, tr Palmer and L. W. Charley 1929.

The teaching of English. 1930.

What the public wants. [1932] (Blue Moon booklet).

Indian spirituality: the travels and teaching of Sivana-rayan, by Mohini Mohan Chatterji. Ed and rev Palmer 1933.

The roving angler. 1933, New York [1933], London 1947 (rev with addns).

The mistletoe child: an autobiography of childhood. 1935.

Post-Victorian poetry. 1938, New York 1940.

The dragon of Tingalam: a fairy comedy. 1945.

The Greenwood anthology of new verse. Compiled by Palmer 1948.

CLERE TREVOR JAMES HERBERT PARSONS
1908–31

Poems. 1932.

Parsons edited, with 'B.B.', Oxford Poetry 1928.

MERVYN LAURENCE PEAKE
1911–68

See col 699, below

RUTH PITTER
b. 1897

§1

First poems. 1920.

First and second poems 1912–1925. Preface by H. Belloc 1927, Garden City NY 1930.

Persephone in Hades. Auch 1931 (100 copies). Single poem.

A mad lady's garland. Preface by H. Belloc 1934, New York [1935].

A trophy of arms: poems 1926–1935. Preface by James Stephens [1936], New York 1936. Omits contents of A mad lady's garland.

The spirit watches. [1939], New York 1940.

The rude potato. 1941. Humorous verse on gardening.

Poem. Southampton 1943 (60 copies). Rptd in next.

The bridge: poems 1939–1944. 1945, New York 1946 (as The bridge: poems 1939–1945).

Ruth Pitter on cats. 1947.

Urania: poems selected from A trophy of arms, The spirit watches and The bridge. 1950.

The ermine: poems 1942–1952. 1953.

Still by choice. 1966.

Poems 1926–1966. 1968.

§2

Gilbert, R. Ruth Pitter. In his Four living poets, Santa Barbara 1944.

Watkin, E. I. Urania: the poetry of Ruth Pitter. In his Poets and mystics, 1953.

Russell, A. (ed). Ruth Pitter: homage to a poet. 1969. Introd by D. Cecil.

WILLIAM CHARLES FRANKLYN PLOMER
b. 1903

See cols 704–5, below.

ALAN PORTER
1899–1942

§1
Poetry

The signature of pain and other poems. 1930, New York 1931.

The sad shepherd: the unfinished pastoral comedy of Ben Jonson, now completed by Porter; with a [biographical] foreword. New York [1944].

Other Works

Poems, chiefly from manuscript, by John Clare. Ed E. Blunden and Porter [1920], New York 1921.

Coal: a challenge to the national conscience. 1927. By various authors, ed Porter.

What life should mean to you, by Alfred Adler. Ed Porter, Boston 1931, London 1932.

The art of being a woman, by Olga Knopf. Ed Porter, Boston 1932, London 1932.

Women on their own, by Olga Knopf. Ed Porter, Boston 1935.

Porter was joint editor of Oxford Poetry 1920 and 1921, and of The Oxford and Cambridge Miscellany, 1920. He was literary editor of Spectator 1924–5 and of T.P.'s Weekly 1928–9.

FRANK TEMPLETON PRINCE
b. 1912

§1
Poetry

Poems. 1938, Norfolk Conn 1938 ([New Directions] Poet of the month).

Soldiers bathing and other poems. 1954.

The stolen heart. San Francisco [1957]. Single poem, rptd in The doors of stone, below.

The doors of stone: poems 1938–1962. 1963. Selection.

Other Works

The Italian element in Milton's verse. Oxford 1954, 1962 (corrected).

Milton. Samson agonistes. Ed Prince 1957.

In defence of English: an inaugural lecture. Southampton 1959.
The poems of Shakespeare. Ed Prince 1960 (New Arden).
Sir Thomas Wyatt, by S. Baldi. Tr Prince 1961 (Br Council pamphlet).
Milton. Paradise lost, books I and II. Ed Prince, Oxford 1962.
Shakespeare: the poems. 1963 (Br Council pamphlet).
Milton. Comus and other poems. Ed Prince 1968.

§2

Inglis, F. Prince and the prospects for poetry. Univ of Denver Quart 1 1966.

KATHLEEN JESSIE RAINE
b. 1908

§1
Poetry

Stone and flower: poems 1935–43. 1943.
Living in time. 1946.
The pythoness and other poems. 1949, New York 1952.
Selected poems. New York 1952 (250 copies). 38 poems selected with one exception from previous books.
The year one. 1952, New York 1953.
Collected poems. 1956, New York 1957.
Christmas 1960. [1960] (priv ptd). Single poem issued as a greetings card.
The hollow hill and other poems, 1960–1964. 1965.
Kathleen Raine and Vernon Watkins: selected by E. Owen. 1968 (Pergamon Poets).
Six dreams and other poems. 1968.

Other Works

Aspects de la littérature anglaise 1918–1945, présentés par Kathleen Raine et Max-Pol Fouchet. Paris 1947.
William Blake. 1951, 1958 (with addns). (Br Council pamphlet).
The letters of Samuel Taylor Coleridge. Selected and with an introd by Kathleen Raine 1950 [1952].
Coleridge. 1953 (Br Council pamphlet).
Coleridge. Poems and prose. Selected with an introd by Kathleen Raine. 1957 (Penguin Poets).
Pinto, V. de S. (ed). The divine vision: studies in the poetry and art of William Blake. 1957. Contains The little girl lost and found and The lapsed soul, by Kathleen Raine.
Poetry in relation to traditional wisdom. 1958. Lecture.
Blake and England. Cambridge 1960. Lecture.
Letters on poetry from W. B. Yeats to Dorothy Wellesley. Introd by Kathleen Raine 1964.
Defending ancient springs. 1967. Essays on literature.
The written word: a speech delivered at the Annual Luncheon of the Poetry Society. 1967 (210 copies).
Blake and tradition. Princeton 1969, London 1969.
Thomas Taylor the Platonist: selected writings, ed with introd by Kathleen Raine and G. M. Harper 1969.
Kathleen Raine tr works by Balzac, Paul Foulquié, Denis de Rougemont and Calderón.

§2

Adams, H. The poetry of Kathleen Raine. Texas Stud in Eng 37 1958.
Foltinek, H. The primitive element in the poetry of Kathleen Raine. E Studies 42 1961.
Mills, R. J. jr. The visionary poetry of Kathleen Raine. Renascence 14 1962.

SIR HERBERT EDWARD READ
1893–1968
See cols 1108–13, below.

HENRY REED
b. 1914

§1
Poetry

A map of Verona: poems. 1946, New York 1947 (as A map of Verona and other poems).

Other Works

The novel since 1939. 1946 (The arts in Britain).
Moby Dick: a play for radio from Herman Melville's novel. 1947.
Perdu and his father, by Paride Rombi; translated from the Italian by Reed. 1954.
Three plays by Ugo Betti: comprising The queen and the rebels, The burnt flower-bed, Summertime. Tr and with a foreword by Reed 1956, New York 1958.
Crime on Goat Island, by Ugo Betti. Tr Reed [1960], San Francisco 1961.
Dino Buzzati. Larger than life. Tr Reed 1962.
Honoré de Balzac. Eugénie Grandet: a new translation by Reed, New York 1964.
Natalia Ginzburg. The advertisement—L'inserzione. Tr Reed 1969.

'JAMES REEVES',
JOHN MORRIS REEVES
b. 1909

§1
Poetry

The natural need. Deyá Majorca, London 1935. With verse preface by L. Riding.
The imprisoned sea. [1949].
The wandering moon. 1950, New York 1960. For children.
The blackbird in the lilac: poems for children. 1952, New York 1959.
The password and other poems. 1952.
A health to John Patch: a ballad operetta. [1957]. For children.
Prefabulous animiles. 1957, New York 1960. With E. Ardizzone. For children.
The talking skull. 1958.
Collected poems 1929–1959. 1960.
Hurdy-gurdy: selected poems. 1961. For children.
Ragged Robin. [1961], New York 1961. For children.
The questioning tiger. 1964.
Selected poems. 1967.
Subsong. 1969.

Other Works

The quality of education: methods and purposes in the secondary curriculum. Ed D. Thompson and Reeves 1947.
Mulcaster market: three plays for young players. 1951.
The Bible in brief: selections from the text of the Authorised Version of 1611, chosen and arranged by Reeves. 1954, New York 1954 (as The Holy Bible in brief: King James text).

The king who took sunshine: a comedy for children in two acts. 1954.

The critical sense: practical criticism of prose and poetry. 1956.

Pigeons and princesses. 1956, New York 1962 (as pt of Sailor Rumbelow and other stories, below). For children.

The idiom of the people: English traditional verse edited with an introduction and notes from the manuscripts of Cecil J. Sharp. 1958, New York 1958.

Mulbridge Manor. 1958. Novel for children.

Teaching poetry: poetry in class from five to fifteen. 1958.

The personal vision. Poetry Supplement, ed Reeves for the Poetry Book Society. 1959.

Titus in trouble. 1959, New York 1960. Story for children.

The everlasting circle: English traditional verse, ed with an introd and notes from the manuscripts of S. Baring-Gould, H. E. D. Hammond and G. B. Gardiner 1960, New York 1960.

The war 1939–1945. Edited by D. Flower and Reeves 1960, New York 1960 (as The taste of courage: the war 1939–1945).

Great English essays, selected and ed Reeves 1961.

Selected poetry and prose of Robert Graves, chosen, introduced and annotated by Reeves 1961.

A short history of English poetry 1340–1940. 1961, New York 1962.

Georgian poetry, selected and introduced by Reeves. 1962 (Penguin Poets).

Sailor Rumbelow and Britannia. 1962, New York 1962 (with contents of Pigeons and princesses, 1956, as Sailor Rumbelow and other stories). For children.

The peddler's dream and other plays. New York 1963.

The story of Jackie Thimble. New York 1964, London 1965. For children.

The strange light. 1964. Stories for children.

The Cassell book of English poetry, selected and introduced by Reeves 1965, New York 1965.

The pillar-box thieves. 1965. Story for children.

Understanding poetry. 1965.

Rhyming Will. 1967. Story for children.

An anthology of free verse. Oxford 1968.

Homage to Trumbull Stickney: poems selected by Reeves and S. Haldane. 1968.

Reeves also wrote a number of school textbooks, mainly on the appreciation of literature; compiled prose and verse anthologies for children; and wrote versions for children of several well-known literary works and traditional and biblical stories. He edited, with J. Bronowski, the series Songs for sixpence, Cambridge 1929, and several other series, including Poetry Bookshelf, *1951–, himself editing the selections from D. H. Lawrence, Donne, Hopkins, Clare, Browning, Coleridge, Emily Dickinson and Swift, and an anthology* The modern poets' world. *He also edited* Unicorn Books, *1960–, himself editing the selection from Stephen Leacock.*

§2

For discussions of Reeves as a writer for children, see Children's Books, *col 810, below.*

A conversation with James Reeves. Review (Oxford) no 11–12 1964.

ANNE BARBARA RIDLER, née BRADBY
b. 1912

§1
Poetry and Verse Plays

Poems. 1939.

A dream observed and other poems. [1941] (Poetry London pamphlet).

Cain: a play in two acts. 1943.

The nine bright shiners. 1943.

The shadow factory: a nativity play. (Mercury 19 Dec 1945). 1946.

Henry Bly and other plays (The mask; The missing bridegroom). 1950. The mask and The missing bridegroom produced at the Watergate, 6 March 1951.

The golden bird and other poems. 1951.

The trial of Thomas Cranmer: a play. 1956. Broadcast 21 March 1956; produced in the University Church, Oxford, May 1956.

A matter of life and death. 1959.

Selected poems. New York 1961.

Who is my neighbour? (The Wayfarers, at the Leeds Civic Theatre, Oct 1961), and How bitter the bread. 1963.

Other Works

Shakespeare criticism 1919–1935, selected with an introd by Anne Bradby. 1936 (WC).

The little book of modern verse, chosen by Anne Ridler. 1941.

Time passes and other poems, by Walter de la Mare, selected and arranged by Anne Ridler. 1942.

Best ghost stories, selected by Anne Ridler. 1945.

The Faber book of modern verse. Ed M. Roberts 1951 (with supplement of new poems chosen by Anne Ridler).

The image of the city and other essays by Charles Williams, selected by Anne Ridler with a critical introduction. 1958.

Charles Williams: selected writings, chosen by Anne Ridler. 1961, Carbondale 1963.

Poems and some letters of James Thomson, edited by Anne Ridler. 1963.

Shakespeare criticism 1935–60, selected with an introduction by Anne Ridler. 1963 (WC).

Best stories of church and clergy: edited with an introduction by C. Bradby and Anne Ridler. 1966.

Thomas Traherne. Poems, centuries and three thanksgivings, edited by Anne Ridler. 1966.

Olive Willis and Downe House: an adventure in education. 1967.

§2

Kliewer, W. Theological form in Anne Ridler's plays. Approach no 52 1964.

Morgan, K. E. 'The holiness of the heart's affections': poetry of Anne Ridler. In her Christian themes in contemporary poets, 1965; also English 16 1966.

Spanos, W. V. The Mercury Theatre poets. In his Christian tradition in modern British verse drama, New Brunswick NJ 1967.

'MICHAEL ROBERTS', WILLIAM EDWARD ROBERTS
1902–48
Bibliographies

Hamilton, R. A select bibliography of the published writings of Roberts. In A portrait of Roberts, ed T. R. Eason and R. Hamilton 1949, §2 below.

§1
Poetry

These our matins. 1930.

Poems. 1936.

Orion marches. 1939.

Collected poems, with an introductory memoir by Janet Roberts [Janet Adam Smith]. 1958. Includes unpbd poems.

Roberts also contributed 5 poems to his anthology New country, *1933, below.*

Other Works

New signatures: poems by several hands, collected by Roberts. 1932.

Elizabethan prose, selected and prefaced by Roberts. 1933.

New country: prose and poetry by the authors of New signatures. 1933. Ed Roberts, with preface, 5 poems and a prose contribution by him.

Critique of poetry. 1934.

Newton and the origin of colours: a study of one of the earliest examples of scientific method. 1934. With E. R. Thomas.

Eberhart, R. Reading the spirit. Introd by Roberts 1936.

The Faber book of modern verse. Ed Roberts 1936, 1951 (with supplement by A. Ridler), 1965 (rev, with supplement by D. Hall).

The modern mind. 1937, New York 1937.

T. E. Hulme. 1938.

The recovery of the west. 1941.

The Faber book of comic verse, compiled by Roberts. 1942.

Belgium and Holland. 1944 (Army Bureau of Current Affairs).

Notes on College history, 1840–1865. College of St Mark and St John, Chelsea. Ed Roberts 1946.

The estate of man. 1951. Ed Janet Adam Smith, Roberts's widow. Unfinished.

§2

Smith, J. A. In her Mountain holiday, 1946.

Eason, T. W. and R. Hamilton (ed). A portrait of Roberts. 1949.

Eliot, T. S. Michael Roberts. New Eng Weekly 13 Jan 1949.

Raine, K. Roberts and the hero myth. Penguin New Writing no 39 1949.

Cattaneo, S. La poesia di Roberts. In Studi e ricerche di letteratura inglese e americana, ed A. Lombardo, vol 1 Milan 1967.

WILLIAM ROBERT RODGERS
1909–69

§1

Awake! and other poems. 1941, New York 1942 (as Awake! and other wartime poems).

The Ulstermen and their country. [1947]. Prose.

Europa and the bull and other poems. 1952, New York 1953.

Ireland in colour: a collection of forty colour photographs, with an introductory text and notes on the illustrations by Rodgers. 1957, New York 1957.

§2

Greacen, R. The poetry of Rodgers. Poetry Quart 12 1950–1.

Bogan, L. War poetry. In her Selected criticism, New York 1955; rptd review of Awake! and other wartime poems.

ISAAC ROSENBERG
1890–1918

Bibliographies

Isaac Rosenberg 1890–1918: a catalogue of an exhibition held at Leeds University May–June 1959, together with the text of unpublished material. [1959]. Includes uncollected verse fragments and letters, paintings etc.

Cohen, J. Rosenberg: the poet's progress in print. Eng Lit in Transition 6 1963.

§1

Night and day. [1912].

Youth. 1915.

Moses: a play. 1916. Includes poems.

Poems, selected and ed G. Bottomley, with an introductory memoir by L. Binyon. 1922.

Collected works: poetry, prose, letters and some drawings, edited by G. Bottomley and D. Harding. 1937. Foreword by S. Sassoon. Includes unpbd verse and contributions to periodicals, some posthumous.

Collected poems. Ed G. Bottomley and D. Harding 1949, New York [1949]. Reimpression of Poems section of Collected works, 1937, above; 'revised'.

§2

Lucas, F. L. Isaac Rosenberg. In his Authors dead & living, 1926.

Roditi, E. Judaism and poetry. Jewish Rev 2 1932.

Harding, D. Aspects of the poetry of Rosenberg. Scrutiny 3 1935; rptd in his Experience into words, 1963.

Leftwich, J. Isaac Rosenberg. Jewish Chron 167 1936.

Gregory, H. The isolation of Rosenberg. Poetry (Chicago) 68 1946.

Bewley, M. The poetry of Rosenberg. Commentary 7 1949.

Daiches, D. Rosenberg: poet. Commentary 10 1950.

Sackton, A. H. Two poems on war: a critical exercise. SE 31 1952. Sassoon's Aftermath and Rosenberg's Break of day in the trenches.

Silkin, J. Anglo-Jewish poetry. Jewish Quart 5 1958.

—— Rosenberg: the war, class and the Jews. Stand 4 1960.

Dickinson, P. A double gift. Listener 11 June 1959.

Lindeman, J. The 'trench poems' of Rosenberg. Literary Rev (Fairleigh Dickinson Univ) 2 1959.

Cohen, J. Rosenberg: from romantic to classic. Tulane Stud in Eng 10 1960.

Hyman, F. C. The worlds of Rosenberg. Judaism 9 1960.

Hobsbaum, P. The road not taken: three poets who died in the first world war. Listener 23 Nov 1961. E. Thomas, Owen, Rosenberg.

Bergonzi, B. Rosenberg and Owen. In his Heroes' twilight: a study of the literature of the Great War, 1965.

Silk, D. Isaac Rosenberg 1890–1918. Judaism 14 1965.

ALAN ROSS
b. 1922

§1
Poetry

Summer thunder. Oxford 1941.

The derelict day: poems in Germany. 1947.

Something of the sea: poems 1942–1952. 1954, Boston 1955.

To whom it may concern: poems 1952–57. 1958.

African negatives. 1962.

North from Sicily: poems in Italy 1961–64. 1965.

Poems 1942–67. 1967.

Other Works

Time was away: a notebook in Corsica. 1948.

The forties: a period piece. 1950.

Poems by John Gay, selected and introduced by Ross. 1950.

Borrowed time: short stories by F. Scott Fitzgerald, selected by A. and J. Ross. 1951.

The gulf of pleasure. 1951. Anthology of Naples.
Poetry 1945–1950. 1951 (The Arts in Britain).
The bandit on the billiard table: a journey through Sardinia. 1954, 1960 (rev as South to Sardinia).
Australia 55: a journal of the MCC tour. 1955.
Abroad: travel stories, chosen with foreword by Ross. 1957.
Cape summer, and the Australians in England. 1957.
The onion man. 1959. For children.
The cricketer's companion. Ed Ross 1960.
Danger on Glass Island. 1960. For children.
Through the Caribbean: the MCC tour of the West Indies, 1959–1960. 1960.
Australia 63. 1963.
The West Indies at Lord's. 1963.
Stories from the London Magazine. Ed Ross 1964.
The wreck of Moni. 1965. For children.
London Magazine stories 3(–5). Ed Ross 1968–70.
Ross tr works by P. Diolé, P.-D. Gaisseau, R. Merle and A. Embiricos. He edited London Mag from 1961.

MARGOT RUDDOCK
1907–51

§1

The lemon tree. Introd by W. B. Yeats 1937.
Many of Margot Ruddock's poems were revised by Yeats, who included some in the Oxford Book of Modern Verse, 1936. Her correspondence with Yeats was ed by R. McHugh as Ah, sweet dancer, 1970.

VICTORIA MARY SACKVILLE-WEST
1892–1962

Bibliographies

Boochever, F. A selected list of writings by and about V. Sackville-West. Bull of Bibliography 16 1938.

§1
Poetry

Poems of west and east. 1917.
Orchard and vineyard. 1921.
The land. 1926.
King's daughter. 1929, Garden City NY 1930.
Duineser Elegien. Elegies from the castle of Duino, tr from the German of R. M. Rilke by V. Sackville-West and E. Sackville-West. 1931 (238 copies).
Invitation to cast out care. 1931 (Ariel Poem).
Sissinghurst. 1931 (500 copies).
[Twenty-three poems]. [1931] (Augustan Books of Poetry). Selection with previously uncollected poems.
Collected poems, volume one. 1933, Garden City NY 1934. No more pbd.
Solitude: a poem. 1938, New York 1939.
Selected poems. 1941. Selection, with 5 new poems.
The garden. 1946, Garden City NY 1946.

Other Works

Heritage. [1919], New York [1919]. Novel.
The dragon in shallow waters. 1921, New York 1922. Novel.
The heir: a love story. [1922] (priv ptd). Single story, rptd in The heir: a love story, below.
The heir: a love story. 1922, New York 1922. 5 stories.
Knole and the Sackvilles. 1922, New York 1923, London 1958 (rev).
The challenge. New York [1923]. Novel.
The diary of the Lady Anne Clifford, with an introductory note by V. Sackville-West. 1923.

Grey Wethers: a romantic novel. 1923, New York [1923].
Seducers in Ecuador. 1924, New York 1925. Story. Rptd 1944, with Gottfried Künstler (1932).
Passenger to Teheran. 1926, New York 1927. Travel.
Aphra Behn: the incomparable Astrea. 1927, New York 1928.
Twelve days: an account of a journey across the Bakhtiari mountains in south-western Persia. 1928, Garden City NY 1928.
Andrew Marvell. 1929.
Granville-Barker, H. (ed). The eighteen-seventies. Cambridge 1929. Contains The women poets of the seventies, by V. Sackville-West.
The Edwardians. 1930, Garden City NY 1930. Novel; dramatized 1960 by R. Gow.
Wellesley D. (ed). The annual: being a selection from the forget-me-nots, keepsakes and other annuals of the nineteenth century. Introd by V. Sackville-West [1930].
All passion spent. 1931, Garden City NY 1931. Novel.
Family history. 1932, Garden City NY 1932. Novel.
Thirty clocks strike the hour and other stories. Garden City NY 1932. 2 stories, The death of noble Godavary and Gottfried Künstler, also pbd separately in Benn's New ninepenny novels series, 1932; Gottfried Künstler rptd 1944 with Seducers in Ecuador (1924).
The dark island. 1934, Garden City NY 1934.
Beginnings, by A. Alington [et al]. 1934. Includes essay by V. Sackville-West on her beginnings as a writer.
Saint Joan of Arc. 1936, Garden City NY 1936, London 1948 (rev).
Joan of Arc. 1937, New York 1938.
Pepita. 1937, Garden City NY 1937. Biographies of Josefa Duran y Ortega and Victoria Sackville-West, Lady Sackville, the author's grandmother and mother.
Some flowers. 1937. Descriptions of garden flowers.
Country notes. 1939, New York 1940.
Country notes in wartime. 1940, New York 1941.
English country houses. 1941 (Britain in Pictures).
Grand canyon. 1942, Garden City NY 1942. Novel.
The eagle and the dove, a study in contrasts: St Teresa of Avila, St Thérèse of Lisieux. 1943, Garden City NY 1944.
Seducers in Ecuador and Gottfried Künstler. 1944 (Penguin).
The Women's Land Army. 1944.
Another world than this: an anthology, compiled by V. Sackville-West and H. Nicolson. 1945.
Alice Meynell. Prose and poetry: centenary volume edited by F. Page [et al] with a biographical & critical introduction by V. Sackville-West. 1947.
Devil at Westease: the story as related by Roger Liddiard. New York 1947. Detective story.
Nursery rhymes. 1947 (Dropmore essays, 550 copies), 1950 (unlimited edn). Essay.
In your garden. 1951. On gardening.
Hidcote Manor garden, Hidcote Bartrim. 1952.
The Easter party. 1953, Garden City NY 1953. Novel.
In your garden again. 1953.
Walter de la Mare and The traveller. 1953 (Warton lecture on English poetry).
More for your garden. 1955.
Even more for your garden. 1958.
A joy of gardening: a selection for Americans. Ed H. I. Popper, New York [1958].
Daughter of France: the life of Anne Marie Louise d'Orléans duchesse de Montpensier 1627–1693, La Grande Mademoiselle. 1959, Garden City NY 1959.
Faces: profiles of dogs; text, V. Sackville-West; photographs, L. Goehr. [1961].
No signposts in the sea. 1961, Garden City NY 1961. Novel.
Victoria Sackville-West's garden book: a collection taken from In your garden, In your garden again, More for your garden, Even more for your garden, by Philippa Nicolson. 1968.

Victoria Sackville-West contributed book reviews to Listener *and* Nation and Athenaeum. *She also contributed* Country notes *regularly to* New Statesman *1938–41, many being rptd in* Country notes, *1939 and* Country notes in wartime, *1940, above. She wrote weekly articles on gardening for* Observer, *many being rptd in* In your garden, *1951,* In your garden again, *1953 etc. above.*

§2

Mais, S. P. B. Victoria Sackville-West. In his Some modern authors, 1923.

Overton, G. The lady of a tradition. Bookman (NY) 57 1923; rptd in his American nights entertainment, New York 1923.

Chesson, W. H. V. Sackville-West. Bookman (London) 65 1924.

Marble, A. R. In her A study of the modern novel, British and American, since 1900, 1928.

Swann, J. H. 'The land'. Papers of the Manchester Lit Club 56 1930.

Walpole, H. V. Sackville-West. Bookman (NY) 72 1930.

Young, G. M. The sweet evening. In his Daylight and champaign, 1937; rptd review of Saint Joan of Arc.

Brodrick, J. Obstinate questionings: a note on the poem Solitude. Month 173 1939.

Church, R. V. Sackville-West: a poet in a tradition. Fortnightly Rev 148 1940; rptd in his Eight for immortality, 1941.

Vallette, J. Victoria Sackville-West. Mercure de France 305 1949.

Nicolson, H. Diaries and letters. 3 vols 1966–8.

SIEGFRIED LORAINE SASSOON
1886–1967

Bibliographies

Muir, P. H. In his Points, 1874–1930, 1931. A check list of some anon and priv ptd items.

Keynes, G. A bibliography of Sassoon. 1962 (Soho Bibliographies). Includes trns. See D. Farmer, Addenda to Keynes's bibliography of Sassoon, PBSA 63 1969.

Siegfried Sassoon: a memorial exhibition [at the Academic Center Library, Univ of Texas]. Catalogue compiled by D. Farmer. Austin [1969].

§1
Poetry

The statements given below of the number of copies of certain books priv ptd for Sassoon by the Chiswick Press occasionally vary from the statements given in Keynes, and are based on information from the records of the Chiswick Press. See the review of Keynes' Bibliography by R. J. Roberts, Book Collector 11 1962.

Poems. 1906 (priv ptd, 50 copies). Anon.

Sonnets and verses. 1909 (priv ptd, 25 [?] copies). Anon.

Sonnets. 1909 (priv ptd, 'probably 50 copies, according to the author' (Keynes)). Anon.

Twelve sonnets. 1911 (priv ptd, 25 copies).

Poems. 1911 (priv ptd, 38 copies).

Melodies. 1912 (priv ptd, 37 copies). Anon.

An ode for music. 1912 (priv ptd, 60 copies).

The daffodil murderer: being the Chantrey Prize Poem, by 'Saul Kain' [i.e. Sassoon]. 1913. Parody of Masefield's The Everlasting mercy.

Discoveries. 1915 (priv ptd, 65 copies).

Morning-glory. [1916] (priv ptd, 11 copies). Anon.

The Redeemer. Cambridge 1916. Rptd from Cambridge Mag 2 1913.

To any dead officer. Cambridge 1917. Rptd from Cambridge Mag 6 1917.

The old huntsman, and other poems. 1917, New York 1918.

Four poems. Cambridge 1918. Rptd from Cambridge Mag 7 1918.

Counter-attack, and other poems. Introd by R. Nichols 1918, New York 1918.

A literary editor for the new London daily newspaper. [1919]. Prospectus for Daily Herald, containing 4 poems rptd from Counter-attack.

Picture-show. Cambridge 1919 (priv ptd), New York 1920 (with 7 additional poems).

The war poems of Siegfried Sassoon. 1919.

Lines written in the Reform Club. 1921.

Recreations. 1923 (priv ptd, 75 copies). Anon.

Lingual exercises for advanced vocabularians, by the author of Recreations. Cambridge 1925 (priv ptd, 99 copies).

Selected poems. 1925.

[Thirty-two poems]. [1926] (Augustan Books of Modern Poetry). Selection.

Satirical poems. 1926, New York 1926, London 1933 (with 5 additional poems).

Nativity. [1927] (Ariel Poem).

The heart's journey. New York and London 1927 (limited edn, anon but with author's autograph signature on title-page), London 1928 (unlimited edn, with 7 additional poems), New York 1929.

To my mother. [1928] (Ariel Poem).

A suppressed poem. 1919 [i.e. 1929?]. The single poem, I'd timed my death in action to the minute, pirated from the first, suppressed edn of Robert Graves' Goodbye to all that, 1929.

On Chatterton: a sonnet. Winchester 1930 (priv ptd, 14 copies).

In Sicily. [1930] (Ariel Poem).

Poems, by 'Pinchbeck Lyre' [i.e. Sassoon]. 1931.

To the red rose. [1931] (Ariel Poem).

Prehistoric burials. New York [1932].

The road to ruin. 1933.

Vigils, by S.L.S. Bristol 1934 (priv ptd, 272 copies) (22 poems), London 1935 (trade edn, 35 poems), New York 1936.

Rhymed ruminations. 1939 (priv ptd, 75 copies), 1940 (trade edn, with 9 additional poems), New York 1941.

Poems newly selected, 1916–1935. 1940.

[Forty-eight poems]. [1943] (Augustan Poets). Selection.

Collected poems. 1947, New York 1949. Contains The old huntsman, Counter-attack, Picture-show, Satirical poems, The heart's journey, The road to ruin, Vigils, Rhymed ruminations. With a few additions and omissions.

Common chords. Stanford Dingley 1950 (107 copies).

Emblems of experience. Cambridge 1951 (75 copies).

The tasking. Cambridge 1954 (priv ptd, 100 copies).

An adjustment, by 'S.S.' Royston 1955 (priv ptd, 150 copies). Foreword by P. Gosse.

Sequences. 1956, New York 1957. 62 poems selected from Common chords, Emblems of experience, The tasking.

Poems by Siegfried Sassoon, selected by D. Silk. Marlborough 1958 (priv ptd, 150 copies).

Lenten illuminations; Sight sufficient. Cambridge 1958 (35 copies).

The path to peace: selected poems. Worcester 1960 (500 copies). Ptd Stanbrook Abbey Press.

Collected poems, 1908–1956. 1961. Contains Collected poems 1947, Common chords (omitting 1 poem, adding To my mother), Emblems of experience, The tasking.

An octave: 8 September 1966. Introd by C. Causley 1966 (priv ptd, 350 copies). 8 poems.

Other Works

Orpheus in Dilœryum. 1908. Anon. 'A sort of Masque' (author).

Hyacinth: an idyll. 1912 (27 copies). A play in prose with 6 pieces in verse.

Amyntas: a mystery. 1912. A short dramatic piece, suppressed by the author. Proof copy in BM.

Memoirs of a fox-hunting man. 1928 (anon), New York 1929 ('by Siegfried Sassoon'), London 1929. Semi-fictional autobiography. *See* also next 2 items.

Memoirs of an infantry officer, by the author of Memoirs of a fox-hunting man. 1930, New York 1930 ('by Siegfried Sassoon'), London 1930.

Sherston's progress. 1936, New York 1936.

The complete memoirs of George Sherston. 1937, Garden City NY 1937 (as The memoirs of George Sherston). Contains Memoirs of a fox-hunting man, Memoirs of an infantry officer, Sherston's progress

The old century and seven more years. 1938, New York 1939, London 1968 (introd by M. Thorpe). Autobiography to 1907.

On poetry. Bristol 1939. Lecture.

The flower show match, and other pieces. 1941. Selections from Memoirs of a fox-hunting man, Memoirs of an infantry officer, Sherston's progress and The old century.

Early morning long ago. 1941 (priv ptd, 50 copies); rptd in next.

The weald of youth. 1942, New York 1942. Autobiography to 1914.

Siegfried's journey, 1916–1920. 1945, New York 1946. Autobiography.

Meredith. 1948, New York 1948. Biography.

Something about myself, by Siegfried Sassoon aged eleven. Worcester 1966 (ptd Stanbrook Abbey Press). From the ms entitled More poems.

Sassoon's contributions to books in the form of forewords etc are generally brief and are listed in Keynes's Bibliography. *28 letters from Sassoon to Sir Sidney Cockerell are included in* The best of friends, *ed V. Meynell 1956. Sassoon was the first literary editor of* Daily Herald.

§2

Mais, S. P. B. In his Books and their writers, 1920.

Wilkinson, M. Siegfried Sassoon. Touchstone 7 1920.

Arns, K. Siegfried Sassoon. Zeitschrift für Französischen und Englischen Unterricht 21 1922.

— Sassoons neue Lyrik. Zeitschrift für Französischen und Englischen Unterricht 28 1929.

Gosse, E. Sassoon's satires. In his Leaves and fruit, 1927.

Blunden, E. Sassoon's poetry. London Mercury 20 1929; rptd in his The mind's eye, 1934.

Graves, R. Goodbye to all that. 1929, 1957 (rev). Includes reminiscences of Sassoon during the first World War.

Murry, J. M. Sassoon's war verses. In his The evolution of an intellectual, 1930. Rptd review.

Darton, F. J. H. From Surtees to Sassoon: some English contrasts. 1931.

Powell, D. In her Descent from Parnassus, 1934.

Pinto, V. de S. Siegfried Sassoon. English 2 1939.

Richard, P. M. Siegfried Sassoon. Cahiers de Paris 8 1940.

Sackton, A. H. Two poems on war: a critical exercise. SE 31 1952. Sassoon's Aftermath and Rosenberg's Break of day in the trenches.

MacCarthy, D. In his Memories, 1953.

Cohen, J. The three roles of Sassoon. Tulane Stud in Eng 7 1957.

Braybrooke, N. Rebel of another generation. Commonweal 67 1958.

Maguire, C. E. Harmony unheard: the poetry of Sassoon. Renascence 11 1959.

Sergeant, H. Sassoon: poet of war. Contemporary Rev 202 1962.

Johnston, J. H. Realism and satire: Sassoon. In his English poetry of the first world war, Princeton 1964.

Bergonzi, B. In his Heroes' twilight: a study of the literature of the Great War, 1965.

Levi, P. Sassoon at eighty. Poetry Rev 57 1966.

Thorpe, M. Sassoon: a critical study. Leyden 1966.

Phillipson, W. Homage to Sassoon. Downside Rev 85 1967.

Jackson, S. The Sassoons. 1968.

EDITH JOY SCOVELL
b. 1907

§1

Shadows of chrysanthemums and other poems. 1944.

The midsummer meadow and other poems. 1946.

The river steamer and other poems. 1956.

SIR OWEN SEAMAN BART.
1861–1936
Selections

Owen Seaman: a selection, with introduction by C. L. Graves. Ed R. S. Clement Brown and M. Sanders 1937.

§1

Paulopostprandials, illustrated by L. Speed. 1883. With H. Monro.

With double pipe. Oxford 1888.

Horace at Cambridge. 1895, 1902 (for 1901) (rev).

Tillers of the sand: being a fitful record of the Rosebery administration from the triumph of Ladas to the decline and fall-off. 1895.

The battle of the bays. 1896.

In cap and bells. 1900 (for 1899).

Victoria: regina, imperatrix; from 'Punch'. [1901].

An ode to Her Majesty the Queen, to be recited at a performance in aid of the Queen Alexandra Fund . . . June 7, 1902. [1902].

When we sleeping beauties awaken, by 'O.S.'. 1903. Lines written for a dinner of the Stage Society.

A harvest of chaff. 1904.

Salvage. 1908.

War-time: verses. 1915, 1915 (with addns).

Made in England: verses. 1916.

From the home front: verses. 1918.

Interludes of an editor. 1929.

Other Works

Pascoe, C. E. (ed). Everyday life in our public schools. 1881. Contains Shrewsbury School, by Seaman.

Oedipus the wreck: or 'To trace the knave', with illustrations by L. Speed and J. D. Batten. Cambridge 1888. Humour.

Borrowed plumes. 1902, New York 1902, London 1916 (with slight addns). Parodies.

Verses and translations by C. S. Calverley, with introduction by Seaman. [1905].

Seaman was editor of Punch 1906–32 *and most of the poems etc collected during these years were originally pbd there.*

§2

Kernahan, C. Seaman of Punch. In his Five more famous living poets, 1928.

Milne, A. A. In his It's too late now: the autobiography of a writer, 1939.

Price, R. G. G. In his A history of Punch, 1957.

EDWARD BUXTON SHANKS
1892–1953

§ 1
Poetry

Songs. 1915.
Poems. 1916.
The queen of China and other poems. 1919, New York 1919.
The island of youth and other poems. [1921].
Fête galante: a dance-dream in one act, after Maurice Baring's story of that name, dramatized and composed by Ethel Smyth. Vienna, New York [1923]. Poetic version by Shanks.
The shadowgraph and other poems. [1925].
Collected poems 1909–1925, arranged in six books. [1926]. Contains most previously pbd verse, but excludes The queen of China. Some revisions and addns.
The beggar's ride: a tragedy in six scenes. [1926]. Included in Poems 1939–1952, below.
Poems 1912–1932. 1933. Selection, with 18 newly collected poems.
The man from Flanders and other poems. 1940 (priv ptd, 250 copies). Most rptd in next.
The night watch for England and other poems. 1942.
Images from the progress of the seasons. 1947 (450 copies).
Poems 1939–1952. 1954. Includes 20 poems from the 2 previous books and others newly collected.

Other Works

Hilaire Belloc: the man and his work, with an introd by G. K. Chesterton. 1916. With C. C. Mandell.
The old indispensables: a romance of Whitehall. 1919. Novel.
The people of the ruins: a story of the English revolution and after. [1920], New York [1920].
First essays on literature. 1923.
The richest man. [1923], New York 1924. Novel.
Whanslaw, H. W. Everybody's theatre and how to make it. [1923]. Introd by Shanks.
Bernard Shaw. 1924, New York 1924.
How to enjoy poetry. Garden City NY 1927.
Second essays on literature. [1927].
Bo and his circle. 1931. Story of the author's dog.
Queer street. 1932, Indianapolis [1933]. Novel.
The enchanted village. 1933, Indianapolis [1933]. Novel.
Welby, T. E. Second impressions, with a biographical introd by Shanks. 1933.
Tom Tiddler's ground. 1934. Indianapolis [1934]. Novel.
Old King Cole. 1936, Indianapolis [1936] (as The dark green circle). Novel.
Edgar Allan Poe. 1937 (EML), New York 1937.
My England. 1938, New York 1938.
Do you know? A question book. 1939.
Rudyard Kipling: a study in literature and political ideas. 1940, New York 1940.
Elizabeth goes home. 1942. Short story.
The universal war and the universal state. 1946 (575 copies). (Dropmore Essays 2).
The dogs of war. 1948 (700 copies). Sequel to Elizabeth goes home, 1942, above.
Selected poems of Swinburne. Ed with an introd by Shanks 1950.
Poems of Robert Browning, selected by Shanks. 1961.
Shanks was the assistant editor of London Mercury *1919–22. He was leader-writer on* Evening Standard *1928–35.*

§ 2

Mégroz, R. L. Edward Shanks. Bookman (London) 64 1923.

FREDEGOND SHOVE,
née MAITLAND
1889–1949

§ 1

Dreams and journeys. Oxford 1918.
Daybreak. Richmond, Surrey 1922.
Christina Rossetti: a study. Cambridge 1931.
Poems. Cambridge 1956. Selection of pbd and unpbd work. Foreword by E. Maitland.

§ 2

Fredegond and Gerald Shove, by Fredegond, with a preface by E. Maitland. Brookthorpe 1952 (priv ptd, 250 copies).

DAME EDITH LOUISA SITWELL
1887–1964

Substantial sales of Edith Sitwell's mss were held at Sotheby's on 12 Dec 1961, 19 June 1962 and 11 May 1964. Most are now in the library of the University of Texas. See also J. Lewis, Edith Sitwell's letters [in the BM], BM Quart 30 1966.

Bibliographies

Balston, T. Sitwelliana 1915–1927: being a handlist of works by Edith, O. and S. Sitwell and of their contributions to certain selected periodicals. 1928 (70 copies).
'Gawsworth, John' (T. I. F. Armstrong). In his Ten contemporaries: notes towards their definitive bibliography, 1932.
Rosenberg, L. D. Edith Sitwell: a critical bibliography 1915–1950. Bull of Bibliography 21 1953–4. Includes reviews.
Fifoot, R. A bibliography of Edith, O. and S. Sitwell. 1963 (Soho Bibliographies). Includes trns of Edith Sitwell's works.

§ 1
Poetry

The mother and other poems. Oxford 1915.
Twentieth-century harlequinade and other poems. By Edith and O. Sitwell. Oxford 1916. 7 poems.
Clowns' houses. Oxford 1918.
The wooden Pegasus. Oxford 1920.
Façade. 1922 (priv ptd, 150 copies). Concert version for voice and orchestra by William Walton performed Jan 1922.
Bucolic comedies. 1923.
The sleeping beauty. 1924, New York 1924.
Troy Park. 1925, New York 1925.
Poor young people. By Edith, O. and S. Sitwell. 1925 (375 copies). 8 poems by Edith Sitwell.
[Eleven poems]. [1926] (Augustan Books of Modern Poetry). Selection.
Elegy on dead fashion. 1926 (225 copies).
Poem for a Christmas card. [1926] (210 copies).
Rustic elegies. 1927, New York 1927.
Popular song. 1928 (Ariel Poem).
Five poems. 1928 (275 copies). Included in Collected poems, 1930, below.
Gold Coast customs. 1929, Boston 1929.
Collected poems. 1930. Selection with some revision and 2 new poems.
In spring. 1931 (priv ptd, 305 copies).
Jane Barston 1719–1746. 1931 (Ariel Poem).
Epithalamium. 1931 (100 copies).
Five variations on a theme. 1933.

Selected poems, with an essay on her own poetry by E. Sitwell. 1936, Boston 1937. Includes 2 previously uncollected poems.

Poems new and old. 1940. Selection, with 2 previously uncollected poems.

Street songs. 1942.

Green song and other poems. 1944, New York [1946].

The weeping babe: motet for soprano solo and mixed choir. [1945]. Music by M. Tippett.

The song of the cold. 1945. Selection, with previously uncollected poems.

The shadow of Cain. 1947.

The song of the cold. New York 1948. Selection with previously uncollected poems, differing greatly from the London edn of 1945, above.

The canticle of the rose: selected poems 1920–1947. 1949, New York 1949 (as The canticle of the rose: poems 1917–49; with same contents, but adding Some notes on my own poetry).

Poor men's music. 1950, Denver 1950.

Façade and other poems 1920–1935. 1950. Selection; introd by J. Lindsay.

Selected poems. 1952 (Penguin Poets). Selection, with previously uncollected poems.

Gardeners and astronomers. 1953, New York 1953 (omitting 4 poems; as Gardeners and astronomers: new poems).

Collected poems. New York [1954], London 1957 (with addns). Selection, with previously uncollected and unpbd poems.

[Twenty-three poems]. 1960 (Pocket Poets). Selection.

The outcasts. 1962.

Music and ceremonies. New York [1963]. Contents of The outcasts, 1962, above, with 4 other poems, 3 unpbd.

Selected poems, chosen with an introd by J. Lehmann. 1965.

Other Works

The contributions to books listed here are a selection; for a more detailed list, see Fifoot, Bibliographies, above.

Children's tales—from the Russian ballet. 1920, [1921 or 1922] (as The Russian ballet gift book).

Poetry and modern poetry. In Yea and nay: a series of lectures and counter-lectures given at the London School of Economics. 1923.

Poetry and criticism. 1925, New York [1926].

Experiment in poetry. In Tradition and experiment in present-day literature: addresses delivered at the City Literary Institute, 1929.

Alexander Pope. 1930, New York 1930.

The pleasures of poetry: a critical anthology. 3 vols 1930–2, New York 1930–2, 1 vol London 1934.

Bath. 1932, New York 1932.

Prose poems from Les illuminations of Arthur Rimbaud. Tr H. Rootham, with an introductory essay by E. Sitwell 1932.

The English eccentrics. 1933, Boston 1933, New York 1957 (rev and enlarged), London 1958.

Aspects of modern poetry. 1934.

Victoria of England. 1936, Boston 1936.

Sitwell, S. Collected poems, with a long introductory essay by E. Sitwell. 1936.

I live under a black sun. 1937, Garden City NY 1938. Novel.

Three eras of modern poetry. In Trio: dissertations on some aspects of national genius, by O., Edith and S. Sitwell, 1938 (Northcliffe Lectures, Univ of London).

The last party: a radio play. In Twelve modern plays, selected by J. Hampden, 1938.

Edith Sitwell's anthology. 1940. English and French poetry, with introd.

Look! the sun. Ed Edith Sitwell 1941. Anthology of poetry.

English women. 1942 (Britain in Pictures).

A poet's notebook. 1943.

Maiden voyage, by Denton Welch. Foreword by Edith Sitwell 1943, New York 1945.

Planet and glow-worm: a book for the sleepless, compiled by Edith Sitwell. 1944. Anthology of verse and prose.

Fanfare for Elizabeth. New York 1946, London 1946. On the childhood of Elizabeth I.

A notebook on William Shakespeare. 1948, Boston 1961.

A book of the winter, compiled by Edith Sitwell. 1950, New York 1951. Anthology of verse and prose.

A poet's notebook. Boston 1950. Contains A poet's notebook, 1943, above, with omissions and revisions, and A notebook on William Shakespeare, 1948, above, with omissions.

The American genius: an anthology of poetry with some prose. Ed Edith Sitwell 1951.

A book of flowers, compiled by Edith Sitwell. 1952. Anthology, including recipes for cordials, scents etc.

Dylan Thomas: a bibliography, by J. A. Rolph. Foreword by Edith Sitwell 1956.

The Atlantic book of British and American poetry. Boston 1958, London 1959. Ed Edith Sitwell.

Roy Campbell. In Hommage à Roy Campbell, Montpellier 1958.

Poems of our time 1900–1960. 1959. Original edn chosen by R. Church and M. Bozman; modern suppl chosen by Edith Sitwell.

The collected poems of Roy Campbell. Vol 3, 1960 (with foreword by Edith Sitwell).

Swinburne: a selection. Ed Edith Sitwell 1960, New York 1960.

Comment on Dylan Thomas. In Dylan Thomas: the legend and the poet, ed E. W. Tedlock 1960.

The queens and the hive. 1962, Boston 1962. On Elizabeth I and Mary Tudor, Mary Queen of Scots, Catharine de' Medici.

Taken care of: an autobiography. 1965, New York 1965.

Edith Sitwell edited and contributed substantially to the 6 'cycles' of Wheels, 1916–21.

Letters

Selected letters. Ed J. Lehmann and D. Parker 1970.

§2

For a checklist of parodies, polemical articles, see Rosenberg, Bibliographies, above.

Graves, R. In his Contemporary techniques of poetry, 1925.

Muir, E. Edith Sitwell. Nation 15 April 1925.

—— Miss Edith Sitwell. Nation 18 Sept 1926; rptd in his Transition, 1926.

Brooks, B. G. The poetry of Edith Sitwell. Fortnightly Rev 119 1926.

Burdett, O. The Sitwells. London Mercury 15 1927.

Gosse, E. Miss Sitwell's poems. In his Leaves and fruit, 1927.

Mégroz, R. L. The three Sitwells: a biographical and critical study. 1927.

Sutton, E. Sitwellismus. Outlook 25 Feb 1928.

Arns, K. Die drei Sitwells. Zeitschrift für Französichen und Englischen Unterricht 28 1929.

Mair, M. Edith Sitwell and her art. Poetry Rev 20 1929.

Williams, C. In his Poetry at present, 1930.

Grigson, G. An examination of the work of Edith Sitwell. Bookman (London) 80 1931.

Powell, D. Edith Sitwell. Life & Letters 6 1931.

—— In her Descent from Parnassus, 1934. Part rptd from Life & Letters, above.

Vines, S. The three Sitwells. In Scrutinies vol 2, ed E. Rickword 1931.

Howarth, R. G. New perceptions, with special reference to the poetry of Edith Sitwell. In A. J. Waldock et al, Some recent developments in English literature, Sydney 1935.

— Walter de la Mare and Edith Sitwell. South African PEN Year Book 1956–7.

— Two modern writers: Ezra Pound and Edith Sitwell. Cape Town 1963.

Gerstmann, I. Die Technik des Bewegungseindrucks in Gedichten Edith Sitwells und Vachel Lindsays. Greifswald 1936.

Wells, H. W. From the Augustans. In his New poets from old, New York 1940. On the Sitwells.

— Gold coast customs reconsidered. College Eng 13 1952.

Hofmann, A. Edith Sitwell: a contribution to the study of modernist poetry. Immensee 1942.

Crowder, R. Mr MacNeice and Miss Sitwell. Poetry 63 1944.

Reed, H. The poetry of Edith Sitwell. Penguin New Writing no 21 1944; rptd in Writers of to-day, ed D. V. Baker 1946.

Bottomley, G. A consideration of Edith Sitwell's Green song. Life & Letters 45 1945.

Bowra, M. The war poetry of Edith Sitwell. Cornhill Mag 161 1945; rptd in A celebration for E. Sitwell, ed J. Garcia Villa [1948], below.

— Edith Sitwell. Monaco 1947.

Gregory, H. The Vita nuova of baroque art in the recent poetry of Edith Sitwell. Poetry 66 1945.

Heath-Stubbs, J. Edith Sitwell: her poetic world. Poetry Quart 8 1946.

Clark, K. On the development of Miss Sitwell's later style. Horizon 16 1947; rptd in next.

Garcia Villa, J. (ed). A celebration for Edith Sitwell. [Norfolk Conn 1948]. Essays by O. Sitwell, S. Spender, C. M. Bowra, F. Prokosch, H. Gregory, J. Lindsay, J. Piper, K. Clark, G. Bottomley, J. Lehmann, A. Waley, C. Morgan, R. Church, G. Stein, J. Russell, L. P. Hartley, W. B. Yeats.

Beach, J. W. Baroque: the poetry of Edith Sitwell. New Mexico Quart Rev 19 1949.

Every, G. Songs of the cold. In his Poetry and personal responsibility, 1949.

Cohen, J. M. Edith Sitwell's development. Spectator 10 Nov 1950.

Lindsay, J. The poetry of Edith Sitwell. Life & Letters 64 1950; rptd as introductory essay to Façade and other poems, 1950, above.

— Meetings with poets: memories of Dylan Thomas, Edith Sitwell [et al]. 1968.

Vallette, J. Note sur le style et l'évolution d'Edith Sitwell. Mercure de France 308 1950.

Jeremy, Sr M. Clown and canticle: the achievement of Edith Sitwell. Renascence 3 1951.

Braybrooke, N. The poetry of Edith Sitwell. Canadian Forum 32 1952.

— Edith Sitwell: poet of the resurrection. America 90 1953.

— The poetry of Edith Sitwell. Irish Ecclesiastical Record 82 1954.

Lehmann, J. Edith Sitwell. 1952 (Br Council pamphlet). Rptd as introd to Selected poems, 1965, above.

— A nest of tigers: Edith, O. and S. Sitwell in their times. 1968.

Nokes, G. and K. Amis. 'Emily-coloured Primulas'. EC 2 1952.

Wykes-Joyce, M. Triad of genius. 1953.

Bogan, L. In her Selected criticism, 1955.

Hassan, I. H. Edith Sitwell and the symbolist tradition. Comparative Lit 7 1955.

Fytton, F. Edith Sitwell: Gothic poet. Catholic World 183 1956.

Cronin, V. The poetry of Edith Sitwell. Month 18 1957.

Julian, Sr M. Edith Sitwell and Dylan Thomas: neo-romantics. Renascence 9 1957.

— Peacocks and pity. Today 12 1957.

Vickery, J. B. The golden bough and modern poetry. Jnl of Aesthetics & Art Criticism 15 1957.

Kelly, J. C. The poems of Edith Sitwell. Studies 47 1958.

Rossi, S. Edith Sitwell. Letterature Moderne 8 1958.

Coles, M. D. The poetry of Edith Sitwell. Contemporary Rev 195 1959.

Edwards, P. D. Watteau and the poets. MLN 74 1959.

Lohmann, B. Gestalt und Funktion des Bildes in W. H. Audens und Edith Sitwells Dichtung zwischen 1940 und 1948. Münster 1960.

Richart, B. Dame Edith's art. Commonweal 69 1960.

Stanford, D. Dame Edith Sitwell and the Transatlantic Muse. Month 24 1960.

Mills, R. J., jr. The poetic roles of Edith Sitwell. Chicago Rev 14 1961.

— Edith Sitwell: a critical essay. Grand Rapids 1966 (Contemporary Writers in Christian Perspective).

Rexroth, K. Poets old and new: Edith Sitwell. In his Assays, [Norfolk Conn] [1961]; rptd review of Collected poems 1954.

Singleton, G. Edith Sitwell: the hymn to life. 1961.

Sandt, Sr M. C. A critique of Edith Sitwell's three poems of the atomic age. New York [1962]. On Dirge for the new sunrise, The shadow of Cain, The canticle of the rose.

Connolly, C. In his Previous convictions, 1963; rptd from Sunday Times; review of Collected poems 1957.

Cattoretti, L. Edith Sitwell e le poesie dell' era atomica. Letture 19 1964.

Robb, M. The growth of a poet. Colorado Quart 13 1964.

Symons, J. Miss Edith Sitwell have and had and heard. London Mag new ser 4 1964.

Cuffel, K. D. The shadow of Cain: themes in Edith Sitwell's later poetry. Personalist 46 1965.

Parker, D. Edith Sitwell. Poetry Rev 56 1965.

Pryce-Jones, A. Edith Sitwell. Commonweal 82 1965.

Welvaert, M-L. The gold-dust imagery of Edith Sitwell. Saint Louis Quart 3 1965.

Lewis, J. Edith Sitwell's letters [in the BM]. BM Quart 30 1966.

Combecher, H. Edith Sitwell: Dirge for a new sunrise. In Die moderne englische Lyrik, ed H. Oppel, Berlin 1967.

Harrington, D. V. The 'metamorphosis' of Edith Sitwell. Criticism 9 1967.

Salter, E. The last years of a rebel: a memoir of Edith Sitwell. 1967.

Brophy, J. D. Edith Sitwell: the symbolist order. Carbondale 1968.

Griffith, P. M. Carolinian conversations: recollections of a visit with Edith Sitwell, March 1957. Nimrod 13 1969.

SIR FRANCIS OSBERT SACHEVERELL SITWELL BART.
1892–1969

Bibliographies

Balston, T. Sitwelliana, 1915–1927: being a handlist of works by Edith, O. and S. Sitwell and of their contributions to certain selected periodicals. 1928 (70 copies).

Fifoot, R. A bibliography of Edith, O. and S. Sitwell, 1963 (Soho Bibliographies). Includes trns of Sitwell's works.

Poetry

Twentieth-century harlequinade and other poems. By Edith and O. Sitwell. Oxford 1916. Includes 2 war poems and The lament of the mole-catcher, by O. Sitwell.

The Winstonburg Line: 3 satires. [1919].

Argonaut and juggernaut. 1919, New York 1920.

At the house of Mrs Kinfoot: consisting of four satires. 1921 (priv ptd, 101 copies). Included in Collected satires and poems, 1931, below.

Out of the flame. 1923, New York 1925.

Poor young people. By Edith, O. and S. Sitwell. 1925 (375 copies). Includes Long winter: 12 songs by O. Sitwell.

Winter the huntsman. [1927]. Rptd from Poor young people, 1925, above.

England reclaimed: a book of eclogues. 1927, Garden City NY 1928. *See* also England reclaimed and other poems, 1949, below.

Miss Mew. Stanford Dingley 1929 (101 copies). 6 poems. Included in next.

Collected satires and poems. 1931.

Three-quarter length portrait of Michael Arlen; with a preface, The history of a portrait, by the author. [1931].

A three-quarter-length portrait of the Viscountess Wimborne. Cambridge 1931 (57 copies).

Mrs Kimber. 1937. 6 poems.

Selected poems, old and new. 1943. Includes 9 previously uncollected poems.

Four songs of the Italian earth. [Pawlet Vermont] 1948 (260 copies); rptd in England reclaimed and other poems, 1949, below.

Demos the emperor: a secular oratorio. 1949.

England reclaimed and other poems. Boston 1949. A different collection from England reclaimed, 1927, above.

Wrack at Tidesend: a book of balnearics, being the second volume of England reclaimed. 1952, New York 1953 (slightly rev).

On the Continent: a book of inquilinics, being the third volume of England reclaimed. 1958.

Poems about people: or England reclaimed. 1965. Collects contents of 3 previous books.

Autobiographies

Left hand, right hand! Boston 1944, London 1945 (as Left hand, right hand! an autobiography: vol 1, The cruel month).

The scarlet tree. Boston 1946, London 1946 (as The scarlet tree: being the second volume of Left hand, right hand! an autobiography).

Great morning! Boston 1947, London 1948 (as Great morning: being the third volume of Left hand, right hand! an autobiography).

Laughter in the next room. Boston 1948, London 1949 (as Laughter in the next room: being the fourth volume of Left hand, right hand! an autobiography).

Noble essences or courteous revelations: being a book of characters and the fifth and last volume of Left hand, right hand! an autobiography. 1950, Boston 1950 (as Noble essences: a book of characters).

Tales my father taught me: an evocation of extravagant episodes. 1962, Boston [1962].

Other Works

The list of books with contributions by Sitwell is selective; for further details see Fifoot, Bibliographies, above.

Who killed Cock-Robin? remarks on poetry, on criticism, and, as a sad warning, the story of Eunuch Arden. 1921.

Triple fugue. 1924, New York [1925]. Stories.

Discursions on travel, art and life. 1925, New York [1925]. C. R. W. Nevinson. 1925. Signed 'O.S.'.

Before the bombardment. 1926, New York [1926]. Novel.

All at sea: a social tragedy in three acts for first-class passengers only. By O. and S. Sitwell; with a preface entitled A few days in an author's life by O. Sitwell. 1927, Garden City NY 1928.

The people's album of London statues. Described by Sitwell, drawn by N. Hamnett. 1928.

The works of Ronald Firbank. Vol 1, 1929 (for Dec 1928). Biographical memoir by Sitwell; rptd, rev, in I. K. Fletcher, Ronald Firbank, 1930, and again (rev) in Firbank's Five novels, 1949.

The man who lost himself. 1929, New York 1930. Novel.

Sober truth: a collection of nineteenth-century episodes, fantastic, grotesque and mysterious, compiled and ed M. Barton and Sitwell. 1930, New York [1930].

Dumb-animal and other stories. 1930, Philadelphia 1931.

Victoriana: a symposium of Victorian wisdom ed and compiled by M. Barton and Sitwell. 1931.

Belshazzar's feast, by William Walton. Text selected and arranged from the Holy Bible by Sitwell. 1931.

Dickens. 1932.

Winters of content: more discursions on travel, art and life. 1932, Philadelphia 1932. *See* also Winters of content and other discursions, 1950, below.

Miracle on Sinai: a satirical novel. 1933, New York [1934], London 1948 (with new preface by the author).

Johnson's England. Ed A. S. Turberville vol 2, Oxford 1933. Contains Taste, by Sitwell and M. Barton.

Brighton. 1935, Boston 1935. With M. Barton.

Penny foolish: a book of tirades and panegyrics. 1935. Miscellaneous essays mainly rptd from Sunday Referee.

Those were the days: panorama with figures. 1938. Novel.

Dickens and the modern novel; The modern novel, its cause and cure. In Trio: dissertations on some aspects of national genius, by O., Edith and S. Sitwell. 1938 (Northcliffe Lectures, Univ of London).

Escape with me! an oriental sketch-book. 1939, New York 1940, London 1948 (with new introd).

Two generations. Ed Sitwell 1940. Reminiscences of Georgiana Caroline Sitwell, afterwards Swinton, and the journal of Florence Alice Sitwell.

Open the door! a volume of stories. 1941, New York 1941.

A place of one's own. 1941. Nouvelle.

Gentle Caesar: a play in three acts. 1942 (for March 1943). With R. J. Minney.

Sing high! sing low! a book of essays. 1944. Mostly rptd, rev, from periodicals.

A letter to my son. 1944. Rptd, rev, from Horizon. On authorship and contemporary life.

The true story of Dick Whittington: a Christmas story for cat-lovers. 1945 (for Feb 1946).

A free house! or the artist as craftsman, being the writings of W. R. Sickert. Ed Sitwell 1947.

Alive—alive oh! and other stories. 1947. Selection from Dumb-animal, 1930, above, and Triple fugue, 1924, above.

The novels of George Meredith and some notes on the English novel. 1947 (Eng Assoc Presidential Address).

Death of a god and other stories. 1949. Mostly rptd from Open the door!, 1941, above; with A place of one's own, 1941, and Staggered holiday.

Sir George Sitwell on the making of gardens. Introd by Sitwell 1949.

Introduction to the catalogue of the Frick collection. [New York] 1949.

Winters of content and other discursions on Mediterranean art and travel. 1950. Contains Winters of content, 1932, chs from Discursions, 1925, and Echoes, a story from Dumb-animal, 1930.

Collected stories. 1953, New York [1953].

The four continents: being more discursions on travel, art and life. 1954, New York [1954].

Fee fi fo fum! a book of fairy stories. 1959.

A place of one's own and other stories. 1961. All rptd from Collected stories, 1953, above.

Pound wise. 1963, Boston, Mass [1963].

§2

Burdett, O. The Sitwells. London Mercury 15 1927.

Mégroz, R. L. The three Sitwells: a biographical and critical study. 1927.

—— In his Five novelist poets of today, 1933.

Arns, K. Die drei Sitwells. Zeitschrift für Französischen und Englischen Unterricht 28 1929.

Williams, C. In his Poetry at present. 1930.

Vines, S. The three Sitwells. In Scrutinies vol 2, ed E. Rickword 1931.

Wells, H. W. From the Augustans. In his New poets from old, New York 1940. On the Sitwells.

Bower, A. A view of Sir Osbert Sitwell. Partisan Rev 15 1948.

Harrison, E. More geese than swans. Queen's Quart 56 1949.

Fulford, R. Osbert Sitwell. 1951 (Br Council pamphlet).

Praz, M. Osbert Sitwell. Paragone 2 1951.

Wykes-Joyce, M. Triad of genius. 1953.

Hartley, L. P. Sir Osbert Sitwell. TLS 6 Aug 1954.

Guimbretière, A. La satire dans les nouvelles de Sir Osbert Sitwell. Études Anglaises 13 1960.

Lehmann, J. A nest of tigers: Edith, O. and S. Sitwell in their times. 1968.

SIR SACHEVERELL SITWELL BART.
b. 1897

Bibliographies

Balston, T. Sitwelliana, 1915–1927: being a handlist of works by Edith, O. and S. Sitwell and of their contributions to certain selected periodicals. 1928 (70 copies).

Fifoot, R. A bibliography of Edith, O. and S. Sitwell. 1963 (Soho Bibliographies). Includes trns of Sitwell's works.

§1
Poetry

The people's palace. Oxford 1918.

Doctor Donne and Gargantua: first canto. 1921 (priv ptd, 101 copies).

The hundred and one harlequins. 1922, New York [1922].

Doctor Donne and Gargantua: canto the second. 1923 (priv ptd, 40 copies).

The parrot. [1923].

The thirteenth Caesar and other poems. 1924, New York 1925.

Poor young people. By Edith, O. and S. Sitwell. 1925 (375 copies). 12 poems by S. Sitwell.

Exalt the eglantine and other poems. 1926 (370 copies).

Doctor Donne and Gargantua: canto the third. Stratford-upon-Avon 1926 (priv ptd, 65 copies).

The cyder feast and other poems. 1927, New York 1927.

[Twenty-five poems.] [1928] (Augustan Books of English Poetry). Selection, adding Two songs, previously unpbd.

Two poems, ten songs. 1929 (275 copies).

Doctor Donne and Gargantua: the first six cantos. 1930.

Canons of giant art: twenty torsos in heroic landscapes. 1933.

Collected poems, with a long introductory essay by Edith Sitwell. 1936. Includes a few previously uncollected or unpbd poems.

Selected poems, with a preface by O. Sitwell. 1948, New York 1948. Includes previously unpbd poems.

48 poems by Sitwell were pbd in Poetry Rev 58 1967.

Other Works

A more detailed list of Sitwell's introductions and other contributions to books can be found in Fifoot, Bibliographies, above.

Southern baroque art: a study of painting, architecture and music in Italy and Spain of the 17th and 18th centuries. 1924, New York 1924, London 1927 (for 1928) (with new preface), 1930 (omitting pt 4, Mexico).

Masters of painting: Antoine Watteau. Foreword by Sitwell 1925.

All summer in a day: an autobiographical fantasia. 1926, New York [1926].

German baroque art. 1927, New York 1928.

All at sea: a social tragedy in three acts for first-class passengers only. By O. and S. Sitwell. 1927, Garden City NY 1928.

A book of towers and other buildings of southern Europe: a series of dry-points engraved by R. Wyndham. 1928 (350 copies). Introd and brief descriptions by Sitwell.

The gothick north: a study of mediaeval life, art and thought. 3 vols 1929–30, 1 vol Boston 1929, London 1938.

Beckford and Beckfordism: an essay. 1930 (265 copies).

Far from my home: stories long and short. 1931.

Spanish baroque art, with buildings in Portugal, Mexico and other colonies. 1931.

Mozart. New York 1932, London 1932.

Liszt. 1934, Boston 1934, London 1955 (rev).

Touching the orient: six sketches. 1934.

A background for Domenico Scarlatti, 1685–1757. 1935.

Dance of the quick and the dead: an entertainment of the imagination. 1936, Boston 1937. On art and miscellaneous subjects.

Conversation pieces: a survey of English domestic portraits and their painters. 1936, New York 1937.

Narrative pictures: a survey of English genre and its painters. 1937, New York 1938.

La vie parisienne: a tribute to Offenbach. 1937, Boston 1938.

Roumanian journey. 1938, New York 1938.

Edinburgh. 1938, Boston 1938. With F. Bamford.

German baroque sculpture. 1938.

Palladian England; George Cruikshank. In Trio: dissertations on some aspects of national genius, by O., Edith and S. Sitwell. 1938 (Northcliffe Lectures, Univ of London).

The romantic ballet in the lithographs of the time. 1938. With C. W. Beaumont.

Massine: camera studies by G. Anthony, with an appreciation by Sitwell. 1939.

Old fashioned flowers. 1939. Illustr J. Farleigh.

Mauretania: warrior, man and woman. 1940.

Poltergeists: an introduction and examination, followed by chosen instances. 1940, New York 1959.

Sacred and profane love. 1940. Reflections on art, travel and miscellaneous subjects.

Valse des fleurs: a day in St Petersburg and a ball at the Winter Palace in 1868. 1941.

Primitive scenes and festivals. 1942.

The homing of the winds and other passages in prose. 1942. Selection, with A sketch of the Scarborough Sands, previously unpbd.

Splendours and miseries. 1943. On art, music and miscellaneous subjects.

British architects and craftsmen: a survey of taste, design and style during three centuries, 1600 to 1830. 1945, 1946 (rev), New York 1946, London 1947 (rev), 1948 (for 1949) (rev), 1960 (rev).

English church monuments 1510 to 1840, by K. A. Esdaile. Introd by Sitwell 1946, New York 1947.

The hunters and the hunted. 1947, New York 1948. On art, birds, music and miscellaneous subjects.

The Netherlands: a study of some aspects of art, costume and social life. [1948], 1952 (rev).

Tropical birds, from plates by John Gould, with an introd and notes on the plates by Sitwell 1948.

The romantic ballet from contemporary prints, with an introd and notes on the prints by Sitwell 1948.

Morning, noon and night in London. 1948. On lithographs by A. Concanen.

Theatrical figures in porcelain: German 18th century. 1949 (The Masque, 9).

Audubon's American birds, from plates by J. J. Audubon, with an introduction and notes on the plates by Sitwell. 1949.

Gallery of fashion 1790–1822 from plates by Heideloff and Ackermann. Ed with an introduction by Sitwell 1949.

Spain. 1950, 1951 (rev), 1961 (rev).

The sacred rites of pride. In Diversion: twenty-two authors on the lively arts, ed J. Sutro 1950.

Cupid and the Jacaranda. 1952. On art and miscellaneous subjects.

Truffle hunt. 1953. Mainly articles entitled 'People and memories' rptd, rev, from Sunday Times.

Fine bird books 1700–1900. 1953. With H. Buchanan and J. Fisher.

Selected works. Indianapolis [1953]. Selected mainly from works on art and travel.

Portugal and Madeira. 1954.

Album de Redouté, with twenty-five facsimile colour plates from the edition of 1824, and a new Redouté bibliography. 1954. With R. Madol.

Old garden roses. Pt 1, 1955. With J. Russell.

Selected works. 1955. A different selection from that of 1953, above, though similar in scope.

Denmark. 1956, New York [1956].

Great flower books, 1700–1900: a bibliographical record of two centuries of finely-illustrated flower books. 1956. With W. Blunt.

Arabesque and honeycomb. 1957, New York 1958. Travel in Persia etc.

Malta. 1958. With T. Armstrong-Jones.

Austria. 1959, New York 1959. Text by Sitwell, photographs by T. Schneiders.

Journey to the ends of time: vol 1, Lost in the dark wood. 1959, New York 1959. 'The problems and mysteries of life and death'.

Bridge of the brocade sash: travels and observations in Japan. [1959], Cleveland [1960].

Golden wall and mirador: from England to Peru. [1961], Cleveland [1961] (as Golden wall and mirador: travels and observations in Peru).

Great houses of Europe. Ed Sitwell [1961]. Photographs by E. Smith.

The red chapels of Banteai Srei, and temples in Cambodia, India, Siam and Nepal. [1962], New York 1963 (as Great temples of the east: the wonders of Cambodia, India, Siam and Nepal).

Great palaces. Introd by Sitwell [1964], New York 1964 (as Great palaces of Europe).

Monks, nuns and monasteries. [1965], New York 1965.

Southern baroque revisited. [1967].

Gothic Europe. 1969.

§ 2

Burdett, O. The Sitwells. London Mercury 15 1927.

Mégroz, R. L. The three Sitwells: a biographical and critical study. 1927.

Arns, K. Die drei Sitwells. Zeitschrift für Französischen und Englischen Unterricht 28 1929.

Williams, C. In his Poetry at present, 1930.

Vines, S. The three Sitwells. In Scrutinies vol 2, ed E. Rickword, 1931.

Sitwell, E. In her Aspects of modern poetry, 1934.

Wells, H. W. From the Augustans. In his New poets from old, New York 1940. On the Sitwells.

Beach, J. W. Rococo: the poetry of Sitwell. Poetry (Chicago) 74 1949.

Wykes-Joyce, M. Triad of genius. 1953.

Smith, J. Shall these bones live?: a note on the poetry of Sitwell. Poetry Rev 58 1967.

Lehmann, J. A nest of tigers: Edith, O. and S. Sitwell in their times. 1968.

SYDNEY GOODSIR SMITH
b. 1915

§ 1
Poetry

Skail wind. Edinburgh 1941.

The wanderer and other poems. Edinburgh 1943.

The deevil's waltz. Glasgow 1946.

Selected poems. Edinburgh 1947.

Under the eildon tree: a poem in XXIV elegies. Edinburgh 1948.

The aipple and the hazel. [Edinburgh] 1951.

So late into the night: fifty lyrics, 1944–1948. 1952.

Cokkils. Edinburgh 1953 (220 copies).

Omens. Edinburgh 1955 (300 copies).

Orpheus and Eurydice: a dramatic poem. Edinburgh 1955.

Figs and thistles. Edinburgh 1959.

The vision of the prodigal son. Edinburgh 1960.

The Wallace: a triumph in five acts. Edinburgh 1960.

Kynd Kittock's land. Edinburgh 1965.

Fifteen poems and a play. Edinburgh 1969.

Other Works

Carotid Cornucopius, caird o the Cannon Gait and voyeur of the Outluik Touer, by Gude Schir Skidderie Smithereens. Glasgow 1947, Edinburgh 1964 (rev and enlarged).

A short introduction to Scottish literature. Edinburgh 1951.

Robert Fergusson 1750–1774. Essays by various hands to commemorate the bicentenary of his birth. Ed Goodsir Smith, Edinburgh 1952.

'Robert Garioch': The masque of Edinburgh. Edinburgh 1954. Contains A pooplick latter, oddrash or mauna-fashtule by Guid Schir Skidderie Smithereens.

Gavin Douglas: a selection from his poetry ed and introduced by S. Goodsir Smith, Edinburgh 1959.

Robert Burns. The merry muses of Caledonia. Ed J. Barke and Goodsir Smith, Edinburgh 1959 (priv ptd), New York 1964, London 1965 (with rearrangement of Burns' text).

Hugh MacDiarmid: a festschrift. Ed K. D. Duval and Goodsir Smith, Edinburgh 1962. Includes MacDiarmid's Three hymns to Lenin by Goodsir Smith.

Bannockburn: the story of the battle and its place in Scotland's history. Ed Goodsir Smith, Stirling [1965]. Includes an extract from his The Wallace.

A choice of Burns's poems and songs. Ed Goodsir Smith. 1966.

Goodsir Smith edited Lines Rev *Jan 1955 to Summer 1956.*

§ 2

Scott, A. Daylight and the dark: Edinburgh in the poetry of Robert Fergusson and Goodsir Smith. Lines 3 1953.

MacCaig, N. The poetry of Goodsir Smith. Saltire Rev 1 1954.

'MacDiarmid, Hugh' (C. M. Grieve). Sydney Goodsir Smith. Edinburgh [1963] (135 copies). An address.

STANLEY SNAITH
b. 1903

April morning. 1926.

A flying scroll. 1928.

The silver scythe. 1933.

North. 1934.

The children's London pageant: stories of a great city. [1935].

Fieldfaring. [1935].

Men against peril. [1936]. Non-fiction.

At grips with Everest. 1937. Non-fiction.

Green legacy. 1937.

Alpine adventure. 1944. Non-fiction.

Stormy harvest: poems of peace and war. 1944.

The inn of night. 1947.

Bygone Bethnal Green. 1948. With G. F. Vale.

The common festival. 1950.

The mountain challenge. 1952. Non-fiction.

CHARLES HAMILTON SORLEY
1895–1915

Bibliographies
Swann, T. B. In his The ungirt runner 1965, §2 below. Includes works by and on Sorley.

§1

Marlborough and other poems. Cambridge 1916, 1916 (rev and enlarged), 1916 (with illustrations in prose), New York 1916, Cambridge 1919 (rearranged, with notes), New York 1919.
[Sixteen poems]. [1931] (Augustan Books of Poetry). Selection.

Letters
Letters from Germany and from the Army. Ed W. R. Sorley, Cambridge 1916 (priv ptd).
The letters of Sorley, with a chapter of biography [by Janet Sorley]. Ed W. R. Sorley, Cambridge 1919, New York 1919.

§2

Moore, T. S. Sorley. In his Some soldier poets, 1919.
Murry, J. M. Lost legions. In his Aspects of literature, 1920.
Lock, D. R. The verse of Sorley. Congregational Quart 6 1928.
Grieg, N. De unge døde: Brooke-Sorley-Owen. Oslo 1932.
Dalglish, D. N. Charles Sorley. Friends Quart Examiner no 284 1937.
Bushnell, A. Charles Hamilton Sorley. Poetry Rev 36 1945.
Jones, J. B. Sorleiana. Swindon Rev 4 1948.
Johnston, J. H. Charles Sorley's 'Bright promise'. West Virginia University Philological Papers 13 1961.
—— Charles Sorley. In his English poetry of the first world war, 1964.
Mackerness, E. D. Charles Hamilton Sorley 1895–1915. Die Neueren Sprachen 10 1961.
Bergonzi, B. Brooke, Grenfell, Sorley. In his Heroes' twilight: a study of the literature of the Great War, 1965.
Swann, T. B. The ungirt runner: Sorley, poet of world war I. Hamden Conn 1965.

WILLIAM SOUTAR
1898–1943
There is a collection of Soutar's mss in the National Library of Scotland.

Bibliographies
Aitken, W. R. William Soutar: bibliographical notes and a checklist. Bibliotheck 1 1957. Lists books, contributions of poetry (selected) and prose to periodicals, and critical references to Soutar.

Collections and Selections
Collected poems, ed with introductory essay by 'Hugh MacDiarmid' (C. M. Grieve) 1948. An incomplete collection, but containing unpbd poems.
Poems in Scots and English, selected by W. R. Aitken. [Edinburgh] 1961. Includes unpbd poems.

§1
Poetry
Gleanings by an undergraduate. Paisley [1923]. Anon, preface signed W.S.
Conflict. 1931.

Seeds in the wind: poems in Scots for children. Edinburgh 1933, London 1943 (rev and enlarged).
The solitary way. Edinburgh 1934.
Brief words: one hundred epigrams. Edinburgh 1935.
Poems in Scots. Edinburgh 1935.
A handful of earth. Edinburgh 1936.
Riddles in Scots. 1937.
In the time of tyrants: poems, with an introductory note on pacifist faith and necessity. Perth 1939 (priv ptd, 100 copies).
But the earth abideth: a verse-sequence. 1943.
The expectant silence. 1944.

Autobiographies
Diaries of a dying man, ed A. Scott. Edinburgh 1954.

§2
Smith, McC. The poetry of Soutar. Poetry Rev 29 1938.
Singer, J. Soutar: people's poet and true Scot. Our Time 4 1944.
'MacDiarmid, Hugh' (C. M. Grieve). William Soutar. Poetry Scotland 2 1945.
Montgomerie, W. Soutar the man. Poetry Scotland 2 1945.
—— William Soutar. Scottish Educational Jnl 24 Dec 1948.
—— Soutar and tradition. New Alliance & Scots Rev 10 1949.
Young, D. Soutar's purpose in poetry. Poetry Scotland 2 1945.
Reid, A. The life story of Soutar. Scotland's Mag 50 1954.
Scott, T. Some poets of the Scottish renaissance. Poetry (Chicago) 88 1956.
Scott, A. Still life: William Soutar 1898–1943. Edinburgh 1958.
Buist, A. Still life: an appreciation of Soutar 1898–1943. Poetry Rev 52 1961.
Goodwin, K. L. Soutar, Adelaide Crapsey and Imagism. Stud in Scottish Lit 3 1965.

CHARLES BERNARD SPENCER
1909–63

§1
Aegean islands and other poems. 1946, New York 1948.
George Seferis. The king of Asine and other poems. Tr from the Greek by Spencer, N. Valaoritis, L. Durrell 1948.
The twist in the plotting: twenty five poems. Reading 1960 (150 copies). Rptd in With luck lasting, below.
With luck lasting. 1963, Chester Springs Pa 1965.
Collected poems. 1965.
Spencer edited Oxford Poetry 1930 (*with S. Spender*) *and* Oxford Poetry 1931 (*with R. Goodman*), *contributing 3 poems to the former and 4 to the latter. He also edited, with L. Durrell and R. Fedden, the periodical* Personal Landscape, *1942–5, and the anthology* Personal landscape, *1945, compiled from it.*

§2
Betjeman, J. L. MacNeice and B. Spencer. London Mag 3 1963–4.
Durrell, L. B. Spencer. London Mag 3 1963–4. Includes 4 poems.

STEPHEN HAROLD SPENDER
b. 1909

Bibliographies

Tolley, A. T. The early published poems of Spender: a chronology. Ottawa 1967.
—— The printing of Auden's Poems (1928) and Spender's Nine experiments. Library 5th ser 22 1967.

Poetry, Plays and Verse Translations

Nine experiments, by S.H.S.: being poems written at the age of eighteen. Hampstead 1928 (30 copies or less), Cincinnati [1964] (rptd in facs).
Twenty poems. Oxford [1930].
Poems. 1933, 1934 (with omissions and many addns), New York 1934.
Vienna. 1934, New York 1935.
Trial of a judge: a tragedy in five acts. (Group Theatre 18 March 1938). 1938, New York 1938.
García Lorca, F. Poems: with English translation by Spender and J. L. Gili. 1939, New York 1939.
Rilke, R. M. Duino elegies: the German text, with an English translation, introduction and commentary by J. B. Leishman and Spender. 1939, New York 1939.
The still centre. 1939.
Selected poems. 1940.
Ruins and visions. 1942, New York 1942.
Selected poems of Federico García Lorca, tr by J. L. Gili and Spender 1943. Selection from Poems, 1939, with alterations.
Spiritual exercises: to Cecil Day Lewis. 1943 (priv ptd, 125 copies); rptd with alterations in next as Spiritual explorations.
Poems of dedication. 1947, New York 1947.
Returning to Vienna 1947: nine sketches. [New York] 1947 (500 copies); rptd with alterations in next.
The edge of being. 1949, New York [1949].
Le dur désir de durer, by Paul Eluard, with the translation in English verse by S. Spender and Frances Cornford. Philadelphia, London 1950.
Rilke, R. M. The life of the Virgin Mary: the German text with an English translation and introd by Spender. 1951, New York 1951.
Sirmione Peninsula. 1954 (Ariel Poem).
Collected poems 1928–1953. 1955, New York [1955]. Selection with extensive revision.
Inscriptions. 1958. 3 short poems ptd in facs of the author's ms.
Schiller's Mary Stuart, tr and adapted by Spender. (Assembly Hall, Edinburgh 2 Sept 1958; Old Vic 17 Sept 1958). 1959.
Selected poems. New York [1964], London 1965 (with slightly different introd). Includes 3 previously uncollected poems.

Other Works

The destructive element: a study of modern writers and beliefs. 1935, Boston 1935.
The burning cactus. 1936. Stories.
Forward from liberalism. 1937, New York [1937].
Danton's death: a play in four acts by George Büchner. Tr Spender and G. Rees 1939.
The new realism: a discussion. 1939.
Pastor Hall: a play in three acts by E. Toller. 1939, New York [1939] (adds Toller and D. Johnston's Blind man's buff). Tr with H. Hunt.
The backward son. 1940. Novel.
Life and the poet. 1942.
Citizens in war—and after. 1945.
European witness. 1946, New York 1946. Impressions of Germany in 1945.
Poetry since 1939. 1946 (The Arts in Britain).

World within world. 1951, New York 1951. Autobiography.
Five tragedies of sex, by F. Wedekind. Tr F. Fawcett and Spender 1952, New York 1952.
Learning laughter. 1952, New York [1953]. On a visit to Israel.
Shelley. 1952 (Br Council pamphlet).
The creative element: a study of vision, despair and orthodoxy among some modern writers. 1953.
The making of a poem. 1955, New York 1962.
Engaged in writing and The fool and the princess. 1958, New York [1958]. 2 short novels.
The imagination of the modern world. Washington 1962. Lectures.
The struggle of the modern. 1963, Berkeley 1963.
Chaos and control in poetry. Washington 1966. Lecture.
The year of the young rebels. 1969, New York 1969.

Principal Works Edited or with Contributions by Spender

Oxford poetry 1929. Oxford 1929. Ed with L. MacNeice; 4 poems by Spender.
Oxford poetry 1930. Oxford 1930. Ed with B. Spencer; 5 poems by Spender.
Poems for Spain. Ed Spender and J. Lehmann 1939. Anthology; introd by Spender.
Jim Braidy: the story of Britain's firemen. By W. Sansom, J. Gordon, S. Spender. 1943.
Botticelli. 1945 (Faber Gallery), New York 1948. Introd and notes by Spender.
A choice of English romantic poetry. Ed Spender, New York 1947.
La Tour du Pin, P. de. The dedicated life in poetry and The correspondence of Laurent de Cayeux. Tr G. S. Fraser with an introd by Spender 1948.
The god that failed: six studies in communism. Ed R. H. S. Crossman 1950. Ch by Spender.
Selected poems of Walt Whitman. Ed Spender 1950.
Europe in photographs [by M. Hürlimann]. Commentary by Spender. 1951.
Great writings of Goethe. Ed Spender, New York 1958.
Great German short stories. Ed Spender, New York [1960].
The writer's dilemma: essays first published in the Times Literary Supplement. Introd by Spender 1961.
The concise encyclopedia of English and American poetry. Ed Spender and D. Hall, New York 1963.
Ghika. Paintings, drawings, sculpture. 1964, Boston 1965. Texts by Spender and P. Leigh Fermor.
Lowry, M. Under the volcano. Introd by Spender 1967.
Spender was joint-editor of Encounter 1953–67. *He contributed to symposia and other collections of essays principally dealing with contemporary literature and the position of the artist in society.*

§2

Glicksberg, C. Poetry and Marxism: three English poets take their stand. UTQ 6 1937. On Auden, Day Lewis and Spender.
Southworth, J. G. Stephen Spender. Sewanee Rev 45 1937; rptd in his Sowing the spring, 1940.
Young, G. M. Out of the twilight: into the fog. In his Daylight and champaign, 1937; rptd review of Forward from liberalism, 1937.
Daiches, D. Poetry of the 1930's: II, W. H. Auden and Spender. In his Poetry and the modern world, 1940.
Hallett, S. Spender's I think continually of those. Explicator 2 1944. See also H. Smith, ibid.
Walcutt, C. C. Spender's The landscape near an aerodrome. Explicator 5 1947.
Waller, J. The human record of Spender. Poetry Quart 11 1949.
Jacobs, W. D. Spender's I think continually of those. MLN 65 1950.
—— The moderate poetical success of Spender. College Eng 17 1956.

Fremantle, A. Stephen Spender. Commonweal 11 May 1951.

Guidi, A. Spender, Praz e Virginia Woolf. Letteratura e Arte Contemporanea 2 1951.

Gerevini, S. L'autobiografia di Spender. Letterature Moderne 4 1953.

Knieger, B. Spender's Awaking. Explicator 12 1954.

Seif, M. The impact of T. S. Eliot on Auden and Spender. South Atlantic Quart 53 1954.

Bogan, L. In her Selected criticism, New York 1955.

Gorlier, C. Maschera e confessione da Yeats a Spender. Paragone 7 1955.

Béra, M.-A. L'autobiographie de Spender. Critique (Paris) no 122 1957.

Fraser, G. S. A poetry of search: Spender. In his Vision and rhetoric, 1959.

Gerstenberger, D. The saint and the circle: the dramatic potential of an image. Criticism 2 1960.

Marcus, M. Walden as a possible source for Spender's The express. Thoreau Soc Bull 75 1961.

Jarka, H. Pre-war Austria as seen by Spender, Isherwood and Lehmann. Proc Pacific Northwest Conference on Foreign Languages 15 1964.

Replogle, J. The Auden group. Wisconsin Stud in Contemporary Lit 5 1964.

Blakeslee, R. C. Three ways past Edinburgh. College Eng 26 1965. On The express. Reply by J. L. Potter, The 'Destined pattern' of Spender's Express, College Eng 27 1966.

Sellers, W. H. Wordsworth and Spender. Stud in Eng Lit 1500-1900 6 1965.

— Spender and Vienna. Humanities Assoc Bull 18 1967.

Cowley, M. In his Think back on us: a contemporary chronicle of the 1930s. Carbondale 1967. On Poems and Vienna.

Gerber, P.-L. and R. J. Gemmett. A conversation with Spender: the creative process. Eng Record 18 1968.

Leardi, M. La poesia di Spender. Eng Miscellany (Rome) 19 1968.

Maxwell-Mahon, W. D. Spender and the struggle of the modern. Unisa Eng Stud 3 1968.

Stanford, D. Stephen Spender, Louis MacNeice, Cecil Day Lewis: a critical essay. Grand Rapids Michigan 1969 (Contemporary Writers in Christian Perspective).

SIR JOHN COLLINGS SQUIRE
1884-1958

Bibliographies

Williams, I. A. Bibliographies of modern authors, 4: Squire and James Stephens. 1922. Prefatory letter by Squire.

Benedikz, B. S. A partial bibliography of the works of Squire. In P. Howarth, Squire: 'most generous of men,' 1963, §2 below.

§1
Poetry

Poems and Baudelaire flowers. 1909.
The three hills and other poems. 1913.
Christmas hymn. 1914 (priv ptd); rptd in next.
The survival of the fittest and other poems. 1916.
Twelve poems. 1916.
The lily of Malud and other poems. 1917.
Poems: first series. 1918, New York 1919. Selection with new poems.
The birds and other poems. 1919, New York 1920.
The moon. [1920], New York 1920.
Poems: second series. New York 1921, London 1922. Collection 1918-21, with new poems.

The rugger match. 1922 (priv ptd, 250 copies). Rptd from previous.
American poems and others. [1923], New York 1923.
A new song of the Bishop of London and the city churches. 1924; rptd in Poems in one volume, 1926, below.
[Eighteen poems]. [1925] (Augustan Books of Modern Poetry). Selection.
Poems in one volume. 1926. Collection including previously unpbd poems.
A face in candlelight and other poems. 1932.
Poems of two wars. 1940.
The symbol. [1940] (priv ptd, 55 copies).
Selected poems. 1948.
Collected poems; with a preface by J. Betjeman. 1959.

Parodies and Humour

Imaginary speeches and other parodies in prose and verse. 1912.
Steps to Parnassus and other parodies and diversions. 1913.
Tricks of the trade. 1917, New York 1917.
Collected parodies. [1921], New York 1922.
The clown of Stratford. Bristol 1926 (priv ptd, 110 copies). Prose play in one act.
Pick-me-up: 13 drawings in colour by I. Fenwick, with rhymed recipes by A. N. Other [i.e. Squire]. 1933.
Weepings and wailings. 1935. Illustr I. Fenwick.

Other Works

Socialism and art. Introd by W. Crane [1907].
William the Silent. 1912.
The gold tree. 1917. Short stories.
Books in general, by 'Solomon Eagle' [i.e. Squire]. [1918], New York 1919. Essays rptd from New Statesman.
Books in general: second series, by 'Solomon Eagle'. [1920], New York 1920. Rptd from New Statesman.
Life and letters. [1920], New York 1920. Essays rptd from Land & Water.
Books in general: third series, by 'Solomon Eagle'. [1921], New York 1922. Rptd from New Statesman.
Books reviewed, by 'Solomon Eagle'. [1922], New York 1923. Rptd from Observer.
Essays at large, by 'Solomon Eagle'. [1922], New York 1923. Rptd mainly from Outlook.
Essays on poetry. [1923], New York 1924.
The Invalids: a chronicle. 1923 (priv ptd). On a cricket club.
The Grub Street nights entertainments. [1924], New York 1924. Short stories.
Life at the Mermaid. [1927]. Short essays, some previously uncollected.
Berkeley Square: a play in three acts, by J. L. Balderston in collaboration with J. C. Squire. [1928] (French's Acting edn), 1929, New York 1929.
Contemporary American authors, by J. C. Squire and associate critics of the London Mercury. Introd by H. S. Canby, New York 1928.
Robin Hood: a farcical romantic pastoral. 1928. With Joan R. Young.
Pride and prejudice: a play in four acts adapted from Jane Austen's novel. 1929. With E. H. Squire.
Sunday mornings. 1930. Articles rptd from Observer.
Speech at the Lewis Carroll centenary exhibition. [1932].
Outside Eden. 1933, New York 1933. Short stories.
Flowers of speech: being lectures in words and forms in literature. 1935. 2 series of broadcast lectures.
Reflections and memories. 1935. Collection of prefaces and sketches.
Shakespeare as a dramatist. 1935.
The hall of the Institute of Chartered Accountants in England and Wales. 1937.
The honeysuckle and the bee: reminiscences. 1937, New York 1937.
Water-music: or a fortnight of bliss. 1939. On a canoe journey.

Works Edited etc by Squire

A selective list (see also endnote, below). Many of the introds contributed by Squire to the works of other authors are rptd in Reflections and memories, *1935, above.*

The collected poems of James Elroy Flecker. 1916, New York 1921.

A book of women's verse. 1921, New York 1921.

Selections from modern poets. 1921, New York 1921.

By-ways round Helicon: a kind of anthology, by Iolo A. Williams, with an introd by Squire 1922.

Hassan, by James Elroy Flecker, with an introd by Squire 1923.

Second selections from modern poets. 1924.

Nimphidia: the court of fayrie, by Michael Drayton. Oxford 1924 (Shakespeare Head Quartos).

Songs from the Elizabethans. 1924, New York 1924.

The comic muse: an anthology of humorous verse. [1925].

The Cambridge book of lesser poets. Cambridge 1927, New York 1927.

Selections from modern poets: a complete edition—first and second series. 1927.

Apes and parrots: an anthology of parodies. 1928, Cambridge Mass 1929.

Last poems, by John Freeman. 1930, New York 1930.

If it had happened otherwise: lapses into imaginary history. 1931, New York 1931 (as If: or history rewritten).

Younger poets of to-day. 1932, 1934 (as Third selections from modern poets).

The Bible treasury: an anthology for everyman. Ed Squire and A. E. Baker 1933.

Third selections from modern poets. 1934. *See* Younger poets of to-day, 1932, above.

Letters, by John Freeman. Ed Gertrude Freeman and Squire 1936, New York 1936.

Cheddar gorge: a book of English cheeses. [1937], New York 1938.

Selected poems of Tennyson. 1947, New York 1947.

Squire founded London Mercury *and edited it 1919–34. For a list of his contributions see Benedikz, Bibliography, above. He was literary editor of* New Statesman *1913–19 (contributing to it as 'Solomon Eagle') and of* Land and Water *1914–20, and contributed weekly articles to* Observer *1921–31. He was general editor of the following series:* English Men of Letters, *1926–30;* English Heritage Ser *(with Viscount Lee of Fareham) 1929–36, (contributing introds to N. Cardus,* Cricket, *1930; E. Blunden,* The face of England, *1932; I. A. Williams,* English folk-song and dance, *1935; and Sir H. Slesser,* The law, *1936);* Rosemary Library *[1937], contributing an introd to W. H. Mallock,* The new republic.

§2

Lynd, R. In his Old and new masters, 1919.

Waugh, A. In his Tradition and change, 1919.

Mais, S. P. B. In his Books and their writers, 1920.

Olivero, F. Due lirici inglesi d'oggi: W. J. Turner e Squire. Nuova Antologia 16 June 1920.

Roberts, R. E. J. C. Squire. Bookman (London) 58 1920.

Maynard, T. The unexpectedness of Squire. Literary Rev 22 Oct 1921.

MacCarthy, D. The younger poets IV: Squire. New Statesman 13 May 1922.

Freeman, J. The poetry of Squire. Bookman (London) 67 1924.

Priestley, J. B. In his Figures in modern literature, 1924.

Davison, E. The poetry of Squire. English Jnl 15 1926.

Arrow, J. Squire v. D. H. Lawrence: a reply to Squire's article in the Observer of March 9th, 1930. 1930.

Howarth, P. Squire: 'most generous of men'. 1963.

Ross, R. H. In his The Georgian revolt: rise and fall of a poetic ideal 1910–22, Carbondale 1965.

Pryce-Jones, A. An honorary John Bull. TLS 19 Dec 1968.

JAMES STEPHENS
1882–1950

Bramsbäck (see Bibliographies, below) lists locations of Stephens mss. The largest holding of literary mss is in the Berg and DeCoursey Fales Collections of New York Public Library. Stephens' correspondence with his agent, J. B. Pinker, is in the Houghton Library, Harvard University.

Bibliographies

Williams, I. A. Bibliographies of modern authors, 4: J. C. Squire and Stephens. 1922.

Saul, G. B. Stephens' contributions to The Irish Review. PBSA 46 1952.

— Descriptive record of Stephens' contributions to Sinn Féin. BNYPL 57 1953; rptd in his Stephens, Yeats and other Irish concerns, New York 1954, §2, below.

Bramsbäck, B. Stephens: a literary and bibliographical study. Upsala 1959 (Upsala Irish Stud 4). Lists mss, unpbd letters, separate pbns, contributions to books, periodicals and newspapers, biography and criticism of Stephens.

Cary, R. Stephens at Colby College. Colby Lib Quart ser 5 no 9 1961.

McFate, P. A holograph notebook and the publication of its contents: a bibliographical note on Stephens. PBSA 57 1963.

— The publication of Stephens' short stories in The Nation. PBSA 58 1964.

The Stephens papers [at Kent State Univ Lib]: a catalogue. Serif 2 1965.

Selections

A Stephens reader, selected with introd by L. Frankenberg, preface by P. Colum, New York 1962, London 1962 (as James Stephens: a selection).

§1
Poetry

Where the demons grin. Dundrum 1908 (Cuala Press broadside 6). Rptd in Insurrections. Stephens contributed poems to later Cuala Press broadsides. For details *see* Bramsbäck (Bibliographies, above).

Insurrections. Dublin 1909, New York 1909.

The lonely god and other poems. New York 1909.

The hill of vision. New York 1912, Dublin 1912, London 1922 (12 poems omitted).

Five new poems. 1913. Ptd by A. T. Stevens for Flying Fame.

Songs from the clay. 1915, New York 1915.

The adventures of Seumas Beg; The rocky road to Dublin. 1915, New York 1915 (as The rocky road to Dublin; The adventures of Seumas Beg). 2 sers of poems.

Green branches. Dublin 1916 (500 copies), New York 1916 (500 copies).

Reincarnations. 1918, New York 1918.

Little things and other poems. Freelands Ky 1924 (priv ptd, 200 copies).

A poetry recital. New York 1925, London 1925.

Collected poems. 1926, New York 1926, London 1954 (with later poems added), New York 1954. Selection, with preface by Stephens.

Optimist. Gaylordsville Conn 1929 (83 copies). Rptd in Collected poems, 1954.

The outcast. 1929 (Ariel Poem).

Theme and variations. New York 1930. Included with addns in next.

Strict joy. 1931, New York 1931.

Kings and the moon. 1938, New York 1938.

Several single poems were pbd in United States as greetings cards, etc.

Other Works

The charwoman's daughter. 1912, Boston [1912] (as Mary, Mary; with introd by P. Colum). Novel.
The crock of gold. 1912, Boston [1912], New York 1942 (introd by C. Fadiman).
Here are ladies. 1913, New York 1913. Stories with 7 poems, 4 of latter rptd in Collected poems, 1954, above.
The demi-gods. 1914, New York 1914. Novel.
The insurrection in Dublin. Dublin 1916, New York 1916.
The poetical works of Thomas MacDonagh. Ed Stephens, 1916, New York [1917?].
Hunger: a Dublin story by 'James Esse' [i.e. Stephens]. Dublin 1918. Included in Etched in moonlight, 1928, below.
Irish fairy tales. 1920, New York 1920.
Deirdre. 1923, New York 1923. Novel.
In the land of youth. 1924, New York 1924. Stories.
Arthur Griffith, journalist and statesman. Dublin [1924?].
Etched in moonlight. 1928, New York 1928. Stories.
On prose and verse. New York 1928. 2 essays. On prose was originally a preface, unpbd, written for French trn of The charwoman's daughter.
Julia Elizabeth: a comedy in one act. New York 1929.
English romantic poets. Ed Stephens, E. L. Beck, R. H. Snow, New York [1933]. Includes essay by Stephens, The poets and poetry of the nineteenth century. Rptd in next.
Victorian and later English poets. Ed Stephens, E. L. Beck, R. H. Snow, New York [1934].
Garrity, D. (ed). Irish stories and tales. New York 1955. Contains A rhinoceros, some ladies, and a horse, by Stephens. According to Bramsbäck, thought to be pt of an unpbd autobiography; rptd in O'Connor, F. (ed), Modern Irish short stories, 1957 (WC).
James, Seumas & Jacques: unpublished writings of James Stephens, chosen and ed with introd by L. Frankenberg. New York 1964, London 1964. Mainly broadcast talks.

Stephens contributed numerous articles to Sinn Féin, *to* Irish Rev *(see G. B. Saul, Bibliographies, above), of which he was associate editor, and to* New Ireland Rev. *Bramsbäck (Bibliographies, above) lists these and also a number of books to which Stephens contributed prefaces or introds.*

§2

Shafer, R. Stephens and the poetry of the day. Forum 50 1913.
Wall, J. AE and Stephens. Poetry Rev 4 1914.
'A.E.' (G. W. Russell). Poetry of Stephens. In his Imaginations and reveries, 1915.
Boyd, E. A. James Stephens. In his Portraits: real and imaginary, New York [1924].
Brulé, A. James Stephens. Revue Anglo-américaine 1 1924.
Marshall, H. P. James Stephens. London Mercury 12 1925.
Weygandt, C. The riddling of Stephens. In his Tuesdays at ten, Philadelphia 1928.
—— Stephens, poet in verse and prose. Irish Rev 1 1934.
Conklin, G. Stephens: prosodist. Eng Jnl 25 1936.
O'Farachaín, R. Faint praise and Stephens. Irish Monthly 67 1939.
Poepping, H. James Stephens: eine Untersuchung über die irische Erneuerungsbewegung in der Zeit von 1900–1930. Halle/Saale 1940.
Henry, N. Stephens' Little things. Explicator 9 1950.
Kemp, L. Stephens' Little things. Explicator 9 1950.
Colum, P. Stephens as a prose artist. Dublin Mag new ser 26 1951.
Marcus, D. One afternoon with Stephens. Irish Writing 14 1951.
Mercier, V. Stephens: his version of pastoral. Irish Writing no 14 1951.

Hatvary, G. E. Re-reading The crock of gold. Irish Writing no 22 1953.
Saul, G. B. On Mercury and reason: the criticism of Stephens. BNYPL 57 1953; rptd in his Stephens, Yeats and other Irish concerns, 1954.
—— Withdrawn in gold. Arizona Quart 9 1953.
—— Stephens, Yeats and other Irish concerns. New York 1954.
Hoult, N. James Stephens. Irish Writing no 27 1954.
Short, C. Stephens' women. Western Humanities Rev 10 1956.
Dunsany, Lord. Four poets: AE, Kipling, Yeats, Stephens. Atlantic Monthly 201 1958.
Kennedy, B. A. Stephens' American diary. Threshold 2 1958.
Martin, A. Stephens: lyric poet. Studies 49 1960; ibid 50 1961.
—— The crock of gold fifty years after. Colby Lib Quart ser 6 no 4 1962.
—— The short stories of Stephens. Colby Lib Quart ser 6 no 8 1963.
Colby Lib Quart ser 5 no 9 1961. A tribute to Stephens 1882–1950, containing:
Gogarty, O. St J. James Stephens.
Bramsbäck, B. Stephens: Dublin-Paris-return.
Cary, R. Stephens at Colby College. [Bibliography].
Loftus, R. J. Stephens: the nation of love. In his Nationalism in modern Anglo-Irish poetry, Madison 1964.
Pyle, H. Stephens: his work and an account of his life. 1965. Includes checklist of books and contributions to books.

RANDALL CARLINE SWINGLER
1909–67

§1

Difficult morning. 1933.
Reconstruction: six poems. Oxford 1933.
No escape. 1937. Novel.
To town. 1939. Novel.
The years of anger. [1946].
The god in the cave. 1950.
The harvest of peace: a cantata [of 8 poems] *was pbd in* California Quart *3 1953. Swingler was for a time literary editor of* Daily Worker, *editor of* Left Rev *1937–8, editor or co-editor of* Our Time *1941–9 (with a gap), and joint editor of* Arena. *He was joint editor of* Circus *1950 and reviewed for* TLS.

JULIAN GUSTAVE SYMONS
b. 1912

§1
Poetry

Confusions about X. [1939].
The second man. 1943.

Other Works

An anthology of war poetry, compiled by Symons. 1942 (Pelican), New York 1942.
The immaterial murder case. 1945, New York 1957. Fiction.
A man called Jones. 1947. Fiction.
Bland beginning: a detective story. 1949, New York 1949.
Selected writings of Samuel Johnson. Ed Symons 1949.
A. J. A. Symons: his life and speculations. 1950.
The thirty-first of February: a mystery novel. 1950, New York [1950] (as The 31st of February).

Charles Dickens. 1951, New York [1951].

Thomas Carlyle: the life and ideas of a prophet. 1952, New York 1952.

The broken penny. 1953, New York [1953]. Fiction.

The narrowing circle. 1954, New York [1954]. Fiction.

Carlyle: selected works, reminiscences and letters. Ed Symons 1955.

Horatio Bottomley: a biography. 1955.

The paper chase. 1956, New York [1957] (as Bogue's fortune). Fiction.

The colour of murder. 1957, New York [1957]. Fiction.

The general strike: a historical portrait. 1957.

The gigantic shadow. [1958], New York [1959] (as The pipe dream). Fiction.

The progress of a crime. 1960, New York [1960]. Fiction.

A reasonable doubt: some criminal cases re-examined. 1960.

The thirties: a dream revolved. 1960.

Murder! Murder! 1961. Stories.

The detective story in Britain. 1962 (Br Council pamphlet).

The killing of Francie Lake. [1962], New York [1962] (as The plain man). Fiction.

Buller's campaign. 1963. On the Boer war.

The end of Solomon Grundy. [1964], New York [1964]. Fiction.

The Belting inheritance. [1965], New York [1965]. Fiction.

England's pride: the story of the Gordon relief expedition. 1965.

Francis Quarles investigates. 1965. Stories.

Crime and detection: an illustrated history from 1840. 1966.

Critical occasions. 1966.

The Julian Symons omnibus. 1967. Introd by Symons. The 31st of February, The progress of a crime, The end of Solomon Grundy.

The man who killed himself. [1967], New York [1967]. Fiction.

The man whose dreams came true. 1968, New York [1968]. Fiction.

Essays and biographies, by A. J. A. Symons. Ed Symons 1969.

Symons founded and edited Twentieth-Century Verse, *1937–9.*

§2

Scarfe, F. Julian Symons: the critic as poet. In his Auden and after, 1942.

RACHEL ANNAND TAYLOR
1876–1960

§1

Poems. 1904.

Rose and vine. 1909.

The hours of Fiammetta: a sonnet sequence. 1910.

Aspects of the Italian Renaissance, with a preface by G. Murray. 1923, New York 1930 (rev and enlarged, as Invitation to Renaissance Italy).

The end of Fiammetta. 1923, New York 1924.

Leonardo the Florentine: a study in personality. 1927, New York 1928 (with a note on the author's work by G. Murray).

Dunbar: the poet and his period. 1931.

§2

Hamilton, W. H. The poetry of Rachel Annand Taylor. Quest 13 1921–2.

Lawrence, D. H. Rachel Annand Taylor. In Lawrence, Ada and G. S. Gelder, Young Lorenzo, 1932.

—— Eight letters to Rachel Annand Taylor. Foreword by M. Ewing. Pasadena 1956.

ARTHUR SEYMOUR JOHN TESSIMOND
1902–62

§1

The walls of glass. 1934.

Voices in a giant city. 1947.

Bewick's Birds: a selection. 1952. Verses by Tessimond.

Selection. 1958. Includes uncollected poems 1947–57.

PHILIP EDWARD THOMAS
1878–1917

The principal collections of Thomas's poetical mss are in BM (see H. I. Bell, Autograph poems of Edward Thomas, BM Quart 12 1938), in Bodley, and in Lockwood Lib, Buffalo. Mss of a few poems, some letters and a substantial number of prose works are in New York Public Library (see J. D. Gordan, New in the Berg Collection, BNYPL 68 1964). For other collections of Thomas's letters see W. Cooke, Edward Thomas, 1970 (§2, below).

Bibliographies

Bibliographies of modern authors: Edward Thomas. London Mercury 2 1920.

Murphy, G. Bibliographies of modern authors II, Edward Thomas. London Mercury 16–17 1927–8.

Eckert, R. P. Edward Thomas: soldier-poet of his race. Amer Book Collector 4 1933.

—— Edward Thomas: a biography and a bibliography. 1937. Includes secondary material.

Muir, P. H. Points, ser 2, 1866–1934. 1934. On 11 of Thomas's books.

Prance, C. A. An Edward Thomas collection. Private Lib 6 1962.

Bodleian Library. Edward Thomas 1878–1917: an exhibition [etc]. Oxford 1968.

Cooke, W. In his Edward Thomas, 1970, §2, below. Includes recent secondary material and notes on the location of mss, on the order of composition of the poems and on the relationships between their various states in ms and in print.

Poetry

Most of the verse pbd by Thomas in his lifetime appeared in anthologies and under the pseudonym 'Edward Eastaway'.

Beautiful Wales, painted by R. Fowler, described by Thomas. 1905. Includes Eluned, by 'Llewelyn the Bard', i.e. Thomas.

This England: an anthology from her writers. Ed Thomas 1915. Includes 2 poems by 'Edward Eastaway', Haymaking and The manor farm.

Six poems, by 'Edward Eastaway'. Flansham [1916] (100 copies; pbd by Pear Tree Press).

An annual of new poetry. 1917. Includes 18 poems by 'Edward Eastaway', 4 previously pbd in Six poems, [1916], above.

Poems by Edward Thomas—'Edward Eastaway'. 1917, New York 1917. 64 poems, including Cock-crow from Six poems, [1916] above.

Last poems. 1918.

Twelve poets: a miscellany of new verse. 1918. 10 poems by Thomas, simultaneously pbd in Last poems, above.

In memoriam: Edward Thomas. 1919. Contains Up in the wind, previously unpbd.

Collected poems. 1920 (containing Poems, 1917 and Last poems, 1918, and one additional poem; foreword by W. de la Mare), New York 1921, London 1928 (with 4 more poems and a few corrections), 1949 (with additional poem, P.H.T.).

[Twenty-four poems]. [1926] (Augustan Books of Modern Poetry). Selection.

Selected poems. Newtown 1927 (275 copies). Introd by E. Garnett contains excerpts from letters.

Two poems. 1927 (85 copies). The lane and The watchers, previously unpbd; rptd in 1928 edn of Collected poems, above.

The trumpet and other poems. 1940. Selection.

[Thirty-three poems]. 1960 (Pocket Poets). Selection by H. Thomas.

Selected poems. Ed R. Skelton 1962.

Selected poems, selected and introduced by R. S. Thomas. 1964.

The green roads: poems for young readers, chosen and introduced by E. Farjeon. 1965, New York 1965 (as The green roads: poems).

Other Works
(including works edited by Thomas)

The woodland life. Edinburgh 1897. Essays and a naturalist's diary.

Horae solitariae. 1902, New York [1902?]. Essays.

Oxford, painted by J. Fulleylove, described by Thomas. 1903, 1922 (rev).

Rose Acre papers. 1904. Essays. See also Rose Acre papers, etc, 1910, below.

Beautiful Wales, painted by R. Fowler, described by Thomas. 1905, 1924 (as Wales). Includes Eluned, a poem by Thomas. See Poetry above.

The heart of England. 1906.

The pocket book of poems and songs for the open air. 1907, New York 1929. Anthology.

The book of the open air. Ed Thomas 1907-[8]. 12 pts bound in 2 vols entitled British country life in spring and summer, and British country life in autumn and winter.

British butterflies and other insects. Ed Thomas 1908. Rptd from The book of the open air, 1907-8, above.

Some British birds. Ed Thomas 1908. Rptd from The book of the open air, 1907-8, above.

Richard Jefferies: his life and work. 1909.

The south country. 1909, 1932 (with introd by Helen Thomas and woodcuts by E. F. Daglish).

Rest and unrest. 1910, New York 1910. Essays.

Rose Acre papers, including essays from Horae solitariae. 1910. 2 essays from Rose Acre papers, 1904, 12 from Horae solitariae, 1902.

Feminine influence on the poets. 1910, New York 1911.

Windsor Castle, described by Thomas, pictured by E. W. Haslehurst. 1910.

Celtic stories. Oxford 1911.

The Isle of Wight, described by Thomas, pictured by E. W. Haslehurst. 1911.

Light and twilight. 1911. Essays.

Maurice Maeterlinck. 1911.

The tenth muse. [1911], 1917 (with memoir of Thomas by J. Freeman). Based on ch 8 of Feminine influence on the poets, 1910, above.

Algernon Charles Swinburne: a critical study. 1912, New York 1912.

George Borrow: the man and his books. 1912.

Lafcadio Hearn. 1912, Boston 1912.

Norse tales. Oxford 1912.

The Icknield Way. 1913, New York 1913.

The country. 1913.

The happy-go-lucky Morgans. 1913. Autobiographical novel.

Walter Pater: a critical study. 1913.

In pursuit of spring. 1914. On a bicycle journey from London to the Quantocks.

Four-and-twenty blackbirds. 1915, 1965 (foreword by H. Thomas), New York 1966 (as The complete fairy tales of Edward Thomas). Expansions of proverbial phrases for children.

The life of the Duke of Marlborough. 1915.

This England: an anthology from her writers. 1915. Includes 2 of Thomas's own poems. See Poetry, above.

The flowers I love: drawings in colour by K. Cameron with an anthology of flower poems selected by Thomas. [1916], New York 1917.

Keats. 1914 (for 1916).

A literary pilgrim in England. 1917, New York 1917.

Cloud Castle and other papers. 1922, New York [1923]. Essays with foreword by W. H. Hudson.

Chosen essays. Newtown 1926 (350 copies). Selection.

Essays of today and yesterday: Thomas. 1926. Selection.

The last sheaf. 1928. Essays rptd from periodicals; foreword by T. Seccombe.

The childhood of Edward Thomas: a fragment of autobiography. 1938. Preface by J. Thomas.

The friend of the blackbird. Flansham 1938 (100 copies, pbd by Pear Tree Press). First pbd in Nation. Rptd from author's corrected copy.

The prose of Edward Thomas, selected by R. Gant. 1948.

Thomas also contributed introds to edns of earlier English prose and verse, including a number of works by Borrow, and to a few other works.

Letters

Garnett, E. Some letters of Edward Thomas. Athenaeum 16, 23 April 1920. 18 letters.

Guthrie, J. To the memory of Edward Thomas. 1937, below. Contains extracts from Thomas's letters to W. H. Hudson.

Moore, J. The life and letters of Edward Thomas. 1939, below. Extracts from nearly 80 letters.

Farjeon, E. Edward Thomas: the last four years. 1958, below. Letters from Thomas to the author.

Letters from Edward Thomas to Gordon Bottomley, ed and introduced by R. G. Thomas. 1968.

§2

Haynes, E. S. P. Edward Thomas. Eng Rev 24 1917; rptd in his Personalia, 1918.

Moore, T. S. Soldier poets III. Eng Rev 27 1918; rptd in his Some soldier poets, 1919.

Wright, H. G. In his Studies in contemporary literature, Bangor 1918. Includes Notes on the life and ancestry of Edward Thomas by his father, P. H. Thomas.

— The sense of the past in Edward Thomas. Welsh Outlook 19 1932.

In memoriam Edward Thomas. 1919. Contributions by V. Locke Ellis, J. W. Haines, W. H. Davies, Julian Thomas.

Huxley, A. Edward Thomas. Athenaeum 24 Sept 1920; rptd in his On the margin, 1923.

Murry, J. M. The poetry of Edward Thomas. In his Aspects of literature, 1920.

Squire, J. C. In his Life and letters, [1920].

— In his Books in general, by 'Solomon Eagle', 3rd ser [1921].

Whicher, G. F. The writings of Edward Thomas. Yale Rev new ser 9 1920.

Van Doren, M. Edward Thomas. Nation 7 Dec 1921.

T., H. [Helen Thomas]. As it was. 1926, New York 1927. An account by the poet's widow of her life with him. The first pbd edn has pp. 53-6 cancelled and an expurgated text substituted, but the American edn has the uncancelled text and an introd by J. M. Murry.

— World without end. 1931. Sequel to As it was. Both books pbd together under this title New York 1931, London 1935 (as As it was: world without end).

— Poets' holiday in the shadow of war. Times 3 Aug 1963.

Herring, R. Edward Thomas. London Mercury 15 1927.

Freeman, J. Edward Thomas. Bookman (London) 74 1928.

Conrad, Mrs Joseph. A personal tribute to the late
P. Gibbon and Edward Thomas. Bookman (London) 78
1930.
Harding, D. W. A note on Nostalgia. Scrutiny 1 1932.
Bonnerot, L. Edward Thomas. Revue Anglo-américaine
11 1934.
Haines, J. W. Edward Thomas: a Welsh poet in Glou-
cestershire. Gloucester Jnl 16 Feb 1935.
These things the poets said. 1935. Poems on Edward
Thomas by several authors, foreword by R. P. Eckert.
Ashton, T. Edward Thomas; from prose to poetry.
Poetry Rev 28 1937.
Eckert, R. P. Edward Thomas: a biography and a biblio-
graphy. 1937.
Guthrie, J. To the memory of Edward Thomas. 1937.
— Edward Thomas in Sussex. Sussex County Mag 13
1939.
Lee, F. A. On patriotism and Edward Thomas. Adelphi
new ser 14 1938.
MacAlister, I. I knew Edward Thomas. Listener 5 Jan
1939.
Moore, J. The life and letters of Edward Thomas. 1939.
Ball, D. Edward Thomas. Cahiers de Paris 8 1940.
Nevinson, H. W. Fame too late. Life & Letters 24 1940.
Bottomley, G. A note on Edward Thomas. Welsh Rev 4
1945.
Bushnell, A. Edward Thomas. Poetry Rev 38 1947.
Hockey, L. W. Edward Thomas and W. H. Davies. Welsh
Rev 7 1948.
Lehmann, J. In his Open night, 1952.
Coombes, H. The poetry of Edward Thomas. EC 3 1953.
— Edward Thomas. 1956.
— Keats and Edward Thomas. EC 8 1958.
— Hardy, de la Mare and Edward Thomas. In Pelican
guide to English literature, ed B. Ford, vol 7; The
modern age, 1961.
Day Lewis, C. The poetry of Edward Thomas. Essays by
Divers Hands 28 1956.
— Edward Thomas. Stand 4 1960.
'Edwards, Oliver'. He went singing. Times 15 March
1956; rptd in his Talking of books, 1957.
Burrow, J. Keats and Edward Thomas. EC 7 1957. On
Thomas's Keats.
Harding, J. Dylan Thomas and Edward Thomas. Con-
temporary Rev 192 1957.
Farjeon, E. Edward Thomas: the last four years; book one
of the memoirs of E. Farjeon. 1958. 3 sections rptd
from London Mag.
Snaith, S. A note on Thomas and 'Eluned'. Listen 3 1958.
With the text of the poem.
Danby, J. F. Edward Thomas. CQ 1 1959.
Lawrence, R. Edward Thomas in perspective. English 12
1959.
Mathias, R. Edward Thomas. Anglo-Welsh Rev 10 1960.
Hobsbaum, P. The road not taken: three poets who died
in the first world war. Listener 23 Nov 1961. Thomas,
Owen, Rosenberg.
Robson, W. W. Edward Thomas's Roads. TLS 23 March
1962.
Scannell, V. Content with discontent: a note on Edward
Thomas. London Mag new ser 1 1962.
— Edward Thomas. 1963 (Br Council pamphlet).
Emslie, M. Spectatorial attitudes. REL 5 1964. On The
watchers.
Jacobs, R. A. Regrets and wishes. Eng Jnl 54 1965. On
The sign-post.
John, A. Edward Thomas: anniversary considerations.
Anglo-Welsh Rev 16 1967.
Cooke, W. Roads to France: the war poetry of Thomas.
Stand 9 1968; rptd in next.
— Edward Thomas: a critical biography. 1970.
Thomas, R. G. Edward Thomas: poet and critic. E & S
21 1968.
Hooker, J. The writings of Edward Thomas. Anglo-Welsh
Rev 18 1969.

RONALD STUART THOMAS
b. 1913

§ 1
Poetry

The stones of the field. Carmarthen 1946.
An acre of land. Newtown [1952].
The minister. Newtown 1953.
Song at the year's turning: poems 1942–1954. Introd by
J. Betjeman 1955. Selection, with 19 new poems.
Poetry for supper. 1958, Chester Springs 1961.
Judgement day. 1960. Single poem in facs of author's ms.
Tares. 1961, Chester Springs 1961.
Penguin modern poets, 1: Lawrence Durrell, Elizabeth
Jennings, R. S. Thomas. 1962. Selection, 27 poems.
The bread of truth. 1963, Chester Springs 1963.
Pietà. 1966.
Not that he brought flowers. 1968.
Roy Fuller and R. S. Thomas, selected by E. Owen. 1968
(Pergamon Poets).

Other Works

The Batsford book of country verse. Ed Thomas 1961.
The Penguin book of religious verse. Ed Thomas 1963.
Selected poems by Edward Thomas. Ed R. S. Thomas
1964.
Words and the poet. Cardiff 1964. Lecture.
A choice of George Herbert's verse. Ed Thomas
1967.
The mountains. New York [1968] (350 copies). Illustr
J. Piper.

§2

Conran, A. The English poet in Wales II, The boys of
summer in their ruin. Anglo-Welsh Rev 10 1960.
Merchant, W. M. R. S. Thomas. CQ 2 1960.
Thomas, R. G. The poetry of R. S. Thomas. REL 3
1962.
— R. S. Thomas. 1964 (Br Council pamphlet). With
L. Clark on Andrew Young.
Hainsworth, J. D. Extremes in poetry: R. S. Thomas and
Ted Hughes. English 14 1963.
Oppel, H. R. S. Thomas: The meeting. In Die moderne
englische Lyrik: Interpretationen, ed H. Oppel, Berlin
1967.
Castay, M.-T. Un poète gallois contemporain: R. S.
Thomas. Caliban 5 1968.

TERENCE TILLER
b. 1916

Poems. 1941.
The inward animal. 1943.
Unarm, Eros. 1947.
Reading a medal and other poems. 1957.
Confessio amantis, The lover's shrift [by] John Gower;
translated into modern English with an introduction by
Tiller. 1963 (Penguin Classics).
Chess treasury of the air. Ed Tiller 1966 (Penguin).
Notes for a myth and other poems. 1968.

RUTHVEN TODD
b. 1914

§ 1
Poetry

Poets of tomorrow, first selection: representing the work
of P. Hewett, H. B. Mallalieu, R. Todd, R. Waller.
1939. 12 poems by Todd.

Ten poems. Edinburgh 1940.
Until now. [1942].
The acreage of the heart. Glasgow 1944 (Poetry Scotland).
The planet in my hand. 1944 (priv ptd), 1946.
A mantelpiece of shells. New York 1955.
Garland for the winter solstice: selected poems. 1961, Boston 1962. Some poems previously uncollected.

Other Works

The laughing mulatto: the story of Alexandre Dumas. [1939].
Over the mountain. 1939, New York 1939. Novel.
Life of William Blake, by Alexander Gilchrist. Ed Todd 1942 (EL).
The lost traveller. 1943. Novel.
Tracks in the snow: studies in English science and art. 1946, New York 1947.
A century of British painters, by Richard and Samuel Redgrave. Ed Todd 1947.
A song to David and other poems by Christopher Smart, selected and with an introduction by Todd 1947.
Poems by William Blake, selected and introduced by Todd 1949.
Loser's choice. New York 1953. Novel.
The tropical fish book. Greenwich Conn 1953.
Trucks, tractors and trailers. New York 1954. For children.
Blake's Dante plates. 1968.
Todd also wrote stories for children, and wrote detective stories as 'R. T. Campbell'.

HENRY TREECE
1911–66
Bibliographies

Kamm, A. In Fisher, M. Henry Treece, 1969, §2 below.

§1
Poetry

38 poems. [1940].
Towards a personal Armageddon. Prairie City Ill 1941.
Invitation and warning. 1942.
Sailing tomorrow's seas: an anthology of new poems by Treece [et al]. Ed M. Lindsay 1944. 3 poems by Treece.
The black seasons. 1945.
Collected poems. New York 1946.
The haunted garden. 1947.
The exiles. 1952.

Novels

The dark island. 1952, New York 1953.
The rebels. 1953.
The golden strangers. 1956, New York 1957, London 1967 (rev).
The great captains. 1956, New York 1956.
Red queen, white queen. 1958, New York 1958.
The master of Badger's Hall. New York 1959, London 1960 (as A fighting man).
Jason. 1961, New York 1961.
Electra. 1963, New York 1963 (as Amber princess).
Oedipus. 1964, New York 1965 (as The eagle king).
The green man. 1966, New York 1966.
Treece also wrote a large number of novels (and a few historical works) for children. For a list of these, see Kamm, Bibliographies, above.

Other Works

The white horseman: prose and verse of the New Apocalypse. Ed J. F. Hendry and Treece 1941.
Wartime harvest: an anthology of prose and verse. Ed

S. Schimanski and Treece 1943. Selected from periodical Kingdom Come.
Air Force poetry. Ed J. Pudney and Treece 1944.
Herbert Read: an introduction to his work by various hands. Ed Treece 1944.
A map of hearts: a collection of short stories. Ed S. Schimanski and Treece [1944].
The crown and the sickle: an anthology, compiled by J. F. Hendry and Treece [1945].
How I see Apocalypse. 1946.
I cannot go hunting tomorrow: short stories. 1946.
Leaves in the storm: a book of diaries. Ed with a running commentary by S. Schimanski and Treece 1947.
Selected poems by A. C. Swinburne. Ed with an introd by Treece 1948.
Dylan Thomas: 'dog among the fairies'. 1949, 1956 (rev), New York 1956.
A new romantic anthology. Ed S. Schimanski and Treece 1949.
Carnival king: a play in three acts. 1955.
The Crusades. 1962, New York 1963.
Treece and Schimanski were editors of Transformation (4 nos 1943–7), a miscellany of prose, poetry and plays. They were also general editors of Transformation Library 1946–7. They were joint editors of Kingdom Come from 1941.

§2

Fisher, M. Henry Treece. In Three Bodley Head Monographs, 1969. Includes Notes on perception and vision by Treece.

ROBERT CALVERLEY TREVELYAN
1872–1951

§1
Poetry and Verse Plays

Mallow and asphodel. 1898.
Polyphemus & other poems. 1901.
Cecilia Gonzaga. 1903. Play.
The birth of Parsival. 1905.
Sisyphus: an operatic fable. 1908.
The bride of Dionysus: a music drama, and other poems. 1912, Edinburgh [1932] (omitting poems).
The new Parsifal: an operatic fable. 1914.
The foolishness of Solomon. 1915.
The death of man. Chicago 1916 (priv ptd, 35 copies).
The pterodamozels: an operatic fable. [1916].
The death of man and other poems. [1919].
Poems and fables. 1925.
The deluge and other poems. 1926.
Cheiron. 1927.
Meleager. 1927. Play.
Three plays: Sulla, Fand, The pearl-tree. 1931.
Rimeless numbers. 1932. With a Note on metre.
Poems. 1934.
Beelzebub and other poems. 1935.
Collected works. 2 vols 1939. Vol 1, Poems, with 7 unpbd poems; vol 2, Plays.
Aftermath. 1941.
From The Shiffolds: Christmas 1946. Dorking [1946].
From The Shiffolds. 1947. Translations; contents different from previous.
Selected poems. Foreword by H. Trevelyan 1953. With 2 unpbd poems.

Other Works

Thamyris: or, is there a future for poetry? [1925], New York [1925]. *See* R. Graves, Another future of poetry, 1926. Reply to Trevelyan's Thamyris.
Translations from Horace, Juvenal and Montaigne; with two imaginary conversations. Cambridge 1940.

Windfalls: notes and essays. 1944. With a dialogue, Thersites.

From the Chinese. Selections from trns of Chinese verse, ed Trevelyan, Oxford 1945.

Translations from Latin poetry. 1949.

Translations from Greek poetry. 1950.

XXI letters: a correspondence between Robert Bridges and R. C. Trevelyan on New verse and The testament of beauty. Stanford Dingley 1955 (68 copies).

Trevelyan also translated works by Aeschylus, Euripides, Leopardi, Lucretius, Sophocles, Theocritus and Vergil.

WALTER JAMES REDFERN TURNER
1889–1946

§1
Poetry

The hunter and other poems. 1916.

The dark fire. 1918.

The dark wind. New York [1920].

In time like glass. 1921.

Paris and Helen. 1921.

Landscape of Cytherea: record of a journey into a strange country. 1923.

The seven days of the sun: a dramatic poem. 1925.

Marigold: an idyll of the sea. 1926.

[Twenty-one poems]. [1926] (Augustan Books of Modern Poetry).

New poems. 1928.

Seven sciagraphical poems. Plaistow 1929 (priv ptd, 65 copies). Rptd in Songs and incantations, 1936, below.

Miss America: Altiora in the Sierra Nevada. 1930, New York 1930.

Pursuit of Psyche. 1931.

Jack and Jill. 1934.

Songs and incantations. 1936.

Selected poems, 1916–1936. 1939.

Fossils of a future time? 1946.

Other Works

Music and life. [1921], New York 1922. Essays.

The man who ate the popomack: a tragi-comedy of love in four acts. Oxford 1922, New York 1923, London 1929 (rev).

Smaragda's lover: a dramatic phantasmagoria. 1924.

Variations on the theme of music. 1924. Essays.

Great names: being an anthology of English and American literature from Chaucer to Francis Thompson. Ed Turner, New York 1926.

Orpheus: or the music of the future. [1926], New York [1926].

The aesthetes. 1927. Philosophical dialogue.

Beethoven: the search for reality. 1927, Garden City NY 1927.

Musical meanderings. 1928, New York 1928. Essays.

A trip to New York and a poem. 1929. Poem entitled Bazin—and at New York.

Eighteenth-century poetry: an anthology. Ed Turner 1931.

Music: a short history. 1932, 1949 (enlarged and illustr).

Facing the music: reflections of a music critic. 1933.

Wagner. 1933, New York 1948.

Berlioz: the man and his work. 1934.

Blow for balloons: being the first hemisphere of the history of Henry Airbubble. 1935. Novel.

Henry Airbubble in search of a circumference to his breath: being the second hemisphere of the history of Henry Airbubble. 1936. Novel.

Music: an introduction to its nature and appreciation. 1936.

Mozart: the man and his works. 1938, New York 1938, London 1965 (rev C. Raeburn).

The duchess of Popocatapetl. 1939. Novel.

English music. 1941 (Britain in Pictures).

Fables, parables and plots: revolutionary stories for the young and old. 1943. Short stories, with a poem, Spring festival.

English ballet. 1944 (Britain in Pictures).

Exmoor village: a general account, based on factual information from Mass-Observation. 1947.

Turner contributed to the 3rd vol of Georgian Poetry, *1917. He was dramatic critic of* London Mercury *1919–23, literary editor of* Daily Herald *1920–3 and literary editor of* Spectator *1942–6. He wrote music criticism for* New Statesman *and* Daily Express. *He edited several series, notably* Britain in pictures *1941–8,* The nations and Britain *[1943–6] and, with S. Shannon,* New excursions into English poetry, *1944–7.*

§2

Olivero, F. Due lirici inglesi d'oggi: Turner e J. C. Squire. Nuova Antologia 16 June 1920.

Warren, C. H. W. J. Turner. Bookman (London) 81 1931.

Haüsermann, H. W. Turner, a Georgian poet. E Studies 25 1943.

—— W. B. Yeats and Turner, 1935–7. E Studies 40 1959. With unpbd letters.

—— Die Streitigkeiten Turners mit H. G. Wells und Arnold Bennett. In Festschrift zum 75. Geburtstag von Theodor Spira, ed H. Viebrock and W. Erzgräber, Heidelberg 1961.

—— The Australian strain in the work of Turner. E Studies 43 1962.

Heddle, E. M. Turner: an Australian writer abroad. Meanjin 6 1947.

MacKerness, E. D. Turner, 1899–1946: the poet as music critic. Canadian Music Jnl 3 1958.

ARTHUR DAVID WALEY
1889–1966

A collection of Waley's papers is in the Library of Rutgers University, New Brunswick NJ. See F. A. Johns, A collection of papers of Waley and Beryl de Zoete, Rutgers Univ Lib Jnl 29 1966. *See also Alison Waley,* Arthur Waley's mss, TLS 2 Nov 1967, *and* Commentary, *ibid, 2 Nov, 7 Dec 1967.*

Bibliographies

Johns, F. A. A preliminary list of the published writings of Waley. Asia Major new ser 7 1959. Includes contributions to books, articles and reviews.

—— A bibliography of Waley. New Brunswick NJ [1968]. Includes books, first appearances of trns, articles, original poetry and prose book reviews, some appearances in anthologies, select list of material on Waley.

§1
Verse Translations

Chinese poems. 1916 (anon, priv ptd, about 50 copies), [1965] (facsimile reprint with note by F. A. Johns).

A hundred and seventy Chinese poems. 1918, New York 1919, London 1962 (as One hundred and seventy Chinese poems [with new introd]).

More translations from the Chinese. 1919, New York 1919.

Japanese poetry: the 'Uta'. Oxford 1919. Trn of poems from the Manyōshū, the Kokinshū and other minor collections.

The Nō plays of Japan; with letters by O. Sickert. 1921, New York 1922 (with abridged introd and additional plates). Trns in verse and prose.

The temple and other poems. 1923, New York 1923. With an introductory essay on early Chinese poetry.

Poems from the Chinese. [1927] (Augustan Books of English Poetry). Selection.

The soul of China, by R. Wilhelm. 1928, New York 1928. Text tr by J. H. Reece, poems by Waley.

Select Chinese verses. Shanghai 1934. With H. A. Giles. Selected from A hundred and seventy Chinese poems, 1918, with Chinese text.

The book of songs [the Shih Ching]. 1937, Boston 1937, London 1954 (with new preface, textual changes and additional notes), New York 1960.

Translations from the Chinese. New York 1941. Contents of A hundred and seventy Chinese poems (omitting 5 poems) and More translations from the Chinese, (omitting 1 poem) with some corrections.

Folk songs from China. 1943. With Tzu-jen Ku and I. Gass. Music arranged by R. Redman.

Chinese poems, selected from 170 Chinese poems, More translations from the Chinese, The temple and The book of songs [with a few addns]. 1946, 1961 (rev, with new poems).

The great summons, by Ch'u Yuan. Honolulu 1949 (100 copies). Rptd from previous.

77 poems, [by] Alberto de Lacerda. Tr Lacerda and Waley 1955. Portuguese and English texts.

Ballads and stories from Tun-huang: an anthology. 1960, New York 1960. Verse and prose trn.

Waley did not collect all his trns. See Section B in Johns' Bibliography (above).

Prose Translations

The tale of Genji [pt 1], by Lady Murasaki. 1925, Boston 1925. Tr from the Japanese.

The sacred tree [The tale of Genji, pt 2]. 1926, Boston 1926.

A wreath of cloud [The tale of Genji, pt 3]. 1927, Boston 1927.

Blue trousers [The tale of Genji, pt 4]. 1928, Boston 1928.

The pillow-book of Sei Shōnagon [selections]. 1928, Boston 1928. Tr from the Japanese.

The lady who loved insects [attributed to Fujiwara no Kanesuke). 1929. Story, included in The real Tripitaka, 1952 (*see* Oriental studies, below). Tr from the Japanese.

The travels of an alchemist: the journey of the Taoist Ch'ang-Ch'un recorded by Li Chih-Ch'ang. 1931 (Broadway Travellers). Tr from the Chinese with introd by Waley.

The lady of the boat [The tale of Genji, pt 5]. 1932, Boston 1932.

The bridge of dreams: being the second volume of The lady of the boat [The tale of Genji, pt 6]. 1933, Boston 1933.

The tale of Genji: a novel in six parts, by Lady Murasaki. 1935, 2 vols Boston 1935.

The analects of Confucius, tr and annotated by Waley 1938, New York 1939.

Monkey, by Wu Ch'êng-ên. 1942, New York 1942 (with introd by Hu Shih). Tr from the Chinese.

Conze, E. (ed). Buddhist texts throughout the ages, newly translated. (Pt 4, Texts from China and Japan, by Waley). Oxford 1954.

Oriental Studies etc
Several of the books below contain prose and verse trns.

The poet Li Po, AD 701–762: a paper read before the China Society. 1919.

An index of Chinese artists represented in the Sub-Department of Oriental Prints and Drawings in the British Museum. 1922.

Zen Buddhism and its relation to art. 1922.

An introduction to the study of Chinese painting. 1923, New York 1923. Includes some verse trns.

The originality of Japanese civilization. 1929, Tokyo 1941 (pamphlet).

A catalogue of paintings recovered from Tun-huang by Sir Aurel Stein. 1931.

The way and its power: a study of the Tao Tê Ching and its place in Chinese thought. 1934. With trn of the text.

Three ways of thought in ancient China. 1939, New York 1954 (slightly abridged). On Chuang Tzu, Mencius and the Realist school with extracts from their works.

In the gallery. Zurich 1949 (priv ptd). Story: rptd in The secret history of the Mongols, 1963, below.

The life and times of Po Chü-i, 772–846 AD. 1949.

The poetry and career of Li Po, 701–762 AD. 1950 (Ethical and Religious Classics of East and West).

The real Tripitaka and other pieces. 1952, New York 1952.

The nine songs: a study of shamanism in ancient China. 1955, New York 1956. With trns of the songs.

Yuan Mei: eighteenth-century Chinese poet. 1956, New York 1957.

The Opium War through Chinese eyes. 1958, New York 1958.

The secret history of the Mongols and other pieces. 1963, New York 1964. Includes trn of 50 poems from the Manyōshū and Ryōjin Hishō, not previously collected.

Hatto, A. T. (ed). Eos: an enquiry into the theme of lovers' meetings and partings at dawn in poetry. Hague 1965. Chinese and Japanese sections by Waley.

Waley contributed introds to trns from Chinese and to other works, including The works of Ronald Firbank, *1929. He contributed a concordance table and notes to the 3rd edn of J. Legge,* Mencius. *He edited* Year book of oriental art and culture, *1924–5. See F. A. Johns, Bibliography, above.*

§2

Aiken, C. Sunt lachrimae rerum: Chinese poetry. In his Scepticisms, 1919.

Mais, S. P. B. A hundred and seventy Chinese poems. In his Books and their writers, 1920; rptd review.

'Solomon Eagle' (J. C. Squire). A translator of genius. In his Essays at large, [1922].

Bates, E. S. In his Modern translation, 1936.

— In his Intertraffic: studies in translation, 1943.

Hsieh Wen-tung. English translations of Chinese poetry. Criterion 18 1938.

Yashiro, Y. Arthur Waley. Bull of Eastern Art 9 1940.

— Arthur Waley. Japan Quart 14 1967.

Teele, R. E. In his Through a glass darkly: a study of English translations of Chinese poetry. Ann Arbor 1949.

Morris, I. Arthur Waley. Encounter 27 1966.

REX WARNER
b. 1905
See cols 761–2, below.

VERNON PHILLIPS WATKINS
1906–67
Most of Watkins' mss are in the BM.

Bibliographies
Two Swansea poets: Dylan Thomas and Watkins; exhibition 3rd–12th July 1969. Swansea [1969]; pbd Swansea Public Libraries.

§1
Poetry
Ballad of the Mari Lwyd and other poems. 1941.

The lamp and the veil. 1945.

The lady with the unicorn. 1948.

Selected poems. Norfolk Conn 1948. From first 2 works, above.

The death bell: poems and ballads. 1954, Norfok Conn 1954.

Heinrich Heine. The North Sea, translated by Watkins. 1955.

Cypress and acacia. 1959, Norfolk Conn [1959].

Affinities. 1962, Norfolk Conn 1963.

Selected poems, 1930–1960. 1967.

Fidelities. 1968.

Kathleen Raine and Vernon Watkins: selected by E. Owen. 1968 (Pergamon Poets).

Other Works

Dylan Thomas. Letters to Vernon Watkins. Ed with an introd by Watkins 1957, New York 1957.

Landmarks and voyages: poetry supplement [pbd Poetry Book Soc] Christmas 1957. Ed Watkins 1957.

Richard Hughes. A high wind in Jamaica, with a foreword by Watkins. New York 1961.

§2

Heath-Stubbs, J. Pity and the fixed stars: an approach to Watkins. Poetry Quart 12 1950.

Conran, A. The English poet in Wales: II, The boys of summer in their ruin. Anglo-Welsh Rev 10 1960.

Raine, K. Watkins: poet of tradition. Anglo-Welsh Rev 14 1964 and Texas Quart 7 1964.

—— Intuition's lightning: the poetry of Watkins. Poetry Rev 59 1968.

DOROTHY VIOLET WELLESLEY, née ASHTON

1889–1956

§1
Poetry

Early poems. By 'M.A.' [i.e. D. Wellesley]. 1913.

Poems. 1920.

Pride and other poems. 1923.

Lost lane. 1925.

Genesis: an impression. 1926.

Matrix. 1928.

Jupiter and the nun. 1932.

Poems of ten years 1924–1934. 1934. Selection with revisions. Includes previously unpbd poems.

Selections from the poems of Dorothy Wellesley. 1936, New York 1936. Introd by W. B. Yeats; includes a new poem, Fire.

Lost planet and other poems. 1942.

The poets and other poems. Tunbridge Wells 1943.

Desert wells. 1946.

Selected poems. 1949.

Rhymes for middle years. 1954.

Early light: the collected poems of Dorothy Wellesley. 1955. Includes previously unpbd poems.

Other Works

The annual: being a selection from the Forget-me-nots, Keepsakes and other annuals of the nineteenth century. Ed Dorothy Wellesley. [1930].

A broadcast anthology of modern poetry. Ed Dorothy Wellesley 1930.

Sir George Goldie, founder of Nigeria: a memoir. 1934.

Letters on poetry from W. B. Yeats to Dorothy Wellesley. 1940, 1964 (with introd by Kathleen Raine). Ed Dorothy Wellesley.

Far have I travelled. 1952. Reminiscences.

Dorothy Wellesley edited the first ser of the Hogarth Living Poets, *was on the editorial committee of the* Britain in Pictures *ser and herself edited the sub-series* The English Poets in Pictures *1941–2. With W. B. Yeats she edited the 1937 series of* Cuala Press broadsides

ALAN CHARLES LAURENCE WHISTLER
b. 1912

§1
Poetry

Children of Hertha & other poems. Oxford 1929.

Armed October and other poems. 1932.

Proletaria, en avant! A poem of socialism. Oxford 1932.

Four walls. 1934, New York 1935.

The emperor heart. 1936, New York 1937.

In time of suspense. 1940.

The burning-glass. 1941 (priv ptd, 50 copies). Rptd in next.

Ode to the sun and other poems. 1942.

Who live in unity. Ramby Camp, Retford 1944 (24 copies), London 1944 (unlimited).

The world's room: the collected poems of Laurence Whistler. 1949. Selection with revisions, and 5 uncollected poems.

The view from this window. 1956.

Audible silence. 1961.

Fingal's cave. [Birmingham] 1963 (180 copies). Single poem.

To celebrate her living. 1967.

For example: ten sonnets in sequence to a new pattern. Birmingham 1969 (160 copies). Rptd from previous.

Way: two affirmations in glass and verse. Cambridge 1969 (275 copies).

Other Works

Sir John Vanbrugh: architect and dramatist 1664–1726. 1938.

Jill Furse: her nature and her poems, 1915–1944. 1945 (150 copies). Memoir of his first wife.

¡Oho! the drawings by Rex Whistler, the words by Laurence Whistler. 1946. Humour.

The English festivals. 1947.

The masque of Christmas: dramatic joys of the festival old and new [with Christmas, his masque, by Ben Jonson]. 1947.

Rex Whistler: his life and his drawings. 1948.

Selected poems of John Keats; ed and introduced by Whistler. 1950.

The engraved glass of Laurence Whistler. Preston Hitchin 1952 (550 copies). Introd by Whistler and 82 plates.

Rex Whistler. The Königsmark drawings, reproduced in facsimile; introd and the story in brief by Whistler. 1952.

The kissing bough: a Christmas custom described by Laurence Whistler. 1953.

The imagination of Vanbrugh and his fellow artists. 1954.

Stowe: a guide to the gardens. 1956, 1968 (rev).

Engraved glass 1952–58. 1959.

The work of Rex Whistler. Ed Whistler and R. Fuller 1960.

The initials in the heart. 1964, Boston 1964. On his marriage to Jill Furse.

§2

Hadfield, J. Artist in glass: the engravings of Whistler. Saturday Book 10 1950.

Whistler glass. Saturday Book 16 1956.

'ANNA WICKHAM',
EDITH ALICE MARY HEPBURN,
née HARPER
1884–1947

§1

Songs of John Oland. 1912 (priv ptd). Anon.
The contemplative quarry. 1915.
The man with a hammer: verses. 1916.
The contemplative quarry and The man with a hammer. Introd by L. Untermeyer, New York 1921.
The little old house. 1921.
[Thirty-six poems.] 1936 (Richards' Shilling selections from Edwardian poets). Includes 30 previously uncollected poems.
A piece by Anna Wickham entitled The spirit of the [D.H.] Lawrence women: a posthumous memoir, *with a biographical introd by D. Garnett, was pbd in Texas Quart 9 1966.*

§2

Grant, J. In her Harold Monro and the Poetry Bookshop, 1967.

CHARLES WALTER STANSBY WILLIAMS
1886–1945

See cols 772–4, below.

SHEILA CLAUDE WINGFIELD
b. 1906

Poems. [1938].
Beat drum, beat heart. 1946.
A cloud across the sun. 1949.
Real people. 1952. Reminiscences.
A kite's dinner: poems 1938–54. 1954. Selection, with some revision.
The leaves darken. [1964].

HUMBERT WOLFE
1885–1940

§1

Poetry, Verse Plays and Verse Translations

London sonnets. Oxford 1920.
Shylock reasons with Mr Chesterton, and other poems. Oxford 1920.
Kensington Gardens. 1924, New York [1927].
Lampoons. 1925.
The unknown goddess. 1925, New York [1925] (with 2 new poems), London 1927.
Humoresque. 1926.
News of the devil. 1926, New York 1926.
[Thirty-four poems.] [1926] (Augustan Books of Modern Poetry). Selection.
Cursory rhymes. 1927, Garden City NY 1928.
Others abide. 1927. Verse trns from the Greek Anthology.
Requiem. 1927, New York [1927].
Veni Creator! 1927 (priv ptd). Rptd in The uncelestial city, 1930, below.
The blind rose. 1928, Garden City NY 1929.
The moon and Mrs Smith. 1928. Christmas card, containing a poem rptd in The uncelestial city, 1930 below.
The silver cat and other poems. New York, London 1928.

Troy. [1928] (Ariel Poem).
Early poems. Oxford 1930, New York 1931. Contains London sonnets and Shylock reasons with Mr Chesterton. With a preface by Wolfe.
Homage to Meleager. New York 1930 (464 signed copies). Verse trns from Greek.
Portrait of Heine. 1930, 1935 (as Selected lyrics of Heine). Trns by Wolfe.
The uncelestial city. 1930, New York 1930.
Snow. 1931.
ABC of the theatre. [1932].
Reverie of policeman: a ballet in three acts. 1933.
Sonnets pour Hélène, by Pierre de Ronsard, with English renderings by Wolfe. 1934, New York 1934.
The fourth of August: a sonnet sequence. 1935.
Stings and wings. 1935.
X at Oberammergau: a poem. 1935.
Cyrano de Bergerac: a translation of Rostand's play. [1937].
Don J. Ewan. 1937.
The silent knight: a romantic comedy in three acts from the Hungarian of Eugene Heltai. 1937.
Out of great tribulation. 1939.
Kensington Gardens in war-time. 1940.
See also A winter miscellany, 1930, *below.*

Other Works

Circular saws. 1923. Short stories.
Labour supply and regulation. Oxford 1923 (Economic and social history of the World War: British ser).
Edward Lear. Ed with introd by Wolfe [1927] (Augustan Books of English Poetry).
The craft of verse: Oxford poetry essay. New York 1928.
Dialogues and monologues. 1928, New York 1929. On literary topics.
The poetical works of Robert Herrick. 4 vols 1928. With a preface by Wolfe.
Selected poems by Swinburne. Introd by Wolfe 1928.
Notes on English verse satire. 1929, New York [1929].
The wall of weeping, by Edmond Fleg. Tr by Wolfe 1929.
Tennyson. 1930.
A winter miscellany [in prose and verse], ed and compiled by Wolfe, to which are added original poems by the editor. 1930, New York 1930.
George Moore. 1931, New York 1932, London 1933 (rev).
Signpost to poetry: an introduction to the study of verse. 1931.
The life of Percy Bysshe Shelley as comprised in The life of Shelley by Thomas Jefferson Hogg, The recollections of Shelley and Byron by Edward John Trelawny, Memoirs of Shelley by Thomas Love Peacock. Introd by Wolfe 2 vols 1933.
Now a stranger. 1933. Autobiography.
Romantic and unromantic poetry. Bristol [1933] (Arthur Skemp memorial lecture).
Portraits by inference. 1934. Reminiscences and sketches of contemporaries.
Ronsard and French romantic poetry: the Zaharoff lecture for 1934. Oxford 1935.
P.L.M.: peoples, landfalls, mountains. 1936. Travel in France.
Personalities: a selection from the writings of A. A. Baumann. Ed Wolfe 1936, New York 1936.
The pilgrim's way. 1936. Anthology, chiefly of poetry, selected by Wolfe.
The upward anguish. 1938. Autobiography. Contains The old man of Königsberg, or, Kant and re-Kant: a Greats Week pantomime, in verse written in part by Wolfe and pbd separately.
Wolfe edited the second ser of Augustan Books of English Poetry.

§2

Gorman, H. Humbert Wolfe. Bookman (New York) 65 1927.
Garrod, H. W. Mr Humbert Wolfe. In his The profession of poetry, 1929.
Arns, K. Humbert Wolfe. Zeitschrift für Französischen und Englischen Unterricht 30 1931.
Gilbert, T. R. Humbert Wolfe. London Quart & Holborn Rev 165 1940.
Shillito, E. A satirist of these days. Christian Century 7 Feb 1940.
Wells, H. W. Humbert Wolfe: a modern English Heine. Sewanee Rev 49 1941.
Bentwich, N. Humbert Wolfe, poet and civil servant. Menorah Jnl 31 1943. Includes 3 poems.
Bushnell, A. Humbert Wolfe. Poetry Rev 34 1943.
Garvin, V. G. Two Observer reviewers: Gerald Gould and Wolfe. English 5 1944.

ANDREW JOHN YOUNG
1885–1971
Bibliographies

Checklist of the writings of Young. In Andrew Young: prospect of a poet, ed L. Clark, 1957, §2 below.
Collected poems, *1960, contains a bibliographical note by L. Clark describing the composition of Young's successive collections of poems.*

§1
Poetry and Verse Plays

Young's first 8 books are described on the title-pages as being 'by A. J. Young'.

Songs of night. [1910].
Cecil Barclay Simpson: a memorial by two friends. Edinburgh 1918. With D. Baillie. Memorial verses by Young.
Boaz and Ruth and other poems. 1920.
The death of Eli and other poems. 1921.
Thirty-one poems. 1922.
The adversary [and Rizpah]. 1923. 2 short verse plays.
The bird-cage. 1926.

The cuckoo clock. [1928].
The new shepherd. 1931.
Winter harvest. 1933.
The white blackbird. 1935.
Collected poems. 1936. Contains Winter harvest and The white blackbird and 17 new poems.
Nicodemus: a mystery, with incidental music by Imogen Holst. 1937. Rptd in Collected poems, 1950, below.
Speak to the earth. 1939.
The green man. 1947.
Collected poems. 1950. Selection, with revisions.
Into Hades. 1952. Rev and rptd in Out of the world and back.
Out of the world and back: Into Hades and A traveller in time. 1958. Two poems.
Quiet as moss: thirty-six poems chosen by L. Clark. 1959, Philadelphia 1963. Selection.
Collected poems, arranged with a bibliographical note by L. Clark. 1960. Collected poems 1950, with 22 addns all previously pbd.
Burning as light: thirty-seven poems chosen by L. Clark. 1967.

Other Works

Sermon by the minister, Rev Andrew J. Young, preached 7th December 1930, the anniversary of The Women's Missionary Association, Hove. Hove 1930.
A prospect of flowers: a book about wild flowers. 1945.
A retrospect of flowers. 1950.
A prospect of Britain, with 20 photographs by J. A. Cash. 1956, New York [1956].
The poet and the landscape. 1962, Philadelphia 1963.
The new Poly-Olbion: topographical excursions with an introductory account of the poet's early days. 1967.

§2

Clark, L. (ed). Andrew Young, prospect of a poet: essays and tributes by fourteen writers. 1957. Essays by J. Arlott, J. Baillie, J. Betjeman, R. Church, C. Hassall, N. Nicholson, V. Meynell, L. Bonnerot, R. Tanner, L. A. G. Strong, the Bishop of Chichester, G. Rostrevor Hamilton, poem by E. Blunden.
Clark, L. Andrew Young. 1964 (Br Council pamphlet). With R. G. Thomas on R. S. Thomas.

R. J. R

3. THE NOVEL

I. GENERAL WORKS

(1) BIBLIOGRAPHIES

Nield, J. A guide to the best historical novels and tales. 1902, 1904 (rev), 1911 (rev), 1929 (rev).

Baker, E. A. A descriptive guide to the best fiction British and American. 1903, 1913 (rev, as A guide to the best fiction in English), 1932 (rev, as A guide to the best fiction English and American; with J. Packman).

Adler, F. H. H. American and British novels of today 1890–1924. Cleveland 1925, 1929 (rev, as American and British novels of our day 1890–1929; with I. Talmage).

Hill, W. C. The overseas empire in fiction: an annotated bibliography. 1930.

Lenrow, E. Reader's guide to prose fiction. New York 1940.

'Queen, Ellery' (F. Dannay and M. B. Lee). The detective short story: a bibliography. Boston 1942.

Gardner, F. M. Sequels. 1947, 1955 (rev), 1967 (rev).

Bleiler, E. F. (ed). The checklist of fantastic literature: a bibliography of fantasy, weird and science fiction books published in the English language. Chicago 1948.

Rouse, H. B. A selective and critical bibliography of studies in prose fiction. JEGP 48–51 1949–52. Covers years 1948–51.

Kerr, E. M. Bibliography of the sequence novel. Minneapolis 1950.

Stallman, R. W. Selected bibliography of criticism of modern fiction. In Critiques and essays on modern fiction 1920–51, ed J. W. Aldridge 1952. See §2, below.

Crawford, J. H. et al. 333: a bibliography of the science-fantasy novel. Providence 1953.

Leclaire, L. A general analytical bibliography of the regional novelists of the British isles 1800–1950. Paris 1954.

Friedman, N. In his Point of view in fiction: the development of a critical concept, PMLA 70 1955. See §2, below.

Gerber, R. An annotated list of English utopian fantasies 1901–51. In his Utopian fantasy, 1955. See §2, below.

Dard, R. Fantastic novels: a check list. Perth W. Australia 1957.

Taylor, W. A. and A. Duggan. Historical fiction. Cambridge 1957 (NBL Reader's Guide).

Bell, I. F. and D. Baird. The English novel 1578–1956: a checklist of twentieth-century criticisms. Denver 1958.

Scholl, R. Science fiction: a selected check-list. Bull of Bibliography 22 1958.

Beer, J. (ed). Der Romanführer: vol 10. Der Inhalt der englischen [etc] Romane und Novellen der Gegenwart. Stuttgart 1959. Contains plot summaries.

Stevenson, L. In his English novel: a panorama, 1960. See §2, below.

Thurston, J. et al. Short fiction criticism: a checklist of interpretation since 1925 of stories and novelettes—American, British, Continental—1800–1958. Denver 1960.

Booth, W. C. In his Rhetoric of fiction, 1961. See §2, below.

Clarke, I. F. The tale of the future: from the beginning to the present day: a check-list. 1961. Futurist literature in England 1644–1960.

Walker, W. S. Twentieth-century short story explication: interpretations, 1900–1960 inclusive, of short fiction since 1800. Hamden Conn 1961, 1967 (rev: brought up to 1966).

Freeman, W. Dictionary of fictional characters. 1963.

McGarry, D. D. and S. H. White. Historical fiction guide: annotated chronological, geographical and topical list of five thousand selected historical novels. New York 1963.

Goetsch, P. and H. Kosok. Literatur zum modernen englischen Roman: eine ausgewählte Bibliographie. In Der moderne englische Roman: Interpretationen, ed H. Oppel 1965. See §2, below.

Souvage, J. A systematic bibliography for the study of the novel. In his Introduction to the study of the novel with special reference to the English novel, 1965. See §2, below.

Bufkin, E. C. The twentieth-century novel in English: a checklist. Athens Georgia 1967.

Cotton, G. B. and H. M. McGill. Fiction guides—general: British and American. 1967.

Bailey, R. W. and D. M. Burton. English stylistics in the twentieth century: prose stylistics. In their English stylistics: a bibliography. Cambridge Mass 1968.

Bennett, J. R. Style in twentieth century British and American fiction: a bibliography. West Coast Rev 2 1968.

Killam, G. D. In his Africa in English fiction 1874–1939, 1968. See §2, below.

(2) HISTORIES AND STUDIES

See also General histories and studies of the literature of the period, cols 3–14, above; and Modern Fiction Studies, *1955 onwards;* Critique: Studies in Modern Fiction, *1956 onwards;* English Fiction in Transition (*later* English Literature in Transition), *1957 onwards; and* Novel: a Forum on Fiction, *1967 onwards. For studies of the best-seller and the popular genres of detective fiction, science fiction, the romantic novel, etc, see Reading, cols 123–30, above. For manuals and guides for the writing of fiction, see Authorship, cols 63–8, above.*

Vowinckel, E. Der englische Roman der Gegenwart. Leipzig 1904, Berlin 1926 (enlarged as Der englische Roman der neuesten Zeit und Gegenwart).

—— Der englische Roman zwischen den Jahrzehnten 1927–35. Berlin 1936.

Horne, C. F. The technique of the novel: the elements of the art, their evolution and present use. New York 1908.

Canby, H. S. The short story in English. New York 1909.

—— A study of the short story. New York 1913, 1935 (rev).

—— Definitions: essays in contemporary criticism. New York 1922.

Cooper, F. T. Some English story tellers: a book of the younger novelists. New York 1912.

Roz, F. Le roman anglais contemporain. Paris 1912.

Grabo, C. H. The art of the short story. New York 1913.

—— The technique of the novel. New York 1928.

Cross, E. A. The short story: a technical and literary study. Chicago 1914.

—— A book of the short story. New York 1934.

James, H. The younger generation. TLS 19 March, 2 April 1914. Rptd, extended and rev, as The new novel, in his Notes on novelists, 1914.
— James and H. G. Wells: a record of their friendship, their debate on the art of fiction, and their quarrel. Ed L. Edel and G. N. Ray 1958.
Pain, B. The short story. [1916].
Phelps, W. L. The advance of the English novel. New York 1916.
Scarborough, D. The supernatural in modern English fiction. New York 1917.
Follett, H. T. and W. Follett. Some modern novelists: appreciations and estimates. New York 1918.
Follett, W. The modern novel: a study of the purpose and the meaning of fiction. New York 1918, 1923 (rev).
George, W. L. A novelist on novels. 1918.
Williams, H. H. Modern English writers: being a study of imaginative literature 1890–1914. 1918, 1925 (rev).
Woolf, V. Modern novels. TLS 10 April 1919; rptd as Modern fiction, in her Common reader, 1925, and in Modern British fiction, ed M. Schorer 1961, below.
— Character in fiction. Criterion 2 1924; rptd as Mr Bennett and Mrs Brown, 1924 (as pamphlet), and in her Captain's death bed, 1950.
— Is fiction an art? New York Herald Tribune 16 Oct 1927. Rptd, rev, as The art of fiction, in her The moment and other essays, 1947.
— Contemporary writers. Ed J. Guiget 1965. Uncollected essays from TLS.
— Collected essays. Ed L. Woolf 4 vols 1966–7. Includes the 3 essays above, also essays on Conrad, Forster, Lawrence, K. Mansfield et al.
Goldring, D. Reputations: essays in criticism. 1920. On Lawrence, Wells, W. Lewis et al.
Johnson, R. B. Some contemporary novelists: women. 1920.
— Some contemporary novelists: men. 1922.
Chevalley, A. D. Le roman anglais de notre temps. 1921. Tr New York 1925.
Lubbock, P. The craft of fiction. 1921.
Starr, M. The future of the novel: famous authors on their methods—a series of interviews with renowned authors. 1921.
Lawrence, D. H. Surgery for the novel, or a bomb. Literary Digest International Book Rev April 1923; rptd in his Phoenix, below.
— Morality and the novel. Calendar of Modern Letters 2 1925; rptd in his Phoenix, below, and in Modern British fiction, ed M. Schorer 1961, below.
— The novel. In his Reflections on the death of a porcupine, Philadelphia 1925; rptd in his Phoenix II: uncollected, unpublished and other prose works, ed W. Roberts and H. T. Moore 1968.
— Why the novel matters. In Phoenix: the posthumous papers of D. H. Lawrence, ed E. D. McDonald 1936.
'Lee, Vernon' (V. Paget). The handling of words and other studies in literary psychology. 1923, Lincoln Nebraska [1968] (with introd by R. A. Gettmann).
Schirmer, W. F. Der englische Roman der neuesten Zeit. Heidelberg 1923.
Brewster, D. and A. Burrell. Dead reckonings in fiction. New York 1924. On Conrad, K. Mansfield, Lawrence et al.
— Adventure or experience: four essays on certain writers and readers of novels. New York 1930. On Maugham, Bennett, V. Woolf et al.
— Modern fiction. New York 1934. A combination and revision of the two earlier books.
Brewster, D. East-west passage: a study in literary relationships. 1954. Russian influence on Forster, V. Woolf, Lawrence, Pritchett et al.
Gould, G. The English novel of to-day. 1924.
Murry, J. M. The break-up of the novel. In his Discoveries, 1924.

— Katherine Mansfield and other literary studies. 1959. Also on H. Williamson.
Speare, M. E. The political novel: its development in England and America. New York 1924.
Ward, A. C. Aspects of the modern short story, English and American. 1924.
Walpole, H. The English novel: some notes on its evolution. Cambridge 1925.
— et al. Tendencies of the modern novel. 1934.
Weygandt, C. A century of the English novel. New York 1925. Scott to Conrad.
Bullett, G. W. Modern English fiction: a personal view. 1926.
Drew, E. A. The modern novel: some aspects of contemporary fiction. New York 1926.
— The novel: a modern guide to fifteen English masterpieces. New York 1963. On Joyce, Lawrence, V. Woolf.
Muir, E. Transition: essays on contemporary literature. 1926. On Joyce, Lawrence, V. Woolf, S. Hudson, Huxley, Contemporary fiction etc.
— The structure of the novel. 1928.
— The decline of the novel. In his Essays on literature and society, 1949, 1965 (rev).
Read, H. The modern novel. In his Reason and romanticism, 1926.
Rickword, C. H. A note on fiction. Calendar of Modern Letters 3 1926; rptd in Towards standards of criticism, ed F. R. Leavis 1933, and in Forms of modern fiction, ed W. V. O'Connor 1948, below.
Williams, O. Some great English novels: studies in the art of fiction. 1926. On W. de Morgan, Somerville and Ross et al.
'Carruthers, John' (J. Y. T. Greig). Scheherazade: or the future of the English novel. 1927.
Eliot, T. S. Le roman anglais contemporain. Nouvelle Revue Française 28 1927.
Forster, E. M. Aspects of the novel. 1927.
— Abinger harvest. 1936. On Conrad, Firbank, V. Woolf et al.
— The development of English prose between 1918 and 1939. Glasgow 1945.
Myers, W. L. The later realism: a study of characterization in the British novel. Chicago 1927.
Priestley, J. B. The English novel. 1927, 1935 (rev).
— Some reflections of a popular novelist. E & S 18 1932.
Ames, V. M. Aesthetics of the novel. Chicago 1928.
— The novel: between art and science. Kenyon Rev 5 1943.
Cross, W. L. The modern English novel. New Haven 1928.
— Four contemporary novelists. New York 1930. On Bennett, Conrad, Galsworthy, Wells.
Marble, A. R. A study of the modern novel, British and American, since 1900. New York 1928.
Overton, G. The philosophy of fiction. New York 1928.
Rickword, E. (ed). Scrutinies. 2 vols 1928–31. Vol 1 on Bennett, Galsworthy, Wells et al; vol 2 on Huxley, Joyce, Lawrence, W. Lewis, V. Woolf et al.
'West, Rebecca' (C. I. Andrews). The strange necessity: essays and reviews. 1928. On Joyce, Bennett et al.
— Ending in earnest: a literary log. New York 1931. Essays from the Bookman (NY). On V. Woolf, Waugh et al.
Zucker, A. E. The genealogical novel: a new genre. PMLA 43 1928.
Braybrooke, P. Philosophies in modern fiction. 1929.
— Some Catholic novelists: their art and outlook. 1931.
Dobrée, B. The lamp and the lute: studies in six modern authors. Oxford 1929, London 1964 (rev, with subtitle Studies in seven authors). On Forster, Lawrence.
Ford, F. M. The English novel from the earliest days to the death of Joseph Conrad. Philadelphia 1929.
— Techniques. Southern Rev 1 1935.
— Portraits from life: memories and criticisms. Boston 1937, London 1938 (as Mightier than the sword).
Jameson, S. The Georgian novel and Mr Robinson. 1929.

—— The novel in contemporary life. Boston 1938.
—— The writer's situation. 1950. The form of the novel, the novelist today, etc.
Messac, R. Le 'détective novel' et l'influence de la pensée scientifique. Paris 1929.
Rotter, A. Der Arbeiterroman in England seit 1880: ein Beitrag zur Geschichte des sozialen Romans in England. Reichenberg 1929.
Garnett, D. Some tendencies of the novel. Symposium 1 1930.
'Mansfield, Katherine' (K. M. Beauchamp). Novels and novelists. Ed J. M. Murry 1930.
Knight, G. C. The novel in English. New York 1931.
Penton, B. Note on form in the novel. In Scrutinies, ed E. Rickword vol 2, 1931.
Beach, J. W. The twentieth-century novel: studies in technique. New York 1932.
Collins, N. The facts of fiction. 1932.
Leavis, Q. D. Fiction and the reading public. 1932.
Lovett, R. M. and H. S. Hughes. The history of the novel in England. Boston 1932.
Marinoff, I. Imagination und Reality: ein Beitrag zur Welt- und Lebensanschauung des englischen Nachkriegsromans. Die Neueren Sprachen 40 1932.
—— Das Lebensgefühl im modernen englischen Roman. Anglia 56 1932.
—— Neue Wertungen im englischen Roman. Leipzig 1932.
Cook, E. C. Reading the novel. Boston 1933.
Edgar, P. The art of the novel from 1700 to the present time. New York 1933.
Mégroz, R. L. Five novelist poets of today. 1933. On de la Mare, L. A. G. Strong, M. Armstrong, O. Sitwell, Lawrence.
Stonier, G. W. Gog Magog and other critical essays. 1933. On Joyce, Lawrence, W. Lewis et al.
Hoops, R. Der Einfluss der Psychoanalyse auf die englische Literatur. Heidelberg 1934.
Leggett, H. W. The idea in fiction. 1934.
Smith, W. H. Architecture in English fiction. New Haven 1934.
Bohlen, A. Lehrer und Schüler im neueren französischen und englischen Schulroman. Die Neueren Sprachen 43 1935.
'Maurois, André' (E. S. W. Herzog). Magiciens et logiciens: essais sur quelques écrivains anglais de notre temps. Paris 1935. Tr H. Miles, New York 1935 (as Prophets and poets). On Conrad, Wells, Lawrence, Huxley et al. 1968 edn, Points of view, adds V. Woolf, Greene.
O'Faolain, S. It no longer matters: or, the death of the English novel. Criterion 15 1935.
—— The modern novel: a catholic point of view. Virginia Quart Rev 11 1935.
—— The short story. 1948.
—— The vanishing hero: studies in novelists of the twenties. 1956. On Huxley, Waugh, Greene, E. Bowen, V. Woolf, Joyce et al.
Uzzell, T. H. New techniques in the novel. English Jnl 24 1935.
—— The technique of the novel. Chicago 1947, New York 1959 (rev).
Daiches, D. New literary values: studies in modern literature. Edinburgh 1936. On Joyce, K. Mansfield.
—— The novel and the modern world. Chicago 1939, 1960 (rev), 1965 (rev).
Henderson, P. The novel today: studies in contemporary attitudes. 1936.
Lawrence, M. The school of femininity. New York 1936, London 1937 (as We write as women). On women novelists.
Ransom, J. C. Characters and character. Amer Rev 6 1936.
—— The content of the novel Amer Rev 7 1936.
—— The understanding of fiction. Kenyon Rev 12 1950.
Stern, M. B. Counterclockwise: flux of time in literature. Sewanee Rev 44 1936.

Verschoyle, D. (ed). The English novelists: a survey of the novel by twenty contemporary novelists. 1936.
Bowen, E. Introduction [to The Faber book of modern stories]. 1937.
—— Collected impressions. 1950. Notes on writing a novel; Women novelists; Forster; Conrad; Lawrence etc.
—— Afterthought: pieces about writing. 1962. Truth and fiction; K. Mansfield; V. Woolf; Forster etc.
Fox, R. W. The novel and the people. 1937.
Gerould, G. H. How to read fiction. Princeton 1937.
—— The patterns of English and American fiction. Boston 1942.
Muller, H. J. Modern fiction: a study of values. New York 1937.
—— Impressionism in fiction: prism vs mirror. Amer Scholar 7 1938.
Belgion, M. The testimony of fiction. Southern Rev 4 1938.
Cruse, A. After the Victorians. 1938. On English readers and popular fiction.
Glicksberg, C. I. Proletarian fiction in England. UTQ 8 1938.
—— Fiction and philosophy. Arizona Quart 13 1957.
—— The numinous in fiction. Arizona Quart 15 1959.
—— The self in modern literature. University Park Pa 1963.
Hoare, D. M. Some studies in the modern novel. 1938.
Swinnerton, F. Variations of form in the novel. E & S 23 1938.
Baker, E. A. The history of the English novel. Vol 10, Yesterday, 1939; for vol 11, see L. Stevenson, Yesterday and after, 1967, below.
Ellis, G. U. Twilight on Parnassus: a survey of post-war fiction and pre-war criticism. 1939.
Elwin, M. Old gods falling. 1939. On best sellers, Bennett, Galsworthy.
Gillam, D. J. Le moi et l'univers: quelques aspects du roman psychologique contemporain en Angleterre. Neuchâtel 1939.
Baker, H. In praise of the novel: the fiction of Huxley, Steinbeck and others. Southern Rev 5 1940.
Blackmur, R. P. Notes on the novel. In his The expense of greatness, New York 1940.
Dataller, R. The plain man and the novel. 1940.
Henkin, L. J. Darwinism in the English novel 1860-1910. New York 1940.
Marriott, J. A. R. English history in English fiction. 1940.
Bates, H. E. The modern short story: a critical survey. 1941.
Bentley, P. E. The English regional novel. 1941.
—— Some observations on the art of narrative. 1946.
Dubois, A. E. The art of fiction. South Atlantic Quart 40 1941.
Dupont, V. L'utopie et le roman utopique dans la littérature anglaise. Paris 1941.
Haycraft, H. Murder for pleasure: the life and times of the detective story. New York 1941.
Monroe, N. E. The novel and society: a critical study of the modern novel. Chapel Hill 1941.
Morrow, C. Le roman irréaliste dans les littératures contemporaines de langues française et anglaise. Toulouse 1941.
Endicott, N. J. The novel in England between the wars. UTQ 12 1942.
Frierson, W. C. The English novel in transition 1885-1940. Norman Okla 1942.
Brooks, C. and R. P. Warren. Understanding fiction. New York 1943, 1959 (rev).
Nicholson, N. Man and literature. 1943. On Bennett, Wells, Lawrence, Huxley, Joyce et al.
Wagenknecht, E. C. Cavalcade of the English novel: from Elizabeth to George VI. New York 1943, 1954 (rev).
Wells, J. M. The artist in the English novel 1850-1919. West Virginia Univ Bull: Philological Stud 4 1943.

Coates, J. B. Ten modern prophets. 1944. On Huxley, Lawrence, Wells.

Fehr, B. Der moderne englische Roman. In his Von Englands geistigen Beständen, Frauenfeld 1944.

Foster-Harris, W. The basic formulas of fiction. Norman Okla 1944.

Tate, A. The post of observation in fiction. Maryland Quart 2 1944.

— Techniques of fiction. Sewanee Rev 52 1944; rptd in his On the limits of poetry, New York 1948; in Forms of modern fiction, ed W. V. O'Connor 1948, below; and in Critiques and essays on modern fiction, ed J. W. Aldridge 1952, below.

Connolly, C. The condemned playground: essays 1927–44. 1945.

— Previous convictions: selected writings of a decade. 1963. On Lawrence, Joyce, Orwell et al.

Frank, J. Spatial form in modern literature. Sewanee Rev 53 1945; rptd in part in Critiques and essays on modern fiction, ed J. W. Aldridge 1952, below.

— The widening gyre. New Brunswick 1963.

Hoffman, F. J. Freudianism and the literary mind. Baton Rouge 1945, 1957 (rev). On Joyce, Lawrence et al.

— The mortal no: death and the modern imagination. Princeton 1964. On Joyce, Lawrence, Conrad, V. Woolf, Forster et al.

Lovecraft, H. P. Supernatural horror in literature. New York 1945.

Auerbach, E. Mimesis: dargestellte Wirklichkeit in der abendländischen Literatur. Berne 1946. Tr W. Trask Princeton 1953 as Mimesis: the representation of reality in Western literature. On V. Woolf, Joyce.

Baker, D. V. (ed). Writers of to-day. Vol 1, 1946. On Huxley, Greene, Joyce, Priestley, Forster et al. Vol 2, 1948. On Maugham, V. Woolf, J. C. Powys, Waugh et al.

Gray, J. On second thought. Minneapolis 1946. On Bennett, Galsworthy, Wells, Huxley, Maugham et al.

Krey, L. Time and the English novel. In Twentieth-century English, ed W. S. Knickerbocker, New York 1946.

McCullough, B. W. Representative English novelists: Defoe to Conrad. New York 1946.

'Orwell, George' (E. A. Blair). Critical essays. 1946, New York (as Dickens, Dali and others). On Wells, Koestler, Wodehouse etc.

Pritchett, V. S. The living novel. 1946, New York 1947, 1964 (rev, with contents of The working novelist below.

— The future of English fiction. Partisan Rev 15 1948.

— Books in general. 1953. On Conrad, Firbank, W. Lewis.

— The working novelist. 1965. On Ford, Galsworthy, Forster, Conrad et al.

Reed, H. The novel since 1939. 1946 (Br Council pamphlet).

Bailey, J. O. Pilgrims through space and time. New York 1947. On scientific and utopian fiction.

Burgum, E. B. The novel and the world's dilemma. New York 1947. On Joyce, V. Woolf, Huxley.

Kempton, K. P. The short story. Cambridge Mass 1947.

Liddell, R. A treatise on the novel. 1947.

— Some principles of fiction. 1953.

Rajan, B. (ed). The novelist as thinker. 1947. On Huxley, Waugh, Isherwood, L. H. Myers et al.

Comfort, A. The novel and our time. 1948.

Leavis, F. R. The great tradition: George Eliot, Henry James, Joseph Conrad. 1948.

— The common pursuit. 1952. On Lawrence, Forster.

— Anna Karenina and other essays. 1967. On Conrad, Lawrence.

Nicolson, M. H. Voyages to the moon. New York 1948.

O'Connor, W. V. (ed). Forms of modern fiction: essays collected in honor of J. W. Beach. Minneapolis 1948. On Joyce, Lawrence, Forster, Huxley, Conrad, V. Woolf, Greene et al.

Schorer, M. Technique as discovery. Hudson Rev 1 1948; rptd in his World we imagine, below; in Forms of modern fiction, ed W. V. O'Connor 1948, above; in Critiques and essays on modern fiction, ed J. W. Aldridge 1952, below; and in Perspectives on fiction, ed J. L. Calderwood and H. E. Toliver 1968, below.

— (ed). Society and self in the novel. New York 1956.

— The novelist in the modern world. Tucson 1957.

— (ed). Modern British fiction. New York 1961. Reprints essays on Conrad, Ford, Forster, Lawrence, Joyce, V. Woolf.

— The world we imagine: selected essays. New York 1968. On Ford, Lawrence et al.

Stafford, J. The psychological novel. Kenyon Rev 10 1948.

Trilling, L. Art and fortune. Partisan Rev 15 1948; rptd in his Liberal imagination, 1950.

— Manners, morals and the novel. Kenyon Rev 10 1948; rptd in his Liberal imagination, 1950, and in Forms of modern fiction, ed W. V. O'Connor 1948, above.

Turner, E. S. Boys will be boys: the story of Sweeney Todd, Deadwood Dick, Sexton Blake, Billy Bunter, Dick Barton et al. 1948, 1957 (rev).

Woodcock, G. The writer and politics. 1948. On Orwell, Greene et al.

Adam, G. F. Three contemporary Anglo-Welsh regional novelists: Jack Jones, Rhys Davies and Hilda Vaughan. Berne 1949.

Allen, W. Reading a novel. 1949, 1956 (rev), 1963 (rev).

— The English novel: a short critical history. 1954.

— The novel today. 1955 (Br Council pamphlet).

— Tradition and dream: the English and American novel from the twenties to our time. 1964, New York 1964 (as The modern novel in Britain and the United States).

Cather, W. On writing: critical studies on writing as an art. New York 1949. On the art of fiction, K. Mansfield etc.

Howe, S. Novels of empire. New York 1949.

Musgrove, S. Anthropological themes in the modern novel. Auckland 1949.

Rahv, P. Image and idea. New York 1949, Norfolk Conn 1957 (rev and enlarged).

— Fiction and the criticism of fiction. Kenyon Rev 18 1956.

Sackville-West, E. Inclinations. 1949. On Conrad, E. Bowen, I. Compton-Burnett.

Simon, I. Formes du roman anglais de Dickens à Joyce. Liège 1949.

West, K. Chapter of governesses: a study of the governess in English fiction 1800–1949. 1949.

West, R. B. and R. W. Stallman (ed). The art of modern fiction. New York 1949. Critical anthology.

Bowling, L. E. What is the stream of consciousness technique? PMLA 65 1950.

Brown, E. K. Rhythm in the novel. Toronto 1950.

De Voto, B. The world of fiction. Boston 1950.

Drummond, A. L. The churches in English fiction. Leicester 1950.

Frye, N. The four forms of prose fiction. Hudson Rev 2 1950; rptd in his Anatomy of criticism, Princeton 1957.

Johnson, P. H. Three novelists and the drawing of character: Snow, Cary and I. Compton-Burnett. E & S new ser 3 1950.

Kiely, B. Modern Irish fiction: a critique. Dublin 1950.

Millett, F. B. Reading fiction. New York 1950.

Phelps, G. Russian realism and English fiction. Cambridge Jnl 3 1950.

— The Russian novel in English fiction. 1956.

Savage, D. S. The withered branch: six studies in the modern novel. 1950.

Wilson, E. Classics and commercials. New York 1950. On Waugh, Joyce, Huxley, Maugham et al.

— The shores of light. New York 1952. On Lawrence, V. Woolf et al.

Brower, R. A. The fields of light: an experiment in critical reading. New York 1951. On V. Woolf, Forster.

Burns, W. The novelist as revolutionary. Arizona Quart 7 1951.

Church, R. The growth of the English novel. 1951.

Davis, R. G. The sense of the real in English fiction. Comparative Lit 3 1951.

Grant, D. The novel and its critical terms. EC 1 1951.

Greene, G. The lost childhood and other essays. 1951. Pt 2: Novels and novelists.

Humphrey, R. Stream of consciousness: technique or genre? PQ 30 1951.

— Stream of consciousness in the modern novel. Berkeley 1954.

Michener, J. A. The conscience of the contemporary novel. In The arts in renewal, ed S. Bradley, Philadelphia 1951.

Neill, S. D. A short history of the English novel. 1951, New York 1964 (rev).

Newby, P. H. The novel 1945–50. 1951 (Br Council pamphlet).

Wagner, H. Der englische Bildungsroman bis in die Zeit des ersten Weltkrieges. Berne 1951.

Aldridge, J. W. (ed). Critiques and essays on modern fiction 1920–51. New York 1952.

— Time to murder and create: the contemporary novel in crisis. New York 1966.

Mayoux, J.-J. L'inconscient et la vie intérieure dans le roman anglais 1905–40. Nancy 1952.

— Vivants piliers: le roman anglo-saxon et les symboles. Paris 1960.

Mendilow, A. A. Time and the novel. 1952.

Morton, A. L. The English utopia. 1952. On Wells, Huxley et al.

'O'Donnell, Donat' (C. C. O'Brien). Maria Cross: imaginative patterns in a group of modern catholic writers. New York 1952. On Greene, O'Faolain, Waugh.

Penzoldt, P. The supernatural in fiction. 1952.

Pongs, H. Im Umbruch der Zeit: das Romanschaffen der Gegenwart. Göttingen 1952, 1956 (rev).

Prescott, O. In my opinion: an inquiry into the contemporary novel. Indianapolis 1952.

Roland, A. A rebirth of values in contemporary fiction. Western Humanities Rev 6 1952.

Gardiner, H. C. Norms for the novel. New York 1953, 1960 (rev).

Gordon, C. Some readings and misreadings. Sewanee Rev 61 1953.

— How to read a novel. New York 1957.

Kettle, A. An introduction to the English novel vol 2: Henry James to the present day. 1953.

Melchiori, G. The moment as a time-unit in fiction. EC 3 1953; rptd in his Tightrope walkers, below.

— The tightrope walkers: studies of mannerism in modern English literature. 1956. On Joyce, H. Green.

Spiel, H. Der Park und die Wildnis: zur Situation der neueren englischen Literatur. Munich 1953.

Strong, L. A. G. Personal remarks. 1953. On Joyce, Forster, E. Bowen et al.

Usborne, R. Clubland heroes: a nostalgic study of some recurrent characters in the romantic fiction of Dornford Yates, John Buchan and Sapper. 1953.

Van Ghent, D. The English novel: form and function. New York 1953. On Conrad, Lawrence, Joyce.

Leclaire, L. Le roman régionaliste dans les îles Britanniques 1800–1950. Paris 1954.

Paul, D. Time and the novelist. Partisan Rev 21 1954.

Pound, E. Literary essays. Ed T. S. Eliot, 1954. On Joyce, W. Lewis.

Raleigh, J. H. The English novel and the three kinds of time. Sewanee Rev 62 1954.

— Victorian morals and the modern novel. Partisan Rev 25 1958.

Blotner, J. L. The political novel. New York 1955.

Bogan, L. Selected criticism. New York 1955. On V. Woolf, E. Bowen, Joyce, I. Compton-Burnett, Forster, Huxley, Conrad, Lawrence et al.

Cazamian, M. L. Le roman et les idées en Angleterre 1860–1914: les doctrines d'action et l'aventure 1880–1914. Paris 1955.

Chatterjee, S. The novel as the modern epic. Calcutta 1955.

— The technique of the modern English novel. Calcutta 1959.

— Problems in modern English fiction. Calcutta 1965.

Edel, L. The psychological novel 1900–50. Philadelphia 1955, New York 1964 (rev, as The modern psychological novel).

Friedman, M. J. Stream of consciousness: a study in literary method. New Haven 1955.

Friedman, N. Forms of the plot. Jnl of General Education 8 1955.

— Point of view in fiction: the development of a critical concept. PMLA 70 1955.

— Criticism and the novel: Hardy, Hemingway, Crane, V. Woolf, Conrad. Antioch Rev 18 1958.

— What makes a short story short? Modern Fiction Studies 4 1958.

Gerber, R. Utopian fantasy: a study of English utopian fiction since the end of the nineteenth century. 1955.

Gold, H. Truth and falsity in the novel. Hudson Rev 8 1955.

— The mystery of personality in the novel. Partisan Rev 24 1957.

Kahler, E. The transformation of modern fiction. Comparative Lit 7 1955.

— The forms of form. Centennial Rev 7 1963.

Meyerhoff, H. Time in literature. Berkeley 1955.

Stanzel, F. Die typischen Erzählsituationen im Roman. Vienna 1955. On Joyce et al.

Tindall, W. Y. The literary symbol. New York 1955.

— The criticism of fiction. Texas Quart 1 1958.

Viebrock, H. Sprachstil und Sprachspiel. (Das Motiv 'Bildergalerie' und seine Funktion im englischen Roman.) Dickens, Meredith, Galsworthy, Morgan. Die Neueren Sprachen new ser 4 1955.

Blake, G. Annals of Scotland 1895–1955: an essay on the twentieth-century Scottish novel. 1956.

Lindsay, J. After the thirties: the novel in Britain and its future. 1956.

'O'Connor, Frank' (M. F. O'Donovan). The mirror in the roadway: a study of the modern novel. New York 1956.

— The lonely voice: a study of the short story. Cleveland 1963.

Pendry, E. D. The new feminism of English fiction: a study in contemporary women-novelists. Tokyo [1956].

Scrutton, M. Addiction to fiction. Twentieth Century 159 1956.

Toynbee, P. Experiment and the future of the novel. In The craft of letters in England, ed J. Lehmann 1956.

Wyndham, F. Twenty-five years of the novel. In The craft of letters in England, ed J. Lehmann 1956.

Coveney, P. Poor monkey: the child in literature. 1957, 1967 (rev, as The image of childhood). On Joyce, V. Woolf, Lawrence.

Enright, D. J. To the Lighthouse or to India? In his Apothecary's shop, 1957. On V. Woolf, Forster.

Green, R. L. Into other worlds: space-flight in fiction, from Lucian to Lewis. 1957.

Howe, I. Politics and the novel. New York 1957. On Conrad, Orwell, Koestler.

— Mass society and post-modern fiction; The fiction of anti-utopia. In his World more attractive, New York 1957.

Lesser, S. O. Fiction and the unconscious. Boston 1957.

McCormick, J. Catastrophe and imagination: an interpretation of the recent English and American novel. 1957.

Meyer, K. R. Zur erlebten Rede im englischen Roman des zwanzigsten Jahrhunderts. Berne 1957. On Bennett, Conrad, Forster, Lawrence, D. Richardson, V. Woolf.

Moore, P. A. Science and fiction. 1957.

Neubert, A. Die Stilformen der 'Erlebten Rede' im neueren englischen Roman. Halle 1957.

Proctor, M. R. The English university novel. Berkeley 1957.

Taylor, W. A. and A. Duggan. Historical fiction. Cambridge 1957 (NBL Reader's Guide).

West, A. Principles and persuasions. New York 1957. On Wells, Orwell, Greene, I. Compton-Burnett et al.

Zabel, M. D. Craft and character: texts, method, and vocation in modern fiction. New York 1957. On Conrad, Forster, Ford, G. Greene.

Aiken, C. A reviewer's ABC. New York 1958. On Lawrence, W. Lewis, K. Mansfield.

Booth, B. A. The novel. In Contemporary literary scholarship, ed L. Leary, New York 1958.

Borinski, L. and G. Krause. Die Utopie in der modernen englischen Literatur. Frankfurt 1958.

Borinski, L. Meister des modernen englischen Romans: Dickens, Galsworthy, H. G. Wells, Joseph Conrad, Virginia Woolf, Aldous Huxley, Graham Greene, George Orwell. Heidelberg 1963.

Brumm, U. Symbolism and the novel. Partisan Rev 25 1958.

Cary, J. Art and reality. Cambridge 1958.

Fricker, R. Der moderne englische Roman. Göttingen 1958, 1964 (rev).

Fuller, E. Man in modern fiction. New York 1958.

— Books with men behind them. New York 1962. On Snow, C. S. Lewis, C. Williams.

Kennedy, M. The outlaws on Parnassus. 1958. On the art of the novel.

Kenner, H. Gnomon: essays on contemporary literature. New York 1958. On Ford, W. Lewis.

— Flaubert, Joyce and Beckett: the stoic comedians. Boston 1962.

Murch, A. E. The development of the detective novel. 1958, 1968 (rev).

Rathburn, R. C. and M. Steinmann (ed). From Jane Austen to Joseph Conrad: essays collected in memory of James T. Hillhouse. Minneapolis 1958.

Stevenson, W. B. Detective fiction. Cambridge 1958 (NBL Reader's Guide).

Tillyard, E. M. W. The epic strain in the English novel. 1958. On Conrad, Bennett, Joyce et al.

Williams, R. Culture and society 1780–1950. 1958. On Lawrence, Orwell.

— Realism and the contemporary novel. In his Long revolution, 1961, 1965 (rev).

Writers at work: the Paris Review interviews. Ser 1, ed M. Cowley, New York 1958. On Forster, Cary, O'Connor. Ser 3, ed A. Kazin, New York 1967. On Waugh.

Allott, M. (ed). Novelists on the novel. 1959.

Brady, C. A. The British novel today. Thought 34 1959.

Davenport, B. et al. The science fiction novel: imagination and social criticism. Chicago 1959.

Davies, H. A mirror of the ministry in modern novels. New York 1959.

Karl, F. R. and M. Magalaner. A reader's guide to great twentieth-century English novels. New York 1959.

Karl, F. R. The contemporary English novel. New York 1962, London 1963 (as A reader's guide to the contemporary English novel).

Mueller, W. R. The prophetic voice in modern fiction. New York 1959.

Reiss, H. S. Style and structure in modern experimental fiction. In Stil- und Formprobleme in der Literatur, ed P. Böckmann, Heidelberg 1959.

Cook, A. The meaning of fiction. Detroit 1960. On Conrad, Lawrence et al.

Gransden, K. W. Thoughts on contemporary fiction. REL 1 1960.

Krieger, M. The tragic vision. New York 1960. On Conrad, Lawrence.

McCarthy, M. The fact in fiction. Partisan Rev 27 1960; rptd in her On the contrary, 1962.

— Characters in fiction. Partisan Rev 28 1961; rptd in her On the contrary, 1962.

May, D. The novelist as moralist and the moralist as critic. EC 10 1960.

Miller, J. E. (ed). Myth and method: modern theories of fiction. Lincoln Nebraska 1960.

Rovit, E. H. The ambiguous modern novel. Yale Rev 49 1960.

Sale, R. (ed). Discussions of the novel. Boston 1960.

Shapiro, C. (ed). Twelve original essays on great English novels. Detroit 1960. On Conrad, Forster, Joyce, Lawrence.

— (ed). Contemporary British novelists. Carbondale 1965. On Powell, Snow et al.

Stevenson, L. The English novel: a panorama. Boston 1960.

— Yesterday and after. New York 1967. Forms vol 11 of E. A. Baker, The history of the English novel.

Wagner, G. Sociology and fiction. Twentieth Century 167 1960.

Bland, D. S. Endangering the reader's neck: background description in the novel. Criticism 3 1961.

Booth, W. C. Distance and point-of-view: an essay in classification. EC 11 1961.

— The rhetoric of fiction. Chicago 1961.

— 'The rhetoric of fiction' and the poetics of fictions. Novel 1 1968.

Cam, H. M. Historical novels. 1961 (Historical Assoc pamphlet).

Dahlberg, E. and H. Read. Truth is more sacred: a critical exchange on modern literature. New York 1961. On Joyce, Lawrence.

Heppenstall, R. The fourfold tradition: notes on the French and English literatures. 1961. On Lawrence, V. Woolf et al.

Lever, K. The novel and the reader. 1961.

Mander, J. The writer and commitment. 1961.

Scholes, R. Approaches to the novel. San Francisco 1961.

— Elements of fiction. New York 1968.

Snow, C. P. Science, politics and the novelist. Kenyon Rev 23 1961.

Stallman, R. W. The houses that James built. East Lansing 1961.

Stewart, D. The ark of God: Studies in five modern novelists. 1961. On Cary, Greene, Huxley, Joyce, R. Macaulay.

Tomlinson, T. B. Literature and history: the novel. Melbourne Critical Rev 4 1961.

Uitti, K. D. The concept of self in the symbolist novel. Hague 1961.

Wilson, A. The novelist and the narrator. In English studies today 2nd ser, ed G. A. Bonnard, Berne 1961.

— The dilemma of the contemporary novelist. In Approaches to the novel, ed J. Colmer 1967, below.

Albérès, R. M. Histoire du roman moderne. Paris 1962.

— Metamorphoses du roman. Paris 1966.

Bruner, J. S. Identity and the modern novel. In his On knowing, Cambridge Mass 1962.

Current-Garcia, E. and W. R. Patrick. Realism and romanticism in fiction. Chicago 1962.

Davies, H. S. Browning and the modern novel. Hull 1962.

Gindin, J. Postwar British fiction: new accents and attitudes. Berkeley 1962.

Gregor, I. and B. Nicholas. The moral and the story. 1962. On Greene, Lawrence.

Hale, N. The realities of fiction. Boston 1962.

Harding, D. W. Psychological processes in the reading of fiction. Brit Jnl of Aesthetics 2 1962.

Hartley, L. P. The novelist's responsibility. E & S new ser 15 1962. Rptd in following item.

— The novelist's responsibility. 1967. Essays on L. H. Myers, C. H. B. Kitchin, the short story, novelist's material etc.

Kermode, J. F. Puzzles and epiphanies: essays and reviews 1958–61. 1962. On Forster, Joyce, Waugh, Greene et al.
— The house of fiction: interviews with seven English novelists. Partisan Rev 30 1963.
— Novel, history and type. Novel 1 1967.
— The sense of an ending: studies in the theory of fiction. New York 1967.
— Continuities. 1968. On Lawrence, Beckett et al.
Kreutz, I. Mr Bennett and Mrs Woolf. Modern Fiction Studies 8 1962.
Kumar, S. K. Bergson and the stream of consciousness novel. 1962.
Noon, W. T. God and man in twentieth-century fiction. Thought 37 1962.
Pascal, R. Tense and novel. MLR 57 1962.
Putt, S. G. Scholars of the heart: essays in criticism. 1962. On Huxley, Forster, F. Reid.
Romberg, B. Studies in the narrative technique of the first-person novel. Stockholm 1962.
Symons, J. The detective story in Britain. 1962.
— Critical occasions. 1966. On Machen, Saki, Orwell, W. Lewis, Snow, Waugh, Powell et al.
Wain, J. The conflict of forms in contemporary English literature: 2 [The novel]. CQ 4 1962; rptd in his Essays on literature and ideas, 1963.
Walsh, C. From Utopia to nightmare. 1962. On Wells, Huxley, Orwell, Waugh et al.
Wilson, C. The strength to dream: literature and the imagination. 1962. On Waugh, Greene, Beckett, Wells, Lawrence et al.
'Burgess, Anthony' (J. B. Wilson). The novel today. 1963 (Br Council pamphlet).
— The novel now: a student's guide to contemporary fiction. 1967.
Church, M. Time and reality: studies in contemporary fiction. Chapel Hill 1963. On Joyce, Huxley, V. Woolf.
Conquest, R. Science fiction and literature. CQ 5 1963.
Cox, C. B. The free spirit: a study of liberal humanism in the novels of George Eliot, Henry James, E. M. Forster, Virginia Woolf, Angus Wilson. 1963.
Freedman, R. The lyrical novel: studies in Hermann Hesse, André Gide and Virginia Woolf. Princeton 1963.
Goldberg, M. A. Chronology, character and the human condition: a reappraisal of the modern novel. Criticism 5 1963.
Guerard, A. J. et al. Perspectives on the novel. Daedalus 92 1963.
Hall, J. The tragic comedians. Bloomington 1963. On Forster, Huxley, Waugh, H. Green, Cary, Hartley, Powell.
— The lunatic giant in the drawing room: the British and American novel since 1930. Bloomington 1968.
Hartt, J. N. The lost image of man. Baton Rouge 1963.
Moody, P. In the lavatory of the Athenaeum: postwar English novels. Melbourne Critical Rev 6 1963.
Moseley, E. M. Pseudonyms of Christ in the modern novel: motifs and methods. Pittsburg 1963. On Conrad, Lawrence, Forster et al.
Shroder, M. Z. The novel as a genre. Massachusetts Rev 4 1963.
Stewart, J. I. M. Eight modern writers. Oxford 1963 (OHEL). On Conrad, Joyce, Lawrence.
West, P. The modern novel. 1963.
— The wine of absurdity. University Park Pennsylvania 1966. On Lawrence, Greene et al.
Adams, K. Notes on concretization. Br Jnl of Aesthetics 4 1964.
Beachcroft, T. O. The English short story. 2 vols 1964.
— The modest art: a survey of the short story in English. 1968.
Beebe, M. Ivory towers and sacred founts: the artist as hero in fiction from Goethe to Joyce. New York 1964.
Hardy, B. The appropriate form: an essay on the novel. 1964.

Hardy, J. E. Man in the modern novel. Seattle 1964. On Conrad, Forster, Lawrence, Joyce, V. Woolf, Waugh et al.
Harris, W. V. Style and the twentieth-century novel. Western Humanities Rev 18 1964.
Lees, F. N. Identification and emotion in the novel: a feature of narrative method. Br Jnl of Aesthetics 4 1964.
Brome, V. Four realist novelists. 1965 (Br Council pamphlet). On E. Pugh, R. Whiteing, W. P. Ridge.
Davie, D. (ed). Russian literature and modern English fiction. Chicago 1965. Essays on influence of Russian writers, and on Galsworthy, Lawrence et al.
Dyson, A. E. The crazy fabric: essays in irony. 1965. On Huxley, Waugh, Orwell et al.
Gillie, C. Character in English literature. 1965.
Greenblatt, S. J. Three modern satirists: Waugh, Orwell and Huxley. New Haven 1965.
Harvey, W. J. Character and the novel. 1965.
Hildick, E. W. Word for word: a study of authors' alterations. 1965. On Lawrence, V. Woolf.
O'Grady, W. On plot in modern fiction: Hardy, James and Conrad. Modern Fiction Stud 11 1965.
Oppel, H. (ed). Der moderne englische Roman: Interpretationen. Berlin 1965.
Scott, N. A. (ed). Forms of extremity in the modern novel. Richmond Va 1965.
— Craters of the spirit: studies in the modern novel. Washington 1968. On Beckett, Greene et al.
Souvage, J. An introduction to the study of the novel with special reference to the English novel. Ghent 1965.
Unterecker, J. E. (ed). Approaches to the twentieth-century novel. New York 1965.
Cohn, D. Narrated monologue: definition of a fictional style. Comparative Lit 18 1966.
Cronin, A. A question of modernity. 1966. On Joyce, Beckett.
French, W. The social novel at the end of an era. Carbondale 1966.
Friedman, A. The turn of the novel. New York 1966. On Conrad, Forster, Lawrence.
Greenberg, A. The death of the psyche: a way to the self in the contemporary novel. Criticism 8 1966.
Kaplan, H. J. The passive voice: an approach to modern fiction. Athens Ohio 1966. On Joyce, Conrad, Lawrence.
Killham, J. The 'second self' in novel criticism. Br Jnl of Aesthetics 6 1966.
Lodge, D. Language of fiction: essays in criticism and verbal analysis of the English novel. 1966.
Mylne, V. Illusion and the novel. Br Jnl of Aesthetics 6 1966.
Scholes, R. and R. Kellogg. The nature of narrative. New York 1966.
Walcutt, C. C. Man's changing mask: modes and methods of characterization in fiction. Minneapolis 1966.
Colmer, J. Form and design in the novel. In Approaches to the novel, ed Colmer, Edinburgh 1967.
Goetsch, P. Die Romankonzeption in England 1880–1910. Heidelberg 1967.
Hoyt, C. A. (ed). Minor British novelists. Carbondale 1967. On A. Machen, C. Williams, R. Macaulay.
Larrett, W. The English novel from Thomas Hardy to Graham Greene. Frankfort 1967.
Rabinovitz, R. The reaction against experiment in the English novel 1950–60. New York 1967. On A. Wilson, Snow.
Sandison, A. The wheel of empire: a study of the imperial idea in some late nineteenth and early twentieth-century fiction. 1967.
Stevick, P. (ed). The theory of the novel. New York 1967.
Troy, W. Selected essays, ed S. E. Hyman. New Brunswick 1967. On Joyce, Lawrence, V. Woolf et al.
Calderwood, J. L. and H. E. Toliver (ed). Perspectives on fiction. New York 1968. Reprints essays on technique of novel.

Goodheart, E. The cult of the ego: the self in modern literature. Chicago 1968. On Lawrence, Joyce et al.

Grossvogel, D. I. Limits of the novel: evolutions of a form from Chaucer to Robbe-Grillet. Ithaca 1968.

Killam, G. D. Africa in English fiction 1874–1939. Ibadan 1968.

McCormack, T. (ed). Afterwords: novelists on their novels. New York 1968.

Mack, M. and I. Gregor (ed). Imagined worlds: essays on some English novels and novelists. 1968. On Conrad, Lawrence, Joyce, Waugh, M. Lowry et al.

Mooney, H. J. and T. F. Staley (ed). The shapeless god: essays on modern fiction. Pittsburgh 1968. On Greene, Waugh et al.

Price, M. The other self: thoughts about character in the novel. In Imagined worlds, ed M. Mack and I. Gregor 1968 (above).

Raban, J. The technique of modern fiction. 1968.

Davis, R. M. (ed). The novel: modern essays in criticism. Englewood Cliffs NJ 1969.

Garrett, P. K. Scene and symbol from George Eliot to James Joyce: studies in changing fictional mode. New Haven 1969.

Realism, reality and the novel. Novel 2 1969. A symposium.

Reinhardt, K. F. The theological novel of modern Europe. New York 1969. On Greene, Waugh et al.

Ross, S. D. Literature and philosophy: an analysis of the philosophical novel. New York 1969.

K.W.

II. INDIVIDUAL NOVELISTS

JOSEPH CONRAD
(JÓZEF TEODOR KONRAD
NAŁECZ KORZENIOWSKI)
1857–1924

The principal collections are at the A.S.W. Rosenbach Foundation, Philadelphia (the bulk of the Conrad mss), Yale Univ (the Keating Conrad Memorial Library), BM (T. J. Wise's Ashley Library). Harvard Univ, Lilly Library Indiana Univ, and the New York Public Library also have collections.

Bibliographies

Principal bibliographies, catalogues etc only. For fuller lists, see the bibliography by Ehrsam, below.

Wise, T. J. A bibliography of the writings of Conrad 1895–1920. 1920 (priv ptd), 1921 (priv ptd, rev and enlarged), 1964.

—— A Conrad library: a catalogue of printed books, manuscripts and autograph letters. 1928 (priv ptd). Pt 2 contains short descriptions of some books on Conrad.

Anderson Galleries. Complete catalogue of the library of John Quinn, vol 1. New York 1924. Auction catalogue.

W. Heffer and Sons. Catalogue of second-hand books, nos 251, 257. Cambridge 1925–6. Books from Conrad's library.

Hodgson & Co. A catalogue of books, manuscripts and corrected typescripts from the library of the late Joseph Conrad. 1925.

American Art Association. The Richard Curle Conrad collection. New York 1927. Auction catalogue.

—— The historic Edward Garnett Conrad-Hudson collection. New York 1928. Auction catalogue.

A Conrad memorial library: the collection of G. T. Keating. Garden City NY 1929. *See* also J. T. Babb, A checklist of additions to a Conrad memorial library 1927–38, Yale Univ Lib Gazette 13 1938, with an article by J. A. Gee on the Keating Conrad Library.

Curle, R. H. P. A handlist of the various books [etc], articles [etc] written about Conrad by R. Curle 1911–31. Brookville 1932 (priv ptd), Port Washington 1964; rptd in Jessie Conrad, Conrad and his circle, 1935.

Beebe, M. Criticism of Conrad: a selected checklist. Modern Fiction Stud 1 1955. Items in English only. Brought up to date, with pruning, Modern Fiction Stud 10 1964.

Lohf, K. A. and E. P. Sheehy. Joseph Conrad at mid-century: editions and studies 1895–1955. Minneapolis 1957. Includes trns. *See* also L. Krzyżanowski, Conrad: a bibliographical note—[Polish] items not listed in Conrad at mid-century. In Joseph Conrad: centennial essays, ed L. Krzyżanowski, New York 1960.

Harvey, D. D. Ford Madox Ford 1873–1939: a bibliography of works and criticism. Princeton 1962. Further details of Conrad's collaborations with F. M. Hueffer [Ford].

Rice, H. C. Additions to the Doubleday collection: Kipling, T. E. Lawrence, Conrad. Princeton Univ Lib Chron 24 1963.

Bojarski, E. A. and H. T. Conrad: a bibliography of masters' theses and doctoral dissertations 1917–63. Lexington 1964.

Ehrsam, T. G. A bibliography of Conrad. Metuchen NJ 1969. Primary and secondary material; includes trns.

Schultheiss, T. Conrad bibliography: the start of the second era. Conradiana 1 1969. Corrections and addns to Ehrsam, above.

Stephens, H. R. Conrad bibliography: a continued checklist. Conradiana 1 1969 onwards.

Collections

Works. Garden City NY 1920–5 (Sun-dial edn, limited to 735 sets), London 1923–8 (Uniform edn). The texts of those vols issued before Conrad's death were rev by the author, and were given prefatory notes except where a note had already been written by Conrad for the earlier, separate edn of a particular text (see §1, below). The collaborations with Hueffer [F. M. Ford], The inheritors and Romance, do not have author's notes; nor does Harvey's Bibliography of Ford, above, mention any textual revisions. The plates of this edn formed the basis for sets subsequently issued by Doubleday in varying numbers of vols, e.g. the Kent, Memorial, Malay, Concord, Canterbury, Personal edns, and for the Dent (London) Collected edn 1946–55. (*See* the textual note in Conrad's secret sharer and the critics, ed B. Harkness [1962], §2 below). Excludes the plays, The nature of a crime (written with F. M. Hueffer), and The sisters. The prefatory notes were also pbd separately as Notes on my books, Garden City NY 1921 (250 copies), London 1921 (250 copies).

Works. 20 vols 1921–7 (Heinemann, limited to 780 sets). Contents same as the Sun-dial edn, but excludes Tales of hearsay and Last essays. Possibly the last state of the texts rev by Conrad for these collected edns of his works. *See* Harkness, op cit.

Notes on my books. Garden City NY 1921, London 1921, 1937 (ed E. Garnett, as Conrad's prefaces to his works). Reprints prefaces from Sun-dial edn.

Complete short stories. [1933].

Three plays: Laughing Anne, One day more and The secret agent. 1934.

Selections

*Of the more recent selections only those with the more signifi-
cant introds are given.*

Wisdom and beauty from Conrad. Ed M. H. M. Capes
1915, [1922], New York [1923].

The shorter tales of Conrad. Garden City NY 1924. Preface by Conrad. Contains Youth, The secret sharer, The
brute, To-morrow, Typhoon, Because of the dollars,
The partner, Falk.

A Conrad argosy. Introd by W. McFee, Garden City NY
1942.

The Conrad reader. Ed A. J. Hoppé 1946, 1947 (as The
Conrad companion).

The portable Conrad. Ed M. D. Zabel, New York 1947.

Sagesse de Conrad. Ed G. Jean-Aubry, Paris 1947.

Four tales. Introd by D. Bone 1949.

Heart of darkness, and The secret sharer. Introd by A. J.
Guerard, New York 1950.

Tales of land and sea. Introd by W. McFee, Garden City
NY 1953.

Tales of the East and West. Ed M. D. Zabel, Garden City
NY 1958.

The shadow-line and two other tales: Typhoon, The
secret sharer. Ed M. D. Zabel, Garden City NY 1959.

Heart of darkness, Almayer's folly and The lagoon. Introd
by A. J. Guerard, New York 1960.

The mirror of the sea, and A personal record. Ed M. D.
Zabel, Garden City NY 1960.

Tales of heroes and history. Ed M. D. Zabel, Garden City
NY 1960.

Tales of the East. Ed M. D. Zabel, Garden City NY 1961.

Typhoon and other tales. Foreword by A. J. Guerard,
New York 1963.

Joseph Conrad on fiction. Ed W. F. Wright, Lincoln
Nebraska [1964].

Almayer's folly and other stories. Afterword by J. Baines,
New York 1965.

§1

*For details of pbn of individual short stories and essays, etc,
in magazines prior to their collection in book form, see the
bibliography by Lohf and Sheehy. For a general discussion of
Conrad's revisions, from ms through serial pbn to book pbn,
in his early works up to and including Lord Jim, see J. D.
Gordan, Conrad: the making of a novelist, 1940, §2, below.
See also the various articles listed in §2, below, discussing
the revision of individual texts.*

Prose Fiction

Almayer's folly: a story of an eastern river. 1895, New
York 1895.

An outcast of the islands. 1896, New York 1896 (bowdler-
ized).

The nigger of the 'Narcissus': a tale of the sea. 1897 (7
copies for copyright purposes, with subtitle 'a tale of
the forecastle') New York 1897 (as The children of the
sea), London 1898 (as The nigger of the 'Narcissus':
a tale of the sea), Garden City NY 1914 (with the preface,
first pbd in New York Dec 1897 and previously suppressed, and with an introd by Conrad 'To my readers in
America'), New York 1951 (introd by M. D. Zabel),
[1965] (introd by H. M. Jones). First pbd in New Rev
Aug–Dec 1897. The preface was ptd separately at Hythe,
1902 (100 copies) and pbd at Garden City NY 1914 (as
Joseph Conrad on the art of writing, with 'to my readers
in America').

Tales of unrest. New York 1898, London 1898. Karain:
a memory; The idiots; An outpost of progress; The
return; The lagoon.

Lord Jim: a tale. Edinburgh 1900, New York 1900 (as
Lord Jim: a romance), London 1917 (as Lord Jim:
a tale; with Author's note), New York 1957 (ed R. D.

Heilman), 1958 (introd by W. F. Wright), Boston 1958
(introd by M. D. Zabel). First pbd in Blackwood's Mag
Oct 1899–Nov 1900 (as Lord Jim: a sketch).

The inheritors: an extravagant story. New York 1901,
London 1901. With F. M. Hueffer [Ford].

Youth: a narrative, and two other stories. Edinburgh
1902, New York 1903, London 1917 (with Author's
note); ed M. D. Zabel, Garden City NY 1959. Youth;
Heart of darkness; The end of the tether.

Typhoon. New York 1902, London 1912. First pbd in
Pall Mall Mag Jan–March 1902 and in Critic (New York)
Feb–May 1902.

Typhoon and other stories. 1903, Garden City NY 1923.
Typhoon; Amy Foster; Falk: a reminiscence; Tomor-
row. The latter 3 stories were pbd in New York 1903 as
Falk; Amy Foster; Tomorrow: three stories.

Romance: a novel. 1903, New York 1904. With F. M.
Hueffer [Ford]. *See* Hueffer's note in The nature of
a crime, below, for details of the collaboration.

Nostromo: a tale of the seaboard. 1904, New York 1904,
London 1918 (with Author's note), New York 1951
(introd by R. P. Warren, rptd in his Selected essays,
New York 1958 and in Stallman, 1960, §2, below)
(Modern Library), 1960 (foreword by F. R. Leavis),
1961 (introd by D. Van Ghent). First pbd in T.P.'s
Weekly 29 Jan–7 Oct 1904.

The secret agent: a simple tale. 1907, New York 1907.
First pbd (shorter version) in Ridgway's (New York)
6 Oct 1906–12 Jan 1907.

A set of six. 1908, Garden City NY 1915. Gaspar Ruiz;
The informer; The brute; An anarchist; The duel (pbd
separately New York 1908 as The point of honor:
a military tale); Il Conde. Gaspar Ruiz rptd separately
with Youth, and with Author's note, 1920.

Under western eyes: a novel. 1911, New York 1911, 1951
(introd by M. D. Zabel, rptd, rev, as Conrad: the threat
to the West, in his Craft and character 1957, §2, below),
1963 (rev and expanded introd by Zabel, rptd in
Mudrick, [1966], §2, below). First pbd in Eng Rev and
North Amer Rev Dec 1910–Oct 1911.

'Twixt land and sea: tales. 1912, New York 1912. A smile
of fortune; The secret sharer; Freya of the Seven
Isles.

Chance: a tale in two parts. Toronto [1913], London 1914,
New York 1914. First pbd in New York Herald
21 Jan–30 June 1912.

Victory: an island tale. Garden City NY 1915, London
1915 (with Author's note). First pbd in Munsey's Mag
Feb 1915 and Star (London) 24 Aug–9 Nov 1915.
A second Author's note, written 1920, appears in the
collected edns of Conrad's Works, above. For Conrad's
connection with the stage adaptation of Victory by
Macdonald Hastings, *see* R. S. Ryf, Conrad's stage
Victory, Modern Drama 7 1964.

Within the tides: tales. 1915, Garden City NY 1916. The
planter of Malata; The partner; The inn of the two
witches; Because of the dollars.

The shadow-line: a confession. 1917, Garden City NY
1917. First pbd in Eng Rev Sept 1916–March 1917.

The arrow of gold: a story between two notes. Garden
City NY 1919, London 1919 (with corrections). First
pbd Lloyd's Mag Dec 1918–Feb 1920.

The tale. 1919 (priv ptd by C. K. Shorter, 25 copies);
rptd in Tales of hearsay, 1925 below.

Prince Roman. 1920 (priv ptd for Conrad, 25 copies); rptd
in Tales of hearsay, 1925, below.

The warrior's soul. 1920 (priv ptd for Conrad, 25 copies);
rptd in Tales of hearsay, 1925, below.

The rescue: a romance of the shallows. Garden City NY
1920, London 1920. First pbd in Land and Water
30 Jan–31 July 1919 and in Romance (New York) Nov
1919–May 1920.

The black mate: a story. Edinburgh 1922 (priv ptd, 50
copies); rptd in Tales of hearsay, 1925, below.

The rover. Garden City NY 1923, London 1923.

The nature of a crime. 1924, Garden City NY 1924. With F. M. Hueffer (US edn gives 'F. M. Ford'). Prefaces by Conrad and Hueffer, and appendix, A note on Romance, by Hueffer. First pbd in Eng Rev April–May 1909 as by 'Ignatz von Aschendorf'.

Suspense: a Napoleonic novel. Garden City NY 1925, London 1925 (introd by R. Curle). First pbd in Hutchinson's Mag Feb–Aug 1925 and in Saturday Rev of Lit 27 June–12 Aug 1925.

Tales of hearsay. With preface by R. B. Cunninghame Graham. 1925, Garden City NY 1925. The warrior's soul; Prince Roman; The tale; The black mate.

The sisters. New York 1928. Unfinished; with introd by F. M. Ford.

The bibliographies by Lohf and Sheehy and by Ehrsam list a number of film adaptations of Conrad's fiction.

Other Works

The mirror of the sea: memories and impressions. 1906, New York 1906. The sections called The 'Tremolino' pbd separately New York 1942.

A personal record. 1912 (as Some reminiscences), New York 1912 (as A personal record), London 1916, 1919 (with Author's note). First pbd in Eng Rev Dec 1908 to June 1909 (as Some reminiscences). The Dec 1908 instalment was pbd as a pamphlet in a limited edn, New York 1908, for copyright purposes.

Joseph Conrad on the art of writing. Garden City NY 1914. *See* The nigger of the 'Narcissus', 1897, Prose Fiction, above.

One day more: a play in one act. (Stage Society 25 June 1905; Birmingham Repertory Th 12 Sept 1918). 1917 (priv ptd by C. K. Shorter, 25 copies), 1919, Garden City NY 1920. Dramatization of Tomorrow, from Typhoon and other stories.

The first news. 1918 (priv ptd by C. K. Shorter, 25 copies). On Poland in 1914. This and all the following articles, essays etc (except London's river) priv ptd as pamphlets 1918–20, were rptd in Notes on life and letters, 1921, below.

'Well done!' 1918 (priv ptd for Shorter, 25 copies). On British seamen.

Anatole France. 1919 (priv ptd for T. J. Wise, 25 copies).

Autocracy and war. 1919 (priv ptd for Wise, 25 copies).

Guy de Maupassant. 1919 (priv ptd for Wise, 25 copies).

Henry James: an appreciation. 1919 (priv ptd for Wise, 25 copies).

The lesson of the collision: a monograph upon the loss of the Empress of Ireland. 1919 (priv ptd for Wise, 25 copies).

London's river. 1919 (priv ptd for Shorter, 25 copies). Rptd from The mirror of the sea.

My return to Cracow. 1919 (priv ptd for Wise, 25 copies).

The North Sea on the eve of war. 1919 (priv ptd for Wise, 25 copies).

The Polish question: a note on the joint protectorate of the western powers and Russia. 1919 (priv ptd by Shorter, 25 copies).

The shock of war: through Germany to Cracow. 1919 (priv ptd for Wise, 25 copies).

Some aspects of the admirable inquiry into the loss of the Titanic. 1919 (priv ptd for Wise, 25 copies).

Some reflections, seamanlike and otherwise, on the loss of the Titanic. 1919 (priv ptd for Wise, 25 copies).

Tales of the sea. 1919 (priv ptd for Wise, 25 copies). On Marryat.

To Poland in war-time: a journey into the east. 1919 (priv ptd for Wise, 25 copies).

Tradition. 1919 (priv ptd for Wise, 25 copies).

Alphonse Daudet. 1920 (priv ptd for Wise, 25 copies).

Anatole France: 'L'île des pingouins'. 1920 (priv ptd for Wise, 25 copies).

Books. 1920 (priv ptd for Wise, 25 copies).

Confidence. 1920 (priv ptd for Wise, 25 copies).

An observer in Malay. 1920 (priv ptd for Wise, 25 copies). Rptd review of Studies in brown humanity, by H. Clifford.

Notes on life and letters. 1921, Garden City NY 1921. With Author's note.

Notes on my books. 1921. *See* Collections, above.

The secret agent: drama in four acts. (Ambassadors 2 Nov 1922). Canterbury 1921 (priv ptd for Conrad, 52 copies), London 1923 (priv ptd, as The secret agent: a drama in three acts).

Simple cooking precepts for a little house by Jessie Conrad, with preface by Conrad. 1921 (priv ptd, 100 copies). The preface only. This and the following articles, essays etc priv ptd as pamphlets, were rptd in Last essays, 1926, below. This item was rptd as Cookery.

The Dover patrol: a tribute. Canterbury 1922 (priv ptd for Wise, 75 copies).

John Galsworthy: an appreciation. Canterbury 1922 (priv ptd for Wise, 75 copies).

Travel: a preface to Into the East, by R. Curle. 1922 (priv ptd for Curle, 20 copies).

Laughing Anne: a play. 1923. Dramatization of Because of the dollars, from Within the tides.

The Torrens: a personal tribute. 1923 (priv ptd for Wise, 20 copies).

Geography and some explorers. 1924 (priv ptd for Wise, 30 copies).

Laughing Anne and One day more: two plays, with an introduction by John Galsworthy. 1924, Garden City NY 1925. Laughing Anne first pbd 1923, One day more 1917.

'Admiralty paper', written by Joseph Conrad. 1925 (priv ptd for Jerome Kern, 93 copies); rptd in Last essays as The unlighted coast.

Notes by Joseph Conrad written in a set of his first editions in the possession of Richard Curle, with an introduction and explanatory comments [by Curle]. 1925 (priv ptd, 100 copies).

Joseph Conrad's diary of his journey up the valley of the Congo in 1890, with introd and notes by R. Curle. 1926 (priv ptd, 100 copies).

Last essays. Introd by Curle. 1926, Garden City NY 1926.

Winawer, B. The book of Job: a satirical comedy. Tr by Conrad 1931.

For details of Conrad's other newspaper and magazine articles and introds, forewords etc to books by other authors, most of which were rptd in Notes on life and letters and Last essays, above, see the bibliographies by Lohf and Sheehy and by Ehrsam.

Letters

A collected edn of Conrad's letters is being compiled by F. R. Karl (see §2, below, F. P. W. McDowell, Review essay: the most recent books on Conrad, Papers on Lang & Lit 4 1968). The following is a list of letters pbd in books, pamphlets and the more substantial periodical articles only. For further references, see the bibliography by Lohf and Sheehy.

Five letters by Conrad written to Edward Noble in 1895. 1925 (priv ptd, 100 copies). With foreword by Noble.

Symons, A. Notes on Conrad, with some unpublished letters. 1925.

The intimate letters of Joseph Conrad. World Today 49 1926–7, World's Work 53 1926–7 (as Conrad's intimate letters to Galsworthy and Wells: the private correspondence of a master of literature).

Jean-Aubry, G. Conrad: life and letters. 2 vols Garden City NY 1927, London 1927. Contains a selection of about 600 letters, including some translated from the Polish.

Conrad's letters to his wife. 1927 (priv ptd, 220 copies). Preface, and some letters, by Jessie Conrad.

To my brethren of the pen. 1927 (priv ptd). Pamphlet containing one letter.

Letters from Conrad, 1895–1924. Ed with introd and notes by E. Garnett, Indianapolis 1928, London 1928. Contains about 300 letters, mostly not included in Jean-Aubry's Life and letters.

Conrad to a friend: 150 selected letters from Conrad to Richard Curle. Ed with introd and notes by Curle 1928, New York 1928 (as Letters: Conrad to Richard Curle), Garden City NY 1928 (as Conrad to a friend). The New York edn has more complete versions of some of the letters.

Letters of Conrad to Stephen and Cora Crane. Amer Bookman 69 1929. Ed C. Bohnenberger and N. M. Hill.

Lettres françaises. Ed G. Jean-Aubry Paris, 1930.

Letters of Conrad to Marguerite Poradowska 1890–1920. Tr from the French, and ed J. A. Gee and P. A. Sturm, New Haven 1940. For French edn see below.

Conrad: letters to William Blackwood and David S. Meldrum. Ed W. Blackburn, Durham NC 1958.

Conrad's Polish background: letters to and from Polish friends. Ed Z. Najder 1964.

Six lettres inédites de Conrad. Ed P. Meykiechel, Nouvelles Littéraires 6 Aug 1964. Letters in French to Emile Briquel.

Lettres de Conrad à Marguerite Poradowska. Ed R. Rapin, Geneva 1966.

Conrad and Warrington Dawson: the record of a friendship. Ed D. B. J. Randall, Durham NC 1968. 60 letters.

Joseph Conrad's letters to R. B. Cunninghame Graham. Ed C. T. Watts 1969.

§2

See also Ford Madox Ford, *cols 569–75, below, and Harvey's bibliography of Ford, above, for further material on Conrad's collaborations with F. M. Hueffer [Ford].*

Books and Chapters in Books

Curle, R. H. P. Joseph Conrad: a study. 1914.
— Conrad: the history of his books. [1924]. Pamphlet. Partly rptd from TLS 30 Aug 1923.
— Conrad's last day. 1924 (priv ptd, 100 copies).
— The personality of Conrad. 1925 (priv ptd, 100 copies).
— The last twelve years of Conrad. 1928.
— A remarkable friendship: Conrad and Galsworthy; The background of Nostromo. In his Caravansary and conversation, 1937.
— Joseph Conrad and his characters: a study of six novels. 1957.
Follett, W. Joseph Conrad: a short study of his intellectual and emotional attitude towards his work and of the chief characteristics of his novels. Garden City NY 1915 (priv ptd).
Freeman, J. Joseph Conrad. In his The moderns: essays in literary criticism, 1916.
Powys, J. C. Joseph Conrad. In his Suspended judgments: essays on books and sensations, New York 1916.
Walpole, H. Joseph Conrad. [1916], 1924 (rev).
Mencken, H. L. Conrad. In his A book of prefaces, New York 1918. Later printings have revisions.
— Conrad. In his Prejudices: fifth series, New York 1926.
Ford, F. M. (formerly Hueffer). To Joseph Conrad. In his English novel from the earliest days to the death of Conrad, Philadelphia 1919.
— Conrad: a personal remembrance. 1924.
Garnett, E. Conrad. In his Friday nights: literary criticisms and appreciations, 1922.
Stauffer, R. M. Conrad: his romantic-realism. Boston 1922.
Sutherland, J. G. At sea with Conrad. 1922. With a foreword by Conrad.
Bendz, E. Conrad: an appreciation. Gothenburg 1923.
Weygandt, C. The art of Conrad. In Schelling anniversary papers, ed A. H. Quinn, New York 1923.

Conrad [Korzeniowski], Jessie. Personal recollections of Conrad. 1924 (priv ptd, 100 copies). Incorporated, rev, in next.
— Conrad as I knew him. 1926.
— Conrad and his circle. 1935. Port Washington 1964 (rptd with R. Curle, A handlist of the various books [etc] written about Conrad by Curle, 1932, Bibliographies, above).
Graham, R. B. C. Inventi portam: Conrad. Cleveland 1924 (priv ptd, 157 copies).
Muir, E. A note on Conrad. In his Latitudes, New York 1924.
Adams, E. L. Conrad: the man. New York 1925.
Jean-Aubry, G. Conrad au Congo. Paris 1925. Tr 1926.
— Conrad: life and letters. 2 vols Garden City NY 1927.
— Vie de Conrad. Paris 1947 (tr as The sea dreamer: a definitive biography of Conrad, 1957).
Symons, A. Notes on Conrad, with some unpublished letters. 1925. Pamphlet.
Zelie, J. S. A burial in Kent. New York 1925. Containing Conrad's answers to questions inserted anonymously into a set of his first edns.
Bullett, G. W. Joseph Conrad. In his Modern English fiction, 1926.
Drew, E. A. Joseph Conrad. In her Modern novel, New York 1926.
Hutchison, P. A. Conrad—alchemist of the sea. In Essays in memory of Barrett Wendell by his assistants, ed W. R. Castle and P. Kaufman, Cambridge Mass 1926.
Mégroz, R. L. A talk with Conrad and a criticism of his mind and method. 1926. Part incorporated in next.
— Conrad's mind and method: a study of personality in art. 1931.
Ruch, G. Zeitverlauf und Erzählerstandpunkt in Conrads Romanen. Herrnstadt in Schlesien 1926.
Twenty letters to Conrad. 1926. Introd and notes by G. Jean-Aubry. Correspondents are Kipling, Gissing, Wells, Crane, Huneker, E. V. Lucas, Galsworthy, James, Bennett, Edward Garnett and Constance Garnett.
Clifford, H. A talk on Conrad and his work. [Colombo] 1927. Pamphlet.
Grabowski, Z. Ze studjów nad Conradem. Poznan 1927.
Middleton, A. S. Tropic shadows: memories of the South Seas, together with reminiscences of the author's sea meetings with Conrad. 1927.
Daniel-Rops, H. Joseph Conrad. In his Carte d'Europe, Paris 1928.
A Conrad memorial library: the collection of G. T. Keating. Garden City NY 1929. With notes on individual books by Conrad by H. M. Tomlinson, H. Clifford, C. Morley, D. Garnett, T. F. Powys, F. M. Hueffer [Ford], L. Powys, M. Austin, Jessie Conrad, L. O'Flaherty, J. C. Powys, S. Burt, A. Machen, D. Bone, R. Curle, N. Munro and G. Jean-Aubry.
Cross, W. L. Conrad. In his Four contemporary novelists, New York 1930.
Galsworthy, J. Two essays on Conrad. Cincinnati 1930 (priv ptd, 93 copies).
Mann, T. Vorwort zu Conrads Roman Der Geheimagent. In his Die Forderung des Tages, Berlin 1930. Tr in his Past masters and other papers, [1933]. Excerpt rptd in Stallman, 1960 below.
Morf, G. The Polish heritage of Conrad. 1930.
O'Flaherty, L. Joseph Conrad: an appreciation. [1930]. Pamphlet.
Walpole, V. Conrad's method: some formal aspects. Capetown 1930. Pamphlet.
Bancroft, W. W. Conrad: his philosophy of life. Philadelphia 1931 (pbd thesis), Boston 1933.
David, M. Conrad: l'homme et l'œuvre. Paris 1931.
MacCarthy, D. Conrad. In his Portraits, 1931.
Price, A. J. An appreciation of Conrad. Newport Mon 1931.

Beach, J. W. Impressionism: Conrad. In his The twentieth-century novel: studies in technique, New York [1932].

Raphael, A. P. Conrad's Faust. In her Goethe the challenger, New York 1932. On Victory.

Bennewitz, H. Die Charaktere in den Romanen Conrads. Greifswald 1933.

Cushwa, F. W. An introduction to Conrad. Garden City NY 1933.

Vetö-Mandl, E. Die Frau bei Conrad. Budapest 1934.

Wüschel, A. Schau und Veranschaulichung der Aussenwelt bei Conrad. Thayngen 1934.

Burkhardt, J. Das Erlebnis der Wirklichkeit und seine künstlerische Gestaltung in Conrads Werk. Marburg 1935.

'Maurois, André' (E. S. W. Herzog). Conrad. In his Magiciens et logiciens, Paris 1935. Tr as Prophets and poets, 1935.

Crankshaw, E. Conrad: some aspects of the art of the novel. 1936.

Forster, E. M. Conrad: a note. In his Abinger harvest, 1936.

Ujejski, J. O Konradzie Korzeniowskim. Warsaw 1936. Tr French, as Joseph Conrad, Paris 1939.

Doubleday, F. Joseph Conrad. In her Episodes in the life of a publisher's wife, New York 1937 (priv ptd, 100 copies).

Stresau, H. Conrad: der Tragiker des Westens. Berlin 1937.

Hoare, D. The tragic in Hardy and Conrad. In her Some studies in the modern novel. 1938.

Mason, J. E. Joseph Conrad. Exeter 1938 (Makers of Literature 3).

Daiches, D. Conrad. In his The novel and the modern world, Chicago 1939, 1960 (rewritten).

— Experience and the imagination: the background of Heart of darkness. In his White man in the tropics: two moral tales—Heart of darkness and The beach of Falesá [R. L. Stevenson]. New York 1962.

Las Vergnas, R. Joseph Conrad. Paris 1938.

— Conrad: romancier de l'exil. Paris 1959.

Gordan, J. D. Conrad: the making of a novelist. Cambridge Mass 1940.

Bradbrook, M. C. Conrad: Poland's English genius. Cambridge 1941.

Retinger, J. H. Conrad and his contemporaries: souvenirs. 1941.

Mélisson-Bubreil, M-R. La personnalité de Conrad. Paris 1943.

— Le vocabulaire maritime de Conrad. Paris 1943.

Pritchett, V. S. A Pole in the Far East. In his The living novel, 1946.

— An emigré. In his Books in general, 1953.

— Conrad. In his The working novelist, 1965.

Guerard, A. J. Joseph Conrad. Norfolk Conn 1947.

— Conrad the novelist. Cambridge Mass 1958.

Leavis, F. R. The great tradition: George Eliot, James, Conrad. 1948.

Stallman, R. W. Life, art and The secret sharer. In Forms of modern fiction, ed W. V. O'Connor, Minneapolis 1948.

— (ed). The art of Conrad: a critical symposium. East Lansing 1960.

Sackville-West, E. The moment of silence. In his Inclinations, 1949.

Simon, I. Conrad. In her Formes du roman anglais de Dickens à Joyce. Liège 1949.

Wright, W. F. Romance and tragedy in Conrad. Lincoln Nebraska 1949.

Warner, O. Joseph Conrad. 1950, 1960 (rev) (Br Council pamphlet).

— Joseph Conrad. 1951 (Men and Books).

Greene, G. Remembering Mr Jones; The domestic background. In his The lost childhood and other essays, 1951. Reviews of Conrad's prefaces to his works, and Jessie Conrad, Joseph Conrad and his circle, rptd from Spectator 17 Sept 1937 and 26 July 1935.

Häusermann, H. W. In his The Genevese background, 1952. Studies of various writers in Geneva including Conrad.

Hewitt, D. J. Conrad: a reassessment. Cambridge 1952, 1969 (rev).

de la Mare, W. At the world's end. In his Private view, 1953. Review of Victory rptd from TLS 30 Sept 1915.

Kettle, A. In his An introduction to the English novel vol 2, 1953. On Nostromo.

Van Ghent, D. In her The English novel: form and function, New York 1953. On Lord Jim.

Wiley, P. L. Conrad's Measure of man. Madison 1955.

Allen, W. Conrad. In his Six great novelists, 1955.

Visiak, E. H. The mirror of Conrad. 1955.

Unger, L. Laforgue, Conrad and T. S. Eliot. In his Man in the name: essays on the experience of poetry, Minneapolis [1956].

Cecil, D. Conrad. In his Fine art of reading, 1957.

De Chastellier, A. Conrad à la recherche de l'amour. Avignon 1957.

Haugh, R. F. Joseph Conrad: discovery in design. Norman Oklahoma 1957.

Howe, I. Conrad: order and anarchy. In his Politics and the novel, New York 1957.

Moser, T. C. Conrad: achievement and decline. Cambridge Mass 1957.

— (ed) Lord Jim. New York 1968. Text and collection of essays.

Tarnawski, W. (ed). Conrad żywy. 1957. Centenary memorial essays: summary in English. Also includes Some reminiscences of my father by John Conrad.

Zabel, M. D. Conrad. In his Craft and character: texts, method and vocation in modern fiction, New York 1957.

Allen, J. The thunder and the sunshine: a biography of Conrad. New York 1958.

— The sea years of Conrad. Garden City NY 1965.

Joseph Conrad Korzeniowski: essays and studies. Warsaw 1958. Rptd from Kwartalnik Neofilologiczny Special no 1–2 1958. Includes R. Curle, My impressions of the Conrad Centenary celebrations; M. C. Bradbrook, Conrad and the tragic imagination; J. Baines, Conrad—raw material into art; I. Vidan, Some aspects of structure in the works of Conrad, and Conrad in Yugoslavia; W. Chwalewik, Conrad and the literary tradition; and essays in Polish, two (S. Helsztyński, Conrad—the man and writer; W. Tarnawski, Conrad's artistic personality and form) with English summaries.

Kenner, H. Conrad and Ford. In his Gnomon: essays on contemporary literature. New York 1958.

Tillyard, E. M. W. Conrad: Nostromo. In his The epic strain in the English novel. 1958.

Tindall, W. Y. Apology for Marlow. In From Jane Austen to Conrad: essays collected in memory of J. T. Hillhouse, ed R. C. Rathburn and M. Steinmann, Minneapolis 1958.

Andreas, O. Joseph Conrad: a study in non-conformity. New York 1959.

Dąbrowska, M. Szkice o Conradzie. Warsaw 1959. Collected essays.

Spoerri-Müller, R. Joseph Conrad: das Problem der Vereinsamung. Winterthur 1959.

Baines, J. Conrad: a critical biography. 1960.

Cook, A. Plot as discovery: Conrad, Dostoevsky and Faulkner. In his The meaning of fiction, Detroit 1960.

Dean, L. F. (ed). Heart of darkness: backgrounds and criticisms. Englewood Cliffs NJ 1960.

Gillon, A. The eternal solitary: a study of Conrad. New York 1960.

— Cosmopolitanism in Conrad's work. In Proceedings of the 4th Congress of the International Comparative Lit Assoc 2 vols Hague 1966.

Guetti, J. The rhetoric of Conrad. Amherst 1960.

— The limits of metaphor: a study of Melville, Conrad and Faulkner. Ithaca 1967.

Harkness, B. (ed). Conrad's Heart of darkness and The critics. San Francisco 1960. Text and collection of essays.
— Conrad's Secret sharer and the critics. Belmont Calif 1962. Text and collection of essays. Contains 2 new articles: D. Curley, Legate of the ideal (rptd in Mudrick 1966, below); R. A. Gettmann and B. Harkness, Morality and psychology in The secret sharer.

Krzyżanowski, L. (ed). Joseph Conrad: centennial essays. New York 1960. Includes A. Janta, Conrad's place and rank in American letters [consists chiefly of answers to a questionnaire]; Krzyżanowski, Conrad's Prince Roman: fact and fiction; P. Mroczkowski, A glance back at the romantic Conrad: The lagoon; A. Janta, A Conrad family heirloom at Harvard [the 'Bobrowska album', containing Tuan Jim: a sketch earlier transcribed by Janta in Tarnawski, W. (ed), Conrad żywy, 1957, above, with slight misnumeration of pages]; Krzyżanowski, Conrad: some Polish documents; Gillon, A. Conrad in present-day Poland; and Krzyżanowski's bibliographical note (see Bibliographies, above). Mostly rptd (rev) from The Polish Review.

Karl, F. R. A reader's guide to Conrad. New York 1960.

Krieger, M. Conrad: action, inaction and extremity. In his The tragic vision: variations on a theme in literary interpretation, New York [1960].

Baarner, P. Stephen Crane and Conrad. In Kleine Beiträge zur amerikanischen Literaturgeschichte. Ed H. Galinsky and H.-J. Lang, Heidelberg 1961.

Brown, D. From Heart of darkness to Nostromo: an approach to Conrad. In Pelican guide to English literature vol 7, The modern age, ed B. Ford 1961.

Jabłkowska, R. Joseph Conrad 1857-1924. Warsaw 1961. In Polish.
— (ed). Joseph Conrad Korzeniowski. Warsaw 1964. Selection of biographical and critical material by and about Conrad. In Polish.

Gurko, L. Conrad: giant in exile. 1962.
— The two lives of Conrad. New York [1965].

Miyazaki, K. Conrad's novels. Tokyo 1962.

Hay, E. K. The political novels of Conrad. Chicago 1963.

Kimbrough, R. (ed). Heart of darkness. New York 1963. Text and collection of essays.

Kocówna, B. (ed). Wspomnienia i studia o Conradzie. Warsaw 1963.

Moseley, E. M. Christ as tragic hero: Conrad's Lord Jim. In his Pseudonyms of Christ in the modern novel, Pittsburgh [1963].

Stewart, J. I. M. Conrad. In his Eight modern writers, Oxford 1963 (OHEL).
— Joseph Conrad. 1968.

Tanner, P. A. Conrad: Lord Jim. 1963 (Studies in English Literature no 12).

Whittemore, R. The fascination of the abomination— Wells, Shaw, Ford, Conrad. In his The fascination of the abomination, New York 1963.

Cox, C. B. Nostromo. Oxford 1964 (Notes on English Literature).

Hoffman, F. J. Violence and decorum [in Stendhal, James, Conrad]. In his The mortal no: death and the modern imagination, Princeton 1964.

Watt, I. Conrad: alienation and commitment. In The English mind: studies in the English moralists presented to Basil Willey, ed H. S. Davies and G. Watson, Cambridge 1964.

Boyle, T. E. Symbol and meaning in the fiction of Conrad. Hague 1965.

Goetsch, P. Conrad: Nostromo. In Der moderne englische Roman: Interpretationen, ed H. Oppel, Berlin 1965.

Miller, J. H. Conrad. In his Poets of reality, 1965.

Najder, Z. Nad Conradem. Warsaw 1965. Essays.

Said, E. W. Conrad—Nostromo: record and reality. In Approaches to the twentieth-century novel, ed J. Unterecker, New York 1965.
— Conrad and the fiction of autobiography. Cambridge Mass 1966.

Craemer, T. Der Stil im Frühwerk Conrads. Hamburg 1966.

Mudrick, M. (ed). Conrad: a collection of critical essays. Englewood Cliffs NJ [1966].

Reinecke, G. F. Conrad's Victory: psychomachy, Christian symbols and theme. In Explorations of literature, ed R. D. Reck, Baton Rouge 1966.

Sherry, N. Conrad's Eastern world. Cambridge 1966.

Theumer, E. Symbolische Erzählstruktur bei Conrad. Bonn 1966.

Fleishman, A. Conrad's politics. Baltimore 1967.

Hodges, R. R. The dual heritage of Conrad. Hague 1967.

Meyer, B. C. Joseph Conrad: a psychoanalytic biography. Princeton 1967.

Rosenfield, C. Paradise of snakes: an archetypal analysis of Conrad's political novels. Chicago 1967.

Sandison, A. Conrad. In his Wheel of empire: a study of the imperial idea in some late nineteenth- and early twentieth-century fiction, 1967.

Wolpers, T. Formen mythisierenden Erzählens in der modernen Prosa: Conrad im Vergleich mit Joyce, Lawrence und Faulkner. In Lebende Antike: Symposium für R. Sühnel, ed H. Meller and H.-J. Zimmermann, Berlin 1967.

Yelton, D. C. Mimesis and metaphor: an inquiry into the genesis and s cope of Conrad's symbolic imagery. The Hague 1967.

Kirschner, P. Conrad: the psychologist as artist. Edinburgh 1968.

Leech, C. The shaping of time: Nostromo and Under the volcano. In Imagined worlds, ed M. Mack and I. Gregor, 1968.

Liljegren, S. B. Conrad as a prober of feminine hearts: notes on the novel The rescue. Uppsala 1968 (Essays and Stud on Eng Lang and Lit).

Sutton, M. (ed). Conrad: The nigger of the Narcissus. New York 1968.

Graver, L. Conrad's short fiction. Berkeley 1969.

Heimer, J. W. Look on—make no sound: Conrad's fiction. In Studies in the humanities, ed W. F. Grayburn, Indiana 1969.

Hoffman, S. de V. Comedy and form in the fiction of Conrad. Hague 1969.

Kuehn, R. E. (ed). Twentieth-century interpretations of Lord Jim: a collection of critical essays. Englewood Cliffs NJ 1969. All essays previously pbd.

Articles in Periodicals

For lists of the early reviews of Conrad's works, see the bibliographies by Lohf and Sheehy and by Ehrsam, above. For a more complete list of explications and other notes, see M. Beebe, Criticism of Conrad, Modern Fiction Stud 10 1964, and Ehrsam, above. Articles in Polish on Conrad are not listed here: for these see Lohf and Sheehy, Ehrsam and Krzyżanowski's supplementary Note, above. For anthologies of articles in Polish, see the books ed B. Kocówna, 1963, and R. Jabłkowska, 1964, above. For a select list of articles in Polish, see the bibliography appended to A. Busza, Conrad's Polish literary background, Antemurale 10 1966, below.

Davray, H.-D. Lettres anglaises. Mercure de France 31 1899.
— Conrad. Mercure de France 1 Oct 1924.

Waliszewski, A. K. Un cas de naturalisation littéraire. Revue des Revues 15 Dec 1903.

Clifford, H. The genius of Conrad. North Amer Rev 178 1904.
— Conrad: some scattered memories. Bookman's Jnl 11 1924.

Galsworthy, J. Conrad: a disquisition. Fortnightly Rev 89 1908; rptd in his Two essays on Conrad, 1930.
— Reminiscences of Conrad. Scribner's Mag 77 1925; rptd in his Castles in Spain, 1927, and in his Two essays on Conrad, above.

Gibbon, P. Conrad, an appreciation. Bookman (London) 39 1911.

Smet, J. de. Conrad. Mercure de France 1 May 1912.

James, H. The younger generation. TLS 19 March, 2 April 1914; rptd, rev and enlarged, in his Notes on novelists, 1914 (as The new novel).

Bendz, E. P. Conrad, sexagenarian. E Stud 51 1918.

Cutler, F. W. Why Marlow? Sewanee Rev 26 1918.

Robertson, J. M. The novels of Conrad. North Amer Rev 208 1918.

Gwynn, S. The novels of Conrad. Edinburgh Rev 231 1920.

McFee, W. The sea—and Conrad. Bookman (New York) 53 1921.

—— Rolling home. Saturday Rev of Lit 1 1924.

—— Conrad after fourteen years. Yale Univ Lib Gazette 13 1938.

Clarke, G. H. Conrad and his art. Sewanee Rev 30 1922.

Ould, H. Conrad's first play. Eng Rev 35 1922.

Curle, R. H. P. Conrad in the East. Yale Rev 12 1923.

—— Conrad's last novel. Bookmark 1 1925.

—— The last of Conrad. Mentor 13 1925.

—— The personality of Conrad. Edinburgh Rev 241 1925.

—— Conrad as a letter-writer. New York Herald Tribune 30 Sept 1928.

—— Conrad: ten years after. Virginia Quart Rev 10 1934. Also in Fortnightly Rev 142 1934.

—— Conrad as I remember him. Contemporary Rev 196 1959.

Jean-Aubry, G. Joseph Conrad et la France. Figaro Supplément Littéraire 21 April 1923.

—— The inner history of Conrad's Suspense. Bookman's Jnl 13 1926.

—— Une idylle de Conrad à l'Ile Maurice. Figaro 14 May 1932.

—— La Pologne dans la vie et l'oeuvre de Conrad. Pologne Littéraire 15 May 1932.

Overton, G. M. In the kingdom of Conrad. Bookman (New York) 57 1923; rptd in his American nights entertainment, New York 1923, and Authors of the day, New York [1924].

Woolf, V. Mr Conrad: a conversation. Nation & Athenaeum 1 Sept 1923; rptd in her Captain's death bed, New York [1950].

—— Conrad. TLS 14 Aug 1924; rptd in her Common reader, 1924.

Allen, C. K. Conrad. Contemporary Rev 125 1924.

Hoffmann, R. Proportion and incident in Conrad and Arnold Bennett. Sewanee Rev 32 1924.

Hommage à Conrad. Nouvelle Revue Française 135 1924. Contributors include Gide (Joseph Conrad, tr in Stallman 1960, above), Valéry, H.-R. Lenormand (Note sur un séjour de Conrad en Corse, excerpt tr in Stallman), G. Jean-Aubry, E. Estaunié, A. Chevrillon, A. Maurois, E. Jaloux, J. Kessel, R. Francillon, R. Fernández (L'art de Conrad, tr in his Messages, 1927, and in Stallman), A. Saugère.

Moult, T. Conrad. Quart Rev (New York) 242 1924.

—— The life and work of Conrad. Yale Rev 14 1925.

Shand, J. Some notes on Conrad. Criterion 3 1924; rptd in Stallman 1960, above.

Shanks, E. Conrad. London Mercury 9 1924; rptd in his Second essays on literature, 1927.

Sholl, A. M. Conrad. Catholic World 119 1924.

Transatlantic Rev 2 1924. Conrad supplement. Contributions by F. M. Ford (subsequently forming pt of his Conrad: a personal remembrance), H.-R. Lenormand, Hemingway, R. McAlwan, E. C. Mayne and A. Potocki.

Chew, S. C. et al. Essays on Suspense. Saturday Rev of Lit 14, 21 Nov 1925.

Conrad, Jessie. Conrad's share in The nature of a crime and his Congo diary. Bookman's Jnl 12 1925.

—— The romance of The rescue. Ibid.

—— Joseph Conrad. Bookmark 1 1925.

—— Conrad's skill as an artist. Saturday Rev of Lit 3 1926.

Davidson, D. Conrad's directed indirections. Sewanee Rev 33 1925.

De Gruyter, J. A master of English: Suspense, by Conrad. E Studies 7 1925.

Gordon, W. Joseph Conrad. Queen's Quart 32 1925.

Hogarth, H. The novels of Conrad. London Quart Rev 143 1925.

Mentor (New York) 13 1925. Conrad memorial no. Contributors: R. Curle, R. H. Platt, C. Morley.

Roberts, C. Conrad: a reminiscence. Bookman (New York) 61 1925. Also in Bookman (London) 69 1925.

Kellett, E. E. A note on Conrad. London Mercury 13 1926; rptd in his Reconsiderations, Cambridge 1928.

Mégroz, R. L. Conrad, man and artist. Bookman (London) 70 1926.

Randall, J. H. Conrad: his outlook on life. Unity (Chicago) 96 1926.

Villard, L. Conrad et les mémorialistes—à propos de Suspense. Rev Anglo-américaine 3 1926.

Blunden, E. A Conrad repository. London Mercury 17 1927.

Golding, H. J. Glimpses of Conrad. Standard 14 1927.

Żeromski, S. Joseph Conrad. Nineteenth Century 101 1927.

Austin, H. P. Conrad and the ironic attitude. Fortnightly Rev 130 1928.

Chevrillon, P. L'homme dans le roman marin de Conrad. Revue Anglo-américaine 5 1928.

Cross, W. L. The illusions of Conrad. Yale Rev 17 1928.

Danchin, F. C. Songs of the sea. Les Langues Modernes 26 1928. Kipling and Conrad.

Follett, W. Conrad 1907–: a humble apology. Bookman (New York) 67 1928.

Ford, F. M. On Conrad's vocabulary. Ibid. Pt subsequently rev and included in his introd to Conrad's The sisters, 1928.

—— Working with Conrad. Yale Rev 18 1929; rptd in his Return to yesterday, 1931.

—— Conrad and the sea. Amer Mercury 35 1935; rptd in his Portraits from life, New York 1937, London 1938 (as Mightier than the sword).

Garnett, E. Conrad. 1, Impressions and beginnings; 2, The long hard struggle for success. Century Mag 115 1928.

Dierlamm, G. Joseph Conrad. Zeitschrift für Französischen und Englischen Unterricht 28 1929.

Douglas, R. My boyhood with Conrad. Cornhill Mag 66 1929.

Fisher, E. E. Conrad as novelist. Holborn Rev 20 1929.

Freissler, E. W. Conrad in Deutschland. Neue Rundschau 40 1929.

Thompson, A. R. The humanism of Conrad. Sewanee Rev 37 1929.

Cox, S. Conrad: the teacher as artist. Eng Jnl 19 1930.

Hicks, G. Conrad after five years. New Republic 8 Jan 1930.

Lütken, O. Conrad in the Congo. London Mercury 22 1930; reply by Jessie Conrad, and rejoinder by Lütken, ibid.

Blüth, R. Conrad et Dostoiweski: le problème du crime et du châtiment. Vie Intellectuelle 10 May 1931.

Braybrooke, P. Conrad: an appreciation. Dublin Rev 189 1931.

Coleman, A. P. Polonisms in the English of Conrad's Chance. MLN 46 1931.

De Tonquédec, J. Le message de Conrad. Études 5 July 1931.

Anthony, I. The illusion of Conrad. Bookman (New York) 74 1932.

Cadot, R. Conrad et le navire. Revue de l'Enseignement des Langues Vivantes 49 1932.

—— Les traits moraux de la mer dans l'oeuvre de Conrad. Revue de l'Enseignement des Langues Vivantes 50 1933.

Hourcade, P. Les hommes de Conrad. Cahiers du Sud 20 1933.

Wellek, R. Joseph Conrad. Eng Post (Prague) 1 1933.

Whiting, G. W. Conrad's revision of six of his short stories. PMLA 48 1933.
— Conrad's revision of Lord Jim. Eng Jnl 23 1934.
— Conrad's revision of The lighthouse in Nostromo. PMLA 52 1937.
Franzen, E. Über Conrad. Neue Rundschau 45 1934.
Strawson, H. Conrad—master mariner and master novelist. London Quart Rev 159 1934.
Wohlfarth, P. Conrad und die Rahmenerzählung. Die Literatur 36 1934.
— Conrad als Geschichtserzähler. Schweizer Rundschau 60 1961.
— Conrad and Germany. German Life & Letters 16 1963.
Wollnick, L. Conrad: en kritisk studie. Edda 34 1934.
Ferguson, J. D. The plot of Conrad's The duel. MLN 50 1935.
Lillard, R. G. Irony in Hardy and Conrad. PMLA 50 1935.
'Maurois, André' (E. S. W. Herzog). Conrad. Revue Hebdomadaire 6, 13 April 1935.
Wood, M. H. A source of Conrad's Suspense. MLN 50 1935.
Glenutt, R. Conrad—twelve years after. Cornhill Mag 154 1936.
Gordan, J. D. The Rajah Brooke and Conrad. SP 35 1938.
— The Ranee Brooke and Conrad. SP 37 1939.
Süskind, W. E. Joseph Conrad. Neue Rundschau 49 1938.
Clemens, F. Conrad's favorite bedside book: Wallace's Malay Archipelago. South Atlantic Quart 38 1939.
— Conrad as a geographer. Scientific Monthly 51 1940.
— Conrad's Malaysia. College Eng 2 1941.
Ehrentreich, A. Verwendung von Leitmotiven bei Conrad. Neuphilologische Monatsschrift 10 1939.
Hohott, C. Über Conrad. Hochland 36 1939.
Fletcher, J. V. Ethical symbolism in Conrad. College Eng 2 1940.
Zabel, M. D. Conrad: The secret sharer. New Republic 21 April 1941.
— Conrad: chance and recognition. Sewanee Rev 53 1945.
Wagenknecht, E. 'Pessimism' in Hardy and Conrad. College Eng 3 1942.
Dąbrowski, M. An interview with Conrad. Amer Scholar 13 1944. Tr A. Jezierski.
Dean, L. F. Tragic pattern in Conrad's Heart of darkness. College Eng 6 1944.
Roditi, E. Trick perspectives. Virginia Quart Rev 20 1944.
Wright, W. F. Conrad's critical views. Research Stud of State College of Washington 12 1944.
— Conrad's The rescue, from serial to book. Research Stud of State College of Washington 13 1945.
— How Conrad tells a story. Prairie Schooner 21 1947.
Brown, E. K. James and Conrad. Yale Rev 35 1945.
Webster, H. T. Conrad: a reinterpretation of five novels. College Eng 7 1945.
— Conrad's changes in narrative conception in the manuscripts of Typhoon and other stories and Victory. PMLA 64 1949.
Morris, R. L. The classical references in Conrad's fiction. College Eng 7 1946.
— Eliot's Game of chess and Conrad's Return. MLN 65 1950.
Halle, L. J. Conrad: an enigma decoded. Saturday Rev of Lit 31 1948.
Martin, E. Conrad, romancier de la mer. Les Langues Modernes 42 1948.
Haugh, R. F. Conrad and revolution. College Eng 10 1949.
— The structure of Lord Jim. College Eng 13 1951.
— Death and consequences: Conrad's attitude toward fate. Univ of Kansas City Rev 18 1952.
'Orwell, George' (E. A. Blair). Conrad's place and rank in English letters. Wiadomości (London) 10 April 1949.
Stallman, R. W. Conrad and The secret sharer. Accent 9 1949; rptd in Stallman, 1960 above.

— The structure and symbolism of Conrad's Victory. Western Rev 13 1949.
— Conrad and The great Gatsby. Twentieth Century Lit 1 1955; rptd in his The houses that James built, East Lansing 1961.
— Conrad criticism today. Sewanee Rev 67 1959; rptd in Stallman, 1960, above.
— Time and The secret agent. Texas Stud in Lit & Lang 1 1959.
Young, V. Conrad: outline for a reconsideration. Hudson Rev 2 1949.
— Trial by water: Conrad's The nigger of the Narcissus. Accent 12 1952.
— Lingard's folly: the last subject. Kenyon Rev 15 1953. Last 2 items rptd in Stallman, 1960, above.
Arcangeli, F. Per un racconto di Conrad. Paragone 1 1950.
Ure, P. Character and imagination in Conrad. Cambridge Jnl 3 1950.
Weber, D. C. Conrad's Lord Jim. Colby Lib Quart 2 1950.
Gatch, K. H. Conrad's Axel. SP 48 1951.
Lehmann, J. On re-reading The rover. World Rev 28 1951; rptd in his The open night, 1952.
Miller, J. E. The nigger of the Narcissus: a re-examination. PMLA 66 1951.
Warren, R. P. Nostromo. Sewanee Rev 59 1951; rptd as introd to Modern Library edn of the novel; as 'The great mirage': Conrad and Nostromo, in his Selected essays, New York 1958; and in Stallman, 1960, above.
Wilson, A. H. The complete narrative of Conrad. Susquehanna Univ Stud 4 1951.
— The great theme in Conrad. Susquehanna Univ Stud 5 1953.
Day, A. G. Pattern in Lord Jim: one jump after another. College Eng 13 1952.
Bachrach, A. G. H. Conrad's western eye. Neophilologus 37 1953.
Bantock, G. H. The two 'moralities' of Conrad. EC 3 1953.
— Conrad and politics. ELH 25 1958.
Jahier, P. L'uomo Conrad. Paragone 4 1953.
Russell, B. Portraits from memory: 5, Conrad. Listener 17 Sept 1953; rptd in his Portraits from memory, 1.
Sherbo, A. Conrad's Victory and Hamlet. N & Q 198 1953.
Benson, C. Conrad's two stories of initiation. PMLA 69 1954. The secret sharer; The shadow line.
Collins, H. R. Kurtz, the cannibals and the second-rate helmsman. Western Humanities Rev 8 1954.
Harkness, B. The epigraph of Conrad's Chance. Nineteenth-Century Fiction 9 1954.
— The secret of The secret sharer bared. College Eng 27 1965.
Mudrick, M. Conrad and the terms of modern criticism. Hudson Rev 7 1954.
— The artist's conscience and The nigger of the Narcissus. Nineteenth-Century Fiction 11 1957.
— The originality of Conrad. Hudson Rev 9 1958-9. Rptd in Mudrick [1966], above.
Bien, H. Conrad und der Anarchismus. Zeitschrift für Anglistik und Amerikakunde 3 1955.
Chaikin, M. Zola and Conrad's The idiots. SP 52 1955.
Feder, L. Marlow's descent into hell. Nineteenth-Century Fiction 9 1955; rptd in Stallman 1960, above.
Hagan, J. The design of Conrad's The secret agent. ELH 22 1955.
Modern Fiction Studies 1 1955. Conrad special no. Contains W. Carroll, The novelist as artist; R. F. Haugh, Conrad's Chance: 'progression d'effet'; W. Lynskey, The role of the silver in Nostromo; J. H. Wills, Adam, Axel and 'Il Conde' (rptd in Stallman, 1960, above); W. F. Wright, 'The truth of my own sensations'; M. Beebe, Criticism of Conrad: a selected checklist.
Schwab, A. T. Conrad's American friend: correspondence with James Huneker. MP 52 1955.
— Conrad's American speeches and his reading from Victory. MP 62 1965.

Thale, J. Marlow's quest. UTQ 24 1955; rptd in Stallman 1960, above.
— The narrator as hero. Twentieth-Century Lit 3 1957. On Heart of darkness and The great Gatsby.
Worth, G. J. Conrad's debt to Maupassant in the preface to The nigger of the Narcissus. JEGP 54 1955.
Cambon, G. Giacobbe e l'angelo in Melville e Conrad. Letteratura 4 1956.
Davis, H. E. Symbolism in The nigger of the Narcissus. Twentieth-Century Lit 2 1956.
Evans, R. O. Conrad's underworld. Modern Fiction Stud 2 1956. On Heart of darkness. Comments by W. B. Stein, ibid, and S. Gross 3 1957. Reply by Evans 3 1957. All rptd in Stallman, 1960, above.
Vidan, I. One source of Conrad's Nostromo. RES 7 1956.
— Rehearsal for Nostromo: Conrad's share in Romance. Studia Romanica et Anglica Zagrabiensia no 12 1961.
— Perspective of Nostromo. Studia Romanica et Anglica Zagrabiensia no 13–14 1962.
— and J. McLauchlan. The politics of Nostromo. EC 17 1967.
Bache, W. B. Nostromo and the Snows of Kilimanjaro. MLN 72 1957.
Burgess, O. N. Conrad: the old and the new criticism. Australian Quart 29 1957.
A critical symposium on Conrad: O. Warner, J. Wain, W. W. Robson, R. Freislich, T. Hopkinson, J. Baines, R. Curle. London Mag 4 1957.
Gross, S. L. Conrad and All the king's men. Twentieth-Century Lit 3 1957.
— Hamlet and Heyst again. N & Q 204 1959.
— The devil in Samburan: Jones and Ricardo in Victory. Nineteenth-Century Fiction 16 1961.
— Conrad's revision of Amy Foster. N & Q 208 1963.
Hough, G. Chance and Conrad. Listener 26 Dec 1957; rptd, enlarged, in his Image and experience, 1960.
Karl, F. R. Conrad's debt to Dickens. N & Q 202 1957.
— Conrad's literary theory. Criticism 2 1960.
— Conrad's waste land: moral anarchy in The secret agent. Four Quarters 9 1960.
— Introduction to the Danse macabre: Conrad's Heart of darkness. Modern Fiction Stud 14 1968.
Kaye, J. B. Conrad's Under western eyes and Mann's Doctor Faustus. Comparative Lit 9 1957.
Kirschner, P. Conrad and the film. Quart of Film, Radio & Television 11 1957.
— Conrad and Maupassant. REL 6 1965.
— Conrad and Maupassant: moral solitude and A smile of fortune. REL 7 1966.
— Conrad: an uncollected article [The silence of the sea]. N & Q 213 1968.
Maser, F. E. The philosophy of Conrad. Hibbert Jnl 56 1957.
Mazzotti, G. Sul 'metodo inversivo' di Conrad. Rivista di Letterature Moderne e Comparate 10 1957.
Miłosz, C. Conrad in Polish eyes. Atlantic Monthly 200 1957. Rptd in Stallman 1960, above.
Mroczkowski, P. Heart of darkness revisited. Roczniki Humanistyczne 6 1957.
— A Polish view of Conrad. Listener 12 Dec 1957.
— The gnomic element in Conrad. Kwartalnik Neofilologiczny no 3 1958.
Peterkiewicz, J. Patriotic irritability: Conrad and Poland. Twentieth-Century Lit 162 1957.
Stein, W. B. Buddhism and the Heart of darkness. Western Humanities Rev 9 1957.
David, H. E. Conrad's revisions of The secret agent: a study in literary impressionism. MLQ 19 1958.
Dowden, W. S. The light and the dark: imagery and thematic development in Conrad's Heart of darkness. Rice Institute Pamphlets 44 1958.
— The 'illuminating quality': imagery and theme in The secret agent. Rice Institute Pamphlets 47 1960.
— Almayer's folly and Lord Jim: a study in the development of Conrad's imagery. Rice Univ Stud 51 1965.

Friedman, N. Criticism and the novel: Hardy...Conrad [et al]. Antioch Rev 18 1958.
Jurg, U. Conrad und das Problem des Selbstverständnisses. Die Neueren Sprachen 8 1958.
Kimpel, B. and T. C. D. Eaves. The geography and history in Nostromo. MP 56 1958.
Knopf, A. A. Conrad: a footnote to publishing history. Atlantic Monthly 201 1958.
Kreisel, H. Conrad and the dilemma of the uprooted man. Tamarack Rev no 7 1958.
Leavis, F. R. Conrad. Sewanee Rev 66 1958.
Levin, G. H. An allusion to Tasso in Conrad's Chance. Nineteenth-Century Fiction 13 1958.
— The scepticism of Marlow. Twentieth-Century Lit 3 1958.
Mayoux, J.-J. Conrad: l'homme et sa liberté; Conrad: l'enfer des consciences. Lettres Nouvelles no 56, 57 1958.
Moynihan, W. T. Conrad's The end of the tether: a new reading. Modern Fiction Stud 4 1958; rptd in Stallman 1960, above.
Watt, I. Conrad criticism and The nigger of the Narcissus. Nineteenth-Century Fiction 12 1958.
— Story and idea in Conrad's The shadow line. CQ 2 1960.
Hainsworth, J. D. An approach to Nostromo. Use of English 10 1959.
Halverson, J. and I. Watt. The original Nostromo: Conrad's source. RES 10 1959.
Kocmanová, J. The revolt of the workers in the novels of Gissing, James and Conrad. Brno Stud in Eng 1 1959.
Krieger, M. Conrad's youth: a naive opening to art and life. College Eng 20 1959.
Morgan, G. Captain Korzeniowski's Prince Roman: natural allusion in Conrad's patriotic tale. Études Slaves et Est-Européennes 4 1959.
— Conrad, Madach et Calderon. Études Slaves et Est-Européennes 4 1959.
— Narcissus afloat. Humanities Assoc Bull 15 1964.
Resink, G. J. De archipel voor Conrad. Bijdragen tot de Taal-, Land- en Volkenkunde 115 1959.
— De excentrieke Lord Jim; Marlow-Almayer-Havelaar; Stuurman Korzeniowski ontmoet Shawlman. De Gids 124 1961. Max Havelaar, by E. Douwes Dekker.
— Jozef Korzeniowski's voornaamste lectuur betreffende Indonesië. Bijdragen tot de Taal-, Land- en Volkenkunde 117 1961.
— Axel Heyst and the second king of the Cocos Islands. E Studies 44 1963.
— Conradiaanse interraciale vriendschappen. Forum der Letteren 6 1965.
— Tristram [Shandy], Max [Havelaar] en Jim. De Nieuwe Stem 20 1965.
— Samburan encantada. E Studies 47 1966.
Sawyer, A. S. Conrad: a centenary review. Canadian Slavonic Papers 4 1959.
Vančura, Z. The negro in the white man's ship: a critica triptych. Prague Stud in English 8 1959.
Widmer, K. Conrad's Pyrrhic victory. Twentieth-Century Lit 5 1959.
Bowen, R. O. Loyalty and tradition in Conrad. Renascence 12 1960.
Brennan, J. X. and S. Gross. The problem of moral values in Conrad and Faulkner. Personalist 41 1960.
Gose, E. B. Cruel devourer of the world's light: The secret agent. Nineteenth-Century Fiction 15 1960.
— Pure exercise of imagination: archetypal symbolism in Lord Jim. PMLA 79 1964.
Greenberg, R. A. The presence of Mr Wang [in Victory]. Boston Univ Stud in Eng 4 1960.
Hay, E. K. Lord Jim: from sketch to novel. Comparative Lit 12 1960.
Herndon, R. The genesis of Conrad's Amy Foster. SP 57 1960.
Holmes, K. S. Lord Jim: Conrad's alienated man. Descant 4 1960.

Hunt, K. W. Lord Jim and The return of the native: a contrast. Eng Jnl 49 1960.

Leiter, L. H. Echo structures: Conrad's The secret sharer. Twentieth-Century Lit 5 1960.

Marsh, D. R. C. Moral judgments in The secret agent. Eng Stud in Africa 3 1960.

Newman, P. B. Conrad and the Ancient mariner. Kansas Mag 1960.

— The drama of conscience and recognition in Lord Jim. Midwest Quart 6 1965.

Stavrou, C. N. Conrad, Camus and Sisyphus. Audience 7 1960.

Wilcox, S. C. Conrad's 'complicated presentations' of symbolic imagery in Heart of darkness'. PQ 39 1960.

Wright, E. C. The defining function of vocabulary in Conrad's The rover. South Atlantic Quart 59 1960.

Beker, M. Virginia Woolf's appraisal of Conrad. Studia Romanica et Anglica Zagrabiensia no 12 1961.

Cossman, A. M. and G. W. Whiting. The essential Jim. Nineteenth-Century Fiction 16 1961.

Kerf, R. Typhoon and The shadow line: a re-examination. Revue des Langues Vivantes no 6 1961.

— The nigger of the Narcissus and the ms version of The rescue. E Studies 44 1963.

— Ethics versus aesthetics: a clue to the deterioration of Conrad's art. Revue des Langues Vivantes 31 1965.

— Symbol hunting in Conradian land. Revue des Langues Vivantes 32 1966.

Lordi, R. J. The three emissaries of evil: their psychological relationship in Conrad's Victory. College Eng 23 1961.

Masback, F. J. Conrad's Jonahs. College Eng 22 1961.

Michel, L. A. The absurd predicament in Conrad's political novels. College Eng 23 1961.

Tillyard, E. M. W. The secret agent reconsidered. EC 11 1961; rptd in Mudrick [1966], above.

Wills, J. H. Conrad's The secret sharer. Univ of Kansas City Rev 28 1961.

— Conrad's Typhoon: a triumph of organic art. North Dakota Quart 30 1962.

— A neglected masterpiece: Conrad's Youth. Texas Stud in Lit & Lang 4 1962.

Allen, J. Conrad's river. Columbia Univ Forum 5 1962.

Brady, M. B. Conrad's whited sepulcher [in Heart of darkness]. College Eng 24 1962; replies by T. C. Kishler and Brady, ibid.

Dike, D. A. The tempest of Axel Heyst. Nineteenth-Century Fiction 17 1962.

Fleischmann, W. B. Conrad's Chance and Bergson's Laughter. Renascence 14 1962.

Freeman, R. Conrad's Nostromo: a source and its use. Modern Fiction Stud 7 1962.

Green, J. D. Diabolism, pessimism and democracy: notes on Melville and Conrad. Modern Fiction Stud 8 1962.

Gross, H. Aschenbach and Kurtz: the cost of civilization. Centennial Rev 6 1962.

Hertz, R. N. The scene of Mr Verloc's murder in The secret agent: a study of Conrad's narrative and dramatic method. Personalist 43 1962.

Hoffmann, C. G. Point of view in The secret sharer. College Eng 23 1962.

McConnell, D. J. The heart of darkness in T. S. Eliot's The hollow men. Texas Stud in Lit & Lang 4 1962.

Smith, D. R. Nostromo and The three sisters. Stud in Eng Lit 1500–1900 2 1962.

Tanner, P. A. Nightmare and complacency: Razumov and the western eye. CQ 4 1962.

— Butterflies and beetles: Conrad's two truths. Chicago Rev 16 1963.

Toliver, H. E. Conrad's Arrow of gold and pastoral tradition. Modern Fiction Stud 8 1962.

Tomlinson, M. Conrad's integrity: Nostromo, Typhoon, The shadow-line. Melbourne Critical Rev no 5 1962.

Beebe, M. The masks of Conrad. Bucknell Rev 11 1963.

Burkhart, C. Conrad the Victorian. Eng Lit in Transition 6 1963.

Day, R. A. The rebirth of Leggatt. Lit & Psychology 13 1963.

Gillon, A. The Jews in Conrad's fiction. Chicago Jewish Forum 22 1963.

— The merchant of Esmeralda: Conrad's archetypal Jew. Polish Rev 9 1964.

— Some Polish literary motifs in the work of Conrad. Slavic & East European Jnl 10 1966.

Goetsch, P. Conrad: The secret agent. Die Neueren Sprachen 12 1963.

Graver, L. Critical confusion and Conrad's End of the tether. Modern Fiction Stud 9 1963–4.

— Conrad's first story. Stud in Short Fiction 2 1965.

Johnson, B. M. Conrad's Karain and Lord Jim. MLQ 24 1963.

— Conrad and Crane's The red badge of courage. Pbns of the Michigan Acad of Science, Arts & Letters 48 1963.

— Conrad's Falk: manuscript and meaning. MLQ 26 1965.

Martin, W. R. The captain of the Narcissus. Eng Stud in Africa 6 1963.

Maxwell, J. C. Conrad and Turgenev: a minor source for Victory. N & Q 208 1963.

Moore, C. Conrad and the novel as ordeal. PQ 42 1963.

Reid, S. A. The 'unspeakable rites' in Heart of darkness. Modern Fiction Stud 9 1963–4; rptd in Mudrick [1966], above.

Ridley, F. H. The ultimate meaning of Heart of darkness. Nineteenth-Century Fiction 18 1963.

Smith, J. O. The existential comedy of Conrad's youth. Renascence 16 1963.

Bojarski, E. A. A window on Conrad's Polish soul. Eng Lit in Transition 7 1964.

— Conrad's sentimental journey. Texas Quart 7 1964.

— Poland looks at Conrad. Books Abroad 39 1965.

— Conrad in Cardiff: impressions 1885–1896. Anglo-Welsh Rev 15 1966.

— Conrad: original ugliness. Polish–American Stud 23 1966.

— A stranger and afraid: Conrad. Eng Stud in Africa 10 1967.

— Conrad at the crossroads; from navigator to novelist, with some new biographical mysteries. Texas Quart 11 1968.

Bruffee, K. A. The lesser nightmare: Marlow's lie in Heart of darkness. MLQ 25 1964.

Hicks, J. H. Conrad's Almayer's folly: structure, theme and critics. Nineteenth-Century Fiction 19 1964.

Hodges, R. R. The four fathers of Lord Jim. Univ Rev (Kansas) 31 1964.

Hoffman, S. de V. Conrad's menagerie: animal imagery and theme. Bucknell Rev 12 1964.

— Scenes of low comedy: the comic in Lord Jim. Ball State Teachers College Forum 5 1964.

— The hole in the bottom of the pail: comedy and theme in Heart of darkness. Stud in Short Fiction 2 1965.

Levine, P. Conrad's blackness. South Atlantic Quart 63 1964.

Maclennan, D. A. C. Conrad's vision. Eng Stud in Africa 7 1964.

McIntyre, A. O. Conrad on conscience and the passions. Univ Rev (Kansas) 31 1964.

— Conrad on the functions of the mind. MLQ 25 1964.

— Conrad on writing and critics. Forum (Houston) 4–5 1964.

Modern Fiction Stud 10 1964. Conrad special no. Contains J. O. Perry, Action, vision or voice: the moral dilemmas in Conrad's tale-telling; S. Tick, The gods of Nostromo; P. Williams, The brand of Cain in The secret sharer; P. Kirschner, Conrad's strong man [Gaspar Ruiz]; J. M. Luecke, Conrad's secret and its agent; J. Zuckerman, Contrapuntal structure in Conrad's Chance; S. Kaehele and H. Gerwan, Conrad's Victory:

a reassessment; T. M. Lorch, The barrier between youth and maturity in the works of Conrad; M. Beebe, Criticism of Conrad: a selected checklist.

Stein, W. B. The heart of darkness: Bodhisattva scenario. Orient-West 9 1964.

—— Conrad's East: time, history, action and 'Maya'. Texas Stud in Lit & Lang 7 1965.

Williams, P. The matter of conscience in Conrad's Secret sharer. PMLA 79 1964.

Wolfe, P. Conrad's Mirror of the sea: an assessment. McNeese Rev 15 1964.

Yates, N. W. Social comment in The nigger of the Narcissus. PMLA 79 1964.

Zuckerman, J. A smile of fortune: Conrad's interesting failure. Stud in Short Fiction 1 1964.

Andreach, R. J. The two narrators of 'Amy Foster'. Stud in Short Fiction 2 1965.

Bass, E. The verbal failure of Lord Jim. College Eng 26 1965.

Cross, D. C. Nostromo: further sources. N & Q 210 1965.

Dudley, E. J. Three patterns of imagery in Conrad's Heart of darkness. Revue des Langues Vivantes 31 1965.

Echerus, W. J. C. James Wait and The nigger of the Narcissus. Eng Stud in Africa 8 1965.

Fleishman, A. The symbolic world of The secret agent. ELH 32 1965.

—— Conrad's last novel. Eng Lit in Transition 12 1969.

Hagopian, J. V. The pathos of Il Conde. Stud in Short Fiction 3 1965.

Hynes, S. Two Rye revolutionists [Conrad and F. M. Ford]. Sewanee Rev 73 1965.

Killam, G. D. Kurtz's country. Lock Haven Rev no 7 1965. Rptd in his Africa in English fiction, 1968.

Kinney, A. F. Jimmy Wait: Conrad's kaleidoscope. College Eng 26 1965.

McCann, C. J. Lord Jim vs. the darkness: the saving power of human involvement. College Eng 27 1965.

Malbone, R. G. 'How to be': Marlow's quest in Lord Jim. Twentieth-Century Lit 10 1965.

Moorthy, P. R. The nigger of the Narcissus. Literary Criterion (Mysore) 7 1965.

Ober, W. U. Heart of darkness: the Ancient mariner a hundred years later. Dalhousie Rev 45 1965.

O'Grady, W. On plot in modern fiction: Hardy, James and Conrad. Modern Fiction Stud 11 1965.

O'Hara, J. D. Unlearned lessons in The secret sharer. College Eng 26 1965.

Scrimgeour, G. J. Jimmy Wait and the dance of death: Conrad's Nigger of the Narcissus. CQ 7 1965.

Simmons, J. L. The dual morality in Conrad's Secret sharer. Stud in Short Fiction 2 1965.

Smith, C. C. Conrad's Chance: a dialectical novel. Thoth 6 1965.

Watts, C. T. A minor source for Nostromo. RES 16 1965.

Whitehead, L. M. Alma renamed Lena in Conrad's Victory. Eng Lang Notes 3 1965.

—— Nostromo: the tragic idea. Nineteenth-Century Fiction 23 1968.

Benson, D. R. Heart of darkness: the grounds of civilization in an alien universe. Texas Stud in Lit & Lang 7 1966.

Busza, A. Conrad's Polish literary background, and some illustrations of the influence of Polish literature on his work. Antemurale 10 1966.

Fraser, G. S. Lord Jim: the romance of irony. CQ 8 1966.

Holland, N. N. Style as character: The secret agent. Modern Fiction Stud 12 1966.

Hudspeth, R. N. Conrad's use of time in Chance. Nineteenth-Century Fiction 21 1966.

Kramer, D. Marlow, myth and structure in Lord Jim. Criticism 8 1966.

McCann, C. J. Setting as a key to the structure and meaning of Nostromo. Research Stud (Washington State Univ) 34 1966.

Maud, R. The plain tale of Heart of darkness. Humanities Assoc Bull 17 1966.

Schneider, D. J. Symbolism in Conrad's Lord Jim: the total pattern. Modern Fiction Stud 12 1966.

Tolley, A. T. Conrad's favorite story. Stud in Short Fiction 3 1966. An outpost of progress.

Tuveson, E. The creed of the confidence man. ELH 33 1966.

Wilding, M. The politics of Nostromo. EC 16 1966.

Zerbini, R. Vita e arte in Conrad. Acme 19 1966.

Allen, V. Memories of Conrad. REL 8 1967.

Cagle, W. R. The publication of Conrad's Chance. Book Collector 16 1967.

Canario, J. W. The harlequin in Heart of darkness. Stud in Short Fiction 4 1967.

Clark, C. C. The Brierly suicide: a new look at an odd ambiguity. Arlington Quart 1 1967.

Crews, F. The power of darkness. Partisan Rev 34 1967.

Curley, D. The writer and his use of material: the case of The secret sharer. Modern Fiction Stud 13 1967.

Geddes, C. Conrad and the fine art of understanding. Dalhousie Rev 47 1967.

—— The structure of sympathy: Conrad and the Chance that wasn't. Eng Lit in Transition 12 1969.

Gilley, L. Conrad's Secret sharer. Midwest Quart 8 1967.

Guidi, A. Struttura e linguaggio di Nostromo. Convivium 35 1967.

Hamer, D. Conrad: two bibliographical episodes. RES 18 1967.

Heimer, J. W. Betrayal, confession, attempted redemption and punishment in Nostromo. Texas Stud in Lit & Lang 9 1967.

—— Patterns of betrayal in the novels of Conrad. Ball State Univ Forum 8 1967.

Kilroy, J. Conrad's 'succès de curiosité': the dramatic version of The secret agent. Eng Lit in Transition 10 1967.

Purdy, S. B. On the relevance of Conrad: Lord Jim over Sverdlovsk [i.e. the 'U-2 incident' of 1 May 1960]. Midwest Quart 9 1967.

Raskin, J. Heart of darkness: the manuscript revisions. RES 18 1967.

Sherry, N. The Greenwich bomb outrage and The secret agent. RES 18 1967.

—— Conrad's ticket-of-leave apostle. MLR 64 1969.

—— Sir Ethelred in The secret agent. PQ 48 1969.

Torchiana, D. The nigger of the Narcissus: myth, mirror and metropolis. Wascana Rev 2 1967.

Walton, J. H. Mr X's 'little joke': the design of Conrad's Informer. Stud in Short Fiction 4 1967.

—— Conrad, Dickens and the detective novel. Nineteenth-Century Fiction 23 1968.

Brady, M. B. The collector-motif in Lord Jim. Bucknell Rev 16 1968.

Conradiana. College Park, Maryland 1968–.

Esslinger, P. M. A theory and three experiments: the failure of the Conrad-Ford collaboration. Western Humanities Rev 22 1968.

Jacobs, R. G. Comrade Ossipon's favourite saint: Lombroso and Conrad. Nineteenth-Century Fiction 23 1968.

Lee, R. The secret agent: structure, theme, mode. Eng Stud in Africa 11 1968.

McDonald, W. R. Conrad as a novelist of moral conflict and isolation. Iowa Eng Yearbook 13 1968.

McDowell, F. P. W. Review essay: the most recent books on Conrad. Papers on Lang & Lit 4 1968.

Ordonez, E. A. Notes on the revisions in An outcast of the Islands. N & Q 213 1968.

Reichard, H. M. The Patusan crises: a revaluation of Jim and Marlow. E Studies 49 1968.

Ursell, G. Conrad and the 'Riversdale'. TLS 11 July 1968. Conrad's quarrel with Capt McDonald.

Ruthven, K. K. The savage god: Conrad and Lawrence. CQ 10 1968.

Smith, D. R. One word more about The nigger of the Narcissus. Nineteenth-Century Fiction 23 1968.

Van Marle, A. The location of Lord Jim's Patusan. N & Q 213 1968.

Young, W. J. Conrad against himself. Critical Rev 11 1968.

Crawford, J. Another look at Youth. Research Stud (Washington) 37 1969.

Dussinger, G. R. The secret sharer: Conrad's psychological study. Texas Stud in Lit & Lang 10 1969.

Fradin, J. I. Conrad's Everyman: The secret agent. Texas Stud in Lit & Lang 11 1969.

Godshalk, W. L. Kurtz as diabolical Christ. Discourse 12 1969.

Hagan, J. Conrad's Under western eyes: the question of Razumov's 'guilt' and 'remorse'. Stud in the Novel (North Texas) 1 1969.

Higdon, D. L. Conrad's Rover: the grammar of a myth. Stud in the Novel (North Texas) 1 1969.

Hurwitz, H. The great Gatsby and Heart of darkness: the confrontation scenes. Fitzgerald-Hemingway Annual 1969.

Kitterer, D. A. Beyond the threshold in Conrad's Heart of darkness. Texas Stud in Lit & Lang 11 1969.

Low, A. Heart of darkness: the search for an occupation. Eng Lit in Transition 12 1969.

Nash, C. More light on The secret agent. Rev of Eng Stud 20 1969.

Rose, A. M. Conrad and the sirens of the decadence. Texas Stud in Lit & Lang 11 1969.

Schwarz, D. R. The self-deceiving narrator of Conrad's Il Conde. Stud in Short Fiction 6 1969.

Smoller, S. J. A note on Conrad's fall and abyss. Modern Fiction Stud 15 1969.

Stephens, R. C. Heart of darkness: Marlow's spectral moonshine. EC 19 1969.

Thomson, G. H. Conrad's later fiction. Eng Lit in Transition 12 1969.

C. P. C.

HERBERT GEORGE WELLS
1866–1946

The most important collection of Wells papers is in the Wells Archive at the Univ of Illinois at Urbana-Champaign.

Bibliographies

Chappell, F. A. A bibliography of Wells. Chicago 1924.

Wells, G. H. A bibliography of the works of Wells, 1893–1925, with some notes and comments. 1925. Enlarged and rev as The works of Wells 1887–1925: a bibliography, dictionary and subject-index, 1926. Includes a chronological list of uncollected stories, articles etc, a brief list of letters to the press, a note on trns and on parodies of Wells.

Weeks, R. P. et al. In Eng Fiction [later Eng Lit] in Transition 1 1957–8 onwards. Secondary material.

Raknem, I. In his H. G. Wells and his critics, 1962. Secondary material, including reviews.

H. G. Wells: a comprehensive bibliography compiled by the H. G. Wells Society. 1966, 1968 (rev). Includes appendices listing Wells' prefaces to books by other writers, simplified versions of his works, his contributions to books and a selection of secondary material. Announces research in progress to record, inter alia, the large amount of Wells' journalism still uncollected.

Levidova, I. and B. M. Parchevskaya. Herbert George Wells: a bibliography of Russian translations and of critical literature in Russia, 1898–1965. Moscow 1966. In Russian.

Thirsk, J. W. H. G. Wells 1866–1946: a centenary booklist. 1966.

G. N. Ray, Wells's contributions to the Saturday Rev, Library 5th ser 16 1961, and M. Timko, Wells's dramatic criticism for the Pall Mall Gazette, Library 5th ser 17 1962, contain important listings of Wells' anonymous journalism for these periodicals.

Collections and Selections

Works: Atlantic edition. 28 vols 1924–7. Texts rev by Wells, special preface by Wells to each vol, also general introd to set.

Works: Essex edition. 24 vols 1926–7.

The door in the wall, and other stories. New York 1911, London 1915 (60 copies from American sheets). Contains The door in the wall, The star, A dream of Armageddon, The cone, A moonlight fable, The diamond maker, The lord of the dynamos, The country of the blind.

Short stories. 1927, Garden City NY 1929, London 1966 (as The complete short stories). Contains The time machine, The story of the last trump (from Boon), and the stories included in The stolen bacillus, The Plattner story, Tales of space and time, Twelve stories and a dream and The country of the blind; also several stories not previously pbd in book form: My first aeroplane (1910), Little mother up the Mörderberg (1910), and The grisly folk (1921). Does not include 3 previously pbd stories: The presence by the fire (1897), Mr Marshall's Doppelgänger (1897), and The loyalty of Esau Common (1902).

Wells' social anticipations. Ed H. W. Laidler, New York 1927.

A quartette of comedies. 1928. Kipps, The history of Mr Polly, Bealby, Love and Mr Lewisham.

The scientific romances. Introd by Wells 1933. The time machine, The island of Dr Moreau, The invisible man, The war of the worlds, The first men in the moon, The food of the gods, In the days of the comet, Men like gods.

Stories of men and women in love. Preface by Wells [1933]. Love and Mr Lewisham, The passionate friends, The wife of Sir Isaac Harman, The secret places of the heart.

Seven famous novels. Preface by Wells, New York 1934. Contents as in The scientific romances (1933), except for omission of Men like gods.

Tales of wonder; Tales of life and adventure; Tales of the unexpected. Introds by F. Wells. 3 vols 1953–4.

Selected short stories. 1958 (Penguin).

H. G. Wells, journalism and prophecy 1893–1946: an anthology. Ed W. W. Wagar, Boston 1964.

The last books of Wells. Ed G. P. Wells 1968. Mind at the end of its tether, The happy turning.

§1

Prose Fiction

For details of the serial pbn of Wells' novels to 1925, see G. H. Wells' bibliography, above, which also gives details of the pbn of Wells' stories in magazines.

The chronic argonauts. Science Schools Jnl April–June 1888. Story, rptd in Bergonzi, The early Wells, 1961, §2 below.

Select conversations with an uncle, now extinct, and two other reminiscences. 1895, New York 1895. 12 'conversations' and 2 short stories, A misunderstood artist, and The man with a nose.

The time machine: an invention. 1895, New York 1895 (as by 'H. S. Wells'), [1895] (as by H. G. Wells), 1935 (with preface by Wells). Based on The chronic argonauts. For various serial versions see Bergonzi, The publication of The time machine, RES 11 1960.

The wonderful visit. 1895, New York 1895. Dramatized by Wells and St John Ervine for production at St Martin's Theatre, London 10 Feb 1921.

The stolen bacillus, and other incidents. 1895. Contains The stolen bacillus; The flowering of the strange orchid; In the Avu observatory; The triumphs of a taxidermist; A deal in ostriches; Through a window; The temptation of Harringay; The flying man; The diamond maker;

Æpyornis island; The remarkable case of Davidson's eyes; The lord of the dynamos; The Hammerpond Park burglary; A moth—genus novo; The treasure in the forest. A moth—genus novo was titled The moth in Short stories (1927), Selections above, and subsequently.

The red room. Chicago 1896 (12 copies, for copyright purposes). Short story rptd in The Plattner story, 1897, below.

The island of Dr Moreau. 1896, New York 1896.

The wheels of chance: a holiday adventure. 1896, New York 1896 (as The wheels of chance: a bicycling idyll). A dramatization, Hoopdriver's holiday, made by Wells 1903-4 was pbd (ed M. Timko) in Eng Lit in Transition 7 1964.

The Plattner story, and others. 1897. Contains The Plattner story; The argonauts of the air; The story of the late Mr Elvesham; In the abyss; The apple; Under the knife; The sea raiders; Pollock and the Porroh man; The red room; The cone; The purple pileus; The jilting of Jane; In the modern vein; A catastrophe; The lost inheritance; The sad story of a dramatic critic; A slip under the microscope.

The invisible man: a grotesque romance. 1897, New York 1897 (with epilogue), London 1900, 1953 (with introd by F. Wells), New York 1967 (introd by B. Bergonzi).

Thirty strange stories. New York 1897. Rpts contents of The Plattner story, and ten stories from The stolen bacillus. Contains 3 hitherto unpbd stories: The reconciliation, The rajah's treasure, Le mari terrible.

The war of the worlds. 1898, New York 1898.

When the sleeper wakes: a story of the years to come. 1899, New York 1899, London [1910] (rev, with preface by Wells, as The sleeper awakes), 1954 (with introd by M. Belgion).

Tales of space and time. 1900 [1899], New York 1899. Contains The crystal egg; The star; A story of the stone age; A story of the days to come; The man who could work miracles.

Love and Mr Lewisham. 1900, New York 1900, London 1954 (with introd by F. Wells).

The first men in the moon. 1901, Indianapolis 1901, London 1954 (with introd by F. Wells).

The sea lady: a tissue of moonshine. 1902, New York 1902 (as The sea lady).

Twelve stories and a dream. 1903, New York 1905. Contains Filmer; The magic shop; The valley of spiders; The truth about Pyecraft; Mr Skelmersdale in fairyland; The story of the inexperienced ghost; Jimmy Goggles the god; The new accelerator; Mr Ledbetter's vacation; The stolen body; Mr Brisher's treasure; Miss Winchelsea's heart; A dream of Armageddon.

The food of the gods, and how it came to earth. 1904, New York 1904, London 1955 (with introd by R. Seth).

A modern utopia. 1905, New York 1905, Lincoln Nebraska 1967 (with introd by M. R. Hillegas).

Kipps: the story of a simple soul. 1905, New York 1905, London 1952 (with introd by E. Shanks).

In the days of the comet. 1906, New York 1906, London 1954 (with introd by F. Wells).

The war in the air, and particularly how Mr Bert Smallways fared while it lasted. 1908, New York 1908.

Tono-Bungay. New York 1908, London 1909, 1953 (with introd by C. E. M. Joad), Boston 1966 (ed B. Bergonzi).

Ann Veronica: a modern love story. 1909, New York 1909.

The history of Mr Polly. 1910, New York 1910, London 1953 (ed F. Wells), Boston 1960 (ed G. N. Ray).

The new Machiavelli. New York 1910, London 1911.

The country of the blind, and other stories. [1911]. Contains The jilting of Jane; The cone; The stolen bacillus; The flowering of the strange orchid; In the Avu observatory; Æpyornis island; The remarkable case of Davidson's eyes; The lord of the dynamos; The moth; The treasure in the forest; The story of the late Mr Elvesham; Under the knife; The sea raiders; The

obliterated man; The Plattner story; The red room; The purple pileus; A slip under the microscope; The crystal egg; The star; The man who could work miracles; A vision of judgment; Jimmy Goggles the god; Miss Winchelsea's heart; A dream of Armageddon; The valley of spiders; The new accelerator; The truth about Pyecraft; The magic shop; The empire of the ants; The door in the wall; The country of the blind; The beautiful suit. Title story pbd separately New York 1915 (priv ptd), London 1939 (rev).

Marriage. 1912, New York 1912.

The passionate friends. 1913, New York 1913, London 1922 (abridged).

The world set free: a story of mankind. 1914, New York 1914, London 1956 (with introd by R. Calder).

The wife of Sir Isaac Harman. 1914, New York 1914.

Boon, the mind of the race, the wild asses of the devil, and the last trump: being a first selection from the literary remains of George Boon, appropriate to the times. Prepared for publication by Reginald Bliss with an ambiguous introduction by H. G. Wells. 1915, New York 1915, London 1920 (naming Wells as author).

Bealby: a holiday. 1915, New York 1915.

The research magnificent. 1915, New York 1915.

Mr Britling sees it through. 1916, New York 1916.

The soul of a bishop: a novel—with just a little love in it—about conscience and religion and the real troubles of life. 1917, New York 1917.

Joan and Peter: the story of an education. 1918, New York 1918.

The undying fire: a contemporary novel. [1919], New York 1919.

The secret places of the heart. 1922, New York 1922.

Men like gods. 1923, New York 1923.

The dream. 1924, New York 1924.

Christina Alberta's father. 1925, New York 1925.

The world of William Clissold: a novel at a new angle. 3 vols 1926, 2 vols New York 1926.

Meanwhile: the picture of a lady. 1927, New York 1927.

Mr Blettsworthy on Rampole Island. 1928, Garden City NY 1928.

The king who was a king: the book of a film. 1929, Garden City NY 1929. The film was never made.

The adventures of Tommy. 1929, New York 1967. For children.

The autocracy of Mr Parham: his remarkable adventure in this changing world. 1930, Garden City NY 1930.

The Bulpington of Blup. [1932], New York 1933.

The shape of things to come: the ultimate resolution. 1933, New York 1933. Partly historical.

Things to come: a film story based on the material contained in his history of the future, The shape of things to come. 1935, New York 1935; rptd in Two film stories, 1940.

The croquet player: a story. 1936, New York 1937.

Man who could work miracles: a film story based on the material contained in his short story [In Tales of space and time]. 1936, New York 1936. Rptd in Two film stories, 1940.

Star begotten: a biological fantasia. 1937, New York 1937.

Brynhild. 1937, New York 1937.

The Camford visitation. 1937.

The brothers: a story. 1938, New York 1938.

Apropos of Dolores. 1938, New York 1938.

The holy terror. 1939, New York 1939.

Babes in the darkling wood. 1940, New York 1940.

All aboard for Ararat. 1940, New York 1941.

You can't be too careful: a sample of life 1901-51. 1941, New York 1942.

The desert daisy. Introd by G. N. Ray, Urbana 1957. Ms (facs) of story written between 1878-80.

The wealth of Mr Waddy: a novel. Ed H. Wilson, Carbondale 1969.

Other Works

For details of the serial pbn of Wells' monographs to 1925 see G. H. Wells' bibliography above, which also gives details of the first pbn of Wells' collected newspaper articles, essays etc.

Text-book of biology. Introd by G. B. Howes. 2 vols [1893]. (University Correspondence College Tutorial ser.) Vol 1 rev 1894; subsequent revisions by A. M. Davies et al, as Text-book of zoology.

Honours physiography. 1893. With R. A. Gregory.

Certain personal matters: a collection of material, mainly autobiographical. 1898 (for 1897). Humorous essays.

Anticipations of the reaction of mechanical and scientific progress upon human life and thought. 1902 (for 1901), New York 1902, London 1914 (with introd by Wells).

The discovery of the future: a discourse delivered to the Royal Institution on January 24th, 1902. 1902, New York 1913.

Mankind in the making. 1903, New York 1904, London 1914 (with introd by Wells).

The future in America: a search after realities. 1906, New York 1906.

Faults of the Fabian. [1906] (priv ptd for Fabian Soc). Pamphlet.

Reconstruction of the Fabian Society. [1906] (priv ptd). Pamphlet.

Socialism and the family. 1906. Booklet.

The so-called science of sociology. 1907. Pamphlet; rptd in An Englishman looks at the world, 1914, below.

This misery of boots. 1907, Boston 1908. Fabian Soc pamphlet.

Will socialism destroy the home? [1907]. Independent Labour Party pamphlet; rptd in next.

New worlds for old. 1908, New York 1908, London 1917 (rev).

First & last things: a confession of faith and rule of life. 1908, New York 1908, London 1917 (rev, with new preface by Wells), 1929 (definitive edn).

Floor games. 1911, Boston 1912.

The great state: essays in construction. 1912, New York 1912 (as Socialism and the great state). By Wells, Lady Warwick et al.

The labour unrest. 1912. Pamphlet; rptd in An Englishman looks at the world, 1914, below.

War and common sense. 1913. Pamphlet; rptd (as The common sense of warfare) in An Englishman looks at the world, 1914 below.

Liberalism and its party: what are we Liberals to do? [1913]. Nat Unionist Assoc pamphlet.

Little wars: a game for boys from twelve years of age to one hundred and fifty, and for that more intelligent sort of girls who like boys' games and books. 1913, Boston 1913, London 1931 (rev).

An Englishman looks at the world: being a series of unrestrained remarks upon contemporary matters. 1914, New York 1914 (as Social forces in England and America).

The war that will end war. 1914, New York 1914. Collected articles first pbd 7–29 Aug 1914.

The end of the armament rings. New York 1914. World Peace Federation pamphlet. Rptd from previous.

The peace of the world. [1915].

The war of socialism. [1915]. Reprint of 2 chs from The war that will end war, 1914 above.

What is coming? A forecast of things after the war. 1916, New York 1916 (as What is coming? A European forecast).

The elements of reconstruction. Introd by Viscount Milner 1916. 6 letters to the Times, signed D.P.

War and the future: Italy, France and Britain at war. 1917, New York 1917 (as Italy, France and Britain at war).

God the invisible king. 1917, New York 1917.

A reasonable man's peace. 1917. Nat Council of Civil Liberties pamphlet; rptd in next.

In the fourth year: anticipations of a world peace. 1918, New York 1918, 1918 (abridged, as Anticipations of a world peace).

British nationalism and the League of Nations. 1918. League of Nations Union pamphlet.

Memorandum on propaganda policy against Germany. [1918]. In Stuart, G., Secrets of Crewe House, 1920; rptd in The common sense of war and peace, 1940, below.

History is one. [Boston 1919]. Pamphlet.

The outline of history, being a plain history of life and mankind. 1920, New York 1920, and numerous rev edns thereafter both in Britain and USA. First pbd in 24 fortnightly parts Nov 1919–Nov 1920, with footnotes by other writers, many of which do not appear in the book edns.

Russia in the shadows. 1920, New York 1921. Sunday Express articles.

The salvaging of civilisation. 1921, New York 1921.

The new teaching of history: with a reply to some recent criticisms of The outline of history. 1921.

Washington and the hope of peace. [1922], New York 1922 (as Washington and the riddle of peace). Articles rptd from New York World.

What H. G. Wells thinks about 'The mind in the making'. New York 1922, London 1923 (rev, as introd to J. H. Robinson's Mind in the making).

University of London Election. [1922]. Electoral letter.

The world, its debts, and the rich men: a speech. 1922. Election address substituted for the previous.

A short history of the world. 1922, New York 1922, and numerous rev edns thereafter.

Socialism and the scientific motive. 1923. Speech.

To the electors of London University general election, 1923, from H. G. Wells, B.Sc., Lond. [1923]. Address.

The Labour ideal of education. 1923. Pamphlet, to accompany preceding item.

A walk along the Thames embankment. 1923. Independent Labour Party booklet. Rptd from pt of ch 1 of New worlds for old, 1908, above.

The story of a great schoolmaster: being a plain account of the life and ideas of Sanderson of Oundle. 1924, New York 1924.

The P.R. Parliament. [1924]. Proportional Representation Soc pamphlet; rptd in next.

A year of prophesying. 1924, New York 1925. Articles, all previously pbd in journals and newspapers.

A forecast of the world's affairs. 1925. Rptd from These eventful years, by J. L. Garvin et al, 2 vols 1924.

Mr Belloc objects to The outline of history. 1926, New York 1926. *See* Belloc's Companion to Mr Wells's Outline of history, 1926, and his Mr Belloc still objects to Mr Wells's Outline of history, 1926.

Democracy under revision: a lecture delivered at the Sorbonne. 1927, New York 1927; rptd in The way the world is going, 1928 below.

Playing at peace. 1927. Nat Council for the Prevention of War pamphlet; rptd in The way the world is going, below.

The way the world is going: guesses and forecasts of the years ahead. 1928, Garden City NY 1929.

The open conspiracy: blue prints for a world revolution. 1928, Garden City NY 1928, London 1930 (rev), 1931 (rev, as What are we to do with our lives?).

The common sense of world peace: an address delivered to the Reichstag. 1929; rptd in After democracy, 1932, below.

Imperialism and the open conspiracy. 1929 (Criterion Miscellany 3).

The science of life: a summary of contemporary knowledge about life and its possibilities. 3 vols 1929–30, 1 vol 1931, 9 vols 1934–7 (corrected, as Science of life ser), 1 vol 1938 (rev). First pbd in 31 fortnightly parts. With J. S. Huxley and G. P. Wells.

The way to world peace. 1930. Pamphlet.

The problem of the troublesome collaborator: an account of certain difficulties in an attempt to produce a work in collaboration [The science of work and wealth], and of the intervention of the Society of Authors therein. Woking 1930 (priv ptd, 175 copies).

Settlement of the trouble between Mr Thring [Secretary of the Society of Authors] and Mr Wells: a footnote to The problem of the troublesome collaborator. [1930] (priv ptd).

What are we to do with our lives?. 1931. *See* The open conspiracy, 1928, above.

The work, wealth and happiness of mankind. 2 vols Garden City NY 1931, 1 vol London 1932, 1934 (rev), Garden City NY 1936 (as The outline of man's work and wealth).

After democracy: addresses and papers on the present world situation. 1932.

What should be done now? New York 1932. Pamphlet. Rptd from After democracy, above.

Experiment in autobiography: discoveries and conclusions of a very ordinary brain since 1866. 2 vols 1934, New York 1934, London 1966 (without portraits).

Stalin-Wells talk: the verbatim record, and a discussion by G. Bernard Shaw, H. G. Wells, J. M. Keynes, Ernst Toller et al. 1934. Pamphlet.

The new America: the new world. 1935, New York 1935. Impressions.

The anatomy of frustration: a modern synthesis. 1936, New York 1936.

The idea of a world encyclopaedia. 1936. Lecture to the Royal Institution; rptd in World brain, 1938 below.

The informative content of education. 1937. Presidential address to the education section of Br Assoc.

World brain. 1938, Garden City NY 1938. Articles and lectures.

Travels of a republican radical in search of hot water. 1939 (Penguin Special).

The fate of Homo sapiens: an unemotional statement of the things that are happening to him now and of the immediate possibilities confronting him. 1939, New York 1939.

The new world order: whether it is obtainable, how it can be attained, and what sort of world a world at peace will have to be. 1940, New York 1940.

The rights of man: or, what are we fighting for? [1940] (Penguin Special).

The common sense of war and peace: world revolution or war unending? 1940 (Penguin Special).

Two hemispheres or one world? 1940. Pamphlet.

Guide to the new world: a handbook of constructive world revolution. 1941.

The outlook for Homo sapiens: an amalgamation and modernization of two books, The fate of Homo sapiens and The new world order. 1942.

Science and the world-mind. 1942.

Phoenix: a summary of the inescapable conditions of world reorganization. 1942.

A thesis on the quality of illusion in the continuity of individual life of the higher metazoa, with particular reference to the species Homo sapiens. [1942] (priv ptd); rptd in '42 to '44, below. An abridgement pbd in Nature 1 April 1944 was rptd as a pamphlet, The illusion of personality.

The conquest of time, by H. G. Wells: written to replace his First and last things. 1942.

The new rights of man. Girard Kansas 1942. Pamphlet.

Crux ansata: an indictment of the Roman Catholic Church. 1943 (Penguin Special).

The Mosley outrage. 1943. Pamphlet.

'42 to '44: a contemporary memoir upon human behaviour during the crisis of the world revolution. 1944. Essays.

The happy turning: a dream of life. 1945.

Mind at the end of its tether. 1945.

There is unrptd journalism from Wells' early years in Science Schools Jnl, Fortnightly Rev, Saturday Rev, Nature,

Univ Correspondent *and* Educational Times. *Much of this is listed by Raknem (see Bibliographies, above). See also the endnote to Bibliographies, above. For Wells' frequent contributions (chs or introds) to books and pamphlets, see bibliographies by G. H. Wells and the H. G. Wells Soc.*

Letters

Edel, L. and G. N. Ray (ed). Henry James and Wells: a record of their friendship, their debate on the art of fiction and their quarrel. Urbana 1958.

Gerber, H. E. (ed). Some letters of Wells, from a private collection. Eng Fiction in Transition 3 1960.

Wilson, H. (ed). Arnold Bennett and Wells: a record of a personal and literary friendship. Urbana 1960.

Gettmann, R. A. (ed). Gissing and Wells: their friendship and correspondence. 1961.

Other sources of Wells letters include W. H. G. Armytage, Sir Richard Gregory, 1957; G. Jean-Aubry, 20 letters to Joseph Conrad, 1926; G. Richards, Memories of a misspent youth, 1932, and Author hunting, 1934; M. Light, Wells and Sinclair Lewis, Eng Fiction in Transition 5 1962; 'Geoffrey West' (G. H. Wells), H. G. Wells: a sketch for a portrait, 1930.

§2
Books and Chapters in Books

Chesterton, G. K. Wells and the giants. In his Heretics, 1905.

Craufurd, A. H. The religion of Wells. 1909.

Scott-James, R. A. In his Personality in literature, 1913.

Beresford, J. D. H. G. Wells. 1915.

Brooks, V. W. The world of Wells. New York 1915.

Archer, W. God and Mr Wells: a critical examination of God the invisible king. 1917.

Sherman, S. P. The utopian naturalism of Wells. In his On contemporary literature, New York 1917.

Slosson, E. E. Wells: scientific futurist. In his Six major prophets, Boston 1917.

Mencken, H. L. The late Mr Wells. In his Prejudices: first series, New York [1919].

Goldring, D. Wells and the war. In his Reputations, 1920.

Guyot, E. H. G. Wells. Paris 1920.

Downey, R. Some errors of Wells: a Catholic's criticism of the Outline of history. 1921, 1933 (rev)

Gomme, A. W. Mr Wells as historian: an inquiry into those parts of Wells' Outline of history which deal with Greece and Rome. Glasgow 1921.

Dark, S. The outline of Wells: the superman in the street. 1922.

Ervine, St J. G. In his Some impressions of my elders, New York 1922.

Hopkins, R. T. H. G. Wells: personality, character and topography. 1922.

Macy, J. A. Wells and utopia. In his Critical game, New York 1922.

Zamyatin, E. I. Gerbert Uells. Peterburg 1922.

Adcock, A. St J. In his Gods of modern Grub Street, 1923.

Brown, I. H. G. Wells. 1923.

Connes, G. A. A dictionary of the characters and scenes in the novels, romances and short stories of Wells. Dijon 1925.

—— Étude sur la pensée de Wells. Strasbourg 1926.

Doughty, F. H. H. G. Wells: educationist. 1926.

Guedalla, P. In his Men of letters, 1927.

Braybrooke, P. Some aspects of Wells. 1928.

Holms, J. In Scrutinies, ed E. Rickword 1928.

'West, Geoffrey' (G. H. Wells). H. G. Wells: a sketch for a portrait. 1930.

Edgar, P. Wells and the modern mind. In his Art of the novel, New York 1933.

Barber, O. H. G. Wells' Verhältnis zum Darwinismus. Leipzig 1934 (Beiträge zur englischen Philologie 27).

Sonnemann, U. Der soziale Gedanke im Werk von Wells. Basle 1934.

Swinnerton, F. Teachers: Shaw and Wells. In his Georgian literary scene, 1934.

Mattick, H. H. G. Wells als Sozialreformer. Leipzig 1935 (Beiträge zur englischen Philologie 29).

Orage, A. R. The marks of Mr Wells. In his Selected essays and critical writings, 1935.

'Caudwell, Christopher' (C. St J. Sprigg). Wells: a study in utopianism. In his Studies in a dying culture, 1938.

Legouis, E. H. G. Wells. In his Dernière gerbe, Paris 1940.

Coates, J. B. In his Ten modern prophets, 1944.

Pritchett, V. S. The scientific romances. In his Living novel, 1946.

Salter, A. Wells: apostle of the world society. In his Personality in politics, 1947.

Lang, H-J. H. G. Wells. Hamburg 1948.

Berneri, M. L. Modern utopias. In his Journey through Utopia, 1950. On A modern utopia, and Men like gods.

Earle, E. M. Wells: British patriot in search of a world state. In Nationalism and internationalism, ed Earle, New York 1950.

Nicholson, N. H. G. Wells. 1950.

Vallentin, A. H. G. Wells: prophet of our day. New York 1950. A collection of book reviews.

—— H. G. Wells: ou la conspiration au grand jour. Paris 1952.

Brome, V. H. G. Wells: a biography. 1951.

—— In his Six studies in quarrelling, 1958. Shaw versus Wells; Shaw and Wells versus Henry Arthur Jones; Henry James versus Wells; Hilaire Belloc versus Wells.

Morton, A. L. In his English Utopia, 1952.

Quennell, P. In his Singular preference, 1952.

Belgion, M. H. G. Wells. 1953 (Br Council pamphlet).

MacCarthy, D. Bennett, Wells and Trollope, and Last words on Wells. In his Memories, 1953.

Gerber, R. In his Utopian fantasy, 1955.

Meyer, M. M. H. G. Wells and his family as I have known them. Edinburgh [1956].

Gregory, H. H. G. Wells: a wreath for the liberal tradition. In New world writing, 11th selection, New York 1957.

Amis, K. Starting points. In his New maps of hell, 1961. On the science-fiction.

Bergonzi, B. The early Wells: a study of the scientific romances. Manchester [1961].

Chaplin, F. K. H. G. Wells: an outline. [1961].

Häusermann, H. W. Die Streitigkeiten W. J. Turners mit Wells und Arnold Bennett. In Festschrift zum 75. Geburtstag von Theodor Spira, ed H. Viebrock and W. Erzgräber, Heidelberg 1961.

Rexroth, K. Henry James and Wells. In his Assays, Norfolk Conn 1961.

Wagar, W. W. H. G. Wells and the world state. New Haven 1961.

Raknem, I. H. G. Wells and his critics. [1962].

Walsh, C. In his From utopia to nightmare, 1962.

Kagarlitsky, Yu. Gerbert Uells: ocherk zhizni i tvorchestva. Moscow 1963. Tr M. Budberg 1966 (as The life and thought of Wells).

Moskowitz, S. The wonders of Wells. In his Explorers of the infinite, New York 1963.

Whittemore, R. The fascination of the abomination: Wells, Shaw, Ford, Conrad. In his Fascination of the abomination, New York 1963.

Borges, J. L. The first Wells. In his Other inquisitions, Austin 1964.

Borinski, L. Wells, Huxley und die Utopie. In Literatur-Kultur-Gesellschaft in England und Amerika: Aspekte und Forschungsbeiträge Friedrich Schubel zum 60. Geburtstag, ed G. Müller-Schwefe and K. Tuzinski, Frankfurt 1966.

Clarke, I. F. In his Voices prophesying war 1763–1984, 1966.

Lodge, D. Tono-Bungay and the condition of England. In his Language of fiction, 1966.

Snow, C. P. In his Variety of men, 1966.

Costa, R. H. H. G. Wells. New York 1967 (Twayne's English Authors).

Hillegas, M. R. The future as nightmare: Wells and the anti-utopians. New York 1967.

Newell, K. B. Structure in four novels by Wells. Hague 1968 (Stud in Eng Lit 48). Love and Mr Lewisham, Kipps, Tono-Bungay, The history of Mr Polly.

Sussman, H. L. In his Victorians and the machine, Cambridge Mass 1968.

Dickson, L. H. G. Wells: his turbulent life and times. 1969.

Róna, E. H. G. Wells. Budapest 1969.

Articles in Periodicals

Review articles and other journalism about Wells are listed in Raknem, H. G. Wells and his critics, 1962, above. For critical material in Russian to 1965, see Levidova and Parchevskaya, under Bibliographies, above.

Bennett, E. A. Wells and his work. Cosmopolitan Mag 33 1902; rptd in his Books and persons, 1917.

Blunt, F. Wells et le style. Nouvelle Revue 30 1904.

Crozier, J. B. Wells as a sociologist. Fortnightly Rev 84 1905.

Hawkins, C. H. Mr Wells: prophet of the new order. Arena 36 1906.

Hobson, J. A. The new aristocracy of Mr Wells. Contemporary Rev 89 1906.

Spender, H. Wells and his work. Pall Mall Gazette 50 1907.

Campbell, W. E. Wells. Catholic World 91 1910.

Seguy, R. Wells et la pensée contemporaine. Mercure de France 95 1911.

Seccombe, T. Wells. Bookman (London) 46 1914.

Lay, W. Wells and his mental hinterland. Bookman (NY) 45 1917.

Roz, F. Les anticipations de M. Wells. Revue des Deux Mondes 41 1917.

Belloc, H. A few words with Mr Wells. Dublin Rev 166 1920. On the Outline of history.

Stewart, H. L. The prophetic office of Mr Wells. International Jnl of Education 30 1920.

Baker, A. E. The religious development of Wells. Living Age 310 1921.

Becker, C. L. Wells and the new history. Amer Historical Rev 26 1921; rptd in his Everyman his own historian, New York 1935.

Dixon, J. M. Wells versus Kipling. Personalist 2 1921.

Rosenbach, E. Wells' Glaube und Geschichtsbetrachtung. Die Neueren Sprachen 29 1921.

Bloch, M. Wells historien. Revue de Paris 4 1922.

Hewlett, M. Mr Wells on the millenium. Forum 67 1922.

Lubbock, P. Bennett and Wells. Independent 108 1922.

Richter, H. H. G. Wells. Anglia 46 1922.

Shanks, E. The work of Mr Wells. London Mercury 5 1922; rptd in his First essays on literature, 1923.

Arns, K. H. G. Wells. Zeitschrift für Französischen und Englischen Unterricht 22 1923.

Royce, E. H. G. Wells. Manchester Quart 168 1923.

Connes, G. A. Wells et l'action. Revue Anglo-américaine 1 1924.

—— La première forme de la Machine à explorer le temps. Ibid.

Trotsky, L. Wells and Lenin. Labour Monthly 6 1924.

Priestley, J. B. H. G. Wells. Eng Jnl 14 1925.

Lawrence, D. H. The world of William Clissold. Calendar 3 1926; rptd in his Phoenix, New York 1936 and in his Selected literary criticism, 1955.

Mellersh, H. E. L. Shaw, Wells and creative evolution. Fortnightly Rev 119 1926.

—— Religion and Mr Wells: his unchanging faith. Socialist Rev 2 1930.

Wells, G. H. The failure of Wells. Adelphi 3 1926.

Cross, W. L. The mind of Wells. Yale Rev 16 1927; rptd (rev) in his Four contemporary novelists, New York 1930

Dandieu, A. Wells et Diderot. Mercure de France 194 1927.

The Wells and Bennett novel. TLS 23 Aug 1928.

McCallum, R. B. History and Mr Wells. New Century 108 1930.

Grattan, C. H. Goodbye to Wells! Outlook 157 1931.

Sherman, S. P. Wells and the Victorians. Bookman (NY) 73 1931.

Lloyd, D. B. The world and Mr Wells. Quart Rev 259 1932.

Mirsky, D. S. Wells and history (1). Criterion 12 1932.

Dawson, C. Wells and history (2). Ibid.

Heard, G. Mr Wells' apocalypse. Nineteenth Century 114 1933.

— Wells: the end of a faith. Saturday Rev of Lit 13 March 1948.

Grabo, C. H. Wells: chronicler, philosopher and seer. New Humanist 7 1934.

Keun, O. Wells—the player. Time & Tide 13–27 Oct 1934.

'Maurois, André' (E. S. W. Herzog). H. G. Wells. Revue Hebdomadaire 23 Feb 1935; rptd in his Magiciens et logiciens, 1935. Tr 1935 as Prophets and poets.

Ford, F. M. (formerly Hueffer). H. G. Wells. Amer Mercury 38 1936; rptd in his Portraits from life, Boston 1937, London 1938 (as Mightier than the sword).

Kauffmann, S. Wells and the new generation: the decline of a leader of youth. College Eng 1 1940.

'Orwell, George' (E. A. Blair). Wells, Hitler and the world state. Horizon 4 1941; rptd in his Critical essays, 1946, New York 1946 (as Dickens, Dali and others).

Sykes, W. J. Is Wells also among the prophets? Queen's Quart 49 1942.

Brown, E. K. Two formulas for fiction: James and Wells. College Eng 8 1946.

Murry, J. M. H. G. Wells. Adelphi 23 1946.

Arnot, R. P. Retrospect on Wells. Modern Quart 2 1947.

Jones, W. S. H. The world of Wells. London Quart & Holborn Rev 172 1947.

Spencer, S. Wells, materialist and mystic. Hibbert Jnl 46 1948.

Bennett, J. W. Galsworthy and Wells. Yale Univ Lib Gazette 28 1953.

Krutch, J. W. Loss of confidence. Amer Scholar 22 1953. Wells and Shaw.

Russell, B. Wells: liberator of thought. Listener 10 Sept 1953; rptd in his Portraits from memory, 1956.

Weeks, R. P. Disentanglement as a theme in Wells's fiction. Papers of Michigan Acad of Science, Arts & Letters 39 1953.

Hyde, W. J. The socialism of Wells. JHI 17 1956.

Starr, W. T. Romain Rolland and Wells. French Rev 30 1957.

West, A. H. G. Wells. Encounter 8 1957; rptd in his Principles and persuasions, New York 1957.

Haight, G. S. Wells's Man of the year million. Nineteenth-Century Fiction 12 1958.

Bergonzi, B. The publication of The time machine. RES 11 1960.

Ray, G. N. Wells tries to be a novelist. Eng Inst Essays 1959, 1960.

— Wells's contributions to the Saturday Review. Library 5th ser 16 1961.

Hillegas, M. R. Cosmic pessimism in Wells' scientific romances. Papers of Michigan Acad of Science, Arts & Letters 26 1961.

Newell, K. D. The structure of Wells's Tono-Bungay. Eng Fiction in Transition 4 1961; rptd in his Structure in four novels by Wells, 1968, above.

Coustillas, P. Gissing and Wells. Études Anglaises 15 1962.

Nickerson, C. C. A note on some neglected opinions of Wells. Eng Fiction in Transition 5 1962.

Timko, M. Wells's dramatic criticism for the Pall Mall Gazette. Library 5th ser 17 1962.

— Wells and 'the most unholy trade'. Eng Lang Notes 1 1964.

Claes, V. De invloed van Wells' God the invisible king op het werk van Pär Lagerkvist. Studia Germanica Gandensia 7 1965.

Hughes, D. Y. Wells: ironic romancer. Extrapolation 6 1965.

— The war of the worlds in the Yellow Press. Journalism Quart 43 1966.

— Wells and the charge of plagiarism. Nineteenth-Century Fiction 21 1966.

Leeper, G. The happy utopias of Huxley and Wells. Meanjin 24 1965.

Poston, L. Tono-Bungay: Wells's unconstructed tale. College Eng 26 1965.

Armytage, W. H. Superman and the system. Riverside Quart 2– 1966–.

Collins, C. Zamyatin, Wells and the Utopian literary tradition. Slavonic East European Rev 44 1966.

Kovalev, Yu. V. Gerbert Uells v sovetskoi kritike 1920-kh godov. (Wells in Soviet criticism of the 1920s.) Vestnik Leningradskogo Univ, ser Istorii, Yazyka i Literatury 21 1966.

Taylor, A. J. P. The man who tried to work miracles. Listener 21 July 1966.

Vernier, J. P. Wells critique. Études Anglaises 19 1966.

Williamson, J. Wells: critic of progress. Riverside Quart 2 1966, 3 1967.

Costa, R. H. Wells' Tono-Bungay: review of new studies. Eng Lit in Transition 10 1967.

Elvin, H. L. Wells 1866–1966. Rationalist Annual 1967.

Lodge, D. Assessing Wells. Encounter 28 1967.

Mullen, R. D. Wells and Victor Rousseau Emanuel: When the sleeper awakes and The messiah of the cylinder. Extrapolation 8 1967.

University of Windsor Rev 2 1967. Wells centennial issue: C. P. Crowley, Failure of nerve: Wells; M. W. Steinberg, Wells as a social critic; E. McNamara, Wells as novelist; V. Brome, Wells as a controversialist; J. K. A. Farrell, Wells as an historian; E. D. Le Mire, Wells and the world of science fiction; J. G. Parr, Wells: his significance in 1966.

Donaghy, H. J. Love and Wells: a Shelleyan search for the epipsyche. Stud in the Lit Imagination 1 1968.

Kazin, A. Wells, America and 'the future'. Amer Scholar 37 1968.

Rogal, S. J. The biographical elements in Tono-Bungay. Iowa Eng Year-book 13 1968.

Scheick, W. J. The thing that is and the speculative if: the pattern of several motifs in three novels by Wells. Eng Lit in Transition 11 1968.

— Reality and the word: the last books of Wells. Eng Lit in Transition 12 1969.

Gilkin, G. Through the novelist's looking-glass. Kenyon Rev 31 1969.

Müllenbrock, H.-J. Nationalismus und Internationalismus im Werk von Wells. Die Neueren Sprachen 18 1969.

Philmus, R. M. The time machine: or, fourth dimension as prophecy. PMLA 84 1969.

Platzner, R. L. Wells' 'Jungle book': the influence of Kipling on The island of Dr Moreau. Victorian Newsletter 36 1969.

Smith, P. The millennial vision of Wells. Jnl of Historical Stud 2 1969.

Thibault, R.-A. Wells et la France. Revue de l'Université d'Ottawa 39 1969.

See also the numerous articles in The Wellsian (Jnl of the H. G. Wells Soc), 1961– and in its supplement, H. G. Wells Soc Bull, 1963–.

C.P.C.

ENOCH ARNOLD BENNETT
1867-1931

The chief collections of Bennett mss are in the New York Public Library (Berg Collection), Indiana Univ (The old wives' tale), University College London (C. K. Ogden Collection), The Arnold Bennett Museum (Stoke-on-Trent), Keele Univ. See J. G. Hepburn, Bennett manuscripts and rare books: a list of holdings, Eng Fiction in Transition 1 1958; N. Emery, Bennett: a bibliography, 1967, below; J. Gordan (ed), Bennett: the centenary of his birth, New York 1968 (exhibition catalogue of selections from the mss and typescripts in the Berg collection).

Bibliographies
Lafourcade, G. In his Arnold Bennett, 1939, below. Includes enumerative list giving contents and publishers, introductions by Bennett and some periodical articles by him; also includes secondary material.
Hepburn, J. G. et al. In Eng Fiction [later Eng Lit] in Transition 1 1957-8 onwards. A running bibliography of secondary material.
Emery, N. Arnold Bennett 1867-1931: a bibliography. Stoke-on-Trent 1967 (Horace Banks Reference Lib: Bibliographical ser 3). Primary material only. Includes unpbd plays and film scenarios, plays based on Bennett's novels and works which have been filmed; also lists unpbd bibliographies and various check-lists, book-trade catalogues and notes of Bennett material.
Hepburn, The art of Bennett, 1963, below, lists 'miscellaneous uncollected writings of some importance', and the footnotes to his edn of the letters 1966-70, below, give information on the serial pbn of uncollected writings, etc.

Collections and Selections
Minerva edition. 7 vols 1926. Anna of the Five Towns; Buried alive; The card; A great man; The regent; Teresa of Watling Street; Whom God hath joined.
The Arnold Bennett calendar. Ed F. Bennett 1911, New York 1912.
Essays of today and yesterday: Bennett. 1926. 8 essays.
Short stories of today and yesterday: Bennett. 1928. 10 stories.
The Arnold Bennett omnibus book. 1931. Contains Riceyman steps, Elsie and the child, Lord Raingo and Accident.
Three plays: The bright island; Cupid and common sense; Sacred and profane love. [1931].
The author's craft and other critical writings. Ed S. Hynes, Lincoln Nebr 1968.

§ I
Prose Fiction
A man from the north. 1898, New York 1898.
The Grand Babylon Hotel: a fantasia on modern themes. 1902, New York 1902 (as T. Racksole and daughter), London 1954 (Penguin; introd by F. Swinnerton). First pbd serially in the Golden penny 2 Feb 1901-.
Anna of the Five Towns: a novel. 1902, New York 1903, London 1954 (Penguin, introd by F. Swinnerton).
The gates of wrath: a melodrama. 1903. First pbd serially in Myra's Jnl 1 Oct 1899-.
Leonora: a novel. 1903, New York 1910.
A great man: a frolic. 1904, New York 1910.
Teresa of Watling Street: a fantasia on modern themes. 1904.
Tales of the Five Towns. 1905.
The loot of cities: being the adventures of a millionaire in search of joy—a fantasia. 1905, [1917] (with additional stories). The 6 stories in 1905 edn first pbd serially in Windsor Mag summer and autumn 1904.

Sacred and profane love: a novel in three episodes. 1905, New York 1911 (rev, as The book of Carlotta; with preface by Bennett).
Hugo: a fantasia on modern themes. 1906, New York 1906. First pbd serially in To-day 3 May-19 July 1905.
Whom God hath joined. 1906, New York 1911.
The sinews of war: a romance of London and the sea. [1906], New York 1906 (as Doubloons). With E. Phillpotts. First pbd serially in T.P.'s Weekly 2 March 1906-.
The ghost: a fantasia on modern themes. 1907, Boston 1907.
The grim smile of the Five Towns. 1907.
The city of pleasure: a fantasia on modern themes. 1907, New York 1915. First pbd serially in Staffordshire Sentinel and other provincial newspapers 6 Jan-14 April 1906.
The statue. 1908, New York 1908. With E. Phillpotts.
Buried alive: a tale of three days. 1908, New York 1910.
The old wives' tale: a novel. 1908, New York [1911] (with preface by Bennett), London 1912, 2 vols 1927 (facs from author's ms), Oxford 1941 (Limited Editions Club, introd by F. Swinnerton, preface by Bennett), 1 vol London 1954 (Penguin, introd by F. Swinnerton), 1964 (introd by A. Sillitoe).
The glimpse: an adventure of the soul. 1909, New York 1909.
Helen with the high hand: an idyllic diversion. 1910, New York 1910. First pbd serially (as The miser's niece) in Star, 12 June 1909-.
Clayhanger. 1910, New York 1910, London 1954 (Penguin, introd by F. Swinnerton). First vol of Clayhanger trilogy.
The card: a story of adventure in the Five Towns. 1911, New York 1911 (as Denry the audacious). The first 3 chs issued New York 1911 as The deeds of Denry the audacious, for copyright purposes. First pbd serially in Times Weekly Edition 4 Feb 1910-.
Hilda Lessways. 1911, New York 1911. 2nd vol of Clayhanger trilogy.
The matador of the Five Towns, and other stories. 1912, New York 1912. The contents of the English and American edns are not identical.
The regent: a Five Towns story of adventure in London. 1913, New York 1913 (as The old Adam). Sequel to The card. First pbd serially in London Mag Nov 1912-, and American Mag Dec 1912-.
The price of love: a tale. 1914, New York 1914. First pbd serially in Harper's Mag Dec 1913-.
These twain. New York 1915, London 1916. 3rd vol of Clayhanger trilogy. First pbd serially in Munsey's Mag Sept-Oct 1915.
The lion's share. 1916, New York 1916. First pbd serially in Metropolitan Mag Oct 1915-.
The pretty lady: a novel. 1918, New York 1918, London 1950 (introd by F. Swinnerton).
The roll-call. 1918, New York 1918.
Mr Prohack. 1922, New York 1922. First pbd serially in Delineator July 1921-Jan 1922 and in Westminster Gazette.
Lilian. 1922, New York 1922. First pbd serially in Cassell's Mag July 1922-.
Riceyman Steps: a novel. 1923, New York 1923, London 1954 (Penguin, introd by F. Swinnerton), 1956 (with Elsie and the child, introd by Michael Sadleir), 1964 (introd by A. Sillitoe [same as introd to Old Wives' tale, above]).
Elsie and the child: a tale of Riceyman Steps, and other stories. 1924, New York 1924.
The Clayhanger family. 1925. Contains Clayhanger, Hilda Lessways and These twain.
Lord Raingo. 1926, New York 1926. First pbd serially in Evening Standard 20 Sept 1926-.
The vanguard: a fantasia. New York [1927], London 1928 (as The strange vanguard: a fantasia).

The woman who stole everything, and other stories. 1927, New York 1927.

Accident. New York 1928, London 1929. First pbd serially (as Train de luxe) in Daily Express 16 July 1928–.

'Piccadilly': story of the film. [1929]. First pbd serially in Film Weekly 22 Oct 1928–.

Elsie and the child. 1929 (limited edn). Short story, first pbd 1924 with other stories.

Imperial Palace. 1930 (1 vol and 2 vols [limited] edns), New York 1930.

The night visitor, and other stories. Garden City NY 1931, London 1931.

Venus rising from the sea. 1931 (350 copies). Short story. See next.

Dream of destiny: an unfinished novel, and Venus rising from the sea [short story]. 1932, New York 1932 (as Stroke of luck, and Dream of destiny: an unfinished novel).

Plays, Libretti etc

Plays are listed in order of production, not of pbn.

Rosalys: a music play for girls in two acts. Libretto by Bennett. (Welsh Girls' School, Ashford Middlesex 27 July 1898). In M. Locherbie-Goff, La jeunesse de Bennett, 1939. See §2, below. Music by J. Brown.

Polite farces for the drawing-room. 1900, New York 1912. Plays: contains The stepmother, A good woman, A question of sex. All reissued separately 1929–30.

Cupid and commonsense: a play in four acts. (Stage Soc, Shaftesbury Th 26 Jan 1908). 1909, New York [1910]. Based on Anna of the Five Towns. With preface on The crisis in the theatre.

What the public wants: a play in four acts. (Aldwych 2 May 1909). 1909, New York 1910.

The honeymoon: a comedy in three acts. (Royalty 6 Oct 1911). 1911, New York 1912.

Milestones: a play in three acts. (Royalty 5 March 1912; Liberty, New York 12 Sept 1912). 1912, New York [1912]. With E. Knoblauch [Knoblock].

The great adventure: a play of fancy in four acts. (Kingsway 25 March 1913). 1913, New York [1913]. Based on Buried alive, 1908, above.

A good woman. (Palace 16 Feb 1914, as Rivals for Rosamund). In Polite farces for the drawing-room, 1900, above.

The title: a comedy in three acts. (Royalty 20 July 1918). 1918, New York 1918.

Judith: a play in three acts, founded on the apocryphal book of Judith. (Kingsway 30 April 1919). 1919, New York 1919.

Sacred and profane love: a play in four acts. (Playhouse, Liverpool 15 Sept 1919; Aldwych 10 Nov 1919). 1919, New York 1920. Based on the novel.

Body and soul: a play in four acts. (Playhouse, Liverpool 15 Feb 1922; Regent, Euston Rd 11 Sept 1922). New York 1921, London 1922.

The love match: a play in five scenes. (Strand 21 March 1922). 1922, New York 1922.

Don Juan de Marana: a play in four acts. 1923 (priv ptd).

London life: a play in three acts and nine scenes. (Drury Lane 3 June 1924). 1924, New York 1924. With E. Knoblock.

The bright island. (Aldwych 15 Feb 1925). 1924 (200 copies), New York 1925, London 1926.

Flora. (Rusholme, Manchester 19 Oct 1927). In Five three-act plays, 1933.

Mr Prohack: a comedy in three acts. (Court 16 Nov 1927). 1927. With E. Knoblock; based on the novel.

Judith: an opera in one act. (Covent Garden 25 June 1929). [1929]. Music by E. Goossens; libretto by Bennett.

The snake-charmer. In Eight one-act plays, 1933.

The Ides of March. In One-act plays for stage and study, ser 8, New York 1934. With F. Alcock.

Don Juan de Mañara: opera in four acts. (Covent Garden 24 June 1937). 1935. Vocal score. Libretto by Bennett, music by E. Goossens. Based on Don Juan de Marana, 1923, above.

For Bennett's unpbd plays and film scenarios, and for plays by other writers based on his novels, see Emery, Bibliography, above. J. G. Hepburn, Letters of Bennett, vol 1 below, p. 59 mentions Bennett and Phillpotts collaborating on a dramatization of Phillpotts' Children of the mist (1898) in 1900, and in 1904 on two plays, Christina (A credit to human nature) and An angel unawares, none of this work being produced.

Other Works

Journalism for women: a practical guide. 1898.

Fame and fiction: an inquiry into certain popularities. 1901, New York 1901.

How to become an author: a practical guide. 1903.

The truth about an author. 1903 (anon), New York 1911 (with preface by Bennett), London 1914. Autobiographical.

Things that interested me: being leaves from a journal. Preface by G. Sturt, Burslem 1906 (priv ptd).

The reasonable life: being hints for men and women. 1907, New York [1911] (expanded, as Mental efficiency and other hints to men and women), London [1912].

Things which have interested me: being leaves from a journal. Preface by A. Hooley 2nd ser, Burslem 1907 (priv ptd, 100 copies).

How to live on 24 hours a day. 1908, 1910 (with preface by Bennett), New York 1910.

The human machine. 1908, New York 1911.

Things which have interested me: 3rd ser, Burslem 1908 (priv ptd, 100 copies). Preface [in French] by M. D. Calvocoressi.

Literary taste: how to form it; with detailed instructions for collecting a complete library of English literature. 1909, New York 1927, London 1937 (with additional lists by F. Swinnerton), 1938 (Penguin, with a further list by F. Swinnerton).

The present crisis: plain words to plain men. Burslem [1910]. A pamphlet against tariff reform.

The feast of St Friend. 1911, New York 1911, London 1914 (as Friendship and happiness: a plea for the feast of St Friend). Essays.

Those United States. 1912, New York 1912 (as Your United States: impressions of a first visit).

How to be happy. New York [1912]. Pamphlet rptd from Metropolitan Mag and rptd in The plain man and his wife, 1913, below.

Paris nights, and other impressions of places and people. 1913, New York 1913.

The plain man and his wife. [1913], New York [1913], New York 1913 (as Married life), London 1916 (as Marriage: the plain man and his wife).

From the log of the Velsa. New York 1914, London 1920. Travel.

Liberty: a statement of the British case. 1914, New York 1914.

The author's craft. 1914, New York 1914.

Over there: war scenes on the western front. 1915, New York 1915.

Wounded. 1915. Wounded Allies' Relief Committee pamphlet.

The Wounded Allies' Relief Committee: a short account of work done. 1915. Pamphlet.

'Wounded Allies' at the Caledonian Market: the greatest war fair. [1916]. Publicity circular.

Books and persons: being comments on a past epoch 1908–11. 1917, New York 1917. Selected articles from New Age, written by 'Jacob Tonson'; with some revisions.

A national responsibility: future employment of the disabled. Manchester 1917. Pamphlet.

The embargo v. the gun. 1918. League of Free Nations Assoc pamphlet.

Independence and sovereignty. [1918]. League of Nations Union pamphlet.

Self and self-management: essays about existing. 1918, New York 1918.

Thoughts on national kitchens. 1918. Pamphlet.

Our women: chapters on the sex-discord. 1920, New York 1920.

Things that have interested me. 1921, New York 1921. This, and subsequent ser with same title, below, are distinct from 3 similar titles priv ptd at Burslem 1906–8, above.

Things that have interested me. 2nd ser 1923, New York 1923.

How to make the best of life. [1923], New York 1923. Essays.

Things that have interested me. 3rd ser 1926, New York 1926.

The savour of life: essays in gusto. 1928, Garden City NY 1928.

Mediterranean scenes: Rome—Greece—Constantinople. 1928. Travel.

The religious interregnum. 1929. Pamphlet.

How to live. Garden City NY 1929. Reprints How to live on 24 hours a day; The human machine; Mental efficiency and other hints to men and women; Self and self-management.

Journal, 1929. 1930, New York 1930 (as Journal of things new and old).

The journals of Arnold Bennett 1896–1928. Ed N. Flower 3 vols 1932–3, New York 1932–3 (rev, as The journal of Arnold Bennett), 1 vol New York 1935. A selection by F. Swinnerton from this and the Journal 1929 pbd 1954 (Penguin).

Florentine journal 1st April–25th May 1910. Introd by S. Sitwell 1967.

For Bennett's few poems, occasional contributions to symposia etc, and for his introds and prefaces to works by other writers, see Emery, Bibliography, above. Bennett contributed regularly to Woman 1894–1900 and was editor thereof 1896–1900; to Academy 1898–1901 (dramatic criticism and reviews); to New Age 1908–11 as 'Jacob Tonson' on Books and persons; to John Bull 1922–3 (miscellaneous articles); and Evening Standard 1926–31 (book reviews). He also contributed to T.P.'s Weekly in the early 1900s and to Daily News during the 1914–18 war. Many of the pieces were collected in the books listed above: for details, see Emery, Bibliography.

Letters

Bennett's letters to his nephew [Richard Bennett], with a preface by F. Swinnerton. New York 1935, London 1936.

Bennett and H. G. Wells: a record of a personal and literary friendship. Ed H. Wilson, Urbana 1960.

Correspondance André Gide—Bennett: vingt ans d'amitié littéraire 1911–31. Ed L. F. Brugmans, Geneva 1964.

Letters of Arnold Bennett. Ed J. G. Hepburn 3 vols 1966–70.

Dorothy Cheston Bennett, Arnold Bennett: a portrait done at home (1935) contains 170 letters from Bennett to the author.

§2

Bettany, F. G. Bennett: an appreciation. Bookman (London) 39 1911.

Howells, W. D. Speaking of Bennett. Harper's Monthly Mag 122 1911.

Cooper, F. T. In his Some English story-tellers, New York 1912.

Murry, J. M. Bennett, Stendhal and the modern novel. Blue Rev Jnl 1 1913.

Scott-James, R. A. In his Personality in literature, 1913.

—— Bennett and Galsworthy. In his Fifty years of English literature, 1951.

Classen, E. The novels of Bennett. Germanisch-romanische Monatsschrift 6 1914.

Bronson-Howard, G. B. Bennett as a melodramatist. Bookman (NY) 42 1915.

Darton, F. J. H. Arnold Bennett. 1915.

Sherman, S. P. Realism of Bennett. Nation 23 Dec 1915; rptd in his On contemporary literature, New York 1917.

Hughes, D. P. The novels of Bennett and Wesleyan Methodism. Contemporary Rev 110 1916.

Cox, S. H. Romance in Bennett. Sewanee Rev 28 1920.

Goldring, D. The Gordon Selfridge of English letters. In his Reputations, 1920.

Ervine, St J. In his Some impressions of my elders, New York 1922.

—— Portrait of Bennett. Listener 22 Sept 1955.

Hind, C. L. In his Authors and I, 1921.

Lubbock, P. Bennett and Wells. Independent 108 1922.

Adcock, A. St J. In his Gods of modern Grub Street, 1923.

Chesterton, G. K. The mercy of Bennett. In his Fancies versus fads, 1923.

Gillet, L. Deux romans de Bennett. Revue des Deux Mondes 15 Feb 1923. Mr Prohack; Lilian.

McIntyre, C. F. Bennett and old age. Personalist 4 1923.

Downs, B. W. Arnold Bennett. North Amer Rev 219 1924.

Follett, H. T. (ed). Arnold Bennett. New York [1924?]. Appreciations by various writers.

Hoffmann, R. Proportion and incident in Conrad and Bennett. Sewanee Rev 32 1924.

Johnson, L. G. Bennett of the Five Towns. 1924.

Priestley, J. B. Mr Arnold Bennett. London Mercury 9 1924.

—— Arnold Bennett. Eng Jnl 14 1925.

Woolf, V. Character in fiction. Criterion 2 1924; rptd as Mr Bennett and Mrs Brown, 1924, and in her The captain's death bed, 1950.

Bennett, Mrs A. M. Arnold Bennett. 1925.

—— My Arnold Bennett. 1931.

Dutton, G. B. Arnold Bennett, showman. Sewanee Rev 33 1925.

Fehr, B. Bennetts Späternte. Anglia Beiblätter 36 1925.

Muir, E. Scrutinies IV: Bennett. Calendar of Modern Letters June 1925; rptd in Scrutinies, ed E. Rickword 1928.

Aas, L. A. Bennett. Copenhagen Tilskueren 43 1926.

Delattre, F. Sur deux ouvrages récents de Bennett. Revue Anglo-américaine 3 1926. Riceyman Steps and Elsie and the child.

Cross, W. L. Bennett of the Five Towns. Yale Rev 18 1928; rptd in his Four contemporary novelists, 1930.

Roberts, R. E. Mr Bennett is interested. In his Reading for pleasure and other essays, 1928.

—— Arnold Bennett. Nineteenth Century 109 1931.

The Wells and Bennett novel. TLS 23 Aug 1928.

'West, Rebecca' (C. I. Andrews). Uncle Bennett. In her Strange necessity, 1928.

—— Bennett himself. New York 1931 (John Day pamphlets 1).

Beardmore, F. G. [Miscellaneous articles on Bennett and the Five Towns]. Sunday Chron 3 Feb–22 Dec 1929, intermittently.

Orage, A. R. In his Art of reading, New York [1930]. Various comments, rptd from New Age.

Byrne, M. St C. Bennett and his critics. National Rev 96 1931.

Ford, F. M. (formerly Hueffer). In his Return to yesterday, 1931.

Gide, A. Arnold Bennett. Nouvelle Revue Française 36 1931.

Hackett, F. Arnold Bennett. Saturday Rev of Lit 2 May 1931.

Maugham, W. S. Arnold Bennett. Life & Letters 6 1931.

—— Living in the Grand Hotel. Saturday Rev of Lit 20 May 1933.

—— In his Vagrant mood, 1952.

Sutton, G. The plays of Bennett. Bookman (London) 81 1931.

Beach, J. W. In his Twentieth-century novel, New York 1932.

Bennett, D. C. Bennett's unfinished novel. Bookman (NY) 75 1932.

—— Bennett: a portrait done at home. 1935.

Hunt, V. Bennett in Paris. Bookman (NY) 75 1932.

Lafourcade, G. Arnold Bennett. Marsyas Dec 1932.

—— The sources of Bennett's Old wives' tale. London Mercury 35 1937.

—— Bennett: a study. 1939.

—— Stendhal et Bennett. Revue de Littérature Comparée 19 1939.

Wagenknecht, E. Arnold Bennett. Virginia Quart Rev 8 1932.

'West, Geoffrey' (G. H. Wells). The problem of Bennett. 1932.

Williams, O. The old wives' tale. National Rev 99 1932.

Wilson, E. Post-war Shaw and pre-war Bennett. New Republic 8 June 1932.

Nishimura, S. On the misers in Bennett's novels. Stud in Eng Lit (Tokyo) 13 1933.

Smith, P. A.B. 1933.

Jaeschke, R. Bennett und Frankreich. Breslau 1934.

Swinnerton, F. In his Georgian scene, New York [1934].

—— In his Swinnerton: an autobiography, Garden City NY 1936.

—— Arnold Bennett. 1950, 1961 (rev) (Br Council pamphlet).

—— Three older novelists. In his Background with chorus, 1956.

—— Star reviewing. In his Figures in the foreground, 1963.

Tillier, L. Bennett: ou de la mutilation volontaire. Revue Anglo-américaine 11 1934.

—— Sur deux chapitres de Clayhanger. Études Anglaises 3 1939.

—— Bennett et ses romans réalistes. Paris 1967.

Wells, H. G. In his Experiment in autobiography, 1934.

Wheatley, E. Bennett's trifles: his novels for the gay middle-aged. Sewanee Rev 42 1934.

Doran, G. In his Chronicles of Barabbas, New York [1935].

Drabert, E. Frauengestalten in Bennetts Romanen. Bonn 1936 (Bonner Studien zur englischen Philologie 28).

Frank Harris to Bennett: fifty-eight letters 1908–10. Merion Station Pa 1936.

Simons, J. B. Bennett and his novels. Oxford 1936.

Muller, H. J. Realism of the center: Bennett, Galsworthy, Maugham. In his Modern fiction, New York 1937.

Massoulard, E. Die romantischen Elemente in Bennett. Bonn 1938 (Bonner Studien zur englischen Philologie 34).

Locherbie-Goff, M. La jeunesse de Bennett (1867–1904). Avesnes-sur-Helpe 1939.

Evans, R. L. Bennett et la France. Modern Languages 21 1940.

Rohrmann, E. Bennetts The lion's share and The silent brothers. Zeitschrift für Neusprachlichen Unterricht 40 1941.

Elwin, M. Bennett and George Moore. TLS 5 Dec 1942.

Koziol, H. Bennett, Galsworthy und Priestley über englische Demokratie. Deutschlands Erneuerung 26 1942.

Tresidder, A. Bennett and the drama. In Studies in speech and drama in honor of A. M. Drummond, ed D. C. Bryant, Ithaca 1944.

Pritchett, V. S. The Five Towns. In his Living novel, 1946.

Allen, W. Arnold Bennett. 1948.

Curtin, F. D. Bennett and after. In If by your art: testament to P. Hunt, ed A. L. Starrett, Pittsburgh 1948.

—— Bennett through biography. Eng Fiction in Transition 1 1958.

Green, A. In her With much love, New York 1948. Reminiscences.

Sitwell, O. In his Laughter in the next room, Boston 1948.

—— In his Noble essences, 1950.

Conacher, W. M. Bennett and the French realists. Queen's Quart 56 1949.

Flower, N. In his Just as it happened, 1950.

Beardmore, G. An Arnold Bennett Museum. John O'London's Weekly 17 Aug 1951.

Dunkel, W. B. The genesis of Milestones. College Eng 13 1952.

Pound, R. Bennett: a biography. 1952.

Sanna, V. Bennett e i romanzi delle Cinque Città. Florence 1953.

Wilson, A. Bennett's novels. London Mag 1 1954.

Pilkington, F. Methodism in Bennett's novels. Contemporary Rev 189 1956.

Wain, J. The quality of Bennett. In his Preliminary essays, 1957.

—— Arnold Bennett. New York 1967 (Columbia Essays on Modern Writers).

Hepburn, J. G. Bennett in Clerkenwell. N & Q 203 1958.

—— Manuscript notes for Lord Raingo. Eng Fiction in Transition 5 1962.

—— Some curious realism in Riceyman Steps. Modern Fiction Stud 8 1962.

—— The art of Bennett. Bloomington 1963.

—— The notebook for Riceyman Steps. PMLA 78 1963.

Tillyard, E. M. W. Middlemarch and Bursley. In his Epic strain in the English novel, 1958.

Hall, J. Bennett: primitivism and taste. Seattle 1959.

Antrim, D. K. Bennett's 24 hour day. Amer Mercury 90 1960.

Ford, J. Bennett country. Stoke-on-Trent 1960 (City of Stoke-on-Trent Information 5).

Roberts, T. R. Bennett's Five Towns origins. Stoke-on-Trent [1960].

Fuchs, K. Raum und Mensch im Werk des Heimatdichters Bennett. Die Neueren Sprachen 10 1961.

Häusermann, W. Die Streitigkeiten W. J. Turners mit Wells und Bennett. In Festschrift zum 75. Geburtstag von Theodor Spira, 1961.

Salisbury, L. A weekend with Bennett. Virginia Quart Rev 37 1961.

Kennedy, J. G. Bennett: Künstler und Bürger. Eng Fiction in Transition 5 1962.

—— Reassuring facts in The pretty lady, Lord Raingo and modern novels. Eng Lit in Transition 7 1964.

Kreutz, I. Mr Bennett and Mrs Woolf. Modern Fiction Stud 8 1962.

Haresnape, G. Pauline Smith and Bennett. Eng Stud in Africa 6 1963.

Hughes, R. Faulkner and Bennett. Encounter 21 1963.

Pommerening, I. Bennett als Literaturkritiker. Giessen 1964.

Barker, D. Writer by trade: a view of Bennett. 1966.

Davis, O. H. The master: a study of Bennett. 1966.

Heywood, C. D. H. Lawrence's Lost girl and its antecedents by George Moore and Bennett. Eng Stud 47 1966.

Warrillow, E. J. D. Bennett and Stoke-on-Trent. Stoke-on-Trent 1966.

Durkin, B. Some new lights on Riceyman Steps. Eng Lit in Transition 10 1967.

Hynes, S. The whole contention between Mr Bennett and Mrs Woolf. Novel 1 1967.

Marriott, F. My association with Bennett. Keele 1967 (Keele Univ Lib Occasional Pbns 3).

Wright, W. F. The comic spirit in Bennett. Kansas Quart 1 1969.

C.P.C.

EDWARD MORGAN FORSTER
1879–1970

The ms of Where angels fear to tread *is in the British Museum, and that of* A passage to India *in the Academic Center of the Univ of Texas. The other major and most minor mss are at King's College, Cambridge. Cf Kirkpatrick's* Bibliography, *below.*

Bibliographies

Gerber, H. E. E. M. Forster: an annotated checklist of writings about him. Eng Fiction in Transition 2 1959.

Beebe, M. and J. Brogunier. Criticism of Forster: a selected checklist. Modern Fiction Stud 7 1961. Based on Gerber's checklist.

Grieff, L. K. E. M. Forster: a bibliography. Bull of Bibliography 24 1964. Checklist of works by Forster.

Kirkpatrick, B. J. A bibliography of Forster. With a foreword by Forster 1965, 1968 (rev) (Soho bibliographies). Includes contributions to periodicals and manifestoes, also letters to the press, interviews, broadcasts and translations.

McDowell, F. P. Forster. Eng Lit in Transition 10–1967–. Supplement to Gerber, above.

Collections and Selections

Uniform edn. 5 vols 1924–6. Novels only: texts as in first edns.

Pocket edn. 8 vols 1947–62.

The collected tales of Forster. New York 1947, London [1948] (as Collected short stories of Forster). Incorporates The celestial omnibus and The eternal moment; includes a preface by Forster which is slightly rev in the English edn.

E. M. Forster: a tribute. With selections from his writings on India. Ed K. Natwar-Singh, New York [1964].

§1
Prose Fiction

Where angels fear to tread. Edinburgh 1905, New York 1920.

The longest journey. Edinburgh 1907, New York 1922, London 1960 (WC), with introd by Forster.

A room with a view. 1908, New York 1911, London 1951 (as play by S. Tait and K. Allott produced at Arts Theatre Cambridge 6 Feb 1950).

Howards End. 1910, New York 1910 (for 1911) (with unauthorized alterations), London 1919, New York 1921 (with text of first English edn).

The celestial omnibus and other stories. 1911, New York 1923. Contains The story of a panic, The other side of the hedge, The celestial omnibus, Other Kingdom, The curate's friend, The road from Colonus. Rptd from Independent Rev, Pall Mall Mag, Albany Rev, Eng Rev.

The story of the siren. Richmond 1920 (Hogarth Press). Short story, rptd in The eternal moment.

A passage to India. 1924, New York 1924, London [1942] (EL) (with foreword and notes by Forster and introd by P. Burra rptd from Nineteenth Century 116 1934), 1957 (with foreword and notes rev); 1960 (as play by S. R. Rau produced at Oxford Playhouse 19 Jan 1960).

The eternal moment and other stories. 1928, New York [1928]. Contains The machine stops, The point of it, Mr Andrews, Co-ordination, The story of the siren, The eternal moment. Rptd from Independent Rev, Oxford & Cambridge Rev, Open Window and Eng Rev.

Extracts from three unfinished novels are given in R. Macaulay, The writings of Forster; Tribute to B. Britten, ed A. Gishford (Arctic summer: fragment of an unfinished novel by Forster); *and* Listener 23 Dec 1948 (Entrance to an unwritten novel). *Forster refers to an unpbd story*, The rock, *in his introd to* The collected tales.

Other Works

Alexandria: a history and a guide. Alexandria 1922, 1938 (rev), New York 1961 (with text of first edn and new introd).

Pharos and Pharillon. Richmond 1923 (Hogarth Press), New York 1923. Articles first pbd in the Egyptian Mail and the Athenaeum.

Anonymity: an enquiry. 1925 (Hogarth essays 12). First pbd in Calendar of modern letters 2 1925, rptd in Two cheers for democracy.

Aspects of the novel. 1927, New York 1927. (Clark lectures 1927).

A letter to Madan Blanchard. 1931 (Hogarth letters 1), New York 1932. Rptd in Two cheers for democracy.

Sinclair Lewis interprets America. [Cambridge Mass 1932]. Priv ptd for H. Taylor, 100 copies. Extract from Our photography: Sinclair Lewis, New York Herald Tribune 28 Apr 1929. Rptd in Abinger harvest.

Goldsworthy Lowes Dickinson. 1934, New York 1934. Biography.

Pageant of Abinger: in aid of the Parish Church Preservation Fund. [Abinger 1934]. Rptd (as Abinger pageant) in Abinger harvest.

Abinger harvest. 1936, New York 1936, London 1936 (without A flood in the office), New York 1947; London 1940 (with rev prefatory note and without Abinger pageant), 1953 (with original prefatory note and Abinger pageant). Articles and reviews rptd from various journals.

England's pleasant land: a pageant play. Westcott Surrey 1938 (synopsis only), London 1940 (full text).

What I believe. 1939 (Hogarth sixpenny pamphlets 1). First pbd, with some omissions, as Two cheers for democracy, in Nation 16 July 1938; rptd in Two cheers for democracy.

Reading as usual. 1939. Broadcast talk rptd from the Listener 21 Sept 1939.

Nordic twilight. 1940 (Macmillan war pamphlets 3).

Virginia Woolf. Cambridge 1942, New York 1942 (Rede lecture 1941). Rptd in Two cheers for democracy.

The development of English prose between 1918 and 1939. Glasgow 1945 (W. P. Ker memorial lecture 1944). Rptd (rev) in Two cheers for democracy.

The new disorder. New York 1949. Essay rptd from Horizon 4 1941.

Two cheers for democracy. 1951, New York 1951. Essays, reviews and broadcasts, mostly rptd from various journals.

Billy Budd: opera in four acts. Music by B. Britten, libretto by Forster and E. Crozier, adapted from the story by H. Melville. 1951, 1962 (rev).

Desmond MacCarthy. Stanford Dingley 1952. Priv ptd (Mill House Press) 72 copies. Tribute first pbd in Listener 26 June 1952.

Reply to Lord Cohen who had proposed the health of [King's] College at Founder's Feast December 6th 1952. [Cambridge 1952]. Mimeographed.

The hill of Devi, being letters from Dewas State Senior. 1953, New York 1953. Reminiscences of India.

'I assert that there is an alternative in humanism'. 1955. Essay first pbd as a letter in Twentieth Century 157 1955.

Battersea Rise. New York [1955] (priv ptd). The first chapter of Marianne Thornton, slightly condensed. Rptd as Daughter dear, London Mag 3 1956.

Marianne Thornton 1797–1887: a domestic biography. 1956, New York 1956.

Tourism v. thuggism. 1957. Review of Portrait of Greece, by Lord Kinross. Offprint from Listener 17 Jan 1957.

E. K. Bennett—Francis—1887–1958. 1959 (priv ptd). Tribute rptd from Caian 55 1958. 300 copies.

A presidential address to the Cambridge humanists, summer 1959. 1963. Mimeographed, 50 copies. Rptd from Univ Humanist Bull 11 1963.

Principal Contributions to Books

Virgil. The Aeneid. Tr E. Fairfax Taylor, introd and notes by Forster 1906, New York 1906 2 vols, London 1957 (with rev introd) 1 vol.

Committee of the International Section of the Labour Research Department. The government of Egypt: recommendations. With notes on Egypt by E. M. Forster. 1920. Pamphlet.

Fay, E. Original letters from India 1779–1815. 1925. Notes by Forster.

Sitwell, C. Flowers and elephants. Foreword by Forster 1927.

Edward Carpenter: in appreciation. Ed G. Beith 1931. Includes Forster's memories of Carpenter.

The life of George Crabbe by his son. Introd by Forster 1933 (WC).

O'Sullivan, M. Twenty years a-growing. Introductory note by Forster 1933.

Anand, M. R. Untouchable: a novel. Preface by Forster 1935.

Aspects of England. 1935. Contributions by W. R. Inge, C. Morgan, H. W. Nevinson and Forster.

Craig, A. The banned books of England. Foreword by Forster 1937.

T. E. Lawrence by his friends. Ed A. W. Lawrence 1937. Contribution by Forster.

Britain and the beast. 1937. Contributions by J. M. Keynes, H. J. Massingham, S. Kaye-Smith, Forster et al.

Bell, J. Essays, poems and letters. Ed Q. Bell 1938. With contributions by J. M. Keynes, D. Garnett, C. Mauron, C. Day Lewis and Forster.

Writers in freedom: a symposium. Ed H. Ould 1942. Contribution by Forster.

British Broadcasting Corporation. Tolstoy's War and peace: introd to the series of broadcasts. 1943. Essay by Forster, similar to his broadcast talk pbd in Listener 13 Jan 1937.

Srinivasa Iyengar, K. R. Literature and authorship in India. Introd by Forster 1943.

Talking to India. By E. M. Forster... and others: a selection of English language broadcasts to India, ed G. Orwell 1943.

Crozier, E. (ed). Sadler's Wells opera books no 3: Benjamin Britten, Peter Grimes. Essays by Britten, Forster, M. Slater, E. Sackville-West. 1945. Forster's essay on Crabbe is a rev version of his essay pbd in Listener 29 May 1941.

Freedom of expression: a symposium. Ed H. Ould 1945. Contribution by Forster.

Dickinson, G. L. Letters from John Chinaman and other essays. Introd by Forster 1946.

The challenge of our time: a series of essays by A. Koestler [et al, including Forster]. 1948. Forster's essay, The point of view of the creative artist, was first pbd in Listener 11 April 1946 and rptd (as The challenge of our time) in Two cheers for democracy.

Mahatma Gandhi: essays and reflections on his life and work. Ed S. Radhakrishnan. 1949. Contribution by Forster.

Desani, G. V. Hali. Foreword by T. S. Eliot and Forster. 1950.

Singh, H. Maura. Introd by Forster 1951.

Futehally, Z. Zohra: a novel. Foreword by Forster, Bombay [1951].

Cambridge anthology. Ed P. Townsend, introd by Forster 1952.

Hermon Ould: a tribute. 1952. Includes a reminiscence by Forster.

Forrest Reid memorial addresses... Belfast 1952. Contribution by Forster.

Reid, F. Tom Barber. Introd by Forster, New York 1955.

The author and the public. 1957 (Speeches at the 28th International PEN Congress 1956). Includes speech by Forster on the art of biography.

Dickinson, G. L. The Greek view of life. Preface by Forster 1957 [4th edn].

The fearful choice: a debate on nuclear policy, conducted by P. Toynbee. 1958. Contribution by Forster.

De Charms, L. Elizabeth of the German garden: a biography. 1958. Includes reminiscences by Forster, taken from an unpbd fuller account. Further reminiscences appeared in Forster's article Recollections of Nassenheide, Listener 1 Jan 1959.

Windham, D. The warm country. Introd by Forster 1960.

Golding, W. Lord of the flies. Introd by Forster, New York 1962.

Lampedusa, G. di. Two stories and a memory. Tr A. Colquhoun, introd by Forster, 1962.

Gishford, A. (ed). Tribute to Benjamin Britten on his fiftieth birthday. 1963. Includes Forster's Arctic summer: fragment of an unfinished novel, read by Forster at Aldeburgh Festival 10 June 1951.

§2
Books and Chapters in Books

Dobrée, B. E. M. Forster. In his The lamp and the lute: studies in six modern authors, 1929.

Hoare, D. M. E. M. Forster. In her Some studies in the modern novel, 1938.

Macaulay, R. The writings of Forster. 1938.

Trilling, L. Forster: a study. Norfolk Conn 1943, London 1967 (rev).

Morton, A. L. Forster and the classless society. In his Language of men, 1945.

Brown, E. K. E. M. Forster. In his Rhythm in the novel, 1950.

Warner, R. E. M. Forster. 1950, 1960 (rev J. Morris) (Br Council pamphlet).

Brower, R. A. The twilight of the double vision: symbol and irony in A passage to India. In his The fields of light, New York 1951.

Johnstone, J. K. The Bloomsbury group: a study of Forster, Strachey, V. Woolf and their circle. 1954.

McConkey, J. The novels of Forster. Ithaca 1957.

Kain, R. M. Vision and discovery in Forster's A passage to India. In Twelve original essays on great English novels. Ed C. Shapiro, Detroit 1958.

Werry, R. R. Rhythm in Forster's A passage to India. In Studies in honor of J. Wilcox. Ed A. D. Wallace and W. O. Ross, Detroit 1958.

Oliver, H. J. The art of Forster. Melbourne 1960.

Turnell, M. The shaping of contemporary literature: Lawrence, Forster, Virginia Woolf. In his Modern literature and the Christian faith, 1961.

Beer, J. B. The achievement of Forster. 1962.

Crews, F. C. Forster: the perils of humanism. Princeton 1962. 2 chs rptd from articles in journals.

Fadda, A. M. Edward Morgan Forster e il decadentismo. Palumbo 1962.

Gransden, K. W. E. M. Forster. 1962 (Writers & Critics).

Shahane, V. A. Forster: a reassessment. Mysore 1962. Some pts rptd from articles in journals.

—— (ed). Perspectives on Forster's Passage to India: a collection of critical essays. New York 1967.

Cox, C. B. Forster's island. In his The free spirit: a study of liberal humanism in the novels of G. Eliot, H. James, Forster, V. Woolf and A. Wilson, 1963.

Hall, J. In his Tragic comedians, Bloomington 1963.

Joseph, D. I. The art of rearrangement: Forster's Abinger harvest. New Haven 1964. (Yale College ser 1).

Natwar-Singh, K. (ed). Forster: a tribute, with selections from his writings on India. New York [1964].

Wilde, A. Art and order: a study of Forster. New York 1964.

Mason, W. H. A passage to India. Oxford 1965 (Notes on Eng Lit).

Moore, H. T. E. M. Forster. New York 1965 (Columbia Essays on Modern Writers).

Panichas, G. A. Forster and D. H. Lawrence: their views on education. In Renaissance and modern studies presented to V. de Sola Pinto, ed R. G. Hibbard, 1965.

Shusterman, D. The quest for certitude in Forster's fiction. Bloomington 1965 (Indiana Univ Pbns, Humanities ser 58).

Stebner, G. Forster: A passage to India. In Der moderne englische Roman ed H. Oppel, Berlin 1965.

Bradbury, M. (ed). Forster: a collection of critical essays. Englewood Cliffs, NJ 1966.

Daleski, H. M. Rhythm and symbolic patterns in A passage to India. In Studies in English language and literature, ed A. Shalvi and A. A. Mendilow, Jerusalem 1966.

Mendilow, A. A. The tragic world of Forster. Ibid.

Stone, W. The cave and the mountain: a study of Forster. Stanford 1966.

Colmer, J. A. (ed). A passage to India. 1967 (Studies in Eng Lit).

Kelvin, N. E. M. Forster. Carbondale 1967.

Kondo, I. (ed). E. M. Forster. Tokyo 1967.

Thomson, G. H. The fiction of Forster. Detroit 1967.

Brander, L. Forster: a critical study. 1968.

Godfrey, D. Forster's other kingdom. Edinburgh 1968.

Moody, P. A critical commentary on Forster's Passage to India. 1968.

McDowell, F. P. W. E. M. Forster. New York 1969.

Stallybrass, O. (ed). Aspects of Forster. 1969.

Articles in Periodicals

Richards, I. A. A passage to Forster. Forum 78 1927.

Shanks, E. Mr E. M. Forster. London Mercury 16 1927.

Woolf, V. The novels of Forster. Atlantic Monthly 140 1927; rptd in her The death of the moth, 1942.

Doughty, H. M. The novels of Forster. Bookman (NY) 75 1932.

Belgion, M. The diabolism of Forster. Criterion 14 1934.

Brown, E. K. Forster and the contemplative novel. UTQ 3 1934.

— The revival of Forster. Yale Rev 33 1944; rptd in Forms of modern fiction, ed W. V. O'Connor, Minneapolis 1948.

Burra, P. The novels of Forster. Nineteenth Century 116 1934; rptd as introd to A passage to India, 1942 (EL).

Bowen, E. E. M. Forster. Spectator 20 March 1936; rptd in her Collected impressions, 1950.

Traversi, D. A. The novels of Forster. Arena 1 1937.

Warren, A. The novels of Forster. American Rev 9 1937; rptd in his Rage for order, Chicago 1948.

Leavis, F. R. E. M. Forster. Scrutiny 7 1938; rptd in his The common pursuit, 1952.

Zabel, M. D. E. M. Forster. Nation 147 1938; rptd in his Craft and character in modern fiction, New York 1957.

Ransom, J. C. E. M. Forster. Kenyon Rev 5 1943.

McLuhan, H. M. Kipling and Forster. Sewanee Rev 52 1944.

Lunan, N. M. The novels of Forster. Durham Univ Jnl 6 1945.

Savage, D. S. E. M. Forster. Now 3–4 [1945]; rptd (rev) in Writers of today, ed D. V. Baker, New York 1947. Enlarged as Examinations of modern authors: 4. E. M. Forster, Rocky Mountain Rev 10 1946; rptd in his The withered branch, 1950.

Waggoner, H. H. Exercises in perspective: notes on the use of coincidence in the novels of Forster. Chimera 3 1945.

Ault, P. Aspects of Forster. Dublin Rev 219 1946.

Brower, R. A. Beyond Forster: 1. The earth. Foreground 1 1946.

Gilomen, W. Fantasy and prophecy in Forster's work. E Studies 27 1946.

Holt, L. E. Forster and Samuel Butler. PMLA 61 1946.

Macaulay, R. E. M. Forster. Listener 12 Dec 1946; rptd in Living writers, ed G. Phelps 1947.

Bentley, P. The novels of Forster. Eng Jnl 37 1948. Also in College Eng 9 1948.

Cecil, D. E. M. Forster. Atlantic Monthly 183 1949; rptd in his Poets and storytellers, 1949.

Boyle, A. Novels of Forster. Irish Monthly 78 1950.

Beaumont, E. Mr E. M. Forster's strange mystics. Dublin Rev 225 1951.

Keir, W. A. S. A passage to India reconsidered. Cambridge Jnl 5 1952.

Berland, A. James and Forster: the morality of class. Cambridge Jnl 6 1953.

Furbank, P. N. and F. J. H. Haskell. E. M. Forster. Paris Rev 1953; rptd in Writers at work: the Paris Rev interviews, ed M. Cowley, New York 1958.

Fussell, P. Forster's Mrs Moore: some suggestions. PQ 32 1953.

Maclean, H. The structure of A passage to India. UTQ 22 1953.

White, G. M. A passage to India: analysis and revaluation. PMLA 68 1953.

Chaudhuri, N. C. Passage from India. Encounter 2 1954.

Johnson, E. H. The intelligent Mr Forster. Personalist 35 1954.

Voorhees, R. J. The novels of Forster. South Atlantic Quart 53 1954.

Allen, G. O. Structure, symbol and theme in Forster's A passage to India. PMLA 70 1955.

Benson, A. R. Forster's dialectic: Howards End. Modern Fiction Stud 1 1955.

Harvey, W. J. Imagination and moral theme in Forster's The longest journey. EC 6 1956.

Wilcox, S. C. The allegory of Forster's 'The celestial omnibus'. Modern Fiction Stud 2 1956.

Zwerding, A. The novels of Forster. Twentieth-Century Lit 2 1957.

Hall, J. Forster's family reunions. ELH 25 1958. Chiefly on Howards End; rptd in his The tragic comedians, Bloomington 1963.

Kermode, F. Mr Forster as a symbolist. Listener 2 Jan 1958; rptd (as The one orderly product) in his Puzzles and epiphanies, 1962. On A passage to India.

Klingopoulos, G. D. Forster's sense of history, and Cavafy. EC 8 1958.

Gransden, K. W. Forster at eighty. Encounter 12 1959.

McDowell, F. P. W. The mild intellectual light: idea and theme in Howards End. PMLA 74 1959.

— Forster's many-faceted universe. Critique (Minneapolis) 4 1960–1.

— Forster's conception of the critic. Tennessee Stud in Lit 10 1965.

— Forster's most recent critics. Eng Lit in Transition 8 1965.

— Forster's theory of literature. Criticism 8 1966.

— Forster: romancer or realist. Eng Lit in Transition 11 1968.

Pedersen, G. Forster's symbolic form. Kenyon Rev 21 1959.

Hale, N. A passage to relationship. Antioch Rev 20 1960.

Hoy, C. Forster's metaphysical novel. PMLA 75 1960. On Howards End.

MacDonald, A. A. Class-consciousness in Forster. Univ of Kansas City Rev 27 1961.

Modern Fiction Stud 7 1961. Special no on Forster. Contains:

Wilde, A. The aesthetic view of life: Where angels fear to tread.

Austin, D. The problem of continuity in three novels of Forster. [The longest journey, A room with a view, Howards End].

Thomson, G. H. Theme and symbol in Howards End.

Hoffman, F. J. Howards End and the bogey of progress.

Dauner, L. What happened in the cave?: reflections on A passage to India.

McDowell, F. P. W. Forster's 'natural supernaturalism': the tales.

Beebe, M. and J. Brogunier. Criticism of Forster: a selected checklist.

Shusterman, D. The curious case of Professor Godbole: A passage to India re-examined. PMLA 76 1961.

Thomson, G. H. Symbolism in Forster's earlier fiction. Criticism 3 1961.

— Thematic symbol in A passage to India. Twentieth-Century Lit 7 1961.

— E. M. Forster and Howard Sturgis. Texas Stud in Lit & Lang 10 1968.

— E. M. Forster, Gerald Heard and Bloomsbury. Eng Lit in Transition 12 1969.

Bradbury, M. Forster's Howards End. CQ 4 1962.

Brander, L. Forster and India. Rev of Eng Lit 3 1962.

Churchill, T. Place and personality in Howards End. Critique (Minneapolis) 5 1962.

Echeruo, M. J. C. Forster and the undeveloped heart. Eng Stud in Africa 5 1962.

Hannah, D. The limitations of liberalism in Forster's work. Eng Miscellany 13 1962.

Hollingworth, K. A passage to India: the echoes in the Marabar Caves. Criticism 4 1962.

Kaiser, R. E. M. Forster: gedankliche Analyse seines Romanes Howards End im Rahmen des Gesamtwerkes. Die Neueren Sprachen 11 1962.

Clubb, R. L. A passage to India: the meaning of the Marabar Caves. College Lang Assoc Jnl 6 1963.

Cooperman, S. The imperial posture and the shrine of darkness: Kipling's The Naulakha and Forster's A passage to India. Eng Lit in Transition 6 1963.

Sorenson, P. E. Forster: a brief memoir. Claremont Quart 11 1963.

Woodward, A. The humanism of Forster. Theoria 20 1963.

Austin, E. A. Rites of passage in A passage to India. Orient-West 9 1964.

Friedman, A. B. Forster, Dostoyevsky, Akutagawa and 'St Peter and his mother'. Eng Lang Notes 1 1964.

Garnett, D. Forster and Galsworthy. REL 5 1964.

Horowitz, E. The communal ritual and the dying god in Forster's A passage to India. Criticism 6 1964.

Nierenberg, E. The prophecy of Forster. Queen's Quart 71 1964.

— The withered priestess: Mrs Moore's incomplete passage to India. MLQ 25 1964.

Boyle, T. E. Adela Quested's delusion: the failure of rationalism in A passage to India. College Eng 26 1965.

Hagopian, J. V. Eternal moments in the short fiction of Forster. College Eng 27 1965.

Howarth, H. Forster and the contrite establishment. Jnl of General Education 17 1965.

Koljevic, S. Forster: sceptic as novelist. Mad River Rev 1 1965.

Missey, J. L. Forster's redemptive siren. Modern Fiction Stud 10 1965.

Thomas, R. and H. Erskine-Hill. A passage to India: two points of view. Anglo-Welsh Rev 15 1965.

Westburg, B. R. Forster's fifth symphony: another aspect of Howards End. Modern Fiction Stud 10 1965.

Goldman, M. Virginia Woolf and Forster: a critical dialogue. Texas Stud in Lit & Lang 7 1966.

Hunt, J. D. Muddle and mystery in A passage to India. ELH 33 1966.

Lucas, J. Wagner and Forster: Parsifal and A room with a view. ELH 33 1966.

Martin, J. S. Mrs Moore and the Marabar Caves: a mythological reading. Modern Fiction Stud 11 1966.

Shahane, V. A. The Marabar Caves: fact and fiction. Amer Notes & Queries 5 1966.

— A visit to Mr E. M. Forster. Quest 53 1967.

Bell, V. M. Comic seriousness in A passage to India. South Atlantic Quart 66 1967.

Confalonieri, M. B. I racconti di Forster. Eng Miscellany 18 1967.

Magnus, J. Ritual aspects of Forster's The longest journey. Modern Fiction Stud 13 1967.

Rawlings, D. Forster: 'prophecy' and the subversion of myth. Paunch 30 1967.

Schmerl, R. B. Fantasy as technique. Virginia Quart Rev 43 1967.

Decap, R. Un roman pascalien: A passage to India. Caliban 5 1968.

Lacotte, C. Études récentes sur Forster. Études Anglaises 20 1968.

Langbaum, R. A new look at Forster. Southern Rev 4 1968.

Moran, R. 'Come, come', 'Boum, boum': easy rhythm in Forster's A passage to India. Ball State Univ Forum 9 1968.

Mukherjee, A. K. The split personality of Forster. Quest 56 1968.

Shonfield, A. The politics of Forster's India. Encounter 30 1968. Reply by H. S. Nelson and G. K. Das, Shonfield and Forster's India, with rejoinder by Shonfield.

Spencer, M. Hinduism in A passage to India. Jnl of Asian Studies 27 1968.

Delbaere-Garant, J. Who shall inherit England? A comparison between Howards End, Parade's end, and Unconditional surrender. E Studies 50 1969.

Gowda, H. H. A. (ed). A garland for Forster. Literary Half-Yearly 1969.

Maskell, D. Style and symbolism in Howards End. EC 19 1969.

Müllenbrock, H-J. Gesellschaftliche Thematik in Forsters Roman Howards End. Anglia 87 1969.

C.P.C.

JAMES AUGUSTINE ALOYSIUS JOYCE
1882–1941

Slocum and Cahoon, Bibliography, below, includes a section on Joyce mss (including unpbd works), and gives locations in public institutions and the Slocum Library. Principal collections are at the BM (Finnegans wake), New York Public Library, Yale Univ (the Slocum Library includes Dubliners), National Library of Ireland (includes A portrait of the artist as a young man, and the Joyce-Léon correspondence), the Rosenbach Foundation (Ulysses), State Univ of New York at Buffalo, and Cornell and Southern Illinois universities.

Bibliographies

Beach, S. Catalogue of a collection containing manuscripts and rare editions of Joyce. Paris [1935].

Roberts, R. F. Bibliographical notes on Joyce's Ulysses. Colophon new ser 1 1936.

O'Hegarty, P. S. A bibliography of Joyce. Dublin 1946. Rptd from Dublin Mag 21 1946.

Parker, A. Joyce: a bibliography of his writings, critical material and miscellanea. Boston 1948. See also White, and Cohn, below.

Spoerri, J. F. Catalog of a collection of the works of Joyce [at the Newberry Lib]. Chicago 1948.

— Finnegans wake: a checklist. Evanston 1953.

— Joyce: books and pamphlets relating to the author and his works. Bibl Soc of the Univ of Virginia Secretary's News Sheet Oct 1955. Suppls Sept 1957, Feb 1964.

Gheerbrant, B. Joyce: sa vie, son oeuvre, son rayonnement. Paris 1949. Joyce material now at State Univ Buffalo: sometimes cited as La Hune catalogue.

White, W. Joyce: addenda to Alan Parker's bibliography. PBSA 43 1949.

— Addenda to Joyce bibliography 1950–3 [and] 1954–7. James Joyce Rev 1 1957.

Slocum, J. J. and H. Cahoon. A bibliography of Joyce 1882–1941. 1953 (Soho Bibliographies). Includes books, contributions to books and periodicals, trns, mss, musical settings, recordings, broadcasts, miscellany.

— A note on Joyce bibliography. Yale Univ Lib Gazette 28 1953.

Connolly, T. E. The personal library of Joyce: a descriptive bibliography. Buffalo 1955. Includes Joyce's notebooks, mss and letters.

Cohn, A. M. An exhibition from the collection of Dr H. K. Croessmann [at Southern Illinois Univ]. Carbondale 1957.

— Further supplement to Joyce bibliography 1950–7. James Joyce Rev 2 1958.

— and H. K. Croessmann. Additional supplement to Joyce bibliography 1950–9. James Joyce Rev 3 1959.

Cohn, A. M. and R. M. Kain. Supplemental Joyce checklist 1962 [etc]. James Joyce Quart 1– 1964– (annually).

Cohn, A. M. Joyce bibliographies: a survey. Amer Book Collector 15 1965.

Scholes, R. E. The Cornell Joyce collection: a catalogue. Ithaca 1961.

Thornton, W. Books and manuscripts by Joyce. Lib Chron of Univ of Texas 7 1961.

Adams, R. M. The bent knife blade: Joyce in the 1960s. Partisan Rev 29 1962.

Spielberg, P. Joyce's manuscripts and letters at the University of Buffalo. Buffalo 1962.

Deming, R. H. A bibliography of Joyce studies. Lawrence 1964 (Univ of Kansas Pbns, Lib ser 18). Includes work pbd to Dec 1961: exhaustive and annotated; supplemented by Cohn and Kain.

Rice, H. C., jr. The Sylvia Beach collection. Princeton Univ Lib Chron 26 1964.

Kain, R. M. Addenda to Deming bibliography. James Joyce Quart 3 1965.

— and A. M. Cohn. Portraits of Joyce: a revised list. James Joyce Quart 3 1966.

Staley, T. F. Joyce scholarship in the 1960s. Papers on Eng Lang & Lit 1 1965. A review-essay.

Beebe, M., P. F. Herring and W. Litz. Criticism of Joyce: a selected checklist. Modern Fiction Stud 15 1969.

Collections and Selections

Collected poems. New York 1936. Chamber music, Pomes penyeach and Ecce puer.

Eliot, T. S. (ed). Introducing Joyce: a selection from Joyce's prose. 1942. Contains The sisters [from Dubliners] and selections from A portrait of the artist, Ulysses and Finnegans wake.

Levin, H. (ed). The portable Joyce. New York 1947, London 1948 (as The essential Joyce), New York 1949 (as The indispensable Joyce), 1966 (rev, as The portable Joyce).

The critical writings of Joyce. Ed E. Mason and R. Ellmann 1959.

§I

For details of ms versions and corrections etc and for the complicated publishing history of Joyce's works, see Slocum and Cahoon, Bibliography, section E.

Et tu Healy! [1891]. No copy known to survive. Verse.

The day of the rabblement. In Two essays, Dublin [1901] (with A forgotten aspect of the university question by F. J. C. Skeffington). Rptd Minneapolis 1957.

The holy office. [Pola 1904 or 1905]. Broadside poem.

Chamber music. 1907, 1918, Boston [1918] (unauthorized), New York 1918, London 1927, ed W. Y. Tindall, New York 1954.

Gas from a burner. Flushing 1912. Broadside poem. Slocum and Cahoon quote S. Joyce as giving Trieste as actual place of printing.

Dubliners. 1914, New York 1916 (English sheets), 1917, London 1926 (with introd by P. Colum), 1967 (corrected text, ed R. Scholes), New York 1967. Stories. Contains The sisters, An encounter, Araby, Eveline, After the race, Two gallants, The boarding house, A little cloud, Counterparts, Clay, A painful case, Ivy

Day in the committee room, A mother, Grace, The dead.

A portrait of the artist as a young man. New York 1916. London [1917] (American sheets), [1918], New York 1928 (with introd by H. Gorman), London 1930; ed J. S. Atherton 1964; ed C. G. Anderson, New York 1964, London 1968. First pbd serially in Egoist 1–2 1914–15. *See* also Stephen hero, 1944 below. *See* The workshop of Daedalus, ed R. Scholes and R. M. Kain, Evanston 1965.

Exiles: a play in three acts. 1918, New York 1918, Norfolk Conn 1945 (with introd by F. Fergusson), New York 1951 (with previously unpbd notes by Joyce and introd by P. Colum), London 1952. First performed, in German, at the Münchener Theater, Munich 1919; in English, at the Neighborhood Playhouse, New York 19 Feb–22 March 1925, and by the Stage Soc at the Regent Theatre 14 and 15 Feb 1926.

Ulysses. Paris 1922, London 1922 (Paris ptd), [New York 1929] (unauthorized), 2 vols Hamburg 1932 (rev S. Gilbert at Joyce's request), New York 1934, 1935 (with introd by S. Gilbert), London 1936. 13 episodes, and pt of 14th, pbd in Little Rev March 1918–Dec 1920; some episodes pbd in Egoist 6 1919; 14 episodes rptd unauthorized in Two Worlds Monthly 1–3 1926–7.

Pomes penyeach. Paris 1927, [Princeton] 1931 (50 copies, for copyright), Cleveland 1931 (priv ptd), London 1932 (Paris ptd), 1933, Oxford [1933] (as The Joyce book, with prologue by J. Stephens, essay by P. Colum and musical settings of each poem), London 1966 (with Ecce puer, The holy office, and Gas from a burner; as Pomes penyeach and other verses).

Work in progress: volume 1. New York 1928 (20 copies, for copyright). Rptd from transition April–Nov 1927.

Work in progress: parts 11 and 12. [New York 1928] (5 copies, for copyright). Rptd from transition March 1928.

Anna Livia Plurabelle: fragment of Work in progress. New York 1928 (with introd by P. Colum), London 1930.

Anna Livia Plurabelle: the making of a chapter. Ed F. H. Higginson 1960.

Work in progress: part 13. [New York 1928] (5 copies, for copyright). Rptd from transition Summer 1928.

Work in progress: part 15. [New York 1929] (5 copies, for copyright). Rptd from transition Feb 1929.

Tales told of Shem and Shaun: three fragments from Work in progress. Paris 1929. Contains The mookse and the gripes, The muddest thick that was ever heard dump, The ondt and the gracehoper. Preface by C. K. Ogden.

Two tales of Shem and Shaun: fragments from Work in progress. 1932. Contains The mookse and the gripes, and The ondt and the gracehoper.

Work in progress: part 18. [New York 1930] (5 copies, for copyright). Rptd from transition Nov 1929.

Haveth childers everywhere: fragment from Work in progress. New York 1930 (Paris ptd), London 1931.

The mime of Mick, Nick and the maggies: a fragment from Work in progress. The Hague 1934.

Storiella as she is syung. 1937 (176 copies). A section of Work in progress.

Finnegans wake. 1939, New York 1939, London 1946 (with list of corrections), New York 1947, London 1950 (incorporating most of the corrections), 1964 (incorporating remainder of corrections), 1966 (abridged by A. Burgess, as A shorter Finnegans wake). Some sections pbd separately from 1928 as Work in progress; *see* above. *See* also J. F. Spoerri, Finnegans wake by Joyce: a check list, Evanston 1953. Corrections of misprints in Finnegans wake was first pbd separately New York 1945.

A first-draft version of Finnegans wake. Ed D. Hayman, Austin 1963.

Pastimes. New York 1941. Facs of a poem in holograph.

Stephen hero: part of the first draft of A portrait of the artist as a young man. Ed with introd by T. Spencer 1944, New York 1944 (US edn differs slightly and is regarded by the editor as superior); ed J. J. Slocum and H. Cahoon, New York 1955, 1963 (with addns).

The early Joyce: the book reviews 1902–03. Ed S. Joyce and E. Mason, Colorado Springs 1955.

Epiphanies. Ed O. A. Silverman, Buffalo 1956. *See also* The workshop of Daedalus, ed Scholes and Kain, 1965.

Scribbledehobble: the ur-workbook for Finnegans wake. Ed T. E. Connolly, Evanston 1961.

The cat and the devil. New York 1964, London 1965. Children's story in the form of a letter to Joyce's grandson dated 10 Aug 1936.

Daniel Defoe. Ed and tr J. Prescott, Buffalo Stud 1 1964. Lecture given in Italian in 1912 at the Università Popolare Triestina.

Giacomo Joyce. Ed R. Ellmann, New York 1968, London 1968. With facs. Written about 1914.

Letters

A collection of letters between Joyce and P. Léon 1930–40 is deposited in the National Library of Ireland but will not be available till 1991.

A., E.L. Joyce to his literary agents. More Books 18 1943. 3 letters on Ulysses.

Levin, H. Carteggio inedito Italo Svevo–James Joyce. Inventario 2 1949.

Letters of Joyce. 3 vols; vol 1, ed S. Gilbert 1957; vols 2–3, ed R. Ellmann 1966; New York 1966 (with corrections to vol 1).

Boyle, K. Letter from Joyce. Tri-Quarterly 8 1967.

Joyce: a hitherto unpublished letter [to H. L. Mencken]. Menckeniana 28 1968.

§2

In view of the enormous quantity of secondary material on Joyce only a selection is given below. It is divided as follows: biographical studies, general studies of Joyce's work as a whole, and studies of individual works (arranged under the particular work). This arrangement corresponds broadly with that of Deming, Bibliography of Joyce Studies, where much fuller listings can be found: such listings of post-1961 material are available in Modern Fiction Stud 15 1969, and in the James Joyce Quart nos given above. Reviews are listed and excerpted in Joyce: the critical heritage, ed R. H. Deming 2 vols 1970.

Biographical

Francini Bruni, A. Joyce intimo spogliato in piazza. Trieste 1922.

— Ricordi personali su Joyce. Nuova Antologia Sept–Dec 1947.

Cecchi, E. Incontro con Ulysses. La Tribuna 2 March 1923; rptd in Europa letteraria 2 1961; and in his Scrittori inglesi e americani, 4th edn Milan 1964.

Clarke, A. 'Stephen Daedalus': author of Ulysses. New Statesman 23 Feb 1924.

Gorman, H. Joyce: his first forty years. New York 1924.

— James Joyce. New York 1940, 1948 (rev).

Colum, P. In his Road round Ireland, 1926.

— A portrait of Joyce. New Republic 66 1931.

— Portrait of Joyce. Dublin Mag new ser 7 1932.

— Working with Joyce. Irish Times 5, 6 Oct 1956.

Anderson, M. In her My thirty years war, New York 1930.

Benco, S. Ricordi di Joyce. Pegaso no 2 1930 and Bookman (New York) 72 1930 (as Joyce in Trieste).

Soupault, P. Autour de Joyce. Bravo (Paris) Sept 1930; rptd in Souvenirs de Joyce, Paris 1945; and in A Joyce yearbook, ed M. Jolas, Paris 1949 (as Recollections of Joyce).

— James Joyce. In his Profils perdus, Paris 1963.

Borach, G. Gespräche mit Joyce. Neue Zürcher Zeitung 3 May 1931; rptd in College Eng 15 1954 (tr J. Prescott).

Lennon, M. J. James Joyce. Catholic World 132 1931.

'Eglinton, John' (W. K. Magee). The beginnings of Joyce. Life & Letters 8 1932; rptd in his Irish literary portraits, 1935.

Paul, E. Farthest north: a study of Joyce. Bookman (New York) 75 1932.

Pound, E. Past history. Eng Jnl 22 1933; rptd in next.

— Pound/Joyce: the letters of Pound to Joyce, with Pound's essays on Joyce. Ed F. Read, New York 1967.

Budgen, F. Joyce and the making of Ulysses. New York 1934, London 1934 (corrected), Bloomington 1960 (rev, with next, but without the London edn corrections).

— Further recollections of Joyce. 1955; rptd (rev) Partisan Rev 23 1956.

— Joyce and Martha Fleischmann: a witness's recollection. Tri-Quarterly 8 1967.

Kerr, A. Joyce en Angleterre. Les Nouvelles Littéraires 11 Jan 1936; rptd in A Joyce miscellany, ed M. Magalaner 1957 (as Joyce in England, tr J. Prescott).

Gogarty, O. St J. As I was going down Sackville Street. 1937.

— The Joyce I knew. Saturday Rev of Lit 23 1941.

— Joyce: a portrait of the artist. In his Mourning became Mrs Spendlove, New York 1948.

— Joyce as a friend of music. Tomorrow 9 1949.

— They think they know Joyce. Saturday Rev of Lit 33 1950; see discussion, ibid.

— Joyce as a tenor. In his Intimations, New York 1950.

— It isn't that time of year at all. Garden City NY 1954.

'Svevo, Italo' (E. Schmitz). James Joyce. Convegno 25 April 1937; tr S. Joyce 1950; rptd with additional material in his Saggi e pagine sparse, 1954.

Griffin, G. Wild geese: pen portraits of famous Irish exiles. 1938.

McAlmon, R. Being geniuses together. 1938, 1968 (rev and with supplementary chs by K. Boyle).

Wilder, T. Essay on Joyce. Poetry 57 1940; rptd as James Joyce 1882–1941, Aurora NY 1944.

Giedion-Welcker, C. et al. In memoriam James Joyce. Zürich 1941.

Giedion-Welcker, C. Joyce in Zürich. Horizon 18 1948.

Gillet, L. Recuerdos de Joyce. Sur Dec 1941, Jan 1942; rptd in his Stèle pour Joyce, Marseilles 1941 and tr G. Markow-Totevy 1958, New York 1958 (as Claybook for Joyce).

Jolas, E. My friend Joyce. Partisan Rev 8 1941; rptd in Partisan reader, New York 1946; and in Joyce: two decades of criticism, ed S. Givens, New York 1948.

Joyce, S. Ricordi di Joyce. Letteratura 5 1941. Tr E. Mason, New York 1950 (as Recollections of Joyce by his brother); and tr F. Giovanelli, Hudson Rev 2 1950.

— Early memories of Joyce. Listener 41 1949.

— Joyce's Dublin. Partisan Rev 19 1952.

— Open letter to Dr Oliver Gogarty. Interim 4 1954.

— My brother's keeper. Ed R. Ellmann, New York 1958.

— In his Dublin diary, ed G. H. Healy, Ithaca 1962.

— The meeting of Svevo and Joyce. Udine 1965.

Léon, P. Souvenir de Joyce. Poésie 5 1942; rptd in A Joyce yearbook ed M. Jolas, Paris 1949 (as In memory of Joyce, tr M. J[olas]).

Antheil, G. Joyce and others. In his Bad boy of music, Garden City NY 1945.

John, A. Fragment of an autobiography, XV. Horizon 13 1946; rptd in his Chiaroscuro, New York 1952.

Curran, C. P. When Joyce lived in Dublin. Vogue 1 May 1947.

— Joyce remembered. New York 1968.

Putnam, S. In his Paris was our mistress, New York 1947.

Edel, L. Joyce: the last journey. Story 32 1948. Also rptd separately, New York 1947.

Levin, H. Joyce's sentimental journey through France and Italy. Yale Rev 38 1949: rptd in his Contexts of criticism, Cambridge Mass 1957.

Gilbert, S. Souvenirs de voyage. Mercure de France 309 1950.

Hutchins, P. Joyce's Dublin. 1950.
— Joyce's world. 1957.
Jolas, M. Joyce en 1939–40. Mercure de France 309 1950.
Noël [Léon], L. Joyce and Paul L. Léon: the story of a friendship. New York 1950.
Pichette, H. Rond-Point, suivi de Joyce au participe futur. Paris 1950.
Hone, J. A recollection of Joyce. Envoy 5 1951.
Byrne, J. F. Silent years: an autobiography, with memoirs of Joyce and our Ireland. New York 1953.
Kenner, H. The trivium in Dublin. Eng Inst Essays 1952, New York 1954.
— Prometheus's diary. Prairie Schooner 32 1958.
Ellmann, R. A portrait of the artist as friend. Kenyon Rev 18 1956; also in Eng Institute Essays 1955, New York 1956.
— Joyce in love. Ithaca 1959.
— James Joyce. New York 1959.
— Eminent domain: Yeats among Wilde, Joyce, Pound, Eliot and Auden. New York 1967.
— Joyce, Irish European. Tri-Quarterly 8 1967.
— and H. Barolini. The curious case of Amalia Popper. New York Rev of Books 20 Nov 1969.
Mason, E. Joyce's shrill note: the Piccolo della Sera articles. Twentieth-Century Lit 2 1956.
Rodgers, W. R. Joyce's wake. Explorations no 5 1956; also in Explorations in communication: an anthology, ed E. Carpenter and M. McLuhan, Boston 1960.
— The Dublin of Joyce. Meanjin 22 1963; also in Harper's Bazaar 96 1963.
Paris, J. Joyce par lui-même. Paris 1957.
Colum, M. and P. Our friend Joyce. Garden City NY 1958.
MacCarvill, E. Les années de formation de Joyce à Dublin. Archives des Lettres Modernes no 12 1958.
Sullivan, K. Joyce among the Jesuits. New York 1958.
Beach, S. Shakespeare and Company. New York 1959.
Morse, J. M. The sympathetic alien: Joyce and Catholicism. New York 1959.
O'Neill, M. J. The Joyces in the Holloway diaries. In A Joyce miscellany: second series, ed M. Magalaner, Carbondale 1959.
O'Connor, U. Joyce and Gogarty: a famous friendship. Texas Quart 3 1960.
— (ed) The Joyce we knew: memoirs by Eugene Sheehy, William G. Fallon, Padraic Colum, Arthur Power. Cork 1967.
Tindall, W. Y. The Joyce country. University Park Pa 1960. Photographs.
Bini, L. Joyce esule ribelle. Letture 16 1961.
Crise, S. Joyce e Trieste. Accademie e biblioteche d'Italia 29 1961.
— Epiphanies and Phadographs: Joyce e Trieste. Milan 1967.
Hoffmeister, A. James Joyce; Osobnost Joyce. In his Podoby, Prague 1961. The latter tr E. Ripellino in Europa Letteraria 2 1962 (as Un incontro di Joyce); both tr (F. Kerel) in his Visages écrits et dessinés, Paris 1964 (as La personnalité de Joyce).
Noon, W. T. Joyce: unfacts, fiction and facts. PMLA 76 1961. See also R. Scholes and Fr. Noon, 79 1964.
White, W. Irish antitheses: Shaw and Joyce. Shavian 2 1961.
Mercanton, J. The hours of Joyce, tr L. C. Parks. Kenyon Rev 24 1962, 25 1963. Accounts of meetings with Joyce. Rptd Lausanne 1967 (as Les heures de Joyce).
Curtayne, A. Portrait of the artist as brother: an interview with Joyce's sister. Critic 21 1963.
Mercure de France 349 1963. Sylvia Beach no. Contributions by S. Beach, C. Connolly, T. S. Eliot, J. Flanner, M. Jolas, V. Larbaud, M. Mohrt, A. Monnier, M. Saillet, A. Spire and W. C. Williams.
Pinguentini, G. Joyce in Italia. Florence 1963.
Scholes, R. (ed). Grant Richards to Joyce. SB 16 1963. Letters.

Bianchini, A. Joyce e l'Italia. Tempo Presente 9 1964.
Neufeld, M. R. Mirrors and photographs in Joyce's Ulysses. November Rev 1 1964.
Reynolds, M. T. Joyce and Nora: the indispensable countersign. Sewanee Rev 72 1964.
Wildi, M. Joyce and Arthur Symons. Orbis Litterarum 19 1964.
Yeats, J. B. On Joyce: a letter, ed D. Torchiana and G. O'Malley. Tri-Quarterly 1 1964.
Power, A. Conversations with Joyce. James Joyce Quart 3 1965.
De Tuoni, D. Ricordo di Joyce a Trieste. Milan 1966.
Freund, G. and V. B. Carleton. Joyce in Paris: his final years. New York 1965. Photographs.
Furbank, P. N. Svevo and Joyce. In his Italo Svevo, 1966.
Núñez, E. Joyce y Victor Llona. Revista Peruana de Cultura 7–8 1966.
Thomson, V. Antheil, Joyce and Pound. In his Virgil Thomson, New York 1966.
Anderson, C. G. Joyce's letters and his use of place. James Joyce Quart 4 1967.
— Joyce and his world. 1967.
Beckson, K. and J. M. Munro (ed). Letters from Arthur Symons to Joyce: 1904–32. James Joyce Quart 4 1967.
Firth, J. (ed). Harriet Weaver's letters to Joyce, 1915–20. SB 20 1967.
— James Pinker to Joyce, 1915–20. SB 21 1968.
Frank, N. In his Mémoire brisée, Paris 1967.
Lewis, W. In his Blasting and bombardiering, Berkeley 1967 (2nd edn, rev).
Livermore, A. Carmen and Ulysses. Music Rev 28 1967.
Recklinghausen, D. von. Joyce: Chronik von Leben und Werk. Frankfurt 1968.
Reid, B. L. The man from New York: John Quinn and his friends. New York 1968.
Trilling, L. Joyce in his letters. Commentary 45 1968.
Read, F. Storicamente Joyce, 1930: Ezra Pound's first Italian essay. Tri-Quarterly no 15 1969. Followed by his trn of E. Pound, Historically Joyce (and censorship).

General Studies

Muir, E. In his Transition: essays on contemporary literature, 1926.
Lewis, W. An analysis of the mind of Joyce. Enemy 1 1927; rptd in his Time and western man, 1927.
O'Faolain, S. Style and the limitations of speech. Criterion 8 1928.
— In his Vanishing hero: studies in the novelists of the twenties, 1956.
'West, Rebecca' (C. I. Andrews). In her Strange necessity, 1928.
Connolly, C. The position of Joyce. Life & Letters 2 1929; rptd in his Condemned playground, 1945.
Dujardin, E. Le monologue intérieure: son apparition, ses origines, sa place dans l'oeuvre de Joyce. Paris 1931.
Eastman, M. In his The literary mind, New York 1931.
Lindsay, J. In Scrutinies vol 2, ed E. Rickword 1931.
Wilson, E. In his Axel's castle, New York 1931.
Duff, C. Joyce and the plain reader. 1932.
Gilbert, S. et al. Homage to Joyce. Transition no 21 1932.
Gilbert, S. The Latin background of Joyce's art. Horizon 10 1944.
— James Joyce. In Writers of today, ed D. V. Baker, 1946; rptd in Joyce: two decades of criticism, ed S. Givens, New York 1948.
Eliot, T. S. In his After strange gods, 1933.
— A message to the fish. Horizon 3 1941; rptd in Joyce: two decades of criticism, ed S. Givens, New York 1948.
Golding, L. James Joyce. 1933.
Stonier, G. W. In his Gog Magog and other critical essays, 1933.
Gorgianni, E. Inchiesta su Joyce. Milan 1934.
Dubois, P. M. Joyce, irlandais. Revue Universelle 61 1935.

Broch, H. Joyce und die Gegenwart. Vienna 1936; rptd in his Gesammelte Werke, Zürich 1955, and in A Joyce yearbook, ed M. Jolas, Paris 1949 (as Joyce and the present age, tr E. and M. Jolas).

Farrell, J. T. In his A note on literary criticism, New York 1936.

More, P. E. In his On being human, Princeton 1936.

Ross, M. Music and Joyce. Chicago 1936.

Colum, M. In her From these roots: the ideas that have made modern literature, New York 1937.

Cazamian, L. L'oeuvre de Joyce. In his Essais en deux langues, Paris 1938; rptd (rev) from Revue Anglo-américaine 2 1924.

Hoare, D. M. Moore and Joyce: a contrast. In her Some studies in the modern novel, 1938.

Mercanton, J. James Joyce. Europe 46 1938.

— In his Poètes de l'univers, Paris 1947.

Miller, H. The universe of death. In his Cosmological eye, Norfolk Conn 1939.

Auden, W. H. Joyce and Richard Wagner. Common Sense 10 1941.

Bowen, E. James Joyce. The Bell 1 1941.

Levin, H. Joyce: a critical introduction. Norfolk Conn 1941, 1960 (rev).

Hope, A. D. The esthetic theory of Joyce. Australasian Jnl of Psychology & Philosophy 16 1943; rptd in Joyce's Portrait: criticisms and critiques, ed T. E. Connolly, New York 1962.

Davies, A. Yr all tud rhagarweiniad i weithiau Joyce. 1944.

Stoll, E. E. In his From Shakespeare to Joyce, New York 1944.

Hendry, J. F. The element of myth in Joyce. Scottish Arts & Letters no 1 1945; rptd in Joyce: two decades of criticism, ed S. Givens, New York 1948.

Hoffman, F. J. Infroyce. In his Freudianism and the literary mind, Baton Rouge 1945, 1957 (rev); rptd in Joyce: two decades of criticism, ed S. Givens, New York 1948.

— The authority of the commonplace: Joyce's Bloomsday. Kenyon Rev 22 1960.

— In his Mortal no: death and the modern imagination, Princeton 1964.

— The harness of reality: Joyce's Stephen Dedalus. In his Imagination's new beginning: theology and modern literature, South Bend 1967.

MacLeod, V. K. Influence of Ibsen on Joyce. PMLA 60 1945, 62 1947 (Addendum).

Strong, L. A. G. Joyce and vocal music. E & S 31 1945.

— The sacred river: an approach to Joyce. 1949.

Burgum, E. B. In his The novel and the world's dilemma, New York 1947.

Rothman, N. L. Thomas Wolfe and Joyce: a study in literary influence. In A Southern vanguard, ed A. Tate, New York 1947.

Givens, S. (ed). Joyce: two decades of criticism. New York 1948, 1963 (with new introd and enlarged bibliography).

Haan, J. den. Joyce: mythe van Erin. Amsterdam 1948, 1967 (rev).

Honig, E. Hobgoblin or Apollo? Kenyon Rev 10 1948.

Bacca, J. D. G. Husserl and Joyce: or theory and practice of the phenomenological attitude. Philosophy & Phenomenological Research 9 1949.

Fleming, R. Quidditas in the tragi-comedy of Joyce. Univ of Kansas City Rev 15 1949.

— Dramatic involution: Tate, Husserl and Joyce. Sewanee Rev 60 1952.

Jolas, M. (ed). A Joyce yearbook. Paris 1949.

Kelly, R. G. Joyce: a partial explanation. PMLA 64 1949.

Ellmann, R. Joyce and Yeats. Kenyon Rev 12 1950.

— The limits of Joyce's naturalism. Sewanee Rev 63 1955.

— A portrait of the artist as friend. Kenyon Rev 18 1956; rptd in Eng Institute Essays 1955, New York 1956.

Savage, D. S. In his Withered branch: six studies in the modern novel, 1950.

Tindall, W. Y. Joyce: his way of interpreting the modern world. New York 1950.

— Joyce and the hermetic tradition. JHI 15 1954.

— A reader's guide to Joyce. New York 1959.

Baker, J. R. Joyce: esthetic freedom and dramatic art. Western Humanities Rev 5 1951.

— Joyce: affirmation after exile. MLQ 18 1957.

'Cass, Andrew' (J. Garvin). Childe Horrid's pilgrimace. Envoy 5 1951.

McLuhan, H. M. Joyce, Aquinas and the poetic process. Renascence 4 1951; rptd in Joyce's Portrait: criticisms and critiques, ed T. E. Connolly, New York 1962.

— A survey of Joyce criticism. Ibid.

— Joyce: trivial and quadrivial. Thought 28 1953.

— Joyce, Mallarmé and the press. Sewanee Rev 62 1954; rptd, with preceding, in his Interior landscape, ed E. McNamara, New York 1969.

Mayoux, J.-J. L'hérésie de Joyce. In Eng Miscellany (Rome) 2 1951.

— Parody and self-mockery in the work of Joyce. Eng Stud Today 3 1964.

— James Joyce. Paris 1965.

Melchiori, G. Joyce and the 18th-century novelists. Eng Miscellany (Rome) 2 1951; rptd in his Tightrope walkers, 1956 (as Joyce and the tradition of the novel).

Russell, F. Joyce and Alexandria. Catacomb 2 1951; rptd in his Three studies in twentieth-century obscurity, Aldington Kent 1954.

Allt, P. Some aspects of the life and works of Joyce. Groningen 1952.

CEA Critic 14 1952. Essays by E. Drew, E. Mason, J. Prescott, D. Johnston, H. Block, K. Rockwell and H. Nemerov.

Huxley, A. and S. Gilbert. Joyce the artificer: two studies of Joyce's method. 1952.

The analyst. 1953 onwards. Includes explications of Ulysses and Finnegans Wake.

Cope, J. I. Joyce: test case for a theory of style. ELH 21 1954.

Guidi, A. Il primo Joyce. Rome 1954.

Hull, W. Shaw on the Joyce he scarcely read. Shaw Bull 1 1954.

Edel, L. The psychological novel 1900–50. Philadelphia 1955, 1964 (rev and enlarged).

Hô, S. (ed). Joisu kenkyû. Tokyo 1955, 1965 (rev and enlarged).

Jones, W. P. Joyce and the common reader. Norman Okla 1955.

Smidt, K. Joyce and the cultic use of fiction. Oslo 1955 (Oslo Stud in Eng no 4).

Beebe, M. Joyce: barnacle goose and lapwing. PMLA 71 1956.

— Ivory towers and sacred founts: the artist as hero in fiction from Goethe to Joyce. New York 1964.

Friedman, M. J. In his Stream of consciousness, New Haven 1956.

Hayman, D. Joyce et Mallarmé. Paris 1956.

— Joyce's critical case: or conscience versus consciousness. PQ 48 1969.

Kenner, H. Dublin's Joyce. 1955 (for 1956).

— Joyce: comedian of the inventory. In his Flaubert, Joyce and Beckett: the stoic comedians, Boston 1963.

— The counterfeiters. Virginia Quart Rev 42 1966.

Magalaner, M. and R. M. Kain. Joyce: the man, the work, the reputation. New York 1956.

Magalaner, M. (ed). A Joyce miscellany. New York 1957; second series, Carbondale 1959; third series, 1962.

Magalaner, M. Time of apprenticeship: the fiction of young Joyce. New York 1959.

Mallam, D. Joyce and Rabelais. Univ of Kansas City Rev 23 1956.

'O'Connor, Frank' (M. O'Donovan). Joyce and dissociated metaphor. In his Mirror in the roadway: a study of the modern novel, New York 1956.

— James Joyce. Amer Scholar 36 1967; rptd from his Short history of Irish literature, 1967.

Peter, J. Joyce and the novel. Kenyon Rev 18 1956.

Deakin, W. Lawrence's attacks on Proust and Joyce. EC 7 1957.

Donoghue, D. Joyce's landscapes. Studies 46 1957.

— Joyce and the finite order. Sewanee Rev 68 1960.

Noon, W. T. Joyce and Aquinas. New Haven Conn 1957 (Yale Univ Stud in Eng).

— Joyce and Catholicism. James Joyce Rev 1 1957.

Rothe, W. James Joyce. Wiesbaden 1957.

Stewart, J. I. M. James Joyce. 1957, 1964 (rev) (Br Council pamphlet).

— In his Eight modern writers, Oxford 1963 (OHEL).

Wilder, T. Joyce and the modern novel. In A Joyce miscellany, ed M. Magalaner, New York 1957.

Bierman, R. Ulysses and Finnegans wake: the explicit, the implicit and the tertium quid. Renascence 11 1958.

Fritz, H. Joyce and existentialism. James Joyce Rev 2 1958.

Howarth, H. In his Irish writers 1880–1940, 1958.

— The Joycean comedy: Wilde, Jonson and others. In A Joyce miscellany: second series, ed M. Magalaner, Carbondale 1959.

Morse, J. M. Baudelaire, Stephen Dedalus and Shem the penman. Bucknell Rev 7 1958.

— Joyce and the early Thomas Mann. Revue de Littérature Comparée 36 1962.

— By and about Joyce. Hudson Rev 21 1968.

De Castris, A. L. Svevo e Joyce. In his Italo Svevo, Pisa 1959.

Glasheen, A. Joyce and the three ages of Parnell. In A Joyce miscellany: second series, ed M. Magalaner, Carbondale 1959.

Hodgart, M. J. C. and M. P. Worthington. Song in the works of Joyce. New York 1959.

Hornik, M. Studies in Joyce: Leopold Bloom-Candaules. Boar's Hill, Oxford 1959.

Jacquot, J. Exégètes et interprètes de Joyce. Études Anglaises 12 1959, 15 1962.

Karl, F. R. and M. Magalaner. In their Reader's guide to great twentieth-century novels, New York 1959.

Von Phul, R. Joyce and the strabismal apologia. In A Joyce miscellany: second series, ed M. Magalaner, Carbondale 1959.

Ara, M. and S. Saeki (ed). Joisu Nyumon. Tokyo 1960.

Bonifacino, V. In his Ensayos beligerantes: Bertrand Russell–Joyce, Montevideo 1960.

Markow-Totevy, G. André Gide et Joyce. Mercure de France 338 1960.

Seward, B. Joyce and synthesis. In her Symbolic rose, New York 1960.

Bamborough, J. B. Joyce and Jonson. REL 2 1961.

Block, H. M. Theory of language in Flaubert and Joyce. Revue de Littérature Comparée 35 1961.

Brooke, J. Proust and Joyce: the case for the prosecution. Adam nos 297–8 1961.

Dahlberg, E. and H. Read. In their Truth is more sacred, New York 1961; rptd from their Literary correspondence, Sewanee Rev 67 1959.

Goldberg, S. L. Joyce and the artist's fingernails. REL 2 1961.

— James Joyce. Edinburgh 1962.

Heppenstall, R. In his Fourfold tradition, 1961.

Litz, W. The art of Joyce: method and design in Ulysses and Finnegans wake. 1961.

— James Joyce. New York 1966.

— Vico and Joyce. In Giambattista Vico: an international symposium, ed G. Tagliacozzo and H. V. White, Baltimore 1969.

Praz, M. James Joyce. Terzo programma no 4 1961.

— Joyce, T. S. Eliot: due maestri dei moderni. Turin 1967.

Stevenson, R. MacDiarmid, Joyce and Busoni. In MacDiarmid: a festschrift, ed K. D. Duval and S. G. Smith, Edinburgh 1961.

Stewart, D. In his The ark of God: studies in five modern novelists, 1961.

Eco, U. Le moyen âge de Joyce, tr L. Bonalami. Tel Quel no 11 1962, no 12 1963.

— Le poetiche de Joyce: dalla Summa al Finnegans wake. Milan 1966.

Kermode, F. Puzzles and epiphanies. In his Puzzles and epiphanies, 1962.

Kumar, S. K. In his Bergson and the stream of consciousness novel, 1962.

Mercier, V. Joyce and the Irish tradition of parody. In his Irish comic tradition, 1962.

Montgomery, N. Proust and Joyce. Dubliner no 4 1962.

Naganowski, E. Telemach w labiryncie świata: o twórczosci Jamesa Joyce'a. Warsaw 1962.

Ryf, R. S. A new approach to Joyce: the portrait of the artist as a guidebook. Berkeley 1962 (Perspectives in Criticism).

Srinivasa Iyengar, K. R. In his Adventure of criticism, Bombay 1962.

Waldron, P. The novels of Joyce. Wellington 1962.

Abel, L. Beckett and Joyce in Endgame. In his Metatheatre, New York 1963.

Arnold, A. James Joyce. Berlin 1963; tr 1969.

Boulez, P. Sonate, que me veux-tu? Tr D. Noakes and P. Jacobs. Perspective of New Music 1 1963.

Church, M. Joyce: time and time again. In her Time and reality: studies in contemporary fiction, Chapel Hill 1963.

Duncan, E. J. Joyce and the primitive Celtic church. Alphabet 7 1963.

García Sabell, D. Joyce i a loita pola comunicación total. In his Ensaios, Vigo 1963.

Majault, J. James Joyce. Paris 1963.

Misra, B. P. Indian inspiration of Joyce. Agra 1963.

Spender, S. Tradition-bound literature and traditionless painting. In his The struggle of the modern, 1963.

Benstock, B. A covey of clerics in Joyce and O'Casey. James Joyce Quart 2 1964.

— The Joyce industry: a critical assessment in the sixties. Southern Rev new ser 2 1966.

Bonheim, H. Joyce's benefictions. Berkeley 1964.

Brennan, J. G. Three philosophical novelists: Joyce, André Gide, Thomas Mann. New York 1964.

Le Breton, G. Le méthode de Joyce. Mercure de France 351 1964.

Oketani, H. Jeimusu Joisu. Tokyo 1964.

Prescott, J. Exploring Joyce. Carbondale 1964.

Stavrou, C. N. The love songs of Swift, Shaw and Joyce. Midwest Quart 6 1964.

Stephens, J. In his James, Seumas and Jacques: unpublished writings of James Stephens, ed L. Frankenberg, New York 1964.

Wais, K. Shakespeare und die neueren Erzähler: von Bonaventura und Manzoni bis Laforgue und Joyce. In Shakespeare, seine Welt—unsere Welt, ed G. Müller-Schwefe, Tübingen 1964.

Weathers, W. A portrait of the broken word. James Joyce Quart 1 1964.

— Joyce and the tragedy of language. Forum (Houston) 4 1967.

Zolla, E. Joyce o l'apoteosi del fantasticare. In his Storica del fantasticara, 1964.

Burgess, A. Here comes everybody: an introduction to Joyce for the ordinary reader. 1965, New York 1965 (as Re Joyce).

Collins, B. L. Progression in the works of Joyce. Wisconsin Stud in Lit no 2 1965.

Egri, P. A survey of criticism on the relation of Joyce and Thomas Mann. Hungarian Stud in Eng 2 1965.

— Joyce and Adrian Leverkühn: decadence and modernity in the Joycean parallels of Mann's Doktor Faustus. Acta Litteraria Academiae Scientiarum Hungaricae 8 1966.

— Joyce és Thomas Mann. Budapest 1967.

Staples, H. B. Joyce and cryptology. James Joyce Quart 2 1965.

Urnov, D. Portret Dzh. Dzhojsa-pisatel ja i 'Proroka'. Znamia 35 1965. Tr in Kunst und Literatur 13 1965 (as Joyce, Schriftsteller und Prophet).

Adams, R. M. Joyce: common sense and beyond. New York 1966.

Goldman, A. The Joyce paradox: form and freedom in his fiction. Evanston 1966.

— James Joyce. 1968 (Profiles in Literature).

Kaplan, H. J. Stoom: the universal comedy of Joyce. In his Passive voice, Athens Ohio 1966.

Klowitter, R. Bergson and Joyce's fictional world. Comparative Lit Stud 3 1966.

Lutter, T. James Joyce. Budapest 1966.

Staley, T. F. (ed). Joyce today: essays on the major works. Bloomington 1966.

Wolff-Windegg, P. Auf der Suche nach dem Symbol: Joyce und W. B. Yeats. Symbolon 5 1966.

Byrd, D. Joyce's method of philosophic fiction. James Joyce Quart 5 1967.

García Pouce, J. Musil y Joyce. Revista de Bellas Artes 13 1967. Pt of this tr B. and E. Carter in James Joyce Quart 5 1968.

Hart, C. Joyce's sentimentality. PQ 46 1967.

Moseley, V. D. Joyce and the Bible. DeKalb Illinois 1967.

O'Brien, D. The conscience of Joyce. Princeton 1967.

O Hehir, B. A Gaelic lexicon for Finnegans wake and glossary for Joyce's other works. Berkeley 1967.

Rubin, L. D., jr. A portrait of a highly visible artist. In his Teller in the tale, Seattle 1967.

Zhanteeva, D. G. Dzheims Dzhois. Moscow 1967.

Bickerton, D. Joyce and the development of the interior monologue. EC 18 1968.

Bredin, H. T. Applied Aquinas: Joyce's aesthetics. Eire-Ireland 3 1968.

Cixous, H. L'exil de Joyce: ou l'art du remplacement. Paris 1968.

Fáj, A. Probable Byzantine and Hungarian models of Ulysses and Finnegans wake. Arcadia 3 1968.

— La filosofia Vichiana in Joyce. Forum Italicum 2 1968.

Ferrendino, J. Joyce and phenomenology. Telos 1 1968.

Goodheart, E. Joyce and the career of the artist-hero. In his Cult of the ego: the self in modern literature, Chicago 1968.

Grossvogel, D. I. Joyce and Robbe-Grillet. In his Limits of the novel, Ithaca 1968.

Halper, N. Marshall McLuhan and Joyce. In McLuhan: pro and con, ed R. Rosenthal, New York 1968.

Helsinger, H. Joyce and Dante. ELH 35 1968.

Levitt, M. P. Shalt be accursed?: the martyr in Joyce. James Joyce Quart 5 1968.

Moore, J. R. Artifices for eternity: Joyce and Yeats. Eire-Ireland 3 1968.

Murillo, L. A. The cyclical night: irony in Joyce and Borges. Cambridge Mass 1968.

Tysdahl, B. J. Joyce and Ibsen: a study in literary influence. Oslo and New York 1968 (Norwegian Stud in Eng).

Furst, L. R. Thomas Mann's interest in Joyce. MLR 64 1969.

Hildesheimer, W. In his Interpretationen, Frankfurt 1969.

Worthington, M. P. Gilbert and Sullivan in the works of Joyce. Hartford Stud in Lit 1 1969.

Epiphanies

Hendry, I. Joyce's Epiphanies. Sewanee Rev 54 1946.

Ziolkowski, T. Joyces Epiphanie und die Überwindung der empirischen Welt in der modernen deutschen Prosa. Deutsche Vierteljahrsschrift für Literaturwissenschaft und Geistesgechichte 35 1961.

Scholes, R. Joyce and the epiphany: the key to the labyrinth? Sewanee Rev 72 1964.

Walzl, F. L. The liturgy of the Epiphany season and the Epiphanies of Joyce. PMLA 80 1965. See R. Scholes, The Epiphanies of Joyce, PMLA 82 1967 and reply by F. L. Walzl, ibid.

Poetry

Zabel, M. D. The lyrics of Joyce. Poetry 36 1930.

Colum, P. Joyce as poet. In The Joyce book, ed H. Hughes, 1933.

Golding, L. A sidelight on Joyce. Nineteenth Century & After 113 1933. On Chamber music.

Tindall, W. Y. Joyce's chambermade music. Poetry 80 1952.

Anderson, C. G. Joyce's Tilly. PMLA 73 1958.

Baker, J. R. Joyce's Chamber music: the exile of the heart. Arizona Quart 15 1959.

Fisher, M. Joyce's Ecce puer: the return of the prodding Gaul. Univ of Kansas City Rev 25 1959.

Wildi, M. The lyrical poems of Joyce. In Language and society: essays presented to Arthur M. Jensen on his seventieth birthday, Copenhagen 1961.

Moseley, V. D. The 'perilous theme' of Chamber music. James Joyce Quart 1 1964.

Doyle, P. A. Joyce's miscellaneous verse. James Joyce Quart 2 1965.

— A concordance to the collected poems of Joyce. New York 1966.

Scholes, R. E. Joyce, Irish poet. James Joyce Quart 2 1965.

Sen, M. K. The poetry of Joyce. Modern Rev (Calcutta) no 118 1965.

Howarth, H. Chamber music and its place in the Joyce canon. In Joyce today, ed T. F. Staley, Bloomington 1966.

Bowen, Z. Goldenhair: Joyce's archetypal female. Lit & Psychology 17 1967.

Staley, T. F. The poet Joyce and the shadow of Swift. In Jonathan Swift: tercentenary essays, ed W. Weathers and T. F. Staley, Tulsa Okla 1967.

Dubliners

Pound, E. Dubliners and Mr Joyce. Egoist 1 1914; rptd in his Pavannes and divisions, 1918; and in Pound/Joyce, ed F. Read, New York 1967.

Levin, R. and C. Shattuck. First flight to Ithaca: a new reading of Joyce's Dubliners. Accent 4 1944; rptd in Joyce: two decades of criticism, ed S. Givens, New York 1948.

Tate, A. Three commentaries. Sewanee Rev 58 1950; rptd in The house of fiction, ed C. Gordon and A. Tate, New York 1950; and in R. Scholes and A. W. Litz (ed), Dubliners, New York 1969.

Magalaner, M. 'The sisters' of Joyce. Univ of Kansas City Rev 18 1952.

— Joyce and the uncommon reader. South Atlantic Quart 52 1953.

— Joyce, Nietzsche and Hauptmann in Joyce's A painful case. PMLA 68 1953.

— The other side of Joyce. Arizona Quart 9 1953. On Clay.

Friedrich, G. Bret Harte as a source for Joyce's The dead. PQ 33 1954.

— The gnomic clue to Joyce's Dubliners. MLN 72 1957.

— The perspective of Joyce's Dubliners. College Eng 26 1965.

Joyce, S. The backgrounds to Dubliners. Listener 25 March 1954.

Blum, M. The shifting point of view: Joyce's The dead and Gordon's Old red. Critique 1 1956.

Ghiselin, B. The unity of Joyce's Dubliners. Accent 16 1956; rptd in Twentieth-century interpretations of Dubliners, ed P. K. Garrett, Englewood Cliffs NJ 1968; and in R. Scholes and A. W. Litz (ed), Dubliners, New York 1969.

Blotner, J. L. Ivy day in the committee room: death without resurrection. Perspective 9 1957.

O Hehir, B. Structural symbol in Joyce's The dead. Twentieth-Century Lit 3 1957; rptd in Joyce's The dead, ed W. T. Moynihan, Boston 1965.

Ruoff, J. A little cloud: Joyce's portrait of the would-be artist. Research Stud (Washington State College) 25 1957.

Ellmann, R. Backgrounds of The dead. Kenyon Rev 20 1958; rptd in his James Joyce, 1959.

Kaye, J. B. The wings of Dedalus: two stories in Dubliners. Modern Fiction Stud 4 1958.

Dadufalza, C. D. The quest of the chalice-bearer in Joyce's Araby. Diliman Rev 7 1959.

Knox, G. Michael Furey: symbol-name in Joyce's The dead. Western Humanities Rev 13 1959.

O'Neill, M. J. Joyce's use of memory in A mother. MLN 74 1959.

Loomis, C. C., jr. Structure and sympathy in Joyce's The dead. PMLA 75 1960; rptd in Joyce's The dead, ed W. T. Moynihan, Boston 1965; in Twentieth-century interpretations of Dubliners, ed P. K. Garrett, Englewood Cliffs NJ 1969; and in R. Scholes and A. W. Litz (ed), Dubliners, New York 1969.

Ryan, M. Dubliners and the stories of Katherine Anne Porter. Amer Lit 31 1960.

Brodbar, H. A religious allegory: Joyce's Little cloud. Midwest Quart 2 1961.

Jackson, R. S. A parabolic reading of Joyce's Grace. MLN 76 1961.

Walzl, F. Patterns of paralysis in Joyce's Dubliners: a study of the original framework. College Eng 22 1961. *See* correspondence, F. Friedrich and F. Walzl, ibid.

— Symbolism in Joyce's Two gallants. James Joyce Quart 2 1965.

— Ambiguity in the structural symbols in Gabriel's vision in Joyce's The dead. Wisconsin Stud in Lit no 2 1965.

— Gabriel and Michael: the conclusion of The dead. James Joyce Quart 4 1966; rptd in R. Scholes and A. W. Litz (ed), Dubliners, New York 1969.

Baker, J. R. Ibsen, Joyce and the living-dead: a study of Dubliners. In James Joyce miscellany: third series, ed M. Magalaner, Carbondale 1962.

Scholes, R. E. Some observations on the text of Dubliners: The dead. SB 15 1962.

— Further observations on the text of Dubliners. SB 17 1964.

— and A. W. Litz (ed). Dubliners: text, criticism and notes. New York 1969.

Stein, W. B. Joyce's Araby: Paradise lost. Perspective 12 1962.

Boyle, R. Two gallants and Ivy day in the committee room. James Joyce Quart 1 1963; rptd in Twentieth-century interpretations of Dubliners, ed P. K. Garrett, Englewood Cliffs NJ 1968.

Egri, P. Thomas Mann és Joyce első világháború alatti novellai. Filológiai Kozlony (Budapest) 9 1963.

'O'Connor, Frank' (M. O'Donovan). Work in progress. In his Lonely voice: a study of the short story, Cleveland 1963; rptd in Twentieth-century interpretations of Dubliners, ed P. K. Garrett, Englewood Cliffs NJ 1968; and in R. Scholes and A. W. Litz (ed), Dubliners, New York 1969.

Reid, S. The beast in the jungle and A painful case: two different sufferings. American Imago 20 1963.

Weber, R. Clay. In Insight II, ed J. V. Hagopian and M. Dolch, Frankfurt 1964.

Carrier, W. Dubliners: Joyce's Dantean vision. Renascence 17 1965.

Connolly, T. E. Joyce's The sisters: a pennyworth of snuff. College Eng 27 1965.

— Marriage divination in Joyce's Clay. Stud in Short Fiction 3 1966.

Kelleher, J. V. Irish history and mythology in Joyce's The dead. Rev of Politics 27 1965.

Moseley, V. D. Two sights for ever a picture in Joyce's The dead. College Eng 26 1965.

— The coincidence of contrarieties in Grace. James Joyce Quart 6 1968.

Moynihan, W. T. (ed). Joyce's The dead. Boston 1965. Text and criticism.

Niemeyer, C. Grace and Joyce's method of parody. College Eng 27 1965.

Stone, H. Araby and the writings of Joyce. Antioch Rev 25 1965; rptd in part in R. Scholes and A. W. Litz (ed), Dubliners, New York 1969.

Atherton, J. S. The Joyce of Dubliners. In Joyce today: essays on the major works, ed T. F. Staley, Bloomington 1966.

Corrington, J. W. Isolation as motif in A painful case. James Joyce Quart 3 1966.

Hutton, V. Joyce's The dead. East West Rev 2 1966.

Newman, F. X. The land of ooze: Joyce's Grace and The book of Job. Stud in Short Fiction 4 1966.

Staley, T. F. Moral responsibility in Joyce's Clay. Renascence 18 1966.

Wright, C. D. Melancholy Duffy and Sanguine Sinico: humors in A painful case. James Joyce Quart 3 1966.

ap Roberts, R. P. Araby and the palimpsest of criticism: or, through a glass eye darkly. Antioch Rev 26 1967.

Benstock, B. Arabesques: third position of concord. James Joyce Quart 5 1967.

Collins, B. L. Joyce's Araby and the extended simile. James Joyce Quart 4 1967; rptd in Twentieth-century interpretations of Dubliners, ed P. K. Garrett, Englewood Cliffs NJ 1968.

Gibbons, T. H. Dubliners and the critics. CQ 9 1967.

Gifford, D. and R. Seidman. Notes for Joyce: Dubliners and A portrait of the artist as a young man. New York 1967.

Madden, D. James Joyce's Clay. Univ Rev (Kansas City) 33 1967.

Rosenberg, B. The crucifixion in The boarding house. Stud in Short Fiction 5 1967.

Ward, D. F. The race before the story: Joyce and the Gordon Bennett Cup automobile race. Eire-Ireland 2 1967.

Cooke, M. G. From comedy to terror: on Dubliners and the development of tone and structure in the modern short story. Massachusetts Rev 9 1968.

Garrett, P. K. (ed). Twentieth-century interpretations of Dubliners. Englewood Cliffs NJ 1968.

Torchiana, D. T. Joyce's Eveline and the Blessed Margaret Mary Alacoque. James Joyce Quart 6 1968.

Beck, W. Joyce's Dubliners: substance, vision, art. Durham NC 1969.

Brandabur, E. The sisters. In Joyce, Dubliners, ed R. Scholes and A. W. Litz, New York 1969.

Hart, C. (ed). Joyce's Dubliners: critical essays. 1969. Essays by J. W. Corrington, J. S. Atherton, F. Senn, C. Hart, Z. Bowen, A. W. Litz, N. Halper, R. Boyle, R. Scholes, A. Glasheen, T. E. Connolly, M. J. C. Hodgart, D. Hayman, R. M. Kain and B. Benstock.

Murphy, M. W. Darkness in Dubliners. Modern Fiction Stud 15 1969.

A Portrait of the Artist as a Young Man and Stephen Hero

Pound, E. At last the novel appears. Egoist 4 1917; rptd in his Literary essays, 1954; and in Pound/Joyce, ed F. Read, New York 1967.

Wells, H. G. Joyce's Portrait of the artist as a young man. New Republic 10 1917; rptd in New Republic anthology, ed G. Conklin 1936, and in C. G. Anderson (ed), Joyce, A portrait of the artist as a young man, New York 1968.

Hueffer, F. M. (later Ford). A haughty and proud generation. Yale Rev 11 1922.

Daiches, D. Joyce: the artist as exile. College Eng 2 1940; rptd (rev) in Forms of modern fiction, ed W. V. O'Connor, Minneapolis 1948.

Spencer, T. Stephen Hero: the unpublished manuscripts of Joyce's A portrait of the artist as a young man. Baton Rouge 1941.

Farrell, J. T. Joyce's A portrait of the artist as a young man. In his League of frightened philistines, New York 1946; rptd with postscript on Stephen Hero in Joyce: two decades of criticism, ed S. Givens, New York 1948.

Levin, H. James Joyce. Atlantic Monthly 178 1946. On Stephen Hero.

MacGregor, G. Artistic theory in Joyce. Life & Letters 54 1947.

Kenner, H. The Portrait in perspective. Kenyon Rev 10 1948; rptd in Joyce: two decades of criticism, ed S. Givens, New York 1948; in Joyce's Portrait: criticisms and critiques, ed T. E. Connolly, New York 1962; and in Twentieth-century interpretations of A portrait of the artist as a young man, ed W. M. Schutte, Englewood Cliffs NJ 1968.

— Joyce's Portrait: a reconsideration. Univ of Windsor Rev 1 1965.

Schorer, M. Technique as discovery. Hudson Rev 1 1948; rptd in his World we imagine, New York 1968.

Fleming, R. G. Joyce: a partial explanation. PMLA 64 1949.

Baker, J. R. Joyce: esthetic freedom and dramatic art. Western Humanities Rev 5 1950; rptd in Portraits of an artist: a casebook on Joyce's A portrait of the artist as a young man, ed W. E. Morris and C. A. Nault, jr, New York 1962.

— Joyce: affirmation after exile. MLQ 18 1957.

Block, H. M. The critical theory of Joyce. Jnl of Aesthetics 8 1950; rptd in Joyce's Portrait: criticisms and critiques, ed T. E. Connolly, New York 1962.

Burke, K. Three definitions. Kenyon Rev 13 1951; rptd in C. G. Anderson (ed), A portrait of the artist as a young man, New York 1968.

Hennig, J. Stephen Hero and Wilhelm Meister: a study of parallels. German Life & Letters 5 1951.

Anderson, C. G. The sacrificial butter. Accent 12 1952; rptd in Joyce's Portrait: criticisms and critiques, ed T. E. Connolly, New York 1962; and in Portraits of an artist: a casebook on A portrait of the artist as a young man, ed W. E. Morris and C. A. Nault, jr, New York 1962.

— A word index to Joyce's Stephen Hero. Ridgefield 1958.

— The text of Joyce's A portrait of the artist as a young man. Neuphilologische Mitteilungen 65 1964.

— (ed). A portrait of the artist as a young man: text, criticism and notes. New York 1968.

Magalaner, M. James Mangan and Joyce's Dedalus family. PQ 31 1952.

Gordon, C. Some readings and misreadings. Sewanee Rev 61 1953; rptd in her How to read a novel, New York 1957.

Mason, E. Joyce's categories. Sewanee Rev 61 1953; rptd in Portraits of an artist: a casebook on Joyce's A portrait of the artist as a young man, ed W. E. Morris and C. A. Nault, jr, New York 1962.

Prescott, J. Joyce's Stephen Hero. JEGP 53 1954.

Jack, J. H. Art and The portrait of an artist. EC 5 1955; rptd in Joyce's Portrait: criticisms and critiques, ed T. E. Connolly, New York 1962.

Feehan, J. (ed). Dedalus on Crete: essays on the implications of Joyce's Portrait. Los Angeles 1956.

Stern, R. G. Proust and Joyce underway: Jean Santeuil and Stephen Hero. Kenyon Rev 18 1956.

Beebe, M. Joyce and Aquinas: the theory of aesthetics. PQ 36 1957; rptd in Joyce's Portrait: criticisms and critiques, ed T. E. Connolly, New York 1962.

— Joyce and Stephen Dedalus: the problem of autobiography. In A Joyce miscellany: second series, ed M. Magalaner, Carbondale 1959.

Morin, E. Joyce as Thomist. Renascence 9 1957.

Seward, B. The artist and the rose. UTQ 26 1957; rptd in her Symbolic rose, New York 1960; in Joyce's portrait: criticisms and critiques, ed T. E. Connolly, New York 1962; and in Twentieth-century interpretations of A portrait of the artist as a young man, ed W. N. Schutte, Englewood Cliffs NJ 1968.

Waith, E. M. The calling of Stephen Dedalus. College Eng 18 1957; rptd in Portraits of an artist: a casebook on Joyce's A portrait of the artist as a young man, ed W. E. Morris and C. A. Nault, jr, New York 1962.

Gerard, A. Le Dédale de Joyce. Revue Nouvelle 27 1958.

Kelleher, J. V. The perceptions of Joyce. Atlantic Monthly 201 1958.

Redford, G. H. The role of structure in Joyce's Portrait. Modern Fiction Stud 4 1958.

Connolly, T. E. Stephen Hero revisited. James Joyce Rev 3 1959.

— (ed). Joyce's Portrait: criticisms and critiques. New York 1962.

Connolly, T. E. Kinesis and stasis: structural rhythm in Joyce's Portrait of the artist as a young man. Univ Rev (Dublin) 3 1966.

Pascal, R. The autobiographical novel and the autobiography. EC 9 1959.

Slocum, J. J. and H. Cahoon. Five more pages of Joyce's Stephen Hero. In A James Joyce miscellany: second series, ed M. Magalaner, Carbondale 1959.

Boyd, E. F. Joyce's hell-fire sermons. MLN 75 1960.

Ellmann, R. Two faces of Edward. In Eng Inst Essays 1959, New York 1960.

Moseley, V. D. Joyce's Grave of boyhood. Renascence 13 1960.

— Stephen Hero: the last of the first. James Joyce Quart 3 1966.

Poss, S. H. A portrait of the artist as beginner. Univ of Kansas City Rev 26 1960.

— A portrait of the artist as hard-boiled messiah. MLQ 27 1966.

Thrane, J. R. Joyce's sermon on hell: its source and its backgrounds. MP 57 1960; rptd in A James Joyce miscellany: third series, ed M. Magalaner, Carbondale 1962.

Booth, W. The problem of distance in A portrait of the artist. In his Rhetoric of fiction, Chicago 1961; rptd in Joyce, A portrait of the artist as a young man, ed C. G. Anderson, New York 1968; and in Twentieth-century interpretations of A portrait of the artist as a young man, ed W. M. Schutte, Englewood Cliffs NJ 1968.

Scholes, R. E. Stephen Dedalus: Eiron and Alazon. Texas Stud in Lit & Lang 3 1961.

— Stephen Dedalus, poet or aesthete? PMLA 79 1964; rptd in C. G. Anderson (ed), A portrait of the artist as a young man, New York 1968.

— and R. M. Kain. (ed). The workshop of Daedalus. Evanston 1965.

Woodward, A. G. Technique and feeling in Joyce's Portrait of the artist as a young man. Eng Stud in Africa 4 1961.

Morris, W. E. and C. A. Nault, jr (ed). Portraits of an artist: a casebook on Joyce's A portrait of the artist as a young man. New York 1962.

Ryf, R. S. A new approach to Joyce: the Portrait of the artist as a guidebook. Berkeley 1962 (Perspectives in Criticism).

Spielberg, P. Joyce's errata for American editions of Portrait of the artist as a young man. In Joyce's Portrait: criticisms and critiques, ed T. E. Connolly, New York 1962.

Doherty, J. Joyce and Hell opened to Christians: the editions he used for his Hell sermons. MP 61 1963.

Andreach, R. J. In his Studies in structure: the stages of the spiritual life in four modern authors. New York 1964.

Brandabur, E. Stephen's aesthetic in A portrait of the artist. In The Celtic cross, ed R. B. Browne, W. J. Roscelli and R. Loftus, Lafayette 1964. See Comment by M. Beebe, ibid.

Hardy, J. E. Joyce's Portrait: the flight of the serpent. In his Man in the modern novel, Seattle 1964.

Hayman, D. A portrait of the artist as a young man and L'éducation sentimentale: the structural affinities. Orbis Litterarum 19 1964.

—— Daedalian imagery in A portrait. In Hereditas: seven essays on the modern experience of the classical, ed F. Will, Austin Texas 1964.

Van Laan, T. F. The meditative structure of Joyce's Portrait. James Joyce Quart 1 1964.

Bates, R. The correspondence of birds to things of the intellect. James Joyce Quart 2 1965.

Erzgräber, W. Joyce: A portrait of the artist as a young man. In Der moderne englische Roman: Interpretationen, ed H. Oppel, Berlin 1965.

Gillie, C. Human subject and human substance: Stephen Dedalus of A portrait of the artist as a young man, Rupert Birkin of Women in love. In his Character in English literature, 1965.

Ranald, M. L. Stephen Dedalus' vocation and the irony of religious ritual. James Joyce Quart 2 1965.

Sprinchorn, E. A portrait of the artist as Achilles. In Approaches to the twentieth-century novel, ed J. Unterecker, New York 1965.

Vogel, J. The consubstantial family of Stephen Dedalus. James Joyce Quart 2 1965.

Walcott, W. D. The paternity of Joyce's Stephen Dedalus. Jnl of Analytical Psychology 10 1965.

Wasson, R. Stephen Dedalus and the imagery of sight: a psychological approach. Lit & Psychology 15 1965.

Forster, J.-P. Joyce, Stephen Hero et Stephen Dedalus. Études de Lettres 9 1966.

Link, F. M. The aesthetics of Stephen Dedalus. Papers on Lang & Lit 2 1966.

Noon, W. T. Portrait of the artist as a young man fifty years after. In Joyce today: essays on the major works, ed T. F. Staley, Bloomington 1966.

Waldron, P. A note on the text of Stephen Hero. James Joyce Quart 3 1966.

Feshbach, S. The slow and dark birth: a study of the organization of A portrait of the artist as a young man. James Joyce Quart 4 1967.

Grayson, T. W. Joyce and Stephen Dedalus: the theory of aesthetics. Ibid.

Gifford, D. and R. Seidman. Notes for Joyce: Dubliners and A portrait of the artist as a young man. New York 1967.

Hancock, L. Word index to Joyce's Portrait of the artist. Carbondale 1967.

Lemon, L. T. A portrait of the artist as a young man: motif as motivation and structure. Modern Fiction Stud 12 1967; rptd in Twentieth-century interpretations of A portrait of the artist as a young man, ed W. M. Schutte, Englewood Cliffs NJ 1968.

Manso, P. The metaphoric style of Joyce's Portrait. Modern Fiction Stud 13 1967.

Naremore, J. Style as meaning in A portrait of the artist. James Joyce Quart 4 1967.

Sharpless, F. P. Irony in Joyce's Portrait: the stasis of pity. James Joyce Quart 4 1967; rptd in Twentieth-century interpretations of A portrait of the artist as a young man, ed W. M. Schutte, Englewood Cliffs NJ 1968.

Egri, P. The function of dreams and visions in A portrait and Death in Venice. James Joyce Quart 5 1968.

Schutte, W. M. (ed). Twentieth-century interpretations of A portrait of the artist as a young man, Englewood Cliffs NJ 1968.

Staley, T. F. A critical study guide to Joyce's Portrait of the artist as a young man. Totawa NJ 1968.

Geckle, G. L. Stephen Dedalus and W. B. Yeats: the making of the villanelle. Modern Fiction Stud 15 1969.

Exiles

Pound, E. Joyce and the modern stage. Drama 6 1916; rptd in Pound/Joyce, ed F. Read, New York 1967.

Rodker, J. et al. Exiles: a discussion of Joyce's play. Little Rev 5 1919.

MacCarthy, D. Joyce's play. New Statesman & Nation 20 Feb 1926; rptd in his Humanities, 1953.

Fergusson, F. Exiles and Ibsen's work. Hound & Horn 5 1932.

Bandler, B. Joyce's Exiles. Hound & Horn 6 1933.

Farrell, J. T. Exiles and Ibsen. In Joyce: two decades of criticism, ed S. Givens, New York 1948; rptd in his Reflections at fifty, New York 1954.

Williams, R. The Exiles of Joyce. Politics & Letters 1 1948.

Von Weber, R. On and about Joyce's Exiles. In Joyce yearbook, ed M. Jolas, Paris 1949.

Kenner, H. Joyce and Ibsen's naturalism. Sewanee Rev 59 1951.

—— Joyce's Exiles. Hudson Rev 5 1952.

Jacquot, J. Réflexions sur les Exiles de Joyce. Études Anglaises 9 1956.

Aitkin, D. J. F. Dramatic archetypes in Joyce's Exiles. Modern Fiction Stud 4 1958.

Douglass, J. W. Joyce's Exiles: a portrait of the artist. Renascence 15 1963.

Adams, R. M. Light on Joyce's Exiles? a new ms, a curious analogue and some speculations. SB 17 1964.

—— The manuscript of Joyce's play. Yale Univ Lib Gazette 39 1964.

Tysdahl, B. J. Joyce's Exiles and Ibsen. Orbis Litterarum 19 1964.

Harmon, M. Richard Rowan, his own scapegoat. James Joyce Quart 3 1965.

Metzger, D. P. Variations on a theme: a study of Exiles by Joyce and the Great god Brown by Eugene O'Neill. Modern Drama 8 1965.

Brivic, S. R. Structure and meaning in Joyce's Exiles. James Joyce Quart 6 1968.

Clark, E. J. Joyce's Exiles. James Joyce Quart 6 1968.

Benstock, B. Exiles: 'Paradox lust' and 'Lost Paladays'. ELH 36 1969.

Ferris, W. R., jr. Rebellion matured: Joyce's Exiles. Eire-Ireland 4 1969.

Ulysses

Hueffer, F. M. (later Ford). Ulysses and the handling of indecencies. Eng Rev 35 1922.

Larbaud, V. James Joyce. Nouvelle Revue Française 18 1922. Tr in Criterion 1 1922 (as The Ulysses of Joyce); rptd in Joyce's Gens du Dublin, Paris 1926.

—— A propos de Joyce et de Ulysses. Nouvelle Revue Française 24 1925.

Bennett, A. Joyce's Ulysses. In his Things that have interested me, 2nd ser 1923; rptd from Outlook (London) 49 1922 and Bookman (New York) 55 1922.

Eliot, T. S. Ulysses, order and myth. Dial 75 1923; rptd in Criticism: the foundation of modern literary judgment, ed M. Schorer et al, New York 1948; in Joyce: two decades of criticism, ed S. Givens, New York 1948; and in The modern tradition, ed R. Ellmann and C. Feidelson, 1965 (with note by Eliot).

Aldington, R. Joyce's Ulysses. In his Literary studies and reviews, 1924; rptd (rev) from Eng Rev 32 1921.

Fehr, B. Joyce's Ulysses. E Studien 60 1926.

Read, H. In his Reason and romanticism: essays in literary criticism, 1926.

Smith, P. J. A key to Ulysses of Joyce. Chicago 1927.

Curtius, E. R. Joyce und sein Ulysses. Neue Schweizer Rundschau 22 1929; tr E. Jolas in Transition no 16–17 1929 (as Technique and thematic development of Joyce).

Damon, S. F. The Odyssey in Dublin. Hound & Horn 3 1929; rptd in Joyce: two decades of criticism, ed S. Givens, New York 1948, 1963 (with postscript).

Gilbert, S. Ulysse, par Joyce. Nouvelle Revue Française 32 1929.
— Joyce's Ulysses. 1930, 1952 (rev).
Morse, B. J. Joyce and Shakespeare. E Studien 65 1930.
Beach, J. W. In his Twentieth-century novel, New York 1932.
Daniel-Rops, H. Une technique nouvelle: le monologue intérieur. Le Correspondant 25 Jan 1932.
Jung, C. G. Ulysses: ein Monolog. Europäische Rev Sept 1932. Rptd in his Wirklichkeit der Seele, Zürich 1934. Tr W. S. Dell, New York 1949; rptd in Nimbus 2 1953.
MacCarthy, D. Joyce's Ulysses. In his Criticism, 1932.
Hentze, R. Die proteïsche Wandlung im Ulysses von Joyce und ihre Spiegelung im Stil. Marburg 1933.
Brewster, D. and A. Birrell. Joyce and Ulysses. In their Modern fiction, New York 1934.
Brown, A. Joyce's Ulysses and the novel. Dublin Mag 9 1934.
Daiches, D. Importance of Ulysses. In his New literary values, 1936.
Baake, J. Das Riesenscherzbuch Ulysses. Bonn 1937.
Hanley, M. (ed). Word index to Joyce's Ulysses. Madison 1937, 1951 (corrected).
Van der Vat, D. G. Paternity in Ulysses. E Studies 19 1937.
Waldock, A. J. A. In his James, Joyce and others, 1937.
Miller-Budnitskaya, R. Joyce's Ulysses. Dialectics no 5 1938.
Lundkvist, A. In his Ikarus' Flykt, Stockholm 1939.
Monnier, A. L'Ulysse de Joyce et le public français. Gazette des Amis des Livres 3 1940; tr S. Beach, Kenyon Rev 8 1946.
— La traduction d'Ulysse. Mercure de France 309 1950.
Visser, G. J. Joyce's Ulysses and Anglo-Irish. E Studies 24 1942.
Koch, V. An approach to the Homeric content of Joyce's Ulysses. Maryland Quart 1 1944.
Meagher, J. A. A Dubliner reads Ulysses. Australian Quart 17 1945.
Zipf, G. K. The repetition of words, time-perspective and semantic balance. Jnl of General Psychology 32 1945.
Bajarlia, J. J. In his Literatura de vanguardia—del Ulises de Joyce y las escuelas poéticas. Buenos Aires 1946.
Kain, R. M. Fabulous voyager: Joyce's Ulysses. Chicago 1947, 1959 (corrected).
— Joyce's Shakespeare chronology. Massachusetts Rev 5 1964.
— The position of Ulysses today. In Joyce today: essays on the major works, ed T. F. Staley, Bloomington 1966.
Blackmur, R. P. The Jew in search of a son. Virginia Quart Rev 24 1948; rptd in his Eleven essays on the European novel, New York 1964.
Rogers, H. E. Irish myth and the plot of Ulysses. ELH 15 1948.
Toynbee, P. A study of Joyce's Ulysses. In Joyce: two decades of criticism, ed S. Givens, New York 1948, 1963.
Heine, A. Shakespeare in Joyce. Shakespeare Assoc Bull 24 1949.
Klein, A. M. The oxen of the sun. Here & Now 1 1949.
— The black panther: a study in technique. Accent 10 1950.
— A shout in the street: an analysis of the second chapter of Joyce's Ulysses. New Directions no 13 1951.
Simon, I. In her Formes du roman anglais de Dickens à Joyce, Liège 1949.
Duncan, E. Unsubstantial father: a study of the Hamlet symbolism in Joyce's Ulysses. UTQ 19 1950.
Edwards, C. R. The Hamlet motif in Joyce's Ulysses. Western Rev 15 1950.
Mayhew, G. Joyce on Shakespeare. Southwestern Jnl 5 1950.
Albert, L. Ulysses, cannibals and freemasons. A.D. 2 1951.
Hall, V., jr. Joyce's use of Da Ponte and Mozart's Don Giovanni. PMLA 66 1951.
Montgomery, N. Joyeux quicum Ulysse. Envoy 5 1951.

Tindall, W. Y. Dante and Mrs Bloom. Accent 11 1951.
Knight, D. The reading of Ulysses. ELH 19 1952.
Peery, W. The Hamlet of Stephen Dedalus. Univ of Texas Stud in Eng 31 1952.
Prescott, J. Notes on Joyce's Ulysses. MLQ 13 1952.
Stein, S. The aesthetics of Joyce's Ulysses. Univ of Kansas City Rev 18 1952.
Loehrich, R. The secret of Ulysses: an analysis of Joyce's Ulysses. McHenry Ill 1953.
Magalaner, M. The anti-semitic limerick incidents and Joyce's Bloomsday. PMLA 68 1953.
— Labyrinthine motif: Joyce and Leo Taxil. Modern Fiction Stud 2 1957.
Stanford, W. B. Ulyssean qualities in Joyce's Leopold Bloom. Comparative Lit 2 1953.
— In his Ulysses theme: a study in the adaptability of a traditional hero. Oxford 1954, 1963 (rev).
Humphrey, R. In his Stream of consciousness in the modern novel, Berkeley 1954.
Thompson, L. A comic principle in Sterne-Meredith-Joyce. Oslo 1954.
Von Abele, R. Ulysses: the myth of myth. PMLA 69 1954.
Edwards, P. Ulysses and the legends. EC 5 1955.
Greenway, J. A guide through Joyce's Ulysses. College Eng 17 1955.
Killeen, J. F. Joyce's Roman prototype. Univ Rev (Dublin) 1 1955; rptd in Comparative Lit 9 1957.
Empson, W. The theme of Ulysses. Kenyon Rev 18 1956; rptd in A Joyce miscellany: third series, ed M. Magalaner, Carbondale 1962.
Litz, W. Early vestiges of Joyce's Ulysses. PMLA 71 1956.
— Joyce's notes for the last episodes of Ulysses. Modern Fiction Stud 4 1958.
— The last adventures of Ulysses. Princeton Univ Lib Chron 28 1967.
Mason, E. The oxen of the sun. Analyst no 10 1956.
Weiss, D. The end of The oxen of the sun. Analyst no 9 1956.
Worthington, M. P. Irish folk songs in Joyce's Ulysses. PMLA 71 1956.
Duncan, J. E. The modality of the audible in Joyce's Ulysses. PMLA 72 1957.
Ellmann, R. Ulysses, the divine nobody. Yale Rev 47 1957; rptd in Twelve original essays on great English novels, ed C. Shapiro, Detroit 1960.
— Ulysses and the Odyssey. E Studies 43 1962.
— Odyssey of a unique book. New York Times Mag 14 Nov 1965.
Epstein, E. L. Cruxes in Ulysses: notes toward an edition and annotation. James Joyce Rev 1 1957.
Jarrell, M. L. Joyce's use of Swift's Polite conversation in the Circe episode of Ulysses. PMLA 72 1957.
Poss, S. Ulysses and the comedy of the immobilized act. ELH 24 1957.
Schutte, W. J. Joyce and Shakespeare: a study in the meaning of Ulysses. New Haven 1957.
Sternfeld, F. W. Poetry and music: Joyce's Ulysses. In Eng Inst Essays 1956, New York 1957.
Steinberg, E. R. A book with a Molly in it. James Joyce Rev 2 1958.
— Introducing the stream-of-consciousness technique in Ulysses. Style 2 1968.
— The Proteus episode: signature of Stephen Dedalus. James Joyce Quart 5 1968.
— Lestrygonians, a pale Proteus? Modern Fiction Stud 15 1969.
Kaye, J. B. A portrait of the artist as Blephen-Stoom. In James Joyce miscellany: second series, ed M. Magalaner, Carbondale 1959.
Morse, J. M. Molly Bloom revisited. Ibid.
Rosenberg, K. Joyce: ein Wanderer ins Reich des Unbewussten. Geist und Zeit no 4 1959.
Sultan, S. The sirens at the Ormond bar: Ulysses. Univ of Kansas City Rev 26 1959.
— The argument of Ulysses. Columbus Ohio 1964.

Lennam, T. The happy hunting ground: Shakespearean dramatis personae in the Scylla and Charybdis episode of Joyce's Ulysses. UTQ 29 1960; rptd in James Joyce miscellany: third series, ed M. Magalaner, Carbondale 1962.

Peradotto, J. J. A liturgical pattern in Ulysses. MLN 75 1960.

Stavrou, C. N. Gulliver's voyage to the land of Dubliners. South Atlantic Quart 59 1960.

—— Mr Bloom and Nikos' [Kazantzakis'] Odysseus. South Atlantic Quart 62 1963.

—— The love songs of Swift, Shaw and Joyce. Midwest Quart 6 1965.

Ahearn, E. J. Religious values in Joyce's Ulysses. Christian Scholar 44 1961.

De Angelis, G. Guida alla lettura dell'Ulisse di Joyce. Milano 1961.

Decker, H. Der innere Monolog: zur Analyse des Ulysses. Akzente 8 1961.

Goldberg, S. L. The classical temper: a study of Joyce's Ulysses. 1961.

Knight, G. W. Lawrence, Joyce and [J.C.] Powys. EC 11 1961.

Parr, M. Joyce—the poetry of conscience: a study of Ulysses. Milwaukee 1961.

Peake, C. Ulysses and some modern criticisms. Literary Half-Yearly 2 1961.

Adams, R. M. Surface and symbol: the consistency of Joyce's Ulysses. New York 1962.

Cambon, G. La traduzione italiana d'Ulisse. Veltro 6 1962.

Cope, J. I. The rhythmic gesture: image and aesthetic in Joyce's Ulysses. ELH 29 1962.

Dundes, A. Re: Joyce—no in at the womb. Modern Fiction Stud 8 1962.

Flora, F. Poesia e impoesia nell'Ulisse di Joyce. Milan 1962.

Kenner, H. Art in a closed field. Virginia Quart Rev 38 1962.

Paley, M. D. Blake in Nighttown. In James Joyce miscellany: third series, ed M. Magalaner, Carbondale 1962.

Plebe, A. L'Ulisse di Joyce e l'estetica dell'arte al quadrato. Giornale Critico della Filosofia Italiana 41 1962.

Clarke, J. Joyce and the Blakean vision. Criticism 5 1963.

Gill, R. The 'corporal works of mercy' as a moral pattern in Joyce's Ulysses. Twentieth-Century Lit 9 1963.

González, M. P. El Ulisse cuarenta años depués. Cuadernos Americanos 22 1963.

Kelly, H. A. Consciousness in the monologues of Ulysses. MLQ 24 1963.

Kuehn, R. E. Mr Bloom and Mr Joyce: a note on heroism in Ulysses. Wisconsin Stud in Contemporary Lit 4 1963.

Leventhal, A. J. The Jew errant. Dubliner 2 1963.

Berger, H. (afterwards Cixous). Stephen, Hamlet, Will: Joyce par delà Shakespeare. Études Anglaises 17 1964.

Hardy, B. Form as end and means in Ulysses. Orbis Litterarum 19 1964.

Lorch, T. L. The relationship between Ulysses and The waste land. Texas Stud in Lit & Lang 6 1964.

Madtes, R. E. Joyce and the building of Ithaca. ELH 31 1964.

Ridgeway, A. Two authors in search of a reader. James Joyce Quart 1 1964. Joyce and Sterne.

Silverstein, N. Magic on the notesheets of the Circe episode. James Joyce Quart 1 1964. See corrections, P. F. Herring (with N. Silverstein) 2 1965.

Boldereff, F. M. A Blakean translation of Joyce's Circe. Trenton 1965.

Davidson, D. Decorum in the novel. Modern Age 9 1965.

Isaacs, N. D. The autoerotic metaphor in Joyce, Sterne, Lawrence, Stevens and Whitman. Lit & Psychology 15 1965.

Killham, J. Ineluctable modality in Joyce's Ulysses. UTQ 34 1965.

Levin, L. L. The Sirens episode as music: Joyce's experiment in prose polyphony. James Joyce Quart 3 1965.

Littmann, M. E. and C. A. Schweighauser. Astronomical allusions, their meaning and purpose, in Ulysses. James Joyce Quart 2 1965.

Peignot, J. Ulysse, ou de l'inattendu considéré comme l'un des beaux-arts. Cahiers des Saisons 10 1965.

Spencer, J. A note on the 'steady monologuy of the interiors'. REL 6 1965.

Tracy, R. Leopold Bloom fourfold: a Hungarian-Hebraic-Hellenic-Hibernian hero. Massachusetts Rev 6 1965.

Benjamin, J.-L. (ed). The Celtic bull: essays on Joyce's Ulysses. Tulsa Okla 1966.

Bennett, J. Z. Unposted letter: Joyce's Leopold Bloom. Bucknell Rev 14 1966.

Blamires, H. The Bloomsday book: a guide through Joyce's Ulysses. 1966.

Briskin, I. O. Some new light on The parable of the plums. James Joyce Quart 3 1966.

Castronovo, D. Touching the much vexed question of stimulants: drinkers and drinking in Joyce's Ulysses. November Rev (Brooklyn) no 3 1966.

Cronin, A. The advent of Bloom. In his A question of modernity, 1966.

Durzak, M. Hermann Broch und Joyce. Deutsche Vierteljahrsschrift für Literaturwissenschaft und Geistesgeschichte 40 1966.

Galloway, D. D. Moses-Bloom-Herzog: Bellow's Everyman. Southern Rev new ser 2 1966.

Jeremić, L. Unutrašnji monolog kod Tolstoja i Džojsa. Delo 12 1966.

Kaplan, H. J. Stoom: the universal comedy of Joyce. In his Passive voice: an approach to modern fiction, Athens Ohio 1966.

Nichols, M. An epochal palimpsest. In The Celtic bull: essays on Joyce's Ulysses, ed J.-L. Benjamin, Tulsa Okla 1966.

Raimond, M. Le monologue intérieur. In his Crise du roman: des lendemains du naturalisme aux années vingt, Paris 1966.

Read, F. Ezra Pound et Joyce: les odysséens, tr P. Alien. L'Herne no 7 1966.

Russell, J. C. A Baedeker to Bloom. James Joyce Quart 3 1966.

Watson, E. A. Stoom-Bloom: scientific objectivity versus romantic subjectivity in the Ithaca episode of Joyce's Ulysses. Univ of Windsor Rev 2 1966.

Bowen, Z. The bronzegold sirensong: a musical analysis of the sirens episode in Joyce's Ulysses. In Literary Monographs vol 1, ed E. Rothenstein and T. K. Dunsheath, Madison 1967.

Bryer, J. R. Joyce, Ulysses and the Little Review. South Atlantic Quart 66 1967.

Cohn, A. M. Joyce's notes on the end of the Oxen of the sun. James Joyce Quart 4 1967.

Costa, R. H. Ulysses, Lowry's Volcano and the Voyage between: a study of an unacknowledged literary kinship. UTQ 36 1967.

Esch, A. Joyce und Homer: zur Fragen der Odysee-Korrespondenzen in Ulysses. In Lebende Antike: Symposium für R. Sühnel, ed H. Meller and H.-J. Zimmermann, Berlin 1967.

Fleishman, A. Science in Ithaca. Wisconsin Stud in Contemporary Lit 8 1967.

Hayman, D. Forms of folly in Joyce: a study of clowning in Ulysses. ELH 34 1967.

Iser, W. Historische Stilformen in Joyce's Ulysses: zur Interpretation des Kapitels The oxen of the sun. In Lebende Antike: Symposium für R. Sühnel, ed H. Meller and H.-J. Zimmermann, Berlin 1967.

Köhler, E. Nausikaa, Danae und Gerty MacDowell: zur Literaturgeschichte des Feuerwerks. In Lebende Antike: Symposium für R. Sühnel, ed H. Meller and H.-J. Zimmermann, Berlin 1967.

McMillan, D. Influences of Gerhart Hauptmann in Joyce's Ulysses. James Joyce Quart 4 1967.

Novak, J. Verisimilitude and vision: Defoe and Blake as influences on Molly Bloom. Carrell 8 1967.

Schoonbroodt, J. Point of view and expressive form in Joyce's Ulysses. Liège 1967.

Senn, F. Seven against Ulysses. James Joyce Quart 4 1967.

— Ulysses in der Übersetzung. Sprache im Technischen Zeitalter 28 1968.

Borel, J. Petite introduction à l'Ulysse de Joyce. Temps Modernes 23 1968.

Briand, P. L., jr. The Catholic mass in Joyce's Ulysses. James Joyce Quart 5 1968.

Brooks, C. Joyce's Ulysses: symbolic poem, biography or novel? In Imagined worlds: essays on some English novels and novelists in honour of John Butt, ed M. Mack and I. Gregor, 1968.

Hart, C. Joyce's Ulysses. Sydney 1968.

Stern, F. C. Pyrrhus, Fenians and Bloom. James Joyce Quart 5 1968.

Thornton, W. Allusions in Ulysses: an annotated list. Chapel Hill 1968.

Timpe, E. F. Ulysses and the archetypal feminine. In Perspectives in literary criticism, ed J. Strelka, University Park Pa 1968.

Wykes, D. The Odyssey of Ulysses. Texas Stud in Lit & Lang 10 1968.

Herring, P. F. The bedsteadfastness of Molly Bloom. Modern Fiction Stud 15 1969.

Finnegans Wake

Jolas, E., E. Paul and R. Sage. First aid to the enemy. transition no 9 1927.

Jolas, E. et al. The revolution of the word (a symposium). Modern Quart 5 1929.

Jolas. E. Elucidation du monomythe de Joyce. Critique 4 1948.

Williams, W. C. A note on the recent work of Joyce. transition no 8 1927.

Beckett, S. et al. Our exagmination round his factification for incamination of Work in progress. Paris 1929, London 1936, Norfolk Conn 1939 (as An exagmination of Joyce). Essays by M. Brion, F. Budgen, S. Gilbert, E. Jolas, V. Llona, R. McAlmon, T. McGreevy, E. Paul, J. Rodker, R. Sage, W. C. Williams, G. V. L. Slingsby, V. Dixon.

Gilbert, S. Thesaurus minusculus: a short commentary on a paragraph of Work in progress. transition no 16–17 1929.

— A footnote to Work in progress. Contempo 15 Feb 1934.

— Sketch of a scenario of Anna Livia Plurabelle. In A James Joyce yearbook, ed M. Jolas, Paris 1949.

Salemson, H. J. Joyce and the new world. Modern Quart 5 1929.

Stuart, M. The Dubliner and his Dowdili: a note on the sublime. transition no 18 1929.

— Joyce after Ulysses. This Quarter 2 1929.

— Mr Joyce's word-creatures. Symposium 2 1931.

Giedion-Welcker, C. Work in progress, translated by E. Jolas. transition no 19–20 1930.

— Die Funktion der Sprache in der heutigen Dichtung. transition no 22 1933.

Ogden, C. K. Joyce's Anna Livia Plurabelle in Basic English. transition no 21 1932.

Leavis, F. R. Joyce and 'the revolution of the word'. Scrutiny 2 1933; rptd in his For continuity, Cambridge 1933; and in The importance of Scrutiny, ed E. Bentley, New York 1948.

Highet, G. The revolution of the word. New Oxford Outlook 1 1934.

Obradovic, A. Die Behandlung der Räumlichkeit im späteren Werk des Joyce. Marburg 1934.

Petitjean, A. M. Joyce et l'absorption du monde par le langage. Cahiers du Sud 11 1934.

— Joyce and mythology: mythology and Joyce, tr M. Jolas. transition no 23 1935.

— Signification de Joyce. Études Anglaises 1 1937.

— El tratamiento del lenguaje en Joyce. Sur no 78 1941.

Symond, R. The third Mr Joyce: comments on Work in progress. London Mercury 29 1934; rptd in Living Age 456 1934.

Bishop, J. P. Finnegans wake. Southern Rev 5 1939; rptd in his Collected essays, New York 1948.

Bogan, L. Finnegans wake. Nation 148 1939 (as Proteus: or Vico's road), 159 1944; rptd in her Selected criticism, New York 1955.

Edel, L. Joyce and his new work. UTQ 9 1939.

Glendinning, A. Commentary [Finnegans wake]. Nineteenth Century & After 126 1939.

Hill, A. A. A philologist looks at Finnegans wake. Virginia Quart Rev 15 1939.

Levin, H. On first looking into Finnegans wake. New directions in prose and poetry, 1939.

Ransom, J. C. The aesthetic of Finnegans wake. Kenyon Rev 1 1939.

Schlauch, M. Linguistic aspects of Work in progress. Washington Square College Rev 3 1939.

— The language of Joyce. Science & Society 3 1939.

Troy, W. Notes on Finnegans wake. Partisan Rev 6 1939; rptd in Joyce: two decades of criticism, ed S. Givens, New York 1948.

Gillet, L. A propos de Finnegans wake. Babel 1 1940.

— Joyce's testament: Finnegans wake, tr D. D. Paige. Quart Rev of Lit 1 1944.

Budgen, F. Joyce's chapters on going forth by day. Horizon 4 1941; rptd in Joyce: two decades of criticism, ed S. Givens, New York 1948.

Colum, P. Notes on Finnegans wake. Yale Rev 30 1941.

Campbell, J. and H. M. Robinson. A skeleton key to Finnegans wake. New York 1944.

— Finnegan the wake. Chimera Spring 1946; rptd in Joyce: two decades of criticism, ed S. Givens, New York 1948.

Chase, R. V. Finnegans wake: an anthropological study. Amer Scholar 13 1944.

Kelleher, J. V. Joyce digested. Accent 5 1945.

— Notes on Finnegans wake. Analyst no 12 1957, no 15 1958.

Tyler, H. Finnegan epic. Circle no 7–8 1946.

Powys, J. C. Finnegans wake. In his Obstinate Cymric, Carmarthen 1947.

Reed, H. Joyce's progress. Orion no 4 1947.

Wilson, E. The dream of H. C. Earwicker. In his Wound and the bow, New York 1947; rptd in Joyce: two decades of criticism, ed S. Givens, New York 1948.

— In his Classics and commercials: a literary chronicle of the forties, New York 1950.

Magalaner, M. Joyce and the myth of man. Arizona Quart 4 1948.

— The myth of man: Joyces Finnegans wake. Univ of Kansas City Rev 16 1950.

Mason, E. C. Zu Joyces Finnegans Wake. Du 8 1948; rptd in his Exzentrische Bahnen, Göttingen 1963.

Ramnoux, C. The Finn cycle: the atmosphere and symbols of a legend. In A Joyce yearbook, ed M. Jolas, Paris 1949.

Thompson, F. Portrait of the artist asleep. Western Rev 14 1950.

Halper, N. Joyce and the Russian general. Partisan Rev 18 1951.

— Joyce and Eliot. Wake Newslitter new ser 2 1965; Nation 31 May 1965 (rev).

— Joyce and Anna Livia. James Joyce Quart 4 1967.

Peery, W. Shakhisbeard at Finnegans wake. Univ of Texas Stud in Eng 30 1951.

Hodgart, M. J. C. Work in progress. Cambridge Jnl 6 1952.

— Shakespeare and Finnegans wake. Ibid 6 1953.

— The earliest sections of Finnegans wake. James Joyce Rev 1 1957.

Ussher, A. Three great Irishmen: Shaw, Yeats, Joyce. 1952.

Montgomery, N. The Pervigilium Phoenicis. New Mexico Quart 23 1953.

Raleigh, J. H. My brother's keeper: Stanislaus Joyce and Finnegans wake. MLN 68 1953.

Glasheen, A. Finnegans wake and the girls from Boston, Mass. Hudson Rev 7 1954.

— A census of Finnegans wake: an index to the characters and their roles. New York 1956.

— Out of my census. Analyst no 17 1959.

— The strange cold fowl in Finnegans wake. Spectrum 1 1961.

— A second census of Finnegans wake. Evanston 1963.

— Part of what the thunder said in Finnegans wake. Analyst no 23 1964.

— The opening paragraphs. Wake Newslitter new ser 2 1965.

— Notes toward a supreme understanding of the use of Finnegan's wake in Finnegans wake. Wake Newslitter new ser 5 1968.

Prescott, J. Concerning the genesis of Finnegans wake. PMLA 69 1954.

Atherton, J. S. Finnegans wake: the gist of the pantomime. Accent 15 1955.

— The books at the wake: a study of literary allusions in Joyce's Finnegans wake. New York 1960.

— Joyce and Finnegans wake. Manchester Rev 9 1961.

— To give down the banks and hark from the tomb! James Joyce Quart 4 1967.

Higginson, F. H. Homer: Vico: Joyce. Kansas Mag 1956.

— Notes on the text of Finnegans wake. JEGP 55 1956.

— (ed). Two letters from Dame Anna Earwicker. Critique 1 1957.

Higginson, F. H. Anna Livia Plurabelle: the making of a chapter. Minneapolis 1960.

Worthington, M. P. American folk songs in Joyce's Finnegans wake. Amer Lit 28 1956.

— Nursery rhymes in Finnegans wake. Jnl of Amer Folklore 70 1957.

Frye, N. Quest and cycle in Finnegans wake. James Joyce Rev 1 1957; rptd in his Fables of identity, New York 1963.

Litz, W. The evolution of Joyce's Anna Livia Plurabelle. PQ 36 1957.

— The making of Finnegans wake. In James Joyce miscellany: second series, ed M. Magalaner, Carbondale 1959.

Manning, M. Passages from Finnegans wake by Joyce: a free adaptation for the theatre. Cambridge Mass 1957 (introd by D. Johnston).

Von Phul, R. Who sleeps at Finnegans wake? James Joyce Rev 1 1957.

— Shaun in Brooklyn. Analyst no 14 1959, no 20 1961.

— Circling the square: a study of structure. In James Joyce miscellany: third series, ed M. Magalaner, Carbondale 1962.

Wagner, G. Wyndham Lewis and Joyce: a study in controversy. South Atlantic Quart 56 1957.

Beechhold, H. F. Finn MacCool and Finnegans wake. James Joyce Rev 2 1958.

Bierman, R. White and pink elephants: Finnegans wake and the tradition of unintelligibility. Modern Fiction Stud 4 1958.

Hayman, D. Dramatic motion in Finnegans wake. Texas Stud in Eng 37 1958.

— From Finnegans wake: a sentence in progress. PMLA 73 1958.

— Notes for the staging of Finnegans wake. In James Joyce miscellany: third series, ed M. Magalaner, Carbondale 1962.

— A list of corrections for the Scribbledehobble. James Joyce Quart 1 1964.

— Tristan and Isolde in Finnegans wake: a study of the sources and evolution of a theme. Comparative Lit Stud 1 1964.

— Pound at the wake or the uses of a contemporary. James Joyce Quart 2 1965.

— The distribution of the Tristan and Isolde notes under Exiles in Scribbledchobble. Wake Newslitter new ser 2 1965.

Boldereff, F. M. Reading Finnegans wake. New York 1959.

— Hermes to his son Thoth: Joyce's use of Giordano Bruno in Finnegans wake. Lawrenceville 1968.

Bonheim, H. The father in Finnegans wake. Studia Neophilologica 31 1959; rptd in his Joyce's benefictions, 1964.

— God and the gods in Finnegans wake. Studia Neophilologica 34 1962; rptd in his Joyce's benefictions, 1964.

— A lexicon of the German in Finnegans wake. Berkeley 1967.

De Campos, A. Um lance de 'des' do Grande Sertão. Revista do livre 4 1959.

— and H. Panorama do Finnegans wake. São Paulo 1962.

Jarrell, M. L. Swiftiana in Finnegans wake. ELH 26 1959.

Kiralis, K. Joyce and Blake: a basic source for Finnegans wake. Modern Fiction Stud 4 1959.

Robinson, H. M. Hardest crux ever. In A James Joyce miscellany: second series, ed M. Magalaner, Carbondale 1959.

Carlson, M. Henrik Ibsen and Finnegans wake. Comparative Lit 12 1960.

Hart, C. Notes on the text of Finnegans wake. JEGP 59 1960.

— Structure and motif in Finnegans wake. 1962.

— A concordance to Finnegans wake. Minneapolis 1963.

— The elephant in the belly: exegesis of Finnegans wake. Wake Newslitter no 13 1963; rptd in Wake digest, ed C. Hart and F. Senn, Sydney 1968.

— Finnegans wake in perspective. In Joyce today: essays on the major works, ed T. F. Staley, Bloomington 1966.

— The hound and the type-bed: further notes on the text of Finnegans wake. Wake Newslitter new ser 3 1966.

— His good smetterling of entymology. Wake Newslitter new ser 4 1967.

— and F. Senn (ed). Wake Newslitter nos 1–18 1962–3, new ser 1 1964–.

—— A Wake digest. Sydney 1968. Essays by A. Glasheen, P. L. Graham, C. Hart, M. J. C. Hodgart, F. Senn et al.

Hart, C. and P. B. Sullivan. Australiana in Finnegans wake. Wake Newslitter no 9 1963.

Misra, B. P. Joyce's use of Indian philosophy in Finnegans wake. Indian Jnl of Eng Stud 1 1960.

Morse, J. M. Burrus, Caseous and Nicholas of Cusa. MLN 75 1960.

— HCE's chase ecstacy. Yale Rev 56 1967.

— Charles Nodier and Finnegans wake. Comparative Lit Stud 5 1968.

Senn, F. Some Zürich allusions in Finnegans wake. Analyst no 19 1960.

— Every klitty of a scolderymeid: sexual-political analogies. Wake Newslitter no 3 1962; rptd in Wake digest, ed C. Hart and F. Senn, Sydney 1968.

— A test-case of over-reading. Wake Newslitter new ser 1 1964.

— Ossianic echoes. Wake Newslitter new ser 3 1966.

— Reading in progress: words and letters in Finnegans wake. Leuvense Bijdragen 57 1968.

Coleman, E. Heliotropical noughttime: light and color in Finnegans wake. Texas Quart 4 1961.

Tello, J. Un experimento joyceano. Revista Nacional de Cultura 29 1961.

Gleckner, R. F. Joyce and Blake: notes toward defining a literary relationship. In A James Joyce miscellany: third series, ed M. Magalaner, Carbondale 1962.

Graham, P. L., P. B. Sullivan and G. F. Richter. Mind your hats goan in! notes on the museyroom episode of Finnegans wake. Analyst no 21 1962, no 22 1962.

Mercier, V. In the wake of the Fianna: some additions and corrections to Glasheen and a footnote or two to Atherton. In A James Joyce miscellany: third series, ed M. Magalaner, Carbondale 1962.

Wilder, T. Giordano Bruno's last meal in Finnegans wake. Wake Newslitter no 6 1962; rptd in Hudson Rev 16 1963. *See* J. P. Dalton, Wake Newslitter no 10 1963.

Visser, G. J. Joyce's prose and Welsh cynghanedd. Neophilologus 47 1963.

Asenjo, F. G. The general problem of sentence structure: an analysis prompted by the loss of subject in Finnegans wake. Centennial Rev 8 1964.

Benstock, B. Americana in Finnegans wake. Bucknell Rev 12 1964.

—— A Finnegans wake address book. James Joyce Quart 2 1965.

—— The gastronome's Finnegans wake. James Joyce Quart 2 1965.

—— Joyce-again's wake. Seattle 1965.

—— Persian in Finnegans wake. MP 44 1965.

—— L. Bloom as dreamer in Finnegans wake. PMLA 82 1967.

—— The reel Finnegans wake. New Orleans Rev 1 1968.

—— Every telling has a taling: a reading of the narrative of Finnegans wake. Modern Fiction Stud 15 1969.

Johnston, D. Clarify begins at: the non-information of Finnegans wake. Massachusetts Rev 5 1964.

Naganowski, E. La nuit au bord du fleuve de la vie: essai d'interpretation de Finnegans wake. Tr E. Veaux, Nouvelles 11 1964. A ch tr from his Telemach w labiryncie świata: o twórczości Joyce'a, Warsaw 1962. *See* General Studies, above.

Staples, H. B. Some notes on the one hundred and eleven epithets of HCE. Wake Newslitter new ser 1 1964; 2 1965.

Thompson, W. I. The language of Finnegans wake. Sewanee Rev 72 1964.

Tysdahl, B. J. and C. Hart. Norwegian captions. Wake Newslitter new ser 1 1964, 2 1965.

—— A Norse hundredlettered name in Finnegans wake. Orbis Litterarum 19 1964.

Bates, R. The feast is a flyday. James Joyce Quart 2 1965.

Broes, A. T. The Bible in Finnegans wake. Wake Newslitter new ser 2 1965.

—— More people at the wake. Wake Newslitter new ser 3 1966, 4 1967.

Christiani, D. H. C. Earwicker the ostman. James Joyce Quart 2 1965.

—— Scandinavian elements in Finnegans wake. Evanston 1965.

Dalton, J. P. and C. Hart (ed). Twelve and a tilly: essays on the occasion of the 25th anniversary of Finnegans wake. 1965. Poem by P. Colum and essays by F. Budgen, F. J. Hoffman, V. Mercier, F. Senn, R. F. Gleckner, J. S. Atherton, J. M. Morse, N. Halper, R. M. Kain, A. W. Litz, D. Hayman, J. P. Dalton (2).

Dalton, J. P. A letter from T. S. Eliot. James Joyce Quart 6 1968.

Kopper, E. A., jr. Some additional Christian allusions in the Wake. Analyst no 24 1965.

—— Saint Patrick in Finnegans wake. Wake Newslitter new ser 4 1967.

O Hehir, B. Anna Livia Plurabelle's Gaelic ancestry. James Joyce Quart 2 1965.

—— The names of Shem and Shaun. Wake Newslitter new ser 1 1964, 3 1966.

—— The name of Humphrey. Wake Newslitter new ser 3 1966.

—— A Gaelic lexicon for Finnegans wake and glossary for Joyce's other works. Berkeley 1967.

Reichert, K. Reise ans Ende des Möglichen: Joyce. In Romananfänge: Versuch zu einer Poetik des Romans, ed N. Miller, Berlin 1965.

Boyle, R. Finnegans wake, page 185: an explication. James Joyce Quart 4 1966.

Epstein, E. L. Interpreting Finnegans wake: a half-way house. James Joyce Quart 3 1966.

Tanner, G. Classical language references in Finnegans wake: a philological commentary with versions. Wake Newslitter new ser 3 1966.

Werckmeister, O. K. Das Book of Kells in Finnegans wake. Neue Rundschau 77 1966.

Paris, J. Finnegans, wake! Tel Quel 30 1967.

Behar, J. McLuhan's Finnegans wake. Denver Quart 3 1968.

Henrici, W. B. Ausspielungen auf Ibsens Dramen in Finnegans wake. Orbis Litterarum 23 1968.

Henseler, D. L. Harpsdichord, the formal principle of HCE, ALP and the cad. James Joyce Quart 6 1968.

Knuth, L. Dutch elements in Finnegans wake pp 75–8 compared with holograph workbook VI.B.46. Wake Newslitter new ser 5 1968.

—— Some notes on Malay elements in Finnegans wake. Wake Newslitter new ser 5 1968.

Schwimmer, H. Die Musik in Finnegans Wake. Melos 35 1968.

Begnal, M. H. The narrator of Finnegans wake. Eire-Ireland 4 1969.

Di Pietro, R. J. A transformational note on a few types of Joycean sentences. Style 3 1969.

Harmon, M. (ed). The Celtic master. Dublin 1969.

Solomon, M. C. Eternal geomater: the sexual universe of Finnegans wake. Carbondale 1969.

Tindall, W. Y. A reader's guide to Finnegans wake. New York 1969.

W. W.

ADELINE VIRGINIA WOOLF, née STEPHEN
1882–1941

The Berg Collection of New York Public Library has an important group of ms notebooks. The ms of Mrs Dalloway *is in BM; that of* Orlando *is at Knole. See Kirkpatrick, below.*

Bibliographies

Toerien, B. J. A bibliography of Virginia Woolf, 1882–1941. Capetown 1943.

Beebe, M. Criticism of Virginia Woolf: a selected checklist. Modern Fiction Stud 2 1956.

Kirkpatrick, B. J. A bibliography of Virginia Woolf. 1957, 1967 (rev) (Soho Bibliographies). Includes contributions to periodicals and newspapers, trns and foreign edns.

Collections and Selections

Works: uniform edition. 17 vols 1929–55.

Virginia Woolf: selections from her essays. Ed W. James [1966] (Queen's Classics).

Collected essays. Ed L. Woolf 4 vols 1966–7, New York 1967.

§ 1
Prose Fiction

The voyage out. 1915, New York 1920 (rev), London 1920 (from American sheets).

Two stories: written and printed by Virginia Woolf and L. S. Woolf. Richmond Surrey 1917 (150 copies). Contains The mark on the wall, by Virginia Woolf, and Three Jews, by Leonard Woolf.

The mark on the wall. Richmond Surrey 1919 (150 copies). First pbd 1917 in Two stories, above; rptd (rev) in Monday or Tuesday, below, and in A haunted house, below.

Kew Gardens. Richmond Surrey 1919 (150 copies). Story; rptd in Monday or Tuesday, below, and in A haunted house, below.

Night and day. 1919, New York 1920.

Monday or Tuesday. Richmond Surrey 1921, New York 1921. Stories; contains A haunted house, A society, Monday or Tuesday, An unwritten novel, The string quartet, Blue and green, Kew Gardens, The mark on the wall.

Jacob's room. Richmond Surrey 1922, New York 1923.

Mrs Dalloway. 1925, New York 1925, 1928 (Modern Lib, with introd by V. Woolf).

To the lighthouse. 1927, New York 1927, London 1938 (EL, introd by D. M. Hoare).

Orlando: a biography. New York 1928 (limited edn), London 1928, New York 1960 (Signet Classics, with afterword by E. Bowen).

The waves. 1931, New York 1931.

The years. 1937, New York 1937.

Between the acts. 1941, New York 1941.

A haunted house, and other short stories. 1943 (for 1944), New York 1944. Contains the stories already pbd in Monday or Tuesday, above, except A society and Blue and green, and adds The new dress, The shooting party, Lappin and Lapinova, Solid objects, The lady in the looking glass, The duchess and the jeweller (all previously pbd in various periodicals), Moments of being, The man who loved his kind, The searchlight, The legacy, Together and apart, A summing up (the last 6 not previously pbd).

Nurse Lugton's golden thimble. 1966. Children's story.

Other Works

F. M. Dostoevsky. Stavrogin's confession and the plan of The life of a great sinner. Tr S. S. Koteliansky and V. Woolf, Richmond Surrey 1922.

Tolstoi's love letters, with a study on the autobiographical elements in Tolstoy's work by P. Biryukov. Tr S. S. Koteliansky and V. Woolf, Richmond Surrey 1923.

Talks with Tolstoy, by A. B. Goldenveizer. Tr S. S. Koteliansky and V. Woolf, Richmond Surrey 1923.

Mr Bennett and Mrs Brown. 1924 (Hogarth Essays 1). First pbd in Criterion 2 1924 (as Character in fiction); rptd in Hogarth essays, New York 1928, and in The captain's death bed, below.

The common reader. 1925, New York 1925, 1948 (with The common reader: second series, in one vol). Essays. American edns include an additional essay, Lives of the obscure III: Miss Ormerod, which does not appear in the English edns.

A room of one's own. New York 1929 (limited edn), London 1929, New York 1929. Essay.

Street haunting. San Francisco 1930. Essay, first pbd in Yale Rev 1927; rptd in The death of the moth, below.

On being ill. 1930 (250 copies). Essay, first pbd in New Criterion, 1926; rptd in Forum 1926 (as Illness: an unexplored mine). This text (slightly rev from periodical texts) rptd in The moment, below.

Beau Brummell. New York 1930. Essay, first pbd in Nation & Athenaeum 1929; rptd in The common reader: second series, below.

A letter to a young poet. 1932 (Hogarth Letters 8). Essay, first pbd in Yale Rev 1932; rptd in The death of the moth, below. See P. Quennell, A letter to Mrs Virginia Woolf (Hogarth Letters 12), 1932.

The common reader: second series. 1932, New York 1932 (as The second common reader), London 1944, New York 1948 (with The common reader: first series, in one vol, as The common reader).

Flush: a biography. 1933, New York 1933. A 'biography' of Elizabeth Barrett Browning's spaniel.

Walter Sickert: a conversation. 1934. Essay, first pbd in Yale Rev 1934 (as A conversation about art); rptd in The captain's death bed, below. Text slightly rev from that in Yale Rev.

The Roger Fry memorial exhibition: an address. Bristol 1935 (125 copies, not for sale); rptd in The moment, below (as Roger Fry).

Three guineas. 1938, New York 1938. On the part that women can play in the prevention of war.

Reviewing. 1939 (Hogarth Sixpenny pamphlets 4). Essay; rptd in The captain's death bed, below.

Roger Fry: a biography. 1940, New York 1940.

The death of the moth, and other essays. 1942, New York 1942.

The moment, and other essays. 1947, New York 1948.

The captain's death bed, and other essays. New York 1950, London 1950.

Hours in a library. New York [1958]. Essay, first pbd in TLS 30 Nov 1916; rptd in Granite and rainbow, below.

Granite and rainbow: essays. 1958, New York 1958.

Contemporary writers, with a preface by Jean Guiguet. 1965, New York 1966. Essays, mostly rptd from TLS.

Books with Introductions by Virginia Woolf

Cameron, J. M. Victorian photographs of famous men and fair women. 1926.

Sterne, L. A sentimental journey. 1928.

Selections autobiographical and imaginative from the works of George Gissing. 1929; rptd in Gissing's By the Ionian sea, 1933.

Recent paintings by Vanessa Bell. [1930]. A catalogue.

Life as we have known it, by co-operative working women. 1931.

Letters and Diaries

A writer's diary: being extracts from the diary of Virginia Woolf. Ed L. Woolf 1953, New York 1954.

Virginia Woolf and Lytton Strachey: letters. Ed L. Woolf and J. Strachey 1956, New York 1956.

§2
Books and Chapters in Books

Collins, J. Two lesser literary ladies of London: Stella Benson and Virginia Woolf. In his The doctor looks at literature, 1923.

Empson, W. In Scrutinies, ed E. Rickword vol 2, 1931.

Badenhausen, I. Die Sprache Virginia Woolfs. Marburg 1932.

Delattre, F. Le roman psychologique de Virginia Woolf. Paris 1932.

Holtby, W. Virginia Woolf. 1932.

Edgar, P. Stream of consciousness: Dorothy Richardson, Virginia Woolf. In his Art of the novel, New York 1933.

Finke, I. Virginia Woolfs Stellung zur Wirklichkeit. Marburg 1933.

Weidner, E. Impressionismus und Expressionismus in den Romanen Virginia Woolfs. Greifswald 1934.

Gruber, R. Virginia Woolf: a study. Leipzig 1935.

Lohmüller, G. Die Frau im Werk Virginia Woolfs. Leipzig 1937.

Daiches, D. In his The novel and the modern world, Chicago 1939.

— Virginia Woolf. 1942, 1963 (rev).

Forster, E. M. Virginia Woolf. Cambridge 1942 (Rede lecture); rptd in his Two cheers for democracy, 1951.

Mortimer, R. In his Channel packet, 1942.

Bennett, J. Virginia Woolf: her art as a novelist. Cambridge 1945, 1964 (rev).

Auerbach, E. Der braune Strumpf. In his Mimesis, Berne 1946; tr W. R. Trask, Princeton 1953. On To the lighthouse.

Newton, D. Virginia Woolf. Melbourne 1946.

Burgum, E. B. Virginia Woolf and the empty room. In his Novel and the world's dilemma, New York 1947.

Chambers, R. L. The novels of Virginia Woolf. Edinburgh 1947.

Beck, W. For Virginia Woolf. In Forms of modern fiction, ed W. V. O'Connor, Minneapolis 1948.

Lehmann, J. Virginia Woolf. In Writers of to-day, vol 2 ed D. Baker 1948.

Blackstone, B. Virginia Woolf: a commentary. 1949.

—— Virginia Woolf. 1952, 1956 (rev) (Br Council pamphlet).

Wiget, E. Virginia Woolf und die Konzeption der Zeit in ihren Werken. Zürich 1949.

Savage, D. S. In his Withered branch, 1950.

Brower, R. A. Something central which permeated Virginia Woolf and Mrs Dalloway. In his Fields of light: an experiment in critical reading, New York 1951.

Chastaing, M. La philosophie de Virginia Woolf. Paris 1951.

Sanna, V. Il romanzo di Virginia Woolf. Florence 1951.

Rantavaara, I. Virginia Woolf and Bloomsbury. Helsinki 1953.

—— Virginia Woolf's The waves. Helsinki 1960.

Johnstone, J. K. The Bloomsbury group: a study of E. M. Forster, Lytton Strachey, Virginia Woolf and their circle. 1954.

Edel, L. The novel as poem. In his Psychological novel 1900–50, 1955.

Friedman, M. J. Dorothy Richardson and Virginia Woolf. In his Stream of consciousness, New Haven 1955.

Pippett, A. The moth and the star: a biography of Virginia Woolf. Boston 1955.

Bell, C. Virginia Woolf. In his Old friends, 1956.

Nathan, M. Virginia Woolf par elle-même. Paris 1956; tr 1961.

Enright, D. J. To the lighthouse or to India? In his Apothecary's shop, 1957.

Hollingsworth, K. Freud and the riddle of Mrs Dalloway. In Studies in honor of John Wilcox, ed A. P. Wallace and W. O. Ross, Detroit 1958.

Brewster, D. Virginia Woolf's London. 1959.

—— Virginia Woolf. 1963.

Woolf, L. Sowing: an autobiography of the years 1880–1904. 1960.

—— Growing: an autobiography of the years 1904–11. 1961.

—— Beginning again: an autobiography of the years 1911–18. 1964.

—— Downhill all the way: an autobiography of the years 1919–39. 1967.

—— The journey not the arrival matters: an autobiography of the years 1939–69. 1969.

Turnell, M. The shaping of contemporary literature: Lawrence, Forster, Virginia Woolf. In his Modern literature and Christian faith, 1961.

Collins, R. G. Virginia Woolf's black arrows of sensation: The waves. Ilfracombe 1962.

Cornwell, E. F. The still point: theme and variations in the writings of T. S. Eliot, Coleridge, Yeats, Henry James, Virginia Woolf and D. H. Lawrence. New Brunswick NJ 1962.

Guiguet, J. Virginia Woolf et son oeuvre. Paris 1962; tr 1965.

Izzo, C. Testimonianze sul Bloomsbury group. In Studi in onore di Vittorio Lugli e Diego Valeri, Venice 1962.

Pasternack, G. Aspekte des Komischen bei Virginia Woolf. Köln 1962.

Freedman, R. The lyrical novel: studies in Hermann Hesse, André Gide and Virginia Woolf. Princeton 1963.

Moody, A. D. Virginia Woolf. Edinburgh 1963 (Writers and Critics).

Hungerford, E. A. The narrow bridge of art: Virginia Woolf's early criticism 1905–25. Ann Arbor 1965.

Schaefer, J. O'B. The three-fold nature of reality in the novels of Virginia Woolf. The Hague 1965.

Thakur, N. C. The symbolism of Virginia Woolf. 1965.

Woodring, C. R. Virginia Woolf. New York 1966.

Cowley, M. Virginia Woolf: England under glass. In his Think back on us, Carbondale 1967.

Brandt, M. Realismus und Realität im modernen Roman: methodologische Untersuchungen zu Virginia Woolfs The waves. Bad Homburg 1968.

Marder, H. Feminism and art: a study of Virginia Woolf. Chicago 1968.

Articles in Periodicals

Bell, C. Virginia Woolf. Dial 76 1924.

Carew, D. Virginia Woolf. London Mercury 14 1926.

Forster, E. M. The novels of Virginia Woolf. New Criterion 4 1926; rptd in his Abinger harvest, 1936 (as The early novels of Virginia Woolf).

Muir, E. Virginia Woolf. Nation & Athenaeum 17 April 1926.

—— Virginia Woolf. Amer Bookman 74 1931.

Murry, J. M. The 'classical' revival. Adelphi 3 1926.

Mortimer, R. Mrs Woolf and Mr Strachey. Amer Bookman 68 1929.

St Jean, R. de. Mrs Dalloway. Revue Hebdomadaire 16 March 1929.

Sutherland, J. R. Virginia Woolf. Br Weekly 24 Oct 1929.

Dottin, P. Les sortilèges de Mrs Virginia Woolf. Revue de France 1 April 1930.

Lanoire, M. Le témoignage de Mrs Dalloway. Les Lettres (Paris) 17 1930.

Mayoux, J-J. A propos d'Orlando de Virginia Woolf. Europe 15 Jan 1930.

—— Le roman de l'espace et du temps: Virginia Woolf. Revue Anglo-américaine 7 1930.

Delattre, F. La durée bergsonienne dans le roman de Virginia Woolf. Revue Anglo-américaine 9 1931.

—— Le nouveau roman de Virginia Woolf. Études Anglaises 1 1937. The years.

Elkan, L. Virginia Woolf: ihre künstlerische Idee und ihre Auffassung der Frau. Der Kreis (Hamburg) 8 1931.

Herrick, R. The works of Mrs Woolf. Saturday Rev of Lit 5 Dec 1931.

Hoare, D. M. Virginia Woolf. Cambridge Rev 16 Oct 1931.

Josephson, M. Virginia Woolf and the modern novel. New Republic 15 April 1931.

Morra, U. Il nuova romanzo inglese: Virginia Woolf. La Cultura Jan 1931.

Nicolson, H. The writing of Virginia Woolf. Listener 18 Nov 1931.

Badt-Strauss, B. Das Werk der Virginia Woolf. Die Literatur 34 1932.

Bradbrook, M. C. Notes on the style of Mrs Woolf. Scrutiny 1 1932.

Daniel-Rops, H. Une technique nouvelle: le monologue intérieur. Correspondant 25 Jan 1932. Joyce and Virginia Woolf.

Masui, J. Virginia Woolf. Le Flambeau (Brussels) 15 1932.

Troy, W. Virginia Woolf. 1, The poetic method; 2, The poetic style. Symposium 3 1932.

—— Virginia Woolf and the novel of sensibility. Perspectives 6 1954; rptd in his Selected essays, New Brunswick NJ 1967.

Peel, R. Virginia Woolf. New Criterion 13 1933.

Burra, P. Virginia Woolf. Nineteenth Century 115 1934.

Roberts, J. H. Towards Virginia Woolf. Virginia Quart Rev 10 1934.

—— Vision and design in Virginia Woolf. PMLA 61 1946.

Beach, J. W. Virginia Woolf. Eng Jnl 26 1937.

Lalou, R. Le sentiment de l'unité humaine chez Virginia Woolf et Aldous Huxley. Europe 15 Oct 1937.

Muller, H. J. Virginia Woolf and feminine fiction. Saturday Rev of Lit 15 1937; rptd in his Modern fiction: a study of values, New York 1937.

Impressions 5 1938. Special no on Virginia Woolf. M. Yourcenar, Sur Virginia Woolf; F. Delattre, Un roman lyrique: The waves; L. Lemonnier, Le dernier roman: The years; L. Pimienta, Virginia Woolf et ses compagnes [K. Mansfield, R. Lehmann, May Sinclair].

Hartley, L. Of time and Mrs Woolf. Sewanee Rev 48 1939.

Monroe, N. E. The inception of Mrs Woolf's art. College Eng 2 1940.

Brooks, B. G. Virginia Woolf. Nineteenth Century & After 130 1941.

Eliot, T. S., R. Macaulay, V. Sackville-West and W. Plomer. Reminiscences of Virginia Woolf. Horizon 3 1941.

Lehmann, R. For Virginia Woolf. Penguin New Writing no 7 1941.

Grant, D. Virginia Woolf. Horizon 3 1941.

Roberts, R. E. Virginia Woolf 1882–1941. Saturday Rev of Lit 12 April 1941.

Smart, J. A. E. Virginia Woolf. Dalhousie Rev 21 1941.

Spender, S. Virginia Woolf: a tribute. Listener 10 April 1941.

Derbyshire, S. H. An analysis of Mrs Woolf's To the lighthouse. College Eng 3 1942.

Howarth, R. G. Dayspring of Virginia Woolf. Southerly 3 1942. On Night and day.

Kronenberger, L. Virginia Woolf as critic. Nation (New York) 17 Oct 1942.

Leavis, F. R. After To the lighthouse. Scrutiny 10 1942. Review of Between the acts.

Mellers, W. H. Virginia Woolf: the last phase. Kenyon Rev 4 1942.

Phelps, G. Virginia Woolf and the Russians. Cambridge Rev 17 Oct 1942.

Turnell, M. Virginia Woolf. Horizon 6 1942.

Wilson, J. S. Time and Virginia Woolf. Virginia Quart Rev 18 1942.

Fishman, S. Virginia Woolf on the novel. Sewanee Rev 51 1943.

Rahv, P. Mrs Brown and Mrs Woolf. Kenyon Rev 5 1943.

Wright, N. Mrs Dalloway: a study in composition. College Eng 5 1944.

Guidi, A. Appunti da una lettura di Virginia Woolf. Mercurio 2 1945.

— Spender, Praz e Virginia Woolf. Letteratura e Arte Contemporanea 2 1951.

Peschmann, H. The world of Virginia Woolf. Wind and the Rain 3 1945.

Smith, L. P. Tavistock Square. Orion 2 1945.

Chiesura, G. A proposita di Mrs Dalloway. Letteratura 8 1946.

Kelsey, E. M. Virginia Woolf and the she-condition. Sewanee Rev 54 1946.

Toynbee, P. Virginia Woolf: a study of three experimental novels. Horizon 14 1946. On Mrs Dalloway, To the lighthouse and The waves.

Plomer, W. A note on Virginia Woolf. Meanjin 6 1947.

— Virginia Woolf's diary. TLS 6 Aug 1954.

Savage, D. S. The mind of Virginia Woolf. South Atlantic Quart 46 1947.

Connolly, C. The novelist as critic. New Yorker 10 April 1948.

Osawa, M. Virginia Woolf and Pater. New Eng and Amer Lit no 1 1948.

Pacey, D. Virginia Woolf as a literary critic. UTQ 17 1948.

Tindall, W. Y. Many-leveled fiction: Virginia Woolf to Ross Lockridge. College Eng 10 1948.

Bowen, E. The achievement of Virginia Woolf. New York Times Book Rev 26 June 1949; rptd in her Collected impressions, 1950.

— The principle of her art was joy. New York Times Book Rev 21 Feb 1954.

Graham, J. W. Time in the novels of Virginia Woolf. UTQ 18 1949.

— A negative note on Bergson and Virginia Woolf. EC 6 1956.

— The caricature value of parody and fantasy in Orlando. UTQ 30 1961.

Bogan, L. Virginia Woolf: the skirting of passion. New Republic 29 May 1950; rptd in her Selected criticism, New York 1955.

Overcarsh, F. L. The lighthouse, face to face. Accent 10 1950.

Rosati, S. Virginia Woolf. Eng Miscellany (Rome) 1 1950.

Wilson, E. Virginia Woolf and Logan Pearsall-Smith. New Yorker 27 May 1950.

De Robertis, D. Virginia Woolf. Paragone 2 1951.

Banti, A. Umanità della Woolf. Paragone 3 1952.

Cazamian, L. La philosophie de Virginia Woolf. Études Anglaises 5 1952.

Lorberg, A. D. Virginia Woolf: benevolent satirist. Personalist 33 1952.

Hafley, J. A reading of Between the acts. Accent 13 1953.

Havard-Williams, P. and M. H. Bateau ivre: the symbol of the sea in Virginia Woolf's The waves. E Studies 34 1953.

— Mystical experience in Virginia Woolf's The waves. EC 4 1954.

— Perceptive contemplation in the work of Virginia Woolf. E Studies 35 1954.

Ridley, H. M. Leslie Stephen's daughter. Dalhousie Rev 33 1953.

Melchiori, G. Il diario di Virginia Woolf. Lo Spettatore Italiano 7 1954.

Sackville-West, V. The landscape of a mind. Encounter 2 1954.

— Virginia Woolf and Orlando. Listener 27 Jan 1955.

Stanzel, F. Die Erzählsituation in Virginia Woolfs Jacob's room, Mrs Dalloway and To the lighthouse. Germanisch-romanische Monatsschrift 4 1954.

Baldanza, F. Orlando and the Sackvilles. PMLA 70 1955. See D. B. Green, Orlando and the Sackvilles: addendum. PMLA 71 1956.

— To the lighthouse again. PMLA 70 1955.

Church, M. Concepts of time in novels of Virginia Woolf and Aldous Huxley. Modern Fiction Stud 1 1955.

Friedman, N. The waters of annihilation: double vision in To the lighthouse. ELH 22 1955.

— Criticism and the novel: Hardy, Woolf [et al]. Antioch Rev 18 1958.

Hungerford, E. A. Mrs Woolf, Freud and J. D. Beresford. Lit & Psychology 5 1955.

— My tunnelling process: the method of Mrs Dalloway. Modern Fiction Stud 3 1957.

Lehmann, J. Working with Virginia Woolf. Listener 13 Jan 1955.

Lombardo, A. Il diario di Virginia Woolf. Convivium 23 1955.

Bevis, D. The waves: a fusion of symbol, style and thought in Virginia Woolf. Twentieth-Century Lit 2 1956.

Blotner, J. L. Mythic patterns in To the lighthouse. PMLA 71 1956; rptd in Myth and literature, ed J. B. Vickery, Lincoln Nebr 1966.

Gamble, I. The secret sharer in Mrs Dalloway. Accent 16 1956.

Hoffman, C. G. The 'real' Mrs Dalloway. Univ of Kansas City Rev 22 1956.

— Fact and fantasy in Orlando: Virginia Woolf's manuscript revisions. Texas Stud in Lit & Lang 10 1968–9.

— From short story to novel: the manuscript revisions of Virginia Woolf's Mrs Dalloway. Modern Fiction Stud 14 1968.

— From lunch to dinner: Virginia Woolf's apprenticeship. Texas Stud in Lit & Lang 10 1969.

— Virginia Woolf's manuscript revisions of The years. PMLA 84 1969.

Modern Fiction Stud 2 1956. Special no on Virginia Woolf. D. Doner, Virginia Woolf: the service of style; J. Hafley, On one of Virginia Woolf's short stories [Moments of being]; C. Hunting, The technique of persuasion in Orlando; F. Baldanza, Clarissa Dalloway's 'party consciousness'; M. Zorn, The pageant in Between the acts; M. Beebe, Criticism of Virginia Woolf: a selected checklist.

O'Faolain, S. Narcissa and Lucifer: an essay on Virginia Woolf and Joyce. New World Writing 1956.

Stürzl, E. Virginia Woolfs Romankunst im Lichte ihres Tagebuches. Die Neueren Sprachen 5 1956.

Brogan, H. O. Science and narrative structure in Jane Austen, Hardy and Virginia Woolf. Nineteenth-Century Fiction 11 1957.

Moloney, M. F. The enigma of time in Proust, Virginia Woolf and Faulkner. Thought 32 1957.

Nathan, M. 'Visualisation' et vision chez Virginia Woolf. Revue des Lettres Modernes 5 1957–8.

Woolf, L. Génie et folie de Virginia Woolf. Revue de Paris 72 1965.

— Virginia Woolf and The waves. Radio Times 28 June 1957.

— Virginia Woolf: writer and personality. Listener 4 March 1965.

Dataller, R. Mr Lawrence and Mrs Woolf. EC 8 1958.

Howlett, J. Journal d'un écrivain. Lettres Nouvelles no 62 1958.

Pedersen, G. Vision in To the lighthouse. PMLA 73 1958.

Samuelson, R. The theme of Mrs Dalloway. Chicago Rev 11 1958.

— Virginia Woolf, Orlando and the feminist spirit. Western, Humanities Rev 15 1961.

— More than one room of her own: Virginia Woolf's critical dilemmas. Western Humanities Rev 19 1965.

Somnath, A. The elegiac strain in Virginia Woolf. Jammu and Kashmir Univ Rev 1 1958.

Beede, M. Virginia Woolf: romantic. North Dakota Quart 27 1959.

Bourniquel, C. Le journal littéraire de Virginia Woolf. Esprit 27 1959.

Brown, R. C. Laurence Sterne and Virginia Woolf: a study in literary continuity. Univ of Kansas City Rev 25 1959.

Cox, C. B. The solitude of Virginia Woolf. CQ 1 1959; rptd in his Free spirit: a study of liberal humanism in the novels of George Eliot, James, Forster, Virginia Woolf and Angus Wilson, 1963.

— Mental images and the style of Virginia Woolf. Critical Stud 3 1968.

Leyburn, E. D. Virginia Woolf's judgment of Henry James. Modern Fiction Stud 5 1959.

Basham, C. Between the acts. Durham Univ Jnl 21 1960.

Borgal, C. Virginia Woolf ou le point de vue de Sirius. Critique (Paris) no 158 1960.

Francis, H. E. Virginia Woolf and The moment. Emory Univ Quart 16 1960.

Kumar, S. K. Virginia Woolf and Bergson's Mémoire par excellence. E Studies 41 1960.

— Memory in Virginia Woolf and Bergson. Univ of Kansas City Rev 26 1960.

— A positive note on Bergson and Virginia Woolf. Literary Criterion (Mysore) 4 1961.

Lund, M. G. The androgynous moment: Woolf and Eliot. Renascence 12 1960.

McIntyre, C. F. Is Virginia Woolf a feminist? Personalist 41 1960.

Simon, I. Some aspects of Virginia Woolf's imagery. E Studies 41 1960.

Beker, M. Virginia Woolf's appraisal of Conrad. Studia Romanica et Anglica Zagrabiensia 12 1961.

Hartman, G. H. Virginia's web. Chicago Rev 14 1961.

Hashmi, S. Indirect style in To the lighthouse. Indian Jnl of Eng Stud 2 1961.

Page, A. A dangerous day: Mrs Dalloway discovers her double. Modern Fiction Stud 7 1961.

Ramsay, W. The claims of language: Virginia Woolf as symbolist. Eng Fiction in Transition 4 1961.

Cohn, R. Art in To the lighthouse. Modern Fiction Stud 8 1962.

German, H. and S. Kaehele. The dialectic of time in Orlando. College Eng 24 1962.

Kaehele, S. and H. German. To the lighthouse: symbol and vision. Bucknell Rev 10 1962.

Kreutz, I. Mr Bennett and Mrs Woolf. Modern Fiction Stud 8 1962.

Moody, A. D. The unmasking of Clarissa Dalloway. REL 3 1962.

Rigo, G. de. The waves di Virginia Woolf. Letterature Moderne 12 1962.

Briffault, H. Virginia Woolf y la revolución novelística. Torre 11 1963.

Delord, J. Virginia Woolf's critical essays. Revue des Langues Vivantes 29 1963.

Irons, E. An evening with Virginia Woolf. New Yorker 30 March 1963.

Koeztur, G. Virginia Woolf and the dilemma of the modern English novel. Annales Universitatis Scientiarum Budapestiensis, Sectio Philologica 4 1963.

Summerhayes, D. Society, morality, analogy: Virginia Woolf's world Between the acts. Modern Fiction Stud 9 1963.

Wilson, A. Evil in the English novel: from George Eliot to Virginia Woolf. Listener 3 Jan 1963.

Beja, M. Matches struck in the dark: Virginia Woolf's moments of vision. CQ 6 1964.

King, M. P. The androgynous mind and The waves. Univ Rev 30 1964.

— The waves and the androgynous mind. Ibid.

Lewis, A. J. From The hours to Mrs Dalloway. BM Quart 28 1964.

Benjamin, A. S. Towards an understanding of the meaning of Virginia Woolf's Mrs Dalloway. Wisconsin Stud in Contemporary Lit 6 1965.

Collet, G-P. Jacques-Emile Blanche and Virginia Woolf. Comparative Lit 17 1965.

Fortin, R. E. Sacramental imagery in Mrs Dalloway. Renascence 18 1965.

Garnett, D. Virginia Woolf. Amer Scholar 34 1965.

Goldman, M. Virginia Woolf and the critic as reader. PMLA 80 1965.

— Virginia Woolf and E. M. Forster: a critical dialogue. Texas Stud in Lit and Lang 7 1966.

Hildick, W. In that solitary room. Kenyon Rev 27 1965.

Weber, R. W. Die Glocken von Big Ben: zur Strukturfunktion der Uhrzeit in Mrs Dalloway. Deutsche Vierteljahrsschrift für Literaturwissenschaft und Geistesgeschichte 39 1965.

De Araujo, V. 'A haunted house'—the shattered glass. Stud in Short Fiction 3 1966.

Gelfant, B. H. Love and conversion in Mrs Dalloway. Criticism 8 1966.

Latham, J. E. The origin of Mrs Dalloway. N & Q 211 1966.

— The model for Clarissa Dalloway: Kitty Maxse. N & Q 214 1969.

— Thessaly and the 'colossal figure' in Mrs Dalloway. Ibid.

Manuel, M. Virginia Woolf as The common reader. Literary Criterion (Mysore) 7 1966.

Wilkinson, A. Y. A principle of unity in Between the acts. Criticism 8 1966.

Hynes, S. The whole contention between Mr Bennett and Mrs Webb. Novel 1 1967.

Marder, H. Beyond the lighthouse: The years. Bucknell Rev 15 1967.

— Virginia Woolf's 'system that did not shut out'. Papers on Lang and Lit 10 1969.

May, K. M. The symbol of 'painting' in Virginia Woolf's To the lighthouse. REL 8 1967.

Rosenberg, S. The match in the crocus: obtrusive art in Virginia Woolf's Mrs Dalloway. Modern Fiction Stud 13 1967.

Batchelor, J. B. Feminism in Virginia Woolf. English 17 1968.

Fromm, H. To the lighthouse: music and sympathy. Eng Miscellany 19 1968.

McConnell, F. D. Death among the apple trees: The waves and the world of things. Bucknell Rev 16 1968.

Franks, G. Virginia Woolf and the philosophy of G. E. Moore. Personalist 50 1969.

Henig, S. D. H. Lawrence and Virginia Woolf. D. H. Lawrence Rev 2 1969.

Payne, M. The eclipse of order: the ironic structure of The waves. Modern Fiction Stud 15 1969.

Roll-Hansen, D. Peter Walsh's seven-league boots: a note on Mrs Dalloway. E Studies 50 1969.

Steele, P. L. Virginia Woolf's spiritual autobiography. Topic 18 1969.

Warner, J. M. Symbolic patterns of retreat and reconciliation in To the lighthouse. Discourse 12 1969.

Watkins, R. Survival in discontinuity: Virginia Woolf's Between the acts. Massachusetts Rev 10 1969.

C.P.C.

DAVID HERBERT LAWRENCE
1885–1930

F. W. Roberts, Bibliography, below, gives (section E) locations of several hundred mss and typescripts. The largest collections are in the libraries of the Univ of California and of the Univ of Texas.

Bibliographies

For a fuller list of bibliographies, catalogues etc see Roberts, below.

McDonald, E. D. A bibliography of the writings of Lawrence. Philadelphia 1925. With secondary material; foreword by Lawrence.

—— The writings of Lawrence 1925–30: a bibliographical supplement. Philadelphia 1931.

Snyder, H. J. A catalogue of English and American first editions, 1911–32, of Lawrence. New York 1932.

Fabes, G. H. Lawrence: his first editions, points and values. 1933.

Aldington, R. Lawrence: a complete list of his works, with a critical appreciation. 1935.

Powell, L. C. The manuscripts of Lawrence: a descriptive catalogue. Foreword by A. Huxley, Los Angeles 1937.

—— Lawrence and his critics: a chronological excursion in bio-bibliography. Colophon 1 1940.

Tedlock, E. W. The Frieda Lawrence collection of Lawrence manuscripts: a descriptive bibliography. Albuquerque New Mexico 1948.

White, W. Lawrence: a checklist, secondary material 1931–50. Detroit 1950.

Roberts, F. W. The manuscripts of Lawrence. Lib Chron Univ of Texas 5 1955.

—— A bibliography of Lawrence. 1963 (Soho Bibliographies). Includes Lawrence's first appearances in print, both in periodical and book form, and traces subsequent significant publishing history; lists his mss, trns and some reviews of his works and books and pamphlets about him.

Tannenbaum, E. Lawrence: an exhibition of first editions, manuscripts etc. Carbondale 1958.

Beebe, M. and A. Tommasi. Criticism of Lawrence: a selected checklist. Modern Fiction Stud 5 1959.

Pinto, V. de S. (ed). Lawrence after thirty years. Nottingham 1960. Exhibition catalogue.

Hepburn, J. G. Lawrence's plays: an annotated bibliography. Book Collector 14 1965.

Beards, R. D. and J. B. Crump. Lawrence: ten years of criticism, 1959–68: a checklist. D. H. Lawrence Rev 1 1968.

Edwards, L. I. Lawrence: a finding list. Nottingham 1968. Lists holdings of Lawrence material in the city, county and university libraries of Nottingham.

Altenberg, B. A checklist of Lawrence scholarship in Scandinavia, 1934–68. D. H. Lawrence Rev 2 1969.

Kai, S. et al. A checklist of Lawrence articles in Japan, 1951–68. Ibid.

Collections and Selections

D. H. Lawrence. Introd by Humbert Wolfe [1928] (Augustan Books of English Poetry).

The plays of Lawrence. 1933. Contains The widowing of Mrs Holroyd, Touch and go, and David.

The ship of death and other poems. 1933. A selection from Last poems; not the same as the 1941 selection of the same title.

The tales of D. H. Lawrence. 1934. 46 selected stories.

Selected poems. 1934.

The spirit of place: an anthology compiled from the prose of D. H. Lawrence. Ed with introd by R. Aldington 1935.

Pornography and so on. 1936. Contains Nettles, Pornography and obscenity, and the introd to The paintings of D. H. Lawrence.

Poems. 2 vols 1939. First collected edn; contains from Collected poems 1928 the sequence Rhyming poems, Look! we have come through! and Birds, beasts and flowers; and from Last poems 1932, Last poems and Appendix of five poems.

Stories, essays and poems. Introd by D. Hawkins 1939 (EL).

The ship of death, and other poems. 1941. A selection; not the same as the 1933 book with same title, above.

Full score: twenty tales. 1943 (Reprint Soc).

The portable Lawrence. Ed with introd by Diana Trilling, New York 1947. A selection from the whole range of Lawrence's writings.

Selected poems. With introd by K. Rexroth, New York [1947].

Selected essays. Introd by R. Aldington 1950 (Penguin).

Selected poems. Chosen with introd by W. E. Williams 1950 (Penguin).

Art and painting. 1951 (Current Affairs 137). 4 essays.

Selected poems. Ed J. Reeves 1951.

The later D. H. Lawrence. New York 1952. Novels, stories, essays 1925–30 selected, with introds, by W. Y. Tindall.

Sex, literature and censorship: essays. Ed H. T. Moore, New York [1953], London 1955 (enlarged, with rev introd).

Complete short stories. 3 vols 1955.

Selected literary criticism. Ed A. Beal 1956.

Short novels. 2 vols 1956.

Complete poems. 3 vols 1957.

Selected poetry and prose. Ed T. R. Barnes 1957.

Love poems, selected by J. Hadfield. 1958.

20 poems. Hampstead 1959 (priv ptd, 65 copies).

Selected tales. Introd by I. Seraillier 1963.

The widowing of Mrs Holroyd and The daughter-in-law. Ed M. Morland 1968.

Lawrence: three plays. 1969 (Penguin, introd by R. Williams).

Lawrence: a selection. Ed R. H. Poole and P. J. Shepherd 1970.

§1

For original serial pbn of separate stories, and for details of the frequent changes of title in all types of Lawrence's writings, see Roberts, Bibliography, above. The contents of vols of stories are set out below: for contents of vols of poems, essays, articles etc see Roberts, Bibliography, above.

The white peacock. New York 1911, London 1911, 1950 (Penguin) (with introd by R. Aldington), Carbondale 1966 (preface by H. T. Moore, text from first English printing with restoration of rev passages from first American edn).

The trespasser. 1912, New York 1912.

Love poems, and others. 1913, New York 1913.

Sons and lovers. 1913, New York 1913, 1922 (with introd by J. Macy), 1951 (with introd by M. Schorer), 1962 (introd by A. Kazin, rptd from Partisan Rev 29 1962). *See* E. W. Tedlock, A final report on the manuscript of Sons and lovers, in his D. H. Lawrence and Sons and Lovers, New York 1965.

The widowing of Mrs Holroyd: a drama in three acts. (Altrincham Feb 1920 (amateur); Kingsway 13 Dec 1926). With introd by E. Bjorkman, New York 1914, London 1914.

The Prussian officer, and other stories. 1914, New York 1916. Contains The Prussian officer, The thorn in the flesh, Daughters of the vicar, A fragment of stained glass,

The shades of spring, Second best, The shadow in the rose garden, Goose Fair, The white stocking, A sick collier, The christening, Odour of chrysanthemums.

The rainbow. 1915 (unexpurgated, suppressed), New York 1915 (expurgated), New York 1924 (unexpurgated), London 1926, 1949 (Penguin, unexpurgated).

Twilight in Italy. 1916, New York 1916 (English sheets), London 1950 (with introd by R. Aldington). Travel sketches.

Amores: poems. [1916], New York 1916.

Look! we have come through! 1917 (expurgated), New York 1918 (English sheets), Marazion 1958 (unexpurgated). Verse.

New poems. 1918, New York 1920.

Bay: a book of poems. 1919.

Touch and go: a play in three acts. 1920, New York 1920. Unperformed.

Women in love. New York 1920 (priv ptd), London [1921], New York 1937 (with Lawrence's Foreword: see below, 1936), London 1951 (with introd by R. Aldington).

The lost girl. 1920, New York 1921, London 1950 (Penguin, with introd by R. Aldington). The first edn has 3 states, involving textual changes; the American 1921 edn has original unaltered text.

Movements in European history. By Lawrence H. Davison [i.e. Lawrence]. 1921, 1925 (illustr, as by D. H. Lawrence), Dublin [1926] (rev). School textbook.

Psychoanalysis and the unconscious. New York 1921, London 1923.

Tortoises. New York 1921. Verse, rptd in Birds, beasts and flowers, below.

Sea and Sardinia. New York 1921, London 1923, 1956 (with introd by R. Aldington). Travel.

Aaron's rod. New York 1922, London 1922, 1950 (Penguin, with introd by R. Aldington).

Fantasia of the unconscious. New York 1922, London 1923 (without epilogue).

England my England, and other stories. New York 1922, London 1924. Contains England my England, Tickets please, The blind man, Monkey nuts, Wintry peacock, You touched me, Samson and Delilah, The primrose path, The horse-dealer's daughter, Fanny and Annie.

The ladybird, The fox, The captain's doll. 1923, New York 1923 (as The captain's doll: three novelettes). The first version of The fox was ed H. T. Moore in his D. H. Lawrence miscellany, Carbondale 1959, London 1961, §2, below.

Studies in classic American literature. New York 1923, London 1924 (without foreword), New York 1962 (as The symbolic meaning: the uncollected versions [i.e. the original versions ptd Nov 1918–July 1921 in Eng Rev and in Nation & Athenaeum] of Studies in classic American literature, ed A. Arnold with preface by H. T. Moore).

Kangaroo. 1923, New York 1923, London 1950 (Penguin, with introd by R. Aldington).

Birds, beasts and flowers: poems. New York 1923, London 1923, 1930 (illustr, with prefaces not pbd elsewhere until Phoenix, 1936).

The boy in the bush. 1924, New York 1924. With M. L. Skinner.

Memoirs of the foreign legion by M.M. [Maurice Magnus]. Introd by Lawrence 1924, New York 1925. The introd is a substantial item in its own right (83 pp.).

St Mawr, together with The princess. 1925, New York 1925 (St Mawr only), London 1950 (Penguin, St Mawr together with The virgin and the gipsy, with introd by R. Aldington). Short novel and story.

Reflections on the death of a porcupine, and other essays. Philadelphia 1925, London 1934.

The plumed serpent (Quetzalcoatl). 1926, New York 1926, 1950 (Penguin, with introd by R. Aldington), New York 1950 (with introd by W. Y. Tindall).

David: a play. (Regent 22 May 1927). 1926, New York 1926.

Sun. 1926 (priv ptd, 100 copies), Paris 1928 (unexpurgated, 165 copies). Story; expurgated text rptd in the Woman who rode away. Roberts (bibliography, above) mentions a spurious text.

Glad ghosts. 1926. Story; rptd in The woman who rode away.

Mornings in Mexico. 1927, New York 1927, London 1950 (with introd by R. Aldington). Travel sketches.

Rawdon's roof. 1928 (Woburn Books 7). Story; rptd in Lovely lady, 1932, below.

The woman who rode away, and other stories. 1928, New York 1928 (with extra story, The man who loved islands), London 1950 (Penguin, with introd by R. Aldington; adds A modern lover and Strike-pay but omits The man who loved islands). Contains Two blue birds, Sun, The woman who rode away, Smile, The border line, Jimmy and the desperate woman, The last laugh, In love, Glad ghosts, None of that.

Lady Chatterley's lover. [Florence] 1928 (priv ptd), Paris 1929 (priv ptd, with My skirmish with Jolly Roger), London 1932 (expurgated), New York 1932, Hamburg 1933 (unexpurgated, with prefatory note by Frieda Lawrence), New York [1944] (as The first Lady Chatterley, with foreword by Frieda Lawrence and ms report by E. Forbes [first edn of first ms version]), New York [1957] (unexpurgated 1928 text; with introd by M. Schorer, rptd in A propos of Lady Chatterley's lover, 1961 (Penguin)), London 1960 (Penguin), 1961 (with introd by R. Hoggart); tr Italian, 1954 (as Le tre Lady Chatterley [i.e. the 3 versions of the novel], with introd by P. Nardi, including the first edn of the 2nd ms version). A description of the 3 versions is given in Schorer's introd. For list of piracies, parodies and forgeries, see Roberts, Bibliography, above.

Collected poems. 2 vols (vol 1, Rhyming poems; vol 2, Unrhyming poems) 1928, New York 1929 (in one vol), London 1932. Preface by Lawrence. Many poems rev and retitled from original appearances; Song of a man who is loved pbd first in this collection.

Sex locked out. 1928 (priv ptd). Article, rptd from Sunday Dispatch, and rptd in Assorted articles, below.

The paintings of D. H. Lawrence. [1929] (priv ptd). Introd by Lawrence.

Pansies: poems. Introd by Lawrence 1929 (expurgated), 1929 (priv ptd, unexpurgated), New York 1929 (expurgated).

My skirmish with Jolly Roger, written as an introduction to and a motivation of the Paris edition of Lady Chatterley's lover. New York 1929, London 1930 (rev, as A propos of Lady Chatterley's lover); rptd in Sex, literature and censorship, Collections above, and in Phoenix II, below.

Pornography and obscenity. 1929 (Criterion Miscellany 5), New York 1930, 1948 (with preface by F. A. Hasratoff); rptd in Sex, literature and censorship, and in Phoenix.

The escaped cock. Paris 1929, London 1931 (as The man who died), New York 1931 (as The man who died) in the Tales of Lawrence, 1934, Collections above.

The life of J. Middleton Murry, by J.C. [Jesus Christ]. 1930 (priv ptd, 50 copies). 5 lines.

Nettles. 1930 (Criterion Miscellany 11). Verse.

Assorted articles. 1930, New York 1930. Mostly from 1928–9.

The virgin and the gipsy. Florence 1930, London 1930, New York 1930; rptd in the Tales of Lawrence, 1934, above.

Love among the haystacks and other pieces, with a reminiscence by D. Garnett. 1930, New York 1933 (with extra piece, Christs in the Tirol). Stories and sketches; contains Love among the haystacks, A chapel among the mountains, A hay hut among the mountains, Once.

Apocalypse. Florence 1931, New York 1931 (with introd by R. Aldington), London 1932.

The triumph of the machine. 1930 (for 1931). Poem; rptd in Last poems, below.

Etruscan places. 1932, New York 1932 (English sheets), London 1950 (Penguin, with introd by R. Aldington). Travel sketches.

Last poems. Ed R. Aldington and G. Orioli, Florence 1932, New York 1933, London 1933.

The lovely lady. 1932 (for 1933), New York 1933. Stories; contains The lovely lady, Rawdon's roof, The rocking-horse winner, Mother and daughter, The blue moccasins, Things, The overtone, The man who loved islands. All previously pbd except The overtone.

We need one another. New York 1933. 2 essays, rptd in Phoenix, below.

A collier's Friday night. (Royal Court 8 Aug 1965). 1934. Play; introd by E. Garnett.

An original poem. 1934 (priv ptd, 100 copies). With note by C. Carswell. 'The wind, the rascal'.

A modern lover. 1934, New York 1934. Stories; contains A modern lover, The old Adam, Her turn, Strike-pay, The witch à la mode, New Eve and old Adam, Mr Noon. Some previously pbd.

Lawrence's unpublished foreword to Women in love. San Francisco 1936 (103 copies).

Phoenix: the posthumous papers. Ed with an introd by E. D. McDonald, New York 1936, London 1936. Contains a great deal not previously pbd in book form, and some ms material.

Fire, and other poems, with a foreword by Robinson Jeffers and a note on the poems by Frieda Lawrence. San Francisco 1940. Mostly previously unpbd.

A prelude, by D. H. Lawrence: his first and previously unrecorded work. Thames Ditton 1949 (priv ptd, 160 copies); rptd in Phoenix II, below. Story, rptd from Nottinghamshire Guardian 7 Dec 1907; foreword by P. B. Wadsworth.

Life. St Ives 1954 (250 copies). Essay, first pbd in Eng Rev Feb 1918; rptd in Phoenix, above.

The man who was through with the world: an unfinished story by Lawrence. Ed J. R. Elliot jr EC 9 1959.

Complete poems. Ed V. de S. Pinto and W. Roberts 2 vols 1964. Poems previously collected, together with uncollected poems from ptd and ms sources, appendices of juvenilia, variants and early drafts; includes all Lawrence's critical introds to his poems. Introd by V. de S. Pinto. Glossary of dialect and foreign words.

The paintings of Lawrence, ed M. Levy, with essays by H. T. Moore, J. Lindsay and H. Read. 1964.

Complete plays. 1965, New York 1965. The widowing of Mrs Holroyd (see above), David (see above), The married man (unperformed), The daughter-in-law (Royal Court 19 March 1967), The fight for Barbara (Mermaid 10 Aug 1967), Touch and go (see above), The merry-go-round (unperformed), A collier's Friday night (see above), Altitude (fragment, unperformed), Noah's flood (fragment, unperformed).

Phoenix II: uncollected, unpublished and other prose works. Ed F. W. Roberts and H. T. Moore 1968. With introd and notes.

Two hitherto unknown pieces by Lawrence. Ed C. E. Baron, Encounter 33 1969. Review of Bithell's Contemporary German poetry, and article, With the guns.

Roberts, F. W. Lawrence, the second 'poetic me': some new material. Renaissance and Modern Stud 14 1970. Poems from the Clarke notebook.

Lawrence edited Signature, *with Murry, for 3 nos (Oct–Nov 1915) and made numerous contributions to periodicals, the most important being* Adelphi, Eng Rev *and* Dial. *He also wrote a number of introds to other authors' books. For details see Roberts, Bibliography, above.*

Translations

All things are possible, by Leo Shestov, authorized translation by S. S. Koteliansky, with a foreword by Lawrence. Tr Lawrence and Koteliansky, 1920.

The gentleman from San Francisco and other stories, by I. A. Bunin, tr S. S. Koteliansky and Leonard Woolf. Richmond 1922. Title story tr by Lawrence and Koteliansky.

Mastro-Don Gesualdo, by Giovanni Verga, tr Lawrence. New York 1923, London 1928 (with introd by Lawrence).

Little novels of Sicily, by Giovanni Verga, tr Lawrence. New York 1925.

Cavalleria rusticana and other stories, by Giovanni Verga, tr and with an introd by Lawrence. London 1928.

The story of Doctor Manente, being the tenth and last story from the Suppers of A. F. Grazzini called Il Lasca. Trn and introd by Lawrence, Florence 1929.

The grand inquisitor, by F. M. Dostoevsky, tr S. S. Koteliansky, with introd by Lawrence. Tr Lawrence and Koteliansky 1930 (300 copies).

Letters

The following list includes major collections only of Lawrence's letters. Roberts, Bibliography, above, includes a large number of other reprintings up to 1962.

Letters. Ed with introd by A. Huxley, 1932.

Brewster, E. and A. Lawrence: reminiscences and correspondence. 1934.

Letters to Bertrand Russell. Ed H. T. Moore, New York [1948].

Letters, selected by R. Aldington. 1950 (Penguin). Introd by A. Huxley.

Selected letters. Ed with introd by Diana Trilling, New York [1958].

Collected letters. Ed with introd by H. T. Moore 2 vols New York [1962].

Lawrence in love: letters from Lawrence to Louie Burrows. Ed with introd by J. T. Boulton, Nottingham 1968.

Centaur letters. Austin Texas 1970. Ed E. D. McDonald. On the Centaur Press edns of Reflections on the death of a porcupine and McDonald's Bibliography, etc.

Letters from Lawrence to Martin Secker 1911–30. Ed Secker, Iver 1970 (priv ptd, 500 copies).

The quest for Rananim: Lawrence's letters to S. S. Koteliansky, 1914–30. Ed with introd by G. J. Zytaruk, Montreal 1970.

§2

For a selection of reviews and comments on Lawrence's works during his life, see Draper, Lawrence: the critical heritage, 1970 below. Some reviews are also listed in Roberts, Bibliography, above.

Books and Chapters in Books

Bickley, F. Some tendencies in contemporary poetry. In New paths, ed C. W. Beaumont and M. T. H. Sadler 1918.

Sadler, M T. H. The young novel. Ibid.

George, W. L. Three young novelists. In his A novelist on novels, 1918.

Aiken, C. In his Scepticisms, New York 1919.

— In his A reviewer's ABC, New York 1958.

Cunliffe, J. W. The new novelists. In his English literature during the last half century, New York 1919.

Waugh, A. In his Tradition and change, 1919.

Goldring, D. The later work of Lawrence. In his Reputations, 1920.

Monro, H. In his Some contemporary poets, 1920.

Chevalley, A. In his Le roman anglais de notre temps, 1921.

Phelps, W. L. In his Advance of English poetry, New York 1921.

Johnson, R. B. In his Some contemporary novelists: men, 1922.

Macy, J. In his Critical game, New York 1922.

Van Doren, C. In his Roving critic, New York 1923.

Brewster, D. and A. Burrell. In their Dead reckonings in fiction, New York 1924.

Douglas, N. Lawrence and Maurice Magnus: a plea for better manners. [Florence] 1924 (priv ptd); rptd in his Experiments, 1925. This refers to Lawrence's introd to Magnus's Foreign legion.

Gould, G. In his English novel of to-day, 1924.

Rosenfeld, P. In his Men seen, New York 1925.

Young, F. B. A note on Lawrence. In The Borzoi, New York 1925.

Drew, E. A. In her Modern novel, New York 1926.

Aldington, R. Lawrence: an indiscretion. Seattle 1927, London 1930 (as D. H. Lawrence).

— In his Artifex, 1935.

— Portrait of a genius but... 1950.

Forster, E. M. In his Aspects of the novel, 1927.

Marble, A. R. In her Study of the modern novel, New York 1928.

Read, H. In his English prose style, 1928.

— and E. Dahlberg. In their Truth is more sacred, 1961.

Swinnerton, F. Lawrence and Norman Douglas. In his A London bookman, 1928.

— Post Freud. In his Georgian scene, New York 1934.

Dobrée, B. In his Lamp and the lute, Oxford 1929.

— In his Modern prose style, 1934.

Wickham, H. In his Impuritans, New York 1929.

Arrow, J. J. C. Squire v. Lawrence. 1930 (pamphlet).

Leavis, F. R. D. H. Lawrence. Cambridge 1930; rptd in his For continuity, Cambridge 1933.

— Lawrence and Professor Irving Babbitt. In his For continuity, Cambridge 1933.

— D. H. Lawrence, novelist. 1955.

— The necessary opposite, Lawrence. In his English literature in our time and the university, 1969.

Lowell, A. The poetry of Lawrence. In her Poetry and poets, Boston 1930.

Murry, J. M. Lawrence: two essays. Cambridge 1930.

— Son of woman: the story of Lawrence. 1931, 1954 (with new introd, as D. H. Lawrence, son of woman).

— Reminiscences of Lawrence. 1933.

— In his Between two worlds, 1935.

— Introd to American edn of E.T., Lawrence: a personal record, New York 1936.

— In his Adam and Eve, 1944.

— Love, freedom and society. 1957. Comparison of the beliefs of Lawrence and Schweitzer.

Potter, S. Lawrence: a first study. 1930.

Ward, A. C. Scourgers and scavengers of society. In The nineteen-twenties, 1930.

'West, Rebecca' (C. I. Andrews). D. H. Lawrence. 1930 (pamphlet); rptd in her Ending in earnest, 1931.

Ford, F. M. (formerly Hueffer). In his Return to yesterday, 1931.

Hughes, G. Lawrence, the passionate psychologist. In his Imagism and the imagists, Stanford 1931.

Huxley, A. To the puritan all things are impure. In his Music at night, 1931.

— In his Olive tree, 1936.

Lawrence, A. and G. S. Gelder. Young Lorenzo: early life of Lawrence, containing hitherto unpublished letters, articles and reproductions of pictures. Florence 1931, London 1932.

Quennell, P. The later period of Lawrence. In Scrutinies, ed E. Rickword 1931.

— Lawrence and Aldous Huxley. In The English novelists, ed D. Verschoyle 1936.

Wesslau, W. Der Pessimismus bei Lawrence. Greifswald 1931.

Abraham, A. Die Kunstform von Lawrences Versdichtungen. Vienna 1932.

Beach, J. W. Impressionism: Lawrence. In his Twentieth-century novel, New York [1932].

— Victorian afterglow. In his Concept of nature in nineteenth-century poetry, New York 1936.

Carswell, C. The savage pilgrimage: a narrative of Lawrence. 1932, 1932 (rev). Reply to J. M. Murry, Son of woman, above.

Carter, F. Lawrence and the body mystical. 1932.

Colin, S. C. Naturalisme et mysticisme chez Lawrence. Paris 1932.

Goodman, R. Footnote to Lawrence. 1932 (pamphlet).

Luhan, M. D. Lorenzo in Taos. New York 1932.

— Taos and its artists. New York 1948.

McCarthy, D. In his Criticism, 1932.

Malraux, A. Preface to L'amant de Lady Chatterley. Paris 1932.

Marinoff, I. In her Neue Wertungen im englischen Roman, Leipzig 1932.

Moore, O. Further reflections on the death of a porcupine. 1932.

Nin, A. Lawrence: an unprofessional study. Paris 1932.

Strachey, J. In his The coming struggle for power, 1932.

Brett, D. Lawrence and Brett: a friendship. Philadelphia [1933].

Corke, H. Lawrence and Apocalypse. 1933.

— Lawrence: the Croydon years. Austin 1965.

Grant, J. L. Male and female. 1933.

Gregory, H. Pilgrim of the Apocalypse: a critical study of Lawrence. New York 1933.

— Lawrence: the posthumous reputation. In Literary opinion in America, ed M. D. Zabel, New York 1937; rptd in his Shield of Achilles, New York 1944.

Joad, C. E. M. In his Guide to modern thought, 1933.

Mégroz, R. L. Lawrence. In his Five novelist poets of today, 1933.

— In The Post-Victorians, 1933.

Rascoe, B. In his Prometheans, New York 1933.

Stonier, G. W. In his Gog Magog and other critical essays, 1933.

Brewster, E. and A. Lawrence: reminiscences and correspondence. 1934.

Brown, I. 'Brother Lawrence' and 'Belly and brain'. In his I commit to the flames, 1934.

Eliot, T. S. In his After strange gods, 1934.

— Foreword to W. Tiverton, Lawrence and human existence, 1951.

— In his To criticize the critic, 1965.

Hoops, R. In his Der Einfluss der Psychoanalyse auf die englische Literatur, Heidelberg 1934.

Jaensson, K. D. H. Lawrence. Stockholm 1934.

Lawrence, Frieda. Not I, but the wind... Santa Fe, New Mexico 1934 (priv ptd), New York 1934. Includes original material by Lawrence.

— Memoirs and correspondence. Ed E. W. Tedlock 1961.

Powell, D. In her Descent from Parnassus, 1934.

Reuter, I. Studien über die Persönlichkeit und die Kunstform von Lawrence. Marburg 1934.

Schickele, R. Liebe und Ärgernis des Lawrence. Amsterdam 1934.

Blackmur, R. P. Lawrence and expressive form. In his Double agent, New York 1935; rptd 1952 in his Language as gesture.

Collis, J. S. An inevitable prophet. In his Farewell to argument, 1935.

E.T. (Jessie Chambers Wood). Lawrence: a personal record. 1935; ed J. D. Chambers 1965 (includes additional material by J. D. Chambers, Helen Corke, J. A. Bramley and May Holbrook).

Fabre-Luce, A. La vie de Lawrence. Paris 1935.

'Maurois, André' (E. S. W. Herzog). In his Magiciens et logiciens, Paris 1935. Tr New York 1935 (as Poets and prophets); rptd 1969 (as Points of view).

Sitwell, O. Portrait of Lawrence. In his Penny foolish, 1935.

Spender, S. Notes on Lawrence. In his Destructive element, 1935.

— In his World within world, 1951.

— Pioneering the instinctive life. In his Creative element, 1953.

Seillière, E. Lawrence et les récentes idéologies allemandes. Paris 1936.

Winter, K. Impassioned pygmies. 1936.

Couaillac, M. Lawrence: essai sur la formation et le développement de sa pensée d'après son oeuvre en prose. Toulouse 1937.

Gomes, E. Lawrence e outres. Porto Allegro Brazil 1937.

Muller, H. J. In his Modern fiction, New York 1937.

Praz, M. In his Studi e svaghi inglesi, Florence 1937.

Reul, P. de. L'oeuvre de Lawrence. Paris 1937.

Wulfsberg, F. Lawrence fra Nottinghamshire. Oslo 1937.

'Caudwell, Christopher' (C. St J. Sprigg). In his Studies in a dying culture, 1938.

Hoare, D. M. The novels of Lawrence. In her Some studies in the modern novel, 1938.

'Kingsmill, Hugh' (H. K. Lunn). D. H. Lawrence. 1938.

Merrild, K. A poet and two painters: a memoir of Lawrence. 1938, 1964 (as With Lawrence in New Mexico).

Peyre, H. Lawrence, le message d'un prophète. In his Hommes et oeuvres du XXᵉ siècle, Paris 1938.

Weidner, I. Botschaftsverkündigung und Selbstausdruck im Prosawerk von Lawrence. Berlin 1938.

Anderson, G. K. and E. L. Walton. In This generation, Chicago 1939.

Daiches, D. In his Novel and the modern world, Chicago 1939, Cambridge 1960 (rev).

— Georgian poetry. In his Poetry and the modern world, Chicago 1940, 1960 (rev).

— D. H. Lawrence. 1963 (priv ptd). Broadcast talk.

Fraenkel, M. The otherness of Lawrence. In his Death is not enough, 1939.

Henderson, P. Birds, beasts and flowers. In his The poet and society, 1939.

Johnsson, M. Lawrence: ett modernt tankeäventyr. Stockholm 1939.

Tindall, W. Y. Lawrence and Susan his cow. New York 1939.

Undset, S. In her Men, women and places, New York 1939.

Beutmann, M. Die Bildwelt Lawrences. Freiburg 1940.

Southworth, J. G. Lawrence: poet. In his Sowing the spring, Oxford 1940.

Wilder, A. N. The primitivism of Lawrence. In his Spiritual aspects of the new poetry, New York 1940.

Bates, H. E. In his Modern short story, 1941.

Miller, H. 'Creative death' and 'Into the future'. In his Wisdom of the heart, Norfolk Conn 1941.

Plowman, M. The significance of Lawrence. In his Right to live, 1942.

Nicholson, N. In his Man and literature, 1943.

Wagenknecht, E. C. Lawrence: pilgrim of the rainbow. In his Cavalcade of the English novel, New York 1943.

Bentley, E. R. In his A century of hero-worship, Philadelphia 1944, London 1947 (as Cult of the superman).

Coates, J. B. In his Ten modern prophets, 1944.

Savage, D. S. Lawrence: a study in dissolution. In his Personal principle, 1944.

Hoffman, F. J. Lawrence's quarrel with Freud. In his Freudianism and the literary mind, Baton Rouge 1945, 1957 (rev).

— and H. T. Moore (ed). The achievement of Lawrence. Norman Okla [1953].

Pritchett, V. S. Sons and lovers. In his Living novel, 1946.

Warner, R. Cult of power. In his Cult of power: essays, 1946.

Nardi, P. La vita di Lawrence. Milan 1947.

Woolf, V. Notes on Lawrence. In her The moment and other essays, 1947.

Evans, B. I. In his English literature between the wars, 1948.

Fergusson, F. Lawrence's sensibility. In Forms of modern fiction, ed W. V. O'Connor, Minneapolis 1948.

Armitage, M. Taos quartet in three movements. New York 1950.

Bowen, E. In her Collected impressions, 1950.

West, A. D. H. Lawrence. 1950.

Auden, W. H. Heretics. In Literary opinion in America, ed M. D. Zabel, New York 1951; rptd in his Dyer's hand, 1962.

— In his Dyer's hand, 1962.

Bynner, W. Journey with genius: recollections and reflections concerning the Lawrences. New York 1951.

De Lucia, D. A proposito de L'amante di Lady Chatterley di Lawrence. Matera 1951.

Kenmare, D. Fire-bird: a study of Lawrence. 1951. Poetry only.

Moore, H. T. The life and works of Lawrence. New York 1951, 1964 (rev, as Lawrence: his life and works).

— The intelligent heart: the story of Lawrence. New York 1954, 1960 (Penguin) (rev).

— Poste restante: a Lawrence travel calendar. Berkeley 1956.

— (ed). A Lawrence miscellany. Carbondale 1959. Contributions by Moore, J. M. Murry, W. Morris, K. Widmer, E. Bergler, M. Mudrick, A. P. Bertocci, V. de Sola Pinto, D. Trilling, K. Mansfield, D. Patmore, B. Patmore, E. Mayer, R. Aldington, M. Green, J. L. Jarrett, R. E. Gajdusek, P. Abel, R. Hogan, N. Abolin, S. R. Weiner, J. Kessler, F. R. Karl, M. Schorer, R. Williams, R. Foster, H. Lindenberger, A. Alvarez, H. Bloom, C. Hassall and K. Shapiro.

Moore, H. T. The prose style of Lawrence. In Langue et littérature: actes du VIIIᵉ Congrès de la Fédération Internationale des Langues et Littératures Modernes, Paris 1961.

— and W. Roberts (ed). Lawrence and his world. 1966.

Pinto, V. de S. Lawrence: prophet of the Midlands. Nottingham 1951 (for 1952).

— The burning bush: Lawrence as religious poet. In Mansions of the spirit: essays in literature and religion, ed G. A. Panichas, New York 1967.

— Blake and Lawrence. In William Blake: essays for S. Foster Damon, ed A. H. Rosenfeld, Providence RI 1969.

Rowse, A. L. Lawrence at Eastwood. In his English past, 1951.

'Tiverton, William' (M. R. Jarrett-Kerr). Lawrence and human existence. Foreword by T. S. Eliot 1951.

Wickramasinghe, M. The mysticism of Lawrence. Colombo 1951.

Asquith, C. In her Remember and be glad, 1952.

Bantock, G. H. Lawrence and the nature of freedom. In his Freedom and authority in education, 1952.

Deutsch, B. In her Poetry in our time, New York 1952.

Scott, N. A. Lawrence: chartist of the via mystica. In his Rehearsals of discompose, New York 1952.

Young, K. D. H. Lawrence. 1952, 1960 (rev), 1963 (rev) (Br Council pamphlet).

Fay, E. Lorenzo in search of the sun: Lawrence in Italy, Mexico and the American southwest. New York 1953.

Highet, G. Lawrence in America. In his People, places and books, New York 1953.

Kettle, A. On The rainbow. In his Introduction to the English novel vol 2, 1953.

Van Ghent, D. B. On Sons and lovers. In her English novel, New York 1953.

Freeman, M. Lawrence: a basic study of his ideas. Gainesville 1955.

Kazin, A. The painfulness of Lawrence. In his Inmost leaf, New York 1955.

Spilka, M. The love ethic of Lawrence. Bloomington 1955.

— (ed). Lawrence: a collection of critical essays. Englewood Cliffs NJ 1963.

Vivante, L. In his A philosophy of potentiality, 1955.

Galinsky, H. Deutschland in der Sicht von Lawrence und Eliot. Wiesbaden 1956. Lecture.

Hough, G. G. The dark sun: a study of Lawrence. 1956.

— Two exiles: Lord Byron and Lawrence. Nottingham 1956. Lecture. Rptd in his Image and experience, 1960.

Price, A. W. Lawrence and Congregationalism. 1956.

Russell, B. In his Portraits from memory, 1956.

—— In his Autobiography vol 2, 1968.

Allen, W. In his English novel, 1957.

Blöcker, G. In his Die neuen Wirklichkeiten, Berlin 1957.

Coveney, P. In his The child in literature, 1957, 1967 (rev, as The image of childhood).

Hess, E. Die Naturbetrachtung im Prosawerk von Lawrence. Berne 1957.

King, R. W. Lawrence: an informal note. Croydon 1957.

Nehls, E. (ed). Lawrence: a composite biography. 3 vols Madison 1957–9. Extracts from memoirs of Lawrence and from Lawrence's own writings arranged chronologically to form a collective biography.

Alvarez, A. In his Shaping spirit, 1958, New York 1958 (as Stewards of excellence).

Arnold, A. Lawrence and America. 1958.

—— Lawrence and German literature. Montreal 1963.

Rees, R. Brave men: a study of Lawrence and Simone Weil. 1958.

Williams, R. In his Culture and society 1780–1950, 1958.

—— Social and personal tragedy: Tolstoy and Lawrence. In his Modern tragedy, 1966.

—— Lawrence: The widowing of Mrs Holroyd. In his Drama from Ibsen to Brecht, 1968.

Karl, F. R. and Magalaner, M. D. H. Lawrence. In their Reader's guide to great twentieth-century English novels, New York 1959.

Krook, D. Messianic humanism: Lawrence's Man who died. In her Three traditions of moral thought, Cambridge 1959.

Rexroth, K. Poetry, regeneration and Lawrence. In his Bird in the bush, New York 1959.

Walsh, W. Ursula in The rainbow; The educational ideas of Lawrence. In his Use of imagination, 1959.

Cook, A. In his The meaning of fiction, Detroit 1960.

Drain, R. L. Tradition and Lawrence. Gröningen 1960 (pamphlet).

Freiberg, L. The unattainable self: Sons and lovers. In Twelve original essays on great English novels, ed K. Shapiro, Detroit 1960.

Krieger, M. In his The tragic vision, New York 1960.

Temple, F.-J. Lawrence: l'oeuvre et la vie. Paris 1960.

Vivas, E. Lawrence: the failure and triumph of art. Evanston 1960.

Beal, A. D. H. Lawrence. Edinburgh 1961 (Writers and Critics).

Heppenstall, R. In his The fourfold tradition: notes on the French and English literatures, 1961.

Lacher, W. L'amour et le divin: Desbordes-Valmore, de Noailles, Lawrence, Morgan. Geneva 1961.

Robson, W. W. Women in love. In Pelican guide to English literature vol 7, The modern age, ed B. Ford 1961; rptd in his Critical essays, 1966.

Rolph, C. H. (ed). The trial of Lady Chatterley. 1961 (Penguin).

Cornwell, E. F. The sex mysticism of Lawrence. In her Still point, New Brunswick 1962.

Gregor, I. and B. Nicholas. In their Moral and the story, 1962. On Lady Chatterley's lover.

Mackenzie, C. In his On moral courage, 1962.

Weiss, D. A. Oedipus in Nottingham: Lawrence. Seattle 1962. Mainly about Sons and lovers.

Widmer, K. The art of perversity: Lawrence's shorter fictions. Seattle 1962.

Goodheart, E. The utopian vision of Lawrence. Chicago 1963.

—— In his Cult of the ego: the self in modern literature, Chicago 1968.

Moynahan, J. The deed of life: the novels and tales of Lawrence. Princeton 1963.

—— (ed). Sons and lovers: text, background and criticism. New York 1968.

Sparrow, J. The censor as aedile. In his Independent essays, 1963.

Stewart, J. I. M. In his Eight modern writers, Oxford 1963 (OHEL).

Tedlock, E. W. Lawrence—artist and rebel: a study of Lawrence's fiction. Albuquerque 1963.

—— (ed). Lawrence and Sons and lovers: sources and criticism. New York 1965.

Draper, R. P. D. H. Lawrence. New York 1964.

—— Satire as a form of sympathy: Lawrence as a satirist. In Renaissance and modern essays presented to V. de S. Pinto, ed G. R. Hibbard 1966.

—— D. H. Lawrence. 1969 (Profiles in Literature).

—— (ed). Lawrence: the critical heritage. 1970.

Gillès, D. Lawrence: ou le puritain scandaleux. Paris 1964.

Gottwald, J. Die Erzählformen der Romane von Aldous Huxley und Lawrence. Munich 1964.

Hardy, B. Truthfulness and schematism: Lawrence. In her Appropriate form: an essay on the novel, 1964.

Holbrook, D. On Lady Chatterley's lover. In his Quest for love, 1964.

Panichas, G. A. Adventure in consciousness: the meaning of Lawrence's religious quest. Hague 1964.

—— Forster and Lawrence: their views on education. In Renaissance and modern essays presented to V. de S. Pinto, ed G. R. Hibbard 1966.

Sinzelle, C. M. The geographical background of the early works of Lawrence. Paris 1964.

Clark, L. D. Dark night of the body: Lawrence's Plumed serpent. Austin 1965.

—— Lawrence, Women in love: the contravened knot. In Approaches to the twentieth-century novel, ed J. E. Unterecker, New York 1965.

Corsani, M. Lawrence e l'Italia. Milan 1965.

Daleski, H. M. The forked flame: a study of Lawrence. 1965.

Ford, G. H. Double measure: a study of the novels and stories of Lawrence. New York 1965.

Gray, R. In his German tradition in literature, 1871–1945, Cambridge 1965.

Hildick, E. W. In his Word for word: a study of authors' alterations, 1965.

Oppel, H. Lawrence: St Mawr. In Der moderne englische Roman, ed H. Oppel, Berlin 1965.

Talon, H. A. Lawrence, Sons and lovers: les aspects sociaux, la vision de l'artiste. Paris 1965.

Enright, D. J. A haste for wisdom: the poetry of Lawrence. In his Conspirators and poets, 1966.

Fedder, N. J. The influence of Lawrence on Tennessee Williams. The Hague 1966.

Friedman, A. Lawrence: 'The wave which cannot halt'. In his Turn of the novel, New York 1966.

Gordon, D. J. Lawrence as a literary critic. New Haven 1966 (Yale Stud in Eng 162).

Harrison, J. R. The reactionaries—Yeats, Lewis, Pound, Eliot, Lawrence: a study of the anti-democratic intelligentsia. 1966.

Kaplan, H. J. The naturalist theology of Lawrence. In his Passive voice: an approach to modern fiction, Athens Ohio 1966.

Lee, B. America, my America. In Renaissance and modern essays presented to V. de S. Pinto, ed G. R. Hibbard 1966.

Marnat, M. David Herbert Lawrence. Paris 1966.

Sagar, K. The art of Lawrence. Cambridge 1966.

Salgado, G. Lawrence: Sons and lovers. 1966 (Stud in Eng Lit).

—— (ed). Lawrence: Sons and lovers. 1969 (Casebook ser).

Vickery, J. B. Myth and ritual in the shorter fiction of Lawrence. In Myth and literature, ed J. B. Vickery, Lincoln Nebraska 1966.

West, P. In his Wine of absurdity, 1966.

Lerner, L. D. The truthtellers: Jane Austen, George Eliot, Lawrence. 1967.

Potts, A. F. Pipings of Pan: Lawrence. In his Elegiac mode, Ithaca 1967.

Clark, R. In his The Huxleys, 1968.

Donoghue, D. In his Ordinary universe: soundings in modern literature, 1968.

Hsia, A. Lawrence: die Charaktere in der Handlung und Spannung seiner Kurzgeschichten. Bonn 1968.

Kinkead-Weekes, M. The marble and the statue: the exploratory imagination of Lawrence. In Imagined worlds: essays on some English novels and novelists in honour of John Butt, ed M. Mack and I. Gregor 1968.

Martz, L. L. Portrait of Miriam: a study in the design of Sons and lovers. Ibid.

Morrison, C. Lawrence and American literature. In her Freud and the critic: the early use of depth psychology in literary criticism, Chapel Hill 1968.

Poole, R. H. Lawrence and education. Nottingham 1968. Pamphlet.

Schorer, M. In his World we imagine: selected essays, New York 1968.

Stoll, J. E. Lawrence's Sons and lovers: self-encounter and the unknown self. Muncie Indiana 1968.

Thody, P. M. W. In his Four cases of literary censorship, Leeds 1968. Lecture.

Cavitch, D. Lawrence and the new world. 1969.

Clarke, C. River of dissolution: Lawrence and English romanticism. 1969.

— (ed). Lawrence: Rainbow and Women in love. 1969 (Casebook ser).

Delavenay, E. Lawrence—l'homme et la genèse de son oeuvre: les années de formation, 1885–1919. Paris 1969. Appendices include unpbd letters etc by Jessie Chambers.

Griffin, E. G. In his John Middleton Murry, New York 1969.

Ileana, C-S. Lawrence as critic. Delhi 1969.

Garrett, P. K. In his Scene and symbol from George Eliot to James Joyce, New Haven 1969.

Meckier, J. Huxley's Lawrencian interlude: the 'Latin compromise' that failed. In his Aldous Huxley: satire and structure, 1969.

Miko, S. J. (ed). Twentieth century interpretations of Women in love. Englewood Cliffs NJ 1969.

Rahv, P. On F. R. Leavis and Lawrence. In his Literature and the sixth sense, Boston 1969.

Rembar, C. The end of obscenity: the trials of Lady Chatterley, Tropic of cancer and Fanny Hill. 1969.

Slade, T. Lawrence. 1969 (Literature in Perspective).

Yudhishtar. Conflict in the novels of Lawrence. Edinburgh 1969.

Cowan, J. C. Lawrence's American journey. Cleveland Ohio 1970.

Articles in Periodicals

James, H. In The younger generation, TLS 19 March, 2 April 1914; rptd in his Notes on novelists, 1914.

Hale, E. E. In The new realists, Independent 30 Aug 1915.

Kuttner, A. New Republic 10 April 1915. Review article on Sons and lovers; rptd in Lawrence: the critical heritage, ed R. P. Draper, 1970. Expanded into article (as A Freudian appreciation), Psychoanalytic Rev 3 1916.

Garnett, E. Art and the moralists: Lawrence's work. Dial 61 1916; rptd in his Friday nights, 1922, and in Lawrence: the critical heritage, ed R. P. Draper, 1970.

— Lawrence: his posthumous papers. London Mercury 35 1937. Review of Phoenix.

Lippmann, W. The crude barbarian and the noble savage. New Republic 15 Dec 1920.

Untermeyer, L. Lawrence. New Republic 11 Aug 1920; rptd in Lawrence: the critical heritage, ed R. P. Draper 1970.

Canby, H. S. A specialist in sex. Literary Rev 3 June 1922; rptd in his Definitions ser 2, New York 1924.

Hueffer, F. M. (afterwards Ford). A haughty and proud generation. Yale Rev 11 1922.

— D. H. Lawrence. Amer Mercury 38 1936; rptd in his Portraits from life, Boston 1937, London 1938 (as Mightier than the sword).

Shanks, E. Lawrence: some characteristics. London Mercury 8 1923; rptd in Lawrence: the critical heritage, ed R. P. Draper 1970.

Gregory, A. Artist turned prophet. Dial 76 1924; rptd ibid.

Muir, E. D. H. Lawrence. Nation 11 Feb 1925; rptd in Nation & Athenaeum 4 July 1925, in his Transition, 1926, and in Lawrence: the critical heritage, ed R. P. Draper 1970.

Richards, I. A. In A background for contemporary poetry, Criterion 3 1925.

Sherman, S. Lawrence cultivates his beard. New York Herald Tribune 14 June 1925; rptd in his Critical woodcuts, New York 1926, and in Lawrence: the critical heritage, ed R. P. Draper 1970.

Aldington, R. Lawrence as poet. Saturday Rev of Lit 1 May 1926; rptd in Lawrence: the critical heritage, ed R. P. Draper 1970.

— D. H. Lawrence. Everyman 3 1930.

— D. H. Lawrence. Das Inselschiff 14 1932.

— Lawrence: ten years after. Saturday Rev of Lit 24 June 1939.

— A wreath for Lawrence. Encounter 14 1960.

Laughing Horse no 13 1926. Special D. H. Lawrence issue.

Eliot, T. S. Le roman anglais contemporain: Lawrence, Woolf, Garnett, Huxley. Nouvelle Revue Française 28 1927; rptd in Lawrence: the critical heritage, ed R. P. Draper 1970.

— Criterion 10 1931. Review of J. M. Murry, Son of woman; rptd ibid.

Lewis, W. Paleface. The Enemy no 2 1927; rptd in his Paleface, 1929.

Squire, J. C. Mr Lawrence's poems. Observer 7 Oct 1928; rptd in his Sunday mornings, 1930, and in Lawrence: the critical heritage, ed R. P. Draper 1970.

Chance, R. Love and Mr Lawrence. Fortnightly Rev 126 1929.

Levinson, A. Un immoraliste vertueux: Lawrence. Nouvelles Littéraires 14 Dec 1929.

Wilson, E. Signs of life: Lady Chatterley's lover. New Republic 3 July 1929; rptd in his Shores of light, New York 1952 and in The achievement of Lawrence, ed F. J. Hoffman and H. T. Moore, Norman Okla 1952, above.

Bennett, A. Lawrence's delusion. Evening Standard 10 April 1930; rptd in Lawrence: the critical heritage, ed R. P. Draper 1970.

Blanche, J-E. Un sensualiste mystique: Lawrence. Nouvelles Littéraires 8 Aug 1930.

— Lawrence et Mabel Dodge. Revue de Paris 39 1932.

Forster, E. M. Nation & Athenaeum 29 March, 12, 26 April 1930. Exchange of letters with Clive Bell and T. S. Eliot on Lawrence.

— D. H. Lawrence. Listener 30 April 1930; rptd in Lawrence: the critical heritage, ed R. P. Draper 1970.

— Spectator 18 April 1931. Review of J. M. Murry, Son of woman.

Gwynn, S. Mr D. H. Lawrence. Fortnightly Rev 127 1930.

Heilbrunn, E. Englische Nachkriegsliteratur: Lawrence. Kunstwort July 1930.

McCarthy, D. Notes on Lawrence. Life & Letters 4 1930.

Monro, H. D. H. Lawrence. Poetry 36 1930.

Powell, D. Lawrence the moralist. Life & Letters 4 1930.

Rosenfeld, P. D. H. Lawrence. New Republic 26 March 1930; rptd in Lawrence: the critical heritage, ed R. P. Draper 1970.

Thomas, J. H. The perversity of Lawrence. Criterion 10 1930.

Trilling, L. Lawrence: a neglected aspect. Symposium 1 1930.

Tunstill, R. D. H. Lawrence. London Mercury 21 1930.

Villiers, B. Lawrence in Mexico. Southwest Rev 15 1930.

Carswell, C. Reminiscences of Lawrence. Adelphi 3 1931.

— Lawrence in his letters. Nineteenth Century 112 1932.

Fluchère, H. D. H. Lawrence. Cahiers du Sud 8 1931.

—— A propos de L'amant de Lady Chatterley. Cahiers du Sud 9 1932.

Kayser, R. Lawrence und sein erotisches Evangelium. Neue Rundschau 42 1931.

Kohler, D. D. H. Lawrence Sewanee Rev 39 1931.

Lalou, R. D. H. Lawrence, romancier anglais. Nouvelles Littéraires 18 April 1931.

—— Le message de Lawrence. Revue du Siècle 1 1933.

Neville, G. H. Early days of Lawrence. London Mercury 23 1931.

Reul, P. de. D. H. Lawrence. Revue de l'Université de Bruxelles 36 1931.

Salmon, H. L. Lawrence and a 'sense of the whole'. Adelphi 2 1931.

Schoenberner, F. D. H. Lawrence. Neue Schweizer Rundschau 24 1931.

——D. H. Lawrence. Das Inselschiff 13 1932.

Sitwell, O. Portrait of Lawrence. Week End Rev 3 1931.

Thompson, A. R. Lawrence: apostle of the dark gods. Bookman (New York) 73 1931; rptd in Lawrence: the critical heritage, ed R. P. Draper 1970.

Adam, G. Le roman humain: Lawrence. Sang Nouveau Aug 1932.

Connolly, C. Under which king? Living Age 341 1932.

Crémieux, B. David-Herbert Lawrence. In Les Annales Politiques et Littéraires 98 1932.

Davy, C. Lawrence and the serpent power. Adelphi 4 1932.

Gillet, L. D. H. Lawrence. Revue des Deux Mondes 1 Dec 1932.

Harding, D. W. In A note on nostalgia, Scrutiny 1 1932.

Kernan, J. Lawrence and the French. Commonweal 16 1932.

Lanoire, M. D. H. Lawrence. Revue de Paris 39 1932.

Leavis, F. R. In The literary mind, Scrutiny 1 1932.

—— In Restatements for critics, Scrutiny 1 1933.

—— Mr Eliot, Mr Wyndham Lewis and Lawrence. Scrutiny 3 1934; rptd in his Common pursuit, 1952.

—— The wild, untutored phoenix. Scrutiny 6 1937; rptd ibid.

—— Keynes, Lawrence and Cambridge. Scrutiny 16 1949; rptd ibid.

—— 'Lawrence scholarship' and Lawrence. Sewanee Rev 71 1963; rptd in his Anna Karenina and other essays, 1967.

Malraux, A. Lawrence et l'éroticisme. Nouvelle Revue Française 38 1932; rptd (tr) in From the NRF: an image of the twentieth century from the Nouvelle Revue Française, ed J. O'Brien, New York 1958.

Pearson, S. V. Psychology of the consumptive. Jnl of State Medicine 40 1932.

Roberts, J. H. The religion of Lawrence. New Humanist 5 1932.

—— Huxley and Lawrence. Virginia Quart Rev 13 1937.

Soames, J. The modern Rousseau. Life & Letters 8 1932.

Sorani, A. Incontri con Lawrence. Pegaso 4 1932.

Anderson, S. A man's song of life. Virginia Quart Rev 9 1933.

Appleby, M. The plumed serpent. Contemporaries Summer 1933.

Chesterton, G. K. In The end of the moderns, London Mercury 27 1933.

Fergusson, F. Lawrence's sensibility. Hound & Horn 6 1933.

Linati, C. Lawrence e l'Italia. Pegaso 5 1933.

Marcel, G. Le testament poétique de Lawrence. Revue du Siècle 1 1933.

Petre, M. D. Some reflections on Lawrence from the Catholic point of view. Adelphi 6 1933.

Trient, R. Lawrence panthéiste et l'antiquité payenne. Cahiers du Sud 10 1933.

Troy, W. Symposium 4 1933. Long review of Letters.

—— The Lawrence of myth. Partisan Rev 4 1938; rptd in The Partisan reader, ed P. Rahv and W. Phillips, New York 1946.

Wellek, R. D. H. Lawrence. Eng Post (Prague) 1 1933.

—— D. H. Lawrence. Listy pro umění a kritiku 1 1933.

Cazamian, L. Lawrence and Katherine Mansfield as letter writers. UTQ 3 1934.

Davis, H. The poetic genius of Lawrence. Ibid.

—— Women in love: a corrected typescript. UTQ 27 1957.

E.T. (Jessie Chambers Wood). The literary formation of Lawrence. European Quart 1 1934.

—— Lawrence's student days. Ibid.

—— Lawrence's literary debut. Ibid.

Guéhenno, J. Le message de Lawrence d'après sa correspondance. Europe 35 1934.

Harrison, A. W. The philosophy of Lawrence. Hibbert Jnl 32 1934.

Powell, S. W. Lawrence as poet. Poetry Rev 25 1934.

Wahl, J. Sur Lawrence. Nouvelle Revue Française 42 1934.

Witcutt, W. P. The cult of Lawrence. Amer Rev 3 1934.

Alexander, H. Lawrence and Huxley. Queen's Quart 42 1935.

Granger, F. The fiend in our universities. Ibid.

Lavrin, J. Sex and eros. Ibid. Rptd in his Aspects of modernism, 1935.

Leaney, A. R. C. Lawrence and politics. Adelphi 10 1935.

Parkes, H. B. Lawrence and Irving Babbitt. Adelphi 9 1935.

Arvin, N. Lawrence and fascism. New Republic 16 Dec 1936.

Delavenay, E. Sur un exemplaire de Schopenhauer annoté par Lawrence. Revue Anglo-américaine 13 1936.

Gurling, F. E. Lawrence's apology for the artist. London Mercury 33 1936.

Friedrich, H. E. Lawrence: Gottsucher und Mystizist. Zeitwende 13 1937.

—— Der Dichter Lawrence. Deutsches Adelsblatt 55 1938.

—— Lawrence: ein Dichter des 'echten Lebens'. Eckart 14 1938.

Moore, H. T. Another side of Lawrence. Reading & Collecting 1 1937.

—— Great unread. Saturday Rev of Lit 2 March 1940.

—— Why not read Lawrence too? Portfolio V [2] 1947.

Tindall, W. Y. Lawrence and the primitive. Sewanee Rev 45 1937.

Wells, H. K. Lawrence and fascism. New Republic 16 June 1937.

Wildi, M. The birth of expressionism in the work of Lawrence. E Studies 19 1937.

Pearce, T. M. The unpublished Lady Chatterley's lover. New Mexico Quart 8 1938.

Bechot, J. Sur Lawrence. Cahiers du Sud 16 1939.

Higashida, C. On the prose style of Lawrence. Stud in Eng Lit (Tokyo) 19 1939.

Marsh, E. A number of people. Harper's Mag 179 1939.

Williams, C. Sensuality and substance. Theology 38 1939.

Freeman, M. Lawrence in Valhalla? New Mexico Quart 10 1940.

Nulle, S. H. Lawrence and the fascist movement. New Mexico Quart 10 1940.

Powell, L. C. Lawrence and his critics: a chronological excursion in bio-bibliography. Colophon 1 1940.

Ruggles, A. M. The kinship of Blake, Vachell Lindsay and Lawrence. Poet Lore 46 1940.

Wood, F. Rilke and Lawrence. Germanic Rev 15 1940.

Magny, C. E. Lawrence, ou le mal du XXe siècle. Esprit 11 1941.

Vivas, E. Lawrence's problems. Kenyon Rev 3 1941.

—— The substance of Women in love. Sewanee Rev 66 1958.

—— The two Lawrences. Bucknell Rev 7 1958.

Bentley, E. R. Lawrence, John Thomas and Dionysos. New Mexico Quart 12 1942.

Mesnil, J. A prophet: Lawrence. Southwest Rev 31 1946. Tr Frieda Lawrence.

Miller, H. The apocalyptic Lawrence. Southwest Rev 31 1946.

Trilling, D. Lawrence: creator and dissenter. Saturday Rev of Lit 7 Dec 1946.
— A letter of introduction to Lawrence. Partisan Rev 25 1958.
Allen, W. Lawrence in perspective. Penguin New Writing No 29 1947.
Auden, W. H. Some notes on Lawrence. Nation (New York) 26 April 1947.
Bartlett, N. The failure of Lawrence. Australian Quart 19 1947.
— Aldous Huxley and Lawrence. Australian Quart 36 1964.
Collins, C. The letters of Lawrence. Politics & Letters 1 1947.
Ghiselin, B. Lawrence and a new world. Western Rev 11 1947.
— Lawrence in Bandol. London Mag 5 1958.
Nardi, P. Le tre redazioni dell' Amante di Lady Chatterley. Tre Venezie 21 1947.
Glicksberg, C. I. Lawrence, the prophet of surrealism. Nineteenth Century 143 1948.
— The poetry of Lawrence. New Mexico Quart 18 1948.
— Lawrence and science. Scientific Monthly 73 1951.
Hoffman, F. J. From surrealism to the apocalypse. ELH 15 1948.
Jeffries, C. Metaphor in Sons and lovers. Personalist 29 1948.
Jones, W. S. H. Lawrence and the revolt against reason. London Quart & Holborn Rev 173 1948.
Fay, E. G. Lawrence in Mexico. Emory Univ Quart 5 1949.
Nicholes, E. L. The simile of the sparrow in The rainbow of Lawrence. MLN 64 1949.
Steinhauer, H. Eros and psyche. Ibid. On Lawrence and O'Neill.
Howe, I. Sherwood Anderson and Lawrence. Furioso Fall 1950; rptd in his Sherwood Anderson, 1951 (for 1952).
Prichard, K. S. Lawrence in Australia. Meanjin 9 1950.
Read, H. An irregular genius: the significance of Lawrence. World Rev new ser 17 1950. Expanded in his Cult of sincerity, 1968.
— On Lawrence. Twentieth Century 165 1959.
Skinner, M. L. Lawrence and The boy in the bush. Meanjin 9 1950.
Bartlett, P. Lawrence's collected poems: the demon takes over. PMLA 66 1951.
Beauvoir, S. de. Lawrence: das komische Privileg des Mannes. Merkur no 5 1951.
Birrell, T. A. Where the rainbow ends: a study of Lawrence. Downside Rev 69 1951.
Danby, J. F. D. H. Lawrence. Cambridge Jnl 4 1951.
Greene, T. Lawrence and the quixotic hero. Sewanee Rev 59 1951.
Lawrence, F. About Lawrence. New Mexico Quart 21 1951.
Dataller, R. Eastwood in Taos. Adelphi 28 1952.
— Elements of Lawrence's prose style. EC 3 1953.
— Mr Lawrence and Mrs Woolf. EC 8 1958.
Ellmann, R. Lawrence and his demon. New Mexico Quart 22 1952.
Leaver, F. B. The man-nature relationship in Lawrence's novels. Univ of Kansas City Rev 19 1953.
Martin, D. Lawrence and Pueblo religion: an inquiry into accuracy. Arizona Quart 9 1953.
Miller, M. Definition by comparison: Chaucer, Lawrence and Joyce. EC 3 1953.
Schoberth, R. W. Lawrence in der zeitgenössischen Kritik. Die Neueren Sprachen 2 1953.
Schorer, M. Two houses, two ways: the Florentine villas of Lewis and Lawrence, respectively. New World Writing 4 1953.
— 'Women in love' and death. Hudson Rev 6 1953.
— On Lady Chatterley's lover. Evergreen Rev 1 1957.
Stewart, D. Immoral books: Lady Chatterley and the Shropshire lad. The European no 1 1953.

Adix, M. Phoenix at Walden: Lawrence calls on Thoreau. Western Humanities Rev 8 1954.
Hafley, J. The lost girl—Lawrence really real. Arizona Quart 10 1954.
Liddell, R. Lawrence and Dr Leavis: the case of St Mawr. EC 4 1954.
Melchiori, G. The lotus and the rose: Lawrence and Eliot's Four quartets. Eng Miscellany (Rome) 5 1954; rptd in his Tightrope walkers, 1956.
Gose, E. B. An expense of spirit. New Mexico Quart 25 1955.
Lainoff, S. The rainbow: the shaping of modern man. Modern Fiction Stud 1 1955.
Maud, R. N. Lawrence: true emotion as the ethical control in art. Western Humanities Rev 9 1955.
Obler, P. C. Lawrence's world of The rainbow. Drew Univ Stud 8 1955.
Parry, A. Lawrence through a Marxist mirror. Western Rev 19 1955.
Spilka, M. The floral pattern in Sons and lovers. New Mexico Quart 25 1955.
— The shape of an arch: a study of Lawrence's Rainbow. Modern Fiction Stud 1 1955.
— Was Lawrence a symbolist? Accent 15 1955.
— Post-Leavis Lawrence critics. MLQ 25 1964.
— Lawrence's quarrel with tenderness. CQ 9 1967.
Wain, J. The teaching of Lawrence. Twentieth Century 157 1955.
Fisher, W. J. Peace and passivity: the poetry of Lawrence. South Atlantic Quart 55 1956.
Gransden, K. W. Rananim: Lawrence's letters to S. S. Koteliansky. Twentieth Century 159 1956.
Murry, J. M. The living dead: 1, Lawrence. London Mag 3 1956.
Stavrou, C. N. Lawrence's 'psychology' of sex. Lit & Psychology 6 1956.
— Blake and Lawrence. Univ of Kansas City Rev 22 1956.
Traversi, D. A. Dr Leavis and the case of Lawrence. Month 15 1956.
Appleman, P. Lawrence and the intrusive knock. Modern Fiction Stud 3 1957.
Cecchetti, G. Verga and Lawrence's translations. Comparative Lit 9 1957.
Deakin, W. Lawrence's attacks on Proust and Joyce. EC 7 1957.
Johnsson, M. Lawrence och hans stad. Vi 38 1957.
Klingopulos, G. D. Lawrence's criticism. EC 7 1957.
Patmore, B. Conversations with Lawrence. London Mag 4 1957.
Pinto, V. de S. Lawrence: letter-writer and craftsman in verse. Nottingham Renaissance & Modern Stud 1 1957.
— Poet without a mask. CQ 3 1961; rptd as introd to Complete poems, ed Pinto and Roberts 1964.
Stanzel, F. Hopkins, Yeats, Lawrence und die Spontaneität der Dichtung. Wiener Beiträge zur englischen Philologie 66 1957.
Swan, M. Lawrence the traveller. London Mag 4 1957.
Abel, P. and R. Hogan. D. H. Lawrence's singing birds. Die Neueren Sprachen 7 1958; rptd in H. T. Moore, A Lawrence miscellany, 1959.
Barzun, J. Lawrence in life and letters. The Griffin 7 1958.
Draper, R. P. Lawrence on mother-love. EC 8 1958.
— Authority and the individual: a study of Lawrence's Kangaroo. CQ 1 1959.
— The defeat of feminism: Lawrence's Fox and The woman who rode away. Stud in Short Fiction 3 1966.
— A short guide to Lawrence studies. Critical Survey 2 1966.
— The sense of reality in the work of Lawrence. Revue des Langues Vivantes 33 1967.
— Form and tone in the poetry of Lawrence. E Studies 49 1968.
Engel, M. The continuity of Lawrence's short novels. Hudson Rev 11 1958.

Gindre, M. Points de vue sur Lawrence. Études Anglaises 11 1958.

Grant, D. England's Phoenix. UTQ 27 1958.

— Hands up, America! REL 4 1963.

Grigson, G. The poet in Lawrence. London Mag 5 1958; rptd in his Poems and poets, 1969.

Smith, G. The doll-burners: Lawrence and Louisa Alcott. MLQ 19 1958.

Snodgrass, W. D. A rocking-horse: the symbol, the pattern, the way to live. Hudson Rev 11 1958.

Widmer, K. Lawrence and the art of nihilism. Kenyon Rev 20 1958.

— Birds of passion and birds of marriage in Lawrence. Univ of Kansas City Rev 25 1959.

— The primitive aesthetic—Lawrence. Jnl of Aesthetics 17 1959.

Williams, R. The social thinking of Lawrence. Univ & Left Rev 4 1958.

Woodcock, G. Mexico and the English novelist. Western Rev 21 1958.

— Tolstoy, Lawrence and tragedy. Kenyon Rev 25 1963.

Bramley, J. A. The significance of Lawrence. Contemporary Rev 195 1959.

— The challenge of Lawrence. Hibbert Jnl 58 1960.

— Lawrence and Miriam. Cornhill Mag no 1024 1960; rptd in E.T., Lawrence: a personal record, ed J. D. Chambers 1965.

Corke, H. Concerning The white peacock. Texas Quart 2 1959.

— Lawrence as I saw him. Nottingham Renaissance & Modern Stud 4 1960.

— Portrait of Lawrence 1909–10. Texas Quart 5 1962.

— The dreaming woman: Helen Corke, in conversation with M. Muggeridge, tells of her relationship with Lawrence. Listener 25 July 1968.

Gifford, H. Anna, Lawrence 'and the law'. CQ 1 1959. See R. Williams, Lawrence and Tolstoy CQ 2 1960, and H. Gifford, Further notes on Anna Karenina, ibid.

Gregor, I. The fox: a caveat. EC 9 1959.

Hogan, R. Lawrence and his critics. Ibid.

Jones, W. M. Growth of a symbol: the sun in Lawrence and Eudora Welty. Univ of Kansas City Rev 25 1959.

Modern Fiction Stud 5 1959. Special Lawrence number. Contains:

Daleski, H. M. The duality of Lawrence.

Hogan, R. The amorous whale: a study in the symbolism of Lawrence.

Moynahan, J. Lawrence's Man who loved islands: a modern fable.

Sale, R. The narrative technique of The rainbow.

Stanford, R. Hardy and Lawrence's White peacock.

Vickery, J. B. Myth and ritual in the shorter fiction of Lawrence; rptd in his Myth and literature: contemporary theory and practice, Lincoln Nebraska 1966.

Widmer, K. Lawrence and the fall of modern woman.

Moynahan, J. Lady Chatterley's lover: the deed of life. ELH 26 1959.

Benedict, J. The Lady Chatterley's lover case. Amer Rev 90 1960.

Cowan, J. C. The function of allusions and symbols in Lawrence's Man who died. Amer Imago 17 1960.

— The symbolic structure of The plumed serpent. Tulane Stud in Eng 14 1965.

— Lawrence's Princess as ironic romance. Stud in Short Fiction 4 1967.

— Lawrence's romantic values: Studies in classic American literature. Ball State Univ Forum 8 1967.

— Lawrence's quarrel with Christianity. Univ of Tulsa Dept of English Monographs 7 1969.

Goodheart, E. Freud and Lawrence. Psychoanalysis and the Psychoanalytic Rev 47 1960.

— Lawrence and the critics. Chicago Rev 16 1963.

— Lawrence and Christ. Partisan Rev 31 1964.

Porter, K. A. A wreath for the gamekeeper. Encounter 14 1960.

Salgado, G. Lawrence as literary critic. London Mag 7 1960.

Tedlock, E. W. Lawrence's annotation of Ouspensky's Tertium organum. Texas Stud in Lit & Lang 2 1960.

Traschen, I. Pure and ironic idealism: Lawrence. South Atlantic Quart 59 1960.

Waterman, A. E. The plays of Lawrence. Modern Drama 2 1960; rptd in Lawrence: a collection of critical essays, ed M. Spilka 1963, above.

Arnold, A. The transcendental element in American literature: a study of some unpublished Lawrence manuscripts. MP 60 1961.

— Lawrence, the Russians and Giovanni Verga. Comparative Lit Stud 2 1965.

— The German letters of Lawrence. Comparative Lit Stud 3 1966.

— Genius with a dictionary: reevaluating Lawrence's translations. Comparative Lit Stud 5 1968.

Baldanza, F. DHL's Song of songs. Modern Fiction Stud 7 1961.

Foster, D. W. Lawrence, sex and religion. Theology 64 1961.

Goldberg, S. L. The rainbow: fiddle-bow and sand. EC 11 1961.

Knight, G. W. Lawrence, Joyce and [J.C.] Powys. EC 11 1961.

Lucas, B. Apropos of England my England. Twentieth Century 169 1961.

Michot, P. Lawrence, a belated apology. Revue des Langues Vivantes 27 1961.

Panichas, G. A. Dostoevsky and Lawrence: their visions of evil. Nottingham Renaissance & Modern Stud 5 1961.

— Voyage of oblivion: the meaning of Lawrence's death poems. Eng Miscellany (Rome) 13 1962.

— Lawrence's Biblical play David. Modern Drama 6 1963.

— Lawrence's war letters. Texas Stud in Lit & Lang 5 1963.

— Lawrence and the ancient Greeks. Eng Miscellany (Rome) 16 1965.

Sawyer, P. W. The religious vision of Lawrence. Crane Rev 3 1961.

Saxena, H. S. The critical writings of Lawrence. Indian Jnl of Eng Stud 2 1961.

— Lawrence and the impressionistic technique. Indian Jnl of Eng Stud 3 1962.

Werner, A. Lawrence and Pascin. Kenyon Rev 23 1961.

Wright, R. Lawrence's non-human analogues. MLN 76 1961.

Beebe, M. Lawrence, sacred fount: the artist theme of Sons and lovers. Texas Stud in Lit & Lang 4 1962.

Busch, G. Kritische These über Lawrence. Wort in der Zeit 8 1962.

Clark, L. D. The habitat of The plumed serpent. Texas Quart 5 1962.

Clements, A. L. The quest for the self in Lawrence's Rainbow. Thoth 3 1962.

Hassall, C. Lawrence and the Etruscans. Trans of Royal Soc of Lit 31 1962.

Kazin, A. Sons, lovers and mothers. Partisan Rev 29 1962.

Kermode, F. Spenser and the allegorists. Proc Br Acad 48 1962. Includes some parallels with Lawrence.

— Lawrence and the apocalyptic types. CQ 10 1968. Rptd in his Continuities, 1968.

Levy, M. and C. Wilson. The paintings of Lawrence. Studio 164 1962.

Longville, T. The longest journey: Lawrence's Phoenix. CQ 4 1962.

Miller, N. The 'success' and 'failure' of Lawrence. Antioch Rev 22 1962.

Myers, N. Lawrence and the war. Criticism 4 1962.

Osgerby, J. R. Lawrence's White peacock. Use of Eng 13 1962.

Ryals, C. de L. Lawrence's Horse-dealer's daughter. Lit & Psychology 12 1962.

Sagar, K. M. The Lawrences and the Wilkinsons. REL 3 1962.

— 'The best I have known': Lawrence's Modern lover and The shades of spring. Stud in Short Fiction 4 1967.

— The genesis of The rainbow and Women in love. D. H. Lawrence Rev 1 1968.

Sparrow, J. Regina v. Penguin Books Ltd: an undisclosed element in the case. Encounter 18 1962. On Lady Chatterley's lover; rptd in his Controversial essays, 1966.

— On Lady Chatterley's lover. EC 13 1963.

Thody, P. Lady Chatterley's lover: a pyrrhic victory. Threshold 5 1962.

Adelman, G. Beyond the pleasure principle: an analysis of Lawrence's Prussian officer. Stud in Short Fiction 1 1963.

Chamberlain, R. L. Pussum, Minette and Africo-nordic symbols in Lawrence's Women in love. PMLA 78 1963.

Empson, W. Lady Chatterley again. EC 13 1963.

Engelberg, E. Escape from the circles of experience: Lawrence's Rainbow as a modern Bildungsroman. PMLA 78 1963.

Englander, A. The Prussian officer: the self divided. Sewanee Rev 71 1963.

Ford, G. H. An introductory note to Lawrence's Prologue to Women in love. Texas Quart 6 1963.

— Shelley or Schiller: a note on Lawrence at work. Texas Stud in Lit & Lang 4 1963.

— The 'wedding' chapter of Lawrence's Women in love. Texas Stud in Lit & Lang 6 1964.

Gurko, L. The lost girl: Lawrence as a Dickens of the Midlands. PMLA 78 1963.

— The trespasser: Lawrence's neglected novel. College Eng 24 1963.

— Kangaroo: Lawrence in transit. Modern Fiction Stud 10 1964.

Tetsumura, H. Lawrence's mysticism: what the moon signifies. Hiroshima Stud in Eng Lang & Lit 9 1963.

Vickery, J. B. The plumed serpent and the eternal paradox. Criticism 5 1963.

Branda, E. S. Textual changes in Women in love. Texas Stud in Lit & Lang 6 1964.

Donald, D. R. The first and final versions of Lady Chatterley's lover. Theoria 22 1964.

Gordon, D. J. Lawrence's quarrel with tragedy. Perspective 13 1964.

— Two anti-puritan puritans: Shaw and Lawrence. Yale Rev 56 1967.

Guttmann, A. Lawrence: the politics of irrationality. Wisconsin Stud in Contemporary Lit 5 1964.

Kessler, J. Lawrence's primitivism. Texas Stud in Lit & Lang 6 1964.

Merivale, P. Lawrence and the modern Pan myth. Ibid; rptd in her Pan the goat-god: his myth in modern times, Cambridge Mass 1969.

Mori, H. Lawrence's imagistic development in The rainbow and Women in love. ELH 31 1964.

Newman, P. B. The natural aristocrat in letters. Kansas Univ Rev 31 1964.

Pearsall, R. B. The second art of Lawrence. South Atlantic Quart 63 1964.

Wilde, A. The illusion of St Mawr: technique and vision in Lawrence's novel. PMLA 79 1964.

Alexander, J. Lawrence's Kangaroo: fantasy, fact or fiction? Meanjin 24 1965.

Ehrstine, J. W. The dialectic in Lawrence. Research Stud 33 1965.

Marks, W. S. The psychology of the uncanny in Lawrence's Rocking-horse winner. Modern Fiction Stud 11 1965.

Mayhall, J. Lawrence: the triumph of texture. Western Humanities Rev 19 1965.

Mitchell, P. T. Lawrence's Sea and Sardinia re-visited. Texas Quart 8 1965.

Sale, R. D. H. Lawrence 1912–16. Massachusetts Rev 6 1965.

Waldron, P. J. The education of Lawrence. Jnl of Australasian Univ Lang & Lit Assoc no 24 1965.

West, P. Lawrence: mystical critic. Southern Rev 1 1965.

White, V. Frieda and the Lawrence legend. Southwest Rev 50 1965.

Zanger, J. Lawrence's three strange angels. Papers on Eng Lang & Lit 1 1965.

Bedient, C. The radicalism of Lady Chatterley's lover. Hudson Rev 19 1966.

Corsani, M. Lawrence traduttore dall' italiano. Eng Miscellany (Rome) 17 1966.

Hudspeth, R. N. Duality as theme and technique in Lawrence's Border line. Stud in Short Fiction 4 1966.

— Lawrence's Odour of chrysanthemums: isolation and paradox. Stud in Short Fiction 6 1969.

Kay, W. G. The cortege of Dionysos: Lawrence and Jean Giono. Southern Quart 4 1966.

Le Breton, G. Lawrence et l'architecture du roman. Preuves no 189 1966.

Littlewood, J. C. F. Lawrence's early tales. Cambridge Quart 1 1966.

— Son and lover. Cambridge Quart 4 1970.

Reddick, B. Sons and lovers: the omniscient narrator. Thoth 7 1966.

Bickerton, D. The language of Women in love. REL 8 1967.

Longman, F. H. Women in love. EC 17 1967.

Remsbury, J. Real thinking: Lawrence and Cézanne. Cambridge Quart 2 1967.

Wasson, R. Comedy and history in The rainbow. Modern Fiction Stud 13 1967.

Weatherby, H. L. Old-fashioned gods: Eliot on Lawrence and Hardy. Sewanee Rev 75 1967.

Zytaruk, G. T. The phallic vision: Lawrence and V. V. Rozanov. Comparative Lit Stud 4 1967.

— Lawrence's reading of Russian literature. D. H. Lawrence Rev 2 1969.

Bain, J. The second coming of Pan: a note on Lawrence's Last laugh. Stud in Short Fiction 6 1968.

Benstock, B. The present recaptured: Lawrence and others. Southern Rev 4 1968.

Conti, G. G. Una lettera inedita di Lawrence. Eng Miscellany (Rome) 19 1968.

Davie, D. On sincerity: from Wordsworth to Ginsberg. Encounter 31 1968.

Dawson, E. W. Love among the mannikins: The captain's doll. D. H. Lawrence Rev 1 1968.

Elsbree, L. Lawrence, homo ludens, and the dance. Ibid.

Fulmer, O. B. The significance of the death of the fox in Lawrence's The fox. Stud in Short Fiction 5 1968.

Gerard, D. E. Glossary of Eastwood dialect words used by Lawrence in his poems, plays and fiction. D. H. Lawrence Rev 1 1968.

Gindin, J. Society and compassion in the novels of Lawrence. Centennial Rev 12 1968.

Hinz, E. J. Lawrence's clothes metaphor. D. H. Lawrence Rev 1 1968.

Howarth, H. Lawrence from island to glacier. UTQ 37 1968.

Keith, W. J. Lawrence's White peacock: an essay in criticism. Ibid.

Latta, W. Lawrence's debt to Rudolph, Baron von Hube. D. H. Lawrence Rev 1 1968.

Madonna, M. Le primitivisme dans Women in love. Les Langues Modernes 62 1968.

Marks, W. S. Lawrence and his rabbit Adolph: three symbolic permutations. Criticism 10 1968.

— The psychology of regression in Lawrence's Blind man. Lit & Psychology 17 1968.

Mendel, S. Shakespeare and Lawrence: two portraits of the hero. Wascana Rev 3 1968.

Michener, R. L. Apocalyptic Mexico: The plumed serpent and The power and the glory. Univ of Kansas City Rev 34 1968.

Morse, S. The phoenix and the desert places. Massachusetts Rev 9 1968.

New, W. H. Character as symbol: Annie's role in Sons and lovers. D. H. Lawrence Rev 1 1968.

Pierle, R. C. Lawrence's Studies in classic American literature: an evaluation. Southern Quart 6 1968.

Roy, K. Sons and lovers or the sin against the Holy Ghost. Modern Rev (Calcutta) April, May 1968.

Ruthven, K. K. The savage god: Conrad and Lawrence. CQ 10 1968.

Schneiderman, L. Notes on Lawrence's Studies in classic American literature. Connecticut Rev 1 1968.

Smailes, T. A. The mythical bases of Women in love. D. H. Lawrence Rev 1 1968.

Smith, B. L. Lawrence's St Mawr: transposition of myth. Arizona Quart 24 1968.

Stilwell, R. L. The multiplying of entities: Lawrence and five other poets. Sewanee Rev 76 1968.

Travis, L. Lawrence: the blood-conscious artist. Amer Imago 25 1968.

Waters, F. Quetzalcoatl versus Lawrence's Plumed serpent. Western Amer Lit 3 1968.

Youngblood, S. Substance and shadow: the self in Lawrence's poetry. D. H. Lawrence Rev 1 1968.

Alexander, J. C. Lawrence and Teilhard de Chardin: a study in agreements. D. H. Lawrence Rev 2 1969.

Barrière, F. Women in love ou le roman de l'antagonisme. Les Langues Modernes 63 1969.

Barry, J. Oswald Spengler and Lawrence. Eng Stud in South Africa 12 1969.

Beards, R. D. Lawrence and the 'Study of Thomas Hardy', his Victorian predecessor. D. H. Lawrence Rev 2 1969

Beker, M. The crown, The reality of peace and Women in love. Ibid.

Boulton, J. T. Lawrence's Odour of chrysanthemums. Renaissance & Modern Stud 13 1969.

Cipolla, E. The last poems of Lawrence. D. H. Lawrence Rev 2 1969.

Hendrick, G. '10' and the phoenix. Ibid.

Henig, S. Lawrence and Virginia Woolf. Ibid.

Junkins, D. Lawrence's Horse-dealer's daughter. Stud in Short Fiction 6 1969

Mason, H. A. Towards an early life of Lawrence. Cambridge Quart 4 1969.

Pirenet, C. La structure symbolique de Women in love. Études Anglaises 22 1969.

Secor, R. Language and movement in Fanny and Annie. Stud in Short Fiction 6 1969.

Weiner, S. R. The rhetoric of travel: the example of Sea and Sardinia. D. H. Lawrence Rev 2 1969.

R.P.D.

GRAHAM GREENE
b. 1904

Bibliographies

Remords, G. Greene: notes bibliographiques. Bulletin de la Faculté des Lettres de Strasbourg 29 1951.

Birmingham, W. Greene criticism: a bibliographical study. Thought 27 1952.

Hargreaves, P. Greene: a selected bibliography. Modern Fiction Stud 3 1957. Lists essays and periodical articles. Supersedes bibliography by same author in Bull of Bibliography 22 1957.

Beebe, M. Criticism of Greene: a selected checklist with an index to studies of separate works. Ibid.

Brennan, N. Bibliography. In Graham Greene, ed R. O. Evans, Lexington 1963. Includes a note on Greene's periodical articles, and his film scripts; also unpbd dissertations on Greene.

Vann, J. D. Graham Greene: a checklist of criticism. Kent, Ohio 1970 (Serif Series: bibliographies and checklists 14).

Collections and Selections

Uniform edition. 1947 onwards. Textual changes from first edns in many cases.

Collected edition. 1970 onwards. With prefaces by Greene.

Three by Graham Greene: This gun for hire; The confidential agent; The Ministry of Fear. New York 1952.

Three plays. 1961. Contains The living room; The potting shed; The complaisant lover. With preface by Greene.

The travel books: Journey without maps; The lawless roads. 1963.

Collected essays. 1969, New York 1969.

§I
Prose Fiction

The man within. 1929, Garden City NY 1929, London 1952 (with note by Greene).

The name of action. 1930, Garden City NY 1931.

Rumour at nightfall. 1931, Garden City NY 1932.

Stamboul train: an entertainment. 1932, Garden City NY 1933 (as Orient express).

It's a battlefield. 1934, Garden City NY 1934, New York 1962 (introd by Greene).

England made me. 1935, Garden City NY 1935, New York 1953 (as The shipwrecked).

The basement room, and other stories. 1935. Contains The basement room (retold as The fallen idol in The third man, and The fallen idol, 1950, below), Brother, A chance for Mr Lever, A day saved, The end of the party, I spy, Jubilee, The lottery ticket, The other side of the border, Proof positive. These were all rptd in Nineteen stories, 1947, below, and with 2 omissions in Twenty-one stories, 1954, below.

The bear fell free. 1935 (limited to 285 copies) (Grayson Books). Story.

This gun for hire: an entertainment. Garden City NY 1936, London 1936 (as A gun for sale), Toronto 1942 (as This Gun, Inc).

Brighton rock: an entertainment. New York 1938, London 1938 (with sub-title 'a novel').

The confidential agent: an entertainment. 1939, New York 1939.

The power and the glory. 1940, New York 1940 (as The labyrinthine ways), New York 1946 (as The power and the glory), London 1963 (introd by Greene, rptd from Introductions to three novels, 1962, below).

The Ministry of Fear: an entertainment. 1943, New York 1943.

Nineteen stories. 1947, New York 1949 (omitting The lottery ticket, adding The hint of an explanation). Includes contents of The basement room, 1935, above, together with The innocent, A drive in the country, Across the bridge, The second death, A little place off the Edgware Road, The case for the defence, When Greek meets Greek, Men at work, Alas poor Maling.

The heart of the matter. 1948, New York 1948.

The third man: an entertainment. New York 1950, London 1950, (with The fallen idol, as The third man, and The fallen idol). The third man was written as a preliminary to the script of the film of the same name. First pbd as story in Amer Mag March 1949. The filmscript with changes by Carol Reed, Orson Welles etc pbd 1969.

The end of the affair. 1951, New York 1951.

Twenty-one stories. 1954, New York 1954. Contents as Nineteen stories, 1947, above, omitting The lottery ticket and The other side of the border, and adding The hint of an explanation, The blue film, Special duties, The destructors.

The quiet American. 1955, New York 1956. First pbd, in Swedish trn, from ms, Stockholm 1955.

Loser takes all: an entertainment. 1955, New York 1957. Pbd as serial in Harper's Mag Oct 1955–Jan 1956.

Our man in Havana. 1958, New York 1958.

A visit to Morin. [1959] (250 copies). First pbd, in French trn, Les Œuvres Libres new ser no 131 1957.

A burnt-out case. 1961, New York 1961. First pbd, in Swedish trn from ms, Stockholm 1960

A sense of reality. 1963, New York 1963. Stories; contains Under the garden, A visit to Morin, Dream of a strange land, A discovery in the woods.

The comedians. 1966, New York 1966.

May we borrow your husband? and other comedies of the sexual life. 1967, New York 1967. Contains May we borrow your husband?, Beauty, Chagrin in three parts, The over-night bag, Mortmain, Cheap in August, A shocking accident, The invisible Japanese gentlemen, Awful when you think of it, Doctor Crombie, The root of all evil, Two gentle people.

Other Works

Babbling April. Oxford 1925. Verse.

The old school: essays by divers hands. Ed Greene 1934. Contains The last word, by Greene.

Journey without maps: a travel book. 1936, Garden City NY 1936, London 1948 (rev).

The lawless roads: a Mexican journey. 1939, New York 1939 (as Another Mexico).

British dramatists. 1942 (Britain in Pictures).

The little train, by Dorothy Craigie [i.e. illustr D. Craigie, text by Greene]. [1946], 1957 (as by Greene), New York 1958. For children.

Why do I write?: an exchange of views between Elizabeth Bowen, Greene and V. S. Pritchett. 1948, New York 1948.

The little fire engine. [1950], New York 1953 (as The little red fire engine). For children.

The lost childhood, and other essays. 1951, New York 1952.

For Christmas. 1951 (limited to 12 copies). 7 poems.

The little horse bus. [1952], New York 1954. For children.

The living room: a play in two acts. (Wyndham's 16 April 1953). 1953, New York 1954, London 1955 (introd by P. Glenville). Slight difference between the endings of the English and US edns. First pbd, in Swedish trn from ms, Stockholm 1952.

Essais catholiques. Paris 1953. 6 essays, tr M. Sibon; 3 not previously pbd in English.

The little steamroller: a story of adventure, mystery and detection. [1953], New York 1955. For children.

Nino Caffé. New York [1953]. Essay on the painter Caffé.

The potting shed: a play in three acts. (Bijou, New York 29 Jan 1957; Globe 5 Feb 1958). New York [1957], London 1958, 1959 (French's Acting Edn).

The spy's bedside book: an anthology ed G. Greene and H. Greene. 1957.

The complaisant lover: a comedy. (Globe 18 June 1959). 1959, New York 1960, London [1961] (French's Acting Edn).

In search of a character: two African journals. 1961, New York 1962. Contains Congo journal, containing material used in A burnt-out case, and Convoy to West Africa.

Introductions to three novels. Stockholm 1962. The power and the glory, The heart of the matter, The end of the affair.

The revenge: an autobiographical fragment. 1963 (priv ptd, 300 copies).

Carving a statue: a play. (Haymarket 17 Sept 1964). 1964, New York 1964.

Greene has contributed to numerous periodicals, notably reviews for Spectator *(1932–45),* London Mercury, Fortnightly Rev, Observer, Time & Tide, Now & Then, Life & Letters, Tablet, New Statesman *and* Evening Standard. *A number of his film criticisms were rptd in* Garbo and the night watchman, *ed A. Cooke 1937. For details of various dramatizations and film scripts from Greene's works, and of original film scripts and other matters relating to Greene's interest in the cinema see section vii of Brennan's bibliography.*

§2
Books and Chapters in Books

Rillo, L. E. The power and the glory: a novel by Greene. Buenos Aires 1946.

Calder-Marshall, A. In Living writers, ed G. Phelps 1947.

Woodcock, G. In his Writer and politics, 1948.

Allen, W. The power and the glory, by Greene. In his Reading a novel, 1949, 1956 (rev), 1963 (rev).

Engel, C. E. In her Esquisses anglaises, Paris 1949.

Madaule, J. Graham Greene. Paris 1949.

Mauriac, F. Graham Greene. In his Mes grands hommes, Monaco 1949; tr as Men I hold great, New York 1951, London 1952 (as Great men).

Rostenne, P. Greene: témoin des temps tragiques. Paris 1949.

Chaigne, L. In his Vies et oeuvres d'écrivains vol 3, Paris 1950.

Allott, K. and M. Farris. The art of Greene. 1951.

Dellevaux, R. Greene et 'Le fond du problème'. Brussels [1951].

Rischik, J. Greene und sein Werk. Berne 1951 (Schweizer anglistische Arbeiten 28).

'O'Donnell, Donat' (C. C. O'Brien). Greene: the anatomy of pity. In his Maria Cross: imaginative patterns in a group of modern Catholic writers, New York 1952.

Prescott, O. Comrades of the coterie: H. Green, Ivy Compton-Burnett, Elizabeth Bowen, Greene. In his In my opinion, Indianapolis 1952.

Albérès, R. M. Greene et la responsabilité. In his Les hommes traqués, Paris 1953.

Fournier, G. Le tourment de Dieu chez les amants de Greene. Toulouse 1953.

— Scobie: ou l'homme victime de sa pitié. Toulouse 1953.

Moeller, C. In his Littérature du XXe siècle et christianisme, Tournai 1953.

Pange, V. de. Graham Greene. Paris 1953.

Mesnet, M. B. Greene and The heart of the matter. 1954.

Sturzl, E. Von Satan zu Gott: religiöse Probleme bei Greene. Vienna 1954.

Wyndham, F. Graham Greene. 1955, 1958 (rev) (Br Council pamphlet).

O'Faolain, S. In his Vanishing hero, 1956.

Atkins, J. A. Graham Greene. 1957, 1966 (rev).

Matthews, R. Mon ami Greene. Paris 1957.

West, A. In his Principles and persuasions, New York 1957.

Davies, H. The confessional and the altar. In his A mirror of the ministry in modern novels, New York 1959. On The power and the glory.

Lewis, R. W. B. Greene: the religious affair. In his Picaresque saint, New York 1959.

Mueller, W. R. Theme of love: Greene's Heart of the matter. In his Prophetic voice in modern fiction, New York 1959.

Gassner, J. Points of return: religion and Greene's Potting shed. In his Theatre at the crossroads, New York 1960.

Kunkel, F. L. The labyrinthine ways of Greene. New York 1960.

Kohn, L. Greene: the major novels. Stanford 1961 (Stanford Honors Essays in Humanities 4).

Stewart, D. In his The ark of God: studies in five modern novelists, 1961.

Browne, E. M. Contemporary drama in the Catholic tradition. In Christian faith and the contemporary arts, ed F. Eversole, Nashville 1962.

Gregor, I. and B. Nicholas. Grace and morality... In their Moral and the story, 1962. On The end of the affair.

Karl, F. R. Greene's demonical heroes. In his Contemporary English novel, New York 1962, London 1963 (as A reader's guide to the contemporary English novel).

Kazin, A. Greene and the age of absurdity. In his Contemporaries, Boston 1962.

Wilson, C. Evelyn Waugh and Greene. In his Strength to dream: literature and the imagination. 1962.

Evans, R. O. (ed). Greene: some critical considerations. Lexington 1963. 14 articles.

Pryce-Jones, D. Graham Greene. 1963 (Writers and Critics).

De Vitis, A. A. Graham Greene. New York 1964 (Twayne's English Authors).

Joselyn, M. Greene's novels: the conscience in the world. In Literature and society, ed B. Slote, Lincoln Nebr 1964.

Stratford, P. Faith and fiction: creative process in Greene and Mauriac. Notre Dame 1964.

Chapman, R. The vision of Greene. In Forms of extremity in the modern novel, ed N. A. Scott, Richmond Va 1965.

Lodge, D. Graham Greene. 1966 (Columbia Essays on Modern Writers).

West, P. In his Wine of absurdity, University Park Pa 1966.

Hall, J. Efficient saints and civilians: Greene. In his Lunatic giant in the drawing room, Bloomington 1968.

Scott, N. A. In his Craters of the spirit: studies in the modern novel, Washington 1968.

Cargas, H. J. (ed). Graham Greene. St Louis 1969 (Christian Critic ser).

Reinhardt, K. F. In his The theological novel of modern Europe, New York 1969.

Articles in Periodicals

Calder-Marshall, A. The works of Greene. Horizon 1 1940; rptd in Little Review anthology, ed D. V. Baker 1943.

Sylvester, H. Graham Greene. Commonweal 25 Oct 1940.

Allen, W. The novels of Greene. Penguin New Writing no 18 1943; rptd in Writers of today, ed D. V. Baker 1946.

— Awareness of evil: Greene. Nation (New York) 21 April 1956.

Zabel, M. D. Graham Greene. Nation (New York) 3 July 1943; rptd (rev) in Forms of modern fiction, ed W. V. O'Connor, Minneapolis 1948; in Critiques and essays on modern fiction 1920–51, ed J. W. Aldridge, New York 1952; and in Zabel's Craft and character in modern fiction, New York 1951.

Brady, C. A. Contemporary Catholic authors: Greene, novelist of good and evil. Catholic Lib World 16 1944.

McCarthy, M. Greene and the intelligentsia. Partisan Rev 11 1944.

Magny, C-E. Graham Greene. Poésie 46 no 32 1946.

Miller, B. Graham Greene. Meanjin 5 1946.

'O'Donnell, Donat' (C. C. O'Brien). An epic of the thirties: Greene. Bell 13 1947. Expanded in Chimera 5 1947.

Rostenne, P. Introduction à Greene. Revue Nouvelle 6 1947.

De Hegedus, A. Greene: the man and his work. World Rev 15 1948 (and Tomorrow 8 1948).

Duché, J. Du rocher de Sysyphe au Rocher de Brighton. Table Ronde no 2 1948.

Jans, A. Greene: entre le péché et l'amour. Empreintes 4 1948.

McLaughlin, R. Greene: saint or cynic? America 79 1948.

Mauriac, F. La puissance et la gloire. Figaro Littéraire 30 Oct 1948 (and Renascence 1 1949).

O'Faolain, S. The novels of Greene: The heart of the matter. Britain Today no 148 1948.

Waugh, E. Felix culpa? Tablet 5 June 1948 (and Commonweal 16 July 1948). On The heart of the matter.

— Heart's own reasons. Commonweal 17 Aug 1951 (and Month 6 1951). On The end of the affair.

Aguirre de Carcer, N. La novela en la Inglaterra actual, II: Greene. Arbor 14 1949.

Allen, W. G. Evelyn Waugh and Greene. Irish Monthly 77 1949.

— The world of Greene. Irish Ecclesiastical Record 71 1949.

Boyle, A. Graham Greene. Irish Monthly 77 1949.

— The symbolism of Greene. Irish Monthly 80 1952.

Connolly, F. X. Inside modern man: the spiritual adventures of Greene. Renascence 1 1949.

Elsen, C. Greene: ou la geste de l'homme traqué. Table Ronde no 14 1949.

Gardiner, H. C. Greene: Catholic shocker. Renascence 1 1949.

Grubbs, H. A. Albert Camus and Greene. MLQ 10 1949.

Hahn, K. J. Graham Greene. Hochland (Munich) 41 1949.

Herling, G. Two sanctities: Greene and Camus. Adam 201 1949.

Hillig, F. Die Kraft und die Herrlichkeit. Stimmen der Zeit 143 1949.

Jouve, R. La damnation de Scobie? Études no 263 1949.

Las Vergnas, R. A propos de Greene. Hommes et Mondes 9 1949.

Lemaitre, H. Un romancier chrétien de l'absurde: Greene. Culture Catholique 4 1949.

Parc, R. de. Saint ou maudit: le prêtre dans La puissance et la gloire. Études no 260 1949.

Schmidthues, K. Greene. Neue Heimat (Berlin) 4 1949.

— Greenes Katholizismus. Wort und Wahrheit 12 1957.

Young, V. Hell on earth: six versions. Hudson Rev 2 1949.

Alloway, L. Symbolism in The third man. World Rev 13 1950.

Braybrooke, N. Graham Greene. Envoy 3 1950; abridged as Greene: a pioneer novelist, College Eng 12 1950 and Eng Jnl 39 1950.

— Greene as critic. Commonweal 6 July 1951.

— Greene and the double man: an approach to The end of the affair. Dublin Rev 226 1952.

Brion, M. Les romans de Greene. Revue des Deux Mondes 6 1950.

Chavardes, M. Greene: ou la nudité de Dieu. Vie Intellectuelle 7 1950.

Fouchet, M-P. Graham Greene. Revue de Paris 57 1950.

Howes, J. Out of the pit. Catholic World 171 1950.

Marshall, B. Greene and Evelyn Waugh. Commonweal 3 March 1950.

Moré, M. Les deux holocaustes de Scobie. Dieu Vivant 16 1950; tr as The two holocausts of Scobie, Cross Currents 2 1951.

Roy, J. H. L'oeuvre de Greene: ou un Christianisme de la damnation. Temps Modernes 52 1950.

Viatte, A. Greene: romancier de la grâce. Revue de l'Université Laval 4 1950.

Cayrol, J. Autour de l'oeuvre de Greene. Revue de la Pensée Française 10 1951.

Crubellier, M. Greene: la tragédie de la pitié. Vie Intellectuelle 12 1951.

Escarpit, R. L'arrière-plan mexicain dans Lawrence et Greene. Langues Modernes 45 1951.

Lohf, K. A. Greene and the problem of evil. Catholic World 173 1951.

Sackville-West, E. The electric hare: some aspects of Greene. Month 6 1951.

— Time-bomb. Month 25 1961. On A burnt-out case.

Traversi, D. Graham Greene. Twentieth Century 149 1951.

Voorhees, R. J. The world of Greene. South Atlantic Quart 50 1951.

— Recent Greene. South Atlantic Quart 62 1963.

Boyle, R. M. Man of controversy. Grail 35 1952.

Dinkins, P. Greene: the incomplete version. Catholic World 176 1952.

Downing, F. Greene and the case for 'disloyalty'. Commonweal 14 March 1952.

Duesberg, J. Un épigone du misérabilisme: Greene. Synthèses no 69 1952.

Herzog, B. Welt unter geschlossenem Himmel: zu den Büchern von Greene. Stimmen der Zeit 151 1952.

Lees, F. N. Greene: a comment. Scrutiny 19 1952.

O'Grady, E. Greene: écrivain eschatologique. Revue de L'Université d'Ottawa 22 1952.

Barra, G. La conversione di Greene. Vita e Pensiero 36 1953.

Cronin, V. Greene's first play. Catholic World 177 1953.

Findlater, R. Greene as dramatist. Twentieth Century 156 1953.

Fowler, A. D. S. Novelist of damnation. Theology 56 1953.

Gregor, I. The new romanticism: a comment on The living room. Blackfriars 34 1953.

Hoggart, R. The force of caricature: aspects of the art of Greene, with particular reference to The power and the glory. EC 3 1953.

Peters, W. The concern of Greene. Month 10 1953.

Shuttleworth, M. and S. Raven. The art of fiction, 3: Graham Greene. Paris Rev 1 1953.

Sordet, E. Signification de Greene. Cahiers Protestants 37 1953.

Fytton, F. Greene: Catholicism and controversy. Catholic World 180 1954.

Grunt, O. P. Grunntrekk i Greenes fortellerkunst. Samtiden 63 1954.

Johnston, J. L. Greene: the unhappy man. Central Lit Mag (Birmingham) 38 1954.

Madaule, J. El misterio del amor en la obra de Greene. Sur no 226 1954.

Battcock, M. The novels of Greene. Norseman 13 1955.

Bouscaren, A. T. France and Greene versus America and Diem. Catholic World 181 1955.

Codey, R. Notes on Greene's dramatic technique. Approach 17 1955.

Cosman, M. An early chapter in Greene. Arizona Quart 11 1955.

—— Disquieted Greene. Colorado Quart 6 1958.

McGowan, F. A. Symbolism in Brighton rock. Renascence 8 1955.

Elistratova, A. Greene and his new novel. Soviet Lit 8 1956.

Ellis, W. D. The grand theme of Greene. Southwest Rev 41 1956.

Freedman, R. Novel of contention: The quiet American. Western Rev 21 1956.

Liebling, A. J. A talkative something-or-other. New Yorker 7 April 1956.

Rahv, P. Wicked American innocence. Commentary 21 1956.

Trilling, D. and P. Rahv. America and The quiet American. Commentary 22 1956.

Bechner, H. Der stille Amerikaner. Stimmen der Zeit 160 1957.

Cassidy, J. America and innocence: Henry James and Greene. Blackfriars 38 1957.

Jefferson, M. E. The heart of the matter: the responsible man. Carolina Quart 9 1957.

Kenny, H. A. Graham Greene. Catholic World 185 1957.

Lewis, R. W. B. The fiction of Greene: between the horror and the glory. Kenyon Rev 19 1957; rptd in his Picaresque saint, New York 1959.

McCormick, J. O. The rough and lurid vision: Henry James, Greene, and the international theme. Jahrbuch für Amerikastudien 2 1957.

Modern Fiction Studies 3 1957. Special Greene no. Contains Lewis, R. W. B., The 'trilogy' of Greene; De Vitis, A. A., Allegory in Brighton rock; Patten, K., The structure of The power and the glory; Spier, U., Melodrama in Greene's End of the affair; Evans, R. O., Existentialism in Greene's Quiet American; Cottrell, B. W., Second time charm: the theatre of Greene; Huber, H. R., The two worlds of Greene; Hargreaves, P., Greene: a selected bibliography; Beebe, M., Criticism of Greene: a selected checklist.

Neis, E. Zum Sprachstil Greenes. Die Neueren Sprachen 6 1957.

Rewak, J. The potting shed: maturation of Greene's vision. Catholic World 186 1957.

De Vitis, A. A. The Church and Major Scobie. Renascence 10 1958.

—— The entertaining Mr Greene. Renascence 14 1961.

—— Greene's Comedians: hollower men. Renascence 18 1966.

Duffy, J. M. The lost world of Greene. Thought 33 1958.

Mesnet, M. B. Le Potting shed de Greene. Études no 296 1958.

Seward, B. Greene: a hint of an explanation. Western Rev 22 1958.

Wassmer, T. A. Greene: literary artist and philosopher-theologian. Homiletic & Pastoral Rev 58 1958 (and Critic 18 1959–60, as Greene: a look at his sinners).

—— Faith and reason in Greene. Studies (Dublin) 48 1959.

—— Sinners of Greene. Dalhousie Rev 39 1959.

Wyatt, E. van R. God in a garden. Critique 1 1958. On The potting shed.

Barlow, G. L'art de Greene. Esprit 27 1959.

Glicksberg, C. I. Greene: Catholicism in fiction. Criticism 1 1959.

Renascence 12 1959. Greene special no. Contains Costello, D. P., Greene and the Catholic press, and The latest in Greene criticism; Hughes, C., Innocence revisited; Hughes, R. E., The quiet American: the case reopened; Murphy, J. P., The potting shed: dogmatic and dramatic effects; Puentevella, R., Ambiguity in Greene.

Happel, N. Formbetrachtung an Greenes short story The hint of an explanation. Die Neueren Sprachen 9 1960.

Hinchcliffe, A. P. The good American. Twentieth Century 168 1960. On The quiet American.

Spinucci, P. L'ultimo dramma di Greene. Humanitas 15 1960.

Browne, E. M. Greene: theatre's gain. Theatre Arts 45 1961.

Hess, W. Greene's travesty on The ring and the book. Catholic World 194 1961. On A burnt-out case.

Highet, G. Our man in purgatory. Horizon (New York) 3 1961. On A burnt-out case.

Kermode, F. Greene's eggs and crosses. Encounter 16 1961; rptd in his Puzzles and epiphanies, 1962. On A burnt-out case.

Lodge, D. Use of key words in the novels of Greene: love, hate and The end of the affair. Blackfriars 42 1961.

—— Greene's Comedians. Commonweal 25 Feb 1966.

Martin, G. Novelists of three decades: E. Waugh, Greene, C. P. Snow. In Pelican guide to English literature vol 7, The modern age, ed B. Ford 1961.

Rolo, C. J. The man and the message. Atlantic 207 1961.

Servotte, H. Bedenkingen bij A burnt-out case. Dietsche Warande en Belfort 106 1961.

Smith, A. J. M. Greene's theological thrillers. Queen's Quart 68 1961.

Stratford, P. Greene: master of melodrama. Tamarack Rev 19 1961. This and the following items incorporated, rev, in his Faith and fiction, 1964, above.

—— The uncomplacent dramatist. Wisconsin Stud in Contemporary Lit 2 1961.

—— Unlocking The potting shed. Kenyon Rev 24 1962.

—— Chalk and cheese: a comparative study of A kiss for the leper, by Mauriac, and A burnt-out case. UTQ 33 1964.

Weyergans, F. La saison des pluies de Greene. Revue Nouvelle 33 1961. On A burnt-out case.

Barnes, R. J. Two modes of fiction: Hemingway and Greene. Renascence 14 1962.

Consolo, D. P. Music as motif: the writing of Brighton rock. Renascence 15 1962.

Ivaschova, V. Legende und Wahrheit über Greene. Zeitschrift für Anglistik und Amerikanistik 10 1962.

Noxon, J. Kierkegaard's stages and A burnt-out case. REL 3 1962.

Dooley, D. J. The suspension of disbelief: Greene's A burnt-out case. Dalhousie Rev 43 1963.

Harmer, R. M. Greene world of Mexico: the birth of a novelist. Renascence 15 1963.

Kunkel, F. L. The priest as scapegoat in the modern Catholic novel. Ramparts 1 1963.

Lerner, L. Graham Greene. CQ 5 1963.

Markovic, V. E. Greene in search of God. Texas Stud in Lit & Lang 5 1963.

Schumann, H. Zum Problem des Anti-Helden in Greenes neueren Romanzen. Wissenschaftliche Zeitschrift der Universität Rostock 12 1963.

Wichert, R. A. The quality of Greene's mercy. College Eng 25 1963.

Déchet, F. Suggestioni e limiti della tematica di Greene. Giornale di Metafisica 19 1964.

Hortmann, W. Greene: the burnt-out Catholic. Twentieth-Century Lit 10 1964.

Jacobsen, J. A Catholic quartet. Christian Scholar 47 1964. Greene, Muriel Spark, Powers, Flannery O'Connor.

Poole, R. C. Greene's indirection. Blackfriars 45 1964.

Ruotolo, L. P. Brighton rock's absurd heroine. MLQ 25 1964.

Simon, J. K. Off the Voie royale: the failure of Greene's A burnt-out case. Symposium 18 1964.

Barratt, H. Adultery as betrayal in Greene. Dalhousie Rev 45 1965.

Boardman, G. R. Greene's Under the garden: aesthetic explorations. Renascence 17 1965.

Marian, I. H. M. Greene's people: being and becoming. Renascence 18 1965.

Sandra, M. The priest-hero in modern fiction. Personalist 46 1965. Greene, Bernanos, Powers, O'Connor.

Taylor, M. A. and J. Clark. Further sources for The second death by Greene. Papers on Eng Lang & Lit 1 1965.

Ibáñez Langlois, J. M. Catolicismo y protestantismo en la novela de Greene. Atlantida no 22 1966.

Jones, J. L. Greene and the structure of the moral imagination. Phoenix 1 1966.

McCall, D. Brighton rock: the price of order. Eng Lang Notes 3 1966.

Wilshire, A. D. Conflict and conciliation. E & S 19 1966.

King, B. Greene's Inferno. Études Anglaises 21 1968.

Michener, R. L. Apocalyptic Mexico: The plumed serpent and The power and the glory. University of Kansas City Rev 34 1968.

Sternlicht, S. The sad comedies: Greene's later novels. Florida Quart 1 1968.

Desmond, J. F. Greene and the eternal dimension. Amer Benedictine Rev 20 1969.

Grob, A. The power and the glory: Greene's argument from design. Criticism 11 1969.

Jones, G. C. Greene and the legend of Péguy. Comparative Lit 21 1969.

King, J. In the lost boyhood of Judas: Greene's early novels of hell. Dalhousie Rev 49 1969.

Knipp, T. R. Gide and Greene: Africa and the literary imagination. Serif 6 1969.

C.P.C.

JOE RANDOLPH ACKERLEY
1896–1967

See col 905, below.

RICHARD ALDINGTON
1892–1962

Bibliographies

Kershaw, A. A bibliography of the works of Aldington from 1915 to 1948. Introd by Aldington 1950. Includes trns.

Parchevskaya, B. M. Richard Oldington: biobibliografichesky ukazatel. Moscow 1965. Includes works tr into Russian and secondary material, including early reviews of Aldington's works.

Schlueter, P. A chronological check list of the books by Aldington. In Richard Aldington: an intimate portrait, ed A. Kershaw and F.-J. Temple 1965. *See* §2 below.

§1

Images 1910–15. [1915], Boston 1916 (as Images old and new), London [1919] (as Images, with additional poems). Verse.

The love poems of Myrrhine and Konallis: a cycle of prose poems. Cleveland 1917 (40 copies), Chicago 1926 (as The love of Myrrhine and Konallis, and other prose poems).

Reverie: a little book of poems for H.D. Cleveland 1917 (50 copies).

Images of desire. 1919. Verse.

Images of war: a book of poems. 1919 (pbd Beaumont Press), 1919 (enlarged, but omitting some of the poems in the Beaumont Press edn, as Images of war).

War and love, 1915–18. Boston 1919. Contains most of Images of desire and Images of war.

The Berkshire Kennet. 1923 (50 copies). Poem.

Exile, and other poems. 1923.

Literary studies and reviews. 1924.

A fool i' the forest: a phantasmagoria. 1925. Verse.

Voltaire. 1925, 1929 (rev). Biography.

French studies and reviews. 1926, New York 1926.

D. H. Lawrence: an indiscretion. Seattle 1927 (Univ of Washington Chapbooks 6), London 1930 (as D. H. Lawrence). Pamphlet.

Collected poems. New York 1928, 1929, 1933 (as Collected poems 1915–23, omitting A fool i' the forest).

Hark the herald. [Paris 1928]. Poem, rptd in Movietones.

Remy de Gourmont: a modern man of letters. Seattle 1928 (Univ of Washington Chapbooks 13).

Death of a hero. New York 1929, London 1929, Paris 1930 (2 vols, unexpurgated), London 1965.

The eaten heart. Chapelle-Réanville 1929 (200 copies), Poem, rptd in The eaten heart [and other poems], 1933 below.

At all costs. 1930. Story, rptd in Roads to glory.

Balls, and Another book for suppression. 1930 (Blue Moon Booklets 7, 100 copies), Westport Conn 1932 (priv ptd, about 100 copies).

Last straws. Paris 1930. Story, rptd in US edn (only) of Soft answers, below.

Love and the Luxembourg. New York 1930, London 1930 (as A dream in the Luxembourg). Poem.

Two stories: Deserter; The lads of the village. 1930; rptd in Roads to glory, below.

Roads to glory. 1930, Garden City NY 1930. Stories.

The colonel's daughter. 1931, Garden City NY 1931.

Stepping heavenward: a record. Florence 1931, London 1931. Story; rptd in Soft answers.

Movietones, invented and set down 1928–1929. [1932?] (priv ptd, 10 copies). Verse.

Soft answers. 1932, Garden City NY 1932. Stories.

All men are enemies: a romance. 1933, Garden City NY 1933.

The eaten heart [and other poems]. 1933.

The poems of Richard Aldington. Garden City NY 1934.

The squire. 1934 (12 copies). Essay.

Women must work. 1934, Garden City NY 1934.

Artifex: sketches and ideas. 1935, Garden City NY 1936.

Life quest. 1935, Garden City NY 1935. Verse.
D. H. Lawrence: a complete list of his works, together with a critical appreciation [1936?]. Pamphlet, not identical with Aldington's earlier work of same title.
Life of a lady: a play. Garden City NY 1936, London [1936] (with subtitle, A play in three acts). With D. Patmore.
The crystal world. 1937, Garden City NY 1938. Verse.
Very heaven. 1937, Garden City NY 1937.
Seven against Reeves: a comedy-farce. 1938, New York 1938. Fiction.
Rejected guest. New York 1939, London 1939 (with note by Aldington on textual differences between US and English edns).
W. Somerset Maugham: an appreciation. New York 1939. Pamphlet.
Life for life's sake: a book of reminiscences. New York 1941, London 1968.
The Duke: being an account of the life and achievements of Arthur Wellesley, 1st Duke of Wellington. New York 1943, London 1946 (as Wellington, [etc]).
The romance of Casanova. New York 1946, London 1947. Fiction.
Four English portraits, 1801–1851. (The grand world of 'Prinney'; The lustrous world of young Disraeli; The strange world of Squire Waterton; The underworld of young Dickens). 1948.
The complete poems. Introd by Aldington 1948.
Jane Austen. Pasadena 1948. Pamphlet.
The strange life of Charles Waterton, 1782–1865. 1949, New York 1949.
Portrait of a genius, but... : the life of D. H. Lawrence. 1950, New York 1950 (as D. H. Lawrence: portrait of a genius, but...).
Ezra Pound and T. S. Eliot: a lecture. Hurst 1954.
Pinorman: personal recollections of Norman Douglas, Pino Orioli and Charles Prentice. 1954.
A. E. Housman and W. B. Yeats: two lectures. Hurst 1955.
Lawrence of Arabia: a biographical enquiry. 1955, Chicago 1955.
Introduction to Mistral. 1956, Carbondale 1960 (with preface by H. T. Moore).
Frauds. 1957. Biography.
Portrait of a rebel: the life and work of Robert Louis Stevenson. 1957.
A letter from Richard Aldington [to G. W. V. Potocki], and a summary bibliography of Count Potocki's published works. Draguignan [1961].
A tourist's Rome. Draguignan [1961]. Sketch.

Aldington pbd a number of trns, mostly from the French, and edited a number of anthologies and works by other authors, including some of the last works of D. H. Lawrence. For details see the bibliographies above.

Letters
Benkovitz, M. J. Nine for Reeves: letters from Richard Aldington. BNYPL 69 1965.

§2
Moore, T. S. In his Some soldier poets, 1919.
Rosenfeld, P. The importance of Aldington. In his By way of art, New York 1928.
Baum, P. F. Mr Richard Aldington. South Atlantic Quart 28 1929.
Hughes, G. In his Imagism and the imagists, Stanford 1931.
McGreevy, T. Richard Aldington: an Englishman. 1931.
Weidlé, V. Les romans de R. Aldington. Vie Intellectuelle 25 Oct 1937.
Snow, C. P. Richard Aldington: an appreciation. 1938.
Wellner, E. Das dichterische Schaffen Aldingtons. Würzburg 1940.

Papajewski, H. Die Lebenskritik Aldingtons. E Studien 74 1941.
Schwalbe, J. Richard Aldington: der literarische und weltanschauliche Weg eines modernen Engländers. Würzburg 1941.
Mossop, D. Un disciple de Gourmont: Aldington. Revue de Littérature Comparée 25 1951.
Moore, H. T. Aldington in his last years. Texas Quart 6 1963.
Kershaw, A. and Temple, F.-J. (ed). Richard Aldington: an intimate portrait. Carbondale 1965.
Bouysson, R. Dulce et decorum est pro patria mori. Caliban 3 1967.
Urnov, M. V. Richard Oldington. Moscow 1968.

WALTER ERNEST ALLEN
b. 1911

§1
Innocence is drowned. 1938.
Blind man's ditch. 1939.
Living space. 1940.
The Black Country. 1946. Topography.
Rogue elephant. 1946, New York 1946.
Arnold Bennett. 1948, Denver 1949.
The festive baked-potato cart, and other stories. 1948.
Writers on writing, selected and introduced by W. Allen. 1948, New York 1949 (as The writer on his art), Boston 1958 (as Writers on writing).
Reading a novel. 1949, 1956 (rev), 1963 (rev).
Dead man over all. 1950, New York 1951 (as Square peg).
Joyce Cary. 1953, 1963 (rev) (Br Council pamphlet).
The English novel: a short critical history. 1954, New York 1955.
The novel today. 1955, 1960 (rev) (Br Council pamphlet).
Six great novelists: Defoe, Fielding, Scott, Dickens, Stevenson, Conrad. 1955.
All in a lifetime. 1959, New York 1959 (as Threescore and ten).
George Eliot. New York 1964, London 1965.
Tradition and dream: the English and American novel from the twenties to our time. 1964, New York 1964 (as The modern novel in Britain and the United States).
The urgent West. 1969, New York 1969.

MICHAEL ARLEN
formerly
DIKRAN KUYUMJIAN
1895–1956

Selections
The ancient sin, and other stories, selected from These charming people, May Fair, The romantic lady. [1930].
The short stories of Arlen. [1933].

§1
The London venture. [1920], New York [1920].
The romantic lady, and other stories. [1921], New York 1921.
'Piracy': a romantic chronicle of these days. [1922], New York [1923].
These charming people. [1923], New York [1924]. Stories.
The green hat: a romance for a few people. [1924], New York [1924], 1925 (acting version). For parodies, see R. Abingdon, The green mat, [1925] and Barry Pain, This charming green hat-fair, [1925].
May Fair (in which are told the last adventures of These charming people). [1925], New York 1925. Stories.
The ace of cads, and other stories. [1927]. Stories from May Fair, above.

Ghost stories. 1927.

The man with the broken nose, and other stories. [1927]. Stories from These charming people, above.

Young men in love. [1927], New York [1927]. For a parody, see 'Melita Noose' [Nora K. Strange], Young women out of love: being a commentary on the genius peculiar to Arlen, 1928.

The zoo: a comedy in three acts. [1927]. With W. Smith.

Lily Christine: a romance. Garden City NY 1928, London 1929.

Babes in the wood. Garden City NY 1929, London [1930]. Stories.

Men dislike women: a romance. 1931, Garden City NY 1931.

A young man comes to London. [1932]. Story.

Good losers: a play in three acts and a prologue. [1933]. With W. Hackett.

Man's mortality: a story. 1933, Garden City NY 1933.

Hell! said the duchess: a bed-time story. 1934, Garden City NY 1934.

The crooked coronet, and other misrepresentations of the real facts of life. 1937, Garden City NY 1937. Stories.

Flying Dutchman. [1939], New York 1939.

§2

Overton, G. M. A reasonable view of Arlen. In his Cargoes for Crusoes, New York 1924.

Washburn, C. C. Sophistication. In his Opinions, New York 1926. On The green hat.

Guggenbühl, H. C. Michael Arlen: Kritiker der englischen Gesellschaft. Affoltern 1937.

ENID BAGNOLD
b. 1889

See cols 908–9 below.

HENRY CHRISTOPHER BAILEY
1878–1961

Selections

Mr Fortune's case book. 1936.

Meet Mr Fortune: a Reggie Fortune omnibus. Garden City NY 1942.

The best of Mr Fortune stories. New York 1943.

§1

My lady of Orange. 1901, New York 1901.

Karl of Erbach: a tale of Lichtenstein and Solgau. New York 1902, London 1903.

The Master of Gray. 1903, New York 1903.

Rimingtons. 1904.

Beaujeu. 1905.

Under castle walls. New York 1906, London 1907 (as Springtime).

Raoul, gentleman of fortune. 1907, New York 1907 (as A gentleman of fortune).

Colonel Stow. 1908, Indianapolis 1908 (as Colonel Greatheart).

The god of clay. 1908, New York 1908.

Storm and treasure. 1910, New York 1910.

The lonely queen. 1911, New York 1911.

The suburban. 1912.

The sea captain. New York 1913, London 1914.

Forty years after: the story of the Franco-German war 1870. 1914 (Daily Telegraph War Books).

The gentleman adventurer. 1914, New York 1915.

The highwayman. 1915, New York 1916.

The gamesters. 1916, New York 1919.

The young lovers. 1917, New York 1929.

The pillar of fire. 1918.

Barry Leroy. 1919, New York 1920.

Call Mr Fortune. 1920, New York 1921. Stories.

His Serene Highness. 1920, New York 1922.

The fool. 1921, New York 1927.

The plot. 1922.

Mr Fortune's practice. 1923, New York 1924. Stories.

The rebel. 1923.

Knight at arms. 1924, New York 1925.

The golden fleece. 1925.

Mr Fortune's trials. 1925, New York 1926. Stories.

The merchant prince. 1926, New York 1929.

Bonaventure. 1927.

Mr Fortune, please. 1927, New York 1928. Stories.

Judy Bovenden. 1928.

Mr Fortune speaking. 1929, New York 1931. Stories.

The Roman eagles. 1929. For children.

Garstons. 1930, Garden City NY 1930 (as The Garston murder case).

Mr Fortune explains. 1930, New York 1931.

Mr Cardonnel. 1931.

Case for Mr Fortune. 1932, Garden City NY 1932. Stories.

The red castle. 1932, Garden City NY 1932 (as The red castle mystery).

The man in the cape. 1933.

Mr Fortune wonders. 1933, Garden City NY 1933. Stories.

Shadow on the wall. 1934, Garden City NY 1934.

Mr Fortune objects. 1935, Garden City NY 1935. Stories.

The sullen sky mystery. 1935, Garden City NY 1935.

Clue for Mr Fortune. 1936, Garden City NY 1936 (as A clue for Mr Fortune).

Black land, white land: a Reginald Fortune detective story. 1937; Garden City NY 1937 (as Black land, white land: a Reggie Fortune novel).

Clunk's claimant. 1937, Garden City NY 1937 (as The twittering bird mystery).

This is Mr Fortune. 1938, New York 1938. Stories.

The great game. 1939, New York 1939.

The Veron mystery. 1939, New York 1939 (as Mr Clunk's text).

The Bishop's crime. 1940, New York 1941.

Mr Fortune here. 1940, New York 1940. Stories.

The little captain. 1941, Garden City NY 1941 (as Orphan Ann).

Dead man's shoes. 1942, Garden City NY 1942 (as Nobody's vineyard: a Joshua Clunk story).

No murder. 1942, Garden City NY 1942 (as The apprehensive dog: a Reggie Fortune novel).

Mr Fortune finds a pig. 1943, Garden City NY 1943.

The cat's whisker: a Reggie Fortune novel. Garden City NY 1944, London [1945] (as Dead man's effects).

Slippery Ann. 1944, Garden City NY 1944 (as The Queen of spades: a Joshua Clunk mystery).

The wrong man. Garden City NY 1945, London [1946].

The life sentence. 1946, Garden City NY 1946.

Honour among thieves. 1947, Garden City NY 1947.

Saving a rope. 1948, Garden City NY 1948 (as Save a rope).

Shrouded death. 1950.

NIGEL MARLIN BALCHIN
1908–70

§1

How to run a bassoon factory: or, business explained. 1934, Boston 1936, London 1950 (with Business for pleasure, and An appreciation of the late Mr Spade by Nigel Balchin). As 'Mark Spade'; humour.

No sky. 1934.

Business for pleasure. 1935, 1950 (with How to run a bassoon factory, and An appreciation of the late Mr Spade by Nigel Balchin, above). As 'Mark Spade'; humour.

Simple life. 1935.

Fun and games: how to win at almost anything. 1936. As 'Mark Spade': humour.

Income and outcome: a study of personal finance. 1936.

Lightbody on liberty. 1936.

Darkness falls from the air. 1942.

The small back room. 1943, Boston 1945.

Mine own executioner. 1945, Boston 1946.

The aircraft builders: an account of British aircraft production 1939–45. 1947.

Lord, I was afraid. 1947.

The Borgia testament. 1948, Boston 1949.

A sort of traitors. 1949, Boston 1950 (as Who is my neighbour?).

The anatomy of villainy. 1950. Essays.

A way through the wood. 1951, Boston 1951.

Sundry creditors. 1953, Boston 1953 (as Private interests).

Last recollections of my Uncle Charles. 1954, New York 1957. Stories.

The worker in modern industry. 1954. Pamphlet.

The fall of the sparrow. 1955, New York 1956 (as The fall of a sparrow).

Seen dimly before dawn. 1962, New York 1962.

Burnt Njal—the irredeemable crime. In Fatal fascination: a choice of crime, by N. Balchin [et al], 1964, Boston 1965.

In the absence of Mrs Petersen. 1966, New York 1966.

Kings of infinite space. 1967, New York 1968.

MAURICE BARING
1874-1945

Bibliographies

Chaundy, L. A bibliography of the first editions of the works of Baring, with poems by Baring. 1925.

Cutler, B. D. and V. Stiles, Maurice Baring. In their Modern British authors: their first editions, 1930.

Collections and Selections

Collected poems. 1911, New York 1911, London 1925 (enlarged), Garden City NY 1925. Includes verse plays.

What I saw in Russia. 1913, 1927 (enlarged). Selections from Baring's books on Russia.

Maurice Baring. [1929]. (Augustan Books of Modern Poetry). 22 selected poems.

Poems 1892–1929. 1930 (priv ptd, 50 copies). Trade edn as Selected poems, 1930.

Unreliable history. 1934, New York 1934. Contains Diminutive dramas, Dead letters, Lost diaries.

Ten diminutive dramas. 1951. Selected from Diminutive dramas.

§1

Hildesheim: quatre pastiches. Paris 1899, London 1924.

The Black Prince, and other poems. 1903 [1902].

Gaston de Foix and other plays. 1903. In verse. For rev version of the title play, see Gaston de Foix 1913, below.

The story of Forget-me-not and Lily of the valley. [1905] (priv ptd, 25 copies), 1909 (trade edn), 1928 (as Forget-me-not and Lily of the valley). For children.

With the Russians in Manchuria. 1905.

Mahasena. Oxford 1905. Verse play.

Sonnets and short poems. Oxford 1906.

Desiderio. Oxford 1906, 1911 (rev). Verse drama.

A year in Russia. 1907, 1917 (rev, with new preface).

Proserpine: a masque. Oxford 1908. In verse.

Russian essays and stories. 1908.

Orpheus in Mayfair, and other stories and sketches. 1909.

Landmarks in Russian literature. 1910.

Dead letters. 1910, Boston 1910. Imaginary letters, rptd from Morning Post.

The glass mender, and other stories. 1910, New York 1911 (as The blue rose fairy book).

Diminutive dramas. 1911, Boston 1911. Rptd from Morning Post.

The Russian people. 1911.

The grey stocking, and other plays. 1911.

Gaston de Foix. Oxford 1913. Text rev from that in Gaston de Foix, and other plays, 1903, above.

Letters from the Near East, 1909 and 1912. 1913. Rptd from Morning Post and Times.

Lost diaries. 1913, Boston 1913. Rptd from The Eye Witness. Fiction.

Palamon and Arcite: a play for puppets. Oxford 1913.

Round the world in any number of days. Boston 1914, London 1919.

The mainsprings of Russia. 1914.

An outline of Russian literature. 1915.

English landscape: an anthology compiled by Baring. 1916.

Translations, found in a commonplace book, edited by 'S.C.' Oxford 1916, London 1918 (as Translations ancient and modern by M. Baring, with additional material), 1925 (with originals which had in fact been written by Ronald Knox et al). Fiction.

In memoriam: Auberon Herbert. Oxford 1917 (priv ptd, 35 copies), 1917 (trade edn).

Poems 1914–17. 1917, 1920 (with addns, as Poems 1914–19).

Manfroy: a play in five acts. 1920 (priv ptd, 25 copies). Rptd in His Majesty's embassy and other plays, 1923 below.

R.F.C., H.Q., 1914–18. 1920, 1930 (as Flying Corps Headquarters 1914–18).

Passing by. 1921.

The puppet show of memory. 1922, Boston 1922. Autobiography.

Overlooked. 1922, Boston 1922.

His Majesty's embassy and other plays. 1923.

A triangle: passages from three notebooks. 1923.

C. 1924, 2 vols Garden City NY 1924.

Punch and Judy and other essays. 1924, Garden City NY 1924.

The Oxford book of Russian verse, chosen by M. Baring. Oxford 1924.

Half a minute's silence, and other stories. 1925, Garden City NY 1926.

Cat's cradle. 1925.

Daphne Adeane. 1926, New York 1927.

Catherine Parr: or, Alexander's horse. Lockport Ill 1927. From Diminutive dramas.

French literature. 1927. Pamphlet.

Last days of Tsarskoe Selo: being the personal notes and memoirs of Count Paul Benckendoff. Tr Baring 1927.

Tinker's leave. 1927, Garden City NY 1928.

Cecil Spencer. 1928 (priv ptd), 1929 (trade edn). Commemorative verse.

Comfortless memory. 1928, Garden City NY 1928 (as When they love).

Forget-me-not and Lily of the valley. 1928. See The story of Forget-me-not and Lily of the valley, 1905, above.

The coat without seam. 1929, New York 1929.

Passing by, and Overlooked. 1929. First pbd separately 1921 and 1922.

Flying Corps Headquarters 1914–18. 1930. See R.F.C., H.Q., 1914–18, 1920, above.

Robert Peckham. 1930, New York 1930.

In my end is my beginning. 1931, New York 1931.

Poems translated from Pushkin by M. Baring. 1931 (priv ptd, 50 copies).

Friday's business. 1932, New York 1933.

Lost lectures: or, the fruits of experience. 1932, New York 1932. Essays.

Sarah Bernhardt. 1933, New York 1934.

The lonely land of Dulwich. 1934, New York 1934.

Darby and Joan. 1935, New York 1936.

Have you anything to declare?: a notebook with commentaries. [1936], New York 1937.

Baring pbd privately pamphlets of verse in small edns, most of the contents of which were rptd in Collected poems, *1925* and Poems 1892–1929. *(See Chaundy, Bibliographies, above.) Some of Baring's letters were ptd in E. Smyth,* Maurice Baring, *1938 and L. Lovat,* Maurice Baring, *1947 (see §2, below). With R. A. Leigh and H. Cornish, Baring edited and largely wrote* The Cambridge ABC *(4 nos, 1894), and with Hilaire Belloc he edited, and largely wrote,* The North Street Gazette *(1 no only, March 1910). He was also co-editor of the* Russian Rev *(1912–14).*

§2

Beerbohm, M. An adramatist. Saturday Rev 6 June 1908; rptd in his Around theatres, 1953. Review of The grey stocking.
Kernahan, C. In his Six famous living poets, 1922.
Darlington, W. A. Three Baring plays. In his Literature in the theatre, 1925; rptd review of His Majesty's embassy and other plays.
Arns, K. Maurice Baring. E Studien 61 1927.
Mainsard, J. Les romans de Baring. Études 198 1929.
Martindale, C. C. Mr Baring's novels. Commonweal 10 1929.
—— Maurice Baring. Catholic World 163 1946.
Ruegg, A. Maurice Baring. Schweizerische Rundschau 30 1930.
Bellessort, A. Maurice Baring. Correspondant 10 March 1931.
Hanighen, F. C. The art of Baring. Bookman (NY) 75 1932.
Alexander, C. Chesterton, Baring, Belloc. In his The Catholic literary revival, Milwaukee [1935].
Chaigne, L. Maurice Baring. Paris [1935].
Las Vergnas, R. Un écrivain catholique anglais: Maurice Baring. Revue des Deux Mondes 15 Oct 1936; rptd in his Portraits anglais, Paris 1937.
Smyth, E. Maurice Baring. 1938.
Marsh, E. In his A number of people, 1939.
Reilly, J. J. The novels of Baring. Catholic World 150 1939. Rptd in his Of books and men, New York 1942.
Ezban, S. Baring et la France. PMLA 60 1945.
Kelly, H. Maurice Baring. Studies 35 1946.
Lovat, L. Baring: a postscript, with some letters and verse. 1947.
Storrs, R. Baring: a recollection. Atlantic Monthly 180 1947.
Albion, G. Catholicism in Baring's 'C'. Month 185 1948.
Mitchell, J. Baring—realist. Twentieth Century 3 1948.
Lodge, D. Baring, novelist: a reappraisal. Dublin Rev 234 1960.
Lefèbve, M. J. L'inactualité de Baring. Revue des Langues Vivantes 31 1965.

JOSEPH ALEXANDER BARON
b. 1917

From the city, from the plough. 1948, New York 1949.
There's no home. 1950, New York 1950 (as The wine of Etna).
Rosie Hogarth. 1951.
With hope, farewell. 1952, New York 1952, London 1962 (as The thunder of peace).
The human kind: a sequence. 1953, New York [1953].
The golden princess. 1954, New York 1954.
Queen of the east. 1956, New York 1956.
Seeing life. 1958.
The lowlife. 1963, New York 1964.
Strip Jack naked. 1966.

HERBERT ERNEST BATES
b. 1905

Bibliographies

'Gawsworth, John' (T. I. F. Armstrong). In his Ten contemporaries: notes toward their definitive bibliography, 2nd ser 1933.

Collections and Selections

Thirty tales. 1934.
Country tales: collected short stories. 1940.
Something in the air: stories by Flying Officer 'X'. 1944.
Thirty-one selected tales. 1947.
Works Evensford edition. 1951–.
Selected short stories chosen and introduced by the author. 1951.
Twenty tales. 1951.
Selected stories. 1957 (Penguin).
Seven by five: stories by H. E. Bates 1926–61. Preface by H. Miller 1963, Boston 1963 (as The best of H. E. Bates).

§1

The last bread: a play in one act. 1926.
The two sisters. 1926, New York 1926.
The seekers. 1926. Stories.
The spring song, and In view of the fact that: two stories. 1927 (priv ptd, 100 copies), San Francisco 1927 (priv ptd, 50 copies).
Day's end, and other stories. 1928.
Song for December. [1928] (priv ptd, 150 copies). Poem.
Seven tales and Alexander. 1929, New York 1930.
Catherine Foster. 1929, New York 1929.
The tree. [1930] (Blue Moon Booklets 3). Story.
The Hessian prisoner. Foreword by E. Garnett 1930 (Furnivall Books 2). Story
Christmas 1930. [1930] (priv ptd). Poem.
Charlotte's Row. 1931.
Holly and sallow. 1931 (100 copies). Poem.
Mrs Esmond's life. 1931 (priv ptd, 300 copies). Story.
A threshing day. 1931. (300 copies). Story.
The black boxer: tales. 1932.
Sally go round the moon. 1932. Story.
A German idyll. Waltham St Lawrence 1932 (307 copies). Story.
The fallow land. 1932, New York 1933.
The story without end, and The country doctor. 1932 (130 copies).
The house with the apricot, and two other tales. 1933.
The woman who had imagination, and other stories. 1934, New York 1934.
Cut and come again: fourteen stories. 1935.
The duet. 1935 (285 copies) (Grayson Books). Story.
Flowers and faces. [Waltham St Lawrence] 1935 (325 copies). On gardening.
The poacher. 1935, New York 1935.
A house of women. 1936, New York 1936.
Through the woods: the English woodlands—April to April. 1936, New York 1936. Essays.
Down the river. 1937, New York 1937. Essays.
Something short and sweet: stories. 1937.
Spella Ho. 1938, Boston 1938.
The flying goat. 1939. Stories.
My Uncle Silas. 1939.
The beauty of the dead, and other stories. 1940.
The seasons and the gardener: a book for children. Cambridge 1940. Non-fiction.
The beauty of the dead and one other short story (The bridge). 1941 (25 copies).
The modern short story: a critical survey. 1941.
The greatest people in the world, and other stories, by Flying Officer 'X'. 1942, New York 1943 (as There's something in the air). Anon.
In the heart of the country. 1942. Essays.

The bride comes to Evensford. 1943. Story.
Country life. 1943 (Penguin). Notes, rptd from Spectator.
How sleep the brave, and other stories, by Flying Officer 'X'. 1943. Anon.
O more than happy countryman. 1943. Essays.
Fair stood the wind for France. Boston 1944, London 1944.
There's freedom in the air: the official story of the allied air forces from the occupied countries. 1944. Anon.
The day of glory: a play in three acts. 1945.
The cruise of the Breadwinner. 1946, Boston 1947.
The tinkers of Elstow. [1946]. Pamphlet history of an ordnance factory.
Otters and men. [1947]. Essay rptd from Down the river, 1937, above
The purple plain. 1947, Boston 1947.
The bride comes to Evensford, and other tales. 1949.
The country heart. 1949. Rev edn of O more than happy countryman, 1943, above, and In the heart of the country, 1942, above.
Dear life. Boston 1949, London 1950.
The jacaranda tree. 1949, Boston 1949.
Edward Garnett. 1950. Biography.
Flower gardening: a reader's guide. 1950 (National Book League pamphlet).
The scarlet sword. 1950, Boston 1951.
Colonel Julian, and other stories. 1951, Boston 1952.
The country of white clover. 1952. Essays.
The face of England. 1952. Non-fiction.
Love for Lydia. 1952, Boston 1953.
The nature of love: three short novels. 1953, Boston 1954.
The feast of July. 1954, Boston [1954].
The daffodil sky. 1955, Boston 1956. Stories.
Pastoral on paper. [1956]. On the Medway Corrugated Paper Company.
The sleepless moon. 1956, Boston [1956].
Death of a huntsman: four short novels. 1957, Boston 1957 (as Summer in Salandar).
Sugar for the horse. 1957. Stories.
The darling buds of May. 1958, Boston 1958.
A breath of French air. 1959, Boston 1959.
The watercress girl, and other stories. 1959, Boston 1960.
An aspidistra in Babylon: four novellas. 1960, Boston 1960 (as The grapes of paradise).
When the green woods laugh. 1960, Boston 1961 (as Hark, hark, the lark).
The day of the tortoise. 1961.
Now sleeps the crimson petal, and other stories. 1961, Boston 1961 (as The enchantress, and other stories).
Achilles the donkey. 1962. Children's story.
A crown of wild myrtle. 1962, New York 1963.
The golden oriole: five novellas. 1962, Boston 1962.
Achilles and Diana. 1963, New York 1963. Children's story.
Oh! to be in England. 1963, New York 1964.
Achilles and the twins. 1964, New York 1965. Children's story.
The fabulous Mrs V. 1964. Stories.
A moment in time. 1964, New York 1964.
The wedding party. 1965. Stories.
The distant horns of summer. 1967.
The four beauties. 1968. Stories.
The white admiral. 1968. Children's story.
The wild cherry tree. 1968. Stories.
The vanished world: an autobiography. 1969–.

RALPH BATES
b. 1899

Sierra. 1933. Stories.
Franz Schubert. 1934, New York 1935. Biography.
Lean men: an episode in a life. 1934, New York 1935, 2 vols London 1938.
The olive field. 1936, New York [1936].

Rainbow fish: four short novels. 1937, New York 1937. Rainbow fish; Death of a virgin; The other land; Dead end of the sky.
The miraculous horde, and other stories. 1939, New York [1939] (as Sirocco, and other stories).
The fields of paradise. New York [1940], London 1941.
The undiscoverables, and other stories. New York 1942.
The dolphin in the wood. 1950, New York 1950.

THOMAS OWEN BEACHCROFT
b. 1902

Collections
Collected stories. 1946.

§1
A young man in a hurry, and other stories. 1934.
Just cats. 1936, New York 1936. Photographs by L. Luard.
You must break out sometimes, and other stories. 1936.
The man who started clean. 1937, New York 1937.
The parents left alone, and other stories. 1940.
Calling all nations. Wembley [1942]. Broadcast talks.
British broadcasting. 1946.
Malice bites back. 1947. Stories.
Asking for trouble. 1948.
A thorn in the heart. 1952.
Goodbye, Aunt Hesther. 1955. Stories.
The English short story. 2 pts 1964 (Br Council pamphlet).
The modest art: a survey of the short story in English. 1968, New York 1968.

SAMUEL BARCLAY BECKETT
b. 1906
See cols 885–906, below.

SIR HENRY MAXIMILIAN BEERBOHM
1872–1956
See cols 1000–3, below.

ADRIAN HANBURY BELL
b. 1901

§1
Corduroy. 1930. Rptd in Silver ley, below.
Silver Ley. 1931, New York 1931.
The cherry tree. 1932, New York 1932.
Folly field. 1933.
The balcony. 1934, New York 1936.
Seasons. 1934. Verse.
Poems. 1935 (30 copies).
By-road. 1937.
Men and the fields. 1939, New York 1939. Non-fiction.
The shepherd's farm. 1939.
Apple acre. 1942, 1964 (rev).
Sunrise to sunset. 1944.
The budding morrow. 1946.
The black donkey. 1949.
The flower and the wheel. 1949.
The path by the window. 1952. Stories.
Music in the morning. 1954.
A young man's fancy. 1955, New York 1956.
A Suffolk harvest. 1956. Non-fiction.
The mill house. 1958.
My own master. 1961. Autobiography.
A street in Suffolk. 1964. Non-fiction.

§2

Warren, C. H. Bell and English farming. Fortnightly Rev new ser 157 1945.
Corduroy country. TLS 17 Sept 1964.

'NEIL BELL',
STEPHEN SOUTHWOLD
1887–1964

The common day. 1915. Verse. As Stephen Southwold.
The seventh bowl. 1930.
The gas war of 1940. 1931, 1934 (as Valiant clay, by Neil Bell), [1940] (as The gas war of 1940, by Neil Bell). First pbd as by 'Miles'.
Life and Andrew Otway. 1931, New York 1932.
Precious porcelain. 1931, New York 1931.
The disturbing affair of Noel Blake. 1932, New York 1932.
The marriage of Simon Harper. 1932.
Bredon and Sons. [1933], Boston 1934.
Death rocks the cradle. 1933.
The lord of life. 1933, Boston 1933.
The truth about my father. 1934.
Winding road. 1934, Boston 1934.
The days dividing. 1935, Boston 1935.
Mixed pickles: short stories. 1935.
The son of Richard Carden. 1935, Boston 1935.
Crocus. 1936, Garden City NY 1937.
Strange melody. 1936, Garden City NY 1936.
Pinkney's garden. Garden City NY [1937], London 1937, [1949] (abridged).
Testament of Stephen Fane. 1937.
Love and Julian Farne. [1938].
One came back. 1938.
The Smallways rub along. 1938.
The abbot's heel. 1939.
Not a sparrow falls. [1939].
So perish the roses. 1940, New York 1940.
The desperate pursuit. 1941. Stories.
The spice of life. 1941. Stories.
Peek's progress. 1942.
The tower of darkness. 1942.
Cover his face: a novel of the life and times of Thomas Chatterton. 1943.
Child of my sorrow. 1944.
The handsome Langleys. 1945.
Alpha and Omega. 1946. Stories.
A romance in lavender. 1946. As Stephen Southwold.
Forgive us our trespasses. 1947.
The governess at Ashburton Hall. 1948.
Immortal dyer. [1948]. As Stephen Southwold.
Who was James Carey? 1949.
I am legion. 1950.
The inconstant wife. [1950]. As Stephen Southwold.
The dark page. 1951.
Three pairs of heels, and twenty-four short stories. [1951].
The flowers of the forest. 1952.
One of the best. 1952.
Custody of the child. 1953.
The secret life of Miss Lottinger: a novela and twenty short stories. 1953.
Who walk in fear. 1953. 3 novels.
Many waters. 1954.
The captain's woman & other stories. 1955.
Luke Branwhite: his joyous life and happy death. 1955.
All my days. 1956.
The endless chain. 1956.
My writing life. 1955 (for 1956). Autobiography.
Love and desire and hate: three short novels and other stories. 1957.
Thy first begotten. 1957.
Who no woman knows. 1957.
The black sheep. 1958.

Forty stories. 1958.
Mrs Rawleigh and Mrs Paradock. 1958.
At the sign of the unicorn. 1959.
Simon Dale. 1959.
Corridor of Venus: thirty-two stories. 1960.
My brother Charles. 1960.
The narrow edge. 1961.
13 Piccadilly. 1961.
Village Casanova, and other stories. 1961.
Portrait of Gideon Power. 1962.
Weekend in Paris. 1962.
I paint your world. 1963.
The story of Leon Barentz. 1963.
This time for love. 1964. Stories.
The house at the crossroads. 1966. Stories.
The ninth Earl of Whitby: a novel and other stories. 1966.

Southwold also wrote, between 1923 and 1947, numerous books for children under his real name.

JOSEPH HILAIRE PIERRE
RENÉ BELLOC
1870–1953

See cols 1004–10, below.

ELEANOR THEODORA
ROBY BENSON
1906–68

Selections

The best stories of Theodora Benson. 1940.

§1

Salad days. 1928, New York 1929.
Glass houses. [1929], New York 1930 (as Anita agrees).
Lobster quadrille. 1930. With B. Askwith.
Shallow water. 1931.
Which way? 1931, Garden City NY 1932.
Seven basketfuls. 1932. With B. Askwith.
Façade. 1933, New York 1933.
Chip, chip, my little horse: the story of an air-holiday. 1934.
Concert pitch. 1934, New York 1934.
Foreigners: or, The world in a nutshell. 1935. With B. Askwith. Humour.
The unambitious journey. 1935. Travel.
Middling through: or, Britain in a nutshell. 1936. With B. Askwith. Humour.
How to be famous: or, The great in a nutshell. 1937. With B. Askwith. Humour.
In the east my pleasure lies. 1938. Travel.
Sweethearts and wives: their part in war. 1942.
The undertaker's wife. 1947.
The man from the tunnel, and other stories. 1950.
London immortals. 1951. Non-fiction.
Rehearsal for death. 1954.

STELLA BENSON
1892–1933

Bibliographies

Gawsworth, J. In his Ten contemporaries: notes toward their definitive bibliographies, 2nd ser 1933.

Collections

Poems. 1935. Contains Twenty, and a selection of other poems made by the author.
Collected short stories. 1936.

§1

I pose. 1915, New York 1916.
This is the end. 1917.
Twenty. 1918, New York 1918. Verse.
Living alone. 1919.
Kwan-Yin. San Francisco 1922 (priv ptd, 100 copies). Play.
The poor man. 1922, New York 1923.
Pipers and a dancer. 1924, New York 1924.
The little world. 1925, New York 1926. Travel.
The awakening: a fantasy. San Francisco 1925. Story.
Goodbye, stranger. 1926, New York 1926.
Worlds within worlds. 1928, New York 1929. Travel.
The man who missed the 'bus. 1928. Story.
Come to Eleuthera. [1929?]. Travel, ed and partly written by Stella Benson.
The far-away bride. New York 1930, London 1931 (as Tobit transplanted).
Hope against hope, and other stories. 1931.
Christmas formula, and other stories. 1932.
Mundos: an unfinished novel. 1935.

§2

Johnson, R. B. In his Some contemporary novelists: women, 1920.
Collins, J. Two lesser literary ladies of London: Stella Benson and Virginia Woolf. In his The doctor looks at literature, 1923.
Mais, S. P. B. In his Some modern authors, 1923.
Bottome, P. Stella Benson. San Francisco 1934 (priv ptd). Booklet.
Roberts, R. E. Portrait of Stella Benson. 1939.
Steinbeck, S. Der ausgesetzte Mensch. Berne 1959.

EDMUND CLERIHEW BENTLEY
1875–1956
Collections

Clerihews complete. [1951].
Trent's case book, with an introduction by B. R. Redman. New York 1953. Contains Trent's last case, Trent's own case, and Trent intervenes.

§1

Biography for beginners. [1905]. As 'E. Clerihew'. Humorous verse.
Trent's last case. [1913], New York 1913 (as The woman in black), London 1929 (rev, as Trent's last case), New York 1930.
Peace year in the City 1918–19; an account of the outstanding events in the City of London during Peace year. 1920 (priv ptd).
More biography. 1929. Humorous verse.
Trent's own case. 1936, New York 1936. With H. W. Allen.
Trent intervenes. 1938, New York 1938. Stories.
Baseless biography. 1939. Humorous verse.
Those days: an autobiography. 1940.
Elephant's work: an enigma. 1950, New York 1950.

PHYLLIS ELEANOR BENTLEY
b. 1894

§1

Pedagomania: or the gentle art of teaching, by 'A Bachelor of Arts'. 1918.
The world's bane, and other stories. 1918.
Environment. 1922, New York 1935.
Cat-in-the-manger. 1923. Sequel to Environment, above.
The partnership. 1928, Boston 1929.

The spinner of the years. 1928, New York [1929].
Carr: being the biography of Philip Joseph Carr, manufacturer. 1929, New York 1933. Fiction.
Sounding brass: a play in one act. Halifax 1930.
Trio. 1930.
Inheritance. 1932, New York 1934.
A modern tragedy. 1934, New York 1934.
The whole of the story. 1935. Stories.
Freedom, farewell! 1936, New York 1936.
Sleep in peace. 1938, New York 1938.
Take courage. 1940, New York 1940 (as The power and the glory).
The English regional novel. 1941.
Manhold. 1941, New York 1941.
Here is America. 1942. Non-fiction.
The rise of Henry Morcar. 1946, New York 1946.
Some observations on the art of narrative. 1946, New York 1947.
The Brontës. 1947, New York 1947.
Colne Valley cloth from the earliest times to the present day. Huddersfield 1947.
Life story. 1948, New York 1948. Fiction.
The Brontë sisters. 1950 (Br Council pamphlet).
Quorum. 1950, New York 1951.
Panorama: tales of the West Riding. 1952, New York 1952.
The house of Moreys: a romance. 1953, New York 1953.
Noble in reason. 1955, New York 1955.
Love and money: seven tales of the West Riding. 1957, New York 1957.
Crescendo. 1958, New York 1958.
Kith and kin: nine tales of family life. 1960, New York 1960.
The young Brontës. [1960], New York [1960].
Committees. 1962 (Collins Nutshell books). Non-fiction.
O dreams, O destinations: an autobiography. 1962, New York 1962.
Enjoy books: reading and collecting. 1964.
Public speaking. 1964 (Collins Nutshell books). Non-fiction.
The adventures of Tom Leigh. 1964, Garden City NY [1964]. For children.
Tales of the West Riding. 1965.
A man of his time. 1966, New York 1966.
Ned Carver in danger. 1967. For children.
Gold pieces. 1968.
The Brontës and their world. 1969, New York 1969.
Ring in the new. 1969.

§2

Lawrence, M. Matriarchs. In her School of femininity, New York 1936, London 1937 (as We write as women).

JOHN DAVYS BERESFORD
1873–1947
Bibliographies

Gerber, H. E. Beresford: a bibliography. Bull of Bibliography 21 1956. With prefatory note on Beresford; includes uncollected stories and essays.

§1

The early history of Jacob Stahl. 1911, Boston [1911]. First vol of Stahl trilogy.
The Hampdenshire wonder. 1911, New York [1917] (as The wonder), London 1948 (with introd by W. de la Mare).
A candidate for truth. 1912, New York 1912. 2nd vol of Stahl trilogy.
Goslings. 1913, New York 1913 (as A world of women).
The house in Demetrius Road. 1914, New York [1914].
The compleat angler: a duologue. [1915] (French's Acting edn). With A. S. Craven.

H. G. Wells. 1915.
The invisible event. 1915, New York [1915]. 3rd vol of Stahl trilogy.
The mountains of the moon. 1915.
Poems by two brothers. 1915. With R. Beresford.
These Lynnekers. 1916, New York [1916].
House-mates. 1916 [1917], New York [1917].
W. E. Ford: a biography. [1917], New York [1917]. With K. Richmond; semi-autobiographical fiction.
God's counterpoint. [1918], New York [1918].
Nineteen impressions. 1918. Stories.
The perfect machine. In English Rev 26 1918. Play, with A. S. Craven.
The Jervaise comedy. [1919], New York 1919.
An imperfect mother. 1920, New York 1920.
Revolution. [1921], New York 1921.
Signs & wonders. Waltham Saint Lawrence 1921, New York 1921. Stories.
The prisoners of Hartling. [1922], New York 1922.
Taken from life. [1922]. Text by Beresford, photographs by E. O. Hoppé. Character sketches.
The imperturbable duchess, and other stories. [1923].
Love's pilgrim. [1923], Indianapolis [1923].
Unity. [1924], Indianapolis [1924].
The monkey-puzzle. [1925], Indianapolis [1925].
That kind of man. [1926], Indianapolis [1926] (as Almost pagan).
The decoy. [1927].
The tapestry. [1927], Indianapolis [1927].
The instrument of destiny: a detective story. [1928], Indianapolis [1928].
All or nothing. [1928], Indianapolis [1928].
Writing aloud. [1928].
Experiment in the novel. In Tradition and experiment in present-day literature: addresses delivered at the City Literary Institute, 1929.
The meeting place, and other stories. 1929.
Real people. [1929].
Love's illusion. 1930, New York 1930.
Seven, Bowsworth. 1930.
An innocent criminal. [1931], New York [1931].
The old people. [1931], New York [1932]. First vol of Three generations trilogy.
The next generation. 1932.
The middle generation. [1932], New York [1933]. 2nd vol of Three generations trilogy.
The inheritor. 1933.
The Camberwell miracle. 1933.
The young people. 1933, New York [1934]. 3rd vol of Three generations trilogy.
The case for faith-healing. 1934.
Peckover. 1934, New York [1935].
On a huge hill. 1935.
Blackthorn winter, and other stories. [1936].
The faithful lovers. [1936], New York [1936].
Cleo. [1937].
The root of the matter: essays by J. D. Beresford [et al]. Ed H. R. L. Sheppard 1937. Human relations, by Beresford.
The unfinished road. [1938].
What I believe. 1938. (I believe: a series of personal statements 1).
Strange rival. 1939.
Snell's folly. [1939].
The idea of God. [1940].
Quiet corner. [1940].
'What dreams may come...' [1941].
A common enemy. [1941].
The benefactor. [1943].
The long view. [1943].
Men in the same boat. [1943]. With E. Wynne-Tyson.
If this were true—. [1944].
The riddle of the tower. [1944]. With E. Wynne-Tyson.
The prisoner. [1946].
The gift. [1947]. With E. Wynne-Tyson.

According to Gerber (Bibliography, above) Beresford wrote one unpbd play, The royal heart, *with A. S. Craven and another*, Howard and son, *with K. Richmond. Among his contributions to periodicals were frequent articles and reviews in the* Westminster Gazette *and* Aryan Path.

§2

Roberts, R. E. J. D. Beresford. Bookman (London) 58 1920.
Mais, S. P. B. In his Why we should read, 1921.
Johnson, R. B. In his Some contemporary novelists; men, 1922.
Adcock, A. St J. In his Gods of modern Grub Street, 1923.
Swinnerton, F. A. Younger novelists. In his The Georgian scene, New York [1934].
Hungerford, E. A. Mrs Woolf, Freud and Beresford. Lit & Psychology 5 1955.
Gerber, H. E. Beresford: the Freudian element. Lit & Psychology 6 1956.

'ANTHONY BERKELEY', 'FRANCIS ILES', ANTHONY BERKELEY COX
1893–1971

Brenda entertains. 1925. Stories. By A. B. Cox.
The family witch: an essay in absurdity. 1925. By A. B. Cox.
Jugged journalism. 1925. Humorous sketches. By A. B. Cox.
The Layton Court mystery. By '?'. 1925, Garden City NY 1929 (as by 'Anthony Berkeley').
The professor on paws. [1926], New York 1927. By A. B. Cox.
The Wychford poisoning case: an essay in criminology. [1926] (anon), Garden City NY 1930 (as by 'Anthony Berkeley').
Mr Priestley's problem. [1927] (by A. B. Cox), 1948 (as by 'Anthony Berkeley').
The mystery at Lovers' cave. New York 1927.
Roger Sheringham and the Vane mystery. [1927], Garden City NY 1928 (as The amateur crime).
The silk stocking murders. [1928], Garden City NY 1928.
The Piccadilly murder. [1929], Garden City NY 1929.
The poisoned chocolates case. [1929], Garden City NY 1929.
The second shot. [1930], Garden City NY [1931].
Malice aforethought: the story of a commonplace crime. 1931, New York 1931. As 'Francis Iles'.
Top storey murder. [1931], Garden City NY [1931].
Before the fact: a murder story for ladies. 1932, Garden City NY 1932, London 1958 (rev). As 'Francis Iles'.
Murder in the basement. 1932, Garden City NY [1932].
Jumping Jenny. 1933, Garden City NY 1933 (as Dead Mrs Stratton).
Lord Peter's Privy Counsel. [1933]. Story, in Ask a policeman, by 'Anthony Berkeley' and others.
O England! 1934. Sociology.
Panic party. 1934, Garden City NY 1934 (as Mr Pidgeon's island).
Trial and error. 1937, Garden City NY 1937.
Not to be taken: a puzzle in poison. 1938, New York 1938 (as A puzzle in poison).
As for the woman: a love story. [1939], New York 1939. As 'Francis Iles'.
Death in the house. 1939, New York 1939.

GERARD HUGH TYRWHITT,
later TYRWHITT-WILSON,
LORD BERNERS
1883–1950

§1

First childhood. 1934, New York [1934]. Autobiography.
The camel: a tale. 1936.
The girls of Radcliff Hall. [Faringdon] [1937] (priv ptd).
By 'Adela Quebec'.
Count Omega. 1941.
Far from the madding war. 1941.
Percy Wallingford and Mr Pidger: two stories. Oxford 1941.
The romance of a nose. 1941.
A distant prospect: a sequel to First childhood. 1945.

§2

Lord Berners. [1922] (Miniature essays). On Berners as a composer. Anon.
Bell, C. [Foreword to] Catalogue of paintings by Lord Berners. 1931.

'GEORGE A. BIRMINGHAM',
JAMES OWEN HANNAY
1865–1950

Selections

Golden sayings from George A. Birmingham. [1915].
The Birmingham bus: containing Spanish gold, The search party, Lalage's lovers, The adventures of Dr Whitty. 1934.

§1

The seething pot. 1905.
Hyacinth. 1906.
Benedict Kavanagh. 1907.
The northern iron. Dublin 1907, London [1913].
The bad times. 1908.
Spanish gold. 1908, New York 1912.
The search party. 1909.
Lalage's lovers. 1911, New York [1911].
The lighter side of Irish life. 1911. Non-fiction.
The major's niece. 1911.
The Simpkins plot. 1911, New York 1912.
Dr Whitty's patient, and Mrs Challmer's public meeting. New York [1912].
The inviolable sanctuary. 1912, New York 1912 (as Priscilla's spies).
The red hand of Ulster. 1912, New York [1912].
The adventures of Dr Whitty. 1913, New York [1913]. Stories.
General John Regan. 1913, New York [1913]; London 1933 as play.
An intolerable honour, and Hygienic and scientific apparatus. New York [1913].
Irishmen all. 1913. Non-fiction.
Miss Mulhall's lecture, and Dr Whitty's honeymoon. New York [1913].
Connaught to Chicago. 1914, New York 1914 (as From Dublin to Chicago: some notes on a tour in America).
The lost tribes. 1914, New York [1914].
Gossamer. 1915, New York [1915].
Minnie's bishop, and other stories of Ireland. 1915, New York [1915].
The island mystery. 1918, New York [1918].
A padre in France. [1918], New York [1919]. Non-fiction.
An Irishman looks at his world. 1919, New York 1919. Non-fiction.

Our casualty, and other stories. [1919], New York 1919.
Up, the rebels! 1919, New York [1919].
Good conduct. 1920.
Inisheeny. 1920.
Adventurers of the night. New York [1921].
Lady Bountiful. 1921, New York 1922. Stories.
The lost lawyer. 1921.
The great-grandmother. 1922, Indianapolis [1923].
A public scandal, and other stories. [1922].
Found money. 1923, Indianapolis [1923].
King Tommy. [1923], Indianapolis [1924].
Send for Dr O'Grady. [1923].
The Grand Duchess. [1924].
Bindon Parva. 1925, Indianapolis [1925].
The gun-runners. [1925].
A wayfarer in Hungary. 1925, New York 1925. Travel.
Goodly pearls. [1926].
The lady of the abbey. Indianapolis 1926.
The smugglers' cave. [1926], Indianapolis [1927].
Spillikins: a book of essays. 1926.
Fidgets. [1927].
Gold, gore & gehenna. Indianapolis [1927].
Now you tell one: stories of Irish wit and humour. 1927.
Ships and sealing-wax. 1927. Essays.
The runaways. 1928, Indianapolis [1928].
The major's candlesticks. 1929, Indianapolis [1929].
Murder most foul! a gallery of famous criminals. 1929.
The hymn tune mystery. 1930, Indianapolis [1931].
Wild justice. 1930, Indianapolis [1930].
Fed up. 1931, Indianapolis [1931].
Elizabeth and the archdeacon. 1932, Indianapolis [1933].
Irish short stories. Ed G. A. Birmingham 1932.
The silver-gilt standard. 1932.
Angel's adventure. 1933.
Pleasant places. 1934. Autobiography.
Two fools. 1934.
Love or money, and other stories. 1935.
Millicent's corner. 1935.
Daphne's fishing. 1937.
Isaiah. 1937.
Mrs Miller's aunt. 1937.
Magilligan Strand. 1938.
Appeasement. 1939.
God's iron: a life of the prophet Jeremiah. 1939, New York 1956 (as The prophet Jeremiah).
Miss Maitland's spy. 1940.
The search for Susie. 1941.
Over the border. 1942.
Poor Sir Edward. 1943.
Lieutenant Commander. 1944.
Good intentions. 1945.
The Piccadilly lady. 1946.
Golden apple. 1947.
A sea battle. 1948.
Laura's bishop. 1949.
Two scamps. 1950.

Hannay also wrote some theological and devotional works under his own name.

ALGERNON HENRY BLACKWOOD
1869–1951

Selections

Ancient sorceries, and other tales. 1927.
Strange stories. 1929.
Algernon Blackwood. 1930, New York 1930 (Short Stories of To-day and Yesterday).
The willows, and other queer tales. 1932.
The tales of Algernon Blackwood. 1938, New York 1939.
Selected tales of Algernon Blackwood: stories of the supernatural and the uncanny. 1942 (Penguin).
Tales of the uncanny and supernatural. 1949.
Selected tales of Algernon Blackwood. [1964].
Tales of the mysterious and macabre. 1967.

§1

The empty house, and other ghost stories. 1906, New York 1915.

The listener, and other stories. 1907, New York 1914.

John Silence, physician extraordinary. 1908, New York 1909. Stories.

The education of Uncle Paul. 1909, New York 1910. For children.

Jimbo: a fantasy. 1909, New York 1909.

The human chord. 1910, New York 1910.

The lost valley, and other stories. 1910, New York 1914.

The centaur. 1911, New York 1911.

Pan's garden: a volume of nature stories. 1912, New York 1912.

A prisoner in fairyland: the book that 'Uncle Paul' wrote. 1913, New York 1913. For children.

Incredible adventures. 1914, New York 1914. Stories.

Ten minute stories. 1914, New York 1914.

The extra day. 1915, New York 1915. For children.

Julius Le Vallon: an episode. 1916, New York 1916.

The wave: an Egyptian aftermath. 1916, New York [1916].

Day and night stories. 1917, New York [1917].

The garden of survival. 1918, New York [1918].

Karma: a re-incarnation play in prologue, epilogue and 3 acts. 1918, New York [1918]. With V. A. Pearn.

The promise of air. 1918, New York [1918].

The bright messenger. 1921, New York [1922].

The wolves of God, and other fey stories. 1921, New York [1921]. With W. Wilson.

Episodes before thirty. 1923, New York [1924], London 1934 (as Adventures before thirty). Autobiographical.

Tongues of fire, and other sketches. 1924, New York [1925].

Through the crack: a play in five scenes. [1925]. With V. A. Pearn.

The dance of death, and other tales. 1927, New York 1928.

Sambo and Snitch. Oxford [1927], New York 1927. Children's story.

Mr Cupboard. Oxford [1928]. Children's story.

Dudley & Gilderoy: a nonsense. 1929, New York [1929].

Full circle. 1929. Story.

By underground. Oxford [1930]. Children's story.

The parrot and the—cat! Oxford [1931]. Children's story; from Dudley & Gilderoy, above.

The Italian conjuror. Oxford [1932]. Children's story.

Maria—of England—in the rain. Oxford [1933]. Children's story.

The fruit stoners: being the adventures of Maria among the fruit stoners. 1934, New York 1935.

Sergeant Poppett and Policeman James. Oxford [1934]. Children's story.

The fruit stoners. Oxford [1935]. Children's story, from The fruit stoners, above.

Shocks. 1935, New York [1935]. Stories.

How the circus came to tea. Oxford [1936]. Children's story.

The doll, and one other. Sauk City Wisconsin 1946. Two stories.

§2

Gilbert, S. Blackwood: novelist and mystic. Transition no 35 1935.

Pentzoldt, P. In his The supernatural in fiction, 1952.

Hudson, D. A study of Blackwood. E & S 14 1961.

GEORGE BLAKE
1893–1961

§1

The mother. Glasgow 1921. Play.

Clyde built. Glasgow 1922. Play.

Vagabond papers. Glasgow 1922. Essays.

Mince Collop close. 1923, New York 1924.

The weaker vessel. Edinburgh 1923. Play.

The wild men. 1925.

Young Malcolm. 1926, New York 1927.

Paper money. 1928, New York 1928 (as Gettin' in society).

The coasts of Normandy. 1929. Story.

The path of glory. 1929, New York 1929.

The press and the public. 1930. Pamphlet.

The seas between. 1930.

Returned empty. 1931.

Sea tangle. 1932.

The heart of Scotland. 1934, 1951 (rev). Topography.

Rest and be thankful. Edinburgh 1934. Essays.

The shipbuilders. 1935, Philadelphia [1936].

David and Joanna. 1936, New York [1936].

Late harvest. 1938.

The valiant heart. [1940], New York 1940.

The constant star. 1945.

The westering sun. 1946.

The five arches. 1947.

Scottish affairs. 1947. Pamphlet.

The paying guest. 1949.

Mountain and flood: the history of the 52nd Lowland Division 1939–46. Glasgow 1950.

The piper's tune. 1950.

Barrie and the Kailyard school. 1951. Criticism.

The voyage home. 1952.

The innocence within. 1955.

Annals of Scotland 1895–1955: an essay on the twentieth-century Scottish novel. [1956].

The last fling. 1957.

The peacock palace. 1958.

The loves of Mary Glen. 1960.

Blake also wrote a number of books and pamphlets on ships and shipbuilding, and histories of various firms connected with shipping.

SIR DAVID WILLIAM BONE
1874–1959
Bibliographies

Skallerup, H. R. Sir David Bone 1874–1959: a selected bibliography. Bull of Bibliography 23 1963. Includes contributions to books and periodicals; also a biographical note, and references to Bone.

§1

The brassbounder. 1910, New York 1911.

'Broken stowage'. 1915, New York [1922]. Stories.

Merchantmen-at-arms. 1919, 1929 (with introd by H. M. Tomlinson), New York 1929. Non-fiction.

The lookoutman. 1923, New York [1923]. Non-fiction.

Capstan bars. Edinburgh 1931, New York [1932]. Sea-shanties, selected and elaborated by Bone.

Merchantman rearmed. 1949. Autobiography.

The Queerfella. 1952.

Landfall at sunset: the life of a contented sailor. 1955. Autobiography.

PHYLLIS BOTTOME
1884–1963
Selections

The best stories of Phyllis Bottome, chosen by D. du Maurier. 1963.

§1

Life the interpreter. 1902.

The master hope. 1904.

Raw material: some characters and episodes among working lads. 1905.
The imperfect gift. 1907.
Crooked answers. 1911. With H. de L. Brock.
The common chord. 1913.
'Broken music'. 1914, Boston 1914.
The captive. 1915.
Secretly armed. 1916, New York 1916 (as The dark tower).
A certain star. 1917.
The derelict [and other stories]. New York 1917, London 1923.
The second fiddle. New York 1917.
Helen of Troy, and Rose. New York 1918.
A servant of reality. [1919], New York 1919.
The crystal heart. New York 1921.
The kingfisher. 1922, New York [1922]. Rptd in The belated reckoning, below.
The victim, and The worm. New York [1923].
The depths of prosperity. [1924]. With Dorothy Thompson.
The perfect wife. New York [1924].
The belated reckoning. New York [1926], London [1927]. Stories.
Old wine. New York [1926], London [1926].
The rat. 1926, New York [1927]. Based on a play by I. Novello and Constance Collier.
The messenger of the gods. New York [1927].
Strange fruit: tales. [1928], Boston 1928.
Tatter'd loving. [1929], Boston 1930.
Windlestraws. [1929], Boston 1929.
Devil's due. Boston 1931, London [1931] (as Wind in his fists).
The advances of Harriet. Boston 1933, London 1933.
Innocence and experience: stories. Boston 1934, London 1935.
Private worlds. Boston 1934, London 1934.
Stella Benson. San Francisco 1934 (priv ptd). Booklet.
Level crossing. New York 1936, London 1936.
The mortal storm. 1937, Boston 1938.
Alfred Adler: a biography. New York [1939], London 1939 (as Alfred Adler: apostle of freedom).
Murder in the bud. 1939, Boston 1939 (as Danger signal).
Heart of a child. 1940, New York [1940] (as The heart of a child).
Masks and faces. 1940, Boston 1940.
Formidable to tyrants. 1941, Boston 1941 (as Mansion House of liberty). England in war-time.
London pride. 1941, Boston 1941.
Within the cup. 1943, Boston 1943 (as Survival).
Austria's contribution towards our new order. 1944. Lecture.
From the life. 1944. Biographical sketches.
Individual countries. 1946. Non-fiction.
The life line. Boston 1946, London 1946.
Search for a soul. 1947, New York 1948. Autobiography.
Fortune's finger: short stories. 1950.
Under the skin. New York [1950], London 1950.
The challenge. 1952. New York 1953. Sequel to Search for a soul, above.
Man and beast. 1953, New York 1954. Stories.
Against whom? 1954, New York 1954 (as The secret stair).
Not in our stars. 1955. Essays.
'Eldorado Jane'. 1956, New York 1957 (as Jane).
Walls of glass. 1958, New York [1958]. Stories.
The goal. 1962, New York [1962]. Autobiography.

§2

Lawrence, M. Matriarchs. In her School of femininity, New York 1936, London 1937 (as We write as women).

ELIZABETH DOROTHEA COLE BOWEN
b. 1899

Bibliographies

Heath, W. In his Elizabeth Bowen, 1961, below. Does not include non-literary works; includes list of reviews.

Collections and Selections

Selected stories. Ed R. Moore 1946.
Collected edition. 1948—.
Early stories. New York 1951. Includes Encounters and Ann Lee's.
Stories. New York 1959. A selection with preface by the author.

§1

Encounters: stories. 1923, 1949 (with preface by the author).
Ann Lee's & other stories. 1926, New York [1928].
The hotel. 1927, New York 1928.
Joining Charles, and other stories. 1929, New York 1929.
The last September. 1929, New York 1929.
Friends and relations. 1931, New York 1931.
She gave him. In Consequences: a complete story in the manner of the old parlour game in nine chapters each by a different author, Waltham St Lawrence 1932.
To the north. 1932, New York 1933.
The cat jumps, and other stories. [1934].
The house in Paris. 1935, New York 1936.
The death of the heart. 1938, New York 1939.
Look at all those roses: short stories. 1941, New York 1941.
Seven winters. Dublin 1942, London 1943, New York 1962 (with Afterthought, below). Reminiscences of childhood.
Bowen's Court. 1942, New York 1942, 1964 (with addns), London 1964. Family history.
English novelists. 1942 (Britain in pictures).
The demon lover and other stories. 1945, New York 1946 (as Ivy gripped the steps, with preface rptd in Collected impressions, below).
Anthony Trollope: a new judgment. 1946, New York 1946. Play; rptd in Collected impressions, below.
How I write my novels, by Elizabeth Bowen [et al]. 1948. Radio interviews, ed T. Jones.
Why do I write? An exchange of views between Elizabeth Bowen, Graham Greene and V. S. Pritchett. 1948, New York 1948.
The heat of the day. 1949, New York 1949.
Collected impressions. 1950, New York 1950. Essays, reviews and prefaces etc.
The Shelbourne: a centre in Dublin life for more than a century. 1951, New York 1951 (as The Shelbourne hotel).
A world of love. 1955, New York 1955.
A time in Rome. 1960, New York 1960. Travel.
Afterthought: pieces about writing. 1962, New York 1962 (with Seven winters, above).
The little girls. 1964, New York 1964.
A day in the dark and other stories. [1965].
The good tiger. New York [1965]. For children.
Eva Trout, or changing scenes. New York 1968, London 1969.

An unpbd play, Castle Anna, *written with John Perry, was first performed in London in 1948. From 1941 Miss Bowen made regular contributions to* Tatler *as its permanent book reviewer. During 1954–61 she was on the editorial board of* London Mag. *She edited the* Faber *book of modern stories, 1937. The preface to this, and to edns of works by various individual authors, were rptd in* Collected impressions *above.*

§2

Greene, Graham. The dark backward: a footnote. London Mercury 32 1935. Special reference to The house in Paris.

Daiches, D. The novels of Elizabeth Bowen. Eng Jnl 38 1949.

Hardwick, E. Elizabeth Bowen's fiction. Partisan Rev 16 1949.

Sackville-West, E. 'Ladies whose bright pens...'. In his Inclinations, 1949. On Elizabeth Bowen and Ivy Compton-Burnett.

Vallette, J. Elizabeth Bowen. Mercure de France 307 1949.

Snow, L. The uncertain 'I': a study of Elizabeth Bowen's fiction. Western Humanities Rev 4 1950.

Brooke, J. Elizabeth Bowen. 1952 (Br Council pamphlet).

Prescott, O. Comrades of the coterie: H. Green, Ivy Compton-Burnett, Elizabeth Bowen, G. Greene. In his In my opinion, Indianapolis 1952.

Strong, L. A. G. Elizabeth Bowen. In his Personal remarks, 1953.

Harkness, B. The fiction of Elizabeth Bowen. Eng Jnl 44 1955.

O'Faolain, S. Elizabeth Bowen: or romance does not pay. In his The vanishing hero, 1956.

Pendry, E. D. Elizabeth Bowen. In his The new feminism of English fiction, Tokyo [1956].

Seward, B. Elizabeth Bowen's world of impoverished love. College Eng 18 1956.

Stokes, E. Elizabeth Bowen: preassumptions or moral angle? Jnl of the Australian Univ Lang & Lit Assoc Sept 1959.

Heath, W. Elizabeth Bowen: an introduction to her novels. Madison 1961.

Van Duyn, M. Pattern and pilgrimage: a reading of The death of the heart. Critique (Minneapolis) 4 1961.

Karl, F. R. The world of Elizabeth Bowen. In his The contemporary English novel, New York 1962, London 1963 (as A reader's guide to the contemporary English novel).

Sharp, M. C. The house as setting and symbol in three novels by Elizabeth Bowen. Xavier Univ Stud 2 1963.

Wagner, G. Elizabeth Bowen and the artificial novel. EC 13 1963.

Greene, George. Elizabeth Bowen: imagination as therapy. Perspective 14 1965.

Rupp, R. H. The post-war fiction of Elizabeth Bowen. Xavier Univ Stud 4 1965.

Saul, G. B. The short stories of Elizabeth Bowen. Arizona Quart 21 1965.

Mitchell, E. Themes in Elizabeth Bowen's short stories. Critique (Minneapolis) 8 1966.

Dorenkamp, A. G. 'Fall or leap': Elizabeth Bowen's The heat of the day. Critique (Minneapolis) 10 1968.

Hall, J. The giant located: Elizabeth Bowen. In his The lunatic giant in the drawing room: the British and American novel since 1930, Bloomington 1968.

Heinemann, A. The indoor landscape in Elizabeth Bowen's The death of the heart. Critique (Minneapolis) 10 1968.

'MARJORIE BOWEN', 'GEORGE R. PREEDY', 'JOSEPH SHEARING', GABRIELLE MARGARET VERE CAMPBELL
1886–1952

This author also wrote children's books, and other fiction as 'John Winch', 'Robert Paye' and under other pseudonyms.

(1) As 'Marjorie Bowen'
Selections

Affairs of men. [1922]. Extracts from various historical novels, selected by the author.

§1

The viper of Milan. 1906, New York 1906.

The glen o' weeping. 1907, New York 1907 (as The master of Stair).

The sword decides! 1908, New York 1908. Founded on the story of Giovanna of Naples.

Black magic: a tale of the rise and fall of Antichrist. 1909.

The leopard and the lily. 1909, New York 1909.

I will maintain. 1910, New York 1911, London 1943 (rev) (Penguin).

Defender of the faith. 1911, New York 1911.

God and the king. 1911, New York 1912.

God's playthings. 1912, New York 1913. Stories.

Lovers' knots. 1912.

The quest of glory. 1912, New York 1912, London 1928 (with new preface).

The rake's progress. 1912.

The soldier from Virginia. New York 1912, London 1915 (as Mr Washington), [1925] (as The soldier from Virginia).

The governor of England. 1913, New York 1914.

A knight of Spain. 1913.

The two carnations. 1913.

Prince and heretic. 1914, New York 1915.

'Because of these things...'. 1915.

The carnival of Florence. 1915, New York 1915.

Shadows of yesterday. 1916, New York 1916. Stories.

'William, by the grace of God—'. 1916, New York 1917, London 1928 (abridged). Sequel to Prince and heretic, above.

Curious happenings. 1917. Stories.

The third estate. 1917, New York 1918.

The burning glass. 1918, New York 1919.

Kings-at-arms. 1918, New York 1919.

Crimes of old London. [1919]. Stories.

Mr Misfortunate. 1919.

The cheats. [1920].

The haunted vintage. [1921].

The pleasant husband, and other stories. [1921].

Roccoco. [1921].

The jest. [1922]. Based on Benelli's La cena delle beffe.

Seeing life!, and other stories. [1923].

Stinging nettles. 1923, Boston 1923.

The presence and the power. 1924.

Five people. 1925.

'Luctor et emergo': being an historical essay on the state of England at the Peace of Ryswyck, 1697. Newcastle-upon-Tyne 1925.

Boundless water. 1926.

Nell Gwyn. [1926], New York 1926 (as Mistress Nell Gwyn), London [1949].

The Netherlands display'd. 1926, New York 1926. Non-fiction.

The seven deadly sins. [1926]. Stories.

Dark Ann, and other stories. 1927.

'Five winds'. [1927].

The pagoda: le pagode de Chanteloup. [1927].

The countess Fanny. [1928].

The golden roof. [1928]. Pt 1 of Renaissance trilogy.

Holland, being a general survey of the Netherlands. 1928, Garden City NY 1929.

The story of the Temple and its associations. [1928].

Sundry great gentlemen. 1928, New York 1928. Biographical essays.

William, Prince of Orange. 1928, New York 1928. Biography.

Dickon. [1929].

The gorgeous lovers, and other tales. 1929.

Sheep's-head & Babylon, and other stories of yesterday and today. 1929.

The third Mary Stuart. 1929. Biography.

The English paragon. [1930].

Exits and farewells. [1930]. Historical essays.

A family comedy, 1840. [1930]. Play.

Old Patch's medley: or, a London miscellany. [1930]. Stories.

Brave employments. 1931.

Grace Latouche and the Warringtons: some nineteenth-century pieces, mostly Victorian. 1931. Stories.

The question. [1931]. Play.

Withering fires. 1931.

Dark Rosaleen. 1932, Boston 1933.

Fond fancy, and other stories. [1932].

Passion flower. [1932].

The shadow on Mockways. [1932].

I dwelt in high places. 1933.

The last bouquet. 1933. Stories.

'Set with green herbs...'. 1933.

The stolen bride. 1933, [1946] (abridged).

The veil'd delight. [1933].

Mary Queen of Scots, daughter of debate. 1934, New York 1935. Biography.

The scandal of Sophie Dawes. 1934, New York 1935. Non-fiction.

The triumphant beast. 1934. Pt 2 of Renaissance trilogy.

Patriotic lady: a study of Emma, Lady Hamilton. 1935, New York 1936.

Peter Porcupine: a study of William Cobbett, 1762–1835. 1935, New York 1935.

Trumpets at Rome. [1936]. Pt 3 of Renaissance trilogy.

William Hogarth, the cockney's mirror. 1936, New York 1936.

Crowns and sceptres: the romance & pageantry of coronations. 1937.

Wrestling Jacob: a study of the life of John Wesley and some members of his family. 1937, 1948 (abridged).

A giant in chains: prelude to revolution—France 1775–91. [1938]. Fiction.

God and the wedding dress. [1938]. Pt 1 of a trilogy.

World's wonder, and other essays. [1938].

The debate continues: being the autobiography of Marjorie Bowen, by Margaret Campbell. 1939.

Ethics in modern art. 1939. Lecture.

Mr Tyler's saints. [1939]. Pt 2 of a trilogy.

The circle in the water. [1939]. Pt 3 of a trilogy.

Exchange Royal. [1940].

Strangers to freedom. 1940.

Today is mine. [1941].

The Church and social progress: an exposition of rationalism and reaction. 1945.

The bishop of hell, and other stories. 1949.

The life of John Knox. 1949. First pbd 1940, as by George R. Preedy.

In the steps of Mary Queen of Scots. 1952. Non-fiction.

The man with the scales. 1954.

(2) As 'George Preedy' or 'George R. Preedy'

General Crack. 1928, New York 1928.

Bagatelle, and some other diversions. 1930, New York 1931. Stories.

Captain Banner. 1930. Play.

The Rocklitz. 1930, New York 1930 (as The prince's darling).

Tumult in the north. 1931, New York 1931.

The devil snar'd. 1932.

The pavilion of honour. 1932.

Violante: Circe and the ermine. 1932.

Dr Chaos and The devil snar'd. 1933.

Double Dallilay. 1933, New York 1934 (as Queen's caprice).

The knot garden. 1933. Stories.

The autobiography of Cornelis Blake, 1773–1810, of Ditton See, Cambridgeshire. 1934. Fiction.

Laurell'd captains. [1935].

The poisoners. [1936].

My tattered loving: the Overbury mystery. 1937.

This shining woman: Mary Wollstonecraft Godwin 1759–97. 1937, New York 1937.

Painted angel. 1938.

Child of chequer'd fortune. 1939. Biography of Marshal de Saxe.

Dove in the mulberry tree. 1939.

The fair young widow. 1939.

The life of John Knox. 1940, 1949 (as by 'Marjorie Bowen').

The life of Rear-Admiral John Paul Jones 1747–92. 1940.

Primula. 1940.

Black man—white maiden. 1941.

Findernes' flowers. 1941.

The courtly charlatan: the enigmatic Comte de St Germain. [1942].

Lyndley waters. 1942.

Lady in a veil. 1943.

The fourth chamber. 1944.

Nightcap and plume. 1945.

No way home. 1947.

The sacked city. 1949.

Julia Ballantyne. 1952.

(3) As 'Joseph Shearing'

Forget-me-not. 1932, New York 1932 (as Lucile Cléry), 1941 (as The strange case of Lucile Cléry).

Album leaf. 1933, New York 1934 (as The spider in the cup).

Moss rose. 1934, New York 1935.

The angel of the assassination. 1935, New York 1935. On Charlotte Corday.

The golden violet. 1936, New York 1941.

The lady and the arsenic. 1937, New York 1944. On Marie Lafarge.

Orange blossoms. 1938. Stories.

Blanche Fury. [1939], New York 1939.

Aunt Beardie. [1940], New York 1941.

Laura Sarelle. 1940, New York 1941 (as The crime of Laura Sarelle).

The fetch. 1942, New York 1942 (as The spectral bride).

Airing in a closed carriage. [1943], New York 1943.

The abode of love. [1945].

For her to see. [1947], New York 1947 (as So evil my love).

Mignonette. New York 1948, London 1949.

Within the bubble. 1950.

To bed at noon. 1951.

'ERNEST BRAMAH',
ERNEST BRAMAH SMITH
1869?–1942

Some of Bramah's mss, typescripts, galleys and page-proofs are in the Humanities Research Center of the Univ of Texas. See W. White, A Bramah biographer's dilemma, below.

Bibliographies

White, W. Some uncollected authors xxxvii: Bramah. Book Collector 13 1964.

Selections

Ernest Bramah. 1929. (Short stories of today and yesterday.) 4 stories from Kai Lung's golden hours, 3 from Max Carrados mysteries, 4 from The specimen case.

The Kai Lung omnibus. 1936. Contains The wallet of Kai Lung, Kai Lung unrolls his mat, and Kai Lung's golden hours.

§1

English farming and why I turned it up. 1894. Autobiographical.

The wallet of Kai Lung. 1900, Boston 1900, London 1923 (with introd by G. Richards). Stories.

The mirror of Kung Ho. 1905, 1929 (with preface by J. C. Squire), New York 1930.

What might have been: the story of a social war. 1907, 1909 (as The secret of the league).

The transmutation of Ling. 1911, New York 1912. Story, first pbd in The wallet of Kai Lung.

Max Carrados. 1914. Detective stories.

Kai Lung's golden hours. With a preface by H. Belloc 1922, New York 1923. Stories.

The eyes of Max Carrados. 1923, New York 1924. Detective stories.

The specimen case. 1924, New York 1925. Stories.

Max Carrados mysteries. 1927. Detective stories.

The story of Wan and the remarkable shrub, and The story of Ching-kwei and the destinies. New York 1927. Both rptd in Kai Lung unrolls his mat.

Kai Lung unrolls his mat. 1928, New York 1928. Stories.

A guide to the varieties and rarity of English regal copper coins: Charles II–Victoria, 1671–1860. 1929.

A little flutter. 1930.

The moon of much gladness, related by Kai Lung. 1932, New York 1937 (as The return of Kai Lung).

The bravo of London. 1934.

Kai Lung beneath the mulberry tree. 1940. Stories.

§2

Mais, S. P. B. In his Some modern authors, 1923.

Richards, G. Author hunting by an old literary sportsman. 1934.

White, W. Kai Lung in America: the critical reception of Bramah. Amer Book Collector 9 1959.

—— A Bramah biographer's dilemma. Amer Book Collector 15 1965.

—— Quest for Bramah: a study in literary detection. In Themes and essays in commemoration of the 70th anniversary of Soong Sil College, Seoul 1967.

JOHN BROPHY
1899–1965

Selections

Selected stories. 1946.

§1

The bitter end. [1928], New York [1928].

Peter Lavelle. 1929, New York 1929.

Pluck the flower. [1929], New York [1929].

Fanfare, and other papers. 1930.

Flesh and blood. 1931.

Thunderclap. 1931.

English prose. 1932.

The rocky road. 1932.

Waterfront. 1934, New York 1934, London 1950 (rev).

The world went mad. 1934, New York [1934].

I let him go. 1935.

The five years: a conspectus of the Great War. 1936.

Ilonka speaks of Hungary. 1936. Non-fiction.

The ramparts of virtue. 1936.

Behold the judge. 1937.

Felicity Greene: the story of a success. 1937.

Man, woman and child. 1938, 1955 (rev, as City of scandals).

Gentleman of Stratford. [1939], New York 1940.

The queer fellow: stories. [1939].

The ridiculous hat. 1939.

Green glory. [1940]. Rptd (rev) in Soldiers of the queen, below.

Green ladies. 1940. Rptd (rev) in Soldiers of the queen, below.

Solitude island. 1941.

Britain needs books. 1942. Booklet.

Immortal sergeant. 1942, New York 1942.

Spear head. 1943, New York 1943.

Target island. 1944.

Britain's Home Guard: a character study. 1945.

The human face. 1945, New York 1946. Non-fiction.

Portrait of an unknown lady. 1945.

City of departures. 1946.

The woman from nowhere. 1946.

Body and soul. 1948. Non-fiction.

Sarah. 1948.

Julian's way. 1949.

The mind's eye: a twelve-month journal. 1949. Non-fiction.

Turn the key softly. 1951.

Windfall. 1951.

Somerset Maugham. 1952, 1958 (rev) (Br Council pamphlet).

The prime of life. 1954.

The nimble rabbit. 1955.

The prince and Petronella. 1956.

Soldiers of the queen. 1957. Contains Green glory and Green ladies, above (rev).

The day they robbed the Bank of England. 1959.

The front door key. 1960.

The human face reconsidered. 1962.

The face in western art. 1963.

The meaning of murder. 1966.

Brophy also wrote a number of manuals for the Home Guard during the Second World War.

JOHN BUCHAN,
1st BARON TWEEDSMUIR
1875–1940

Numerous mss are in the Buchan collection at Queen's University Kingston (Ontario). See Wilmot, Bibliographies, below.

Bibliographies

Hanna, A. John Buchan 1875–1940: a bibliography. Hamden Conn 1953. Includes contributions to books and periodicals, and a checklist of criticism and trns of Buchan's works.

—— A Buchan collection [Beinecke collection, Yale]. Yale Univ Lib Gazette 37 1962.

Wilmot, B. C. A checklist of works by and about Buchan in the Buchan collection, Queen's University, Kingston Ontario 1958. Includes mss of pbd and unpbd works.

Cox, J. R. John Buchan, Lord Tweedsmuir: an annotated bibliography of writings about him. Eng Lit in Transition 9 1966. Exhaustive; mostly reviews and press notices.

—— Ibid 10 1967. Books, articles and reviews.

Collections and Selections

The thirty-nine steps and other tales. Paris [1917]. Also contains The power-house; The king of Ypres; Basilissa; Divus Johnston. (Nelson's Continental Library).

The thirty-nine steps and The power-house. [1922].

The four adventures of Richard Hannay. [1930]. Contains The thirty-nine steps; Greenmantle; Mr Standfast; The three hostages.

The adventures of Sir Edward Leithen. [1933]. Contains Sing a song of sixpence; The power-house; The dancing floor; John Macnab; The gap in the curtain.

Men and deeds. 1935. Contains The causal and the casual in history; Julius Caesar; The massacre of Glencoe; Gordon at Khartoum; Montrose and leadership; Lord Rosebery; The Kirk in Scotland.

Four tales. Edinburgh 1936. Contains The thirty-nine steps; The power-house; The watcher by the threshold; The moon endureth.

The adventures of Dickson McCunn. 1937. Contains Huntingtower; Castle Gay; The house of the four winds.

Five-fold salute to adventure: an omnibus volume of historical novels. 1939. Contains The blanket of the dark; Witch wood; Salute to adventurers; Midwinter; The free fishers.

Adventurers of Richard Hannay. Boston 1939. Contains The thirty-nine steps; Greenmantle; Mr Standfast.

Adventurers all: Sir Richard Hannay, Sir Edward Leithen [et al]. Boston 1942. Contains Huntingtower; John Macnab; The three hostages.

The clearing house; a survey of one man's mind: a selection from the writings of John Buchan arranged by Lady Tweedsmuir, with preface by Gilbert Murray. 1946.

Life's adventure: extracts from the works of Buchan compiled by S. Tweedsmuir. 1947.

The power-house and The frying-pan and the fire. 1961. Second item first pbd in The Runagates Club, 1928.

§ 1

For details (incomplete) of the first pbn of Buchan's fiction in magazines see Hanna, Bibliographies, above. See also J. A. Smith, Buchan: a biography, 1965, §2, below.

Sir Quixote of the moors: being some account of an episode in the life of the Sieur de Rohaine. 1895, New York 1895.

Scholar gipsies. 1896. Essays.

Sir Walter Raleigh: the Stanhope essay. 1897. Oxford 1897.

John Burnet of Barns: a romance. 1898, New York 1898.

The Pilgrim Fathers: the Newdigate prize poem, 1898. Oxford 1898.

Brasenose College. 1898 (College histories: Oxford).

Grey weather: moorland tales of my own people. 1899.

A lost lady of old years: a romance. 1899.

The half-hearted. 1900, Boston 1900.

The watcher by the threshold, and other tales. Edinburgh 1902, New York 1918 (with additional tales).

The African colony: studies in the reconstruction. Edinburgh 1903.

The law relating to the taxation of foreign income. 1905.

A lodge in the wilderness. Edinburgh 1906. Anon.

Some eighteenth century byways, and other essays. Edinburgh 1908.

Prester John. 1910, New York 1910 (as The great diamond pipe).

Sir Walter Raleigh. 1911, New York 1911. For children.

The moon endureth: tales and fancies. Edinburgh 1912, New York 1912 (omitting several tales).

The marquis of Montrose. 1913, New York [1913].

Andrew Jameson, Lord Ardwall. Edinburgh 1913.

Britain's war by land. [1915] (Oxford pamphlets 1914–15).

Nelson's history of the war. [1915–19] (24 vols), [1921–2] (4 vols, as A history of the Great War), Boston 1922 (8 vols autographed edn, 4 vols standard edn).

The battle of Jutland. [1916]. A ch from Nelson's history of the war, above.

The battle of the Somme. [1916, 1917], New York [1917]. Chs from Nelson's history of the war, above.

A history of the British navy during the war. Adapted from Buchan's History of the war by H. C. O'Neill, 1918.

Episodes of the Great War. 1936. This and the next two items are selections from History of the war, above.

Naval episodes of the Great War. 1938.

Unchanging Germany. [1939].

The achievement of France. 1915. Articles rptd from Times.

The thirty-nine steps. Edinburgh 1915, New York 1915.

Salute to adventurers. [1915], Boston 1915.

Ordeal by marriage: an eclogue. 1915.

The power-house. Edinburgh 1916, New York [1916].

The battle of Jutland. 1916. *See* Nelson's history of the war 1915–19, above.

Greenmantle. 1916, New York 1916.

The battle of the Somme. [1916–17]. *See* Nelson's History of the war, above.

The British front in the west. 1916. Pamphlet.

Poems, Scots and English. 1917, 1936 (rev and enlarged).

A history of the British navy during the war. 1918. *See* Nelson's history of the war [1915–19], above.

Mr Standfast. 1918, New York 1919.

These for remembrance. 1919 (priv ptd). Reminiscences of friends killed in the war.

The island of sheep, by 'Cadmus' and 'Harmonia' [i.e. John and Susan Buchan]. 1919, Boston 1920. Non-fiction: for novel of same title, *see* 1936.

The battle-honours of Scotland, 1914–18. Glasgow [1919].

The history of the South African forces in France. [1920].

Francis and Riversdale Grenfell: a memoir. 1920.

The path of the king. [1921], New York 1921.

Huntingtower. 1922, New York [1922].

A book of escapes and hurried journeys. 1922, Boston 1923.

The last secrets: the final mysteries of exploration. 1923, Boston 1924.

Midwinter: certain travellers in old England. [1923], New York [1923].

Days to remember: the British empire in the Great War. 1923. With H. Newbolt.

Some notes on Sir Walter Scott. 1924 (Eng Assoc pamphlet).

The three hostages. [1924], Boston 1924.

Lord Minto: a memoir. 1924.

The history of the Royal Scots Fusiliers 1678–1918. 1925.

John Macnab. 1925, Boston 1925.

The man and the book: Sir Walter Scott. 1925.

Two ordeals of democracy. Boston 1925. Lecture, On the American Civil War and the First World War.

The dancing floor. 1926, Boston 1926.

Homilies and recreations. [1926]. Essays.

Witch wood. 1927, Boston 1927.

The Runagates Club. 1928, Boston 1928. Stories.

Montrose. 1928, Boston 1928, London 1957 (WC, with introd by K. Feiling).

The courts of the morning. 1929, Boston 1929.

The causal and the casual in history. Cambridge 1929 (Rede lecture).

The Kirk in Scotland 1560–1929. [1930].

Montrose and leadership. 1930 (Walker Trust lectures on leadership 1).

The revision of dogmas. Ashridge [1930?]. Lecture.

Castle Gay. 1930, Boston 1930.

Lord Rosebery 1847–1930. 1930. Rptd from Proc Br Acad.

The blanket of the dark. 1931, Boston 1931.

The novel and the fairy tale. 1931 (Eng Assoc pamphlet).

Sir Walter Scott. 1932, New York 1932.

The gap in the curtain. 1932, Boston 1932.

Julius Caesar. 1932, New York 1932.

The magic walking-stick. 1932, Boston 1932.

The massacre of Glencoe. 1933, New York 1933.

A prince of the captivity. 1933, Boston 1933.

Andrew Lang and the border. 1933 (Andrew Lang lecture 1932).

The margins of life. 1933 (Birkbeck College foundation oration).

The free fishers. 1934, Boston 1934.

Gordon at Khartoum. 1934.

Oliver Cromwell. 1934, Boston 1934.

The King's grace: 1910–35. 1935, Boston 1935 (as The people's king: George V), London 1936 (with second epilogue).

The house of the four winds. 1935, Boston 1935.

Episodes of the Great War. 1936. *See* Nelson's history of the war 1915–19, above.

The island of sheep. 1936, Boston 1936 (as The man from the Norlands).

Augustus. 1937, Boston 1937.
Naval episodes of the Great War. 1938. *See* Nelson's history of the war 1915–19, above.
Unchanging Germany. 1939. *See* Nelson's history of the war 1915–19, above.
Memory hold-the-door. 1940, Boston 1940 (as Pilgrim's way: an essay in recollection). Autobiography. The ch My America was rptd by the British Library of Information, New York 1940.
Comments and characters, ed with an introd by W. F. Gray. 1940. A selection of Buchan's contributions to the Scottish Rev.
Canadian occasions: addresses by Lord Tweedsmuir. Toronto 1940, London 1941.
Sick heart river. 1941, Boston 1941 (as Mountain meadow, with introduction by H. Swiggett).
The long traverse. 1941, Boston 1941 (as Lake of gold).

Many more of Buchan's political and other public addresses were pbd separately as pamphlets. See Hanna, Bibliography, above. Buchan edited The northern muse: an anthology of Scots vernacular poetry *1922, and* The long road to victory *and* Great hours in sport, *the latter two anthologies forming the 2 vols of* John Buchan's Annual, *1920, 1921. Buchan also edited* The nature of to-day: a new history of the world, *12 vols 1923, 1924. As chief literary adviser and, later, director of Thomas Nelson & Son 1907–29 Buchan edited a number of that publisher's series and encyclopaedias. See J. A. Smith,* Buchan: a biography, *1965, below. For other books ed Buchan see Hanna, Bibliographies, above. Buchan was on the staff of* Spectator *1903–6, edited* Scottish Rev *1907–8, wrote the 'Atticus' column in* Sunday Times *1930–35 and a fortnightly article in* Graphic *1930–2.*

§2

Hodge, D. John Buchan. Bookman (London) 51 1916.
Collins, J. P. The idealism of Buchan. Bookman (London) 62 1922.
Adcock, A. St J. In his Gods of modern Grub Street, 1923.
'MacDiarmid, Hugh' (C. M. Grieve). John Buchan. Scottish Educational Jnl 19 June 1925. Rptd in his Contemporary Scottish Studies, 1926.
Lockhart, J. G. John Buchan, M.P. In his The feet of the young men, 1928.
Church, L. F. John Buchan. London Quart & Holborn Rev 165 1940.
N., G. A scholar-gipsy who became viceroy. Friends' Quart Examiner 74 1940.
Greene, G. The last Buchan. Spectator 18 May 1941. Rptd in his The lost childhood, 1951.
Hankins, K. John Buchan classicist. Classical Jnl 37 1941.
Greenslet, F. Portrait of a friend. In his Under the bridge, Boston 1943.
'Douglas, O.' (A. Buchan). In her Unforgettable, unforgotten, 1945.
Buchan, S. et al. Buchan, by his wife and friends. 1947.
Moskowitz, S. Buchan: a possible influence on Lovecraft. Fantasy Commentator 2 1948.
Turner, A. C. Mr Buchan, writer. 1949.
Usborne, R. Clubland heroes: a nostalgic study of some recurrent characters in the romantic fiction of Dornford Yates, Buchan and Sapper. 1953.
Markham, V. A man of many gifts. In her Friendship's harvest, 1956.
Bloomingdale, L. G. Buchan: author and statesman. Books at Brown 18 1958.
Raymond, J. The novels of Buchan. In his England's on the anvil! 1958.
Himmelfarb, G. Buchan: an untimely appreciation. Encounter 15 1960.
—— Buchan, the last Victorian. In her Victorian minds, 1968.
Ridley, M. R. A misrated author? In his Second thoughts, 1965.

Schubert, L. Almost real reality: Buchan's visible world. Serif 2 1965.
Smith, J. A. Buchan: a biography. 1965.
Cox, J. R. The genie and his pen: the fiction of Buchan. Eng Lit in Transition 9 1966.
Scott, J. D. Buchan and the British Guermantes. New Republic 30 April 1966.
Weaver, R. Visible devils. Reporter 10 March 1966. Evil in Buchan.
Sandison, A. In his Wheel of empire, 1967.

GERALD WILLIAM BULLETT
1893–1958
Collections and Selections
Gerald Bullett. 1929 (Short Stories of Today and Yesterday). Selection.
Twenty-four tales. 1938. Selected by the author, and includes 5 previously unpbd stories.
Selected stories. Dublin 1947.
Collected poems. Preface by E. M. W. Tillyard 1959.

§1

Dreams o' mine. 1915. Verse.
The progress of Kay: a series of glimpses. 1916.
Mice, & other poems. Cambridge 1921.
The innocence of G. K. Chesterton. 1923.
The street of the eye, and nine other tales. 1923.
Mr Godly beside himself. 1924, New York 1925, London 1926 (as play).
Walt Whitman: a study and a selection. 1924.
The baker's cart, and other tales. 1925.
Modern English fiction: a personal view. 1926.
The panther. 1926.
The Spanish caravel. 1927, 1935 (as The happy mariners), New York 1936. Story for children.
Dreaming. 1928, New York 1929. Essay.
The history of Egg Pandervil: a pure fiction. 1928, New York 1929. Rptd in The Pandervils, below.
The world in bud: tales. 1928.
Nicky, son of Egg. 1929, New York 1929. Rptd in The Pandervils, below.
Germany. 1930.
The Pandervils. 1930, 1943 (rev).
Marden Fee. 1931, New York 1931.
Remember Mrs Munch. 1931.
Helen's lovers, and other tales. 1932.
I'll tell you everything: a frolic. 1933, New York 1933. With J. B. Priestley.
The quick and the dead. 1933, New York 1933.
The bubble: a satire on the world of letters. 1934. Verse.
Eden river. 1934.
The jury. 1935, New York 1935, London 1957 (rev).
The story of English literature. 1935.
The snare of the fowler. 1936, New York 1936.
Poems in pencil. 1937.
The bending sickle. 1938, New York 1938.
Problems of religion. 1938.
A man of forty. 1940, New York 1940.
When the cat's away. 1940, New York 1941.
Winter solstice. Cambridge 1943.
Achievement in feeding Britain. [1944].
The Elderbrook brothers. 1945.
The golden year of Fan Cheng-ta: a Chinese rural sequence. Cambridge 1946.
Judgment in suspense. 1946.
George Eliot: her life and books. 1947.
Men at high table & The house of strangers. 1948.
Cricket in heaven. 1949.
Poems. Cambridge 1949.
The English mystics. 1950.
Sydney Smith: a biography & a selection. 1951.
News from the village. Cambridge 1952. Verse.

The trouble at Number seven. 1952.
The alderman's son. 1954.
Windows on a vanished time. 1955.
One man's poison. 1956. As 'Sebastian Fox'. Detective
story.
The daughters of Mrs Peacock. 1957.
Odd woman out. 1958. As 'Sebastian Fox'. Detective
story.
The Peacock brides. 1958.
Ten-minute tales, and some others. Foreword by S.
Jameson 1959.

THOMAS BURKE
1886–1945

Bibliographies
'Gawsworth, John' (T. I. F. Armstrong). In his Ten
contemporaries: notes toward their definitive bibliography, ser 2 1933. With prefatory essay by Burke.

Selections
Broken blossoms: a selection of stories from Limehouse
nights. 1920.
In Chinatown: more stories from Limehouse nights. 1921.
Thomas Burke. 1928 (Essays of Today and Yesterday).
The best stories of Thomas Burke. Ed 'John Gawsworth'
(T. I. F. Armstrong) 1950.

§1
Verses. [1910] (priv ptd, 25 copies).
Pavements and pastures: a book of songs. [1912] (priv ptd,
100 copies).
Nights in town: a London autobiography. 1915, New
York 1916 (as Nights in London). Essays.
Limehouse nights: tales of Chinatown. 1917 (for 1916),
New York 1917.
London lamps: a book of songs. 1917.
Twinkletoes: a tale of Chinatown. 1917, New York 1918.
Out and about: a note-book of London in war-time. 1919,
New York 1919 (as Out and about London).
The song book of Quong Lee of Limehouse. 1920, New
York 1920.
The outer circle: rambles in remote London. 1921, New
York 1921.
Whispering windows: tales of the waterside. 1921, New
York [1921] (as More Limehouse nights).
The London spy: a book of town travels. 1922, New York
[1922].
The wind and the rain: a book of confessions. 1924, New
York [1924].
East of Mansion House. New York [1926], London 1928.
Stories.
The sun in splendour. New York [1926], London 1927.
The Bloomsbury wonder. 1929. Stories.
The flower of life. 1929, Garden City NY 1930.
The English inn. 1930, 1931 (with introd by A. P.
Herbert), 1947 (rev).
The pleasantries of Old Quong. 1931, Boston 1931 (as
A tea-shop in Limehouse). Stories.
Go, lovely rose. New York 1931 (100 copies).
City of encounters: a London divertissement. 1932, Boston
1932. Essays.
The real East End. 1932. Essays.
The beauty of England. 1933.
London in my time. 1934.
Billy and Beryl in Chinatown. 1935. For children.
Night pieces: eighteen tales. 1935.
Billy and Beryl in old London. 1936. For children.
Billy and Beryl in Soho. 1936. For children.
Murder at Elstree: or, Mr Thurtell and his gig. 1936.
Vagabond minstrel: the adventures of Thomas Dermody.
1936.
Will someone lead me to a pub? 1936. Essays.

Dinner is served! or, eating round the world in London.
1937.
The Winsome Wench: a story of a London inn 1825–1900.
1938. Fiction.
Abduction: a story of Limehouse. 1939.
Living in Bloomsbury. 1939. Essays.
The streets of London through the centuries. 1940, New
York 1940.
English night-life from Norman curfew to present black-
out. 1941, New York 1946.
Victorian grotesque. 1941.
Travel in England from pilgrim and pack-horse to light
car and plane. 1942, New York 1946.
English inns. 1943 (Britain in Pictures).
Dark nights. [1944]. Stories.
The English and their country. [1945].
The English townsman, as he was and as he is. 1946, New
York 1947.
Son of London. [1946]. Essays and reminiscences.
Burke also edited prose and verse anthologies.

§2
Adcock, A. St J. In his The glory that was Grub Street,
1928.

MARY FRANCIS BUTTS
1892–1937

§1
Speed the plough, and other stories. 1923.
Ashe of Rings. Paris 1925, New York 1926, London 1933
(rev).
Armed with madness. 1928, New York 1928.
Imaginary letters. Paris 1928 (250 copies).
Death of Felicity Taverner. 1932.
Several occasions. 1932. Stories.
Traps for unbelievers. 1932. Essay.
Warning to hikers. 1932. Pamphlet; non-fiction.
The Macedonian. 1933.
Scenes from the life of Cleopatra. 1935. Fiction.
The crystal cabinet: my childhood at Salterns. 1937.
Last stories. 1938.

§2
Hope, D. Mary Butts, fire-bearer. 1937 (Sennen pamphlet
1).

ARTHUR CALDER-MARSHALL
b. 1908

About Levy. 1933, New York 1934.
Two of a kind. 1933.
At sea. 1934, New York 1934.
A crime against Cania. 1934 (250 copies). Story.
Challenge to schools: a pamphlet on public school
education. 1935.
Dead centre. 1935.
A pink doll. 1935 (285 copies). Story.
The changing scene. 1937. Essays on contemporary
English society.
A date with a duchess, and other stories. 1937.
Pie in the sky. 1937, New York 1937.
Glory dead. 1939. Impressions of Trinidad.
The way to Santiago. 1940, New York [1940].
The book front. 1947. Non-fiction.
The watershed. 1947. Experiences in Yugoslavia
1945–6.
A man reprieved. 1949.
The magic of my youth. 1951. Reminiscences.

Occasion of glory. 1955.

No earthly command: being an enquiry into the life of Vice-Admiral the Reverend Alexander Riall Wadham Woods. 1957.

The man from Devil's Island. 1958.

The fair to middling: a mystery. 1959.

Havelock Ellis: a biography. 1959, New York 1960 (as The sage of sex).

Lone wolf: the story of Jack London. 1961, New York 1962.

The scarlet boy. 1961, New York 1962.

The enthusiast: an enquiry into the life [etc] of the Rev Joseph Leycester Lyne, alias Fr Ignatius. 1962.

The innocent eye: the life of Robert J. Flaherty. 1963.

Wish you were here: the art of Donald McGill. 1966.

GILBERT CANNAN
1884-1955

§1

Peter Homunculus. 1909, New York 1909.

Devious ways. 1910.

Little brother. 1912.

Four plays: James and John (Haymarket 27 March 1911); Miles Dixon, (Gaiety, Manchester 21 Nov 1910); Mary's wedding (Coronet 6 May 1912); A short way with authors (Cosmopolis 26 May 1913). 1913, Boston [1920] (separately).

The joy of the theatre. 1913.

Round the corner: being the life and death of Francis Christopher Folyat. 1913, New York 1913.

Love. 1914. Non-fiction.

Old Mole: being the surprising adventures in England of Herbert Jocelyn Beenham M.A. 1914, New York 1914.

Satire. [1914]. Non-fiction.

Adventurous love, and other verses. 1915.

Samuel Butler: a critical study. 1915.

Windmills: a book of fables. 1915.

Young Earnest: the romance of a bad start in life. 1915, New York 1915.

Mendel: a story of youth. 1916, New York [1916].

Three pretty men. 1916, New York [1916] (as Three sons and a mother).

Everybody's husband. (Birmingham Repertory 14 April 1917). 1917, [1927] (French's Acting edn). Play, rptd in Seven plays, 1923, below.

Freedom, 1917. Non-fiction.

Noel: an epic in ten cantos. 3 pts [1917-18] [only cantos 1-4 pbd], 1922 (as Noel: an epic in seven cantos).

The stucco house. 1917, New York 1918.

Mummery: a tale of three idealists. [1918], New York [1919].

The anatomy of society. 1919. Non-fiction.

Pink roses. 1919, New York [1919].

Time and eternity: a tale of three exiles. 1919, New York 1920.

The release of the soul. 1920. Essay.

Pugs and peacocks. [1921].

Annette and Bennett. [1922], New York 1923.

Sembal. [1922], New York 1924.

Letters from a distance. 1923. Articles rptd from New York Freeman.

Seven plays. 1923. Everybody's husband; The fat kine and the lean; In the park; Someone to whisper to; The same story; Pierrot in hospital; The polite art of conversation.

The house of prophecy. 1924, New York 1924.

Cannan also made a number of trns from the French, including Rolland, Jean Christophe, and Russian and German. He was dramatic critic of the Star 1909-10.

§2

Goldring, D. In his Reputations, 1920.

Johnson, R. B. In his Some contemporary novelists: men, 1922.

Mais, S. P. B. In his Some modern authors, 1923.

CATHERINE ROXBURGH CARSWELL, née MACFARLANE
1879-1946

Open the door! 1920, New York 1920.

The camomile: an invention. 1922, New York [1922].

The life of Robert Burns. 1930, New York [1931], London 1951 (with additional illustrations).

The savage pilgrimage: a narrative of D. H. Lawrence. 1932, 1932 (rev), New York [1932]. *See* Murry, J. M., Murry and Mrs Carswell, in his Reminiscences of D. H. Lawrence, 1933. The first edn of The savage pilgrimage was withdrawn.

Robert Burns. 1933, New York 1933.

The Fays of the Abbey Theatre. 1935. With W. G. Fay.

The tranquil heart: portrait of Giovanni Boccaccio. 1937, New York [1937].

Lying awake: an unfinished autobiography and other posthumous papers. Ed with introd by J. Carswell 1950.

ARTHUR JOYCE LUNEL CARY
1888-1957

The James M. Osborn collection of Cary mss is in the Bodleian Library. See A. Wright, Cary's unpublished work, London Mag 5 1958, and Cary: fragments of an oeuvre, International Literary Annual 1 1958.

Bibliographies

Wright, A. In his Joyce Cary, 1958.

Meriwether, J. B. The books of Cary: a preliminary bibliography of English and American editions. Texas Stud in Lit & Lang 1 1959.

Bloom, R. In his The indeterminate world: a study of the novels of Cary. Philadelphia [1962].

Beebe, M. et al. Criticism of Cary: a selected checklist. Modern Fiction Stud 9 1963.

Reed, P. J. Cary: a selected checklist of criticism. Bull of Bibliography 25 1968.

Fisher, B. Cary's published writings. Bodleian Lib Record 8 1970.

Collections

Carfax edition. 1951-. Reprints of the novels, with a prefatory essay by the author to each novel up to and including Prisoner of grace (the last pbd in this edn during the author's lifetime).

The case for African freedom and other writings on Africa. Ed C. Fyfe, Austin [1962].

§1

Verse. Edinburgh 1908. Signed: Arthur Cary.

Aissa saved. 1932, New York [1962].

An American visitor. 1933, New York 1961.

The African witch. 1936, New York 1936.

Castle Corner. 1938, New York 1963.

Power in men. 1939, Seattle 1963 (with introd by H. Adams). Non-fiction.

Mister Johnson. 1939 [1951] (with prefatory essay by Cary rptd in the Carfax edn).

Charley is my darling. 1940, New York 1960.

A house of children. 1941, New York [1956].

The case for African freedom. 1941 (with foreword by 'George Orwell'), 1944 (rev, omitting foreword).

Herself surprised. 1941, New York 1948, 1961 (with critical and biographical material by A. Wright). First bk of a trilogy.

To be a pilgrim. 1942 New York 1949. 2nd bk of a trilogy.

Process of real freedom. 1943. Pamphlet.

The horse's mouth. 1944, New York 1950, London 1957 (rev, with the preface to the Carfax edn and the discarded ch The old strife at Plant's, ed A. Wright), New York 1959 (with introd by A. Wright). 3rd bk of a trilogy.

Marching soldier. 1945. Verse.

The moonlight. 1946, New York 1947.

Britain and West Africa. 1946, 1947 (rev).

The drunken sailor: a ballad-epic. 1947.

A fearful joy. 1949, New York [1950].

Prisoner of grace. 1952, New York 1952. First bk of a trilogy.

Except the Lord. New York 1953, London 1953. 2nd bk of a trilogy.

Not honour more. 1955, New York 1955. 3rd bk of a trilogy.

The old strife at Plant's. Oxford 1956 (priv ptd, 100 copies). A discarded ch from The horse's mouth. Rptd in the 1957 edn of the novel.

Art & reality. Cambridge 1958, New York 1958. Clark lectures, 1956.

First trilogy. New York [1958]. Contains Herself surprised; To be a pilgrim; The horse's mouth. With preface by Cary.

The captive and the free. Introd D. Cecil, ed W. Davin, New York 1959, London 1959.

Spring song and other stories. 1960, New York 1960. With 5 hitherto unpbd stories.

Memoir of the Bobotes. Austin 1960 (introd J. B. Meriwether), London 1964 (foreword by W. Allen). Reminiscences of the First Balkan War.

Cary also pbd, under the pseudonym 'Thomas Joyce', 10 short stories in the Saturday Evening Post, *1920, 3 in* Strand Mag *1921 and 1923, and 1 in* Hutchinson's Mag *1921. Not rptd in* Spring Song *1960.*

§2

Johnson, P. H. Joyce Cary. Modern Reading 16 1947; rptd in Little reviews anthology, ed D. V. Baker 1949.
—— Three novelists and the drawing of character: C. P. Snow, Cary and Ivy Compton-Burnett. E & S new ser 3 1950. Mainly on the first trilogy.

Allen, W. The horse's mouth. In his Reading a novel, 1949.
—— Joyce Cary. 1953, 1963 (rev) (Br Council pamphlet).
—— Joyce Cary. New Statesman & Nation 6 April 1957.

Adam International Rev 18 1950. Special Cary issue. Contains several of his articles on the novel, also:
Cecil, D. The novelist at work: a conversation between Cary and Cecil.
Owen, B. E. The supremacy of the individual in the novels of Cary.
Schorer, M. The 'socially extensive' novel.

Monas, S. What to do with a drunken sailor. Hudson Rev 3 1950. On the first trilogy and A fearful joy.

Prescott, O. Two modern masters: Cozzens, Cary. In his In my opinion, Indianapolis 1952.

Van Horn, R. G. Freedom and imagination in the novels of Cary. Midwest Jnl 5 1952.

Collins, H. R. Joyce Cary's troublesome Africans. Antioch Rev 13 1953.

Kettle, A. Cary: Mister Johnson. In his An introduction to the English novel, vol 2 1953.

Burrows, J. and A. Hamilton. The art of fiction 7: Joyce Cary. Paris Rev no 7 1954; rptd in Writers at work: the Paris Review interviews, ed M. Cowley, New York 1958.

Craig, D. Idea and imagination: a study of Cary. Fox (Aberdeen) [1954].

Hardy, B. Form in Cary's novels. EC 4 1954.

King, C. Joyce Cary. Canadian Forum 33 1954.
—— Cary and the creative imagination. Tamarack Rev no 10 1959.

Woodcock, G. Citizens of Babel: a study of Cary. Queen's Quart 63 1956.

Bettman, E. R. Cary and the problem of political morality. Antioch Rev 17 1957.

Seymour-Smith, M. Zero and the impossible. Encounter 9 1957.

Steinbrecher, G. Cary: master novelist. College Eng 18 1957.

Garant, J. Cary's portrait of the artist. Revue des Langues Vivantes 24 1958. On The horse's mouth.

Hall, A. The African novels of Cary. Standpunte 12 1958.

Moore, G. Mister Johnson reconsidered. Black Orpheus 4 1958.

Ryan, M. An interpretation of Cary's The horse's mouth. Critique (Minneapolis) 2 1958.

Wright, A. Cary: a preface to his novels. 1958.
—— Cary's unpublished work. London Mag 5 1958.
—— Cary: fragments of an oeuvre. International Literary Annual 1 1958.

Adams, H. Blake and Gulley Jimson: English symbolists. Critique (Minneapolis) 3 1959.
—— Cary: posthumous volumes and criticism to date. Texas Stud in Lit & Lang 1 1959.
—— Cary's three speakers. Modern Fiction Stud 5 1959. On the first trilogy.
—— Cary's swimming swan. Amer Scholar 29 1960.

Case, E. The free world of Cary. Modern Age 3 1959.

Cosman, M. The protean Cary. Commonweal 69 1959.

Hamilton, K. Boon or thorn? Cary and Beckett on human life. Dalhousie Rev 38 1959. On the first trilogy.

Hoffmann, C. G. Cary and the comic mask. Western Humanities Rev 13 1959. This and subsequent articles incorporated (rev) in his Cary: the comedy of freedom, Pittsburgh 1964.

Holloway, J. Cary's fiction: modernity and sustaining power. TLS 7 Aug 1959; rptd in his The colours of clarity, 1964.

French, W. G. Cary's American Rover girl. Texas Stud in Lit & Lang 2 1960. On An American visitor.

Karl, F. R. Cary: the moralist as novelist. Twentieth-Century Lit 5 1960; rptd in his The contemporary English novel, New York 1962, London 1963 (as A reader's guide to the contemporary English novel).

Kerr, E. M. Cary's second trilogy. UTQ 29 1960.

Mahood, M. M. Cary in Africa 1913–20. New Statesman & Nation 1 Oct 1960.
—— Cary's Africa. 1964.

Meriwether, J. B. A note on Verse: Cary's first book. Lib Chronicle of Univ of Texas 6 1960.

Mustanoja, T. F. Two painters: Cary and Gulley Jimson. Neuphilologische Mitteilungen 61 1960.

Starkie, E. Cary: a personal portrait. Virginia Quart Rev 37 1961; rptd (rev) in Essays by Divers Hands 32 1963.

Stewart, D. Cary: Protestantism. In his The ark of God: studies in five modern novelists, 1961.

Bloom, R. The indeterminate world: a study of the novels of Cary. Philadelphia [1962].

Barba, H. Cary's image of the African in transition. Univ of Kansas City Rev 29 1963.

Hall, J. Directed restlessness: Cary. In his The tragic comedians: seven modern British novelists, Bloomington 1963.

Modern Fiction Studies 9 1963. Special Cary no. Contains:
Wright, A. A note on Cary's reputation.
Stevenson, L. Cary and the Anglo-Irish tradition.
Hoffmann, C. G. 'They want to be happy': Cary's unfinished Castle Corner series.
Fyfe, C. The colonial situation in Mister Johnson.
Stockholder, F. The triple vision in Cary's first trilogy.
Garrett, G. The major poetry of Cary.

Foster, M. Fell of the lion, fleece of the sheep.
Mitchell, G. Cary's Prisoner of grace.
Teeling, J. Cary's moral world.
Beebe, M. et al. Criticism of Cary: a select checklist.
Pittock, M. Cary: a fearful joy. EC 13 1963.
Lyons, R. S. Narrative method in Cary's To be a pilgrim. Texas Stud in Lit & Lang 6 1964.
Shapiro, S. Leopold Bloom and Gulley Jimson: the economics of survival. Twentieth Century Lit 10 1964.
—— Cary's To be a pilgrim: Mr Facing-both-ways. Texas Stud in Lit & Lang 8 1966.
Weintraub, S. Castle Corner: Cary's Buddenbrooks. Wisconsin Stud in Contemporary Lit 5 1964.
Adams, R. H. Freedom in The horse's mouth. College Eng 26 1965.
Larsen, G. L. The dark descent: social change and moral responsibility in the novels of Cary. 1965.
O'Connor, W. Van. Joyce Cary. New York 1966 (Columbia Essays on Modern Writers).
Salz, P. J. The philosophical principles in Cary's work. Western Humanities Rev 20 1966.
Watson, K. The captive and the free: artist, child and society in the world of Cary. English 16 1966.
Battaglia, F. J. Spurious Armageddon: Cary's Not honour more. Modern Fiction Studies 13 1967.
Bède, J. L'expression par la trilogie chez Cary. Caliban 3 1967.
Ferrien, P. H. Cary. Études Anglaises 20 1967.
Galligan, E. L. Intuition and concept: Cary and the critics. Texas Studies in Lit & Lang 8 1967.
Moody, P. R. Road and bridge in Cary's African novels. Bull of Rocky Mountain Modern Lang Assoc 21 1967.
Schoonbroodt, J. Cary. Dietsche Warande en Belfort 112 1967.
Eastman, R. Historical grace in Cary's A fearful joy. Novel 1 1968.
Foster, M. Cary: a biography. Boston 1968.
Wolkenfeld, J. Cary: the developing style. New York 1968.
Brawer, J. The triumph of defeat: a study of Cary's first trilogy. Texas Studies in Lit & Lang 10 1969.
Reed, P. J. Holding back: Cary's To be a pilgrim. Contemporary Lit 10 1969.
Smith, B. R. Moral evaluation in Mister Johnson. Critique (Minneapolis) 11 1969.

GILBERT KEITH CHESTERTON
1874–1936
See cols 1021–8, below.

ROBERT ERSKINE CHILDERS
1870–1922

Bibliographies
O'Hegarty, P. S. Bibliographies of 1916 and the Irish Revolution: no 16 Childers. Dublin Mag new ser 23 1948. Rptd separately 1948 as A bibliography of the books of Childers.

§ 1
The riddle of the sands: a record of secret service recently achieved. Ed [i.e. written] Erskine Childers 1903, New York 1915.

Childers also wrote a number of works on military history and Irish politics.

§ 2
Williams, B. Childers: a sketch. 1926 (priv ptd).

DAME AGATHA MARY CLARISSA CHRISTIE
(afterwards MALLOWAN)
b. 1890

Bibliographies
Ramsey, G. C. In his Agatha Christie, 1967, below. Includes notes of some of the many collections, 'omnibuses' and other selections from Agatha Christie's work.

§ 1
This list is based on Ramsey, above. It excludes the occasional reprinting of a single short story originally pbd in one of the collections listed below. Plays are listed in order of production.

The mysterious affair at Styles: a detective story. 1920.
The secret adversary. 1922, New York 1922.
The murder on the links. 1923, New York 1923.
The man in the brown suit. 1924, New York 1924.
Poirot investigates. 1924, New York 1925. Stories.
The secret of Chimneys. 1925, New York 1925.
The murder of Roger Ackroyd. 1926, New York 1926. Dramatized by M. Morton as Alibi, Prince of Wales 15 May 1928; pbd 1929 (French's Acting edn).
The big four. [1927], New York 1927.
The mystery of the Blue Train. [1928], New York 1928.
Partners in crime. 1929, New York [1929]. Chs 11–22 pbd London 1933 as The Sunningdale mystery. Stories.
The Seven Dials mystery. [1929], New York 1929.
The under dog, by A. Christie, and Blackman's wood, by E. Phillips Oppenheim. [1929], [1936] (as Two thrillers).
Black coffee: a play in three acts. (Embassy 8 Dec 1930; St Martin's 9 April 1931). 1934, [1952] (French's Acting edn).
The murder at the vicarage. [1930], New York 1930. Dramatized by M. Charles and B. Toy, Playhouse 16 Dec 1949; pbd 1950 (French's Acting edn).
The mysterious Mr Quin. 1930, New York 1930. Also pbd as The passing of Mr Quin. Stories.
The Sittaford mystery. 1931, New York 1931 (as The murder at Hazelmoor).
Peril at End House. [1932], New York 1932. Dramatized by A. Ridley, Vaudeville 1 May 1940; pbd [1945] (French's Acting edn).
The thirteen problems. 1932, New York 1933 (as The Tuesday Club murders), London 1953 (as Miss Marple and the thirteen problems) (Penguin). Stories.
The hound of death and other stories. [1933].
Lord Edgware dies. [1933], New York 1933 (as Thirteen at dinner).
The Sunningdale mystery. 1933. *See* Partners in crime, 1929, above.
The Listerdale mystery, and other stories. 1934. The story Philomel cottage, dramatized by F. Vosper as Love from a stranger, Wyndham's 2 Feb 1936; New 31 March 1936; pbd 1936 (French's Acting edn).
Murder in three acts. New York [1934], London [1935] (as Three act tragedy).
Murder on the Orient Express. [1934], New York 1934 (as Murder in the Calais coach).
Parker Pyne investigates. 1934, New York 1934 (as Mr Parker Pyne, detective). Stories.
Why didn't they ask Evans? [1934], New York 1935 (as The boomerang clue).
Death in the clouds. [1935], New York 1935 (as Death in the air).
The ABC murders. [1936], New York 1936.
Cards on the table. [1936], New York 1937.
Murder in Mesopotamia. [1936], New York 1936.
Dead man's mirror. New York 1937. Stories.
Death on the Nile. 1937, New York 1938. Dramatized as Hidden horizon, Wimbledon 9 April 1945, renamed Murder on the Nile, Ambassadors 19 March 1946; pbd 1948 (French's Acting edn).

Dumb witness. [1937], New York 1937 (as Poirot loses a client). Also pbd as Murder at Littlegreen House, and Mystery at Littlegreen House.

Murder in the mews, and other stories. [1937]. Includes stories in Dead man's mirror, above, together with The incredible theft.

Appointment with death. [1938], New York 1938. Dramatized, Piccadilly 31 March 1945; pbd 1956 (French's Acting edn).

Hercule Poirot's Christmas. 1939 (for 1938), New York 1939 (as Murder for Christmas), 1947 (as A holiday for murder).

Murder is easy. [1939], New York 1939 (as Easy to kill).

The regatta mystery, and other stories. New York 1939.

Ten little niggers. [1939], New York 1940 (as And then there were none). Also pbd as Ten little Indians, and The nursery rhyme murders. Dramatized, Wimbledon 20 Sept 1943, St James 17 Nov 1943; pbd 1944 (French's Acting edn).

One, two, buckle my shoe. 1940, New York 1941 (as The patriotic murders).

Sad cypress. [1940], New York 1940.

Evil under the sun. 1941, New York 1941.

N or M? 1941, New York 1941.

The body in the library. 1942, New York 1942.

Five little pigs. 1942, New York 1942 (as Murder in retrospect). Dramatized as Go back for murder, Duchess 23 March 1960; pbd 1960 (French's Acting edn).

The moving finger. New York 1942, London 1943.

Towards zero. 1944, Philadelphia 1944. Also pbd as Come and be hanged. Dramatized by the author and G. Verner, St James's 4 Sept 1956; pbd New York 1957 (Dramatists Play Service), London 1958 (French's Acting edn).

Death comes as the end. 1945.

Sparkling cyanide. 1945, New York 1945 (as Remembered death).

The hollow. 1946, New York 1946 (as Murder after hours). Dramatized, Fortune 7 June 1951; pbd 1952 (French's Acting edn).

A holiday for murder. New York 1947. See Hercule Poirot's Christmas, 1939, above.

The labours of Hercules. 1947, New York 1947. Stories.

Taken at the flood. 1948, New York 1948 (as There is a tide).

The witness for the prosecution, and other stories. New York 1948. Title story dramatized, Winter Garden 28 Oct 1953; pbd in Famous plays of 1954, and separately (French's Acting edn), New York 1954.

Crooked house. 1949, New York 1949.

A murder is announced. 1950, New York 1950.

Three blind mice, and other stories. New York [1950?]. Also pbd as The mousetrap and other stories; title story dramatized as The mousetrap, Ambassadors 25 Nov 1952; pbd 1956 (French's Acting edn).

Blood will tell. New York [1951], London 1952 (as Mrs McGinty's dead), New York 1952.

They came to Baghdad. 1951, New York 1951.

The under dog, and other stories. New York 1951. Title story first pbd 1929.

They do it with mirrors. 1952, New York 1952 (as Murder with mirrors).

After the funeral. 1953, New York 1953 (as Funerals are fatal), London 1963 (wrapper title Murder at the gallop).

Miss Marple and the thirteen problems. 1953. See The thirteen problems, 1932, above.

A pocket full of rye. 1953, New York [1953].

Spider's web: a play in three acts. (Savoy 13 Dec 1954). [1957] (French's Acting edn).

Destination unknown. 1954, New York 1955 (as So many steps to death).

Hickory, dickory, dock. 1955, New York 1955 (as Hickory, dickory, death).

Dead man's folly. [1956], New York 1956.

4.50 from Paddington. 1957, New York 1957 (as What Mrs McGillicuddy saw!), 1961 (as Murder she said).

The unexpected guest. (Duchess 12 Aug 1958). [1958] (French's Acting cdn).

Verdict: a play in two acts. (Strand 22 May 1958). 1958, [1958] (French's Acting edn).

Ordeal by innocence. [1958], New York 1959.

Cat among the pigeons. [1959], New York 1960.

The adventures of the Christmas pudding, and a selection of entrées. [1960]. Stories.

Double sin, and other stories. New York 1961.

The pale horse. [1961], New York 1962.

Afternoon at the seaside; The patient; The rats. (Duchess 20 Dec 1962). Three one-act plays; pbd separately [1963] (French's Acting edn).

The mirror crack'd from side to side. [1962], New York [1963] (as The mirror crack'd).

The clocks. [1963].

Murder at the gallop. 1963. See After the funeral, 1953, above.

A Caribbean mystery. 1964.

At Bertrams Hotel. 1965, New York 1966.

Third girl. 1966, New York 1968.

By the pricking of my thumbs. 1968, New York 1968.

Hallowe'en party. 1969.

Agatha Christie has also written novels under the pseudonym Mary Westmacott, and books on archaeological experiences in Syria, also stories and poems, under the name Agatha Christie Mallowan.

§2

Allingham, M. [Review of A murder is announced]. New York Times Book Rev 4 June 1950.

Dennis, N. Genteel queen of crime. Life Mag 14 May 1956.

Ramsey, G. C. Perdurable Agatha. New York Times Book Rev 21 Nov 1965.

—— Agatha Christie: mistress of mystery. New York [1967].

Wyndham, F. The algebra of Agatha Christie. Sunday Times 27 Feb 1966.

Behre, F. E. O. Studies in Agatha Christie's writings: the behaviour of 'a good—great—deal', 'a lot', 'lots', 'much', 'plenty', 'a good—great—many'. Stockholm 1967 (Gothenburg Stud in English).

RICHARD THOMAS CHURCH
1893–1972

See cols 246–8, above.

JOHN HENRY NOYES COLLIER
b. 1901

Bibliographies

'Gawsworth, John' (T. I. F. Armstrong). In his Ten contemporaries: notes toward their definitive bibliography, 2nd ser 1933. With a note on writing by Collier.

§1

His monkey wife: or, married to a chimp. 1930, New York 1931.

Gemini: poems. 1931.

No traveller returns. 1931 (210 copies). Story.

An epistle to a friend. 1932 (priv ptd, 99 copies).

Green thoughts. 1932. Story.

Just the other day: an informal history of Great Britain since the war. 1932, New York 1932. With I. Lang.

Tom's a-cold. 1933, New York 1933 (as Full circle).

Defy the foul fiend: or, the misadventures of a heart. 1934, New York 1934.

The devil and all. [1935]. Stories.

Variation on a theme. 1935 (285 copies). Story.
Witch's money. New York 1940. Story.
Presenting moonshine. 1941, New York 1941. Stories.
The touch of nutmeg, and more unlikely stories. New York [1943]. Some stories previously pbd in Presenting moonshine, above.
Fancies and goodnights. New York 1951, 1961 (foreword by M. Hadas). Stories.
Pictures in the fire. 1958.

ALEXANDER COMFORT
b. 1920

See cols 249–50, above.

DAME IVY COMPTON-BURNETT
1892–1969

Collected edition. 1948–.

§1

Dolores. Edinburgh 1911.
Pastors and masters: a study. 1925.
Brothers and sisters. 1929, New York [1929].
Men and wives. 1931, New York [1931].
More women than men. 1933, New York 1965 (with A family and a fortune, below).
A house and its head. 1935.
Daughters and sons. 1937, New York 1938.
A family and a fortune. 1939, New York 1965 (with More women than men, above).
Parents and children. 1941.
Elders and betters. 1944.
Manservant and maidservant. 1947, New York 1948 (as Bullivant and the Lambs).
Two worlds and their ways. 1949, New York 1949.
Darkness and day. 1951, New York 1951.
The present and the past. 1953, New York 1953.
Mother and son. 1955, New York 1955.
A father and his fate. 1957, New York 1958.
A heritage and its history. 1959, New York 1960.
The mighty and their fall. 1961, New York 1962.
A god and his gifts. 1963, New York 1964.

§2

Strachey, R. The works of Ivy Compton-Burnett. Life & Letters 12 1935.
A conversation between I. Compton-Burnett and M. Jourdain. Orion 1 1945.
Liddell, R. The novels of I. Compton-Burnett. In his A treatise on the novel, 1947.
—— The novels of I. Compton-Burnett. 1955.
Sackville-West, E. 'Ladies whose bright pens...'. In his Inclinations, 1949. On Elizabeth Bowen and Ivy Compton-Burnett.
Bowen, E. In her Collected impressions, 1950.
Burkhart, C. I. Compton-Burnett: a note on the conventions. Western Rev 14 1950.
—— I. Compton-Burnett. 1965.
Hansford-Johnson, P. Three novelists and the drawing of character: C. P. Snow, J. Cary, Ivy Compton-Burnett. E & S new ser 3 1950.
—— I. Compton-Burnett. 1951 (Br Council pamphlet).
Prescott, O. Comrades of the coterie: H. Green, I. Compton-Burnett, Elizabeth Bowen, G. Greene. In his In my opinion, Indianapolis 1952.
Amis, K. One world and its way. Twentieth Century 158 1955.
Wilson, A. Ivy Compton-Burnett. London Mag 2 1955.
Snow, L. 'Good is bad condensed': Ivy Compton-Burnett's view of human nature. Western Humanities Rev 10 1956.

West, A. In his Principles and persuasions, New York 1957.
Cranston, M. Lettres Nouvelles 6 1958.
Mackworth, C. Les romans d'Ivy Compton-Burnett. Critique (Paris) 14 1958.
Greenfield, S. B. Pastors and masters: the spoils of genius. Criticism 2 1960.
Jefferson, D. W. A note on Ivy Compton-Burnett. REL 1 1960.
Las Vergnas, R. Revue de Paris 67 1960.
McCabe, B. Ivy Compton-Burnett: an English eccentric. Critique (Minneapolis) 3 1960.
Preston, J. The matter in a word. EC 10 1960. On A heritage and its history.
Frischknecht, R. Ivy Compton-Burnett: kritische Betrachtung ihrer Werke. Winterthur 1961.
Gold, J. Exit everybody: the novels of Ivy Compton-Burnett. Dalhousie Rev 42 1962.
Karl, F. R. The intimate world of Ivy Compton-Burnett. In his The contemporary English novel, New York 1962, London 1963 (as A reader's guide to the contemporary English novel).
Baldanza, F. Ivy Compton-Burnett. New York [1964] (Twayne's English Authors).
Curtis, M. M. The moral comedy of Miss Compton-Burnett. Wisconsin Stud in Contemporary Lit 5 1964.
Iser, W. Ivy Compton-Burnett: A heritage and its history. In Der moderne englische Roman, ed H. Oppel, Berlin 1965.
McCarthy, M. The inventions of Ivy Compton-Burnett. Encounter 27 1966.
Kattan, N. Le monde cruel d'Ivy Compton-Burnett. Liberté 10 1968.

ALFRED EDGAR COPPARD
1878–1957
Bibliographies

Schwartz, J. The writings of Coppard. 1931. Foreword and notes by Coppard: includes introds, trns and contributions to periodicals.
Fabes, G. H. The first editions of Coppard [et al]. 1933.

Collections and Selections

Collected poems. 1928, New York 1928.
Fares please!: an omnibus. 1931. Includes contents of The black dog, The field of mustard, Silver circus, below.
Selected tales. 1946.
The collected tales. New York 1948.

§1

Adam & Eve & pinch me: tales. Waltham St Lawrence 1921, New York 1922.
Clorinda walks in heaven: tales. Waltham St Lawrence 1922.
Hips & haws: poems. Waltham St Lawrence 1922.
The black dog, and other stories. 1923, New York 1923.
Fishmonger's fiddle: tales. 1925, New York 1925.
The field of mustard: tales. 1926, New York 1927.
Pelagea, and other poems. Waltham St Lawrence 1926.
Yokohama garland, and other poems. Philadelphia 1926.
Silver circus: tales. 1928, New York 1929.
Count Stefan. [Waltham St Lawrence] 1928. Story.
The Gollan. 1929 (priv ptd, 75 copies). Story.
The higgler. Chelsea NY 1930 (39 copies). Story, rptd from Fishmonger's fiddle, above.
The hundredth story of A. E. Coppard. Waltham St Lawrence 1930.
The man from Kilsheelan. 1930. Story, rptd (rev) from The black dog, above.
Pink furniture: a tale for lovely children with noble natures. 1930, New York [1930].
Easter day: a poem. 1931.

Nixey's harlequin: tales. 1931, New York 1932.
Crotty Shinkwin [and] The beauty spot. Waltham St
Lawrence 1932. Stories.
Rummy: the noble game, expounded in prose, poetry,
diagram and engraving by Coppard and R. Gibbings.
Waltham St Lawrence 1932, Boston 1933.
Dunky Fitlow: tales. 1933.
Ring the bells of heaven. 1933. Story.
Emergency exit. New York [1934]. Story.
Cherry ripe: poems. Chepstow 1935, Windham Conn
1935.
Polly Oliver: tales. 1935.
The ninepenny flute: twenty-one tales. 1937.
Tapster's tapestry. 1938 (75 copies).
You never know, do you? and other tales. 1939.
Ugly Anna, and other tales. 1944.
Fearful pleasures. Sauk City 1946, London 1951. Stories.
Dark-eyed lady: fourteen tales. 1947.
Lucy in her pink jacket. 1954. Stories.
It's me, O Lord! 1957. Autobiography.

§2

Saul, G. B. A. E. Coppard: his life and his poetry.
Philadelphia 1932.
Jehin, A. Remarks on the style of Coppard. 1944.
'O'Connor, Frank' (M. F. O'Donovan). The price of
freedom. In his The lonely voice: a study of the short
story, Cleveland 1963.

ARCHIBALD JOSEPH CRONIN
b. 1896

Selections

Complete novels. New York 1967. Contains The northern
light, Green years, Shannon's way.

§1

Hatter's castle. 1931, Boston 1931.
Three loves. 1932, Boston 1932.
Grand canary. 1933, Boston 1933.
The stars look down. 1935, Boston 1935.
The citadel. 1937, Boston 1937.
Jupiter laughs: a play in three acts. Boston 1940, London
1941.
The keys of the kingdom. Boston 1941, London 1942.
The green years. Boston 1944, London 1945, Boston 1960
(with Shannon's way, below).
Shannon's way. 1948, Boston 1948, 1960 (with The green
years, above). Sequel to The green years.
The Spanish gardener. 1950, Boston 1950.
Adventures in two worlds. 1952, New York [1952]. Auto-
biography.
Beyond this place. 1953, Boston 1953.
Crusader's tomb. 1956, Boston 1956 (as A thing of beauty).
The innkeeper's wife. New York 1958. Story.
The northern light. 1958, Boston 1958.
The Judas tree. 1961, Boston 1961.
A song of sixpence. 1964, Boston 1964.
A pocketful of rye. 1969, Boston 1969.

§2

Davies, H. Pilgrims, not strangers: Maugham, Cronin,
Alan Paton. In his A mirror of the ministry in modern
novels, New York 1959. On Grand canary; The keys of
the kingdom.

'CLEMENCE DANE',
WINIFRED ASHTON
1887?–1965

See cols 927–9, below.

RHYS DAVIES
b. 1903

Bibliographies

'Gawsworth, John' (T. I. F. Armstrong). In his Ten
contemporaries: notes toward their definitive bibliography, 1932. With a note by Davies, Writing about the
Welsh.
In Wales no 3 1937.

Collections and Selections

Selected stories. 1945.
Boy with a trumpet. 1949, Garden City NY 1951. Selected
stories: introd by B. Moon.
The collected stories of Rhys Davies. 1955.

§1

The song of songs, and other stories. [1927] (priv ptd, 100
copies).
The withered root. 1927, New York [1928].
Aaron. 1927 (priv ptd, 100 copies).
A bed of feathers. [1929].
Rings on her fingers. 1930, New York [1930].
Tale. [1930] (Blue Moon booklet).
The stars, the world, and the women. Foreword by
L. O'Flaherty 1930.
Arfon. [1931].
A pig in a poke: stories. 1931.
A woman. 1931 (165 copies).
The woman among women. 1931 (Blue Moon Christmas
poem).
Count your blessings. 1932.
Daisy Matthews, and three other tales. Waltham St
Lawrence 1932.
The red hills. 1932, New York 1933.
Love provoked. 1933.
Honey and bread. 1935.
One of Norah's early days. 1935 (285 copies). Story.
The skull. Chepstow 1936 (110 copies). Story.
The things men do: short stories. 1936.
My Wales. 1937, New York 1938. Non-fiction.
A time to laugh. 1937, New York [1938].
Jubilee blues. 1938.
Sea urchin: adventures of Jorgen Jorgensen. 1940. Bio-
graphy.
Under the rose. 1940.
Tomorrow to fresh woods. 1941.
A finger in every pie. 1942. Stories.
The story of Wales. 1943 (Britain in Pictures).
The black Venus. 1944, New York 1946.
The trip to London: stories. 1946, New York 1946.
The dark daughters. 1947, Garden City NY 1948.
Marianne. 1951, Garden City NY 1952.
The painted king. 1954, Garden City NY 1954.
No escape: a play in three acts. 1955. With A. Batty;
based on Under the rose, above.
The perishable quality. 1957.
The darling of her heart, and other stories. 1958.
Girl waiting in the shade. 1960.
The chosen sea, and other stories. 1967.
Print of a hare's foot: an autobiographical beginning.
1969, New York 1969.

§2

Mégroz, R. L. Rhys Davies: a critical sketch. 1932.
Adam, G. F. In his Three contemporary Anglo-Welsh
novelists, Berne 1950.

GEORGE WARWICK DEEPING
1877–1950
Selections

Stories of love, courage and compassion. New York 1930.

§1

Uther & Igraine. 1903, New York 1903.
Love among the ruins. 1904, New York 1904.
The seven streams. 1905.
The slanderers. New York 1905, London 1907.
Bess of the woods. 1906.
A woman's war. 1907.
Bertrand of Brittany. New York 1908, London 1908.
Mad Barbara. 1908, New York 1909.
The red saint. 1909, New York 1940.
The return of the petticoat. 1909, 1913 (rev).
The lame Englishman. 1910.
The rust of Rome. 1910.
Fox farm. 1911, New York [1911], 1933 (as The eyes of love).
Joan of the tower. 1911.
Sincerity. 1912, New York 1912 (as The strong hand), 1932 (as The challenge of love).
The house of spies. 1913, New York 1913.
The white gate. 1913, New York 1914.
The king behind the king. 1914, New York 1914.
The pride of Eve. 1914.
Marriage by conquest. 1915, New York 1915.
Unrest. 1916, New York 1916 (as Bridge of desire).
Martin Valliant. 1917, New York 1917.
Valour. 1918, New York 1934.
Countess Glika, and other stories. 1919.
Second youth. 1919, New York 1932 (as The awakening).
The prophetic marriage. 1920.
The house of adventure. 1921, New York 1922.
Lantern lane. 1921.
Orchards. 1922, New York 1933 (as The captive wife).
Apples of gold. 1923.
The secret sanctuary: or the saving of John Stretton. 1923.
Suvla John. 1924.
Three rooms. 1924.
Sorrell and son. 1925, New York 1926.
Doomsday. 1927, New York 1927.
Kitty. 1927, New York 1927.
Old Pybus. 1928, New York 1928.
Martyrdom. [1929]. Story, pbd with The house behind the Judas tree, by G. Frankau, and Forbidden music, by E. Mannin. Reissued 1936 as Three stories of romance.
Roper's Row. 1929, New York 1929.
Exiles. 1930, New York 1930 (as Exile).
The road. 1931, New York 1931 (as The ten commandments).
The awakening. New York 1932. See Second youth, above.
The challenge of love. New York 1932. See Sincerity, above.
Old wine and new. 1932, New York 1932.
Smith. 1932, New York 1932.
The black sheep. 1933, New York 1933.
The captive wife. New York 1933. See Orchards, above.
The eyes of love. New York 1933. See Fox farm, above.
The man on the white horse. 1934, New York 1934.
Seven men came back. 1934, New York 1934.
Sackcloth into silk. 1935, New York 1935 (as The golden cord).
Two in a train, and other stories. 1935.
No hero—this. 1936, New York 1936.
Blind man's year. 1937, New York 1937.
These white hands. New York 1937.
The woman at the door. 1937, New York 1937.
The malice of men. 1938, New York 1938.
Fantasia. 1939, New York 1939 (as Bluewater).

Shabby summer. 1939, New York 1939 (as Folly island).
The man who went back. 1940, New York 1940.
The shield of love. New York 1940.
Corn in Egypt. 1941, New York 1942.
The dark house. 1941, New York 1941.
I live again. 1942, New York 1942.
Slade. 1943, New York 1943.
Mr Gurney and Mr Slade. 1944, New York 1944 (as The cleric's secret).
Reprieve. 1945, New York 1945.
The impudence of youth. 1946, New York 1946.
Laughing house. 1946, New York 1946.
Portrait of a playboy. 1947, New York 1948 (as The playboy).
Paradise Place. 1949.
Old mischief. 1950.
Time to heal. 1952.
Man in chains. 1953.
The old world dies. 1954.
Caroline Terrace. 1955.
The serpent's tooth. 1956.
The sword and the cross. 1957.

'E. M. DELAFIELD',
EDMÉE ELIZABETH MONICA
DE LA PASTURE
1890–1943

Bibliographies

'Gawsworth, John' (T. I. F. Armstrong). In his Ten contemporaries: notes toward their definitive bibliography, 2nd ser 1933. With a Note by the way by E. M. Delafield.

Selections

The provincial lady at home and abroad. 1935. Contains Diary of a provincial lady, The provincial lady goes further, The provincial lady in America.
The provincial lady, with a foreword by Kate O'Brien. 1947. Contents as above, with The provincial lady in wartime.
The provincial lady. 1951. Contains Diary of a provincial lady, The provincial lady goes further, ed and abridged by L. Lewis.

§1

Zella sees herself. 1917.
The war-workers. 1918, New York 1918.
The pelicans. 1918, New York 1919.
Consequences. [1919], New York 1919.
Tension. [1920], New York 1920.
The heel of Achilles. [1921].
Humbug. [1921], New York 1922.
The optimist. [1922], New York 1922.
A reversion to type. [1923], New York 1923.
Mrs Harter. [1924], New York [1925].
Messalina of the suburbs. [1924] (with stories and a one-act play), 1929 (alone).
The chip and the block. [1925], New York [1926].
Jill. [1926], New York [1927].
The entertainment. [1927], New York [1927]. Stories.
The way things are. [1927], New York [1928].
The suburban young man. [1928].
What is love? 1928, New York 1929 (as First love).
Women are like that: short stories. 1929.
Turn back the leaves. 1930, New York 1930.
Diary of a provincial lady. 1930.
Challenge to Clarissa. 1931, New York [1931] (as House party).
To see ourselves: a domestic comedy in three acts. In Famous plays of 1931, 1931, New York [1932].
Thank heaven fasting. 1932.

The provincial lady goes further. 1932, New York 1933 (as The provincial lady in London).
Gay life. 1933.
General impressions. 1933. Essays.
The glass wall: a play in three acts. 1933.
The provincial lady in America. 1934.
The Bazalgettes. 1935. Anon.
Faster! faster! 1936.
As others hear us: a miscellany. 1937. Stories.
Ladies and gentlemen in Victorian fiction. 1937, New York [1937].
Nothing is safe. 1937 ,New York 1937.
Straw without bricks: I visit Soviet Russia. 1937, New York 1937 (as I visit the Soviets).
When women love. New York 1938, London 1939 (as Three marriages). Stories.
Love has no resurrection, and other stories. 1939.
People you love. [1940]. On the status of the family under Nazism.
The provincial lady in war-time. 1940, New York [1940].
No one now will know. 1941, New York [1944].
Late and soon. 1943, New York 1943.

§2

Johnson, R. B. In his Some contemporary novelists: women, 1920.
Lawrence, M. Sophisticated ladies. In her School of femininity, New York 1936, London 1937 (as We write as women).

WALTER JOHN DE LA MARE
1873–1956
See cols 256–62, above.

WILLIAM FREND DE MORGAN
1839–1917

§1

Report on the feasibility of a manufacture of glazed pottery in Egypt. Cairo 1894.
Joseph Vance: an ill-written autobiography. 1906, New York 1906, London 1954 (with introd by A. C. Ward) (WC).
Alice-for-short: a dichronism. New York 1907, London 1907.
Somehow good. 1908, New York 1908.
It can never happen again. 2 vols 1909, 1 vol New York 1909.
An affair of dishonour. 1910, New York 1910.
A likely story. 1911, New York 1911.
When ghost meets ghost. [1914], New York 1914.
The old madhouse. 1919, New York 1919. Completed by Mrs E. de Morgan.
The old man's youth and the young man's old age. 1920, New York 1920. Completed by Mrs E. de Morgan.

§2

Phelps, W. L. In his Essays on modern novelists, New York 1910.
Cooper, F. T. In his Some English story tellers, New York 1912.
Follett, H. T. and W. In their Some modern novelists, New York 1918.
Seymour, F. W. William de Morgan: a post-Victorian realist. Chicago 1920.
Hale, W. T. William de Morgan and the greater early Victorians. Bloomington 1921 (Indiana Univ Stud 50).
Hewlett, M. The de Morgans. In his Extemporary essays, 1922.

Stirling, A. M. D. W. William de Morgan and his wife. 1922.
Utter, R. P. In his Pearls and pepper, New Haven 1924.
Ellis, S. M. In his Mainly Victorian, 1925.
Williams, O. The novels of de Morgan. In his Some great English novels; studies in the art of fiction, 1926.

NIGEL FORBES DENNIS
b. 1912

§1

Boys and girls come out to play. 1949, Boston 1949 (as A sea change).
Cards of identity. 1955, New York 1955.
Two plays and a preface. [1958], New York [1958]. Contains dramatized version of Cards of identity, and The making of Moo.
August for the people: a play in two acts. [1962].
Dramatic essays. [1962].
Jonathan Swift: a short character. New York 1964, London 1965.
A house in order. [1966], New York 1966.

§2

Engelborghs, M. Nigel Dennis and Kingsley Amis. Dietsche Warande en Belfort 9 1957.
Peake, C. Cards of identity: an intellectual satire. Literary Half-Yearly 1 1960.
Watt, I. Very funny...unbelievably tough. New Republic 29 Aug 1960.
Karl, F. R. The still comic music of humanity: the novels of A. Powell, A. Wilson and Dennis. In his The contemporary English novel, New York 1962, London 1963 (as A reader's guide to the contemporary English novel).
Ewart, G. Nigel Dennis—identity man. London Mag 3 1963.
Wellwarth, G. E. The new English dramatists: the traditionalists—N. Dennis. In his The theater of protest and paradox, New York 1964.

HUGH DE SÉLINCOURT
1878–1951

A boy's marriage. 1907, New York 1907.
The strongest plume. 1907, New York 1907.
Great Ralegh. 1908. Non-fiction.
The high adventure. 1908, New York 1908.
The way things happen. 1909, New York 1909.
Oxford from within. 1910. Non-fiction.
A fair house. 1911, New York 1911.
A daughter of the morning. 1912. Pt 1 of trilogy.
Pride of body. [1914]. Articles on health rptd mostly from Daily Mail.
Realms of day. [1915]. Pt 2 of trilogy.
A soldier of life. 1916, New York 1917.
Nine tales. 1917, New York 1918. With introd by H. Child.
Women and children. 1921.
The cricket match. 1924.
One little boy. New York 1924.
Young mischief and the perfect pair. New York 1925.
Young 'un. 1927.
Never in vain: a dream of friendship. 1929.
Mr Buffum. 1930.
Evening light: being the life and letters of Susan Rivarol, as related by Professor Owen Mansfield. 1931. Pt 3 of trilogy.
The game of the season. 1931.
'Over!': some personal remarks on the game of cricket. 1932.
Moreover: reflections on the game of cricket. 1934.

Studies from life. 1934. Biographical sketches.
The Saturday match. 1937. Stories.
Gauvinier takes to bowls. 1949, New York 1949.

KATHERINE HELEN MAUD MARSHALL DIVER
1867–1945

Selections

Four complete novels. 1930. Contains Unconquered, Strange roads, The strong hours, Captain Desmond VC.
The men of the frontier force. 1930. Contains rev edn of Captain Desmond VC, The great amulet, Desmond's daughter.

§1

Captain Desmond, VC. 1907, New York 1910, 1914 (rev), London 1915.
The great amulet. 1908, New York 1910, 1914 (rev), London 1914.
Candles in the wind. 1909, New York 1909, London 1931 (rev and abridged).
The Englishwoman in India. 1909. Non-fiction.
Lilamani: a study in possibilities. 1911, New York 1911 (as Awakening).
The hero of Herat [Eldred Pottinger]: a frontier biography in romantic form. 1912, New York 1913.
The judgment of the sword: the tale of the Kabul tragedy, and of the part played therein by Major Eldred Pottinger. 1913, New York 1913.
Sunia: and other stories. 1913, New York 1913.
Desmond's daughter. 1916, New York 1916.
Unconquered. 1917, New York 1917.
Strange roads. 1918.
The strong hours. 1919. Sequel to Strange roads, above.
Far to seek: a romance of England and India. 1921, Boston 1921.
Lonely furrow. 1923, Boston 1923.
Siege perilous, and other stories. 1924, Boston 1924.
Coombe St Mary's. 1925, Boston 1925.
But yesterday—. 1927, New York 1927.
Together. [1928].
A wild bird. 1929, Boston 1929.
Ships of youth: a study of marriage in modern India. 1931, Boston 1931.
The singer passes: an Indian tapestry. 1934, New York 1934.
Kabul to Kandahar. 1935. On the second Afghan war.
Honoria Lawrence: a fragment of Indian history. 1936, Boston 1936. Biography.
The dream prevails. 1938, Boston 1938.
Sylvia Lyndon: a novel of England. 1940, Boston 1940.
Royal India: a descriptive and historical account of India's fifteen principal states and their rulers. 1942, New York 1942.
The unsung: a record of British services in India. 1945.

GEORGE NORMAN DOUGLAS [DOUGLASS]
1868–1952

Bibliographies

Stonehill, C. A. A bibliography of Douglas. 1926. Suppl to Bookman's Jnl.
McDonald, E. D. A bibliography of the writings of Douglas. Philadelphia 1927. With notes by Douglas.
Woolf, C. and A. Anderson. Bibliographical catalogue of the Douglas memorial exhibition June 1952 at Edinburgh Central Library. Edinburgh [1952].
Woolf, C. A bibliography of Douglas. 1954, 1954 (rev) (Soho Bibliographies). Includes trns and Douglas' contributions to periodicals.

—— Notes on the bibliography of Douglas. Edinburgh 1955 (priv ptd, 95 copies).
Douglas's own Late harvest (*1946*) *contains much bibliographical comment.*

Selections

Three of them. 1930. One day, Nerinda, On the herpetology of the Grand Duchy of Baden.
An almanac. Lisbon 1941 (priv ptd, 25[?] copies), London 1945. Extracts chosen by the author.
Norman Douglas: a selection from his works. With introd by D. M. Low 1955.

§1
Prose Fiction

Unprofessional tales. 1901. By 'Normyx' (i.e. Douglas and his wife Elsa FitzGibbon).
South wind. 1917, New York 1918, [1925] (with new introd) (Modern Lib), London 1942 (abridged, and with introductory note by Douglas), 1946 (with ch divisions and introductory letter by W. King).
They went. 1920, 1921 (abridged, with introductory letter by Douglas), New York 1921.
In the beginning. Florence 1927 (priv ptd), London 1928 (expurgated), New York 1928 (unexpurgated), London 1953.
The angel of Manfredonia. San Francisco 1929 (225 copies). Story, from Old Calabria, below.
Nerinda, 1901. Florence 1929, New York [1929]. Story rptd (rev) from Unprofessional tales, above.

Other Works

Siren land. 1911, New York 1911, London 1923 (rev), New York 1923, London 1957 (with Fountains in the sand, below), New York 1957. Travel.
Fountains in the sand: rambles among the oases of Tunisia. 1912, New York 1912, London 1944 (rev, Penguin), 1957 (with Siren land, above), New York 1957.
Old Calabria. 1915, Boston 1915, New York 1928 (with introd) (Modern Lib), 1938 (with new introd) (WC), London 1955 (with introd by J. Davenport), New York 1956.
London street games. 1916, 1931 (rev).
Alone. 1921, New York 1922. On Italy.
Together. 1923, New York 1923. On the Vorarlberg.
D. H. Lawrence and Maurice Magnus: a plea for better manners. [Florence] 1924 (priv ptd); rptd (rev) in Experiments, below (New York and London edns only). Written in connection with Lawrence's introd to Magnus's Memoirs of the Foreign Legion, 1924.
Experiments. [Florence] 1925 (priv ptd), New York 1925, London 1925. Essays.
Birds and beasts of the Greek anthology. Florence 1927 (priv ptd), London 1928 (rev), New York 1929 (with foreword by W. A. Percy).
Some limericks collected for the use of students and ensplendour'd with introduction, geographical index and with notes explanatory and critical by N. Douglas. [Florence] 1928 (priv ptd, 110 copies), [New York] 1928 (priv ptd, 750 copies), London 1969 (as The Norman Douglas limerick book). For the various intervening continental etc edns, piracies etc, *see* Woolf's bibliography, above.
How about Europe?: some footnotes on East and West. Florence 1929 (priv ptd), New York 1930 (as Goodbye to western culture), London 1930.
One day. Chapelle-Réauville 1929. On Athens; rptd in Three of them (1930, Selections, above).
Capri: materials for a description of the island. Florence 1930. Collects 8 pamphlets priv ptd between 1904 and 1915; for details *see* Woolf's bibliography, above.
Paneros: some words on aphrodisiacs and the like. Florence 1930 (priv ptd), London 1931, New York 1932.

Summer islands: Ischia and Ponza. [1931], New York 1931, London 1942 (for 1944) (with introductory letter by Douglas); rptd (with omissions) in Late harvest, 1946, below.

Looking back: an autobiographical excursion. 2 vols 1933, New York [1933], 1 vol 1934.

Late harvest. 1946, 1947 (with addns). Comments on his work, with reprints of essays and reviews.

Footnote on Capri. 1952, New York 1952. Essay, accompanying photographs by Islay Lyons.

Venus in the kitchen: or love's cookery book, by 'Pilaff Bey', ed by N. Douglas, introd by G. Greene. 1952, New York 1953. By Douglas and Orioli. *See* Woolf's bibliography, above.

For details of Douglas's papers on natural science between 1892 and 1895 see Woolf's bibliography. Douglas contributed frequently to Eng Rev *1909–16, mostly reviews.*

Letters
Palmer, A. Some Douglas letters. REL 6 1965.

§2
Lindsay, J. Douglas: an essay in humanistic values. London Aphrodite 1 1929.

Tomlinson, H. M. Norman Douglas. 1931, 1952 (rev).

Wheatley. E. D. Norman Douglas. Sewanee Rev 40 1932.

'MacGillivray, Richard' (R. M. Dawkins). Norman Douglas. Florence 1933, London 1952 (rev, as by R. M. Dawkins).

Webster, H. T. Douglas: a reconsideration. South Atlantic Quart 49 1950.

Davenport, J. Norman Douglas. Twentieth Century 151 1952.

—— Norman Douglas. Atlantic Monthly 194 1954.

Flint, R. W. Norman Douglas. Kenyon Rev 14 1952.

Fitzgibbon, C. Norman Douglas: a pictorial record. 1953.

Macpherson, K. Omnes eodem cogimur. 1953 (priv ptd).

Aldington, R. Pinorman: personal recollections of Douglas, Pino Orioli and C. Prentice. 1954.

Cunard, N. Grand man: memories of Douglas. 1954.

Greenlees, I. Norman Douglas. 1957 (Br Council pamphlet).

Swan, M. Douglas and the southern world. In his Small part of time, 1957.

Lindeman, R. Norman Douglas. New York 1965 (Twayne's English Authors).

Leary, L. Norman Douglas. New York 1968 (Columbia Essays on Modern Writers).

DAME DAPHNE DU MAURIER
b. 1907

Selections
Early stories. 1954.

The Daphne du Maurier omnibus. 1956, Garden City NY 1961 (as Three romantic novels of Cornwall). Contains Frenchman's Creek, Jamaica Inn, Rebecca.

The treasury of du Maurier short stories. 1960.

The Daphne du Maurier tandem. 1964. Contains Mary Anne, My cousin Rachel.

Duet: The flight of the falcon; The scapegoat. Garden City NY 1968.

§1
The loving spirit. 1931, Garden City NY 1931.

I'll never be young again. 1932, Garden City NY 1932.

The progress of Julius. 1933, Garden City NY 1933.

Gerald: a portrait. 1934, Garden City NY 1935. Biography of Gerald du Maurier.

Jamaica Inn. 1936, Garden City NY 1936.

The du Mauriers. 1937, Garden City NY 1937. Biography.

Rebecca. 1938, New York 1938, London 1940 (as play), New York 1943.

Come wind, come weather. 1940, New York 1941. Stories.

Happy Christmas. New York 1940, London [1943]. Story.

Frenchman's Creek. 1941, Garden City NY 1942.

Consider the lilies. [1943]. Story.

Escort. 1943. Story. Rptd in Nothing hurts for long, and Escort, below.

Hungry hill. 1943, Garden City NY 1943.

Nothing hurts for long, and Escort. 1943. 2 stories.

Spring picture. [1944], New York 1944. Story.

Leading lady. [1945]. Story.

London and Paris. 1945.

The years between: a play in two acts. 1945, Garden City NY 1946.

The king's general. 1946, Garden City NY 1946.

The parasites. 1949, Garden City NY 1950.

September tide: a play in three acts. 1949, Garden City NY 1950.

My cousin Rachel. 1951, Garden City NY 1952.

The apple tree: a short novel and some stories. 1952, Garden City NY 1953 (as Kiss me again, stranger).

Mary Anne. 1954, Garden City NY 1954.

The scapegoat. 1957, Garden City NY 1957.

Breaking point: eight stories. 1959, Garden City NY 1959.

The infernal world of Branwell Brontë. 1960, Garden City NY 1961. Non-fiction.

The glass-blowers. 1963, Garden City NY 1963.

The flight of the falcon. 1965, Garden City NY 1965.

Vanishing Cornwall. 1967.

The house on the strand. 1969, Garden City NY 1969.

§2
Stockwell, L. Best sellers and the critics: a case history. College Eng 16 1955.

LAWRENCE GEORGE DURRELL
b. 1912
See cols 266–71, above.

DAVID CARADOC EVANS
1878–1945

§1
My people: stories of the peasantry of West Wales. [1915], New York 1915, 1918 (as My own people).

Capel Sion. [1917], New York 1918. Stories.

My neighbours. 1919, New York 1920 (as My neighbors: stories of the Welsh people).

Taffy: a play of Welsh village life in three acts. [1923].

Nothing to pay. 1930, New York [1930].

Wasps. 1933.

This way to heaven. 1934.

Pilgrims in a foreign land. 1942. Stories.

Morgan Bible. 1943.

The earth gives all and takes all. 1946. Stories; with a memoir of Evans by G. H. Green.

Mother's marvel. [1949].

§2
Smith, P. J. In his For the love of books, 1934.

Green, G. H. A memoir of Evans. In Evans's The earth gives all and takes all, 1946, above.

'Sandys, Oliver' (Marguerite Evans). Caradoc Evans. [1946].

Jones, G. In his The dragon has two tongues, 1968.

'MARGIAD EVANS', PEGGY EILEEN ARABELLA WILLIAMS
1909–58

Bibliographies
In Wales no 5 1938.

§1
Country dance. 1932.
The wooden doctor. Oxford 1933.
Turf or stone. Oxford 1934.
Creed. Oxford 1936.
Autobiography. Oxford 1943, London 1952 (rev).
Poems from obscurity. 1947.
The old and the young. 1948.
A ray of darkness. 1952, New York 1953. Memoirs.
A candle ahead. 1956.

§2
Savage, D. S. Margiad Evans. In his The withered branch, 1950.

ARTHUR ANNESLEY RONALD FIRBANK
1886–1926

Bibliographies
Muir, P. H. A bibliography of the first edns of books by Firbank. Bookman's Jnl 3rd ser 15 no 3 (suppl) 1927.
Horder, T. M. More Ronald Firbank. TLS 28 April 1961. A note on the discovery of the ms of The new rythum.
Benkovitz, M. J. A bibliography of Ronald Firbank. 1963 (Soho bibliographies). With extensive notes on the often complicated publishing history. Also lists Firbank's contributions to periodicals and the surviving mss and typescripts.
Davis, R. M. Firbank: a selected bibliography of criticism. Bull of Bibliography 26 1969.

The catalogue of Sotheby and Co's sale on 12 Dec 1961 contains full details of a number of Firbank letters and other mss, the property of T. Firbank. Seven of the Valmouth notebooks are now at the Univ of Texas, Austin, another is in the Berg Collection, New York Public Library and the Caprice notebooks are at Harvard (see N. W. Alford, Seven notebooks of Firbank, Lib Chronicle of the Univ of Texas 8 1967).

Collections and Selections
Works. 6 vols 1929–34, 5 vols New York 1929. Introd by A. Waley, biographical memoir by O. Sitwell. Based on first edns, with minor textual revisions, except for Odette for which 1916 edn was used. Vol 6 of the English edn, The artificial princess, was not added to the New York edn. Excludes A study in temperament and other early pieces rptd in The new rythum, below.
Rainbow edition (new edn). 8 vols 1929–30, 1940 with 9th vol (The artificial princess). Texts as in Works. Excludes Odette and Santal.
Extravaganzas. New York 1935. Contains The artificial princess and The eccentricities of Cardinal Pirelli. Texts as in 1st edns.
Omnibus edition. 2 vols i.e. Five novels 1949 (with introd by O. Sitwell), Norfolk Conn 1949; Three novels 1950 (with introd by E. Jones), Norfolk Conn 1951. Texts as in Works.
The complete Ronald Firbank. 1961 (preface by A. Powell), Norfolk Conn 1961. Texts as in Works with minor textual corrections, except for texts of Santal and The artificial princess, which are those of the 1st edns.

Two novels. Norfolk Conn 1962. Contains The flower beneath the foot and Prancing nigger. Texts as in 1st edns. With a chronology of Firbank by M. J. Benkovitz.

§1
Odette d'Antrevernes and A study in temperament. 1905. Short stories. 1st story pbd separately 1916 with slight textual revisions (as Odette: a fairy tale for weary people).
Vainglory. 1915, New York [1925] (rev).
Inclinations. 1916.
Odette: a fairy tale for weary people. 1916. See Odette d'Antrevernes above.
Caprice. 1917.
Valmouth: a romantic novel. 1919, 1956 (text as in Works), New York 1956. Unrevised version of ch 8 first pbd in Art & Letters new ser 2 1919 (as Fantasia for orchestra in F sharp minor).
The Princess Zoubaroff: a comedy. 1920. First performed June 1951 at the Watergate Theatre.
Santal. 1921, New York [1955]. Story.
The flower beneath the foot: being a record of the early life of St Laura de Nazianzi and the times in which she lived. 1923, New York [1924] (corrected, with preface by Firbank).
Prancing nigger. New York 1924 (with introd by C. van Vechten), London 1924 (as Sorrow in sunlight, corrected and without the introd), 1931 (as Prancing nigger, with minor revisions i.e. the 1929 Works text). Unrevised version of ch 11 first pbd in Reviewer (Richmond Va) 4 1923 (as A broken orchid).
Concerning the eccentricities of Cardinal Pirelli. 1926.
The artificial princess. Introd by C. Kennard 1934.
A letter from Arthur Ronald Firbank to Madame Albani: written 1902–3 and found amongst her papers after her death. [1934].
The new rythum and other pieces. 1962 (with introd by A. Harris), Norfolk Conn 1963. Contains, in addition to the unfinished title novel, A study in temperament, Lady Appledore's mésalliance, Impression d'automne and a miscellany of unpbd juvenilia.
The wind and the roses. Introd by M. Benkovitz 1965.
Far away. Introd by M. Benkovitz, Iowa 1966.

Firbank is often credited with the authorship of Count Fanny's nuptials 1907, but the attribution rests on hearsay. See Benkovitz's bibliography, above.

§2
Van Vechten, C. Ronald Firbank. Double Dealer 3 1922.
Wilson, E. Late violets from the nineties. Dial 75 1923; rptd in his The shores of light, New York 1952.
— Firbank and Beckford. New Republic 8 Sept 1926; rptd in his The shores of light, New York 1952.
— A revival of Firbank. New Yorker 10 Dec 1949; rptd in his Classics and commercials, New York 1950.
Waugh, E. Ronald Firbank. Life & Letters 2 1929.
Fletcher, I. K. Ronald Firbank. 1930. With personal reminiscences by Lord Berners, V. B. Holland, A. John and O. Sitwell.
Richards, G. Ronald Firbank. In his Author hunting, 1934.
Forster, E. M. Ronald Firbank. In his Abinger harvest, 1936.
Connolly, C. Anatomy of dandyism. In his Enemies of promise, 1938.
Dickinson, P. A note on Firbank 1886–1915–1926. In The Windmill, ed R. Moore and E. Lane 1946.
Pritchett, V. S. Firbank. New Statesman 7 Jan 1950; rptd in his Books in general, 1953.
Sitwell, O. Ronald Firbank. In his Noble essences, 1950.
Brooke, J. Ronald Firbank. 1951.
— Firbank and J. Betjeman. 1962 (Br Council pamphlet).
Hafley, J. Ronald Firbank. Arizona Quart 12 1956.
Benkovitz, M. J. Firbank in New York. BNYPL 63 1959.

—— Firbank in periodicals. PBSA 54 1960.
—— Notes towards a chapter of biography: Lord Alfred Douglas and Firbank. BNYPL 67 1963.
—— Ronald Firbank: a biography. New York 1969.
Auden, W. H. Firbank and an amateur world. Listener 8 June 1961.
Duck, D. Ronald Firbank. In Frederick Rolfe and others: a miscellany of essays, Aylesford 1961.
Duckworth, G. Puzzles in Firbank. TLS 28 April 1961.
Braybrooke, N. Ronald Firbank 1886–1926. Dalhousie Rev 42 1962.
—— Thorns and vanities: Firbank revisited. Encounter 31 1968.
Alford, N. W. Seven notebooks of Firbank. Lib Chron of Univ of Texas 8 1967.
Davis, R. M. From artifice to art: the technique of Firbank's novels. Style 2 1968.
—— 'Hyperaesthesia with complications': the world of Firbank. Rendezvous 3 1968.
—— The text of Firbank's Vainglory. PBSA 63 1969.
Woodward, A. G. Ronald Firbank. English Studies in Africa 11 1968.

FORD MADOX FORD
formerly
JOSEPH LEOPOLD FORD
HERMANN MADOX HUEFFER
1873–1939

According to Harvey's bibliography, below, important collections of Ford mss and letters are in Mrs J. Loewe's private collection (Pasadena), the Brustlein deposit at Princeton Univ, E. Naumburg's private collection (New York), Yale Univ Library and Virginia Univ Library. For details of these and other mss and letters see Harvey.

Bibliographies

Ford Madox Hueffer. New Age 7 1910 (Bibliography of Modern Authors 24).
Ford Madox Hueffer. In A bibliography of modern poetry with notes on some contemporary poets. Chapbook 2 1920.
Gerber, H. Ford Madox Ford: an annotated checklist of writings about him. Eng Fiction in Transition 1 1958. Supplement by F. MacShane in Eng Fiction in Transition 4 1961.
—— Ford Madox Ford. In Bibliography, news and notes. Eng Fiction in Transition 1 1958 and subsequent vols.
MacShane, F. Ford Madox Ford: collections of his letters, collections of his manuscripts, periodicals publications by him, his introductions, prefaces and miscellaneous contributions to books by others. Eng Fiction in Transition 4 1961. The lists of articles and of contributions to books by others are selective.
Harvey, D. D. Ford Madox Ford 1873–1939: a bibliography of works and criticism. Princeton 1962. Exhaustive and annotated, including reviews, with extensive quotation from Ford's uncollected journalism as well as from a large quantity of secondary material concerned only incidentally with Ford.
Beebe, M. and R. G. Johnson. Criticism of Ford: a selected checklist. Modern Fiction Stud 9 1963.
Armato, P. Ford Madox Ford. Eng Lit in Transition 10 1967. Continues Gerber and MacShane above.

Collections and Selections

Collected poems. 1914 [1913]. Signed F. M. Hueffer. With a preface by the author.
Collected poems. New York 1936.
Parade's end, with an introd by R. Macauley. New York 1950. The Tietjens tetralogy in 1 vol.
The Bodley Head Ford Madox Ford. Ed and introd G. Greene 5 vols 1962–71. Includes The good soldier,

The fifth queen trilogy, the Tietjens tetralogy and selected poems and reminiscences.
Critical writings. Ed F. MacShane, Lincoln Nebraska 1964.

§1

All works before The Marsden case *1923 (except pseudonymous ones) are signed Ford Madox Hueffer.*

Prose Fiction

The brown owl: a fairy story. 1892 [1891], New York 1891.
The feather. 1892, New York 1892. Fairy story.
The shifting of the fire. 1892.
The queen who flew. 1894. Fairy story.
The inheritors: an extravagant story. New York 1901, London 1901. With Joseph Conrad.
Romance: a novel. 1903, New York 1904. With Conrad.
The benefactor: a tale of a small circle. 1905.
The fifth queen and how she came to court. 1906. First of The fifth queen trilogy.
Christina's fairy book. [1906]. Fairy stories.
Privy seal: his last venture. 1907. Second of The fifth queen trilogy.
An English girl: a romance. [1907].
The fifth queen crowned: a romance. 1908. Third of The fifth queen trilogy: dramatisation by Ford and F. N. Connell performed at Kingsway Theatre March 1909.
Mr Apollo: a just possible story. [1908].
The Half moon: a romance of the old world and the new. 1909, New York 1909. Planned as part of a trilogy called The three ships; neither of the other pts pbd.
A call: the tale of two passions. 1910. Rptd from Eng Rev 1909 with addn of an 'Epistolary epilogue'.
The portrait. [1910].
The Simple Life Limited. 1911, New York 1911. Satire, under the pseudonym 'Daniel Chaucer'.
Ladies whose bright eyes: a romance. 1911, New York 1911, Philadelphia 1935 (rev).
The panel: a sheer comedy. 1912, Indianapolis [1913] (rev and expanded as Ring for Nancy).
The new Humpty-Dumpty. 1912, New York 1912. Satire, under the pseudonym of 'Daniel Chaucer'.
Mr Fleight. 1913. Satire.
The young Lovell: a romance. 1913.
The good soldier: a tale of passion. 1915, New York 1915, New York 1927 (with preface by Ford), London 1928, New York 1951 (with essay by M. Schorer). The first part of this novel appeared, in somewhat different form, in Blast, 20 June 1914, as The saddest story.
The Marsden case: a romance. [1923].
Some do not—a novel. [1924], New York 1924, London 1948 (with preface by R. A. Scott-James). First of the Tietjens tetralogy.
The nature of a crime. [1924], New York 1924. With Conrad; originally pbd in Eng Rev 1909.
No more parades. [1925], New York [1925], London 1948 (with same preface by Scott-James as to Some do not). Second of the Tietjens tetralogy.
A man could stand up—a novel. [1926], New York 1926, London 1948 (with Scott-James' preface as in Some do not). Third of the Tietjens tetralogy.
The last post. New York 1928, London 1928 (as Last post), London 1948 (with Scott-James' preface as in Some do not). Fourth of the Tietjens tetralogy.
A little less than gods: a romance. [1928], New York 1928.
When the wicked man. New York [1931], London 1932.
The rash act: a novel. New York 1933, London 1933.
Henry for Hugh: a novel. Philadelphia 1934.
Vive le roy: a novel. Philadelphia 1936, London 1937.

An unpbd novel, That same poor man, *exists in ms in the Brustlein deposit at Princeton.*

Other Writings

The questions at the well, with sundry other verses for notes of music. By 'Fenil Haig' [i.e. Ford]. 1893.

Ford Madox Brown: a record of his life and work. 1896.

Poems for pictures and for notes of music. 1900.

The Cinque Ports: a historical and descriptive record. 1900.

Rossetti: a critical essay on his art. [1902], New York [1902].

The face of the night: a second series of poems for pictures. 1904.

The soul of London: a survey of a modern city. 1905.

Hans Holbein the younger: a critical monograph. [1905], New York [1905].

The heart of the country: a survey of a modern land. 1906.

England and the English: an interpretation. New York 1907. Contains The soul of London, The heart of the country and The spirit of the people.

From inland and other poems. 1907.

The Pre-Raphaelite brotherhood: a critical monograph. [1907], New York [1907].

The spirit of the people: an analysis of the English mind. 1907. Previously pbd in U.S.A. only, in England and the English, above.

Songs from London. 1910. Poems.

Ancient lights and certain new reflections. 1911, New York 1911 (as Memories and impressions: a study in atmospheres). Reminiscences.

The critical attitude. 1911. Essays, originally in Eng Rev.

High Germany: eleven sets of verse. 1911 [1912].

This monstrous regiment of women. [1913]. Suffragette pamphlet.

The desirable alien: at home in Germany. 1913. With V. Hunt. Travel.

Henry James: a critical study. 1913 [1914].

Antwerp. [1915]. Poem.

When blood is their argument: an analysis of Prussian culture. 1915. Anti-German war propaganda.

Between St Dennis and St George: a sketch of three civilisations. 1915. Anti-German war propaganda.

Zeppelin nights: a London entertainment. 1916 [1915]. With V. Hunt. Historical sketches.

On heaven, and poems written on active service. 1918.

A house: modern morality play. 1921 (Chapbook 21). Poem.

Thus to revisit: some reminiscences. 1921.

Women and men. Paris 1923. Essays originally pbd in Little Rev.

Mister Bosphorus and the Muses. [1923]. Poem.

Joseph Conrad: a personal remembrance. 1924, Boston 1924.

A mirror to France. [1926]. Impressions.

New poems. New York 1927.

New York is not America. [1927]. New York 1927. Impressions.

New York essays. New York 1927. Rptd from various American journals.

The English novel from the earliest days to the death of Conrad. Philadelphia 1929, London 1930.

No enemy: a tale of reconstruction. [New York 1929]. Disguised autobiography.

Return to yesterday (reminiscences 1894–1914). 1931, New York 1932.

It was the nightingale. Philadelphia 1933, London 1934. Reminiscences, from 1918.

Provence: from minstrels to the machine. Philadelphia 1935, London 1938. Impressions.

Great trade route. New York 1937, London 1937. Impressions.

Portraits from life: memories and criticisms [of various authors]. New York 1937, London 1938 (as Mightier than the sword). Most of these essays first pbd in American Mercury.

The march of literature from Confucius to modern times. New York 1938, London 1939.

Principal Prefaces, Contributions to Books, and Translations

Maupassant, G. de. Stories from De Maupassant. Tr E.M. [Elsie Martindale]. 1903. Preface by Ford.

Chesson, N. Dirge for Aoine and other poems. Introd by Ford 1906.

Hutchings, W. W. London town past and present. With a chapter on the future in London by Ford. 2 vols 1909.

Hunt, A. and V. The governess. With a preface by Ford 1912.

Loti, P. The trail of the barbarians, being L'outrage des barbares. Tr Ford 1917.

Transatlantic stories. Selected from the Transatlantic Rev. With an introd by Ford 1926.

Rhys, J. The left bank and other stories. 1927. Preface.

Asch, N. Love in Chartres. 1927. Introd.

Chadbourne, M. Vasco. Tr E. Sutton, New York 1928. Preface.

Conrad, J. The sisters. New York 1928. Introd.

Carco, F. Perversity. Chicago 1928. Tr Ford [or J. Rhys?].

Morrow's almanack for 1929. Ed B. Rascoe, New York 1928. In vino, by Ford.

Acland, P. All else is folly: a tale of war and passion. With a note by way of preface by Ford. New York 1929.

A Conrad memorial library: the collection of George T. Keating. New York 1929. Includes chapter by Ford on the collaboration in The inheritors.

Defoe, D. The life and strange surprising adventures of Robinson Crusoe. San Francisco 1930. Introd.

Imagist anthology 1930. New York [1930], London 1930. Foreword by Ford, also 3 poems.

Shipp, H. (ed). The English Review book of short stories. 1932. Foreword.

Hemingway, E. A farewell to arms. New York 1932. Introd.

The cantos of Ezra Pound: some testimonials by E. Hemingway, Ford, T. S. Eliot, H. Walpole, A. MacLeish, J. Joyce et al. New York 1933. Ford was apparently the organizer of the tribute.

Béhaine, R. The survivors. Tr E. Crankshaw, preface by Ford, Boston 1938.

Ford edited the English Review *for 15 months from its foundation in Dec 1908, and also the* Transatlantic Review *for 1924.*

Letters

Bartlett, P. Letters of Ford Madox Ford. Saturday Rev of Lit 2 Aug 1941.

Letters of Ford Madox Ford. Ed R. M. Ludwig, Princeton 1965.

See Harvey's bibliography for details of other letters.

§2

Books and Chapters in Books

Sturgeon, M. C. In her Studies of contemporary poets, 1916, 1920 (rev and enlarged).

Monro, H. In his Some contemporary poets, 1920.

Hunt, V. The flurried years. 1926, New York 1926 (rev) (as I have this to say). Reminiscences of Ford.

Jean-Aubry, G. Joseph Conrad: life and letters. 2 vols Garden City NY 1927.

Huddleston, S. Bohemian literary and social life in Paris. 1928, Philadelphia 1928 (as Paris salons, cafés, studios).

Goldring, D. People and places. Boston 1929.

— Odd man out: autobiography of a propaganda novelist. 1935.

— South Lodge: reminiscences of V. Hunt, Ford and the English Review circle. 1943.

— The last pre-Raphaelite: the life and writings of Ford. 1948, New York 1949 (as Trained for genius).

Marshall, A. Out and about. 1933. Reminiscences of Ford.

Wells, H. G. Experiment in autobiography. 2 vols 1934.

Conrad, Jessie. Joseph Conrad and his circle. 1935.

Jepson, E. Memoirs of an Edwardian. 1938.

Aldington, R. Life for life's sake. New York 1941. Includes reminiscences of Ford.

Bowen, S. Drawn from life: reminiscences. 1941.

Putnam, S. Paris was our mistress. New York 1947. Reminiscences of Ford.

Pound, E. The letters of Ezra Pound ed D. D. Paige, New York 1950.

Coffman, S. K. Imagism: a chapter for the history of modern poetry. Norman 1951.

Kenner, H. Digression in French prose. In his The poetry of Ezra Pound, Norfolk Conn 1953.

Garnett, D. The golden echo. 1953. Includes reminiscences of Ford.

Allen, W. The English novel. 1954.

Young, K. Ford Madox Ford. 1956 (Br Council pamphlet).

Baines, J. Joseph Conrad: a critical biography. 1960.

Cassell, R. A. Notes on the labyrinth of design in The good soldier. In Modern British fiction, ed M. Schorer 1961. Rev and expanded in his Ford Madox Ford.
— Ford Madox Ford: a study of his novels. Baltimore 1961.

Meixner, J. A. Ford Madox Ford's novels: a critical study. Minneapolis 1962.

Wiley, P. L. Novelist of three worlds: Ford Madox Ford. Syracuse NY 1962.

Gordon, C. A good soldier: a key to the novels of Ford, with a select bibliography by H. Gerber. Davis California 1963.

Whittemore, R. The fascination of the abomination: Wells, Shaw, Ford, Conrad. In his The fascination of the abomination, New York 1963.

Gordon, A., jr. The invisible tent: the war novels of Ford Madox Ford. Austin 1964.

Lid, R. W. Ford Madox Ford: the essence of his art. Berkeley 1964.

MacShane, F. The life and work of Ford Madox Ford. 1964.

Ohmann, C. B. Ford Madox Ford: from apprentice to craftsman. Middletown Conn 1964.

Hoffmann, C. G. Ford Madox Ford. New York 1967.

Leer, N. The limited hero in the novels of Ford. East Lansing 1967.

Poli, B. J. Ford Madox Ford and The Transatlantic Review. 1968.

Articles in Periodicals

Pound, E. Mr Hueffer and the prose tradition in verse. Poetry (Chicago) 4 1914; rptd in his Pavannes and divisions, New York 1918; Polite essays, 1937; and Literary essays, 1954.
— Ford Madox Ford: obit. Nineteenth Century and After 126 1939; rptd in Furioso 1 1940 and New Directions 7 1942 below.
— Madox Ford at Rapallo. Mood (St Louis) no 24 1950; rptd in his Pavannes and divagations, 1958.

Bonner, M. Ford Madox Hueffer: impressionist. Bookman (New York) 44 1916.

Aiken, C. The function of rhythm. Dial 65 1918. On Ford's On heaven; rptd in his Scepticisms, New York 1919 (as The function of rhythm: Ford Madox Hueffer).

'Lucius' (Douglas Goldring). On heaven. New Ireland 6 1918. Review article rptd and expanded in his Reputations, 1920.

Price, L. M. Ford Madox Hueffer. Poet Lore 31 1920.
— Ford Madox Ford. Univ of California Chron 27 1925.

Gorman, H. Ford Madox Ford: a portrait in impressions. Bookman (New York) 67 1928.
— Ford Madox Ford: the personal side. Harper's Bazaar 84 1950. Different from his article of the same title in the Princeton Univ Lib Chron symposium on Ford, 1948, below.

Hicks, G. Ford Madox Ford: a neglected contemporary. Bookman (New York) 72 1930; rptd in New Directions 7 1942, below.

Zabel, M. D. [Review of Return to yesterday]. Nation (NY) 6 April 1932.
— [Review of Goldring, D. Trained for genius]. Nation (NY) 30 July 1949; rptd with the above, and with addns, as Ford Madox Ford: yesterday and after, in his Craft and character in modern fiction, New York 1957.

Bishop, J. P. The poems of Ford. Poetry (Chicago) 50 1937; rptd in his Collected essays, 1948.

Greene, G. Ford Madox Ford. Spectator 7 July 1939. Obituary essay, rptd in his The lost childhood, 1951.
— Last post? TLS 16 Sept 1965.

Homage to Ford Madox Ford: a symposium. New Directions 7 1942. Brief memoirs of Ford, and tributes to him, by 23 writers.

Ford Madox Ford symposium. Princeton Univ Lib Chron 9 1948. Contains:

Naumburg, E. A collector looks at Ford.
— A catalogue of my Ford collections.

Gorman, H. Ford: the personal side.

Blackmur, R. P. The king over the water: notes on the novels of Hueffer.

Schorer, M. The good novelist in The good soldier, rptd in Horizon 20 1949 and (as An interpretation), in The good soldier, New York 1951.

Macauley, R. The good Ford. Kenyon Rev 11 1949; rptd in The Kenyon critics, ed J. C. Ransom, Cleveland 1951; rev portion pbd as introd to Parade's end, New York 1950.
— The man who talked too well. Vogue 116 1950. Reminiscences of Ford.
— The dean in exile: notes on Ford. Shenandoah 4 1953. More reminiscences.
— Observations on technique: some notes on a lecture given by Ford at Olivet College June 1938. Shenandoah 4 1953.
— A moveable myth. Encounter 23 1964. Hemingway and Ford.

Gordon, C. Parade's end. New York Times Book Rev 17 Sep 1950; rptd (as The story of Ford Madox Ford) in Highlights of modern literature, ed F. Brown, New York 1954.
— The elephant. Sewanee Rev 74 1966. Reviews Ford criticism 1950–66.

Kenner, H. Remember that I have remembered. Hudson Rev 3 1951. Mainly on Parade's end.
— Conrad and Ford. Shenandoah 3 1952; rptd in his Gnomon, [New York] 1958.

Williams, W. C. Parade's end. Sewanee Rev 59 1951; rptd in his Selected essays, New York 1954.

Firebaugh, J. J. Tietjens and the tradition. Pacific Spectator 6 1952.

Bornhauser, F. Ford as art critic. Shenandoah 4 1953.

Gose, E. B. Reality to romance: a study of Ford's Parade's end. College Eng 17 1956.
— The strange irregular rhythm: an analysis of The good soldier. PMLA 72 1957.

Walter, E. V. The political sense of Ford. New Republic 26 March 1956.

Whigham, P. Ford Madox Ford. European 10 1957.

Bradbury, M. The English Review. London Mag 5 1958.

Scott-James, R. A. Ford Madox Ford when he was Hueffer. South Atlantic Quart 57 1958.

Hafley, J. The moral structure of The good soldier. Modern Fiction Stud 5 1959.

Isaacs, N. D. Ford Madox Ford and the Tietjens fulfilment. Lock Haven Bull 1 1959.
— The narrator of The good soldier. Eng Fiction in Transition 6 1963.

Seiden, M. Ford Madox Ford and his tetralogy. London Mag 6 1959.
— Persecution and paranoia in Parade's end. Criticism 8 1966.

Auden, W. H. Il faut payer. Mid-Century no 22 1961. On Parade's end.

Cassell, R. A. The two Sorrells of Ford. MP 59 1961. Expanded from his book on Ford pp 90–106.

Cox, J. T. Ford's passion for Provence. ELH 28 1961. On The good soldier.

Hynes, S. The epistemology of The good soldier. Sewanee Rev 69 1961.

—— Two Rye revolutionists. Sewanee Rev 73 1965. Ford and Conrad.

Ludwig, R. M. The ms of Ford's It was the nightingale. Princeton Univ Lib Chron 22 1961.

—— The reputation of Ford. PMLA 76 1961.

MacShane, F. Ford Madox Ford and his contemporaries: the techniques of the novel. Eng Fiction in Transition 4 1961.

Bender, T. K. The sad tale of Dowell: Ford's The good soldier. Criticism 4 1962.

The conscious artist. TLS 15 June 1962. Critical commentary in the form of a review article.

Pritchett, V. S. Fordie. New Statesman 22 June 1962; rptd in his The working novelist, 1965.

Hill, A. G. The literary career of Ford. CQ 5 1963.

Modern Fiction Studies 9 1963. Ford Madox Ford special no. Contains:

Harvey, D. D. Pro patria mori: the neglect of Ford's novels in England.

Hynes, S. Ford and the spirit of romance.

Griffith, M. A double reading of Parade's end.

Wiesenfarth, J. Criticism and the semiosis of The good soldier.

McFate, P. and B. Golden. The good soldier: a tragedy of self-deception.

Ray, R. J. Style in The good soldier.

Gordon, A., jr. At the edge of silence: The good soldier as war novel. [Rptd in his The invisible tent: the war novels of Ford, 1964].

Andreach, R. J. Ford's The good soldier: the quest for permanence and stability. Tennessee Stud in Lit 10 1965.

Henigan, T. J. The desirable alien: a source for Ford's The good soldier. Twentieth-Century Lit 11 1965.

McCaughey, G. S. The mocking bird and the tomcat: an examination of Ford's The good soldier. Humanities Assoc Bull 16 1965.

Wagner, G. Ford Madox Ford: the honest Edwardian. Carleton Misc 6 1965; EC 17 1967.

Baernstein, J. A. Image, identity and insight in The good soldier. Critique 9 1966.

Braybrooke, N. The walrus and the windmill: a study of Ford. Sewanee Rev 74 1966.

Hanzo, T. A. Downward to darkness. Sewanee Rev 74 1966.

Hoffmann, C. G. Ford's manuscript revisions of The good soldier. Eng Lit in Transition 9 1966.

Kashner, R. J. Tietjens' education: Ford's tetralogy. CQ 8 1966.

Bartlett, P. Ford: a profile. Queen's Quart 74 1967.

Bergonzi, B. The reputation of Ford. New Blackfriars 48 1967.

Bort, B. D. The good soldier: comedy or tragedy? Twentieth-Century Lit 12 1967.

Huntley, H. R. Flaubert and Ford: the fallacy of le mot juste. Eng Lang Notes 4 1967.

—— The good soldier and Die Wahlverwandtschaften. Comparative Lit 19 1967.

Barnes, D. R. Ford and the 'slaughtered saints': a new reading of The good soldier. Modern Fiction Stud 14 1968.

Esslinger, P. M. A theory and three experiments: the failure of the Conrad-Ford collaboration. Western Humanities Rev 22 1968.

Delbaere-Garant, J. Who shall inherit England? a comparison between Howards End, Parade's end, and Unconditional surrender. E Studies 50 1969.

Johnson, A. S. Narrative form in The good soldier. Critique 11 1969.

Mosher, H. F. Wayne Booth and the failure of rhetoric in The good soldier. Caliban 6 1969.

CECIL SCOTT FORESTER
1899–1966

Selections

Captain Hornblower, RN. 1939, Boston 1939 (as Captain Horatio Hornblower). Contains The happy return; A ship of the line; Flying colours.

Rifleman Dodd and The gun. New York 1942.

Cadet edition of Hornblower. 4 vols 1954–5, Boston 1965. Stories selected from the novels by G. P. Griggs. Contains Hornblower goes to sea; Hornblower takes command; Hornblower in captivity; Hornblower's triumph.

The young Hornblower: three complete novels. Boston 1960, London 1964. Mr Midshipman Hornblower; Lieutenant Hornblower; Hornblower and the Atropos.

Captain Hornblower RN. 1965. Hornblower and the Hotspur; The happy return; A ship of the line.

Admiral Hornblower omnibus. 1966.

§1

Napoleon and his court. 1924.

The paid piper. 1924.

A pawn among kings. 1924.

Josephine, Napoleon's empress. 1925, New York 1925.

Payment deferred. 1926, Boston 1942.

Love lies dreaming. 1927, Indianapolis [1927].

Victor Emmanuel II and the union of Italy. 1927, New York 1927.

The wonderful week. 1927, Indianapolis [1927] (as One wonderful week).

Louis XIV, King of France and Navarre. 1928.

The shadow of the hawk. 1928, Indianapolis [1928] (as The daughter of the hawk).

Brown on resolution. 1929, New York 1929 (as Single-handed).

Nelson. 1929, Indianapolis [1929] (as Lord Nelson).

The voyage of the Annie Marble. 1929. Travel.

The Annie Marble in Germany. 1930. Travel.

Plain murder. 1930, New York 1954.

Two-and-twenty. 1931, New York 1931.

U97: a play in three acts. 1931.

Death to the French. 1932.

The gun. 1933, Boston 1933.

Nurse Cavell: a play in three acts. 1933. With C. E. Bechhofer Roberts.

The peacemaker. 1934, Boston 1934.

The African Queen. 1935, Boston 1935, New York 1963 (with new foreword by author).

The general. 1936, Boston 1936.

Marionettes at home. 1936. Non-fiction.

The happy return. 1937, Boston 1937 (as Beat to quarters).

Flying colours. 1938, Boston 1939.

A ship of the line. 1938, Boston 1938.

The earthly paradise. 1940, Boston 1940 (as To the Indies).

The captain from Connecticut. 1941, Boston 1941.

Poo-poo and the dragons. 1942, Boston 1942. For children.

The ship. 1943, Boston 1943.

The commodore. 1945, Boston 1945 (as Commodore Hornblower).

Lord Hornblower. 1946, Boston 1946.

The sky and the forest. 1948, Boston 1948.

Mr Midshipman Hornblower. 1950, Boston 1950.

Randall and the river of time. Boston 1950, London 1951.

Lieutenant Hornblower. 1952, Boston 1952.

The Barbary pirates. New York 1953, London 1956. For children.

Hornblower and the Atropos. 1953, Boston 1953.

The adventures of John Wetherell, ed with an introd by Forester. 1953.

The nightmare. 1954, Boston 1954.

The good shepherd. 1955.

The age of fighting sail: the story of the naval war of 1812. Garden City NY 1956, London 1957 (as The naval war of 1812).

Hornblower in the West Indies. 1958, Boston 1958 (as Admiral Hornblower in the West Indies).

Hunting the Bismarck. 1959, Boston 1959 (as The last nine days of the Bismarck). A fictional account.

Hornblower and the Hotspur. 1962, Boston 1962.

The Hornblower companion. 1964, Boston 1964. Contains autobiographical notes.

William Joyce. In Fatal fascination: a choice of crime, by N. Balchin, Forester [et al], 1964, Boston 1965.

Hornblower and the crisis: an unfinished novel. 1967.

Long before forty. 1967, Boston 1968. Autobiography to the age of 31. Contains autobiographical notes rptd from The Hornblower companion, 1964.

The man in the yellow raft. 1969, Boston 1969. Short stories.

ELLEN THORNEYCROFT FOWLER
1860–1929

§1

Verses grave and gay. 1891.

Verses wise or otherwise. 1895, 1905 (including Verses grave and gay).

Cupid's garden. 1897. Stories.

Concerning Isabel Carnaby. 1898, New York 1899.

A double thread. 1899, New York 1899.

The Farringdons. 1900, New York 1900.

Love's argument, and other poems. 1900, New York 1901.

The angel and the demon, and other stories. 1901.

How to make an angel. [1901]. Temperance tract.

Sirius, and other stories. 1901, New York 1901 (as Sirius: a volume of fiction).

Fuel of fire. 1902, New York 1902.

Place and power. 1903, New York 1903.

Kate of Kate Hall. 1904, New York 1904. With A. L. Felkin.

In subjection. 1906, New York 1906 (as The subjection of Isabel Carnaby).

Miss Fallowfield's fortune. 1908, New York 1908.

The wisdom of folly. 1910.

Her ladyship's conscience. [1913].

Ten degrees backward. 1915, New York 1915.

Beauty and bands. 1920.

The lower pool. [1923].

Signs and wonders. [1926].

The Isabel Carnaby birthday book [*1900*] *is a selection of sayings from the first 3 novels arranged by E. D. Barrington.*

§2

The novels of E. T. Fowler. Living Age 226 1900.

The author of The Farringdons: an enquiry. Academy 58 1900.

Williams, J. E. H. Ellen Thorneycroft Fowler. Bookman (London) 18 1900.

GILBERT FRANKAU
1884–1952

Collections and Selections

The poetical works of Gilbert Frankau. 2 vols 1923.

The Peter Jackson omnibus. [1932].

Gilbert Frankau's romances. [1933]. Contains The love story of Aliette Brunton, Gerald Cranston's lady, Life—and Erica.

Gilbert Frankau's escape to yesterday: a miscellany of tales. [1942].

Selected verses. 1943.

The definitive edition of Gilbert Frankau's novels and short stories. 18 vols [1945–9]. A few of the texts have minor corrections.

§1

Eton echoes: a volume of humorous verse. 1901.

The XYZ of bridge. [1906]. Humorous verse.

One of us: a novel in verse. 1912, New York [1912] (as Jack—one of us).

'Tid'apa': what does it matter? New York 1914, London 1915. Verse.

The guns. 1916, New York 1916 (as A song of the guns). Verse.

How rifleman Brown came to Valhalla. New York 1916. Verse.

The city of fear, and other poems. 1917.

The woman of the horizon: a romance of nineteen-thirteen. 1917, New York 1923.

The judgement of Valhalla. 1918, New York 1918. Verse.

One of them: a novelette in verse. 1918.

The other side, and other poems. New York 1918.

Peter Jackson, cigar merchant: a romance of married life. 1920, New York 1920.

The seeds of enchantment. [1921], Garden City NY 1921.

The love story of Aliette Brunton. 1922, New York 1922.

Men, maids and mustard pot: a collection of tales. 1923 New York [1924].

Gerald Cranston's lady: a romance. 1924, New York [1924].

Life—and Erica: a romance. New York [1924], London [1925].

The dominant type of man. 1925. Essay, on cigar smokers.

Masterson: a study of an English gentleman. [1925], New York 1926.

My unsentimental journey. [1926].

Twelve tales. [1927].

So much good. [1928].

Dance, little gentleman! [1929], New York 1930.

The house behind the Judas tree. [1929]. Story, pbd with Martyrdom, by W. Deeping, and Forbidden music, by E. Mannin. Reissued 1936 as Three stories of romance.

Martin Make-Believe: a romance. [1930], New York 1931.

Concerning Peter Jackson and others. [1931].

Christopher Strong: a romance. [1932], New York [1932].

The lonely man: a romance of love and the Secret Service. [1932], New York [1933].

Wine, women and waiters. [1932]. Stories.

Everywoman. New York [1933], London [1934].

Secret services. [1934]. Short stories.

Three Englishmen: a romance of married lives. [1935], New York 1935.

Farewell romance. 1936, New York 1936.

Experiments in crime, and other stories. [1937], New York 1937.

More of us, being the present-day adventures of 'One of us': a novel in verse. 1937, New York [1951].

The dangerous years: a trilogy. 1937, New York 1938.

Royal regiment: a drama of contemporary behaviours. 1938, New York 1939.

Gilbert Frankau's self-portrait: a novel of his own life. [1940], New York 1940.

Winter of discontent. [1941], New York 1942 (as Air Ministry Room 28).

World without end. [1943], New York 1943.

Michael's wife. 1948, New York 1948.

Son of the morning. 1949.

Oliver Trenton, KC. 1951.

Unborn tomorrow: a last story. 1953.

§2

Braybrooke, P. In his Novelists: we are seven, 1926.

RONALD FRASER
(SIR ARTHUR RONALD FRASER)
b. 1888

§1

The flying draper. 1924, 1931 (rev).
Landscape with figures. 1925, New York 1926, London 1952 (rev).
Flower phantoms. 1926, New York 1926.
The vista. 1928.
Rose Anstey. 1930.
Marriage in heaven. 1932, New York 1933.
Tropical waters. 1933.
The ninth of July. 1934.
Surprising results. 1935.
A house in the park. 1937.
Bird under glass. 1938.
Miss Lucifer. 1939.
Financial times. 1942.
The fiery gate. 1943.
Circular tour. 1946.
Maia. 1948.
Sun in Scorpio. 1949.
Beetle's career. 1951.
Glimpses of the sun. 1952.
Latin America: a personal survey. 1953.
Bell from a distant temple. 1954.
Flight of wild geese. 1955.
Lord of the east. 1956.
The wine of illusion. 1957.
Jupiter in the chair. 1958.
A visit from Venus. 1958.
Trout's testament. 1960.
City of the sun. 1961.

ROY BROADBENT FULLER
b. 1912
See col 278, above.

JOHN GALSWORTHY
1867–1933

The Univ of Birmingham Library contains Galsworthy's own collection of mss (see Catalogue pbd by the Library 1967). The ms of The Forsyte Saga is in the BM.

Bibliographies

Marrot, H. V. A bibliography of the works of Galsworthy. 1928. Includes Galsworthy's contributions to books and periodicals.
Fabes, G. H. Galsworthy: his first editions. 1932.
Bennett, J. W. Galsworthy and H. G. Wells. Yale Univ Lib Gazette 28 1953. On the Yale Galsworthy collection.
Gerber, H. E. Galsworthy: an annotated bibliography of writings about him. Eng Fiction in Transition 1 1958. Continued by E. E. Stevens in Eng Lit in Transition 7 1964, 10 1967.
Vsesoyuznaya Gosudarstvennaya Biblioteka Inostrannoi Literatury. Dzhon Golsuorsi: bio-bibliografichesky ukazatel'. Moscow 1958. Includes Russian trns and secondary material in Russian.

Collections and Selections

See also Marrot's bibliography, above, for a note on various cheap and uniform edns.

Plays. 7 sers 1909–30. Sers 1–6 pbd New York 1909–26.
Works: Manaton edition. 30 vols New York 1922–36, London 1923–35. Contains prefaces specially written by the author for this edn, and other prefaces by Ada Galsworthy.
Novels, tales and plays of Galsworthy: Devon edition. 18 vols New York 1926–7.
Works: Grove edition. 26 vols 1927–34.
Collected poems. Ed A. Galsworthy [1934], New York 1934.

Some slings and arrows from Galsworthy, selected by E. E. Morton. 1914.
Representative plays by Galsworthy, with an introd by G. P. Baker. New York [1924]. Contains The silver box, Strife, Justice, The pigeon, A bit o'love, Loyalties.
Caravan: the assembled tales of Galsworthy. 1925, New York 1925.
Plays. New York and London 1928. 25 plays.
Candelabra: selected essays and addresses. 1932 (in Grove edn, above), New York 1933.
Worshipful society. New York 1932. The country house, Fraternity, The patrician.
Ex libris John Galsworthy. 1933. Selection made by the author and A. Galsworthy.
Three novels of love. New York 1933. The dark flower, Beyond, Saint's progress.
Forsytes, Pendyces and others. 1935, New York 1935. Essays and stories, selected by A. Galsworthy.
Selected short stories. Ed T. W. Moles 1935.
Ten famous plays. [1941].
The Galsworthy reader. Ed A. West, New York 1968.

§1
Prose Fiction

From the four winds, by John Sinjohn [i.e. Galsworthy]. 1897. Stories.
Jocelyn, by John Sinjohn. 1898.
Villa Rubein, by John Sinjohn. 1900, New York 1908 (as by Galsworthy), London 1909 (rev, with A man of Devon, below).
A man of Devon, by John Sinjohn. 1901. Stories; rptd (rev) in 1909 edn of Villa Rubein, above.
The island Pharisees. 1904, 1908 (rev).
The man of property. 1906, New York 1906, [1964] (Limited Editions Club, introd by E. Waugh); rptd in The Forsyte saga, 1922, below.
The country house. 1907, New York 1907.
A commentary. 1908, New York 1908. Stories.
Fraternity. 1909, New York 1909.
A motley. 1910, New York 1910. Stories.
The patrician. 1911, New York 1911, [1926] (introd by B. Perry).
The dark flower. 1913, New York 1913.
The little man, and other satires. New York 1915, London 1915. Stories.
The Freelands. 1915, New York 1915.
Beyond. New York 1917, London 1917, 1923 (rev).
Five tales. New York 1918, London 1918, 1920 (2 vols, The first and the last; The stoic), New York 1965 (as The apple tree and other tales). Includes Indian summer of a Forsyte, rptd in The Forsyte saga, below.
The burning spear: being the adventures of Mr John Lavender in time of war, recorded by A.R.P—M. 1919, New York 1923 (as by Galsworthy, with foreword by him).
Saint's progress. New York 1919, London 1919.
Tatterdemalion. 1920, New York 1920. Stories.
In Chancery. 1920, New York 1920; rptd in The Forsyte saga, below.
Awakening. New York [1920], London [1920]; rptd in The Forsyte saga, below.
To let. New York 1921, London 1921; rptd in The Forsyte saga, below.
The Forsyte saga. New York 1922, London 1922, 1933 (with preface by A. Galsworthy), New York 1933.
Captures. 1923, New York 1923. Stories.
The white monkey. New York 1924, London 1924. Rptd in A modern comedy, 1929, below.

Abracadabra and other satires. 1924. Stories first pbd in The little man and other satires, above.

The silver spoon. 1926, New York 1926. Rptd in A modern comedy, below.

Two Forsyte interludes: A silent wooing; Passers by. 1927, New York 1938.

Swan song. New York 1928, London 1928. Rptd in A modern comedy, below.

Four Forsyte stories. New York 1929, London 1929.

A modern comedy. 1929, New York 1929. The white monkey, The silver spoon, Swan song.

On Forsyte 'change. 1930, New York 1930. Stories.

Soames and the flag. 1930, New York 1930.

Maid in waiting. 1931, New York 1931. This and the next two items rptd in End of the chapter, 1934 below.

Flowering wilderness. 1932, New York 1932.

Over the river. 1933, New York 1933 (as One more river).

The apple tree. New York 1934. Story, first pbd in Five tales, 1918.

End of the chapter. New York 1934, London 1935. Maid in waiting, Flowering wilderness, Over the river

'Corduroys', by John Sinjohn. Kansas City 1937 (priv ptd).

The rocks, by John Sinjohn. Kansas City 1937 (priv ptd).

'Nyasha. Kansas City 1939 (priv ptd, 30 copies). Story.

Plays

Plays are listed in order of production, where known.

The silver box: a comedy in three acts. (Royal Court 25 Sept 1906). In Plays ser 1, 1909, Collections, above; pbd separately New York 1909, London 1910.

Joy: a play on the letter I in three acts. (Savoy 24 Sept 1907). In Plays ser 1, 1909, Collections, above; pbd separately 1910.

Strife: a drama in three acts. (Duke of York's 9 March 1909). In Plays ser 1, 1909, Collections, above; pbd separately 1910, New York 1920.

Justice: a tragedy in four acts. (Duke of York's 21 Feb 1910). 1910, New York 1910.

The little dream: an allegory in six scenes. (Gaiety, Manchester 15 April 1911; Court 28 Oct 1912). New York 1911, London [1911], [1912] (rev).

The pigeon: a fantasy in three acts. (Royalty 30 Jan 1912). 1912, New York 1912.

The eldest son: a domestic drama in three acts. (Kingsway 25 Nov 1912). 1912, New York 1912.

The fugitive: a play in four acts. (Royal Court 16 Sept 1913). 1913.

The mob: a play in four acts. (Coronet 20 April 1914). 1914, New York 1914.

A bit o' love: a play in three acts. (Kingsway 25 May 1915). 1915, New York 1915.

The foundations: an extravagant play in three acts. (Royalty 26 June 1917). 1920, New York 1920.

The skin game: a tragi-comedy in three acts. (St Martin's 21 April 1920). 1920, New York 1920.

A family man: in three acts. (Comedy 2 June 1921). 1922, New York 1922.

Six short plays. 1921, New York 1921. Contains The first and the last; The little man; Hall-marked; Defeat; The sun; Punch and go.

Loyalties: a drama in three acts. (St Martin's 8 March 1922). 1922.

Defeat: a play in one act. (Everyman 17 April 1922). In Six short plays, 1921, above.

Windows: a comedy in three acts for idealists and others. (Royal Court 25 April 1922). 1922, New York 1923.

The forest: a drama in four acts. (St Martin's 6 March 1924). 1924, New York 1924.

Old English: a play in three acts. (Haymarket 21 Oct 1924). 1924, New York 1925.

The show: a drama in three acts. (St Martin's 1 July 1925). 1925, New York 1925.

Punch and go: a comedy. (Everyman 24 May 1926). In Six short plays, 1921, above.

Escape: an episodic play in a prologue and two parts. (Ambassadors 12 Aug 1926). 1926. For the discarded Episode VII, *see* The winter garden, 1935, below.

Exiled: an evolutionary comedy in three acts. (Wyndham's 19 June 1929). 1929.

The roof: a play in seven scenes. (Vaudeville 5 Nov 1929). 1929, New York 1931.

The little man: a farcical morality in three scenes. (Little 19 June 1934). In Six short plays, 1921, above; pbd separately 1924.

The winter garden: four dramatic pieces. 1935. The winter garden; Escape—episode VII; The golden eggs; Similes.

Other Works

A commentary. 1908. Sketches.

A justification of the censorship of plays. 1909. Pamphlet.

Horses in mines. [1910]. Rptd from Times.

A motley. 1910, New York 1910. Essays.

The spirit of punishment. 1910. Rptd, rev, from Daily Chron.

For love of beasts. 1912. Rptd from Pall Mall Gazette.

The inn of tranquillity. New York 1912, London 1912. Essays.

Moods, songs & doggerels. New York 1912, London 1912.

'Gentles, let us rest'. [1913]. Rptd from Nation.

The slaughter of animals for food. [1913]. Rptd from Daily Mail.

Treatment of animals. [1913]. Speech.

Memories. 1914, New York 1914. First pbd in the Inn of tranquillity, 1912.

A sheaf. 1916, New York 1916. Essays.

Your Christmas dinner is served! 1916. Leaflet, issued by the National Committee for Relief in Belgium.

The land: a plea. [1917]. Pamphlet.

Addresses in America. New York 1919, London 1919.

Another sheaf. 1919, New York 1919. Essays.

Five poems. New York 1919 (priv ptd, 10 copies).

To the Cliff-Dwellers [of Chicago]: an address. Chicago 1919 (priv ptd).

The bells of peace. Cambridge 1921. Poem.

International thought. Cambridge 1923. Pamphlet.

Memorable days. 1924 (priv ptd, 60 copies). Pamphlet; autobiographical.

On expression. 1924 (English Assoc presidential address).

Is England done? Hove 1925 (priv ptd, 60 copies). Rptd from Sunday Times.

A talk on playing the game with animals and birds. [1926.]

Verses new and old. 1926, New York [1926].

Castles in Spain & other screeds. 1927, New York 1927. Essays.

The way to prepare peace. 1927 (priv ptd, 20 copies). Rptd from Daily Mirror.

Mr Galsworthy's appeal for the miners. [1928]. Rptd from Manchester Guardian Weekly.

The plight of the miners: a national danger: Mr Galsworthy's suggestions. [1928]. Rptd from Manchester Guardian.

A rambling discourse. 1929. Address to the Associated Societies of Edinburgh University.

Two essays on Conrad. Cincinnati 1930 (priv ptd).

The creation of character in literature. Oxford 1931 (Romanes lecture).

'Literature and life'. Princeton 1931. Lecture.

[Forty poems]. [1932] (Augustan Books of Poetry).

Author and critic. New York 1933. Booklet.

Glimpses & reflections. 1937. Miscellaneous papers.

Address to the PEN Club (Brussels June 1927). Kansas City 1939 (priv ptd, 30 copies).

Many of Galsworthy's works were first pbd in various periodicals: see Marrot's bibliography for details to 1928.

Letters

Autobiographical letters of Galsworthy: a correspondence with Frank Harris, hitherto unpublished. New York 1933.

Letters from Galsworthy 1900–1932. Ed E. Garnett 1934.

Wilson, A. B. Galsworthy's letters to Leon Lion. Hague 1968 (Stud in Eng Lit 15).

§2

A list of secondary material in Russian appears in Dzhon Golsuorsi: bio-bibliograficheskesky ukazatel', *1958. See* Bibliographies, *above.*

Books and Chapters in Books

Cooper, F. T. In his Some English story tellers, New York 1912.

Kaye-Smith, S. John Galsworthy. 1916.

Schrey, K. Galsworthy und die besitzenden Klassen Englands. Marburg 1917.

Trumbauer, W. H. Gerhart Hauptmann and Galsworthy. Philadelphia 1917.

Chevrillon, A. In his Trois études de littérature anglaise, Paris 1922. Tr 1923.

Conrad, J. Galsworthy: an appreciation. Canterbury 1922; rptd in his Last essays, 1926.

Ervine, St J. In his Some impressions of my elders, 1922.

— In Great democrats, ed A. B. Brown 1934.

Adcock, A. St J. In his Gods of modern Grub Street, 1923.

Mais, S. P. B. In his Some modern authors, 1923.

Coats, R. H. John Galsworthy as a dramatic artist. 1926.

Lawrence, D. H. In Scrutinies, ed E. Rickword 1928; rptd in his Phoenix, New York 1936.

Marrot, H. V. A note on Galsworthy, dramatist. 1928.

— The life and letters of Galsworthy. 1935.

Schalit, L. John Galsworthy. Berlin 1928. Tr 1929.

Leimert, E. Viktorianismus bei Galsworthy. Marburg 1930.

Ford, F. M. (formerly Hueffer). It was the nightingale. 1933. Includes reminiscences of Galsworthy.

Guyot, E. John Galsworthy 1: Le romancier. Paris 1933. No more pbd.

Heraucourt, W. Die Darstellung des englischen National-charakters in Galsworthys Forsyte Saga. Marburg 1933.

Rohmer, C. Buddenbrooks und The Forsyte Saga. Nördlingen 1933.

Walpole, H. In The Post-Victorians, 1933.

Delattre, F. Le roman social de Galsworthy, Paris 1934.

Jopp, G. Die Modifikation des Verbalbegriffs bei Galsworthy. Marburg 1934.

Ould, H. John Galsworthy. 1934.

Swinnerton, F. In his Georgian scene, New York 1934, London 1935 (as The Georgian literary scene).

Arns, L. Galsworthy und die Krisis des Industrialismus. Düren 1935.

Davies, S. H. Galsworthy the craftsman: final studies in the original manuscripts of the Forsyte chronicles. [Swansea 1935] (priv ptd).

Kroener, J. Die Technik des realistischen Dramas bei Ibsen und Galsworthy. Leipzig 1935 (Beiträge zur englischen Philologie 28).

Rabius, W. Die innere strukturelle Verwandschaft von Galsworthys Forsyte Saga und den isländischen Sagas. Marburg 1935.

Zimmermann, I. Stilistischer Wert der progressiven Form in Galsworthys Werken. Bochum 1935.

Reynolds, M. E. Memories of Galsworthy, by his sister. 1936.

Schmitz, W. Der Mensch und die Gesellschaft im Werke Galsworthys. Bochum 1936.

Burbiel, E. Die Kunst der Charakterdarstellungen in Galsworthys Forsyte Saga. Borna-Leipzig 1937.

Curle, R. A remarkable friendship: Conrad and Galsworthy. In his Caravansary and conversation, 1937.

Galsworthy, A. In her Over the hills and far away, 1937.

Muller, H. J. Realism of the center: Bennett, Galsworthy, Maugham. In his Modern fiction, New York 1937.

Gese, G. Galsworthy als sozialer Kritiker und Reformer. Greifswald 1938.

Radtke, W. Ironie und Humor in Galsworthys Forsyte-zyklus. Lengerich 1938.

Dupont, V. Galsworthy: the dramatic artist. Paris 1942.

Smith, J. H. The short stories of Galsworthy. Rotterdam 1947.

Mottram, R. H. John Galsworthy. 1953 (Br Council pamphlet).

— For some we loved: an intimate portrait of Ada and John Galsworthy. 1956.

Takahashi, G. Studies in the works of Galsworthy. Tokyo 1954, 1956 (rev).

Ross, W. O. Galsworthy: aspects of an attitude. In Studies in honor of J. Wilcox, ed A. D. Wallace and W. O. Ross, Detroit 1958.

Choudhuri, A. D. Galsworthy's plays: a critical survey. Calcutta 1961.

Barker, D. The man of principle: a view of Galsworthy. 1963.

Fricker, R. Galsworthy: Justice. In Das moderne englische Drama, ed H. Oppel, Berlin 1963.

Morris, M. My Galsworthy story. 1967. Includes letters from Galsworthy.

Sauter, R. Galsworthy the man: an intimate portrait. 1967.

Holloway, D. John Galsworthy. [1968].

Articles in Periodicals

Macartney, M. H. H. The novels of Galsworthy. Westminster Rev 171 1909.

Bjorkman, E. Galsworthy: an interpreter of modernity. Rev of Reviews 43 1911; rptd in his Is there anything new under the sun?, 1913.

Cazamian, M. La pensée de Galsworthy. Revue du Mois 15 1913.

d'Hangest, G. La nature dans l'oeuvre de Galsworthy. Revue Germanique 9 1913.

Howe, P. P. Galsworthy as dramatist. Fortnightly Rev 94 1913.

Skemp, A. R. The plays of Galsworthy. E & S 4 1913.

Storer, E. Dramatists of today: Galsworthy. Br Rev 4 1913.

Hale, E. E. John Galsworthy. Dial 59 1915.

Follett, H. T. and W. John Galsworthy. Atlantic Monthly 118 1916.

Courtney, W. L. Galsworthy as a dramatist. Fortnightly Rev 111 1922.

Lockert, L. Some of Galsworthy's heroines. North Amer Rev 215 1922.

Lugli, V. John Galsworthy. Nuova Antologia 57 1922.

Wilson, A. C. The Forsyte family. Manchester Quart 41 1922.

Cobley, W. D. John Galsworthy. Manchester Quart 42 1923.

Gould, G. Galsworthy as a novelist. Bookman (London) 65 1923.

Lemonnier, L. Galsworthy et quelques auteurs français. Mercure de France 161 1923.

Overton, G. Galsworthy's secret loyalties. Bookman (New York) 57 1923.

Shanks, E. John Galsworthy. London Mercury 8 1923.

Martin, D. Galsworthy as artist and reformer. Yale Rev 14 1924.

Priestley, J. B. John Galsworthy. English Jnl 14 1925.

Steinermayr, F. C. Der Werdegang von Galsworthys Welt- und Kunstanschauung. Anglia 49 1925–6.

Simrell, V. E. Galsworthy: the artist as propagandist. Quart Jnl of Speech Education 13 1927.

Wolff, L. Galsworthy: conteur. Revue Anglo-américaine 5 1927.

Knapp, O. John Galsworthy. Hochland 26 1928–9.

Stranik, E. John Galsworthy. Neue Schweizer Rundschau 21 1928.

Weltzien, E. Galsworthys Dramen als kulturkundliche Lesestoffe. Zeitschrift für Französischen und Englischen Unterricht 27 1928.

Cross, W. The Forsytes. Yale Rev 19 1929; rptd in his Four contemporary novelists, New York 1930.

Funke, O. Zur 'Erlebten Rede' bei Galsworthy. E Studien 64 1929.

Shipp, H. The art of Galsworthy. Eng Rev 49 1929.

Duffin, H. C. The rehabilitation of Soames Forsyte. Cornhill Mag 68 1930.

Gary, F. Galsworthy and the Poetics. Symposium 1 1930.

Mann, T. An impression of Galsworthy. Virginia Quart Rev 6 1930.

Russell, F. T. Ironic Galsworthy. Univ of California Chron 32 1930.

Austin, H. P. John Galsworthy. Dublin Rev 189 1931.

Bruyn, J. de. John Galsworthy. Dietsche Warande en Belfort 32 1932.

'Daniel-Rops' (J. C. H. Petiot). Le prix Nobel: Galsworthy. Vie Intellectuelle 18 1932.

Jaloux, E. John Galsworthy. Revue de Paris 39 1932.

Bates, E. S. John Galsworthy. Eng Jnl 22 1933.

Ford, F. M. (formerly Hueffer). Galsworthy and George Moore. Eng Rev 57 1933.

—— John Galsworthy. Amer Mercury 37 1936; rptd in his Portraits from life, New York 1937, London 1938 (as Mightier than the sword).

James, S. B. A contrast in sagas: Undset and Galsworthy. Month 161 1933.

Michel-Côte, P. Galsworthy et le traditionalisme anglais. Revue Hebdomadaire new ser 29 1933.

Moses, M. J. John Galsworthy. North Amer Rev 235 1933.

Siegel, P. Galsworthys Strife in der mathematischen Oberprima. Die Neueren Sprachen 41 1933.

Sparrow, J. John Galsworthy. London Mercury 28 1933.

Véron, J. Galsworthy through French eyes. Cornhill Mag 74 1933.

Watson, E. H. Galsworthy the novelist. Eng Rev 56 1933.

Colenutt, R. The world of Galsworthy's fiction. Cornhill Mag 149 1934.

Krause, G. Das Verhältnis der Menschen zum Besitz in Galsworthys Forsyte Saga. Neuphilologische Mitteilungen 35 1934.

Brash, W. B. John Galsworthy. London Quart 160 1935.

Mark, H. Die Verwendung der Mundart und des Slang in den Werken von Galsworthy. Sprache und Kultur der Germanischen und Romanischen Völker 23 1936.

Dierlam, G. Galsworthy als Dramatiker. Germanisch-Romanische Monatsschrift 28 1940.

Wagenknecht, E. The selfish heroine: Thackeray and Galsworthy. College Eng 4 1942.

Kain, R. M. Galsworthy, the last Victorian liberal. Madison Quart 4 1944.

Grove, F. P. Morality in The Forsyte saga. UTQ 15 1945.

Faure, F. Galsworthy et les littératures étrangères. Revue de Littérature Comparée 22 1948.

Eaker, J. G. Galsworthy and the modern mind. PQ 29 1950.

Freeman, J. C. Whyte-Melville and Galsworthy's 'Bright beings'. Nineteenth-Century Fiction 5 1950.

Bennett, J. W. Galsworthy and H. G. Wells. Yale Lib Gazette 28 1953.

Hamilton, R. Galsworthy: a humanitarian prophet. Quart Rev 291 1953.

—— The Forsyte saga. Quart Rev 304 1966.

Harkness, B. Conrad on Galsworthy: the time scheme of Fraternity. Modern Fiction Stud 1 1955.

Thienova, I. Der kritische Realismus bei Galsworthy. Zeitschrift für Anglistik und Amerikanistik 3 1955.

Poettgen, H. and K. H. Stader. Galsworthys The man who kept his form. Die Neueren Sprachen 4 1956.

Schloesser, A. Galsworthys Bedeutung als Dramatiker. Zeitschrift für Anglistik und Amerikanistik 5 1957.

Pallette, D. Young Galsworthy: the forging of a satirist. MP 56 1959.

Zumwatt, E. E. The myth of the garden in Galsworthy's Apple tree. Research Stud (Washington) 27 1959.

Bache, W. B. Justice: Galsworthy's dramatic tragedy. Modern Drama 3 1960.

Croft-Cooke, R. Grove Lodge. Cornhill Mag 173 1962. Reminiscences of Galsworthy.

Garnett, D. E. M. Forster and Galsworthy. REL 5 1964.

Scrimgeour, G. J. Naturalist drama and Galsworthy. Modern Drama 7 1964.

Van Egmond, P. Naming techniques in Galsworthy's Forsyte saga. Names 16 1968.

DAVID GARNETT
b. 1892

§1

Dope-darling, by Leda Burke [i.e. Garnett]. [1919].

Lady into fox. 1922, New York 1923, London 1928 (with A man in the zoo, below), New York 1966 (with note by author and introd by V. Starrett).

A man in the zoo. 1924, New York 1924, London 1928 (with Lady into fox, above).

The sailor's return. 1925, New York 1925, London 1948 (with Beany-eye, below).

Go she must! 1927, New York 1927.

The old dovecote, and other stories. 1928.

No love. 1929, New York 1929.

The grasshoppers come. 1931, New York [1931].

A rabbit in the air: notes from a diary kept while learning to handle an aeroplane. 1932.

A terrible day. 1932.

Pocahontas: or, the nonpareil of Virginia. 1933, New York [1933]. Biography.

Beany-eye. 1935, New York [1935], London 1948 (with The sailor's return, above).

The letters of T. E. Lawrence. Ed Garnett 1938, New York 1939, London 1952 (as Selected letters of T. E. Lawrence).

War in the air: September 1939 to May 1941. 1941, Garden City NY 1941.

The essential T. E. Lawrence, selected by Garnett. 1951, New York 1951.

The golden echo. 1953, New York 1954. Autobiography.

Aspects of love. 1955, New York 1956.

The flowers of the forest. 1955, New York 1956. Autobiography; sequel to The golden echo, above.

A shot in the dark. 1958, Boston 1958.

A net for Venus. 1959.

The familiar faces. 1962, New York 1963. Autobiography: sequel to The flowers of the forest, above.

Two by two: a story of survival. 1963, New York 1964.

Ulterior motives. 1966, New York 1967.

Letters

The [T.H.] White/Garnett letters. Ed Garnett 1968, New York 1968.

§2

Irwin, W. R. The metamorphoses of Garnett. PMLA 73 1958.

WALTER LIONEL GEORGE
1882–1926

Selections

The selected short stories of W. L. George. 1927.

§1

Engines of social progress. 1907. Non-fiction.
France in the twentieth century. 1908, New York 1909.
Labour and housing at Port Sunlight. 1909.
A bed of roses. 1911, New York [1919].
The city of light: a novel of modern Paris. 1912, New York 1912.
Israel Kalisch. 1913, New York 1913 (as Until the day break).
Woman and to-morrow. 1913, New York 1913. Non-fiction.
Dramatic actualities. 1914. Essays.
The making of an Englishman. 1914, New York 1914, Boston 1916 (as The little beloved).
The second blooming. 1914, Boston 1915.
Anatole France. 1915, New York 1915.
Olga Nazimov, and other stories. 1915. Stories, some in collaboration with Helen George.
The intelligence of woman. Boston 1916, London 1917. Non-fiction.
The strangers' wedding: the comedy of a romantic. Boston 1916, London 1916.
A novelist on novels. [1918], Boston 1918 (as Literary chapters).
Blind alley. 1919, Boston 1919.
Eddies of the day. 1919. Essays.
Caliban. 1920, New York [1920].
The confession of Ursula Trent. 1921, New York 1921 (as Ursula Trent).
Hail Columbia!: random impressions of a conservative English radical. New York 1921, London 1923.
A London mosaic. 1921, New York 1921.
The stiff lip. 1922, New York 1922 (as Her unwelcome husband).
One of the guilty. 1923, New York [1923].
How to invest your money. 1924.
The triumph of Gallio. 1924, New York 1924.
The story of woman. 1925, New York 1925. Non-fiction.
Children of the morning. 1926, New York 1927.
Gifts of Sheba. 1926, New York 1926.
Historic lovers. [1926]. Non-fiction.
The ordeal of Monica Mary. [1927].

§2

Harris, F. W. L. George. In his Contemporary portraits, 3rd ser New York [1920].
Hind, C. L. W. L. George. In his More authors and I, 1922.
Johnson, R. B. W. L. George. In his Some contemporary novelists: men, 1922.

WILLIAM ALEXANDER GERHARDIE
b. 1895

Mr Gerhardie formerly used the spelling Gerhardi

Collections

Collected uniform revised edition. 1947–. Vol 1, Futility, contains an introd by the author, including 'My literary credo'; vol 7, Of mortal love, has a prefatory note stating that while other vols were textually emended, this has 'undergone considerable structural alteration'.

§1

Futility: a novel on Russian themes. [1922], New York 1922.
Anton Chehov: a critical study. [1923], New York 1923.
The polyglots. [1925], New York 1925.
A bad end. 1926. Story, rptd in Pretty creatures, below.
Perfectly scandalous: or 'The immortal lady'. 1927, 1929 (as Donna Quixote: or Perfectly scandalous). Play.

The vanity-bag. 1927. Story rptd in Pretty creatures, below.
Pretty creatures. 1927, New York 1927. Stories.
Jazz and Jasper: the story of Adams and Eva. [1928], New York 1928 (as Eva's apples), London 1947 (rev, as My sinful earth).
Pending heaven. 1930, New York 1930.
Memoirs of a polyglot. 1931, New York 1931. Autobiography.
The memoirs of Satan. 1932, Garden City NY 1933. With B. Lunn.
The Casanova fable: a satirical revaluation. 1934. Non-fiction; with 'Hugh Kingsmill'.
Resurrection. 1934, New York [1934].
Meet yourselves as you really are. 1936, 1962 (rev) (Penguin). With Prince Leopold zu Loewenstein. Adapted by V. Rosen, New York 1955 (as Analyze yourself).
Of mortal love. 1936.
My wife's the least of it. 1938.
The Romanovs. New York [1939], London 1940. Non-fiction.

§2

Mais, S. P. B. In his Some modern authors, 1923.
MacCarthy, D. The artistic temperament. In his Criticism, 1932. On Memoirs of a polyglot.
Putt, S. G. Comedy of the poetic present: Gerhardi. In his Scholars of the heart, 1962.

'LEWIS GRASSIC GIBBON', JAMES LESLIE MITCHELL
1901–35

§1

Hanno: or the future of exploration. 1928, New York 1928. As Mitchell; non-fiction.
Stained radiance: a fictionist's prelude. [1930]. As Mitchell.
The thirteenth disciple: being portrait and saga of Malcolm Maudslay in his adventure through the dark corridor. [1931]. As Mitchell.
The calends of Cairo. [1931], Indianapolis [1931] (as Cairo dawns). As Mitchell.
Three go back. [1932], Indianapolis [1932]. As Mitchell.
The lost trumpet. [1932], Indianapolis [1932]. As Mitchell.
Sunset song. 1932, New York [1933]. First pt of trilogy, A Scots quair, below. As Gibbon.
Persian dawns, Egyptian nights: two story-cycles. [1933]. As Mitchell.
Image and superscription. 1933. As Mitchell.
Cloud Howe. 1933, Garden City NY 1934. 2nd pt of trilogy. As Gibbon.
Spartacus. 1933. As Mitchell.
Niger: the life of Mungo Park. Edinburgh 1934. As Gibbon.
The conquest of the Maya. 1934, New York 1935. Non-fiction. As Mitchell.
Gay hunter. 1934. As Mitchell.
Scottish scene: or the intelligent man's guide to Albyn. 1934. As Gibbon; with 'Hugh MacDiarmid' (C. M. Grieve).
Grey granite. 1934, Garden City NY 1935. 3rd pt of trilogy. As Gibbon.
Nine against the unknown: a record of geographical exploration, by J. L. Mitchell and Lewis Grassic Gibbon. 1934, Garden City NY 1936 (As Earth conquerors), New York 1942 (as The lives and achievements of the great explorers).
A Scots quair: novels forming the trilogy Sunset song, Cloud Howe, Grey granite. Foreword by I. Brown 1946. As Gibbon.

A Scots hairst: essays and short stories. Ed I. S. Munro 1967. Rptd from Scottish scene, 1934, with other hitherto uncollected or unpbd essays, poems and stories.

§2

'MacDiarmid, Hugh' (C. M. Grieve). Lewis Grassic Gibbon. Scottish Art & Letters no 2 1946; rptd in Modern British writing, ed D. V. Baker, New York 1947.
— Lewis Grassic Gibbon 1901-1935. Our Time 7 1948.
Macdonald, A. A. Gibbon and the regional whole. Dalhousie Rev 39 1960.
Walch, G. Bemerkungen zu Gibbons A Scots quair. Zeitschrift für Anglistik und Amerikanistik 10 1962.
Macaree, D. Myth and allegory in Gibbon's A Scots quair. Stud in Scottish Lit 2 1964.
Munro, I. S. Leslie Mitchell: Lewis Grassic Gibbon. Edinburgh 1966. With list of Mitchell's works.

STELLA DOROTHEA GIBBONS
b. 1902

Collections
Collected poems. 1950.

§1

The mountain beast and other poems. 1930.
Cold Comfort Farm. 1932.
Bassett. 1934.
The priestess, and other poems. 1934.
Enbury Heath. 1935.
The untidy gnome. 1935. For children.
Miss Linsey and Pa. 1936.
Roaring tower and other short stories. 1937.
The lowland Venus, and other poems. 1938.
Nightingale wood. 1938.
My American: a romance. 1939, New York 1940.
Christmas at Cold Comfort Farm, and other stories. 1940.
The rich house. 1941.
Ticky. 1943.
The bachelor. 1944, New York 1944.
Westwood: or, the gentle powers. 1946, New York 1946 (as The gentle powers).
Conference at Cold Comfort Farm. 1949.
The matchmaker. 1949.
The Swiss summer. 1951.
Fort of the bear. 1953.
Beside the pearly water. 1954.
The shadow of a sorcerer. 1955.
Here be dragons. 1956.
White sand and grey sand. [1958].
A pink front door. [1959].
The weather at Tregulla. [1962].
The wolves were in the sledge. 1964.
The charmers. 1965.
Starlight. 1967.
The snow-woman. 1969.

SIR PHILIP HAMILTON GIBBS
1877-1962
See cols 1164-6, below.

ELINOR SUTHERLAND GLYN
1864-1943

§1

Many of Elinor Glyn's novels were serialized before pbn in book form, notably in Nash's Mag and Cosmopolitan.

The visits of Elizabeth. 1900, New York 1901.
Reflections of Ambrosine. 1902, New York 1902 (as The seventh commandment).

The damsel and the sage. 1903, New York 1903.
The vicissitudes of Evangeline. 1905, New York 1905 (as Red hair).
Beyond the rocks. 1906, New York 1906.
Three weeks. 1907, New York 1907.
The sayings of Grandmamma and others, from the works of Elinor Glyn. 1908, New York 1908.
Elizabeth visits America. 1909, New York 1909.
His hour. 1910, New York 1910. Some later edns titled When the hour came, or When his hour came.
The reason why. 1911, New York 1911.
Halcyone. 1912, New York 1912. Some American edns titled Love itself.
The contrast, and other stories. 1913.
The point of view. New York 1913. Story, also pbd in The contrast, above.
The sequence, 1905-12. 1913, New York 1913 (as Guinevere's lover).
Letters to Caroline. 1914, New York 1914 (as Your affectionate godmother).
The man and the moment. New York 1914, London 1915.
Three things. 1915, New York [1915]. Articles.
The career of Katherine Bush. New York 1916, London 1917.
Destruction. 1918. Non-fiction.
The price of things. [1919], New York 1919 (as Family), Auburn NY 1924 (as The price of things).
Points of view: from the works of Elinor Glyn. [1920].
The philosophy of love. [1920]. Articles.
The Elinor Glyn system of writing. 4 vols Auburn NY [1922].
Man and maid—renaissance. 1922, Philadelphia 1922.
The great moment. 1923, Philadelphia 1923.
The philosophy of love. Auburn NY [1923], London [1928] (as Love—what I think of it). Not the same as The philosophy of love, 1920, above.
Six days. 1924, Philadelphia 1924.
Letters from Spain. 1924. Travel.
This passion called love. 1925, Auburn NY [1925].
Love's blindness. 1926, Auburn NY [1926].
The wrinkle book: or how to keep looking young. 1927, New York [1928] (as Eternal youth).
It, and other stories. 1927, New York [1927].
The flirt and the flapper: dialogue. 1930.
Glorious flames. 1932, New York [1933]. Based on the film script for The price of things, above.
Love's hour. 1932, New York [1932].
Saint or satyr? and other stories. 1933, New York [1933] (as Such men are dangerous).
Sooner or later. 1933, New York 1935.
Did she? 1934.
Romantic adventure. 1936, New York 1937. Autobiography.
The third eye. 1940.

Elinor Glyn also wrote a number of film-scripts, most of which were based on her novels and stories. For details see 'Anthony Glyn' (G. L. S. Davson), Elinor Glyn, below.

§2

Bennett, A. In his Books and persons, 1917.
'Glyn, Anthony' (G. L. S. Davson). Elinor Glyn. 1955, 1968 (rev).
Mosley, L. O. In his Curzon: the end of an epoch, 1960.

MARGARET RUMER GODDEN
b. 1907

§1

Chinese puzzle. 1936.
The lady and the unicorn. 1937.

Black narcissus. 1939, Boston 1939.
Gypsy, gypsy. 1940, Boston 1940.
Breakfast with the Nikolides. 1942, Boston 1942.
Rungli-Rungliot. 1943, Boston 1946, London 1961 (as Thus far and no further). Travel in the Himalayas.
Bengal journey: a story of the part played by women in the province 1939-45. 1945.
A fugue in time. 1945, Boston 1945 (as Take three tenses).
The river. 1946, Boston 1946.
The dolls' house. 1947, New York 1948. For children.
A candle for St Jude. 1948, New York 1948.
In Noah's ark. 1949, New York 1949. Verse.
A breath of air. 1950, New York 1951.
The mousewife. New York 1951, London 1951. For children, adapted from a story in Dorothy Wordsworth's Journals.
Kingfishers catch fire. 1953, New York 1953.
Impunity Jane: the story of a pocket doll. New York 1954, London 1955. For children.
An episode of sparrows. New York 1955, London 1956.
Hans Christian Andersen. 1955, New York 1955. Biography.
The fairy doll. 1956, New York 1956. For children.
Mooltiki, and other stories and poems of India. 1957, New York 1957.
Mouse House. New York 1957, London 1958. For children.
The greengage summer. 1958, New York 1958.
The story of Holly and Ivy. 1958, New York 1958. For children.
Candy floss. 1960, New York 1960. For children.
China court. 1961, New York 1961.
Miss Happiness and Miss Flower. 1961, New York 1961. For children.
St Jerome and the lion. 1961, New York 1961. Verse. For children.
The battle of the Villa Fiorita. 1963, New York 1963.
Little plum. 1963, New York 1963. For children.
Home is the sailor. 1964, New York 1964. For children.
Two under the Indian sun. 1966, New York 1966. Autobiography; with J. Godden.
The kitchen Madonna. 1967, New York 1967. For children.
Swans and turtles. 1968, New York 1968 (as Gone: a thread of stories). Stories.
In this house of Brede. 1969, New York 1969.
The lady and the unicorn. 1969.
Operation Sappacik. 1969, New York 1969.

§2

Hartley, L. The Indian novels of Rumer Godden. Mahfil (Chicago) 3 1966.

LOUIS GOLDING
1895–1958

§1

Sorrow of war. 1919. Verse.
Forward from Babylon. 1920, New York 1921, London 1932 (rev), New York 1932.
Shepherd singing ragtime, and other poems. [1921].
Prophet and fool: a collection of poems. New York [1923].
Seacoast of Bohemia. 1923, New York 1924.
Sunward. 1924, New York 1924. Travel in Italy.
Day of atonement. 1925, New York 1925.
Sicilian noon. 1925, New York 1925. Travel.
Luigi of Catanzaro. 1926 (priv ptd, 100 copies). Story, rptd in Pale blue nightgown, 1944, below.
The miracle boy. 1927, New York 1927.
Store of ladies. 1927, New York 1927.

Those ancient lands: being a journey to Palestine. 1928, New York 1928.
The prince or somebody. 1929, New York 1929.
Adventures in living dangerously. 1930. Autobiography.
Give up your lovers. 1930, New York 1930.
A letter to Adolf Hitler. 1932. Essay, on anti-semitism.
Magnolia Street. 1932, New York 1932.
James Joyce. 1933 (Modern writers and playwrights).
Black frailty. 1934 (75 copies), 1944.
The Doomington wanderer: a book of tales. 1934, New York 1935 (as This wanderer). A selection, The call of the land, and other stories, pbd 1944.
Five silver daughters. 1934, New York 1934.
Poems drunk and drowsy. 1934.
Terrace in Capri: an imaginary conversation with Norman Douglas. 1934 (75 copies).
The Camberwell beauty. 1935, New York 1935.
Adventures in architecture. 1936 (40 copies).
Pale blue nightgown. 1936 (60 copies). Story, rptd in collection of same title, 1944, below.
The pursuer. 1936, New York 1936.
The dance goes on. 1937, New York 1937.
In the steps of Moses the lawgiver. 1937, New York 1938. Travel.
The Song of Songs. 1937 (178 copies). Verse play adapted from biblical text.
In the steps of Moses the conqueror. 1938, New York 1938. Travel.
Hitler through the ages. [1939]. On antisemitism.
The Jewish problem. 1939, New York 1939 (Penguin special).
Mr. Emmanuel. 1939, New York 1939.
The world I knew. [1940], New York 1940. Autobiography.
Who's there within? 1942.
In the steps of Moses. Philadelphia 1943. Contains the 2 In the steps of Moses titles, above.
No news from Helen. [1943], New York 1943.
The man in the white tie, and other stories. 1944.
Pale blue nightgown: a book of tales. [1944].
The vicar of Dunkerly Briggs. 1944. Stories.
Bert and Mary, and other stories. 1945.
The glory of Elsie Silver. New York 1945, London [1946].
Louis Golding goes travelling. 1945.
Swoop of the falcon. Brighton [1945]. Story.
Three jolly gentlemen. [1947].
The dark prince: a short novel. [1948].
My boxing tales: short stories. [1948].
My sporting days and nights. [1948]. Sketches.
Honey for the ghost. [1949], New York 1949.
The dangerous places. 1951.
The bare-knuckle breed. 1952, New York 1954. On boxing.
The loving brothers. 1952.
To the quayside. 1954.
Goodbye to Ithaca. 1955, New York 1958. Travel.
Mario on the beach, and other tales. 1956.
Mr Hurricane. 1957.
The little old admiral. 1958, New York 1958.

§2

Simons, J. B. Louis Golding: a memoir. [1958].

ROBERT BONTINE CUNNINGHAME GRAHAM
1852–1936

See cols 1318–19, below.

KENNETH GRAHAME
1859–1932
Bibliographies
Green, R. L. Kenneth Grahame. TLS 9 June 1945. Describes books and lists contributions to periodicals.
Green, P. In his Kenneth Grahame, [1959], §2, below. Based on the above; adds critical references.

Collections and Selections
The Kenneth Grahame book. 1932. Introductory note by E. Grahame. Contains The golden age, Dream days, The wind in the willows.
The reluctant dragon, and other stories from The golden age and Dream days. 1936, New York [1938].
The Kenneth Grahame day book. 1937. Compiled by Margery Coleman.
Pagan papers, and The headswoman. 1938.
The golden age and Dream days. Foreword by N. Lewis 1962, Philadelphia 1965.

§1
Pagan papers. 1894 (for 1893), 1898 (omitting Golden age stories). Essays and stories.
The golden age. 1895, Chicago 1895. Stories, some previously pbd in Pagan papers.
Dream days. 1898.
The headswoman. 1898. Story.
The wind in the willows. 1908, New York 1908, 1940 (with introd by A. A. Milne) (Limited Editions Club). Dramatized by A. A. Milne (as Toad of Toad Hall) 1929, New York 1929.
The Cambridge book of poetry for children. Ed Grahame, Cambridge 1916, New York [1916], Cambridge 1932 (rev), New York [1933].
First whisper of The wind in the willows. Ed with introd by E. Grahame 1944, Philadelphia 1945. Unpbd stories.
Bertie's escapade. 1949, Philadelphia 1949. Story rptd from First whisper of The wind in the willows.

Some unpbd pieces by Grahame, together with some previously uncollected contributions to periodicals, are ptd in P. R. Chalmers, Kenneth Grahame, §2, below.

§2
Parker, W. M. The children's advocate: Grahame. In his Modern Scottish writers, 1917.
Milne, A. A. A household book. In his Not that it matters, 1919.
Hind, C. L. In his Authors and I, 1921.
Chalmers, P. R. Grahame: life, letters and unpublished work. 1933.
Fyrth, D. M. Etude littéraire: Grahame. Paris 1937.
Swinnerton, F. A. Bedside book. In his Tokefield papers old and new, 1949. On The wind in the willows.
Graham, E. The story of The wind in the willows. [1950].
—— Kenneth Grahame. 1963 (Bodley Head Monograph).
Green, P. Kenneth Grahame 1859–1932: a study of his life, work and times. [1959].

ROBERT VON RANKE GRAVES
b. 1895
See cols 201–7, above.

FREDERICK LAWRENCE GREEN
1902–53
Julius Penton. 1934.
On the night of the fire. 1939, New York 1939.
The sound of winter. 1940.

Give us the world. 1941.
Music in the park. 1942.
A song for the angels. 1943.
On the edge of the sea. 1944.
Odd man out. 1945, New York 1947, London 1950 (as film, with R. C. Sherriff, in Three British screenplays, ed R. Manvell).
A flask for the journey. 1946, New York 1948.
A fragment of glass. 1947.
Mist on the waters. 1948, New York 1949.
Clouds in the wind. 1950, New York 1951.
The magician. 1951, New York 1951.
Ambush for the hunter. 1952, New York 1953.

'HENRY GREEN',
HENRY VINCENT YORKE
b. 1905

§1
Blindness. 1926, New York [1926].
Living. 1929.
Party going. 1939, New York 1951.
Pack my bag: a self-portrait. 1940.
Caught. 1943, New York 1950.
Loving. 1945, New York 1949.
Back. 1946, New York 1950.
Concluding. 1948, New York 1951.
Nothing. 1950, New York 1950.
Doting. 1952, New York 1952.

According to Green (London Mag, Green special no, 6 1959, *below*) *there is an unfinished novel*, Mood, *which followed* Blindness, *above.*

§2
Allen, W. An artist of the thirties. Folios of New Writing 3 1941.
—— Henry Green. Penguin New Writing no 25 1945.
—— Greening. New Statesman 2 May 1959.
Bain, B. Henry Green: the man and his work. World Rev new ser no 3 1949.
Toynbee, P. The novels of Green. Partisan Rev 16 1949.
Weaver, R. L. The novels of Green. Canadian Forum 30 1951.
Dennis, N. The double life of Green. Life 4 Aug 1952.
Prescott, O. Comrades of the coterie: Green, I. Compton Burnett, E. Bowen, G. Greene. In his In my opinion, Indianapolis 1952.
Phelps, R. The vision of Green. Hudson Rev 5 1953.
Vinaver, M. Essai sur un roman. Lettres Nouvelles June, July 1953. On Loving.
Applegate, J. Something about Green. New Mexico Quart 25 1955.
Melchiori, G. The abstract art of Green. In his The tight-rope walkers, 1956.
Stokes, E. Henry Green: dispossessed poet. Australian Quart 28 1956.
—— The novels of Green. 1959.
Hall, J. The fiction of Green: paradoxes of pleasure-and-pain. Kenyon Rev 19 1957; rptd in his The tragic comedians, Bloomington 1963.
Green, H. The art of fiction 20. Paris Rev no 19 [1958]. An interview with T. Southern; rptd in Writers at work: the Paris Review interviews, ser 2 1963.
London Mag 6 1959. Green special no. Contains:
Green, H. An unfinished novel [i.e. Mood].
Ross, A. Green, with envy: critical reflections and an interview.
Quinton, A. A French view of Loving. [On Vinaver's 1953 article].
Weatherhead, A. K. Structure and texture in Green's latest novels. Accent 19 1959.
—— A reading of Green. Seattle 1961.

Cosman, M. The elusive Green. Commonweal 72 1960.
Davidson, B. The world of Loving. Wisconsin Stud in Contemporary Lit 1 1960.
Labor, E. Henry Green's web of loving. Critique (Minneapolis) 4 1960; reply by T. Churchill, ibid.
Russell, J. Henry Green: nine novels and an unpacked bag. New Brunswick 1960.
—— There it is. Kenyon Rev 26 1964. On Green in retirement.
Welty, E. Henry Green: a novelist of the imagination. Texas Quart 4 1961.
Karl, F. R. Normality defined: the novels of Green. In his The contemporary English novel, New York 1962, London 1963 (as A reader's guide to the contemporary English novel).
Odom, K. C. Symbolism and diversion: birds in the novels of Green. Descant 6 1962.
Shapiro, S. A. Henry Green's Back: the presence of the past. Critique (Minneapolis) 7 1964.
Johnson, B. Henry Green's comic symbolism. Ball State Univ Forum 6 1965.
Southern, T. Henry Green et l'art du roman. Lettres Nouvelles 13 1965. Interview.
Taylor, D. S. Catalytic rhetoric: Green's theory of the modern novel. Criticism 7 1965.
Ryf, R. S. Henry Green. New York 1967 (Columbia Essays on Modern Writers).
Turner, M. The imagery of Wallace Stevens and Green. Wisconsin Studies in Contemporary Lit 8 1967.

NEIL MILLER GUNN
b. 1891

Selections

Storm and precipice, and other pieces. 1942.

§1

The grey coast. 1926, Boston 1926.
Hidden doors. Edinburgh 1929. Stories.
Morning tide. Edinburgh 1931, New York [1931].
Back home. Glasgow 1932. Play.
The lost glen. Edinburgh 1932.
Sun circle. Edinburgh 1933.
Butcher's broom. Edinburgh 1934, New York [1935] (as Highland night).
Whisky & Scotland: a practical and spiritual survey. 1935.
Highland river. Edinburgh 1937, Philadelphia [1937].
Choosing a play: a comedy of community drama. Edinburgh [1938].
Off in a boat. 1938. Travels, West coast of Scotland.
Net results. [1939]. Play.
Old music. [1939]. Play.
Wild geese overhead. 1939.
Second sight. 1940.
The silver darlings. 1941, New York 1945.
Young Art and old Hector. 1942, New York 1944.
The serpent. 1943, New York 1944 (as Man goes alone).
The green isle of the great deep. 1944.
The key of the chest. 1945, New York 1946.
The drinking well. 1946, New York 1947.
The shadow. 1948.
The silver bough. 1948.
Highland pack. 1949. Travel.
The lost chart. 1949.
The white hour, and other stories. 1950.
The well at the world's end. 1951.
Blood hunt. 1952.
The other landscape. 1954.
The atom of delight. 1956. Autobiography.

MARGUERITE RADCLYFFE HALL
1883?–1943

§1

'Twixt earth and stars: poems. 1906.
A sheaf of verses. 1908.
Poems of the past & present. 1910.
Songs of three counties, and other poems. Introd by R. B. Cunninghame-Graham 1913.
The forgotten island. 1915. Verse.
The forge. 1924.
The unlit lamp. 1924, New York 1929.
A Saturday life. 1925, New York 1930.
Adam's breed. 1926, Garden City NY 1926.
The well of loneliness. 1928, Paris 1928, New York [1928] (with commentary by Havelock Ellis), London 1949 (without commentary). The first English edn was withdrawn 22 Aug 1928, but the Paris edn was ptd from stereos of the type.
The master of the house. 1932, New York 1932.
Miss Ogilvy finds herself. 1934, New York [1934]. Stories.
The sixth beatitude. 1936, New York [1936].

§2

'West, Rebecca' (C. I. Andrews). Concerning the censorship. In her Ending in earnest, Garden City NY 1931. On The well of loneliness.
Lawrence, M. Priestesses. In her School of femininity, New York 1936, London 1937 (as We write as women).
Troubridge, U. V. The life and death of Radclyffe Hall. 1961.
Brittain, V. Radclyffe Hall: a case of obscenity? 1968.

ANTHONY WALTER PATRICK HAMILTON
1904–62

See cols 949–50, below.

'JOHN HAMPSON', JOHN FREDERICK NORMAN HAMPSON SIMPSON
1901–55

§1

Saturday night at the Greyhound. 1931, New York 1931.
The sight of blood. 1931. Story.
Two stories: The mare's nest; The long shadow. 1931.
O Providence. 1932.
Strip Jack naked. 1934, New York [1934] (as Brothers and lovers).
Man about the house. 1935 (285 copies). Story.
Family curse. 1936, New York 1936.
The Larches. 1938. With L. A. Pavey.
Care of 'The Grand'. 1939.
The English at table. 1944 (Britain in Pictures).
A bag of stones. 1952.

JAMES HANLEY
b. 1901

Selections

Selected stories. Dublin 1947.
Collected stories. 1953. A selection.

§1

Drift. 1930.
The German prisoner: a tale, with introd by R. Aldington. [1930] (priv ptd, 500 copies).

A passion before death: a tale. 1930 (priv ptd, 200 copies).

Boy. 1931 (unexpurgated), 1931 (expurgated trade edn), New York 1932. The US edn has some textual differences.

The last voyage, with foreword by R. Aldington. 1931. Story.

Men in darkness: five stories. 1931, New York 1932.

Aria & finale. 1932. Stories.

Ebb and flood. 1932.

Stoker Haslett: a tale. 1932.

Captain Bottell. 1933.

Quartermaster Clausen. 1934. Stories.

Resurrexit Dominus. 1934 (priv ptd, 110 copies).

At bay. 1935 (285 copies). Story, rptd in vol of same title, below, 1944.

The Furys. 1935, New York 1935. First vol of Furys Chronicle.

Stoker Bush. 1935, New York 1936.

The secret journey. 1936, New York 1936. 2nd vol of Furys Chronicle.

Broken water: an autobiographical excursion. 1937.

Grey children: a study in humbug and misery. 1937. Unemployment among South Wales coalminers.

Half an eye: sea stories. 1937.

Hollow sea. 1938.

People are curious. 1938. Stories.

Between the tides. 1939, Dublin [?1949] (as Towards horizons, by 'James Bentley').

Our time is gone. 1940, 1949 (rev). 3rd vol of Furys Chronicle.

The ocean. 1941, New York 1941.

No directions. 1943.

Sailor's song. 1943.

At bay. 1944. Stories.

Crilley, and other stories. 1945.

What Farrar saw. 1946.

Emily. 1948.

A walk in the wilderness. 1950. Stories.

Winter song. 1950. 4th vol of Furys Chronicle.

The house in the valley. 1951. As by 'Patric Shone'.

The closed harbour. 1952, New York 1953.

Don Quixote drowned. 1953. Stories.

The Welsh sonata: variations on a theme. 1954.

Levine. 1956, New York 1956.

An end and a beginning. 1958, New York 1958.

Say nothing. 1962, New York 1962.

The inner journey. 1965, New York 1965. Play.

Plays one. 1968. Contains The inner journey, and A stone flower.

The face of winter. 1969 (99 copies).

§2

Stokes, E. The novels of Hanley. Melbourne 1964.

LESLIE POLES HARTLEY
b. 1895

Bibliographies

Bien, P. A Hartley bibliography. Adam 29 1961. Includes contributions to books and periodicals and translations of Hartley's books.

Collections

Eustace and Hilda: a trilogy. 1958, New York 1958. Contains The shrimp and the anemone; The sixth heaven; Eustace and Hilda; and the story, Hilda's letter. With slight textual changes (see Bien, 1963, §2, below). Introd by D. Cecil.

Collected short stories. 1968. Introd by D. Cecil. Simonetta Perkins, The travelling grave, Two for the river, The white wand.

§1

Night fears, and other stories. 1924. Mostly rptd from Oxford Chron and Oxford Outlook.

Simonetta Perkins. 1925, New York 1926. Story.

The killing bottle. 1932. Stories.

The shrimp and the anemone. 1944, New York 1945 (as The west window).

The sixth heaven. 1946, New York 1947.

Eustace and Hilda. 1947.

The travelling grave, and other stories. Sauk City 1948, London 1951. Includes various stories rptd from Night fears and The killing bottle.

The boat. 1949, New York 1950.

My fellow devils. 1951.

The go-between. 1953, New York 1954, London 1963 (with introd by Hartley).

The white wand, and other stories. 1954. Includes various stories rptd from Night fears and The killing bottle.

A perfect woman. 1955, New York 1956.

The hireling. 1957, New York 1958.

Facial justice. 1960, Garden City NY 1961.

Two for the river, and other stories. 1961.

The brickfield. 1964.

The betrayal. 1966.

The novelist's responsibility. 1967. Essays.

Poor Clare. 1968.

The love-adept: a variation on a theme. 1969.

Hartley contributed regularly to several journals. See Bien, below, p. 282.

§2

Closs, A. Hartley. Die Neueren Sprachen 6 1957.

Vernier, J.-P. La trilogie romanesque de Hartley. Études Anglaises 13 1960.

Adam International Rev 29 1961. Special Hartley no. Contains:
  Grindea, M. Un maître du roman anglais.
  Bloomfield, P. L.P.H.: short note on a great subject.
  Kitchin, C. H. B. Leslie Hartley: a personal angle.
  Brion, M. Le surprenant Mr Hartley.
  Hartley, L. P. De la responsabilité du romancier. A trn of a lecture given at the 1957 Aldeburgh Festival.
  —— The face. [Story].
  —— A very present help. [Story].
  Bien, P. A Hartley bibliography.

Webster, H. C. The novels of Hartley. Critique (Minneapolis) 4 1961.

Bloomfield, P. L. P. Hartley. 1962. (Br Council pamphlet). With B. Bergonzi on Anthony Powell.

Bien, P. L. P. Hartley. 1963.

Hall, J. Games of apprehension: Hartley. In his The tragic comedians, Bloomington 1963.

Kreutz, I. L. P. Hartley, who are U? or: luncheon in the lounge. Kenyon Rev 25 1963. Vocabulary of A perfect woman.

Davison, R. A. Graham Greene and Hartley: The basement room and The go-between. N & Q 211 1966.

'IAN HAY',
JOHN HAY BEITH
1876–1952

Collections

The writings of Ian Hay: Argyll edition. 10 vols Boston 1921.

§1

Plays are listed in order of production, where known; otherwise, of pbn.

'Pip': a romance of youth. 1907, Boston 1917.

'The right stuff': some episodes in the career of a North Briton. 1908, Boston 1910.

A man's man. 1909, Boston 1910.

A safety match. 1911, Boston 1911. Dramatized, Strand 13 Jan 1921, pbd 1927 (French's Acting Edn).

The crimson cocoanut, and other plays (A late delivery; The missing card). Boston 1913. The crimson cocoanut pbd separately 1928 (French's Acting Edn).

Happy-go-lucky. 1913, Boston 1913. Dramatized as Tilly of Bloomsbury, Apollo 10 July 1919, pbd 1922 (French's Acting Edn).

A knight on wheels. 1914, Boston 1914.

The lighter side of school life. 1914, Boston 1915. Articles, rptd from Blackwood's Mag.

The first hundred thousand: being the unofficial chronicle of a unit of 'K(1)' (Kitchener's First Army). 1915, Boston 1916.

Scally: the story of a perfect gentleman. Boston 1915, London 1932. Story, rptd in The lucky number, 1923, below.

Carrying on—after the first hundred thousand. 1917, Boston 1917 (as All in it: K(1) carries on).

Getting together. 1917, Garden City NY 1917. On the U.S. and Great Britain in the European War.

The oppressed English. Garden City NY 1917.

The last million. [1919], Boston 1919. On the US Army.

The willing horse. [1921], Boston 1921.

The happy ending: a play in three acts. (St James's 30 Nov 1922). [1927] (French's Acting Edn).

The lucky number. [1923], Boston 1923. Stories.

The sport of kings: a domestic comedy in three acts. (Savoy 9 Sept 1924). [1926] (French's Acting Edn).

'The Liberry'. Boston 1924.

The shallow end. 1924, Boston 1924. Essays and sketches.

Paid with thanks. [1925], Boston 1925 (as Paid in full).

Half-a-sovereign. [1926], Boston 1926.

The ship of remembrance, Gallipoli-Salonica. [1926].

A damsel in distress: a comedy in three acts. (New 13 Aug 1928). [1930] (French's Acting Edn). With P. G. Wodehouse, adapted from Wodehouse's novel.

A blank cartridge: a farce. [1928] (French's Acting Edn).

Personally or by letter: a little comedy. [1928] (French's Acting Edn).

The poor gentleman. 1928, Boston 1928.

Treasure trove: a fantasy. [1928] (French's Acting Edn).

Baa, baa, black sheep: a farcical comedy in three acts. (New 22 April 1929). [1930] (French's Acting Edn). With P. G. Wodehouse.

The middle watch: a romance of the Navy in three acts. (Shaftesbury 12 Aug 1929). [1931] (French's Acting Edn). As novel 1930, Boston 1930. With S. King-Hall.

A song of sixpence: a Scottish comedy. (Daly's 17 March 1930). [1930] (French's Acting Edn). With G. Bolton.

Leave it to Psmith: a comedy of youth, love and misadventure in three acts. (Shaftesbury 29 Sept 1930). [1932] (French's Acting Edn). With P. G. Wodehouse.

Mr Faint-heart: a romantic comedy in three acts. (Shaftesbury 20 April 1931). [1931] (French's Acting Edn).

The midshipmaid: a naval manoeuvre in three acts. (Shaftesbury 10 Aug 1931). [1932] (French's Acting Edn). With S. King-Hall. Pbd 1933 as novel, by Hay alone.

Their name liveth: the book of the Scottish National War Memorial. 1931.

Orders are orders: a military diversion in three acts. (Shaftesbury 9 Aug 1932). [1933] (French's Acting Edn). With A. Armstrong.

A present from Margate: a frivolous comedy in three acts. (Shaftesbury 14 Dec 1933). [1934] (French's Acting Edn). With A. E. W. Mason.

Find the lady: a comedietta in one act. [1933] (French's Acting Edn).

The great wall of India. 1933, Boston 1933.

It is quicker to telephone: a comedy in one act. [1933] (French's Acting Edn).

Admirals all: an amphibious adventure in three acts. (Shaftesbury 6 Aug 1934). [1935] (French's Acting Edn). With S. King-Hall.

David and destiny. 1934, Boston 1934.

Lucky dog. 1934.

Right of search: a comedy in one act. [1935] (French's Acting Edn).

Housemaster. 1936, Boston 1937, London [1938] (as play, Apollo 12 Nov 1936) (French's Acting Edn), New York 1938 (as play, with title Bachelor born) (French's Standard Library Edn).

The King's service: an informal history of the British infantry soldier. 1938, 1942 (abridged, as The British infantryman).

Little ladyship: a comedy in three acts. (Kings Glasgow 16 Jan 1939). [1941] (French's Acting Edn). Pbd 1941 as novel.

Stand at ease: stories and memories. 1940.

The battle of Flanders, 1940. 1941.

America comes across. 1942.

The unconquered isle: the story of Malta GC. 1943, New York 1943 (as Malta epic).

A flat and a sharp: a domestic complication in one act. [1944] (French's Acting Edn).

Burglar alarm: a midnight adventure in one act. [1945] (French's Acting Edn).

Peaceful invasion. 1946.

The Post Office went to war. 1946.

Off the record: a naval comedy in three acts. (King's, Edinburgh 17 March 1947; Apollo 3 June 1947). [1949] (French's Acting Edn). With S. King-Hall.

The fourpenny box: a play in one act. [1947] (French's Acting Edn).

Let my people go. 1948. Play.

Arms and the men. 1950. War history.

The Royal Company of Archers 1676-1951. 1951.

The commissioner's bungalow: a play in three acts. [1952] (French's Acting Edn). With J. Smyth.

One hundred years of Army nursing. 1953.

§2

Braybrooke, P. In his Novelists: we are seven, 1926.
—— In his Philosophies in modern fiction, 1929.
Adcock, A. St J. In his Glory that was Grub Street, 1928.

SIR ALAN PATRICK HERBERT
1890-1971

See cols 288-90, above.

MAURICE HENRY HEWLETT
1861-1923

Bibliographies

Muir, P. H. A bibliography of the first editions of books by Hewlett. Bookman's Jnl 15 1927.
—— Points 1874-1930. 1931. Contains corrections to the above.

Cutler, B. D. and V. Stiles. In their Modern British authors: their first editions, New York 1930.

Sutherland, A. B. In his Maurice Hewlett, Philadelphia 1938. Includes trns of Hewlett's novels; reviews, prefaces and speeches by Hewlett; a list of secondary material including reviews; and, in the footnotes to the text of the book, details of first pbn of Hewlett's work in various jnls. Supersedes bibliography by Sutherland in Bull of Bibliography 15 1935.

Selections

Maurice Hewlett. [1926] (Augustan Books of Modern Poetry).

§1

Earthwork out of Tuscany: being impressions and translations. 1895, 1899 (rev, with new preface), New York 1900, London 1901 (rev). Essays.

A masque of dead Florentines. 1895. Verse.

Songs and meditations. 1896.

The forest lovers. 1898, New York 1898.

Pan and the young shepherd. 1898, 1906 (abridged). Verse play.

Quattrocentisteria: how Sandro Botticelli saw Simonetta in the spring. Portland Maine 1898. First pbd in Earthwork out of Tuscany, above.

Little novels of Italy. 1899, New York 1899.

The life and death of Richard Yea-and-nay. 1900, New York 1900.

New Canterbury tales. 1901, New York 1901.

The queen's quair: or the six years' tragedy. 1904, New York 1904.

The road in Tuscany. 2 vols 1904, New York 1904, 1 vol London 1906. Travel.

Fond adventures: tales of the youth of the world. 1905, New York 1905.

The fool errant: being the memoirs of Francis-Antony Strelley Esq, citizen of Lucca. 1905, New York 1905.

The stooping lady. 1907, New York 1907.

The Spanish jade. 1908, New York 1908.

Halfway house: a comedy of degrees. 1908, New York 1908. 1st part of a trilogy.

Letters to Sanchia. 1908 (priv ptd), 1910 (rev, as Letters to Sanchia upon things as they are), New York 1910. Incorporated into Open country, below.

A sacrifice at Prato. Englewood NJ 1908 (80 copies). First pbd in Earthwork out of Tuscany, above.

Artemision: idylls and songs. 1909, New York 1909.

Open country: a comedy with a sting. 1909, New York 1909. 2nd pt of trilogy.

The ruinous face. New York 1909. Story.

Rest harrow: a comedy of resolution. 1910, New York 1910. 3rd pt of trilogy.

The agonists: a trilogy of God and man. 1911, New York 1911. Verse plays.

The birth of Roland. Chicago [1911]. Story.

Brazenhead the great. 1911, New York 1911. One section, The captain of Kent, first pbd in Fond adventures, above, as Brazenhead the great.

The song of Renny. 1911, New York 1911.

Songs of loss. [c. 1911] (priv ptd). Anon.

Mrs Lancelot: a comedy of assumptions. 1912, New York 1912.

Bendish: a study in prodigality. 1913, New York 1913.

Helen redeemed, and other poems. 1913, New York 1913.

Lore of Proserpine. 1913, New York 1913. Essays and stories.

Sing-songs of the war. 1914.

The wreath. 1914 (priv ptd, 25 copies).

A ballad of The Gloster and The Goeben. [1914]. Broadside.

The little Iliad. 1915, Philadelphia 1915.

A lovers' tale. 1915, New York 1916.

Frey and his wife. 1916, New York 1916.

Gai saber: tales and songs. 1916, New York 1916. Verse.

Love and Lucy. 1916, New York 1916.

The song of the plow, being the English chronicle. 1916, New York 1916.

The loving history of Peridore and Paravail. [1917]. Verse.

Thorgils of Treadholt. 1917, New York 1917 (as Thorgils).

Gudrid the fair. 1918, New York 1918.

The village wife's lament. 1918, New York 1918. Verse.

The outlaw. 1919, New York 1920.

Flowers in the grass—Wiltshire plainsong. 1920.

In a green shade: a country commentary. 1920.

The light heart. 1920, New York 1920.

Mainwaring. New York 1920, London [1921].

Wiltshire essays. 1921.

Extemporary essays. 1922.

Last essays. 1924.

Letters

The letters of Maurice Hewlett: to which is added A diary in Greece, 1914. Ed L. Binyon 1926. With memoir by E. Hewlett.

§2

Conrad, H. Maurice Hewlett. Preussische Jahrbücher 105 1901.

Lyttelton, E. Maurice Hewlett. National Rev 37 1901.

Bronner, M. Hewlett as a poet. Critic 43 1903.

—— Hewlett: being a critical review of his prose and poetry. Boston 1910.

Harrison, F. Maurice Hewlett. In his Memories and thoughts, 1906.

Davray, H. D. Amours charmantes et cruelles. Mercure de France 74 1908. On Little novels of Italy.

Cooper, F. T. Maurice Hewlett. In his Some English story tellers, New York 1912.

Monro, H. Hewlett as poet. Poetry Rev 1 1912.

O'Reardon, B. Maurice Hewlett. Sewanee Rev 21 1913.

Hervey, J. L. The decline and fall of Hewlett. Dial 61 1916.

Freeman, J. The 'English' poems of Hewlett. Quart Rev 236 1921.

—— Maurice Hewlett. In his English portraits and essays, 1924.

'Lee, Vernon' (V. Paget). Maurice Hewlett. In her The handling of words, 1923.

Priestley, J. B. Hewlett's later verse and prose. London Mercury 8 1923; rptd in his Figures in modern literature, 1924.

Squire, J. C. Maurice Hewlett. Observer 17 June 1923. Rptd in his Sunday mornings, 1930.

—— Hewlett's essays. Observer 13 April 1924. Rptd in his Sunday mornings, 1930.

Gwynn, S. Maurice Hewlett. Edinburgh Rev 239 1924.

Graham, W. H. Maurice Hewlett. Fortnightly Rev new ser 118 1925.

Weygandt, C. Maurice Hewlett, 'poet of sorts'? In his A century of the English novel, New York 1925.

Boileau, H. T. Hewlett and the romance of the Renaissance. In his Italy in the post-Victorian novel, Philadelphia 1931.

Allen, R. B. Hewlett's retold sagas. In his Old Icelandic sources in the English novel, Philadelphia 1932.

Church, R. Hewlett reconsidered. Fortnightly Rev new ser 135 1934.

Sutherland, A. B. Hewlett: historical romancer. Philadelphia 1938.

ROBERT SMYTHE HICHENS
1864–1950

§1

The coastguard's secret. 1886.

The green carnation. 1894, New York 1894. Anon.

After tomorrow, and The new love; by the author of The green carnation. New York [1895].

An imaginative man. 1895, New York 1895.

The folly of Eustace, and other stories. 1896, New York 1896.

Byeways. New York 1897, London 1898. Stories.

Flames: a London phantasy. 1897, Chicago 1897.

The Londoners: an absurdity. 1898, Chicago 1898.

The daughters of Babylon. 1899. With W. Barrett.

The slave. 1899, Chicago 1899.

Tongues of conscience. 1900, New York [1900]. Stories.

The prophet of Berkeley Square: a tragic extravaganza. 1901, New York 1901.
Felix: three years in a life. 1902, New York 1903.
The garden of Allah. 1904, New York [1904].
The woman with the fan. 1904, New York 1904.
The black spaniel, and other stories. 1905, New York 1905.
The call of the blood. 1906, New York 1906.
Barbary sheep. New York 1907, London 1909.
Egypt and its monuments. 1908, New York 1908, London 1910 (as The spell of Egypt; without illustrations), New York 1911. Non-fiction.
A spirit in prison. 1908, New York 1908.
Bella Donna. 1909, New York 1909, London [1927] (abridged).
The knock on the door. 1909, Philadelphia 1909.
The Holy Land. 1910, New York 1910. Travel.
The dweller on the threshold. 1911, New York 1911.
The fruitful vine. 1911, New York 1911, London [1918] (abridged).
The Near East. 1913, New York 1913. Travel.
The way of ambition. 1913, New York 1913.
The Hindu. New York [1917]. Story.
In the wilderness. 1917, New York [1917].
Mrs Marden. [1919], New York [1919].
Snake-bite, and other stories. 1919, New York [1919].
The spirit of the time. 1921, New York [1921].
December love. 1922, New York 1922.
The last time, and other stories. [1923], New York [1924].
After the verdict. 1924, New York [1924].
The god within him. 1926, New York 1926 (as The unearthly).
The bacchante and the nun. 1927, New York 1927 (as The bacchante).
The streets, and other stories. [1928].
Dr Artz. [1929], New York 1929.
On the screen. 1929.
The bracelet. 1930, New York 1930.
The gates of paradise, and other stories. 1930.
The first Lady Brendon. 1931, Garden City NY 1931.
My desert friend and other stories. 1931.
Mortimer Brice: a bit of his life. 1932, Garden City NY 1932.
The Paradine case. 1933, Garden City NY 1933, 2 vols London 1938 (Penguin).
The gardenia, and other stories. [1934].
The power to kill. 1934, Garden City NY 1934.
The afterglow, and other stories. 1935.
'Susie's' career. 1935, Garden City NY 1936 (as The pyramid).
The sixth of October. 1936, Garden City NY 1936.
Daniel Airlie. 1937, Garden City NY 1937.
The journey up. 1938, New York 1938.
Secret information. [1938], Garden City NY 1938.
That which is hidden. 1939, New York 1940.
The million: an entertainment. 1940, New York 1941.
Married or unmarried. 1941.
A new way of life. [1942], Garden City NY 1942.
Veils. [1943], Philadelphia 1944 (as Young Mrs Brand).
Harps in the wind. 1945, Philadelphia 1945 (as The woman in the house).
Incognito. [1947], New York 1948.
Too much love of living. Philadelphia 1947, London 1948.
Yesterday. 1947. Autobiography.
Beneath the magic. [1950], Philadelphia 1950 (as Strange lady).
The man in the mirror, and other stories. 1950.
The mask. 1951.
Nightbound. 1951.

§2

Adcock, A. St J. In his The glory that was Grub Street, 1928.

JAMES HILTON
1900–54
Selections

Three famous novels. New York [1957]. Lost horizon, Goodbye Mr Chips, Random harvest.

§1

Catherine herself. 1920.
Storm passage. 1922.
The passionate year. 1923, Boston 1924.
The dawn of reckoning. 1925, New York 1937.
The meadows of the moon. 1926, Boston 1927.
Terry. 1927.
The silver flame. 1928.
And now goodbye. 1931, New York 1932.
Murder at school. 1931 (by 'Glen Trevor'), New York 1933 (as Was it murder?), 1935 (as by James Hilton).
Contango. 1932, New York 1932 (as Ill wind).
Rage in heaven. New York 1932.
Knight without armour. 1933, New York 1934 (as Without armor).
Lost horizon. 1933, New York 1933.
Good-bye, Mr Chips. 1934, Boston 1934, London 1938 (as play, with B. Burnham).
We are not alone. 1937, Boston 1937.
To you, Mr Chips. 1938. Stories, with a chapter of autobiography.
Mr Chips looks at the world. [Los Angeles 1939]. Lecture.
Random harvest. 1941, Boston 1941.
The story of Dr Wassell. Boston 1943, London 1944.
So well remembered. Boston 1945, London 1947.
Nothing so strange. Boston 1947, London 1948.
Twilight of the wise. [1949]. Story.
Morning journey. 1951, Boston 1951.
Time and time again. 1953, Boston 1953.

CONSTANCE HOLME
1880–1955
Bibliographies

Rota, B. Book Collector 5 1956. Includes 4 priv ptd items.

§1

Crump folk going home. 1913, 1934 (with preface by the author) (WC).
The lonely plough. 1914, 1931 (with preface by the author) (WC).
The old road from Spain. 1916, 1932 (with preface by the author) (WC).
Beautiful end. 1918, 1935 (WC).
The splendid fairing. 1919, 1933 (WC).
The trumpet in the dust. 1921, 1933 (WC).
The things which belong—. 1925, 1934 (WC).
He-who-came? 1930, 1936 (WC).
Four one-act plays. Kirkby Lonsdale [1932].
'I want!': a fantasy in three acts. In Five three-act plays, 1933.
The wisdom of the simple, and other stories. 1937 (WC).

§2

Brown, A. L. Constance Holme 1880–1955. Serif 1 1964, With hitherto unpbd sketch, That's easy!, by C. Holme.

WINIFRED HOLTBY
1898–1935
Bibliographies

Handley-Taylor, G. Winifred Holtby: a concise and selected bibliography, together with some letters. 1955.

§1

My garden, and other poems. 1911.
Anderby wold. 1923.
The crowded street. 1924.
The land of green ginger. 1927, New York 1928.
Eutychus, or the future of the pulpit. 1928, New York 1928. (Today and Tomorrow ser). Essay.
A new voter's guide to party programmes: political dialogues. 1929.
Poor Caroline. 1931, New York 1931.
Virginia Woolf. 1932.
The astonishing island. 1933, New York 1933. Satire.
Mandoa! Mandoa! a comedy of irrelevance. 1933, New York 1933.
Truth is not sober. 1934, New York 1934. Stories.
Women and a changing civilisation. 1934, New York 1935.
The frozen earth, and other poems. 1935.
South Riding: an English landscape. 1936, 1936 (limited edn with introd by V. Brittain), New York 1936 (with epitaph by V. Brittain). Fiction.
Pavements at Anderby: tales of 'South Riding' and other regions. Ed H. S. Reid and V. Brittain 1937, New York 1938.
Take back your freedom. 1939. Play, with N. Ginsbury.

Letters

Letters to a friend. Ed A. Holtby and J. McWilliam 1937, New York 1938.
Letters. In G. Handley-Taylor, Winifred Holtby, 1955, Bibliographies above.
Selected letters of Winifred Holtby and Vera Brittain 1930–1938. Ed V. Brittain and G. Handley-Taylor 1960.

§2

Mackworth, M. H. In her Notes on the way, 1937.
White, E. E. M. Winifred Holtby as I knew her. [1938].
Brittain, V. Testament of friendship: the story of W. Holtby. 1940.

NORAH HOULT
b. 1898
Selections

Selected stories. 1946.

§1

Poor women. 1928, New York 1929. Stories.
Time, gentlemen, time! 1930, New York 1930 (as Closing hour).
Violet Ryder. [1930].
Apartments to let. 1931, New York 1932.
Ethel. 1931. Story, first pbd in Poor women, above.
Youth can't be served. 1933, New York 1934.
Holy Ireland. 1935, New York [1936].
Coming from the fair: being book two of Holy Ireland. 1937, New York [1937].
Nine years is a long time. [1938]. Stories.
Four women grow up. 1940.
Smilin' on the vine. 1941.
Augusta steps out. 1942.
Scene for death. 1943.
There were no windows. 1944, New York 1947.
House under Mars. 1946.
Farewell happy fields. 1948.

Cocktail bar. 1950. Stories.
Frozen ground. 1952.
Sister Mavis. 1953.
A death occurred. 1954.
Journey into print. 1954, New York 1954.
Father Hone and the television set. 1956.
Father and daughter. 1957.
Husband and wife. 1959.
The last days of Miss Jenkinson. 1962.
A poet's pilgrimage. 1966.
Only fools and horses work. 1969.

GEOFFREY EDWARD WEST HOUSEHOLD
b. 1900

The terror of Villadonga. [1936], Boston 1936 (as The Spanish cave), London 1940. For children.
The third hour. 1937, Boston 1938.
The salvation of Pisco Gabar, and other stories. 1938, Boston 1940.
Rogue male. 1939, Boston 1939, New York 1942 (as Man hunt).
Arabesque. 1948, Boston 1948.
The high place. 1950, Boston 1950.
A rough shoot. Boston 1951, London 1951.
A time to kill. Boston 1951, London 1952.
Tales of adventurers. 1952, Boston 1952.
The exploits of Xenophon. New York 1955, London 1961 (as Xenophon's adventure). For children.
Fellow passenger. 1955, Boston 1955.
Against the wind. 1958, Boston 1959. Autobiography.
The brides of Solomon, and other stories. 1958, Boston 1958.
Watcher in the shadows. 1960, Boston 1960.
Thing to love. 1963, Boston 1963.
Olura. 1965, Boston 1965.
Sabres on the sand, and other stories. 1966, Boston 1966.
The courtesy of death. 1967, Boston 1967.
Prisoner of the Indies. 1967, Boston 1967. For children.
Dance of the dwarfs. 1968, Boston 1968.

'STEPHEN HUDSON', SYDNEY SCHIFF
1868–1944

About 950 letters written to Schiff and his wife Violet are in BM. See M. A. F. Borrie, The Schiff papers, BM Quart 31 1966, and G. D. Painter, Proust's letters to Sydney and Violet Schiff, BM Quart 32 1968.

Bibliographies

'Gawsworth, John' (T. I. F. Armstrong). In his Ten contemporaries: notes toward their definitive bibliography, 1932.

§1

For the interrelations between Hudson's novels see Boll, in Richard, Myrtle and I, [1962], below.

Concessions. 1913. As Sydney Schiff.
War-time silhouettes. 1916.
Richard Kurt. 1919.
Elinor Colhouse. 1921, New York 1922.
In sight of chaos, by H. Hesse. Tr Hudson, Zürich 1923.
Prince Hempseed. 1923.
Tony. 1924, New York 1924.
Myrtle. 1925, New York 1925.
Richard, Myrtle and I. New York 1926, London 1926, Philadelphia [1962] (ed Violet Schiff, with biographical note and critical essay by T. E. M. Boll).
Céleste and other sketches. 1930.

A true story in three parts and a postscript. [1930], New York 1930, London 1948 (rev and enlarged).
Time regained, by M. Proust. Tr Hudson 1931.
The other side. 1937.

§2

Muir, E. In his Transition, 1926.
Boll, T. E. M. Biographical note and a critical essay [on Hudson]. In Richard, Myrtle and I, [1962], above.

RICHARD ARTHUR WARREN HUGHES
b. 1900

Selections
Richard Hughes: an omnibus. New York 1931.

§1

Gipsy-night, and other poems. Waltham St Lawrence [1922], Chicago 1922 (63 copies).
The sisters' tragedy. Oxford 1922. Play.
The sisters' tragedy, and three other plays. 1924, New York 1924 (as A rabbit and a leg: collected plays), London 1966 (as Plays).
Confessio juvenis: collected poems. 1926.
A moment of time. 1926. Stories.
A high wind in Jamaica. 1929, New York 1929 (as The innocent voyage, with introd by I. Paterson), [1932] (as A high wind in Jamaica) (Modern Lib).
Burial, and The dark child. 1930 (priv ptd, 60 copies). Poem and children's story.
The spider's palace and other stories. 1931, New York 1932. For children.
In hazard: a sea story. 1938, New York 1938, London 1953 (ed and abridged by author), New York 1966 (with new introd by author).
Don't blame me! and other stories. 1940. For children.
The administration of war production. 1955 (History of the Second World War). With J. D. Scott.
The fox in the attic. 1961, New York [1962]. Vol 1 of The human predicament.
Gertrude's child. New York 1966, London 1967. For children.
Hong Kong. 1968.

§2

Bosano, J. Études Anglaises 16 1963.
Henighan, T. J. Nature and convention in A high wind in Jamaica. Critique (Minneapolis) 9 1967.
Woodward, D. H. The delphic voice: Hughes's A high wind in Jamaica. Papers on Lang & Lit 3 1967.
Brown, D. R. A high wind in Jamaica: comedy of the absurd. Ball State Univ Forum 9 1968.

ISOBEL VIOLET HUNT
1866–1942

§1

The maiden's progress: a novel in dialogue. 1894, New York 1894.
A hard woman: a story in scenes. 1895, New York 1895.
The way of marriage. 1896.
Stories and play stories, by V. Hunt [et al]. 1897. A collection, mostly rptd from Chapman's Mag.
Unkist, unkind! 1897, New York 1898.
The human interest: a study in incompatibilities. 1899, Chicago 1899.
Affairs of the heart. 1900. Stories.
The celebrity at home. 1904.
Sooner or later: the story of an ingenious ingénue. 1904.
The cat. 1905, 1910 (as The life story of a cat).

The workaday woman. [1906].
White rose of weary leaf. 1908.
The wife of Altamont. 1910.
The doll: a happy story. [1911].
Tales of the uneasy. 1911.
The governess, by Mrs Alfred Hunt and V. Hunt, with a preface by F. M. Hueffer. 1912.
The celebrity's daughter. 1913, New York 1914.
The desirable alien: at home in Germany, with preface and two additional chapters by F. M. Hueffer. 1913.
The house of many mirrors. 1914.
Zeppelin nights: a London entertainment. 1916 [1915]. With F. M. Hueffer [F. M. Ford], and mostly written by him. See D. D. Harvey, Ford Madox Ford: a bibliography, Princeton 1962.
Their lives. 1916.
The last ditch. 1918.
Their hearts. 1921.
The tiger skin. 1924. First pbd in Tales of the uneasy, above.
More tales of the uneasy. 1925.
The flurried years. [1926], New York [1926] (as I have this to say). Autobiography.
The wife of Rossetti: her life and death. 1932, New York [1932].

§2

Aldington, R. Violet Hunt. Egoist 1 Jan 1914.
Sinclair, M. The novels of Violet Hunt. English Rev 34 1922.
Adcock, A. St J. In his The glory that was Grub Street, 1928.
Goldring, D. South Lodge: reminiscences of Violet Hunt, Ford and the English Review circle. 1943.
— Violet Hunt. Windmill no 7 1947.
Henighan, T. J. Desirable alien: a source for F. M. Ford's The good soldier. Twentieth-Century Lit 11 1965.
Mizener, A. The lost poems of Violet Hunt. Cornell Lib Jnl 3 1967.

ARTHUR STUART MENTETH HUTCHINSON
1879–1971

§1

Once aboard the lugger: the history of George and his Mary. 1908, New York [1908].
The happy warrior. 1912, Boston 1913.
The clean heart. [1914], Boston 1914.
If winter comes. [1921], Boston 1921, London [1928] (as play, with B. M. Hastings). For a parody, see B. E. O. Pain, If summer don't, [1922], New York 1922 (as If winter don't).
This freedom. 1922, Boston 1922.
The eighth wonder, and other stories. [1923], Boston 1923.
One increasing purpose. [1925], Boston 1925.
The uncertain trumpet. [1929], Boston 1929.
The book of Simon. 1930, Boston 1930. Impressions of his son.
The golden pound, and other stories. [1930].
Big business. 1932, Boston 1932.
The soft spot. 1933, Boston 1933.
A year that the locust—. 1935. Memoirs.
As once you were. 1938, Boston 1938.
He looked for a city. 1940, New York [1941].
It happened like this. New York 1942, London 1943.
Bring back the days. 1958. Autobiography.
Of Swinburne. [Bethesda Md] 1960 (160 copies). Pamphlet.

§2

Adcock, A. St J. In his Gods of modern Grub Street, 1923.
Mais, S. P. B. In his Some modern authors, 1923.

RAY CORYTON HUTCHINSON
b. 1907

§1

Thou hast a devil: a fable. 1930.
The answering glory. 1932, New York 1932.
The unforgotten prisoner. 1933, New York 1934.
One light burning. 1935, New York 1935.
Shining scabbard. 1936, New York 1936.
Testament. 1938, New York 1938.
The fire and the wood. 1940, New York [1940].
Interim. 1945, New York 1945. Reminiscences.
Elephant and Castle: a reconstruction. 1949, New York 1949.
Recollection of a journey. 1952, New York 1952 (as Journey with strangers).
The stepmother. 1955, New York [1955].
March the ninth. 1957, New York 1957.
Image of my father. 1961, New York 1962 (as The inheritor).
A child possessed. 1964, New York 1964.
Johanna at daybreak. 1969.

ALDOUS LEONARD HUXLEY
1894–1963

Many Huxley mss are in the Library of the Univ of California at Los Angeles. See Wickes, Bibliographies, below.

Bibliographies

Muir, P. H. and B. Van Thal. Bibliographies of the first editions of books by Huxley and T. F. Powys. 1927. Includes contributions to periodicals.

Duval, H. R. Aldous Huxley: a bibliography. New York 1939. Includes contributions to periodicals.

The writings of Huxley 1916–43. Los Angeles 1943 (500 copies for presentation). Catalogue of an exhibition of the Zeitlin collection at the Library of Univ of California.

Eschelbach, C. J. and J. L. Shober. Aldous Huxley: a bibliography 1916–59. Foreword by Huxley. Berkeley 1961. Includes full lists of original publication of essays, articles etc., newspaper contributions and reviews; also a section of secondary material, including unpbd dissertations.

Clareson, T. D. and C. S. Andrews. Huxley: a bibliography 1960–4. Extrapolation 6 1964. Continues Eschelbach and Shober's bibliography.

Wickes, G. (ed). Aldous Huxley at UCLA: a catalogue of the mss in the Aldous Huxley collection, with the texts of three unpublished letters. Los Angeles 1964.

Collections and Selections

Collected edition. 1946 onwards.
Rotunda: a selection from the works of Huxley. 1932. Fiction, verse, drama, essays.
Retrospect: an omnibus of Huxley's books. Garden City NY 1933. Contains Crome yellow and Brave new world (both complete), a selection of short stories and verse, and some essays.
Stories, essays and poems. 1937 (EL).
Twice seven: fourteen selected stories. 1944 (Reprint Soc). Includes one story, Sir Hercules, not previously pbd.
Verses and a comedy: early poems; Leda; The cicadas; The world of light. 1946. Pt of the Collected edn, see above.
The world of Aldous Huxley: an omnibus of his fiction and non-fiction over three decades. Ed with introd by C. J. Rolo, New York 1947.

Collected short stories. 1957, New York 1957. Omits After the fireworks, Two or three graces, Happy families, The farcical history of Richard Greenow.
Collected essays. New York 1959, London 1960. A selection only. Preface by Huxley.
On art and artists. Ed M. Philpson, New York 1960, London 1960. Preface by Huxley.

§1

Many of Huxley's books appeared in limited edns as well as trade edns. The first ch of an unfinished novel is printed in L. A. Huxley, The timeless moment, 1968, pp. 212–38.

Prose Fiction

Limbo. 1920, New York 1920. Stories. Contains The farcical history of Richard Greenow, Happily ever after, Eupompus gave splendour to art by numbers, Happy families, Cynthia, The bookshop, The death of Lully.
Crome yellow. 1921, New York 1922.
Mortal coils. 1922, New York 1922. Stories. Contains The Gioconda smile, Permutations among the nightingales [a play], The Tillotson banquet, Green tunnels, Nuns at luncheon.
Antic hay. 1923, New York 1923.
Little Mexican, and other stories. 1924, New York 1924 (as Young Archimedes). Contains Uncle Spencer, Little Mexican, Hubert and Minnie, Fard, The portrait, Young Archimedes.
Those barren leaves. 1925, New York 1925.
Two or three graces, and other stories. 1926, New York 1926. Contains Two or three graces, Half-holiday, The monocle, Fairy godmother.
Point counter point. 1928, Garden City NY 1928, New York 1947 (introd by H. Watts).
Brief candles: stories. 1930, Garden City NY 1930; Contains Chawdron, The rest cure, The Claxtons, After the fireworks.
Brave new world. 1932, Garden City NY 1932, New York 1946 (with foreword by Huxley) 1950 (introd by C. J. Rolo), 1960 (foreword by Huxley).
Eyeless in Gaza. 1936, New York 1936.
The Gioconda smile. 1938 (Zodiac Books). Story, first pbd in Mortal coils.
After many a summer. 1939, New York 1939 (as After many a summer dies the swan).
Time must have a stop. New York 1944, London 1945.
Ape and essence. New York 1948, London 1949.
The genius and the goddess. 1955, New York 1955.
Island. 1962, New York 1962.
The crows of pearblossom. New York 1967, London [1968]. Children's story.

Other Works

The burning wheel. Oxford 1916. Verse.
Jonah. Oxford 1917 (50 copies). Verse.
The defeat of youth, and other poems. Oxford 1918.
Leda. 1920, New York 1920. Verse.
On the margin: notes and essays. 1923, New York 1923.
The discovery: a comedy in five acts written by Mrs Frances Sheridan: adapted for the modern stage by Huxley. (RADA 4 May 1924). 1924.
Along the road: notes and essays of a tourist. 1925, New York 1925.
Selected poems. Oxford 1925, New York 1925.
Essays new and old. 1926, New York 1927. Some essays rptd from On the margin and Along the road.
Jesting Pilate: the diary of a journey. 1926, New York 1926 (as Jesting Pilate: an intellectual holiday). Travel.
Proper studies. 1927, Garden City NY 1928. Essays.
Arabia infelix, and other poems. New York 1929, London 1929.
Do what you will: essays. 1929, Garden City NY 1929.
Holy face, and other essays. 1929.
Apennine. Gaylordsville 1930 (91 copies). Poem; rptd in The cicadas.

Vulgarity in literature: digressions from a theme. 1930, New York 1966.

Music at night, and other essays. 1931, New York 1931.

The world of light: a comedy in three acts. (Royalty, 30 March 1931), 1931, Garden City NY 1931.

The cicadas, and other poems. 1931, Garden City NY 1931.

The letters of D. H. Lawrence, ed and with an introd by A. Huxley. 1932, New York 1932.

Texts and pretexts: an anthology with commentaries. 1932, New York 1933.

T. H. Huxley as a man of letters. [1932] (Huxley memorial lecture). Rptd in The olive tree, below.

Beyond the Mexique bay. 1934, New York 1934. Travel.

1935...peace? [1936]. Leaflet for Friends Peace Committee.

The olive tree, and other essays. 1936, New York 1937.

What are you going to do about it?: the case for constructive peace. 1936, New York 1936, London 1936 (as The case for constructive peace). Reply by C. Day Lewis, We're not going to do nothing, 1936.

An encyclopaedia of pacifism. Ed Huxley 1937, New York 1937.

Ends and means: an enquiry into the nature of ideals and into the methods employed for their realization. 1937, New York 1937.

The most agreeable vice. Los Angeles 1938. Essay on reading.

Words and their meanings. Los Angeles [1940] (100 copies).

Grey eminence: a study in religion and politics. 1941, New York 1941. A biography of Father Joseph, Capuchin.

The art of seeing. New York 1942, London 1943.

The perennial philosophy. New York 1945, London 1946. Anthology of mysticism, with commentary.

Science, liberty and peace. New York 1946, London 1947.

The Gioconda smile: a play. (New, 3 June 1948). 1948, New York 1948 (as Mortal coils). London 1949 (French's Acting Edn). Based on Huxley's own story.

Prisons: with the 'Carceri' etchings by Piranesi. [1949], Los Angeles 1949.

Themes and variations. 1950, New York 1950. Essays.

The devils of Loudun. 1952, New York 1952.

Joyce the artificer: two studies of Joyce's method. 1952 (priv ptd, 90 copies). With S. Gilbert.

A day in Windsor. 1953. With J. A. Kings.

The French of Paris. Paris [1953]. Text accompanying photographs by S. H. Roth.

The doors of perception. 1954, New York 1954, London 1959 (with Heaven and hell).

Adonis and the alphabet, and other essays. 1956, New York 1956 (as Tomorrow and tomorrow and tomorrow, and other essays).

Heaven and hell. 1956, New York 1956, London 1959 (with The doors of perception).

Brave new world revisited. New York 1958, London 1959.

Literature and science. 1963, New York 1963.

The politics of ecology: the question of survival. Santa Barbara 1963 (Center for the Study of Democratic Institutions. Occasional paper).

Letters

Letters of Aldous Huxley. Ed G. Smith 1969.

§2

Books and Chapters in Books

Mais, S. P. B. The poems of Huxley. In his Why we should read, 1921.

Overton, G. M. The twentieth-century Gothic of Huxley. In his Cargoes for Crusoes, New York 1924.

Muir, E. In his Transition: essays on contemporary literature, 1926.

Adcock, A. St J. In his The glory that was Grub Street 1928.

Weaver, R. et al. Huxley: satirist and humanist. Garden City NY 1928.

Butts, M. In Scrutinies vol 2, ed E. Rickword 1931.

Chapman, J. B. Genealogy of Huxley and some others. Foreword by Huxley 1931 (50 copies).

Lloyd, R. B. The undisciplined life: an examination of Huxley's recent works. 1931.

Beach, J. W. Counterpoint: Huxley. In his Twentieth-century novel, New York 1932.

MacCarthy, D. In his Criticism, 1932.

— The stage and the spirits. In his Humanities, 1953. On the world of light.

Garman, D. Those barren leaves. In Towards standards of criticism, ed F. R. Leavis 1933.

Brewster, D. and A. Burrell. Huxley's Point counter point and André Gide's Counterfeiters. In their Modern fiction, New York 1934.

Vann, G. On being human: St Thomas and Huxley. 1934.

Henderson, A. J. Aldous Huxley. 1935.

Joad, C. E. M. Huxley and the dowagers. In his Return to philosophy, 1935.

— Huxley and the nature of the universe. In his The recovery of belief, 1952.

'Maurois, André' (E. S. W. Herzog). In his Magiciens et logiciens, Paris 1935; tr 1935 (as Prophets and poets).

Quennell, P. D. H. Lawrence and Huxley. In English novelists, ed D. Verschoyle 1936.

— In Living writers, ed G. Phelps 1947.

Lovett, R. M. Vanity Fair up to date. In Literary opinion in America, ed M. D. Zabel, New York 1937. On Point counter point.

Muller, H. J. Apostles of the lost generation: Huxley, Hemingway. In his Modern fiction, New York 1937.

Poschmann, W. Das kritische Weltbild bei Huxley. Düsseldorf 1937.

Bredsdorff, M. Aldous Huxley. Copenhagen 1938.

Plesner, K. F. En kynisk idealist: Huxley. Copenhagen 1938.

Daiches, D. In his The novel and the modern world, Chicago 1939.

Buck, P. M. Sight to the blind: Huxley. In his Directions in contemporary literature, New York 1942.

Baldensperger, F. Les petits illogismes d'un grand romancier: une hypothèse historique de Huxley. In Essays in honor of Albert Feuillerat, ed H. Peyre, New Haven 1943.

Nicholson, N. Henry de Montherlant, Huxley and others. In his Man and literature, 1943.

Rillo, L. E. Huxley and T. S. Eliot. Buenos Aires 1943.

Coates, J. B. In his Ten modern prophets, 1944.

Bowersox, H. C. Huxley: the defeat of youth. Chicago 1946.

Brunius, T. Huxley: en studie. Stockholm 1947.

Gérard, A. À la rencontre de Huxley. Liège 1947.

Savage, D. S. Mysticism and Huxley: an examination of Heard–Huxley theories. Yonkers 1947.

Jouguelet, P. Aldous Huxley. Paris 1948.

Nordhjem, B. Aldous Huxley. Copenhagen 1948.

Eaton, G. Monk at large: Huxley. In his The richest vein, 1949.

Heintz-Friedrich, S. Aldous Huxley: Entwicklung seiner Metaphysik. Berne 1949.

Bowen, E. Huxley's essays. In her Collected impressions, 1950. On The olive tree.

Brooke, J. Aldous Huxley. 1954, 1958 (rev) (Br Council pamphlet).

Moeller, C. Huxley: ou la religion sans amour. In his Littérature du XXᵉ siècle et Christianisme, Tournai 1954.

Chatterjee, S. Huxley: a study. Calcutta 1955.

Hull, J. Huxley: the growth of a personality. Zürich 1955.

Ueda, T. A study of Huxley. Tokyo 1955.

Atkins, J. A. Huxley: a literary study. 1956, 1967 (rev).

Narita, S. Aldous Huxley. Tokyo 1956.

O'Faolain, S. Huxley and Waugh: or, I do not think, therefore I am. In his Vanishing hero, 1956.

Hines, B. The social world of Huxley. Loretto Pa 1957.

Stewart, D. Huxley—mysticism. In his Ark of God: studies in five modern novelists, 1961.

Ghose, S. Huxley: a cynical salvationist. 1962.

Putt, S. G. The limitations of intelligent talk: Huxley's essays. In his Scholars of the heart, 1962.

Walsh, C. In his From utopia to nightmare, 1962.

Hall, J. In his The tragic comedians, Bloomington 1963.

Holz, L. Methoden der Meinungsbeeinflussung bei Orwell und Huxley. Hamburg 1963.

Morand, C. Los adolescentes en la obra narrativa de Huxley. Santiago 1963.

Gottwald, J. Die Erzählformen der Romane von Huxley und D. H. Lawrence. Munich 1964.

Henderson, A. J. Aldous Huxley. New York 1964.

Aldous Huxley, 1894–1963: a memorial volume. Ed J. Huxley 1965.

Greenblatt, S. J. Three modern satirists: Waugh, Orwell and Huxley. New Haven 1965.

Borinski, L. Wells, Huxley und die Utopie. In Literatur-Kultur-Gesellschaft in England und Amerika: Aspekte und Forschungsbeiträge Friedrich Schubel zum 60. Geburtstag, ed G. Müller-Schwefe und K. Tuzinski, Frankfurt 1966.

Jog, D. V. Huxley the novelist. Bombay 1966.

Bowering, P. Huxley: a study of the major novels. 1968.

Clark, R. W. The Huxleys. 1968.

Huxley, L. A. This timeless moment: a personal view of Huxley. New York 1968.

Witschel, G. Rausch und Rauschgift bei Baudelaire, Huxley, Benn und Burroughs. Bonn 1968.

Meckier, J. Huxley: satire and structure. 1969.

Watts, H. H. Aldous Huxley. New York 1969 (Twayne's English Authors).

Articles in Periodicals

MacCarthy, D. The poetry of Huxley. Living Age 307 1920.

— Notes on Huxley. Life & Letters 5 1930.

Weaver, R. Aldous Huxley. Bookman (New York) 60 1924.

Eliot, T. S. Le roman anglais contemporain (D. H. Lawrence, V. Woolf, D. Garnett, Huxley). Nouvelle Revue Française 28 1927.

Freeman, J. Aldous Huxley. London Mercury 15 1927.

Logé, M. Trois romanciers anglais: Arthur Machen, Huxley, T. F. Powys. Revue Politique et Littéraire 65 1927.

Cajumi, A. Il nuovo romanzo inglese: Huxley. La Cultura Aug 1929.

Joad, C. E. M. Philosophy and Huxley. Realist 1 1929.

Drieu La Rochelle, P. A propos d'un roman anglais. Nouvelle Revue Française 35 1930. On Point counter point.

'Maurois, André' (E. S. W. Herzog). Huxley's progress. Living Age 339 1930.

Thorp, M. F. Is Huxley unhappy? Sewanee Rev 38 1930.

Dottin, P. Aldous Huxley: un romancier du monde où l'on s'ennuie. Revue de France 11 1931.

Kooistra, J. Aldous Huxley. E Studies 13 1931.

Mönch, W. Der Acte gratuit und das Schicksalsproblem bei André Gide und Huxley. Zeitschrift für französischen und englischen Unterricht 30 1931.

Vallette, J. Aldous Huxley: histoire d'un évolution. Revue Anglo-américaine 8 1931.

Connolly, C. Under which king? Living Age 341 1932.

Petre, M. D. Bolshevist ideals and the brave new world. Hibbert Jnl 31 1932.

Bethell, P. The philosophy in the poetry of Huxley. Poetry Rev 24 1933.

Häusermann, H. W. Huxley as a literary critic. PMLA 48 1933.

Mainsard, J. Huxley: moraliste. Études no 214 1933.

Houston, P. H. The salvation of Huxley. Amer Rev 4 1934.

Lanoire, M. Aldous Huxley. Revue de Paris 1 Sept 1934.

Webster, H. C. Facing futility: Huxley's really brave new world. Sewanee Rev 42 1934.

Young, G. M. The emotions and Huxley. Life & Letters 10 1934.

Alexander, H. Lawrence and Huxley. Queen's Quart 42 1935.

Hogarth, B. Huxley as music critic. Musical Times 76 1935.

Rogers, W. H. Huxley's humanism. Sewanee Rev 43 1935.

Steen, E. B. Aldous Huxley. Edda 35 1935.

Ueda, T. Theory and practice: Huxley's ideal of perfected humanity. Stud in English Lit (Tokyo) 15 1935.

Villard, L. Huxley et ses romans. Revue des Cours et Conférences 30 May 1935.

Bentley, P. The structure of Eyeless in Gaza. London Mercury 34 1936.

Blom, E. The musician in Huxley. Chesterian 17 1936.

Castier, J. De la culture scientifique d'Aldous Huxley. Revue Politique et Littéraire 74 1936.

— Les héroines d'Aldous Huxley et son évolution psychologique. Revue Politique et Littéraire 75 1937.

— Aldous Huxley: sociologue. Revue Politique et Littéraire 76 1938.

Hart, E. P. Huxley's Eyeless in Gaza. Adelphi 13 1936.

Maynard, T. Huxley: moralist. Catholic World 144 1936.

Stevens, G. Huxley's man of good will. Saturday Rev of Lit 11 July 1936. On Eyeless in Gaza.

Ament, W. S. Jesting Huxley waiting for an answer. Personalist 18 1937.

Chesterton, G. K. Huxley heritage. Amer Rev 8 1937.

Hoops, R. Die Weltanschauung Huxleys. E Studien 72 1937.

Kirkwood, M. M. The thought of Huxley. UTQ 6 1937.

Lalou, R. Le sentiment de l'unité humaine chez Virginia Woolf et Huxley. Europe 15 Oct 1937.

— Les fins et les moyens d'Aldous Huxley. Études Anglaises 2 1938.

Neumann, H. Huxley and H. G. Wells seek religion. Standard 23 1937.

Roberts, J. H. Huxley and Lawrence. Virginia Quart Rev 13 1937.

Thiébaut, M. Trois romanciers étrangers: Huxley, Morgan, Caldwell. Revue de Paris 1 Dec 1937.

Bedoyère, M. de la. Huxley's challenge. Dublin Rev 202 1938.

Cairns, D. Huxley: cosmology and ethic. Expository Times 50 1938.

— Why Mr Aldous Huxley is not a Christian. Ibid.

Dalglish, D. N. Huxley's poetry. London Mercury 38 1938.

Hartz, H. Les influences françaises dans l'oeuvre d'Aldous Huxley. Bulletin de la Faculté des Lettres de Strasbourg 17 1938–9.

Kanters, R. Aldous Huxley jugé par Blaise Pascal. Cahiers du Sud no 210 1938.

Estrich, H. W. Jesting Pilate tells the answer: Huxley. Sewanee Rev 47 1939.

Glicksberg, C. I. The intellectual pilgrimage of Huxley. Dalhousie Rev 19 1939.

— Huxley: art and mysticism. Prairie Schooner 27 1953.

— Huxley: the experimental novelist. South Atlantic Quart 52 1953.

Kohn-Bramstedt, E. Intellectual as ironist: Huxley and Thomas Mann. Contemporary Rev 155 1939.

Temple, R. Z. Aldous Huxley et la littérature française. Revue de Littérature Comparée 19 1939.

Baker, H. In praise of the novel: the fiction of Huxley, Steinbeck and others. Southern Rev 5 1940.

Merton, T. Huxley's pantheon. Catholic World 152 1940.

Orrell, H. M. Huxley as novelist. New Republic 15 Jan 1940.

Spencer, T. Huxley: the latest phase. Atlantic Monthly 165 1940.

Burgum, E. B. Huxley and his dying swan. Antioch Rev 2 1942; rptd in his The novel and the world's dilemma, New York 1947.

Lorus, P. L'Inde vue par Huxley. Revue des Deux Mondes 70 1942.

Tindall, W. Y. The trouble with Huxley. Amer Scholar 11 1942.

Chase, R. The Huxley–Heard paradise. Partisan Rev 10 1943.

Wilson, E. Huxley in the world beyond time. New Yorker 2 Sept 1944; rptd in his Classics and commercials, New York 1950.

Hoffman, F. J. Huxley and the novel of ideas. College Eng 8 1946; rptd in Forms of modern fiction ed W. V. O'Connor, Minneapolis 1948.

Orsini, N. Aldous Huxley. Belfagor 1 1946.

Webster, H. T. Huxley: notes on a moral evolution. South Atlantic Quart 45 1946.

Wilson, R. H. Brave new world as Shakespeare criticism. Shakespeare Assoc Bull (New York) 21 1946.

— Versions of Brave new world. Lib Chron of Univ of Texas 8 1968.

Nicholson, N. Huxley and the mystics. Fortnightly 161 1947.

Rolo, C. J. Aldous Huxley. Atlantic Monthly 180 1947; rptd as introd to The world of Aldous Huxley, 1947, Collections and Selections, above.

Savage, D. S. Huxley and the dissociation of personality. Sewanee Rev 55 1947; rptd in The novelist as thinker, ed B. Rajan 1947; in Savage's The withered branch, 1950; and in Critiques and essays in modern fiction, ed J. W. Aldridge, New York 1952.

Hamilton, R. The challenge of Huxley: the perennial philosophy. Horizon 17 1948.

Bode, H. Die Wandlung Huxleys. Literarische Revue (Munich) 4 1949.

Bullough, G. Aspects of Huxley. E Studies 30 1949.

Gérard, J. Huxley et notre génération. Revue Générale Belge 41 1949.

Perruchot, H. Les hommes et leurs oeuvres: l'évolution spirituelle d'Aldous Huxley. Synthèses 1 1949.

Voorhees, R. J. The perennial Huxley. Prairie Schooner 23 1949.

Woodcock, G. Huxley: the man and his work. World Rev 4 1949.

Bald, R. C. Huxley as a borrower. College Eng 11 1950.

Jones, J. Utopias as dirge. Amer Quart 2 1950.

Le Roy, G. C. A.F. 632 to 1984. College Eng 12 1950.

Godfrey, D. R. The essence of Huxley. E Studies 32 1951.

Salvan, J. L. Le scandale de la multiplicité des consciences chez Huxley, Sartre et Simone de Beauvoir. Symposium 5 1951.

Hart, H. N. Aldous Huxley. Catholic World 175 1952.

Maini, D. S. Huxley: a study in disintegration. Indian Rev 54 1953.

King, C. A. Huxley's way to God. Queen's Quart 61 1954.

— Huxley and music. Queen's Quart 70 1963.

Matson, F. W. Aldous and heaven too: religion among the intellectuals. Antioch Rev 14 1954.

Sutherland, A. Huxley's mind at large. Twentieth Century 155 1954. The doors of perception.

Zolla, E. Huxley and the doom of reason. Letterature Moderne 5 1954.

Church, M. Concepts of time in novels of Virginia Woolf and Huxley. Modern Fiction Stud 1 1955.

— Huxley's attitude toward duration. College Eng 17 1956. Both rptd in her Time and reality, 1963.

Stürzl, E. Aldous Huxley: Zeitgebundenheit und Zeitlosigkeit seines Werkes. Stimmen der Zeit 156 1955.

— Aldous Huxleys Gedanken über die Sprache. Germanisch–Romanische Monatsschrift 39 1958.

Vein, I. Huxley as musical critic. Chesterian 29 1955.

Waugh, E. et al. A critical symposium on Huxley. London Mag 2 1955. Contains Youth at the helm and pleasure at the prow, by E. Waugh; The house party novels, by A. Wilson; The teacher emerges, by F. Wyndham; Tracts against materialism, by J. Wain; and Electrifying the audience, by P. Quennell.

Blocker, G. Huxley und die Gnade. Merkur 10 1956.

Barzun, J. The anti-modern essays of Huxley. London Mag 4 1957.

Ehrenpreis, I. Orwell, Huxley, Pope. Revue des Langues Vivantes 23 1957.

Kessler, M. Power and the perfect state: a study in disillusionment as reflected in Orwell's Nineteen eighty-four and Huxley's Brave new world. Political Science Quart 72 1957.

Vickery, J. B. Three modes and a myth. Western Humanities Rev 12 1958.

Wilson, C. Existential criticism and the work of Huxley. London Mag 5 1958.

Baldanza, F. Point counter point: Huxley on the human figure. South Atlantic Quart 58 1959.

Bataller Ferrandiz, J. Aldous Huxley y la novela. Revista de Literatura 16 1959.

Nagarajan, S. Religion in three recent novels of Huxley. Modern Fiction Stud 5 1959. After many a summer, Time must have a stop, The genius and the goddess.

Schmerl, R. B. Huxley's social criticism. Chicago Rev 13 1959.

— The two future worlds of Huxley. PMLA 77 1962.

Cary, R. Huxley, Vernon Lee and the genius loci. Colby Lib Quart 5 1960.

Enroth, C. Mysticism in two of Huxley's early novels. Twentieth-Century Lit 6 1960. Antic hay, and Brave new world.

Stewart, D. Significant modern writers: Huxley. Expository Times 71 1960.

Wickes, G. and R. Grazer. A conversation with Huxley. Claremont Quart 8 1960.

Clareson, T. D. The classic: Huxley's Brave new world. Extrapolation 2 1961.

Dyson, A. E. Huxley and the two nothings. CQ 3 1961; rptd in his Crazy fabric, 1965.

Hoffmann, C. G. The change in Huxley's approach to the novel of ideas. Personalist 42 1961.

Holmes, C. M. Huxley's struggle with art. Western Humanities Rev 15 1961.

— The early poetry of Huxley. Texas Stud in Lit & Lang 8 1966.

Jones, M. The Iago of Brave new world. Western Humanities Rev 15 1961.

Karl, F. R. The play within the novel in Antic hay. Renascence 13 1961.

Richards, D. Four utopias. Slavonic and East European Rev 40 1961. Dostoevsky's Legend of the Grand Inquisitor; Zamyatin's We; Brave new world; Orwell's 1984.

Grushow, I. Brave new world and The tempest. College Eng 24 1962.

Quinn, J. H. The philosophical phases of Huxley. College Eng 23 1962.

Salter, K. W. and A. E. Dyson. Aldous Huxley. CQ 4 1962.

Pritchett, V. S. Aldous Huxley. New Statesman 6 Dec 1963.

Stewart, D. H. Huxley's Island. Queen's Quart 70 1963.

Bartlett, N. Huxley and D. H. Lawrence. Australian Quart 36 1964.

Ketser, G. Huxley: a retrospect. Revue des Langues Vivantes 30 1964.

Nazareth, P. Huxley and his critics. Eng Stud in Africa 7 1964.

Poisson, J. R. Hommage à Aldous Huxley. Études Anglaises 17 1964.

Heard, G. The poignant prophet. Kenyon Rev 27 1965.

Huxley, J. My brother Aldous. Humanist 25 1965.

Kennedy, R. S. Huxley: the final wisdom. Southwest Rev 50 1965.

Leeper, G. The happy utopias of Huxley and H. G. Wells. Meanjin 24 1965.

Miles, O. T. Three authors in search of a character. Personalist 6 1965.

Birnbaum, M. Huxley's animadversions upon sexual love. Texas Stud in Lit & Lang 8 1966.

—— Huxley's conception of the nature of reality. Personalist 47 1966.

—— Huxley's quest for values: a study in religious syncretism. Comparative Lit Stud 3 1966.

—— Huxley's treatment of nature. Hibbert Jnl 64 1966.

—— Huxley's views on education. Xavier Univ Stud 6 1967.

—— Huxley: an aristocrat's comments on popular culture. Jnl of Popular Culture 2 1968.

Firchow, P. E. The satire of Huxley's Brave new world. Modern Fiction Stud 12 1966.

Meckier, J. Huxley: satire and structure. Wisconsin Stud in Contemporary Lit 7 1966.

Wajc-Tenenbaum, R. Huxley and D. H. Lawrence. Revue des Langues Vivantes 32 1966.

Yoder, E. M. Huxley and his mystics. Virginia Quart Rev 42 1966.

Bentley, J. Huxley's ambivalent responses to the ideas of Lawrence. Twentieth-Century Lit 13 1967.

Margolin, J.-C. Erasme et Huxley. Moreana 15–16 1967.

Thomas, W. K. Brave new world and the Houyhnhnms. Revue de l'Université d'Ottawa 37 1967.

Dommergues, A. Aldous Huxley: une oeuvre de jeunesse, Crome yellow. Études Anglaises 21 1968.

McMichael, C. T. Huxley's Island: the final version. Studi Linguistici Italiani 1 1968.

Misra, C. S. P. and N. Satin. The meaning of life in Huxley. Midwest Quart 9 1968.

Watt, D. J. Vision and symbol in Huxley's Island. Twentieth-Century Lit 14 1968.

Farmer, D. A note on the text of Huxley's Crome yellow. PBSA 63 1969.

Watson, D. S. Point counter point: the modern satiric novel a genre? Satire Newsletter 6 1969.

'MICHAEL INNES',
JOHN INNES MACKINTOSH
STEWART
b. 1906

Selections

Appleby intervenes: three tales from Scotland Yard. New York 1965. One-man show [i.e. A private view]; A comedy of terrors [i.e. There came both mist and snow]; The secret vanguard.

§ I

Death at the President's lodging. 1936, New York 1937 (as Seven suspects).

Hamlet, revenge! 1937, New York 1937.

Lament for a maker. 1938, New York 1938.

Stop press. 1939, New York 1939 (as The spider strikes).

The secret vanguard. 1940, New York 1941.

There came both mist and snow. 1940, New York 1940 (as A comedy of terrors).

Appleby on Ararat. 1941, New York 1941.

The daffodil affair. 1942, New York 1942.

The weight of the evidence. New York 1943, London 1944.

Appleby's end. 1945, New York 1945.

From London far. 1946, New York 1946 (as The unsuspected chasm).

What happened at Hazlewood. 1946, New York 1946.

A night of errors. New York 1947, London 1948.

Character and motive in Shakespeare. 1949, New York 1949. As J. I. M. Stewart.

The journeying boy. [1949], New York 1949 (as The case of the journeying boy).

Three tales of Hamlet. 1950. With R. Heppenstall. Contains The hawk and the handsaw and The mysterious affair at Elsinore, by Innes.

Operation Pax. 1951, New York 1951 (as The paper thunderbolt).

A private view. 1952, New York 1952 (as One-man show).

Christmas at Candleshoe. 1953, New York 1953.

Appleby talking. 1954, New York 1954 (as Dead man's shoes). Stories.

Mark Lambert's supper. 1954. As J. I. M. Stewart.

The guardians. 1955, New York 1957. As J. I. M. Stewart.

The man from the sea. 1955, New York 1955.

Appleby plays chicken. 1956, New York 1957 (as Death on a quiet day).

Appleby talks again. 1956, New York 1957. Stories.

Old Hall, New Hall. 1956, New York 1956 (as A question of queens).

James Joyce. 1957, 1960 (rev) (Br Council pamphlet). As J. I. M. Stewart.

A use of riches. 1957, New York 1957. As J. I. M. Stewart.

The long farewell. 1958, New York 1958.

Hare sitting up. 1959, New York 1959.

The man who wrote detective stories, and other stories. 1959, New York 1959. As J. I. M. Stewart.

The new Sonia Wayward. 1960, New York 1960 (as The case of Sonia Wayward), 1962 (as The last of Sonia Wayward).

The man who won the pools. 1961, New York 1961. As J. I. M. Stewart.

Silence observed. 1961, New York 1961.

A connoisseur's case. 1962, New York 1962 (as The Crabtree affair).

Eight modern writers. Oxford 1963 (OHEL). As J. I. M. Stewart.

The last Tresilians. 1963, New York 1963. As J. I. M. Stewart.

Thomas Love Peacock. 1963 (Br Council pamphlet). As J. I. M. Stewart.

Money from Holme. 1964, New York 1965.

An acre of grass. 1965, New York 1966. As J. I. M. Stewart.

The Aylwins. 1966, New York 1967. As J. I. M. Stewart.

The bloody wood. 1966, New York 1966.

A change of heir. 1966, New York 1966.

Rudyard Kipling. 1966, New York 1966. As J. I. M. Stewart.

Vanderlyn's kingdom. 1967, New York 1968. As J. I. M. Stewart.

Appleby at Allington. 1968.

Joseph Conrad. 1968. As J. I. M. Stewart.

Cucumber sandwiches, and other stories. 1969. As J. I. M. Stewart.

A family affair. 1969.

MARGARET EMMA FAITH IRWIN
?– 1967

How many miles to Babylon? 1913.

Come out to play. 1914.

Out of the house. 1916.

The happy man: a sketch for acting. 1921.

Still she wished for company. 1924.

These mortals. 1925.

Knock four times. 1927.

South Molton Street. 1927. Non-fiction.

Fire down below. 1928.

None so pretty. 1930.

Royal flush: the story of Minette. 1932. Biography of Henrietta Anna, Consort of Philip, Duke of Orleans.

Check to the King of France: an historical play in one act. [1933].

Minette: an historical play in one act. [1933].

Save the children: a play in one act. [1933].

The proud servant: the story of Montrose. 1934. Fiction.

Madame fears the dark: seven stories and a play. 1935.

The stranger prince: the story of Rupert of the Rhine. 1937. Biography.

The bride: the story of Louise and Montrose. 1939. Fiction.

Mrs Oliver Cromwell, and other stories. 1940.

The gay galliard: the love story of Mary Queen of Scots. 1941. Fiction.

Young Bess. 1944. Pt 1 of The story of Elizabeth Tudor. Fiction.

Elizabeth, captive princess. 1948. Pt 2 of The story of Elizabeth Tudor.

Bloodstock, and other stories. 1953.

Elizabeth and the prince of Spain. 1953. Pt 3 of The story of Elizabeth Tudor.

That great Lucifer: a portrait of Sir Walter Raleigh. 1960.

CHRISTOPHER WILLIAM BRADSHAW ISHERWOOD
b. 1904

Bibliographies

Westby, S. and Clayton, M. B. Christopher Isherwood: a bibliography 1923–67. Los Angeles 1968.

§1

All the conspirators. 1928, New York 1958.

The memorial: portrait of a family. 1932, Norfolk Conn 1946.

Mr Norris changes trains. 1935, New York 1935 (as The last of Mr Norris).

The dog beneath the skin: or, where is Francis? a play in three acts. (Westminster Theatre 12 Jan 1936). 1935, New York 1935. With W. H. Auden.

The ascent of F6: a tragedy in two acts. (Mercury Theatre 26 Feb 1937). 1936, New York 1937 (rev), London 1937 (2nd edn again rev). With W. H. Auden.

Sally Bowles. 1937. Story.

Lions and shadows: an education in the twenties. 1938, Norfolk Conn 1947. Autobiographical.

On the frontier: a melodrama in three acts. (Arts Theatre, Cambridge 14 Nov 1938). 1938, New York [1939]. With W. H. Auden.

Goodbye to Berlin. 1939, New York 1939. Stories.

Journey to a war. 1939, New York [1939]. Travel in China; with W. H. Auden.

Vedanta for the western world. Ed with introd by C. Isherwood, Hollywood 1945, London 1948.

Prater violet. New York 1945, London 1946.

The Berlin stories. New York 1946, 1954 (with new preface by the author). Contains The last of Mr Norris and Goodbye to Berlin.

The condor and the cows. New York 1949, London 1949. Travel in S. America.

Vedanta for modern man. Ed with introd by C. Isherwood, New York 1951, London 1952.

The world in the evening. New York 1954, London 1954.

Great English short stories. Ed with foreword and introd by C. Isherwood. New York 1957.

Down there on a visit. New York 1962, London 1962.

A single man. New York 1964, London 1964.

Ramakrishna and his disciples. New York 1965, London 1965.

Exhumations: stories, articles, verses. New York 1966, London 1966.

A meeting by the river. New York 1967, London 1967.

§2

Spender, S. The poetic dramas of Auden and Isherwood. New Writing new ser 1 1938.

Bantock, G. H. The novels of Isherwood. In The novelist as thinker, ed B. Rajan, Focus 4 1947.

Moore, G. Three who did not make a revolution. Amer Mercury 74 1952. Auden, Spender, Isherwood.

Mayne, R. The novel and Mr Norris. Cambridge Jnl 6 1953.

Breit, H. Christopher Isherwood. In his The writer observed, Cleveland 1956.

Weisgerber, J. Les romans et récits de C. Isherwood. Revue de l'Université de Bruxelles 10 1957.

Kermode, F. The interpretation of the times. Encounter 15 1960. Rptd in his Puzzles and epiphanies, 1962. Mainly on The world in the evening and The memorial.

Maes-Jelinek, H. The knowledge of man in the works of Isherwood. Revue des Langues Vivantes 26 1960.

Gerstenberger, D. L. Poetry and politics: the verse drama of Auden and Isherwood. Modern Drama 5 1962.

Stebner, G. W. H. Auden and C. Isherwood: The ascent of F6. In Das moderne englische Drama, ed H. Oppel, Berlin 1963.

Jarka, H. Pre-war Austria as seen by Spender, Isherwood and Lehmann. Proc Pacific Northwest Conference on Foreign Languages 15 1964.

Wickes, G. An interview with Isherwood. Shenandoah 16 1965.

Mitchell, B. W. H. Auden and Isherwood: the 'German influence'. Oxford German Stud 1 1966.

Bruehl, W. J. Polus naufrangia: a key symbol in The ascent of F6. Modern Drama 10 1967.

Pérez Minik, D. Isherwood: un novelista famoso pero frustrado. Insula 23 1968.

Valgemae, M. Auden's collaboration with Isherwood on A dog beneath the skin. HLQ 31 1968.

See also under W. H. Auden, cols 207–20 above, for additional items on Isherwood's collaborations with Auden.

WILLIAM WYMARK JACOBS
1863–1943

Bibliographies

Osborne, E. A. Epitome of a bibliography of Jacobs. Amer Book Collector 5 1934.

In P. H. Muir, Points, ser 2 1934.

Collections and Selections

Fifteen stories. 1926.

[Selected stories]. 1928 (Short Stories of Today and Yesterday).

Snug harbour: collected stories. New York 1931. Selection.

The night-watchman and other longshoremen. 1932. Deep waters; Sea whispers; Captains all; Night watches; Ship's company. Contains a story, Love letters, not previously collected.

W. W. Jacobs. 1933 (Methuen's Lib of Humour, ed E. V. Knox).

Cruises and cargoes: a W. W. Jacobs omnibus. 1934. Many cargoes; Sea urchins; Light freights; Odd craft; Short cruises.

Six collected one-act plays. [1937].

Selected short stories. Ed D. K. Roberts 1959.

§1

Plays are listed in order of date of production, where known; otherwise of pbn.

Many cargoes. 1896, New York [1897]. Stories.

The skipper's wooing, and The brown man's servant. 1897, New York [1897]. Stories.

Sea urchins. 1898, New York [1898] (as More cargoes). Stories.

A master of craft. New York [1900], London 1900.

Light freights. 1901, New York 1901. Stories.

At Sunwich Port. 1902, New York 1902.

The lady of the barge, and other stories. New York 1902, London 1902. Includes The monkey's paw; *see* next.

The monkey's paw: a story in three scenes. (Haymarket 6 Oct 1903). [1910] (Lacy's Acting Edn), [1910] (French's Acting Edn). Dramatized by L. N. Parker.

Odd craft. [1903], New York 1903. Stories.

Beauty and the barge: a farce in three acts. (New 30 Aug 1904). [1910] (French's Acting Edn). With L. N. Parker.

Dialstone Lane. 1904, New York 1904.

Captains all. 1905, New York 1905. Stories.

The boatswain's mate: a play in one act. [1907] (Lacy's Acting Edn). With H. C. Sargent.

Short cruises. 1907, New York 1907. Stories.

The changeling: a play in one act. [1908] (Lacy's Acting Edn). With H. C. Sargent.

The ghost of Jerry Bundler. [1908] (Lacy's Acting Edn). Play; with C. Rock.

The grey parrot. [1908] (Lacy's Acting Edn). Play; with C. Rock.

Salthaven. 1908, New York 1908.

Admiral Peters: a comedy in one act. [1909] (Lacy's Acting Edn). With H. Mills.

Sailor's knots. 1909, New York 1909. Stories.

Ship's company. [1911], New York 1911. Stories.

A love passage: a comedy in one act. (Little 3 Feb 1913). [1913] (Lacy's Acting Edn). With P. E. Hubbard.

In the library. (Little 3 Feb 1913). [1913] (Lacy's Acting Edn). Play; with H. C. Sargent.

Night watches. 1914, New York 1914. Stories.

Keeping up appearances: a farce in one act. (Savoy 17 April 1915). [1919] (French's Acting Edn).

The castaways. 1916, New York 1917.

Deep waters. [1919], New York 1919. Stories.

The castaway: a farce in one act. [1924] (French's Acting Edn). With H. C. Sargent.

Establishing relations: a comedy. [1925] (French's Acting Edn).

Sea whispers. [1926], New York 1926. Stories.

The warming pan: a comedy in one act. [1929] (French's Acting Edn).

A distant relative: a comedy in one act. [1930] (French's Acting Edn).

Master mariners. [1930]. Play.

Matrimonial openings: a comedy in one act. [1931] (French's Acting Edn).

Dixon's return: a comedy in one act. [1932] (French's Acting Edn).

Double dealing: a comedy in one act. [1935] (French's Acting Edn).

The last 6 plays were rptd in Six collected one-act plays, *1937. See Selections, above.*

§2

Bennett, A. Jacobs and Aristophanes. In his Books and persons, 1917.

Priestley, J. B. In his Figures in modern literature, 1924.

Chesterton, G. K. In his Handful of authors, 1953.

Pritchett, V. S. In his Books in general, 1953.

MONTAGUE RHODES JAMES
1862–1936

Bibliographies

Scholfield, A. F. In S. G. Lubbock, A memoir of James, Cambridge 1939. *See* §2, below. Includes contributions to books and periodicals.

Osborne, E. A. Bibliographical notes. Book Handbook no 4 1947. Appended to L. J. Lloyd, The ghost stories of James. *See* §2, below.

Cox, J. R. James: an annotated bibliography of writings about him. Eng Lit in Transition 12 1969.

Collections and Selections

The collected ghost stories of James. 1931, New York 1931.

Best ghost stories. Cleveland 1944.

§1

Ghost-stories of an antiquary. 1904, New York 1919.

More ghost stories of an antiquary. 1911, New York 1911, London 1959 (as More ghost stories) (Penguin).

A thin ghost, and others. 1919, New York 1920.

The five jars. 1922, New York 1922. Story.

A warning to the curious, and other ghost stories. 1925, New York 1925.

Eton and King's: recollections, mostly trivial, 1875–1925. 1926.

Wailing well. Stanford Dingley 1928 (157 copies). Story.

James contributed an introd on ghost stories to V. H. Collins, Ghosts and marvels, 1924. For his numerous works on palaeography, biblical scholarship etc see Scholfield, Bibliographies, above.

Letters

Letters to a friend. Ed G. McBryde 1956.

§2

Butte, M. The art of James. London Mercury 29 1934.

Gaselee, S. Montague Rhodes James. [1937]. Rptd from Proc Br Acad 22 1936.

Lubbock, S. G. A memoir of James. Cambridge 1939.

Lloyd, L. J. The ghost stories of James. Book Handbook no 4 1947.

Penzoldt, P. In his The supernatural in fiction, 1952.

Cox, J. R. Ghostly antiquary: the stories of James. Eng Lit in Transition 12 1969.

See also Cox, Bibliographies, above.

MARGARET STORM JAMESON
b. 1897

§1

The pot boils. 1919.

The happy highways. 1920, New York 1920.

Modern drama in Europe. [1920].

The clash. 1922, Boston 1922.

Lady Susan and life: an indiscretion. 1923.

The pitiful wife. 1923, New York 1924.

Three kingdoms. 1926, New York 1926.

The lovely ship. 1927, New York 1927. Vol 1 of trilogy, The triumph of time, 1932, below.

Farewell to youth. 1928, New York 1928.

Full circle: a play in one act. Oxford 1928.

The Georgian novel and Mr Robinson. 1929, New York 1929.

The decline of merry England. 1930, Indianapolis [1930].

The voyage home. 1930, New York 1930. Vol 2 of trilogy, The triumph of time, below.

A richer dust... 1931, New York 1931. Vol 3 of trilogy, The triumph of time, below.

The single heart. 1932. Rptd in A day off, 1959, below.

That was yesterday. 1932, New York 1932.

The triumph of time. 1932.

A day off. 1933. Rptd in A day off, 1959, below.

No time like the present. 1933, New York 1933. Autobiography.

Women against men. New York 1933. 3 stories.
Company parade. 1934, New York 1934. Vol 1 of trilogy, The mirror in darkness.
Love in winter. 1935, New York 1935. Vol 2 of trilogy, The mirror in darkness.
The soul of man in an age of leisure. 1935. Pamphlet.
In the second year. 1936, New York 1936.
None turn back. 1936. Vol 3 of trilogy, The mirror in darkness.
Delicate monster. 1937.
The moon is making. 1937, New York 1938.
Here comes a candle. 1938, New York 1939.
The novel in contemporary life. Boston [1938].
Civil journey. 1939. Articles rptd from periodicals.
Farewell night, welcome day. 1939, New York 1939 (as The captain's wife).
Cousin Honoré. 1940, New York 1941.
Europe to let: the memoirs of an obscure man. 1940, New York 1940.
The fort. 1940, New York 1941.
The end of this war. 1941 (PEN books).
Then we shall hear singing: a fantasy in C major. 1942, New York 1942.
Cloudless May. 1943, New York 1944.
The journal of Mary Hervey Russell. 1945, New York 1945.
The other side. 1946, New York 1946.
Before the crossing. 1947, New York 1947.
The black laurel. 1947.
The moment of truth. 1949, New York 1949.
The writer's situation, and other essays. 1950.
The green man. 1952, New York 1953.
The hidden river. 1955, New York 1955, London [1957] (as play by R. and A. Goetz).
The intruder. 1956, New York 1956.
A cup of tea for Mr Thorgill. 1957, New York 1957.
A Ulysses too many. 1958, New York 1958 (as One Ulysses too many).
A day off: two short novels and some stories. 1959.
Last score: or the private life of Sir Richard Ormston. 1961, New York 1961.
Morley Roberts: the last eminent Victorian. 1962. Biography.
The road from the monument. 1962, New York 1962.
A month soon goes. 1963, New York 1963.
The Aristide case. 1964, New York 1964 (as The blind heart).
The early life of Stephen Hind. 1966, New York 1966.
The white crow. 1968, New York 1968.
Journey from the north: autobiography. 1969–.

§2

Adcock, A. St J. In his The glory that was Grub Street, 1928.
Lawrence, M. Matriarchs. In her School of femininity, New York 1936, London 1937 (as We write as women).

FRYNIWYD MARSH TENNYSON JESSE
189?–1958

§1

The Milky Way. 1913, New York [1914].
Beggars on horseback. 1915.
Secret bread. 1917, New York [1917].
The sword of Deborah: first-hand impressions of the British women's army in France. 1919, New York [1919].
The happy bride. 1920, New York [1920]. Verse.
The white riband: or, a young female's folly. 1921, New York [1921].

Murder and its motives. 1924, New York 1924, London 1952 (rev).
Anyhouse: a play in three acts. 1925.
Tom fool. 1926, New York 1926.
Moonraker: or, the female pirate and her friends. 1927, New York 1927.
Many latitudes. 1928, New York 1928. Stories.
The lacquer lady. 1929, New York 1930.
The Solange stories. 1931, New York 1931.
A pin to see the peepshow. 1934, Garden City NY 1934.
Sabi pas: or, I don't know. 1935. On her animals.
Act of God. 1937, New York 1937.
London front: letters written to America, August 1939–July 1940. 1940, New York 1941. With H. M. Harwood.
The saga of 'San Demetrio' (a tanker). 1942, New York 1942. Non-fiction.
While London burns: letters written to America July 1940–June 1941. 1942. With H. M. Harwood.
The story of Burma. 1946.
Comments on Cain. 1948. On murder trials.
The alabaster cup. 1950.
The dragon in the heart: a love story. 1956.

For details of the plays written by F. T. Jesse in collaboration with H. M. Harwood, see H. M. Harwood, cols 951–2, below.

§2

Smith, P. J. Collecting in English pastures. In his For the love of books, 1934.

PAMELA HANSFORD JOHNSON
b. 1912

§1

Symphony for full orchestra. 1934 (Sunday Referee Poets, 1).
This bed thy centre. 1935, New York [1935], London 1961 (with preface by the author).
Blessed above women. 1936, New York [1936].
Here to-day. 1937.
World's end. 1937, New York [1938].
The monument. 1938, New York [1938].
Girdle of Venus. 1939.
Too dear for my possession. 1940, New York 1940. First vol of trilogy.
The family pattern. 1942.
Winter quarters. 1943, New York 1944.
The Trojan brothers. 1944, New York 1945.
An avenue of stone. 1947, New York 1948. 2nd vol of trilogy.
Thomas Wolfe: a critical study. 1947, New York 1948 (as Hungry Gulliver: an English critical appraisal of Thomas Wolfe), 1963 (as The art of Thomas Wolfe).
A summer to decide. 1948. 3rd vol of trilogy.
The Philistines. 1949.
Corinth House: a play in three acts. [1950], Boston 1950, London 1954 (with an essay on the future of prose-drama).
Family party. [1951]. Play, with C. P. Snow.
Her best foot forward. [1951]. Play, with C. P. Snow.
I. Compton-Burnett. 1951 (Br Council pamphlet).
The pigeon with the silver foot. [1951]. Play, with C. P. Snow.
Spare the rod. [1951]. Play, with C. P. Snow.
The supper dance. [1951]. Play, with C. P. Snow.
To murder Mrs Mortimer. [1951]. Play, with C. P. Snow.
Catherine Carter. 1952, New York 1952.
An impossible marriage. 1954, New York 1955.
The last resort. 1956, New York 1957 (as The sea and the wedding).

Six Proust reconstructions. 1958, Chicago 1958 (as Proust recaptured).
The humbler creation. 1959, New York 1960.
The unspeakable Skipton. 1959, New York 1959.
An error of judgement. 1962, New York [1962].
Night and silence—who is here?: an American comedy. 1963, New York 1963.
Cork Street, next to the hatter's: a novel in bad taste. 1965, New York 1965.
On iniquity: some personal reflections arising out of the Moors murder trial. 1967.
The survival of the fittest. 1968, New York 1968.

Pamela Hansford Johnson contributed an essay, The novel of Marcel Proust *to Proust's* Letters to his mother, *tr and ed G. D. Painter, 1956. She translated, with G. Black, J. Anouilh*, La répétition (*as* The rehearsal) *1961.*

§2

Raymond, J. A Corvo of our day. In his The doge of Dover, 1960.
Quigly, I. Pamela Hansford Johnson. 1968 (Br Council pamphlet).

DAVID MICHAEL JONES
b. 1895

See col 292, above.

SHEILA KAYE-SMITH
1887–1955

§1

The tramping Methodist. 1908, New York 1922.
Starbrace. 1909, New York 1926.
Spell land: the story of a Sussex farm. 1910, New York 1926.
Isle of thorns. 1913, New York 1924.
Three against the world. 1914, Philadelphia 1914 (as The three furlongers), New York 1929 (as Three against the world).
Willow's forge, and other poems. 1914.
John Galsworthy. 1916, New York 1916. Criticism.
Sussex gorse: the story of a fight. 1916, New York 1916.
The challenge to Sirius. 1917, New York 1918.
Little England. 1918, New York 1919 (as The four roads).
Tamarisk town. 1919, New York [1920].
Green apple harvest. 1920, New York [1921].
Joanna Godden. 1921, New York [1922].
The end of the house of Alard. 1923, New York [1923].
Saints in Sussex. Birmingham 1923, London 1926 (with two plays, The child born at the plough and The shepherd of Lattenden), New York 1927.
Anglo-Catholicism. 1925.
The George and the Crown. 1925, New York [1925].
The mirror of the months. 1925, New York 1931. Essays.
Joanna Godden married, and other stories. 1926, New York 1926.
Iron and smoke. 1928, New York [1928].
A wedding morn: a story. 1928.
Mrs Adis: a tragedy in one act, with The mock-beggar, a comedy in one act. [1929]. With J. Hampden.
Sin. 1929. Essays.
The village doctor. 1929, New York [1929].
Shepherds in sackcloth. 1930, New York 1930.
The history of Susan Spray, the female preacher. 1931, New York 1931 (as Susan Spray).
Songs late and early. 1931.
The children's summer. 1932, New York 1932 (as Summer holiday).
The ploughman's progress. 1933, New York 1933 (as Gipsy waggon).

Gallybird. 1934, New York 1934.
Superstition corner. 1934, New York 1934, Chicago 1955 (with preface by G. B. Stern).
Selina is older. 1935, New York 1935 (as Selina).
Rose Deeprose. 1936, New York 1936.
Three ways home. 1937, New York 1937. Autobiographical essays.
Dropping the hyphen: a story of a conversion. 1938.
Faithful stranger, and other stories. 1938, New York 1938.
The valiant woman. New York 1938, London 1939.
Ember lane: a winter's tale. 1940, New York [1940].
The hidden son. 1941, New York 1942 (as The secret son).
Talking of Jane Austen. 1943, New York 1944 (as Speaking of Jane Austen). With G. B. Stern.
Tambourine, trumpet and drum. 1943, New York 1943.
Kitchen fugue. 1945, New York 1945. Essays.
The Lardners and the Laurelwoods. New York 1947, London 1948.
The happy tree. New York 1949, London 1950 (as The treasures of the snow).
More about Jane Austen. New York 1949, London 1950 (as More talk of Jane Austen). With G. B. Stern.
Mrs Gailey. 1951, New York 1951.
Quartet in heaven. 1952, New York 1952. Biographical studies.
Weald of Kent and Sussex. 1953. Topography.
The view from the parsonage. 1954, New York 1954.
All the books of my life: a bibliobiography. 1956, New York 1956.

§2

Ellis, S. M. Novelist of Sussex: Miss Sheila Kaye-Smith. Worthing Observer 28 March 1914; rptd in his Mainly Victorian, 1925.
Johnson, R. B. In his Some contemporary novelists: women, 1920.
Mais, S. P. B. In his Why we should read, 1921. On Sussex gorse.
Adcock, A. St J. In his Gods of modern Grub Street, 1923.
Haydon, W. Sheila Kaye-Smith: a personal note. Bookman (London) 63 1923.
Quigley, J. Sheila Kaye-Smith. Fortnightly Rev 114 1923.
Roberts, R. E. Sheila Kaye-Smith. Bookman (London) 63 1923.
Allen, F. Sheila Kaye-Smith in and out of fiction. International Book Rev 2 1924.
Malone, A. E. Sheila Kaye-Smith: a novelist of the farm. Living Age 323 1924.
—— The novelist of Sussex: Sheila Kaye-Smith. Fortnightly Rev 120 1926.
Hopkins, R. T. Sheila Kaye-Smith and the Weald country. 1925.
Kernahan, C. Sheila Kaye-Smith as a poet. Nineteenth Century 97 1925; rptd in his Five more famous living poets, 1928.
Stern, G. B. The heroines of Sheila Kaye-Smith. Yale Rev 15 1925.
Villard, L. Sheila Kaye-Smith et les 'romans de Sussex'. Revue Anglo-américaine 3 1926.
Arns, K. Sheila Kaye-Smith. Zeitschrift für französischen und englischen Unterricht 26 1927.
Braybrooke, P. In his Some goddesses of the pen, 1928.
—— Sheila Kaye-Smith and her realism. In his Some Catholic novelists, 1931.
Knapp, I. In her Die Landschaft im modernen englischen Frauenroman, Brno 1935.

MARGARET MOORE KENNEDY
1896–1967

A century of revolution, 1789–1920. 1922.
The ladies of Lyndon. 1923, Garden City NY 1925.

The constant nymph. 1924, Garden City NY 1925. Dramatized (with B. Dean) as The constant nymph: a play in three acts (New 23 Sept 1926), 1926, New York 1926; French's Acting Edn 1930; French adaptation by J. Giraudoux, Paris 1934. Film versions: silent, 1928; talking 1934 (produced by Dean), 1943.

A long week-end. 1927, Garden City NY 1927 (110 copies). Story.

Red sky at morning. 1927, Garden City NY 1927.

Come with me: a play in three acts. (New 26 April 1928). 1928. With B. Dean.

Dewdrops. 1928. Story.

The game and the candle. 1928. Story.

The fool of the family: continuing the story of Sanger's circus from The constant nymph. 1930, Garden City NY 1930.

Return I dare not. 1931, Garden City NY 1931.

A long time ago. 1932, Garden City NY 1932.

Escape me never! a play in three acts. (Apollo 8 Dec 1933). 1934, Garden City NY 1935.

Together and apart. 1936, New York 1937.

The Midas touch. 1938, New York 1939.

Autumn. (St Martin's 15 Oct 1937). With G. Ratoff. In Five plays of our times, ed S. Box [1939]. Adapted from I. Surguchev; pbd separately [1940].

Where stands a wingèd sentry. New Haven 1941. Journal May–Sept 1940.

The mechanized muse. 1942. On the cinema.

Who will remember? Chicago 1946. Play.

The feast. 1950, New York 1950.

Jane Austen. 1950, Denver 1952, London 1957 (rev).

Lucy Carmichael. New York [1951], London 1951.

Troy chimneys. New York [1952], London 1953.

The oracles. 1955, New York 1955 (as Act of God).

The heroes of Clone. 1957, New York 1957 (as The wild swan).

The outlaws on Parnassus. 1958, New York 1960. Critical essays.

A night in Cold Harbour. 1960, New York 1960.

The forgotten smile. 1961, New York 1962.

Not in the calendar: the story of a friendship. 1964, New York 1964.

Women at work. 1966. Stories: The little green man; Three-timer.

Margaret Kennedy also wrote an unpbd play, Happy with either *(St James's 22 April 1948).*

'HUGH KINGSMILL',
HUGH KINGSMILL LUNN
1889–1949

See cols 1065–6, below.

CLIFFORD HENRY BENN KITCHIN
1895–1967

Curtains. Oxford 1919. Verse.

Winged victory. Oxford [1921]. Verse.

Streamers waving. 1925.

Mr Balcony. 1927.

Death of my aunt. 1929, New York 1930.

The sensitive one. 1931.

Crime at Christmas. 1934, New York 1935.

Olive E. 1937.

Birthday party. 1938.

Death of his uncle. 1939.

The auction sale. 1949, New York 1949.

The Cornish fox. 1949.

Jumping Joan, and other stories. 1954.

The secret river. 1956.

Ten Pollitt Place. 1957.

The book of life. 1960, New York 1961.

ARTHUR KOESTLER
b. 1905

Collections

Danube edition. 1965–. Contains additional prefaces, or postscripts, to the individual works, with occasional textual revision.

§1

Menschenopfer unerhört: Schwarzbuch über Spanien. Paris 1937.

Spanish testament. 1937. Pt 1, an adaptation of Menschenopfer unerhört; pt 2, entitled Dialogue with death. Tr T. and P. Blewitt. German original, Ein spanisches Testament, pbd Zürich 1938. Autobiographical.

The gladiators. Tr E. Simm 1939, New York 1939.

Darkness at noon. Tr D. Hardy 1940, New York 1941, 1961 (with foreword by P. Viereck).

Scum of the earth. 1941, New York 1941, London 1955 (corrected, with preface by Koestler). Autobiographical.

Dialogue with death [pt 2 of Spanish testament, 1937]. 1942, New York 1942, London [1954] (corrected against the original German version, Zürich 1938, with preface by Koestler).

Arrival and departure. 1943, New York 1943.

Twilight bar: an escapade in four acts. 1945, New York 1945. Play.

The yogi and the commissar, and other essays. 1945, New York 1945.

Thieves in the night: chronicle of an experiment. 1946, New York 1946.

What the modern world is doing to the soul of man. In The challenge of our time: a series of essays by Koestler [et al], 1948.

Insight and outlook: an inquiry into the common foundations of science, art and social ethics. 1949, New York 1949.

Promise and fulfilment: Palestine 1917–49. 1949, New York 1949.

The god that failed: six studies in communism by Koestler [et al]. Ed R. H. S. Crossman 1950, New York 1950.

The age of longing. 1951, New York 1951.

Arrow in the blue: an autobiography. 1952, New York 1952.

The invisible writing: being the second volume of Arrow in the blue. 1954, New York 1954.

The trail of the dinosaur, and other essays. 1955, New York 1955.

Reflections on hanging. 1956, New York 1957.

The sleepwalkers: a history of man's changing vision of the universe. 1959, New York 1959. Pt 4, The watershed [a biography of Johannes Kepler] pbd separately Garden City NY 1960, London 1961.

The lotus and the robot. 1960, New York 1961.

Hanged by the neck: an exposure of capital punishment in England. 1961, Baltimore 1961. With 'C. H. Rolph' (C. R. Hewitt).

Suicide of a nation? An enquiry into the state of Britain today. Ed with introd by Koestler 1963, New York 1964.

The act of creation. 1964, New York 1964. Non-fiction.

The ghost in the machine. 1967, New York 1968. Non-fiction.

Drinkers of infinity: essays 1955–67. 1968, New York 1969.

From 1934 to 1939, under the pseudonym 'Dr A. Costler', Koestler collaborated in the writing of some French works of popular sexology. See 'Introducing Dr Costler' *in* The invisible writing, *1954, above.*

§2

Davis, R. G. Sharp horns of Koestler's dilemmas: difficulty of reconciling ends and means. Antioch Rev 4 1944.

Rahv, P. Testament of a homeless radical. Partisan Rev 12 1945; rptd (rev and enlarged) as Koestler and homeless radicalism, in his Image and idea, New York 1949.

Smith, R. D. Detours and oases: a note on Koestler. Orion 2 1945.

Mortimer, R. Arthur Koestler. Cornhill Mag 192 1946.

'Orwell, George' (E. A. Blair). Arthur Koestler. In his Critical essays, 1946.

Stanford, D. Arthur Koestler. In Writers of today, ed D. V. Baker 1946.

Braatøy, T. Koestler og psykoanalysen. Oslo 1947.

Glicksberg, C. I. Koestler and Communism. Queen's Quart 53 1947.

Pritchett, V. S. Arthur Koestler. Horizon 15 1947. Rptd (as The art of Arthur Koestler) in his Books in general, 1953.

— Koestler: a guilty figure. Harper's Mag 196 1948.

Rivett, K. In defence of Koestler. Australian Quart 19 1947.

Waugh, E. The Jesuit who was Thursday: villains, by Mrs Trollope, Chesterton and Koestler. Commonweal 45 1947.

Bantock, G. H. Arthur Koestler. Politics & Letters 1 1948.

Garaudy, R. Arthur Koestler. In his Une littérature de fossoyeurs, Paris 1948. Tr (as Literature of the grave-yard: Sartre, Mauriac, Malraux, Koestler) New York 1948.

Nedava, J. Arthur Koestler. 1948.

Birkenfeld, G. Die Deutschen und Koestler. Der Monat (Munich) 1 1949.

Edman, I. Koestler als Philosoph. Ibid.

Haerdter, R. Der Mensch ohne Mythos und Illusionen. Die Gegenwart (Freiburg) 4 1949.

Klingopulos, G. D. Arthur Koestler. Scrutiny 16 1949.

Lasky, M. J. Arthur Koestler. Colloquium 3 1949.

Lerner, M. Koestler on terrorism. In his Actions and passions, New York 1949. On Thieves in the night.

Reitz, H. Arthur Koestler. Welt und Wort 149 1949.

Downing, F. Koestler revisited. Commonweal 53 1951.

— Koestler's Dialogue with death. Commonweal 54 1951.

Fischer, M. Koestler's longing and despair. Commonweal 53 1951.

Redman, B. R. Koestler: radical's progress. College Eng 13 1951.

Ashe, G. Koestler and the infinite. Commonweal 56 1952.

Prescott, O. The political novel: Warren, Orwell, Koestler. In his In my opinion, Indianapolis 1952.

Hayman, R. The hero as revolutionary: an assessment of Koestler's novels. London Mag 2 1955.

Atkins, J. Arthur Koestler. 1956.

Howe, I. Malraux, Silone, Koestler. In his Politics and the novel, New York 1957.

Geering, R. G. Darkness at noon and Nineteen eighty four: a comparative study. Australian Quart 30 1958.

Kahn, L. Koestler and the Jews. Chicago Jewish Forum 18 1960.

Strachey, J. The strangled cry. Encounter 15 1960; rptd in his The strangled cry, 1962. On Darkness at noon.

Beum, R. Epigraphs for Rubashov: Koestler's Darkness at noon. Dalhousie Rev 42 1962.

Huber, P. Koestlers Werk in literarischer Sicht. Zürich 1962.

Kadt, J. de. Arthur in Wonderland: Koestler's Act of creation. Tirade (Antwerp) 8 1964.

Toulmin, S. Koestler's Act of creation. Encounter 23 1964.

Calder, J. Chronicles of conscience: a study of Orwell and Koestler. 1968.

Dahm, E. Den unge Koestler. Horisont 15 1968.

Nott, K. Koestler and his critics. Encounter 30 1968.

Steele, P. Darkness at noon. Critical Rev 12 1969.

ROSAMOND NINA LEHMANN
b. 1903

Bibliographies

Gustafson, M. T. Rosamond Lehmann: a bibliography. Twentieth Century Lit 4 1959. Includes trns of works, contributions to periodicals and some secondary material.

§1

Dusty answer. 1927, New York 1927.
A note in music. 1930, New York [1930].
A letter to a sister. 1931, New York [1932] (Hogarth Letters 3).
Invitation to the waltz. 1932, New York [1932].
The weather in the streets. 1936, New York [1936].
No more music: a play in three acts. [1939], New York 1939.
The ballad and the source. 1944, New York 1945.
The gipsy's baby, and other stories. 1946, New York 1946.
The echoing grove. 1953, New York 1953.
The swan in the evening: fragments of an inner life. 1967, New York 1968.
Rosamond Lehmann was one of the editors of the first 3 vols of Orion: a miscellany, 1945–6. She also edited, with extensive commentary, A man seen afar, by W. T. Pole, 1965.

§2

Dangerfield, G. Rosamond Lehmann and the perilous enchantment of things past. Bookman (New York) 76 1933.

Warner, O. Rosamond Lehmann. Bookman (London) 87 1934.

Bowen, E. Island life. New Statesman 5 March 1938. Review article on No more music, rptd in her Collected impressions, 1950.

— The modern novel and the theme of love. New Republic 11 May 1953. Review article on The echoing grove, rptd in her Afterthought, 1962.

Shuman, R. B. Personal isolation in the novels of Rosamond Lehmann. Revue des Langues Vivantes 26 1960.

Lestourgeion, D. E. Rosamond Lehmann. New York 1965.

ADA LEVERSON
1862–1933

Collections

The little Ottleys, with a foreword by C. MacInnes. 1962, New York 1962. Contains Love's shadow, Tenterhooks, Love at second sight.

§1

The twelfth hour. 1907.
Love's shadow. 1908.
The limit. 1911, New York 1951.
Tenterhooks. [1912].
Bird of paradise. 1914, New York 1952.
Love at second sight. 1916.
Letters to the Sphinx from Oscar Wilde, with reminiscences of the author by A. Leverson. 1930.

§2

Brown, J. M. Edwardian Sphinx. In his As they appear, New York 1952.

Wyndham, V. The Sphinx and her circle: a biographical sketch of Ada Leverson 1862–1933. 1963.

Pritchett, V. S. The Knightsbridge kennels. In his The living novel, New York 1964, London 1965 (as The working novelist).

ALUN LEWIS
1915–44

See col 298, above.

CECIL DAY-LEWIS
1904–72

See cols 253–6, above.

CLIVE STAPLES LEWIS
1898–1963

See cols 1073–8, below.

PERCY WYNDHAM LEWIS
1882–1957

The Carlow collection of Lewisiana is at the State Univ of New York, Buffalo. For details of the Lewis collection at Cornell Univ, see W. K. Rose, Wyndham Lewis at Cornell: a review of the Lewis papers presented to the university by W. G. Mennen, Ithaca 1961.

Bibliographies

'Gawsworth, John' (T. I. F. Armstrong). In his Apes, japes and Hitlerism, 1932, below.

Todd, R. A check-list of books and articles by Lewis. Twentieth-century Verse 9 1938.

Kenner, H. In his Wyndham Lewis, 1954, below.

Wagner, G. In his Wyndham Lewis, 1957, below. Includes the numerous contributions to periodicals, and a section of secondary material.

Selections

Wyndham Lewis the artist: from Blast to Burlington House, 1939. Contains his writings on art from Blast and The tyro; The Caliph's design; and a retrospective survey by Lewis of his career as a painter.

A soldier of humour and selected writings. Ed R. Rosenthal, New York 1966.

Wyndham Lewis: an anthology of his prose. Ed E. W. F. Tomlin 1969.

§I

Blast: review of the great English vortex. No 1, 1914: no 2, 1915. Ed and largely written by Lewis; no 1 contains the first version of The enemy of the stars, pbd separately (rev) in 1932.

The ideal giant; The code of a herdsman; Cantelman's springmate. [1917] (priv ptd for Little Rev, 50 copies). Play; criticism; story.

Tarr. New York 1918, London 1918, 1928 (rev). Expanded from version serialized in Egoist, April 1916 to Nov 1917.

Harold Gilman: an appreciation. 1919. With L. F. Fergusson. Art criticism.

The Caliph's design: architects! where is your vortex? 1919; rptd (rev) in Wyndham Lewis the artist, 1939. *See* Selections, above.

The tyro: a review of the arts of painting, sculpture and design. no 1, 1921; no 2, 1922. Ed Lewis, with contributions by him.

The art of being ruled. 1926, New York 1926.

The enemy: a review of art and literature. Nos 1 and 2, 1927; no 3, 1929. Ed and largely written by Lewis.

The lion and the fox: the rôle of hero in the plays of Shakespeare. 1927, New York 1927.

Time and western man. 1927, New York [1928] (with new preface). Bk 1 first pbd in Enemy no 1.

The wild body: a soldier of humour and other stories. 1927, New York [1928]. Some stories first pbd in Little Rev.

The Childermass: section 1. 1928, New York 1928, London 1956 (rev) (as bk 1 of The human age, 1955 below).

Paleface: the philosophy of the 'melting pot'. 1929. Part first pbd in Enemy, no 2.

The apes of God. 1930, New York 1932, London 1955 (with introd by Lewis). Part first pbd in Criterion 2 1924.

Satire & fiction: preceded by The history of a rejected review (Have with you to Great Queen Street!), by R. Campbell. 1930. (Enemy pamphlets 1). In defence of The apes of God.

Hitler. 1931. Articles, rptd from Time & Tide 17 Jan to 14 Feb 1931.

The diabolical principle and The dithyrambic spectator. 1931. Rptd from Calendar of Modern Letters 1 1925 and Enemy no 3.

Doom of youth. New York 1932, London 1932 (withdrawn). Articles rptd from Time & Tide 13 June–25 July 1931.

Filibusters in Barbary: record of a visit to the Sous. 1932, New York 1932. Rptd from Everyman Oct 29 1931–7 Jan 1932.

Enemy of the stars. 1932. Play, heavily rev from the original text pbd in Blast no 1, with appended essay The physics of the not-self, rptd (rev) from Chapbook no 40, 1925.

Snooty baronet. 1932.

The old gang and the new gang. 1933. Pamphlet to replace the withdrawn English edn of Doom of youth.

Engine-fight talk; The song of the militant romance; If so the man you are; One-way song: Envoi. (Cover and half-title: One-way song). 1933, 1960 (as One-way song, with foreword by T. S. Eliot). Poems.

Men without art. 1934, New York 1964. Essays.

Left wings over Europe: or how to make a war about nothing. 1936.

The roaring queen. 1936 (withdrawn before pbn).

Count your dead: they are alive! or, a new war in the making. 1937. Political commentary in fictional form.

The revenge for love. 1937, Chicago 1952.

Blasting and bombardiering. 1937, 1967 (preface by A. Wyndham Lewis with additional chs). Autobiography 1914–26. Reprints parts of Blast, with minor revision.

The Mysterious Mr Bull. 1938. Social criticism.

The Jews: are they human? 1939.

The Hitler cult, and how it will end. 1939.

America, I presume. New York [1940].

The vulgar streak. 1941.

Anglosaxony: a league that works. Toronto [1941]. Pamphlet.

America and cosmic man. 1948, Garden City NY 1949.

Rude assignment: a narrative of my career up-to-date. [1950].

Rotting Hill. 1951, Chicago 1952. Stories.

The writer and the absolute. 1952.

Self condemned. 1954, Chicago 1955. Semi-autobiographical.

The demon of progress in the arts. 1954, Chicago 1955.

The human age: bk 2, Monstre gai; bk 3, Malign fiesta. 2 vols 1955. Bk 1, The Childermass, 1956 (rev from version pbd 1928). The Childermass, adapted by D. G. Bridson, broadcast BBC Third Programme 18 June 1951; Monstre gai and Malign fiesta, adapted by Bridson and Lewis, broadcast 24, 26, 28 May 1955. *See* Bridson in Agenda 7–8 1969–70 (§2, below).

The red priest. 1956.

Letters

The letters of Wyndham Lewis. Ed W. K. Rose 1963, Norfolk Conn 1964.

The Wyndham Lewis special issue of Agenda 7–8 1969–70, below, prints excerpts from Hoodopip and Joint, sections of the uncompleted Man of the world (see prefatory notes by H. Kenner). Lewis also pbd drawings and wrote introds to various art exhibition catalogues. For details of these see Wagner's bibliography, above.

§2

Aldington, R. Blast. Egoist 1 1914.

Pound, E. Wyndham Lewis. Egoist 1 1914.

— Art notes, by 'B. H. Dias' [i.e. E. Pound]: Lewis at the Goupil. New Age 20 Feb 1919; rptd (as The war paintings of Lewis) in Agenda 7–8 1969–70 (Lewis special issue), below.

— In his Instigations, 1920; rptd in his Literary essays, 1954.

— Augment of the novel. New Directions 6 1941; rptd in Agenda 7–8 1969–70, below.

Eliot, T. S. Tarr. Egoist 5 1918.

— A note on Monstre gai. Hudson Rev 7 1955.

— Wyndham Lewis. Hudson Rev 10 1957.

'West, Rebecca' (C. I. Andrews). Tarr. Nation 10 Aug 1918; rptd in Agenda 7–8 1969–70, below.

Golding, D. The author of Tarr. In his Reputations, 1920.

'Five'. Wyndham Lewis's 'Enemy'. Experiment (Cambridge) no 3 1929.

Porteus, H. G. Wyndham Lewis. Twentieth Century 2 1931.

— Wyndham Lewis: a discursive exposition. 1932.

Rickword, E. In Scrutinies vol 2, ed E. Rickword 1931.

'Gawsworth, John' (T. I. F. Armstrong). Apes, japes and Hitlerism: a study and bibliography of Lewis. 1932.

Linati, C. In his Scrittori anglo-americani d'oggi, Milan 1932.

Stone, G. The ideas of Lewis. American Rev 1, 2 1933.

Stonier, G. W. In his Gog Magog and other critical essays, 1933.

Leavis, F. R. Mr Eliot, Lewis and Lawrence. Scrutiny 3 1934; rptd in his Common pursuit, 1952.

Lewis, W. Mr Wyndham Lewis. In his own Men without art, 1934.

Sitwell, E. Pastors and masters. In her Aspects of modern poetry, 1934. On One-way song.

Spender, S. The great without. In his Destructive element, 1935. Lewis as satirist.

Frye, H. N. Lewis: anti-Spenglerian. Canadian Forum 16 1936.

— Neo-classical agony. Hudson Rev 10 1958.

Twentieth-Century Verse. Wyndham Lewis double no, 6–7 1937. Contains G. Armitage, A note on The wild body; J. Beevers, I read Lewis; T. W. Earp, The Leicester Galleries exhibition; T. S. Eliot, The lion and the fox; G. Jones, Satiric eye; C. Lambert, An objective self-portrait; H. B. Mallalieu, Social force; H. G. Porteus, Eyes front (ideogram); K. Rhys, Celtic view; D. S. Savage, Lewis and Lawrence; G. W. Stonier, That taxi-driver; J. Symons, Notes on One-way song; R. Todd, Comments on a critic; E. W. F. Tomlin, The philosopher-politician; R. Warner, Extract from a letter.

Duncan, R. Blast and about and about. Townsman 1 1938.

Hennecke, H. Lewis: Vision und Satire. Europäische Revue 14 1938.

Rothenstein, J. Great British masters: 26, Wyndham Lewis. Picture Post 25 March 1939.

— Modern English painters: Lewis to Moore. 1956.

Fjelde, R. Time, space and Lewis. Western Rev 15 1951.

Grigson, G. A master of our time: a study of Lewis. 1951.

Handley-Read, C. (ed). The art of Wyndham Lewis. 1951. Lewis' pictorial art.

Pritchett, V. S. The eye-man. New Statesman 21 Jul 1951; rptd in his Books in general, 1953.

Shenandoah 4 1953. Wyndham Lewis no. Contains: R. Campbell, A note on W.L.; H. M. McLuhan, Lewis: his theory of art and communication; M. Mudrick, The double-artist and the injured party; P. Russell, Lewis today.

Kenner, H. Wyndham Lewis. Norfolk Conn 1954 (Makers of Modern Literature).

— The last European. Canadian Lit no 36 1968.

Ayrton, M. Tarr and flying feathers. Shenandoah 7 1955.

Kirk, R. Lewis's first principles. Yale Rev 44 1955; rptd in his Beyond the dreams of avarice, Chicago 1956.

Tomlin, E. W. F. Wyndham Lewis. 1955 (Br Council pamphlet).

Carter, T. H. The human age. Kenyon Rev 18 1956.

— 'An universal prey': a footnote to The lion and the fox. Shenandoah 9 1958.

Mayoux, J-J. Lewis: ou J'ai du génie. Études Anglaises 9 1956.

Roberts, W. The resurrection of vorticism and the apotheosis of Lewis at the Tate. 1956.

Wagner, G. Lewis's inhuman tetralogy: an introduction to The human age. Modern Fiction Stud 2 1956.

— Lewis and Joyce: a study in controversy. South Atlantic Quart 56 1957.

— Wyndham Lewis: a portrait of the artist as the enemy. New Haven 1957.

Fraser, G. S. Lewis: an energy of mind. Twentieth Century 161 1957.

Holloway, J. Lewis: the massacre and the innocents. Hudson Rev 10 1957; rptd in his Charted mirror, 1960.

Stanford, D. Lewis: a valedictory. Month 17 1957.

— Wyndham Lewis. Contemporary Rev no 1096 1957.

Symons, J. Meeting Lewis. London Mag 4 1957.

Allen, W. Lonely old volcano: the achievement of Lewis. Encounter 21 1963.

Coffey, W. Lewis: enemy of the rose. Ramparts 2 1963.

Rose, W. K. Lewis in his letters. Ramparts 2 1963.

— Ezra Pound and Lewis: the crucial years. Southern Quart 4 1968; rptd in Agenda 7–8 1969–70 (Lewis special issue), below.

Wiebe, D. E. Lewis and the picaresque novel. South Atlantic Quart 62 1963.

Greene, G. The wars of Lewis. Commonweal 8 May 1964.

Harrison, J. R. In his Reactionaries, 1966.

Lafourcade, B. Lewis au Purgatoire. Études Anglaises 19 1966.

Canadian Literature no 35 1968. Contains: Anon. Lewis in Canada; C. J. Fox, The wild land; J. S. Murphy, Lewis at Windsor; L. Pierce, A recollection of Lewis; W. K. Rose, Exile's letter; S. Watson, Canada and Lewis the artist.

Pritchard, W. H. Wyndham Lewis. New York 1968 (Twayne's English Authors).

Agenda 7–8 1969–70 Wyndham Lewis special issue. Contains: M. Seymour-Smith, Lewis as an imaginative writer; I. A. Richards, A talk on The Childermass; P. Palmer, The human age; P. Dale, Self condemned; J. Symons, The thirties novels; E. Pound, Augment of the novel; T. Materer, The apes of God; 'Rebecca West', Tarr; P. Dale, The revenge for love; W. Michel, Lewis the painter; E. Pound, The war paintings; E. Gray, Lewis and the modern crisis of painting; H. G. Porteus, Anthologies of Lewis; E. W. F. Tomlin, Time and western man; C. H. Sisson, The politics of Lewis; W. K. Rose, Pound and Lewis; K. Cox, Dualism and 'les autres'; W. Pritchard, Lawrence and Lewis; A. Bold, One-way song; A. Sala, Vorticism and Futurism; D. G. Bridson, The making of the human age; H. G. Porteus, A man apart; H. Kenner, Excerpts from The man of the world, Note on Joint (*see* footnote to §1, above).

DAVID LINDSAY
1876–1945

§1

A voyage to Arcturus. 1920, 1946 (with note by E. H. Visiak).

The haunted woman. 1922.

Sphinx. 1923.
Adventures of Monsieur de Mailly. 1926, New York 1927
(as A blade for sale).
Devil's tor. 1932.

§2

Pick, J. B. The work of Lindsay. Studies in Scottish Lit 1
1964.
— C. Wilson and E. H. Visiak. The strange genius of
Lindsay: an appreciation. 1970.

JACK LINDSAY
b. 1900

Fauns and ladies. Kirribilli, New South Wales 1923.
Verse.
Helen comes of age: three plays. 1927. Verse.
Marino Faliero: a tragedy. 1927. Verse.
William Blake: creative will and the poetic image. 1927,
1929 (rev).
Dionysos—Nietzsche contra Nietzsche: an essay in lyrical
philosophy. [1928].
Hereward: a play. [1930].
The passionate neatherd: a lyric sequence. [1930]. Some
poems of which proofs are extant were previously ptd in
Sydney, but not pbd.
Cressida's first lover: a tale of ancient Greece. 1931, New
York 1932.
Caesar is dead. 1934.
Rome for sale. 1934, New York 1934.
Despoiling Venus. 1935.
Last days with Cleopatra. 1935.
The Romans. 1935.
Runaway. 1935. For children.
Storm at sea. 1935.
Adam of a new world. 1936.
Come home at last. 1936.
Marc Antony: his world and his contemporaries. 1936.
Rebels of the goldfields. 1936.
Shadow and flame. 1936. As by 'Richard Preston'.
The wanderings of Wenamen, 1115–1114 B.C. 1936.
The anatomy of spirit: an inquiry into the origins of
religious emotions. 1937.
End of Cornwall. 1937. By 'Richard Preston'.
John Bunyan: maker of myths. 1937.
Sue Verney. 1937.
1649: a novel of a year. 1938.
To arms! A story of ancient Gaul. 1938.
Brief light: a novel of Catullus. 1939.
England, my England...[1939]. Political.
Lost birthright. 1939.
A short history of culture. 1939.
Hannibal takes a hand. 1941.
Light in Italy. 1941.
The stormy violence. 1941.
Into action: the battle of Dieppe. 1942. Verse.
We shall return: a novel of Dunkirk and the French cam-
paign. 1942.
Beyond terror: a novel of the battle of Crete. 1943.
Perspective for poetry. 1944.
Second front: poems. 1944.
The barriers are down: a tale of the collapse of a civilisa-
tion. 1945.
British achievement in art and music. [1945].
Hullo stranger. 1945.
Time to live. 1946.
The subtle knot. 1947.
Men of forty-eight. 1948.
Mulk Raj Anand: a critical essay. Bombay 1948.
Song of a falling world: culture during the break-up of the
Roman empire A.D. 350–600. 1948.
Clue of darkness. 1949.
Marxism and contemporary science: the fullness of life.
1949.

Charles Dickens: a biographical and critical study. 1950,
New York 1950.
Fires in Smithfield: a novel of Mary Tudor's days. 1950.
Peace is our answer. 1950. Verse.
Three letters to Nicolai Tikhonov. 1950. Verse.
A world ahead: journal of a Soviet journey. [1950].
The passionate pastoral. 1951.
Byzantium into Europe. 1952. History.
Betrayed spring. 1953.
Rising tide. 1953.
Rumanian summer: a view of the Rumanian People's
Republic. 1953. With M. Cornforth.
Civil war in England. 1954. History.
The moment of choice: a novel of the British way. 1955.
After the 'thirties: the novel in Britain and its future. 1956.
George Meredith: his life and work. 1956.
The Romans were here: the Roman period in Britain and
its place in our history. 1956.
The great oak: a story of 1549. 1957.
A local habitation. 1957.
Three elegies. Sudbury Suffolk 1957. Verse.
Arthur and his times: Britain in the dark ages. 1958.
The discovery of Britain. [1958]. Archaeology.
Life rarely tells. 1958. Autobiography to 1921.
1764: the hurlyburly of daily life exemplified in one year
of the eighteenth century. 1959.
The revolt of the sons. 1960.
The roaring twenties. 1960. Autobiography 1921–6.
The writing on the wall. 1960. On Pompeii.
All on the never-never. 1961.
Death of the hero: French painting from David to Dela-
croix. [1961].
Fanfrolico and after. 1962. Autobiography.
Our Celtic heritage. [1962].
A short history of culture from prehistory to the Renas-
cence. 1962, New York 1963. A different work from
A short history of culture, 1939, above.
The way the ball bounces. 1962.
Daily life in Roman Egypt. 1963.
Masks and faces. 1963.
Choice of times. 1964.
Nine days' hero: Wat Tyler. 1964.
Leisure and pleasure in Roman Egypt. 1965.
Our Anglo-Saxon heritage. [1965].
Thunder underground: a story of Nero's Rome. 1965.
The clashing rocks: a study of early Greek religion and
culture. 1966.
J. M. W. Turner: his life and work. [1966].
Our Roman heritage. [1967].
The ancient world: manners and morals. 1968.
Meetings with poets: memories of Dylan Thomas, Edith
Sitwell, Louis Aragon, Paul Eluard, Tristan Tzara.
1968. Reminiscences.
Men and gods on the Roman Nile. 1968.
Cézanne: his life and art. Greenwich Conn 1969.

ERIC ROBERT RUSSELL
LINKLATER
b. 1899

Collections

The Orkney edition. 1950–.
The stories of Eric Linklater. 1968, New York 1969.

§1

Poobie. Edinburgh 1925 (Porpoise Press broadsheets).
Verse.
Poet's pub. 1929, New York [1930].
White-maa's saga. 1929.
A dragon laughed, and other poems. 1930.
Ben Jonson and King James: biography and portrait. 1931.
Juan in America. 1931, New York [1931].

The men of Ness: a saga of Thorlief Coalbiter's sons. 1932, New York [1933].

The crusader's key. [1933], New York 1933. Story, rptd in God likes them plain, below.

Mary Queen of Scots. 1933, New York 1933.

The devil's in the news: a comedy to be played with occasional music. 1934.

Magnus Merriman. 1934, New York [1934].

The revolution. 1934. Three stories, rptd in God likes them plain, below.

Robert the Bruce. 1934, New York 1934.

God likes them plain: short stories. 1935.

The lion and the unicorn: or, what England has meant to Scotland. 1935.

Ripeness is all. 1935, New York [1935].

Juan in China. 1937, New York [1937].

The sailor's holiday. 1937, New York [1938].

The impregnable women. 1938, New York [1938].

Judas. 1939, New York [1939].

The cornerstones: a conversation in Elysium. 1941 (War Pamphlet ser).

The defence of Calais. 1941 (Army at War ser).

The man on my back: an autobiography. 1941.

The northern garrisons. 1941, Garden City NY 1941 (Army at War ser).

The Highland Division. 1942 (Army at War ser).

The raft, and Socrates asks why: two conversations. 1942.

Crisis in heaven: an Elysian comedy. 1944. Play.

The great ship, and Rabelais replies: two conversations. 1944.

The wind on the moon: a story for children. 1944, New York 1944.

Private Angelo. 1946, New York 1946.

The art of adventure. 1947. Essays.

Sealskin trousers, and other stories. 1947.

The pirates in the deep green sea: a story for children. 1949.

A spell for old bones. 1949, New York 1950.

Love in Albania: a comedy in three acts. [1950].

Mr Byculla. 1950, New York 1951.

The thistle and the pen: an anthology of modern Scottish writers chosen and introduced by E. Linklater. 1950.

Two comedies: Love in Albania, and To meet the Mac-Gregors 1950.

The campaign in Italy. 1951. Second World War 1939–45.

Laxdale Hall. 1951, New York 1952.

The Mortimer touch: a farcical comedy. [1952].

Our men in Korea. 1952. Non-fiction.

The house of Gair. 1953, New York 1954.

A year of space: a chapter in autobiography. 1953, New York 1953.

The faithful ally. 1954, New York [1954] (as The sultan and the lady).

The ultimate Viking. 1955, New York 1956. Sweyn Asleifsson and the Icelandic sagas.

The dark of summer. 1956, New York 1957.

A sociable plover, and other stories and conceits. 1957.

Breakspear in Gascony. 1958. Play.

Karina with love. 1958. For children.

Position at noon. 1958, New York 1959 (as My fathers and I).

The merry muse. 1959, New York 1960.

Edinburgh. 1960, New York 1961.

Roll of honour. 1961.

Husband of Delilah. 1962, New York 1963.

A man over forty. 1963.

The murder of Darnley. In Fatal fascination: a choice of crime, by N. Balchin, Linklater [et al], 1964, Boston 1965.

Orkney and Shetland: an historical, geographical, social and scenic survey. 1965.

The prince in the heather. [1965], New York 1966. The escape of the Young Pretender after Culloden.

The conquest of England. 1966, Garden City NY 1966. Non-fiction.

A terrible freedom. 1966.

The survival of Scotland 1968, New York 1968.

'RICHARD LLEWELLYN', RICHARD DAFYDD VIVIAN LLEWELLYN LLOYD
b. 1907?

Poison pen: a play in three acts. [1938].

How green was my valley. 1939, New York 1940.

None but the lonely heart. 1943, New York 1943, 1969 (with new chapters completing the work).

A few flowers for Shiner. 1950, New York 1950.

A flame for doubting Thomas. New York 1953, London 1954.

The witch of Merthyn. Garden City NY 1954, London 1955 (as Sweet witch).

The flame of Hercules. Garden City NY 1955, London 1957.

Mr Hamish Gleave. 1956, Garden City NY 1956.

Warden of the smoke and bells. Garden City NY 1956, London 1958.

Chez Pavan. Garden City NY 1958, London 1959.

Up, into the singing mountain. Garden City NY 1960, London 1963. Sequel to How green was my valley.

A man in a mirror. Garden City NY 1961, London 1964.

Sweet morn of Judas' Day. Garden City 1964, London 1965.

And I shall sleep...down where the moon is small. Garden City NY 1966, London 1966 (as Down where the moon is small). Sequel to Up, into the singing mountain.

The end of the rug. Garden City NY 1968, London 1969.

But we didn't get the fox. Garden City NY 1969.

WILLIAM JOHN LOCKE
1863–1930

§I

At the gate of Samaria. New York 1894, London 1895.

The demagogue and Lady Phayre. New York [1895], London 1896.

A study in shadows. 1896, New York 1896 (as Some women and a man).

Derelicts. 1897, New York 1897.

Idols. 1898, New York 1899.

The white dove. 1900, New York 1900.

The usurper. 1902, New York 1902.

Where love is. 1903, New York 1903.

The morals of Marcus Ordeyne. 1905, New York 1905.

The beloved vagabond. New York 1906, London 1907.

Flower o' the rose: a romantic play. 1909 (50 copies).

Septimus. 1909, New York 1909.

A Christmas mystery: the study of three wise men. New York 1910, London 1922. Story.

Simon the jester. 1910, New York 1910.

The glory of Clementina Wing. 1911, New York 1911 (as The glory of Clementina).

The joyous adventures of Aristide Pujol. 1912, New York 1912.

Stella maris. 1913, New York 1913.

The fortunate youth. 1914, New York 1914.

Jaffery. 1915, New York 1915.

Morals for the young. 1915, New York 1915. As by 'Marcus'. Humorous verse.

Far-away stories. 1916, New York 1916.

Viviette. New York 1916.

The wonderful year. 1916, New York 1916.

The red planet. 1917, New York 1917.

The rough road. 1918, New York 1918.
The house of Baltazar. 1920, New York 1920.
The apostle. 1921, New York 1921.
The mountebank. 1921, New York 1921.
The tale of Triona. 1922, New York 1922.
Moordius & Co. 1923, New York 1923 (as The lengthened shadow).
The coming of Amos. 1924, New York 1924.
The golden journey of Mr Paradyne. 1924, New York 1924. Story.
The great Pandolfo. 1925, New York 1925.
The old bridge. 1926, New York 1926 (as Perella).
Stories near and far. 1926, New York 1927.
The kingdom of Theophilus. 1927, New York 1927.
Joshua's vision. 1928, New York 1928.
Ancestor Jorico. 1929, New York 1929.
The town of Tombarel. 1930, New York 1930.
The shorn lamb. New York 1930, London 1931.

Locke also wrote a number of unpbd plays, some of which were based on his novels.

§2

Cooper, F. T. In his Some English story-tellers: a book of the younger novelists, New York 1912.
Hind, C. L. In his Authors and I, 1921.
Adcock, A. St J. In his Gods of modern Grub Street, 1923.
'Lacon' (E. H. L. Watson). In his Lectures to living authors, 1925.
Hamilton, C. In his People worth talking about, 1933.

MARIE ADELAIDE BELLOC LOWNDES, née BELLOC
1868–1947

Collections

Novels of mystery: The lodger; The story of Ivy; What really happened. New York 1933.
Murder omnibus: Another man's wife; The Chianti flask; Who rides on a tiger. New York 1936.

§1

H.R.H. The Prince of Wales: an account of his career. 1898 [anon], New York 1898, London 1901 (rev) (as His Most Gracious Majesty King Edward VII, by Mrs Belloc Lowndes).
The philosophy of the Marquise. 1899. Sketches and dialogues.
T.R.H. The Prince and Princess of Wales. 1902. Anon.
The heart of Penelope. 1904, New York 1915.
Barbara Rebell. 1905, New York 1907.
The pulse of life: a story of a passing world. 1908, New York 1909.
The uttermost farthing. 1908, New York [1910].
Studies in wives. 1909, New York [1910]. Stories.
When no man pursueth: an everyday story. 1910, New York 1911.
Jane Aglander. 1911, New York 1911.
The chink in the armour. 1912, New York 1912, London 1935 (as The house of peril).
Mary Pechell. 1912, New York 1912.
The lodger. 1913, New York 1913.
The end of her honeymoon. New York 1913, London 1914.
Studies in love and terror. 1913, New York 1913. Stories.
Noted murder mysteries. 1914. As by 'Philip Curtin'. Non-fiction.
Told in gallant deeds: a child's history of the War. 1914
Good old Anna. 1915, New York 1916.
Price of Admiralty. 1915. 2 stories from Studies in love and terror.
The Red Cross barge. 1916, New York 1918.

Lilla: a part of her life. 1916, New York [1917].
Love and hatred. 1917, New York [1917].
Out of the war? 1918, 1934 (as The gentleman anonymous).
From the vasty deep. [1920], New York [1921] (as From out the vasty deep).
The lonely house. 1920, New York [1920].
What Timmy did. [1921], New York [1922].
Why they married. 1923. Stories. A different work from Why they married pbd with Price of Admiralty, 1915, above.
The Terriford mystery. [1924], Garden City NY 1924.
Bread of deceit. [1925], Garden City NY 1928 (as Afterwards). Stories.
Some men and women. [1925], Garden City NY 1928. Stories.
What really happened. 1926, Garden City NY 1926, London 1932 (as play, What really happened).
The story of Ivy. 1927, Garden City NY 1928.
Thou shalt not kill. 1927.
Cressida: no mystery. 1928, New York 1930.
Duchess Laura: certain days of her life. 1929, New York 1933 (as The duchess intervenes).
Love's revenge. [1929].
One of those ways. 1929, New York 1929.
The key: a love drama in three acts. 1930.
With all John's love: a play in three acts. 1930.
Letty Lynton. 1931, New York [1931].
Vanderlyn's adventure. New York [1931], London 1937 (as The house by the sea).
Why be lonely? A comedy in three acts. 1931. With F. S. A. Lowndes.
Jenny Newstead. 1932, New York 1932.
Love is a flame. 1932.
The reason why. 1932.
Duchess Laura: further days of her life. New York 1933.
Another man's wife. 1934, New York 1934.
The Chianti flask. New York 1934, London 1935.
Who rides on a tiger. New York 1935, London 1936.
And call it accident. New York 1936, London 1939 (as And call it an accident).
The second key. New York 1936, London [1939] (as The injured lover).
The marriage-broker. 1937, New York 1937 (as The fortune of Bridget Malone).
The Empress Eugenie: a three-act play. New York 1938.
Motive. [1938], New York 1938 (as Why it happened).
Lizzie Borden: a study in conjecture. New York 1939, London [1940].
Reckless angel. New York 1939.
The Christie diamond. New York 1940, London [1940].
Before the storm. New York 1941.
'I, too, have lived in Arcadia': a record of love and childhood. 1941, New York 1942. Autobiography.
What of the night? New York 1943. Short stories.
Where love and friendship dwelt. 1943, New York 1943. Autobiography.
The merry wives of Westminster. 1946. Autobiography.
A passing world. 1948. Autobiography.
She dwelt with beauty. 1949.
The young Hilaire Belloc. New York 1956.

CLARENCE MALCOLM LOWRY
1909–57

Lowry's literary mss are in the library of the University of British Columbia.

Bibliographies

Birney, E. Lowry, 1909–57: a bibliography. Canadian Lit nos 8, 9, 1961.

Selections

Selected poems. San Francisco 1962, Lowestoft 1962. Ed E. Birney.

§1

Ultramarine. 1933, 1963 (rev).

Under the volcano. New York 1947, London 1947, Paris 1949 (French trn, with preface tr from Lowry's notes; this was tr into English by G. Woodcock, Canadian Lit no 9 1961), London 1967 (with foreword by S. Spender).

Hear us, O Lord, from heaven thy dwelling place. Philadelphia 1961, London 1962. Stories.

Dark as the grave wherein my friend is laid. New York 1968, London 1969. Ed D. Day and M. B. Lowry.

Lunar caustic. 1968. Ed E. Birney and M. B. Lowry; foreword by C. Knickerbocker. First pbd in Paris Rev no 29 1963.

Letters

Selected letters of Lowry. Philadelphia 1965, London 1967. Ed H. Breit and M. B. Lowry.

For an unpbd novel, October Ferry to Gabriola, *see Birney, Bibliography, above.*

§2

The second part (and supplements) of Birney's bibliography, above, has a comprehensive list of reviews etc.

Lettres Nouvelles no 5 1960. Lowry no. Contains:
Nadeau, M. Lowry.
Francillon, C. Malcolm, mon ami.
Fouchet, M.-P. No se puede...
Myrer, A. Le monde au-dessous du volcano.
Spriel, S. Le cryptogramme Lowry.
Carroy, J.-R. Obscur présent, le feu.
Bonnefoi, G. Souvenir de Quauhnahuac.

Birney, E. The unknown poetry of Lowry. Br Columbia Literary Quart 24 1961.
— Lowry: poète méconnu. Lettres Nouvelles Oct 1962.
Canadian Lit no 8 1961. Lowry no. Contains:
Fouchet, M.-P. No se puede...
Heilman, R. B. The possessed artist and the ailing soul.
Kirk, D. More than music: glimpses of Lowry.
Woodcock, G. Under Seymour Mountain.
McConnell, W. Recollections of Lowry. In Masks of fiction, ed A. J. M. Smith, Toronto 1961.
Prairie Schooner 37 1963. Lowry no. Contains:
Birney, E. Against the spell of death.
Day, D. Of tragic joy.
Edelstein, J. M. On re-reading Under the volcano.
Hirschman, J. Kabbala/Lowry etc.
Knickerbocker, C. The voyages of Lowry.
Markson, D. Myth in Under the volcano.
Noxon, G. Lowry: 1930.
Romijn Meijer, H. Lowry. Tirade 7 1963.
Allen, W. The masterpiece of the forties. In On contemporary literature, ed R. Kostelanetz, New York 1964.
Chittick, V. L. O. Ushant's [Conrad Aiken's] Lowry. Queen's Quart 71 1964.
Christella Marie, Sr. Under the volcano: a consideration. Xavier Univ Stud 4 1965.
Kilgallin, A. R. Eliot, Joyce and Lowry. Canadian Author & Bookman 40 1965.
— Faust and Under the volcano. Canadian Lit no 26 1965.
Kim, S. Les oeuvres de Lowry. Études Anglaises 18 1965.
— Par l'eau et le feu: deux oeuvres de Lowry. Ibid. On Ultramarine and Hear us, O Lord.
Magee, A. P. The quest for love. Emeritus 1 1965.
Knickerbocker, C. Lowry in England. Paris Rev no 38 1966.
— Lowry à vingt ans. Lettres Nouvelles Mar/Apr 1967.
Rapin, R. Sur l'art de Lowry dans Under the volcano. In Mélanges offerts à Monsieur Georges Bonnard, Geneva 1966.
Costa, R. H. Ulysses, Lowry's Volcano and the Voyage [Conrad Aiken's Blue voyage] between: a study of an unacknowledged literary kinship. UTQ 36 1967.

Edwards, D. The short fiction of Lowry. Tulane Stud in Eng 15 1967.
Stern, J. Lowry: a first impression. Encounter 29 1967.
Barnes, J. The myth of Sisyphus in Under the volcano. Prairie Schooner 42 1968.
Day, D. Lowry: Oscuro como la tumba donde mi amigo yace. Revista Nacional de Cultura 29 1968.
Edmonds, D. Under the volcano: a reading of the 'immediate level'. Tulane Stud in Eng 16 1968.
Wild, B. Lowry: a study of the sea metaphor in Under the volcano. Univ of Windsor Rev 4 1968.
Doyen, V. Elements towards a spatial reading of Under the volcano. E Studies 50 1969.
Fernandez, D. Lowry et le feu infernal. Preuves nos 215–16 1969.

PERCY LUBBOCK
1879–1965

See col 1079, below.

DAME EMILIE ROSE MACAULAY
1881–1958

Selections

Three novels. [1928]. Orphan island; Told by an idiot; Crewe train.

§1

Abbots Verney. 1906.
The furnace. 1907.
The secret river. 1909.
The valley captives. 1911, New York 1911.
The lee shore. [1912], New York [1912].
Views and vagabonds. 1912, New York 1912.
The making of a bigot. [1914].
The two blind countries. 1914. Verse.
Non-combatants and others. 1916.
What not: a prophetic comedy. 1918.
Three days. 1919. Verse.
Potterism: a tragi-farcical tract. 1920, New York [1920].
Dangerous ages. 1921, New York [1921].
Mystery at Geneva. [1922], New York 1923.
Told by an idiot. [1923], New York [1923], London 1965 (introd by R. Mortimer).
Orphan island. [1924], New York [1925].
A casual commentary. 1925, New York 1926. Essays.
Catchwords and claptrap. 1926. Essays.
Crewe train. [1926], New York 1926.
[Twenty-two poems]. [1927] (Augustan Books of English Poetry).
Keeping up appearances. [1928], New York 1928 (as Daisy and Daphne).
Staying with relations. 1930, New York [1930].
Some religious elements in English literature. 1931, New York [1931].
They were defeated. 1932, New York 1932 (as The shadow flies). Non-fiction.
Going abroad. 1934, New York 1934.
Milton. 1934, New York 1935, London 1957 (rev), New York 1957.
Personal pleasures. 1935, New York 1936.
I would be private. 1937, New York 1937.
An open letter to a non-pacifist. [1937]. Rptd from Time & Tide.
The writings of E. M. Forster. 1938, New York 1938.
And no man's wit. [1940], Boston 1940.
Life among the English. 1942 (The British People in Pictures).
They went to Portugal. 1946. On English visitors to Portugal.
Fabled shore: from the Pyrenees to Portugal. 1949, New York 1951.

The world my wilderness. 1950, Boston 1950.
Pleasure of ruins. 1953. Non-fiction.
The towers of Trebizond. 1956, New York 1957.

Letters

Letters to a friend 1950-2. Ed C. B. Smith 1961, New York 1962. To J. H. C. Johnson.
Last letters to a friend 1952-8. Ed C. B. Smith 1962, New York 1963. To J. H. C. Johnson.
Letters to a sister. Ed C. B. Smith 1964, New York 1964. To Jean Macaulay. Includes a fragment of a novel, Venice besieged.

§2

Bruessow, M. Zeitbedingtes in den Werken Rose Macaulays. Greifswald 1934.
Lawrence, M. Go-getters. In her School of femininity, New York 1936, London 1937 (as We write as women).
Wahl, I. Gesellschaftskritik und Skeptizismus bei Rose Macaulay. Tübingen 1936.
Hollis, C. Rose Macaulay. Library Jnl 7 Nov 1958.
Nicolson, H. et al. The pleasures of knowing Rose Macaulay. Encounter 12 1959.
Stewart, D. In his The ark of God: studies in five modern novelists, 1961.
Bensen, A. R. The skeptical balance: a study of Rose Macaulay's Going abroad. Papers of Michigan Acad of Science, Arts & Letters 48 1963.
Lockwood, W. J. In Minor British novelists ed C. A. Hoyt, Carbondale 1967.
Swinnerton, F. Rose Macaulay. Kenyon Rev 29 1967.

ARCHIBALD GORDON MACDONELL
1895–1941

The factory on the cliff. 1928. As 'Neil Gordon'.
The new gun-runners. New York [1928]. As 'Neil Gordon'.
The professor's poison. 1928, New York [1928]. As 'Neil Gordon'.
The seven stabs. 1929, New York 1930. As 'John Cameron'.
The silent murders. 1929, New York 1930. As 'Neil Gordon'.
The Big Ben alibi. 1930. As 'Neil Gordon'.
Murder in Earl's Court. 1931. As 'Neil Gordon'.
Body found stabbed. 1932. As 'John Cameron'.
England, their England. 1933, New York 1933 (with foreword by C. Morley), London 1942 (with preface by J. C. Squire). Non-fiction.
The Shakespeare murders. [1933], New York [1933]. As 'Neil Gordon'.
How like an angel! 1934, New York 1935.
Napoleon and his marshals. 1934, New York 1934. Non-fiction.
A visit to America. 1935, New York 1935. Travel.
Lords and masters. 1936, New York 1937.
My Scotland. 1937, New York 1937. Non-fiction.
Autobiography of a cad. 1938. Novel.
Flight from a lady. 1939. Travel, in fictional form.
The Spanish pistol, and other stories. 1939.
What next, baby? or, shall I go to Tanganyika? 1939. Play.
The crew of the Anaconda. 1940.
The fur coat. 1943. Play.
The village cricket match. 1950. Rptd from England, their England, above.

WILLIAM MORLEY PUNSHON
MCFEE
1881–1966

Bibliographies

Babb, J. T. A bibliography of the writings of McFee, with an introduction and notes by McFee. Garden City NY

1931. Includes contributions to periodicals and books and a listing of secondary material.

§1

Letters from an ocean tramp. 1908, Garden City NY 1921 (rev, as An ocean tramp, with preface by McFee).
Aliens. 1914, New York [1914], Garden City NY 1918 (rev, with preface by McFee).
Casuals of the sea: the voyage of a soul. 1916, New York 1916, Garden City NY 1929 (with preface by C. Morley).
A Port Said miscellany. Boston 1918. Story. Rptd in Harbours of memory, 1921, below.
Captain Macedoine's daughter. Garden City NY 1920, London 1920 [1921].
A six-hour shift. Garden City NY 1920.
Harbours of memory. Garden City NY 1921, London 1921. Essays and stories.
An engineer's note book: essays on life and letters. New York 1921. Rptd in Swallowing the anchor, 1925, below.
Captain Macedoine cocktail. [New York 1921] (priv ptd, 12 copies), 1930 (50 copies). Extract from a letter to Morley from McFee.
Command. Garden City NY 1922, London 1922.
The gates of the Caribbean. Boston 1922. Travel.
Race. Garden City NY 1924, London 1924.
Swallowing the anchor. Garden City NY 1925, London 1925. Essays and reviews.
Sunlight in New Granada. Garden City NY 1925, London 1925. Travel.
The life of Sir Martin Frobisher. New York 1928, London 1928 (as Sir Martin Frobisher).
Pilgrims of adversity. Garden City NY 1928, London 1928.
Sailors of fortune. Garden City NY 1929, London 1930. Stories.
North of Suez. Garden City NY 1930, London 1930.
Born to be hanged. Gaylordsville 1930 (priv ptd, 91 copies).
The harbourmaster. Garden City NY 1932, London 1932.
No castles in Spain. Garden City NY 1933, London 1933.
The reflections of Marsyas. Gaylordsville 1933. Includes autobiographical material.
More harbours of memory. Garden City NY 1934, London 1934. Essays.
The beachcomber. Garden City NY 1935, London 1935.
Sailor's wisdom. 1935. Essays and stories.
Sailor's bane. Philadelphia 1936. Story.
Derelicts. New York 1938, London 1939.
Watch below: a reconstruction in narrative form of the golden age of steam. New York [1940], London 1940.
Spenlove in Arcady. New York [1941], London 1942.
Ship to shore. New York 1944, London 1945.
In the first watch. New York 1946, London 1946. Autobiography.
Family trouble. New York 1949, London 1949.
The law of the sea. Philadelphia 1950, London 1951.
The adopted. 1952.

§2

Mais, S. P. B. In his Some modern authors, 1923.
Maule, H. E. McFee: a biographical sketch. New York 1923.
Leatherby, J. N. McFee: writing engineer. Prairie Schooner 23 1949.

ARTHUR LLEWELYN JONES
MACHEN
1863–1947

Bibliographies

Danielson, H. Machen: a bibliography. 1923. With notes by Machen and introd by H. Savage.

Van Patten, N. Machen: a bibliographical note. Queen's Quart 33 1926.
—— Machen bibliography. Reading and Collecting 1 1937.
Jordan-Smith, P. Some Machen items not included in Danielson's bibliography. In his For the love of books, New York 1934.
Goldstone, A. and W. D. Sweetser. A bibliography of Machen. Austin [1965]. Includes Machen's trns and his contributions to books and periodicals, also secondary material.

Various Machen collections in the United States are briefly mentioned in J. K. Vodrey, Arthur Machen, Princeton Univ Lib Chron 26 1965.

Collections and Selections

The Caerleon edition of the works of Machen. 9 vols 1923.
Tales of horror and the supernatural, ed with introd by P. Van Doren Stern, New York 1948, London 1949 (omitting introd and several tales), 1964 (contents as in New York 1948 edn).
The strange world of Machen. New York 1960.
The novel of the Black Seal and other stories; The novel of the white powder and other stories. 2 vols 1965.

§ I

For details of the first pbn of Machen's works in magazines, see Goldstone and Sweetser, bibliography, above.

Eleusinia, by a former member of H[ereford] C[athedral] S[chool]. Hereford 1881. Verse.
The anatomy of tobacco: or smoking methodised, divided and considered after a new fashion, by Leolinus Siluriensis. 1884, New York, London 1926 (with introd by Machen).
A chapter from the book called The ingenious gentleman Don Quijote de la Mancha which by some mischance has not till now been printed. [1887]. Pamphlet, rptd (as The priest and the barber) in The shining pyramid, 1923, below. Anon.
The chronicle of Clemendy: or the history of the IX joyous journeys. Carbonnek [i.e. London] 1888, Carbonnek [i.e. New York] 1923 (with introd by Machen), London 1925 (with different introd by Machen), New York 1926. Stories.
Thesaurus incantatus—the enchanted treasure: or the spagyric quest of Beroaldus Cosmopolita, in which is sophically and mystagorically declared the first matter of the stone. [1888]. Rptd (as The spagyric quest of Beroaldus Cosmopolita) in The shining pyramid, 1923, below. Anon.
The great god Pan, and The inmost light. 1894, Boston 1894, London [1916] (with introd by Machen and omitting The inmost light). Stories, rptd in The house of souls, 1906, below.
The three impostors: or the transmutations. 1895, Boston 1895, New York 1923 (with introd by Machen and omitting the story The iron maid, but including The red hand, not in first edns). Stories, rptd in The house of souls, 1906, below.
Hieroglyphics. 1902, 1912 (rev), New York 1913, London 1960 (with introd by M. Bishop). 'A note upon ecstasy in literature.'
The house of the hidden light, manifested and set forth in certain letters communicated from a lodge of the adepts by the high fratres Filius Aquarum [Machen] and Elias Aetista [A. E. Waite]. Zion [i.e. London] 1904 (priv ptd).
The house of souls. 1906, New York 1922 (omitting The three impostors and The red hand), 1923 (with introd by Machen), London 1923 (with note by Machen). Stories.
Dr Stiggins: his views and principles. 1906, New York 1925 (with introd by Machen). Satire.
The hill of dreams. 1907, New York 1923 (with introd by Machen), London 1968 (with introd by Lord Dunsany).

The angels of Mons—The bowmen and other legends of the war, with an introduction by the author. 1915, 1915 (rev, with two additional stories), New York 1915 (with contents as in first English edn). Stories. *See* H. Begbie, On the side of the angels: a reply to A. Machen, 1915; T. W. H. Crosland, Find the angels—the showmen: a legend of the war, 1915; G. P. B. Kerry, Guardian angels [a reply to Machen], Eastbourne 1915; I. E. S. Taylor, Angels, saints and bowmen of Mons: an answer to Machen and Begbie, 1916.
The great return. 1915.
The terror: a fantasy. 1917, New York [1917] (as The terror: a mystery), London 1927 (rev), New York 1964 (with introd by V. Starrett).
War and the Christian faith. 1918.
The secret glory. [1922], New York 1922.
Far off things. 1922 (100 copies), New York 1922, London [1922] (trade edn). Rptd in The autobiography of Machen, 1951.
Things near & far. 1923, New York 1923. Rptd in The autobiography of Machen, 1951.
The grande trouvaille: a legend of Pentonville. [1923] (priv ptd). Pamphlet.
The shining pyramid. Chicago 1923. Introd by V. Starrett. Stories and essays. Contents differ from 1924 book of same title.
The collector's craft. [1923] (priv ptd). Pamphlet.
Strange roads. (With The gods in spring). 1923, 1924 (with introd by Machen). 2 articles.
Dog and duck. New York 1924, London 1924 (as Dog and duck: a London calendar et cætera). Articles.
The London adventure: or the art of wandering. 1924, New York 1924 (subtitled An essay in wandering).
The glorious mystery, ed V. Starrett. Chicago 1924. Essays and stories.
Precious balms. 1924. Review articles of his own works.
Ornaments in jade. New York 1924. Stories, some previously pbd in The glorious mystery and The shining pyramid (1923).
The shining pyramid. Introd by Machen 1924 (limited edn), 1925, New York 1925. Stories.
A preface to Casanova, Escape from the leads. 1925 (priv ptd, 25 copies). Rptd in Machen's trn of Casanova, Escape from the leads, 1925.
The Canning wonder. 1925, New York 1926. On the case of Elizabeth Canning 1753-4.
Dreads and drolls. 1926, New York 1927. Articles.
Notes and queries. 1926. Articles.
Parish of Amersham. [Amersham] 1930. Anon pamphlet.
Tom o' Bedlam and his song. [Glen Rock Pa] 1930.
Beneath the barley: a note on the origins of Eleusinia. 1931 (priv ptd, 25 copies).
In the 'eighties: a reminiscence of the Silurist put down by him. Amersham 1931 (priv ptd, 10 copies), London 1933 (50 copies). Anon pamphlet.
An introduction to John Gawsworth, Above the river. [1931] (priv ptd, 12 copies). Rptd in Gawsworth, Above the river, 1931.
The glitter of the brook. Dalton Ga 1932 (priv ptd, 10 copies). Stories.
The rose garden. [Stanford]. 1932 (priv ptd, 50 copies). Story rptd from The glorious mystery, 1924, above.
The green round. 1933.
The cosy room and other stories. 1936. Mostly previously pbd in various collections.
The children of the pool, and other stories. [1936].
The autobiography of Machen, ed with introd by M. Bishop. 1951. Contains Far off things, Things near and far.
Bridles & spurs, with preface by N. Van Patten. Cleveland 1951. Essays, mostly written between 1931 and 1934.
A critical essay by Machen: his thoughts on A bookman's diary, by J. A. Hammerton. Lakewood Ohio 1953 (priv ptd, 50 copies).

A receipt for fine prose. [New York] 1956 (priv ptd, 2 copies).

A note on poetry. [Wichita 1959] (priv ptd, 50 copies). Essay first pbd in The Wind and the Rain 2 1943.

From the London Evening News, with introduction by J. H. S[tewart], jr. Wichita 1959 (priv ptd, 50 copies). 3 articles, first pbd 1921.

An excellent ballad of the armèd man. 1963 (priv ptd, 40 copies). First pbd Poetry Rev 41 1950.

Letters

A few letters from Arthur Machen [to M. Havens]. Cleveland 1932.

A.L.S.: an unimportant exchange of letters between Machen and J. H. Stewart jr. Wichita 1956 (priv ptd, 50 copies).

For bibliographical details of Machen's trns, including the Heptameron of Marguerite of Navarre (*1886*) *and* The memoirs of Casanova (*1894*), *see Goldstone and Sweetser, bibliography, above. The bibliography also contains full listings of Machen's large number of contributions to* Academy *and* Evening News.

§2

Milbank, A. Mr Machen's place among contemporary writers. Academy 73 1907.

Watkins, A. A brilliant O.H. Herefordian 67 1911.

Starrett, V. Machen and the angels of Mons. Open Court 32 1918.

— Machen: a novelist of ecstasy and sin. Chicago 1918.

Garland, H. Machen and his collected books. Bookman's Jnl 7 1922.

Jordan-Smith, P. A little journey to the home of Machen. Wave 1 1922.

— Black magic: an impression of Machen. In his On strange altars, 1923.

Roberts, R. E. Machen. Bookman (London) 62 1922.

— Machen. Sewanee Rev 32 1924.

Ellis, S. M. In Current literature. Fortnightly Rev new ser 113 1923; rptd as Arthur Machen, in his Mainly Victorian, 1925.

Hillyer, R. Machen. Yale Rev 13 1923.

— Machen. Atlantic Monthly 179 1947.

Mais, S. P. B. In his Some modern authors, 1923.

Savage, H. Machen: a personal sketch of the famous writer. Book Notes 1 1923.

Van Vechten, C. Literary Digest International Book Rev 1 1923. Rptd in his Excavations, New York 1926.

Wright, C. The mystery of Machen. Double Dealer March–April 1923.

Wells, G. H. A Welsh border writer. Welsh Outlook 11 1924.

Gunther, J. The truth about Machen. Bookman (NY) 61 1925.

Shiel, M. P. Machen. In Borzoi: 1925, New York 1925; rptd in his Science, life and literature, 1950.

Adcock, A. St J. In his The glory that was Grub Street, 1928.

West, G. Machen, visionary and master of prose. Everyman 2 1929.

Van Patten, N. James Branch Cabell and Machen: certain analogies between their early works. Hesperian, Summer 1930.

'Gawsworth, John' (T. I. F. Armstrong). Siluria. In his Fifteen poems: three friends, 1931.

— Priest of the mysterious. New Eng Weekly 5 Nov 1936.

Cazamian, M. L. Machen: théoricien de l'esthétisme. Revue Anglo-américaine 12 1935; rptd in her Le roman et les idées en Angleterre, vol 2, Paris 1935.

Derleth, A. A note on Machen. Reading & Collecting 1 1937.

Jepson, E. A. In his Memories of an Edwardian and neo-Georgian, 1937.

Waite, A. E. In his Shadows of life and thought, 1938.

Lynch, H. Arthur Machen. Sewanee Rev 47 1939.

Gekle, W. F. Machen, weaver of fantasy. Millbrook NY 1949.

— A Machen miscellany. Ed W. F. Gekle [New York] 1957.

Lejeune, A. An old man and a boy: memories of Machen. Listener 29 March 1956.

Martineau, H. P.-J. Toulet et Machen. Paris 1957.

Pauwels, L. and J. Bergier. In their Le matin des magiciens: introduction au réalisme fantastique, Paris 1960, London 1963 (as The dawn of magic).

Peterley, D. In his Peterley harvest, 1960.

Sewell, B. (ed). Arthur Machen. Llandeilo 1960. Articles rptd from Aylesford Rev 2 1959–60.

Tyler, R. L. Machen: the minor writer and his function. Approach no 35 1960.

— The superannuation of Machen. Western Humanities Rev 14 1960.

The Arthur Machen Jnl vol 1 no 1 1963. All pbd. Includes notes by various authors on Machen.

Reynolds, S. A. and W. E. Charlton. Machen: a short account of his life and works. 1963.

Sweetser, W. D. Arthur Machen. New York 1964.

John, A. Machen and the angels of Mons. Anglo-Welsh Rev 14 1964–5.

Matteson, R. S. Machen: a vision of an enchanted land. Personalist 46 1965.

Nash, B. In Minor British novelists, ed C. A. Hoyt, Carbondale 1967.

DENIS GEORGE MACKAIL
1892–1971

§1

What next? 1920, Boston 1921.

Romance to the rescue. 1921, Boston 1921.

Bill the bachelor. 1922, Boston 1922.

According to Gibson. [1923], Boston 1923. Stories.

Summertime. 1923, Boston 1924.

The 'Majestic' mystery. 1924, Boston 1924.

Greenery Street. 1925, Boston 1925.

The fortunes of Hugo. 1926, Boston 1926.

The flower show. 1927, Boston 1927.

Tales from Greenery Street. 1928, Boston 1928.

Another part of the wood. 1929, Boston 1929.

How amusing! and a lot of other fables. 1929, Boston 1929.

The young Livingstones. 1930, Boston 1930.

The square circle. [1930], Boston 1931.

David's day. 1932, Boston 1932.

Ian and Felicity: or, Peninsula Place. 1932, Garden City NY 1932 (as Peninsula Place: being the adventures of Ian and Felicity).

Chelbury Abbey. 1933, Garden City NY 1934.

Having fun: more non-stop stories. 1933.

Summer leaves. 1934, Garden City NY 1934.

The wedding. 1935, Garden City NY 1935.

Back again. 1936, Garden City NY 1936.

Jacinth: or, being an uncle. 1937.

London lovers and a whole heap of shortish stories. 1938.

Morning, noon and night. 1938.

The story of J.M.B.: a biography. 1941, New York 1941 (as Barrie: the story of J.M.B.).

Life with Topsy. 1942. Reminiscences 1927–39.

Upside-down: or, love among the ruins. [1943].

Ho! or, how it all strikes me. [1944]. Autobiographical essays.

Tales for a godchild. [1944]. For children.

Huddleston House: a period piece. [1945].

Our hero: pages from the life of S. W. Glazebrook. [1947].

We're here! or, the adventures of Milford and Bailey. [1947].
Where am I? or, a stranger here myself. [1948]. Autobiographical sketches.
By auction. [1949].
Her ladyship. [1949].
It makes the world go round: or, St Valentine's Day. [1950].

STEPHEN MCKENNA
1888–1956

§ 1

The reluctant lover. 1912, Philadelphia 1913.
Sheila intervenes. 1914, New York 1920.
The sixth sense. 1915, New York [1921].
Ninety-six hours' leave. 1917, New York [1917].
Sonia: between two worlds. 1917, New York [1917].
Midas and son. 1919, New York [1919].
Sonia married. [1919], New York [1919].
Lady Lilith: being the first part of The sensationalists. [1920], New York [1920].
The education of Eric Lane: being the second part of The sensationalists. [1921], New York [1921].
The secret victory: being the third part of The sensationalists. [1921], New York [1922].
While I remember. 1921, New York [1921]. Reminiscences.
The confession of a well-meaning woman. 1922, New York [1922].
Soliloquy. [1922], New York [1923].
Tex: a chapter in the life of Alexander Teixeira de Mattos. 1922, New York 1922.
By intervention of providence. 1923, Boston 1923. Travel in West Indies.
The commandment of Moses. [1923], New York [1923].
Vindication. 1923, Boston 1924.
Tales of intrigue and revenge. [1924], Boston 1925.
To-morrow and to-morrow. [1924], Boston 1924.
An affair of honour. 1925, Boston 1925.
The oldest god. 1926, Boston 1926.
Saviours of society: being the first part of The realists. 1926, Boston 1926.
The secretary of state: being the second part of The realists. 1927, Boston 1927.
Due reckoning: being the third and last part of The realists. 1927, Boston 1928.
The shadow of Guy Denver. 1928, New York 1929.
The unburied dead. 1928, New York 1928 (as Divided allegiance).
The Datchley inheritance. 1929, New York 1929.
Happy ending. 1929, New York 1929 (as Between the lines).
The cast-iron duke. 1930, New York 1931.
The redemption of Morley Darville. 1930, New York 1930.
Beyond hell. 1931, New York 1932.
Dermotts rampart. 1931, New York 1931.
Pandora's box, and other stories. 1932.
Superstition. [1932].
The way of the phoenix. 1932, New York 1932.
Magic quest. [1933].
Namesakes. [1933].
Portrait of His Excellency. [1934].
The undiscovered country. [1934].
Sole death. [1935].
Lady Cynthia Clandon's husband. [1936].
While of sound mind. [1936].
The home that Jill broke. [1937].
Last confession. [1937].
Breasted Amazon. [1938].
A life for a life. [1939].
Mean sensual man. [1943], New York [1943].

Reginald McKenna 1863–1943: a memoir. 1948.
Not necessarily for publication. [1949].
Pearl wedding. 1951, New York 1951.
Life's eventime. 1954.
That dumb loving. 1957.
A place in the sun. 1962.

§ 2

Mais, S. P. B. In his Books and their writers, 1920.
Adcock, A. St J. In his Gods of modern Grub Street, 1923.
Overton, G. M. Confessions of a well-meaning young man. In his Authors of the day, 1924.

SIR EDWARD MONTAGUE COMPTON MACKENZIE
b. 1883

There is a collection of Mackenzie's mss in Texas Univ Library.

Bibliographies
Danielson, H. Bibliographies of modern authors XV: Mackenzie. Bookman's Jnl 3 1920.

§ 1
Prose Fiction
The passionate elopement. 1911, New York 1911, London 1953 (with foreword by Mackenzie).
Carnival. 1912, New York 1912, London 1951 (with foreword by Mackenzie).
Sinister Street. 2 vols 1913–14, New York 1913–14 (vol 1 as Youth's encounter, vol 2 as Sinister Street), 1 vol London 1949 (with foreword by Mackenzie).
Guy and Pauline. 1915, New York 1915 (as Plashers Mead), London 1938 (WC, with introd by Mackenzie).
The early life and adventures of Sylvia Scarlett. 1918, New York 1918.
Poor relations. 1919, New York [1919].
Sylvia and Michael: the later adventures of Sylvia Scarlett. 1919, New York 1919.
The vanity girl. 1920, New York [1920].
Rich relatives. 1921, New York [1921].
The altar steps. 1922, New York [1922], London 1956 (with foreword by J. Betjeman).
The parson's progress. 1923, New York [1924]. Sequel to The altar steps.
The seven ages of woman. 1923, New York [1923].
The heavenly ladder. 1924, New York [1924]. Sequel to The parson's progress.
The old men of the sea. 1924, New York 1924, London 1963 (with new preface, as Paradise for sale).
Santa Claus in summer. 1924, New York 1925. For children.
Coral: a sequel to Carnival. 1925, New York [1925].
Fairy gold. 1926, New York [1926].
The life and adventures of Sylvia Scarlett. 1927, 1950 (as The adventures of Sylvia Scarlett, with foreword by Mackenzie). Contains the two Sylvia Scarlett novels.
Mabel in Queer Street. Oxford [1927]. For children.
Rogues and vagabonds. 1927, New York [1927].
Vestal fire. 1927, New York [1927].
Extraordinary women: theme and variations. 1928, Garden City NY 1928, London 1929 (abridged), 1953 (with foreword by Mackenzie).
Extremes meet. 1928, Garden City NY 1928.
The unpleasant visitors. Oxford [1928]. For children.
The adventures of two chairs. Oxford [1929]. For children.
The three couriers. 1929, Garden City NY 1929.
April fools: a farce of manners. 1930, Garden City NY 1930.
The enchanted blanket. Oxford [1930]. For children.

Told. Oxford 1930, New York 1930. Children's stories and verse.

Buttercups and daisies. 1931, Garden City NY 1931 (as For sale).

The conceited doll. Oxford [1931]. For children.

Our street. 1931, Garden City NY 1932.

The fairy in the window-box. Oxford [1932]. For children.

The dining-room battle. Oxford [1933]. For children.

Water on the brain. 1933, Garden City NY 1933.

The darkening green. 1934, Garden City NY 1934.

The enchanted island. Oxford [1934]. For children.

Figure of eight. 1936.

The naughtymobile. Oxford [1936]. For children.

The four winds of love:

The east wind of love. 1937, New York 1937 (as The east wind).

The south wind of love. 1937, New York 1937.

The west wind of love. 1940, New York 1940.

West to north. 1940, New York 1941.

The north wind of love: book one. 1944, New York 1945.

The north wind of love: book two. 1945, New York 1946 (as Again to the north).

The stairs that kept on going down. Oxford [1937]. For children.

The monarch of the glen. 1941, Boston 1951.

The red tapeworm. 1941.

Keep the Home Guard turning. 1943.

Whisky galore. 1947, Boston 1950 (as Tight little island).

Hunting the fairies. 1949.

The rival monster. 1952.

Ben Nevis goes east. 1954.

Thin ice. 1956, New York 1957.

Rockets galore. 1957.

The lunatic republic. 1959.

Mezzotint. [1961].

Paradise for sale. 1963. See above, The old men of the sea, 1924.

Little cat lost. 1965, New York [1965]. For children.

The stolen soprano. 1965.

Paper lives. 1966.

The strongest man on earth. 1968. On Heracles; for children.

The secret island. 1969. For children.

Other Works

Poems. Oxford 1907.

Kensington rhymes. 1912. For children.

Gramophone nights. 1923. With A. Marshall.

Gallipoli memories. 1929, Garden City NY 1930. First vol of war memoirs.

First Athenian memories. 1931. Second vol of war memoirs.

Address delivered in the St Andrew's Hall on January 29th 1932 on the occasion of his installation as Rector [of Glasgow Univ]. Glasgow 1932.

Greek memories. 1932, 1939 (with postscript). 3rd vol of war memoirs.

Prince Charlie: de jure Charles III, King of Scotland, England, France and Ireland. 1932, New York 1933.

Unconsidered trifles. 1932. Essays.

Literature in my time. 1933.

The lost cause: a Jacobite play. 1933.

Reaped and bound. 1933. Essays.

Marathon and Salamis. 1934.

Prince Charlie and his ladies. 1934, New York 1935.

Catholicism and Scotland. 1936.

Pericles. 1937.

The Windsor tapestry. 1938, New York 1938, London 1952 (rptd with index). On the Duke of Windsor.

A musical chair. 1939. Articles rptd from the Gramophone.

Ægean memories. 1940. 4th vol of war memoirs.

Calvary. 1942. Reflections on the war etc. With F. Compton Mackenzie.

Mr Roosevelt. 1943, New York 1944.

Wind of freedom: the history of the invasion of Greece by the Axis Powers 1940–1. 1943.

Dr Benes. 1946.

The vital flame. 1947. On the gas industry.

All over the place. 1948. Travel.

Eastern epic: vol 1, Defence. 1951. On the Indian Army in World War II.

The house of Coalport 1750–1950. 1951. The Coalport China Company.

I took a journey: a tour of National Trust properties. 1951.

The Queen's house: a history of Buckingham Palace. [1953].

The Savoy of London. 1953.

Echoes. 1954. Broadcast talks.

Realms of silver: one hundred years of banking in the East. 1954. The Chartered Bank of India, Australia and China.

My record of music. 1955, New York 1956.

A posy of sweet months. [1955] (priv ptd).

Sublime tobacco. 1957, New York 1958.

Cats' company. [1960], New York [1961].

Greece in my life. 1960.

Catmint. 1961, New York 1962.

On moral courage. 1962, Garden City NY (as Certain aspects of moral courage).

Look at cats. 1963.

My life and times: octave 1–10. 1963–71.

Robert Louis Stevenson. 1968.

Mackenzie founded The Gramophone *1923 and edited it for many years.*

§2

Goldring, D. Three Georgian novelists. In his Reputations, 1920.

Mais, S. P. B. The genius of Mackenzie. In his Books and their writers, 1920.

Johnson, R. B. In his Some contemporary novelists: men, 1922.

Adcock, A. St J. In his Gods of modern Grub Street, 1923.

Freeman, J. In his English portraits and essays, 1924.

Robertson, L. Compton Mackenzie: an appraisal of his literary work. 1954.

Young, K. Compton Mackenzie. 1968 (Br Council pamphlet).

FREDERIC MANNING
1882–1935

§1

The vigil of Brunhild: a narrative poem. 1907.

Scenes and portraits. 1909, New York 1909, London 1930 (rev), New York 1931. Stories.

Poems. 1910.

Eidola. 1917, New York 1918. Verse.

Poetry in prose. In Poetry and prose: three essays by T. S. Eliot, F. Manning, R. Aldington, 1921 (Chapbook 22).

The life of Sir William White. 1923, New York 1923. Biography.

Epicurus's morals, with introductory essay by Manning. 1926.

The middle parts of Fortune: Somme and Ancre, 1916. 2 vols 1929, 1930 (abridged) (as Her privates we), New York 1930; ed E. Blunden 1964. The middle parts of Fortune pbd anon; Her privates we pbd as by 'Private 19022'.

§2

Bergonzi, B. In his Heroes' twilight: a study of the literature of the Great War, 1965.

OLIVIA MANNING

The wind changes. 1937, New York 1938.
The remarkable expedition: the story of Stanley's rescue of Emin Pasha from equatorial Africa. 1947, Garden City NY 1947 (as The reluctant rescue).
Growing up. 1948. Stories.
Artist among the missing. 1949.
The dreaming shore. 1950. Travel, West coast of Ireland.
School for love. 1951.
A different face: a novel. 1953, New York 1957.
The doves of Venus: a novel. 1955, New York 1956.
My husband Cartwright. 1956. Stories.
The great fortune. 1960, Garden City NY 1961. Vol 1 of The Balkan trilogy.
The spoilt city. 1962, Garden City NY 1962. Vol 2 of The Balkan trilogy.
Friends and heroes. 1965, Garden City NY 1966. Vol 3 of The Balkan trilogy.
Extraordinary cats. 1967. Non-fiction.
A romantic hero, and other stories. 1967.
The play room. 1969, New York 1969 (as The Camperlea girls).

'KATHERINE MANSFIELD', KATHLEEN MANSFIELD BEAUCHAMP
1888–1923

Bibliographies

Stonehill, C. A. and F. W. In their Bibliographies of modern authors ser 2, 1925. To 1924.
Mantz, R. C. The critical bibliography of Katherine Mansfield. Introd by J. M. Murry 1931. Includes details of original periodical pbn of stories and uncollected contributions to periodicals, also 2 sketches, Perambulations and About Pat. Corrected in some details by S. Berkman, Katherine Mansfield, 1951, §2, below.
Mansfieldiana: a brief Katherine Mansfield bibliography. Introd by G. N. Morris, Wellington 1948 (New Zealand Collectors' Monographs 3).

Collections and Selections

The short stories of Katherine Mansfield. Introd by J. M. Murry, New York 1937.
Collected stories of Katherine Mansfield. 1945.
Stories by Katherine Mansfield: a selection made by J. M. Murry. New York 1930.
The garden party and other stories. 1939 [1947]. Ptd at Verona, limited edn. Different work from The garden party and other stories, 1922, below.
Selected stories. Ed D. M. Davin 1953 (WC).
Stories. Ed E. Bowen, New York 1956, London 1957 (as 34 short stories).

§1

In a German pension. [1911], 1926 (introd by J. M. Murry), New York 1926. Stories. Contains The child-who-was-tired, Germans at meat, The baron, The Luft Bad, At Lehmann's, Frau Brechenmacher attends a wedding, The sister of the baroness, Frau Fischer, A birthday, The modern soul, The advanced lady, The swing of the pendulum, A blaze. All previously pbd in New Age except last 3.
Prelude. Richmond Surrey [1918]. Story; rptd in Bliss, and other stories, below.
Je ne parle pas français. Hampstead 1919 (priv ptd). Story; rptd in Bliss, and other stories, below.

Bliss, and other stories. 1920, New York 1921. Contains The wind blows, The little governess, Mr Reginald Peacock's day, Feuille d'album, A dill pickle, Prelude, Bliss, Pictures, Je ne parle pas français, The man without a temperament, Revelations, The escape, Sun and moon, Psychology. All except Psychology previously pbd, either separately or in various periodicals.
The garden-party, and other stories. 1922, New York 1922. Contains Bank Holiday, The young girl, Miss Brill, The lady's maid, The stranger, The life of Ma Parker, The daughters of the late Colonel, Mr and Mrs Dove, An ideal family, Her first ball, The voyage, Marriage à la mode, At the bay, The garden-party, The singing lesson. All except The singing lesson previously pbd in various periodicals.
The dove's nest, and other stories. Introd by J. M. Murry 1923, New York 1923. Contains The doll's house, Taking the veil, The fly, Honeymoon, A cup of tea, The canary (all previously pbd in various periodicals); and 15 stories unfinished at the author's death: A married man's story, The dove's nest, Six years after, Daphne, Father and the girls, All serene, A bad idea, A man and his dog, Such a sweet old lady, Honesty, Susannah, Second violin, Mr & Mrs Williams, Weak heart, Widowed.
Poems. 1923, New York 1924, London 1930 (with 2 more poems).
Something childish, and other stories. [1924], New York 1924 (as The little girl, and other stories). Contains The journey to Bruges, A truthful adventure, The woman and the store, How Pearl Button was kidnapped, The little girl, New dresses, Ole Underwood, Pension Séguin, Millie, Violet, Bains turcs, Two tuppenny ones please, Late at night, The black cap, Sixpence, Poison, A suburban fairy tale, Something childish but very natural, The tiredness of Rosabel, See-saw, Carnation, An indiscreet journey, Spring pictures, This flower, The wrong house. All except the last 5 previously pbd in various periodicals.
Reminiscences of Leonid Andreyev by Maxim Gorky. Tr K. Mansfield and S. S. Koteliansky, New York 1928, London [1931].
The aloe. Introd by J. M. Murry 1930, New York 1930. The original longer version of Prelude, written in 1916.
Novels and novelists. Ed J. M. Murry 1930. Reprints book reviews from Athenaeum 1919–20.
A fairy story. Stanford 1932 (priv ptd, 25 copies). Issued by Stanford Univ Library.
To Stanislaw Wyspianski. 1938 (priv ptd, 100 copies). Poem dated Jan 1910.
The scrapbook of Katherine Mansfield. Ed J.M.M[urry] 1939, New York 1940.

For the unfinished novel Maata, *see P. A. Lawlor*, The mystery of Maata, *Wellington 1946. Katherine Mansfield contributed numerous stories to* New Age, *and later to magazines she edited with Murry 1912–15*: Rhythm, Blue Rev *and* Signature.

Letters, Diaries etc

The journal of Katherine Mansfield. Ed J. M. Murry 1927, New York 1927, London 1954 (with introd replaced by short preface, and with some textual addns).
The letters of Katherine Mansfield. Ed J. M. Murry 2 vols 1928, New York 1929.
Katherine Mansfield's letters to John Middleton Murry 1913–22. Ed Murry 1951, New York 1951. Passages omitted in 1928 edn restored.
Forty-six letters. Adam no 300 1965. Letters to A. E. Rice and to Mr and Mrs S. Schiff.

§2

For a fuller list of explications of particular short stories, see W. S. Walker, Twentieth-century short story explication, *Hamden Conn 1967.*

Squire, J. C. Miss Mansfield's stories. In his Books reviewed, 1922.

Armstrong, M. The art of Katherine Mansfield. Fortnightly Rev new ser 113 1923.

Collins, J. Two literary ladies of London: Katherine Mansfield and Rebecca West. In his The doctor looks at literature, New York [1923].

Lynd, S. Katherine Mansfield. Weekly Westminster Gazette 20 Jan 1923.

Mais, S. P. B. In his Some modern authors, 1923.

Moult, T. Katherine Mansfield. Bookman (London) 63 1923.

Murry, J. M. Katherine Mansfield. New York Evening Post Literary Rev 17 Feb 1923.
— Katherine Mansfield, Stendhal and style. Adelphi 1 1923.
— A month after. Ibid.
— Between two worlds: an autobiography. 1935.
— The isolation of Katherine Mansfield. Adelphi 23 1947.
— A friend in need to Katherine Mansfield. Adelphi 24 1948.
— Katherine Mansfield and other literary portraits. 1949.
— Katherine Mansfield in France. Atlantic Monthly 184 1949.
— Katherine Mansfield and other literary studies. 1959.

Brewster, D. and A. Burrell. In their Dead reckonings in fiction, New York 1924. Chekhov and Katherine Mansfield compared.

Gillet, L. Katherine Mansfield. Revue des Deux Mondes 15 Dec 1924.
— Les lettres de Katherine Mansfield. Revue des Deux Mondes 1 May 1929.
— 'Kass': ou la jeunesse de Katherine Mansfield. Revue des Deux Mondes 15 Jan 1934.

Hartley, L. P. Katherine Mansfield. Spectator 6 Sept 1924. On Something childish.

Orage, A. R. Talks with Katherine Mansfield. Century Mag 87 1924; rptd in his Selected essays, 1935.

Huxley, A. The traveller's eye view. Nation & Athenaeum 16 May 1925.

Bullett, G. In his Modern English fiction, 1926.

Freeman, K. The art of Katherine Mansfield. Canadian Forum 7 1927.

Hubbell, G. S. Katherine Mansfield and Kezia. Sewanee Rev 35 1927.

Woolf, V. A terribly sensitive mind. New York Herald Tribune 19 Sept 1927; rptd in her Granite and rainbow, 1958, and in Collected essays vol 1, 1966. Review of The journal of Katherine Mansfield.

Shanks, E. Katherine Mansfield. London Mercury 17 1928.

Wagenknecht, E. Katherine Mansfield. Eng Jnl 17 1928.
— Dickens and Katherine Mansfield. Dickensian 26 1929; rptd in his Dickens and the scandalmongers, Norman Oklahoma 1965.

Harper, G. M. Katherine Mansfield. Quart Rev 253 1929; rptd in his Literary appreciations, Indianapolis 1937.

Marcel, G. Katherine Mansfield. Nouvelle Revue Française 32 1929.

Williams, O. Katherine Mansfield. New Criterion 8 1929.

Stanley, C. W. The art of Katherine Mansfield. Dalhousie Rev 10 1930.

Van Kranendonk, A. G. Katherine Mansfield. E Studies 12 1930.

Bertrand, G. P. L'attitude spirituelle de Katherine Mansfield. Cahiers du Sud 18 1931.

Cox, S. The fastidiousness of Katherine Mansfield. Sewanee Rev 39 1931.

Cremieux, B. Katherine Mansfield. Annales Politiques et Littéraires 15 Sept 1931.

Deffrennes, P. L'homme et sa plume: la correspondance de Katherine Mansfield. Etudes 209 1931.

Jean-Aubry, G. Katherine Mansfield. Revue de Paris 6 1931.

'Olgivanna' (Mrs F. Lloyd Wright). The last days of Katherine Mansfield. Bookman (New York) 73 1931.

Vowinckel, E. Katherine Mansfield. Zeitschrift für Französischen und Englischen Unterricht 30 1931.

Beauchamp, H. Katherine Mansfield's career. Saturday Rev of Lit 30 Sept 1933.
— In his Reminiscences and recollections, New Plymouth 1937.

Bompard, J. Sur une jeune femme morte: Katherine Mansfield. Grande Revue 140 1933.

Mantz, R. E. and J. M. Murry. The life of Katherine Mansfield. 1933.

Tasset-Nissolle, E. Katherine Mansfield (1888–1923). Le Correspondant 25 Sept 1933.

Thiébaut, M. Katherine Mansfield. Revue de Paris 8 1933.

Barretta, R. W. Les petites servantes méridionales vues par Katherine Mansfield. Revue Hebdomadaire 15 Sept 1934.

Burrell, M. In his Crumbs are also bread, 1934.

'Carco, Francis' (F. C. Tusoli). Souvenirs sur Katherine Mansfield. Paris 1934.

Cazamian, L. D. H. Lawrence and Katherine Mansfield as letter-writers. UTQ 3 1934.

D'Escola, M. Katherine Mansfield. Revue Bleue 1 Sept 1934.

Clarke, I. C. In her Six portraits, 1935.

Haffner, H. Der Charakter der Frau bei Katherine Mansfield. Tübingen 1935.

'Maurois, André' (E. S. W. Herzog). In his Magiciens et logiciens, Paris 1935. Tr as Prophets and poets, 1935.

Schneider, E. Katherine Mansfield and Chekhov. MLN 50 1935.

Cather, W. In her Not under forty, New York 1936.

Daiches, D. The art of Katherine Mansfield. In his New literary values, 1936.
— Katherine Mansfield and the search for truth. In his Novel and the modern World, Chicago 1939.

Lang, W. Sprache und Stil in Katherine Mansfields Kurzgeschichten. Leipzig 1936.

Muffang, M. L. Katherine Mansfield: sa vie, son oeuvre, sa personnalité. Paris 1936.

Sewell, A. Katherine Mansfield: a critical essay. Auckland 1936.

Guéritte, M. T. K.M. and music. Chesterian 18 1937.

Orton, W. In his The last romantic, 1937.

Porter, K. A. The art of Katherine Mansfield. Nation 23 Oct 1937.

Wiegelmann, T. Das Weltbild der Katherine Mansfield. Bonn 1937.

Hoare, D. M. In her Some studies in the modern novel, 1938.

Blanchet, A. Le secret de Katherine Mansfield. Etudes 241 1939.

Bordeaux, H. Le souvenir de Katherine Mansfield. Revue Hebdomadaire 17 June 1939. See also H. Sellon, ibid 1 July

Jacoubet, E. Un curieux exemple d'identité littéraire: Katherine Mansfield et Tchekhov. Études Anglaises 3 1939.

Marsh, E. In his A number of people: a book of reminiscences. 1939.

A writer's sanctuary: Katherine Mansfield with her scrapbook. TLS 28 Oct 1939.

Citron, P. Katherine Mansfield et la France. Revue de Littérature Comparée 20 1940.

Moorman, L. J. In his Tuberculosis and genius, Chicago 1940.

Whitridge, A. Katherine Mansfield. Sewanee Rev 48 1940.

Nelson, A. Katherine Mansfield: artist in miniature. Yale Literary Mag 106 1941; rptd in R. B. West and R. W. Stallman (ed), The art of modern fiction, New York

1949, and in R. W. Stallman and R. E. Watters (ed), The creative reader, New York 1954.

White, N. G. Daughter of time: the life of Katherine Mansfield in novel form. New York 1942.

Morris, G. N. Katherine Mansfield in fiction. New Zealand Mag 22 1943.

— The early work of Katherine Mansfield. New Zealand Mag 22 1943.

— Katherine Mansfield in ten languages. New Zealand Mag 23 1944.

— Katherine Mansfield: the New Zealand period. History & Bibliography (Christchurch) no 1 1948.

— Katherine Mansfield: early London days. History & Bibliography no 2 1948.

— Katherine Mansfield: the last ten years. History & Bibliography no 3 1948.

— Her unlucky star: some thoughts on the inner life of Katherine Mansfield. New Zealand Mag 28 1949.

Le Rolle, V. et al. Katherine Mansfield. Angers 1945.

Eustace, C. J. In his An infinity of questions: a study of the religion of art and the art of religion in the lives of five women, 1946.

Friis, A. Katherine Mansfield: life and stories. Copenhagen 1946.

Kafian, A. The last days of Katherine Mansfield. Adelphi 23 1946.

Lenoël, O. La vocation de Katherine Mansfield. Paris 1946.

Marion, B. A la rencontre de Katherine Mansfield. Brussels 1946.

Pritchett, V. S. Katherine Mansfield and the short story. New Zealand Listener 15 1946.

Verney, A. Histoire de Katherine Mansfield. France Libre 1946.

Bosanquet, B. Life should be glorious: a new view of Katherine Mansfield as revealed in her stories. New Zealand Mag 26 1947.

La Marche, G. Equipe Murry–Mansfield. Carnets Victoriens 12 1947.

Van Weddingen, M. Lumière de Katherine Mansfield. Revue Générale Belge no 45 1949.

Villard, L. Katherine Mansfield. Langues Modernes 43 1949.

Andree, M. Das Lebensgefühl der Katherine Mansfield. Münster 1950.

Lawlor, P. A. The loneliness of Katherine Mansfield. Wellington 1950.

— In his Books and bookmen, New Zealand and overseas. Wellington 1954.

Merlin, R. Le drame secret de Katherine Mansfield. Paris 1950.

Almedingen, E. M. Chekhov and Katherine Mansfield. TLS 19 Oct 1951. Correspondence to 16 Nov 1951, with contributions from Murry, Sylvia Berkman, Aloers and A. E. Coppard.

Berkman, S. Katherine Mansfield: a critical study. New Haven 1951.

Christen, M. Katherine Mansfield: de la Nouvelle Zélande à Fontainebleau. Niort 1951.

Shaw, H. Katherine Mansfield. Meanjin 10 1951.

'Dominique, Jean' (M. Closset). Katherine Mansfield. Brussels 1952.

Spiel, H. Katherine Mansfield. Der Monat 4 1952.

— In her Der Park und die Wildnis: zur Situation der neueren englischen Literatur, Munich 1953.

Alpers, A. Katherine Mansfield: a biography. New York 1953.

Dinkins, P. Katherine Mansfield: the ending. Southwest Rev 38 1953.

Hynes, S. Katherine Mansfield: the defeat of the personal. South Atlantic Quart 52 1953.

Seiler, A. J. P. Ausblick ins Unbekannte: Hinweis auɪ Katherine Mansfield. Schweizer Rundschau 4–5 1953.

Arland, M. Katherine Mansfield: ou la grace d'écrire. Nouvelle Revue Française 4 1954.

Belitt, B. The short stories of Katherine Mansfield. In E. C. Wagenknecht, A preface to literature, New York 1954.

Gordon, I. A. Katherine Mansfield. 1954 (Br Council pamphlet).

Wright, C. T. Darkness as a symbol in Katherine Mansfield. MP 51 1954.

— Genesis of a short story. PQ 34 1955. The fly.

— Katherine Mansfield and the 'secret smile'. Lit & Psychology 5 1955.

— Katherine Mansfield's boat image. Twentieth-Century Lit 1 1955.

— Katherine Mansfield's father image. In The image of the work, ed B. H. Lehman et al, Berkeley 1955.

— Katherine Mansfield's dog image. Lit & Psychology 10 1960. On Bliss.

Clarke, B. Katherine Mansfield's illness. Proc Royal Soc of Medicine 48 1955.

Kirkwood, H. Katherine Mansfield. Canadian Forum 35 1955.

Palmer, V. Katherine Mansfield. Meanjin 14 1955.

Bowen, E. A living writer. Cornhill Mag 169 1956; rptd as preface in Thirty four short stories by Katherine Mansfield, 1951 (see §1, above) and in Afterthought, 1962.

Corin, F. Creation of atmosphere in Katherine Mansfield's stories. Revue des Langues Vivantes 22 1956.

Garlington, J. Katherine Mansfield: the critical trend. Twentieth-Century Lit 2 1956.

— An unattributed story of Katherine Mansfield? MLN 71 1956. The mating of Gwendolen, New Age 2 Nov 1911.

Walker, W. The unresolved conflict in The garden-party. Modern Fiction Stud 3 1957.

'Hudson, Stephen' (S. Schiff). First meetings with Katherine Mansfield. Cornhill Mag 170 1958.

Taylor, D. S. and D. A. Weiss. Crashing The garden party. Modern Fiction Stud 4 1958.

Allbright, R. Katherine Mansfield and Wingley. Folio 24 1959. On her cats.

Distel, M. Katherine Mansfields Erzählung Je ne parle pas français: ein Beitrag zur Interpretation anhand der Originalfassung. Die Neueren Sprachen 8 1959.

Murry, M. M. Katherine Mansfield and J. M. Murry. London Mag 6 1959.

Selver, P. In his Orage and the New Age circle: reminiscences and reflections, 1959.

Kleine, D. W. Katherine Mansfield and The prisoner of love. Critique (Minneapolis) 3 1960. On The man without a temperament.

— The Chekhovian source of Marriage à la mode. PQ 42 1963.

— The garden party: a portrait of the artist. Criticism 5 1963.

— Eden for insiders: Mansfield's New Zealand. College Eng 27 1965.

Monnet, A. M. Katherine Mansfield. [Paris 1960].

Schwinn, L. Katherine Mansfield. Hochland 53 1961.

Thomas, J. D. Symbolism and parallelism in The fly. College Eng 22 1960–1.

Bateson, F. W. and B. Shahevitch. Katherine Mansfield's The fly: a critical exercise. EC 12 1962. With replies.

Brophy, B. Katherine Mansfield. London Mag 2 1962; rptd in her Don't never forget, 1966, and in Michigan Quart Rev 5 1966 (as Katherine Mansfield's self-depiction).

Sutherland, R. Katherine Mansfield: plagiarist, disciple or ardent admirer? Critique (Minneapolis) 5 1962. Comparison with Chekhov.

Leeming, O. A. Katherine Mansfield's sisters; Katherine Mansfield and her family; Katherine Mansfield's rebellion; Katherine Mansfield in Europe. New Zealand Listener 1 March–11 April 1963. Series of articles.

Swinnerton, F. A. In his Figures in the foreground, 1963.

Hagopian, J. T. Capturing Mansfield's Fly. Modern Fiction Stud 9 1963–4.

Davis, R. M. The unity of The garden party. Stud in Short Fiction 2 1964.

Madden, D. Katherine Mansfield's Miss Brill. Univ Rev (Kansas City) 31 1964.

Willy, M. Three women diarists: Celia Fiennes, Dorothy Wordsworth, Katherine Mansfield. 1964 (Br Council pamphlet).

Boyle, T. E. The death of the boss: another look at Katherine Mansfield's The fly. Modern Fiction Stud 11 1965.

Daly, S. R. Katherine Mansfield. New York 1965.

Boyer, P. K. Mansfield: l'oeuvre romanesque? Esprit 10 1966.

Aubrion, M. K. Mansfield ou le rêve fracassé. Revue Générale Belge June 1967.

Hormasji, N. Katherine Mansfield: an appraisal. Auckland 1967.

Schwendimann, M. A. Katherine Mansfield: ihr Leben in Darstellung und Dokumenten. Munich 1967.

Yanson, M. M. The problems of style of Katherine Mansfield's mature stories and her views on literary skill. Riga 1967. In Russian.

Gateau, A.-M. Poétesse, musicienne et peintre d'un moment éphémère: ou Katherine Mansfield impressionniste. Caliban 5 1968.

—— Katherine Mansfield impressioniste: ou, quand et comment se déroulent les nouvelles de K. Mansfield. Caliban 6 1969.

Iversen, A. A reading of Katherine Mansfield's The garden party. Orbis Litterarum 23 1968.

Schahevitch, B. From simile to short story: on K. Mansfield's The fly. Hasifrut 1 1968. In Hebrew; English summary.

Haferkamp, B. Zur Bildersprache Katherine Mansfields. Die Neueren Sprachen 18 1969.

'LOUIS MARLOW',
LOUIS UMFREVILLE WILKINSON
1881–1968

§1

The puppets' dallying. 1905.

Blasphemy and religion: a dialogue about J. C. Powys, Wood and stone, and T. Powys, The soliloquy of a hermit. New York [1916]. Pamphlet, as Wilkinson.

The buffoon. 1916, New York 1916. As Wilkinson.

A chaste man. New York 1917, London 1918. As Wilkinson.

Brute gods. New York 1919, London 1920. As Wilkinson.

Mr Amberthwaite. 1928, New York 1929.

Love by accident: a tragi-farce. 1929, Garden City NY 1930.

Two made their bed. 1929. Preface by W. S. Maugham.

The lion took fright. 1930, Garden City NY 1931.

Swan's milk. 1934.

Fool's quarter-day. 1935.

Welsh ambassadors: Powys lives and letters. 1936.

The devil in crystal. 1944.

The brothers Powys. [Cincinnati] 1946. Lecture, as Wilkinson.

Forth, beast! 1946.

Sackville of Drayton. 1948. Biography.

Seven friends. 1953. On Wilde, Frank Harris, Aleister Crowley, the Powys brothers, and Maugham.

§2

Harris, F. Louis Wilkinson. In his Contemporary portraits, 3rd series, 1920.

JOHN EDWARD MASEFIELD
1878–1967

See cols 306–13, above.

ALFRED EDWARD WOODLEY MASON
1865–1948

Bibliographies

Green, R. L. In his A. E. W. Mason, 1952, §2 below. Includes dates of performance of plays and a note on uncollected stories and miscellaneous writings.

Selections

The A. E. W. Mason omnibus: Inspector Hanaud's investigations. 1931. Contains At the Villa Rose, The house of the arrow, The prisoner in the opal.

§1

Blanche de Malétroit: a play in one act founded upon the story by R. L. Stevenson. [1894].

A romance of Wastdale. 1895, New York 1895.

The courtship of Morrice Buckler: a romance. 1896.

Lawrence Clavering. 1897, New York 1897.

The philanderers. 1897, New York 1897.

Miranda of the balcony. 1899, New York 1899.

Parson Kelly. New York 1899, London 1900. With A. Lang.

The watchers (Arrowsmith's Christmas Annual 1899). Bristol 1899, New York 1899.

Clementina. 1901, New York 1901.

Ensign Knightley, and other stories. 1901, New York 1901.

The four feathers. 1902, New York 1902.

The truants. 1904, New York 1904.

The broken road. 1907, New York 1907.

Running water. 1907, New York 1907.

At the Villa Rose. 1910, New York 1910. Dramatized as At the Villa Rose: a play in four acts, [1928].

The clock. New York 1910. Story, rptd in The four corners of the world, below.

Making good. New York 1910. Story.

The turnstile. [1912], New York 1912.

The witness for the defence. 1913, New York 1914. Dramatized as The witness for the defence: a play in four acts, [1913], New York [1913].

Green stockings: a comedy in three acts. [1914], New York [1914].

The affair at the Semiramis Hotel. New York 1917. Story, rptd in The four corners of the world, below.

The four corners of the world. 1917, New York 1917. Stories.

'The episode of the thermometer'. New York 1918. Story.

The Royal Exchange: a note on the occasion of the bicentenary of the Royal Exchange Assurance. [1920].

The summons. [1920], New York 1920.

The winding stair. [1923], New York 1923.

The house of the arrow. [1924], New York 1924.

No other tiger. 1927, New York 1927.

The prisoner in the opal. [1928], Garden City NY 1928.

The dean's elbow. 1930, Garden City NY 1931.

The three gentlemen. 1932, Garden City NY 1932.

The sapphire. 1933, Garden City NY 1933.

Dilemmas. 1934, Garden City NY 1935. Stories.

A present from Margate: a frivolous comedy in three acts. [1934]. With I. Hay.

Sir George Alexander and the St James' Theatre. 1935, New York 1935.

They wouldn't be chessmen. 1935, Garden City NY 1935.

Fire over England. 1936, Garden City NY 1936.

The drum. 1937, Garden City NY 1937. Story.

Königsmark. 1938, New York 1939.

The secret fear. New York 1940. Story.
The life of Francis Drake. 1941, Garden City NY 1942.
Musk and amber. 1942, Garden City NY 1942.
The house in Lordship Lane. 1946, New York 1946.

§2

Adcock, A. St J. In his Gods of modern Grub Street, 1923.
Green, R. L. A. E. W. Mason. 1952.

WILLIAM SOMERSET MAUGHAM
1874–1965
Bibliographies

Bason, F. T. A bibliography of the writings of Maugham. Preface by Maugham 1931.
Jonas, K. W. A bibliography of the writings of Maugham. South Hadley Mass 1950. Includes contributions to books and periodicals, trns of Maugham's books and mss locations; lists of secondary material include unpbd dissertations.
—— More Maughamiana. PBSA 44 1950. Also pbd separately. Suppl, Icelandic trns of Maugham, by N. Van Patten, PBSA 45 1951.
—— A note on Maugham collections. In his World of Somerset Maugham, 1959. See §2, below.
Stott, R. T. Maughamiana: the writings of Maugham. 1950. Includes contributions to books and periodicals, trns of Maugham's works and a section of secondary material. For additional Swedish trns, see A. Runnquist, Maughamiana, TLS 10 March 1950.
—— The writings of Maugham. 1956, with suppls 1961 and 1964. Main work is fully descriptive of Maugham's works: secondary material is listed in suppls.
Mander, R. and J. Mitchenson. In their Theatrical companion to Maugham: a pictorial record of the first performances of the plays of Maugham, [1955]. See §2, below. Includes lists of adaptations by other writers; film versions of the plays, stories and novels; trns and broadcasts.
Wing, D. G. The manuscript of Maugham's On a Chinese screen. Yale Univ Lib Gazette 29 1955.
Stanford University Library. A comprehensive exhibition of the writings of Maugham: a catalogue compiled by J. T. Bender, with a preface by Maugham. Stanford 1958.
Kendall, L. H. The first edition of The moon and sixpence. PBSA 55 1961.
Davies, H. M. P. The King's School Canterbury: the Somerset Maugham Library. Études Anglaises 16 1963.

Collections and Selections

Collected edition. 1931–. Prefaces by the author, many titles rev from previous edns. Plays issued in 6 vols 1931–4, under the title Plays by W. Somerset Maugham. See also Collected plays, 1952, below.
East and west: the collected short stories. Garden City NY 1934, London 1934 (as Altogether). Preface by the author; English edn contains D. MacCarthy's Appreciation (see §2, below).
The favorite short stories of Maugham. Garden City NY 1937.
Six comedies. Garden City NY [1937]. Preface by the author; contains The unattainable, Home and beauty, The circle, Our betters, The constant wife, The breadwinner. The first 2 pbd here for the first time in America.
The round dozen: a collection of his stories selected by W. Somerset Maugham. [1939].
The Somerset Maugham sampler. Ed J. Weidman, Garden City NY 1943. Rptd as The Somerset Maugham pocket book. Contains Cakes and ale, The circle, and a selection of stories, travel sketches and essays.

East of Suez: great stories of the tropics. New York 1948. Excerpts from On a Chinese screen, and stories from The casuarina tree.
Here and there. 1948. A collection of stories.
Quartet: four stories. 1948, New York 1949. The facts of life, The alien corn, The kite, The colonel's lady; with film scripts by R. C. Sherriff.
The Maugham reader. Introd by G. Wescott, New York 1950.
Trio: stories by Maugham; screen adaptation by Maugham, R. C. Sherriff and Noel Langley. 1950, New York 1950. The verger, Mr Know-all, Sanatorium.
Encore: stories by Maugham; screen adaptation by T. E. B. Clarke, A. Macrae and E. Ambler. 1951. The ant and the grasshopper, Winter cruise, Gigolo and Gigolette.
The complete short stories. 3 vols 1951, 2 vols New York 1952. With prefaces by the author.
Collected plays. 3 vols 1952. First pbd in 6 vols 1931–4 as part of Collected edn.
The world over: stories of manifold places and people. Garden City NY 1952.
Selected novels. 3 vols 1953. With prefaces by the author.
Mr Maugham himself, selected by J. Beecroft. Garden City NY 1954.
The partial view. 1954. Contains The summing up and A writer's notebook, with a new preface.
The travel books. 1955. On A Chinese screen, The gentleman in the parlour, Don Fernando. With new preface.
Best short stories of Somerset Maugham, selected with introd by J. Beecroft, New York 1957 (Modern Library).
Husband and wives: nine stories, selected with an introduction by R. A. Cordell. New York [1963].
Selected plays. 1963 (Penguin Plays). Sheppey, The sacred flame, The circle, The constant wife, Our betters.
Selected prefaces and introductions. Garden City NY 1963, London [1964].
A Maugham twelve: stories selected with introd by A. Wilson. 1966.
Wit and wisdom of Maugham. Ed C. Hewetson 1966.
Essays on literature. 1967 (Signet Modern Classics).
A baker's dozen: thirteen short stories. 1969.
A second baker's dozen: thirteen short stories. 1970.

§1

Prose Fiction

Liza of Lambeth. 1897, New York 1921, London 1930 (with preface by Maugham), 1947 (with expanded preface).
The making of a saint: a romance of medieval Italy. Boston 1898, London 1898.
Orientations: short stories. 1899.
The hero. 1901.
Mrs Craddock. 1902, New York 1920, London 1928 (rev).
The merry-go-round. 1904, New York 1904.
The land of the Blessed Virgin: sketches and impressions in Andalusia. 1905, New York 1920, 1921 (as Andalusia: sketches and impressions).
The bishop's apron: a study in the origins of a great family. 1906. Novel version of the play Loaves and fishes, 1911.
The explorer. 1908 (for 1907), Boston 1908.
The magician. 1908, New York 1909.
Of human bondage. New York 1915, London 1915, New Haven 1938 (introd by T. Dreiser), New York 1956 (Modern Library edn, introd by R. A. Cordell), 1967 (abridged, introd by Maugham).
The moon and sixpence. 1919, New York [1919], [1941] (with excerpts from author's letters).
The trembling of a leaf: little stories of the South Sea Islands. New York 1921, London 1921, [1928] (as Sadie Thompson and other stories of the South Seas), New York 1932 (as Rain and other stories of the South Sea islands).

On a Chinese screen. New York [1922], London 1922. Travel.

The painted veil. New York 1925, London 1925.

The casuarina tree: six stories. 1926, New York 1926, London [1930] (as The letter: stories of crime).

Ashenden: or the British agent. 1928, New York 1928. Stories.

Cakes and ale: or the skeleton in the cupboard. 1930, New York 1930, 1950 (with preface by Maugham), London 1954.

The gentleman in the parlour: a record of a journey from Rangoon to Haiphong. 1930, Garden City NY 1930.

Six stories written in the first person singular. Garden City NY 1931, London 1931.

The book-bag. Florence 1932. Story, rptd in Ah King.

The narrow corner. 1932, New York 1932.

Ah King: six stories. 1933, Garden City NY 1933.

The judgment seat. 1934. Story, rptd in Cosmopolitans.

Don Fernando: or variations on some Spanish themes. 1935, Garden City NY 1935, London 1950 (rev). Travel and criticism.

Cosmopolitans. Garden City NY 1936, London 1936 (with subtitle, Very short stories).

My South Sea island. Chicago 1936 (50 copies). Travel, rptd from Daily Mail 31 Jan 1922.

Theatre. Garden City NY 1937, London 1937.

The summing up. 1938, Garden City NY 1938. See Collections, above, The partial view, 1954.

Christmas holiday. [1939], New York 1939.

Princess September and the nightingale. 1939. Rptd from The gentleman in the parlour, 1930, above.

Books and you. 1940, Garden City NY 1940. Essays rptd from Saturday Evening Post.

France at war. 1940, New York 1940. Essay.

The mixture as before: short stories. 1940, New York 1940, 1947 (as Great stories of love and intrigue).

Strictly personal. Garden City NY 1941, London 1942. Autobiography, previously serialised in Saturday Evening Post 29 March–12 April 1941 (as Novelist's flight from France).

Up at the villa. New York 1941, London 1941. Previously serialised in Red Book Mag as The villa on the hill.

The hour before dawn. Garden City NY 1942.

The unconquered: a short story. New York 1944; rptd (rev) in Creatures of circumstance, 1947, below.

The razor's edge. Garden City NY 1944, London 1944.

Of human bondage, with a digression on the art of fiction: an address. Washington 1946. On the occasion of presenting the original ms to the Library of Congress.

Then and now. 1946, Garden City NY 1946.

Creatures of circumstance: short stories. 1947, Garden City NY 1947.

Catalina: a romance. 1948, Garden City NY 1948. First pbd serially in The Windmill 1948.

Great novelists and their novels: essays on the ten greatest novels of the world and the men and women who wrote them. Philadelphia [1948], London 1954 (rev as Ten novels and their authors), Garden City NY 1955 (rev, as The art of fiction). Essays, originally pbd in Atlantic Monthly 1947–8 except that on Tolstoy.

A writer's notebook. 1949, Garden City NY 1949; rptd in The partial view (see Collections, above, 1954).

The writer's point of view. 1951. National Book League lecture.

The vagrant mood: six essays. 1952, Garden City NY 1953.

Points of view. 1958, Garden City NY 1959. Essays.

Purely for my pleasure. 1962, Garden City NY 1963. On his art collection.

Many of Maugham's short stories were first pbd in various magazines: for a listing of these see Jonas, bibliography, above. Maugham was joint editor, with L. Housman, of the periodical Venture: an annual of art and literature, *2 vols 1903–5.*

Plays

Plays are listed in order of production, not of pbn.

Schiffbrüchig. (Schall und Rauch, Berlin 3 Jan 1902). Not pbd. English version, Marriages are made in heaven: a play in one act, pbd in Venture 1 1903.

A man of honour: a play in four acts. (Stage Soc, at the Imperial 22 Feb 1903). 1903, Chicago [1912]. Also pbd as suppl to Fortnightly Rev March 1903.

Mademoiselle Zampa: a new one-act farce. (Avenue 18 Feb 1904). Not pbd.

Lady Frederick: a comedy in three acts. (Court 26 Oct 1907). 1912, Chicago 1912, London [1947] (French's Acting Edn).

Jack Straw: a farce in three acts. (Vaudeville 26 March 1908). 1912, Chicago 1912.

Mrs Dot: a farce in three acts. (Comedy 27 April 1908). 1912, Chicago 1912.

The explorer: a melodrama in four acts. (Lyric 13 June 1908). 1912, Chicago [1912].

Penelope: a comedy in three acts. (Comedy 9 Jan 1909). 1912, Chicago [1912].

The noble Spaniard: a comedy in three acts, adapted from the French of Grenet-Dancourt. (New Royalty 20 March 1909). 1953 (Evans' Acting Edn).

Smith: a comedy in four acts. (Comedy 30 Sept 1909). 1913, Chicago [1913].

The tenth man: a tragic comedy in three acts. (Globe 24 Feb 1910). 1913, Chicago [1913].

Grace: a play in four acts. (Duke of York's 15 Oct 1910). Pbd as Landed gentry: a comedy in four acts 1913, Chicago [1913].

Loaves and fishes: a comedy in four acts. (Duke of York's 24 Feb 1911). 1924.

The perfect gentleman: an adaptation of Molière's Le bourgeois gentilhomme. (His Majesty's 27 May 1913). Not pbd.

The land of promise: a comedy in four acts. (Lyceum, New York 25 Dec 1913; Duke of York's 26 Feb 1914). 1913, New York 1923.

Caroline: a light comedy in three acts. (New 8 Feb 1916). Pbd 1923 as The unattainable: a farce in three acts.

Our betters: a comedy in three acts. (Hudson, New York 12 March 1917; Globe 12 Sept 1923). 1923, New York 1924.

Love in a cottage. (Globe 26 Jan 1918). In 4 acts; not pbd.

Caesar's wife: a comedy in three acts. (Royalty 27 March 1919). 1922, New York 1923.

Home and beauty: a farce in three acts. (Playhouse 30 Aug 1919; Booth, New York 8 Oct 1919, as Too many husbands). 1923, [1951] (French's Acting Edn).

The unknown: a play in three acts. (Aldwych 9 Aug 1920). 1920, New York 1920.

The circle: a comedy in three acts. (Haymarket 3 March 1921). 1921, New York 1921, London 1948 (French's Acting Edn).

East of Suez: a play in seven scenes. (His Majesty's 2 Sept 1922). 1922, New York 1922.

The camel's back: a new farce in three acts. (Vanderbilt, New York 13 Nov 1923; Playhouse 31 Jan 1924). Not pbd.

The constant wife: a comedy in three acts. (Maxine Elliott, New York 29 Nov 1926; Strand 6 April 1927). New York [1927], London 1927, [1949] (French's Acting Edn).

The letter: a play in three acts. (Playhouse 24 Feb 1927). 1927, New York 1927, London 1949 (French's Acting Edn). Dramatization of the story pbd in the preceding year.

The sacred flame: a play in three acts. (Henry Miller, New York 19 Nov 1928; Playhouse 8 Feb 1929). New York 1928, London 1928, 1948 (French's Acting Edn).

The breadwinner: a comedy in one act. (Vaudeville 30 Sept 1930). 1930, Garden City NY 1931, London 1948 (French's Acting Edn).

For services rendered: a play in three acts. (Globe 1 Nov 1932). 1932, Garden City NY 1933, London [1948] (French's Acting Edn).

The mask and the face: a satire in three acts, tr from a play by L. Chiarelli. (Fifty-Second Street Th, New York 8 May 1933). Not pbd.

Sheppey: a play in three acts. (Wyndham's 14 Sept 1933). 1933, 1948 (French's Acting Edn).

According to Mander and Mitchenson (see Bibliographies, above) Maugham wrote in 1924 a play in 3 acts, The road uphill, which was never produced. For plays adapted from Maugham's novels and stories, see Mander and Mitchenson.

§2

Eaton, W. P. A playwright who stumbled into fame. Harper's Weekly 10 Oct 1908.

Beerbohm, M. Maugham. Saturday Rev 9 Jan 1909.

Dreiser, T. As a realist sees Of human bondage. New Republic 5 1915; rptd in New Republic Anthology 1915–35, New York 1936.

Adcock, A. St J. In his Gods of modern Grub Street, 1923.

Mais, S. P. B. In his Some modern authors, 1923.

Walkley, A. B. In his More prejudice, 1923. On East of Suez.

Overton, G. M. The heterogeneous magic of Maugham. In his Authors of the day, 1924.

Sutton, G. W. In his Some contemporary dramatists, 1924.

Towne, C. H. (et al). W. Somerset Maugham: novelist, essayist, dramatist. New York 1925. Also includes an article by Maugham, To a young novelist.

Dottin, P. Le réalisme de Maugham. Revue de France 1 June 1926.

— Maugham et ses romans. Paris 1928.

— Le théâtre de Maugham. Paris 1937.

Morgan, L. In her writers at work, 1927.

Brewster, D. and J. A. Burrell. Time passes. In their Adventure or experience, New York 1930. On Of human bondage.

MacCarthy, D. Maugham, the English Maupassant: an appreciation. Nash's Pall Mall Mag 93 1933. Pbd separately 1934.

— Maugham and Noel Coward. In his Humanities, 1953.

— Theatre. 1954. Reprints various reviews of Maugham's plays.

Marchand, L. A. The exoticism of Maugham. Revue Anglo-américaine 10 1933; rptd in The Maugham enigma, ed K. W. Jonas, New York 1954, below.

Quéry, S. La philosophie de Maugham. Paris 1933.

Swinnerton, F. A. Black and white. In his Georgian scene, 1934.

— Maugham as a writer. John o' London's Weekly 22 Jan 1954; rptd in The world of Somerset Maugham, ed K. W. Jonas 1959, below.

— Maugham at eighty. Saturday Rev 23 Jan 1954; rptd in Saturday Review gallery, ed J. Winterich, New York 1959.

— In his Figures in the foreground, 1963.

Williams, O. Realistic prose drama: Maugham's last plays. Nat Rev 102 1934.

Ervine, St J. Maugham the playwright. Life & Letters 11 1935; rptd in The world of Maugham, ed K. W. Jonas 1959, below.

Greene, G. Spanish gold. Spectator 21 June 1935. On Don Fernando; rptd in The Maugham enigma, ed K. W. Jonas, New York 1954, below.

McIver, C. S. Maugham: a study of technique and literary sources. Philadelphia 1936.

Mackay, L. A. Maugham. Canadian Forum 16 1936.

Schreiber, G. In his Portraits and self-portraits, 1936.

Cordell, R. A. W. Somerset Maugham. New York 1937.

— Maugham at eighty. College Eng 15 1954.

— Maugham: lucidity versus cunning. Eng Fiction in Transition 1 1958.

— The theatre of Maugham. Modern Drama 1 1959.

— Somerset Maugham: a biographical and critical study. Bloomington 1961, 1969 (lengthened).

Flement, A. Cap Ferrat: Maugham. Revue de Paris 15 Oct 1937.

Muller, H. J. Realism of the center: Bennett, Galsworthy, Maugham. In his Modern fiction, New York 1937.

Sée, E. Le théâtre de Maugham. Revue de France 15 Sept 1937.

Ward, R. H. W. Somerset Maugham. 1937.

Brown, J. M. Maugham and Coward compared. In his Two on the aisle, New York 1938.

Aldington, R. W. Somerset Maugham: an appreciation. New York 1939.

Kruschwitz, H. Die Rassenfrage in Maughams Alien corn. Zeitschrift für Neusprachlichen Unterricht 38 1939–40.

— Die Darstellung der englischen Gesellschaft in Maughams Lustspiel Jack Straw. Ibid.

Savini, G. Das Weltbild in Maughams Dramen. Erlangen 1939.

Waugh, E. The technician. Spectator 17 Feb 1939; rptd in The Maugham enigma, ed K. W. Jonas, New York 1954, below.

Aas, L. W. Somerset Maugham. Samtiden 51 1940.

Spencer, T. Maugham: an appreciation. College Eng 2 1940; rptd in The Maugham enigma, ed K. W. Jonas, New York 1954, below.

Van Gelder, R. Mr Maugham on the essentials of writing. New York Times Book Rev 24 Nov 1940; rptd in his Writers and writing, New York 1946.

Montague, C. M. William Somerset Maugham. Poet Lore 47 1941.

Carbuccia, H. Adieu à mon ami anglais. Paris 1942.

Scully, F. In his Rogues' gallery, Hollywood 1943.

Bason, F. T. Mr Somerset Maugham. Saturday Book 5 1945.

— Fred Bason's diary. 1950.

Connolly, C. The art of being good. In his Condemned playground, 1945. On The razor's edge.

Pfeiffer, K. G. Maugham—as I know him. Redbook Mag May 1945.

— Maugham: a candid portrait. New York 1959.

Stokes, S. W. Maugham: his attitude towards the drama and his dictum on the theatre. Theatre Arts Mag 29 1945; rptd in Theatre arts anthology, ed R. Gilder 1950.

Mr Somerset Maugham. TLS 27 April 1946.

Paul, D. Maugham and two myths. Cornhill Mag 162 1946; rptd in The Maugham enigma, ed K. W. Jonas, New York 1954, below.

Ross, W. O. Maugham: theme and variations. College Eng 8 1946; rptd in The Maugham enigma, ed K. W. Jonas, New York 1954, below.

Webster, H. T. The possible influence of Gissing's Workers in the dawn on Maugham's Of human bondage. MLQ 7 1946.

Wilson, E. The apotheosis of Maugham. New Yorker 8 June 1946; rptd in his Classics and commercials, New York 1950.

Hichens, R. In his Yesterday [autobiography], 1947.

Wescott, G. Maugham and posterity. Harper's Mag 195 1947; rptd in The world of Maugham, ed K. W. Jonas 1959, below, and in Wescott's Images of truth, New York 1962.

'Marlow, Louis' (L. U. Wilkinson). Somerset Maugham. In Writers of today 2nd ser, ed D. V. Baker 1948.

— In his Seven friends, 1953.

Gordon, C. Notes on Chekhov and Maugham. Sewanee Rev 57 1949.

Angoff, C. Maugham. American Mercury 70 1950.

Morgan, C. Maugham's workshop. Spectator 7 Oct 1950; rptd in The Maugham enigma, ed K. W. Jonas, New York 1954, below.

Mustanoja, T. F. Maugham portrays Henry James. Neuphilologische Mitteilungen 52 1951.

Spence, R. Maugham's Of human bondage: the making of a masterpiece. Univ Pennsylvania Chron 17 1951.

Brophy, J. Somerset Maugham. 1952, 1958 (rev) (Br Council pamphlet).

Kronenberger, L. Maugham. In his Thread of laughter: chapters on English stage comedy, New York 1952.

Papajewski, H. Die Welt-, Lebens- und Kunstanschauung Maughams. Cologne 1952.

Cosman, M. A pattern of doubt. Arizona Quart 9 1953.
— Maugham as footnote. Pacific Spectator 10 1956.

Jonas, K. W. Maugham. Archiv für das Studium der Neueren Sprachen 189 1953.
— (ed). The Maugham enigma. New York 1954. Rptd articles, many listed separately above.

Jonas, K. W. The gentleman from Cap Ferrat. New Haven 1956; rptd in his World of Maugham, 1959, below.
— The Center of Maugham Studies. Stechert Hafner Book News 13 1959.
— Maugham: an appreciation. Books Abroad 33 1959.
— (ed). The world of Maugham. 1959. Preface by Maugham; contains, in addition to various rptd articles listed separately above, a note by Jonas on Maugham collections, an article by Jonas on Maugham and the East and one by M. C. Kuner on Maugham and the West.

Duesberg, J. Les 80 ans de Maugham. Synthèses March 1954.

Engelborghs, M. Maugham en de populariteit van zijn romans. Dietsche Warande en Belfort July 1954.

John o' London's Weekly 22 Jan 1954. An issue largely devoted to Maugham.

Krim, S. Somerset Maugham. Commonweal 61 1954.
— Maugham the artist. Ibid.

Maugham, F. H. At the end of the day. 1954. Reminiscences.

Nakano, Y. et al. Studies of Maugham. Tokyo 1954.

Natan, A. Somerset Maugham. Deutsche Rundschau 80 1954.

Waugh, A. Maugham at eighty. Encounter 2 1954.

Dobrinsky, J. Aspects biographiques de l'oeuvre de Maugham: l'enfance. Études Anglaises 8 1955.
— Les débuts de Maugham au théâtre. Études Anglaises 10 1957.

Doner, D. Spinoza's Ethics and Maugham. Univ of Kansas City Rev 21 1955.

Mander, R. and J. Mitchenson. Theatrical companion to Maugham: a pictorial record of the first performances of the plays of Maugham, with an appreciation of Maugham's dramatic works by J. C. Trewin. [1955].

Breit, H. Maugham and Evelyn Waugh. In his Writer observed, 1956.

Fielden, J. S. Mrs Beamish and The circle. Boston Univ Stud in Eng 2 1956.
— Maugham on the purpose of drama. Educational Theatre Jnl 10 1958.
— The Ibsenite Maugham. Modern Drama 4 1961.

Ueda, T. Somerset Maugham. Tokyo 1956.

Grötz, A. Maughams Erzählung The outstation: ein Beitrag zur Gentleman Thematik. Die Neueren Sprachen 6 1957.

Highet, G. The magician. In his Talents and geniuses, New York 1957.

Jensen, S. A. Maugham: some aspects of the man and his work. Oslo 1957.

Zabel, M. D. A cool hand. In his Craft and character in modern fiction, New York 1957. On Up at the villa.

Davies, H. Pilgrims not strangers. In his A mirror of the ministry in modern novels, New York 1959. On Rain.

Hassall, C. Edward Marsh. 1959. Includes some unpbd Maugham letters.

Viswanath, G. V. The novels of Maugham. Quest (Bombay) no 23 1959.

Brown, A. B. Substance and shadow: the originals of the characters in Cakes and ale. Papers of Michigan Acad of Sciences, Arts & Letters 45 1960.

Boothby, R. J. The Maugham 'legend'. In his My yesterday, your tomorrow, 1962.

Brander, L. Maugham: a guide. Edinburgh 1963.

Belloc, E. The stories of Maugham. Month 217 1964.

Redlin, R. Maugham: On a Chinese screen. Die Neueren Sprachen 13 1964.

Menard, W. The two worlds of Maugham. Los Angeles [1965].
— Maugham and Gauguin. Michigan Quart Rev 7 1968.
— Maugham in Hollywood. Ibid.

Heywood, C. Maugham's debt to Madame Bovary and Miss Braddon's The doctor's wife. Études Anglaises 19 1966.
— Two printed texts of Maugham's Mrs Craddock. Eng Lang Notes 5 1967. Effect of censorship.

Kanin, G. Remembering Mr Maugham. Introd by Noel Coward 1966.

Maugham, R. Somerset and all the Maughams. 1966.

Moskovit, L. Maugham's Outstation: a single serious effect. Univ of Colorado Stud: Ser in Lang & Lit 10 1966.

Naik, M. K. W. Somerset Maugham. Norman Oklahoma 1966.

Nichols, B. A case of human bondage. 1966. A memoir.

Pollock, J. Maugham and his work. Quart Rev 204 1966.

Barnes, R. E. The dramatic comedy of Maugham. Hague 1968 (Stud in Eng Lit 32).

WILLIAM BABINGTON MAXWELL
1866–1938

§1

Tales of the Thames. 1892. Stories.

The Countess of Maybury; Between you and I. 1901. Stories.

Fabulous fancies. 1903. Stories.

The ragged messenger. 1904, New York 1904.

Vivien. 1905, Buffalo 1905.

The guarded flame. 1906, New York 1906.

Hill Rise. New York [1907], London 1908.

Odd lengths. 1907. Stories.

Seymour Charlton. 1909, New York 1909.

The last man in. 1910, Boston 1912. Play.

The naked truth: a farcical comedy in three acts. 1910, New York [1910]. With 'George Paston' (E. M. Symonds).

The rest cure. 1910, New York 1910.

Mrs Thompson. 1911, New York 1911.

General Mallock's shadow. 1912, New York 1913.

In cotton wool. 1912, New York 1912.

The devil's garden. 1913, Indianapolis 1914.

The mirror and the lamp. 1918, Indianapolis [1918].

Glamour. Indianapolis [1919].

The great interruption. [1919], Indianapolis [1919] (as Life can never be the same). Stories.

A man and his lesson. [1919], Indianapolis [1919].

A remedy against sin. [1920], New York 1920 (as For better, for worse).

A little more: a morality. [1921], New York 1922.

Spinster of this parish. 1922, New York 1922.

The day's journey. 1923, Garden City NY 1923.

Elaine at the gates. 1924, Garden City NY 1924.

Children of the night. 1925. Stories.

Fernande. 1925, New York 1925.

Life: a study of self. Garden City NY 1925, London 1926.

Gabrielle: a romance. 1926, New York 1926.

The case of Bevan Yorke. 1927, Garden City NY 1927 (as Bevan Yorke).

We forget because we must. [1928], Garden City NY 1928.

Himself and Mr Raikes. 1929, Garden City NY 1929 (as The man who pretended).
Like shadows on the wall. [1929]. Stories.
To what green altar? [1930], Garden City NY 1930.
The concave mirror. 1931, New York 1931.
Amos the wanderer. 1932, New York 1932.
This is my man. 1933, New York 1933.
And Mr Wyke Bond. [1934], New York 1935.
The people of a house. 1934, New York 1934.
Tudor Green. 1935, New York 1936. First vol of series Men and women.
The emotional journey. 1936, New York 1937. 2nd vol of Men and women.
Jacob's ladder, and other stories. [1937].
Time gathered: autobiography. [1937], New York [1938].
Everslade. 1938. 3rd vol of Men and women.

§2

Adcock, A. St J. In his Gods of modern Grub Street, 1923.
'Lacon' (E. H. L. Watson). In his Lectures on living authors, 1925.
Braybrooke, P. In his Novelists: we are seven, 1926.

ETHEL COLBURN MAYNE
187?–1941

The clearer vision. 1898.
Jessie Vandeleur. 1902.
The fourth ship. 1908.
Enchanters of men. 1909, Philadelphia [1909]. Biographical sketches.
The romance of Monaco and its rulers. 1910, New York 1910.
Things that no one tells. 1910. Stories.
Byron. 2 vols 1912, New York 1912 (1 vol), London 1924 (rev), New York 1924.
Browning's heroines. 1913, New York 1914.
Gold lace: a study of girlhood. 1913.
One of our grandmothers. 1916.
Come in. 1917. Stories.
Blindman. 1919. Stories.
Nine of hearts. 1923, New York 1923. Stories.
Inner circle. 1925, New York 1925. Stories.
The life and letters of Anne Isabella, Lady Noel Byron. 1929, New York 1929.
A Regency chapter: Lady Bessborough and her friendships. 1939.

Ethel C. Mayne contributed stories to Yellow Book *and* Chapman's Magazine, *1895–6, as 'Frances E. Huntly'. She also pbd a number of trns.*

VIOLA MEYNELL
1886–1956

Collections

Collected stories. 1957.

§1

Martha Vine: a love story of a simple life. 1910.
Cross-in-Hand Farm. [1911].
Lot Barrow. 1913, Boston 1913.
Modern lovers. 1914, Boston [1914].
Columbine. 1915, New York 1915.
Narcissus. 1916, New York 1916.
Julian Grenfell. [1917]. Rptd from Dublin Rev.
Second marriage. 1918, New York 1919.
Verses. 1919.
Antonia. 1921.
Young Mrs Cruse. 1924, New York 1925. Stories.

A girl adoring. 1927, New York [1928].
Alice Meynell: a memoir. 1929, New York 1929.
The frozen ocean and other poems. 1930.
Follow thy fair sun. 1935.
Kissing the rod and other stories. 1937.
First love and other stories. 1947.
Ophelia. 1951.
Francis Thompson and Wilfred Meynell: a memoir. 1952, New York 1953.
Louise, and other stories. 1954.

§2

Johnson, R. B. Viola Meynell. In his Some contemporary novelists: women, 1920.
Bogan, L. Viola Meynell. In Literary opinion in America, ed M. D. Zabel, New York 1937.
Maguire, C. E. Another Meynell. Renascence 11 1959.

RICHARD BARHAM MIDDLETON
1882–1911

Bibliographies

Savage, H. In his Richard Middleton, 1922, below. Includes a list of articles on Middleton.
See also The pantomime man (below).

Collections and Selections

The pantomime man. Ed with foreword by 'John Gawsworth' (T. I. F. Armstrong), introd by A. Douglas 1933. Contains A diary of youth [1903–5], Tales and fantasies [17 stories], A poet's holiday [essays], Literary papers, Occasional pieces and descriptive bibliography.
Richard Middleton. Ed 'John Gawsworth' (T. I. F. Armstrong) 1937. Selected poems.

§1

The ghost ship & other stories, with an introduction by A. Machen. Ed H. Savage 1912, New York 1912.
The day before yesterday. Ed H. Savage 1912, New York 1913. Childhood sketches.
Poems & songs, with an introduction by H. Savage. 2 ser 1912, New York 1912–13.
Monologues. Ed H. Savage 1913, New York 1914. Essays.
The district visitor, with a short sketch of his [i.e. Middleton's] life. Baltimore 1924. Play.

Most of Middleton's writings were first pbd in Academy, Eng Rev *and* Vanity Fair.

Letters

Richard Middleton's letters to Henry Savage, with introd and comments by the recipient. 1929.

§2

Harris, F. Richard Middleton ad memoriam. Rhythm 2 1912; rptd in his Contemporary portraits ser 1, 1915.
Mais, S. P. B. Richard Middleton. Fortnightly Rev new ser 100 1916; rptd in his From Shakespeare to O. Henry, 1923.
Savage, H. Richard Middleton: the man and his work. 1922. Includes list of earlier articles by Savage on Middleton.
Starrett, V. Two suicides (Crackanthorpe and Middleton). In his Buried Caesars, 1923.
Chapman, J. A. Richard Middleton. In his Papers on Shelley, Wordsworth and others, 1929.

C.P.C.

ALAN ALEXANDER MILNE
1882–1956

Selections

[Selected works]. 7 vols [1926] (Minerva Edns of Modern Authors). The Red House mystery, and the collections of essays and sketches only.

A. A. Milne. 1933 (Methuen's Lib of Humour).

§I
Fiction, Prose and Verse

Lovers in London. 1905.

The day's play. 1910. Sketches and verse rptd from Punch.

The holiday round. 1912. Sketches rptd from Punch.

Once a week. 1914, New York [1925]. Sketches rptd from Punch.

Happy days. New York [1915]. Sketches rptd from Punch.

Not that it matters. 1919, New York [1920]. Essays.

If I may. 1920, New York [1921]. Essays.

Mr Pim. [1921], New York 1922, London 1929 (as Mr Pim passes by). Based on the play; see below.

The sunny side. 1921, New York 1922. Sketches and verse mainly rptd from Punch.

The Red House mystery. 1922, New York [1922], 1926 (with introd by Milne).

For the luncheon interval: cricket and other verses. 1925.

The ascent of man. 1928.

By way of introduction. 1929, New York [1929]. Prefaces, reviews and essays.

The secret, and other stories. New York 1929.

Those were the days: The day's play; The holiday round; Once a week; The sunny side. 1929. The collected Punch writings, with 'Prelude' by Milne.

When I was very young. 1930, New York 1930. Autobiography, illustr E. H. Shepard.

Two people. 1931, New York 1931.

Four days' wonder. 1933, New York [1933].

Peace with honour: an enquiry into the War Convention. 1934, New York [1934] (with special preface for the American edn), London 1935 (enlarged), New York 1935.

It's too late now: the autobiography of a writer. 1939, New York 1939 (as Autobiography).

Behind the lines. 1940, New York [1940]. Verse.

War with honour. 1940 (Macmillan War pamphlets).

War aims unlimited. 1941. Pamphlet.

Chloe Marr. 1946, New York 1946.

Going abroad? [1947]. Pamphlet on travel.

Birthday party, and other stories. New York 1948, London 1949.

Books for children. 1948 (National Book League Reader's Guide).

The Norman church. 1948. Verse.

A table near the band, and other stories. 1950, New York 1950.

Year in, year out. 1952. Monthly calendar of reminiscences, sketches and essays, illustr E. H. Shepard.

Milne was assistant editor of Punch *1906–14.*

Children's Books

Once on a time. 1917, New York 1922.

Make-believe: a children's play in a prologue and three acts, the lyrics by C. E. Burton. (Lyric, Hammersmith 24 Dec 1918). In Second plays, 1921, below (with new prologue and without lyrics); pbd separately 1925 (French's Acting Edn) (with lyrics).

When we were very young. 1924, New York [1924]. Verse.

A gallery of children. 1925, Philadelphia [1925]. Stories.

Winnie-the-Pooh. 1926, New York 1926. Stories.

Now we are six. 1927, New York [1927]. Verse.

The house at Pooh Corner. 1928, New York [1928]. Stories.

Toad of Toad Hall: a play from Grahame's book The wind in the willows. (Lyric 17 Dec 1930). 1929, New York 1929, London [1932] (French's Acting Edn).

Prince Rabbit, and the princess who could not laugh. 1966, New York 1966.

Milne pbd a number of selections of his children's stories and verse under various titles.

Plays

Plays are listed in order of production where known.

Wurzel-Flummery: a comedy in two acts. (New 7 April 1917). [1921] (French's Acting edn). Rev version in one act pbd in First plays, 1919, below, and pbd separately 1922 (French's Acting Edn).

Belinda: an April folly in three acts. (New 8 April 1918). In First plays, 1919, below. Pbd separately 1922 (French's Acting Edn).

The boy comes home: a comedy in one act. (Victoria Palace 9 Sept 1918). In First plays, 1919, below. Pbd separately 1926 (French's Acting Edn).

Make-believe. 1918. *See* above, Children's books.

The Camberley triangle: a comedy in one act. (Coliseum 8 Sept 1919). In Second plays, 1921, below. Pbd separately 1925 (French's Acting Edn).

First plays. 1919, New York 1930. Wurzel-Flummery; The lucky one; The boy comes home; Belinda; The red feathers.

Mr Pim passes by: a comedy in three acts. (Gaiety, Manchester 1 Dec 1919; New 5 Jan 1920). In Second plays, 1921, below. Pbd separately 1921 (French's Acting Edn). For the novel *see* Fiction, etc, above.

The romantic age: a comedy in three acts. (Comedy 18 Oct 1920). In Second plays, 1921, below. Pbd separately 1922 (French's Acting Edn).

The stepmother: a play in one act. (Alhambra 16 Nov 1920). In Second plays, 1921, below. Pbd separately 1921 (French's Acting Edn).

Second plays. 1921. Make-believe; Mr Pim passes by; The Camberley triangle; The romantic age; The stepmother.

The great Broxopp: four chapters in her life—a comedy. (Punch and Judy, New York 14 Nov 1921; St Martin's 6 March 1923). In Three plays, 1922, below.

The truth about Blayds: a comedy in three acts. (Globe 20 Dec 1921). In Three plays, 1922, below. Pbd separately 1923 (French's Acting Edn).

The Dover road: a comedy in three acts. (New Bijou 23 Dec 1921; Haymarket 7 June 1922). In Three plays, 1922, below. Pbd separately 1923 (French's Acting Edn).

The lucky one. (Garrick, New York 20 Nov 1922). In First plays, 1919, above.

Three plays: The Dover road; The truth about Blayds; The Great Broxopp. New York 1922, London 1923.

Success. (Haymarket 21 June 1923; Charles Hopkins, New York 4 March 1931, as Give me yesterday). In Four plays, 1926 below.

The artist: a duologue. [1923].

To have the honour: a comedy in three acts. (Wyndham's 22 April 1924; Lyceum, New York 25 Feb 1929, as To meet the prince). [1925] (French's Acting Edn).

The man in the bowler hat: a terribly exciting affair. (New York Belasco 5 May 1924). [1923] (French's Acting Edn).

Ariadne, or business first: a comedy in three acts. (Garrick, New York 25 Feb 1925; Haymarket 22 April 1925). [1925] (French's Acting Edn).

Portrait of a gentleman in slippers: a comedy in one act. (Liverpool Repertory 4 Sept 1926). In Four plays, 1926, below.

Four plays. 1926. To have the honour; Ariadne; Portrait of a gentleman in slippers; Success.

Miss Marlow at play: a one-act comedy. (Coliseum 11 April 1927). [1936] (French's Acting Edn).

The ivory door: a legend in a prologue and three acts. (Charles Hopkins, New York 18 Oct 1927; Haymarket 17 April 1929). New York 1928, London 1929, [1930] (French's Acting Edn).

The fourth wall: a detective story in three acts. (Haymarket 29 Feb 1928; Charles Hopkins, New York 27 Nov 1928, as The perfect alibi). New York [1929], London [1930] (French's Acting Edn).

Toad of Toad Hall. 1929. *See* above, Children's books.

Michael and Mary: a play in three acts. (St James's, New York 1 Feb 1930). 1930, [1932] (French's Acting Edn).

Four plays: Michael and Mary; To meet the prince; The perfect alibi; Portrait of a gentleman in slippers. New York 1932.

Other people's lives: a play in three acts. (Wyndhams 11 July 1933). [1935] (French's Acting Edn).

Sarah Simple: a comedy in three acts. (Garrick 4 May 1937). [1939] (French's Acting Edn).

Miss Elizabeth Bennet: a play from Pride and prejudice (People's Palace 3 Feb 1938). 1936.

The ugly duckling: a play in one act. [1941] (French's Acting Edn).

Before the Flood: a play in one act. [1951] (French's Acting Edn).

Milne also wrote the following unpbd plays: Let's all talk about Gerald (*Arts 11 May 1928*); They don't mean any harm (*Charles Hopkins, New York 23 Feb 1932*); Gentleman unknown (*St James's 16 Nov 1928*).

M.P.

NAOMI MARY MARGARET MITCHISON, née HALDANE
b. 1897

The conquered. 1923.
When the bough breaks and other stories. 1924.
Cloud cuckoo land. 1925, New York [1926].
The laburnum branch. 1926. Verse.
Anna Comnena. 1928. Biography.
Black Sparta: Greek stories. 1928, New York [1928].
Nix-nought-nothing: four plays for children. 1928.
Barbarian stories. 1929, New York 1929.
Comments on birth control. 1930.
The hostages. 1930, New York [1931]. Children's stories.
Boys and girls and gods. 1931. For children.
The corn king and the spring queen. 1931, New York 1961 (as The barbarian).
The price of freedom. 1931. Play, with L. E. Gielgud.
The powers of light. [1932].
The delicate fire: short stories and poems. 1933, New York 1933.
The home and a changing civilisation. 1934.
Naomi Mitchison's Vienna diary. 1934, New York 1934.
Beyond this limit; pictures by Wyndham Lewis and words by N. Mitchison. 1935.
We have been warned. 1935, New York 1936.
The fourth pig: stories and verses. 1936.
An end and a beginning, and other plays. 1937.
Socrates. 1937. With R. H. S. Crossman.
The moral basis of politics. 1938.
The Alban goes out. [Harrow] 1939. Verse.
As it was in the beginning. 1939. Play, with L. E. Gielgud.
The blood of the martyrs. 1939.
Historical plays for schools. [1939].
The kingdom of heaven. 1939. Non-fiction.
The bull calves. 1947.
Nix-nought-nothing, and Elfin Hall: two plays for children. 1948.
Men and herring: a documentary. Edinburgh 1949. With D. Macintosh.
The big house. 1950. For children.
Spindrift. [1951]. Play, with D. Macintosh.

Lobsters on the agenda. 1952.
Travel light. 1952.
Graeme and the dragon. 1954. For children.
The swan's road. 1954. On the Vikings. For children.
The land the ravens found. 1955. For children.
To the Chapel Perilous. 1955.
Little boxes. 1956. For children.
Behold your king. [1957].
The far harbour. 1957. For children.
Five men and a swan. 1957. Stories and verse.
Other people's worlds. 1958. On Ghana and Nigeria.
Judy and Lakshmi. 1959. For children.
The rib of the green umbrella. 1960. For children.
The young Alexander the Great. 1960. For children.
A fishing village on the Clyde. 1961. With G. W. L. Paterson.
Karensgaard: the story of a Danish farm. 1961. For children.
Presenting other people's children. [1961]. Non-fiction.
Memoirs of a spacewoman. 1962.
The young Alfred the Great. [1962], New York 1963. For children.
The fairy who couldn't tell a lie. 1963. For children.
Ketse and the chief. 1965. For children.
When we become men. 1965.
The conquered land. 1966.
Friends and enemies. 1966, New York 1968. For children.
Return to the fairy hill. 1966, New York 1966. Travel.
The big surprise. 1967. For children.
Highland holiday. Wellington 1967. For children.
African heroes. 1968, New York 1969. For children.
Don't look back. 1969. For children.
The family at Ditlabeng. 1969. For children.

NANCY FREEMAN MITFORD
b. 1904

Selections
The Nancy Mitford omnibus. 1956. The pursuit of love, Love in a cold climate, The blessing.

§1

Highland fling. 1931.
Christmas pudding. 1932.
Wigs on the green. 1935.
Pigeon pie: a wartime receipt. 1940, New York 1959.
The pursuit of love. 1945, New York 1946.
Love in a cold climate. 1949, New York 1949.
The Princesse de Cleves [by] Madame de Lafayette. Tr N. Mitford 1950, 1962 (rev) (Penguin).
The blessing. 1951, New York 1951.
The little hut, by A. Roussin, adapted from the French by N. Mitford. 1951.
Madame de Pompadour. 1954, 1968 (rev), New York 1968. Biography.
Noblesse oblige: an enquiry into the identifiable characteristics of the English aristocracy by A. S. C. Ross, N. Mitford [et al]. 1956, New York 1956.
Voltaire in love. 1957, New York 1957. Biography.
Don't tell Alfred. 1960, New York 1961.
The water beetle. 1962, New York [1962]. Essays.
The Sun King. 1966, New York 1966. On Louis XIV.

NICHOLAS JOHN TURNEY MONSARRAT
b. 1910

§1

Think of to-morrow. [1934].
At first sight. [1935].

The whipping boy. [1937].
This is the schoolroom. 1939, New York 1940.
H.M. Corvette. 1942, Philadelphia 1943. Reminiscences.
East coast corvette. 1943, Philadelphia 1943. Reminiscences.
Corvette command. 1944. Reminiscences.
Leave cancelled. New York 1945. Rptd in Depends what you mean by love, 1947, below.
Three corvettes. 1945, 1953 (with rev foreword). Reissue of H.M. Corvette, East coast corvette and Corvette command, above.
H.M. Frigate. 1946. Reminiscences.
Depends what you mean by love. 1947, New York 1948. Stories.
My brother Denys. 1948, New York 1948. Reminiscences.
The cruel sea. 1951, New York 1951.
H.M.S. Marlborough will enter harbour. 1952. First pbd in Depends what you mean by love, 1947, above.
The story of Esther Costello. 1953, New York 1953.
Castle Garac. New York 1955.
The tribe that lost its head. 1956, New York 1956.
The ship that died of shame, and other stories. 1959, New York 1959.
The nylon pirates. 1960, New York 1960.
The white rajah. 1961, New York 1961.
The time before this. 1962, New York 1962. Pt of his Signs of the times ser.
Smith and Jones. 1963, New York 1963. Pt of his Signs of the times ser.
To Stratford with love. Toronto [1963]. On the Stratford, Ontario, Shakespeare Festival.
A fair day's work. 1964, New York 1964. Pt of his Signs of the times ser.
The pillow fight. 1965, New York 1965.
Something to hide. 1965, New York 1966. Pt of the Signs of the times ser.
Life is a four-letter word. 1966–. Autobiography.
Richer than all his tribe. 1968, New York 1969.

§2

Jarrett, T. D. The talent of Monsarrat. Eng Jnl 45 1956.

CHARLES EDWARD MONTAGUE
1867–1928
Selections
C. E. Montague. 1926 (Essays of Today and Yesterday).

§1

The Manchester stage 1880–1900: criticisms reprinted from the Manchester Guardian. [1900]. By Montague et al.
William Thomas Arnold, journalist and historian. Manchester 1907, New York 1907. With Mrs Humphry Ward.
A hind let loose. 1910.
Dramatic values. 1911, New York 1911, London 1925 (rev), New York 1925. Essays.
The morning's war: a romance. 1913, New York 1913.
The front line. 1916. Pamphlet on 1914–18 war.
The western front; drawings by Muirhead Bone, with text by C. E. Montague. 2 vols 1917.
Notes from Calais base, and pictures of its many activities. 1918. Pamphlet on 1914–18 war.
Disenchantment. 1922, New York 1922. Essays.
Fiery particles. 1923, New York 1923. Stories.
The right place: a book of pleasures. 1924, New York 1924. Essays.
Rough justice. 1926, New York 1926.
Right off the map. 1927, New York 1927.

Action, and other stories. 1928, New York 1929.
A writer's notes on his trade. Introd by H. M. Tomlinson. 1930, New York 1930. Essays.

§2

Cooper, A. P. In her Authors and others, New York 1927.
Elton, O. C. E. Montague: a memoir. 1929. Contains letters and some uncollected fragments.

CHARLES LANGBRIDGE MORGAN
1894–1958
Bibliographies
Fabes, G. The first editions of A. E. Coppard, A. P. Herbert and Morgan. 1933.

§1

The gunroom. 1919.
My name is Legion. 1925, New York 1925.
Portrait in a mirror. 1929, New York 1929.
The fountain. 1932, New York 1932.
Epitaph on George Moore. 1935, New York 1935.
Sparkenbroke. 1936, New York 1936.
The flashing stream: a play. (Lyric 1 Sept 1938); 1938 (with an essay, On Singleness of mind), New York 1938, London 1948 (rev).
The voyage. 1940, New York 1940.
The empty room. 1941, New York 1941.
Ode to France. [1942].
Du génie français. Paris 1943. Pamphlet.
The house of Macmillan 1843–1943. 1943, New York 1944.
Reflections in a mirror. First ser 1944, 2nd ser 1946.
The artist in the community. Glasgow 1945 (W. P. Ker memorial lecture).
The judge's story. 1947, New York 1947.
The liberty of thought and the separation of powers: a modern problem considered in the context of Montesquieu. 1948 (Zaharoff lecture).
The river line. 1949, New York 1949. First pbd serially in Woman's Home Companion Sept, Oct 1948 (as Edge of happiness); adapted as a play 1952, New York 1952 (with a preface by the author, On transcending the age of violence); first performed Lyric, Hammersmith 2 Sept 1952, Strand 28 Oct 1952.
A breeze of morning. 1951, New York 1951.
Liberties of the mind. 1951, New York 1951. Essays.
The burning glass: a play. (Royal, Brighton 18 Jan 1954; Apollo 18 Feb 1954). 1953 (with a preface, On power over nature), New York 1953, London 1955 (rev).
Dialogue in novels and plays. Aldington [1954], Philadelphia 1954 (Herman Ould Memorial Lecture).
On learning to write. 1954 (Eng Assoc Presidential Address).
Challenge to Venus. 1957, New York 1957.
The writer and his world: lectures and essays. 1960.

Letters
Selected letters, ed E. Lewis. 1967.

§2

Bonnerot, L. Essai sur les romans de Morgan. Revue Anglo-américaine 10 1932.
—— Essai sur le dernier roman de Morgan: Sparkenbroke. Études Anglaises 1 1937.
Gillet, L. Un romancier anglais: Morgan. Revue des Deux Mondes 1 July 1933.
—— Le singulier voyage de Morgan. Revue des Deux Mondes 15 March 1942.
Hourcade, P. Morgan et le roman de la connaissance spirituelle. Cahiers du Sud 21 1934.

Fehr, B. Sparkenbroke und die platonische Idee in England. Die Tatwelt 13 1937.

Michel-Côte, P. Sparkenbroke ou le climat de la pensée anglaise. Revue Hebdomadaire 30 April 1938.

Pintschovius, K. Menschliche Atmosphäre: Gedanken zu Morgans Romanen. Die Neue Rundschau 49 1938.

Sehrt, E. T. Morgans Begriff vom Wesen der Kunst. Germanisch-romanische Monatsschrift 26 1938.

Chastaing, M. L'imagination chez Morgan. Vie Intellectuelle 25 April 1939.

Delere, O. Metaphysik und Ethik in den Werken von Morgan. Bonn 1939.

Madaule, J. Morgan ou la recherche du paradis perdu. Esprit 1 June 1939.

Simon, P.-H. Essai d'une critique chrétienne de Morgan. Vie Intellectuelle 25 April 1939.

Dockhorn, K. Morgan und Hegel. E Studien 74 1940/41.

Héraucourt, W. Morgan: The flashing stream. Ibid.

Papajewski, H. Das Problem der Wirklichkeit bei Morgan. Berlin 1940.

Brie, F. Morgans jüngste Entwicklung. Anglia Beiblatt 53 1942.

Lesort, P.-A. Morgan et l'unité de l'esprit. Cahiers du Sud 29 1942.

Gérard, A. Charles Morgan. Brussels 1943.

— Morgan et l'amour. Tijdschrift voor Levende Talen 9 1943.

— Le thème de la mort dans l'oeuvre de Morgan. Tijdschrift voor Levende Talen 9 1943.

Viebrock, H. Die Bedeutung der Einbildungskraft bei Morgan. Germanisch-romanische Monatsschrift 31 1943.

Vincent, M. A la rencontre de Morgan. Brussels 1947.

Bethell, S. L. Morgan and the nature of criticism. In his Essays on criticism and the English tradition, 1948.

Guyard, M. F. Morgan en France. Revue de Littérature Comparée 23 1949.

Fischer, W. Zu Morgans künstlerischer Entwicklung. Forschungen und Fortschritte 26 1950.

Harding, J. N. Morgan and Browning. Hibbert Jnl 51 1952.

— Morgan and the metaphysic of evil. Contemporary Rev 198 1960.

Effelberger, H. Der literarische Esoteriker Morgan. Die Neueren Sprachen 4 1955.

Duffin, H. C. Morgan's novels. Contemporary Rev 193 1958.

— The novels and plays of Morgan. 1959.

Stanford, D. Un jugement anglais sur Morgan. Études 296 1958.

Vallette, J. Hommage à Morgan. Mercure de France 332 1958.

Madariaga, S. Notice sur la vie et les travaux de Morgan. Paris 1960.

Iklé, C. A. P. Individualität und Transzendenz bei Morgan. Zürich 1961. With bibliography.

Pange, V. de. Charles Morgan. Paris [1962]. With bibliography.

Riesner, D. Morgan: Portrait in a mirror. In Der moderne englische Roman, ed H. Oppel, Berlin 1965.

Cazamian, L. Sparkenbroke de Morgan. Études Anglaises 19 1966.

Calder-Marshall, A. Morgan's Gunroom. TLS 21 Nov 1968.

NANCY AGNES BRYSSON MORRISON
b. 190?

Breakers. 1930.
Solitaire. 1932.
The gowk storm. 1933.
The strangers. 1935.
When the wind blows. 1937.

These are my friends. [1946]. Verse.
The winnowing years. 1949.
The hidden fairing. 1951.
The keeper of time. Edinburgh 1953. On the 12 apostles: for children.
The following wind. 1954.
The other traveller. 1957.
They need no candle: the men who built the Scottish Kirk. 1957, Richmond Va 1957.
Mary, Queen of Scots. 1960, New York 1960.
Thea. New York 1962, London 1963.
The private life of Henry VIII. 1964, New York 1964.
Haworth harvest: the lives of the Brontës. 1969, New York 1969.

RALPH HALE MOTTRAM
1883-1971
Bibliographies

Fabes, G. H. The first editions of Mottram. 1934. Includes works containing contributions by Mottram. With a note, How The Spanish farm came to be written, by Mottram.

§I

Repose, and other verses. 1907. As 'J. Marjoram'.
New poems. 1909. As 'J. Marjoram'.
The Spanish farm. 1924, New York 1924. Vol 1 of trilogy.
Sixty-four, ninety-four. 1925, New York 1925. Vol 2 of trilogy.
The crime at Vanderlinden's. 1926, New York 1926. Vol 3 of trilogy.
The Spanish farm trilogy 1914-18. 1927, New York 1927. With 3 'connecting pieces': D'Archeville; The winner; The stranger.
Our Mr Dormer. 1927.
The apple disdained. 1928. Story, rptd in The headless hound.
The English miss. 1928, New York 1928.
Ten years ago: armistice & other memories, forming a pendant to The Spanish farm trilogy. 1928, New York 1929 (as Armistice and other memories). Sketches and stories.
The boroughmonger. 1929, Boston 1929.
A history of financial speculation. 1929, Boston 1929.
Three personal records of the war. 1929, New York 1930 (as Three men's war). With J. Easton and E. Partridge.
Europa's beast. 1930, New York 1930 (as A rich man's daughter).
Miniature banking histories. 1930.
The new providence. 1930. Story.
The old man of the stones: a Christmas allegory. [1930]. Story.
Poems new and old. 1930.
Castle island. 1931, New York 1931.
The headless hound, and other stories. 1931.
John Crome of Norwich. 1931.
The lost Christmas presents. 1931. Story.
Home for the holidays. 1932.
Dazzle. 1932.
Through the Menin Gate. 1932. Reminiscences.
East Anglia: England's eastern province. 1933.
A good old fashioned Christmas. 1933. Story.
The Lame Dog. 1933, New York 1933 (as At the sign of The Lame Dog).
Bumphrey's. 1934.
Strawberry time, and The banquet. 1934.
The banquet. 1934. With other stories.
Early morning. [1935].
Flower Pot End. 1935.
Journey to the western front: twenty years after. 1936.
Portrait of an unknown Victorian. 1936. Biography of James Mottram.
The Westminster Bank 1836-1936. 1936.

Noah. 1937 (Biblical biographies 9).
Old England: illustrated by English paintings of the 18th and early 19th centuries. 1937.
Success to the mayor: a narrative of the development of local self-government in a provincial centre, Norwich, during eight centuries. 1937.
Time to be going. [1937].
Autobiography with a difference. 1938.
There was a jolly miller. [1938].
Miss Lavington. [1939].
Traders' dream: the romance of the East India Company. New York 1939.
You can't have it back! [1939].
Bowler hat: a last glance at the old country banking. 1940.
The ghost and the maiden. [1940].
The Norwich players. Norwich [1940].
The world turns slowly round. [1942].
The Corbells at war. [1943].
Buxton the liberator. [1946]. Life of Sir Thomas Fowell Buxton.
Visit of the princess: a romance of the nineteen-sixties. [1946].
Hibbert Houses. 1947. On welfare centres for the Services.
The gentleman of leisure: a romance. [1948].
The glories of Norwich Cathedral. 1948.
Norfolk. 1948 (Vision of England).
Come to the bower. [1949].
Through five generations: the history of the Butterley Company. 1950. With C. Coote.
One hundred and twenty-eight witnesses. 1951.
The Broads. 1952.
The part that is missing. 1952.
If stones could speak: an introduction to an almost human family. 1953. On Norwich.
John Galsworthy. 1953 (Br Council pamphlet).
The City of Norwich museums 1894–1954: a diamond jubilee record. 1954. Pamphlet.
The window seat: or life observed by R. H. Mottram. 1954.
Over the wall. 1955.
For some we loved: an intimate portrait of Ada and John Galsworthy. 1956.
Scenes that are brightest. 1956.
Another window seat: or life observed by R. H. Mottram; vol 2, 1919–53. 1957.
No one will ever know: or the hidden life of Gregory Wantage. 1958.
Vanities and verities. 1958. Reminiscences.
Young man's fancies. 1959.
Musetta. 1960.
Time's increase. 1961.
To hell, with Crabb Robinson. 1962.
Happy birds. 1964.
Maggie Mackenzie. 1965.
The speaking likeness. 1967.
Behind the shutters. 1968.
Twelve poems. Stoke Ferry Norfolk 1968 (priv ptd).
The twentieth century: a personal record. 1969.

EDWIN MUIR
1887–1959

See cols 316–19 above.

WILLA MUIR
(WILHELMINA JOHNSTONE MUIR, née ANDERSON)
1890–1970

Women: an enquiry. 1925 (Hogarth Essays 10), New York 1926.
Five songs from the Auvergnat, done into modern Scots. Warlingham 1931 (100 copies).

Imagined corners. 1931, New York [1931].
Mrs Ritchie. [1933].
Mrs Grundy in Scotland. 1936. Non-fiction.
Living with ballads. 1965, New York 1965. Non-fiction.
Belonging: a memoir. 1968.
Laconics, jingles, and other verses. 1969 (priv ptd).

Willa Muir made a number of trns in collaboration with Edwin Muir, particularly of various works by Kafka. For details see Edwin Muir, col 318, above, and E. W. Mellown, Bibliography of the writings of E. Muir, University Alabama [1964], London 1966 (rev). Willa Muir also tr a number of novels under the pseudonym 'Agnes Neill Scott'; for details see Mellown.

LEOPOLD HAMILTON MYERS
1881–1944

§1

Arvat: a dramatic poem in four acts. 1908.
The Orissers. 1922, New York 1922.
The 'Clio'. 1925, New York 1925.
The near and the far. 1929, New York [1930].
Prince Jali. 1931, New York 1931. Continues The near and the far, above.
The root and the flower. 1935, New York 1935. Contains The near and the far and Prince Jali, both rev, with a new third part, Rajah Amar.
Strange glory. 1936, New York [1936].
The pool of Vishnu. 1940, New York [1940]. Conclusion of The root and the flower, above.
The near and the far: containing The root and the flower and The pool of Vishnu, above. 1940 (Book Society), 1943, New York 1947, London 1956 (with introd by L. P. Hartley).

§2

Harding, D. W. The work of Myers. Scrutiny 3 1934.
Van Doren, M. Connoisseur of character. In his The private reader, 1942.
Prescott, O. Four great novels. In his In my opinion, 1952.
Strong, L. A. G. In his Personal remarks, 1953.
Bantock, G. H. L. H. Myers: a critical study. 1956.
Simon, I. The novels of Myers. Brussels 1956.
Bottrall, R. L. H. Myers. REL 2 1961.

PERCY HOWARD NEWBY
b. 1918

§1

A journey to the interior. 1945, Garden City NY 1946.
Agents and witnesses. 1947, Garden City NY 1947.
The spirit of Jem. 1947. For children.
Mariner dances. 1948.
The loot runners. 1949. For children.
The snow pasture. 1949.
Maria Edgeworth. 1950, Denver 1950. Criticism.
The young may moon. 1950, New York 1951.
The novel 1945–50. 1951 (Br Council pamphlet).
A season in England. 1951, New York 1952.
A step to silence. 1952.
The retreat. 1953, New York 1953.
The picnic at Sakkara. 1955, New York 1955.
Revolution and roses. 1957, New York 1957.
Ten miles from anywhere and other stories. 1958.
A guest and his going. 1959, New York 1960.
The Barbary light. 1962.
One of the founders. 1965, Philadelphia 1965.
The Third Programme. 1965. Lecture.
Something to answer for. 1968, Philadelphia 1969.

§2

Watts, H. H. Newby: experience as farce. Perspective (St Louis) 10 1958.

Dickerson, L. Portrait of the artist as a Jung man. Kenyon Rev 21 1959.

A novelist on his own. TLS 6 April 1962.

Karl, F. R. The novel as moral allegory: the fiction of Golding, Iris Murdoch, Warner, Newby. In his The contemporary English novel, New York 1962, London 1963 (as The reader's guide to the contemporary English novel).

Bufkin, E. C. Quest in the novels of Newby. Critique (Minneapolis) 8 1965.

JOHN BEVERLEY NICHOLS
b. 1899

Prelude. 1920.

Patchwork. 1921, New York 1922.

Self. 1922.

25: being a young man's candid recollections of his elders and betters. [1926], New York [1926].

Are they the same at home? 1927, New York [1927]. Impressions.

Crazy pavements. 1927, New York [1927].

The star-spangled manner. 1928, Garden City NY 1928. Autobiography.

Women and children last. 1931, Garden City NY 1931. Non-fiction.

Down the garden path. 1932, Garden City NY [1932]. Non-fiction.

Evensong. 1932, Garden City NY 1932. Adapted as play, with E. Knoblock, 1933.

For adults only. 1932, Garden City NY 1933.

Cry havoc! 1933, Garden City NY 1933. Non-fiction.

Failures: three plays. 1933. The stag, Avalanche, When the crash comes.

A thatched roof. 1933, Garden City NY [1933]. Non-fiction.

A village in a valley. 1934, Garden City NY 1934. Non-fiction.

How does your garden grow? 1935. Broadcast talks by Nichols et al.

Mesmer: a play in three acts. 1935.

The fool hath said. 1936, Garden City NY 1936. Non-fiction.

No place like home. 1936, Garden City NY 1936. Travel.

News of England: or a country without a hero. 1938, New York 1938. Non-fiction.

Green grows the city: the story of a London garden. 1939, New York [1939].

Revue. 1939, New York 1939.

Men do not weep. 1941, New York 1942. Stories.

Verdict on India. 1944, New York 1944. Non-fiction.

The tree that sat down. 1945, 1960 (abridged with The stream that stood still, 1948, below), New York 1966. For children.

The stream that stood still. 1948, 1960 (abridged, with The tree that sat down, 1945, above), New York 1966. For children.

All I could never be: some recollections. 1949, New York 1952.

Shadow of the vine: a play in three acts. 1949.

Yours sincerely. 1949. Essays; with Monica Dickens.

The mountain of magic: a romance for children. 1950.

Uncle Samson. 1950. Travel in USA.

Merry Hall. 1951, New York 1953. Non-fiction.

A pilgrim's progress. 1952. Non-fiction.

Laughter on the stairs. 1953, New York 1954. Non-fiction.

No man's street. 1954, New York 1954.

The moonflower. 1955, New York 1955 (as The moonflower murder).

Death to slow music. 1956, New York 1956.

Sunlight on the lawn. 1956, New York [1956]. Non-fiction.

The rich die hard. 1957, New York 1958.

The sweet and twenties. [1958], New York 1958. Non-fiction.

Cats' ABC. 1960, New York 1960.

Murder by request. 1960, New York 1960.

Beverley Nichols' Cats' XYZ. 1961, New York 1961.

Garden open today. 1963, New York 1963. Non-fiction.

Forty favourite flowers. 1964, New York 1965.

A case of human bondage. 1966, New York 1966. On Somerset Maugham.

Powers that be. 1966, New York 1966. Non-fiction.

The art of flower arrangement. 1967, New York 1967.

Garden open tomorrow. 1968, New York 1969. Non-fiction.

The sun in my eyes: or how not to go round the world. 1969. Travel.

WILLIAM EDWARD NORRIS
1847-1925

The English first edns of most of Norris' novels up to 1896 were pbd in 2 or 3 vols, the American edns being pbd in one vol.

Heaps of money. 1877, New York 1877.

Mademoiselle de Mersac. 1880, [New York 1880].

Matrimony. 1881, New York 1884.

No new thing. 1883, New York 1883.

Thirlby Hall. 1883, New York 1884.

Adrian Vidal. 1885, New York 1885.

A man of his word, and other stories. 1885, New York 1885.

That terrible man. New York 1885.

A bachelor's blunder. 1886, New York 1886.

Her own doing. New York 1886.

My friend Jim. 1886, New York 1886.

Major and minor. 1887.

Chris. 1888, New York 1888.

The rogue. 1888, New York 1888.

Miss Shafto. 1889, New York 1889.

Mrs Fenton: a sketch. 1889, New York 1889.

The baffled conspirators. 1890, New York [1890].

Marcia. 1890, New York 1890.

Misadventure. 1890, New York 1890.

Jack's father, and other stories. 1891, New York [1891].

Miss Wentworth's idea. 1891, New York [1891].

Mr Chaine's sons. 1891, New York [1891].

The mysterious Mrs Wilkinson, and other stories. New York [1891].

His Grace. 1892, New York [1892].

The Countess Radna. New York [1893].

A deplorable affair. 1893.

Matthew Austin. 1894.

Saint Ann's. 1894, New York [1895].

A victim of good luck. 1894, New York 1894.

Billy Bellew. 1895, New York 1895.

The despotic lady, and others. 1895, Philadelphia 1895. Stories.

The spectre of Strathannan. 1895.

Clarissa Furiosa. New York 1896, London 1897.

The dancer in yellow. 1896, New York 1896.

The fight for the crown. New York 1897, London 1898.

Marietta's marriage. 1897, New York 1897.

The widower. 1898.

Giles Ingilby. 1899, Philadelphia 1899.

The flower of the flock. 1900, New York 1900.

An octave. 1900. Stories.

The embarrassing orphan. 1901, Philadelphia [1904] (as An embarrassing orphan).

His own father. 1901.

The credit of the county. 1902, New York 1902.
Lord Leonard the luckless. 1903, New York 1903.
Nature's comedian. 1904, New York 1904.
Nigel's vocation. 1904.
Barham of Beltana. 1905, New York 1905.
Lone Marie. 1905.
Harry and Ursula: a story with two sides to it. 1907.
The square peg. 1907.
Pauline. 1908, New York 1910.
The perjurer. 1909.
Not guilty. 1910.
Vittoria Victrix. 1911.
Paul's paragon. 1912, New York 1912.
The right honourable gentleman. 1913, New York 1913.
Barbara and company. 1914.
Troubled Tranton. 1915, New York 1916.
Proud Peter. 1916, New York 1916.
Brown amber. 1917.
The fond fugitive. 1917.
The narrow strait. 1918.
The obstinate lady. [1919], New York 1919.
The triumphs of Sara. 1920.
Tony the exceptional. [1921].
Sabine and Sabina. [1922].
Next of kin. [1923].
The conscience of Gavin Blane. [1924].
Trevalion. [1925].
Adrienne of Auxelles. [1926].

'FLANN O'BRIEN', BRIAN O'NOLAN
1911–66

§1

At Swim-two-birds. 1939, New York 1951.
An béal boċt: nó, An milleánach. Dublin 1941. As by 'Myles na gCopaleen'.
Faustus Kelly. Dublin 1943. Play, first performed at the Abbey, Dublin 1943.
The hard life: an exegesis of squalor. 1961, New York 1962.
The Dalkey archive. 1964, New York 1965.
The third policeman. 1967, New York 1968.
The best of Myles: a selection from 'Cruiskeen lawn'. Ed K. O'Nolan 1968, New York 1968. Articles written for the Irish Times 1940–66 under pseud 'Myles na gCopaleen'.

O'Brien also wrote an unfinished novel, The great sago saga; *a sketch*, Thirst (*Gate Theatre, Dublin 1942, rewritten for radio and television); and adapted Capek's* Insect play *(1943).*

§2

Wain, J. 'To write for my own race': the fiction of O'Brien. Encounter 29 1967.

KATE O'BRIEN
b. 1897

§1

Distinguished villa. 1926. Play.
Without my cloak. 1931, Garden City NY 1931.
The ante-room. 1934, Garden City NY 1934.
Mary Lavelle. 1936, Garden City NY 1936.
Farewell, Spain. 1937, Garden City NY 1937. Travel.
Pray for the wanderer. 1938, New York 1938.
The land of spices. 1941, Garden City NY 1941.
English diaries and journals. 1943 (Britain in Pictures).
The last of summer. 1943, Garden City NY 1943.

That lady. 1946, New York 1946 (as For one sweet grape). Dramatized as That lady: a romantic drama, New York [1949].
Teresa of Avila. 1951, New York 1951. Biography.
The flower of May. [1953], New York 1953.
As music and splendour. 1958, New York 1958.
My Ireland. 1962, New York 1962. Topography.
Presentation parlour. 1963. Autobiography.

§2

Lawrence, M. Matriarchs. In her The school of femininity, New York 1936, London 1937 (as We write as women).
Nathan, G. J. That lady. In his Theatre book of the year 1949–50, New York 1950.

'FRANK O'CONNOR', MICHAEL FRANCIS O'DONOVAN
1903–66

Bibliographies

Brenner, G. Frank O'Connor 1903–66: a bibliography. West Coast Rev 2 1967.
Sheehy, M. (ed). Michael/Frank: studies on O'Connor with a bibliography of his writings. Dublin 1969.

Selections

Selected stories. Dublin 1946.
Stories by Frank O'Connor. New York 1956.
My Œdipus complex, and other stories. 1963.

§1

Many of O'Connor's vols of stories contain items rptd from earlier vols. See Brenner, Bibliography, above.

Guests of the nation. 1931, New York 1931.
The saint and Mary Kate. 1932, New York 1932.
Bones of contention and other stories. 1936, New York 1936.
Three old brothers and other poems. 1936.
The big fellow: a life of Michael Collins. 1937, New York 1937 (as Death in Dublin: Michael Collins and the Irish revolution), Dublin 1965 (rev, as The big fellow: Michael Collins and the Irish revolution).
In the train [1937]. In The genius of the Irish theater, ed S. Barnet et al, New York 1960. Play; with H. Hunt.
Dutch interior. 1940, New York 1940.
Three tales. Dublin 1941 (250 copies).
A picture book. Dublin 1943 (480 copies). Descriptions of Ireland.
Crab apple jelly: stories and tales. 1944, New York 1944.
Towards an appreciation of literature. Dublin 1945.
The art of the theatre. Dublin 1947.
The common chord: stories and tales. 1947, New York 1948.
Irish miles. 1947. Topography.
The road to Stratford. 1948, Cleveland 1960 (rev, as Shakespeare's progress).
Leinster, Munster and Connaught. [1950], New York 1950. Topography.
Traveller's samples: stories and tales. 1951, New York 1951.
The stories of Frank O'Connor. New York 1952, London 1953.
More stories. New York 1954.
The mirror in the roadway: a study of the modern novel. New York 1956, London 1957.
Domestic relations: short stories. 1957, New York 1957.
An only child. 1961, New York 1961. Autobiography.
The lonely voice: a study of the short story. Cleveland 1963, London 1963.
Collection two. 1964. Stories.

The backward look: a survey of Irish literature. 1967.
My father's son. [1968], New York 1969. Autobiography.
Collection three. 1969. Stories.

Translations from the Irish

The wild bird's nest. Dublin 1932 (250 copies).
Lords and commons. Dublin 1938 (250 copies).
The fountain of magic. 1939. Includes previous 2 vols, with preface.
E. O'Connell. A lament for Art O'Leary. Dublin 1940 (130 copies).
The midnight court: a rhythmical Bacchanalia from the Irish of Bryan Merriman. London and Dublin 1945.
Kings, lords and commons: an anthology from the Irish. New York 1959, London 1961. Includes trns, some rev from earlier vols, above, with new trns.
The little monasteries: poems. Dublin 1963. Some trns rev from earlier vols.
A golden treasury of Irish poetry A.D. 600 to 1200. 1967. With D. Greene.

O'Connor wrote the unpbd plays, The invincibles, Moses' rock (*both with H. Hunt*) *and* Time's pocket. *He also edited* Modern Irish short stories, *1957* (*WC*), *and* A book of Ireland, *1959* (*Collins National Anthologies*).

§2

Hackett, F. O'Connor's art. In his On judging books, 1947.
Kavanagh, P. Coloured balloons: a study of O'Connor. Bell 15 1947.
Breit, H. In his Writer observed, 1956.
Fowler, A. Challenge to mood in O'Connor. Approach 23 1957.
Whittier, A. Paris Rev no 17 1958.
Weiss, D. Freudian criticism: O'Connor as paradigm. Northwest Rev 2 1959.
Hennig, J. O'Connor and Goethe. Goethe 24 1962.
Saul, G. B. A consideration of O'Connor's short stories. Colby Lib Quart ser 6 1963.
Sealy, D. Translations of O'Connor. Dubliner 2 1963.
McAleer, E. C. O'Connor's Oedipus trilogy. Hunter College Stud no 2 1965.
Flanagan, T. Frank O'Connor 1903–66. Kenyon Rev 28 1966.
Brenner, G. O'Connor's imprudent hero. Texas Studies in Lit & Lang 10 1968.
Cooke, M. G. O'Connor and the fiction of artlessness. Univ Rev (Dublin) 5 1968.
Sheehy, M. (ed). Michael/Frank: studies on O'Connor. Dublin 1969.

SEÁN O'FAOLÁIN
b. 1900

Selections

The finest stories of Seán O'Faoláin. Boston 1957, London 1958 (as The stories of Seán O'Faoláin).

§1

Midsummer madness and other stories. 1932, New York 1932.
The life story of Eamon de Valera. Dublin 1933.
A nest of simple folk. 1933, New York 1934.
Constance Markievicz, or the average revolutionary: a biography. 1934, 1968 (rev).
There's a birdie in the cage. 1935. Story, rptd in A purse of coppers, below. 285 copies.
Bird alone. 1936, New York 1936.
A born genius: a short story. Detroit 1936. Rptd in A purse of coppers, below.
A purse of coppers: short stories. 1937, New York 1938.

King of the beggars: a life of Daniel O'Connell. 1938, New York 1938.
She had to do something: a comedy in three acts. 1938.
De Valera. 1939 (Penguin).
Come back to Erin. 1940, New York 1940.
An Irish journey. 1940, New York 1940. Non-fiction.
The great O'Neill: a biography of Hugh O'Neill, Earl of Tyrone 1550–1616. 1942, New York 1942.
The story of Ireland. 1942, New York 1943 (Britain in Pictures).
The Irish. 1947 (Pelican), New York 1949, London 1969 (rev).
Teresa, and other stories. 1947, New York 1948 (as The man who invented sin).
The short story. 1948, New York 1951.
A summer in Italy. 1949, New York 1950. Non-fiction.
Newman's way. 1952, New York 1952. Biography.
South to Sicily. 1953, New York 1953 (as Autumn in Italy).
The vanishing hero: studies in novelists of the twenties. 1956, Boston 1957.
I remember, I remember. Boston 1961, London 1962. Stories.
Vive-moi! an autobiography. Boston 1964, London 1965.
The heat of the sun: stories and tales. 1966, Boston 1966.

§2

'O'Donnell, Donat' (C. C. O'Brien). In his Maria Cross: imaginative patterns in a group of modern Catholic writers, New York 1952.
Saul, G. B. The brief fiction of O'Faolain. Colby Lib Quart ser 7 1965.
Doyle, P. A. Sean O'Faolain as a novelist. South Atlantic Quart 66 1967.
—— Chekhov in Erin: O'Faolain's career as a short story writer. Four Quarters 17 1968.
—— Sean O'Faolain. New York 1968.
Harmon, M. Sean O'Faolain: a critical introduction. Notre Dame 1967.

LIAM O'FLAHERTY
b. 1897

Bibliographies

'Gawsworth, John' (T. I. F. Armstrong). In his Ten contemporaries, 2nd ser, 1933. With autobiographical note by O'Flaherty.
Doyle, P. A. A Liam O'Flaherty checklist. Twentieth-Century Lit 13 1967. Includes contributions to periodicals.

Selections

The short stories of O'Flaherty. 1937.
The stories of O'Flaherty. Introd V. Mercier, New York 1956.
Selected stories. Ed D. A. Garrity, New York 1958.

§1

Thy neighbour's wife. 1923, New York [1924].
The black soul. 1924.
Spring sowing. 1924. Stories.
The informer. 1925, New York 1925, 1961 (with afterword by D. MacDonagh).
Civil war. 1925 (priv ptd, 100 copies). Story. Rptd in The tent, 1926, below.
The terrorist. 1926 (priv ptd, 100 copies). Story. Rptd in The tent.
Darkness: a tragedy in three acts. 1926 (priv ptd, 100 copies).
The tent [and other stories]. 1926.
Mr Gilhooley. 1926, New York [1927].
The child of God. 1926 (priv ptd, 100 copies). Story. Rptd in The mountain tavern, 1929, below.

The life of Tim Healy. 1927, New York [1927].
The fairy-goose, and two other stories. New York 1927, London 1927.
The assassin. 1928, New York [1928].
Red Barbara, and other stories. New York 1928, London 1928.
The mountain tavern, and other stories. 1929, New York [1929].
A tourist's guide to Ireland. [1929].
The house of gold. 1929, New York [1929].
The return of the brute. 1929, New York 1930.
Joseph Conrad: an appreciation. [1930] (Blue Moon booklets 1).
Two years. 1930, New York [1930]. Autobiographical.
The ecstasy of Angus. 1931 (priv ptd). Story.
A cure for unemployment. 1931 (Blue Moon booklets 8).
I went to Russia. 1931, New York [1931].
The puritan. 1931, New York [1932].
The wild swan, and other stories. Foreword by R. Davies 1932.
Skerrett. 1932, New York 1932.
The martyr. 1933, New York 1933.
Shame the devil. 1934. Autobiographical.
Hollywood cemetery. 1935.
Famine. 1937, New York [1937].
Land. 1946, New York 1946.
Two lovely beasts, and other stories. 1948, New York 1950.
Insurrection. 1950, Boston 1951.
Dúil [Desire]. Baile Atha Cliath [Dublin] 1953. Stories.

§2

Troy, W. The position of O'Flaherty. Bookman (NY) 69 1929.
Warren, C. H. Liam O'Flaherty. Bookman (London) 77 1930.
Steinemann, J. von. Irische Geschichten: Novellen von O'Flaherty. Neue Rundschau 42 1931.
Paul-Dubois, L. Un romancier-réaliste en Erin: O'Flaherty. Revue des Deux Mondes 21 1934.
O'Faolain, S. Don Quixote O'Flaherty. London Mercury 37 1937; rptd (rev) in The Bell 2 1941.
— Liam O'Flaherty. In D. V. Baker (ed), Writers of today vol 2, 1948.
Griffin, G. In his The wild geese, 1938.
Hackett, F. O'Flaherty as novelist. In his On judging books, New York 1947.
Kiely, B. O'Flaherty: a story of discontent. Month new ser 2 1949.
Saul, G. B. A wild sowing: the short stories of O'Flaherty. REL 4 1963.
Mercier, V. Man against nature: the novels of O'Flaherty. Wascana Rev 1 1966.
Murray, M. H. O'Flaherty and the speaking voice. Stud in Short Fiction 5 1968.

'RICHARD OKE', NIGEL MILLETT

Frolic wind. 1929, New York 1930. Adapted as play by R. Pryce, 1935.
Wanton boys. 1932.
India's coral strand. 1934.
The boy from Apulia. 1936. Biography of Frederick II.
Strange island story. 1939.

SEUMAS O'KELLY
1881–1918

Bibliographies

O'Hegarty, P. S. Bibliographies of 1916 and the Irish Revolution—4: Seumas O'Kelly. Dublin Mag new ser 9 1934; rptd separately as A bibliography of books by Seumas O'Kelly, Dublin 1934 (25 copies).

Selections

A land of loneliness and other stories. Ed E. Grennan, Dublin 1969.

§1

By the stream of Killmeen. Dublin 1906. Stories and sketches.
The matchmakers: a comedy in one act. Dublin 1908.
The shuiler's child: a tragedy in two acts. Dublin 1909.
Three plays: The homecoming; The stranger; The matchmakers. Dublin 1912. The stranger is a rev version of an unpbd play, The flame on the hearth.
The bribe: a play in three acts. Dublin 1914.
The lady of Deerpark. 1917, [1944] (abridged).
Waysiders: stories of Connacht. Dublin, London 1917, New York 1918.
Ranns and ballads. Dublin 1918.
The golden barque, and The weaver's grave. Dublin, London 1919.
Meadowsweet: a comedy in one act. Naas [1919].
The Parnellite: a play in three acts. Naas [1919].
The leprechaun of Killmeen. Dublin [1920].
Hillsiders. Dublin, London 1921. Stories.
The weaver's grave. Dublin [1922], 1965 (introd by P. Colum). First pbd with The golden barque 1919.
Wet clay. Dublin, London 1922, New York 1923.

Another one-act comedy, Driftwood, *was pbd in the Dublin Mag 1 1923. O'Kelly was successively editor of* Southern Star (Skibbereen), Leinster Leader, Dublin Saturday Post *and* Sinn Fein Nationality.

EDITH MAUD OLIVIER
1879(?)–1948

§1

The love-child. 1927, New York 1927.
Secrets of some Wiltshire housewives: a book of recipes. Warminster [1927].
As far as Jane's grandmother's. 1928, New York 1928.
The underground river. [1928]. Children's story.
Moonrakings. Warminster 1930. Wiltshire stories.
The triumphant footman: a farcical fable. 1930, New York 1930.
Dwarf's blood. 1931, New York 1931.
The seraphim room. 1932, New York 1933 (as Mr Chilvester's daughters).
The eccentric life of Alexander Cruden. 1934, New York 1934 (as Alexander the corrector: the eccentric life of Alexander Cruden).
Mary Magdalen. 1934, New York 1935. Biography.
Without knowing Mr Walkley: personal memories. 1938.
Country moods and tenses: a non-grammarian's chapbook. 1941.
Night thoughts of a country landlady: being the pacific experiences of Miss Emma Nightingale in time of war. 1943.
Four Victorian ladies of Wiltshire, with an essay on those leisured ladies. 1945.
Wiltshire. 1951 (County books).

CAROLA MARY ANIMA OMAN (LADY LENANTON)
b. 1897

The Menin road and other poems. 1919.
Princess Amelia. 1924, New York 1924.
The road royal. 1924, New York 1924.
King heart. 1926.

Mrs Newdigate's window. 1927, New York 1927. As C. Lenanton.
The holiday. 1928, New York 1928. As C. Lenanton.
Crouchback. [1929], New York 1929.
Miss Barrett's elopement. [1929], New York 1930. As C. Lenanton.
'Fair stood the wind...'. 1930. As C. Lenanton.
Major Grant. [1931], New York 1932.
The empress. 1932, New York 1932.
The best of his family. 1933.
Over the water. 1935.
Prince Charles Edward. 1935 (Great Lives).
Ferry the fearless. 1936. For children.
Henrietta Maria. 1936, New York 1936. Biography.
Johel. 1937, New York 1937. For children, sequel to Ferry the fearless, above.
Robin Hood, the prince of outlaws. 1937, New York 1937. For children.
Elizabeth of Bohemia. 1938, 1964 (rev). Biography.
Alfred, king of the English. 1939, New York 1940. For children.
Baltic spy. [1940]. For children.
Nothing to report. 1940.
Britain against Napoleon. 1942, Garden City NY 1942 (as Napoleon at the Channel).
Somewhere in England. 1943. Non-fiction.
Nelson. Garden City NY 1946, London [1947]. Biography.
Sir John Moore. 1953. Biography.
Lord Nelson. 1954 (Brief Lives).
David Garrick. [1958]. Biography.
Mary of Modena. 1962. Biography.
Ayot Rectory. 1965. Biography of Mary Sneade Brown, based on the ms memoir by her daughter Ellen Olive.
Napoleon's viceroy, Eugène de Beauharnais. 1966. Biography.
The Gascoyne heiress: the life and diaries of Frances Mary Gascoyne-Cecil 1802–39. 1968.

GEORGE OLIVER ONIONS
(later GEORGE OLIVER)
1873–1961

Bibliographies

'Gawsworth, John' (T. I. F. Armstrong). Oliver Onions. In his Ten contemporaries: notes toward their definitive bibliography, 2nd ser 1933.

Collections and Selections

Collected ghost stories. 1935. Includes contents of Widdershins, Ghosts in daylight, The painted face.
Bells rung backward. 1953. 5 stories from Collected ghost stories.

§1

The compleat bachelor. 1900, New York 1901.
Tales from a far riding. 1902.
The odd-job man. 1903.
Back o' the moon, and other stories. 1906.
The drakestone. 1906.
Admiral Eddy. 1907. Stories.
Pedlar's pack. 1908.
Draw in your stool. 1909. Stories.
Little devil doubt. 1909.
The exception. 1910, New York 1911.
Good boy seldom: a romance of advertisement. 1911.
Widdershins. 1911. Stories.
In accordance with the evidence. 1912, New York 1913. Pt 1 of trilogy: see Whom God hath sundered, 1925, below.
The debit account. 1913, New York 1913. Pt 2 of trilogy.
The story of Louie. 1913, New York 1914. Pt 3 of trilogy.

The two kisses: a tale of a very modern courtship. 1913, New York 1913.
A crooked mile. 1914, New York 1914. Sequel to The two kisses, above.
Gray youth: the story of a very modern courtship and a very modern marriage. New York 1914. Contains The two kisses and A crooked mile.
Mushroom town. 1915 [1914], New York 1914.
The new moon: a romance of reconstruction. [1918].
A case in camera. Bristol 1920, New York 1921.
The tower of oblivion. [1921], New York 1921.
Peace in our time. 1923.
Ghosts in daylight. 1924. Stories.
The spite of heaven. 1925, New York 1926.
Whom God hath sundered: a trilogy. 1925, New York 1926. In accordance with the evidence, The debit account and The story of Louie, above, rewritten as one story.
Cut flowers. 1927.
The painted face. 1929. Stories.
The open secret. 1930, Boston 1930.
A certain man. 1931.
Catalan circus. 1934.
The hand of Kornelius Voyt. 1939.
The Italian chest, and other stories. 1939.
Cockcrow: or, anybody's England. 1940.
The story of ragged Robyn. 1945.
Poor man's tapestry. 1946.
Arras of youth. 1949.
A penny for the harp. 1952.
A shilling to spend. 1965.

'GEORGE ORWELL',
ERIC ARTHUR BLAIR
1903–50

The Orwell Archive at University College London contains letters, mss and unpbd material, and attempts completeness in work pbd by and on Orwell. Other collections of letters are in the Berg Collection, New York Public Library, and the Humanities Research Center, University of Texas.

Bibliographies

Zeke, Z. G. and W. White. George Orwell: a selected bibliography. Boston 1962. Rptd from Bull of Bibliography 23 1961–2.
McDowell, M. J. Orwell: bibliographical addenda. 2 pts, Bull of Bibliography 23, 24 1963.
Willison, I. R. and I. Angus. Orwell: bibliographical addenda. Bull of Bibliography 24 1965.

Collections and Selections

A collection of essays. Garden City NY 1954.
The Orwell reader: fiction, essays and reportage. Introd by R. H. Rovere. New York 1956.
Selected essays. 1957, 1962 (as Inside the whale, and other essays) (Penguin).
Selected writings. Ed G. Bott 1958 (Twentieth Century Series).
Collected essays. 1961, 1961 (2nd edn) (adds Rudyard Kipling, and Reflections on Gandhi).
Decline of the English murder, and other essays. 1965 (Penguin).
See also Collected essays, journalism and letters, ed Sonia Orwell and I. Angus 1968, §1 below.

§1

The chronologies appended to each vol of Collected essays, 1968 below, give details of the publishing history of Orwell's books.

Down and out in Paris and London. 1933, New York 1933. Autobiographical.

Burmese days. New York 1934, London 1935 (with slight alterations), 1944 (restoring original text) (Penguin).
A clergyman's daughter. 1935, New York 1936.
Keep the aspidistra flying. 1936, New York 1956.
The road to Wigan pier. 1937, 1937 (Left Book Club edn, with foreword by V. Gollancz), New York 1958 (with Gollancz's foreword), London 1965 (with introd by R. Hoggart).
Homage to Catalonia. 1938, New York 1952 (with introd by L. Trilling).
Coming up for air. 1939, New York 1950.
Inside the whale, and other essays. 1940.
The lion and the unicorn: socialism and the English genius. 1941 (Searchlight Books 1).
Animal farm: a fairy story. 1945, New York 1946, 1956 (with introd by C. M. Woodhouse), London 1960 (with introd by L. Brander).
Critical essays. 1946, New York 1946 (as Dickens, Dali and others: studies in popular culture).
James Burnham and the managerial revolution. 1946. First pbd in Polemic as Second thoughts on James Burnham.
The English people. 1947 (Britain in Pictures).
Politics and the English language. Evansville Indiana 1947. First pbd in Horizon.
Nineteen eighty-four. 1949, New York 1949, 1961 (with afterword by E. Fromm), 1963 (ed I. Howe, with sources and selected criticism), London 1965 (with introd by S. Spender).
Shooting an elephant, and other essays. 1950, New York 1950.
Such, such were the joys. New York 1953, London 1953 (as England your England, and other essays). The London edn omits 'Such such were the joys' and adds North and south, and Down the mine (both from The road to Wigan pier).
The collected essays, journalism and letters of George Orwell. Ed S. Orwell and I. Angus 4 vols 1968, New York 1968. Includes the contents of Critical essays, Shooting an elephant, Such such were the joys, The lion and the unicorn, and The English people; and over 200 pieces of uncollected journalism, 236 letters, 5 notebooks and diaries and 4 poems.

Editions, Introductions and Contributions by Orwell

The betrayal of the Left. Ed V. Gollancz 1941. Contains Fascism and democracy, and Patriots and revolutionaries.
Victory or vested interest? By G. D. H. Cole [et al]. 1942. Contains Culture and democracy.
Talking to India, by E. M. Forster [et al]: a selection of English language broadcasts to India. Ed Orwell 1943. Contains The rediscovery of Europe.
Love of life, and other stories, by J. London. Introd by Orwell 1946.
British pamphleteers: 1, From the sixteenth century to the French revolution. Ed Orwell and R. Reynolds 1948. Introd by Orwell.
With T. R. Fyvel, Orwell edited a series of 10 Searchlight books 1941–3. He wrote forewords for 2 of them: The end of the 'old school tie', by T. C. Worsley, and The case for African freedom, by J. Cary. He was literary editor of Tribune 1943–45, writing the weekly column 'As I please' (after his resignation irregularly till 1947). He contributed regularly to Adelphi 1930–35, New English Weekly 1935–40, Time and Tide 1936–43, Observer and Manchester Evening News 1943–46. See the chronologies appended to each vol of Collected essays, 1968, §1, above.

§2

Books and Chapters in Books

Connolly, C. A Georgian boyhood. In his Enemies of promise, 1938, New York 1948 (rev).
— In his Previous convictions, 1963.
Pritchett, V. S. In Living writers: critical studies broadcast in the BBC Third Programme, ed G. Phelps 1947.
Churchill, R. C. In his Disagreements: a polemic on culture in the English democracy, 1950.
— In his A short history of the future, 1955.
Lewis, W. Orwell: or two and two make four. In his The writer and the absolute, 1952.
Prescott, O. The political novel: Warren, Orwell, Koestler. In his In my opinion: an enquiry into the contemporary novel, Indianapolis 1952.
Hopkinson, T. George Orwell. 1953, 1955 (rev), 1962 (rev) (Br Council pamphlet).
Spender, S. In his The creative element: a study of vision, despair and orthodoxy among some modern writers, 1953.
Atkins, J. A. Orwell: a literary study. 1954.
Brander, L. George Orwell. 1954.
Highet, G. The outsider. In his A clerk of Oxenford, New York 1954.
O'Casey, S. Rebel Orwell. In his Sunset and evening star, 1954.
Deutscher, I. 1984: the mysticism of cruelty. In his Heretics and renegades, 1955, New York 1957 (as Russia in transition).
Gerber, R. In his Utopian fantasy, 1955.
Hollis, C. A study of Orwell, the man and his works. 1956.
Leyburn, E. D. Future worlds. In her Satiric allegory: mirror of man, New Haven 1956.
Russell, B. Symptoms of Orwell's 1984. In his Portraits from memory, 1956.
Amis, K. In his Socialism and the intellectuals, 1957 (Fabian Tract).
Williams, R. In his Culture and society 1780–1950, 1958.
Slater, J. The fictional values of 1984. In Essays in literary history, ed R. Kirk and C. F. Main, New Brunswick NJ 1960.
Thompson, E. P. Outside the whale. In Out of apathy, ed E. P. Thompson 1960.
Warburg, F. J. In his An occupation for gentlemen, 1959. Reminiscences of Orwell by his publisher.
Rees, R. Orwell: fugitive from the camp of victory. 1961, Carbondale 1962 (with preface by H. T. Moore).
Voorhees, R. J. The paradox of Orwell. Lafayette Indiana 1961 (Purdue Univ Stud).
Karl, F. R. Orwell: the white man's burden. In his The contemporary English novel, New York 1962, London 1963 (as A reader's guide to the contemporary English novel).
Walsh, C. In his From utopia to nightmare, 1962.
Borinski, L. In his Meister des modernen englischen Romans, Heidelberg 1963.
Holz, L. Methoden der Meinungsbeeinflussung bei Orwell und Huxley. Hamburg 1963.
Kateb, G. In his Utopia and its enemies, New York 1963.
Carnall, G. Saints and human beings: Orwell, Osborne and Gandhi. In Essays presented to A. G. Stock, ed R. K. Kaul, Rajasthan 1965.
Dyson, A. E. Orwell: irony as prophecy. In his The crazy fabric, 1965.
Greenblatt, S. J. Three modern satirists: Waugh, Orwell and Huxley. New Haven 1965.
Thomas, E. M. Orwell. Edinburgh 1965 (Writers and Critics).
Lang, H. J. Orwells dialektischer Roman—1984. In Rationalität-Phänomenalität-Individualität: Festgabe für H. and M. Glockner, ed W. Ritzel, Bonn 1966.

Woodcock, G. The crystal spirit: a study of Orwell. Boston 1966, London 1967 (abridged).

Hillegas, M. R. In his The future as nightmare: H. G. Wells and the anti-utopias, New York 1967.

Oxley, B. T. George Orwell. 1967 (Literature in Perspective).

Calder, J. Chronicles of conscience: a study of Orwell and Koestler. 1968.

Hooning, Th. J. Orwell in zijn tijd. Meppel 1968.

Wulfsberg, F. George Orwell. [Oslo] 1968. In Norwegian.

Alldritt, K. The making of Orwell: an essay in literary history. 1969.

Lee, R. A. Orwell's fiction. Notre Dame 1969.

Articles in Periodicals

Martindale, C. C. Why not our ally? Orwell and his solution of our social problems. Month 173 1939.

Miller, J. E. Orwell and our times. Million 2 1945.

Woodcock, G. Orwell: 19th-century Liberal. Politics 3 1946; rptd in his The writer and politics, 1948.

— Orwell and conscience. World Rev April 1950.

— Recollections of Orwell. Northern Rev 6 1953.

World Rev June 1950. Special Orwell no. Contains S. Schimanski, Editorial; B. Russell, Orwell; T. R. Fyvel, A writer's life; The unpublished notebooks of Orwell; Revaluations by M. Muggeridge (Burmese days), J. Beavan (The road to Wigan Pier), S. Spender (Homage to Catalonia), T. Hopkinson (Animal Farm), H. Read (1984), A. Huxley (A footnote about 1984).

Ashe, G. The servile state in fact and fiction. Month 4 1950.

— Second thoughts on 1984. Ibid.

— A note on Orwell. Commonweal 1 June 1951.

Birrell, T. A. Is integrity enough? A study of Orwell. Dublin Rev 225 1950.

Davet, Y. Orwell et notre temps. Table Ronde no 29 1950.

Duesberg, J. Les anticipations de M. Orwell. Synthèses (Brussels) April 1950.

Forster, E. M. George Orwell. Listener 2 Nov 1950; rptd in his Two cheers for democracy, 1951.

Jones, J. Utopias as dirge. Amer Quart 2 1950.

Koestler, A. A rebel's progress. Observer 29 Jan 1950; rptd in his The trail of the dinosaur, 1955.

Le Roy, G. C. A.F. 632 to 1984. College Eng 12 1950. Huxley's Brave new world and 1984.

Pritchett, V. S. Orwell: an appreciation. New York Times Book Rev 5 Feb 1950; rptd in Highlights of modern literature, ed F. Brown, New York 1954.

Rosenfeld, I. Decency and death. Partisan Rev 17 1950.

— Gentleman George. Commentary 21 1956; both rptd in his An age of enormity, Cleveland 1962.

Siepman, E. O. Farewell to Orwell. Nineteenth Century and After 147 1950.

Waard, H. de. Orwell en Epictetus. Nieuwe Stem 5 1950.

Wulfsberg, F. George Orwell. Norseman March–April 1950.

Allen, W. George Orwell. Year's Work in Lit 1950, 1951.

Braybrooke, N. The two poverties: Léon Bloy and Orwell. Tablet 7 April 1951.

— George Orwell. Fortnightly 169 1951.

— Orwell: an English Radical in the Christian tradition. Christus Rex 7 1953.

— George Orwell. Catholic World 178 1953.

Fyvel, T. R. Wingate, Orwell and the 'Jewish question'. Commentary 11 1951.

— Orwell and Blair: glimpses of a dual life. Encounter 13 1959.

Hamilton, K. M. Chesterton and Orwell: a contrast in prophecy. Dalhousie Rev 31 1951.

Pampaloni, G. Ritratto sentimentale di Orwell. Il Ponte 7 1951.

Trilling, L. Orwell and the politics of truth. Commentary 13 1952; rptd as introd to Homage to Catalonia, 1952, above, and in his Opposing self, New York 1955.

North, R. George Orwell. Visva-Bharati Quart 19 1953.

Bondy, F. Orwell: oder Common sense als Paradox. Der Monat 6 1954.

Cosman, M. Orwell's terrain. Personalist 35 1954.

— Orwell and the autonomous individual. Pacific Spectator 9 1955.

Glicksberg, C. I. The literary contribution of Orwell. Arizona Quart 10 1954.

Krause, G. Orwells Utopie 1984. Die Neueren Sprachen 3 1954.

Rieff, P. Orwell and the post-liberal imagination. Kenyon Rev 16 1954.

Crowcroft, P. Politics and writing: the Orwell analysis. New Republic 3 Jan 1955.

Heppenstall, R. Memoirs of Orwell: The shooting stick; Orwell intermittent. Twentieth Century 157 1955; both rptd (rev) in his Four absentees: reminiscences of Eric Gill, Orwell, Dylan Thomas and J. Middleton Murry, 1960.

Lewis, C. S. George Orwell. Time & Tide 8 Jan 1955.

Peters, R. A boy's view of Orwell. Listener 22 Sept 1955.

Willison, I. Orwell's bad good books. Twentieth Century 157 1955.

Wadsworth, F. W. Orwell as a novelist. Univ of Kansas City Rev 22 1955–6.

Dutscher, A. Orwell and the crisis of responsibility. Contemporary Issues 8 1956.

Gleckner, R. F. 1984 or 1948? College Eng 18 1956.

Howe, I. Orwell: history as nightmare. Amer Scholar 25 1956; rptd in his Politics and the novel, New York 1957.

King, C. The politics of Orwell. UTQ 26 1956.

Smith, W. D. George Orwell. Contemporary Rev 189 1956.

Thirlby, P. Orwell as a Liberal. Marxist Quart 3 1956.

Walsh, J. An appreciation of an individualist writer. Ibid.

West, A. Hidden damage. New Yorker 31 1956; rptd in his Principles and persuasions, New York 1957.

Ehrenpreis, I. Orwell, Huxley, Pope. Revue des Langues Vivantes (Brussels) 23 1957.

Elliott, G. P. A failed prophet. Hudson Rev 10 1957.

Kessler, M. Power and the perfect state: a study in disillusionment as reflected in Orwell's 1984 and Huxley's Brave new world. Political Science Quart 72 1957.

Park, M. van. Aspecten van Orwell. Vlaamse Gids 41 1957.

Potts, P. Don Quixote on a bicycle: in memoriam George Orwell. London Mag 4 1957; rptd in his Dante called you Beatrice, 1960.

Wain, J. Orwell in perspective. New World Writing 12 1957.

— Here lies Lower Binfield. Encounter 17 1961; both rptd in his Essays on literature and ideas, 1963.

— Orwell and the intelligentsia. Encounter 31 1968.

Cami, B. Orwell: enkele kanttekeningen. Nieuw Vlaams Tijdschrift 1 1958.

Geering, R. G. Darkness at noon and 1984. Australian Quart 30 1958.

Gérard, A. Orwell et l'utopie de notre temps. Revue Générale Belge 94 1958.

Gürster, E. von. Orwells Bedeutung für unsere Zeit. Hochland 50 1958.

Trocchi, A. A note on Orwell. Evergreen Rev 2 1958.

Elsbree, L. The structured nightmare of 1984. Twentieth Century Lit 5 1959.

Green, M. British decency. Kenyon Rev 21 1959; rptd in his A mirror for Anglo-Saxons, New York 1960.

Harris, H. J. Orwell's essays and 1984. Twentieth-Century Lit 4 1959.

Scott, N. A. The example of Orwell. Christianity & Crisis 19 1959.

Spence, J. E. Orwell. Theoria 13 1959.

Fen, E. Orwell's first wife. Twentieth Century 168 1960.

Geste (Leeds Univ) 6 1960. Special Orwell no. Contains: W. Kendall, David and Goliath: a study of the political ideas of Orwell; M. Beker, The duality of Orwell;

M. Maddison, At the crossroads of ideology [on Animal Farm]; R. N. Coe, 1984 and the anti-Utopian tradition.

Griffin, C. W. Orwell and the English language. Audience 7 1960.

Mander, J. Orwell's politics. Contemporary Rev 197 1960; rptd (rev) with title 'One step forward: two steps back' in his The writer and commitment, 1961.

Morris, J. 'Some are more equal than others': a note on Orwell. Penguin New Writing 40 1960.

Strachey, J. The strangled cry. Encounter 15 1960; rptd in his The strangled cry, 1962. Koestler, Orwell, Whittaker Chambers, Pasternak.

Way, B. Orwell: the political thinker we might have had. Gemini/Dialogue 3 1960.

Wollheim, R. Orwell reconsidered. Partisan Rev 27 1960.

Yorks, S. Orwell: seer over his shoulder. Bucknell Rev 9 1960.

Beker, M. Orwell i kriza gradjanskog liberalizma. Naše Teme (Zagreb) 5 1961.

— The ambivalence of Orwell. Studia Romanica et Anglica Zagrabiensia 13–14 1962.

Müller-Tochtermann, H. Orwell und die Sprachpflege in England. Muttersprache 71 1961.

'O'Donnell, Donat' (C. C. O'Brien). Orwell looks at the world. New Statesman 26 May 1961; rptd in C. C. O'Brien, Writers and politics, 1965.

Quintana, R. Orwell: the satiric resolution. Wisconsin Stud in Contemporary Lit 2 1961.

Richards, D. Four Utopias. Slavonic & East European Rev 40 1961. Dostoevsky's Legend of the Grand Inquisitor; Zamyatin's We; Huxley's Brave new world; 1984.

Thompson, F. H. jr. Orwell's image of the man of good will. College Eng 22 1961. Winston Smith in 1984.

Walter, N. Orwell: an accident in society. Anarchy 1 1961.

McDowell, J. 1984 and Soviet reality. Univ of California Graduate Jnl no 1 1962.

Shibata, T. The road to nightmare: an essay on Orwell. Stud in Eng Lit & Lang (Kyushu Univ) no 12 1962.

Stevens, A. W. Orwell and southeast Asia. Yearbook of Comparative & General Lit 1962.

Thale, J. Orwell's modest proposal. CQ 4 1962. 1984.

Wicker, B. An analysis of Newspeak. Blackfriars 43 1962.

Nott, K. Orwell's 1984. Listener 31 Oct 1963.

Symons, J. Orwell: a reminiscence. London Mag 3 1963. Rptd in his Critical occasions, 1966.

Fixler, M. Orwell and the instrument of language. Iowa Eng Yearbook 9 1964.

Colquitt, B. F. Orwell: traditionalist in Wonderland. Discourse 8 1965.

Füger, W. Wie entsteht ein Gedicht? ein indirekter Beitrag Orwells zur Dichtungstheorie des 20. Jahrhunderts. Die Neueren Sprachen 14 1965.

Hoggart, R. Orwell and The road to Wigan Pier. CQ 7 1965. Rptd as introd to The road to Wigan Pier, 1965, above.

Mellichamp, L. Orwell and the ethics of revolutionary politics. Modern Age (Chicago) 9 1965.

Fitzgerald, J. J. Orwell's social compassion. Discourse 9 1966.

Foley, J. and J. Ayer. Orwell in English and Newspeak: a computer translation. CCC: College Composition & Communication 17 1966.

Gulbin, S. Parallels and contrasts in Lord of the flies and Animal farm. English Jnl 55 1966.

Keskinen, K. Shooting an elephant—an essay to teach. English Jnl 55 1966.

Burns, W. Orwell: our responsible Quixote. West Coast Rev 2 1967.

Hooning, T. J. Woodcock's Orwell. Tirade 11 1967.

Lutman, S. Orwell's patriotism. Jnl of Contemporary History 2 1967.

Molina Quirós, J. 1984: fuentes literarias. Filología Moderna (Madrid) 6 1967.

Ranald, R. A. Orwell and the mad world: the anti-universe of 1984. South Atlantic Quart 66 1967.

Schmerl, R. B. Fantasy as technique [in E. M. Forster and Orwell]. Virginia Quart Rev 43 1967.

Smilde, R. How many years to 1984. Anarchy 7 1967.

Warncke, W. W. The permanence of Orwell. Univ Rev (Kansas City) 33 1967.

— Orwell's critical approach to literature. Southern Humanities Rev 2 1968.

Armytage, W. H. The disenchanted mecanophobes in twentieth century England. Extrapolation 9 1968.

Barr, A. The paradise behind 1984. Eng Miscellany 19 1968.

Smith, M. The wall of blackness: a psychological approach to 1984. Modern Fiction Studies 14 1968.

'JOHN OXENHAM',
WILLIAM ARTHUR DUNKERLEY
1852–1941

Selections

The 'John Oxenham' book of daily readings, compiled by A. Andrews-Dale. [1920].

Selected poems. 1924.

Selected poems. New York [1948]. Ed C. L. Wallis, with biographical sketch by E. Oxenham.

§1

God's prisoner: the story of a crime, a punishment, a redemption. 1898, New York 1899.

A princess of Vascovy. New York 1899, London 1900.

Rising fortunes: the story of a man's beginnings. 1899, New York 1899.

Our Lady of Deliverance. 1901, New York 1901.

Bondman free. New York 1902, London 1903.

John of Gerisau. 1902.

Under the iron flail. 1902.

Barbe of Grand Bayou. 1903, New York 1903.

Flowers of the dust. New York 1903, London [1915].

The very short memory of Mr Joseph Scorer, and other seaside experiences. 1903.

Hearts in exile. 1904, New York 1904.

A weaver of webs. 1904.

The gate of the desert. 1905.

White fire. 1905.

Giant circumstance. 1906.

Profit and loss. 1906.

Carette of Sark. 1907, New York 1907 (as A man of Sark).

The long road. 1907, New York 1907.

Pearl of Pearl island. 1908.

The song of Hyacinth, and other stories. 1908.

Great-heart Gillian. [1909].

My lady of Shadows. 1909.

Lauristons. 1910.

A maid of the silver sea. [1910].

The book of the words of the pageant of darkness and light. New York [1911], London [1923]. Verse.

The coil of Carne. 1911, New York 1911.

Their high adventure. [1911], New York 1911 (as The high adventure).

Mr Cherry. 1912, 1937 (as Mr Cherry retired?!).

Queen of the guarded mounts. [1912], New York 1912.

The quest of the golden rose. 1912.

Bees in amber: a little book of thoughtful verse. 1913, New York 1913.

Mary All-alone. 1913.

Red wrath. [1913], New York 1914.

Broken shackles. 1914, New York 1915.

Maid of the mist. [1914], New York 1914.

'Policeman X', the man who did not dare—and after! 1914. Verse.

'All's well!': some helpful verse for these dark days of war. 1915.

A little Te Deum of the commonplace. [1915].

Ad finem: when will the war end? and how? 1916. Poem.

Corner island. 1916.

The cradle of Our Lord. [1916]. Verse.

Everywoman and war. [1916]. Pamphlet.

The King's high way: some more helpful verse. 1916, New York [1916].

My lady of the moor. 1916.

'1914'. 1916.

The fiery cross: some verse for to-day and to-morrow. 1917, New York [1918].

The loosing of the lion's whelps, and other stories. 1917.

The vision splendid: some verse for the times and the times to come. 1917, New York 1917.

Be of good cheer! [1918]. Essay.

Hearts courageous. 1918. Verse.

High altars: the battlefields of France and Flanders as I saw them. 1918, New York [1918].

'Inasmuch': some thoughts concerning the wreckage of the war. 1918.

'All clear!': a book of verse commemorative of the great peace. 1919, New York [1919].

Winds of the dawn: some commonsense occasional papers for the times. 1919.

'Gentlemen—the King!': a book of introduction. 1920, Boston [1928]. Verse.

The sacraments of fire, water. [1920]. Verse.

Chaos, and the way out. 1923. Verse.

A hazard in the blue. [1923].

The cedar box. 1924.

Chaperon to Cupid. 1924.

The perilous lovers: an idyll of Sercq. 1924.

The wonders of Lourdes. 1924. Non-fiction.

The hidden years. 1925.

Scala sancta. 1925.

The man who would save the world. 1927.

The recollections of Roderic Fyfe. 1927.

First prayers: a manual of help for parents. 1928. With R. Dunkerley.

The hawk of Como. 1928.

God's candle. 1929. Non-fiction.

The pageant of the King's children: eight scenes and a processional tableau. [1930]. With R. Dunkerley.

The splendour of the dawn. 1930.

Cross-roads: the story of four meetings. 1931.

A saint in the making: the story of the Curé d'Ars. 1931.

The master's golden years. New York 1932, London 1932 (as Anno domini).

God and Lady Margaret. 1933.

Christ and the third wise man. 1934. Non-fiction.

Lake of dreams. 1940. With E. Oxenham.

Wide horizons: some selected verse for these times. 1940.

Out of the body: a plain man's parable of the life to come. 1941. With E. Oxenham.

§2

'Oxenham, Erica' (E. Dunkerley). 'J.O.' 1942.

— Scrap-book of J.O. 1946.

Parr, O. K. My chief knight, John Oxenham. [1943].

BARRY ERIC ODELL PAIN
1864–1928

Collections and Selections

Collected tales. Vol 1, 1916, New York 1916. No more pbd.

Barry Pain. [Selected essays]. 1926 (Essays of Today and Yesterday).

Barry Pain. [Selected stories]. 1928 (Short Stories of Today and Yesterday).

Humorous stories. 1930. Contains 'Eliza'; Mrs Murphy; Edwards; Me and Harris; Confessions of Alphonse; Innocent amusements; Robinson Crusoe's return; The diary of a baby; Tamplin's tales of his family; Marge Askinforit.

More stories. 1930. Contains In a Canadian canoe; The octave of Claudius; The memoirs of Constantine Dix; The exiles of Faloo; An exchange of souls.

The Eliza books. 1931.

Barry Pain. [Selections]. 1934 (Methuen's Library of Humour).

§1

In a Canadian canoe, and other stories. 1891.

Playthings and parodies. 1892, New York [1892].

Stories and interludes. 1892, New York 1892. In verse and prose.

Graeme and Cyril. 1893.

The kindness of the Celestial, and other stories. 1894.

The octave of Claudius. 1897.

The romantic history of Robin Hood. 1898.

Wilmay, and other stories of women. 1898.

'Eliza'. 1900, Boston [1904].

Another Englishwoman's love-letters. 1901, New York 1901. Parody of An Englishwoman's love-letters.

De omnibus, by the conductor. 1901.

Nothing serious. 1901. Stories.

Stories in the dark. 1901.

'Two': a story of English schoolboy life. New York [1901].

The one before. 1902, New York 1902.

Eliza's husband. 1903.

Little entertainments. 1903.

Curiosities. 1904.

Deals. 1904. Stories.

Lindley Kays. 1904.

Three fantasies. 1904.

The memoirs of Constantine Dix. 1905.

Robinson Crusoe's return. [1906], 1921 (rev, as The return of Robinson Crusoe).

Wilhelmina in London. 1906.

The diary of a baby: being a free record of the unconscious thought of Rosalys Ysolde Smith, aged one year. 1907.

First lessons in story-writing. 1907 (London Correspondence College Booklet).

The shadow of the unseen. 1907. With J. Blyth.

The luck of Norman Dale. 1908. With J. Blyth.

The gifted family. 1909.

Proofs before pulping. [1909].

The exiles of Faloo. 1910.

Eliza getting on. 1911.

An exchange of souls. 1911.

Here and hereafter. 1911.

Stories in grey. [1911].

Exit Eliza. 1912.

The new Gulliver, and other stories. [1912].

Stories without tears. 1912.

Eliza's son. 1913.

Mrs Murphy. [1913].

Futurist fifteen: an old Moore or less accurate forecast of certain events in the year 1915. [1914].

One kind and another. 1914.

Edwards. [1915].

Me and Harris. [1916].

The short story. [1916] (Art and Craft of Letters).

Confessions of Alphonse. [1917].

Innocent amusements. [1918]. Stories.

The Problem Club [1919].

The death of Maurice. [1920].

Marge Askinforit. [1920].

Going home: being the fantastic romance of the girl with angel eyes and the man who had wings. [1921].

If summer don't. [1922], New York 1922 (as If winter don't). Parody of A. S. M. Hutchinson's If winter comes.

Tamplin's tales of his family. [1924].

This charming green hat-fair. [1925]. Parody of M. Arlen's Green hat.
Dumphry. 1927.
The later years. 1927.

MERVYN LAURENCE PEAKE
1911–68

§1

Captain Slaughterboard drops anchor. 1939, 1945 (rev), 1967 (rev), New York 1967. Story for children.
Shapes and sounds. [1941]. Verse.
Rhymes without reason. 1944.
The craft of the lead pencil. 1946. Non-fiction.
Titus Groan. 1946, New York 1946 (as Titus Groan: a Gothic novel).
Letters from a lost uncle. 1948. Story for children.
Drawings by Mervyn Peake. 1949 (for Sept 1950).
The glassblowers. 1950. Verse.
Gormenghast. 1950. Sequel to Titus Groan, above.
Mr Pye. 1953.
Figures of speech. 1954. Humorous drawings.
Sometime, never: three tales of imagination by W. Golding, J. Wyndham, M. Peake. 1956. Contains Boy in darkness, by Peake.
Titus alone. 1959. Sequel to Titus Groan and Gormenghast, above.
The rhyme of the flying bomb. 1962.
Poems and drawings. 1965 (150 copies).
A reverie of bone and other poems. 1967 (320 copies).

Peake illustrated most of his books. He also illustrated books by other authors. A play, The wit to woo, was produced at the Arts Theatre 12 March 1957.

§2

Sarzano, F. The book illustrations of Mervyn Peake. Alphabet & Image no 1 1946.
Morgan, E. The walls of Gormenghast: an introduction to the novels of Peake. Chicago Rev 14 1960.
Gilmore, M. A world away: a memoir of Peake. 1970.

EDEN PHILLPOTTS
1862–1960

Bibliographies

Hinton, P. Phillpotts: a bibliography of first editions. Birmingham 1931. Includes a list of books with contributions by Phillpotts.

Collections and Selections

The Phillpotts calendar: a quotation from the work of Phillpotts for every day in the year, selected by H. C. Palmer. [1915].
One hundred pictures from Phillpotts, selected by L. H. Brewitt. 1919.
[Selected poems]. [1926] (Augustan Books of Modern Poetry).
Devonshire plays. 1927. Contains The farmer's wife; Devonshire cream; Yellow sands.
The Widecombe edition of the Dartmoor novels. 20 vols 1927–8. Includes 2 vols of stories. Preface to vol 1 by A. Bennett. Texts of novels were rev, and sometimes abridged, by the author for this edn; some stories first pbd in book form in this edn.
[Selected stories]. 1929 (Short Stories of Today and Yesterday).
The complete human boy: comprising The human boy, The human boy again, The human boy and the war, A human boy's diary, From the angle of seventeen. [1930].

Dartmoor omnibus: containing Orphan Dinah, The three brothers, Children of men, The whirlwind. [1933].
West Country plays. 1933. Contains Buy a broom; A cup of happiness; The good old days.

§1

My adventure in the Flying Scotsman: a romance of London and North-Western Railway shares. 1888. Stories.
The end of a life. Bristol [1891].
Folly and fresh air. 1891, New York 1892, London 1899 (rev).
A tiger's cub. Bristol [1892].
Summer clouds, and other stories. [1893].
In sugar-cane land. [1894]. Travel in the West Indies.
Some every-day folks. 3 vols 1894, 1 vol 1894, New York 1895.
A deal with the devil. 1895.
A breezy morning. (Grand, Leeds 27 April 1891). 1895 (French's Acting Edn). Comedy.
The prude's progress. (Theatre Royal, Cambridge 16 May 1895). 1895, 1900 (rev). Comedy. With J. K. Jerome.
Down Dartmoor way. 1896.
My laughing philosopher. 1896.
Lying prophets. 1897, New York 1898. Text of American edn differs considerably.
Children of the mist. 1898, New York 1899.
Loup-garou! 1899. Stories.
A golden wedding. (Haymarket 30 Nov 1898). 1899 (French Acting Edn). Comedy. With C. Groves.
The human boy. 1899, New York 1900.
A pair of knickerbockers. (St George's Hall 26 Dec 1899). [1900] (French's Acting Edn), New York [1900] (French International Edn), Farce.
Sons of the morning. 1900, New York 1900.
The good red earth. Bristol 1901, New York 1901, Bristol [1904] (as Johnny Fortnight), 1920 (rev).
The striking hours. 1901, New York [1901]. Stories.
Fancy free. 1901. Stories.
The river. 1902, New York 1902.
The transit of the red dragon, and other tales. Bristol 1903.
The golden fetich. 1903, New York 1903.
My Devon year. 1904 (for 1903). Essays.
Johnny Fortnight. [1904]. *See* The good red earth, 1901, above.
The American prisoner. 1904, New York 1904.
The farm of the dagger. 1904, New York 1904.
The secret woman. 1905, New York 1905. Dramatized 1912.
Knock at a venture. 1905, New York 1905. Stories.
Up-along and down-along. 1905. Verse.
The Portreeve. 1906, New York 1906.
The unlucky number. [1906]. Stories.
My garden. 1906. Essays.
The poacher's wife. 1906, New York 1906 (as Daniel Sweetland).
The sinews of war: a romance of London and the sea. [1906], New York 1906 (as Doubloons). With A. Bennett.
The whirlwind. 1907, New York 1907.
The folk afield. 1907, New York 1907. Stories.
The mother. 1908, New York 1908 (as The mother of the man). Dramatised 1913.
The statue. 1908, New York 1908. With A. Bennett.
The human boy again. 1908.
The virgin in judgment. 1908, New York 1908, London 1911 (abridged, as A fight to a finish), 1948 (with introd by L. A. G. Strong, as The virgin in judgement).
The three brothers. 1909, New York 1909.
The fun of the fair. 1909.
The haven. 1909, New York 1909.
The thief of virtue. 1910, New York 1910, London 1952 (with introd by F. Swinnerton).
Tales of the tenements. 1910, New York 1910.

The flint heart: a fairy story. 1910, New York [1910], London 1922 (rev).

A fight to a finish. 1911. *See* The virgin in judgment, 1908, above.

Wild fruit. 1911. Verse.

Demeter's daughter. 1911, New York 1911.

The beacon. 1911, New York 1911.

Dance of the months. 1911. Sketches and verse.

The secret woman. (Kingsway 22 Feb 1912). 1912, New York 1914, London 1935 (rev). Tragedy.

The forest on the hill. 1912, New York 1912.

The Iscariot. 1912, New York 1912. Verse.

The three knaves. 1912. Mystery.

From the angle of seventeen. 1912. Pt of the Human boy ser.

The lovers: a romance. 1912, Chicago [1912].

Curtain raisers. 1912. The point of view (St George's House 18 Nov 1913); Hiatus (Gaiety, Manchester 22 Sept 1913); The carrier-pigeon (Royalty, Glasgow 17 April 1913).

Widecombe fair. 1913, Boston 1913, London 1947 (with introd by L. A. G. Strong).

The old time before them. 1913, [1921] (rev as Told at 'The Plume'). Stories.

The joy of youth: a comedy. 1913, Boston 1913. Novel.

The shadow. (Gaiety, Manchester 6 Oct 1913). 1913, New York 1914. Tragedy.

The mother. (Liverpool Repertory Th 22 Oct 1913). 1913, New York 1914.

Three plays. 1913. The secret woman; The shadow; The mother.

The master of Merripit. 1914.

The judge's chair. 1914. Stories.

Faith Tresilion. New York 1914, London 1916.

Brunel's tower. 1915, New York 1915.

My shrubs. 1915. Essays.

The angel in the house. (Savoy 3 June 1915). [1915] (French's Acting Edn). Comedy. With B. M. Hastings.

Old Delabole. 1915, New York 1915.

The human boy and the war. 1916, New York 1916.

The green alleys: a comedy. 1916, New York 1916. Novel.

'Delight'. 1916. Verse.

The girl and the faun. 1916, Philadelphia 1917. Fairy story.

The farmer's wife. (Birmingham Repertory Th 11 Nov 1916). [1916], 1929 (rev, French's Acting Edn). Comedy.

The nursery—Banks of Colne. 1917, New York 1917 (as The banks of Colne).

Plain song 1914–16. 1917. Verse.

The chronicles of St Tid. 1917, New York 1918.

The spinners. 1918, New York 1918.

A shadow passes. 1918. Sketches and verse.

Storm in a teacup. 1919, New York 1919.

St George and the dragons. (Birmingham Repertory Th 30 March 1918). 1919, Boston 1929 (as The bishop's night out). Comedy.

Evander. 1919, New York 1919. Fable.

Miser's money. 1920, New York 1920.

As the wind blows. 1920, New York 1920. Verse.

A West Country pilgrimage. 1920. Essays and verse.

Orphan Dinah. 1920, New York 1921.

Told at 'The Plume'. [1921]. *See* The old time before them, 1913, above.

The bronze Venus. 1921.

Eudocia: a comedy royal. 1921, New York 1921. Dramatized (as A comedy royal) 1925.

A dish of apples. [1921]. Verse.

The grey room. New York 1921, London [1922]. Mystery.

Pan and the twins. 1922, New York 1922. Fairy story.

Pixies' plot. 1922. Verse.

The red Redmaynes. New York 1922, London [1923]. Mystery.

Number 87. 1922, New York 1922. As 'Harrington Hext'. Mystery.

Black, white and brindled. 1923, New York 1923. Satires.

Children of men. 1923, New York 1923.

The market-money. 1923 (Repertory plays). Tragedy.

The lavender dragon. 1923, New York 1923. Fairy story.

Cherry-stones. 1923, New York 1924. Verse.

The thing at their heels. 1923, New York 1923. As 'Harrington Hext'. Mystery.

Cheat-the-boys. 1924, New York 1924.

A human boy's diary. 1924, New York 1924.

Thoughts in prose and verse. 1924.

Bedrock. (Gaiety, Manchester Oct 1916). 1924. Comedy. With B. M. Hastings.

Redcliff. [1924], New York 1924.

The treasures of Typhon. 1924. Fairy story.

A harvesting. 1924. Verse.

Who killed Diana? 1924, New York 1924 (as Who killed Cock Robin?)

A comedy royal. 1925 (priv ptd), 1932 (rev). Dramatization of Eudocia, 1921, above.

Devonshire cream. (Birmingham Repertory Th 20 Dec 1924). 1925, New York 1925, London [1930] (French's Acting Edn). Comedy.

A voice from the dark. [1925], New York 1925. Mystery.

Up hill, down dale. [1925], New York 1926. Stories.

George Westover. [1925], New York 1926.

Circe's island, and The girl and the faun. 1926. The girl and the faun first pbd 1916.

The Marylebone miser. [1926], New York 1926 (as Jigsaw).

Peacock House, and other mysteries. [1926].

The miniature. 1926, New York 1927. Fable.

A Cornish droll. [1926].

Yellow sands. (Haymarket 3 Nov 1926). 1926, New York 1927, London [1950] (French's Acting Edn). Comedy. With A. Phillpotts.

Brother man. 1926. Verse. Vol 20 of Widecombe edn (stories) also has this title.

The blue cornet. (Court 23 Feb 1927). 1927. Comedy.

The jury. [1927], New York 1927.

It happened like that. [1927]. Stories.

Arachne. 1927. Fable.

The ring fence. [1928], New York 1928.

Brother beast. 1928. Verse.

Three short plays. 1928. Contains The market-money (tragedy) [first pbd 1923]; Something to talk about; The purple bedroom (Court 3 May 1926) (comedy).

Goodwill. 1928. Verse.

The runaways. (Birmingham Repertory Th 1 Sept 1928). 1928. Comedy.

A West Country sketchbook [1928]. Essays from Dance of the months (1911) and A West Country pilgrimage (1920) with one new essay.

The bishop's night out. Boston 1929. *See* St George and the dragons, 1919, above.

Tryphena. [1929], New York 1929.

For remembrance. 1929 (priv ptd, 25 copies). Verse.

The torch, and other tales. [1929], New York 1929.

A hundred sonnets. 1929.

Buy a broom. 1929. Comedy.

The apes. 1929, New York 1929. Fable.

The three maidens. [1930], New York 1930.

A hundred lyrics. 1930.

Alcyone: a fairy story. 1930.

Cherry Gambol, and other stories. [1930].

Jane's legacy: a folk play. (Birmingham Repertory Th 24 Oct 1925). 1931, [1932] (French's Acting Edn).

Found drowned. [1931], New York 1931.

Essays in little. [1931].

Stormbury. [1931], New York 1932.

Becoming. 1932. Verse.

Bert: a play in one act. [1932]. (French's Acting Edn).

Bred in the bone. [1932], New York 1932. First pt of trilogy The book of Avis, below.

The Broom squires. 1932, New York 1932.

A clue from the stars. [1932], New York 1932. Mystery.

The good old days. [1932]. Comedy. With A. Phill-potts.

The captain's curio. [1933], New York 1933.

A cup of happiness. (Royalty 24 Dec 1932). 1933. Comedy.

Mr Digweed and Mr Lumb. [1933], New York 1934.

Nancy Owlett. 1933, New York 1933.

Song of a sailor man: narrative poem. 1933.

They could do no other. [1933]. Stories.

Witch's cauldron. [1933], New York 1933. 2nd pt of trilogy The book of Avis, below.

A shadow passes: being the third and last part of the book of Avis. [1933], New York 1934.

Minions of the moon. [1934], New York 1935.

The oldest inhabitant: a comedy. [1934], New York 1934. Novel.

Portrait of a gentleman. [1934].

A year with Bisshe-Bantam. 1934. Rural life.

Ned of the Caribbees. [1935].

Physician heal thyself. [1935], New York 1936 (as The anniversary murder). Mystery.

Sonnets from nature. 1935.

The wife of Elias. [1935], New York 1937. Mystery.

The book of Avis: a trilogy comprising Bred in the bone, Witch's cauldron, A shadow passes. [1936].

A close call. [1936], New York 1936.

Once upon a time. [1936]. Stories.

The owl of Athene. 1936. Fable.

The white camel. 1936, New York 1938. For children.

Wood-nymph. [1936], New York [1937].

A Dartmoor village. 1937. Verse.

Farce in three acts. [1937]. Novel.

Lycanthrope: the mystery of Sir William Wolf. 1937, New York 1938. Novel.

Dark horses. [1938].

Golden island. 1938. Children's story.

Portrait of a scoundrel. 1938, New York 1938.

Saurus. 1938. Fable.

Monkshood. 1939, New York 1939. Mystery.

Tabletop. New York 1939.

Thorn in her flesh. 1939.

Awake Deborah! 1940, New York 1941. Mystery.

Chorus of clowns. 1940.

Goldcross. 1940.

A mixed grill. 1940. Essays.

A deed without a name. [1941], New York 1942.

Ghostwater. 1941.

Flower of the gods. [1942], New York 1943.

Miniatures. 1942. Verse.

Pilgrims of the night. [1942].

A museum piece. [1943].

At the 'bus-stop: a duologue for two women. 1943.

The changeling. [1944].

They were seven: a mystery. [1944], New York 1945.

The drums of Dombali. [1945].

Swinburne. Port Hueneme Cal 1945. Fac of author's ms of poem first pbd in Athenaeum 24 April 1909.

Quartet. [1946].

There was an old woman. [1947].

The enchanted wood. 1948. Verse.

Fall of the house of Heron. [1948].

Address unknown. [1949].

Dilemma. [1949].

The waters of Walla. [1950]. Dramatized (as The orange orchard) 1951.

From the angle of 88. 1951. Autobiography.

The orange orchard. [1951] (French's Acting Edn). With N. Price; based on The waters of Walla, above.

Through a glass darkly. 1951.

George and Georgina. 1952. Mystery.

The hidden hand. 1952.

His brother's keeper. 1953.

One thing and another. 1954. Memoirs, sketches, verse.

The widow Garland. 1955.

Connie Woodland. 1956.

Giglet market. 1957.

There was an old man. 1959.

Some of Phillpotts' stories were repbd by the Todd Publishing Co in their Bantam and Polybooks series. According to Hinton's Bibliography, three titles, Little silver chronicles, The devil's tight-rope and The mound by the way, copies of which were deposited in the Library of Congress in 1900, were not in fact pbd. Many of Phillpotts' plays were not pbd (see Trewin in W. Girvan, Eden Phillpotts, 1953, below). The Enciclopedia dello Spettacolo lists The policeman (Lyric Hall, Ealing 12 Jan 1887); A Platonic attachment (the same 20 Feb 1889); Allendale (Strand 14 Feb 1893); The MacHaggis (Globe 25 Feb 1897: with J. K. Jerome); My lady's mill (Lyric 2 July 1928: with A. Phillpotts); Hinton adds, with no details of performance, The Counsellor's wife; The dentist (with C. Groves); His lordship (with G. B. Burgin). J.G. Hepburn, Letters of Arnold Bennett vol 1 1966, p. 59, mentions Bennett and Phillpotts collaborating on a dramatisation of Children of the mist in 1900, and in 1904 on two plays, Christina (A credit to human nature) and An angel unawares, none of this work ever being produced.

§2

Colbron, G. I. The quality of Phillpotts. Forum (New York) 39 1908.

Howells, W. D. The fiction of Phillpotts. North Amer Rev 190 1909.

Cooper, F. T. In his Some English story tellers, New York 1912.

Evans, C. S. Phillpotts and the epic of Dartmoor. Bookman (London) 49 1916.

Follett, H. T. and W. Follett. In their Some modern novelists, New York 1918.

Gorman, H. S. A Dartmoor cycle. In his Procession of works, Boston 1923.

Meadowcroft, C. W. The place of Phillpotts in English peasant drama. Philadelphia 1924.

Jordan-Smith, P. In his For the love of books, New York 1934.

Gottschalk, E. Der Dartmoor Cyklus von Phillpotts. Quakenbrück 1935.

Timms, C. The humanity of Phillpotts. London Quart & Holborn Rev 176 1951.

Girvan, W. (ed). Phillpotts: an assessment and a tribute. 1953. Contains:
Strong, L. A. G. The Dartmoor novels.
Price, N. The fruits of Eden.
Pound, R. Phillpotts and Arnold Bennett.
Knox, E. V. The human boy.
Trewin, J. C. Phillpotts the dramatist.
Foot, I. A Westcountryman's tribute.
Rosland, J. Phillpotts's detective fiction.

WILLIAM CHARLES FRANKLYN PLOMER

b. 1903

Collections and Selections

Selected poems. 1940.

A choice of ballads. 1960 (priv ptd).

Collected poems. 1960.

§1

Turbott Wolfe. 1926, New York [1926], London 1965 (with introd by L. van der Post), New York 1965.

I speak of Africa. 1927. Contains 3 short novels: Portraits in the nude, Uda Masondo, Black peril; 7 short stories; 2 plays for puppets.

Notes for poems. 1927.

The family tree. 1929. Verse

Paper houses. 1929, New York 1929. Stories.

Sado. 1931, New York [1932] (as They never came back).
The case is altered. 1932, New York [1932].
The fivefold screen. 1932, New York 1932. Verse.
Cecil Rhodes. 1933, New York 1933.
The child of Queen Victoria, and other stories. 1933.
The invaders. 1934.
Ali the lion: Ali of Tebeleni, pasha of Jannina, 1741-1822. 1936.
Visiting the caves. 1936. Verse.
Double lives: an autobiography. 1943, New York 1956.
Curious relations. By 'William d'Arfey' [A. Butts]. Ed W. Plomer. 1945, New York 1947. Stories.
The Dorking thigh and other satires. 1945. Verse.
Four countries. 1949. Stories, some rptd from I speak of Africa, Paper houses, The child of Queen Victoria.
Museum pieces. 1952, New York [1954].
Gloriana: opera in 3 acts. Libretto by W. Plomer. [1953].
A shot in the park. 1955, New York 1955 (as Borderline ballads). Verse.
At home: memoirs. 1958, New York [1958].
Conversation with my younger self. Ewelme 1963 (priv ptd, 25 copies).
Curlew river: a parable for church performance, set to music by B. Britten. 1964. Based on the Japanese No play, Sumidagawa, by Juro Motomasa.
The burning fiery furnace: second parable for church performance, set to music by B. Britten. 1966.
Taste and remember. 1966. Verse.
The prodigal son: third parable for church performance, set to music by B. Britten. 1968.

Plomer edited a number of diaries, Japanese lady in Europe, *by H. Ichikawa, 1937*; Kilvert's diary: selections from the diary of the Rev Francis Kilvert, *3 vols 1938-40; and* A message in code: the diary of Richard Rumbold 1932-60, *[1964]. With Roy Campbell he edited the magazine* Voorslag, *Durban 1926-7.*

§2

Bartelme, E. Moments of beauty and of high idealism. Commonweal 65 1956.
Moss, H. Over the border. Poetry (Chicago) 88 1956.
Barkham, J. Refugee from the dark cave. Saturday Rev 16 Feb 1957.
van der Post, L. The Turbott Wolfe affair. Cornhill no 1043 1965. Adapted from his introd to Turbott Wolfe, 1965.
Doyle, J. R. William Plomer. New York 1969.

ANTHONY DYMOKE POWELL
b. 1905

§1

Afternoon men. 1931, Boston 1963.
Venusberg. 1932, New York 1952 (with Agents and patients, below, as Two novels).
From a view to a death. 1933.
Caledonia: a fragment. 1934 (priv ptd). Verse satire.
Agents and patients. 1936, New York 1952 (with Venusberg, above, as Two novels).
What's become of Waring? 1939, Boston 1963.
John Aubrey and his friends. 1948, New York 1948, London 1963 (rev), New York 1963. Non-fiction.
A question of upbringing. 1951, New York 1951. This and the following novels form part of the Music of time sequence.
A buyer's market. 1952, New York 1953.
The acceptance world. 1955, New York [1955].
At Lady Molly's. 1957, Boston [1957].
Casanova's Chinese restaurant. 1960, Boston 1960.
A dance to the music of time. 1962, Boston 1962. Contains A question of upbringing, A buyer's market and

The acceptance world, above.
The kindly ones. 1962, Boston 1962.
A dance to the music of time: second movement. Boston 1964. Contains At Lady Molly's, Casanova's Chinese Restaurant, The kindly ones, above.
The valley of bones. 1964, Boston 1964.
The soldier's art. 1966, Boston 1966.
The military philosophers. 1968, Boston 1969.

Powell edited Barnard letters 1778-1824, *1928*; Novels of high society from the Victorian age, *1947*; Brief lives and other selected writings by John Aubrey, *1949. He contributed a preface to* The complete Ronald Firbank, *1961.*

§2

Raymond, J. Isherwood and Powell. Listener 16 Dec 1954.
Voorhees, R. J. Powell: the first phase. Prairie Schooner 28 1954.
—— The music of time: themes and variations. Dalhousie Rev 42 1962.
Arau, A. A handful of dust. New Republic 134 1956.
Leclaire, L .A. Powell: biographie spirituelle d'une génération. Études Anglaises 9 1956.
Brownjohn, A. The social comedy of Powell. Gemini no 2 1957.
Schlesinger, A.Waugh à la Proust. New Republic 139 1958.
Vinson, J. Powell's Music of time. Perspective (St Louis) 10 1958.
Webster, H. C. A dance of British eccentrics. New Leader 41 1958.
Hynes, S. Novelist of society. Commonweal 70 1959.
Brooke, J. From Wauchop to Widmerpool. London Mag 7 1960.
Mizener, A. A dance to the music of time: the novels of Powell. Kenyon Rev 22 1960.
—— The novel and nature in the twentieth century: Powell and Cozzens. In his The sense of life in the modern novel, Boston 1964.
A Who's who of the Music of time. Time & Tide 2, 9 July 1960.
Bergonzi, B. Anthony Powell. 1962. With P. Bloomfield on L. P. Hartley (Br Council pamphlet).
—— Powell 9/12. CQ 11 1969.
Hall, J. The uses of polite surprise. EC 12 1962; rptd in his The tragic comedians, Bloomington 1963.
Karl, F. R. The still comic music of humanity: the novels of Powell, A. Wilson and N. Dennis. In his The contemporary English novel, New York 1962, London 1963 (as A reader's guide to the contemporary English novel).
Quesenbery, W. D. Powell: the anatomy of decay. Critique (Minneapolis) 7 1964.
Radner, S. Powell's early novels: a study in point of view. Renascence 16 1964.
McCall, R. G. Powell's gallery. College Eng 27 1965.
Russell, J. Quintet from the 30s: Powell. Kenyon Rev 27 1965.
Zigerell, J. J. Powell's Music of time: chronicle of a declining establishment. Twentieth Century Lit 12 1966.
Woodward, A. G. The novels of Powell. English Stud in Africa 10 1967.
Herring, H. D. Powell: a reaction against determinism. Ball State Univ Forum 9 1968.
Morris, R. K. The novels of Powell. Pittsburgh 1968.

JOHN COWPER POWYS
1872-1963

For some details of the locations of various Powys mss, see introd to Langridge's bibliography, below.

Bibliographies

Muir, P. H. Bibliographical check list of Powys. In his Points: ser 2, 1866-1934. 1934.

Siberell, L. E. A bibliography of the first editions of Powys. Introd by Powys, Cincinnati, 1934.

Siberell, L. E. and P. H. Muir. A check list of the books of Powys. In 'Louis Marlow', Welsh ambassadors, 1936, below.

Langridge, D. W. Powys: a record of achievement. 1966. Includes contributions to periodicals, reviews of Powys' works and other recording material: also prints lecture-synopses and a number of early poems.

Anderson, A. J. Powys: a bibliography. Bull of Bibliography 25 1967. Primary and secondary material.

Selections

John Cowper Powys: a selection from his poems. Ed K. Hopkins 1964.

§1

Odes and other poems. 1896.

Poems. 1899.

The war and culture: a reply to Professor Münsterberg. New York 1914, London 1915 (as The menace of German culture). Reply to Münsterberg's War and America.

Visions and revisions: a book of literary devotions. New York 1915, London 1915, 1955 (with new introd by Powys). Critical essays.

Wood and stone: a romance. New York 1915, London 1917.

Confessions of two brothers: J. C. Powys, Llewellyn (sic) Powys. Rochester NY 1916.

Wolf's-bane: rhymes. New York 1916, London [1916].

One hundred best books, with commentary and an essay on books and reading. New York 1916.

Rodmoor: a romance. New York 1916.

Suspended judgments: essays on books and sensations. New York 1916. Some of these essays were rptd individually from 1923 at Girard Kansas in the Little Blue Book series.

Mandragora: poems. New York 1917.

The complex vision. New York 1920. Philosophy.

Samphire. New York 1922. Verse.

The art of happiness. Girard Kansas [1923]. Differs from 1935 book with same title.

Psychoanalysis and morality. San Francisco 1923.

Ducdame. New York 1925, London 1925.

The religion of a sceptic. New York 1925.

The secret of self development. Girard Kansas 1926. Essay.

The art of forgetting the unpleasant. Girard Kansas 1928. Essays.

Wolf Solent. 2 vols New York 1929, 1 vol London 1929, 1961 (with preface by Powys).

The meaning of culture. New York [1929], London 1930, New York 1939 (enlarged, with introd and conclusions by Powys), London 1940.

Debate! Is modern marriage a failure? New York 1930. With Bertrand Russell.

The owl, the duck, and—Miss Rowe! Miss Rowe! Chicago 1930 (250 copies).

In defence of sensuality. New York 1930, London 1930.

Dorothy M. Richardson. 1931. Expanded from articles in Adelphi 2 1931.

A Glastonbury romance. New York 1932, London 1933, 1955 (with preface by Powys).

A philosophy of solitude. New York 1933, London 1933 (with introd by Powys).

Autobiography. New York 1934, London 1934, 1967 (introd by J. B. Priestley).

Weymouth sands. New York 1934, London 1935 (as Jobber Skald), 1963 (as Weymouth sands). 1935 edn has changes in personal and place-names, restored in 1963.

The art of happiness. New York 1935, London 1935. Differs from 1923 book with same title.

Maiden Castle. New York 1936, London 1937, 1966 (with preface by M. Elwin).

Morwyn: or the vengeance of God. 1937.

The enjoyment of literature. New York 1938, London 1938 (with variations, as The pleasures of literature).

Owen Glendower: an historical novel. 2 vols New York [1940], 1 vol London 1941.

Mortal strife. 1942. Philosophy.

The art of growing old. 1944.

Pair Dadeni: or, 'The cauldron of rebirth'. Carmarthen 1946. Rptd from Wales 6 1946.

Dostoievsky, 1947.

Obstinate Cymric: essays 1935–47. Carmarthen 1947.

Rabelais: his life, the story told by him, selections therefrom newly translated, and an interpretation of his genius and his religion. 1948, New York 1951.

Porius: a romance of the dark ages. 1951, New York 1952.

The inmates. 1952, New York 1952.

In spite of: a philosophy for everyman. 1953, New York 1953.

Atlantis. 1954.

Lucifer: a poem. 1956. Written 1906.

The brazen head. 1956.

Up and out. 1957. Contains Up and out: a mystery tale; The mountains of the moon: a lunar love story.

Homer and the aether. 1959. Adaptation of the Iliad.

All or nothing. 1960.

Letters

Letters from Powys to Clifford Tolchard. World Rev no 17 1950.

Tolchard, C. Letters from John Cowper Powys. Meanjin 23 1964. Selection, with additional letter, of the above.

Letters of Powys to Louis Wilkinson 1935–56. Preface by L. Wilkinson 1958.

§2

'Marlow, Louis' (L. U. Wilkinson). Blasphemy and religion: a dialogue about J. C. Powys' Wood and stone, and T. Powys' Soliloquy of a hermit. New York [1916]. As Wilkinson.

—— The buffoon. 1916. J. C. Powys is 'Jack Welsh' in this novel. As Wilkinson.

—— In his Swan's milk, 1934.

—— Welsh ambassadors: Powys lives and letters. 1936

—— In his Forth, beast! 1946. Continuation of Swan's milk above.

—— The brothers Powys. [Cincinnati] 1946 (for 1947). Rptd in Essays by Divers Hands 24 1948. As Wilkinson.

—— In his Seven friends, 1953.

Deacon, W. A. John Cowper Powys. Montreal Univ Mag 18 1919.

Durant, W. J. In his Adventures in genius, New York 1931.

Gillis, J. M. Powys on Catholicism; Solitude for moderns, In his This our day, New York 1933.

Delafield, E. M. Romantic Glastonbury. Essays of the Year 1933–4, 1934.

Arns, K. Die Geschwister Powys. E Studien 69 1935.

Ward, R. H. The Powys brothers. 1935.

Powys, L. C. In his The joy of it, 1937. Reminiscences.

—— The Powys family. Welsh Rev 7 1948; rptd separately, West Pennard 1952.

—— Still the joy of it. 1956.

Derry, W. C. John Cowper Powys: an interpretation. Boston 1938.

Govan, G. E. The Powys family. Sewanee Rev 46 1938.

Wahl, J. Un défenseur de la vie sensuelle: Powys. Revue de Métaphysique et de Morale 46 1939; rptd in his Poésie, pensée, perception, Paris 1948.

—— John Cowper Powys. Lettres Nouvelles 60 1958.

Chaning-Pearce, M. 'Facilis descensus Averni'. In his Terrible crystal, 1940. On Lawrence and Powys.

Hentschel, C. Powys and the 'Gretchen-cult'. Studia Neophilologica 15 1941.

Powys, Llewelyn. Letters. Selected and ed L. Wilkinson 1943. Many letters to J. C. Powys.

Elwin, M. The life of Llewelyn Powys. 1946. Many references to J. C. Powys.

—— In Writers of today ed D. V. Baker, 1948.

Hopkins, K. Powys: the man and his work. World Rev March 1948.

—— The Powys brothers: a biographical appreciation. 1967.

Dock Leaves, Spring 1956. Powys no. Contains: R. Garlick, Editorial note; J. Hanley, The man in the corner; K. Hopkins, A note on the poetry of J. C. Powys; R. Mathias, Gwlad-yr-hat [On A Glastonbury romance]; H. Menai, J.C.P. [Poem]; G. D. Painter, The oar and the winnowing-fan.

Anderson, J. R. Powys' Lucifer: an appreciation. Dublin Mag 32 1957.

Gregory, A. A famous family. London Mag 5 1958.

Kehr, W. John Cowper Powys. Marburg 1958.

New Chapter 1 1958. Powys no. Contains: J. Norbury, The life and the legend: an etching of an artist in solitude; J. Powys: a tribute (Contributions in prose and verse by A. Wilson, R. Garlick, G. W. Knight, K. Hopkins, G. D. Painter and H. Menai).

Jones, B. J. C. Powys: some notes on his life and writings. Dorset Year Book 1959-60, 1959.

—— John Cowper Powys. [Dorchester 1962] (Dorset Worthies 3).

Cavaliero, C. On the frontier: J. C. Powys. Theology 64 1961.

Knight, G. W. Lawrence, Joyce and Powys. EC 11 1961.

—— The Saturnian quest: a chart of the prose works of Powys. 1964.

Churchill, R. C. The Powys brothers. 1962 (Br Council pamphlet).

Collins, H. P. The largeness of Powys. Contemporary Rev 202 1962.

—— John Cowper Powys: old earth-man. 1966.

Hardy, E. John Cowper Powys: a tribute and impression in his 91st year. Aylesford Rev 5 1962-3.

Aury, D. John Cowper Powys. Nouvelle Revue Française 11 1963.

Gresset, M. John Cowper Powys. Mercure de France 349 1963.

—— J. C. Powys: notre contemporain. Preuves no 163 1964.

—— Les rites matinaux de Powys. Cahiers du Sud 53 1966.

—— Le rôle de l'humeur dans la création littéraire de Powys. Actes du 4e Congrès des Anglicistes de l'Enseignement Supérieur (Lille) 1966.

—— John Cowper Powys. Nouvelle Revue Française 16 1968.

Hanbury, M. J. C. Powys and some Catholic contacts. Month 30 1963.

Myers, M. [Editorial on Powys]. Anglo-Welsh Rev 13 1963.

Review of English Literature. Jan 1963. J. C. Powys no. Contains: A. N. Jeffares, Editorial; A. Wilson, 'Mythology' in Powys's novels; H. Miller, The immortal bard; J. B. Priestley, The happy introvert; D. Aury, Reading Powys; I. C. Peate, John Cowper Powys: letter writer; G. W. Knight, Owen Glendower.

Wilson, C. The swamp and the desert: notes on J. C. Powys and Hemingway. Aylesford Rev 6 1964.

André, R. La sensibilité de Powys. Nouvelle Revue Française 13 1965.

Davies, F. J. C. Powys et le roi Lear. Lettres Nouvelles 13 1965.

Pritchett, V. S. The mysteries of J. C. Powys. New Statesman 2 April 1965.

Raddatz, F. J. Verstellte Wirklichkeiten: Mythos und Realität im Werke des J. C. Powys. Frankfurter Hefte 20 1965.

Adkinson, R. V. A short guide to Powysland. Revue des Langues Vivantes 32 1966.

Philobiblon (Colgate Univ Lib) no 8 1966. J. C. Powys special issue. Contains: Powys: an Englishman up-state; L. Wilkinson, The brothers Powys; R. Speirs, A man from the west country; K. Hopkins, A visit to Powys July 1937; M. Elwin, Powys: publishing his later works; T. Davies, The Powys family.

Réda, J. L'insaisissable: notes sur l'Autobiographie de J. C. Powys. Cahiers du Sud 53 1966.

Fernandez, D. J. C. Powys: ou la persistance oedipienne. Preuves no 196 1967.

De Wet, O. Visit to J. C. Powys. Texas Quart 11 1968.

Mayoux, J.-J. L'extase et la sensualité: J. C. Powys et Wolf Solent. Critique 24 1968.

Robillard, D. Landscape with figures: the early fiction of J. C. Powys. Stud in the Literary Imagination 1 1968.

Breckon, R. John Cowper Powys: the solitary giant. 1969.

Cartianu, V. Izvoare străvechi de inspiraţie comună în operele lui Powys şi Lucian Blaga. Viaţa Romanească 22 1969.

—— Raportul om-natură în opera lui Powys. Ibid.

LLEWELYN POWYS
1884-1939

See cols 1105-7, below.

THEODORE FRANCIS POWYS
1875-1953

Bibliographies

Muir, P. H. and B. Van Thal. Bibliographies of the first editions of books by Aldous Huxley and Powys. 1927. Includes contributions to periodicals. Rptd in 'Louis Marlow', Welsh ambassadors, 1936, below.

Hutchinson, C. G. A check-list of Powys. Bookman (London) 83 1933. Lists some unpbd material.

Riley, A. P. A bibliography of Powys. Hastings 1967. Includes translations, contributions to periodicals and anthologies, unpbd material, and a select list of secondary material.

Selections

God's eyes a-twinkle: an anthology of the stories of T. F. Powys. With preface by C. Prentice 1947.

§1

Some of Powys' stories were issued in limited edns of a few hundred copies; many stories were previously pbd in periodicals; some were pbd in periodicals and anthologies and have not yet been collected.

An interpretation of Genesis. [1907] (priv ptd, 100 copies), 1929, New York 1929.

The soliloquy of a hermit. New York 1916, London 1918 (as Soliloquies of a hermit), 1926 (rev).

The left leg: containing The left leg, Hester Dominy, Abraham men. 1923, New York 1923. Stories, previously unpbd.

Black bryony. 1923, New York 1923.

Mark only. [1924], New York 1924.

Mr Tasker's gods. 1925, New York 1925.

Mockery Gap. 1925, New York 1925.

A stubborn tree. 1926 (priv ptd, 100 copies). Story.

Innocent birds. 1926, New York 1926.

Feed my swine. 1926 (priv ptd, 100 copies). Story; rptd in The white paternoster, below.

A strong girl, and The bride: two stories. 1926 (priv ptd, 100 copies). A strong girl was previously unpbd; The bride was rptd in The white paternoster, below.

What lack I yet? 1927 (priv ptd, 100 copies), San Francisco 1927 (35 copies). Story, rptd in The white paternoster, below.

Mr Weston's good wine. 1927 (660 copies), New York 1928 (first trade edn), London 1928.

The rival pastors. 1927 (priv ptd, 100 copies). Story, rptd in The white paternoster, below.

The house with the echo: twenty-six stories. 1928, New York 1928.

The dewpond: a story. 1928 (Woburn Books 2). Not previously pbd; rptd in Bottle's path, below.

Fables. New York 1929, London 1929 (750 copies), 1930, 1934 (as No painted plumage). 19 stories not previously pbd.

Christ in the cupboard. 1930 (Blue Moon booklet 5). Story, rptd in The white paternoster, below.

The key of the field. 1930 (Furnival Books 1). With foreword by S. Townsend Warner. Story not previously pbd; rptd in Bottle's path, below.

Kindness in a corner. 1930, New York 1930.

The white paternoster, and other stories. 1930, New York 1931. Some stories not previously pbd.

Uriah on the hill. Cambridge 1930 (Minority pamphlet 2). Story, not previously pbd.

Uncle Dottery: a Christmas story. Bristol 1930. Not previously pbd.

The only penitent. 1931. Story; rptd in Bottle's path, below.

When thou wast naked: a story. Waltham St Lawrence 1931; rptd in Bottle's path, below.

Unclay. 1931, New York 1932.

The tithe barn, and The dove & the eagle. 1932. Stories; The dove and the eagle was rptd in Bottle's path, below.

The two thieves: In good earth, God, The two thieves. 1932, New York 1933. Stories.

Captain Patch: twenty-one stories. 1935. The shut door not previously pbd.

Make thyself many. 1935 (285 copies). Story; rptd in No want of meat, sir!, ed J. Hackney 1936.

Goat Green; or the better gift. 1937. Story; rptd in Bottle's path (as The better gift).

Bottle's path, and other stories. 1946.

Rosie Plum, and other stories. Ed F. Powys 1966, New York 1966.

Come and dine, and Tadnol. Ed A. P. Riley, Hastings 1967. 2 stories not previously pbd.

13 letters to L. C. Powys and Elizabeth Myers are ptd in Theodore: essays on T. F. Powys, ed B. Sewell 1964, below. Numerous letters are quoted in 'Louis Marlow', Welsh ambassadors, 1936, below.

§2

'Marlow, Louis' (L. U. Wilkinson). Blasphemy and religion: a dialogue about J. C. Powys, Wood and stone, and T. Powys, Soliloquy of a hermit. New York [1916]. As Wilkinson.

—— Welsh ambassadors: Powys lives and letters. 1936.

—— The brothers Powys. [Cincinnati] 1946 (for 1947). Rptd in Essays by Divers Hands 24 1948. As Wilkinson

—— In his Seven friends, 1953.

Warren, C. H. The novels of T. F. Powys. Criterion 7 1928.

Hunter, W. The novels and stories of T. F. Powys. Cambridge 1930 (Minority pamphlets 3).

Leavis, F. R. T. F. Powys. Cambridge Rev 9 May 1930. Review of Kindness in a corner.

Callander, E. T. F. Powys: an appreciation. Library Assistant 24 1931.

Lawson, J. C. T. F. Powys: an appreciation. King's College (London) Rev 33 1932; rptd as pamphlet Yeovil 1954.

Hutchinson, C. G. T. F. Powys. Bookman (London) 83 1933.

Fluchère, H. T. F. Powys. Cahiers du Sud no 159 1934.

MacCampbell, D. The art of Powys. Sewanee Rev 42 1934.

Powys, J. C. In his Autobiography, 1934

Arns, K. Die Geschwister Powys. E Studien 69 1935.

Ward, R. H. The Powys brothers. 1935.

Powys, L. C. In his The joy of it, 1937. Reminiscences.

—— The Powys family. Welsh Rev 7 1948; rptd separately, West Pennard 1952.

—— In his Still the joy of it, 1956.

Govan, G. E. The Powys family. Sewanee Rev 46 1938.

Kranendank, A. G. van. Theodore Powys. E Studies 26 1944.

Ferriday, P. In two worlds: the novels of T. F. Powys. The Bridge (Cambridge) 1 1946.

Churchill, R. C. The path of T. F. Powys. Critic (Mistley) 1 1947.

—— The Powys brothers. 1962 (Br Council pamphlet).

Kermode, F. The art of T. F. Powys: ironist. Welsh Rev 6 1947.

Powys, F. The quiet man of Dorset: T. F. Powys. Adelphi 31 1954.

Steinmann, M. The symbolism of T. F. Powys. Critique (Minneapolis) 1 1957.

—— Water and animal symbolism in T. F. Powys. E Studies 41 1960.

Gregory, A. A famous family. London Mag 5 1958.

Carr, W. I. Reflections on T. F. Powys. Delta (Cambridge) 19 1960; rptd in English 15 1964 (as T. F. Powys: a comment).

Coombes, H. T. F. Powys. 1960.

Holbrook, D. Two Welsh writers: T. F. Powys and Dylan Thomas. In Pelican guide to English literature vol 7, The modern age, ed B. Ford 1961.

Hopkins, K. The second brother: a note on T. F. Powys. REL 4 1963.

—— The Powys brothers: a biographical appreciation. 1967.

Sewell, B. (ed). Theodore: essays on T. F. Powys. Aylesford 1964. Also contains a story by Powys, The useless woman, and a number of letters.

Las Vergnas, R. Powys: l'homme tranquille du Dorset. Revue de Paris 72 1965.

Philobiblon (Colgate Univ Lib) no 8 1966. J. C. Powys special issue. Includes L. Wilkinson, The brothers Powys; T. Davies, The Powys family.

Riley, A. P. The original end of Mr Weston's good wine. REL 8 1967.

JOHN BOYNTON PRIESTLEY
b. 1894

A substantial collection of Priestley typescripts is in the University of Texas Humanities Research Center Library. See L. J. Teagarden, The J. B. Priestley Collection, Lib Chron of Univ of Texas 7 1963.

Bibliographies

Jones, L. A. The first editions of Priestley. Bookman (London) 80 1931.

Löb, L. In his Mensch und Gesellschaft bei Priestley, Berne [1962]. See §2, below.

University of Texas Humanities Research Center. A writer's life (J. B. Priestley: an exhibition of mss and books). Austin 1963. Catalogue compiled by L. J. Teagarden.

Collections and Selections

Works. 5 vols 1931–7. The good companions; Angel Pavement (both with introd by Priestley); Adam in moonshine and Benighted (in 1 vol); Three plays [Dangerous corner, Eden End, Cornelius] and a preface (pbd separately New York 1935); Self-selected essays.

Plays. 3 vols 1948–50, New York 1950–2 (vol 1 as Seven plays).

[Selected essays]. 1926 (Essays of Today and Yesterday).
Four-in-hand. 1934. Contains Adam in moonshine; Laburnum Grove; The roundabout and a selection of essays; stories and miscellaneous prose pieces.
Two time plays. 1937. Contains Time and the Conways; I have been here before.
Four plays. 1944. Contains Music at night; The long mirror; They came to a city; Desert highway.
Three time plays. 1947. Contains Dangerous corner; Time and the Conways; I have been here before.
Going up: stories and sketches. 1950.
The Priestley companion: a selection from the writings. Introd by I. Brown 1951 (Penguin).
All about ourselves, and other essays, chosen and introduced by E. Gillett. 1956.
Essays of five decades. Selected with preface by S. Cooper, Boston 1968, London 1969.
The world of J. B. Priestley: chosen and introduced by D. G. MacRae. 1968.

§1

The chapman of rhymes. 1918.
Brief diversions: being tales, travesties and epigrams. Cambridge 1922. Many items rptd from Cambridge Rev.
Papers from Lilliput. Cambridge 1922. Essays rptd from various periodicals.
I for one. 1923, New York 1924. Essays rptd from Challenge.
Figures in modern literature. 1924, New York 1924. Essays, mostly rptd from London Mercury.
The English comic characters. 1925, New York 1925. Essays.
George Meredith. 1926 (EML), New York 1926.
Talking. 1926, New York 1926.
Adam in moonshine. 1927, New York 1927.
Benighted. 1927, New York 1928 (as The old dark house).
The English novel. 1927, 1935 (rev).
Open house: a book of essays. 1927, New York 1927. Rptd from Saturday Rev.
Thomas Love Peacock. 1927 (EML), New York 1927, London 1966 (introd by J. I. M. Stewart).
Apes and angels: a book of essays. 1928.
The balconinny, and other essays. 1929, New York 1930. Rptd from Saturday Rev.
English humour. 1929, New York 1929 (English Heritage ser).
Farthing Hall. 1929, Garden City NY 1929. With H. Walpole.
The good companions. 1929, New York 1929. For the dramatization, with E. Knoblock, see Plays, below.
Angel Pavement. 1930, New York 1930.
The town major of Miraucourt. 1930. Story.
Far away. 1932, New York 1932.
Self-selected essays. 1932, New York 1932. More than half previously uncollected.
Albert goes through. 1933, New York 1933. Story.
I'll tell you everything: a frolic. 1933, New York 1933. With G. Bullett.
Wonder hero. 1933, New York 1933.
English journey: being a rambling but truthful account of what one man saw and heard and felt and thought during a journey through England during the autumn of the year 1933. 1934, New York 1934.
They walk in the city: the lovers in the stone forest. 1936, New York 1936.
Midnight on the desert: a chapter of autobiography. 1937, New York 1937.
The doomsday men: an adventure. 1938, New York 1938.
Let the people sing. 1939, New York 1940.
Rain upon Godshill: a further chapter of autobiography. 1939, New York 1939.
Britain speaks. New York 1940. Based on broadcast talks.
Postscripts. 1940. Broadcast talks.
Out of the people. 1941, New York 1941. Politics.

Black-out in Gretley: a story of—and for—wartime. 1942, New York 1942.
Britain at war. New York 1942.
British women go to war. [1943].
Daylight on Saturday: a novel about an aircraft factory. 1943, New York 1943.
Here are your answers. [1944]. Pamphlet.
Manpower. 1944.
Letter to a returning serviceman. 1945. Pamphlet.
Three men in new suits. 1945, New York 1945.
Bright day. 1946, New York 1946, London 1966 (EL) (with new introd by Priestley).
The new citizen. [1946]. Pamphlet.
Russian journey. 1946. Pamphlet.
The secret dream: an essay on Britain, America and Russia. 1946. Based on broadcast talks.
The arts under socialism. 1947.
Jenny Villiers: a story of the theatre. 1947, New York 1947.
Theatre outlook. 1947.
Delight. 1949, New York 1949.
Festival at Farbridge. 1951, New York 1951 (as Festival).
The other place, and other stories of the same sort. 1953, New York [1953].
Low notes on a high level: a frolic. 1954, New York [1954].
The magicians. 1954, New York 1954.
Journey down a rainbow. 1955, New York [1955]. With J. Hawkes. Travel in New Mexico and Texas.
The writer in a changing society. Aldington 1956. Lecture.
The art of the dramatist: a lecture together with appendices and discursive notes. 1957.
Thoughts in the wilderness. 1957, New York [1957].
Topside, or the future of England: a dialogue. 1958.
The story of theatre. [1959], Garden City NY [1959] (as The wonderful world of the theatre); London 1969 (rev), Garden City NY 1969. For children.
Literature and western man. 1960, New York 1960.
William Hazlitt. 1960 (Br Council pamphlet).
Charles Dickens: a pictorial biography. [1961], New York 1962.
Saturn over the water. 1961, Garden City NY 1961.
Margin released: a writer's reminiscences and reflections. 1962, New York [1962].
The shapes of sleep: a topical tale. 1962, Garden City NY 1962.
Man and time. 1964, Garden City NY 1964. Philosophy.
Sir Michael and Sir George: a tale of COMSA and DISCUS and the New Elizabethans. 1964, Boston [1964] (with sub-title: a comedy of the New Elizabethans).
Lost empires: being Richard Herncastle's account of his life on the variety stage. 1965, Boston 1965.
The moments, and other pieces. 1966. Essays.
Salt is leaving. 1966.
It's an old country. 1967, Boston 1967.
All England listened: the wartime broadcasts of J. B. Priestley. Introd by E. Sevareid, New York 1968.
The image men (Out of town; London end). 2 vols 1968, 1 vol Boston 1969.
Trumpets over the sea: being a rambling and egotistical account of the London Symphony Orchestra's engagement at Daytona Beach, Florida, in July–August 1967. 1968.
The prince of pleasure and his regency 1811–20. 1969, New York 1969.

Plays

Plays are listed in order of production, where known

The good companions: a play in two acts. (His Majesty's 14 May 1931). [1935] (French's Acting Edn). With E. Knoblock: based on the novel, 1929 above.
Dangerous corner: a play in three acts. (Lyric 17 May 1932). 1932, New York 1932, London [1933] (French's Acting Edn).

The roundabout: a comedy in three acts. (Playhouse, Liverpool 14 Dec 1932). [1933] (French's Acting Edn), 1933.

Laburnum Grove: an immoral comedy in three acts. (Duchess 28 Nov 1933). 1934, [1935] (French's Acting Edn).

Eden End: a play in three acts. (Duchess 13 Sept 1934), 1934, [1935] (French's Acting Edn).

Cornelius: a business affair in three transactions. (Duchess 20 March 1935). 1935, [1936] (French's Acting Edn).

Duet in floodlight: a comedy. (Apollo 4 June 1935). 1935.

Bees on the boat deck: a farcical tragedy in two acts. (Lyric 5 May 1936). 1936, [1936] (French's Acting Edn).

Spring tide: a play in three acts. (Duchess 15 July 1936). [1936], [1937] (French's Acting Edn). With G. Billam.

I have been here before: a play in three acts. (Royalty 22 Sept 1937). 1937, New York 1938, London 1939 (French's Acting Edn).

Time and the Conways: a play in three acts. (Duchess 26 Aug 1937). 1937, New York 1938, London 1939 (French's Acting Edn).

People at sea: a play in three acts. (Apollo 24 Nov 1937). 1937, [1938] (French's Acting Edn).

Mystery at Greenfingers: a comedy of detection. 1937. Test piece for News Chron Amateur Dramatic Contest.

Music at night. (Malvern Festival April 1938; Westminster 10 Oct 1939). In Three plays, 1943, below. Pbd separately 1947 (French's Acting Edn).

When we are married: a Yorkshire farcical comedy. (St Martin's 11 Oct 1938). [1938], [1940] (French's Acting Edn).

Johnson over Jordan: the play and all about it—an essay. (New 22 Feb 1939). 1939, New York [1939], [1941] (French's Standard Library Edn, with subtitle, A modern morality play in three acts).

The long mirror. (Playhouse, Oxford March 1940; Gateway 6 Nov 1945). In Three plays, 1943, below. Pbd separately 1947 (French's Acting Edn).

Goodnight children: a comedy of broadcasting. (New 5 Feb 1942). In Three comedies, 1945, below.

They came to a city. (Globe 21 April 1943). In Three plays, 1943, below. Pbd separately 1944 (French's Acting Edn).

Desert highway: a play in two acts and an interlude. (Theatre Royal, Bristol 13 Dec 1943; Playhouse 10 Feb 1944). 1944, [1944] (French's Acting Edn).

Three plays. 1943. Music at night; The long mirror; They came to a city.

How are they at home?: a topical comedy in two acts. (Apollo 4 May 1944). [1945] (French's Acting Edn).

The golden fleece: a comedy in three acts. In Three comedies, 1945, below. Pbd separately 1948 (French's Acting Edn). Performed under the title Bull market at the Bradford Civic Theatre and the Glasgow Citizens Theatre, 1944.

Three comedies. 1945. Goodnight children; The golden fleece; How are they at home?

Jenny Villiers: a play in two acts. (Theatre Royal, Bristol March 1946). Not pbd.

An inspector calls: a play in three acts. (New 1 Oct 1946). 1947, [1948] (French's Acting Edn).

Ever since paradise: an entertainment chiefly referring to love and marriage, in three acts. (New 4 June 1947). [1949] (French's Acting Edn).

The linden tree: a play in two acts and four scenes. (Duchess 15 Aug 1947). 1948, New York 1948, London [1948] (French's Acting Edn).

The Rose and Crown: a play in one act. 1947 (French's Acting Edn).

Home is tomorrow: a play in two acts. (Princes, Bradford 17 Oct 1948; Cambridge 4 Nov 1948). 1949, [1950] (French's Acting Edn).

The high Toby: a play for the toy theatre. [1948].

Summer day's dream: a play in two acts. (Prince's, Bradford 8 Aug 1949; St Martin's 8 Sept 1949). [1950] (French's Acting Edn).

The Olympians: opera in three acts. (Covent Garden 29 Sept 1949). [1950]. Music by Bliss. Vocal score.

Bright shadow: a play of detection in three acts. (Coliseum, Oldham 3 April 1950; Intimate, Palmers Green 10 April 1950). 1950 (French's Acting Edn).

Treasure on Pelican: a play in three acts. (Prince of Wales, Cardiff 4 Feb 1952). 1953 (for 1954) (Evans Plays).

Dragon's mouth: a dramatic quartet in two parts. (Festival, Malvern 13 April 1952; Winter Garden 13 May 1952). 1952, [1953] (French's Acting Edn). With J. Hawkes.

Mother's day: a comedy in one act. [1933] (French's Acting Edn).

Private rooms: a one act comedy in the Viennese style. [1953] (French's Acting Edn).

Try it again: a one act play. [1953] (French's Acting Edn).

The white countess. (Gaiety, Dublin 16 Feb 1954; Saville 24 March 1954). With J. Hawkes. Unpbd.

A glass of bitter: a play in one act. [1954] (French's Acting Edn).

The scandalous affair of Mr Kettle and Mrs Moon: a comedy in three acts. (Pleasure Gardens, Folkestone 22 Aug 1955; Duchess 1 Sept 1955). [1956].

Take the fool away. (Burgtheater, Vienna Feb 1956; Playhouse, Nottingham 28 Sept 1959). Unpbd.

These our actors. (Citizens, Glasgow 1 Oct 1956). Unpbd.

The glass cage: a play in two acts. (Piccadilly 26 April 1957). [1958] (French's Acting Edn).

A severed head: a play in three acts. (Criterion 27 June 1963). With Iris Murdoch; based on her novel of same title.

The pavilion of masks. (Old Vic, Bristol 7 Oct 1963). Unpbd.

Priestley also wrote a number of film scripts. See L. Löb, Bibliographies, above.

§2

Mann, D. L. Priestley: servant of the comic spirit. Bookman (New York) 73 1931.

Shanks, E. Mr Priestley's novels. London Mercury 26 1932.

Frederick, J. T. Priestley: all-round man of letters on the 18th century plan. Eng Jnl (College edn) 27 1938.

Zur Megede, G. Wort- und Gestaltungskunst bei Priestley. Marburg 1938.

Riese, T. Priestley und das achtzehnte Jahrhundert. E Studien 74 1941.

Whidden, R. W. Priestley and his novels. Queen's Quart 48 1941.

Lindsay, J. In Writers of to-day, ed D. V. Baker, 1946.

Pogson, R. Priestley and the theatre. Clevedon 1947.

Nigot, G. Trois aspects de Priestley. Études Anglaises 7 1954.

— Le théâtre de Priestley. Études Anglaises 10 1957.

Brown, I. J. B. Priestley. 1957, 1964 (rev) (Br Council pamphlet).

Smith, G. Time alive: Dunne and Priestley. South Atlantic Quart 56 1957.

Stürzl, E. Die Zeit in den Dramen Priestleys. Germanisch-romanische Monatsschrift 38 1957.

Hughes, D. J. B. Priestley: an informal study of his work. 1958.

Löb, L. Mensch und Gesellschaft bei Priestley. Berne [1962].

Schloesser, A. A critical survey of some of Priestley's plays. Zeitschrift für Anglistik und Amerikanistik 10 1962.

Dietrich, G. Priestleys Angel Pavement in soziologischer Sicht. Wissenschaftliche Zeitschrift der Martin-Luther-Universität Halle-Wittenberg 13 1964.

Evans, G. L. Priestley: the dramatist. 1964.

Fuchs, K. J. B. Priestley. Die Neueren Sprachen 15 1966.

Oetting, W. Priestley—An inspector calls: eine Erörterung des Schauspielschlusses. Die Neueren Sprachen 15 1966.

Rogers, I. A. The time plays of Priestley. Extrapolation 10 1968.

VICTOR SAWDON PRITCHETT
b. 1900

Selections

Collected stories. 1956. Includes contents of You make your own life and It may never happen, below, with some others.

The sailor, Sense of humour and other stories. New York 1956.

§1

Marching Spain. 1928. Non-fiction.
Clare Drummer. 1929.
The Spanish virgin and other stories. 1930.
Shirley Sanz. 1932, Boston 1932 (as Elopement into exile).
Nothing like leather. 1935, New York 1935.
Dead man leading. 1937.
You make your own life. 1938. Stories.
In my good books. 1942. Essays.
It may never happen & other stories. 1945, New York 1947.
Build the ships: the official story of the shipyards in war-time. 1946.
The living novel. 1946, New York 1947, 1964 (rev, with contents of The working novelist, below, as The living novel & later appreciations). Essays.
Why do I write?: an exchange of views between Elizabeth Bowen, Graham Greene and V. S. Pritchett. 1948, New York 1948.
Mr Beluncle. 1951, New York 1951.
Books in general. 1953, New York 1953. Essays.
The Spanish temper. 1954, New York 1954. Non-fiction.
When my girl comes home. 1961, New York 1961. Stories.
London perceived. [1962], New York 1962. Topography.
The key to my heart: a comedy in three parts. 1963, New York 1964. Stories.
Foreign faces. 1964, New York 1964 (as The offensive traveller). Travel.
New York proclaimed. [1965], New York 1965. Topography.
The working novelist. 1965. Essays.
Dublin: a portrait. 1967. Topography.
A cab at the door: an autobiography. 1968, New York 1968.
Blind love, and other stories. 1969.

Many of Pritchett's stories and essays were first pbd in New Statesman (*of which he was literary editor for two years shortly after World War II*).

EDWIN WILLIAM PUGH
1874–1930

§1

A street in Suburbia. 1895, New York 1895. Sketches.
The man of straw. 1896.
King Circumstance. 1898, New York 1898. Stories.
The rogue's paradise: an extravaganza. 1898. With C. Gleig.
Tony Drum: a Cockney boy. 1898, New York 1898.
Mother-sister. 1900.
The heritage. 1901. With G. Burchett.
The stumbling-block. 1903, New York 1903.
The fruit of the vine: being the autobiography in outline of Gideon Bolsover, compiled from George Barnard's mss. 1904. Fiction.

The purple head: a romance of the twentieth century. 1905.
The spoilers. 1906.
The shuttlecock. 1907.
The broken honeymoon. 1908.
Charles Dickens: the apostle of the people. 1908.
The enchantress. 1908.
Peter Vandy: a biography in outline. 1909. Fiction.
The mocking bird: an entertainment. Compiled by Mrs Lorimer Wake, with spelling, stops, grammar and literary graces by E. Pugh. 1910.
The Charles Dickens originals. 1912, New York 1912.
The city of the world: a book about London and the Londoner. 1912.
Harry the Cockney. [1912].
The proof of the pudding. 1913.
Punch and Judy. 1913, Indianapolis 1914.
The Cockney at home: stories and studies of London life and character. 1914.
The phantom peer: an extravaganza. 1914.
The quick and the dead: a tragedy of temperaments. 1914.
A book of laughter. 1916.
Slings and arrows: a book of essays. 1916.
The eyes of a child. 1917.
The great unborn: a dream of to-morrow. 1918.
The way of the wicked. [1921].
The secret years: further adventures of Tobias Morgan. 1923.
The world is my oyster. 1924.
Empty vessels. 1926.

§2

Adcock, S. St J. In his Glory that was Grub Street, 1928.
Boll, T. E. M. The works of Pugh: a chapter in the novel of humble London life. Philadelphia 1934.
Brome, V. In his Four realist novelists, 1965 (Br Council pamphlet).

BARBARA MARY CRAMPTON PYM
b. 1913

§1

Some tame gazelle. 1950.
Excellent women. 1952.
Jane and Prudence. 1953.
Less than angels. 1955, New York 1957.
A glass of blessings. 1958.
No fond return of love. 1961.

ARTHUR MICHELL RANSOME
1884–1967

Bibliographies

Rota, A. Some uncollected authors: Arthur Ransome. Book Collector 8 1959.

§1

The souls of the streets, and other little papers. 1904.
The stone lady, ten little papers, and two mad stories. 1905.
Pond and stream. [1906].
The child's book of the seasons. [1906].
The things in our garden. [1906].
Highways and byways in fairyland. [1906].
Bohemia in London. 1907, New York 1907, London 1912 (rev).
A history of story-telling: studies in the development of narrative. 1909.
Edgar Allan Poe: a critical study. 1910, New York 1910.
The imp and the elf and the ogre. 1910. Reprints (rev) Pond and stream, The child's book of the seasons, The things in our garden.

The hoofmarks of the faun. 1911. Stories.
Oscar Wilde: a critical study. 1912, 1913 (rev), New York 1913.
Portraits and speculations. 1913.
The elixir of life. 1915.
Old Peter's Russian tales. 1916, New York 1917, London [1938] (with new preface).
Aladdin and his wonderful lamp, in rhyme. [1919].
Six weeks in Russia in 1919. 1919, New York 1919 (as Russia in 1919).
The soldier and death: a Russian folk tale told in English. 1920, New York 1922.
The crisis in Russia. 1921, New York 1921.
'Racundra's' first cruise. 1923, New York 1923. Autobiographical.
The Chinese puzzle. 1927. Non fiction.
Rod and line: essays, together with Aksakov on fishing. 1929.
Swallows & Amazons. 1930, Philadelphia 1931.
Swallowdale. 1931, Philadelphia 1932.
Peter Duck. 1932, Philadelphia [1933].
Winter holiday. 1933, Philadelphia [1934].
Coot club. 1934, Philadelphia [1935].
Pigeon post. 1936, Philadelphia [1937].
We didn't mean to go to sea. 1937, New York 1938.
Secret water. 1939, New York 1940.
The big six. 1940, New York 1941.
Missee Lee. 1941, New York 1942.
The Picts and the martyrs: or not welcome at all. 1943, New York 1943.
Great Northern? 1947, New York 1948.
Fishing. Cambridge 1955 (National Book League Reader's Guide).
Mainly about fishing. 1959.

§2

Shelley, H. Arthur Ransome. 1960, 1968 (rev).

For further discussion of Ransome as a writer for children, see col 797, below.

SIR HERBERT EDWARD READ
1893–1968
See cols 1108–13, below.

FORREST REID
1875–1947

Bibliographies
Burlingham, R. In his Forrest Reid, 1953, below. Includes contributions to periodicals.
City of Belfast Public Libraries. Forrest Reid: an exhibition of books and manuscripts September 2nd–23rd 1953. 1953 (duplicated), 1954 (priv ptd).

§1
The kingdom of twilight. 1904.
The garden god: a tale of two boys. 1905.
The Bracknels: a family chronicle. 1911. *See* also Denis Bracknel, below.
Following darkness. 1912. *See* also Peter Waring, below.
The gentle lover: a comedy of middle age. 1913.
At the door of the gate. 1915, Boston 1916.
W. B. Yeats: a critical study. 1915.
The spring song. 1916, Boston 1917.
A garden by the sea: stories and sketches. Dublin and London 1918. Also includes verse.
Pirates of the spring. Dublin and London 1919, Boston 1920.
Pender among the residents. [1922], Boston 1923.
Apostate. 1926, Boston 1926. Autobiography.

Demophon: a traveller's tale. 1927.
Illustrators of the sixties. 1928. On the illustration of books and periodicals.
Walter de la Mare: a critical study. 1929.
Uncle Stephen. 1931.
Brian Westby. 1934.
The retreat: or the machinations of Henry. 1936.
Peter Waring. 1937. A rewritten version of Following darkness, 1912, above.
Private road. 1940. Autobiography.
Retrospective adventures. 1941. Essays and stories.
Notes and impressions. Newcastle Co Down 1942.
Poems from the Greek Anthology. Tr Reid 1943.
Young Tom: or very mixed company. 1944.
The milk of paradise: some thoughts on poetry. 1946.
Denis Bracknel. 1947. A 'completely rewritten' version of The Bracknels, 1911, above.

§2

Ellis, S. M. Bookman (London) 57 1920; rptd in his Mainly Victorian, 1925.
Forster, E. M. In his Abinger harvest, 1936.
—— In his Two cheers for democracy, 1951.
Boyd, J. The achievement of Reid. Dublin Mag 20 1945.
Forrest Reid memorial: addresses [by E. M. Forster, W. de la Mare, S. Gilbert]. 1952.
Burlingham, R. Forrest Reid: a portrait and a study. 1953.
Putt, S. G. Pan in Ulster: Reid. In his Scholars of the heart, 1962.

STEPHEN SYDNEY REYNOLDS
1881–1919

§1

Devizes and round about. [1906] (Mate's Illustrated Guides).
The holy mountain: a satire on tendencies. 1910 [1909], New York 1909.
A poor man's house. 1909, New York 1909.
Alongshore: where man and the sea face one another. 1910, New York 1910. Non-fiction.
Seems so!: a working-class view of politics. 1911. With Bob and Tom Woolley.
How 'twas: short stories and small travels. 1912.
The lower deck: the Navy and the nation. 1912.

Letters
Letters of Stephen Reynolds. Ed H. Wright 1923.

§2

Squire, J. C. In his Books in general, 3rd ser 1921.

JEAN RHYS
b. 1894

The left bank and other stories, with a preface by F. M. Ford. 1927.
Postures. 1928, New York 1929 (as Quartet).
After leaving Mr Mackenzie. 1931, New York 1931.
Voyage in the dark. 1934, New York 1935.
Good morning, midnight. 1939.
The wide Sargasso Sea. 1966, New York 1967. With introd by F. Wyndham.
Tigers are better-looking. 1968. Stories.

DOROTHY MILLER RICHARDSON
1873–1957

Bibliographies

'Gawsworth, John' (T. I. F. Armstrong). In his Ten contemporaries: notes towards their definitive bibliographies, ser 2 1933.

Prescott, J. Preliminary checklist of the periodical articles of Dorothy Richardson. In Studies in honor of John Wilcox, ed A. D. Wallace and O. W. Ross, Detroit 1958.

Blake, C. R. In his Dorothy Richardson, Ann Arbor 1960, below.

Glikin, G. Checklist of writings by Dorothy Richardson; Dorothy Richardson: an annotated bibliography of writings about her. Eng Lit in Transition 8 1965.

§1

The Quakers past and present. 1914, New York 1914.
Gleanings from the works of George Fox. [1914] (Religion of Life ser).
Pilgrimage. Originally pbd as separate vols, as follows:
Pointed roofs. 1915, New York 1916. With introd by J. D. Beresford.
Backwater. 1916, New York 1917.
Honeycomb. 1917, New York 1919.
Interim. 1919, New York 1920. Serialized in Little Rev 6–7 1919–20.
The tunnel. 1919, New York 1919.
Deadlock. 1921, New York 1921 (with foreword by W. Follett).
Revolving lights. 1923, New York 1923.
The trap. 1925, New York 1925.
Oberland. 1927, New York 1928.
Dawn's left hand. 1931, New York 1931.
Clear horizon. 1935, New York 1936.
Collected edn, with final section Dimple hill, and with foreword by the author 4 vols 1938, New York 1938, London 1967 (with introd by W. Allen and a final section, March moonlight, previously unpbd in book form).
John Austen and the inseparables. 1930. Essay on book illustration.

Dorothy Richardson's trns are listed by Gawsworth and Glikin (Bibliographies, above) and 7 letters were ptd by J. Prescott in Yale Univ Lib Gazette 33 1959.

§2

Sinclair, M. The novels of Dorothy Richardson. Egoist 5 1918.
—— The novels of Dorothy Richardson. Little Rev 4 1918. Differs from Egoist article.
Johnson, R. B. In his Some contemporary novelists: women, 1920.
Mais, S. P. B. In his Books and their writers, 1920.
Hyde, L. The work of Dorothy Richardson. Adelphi 2 1924.
Powys, J. C. Dorothy M. Richardson. 1931.
Beach, J. W. Imagism: Dorothy Richardson. In his Twentieth century novel, New York 1932.
Edgar, P. Stream of consciousness: Dorothy Richardson, Virginia Woolf. In his Art of the novel, New York 1933.
Kulemeyer, G. Studien zur Psychologie im neuen englischen Roman: D. Richardson und J. Joyce. Bottrop 1933.
Eagelson, H. Pedestal for statue: the novels of Dorothy Richardson. Sewanee Rev 42 1934.
Buck, E. Die Fabel in Pointed roofs von Dorothy Richardson. Istanbul 1937.
Fitzgerald, E. Dorothy M. Richardson. Life & Letters Today 17 1937.
Church, R. An essay in estimation of Dorothy Richardson's Pilgrimage. [1938]. Pamphlet.

Gregory, H. Dorothy Richardson reviewed. Life & Letters Today 21 1939.
—— Dorothy Richardson: an adventure in self-discovery. New York 1967.
Maisel, E. M. Dorothy M. Richardson's Pilgrimage. Canadian Forum 19 1939.
Kelly, R. G. The strange philosophy of Dorothy Richardson. Pacific Spectator 8 1954.
Friedman, M. J. Dorothy Richardson and Virginia Woolf. In his Stream of consciousness, New Haven 1955.
Stanford, D. Dorothy Richardson's novels. Contemporary Rev 192 1957.
Edel, L. Dorothy M. Richardson 1882–1957. Modern Fiction Stud 4 1958.
—— In his The modern psychological novel, New York 1964.
Trickett, R. The living dead. V: Dorothy Richardson. London Mag 6 1959.
Blake, C. R. Dorothy Richardson. Ann Arbor [1960].
Kumar, S. K. Dorothy Richardson and Bergson's durée. Indian Jnl of Eng Stud 1 1960.
—— In his Bergson and the stream of consciousness novel, 1962.
Glikin, G. Dorothy M. Richardson: the personal 'pilgrimage'. PMLA 78 1963.
—— Variations on a method. James Joyce Quart 2 1964.
Rose, S. The unmoving center: consciousness in Dorothy Richardson's Pilgrimage. Contemporary Lit 10 1969.

WILLIAM PETT RIDGE
1857–1930

§1

Eighteen of them: singular stories. [1894]. As 'Warwick Simpson'.
A clever wife. 1895, New York 1896.
Minor dialogues. Bristol [1895]. Stories.
Telling stories, from 'St James Gazette'. 1895.
An important man, and others. 1896. Stories.
The second opportunity of Mr Staplehurst. [1896].
Secretary to Bayne, M.P. 1897, New York 1898.
Mord Em'ly. 1898, New York 1898 (as Mordemly), 1898 (as By order of the magistrate).
Three women and Mr Frank Cardwell. 1898.
Outside the radius: stories of a London suburb. 1899, New York 1900.
A son of the state. New York 1899, London 1900.
A breaker of laws. 1900, New York 1900.
London only: a set of common occurrences. 1901.
'Erb'. New York 1902, London 1903 (as 'Erb).
Lost property: the story of Maggie Cannon. 1902.
Up side streets. 1903. Stories.
George and The general. [1904]. Stories.
Next door neighbours. 1904. Stories.
Mrs Galer's business. 1905.
On company's service. 1905. Stories.
The Wickhamses. 1906, New York 1915.
Name of Garland. 1907.
Nearly five million. 1907. Stories.
Sixty-nine Birnam Road. [1908].
Speaking rather seriously. 1908. Essays.
Splendid brother. 1909.
Thomas Henry. [1909].
Light refreshment. 1910. Stories.
Nine to six-thirty. 1910.
Table d'hôte. [1911]. Stories.
Thanks to Sanderson. 1911.
Devoted Sparkes. 1912.
Love at Paddington. 1912.
Mixed grill. 1913, New York 1913. Stories.
The Remington sentence. 1913.
The happy recruit. 1914, New York 1915.

Book here. 1915. Stories.
The Kennedy people. 1915, New York 1916.
Madame Prince. 1916, New York 1917.
On toast. 1916. Stories.
The amazing years. 1917.
Old and happy. 1918. On the printing trade, with 2 stories.
Special performances. 1918. Stories.
Top speed. 1918.
The bustling hours. 1919.
Just open. [1920]. Stories.
Well-to-do Arthur. 1920.
Bannerton's agency. 1921.
Richard triumphant. 1922.
The lunch basket. 1923. Stories.
Miss Mannering. 1923.
A story-teller: forty years in London. [1923], New York 1924. Autobiography.
Leaps and bounds. 1924. Stories.
Rare luck. 1924.
I like to remember. [1925], New York 1926. Autobiography.
Just like Aunt Bertha. 1925.
London please: four Cockney plays. [1925], New York 1925.
Ernest escaping. 1926.
London types taken from life. 1926. Sketches.
Our Mr Willis. [1926]. Story.
Easy distances. 1927. Stories.
Hayward's flight. 1927.
The two Mackenzies. 1928.
Affectionate regards. 1929.
The slippery ladder. 1929.
Eldest Miss Collingwood. 1930.
Led by Westmacott. 1931.

§2

Adcock, A. St J. In his The glory that was Grub Street, 1928.
Brome, V. In his Four realist novelists, 1965 (Br Council pamphlet).

CECIL EDRIC MORNINGTON ROBERTS
b. 1892

Selections

The Pilgrim cottage omnibus. 1938. Pilgrim cottage; The guests arrive; Volcano. With foreword by Roberts.
Selected poems 1910–60. 1960.

§1

The youth of beauty and other poems. 1915.
War poems. 1916.
The Chelsea cherub. 1917.
Twenty-six poems. 1917.
A week with the Fleet: impressions. [1917].
Charing Cross and other poems of the period. 1919.
Training the airmen. 1919.
Poems. New York [1920].
A tale of young lovers: a tragedy in 4 acts. 1922.
Scissors: a novel of youth. 1923, New York 1923.
Sails of sunset. 1924, New York 1924.
The love rack. 1925, New York 1925.
Little Mrs Manington. [1926], New York [1926].
The diary of Russell Beresford. 1927, New York 1927, London 1938 (rev).
Sagusto. [1927], Garden City NY 1928.
David and Diana. [1928], New York 1929 (as Goose fair).
Indiana Jane. 1929, New York 1930.
Pamela's spring song. 1929, New York 1930.
Havana bound. 1930, New York 1930.
Bargain basement. 1931, New York 1932.
Half way: an autobiography. 1931, New York 1931.

Alfred Fripp. 1932. Biography.
Spears against us. [1932], New York 1932.
Pilgrim cottage. 1933, New York 1933.
Gone rustic. 1934, New York 1934. Rural impressions.
The guests arrive. 1934, New York 1935.
Gone rambling. 1935, New York 1935. Travel.
Volcano. 1935, New York 1936.
Gone afield. 1936, New York 1936. Travel.
Gone sunwards. 1936, New York 1936. Travel.
Victoria four thirty. 1937, New York 1939.
They wanted to live. 1939, New York 1939.
And so to Bath. 1940, New York 1940. Travel.
A man arose. 1941, New York 1941. Poem on Winston Churchill.
One small candle. 1942, New York 1942.
So immortal a flower. 1944, New York 1944 (as The labyrinth).
And so to America. 1946, Garden City NY 1947. Travel.
Eight for eternity. 1947, Garden City NY 1948.
And so to Rome. 1950, New York 1950. Travel.
A terrace in the sun. 1951, New York 1951.
One year of life: some autobiographical pages. 1952, New York [1952].
The remarkable young man. 1954, New York 1954.
Portal to paradise: an Italian excursion. 1955, New York 1955.
Love is like that. 1957, New York 1958.
Wide is the horizon. 1962, New York 1962.
The grand cruise. 1963. Travel.
A flight of birds. 1965, New York 1966. Short stories.
The growing boy: being the first book of an autobiography, 1892–1908. 1967.
The years of promise: being the second book of an autobiography 1908–19. 1968.

FREDERICK WILLIAM SERAFINO AUSTIN LEWIS MARY ROLFE ('BARON CORVO')
1860–1913

Bibliographies

Woolf, C. Some uncollected authors: Frederick Rolfe. Book Collector 4 1955.
— A bibliography of Frederick Rolfe, Baron Corvo. 1957, 1969 (rev) (Soho Bibliographies). Includes contributions to books and periodicals.

§1

Tarcissus: the boy martyr of Rome in the Diocletian persecution. By F.W.R. [1880]. Verse.
Stories Toto told me. 1898, New York 1898. First pbd in Yellow Book.
The attack on St Winefride's well: or Holywell gone mad. [1898]. Anon; attributed to Corvo by Woolf.
In his own image. 1901, 1924 (with introd by S. Leslie), New York 1925. Stories.
Chronicles of the House of Borgia. 1901, New York 1901, 1931 (as A history of the Borgias, with introd by S. Leslie).
Hadrian the seventh. 1904, New York 1925, 1953 (with introd by H. Weinstock). Adapted as play, The play of Hadrian the seventh, by P. Luke, 1968, New York 1969.
Don Tarquinio: a kataleptic phantasmatic romance. 1905.
The weird of the wanderer: being the papyrus records of some incidents in one of the previous lives of Mr Nicholas Crabbe here produced by Prospero and Caliban. 1912. With C. H. C. Pirie-Gordon.
The bull against the enemy of the Anglica-race. 1929 (priv ptd, 50 copies). Attack on Northcliffe, rptd in Symons, Quest for Corvo, §2, below (1955 edn only).
The desire and pursuit of the whole: a romance of modern Venice. 1934 (with introd by A. J. A. Symons), 1953 (with foreword by W. H. Auden), New York 1953.

Hubert's Arthur: being certain curious documents found among the literary remains of Mr N.C., here produced by Prospero and Caliban. Introd by A. J. A. Symons 1935.

Three tales of Venice. [1950] (150 copies). First pbd in Blackwood's Mag 1913.

Amico di Sandro: a fragment of a novel. 1951 (priv ptd, 150 copies).

The cardinal prefect of propaganda, and other stories. 1957. Introd by C. Woolf; first pbd in various periodicals. 250 copies.

Nicholas Crabbe: or the one and the many. Ed with introd by C. Woolf 1958.

A fragment of a hitherto unpublished theological discourse. In Frederick Rolfe and others, Aylesford Rev 4 1961.

Don Renato: an ideal content. Ed with introd by C. Woolf 1963 (200 copies).

Letters

Letters to Grant Richards. Hurst 1952.

Letters to C. H. C. Pirie-Gordon. Ed with introd by C. Woolf and epilogue by Pirie-Gordon 1959.

Letters to Leonard Moore. Ed with introd by C. Woolf and B. W. Korn, and epilogue by L. Moore 1960.

Letters to R. M. Dawkins. Ed with introd by C. Woolf and epilogue by L. M. Ragg 1962.

Without prejudice: one hundred letters to John Lane. Ed with introd and epilogue by C. Woolf 1963 (priv ptd).

The Venice letters; selected, ed and with an introd by C. Woolf. In Art & Literature no 5 1965.

§2

Leslie, S. In London Mercury 8 1923; rptd (enlarged) as introd to Corvo's In his own image, 1924.

Lawrence, D. H. In Adelphi 3 1925; rptd in his Phoenix, New York 1936.

Symons, A. J. A. Frederick Baron Corvo. 1927 (Sette of Odd Volumes 81).

—— In Life & Letters 1 1928.

—— The quest for Corvo. 1934, 1952 (introd by N. Birkett, memoir by S. Leslie, appendix of Holywell letters), 1955 (preface by J. Symons and 2 appendices).

Bainbridge, H. C. Corvo the enigma. In his Twice seven, 1933.

Greene, G. Spectator 16 Feb 1934; rptd in his Lost childhood, 1951.

Hunter-Blair, D. More light on Baron Corvo. London Mercury 19 1934.

O'Sullivan, V. The gall of human kindness. Dublin Mag Jan 1935.

Symons, J. The battle of Holywell: a story of Corvo. Saturday Book 5 1945.

Woolf, C. and B. Sewell (ed). Corvo 1860–1960: a collection of essays by various hands. Aylesford 1961 (300 copies), London 1965 (as New quests for Corvo). Introd by P. Hansford Johnson.

Woolf, C. and B. Sewell. The clerk without a benefice: a study of Fr Rolfe Baron Corvo's conversion and vocation. Aylesford 1964.

Johnson, P. H. The fascination of the paranoid personality: Baron Corvo. Essays & Studies 16 1963.

Weeks, D. Rolfe in Scotland and Wales. Serif 4 1967.

De Marco, S. L'opera narrativa di Rolfe. Rivista di Letterature Moderne e Comparate 21 1968.

NAOMI GWLADYS ROYDE-SMITH
188?–1964

The tortoiseshell cat. 1925, New York 1925.
The housemaid. 1926, New York 1926.
A balcony. 1927, Garden City NY 1928. Play.
John Fanning's legacy. 1927.
Skin-deep: or portrait of Lucinda. 1927, New York 1927.
Children in the wood. 1928, New York 1928 (as In the wood).

The lover. 1928, New York 1929.
Summer holiday: or Gibraltar. 1929, New York 1929 (as Give me my sin again).
The island: a love story. 1930, New York 1930.
Pictures and people: a transatlantic criss-cross between R. Hinks and N. Royde-Smith during 1930. 1930, New York 1931.
The delicate situation. 1931, New York 1931.
The double heart: a study of Julie de Lespinasse. 1931.
The mother. 1931, Garden City NY 1932.
Mrs Siddons. 1931. Play.
The bridge. 1932, Garden City NY 1933.
Incredible tale. 1932.
Madam Julia's tale, and other queer stories. 1932.
David. 1933, New York 1934.
Pilgrim from Paddington: the record of an experiment in travel. [1933].
The queen's wigs. 1934, New York 1934.
Van lords: or the sport of removing. 1934. Sequel to Pilgrim from Paddington, above.
Jake. 1935, New York 1935.
All star cast. 1936, New York 1936.
For us in the dark. 1937, New York 1937.
Miss Bendix. 1938, 1947 (rev).
The younger Venus. 1938, New York 1939.
The altar-piece: an Edwardian mystery. 1939, New York 1939.
Urchin moor. 1939.
Jane Fairfax. 1940.
Outside information: being a diary of rumours collated by N. Royde-Smith. 1941.
The unfaithful wife: or scenario for Gary. 1941.
Mildensee. 1943.
Fire-weed. 1944.
The state of mind of Mrs Sherwood: a study. 1946.
Love in Mildensee. 1948.
The iniquity of us all. 1949.
Rosy Trodd. 1950.
The new rich. 1951.
She always caught the post. 1953.
Melilot. 1955.
Love at first sight: a story of three generations. 1956.
The whistling chambermaid. 1957.
How white is my sepulchre. [1958].
A blue rose. 1959.
Love and a birdcage. 1960.

EDWARD CHARLES SACKVILLE-WEST
b. 1901

§1

Piano quintet. 1925, New York 1925.
The ruin: a Gothic novel. 1926, New York 1927.
The apology of Arthur Rimbaud: a dialogue. 1927. Essay.
Mandrake over the water-carrier. 1928.
Simpson: a life. 1931, New York 1931 London 1951 (rev). Fiction.
The sun in Capricorn: a recital. 1934.
A flame in sunlight: the life and work of Thomas de Quincey. 1936, New Haven Conn 1936 (as Thomas de Quincey).
Graham Sutherland. 1943, 1955 (rev). (Penguin Modern Painters).
The rescue: a melodrama for broadcasting based on Homer's Odyssey. 1945.
And so to bed: an album compiled from his BBC feature by E. Sackville-West. 1947.
Inclinations. 1949. Essays, rptd (rev) from various jnls.

§2

Brooke, J. The novels of Sackville-West. Month 6 1951.

VICTORIA MARY
SACKVILLE-WEST
1892–1962

See cols 335–7, above.

MICHAEL SADLEIR
(MICHAEL THOMAS HARVEY
SADLER)
1888–1957

See cols 1116–8, below.

'SAKI',
HECTOR HUGH MUNRO
1870–1916

Collections and Selections

The works of Saki. 8 vols 1926–7, New York 1927–9. Does not include The rise of the Russian empire. With introds by various authors; for details *see* §1 below.
The short stories of Saki complete, with introduction by C. Morley. New York 1930, [London] 1930.
The novels and plays of Saki. 1933, New York 1933.
Selected stories. 1939.
The best of Saki, with introd by G. Greene. 1950, New York 1961.
76 short stories, comprising Reginald, The chronicles of Clovis, The toys of peace, with introd by E. V. Knox. 1956.
The Bodley Head Saki, selected and introduced by J. W. Lambert. 1963, 2 vols [The unbearable Bassington and other stories; Saki: selected from Beasts and super-beasts, and other stories] 1965.

§1

The rise of the Russian empire. 1900.
The Westminster Alice. 1902, 1927 (Works, introd by J. A. Spender), New York 1929. Political satires, rptd from Westminster Gazette.
Reginald. 1904, 1921 (with Reginald in Russia), New York 1921, London 1926 (Works, introd by H. Walpole), New York 1928.
Reginald in Russia and other sketches. 1910, 1921 (with Reginald), New York 1921, London 1926 (Works, introd by H. Walpole), New York 1928. Stories, with playlet The baker's dozen.
The chronicles of Clovis. 1912, New York 1912, London 1926 (Works, introd by A. A. Milne), New York 1927. Stories.
The unbearable Bassington. 1912, New York 1912, London 1926 (Works, introd by M. Baring), New York 1927, London 1947 (with introd by E. Waugh).
When William came: a story of London under the Hohenzollerns. 1914, New York 1914, London 1926 (Works, introd by Lord Charnwood), New York 1929.
Beasts and super-beasts. 1914, New York 1914, London 1926 (Works, introd by H. W. Nevinson), New York 1928. Stories.
The toys of peace, and other papers, with a memoir by R. Reynolds. 1919, New York 1919, London 1926 (Works, introd by G. K. Chesterton), New York 1928. Stories.
The square egg, and other sketches, with three plays; with a biography by his [i.e. Saki's] sister. 1924, 1926 (Works, introd by J. C. Squire), New York 1929.
The miracle-merchant. In One-act plays for stage and study, 8th ser ed Alice Gerstenberg, New York 1934. Not separately pbd.

§2

Mais, S. P. B. The humour of Saki. In his Books and their writers, 1920.
Cobley, W. D. The tales of Saki. Papers of the Manchester Literary Club 47 1921.
Porterfield, A. Saki. London Mercury 12 1925.
Hartley, L. P. Saki. Bookman (London) 71 1927.
Milne, A. A. Introducing Saki. In his By way of introduction, 1929; rptd from his introd to Chronicles of Clovis, in The works of Saki, above.
Morley, C. Saki. In his Internal revenue, New York 1933. Rptd from his introd to The short stories, in The works of Saki, above.
Drew, E. Saki. Atlantic Monthly 166 1940.
Gore, J. Saki. In English wits, ed L. Russell 1940.
Greene, G. The burden of childhood. In his The lost childhood, 1951; rptd from The best of Saki, above.
Hudson, D. A little master. Spectator 30 May 1952. Correspondence followed during June from G. Greene and E. Munro.
Pritchett, V. S. The performing lynx. New Statesman 5 Jan 1957; rptd in his Working novelist, 1965.
Drake, R. The sauce for the asparagus. Saturday Book 20 1960. On the humorous stories.
— Saki: some problems and a bibliography. Eng Fiction in Transition 5 1962.
— Saki's ironic stories. Texas Stud in Lit & Lang 5 1963.
Spears, G. J. The satire of Saki. New York [1963].
Overmyer, J. 'Turn down an empty glass'. Texas Quart 7 1964.
Gillen, C. H. H. H. Munro—Saki. New York [1969] (Twayne's English Authors).

WILLIAM SANSOM
b. 1912

Selections

Selected short stories, chosen by the author. 1960.
The stories of William Sansom, with an introd by E. Bowen. [1963], Boston 1963.

§1

Jim Braidy: the story of Britain's firemen. 1943. With J. Gordon and S. Spender.
Fireman Flower and other stories. 1944, New York 1945.
Three: stories. 1946, New York 1947.
Westminster in war. 1947. Historical.
The equilibriad. 1948. Story.
Something terrible, something lovely. 1948, New York 1954. Stories.
South: aspects and images from Corsica, Italy and Southern France. 1948, New York 1950. Stories.
The body. 1949, New York 1949.
The passionate north. [1950], New York 1953. Stories.
The face of innocence. 1951, New York 1951.
A touch of the sun. 1952, New York 1958. Stories.
It was really Charlie's castle. 1953. Children's story.
The light that went out. 1953. Children's story.
Pleasures strange and simple. 1953. Essays.
A bed of roses. 1954, New York 1954.
Lord love us. 1954. Stories.
A contest of ladies. 1956, New York 1956.
The loving eye. 1956, New York [1956].
Among the dahlias, and other stories. 1957. Stories.
The cautious heart. 1958, New York 1958.
The icicle and the sun. 1958, New York 1959. Travel in Scandinavia and Finland.
The bay of Naples: introduction and commentaries. 1960, New York 1960. Photographs by K. Otto-Wasow.
Blue skies, brown studies. 1961, Boston 1961. Travel.

The last hours of Sandra Lee. 1961, Boston 1961, London 1964 (as The wild affair).
Away to it all. 1964, New York 1966. Travel.
The ulcerated milkman. 1966, New York 1966. Stories.
Christmas. 1968, New York 1968 (as A book of Christmas).
The Grand Tour today. 1968.
The vertical ladder, and other stories. 1969.

Sansom edited an anthology, Choice: some new stories and prose, *1946*; *and, with introd*, The tell-tale heart and other stories, by E. A. Poe, *1948*.

§2

Mason, R. The promise of Sansom. Wind & the Rain 3 1946; rptd in Modern British writing, ed D. V. Baker, New York 1947.
Vickery, J. B. Sansom and logical empiricism. Thought 36 1961.
Neumeyer, P. F. Kafka and Sansom. Wisconsin Stud in Contemporary Lit 7 1966.

'SAPPER',
HERMAN CYRIL McNEILE
1888–1937

Selections
John Walters. [1927]. Stories rptd from The lieutenant and others; The human touch; No man's land.
Bull-dog Drummond: his four rounds with Carl Peterson. [1929], New York 1930 (as Four rounds of Bull-dog Drummond). Contains Bull-dog Drummond; The black gang; The third round; The final count.
Sapper's war stories, collected in one volume. [1930].
51 stories by Sapper: his one-man omnibus of thrill and adventure. 1934.
Bull-dog Drummond double-header. Garden City NY 1937. Contains The third round, and The final count.

§1

The lieutenant and others. 1915. Stories.
Sergeant Michael Cassidy, RE. 1915, New York [1916] (as Michael Cassidy, Sergeant).
Men, women and guns. 1916, New York [1916]. Stories.
No man's land. 1917, New York [1917]. Stories.
The human touch. 1918, New York [1918]. Stories.
Mufti. 1919, New York [1919]. As McNeile.
Bull-dog Drummond. [1920], New York [1920]. As McNeile. As play, adapted by Sapper and G. Du Maurier, London [1925] (French's Acting Edn).
The man in ratcatcher, and other stories. [1921], New York [1921]. As McNeile.
The black gang. [1922], New York [1922]. As McNeile.
The dinner club: stories. [1923], New York [1923]. As McNeile.
Jim Maitland. [1923], New York [1924]. As McNeile.
The third round. [1924], New York 1924, [1924] (as Bull-dog Drummond's third round). As McNeile.
Out of the blue. 1925, New York [1925]. Stories.
The final count. [1926], New York [1926].
Jim Brent. [1926].
Shorty Bill. [1926].
Word of honour. [1926], New York [1926]. Stories.
The saving clause. [1927].
The female of the species. [1928], Garden City NY 1928, New York 1943 (as Bulldog Drummond—and the female of the species).
Temple Tower. 1929, Garden City NY 1929.
The finger of fate. [1930], Garden City NY [1931]. Stories.
Tiny Carteret. [1930], Garden City NY 1930.
The island of terror. 1931.

The return of Bull-dog Drummond. 1932, Garden City NY [1932] (as Bulldog Drummond returns).
Bulldog Drummond strikes back. Garden City NY 1933, London 1934 (as Knock-out).
Ronald Standish. 1933.
When Carruthers laughed. 1934.
Bulldog Drummond at bay. 1935, Garden City NY 1935.
Ask for Ronald Standish. 1936, New York 1936. Stories.
Challenge: a Bulldog Drummond novel. 1937, Garden City 1937.

A number of individual stories were pbd separately in America. After McNeile's death the Bulldog Drummond ser was continued, under the 'Sapper' pseudonym, by Gerard T. Fairlie.

§2
Usborne, R. In his Clubland heroes, 1953.

DOROTHY LEIGH SAYERS
1893–1957

Bibliographies
Sandoe, J. Contribution towards a bibliography of Dorothy L. Sayers. Bull of Bibliography 18 1944.

Selections
The Dorothy L. Sayers omnibus. 1933. The five red herrings, Strong poison, Lord Peter views the body.
The Dorothy L. Sayers omnibus. New York 1934. Whose body?, The unpleasantness at the Bellona Club, Suspicious characters, [i.e. The five red herrings].
Four sacred plays. 1948, Boston 1948. The zeal of thy house, The devil to pay, He that should come, The just vengeance.
The new Sayers omnibus. 1956. The five red herrings, Have his carcase, Murder must advertise.
The Sayers tandem. 1957. The Nine Tailors, Busman's honeymoon.
A treasury of Sayers stories. 1958.
The Sayers holiday book. 1963. Gaudy night, Strong poison, In the teeth of the evidence.
The Lord Peter omnibus. 1964. Clouds of witness, Unnatural death, The unpleasantness at the Bellona Club.

§1

Op 1. Oxford 1916, New York 1916. Verse.
Catholic tales and Christian songs. Oxford 1918, New York 1918. Verse.
Whose body? 1923, New York [1923].
Clouds of witness. 1926, New York 1927, 1938 (with The documents in the case).
Unnatural death. 1927, New York 1928 (as The Dawson pedigree), 1938 (with Lord Peter views the body).
Lord Peter views the body. 1928, New York 1929, 1938 (with The Dawson pedigree).
The unpleasantness at the Bellona Club. 1928, New York 1928.
The documents in the case. 1930, New York 1931, 1938 (with Clouds of witness). With 'Robert Eustace' [E Rawlins].
Strong poison. 1930, New York 1930, 1936 (with Have his carcase).
The five red herrings. 1931, New York 1931 (as Suspicious characters.)
The floating admiral, by certain members of the Detection Club [D. L. Sayers et al]. 1931.
Have his carcase. 1932, New York 1932, 1936 (with Strong poison).
Ask a policeman. [1933]. By A. Berkeley, D. L. Sayers et al.

Hangman's holiday. 1933, New York 1933, 1938 (with Murder must advertise).

Murder must advertise: a detective story. 1933, New York 1933, 1938 (with Hangman's holiday,).

The Nine Tailors. 1934, New York 1934.

Gaudy night. 1935, New York 1936.

Papers relating to the family of Wimsey. Ed 'Matthew Wimsey' [D. L. Sayers] [c .1935] (priv ptd).

The murder of Julia Wallace. In The anatomy of murder: famous crimes considered by members of the Detection Club, 1936, New York 1937.

Busman's honeymoon: a love story with detective interruptions. 1937, New York [1937]. As play, with M. St C. Byrne, (Comedy 16 Dec 1936); in Famous plays of 1937, 1937.

The zeal of thy house. (Chapter House, Canterbury 12 June 1937; Westminster 29 March 1938). 1937, New York 1937. Verse play.

The greatest drama ever staged. 1938. On Easter.

He that should come: a nativity play in one act. (BBC Radio 25 Dec 1938). 1939.

The devil to pay: being the famous history of John Faustus [etc]: a stage-play. (Chapter House, Canterbury 10 June 1939; His Majesty's 20 July 1939). Canterbury 1939 (Acting Edn for the Festival of the Friends of Canterbury Cathedral), London 1939, New York 1939.

Double death: a murder story, by D. L. Sayers [et al]. 1939.

In the teeth of the evidence, and other stories. 1939, New York 1940.

Strong meat. 1939. Religious tract.

Begin here: a war-time essay. 1940, New York 1941.

Creed or chaos? [1940]. Lecture.

The mind of the maker. 1941, New York 1942. Religious tract.

The mysterious English. 1941 (Macmillan War pamphlets 10).

Why work? 1942. Lecture.

The man born to be king: a play-cycle on the life of Our Lord and Saviour Jesus Christ, written for broadcasting. Presented by the British Broadcasting Corporation Dec 1941–Oct 1942. 1943, New York 1949.

The other six deadly sins. 1943. Lecture.

Even the parrot: exemplary conversations for enlightened children. 1944.

The just vengeance: the Lichfield Festival Play for 1946. (Lichfield Cathedral 15 June 1946). 1946.

Unpopular opinions: twenty-one essays. 1946, New York 1947.

Creed or chaos? and other essays in popular theology. 1947, New York 1949.

The lost tools of learning. 1948. Lecture.

The emperor Constantine: a chronicle. 1951, New York 1951. Play.

Introductory papers on Dante. 1954, New York 1954. Preface by B. Reynolds.

Further papers on Dante. 1957, New York 1957.

The poetry of search and the poetry of statement, and other posthumous essays on literature, religion and language. 1963, New York 1969.

Dorothy Sayers tr Dante's Inferno *and* Purgatorio, *Thomas the Troubadour's* Romance of Tristan, *and also* The song of Roland.

§2

Nott, K. Lord Peter views the soul. In her Emperor's clothes, 1953.

Weales, G. C. In his Religion in modern English drama, Philadelphia 1961.

Moorman, C. The suburbs of the city: Eliot and D. L. Sayers. In his Precincts of felicity: the Augustinian city of the Oxford Christians, Gainesville 1966.

Thurmer, J. The theology of D. L. Sayers. Church Quart Rev 168 1967.

Heilbrun, C. G. Sayers, Lord Peter and God. Amer Scholar 37 1968.

JOHN DICK SCOTT
b. 1917

§1

The cellar. 1947, New York 1948 (as Buy it for a song).

The margin. 1949, New York 1950.

The way to glory, or the last night of the holidays: a love story. 1952, New York 1952.

The end of an old song. 1954, New York 1954.

The administration of war production. 1955. With R. Hughes.

Life in Britain. 1956, New York 1956. Non-fiction.

Siemens Brothers 1858–1958: an essay in the history of industry. [1958].

Look at post offices. 1962 (Look Books).

Vickers: a history. [1962].

The pretty penny: an adventure story. 1963, New York 1964.

BEATRICE KEAN SEYMOUR
18?–1955

Invisible tides. 1919, New York 1921.

Intrusion. 1921, New York 1922.

The hopeful journey. 1923, New York 1923.

The romantic tradition. 1925, New York 1925 (as Unveiled).

The last day. 1926, New York 1926.

Three wives. 1927, New York 1927.

Youth rides out. 1928, New York 1929.

False spring. 1929, New York 1930.

But not for love. 1930, New York 1931.

Maids and mistresses. 1932, New York 1932.

Daughter to Philip. 1933, New York 1933.

Interlude for Sally: being some further chapters in the life of Sally Dunn. 1934, New York 1934.

Frost at morning. 1935, Boston 1935.

Summer of life. 1936, Boston 1936.

The happier Eden. 1937, Boston 1937.

Jane Austen: study for a portrait. 1937.

The chronicles of Sally. 1940. Contains Maids and mistresses, Interlude for Sally, Summer of life.

Fool of time. 1940, New York 1941.

The unquiet field. 1940, New York 1940.

Happy ever after —. 1941, New York 1942.

Return journey. 1942, New York 1943.

Buds of May. 1943.

Joy as it flies. 1944.

Tumbled house. 1946.

The children grow up. 1947.

Family group. 1947.

The second Mrs Conford. 1951.

The wine is poured... 1953.

The painted lath. 1955.

ROBERT CEDRIC SHERRIFF
b. 1896

See col 979, below.

MATTHEW PHIPPS SHIEL
1865–1947
Bibliographies

'Gawsworth, John' (T. I. F. Armstrong). M. P. Shiel. In his Ten contemporaries: notes toward their definitive bibliographies, 1932. With preface by Shiel, The inconsistency of a novelist.

Morse, A. R. The works of M. P. Shiel: a study in bibliography. Los Angeles 1948.

Selections

The best short stories of M. P. Shiel. 1948. Selected by 'John Gawsworth' (T. I. F. Armstrong).

§1

The London 1929 rev edns of Cold Steel, The lord of the sea, The purple cloud, The last miracle, *and* The dragon (*entitled* The yellow peril) *have the series title* The novels of M. P. Shiel. *Some details of Shiel's rewriting of his stories and their previous appearances in periodicals are given in A. R. Morse, Bibliography, above.*

Prince Zaleski. 1895, Boston 1895. Stories.
The rajah's sapphire. 1896.
Shapes in the fire: being a mid-winter night's entertainment in two parts and an interlude. 1896, Boston 1896. Stories.
The yellow danger. 1898, New York 1899 (rev).
Contraband of war: a tale of the Hispano-American struggle. 1899, 1914 (rev).
Cold steel. 1899, New York 1900, London 1929 (rev), New York 1929.
The man-stealers: an incident in the life of the Iron Duke. 1900, Philadelphia 1900, London 1908 (rev).
The lord of the sea. 1901, New York 1901, London 1913 (rev), New York 1924 (rev, with introd by C. Van Vechten), London 1929 (without introd).
The purple cloud. 1901, 1929 (rev), New York [1930]
The weird o' it. 1902.
Unto the third generation. 1903.
The evil that men do. 1904.
The lost viol. New York 1905, London 1908 (slight corrections).
The yellow wave. 1905.
The last miracle. 1906, 1929 (rev).
The white wedding. [1908].
The isle of lies. [1908].
This knot of life. [1909].
The pale ape, and other pulses. [1911]. Stories.
The dragon. 1913, 1929 (rev, as The yellow peril).
Children of the wind. 1923, New York 1923.
How the old woman got home. 1927, New York 1928.
Here comes the lady. [1928]. Stories.
Dr Krasinski's secret. New York [1929], London [1930].
The black box. New York [1930], London 1931.
Say Au r'voir but not goodbye. 1933.
This above all. New York [1933], London 1943 (as Above all else; with slight corrections).
The invisible voices. 1935. Stories. With 'John Gawsworth' (T. I. F. Armstrong).
M. P. Shiel. (Richards' shilling selections from Edwardian poets). 1936. Ed 'John Gawsworth' (T. I. F. Armstrong).
The young men are coming! 1937.
Science, life and literature. 1950. With foreword by 'John Gawsworth' (T. I. F. Armstrong). Essays.
An address to the Horsham Rotary Club, November 27th 1938. Aylesford Rev 7 1965.

For details of Shiel's contributions to the novels of Louis Tracy (some pbd as by 'Gordon Holmes') see A. R. Morse, Bibliography, above.

§2

Tytheridge, A. An uncrowned lord of language: an appreciation of the literary work of Shiel. Nichi-Nichi (Tokyo) 16, 17, 18, 19, 21, 22, 23, 24 July 1924.
Van Vechten, C. In his Excavations, New York 1926; rpt of introd to 1924 edn of The lord of the sea.
Estraubs, E. The purple cloud and its author. London Mercury 20 1929.
Billings, H. W. Shiel: a collection and comments. Univ of Texas Lib Chron 6 1958.
Sewell, B. M. P. Shiel. Aylesford Rev 7 1965.

'NEVIL SHUTE', NEVIL SHUTE NORWAY
1899–1960

Selections

Three of a kind: Requiem for a Wren; An old captivity; Pastoral. 1962.

§1

Marazan. 1926.
So disdained. 1928, Boston 1928 (as The mysterious aviator).
Lonely road. 1932, New York 1932.
Ruined city. 1938, New York 1938 (as Kindling).
What happened to the Corbetts. [1939], New York 1939 (as Ordeal).
Landfall: a Channel story. 1940, New York 1940.
An old captivity. 1940, New York 1940.
Pied piper. 1942, New York 1942, London 1956 (abridged).
Pastoral. 1944, New York 1944.
Most secret. 1945, New York 1945.
Vinland the good. 1946, New York 1946. Film-play.
The chequer board. 1947, New York 1947.
No highway. 1948, New York 1948, London 1953 (abridged).
A town like Alice. 1950, New York 1950 (as The legacy).
Round the bend. 1951, New York 1951.
The far country. 1952, New York 1952.
In the wet. 1953, New York 1953.
Slide rule: the autobiography of an engineer. 1954, New York 1954.
Requiem for a Wren. 1955, New York 1955 (as The breaking wave).
Beyond the black stump. 1956, New York 1956.
On the beach. 1957, New York 1957.
The rainbow and the rose. 1958, New York 1958.
Trustee from the toolroom. 1960, New York 1960.
Stephen Morris. 1961, New York 1961.

ETHEL SIDGWICK
1877–1970

§1

Thackeray's Rose and the ring, dramatized in two acts by Ethel Sidgwick. 1909. Rptd in Four plays for children, 1913, below.
Promise. 1910, Boston 1912.
Le gentleman: an idyll of the quarter. 1911, Boston 1912.
Herself. 1912, Boston [1912].
Four plays for children: The rose and the ring; The goody-witch; The goosegirl; Boots and the north wind. 1913.
Succession: a comedy of the generations. 1913, Boston [1913]. Sequel to Promise.
A lady of leisure. 1914, Boston [1914].
Duke Jones: a sequel to A lady of leisure. 1914, Boston 1915.
The accolade. 1915, Boston [1916].
Hatchways. 1916, Boston [1916].
Jamesie. 1918, Boston [1918].
Madam. 1921, Boston [1921].
Two plays for schools: The three golden hairs; The robber bridegroom. 1922, Boston [1922] (as The three golden hairs).
Restoration: the fairy-tale of a farm. 1923, Boston [1923].
Laura: a cautionary story. 1924, Boston [1924].
Fairy-tale plays: The elves and the shoemaker; Riquet with the tuft. 1926.
The bells of Shoreditch. 1928, New York 1928 (as When I grow rich).

Dorothy's wedding: a tale of two villages. 1931, New York 1931 (as A tale of two villages).

Mrs Henry Sidgwick: a memoir by her niece. 1938.

§2

Roberts, R. E. Ethel Sidgwick. Bookman (London) 46 1914.

Sergeant, E. S. The novels of Ethel Sidgwick. New Republic 17 April 1915.

Mann, D. Ethel Sidgwick and her art. Book News Monthly 36 1917.

Salmon, A. L. Ethel Sidgwick: an appreciation. Book News Monthly 36 1917.

Johnson, R. B. In his Some contemporary novelists: women, 1920.

MAY SINCLAIR
(MARY AMELIA ST CLAIR SINCLAIR)
1863–1942

The surviving papers of May Sinclair, including unpbd works, are now in the Univ of Pennsylvania Library. See T. E. M. Boll, On the May Sinclair collection, Univ of Pennsylvania Lib Chron 27 1961.

§1

Essays in verse. 1891.

Audrey Craven. 1897, New York 1906.

Mr & Mrs Nevill Tyson. 1898, New York 1906 (as The Tysons).

Two sides of a question. 1901.

The divine fire. 1904, New York 1904.

Superseded. New York 1906. First pbd in Two sides of a question, 1901.

The helpmate. 1907, New York 1907.

The judgment of Eve. New York 1907. Story rptd in The judgment of Eve and other stories, 1914, below.

Kitty Tailleur. 1908, New York 1908 (as The immortal moment).

The creators: a comedy. 1910, New York 1910.

Feminism. 1912. Suffragette pamphlet.

The flaw in the crystal. New York [1912]. Rptd in Uncanny stories, 1923, below.

The three Brontës. 1912, Boston 1912, London 1914 (with introd by author), New York [1914].

The combined maze. 1913, New York 1913.

The judgment of Eve and other stories. 1914.

The return of the prodigal. New York 1914. Stories; contents as in The judgment of Eve and other stories, above, with the addn of The cosmopolitan, first pbd in Two sides of a question, 1901, above, and with the omission of The judgment of Eve.

The three sisters. 1914, New York 1914.

A journal of impressions in Belgium. 1915, New York 1915.

Tasker Jevons: the real story. 1916, New York [1916] (as The belfry).

A defence of idealism: some questions and conclusions. 1917, New York 1917.

The tree of heaven. 1917, New York 1917.

Mary Olivier: a life. 1919, New York 1919.

The romantic. [1920], New York 1920.

Mr Waddington of Wyck. 1921, New York 1921.

Anne Severn and the Fieldings. 1922, New York 1922.

Life and death of Harriett Frean. [1922], New York 1922.

The new idealism. 1922, New York 1922. Non-fiction.

Uncanny stories. [1923], New York 1923.

Arnold Waterlow: a life. [1924], New York 1924.

A cure of souls. [1924], New York 1924.

The dark night. 1924, New York 1924.

The rector of Wyck. [1925], New York 1925.

Far end. [1926], New York 1926.

The Allinghams. [1927], New York 1927.

History of Anthony Waring. [1927], New York 1927.

Fame. 1929. Story, rptd in Tales told by Simpson, below.

Tales told by Simpson. [1930], New York 1930.

The intercessor and other stories. [1931], New York 1932.

According to Boll, Univ of Pennsylvania Lib Chron 27 1961 (*above*), *May Sinclair was the author of* Nakiketos and other poems *by 'Julian Sinclair', 1886.*

§2

Cooper, F. T. In his Some English storytellers, New York 1912.

Wellington, A. Artist of the supernormal. Dial 63 1917.

Johnson, R. B. In his Some contemporary novelists; women, 1920.

Scott, C. A. D. May Sinclair. Bookman (NY) 52 1920.

Lovett, R. M. Miss Sinclair's later work. Dial 71 1921.

Adcock, A. St J. In his Gods of modern Grub Street, 1923.

Bosschère, J. de. Charity in the work of May Sinclair. Yale Rev 14 1924.

Brewster, D. and A. Burrell. New light on old virtues: May Sinclair. In their Dead reckonings in fiction, New York 1924; rptd, rev, in their Modern fiction, New York 1934.

— Post-Freudian apronstrings. Ibid.

Braybrooke, P. In his Novelists: we are seven, 1926. Also in his Philosophies in modern fiction, 1929.

Tannière, E. L'œuvre récente de May Sinclair. Revue Anglo-américaine 7 1929.

Hoops, R. In his Der Einfluss der Psychoanalyse auf die englische Literatur, 1934.

Boll, T. E. M. May Sinclair and the Medico-Psychological Clinic of London. Proc of the American Philosophical Soc 106 1962.

SIR FRANCIS OSBERT
SACHEVERELL SITWELL, BART
1892–1969

See cols 346–9, above.

JOHN COLLIS SNAITH
1876–1936

§1

Mistress Dorothy Marvin: being excerpts from the memoirs of Sir Edward Armstrong of Copeland Hall. 1895, New York 1896. Fiction.

Fierceheart the soldier. 1897, New York 1897.

Lady Barbarity: a romantic comedy. 1899, New York 1899.

Willow the king: the story of a cricket match. [1899].

Patricia at the inn. 1901 (Arrowsmith's Christmas Annual 1901), New York [1906].

The wayfarers. 1902, New York 1902 (as Love's itinerary).

Broke of Covenden. 1904, Boston 1905, London 1914 (rev), Boston 1914.

Henry Northcote. 1906, Boston 1906.

William Jordan, junior. 1907, New York 1908.

Araminta. 1909, New York 1909, Bristol 1921 (rev).

Fortune. 1910, New York 1910.

Mrs Fitz. 1910, New York 1910.

The principal girl. 1912, New York 1912.

An affair of state. 1913, Garden City NY 1913.

Anne Faversham. New York 1914, London 1915 (as The great age).

The sailor. 1916, New York 1916.

The coming. 1917, New York 1917.

Mary Plantagenet: an improbable story. 1918.

The time spirit. New York 1918.

Love lane. 1919.
The undefeated. New York 1919.
The adventurous lady. [1920], New York 1920.
The council of seven. [1921], New York 1921.
The Van Roon. New York 1922, London [1925].
The crime of Constable Kelly. [1924].
Time and tide. [1924], New York 1924 (as There is a tide).
Thus far. [1925], New York 1925.
What is to be. 1926, New York 1926.
The hoop. [1927], New York 1927.
Surrender. [1928], New York 1928.
Cousin Beryl. 1929, New York 1929.
The unforeseen. 1930, New York 1930.
Indian summer. 1931, New York 1931.
But even so... [1935], New York 1935.
Curiouser and curiouser. [1935], New York 1936 (as Lord Cobbleigh disappears).
One of the ones. [1937].

§2

Tennyson, C. B. L. In his Life's all a fragment, 1953.

CHARLES PERCY SNOW, BARON SNOW
b. 1905

Bibliographies
Stone, B. In R. Greacen, The world of Snow, 1962, §2 below.
Rabinovitz, R. In his The reaction against experiment in the English novel, 1967, §2 below.

Selections
C. P. Snow—a spectrum: science, criticism, fiction. Ed S. Weintraub, New York [1963].

§1

Death under sail. 1932, New York [1932], London 1959 (rev).
New lives for old. 1933. Anon.
The search. 1934, Indianapolis [1935], London 1958 (rev and abridged).
Richard Aldington: an appreciation. 1938. Pamphlet.
Strangers and brothers. 1940, New York 1958. This and the following novels form the Strangers and brothers sequence.
The light and the dark. 1947, New York [1947].
Time of hope. 1949, New York 1950.
The masters. 1951, New York 1951. Dramatized by R. Millar: see The affair [and other plays], 1964, below.
The new men. 1954, New York 1955. Dramatized by R. Millar: see The affair [and other plays], 1964, below.
Homecomings. 1956, New York 1956 (as Homecoming).
The conscience of the rich. 1958, New York 1958.
The two cultures and the scientific revolution. Cambridge 1959 (Rede lecture), 1964 (with A second look), New York 1964. See also A. C. Lovell et al, Encounter 13 1959; F. R. Leavis, Two cultures? The significance of C. P. Snow, 1962; D. K. Cornelius and E. St Vincent (ed), Cultures in conflict: perspectives on the Snow-Leavis controversy, Chicago [1964].
The affair. 1960, New York 1960. Dramatized by R. Millar: see The affair [and other plays], 1964, below.
Science and government. 1961, Cambridge Mass 1961, New York 1963 (with new appendix), London 1963 (Godkin lectures at Harvard University).
Magnanimity. 1962. Rectorial address, University of St Andrews.
A postscript to Science and government. 1962.
Recent thoughts on the two cultures. [1962]. Lecture.
The affair; The new men; The masters: three plays by R. Millar with preface by Snow. 1964.
Corridors of power. 1964, New York 1964.

Variety of men. 1967, New York [1967]. Biographical sketches.
Sleep of reason. [1968], New York 1969.
The state of seige. New York 1969. Lectures.
Last things. 1970. Final novel in Strangers and brothers sequence.

Snow collaborated in a series of one-act plays with Pamela Hansford Johnson (q.v.), contributed to Proc Royal Soc 1928-35, and edited Cambridge Library of Modern Science 1938-48.

§2

B. Stone, Bibliography, above, contains a selection of reviews of Snow's writings.
Johnson, P. H. Three novelists and the drawing of character: Snow, J. Cary, Ivy Compton Burnett. E & S new ser 3 1950.
Wagner, G. Writer in the welfare state. Commonweal 65 1956.
Greacen, R. Profile of Snow. Humanist 73 1958.
— The world of Snow. Texas Quart 4 1961.
— The world of Snow. 1962.
Stanford, R. Personal politics in the novels of Snow. Critique (Minneapolis) 2 1958.
— The achievement of Snow. Western Humanities Rev 16 1962.
Cooper, W. C. P. Snow. 1959 (Br Council pamphlet).
Bergonzi, B. The world of Lewis Eliot. Twentieth Century 167 1960.
Kermode, F. Beckett, Snow and pure poverty. Encounter 15 1960; rptd in his Puzzles and epiphanies, 1962.
Millgate, M. Structure and style in the novels of Snow. REL 1 1960.
Stanford, D. C. P. Snow: the novelist as fox. Meanjin 19 1960.
— A disputed master: Snow and his critics. Month 29 1963.
Thale, J. Snow: the art of worldliness. Kenyon Rev 22 1960.
— C. P. Snow. Edinburgh 1964 (Writers & Critics).
Turner, I. Above the Snow-line: the sociology of Snow. Overland Aug 1960.
Dennis, N. Under the combination room. Encounter 17 1961.
Finkelstein, S. The art and science of Snow. Mainstream 14 1961.
Martin, G. Novelists of three decades: E. Waugh, G. Greene, Snow. In The modern age, ed B. Ford, vol 7).
Putt, S. G. Technique and culture. E & S new ser 14 1961.
— The Snow-Leavis rumpus. Antioch Rev 23 1963.
Fuller, E. Snow: spokesman of two communities. In his Books with men behind them, New York 1962.
Green, M. A literary defence of The two cultures. Kenyon Rev 24 1962; rptd in his Science and the shabby curate of poetry, 1964.
Halio, J. L. Snow's literary limitations. Northwest Rev Winter 1962.
Hamilton, K. Snow and political man. Queen's Quart 69 1962.
Karl, F. R. The politics of conscience: the novels of Snow. In his The contemporary English novel, New York 1962, London 1963 (as A reader's guide to the contemporary English novel).
— C. P. Snow: the politics of conscience. Carbondale [1963].
Kazin, A. A brilliant boy from the Midlands. In his Contemporaries, New York 1962.
Lehan, R. The divided world: The masters examined. In Six contemporary novels, ed W. O. S. Sutherland, Dallas 1962.
Mandel, E. W. Snow's fantasy of politics. Queen's Quart 69 1962.

Nott, K. The type to which the whole creation moves? Further thoughts on the Snow saga. Encounter 18 1962.

Hall, W. The humanism of Snow. Wisconsin Stud in Contemporary Lit 4 1963.

Vogel, A. W. The academic world of Snow. Twentieth-Century Lit 9 1963.

Adams, R. Pomp and circumstance: Snow. Atlantic Monthly 214 1964.

Jaffa, H. C. Snow: portrait of a man as an adult. Humanist 24 1964.

Wall, S. Reputations 10: the novels of Snow. London Mag new ser 4 1964.

Burgess, A. Powers that be. Encounter 24 1965.

Davis, R. G. C. P. Snow. New York 1965.

Smith, L. W. Snow as novelist: a delimitation. South Atlantic Quart 64 1965.

Trilling, L. The Leavis–Snow controversy. In his Beyond culture, 1965.

Watson, K. Snow and The new men. English 15 1965.

Fietz, L. Cambridge und die Diskussion um das Verhältnis von Literatur und Naturwissenschaft. In Literatur-Kultur-Gesellschaft in England und Amerika, ed G. Müller-Schwefe und K. Tuzinski, Frankfurt 1966.

Hand, H. E. The paper curtain: the divided world of Snow and Leavis revisited. Jnl of Human Relations 14 1966.

Ketels, V. B. Shaw, Snow and the new man. Personalist 47 1966.

Macdonald, A. Imagery in Snow. Univ Rev 32–3 1966.

Murray, B. O. Snow: grounds for reappraisal. Personalist 47 1966.

Rabinowitz, R. Snow as literary critic; Snow as novelist. In his The reaction against experiment in the English novel 1950–60, 1967.

— Snow vs the experimental novel. Columbia Univ Forum 10 1967.

EDITH ŒNONE SOMERVILLE
1858–1949
and
'MARTIN ROSS'
(VIOLET FLORENCE MARTIN)
1862–1915

Mss described as 'The Somerville and Ross papers' were sold at Sotheby's on 9 July 1968. Some mss of Violet Martin were sold at Sotheby's on 10 Dec 1968. Many were acquired at both sales by Queen's Univ Belfast.

Bibliographies

Hudson, E. A bibliography of the first editions of the works of Somerville and Ross, with explanatory notes by E. Œ. Somerville. New York 1942 (300 copies).

Vaughan, R. Bibliography. In G. Cummins, Dr E. Œ. Somerville, §2, below.

Collections and Selections

Collected edition. 7 vols 1910. Some experiences of an Irish R.M; Further experiences of an Irish R.M.; All on the Irish shore; Some Irish yesterdays; An Irish cousin; The real Charlotte; The silver fox.

The Hitchcock edition of Somerville and Ross. 7 vols New York 1927 (priv ptd). Some experiences of an Irish R.M.; Further experiences of an Irish R.M.; In Mr Knox's country; Dan Russel the fox; All on the Irish shore; Wheel tracks; Irish memories.

The Irish R.M., and his experiences. 1928, 1956 (as The Irish R.M. complete). Contains all the Irish R.M. stories.

Experiences of an Irish R.M. 1944. Some experiences of an Irish R.M.; Further experiences of an Irish R.M.

Maria, and some other dogs, ed and illustrated by E. Œ. Somerville. 1949. Selected dog stories from the works of Somerville and Ross.

§1

For the nature of the collaboration after 1915 between Somerville and Ross, see Collis, §2, below.

An Irish cousin. 2 vols 1889 (as by 'Geilles Herring' and Martin Ross), 1889 (as by 'Viva Graham' and Martin Ross), 1903 (rev, as by Somerville and Ross).

Naboth's vineyard. 1891.

In the vine country. 1893. Travel in France.

Through Connemara in a governess cart, by the authors of An Irish cousin. 1893.

The real Charlotte. 3 vols 1894, 1 vol [1919].

Beggars on horseback: a riding tour in North Wales. 1895. As by Ross and Somerville.

The silver fox. 1898 (as by Ross and Somerville), 1902 (rev), [1919] (as by Somerville and Ross).

Some experiences of an Irish R.M. 1899. Stories.

A Patrick's Day hunt. [1902]. Story by Ross, illustr Somerville.

All on the Irish shore: Irish sketches. 1903.

Slipper's ABC of foxhunting. 1903. Drawings and verse by Somerville.

Some Irish yesterdays. 1906, New York 1906. Essays.

Further experiences of an Irish R.M. 1908, New York 1908. Stories.

Dan Russel the fox: an episode in the life of Miss Rowan. 1911, New York 1912.

The story of the discontented little elephant. 1912, New York 1912. Children's story, by Somerville.

In Mr Knox's country. 1915. Irish R.M. stories.

Irish memories. 1917, New York 1918. Autobiography.

Mount music. 1919, New York 1920.

Stray-aways. 1920. Essays.

An enthusiast. 1921, New York 1921.

Wheel-tracks. 1923.

The big house of Inver. 1925, Garden City NY 1925.

French leave. 1928, Boston 1928.

The States through Irish eyes. Boston 1930, London 1931. By Somerville.

An incorruptible Irishman: being an account of Chief Justice Charles Kendal Bushe and of his wife, Nancy Crampton, and their times, 1767–1843. 1932, Boston 1932.

The smile and the tear. 1933, Boston 1933. Essays.

Little Red Riding Hood in Kerry. 1934 (priv ptd, 100 copies). Story, rptd in The sweet cry of hounds, below.

The sweet cry of hounds. 1936, Boston 1937. Stories.

Sarah's youth. 1938.

Records of the Somerville family of Castlehaven and Drishane from 1174 to 1940. Cork 1940 (priv ptd, 200 copies). By E. Œ. Somerville and B. T. Somerville.

Notions in garrison. 1941. Essays.

'Happy days!' essays of sorts. 1946.

Miss Somerville edited the Mark Twain birthday book, *1885, and* Notes of the horn: hunting verse, old and new, *1934.*

§2

Lucas, E. V. Two ladies. In his Cloud and silver, 1916.

Williams, O. A little classic. In his Some great English novels, 1926.

Pritchett, V. S. The Irish R.M. In his The living novel, 1946.

Cummins, G. Dr E. Œ. Somerville: a biography. 1952.

O'Brien, C. C. Somerville and Ross. In his Writers and politics, 1965.

Flanagan, T. The big house of Ross-Drishane. Kenyon Rev 28 1966.

Collis, M. Somerville and Ross: a biography. 1968.

Institute of Irish Studies, The Queen's University Belfast. Somerville and Ross: a symposium. Belfast 1969.

ROBERT HOWARD SPRING
1889–1965
Collections
The Fairwater edition. 1964-.

§1

Darkie and Co. 1932. For children.
Shabby tiger. 1934, New York [1935].
Rachel Rosing. 1935, New York [1936].
Sampson's circus. 1936. For children.
Book parade. 1938. Essays and reviews.
O Absalom! 1938, New York 1938 (as My son, my son!), London 1957.
Heaven lies about us: a fragment of infancy. 1939, New York 1939. Autobiography.
Tumbledown Dick: all people and no plot. 1939, New York 1940. For children.
All they like sheep. 1940. On German propaganda.
Fame is the spur. 1940, New York 1940.
This war we wage. 1941. Non-fiction, with Herbert Morrison and E. M. Delafield.
In the meantime. 1942. Autobiography.
Hard facts. 1944, New York 1944.
And another thing—. 1946, New York 1946. The author's religious experiences.
Dunkerleys. 1946, New York 1947. Sequel to Hard facts.
There is no armour. 1948, New York [1948].
Christmas honeymoon. [1949].
The houses in between. 1951, New York 1952.
Jinny Morgan: a play in 3 acts. 1952 (acting edn). Rptd in Three plays, below.
A sunset touch. 1953, New York 1953.
Three plays: Jinny Morgan; The gentle assassin; St George at the Dragon. 1953.
These lovers fled away. 1955, New York 1955.
Time and the hour. 1957, New York [1957].
All the day long. 1959, New York 1960.
I met a lady. 1961, New York 1961.
Winds of the day. 1964, New York 1965.

§2

Spring, M. H. Howard. 1967.

WILLIAM OLAF STAPLEDON
1886–1950
Selections
To the end of time. Ed B. Davenport, New York 1953. Contains Last and first men; Star maker; Odd John; Sirius; The flames.

§1

Latter-day psalms. Liverpool 1914.
A modern theory of ethics: a study of the relations of ethics and psychology. 1929, New York 1929.
Last and first men: a story of the near and far future. 1930, New York 1931.
Last men in London. 1932.
Waking world. 1934. Non-fiction.
Odd John: a story between jest and earnest. 1935, New York 1936.
Star maker. 1937.
New hope for Britain. 1939. Non-fiction.
Saints and revolutionaries. 1939. Non-fiction.
Beyond the 'isms'. 1942 (Searchlight Books).
Darkness and the light. 1942.
Old man in new world. 1944. Story.
Sirius: a fantasy of love and discord. 1944.
The seven pillars of peace. [1944]. Pamphlet.

Death into life. 1946. Non-fiction.
Youth and tomorrow. 1946. Non-fiction.
The flames: a fantasy. 1947.
Worlds of wonder: three tales of fantasy. Reading Pa 1949. The flames; Death into life; Old man in new world.
A man divided. 1950.
The opening of the eyes. Ed A. Z. Stapledon 1954. Non-fiction.

CHRISTINA ELLEN STEAD
b. 1902

§1

The Salzburg tales. 1934, New York 1934.
Seven poor men of Sydney. 1934, New York 1935.
The beauties and furies. 1936, New York 1936.
House of all nations. 1938, New York [1938].
The man who loved children. New York 1940, London 1941, New York 1965 (with introd by R. Jarrell), London 1966.
For love alone. New York 1944, London 1945.
Letty Fox, her luck. New York 1946, London 1947.
A little tea, a little chat. New York 1948.
The people with the dogs. Boston 1952.
Dark places of the heart. New York 1966, London 1967 (as Cotters' England).
The puzzle-headed girl: four novellas. New York 1967. The puzzle-headed girl; The Dianas; The right-angled creek; Girl from the beach.

§2

Geering, R. G. Christina Stead. Melbourne 1969. Lists other criticism and biography.

JAMES STEPHENS
1882–1950
See cols 360–2, above.

GLADYS BERTHA STERN
b. 1890

§1

Pantomime. 1914.
'See-saw'. 1914.
Two and threes. 1916.
Grand chain. 1917.
A marrying man. 1918.
Children of no man's land. 1919, New York 1921 (as Debatable ground).
Larry Munro. 1920, New York 1921 (as The china shop), 1926 (with introd by W. Follett).
The room. 1922, New York 1922.
The back seat. 1923, New York 1923.
Smoke rings. 1923, New York 1924.
Tents of Israel. 1924, New York 1925 (as The matriarch), London 1948. Dramatized as The matriarch, [1931].
Thunderstorm. 1925, New York 1925.
A deputy was king. 1926, New York 1926.
The happy meddler. 1926. With G. Holdsworth.
Bouquet. 1927, New York 1927. Travel in France.
The dark gentleman. 1927, New York 1927.
Jack a' Manory. 1927. Stories.
Debonair: the story of Persephone. 1928, New York 1928.
Modesta. New York 1929.
Petruchio. 1929.

The slower Judas. New York 1929. Stories.
Mosaic. 1930, New York 1930.
The man who pays the piper. [1931]. Play.
The shortest night. 1931, New York 1931.
Little red horses. 1932, New York 1932 (as The rueful mating).
Long-lost father: a comedy. 1932, New York 1933. Fiction.
The Rakonitz chronicles. 1932. Contains Tents of Israel, A deputy was king, Mosaic.
The Augs: an exaggeration. 1933, New York 1934 (as Summer's play).
Pelican walking. 1934. Stories.
Shining and free: a day in the life of the matriarch. 1935.
The matriarch chronicles. New York 1936. With preface by the author. The matriarch; A deputy was king; Mosaic; Shining and free.
Monogram. 1936, New York 1936. Reminiscences.
Oleander river. 1937, New York 1937.
The ugly dachshund. 1938, New York 1938.
Long story short: a collection. 1939.
The woman in the hall. 1939, New York 1939.
A lion in the garden. 1940, New York 1940.
Another part of the forest. 1941, New York 1941. Reminiscences.
Dogs in an omnibus. 1942.
The young matriarch. 1942, New York 1942.
Talking of Jane Austen. 1943, New York 1944 (as Speaking of Jane Austen). With S. Kaye-Smith.
Trumpet voluntary. 1944, New York 1944.
The reasonable shores. 1946, New York 1946.
No son of mine. 1948, New York 1948.
Benefits forgot. 1949, New York 1949. Reminiscences.
A duck to water. 1949, New York 1950.
More about Jane Austen. New York 1949, London 1950 (as More talk of Jane Austen). With S. Kaye-Smith.
Gala night at 'The Willows'. [1950]. Play, with R. C. Cooke.
Ten days of Christmas. 1950, New York 1950.
The donkey shoe. 1952, New York 1952.
Robert Louis Stevenson. 1952 (Br Council pamphlet).
A name to conjure with. 1953, New York [1953]. Autobiography.
Raffle for a bedspread. 1953. Play.
All in good time. 1954, New York 1954. Religious autobiography.
He wrote Treasure island: the story of Robert Louis Stevenson. 1954, New York 1954 (as Robert Louis Stevenson).
Johnny Forsaken. 1954, New York 1954.
For all we know. 1955, New York 1956.
The way it worked out: a sequel to All in good time. 1956, New York 1957.
And did he stop and speak to you? 1957, Chicago 1958. Biographies of friends of the author.
Seventy times seven. 1957, New York 1957.
The patience of a saint: or example is better than precept. 1958.
Unless I marry. 1959, New York 1959.
Bernadette. Edinburgh [1960]. Biography for children.
One is only human. Chicago 1960. Religious essay.
Credit title. Edinburgh [1961]. For children.
The personality of Jesus. Garden City NY 1961. For children.
Dolphin Cottage. 1962.
Promise not to tell. 1964.

§2

Lawrence, M. Go-getters. In her School of femininity, New York 1936, London 1937 (as We write as women).

LEONARD ALFRED GEORGE STRONG
1896–1958

Bibliographies

'Gawsworth, John' (T. I. F. Armstrong). L. A. G. Strong. In his Ten contemporaries: notes toward their definitive bibliography. 2nd series 1933. With a note by Strong on his beginnings in literature.

Collections and Selections

Selected poems. 1931, New York 1932.
Travellers: thirty-one selected short stories. 1945. Preface by F. Swinnerton.
Three novels. 1950. The garden; Corporal Tune; The seven arms.
The body's imperfection: the collected poems. 1957.

§1
Prose Fiction

Doyle's rock, and other stories. Oxford 1925.
Dewer rides. 1929, New York 1929.
Patricia comes home. Oxford [1929]. Children's story.
The English captain, and other stories. 1929, New York 1931.
The jealous ghost. 1930, New York 1930.
The old Argo. Oxford [1931]. Children's story.
The garden. 1931, New York 1931.
The big man. 1931. Story, rptd in Travellers, above.
The brothers. 1932, New York 1932.
Don Juan and the wheelbarrow. 1932, New York 1933. Stories.
King Richard's land: a tale of the Peasants' Revolt. 1933, New York 1934. For children.
Sea wall. 1933, New York 1933.
Corporal Tune. 1934, New York 1934.
Fortnight south of Skye. Oxford [1934], New York 1935. For children.
The westward rock. Oxford [1934]. Children's story.
Mr Sheridan's umbrella. [1935]. For children.
The seven arms. 1935, New York 1935.
Tuesday afternoon, and other stories. 1935.
The last enemy: a study of youth. 1936, New York 1936.
Two stories. [1936] (60 copies). Coming to tea (rptd in Travellers, above); While the going is good.
The fifth of November. 1937. For children.
The swift shadow. 1937, New York 1937 (as Laughter in the west).
The nice cup o' tea. 1938. Story, issued as Christmas greeting. Rptd in Travellers, above.
Odd man in. 1938. For children.
Evening piece. [1939]. Story, issued as a Christmas greeting. Anon; rptd in Travellers, above.
The open sky. 1939, New York 1939.
Sun on the water, and other stories. 1940.
They went to the island. 1940. For children.
Wrong foot foremost. [1940], New York 1940. For children.
The bay. 1941, Philadelphia 1942.
House in disorder. 1941. For children.
Slocombe dies. 1942.
The unpractised heart. 1942.
All fall down. 1944, New York 1944.
The director. 1944.
Othello's occupation. 1945, New York 1945 (as Murder plays an ugly scene).
Sink or swim. 1945. For children.
The doll. Leeds 1946. Story.
Trevannion. 1948.
Which I never: a police diversion. 1950, New York 1950.
Darling Tom, and other stories. 1952. Preface by the author on the short story.

The hill of Howth. 1953.
Deliverance. 1955.
Light above the lake. 1958.
Treason in the egg: a further police diversion. [1958].

Other Works

Dublin days. Oxford 1921 [24 poems], New York 1923 [42 poems].
The Lowery road. Oxford 1923, New York 1924. Verse.
Eighty poems: an anthology. Ed L. A. G. Strong, Oxford 1924.
Difficult love. Oxford 1927. Verse.
At Glenan Cross: a sequence, Christmas 1928. Oxford 1928 (100 copies). Verse. Rptd in Northern light, below.
Northern light. 1930 (275 copies). Verse.
Common sense about poetry. 1931, New York 1932.
Amalia, ye aged sow. Oxford [1932]. Verse, for children. Preceded by The Italian conjuror, a story by A. Blackwood.
A defence of ignorance. New York 1932 (200 copies). Essay.
A letter to W. B. Yeats. 1932 (Hogarth Letters).
Life in English literature: an introduction for beginners. 3 vols 1932, 1 vol 1932 (as Outline of English literature), Boston 1934 (as Life in English literature, ed for American schools by R. Thomas). With M. Redlich.
The hansom cab and the pigeons: being random reflections upon the Silver Jubilee of King George V. 1935.
Call to the swan. 1936. Verse.
Common sense about drama. 1937, New York 1937.
Henry of Agincourt. 1937. For children.
The man who asked questions: the story of Socrates. 1937. For children.
The minstrel boy: a portrait of Tom Moore. 1937, New York 1937.
Shake hands and come out fighting. 1938. On boxing reminiscences.
The absentee. 1939. Play.
Trial and error. 1939. Play.
English for pleasure. 1941. Schools broadcasts.
John McCormack: the story of a singer. 1941, New York 1941.
John Millington Synge. 1941 (PEN Books).
A new anthology of modern verse 1920-40, chosen and with introd by C. Day Lewis and L. A. G. Strong. 1941.
An informal English grammar. 1943.
Authorship. [1944] (Ross Careers Books).
A tongue in your head. 1945. On the speaking of English.
Light through the cloud. [1946]. Account of a mental home, The Retreat, York
Maud Cherrill. 1949, New York 1950 (Personal Portraits).
The sacred river: an approach to James Joyce. 1949, New York 1951.
John Masefield. 1952 (Br Council pamphlet).
Personal remarks. 1953, New York 1954. Literary essays.
The writer's trade. 1953.
It's not very nice: a comedy in one act for women. [1954].
The story of sugar. 1954.
Dr Quicksilver 1660-1742. the life and times of Thomas Dover MD. 1955.
The flying angel: the story of the missions to seamen. 1956.
The rolling road: the story of travel on the roads of Britain and the development of public passenger transport. 1956.
A brewer's progress 1757-1957: a survey of Charrington's brewery. 1957 (priv ptd).
Courtauld Thomson: a memoir. 1958.
Instructions to young writers. 1958.
Green memory. 1961. Autobiography to 1924.

Some of Strong's verses were issued privately as Christmas greetings (see Gawsworth's bibliography). Strong edited the selections The best poems of 1923(-25), Boston [1924-6]. He also edited the series The Gollancz books for schools, 1935, Methuen's One-act plays 1939-49, and from 1934 to 1935 he edited the Nelson novels.

§2

Mégroz, R. L. In his Five novelist poets of to-day, 1933.

FRANK ARTHUR SWINNERTON
b. 1884

Collections

The novels of Swinnerton: uniform edition. 1934-. With prefatory notes.

§1

The merry heart: a gentle melodrama. 1909, Garden City NY 1929.
The young idea: a comedy of environment. 1910, Garden City NY 1930.
The casement: a diversion. 1911, New York 1927.
George Gissing: a critical study. [1912], New York [1923], London 1924 (with preface by author).
The happy family. 1912, New York [1912].
On the staircase. 1914, New York [1914].
R. L. Stevenson: a critical study. 1914, New York [1923].
The chaste wife. 1916, New York [1917].
Nocturne. 1917, New York [1917], London 1918 (with preface by H. G. Wells), 1937 (WC, with introd by author).
Shops and houses. 1918, New York [1918].
Women. 1918, New York 1919. Non-fiction. Anon.
September. 1919, New York [1919].
Coquette. 1921, New York [1921].
The three lovers. New York [1922], London 1923.
Young Felix. [1923], New York [1923].
The elder sister. [1925], New York [1925].
Summer storm. [1926], New York [1926].
Tokefield papers. 1927, New York [1927], London 1949 (enlarged, as Tokefield papers old and new). Essays.
A brood of ducklings. [1928], Garden City NY 1928.
A London bookman. 1928. Selection of articles written for New York Bookman.
Sketch of a sinner. Garden City NY 1929, London 1930.
Authors and the book trade. 1932, New York 1932, London 1933 (with new preface).
The Georgian house. Garden City NY 1932, London [1933]. Fiction.
Elizabeth. [1934], Garden City NY 1934.
The Georgian scene: a literary panorama. New York [1934], London 1935 (as The Georgian literary scene), 1938 (EL, rev), 1950 (rev), 1969 (rev).
Swinnerton: an autobiography. Garden City NY 1936, London 1937.
The university of books. 1936. With A. Huxley et al.
An anthology of modern fiction. 1937. Ed Swinnerton.
Harvest comedy: a dramatic chronicle. [1937], Garden City NY 1938.
The reviewing and criticism of books. 1939. Lecture.
The two wives. [1940], New York 1940.
The fortunate lady: a dramatic chronicle. [1941], Garden City NY 1941.
Thankless child. [1942], Garden City NY 1942.
A woman in sunshine. [1944], Garden City NY 1945.
English maiden: parable of a happy life. [1946].
The cats and Rosemary. New York 1948, London 1950.
A faithful company: a winter's tale. [1948].
The doctor's wife comes to stay. [1949].
Arnold Bennett. 1950, 1961 (rev) (Br Council pamphlet).
A flower for Catherine. 1950.
The bookman's London. 1951, Garden City NY 1952.
Londoner's post: letters to Gog and Magog. 1952. Essays.
Master Jim Probity. 1952, Garden City NY 1953 (as An affair of love).
A month in Gordon Square. 1953, Garden City NY 1954.
The Sumner intrigue. 1955, Garden City NY 1955.

The adventures of a manuscript: being the story of The ragged-trousered philanthropists. 1956.
Authors I never met. 1956.
Background with chorus: a footnote to changes in English literary fashion between 1901 and 1917. 1956, New York [1956].
The woman from Sicily. 1957, Garden City NY 1957.
A tigress in Prothero. 1959, Garden City NY 1959 (as A tigress in the village).
The Grace divorce. 1960, Garden City NY 1960.
Death of a highbrow. 1961, Garden City NY 1962.
Figures in the foreground: literary reminiscences 1917-40. 1963, Garden City NY 1964.
Quadrille. 1965, Garden City NY 1965.
A galaxy of fathers. 1966, Garden City NY 1966. Biographies.
Sanctuary. 1966, Garden City NY 1967.
The bright lights. 1968, New York 1968.
Reflections from a village. 1969, Garden City NY 1969.
Swinnerton pbd edns of Arnold Bennett, Literary taste, *1937 and 1938, and a selection from his* Journals, *1954 (Penguin).*

§2

Swinnerton: personal sketches by Arnold Bennett, H. G. Wells, G. M. Overton. New York [1920].
Johnson, R. B. In his Contemporary novelists: men, 1922.
Collins, J. Swinnerton and his books. In his Taking the literary pulse, 1924.
Overton, G. M. Swinnerton: analyst of lovers. In his Authors of the day, New York 1924.
Rotter, A. Swinnerton und Gissing: eine kritische Studie. Brno 1930.

JULIAN GUSTAVE SYMONS
b. 1912

See cols 362-3, above.

ANGELA MARGARET THIRKELL
1890–1961

Selections

An Angela Thirkell omnibus, with introd by E. Bowen. 1966. Ankle deep; High rising; Wild strawberries.
A second Angela Thirkell omnibus. 1967. August folly; Summer half; Pomfret Towers.
The Brandons, and others. 1968. The Brandons; Before lunch; Cheerfulness breaks in.

§1

Three houses. 1931, New York 1931. Memoirs of childhood.
Ankle deep. 1933, New York 1933.
High rising. 1933, New York 1933.
The demon in the house: stories of Tony Moreland. 1934, New York 1935.
Trooper to the Southern Cross. 1934, 1935 (as What happened on the boat). As 'Leslie Parker'.
Wild strawberries. 1934, New York 1934.
The grateful sparrow, and other stories. 1935, New York 1936. For children, adapted from the German.
O these men, these men! 1935.
August folly. 1936, New York 1937.
The fortunes of Harriette: the surprising career of Harriette Wilson. 1936, New York 1936 (as Tribute for Harriette).
Coronation summer. 1937, New York 1937.
Summer half. 1937, New York 1938.
Pomfret Towers. 1938, New York 1938.
Before lunch. 1939, New York 1940.
The Brandons. 1939, New York 1939.

Cheerfulness breaks in: a Barsetshire war survey. 1940, New York 1941.
Northbridge Rectory. [1941], New York 1942.
Marling Hall. 1942, New York 1942.
Growing up. 1943, New York 1944.
The headmistress. 1944, New York 1945.
Miss Bunting. 1945, New York 1946.
Peace breaks out. 1946, New York 1947.
Private enterprise. 1947, New York 1948.
Love among the ruins. 1948, New York 1948.
The old Bank House. 1949, New York 1949.
County chronicle. 1950, New York 1950.
The duke's daughter. 1951, New York 1951.
Happy returns. 1952, New York 1952 (as Happy return).
Jutland Cottage. 1953, New York 1953.
What did it mean? 1954, New York 1954.
Enter Sir Robert. 1955, New York 1955.
Never too late. 1956, New York 1956.
A double affair. 1957, New York 1957.
Close quarters. 1958, New York 1958.
Love at all ages. 1959, New York 1959.
Three score and ten. 1961. With C. A. Lejeune.

§2

McInnes, G. In his The road to Gundagai. 1965. Reminiscences of his mother, A. Thirkell.

DYLAN MARLAIS THOMAS
1914–53

See cols 220–30, above.

A. G. THORNTON

An astronomer at large. 1924, New York 1924.
John comes home. [1927].
Summer sowing. [1927].

JOHN RONALD REUEL TOLKIEN
b. 1892

Bibliographies

West, R. C. An annotated bibliography of Tolkien criticism. Extrapolation 10 1968.
—— Tolkien criticism: an annotated checklist. Kent (Ohio) 1970. Includes Tolkien's own writings.

§1
Prose Fiction and Verse

Songs for the philologists. 1936 (priv ptd). With E. V. Gordon et al.
The hobbit: or, there and back again. 1937, Boston 1938, London 1951 (rev), Boston 1961, London 1966 (rev), New York 1966.
Farmer Giles of Ham. 1949, Boston 1950.
The lord of the rings: pt 1, The fellowship of the ring, 1954, Boston 1954; pt 2, The two towers, 1954, Boston 1955; pt 3, The return of the king, 1955, Boston 1956. The whole rev, with explanatory matter, London 1966, Boston 1967, 1 vol London 1968.
The adventures of Tom Bombadil and other verses from The red book. 1962, Boston 1963.
Tree and leaf. 1964, Boston 1965. Contains On fairy stories (Andrew Lang lecture, 1938) and Leaf by Niggle [a story].
Smith of Wotton Major. 1967, Boston 1967.

Other Works

A middle English vocabulary, designed for use with Sisam's Fourteenth Century verse & prose. Oxford 1922.

Sir Gawain & the Green Knight. Ed Tolkien and E. V. Gordon, Oxford 1925, 1967 (rev H. Davis).

Beowulf: the monsters and the critics. [1937] (Gollancz memorial lecture 1936).

The English text of the Ancrene Riwle: Ancrene Wisse. Ed Tolkien from ms Corpus Christi College Cambridge 402, 1962 (EETS 249).

Tolkien also edited, with others, the first 7 Oxford English monographs, 1940–59.

§2

Wilson, E. Oo, those awful orcs. Nation 182 1956. Rptd in his The bit between my teeth, New York 1965.

Irwin, W. R. There and back again: the romances of Williams, Lewis and Tolkien. Sewanee Rev 69 1961.

Fuller, E. The lord of the hobbits: Tolkien. In his Books with men behind them, New York 1962.

Reilly, R. J. Tolkien and the fairy story. Thought 38 1963.

Sale, R. England's Parnassus: Lewis, Williams and Tolkien. Hudson Rev 17 1964.

The Tolkien Journal. 1965 onwards.

Moorman, C. W. In his The precincts of felicity: the Augustinian city of the Oxford Christians. Gainesville 1966.

Ryan, J. S. German mythology applied—the extension of the literary folk memory. Folklore 77 1966.

Hayes, N. and N. Renshaw. Of hobbits: The lord of the rings. Critique (Minneapolis) 9 1967.

Mankata Studies in English no 2 1967. Tolkien special no: 10 critical essays.

Ottevaere-van Praag, G. Retour à l'épopée de mythologie: Le maître des anneaux. Revue des Langues Vivantes 33 1967.

Thomson, G. H. The lord of the rings: the novel as traditional romance. Wisconsin Stud in Contemporary Lit 8 1967.

Woods, S. H. Tolkien and the hobbits. Cimarron Rev 1 1967.

Auden, W. H. Good and evil in The lord of the rings. CQ 10 1968.

Isaacs, N. D. and R. A. Zimbardo, (ed). Tolkien and the critics: essays on The lord of the rings. Notre Dame 1968.

Léaud, F. L'épopée religieuse de Tolkien. Études Anglaises 20 1968.

Miesel, S. L. Some motifs and sources for The lord of the rings. Riverside Quart 3 1968.

—— Some religious aspects of The lord of the rings. Ibid.

Norton, J. Tolkien, Beowulf and the poet: a problem in point of view. E Studies 48 1968.

Ratliff, W. E. and C. G. Flinn. The hobbit and the hippie. Modern Age 12 1968.

Wojcik, J. S. Tolkien and Coleridge: remaking of the 'green earth'. Renascence 20 1968.

Carter, I. Tolkien: a look behind The lord of the rings. New York 1969.

Hillegas, M. R. (ed). Shadows of the imagination: the fantasies of C. S. Lewis, Tolkien, and C. Williams. Carbondale 1969.

Kilby, C. S. The lost myth. Arts in Society 6 1969.

Stimpson, C. R. J. R. R. Tolkien. New York 1969.

HENRY MAJOR TOMLINSON
1873–1958

Selections

H. M. Tomlinson: a selection from his writings, made by K. Hopkins. 1953.

§1
Prose Fiction

Gallions Reach. 1927, New York 1927.

Illusion, 1915. New York 1928, London 1929. Story, rptd in All our yesterdays, below.

All our yesterdays. 1930, New York 1930.

The snows of Helicon. 1933, New York 1933.

All hands! 1937, New York 1937 (as Pipe all hands).

The day before. New York [1939], London 1940.

Ports of call. 1942 (31 copies). Story.

Morning light: the islanders in the days of oak and hemp. 1946, New York 1947.

The haunted forest. 1951. Children's story.

The trumpet shall sound. 1957, New York 1957.

Other Works

The sea and the jungle. 1912, New York 1913, 1930 (with foreword by Tomlinson). Travel.

Old junk. 1918, New York 1923, London 1933 (rev). Essays.

London river. 1921, New York 1921, London 1951 (rev). Essays.

Waiting for daylight. 1922, New York 1922. Essays.

Tidemarks: some records of a journey to the beaches of the Moluccas and the forest of Malaya in 1923. 1924, New York 1924.

Gifts of fortune, and hints for those about to travel. 1926, New York 1926. Essays.

Under the red ensign. 1926, New York 1927 (as The foreshore of England), London 1932 (rev, with new introd and extra ch). Travel.

A brown owl. Garden City NY 1928 (107 copies). Essay, rptd in Out of soundings, below.

Côte d'or. 1929. Essay, rptd in Out of soundings, below.

Thomas Hardy. New York 1929. Essay.

War books. Cleveland 1929 (215 copies). Lecture.

Between the lines. Cambridge Mass 1930 (160 copies). Lecture, on modern tendencies in literature.

Great sea stories of all nations. Ed with introd by Tomlinson 1930, Garden City NY 1930.

Norman Douglas. 1931, New York 1952, London 1952 (rev).

Out of soundings. 1931, New York 1931. Essays.

An illustrated catalogue of rare books on the East Indies, and A letter to a friend. 1932 (150 copies).

Below London Bridge. 1934, New York 1935, London 1951 (rev, as pt of rev edn of London river). With H. C. Tomlinson.

South to Cadiz. 1934, New York 1934. Travel.

Mars his idiot. 1935, New York 1955. Essays.

An anthology of modern travel writing. Ed Tomlinson 1936.

The wind is rising. 1941, Boston 1942. War memoirs.

The turn of the tide. 1945, New York 1947. War memoirs.

The face of the earth. 1950, Indianapolis 1951. Travel essays.

Malay waters. 1950. Travel.

The wreck of the Serica, by Thomas Cubbin. 1950 (300 copies). Ed Tomlinson.

Trinity Congregational Church, Poplar. 1952 (priv ptd). Pamphlet.

A mingled yarn: autobiographical sketches. 1953, Indianapolis 1953.

§2

Lynd, R. In his Books and authors, 1923.

Mayer, F. P. Tomlinson: the eternal youth. Virginia Quart Rev 4 1928.

Hodgson, S. In his Portraits and reflections, 1929.

Gay, A. A. Tomlinson: essayist and traveller. In Studies in honor of J. Wilcox, ed A. D. Wallace and W. O. Ross, Detroit 1958.

THEODORE PHILIP TOYNBEE
b. 1916

§1

The savage days. 1937.

A school in private. 1941.

The barricades. 1943, Garden City NY 1944.
Tea with Mrs Goodman. 1947, Garden City NY 1947 (as Prothalamium).
The garden to the sea. 1953, Garden City NY 1954.
Friends apart: a memoir of Esmond Romilly & Jasper Ridley in the thirties. 1954.
Fearful choice: a debate on nuclear policy. 1958, Detroit 1959. With others.
Pantaloon: or, the valediction. 1961, New York 1961. Verse.
Comparing notes: a dialogue across a generation. 1963. With A. J. Toynbee.
Thanatos: a modern symposium. 1963. Fiction, with M. Richardson.
Two brothers: the fifth day of the valediction of Pantaloon. 1964. Verse.
A learned city. 1966. Verse.
Views from the lake: the seventh day of the valediction of Pantaloon. 1968. Verse.

HENRY TREECE
1911–66
See cols 369–70, above.

'ROBERT TRESSELL', ROBERT NOONAN
1870–1911

§1

The ragged-trousered philanthropists. 1914 (ed and abridged by Jessie Pope, as by 'Robert Tressall'), New York [1914], London 1918 (further abridged), 1955 (ed F. C. Ball, full text based on the original ms, as by 'Robert Tressell'), New York 1962.

§2

Ball, F. C. Tressell of Mugsborough. 1951.
Swinnerton, F. A. The adventures of a manuscript: being the story of The ragged-trousered philanthropists. 1956.
Woolf, C. A masterpiece restored. Aylesford Rev 2 1958.
Mitchell, J. B. The ragged-trousered philanthropists: cornerstone of a proletarian literary culture and of socialist realism in English literature. Zeitschrift für Anglistik und Amerikanistik 10 1962.
— Robert Tressell and The ragged-trousered philanthropists. 1969.
Mayne, B. The ragged-trousered philanthropists: an appraisal of an Edwardian novel of social protest. Twentieth Century Lit 13 1967.
Nazareth, P. A committed novel. Transition (Kampala) 6 1967.

WALTER JAMES REDFERN TURNER
1889–1946
See cols 371–2, above.

EDWARD FALAISE UPWARD
b. 1903

Selections
The railway accident, and other stories. 1969. Includes Journey to the border.

§1

The colleagues; Sunday. In New country, ed M. Roberts 1933. Stories.
Sketch for a Marxist interpretation of literature. In The mind in chains, ed C. Day Lewis 1937.

Journey to the border. 1938.
The falling tower. In Folios of new writing, ed J. Lehmann 1941. Essay.
New order. In Penguin New Writing 14 1942. Prose-poem.
The railway accident. In New Directions 11 1949. Story.
In the thirties. 1962. First pt of a trilogy provisionally titled Poet and party. Part of ch 1 first pbd in London Mag 8 1961.
The rotten elements. 1969. 2nd pt of trilogy.

§2

Spender, S. Upward, Kafka and Van der Post. In his The destructive element, 1935.
Isherwood, C. Lions and shadows. 1938. Reminiscences of Upward ('Allen Chalmers').
Sellers, W. H. Edward Upward: an introduction. Dalhousie Rev 43 1963.

HORACE ANNESLEY VACHELL
1861–1955

Selections
Triplets: an omnibus containing Virgin; Out of great tribulation; Into the land of Nod. [1933].

§1

Judge Ketchum's romance. New York [1895], London 1896 (as The romance of Judge Ketchum).
The model of Christian Gray: a study of certain phases of life in California. 1895.
The quicksands of Pactolus. 1896, New York 1896.
A drama in sunshine. 1898.
The procession of life. 1899, New York 1899.
John Charity: a romance of yesterday. 1900, New York 1901.
Life and sport on the Pacific slope. 1900, New York 1901, London 1908 (as Sport and life on the Pacific slope). Non-fiction.
The shadowy third: a study of a temperament. 1902.
The pinch of prosperity: a study of some twisted lives. 1903.
Brothers: the true history of a fight against odds. 1904, New York 1905.
The hill: a romance of friendship. 1905, New York 1906.
The face of clay: an interpretation. 1906, New York 1906.
Her son: a chronicle of love. 1907, New York 1907.
The turn of the tide. New York [1908].
The waters of Jordan. 1908.
An impending sword: an adventure by the sea. 1909.
The paladin, as beheld by a woman of temperament. 1909, New York 1909.
The other side: the record of certain passages in the life of a genius. [1910], New York 1910.
John Verney. 1911, New York [1911].
Blinds down: a chronicle of Charminster. 1912, New York [1912].
Bunch grass: a chronicle of life on a cattle ranch. 1912, New York 1912.
Jelf's. 1912, New York 1912. Play.
Loot from the temple of Fortune. 1913, New York 1914. Stories.
Quinneys'. 1914, New York [1914], London 1915 (as play), [1920] (acting edn).
Spragge's canyon: a character study. 1914, New York [1915].
Searchlights. 1915. Play.
The case of Lady Camber. 1916. Play.
Pepper and salt. 1916. Selected sayings.
The triumph of Tim: the life history of a chameleon. 1916, New York [1916].

Fishpingle: a romance of the countryside. 1917, New York [1917], London [1931] (as play), New York 1931.
Some happenings. 1918, New York [1918]. Stories.
The soul of Susan Yellam: a record. 1918, New York [1918].
The fourth dimension. 1920, New York [1920].
Whitewash. 1920, New York [1920].
Blinkers. 1921, New York [1921].
Change partners. [1922], New York [1923].
Fellow-travellers. 1923. Reminiscences.
The yard. [1923], New York 1923.
Leaves from Arcady. 1924. Stories.
Plain Jane. New York [1924]. Stories.
Quinney's adventures. 1924, New York [1924].
Evarannie. Boston 1925. Play.
Watlings for worth: a romance of an emporium. 1925, New York 1925 (as Watling's).
Mr Allen. 1926, New York 1926 (as The Mote House mystery). With 'Archibald Marshall' [Arthur H. Marshall].
A woman in exile. [1926], New York 1926.
Dew of the sea, and other stories. 1927, New York [1927].
Miss Torrobin's experiment. 1927, New York 1928 (as Men are so selfish!).
The actor: a chronicle. 1928.
The homely art. [1928]. Essay on furnishing.
The enchanted garden, and other stories. 1929.
The leading man. New York 1929.
Virgin: the record of certain passages in the life of a young lady. [1929].
The best of England. 1930, New York 1930. Non-fiction.
Out of great tribulation. [1930].
Plus fours. [1930]. Play, with H. Simpson.
At the sign of the grid. 1931. Stories.
Into the land of Nod. [1931].
Experiences of a Bond Street jeweller. 1932. Stories.
The fifth commandment: a commentary upon certain phases of modern domestic life. [1932].
This was England: a countryside calendar. 1933. Non-fiction.
Vicar's walk. 1933.
The disappearance of Martha Penny. 1934, Boston 1934 (as Nether Applewhite).
The old guard surrenders. 1934.
Arising out of that: being an eye-witness account of the life of the inhabitants of the village of Venner. 1935. Fiction.
Moonhills. 1935.
When sorrows come. 1935.
Joe Quinney's Jodie. 1936. Stories.
My vagabondage: a pot-pourri and causerie. 1936. Non-fiction.
Distant fields: a writer's autobiography. 1937.
The golden house: a romance of Bath. 1937.
Lord Samarkand. 1938.
Quinney's for quality. 1938. Stories.
Where fancy beckons: an arm-chair vagabondage. 1938.
Phoebe's guest house. 1939.
Great chameleon: a biographical romance. [1940].
Little tyrannies. 1940. Essays.
Black squire. [1941].
Gift from God. 1942.
The wheel stood still. 1943.
Hilary Trent. 1944.
Averil. 1945.
Eve's apples. [1946].
Farewell yesterday. [1946].
Now came still evening on. 1946. Autobiography.
Rebels. [1947].
Children of the soil: a West Country romance. [1948].
Quiet corner. [1948].
Twilight grey. 1948. Autobiography.
Golden slippers. 1949.
In sober livery. 1949. Autobiography.
Methuselah's diary. [1950]. The author's diary from July to October 1948.

More from Methuselah. 1951.
The lamp of Golconda. 1952.
Quests: the adventures & misadventures of a collector. 1954.

§2

'Lacon' (E. H. L. Watson). In his Lectures to living authors, 1925.

RICHARD HORATIO EDGAR WALLACE
1875–1932

Bibliographies
Lofts, W. O. G. and D. Adley. The British bibliography of Wallace. 1969.

Selections
Forty-eight short stories. [1929]. Rptd from The cat burglar, Fighting Snub Reilly, The prison-breakers, The little green man, Circumstantial evidence, The governor of Chi-Foo.
The mammoth mystery book. Garden City NY 1929. The gaol-breakers, The just men of Cordova, A king by night.
The Edgar Wallace police van. 1930. The green archer, The forger, The double, The Flying Squad.
Four complete novels. [1930], [1933] (as The Edgar Wallace souvenir book). The Four Just Men, Eve's island, The clue of the twisted candle, The man who knew.
Edgar Wallace—second book: four complete novels. [1931]. Nobby, Smithy, Tam, Bones of the river.
The Edgar Wallace race special. [1932]. Educated Evans, More educated Evans, Good Evans!, The calendar.
The Scotland Yard book of Edgar Wallace: an omnibus. Garden City NY [1932].
An Edgar Wallace foursome. [1933]. The man from Morocco, Captains of souls, The hand of power, The mixer.
The black. [1935]. The reporter, The iron grip.
The Edgar Wallace reader of mystery and detection. New York 1943.

§1

Details of Wallace's frequent use of alternative titles for the same work are taken from the bibliography by Lofts and Adley, above. See also Lofts and Adley for details of the serial pbn of Wallace's novels and stories. Plays are listed in order of production, where known.

The mission that failed! A tale of the [Jameson] raid and other poems reprinted from the Owl. Cape Town 1898.
War! and other poems. Cape Town [1900].
Writ in barracks. 1900. Verse.
Unofficial despatches. [1901]. On the Boer war. Rptd from Daily Mail.
The Four Just Men. 1905, Boston [1920].
'Smithy'. 1905.
Angel Esquire. Bristol [1908], New York 1908, Oxford 1966 (rev).
The council of justice. 1908.
Captain Tatham of Tatham Island. 1909, 1916 (as The island of galloping gold), [1926] (as Eve's island).
Smithy abroad: barrack room sketches. 1909.
The duke in the suburbs. 1909.
The nine bears. 1910, New York 1911 (as The other man), Cleveland 1930 (as Silinski: master criminal), London 1964 (as The cheaters).
Sanders of the river. 1911, Garden City NY 1930. Stories.
The people of the river. 1912. Stories.
Private Selby. 1912.
The fourth plague. 1913, Garden City NY 1930.
Grey Timothy. 1913, 1914 (as Pallard the punter).
The river of stars. 1913.
The admirable Carfew. 1914. Stories.

Bosambo of the river. 1914. Stories.
Famous Scottish regiments. [1914] (Our Fighting Forces 4). Pamphlet.
Field Marshal Sir John French and his campaigns. [1914] (Britain's Great Men). Pamphlet.
Heroes all: gallant deeds of the war. [1914].
Smithy's friend Nobby. 1914, [1916] (as 'Nobby'). Stories.
The standard history of the war. 4 vols [1914–15].
'Bones': being further adventures in Mr Commissioner Sanders' country. 1915. Stories.
Kitchener's army and the Territorial forces: the full story of a great achievement. 6 pts [1915].
The man who bought London. 1915.
The melody of death. 1915 (anon, as By the author of The four just men), [1928] (as by Wallace).
'1925': the story of a fatal peace. 1915.
'Smithy' and the Hun. 1915. Stories.
War of the nations. Vols 2–11 [1915–19]. Pbd in pts. Vol 1 by W. Le Queux.
The clue of the twisted candle. Boston [1916], London [1918].
A debt discharged. 1916.
The island of galloping gold. 1916. See Captain Tatham of Tatham Island, 1909, above.
'Nobby'. [1916]. See Smithy's friend Nobby, 1914, above.
The tomb of Ts'in. 1916.
The just men of Cordova. 1917.
Kate plus 10. Boston [1917], London 1919 (as Kate plus ten).
The keepers of the king's peace. 1917. Stories.
The secret house. 1917, Boston [1919].
Down under Donovan. [1918].
Lieutenant Bones. 1918. Stories.
Tam o' the scouts. 1918, Boston [1919], London [1928], (as Tam).
Those folk of Bulboro. 1918.
The adventures of Heine. 1919. Stories.
The fighting scouts. 1919. Stories.
The green rust. 1919, Boston [1920] (as Green rust).
The man who knew. [1919].
The daffodil mystery. 1920, Boston [1921] (as The daffodil murder).
Jack o' judgment. [1920], Boston [1921].
Bones in London. 1921. Stories.
The book of all-power. 1921.
The law of the Four Just Men. [1921]. Stories.
The angel of terror. [1922], Boston [1922].
Captains of souls. Boston [1922], London 1923, 1969 (rev).
The crimson circle. [1922], 1968 (rev).
The flying Fifty-Five. [1922], 1968 (rev).
Mr Justice Maxell. 1922. Also pbd as Take-a-chance Anderson.
Sandi the king-maker. 1922.
The valley of ghosts. 1922, Boston [1923], London 1967 (rev).
Bones of the river. [1923]. Stories.
The books of Bart. [1923].
Chick. 1923. Stories.
The clue of the new pin. [1933], Boston [1923].
The green archer. [1923], Boston [1924], New York 1965 (introd by V. Starrett).
The missing million. 1923, Boston [1925].
The dark eyes of London. 1924, Garden City NY 1929. Also pbd as The croakers.
Double Dan. [1924], Boston [1924] (as Diana of Kara-Kara). As play (Savoy 7 May 1927), unpbd.
Educated Evans. [1924], Oxford 1966 (rev). Stories.
The face in the night. [1924], Garden City NY 1929. Also pbd as The diamond men and The ragged princess.
Flat 2. Garden City NY 1924, London [1927].
Room 13. 1924.
The sinister man. [1924], Boston [1925].
The three oak mystery. 1924.

The black Avons. 4 vols 1925. How they fared in the time of the Tudors; Roundhead and Cavalier; From Waterloo to the Mutiny; Europe in the melting pot.
Blue hand. 1925, Boston 1926. Also pbd as Beyond recall.
The daughters of the night. [1925].
The fellowship of the frog. 1925.
The gaunt stranger. [1925], [1926] (rev, as The Ringer), Garden City NY 1926, London [1929] (as play, Wyndham's 1 May 1926), [1929] (French's Acting Edn). Also pbd as Police work.
The hairy arm. Boston [1925], London 1926 (as The avenger). Also pbd as The extra girl.
A king by night. 1925, Garden City NY 1926.
The mind of Mr J. G. Reeder. [1925], Garden City NY 1929 (as The murder book of J. G. Reeder). Stories.
The strange countess. [1925], Boston [1926]. Also pbd as The sins of the mother.
Barbara on her own. [1926].
The black abbot. [1926], Garden City NY 1927.
The day of uniting. [1926], Garden City NY 1926.
The door with seven locks. [1926], Garden City NY 1926.
Eve's island. [1926]. See Captain Tatham of Tatham Island, 1909, above.
The joker. [1926], Garden City NY [1932] (as The colossus). Also pbd as The Park Lane mystery.
The man from Morocco. 1926, Garden City NY 1930 (as The black). Also pbd as Souls in shadow.
The million-dollar story. [1926].
More educated Evans. [1926]. Stories.
The Northing tramp. [1926], Garden City NY 1929.
Penelope of the 'Polyantha'. [1926].
People: a short autobiography. 1926, Garden City NY 1929, London 1929 (as Edgar Wallace: a short autobiography). Also pbd as Edgar Wallace, by himself.
The Ringer. [1926]. See The gaunt stranger, [1925], above.
Sanders. [1926], Garden City NY 1930 (as Mr Commissioner Sanders). Stories.
The square emerald. [1926], Garden City NY 1927 (as The girl from Scotland Yard). Also pbd as The woman.
The terrible people. [1926], Garden City NY 1926. Also pbd as The gallows' hand.
The Three Just Men. [1926], Garden City NY 1929.
We shall see! [1926], Garden City NY 1931 (as The gaolbreakers).
The yellow snake. [1926]. Also pbd as The black tenth.
Big foot. 1927.
The brigand. [1927]. Stories.
The feathered serpent. [1927], Garden City NY 1928. Also pbd as Inspector Wade, and as Inspector Wade and the feathered serpent.
The forger. 1927, Garden City NY 1928 (as The clever one). Also pbd as The counterfeiter.
Good Evans! [1927], [1929] (as The educated man—Good Evans!). Stories.
The hand of power. [1927], New York 1930. Also pbd as The proud sons of Ragusa.
The man who was nobody. 1927.
The mixer. 1927. Stories.
Number six. [1927]. Also pbd as Number six and the Borgia.
The squeaker. [1927], Garden City NY 1928 (as The squealer), London [1929] (as play, The squeaker, Apollo 29 May 1928). Also pbd as The sign of the leopard.
The terror. (Lyceum 11 May 1927). [1929]. Play.
Terror Keep. [1927], Garden City NY 1927.
This England. [1927]. Short pieces rptd from Morning Post.
Again Sanders. [1928], Garden City NY [1931]. Stories.
Again the Three Just Men. [1928], Garden City NY 1931 (as The law of the Three Just Men). Also pbd as Again the Three. Stories.
The double. [1928], Garden City NY 1928. Also pbd as Sinister halls.
Elegant Edward. [1928]. Stories.

The Flying Squad. [1928], Garden City NY 1929, London [1929] (as play, Lyceum 7 June 1928).

The gunner. 1928, Garden City NY 1929 (as Gunman's bluff). Also pbd as Children of the poor.

The man who changed his name. (Apollo 14 March 1928). [1929], Garden City NY 1934. Play.

The orator. [1928]. Stories.

Tam. [1928]. *See* Tam o' the scouts, 1918, above.

The thief in the night. 1928, 1962 (with 5 stories rptd from previous collections).

The twister. 1928, Garden City NY 1929, London 1966 (rev).

Again the Ringer. [1929], Garden City NY [1931] (as The Ringer returns). Stories.

The big four. [1929]. Also pbd as Crooks of society. Stories.

The black. [1929], Garden City NY 1930. Also pbd as Blackmailers I have foiled. Stories. Different from identical title pbd Garden City NY in same year: *see* The man from Morocco, 1926, above.

The cat burglar. [1929]. Stories, all rptd in Forty-eight short stories, 1929, Collections, above.

Circumstantial evidence. [1929]. Stories all rptd in Forty-eight short stories, 1929, Collections, above.

The educated man—Good Evans! [1929]. *See* Good Evans!, [1927], above.

Fighting Snub Reilly. [1929]. Stories, all rptd in Forty-eight short stories, 1929, Collections, above.

For information received. [1929]. Stories.

Four square Jane. [1929]. Also pbd as The fourth square.

The ghost of Down Hill, and The queen of Sheba's belt. [1929]. Stories.

The golden Hades. 1929. Also pbd as Stamped in gold.

The governor of Chi-Foo. [1929], Cleveland [1933]. Stories, all rptd in Forty-eight short stories, 1929, Collections, above.

The green ribbon. [1929], Garden City NY 1930, London 1969 (rev).

The india-rubber men. [1929], Garden City NY 1930, London 1969 (rev).

The lady of Little Hell. [1929]. Stories.

The little green man. [1929]. Stories, all rptd in Forty-eight short stories, 1929, Collections, above.

The lone house mystery. [1929]. Stories.

The murder book of J. G. Reeder. Garden City NY 1929. *See* The mind of Mr J. G. Reeder, [1925], above.

Planetoid 127, and The Sweizer pump. 1929. Long stories.

The prison-breakers. [1929]. Stories, all rptd in Forty-eight short stories, 1929, Collections, above.

Red aces: being three cases of Mr Reeder. [1929], Garden City NY 1930. Stories.

The reporter. [1929]. Also pbd as Wise Y. Symon. Stories.

The terror. [1929]. *See* also play version, [1927], above.

The black. Garden City NY 1930. *See* The man from Morocco, 1926, above. Different from The black [1929], above.

The calendar. 1930, Garden City NY [1931], London [1932] (as play, Wyndhams 18 Sept 1929) (French's Acting Edn).

The clue of the silver key. 1930, Garden City NY 1930 (as The silver key).

The iron grip. [1930]. Also pbd as Wireless Bryce. Stories.

Killer Kay. [1930?]. Stories.

The lady called Nita. [1930?]. Stories.

The lady of Ascot. [1930], 1968 (rev).

Mr Commissioner Sanders. Garden City NY 1930. *See* Sanders, [1926], above.

The mouthpiece: a play. (Wyndhams 20 Nov 1930). Unpbd. Pbd as novel, with R. G. Curtis, [1935], New York [1936].

Mrs William Jones & Bill. [1930?]. Stories.

On the spot: a play. (Wyndhams 2 April 1930). Unpbd. Pbd as novel, 1931, Garden City NY [1931], London 1969 (rev).

Silinski: master criminal. Cleveland 1930. *See* The nine bears, 1910, above.

White face. 1930, Garden City NY [1931].

The case of the frightened lady: a play in three acts. (Wyndhams 18 Aug 1931). [1932] (French's Acting Edn).

The coat of arms. [1931], Garden City NY [1932] (as The Arranways mystery), London 1969 (rev).

The devil man. [1931], Garden City [1931]. Also pbd as Sinister-Street, The life and death of Charles Peace, and Silver steel.

The gaol-breakers. 1931 *See* We shall see!, [1926], above.

The law of the Three Just Men. Garden City NY [1931]. *See* Again the Three Just Men, [1928], above.

The man at the Carlton. [1931], Garden City NY [1932]. Also pbd as His devoted squealer, and The mystery of Mary Grier.

On the spot. 1931. *See* play version, 1930, above.

The colossus. [1932]. *See* The joker, [1926], above.

The frightened lady. 1932, Garden City NY 1933 (as The mystery of the frightened lady). Based on the play. Also pbd as Criminal at large.

The green pack: a play in three acts. (Wyndhams 9 Feb 1932). [1933] (French's Acting Edn), Garden City NY 1933.

The guv'nor, and other stories [The man who passed; The treasure house; The shadow man]. 1932, Garden City NY [1932] (as Mr Reeder returns). The guv'nor and The man who passed pbd separately as The guv'nor [1933]; The treasure house and The shadow men pbd separately as Mr J. G. Reeder returns [1934], 1965 (rev).

My Hollywood diary. [1932].

Sergeant Sir Peter. 1932, Garden City NY 1933, London [1962] (as Sergeant Dunn CID). Stories.

The steward. [1932]. Stories.

When the gangs came to London. [1932], Garden City NY [1932], London 1969 (rev). Also pbd as Scotland Yard's Yankee Dick, and The gangsters come to London.

The guv'nor. [1933]. *See* The guv'nor, and other stories, 1932, above.

The last adventure. [1934]. Stories.

Mr J. G. Reeder returns. [1934]. *See* The guv'nor, and other stories, 1932, above.

The woman from the east, and other stories. [1934].

The mouthpiece. [1935]. With R. Curtis. *See* play version, 1930, above.

Sergeant Dunn CID. [1962]. *See* Sergeant Sir Peter, 1932, above.

The undisclosed client. [1963]. Stories, including 9 not previously pbd in book form.

The cheaters. 1964. *See* The nine bears, 1910, above.

Many of Wallace's stories have not yet been collected in book form: for details see Lofts and Adley, Bibliography, above. For some details of Wallace's unpbd plays, reviews etc see M. Lane, Edgar Wallace, 1964, below.

§2

Curtis, R. G. Edgar Wallace—each way. [1932].

Wallace, E. V. Edgar Wallace. [1932].

Lane, M. Edgar Wallace: the biography of a phenomenon. [1938], 1964 (rev).

SIR HUGH SEYMOUR WALPOLE
1884–1941

The mss of Rogue Herries, Judith Paris, The fortress, Vanessa, The bright pavilions *and* Katherine Christian *are in the Fitz Park Museum, Keswick; those of* Joseph Conrad *and* The crystal box *are in the Hugh Walpole Collection at King's School Canterbury; that of* A silly old fool *is in the BM (Ashley Library), and that of* The green mirror *in the Berg Collection, New York Public Library. The mss of* The Duchess of Wrexe, The captives *and* Wintersmoon *are in the Library of Congress (see F. R. Goff,* The Hersholt gift of works of Walpole and Sinclair Lewis, *Lib of Congress Quart Jnl of Current Acquisitions 11 1954).*

Collections and Selections

Works. Cumberland edition. 30 vols 1934–40. Mostly reissues of earlier edns, with new prefaces by the author.

A Hugh Walpole anthology, selected by the author. [1921].

Four fantastic tales. 1932. Maradick at forty; The prelude to adventure; Portrait of a man with red hair; Above the dark circus. With a preface by the author.

The Jeremy stories. 1941. Jeremy, Jeremy and Hamlet, Jeremy at Crale.

§ 1

The wooden horse. 1909, New York 1915.

Maradick at forty: a transition. 1910.

Mr Perrin and Mr Traill: a tragi-comedy. 1911, New York 1911 (as The gods and Mr Perrin), London 1935 (with preface by Walpole).

The prelude to adventure. 1912, New York 1912, London 1938 (WC, with new introd by Walpole).

Fortitude: being a true and faithful account of the education of an explorer. 1913, New York [1913], 1930 (with introd by Walpole).

The Duchess of Wrexe, her decline & death: a romantic commentary. 1914, New York [1914].

The golden scarecrow. 1915, New York 1915. Stories.

The dark forest. 1916, New York [1916].

Joseph Conrad. [1916], 1924 (rev).

The green mirror: a quiet story. New York [1917], London 1918.

Jeremy. 1919, New York [1919].

The secret city: a novel in three parts. 1919, New York [1919].

The art of James Branch Cabell. New York 1920.

The captives: a novel in four parts. 1920, New York [1920].

The thirteen travellers. [1921], New York [1921]. Stories.

The young enchanted: a romantic story. 1921, New York [1921].

The cathedral. 1922, New York [1922], London 1937 (as play).

Jeremy and Hamlet. 1923, New York [1923].

The crystal box. Glasgow 1924.

The old ladies. 1924, New York [1924]. Dramatized by R. Ackland 1935.

The English novel: some notes on its evolution. Cambridge 1925 (Rede Lecture).

Portrait of a man with red hair: a romantic macabre. 1925, New York [1925]. Dramatized by B. Levy 1928.

Harmer John: an unworldly story. 1926, New York [1926].

Reading: an essay. 1926, New York 1926.

Jeremy at Crale. 1927, New York [1927].

Anthony Trollope. 1928 (EML), New York 1928.

My religious experience. 1928 (Affirmations ser). Booklet.

The silver thorn: a book of stories. 1928, Garden City NY 1928.

Wintersmoon: passages in the lives of two sisters, Janet and Rosalind Grandison. 1928, Garden City NY 1928.

Farthing Hall. 1929, Garden City NY 1929. With J. B. Priestley.

Hans Frost. 1929.

Rogue Herries. 1930, Garden City NY 1930. First vol of the Herries chronicle.

Above the dark circus: an adventure. 1931, Garden City NY 1931 (as Above the dark tumult).

Judith Paris. 1931, Garden City NY 1931. 2nd vol of the Herries chronicle.

The apple trees: four reminiscences. Waltham St Lawrence 1932.

The fortress. 1932, Garden City NY 1932. 3rd vol of the Herries chronicle.

A letter to a modern novelist. 1932 (Hogarth Letters 9).

The Waverley pageant; the best passages from the novels of Sir Walter Scott selected with critical introductions by Walpole. 1932.

All Souls' night: a book of stories. 1933, Garden City NY 1933.

Vanessa. 1933, Garden City NY 1933. 4th vol of the Herries chronicle.

Captain Nicholas: a modern comedy. 1934, Garden City NY 1934.

Cathedral carol service. 1934. An episode from The inquisitor, 1935, below.

Claude Houghton: appreciations. 1935. With 'Clemence Dane' (W. Ashton). Non-fiction.

The inquisitor. 1935, Garden City NY 1935.

A prayer for my son. 1936, Garden City NY 1936.

John Cornelius: his life and adventures. 1937, Garden City NY 1937.

Head in green bronze and other stories. 1938, Garden City NY 1938.

The joyful Delaneys. 1938, New York 1938.

The Haxtons: a play in three acts. [1939].

The sea tower: a love story. 1939, New York 1939.

The Herries chronicle: Rogue Herries, Judith Paris, The fortress, Vanessa. 1939.

Roman fountain. 1940, New York 1940. Travel.

The bright pavilions. 1940, New York 1940. 5th vol of the Herries chronicle.

A note by Hugh Walpole on the origins of the Herries chronicle, together with a bibliography, notes on The bright pavilions and the first four volumes of the Herries chronicle. New York 1940.

The freedom of books. [1940]. Pamphlet.

The blind man's house: a quiet story. 1941, Garden City NY 1941.

Open letter of an optimist. 1941 (Macmillan War pamphlets 9).

The killer and the slain: a strange story. 1942, Garden City NY 1942.

Katherine Christian. Garden City NY 1943, London 1944. 6th vol of the Herries chronicle, unfinished.

Women are motherly. 1943. Non-fiction.

Mr Huffam and other stories. 1948.

Letters, Diaries etc

Extracts from a diary. Glasgow 1934 (priv ptd, 100 copies).

§ 2

Goldring, D. Hugh Walpole. Egoist Jan/Feb 1919; rptd in his Reputations, 1920.

Hergesheimer, J. Hugh Walpole: an appreciation, together with notes and comments on the novels. New York 1919.

Hind, C. L. In his Authors and I, 1921.

Johnson, R. B. In his Some contemporary novelists: men, 1922.

Bidwell, E. J. A twentieth-century Trollope? Queen's Quart 30 1923. On The cathedral.

Dutton, G. B. Romance and Mr Walpole. Sewanee Rev 31 1923.

Mais, S. P. B. In his Some modern authors, 1923.

Overton, G. M. (ed). Hugh Walpole: appreciations by J. Conrad, A. Bennett and J. Hergesheimer. New York 1923.

—— The courage of Walpole. In his Authors of the day, New York 1924.

'Lacon' (E. H. L. Watson). In his Lectures to living authors, 1925.

Braybrooke, P. In his Novelists: we are seven, 1926.

—— In his Philosophies in modern fiction, 1929.

Priestley, J. B. Hugh Walpole. Eng Jnl 17 1928.

'Dane, Clemence' (W. Ashton). Tradition and Walpole. New York 1929.

Dottin, P. L'œuvre de Walpole. Revue de France 1 Feb 1932.

Marinoff, I. Hugh Walpole. Anglia 56 1932.

Arns, K. Hugh Walpole. Zeitschrift für französischen und englischen Unterricht 32 1933.

Gassmann, W. Der Viktorianismus bei Walpole. Marburg 1933.

Steen, M. Hugh Walpole: a study. 1933.

Ferguson, R. Canons of taste after Walpole. In her Celebrated sequels, 1934.

Schreiber, G. In his Portraits and self-portraits, Boston 1936.

Ebert, H. Erlebnis und Gestalt in den Romanen Walpoles. Erlangen 1937.

Bescou, Y. Une famille anglaise de 1720 à 1920. Revue de l'Enseignement des Langues Vivantes Nov 1938.

Schlötke, C. Hugh Walpoles Herriesfamilie in ihrer erbbiologischen Bedeutung. Neuphilologische Monatsschrift 9 1938.

Goetze, M. Studien über das 'Image' bei Walpole. Marburg 1939.

Ratzmann, H. M. R. Das Willensproblem bei Walpole. Greifswald 1939.

Church, L. F. Sir Hugh Walpole. London Quart & Holborn Rev 166 1941.

Roberts, R. E. Hugh Walpole 1884–1941. Saturday Rev of Lit 24 1941.

Wall, A. Sir Hugh Walpole and his writings. Wellington 1947.

Hart-Davis, R. Hugh Walpole: a biography. 1952.

West, A. Waiting for Mr Right. New Yorker 23 Aug 1952; rptd in his Principles and persuasions, New York 1957.

Boué, A. Une biographie de Walpole. Études Anglaises 6 1953.

Waugh, A. The nail in the coffin: the curious fate of Walpole. Harper's Mag 207 1953.

Muir, P. H. Sir Hugh Walpole (Bibliomanes 2). Book Collector 4 1955.

Swinnerton, F. A. In his Figures in the foreground, 1963.

REX WARNER
b. 1905

Bibliographies

McLeod, A. L. In his The achievement of Rex Warner, Sydney 1965, §2 below. Includes Warner's contributions to books, periodicals (including reviews), radio and television.

Selections

The stories of the Greeks. 1968. Men and gods; Greeks and Trojans; The vengeance of the gods.

§1

The kite. Oxford 1936, London 1963 (rev). Children's story.

Poems. 1937, New York 1938, London 1945 (rev, as Poems and contradictions), New York 1945.

The wild goose chase. 1937, New York 1937.

The professor. 1938, New York 1939.

The aerodrome: a love story. 1941, New York 1946, London 1966 (with introd by A. Wilson), New York 1966.

Why was I killed?: a dramatic dialogue. 1943, New York 1944 (as Return of the traveller).

English public schools. 1945 (Britain in Pictures).

The cult of power: essays. 1946, New York 1947.

John Milton. 1949, New York 1950.

Men of stones: a melodrama. 1949, Philadelphia 1950.

E. M. Forster. 1950, [1960] (rev) (Br Council pamphlet).

Views of Attica and its surroundings. 1950.

Ashes to ashes: a post-mortem on the 1950–1 Tests. 1951.

Greeks and Trojans. 1951, East Lansing 1953.

Escapade: a tale of Average. 1953.

Eternal Greece. New York 1953, London [1953].

The vengeance of the gods. 1954, East Lansing 1955. Stories adapted from Euripides.

Athens. 1956, New York 1956.

The Greek philosophers. 1958, New York 1958.

The young Caesar. 1960, Boston 1960. Historical novel.

Imperial Caesar. 1960, Boston 1960. Historical novel.

Look at birds. 1962. For children.

Pericles the Athenian. 1963, Boston 1963. Historical novel.

The converts. 1967.

Julius Caesar. 1967. Contains The young Caesar and Imperial Caesar, above.

Warner has pbd a number of trns: Euripides, Medea (*1944*), Hippolytus (*1949*) *and* Helen (*1951*); Aeschylus, Prometheus bound (*1947*); Xenophon, Anabasis (*1948*); Thucydides, Peloponnesian war (*1954*); *a selection of stories from* Ovid (Men and gods, *1950*); 6 Lives of Plutarch (The fall of the Roman republic, *1958*); War commentaries of Caesar (*1960*); St Augustine, Confessions (*1963*); *and from modern Greek*, Seferis, Poems (*1960*) *and his* On the Greek style (*1966*).

§2

Focus one, ed B. Rajan and A. Pearse. 1945. Symposium on Kafka and Warner; contains:

Atkins, J. On Warner; rptd in The achievement of Warner, ed A. L. McLeod, 1965, below.

Harrison, T. Warner's writing.

Rajan, B. Kafka—a comparison with Warner; rptd in The achievement of Warner.

Stonier, G. W. The new allegory.

Woodcock, G. Kafka and Warner; rptd in The achievement of Warner.

Mason, R. The novels of Warner. Adelphi 21 1945.

Pritchett, V. S. Our Time 4 1945; rptd in Modern British writing, ed D. V. Baker, New York 1947, and in The achievement of Warner.

Gorlier, C. Paragone 2 1951.

Drenner, D. V. R. Kafka, Warner and the cult of power. Kansas Mag 1952.

De Vitis, A. A. Warner and the cult of power. Twentieth-Century Lit 6 1960; rptd in The achievement of Warner.

McLeod, A. L. Rex Warner: writer. Sydney 1960.

—— (ed). The achievement of Warner. Sydney 1965.

McLeod, A. L. and E. Wyland. A concordance to the poems of Warner. Lock Haven 1966 (priv ptd).

Maini, D. S. Warner's political novels: an allegorical crusade against fascism. Indian Jnl of Eng Stud 2 1961; rptd in The achievement of Warner.

Karl, F. R. The novel as moral allegory: the fiction of Golding, Iris Murdoch, Warner and Newby. In his The contemporary English novel, New York 1962, London 1963 (as A reader's guide to the contemporary English novel).

Nandakumar, P. In her The glory and the good, 1965.

Churchill, T. Warner: homage to necessity. Critique (Minneapolis) 10 1967.

SYLVIA TOWNSEND WARNER
b. 1893

The espalier. 1925, New York 1925. Verse.

Lolly Willowes: or, the loving huntsman. 1926, New York 1926.

Mr Fortune's maggot. 1927, New York 1927.

The maze: a story to be read aloud. 1928.

Time importuned. 1928, New York 1928. Verse.

Some world far from ours, and 'Stay, Corydon, thou swain'. 1929. Stories.

The true heart. 1929, New York 1929.

Elinor Barley. 1930, Chicago 1930. Story.

A moral ending, and other stories. 1931.

Opus 7. 1931, New York 1931. Verse.
Rainbow. New York 1932. Verse.
The salutation. 1932, New York 1932. Stories.
Whether a dove or a seagull. New York 1933, London 1934. Verse, with V. Ackland.
More joy in heaven, and other stories. 1935.
Summer will show. 1936. New York 1936.
After the death of Don Juan. 1938, New York 1939.
The cat's cradle-book. New York 1940, London 1960. Stories.
A garland of straw, and other stories. 1943, New York 1943.
The museum of cheats, and other stories. 1947, New York 1947.
The corner that held them. 1948.
Somerset. 1949. Topography.
Jane Austen 1775–1817. 1951, 1957 (rev) (Br Council pamphlet).
The flint anchor. 1954, New York 1954.
Winter in the air, and other stories. 1955, New York 1956.
Boxwood: sixteen engravings by R. Stone illustrated in verse by S. T. Warner. 1958 (priv ptd), 1960 (as Boxwood: twenty-one engravings).
A spirit rises. 1962, New York 1962.
Sketches from nature. Wells, London 1963. Reminiscences.
A stranger with a bag, and other stories. 1966, New York 1966 (as Swans on an autumn river).
T. H. White: a biography. 1967, New York 1968.

ALEC WAUGH
(ALEXANDER RABAN WAUGH)
b. 1898

The loom of youth. 1917, New York 1920.
Resentment: poems. 1918.
The prisoners of Mainz. 1919, New York 1919.
Pleasure. 1921.
The lonely unicorn. 1922.
Public school life: boys, parents, masters. [1922].
Roland Whateley. New York 1922.
Myself when young: confessions. 1923, New York 1924.
Card castle. 1924.
Kept: a story of post-war London. 1925, New York [1925].
Love in these days: a modern story. 1926, New York [1927].
On doing what one likes. 1926. Essays.
The last chukka: stories of east and west. 1928.
Nor many waters. 1928.
Portrait of a celibate. Garden City NY 1929.
Three score and ten. 1929, Garden City NY 1930.
The coloured countries. 1930, New York [1930] (as Hot countries), London 1948. Travel.
'Sir' she said. 1930, New York [1930].
'Most women...'. 1931, New York [1931]. Non-fiction.
So lovers dream. 1931.
Leap before you look. 1932, New York 1933, London 1934 (rev).
No quarter. 1932.
That American woman. New York [1932].
Thirteen such years. 1932, New York [1932].
Tropic seed. New York [1932].
Playing with fire. 1933.
Wheels within wheels: a story of the crisis. 1933, New York [1933] (as The golden ripple).
The Balliols. 1934, New York [1934].
Pages in woman's life: a group of stories. 1934.
Jill Somerset. 1936, New York [1936].
Eight short stories. 1937.
Going their own ways: a story of modern marriage. 1938, New York [1939].
No truce with time. 1941, New York [1941].
His second war. 1944.

The sunlit Caribbean. 1948, New York 1949 (as The sugar islands), London 1953 (rev, with original title). Travel.
These I would choose: a personal anthology. 1948.
Unclouded summer: a love story. 1948, New York 1948.
The Lipton story: a centennial biography. Garden City NY 1950, London 1951.
Where the clocks strike twice. New York 1951, London 1952 (as Where the clocks chime twice). Travel.
Guy Renton: a London story. New York 1952, London 1953.
Island in the sun. New York 1955, London 1956.
Merchants of wine: being a centenary account of the fortunes of the House of Gilbey. 1957.
The sugar islands: a collection of pieces written about the West Indies between 1928 and 1953. 1958, New York [1959] (as Love and the Caribbean: tales, characters and scenes of the West Indies).
In praise of wine. 1959. Non-fiction.
Fuel for the flame. 1960, New York 1960.
My place in the bazaar. 1961, New York 1961.
The early years of Alec Waugh. 1962, New York 1963.
A family of islands: a history of the West Indies from 1492 to 1898. 1964, Garden City NY 1964.
The mule on the minaret. 1965, New York 1965.
My brother Evelyn, and other profiles. 1967, New York 1968.
Wines and spirits. New York 1968.

EVELYN ARTHUR ST JOHN WAUGH
1903–66

Bibliographies

Doyle, P. A. Waugh: a bibliography. Bull of Bibliography 22 1956.
Linck, C. E. Works of Waugh, 1910–30. Twentieth Century Lit 10 1964.
Kosok, H. Waugh: a checklist of criticism. Twentieth-Century Lit 11 1966.
Evelyn Waugh Newsletter. 1967 onwards. Includes suppls to Doyle, Linck and Kosok.
Farr, D. P. Waugh: a supplementary bibliography. Bull of Bibliography 26 1969. Primary material only.

Selections

Tactical exercise. Boston 1954. Includes Work suspended, Love among the ruins, and stories from Mr Loveday's little outing.
The world of Waugh, selected and ed C. J. Rolo. Boston 1958.

§1

The world to come: a poem in three cantos. 1916 (priv ptd).
PRB: an essay on the Pre-Raphaelite Brotherhood 1847–54. 1926 (priv ptd).
Decline and fall: an illustrated novelette. 1928, Garden City NY 1929, London 1962 (rev, with new preface).
Rossetti: his life and works. 1928, New York 1928.
Labels: a Mediterranean journal. 1930, New York [1930] (as A bachelor abroad: a Mediterranean journal).
Vile bodies. 1930, New York [1930], London 1965 (rev, with new preface).
Remote people. 1931, New York [1932] (as They were still dancing). Travel.
Black mischief. 1932, New York [1932], London 1962 (rev, with new preface).
A handful of dust. 1934, New York [1934], London 1964 (rev, with new preface).
Ninety-two days: the account of a tropical journey through British Guiana and part of Brazil. 1934, New York [1934].
Edmund Campion. 1935, New York 1935, Boston 1946 (rev), London 1947, 1961 (with new material).

Mr Loveday's little outing, and other sad stories. 1936, Boston 1936.

Waugh in Abyssinia. 1936, New York 1936.

Scoop: a novel about journalists. 1938, Boston 1938, London 1964 (rev, with new preface).

Robbery under law: the Mexican object-lesson. 1939, Boston 1939 (as Mexico: an object lesson).

Put out more flags. 1942, Boston 1942, London 1967 (rev with new preface).

Work suspended: two chapters of an unfinished novel. 1942, 1949 (rev as Work Suspended and other stories).

Brideshead revisited: the sacred and profane memories of Captain Charles Ryder. 1945, Boston 1945, London 1960 (rev, with new preface).

When the going was good. 1946, Boston 1947. Travel; selections from Labels, Remote people, Ninety-two days, Waugh in Abyssinia.

Scott-King's modern Europe. 1947, Boston 1949.

Wine in peace and war. 1947.

The loved one: an Anglo-American tragedy. [1948], Boston 1948, London 1965 (rev, with new preface).

A selection from the occasional sermons of the Right Reverend Monsignor R. A. Knox. Ed Waugh 1949.

Helena. 1950, Boston 1950.

Men at arms. 1952, Boston 1952, London 1965 (rev, as pt of Sword of honour, 1965, below).

The holy places. 1952. Essays.

Love among the ruins: a romance of the near future. 1953.

Officers and gentlemen. 1955, Boston 1955, London 1965 (rev, as pt of Sword of honour, 1965, below).

The ordeal of Gilbert Pinfold: a conversation piece. 1957, Boston 1957.

The life of Ronald Knox. 1959.

A tourist in Africa. 1960, Boston 1960. Travel.

Unconditional surrender: the conclusion of Men at arms and Officers and gentlemen. 1961, Boston 1962 (as The end of the battle), London 1965 (rev, as pt of Sword of honour, 1965, below).

Basil Seal rides again: or, the rake's regress. 1963, Boston 1963.

A little learning: the first volume of an autobiography. 1964, Boston 1964.

Sword of honour. 1965, Boston 1965. A recension by the author, into a single narrative, of Men at arms, Officers and gentlemen, and Unconditional surrender.

Letters

Evelyn Waugh: letters (and post-cards) to Randolph Churchill. Encounter 31 1968.

§2

'West, Rebecca' (C. I. Andrews). In her Ending in earnest: a literary log, 1931.

Dennis, N. Waugh: the pillar of Anchorage House. Partisan Rev 10 1943.

Wilson, E. Never apologize, never explain: the art of Waugh. New Yorker 4 March 1944; rptd in his Classics and commercials, New York 1950.

— Splendors and miseries of Waugh. New Yorker 13 July 1946; rptd in Classics and commercials.

Brady, C. A. Waugh: Shrove Tuesday motley and Lenten sackcloth. Catholic Lib World 16 1945.

Macaulay, R. Evelyn Waugh. Horizon 14 1946; rptd in Writers of today, ed D. V. Baker 2 1948.

'O'Donnell, Donat' (C. C. O'Brien). The pieties of Waugh. Bell 13 1946. Reply by T. J. Bannington, Mr Waugh's pieties, ibid. Rptd in Kenyon Rev 9 1947; in The Kenyon critics, ed J. C. Ransom 1951; and in O'Donnell's Maria Cross: imaginative patterns in a group of modern Catholic writers, New York 1952.

Betjeman, J. Waugh: a critical study. In Living writers, ed G. Phelps 1947.

Linklater, E. In his Art of adventure, 1947.

Savage, D. S. The innocence of Waugh. Focus 4 1947; rptd (rev) in Western Rev 14 1950.

Martindale, C. C. Back again to 'Brideshead'. Twentieth Century (Melbourne) 2 1948.

Wecter, D. On dying in Southern California. Pacific Spectator 2 1948. On The loved one.

Allen, W. G. Waugh and Graham Greene. Irish Monthly 77 1949.

Bayley, J. Two Catholic novelists. Nat Rev 132 1949. On The loved one.

Grace, W. J. Waugh as a social critic. Renascence 1 1949.

Griffiths, J. Waugh's problem comedies. Accent 9 1949.

Voorhees, R. J. Waugh revisited. South Atlantic Quart 48 1949.

— Waugh's war novels. Queen's Quart 65 1958.

Woodcock, G. Waugh: the man and his work. World Rev 1 1949.

Boyle, A. Evelyn Waugh. Irish Monthly 78 1950.

Dever, J. Echoes of two Waughs. Commonweal 27 Oct 1950. On Helena.

Marshall, B. Graham Greene and Waugh. Commonweal 3 March 1950.

Cronin, A. A tribute to Waugh. Envoy 5 1951.

Menen, A. The baroque and Mr Waugh. Month 5 1951.

Beer, O. F. Englische Gegenwartsliteratur: Waugh. Universitas 7 1952.

Braybrooke, N. Waugh and Blimp. Blackfriars 38 1952.

— Evelyn Waugh. Fortnightly 171 1952.

— Evelyn Waugh: an interim study. Books on Trial 10 1956.

— Evelyn Waugh en uniforme. Vie Intellectuelle 27 1956. On Sword of honour.

Prescott, O. Satirists: Waugh, Marquand. In his In my opinion, Indianapolis 1952.

Beattie, A. M. Evelyn Waugh. Canadian Forum 33 1953.

Blumenberg, H. Eschatologische Ironie: über die Romane Waughs. Hochland 46 1953.

Boyle, R. Waugh: master of satire. Grail 35 1953.

Spender, S. The world of Waugh. In his The creative element, 1953.

Spiel, H. Enfant terrible des Katholizismus. In her Der Park und die Wildnis: zur Situation der neueren englischen Literatur, Munich 1953.

Carstensen, B. Waugh und E. Hemingway. Archiv für das Studium der Neueren Sprachen und Literaturen 190 1954.

Hollis, C. Evelyn Waugh. 1954 (Br Council pamphlet).

Mikes, G. In his Eight humourists, 1954.

Rolo, C. J. Waugh: the best and the worst. Atlantic Monthly 194 1954.

Skerle, L. Das Wesen der Satire Waughs. Graz 1954.

Chastaing, M. Ein Satiriker in Stichworten: Waughs gesellschaftskritische Romane. Wort und Wahrkeit 10 1955.

Dauch, A. Das Menschenbild in den Werken Waughs. Cologne 1955.

Deschner, K. In Christliche Dichter der Gegenwart, ed H. Friedmann and O. Mann, Heidelberg 1955.

Fytton, F. Waugh-fare. Catholic World 181 1955.

Breit, H. In his Writer observed, 1956.

— Maugham and Waugh. Ibid.

Cosman, M. The nature and work of Waugh. Colorado Quart 4 1956.

De Vitis, A. A. Roman holiday: the Catholic novels of Waugh. New York 1956.

Marcus, S. Waugh and the art of entertainment. Partisan Rev 23 1956.

O'Faolain, S. Huxley and Waugh: or I do not think, therefore I am. In his Vanishing hero, 1956.

Lapicque, F. La satire dans l'œuvre de Waugh. Études Anglaises 10 1957.

Doyle, P. A. The politics of Waugh. Renascence 11 1958.

— Waugh: a critical essay. Grand Rapids 1969 (Contemporary writers in Christian perspective).

Stopp, F. J. Waugh: portrait of an artist. 1958.

Stürzl, E. Waughs Romanwerk: makabre Farce oder menschliche Komödie? Die Neueren Sprachen 8 1959.

Dyson, A. E. Waugh and the mysteriously disappearing hero. CQ 2 1960; rptd in his Crazy fabric, 1965.

Kermode, F. Waugh's cities. Encounter 15 1960; rptd in his Puzzles and epiphanies, 1962.

Green, M. British comedy and the British sense of humour: Shaw, Waugh and Amis. Texas Quart 4 1961.

Green, P. Du côté de chez Waugh. REL 2 1961.

Hall, J. The other post-war rebellion: Waugh twenty-five years after. ELH 28 1961; rptd as Stylized rebellion: Waugh, in his Tragic comedians, Bloomington 1963.

Martin, G. Novelists of three decades: Waugh, Greene, C. P. Snow. In Pelican guide to English literature vol 7, The modern age, ed B. Ford 1961.

Sheehan, E. A weekend with Waugh. Cornhill Mag 171 1961.

Wasson, R. A handful of dust: critique of Victorianism. Modern Fiction Stud 7 1961.

Corr, P. Waugh: sanity and Catholicism. Studies 51 1962.

Hines, L. Waugh and his critics. Commonweal 13 April 1962.

Karl, F. R. The world of Waugh: the normally insane. In his Contemporary English novel, New York 1962, London 1963 (as A reader's guide to the contemporary English novel).

Kleine, D. W. The cosmic comedies of Waugh. South Atlantic Quart 61 1962.

Nichols, J. W. Romantic *and* realistic: the tone of Waugh's early novels. College Eng 24 1962.

Tysdahl, B. The bright young things in the early novels of Waugh. Edda 62 1962.

Wilson, C. Waugh and Graham Greene. In his Strength to dream: literature and the imagination, 1962.

Benedict, S. H. The Candide figure in the novels of Waugh. Papers of Michigan Acad of Sciences, Arts & Letters 48 1963.

Bergonzi, B. Evelyn Waugh's gentlemen. CQ 5 1963.

Cecchin, G. Echi di T. S. Eliot nei romanzi di Waugh. Eng Miscellany (Rome) 14 1963.

Kernan, A. B. The wall and the jungle: the early novels of Waugh. Yale Rev 53 1963.

Jebb, J. The art of fiction 30: Waugh. Paris Rev 30 1963. Interview.

Bradbury, M. Evelyn Waugh. Edinburgh 1964 (Writers & Critics).

Hardy, J. E. Brideshead revisited: God, man and others. In his Man in the modern novel, Seattle 1964.

La France, M. Context and structure of Waugh's Brideshead revisited. Twentieth-Century Lit 10 1964.

Lorda Alaïz, F. M. De romanschrijver Waugh. Raam no 12 1964.

Davis, R. M. Waugh's early work: the formation of a method. Texas Stud in Lit & Lang 7 1965.

—— Waugh on the art of fiction. Papers on Lang & Lit 2 1966.

—— The mind and art of Waugh. Papers on Lang & Lit 3 1967.

—— Textual problems in the novels of Waugh. PBSA 62 1968.

—— (ed). Evelyn Waugh. St Louis 1969 (Christian Critic ser).

Delasanta, R. and D'Avanzo, M. L. Truth and beauty in Brideshead revisited. Modern Fiction Stud 11 1965.

Greenblatt, S. J. Three modern satirists: Waugh, Orwell and Huxley. New Haven 1965.

Greene, George. Scapegoat with style: the status of Waugh. Queen's Quart 71 1965.

Carens, J. F. The satiric art of Waugh. Seattle 1966.

Hinchcliffe, P. Fathers and children in the novels of Waugh. UTQ 35 1966.

Servotte, H. Evelyn Waugh 1903–66. Dietsche Warande en Belfort 111 1966.

Churchill, T. The trouble with Brideshead revisited. MLQ 28 1967.

Donaldson, F. Waugh: portrait of a country neighbour. 1967.

Evelyn Waugh Newsletter. 1967 onwards.

Harty, E. R. Brideshead re-read: a discussion of some of the themes of Waugh's Brideshead revisited. Unisa Eng Stud 3 1967.

Jervis, S. A. Waugh, Vile bodies, and the younger generation. South Atlantic Quart 66 1967.

Waugh, A. My brother Evelyn, and other profiles. 1967.

Howarth, H. Quelling the riot: Waugh's progress. In The shapeless god: essays on modern fiction, ed H. J. Mooney and T. F. Staley, Pittsburgh 1968.

Rutherford, A. Waugh's Sword of honour. In Imagined worlds: essays on some English novels and novelists in honour of John Butt, ed M. Mack and I. Gregor, 1968.

Semple, H. E. Waugh's modern crusade. Eng Stud in Africa 11 1968.

Wiley, P. W. Evelyn Waugh. Contemporary Lit 9 1968.

Costello, P. An idea of comedy and Waugh's Sword of honour. Kansas Quart 1 1969.

Delbaere-Garant, J. 'Who shall inherit England?': a comparison between Howards End, Parade's end and Unconditional surrender. E Studies 50 1969.

Farr, D. P. Waugh: tradition and a modern talent. South Atlantic Quart 68 1969.

Linck, C. E. and R. M. Davis. The bright young people in Vile bodies. Papers on Lang & Lit 5 1969.

Reinhardt, K. F. Waugh: Christian gentleman. In his Theological novel of modern Europe, New York 1969.

Schlüter, K. Kuriose Welt im modernen englischen Roman: dargestellt an ausgewählten Werken von Waugh und Angus Wilson. Berlin 1969.

Wooton, C. Waugh's Brideshead revisited: war and limited hope. Midwest Quart 10 1969.

GLADYS MARY WEBB, née MEREDITH
1881–1927

Bibliographies

Sanders, C. Mary Webb: an annotated bibliography of writings about her. Eng Lit in Transition 9 1966.

Collections and Selections

The collected works of Mary Webb. 7 vols 1928–29, 6 vols New York 1929 (omitting The golden arrow). With introds by various authors. Texts rptd in Sarn edn 7 vols 1937.

The spring of joy: poems, some prose pieces and the unfinished novel Armour wherein he trusted. 1937, New York 1937. With introds as in Collected works.

A Mary Webb anthology. 1939, New York 1940. Selected by H. B. L. Webb.

The essential Mary Webb, selected and introduced by M. Armstrong. 1949.

Fifty-one poems hitherto unpublished in book form. 1946, New York 1947.

§I

The golden arrow. 1916, New York 1935.

Gone to earth. 1917, New York [1917].

The spring of joy: a little book of healing. 1917.

The house in Dormer Forest. [1920], New York 1921.

Seven for a secret: a love story. 1922, New York [1923].

Precious bane. 1924, New York 1926.

Poems, and The spring of joy. 1928, New York [1929]. Issued as a vol in the Collected works, above.

Armour wherein he trusted: a novel and some stories. 1929, New York [1929].

The Chinese lion. 1937. Story.

§2

Adcock, A. St J. Mary Webb. In his The glory that was Grub Street, 1928.
Pugh, E. Mary Webb. Bookman (London) 74 1928.
Marshall, H. P. Mary Webb. Edinburgh Rev 249 1929.
Chappell, W. R. The Shropshire of Mary Webb. 1930.
Addison, H. Mary Webb: a short study of her life and work. 1931.
Bury, A. An impression of Mary Webb. Sufi Quart 7 1931.
Chapman, G. Mary Webb. London Mercury 23 1931.
Hecht, H. Der Sündenesser. Englische Studien 67 1932. On Precious bane.
Moult, T. Mary Webb: her life and work. 1932.
Collard, L. Mary Webb. Contemporary Rev 143 1933.
Peake, E. The religious teaching of Mary Webb. Congregational Quart 11 1933.
Schneider, G. Die Verwendung und Bedeutung der Folklore in den Romanen von Mary Webb. Göttingen 1934.
Knapp, I. In her Die Landschaft im modernen englischen Frauenroman, Tübingen 1935.
Tiemann, M. Naturbetrachtung und Weltanschauung in den Werken von Mary Webb. Greifswald 1936.
Magdinier, M. Mary Webb: apôtre et poète de la pitié. Études 233 1937.
Evans, C. Mary Webb. Colophon 3 1938.
Marinoff, I. Die Romane Mary Webbs. Anglia 60 1938.
Pitfield, R. L. The Shropshire lass and her goitre: some account of Mary Meredith Webb and her works. Annals of Medical History ser 3, 4 1942.
Byford-Jones, W. Shropshire haunts of Mary Webb. Shrewsbury 1948.
Wrenn, D. P. H. Goodbye to morning: a biographical study of Mary Webb. Shrewsbury 1964.
Sanders, C. Mary Webb: an introduction. Eng Lit in Transition 9 1966.
— The golden arrow: Mary Webb's 'Apocalypse of love'. English Lit in Transition 10 1967.
Davis, W. E. The poetry of Mary Webb: an invitation. English Lit in Transition 11 1968.
Dassié, M. Mary Webb's contributions to The Bookman. Caliban 6 1969.

MAURICE DENTON WELCH
1914–48

A collection of Welch mss is in the library of the Univ of Texas. The ms of Maiden Voyage *is in the BM.*

Selections

Denton Welch: extracts from his published works, ed with an introd by J. Brooke. 1963.

§1

Maiden voyage, with a foreword by E. Sitwell. 1943, New York 1945. Autobiography.
In youth is pleasure. 1944, New York 1946.
Brave and cruel, and other stories. 1948.
A voice through a cloud. 1950, [Austin Texas 1966].
A last sheaf. Ed E. Oliver 1951. Stories and poems.
I left my grandfather's house: an account of his first walking tour, with an introduction by H. Roeder. 1958 (priv ptd).

Diaries

The Denton Welch journals, edited with an introduction by J. Brooke. 1952.

§2

Cranston, M. Denton Welch. Nineteenth Century 148 1950.
Cohn, R. A few novel techniques of Denton Welch. Perspective (St Louis) 10 1958.
Brooke, J. The dual role: Welch as painter and writer. Texas Quart 7 1964.
Braybrooke, N. Savage wars: a study of the journals of W. N. P. Barbellion and Welch. Quest (New York) 1 1966.

ANTHONY PANTHER WEST
b. 1914

Gloucestershire. 1939, 1952 (rev) (Shell Guides).
On a dark night. 1949, Boston 1950 (as The vintage).
D. H. Lawrence. 1950.
Another kind. 1951, Boston 1952.
The crusades. New York 1954, London 1967 (as All about the crusades).
Heritage. New York 1955.
Principles and persuasions. New York 1957, London 1958. Literary essays.
The trend is up. New York 1960, London 1961.
Elizabethan England. 1965, New York 1965.

DAME 'REBECCA WEST', CICILY ISABEL ANDREWS
b. 1892

Bibliographies

Hutchinson, G. E. A preliminary list of the writings of Rebecca West. New Haven 1957.

§1

Henry James. 1916, New York 1916.
The return of the soldier. 1918, New York 1918. Dramatized by J. van Druten 1928.
The judge. [1922], New York 1922.
The strange necessity: essays and reviews. 1928, Garden City NY 1928.
Harriet Hume: a London fantasy. 1929, Garden City NY 1929.
Lions and lambs: caricatures by Low, with interpretations by 'Lynx' [i.e. Rebecca West]. New York 1929.
D. H. Lawrence. 1930, New York 1930 (275 copies, as Elegy: an in memoriam tribute to D. H. Lawrence).
Arnold Bennett himself. New York [1931]. Pamphlet.
Ending in earnest: a literary log. Garden City NY 1931. Essays rptd from Bookman (NY).
A letter to a grandfather. 1933 (Hogarth Letters).
St Augustine. 1933, New York 1933.
The modern 'Rake's progress': words by Rebecca West, paintings by David Low. 1934. Satire.
The harsh voice: four short novels. 1935, Garden City NY 1935.
The thinking reed. [1936], New York 1936.
Black lamb and grey falcon: the record of a journey through Yugoslavia in 1937. 2 vols New York 1941, London 1942.
The meaning of treason. New York 1947, London 1949, 1952 (rev), New York 1964, London 1965 (rev, Penguin).
A train of powder. 1955, New York 1955. Non-fiction.
The court and the castle: some treatments of a recurrent theme. New Haven 1957, London 1958. Essays.
The fountain overflows. 1957, New York 1957.
The Vassall affair. [1963]. Non-fiction.
The birds fall down. 1966, New York 1966.
McLuhan and the future of literature. 1969.

§2

Collins, J. Two literary ladies of London: Katherine Mansfield and Rebecca West. In his The doctor looks at literature, New York 1923.

Braybrooke, P. In his Philosophies in modern fiction, 1929.

Ellmann, M. The Russians of Rebecca West. Atlantic Monthly 218 1966.

Enright, D. J. Rebecca West's novels. New Statesman 4 Nov 1966.

Rainer, D. Rebecca West, disturber of the peace. Commonweal 10 May 1968.

TERENCE HANBURY WHITE
1906–64

§1

The green bay tree: or the wicked man touches wood. Cambridge 1929. Verse.

Loved Helen and other poems. 1929.

Dead Mr Nixon. 1931. With R. McNair Scott.

Darkness at Pemberley. 1932, New York [1933].

First lesson. 1932, New York 1933. As by 'James Aston'.

They winter abroad. 1932, New York 1932. As by 'James Aston'.

Farewell Victoria. 1933, New York 1934.

Earth stopped: or Mr Marx's sporting tour. 1934.

Gone to ground. 1935.

England have my bones. 1936, New York 1936. Essays.

Burke's steerage: or the amateur gentleman's introduction to noble sports and pastimes. [1938].

The sword in the stone. 1938, New York 1939. Rptd in The once and future king, 1958, below.

The witch in the wood. New York 1939, London [1940]. Rptd (as The queen of air and darkness) in The once and future king, below.

The ill-made knight. New York 1940, London 1941. Rptd in The once and future king, below.

Mistress Masham's repose. New York [1946], London 1947.

The elephant and the kangaroo. New York [1947], London 1948.

The age of scandal: an excursion through a minor period. 1950, New York 1950. Non-fiction.

The goshawk. 1951, New York, 1952. Non-fiction.

The scandalmonger. 1952, New York 1952. Non-fiction.

The book of beasts: being a translation from a Latin bestiary made and edited by T. H. White. 1954, New York [1954].

The master: an adventure story. 1957, New York 1957. For children.

The once and future king. 1958, New York 1958. Contains The sword in the stone; The queen of air and darkness; The ill-made knight; The candle in the wind.

The godstone and the blackymor. 1959, New York 1959 (as A western wind). Travel.

Verses. Alderney 1962 (priv ptd, 100 copies).

America at last: the American journal of T. H. White. New York [1965].

S. T. Warner's T. H. White, 1967 below contains a list of White's unpbd works, including several complete novels.

Letters

The White/Garnett letters, ed D. Garnett. 1968, New York 1968.

§2

Hugh-Jones, S. A visible export: T. H. White, Merlyn's latest pupil. TLS 7 Aug 1959.

Dunn, S. P. Mr White, Mr Williams and the matter of Britain. Kenyon Rev 24 1962.

Cameron, J. R. T. H. White in Camelot: the matter of Britain revitalized. Humanities Assoc Bull 16 1965.

Floyd, B. A critique of White's The once and future king. Riverside Quart 1–2, 1965–66.

Warner, S. T. T. H. White: a biography. 1967.

CHARLES WALTER STANSBY WILLIAMS
1886–1945

Bibliographies

Ridler, A. Bibliography. In The image of the city, 1958, Collections and Selections, below.

Dawson, L. R. jr. A checklist of reviews by Williams. PBSA 55 1961.

Shideler, M. M. Bibliography. In her The theology of romantic love, New York 1962, §2, below.

Collections and Selections

The image of the city, and other essays. Selected by A. Ridler with a critical introduction. 1958.

Selected writings, chosen by A. Ridler. 1961.

Collected plays. 1963. With introd by J. Heath-Stubbs.

§1

The silver stair. [1912]. Verse.

Poems of conformity. 1917.

Christian symbolism, by Michal [i.e. Mrs Charles] Williams. 1919. Some passages were by Williams.

Divorce. 1920. Verse.

The moon: a cantata prepared from the airs of Purcell by W. G. Whittaker, the words by C. Williams. [1923].

Windows of night. [1924]. Verse.

The masque of the manuscript. 1927 (priv ptd, 100 copies). Music by H. J. Foss.

An urbanity. [1927?] (priv ptd). Verse.

A myth of Shakespeare. 1928. Verse play.

The masque of perusal. 1929 (priv ptd, 100 copies). Music by H. J. Foss.

Heroes and kings. 1930. Verse.

War in heaven. 1930, New York 1949.

Poetry at present. Oxford 1930.

Many dimensions. 1931, New York 1949.

Three plays. 1931. Contains The witch; The chaste wanton; The rite of the Passion. Also includes some previously pbd verse.

The place of the lion. 1931, New York 1951.

The greater trumps. 1932, New York 1950.

The English poetic mind. Oxford 1932, New York 1963.

Shadows of ecstasy. 1933, New York 1950.

Bacon. 1933.

Reason and beauty in the poetic mind. Oxford 1933.

James I. 1934, 1951 (with introd by D. L. Sayers), New York 1953.

Rochester. 1935.

The rite of the Passion. 1936. First pbd in Three plays, 1931, above.

Queen Elizabeth. 1936.

Cranmer of Canterbury. 1936 (acting edn), 1936 (full text, as Thomas Cranmer of Canterbury). Verse play.

Descent into hell. 1937, New York 1949.

Stories of great names. 1937.

Henry VII. 1937.

He came down from heaven. 1938. Theology.

Taliessin through Logres. 1938. Verse.

The descent of the dove: a short history of the Holy Spirit in the Church. 1939, New York 1939, 1956 (introd W. H. Auden).

Judgement at Chelmsford: a pageant play. 1939.

The way of exchange. 1941. Theological pamphlet.

Religion and love in Dante: the theology of romantic love. [1941]. Pamphlet.

Witchcraft. 1941, New York 1959.
The forgiveness of sins. 1942. Theology.
The figure of Beatrice: a study of Dante. 1943, New York 1961.
The region of the summer stars. 1944. Verse.
All Hallows' Eve. 1945, New York 1948 (introd by T. S. Eliot).
The house of the octopus. 1945. Verse play.
Flecker of Dean Close. 1946.
The figure of Arthur. In Arthurian torso, ed C. S. Lewis, 1948. Verse (fragment).
Seed of Adam, and other plays, with introduction by A. Ridler. 1948. Contains Seed of Adam; The death of Good Fortune; The house by the stable; Grab and Grace.

Williams edited Poems of G. M. Hopkins, *1930 and* Letters of Evelyn Underhill, *1943. For various other books and anthologies ed Williams, see Ridler and Shideler, Bibliographies, above. For Williams' articles and reviews contributed to periodicals and newspapers, in particular* News Chronicle, Sunday Times *and* Time & Tide, *see Ridler, Shideler and also the checklist by Dawson, above.*

§2

Maynard, T. The poetry of Williams. North American Rev 210 1919.
— Williams: Pan and pan-anglicanism. In his Our best poets, New York 1922.
Mason, E. Williams and his work. Bookman (London) 68 1925.
Mehdi Imam, S. C. Williams: cosmic love. In his The poetry of the invisible, 1937.
Power, M. J. Charles Williams. In her Poets at prayer, New York 1938.
Lewis, C. S. A sacred poem. Theology 38 1939. On Taliessin through Logres.
— Preface. In Essays presented to Charles Williams, ed C. S. Lewis,1947.
— Williams and the Arthuriad. In his Arthurian torso, 1948.
Stuart, M. Taliessin through Logres. The Wind & the Rain 1 1941.
Eliot, T. S. The significance of Williams. Listener 19 Dec 1946. Rptd (rev) as introd to All Hallows' Eve, New York, 1948, §1, above.
Pitt, V. Williams: the affirmation of images. Mandrake 3 1946.
Diggle, M. The mathematics of the soul. Poetry London no 11 1947.
Heath-Stubbs, J. The poetic achievement of Williams. Ibid.
— Charles Williams. 1955 (Br Council pamphlet).
Every, G. Charles Williams. Theology 51 1948; rptd in his Poetry and personal responsibility, 1949.
Parsons, G. The spirit of Williams. Atlantic Monthly 184 1949.
Engel, C. Williams: un mystique protestant. Réforme 24 June 1950.
Winship, G. P. jr. This rough magic: the novels of Williams. Yale Rev 40 1950.
Borrow, A. The affirmation of images. Nine 3 1952. On the novels.
Brown, R. M. Williams, lay theologian. Theology Today 10 1953.
Crowley, C. P. The structural patterns of Williams' Descent into hell. Papers of the Michigan Acad of Science Arts & Letters 39 1953.
— The Grail poetry of Williams. UTQ 25 1956.
Evans, D. W. T. S. Eliot, Williams, and the sense of the occult. Accent 14 1954.
Gigrich, J. P. An immortality for its own sake: a study of the concept of poetry in the writings of Williams. Washington 1954.
Davies, R. T. Williams and romantic experience. Études Anglaises 8 1955.

Cavaliero, G. The way of affirmation: a study of the writings of Williams. Church Quart Rev 157 1956.
Conquest, R. The art of the enemy. EC 7 1957. With later comments by various hands.
Moorman, C. W. Myth in the novels of Williams. Modern Fiction Stud 3 1957.
— Arthurian triptych: mythic materials in Williams, Lewis and Eliot. Berkeley 1960.
— Zion and Gomorrah: Williams. In his The precincts of felicity: the Augustinian city of the Oxford Christians, Gainesville 1966.
Sayers, D. L. The poetry of the image in Dante and Williams. In her Further papers on Dante, 1957.
Beaumont, E. Williams and the power of Eros. Dublin Rev no 479 1959.
Hadfield, A. M. An introduction to Williams. 1959.
Spacks, P. M. Williams: a novelist's pilgrimage. Religion in Life 29 1960.
Irwin, W. R. There and back again: the romances of Williams, Lewis and Tolkien. Sewanee Rev 69 1961.
Weales, G. C. In his Religion in modern English drama, Philadelphia 1961.
Dunn, S. P. Mr White, Mr Williams and the matter of Britain. Kenyon Rev 24 1962.
Fuller, E. Many dimensions: the images of Williams. In his Books with men behind them, New York 1962.
Shideler, M. M. The theology of romantic love: a study in the writings of Williams. New York 1962.
— Williams: a critical essay. Grand Rapids Mich 1966.
Spanos, W. V. Williams' Judgement at Chelmsford: a study in the aesthetic of sacramental time. Christian Scholar 45 1962.
— Williams' Seed of Adam: the existential flight from death. Ibid 49 1966.
Wright, E. Theology in the novels of Williams. Stanford 1962 (Stanford Honors Essays in Humanities 6).
Lalande, M. Williams' pattern of time in Descent into hell. Renascence 15 1963.
Carmichael, D. Love and rejection in Williams. Universitas (Wayne State Univ) 2 1964.
Dawson, L. R. Reflections of Williams on fiction. Ball State Teachers College Forum 5 1964.
Sale, R. England's Parnassus: Lewis, Williams and Tolkien. Hudson Rev 17 1964.
Sharpe, E. J. Williams och den engelska kristendomsromanen. Vår Lösen 56 1965.
Versinger, G. Charles Williams. Études Anglaises 18 1965.
Davidson, C. Williams and religious drama. Religious Theatre 5 1967.
— Williams' All Hallows' Eve: the way of perversity. Renascence 20 1968.
Huttar, C. A. Williams: novelist and prophet. Gordon Rev 10 1967.
McMichael, B. Hell is oneself: an examination of the concept of damnation in Williams' Descent into hell. Stud in the Literary Imagination 1 1968.
Sellery, J. Fictive modes in Williams' All Hallows' Eve. Genre 1 1968.
Thrash, L. G. A source for the redemption theme in The cocktail party [Williams' The greater trumps]. Texas Studies in Lit and Lang 9 1968.
Hillegas, M. R. (ed). Shadows of the imagination: the fantasies of Lewis, Tolkien and Williams. Carbondale 1969.

HENRY WILLIAMSON
b. 1895

Bibliographies

Girvan, I. W. A bibliography and a critical survey of the works of Williamson, together with authentic bibliographical annotations by another hand [? Williamson]. Chipping Campden 1931.

Selections

As the sun shines. 1941. With notes by Williamson.
The Henry Williamson animal saga. 1959. Contains
Tarka the otter, Salar the salmon, The epic of Brock the
badger, Chakchek the peregrine.

§1

Prose Fiction

The beautiful years. [1921], 1929 (rev), New York [1929].
Book 1 of The flax of dream sequence.
Dandelion days. [1922], 1930 (rev), New York [1930].
Book 2 of The flax of dream sequence.
The peregrine's saga, and other stories of the country
green. [1923], New York [1925] (as Sun brothers).
The dream of fair women: a tale of youth after the Great
War. [1924], New York [1924], London 1931 (rev),
New York [1931]. Book 3 of The flax of dream sequence.
The old stag. 1926. Stories.
Stumberleap: a story taken from The old stag [1926].
Tarka the otter. 1927, New York 1928.
The pathway. 1928, 1929 (rev), New York [1929]. Book 4
of The flax of dream sequence.
The patriot's progress: being the vicissitudes of Pte John
Bullock. 1930, New York [1930].
The gold falcon; or The haggard of love. 1933 (anon),
1947.
The star-born, with an introduction [i.e. written] by
H. Williamson 1933, 1948 (rev). 'Pendant' to The flax
of dream sequence.
Salar the salmon. 1935, Boston 1936.
The flax of dream. 1936. 4 novels first pbd separately
(here rev). See above.
The Phasian bird. 1948, Boston 1950.
Scribbling lark. 1949.
The dark lantern. 1951, 1962 (rev). This and the following
novels form the sequence A chronicle of ancient sun-
light.
Donkey boy. 1952, 1962 (rev).
Tales of moorland and estuary. 1953. Stories.
Young Phillip Maddison. 1953, 1962 (rev).
How dear is life. 1954, 1963 (rev).
A fox under my cloak. 1955, 1963 (rev).
The golden virgin. 1957, 1963 (rev).
Love and the loveless. 1958, 1963 (rev).
A test to destruction. 1960, 1964 (rev).
The innocent moon. 1961, 1965 (rev).
It was the nightingale. 1962, 1965 (rev).
The power of the dead. 1963, 1966 (rev).
The phoenix generation. 1965, 1967 (rev).
A solitary war. 1966.
Lucifer before sunrise. 1967.
The gale of the world. 1969.

Other Works

The lone swallows. [1922], New York [1926] (as The lone
swallows and other essays of the country green), London
1933 (enlarged, as The lone swallows and other essays of
boyhood and youth). Essays.
The Ackymals. San Francisco 1929 (225 copies). Essay,
rptd (rev) in The village book, 1930, below.
The linhay on the downs. 1929. Essays.
The wet Flanders plain. [1929], 1929 (rev), New York
[1929]. Account of visit to the battlefields.
The village book. 1930, New York [1930]. Essays.
The wild red deer of Exmoor: a digression on the logic and
ethics and economics of stag-hunting in England today.
1931. Pamphlet.
The labouring life. 1932, New York [1933] (as As the sun
shines). Sequel to The village book, 1930, above.
On foot in Devon: or Guidance and gossip, being a mono-
logue in two reels. 1933.
The linhay on the downs, and other adventures in the old
and the new world. 1934. Essays.

Devon holiday. 1935. Semi-autobiographical.
Richard Jefferies. Selections. Ed. Williamson 1937.
Goodbye West Country. 1937, Boston 1938. Diary.
The children of Shallowford. 1939, 1959 (rev). Auto-
biographical.
Genius of friendship: T. E. Lawrence. 1941.
The story of a Norfolk farm. 1941. Autobiographical.
Norfolk life. 1943. With L. R. Haggard.
Life in a Devon village. 1945. This, and the following,
compiled from material gathered together in The village
book, 1930, above, and The labouring life, 1932, above.
Tales of a Devon village. 1945.
The sun in the sands. 1945. Semi-autobiographical.
A clear water stream. 1958. Essays.
In the woods. Llandeilo 1960. Autobiographical essay.

§2

West, H. F. The dreamer of Devon. 1932.
Elwin, M. In Modern British writing, ed D. V. Baker,
1947.
Murry, J. M. In his Katherine Mansfield and other
literary studies, 1959.
Bergonzi, B. Later observations. In his Heroes' twilight:
a study of the literature of the Great War, 1965.
Sewell, B. Some thoughts on The flax of dream. Aylesford Rev 7 1965.

ANGUS FRANK JOHNSTONE WILSON
b. 1913

Bibliographies

McDowell, F. P. The Angus Wilson collection. Books at
Iowa 10 1969.
— and E. S. Graves. The Angus Wilson manuscripts in
the University of Iowa libraries. Iowa City 1969.

Selections

Death dance. New York 1969. Stories from The wrong
set; Such darling dodos; A bit off the map.

§1

The wrong set, and other stories. 1949, New York 1950.
Such darling dodos, and other stories. 1950, New York
1951.
Emile Zola: an introductory study of his novels. 1952,
New York 1952, London 1964 (rev).
Hemlock and after. 1952, New York 1952.
For whom the cloche tolls: a scrap-book of the twenties.
1953. Illustr P. Jullian.
Anglo-Saxon attitudes. 1956, New York 1956.
The mulberry bush: a play in three acts. 1956.
A bit off the map, and other stories. 1957, New York 1957.
The middle age of Mrs Eliot. 1958, New York 1959.
The old men at the zoo. 1961, New York 1961.
The wild garden: or, speaking of writing. 1963, Berkeley
1963.
Late call. 1964, New York 1965.
Tempo: the impact of television on the arts. [1964].
No laughing matter. 1967.

For a selective list of Wilson's uncollected essays and criticism,
see J. L. Halio, Angus Wilson, 1964, below.

§2

Kermode, F. Mr Wilson's people. Spectator 21 Nov
1958; rptd in his Puzzles and epiphanies, 1962.
Millgate, M. In M. Cowley (ed), Writers and their work:
the Paris Review interviews, 1958.
Cockshut, A. O. J. Favoured sons: the moral world of
Wilson. EC 9 1959.
Scott-Kilvert, I. Angus Wilson. REL 1 1960.

Cox, C. B. The humanism of Angus Wilson: a study of Hemlock and after. CQ 3 1961.
— The free spirit: a study of liberal humanism in the novels of George Eliot, H. James, E. M. Forster, Virginia Woolf and Wilson. 1963.
Mander, J. G. A house divided. In his The writer and commitment, 1961. On the short stories.
Gindin, J. J. Angus Wilson's qualified nationalism. In his Postwar British fiction, Berkeley 1962.
Halio, J. L. The novels of Angus Wilson. Modern Fiction Stud 8 1962.
— Angus Wilson. Edinburgh 1964 (Writers & Critics).
Karl, F. R. The still comic music of humanity: the novels of A. Powell, Wilson and N. Dennis. In his The contemporary English novel, New York 1962, London 1963 (as A reader's guide to the contemporary English novel).
Schlüter, K. Angus Wilson: The middle age of Mrs Eliot. In Der moderne englische Roman, ed H. Oppel, Berlin 1965.
— Kuriose Welt im modernen englischen Roman: dargestellt an ausgewählten Werke von Evelyn Waugh und Wilson. Berlin 1969.
Smith, W. J. Angus Wilson's England. Commonweal 82 1965.
Bradbury, M. The short stories of Wilson. Stud in Short Fiction 3 1966.
Poston, L. A conversation with Wilson. Books Abroad 40 1966.
Rabinovitz, R. In his The reaction against experiment in the English novel, 1950-60. New York 1967.
Drescher, H. W. Wilson: an interview. Die Neueren Sprachen 17 1968.
Katona, A. Wilson's fiction and its relation to the English tradition. Acta Litteraria Academiae Scientiarum Hungaricae 10 1968.
Servotte, H. Experiment en traditie: Wilson's No laughing matter. Dietsche Warande en Belfort 113 1968.
— A note on the formal characteristics of No laughing matter. E Studies 50 1969.
Delpech, J. Les masques d'Angus Wilson. Nouvelles Littéraires 10 Apr 1969.
Gransden, K. W. Angus Wilson. 1969 (Br Council pamphlet).

'ROMER WILSON',
FLORENCE ROMA MUIR WILSON
1891–1930

§1

Martin Schüler. [1918], New York 1919, 1928 (with introd by M. Sinclair).
If all these young men. 1919.
The death of society: conte de fée premier. 1921, New York [1921], 1928 (with introd by H. Walpole).
The grand tour. 1923, New York 1923 (as The grand tour of Alphonse Marichaud).
Dragon's blood: conte de feé deuxième. [1926], New York 1926.
Greenlow. 1927, New York 1927.
Latter-day symphony. 1927, New York 1927.
The social climbers: a Russian middle-class tragedy in four acts. 1927.
All alone: the life and private history of Emily Jane Brontë. 1928, New York 1928 (as The life and private history of Emily Jane Brontë).
The hill of cloves: a tract on true love, with a digression upon an invention of the devil. 1929.
Tender advice. 1935. Stories.

§2

Shanks, E. Romer Wilson: some observations. London Mercury 22 1930.

PELHAM GRENVILLE WODEHOUSE
b. 1881
Bibliographies
Usborne, R. In his Wodehouse at work, 1961. See §2, below.

Collections and Selections
Autograph edition. 1956-.

Jeeves omnibus. 1931, 1967 (with 3 additional stories, as The world of Jeeves). Stories in this collection were rev by author for it.
Nothing but Wodehouse. Ed O. Nash, Garden City NY 1932.
P. G. Wodehouse. 1934 (Methuen's Library of Humour).
Mulliner omnibus. 1935.
Week-end Wodehouse. Introd by H. Belloc, 1939, New York 1939.
Wodehouse on golf. New York 1940.
The best of Wodehouse. Introd by S. Meredith, New York 1949.
Selected stories. Ed with introd by J. W. Aldridge, New York [1958] (Modern Library).
The most of P. G. Wodehouse. New York 1960.

§1

The pothunters. 1902. School story.
A prefect's uncle. 1903. School story.
Tales of St Austin's. 1903. School stories.
The gold bat. 1904. School story.
William Tell told again. 1904. For children.
The head of Kay's. 1905. School story.
Love among the chickens. 1906, New York 1909, London 1921 (rev).
The white feather. 1907. School story.
Not George Washington. 1907. With H. Westbrook. Facetiae.
The Globe by the way book: a literary quick-lunch for people who have only got five minutes to spare. [1908]. With H. Westbrook. Facetiae.
The swoop: or how Clarence saved England: a tale of the great invasion. 1909.
Mike: a public school story. 1909, 1935 (2nd half only, as Enter Psmith), New York 1935, London 1953 (complete and rev in 2 vols as Mike at Wrykyn and Mike and Psmith). Mike and Psmith pbd separately New York 1969.
A gentleman of leisure. 1910, New York 1910 (as The intrusion of Jimmy).
Psmith in the City: a sequel to Mike. 1910.
The prince and Betty. 1912, New York [1912].
The little nugget. 1913, New York [1914].
The man upstairs, and other stories. 1914.
Something fresh. 1915, New York 1915 (as Something new).
Psmith, journalist. 1915. Revised version of The prince and Betty.
Uneasy money. New York 1916, London 1917.
The man with two left feet, and other stories. 1917, New York [1933].
Piccadilly Jim. New York 1917, London [1918].
My man Jeeves. [1919]. Stories.
A damsel in distress. 1920 [i.e. 1919], New York 1919.
Their mutual child. New York 1919, London 1920 (as The coming of Bill).
The little warrior. New York 1920, London 1921 (as Jill the reckless).
The indiscretions of Archie. 1921, New York [1921].
The clicking of Cuthbert. 1922, New York [1924] (as Golf without tears). Stories.
The girl on the boat. 1922, New York [1922] (as Three men and a maid).
The adventures of Sally. 1923 [i.e. 1922], New York [1923] (as Mostly Sally).

The inimitable Jeeves. 1923, New York [1923] (as Jeeves).

Leave it to Psmith. 1924 [i.e. 1923], New York [1924].

Ukridge. 1924, New York [1926] (as He rather enjoyed it). Stories.

Bill the conqueror. 1924, New York [1925].

Carry on, Jeeves! 1925, New York [1927]. Stories, 4 rptd from My man Jeeves, 1919, above.

Sam the sudden. 1925, New York [1925] (as Sam in the suburbs).

Hearts and diamonds: a new light opera adapted from The Orlov by E. Marischka and B. Gramichstaedten. English adaptation by Wodehouse and L. Wylie. (Strand 1 June 1926). [1926].

The heart of a goof. 1926, New York [1927] (as Divots). Stories.

Good morning, Bill: a three act comedy based on the Hungarian of L. Fodor. (Devonshire Park, Eastbourne 7 Nov 1927; Duke of York's 28 Nov 1927). 1928.

The small bachelor. 1927, New York [1927].

Meet Mr Mulliner. 1927, Garden City NY 1928. Stories.

The three musketeers. Book by W. A. Macguire, lyrics by Wodehouse and C. Grey. (Lyric 13 March 1928). [1937].

A damsel in distress: a comedy in three acts. (New 13 Aug 1928). [1930] (French's Acting Edn). Adapted from the novel; with 'Ian Hay' (J. H. Beith).

Money for nothing. 1928, Garden City NY 1928.

Baa, baa, black sheep: a farcical comedy in three acts. (New 22 April 1929). [1930] (French's Acting Edn). With 'Ian Hay' (J. H. Beith).

Candle-light: a comedy in three acts by S. Geyer, adapted by Wodehouse. (Empire, New York 1929). New York [1934] (French's Standard Acting Edn).

Mr Mulliner speaking. 1929, Garden City NY 1930. Stories.

Summer lightning. 1929, Garden City NY 1929 (as Fish preferred), London 1929 (US printing, as Fish deferred).

Leave it to Psmith: a comedy of youth, love and misadventure in three acts. (Shaftesbury 29 Sept 1930). [1932] (French's Acting Edn). Adapted from the novel. With 'Ian Hay' (J. H. Beith).

Very good, Jeeves! 1930, Garden City NY 1930.

Big money. 1931, Garden City NY 1931.

If I were you. 1931, Garden City NY 1931.

Doctor Sally. 1932.

Hot water. 1932, Garden City NY 1932.

Louder and funnier. 1932. Essays.

Mulliner nights. 1933, Garden City NY 1933. Stories.

Heavy weather. 1933, Boston 1933.

Thank you, Jeeves. 1934, Boston 1934.

Right ho, Jeeves. 1934, Boston 1934 (as Brinkley Manor).

Anything goes: a musical comedy. (Palace 14 June 1935). [1936] (French's Acting Edn). With G. Bolton.

Enter Psmith. 1935. See Mike, 1909, above.

Blandings Castle and elsewhere. 1935, Garden City NY 1935. Stories.

The luck of the Bodkins. 1935, Boston 1936.

Young men in spats. 1936, Garden City NY 1936. Stories.

Laughing gas. 1936, Garden City NY 1936.

Lord Emsworth and others. 1937, Garden City NY 1937 (as The crime wave at Blandings). Stories.

Summer moonshine. Garden City NY 1937, London 1938.

The code of the Woosters. 1938, Garden City NY 1938.

Uncle Fred in the springtime. 1939, Garden City NY 1939.

Eggs, beans and crumpets. 1940, Garden City NY 1940. Stories.

Quick service. 1940, Garden City NY 1940.

Money in the bank. Garden City NY 1942, London [1946].

Joy in the morning. Garden City NY 1946, London [1947].

Full moon. [1947], Garden City NY 1947.

Spring fever. [1948], Garden City NY 1948.

Uncle Dynamite. [1948].

The mating season. [1949], New York 1949.

Nothing serious. [1950], Garden City NY 1951. Stories.

The old reliable. 1951, Garden City NY 1951.

Barmy in wonderland. 1952, Garden City NY 1952 (as Angel cake).

Pigs have wings. 1952, Garden City NY 1952.

Bring on the girls: the improbable story of our life in musical comedy, with pictures to prove it. New York 1953, London 1954. With G. Bolton.

Mike at Wrykyn; Mike and Psmith. 1953. See Mike, 1909, above.

Ring for Jeeves. 1953, New York 1954 (as The return of Jeeves).

Jeeves and the feudal spirit. 1954, New York 1955 (as Bertie Wooster sees it through).

America, I like you. New York 1956, London 1957 (as Over seventy: an autobiography with digressions).

Come on Jeeves: a farcical comedy in three acts. 1956 (Evans Plays). With G. Bolton.

French leave. 1955 [i.e. 1956], New York 1959.

Something fishy. 1957, New York 1957 (as The butler did it).

Cocktail time. 1958, New York 1958.

A few quick ones. 1959, New York 1959. Stories.

Jeeves in the offing. 1960, New York 1960 (as How right you are, Jeeves).

Ice in the bedroom. 1961, New York 1961.

Service with a smile. New York 1961, London 1962.

Stiff upper lip, Jeeves. 1963, New York 1963.

Frozen assets. 1964, New York 1964 (as Biffen's millions).

The brinkmanship of Galahad Threepwood: a Blandings Castle novel. New York 1965, London 1965 (as Galahad at Blandings).

Plum pie. 1966, New York 1967. Stories.

The purloined paperweight. New York 1967, London 1967 (as Company for Henry).

Do butlers burgle banks? 1968, New York 1968.

A pelican at Blandings. 1969.

Letters

Performing flea: a self-portrait in letters. 1953, 1961 (with the text of Wodehouse's five Berlin broadcasts; Penguin), New York 1962 (as Author! author!). Letters to W. T. Townend, ed Townend.

For details of Wodehouse's unpbd dramatic, musical comedy and film scripts, see appendices to Usborne, Wodehouse at work, 1961.

§2

Hayward, J. P. G. Wodehouse. In The Saturday Book 1941-2, 1941.

Churchill, R. C. The innocence of Dr Wooster. Scrutiny 11 1943.

'Orwell, George' (E. A. Blair). In defence of Wodehouse. Windmill no 2 1945; rptd in his Critical essays, 1946, New York 1946 (as Dickens, Dali & others).

Lardner, J. Wodehouse past and present. New Yorker 22 May 1948.

Ryan, A. P. Wooster's progress. New Statesman 20 June 1953.

Aldridge, J. W. P. G. Wodehouse: the lesson of the young master. New World Writing no 13 1958; rptd as introd to Selected stories, New York 1958.

Stevenson, L. The antecedents of Wodehouse. Arizona Quart 5 1959.

Usborne, R. Wodehouse at work: a study of the books and characters. 1961.

Waugh, E. An act of homage and reparation to Wodehouse. Sunday Times 14 July 1961.

Olney, C. Wodehouse and the poets. Georgia Rev 16 1962.

Voorhees, R. J. The jolly old world of Wodehouse. South Atlantic Quart 61 1962.

—— P. G. Wodehouse. New York 1966 (Twayne's English Authors).

Hall, R. A., jr. Wodehouse and the English language. Annali Istituto Universitario Orientale (Napoli), Sezione Germanica 7 1964.

— Incongruity and stylistic rhythm in Wodehouse. Annali Istituto Universitario Orientale (Napoli), Sezione Germanica 11 1968.

French, R. B. D. P. G. Wodehouse. Edinburgh 1966 (Writers & Critics).

Jaggard, G. Wooster's world: a companion to the Wooster–Jeeves cycle of Wodehouse, containing a modicum of honey from the Drones. 1967.

— Blandings the blest and the blue blood: a companion to the Blandings Castle saga of Wodehouse. 1968.

'DORNFORD YATES', CECIL WILLIAM MERCER
1885–1960

§1

The brother of Daphne. 1914.
The courts of idleness. 1920.
Anthony Lyveden. 1921.
Berry and Co. 1921, New York 1928.
Jonah and Co. 1922, New York 1927, London 1936 (with prologue and epilogue omitted).
Valerie French. 1923.
And five were foolish. 1924.
As other men are. 1925.
The stolen march. 1926, New York 1933.
Blind corner. [1927], New York 1927.
Perishable goods. 1928, New York 1928.
Blood royal. [1929], New York 1930.
Maiden stakes. 1929.
Fire below. 1930.
Adèle and Co. New York 1931, London [1932].
Safe custody. [1932], New York 1932.
Storm music. 1934, New York 1934.
She fell among thieves. 1935, New York [1935].
And Berry came too. [1936], New York [1936].
She painted her face. 1937, New York 1937.
This publican. 1938, Garden City NY 1938 (as The devil in satin).
Gale warning. 1939, New York 1940.
Shoal water. 1940.
Period stuff. 1942.
An eye for a tooth. 1943, New York 1944.
The house that Berry built. 1945, New York 1945.
Red in the morning. 1946, New York 1946 (as Were death denied).
The Berry scene. 1947, New York [1947].
Cost price. 1949, New York [1949] (as The laughing bacchante).
Lower than vermin. 1950.
As Berry and I were saying. 1952.
Ne'er-do-well. 1954.
Wife apparent. 1956.
B-Berry and I look back. [1958].

§2

Usborne, R. In his Clubland heroes, 1953.

EMILY HILDA YOUNG
1880–1949

§1

A corn of wheat. 1910,
Yonder. 1912, New York 1913.
Moor fires. 1916, New York 1927.
The bridge dividing. 1922, 1927 (as The Misses Mallett—the bridge dividing), New York 1927 (as The Malletts).

William. 1925, New York 1925, [1941] (with foreword by C. van Doren).
The vicar's daughter. 1928, New York [1928].
Miss Mole. 1930, New York [1930].
Jenny Wren. 1932, New York [1933].
The curate's wife. 1934, New York [1934].
Celia. 1937, New York [1938].
Caravan island. 1940. For children.
River holiday. 1942. For children.
Chatterton Square. 1947.

§2

Mais, S. P. B. In his Some modern authors, 1923. On The bridge dividing.
Lawrence, M. Sophisticated ladies. In her School of femininity, New York 1936, London 1937 (as We write as women).

FRANCIS BRETT YOUNG
1884–1954

Collections

The Francis Brett Young omnibus. [1932]. Contains The black diamond, The young physician, The red knight.
The works of Francis Brett Young: Severn edition. 1934–. Many of the vols have prefatory notes by Young.

§1

Undergrowth. 1913, New York 1920. With E. B. Young.
Deep sea. 1914.
Robert Bridges: a critical study. 1914.
The dark tower. 1915, New York 1926.
The iron age. 1916.
Five degrees south. 1917. Verse.
Marching on Tanga: with General Smuts in East Africa. 1917, New York 1918, London 1919 (rev).
The crescent moon. 1918, New York 1919.
Captain Swing: a romantic play of 1830. [1919]. With W. E. Stirling.
Poems 1916–18. [1919], New York 1920.
The young physician. 1919, New York 1920.
The tragic bride. [1920], New York 1921.
The black diamond. [1921], New York 1921.
The red knight. [1921], New York 1922.
Pilgrim's rest. [1922], New York 1923.
Cold harbour. [1924], New York 1925.
Woodsmoke. [1924], New York 1924.
Sea horses. 1925, New York 1925.
Portrait of Clare. 1927, New York 1927 (as Love is enough).
The furnace. 1928, New York 1929. Play; with W. Armstrong.
The key of life. 1928, New York 1928.
My brother Jonathan. 1928, New York 1928.
Black roses. 1929, New York 1929.
Jim Redlake. 1930, New York 1930 (as The Redlakes).
Mr and Mrs Pennington. 1931, New York 1931.
Blood oranges. 1932. Story.
The house under the water. 1932, New York 1932.
The cage bird & other stories. 1933, New York 1933.
This little world. 1934, New York 1934.
White ladies. 1935, New York 1935.
Far forest. 1936, New York 1936.
Portrait of a village. 1937, New York 1938.
They seek a country. 1937, New York 1937.
The Christmas box. [1938].
Dr Bradley remembers. 1938, New York 1938, London 1940 (with preface).
The city of gold. 1939, New York 1939.
Cotswold honey and other stories. 1940, New York 1940 (as The ship surgeon's yarn and other stories).
Mr Lucton's freedom. 1940, New York 1940 (as Happy highway).

A man about the house: an old wives' tale. [1942], New York 1942.

The island. 1944, New York 1946. Verse.

In South Africa. 1952. Travel.

Wistanlow. 1956. Unfinished. Pbd as pt of the Severn edn, above.

§2

Mais, S. P. B. The poems of Francis Brett Young. In his Why we should read, 1921.

Twitchett, E. G. Francis Brett Young. 1935.

Young, J. B. Francis Brett Young: a biography. 1962. C.P.C.

III. CHILDREN'S BOOKS

Alphabet books, didactic works, traditional rhymes and stories, picture books have been included where they can be seen to have introduced a new or unusual approach that may have influenced the child's response to books and reading during this period. For a fuller listing of material on comics, etc, see the section on Popular Genres, cols 123–4, above.

The more voluminous writers are represented by a selection of books typical of their work, but every effort has been made to include their earliest publications in book form. In the case of authors whose major contribution to children's literature has been after 1950 only a summary has been given of their development beyond this date. Authors whose date of birth has not been found have been given a conjectural date determined by the date of their first published work. This takes the form (b. c. [date]). Similarly, uncertainty about the date of an author's death has been signalled by a query.

In a number of entries abridgements, changes of format or changes of illustrator have been regarded as sufficient grounds to register a further edition-date, even though there may have been no textual change. These further edns are normally unannotated beyond the standard abbreviation 'rev'. Publication in America is noted, even where there was no separate American edition.

(1) GENERAL WORKS

Guides to Sources

School Library Association. A list of general reference books suitable for school libraries, and a list of books on librarianship and library technique. 1950, 1954 (rev). Contains sections on book selection, children's reading tastes and current book lists.

Eyre, F. Notes for a bibliography. Junior Bookshelf 16 1952.

Crouch, M. Books about children's literature. 1963, 1966 (rev).

Haviland, V. Children's literature: a guide to reference sources. Washington 1966.

Pellowski, A. The world of children's literature. New York 1968.

Field, C. W. Subject collections in children's literature [in USA and Canada]. New York 1969.

Bibliographies of Children's Books

Cannons, H. G. T. Descriptive handbook of juvenile literature. 1906.

Field, W. T. Fingerposts to children's reading. Chicago 1907, 1911 (rev), Boston 1928 (rev, as A guide to literature for children).

H. W. Wilson Co. Children's catalog. New York 1909–. In progress. Pbd intermittently.

Stevenson, L. A child's bookshelf: suggestions on children's reading, with an annotated list of books on heroism, service, patriotism, friendliness, joy and beauty. 1917, 1918 (rev), 1922 (rev).

Smith, L. H. Books for boys and girls. Toronto 1927, 1940 (rev J. Thomson), 1954 (rev); 1966 (rev M. Bagshaw); suppls 1958, 1963.

National Book Council. Readers guides. From 1928 onwards classified lists of new and forthcoming children's books were issued. Many other ephemeral lists, exhibition catalogues etc were pbd after 1944 when the National Book Council became the National Book League. An important retrospective list for the period 1900–50 is British children's books, 1964.

Mahony, B. E. and E. Whitney. Realms of gold in children's books. New York 1929. Suppl: Five years in children's books, New York 1936.

Nowell, C. Books to read. 1930; suppl 1932; both vols rev W. C. B. Sayers as Books for youth, 1936.

Children's Book Club [Harrods Ltd]. Six to sixteen: what they read. 1933, 1934 (rev), 1938 (rev). Catalogue of the circulating library.

Vallance, R. Christmas plays for children. Junior Bookshelf 1 1936. Further listings of various types of play in subsequent issues.

Hill, R. A. and E. de Bondeli. Children's books from foreign languages: English translations from published and unpublished sources. New York 1937. Among translations noted are books by such influential authors as Brunhoff (France); Kästner, Tetzner (Germany); Fabricius (Holland); Beskow, Lagerlöf (Sweden); Carrick and Chukovsky (Russia).

Lines, K. M. Books for young people. 1937.

—— Four to fourteen: a catalogue of books for boys and girls. 1938, Cambridge 1950 (rev), 1956 (rev).

Faraday, J. G. Twelve years of children's books. Birmingham 1939.

Steel, M. Books you'll enjoy. 1939.

Brewton, J. E. and S. W. Index to children's poetry. New York 1942. First suppl New York 1954; 2nd suppl New York 1965.

Eaton, A. T. Treasure for the taking. New York 1946, 1957 (rev). Supplementary list to her Reading with children, New York 1940, col III, below.

Milne, A. A. Books for children: a reader's guide. 1948.

Beresford, R. What shall I read? 1950. Teacher's companion to an educational book, which nonetheless discusses contemporary children's books.

Library Association. Books for young people: group 1, under eleven, 1952, 1954 (rev); group 2, eleven to thirteen plus, 1952, 1954 (rev); group 3, fourteen to seventeen, 1957.

Ramsey, E. Folklore for children and young people. Philadelphia 1952.

Woodfield and Stanley. Books for young readers: pt 1 for children under ten: pt 2 for children from ten to fourteen. Huddersfield [1953].

Pierpont Morgan Library. Children's literature: books and mss. New York 1954. Exhibition catalogue.

Shute, N. Favourite books for boys and girls. 1955.

St John, J. The Osborne collection of early children's books, 1566–1910. Toronto 1958. Suppl: A chronicle of Boys' and Girls' House, Toronto 1964. *See also* K. M.

Lines, Boys' and Girls' Book House, Toronto, Junior Bookshelf 3 1938; J. St John, The Osborne collection, Top of the News 10 1954; and B. W. Alderson, Friendly recognition, Children's Book News 5 1969.

Thwaite, M. F. (ed). Children's books of this century. 1958. Catalogue of a collection begun by the Library Assoc, Youth Libraries Section.

Sunday Times. The one hundred best books for children. 1958.

Kent County Library. Children's books before 1900. Maidstone 1960 (typescript); suppl 1963 includes important addns pbd after 1900.

New York Public Library. Children's books 1910–60. New York 1960.

Shaw, J. M. Childhood in poetry. Tallahassee, Florida 8 vols 1962–6; Detroit 5 vols 1967 (rev).

Smith, D. V. Fifty years of children's books 1910–60. Champaign Ill [1963].

Good, D. A catalogue of the Spencer collection of early children's books and chapbooks. Preston 1967.

International Youth Library, Munich. [Catalogues of the collection.] Boston 1968.

Haviland, V. and W. J. Smith (ed). Children and poetry: a selective annotated bibliography. Washington 1969.

Victoria & Albert Museum. What the children like: a selection of children's books, toys and games from the Renier Collection. 1970. Exhibition catalogue.

Histories and Surveys

Ford, R. Children's rhymes, children's games, children's songs, children's stories. Paisley 1903.

Brown, J. D. Books for very young children. Lib World 9 1907.

Moses, M. J. Children's books and reading. New York 1907, 1924 (rev).

Briggs, I. Should children's reading be restricted? Lib Assoc Record 13 1911.

Hunt, C. W. What shall we read to the children? Boston 1915.

Moore, A. C. Roads to childhood. New York 1920. Sequels are: New roads to childhood, New York 1923; Cross-roads to childhood, New York 1926. An expanded collection is in My roads to childhood, New York 1939, Boston 1961 (rev).

—— The three owls. Bks 1–3 New York 1925–31.

—— and B. M. Miller (ed). Writing and criticism. Boston 1951.

Barnes, W. The children's poets: analysis and appraisals of the greatest English and American poets for children. New York 1924.

Bett, H. Nursery rhymes and tales: their origin and history. [1924].

—— The games of children: their origin and history. 1929.

Cammaerts, E. The poetry of nonsense. 1925.

Eaton, A. T. On reading aloud. Horn Book 1 1925.

—— Reading with children. New York 1940.

Bonner, Mary G. A parents' guide to children's reading. New York 1926.

Terman, L. M. and M. Lima. Children's reading: a guide. New York 1926. Contains extensive bibliographies.

Becker, M. L. Adventures in reading. Philadelphia 1927, 1946 (rev).

—— First adventures in reading. New York 1936, London 1937 (as Choosing books for children). Contains extensive bibliographies.

Gardner, E. E. and E. Ramsey. A handbook of children's literature. Chicago 1927.

International Bureau of Education. Littérature enfantine et collaboration internationale: children's books and international goodwill. Geneva 1929, 1932 (rev).

—— Les périodiques pour la jeunesse. Geneva 1936. Includes British periodicals for young people.

Darton, F. J. H. Children's books in England: five centuries of social life. Cambridge 1932, ed K. M. Lines, Cambridge 1958 (rev).

Hansard, G. Old books for the new young. 1932. Young person's comment on contemporary attitudes to reading 'classics'.

Hazard, P. Les livres, les enfants et les hommes. Paris 1932; tr M. Mitchell, Boston 1944 (as Books, children and men).

Freeman, G. La V. and R. S. The child and his picture book: a discussion of the preferences of the nursery child. Chicago 1933.

Chaundler, C. The children's author. 1934.

Kunitz, S. J. and H. Haycraft. The junior book of authors. New York 1934, 1951 (rev). Suppl M. Fuller, More junior authors, New York 1963.

Mégroz, R. L. English poetry for children: a tract for the times. Wisbech 1934.

Böckheler, L. Das englische Kinderlied. Leipzig 1935.

Wilson, J. G. Books and children. In The family book, 1935.

The publisher chooses. Junior Bookshelf 1936–8. Series of accounts by publishers of significance in children's book publishing at this period.

Stern, C. M. The reading interests of children. Lib Assoc Record 38 1936.

Allen, G. W. To market, to market to buy a fat book. Junior Bookshelf 1 1937. Criticism of low standards in the children's departments of English bookshops.

Crozier, G. The blind child and his books. Junior Bookshelf 1 1937.

Dalgleish, A. First experiences with literature. New York 1937.

Reynolds, J. D. Why story hours? Junior Bookshelf 2 1937.

Sayers, W. C. B. An appreciation [of the first issue of Junior Bookshelf]. Junior Bookshelf 1 1937. Stresses need for stronger criticism of poor books.

Leyland, E. Organising an intermediate department. Junior Bookshelf 3 1938. Provision of literature for adolescents in public libraries.

—— Meet your authors. 1963.

McCulloch, D. Books and broadcasting. Junior Bookshelf 2 1938.

Macpherson, M. R. Children's poetry index. Boston 1938.

Sheffield City Libraries. A survey of children's reading. Sheffield 1938.

'A teacher'. Apologia pro vita sua. Junior Bookshelf 3 1939. Attack on librarians and defence of teachers as trained workers with children; reply by B. M. Makepeace 4 1939.

Vale, G. F. The writing, reading and selection of children's books. Lib Assoc Record 41 1939.

Jenkinson, A. J. What do boys and girls read? An investigation into reading habits. 1940, 1946 (rev). See also W. J. Scott, Reading, film and radio tastes of high school boys and girls, Wellington 1947; R. Jay in Ford, Young writers, young readers, 1960, below; and K. Friedlander, Children's books and their function in latency and pre-puberty, American Imago 3 1942, abridged in New Era in Home & School 39 1958.

'George Orwell' (E. A. Blair). Boys' weeklies. Horizon 1 1940; rptd (rev) in Critical essays, 1946; reply by 'Frank Richards' (C. Hamilton), Horizon 1 1940. The 2 pieces together in Collected essays, ed S. Orwell and I. Angus vol 1, 1968.

Thomson, J. S. M. Stories in middle school English. School Lib Rev 2 1940.

'Peter Parley'. A five years record: recollections of some notable books of the years 1937 to 1941. Junior Bookshelf 5 1941.

Carrington, N. A new deal in juveniles. Junior Bookshelf 6 1942. On the planning of the first Puffin Picture Books.

—— Children's books by auto-litho. Br Book News 1945.

—— Ten years of picture book making. Junior Bookshelf 10 1946.

—— A century of Puffin Picture Books. Penrose Annual 51 1957.

National Book Council. An experiment with youth: report on children's book weeks. 1942.

Colwell, E. H. Stories about dolls. Junior Bookshelf 7 1943.

— Children's books today. Lib Assoc Record 54 1952.

Graham, E. Poetry and children. Junior Bookshelf 7 1943.

— The Carnegie Medal and its winners. Junior Bookshelf 8 1944.

— Children's books in Britain today. Br Book News 1945.

— Nonsense in children's literature. Junior Bookshelf 9 1945.

— How I look at children's books. Junior Bookshelf 14 1950.

— Children's books 1927–63. Books no 346 1963.

Osborne, E. Animals in books. Junior Bookshelf 9 1945.

Green, R. L. Tellers of tales. Leicester 1946, 1953 (rev), London 1965 (rev), 1969 (rev).

White, D. N. About books for children. Wellington 1946.

— Books before five. 1954.

Arbuthnot, M. H. Children and books. Chicago 1947, 1957 (rev), 1964 (rev).

Tolkien, J. R. R. On fairy stories. In Essays presented to Charles Williams, 1947; rptd in his Tree and leaf, 1964.

Waugh, C. The comics. New York 1947.

Nesbitt, E. Books for today's children. Horn Book 26 1948.

Trease, G. Tales out of school. 1948, 1964 (rev).

— Enjoying books. 1951.

Turner, E. S. Boys will be boys: the story of Sweeney Todd, Deadwood Dick, Sexton Blake et al. 1948, 1957 (rev).

Smith, J. A. Children's books. Future 4 1949. Questions how far we have adequately replaced the Victorian idea that children's books should deal in moral values.

The children's author. Author 61 1950.

Larrick, N. Design in children's books. Lib Jnl 75 1950.

Lines, K. The sugared pill. School Lib Rev new ser 5 1950. Critique of fictional approach to non-fiction.

Nightall, A. D. Typography and the child. School Lib Rev new ser 5 1950.

Opie, I. and P. The Oxford dictionary of nursery rhymes. 1951.

— The lore and language of school children. 1959.

— Children's games in street and playground. 1969. Includes many references to popular and traditional rhymes etc.

Whitehouse, W. H. S. Medal winning books: the Newbery, Caldecott and Carnegie Medal awards. Birmingham 1951.

Williams, A. R. The magazine reading of secondary school children. Br Jnl of Educational Psychology 21 1951.

Bauchard, P. The child audience. Paris 1952. A report on press, film and radio for children.

Butler, J. W. Reading and securing the co-operation of parents. Librarian 61 1952.

Children's periodicals. Lib Assoc Record 54 1952.

Eyre, F. Twentieth-century children's books. 1952.

Lewis, C. S. On three ways of writing for children. Proc of Annual Conference, Lib Assoc 1952; rptd in Only connect, 1969, below.

Beresford, R. Children's reading. School Librarian 6 1953.

Briggs, K. M. The personnel of fairyland. Oxford 1953.

Meigs, C. et al. A critical history of children's literature New York 1953, 1969 (rev). See E. F. Walbridge et al, A critical history of children's literature critically considered, New York 1954.

Reeves, J. Counterfeit poetry and the adolescent. Use of Eng 4 1953.

— Writing for children. Proc of Annual Conference, Lib Assoc 1958.

— Did Emil start something? School Librarian 9 1959. Influence of Emil and the detectives.

Smith, L. H. The unreluctant years: a critical approach to children's literature. Chicago 1953.

Lewis, C. Writing for young children. New York 1954.

Stevens, F. M. The choice of poetry for children. Use of Eng 5 1954.

Wertham, F. The seduction of the innocent. New York 1954. Attack on the publication of horror comics.

Hildick, E. W. Boys' weeklies since Orwell. Jnl of Education 87 1955.

— Children and fiction: a critical study in depth. 1970.

Pumphrey, G. H. Children's comics: a guide for parents and teachers. 1955.

From comics to—well... Use of Eng 8 1956. Report on the conference on 'From comics to classics' held in London, 1956.

Klausmeier, R. G. Das englische, französische und schweizerische Jugendbuch. In Probleme der Jugendliteratur, Düsseldorf 1956. Report on the second Literaturpädagogischen Tagung 'Begegnung mit dem Buch' held at Düsseldorf 1955.

Library Association. Chosen for children: an account of the books which have been awarded the Library Association Carnegie Medal 1936–57. 1957, 1967 (rev).

Thompson, R. Frightfully super places. Jnl of Education 89 1957. Girls school stories.

Hürlimann, B. Europäische Kinderbücher in drei Jahrhunderten. Zürich 1959, 1963 (rev), 1969 (rev); tr B. W. Alderson 1967 (as Three centuries of children's books in Europe).

Ford, B. (ed). Young writers, young readers. 1960, 1963 (rev). Articles by various authors rptd from Jnl of Education.

Fisher, M. Intent upon reading. Leicester 1961, 1964 (rev).

Pickard, P. M. I could a tale unfold: violence, horror and sensationalism in stories for children. 1961.

Cameron, E. The green and burning tree. Boston 1962.

Crouch, M. S. Treasure seekers and borrowers: children's books in Britain 1900–60. 1962, 1970 (rev).

Taylor, J. K. G. The social background of children's fiction. School Librarian 11 1962.

Chukovsky, K. I. Ot dvukh do pyati. Moscow 1925; tr M. Morton. Berkeley 1963 (as From two to five).

Smith, D. V. Fifty years of children's books 1910–60: trends, backgrounds, influences. Champaign 1963.

Doyle, B. The who's who of boys' writers and illustrators. 1964.

— The who's who of children's literature. 1968.

Viguers, R. H. Margin for surprise. Boston 1964. Essays etc on aspects of children's literature.

Ward, M. E. and D. A. Marquardt. Authors of books for young people. New York 1964; suppl 1967.

Bodger, J. How the heather looks: a joyous journey to the British sources of children's books. New York 1965.

Townsend, J. R. Written for children: an outline of English children's literature. 1965.

Ellis, A. E. How to find out about children's literature. 1966, 1968 (rev).

— A history of children's reading and literature. 1967.

— Public library services for children in England and Wales during the Edwardian period. Lib Assoc Record 71 1969; 1915–27, 72 1970; 1928–42, 73 1971.

King, A. and A. F. Stuart. The house of Warne. 1966.

Robinson, E. R. (ed). Readings about children's literature. New York 1966. Articles rptd from various periodicals.

Cox, J. What has happened to the annual? Books no 372 1967.

Fenwick, S. I. (ed). A critical approach to children's literature. Chicago 1967. Papers of the 31st Annual Conference of the Univ of Chicago Graduate Library School 1966.

Peel, M. Seeing to the heart: English and imagination in the junior school. 1967.

Bechtel, L. S. Books in search of children: speeches and essays selected and introduced by V. Haviland. New York 1969, London 1970.

Egoff, S., Stubbs G. T. and L. F. Ashley (ed). Only connect: readings on children's literature. Toronto 1969.

Hildebrandt, R. Nonsense–Aspekte der englischen Kinderliteratur. Weinheim 1970.

Klingberg, G. The fantastic tale for children: a genre study from the viewpoints of literary and educational research. Gothenburg 1970.

Illustration of Children's Books

A select list. For fuller bibliographies see the vols by Crouch and Haviland, col 783, above, and Hürlimann, 1965, below.

Miller, B. M. and E. Whitney (ed). Contemporary illustrators of children's books. Boston 1930.

Victoria and Albert Museum. Catalogue of the exhibition of illustrated books for children (Historical section). Introd by E. V. Lucas 1932.

Mahony, B. E. et al. Illustrators of children's books 1744–1945. Boston 1947; suppls 1946–66, Boston 1958, 68.

Smith, J. A. Children's illustrated books. 1948.

Thomas, D. Children's book illustration in England. Penrose Annual 56 1962.

Hürlimann, B. Die Welt im Bilderbuch. Zürich 1965; tr B. W. Alderson 1968 (as Picture book world).

Klemin, D. The art of art for children's books. New York 1966.

Storytelling

For the extensive coverage of this subject in USA see the bibliography in Haviland, col 783, above.

Ransome, A. A history of story-telling: studies in the development of narrative. 1909.

Shedlock, M. L. The art of story telling. New York 1915, 1952 (rev, as The art of the story-teller).

Clark, E. Stories to tell and how to tell them. 1917.

Cather, K. D. Educating by storytelling. New York 1918.

Bone, W. A. Children's stories and how to tell them. 1923, 1930 (rev).

Burrell, A. A guide to storytelling. 1926.

Turnbull, E. L. (ed). The teacher's omnibus of stories to tell. 1936.

Sawyer, R. The way of the storyteller. New York 1942, 1962 (rev). *See also* V. Haviland, Ruth Sawyer, 1965.

Cook, E. The ordinary and the fabulous. Cambridge 1969.

Jones, A. and J. Buttrey. Children and stories. Oxford 1970.

Reviewing Journals etc

In addition to seasonal reviews in general literary journals and newspapers, the period has seen the emergence of several periodicals which have been primarily devoted to children's literature. Most carry general articles as well as reviews.

Times Literary Supplement. 1902 onwards. From 1949 there have been two, and from 1968 four, special issues each year devoted to children's books.

The Horn Book Magazine. Boston 1924 onwards. Selections of important articles rptd in A Horn Book sampler 1924–48, Boston 1959, and Horn Book reflections 1949–66, Boston 1969.

Junior Bookshelf. Huddersfield 1936 onwards.

The School Library Review. 1936–53.

The School Librarian. 1937 onwards.

American Library Association. Top of the News. Chicago 1942 onwards.

International Board on Books for Young People. Bookbird. Vienna 1958 onwards.

Library Association. Youth Library Group News. 1958 onwards.

Growing Point. Northampton 1962 onwards.

Children's Book News. 1964–70. As New Books from May 1964–August 1965.

Children's Literature in Education. 1969 onwards.

Signal. Stroud 1969 onwards.

(2) WRITERS OF THE PERIOD

Hudson, William Henry (1841–1922). A little boy lost. 1905, New York 1918.
 See vol 3, col 1059.

Grahame, Kenneth (1859–1932).
 See vol 3, cols 1097–8, and col 593, above.

Brooke, Leonard Leslie (1862–1940). Johnny Crow's garden. 1903, New York 1903. A poem.

—— Johnny Crow's party. 1907, New York 1909. A poem.

—— Johnny Crow's new garden. 1935, New York 1935. A poem.
 See special issue of Horn Book 17 1941.

Fitzpatrick, Sir James Percy (1862–1931). Jock of the bushveld. 1907, New York 1907.

James, Montague Rhodes (1862–1936). The five jars. 1922, New York 1922.
 See cols 621–2, above.

Finnemore, John (1863–?). Boys and girls of other days. 1898.

—— Fairy stories from the little mountain. 1899.

—— Two boys in wartime. 1900.

—— The story of a scout. 1903.

—— Three school chums. 1907.
 Also many other adventure and school stories, especially the Teddy Lester *books.*

Rouse, William Henry Denham (1863–1950). Tom Noddy the noodle, with other fools and wise men not a few. 1928.

Rhys, Grace (née Little) (1865–1929). In wheelabout and cockalone. 1918, New York 1918.

Marshall, Archibald (1866–1934). Wooden: a fairy tale. [1920], New York 1920 (as Peggy in toyland); London 1928 (rev, as Young Peggy in toyland).

—— Jimmy, the new boy. [1923], 1938 (rev).

—— Simple stories. 1927, New York 1927.

—— Simple people. 1928, 1968 (rev).

—— Simple stories from Punch. 1930.

—— The birdikin family. 1932.

—— The dragon, illustr E. Ardizzone. 1966. (Taken from Simple stories from Punch).

Potter, Beatrix (1866–1943).
 See vol 3, cols 1098–9.

Wells, Herbert George (1866–1946). Floor games. 1911, Boston 1912.

—— Little wars: a game for boys from twelve years of age to one hundred and fifty, and for that more intelligent sort of girls who like boys games and books. 1913, Boston 1913, London 1931 (rev).

—— The adventures of Tommy. 1929, 1967 (rev), New York 1967.
 See cols 417–28, above.

Avery, Charles Harold (1867–1943). A boy all over. [1896].

—— Frank's first term: or making a man of him. 1896.

—— No surrender. 1933.
 Also many other adventure and school stories.

Benson, Edward Frederic (1867–1940). David Blaize. 1916, New York 1916.

—— David Blaize and the blue door. 1918, New York 1919.

—— David of King's. 1924, New York 1924 (as David Blaize of King's).

Brazil, Angela (1868–1947). A terrible tomboy. 1904.

—— The third class at Miss Maye's. 1909, [1908].

—— Bosom friends: a seaside story. [1910].

—— The nicest girl in the school. 1910.
 Also many other schoolgirl stories up to The school on the loch, *[1946]. See her* My own schooldays, *1925; G. Marsh, Angela Brazil, Junior Bookshelf 12 1948.*

Blackwood, Algernon (1869–1951). Sambo and Snitch. Oxford [1927], New York 1927.
—— Mr Cupboard. Oxford [1928].
—— The Italian conjuror. Oxford [1932].
—— Maria—of England—in the rain. Oxford [1933].
—— Sergeant Poppett and Policeman James. Oxford [1934].
—— The fruit stoners. Oxford [1935].
—— How the circus came to tea. Oxford [1936].
—— The adventures of Dudley and Gilderoy. 1941. Adapted by M. B. Cothren from Dudley and Gilderoy, 1929.
    See cols 530–1, above.

Creswell, Harry Bulkeley (1869–1960). Marytary. 1928, 1950 (rev).
—— Johnny and Marytary. 1936.

Tarn, Sir William Woodthorpe (1869–1951). The treasure of the Isle of Mist. 1919, New York 1920, London 1921 (rev), 1938 (with plates), 1950.
    See E. Yates, The isle of mist. Horn Book 14 1938.

Smith, Edward Augustin Wyke (1871–?). Bill of the Bustingforths. 1921.
—— The last of the baron. [1921].
—— Some pirates and Marmaduke. 1921.
—— The marvellous land of Snergs. 1927.

Brereton, Frederick Sadleir (1872–1957). With shield and assegai: a tale of the Zulu war. 1900 [1899].
—— With rifle and bayonet: a story of the Boer war. [1900].
—— In the king's service: a tale of Cromwell's invasion of Ireland. 1901, [1900].
    Also many other adventure stories.

Dawson, Alec John (1872–1951). Finn the wolfhound. 1908, Leicester 1962 (abridged).
—— Jan: a dog and a romance. New York 1915, London 1917 (as Jan: son of Finn), Leicester 1963 (abridged).

Nicholson, William (1872–1949). An alphabet. 1898.
—— Clever Bill. [1926], New York [1926]; London 1958 (rev).
—— The pirate twins. [1929], New York [1929].

Robinson, William Heath (1872–1944). The adventures of Uncle Lubin. 1902, 1925 (rev), New York 1925.
—— Bill the minder. 1912, New York 1912.
    See his My line of life, 1938; G. W. L. Day, The life and art of Heath Robinson, 1947.

De la Mare, Walter (1873–1956). Songs of childhood. 1902 (as by 'Walter Ramal'), 1916 (rev), New York 1916.
—— The three mulla-mulgars. 1910, New York 1919, London 1935 (as The three royal monkeys), New York 1948.
—— A child's day. 1912, 1920, New York 1923. Poems.
—— Peacock pie. 1913, New York 1920. 6 other edns with various illustrators. The 1924 edn included 10 rhymes not again rptd until 1969.
—— Crossings. 1921, New York 1923; London 1923 [1924] (rev), 1942 (rev). A play.
—— Story and rhyme. 1921, New York 1921.
—— Down-adown-derry. 1922, New York 1922. Poems.
—— Broomsticks and other tales. 1925, New York 1925.
—— Miss Jemima. Oxford [1925], New York 1935, 1940 (as The story of Miss Jemima).
—— Lucy. Oxford [1927]. First pbd in Broomsticks, above.
—— Old Joe. Oxford [1927].
—— Stuff and nonsense. 1927, New York 1927, London 1946 (rev). Poems.
—— Stories from the Bible. 1929, New York 1929, London 1933, 1947.
—— Poems for children. 1930.
—— The Dutch cheese. New York 1931.
—— The Lord Fish and other tales. [1933].
—— This year, next year. 1937, New York 1937. Poems.
—— Bells and grass. 1941, New York 1942. Poems.
—— The old lion and other stories. 1942.
—— The magic jacket and other stories. 1943.

—— Collected rhymes and verses. 1944 (illustr B. Wolpe), New York 1947 (as Rhymes and verses), London 1970 (rev, illustr E. Le Cain).
—— The scarecrow and other stories. 1945.
—— The Dutch cheese and other stories. 1946.
—— Collected stories for children. 1947.
    See special issue of Horn Book 18 1942, and also E. Graham, The riddle of de la Mare, Junior Bookshelf 12 1948; Nat Book League, Walter de la Mare: a checklist, Cambridge 1956; L. Clark, Walter de la Mare, 1960, 1968 (rev); and cols 256–62, above.

Graham, Harry (1874–1936). Ruthless rhymes for heartless homes. [1899], New York 1901.
—— More ruthless rhymes for heartless homes. [1930], New York 1930.
—— Happy families: a story for the young of all ages. 1934.

Tourtel, Mary (1874–1948). A horse book. 1901, New York 1901.
—— Three little foxes. 1903.
—— The adventures of the little lost bear. [1921].
—— The little bear and the fairy child. [1922].
—— The little bear and the ogres. [1922].
—— Rupert: little bear's adventures. 1924–? (The Rupert Library).
    Also many other Rupert books, annuals etc. See L. Sherwood, Mary Tourtel's Rupert, TLS 3 Oct 1968.

Corbett, James Edward (1875–1955). Man-eaters of Kumaon. 1944, New York 1944.
—— The man-eating leopard of Rudraprayag. 1948, New York 1948.
—— The temple tiger. 1954, New York 1954.

Dunne, John William (1875–1949). The jumping lions of Borneo. 1937, New York 1938.
—— An experiment with St George. 1939.
    See cols 1250–1, below.

Darwin, Bernard Richard Meirion (1876–1961) and Elinor Mary Darwin (née Monsell). Elves and princesses. 1913.
—— The tale of Mr Tootleoo. 1925, New York 1926.
—— Tootleoo two. 1927, New York 1928.
—— Oboli, Boboli and little Joboli. 1938.
—— Ishybushy and Topknot. 1946.
    See cols 1314–15, below.

'Frank Richards' (Charles Harold St John Hamilton) (1876–1961). *Contributed to the following periodicals under the following surnames:* Pluck *as* 'Martin Clifford'; Gem *as* 'Martin Clifford'; Magnet *as* 'Frank Richards'; Boys' Friend *as* 'Owen Conquest' *and* 'Ralph Redway'; School Friend *as* 'Hilda Richards'. *For details of these periodicals see section* (5), *below. Among pbns in book form are:*
    Billy Bunter at Greyfriars School. 1947.
    Billy Bunter's barring-out. 1948.
    and many other Billy Bunter titles. Also many other stories of school and adventure pbd in books, magazines and annuals. Several bound facsimile reprints of stories serialized in Magnet commenced pbn in 1969. See criticism by 'George Orwell' in col 786, above, 1940; also 'Frank Richards', Autobiography, 1952; D. Holbrook, Greyfriars behind the gashouse, Use of Eng 9 1959 (a comparison of Richards and Hildick); J. S. Butcher, Greyfriars School: a prospectus, 1965; Bunter the bulwark, TLS 7 Oct 1965; F. Fytton, William Brown and Harry Wharton, London Mag 7 1967.

Westerman, Percy Francis (1876–1960). A lad of grit: a story of Restoration times. [1908].
—— The flying submarine. 1912.
—— The scouts of Seal Island. 1913, New York 1922.
—— Building the Empire: a story of the North West Frontier. [1914].
—— The dreadnought of the air. [1914].
—— The Fritz strafers. [1918], 1931 (as Keepers of the narrow seas).
—— Under the white ensign. [1918].
    Also many other stories of derring-do.

Fyleman, Rose (1877–1957). Fairies and chimneys. 1918, New York 1920. Poems.
— Fairy green. 1919, New York 1923. Poems.
— Forty good-night tales. 1923, New York 1924.
— Letty. 1926, New York 1927.
— Garland of Rose's: collected poems. 1928.
— Gay go up. 1929, New York 1930.
— Jeremy Quince. 1933.
— Hob and Bob: a tale of two goblins. 1944.
— Punch and Judy. 1944. Play ed R. Fyleman.
— Adventure with Benghazi. 1946.
— Rhyme book for Adam. 1949.
    Also other fairy books and collections of tales. See her Poetry for children then and now, Lib Assoc Record 1934; Writing verse for children, Horn Book 13 1937; and her A few words, Junior Bookshelf 1 1937.
Goodyear, Robert Arthur Hanson (1877–1948). Forge of Foxenby. 1920.
    Also many other stories of school life.
Coppard, Alfred Edgar (1878–1957). Pink furniture: a tale for lovely children with noble natures. 1930, New York [1930].
— The fairies return: or new tales for old. 1934.
    See cols 556–7, above.
Masefield, John (1878–1967). A book of discoveries. 1910, New York 1910.
— Martin Hyde, the Duke's messenger. 1910, Boston 1910.
— Jim Davis: or the captive of the smugglers. 1911, New York 1912.
— The midnight folk. 1927, New York 1927.
— The box of delights. 1935, New York 1935.
    See M. Fisher, John Masefield, 1963; also cols 306–13, above.
Thomas, Philip Edward (1878–1917). Four and twenty blackbirds. 1915, 1965 (introd by Helen Thomas).
    See cols 364–7, above.
Coke, Desmond Francis Talbot (1879–1931). The bending of a twig. 1906, 1909 (rev).
— The comedy of age. 1906.
— The call. 1907.
— The house prefect. 1908.
— Wilson's. 1911.
Ault, Norman (1880–1950). Sammy and the Snarlywink. 1904. With L. Ault.
— The podgy book of tales. 1907. With L. Ault.
— Dreamland shores: a book of verse for children and others. 1920.
Doorly, Victoria Eleanor Louise (1880–1950). The insect man. Cambridge 1936, New York 1937, London 1942 (rev).
— The microbe man. Cambridge 1938, London 1943 (rev), 1946 (rev).
— The radium woman. 1939, New York [1954].
— The story of France. 1944, New York [1948].
— Ragamuffin king. 1948.
Noyes, Alfred (1880–1958). The secret of Pooduck Island. New York 1943, London [1946].
    See cols 321–3, above.
Williams, E. G. Harcourt (1880–1957). Four fairy plays. [1920], New York [1920]. *Also other plays and dramatic adaptations for children.*
— Tales from Ebony, illustr C. F. Tunnicliffe. 1934, New York 1935.
Williams, Margery Winifred (afterwards Bianco) (1880–1944). The velveteen rabbit, illustr W. Nicholson. 1922, New York 1922.
— Poor Cecco. 1925, New York 1925.
— The candlestick. New York 1929.
— A street of little shops. New York 1932.
— The hurdy-gurdy man. New York 1933, London 1933.
— Rufus the fox: adapted from the French of Samivel. New York 1937, London 1937.
— Bright morning. New York 1942, London [1945].

— Forward, commandos. New York 1944, London 1947.
Young, Emily Hilda (1880–1949). Caravan island. 1940.
— River holiday. 1942.
    See cols 781–2, above.
Cradock, Mrs. Henry Cowper (c. 1880–?). Josephine and her dolls. 1916 (for 1915).
— Everyday stories to tell to children. 1919, Philadelphia [1920].
— Where the dolls lived. [1919].
— Peggy and Joan. [1922].
— Adventures of a Teddy Bear. 1934.
    Also other Josephine and Teddy Bear books.
Hadath, John Edward Gunby (c. 1880–1954). The fears of Foozle. 1913.
— Paying the price. [1913].
— Schoolboy grit. 1913.
— The last of his line. [1914].
— Carey of Cobhouse. 1928.
— The march of time. 1946.
— Honours easy. 1953.
    Also many other school stories.
'Herbert Strang' (George Herbert Ely) (c. 1880–1958) and C. James L'Estrange (c. 1880–1947). Tom Burnaby: a story of Uganda and the great Congo forest 1904, New York 1904.
— Kobo. 1905, New York 1905.
— Brown of Moukden: a story of the Russo-Japanese war. 1906.
    Early examples of the work of an 'author' who wrote numerous historical and adventure stories and edited many anthologies and popular series (e.g. Herbert Strang's Library 1909–?).
Webb, Marion St John (née Adcock) (c. 1880–1930). The littlest one. 1914, New York 1927. Poems.
— Knock three times. 1917, New York [1918].
— The girls of Chequertrees. 1918.
— Eliz'beth Phil and me. 1919.
— The house with the twisting passage. 1922.
— The flower fairies. [1923].
— The littlest one again. 1923. Poems.
— The little round house. 1924.
— The magic lamplighter. 1926.
— The littlest one, his book. 1927. Comprises The littlest one, and The littlest one again, with additional verses.
— The littlest one's third book. 1928. Poems.
— John and me and the Dickory Dog. 1930.
— Twice ten. 1931.
Ashford, Daisy (1881–1972). The young visiters: or Mr Salteena's plan. 1919, New York 1919. London 1951 (illustr H. Corlass), 1956 (illustr D. Brough).
— Daisy Ashford: her book. 1920, New York 1920. Selections 1965, 1966.
'Richard Bird' (Walter Barradell-Smith) (1881–?). The rival captains. 1916.
— The sporting house. 1921.
— School House v The Rest. 1928.
— The Wharton Medal. 1929.
— Terry takes charge. 1931.
    Also other school stories.
Evans, Edward Radcliffe Garth Russell (1881–?). Adventures of Peter. 1924.
— To sweep the Spanish main. 1930.
— For the white cockade. 1931.
— Ghosts of the Scarlet Fleet. 1932, New York 1932.
— The ghostly galleon. 1933.
Farjeon, Eleanor (1881–1965). Nursery rhymes of London Town. 1916.
— More nursery rhymes of London Town. 1917.
— All the way to Alfriston. 1918. Poems.
— Singing games for children. [1919], New York [1919].
— Martin Pippin in the apple orchard. 1921 (illustr C. E. Brock), New York 1922, London 1952 (rev, illustr R. Kennedy).
— Tunes of a penny piper. 1922.

—— All the year round. [1923]. Poems.
—— Tom Cobble. Oxford [1923].
—— The country child's alphabet. 1924.
—— Mighty men. 2 pts Oxford 1924–5, New York 1926, 1 vol Oxford [1928].
—— The town child's alphabet. 1924.
—— Nuts and may. [1926].
—— The wonderful knight. Oxford [1927] (illustr D. Pailthorpe), London 1967 (rev, illustr L. B. Acs).
—— A bad day for Martha. Oxford [1928].
—— Kaleidoscope. 1928, 1963 (rev, illustr E. Ardizzone).
—— The tale of Tom Tiddler. [1929], New York 1930.
—— Tales from Chaucer. 1930 (illustr W. R. Flint), New York 1932, London 1959 (rev, illustr M. Walters).
—— The old nurse's stocking basket. [1931] (illustr E. Whydale), New York 1931, London 1941 (rev, illustr P. Gough), 1965 (rev, illustr E. Ardizzone).
—— Perkin the pedlar. 1932 (illustr C. Leighton), 1956 (rev, illustr D. Masterman).
—— Ameliaranne's prize packet. 1933, Philadelphia 1933 (as Ameliaranne and the magic ring).
—— Over the garden wall. 1933.
—— Ameliaranne's washing day. 1934, Philadelphia 1934.
—— Jim at the corner. Oxford 1934 (illustr J. Mountfort), New York 1934 (as The old sailor's yarn box), London 1958 (illustr E. Ardizzone), New York 1958 (as Jim at the corner).
—— And I dance mine own child. Oxford [1935].
—— Jim and the pirates. Oxford [1936], London 1967 (rev, illustr J. Palmer).
—— Kings and queens. 1936, 1953 (rev). With H. Farjeon.
—— Ten saints. New York 1936, London 1953.
—— Martin Pippin in the daisy field. 1937, New York 1938, London 1954 (rev), 1964 (rev). Uses some stories pbd earlier.
—— Sing for your supper. [1938]. Poems.
—— Grannie Gray. 1939 (illustr J. J. Farjeon), 1956 (illustr P. Fortnum).
—— The new book of days. [1941], New York [1941].
—— Cherrystones. 1942. Poems rptd in Then there were three, 1958.
—— The mulberry bush. 1945. Poems rptd in Then there were three, 1958.
—— The glass slipper. 1946. A play.
—— The starry floor. 1949. Poems rptd in Then there were three, 1958.
—— Mrs Malone. [1950] (illustr D. Knight), 1962 (illustr E. Ardizzone), New York 1962.
—— Silver-sand and snow. 1951. A collection of poems previously pbd elsewhere.
—— The silver curlew. 1953, New York 1954.
—— The little book room. 1955, New York 1956. Short stories previously pbd elsewhere.
—— The children's bells. 1957. New York 1960. A selection of her poetry for children.
—— Then there were three. 1958, New York 1962.
—— Italian peepshow. 1960.
—— Mr Garden. 1966.
—— Around the seasons. 1969. Poems previously pbd elsewhere.
    See Eleanor Farjeon: a handlist of the collection of her works in the Camden Public Libraries, *1968*; E. H. Colwell, Eleanor Farjeon, *1961*. *Also her* A nursery in the nineties, *1935, 1960 (rev)*.
McKay, Herbert (b. 1881). Anne, and Anne's island. 1929.
—— Noah and rabbit. 1931, New York 1932.
—— This duck and that duck. [1944].
—— The ark afloat. 1951.
    And other stories and factual books for children.
Wodehouse, Pelham Grenville (b. 1881). The pothunters. 1902.
—— A prefect's uncle. 1903.
—— Tales of St Austin's. 1903.
—— The gold bat. 1904.

—— William Tell told again. 1904.
—— The head of Kay's. 1905, New York 1922.
—— The white feather. 1907.
—— Mike: a public school story. 1909. Chs 30–59 pbd as Enter Psmith, 1935, New York 1935. Pts 1 and 2 pbd as Mike at Wrykin, and Mike and Psmith, 1953 (rev).
—— The swoop. 1909.
—— The little nugget. 1913, New York 1914.
    See Wodehouse minor [Wodehouse's school stories], *Times Educational Suppl 30 March 1956*; *and cols 778–81, above.*
Armstrong, Martin Donisthorpe (b. 1882). Said the cat to the dog. 1945.
—— Said the dog to the cat. 1948.
Charles, Robert H. (1882–?). A roundabout turn, illustr L. L. Brooke. [1930].
Joyce, James (1882–1941). The cat and the devil. New York 1964, London 1965.
    See cols 444–72, above.
Milne, Alan Alexander (1882–1956). Once on a time. 1917, New York 1922.
—— When we were very young. 1924, New York 1924. Poems.
—— Make-believe: a children's play. 1925, New York 1925.
—— Winnie-the-Pooh. 1926, New York 1926.
—— Now we are six. 1927, New York 1927. Poems.
—— The house at Pooh Corner. 1928, New York 1928.
—— Toad of Toad Hall: a play from K. Grahame's book The wind in the willows. 1929, New York 1929.
—— Prince Rabbit and the princess who could not laugh. 1966, New York 1966.
    See E. Farjeon, A. A. Milne, *Junior Bookshelf 20 1956*; *and cols 671–3, above.*
Walker, Kenneth Macfarlane (b. 1882). The log of the ark. 1923, New York 1926 (as What happened in the ark), London 1934 (rev), 1958 (rev). With G. Boumphrey.
—— On being a father. 1928.
—— The young Jacobites. 1949.
Woolf, Adeline Virginia (1882–1941). Nurse Lugton's golden thimble. 1966.
    See cols 472–81, above.
'Kitty Barne' (Marion Catherine Barne, afterwards Streatfeild) (1883–1957). Timothy's garden: a children's play. [1912].
—— Celandine's secret: a children's play. [1914].
—— The Easter holidays. 1935, New York 1949 (as The secret of the sandhills), London [1955].
—— She shall have music. 1938, New York 1939.
—— Family footlights. 1939, New York 1939.
—— Visitors from London. 1940, New York 1940.
—— We'll meet in England. 1942, New York 1943, London 1962 (rev).
—— Three and a pigeon. 1944, New York 1944.
—— In the same boat. 1945, New York 1945.
—— Musical honours. 1947, New York 1947.
—— Dusty's windmill. 1949, New York 1950 (as The windmill mystery).
—— Roly's dogs. 1950.
—— Barbie. 1952.
—— Rosina Copper. 1954, New York 1956.
—— Cousin Beatie learns the fiddle. Oxford 1955.
—— Tann's boarders. 1955.
—— Rosina and son. 1956.
Mackenzie, Sir Edward Montague Compton (b. 1883). Kensington rhymes. 1912.
—— Santa Claus in summer. 1924, New York 1925, London 1960 (rev).
—— Mabel in Queer St. Oxford [1927]. First of 10 contributions to Blackwell's series of Continuous readers. The last was The stairs that kept going down, Oxford [1937], London 1967 (rev).
—— Told: children's tales and verses. Oxford [1930], New York 1930.
—— Little cat lost. 1965, New York 1965.

—— The strongest man on earth. 1968.
See cols 650–2, above.

Chesterman, Hugh (1884–?). In England once. Oxford [1926].
—— Proud Sir Prim and other verses. Oxford [1926].
—— The odd spot. Oxford [1928].
—— The first boy in the world and other stories from the Old Testament. 1933.
—— The highway, illustr W. Hodges. 1935.
—— A maid in armour. London [1936], New York [1936].
—— Playing with history. 1936. Plays.
—— Seven for a secret. Oxford [1937].
—— Drums across the water. [1939], New York [1939].
—— Crusaders. Oxford 1946.

Budden, John (1884–1967). Jungle John. 1927, New York 1927, London 1944 (rev).
—— Further adventures of Jungle John. 1929, New York 1929.
—— Charlie the fox. 1932, New York 1932.

Evens, George Bramwell (1884–1943). A Romany in the fields. 1929.
—— A Romany and Raq. 1930.
—— A Romany in the country. 1932.
—— Out with Romany. 1933.
Also other stories linked to the 'Romany' radio programmes. See E. Evens, Through the years with Romany, 1946.

Heward, Constance (1884–1968). Ameliaranne and the green umbrella. 1920, Philadelphia 1920, London 1967 (rev).
Also other Ameliaranne books and many other stories for young children.

Ransome, Arthur Michell (1884–1967). The child's book of the seasons. 1906.
—— The things in our garden. 1906.
—— Pond and stream. 1906.
—— Highways and byways in fairyland. [1906].
—— The imp and the elf and the ogre. 1910. One vol edn (rev) of the first 3 vols above.
—— Old Peter's Russian tales. 1916, New York 1917.
—— Aladdin and his wonderful lamp, in rhyme. [1919].
—— The soldier and death. 1920, New York 1922.
—— Swallows and Amazons. 1930, Philadelphia 1931, London 1931 (illustr C. Webb), 1938 (illustr author).
—— Swallowdale. 1931 (illustr C. Webb), Philadelphia 1932, London 1938 (illustr author).
—— Peter Duck. 1932, Philadelphia 1933.
—— Winter holiday. 1933, Philadelphia 1934.
—— Coot club. 1934, Philadelphia 1935.
—— Pigeon post. 1936, Philadelphia 1937.
—— We didn't mean to go to sea. 1937, New York 1938.
—— Secret water. 1939, New York 1940.
—— The big six. 1940, New York 1941.
—— Missee Lee. 1941, New York 1942.
—— The Picts and the Martyrs. 1943, New York 1943.
—— Great Northern? 1947, New York 1948.
See A. Ransome, Swallows and Amazons—how it came to be written, Horn Book 7 1931; tributes to Ransome, Junior Bookshelf 1 1937, 28 1964; G. Bott, Ransome, School Librarian 10 1960; H. Shelley, Arthur Ransome, 1960, 1968 (rev); Ransome: charting the course, TLS 28 Nov 1965 (rptd in Only connect, 1969); S. Simsova, In search of Swallowdale, Children's Book News 5 1970; and cols 718–19, above.

Uttley, Alison (b. 1884). The squirrel, the hare and the little grey rabbit. 1929. First of a long series of Little grey rabbit tales.
—— Moonshine and magic. 1932.
—— The adventures of Peter and Judy in Bunnyland. [1935].
—— Candlelight tales. 1936.
—— Mustard pepper and salt. 1938.
—— Tales of the four pigs and Brock the Badger. 1939.

—— A traveller in time. 1939, New York 1940.
—— The adventures of Sam Pig. 1940. First of several Sam Pig books.
—— Cuckoo cherry tree. 1943.
—— The spice woman's basket and other tales. 1944.
—— The washerwoman's child: a play on the life and stories of Hans Christian Andersen. 1946.
—— The cobbler's shop. 1950.
—— Macduff. 1950.
Also many other stories for children. See E. Graham, Alison Uttley: an appreciation, Junior Bookshelf 5 1941; A. Uttley, Books and reading, Junior Bookshelf 8 1944.

Walpole, Sir Hugh Seymour (1884–1941). Jeremy. 1919.
—— Jeremy and Hamlet. 1923.
—— Jeremy at Crale. 1927.
See cols 758–61, above.

Batchelor, Margaret (b. c. 1884). Six Devonshire dumplings. [1910].
—— Morwenna's prince. [1912].
—— Sallie's children. 1912.
—— A little Rhodesian. [1922].
Also 2 other Rhodesian stories.

James, Grace (1885–1965). Green willow and other Japanese fairy tales. 1910.
—— The dancing shoes: a play for children. 1921.
—— The cucumber king: a Chinese play. 1924.
—— John and Mary. 1935. First of a series of John and Mary books, up to John and Mary revisit Rome, 1963.
See her The real John and Mary, Junior Bookshelf 8 1944; and her John and Mary's aunt, 1950.

Oxenham, Elsie (b. c. 1885–1960). Goblin island. [1907].
—— A princess in tatters. [1908].
—— The conquest for Christine. [1909].
—— The girl who wouldn't make friends. [1909].
—— Mistress Nanciebell. 1910.
—— Girls of the Hamlet Club. 1914.
—— At school with the roundheads. 1915.
—— Expelled from school. [1919].
—— The Abbey girls. [1920].
Also many other Abbey School books and other stories for girls. See L. Muir, Fifty years of the Hamlet Club, Junior Bookshelf 19 1966.

Wolfe, Humbert (1885–1940). Cursory rhymes. 1927, New York 1928.
See cols 377–9, above.

Chaundler, Christine (b. c. 1885–?). The magic kiss: a picture story-book for children. [1916].
—— Little Squirrel Tickletail. [1917].
—— The reputation of the upper fourth. [1919].
—— Ronald's burglar. [1919].
—— Pat's third term. 1920 (for 1919).
Also many other stories for girls.

Lofting, Hugh (1886–1947). The story of Dr Dolittle. New York 1920, London 1922.
—— The voyages of Dr Dolittle. New York 1922, London 1923.
—— Dr Dolittle's post office. New York 1923, London 1924.
—— The story of Mrs Tubbs. New York 1923, London 1924.
—— Porridge poetry. New York 1924, London 1925.
—— Dr Dolittle's circus. New York 1924, London 1925.
—— Dr Dolittle's zoo. New York 1925, London 1926.
—— Dr Dolittle's caravan. New York 1926, London 1927.
—— Dr Dolittle's garden. New York 1927, London 1928.
—— Dr Dolittle in the moon. New York 1928, London 1929.
—— Noisy Norah. New York 1929, London 1929.
—— The twilight of magic. New York 1930, London 1930.
—— Gub Gub's book. New York 1932, London 1932.
—— Dr Dolittle's return. New York 1933, London 1933.
—— Dr Dolittle's birthday book. New York 1935.
—— Tommy, Tilly and Mrs Tubbs. New York 1936, 1937, (rev), London 1937.

—— Dr Dolittle and the secret lake. Philadelphia 1948, London 1949.

—— Dr Dolittle and the green canary. Philadelphia 1950, London 1951.

—— Dr Dolittle's Puddleby adventures. Philadelphia 1952, London 1953.

—— Dr Dolittle: a treasury. Philadelphia 1967, London 1968.

> See *J. F. Halbert*, Lofting: an appreciation, *Junior Bookshelf 1 1936*; *E. H. Colwell*, Lofting: an appreciation, *Junior Bookshelf 11 1947*; *J. Coleman*, Supervet, *New Statesman 26 May 1967*; *E. Blishen*, Hugh Lofting, *1968*.

'Marjorie Bowen' (Gabrielle Margaret Vere Campbell) (1886–1952). The winged trees: a tale for boys. Oxford 1928.

—— The lady's prisoner. Oxford [1929].

—— Mademoiselle Maria Gloria. Oxford [1929].

—— The trumpet and the swan. 1938.

> See cols 535–8, above.

Rieu, Émile Victor (b. 1887). Cuckoo calling: a book of verse for youthful people. 1933.

—— The flattered flying fish and other poems. 1962, New York 1962.

'E. H. Visiak' (Edward Harold Physick) (b. 1887). The haunted island. 1910, 1946 (rev).

Eliot, Thomas Stearns (1888–1965). Old Possum's book of practical cats. 1939, New York 1939, London 1940 (illustr N. Bentley).

> See cols 157–201, above.

Bagnold, Enid, afterwards Lady Roderick Jones (b. 1889). Alice and Thomas and Jane. 1930, New York 1931. Adapted by V. Beringer as a play, 1934.

—— National Velvet. 1935, New York 1935.

> See cols 908–9, below.

Gibbings, Robert John (1889–1958). Coconut island. 1936.

> See *M. McLeish*, Book illustrators of today, 1: Gibbings, *Junior Bookshelf 4 1940*.
> See col 1317, below.

Spring, Robert Howard (1889–1965). Darkie and co. 1932.

—— Sampson's circus. 1936.

—— Tumbledown Dick. 1939, New York 1940.

> See his Why Sampson's circus? *Junior Bookshelf 1 1937*; *and col 741, above*.

Waddell, Helen Jane (1889–1965).

—— The fairy ring (ten books of fairy tales for standards 1–11). 10 pts 1921. Anon, texts simplified by another hand. Selection (with some additional unpbd tales), ed E. Colwell, restoring the original texts, pbd 1969 as The princess Splendour and other stories.

—— Beasts and saints. 1934, New York 1934.

—— Stories from Holy Writ. 1949, New York 1950.

> See cols 1127–8, below.

Baker, Margaret (1890–?). The black cats and the tinker's wife. [1923], New York 1923.

—— The dog, the brownie and the bramble patch. New York 1924, London [1926].

—— The little girl who curtsied to the owl. 1925, New York 1925.

—— Pedlar's ware. 1925, New York 1925.

—— Four times once upon a time. New York 1926.

> *Also many other tales for young children. See her* On writing stories, *Junior Bookshelf 2 1937*.

Crompton, Richmal (1890–1969). Just – William. [1922].

—— More William. 1923.

—— William again. 1923.

> *Also many other William books including* Just – William: the story of the film, *1939*.

—— Jimmy. 1949.

> See *F. Fytton*, William Brown and Harry Wharton, *London Mag 7 1967*.

Wilkins, William Vaughan (1890–1959). After bath. 1945.

Bruce, Dorita Fairlie (b. c. 1890). The senior prefect. 1921.

—— Dimsie moves up. 1921.

—— Dimsie moves up again. 1922.

> *Also many other girls' school stories.*

Hann, Dorothy (b. c. 1890). Peg's patrol. [1924].

—— Smiler, a girl guide. 1925.

—— The pluck of the coward. 1926.

> *Also many other stories for girls.*

Mills, Clifford (b. c. 1890). Where the rainbow ends: a fairy story. [1912], 1932 (rev).

Cleaver, Hylton Reginald (1891–1961). The Harley first XI. 1920 (for 1919).

—— Brother o' mine. 1920 (for 1919).

—— Captains of Harley. 1921.

—— Roscoe makes good. 1921.

> *Also many other school stories.*

Haldane, John Burdon Sanderson (1892–1964). My friend Mr Leakey. 1937, New York 1938.

> See cols 1253–4, below.|

Rae, Gwynedd (b. 1892). Mostly Mary. 1930, New York 1931.

—— All Mary. 1930.

> *Also several other books about Mary Plain.*

Tolkien, John Ronald Reuel (b. 1892). The Hobbit. 1937, Boston 1938, London 1951 (rev), Boston 1961, London 1966 (rev).

—— Leaf by Niggle. 1947; rptd in Tree and leaf 1964, Boston 1965.

—— Farmer Giles of Ham. 1949, Boston 1950.

—— The fellowship of the ring. 1954, Boston 1954.

—— The two towers. 1954, Boston 1954.

—— The return of the king. 1955, Boston 1956.

> The above 3 books rptd in one vol London 1968 (as The Lord of the rings).

—— The adventures of Tom Bombadil. 1962. Poems.

—— Smith of Wooton Major. 1967.

> See *M. Crouch*, Another don in wonderland, *Junior Bookshelf 17 1954*; *W. H. Auden*, A world imaginary but real, *Encounter 1954*; *E. Wilson*, Oo those awful orcs, *Nation 182 1956*; *M. J. Storm*, Mirkwood revisited, *Books no 349 1963*; *Reilly*, Tolkien and the fairy story, *Thought 1963*; *L. Eiseley*, The elvish art of enchantment, *Horn Book 41 1965*; *N. D. Isaacs and R. A. Zimbardo (ed)*, Tolkien and the critics, *Indiana 1968 (Essays on his* Lord of the rings). *M. Wood*, Tolkien's fictions, *New Society 27 March 1969*; *and cols 748–9, above*.

Walmsley, Leo (b. 1892). The silver blimp. [1921].

Barclay, Vera Charlesworth (b. 1893). Danny the detective: a story for wolf-cubs. 1918, New York 1918.

> *Also other stories for cubs and scouts.*

—— Jane will you behave. 1936.

> *Also other stories about Jane.*

—— They went to the sea. [1946].

—— They met a wizard. [1947].

—— They found an elephant. 1950.

Church, Richard Thomas (1893–1972). A squirrel called Rufus. 1941, Philadelphia 1946.

—— The cave. 1950, New York 1951 (as Five boys in a cave), London 1953 (rev).

—— Dog Toby. [1953], New York 1958.

—— Down river. New York 1957, London 1958.

—— The bells of Rye. 1960, New York 1961.

> *Also other stories for children, see cols 246–8, above.*

Englefield, Cicely (1893–1970). George and Angela. 1932.

—— Katie the caterpillar. 1933, New York 1937.

—— Billie Winks. 1934.

> *Also other stories for children.*

Harnett, Cynthia Mary (b. 1893). The great house. 1949.

—— The wool-pack. 1951, New York 1953 (as Nicholas and the wool-pack).

—— Ring out Bow bells. 1953, New York 1954 (as The drawbridge gate).

—— The green popinjay. Oxford 1955.

—— Stars of fortune. 1956, New York 1956.

—— The load of unicorn. 1959, Cleveland 1960 (as Caxton's challenge).
—— Monasteries and monks. 1963.
See her From the ground upwards, *Horn Book 37 1961; see also E. Colwell, Cynthia Harnett, Junior Bookshelf 21 1957.*
Johns, William Earl (1893–1968). Wings: a book of flying adventures. [1931]. Ed Johns.
—— The Camels are coming. [1932].
—— The cruise of the Condor. [1933].
—— 'Biggles' of the Camel Squadron. [1934].
Also many other adventure stories. See K. E. Bush, The Biggles books, Junior Bookshelf 7 1943; T. R. Barnes, Biggles and the adult world, Jnl of Education 88 1956, rptd in Young writers, young readers, ed B. Ford 1960; E. Roe, The mystery of the famous two: or Biggles and Blyton in South Australia, Australian Lib Jnl 12 1963.
Morton, John Bingham (b. 1893). The death of the dragon. 1934.
See cols 1088–9, below.
Best, Oswald Herbert (b. 1894). Garram the hunter. New York 1930, London 1935.
—— Garram the chief. New York 1932, London 1935.
—— Flag of the desert. New York 1936, Oxford 1937.
Also other tales of adventure.
Boumphrey, Geoffrey Maxwell (1894–1969). The story of Mr Bell. Oxford [1929].
Bullett, Gerald (1894–1958). The Spanish caravel. 1927, 1935, (rev, as The happy mariners) New York 1936.
—— Remember Mrs Munch 1931, 1940 (rev).
See cols 544–5, above.
De Sélincourt, Aubrey (1894–1962). Family afloat. 1940.
—— Three green bottles. 1941.
—— One good tern. 1943.
—— One more summer. 1944.
—— Micky. 1948.
Also further adventure stories.
Huxley, Aldous Leonard (1894–1963). The crows of Pearblossom. New York 1967, London 1968.
See cols 609–17, above.
Williams-Ellis, Mary Amabel Nassau, née Strachey (b. 1894). But we know better. 1926.
—— Ottik's book of stories. 1939.
Also re-tellings of traditional tales.
Barker, Cicely Mary (b. 1895). Flower fairies of the spring. 1923.
—— Flower fairies of the summer. 1925.
—— Flower fairies of the autumn. 1926.
—— The book of the flower fairies. 1927.
—— Old rhymes for all times. 1928, New York 1932.
—— When spring came in at the window. 1942. One-act play.
Also many other Flower fairy books and other picture books.
Brent-Dyer, Elinor (1895–1969). A head girl's difficulties. 1923.
—— The school at the Chalet. 1925. First of a long series of Chalet School stories, up to Two Sams at the Chalet School, 1967.
Also many other books for girls.
Graves, Robert von Ranke (b. 1895). The penny fiddle. 1960, Garden City NY 1961. Collection of poems written for children and pbd in books and journals 1917–60.
—— Greek gods and heroes. Garden City NY 1960, London 1961 (as Myths of ancient Greece).
—— The siege and fall of Troy. 1962, Garden City NY 1963.
—— The big green book. New York 1962, London 1963.
—— Ann at Highwood Hall. 1964. Further poems for children.
—— Two wise children. New York 1966, London 1967.

—— The poor boy who followed his star, and children's poems. 1968.
See cols 201–7, above.
Johnston, Arnrid (b. 1895). Pigwiggin, his dashing career. 1938.
—— Animal families and where they live. [1939].
—— Animals we use. 1948, New York 1948.
Manning-Sanders, Ruth (b. 1895). Children by the sea. 1938, New York 1939 (as Adventure may be anywhere).
—— Elephant. New York 1938, London 1940.
—— Mystery at Pennarth. 1940, New York 1941.
—— Circus book. 1947, New York 1948.
—— Swan of Denmark: the story of Hans Christian Andersen. 1949, New York 1950.
—— Peter and the piskies. 1958.
—— Circus boy. 1960.
—— The smugglers. 1962.
Also many other stories, anthologies, folk-tale collections etc.
Webb, Clifford (b. 1895). The story of Noah. 1931, New York 1932.
—— Butterwick farm. 1933, New York 1933.
—— A jungle picnic. 1934, New York 1934.
—— The North Pole before lunch. 1936, New York 1936.
—— Animals from everywhere. 1938, New York 1938.
See Clifford Webb—artist, author. *Horn Book 12 1936.*
Hall, Alice (b. c. 1895–?). The cat, the dog and the dormouse, and other stories. [1925].
—— The runaway road. 1933.
Munro, Elsie Smeaton (b. c. 1895–?). Topsy turvy tales. 1923.
Power, Rhoda Dolores le Poer (c. 1895–?). Boys and girls of history. Cambridge 1926, New York 1927, London 1967 (rev). With E. E. Power.
—— More boys and girls of history. Cambridge 1928. With E. E. Power.
—— Great people of the past. Cambridge 1932, New York 1932.
—— Stories from everywhere. [1943], 1969 (rev).
—— Rhoda Power's ten minute tales. [1943], 1954 (as Ten minute tales and dialogue stories).
—— Here and there stories. 1945.
—— Redcap runs away. 1952, Boston 1953.
—— We were there. 1955.
—— We too were there. 1956.
Skipper, Mervyn (b. c. 1895–?). The meeting pool. 1929, New York 1929 (as The jungle meeting pool).
—— The white man's garden. 1930.
—— The fooling of King Alexander. 1967 (illustr G. Chapman). Picture story taken from previous book.
Todd, Barbara Euphan (b. c. 1895–?). The 'normous Saturday fairy book. 1924.
—— The 'normous Sunday fairy book. 1925. Both with M. Royce and M. Meighn.
—— The very good walkers. 1925. With M. Royce.
—— Hither and thither. 1927.
—— Mr Blossom's shop. 1929.
—— The happy cottage. 1930. With M. Royce.
—— Worzel Gummidge: or the scarecrow of Scatterbrook. 1936.
—— Worzel Gummidge again. 1937.
Further Worzel Gummidge stories up to Detective Worzel Gummidge, 1963. *A selection pbd New York 1947.*
—— The house that ran behind. 1943. With E. Boumphrey.
Also other stories for young children.
Boumphrey, Esther, née Grandage (1896–?). The Hoojibahs. 1929.
—— The Hoojibahs and Mr Robinson. 1931.
—— Hoojibahs and humans. 1949.
Brisley, Joyce Lankester (b. 1896). Milly-Molly-Mandy stories. 1928.

—— More of Milly-Molly-Mandy. 1929.
—— Lamb's-tails and suchlike: verses and sketches. 1930, Philadelphia 1930.
—— Further doings of Milly-Molly-Mandy. 1932.
—— The dawn shops. 1933.
—— Marigold in Godmother's house. 1934.
—— Bunchy. 1937.
—— Three little Milly-Molly-Mandy plays. 1938.
—— My Bible book. 1940.
Also other tales for young children.

Graham, Eleanor (b. 1896). The night adventures of Alexis. 1925.
—— High days and holidays. 1932, New York 1933 (as Happy holidays).
—— Six in a family. 1935.
—— The children who lived in a barn. 1938.
—— Head o' mey. 1947.
See her How I look at children's books, *Junior Bookshelf 2 1938; also the tributes in Junior Bookshelf 26 1962.*

Lewis, Hilda (b. 1896). The ship that flew. 1939, New York 1958.
—— The gentle falcon. 1952, New York 1957.
—— Here comes Harry. 1960, New York 1960.
—— Harold was my king. 1968.

Strong, Leonard Alfred George (1896–1958). Patricia comes home. Oxford [1929].
—— The old Argo. Oxford [1931].
—— Amelia ye aged sow. Oxford [1932]. Verse.
—— King Richard's land. 1933, New York 1934.
—— Fortnight south of Skye. Oxford 1934, New York 1935.
—— Mr Sheridan's umbrella. 1935, New York 1935.
—— The fifth of November. 1937, 1965 (rev).
—— Henry of Agincourt. 1937.
—— The man who asked questions. 1937.
—— They went to the island. 1940.
—— Wrong foot foremost. 1940.
—— House in disorder. 1941.
—— Sink or swim. 1945.
See also his Instructions to young writers, *1958; and cols 744–6, above.*

Dickinson, William Croft (1897–1964). Borrobil. 1944.
—— The eildon tree. 1947.

Mitchison, Naomi Margaret (née Haldane) (b. 1897). Black Sparta. 1928, New York 1928.
—— Nix-nought-nothing: four plays for children. 1928.
—— Boys and girls and gods. 1931.
—— The corn king and the spring queen. 1931.
—— The big house. 1950.
—— Graeme and the dragon. 1954.
—— The swan's road. 1954.
—— The land the ravens found. 1955.
—— Little boxes. 1956.
—— The far harbour. 1957.
—— Judy and Lakshmi. 1959.
—— The rib of the green umbrella. 1960.
—— Karensgaard. 1961.
—— The fairy who couldn't tell a lie. 1963.
—— Ketse and the chief. 1965.
See her The writer and the child, *New Statesman 12 Feb 1955; and her* Children and books, *Books no 304 1956; and cols 673–4, above.*

Oman, Carola Mary Anima (b. 1897). Ferry the fearless. 1936.
—— Johel. 1937.
See cols 688–9, above.

Streatfeild, Noel (b. 1897). The children's matinée. 1934. 8 plays for children.
—— Ballet shoes. 1936, New York 1937.
—— Tennis shoes. 1937, New York 1938.
—— The circus is coming. 1938, New York 1939 (as Circus shoes).
—— Dennis the dragon. 1939.
—— The house in Cornwall. 1940.

—— The children of Primrose Lane. 1941, New York 1941 (as The stranger in Primrose Lane).
—— Harlequinade, illustr C. Hutton. 1943.
—— Curtain up. 1944, New York 1945 (as Theatre shoes).
—— Party frock. 1946, New York 1947 (as Party shoes).
—— The painted garden. 1949, New York 1949 (as Movie shoes).
—— White boots. 1951, New York 1951 (as Skating shoes).
—— The Bell family. 1954.
Also many other family and adventure stories for children. See her Myself and my books, *Junior Bookshelf 3 1939; E. M. Exley*, Noel Streatfeild: Carnegie Medal winner, *Junior Bookshelf 3 1939; B. K. Wilson*, Noel Streatfeild, *1961.*

Cannan, Joanna Maxwell (afterwards Pullein-Thompson) (1898–1961). A pony for Jean. 1936, New York 1937, Leicester 1970 (rev).
—— We meet our cousins. 1937.
—— Another pony for Jean. 1938.
—— London pride. 1939.
—— More ponies for Jean. 1943.
—— Hamish. 1944, New York 1944.
—— They bought her a pony. 1944.
—— I wrote a pony book. 1950. A tale.
—— Gaze at the moon. 1957.

Hale, Kathleen (b. 1898). Orlando, the marmalade cat: a camping holiday. [1938], New York [1938]. First of many books about Orlando, up to Orlando and the three Graces, 1965.
—— Henrietta the faithful hen. 1943, New York 1943.
See Book illustrators of today 2: Kathleen Hale, *Junior Bookshelf 11 1947.*

Hatch, Richard Warren (b. 1898). The curious lobster. [1937], New York 1937.
—— The curious lobster's island. New York 1939, London 1940.
—— All aboard the Whale. New York 1942, London 1944.

Hutton, Clarke (b. 1898). The hare and the tortoise. [1939].
—— A country ABC. [1940].
—— Punch and Judy: an acting book. [1942].
—— A picture history of Britain. 1945, Boston 1946.
—— The tale of Noah and the flood. [1946].

Lewis, Clive Staples (1898–1963). The lion, the witch and the wardrobe. 1950, New York 1950.
—— Prince Caspian. 1951, New York 1951.
—— The voyage of the Dawn Treader. 1952, New York 1952.
—— The silver chair. 1953, New York 1953.
—— The horse and his boy. 1954, New York 1954.
—— The magician's nephew. 1955, New York 1955.
—— The last battle. 1956, New York 1956.
See his On three ways of writing for children, *Proc of Annual Conference, Lib Assoc 1952, rptd in Only connect, Toronto 1969; M. S. Crouch*, Chronicles of Narnia, *Junior Bookshelf 20 1956; L. H. Smith*, News from Narnia, *Bull of Canadian Lib Assoc 15 1958, rptd in Only connect, Toronto 1969; R. L. Green*, C. S. Lewis, *1963; M. Hutton*, C. S. Lewis, *School Librarian 12 1964; P. Lively*, The wrath of God: an opinion on the Narnia books, *Use of Eng 20 1968; and cols 1073–8, below.*

Lynch, Patricia Nora (b. 1898). The green dragon. [1925].
—— The cobbler's apprentice. 1930.
—— The turf-cutter's donkey. 1934, New York 1935.
—— The turf-cutter's donkey goes visiting. 1935, New York 1936 (as The donkey goes visiting).
—— King of the tinkers. 1938, New York 1938.
—— The grey goose of Kilnevin. 1939, New York 1943.
—— Fiddler's quest. 1941, New York 1943.
—— Long ears. 1943.
—— Brogeen and the stepping stones. 1947.
Also many other stories for children. See her A storyteller's childhood, *1947; also E. Graham*, Patricia

Lynch: an appreciation, *Junior Bookshelf 7 1943*; *T. Deevy*, Patricia Lynch: a study, *Junior Bookshelf 13 1949*.

Blyton, Enid Mary (c. 1898–1968). Child whispers. [1922], 1923 (rev).
— Real fairies. 1923.
— Enid Blyton's book of fairies. [1924]. Also Bunnies [1925]; and Brownies [1926].
— Silver and gold. [1925], New York 1928.
— The play's the thing. [1927].
— Let's pretend. [1928].
— Cheerio! a book for boys and girls. [1933].
— Five minute tales. 1933.
— The tale of Mr Wumble. [1935].
— Adventures of the wishing chair. 1937.
— Mr Galliano's circus. [1938].
— The secret island. Oxford 1938.
— The wishing bean and other plays. Oxford 1939.
— The little tree-house, being the adventures of Josie, Bun and Click. [1940].
— Mister Meddle's mischief. 1940.
— The naughtiest girl in the school. 1940.
— The adventurous four. 1941.
— Five o'clock tales. 1941.
— The twins at St Clare's. 1941.
— Five on a treasure island. 1942.
— Hello Mr Twiddle! 1942.
— Mary Mouse and the doll's house. Leicester 1942.
— Dame Slap and her school. [1943].
— The magic Faraway Tree. 1943.
— The mystery of the burnt cottage. 1943.
— The island of adventure. 1944.
— Rainy day stories. 1944.
— Children at Happy House. Oxford 1946.
— First term at Malory Towers. 1946.
— Little Noddy goes to Toyland. 1949.
— The Rockingdown mystery. [1949].
— The secret seven. Leicester 1949.
A representative selection of the stories of a prolific writer. See her Story of my life, *1952, and* Enid Blyton: a complete list of books, *Glasgow 1956. Also J. Dohm*, Enid Blyton and others: an American view, *Jnl of Education 87 1955, rptd in* Young writers, young readers, *ed B. Ford 1960; C. Welch*, Dear Little Noddy: a parent's lament, *Encounter 10 1958; E. Roe*, The mystery of the famous two: or Biggles and Blyton in South Australia, *Australian Lib Jnl Sept 1963; E. Blishen*, Who's afraid of Enid Blyton, *Where 32 1967*; Problems, *Use of Eng 18 1966*.

Atkinson, Mary Evelyn (b. 1899). August adventure. 1936.
— Mystery manor. 1937.
— The compass points north. 1938.
— Smuggler's gap. 1939.
— Going gangster. 1940.
— Crusoe Island. 1941.
Also other family adventure stories. See her For the authors of tomorrow, *Junior Bookshelf 8 1944*.

'Peter Dawlish' (James Lennox Kerr) (b. 1899). The Blackspit smugglers. 1935. As by 'Lennox Kerr'.
— Captain Peg-leg's war. 1939.
— Peg-leg and the fur pirates. 1939. *And other* Peg-leg *books*.
— Dauntless finds her crew. 1947. *And other* Dauntless *books*.

Forester, Cecil Scott (1899–1966). Poo-poo and the dragons. 1942, Boston 1942.
See cols 576–7, above.

Hunter, Norman (b. 1899). The bad barons of Crashbania. Oxford [1932].
— The incredible adventures of Professor Branestawm. 1933.
— Professor Branestawm's treasure hunt. 1937.
— Larky legends. 1938, 1969 (rev as The dribblesome teapots).

— The peculiar triumph of Professor Branestawm. 1970.

Linklater, Eric (b. 1899). The wind on the moon. 1944, New York 1944.
— The pirates in the deep green sea. 1949.
See cols 636–8, above.

Nichols, Beverley (b. 1899). The tree that sat down. 1945.
— The stream that stood still. 1948. Abridged with the previous vol in one vol 1960.
— The mountain of magic. 1950.
See cols 681–2, above.

'A. Stephen Tring' (Laurence Meynell) (b. 1899). The old gang. 1947.
— Penny dreadful. 1949.
— The cave by the sea. 1950.
— Barry's exciting year. 1951.

Ardizzone, Edward Jeffrey Irving (b. 1900). Little Tim and the brave sea captain. 1936, New York 1936, London 1944 (rev), 1955 (rev), New York 1961.
— Lucy Brown and Mr Grimes. [1937], New York [1937], London 1970 (rev).
— Tim and Lucy go to sea. [1938], New York [1938], London 1944 (rev), 1958 (rev), New York 1961.
— Nicholas and the fast moving Diesel. [1947], 1959 (rev), New York 1959.
— Paul, the hero of the fire. 1948, Boston 1949, London 1962 (rev), New York 1963.
— Diana and her rhinoceros. 1964, New York 1964.
— The wrong side of the bed. New York 1969, London 1970 (as Johnny's bad day).
Also other picture story books. See his About Tim and Lucy, *Horn Book 14 1938*; The born illustrator, *Motif 1 1958; and* The young Ardizzone, *1970*.

Goudge, Elizabeth (b. 1900). The fairies' baby. Amersham 1919.
— Sister of the angels. 1939, New York 1939.
— Smoky house. 1940, New York 1940.
— Henrietta's house. 1942, New York 1942 (as The blue hills).
— The little white horse. 1946, New York 1947.
— Make believe. 1949.
— The valley of song. 1951.
— Linnets and Valerians. 1964.
See her Today and tomorrow; *and E. H. Colwell*, Elizabeth Goudge, *Junior Bookshelf 11 1947*.

Household, Geoffrey (b. 1900). The terror of Villadonga. 1936, Boston 1936 (rev, as The Spanish cave).
— The exploits of Xenophon. New York 1955, London 1961 (rev as Xenophon's adventure).
— Prisoner of the Indies. 1968.
See col 606, above.

Hughes, Richard (b. 1900). The spider's palace. 1931, New York 1932.
— Don't blame me and other stories. 1940, New York 1940.
— Gertrude's child. New York 1966, London 1967.
See col 607, above.

Leighton, Clare Veronica Hope (b. 1900). The musical box. 1932, New York 1932, [1936] (rev).
— The wood that came back. [1934], Poughkeepsie [1935].

Lindsay, Jack (b. 1900). Runaway. 1935.
See cols 635–6, above.

Suddaby, William Donald (1900–64). Lost men in the grass. 1940 (as by 'Alan Griff').
— The star raiders. 1950.
— The death of metal. 1952.
— Merry Jack Jugg, highwayman. 1954.
— Village fanfare. 1954.
— The moon of snowshoes. 1956.
— Prisoners of Saturn. 1957.
— Crowned with wild olive. 1961.
— The tower of Babel. 1962.
— A bell in the forest. 1964.

Beaman, Sydney George Hulme (b. c. 1900–?). Aladdin. 1924, New York 1925.
— The seven voyages of Sinbad the Sailor. 1926, New York 1926.
— Tales from Toytown. 1928, New York 1930 (as Ernest the policeman).
— John Trusty. 1929.
— Wireless in Toytown. 1930.
— Stories from Toytown. 1938.
— The adventures of Larry the Lamb. 1942.
Also various other books based on 'Trusty' and 'Toytown' ideas, including the Toytown *series 1957–.*
Elder, Josephine (b. c. 1900–?). Erica wins through. [1924].
— The scholarship girl. [1925].
— The scholarship girl at Cambridge. [1926].
— Thomasina Toddy. [1927].
— Eveline finds herself. 1929.
— Barbara at school. [1930].
— Cherry-tree perch. 1939.
— Strangers at the Farm School. 1940.
Also other stories for girls.
'Golden Gorse' (Mrs M. A. Wace) (b. c. 1900–?). Moorland Mousie. 1929, New York 1929.
— Older Mousie. 1932, New York 1932.
— Janet and Felicity. 1937.
— Mary in the country. 1955.
McGregor, Reginald James (b. c. 1900–?). The laughing pirate. [1927].
— The secret jungle. [1928].
— The young detectives. 1934.
— The secret of Dead Man's Cove. 1937.
— The dragon and the mosquito. 1938.
— Chi–Lo the admiral. 1940.
— The adventures of Grump. 1946.
Also other tales and plays for children.
Reed, Langford (b. c. 1900–?). Nonsense tales for the young (from seven to seventy). 1927.
Pye, Virginia (b. 1901). Red-letter holiday. 1940.
— Snow bird. 1941.
— Primrose Polly. 1942.
— Half-term holiday. 1943.
Also other stories for children.
Saville, Leonard Malcolm (b. 1901). Mystery at Witchend. 1943.
— Seven white gates. 1944.
— The gay dolphin adventure. 1945.
Also many other stories, nature books etc for children. See R. Manning, A book is a book is a book. *Signal 3 1970.*
Gibbons, Stella Dorothea (b. 1902). The untidy gnome. 1935, New York 1935.
See col 589, above.
Hogg, Garry Lester (b. 1902). The muddle-headed postman. 1937.
— Explorers awheel. 1938. *Also other* Explorers *vols.*
— The secret of the shuttered lodge. 1941.
— Climber's glory. 1961.
Marx, Enid (b. 1902). Bulgy the barrage balloon. 1941.
— Nelson, the kite of the King's Navy. [1942].
— The pigeon ace. [1943].
— The little white bear. [1946].
— Slithery Sam. 1947.
Pardoe, Margot Mary (b. 1902). The far island. 1936.
— Four plus Bunkle. 1939. *Also many other* Bunkle *books.*
— The boat seekers. 1953.
— Charles arriving. 1954.
— Argle's mist. 1956, New York 1957 (as Curtain of mist).
Also other stories for children.
Strachey, Richard Philip Farquhar (b. 1902). Little Reuben stories. [1944].
— Buttercup trail. [1948].
— Moonshine. 1953.

'Vipont, Elfrida' (Elfrida Vipont Foulds) (b. 1902). Colin writes to Friends House. 1934, 1957 (rev).
— Blow the man down. 1939, Philadelphia 1952. As by 'Charles Vipont'.
— The lark in the morn. 1948, Indianapolis 1951.
— The lark on the wing. 1950, Indianapolis 1951.
— Sparks among the stubble. 1950.
— The heir of Craigs. 1955. As by 'Charles Vipont'.
— The family of Dowbiggins. 1955, Indianapolis 1955.
Also other stories for children.
Armstrong, Richard (b. 1903). The mystery of Obadiah. 1943.
— Sabotage at the forge. 1946.
— Sea change. 1948.
Also many other adventure stories for boys.
'Bettina' (Bettina Ehrlich, née Bauer) (b. 1903). Poo-Tsee, the water tortoise. 1943.
— Carmelo. 1945.
— Cocolo. 1945, New York 1948.
— A horse for the island. New York 1952, London 1953.
— Angelo and Rosaline. 1957.
Also other picture story books.
Haskell, Arnold Lionel David (b. 1903). Felicity dances. 1937, Philadelphia 1938.
Norton, Mary, née Pearson (b. 1903). The magic bedknob. New York 1943, London 1945.
— Bonfires and broomsticks. 1947. The foregoing books pbd, rev, in one vol as Bed-knob and broomstick, 1957, New York 1957.
— The borrowers. 1952, New York 1953.
— The borrowers afield. 1955, New York 1955.
— The borrowers afloat. 1959, New York 1959.
— The borrowers aloft. 1961, New York 1961.
See C. Field, Mary Norton, School Librarian 11 1963.
Bone, Stephen (1904–58) and Mary Adshead (afterwards Mrs S. Bone (b. 1904)). The little boy and his house. 1936, Philadelphia 1937, London 1950 (rev).
— The silly snail and other stories. 1942.
— The little boys and their boats. 1953.
Day-Lewis, Cecil (1904–72). Dick Willoughby. Oxford [1933], New York 1938.
— Poetry for you. Oxford 1944, New York 1947.
— The Otterbury incident. 1948, New York 1949.
See cols 253–6, above.
Greene, Graham (b. 1904). The little train. 1946, 1957 (rev), New York 1958. The 1946 edn was pbd under the name of the illustrator, Dorothy Craigie.
— The little fire engine. 1950, New York 1953 (as The little red fire engine), London 1961 (rev).
— The little horse bus. 1952, New York 1954.
— The little steam roller. 1953, New York 1955.
See cols 503–12, above.
Jones, Harold (b. 1904). The visit to the farm. [1941].
— The enchanted night. 1947.
King-Hall, Magdalen (b. 1904). Jehan of the ready fists. [1936].
— Sturdy rogue. 1941, Philadelphia 1945.
'B.B.' (Denys James Watkins-Pitchford) (b. 1905). The little grey men. 1942, 1946 (rev), New York 1949, London 1952 (rev), 1969 (rev).
— Brendon Chase. 1944, New York 1945.
— B.B.'s fairy book: Meeting Hill. 1946.
— Down the bright stream. 1948, 1969 (rev).
— The Forest of Boland light railway. 1955, New York 1957 (as The forest of the railway).
Coats, Alice Margaret (b. 1905). The story of Horace. [1937], New York [1939].
— The travels of Maurice. [1939].
Harris, Mary Kathleen (1905–66). Gretel at St Brides. 1941.
— The wolf. 1946, New York 1955 (rev).
— The niche over the door. 1948.
— Henrietta of St Hilary's. 1953.
— Emily and the headmistress. 1958.
— Seraphina. 1960.

—— Penny's way. 1963.
—— The bus girls. 1965.
—— Jessica on her own. 1968.
　　See Mary K. Harris: the real world of school. *TLS 5 Dec 1968.*
Warner, Rex (b. 1905). The kite. Oxford 1936, London 1963 (rev).
　　See cols 761–2, above.
Castellain, Lois (b. c. 1905). Adolphus. 1939.
—— Moidi the refugee cow. [1941].
Emett, Mary (b. c. 1905) and Rowland (b. 1906). Anthony and Antimacassar. [1943].
Lovell, Dorothy Ann (b. c. 1905). Stories of the Hoppity-Pops. [1938].
—— Toby Twinkle. 1939.
—— The dip bucket. 1941.
—— The strange adventure of Emma. 1941.
—— The mystery of the bronze frog. 1942.
—— Rufus the seafaring rat. 1948.
　　And other stories for children.
Rochester, George Ernest (b. c. 1905). The flying spy. [1935].
—— The freak of St Freda's. [1936].
—— Pirates of the air. [1936].
　　Also many other adventure tales.
Tozer, Katharine (b. c. 1905). The wanderings of Mumfie. 1935.
—— Here comes Mumfie. 1936. *And other* Mumfie *books.*
—— Noah: the story of another ark. 1940.
—— The adventures of Alfie. 1941.
Borer, Mary Irene Cathcart (b. 1906). Kilango. 1936.
—— Adventure in August. 1937.
—— The Sinclair family. 1937.
—— Taha the Egyptian. 1937.
　　And other stories for children.
Travers, Pamela Lyndon (b. 1906). Mary Poppins. 1934, New York 1934.
—— Mary Poppins comes back. 1935, New York 1935. The foregoing books pbd in one vol New York 1937, London 1940.
—— I go by sea, I go by land. 1941, New York 1941.
—— Mary Poppins opens the door. New York 1943, London 1944.
—— Mary Poppins in the park. 1952, New York 1952.
—— Mary Poppins from A to Z. New York 1962, London 1963.
—— The fox in the manger. New York 1962, London 1963.
White, Terence Hanbury (1906–64). The sword in the stone. 1938, New York 1939.
—— The witch in the wood. New York 1939, London [1940].
—— The ill-made knight. New York 1940, London 1941.
—— Mistress Masham's repose. New York [1946], London 1947.
—— The master. 1957, New York 1957.
　　See cols 771–2, above.
'Philip Woodruff' (Philip Mason) (b. 1906). The sword of Northumbria. 1948.
—— The island of Chamba. 1950.
Collins, Norman Richard (b. 1907). Black ivory. 1948, New York 1948.
Godden, Margaret Rumer (b. 1907). The dolls' house. 1947, New York 1948.
—— The mousewife. New York 1951, London 1951.
—— Impunity Jane. New York 1954, London 1955.
—— The fairy doll. 1956, New York 1956.
—— Mouse house. New York 1957, London 1958.
—— The story of Holly and Ivy. 1958, New York 1958.
—— Candy floss. 1960, New York 1960.
—— Miss Happiness and Miss Flower. 1961, New York 1961.
　　Also other stories for children. See N. Culpan, Rumer Godden, *School Librarian 8 1956; and cols 590–1, above.*

Grant, Joan Marshall (b. 1907). The scarlet fish and other stories. 1942.
—— Redskin morning. 1944.
Hatt, Ella Mary (1907–72). Callers at our house. 1945. Illustr L. Wood.
—— Priscilla the Paddington mouse. 1946.
—— The cat with a guinea to spend. 1947.
—— The house that was no-one's affair. 1947.
Lewitt, Jan (b. 1907) and George Him (b. 1900). The football's revolt. 1939.
—— Blue Peter. 1943.
—— Five silly cats. [1944].
　　Jan Lewitt pbd The vegetabull, *1956, under the pseudonym 'J. Le Witt'.*
Ainsworth, Ruth Gallard (b. 1908.) Tales about Tony. 1936.
—— The gingerbread house. 1938.
—— Mr Popcorn's friends. 1938.
—— The ragamuffins. 1939.
—— Richard's first term. [1940].
—— All different: poems for children. 1945.
　　And many other poems and stories for young children.
Kiddell-Monroe, Joan (b. 1908). In his little black waistcoat. 1939, 1947 (rev).
—— His little black waistcoat to China. 1940.
—— Ingulabi. [1943].
—— Little skunk. [1943].
—— Wau-wau the ape. 1947.
—— The irresponsible goat. 1948.
—— In his little black waistcoat to India. 1948.
—— In his little black waistcoat to Tibet. 1949.
　　See Book illustrators of today, 3: Joan Kiddell-Monroe, *Junior Bookshelf 11 1947.*
Hodges, Cyril Walter (b. 1909). Columbus sails. 1939, New York 1939.
—— The namesake. 1964, New York 1964.
—— The marsh king. 1967, New York 1967.
Redlich, Monica (b. 1909). Jam tomorrow. 1937.
—— Five farthings: a London story. 1939.
'James Reeves' (John Morris Reeves) (b. 1909). The wandering moon. 1950, 1957 (rev), New York 1960. Poems.
—— The blackbird in the lilac. 1952, New York 1959. Poems.
—— Pigeons and princesses. 1956.
—— Prefabulous animiles. 1957, New York 1960. Poems.
—— Mulbridge Manor. 1958.
—— Titus in trouble. 1959, New York 1960.
—— Ragged Robin. [1961], New York 1961. Poems.
　　Also other plays, stories and adaptations for children. See M. Hutton, Reeves, *School Librarian 14 1966; D. Butts,* Reeves: the truthful poet, *Junior Bookshelf 30 1966; B. W. Alderson,* The big transmitter, *Children's Book News 3 1968; and cols 330–1, above.*
Trease, Robert Geoffrey (b. 1909). Bows against the barons. 1934, Moscow 1934, New York 1934, Leicester 1966 (rev).
—— Comrades for the charter. 1934, Moscow 1935.
—— The unsleeping sword. 1934.
—— The call to arms. 1935.
—— Missing from home. 1936.
—— Mystery on the moors. 1937.
—— The dragon who was different, and other plays for children. 1938.
—— In the land of the mogul. Oxford 1938.
　　Also many other historical and adventure stories. See his Why write for children?, *School Librarian 10, and his* A writer's working bookshelf, *Books no 334 1961. See also M. Meek,* Geoffrey Trease *1960, 1968 (rev), and School Librarian 13 1965.*
'Diana Ross' (Diana Denney) (b. 1910). The story of the beetle who lived alone. [1941].
—— Uncle Anty's album. 1941. With A. Denney.
—— The golden hen and other stories. 1942.
—— The little red engine gets a name, illustr Lewitt-Him, 1942. First of many Little red engine books, all subsequently illustr L. Wood.

—— The wild cherry. 1943.
—— Nursery tales. 1944.
—— Whoo, whoo the wind blew. 1946.
 Also many other stories for young children.
Treadgold, Mary (b. 1910). We couldn't leave Dinah. 1941, New York 1941 (as Left till called for).
—— No ponies. 1946.
—— The Polly Harris. 1949, New York 1951 (as The mystery of the Polly Harris), London 1968 (rev).
—— The heron ride. 1962.
—— The winter princess. Leicester 1962.
 Also several subsequent pbns for children. See her Why I write books, *Junior Bookshelf 6 1942.*
Balfour, Margaret Melville (c. 1910–40). The vanishing mayor of Padstow. 1938.
Binyon, Helen (b. c. 1910) and Margaret. The birthday party. 1940.
—— A country visit. 1940.
—— A day at the sea. 1940.
—— Polly and Jane. 1940.
 Also other picture books for young children.
Fox-Smith, Cicely (b. c. 1910). The ship aground: a tale of adventure. 1940.
—— Painted ports. 1948.
—— Knave-go-by: the adventures of Jacky Nameless. 1951.
—— The valiant sailor. 1955, New York 1957.
Garnett, Eve (b. c. 1910). The family from One End St. 1937, New York 1939.
—— In and out and round about: stories of a little town. 1948.
—— Further adventures of the family from One End Street. 1956, New York 1956.
—— Holiday at the Dew Drop Inn. 1962, New York 1962.
 See her The how and why of the Ruggleses, *Junior Bookshelf 2 1938.*
Hickey, Theodosia Frances Wynne (b. c. 1910). The unexpected adventure. 1935.
—— Bulldog Sheila. 1936, New York 1936.
—— The hand: or mystery at Number Ten. 1937.
—— Alice and James discover their country. 1941.
—— Adventure at Littleacres. 1947.
'Elizabeth Kyle' (Agnes Mary Robertson Dunlop) (b. c. 1910). Visitors from England. 1941.
—— Vanishing island. 1943.
 Also many other stories.
Lewis, Lorna (b. c. 1910). The adventures of Toutou the little French poodle. [1934].
—— The dog with plush paws. [1936].
—— Puppy and the cat Hodge. [1938], New York 1940 (as Puppy and the cat).
—— Holiday luck. 1939.
—— Tea and hot bombs. 1943.
—— Feud in the factory. 1944.
—— Mystery at Lock House. 1947.
 Also other books.
Moncrieff, Ann Scott (b. c. 1910). Aboard the Bulger. 1935.
—— The white drake and other tales. 1936.
—— Auntie Robbo. New York 1941, London [1959].
Needham, Violet (b. c. 1910). The black raiders. 1939.
—— The emerald crown. 1940.
—— The stormy petrel. 1942.
—— The horn of Merlyns. 1943.
 Also other Ruritanian romances. See L. Salway, Survival of the fittest, *Children's Book News 4 1969.*
Rhys, 'Mimpsy' (Mary) (b. c. 1910). Mr Hermit crab: a tale for children by a child. New York 1929, London 1935.
Scales, Catherine (b. c. 1910). Gay company. 1938.
—— Nugger nonsense. 1939.
Awdrey, Wilbert Vere (b. 1911). The three railway engines. 1945.
—— Thomas the tank engine. 1946.

—— James the red engine. 1947. *And other books in the* Railway *series.*
—— Belinda the beetle. 1958.
 See D. Butts, The Reverend's railways, *Books no 358 1965.*
Drummond, Violet Hilda (b. 1911). Phewtus the squirrel. [1939], 1966 (rev).
—— Mrs Easter's parasol. 1944.
—— Miss Anna Truly. 1945, New York 1949.
—— Lady Talavera. 1946.
—— The charming taxi-cab. 1947.
—— The mountain that laughed. 1947.
—— Tidgie's innings. 1947, 1966 (rev).
—— The flying postman. 1948, New York 1949, London 1964 (rev).
—— Mrs Easter and the storks. 1957, New York 1959.
—— Little Laura books. 1960 onwards.
 See G. A. Hogarth, V. H. Drummond, *Horn Book 24 1948; M. S. Crouch,* Tribute to V. H. Drummond, *Junior Bookshelf 13 1949.*
Langley, Noel (b. 1911). The tale of the land of green ginger. 1937, 1947 (rev), 1966 (rev).
—— The true and pathetic history of Desbarollda the waltzing mouse. 1947.
Peake, Mervyn Laurence (1911–68). Captain Slaughterboard drops anchor. 1939, 1945 (rev), 1967 (rev), New York 1967.
—— Letters from a lost uncle. 1948.
 See col 699, above.
Williams, Ursula Moray (b. 1911). Jean-Pierre. 1931.
—— For Brownies. 1932.
—— The autumn sweepers. 1933.
—— Grandfather. 1933.
—— The pettabomination. 1933, 1948 (rev).
—— Kelpie, the gypsies' pony. 1934, Philadelphia 1935.
—— Tales for the sixes and sevens. 1936.
—— Elaine of La Signe. 1937, Philadelphia 1939 (as Elaine of the mountains).
—— The adventures of the little wooden horse. 1938, Philadelphia 1939.
—— Gobbolino the witch's cat. 1942.
 Also many other stories for children.
Buckeridge, Anthony Malcolm (b. 1912). Jennings goes to school. 1950.
—— Rex Milligan's busy term. 1953.
 Also other books about Jennings and Milligan.
Edwards, Monica Le Doux (b. 1912). No mistaking Corker. 1947.
—— Wish for a pony. 1947.
—— The summer of the great secret. 1948.
—— The midnight horse. 1949, New York 1950.
—— The black hunting whip. 1950.
 Also other stories for girls.
Fuller, Roy Broadbent (b. 1912). Savage gold. 1946.
—— With my little eye: a mystery story for teenagers. 1948, New York 1957.
 See col 278, above.
Serraillier, Ian (b. 1912). Thomas and the sparrow. 1946. Poems.
—— They raced for treasure. 1946.
—— Flight to adventure. 1947.
—— Captain Bounsaboard and the pirates. 1949.
—— The tale of the monster horse. 1950. A poem.
—— There's no escape. 1950.
—— Belinda and the swans. 1952. Poems.
—— The silver sword. 1956, New York 1959.
 Also other stories, poetry, adaptations etc for children.
'Ralph Hammond' (Hammond Innes) (b. 1913). Cocos gold. 1950, New York 1950.
—— Isle of strangers. 1951, Philadelphia 1953 (as Isle of peril).
—— Saracen's tower. 1952, Philadelphia 1954 (as Cruise of danger).
—— Black gold on the Double Diamond. 1953.

Cross, John Keir (1914–67). Studio J investigates. 1944. This and the following 2 items pbd under the pseudonym 'Stephen MacFarlane'.
—— Detectives in greasepaint. 1944.
—— Mr Bosanko, and other stories. 1944.
—— The white magic. 1947.
—— Blackadder. 1950, New York 1951.
  Also other stories of mystery and adventure.
Allan, Mabel Esther (b. 1915). The adventurous summer. 1948.
—— The Glen Castle mystery. [1948].
—— The Wyndhams went to Wales. 1948.
  Also many other stories for girls. See her Reviewing of children's books, Books no 346 1963.
Collas, Clare (b. 1915). Four's company. 1942
—— The flying village. 1943.
—— The blue-coated heron. 1944.
—— A penny for the guy. 1945.
'Kathleen Fidler' (Kathleen Annie Goldie) (b. 1915). The borrowed garden. 1944.
—— Fingal's ghost: an adventure story based on a radio play. [1945].
—— The Brydens at Smugglers' Creek. 1946, 1952 (rev).
—— The Kathleen Fidler omnibus. [1946].
—— The mysterious Mr Simister. 1947.
Dehn, Olive (b. c. 1915). Tales of Sir Benjamin Bulbous, Bart. Oxford 1935.
—— The basement bogle. Oxford [1937].
—— The nixie from Rotterdam. Oxford [1937].
—— Tales of the Taunus mountains. Oxford [1937].
—— The well-behaved witch. Oxford [1937].
—— Come in. Oxford 1946.
—— Folk tales. Leeds [1948].
—— Higgly-piggly farm. 1957.
—— The pike dream. 1958.
—— The caretakers. 1960.
  Also other stories.
Forest, Antonia (b. c. 1915). Autumn term. 1948.
—— The Marlows and the traitor. 1953.
—— Falconer's lure. 1957.
—— End of term. 1959.
—— Peter's room. 1961.
—— The Thursday kidnapping. 1963.
—— The thuggery affair. 1965.
—— The ready-made family. 1967.
Lowndes, Joan Selby (b. c. 1915). The story of Firebrand. 1941 (for 1940).
—— The story of Edwin. 1944.
—— Canterbury gallop. 1945.
—— Mail coach. 1945.
—— Bronze eagles. 1946.
—— Royal chase. 1947.
—— Tudor star. 1949.
—— Night hawk. 1950.
  Also other stories.
Ridge, Antonia Florence (b. c. 1915). The handy elephant and other stories. 1946.
—— Rom-bom-bom and other stories. 1946.
—— Hurrah for Muggins and other stories. 1947.
—— Jan and his clogs. [1951], New York [1952].
—— Puppet plays for children. 1953.
—— Never run from the lion. 1958, New York 1959.
—— The poppenkast: or how Jan Klaassen cured the sick king—a play for children. 1958.
  Also other stories and plays for children.
Townend, Jack (b. c. 1915). A railway ABC. [1942], New York 1945 (as Railroad ABC).
—— Ben. 1944.
—— Jenny the jeep. 1944.
—— A story about ducks. 1945.
Wilson, Anthony Eldred Clifford (b. 1916). Norman Bones, detective. 1949, New York 1951.
—— Norman and Henry Bones the boy detectives. 1952.

—— Norman and Henry Bones investigate. 1953, New York 1954 (as Norman and Henry investigate).
—— Mystery tour. New York 1954.
Baker, Margaret Joyce (b. 1918). The fighting cocks. 1949.
—— 'Nonsense' said the tortoise. Leicester 1949, New York [1950] (as Homer the tortoise). Leicester 1954 (rev).
—— Four farthings and a thimble. 1950, New York 1950.
—— A castle and sixpence. 1951, New York 1951.
  Also many other subsequent books for children.
Charlton, Yvonne Moyra Graham (b. 1918). Tally-ho: the story of an Irish hunter. London 1930, New York 1930.
—— Patch: the story of a mongrel. 1931.
—— The midnight steeple chase. 1932.
—— Three white stockings. [1933], New York [1933].
—— Pendellion. 1948.
  Also other stories for girls.
Newby, Percy Howard (b. 1918). The spirit of Jem. 1947.
—— The loot runners. 1949.
  See cols 680–1, above.
'David Severn' (David Storr Unwin) (b. 1918). Rick afire! 1942.
—— A cabin for Crusoe. 1943, Boston 1946.
—— Waggon for five. 1944, Boston 1947.
—— Hermit in the hills. 1945.
—— Drumbeats! 1953.
  Also other tales of adventure for children.
'Cam' (Barbara Mary Campbell) (b. c. 1920). The story of Barbara Lamb. 1944.
—— The story of Buttercup Fairy. 1945, New York [1953?].
—— The story of Margaret Field-mouse. 1946.
  Also other picture books.
Clark, Audrey (b. c. 1920). The Vedor sampler: a tale of Czechoslovakia and its brave children. 1944.
Craigie, Dorothy (b. c. 1920). Summersalt's circus. 1947.
—— The voyage of Luna I. 1948. New York 1949. As by 'David Craigie'.
—— Dark Atlantis. 1951 (for 1952), New York 1953. As by 'David Craigie'.
—— The little balloon. [1953].
—— Milk of the river. 1960. As by 'David Craigie'.
  Also other picture story books. The little train, 1946, pbd under Dorothy Craigie's name as illustrator, was later reissued as by Graham Greene. See col 808, above.
Hughes, Gwilym Fielden (b. c. 1920). The adventures of Bill Holmes. 1950.
—— Bill Holmes and the red panthers. 1953.
—— Bill Holmes and the fortune teller. 1955.
Stebbing, Hilary (b. c. 1920). Maggie the streamlined taxi. 1943, New York 1943.
—— Monty's new house. 1944, New York 1944.
—— The silly rabbits. [1944], New York [1944].
—— Freddy and Ernest, the dragons of Wellbottom Poggs. 1946, New York 1946.
Hull, Katharine (b. 1922) and Pamela Whitlock (b. 1921). The far-distant Oxus. 1937, New York 1938. Introd by Arthur Ransome.
—— Escape to Persia. 1938, New York 1939.
—— Oxus in summer. 1939, New York 1940.
—— Crowns. 1947.
Brown, Pamela (b. 1924). The swish of the curtain. 1941, Philadelphia [1943].
—— Golden pavements. 1947.
—— Blue door venture. 1949.
—— The children of Camp Fortuna. [1949]. Play.
—— To be a ballerina. 1950.
  Also many subsequent pbns for children.
Pullein-Thompson, Christine (b. 1930), Diana and Josephine. It began with Picotee. 1946.

C. Pullein-Thompson subsequently pbd We rode to the sea, 1948, *and many other pony stories; D. Pullein-Thompson,* I wanted a pony *1946, and many other pony stories; and J. Pullein-Thompson,* Six ponies, *1946, and many other pony stories.*

Herald, Kathleen Wendy (b. c. 1933). Sabre, the horse from the sea. 1948.
— The Mandrake, a pony. 1949.
— Crab the roan. 1953.
Also later books, pbd under the name K. M. Peyton.

(3) ANTHOLOGIES

A select list of collections of traditional rhymes, poetry and stories, written or compiled specifically for children, arranged according to date of pbn of first vol by each editor.

Gosset, A. L. J. (ed). Lullabies and baby songs: a posy for mothers. 1900.
— Lullabies of the four nations [i.e. England, Wales, Ireland, Scotland]. 1915.
Ingpen, R. (ed). One thousand poems for children. [1903], Philadelphia [1903], [1920] (rev), [1923] (rev).
— A choice of the best poems for the young. 1922.
— Nursery rhymes for certain times: a collection based upon one made by R. Ingpen. Ed A. M. Ingpen and M. Grenside, introd by W. de la Mare, 1946.
Brooke, L. L. (ed and illustr). The tailor and the crow [1911], New York [1911].
— The man in the moon. [1913].
— A nursery rhyme picture book. [1913], New York [1914].
— Oranges and lemons. [1913].
— Ring o' roses. [1922].
Rackham, A. (ed and illustr). Mother Goose: the old nursery rhymes. [1913], New York 1913.
Potter, H. B. (ed and illustr). Appley Dappley's nursery rhymes. [1917].
— Cecily Parsley's nursery rhymes. [1922].
Fraser, C. L. (ed and illustr). Nursery rhymes with pictures. [1919], New York [1922].
Rhys, G. (ed). The children's garland of verse. 1921, New York 1921.
de la Mare, W. (ed). Come hither. 1923, New York [1923], London 1928 (rev), New York [1928], 1957 (rev), London 1960 (rev).
— Tom Tiddler's ground. [1932], [1961] (rev), New York [1962].
Wayne, P. (ed). A child's book of lyrics. 1923.
Fowler, E. L. For your delight. 1924.
Walter, L. E. (ed). Mother Goose's nursery rhymes. 1924.
Compton, J. (ed). Open sesame: a collection of poems and rhymes for children. 1925.
— Magic sesame: a collection of poems for boys and girls. 1932.
Reed, L. (ed). Nonsense verses: an anthology. [1925], New York 1926 (as A book of nonsense verse).
— Nonsense tales for the young. 1927.
— The child's own limerick book. 1932.
Asquith, Lady C. and E. Bigland (ed). The Princess Elizabeth gift book. [1935].
Fyleman, R. (ed). Joy Street poems. Oxford [1927].
— Widdy-widdy-wurkey: nursery rhymes from many lands. Oxford 1935, New York 1935 (as Picture rhymes from foreign lands).
— Here we come a'piping. 2 vols Oxford [1936]; vol 1, New York [1937]; vol 2, New York [1938] (as A'piping again).
— Bells ringing. Oxford 1938, New York [1939].
— Pipe and drum. Oxford 1939.
— Over the tree tops: nursery rhymes from many lands. Oxford 1949.
Graves, R. (ed). The less familiar nursery rhymes. [1927] (Augustan Books of English Poetry).

Swabey, M. (ed). A book of nursery rhymes. 1928.
Budd, F. E. (ed). A book of lullabies 1300–1900. 1930.
Graham, E. (ed). Welcome Christmas. 1931, New York [1932].
Daglish, A. and E. Rhys (ed). The land of nursery rhyme. 1932, New York [1932].
Grahame, K. (ed). The Cambridge book of poetry for children. Cambridge 1916, New York [1916], Cambridge 1932 (rev), New York [1933].
Blackwell, B. (ed). Fairings in plenty: a book of songs for children. Oxford [1933].
MacBain, J. M. (ed). The London treasury of nursery rhymes. [1933].
— The book of a thousand poems. [1942].
Vallance, R. (ed). The youngest omnibus. 1934.
Pocock, G. N. (ed). A poetry book for boys and girls. 1933, New York [1933].
— A story book for boys and girls. 1936.
Wood, L. (ed and illustr). The old nursery rhymes. [1933].
Sussams, T. W. and W. E. Jarrett (ed). Modern verse for town boys and girls. 1934.
Auden, W. H. and J. W. P. Garrett (ed). The poet's tongue. 2 vols 1935.
Mégroz, I. and R. L. (ed). Modern poems for children. Wisbech 1935.
Day-Lewis, C. (ed). The echoing green. 3 vols Oxford 1937.
Lines, K. (ed). Stories for girls. 1938, 1957 (rev).
— Stories for Christmas. 1939.
— The ten minute story book. [1943].
Evans, J. R. (ed). The junior week-end book. 1939.
Marx, E. (ed). The Zodiac book of nursery rhymes. 1939, New York 1940.
— A book of rigmaroles and jingle rhymes. [1945].
Peake, M. (ed and illustr). Ride a cock-horse and other nursery rhymes. 1940.
Hutton, C. (ed and illustr). Fifteen nursery rhymes. [1941].
Farjeon, E. (ed). The new book of days. 1941, New York [1941].
Sitwell, E. (ed). Look! the sun. 1941.
Carton, J. (ed). A child's garland. 1942.
Green, M. C. (ed and illustr). Stars and primroses. 1945.
— Magic lanterns. 1949.
Montgomerie, N. and W. (ed). Scottish nursery rhymes. 1946.
— Sandy Candy and other Scottish nursery rhymes. 1948.
Bebbington, W. G. A tale told: an anthology of narrative poems. 1947.
Opie, I. and P. I saw Esau: traditional rhymes of youth. 1947.
Barclay, D. D. C. (ed). Spirit of youth. 1948.
Cross, J. K. (ed). The children's omnibus. [1948].
'Stanley, Arthur' (A. S. Megaw). The bedside book for children. 1949.
Gullen, F. D. Traditional number rhymes and games. 1950. A collection compiled for the Panel on Early Number Teaching of the Scottish Council for Research in Education.

(4) TRADITIONAL TALES

A select list of collections, showing edns of some importance either for their illustrations or for special characteristics in their compilation or translation. 'Classic' authors and themes apart, little attempt has been made to include even representative vols of the many English edns of foreign folk and fairy tales. Many of these may be found listed in the bibliographies in cols 783–5, above; detailed lists are also given in M. F. Austin, Some editions of children's classics, Junior Bookshelf 3 1938 and in H. J. B. Woodfield, Folk tales round the world, Junior Bookshelf 3 1939.

Aesop. A child's Aesop. 1902; Fables told to the children, [1906], New York [1908]; Fables, tr V. S. Vernon-Jones, illustr A. Rackham 1912; another trn, illustr C. Folkard 1912; another trn, introd by E. Rhys [1913], New York [1913]; another trn, illustr P. A. Terry [1925]; another trn, illustr A. Johnston [1944].

Andersen, H. C. Fairy tales. Tr H. L. Braeckstad, illustr H. Tegner 1900; another trn, illustr H. M. Brock 1905; retold by M. Macgregor [1906], New York [1908?]; another trn, illustr E. Dulac 1911; another trn, illustr W. H. Robinson 1913, Boston 1931; rev and tr W. A. and J. K. Craigie 1914 (for 1913), New York 1914; Forty stories, tr M. R. James 1930, 1953 (rev) (as Forty-two stories), New York [1959] (as Forty-two stories); another trn, selected and illustr A. Rackham 1932, Philadelphia 1932; another trn, illustr R. Whistler 1935, New York 1926; Four tales, tr R. P. Keigwin, illustr G. Raverat, Cambridge 1935.
  For fuller accounts of English edns see Library of Congress, Catalogue of the Jean Hersholt Collection, Washington 1954, and National Book League catalogue of the Jubilee Exhibition, 1955.
Arabian nights entertainments. 1903 (as A child's Arabian nights, illustr W. H. Robinson); ed E. Dixon, illustr J. D. Batten 1907, New York 1907; retold L. Housman, illustr E. Dulac 1907, New York [1907]; illustr C. Folkard 1913.
Basile, G. B. Stories from the Pentamerone. Ed E. F. Strange, illustr W. Goble 1911.
Brock, H. M. (ed and illustr). The fairy library. [1907], [1914] (rev, as The book of fairy tales), 1934 (rev, as The book of nursery tales).
Brooke, L. L. (ed and illustr). The story of the three little pigs. [1904].
— Tom Thumb. [1904].
— The golden goose book. [1905].
Byrne, M. St C. Havelok the Dane. 1929.
Dane, C. One hundred enchanted tales. 1937.
Darton, F. J. H. (ed). The merry tales of the wise men of Gotham. 1907.
— A wonder book of old romance. 1907, New York [1907].
— A wonder book of beasts. [1909], New York [1909].
Davidson, N. J. (ed). A knight errant and his doughty deeds, the story of Amadis of Gaul. 1911.
de la Mare, W. (ed). Told again. 1927, New York 1927, London 1959 (as Tales told again), New York [1959].
— Stories from the Bible. 1929, New York 1929.
— Animal stories. 1939, New York 1940.
Dulac, E. (ed and illustr). Edmund Dulac's fairy book: fairy tales of the allied nations. [1916], New York [1916].
— (ed and illustr). Picture book for the French Red Cross. 1916.
Farjeon, E. Mighty men. 2 pts Oxford 1924, New York 1926, 1 vol Oxford [1928].
— Paladins in Spain. 1937.
— The wonders of Herodotus. 1937.
Fyleman, R. (ed). Folk tales from many lands. 1939.
— Punch and Judy. 1944.
Glover, W. J. British fairy and folk tales. 1920.
The allies' fairy book. Introd by E. Gosse, illustr A. Rackham [1916], Philadelphia [1916].

Grimm, J. W. and W. C. Fairy tales, tr E. Lucas, illustr A. Rackham 1900, Philadelphia 1902; another tr, illustr L. L. Brooke [1905], New York [1911] (as The house in the wood); tr L. L. Weedon, illustr C. Robinson [1910]; another tr, illustr C. Folkard [1911]; illustr M. Peake 1946 (as Household tales).
Hauff, W. Fairy tales. Tr C. McDonnell [1903]; tr S. Thesiger 1905; tr L. L. Weedon, illustr A. A. Dixon [1910], New York 1910.
— Caravan tales. Adapted by J. G. Hornstein, illustr N. Ault [1912], New York [1912].
— Eastern fairy tales. Ed R. Ingram 1949.
Homeric tales. Harrison, G. B. The wanderings of Ulysses. 1937.
— New tales of Troy. 1940.
De Selincourt, A. Odysseus the wanderer. 1950.
King Arthur. Macleod, M. The book of King Arthur and his noble knights [from Malory]. 1900, Philadelphia 1949.
Clay, B. Stories from Le Morte Darthur and the Mabinogion. 1901.
Haydon, A. L. Stories of King Arthur, illustr A. Rackham 1910, New York 1910.
Gilbert, H. King Arthur's knights, illustr W. Crane 1911.
Pollard, A. W. The romance of King Arthur, illustr A. Rackham 1917.
Hampden, J. Knights of the round table. [1930].
Harrison, G. B. New tales from Malory, illustr C. W. Hodges 1939.
Macdonald, V. M. (ed). Nursery tales. 1929.
Macleod, M. A book of ballad stories. [1906], New York [1906]. And many other retellings.
Mother Goose's nursery tales. Illustr C. Folkard 1923.
Perrault, C. The sleeping beauty and other tales, illustr J. Hassall [1912].
— Fairy tales, illustr C. Robinson [1913], New York [1916].
— McGill, H. M. Perrault's tales of long ago. 1949.
— Fairy tales. Tr N. Denny 1950 (for 1951).
Power, R. How it happened: myths and folk-tales. Cambridge 1930.
Rackham, A. The Arthur Rackham fairy book. 1933, Philadelphia [1933].
Rhys, B. A book of ballads. 1929.
Rhys, E. Fairy gold. 1906, New York 1906.
— The English fairy book. 1912, New York [1912].
Robin Hood. Finnemore, J. The story of Robin Hood. 1909, New York 1929 (as Robin Hood and his merry men).
Macleod, M. Robin Hood and his merry men. [1909].
Gilbert, H. Robin Hood and the men of the greenwood. Illustr W. Crane 1912; illustr W. C. and H. M. Brock [1932]; illustr F. Godwin, New York 1932; illustr G. Williams, Philadelphia [1948].
Chesterman, H. Told in Sherwood. 1931.
Trease, G. Bows against the barons. 1934, Leicester 1966 (rev).
Oman, C. Robin Hood, prince of outlaws. 1937, New York 1937.
Gilson, C. J. L. Robin of Sherwood. 1940.
Suddaby, N. D. New tales of Robin Hood 1950, 1967 (rev).
Sutcliff, R. Chronicles of Robin Hood. 1950.
Steel, F. A. English fairy tales. 1918, New York 1918.
Thirkell, A. M. The grateful sparrow and other tales, taken from the German. 1935.
[Vernaleken, F. T.]. Heath Robinson's book of goblins. 1935.
Williams, H. Tales from Ebony. 1934, New York [1935].
Williams-Ellis, A. Fairies and enchanters: a new book of old English stories. 1933, New York 1934.

(5) PERIODICALS

See also W. O. G. Lofts and D. J. Adley, Old boys' books: a complete catalogue, *1970.*

Comic cuts. 1890–1953. Became a children's paper c. 1914. Finally incorporated with Knock-out.

Illustrated chips. 1890–1953. Became a children's paper c. 1914. Finally incorporated with Film Fun.

Wonder 1892–3 Continued as Funny wonder 1893–1901; Wonder 1901–2; Jester and wonder 1902–12; Jester 1912–20; Jolly jester 1920–4; Jester 1924–40.

Pluck. 1894–1916.

Boys friend. 1895–1927.

Butterfly. 1904–40.

Puck. 1904–40. Became a children's paper c. 1914. Finally incorporated with Sunbeam.

The gem library. 1907–29. Continued as The gem 1929–39. Incorporated in Triumph.

Children's encyclopaedia. 1908–10. Continued as New children's encyclopaedia 1910–11; Children's magazine 1911–14; My children's magazine 1914–15; My magazine 1915–33.

The magnet library. 1908–29. Continued as The magnet 1929–40. Incorporated with Knock-out.

The scout. 1908–66.

Rainbow. 1914–56. Incorporated with Tiny tots, below.

Children's newspaper. 1919–1965.

The school friend. 1919–29. Continued as Schoolgirl 1929–40.

Tiger Tim's tales. 1919–20. Continued as Tiger Tim's weekly 1920–40.

Chicks own. 1920–57. Incorporated with Play-hour.

Film fun. 1920–62. Incorporated with Buster as Buster and film fun.

Adventure. 1921–61. Incorporated with Rover as Rover and adventure.

The guide. 1921 onwards.

Champion. 1922–55. Incorporated with Tiger.

Rover 1922–61.

Sunbeam. 1922–40. Incorporated with Tiny tots.

The merry-go-round. Oxford 1923–39.

Joy Street. [An annual]. Oxford 1923–37.

Triumph. 1924–40. Incorporated with Champion.

Playbox. 1925–55. Incorporated with Jack and Jill.

The schoolboy's own library. 1925–40.

Sunny stories for little folks. 1926–36. New series 1937–?

Joker. 1927–40. Incorporated with Chips.

Larks. 1927–40. Incorporated with Knock-out.

Tiny tots. 1927–59. Incorporated with Playhour.

Modern boy. 1928–39.

Skipper. 1930–41.

The hotspur. 1933–59. As The new hotspur 1959 onwards.

Jingles. 1934–40. Continued as Jingles and golden 1940–3; Jingles 1943–54. Incorporated with TV fun.

Tip top. 1934–54. Incorporated with TV fun.

Mine: a magazine for all who are young. 1935–6.

Mickey Mouse weekly. 1936–55. Continued under various titles to 1959.

Dandy comic. 1937–50. Continued as The dandy 1950 onwards.

Beano comic. 1938–50. Continued as The beano 1950 onwards.

Radio fun. 1938–61. Incorporated with Buster.

The knock-out comic. 1939–63. Incorporated with Valiant.

Magic comic. 1939–41.

Collins for boys and girls 1949–50. As Collins the magazine for boys and girls 1950–1. Continued under various titles and in production since 1958 as Elizabethan.

Eagle. 1950–69. Incorporated with Lion.

B. W. A.

4. DRAMA

I. GENERAL WORKS

(1) BIBLIOGRAPHIES

French, Samuel, Ltd. Descriptive catalogue of plays and dramatic works [later, Guide to selecting plays]. [1891?] onwards. Annually.

Adams, W. D. A dictionary of the drama. Vol 1 (A–G) 1904.

Green room book: or Who's who on the stage—an annual bibliographical record of the dramatic, musical and variety world. 1906–9. Continued as Who's who in the theatre: a bibliographical record of the contemporary stage, 1912 onwards.

Mulliken, C. A. Reading list on modern dramatists. Bull of Bibliography 5 1907.

The Stage year book. 1908–28; 1949 onwards.

'Clarence, Reginald' (H. J. Eldridge). The Stage cyclopaedia: a bibliography of plays. 1909. An alphabetical list of plays, with theatres and dates of first London productions.

The Stage guide. 1912, 1946 (rev).

Lower, H. E. and G. H. Milne. Dramatic books and plays published during 1912–16. Boston Mass 1913–17.

Foshay, F. E. Twentieth-century drama: pt 1, English drama; pt 2, Irish drama. Bull of Bibliography 8 1915.

Boston Public Library. Catalogue of the Allen A. Brown Collection of books relating to the stage. Boston 1919. A bibliography of English drama from 1890 to 1920. Lib Assoc Record 24 1922.

Logasa, H. and W. Ver Nooy. An index to one-act plays. 2 vols Boston 1924. Suppls 1–5 (1924–64), 1932–66.

Clark, B. H. A study of the modern drama: a handbook for the study and appreciation of the best plays, European, English and American, of the last half century. New York 1925, 1938 (rev and brought up to date).

Firkins, I. T. E. Index to plays, 1800–1926. New York 1927. Suppl New York 1935.

Fay, W. G. A short glossary of theatrical terms. 1930.

Gilder, R. A theatre library: a bibliography of 100 books relating to the theatre. New York 1932. For addns, see Booklist 33 1937. Continued by R. Stallings and P. Myers as A guide to theatre reading, New York 1949.

Gilder, R. and G. Freedley. Theatre collections in libraries and museums: an international handbook. New York 1936.

Library Association, County Libraries Section. Modern drama, 1900–38: a select list of plays published since 1900 and of works on dramatic theory and other related subjects. 1939. Suppl 1939–45, 1946.

Nathan, G. J. Encyclopaedia of the theatre. New York 1940.

Sobel, B. (ed). New theatre handbook and digest of plays. New York 1940, with frequent subsequent revisions.

Ottemiller, J. H. Index to plays in collections: an author and title index to plays appearing in collections published between 1900 and 1942. New York 1943, 1964 (4th edn, brought up to 1962).

Index to full length plays, 1895 to 1925 (1926 to 1944; 1944 to 1964). Ed R. G. Thomson [and N. O. Ireland] 3 vols Boston [1946]–65.

Revue d'histoire du théâtre. Bibliographie. 1948 onwards. Annually.

International Theatre Institute. World premieres. Paris 1949–64. Lists details of first productions of plays. Incorporated in World Theatre 1965 onwards.

Theatre world annual. 1949 onwards.

The year's work in the theatre. Ed J. C. Trewin 3 vols 1949–51.

Byrne, M. St C. (ed). British drama, history and criticism. 1950.

Downer, A. S. The British drama: a handbook and brief chronicle. New York [1950].

Loewenberg, A. The theatre of the British Isles excluding London: a bibliography. 1950.

The player's library: the catalogue of the Library of the British Drama League. 1950. Suppls 1–3, 1951–6. Lists contents of anthologies and collected volumes of plays.

Downs, H. (ed). Theatre and stage. 2 vols 1951 (2nd edn).

The Oxford companion to the theatre. Ed P. Hartnoll 1951, 1957 (rev), 1967 (rev).

Sherman, R. L. Actors and authors, with composers and managers who helped to make them famous: a chronological record and brief biography of theatrical celebrities from 1750 to 1950. Chicago 1951.

Baker, B. M. The theatre and allied arts: a guide to books dealing with the history, criticism and technic of the drama and theatre and related arts and crafts. New York 1952.

Granville, W. A dictionary of theatrical terms. 1952.

Library Association. County Libraries Group. Reader's guide to books on stagecraft and the theatre. 1952, 1965 (rev).

Nagler, A. M. A source book in theatrical history. Magnolia Mass 1952.

Play index 1949–52 (1953–60; 1961–7). 3 vols New York 1953–68.

Enciclopedia dello spettacolo. 10 vols and appendix. Rome 1954–68.

Clunes, A. British theatre history. Cambridge 1955 (National Book League Reader's Guides).

Kahn, A. M. C. The British theatre: a select [book] list. 1955.

—— (ed). Library Association. Reference and Special Libraries Section. Library resources in the Greater London area, no 4: theatre collections. 1955.

Trewin, J. C. Verse drama since 1800. Cambridge 1956 (National Book League Reader's Guides).

Encyclopédie du théâtre contemporain, 1850–1950. Ed G. Queant 2 vols Paris 1957–9.

Guide to the performing arts: index to articles and illustrations pertaining to the performing arts in American and foreign periodicals. New York 1957 onwards.

Tulane Drama Review. Books and theatre. 1958 onwards. Annually.

Rae, K. and R. Southern. International vocabulary of technical theatre terms in eight languages. Brussels 1959.

Deane, H. F. W. and Sons. Plays and their plots. [1960]. Details of Deane's Series of Plays.

International Federation of Library Associations. Performing arts collections: an international handbook. Paris 1960, 1967 (as Performing arts libraries and museums of the world).

Modern Drama. 1960 onwards. Contains an annual selective bibliography of works published in English.

Ryan, P. M. History of the modern theatre: a selective bibliography. Tucson 1960.

Bowman, W. P. and R. H. Ball. Theatre language: a dictionary of terms in English of the drama and stage from medieval to modern times. New York 1961.

Zamora, J. G. Historia del teatro contemporáneo. 4 vols Barcelona 1961–7.

Stratman, C. J. A bibliography of British dramatic periodicals, 1720–1960. New York 1962. Revision in progress.

Burton, E. J. The student's guide to British theatre and drama. 1963.

Santaniello, A. E. Theatre books in print. New York 1964, 1967 (rev).

Carlson, M. Modern drama: a selected bibliography of bibliographies. Modern Drama 8 1965.

Dramatic Index, 1909–49: a cumulation of the Dramatic Index, covering articles and illustrations concerning the stage and its players in the periodicals of America and England and including the dramatic books of the year. Ed F. W. Faxon [et al] 2 vols Boston 1965.

Melchinger, S. The concise encyclopedia of modern drama. 1966.

Sharp, H. S. and M. Z. Index to characters in the performing arts: pt 1, non-musical plays. 2 vols New York 1966–. In progress.

Taylor, J. R. Penguin dictionary of the theatre. 1966.

The Thames and Hudson Encyclopaedia of the arts. 1966.

Adelman, I. and R. Dworkin. Modern drama: a checklist of critical literature on 20th-century plays. Metuchen NJ 1967.

Cheshire, D. Theatre: history, criticism and reference. 1967.

New York Public Library. Catalog of the theatre and drama collections. Boston 1967.

Palmer, H. H. and A. J. Dyson. European drama criticism. Hamden Conn 1968.

Theatre documentation. 1968 onwards.

Litto, F. M. American dissertations on the drama and the theatre: a bibliography. Kent State Univ Press 1969.

Gassner, J. and E. Quinn (ed). The reader's encyclopedia of world drama. 1970.

Patterson, C. A. (ed). Plays in periodicals: an index to English language scripts in twentieth century journals. Boston [1971?].

N.H.

(2) THEATRICAL PERIODICALS

See also the lists of more specialized periodicals relating to the Theatre outside London, the Music Hall etc under the appropriate subheading below. These, and the main list here, are based on C. J. Stratman, A bibliography of British dramatic periodicals, New York 1962 (revision in progress). The many 'one-shot' theatrical periodicals which appeared during the period, and periodicals dealing with marginal subjects such as accommodation for actors, are not included below. For details of these, see Stratman's bibliography.

The era. Vols 1–103, 30 Sept 1838–21 Sept 1939. Weekly.

The sporting times ('The pink 'un'): a chronicle of racing, literature, art and the drama. Nos 1–3559, 11 Feb 1865–5 Dec 1931. Weekly

Era almanac. Vols 1–2, 1868–9, continued as The era almanac and annual, vols 3–41, 1870–1919. Ed F. Ledger.

Entr'acte. Nos 138–1974, 24 Feb 1872–26 April 1907. Started as London entr'acte, 1869. Weekly.

The illustrated sporting and dramatic news. Nos 1–3576, 28 Feb 1874–22 Jan 1943. Continued as Sport and country, 5 Feb 1943–16 Oct 1957. Continued as Farm and country, 30 Oct 1957 onwards. Weekly.

The stage directory. Nos 1–14, 1 Feb 1880–1 March 1881. Continued as The stage, 25 March 1881 onwards.

The music hall and theatre review. 16 Feb 1889–5 Sept 1912. Weekly.

The author: the organ of the Society of Authors. May 1890–July 1926. Continued as The author, playwright and composer, Oct 1926–Winter 1948. Continued as The author, Spring 1949 onwards. Began monthly and continued quarterly.

The dramatic world. Vol 1 no 1–vol 9 no 93, Nov 1894–Aug 1902. Continued as Society and dramatic world, 1 Sept 1902–May 1916. Monthly.

The dramatic times. Nos 1–13, 2 Feb–14 Sept 1895. New series nos 1–5, 12 April–5 July 1919. Irregular.

The musical world and dramatic observer. Vols 1–10, 6 Feb 1895–11 Feb 1904. Irregular.

Critique: a journal devoted to things theatrical and matters musical. 1 Oct 1898–July 1902. Monthly.

Beltaine: an occasional publication. (The Organ of the Irish Literary Theatre). Nos 1–3, May 1899–April 1900. Irregular. Ed W. B. Yeats.

Dramatic criticism. Vols 1–5, 1899–1905. No vols pbd 1901 or 1903. These vols contain articles by T. Grein, previously pbd in other periodicals.

The Stage Society annual report. Vols 1–21, 1899/1900–1920/1921.

London theatre entertainment and concert guide. Nos 1–16, 7 July 1900–23 Feb 1901. Continued as The London theatre, concert and fine art guide nos 7–623, 2 March 1901–19 Oct 1912. Weekly.

The playgoer. Vol 1 no 1–vol 5 no 28, Oct 1901–April 1904. Monthly. Ed Fred Dangerfield (S. J. Adair Fitzgerald).

Samhain, an occasional review: edited for the Irish Literary Theatre. Dublin. Nos 1–7, Oct 1901–Nov 1908. (Suspended, Dec 1905–Nov 1906). Irregular. Ed W. B. Yeats.

The tatler: an illustrated journal of society and the stage. Vol 1 no 1–vol 58 no 2053, 3 July 1901–30 Oct 1940. Continued as The tatler and bystander no 2054, 6 Nov 1940 onwards. Weekly.

The play pictorial: an illustrated monthly journal. Vol 1 no 1–vol 75 no 446, April 1902–Sept 1939. Monthly. In vol 5, no 29, are incorporated The play, The play souvenir, The stage souvenir.

International theatre. Paris and London. Nos 1–6, Jan–June 1903. Monthly.

The London stage annual. [1903] onwards. Annual. Ed Sidney Dark.

The programme: a weekly journal. Nos 1–47, 12 Oct 1903–29 Aug 1904. Weekly.

The stage society news. Nos 1–26, Nov 1903–May 1907.

To-day's London guide. Nos 1–320, 6 Feb 1904–1 April 1910. Weekly.

London record. Vol 1, nos 1–5, 29 June–27 July 1904. Weekly.

The play: an illustrated monthly. Vol 1, nos 1–6, 1904. Continued as The play pictorial, nos 1–6, 1905. Monthly. The issues are not dated.

The playhouse. Nos 1–20, 17 Dec 1904–27 April 1905. Weekly.

The theatre. Nos 1–3, 1 Nov 1904–1 Jan 1905. Monthly.

The actor illustrated: a monthly review of the stage. Vol 1, nos 1–13, Jan 1905–Jan 1906. Monthly. 1 Oct 1904 is a registration issue.

The circle: a monthly periodical of art, music and the drama. Vol 1, nos 1–15, March 1905–May 1906. Monthly. Ed R. Percy March–Dec 1905, Rose D'Evelyn Jan–May 1906.

The Millgate monthly. Manchester. Vol 1 no 1–vol 40 no 458, Oct 1905–May/June 1945. Continued as Playgoer and Millgate, vols 40–46, nos 459–503, July/Aug 1945–Jan/Feb 1951. Continued as Millgate and playgoer, new series vol 1 no 1–vol 2 no 14, April 1951–Spring 1953. Monthly and bimonthly.

The arrow. Dublin. (Pbd by the Abbey Theatre.) Nos 1–5, 20 Oct 1906–25 Aug 1909, Summer 1939. Suspended, 1909–38. Irregular.

The green room book: or, Who's who on the stage. Vols 1–4, 1906–9. Continued as Who's who in the theatre,

1912 onwards. Annual. Edns have appeared in 1912, 1914, 1916, 1922, 1925, 1930, 1933, 1936, 1939, 1947, 1952, 1957, 1961, 1967. The early edns of Who's who on the stage were ed John Parker, editor of The green room book, 1908–9.

The performer: official organ of the Variety Artistes' Federation. Vol 1 no 1–vol 105 no 2674, 29 March 1906–26 Sept 1957. Weekly. Special Christmas number, Performer annual, 1907–32

Stage and sport. Nos 1–8, 1 Jan–23 June 1906. Irregular. The variety theatre annual. Vol 1, 1906/7.

The performer annual. 1907–32. Special Christmas number.

The planet: a journal of social, literary, political, dramatic and topical interest. Nos 1–216, 2 March 1907–11 April 1911. Weekly.

The Robert Arthur theatres illustrated journal programme. Nos 1–21, 1907–8.

What's on. Vol 1 no 1–vol 47 no 598, 9 Feb 1907–13 Sept 1919. Weekly with exceptions: in 1919 only 3 issues.

The Stage year book, with which is included the stage provincial guide. Vols 1–21, 1908–28; 1949 onwards. Annual. Ed Lionel Carson.

The prompter. Vol 1, nos 1–2, Dec 1909–Jan 1910. Continued as The prompter: the organ of the amateur stage, vol 1, nos 3–9, Feb–Sept 1910. Continued as The prompter: the official organ of the Dramatic Clubs' Association, vol 1, nos 10–12, Oct–Dec 1910. Continued as The prompter: the organ of the amateur stage, vol 2, nos 1–2, Jan–Feb 1911. Monthly. (Nos 1–14). Ed F. Wood Oct 1910–Feb 1911.

The theatre. Vol 1, nos 1–6, 1909. Continued as The playgoer and society illustrated. New series vol 1 no 1–vol 9 no 51, 1–9 Oct/Nov 1909–14 Jan 1914. Monthly. Ed C. Young.

Lotinga's weekly: an illustrated journal of sports and drama. Nos 1–227, 12 March 1910–18 July 1914. Weekly. Including registration issues dated, 29 Aug 1914–17 Aug 1918.

The Thalia diary and directory of concert parties and entertainers. [Vols 1–6], 1910–15. Annual.

The weekly playgoer. Nos 1–26, 22 March–13 Sept 1911. Weekly.

The independent theatre goer. Nos 1–6, 1 Nov 1912–April 1913. Monthly. Conducted by J. T. Grein and Herman Klein.

The Stage guide. 1912. Ed L. Carson; rev edn compiled by A. W. Tolmie 1946.

Theatreland. Vol 1, nos 1–12, 25 Sept 1912–12 March 1913. Biweekly.

The blue review: literature, drama, art, music. Vol 1 nos 1–3, May–July 1913. Monthly. Supersedes Rhythm: art, music, literature. Ed J. Middleton Murry.

The 'Iris' guide to London's amusements. Nos 1–55, 4 Oct 1913–Oct 1915. Weekly, biweekly, monthly.

The London program. A daily index of forthcoming events and fixtures of general interest in the metropolis. Nos 1–16, 22 Nov 1913–13 March 1914. Continued as The London program: a weekly index of all forthcoming events and fixtures of general interest in the metropolis, nos 17–21, 20 March–18 April 1914. Continued as The London program, The weekly herald, etc, nos 22–30, 25 April–20 June 1914. Weekly.

Poetry and drama. Vol 1 no 1–vol 2 no 8, March 1913–Dec 1914. Quarterly. Superseded by Chapbook July 1914. Ed H. Monro.

Guide to selecting plays. 1914–65. Annual. Continued as The complete guide to selecting plays, 1966/7 onwards. Some years have supplementary sections added.

The London Shakespeare League journal. Vol 1 nos 1–8, Oct 1914–May 1915. Continued as Shakespeare League journal, vol 1 no 9–vol 8 no 6, June 1915–Oct 1922. Continued as The Shakespeare journal, vol 8 no 7–vol 12 no 3, Nov 1922–Christmas 1926. Monthly (irregular. Some years Aug–Sept form one issue; some years the August issue is omitted). Ed S. D. Headlam Nov 1917–June 1922, Herbert Farjeon July 1922–July/Aug 1925, Lionel Millard Nov–Christmas 1925.

The theatre, music hall and cinema blue book for 1917: a list of public amusement companies with full financial particulars of interest to investors. Vol 1, 1917. Continued as The theatre, music hall and cinema companies' blue book, vols 2–13, 1918–29/30. Annual.

Poetry: a magazine of new lyrics. Vol 1 no 1–vol 8 no 74, 1917(?)–April/May(?) 1925. Monthly with a few exceptions. Continued as Poetry and the play, vol 8 no 75–vol 13 no 90, 1925–31. Monthly irregular; then quarterly irregular. Organ of the Poetry League, July 1926–Winter 1930. Title and place of pbn vary.

Arts gazette: drama, music, art, literature. No 1, 1 Feb 1919. New series nos 1–41, 18 March 1922–24 Feb 1923. Weekly. Ed J. T. Grein and L. Dunton Green.

Drama: a magazine of the theatre and allied arts. (Organ of British Drama League). Nos 1–6, July 1919–July 1920. Bimonthly. Continued as Drama: the journal of the British Drama League. New series vol 1 no 1–vol 17 no 10, Nov 1920–July/Sept 1939. Continued as Drama: the quarterly theatre review. Summer 1946 onwards. Quarterly. From Oct 1939–Feb 1946 see War-time drama.

The L.A.G.: or London amusement guide: with complete index of entertainments, sports etc. Vol 1, no 1–vol 2, no 8. Numbering begins with vol 1, no 5, [5 Sept 1919] May 1919–Aug 1920. Continued as London (official) amusement guide. Vol 2 no 9–vol 4 no 4, Sept 1920–March 1922. Monthly. Subtitle varies.

Theatre-craft: a book of the new spirit in the theatre. Nos 1–5, 1919?–1921? Quarterly. Merged into English review. Issues are not dated.

The magazine programme: always enjoyed—never destroyed. Nos 1–1273, 1924–10 July 1939. Weekly, irregular. Plays performed at the London theatres.

The theatre world and illustrated stage review. Vol 1 no 1–vol 4 no 20, Feb 1925–Sept 1926. Monthly. Absorbed Theatre and film illustrated. Ed S. Bickers to no 6, then 'S.T.H.'.

The ball room: theatre and dancing news. Vol 1 nos 1–12, Jan–Dec 1926. Monthly. Ed W. Edmund Querry.

The Festival Theatre review. Cambridge. Vol 1 no 1–vol 3 no 63, Nov 1926–June 1929. Continued as The Festival Theatre programme, vol 1 no 1–vol 2 no 7, Oct 1929–30. Continued as Festival Theatre review, vol 4 no 64–vol 6 no 87, 1930–1. Continued as Festival Theatre programme, nos 2–8. No 1 is really vol 6, no 87, of above, Jan–June 1932. Continued as Festival-Gate review, vol 6 nos 87 (sic)–94, Oct–Dec 1932. Continued as Festival review, vol 6, nos 95–109, 16 Jan–5 June 1933. Continued as Festival Theatre (new lease) programme, nos 1–49, Oct 1933–June 1935. Monthly. Suppl, The Festival Theatre review'd, 20 May 1927.

'The spotlight' casting directory for stage and screen. Nos 1–90, Aug 1927–July 1952. Quarterly, nos 1–61, Aug 1927–Sept 1942. 3 times a year nos 62–89, 1942–51. Beginning with no 71, Jan 1946, each number has 2 pts. Continued as 'The spotlight' casting directory for stage, screen, radio and television, nos 91–109, Jan 1953–Spring 1962. Beginning with no 102, Autumn 1958, each number has 4 pts. Continued as Spotlight, no 110, Autumn 1962 onwards. Twice a year beginning with no 89 Jan 1952.

The dancer. (Official journal of the British Ballet Organization). Vol 1 no 1–vol 10 no 12, [Jan] 1928–Dec 1937. Monthly. Ed Louisa Kay Espinosa.

Plays and players. Vol 1 no 1–vol 3 no 24, 19 Oct 1929–19 Sept 1933. Monthly.

The week-end review of politics, books, the theatre, art and music. Vol 1 no 1–vol 8 no 200, 15 March 1930–6 Jan 1934. Weekly. Incorporated with New statesman.

Who's who in dancing. 1932. Ed A. Haskell and P. J. S. Richardson.

Poetry quarterly (and dramatic review). Vol 1 nos 1–6, Spring 1933–Spring 1934. Title varies.

The theatre illustrated quarterly: a quarterly illustrated guide and souvenir of the theatre. Vol 1 no 1–vol 3 no 12, Spring 1933–Winter 1935.

The modern dance. Vol 1 no 1–vol 4 no 3, 1934–Dec 1937. Continued as The modern dance and the dancer, vol 4 no 4–vol 31 no 8, Jan 1938–June 1965. Monthly.

Friendship. Kettering. Vol 1 no 1–vol 2 no 15, Aug 1937–Oct 1938. Monthly. Ed Mollie Moncrieff Hart Dec 1937–Oct 1938.

The theatre. Nos 1–4, 26 May–16 July 1937. Biweekly.

Weekly sporting review. Nos 1–145, 350–629, 20 March 1937–1 June 1940; 23 Feb 1946–14 July 1951. Continued as Show business and the weekly sporting review, nos 630–741, 21 July 1951–4 Sept 1953. Continued as Weekly sporting review and show business, nos 742–1094, 11 Sept 1953–10 June 1960. Also Christmas and New Year edns, 1948–9–1952–3. Annual.

Theatrecraft. Nos 1–32, Dec 1938–[1942]. (The last dated number is Oct/Nov 1941, no 31). Monthly: nos 1–28, Dec 1938–March 1941. Quarterly: nos 29–32, June 1941–[2]. No 32 really incorporates the Newsletter. Ed J. Bourne.

New theatre: a magazine devoted to the interests of the modern theatre and associated arts. Vol 1 nos 1–2, Aug–Sept 1939. Monthly. Suspended publication, Sept 1939–Dec 1945. Then continued vols 2–5, nos 1–44, Jan 1946–July 1949.

War-time drama: an occasional bulletin from the British Drama League. Nos 1–39, Oct 1939–Feb 1946. Irregular. Issued during the temporary suspension, due to the war, of Drama: a monthly record of the theatre in town and country at home and abroad. The subtitle varies slightly. Nos 35–36, May–July 1945, the title is, VE-time drama; No 37, Oct 1945, the title is, VJ-time drama; Nos 38–39, Nov 1945–Feb 1946, the title is, Interim drama.

Theatre notebook: a quarterly of notes and research. Vol 1, 1945 onwards. Quarterly. Includes The bulletin of the Society for Theatre Research.

Behind the scenes. Nos 1–11, Dec 1946–Dec 1947. Monthly.

British theatre. 1946. Annual.

Christian drama. (Religious Drama Society of Great Britain). Published for the Religious Drama Society by the Society for Promoting Christian Knowledge. Vol 1 no 1–vol 5 no 1, Nov 1946–Spring 1963. 3 issues a year.

The lantern. Vol 1 nos 1–8, Aug 1946–March 1947. Continued as The lantern: stage, screen, radio, the arts, nos 9–[13] June/July–Nov 1947. Monthly.

The masque, a theatre notebook. Nos 1–9, Dec 1946–9. Irregular. Ed Lionel Carter.

Theatre newsletter. Vol 1 no 1–vol 6 no 139, 15 July 1946–19 Jan 1952. Continued as Theatre, vol 6 no 140–vol 7 no 166, 2 Feb 1952–14 Feb 1953. Ed Ossia Trilling 1946–50, Ray Walker 1951–3. Biweekly, slightly irregular.

Theatre today. Nos 1–7, March 1946–Jan 1949. Continued as Film and theatre today, no 8, Aug 1949. Irregular. Ed M. Slater.

The ballet annual: a record and year book of the ballet. Vols 1–18, 1947–64. Annual. Ed A. L. Haskell vols 1–14, A. L. Haskell, Mary Clarke vols 15–18.

Exits and entrances. Nos 1–6, Jan 1947–Jan 1950. Organ of the Durham County Drama Association. Irregular.

Stage and screen miscellany. Vol 1 no 1, Spring 1947. Continued as Stage and screen, [no 2], Summer 1947. Quarterly. Ed P. Noble.

Dobson's theatre year book. Vol 1, 1948–9. Annual. Ed J. Andrews and Ossia Trilling.

Theatre digest. Nos 1–8, 1948–50. The issues are not dated. Nos 2–6 are published quarterly; no 8 is published bimonthly. Ed A. Merryn and G. K. Jeanette nos 1–3, G. K. Jeanette nos 4–8.

The year's work in the theatre. Vols 1–3, 1948–9–1950–1. Annual. Ed J. C. Trewin.

Dance and dancers. Vol 1 no 1 – vol 13 no 12, Jan 1950–Dec 1962. Ed P. Williams.

Opera. Feb 1950 onwards.

Spotlight: a bulletin on the activities of the Hall Green Little Theatre. Birmingham. Nos 1–5, 1950–4. Irregular.

Theatre guild review. Birmingham, Sept 1950 onwards. Monthly. Nos 1–219 (Nov 1965) ed Jack Bishop.

C. J. S. assisted by P. D.

(3) COLLECTIONS OF PLAYS

Collections of plays for school or other amateur production are omitted, as are other popular reprint collections. The contents of anthologies are listed in J. H. Ottemiller, Index to plays in collections (see Bibliographies, above); and in The player's library: the catalogue of the library of the British Drama League (ibid) which also lists contents of collected vols of an author's plays. Guides to play selection were pbd by Samuel French Ltd (annually); by R. Stacey (1951/2–); and by Deane & Co (1960).

Plays of today and tomorrow. 9 vols 1909–13.

Moses, M. J. (ed). Representative British dramas, Victorian and modern. Boston 1918, 1931 (rev).

Contemporary British dramatists [series]. 1923–33[?].

Dickinson, T H. and J. R. Crawford (ed). Contemporary plays. Boston [c. 1925].

Plays of today. 3 vols 1925–30.

Marriott, J. W. (ed). One-act plays of today, 1st[–6th] series 1927–34.

— [et al]. The best one-act plays of 1931 [and later years]. 1932 onwards.

Marriott, J. W. (ed). Great modern British plays. 1932.

Pence, R. W. (ed). Dramas by present-day writers. New York [c. 1927].

Bishop, G. W. (ed). Year Book Press Series of plays. [1929]–1946.

[Bishop, G. W. ed]—The 'Embassy' series of plays. 1935 onwards.

Canfield, C. (ed). Plays of the Irish renaissance, 1880–1930. New York 1929.

— Plays of changing Ireland. New York 1936.

Cordell, R. A. (ed). Representative modern plays. New York 1929.

Famous plays of today [and of 1931–9]. 14 vols 1929–39.

Tucker, S. M. (ed). Twenty-five modern plays. New York 1931, rev A. S. Downer 1948, 1953 (rev).

Bourne, J., W. Armstrong [et al] (ed). 8 new one-act plays of 1933[–1939]. 1st[–7th] series 1933–9.

Chandler, F. W. and R. A. Cordell (ed). Twentieth-century plays, British. New York 1934, 1939 (rev), 1941 (rev and enlarged).

My best play: an anthology of plays chosen by their own authors. 1934.

Reid, J. M. (ed). Scottish one-act plays. Edinburgh 1935.

Drinkwater, J. (ed). A book of one-act plays. [1936].

Ward, R. H. (ed). Ten peace plays. [1938].

Anderson, G. K. and E. L. Walton (ed). This generation: a selection of British and American literature from 1914 to the present. Chicago [1939], [1949] (rev).

Five great modern Irish plays. Foreword by G. J. Nathan, New York 1941.

Hatcher, H. H. (ed). Modern British dramas New York 1941.

Cerf, B. A. and V. H. Cartmell (ed). Sixteen famous British plays. New York [1942].

Ferguson, J. A. (ed). Modern one-act plays. 1942 (Penguin).

Powell, J. and K. Bainbridge (ed). Embassy successes. 3 vols 1946–8.

Durham, W. H. and J. W. Dodds (ed). British and American plays, 1830–1945. New York 1947.

Thompson, E. J. (ed). The drama library. 1949 onwards.

Trewin, J. C. (ed). Plays of the year, 1948–9 [etc]. 1949 onwards.

Warnock, R. (ed). Representative modern plays, British. Chicago [1953].

Modern plays. Introd by J. Hadfield 1956.

Browne, E. M. (ed). Four modern verse plays. 1957 (Penguin).

— Three Irish plays. 1959 (Penguin).

Granada TV network. Manchester plays: television adaptations of six plays recalling the Horniman period at the Gaiety Theatre, Manchester. 1962.

Weales, G. (ed). Edwardian plays. New York [1962].

Armstrong, W. A. (ed). Classic Irish drama. 1964 (Penguin).

Charlton, J. M. (ed). Pan book of one-act plays. 1965.

— Plays of the thirties. 2 vols 1966–7.

Hogan, R. (ed). Seven Irish plays, 1946–64. Minneapolis 1967.

Rowell, G. (ed). Late Victorian plays, 1890–1914. 1968 (WC).

N.H.

(4) HISTORIES AND STUDIES

General

Archer, W. See his regular contributions to World 1900–6; Daily Chron 1900–10; Morning Leader 1901–12; Tribune 1906–8; Nation (London) 1908–10; Nation (New York) 1914–18.

— Playmaking: a manual of craftsmanship. 1912, New York 1960 (introd by J. Gassner).

— The old drama and the new. 1923. See TLS 7 June 1923; E. E. Stoll, MLR 20 1925.

Grein, J. T. Dramatic criticism. Vol 2, Premières of the year, 1900; vol 3, 1900–1, 1902; vol 4, 1902–3, 1904; vol 5, 1903, 1905.

— The world of the theatre: impressions and memoirs, March 1920–1. 1921.

— The new world of the theatre 1923–4. Preface by G. K. Chesterton 1924.

See also his regular contributions to Illustr London News 1927–35.

Walkley, A. B. See his regular contributions to Times 1900–26.

— Dramatic criticism: three lectures delivered at the Royal Institution. 1903.

— Drama and life. 1907.

— Theatre and the war. Cornhill 47 1919.

— Drama with a mission. Forum 66 1921.

— Pastiche and prejudice. 1921.

— More prejudice. 1923.

— Still more prejudice. 1925.

Annual Register 1901–. Includes section on the theatre.

Hooper, W. E. The stage in the year 1900. 1901.

Moore, T. S. The renovation of the theatre. Monthly Rev 7 1902.

— W. B. Yeats and T. Sturge Moore: their correspondence 1901–37, ed U. Bridge. 1953.

Speer, J. C. The ethical outlook of the current drama. Toronto 1902.

Bourdon, G. Les théâtres anglais. Paris 1903.

Platt, A. The stage in 1902. 1903.

Symons, A. Plays, acting and music. 1903.

Williamson, D. The state of the stage. 1903.

Jones, H. A. The foundations of a national drama. 1904, 1913 (rev).

— Talks with playgoers. 1913.

— Theatre of ideas. 1914.

— The urgent question of the British theatre. Living Age 301 1919.

— Plays with a purpose. Living Age 320 1924.

Kerr, A. Das neue Drama. Berlin 1905.

Borsa, M. Il teatro inglese contemporaneo. Milan 1906; tr (as The English stage of today) 1908.

Hale, E. E. Dramatists of today. 1906.

Huneker, J. Iconoclasts: a book of dramatists. 1906.

Craig, G. Some evil tendencies of the modern theatre. Mask 1 1908.

— Tolerance in criticism. Mask 1 1909.

— On the art of the theatre. 1911.

— The theatre advancing. 1921.

Dunn, S. G. The revival of drama. Westminster Rev 171 1909.

Gwynn, S. Poetry and the stage. Fortnightly Rev 85 1909.

Sharp, E. F. A short history of the English stage from its beginnings to the summer of the year 1908. 1909.

Eaton, W. P. Great acting and the modern drama. Scribner's 47 1910.

Spence, E. F. Our stage and its critics. 1910.

Carric, A. The English stage in 1911. Mask 3 1911.

Creizenach, A. Geschichte des neueren Dramas. Halle 1911.

Dukes, A. Modern dramatists. 1911.

— The youngest drama: studies of fifty dramatists. 1923.

— Der neue Geist im englischen Theater. Theater der Welt 1 1937.

— The scene is changed. 1942.

See also his regular contributions to Theatre Arts Monthly 1924–45.

Henderson, A. The new drama in England. Forum 45 1911.

— European dramatists. Cincinnati 1913 (includes Shaw and Granville Barker), New York 1926 (adds Galsworthy).

— The changing drama. 1914, New York 1919 (rev).

— The drama after the war. South Atlantic Quart 19 1920.

Irving, L. The plight of the serious drama. Fortnightly Rev 89 1911.

Montague, C. E. Dramatic values. 1911, New York 1925 (rev).

Norton, C. Modern drama and opera. Boston 1911.

Palmer, J. Aristotle and the modern drama. Saturday Rev 28 Oct 1911.

— The future of the theatre. 1913. See S. Grundy, The play of the future by a playwright of the past: a glance at The future of the theatre by J. Palmer, 1914.

— If I were still a dramatic critic. Nineteenth Century 101 1927.

— Studies in the contemporary theatre. 1927.

Plowman, M. Hopes and fears for modern drama. Academy 80 1911.

Russell, E. R. The theatre and things said about it. Liverpool 1911.

Semar, J. To save the theatre in England. Mask 4 1911.

The stage of the future. Academy 80 1911.

Symposium on the position of the theatre in England. Mask 4 1911.

Woman in modern drama. Review of Reviews 43 1911.

Abercrombie, L. The function of poetry in drama. Poetry Rev 1 1912.

Barley, J. W. The morality motive in contemporary English drama. Mexico, Missouri 1912.

Carter, H. The new spirit in drama and art. 1912.

— The new spirit in the European theatre 1914–24: a comparative study of the changes effected by the war and revolution. 1925.

Dickinson, T. H. Drama of intellectualism. Drama (Chicago) no 7 1912.

— Insurgent theatre. New York 1917.

—— The contemporary drama of England. Boston 1917, 1931 (rev).

—— An outline of contemporary drama. Boston 1927.

—— et al. The theatre in a changing Europe. 1938.

English drama at the beginning of the twentieth century. Saturday Rev 20 Jan 1912.

Figgis, D. The vitality of the drama. In his Studies and appreciations, 1912.

'Flavius Secundus'. Antidrama: a diatribe. Westminster Rev 177 1912.

Galsworthy, J. Some platitudes concerning drama. In his Inn of tranquillity, 1912.

—— The new spirit in the drama. Living Age 277 1913.

Gibson, W. W. Some thoughts on the future of poetic drama. Poetry Rev 1 1912.

Grau, R. The stage in the twentieth century. New York 1912.

Ivanof, V. The theatre of the future. Eng Rev 10 1912 (tr S. Graham).

Macfall, H. The puritan and the theatre. Eng Rev 10 1912.

McNeill, W. E. Shakespeare and the modern drama. Queen's Quart 19 1912.

Oliver, R. E. The English stage: its origin and modern developments. 1912.

Yeats, W. B. The cutting of an agate. New York 1912, London 1919 (enlarged); rptd in his Essays and introductions, 1961.

—— Per amica silentia lunae. 1918; rptd in his Mythologies, 1962.

—— The trembling of the veil. 1922 (priv ptd); rptd in The autobiography of W. B. Yeats, New York 1938.

—— Essays. 1924.

—— Wheels and butterflies. 1934 (plays with introds). Introds rptd in his Explorations, 1962.

—— Dramatis personae. Dundrum 1935; rptd in The autobiography of W. B. Yeats, New York 1938.

—— Essays 1931 to 1936. Dundrum 1937.

—— The autobiography of W. B. Yeats. New York 1938.

—— Florence Farr, Bernard Shaw and W. B. Yeats. Ed C. Bax, Dundrum 1941.

—— W. B. Yeats and T. Sturge Moore: their correspondence 1901–37. Ed U. Bridge 1953.

—— Letters of W. B. Yeats. Ed A. Wade 1954.

—— Essays and introductions. 1961. Includes The cutting of an agate, later essays and introds.

Andrews, C. The drama today. 1913.

Cannan, G. The joy of the theatre. 1913.

—— The decline and fall of the English theatre. Poetry & Drama 8 1914.

—— The English theatre during and after the war. Theatre Arts Monthly 4 1920.

—— Hope for the drama. Sewanee Rev 30 1922.

—— All eyes on the threatre 1924. Sewanee Rev 32 1924.

Courtney, W. L. Realistic drama. Fortnightly Rev 93 1913; rptd in his Old saws and modern instances, 1918.

Howe, P. P. Dramatic portraits. 1913.

Hunt, E. R. The play of today: studies in play structure for the student and theatre-goer. 1913.

Poel, W. Poetry in drama. Contemporary Rev 104 1913.

—— Trade in drama. Contemporary Rev 106 1914.

—— What is wrong with the stage: some notes on the English theatre from the earliest times to the present day. 1920.

—— Poetry and drama. Mask 12 1927.

Browne, M. New rhythmic drama. Drama (Chicago) 16 1914.

Chandler, F. W. Aspects of modern drama. 1914.

Cheney, S. W. The new movement in the theatre. New York 1914.

Forbes-Robertson, J. The theatre of yesterday, today and tomorrow. Century 87 1914.

Goldman, E. The social significance of the modern drama. 1914.

Hamilton, C. M. Studies in stagecraft. New York 1914.

—— Problems of the playwright. New York 1917.

—— Conversations on contemporary drama. New York 1924.

Kilian, E. Aus der Praxis der modernen Dramaturgie. Munich 1914.

Sell, H. B. What is it all about? A sketch of the new movement in the theatre. New York 1914.

Clark, B. H. The British and American drama of today. New York 1915.

—— A study of the modern drama. New York 1925, 1938 (rev).

—— Contemporary English dramatists. Eng Jnl 15 1926.

—— The modern drama. Chicago 1927.

—— A new note in the crook play. Drama 18 1928.

—— and G. Freedley. A history of modern drama. New York 1947.

Leatham, J. The blight of Ibsenism: an analysis of the first of the immoralists. Cottingham 1915.

Lewisohn, L. The renaissance of the English drama. In his Modern drama: an essay in interpretation, New York 1915.

—— The British drama of today. Nation (New York) 5 July 1922.

—— The drama and the stage. New York 1922.

Moderwell, H. K. Modern English dramatists. In his The theatre of today, New York 1915.

Streatfield, G. S. The modern society play. 1915.

Jenkins, W. E. Before and after Ibsen. Chicago 1916.

Neustadtl, V. Ethische Prinzipien in Dramen der Neuzeit. New York 1916.

Pound, E. Mr James Joyce and the modern stage. Drama (Chicago) 21 1916.

Agate, J. Buzz! buzz! Essays of the theatre. 1918.

—— At half-past eight: essays of the theatre 1921–2. 1923.

—— The contemporary theatre, 1923. 1924.

—— The contemporary theatre, 1924. Introd by N. Coward. 1925.

—— The contemporary theatre, 1925. 1926.

—— The contemporary theatre, 1926. Introd by A. Bennett. 1927.

—— [Selected essays]. 1926. (Essays of today and yesterday).

—— A short view of the English stage 1900–26. 1926.

—— Playgoing: an essay. 1927.

—— The contemporary theatre, 1924–7. 4 vols 1928.

—— My theatre talks. 1933.

—— First nights. 1934.

—— More first nights. 1937.

—— The amazing theatre. 1939.

—— The contemporary theatre, 1944–5. 1946.

—— Those were the nights: an anthology of criticism, 1880–1906. Ed Agate 1947.

See also his regular contributions to Sunday Times 1923–47.

Phelps, W. L. The twentieth-century theatre: observations on the contemporary English and American stage. New York 1918.

—— Essays on modern dramatists. New York 1921.

Brown, I. See his regular contributions to Manchester Guardian 1919–35, Saturday Rev 1923–30, Observer 1929–54, Illustr London News 1935–40.

—— The dramatist in danger. In Theatre: essays on the arts of the theatre, ed E. J. R. Isaacs, Boston 1927.

—— Now on view. 1929.

—— The spirit of the age in drama. Fortnightly Rev 128 1930.

—— The critical faculty. In Theatre and stage, ed H. Downs 1934.

—— Serious theatre and its critics. New Statesman 21 Jan 1939.

—— Dramatic criticism—is it possible? Theatre Arts Monthly 24 1940; rptd in Theatre Arts anthology, New York 1950.

—— The difficulties of dramatic criticism. Essays by Divers Hands 19 1942.

—— Can there be a revival of poetic drama in the modern theatre? Essays by Divers Hands 23 1947.

—— Theatre 1954–5. 1955.

—— Theatre 1955–6. 1956.

—— What is a play? 1964.

Eliot, T. S. 'Rhetoric' and poetic drama. 1919; rptd in his Selected essays, 1933.

—— The possibility of a poetic drama. In his Sacred wood, 1920.

—— A dialogue on poetic drama. 1928. Introd to Dryden's Of dramatick poesie; rptd (as A dialogue on dramatic poetry) in his Selected essays, 1933.

—— Audiences, producers, plays, poets. New Verse 18 1935.

—— Five points on dramatic writing: a letter to Ezra Pound. Townsman 1 1938; rptd in J. Isaacs, An assessment of twentieth-century literature, 1951.

—— The aims of poetic drama: presidential address to the Poets' Theatre Guild. 1949; rptd in his Selected essays, 1951.

—— The aims of poetic drama. Adam International Rev 200 1949 (substantially different from above).

—— Poetry and drama. 1951; rptd with an additional note in his On poetry and poets, 1957.

—— The three voices of poetry. 1953; rptd in his On poetry and poets, 1957.

—— Religious drama: mediaeval and modern. New York 1954. An address delivered in 1937.

Franc, M. A. Ibsen in England. 1919.

Gheusi, P. B. Guerre et théâtre 1914–18. Nancy 1919.

Morrison, G. E. The reconstruction of the theatre. 1919.

Turner, W. J. The movement for better drama. London Mercury Nov 1919.

—— The poetic drama. London Mercury Dec 1919.

Darlington, W. A. *See* his regular contributions to Daily Telegraph 1920–68, New York Times 1939–60.

—— Through the fourth wall. 1922.

—— Literature in the theatre, and other essays. 1925.

—— Accent on age. Theatre Arts Monthly 21 1937.

—— The actor and his audience. 1949.

—— Six thousand and one nights: forty years a critic. 1960.

Hughes, G. Concerning a theatre of the people. Drama 11 1920.

—— The modern drama. Scripps College Papers 11 1930.

Jameson, S. Modern drama in Europe. 1920.

Ross, C. A note on the lack of theatricality in modern realistic drama. Drama 10 1920.

Arns, K. Englische Theatermisstände und Reformpläne. Zeitschrift für Französischen und Englischen Unterricht 20 1921.

—— Neues zur englischen Theaterreform. Ibid 22 1923.

—— Reformen und Reformpläne im englischen Theaterwesen. Ibid 24 1926.

—— Moderne englische Dramaturgie und Theaterkritik. Ibid 25 1926.

Hampden, W. The changing drama. Drama 11 1921.

Knapp, J. L. Symbolistic drama of today. Poet Lore 32 1921.

MacGowan, K. The theatre of tomorrow. [1921].

Bakshy, A. The theatre unbound. Eng Rev 34 1922.

Constance, J. M. Some tendencies of the English-speaking drama. Poet Lore 33 1922.

Drew, E. A. The prospects for tragic drama. Freeman 5 1922.

—— The moderns. In her Discovering drama, 1937.

Ervine, St J. The realistic test in drama. Yale Rev 11 1922.

—— Daring new plays in London. Theatre 43 1926.

—— The drama in the doldrums. Shakespeare Rev 1 1928.

—— How to write a play. 1928.

—— Exit, the theatre! Saturday Rev of Lit 23 Feb 1929.

—— The theatre in my time. 1933.

—— The wars and the drama. Fortnightly Rev 148 1940.

Granville-Barker, H. The exemplary theatre. 1922.

—— On dramatic method: being the Clark lectures for 1930. 1931.

—— The study of drama. Cambridge 1934. Lecture.

—— On poetry in drama. 1937 (Romanes lecture).

—— The use of the drama. Princeton 1945.

Ould, H. The contemporary theatre. Eng Rev 34, 35 1922.

—— Das englische Theater seit dem Kriege. Die Literatur 27 1925.

—— The art of the play. 1938.

Shipp, H. The contemporary theatre. Eng Rev 34 1922.

—— Present-day tendencies. Eng Rev 40 1925.

—— British theatre: should it make a pretence of reality? Eng Rev 45 1927.

—— The theatre today. Nat Rev 97 1931.

Young, S. Poetic drama. New Republic 30 1922.

—— Realism and the theatre. Yale Rev 16 1926.

Barnes, J. H. The drama of today. Nineteenth Century 93 1923.

Benavente, J. The playwright's mind. Yale Rev 13 1923.

Boynton, P. H. The drama. Eng Jnl 12 1923.

Farjeon, H. An apology for 'bad' plays. Saturday Rev 27 Oct 1923.

Glover, H. Drama and mankind: a vindication and a challenge. 1923.

McBrien, P. Ibsenism. Catholic World 118 1923.

Milne, A. A. Dramatic art and craft. Nation-Athenaeum 27 Oct 1923.

Morris, L. The changing art of the modern playwright. Lit Digest International Book Rev 1 1923.

What ails the theatre? Blackwood's Mag 213 1923.

Wilde, P. The craftsmanship of the one-act play. Boston 1923.

Beerbohm, M. Around theatres, 1898–1910. 2 vols 1924; rptd in 1 vol 1953.

—— Mainly on the air. 1946.

—— More theatres. 1898–1903. 1969.

—— Last theatres. 1970.

Capek, K. The English theatre. Saturday Rev 2 Aug 1924.

Carroll, S. W. Some dramatic opinions. 1924.

Faulkner, J. W. H. The theatre: ideas and ideals. 1924.

Jourdain, E. F. The drama in Europe in theory and practice. 1924.

Monkhouse, A. The words and the play. E & S 11 1924.

Morgan, A. E. Tendencies of modern English drama. 1924.

Rothe, H. Das moderne englische Theater. Das Tagebuch 5 1924.

Sutton, G. Some contemporary dramatists. 1924.

Vernon, F. The twentieth-century theatre. Introd by J. Drinkwater 1924.

Balmforth, R. The ethical and religious value of the drama. 1925.

—— The problem play and its influence on modern thought and life. New York 1928.

Bonner, G. H. The present state of the drama. Nineteenth Century 97 1925.

Disher, W. The influence of the nursery on the stage. Fortnightly Rev 117 1925.

Dobrée, B. Timotheus: or, The future of the theatre. 1925.

—— Histriophone: a dialogue on dramatic diction. 1925.

—— Plays ancient and modern. Nation (New York) 24 July 1926.

—— The idea of drama. Nation-Athenaeum 5 Feb 1927.

—— Contemporary English drama. Queen's Quart 41 1934.

Drury, F. K. W. Viewpoints in modern drama. Chicago 1925.

Greenwood, G. A. 'This England' on the contemporary stage: the play as a mirror of modern life. World Today 45 1925.

Hughes, R. New trends in the theatre. Forum 73 1925.

Moore, J. B. The comic and the realistic in English drama. Chicago 1925.

Nicoll, A. In his British drama, 1925, 1932 (rev), 1947 (rev), 1962 (rev).

—— The development of the theatre: a study of theatrical art from the beginnings to the present day. 1927, 1937 (rev), 1958 (rev), 1966 (rev).

—— The theory of drama. 1930.

—— In his World drama: from Aeschylus to Anouilh, 1949.

Cunliffe, J. W. Modern English playwrights: a short history of English drama from 1825. New York 1927.

Drinkwater, J. The gentle art of theatre-going. 1927, Boston and New York 1927 (as The art of theatre-going).

Nathan, G. J. The English theatre. Amer Mercury 12 1927.

—— The English stage criticized by G. J. Nathan. Literary Digest 25 July 1931.

—— Testament of a critic. New York 1931.

Newton, C. Crime and the drama: or dark deeds dramatized. 1927.

Rubinstein, H. F. What isn't wrong with the drama. 1927.

Van Druten, J. The sex play. Theatre Arts Monthly 11 1927.

—— Small souls and great plays. Ibid.

Dunsany, Lord. Good plays and bad—why? Theatre 48 1928.

—— Drama. 1945 (Donnellan lectures 3).

Frank, W. Modern drama. Dial 85 1928.

Kaucher, D. J. Modern dramatic structure. Univ of Missouri Stud 3 1928.

Mahr, A. C. Dramatische Situationsbilder und Bildtypen: eine Studie zur Kunstgeschichte des Dramas. Stanford Univ Pbns in Lang & Lit 4 1928.

Baker, G. P. Rhythm in recent dramatic dialogue. Yale Rev 19 1929.

Bottomley, G. Poetry seeks a new home. Theatre Arts Monthly 13 1929.

—— Poetry and the contemporary theatre. E & S 19 1933.

—— Choric speech and the stage. Theatre Arts Monthly 19 1935.

—— Choric drama. Theatre Arts Monthly 26 1942.

—— A note on poetry and the stage. [1944?].

—— A stage for poetry: my purposes with my plays. Kendal 1948 (priv ptd).

—— Poet and painter: being the correspondence between Bottomley and Paul Nash, 1910–46. 1955.

Carpenter, B. The way of the drama: a study of dramatic forms and moods. New York 1929.

Eastman, F. The why and how of religious drama. Drama (Chicago) 19 1929.

—— Christ and the drama: a study of the influence of Christ on the drama of England and America. New York 1947.

Ellehauge, M. Nogle Hovedtyper indenfor det moderne irske Drama. Nordisk Tidskrift for Litteraturforskning 29 1929.

—— Striking figures among modern English dramatists. 1931.

—— The initial stages in the development of the English problem-play. Englische Studien 66 1932.

Flanagan, H. Shifting scenes of the modern European theatre. 1929.

McIntyre, C. F. The word 'universality' as applied to drama. PMLA 44 1929.

Thorndike, A. H. English comedy. New York 1929.

Brighouse, H. News of the English theatre. Drama (Chicago) 21 1930.

—— Review of the English theatre. Drama (Chicago) 21 1931.

Cargill, O. Drama and liturgy. New York 1930. Columbia Univ Stud in English & Comparative Lit.

Fornelli, G. Tendenze e motivi nel dramma inglese moderno e contemporaneo. Florence [1930].

Guthrie, J. The chamber drama: being an introductory treatise on the presentation of a new form of dramatic art. Flansham, Sussex 1930.

Meissner, P. Kulturprobleme des modernen englischen Dramas. Zeitschrift für Französischen und Englischen Unterricht 29 1930.

Sherriff, R. C. In defence of realism. Theatre Arts Monthly 14 1930.

The theatre since the war. TLS 24 April 1930.

Bernstein, H. Women and the theatre. Saturday Rev 29 Aug 1931.

Browne, E. M. The church and drama. Church Quart Rev 113 1931.

—— The one-act play. Theatre Arts Monthly 21 1937.

—— Drama's return to religion. Theatre Arts Monthly 41 1957.

—— Verse in the modern English theatre. Cardiff 1963.

De Smet, R. Le théâtre anglais depuis la guerre. Revue de Paris 1 Dec 1931.

—— Le théâtre contemporain en Angleterre. Revue de Paris 15 Sept 1932.

—— Le mouvement dramatique en Angleterre. Revue de Paris 1 Sept 1933, 1 Oct 1934, 1 Oct 1935.

—— Le théâtre en Angleterre. Revue de Paris 1 Dec 1937, 1 Dec 1939.

Geddes, V. The rebirth of drama. Drama (Chicago) 21 1931.

Hopkins, C. Modern trends in the theatre. Drama (Chicago) 21 1931.

Hutchens, J. Comedy in the saddle. Theatre Arts Monthly 15 1931.

—— The reviving theatre. Current History 44 1936.

Marriott, J. W. In his The theatre, 1931.

—— Modern drama. 1934.

Reynolds, G. F. Literature for an audience. SP 28 1931.

—— British and American theater: a personal tour. Western Humanities Rev 4 1949–50.

Bruestle, B. S. The 'fool of nature' in the English drama of our day. Philadelphia 1932.

Cordell, R. Henry Arthur Jones and the modern drama. New York 1932.

Harris, M. The case for tragedy: being a challenge to those who deny the possibility of a tragic spirit in the modern world. 1932.

Krutch, J. W. The drama as a social force. Nation (New York) 20 April 1932.

—— 'Modernism' in modern drama: a definition and estimate. New York 1953.

Rosenberg, H. Character change and the drama. Symposium 3 1932.

—— Poetry and the theatre. Poetry 57 1941.

Trewin, J. C. See his regular contributions to Morning Post 1932–7, Observer 1937–53, Illustr London News 1947–8.

—— The English theatre. 1948.

—— Plays in performance. Drama new ser 15 1949.

—— (ed). The year's work in the theatre, 1948–51, 3 vols 1949–51.

Trewin, J. C. Drama 1945–50. 1951.

—— Theatre since 1900. 1951.

—— Dramatists of today. 1953.

—— Verse drama since 1800. 1956. (National Book League Reader's Guide).

—— The night has been unruly. 1957.

—— The gay twenties: a decade of the theatre. 1958.

—— The turbulent thirties: a further decade of the theatre. 1960.

Adams, M. A roster of new playwrights. Theatre Arts Monthly 17 1933.

Angus, W. Expressionism in the theatre. Quart Jnl of Speech 19 1933.

Courtneidge, R. The future of the theatre. Quart Rev 260 1933.

Godfrey, P. Back-stage: a survey of the contemporary English theatre from behind the scenes. 1933.

Hanmer, G. V. The theatre's malady. Saturday Rev 20 July 1933.

Jones, J. B. The 'new deal' demanded by modern drama. Quart Jnl of Speech 19 1933.

Lenormand, H. R. Le théâtre d'aujourd'hui et les Elizabéthains. Cahiers du Sud 10 1933.

Sladen-Smith, F. Drama and the people. Spectator 18 Aug 1933.

Davies, H. S. Realism in the drama. Cambridge 1934.

Downs, H. (ed). Theatre and stage. 1934, 1951 (2 vols).

Downs, H. Theatregoing. 1951.

—— The critic in the theatre. 1953.

Hawkins, D. The poet in the theatre. New Criterion 14 1934.

Pellizzi, C. Il teatro del novecento: vol 3, Il teatro inglese. Milan 1934; tr as English drama: the last great phase, 1935.

Sommerfield, J. Behind the scenes. 1934.

Thouless, P. Modern poetic drama. 1934.

Clarke, A. The problem of verse drama today. London Mercury 33 1935.

Jennings, H. The theatre. In The arts today, ed G. Grigson 1935.

Komisarjevsky, T. The theatre and a changing civilization. 1935.

Myers, H. A. The tragic attitude toward value: a study and comparison of Greek, Elizabethan and modern tragedies. International Jnl of Ethics 45 1935.

New poetic drama. TLS 24 Jan 1935.

Priestley, J. B. Audiences and critics. Spectator 19 April 1935.

—— Theatre outlook. 1947.

—— The art of the dramatist: together with appendixes and discursive notes. 1957.

—— In his Margin released, 1962.

Thorogood, H. The English theatre in 1910 and today. Eng Rev 60 1935.

Williamson, H. R. The theatre of tomorrow. Fortnightly Rev 144 1935.

Hardwicke, C. The drama of tomorrow. 1936 (Rede lecture).

Lavrin, J. Aspects of modernism from Wilde to Pirandello. 1936.

Ross, M. M. The theatre and the social confusion. UTQ 5 1936.

Toller, E. British free people's theatre. New Statesman 12 Sept 1936. Discussion ibid 19, 26 Sept 1936.

Elvin, R. Le théâtre en Angleterre. Le Mois Jan 1937.

Jenkins, A. Review of thirty years ago. Drama 15 1937.

Kemény, Z. E. Angol Szinész-Drámaírók. Budapest 1937.

O'Casey, S. The flying wasp: a laughing look-over of what has been said about the things of the theatre by the English dramatic critics. 1937.

—— In his Rose and Crown, 1952.

—— Blasts and benedictions: articles and stories. Ed R. Ayling 1967.

Strong, L. A. G. Commonsense about drama. 1937.

Vočadlo, O. J. Vodák o moderním anglickém dramatu. In Jindřich Vodák, Pocta k jeho sedmdesátinám, Prague 1937.

Wilson, N. S. In his European drama, 1937.

Britannia book of the year. 1938-. Includes a survey of the preceding year's theatre work.

'Dataller, Roger' (A. A. Eaglestone). Drama and life. 1938.

Griffith, H. Can the drama have social significance? Fortnightly Rev 143 1938.

Whitfield, G. J. N. In An introduction to drama, 1938.

Whitworth, G. Theatre in action. New York 1938.

—— The theatre of my heart. 1938.

—— The theatre and the nation. 1939.

Auden, W. H. The outlook for 'poetic drama'. Bulletin de l'Association France–Grande Bretagne 22 1939.

Block, A. The changing world in plays and theatre. Boston 1939.

British drama. TLS 12 Aug 1939.

Flewelling, R. T. Tragic drama—modern style. Personalist 20 1939.

Kozlenko, W. (ed). The one-act play: a discussion of the technique, scope and history of the contemporary short drama. 1939.

Littlewood, S. R. Dramatic criticism. Foreword by B. Jackson 1939.

—— Fifty years of criticism. Drama new ser 8 1948.

—— The art of dramatic criticism. 1952.

MacCarthy, D. The theatre during the last war. New Statesman 23 Sept 1939. Correspondence, 30 Sept 1939.

—— Drama. 1940. Dramatic criticisms from 1913–35.

—— Drama. New Statesman 11 Sept 1943.

—— Murder in the theatre. New Statesman 29 April 1944.

—— Theatre. 1954.

Talbot, A. J. Craft in playwriting. 1939.

Allensworth, J. The effectiveness of the one-act play. Quart Jnl of Speech 26 1940.

Drama in the dark. TLS 12 Oct 1940.

Fricker, R. Das historische Drama in England von der Romantik bis zur Gegenwart. Bern 1940.

—— Das moderne englische Drama. Göttingen 1964.

Gassner, J. Masters of the drama: the story of the theatre from primitive man to the present day. 1940, 1954 (rev).

—— Fabianism and the British playwrights. Theatre Arts Monthly 35 1951.

—— The theatre in our times. New York 1954.

—— Forms of modern drama. Comparative Lit 7 1955.

—— Form and idea in modern theatre. New York 1956.

—— (ed). Ideas in the drama. New York 1964.

Kernodle, G. R. England's religious drama movement. College Eng 1 1940.

Lombard, E. H. Plot, character and action: a study of dramatic theory and practice. 1940.

Owen, H. The playwright's craft. 1940.

Vital drama. TLS 13 April 1940.

Frenz, H. Die Entwicklung des sozialen Dramas in England vor Galsworthy. Bleicherode-am-Harz 1941.

Gielgud, J. A living theatre. New Statesman 19 April 1941. Correspondence, 26 April 1941.

—— Tradition, style and the theatre today. Scandinavian Stud 4 1951.

Knight, G. W. Britain as dramatic artist. TLS 5 April 1941.

Nethercot, A. H. The drama of ideas. Sewanee Rev 49 1941.

Schmidt, D. Über die Inselkultur: mit einem Blick auf den Niedergang des englischen Theaters. Die Bühne 4 1941.

Speckbaugh, P. F. Poetic drama. Spirit 8 1941.

Zinner, E. P. Leo Tolstoy and the English drama at the end of the nineteenth and the beginning of the twentieth century. Trans Hertzen State Pedagogical Inst in Leningrad 5 1941.

Ellis-Fermor, U. M. Masters of reality. 1942.

—— The frontiers of drama. 1945.

Short, E. Theatre cavalcade: from Irving to 1939. 1942.

—— Sixty years of theatre. 1951.

—— The British drama grows up. Quart Rev 295 1957.

Smith, W. Mystics in the modern theatre. Sewanee Rev 50 1942.

Goldsmith, A. Playwrights of the future. Horizon 7 1943.

Norwood, G. English drama: its development from 1914 to 1939. Dalhousie Rev 22 1943.

Redgrave, M., J. B. Priestley, A. West and H. Wilson. Actor and critic. New Statesman 4 Sept–16 Oct 1943. Series of articles.

Scotney, N. Theatre prospect. Spectator 22 Dec 1944.

Bax, C. Whither the theatre? 1945.

—— Plays in performance. Drama new ser 11 1948.

Bentley, E. Drama now. Princeton Rev 12 1945.

—— The playwright as thinker: a study of drama in modern times. New York 1946.

—— Theory and theatre. Theatre Arts Monthly 31 1947.

—— The modern theatre: a study of dramatists and the drama. 1948.

Bridie, J. The British drama. Glasgow 1945.

Brook, D. The romance of the English theatre. 1945.

Dean, B. The theatre in reconstruction. Tonbridge 1945.

Robinson, L. Towards an appreciation of the theatre. 1945.

Hope-Wallace, P. Plays in performance. Drama new ser 1 1946 and following issues, new ser 4 1947 and following issues, new ser 8 1948 and following issues, new ser 12 1949 and following issues.

— The theatre. In The Baldwin age, ed J. Raymond 1960.

Hudson, L. Twentieth-century drama. 1946.

— Life and the theatre. 1949.

— The English stage 1850–1950. 1951.

Noble, P. British theatre. British yearbooks, 1946.

Peacock, R. The poet in the theatre. 1946.

— The art of drama. 1957.

Hobson, H. See his regular contributions to Sunday Times 1947–; rptd in next 2 items.

— Theatre. 1948.

— Theatre 2. 1950.

— Verdict at midnight: sixty years of dramatic criticism. 1952.

— The theatre now. 1953.

McCollom, W. G. Illusion in poetic drama. Jahrbuch für Amerikastudien 5 1947.

Macqueen-Pope, W. J. Carriages at eleven: the story of the Edwardian theatre. 1947.

Mallinson, V. The English theatre. Revue des Langues Vivantes 13 1947.

Pogson, R. Theatre between wars 1919–39. Clevedon 1947.

Stamm, R. Von Theaterkrisen und ihrer Überwindung. Zürich 1947.

— Geschichte des englischen Theaters. Bern 1951.

— Zwischen Vision und Wirklichkeit. Bern 1964. Includes essays on Eliot and Fry.

Fay, G. The British theatre today. World Rev Nov 1948.

Hassall, C. Notes on the verse drama. The Masque 6 1948.

Speaight, R. Drama since 1939. 1948.

— The Christian theatre. 1960.

Thomas, G. The theatre alive. 1948.

Worsley, T. C. See his contributions to New Statesman 1948–9.

— The fugitive art: dramatic commentaries 1947–51. 1952.

— The task of the dramatic critic. Listener 12 Nov 1953.

Arnold, P. From the dream in Aeschylus to the surrealist theatre. Jahrbuch für Amerikastudien 7 1949.

Carr, P. C. The London theatre in 1900. Listener 6 Jan 1949.

Cotes, P. No star nonsense. 1949.

Clurman, H. Preface to the younger dramatists. Neue Rundschau 121 1949.

— Lies like truth. New York 1958.

Dobson's theatre year book, 1948. 1949.

Downer, A. S. The life of our design: the function of imagery in the poetic drama. Hudson Rev 2 1949.

Heyningen, C. van. The theatre in England. Standpunkte 4 1949.

Highet, G. The re-interpretation of the myths as plays. Vancouver Quart Rev 25 1949.

Jeans, R. Writing for the theatre. 1949.

Lindsay, A. The theatre. 1949.

Percy, E. The art of the playwright. 1949.

Reynolds, E. Modern English drama: a survey of the theatre from 1900. Foreword by A. Nicoll 1949, 1950 (rev).

Wilson, A. E. Post-war theatre 1945–9. 1949.

— Edwardian theatre. 1951.

Armstrong, W. A. Modern developments in the British theatre. Neuphilologische Mitteilungen 51 1950.

Brook, P. The contemporary theatre: the vitality of the English stage. Listener 4 May 1950.

Cusack, E. D. What is wrong with the English playwright? Meanjin 9 1950.

Fry, C. The contemporary theatre: a playwright speaks. Listener 23 Feb 1950.

— Comedy. Adelphi 27 1950.

— An experience of critics. 1952.

— Poetry in the theatre. Saturday Rev 21 March 1953.

Gilder, R. (ed). Theatre Arts anthology. New York 1950, 1965 (rev).

Greenwood, O. The playwright: a study of form, method and tradition in the theatre. 1950.

Mizener, A. Poetic drama and the well-made play. New York 1950 (Eng Inst Essays 1949).

Prior, M. E. Poetic drama: an analysis and a suggestion. Ibid.

Fluchère, H. The function of poetry in drama. In English studies today, ed C. L. Wrenn and G. Bullough 1951.

Frye, N. A conspectus of dramatic genres. Kenyon Rev 13 1951; rptd in his Anatomy of criticism, Princeton 1957.

Isaacs, J. Assessment of twentieth-century literature. 1951. Includes ch on T. S. Eliot and poetic drama.

Williams, R. Criticism into drama 1888–1950. EC 1 1951.

— Drama from Ibsen to Eliot. 1952, 1964 (rev) (Peregrine), 1968 (rev, as Drama from Ibsen to Brecht).

— Modern tragedy. 1966.

Williamson, A. Theatre of two decades. 1951.

de Gruyter, D. Toneel in Engeland. Nieuw Vlaams Tijdschrift June 1952.

'Findlater, Richard' (K. B. F. Bain) The unholy trade. 1952.

— The shrinking theatre. Twentieth Century 165 1959.

Lamm, M. Modern drama. 1952. Includes Shaw and Galsworthy.

Melchiori, G. Panorama del teatro di poesia in Inghilterra. Lo Spettatore Italiano 5 1952.

Testing times for dramatists. TLS 29 Aug 1952.

Blau, H. A character study of drama. Jnl of Aesthetics & Art Criticism 13 1954.

— Language and structure in poetic drama. MLQ 18 1957.

Goacher, D. Modern poetic drama. Listener 16 Dec 1954.

Grossvogel, D. I. The plight of the comic author and some new departures in contemporary comedy. Romanic Rev 45 1954.

Mason, H. J. Classical myth in modern drama. Emory Univ Quart 10 1954.

Whiting, F. M. An introduction to the theatre. 1954, 1961 (rev).

Knoblock, E. The playwright's progress. Listener 2 June 1955; rptd in his Kismet and other plays, 1957.

Wimsatt, W. K. (ed). English stage comedy. New York 1955 (Eng Inst Essays 1954).

Borinski, L. Shaw und die Stilexperimente des frühen 20. Jahrhunderts. Die Neueren Sprachen 5 1956.

Fechter, P. Das europäische Drama: Geist und Kultur im Spiegel des Theaters. 3 pts. Mannheim 1956–8.

Henn, T. The harvest of tragedy. 1956.

Lumley, F. Trends in twentieth-century drama: a survey since Ibsen and Shaw. 1956, 1960 (rev), 1967 (rev, as New trends in twentieth-century drama).

Michel L. The possibility of a Christian tragedy. Thought 31 1956.

Rebora, P. Teatro inglese contemporaneo. Nuova Antologia Feb 1956.

Hunter, F. J. The value of time in modern drama. Jahrbuch für Amerikastudien 16 1957.

Janković, M. Engelska poetska drama dvadesetog stoljeća. Umjetnost riječi 2 1957.

Swete Alisoun. TLS 25 Jan 1957. Decline of the heroine in modern drama.

Poulenard, E. Le modernisme au théâtre. Études Anglaises 10 1957.

Cheney, S. The theatre. 1958.

Milstead, J. The structure of modern tragedy. Western Humanities Rev 12 1958.

Pollock, J. Curtain up. 1958.

Popkin, H. The drama. In Contemporary literary scholarship: a critical review, ed L. Leary, New York 1958.

Tulane Drama Review: annual review of books and theatre. 1958–.

Bullough, G. Poetry in modern English drama. Cairo Stud in Eng 1959.

Donoghue, D. The third voice: modern British and American verse drama. Princeton 1959.

Kindermann, H. Das europäische Theater der Jahrhundertwende: eine Umriss-Skizze. Maske und Kothurn 5 1959.

Büttner, L. Das europäische Drama von Ibsen bis Zuckmayer: dargestellt an Einzelinterpretationen. Frankfurt 1960.

Cole, T. (ed). Playwrights on playwriting: the meaning and making of modern drama from Ibsen to Ionescu. 1960.

Courtneidge, R. The future of the theatre. Quart Rev 260 1960.

Ellmann, R. (ed). Edwardians and late Victorians. New York 1960 (Eng Inst Essays 1959).

Gerstenberger, D. Perspectives of modern verse drama. Modern Drama 3 1960.

Styan, J. L. The elements of drama. 1960.
— The dark comedy. 1962.
— The dramatic experience: a guide to the reading of plays. 1965.

Weales, G. The Edwardian theater and the shadow of Shaw. New York 1960 (Eng Inst Essays 1959).
— Religion in modern English drama. Philadelphia 1961.

Churchill, R. C. The comedy of ideas: cross-currents in the fiction and drama of the twentieth century. In Pelican guide to English literature vol 7, ed B. Ford 1961.

Dane, C. Approaches to drama. 1961. Presidential address to Eng Assoc.

Dietrich, M. Das moderne Drama: Strömungen — Gestalten — Motive. Stüttgart 1961.

Franzen, E. Formen des modernene Dramas: von der Illusionsbühne zum Antitheater. Munich 1961.

Die Rebellion gegen das Überlebte in der Dramatik des 20. Jahrhunderts von Shaw bis Ionesco. Universitas 16 1961.

Steiner, G. The death of tragedy. 1961.

Tynan, K. Curtains. 1961.

Contemporary theatre. Stratford-upon-Avon Studies 4, 1962. Ed J. R. Brown and B. A. Harris.

Gascoigne, B. Twentieth-century drama. 1962.

Wickham, G. Drama in a world of science. 1962.

Corrigan, R. W. (ed). Theatre in the twentieth century. New York 1963. Anthology of criticism from Tulane Drama Rev.

Douglas, R. The failure of English realism. Tulane Drama Rev 7 1963.

Gowda, H. H. A. The revival of English poetic drama. Bangalore 1963.

Oppel, H. (ed). Das moderne englische Drama. Berlin 1963.

Brooke, N. The characters of drama. CQ 6 1964.

Freedman, M. (ed). Essays in the modern drama. Boston 1964.

Morgan, M. M. Strindberg and the English theatre. Modern Drama 7 1964–5.

Bogard, T. and W. I. Oliver (ed). Modern drama: essays in criticism. New York 1965.

Bradbrook, M. C. English dramatic form: a history of its development. 1965.

Brustein, R. The theatre of revolt: an approach to modern drama. 1965.

Merchant, W. M. Creed and drama: an essay in religious experience. 1965.

Martin, W. The new drama. In his New age under Orage, Manchester 1067.

Spanos, W. V. The Christian tradition in modern British verse drama: the poetics of sacramental time. New Brunswick NJ 1967.

Jurak, M. Glavna problematika območja v angleški poetič-nopolitični dramatiki v letih 1930–40. Univerza v Ljubljani 1968. In Slovenian; summary in English.
— English political verse drama of the thirties: revision and alteration. Acta Neophilologica (Ljubljana) 1 (1968).

Roston, M. Biblical drama in England. 1968.

Russell Taylor, J. The rise and fall of the well-made play. 1968.

Reminiscences

See also (9) *Actors and Acting: Biographies and Reminiscences, below.*

Barrington, R. More Rutland Barrington. 1911.

Cannan, G. Joy of the theatre. 1913.

Hibbert, H. G. Fifty years of a Londoner's life. 1916.
— A playgoer's memories. Foreword by W. Archer. 1920.

de Guerbel, G. and R. Whiting. Both sides of the curtain. 1918.

Watson, A. E. T. A sporting and dramatic career. 1918.

Furniss, H. My Bohemian days. 1919.

Rendle, T. McD. Swings and roundabouts. 1919.

Scott, C. M. Old days in Bohemian London. New York 1919.

Stratton, C. Diary of a modern playgoer. Drama 2 1920.

Maine, B. Receive it so: being a series of reactions to incidents of the theatre and concert-hall. 1926.

Walbrook, H. M. A playgoer's wanderings. 1926.

Desmond, S. London nights of long ago. 1927.

Newton, H. C. Cues and curtain calls: being the theatrical reminiscences of H. Chance Newton ('Carados' of the Referee). 1927.

Drinkwater, J. Discovery: being the second book of an autobiography 1897–1913. 1932.

Henderson, D. L. Diary of a stage-struck. 1932.

Douglass, A. Footlight reflections. 1934.

'Anstey, F.' (T. A. Guthrie). A long retrospect. 1936.

Royde-Smith, N. All star cast. 1936.

Reminiscences of 1920. Theatre World 28 1937.

Reminiscences of wartime days of 1917. Theatre World 28 1937.

Bancroft, G. P. Stage and bar: recollections, with a preface by N. Birkett. 1939.

Booth, J. B. Life, laughter and brass hats. 1939.
— The days we knew. Foreword by C. B. Cochran, 1943.

Memories of the London theatre 1914–1918. Theatre World 32 1939.

Newman, K. O. Two hundred and fifty times I saw a play: or, Authors, actors and actresses. 1944.

Ripley, A. C. Spectacle: a book of things seen. 1945.

Middleton, G. These things are mine: the autobiography of a journeyman playwright. New York 1947.

Baxter, A. First nights and noises off. 1949.

Gibbs, H. Theatre tapestry. 1949.

Gray, C. Musical chairs: or, between two stools. 1949.

Barnes, K. Welcome, good friends. Ed P. Hartnoll 1958.

Roberts, S. Edwardian retrospect. 1963.

Accounts of London Theatres and Companies

Wyndham, G. Alhambra memories. Saturday Rev 10 June 1933.

Shavian productions at the Bedford Theatre. Theatre World 45 1949.

Barker, F. The house that Stoll built. 1957. Coliseum.

MacCarthy, D. The Court Theatre 1904–7: a commentary and criticism. 1907.

The Court Theatre under the direction of J. B. Fagan opened as a Shakespeare playhouse. Saturday Rev 11 Dec 1920.

Pearson, H. A great theatrical management: Granville Barker and J. E. Vedrenne at the Court Theatre. Listener 28 Oct 1954.

Weintraub, S. J. E. Vedrenne and H. Granville Barker. Shaw Bull 2 1959. Court Theatre.

Johns. E. The story of the Royal Opera House, Covent Garden. Theatre World 32 1939.

Littlefield, J. Covent Garden theatre reopens. Theatre Arts Monthly 30 1946.

Severn, M. Sadler's Wells ballet at Covent Garden. 1947.

Shawe-Taylor, D. Covent Garden. 1948.

— The future of Covent Garden. New Statesman 7, 14 Aug 1948.

Pemberton, T. E. The Criterion Theatre 1875–1903. 1903.

Johns, E. The story of the Criterion Theatre. Theatre World 32 1939.

Forbes-Winslow, D. Daly's: the biography of a theatre. 1944.

Drury Lane Centenary. Illustrated London News 19 Oct 1912.

Parker, L. N. The pageant of Drury Lane Theatre 1663–1918. 1918.

Lawrence, W. J. Drury Lane rejuvenation. Graphic 15 April 1922.

Swaffer, H. Past and present glories of Drury Lane. Graphic 22 April 1922.

What is to be done with Drury Lane. Graphic 23 Aug 1924.

Johns, E. Three centuries of Drury Lane spectacle. Theatre World 27 1937.

— The story of the Theatre Royal, Drury Lane. Theatre World 32 1939.

Macqueen-Pope, W. Theatre Royal, Drury Lane. 1946.

Johns, E. The story of the Duke of York's Theatre. Theatre World 33 1940.

Hollingshead, J. "Good old Gaiety": an historiette and remembrance. 1903.

Mantle, B. The Gaiety season at London. Munsey's Mag 52 1912.

Jupp, J. The Gaiety stage door: thirty years' reminiscences of the theatre. 1923.

Macqueen-Pope, W. Gaiety: theatre of enchantment. 1949.

Maude, C. The Haymarket Theatre: some records and reminiscences. 1903.

Leverton, W. H. Through the box-office window: memories of fifty years at the Haymarket Theatre. 1932. With J. B. Booth.

Johns, E. The story of the Theatre Royal, Haymarket. Theatre World 33 1940.

John Gielgud's new repertory plans for the Haymarket Theatre. Theatre World 40 1944.

Opening productions of the Haymarket Theatre. Ibid.

Gielgud, J. London repertory: the Haymarket and the New Theatre seasons. Theatre Arts Monthly 29 1945.

Macqueen-Pope, W. Haymarket: theatre of perfection. 1948.

Johns, E. The story of His Majesty's Theatre. Theatre World 33 1940.

Macqueen-Pope, W. The story of His Majesty's. Drama 13 1949.

Jennings, R. Irving first nights at the Lyceum Theatre. Nineteenth Century 138 1945.

Wilson, A. E. The Lyceum 1771–1945. 1952.

Playfair, N. The story of the Lyric Theatre, Hammersmith. 1925.

— Hammersmith hoy: a book of minor revelations. 1930.

Shaw productions at the Lyric Theatre. Theatre World 41 1945.

Smith, C. The Lyric Theatre. Theatre Arts Monthly 31 1947.

Hamilton, C. English historical matinees at the New Theatre. Bookman (New York) 33 1911.

Gielgud, J. London repertory: the Haymarket and the New Theatre seasons. Theatre Arts Monthly 29 1945.

Booth, J. The Old Vic: a century of theatrical history, 1816–1916. 1917.

Lawrence, C. E. The Old Vic. Nineteenth Century 96 1924.

The re-opening of the Old Vic. Spectator 8 Nov 1924.

Hamilton, C. and L. Baylis. The Old Vic. 1926.

Phillips, H. A. The popularity of Old Vic bills. Theatre 44 1926.

Westwood, D. These players: a diary of the Old Vic. Introd by L. Baylis 1926.

Smaltz, A. G. The Old Vic Theater: the people's theater of England. Drama (Chicago) 19 1929.

Williams, H. Four years at the Old Vic, 1929–33. 1935.

— (ed). Vic-Wells: the work of Lilian Baylis. 1938.

Williams, H. Old Vic saga. 1949.

The Old Vic season 1935–6. Play Pictorial 67 1936.

Drake, D. The Old Vic, 1936–7 season. Play Pictorial 70 1937.

Ervine, St J. New Vics for old. London Mercury 37 1938.

The popularity of the Old Vic. Theatre World 30 1938.

Thorndike, S. and R. Lilian Baylis. 1938.

Dukes, A. The story of the Old Vic. Theatre Arts Monthly 24 1940.

Vickers, J. The Old Vic in photographs, with introd by J. Burrell. 1940.

Guthrie, T. The Old Vic Theatre Company tours outside areas. Spectator 18 April 1941.

Wartime story of the Old Vic and Sadler's Wells companies. Theatre World 37 1941.

The work of the Old Vic Panzer Theatre. Theatre Arts Monthly 26 1942.

The Old Vic Theatre Company in repertory. Theatre World 40 1944.

The opening productions of the Old Vic repertory company at the New Theatre. Theatre World 40 1944.

Dent, E. J. A theatre for everybody: the story of the Old Vic and Sadler's Wells. 1945.

The Old Vic Theatre Company: second season. Theatre World 41 1945.

Choate, E. and J. V. Matthews. The Old Vic: the statistics. Theatre Arts Monthly 30 1946.

Productions by the Old Vic Theatre Company. Theatre World 42 1946.

Johns, E. Youth at the helm: George Devine discusses the aims of the Young Vic. Theatre World 43 1947.

McKown, R. The Old Vic Theatre Company's new home: West End or Waterloo Road? Ibid.

Old Vic Theatre Company productions. Ibid.

St Denis, M. The Old Vic Theatre Centre. Theatre Arts Monthly 31 1947.

Macartney, K. The Old Vic season. Meanjin 7 1948.

Miller, T. (ed). The Old Vic Theatre Company: a tour of Australia and New Zealand. 1948.

Williamson, A. Old Vic drama: a twelve years' study of plays and players, 1934–47. 1948. Foreword by S. Thorndike.

— and C. Landstone. Old Vic drama, 1947–57. 1957.

Olivier, L. and M. St Denis. Five seasons of the Old Vic Theatre Company: a scrapbook record of production for 1944–9. 1949.

Hale, L. The Old Vic 1949–50. 1950. With a contribution by P. Hope-Wallace.

Clarke, M. Shakespeare at the Old Vic, 1956–7. 1957.

— Shakespeare at the Old Vic, 1957–8. 1958.

Phillips, E. Memories of the Old Vic. Listener 14 Feb 1957.

Command performance at the Palladium Theatre. Illustrated London News 6 Nov 1948.

Bevan, I. Top of the bill: the story of the London Palladium. 1952.

Morice, G. Some fresh notes on the Royal West London Theatre in the nineteenth and twentieth centuries. N & Q 188 1945.

Turner, W. J. At Sadler's Wells. New Statesman 24 Oct 1936.

Armitage, J. M. Sadler's Wells theatre: 1936/7 season. Play Pictorial 70 1937.

Hussey, D. Sadler's Wells and a national theatre. Spectator 8 Oct 1937.

The work of Sadler's Wells. Theatre World 30 1938.

Arundell, D. The story of Sadler's Wells 1683–1964. 1965.

Maddick, E. D. Scala Theatre, 1904. 1905.

Mason, A. E. W. Sir George Alexander and the St James's Theatre. 1935.

Sears, W. P., jr. London's St James's Theater passes the century mark. Eng Jnl 25 1936.

Johns, E. The story of St James's Theatre. Theatre World 33 1940.

Macqueen-Pope, W. St James's: theatre of distinction. 1958.

Duncan, B. The St James's Theatre: its strange and complete history, 1835–1957. 1964.

Priestley, J. B. Plans for our Westminster season. Drama 17 1938.

Belden, K. D. The story of the Westminster Theatre. 1965.

Mayes, R. The romance of London theatres. 1930.

St Clare Byrne, M. (ed). Studies in English theatre history. 1952.

Mander, R. and J. Mitchenson. The theatres of London. 1961, 1963 (rev).

—— The lost theatres of London. 1968.

Howard, D. London theatres and music halls. 1970.
M. T.

(5) THE THEATRE OUTSIDE LONDON

See also A. Loewenberg, The theatre of the British Isles excluding London: a bibliography, *1950*.

The provincial theatre; The repertory movement

Jones, H. A. The drama in the English provinces. Nineteenth Century 49 1901.

—— Municipal and repertory theatres. 1913. Lecture.

Garrett, E. The repertory theatre in England. Nation (New York) 5 Aug 1909.

Howe, P. P. The repertory theatre. 1910.

Dean, B. The repertory theatre. Liverpool 1911.

Palmer, J. L. The future of repertory. In his Future of the theatre, 1913.

Dukes, A. The English scene: little theatres in big cities. Theatre Arts Monthly 16 1932.

Gregson, J. R. Northern repertory theatre. Theatre Arts Monthly 16 1932.

Chisholm, C. Repertory. 1934.

Jackson, B. Twenty-five years of repertory. Listener 23 Feb 1938.

Armstrong, W. The repertory adventure. Listener 16 June 1938.

Dent, A. Repertory enjoys a boom: the provincial theatre in wartime. Listener 16 Sept 1943.

Duff, J. Repertory theatres. Spectator 15 Oct 1943. Discussion 22, 29 Oct 1943.

Marshall, N. The other theatre. 1947.

Council of Repertory Theatres. The repertory movement in Great Britain. 1968.

The Theatre in Particular Cities and Areas

Birmingham

Pollack, O. The theatres of Great Britain: Birmingham. Playgoer 1 1901.

Levy, E. L. Birmingham theatrical reminiscences. Birmingham [1902].

Matthews, B. A history of the Birmingham Repertory Theatre. 1924.

Rodway, P. I. I. and L. H. Slingsby. Philip Rodway and a tale of two theatres. Birmingham 1934.

Kemp, T. C. Birmingham Repertory Theatre. 1943, 1948 (rev).

Fraser, M. F. K. Alexandra Theatre. [1948].

Bristol

Board, M. E. The story of the Bristol stage 1490–1925. [1926].

Williamson, A. M. and C. Landstone. The Bristol Old Vic: the first ten years. [1957].

Cambridge

John, V. The festival theatre in England. Theatre Arts Monthly 13 1929.

Cooke, A. The Cambridge Festival Theatre. Theatre Arts Monthly 15 1931.

Marshall, N. The Festival Theatre Cambridge. In his Other theatre, 1947.

Exeter

Saunders, R. G. A year's drama in a provincial town. Drama new ser 6 1927.

Delderfield, E. R. Cavalcade by candlelight: the story of Exeter's five theatres 1725–1950. Exmouth 1950.

Huddersfield

Chadwick, S. Theatre Royal: the romance of the Huddersfield stage. Huddersfield 1941.

Leeds

Dunning, A. The drama and the people: what the Civic Playhouse is doing in Leeds. Millgate Monthly 21 1926.

Talbot, G. Leeds Civic Playhouse. Theatre Arts Monthly 15 1931.

Liverpool

Goldie, G. W. The Liverpool Repertory Theatre 1911–34. Liverpool 1935.

Dukes, A. The Playhouse, Liverpool. Theatre Arts Monthly 22 1938.

Manchester

Sladen-Smith, F. Reminiscences of a Mancunian playgoer. Drama 1 1919.

—— The unnamed society. Drama new ser 13 1949.

Pogson, R. Miss Horniman and the Gaiety Theatre, Manchester. 1952.

Margate

Morley, M. Margate and its theatres 1730–1965. 1966.

Newcastle-upon-Tyne

Veitch, N. The People's: being a history of the People's Theatre, Newcastle upon Tyne, 1911–39. Gateshead 1950.

Northampton

Dyas, A. Adventure in repertory: Northampton Repertory Theatre, 1927–48. Northampton 1948.

Warwick, L. Death of a theatre: a history of the New Theatre, Northampton. Northampton 1960.

Norwich

Stephenson, A. The Maddermarket Theatre. Drama new ser 30 1923.

Oxford

Marshall, N. J. B. Fagan and the Oxford Playhouse. In his Other theatre, 1947.

Sweeting, E. The Oxford Playhouse 1923–68. Oxford 22 1968.

Sheffield

Seed, T. A. The Sheffield Repertory Theatre. 1959.

Wallasey

Farquar, D. The history of Wallasey Theatre. 1950.

Welwyn Garden City

Craig, E. G. Theatres for all: notes on the new theatre at Welwyn. Mask 14 1928.

Windsor

Counsell, J. Counsell's opinion. Windsor 1963.

Northern Ireland

Kennedy, D. and J. Loudan. The Ulster region and the theatre. Lagan 4 1947.

Tomelty, J. The theatre in Northern Ireland. Drama new ser 28 1953.

Scotland

Leclercq, R. Un mouvement de renaissance théâtrale en Ecosse. Revue Anglo-américaine 3 1926.

Marshall, N. The theatre in Scotland. Drama new ser 4 1926.

Sutherland, D. A year of Scottish drama. Drama new ser 7 1929.

Fay, W. G. Drama in Scotland. Drama new ser 9 1930.

Bridie, J. The theatre in Scotland. Spectator 28 May 1932.

Brown, I. Wales and Scotland: the tributary theatre. Theatre Arts Monthly 23 1939.

Bannister, W. The foundation of the modern Scottish theatre. In International theatre, ed J. Andrews and O. Trilling 1949.

— James Bridie and the Scottish theatre. In her James Bridie and his theatre, 1955.

Cuthbertson, I., A. Leigh and M. Lyons. (ed). A conspectus to mark the Citizens' 21st anniversary as a living theatre in Gorbals Street Glasgow. Glasgow 1964.

Wales

Colwin, J. The drama in Wales. Drama 1 1919.

Hart, O. E. The drama in modern Wales. Philadelphia 1928.

Williams, R. J. A national drama for Wales. Drama new ser 9 1931.

Hughes, R. The theatre in Wales. Bookman (London) 87 1934.

Brown, I. Wales and Scotland: the tributary theatre. Theatre Arts Monthly 23 1939.

Price, C. Towards a national theatre for Wales. Anglo Welsh Rev 12 1962.

Travelling theatre

Elder, E. M. Plays in the villages: some experiences of the Arts League of Service. Drama new ser 25 1923.

— Travelling players: the story of the Arts League of Service. 1939.

Bottomley, G. Theatre on wheels: England—Arts League of Service. Theatre Arts Monthly 13 1929.

Wartime

Kingston, G. Repertory with the BRADC at Cologne. Fortnightly Rev 110 1921.

Ashwell, L. Modern troubadours: a record of the concerts at the front. 1922.

Browne, H. Pilgrim story: the Pilgrim Players 1939–43. 1945.

Dean, B. The theatre at war. 1956.

The Shakespeare Memorial Theatre, Stratford-upon-Avon

Buckley, R. R. The Shakespeare revival and the Stratford-upon-Avon movement. 1911. Contains A. Hutchinson. The Shakespeare Memorial Theatre at Stratford-upon-Avon: a record of its work.

Jaggard, W. Shakespeare memorial, Stratford-on-Avon: fifty years retrospect. Stratford-upon-Avon [1926].

The Shakespeare Memorial Theatre: prospect and retrospect. Drama new ser 7 1928.

Day, M. C. and J. C. Trewin. The Shakespeare Memorial Theatre. 1932.

Jellicoe, G. A. The Shakespeare Memorial Theatre. 1933.

Chesterton, A. K. Brave enterprise: a history of the Shakespeare Memorial Theatre. 1934.

Brown, I. and G. Fearon. Amazing monument. 1939.

Marshall, N. The Shakespeare Memorial Theatre. In his Other theatre, 1947.

Garrett, J. Stratford and the nation. Spectator 16 Jan 1948.

Trewin, J. C. The story of Stratford upon Avon. 1950.

Kemp, T. C. and J. C. Trewin. The Stratford Festival. Birmingham 1953.

Jaggard, G. The old memorial theatre. In his Stratford mosaic, 1960.

Festival Drama

Boughton, R. A national music-drama: The Glastonbury Festival. Proc Musical Assoc 44 1918.

— The Glastonbury festival movement. In Somerset and the drama, ed S. R. Littlewood 1922. Pbd separately 1922.

John, V. The festival theatre in England. Theatre Arts Monthly 13 1929.

Box, S. The drama festival. In The amateur stage, ed P. Carlton 1939.

Boas, F. S. The Malvern theatrical festival 1929–39. Queen's Quart 47 1940.

Adam, K. Festivals of Britain. Fortnightly Rev 164 1948.

Hurd, M. Immortal hour: the life and period of Rutland Boughton. 1962.

— The Glastonbury festivals: 1914–26. Theatre Notebook 17 1963.

L.O.

Periodicals

Where the place of pbn is clearly indicated by the title, it is not cited in the imprint.

London entr'acte. Nos 1–88, 1869–11 March 1871. Continued as London and provincial entr'acte, nos 89–137, 18 March 1871–17 Feb 1872. Continued as Entr'acte, nos 138–1974, 24 Feb 1872–26 April 1907. Weekly.

What's on. Manchester. 1889–? [Nos 343–555, 11 May 1896–4 June 1900]. Weekly.

The prompter. Liverpool. Nos 1–7, [1899]–29 Jan 1900. Ed W. Henderson.

The caste: being a weekly record of Birmingham plays and players. Nos 1–4, 5–26, March 1900. Weekly.

Bristol and Clifton amusements etc. Bristol. Nos 1–157, 10 Dec 1900–7 Dec 1903. Weekly.

John Waddington's annual: the book for the playgoer. Leeds 1901. Annual.

Paignton's amusements and visitor's guide. Nos 1–416, 18 May 1903–10 Sept 1939. Not pbd between 1916 and 1919. Many discrepancies in numbering.

Liverpool and district programme [etc]. Vol 1 no 1–vol 5 no 16, 14 Sept 1903–12 March 1906. 1903 lacks 14 and 21 Dec. Weekly.

Liverpool entertainment and pleasure programme. Sept 1903–26 Aug 1904. Continued as Smith's Liverpool weekly, 2 Sept 1904–20 Sept 1907.

Stage and field: a herald of events…in Manchester and district. Manchester. Nos 1–55, 28 Nov 1904–15 March 1906. Biweekly.

Plays and players. Liverpool 1904. Annual. The annual of Smith's Liverpool weekly.

Glasgow programme and list of entertainments. Nos 1–19, 30 Jan–5 June 1905. Continued as Glasgow programme, nos 20–1311, June 1905–15 May 1922. Continued as Glasgow and district entertainment guide, May 1922–26 Sept 1927. Continued as Glasgow entertainment guide, 7 Nov 1927–6 Oct 1930. Weekly.

The Millgate monthly. Oct 1905–Spring 1953. Various titles. *See* col 824, above.

Birmingham programme of amusements. Birmingham. Vol 1 no 1–vol 10 no 133, 15 Jan 1906–27 July 1908. Continued as Midland amusements, vol 10 no 134–vol 29 no 416, 3 Aug 1908–27 Dec 1913. Continued as ｜What's doing, vol 30 no 417–vol 32 no 569, 3 Jan 1914–6 Jan 1917. Weekly.

Brighton entertainments and pleasure programme. Nos 1–39, 9 June 1906–2 March 1907. Continued as Brighton programme, nos 40–960, 9 March 1907–26 July 1924. Continued as Brighton weekly programme, nos 961–1383, 2 Aug 1924–11 Nov 1933. Continued as Illustrated sporting mail and Brighton weekly programme, nos 1384–5, 18–25 Nov 1933. Continued as Brighton illustrated sporting mail and weekly programme, nos 1386–1503, 2 Dec 1933–29 Feb 1936. Continued as The Brighton weekly programme, nos 1505–38, 7 March–27 Oct 1936 (no 1504 omitted in numbering).

The magazine programme: Grand Theatre magazine programme. Swansea. Vol 1 no 42–vol 3 no 7, 20 Aug 1906–30 Dec 1907. New series incorporating Laughter, vol 1 no 1–vol 4 no 49, 6 Jan 1908–26 Dec 1911. Weekly.

Bournemouth visitors' programme of daily events. 8 June 1907–16 Oct 1909. Continued as Bournemouth visitors' daily events, 23 Oct 1909–25 March 1912. Continued as Bournemouth visitors' daily events guide, 1 April–30 Sept 1912. Continued as Bournemouth and district visitors' and residents' weekly guide to daily events, 7 Oct 1912–31 Aug 1914.

Liverpool theatrical news. Nos 1–49, 29 July 1907–29 June 1908. Weekly.

Prompt box: the official organ of the Liverpool Stage Club. Nos 1–3, [Oct]–2 Nov 1907. Weekly.

Lancashire stage-land. Manchester. Nos 1–6, 1 Feb–7 March 1908. Continued as Stageland, nos 7–21, 14 March–20 June 1908. Weekly.

Eastbourne programme of entertainments and general fixtures and accommodation register. Nos 1–145, 18 April 1908–3 Feb 1917, weekly, irregular. Continued as Today in Eastbourne, nos 146–460, 10 Feb 1917–27 Jan 1923. Continued as Eastbourne mirror, vol 1 no 1–vol 5 no 215, 7 Feb 1923–13 Feb 1927. Continued as Eastbourne courier, vol 1, 5 March 1927 onwards.

The Stage year book, with which is included the stage provincial guide. Vols 1–21, 1908–28; 1949 onwards. Annual.

What's on in Southampton. Nos 1–1314, 26 Dec 1908–7 April 1934. Weekly.

The Manchester playgoer. (Organ of the Manchester Playgoers' Club). Manchester. Vols 1–2, April 1910–May 1912. New ser, Sept 1912–July 1914. Approximately quarterly, but varying from two to eight-month intervals. Ed O. R. Drey from 1912.

The scallop-shell: the Pilgrim review: the organ of the Pilgrim Players. Birmingham. Nos 1–2, Feb, April 1911. Ed J. Drinkwater.

Exeter day by day. Nos 1–19, June 1911–April 1914. Bimonthly.

The independent theatre goer. Nos 1–6, Nov 1912–April 1913. Monthly. Conducted by J. T. Grein and H. Klein.

Season's concert and entertainment calendar. Leeds. 1912–13. Sometime after 1924 the title changed to Concert, lecture, dramatic guide, 1933–8. Annual. The issues were not intended to form vols.

The entertainer: Scotland's amusements weekly, theatrical, vaudeville. Glasgow. Vol 1 no 1–vol 7 no 285, 4 Oct 1913–15 March 1919.

Theatre de luxe gazette. Glasgow. Nos 1–3, Oct 1914–27 Dec 1915. Monthly.

The Bristol playgoer. (Organ of the Bristol Playgoers' Club). Nos 21, 22, April 1915, March 1924.

The Playgoers' Club journal. (Organ of the Manchester Playgoers' Club). Manchester. Vols 1–13, Nov 1915–Sept 1934. Monthly from Oct to March, except Oct 1923–March 1924 bimonthly.

Scottish musical magazine and Scottish drama. Edinburgh. Vol 1 no 1–vol 12 no 137, Sept 1919–Jan 1931. Monthly.

The Liverpool programme of entertainments. Nos 1–17, ?–18 Oct 1920. Continued as Liverpool and Merseyside programme of entertainments, nos 18–40, 25 Oct 1920–11 July 1921. Weekly.

What's on in Coventry and district. Coventry. Vol 1 nos 1–34, 30 Sept 1921–22 July 1922. Weekly, irregular.

The gong. (Pbd by the Birmingham Repertory Theatre). Nos 1–11, Dec 1921–Dec 1922. Monthly. Ed Alan Bland.

What's on in Birmingham. Vol 1 no 1–vol 2 no 113, 4 March 1922–26 May 1924. Weekly.

Glasgow and district entertainments guide. Vol 1 no 1–vol 6 no 281, 15 May 1922–28 Sept 1927. Weekly.

Cambridge guide to 'What's on?'. Nos 1–209, 19 Oct 1922–24 Dec 1926. Weekly.

Clacton visitors' guide. Clacton. Nos 1–106, 21 May 1923–18 Sept 1926. Weekly but irregular.

The Scottish player. (Issued by the Scottish National Theatre Society). Glasgow. Vols 1–4, July ? 1923–April 1926. Monthly.

Oldham amusements and shopping programme. Nov 1923–March 1926. Monthly.

The municipal player: a magazine for mummers. Birmingham. Vols 1–3, May 1924–June 1926. New series vols 1–4, Sept 1927–Aug 1931. Monthly.

Leeds playgoer. Bradford. Nos 1–6, Oct 1924–March 1925. Monthly. Ed F. W. Harland Edgcumbe.

Playgoer. (Playhouse, Liverpool). Liverpool. Nos 1–12, Oct 1924–March 1926. Irregular.

The Manchester playgoer: a monthly review of the stage, screen and sport. Nos 1–5, March–July 1925. Monthly.

Birmingham Repertory Theatre news-letter. Nos 1–8, April 1925–June 1926. Irregular. By A. Bland.

The Midlander...sport, drama, and society etc. Birmingham. Vol 1 no 1–vol 5 no 10, Oct 1925–Nov 1930. Monthly.

The show: King's Theatre, Southsea, monthly programme. Nos 1–12, Nov 1925–Oct 1926. Ed C. Clarke. [Registration issue, 25 June 1925, ed A. Collins].

Theatrical news. Liverpool. Nos 1–8, 23 June–11 Aug 1926. Continued as Theatrical observer, nos 1–10, 18 Aug–20 Oct 1926. Weekly.

What's on in Maidstone. Nos 1–11, 26 Feb–12 May 1927. Continued as Maidstone and district what's on, nos 12–282, 19 May 1927–14 July 1932. Continued as Maidstone day by day, nos 283–690, 21 July 1932–6 June 1940. Continued as Maidstone and district day by day, nos 691–877, 10 Nov 1947–Nov 1963. Weekly, irregular.

The Alexandra journal: a monthly record of the activities of Leon Salberg's Repertory Company of Birmingham. Vol 1 no 1–vol 4 no 43, Oct 1927–July 1932. Irregular.

The Glasgow entertainment guide. Vol 1 no 1–vol 2 no 151, 7 Nov 1927–6 Oct 1930. Weekly.

What's on in Tottenham. Nos 1–75, Aug 1928–Feb 1935. Monthly.

Hardey's universal theatrical directory. Cheltenham. 1928.

The St Pancras People's Theatre magazine. 1928–?

The Royal tatler: gossip about coming attractions at the Theatre Royal, Birmingham. Nos 1–44, March 1929–Dec 1936; nos 1–15, Nov 1936–Aug/Sept 1939, then April/May 1947–Dec 1948? Irregular.

The Prince of Wales courier. (Prince of Wales Theatre, Birmingham). Nos 1–31, July 1929–March 1934. Irregular.

The Rep. (Repertory Theatre, Newcastle upon Tyne). Vol 1 nos 1–9, Jan–May 1930; vol 2 nos 1–12, Aug 1930–Jan 1931. Biweekly.

The Arcadia, Doncaster, monthly post. (Arcadia Theatre, Doncaster). Vol 1 no 1–vol 2 no 12, June 1930–May 1931.

The Scottish stage. (Scottish Community Drama Association). Glasgow. Vol 1 no 1–vol 4 no 37, Sept 1930–May 1934. Monthly.

The Erith, Belvedere and district free press and entertainment guide. London-Bexley. Vol 1 no 1–vol 17 no 364, 15 Nov 1930–30 Oct 1937; weekly. Continued as The Bexley and Erith bulletin, vol 17 no 365–vol 19 no 385, Dec 1937–Aug 1939. Monthly.

The Malvern Theatre's monthly post. 1930–?

What's on in Sheffield and district. Sheffield. Nos 1–12, Jan–Dec 1931. Monthly.

Repertory, a journal of drama and ideas. (Oxford Repertory Co.). Vol [1] no 1–vol 4 no 5, 18 April 1931–29 May 1933 (suspended Dec 1931–early Jan 1933?). By vol 4, no 1 becomes 'organ of the Playhouse Guild'. Ed Thea Holme and then Stamford Holme. Weekly.

The occasional magazine: dealing with theatrical matters in general and the Birmingham Repertory Theatre in particular. Vol 1 no 1–vol 2 no 7, Sept 1932–Jan 1934. Irregular. Ed G. Courtney nos 1–2, F. R. H. Bolton nos 3–6.

The Courier. (Manchester Opera House). Manchester. Nos 1–6, May–Dec 1932. Monthly. Irregular.

Sheffield Repertory Company, Repertory news. Nos 1–90, 15 Sept 1934–Aug 1938. Continued as Playhouse news, nos 91–121, 1 Sept 1938–6 April 1940. Biweekly. Pbd before each production.

The Oxford Repertory Company Limited: annual report and statement of accounts. [Nos 1–2], 1934–5, 1936–7. Apparently not issued 1935–6.

Rep. (Westminster and Croydon Theatre). Croydon. 1934–?

Theatre Royal: Brighton Repertory Theatre magazine. Brighton. Nos 1–5, Feb–May, July 1935. Monthly.

The Hippodrome tatler. Coventry. Vol 1 no 1–vol 3 no 22, July 1935–Sept 1939. Continued as Theatre news, vol 4, nos 23–8, Nov 1939–April 1940. Monthly.

The Manchester Repertory Theatre magazine. Vols 1–2, 1935–6, 1937–8. Annual.

The Highbury Players' bulletin. Sutton Coldfield. Nos 1–17, March 1936–July 1937. Continued as The Highbury bulletin, Aug 1937 onwards. Monthly.

What's on in the city, Manchester, Salford and districts. Manchester. [Vol 1 no 1]–vol 7 no 80, April/May 1936–Nov 1942. Monthly.

The Southampton repertory magazine. Nos 1–5, Aug–Dec 1936. Monthly.

Garrick magazine: a periodical for the members of the Altrincham Garrick Society. London. Vol 1 nos 1–7, Oct 1936–Nov 1937. Bimonthly (irregular).

The 'little' magazine: a monthly publication dedicated to the interests of the Southport Dramatic Club and the Little Theatre. Southport. Nos 1–10, 1937–9. Monthly (irregular).

The Oldham Repertory Club. Nos 1–3, April–June 1938. Monthly.

Theatre forum, a bimonthly magazine. Oxford. Nos 1–4, June/July 1938–Dec 1938/Jan 1939.

The repertory world. York. 1939.

Merseyside Unity Theatre: membership bulletin. Liverpool. 1940–8. New series, Sept 1948–? Monthly (occasionally bimonthly).

What's on in Birmingham. Nos 1–135, 21 Nov 1943–23 June 1946. Continued as What's on in Birmingham, programme of events in the city, pbd by the City of Birmingham Information Department, 30 June 1946 onwards. Weekly.

The prompter: the bulletin of the Citizens' Theatre Society. Glasgow. Nos 1–89, Nov 1943–Jan 1957. (Title adopted with no 7, the earlier issues being unnamed). Monthly, irregular.

Theatre. (Bradford Civic Playhouse). Nos 1–11, July 1945–Winter 1948. 3 issues a year.

The prompter. (Southampton Theatre Guild). Oct 1945–? Monthly.

The gen. East Barnet. 1945?–? (No dates appear in vol 1 nos 1–12; vol 2 no 1 is dated Dec 1946). Ed H. Stanley.

Scots theatre (Glasgow Unity Theatre). Nos 1–6, Sept 1946–May 1947. Monthly. Ed W. M. Coulter and Donald Cameron nos 2–4, Donald Cameron nos 5–6.

What's on?: the Manchester entertainment guide. Nos 1–12, 14 Dec 1946/11 Jan 1947–13 Dec 1948/9 Jan 1949. Bimonthly.

The green room mirror. Portsmouth. Nos 1–4, Spring 1946–Summer 1947.

Proscenium (Erith Theatre Guild). London. Vol 1 no 1–vol 4 no 15, autumn 1946–autumn/winter 1950. Quarterly, irregular.

Con brio: a Scots magazine for the modern music lover. Glasgow. Vol 1 no 1, 1946. Continued as Con brio: the modern magazine for music lovers, vol 1 nos 2–3, [1947–8]. Continued as Scottish music and drama, incorporating 'Con brio', nos [4]–6, 1949–51. With no 6, 1951, becomes an annual.

Bristol diary of events. Nos 1–49, July 1947–July 1951. Monthly.

Spotlight: the journal of the Swindon and District Theatre Guild. 1947 onwards. Monthly.

The Tyneside Phoenix: journal of the People's Theatre Arts Group. Newcastle upon Tyne. Nos 1–18, Spring 1947–autumn 1952. 3 issues a year.

The living theatre. (Darlington Repertory Theatre). Nos 1–12, March 1948–March 1949. Monthly.

Mercury: a review of the arts in Wessex: the journal of the Winter Gardens Society. Bournemouth. Nos 1–9, Oct 1948–Oct 1950. Quarterly. Ed J. Evans.

Civic entertainment: theatre, music, visual arts. London. Vols 1–2, nos 1–10, Nov/Dec 1948–March/April 1950. Bimonthly.

Scottish drama year book. Edinburgh. 1948. Continued as Scottish drama: the Scottish drama year book, 1950. Annual. Ed J. House 1948–9, J. House and G. O. Cribbes 1950.

Shakespeare Memorial Theatre: a photographic record. 1948/9–1959.

What's on in the west country. Weston-super-Mare. Vol 1, nos 1–4, 27 March/9 April–8/21 May 1949. Continued as Events in the west, 22 May/14 June 1949–Jan 1958. Continued as Events in Bristol, vol 9 no 121–vol 18 no 225, Feb 1958–Oct 1966. Continued as Events in Bristol and Cardiff, vol 18, no 226, Nov 1966 onwards. Monthly.

What's on in Ealing. Nos 1–25, Oct [1949]–autumn and Christmas number 1951. Monthly.

Southport playbill: the magazine of the Southport Repertory Company. Nos 1–2, 1949.

Repertory: a weekly magazine devoted to the interests of repertory. Halifax. Vol 1, nos 1–10, 2 Jan–6 March 1950. Ed Angus MacInnes.

Intimate theatre group news letter. Sutton Coldfield. No 1, March 1950.

Proscenium. (Ipswich Theatre Club). Ipswich. Vol 1 no 1–vol 3 no 4, Dec 1950–4. Quarterly (irregular). No issues in 1952, except Winter, 1952–3. One issue in 1954. In all, 11 issues.

Scottish drama. Edinburgh. Vol 1, 1950. Annual. Incorporates Scottish drama year book.

Festival Drama Periodicals

Festival Theatre review. Cambridge. Vol 1 no 1–vol 3 no 63. Nov 1926–June 1929. Continued as Festival Theatre programme, vol 1 no 1–vol 2 no 7, 12 Oct 1929–30. Continued as Festival Theatre review, vol 4 no 64–vol 6 no 87, 1930–1. Continued as Festival Theatre programme, vol 6, no 87, new series, nos 2–8, Jan–June 1932. Continued as Festival-Gate review, vol 6 nos 87(sic)–94 Oct–Dec 1932. Continued as Festival review, vol 6 nos 95–109, 16 Jan–5 June 1933. Continued as Festival Theatre (new lease) programme, nos 1–49, Oct 1933–June 1935. Monthly. Suppl: The Festival Theatre review'd, 20 May 1927.

Malvern Festival. Worthing 1929–39. Annual.

The Malvern theatre's monthly post. Malvern 1930–?

Scottish music and drama: an annual review published during the Edinburgh Festival. 1946 onwards. Annual.

Festival news, published for the International Festival of Music and Drama. Edinburgh. Nos 1–4, 1947–50. Annual?

C. J. S. assisted by P. D.

(6) THE THEATRE IN IRELAND

For the earlier twentieth century (Yeats, Synge etc) see Vol 3.

Bibliographies

O'Brien, M. N. Irish plays. New York 1938.
Macnamara, B. Abbey plays 1899–1948. Dublin 1949.
O'Mahony, M. Progress guide to Anglo-Irish plays. Dublin 1960.

Critical and Historical Works

Malone, A. E. The decline of the Irish drama. Nineteenth Century 97 1925.
— The Irish drama. 1929.
Clark, B. H. The Irish drama. In his Study of the modern drama, New York 1926, 1928 (rev), 1938 (rev).
Yeats, W. B. A defence of the Abbey theatre. Dublin Mag new ser 1 1926.
Byrne, D. The story of Ireland's national theatre. Dublin 1929.
Hobson, B. (ed). The Gate Theatre. Dublin 1934.
Macardle, D. Experiment in Ireland. Theatre Arts Monthly 18 1934.
Fay, W. G. and C. Carswell. The Fays of the Abbey theatre: an autobiographical record. 1935.
Wieczorek, H. Irische Lebenshaltung im neuen irischen Drama. Sprache und Kultur der Germanischen und Romanischen Völker 26 1937.
Robinson, L. (ed). The Irish Theatre. 1939.
O'Casey, S. Autobiographies. 6 vols 1939–54.
Fox, R. M. [A series of articles on the contemporary Irish theatre]. Theatre Arts Monthly 24–31 1940–7.
Nathan, G. J. Lament for Irish playwrights. Amer Mercury 52 1941.
Gregory, A. Lady Gregory's journals 1916–30. Ed L. Robinson 1946.
MacLiammoir, M. All for Hecuba. 1946, 1961 (rev).
— Theatre in Ireland. Dublin 1950, 1964 (rev).
Carroll, P. V. The Irish theatre: post war. In International theatre, ed J. Andrews and O. Trilling, 1949.
Kavanagh, P. The story of the Abbey Theatre. New York 1950.
Cole, A. The Gate influence on Dublin theatre. Dublin Mag new ser 29 1953.

Edwards, H. The mantle of Harlequin. Dublin 1958.
Fay, G. F. A. The Abbey Theatre: cradle of genius. 1958.
Jordan, J. The Irish theatre. In Contemporary theatre, ed J. R. Brown 1962 (Stratford-upon-Avon Stud 4).
Blaghd, E. dc. The Abbey Theatre. Dublin 1963.
Skelton, R. and D. R. Clark (ed). Irish renaissance. Amherst 1965.
Hogan, R. After the Irish renaissance. Minneapolis 1967.
Hogan, R. and M. J. O'Neill (ed). Joseph Holloway's Abbey Theatre. Carbondale 1967.
McCann, S. (ed). The story of the Abbey. 1967.
Thompson, W. I. The imagination of an insurrection: Dublin, Easter 1916. New York 1967.

L. O.

Periodicals

Beltaine: an occasional publication. (Organ of the Irish Literary Theatre). Nos 1–3, May 1899–April 1900. Irregular. Ed W. B. Yeats.
The Irish playgoer and amusement record. Dublin. Vol 1 no 1–vol 2 no 30, 9 Nov 1899–31 May 1900. Weekly.
Samhain: an occasional review. Dublin. Nos 1–7, Oct 1901–Nov 1908; suspended Dec 1905–Nov 1906. Irregular. Ed for the Irish Literary Theatre by W. B. Yeats.
The arrow. (Pbd by Abbey Theatre). Dublin. Nos 1–5, 20 Oct 1906–25 Aug 1909, Summer 1939. Suspended 1909–38. Irregular.
The Irish limelight: the only Irish journal devoted to cinema and theatrical topics. Dublin. Vol 1 no 1–vol 3 no 10, Jan 1917–Oct 1919. Later issues devoted only to cinema.
Motley. (The Dublin Gate Theatre magazine). Vol 1 no 1–vol 3 no 4, March 1932–May 1934. Monthly. Ed M. Manning.
Commentary. Dublin. Nov 1941–April 1947. Monthly. *See* col 1375, below.
Cinema and theatre annual review and directory of Ireland. Dublin 1947.

C. J. S.

(7) MUSIC HALL, MUSICAL COMEDY, PANTOMIME ETC

See bibliographies in Scott, 1946; Pulling, 1952; Howard, 1970, below. Some material has been included from areas adjacent to the subject; for fuller bibliographies of these see C. W. Beaumont, A bibliography of dancing, 1929; Complete book of ballets, 1937, 1949 (rev), 1951 (rev); and Supplement to Complete book of ballets, 1942, 1945 (with index); R. T. Stott, Circus and allied arts: a world bibliography 1500–1959, 3 vols Derby 1958–62 and A bibliography of books on the circus in England from 1773–1964, Derby 1964; F. S. Forrester, Ballet in England: a bibliography and survey c. 1700–June 1966, 1968.

Leno, D. Dan Leno, hys booke. 1899, ed J. Duncan 1968.
Bourdon, G. Les théâtres anglais. Paris 1903. Appendix, music halls functioning in 1903.
Jones, H. A. The licensing chaos in theatres and music halls. In his Foundations of a national drama, 1904, 1913 (rev).
— An open letter to the Right Honble Winston Churchill, M.P. [1910]. Advocating measures to legalize the production of plays at music halls.
Morton, W. H. and H. C. Newton (eds). Sixty years stage service: being a record of the life of Charles Morton, the father of the halls. 1905.
Wood, J. H. Dan Leno. 1905.
Allan, M. My life and dancing. 1908.

Williams, B. An actor's story. 1909.
— Bransby Williams, by himself. 1954.
Grossmith, W. From studio to stage: reminiscences. 1913.
Naylor, S. Gaiety and George Grossmith: random reflections on the serious business of enjoyment. 1913.
Hibbert, H. G. Fifty years of a Londoner's life. 1916.
— A playgoer's memories. Foreword by W. Archer 1920.
Lauder, H. A minstrel in France. [1918].
Parker, L. N. The pageant of Drury Lane Theatre 1663–1918. 1918.
— Several of my lives. 1928.
Sadler, M. Musical comedy's eleventh hour. Drama 1 1920.
Sutton, G. The art of Grand Guignol. Bookman (London) 60 1921.
— The shocking business in the Adelphi. In his Some contemporary dramatists, 1924. Account of Grand Guignol seasons in London.
Eliot, T. S. Marie Lloyd. Dial 73 1922; rptd (rev) in Criterion 1 1923 (as In memoriam: Marie Lloyd); and in his Selected essays, 1932 (as Marie Lloyd).
Haddon, A. Green room gossip. 1922. Contains account of interview with Harry Lauder.
— The story of the music hall: from cave of harmony to cabaret. 1924.

Agate, J. E. At half past eight: essays of the theatre 1921–2. 1923. Contains essay on death of Marie Lloyd.
—— Immmoment toys: a survey of light entertainment on the London stage 1920–43. 1945.
See Agate's collected reviews and criticism, cols 997–8, below, for further accounts of performers in music hall and allied arts.

Jupp, J. The Gaiety stage door: thirty years' reminiscences of the theatre. 1923.

Whanslaw, H. W. Everybody's theatre. 1923. On puppet theatre.

Beerbohm, M. Around theatres. 2 vols 1924, New York 1930, 1 vol London and New York 1953. Articles from Saturday Rev 1898–1910.
—— More theatres, 1898–1903. 1969.
—— Last theatres. 1970.

Booth, J. B. ('Costs'). Old Pink 'Un days. 1924.
—— 'Master' and men: Pink 'Un yesterdays. 1926.
—— London town. 1929.
—— Pink parade. Foreword by C. B. Cochran 1933.
—— A 'Pink 'Un' remembers. Foreword by C. B. Cochran 1937.
—— Sporting times: the Pink 'Un world. 1938.
—— The days we knew. 1943.
—— (ed). Seventy years of song. [1943]. Foreword by M. Beerbohm.
—— Palmy days. 1957.

Harker, J. In his Studio and stage, 1924. Introd by J. Forbes-Robertson.

Calthrop, D. C. Music hall nights. 1925.
—— Punch and Judy: a corner in the history of entertainment. 1926.
—— My own trumpet: being the story of my life. 1935.

Cochran, C. B. The secrets of a showman. 1925.
—— Review of revues, and other matters. 1930.
—— I had almost forgotten: random revelations. Preface by A. P. Herbert 1932.
—— Cock-a-doodle-do. 1941.
—— Showman looks on. 1945.

Disher, M. W. Clowns and pantomimes. 1925.
—— Anecdotes and intimacies. Music Hall Memories 16 Oct 1935 onwards. Series, on various music halls etc.
—— Winkles and champagne: comedies and tragedies of the music hall. 1938.
—— Fairs, circuses and music halls. 1942.
—— Melodrama: plots that thrilled. 1954.

Playfair, N. The story of the Lyric Theatre, Hammersmith. 1925. Introd by A. Bennett. Appendix gives list of comic operas etc at the Lyric 1918–23.
—— Hammersmith hoy: a book of minor revelations. 1930.

Glover, J. M. Hims ancient and modern: being the third book of Jimmy Glover. 1926. On London entertainments, including variety.

Sterne, A. and A. de Bear. The comic history of the Co-optimists. 1926.

Thompson, W. H. (Billy Merson). Fixing the stoof oop. [1926]. Reminiscences of variety and musical comedy.

Isaacs, S. C. The law relating to theatres, music halls, and other public entertainments, and to the performers therein, including the law of musical and dramatic copyright, etc. 1927.

Newton, H. C. Cues and curtain calls: being the theatrical reminiscences of H. Chance Newton ('Carados' of the Referee). 1927
—— Idols of the 'Halls': being my music hall memories. Foreword by O. Stoll 1928.

Roberts, A. Fifty years of spoof. 1927. With list of Roberts's principal rôles.

Duncan, I. My life. 1928.

Reynolds, H. Minstrel memories: the story of the burnt cork minstrelsy in Great Britain from 1836–1927. [1928].

Asche, O. His life, by himself. 1929.

Collier, C. Harlequinade. Preface by N. Coward 1929. Contains account of meeting with Dan Leno.

Priestley, J. B. Little Tich. In his Balconinny and other essays, 1929.
—— Music halls. In his Moments and other pieces, 1966.

Coffin, H. Hayden Coffin's book: packed with acts and facts. 1930.

Courtneidge, R. I was an actor once. [1930]. Contains a Dulac drawing of The Arcadians.

Gray, G. ('The Fighting Parson'). Vagaries of a vagabond. 1930.

Graves, G. Gaieties and gravities: autobiography of a comedian. 1931.

McKechnie, S. Popular entertainment through the ages. 1931.

Alltree, G. W. Footlight memories. [1932]. Recollections of music hall and stage life.

Burke, T. The real East End. 1932.

Collins, J. The maid of the mountains: her story. 1932.

Wilson, A. E. Penny plain, twopence coloured: a history of the juvenile drama. 1932. Foreword by C. B. Cochran. *See* also C. D. Williams, Index to illustrations shown in Wilson's Penny plain, twopence coloured, [1940].
—— Christmas pantomime: the story of an English institution. 1934, New York 1935 (as King Panto).
—— Theatre guyed: the Baedeker of Thespia. 1935.
—— Pantomime pageant: a procession of harlequins, clowns, comedians, principal boys etc. New York 1946.
—— The story of pantomime. 1949.
—— Half a century of entertainment. [1950]. Illustrated from Mander and Mitchenson collection.
—— Edwardian theatre. 1951.
—— Prime minister of mirth: the biography of Sir George Robey, CBE. 1956.

Robey, G. Looking back on life. 1933.

Croxton, A. Crowded nights and days: an unconventional pageant. [1934].

Lupino, S. From the stocks to the stars: an unconventional autobiography. 1934.

Tilley, V. Recollections. [1934].

Boardman, W. H. ('Billy'). Vaudeville days. Ed D. Whitelaw 1935.

Greenwall, H. J. The strange life of Willy Clarkson: an experiment in biography. 1936.

Jacob, N. 'Our Marie' [Marie Lloyd]. 1936.

Coward, N. Present indicative. 1937.

Foster, F. Clowning through. 1937.

Playfair, G. My father's son. 1937.

Brown, I. The English drolls. Theatre Arts Monthly 22 1938. *See* also Brown's collected criticism and reviews, cols 1014–15, below.

Short, E. H. and A. Compton-Rickett. Ring up the curtain. 1938.

Eustis, M. High jinks at the Music Box: Noel Coward rehearses Beatrice Lillie in Set to music. Theatre Arts Monthly 23 1939.

Foster, G. Spice of life: sixty-five years in the glamour world. 1939. Chs on Marie Lloyd, Harry Lauder, and on business side of variety.

Hicks, S. Me and my missus: fifty years on the stage. 1939.

Anderson, A. B. Old London theatres and music halls. N & Q 180 1941; reply by W. Jaggard 181 1941.

Farjeon, H. Herbert Farjeon omnibus. 1942. Sketches rptd from magazines, and lyrics from his revues.

Short, E. H. Theatrical cavalcade. 1942.
—— Fifty years of vaudeville 1894–1945. 1946.
—— Sixty years of theatre. 1951.

Anderson, J. (ed). Late joys at the Players' Theatre. 1943.

Forbes-Winslow D. Daly's: the biography of a theatre. 1944.

Lane, L. How to become a comedian. 1945.

Felstead, S. T. Stars who made the halls: a hundred years of English humour, harmony and hilarity. 1946.

Lawrence, G. A star danced. 1946.

Scott, H. The early doors: origins of the music hall. 1946.

Speaight, G. Juvenile drama: the history of the English toy theatre. 1946, 1969 (rev).

— Pantomime. Theatre Notebook 5 1951.

Tyrwhitt-Drake, G. The English circus and fair ground. 1946.

Batchelder, M. H. The puppet theatre handbook. New York 1947. With bibliography.

Forsyth, G. Notes on pantomime, with a list of Drury Lane pantomimes, 1870–1914. Theatre Notebook 2 1947.

Macqueen-Pope, W. Carriages at eleven: the story of the Edwardian theatre. 1947. Includes musical comedies.

— The melodies linger on: the story of the music hall. [1950].

— Ghosts and greasepaint: a story of the days that were. 1951.

— Ivor: the story of an achievement. 1951. Biography of Ivor Novello.

— Fortune's favourite: the life and times of Franz Lehár. 1953. With D. L. Murray.

— Shirtfronts and sables. 1953. On musical comedy, pantomime etc.

— Nights of gladness. 1956. On musical plays and comic operas.

— Queen of the music halls: being the dramatized story of Marie Lloyd. [1957].

— The footlights flickered. 1959. On musical comedies etc in London, 1920–9.

See also entries under Macqueen-Pope in Histories of Individual Theatres, cols 842–5, above.

Magriel, P. (ed). Isadora Duncan. New York 1947. Includes G. Craig's studies for 6 dance movements, and bibliography of I. Duncan.

Blackham, O. Puppets into actors. 1948.

— Shadow puppets. 1960.

Henson, L. Yours faithfully: an autobiography. 1948.

Fergusson, L. Old time music hall comedians. 1949.

Goodhart-Rendel, H. S. Edwardian musical comedy. Listener 17 Nov 1949.

Kavanagh, H. E. Tommy Handley. 1949.

Stead, P. J. Mr Punch. 1950.

Gorham, M. Showmen and suckers: an excursion on the crazy fringe of the entertainment world. 1951. Illustr E. Ardizzone.

Graves, C. P. R. The Cochran story: a biography of Sir Charles Blake Cochran, Kt. [1951].

Noble, P. Ivor Novello: man of the theatre. 1951.

Rose, Clarkson (Arthur Rose). With a twinkle in my eye. 1951. Autobiography.

— Beside the seaside. 1960.

— Red plush and greasepaint: a memory of the music hall from the nineties to the sixties. 1964.

Warner, J. Funny occupations as performed by Jack Warner. [1951].

Bevan, I. Top of the bill: the story of the London Palladium. 1952.

— Royal performance: the story of royal theatre going. 1954.

Clinton-Baddeley, V. C. The burlesque tradition in the English theatre after 1660. 1952.

— In his All right on the night, 1954.

— Some pantomime pedigrees. 1963.

Le Roy, G. Music hall stars of the nineties. 1952. Includes accounts of Harry Lauder, Lupino etc.

Pulling, C. They were singing: and what they sang about. 1952.

Sheridan, P. Late and early joys at the Players' Theatre. 1952.

Courtneidge, C. Cicely. 1953.

Wodehouse, P. G. and G. R. Bolton. Bring on the girls: the improbable story of our life in musical comedy, with pictures to prove it. New York 1953.

Parker, A. Pageants. 1954.

Reeve, A. Take it for a fact. 1954. Autobiography.

Edwards, J. K. O'N. Take it from me. 1955.

Terriss, E. Just a little bit of string. 1955. Reminiscences.

Barker, E. Steady, Barker! 1956.

Niklaus, T. Harlequin Phoenix: or the rise and fall of a bergamask rogue. 1956. Refers to Mime Theatre Company.

Barker, F. The house that Stoll built. 1957.

'Grock' (i.e. A. Wettach). Grock: king of clowns. 1957. First pbd Stuttgart 1957 (as Nit M-ö-ö-ö-glich).

White, J. Born to star: the Lupino Lane story. 1957.

Beaumont, C. W. Puppets and puppetry. 1958. Photographs of European and American puppets, with short general history.

Nichols, B. The sweet and twenties. 1958.

Trewin, J. C. In his The gay twenties: a decade of the theatre, 1958. Pictures by Mander and Mitchenson. Foreword by N. Coward.

Behrman, S. N. Conversation with Max. 1960. Max Beerbohm reminiscing on music hall artists among others.

Browse, L. Sickert. 1960. Includes Sickert's sketches etc of music halls.

Fields, G. Sing as we go. 1960.

Gresham, W. L. Houdini. 1960.

Flanagan, B. My crazy life. 1961.

Mander, R. and J. Mitchenson. The theatres of London. 1961, 1963 (rev).

— British music hall: a story in pictures. 1965. Illustrated from Mander and Mitchenson collection. Foreword by J. Betjeman. Contains cast lists for Royal Variety performances 1912–64.

— The lost theatres of London. 1968.

— Musical comedy: a story in pictures. Foreword by N. Coward 1969.

Polyakov, N. P. Coco the clown: by himself. 1962 (rev).

Chaplin, C. My autobiography. 1964.

Fletcher, G. The magic of the Halls. In his London overlooked, 1964.

Binyon, H. Puppetry today. 1966.

British Film Institute. British music hall. [1966?] (The Film as a Record of Contemporary Life 1). A catalogue of music hall turns.

Shaw, C. and A. Oates. A pictorial history of the art of female impersonation. 1966.

McInnes, C. Sweet Saturday night. 1967.

Mills, C. B. Bertram Mills circus. 1967.

Van Damm, S. We never closed. 1967. History of the Windmill Theatre.

Baker, R. Drag: a history of female impersonation on the stage. 1968.

Christopher, M. Houdini: the untold story. 1969.

Grun, B. Gold and silver. 1970. Biography of Lehar.

Howard, D. London theatres and music halls 1850–1950. 1970.

See Accounts of London Theatres, cols 842–6, above, for histories of other theatres associated with the music hall and allied forms.

K. J. W.

Periodicals

The era. Vols 1–103, 30 Sept 1838–21 Sept 1939. Weekly.

The sporting times ('The pink 'un'): a chronicle of racing, literature, art, and the drama. Nos 1–3559, 11 Feb 1865–5 Dec 1931. Weekly.

Era almanac. Vols 1–2, 1868–9. Continued as The era almanac and annual, vols 3–41, 1870–1919. Conducted by F. Ledger.

Entr'acte. Nos 138–1974, 24 Feb 1872–26 April 1907. Started as London entr'acte, 1869. Weekly.

The entr'acte almanack and theatrical and music hall annual. Vols 1–34, 1873–1906.

The stage directory. Nos 1–14, 1 Feb 1880–1 March 1881. Continued as The stage, no 1, 25 March 1881 onwards; The Stage guide, 1912; The Stage year book, 1908–28, 1949 onwards. *See* below.

The Mohawk minstrels' 'nigger' dramas, dialogues and drolleries. No 1, 1888. Continued as The Mohawk minstrels' annual, nos 2–10. Continued as Francis & Day's 11th/12th book of dialogues [no 12, 1910]. Ed C. Townley (?) no 1, T. Little nos 2–10.

The music hall and theatre review. Vol 1 no 1–vol 3 no 1229, 16 Feb 1889–5 Sept 1912. Weekly.

Will A. Bradley's pantomime annual. Liverpool. Vols 1–4, 1900/1–1904. Ed 'Dromio'.

Showman; an illustrated journal for showmen and all entertainers. Vol 1 no 1–vol 4 no 69, Sept 1900–28 March 1902; then incorporated in The music hall and theatre review. Weekly.

The hippodrome: an illustrated vaudeville magazine. 1901–?

The playlet and monologue magazine. Nos 1–5, [1901]. Not dated; 'monthly' appears on first issue. Conducted by C. D. Hickman.

The international entertainer: the variety artistes' illustrated magazine. Vol 1 nos 1–2, April–May 1902. Monthly Ed A. C. Lyster.

PAD: patter and dialogue for ventriloquists, conjurors, raconteurs, minstrels, pierrots, single-handed comedians, cross-talkers, and burlesque-double turns. No 1, [1902]. Incorporated in, The playlet and monologue magazine. Conducted by C. D. Hickman.

The stage souvenir: an illustrated monthly journal, with a real photograph as a supplement. Nos 1–4, 1903. Monthly. Issues not dated. Ed F. Dangerfield.

Music hall pictorial and variety stage. Nos 1–3, Dec 1904–[Feb 1905]. Monthly. Not dated after first issue.

The magician: a monthly journal devoted to magic, spiritualism, hypnotism and human progress. Liverpool/London. Vol 1 no 1–vol 35 no 9, Dec 1904–Aug 1939.

The play: an illustrated monthly. Vol 1 nos 1–6, 1904. Continued as The play pictorial, nos 1–6, 1905. Monthly.

R. Douglas Cox's theatrical and C. Douglas Stuart's variety directory. [1904].

Variety stage illustrated. Nos 1–3, 16–30 Jan 1905. Weekly.

The variety theatre. Vol 1 no 1–vol 3 no 33, 12 May 1905–5 Jan 1906. Weekly.

The green room book: or Who's who on the stage. Vols 1–4, 1906–9. Continued as Who's who in the theatre, 1912 onwards. Annual edns in 1912, 1914, 1916, 1922, 1925, 1930, 1933, 1936, 1939, 1947, 1952, 1957, 1961, 1967. 1916 edn contains suppl, Who's who in variety. Early edns of Who's who on the stage ed J. Parker, editor of The green room book, 1908–9.

Variety time table and programme. Nos 1–44, 26 Feb–31 Dec 1906. Weekly.

The performer: official organ of the Variety Artistes' Federation. Vol 1 no 1–vol 105 no 2674, 29 March 1906–26 Sept 1957. Weekly. Special Christmas number, Performer annual, 1907–32.

The variety theatre annual. Vol 1, 1906/7.

The performer annual. 1907–32. Special Christmas number.

The Stage year book: with which is included the stage provincial guide. Vols 1–21, 1908–28; 1949 onwards. Ed L. Carson.

The Thalia diary and directory of concert parties and entertainers. [Vols 1–6], 1910–15. Annual.

The Stage guide. 1912. Ed L. Carson. Rev edn ed A. W. Tolmie 1946.

Sunday chronicle: pantomime annual. Nos 1–19, London and Manchester 1912/13–1930/31, Continued as Sunday Chronicle: pantomime and amusement annual, no 20, 1931/2. Ed 'Bayard'.

Pantomime and vaudeville favourites. [1913]–? Ed W. Goldston.

Universal musical and dramatic directory. 1913. English edn of Annuaire des artistes.

The Thalia diary and directory for music halls and music-hall artists. 1914.

The theatre, music hall and cinema blue book for 1917: a list of public amusement companies with full financial particulars of interest to investors. Vol 1, 1917. Continued as The theatre, music hall and cinema companies' blue book, vols 2–13, 1918–29/30. Annual.

The grand guignol annual review. (Little Theatre). 1921.

The theatre world and illustrated stage review. Vol 1 no 1–vol 4 no 20, Feb 1925–Sept 1926. Monthly. Absorbed Theatre and film illustrated. Ed Sheridan Bickers to no 6, July 1925, then 'S.T.H.'.

'The spotlight' casting directory for stage and screen. Nos 1–90, Aug 1927–July 1952. Quarterly, nos 1–61, Aug 1927–Sept 1942. 3 times a year, nos 62–89, 1942–51. From no 71, Jan 1946, each issue has 2 pts. From no 89, Jan 1952, twice a year. Continued as 'The spotlight' casting directory for stage, screen, radio and television, nos 91–109, Jan 1953–spring 1962 (from no 102, autumn 1958, each issue has 4 pts). Continued as Spotlight, no 110, Autumn 1962 onwards. Twice a year from no 89, Jan 1952.

Theatre and film illustrated. Vol 1 no 1–vol 4 no 24, Feb 1928–March 1930. Monthly. Incorporated in Theatre world.

The 'spotlight' year book. Vols 1–3, 1931–3. Ed W. K. Moss.

Variety, music, stage and film news. Vol 1 no 1–vol 5 no 106, 2 Sept 1931–6 Sept 1933. Continued as Variety, cabaret, film news, vol 6 no 107–vol 8 no 251, 13 Sept 1933–18 June 1936. Weekly.

Amusement world: a weekly journal for amusement centres, seaside and pleasure proprietors. Vol 1 no 1, 22 Jan 1932. Continued as Amusement world: professional amusement caterers, showmen, and public entertainers, vol 1 nos 2–7, 29 Jan–4 March 1932. Weekly.

The dancer and cabaret. Vol 1 nos 1–6, July–Dec 1932. Monthly. Continued as Dancing and film news.

Who's who in dancing. 1932. Ed A. Haskell and P. J. S. Richardson.

Garroway's directory of concert and variety artistes. 1934.

The modern dance. Vol 1 no 1–vol 4 no 3, 1934–Dec 1937. Continued as The modern dance and the dancer, vol 4 no 4–vol 31 no 8, Jan 1938–June 1965. Monthly.

NODA bulletin: the official organ of the National Operatic & Dramatic Association. Vol 1 no 1, Sept 1935 onwards. Irregular. 3 issues a year from 1946 to the present.

British Puppet and Model Theatre Guild: wartime bulletin. Nos 1–17, 1939–45. Irregular. Continued as The puppet master: the journal of the British Puppet and Model theatre Guild, Jan 1946 onwards. Ed A. E. Peterson.

The model stage: the quarterly magazine of Pollock's Toy Theatre Club. Nos 1–3, 1946?–50. Quarterly, irregular.

Show world. Nos 1–517, 11 Sept 1946–12 Jan 1957. Continued as Show world and film and t.v. advertiser, nos 518–25, 19 Jan–9 March 1957. Continued as Show world, film, radio, record and t.v. advertiser, nos 526–35, 16 March–10 Aug 1957. Weekly.

Variety fare. Vol 1 no 1–vol 3 no 2, May 1946–Aug 1947. Continued as Night-life, vol 3 no 3–vol 4 no 2, Sept 1947–April 1948.

The green register, 1946–7: a comprehensive index and register of theatrical artists of stage, screen, radio, music. [1947]. Called a 'Confidential issue to the theatrical profession'.

Stage and screen miscellany. Vol 1 no 1, Spring 1947. Continued as Stage and screen no 2, Summer 1947. Quarterly. Ed P. Noble.

The Laban Art of Movement Guild: news sheet. [Nos 1]–36, [1948]–May 1966. Irregular. Ed B. Ellis.

Movement: an international magazine. (Laban Art of Movement Guild). Vol 1 nos 1–2, Summer–Winter 1948. Quarterly. Ed G. Deckmann.

British puppet theatre. Vol 1 no 1–vol 3 no 5, Dec 1949–Jan 1953. Monthly.

Spotlight: stage and screen casting directory: American and European edition. 1949. Annual.

Theatre world annual: a pictorial review of West End productions. 1949/50 onwards.

Dance and dancers. Vol 1 no 1–vol 13 no 12, Jan 1950–Dec 1962. Monthly. Ed P. Williams.

Stage and variety artistes guide and handbook. Vol 1, 1950. Annual.

C. J. S. assisted by P. D.

(8) RADIO AND TELEVISION DRAMA AND ADAPTATIONS

See also Book Production (Literature, Society and Communication: Relations with other media, and Authorship: manuals and guides) cols 53–60 and 63–8, above.

Enser, A. G. S. Filmed books and plays: a list of books and plays from which films have been made, 1928–49. 1951. Suppls 1952, onwards.

British Broadcasting Corporation. British broadcasting. 1958. A bibliography.

Collison, R. Broadcasting in Britain: a bibliography. 1961. (National Book League. Reader's guide).

Farquharson, J. Picture plays and how to write them. 1916.

Weston, H. In his The art of photo-play writing, 1916.

Ball, E. H. In his Cinema plays: how to write them, 1917.

Jones, H. A. The dramatist and the photo play. Mentor 9 1921.

Shaw, G. B. and A. Henderson. Drama, the theatre and the films. Fortnightly Rev 122 (new ser 116) 1924.

Darlington, W. A. In his Literature in the theatre, and other essays, 1925.

Granville-Barker, H. On translating plays. Essays by Divers Hands 5 1925.

Lea, G. Radio drama and how to write it. 1926.

Berkeley, R. C. Machines: a symphony of modern life. 1927. Includes correspondence with BBC, and preface on writing for radio.

Peach, L. du G. Broadcast sketches. 1927, with preface on radio drama. Several other vols of broadcast sketches by Peach contain same preface.

Ervine, St J. In his How to write a play, 1928.

Dukes, A. Play translation. Author 41 1930.

— From studio theatre to television. Theatre Arts Monthly 21 1937.

— Televised drama so far: the English scene. Theatre Arts Monthly 22 1938.

Denison, M. The broadcast play. Theatre Arts Monthly 15 1931.

Guthrie, T. Squirrel's cage, and two other microphone plays [Matrimonial views; The flowers are not for you to pick]. 1931. Introd by Guthrie on possibilities of radio drama; rptd in P. R. Smith (ed), On the air, Sydney 1959.

Hazlitt, H. Pictures from plays. Nation 30 Sept 1931.

Fawcett, L. In his Writing for the film, 1932.

Gielgud, V. How to write broadcast plays; with three examples: Friday morning, Red tabs, and Exiles. [1932].

— Radio play in the age of television. Theatre Arts Monthly 21 1937.

— Foreword to P. Hamilton, Money with menaces and To the public danger: two radio plays, 1939.

— Radio theatre: plays specially written for broadcasting selected by V. Gielgud, 1946, with an essay by Gielgud on the technique of writing for radio.

— Years of the locust. 1947. Autobiography.

— The right way to radio playwriting. Kingswood, Surrey [1948]. Includes ch on television.

— British radio drama 1922–56: a survey. 1957. Contains chs (rev) from Radio theatre and Years of the locust.

— Years in a mirror. 1965.

Wyatt, E. V. The stage and the screen. Catholic World 135 1932.

Knowles, D. In her The censor, the drama and the film, 1900–34. 1934.

Sieveking, L. The stuff of radio. Introd by R. Hughes 1934.

Times 14 Aug 1934. Special broadcasting number.

Wilson, C. W. Writing for broadcasting. 1935.

Nicoll, A. Film and theatre. New York 1936. With bibliography.

— Literature and the film. Eng Jnl 26 1937.

Thomas, H. The brighter blackout book. 1939. Includes scripts of radio plays.

Lambert, R. S. Ariel and all his quality. 1940.

Sayers, D. L. The man born to be king: a play-cycle on the life of our Lord and Saviour Jesus Christ, written for broadcasting. 1943. With introd and production notes by author and producer, and foreword by the Director of Religious Broadcasting.

MacNeice, L. Christopher Columbus: a radio play. 1944. Introd on technique of writing for radio.

— The dark tower and other radio scripts. 1947. Introd on radio drama and notes on each script.

— Persons from Porlock and other plays for radio. 1969. Introd on MacNeice and radio drama by W. H. Auden.

Bax, C. and L. M. Lion. Hemlock for eight: a radio play. 1946. Preface by Bax on writing radio plays, preface by Lion on radio monopoly as a threat to drama and literature.

Constanduros, M. Shreds and patches. 1946. Autobiography with chs on early days at BBC.

Henderson, D. The trial of Lizzie Borden and other radio plays. [1946]. Foreword by H. Hobson on radio drama.

Johnston, D. Television: the present and the future. In J. E. Morpurgo (ed), Penguin parade, 2nd ser 1, 1947.

Kennedy, M. M. The mechanised muse. 1947.

Kevin, D. Radio play writing. 1947. Script of In pastures green, with some comments on writing radio plays.

Reed, H. Moby Dick: a play for radio, from Herman Melville's novel. 1947. Preface discusses problems of adaptation.

Five radio plays. 1948. Introd by V. Gielgud on radio plays.

Hatton, C. Radio plays and how to write them. 1948.

White, M. and F. Stock. In their Right way to write for the films, Kingswood, Surrey 1948.

Felton, R. F. The radio play: its technique and possibilities. 1949.

Gorham, M. Television: medium of the future. 1949.

— Broadcasting and television since 1900. 1952.

Tilsley, F. Television story. [1949]. (BBC pbn).

Vardac, A. N. Stage to screen: theatrical method from Garrick to Griffith. 1949.

Gilliam, L. (ed). BBC features. 1950.

Wright, B. Film making and screen writing. Author 60 1950; reply by M. Slater, 61 1950.

James, C. F. The story of the Performing Right Society. 1951.

Williams, S. Plays on the air: a survey of drama broadcasts. 1951.

Literature and the lively arts. TLS 14 Nov 1952. See also correspondence in succeeding issues, L. MacNeice, P. Dickinson and others.

Weisman, H. M. An investigation of methods and techniques in the dramatization of fiction. Speech Monographs 19 1952.

Ackland, R. The celluloid mistress: or, the custard pie of Dr Caligari. 1954. With E. Grant.

Mander, R. and J. Mitchenson. Shaw and the films. In their Theatrical companion to Shaw, [1954].

Trewin, J. C. We'll hear a play. BBC Quart 9 1954.

Knoblock, E. The playwright's progress. Listener 2 June 1955; rptd in his Kismet and other plays, 1957.

Hughes, R. The birth of radio drama. Atlantic Monthly 200 1957.

Maschwitz, E. No chip on my shoulder. 1957.

Thorp, M. F. Shakespeare and the movies. Shakespeare Quart 9 1958.

McWhinnie, D. The art of radio. 1959.

Briggs, A. The history of broadcasting in the United Kingdom: vol 1, The birth of broadcasting, 1961; vol 2, The golden age of wireless, 1965.

Costello, D. P. The serpent's eye: Shaw and the cinema. Notre Dame [1965]. Includes list of films made from Shaw's plays, scenes for film version of The devil's disciple, sound track version of Act 5 of Pygmalion and screen play for a projected film version of Arms and the man.

Minney, R. J. Gradual conversion to films. In his Bogus image of Bernard Shaw, 1969.

Periodicals

Radio times. 28 Sept 1923 onwards.

The broadcast listeners' year book. 1924.

The listener. (Pbd by the BBC). Nos 1–1605, 16 Jan 1929–31 Dec 1959. Continued as The listener and BBC television review, no 1606, 7 Jan 1960 onwards. Weekly.

BBC handbook 1928–9; continued as BBC year book 1930–4; continued as BBC annual 1935–7; continued as BBC handbook 1938–42; continued as BBC yearbook 1943–52; not pbd 1953–4; continued as BBC handbook 1955 onwards.

Who's who in broadcasting. 1933–?

Who's who on the wireless. 1934–?

Ariel: the BBC staff magazine. 1936 onwards.

BBC quarterly. Vol 1 no 1–vol 9 no 3, 1946–54.

The radio digest. 1946–?

Television. Vols 1–4, 1946–9; continued as Television and the viewers, vol 5–? 1950–?

British television year book. 1947/8–? Ed A. Gray.

Scan: the television journal. Vol 1 no 1–vol 3 no 8, May 1948–Dec 1950. Continued, with Television news, as Scan television news, vol 3 no 9–vol 4 no 2, Jan–June 1951; continued as Television news, vol 4 no 3–vol 6, July 1951–3.

Television news. Vol 1 no 1–vol 2 no 2, Nov 1948–Dec 1949. Incorporated in Scan, above.

K.J.W.

(9) ACTORS AND ACTING

Biographies and Reminiscences

Pemberton, T. E. Ellen Terry and her sisters. 1902.

—— Sir Charles Wyndham. 1904.

Brereton, A. The Lyceum and Henry Irving. 1903.

—— Henry Irving. 1905.

Bancroft, M. E. and S. B. The Bancrofts. 1909.

Hicks, S. Seymour Hicks: twenty-four years of an actor's life. 1910.

—— Hail fellow, well met. 1949.

Frohman, D. Memories of a manager. 1911.

Walbrook, H. M. Nights at the play. 1911.

Grossmith, W. From studio to stage: reminiscences of Weedon Grossmith. 1913.

Naylor, S. Gaiety and George Grossmith: random reflections on the serious business of enjoyment. 1913.

Howe, P. P. Dramatic portraits. 1913.

Tree, H. B. Thoughts and afterthoughts. 1913. See also M. Beerbohm, Herbert Beerbohm Tree, 1920; H. Pearson, Beerbohm Tree: his life and laughter, 1956.

Irving, H. B. The amusement of the people. 1916. A lecture. See also A. Brereton, 'H.B.' and Lawrence Irving, 1922.

Sothern, E. H. My remembrances. 1917.

Haddon, A. Greenroom gossip. 1922.

Harker, J. C. Studio and stage. 1924.

Forbes-Robertson, J. F. A player under three reigns. 1925.

Barrymore, J. Confessions of an actor. Indianapolis 1926.

Compton, F. Rosemary: some remembrances. 1926.

Maude, C. Behind the scenes with Cyril Maude. 1927.

Arliss, G. On the stage: an autobiography. 1928.

Asche, O. His life, by himself. 1929.

Collier, C. Harlequinade: the story of my life. 1929.

Benson, F. My memoirs. 1930.

Courtneidge, R. I was an actor once. 1930.

Graham, J. An old stock actor's memories. 1930.

Harvey, J. M. Autobiography. 1930. See also M. W. Disher, The last romantic: authorised biography of J. Martin-Harvey, 1948.

Playfair, N. Hammersmith hoy: a book of minor revelations. 1930.

Hardwicke, C. Let's pretend; recollections and reflections of a lucky actor. 1932.

McCarthy, L. Myself and friends. 1933.

Robey, G. Looking back on life. 1933.

Sutro, A. Celebrities and simple souls. 1933.

Du Maurier, D. Gerald [du Maurier]: a portrait. 1934.

Lupino, S. From the stocks to the stars. 1934.

Blow, S. The ghost walks on Fridays: in and out of the stage door. 1935.

—— Through stage doors. 1938.

Fay, W. G. and C. Carswell. The Fays of the Abbey Theatre. 1935.

Mason, A. E. W. Sir George Alexander and the St James's Theatre. 1935.

Williams, H. Four years at the Old Vic 1929–33. 1935.

Arthur, G. From Phelps to Gielgud. 1936.

Ashwell, L. Myself a player. 1936.

Bolitho, H. Marie Tempest. 1936.

Greenwall, H. J. The strange life of Willy Clarkson. 1936.

Coward, N. Present indicative. 1937. See also list of his works, cols 924–7, below.

Playfair, G. My father's son. 1937.

Adam, R. Overture and beginners. 1938.

Lanchester, E. Charles Laughton and I. 1938.

Lehmann, L. Wings of song: an autobiography. 1938.

Loraine, V. Robert Loraine. 1938.

Pearson, H. Thinking it over. 1938.

—— The last actor-managers. 1950.

Fairbrother, S. Through an old stage door. 1939.

Gielgud, J. Early stages. 1939.

—— Stage directions. 1963. See also R. Gilder, John Gielgud's Hamlet, 1937; H. Fordham, John Gielgud, 1952; R. L. Sterne, John Gielgud directs Richard Burton in Hamlet, 1968.

Robbins, E. Both sides of the curtain. 1940.

Darlington, W. A. I do what I like. 1941.

Agate, M. Madame Sarah [Bernhardt]. 1945. See also C. O. Skinner, Madame Sarah, Boston 1967.

Bax, C. (ed). All the world's a stage: theatrical portraits. 1946.

—— Some I knew well. 1951.

Lawrence, G. A star danced. 1946.

MacLiammoir, M. All for Hecuba: an Irish theatrical

autobiography. 1946. *See* also list of his works, cols 964–5, below.

Gielgud, V. Years of the locust. 1947.

Gill, M. See the players. 1948.

Henson, L. Yours faithfully: an autobiography. 1948.

Lion, L. M. Surprise of my life. 1948.

Whitworth, G. Harley Granville-Barker: reprint of a broadcast. 1948. *See* also C. B. Purdom, Harley Granville Barker, 1955.

Cotes, P. No star nonsense. 1949.

Maltby, H. F. Ring up the curtain. 1950.

Macqueen-Pope, W. Ghosts and greasepaint. 1951.

— Back numbers. 1954.

— Give me yesterday. 1957.

Noble, P. Ivor Novello: men of the theatre. 1951.

— The fabulous Orson Welles. 1957.

Bankhead, T. Tallulah: my autobiography. 1952.

Matthews, A. E. Matty: an autobiography. 1952.

Barker, F. The Oliviers: a biography. 1953.

Stokes, S. Without veils: intimate biography of Gladys Cooper. 1953.

Tynan, K. Alec Guinness. 1953.

Trewin, J. C. Edith Evans. 1954.

— Sybil Thorndike. 1956.

— Robert Helpmann. 1957.

— Margaret Rutherford. 1959.

— Paul Scofield. 1959.

— Robert Donat. 1965.

Williams, B. Bransby Williams by himself. 1954.

Dunbar, J. Flora Robson. 1956.

Keown, E. Peggy Ashcroft. 1956.

Williamson, A. Paul Rogers. 1956.

'Findlater, Richard' (K. B. F. Bain). Emlyn Williams: an illustrated study of his work. 1957. *See* also E. Williams, George: an early autobiography, 1961.

— Michael Redgrave—actor. 1957.

Travers, B. Vale of laughter. 1957.

Hobson, H. Ralph Richardson. 1958. *See* also Ralph Richardson looks back, Sunday Times, 3 July 1960.

Dent, A. Mrs Patrick Campbell. 1961.

Marinacci, E. Leading ladies: theatrical portraits. 1962.

Morley, R. Responsible gentleman. 1967.

The Art of Acting

Armstrong, C. F. The actor's companion. 1912.

Gillette, W. The illusion of the first time in acting. Introd by G. Arliss 1915.

Dean, B. The actor and his workshop. 1922. Lecture at Victoria and Albert Museum during International Theatre Exhibition.

Bernhardt, S. The art of the theatre. 1924.

Bosworth, H. Technique in dramatic art. New York 1926, 1934 (rev).

Barry, P. B. How to succeed on the stage: a practical handbook to the actor's profession. 1927.

O'Neill, R. M. The science and art of speech and gesture: founded on the life work of Delsarte. 1927.

Behnke, K. E. Speech and movement on the stage. 1930.

Crauford, L. Acting: its theory and practice. 1930.

Jennings, H. The actor's craft. 1930.

Benson, F. I want to go on the stage. Do? Don't? How? 1931.

Hicks, S. Acting: a book for amateurs. 1931.

Coquelin, B. C. The art of the actor. Tr E. Fogerty, 1932.

Boleslavsky, R. Acting: the first 6 lessons. New York 1933.

Lewis, E. The producer and the players. 1933.

Selden, S. A player's handbook: theory and practice of acting. New York 1934.

Mackenzie, F. The amateur actor. 1935, 1936 (rev).

Stanislavsky, C. An actor prepares. Tr E. R. Hapgood, New York 1936.

— Building a character. Tr E. R. Hapgood, New York 1949.

See also Acting: a handbook of the Stanislavsky method, ed T. Cole, New York 1947; D. Magarshack, Stanislavsky on the art of the stage, 1950; O. Edwards, The Stanislavsky heritage, 1966; S. Moore, The Stanislavsky system, 1966.

D'Angelo, A. The actor creates. New York 1939.

Speaight, R. Acting: its idea and tradition. 1939.

Seyler, A. and S. Haggard. The craft of comedy: a correspondence. 1943.

Lane, L. How to become a comedian. 1945.

Jeayes, A. Letter to a young actor. 1946.

Albright, H. D. Working up a part. Boston 1947.

Cole, T. and H. K. Chinnoy. Actors on acting. New York 1949.

Darlington, W. A. The actor and his audience. 1949.

Laban, R. van. The mastery of movement on the stage. 1950, 1960 (rev and enlarged by L. Ullmann, as The mastery of movement).

Vanbrugh, I. Hints on the art of acting: talks to students of the Royal Academy of Dramatic Art. 1951.

Redgrave, M. The actor's ways and means. 1953.

— Mask or face. 1958.

Lane, Y. The psychology of the actor. 1959.

Saint-Denis, M. Theatre: the rediscovery of style. 1960.

Fishman, M. The actor in training. 1961.

Duerr, E. The length and depth of acting. New York 1962.

Funke, L. and J. E. Booth. Actors talk about acting. 1962.

Gray, D. and M. Denison. The actor and his world. 1964.

Burton, H. (ed). Great acting: BBC TV interviews. 1967.

Hobbs, W. The technique of the stage fight. 1968.

G.A.

Periodicals

The Stage directory. Nos 1–14, 1 Feb 1880–1 March 1881. Continued as The stage, no 1, 25 March 1881 onwards.

Plays and players. Liverpool 1904. Annual of Smith's Liverpool weekly.

The actor illustrated: a monthly review of the stage. Vol 1 nos 1–13, Jan 1905–Jan 1906. Registration issue 1 Oct 1904.

The performer: official organ of the Variety Artistes' Federation. Vol 1 no 1–vol 105 no 2674, 29 March 1906–26 Sept 1957. Special Christmas number, Performer annual 1907–32.

The Stage year book. 1908–28; 1949 onwards.

The Stage guide. 1912, 1946 (rev).

Actresses' Franchise League. [Annual report 1912–13]. 1913.

'A.A.': the official organ of the Actors' Association. Vol 1 no 1–vol 2 no 11, Jan 1917–Dec 1918. Continued as The actor for player and public, vol 1 no 1–vol 3 no 8, Jan 1919–July 1922. Monthly.

The Actors' Association yearbook. 1917.

The performer handbook. [1921]. Ed John Warr.

The Scottish player. (Issued by the Scottish National Theatre Society) Glasgow. Vols 1–4, July? 1923–April 1926. Monthly.

Stage props. 1923. Annual. Ed G. du Maurier.

The municipal player: a magazine for mummers. Birmingham. Vols 1–3, May 1924–June 1926. New series vols 1–4, Sept 1927–Aug 1931. Monthly.

Theatre world and illustrated stage review. Vol 1 no 1–vol 4 no 20, Feb 1925–Sept 1926. Monthly. Absorbed into Theatre and film illustrated.

'The spotlight' casting directory for stage and screen. Nos 1–90, Aug 1927–July 1952. Quarterly, nos 1–61, Aug 1927–Sept 1942; 3 times a year, nos 62–89, 1942–52 (from no 71 each issue has 2 pts); from 89, Jan 1952 twice a year. Continued as 'The spotlight' casting directory for stage, screen, radio and television, nos 91–109, Jan 1953–spring 1962 (from no 102, autumn 1958, each issue has 4 pts).

The theatrical manager, with which is incorporated The acting manager and musical director: the official organ of the Association of Touring and Producing Managers. Vol 1 no 1–vol 2 no 18, Dec 1928–Jan 1931. Monthly at first, then irregular.

Hardey's universal theatre directory. Cheltenham 1928.

Plays and players. Vols 1–3, 19 Oct 1929–19 Sept 1933. Monthly.

The call board: the quarterly organ of Actors' Church Union. Nos 1–32, Feb 1930–Nov 1937.

The red stage: organ of the Workers' Theatre Movement. Nos 1–5, Nov 1931–April/May 1932. Continued as New red stage, nos 6–7, June/July–Sept 1932. Irregular.

The spotlight yearbook. Vols 1–3, 1931–3. Ed W. Keith Moss.

British Actors' Equity…annual report. 1931/2–1932/3. Continued as What Equity is doing, 1935/6 onwards. Annual.

Stage stars of today, portrayed by theatre world. First ser [1932].

Unemployed drama news; introductory issue. 1936. Ed Kathleen Edwards.

The call sheet: a casting directory of small-part players. Vol 1 nos 1–3, July 1937–38? Also autumn suppl for 1937. Quarterly. Irregular.

The London artiste: the medium between the artiste and the booker. Vols 1–9 no 3, 1945–Feb 1954. Continued as The London artiste and general advertiser, vol 9 nos 4–5, March–April 1954.

Theatre mirror. Issued by the New Yiddish Theatre Beth am. In English and Yiddish. Vol 1 no 1–vol 2 no 16, March 1946–June/July 1947. Monthly. Nos 15–16 form a combined issue.

British theatre. 1946. Annual.

The green register: a comprehensive index and register of theatrical artists of stage, screen, radio and music. 1946–7.

The artistes bulletin. Nos 1–2, Dec 1947. Feb 1948. Ed Cary Ellison.

Spotlight-contacts: stage and screen. Jan 1949 onwards. 3 issues a year to no 30, Oct 1958; 2 issues a year since no 31, April 1959.

Spotlight: stage and screen casting directory: American and European edition. 1949. Annual.

Theatre world annual: a pictorial review of West End productions. 1949/50 onwards.

Stage and variety artistes guide and handbook. Vol 1, 1950. Annual.

C.J.S.

(10) PRODUCERS AND THE ART OF PRODUCTION

Items pbd abroad are included because of their influence on producers and the art of production in this country during the period, or because they discuss techniques common to the art of production in various countries during the period.

Craig, E. G. The art of the theatre. 1905. *See* also list of his works, cols 1031–2, below.

Carter, H. The theatre of Max Reinhardt. 1914.

— The new spirit in the European theatre 1914–24. 1925.

— The new spirit in the Russian theatre 1917–28. 1929.

Copeau, J. L'école du Vieux-Colombier. Cahiers du Vieux-Colombier no 2 1921.

— Souvenirs du Vieux-Colombier. Paris 1931; *see* also W. D. Frank, The art of the Vieux Colombier, New York 1918; M. Kurtz, Jacques Copeau, Paris 1950.

— La mise en scène. Encyclopédie Francaise vol 17 1935.

Shaw, G. B. On the art of rehearsal. Arts League of Service Annual 1921–2 [1922]. *See* also list of his works, vol 3 cols 1169–74.

Granville-Barker, H. The exemplary theatre. 1922.

— Shakespeare and modern stagecraft. Yale Rev 15 1926. *See* also list of his works, cols 944–5, below.

Waxman, S. M. Antoine and the théâtre-libre. Cambridge Mass 1926.

Komisarjevsky, T. Myself and the theatre. 1929.

Piscator, E. Das politische Theater. Berlin 1929.

Purdom, C. B. Producing plays. 1930, 1940 (rev), 1951 (rev).

Antoine, A. Le théâtre. Paris 1932.

Browne, E. M. The production of religious plays. 1932.

— [et al]. Putting on a play. 1936.

Guthrie, T. Theatre prospect. 1932.

— The producer's job. Listener 20 March 1941.

Lugné-Poë, A. Sous les étoiles: souvenirs de théâtre 1902–12. Paris 1933.

Houghton, N. Moscow rehearsals: an account of methods of production in the Soviet Theatre. New York 1936.

Nemirovich-Danchenko, V. My life in the Russian theatre. Boston 1936.

Adler, H. The method of Michel Saint-Denis. London Mercury 39 1938.

Artaud, A. Le théâtre et son double. Paris 1938.

Pitöeff, G. Notre théâtre. Paris 1940.

Owen, A. C. The art of play directing: a tentative bibliography. Boston 1943.

Masefield, J. A Macbeth production. 1945.

Dullin, C. Souvenirs et notes de travail d'un acteur. Paris 1946.

Marshall, N. The other theatre. 1947.

— The producer and the play. 1957.

Barrault, J.-L. Réflexions sur le théâtre. Paris 1949. Tr 1951.

Brecht, B. A little organum for the theatre. Accent Winter 1951.

Jones, M. Theatre-in-the-round. New York 1951.

Daubeny, P. Stage by stage. 1952.

Jouvet, L. Témoignages sur le théâtre. Paris 1952.

Cole, T. and H. K. Chinoy (ed). Directing the play: a source book of stagecraft. Indianapolis 1953, 1964 (rev, as Directors on directing). *See* bibliography for periodical material on this subject.

Hunt, H. S. The director in the theatre. 1954.

Speaight, R. William Poel and the Elizabethan revival. 1954.

Saint-Denis, M. Theatre: the rediscovery of style. 1960.

Chekhov, M. To the director and playwright, compiled and written by C. Leonard, New York 1963.

Brook, P. The empty space. 1968.

Fernald, J. Sense of direction. 1968.

Roose-Evans, J. Directing a play. 1968.

G.A.

(11) THEATRE DESIGN AND TECHNICAL PRACTICE; STAGE DESIGN AND SCENIC METHOD

Items pbd before 1900, or pbd abroad, are included because of their influence on domestic theatre design, etc, of the period, or because they discuss techniques common to theatre design etc in various countries during the period.

Theatre Design and Technical Practice

Moynet, J. L'envers du théâtre: machines et decorations. Paris 1873.

Moynet, G. La machine théâtrale: trucs et décors. Paris 1893.

Buckle, J. G. Theatre construction and maintenance. 1888.

Birkmire, W. H. Planning and construction of American theatres. New York 1896.

Sachs, E. O. and E. A. E. Woodrow. Modern opera houses and theatres. 3 vols 1896–8. With suppl on stage construction.

Freeman, J. R. On the safeguarding of life in theaters. New York 1906.

Hammitzsch, M. Der moderne Theaterbau. Berlin 1906.

Kinsila, E. B. Modern theatre construction. New York 1917.

Cheney, S. The open-air theatre. New York 1918.

Pichel, I. On building a theatre: stage construction and equipment for small theatres, schools and community buildings. New York 1920.

— Modern theatres. New York 1925.

Young, S. Theatre practice. New York 1926.

Zucker, P. Theater und Lichtspielhäuser. Berlin 1926.

Isaacs, E. J. R. (ed). Theatre: essays on the arts of the theatre. Boston 1927. Contains 2 chs on architecture by S. Cheney and L. Mumford.

— (ed). Architecture for the new theatre. New York 1935.

Sexton, R. W. and B. F. Betts. American theatres of today. 2 vols New York 1927–30.

Urban, J. Theatres. New York 1929.

Moreau, C. Theatres and cinemas. Paris 1930.

Shand, P. M. Modern theatres and cinemas. 1930.

McCandless, S. R. A method of lighting the stage. New York 1932, 1939 (rev), 1947 (rev).

Jellicoe, G. A. The Shakespeare Memorial Theatre. Stratford-upon-Avon 1933.

Moretti, B. Teatri. Milan 1936.

Southern, R. Stage setting for amateurs and professionals. 1937.

— The open stage, and the modern theatre in research and practice. 1953.

Theatre Arts Prints. Ser 4, Stages of the world. New York 1941, 1949 (rev).

Bagenal, P. H. E. Practical acoustics and planning against noise. 1942.

Hughes, G. The Penthouse Theatre: its history and technique. New York 1942, Seattle 1950 (rev).

Applebee, L. The evolution of stage lighting. Jnl of Royal Soc of Arts 2 Aug 1946.

Report of the Oxford University Drama Commission, with supplementary architectural report by F. Gibberd. 1948.

Corry, P. Stage planning and equipment for multi-purpose halls in schools, little theatres, civic theatres etc. 1949. With frequent subsequent revisions and variations in title.

— Lighting the stage. 1954, 1958 (rev), 1961 (rev).

Robinson, H. W. An approach to theatre planning. Educational Theatre Jnl 1 1949.

Bentham, F. Stage lighting. 1950, 1957 (rev).

Theatre planning: a symposium. Educational Theatre Jnl 2 1950.

Jones, M. Theatre-in-the-round. New York 1951.

Cole, W. Some contemporary trends in theatre architecture. Educational Theatre Jnl 7 1955.

Vilar, J. De la tradition théâtrale. Paris 1955.

Boyle, W. P. Central and flexible staging. Berkeley and Los Angeles 1956.

Leacroft, R. Actor and audience. 1960.

Mander, R. and J. Mitchenson. The theatres of London. 1961, 1963 (rev).

— The lost theatres of London. 1968.

Schlemmer, O. The theatre of the Bauhaus. Middletown Conn 1961.

Joseph, S. (ed). Adaptable theatres: a report of the proceedings at the third biennial congress of the Association Internationale des Techniciens de Théâtre. 1962.

Joseph, S. Planning for new forms of theatre. 1962, 1966 (rev).

— (ed). Actor and architect. Manchester 1964.

Joseph, S. Theatre in the round. 1967.

— New theatre forms. 1968.

Ford Foundation. The ideal theatre—eight concepts: an exhibition of designs and models resulting from the Foundation's program of theater design. 1962.

Bornemann, F. (ed). Modern theatre architecture in Germany since 1945. [1968?]. Travelling exhibition catalogue.

Stage Design and Scenic Method

Ferrari, G. La scenografia. Milan 1902.

Craig, E. G. The art of the theatre. 1905. *See* also list of his works, cols 1031–2, below.

Carter, H. The new spirit in drama and art. 1912.

Goncharova, N. L'art décoratif théâtral moderne. Paris 1919.

Rutherston, A. Decoration in the art of the theatre. 1919.

Appia, A. L'oeuvre d'art vivant. Paris 1921; tr 1960. *See* also W. R. Volbach, Adolphe Appia, Middletown Conn 1968.

MacGowan, K. The theatre of tomorrow. New York [1921].

— Continental stagecraft. New York [1922]. Plates by R. E. Jones.

Drinkwater, J. and A. Rutherston. Claude Lovat Fraser. 1923.

Geddes, N. B. Project for the staging of the Divine Comedy of Dante. New York 1924.

Jones, R. E. Drawings for the theatre. New York 1925.

— The dramatic imagination: reflections and speculations on the art of the theatre. New York [1941].

Gray, T. Dance drama. Cambridge 1926.

Sheringham, G. and J. Laver. Design in the theatre. Studio Winter no 1927.

Polunin, V. The Continental method of scene painting. 1927.

Cheney, S. Stage decoration. 1928.

Fuerst, W. R. and S. J. Hume. XXth century stage decoration. 2 vols. 1928.

Komisarjevsky, T. The costume of the theatre. 1931.

— and L. Simonson. Settings and costumes of the modern stage. Studio Winter no 1933.

Moussinac, L. The new movement in the theatre: a survey of recent developments in Europe and America. 1931.

Simonson, L. The stage is set. New York [1932].

— The art of scenic design. New York 1950.

Messel, O. Stage designs and costumes. 1933.

Nicoll, A. Film and theatre. New York 1936.

Oenslager, D. Scenery then and now. New York 1936.

Burris-Meyer, H. and E. C. Cole. Scenery for the theatre. Boston 1938.

Zinkeisen, D. Designing for the stage. 1938.

Walker, H. R. M. Stage and film décor. 1940.

Beaumont, C. W. Ballet design past and present. 1946.

McDowell, J. H. History of the development of the box set. Theatre Annual 1946.

Forman, R. Scene painting. 1950.

Whistler, R. Designs for the theatre. 3 pts 1950. With appreciations by C. Beaton, J. Laver, L. Whistler.

Laver, J. Drama: its costume and décor. 1951.

Hainaux, R. Stage design throughout the world since 1935. 1956.

— Stage design throughout the world since 1950. 1964.

Parker, W. O. and H. K. Smith. Scene design and stage lighting. New York 1963.

Joseph, S. Scene painting and design. 1964.

'Motley' (E. Montgomery, S. Devine, M. Harris). Designing and making stage costumes. 1964.

Mielziner, J. Designing for the theatre. New York 1965.

Warre, M. Designing and making stage scenery. 1966.

Rowell, K. Stage design. 1968.

G.A.

(12) ECONOMICS AND ORGANIZATION OF THE THEATRE

For handbooks etc on the technique of writing plays which often contain material on economics and organization, see The players' library: the catalogue of the Library of the British Drama League, *1950. Suppls 1951–6.*

Granville-Barker, H. Scheme and estimates for a National Theatre. 1904 (priv ptd), 1907 (as A National Theatre: schemes and estimates). With W. Archer. Rewritten by Barker alone as A National Theatre, 1930.

— The exemplary theatre. 1922.

Jones, H. A. The foundations of a national drama. 1904, 1913 (rev).

— Municipal and repertory theatres. 1913. Lecture.

Shaw, G. B. In A National Theatre: its advantages and disadvantages. Mask 2 1909–10. Symposium, with contributions by G. Craig, M. Harvey and others.

— The National Shakespeare Theatre and the new repertory theatre. Times 10 May 1909.

— National Theatre. Drama 8 nos 13 and 15 1930.

— In his Bernard Shaw's letters to Granville Barker, ed C. B. Purdom 1956. See R. F. Bosworth, Shaw recordings at the BBC, in Shaw Rev 7 1964. Includes account of Shaw's recorded speech at National Theatre ceremony, 1938.

Dean, B. The repertory theatre. Liverpool 1911.

— The theatre in reconstruction. 1945.

— The theatre at war. 1956. History of the Entertainments National Service Association.

Palmer, J. The future of the theatre. 1913.

Settle, A. T. and F. H. Baber. The law of public entertainments: theatres, music and dancing, stage plays, cinematographs, copyright, Sunday performances, children, theatrical cases and specimen contracts. 1915.

Dickinson, T. H. New organisation. In his Contemporary drama of England, Boston 1917, 1931 (rev).

Harvey, M. The case for a National Theatre. Drama 1 1919.

Archer, W. The foundation of the National Theatre. 1921.

Grein, J. T. In his The world of the theatre, 1921.

— In his The new world of the theatre, 1924.

Barbor, H. R. The theatre: an art and an industry. 1924. Introd by S. Thorndike and C. B. Cochran.

Drama. New ser nos 40 and 43 1924. Winning designs for National Theatre in British Drama League competition. With notes by H. Granville-Barker.

Ervine, St J. The organised theatre: a plea in civics. 1924.

Isaacs, S. C. The law relating to theatres, music halls, and other public entertainments, and to the performers therein, including the law of musical and dramatic copyright, etc. 1927.

Ashwell, L. In her The stage, 1929.

Page, D. S. The law of the amateur stage. 1929.

Robinson, L. Recipe for a National Theatre. Realist 1 1929.

Stanton, S. E. Theatre management: a manual of the business of the theatre, including full texts of authors' and actors' standard contracts. New York 1929. Includes material relevant to the English theatre.

Drinkwater, J. Art and the state. 1930.

Whitworth, G. The theatre of my heart. 1930, 1938 (rev).

— The theatre and the nation. 1939. Lecture to the Royal Institution.

— The making of a National Theatre. 1951.

British Actors' Equity. Annual report 1931/32–1932/33; continued as What equity is doing, 1935/36 onwards. *See* also pamphlets on various topics prepared for British Actors' Equity Association.

Playfair, N. Theatre and the films. Eng Rev 52 1931. Discusses theatre subsidies.

Theatre managers and film rights. Author 41 1931. Symposium, with contributions by Shaw, B. Jackson, Drinkwater etc.

Guthrie, T. Theatre prospect. 1932.

Leverton, W. H. Through the box-office window: memories of fifty years at the Haymarket Theatre. 1932. With J. B. Booth.

Brown, I. Policy and entertainment. Fortnightly Rev 147 (new ser 141) 1937. Subsequently priv ptd for the League of Audiences.

— Amazing monument: a short history of the Shakespeare industry. 1939. With G. Fearon.

Hussey, D. Sadler's Wells and a National Theatre. Spectator 8 Oct 1937.

Dukes, A. London blackout. Theatre Arts Monthly 23 1939.

— In his The scene is changed, 1942.

Isaacs, E. J. R. National Theatre 1940: a record and a prophecy. Theatre Arts Monthly 24 1940.

Donisthorpe, S. In her Show business, 1943.

Nicoll, A. 'In association with CEMA'. Theatre Arts Monthly 28 1944.

Arts Council of Great Britain. Annual reports 1945 onwards.

— The first ten years 1945/56. 1956. See also the Council's monthly bulletins, and regular catalogues of its pbns.

Browne, H. Pilgrim story: the Pilgrim Players, 1939–1943. 1945. With ch on the organization by E. M. Browne.

Dent, E. J. A theatre for everybody: the story of the Old Vic and Sadler's Wells. 1945.

Porterfield, R. and R. Breen. Toward a National Theatre. Theatre Arts Monthly 29 1945. Refers to CEMA.

Agate, J. In his Contemporary theatre, 1944–5, 1946.

Stokes, L. The English spotlight: a joyful birth (of a National Theatre). Theatre Arts Monthly 30 1946.

Marshall, N. The other theatre. 1947.

Priestley, J. B. Theatre outlook. 1947.

Rees, L. International Theatre Institute. Author 58 1947.

Andrews, J. and Trilling, O. (eds). International Theatre. 1949. Includes W. A. Darlington, The commercial theatre in London; C. Landstone, The Arts Council of Great Britain; O. Trilling, The other theatre; Sir Barry Jackson, The problem of Stratford-upon-Avon.

Reynolds, E. In his Modern English drama, 1949, 1950 (rev).

White, T. A. B. Copyright. 1949.

Drama and discussion in international understanding. Quart Jnl of Speech 36 1950.

Landstone, C. Notes on civic theatres. [1950]. Rptd from Arts Council bulletin.

— Off-stage: a personal record of the first twelve years of State sponsored drama in Great Britain. [1953].

Monsey, D. Worm's eye view: the story of a freak success. Picture Post 20 May 1950. Discusses the financial aspects.

Willis, T. Playwrights and the contemporary theatre. Author 60 1950. Discusses organisation of League of Dramatists.

James, C. F. The story of the Performing Right Society. 1951.

'Findlater, Richard' (K. B. F. Bain). The unholy trade. 1952.

—— The empty site. Drama new ser no 46 1957.

—— In his The future of the theatre, 1959. Fabian tract no 317.

Federation of Theatrical Unions. Theatre ownership in Britain. 1953.

Melvill, H. In his Theatrecraft: the A to Z of show business, 1954.

Ivamy, E. R. H. Show business and the law. 1955.

Towards a National Theatre: the Encore Symposium. Encore 7 1956.

Herbert, A. P. 'No fine on fun': the comical history of the Entertainments Duty. 1957.

The hundred and ten years' war: a tiny history for beginners (of a National Theatre). Encore 12 1958.

The British Drama League 1919–59. 1959.

Burton, E. J. In his Students' guide to British theatre and drama, 1963.

National Theatre. The National Theatre at the Old Vic. 1966.

Cole, M. In her Fogie, 1967. Biography of Elsie Fogerty, including account of her work for the National Theatre.

Council of Repertory Theatres. The repertory movement in Great Britain. 1968.

Brown, J. R. In his Effective theatre: a study with documentation, 1969.

Sweeting, E. Theatre administration. 1969.

Whitworth, R. The first fifty years. Drama no 95 1969.

K.J.W.

Periodicals

The author: the organ of the Society of Authors, (Playwrights and Composers). Vols 1–36, May 1890–July 1926. Continued as Author, playwright and composer, vols 37–59, Oct 1926–Winter 1948. Continued as The author, vol 60, Spring 1949 onwards.

The Stage Society annual report. Vols 1–21, 1899/1900–1920/1921.

The stage staff journal. Vol 1 no 1–vol 2 no 17, Dec 1901–March 1904. Monthly.

Proprietors and managers reference book. No 1, 1904–5.

The theatrical employees journal. Nos 1–12, Oct 1904–Sept 1905. Monthly.

Actresses' Franchise League. Annual report, 1912–13. 1913.

'A.A.': the official organ of the Actors' Association. Vol 1 no 1–vol 2 no 11, Jan 1917–Dec 1918. Continued as The actor for player and public, vol 1 no 1–vol 3 no 8, Jan 1919–July 1922. Monthly.

The Actors' Association yearbook. 1917.

The theatre, music hall and cinema blue book for 1917: a list of public amusement companies with full financial particulars of interest to investors. Vol 1, 1917. Continued as The theatre, music hall and cinema companies' blue book, vols 2–13. 1918–29/30. Annual.

NATE Journal. (National Association of Theatrical Employees). Letchworth. Nos 1–11, Jan–Nov 1921. Continued as The amusement workers news, London, vol 1 no 1–vol 4 no 105, Jan 1922–Jan 1931. Monthly. Not pbd, Nov 1922–Jan 1923.

The performing right gazette: official organ of the Performing Right Society. Vol 1 no 1–vol 6 no 9, July 1922–July 1939, quarterly. Continued as The Performing Right Society emergency bulletin, nos 1–9, Oct 1939–Feb 1943. Irregular. Continued with sub-title variation, nos 10–13, April 1943–Aug 1944. Continued as The Performing Right Society bulletin, nos 14–17 Aug 1945–Aug 1947. Continued as Performing Right bulletin, nos 18–25, April 1948–Sept 1954. Continued as Performing Right, nos 26–44, Sept 1955–Oct 1966 (nos 33 onwards, twice a year). Ed E. Crozier.

TMA monthly report. (Theatrical Managers' Association). Vols 1–7, April 1922–May 1929. Continued as Theatre managers journal, vols 8–22, 1929–44. Continued as Theatre industry journal, vols 23–6, 1945–8. Continued as Theatre industry, vols 27–38, 1949–March 1960. Monthly.

The manager and stage business gazette: a weekly journal devoted exclusively to the interests of managers resident and touring. Preston. Nos 1–14, 20 May–19 Aug 1925. Weekly. Nos 4–8 at Manchester.

Argus: political, financial, satirical and theatrical. Nos 1–15, Oct 1925–Dec 1926. Monthly.

The theatrical manager, with which is incorporated The acting manager and musical director: official organ of the Association of Touring and Producing Managers. Vol 1 no 1–vol 2 no 18, Dec 1928–Jan 1931. Monthly at first, then irregular.

The theatrical artistes road book and medical list. Nos 1–5, 1929–39. Irregular.

The red stage: organ of the Workers' Theatre Movement. Vol 1 nos 1–5, Nov 1931–April/May 1932. Continued as New red stage, nos 6–7, June/July–Sept 1932. Irregular.

The spotlight year book. Vols 1–3, 1931–3. Ed W. Keith Moss.

British Actor's Equity...annual report. 1931/2–1932/3. Continued as What Equity is doing, 1935/6 onwards. Annual.

The authors', playwrights', and composers' handbook for 1935 (etc). Vols 1–6, 1935–40. Annual. Compiled and ed by D. Kilham Roberts.

Unemployed drama news. 1936. Ed Kathleen Edwards.

The call sheet: a casting directory of small-part players. Vol 1 nos 1–3, July 1937–8? Also, autumn suppl for 1937. Quarterly, irregular.

Performwritings: PRS (Performing Right Society) Staff magazine. Vols 1–2 no 3, Oct 1938–Oct 1948. Irregular.

CEMA bulletin. (Title varies slightly). Nos 1–62, May 1940–June 1945. Continued as Arts Council of Great Britain monthly bulletin, nos 64–71, Aug 1945–March 1946. Continued as Arts Council bulletin, nos 72–140, April 1946–Dec 1951.

Equity letter: a bi-monthly report to the members of the British Actors' Equity Association. Nos 1–23, March 1947–July 1951. With no 24, becomes a quarterly, Oct 1951–Feb 1966. Continued as Equity letter, a report to the members of the British Actors' Equity Association, no 59, Jan 1967 onwards.

Spotlight-contacts: stage and screen. Jan 1949 onwards. 3 issues a year to no 30, Oct 1958; 2 issues a year since no 31, April 1959.

Spotlight: stage and screen casting directory, American and European edition. No 1, London 1949.

Stage and variety artistes guide and handbook. Vol 1, 1950. Annual.

C.J.S.

(13) THEATRE CENSORSHIP

Nicholson, W. The struggle for a free stage. 1906.

Deputation waits on Home Secretary of England and presents a case for improvement of censorship of plays. Theatre 8 1908.

G., G.M. The stage censor: a historical sketch, 1544–1907. 1908.

Beerbohm, M. The censorship report. Saturday Rev 20 Nov 1909.

Censorship of the drama. Spectator 4 Dec 1909.

English authors oppose present form of censorship. Literary Digest 39 1909.

Garnett, E. Censorship of public opinion. Fortnightly Rev 86 1909.

J. K. Jerome on the censor. Munsey's Mag 41 1909.

Jones, H. A. The censorship muddle and a way out of it: a letter addressed to the Rt Hon Herbert Samuel. 1909.

Kingston, G. How we came to be censored by the state. Nineteenth Century 65 1909.

Report of the Joint Parliamentary Committee. Literary Digest 39 1909.

Censorship and licensing. 1910. Printed by The Stage.

Dramatic censorship. Spectator 8 Oct 1910.

Housman, L. A King's proctor for plays. Fortnightly Rev 88 1910.

— My thirty-five years' fight with the censor. Living Age 353 1937.

How England regulates the drama. Current Lit 48 1910.

Report from the Joint Select Committee of the House of Lords and the House of Commons on stage plays—censorship. 1910.

Report of the censorship enquiring committee. Mask 2 1910.

Suppression of plays. Collier's Mag 45 1910.

Tree, V. Censorship of stage plays. Nineteenth Century 67 1910.

J. Palmer. The dear old Charley censorship. Saturday Rev 2 Dec 1911.

— The censor and the theatres. 1912.

The censorship scandal. Eng Rev 10 1912.

England's censorship mania. Literary Digest 44 1912.

The English and their censor. Current Lit 52 1912.

Galsworthy, J. About censorship. In his Inn of tranquillity, 1912.

Literature and morals in England. Nation (New York) 29 Feb 1912.

The new examiner of plays, Mr C. Brookfield. Rev of Reviews 45 1912.

Fowell, F. and F. Palmer. Censorship in England. 1913.

Skinner, C. Views on censorship. Drama (Chicago) 17 1914.

Dickinson, T. Theory and practice of censorship. Drama (Chicago) 18 1915.

Conrad, J. The censor of plays. In his Notes on life and letters, 1921.

English censorship. Nation (New York) 19 Aug 1925.

Street, G. S. The censorship of plays. Fortnightly Rev 118 1925.

Stopes, M. C. C. A banned play (Vectia) and a preface on the censorship. 1926.

Farjeon, H. Censorship. Graphic 19 Feb 1927.

Fricker, R. H. Stage censorship: past, present and future. Theatre 45 1927.

Bennett, A. Censorship in England. World Today 51 1928.

Hicks, W. J. Do we need a censor? 1929.

Beman, L. T. Selected articles on censorship of the theatre and moving pictures. New York 1931.

Liveright, A. The history of censorship. Drama (Chicago) 21 1931.

Griffith, H. The censor as Nazi apologist. New Statesman 14 April 1934.

Knowles, D. The censor, the drama and the film, 1900–34. 1934. See review, TLS 5 July 1934.

McKown, R. The Lord Chamberlain's powers and his critics. Theatre World 22 1934.

Johns, E. Duties of the Lord Chamberlain concerning the theatre. Theatre World 25 1936.

Disher, W. W. England: the throne is the censor. Theatre World 25 1937.

Brown, J. M. Wishful banning. Saturday Rev of Lit 12 March 1949; discussed, 9 April, 21 May 1949.

Bernard Shaw's letters to Granville Barker. Ed C. B. Purdom 1956. Includes letters on censorship.

'Findlater, Richard' (K. B. F. Bain). Banned! a review of theatrical censorship in Britain. 1967.

Hynes, S. The theater and the Lord Chamberlain. In his Edwardian turn of mind, Princeton 1968.

M.T.

(14) AMATEUR DRAMA; DRAMA AND EDUCATION

Amateur Drama

Drama in the village. Blackwood's Mag 179 1906.

Maxwell, G. Revival of the folk-drama. Nineteenth Century 62 1907.

Kingston, G. Repertory with the BRADC at Cologne. Fortnightly Rev 110 1921.

Garrett, A. E. The new amateur movement in Manchester. Eng Rev 34 1922.

Gilbert, B. King Lear at Hordle and other rural plays. 1922.

Littlewood, S. R. (ed). Somerset and the drama. 1922.

A short history of Bristol's Little Theatre 1923–5. Bristol 1925.

Hayes, J. J. The little theatre movement in Ireland. Drama (Chicago) 16 1926.

Bishop, G. W. (ed). The amateur dramatic year book. 1928 onwards.

Clark, T. H. Amateurs. In his Drama in Gloucestershire, 1928.

Sladen-Smith, F. The future of the amateur movement. Drama new ser 7 1929.

— Drama and the people. Spectator 18 Aug 1933.

Purdom, C. B. Producing plays. 1930, 1940 (rev), 1951 (rev).

Wilson, R. A. The small stage and its equipment. 1930.

Miller, A. I. The independent theatres of England. In his Independent theatres in Europe, New York 1931.

Whitworth, G. The amateur movement in England. Theatre Arts Monthly 15 1931.

— Drama and the people. Spectator 1 Sept 1933.

Peach, L. du G. An English village theatre. [Great Hucklow] Theatre Arts Monthly 16 1932.

— Amateur drama and the community. Further Education 2 1949.

— Twenty-five years of play producing 1927–52. 1952. The Village Players, Great Hucklow.

Waugh, A. Fifty years of amateur acting. Fortnightly Rev 131 1932.

Glechan, E. Ashdown Forest Pageant. Sussex County Mag 16 March 1933.

Mackinlay, L. S. Fresh fields for amateurs. Bookman (London) 84 1933.

Marshall, N. Where the amateur movement fails. Ibid.

— The amateur theatre. In his Other theatre, 1947.

Newton, R. Are the English amateurs growing up? Theatre Arts Monthly 17 1933.

Rigby, C. Maddermarket Mondays. Norwich 1933.

Barnes, T. R. The Maddermarket Theatre. Scrutiny 4 1935.

Monck, N. The Norwich players. Listener 2 Jan 1935.

Kelly, M. How to make a pageant. 1936.

— Village theatre. 1939.

Irvine, C. Drama for dumb-bells: a critic's survey of the Scottish amateur stage. Scot's Mag 28 1938.

Carlton, P. (ed). The amateur stage. 1939.

Gyseghem, A. V. A pageant for Welsh miners. Theatre Arts Monthly 23 1939.

Ellis-Fermor, U. Shelter drama. English 3 1941.

Twenty five years of the British Drama League 1919–44. 1944.

Randle, M. and J. English (ed). Highbury Little Theatre. 1946.

Dobrée, B. The amateur and the theatre. 1947.

Barty-King, H. Whitworth and the [British Drama] League. Theatre Arts 32 1948.

Emmet, A. Britain's 'Little Theatres'. Listener 15 Dec 1949.

James, D. G. Amateur drama and the community. Adult Education 14 1951.

Brewer, R. Thirty years of Welwyn drama. Town & Country Planning 20 1952.

Guthrie, T. Aesthetic values in the amateur theatre. Drama new ser 24 1952.

Melvill, H. A complete guide to amateur dramatics. 1957.

The British Drama League: 1919–59. 1959.

Baker, D. V. The Minack Theatre. 1960.

Rendle, A. Everyman and his theatre. 1968.

L. O.

Periodicals

The stroller: a journal devoted to amateur, dramatic and musical societies. Nos 1–3/4, Oct 1905–Jan 1905–6.

The amateur stage. Nos 1–4, 1 Nov 1906–1 Feb 1907. Monthly.

Drama: a magazine of the theatre and allied arts (British Drama League). Nos 1–6, July 1919–July 1920. Bi-monthly. Continued as Drama: the journal of the British Drama League, new series vol 1 no 1–vol 17 no 10, Nov 1920–July/Sept 1939. Continued as Drama: the quarterly theatre review, Summer 1946 onwards.

The National Amateur Operatic and Dramatic Association directory and constitution. Cheltenham. 1921/2–1925/6. Continued as National Operatic and Dramatic Association year book, 1926/7–1930/1. Continued as Year book, 1931–39/40, 1948–56. Continued as The National Operatic and Dramatic Association...directory, 1957–60. Continued as Year book, 1961 onwards.

The amateur stage. Vol 1 no 1–vol 4 no 48, Jan 1926–Dec 1929. (Includes a registration number, listed as vol 1, no 1, and dated, Nov 1925. This number is termed a weekly, is ed F. Lloyd, and is ptd for National Amateur Operatic and Dramatic Association.)

Y llwyfan (Magazine of the Welsh Drama League). Swansea. Nos 1–8, Dec 1927–Feb/March 1929.

The amateur dramatic year book and community theatre handbook. 1928–9. Ed G. W. Bishop.

Amateur stage. Vol 1 no 1–vol 3 no 13, Dec 1932–Dec 1933. Monthly. (Suppl to, and continued in, Theatre world.)

Southport Dramatic Club magazine. Southport. No 1, Sept 1932.

The amateur theatrical review, incorporating the South-port Dramatic Club magazine. No 1, March 1933.

The amateur theatre and playwright's journal. Vol 1 no 1–vol 5 no 102, 31 Jan 1934–30 Sept 1938. Incorporated Scottish stage. Biweekly, Sept–April; monthly, May–Aug.

The Scottish amateur theatre and playwright's journal. Vol 1 no 1–vol 5 no 102, 1934–30 Sept 1938. Bi-monthly.

War-time drama: an occasional bulletin from the British Drama League. Nos 1–39 (no 32 repeated in numbering) Oct 1939–Feb 1946. Irregular. Issued during the temporary suspension of Drama: a monthly record of the theatre in town and country at home and abroad. Subtitle varies.

Script: the journal of the Association of Ulster Dramatic Societies. Belfast. Nos 1–4, Feb–June 1945. New ser Sept 1945–May 1948. Monthly.

Footlights. Coventry. Vol 1 no 1–vol 7 no 68, March 1945–June/July 1951. Monthly. Formerly Coventry amateur stage: a magazine of amateur drama and opera.

Christian drama. (Religious Drama Society of Great Britain). Vols 1–5, no 1, Nov 1946–Spring 1963. 3 issues a year.

The amateur stage. Vol 1 no 1–vol 3 no 12, Sept 1946–Dec 1948. Continued as The amateur stage: the national independent monthly magazine for the amateur player, producer and playwright, vol 4, nos 1–8, Jan–Aug 1949. Continued as The amateur stage: the only national independent magazine for the amateur theatre, vol 4 no 9–vol 5 no 3, Sept 1949–March 1950. Continued as The amateur stage, vol 5 no 4–vol 10 no 12, April 1950–Dec 1955. Monthly. Ed George Taylor.

Call boy. (Bristol Guild of Players monthly magazine). 1946.

Exits and entrances: organ of the Durham County Drama Association. Nos 1–6, Jan 1947–Jan 1950.

Footlights. (Gloucester Theatre Guild). Gloucester. Nos 1–2, March–April 1948.

'Broadcast'. Nos 1–2, [1948]–5 March 1948. Continued as Greek drama (amateur players) broadsheet, nos 3–4, April–May 1948. Monthly.

BDTG bulletin. (Birmingham District Theatre Guild). Nos 1–8, July 1948–Jan 1950; continued as Theatre guild review, Sept 1950 onwards.

Little theatre news. Portsmouth. No 1, 1948.

Folk Dance and Song

The English Folk-Dance Society's journal. Vol 1 nos 1–2, May 1914–April 1915. Annual. Continued as The journal of the English Folk Dance Society, ser 2, nos 1–4, 1927–31. No issue pbd in 1929. Ed Percival Lucas.

EFDS news. Vol 1, nos 1–6, Jan 1921–Nov 1923. Continued as EFDS news: the magazine of the English Folk Dance Society vols 1–4, nos 7–47, May 1924–June 1936. Superseded by English dance and song. 2 issues a year, nos 1–15, Jan 1921–Sept 1927; 3 issues a year, nos 16–37, Feb 1928–Sept 1934; 6 issues a year, nos 38–43, Jan–Dec 1935; 4 issues a year, nos 44–47, Jan–June 1936. Incorporated Bulletin of the English folk dance.

Journal of the English Folk Dance and Song Society. Vol 1 no 1–vol 2 no 4. International Festival number, 1935. Ed Frank Howes. Annual.

English dance and song: the magazine of the English Folk Dance and Song Society. Sept 1936 onwards. Monthly and bimonthly. Supersedes English Folk Dance Society news.

English Folk Dance and Song Society bulletin. Nos 1–13, April 1948–May 1950. Irregular.

C.J.S.

Drama and Education

Tatham, G. B. The ADC. In Fasciculus Ioanni Willis Clark dictatus, Cambridge 1909.

Mackinnon, M. A. The Oxford amateurs: a short history of theatricals at the University. 1910.

Cook, H. C. The play way. 1917.

Lee, S., B. Greet and E. Fogerty. The educational value of the drama. Drama 1 1920.

McElwain, J. Drama and the soldier: practical work under the new army education scheme. Ibid.

Gilpin, E. M. The dramatic sense as a factor in education. Ibid.

Rhodes, R. C. Playmaking in school. Drama new ser 5 1921.

Hall, G. The university and the stage. Drama new ser 12 1921; reply by A. Stewart, ibid.

C., T. F. The value of acting plays at public schools. Drama new ser 32 1923.

HMSO. The drama in adult education: a report by the Adult Education Committee of the Board of Education. 1926.

Davis, C. The Welsh Drama League. Drama new ser 6 1928.

Blackie, J. H., M. Gullan, M. Scott, M. Shairp and L. Stokes. The play in the school. Drama new ser 7 1929. A series of articles.

Dost, G. Der neue dramatische Geist in England und das nationale Erziehungs-System. Die Neueren Sprachen 37 1929.

Motter, T. H. V. The school drama in England. 1929.

Barnes, K. The Royal Academy. Theatre Arts 29 1945.

Report of the Oxford Drama Commission. Oxford 1945. By N. Coghill et al.

Educational Drama Association. The children's theatre. Birmingham 1948.

Annan, N. G. The Marlowe Society tradition. Cambridge Jnl 3 1950.

James, D. G. (ed). The universities and the theatre. 1952 (Colston Papers 4).

Lobb, K. M. The drama in school and church. 1955.

Coggin, P. A. Drama and education. 1956.

L.O.

Periodicals

Journal of the Leeds College of Music, Drama and Art. Leeds. Vols 1–10, Jan 1897–Oct 1906. Continued as Leeds triad, new series, vols 1–5, Jan 1907–July 1911; vol 6, May–Dec 1912. Quarterly.

The maskerpiece: an educational magazine profusely illustrated, showing the link of literature and drama of all ages in the mask and the name. Nos 1–2, Nov 1922–Feb 1923. 3 issues a year proposed. Ed Sinori Levi.

Rada news: Royal Academy of Dramatic Art. 1923.

The link: the journal of the Association of Teachers of the revived Greek dance, The Z Club, the Ginner-Mawer school, etc. Vol 1 no 1–vol 5 no 16, Jan 1924–Oct 1934. New series vol 1 no 1–vol 3 no 15, Jan 1935–July 1940. Irregular.

British Puppet and Model Theatre Guild, wartime bulletin. Nos 1–17, 1939–45. Irregular. Continued as The puppet master: the journal of the British Puppet and Model Theatre Guild. Jan 1946 onwards. Ed Arthur E. Peterson.

British Puppet and Model Theatre Guild junior news. Worcester. Nos 1–2, 1941–2.

Puppet year book: Educational Puppetry Association. Nos 1–2, 1944/5–1946. No 1 ed Ellen M. Marks; no 2 ed Ellen M. Codlin.

Puppet post: the quarterly journal of the Educational Puppetry Association. Spring 1947 onwards. Quarterly 1947–Winter 1951/2. 2 issues a year, 1952 onwards. Ed F. Hook, Spring 1947, M. R. Poulter, Winter 1947–Autumn 1951, D. Hawkes, Winter 1951/2–Spring 1954, A. R. Philpott, Spring 1955–Spring 1958. No editor's name thereafter.

Theatre in education. Nos 1–28 1947–51.

British puppet theatre. Vol 1 no 1–vol 3 no 5, Dec 1949–Jan 1953. Monthly.

Creative drama. (Educational Drama Association). Vol 1 no 1, 1949 onwards.

C.J.S

II. INDIVIDUAL DRAMATISTS

Plays are listed in order of date of production, where known, otherwise of pbn. For theatres, the word 'theatre' has been omitted, except in the case of 'Theatre Royal'. 'Court' refers to the 'Court Theatre', London, even for the period during which it was called 'The Royal Court Theatre'. The abbreviations Lacy, French, Deane, Evans, London Play Co, Dramatists Play Service refer to the acting edns of plays issued by these publishers, and Guild to the acting edns of plays issued by the English Theatre Guild Ltd.

For certain Irish dramatists established early in the century, such as George Fitzmaurice, Lennox Robinson, St John Ervine, see vol 3, cols 1939–48.

SEAN O'CASEY
1880–1964

Major collection of mss notebooks, typescript drafts of plays and prose writings in the Berg Collection, New York Public Library. Important letters are in Cornell Univ and Texas Univ Libraries. Private journals, notebooks, correspondence are in the possession of the dramatist's widow.

Bibliographies

Brandstädter, O. Eine O'Casey-Bibliographie. Zeitschrift für Anglistik und Amerikanistik 2 1954.

Levidova, I. M. and B. M. Parchevskaya. Shon O'Keisi biobibliograficheskii ukazatel'. Moscow 1964. Contains list of O'Casey's books and articles pbd in USSR.

Carpenter, C. A. Sean O'Casey studies through 1964. Modern Drama 10 1967.

Collections and Selections

Five Irish plays: Juno and the paycock; The shadow of a gunman; The plough and the stars; The end of the beginning; A pound on demand. 1935.

Collected plays. 4 vols 1949–51, New York 1957–9. Within the gates is extensively rev, The silver tassie, Purple dust and Red roses for me are slightly rev.

Selected plays. New York 1954. With foreword by O'Casey. The shadow of a gunman, Juno and the paycock, The plough and the stars, The silver tassie, Within the gates, Purple dust, Red roses for me, Bedtime story, Time to go. Texts identical with Collected plays edn.

Mirror in my house: the autobiographies of Sean O'Casey. 2 vols New York 1956, London 1963 (as Autobiographies).

Three plays. 1957. The shadow of a gunman, Juno and the paycock, The plough and the stars.

Five one-act plays. 1958. The end of the beginning, A pound on demand, Hall of healing, Bedtime story, Time to go.

Three more plays. 1965, New York 1965. The silver tassie, Purple dust, Red roses for me. Text is that of Collected plays edn with further minor revisions to Red roses for me.

The Sean O'Casey reader: plays, autobiographies, opinions. Ed B. A. Atkinson 1968, New York 1968.

§ 1

The sacrifice of Thomas Ashe. Dublin 1918.
The story of Thomas Ashe. Dublin 1918.
Songs of the wren. 2 ser Dublin 1918.

More wren songs. Dublin 1918.

The story of the Irish Citizen Army. By 'P. O Cathasaigh' [i.e. O'Casey]. 1919.

The shadow of a gunman: a tragedy in two acts. (Abbey, Dublin 12 April 1923; Court 27 May 1927). In Two plays, 1925, below. Pbd separately 1932 (French).

Kathleen listens in: a phantasy in one act. (Abbey, Dublin 1 Oct 1923). In Feathers from the green crow, 1962, below.

Juno and the paycock: a tragedy in three acts. (Abbey, Dublin 3 March 1924; Royalty 16 Nov 1925). In Two plays, 1925, below. Pbd separately 1932 (French).

Nannie's night out: a comedy in one act. (Abbey, Dublin 29 Sept 1924). In Feathers from the green crow, 1962, below.

Two plays: Juno and the paycock; The shadow of a gunman. 1925, New York 1925.

The plough and the stars: a tragedy in four acts. (Abbey, Dublin 8 Feb 1926, Fortune 12 May 1926). 1926, New York 1926, London [1932] (French).

The silver tassie: a tragi-comedy in four acts. (Apollo 11 Oct 1929). 1928, New York 1928. Rev stage version in Collected plays vol 2, above.

Within the gates: a play of four scenes in a London park. (Royalty 7 Feb 1934). 1933, New York 1934. Rev stage version in Collected plays vol 2, above.

Windfalls: stories, poems, and plays. 1934, New York 1934. Includes The end of the beginning and A pound on demand.

The end of the beginning: a comedy in one act. (Abbey, Dublin 8 Feb 1937; 'Q' 16 Oct 1939). In Windfalls, 1934, above.

The flying wasp: a laughing look-over of what has been said about the things of the theatre by the English dramatic critics, with many merry and amusing comments thereon, with some shrewd remarks by the author on the wise, delicious and dignified tendencies in the theatre of to-day. 1937, New York 1937.

A pound on demand: a sketch in one act. ('Q' 16 Oct 1939). In Windfalls, 1934, above.

I knock at the door: swift glances back at things that made me. 1939, New York 1939. 1st vol of autobiography.

The star turns red. (Unity 12 March 1940). 1940. Slightly rev in Collected plays vol 2, above.

Pictures in the hallway. 1942, New York 1942. 2nd vol of autobiography.

Red roses for me: a play in four acts. (Olympia, Dublin 15 March 1943; Embassy 26 Feb 1946). 1942, New York 1943. Rev text in Collected plays vol 3, above; further revision pbd New York 1956 (Dramatists Play Service) and in Three more plays, 1965, above.

Purple dust: a wayward comedy in three acts. (People's Theatre, Newcastle-on-Tyne 16 Dec 1943; Mermaid 15 Aug 1962). 1940, New York [1957] (rev) (Dramatists Play Service).

Drums under the windows. 1945, New York 1946. 3rd vol of autobiography.

Oak leaves and lavender: or, A warld on wallpaper. (Lyric 13 May 1947). 1946, New York 1947.

Cock-a-doodle dandy. (People's Theatre, Newcastle-on-Tyne 10 Dec 1949; Court 17 Sept 1959). 1949.

Inishfallen, fare thee well. 1949, New York 1949. 4th vol of autobiography.

Bedtime story: an Anatole burlesque in one act. (Jugoslav-American Hall, New York 7 May 1952). In Collected plays vol 4, above.

Hall of healing: a sincerious farce in one scene. (Jugoslav-American Hall, New York 7 May 1952; Unity 22 May 1953). In Collected plays vol 3, above.

Time to go: a morality comedy in one act. (Jugoslav-American Hall, New York 7 May 1952; Unity 22 May 1953). In Collected plays vol 4, above.

Rose and crown. 1952, New York 1952. 5th vol of autobiography.

Sunset and evening star. 1954, New York 1954. 6th vol of autobiography.

The bishop's bonfire: a sad play within the tune of a polka. (Gaiety, Dublin 28 Feb 1955, Mermaid 26 July 1961). 1955, New York 1955.

The green crow. New York 1956, London 1957. Essays and stories; London edn includes 2 additional essays.

The drums of father Ned: a mickrocosm of Ireland. (Little Th, Lafayette Ind 25 April 1959; Queen's, Hornchurch 8 Nov 1960; Olympia, Dublin 6 June 1966). 1960, New York 1960.

Behind the green curtains (Univ of Rochester NY 5 Dec 1962; Theater der Stadt, Cottbus 20 Nov 1965), Figuro in the night (Th de Lys, New York 30 Oct 1962), The moon shines on Kylenamoe (Theater de Lys, New York 30 Oct 1962): three plays. 1961, New York 1961.

Feathers from the green crow: Sean O'Casey 1905–1925. Ed R. Hogan, Columbia Mo 1962, London 1963. Essays, poems, stories, plays. Includes Kathleen listens in and Nannie's night out.

Under a colored cap: articles merry and mournful with comments and a song. 1963, New York 1963.

Blasts and benedictions: articles and stories. Ed R. Ayling 1967, New York 1967.

O'Casey also pbd many articles in English, Irish, US and Russian jnls. His works have been tr into French, German, Russian, Polish, Swedish, Bulgarian, Dutch, Hungarian, Estonian, Rumanian, Italian and Spanish. His Letters, 3 vols ed D. Krause, are due for pbn in 1972–3.

§2

Brugère, R. O'Casey et le théâtre irlandais. Revue Anglo-américaine 3 1926.

Shipp, H. The art of O'Casey. Eng Rev 42 1926.

O'Hegarty, P. S. A dramatist of new born Ireland. North Amer Rev 224 1927.

Malone, A. E. In his Irish drama 1896–1928, 1929.

Bergholz, H. Sean O'Casey. E Studien 65 1930.

Gwynn, S. In his Irish literature and drama in the English language, 1936.

Wittig, K. Sean O'Casey als Dramatiker. Halle 1937.

Starkie, W. Sean O'Casey. In The Irish theatre, ed L. Robinson 1939.

Smet, R. de. O'Casey et la tragédie des tenements. Revue des Vivants 8 1940.

Smith, W. The dying god in the modern theatre. Rev of Religion 5 1941.

Woodbridge, H. E. Sean O'Casey. South Atlantic Quart 40 1941.

O'Faoláin, S. The strange case of O'Casey. Bell 6 1943.

— Too many drums. Bell 11 1945.

Aickman, R. F. O'Casey and the striker. Nineteenth Century 830 1946.

Robinson, L. (ed). Lady Gregory's journals 1916–30. 1946.

— Ireland's Abbey Theatre: a history 1899–1951. 1951.

Heilman, R. B. Definitions needed. Quart Rev of Lit 4 1947.

Johnston, D. In Living writers: critical studies broadcast in the BBC Third Programme, ed G. Phelps 1947.

Nicholson, H. The O'Casey horn of plenty. In his A voyage to wonderland and other essays, 1947.

Boas, G. The drama of O'Casey. College Eng 10 1948.

Colum, P. The narrative writings of O'Casey. Irish Writing 6 1948.

Koslow, J. The green and the red: O'Casey, the man and his plays. New York 1950, 1966 (rev, as O'Casey: the man and his plays).

Findlater, R. In his Unholy trade, 1952.

Williams, R. The colour of O'Casey. In his Drama from Ibsen to Eliot, 1952, 1968 (rev, as Drama from Ibsen to Brecht).

Ellis-Fermor, U. In her Irish dramatic movement, 1954 (rev).

Gassner, J. The prodigality of O'Casey. In his Theatre in our times, New York 1954.

Jordan, J. The indignation of O'Casey. Irish Writing 29 1954.

—— A world in chassis. Univ Rev (Dublin) 1955.

—— The Irish theatre: retrospect and premonition. In Contemporary theatre, ed J. R. Brown and B. Harris 1962 (Stratford-upon-Avon Stud 4).

O'Maoláin, M. An ruathar úd agus an deachaigh leis. Feasta 8 1955.

Baggett, P. O'Casey's development of a basic theme. Dublin Mag 31 1956.

Mercier, V. The riddle of O'Casey: decline of a playwright. Commonweal 64 1956.

—— O'Casey alive. Hudson Rev 13 1961.

Magalaner, M. O'Casey's autobiography. Sewanee Rev 65 1957.

Ayling, R. F. Rowdelum randy: O'Casey and his critics. Enquiry 1 1958.

—— Nannie's night out. Modern Drama 5 1962.

—— Feathers flying: politics in the early life and thought of O'Casey. Dubliner 3 1964.

—— The autobiographies of O'Casey. Research Stud 37 1969.

—— A note on O'Casey's manuscripts and his working methods. BNYPL 73 1969.

—— (ed). Sean O'Casey. 1969 (Modern Judgments).

Barzun, J. O'Casey at your bedside. Tulane Drama Rev 2 1958.

Fréchet, R. O'Casey: un épisode de la vie du théâtre irlandais. In Le théâtre moderne: hommes et tendances, ed J. Jacquot, Paris 1958.

Habart, M. Introduction à Sean O'Casey. Théâtre Populaire 34 1959.

Robinson, E. Juno and the paycock: an introduction. Use of Eng 11 1959.

Armstrong, W. A. History, autobiography and The shadow of a gunman. Modern Drama 2 1960.

—— The sources and themes of The plough and the stars. Modern Drama 4 1961.

—— The Irish point of view: the plays of O'Casey, Brendan Behan and Thomas Murphy. In his Experimental drama, 1963.

—— Sean O'Casey. 1967 (Br Council pamphlet).

Coston, H. O'Casey: prelude to playwriting. Tulane Drama Rev 5 1960.

Duranteau, J. Notes sur le théâtre de Sean O'Casey. Critique (Paris) 16 1960.

Hogan, R. The experiments of O'Casey. New York 1960.

—— In his After the Irish renaissance: a critical history of the Irish drama since The plough and the stars, Minneapolis 1967.

—— and M. J. O'Neill (ed). Joseph Holloway's Abbey Theatre: a selection from his unpublished journal. Carbondale 1967.

Knight, G. W. The drums of father Ned by O' Casey. Stand 4 1960; rptd in his Christian renaissance, 1962 (rev) (as Ever a fighter: on O'Casey's Drums of father Ned).

—— In his Golden labyrinth: a study of British drama, 1962.

Krause, D. O'Casey: the man and his work. 1960.

—— The rageous Ossean: patron-hero of Synge and O'Casey. Modern Drama 4 1961.

—— O'Casey 1880–1964. Massachusetts Rev 6 1965.

—— O'Casey and Yeats and the druid. Modern Drama 11 1967.

—— A self-portrait of the artist as a man: O'Casey's letters. Dublin 1968 (New Dolmen Chapbooks 6).

Coxhead, E. In her Lady Gregory: a literary portrait, 1961, 1966 (rev).

De Baun, V. C. O'Casey and the road to Expressionism. Modern Drama 4 1961.

Rollins, R. G. O'Casey, O'Neill and the Expressionism in Within the gates. West Virginia Univ Philological Papers 13 1961.

—— O'Casey, O'Neill and Expressionism in The silver tassie. Bucknell Rev 10 1962.

—— Dramatic symbolism in O'Casey's Dublin trilogy. West Virginia Univ Philological Papers 15 1966.

—— Form and content in O'Casey's Dublin trilogy. Modern Drama 8 1966.

—— O'Casey and Synge: the Irish hero as playboy and gunman. Arizona Quart 22 1966.

—— Shaw and O'Casey: John Bull and his other island. Shaw Rev 10 1967.

Spinner, K. Die alte Dame sagt Nein! drei irische Dramatiker: L. Robinson, O'Casey, D. Johnston. Berne 1961.

Worth, K. J. O'Casey's dramatic symbolism. Modern Drama 4 1961.

Brandt, G. W. Realism and parables: from Brecht to Arden. In Contemporary theatre, ed J. R. Brown and B. Harris 1962 (Stratford-upon-Avon Stud 4).

Daniel, W. C. Patterns of Greek comedy in O'Casey's Purple dust. BNYPL 66 1962.

Lewis, A. Irish romantic realism—O'Casey: Red roses for me. In his Contemporary theatre: the significant playwrights of our time, New York 1962.

Ritchie, H. M. The influence of melodrama on the early plays of O'Casey. Modern Drama 5 1962.

Cowasjee, S. O'Casey: the man behind the plays. Edinburgh 1963, 1965 (rev).

—— O'Casey seen through Holloway's diary. REL 6 1965.

—— Sean O'Casey. Edinburgh 1966 (Writers and Critics).

—— The juxtaposition of tragedy and comedy in the plays of O'Casey. Wascana Rev 2 1967.

Druzina, M. V. Shon O'Keisi—dramaturg. Moscow 1963.

—— Dramaturgiya Shona O'Keisi. Leningrad 1965.

Esslinger, P. M. O'Casey and the lockout of 1913. Modern Drama 6 1963.

—— The Irish alienation of O'Casey. Eire-Ireland: a Jnl of Irish Stud 1 1966.

Fricker, R. O'Casey: Juno and the paycock. In Das moderne englische Drama: Interpretationen, ed H. Oppel, Berlin 1963.

Reid, A. The legend of the green crow. Drama Survey 3 1963.

Benstock, B. A covey of clerics in Joyce and O'Casey. James Joyce Quart 2 1964.

Freedman, M. The modern tragicomedy of Wilde and O'Casey. College Eng 25 1964; rptd in his Moral impulse: modern drama from Ibsen to the present, Carbondale 1967.

Kosok, H. Sean O'Casey 1880–1964. Die Neueren Sprachen 13 1964.

Rees, L. Remembrance of things past: on meeting O'Casey. Meanjin Quart 23 1964.

Edwards, A. C. (ed). The Lady Gregory letters to O'Casey. Modern Drama 8 1965.

Fallon, G. O'Casey: the man I knew. 1965.

Goldstone, H. The unevenness of O'Casey: a study of Within the gates. Forum 4 1965.

McHugh, R. The legacy of O'Casey. Texas Quart 8 1965.

O'Connor, U. Inishfallen, fare thee well. Dublin Mag 4 1965.

Sarukhanyan, A. P. Tvorchestvo Shona O'Keisi. Moscow 1965.

McCann, S. (ed). The world of O'Casey. 1966.

'Hugh MacDiarmid' (C. M. Grieve). In his Company I've kept: essays in autobiography, 1966.

Malone, M. Red roses for me: fact and symbol. Modern Drama 9 1966.

—— The plays of O'Casey. Carbondale 1969.

Parker, R. B. Shaw and O'Casey. Queen's Quart 73 1966.

Snoddy, O. O'Casey as troublemaker. Eire-Ireland: a Jnl of Irish Stud 1 1966.

Carpenter, C. A. O'Casey studies through 1964. Modern Drama 10 1967.

Harman, B. J. and R. G. Rollins. Mythical dimensions in O'Casey's Within the gates. West Virginia Univ Philological Papers 16 1967.

'Frank O'Connor' (M. F. O'Donovan). In his Short history of Irish literature: a backward look, 1967.

Smith, B. L. Satire in O'Casey's Cock-a-doodle dandy. Renascence 19 1967.

— Satire in The plough and the stars. Ball State Univ Forum 10 1969.

Thompson, W. I. In his Imagination of an insurrection, Dublin, Easter 1916, 1967.

Todd, R. M. The two published versions of O'Casey's Within the gates. Modern Drama 10 1968.

Völker, K. Irisches Theater 2: O'Casey. Hanover 1968.
R. A.

SAMUEL BARCLAY BECKETT
b. 1906

Bibliographies

Cohn, R. A checklist of Beckett criticism. Perspective 11 1959.

In Cahiers Renaud-Barrault 44 1963.

Bryer, J. R. Critique de Beckett: selection bibliographique. In Configuration critique de Beckett, ed M. J. Friedman, Paris 1964; tr and rev in Beckett now, ed M. J. Friedman, Chicago 1970.

Webb, E. Critical writings on Beckett: a bibliography. West Coast Rev 1 1966.

In Biblio 35 1967.

Freeman, E. T. Beckett on the Mississippi. Manuscripts 20 1968. Notes differing ms versions of some of Beckett's works.

Reid, A. In his All I can manage, more than I could, 1968. Contains a chronology of the plays, including dates of production.

Janvier, L. In his Beckett par lui-même, Paris 1969. Lists recordings and films.

Federman, R. and J. Fletcher. Beckett: his works and his critics. Berkeley and Los Angeles 1970. Includes unpbd works, textual variants, Beckett's writings in jnls, including extracts from novels and stories, and his trns of works other than his own. Lists theatre and other reviews and criticism of Beckett on the BBC, 1955–65. Notes locations of some mss, with transcripts of 10 drafts of Bing.

For additional European criticism, see R. Oliva, 1967, and K. Schoell, 1967, below.

Collections and Selections

Molloy—Malone dies—The unnamable: a trilogy. 1959, Paris 1959, New York 1959.

Krapp's last tape and other dramatic pieces. New York 1960. All that fall; Embers; Act without words 1 and 2.

Poems in English. 1961, New York 1963. Whoroscope; Echo's bones; Cascando; Saint-Lô; Beckett's English trns of 4 French poems, with facing French texts.

End of day: an entertainment from the works of Beckett. (Gaiety, Dublin 5 Oct 1962; New Arts 16 Oct 1962). 1962. Selections from Waiting for Godot; Endgame; Krapp's last tape; All that fall; From an abandoned work; Watt; The unnamable; Act without words 1.

Dramatische Dichtungen. 2 vols Frankfurt 1963–4. Vol 1 contains plays originally written in French, with Beckett's English trns and German trns by E. Tophoven. Vol 2 contains plays originally written in English, with Beckett's French trns and German trns by E. and E. Tophoven.

Proust; Three dialogues—Beckett and G. Duthuit. 1965.

A Beckett reader. Ed J. Calder 1967.

§ 1

Beckett translated his own works, either alone or in collaboration, from English into French and French into English, and such trns are listed separately, below.

Dante... Bruno, Vico... Joyce. In Our exagmination round his factification for incamination of work in progress, Paris 1929, London 1936, Norfolk Conn 1939 (as An exagmination of J. Joyce: analyses of the Work in progress).

From the only poet to a shining whore. In H. Crowder, Henry—music, Paris 1930.

Whoroscope. Paris 1930; London 1961, New York 1963 (in Poems in English, above).

Casket of pralinen for a daughter of a dissipated mandarin; Hell crane to starling; Text; Yoke of liberty. In The European caravan: an anthology of the new spirit in European literature, ed S. Putnam et al, New York 1931.

Proust. 1931, New York [1957].

More pricks than kicks. 1934. Dante and the lobster; Fingal; Ding-dong; A wet night; Love and Lethe; Walking out; What a misfortune; The Smeraldina's billet doux; Yellow; Draff.

Echo's bones and other precipitates. Paris 1935; London 1961, New York 1963 (in Poems in English, above).

Murphy. 1938, New York [1957].

Murphy. [Paris] 1947. French trn by Beckett, with A. Péron, of preceding.

Assumption; Malacoda. In Transition workshop, New York 1949.

Malone meurt. [Paris] 1951; English trn, Malone dies, 1956, below.

Molloy. Paris 1951, 1963 (with L'expulsé; introd by B. Pingaud). Adapted for stage as Molloy (L'Atelier, Geneva 1 Nov 1965); English trn, Molloy, 1955, below.

En attendant Godot: pièce en deux actes. (Théâtre de Babylone, Paris 5 Jan 1953). [Paris] 1952, New York 1963 (ed G. Brée and E. Schoenfeld), London 1966 (with introd and notes in English by C. Duckworth), New York 1967; English trn, Waiting for Godot, 1955, below.

L'innommable. [Paris] 1953. English trn, The unnamable, 1958, below.

Watt. Paris 1953, New York 1959, London 1963; French trn, Watt, 1968, below.

Waiting for Godot: a tragicomedy in two acts. (Arts 3 Aug 1955; Criterion 12 Sept 1955). New York [1954], London 1956, [1957] French, 1965 (rev and unexpurgated). Trn by Beckett of En attendant Godot, 1953, above. A mimeographed script of the radio version performed by BBC Third Programme, 27 April 1960, pbd 1960.

Molloy. Paris 1955, New York 1955, London 1959 (with Malone dies and The unnamable. See Collections, above). English trn by P. Bowles, with Beckett, of Molloy, 1951, above.

Nouvelles et Textes pour rien. Paris 1955. Contains Nouvelles (L'expulsé; Le calmant; La fin) and Textes pour rien 1–13. English trn, Stories and Texts for nothing, New York, 1967, below. Trns of the following were pbd separately; Texte 3, 1960, below; L'expulsé and La fin, 1963, below.

Malone dies. New York [1956], London 1958. Trn by Beckett of Malone meurt, 1951, above.

All that fall: a play for radio. (BBC Third Programme 13 Jan 1957). 1957, New York 1957. French trn, Tous ceux qui tombent, 1959, below.

Acte sans paroles. (Court 3 April 1957; Studio des Champs Elysées, Paris 26 April 1957). Paris 1957 (with Fin de partie). Music by J. Beckett.

Act without words: a mime for one player. 1958 (with Endgame), New York 1958. English trn, by Beckett, of preceding.

Fin de partie. (Court 3 April 1957; Studio des Champs Elysées, Paris 26 April 1957). Paris 1957 (with Acte sans paroles), London 1970 (ed J. and B. S. Fletcher). English trn, Endgame, 1958, below.

From an abandoned work. (BBC Third Programme 14 Dec 1957). 1958. French trn, D'un ouvrage abandonné, 1967, below.

Endgame: a play in one act. (Cherry Lane Theatre, New York 28 Jan 1958; Court 28 Oct 1958). 1958 (with Act without words), New York 1958. Trn by Beckett of Fin de Partie, 1957, above.

Krapp's last tape. (Court 28 Oct 1958). 1959 (with Embers), New York 1960 (in Krapp's last tape and other dramatic pieces; see Collections, above). French trn, La dernière bande, 1960, below.

Bram van Velde. Paris 1958 (with G. Duthuit and J. Putman), Turin and Paris 1961 (rev). Includes Beckett's trns of extracts from Three dialogues (with G. Duthuit), first pbd in Transition Forty-nine 5 1949, and Peintres de l'empêchement, first pbd in Derrière le Miroire 11 & 12 1948. English trn, Bram van Velde, 1960 below.

The unnamable. New York 1958, London 1959 (with Molloy and Malone dies; see Collections, above). Trn by Beckett of L'innommable, 1953, above.

Embers. (BBC Third Programme 24 June 1959). 1959 (with Krapp's last tape), New York 1960 (in Krapp's last tape and other dramatic pieces; see Collections, above). French trn, Cendres, 1966, below (pbd 1960).

Tous ceux qui tombent. (ORTF, Paris 19 Dec 1959). Paris 1957. Trn by R. Pinget, with Beckett, of All that fall, 1957, above.

Henri Hayden: recent paintings. Foreword by Beckett 1959. Rptd from Les Cahiers d'Art-Documents 22 1955.

Gedichte. Wiesbaden 1959. Contains Echo's bones, and uncollected poems in French, with German trns.

Act without words 2: a mime for two players. (Institute of Contemporary Arts 25 Jan 1960). In Krapp's last tape and other dramatic pieces, New York 1960 (see Collections, above); London 1967 (in Eh Joe and other writings). French trn by Beckett, Acte sans paroles 2: pour deux personnages et un aiguillon, in Dramatische Dichtungen, Frankfurt 1963 (see Collections above). Also pbd in Comédie et actes divers, 1966, below.

La dernière bande. (Théâtre Récamier, Paris 22 March 1960). Paris 1960 (with Cendres). Trn by P. Leyris, with Beckett, of Krapp's last tape, 1958, above; adapted as an opera, Krapp: ou la dernière bande, by M. Mihalovici (TNP, Paris 13 Feb 1961).

Bram van Velde. New York 1960. English trn by Beckett, with O. Classe, of Bram van Velde, 1958, above.

Stories and Texts for nothing, 3. In Great French short stories, ed G. Brée, New York 1960. English trn by A. Bonner, with Beckett, of Texte 3 in Nouvelles et Textes pour rien, 1955, above.

Happy days: a play in two acts. (Cherry Lane Theatre, New York 17 Sept 1961; Court 1 Nov 1962). New York 1961, London 1962. French trn, Oh les beaux jours, 1963, below.

Comment c'est. Paris 1961. English trn, How it is, 1964, below.

Words and music. (BBC Third Programme 13 Nov 1962). 1964 (In Play and two short pieces for radio, 1964, below) New York 1968 (in Cascando and other short dramatic pieces, below). Music by J. Beckett. French trn, Paroles et musique, 1966, below.

Text; Ooftish. In R. Cohn, Beckett: the comic gamut, New Brunswick NJ 1962 (see §2 below). Uncollected pieces. Text first pbd New Rev April 1932; Ooftish first pbd transition no 27 1938.

Play: a play in one act. (Ulmer Theater, Ulm-Donau 14 June 1963 [in German trn, Spiel, by E. Tophoven]; Cherry Lane Theatre, New York 4 Jan 1964; Old Vic 7 April 1964). In Play and two short pieces for radio, 1964, below; New York 1968 (in Cascando and other dramatic pieces, below). German trn first pbd in Theater Heute 7 1963.

Cascando: pièce radiophonique pour musique et voix. (ORTF, Paris 13 Oct 1963). In Dramatische Dichtungen, Frankfurt 1963 (see Collections, above). Also pbd in Comédie et actes divers, Paris 1966, below. Music by M. Mihalovici. English trn, Cascando, 1964, below.

Oh les beaux jours: pièce en deux actes. (Odéon, Paris 21 Oct 1963). Paris 1963. French trn by Beckett of Happy days, 1961, above.

The end. In Writers in revolt, New York 1963; rptd in Stories and Texts for nothing, New York 1967, below. English trn by R. Seaver, with Beckett, of La fin (in Nouvelles et Textes pour rien), 1955, above.

The expelled. In The existential imagination, ed F. R. Karl and L. Hamalian, Greenwich, Conn 1963. English trn by R. Seaver, with Beckett, of L'expulsé (in Nouvelles et Textes pour rien), 1955, above.

Comédie: un acte. (Pavillon de Marsan, Paris 14 June 1964). In Dramatische Dichtungen, Frankfurt 1963 (see Collections, above). Also pbd in Comédie et actes divers, Paris 1966, below. French trn by Beckett of Play, 1963, above, with note on alternative method of using spotlight. Film version at Venice Biennale, Aug 1966.

Cascando: a radio piece for music and voice. (BBC Third Programme 28 Oct 1964). In Play and two short pieces for radio, 1964, below; New York 1968 (in Cascando and other short dramatic pieces, below). English trn by Beckett of Cascando, 1963, above.

How it is. [1964], New York 1964. English trn by Beckett of Comment c'est, 1961, above.

Play and two short pieces for radio. 1964. Words and music; Cascando.

Come and go: a dramaticule. (Schiller Theater, Berlin Sept 1965 [in German trn]); Abbey [Peacock] Theatre, Dublin 28 Feb 1968). Frankfurt 1966 (in Beckett: aus einem aufgegebenen Werk und kurze Spiele, [with German trn]), London 1967, New York 1968 (in Cascando and other short dramatic pieces). German trn by H. M. Ehardt pbd separately Stuttgart 1968, with facs of Beckett's ms in English. French trn, Va et vient, 1966, below.

Film. (Venice Biennale 4 Sept 1965). In Eh Joe and other writings, 1967, below; New York 1968 (in Cascando and other short dramatic pieces, below), 1969 (with scenario, illustrations of production shots and essay by the director, A. Schneider).

A tribute to Aldington. In R. Aldington: an intimate portrait, ed A. Kershaw and F.-J. Temple, Carbondale [1965].

Imagination morte imaginez. Paris 1965.

Imagination dead imagine. 1965. Trn by Beckett of preceding.

Va et vient. (Odéon, Paris 28 Feb 1966). In Comédie et actes divers, Paris 1966, below. French trn by Beckett of Come and go, 1965, above.

Cendres: pièce radiophonique en un acte (ORTF, Paris 8 May 1966). Paris 1960 (with La dernière bande). Trn by R. Pinget, with Beckett, of Embers, 1959, above.

Eh Joe: a piece for television. (BBC Television 4 July 1966). In Eh Joe and other writings, 1967, below; New York 1968 (in Cascando and other short dramatic pieces, below). French trn, Dis Joe, 1968, below.

Assez. Paris. 1966. English trn, Enough, in No's knife, 1967, below.

Bing. Paris 1966. English trn, Ping, ibid.

Comédie et actes divers. Paris 1966. Va et vient; Cascando; Paroles et musique; Dis Joe; Acte sans paroles 2.

Paroles et musique: pièce radiophonique. Paris 1966. In Comédie et actes divers, Paris 1966, above. French trn by Beckett of Words and music, 1962, above.

Dans le cylindre. Biblio 35 1967. Fragment, from the same 'matrix' as L'issue.

D'un ouvrage abandonné. Paris [1967]. French trn by L. and A. Janvier, with Beckett, of From an abandoned work, 1957, above.

Eh Joe and other writings. 1967. Act without words 2; Film.

No's knife: collected shorter prose 1945–66. 1967. Contains Stories and Texts for nothing (1967, below) and From an abandoned work; Residua of unfinished novels

(Enough; Imagination dead imagine; Ping). The following were tr by Beckett for this edn: The calmative (from Le calmant, 1955); Enough (from Assez, 1966); Ping (from Bing, 1966).

Stories and Texts for nothing. New York 1967. English trn by Beckett (The end and The expelled with R. Seaver) of Nouvelles et Textes pour rien, 1955 above.

Têtes-mortes. Paris 1967. Contains D'un ouvrage abandonné; Assez; Imagination morte imaginez; Bing.

Cascando and other short dramatic pieces New York 1968. Words and music; Eh Joe; Play; Come and go; Film.

Dis Joe: pièce pour la télévision. (ORTF, Paris 2 Feb 1968). In Comédie et actes divers, Paris 1966, above.

L'issue. Paris 1968. Fragment, from the same 'matrix' as Dans le cylindre, with 6 illustrations by Arikha.

Poèmes. Paris 1968.

Watt. Paris 1968. French trn by L. and A. Janvier, with Beckett, of Watt, 1953, above.

Sans. Paris 1969.

Lessness. 1970. Trn by Beckett of preceding.

Letters

Fourteen letters [from Beckett to A. Schneider]. Village Voice 19 March 1958; rptd in the Village Voice reader, ed D. Wolf and E. Fancher, New York 1962.

§2

Muir, E. Listener 4 July 1934. Review of More pricks than kicks.
— Listener 16 March 1938. Review of Murphy.
Thomas, D. New English Weekly 17 March 1938. Review of Murphy.
Gorman, H. In his James Joyce, New York 1941.
Guggenheim, P. In her Out of this century, New York 1946.
— In her Confessions of an art addict, New York 1960.
Bataille, G. Le silence de Molloy. Critique 7 1951.
Nadeau, M. Beckett: l'humour et le néant. Mercure de France 312 (no 1056) 1951; rptd in his Littérature présente, Paris 1952; tr and rptd in Twentieth century views 1965, below.
— Beckett: ou le droit au silence. Temps Modernes 7 1952.
— 'La dernière' tentative de Beckett. Lettres Nouvelles 1 1953.
— Beckett: la tragédie transposée en farce. Avant-Scène no 156 1957.
— Comment c'est. L'Express 26 Jan 1961.
— In his Roman français depuis la guerre, Paris 1965; tr 1967.
Pingaud, B. Molloy. Esprit 19 1951.
— Molloy, douze ans après. Temps Modernes 18 1963; rptd as introd to 1963 edn of Molloy, above.
Pouillon, J. Molloy. Temps Modernes 7 1951.
Seaver, R. Beckett: an introduction. Merlin 1 1952.
— Beckett. Nimbus 2 1953.
Anouilh, J. Godot ou le sketch des Pensées de Pascal traité par les Fratellini. Arts-Spectacles 400 1953.
— Du chapitre des chaises. Figaro Littéraire 23 April 1956.
Belmont, G. Un classicisme retrouvé. Table Ronde 62 1953.
— Lettre de Londres: avec Fin de partie Beckett a atteint la perfection classique. Arts-Spectacles 614 1957.
— Beckett: l'honneur d'être homme. Arts 821 1961.
Blanchot, M. Ou maintenant? Qui maintenant? Nouvelle Nouvelle Revue Française 2 1953; rptd in his Le livre à venir, Paris 1959; tr Evergreen Rev 2 1959 and rptd in R. Kostelanetz 1964, below.
— A rose is a rose. Nouvelle Revue Française 11 1963.
Dort, B. En attendant Godot: pièce de Beckett. Temps Modernes 8 1953.
— Sur une avant-garde: Adamov et quelques autres. Théâtre d'Aujourd'hui 3 1957.

Grenier, J. Beckett: un monument singulier. Arts-Spectacles 418 1953.
Hartley, A. Beckett. Spectator 23 Oct 1953.
Josbin, R. Chronique du théâtre. Etudes 278 1953; tr (as Waiting for Godot) in Crosscurrents 6 1956.
Leventhal, A. J. Nought into zero. Irish Times 24 Dec 1953.
— Beckett's En attendant Godot. Dublin Mag 30 1954.
— Beckett, poet and pessimist. Listener 9 May 1957.
— Close of play: reflections on Beckett's new work for the French theatre [Fin de partie]. Dublin Mag 32 1957.
— The Beckett hero. Critique 7 1965; rptd in Twentieth century views 1965, below. French version, Le héros de Beckett, in Lettres Nouvelles 12 1964.
Mauroc, D. The new French literary avant-garde. Points 17 1953.
Robbe-Grillet, A. Beckett; auteur dramatique. Critique 9 1953; rptd (rev) in his Pour un nouveau roman, Paris 1963; tr 1965 (as Towards a new novel).
Ryan, S. Beckett. Icarus 3 1953.
Salacrou, A. Ce n'est pas un accident mais un réussite. Arts-Spectacles 400 1953.
Simon, A. Beckett et les rendez-vous manqués. Esprit 21 1953.
— Le degré zéro du tragique. Esprit 31 1963.
Beigbeder, M. Le théâtre à l'âge métaphysique. Age Nouveau 9 1954.
— In his Le théâtre en France depuis la libération, [Paris 1959].
Bjurström, C. G. Beckett. Bonniers Litterära Magasin 23 1954.
Franzen, E. Einführung zu Molloy. Merkur no 73 1954.
— In his Formen des modernen Dramas, Munich 1961.
Hogan, T. The reversed metamorphosis. Irish Writing 26 1954.
Horst, K. A. Molloy: oder die Psychologie des Clowns. Merkur no 86 1954.
— In his Das Spektrum des modernen Romans, Munich 1960.
Kennebeck, E. The moment of cosmic ennui. Commonweal 31 Dec 1954.
Kern, E. Drama stripped for inaction: Beckett's Godot. Yale French Stud no 14 1954.
— Beckett: Dionysian poet. Descant 3 1959.
— Beckett's knight of infinite resignation. Yale French Stud no 29 1962.
Micha, R. Une nouvelle littérature allégorique. Nouvelle Nouvelle Revue Française 3 1954.
Montgomery, N. No symbols where none intended. New World Writing 5 1954.
Onimus, J. L'homme égaré: notes sur le sentiment d'égarement dans la littérature actuelle. Etudes 283 1954; rptd in his Face au monde actuel, Paris 1962.
— Beckett. Bruges 1967.
— Beckett: le clochard et l'asile. Revue Générale Belge 103 1968.
A[ron], S. Balzac a-t-il inspiré En attendant Godot? Figaro Littéraire 17 Sept 1955.
Dhomme, S. Des auteurs à l'avant-garde du théâtre. Cahiers Renaud-Barrault 3 1955.
Duvignaud, J. Die avantgardische Pariser Schule. Dokumente 11 1955.
Expatriate writers in Paris. TLS 27 May 1955.
Frank, N. Scherzi di Beckett. Il Mondo 4 Oct 1955.
Hope-Wallace, P. Beckett. Time and Tide 13 Aug 1955.
Mercier, V. Beckett and the search for self. New Republic 19 Sept 1955.
— A Pyrrhonian eclogue. Hudson Rev 7 1955.
— Godot, Molloy et cie. New Statesman 3 Dec 1955.
— The uneventful event. Irish Times 18 Feb 1956.
— Savage humor. Commonweal 17 May 1957.
— How to read Endgame. Griffin 8 1959.
— The mathematical limit. Nation 14 Feb 1959.
— Beckett and the Sheela-na-gig. Kenyon Rev 23 1961.

—— In his Irish comic tradition, Oxford 1962.

Rattigan, T. Aunt Edna waits for Godot. New Statesman 15 Oct 1955.

Rousseaux, A. L'homme désintégré de Beckett. In his Littérature du XXIème Siècle, Paris 1955.

Worsley, T. C. Cactus land. New Statesman 13 Aug 1955.

Anders, G. Sein ohne Zeit: zu Beckett's Stück En attendant Godot. In his Die Antiquiertheit des Menschen: über die Seele im Zeitalter der zweiten industriellen Revolution, Munich 1956. Extract tr and rptd in Twentieth century views 1965, below.

Barrett, W. Real love abides. New York Times Book Rev 16 Sept 1956.

—— The works of Beckett hold clues to an intriguing riddle. Saturday Rev of Lit 8 June 1957.

—— How I understand less and less every year. Columbia Univ Forum 2 1959.

Beckett, J. Waiting for Godot. Meanjin 15 1956.

Bentley, E. The talent of Beckett. New Republic 14 May 1956; rptd, with addn, Postscript 1967, in Casebook on Waiting for Godot 1967, below.

—— In his What is theatre, Boston 1956.

—— In his The life of the drama, New York 1964.

Bollnow, O. F. Beckett. Antares 4 1956.

Bonnefoi, G. Textes pour rien? Lettres Nouvelles no 36 1956.

Davin, D. Beckett's Everymen. Irish Writing 34 1956.

Fraser, G. S. They also serve. TLS 10 Feb 1956 (anon); rptd in English critical essays, D. Hudson (ed), 1958 (as Waiting for Godot). See also correspondence in TLS between 24 Feb and 6 April 1956.

—— 'Modernity' in the drama. In his Modern writer and his world, 1964.

Gibbs, W. Enough is enough is enough. New Yorker 5 May 1956.

Gold, H. Beckett: style and desire. Nation 10 Nov 1956.

Goth, M. In her Franz Kafka et les lettres françaises, Paris 1956.

Gregory, H. Beckett's dying gladiators. Commonweal 26 Oct 1956; rptd in his Dying gladiators and other essays, New York 1961.

—— Prose and poetry in Beckett. Commonweal 30 Oct 1959.

Hayes, R. Nothing. Commonweal 25 May 1956.

Hobson, H. Beckett: dramatist of the year. International Theatre Annual 1956.

—— Godot and after. In Encore: the Sunday Times book, ed L. Russell, 1963.

Johnston, D. Waiting with Beckett. Irish Writing 34 1956; rptd in Casebook on Waiting for Godot 1967, below.

L., J. En attendant Godot de Beckett, au Théâtre Hébertot. Figaro Littéraire 30 June 1956.

Levy, A. The long wait for Godot. Theatre Arts 40 1956; rptd in Casebook on Waiting for Godot 1967, below.

Loy, J. R. 'Things' in recent French literature. PMLA 71 1956.

Magny, O de. Beckett: ou Job abandonné. Monde Nouveau-Paru 11 1956.

—— Panorama d'une nouvelle littérature romanesque: voici dix romanciers. Esprit 26 1958.

—— Ecriture de l'impossible. Lettres Nouvelles 13 1963.

Mauriac, C. Beckett. Preuves no 61 1956; rptd (rev) in his L'alittérature contemporaine, Paris 1958 (tr 1959 as The new literature).

—— Beckett est aussi un poète. Figaro 3 Feb 1960.

Muller, A. Techniques de l'avant-garde. Théâtre Populaire 18 1956.

O'Casey, S. Not waiting for Godot. Encore 6 1956; rptd in his Blasts and benedictions, ed R. Ayling 1967.

Paris, J. The clock struck 29. Reporter 4 Oct 1956.

—— L'engagement d'aujourd'hui. Liberté 3 1961.

Paulding, G. Beckett's new tale: Malone dies. New York Herald Tribune Book Rev 16 Sept 1956.

Poulet, R. In his La lanterne magique, Paris 1956.

Pronko, L. C. Puzzling about Godot. TLS 13 April 1956 (anon).

—— Beckett, Ionesco, Schéhadé: the avant-garde theatre. Modern Lang Forum 42 1958.

—— Beckett. In his Avant-garde: the experimental theatre in France, Berkeley [1962].

Rainoird, M. En attendant Godot. Monde Nouveau-Paru 11 1956.

Rexroth, K. The point is irrelevance. Nation 14 April 1956; rptd in his Bird in the bush, Norfolk Conn 1959.

—— Beckett and the importance of waiting. In his Bird in the bush, Norfolk Conn 1959.

Shenker, I. Moody man of letters. New York Times 6 May 1956.

Vannier, J. Langages de l'avant-garde. Théâtre Populaire 18 1956.

—— Beckett: Fin de partie. Théâtre Populaire 25 1957.

Alter, A. En attendant Godot n'était pas une impasse: Beckett le prouve dans sa seconde pièce. Figaro Littéraire 12 Jan 1957.

Briggs, R. Beckett's world in waiting. Saturday Rev of Lit 8 June 1957.

Chapsal, M. Un célèbre inconnu. L'Express 8 Feb 1957.

—— Le jeune roman. L'Express 12 Jan 1961.

Christie, E. Det absurde drama: tanker omkring Becketts Waiting for Godot. Samtiden 66 1957.

Codignola, L. Il teatro della guerra fredda. Tempo Presente 2 1957.

—— Il grigio di Beckett. Il Mondo 13 June 1961.

Dreyfus, D. Vraies et fausses énigmes. Mercure de France 331 (no 1130) 1957.

Fiedler, L. Search for peace in a world lost. New York Times Book Rev 14 April 1957.

Gessner, N. Die Unzulänglichkeit der Sprache: eine Untersuchung über Formzerfall und Beziehungslosigkeit bei Beckett. Zürich 1957.

Gray, R. Waiting for Godot: a Christian interpretation. Listener 24 Jan 1957.

Hansen-Löve, F. Beckett oder die Einübung ins Nichts. Hochland 50 1957.

Ionesco, E. In his There is no avant-garde theater, Evergreen Rev 1 1957. French version in his Notes et contre-notes, Paris 1962.

Jessup, B. About Beckett, Godot and others. Northwest Rev 1 1957.

Lee, W. The bitter pill of Beckett. Chicago Rev 10 1957.

In Letters of James Joyce, ed S. Gilbert, R. Ellmann, 3 vols 1957–66.

Logue, C. For those still standing. New Statesman 14 Sept 1957.

Mackworth, C. French writing today: Les coupables. Twentieth Century 161 1957.

Marcel, C. Atomisation du théâtre. Nouvelles Littéraires 20 June 1957.

Mayoux, J.-J. Le théâtre de Beckett. Etudes Anglaises 10 1957; tr and rptd in Perspective 11 1959, below.

—— Beckett et l'univers parodique. In his Vivants piliers, Paris 1960; tr and rptd in Twentieth century views 1965, below.

—— Über Beckett. Frankfurt 1966. Incorporates earlier articles. Contains bibliography by J. Fletcher, rev version of bibliography in his The novels of Beckett, 1964, below.

—— Beckett et l'humour. Cahiers Renaud-Barrault 53 1967.

—— Beckett: homme de théâtre. Biblio 35 1967.

—— Beckett et les chemins de l'expressionisme. Langues Modernes 61 1967.

Middleton, C. Zur Entdeckung neuer Wirklichkeit: Randnotizen zu den Romanen von Beckett. Akzente 4 1957.

Norès, D. La condition humaine selon Beckett. Théâtre d'Aujourd'hui 3 1957.

—— Un théâtre de la mémoire et de l'oubli. Lettres Nouvelles 8 1960.

—— Une nouvelle voix dans le théâtre de Beckett. Lettres Nouvelles 11 1964.

Sastre, A. Siete notas sobre Esperando a Godot. Primer Acto 1 1957; tr and rptd in Casebook on Waiting for Godot 1967, below.

Selz, J. L'homme finissant de Beckett. Lettres Nouvelles 5 1957; rptd in his Le dire et le faire ou les chemins de la création, Paris 1964.

The play's the thing. San Quentin News 28 Nov 1957.

The train stops. TLS 6 Sept 1957.

Vahanien, G. The empty cradle. Theology Today 13 1957.

Vigée, C. Les artistes de la faim. Comparative Lit 9 1957.

Walker, R. Shagreen, Shamrock. Listener 24 Jan 1957; rptd in Weiss 1964, below.

—— In the rut. Listener 19 Dec 1957.

—— Love, chess, and death: Beckett's double bill. Twentieth Century 164 1958.

—— Beckett's Play. TLS 16 April 1964.

Wilson, C. In his Religion and the rebel, 1957.

—— In his The strength to dream, 1962.

—— In his Beyond the outsider, Boston 1965.

Allsop, K. In his Angry decade: a survey of the cultural revolt of the nineteen fifties, 1958.

Bachmann, G-H. Die Hoffnung am Strick: Notizen zu Beckett und Bézart. Antares 6 1958.

—— Französische Stücke in Deutschland. Theater der Zeit 8 1961.

Barbour, T. Beckett and Ionesco. Hudson Rev 11 1958.

Boisdeffre, P. de. In his Une histoire vivante de la littérature d'aujourd'hui, Paris 1958, 1964 (rev).

—— In his Dictionnaire de littérature contemporaine, Paris 1962.

Bowles, P. How Beckett sees the universe: Molloy. Listener 19 June 1958.

Brooke-Rose, C. Beckett and the anti-novel. London Mag 5 1958.

Calendoli, G. Il giuoco di Beckett al margine dell'ermetismo. Fiera Letteraria 21 Sept 1958.

—— Personaggi atomizzati nel teatro di Beckett. Fiera Letteraria 1 Oct 1961.

Chiaromonte, N. Beckett e la fine del mondo. Il Mondo 16 Sept 1958.

Cimatti, P. Beckett uomo zero. Fiera Letteraria 19 Jan 1958.

—— L'ironia di Beckett. Fiera Letteraria 6 Mar 1960.

Clurman, H. In his Lies like truth, New York 1958.

—— In his Naked image, New York 1966.

Curtis, A. In his Mood of the month—4. London Mag 5 1958.

Davie, D. Kinds of comedy: All that fall. Spectrum 2 1958.

Dobrée, B. The London theatre. Sewanee Rev 66 1958.

Driver, T. F. Out in left field. Christian Century 75 1958.

—— Rebuke to nihilism. Christian Century 77 1960.

—— Unsweet song. Christian Century 78 1961.

—— Beckett by the Madeleine. Columbia Univ Forum 4 1961; rptd in Weiss 1964, below; tr and rptd in P. Mélèse, Beckett 1966, below. Interview with Beckett.

—— Apostle of failure? New York Times Book Rev 23 Jan 1966.

Fowlie, W. A. Fallen out of the world. New York Herald Tribune 23 Nov 1958.

—— The new French theatre. Sewanee Rev 67 1959.

—— In his Dionysus in Paris, New York 1960.

—— The French novel: quests and questions. In contemporary European novelists, ed S. Mandel, Carbondale 1968.

Godot gets around. Theatre Arts 42 1958.

Gransden, K. W. The dustman cometh. Encounter 11 1958.

Grossvogel, D. I. Beckett. In his Self-conscious stage in modern French drama, New York 1958, 1961 (as Twentieth century French drama).

—— Beckett: the difficulty of dying. In his Four playwrights and a postscript: Brecht–Ionesco–Beckett–Genet, Ithaca 1962.

Hicks, G. Beckett's world. Saturday Rev of Lit 4 Oct 1958.

Lebesque, M. Le théâtre aux enfers: Artaud, Beckett et quelques autres. Cahiers Renaud-Barrault 6 1958. See also his Artaud et le théâtre de notre temps, Paris 1958.

Lukacs, G. In his Wider den missverstandenen Realismus, Hamburg [1958]; tr 1963 (as The meaning of contemporary realism).

McCoy, C. Waiting for Godot: a biblical appraisal. Florida Rev 2 1958.

Messenger of gloom. Observer 9 Nov 1958.

Nicoletti, G. Théâtre d'aujourd'hui: Ionesco et Beckett. Biennale di Venezia 8 1958.

Noon, W. T. Modern literature and the sense of time. Thought 33 1958–59.

—— God and man in twentieth-century fiction. Thought 37 1962.

Paradise of indignity. TLS 28 March 1958.

Pearson, G. The monologue of Beckett. Spectator 11 April 1958.

Picchi, M. Beckett: introduzione. Fiera Letteraria 29 June 1958.

—— Beckett: Malone muore. Fiera Letteraria 30 Nov 1958.

—— Lettera romana: conclusione su Beckett. Fiera Letteraria 4 Jan 1959.

de Say, A. Rouissillon. L'Arc 2 1958.

Schneider, A. Waiting for Beckett: a personal chronicle. Chelsea Rev 1 1958; rptd (rev) in Casebook on Waiting for Godot 1967, below.

—— Reality is not enough. Tulane Drama Rev 9 1965.

Schumack, M. Why they wait for Godot. New York Times Mag 21 Sept 1958.

Spender, S. Lifelong suffocation. New York Times Book Rev 12 Oct 1958.

—— What is man's life, a joke or something sacred? New York Times Book Rev 25 Feb 1962.

—— In his With Lukács in Budapest, Encounter 23 1964.

Thiébaut, M. Le 'nouveau roman'. Revue de Paris 65 1958.

Tindall, W. Y. Beckett's bums. Critique (Minneapolis) 2 1958; priv ptd London 1960.

—— Beckett. New York 1964 (Columbia Essays on Modern Writers).

Abel, L. Joyce the father, Beckett the son. New Leader 14 Dec 1959; rptd in his Metatheatre: a new view of dramatic form, New York 1963.

Bajini, S. Beckett: o l'emblema totale. Il Verri 3 1959.

Barr, D. One man's universe. New York Times Book Rev 21 June 1959.

Brick, A. The madman in his cell: Joyce, Beckett, Nabokov and the stereotypes. Massachusetts Rev 1 1959.

—— A note on perception and communication in Beckett's Endgame. Modern Drama 4 1961.

Bull, P. C. I know the face, but... 1959. By the original English Pozzo.

Cohn, R. Still novel. Yale French Stud no 24 1959.

—— A note on Beckett, Dante and Geulincx. Comparative Lit 12 1960.

—— The comedy of Beckett. Yale French Stud no 23 1960.

—— Waiting is all. Modern Drama 3 1960.

—— Watt in the light of The castle. Comparative Lit 13 1961.

—— Beckett: the comic gamut. New Brunswick [1962]. Incorporates articles from Accent and PMLA, 1960 and 1961.

—— Comment c'est: de quoi rire. French Rev 35 1962.

—— Plays and players in the plays of Beckett. Yale French Stud no 29 1962.

—— Philosophical fragments in the works of Beckett. Criticism 6 1964; rptd in Twentieth century views 1965, below.

— The absurdly absurd: avatars of Godot. Comparative Lit 2 1965.

— The plays of Yeats through Beckett coloured glasses. Threshold 19 1965.

— Tempest in an Endgame. Symposium 19 1965.

— Beckett for comparatists: a review essay of books published in the last two years. Comparative Lit 3 1966.

— Joyce and Beckett: Irish cosmopolitans. In Proc of 4th Congress of International Comparative Lit Assoc, ed F. Jost, 1967.

— 'Theatrum mundi' and contemporary theatre. Comparative Drama 1 1967.

— Beckett's recent residua. Southern Rev 5 1969.

— In her Currents in contemporary drama, Bloomington 1969. See also Perspective 11 1959, Modern Drama 9 1966, Beckett issue, ed R. Cohn, and Casebook on Waiting for Godot, ed R. Cohn 1967.

Drews, W. Die grossen Unsichtbaren, 7: Godot. Theater der Zeit 6 1959.

Eastman, R. M. The strategy of Beckett's Endgame. Modern Drama 2 1959.

— Beckett and Happy days. Modern Drama 6 1964.

Ellmann, R. In his James Joyce, New York 1959. Contains Home olga, an acrostic poem on Joyce's name, first pbd in Contempto 3 1934.

Friedman, M. J. The achievement of Beckett. Books Abroad 33 1959.

— Beckett and the nouveau roman. Wisconsin Stud in Contemporary Lit 1 1960.

— The creative writer as polyglot; Larbaud and Beckett. Trans Wisconsin Acad of Sciences, Arts and Letters 49 1960.

— The novels of Beckett: an amalgam of Joyce and Proust. Comparative Lit 12 1960.

— A note on Leibniz and Beckett. Romance Notes 4 1963.

— Les romans de Beckett et la tradition du grotesque. In Un nouveau roman?, ed J. H. Matthews, Paris 1964.

— Beckett criticism: its early prime. Symposium 21 1967.

— Molloy's 'sacred' stones. Romance Notes 9 1967. See also Revue des Lettres Modernes 100 1964; Configuration critique: Beckett, ed Friedman, below.

Giraud, R. Unrevolt among the unwriters in France today. Yale French Stud no 24 1959.

Hamilton, K. Boon or thorn? J. Cary and Beckett on human life. Dalhousie Rev 38 1959.

— Negative salvation in Beckett. Queen's Quart 69 1962.

Kesting, M. In her Das epische Theater: zur Struktur des modernen Dramas, Stuttgart 1959.

— Das Romanwerk Becketts. Neue Deutsche Hefte 9 1962.

Lamont, R. C. The metaphysical farce: Beckett and Ionesco. French Rev 32 1959.

— Death and tragi-comedy: three plays of the new theatre. [Happy days: Exit the king; Gallows humour.] Massachusetts Rev 6 1965.

Maciel, L. C. Beckett e a solidão humana. Pôrto Alegre 1959.

Mailer, N. A public notice on Waiting for Godot. In his Advertisements for myself, New York 1959.

Miller, K. Beckett's voices. Encounter 13 1959.

Mills, R. J. Beckett's man. The Christian Century 76 1959.

Monticelli, R. de. L'ultima avanguardia. Sipario 164 1959.

Perspective 11 1959. Beckett issue, ed R. Cohn. Contains: R. Cohn, Preliminary observations on Beckett; H. Kenner, The Cartesian centaur; S. J. Mintz, Beckett's Murphy: a 'Cartesian novel'; J. Hoefer, Watt (rptd in Twentieth century views, 1965, below); E. Kern, Moran-Molloy: the hero as author; R. Cohn, A checklist of Beckett criticism. Also rptd article by J.-J. Mayoux 1957, above.

Politzer, H. The egghead waits for Godot. Christian Scholar 42 1959.

Pullini, G. and R. Casarotto. Da patroni griffi a Beckett, a Venezia. Letterature Moderne 9 1959.

Raes, H. Beckett in Amerika. Vlaamse Gids 43 1959.

Strauss, W. A. Dante's Belacqua and Beckett's tramps. Comparative Lit 11 1959.

The anti-novel in France. TLS 13 Feb 1959.

Unterecker, J. Beckett's no-man's land. New Leader 18 May 1959.

— Notes on Off-Broadway Theater. Evergreen Rev 2 1959.

Verkein, L. Wachten met Beckett. Vlaamse Gids 43 1959.

— Beckett: een classicus van de avant-garde? Vlaamse Gids 45 1961.

Abirached, R. Beckett. In Ecrivains d'aujourd'hui, ed B. Pingaud, Paris 1960.

— La voie tragique de Beckett. Etudes 320 1964.

Benítez-Claros, R. Teatro europeo del existencialismo al antiteatro. Revista de la Universidad de Madrid 34 1960.

Blau, H. Meanwhile, follow the bright angels. Tulane Drama Rev 5 1960.

— The popular, the absurd, and the entente cordiale. Tulane Drama Rev 5 1961.

— Windlasses and assays of bias. Encore 9 1962.

— Counterforce 2: notes from the underground. In his Impossible theatre: a manifesto, New York 1964.

— Politics and the theatre. Wascana Rev 2 1967.

Chadwick, C. Waiting for Godot: a logical approach. Symposium 14 1960.

Champigny, R. Interprétation de En attendant Godot. PMLA 75 1960; tr and rptd in Casebook on Waiting for Godot 1967, below.

— In his Le genre dramatique, Monaco 1965.

Closs, A. Formprobleme und Möglichkeiten zur Gestaltung der Tragödie in der Gegenwart. Stil- und Formprobleme 5 1960.

Cmarada, C. Malone dies: a round of consciousness. Symposium 14 1960.

Coleman, J. Under the jar. Spectator 8 April 1960.

Delye, H. Beckett: ou la philosophie de l'absurde. Aix-en-Provence 1960.

Esslin, M. The theatre of the absurd. Tulane Drama Rev 4 1960; rptd in Freedman 1964, below.

— Beckett: the search for the self. In his The theatre of the absurd, New York 1961, London 1968 (rev).

— Beckett. In The novelist as philosopher, ed J. Cruikshank 1962.

— Forget the dustbins. Plays and Players Nov 1962.

— Godot and his children: the theatre of Beckett and Pinter. In Experimental drama, ed W. A. Armstrong 1963.

See also Twentieth century views—Beckett: a collection of critical essays, ed Esslin 1965, below.

Fanizza, F. La parola e il silenzio nel Innommable di Beckett. Aut Aut 60 1960.

Frye, N. The nightmare life in death. Hudson Rev 13 1960.

Gassner, J. Beckett: Waiting for Godot. In his Theatre at the crossroads, New York 1960.

Gerard, M. Molloy becomes unnamable. X: a quarterly review 1 1960.

Grillo, G. Beckett fra anti-teatro e anti-romanzo. Idea 16 1960.

Harvey, L. E. Art and the existential in En attendant Godot. PMLA 75 1960; rptd in Casebook on Waiting for Godot 1967, below.

— Beckett on life, art, and criticism. MLN 80 1965.

Hooker, W. Irony and absurdity in the avant-garde theatre. Kenyon Rev 22 1960; rptd in Freedman 1964, below.

Kermode, F. Beckett, C. P. Snow and pure poverty. Encounter 15 1960; rptd in his Puzzles and epiphanies, 1962.

—— The new apocalyptists. Partisan Rev 33 1966.

Metman, E. Reflections on Beckett's plays. Jnl of Analytical Psychology 5 1960; rptd in Twentieth century views 1965, below.

Miller, J. H. The anonymous walkers. Nation 23 April 1960.

Moore, J. R. A farewell to something. Tulane Drama Rev 5 1960.

—— Some night thoughts on Beckett. Massachusetts Rev 8 1967.

Olles, H. Beckett. Welt und Wort 15 1960; rptd in Lexikon der Weltliteratur im 20. Jahrhundert, Freiburg 1960.

Popkin, H. Williams, Osborne, or Beckett? New York Times Mag 13 Nov 1960; rptd in Freedman 1964, below.

Pritchett, V. S. An Irish Oblomov. New Statesman 2 April 1960; rptd in his Living novel, New York 1964.

Thibaudeau, J. Un théâtre de romanciers. Critique 16 1960.

Trilogy. TLS 17 June 1960.

Zeltner-Neukomm, G. In her Das Wagnis des französischen Gegenwartsromans: die neue Welterfahrung in der Literatur, Hamburg 1960.

Adorno, T. W. Versuch das Endspiel zu verstehen. In his Noten zur Literatur 2, Frankfurt 1961; tr and rptd in Twentieth century interpretations of Endgame 1969, below.

Alvarez, A. Poet waiting for Pegasus. Observer 31 Dec 1961.

—— Audience of captives. New Statesman 1 June 1962.

Aubarède, G.d'. En attendant... Beckett. Nouvelles Littéraires 16 Feb 1961; tr (as Waiting for Beckett), Trace 42 1961.

Bialos, A. Beckett. Studies in Lit 1 1961.

Blanzat, J. Les romans de Beckett. Figaro Littéraire 13 May 1961.

Boyle, K. Molloy: icon of the negative. Westwind 5 1961.

Butler, M. Anatomy of despair. Encore 8 1961.

Corrigan, R. The theatre in search of a fix. Tulane Drama Rev 5 1961; rptd in Theatre in the twentieth century, ed Corrigan, New York 1963.

Fitch, B. T. Narrateur et narration dans la trilogie romanesque de Beckett. Bull des Jeunes Romanistes 3 1961.

Flood, E. A reading of Beckett's Godot. Culture 22 1961.

Fournier, E. Pour que la boue me soit contée... Critique 17 1961.

'Genet' (i.e. J. Flanner). Letter from Paris. New Yorker 4 March 1961; rptd in Paris journal 1944–65, ed W. Shawn, New York 1965.

Gilman, R. The stage: Beckett's Happy days. Commonweal 13 Oct 1961.

Gresset, M. Le 'parce que' chez Faulkner et le 'donc' chez Beckett. Lettres Nouvelles no 9 1961.

—— Création et cruauté chez Beckett. Tel Quel 15 1963.

Grillandi, M. Beckett. L'Italia che Scrive 44 1961.

Guicharnaud, J. Existence on stage: Beckett. In his Modern French theatre from Giraudoux to Beckett, New Haven 1961, 1967 (rev).

—— The 'R' effect. L'Esprit Créateur 2 1962.

Heppenstall, R. In his The fourfold tradition, London 1961.

—— In his The intellectual part, 1963.

Hesse, E. Die Welt des Beckett. Akzente 8 1961.

Iser, W. Becketts dramatische Sprache. Germanisch-Romanische Monatsschrift 11 1961; tr and rptd in Modern Drama 9 1966, Beckett issue, below.

Karl, F. R. Waiting for Beckett: quest and re-quest. Sewanee Rev 69 1961; rptd in his Contemporary English novel, New York 1962, London 1963 (A reader's guide to the contemporary English novel).

Kenner, H. Beckett: a critical study. New York 1961, Berkeley 1968 (rev). Substantially summarizes articles pbd in various journals 1958–61.

—— Flaubert, Joyce and Beckett: the stoic comedians. Boston [1962].

Kramer-Badoni, R. Die Annihilierung des Nihilismus: ein Versuch über Beckett. Forum 8 1961.

Lancelotti, M. A. Observaciones sobre Molloy. Sur 273 1961.

Lees, F. N. On Beckett and Schopenhauer. Memoirs and Proc of Manchester Lit & Phil Society 1961–2.

Lennon, P. Beckett's month. Manchester Guardian Weekly 8 June 1961.

Life in the mud. TLS 7 April 1961.

The long wait. TLS 5 May 1961.

Marmori, G. Il fango di Beckett. Il Mondo 21 March 1961.

Perniola, M. Beckett e la scrittura esistenziale: commento a L'innominabile. Tempo Presente 6 1961.

Piatier, J. Le Monde 11 Feb 1961. Review of Comment c'est.

Rindauer, G. Endspiel und neuer Anfang. Forum 8 1961.

Romulus, H. Beckett, positiv. Theater Heute 2 1961.

Tallmer, J. The magic box. Evergreen Rev 5 1961.

Touchard, P.-A. Le théâtre de Beckett. Revue de Paris 68 1961.

Tynan, K. In his Curtains, New York 1961.

—— In his Tynan right and left, 1967.

Wellwarth, G. E. Life in the void: Beckett. Univ of Kansas City Rev 28 1961; rptd in his Theatre of protest and paradox, New York 1964.

Willcock, J. R. Nulla da fare. Il Mondo 17 Oct 1961.

Yerlès, P. Le théâtre de Beckett. Revue Nouvelle 33 1961.

Zamora, J. G. In his Historia del theatro contemporáneo, Barcelona 1961.

Albérès, R. M. In his Histoire du roman moderne, Paris 1962.

Ashmore, J. Philosophical aspects of Beckett. Symposium 16 1962.

Ashworth, A. New theatre: Ionesco, Beckett, Pinter. Southerly 22 1962.

Butler, H. L. Balzac and Godeau, Beckett and Godot: a curious parallel. Romance Notes 3 1962.

Chambers, R. Beckett and the padded cell. Meanjin 21 1962.

—— Beckett's brinkmanship. Jnl of the Australasian Lang & Lit Assn 19 1963; rptd in Twentieth century views 1965, below.

—— Vers une interprétation de Fin de partie. Studi Francesi 11 1967. Tr, rev and rptd in Twentieth century interpretations of Endgame 1969, below.

Coffey, B. Memory's Murphy maker: some notes on Beckett. Threshold 17 1962.

The core of the onion. TLS 21 Dec 1962.

Donoghue, D. The play of words. Listener 12 July 1962.

Dukore, B. F. Gogo, Didi and the absent Godot. Drama Survey 1 1962; reply by T. Marcus, Feb 1963 and riposte by Dukore, May 1963.

—— Beckett's play, Play. Educational Theatre Jnl 17 1965.

—— The other pair in Waiting for Godot. Drama Survey 7 1968–9.

Fasano, G. Beckett. Belfagor 17 1962.

Fletcher, D. Molloy for Prime Minister. Left Wing Nov 1962.

Fletcher, J. Beckett et Swift: vers une étude comparée. Annales Publiées par la Faculté des Lettres de Toulouse 11 (Littératures 10) 1962.

—— Balzac and Beckett revisited. French Rev 37 1963.

—— Beckett et Proust. Caliban 1 1964.

—— Beckett's verse: influences and parallels. French Rev 37 1964.

—— The novels of Beckett. 1964. With bibliography.

—— Sur un roman inédit de Beckett. Annales (Toulouse) Littératures 12 1965.

—— Beckett's art. 1967. Incorporates rev versions of articles in Nottingham French Stud, Caliban, New Durham, Comparative Lit, Modern Drama, Listener, Twentieth century views, ed Esslin.

—— The arrival of Godot. MLR 64 1969.

Gascoigne, B. In his Twentieth-century drama, 1962.

Glicksberg, C. I. Beckett's world of fiction. Arizona Quart 18 1962; rptd (rev) in his The self in modern literature, Philadelphia 1963.

— The lost self in modern literature. Personalist 43 1962. Rptd ibid.

Hamilton, C. Portrait in old age: the image of man in Beckett's trilogy. Western Humanities Rev 16 1962.

Hayman, D. Beckett. In Six contemporary novelists, ed W. O. S. Sutherland, Austin 1962; slightly rev version tr and rptd in Revue des Lettres Modernes 100 1964, Configuration critique: Beckett, below.

Hoffman, F. J. Beckett: the language of self. [Carbondale] 1962; extracts tr and rptd in Revue des Lettres Modernes 100 1964, Configuration critique: Beckett, below.

Hubert, R. R. The couple and the performance in Beckett's plays. Esprit Créateur 2 1962.

Hughes, C. Beckett and the game of life. Catholic World 195 1962.

— Beckett's world: wherein God is continually silent. Critic 20 1962.

Key-Åberg, S. Om absurdismen. Ord och Bild 71 1962.

Kott, J. Le roi Lear, autrement dit Fin de partie. Temps Modernes 194 1962; rptd in his Shakespeare notre contemporain, Paris 1962 (first pbd in Polish, 1961), London 1964 as Shakespeare our contemporary; English trn, King Lear or Endgame, in Evergreen Rev 33 1964.

— A note on Beckett's realism. Tulane Drama Rev 10 1966.

Lappalainen, A. Under Becketts presenning. Ord och Bild 71 1962.

Lewis, A. The theatre of the 'absurd'. In his Contemporary theatre, New York 1962.

Macksey, R. The artist in the labyrinth: design or Dasein? MLN 77 1962.

Marowitz, C. A quick walk away from Beckett. Village Voice 7 1962.

— A view from the gods. Encore 10 1963.

— Play. Encore 11 1964.

Morse, M. J. The contemplative life according to Beckett. Hudson Rev 15 1962.

— The choreography of 'The new novel'. Hudson Rev 16 1963.

— The ideal core of the onion: Beckett's criticism. French Rev 38 1964.

— The case for irrelevance. College Eng 30 1968.

Oates, J. C. The trilogy of Beckett. Renascence 14 1962.

Radke, J. J. The theatre of Beckett. Yale French Stud no 29 1962.

Reid, A. Beckett and the drama of unknowing. Drama Survey 2 1962.

— All I can manage, more than I could. Dublin 1968.

Rickels, M. Existential themes in Beckett's Unnamable. Criticism 4 1962.

Simpson, A. Beckett and Behan, and a theatre in Dublin. 1962.

Smith, H. A. Dipsychus among the shadows. In Contemporary theatre, ed J. R. Brown 1962, 1968 (rev).

Styan, J. L. In his Dark comedy, 1962.

Sypher, W. In his Loss of the self in modern literature and art, New York 1962.

Weales, G. The language of Endgame. Tulane Drama Rev 6 1962.

Wolf, D. and E. Fancher (eds). Village Voice reader. New York 1962. Reviews, essays and letters by J. Tallmer, N. Mailer and others.

Angus, W. Modern theatre reflects the times. Queen's Quart 70 1963.

Bloch-Michel, J. In his Le présent de l'indicatif, Paris 1963.

Brée, G. Beckett's abstractors of quintessence. French Rev 36 1963.

Brown, J. R. Beckett's Shakespeare. CQ 5 1963.

Cahiers Renaud-Barrault 44 1963. Beckett issue, ed G. Brée. Includes R. N. Coe, Le dieu de Beckett; R. Chambers, Beckett, homme des situations limitées; O de Magny, Beckett et la farce métaphysique.

Corvin, M. In his Le théâtre nouveau en France, Paris 1963.

Dennis, N. No view from the toolshed. Encounter 20 1963.

— Burying Beckett alive. Show 3 1963.

Frisch, J. E. Endgame: a play as poem. Drama Survey 3 1963.

Halldén, R. et al. Ett samtal om Beckett. Ord och Bild 72 1963.

Hesla, D. H. The shape of chaos: a reading of Beckett's Watt. Critique (Minneapolis) 6 1963.

Macron, M. Oh les beaux jours de Beckett. Signes du Temps 3 1963.

Magnan, J-M. Beckett: ou les chaînes et relais du néant. Cahiers du Sud 50 1963.

Marinello, L. J. Beckett's Waiting for Godot: a modern classic affirming man's dignity and nobility and ultimate salvation. Drama Critique 6 1963.

Marissel, A. Beckett. Paris [1963]. Incorporates article from Esprit.

Rhodes, S. A. From Godeau to Godot. French Rev 36 1963.

Seipel, H. Untersuchungen zum experimentellen Theater von Beckett und Ionesco. Bonn 1963.

Warhaft, S. Threne and theme in Watt. Wisconsin Stud in Contemporary Lit 4 1963.

Wellershoff, D. 'Der Gleichgültige': Versuche über Hemingway, Camus, Benn und Beckett. Cologne 1963; extract (tr as Failure of an attempt at de-mythologisation: Beckett's novels) rptd in Twentieth century views 1965, below.

Wendt, E. Spiel in Urnen: die Aufführung des Monats, Becketts neues Stück Spiel in Ulm. Theater Heute 4 1963.

— Die Moderne und die Ersatz-Moderne. Theater Heute 6 1965.

Arnold, B. Beckett. Dubliner 3 1964.

Büchler, F. Notizen zum Werk Becketts. Die Neue Rundschau 75 1964.

Coe, R. N. Beckett. Edinburgh 1964 (Writers and Critics).

— God and Beckett. Meanjin 24 1965.

— Les anarchistes de droite: Ionesco, Beckett, Genet, Arrabal. Cahiers Renaud-Barrault 67 1968.

Cohen, R. S. Parallels and the possibility of influence between Simone Weil's Waiting for God and Beckett's Waiting for Godot. Modern Drama 6 1964.

Davis, R. Radio and Beckett. Prompt 5 1964.

Ewart, G. Play. London Mag 4 1964.

Freedman, M. (ed). Essays in the modern drama. Boston 1964. Includes rptd articles by H. Popkin, 1960 above, M. Esslin, 1960 above, W. Hooker, 1960 above.

Furbank, P. N. Beckett's purgatory. Encounter 22 1964.

Gross, J. Amazing reductions. Encounter 23 1964.

Hainsworth, J. D. Shakespeare, son of Beckett? MLQ 25 1964.

Hambro, C. Beckett's 'romantrilogi'. Vinduet 18 1964.

Harward, T. B. (ed). In his European patterns, Dublin 1964.

Jacobsen, J. and Mueller, W. R. The testament of Beckett. New York 1964. Incorporates articles from Prairie Schooner, and Man in the modern theatre, ed N. A. Scott, 1965.

— The absurd guest. Kenyon Rev 29 1967.

Kostelanetz, R. (ed). On contemporary literature. New York 1964. Includes rptd article by Blanchot, 1953 above and article by Federman, Beckett and the fiction of mud.

Lewis, J. Beckett and the decline of Western civilisation. Marxism Today 8 1964.

Lyons, C. R. Beckett's Endgame: an anti-myth of creation. Modern Drama 7 1964.

— Some analogies between the epic Brecht and the absurdist Beckett. Comparative Drama 1 1967–8.

Peake, C. Waiting for Godot and the conventions of the drama. Prompt 4 1964.

Pevel, H. Résonances mallarméennes du nouveau roman. Médiations 7 1964.

Rechtien, Br. J. Time and eternity meet in the present. Texas Stud in Lit & Lang 6 1964.

Revue des Lettres Modernes 100 1964, Configuration critique: Beckett, ed M. J. Friedman. Contains: B. Morrissette, Les idées de Robbe-Grillet sur Beckett; E. Kern, Beckett et les poches de Lemuel Gulliver; G. Brée, L'étrange monde des 'grands articulés'; R. Lamont, La farce métaphysique de Beckett; R. Champigny, Les aventures de la première personne; L. E. Harvey, Beckett: initiation du poète; J. R. Bryer, Critique de Beckett: sélection bibliographique. Also rptd articles by Hoffman, Hayman 1962, above. Rev English version, Beckett now, Chicago 1970, with following addns; R. Cohn, The laughter of sad Sam Beckett: J. Fletcher, Interpreting Molloy; R. Federman, Beckettian paradox: who is telling the truth?

Ricks, C. Beckett and the lobster. New Statesman 14 Feb 1964.

—— The roots of Beckett. Listener 17 Dec 1964.

—— Mr Artesian. Listener 3 Aug 1967.

Romano, A. Le 'poesie inglesi' di Beckett. Fiera Letteraria 11 Oct 1964.

Rovatti, P. Note sul teatro di Beckett. Aut Aut 81 1964.

Senneff, S. F. Song and music in Beckett's Watt. Modern Fiction Stud 10 1964.

'Talk of the town'. New Yorker 8 Aug 1964. Account of Film, made in New York, summer 1964.

Trussler, S. Happy days: two productions and a text. Prompt 4 1964.

Verdot, G. Recherche de Beckett chez ceux qui l'ont découvert les premiers. Paris-Théâtre 206 1964.

Weiss, S. I. (ed). Drama in the modern world: plays and essays. Boston 1964. Includes rptd articles by Walker, 1959 above and Driver, 1961 above.

Wendler, H. W. Graveyard humanism. Southwest Rev 49 1964.

Wilson, R. N. Beckett: the social psychology of emptiness. Jnl of Social Issues 20 1964.

Brook, P. Endgame as King Lear. Encore 12 1965.

—— Mit Beckett leben. Theater Heute 6 1965.

—— In his The empty space, 1968.

Brustein, R. In his Seasons of discontent, New York 1965.

Chiari, J. In his Landmarks of contemporary drama, 1965.

Federman, R. Journey to chaos: Beckett's early fiction. Berkeley and Los Angeles 1965. Incorporates rev versions of articles in Arizona Quart, French Rev and On Contemporary literature, ed R. Kostelanetz, New York 1964. With bibliography.

—— Film. Film Quart 20 1966–7.

—— Beckett ou le bonheur en enfer. Symposium 21 1967.

—— Le bonheur chez Beckett. Esprit 35 1967.

Francis, R. L. Beckett's metaphysical tragicomedy. Modern Drama 8 1965.

MacGowran, J. Why actors are fascinated by Beckett's theatre. The Times 27 Jan 1965.

MacNeice, L. In his Varieties of parable, Cambridge 1965.

Rosi, L. Beckett e il teatro dell' assurdo. Cenobio 14 1965.

Roy, C. In his L'amour du théâtre, Paris 1965.

Scott, N. A. Beckett. 1965. Incorporates article from Centennial Rev 1962.

Twentieth century views—Beckett: a collection of critical essays, ed M. Esslin, Englewood Cliffs NJ [1965]. Includes rptd articles and lectures by J. Fletcher, M. Nadeau, A. J. Leventhal, J. Hoefer, J-J. Mayoux, D. Wellershoff, E. Metman, G. Anders, R. Chambers, R. Cohn, above.

Vold, J. E. Beckett's romaner. Samtiden 74 1965.

Alpaugh, D. J. Negative definition in Beckett's Happy days. Twentieth Century Lit 11 1966.

Bersani, L. No exit for Beckett. Partisan Rev 33 1966.

Chase, N. C. Images of man: Le malentendu and En attendant Godot. Wisconsin Stud in Contemporary Lit 7 1966.

Cooney, S. Beckett's Murphy. Explicator 25 1966.

Cronin, A. In his A question of modernity, 1966.

Duckworth, C. The making of Godot. Theatre Research 7 1966.

Edström, M. Ansiktet pa väggen. Ord och Bild 75 1966.

Greenberg, A. The death of the psyche: a way to the self in the contemporary novel. Criticism 8 1966.

Hecht, W. Brecht 'und' Beckett. Theater der Zeit 14 1966.

Hildesheimer, W. Wer war Mozart?—Beckett's Spiel: über das absurde Theater. Frankfurt 1966.

Janvier, L. Pour Beckett. Paris [1966].

—— Réduire à la parole. Cahiers Renaud-Barrault 53 1966.

—— Beckett et ses fables. Biblio 35 1967.

—— Le lieu du retrait de la blancheur de l'echo. Critique 23 1967.

—— Beckett: la plaie et le couteau. Le Monde 17 Jan 1968.

—— Beckett par lui-même. Paris [1969].

—— Les difficultés d'un séjour. Critique 25 1969.

Kaiser, J. Am Rande dessen, was sagbar ist: zum 60. Geburstag des Dichters Beckett. Universitas (Stuttgart) 21 1966.

Mélèse, P. Beckett. Paris 1966.

Modern Drama 9 1966. Beckett issue, ed R. Cohn. Contains: D. J. Alpaugh, The symbolic structure of Beckett's All that fall; A. Atkins, A note on the structure of Lucky's speech; C. M. Brooks, The mythic pattern in Waiting for Godot; R. Cohn, Acting for Beckett: The beginnings of Endgame; J. Dubois, Beckett and Ionesco: the tragic awareness of Pascal and the ironic awareness of Flaubert; J. Fletcher, Action and play in Beckett's theatre: Roger Blin at work; M. J. Friedman, 'Critic!'; R. R. Hubert, Beckett's Play between poetry and performance; E. Kern, Beckett and the spirit of the Commedia dell' Arte; J-J. Mayoux, Beckett and expressionism; G. Mihaly, Beckett's Godot and the myth of alienation [rptd from New Hungarian Quart 24 1966]; R. A. Oberg, Krapp's last tape and the Proustian vision; R. Schechner, There's lots of time in Godot [rptd in Casebook on Waiting for Godot 1967, below]; J. J. Sheedy, The comic apocalypse of King Hamm. Also rptd article by W. Iser 1961, above.

Moore, H. T. The mud and ashcan world of Beckett. In his Twentieth-century French literature since world war 2, Carbondale 1966.

Parker, R. B. The theory and theatre of the absurd. Queen's Quart 73 1966.

Serrau, G. In her Histoire du 'nouveau théâtre', Paris 1966.

Tagliaferri, A. Il concreto e l'astratto in Beckett. Il Verri 20 1966.

—— Beckett e l'iperdeterminazione letteraria. Milan 1967.

Williams, R. Tragic deadlock and stalemate. In his Modern tragedy, 1966.

—— Waiting for Godot. In his Drama from Ibsen to Brecht, 1968.

Worth, K. J. Yeats and the French drama. Modern Drama 8 1966. Yeats and Beckett.

Atkins, A. Lucky's speech in Waiting for Godot: a punctuated sense-line arrangement. Education Theatre Jnl 19 1967. See also Modern Drama 9 1966, above.

Ballardini, V. Beckett: écrivain irlandais. Langues Modernes 61 1967.

Beckett at sixty: a festschrift. 1967. Introd by J. Calder. Symposium of reminiscences, tributes and new criticism. Pt 1: reminiscences. A. J. Leventhal, The thirties; M. Jolas, A Bloomlein for Sam; J. Lindon, First meeting with Beckett; M. Mihalovici, My collaboration with Beckett; J. MacGowran, Working with Beckett: H. Hobson, The first night of Waiting for Godot; J. Fletcher, In search of Beckett; A. Schneider, Waiting for Beckett. Part II: critical examinations. M. Esslin, Beckett's poems; H. Kenner, Progress report 1962–65; M. Renaud, Beckett the magnificent; R. Pinget, My dear Sam; H. Pinter, Beckett; C. Monteith, Personal note; F. Arrabal, In connection with Beckett; P. Staib, A propos Beckett; A. Higgins, Tribute; M. Hutchinson, All the livelong way; A. Simpson, Beckett; J. Herbert, A letter; G. Devine, Last tribute.

Beckett: en artikkelsamling. Maerli, T. (ed). Oslo 1967. Includes A-L. Amadou, Fra J-P. Sartres romanverden til Becketts tragiske univers; S. S. Ulriksen, Beckett og den 'absurde tradisjon'; K. Broch, Når stillstanden blir drama; A. Despard, Sluttspill?; O. M. Ellingsen, Happy days: som et drama om uforløst kjærlighet, liv og død; J. E. Vold, Malones blyant; T. Frost, Becketts romaner —en eftertanke; T. Winther, Beckett om kunstnere og deres verk.

Berlin, N. Beckett and Shakespeare. French Rev 40 1967.

Borréli, G. Beckett et le sentiment de la déréliction. In Le théâtre moderne depuis la deuxième guerre mondiale, ed. J. Jacquot Paris 1967.

Capone, G. Drammi per voci: D. Thomas, Beckett, Pinter. Bologna 1967.

Casebook on Waiting for Godot: the impact of Beckett's modern classic; reviews, reflections and interpretations. Ed R. Cohn, New York 1967. Includes rptd articles by E. Bentley, D. Johnston, A. Schneider, A. Simpson, G. Serrau, A. Levy, A. Sastre, D. Suvin, R. Champigny, L. E. Harvey, R. Schechner and 2 specially written articles, S-E. Case, Image and Godot; J. J. Sheedy, The net.

Cattanei, G. Beckett. Florence 1967.

Domenach, J-M. In his Retour du tragique, Paris 1967.

Erickson, J. D. Objects and systems in the novels of Beckett. Esprit Créateur 7 1967.

Gaddis, M. The purgatory metaphor of Yeats and Beckett. London Mag 7 1967.

Geerts, L. Beckett vertaald: de dramatiek von de herin-nering. Dietsche Warande en Belfort 12 1967.

Hassan, I. The literature of silence: from Miller to Beckett and Burroughs. Encounter 28 1967.
— The literature of silence: Miller and Beckett. New York 1968.

Hodgart, M. Saint Beckett. New York Rev of Books 7 Dec 1967.

Kolve, V. A. Religious language in Waiting for Godot. Centennial Rev 11 1967.

Leroux, N. Pour Beckett. Etudes Françaises 3 1967.

Lumley, F. The case against Beckett. In his New trends in twentieth century drama, 1967.

Maierhöfer, F. Becketts forcierte Negation. Stimmen der Zeit 18 1967.

O'Brien, J. Beckett and Gide: an hypothesis. French Rev 40 1967.

Oliva, R. Beckett: prima del silenzio. Milan 1967.

O'Neill, J. P. The absurd in Beckett. Personalist 48 1967.

Schoell, K. Das Theater Becketts. Munich 1967.
— The chain and the circle: a structural comparison of Waiting for Godot and Endgame. Modern Drama 11 1968.

Schramm, U. In his Fiktion und Reflexion: Überlegungen zu Musil und Beckett, Frankfurt 1967.
— Kritik der Theorie vom 'Kunstwerk als Negation': Beobachtungen an Becketts Endspiel und an Bildern von Vasarely und Fontana. Philosophisches Jahrbuch der Görres-Gesellschaft 76 1969.

Schwarz, N. Zeitproblematik in Becketts En attendant Godot. Die Neueren Sprachen 16 1967.

Solomon, P. H. Beckett's Molloy: a dog's life. French Rev 41 1967.
— Lousse and Molloy: Beckett's bower of bliss. Austra-lian Jnl of French Stud 6 1969.

Stamirowska, K. The conception of a character in the works of Joyce and Beckett. Kwartalnik Neofilogiczny 14 1967.

Suvin, D. Beckett's purgatory of the individual: or the three laws of thermodynamics. Tulane Drama Rev 11 1967; rptd in Casebook on Waiting for Godot 1967, above.

Thiel, A. La condition tragique chez Beckett. Revue Nouvelle 45 1967.

Todd, R. E. Proust and redemption in Waiting for Godot. Modern Drama 10 1967.

Torrance, R. M. Modes of being and time in the world of Godot. MLQ 28 1967.

Balotă, N. Aşteptarea lui Beckett. Secolul 3 1968.

Beckett up the pole. TLS 16 May 1968.

Brereton, G. In his Principles of tragedy, 1968.

Büttner, G. In his Absurdes Theater und Bewusstseins-wandel, Berlin-Wilmersdorf [1968].

Cleveland, L. O. Trials in the soundscape: the radio plays of Beckett. Modern Drama 11 1968.

Curnow, D. H. Language and theatre in Beckett's 'English' plays. Mosaic 2 1968.

Dimić, M. Godou. Delo 14 1968.

Douglas, D. The drama of evasion in Waiting for Godot. Komos 1 1968.

Easthope, A. Hamm, Clov, and dramatic method in Endgame. Modern Drama 10 1968; rptd in Twentieth century interpretations of Endgame 1969, below.

Ellingsen, O. M. Söken og anti-söken i Becketts verden. Vinduet 22 1968.

Evers, F. Beckett: the incurious seeker. Dublin Mag 7 1968.

Freeman, E. T. Beckett on the Mississippi. Manuscripts 20 1968.

Gilbert, S. M. All the dead voices: a study of Krapp's last tape. Drama Survey 6 1968.

Hampton, C. C., jr. Beckett's Film. Modern Drama 11 1968.

Harrison, R. Beckett's Murphy. Athens, Georgia 1968.

Hayman, R. Beckett. 1968 (Contemporary Playwrights ser).

Hensel, G. Beckett. Velber bei Hannover 1968.

Lodge, D. Some Ping understood. Encounter 30 1968.

Lombardi, T. W. Who tells who Watt? Chelsea 22–3 1968.

Ludvigsen, C. Beckett og Fontane: Ennspeciel kilde til visse temaer i Becketts senere dramatik. In Festschrift til Jens Krusse, ed Albeck et al, Aarhus 1968.

O'Nan, M. Beckett's Lucky: damned. Athens Georgia 1968. Pamphlet.
— In her Role of mind in Hugo, Faulkner, Beckett and Grass, New York 1969.

Palmer, T. Artistic privilege. London Mag 8 1968.

Steiner, G. Of nuance and scruple. New Yorker 27 April 1968.

Tassing, E. Beckett. In Fremmede digtere i det 20. århundrede, ed S. M. Kristensen, vol 3, Copenhagen 1968.

Trousdale, M. Dramatic form: the example of Godot. Modern Drama 11 1968.

Vasilev, G. Antiteatărăt na Beket. Nyelvtudományi Közlemények 10 1968.

Webner, H. L. Waiting for Godot and the new theology. Renascence 21 1968.

Wernick, R. The three kings of Bedlam. Life 2 Feb 1968.

Bajomée, D. Lumière, ténèbres et chaos dans L'innom-mable de Beckett. Lettres Romanes 23 1969.

Bensky, R. La symbolique du mime dans le théâtre de Beckett. Lettres Nouvelles Sept–Oct 1969.

Bernal, O. Langage et fiction dans le roman de Beckett. Paris 1969.

Burns, G. L. The storyteller and the problem of language in Beckett's fiction, MLQ 30 1969.

Twentieth century interpretations of Endgame, ed B. G. Chevigny. Englewood Cliffs NJ 1969. Includes rptd articles by T. W. Adorno 1961, above; A. Easthope 1968, above; R. Chambers 1962, above, and specially written article by R. M. Goldman, Endgame and its score keepers.

Dubois, J. Deux représentations de la société dans le nouveau théâtre. Revue d'Histoire du Théâtre 21 1969.

Egebak, N. Beckett palimpsest. Copenhagen 1969.

Findlay, R. R. Confrontation in waiting: Godot and the Wakefield play. Renascence 21 1969.

Fischer, E. Beckett: Play and Film. Mosaic 2 1969.

Lahr, J. Notes on the cowardly lion. New York 1969.
Biography of B. Lahr, the original American Estragon.
Murch, A. C. Les indications scéniques dans le nouveau théâtre: Fin de partie de Beckett. Australian Jnl of French Stud 6 1969.
Niemi, I. Calibanin shakki. Parnasso 19 1969. On Fin de partie.
Oster, R. Hamm and Hummel: Beckett and Strindberg on the human condition. Scandinavian Stud 41 1969.
Perche, L. Beckett: l'enfer à notre portée. Paris 1969.

Robinson, M. The long sonata of the dead. 1969.
Robles, M. Cain: an unfortunate? Modern Languages 50 1969. Cain in Unamuno, Baudelaire, Beckett and Steinbeck.
Shapiro, B. Toward a psychoanalytic reading of Beckett's Molloy, 1 & 2. Lit & Psychology 19 1969.
Taylor, A. The minimal affirmation of Godot. Critical Rev 12 1969.
Zelivan, P. Experiment Becketta. Proměny 6 1969.

K.J.W.

LASCELLES ABERCROMBIE
1881–1938
See cols 995–7, below.

JOE RANDOLPH ACKERLEY
1896–1967

§1

Poems by four authors. Cambridge 1923. J. R. Ackerley, A. Y. Campbell, E. Davidson, F. Kendon.
The prisoners of war: a play in three acts. (Court 5 July 1925). 1925.
Escapers all: being the personal narratives of fifteen escapers from war-time prison camps 1914–18. Ed Ackerley, 1932.
Hindoo holiday: an Indian journal. 1932, New York 1932, London 1952 (with addns).
My dog Tulip. 1956.
We think the world of you. 1960, New York 1961. Fiction.
My father and myself. 1968. Autobiography.

§2

Valgemae, M. Auden's collaboration with Isherwood in The dog beneath the skin. HLQ 31 1968. Refers to Isherwood's borrowings from The prisoners of war.

RODNEY ACKLAND
b. 1908

§1

Improper people: a play. (Arts 9 Oct 1929). 1930.
Dance with no music: a play in four acts. (Arts 23 June 1930). 1933 Deane.
Strange orchestra: a play in three acts. (Embassy 30 June 1931). 1932, [1933] French.
Birthday: a play in three acts. (Cambridge 2 Feb 1934). [1935] French.
The old ladies: a play in three acts. (New 3 April 1935). 1935, 1950 French. Adapted from the novel by H. Walpole.
After October: a play in three acts. (Arts 21 Feb 1936). 1936, [1937] French.
The dark river. (Whitehall 19 Oct 1943). [1942] French. With preface by R. Sanvic.
Dostoievsky's Crime and punishment: dramatized by R. Ackland. (Wimbledon 18 June 1946, New 26 June 1946). [1948].
Bond Street, by W. Mannon: adapted from screen play by A. de Grunwald, based on stories by T. Rattigan, R. Ackland and de Grunwald. 1948.
The diary of a scoundrel: adapted from a comedy by A. N. Ostrovsky. (Birmingham Repertory 1949; Arts 19 Oct 1949). [1951] French.

Before the party: a play in two acts. (St Martin's 26 Oct 1949). In Plays of the year 1949. Pbd separately 1950 (French).
The celluloid mistress: or The custard pie of Dr Caligari. 1954. With E. Grant. Autobiography.
A dead secret. (Piccadilly 30 May 1957). [1958] French.
'Farewell, farewell, Eugene'. (Garrick 5 June 1959). 1960 French. By J. Vari, adapted by Ackland.
Ackland wrote several unpbd plays and adaptations, including screen plays. Plays include Marion-Ella (*Player's 30 June 1930*); Plot twenty one (*Embassy 22 Oct 1936*); Remembrance of things past (*Globe 30 Oct 1938*); The pink room: or The escapists (*Lyric, Hammersmith 18 June 1952*); *and* The other place (*Questors, Ealing 1964. Stage adaptations include* Ballerina (*Gaiety 10 Oct 1933*) *from Lady E. Smith's novel;* The white guard (*Ambassadors 11 March 1934*), *from a play by M. Bulgakov;* Yes, my darling daughter (*St James's 3 June 1937*) *from a comedy by M. Reed;* Sixth floor (*St James's 22 May 1939*), *from a play by A. Gehri; and* Blossom time (*Lyric 17 March 1942*), *with music by Schubert. Screen plays include* The old ladies (*from H. Walpole's novel, later adapted by Ackland for stage*), Yellow sands (*from E. Phillpott's novel*), George and Margaret (*from G. Savory's play*), Bank holiday, The silent battle, Thursday's child. *In collaboration with R. Newton, he wrote* Cupid and Mars (*Arts 1 Oct 1947*) *and* A multitude of sins *in 1951. His radio scenario for* Heathcliff, *an adaptation of Wuthering Heights by C. Cox, was broadcast by the BBC, 28 Jan 1967.*

§2

Marshall, N. The plays of Ackland. London Mag 5 1965.

MICHAEL ARLEN
(formerly DIKRAN KUYUMJIAN)
1895–1956
See cols 514–15, above.

'ANTHONY ARMSTRONG',
GEORGE ANTHONY ARMSTRONG
WILLIS
b. 1897

Selections

Selected warriors. 1932. Selections from Warriors at ease and Warriors still at ease.
Anthony Armstrong. 1934 (Methuen's Lib of Humour).
Warriors paraded: a military omnibus from Warriors at ease, Warriors still at ease, Easy warriors, Livestock in barracks, Captain Bayonet and others. 1938.

§1

Well caught: a criminal comedy in three acts. (Strand 8 Dec 1929). [1932].

In the dentist's chair: a one act thriller. (Players' 3 Feb 1931). [1933] French.

At 'The coach and horses': a play in one act. [1931] Deane.

Orders are orders: a military diversion in three acts. (Shaftesbury 9 Aug 1932). [1933] French. With 'Ian Hay' (J. H. Beith).

Ten minute alibi: a play in three acts. (Embassy 2 Jan 1933). 1933, New York [1934] French, London [1935] London Play Co. Pbd 1934 as novel, with H. Shaw.

Without witness. (Embassy 26 Dec 1933). 1934. With H. Simpson.

Eleventh hour: a drama in one act. [1933] London Play Co.

Sitting on a fence: a three-door diversion. 1935 London Play Co.

Mile-away murder: a detective play in three acts. (Duchess 2 April 1937). [1937].

Bad show; Gloves rubber. In Smile please, 1946 French. One-act plays.

Here we come gathering: a comedy. (High Wycombe Repertory 15 Jan 1950). [1952], [1953] French. With P. King.

Bellamy: a comedy-farce in three acts. (Trøndelag, Norway 19 March 1959). 1960 French. With A. Ridley.

The prince who hiccupped. In The theatre window: plays for schools, vol 2, ed W. T. Cunningham, 1953.

A demonstrator on trial. Belton, Great Yarmouth [1968]. One-act play.

Armstrong wrote several unpbd plays, including the following: Full house (*Faculty 16 Dec 1930*); The three pigeons (*1938*); Business with royalty (*Croydon Repertory 23 April 1934*) [*adapted from Diktatur der Frauen by F. Heller and A. Schalt*]; In the course of the evening (*1939*); Stephanie stays a week (*1939*); Happy ever after (*1943*); The running man (*1949*).

Essays, Sketches etc

Warriors at ease. 1926.
Percival and I. 1927.
How to do it. 1928.
Warriors still at ease. 1928.
Livestock in barracks. 1929.
Percival at play. 1929.
Me and Frances. 1930.
Taxi!: being a not too serious book about London taxicabs and drivers, with a few remarks on their foreign cousins. [1930].
Two legs and four. 1930.
Apple and Percival. 1931.
Yesterdailies: being some extracts from the press of the past. 1931.
Britisher on Broadway. 1932.
Easy warriors. 1932.
The prince who hiccupped, and other tales: being some fairy stories for grown-ups. 1932.
While you wait: humorous essays. 1933.
Thoughts on things: humorous essays. 1935.
Cottage into house. [1936].
The after-breakfast book. 1937.
Captain Bayonet and others. 1937.
The laughter omnibus: taken from Punch by A. Armstrong. 1937.
Science in the army: a brief account of the scientific training and technical work of the soldier today, as illustrated by a special War Office exhibition held at the Science Museum Nov 1938–Feb 1939. 1938.
Laughter parade. 1940. Anthology, ed Armstrong.
Nothing to do with the war. 1940.
We like the country. 1940.
Village at war. 1941.
Warriors at war. 1941.
Plonk's party of ATC, etc. 1942. Illustr 'Raff' (W. Hooper).
Prune's progress: the genealogical tree of Pilot-Officer Percy Prune, pictured by 'Raff'. [1942].

Nice types. 1943. With 'Raff'.
Good egg! flights of fancy. 1944. Illustr F. Robinson.
More nice types. 1944. With 'Raff'.
Prangmere mess and other tales. 1945.
Whiskers will not be worn. 1945. With 'Raff'.
Goodbye, nice types! 1946. With 'Raff'.
We keep going. 1946.
England our England: a vague and unauthenticated guide to some English towns. 1948.
My friend Serafin. 1949.
Sappers at war. Aldershot 1949. Illustr 'Raff'.
The year at Margarets. 1953.
Saying your prayers: an approach to Christian prayer. 1957.

Armstrong also pbd several novels, including thrillers. He was a regular contributor to Punch *1925–32 under the initials AA.*

'OSCAR ASCHE',
JOHN STANGER HEISS
1871–1936

§1

Chu Chin Chow: a musical tale of the East. (His Majesty's 31 Aug 1916). 1931 French. Based on Ali Baba and the forty thieves. *See* Chu-Chin-Chow: the story of the play. By H. Simpson [1916].

Oscar Asche: his life. [1929].

The joss sticks of Chung. [1930]. Fiction.

The saga of Hans Hansen. [1930]. Fiction.

Asche wrote the scenario for the musical play, Cairo (*His Majesty's 15 Oct 1921*), *and collaborated on scenarios of* Count Hannibal *and* Eastward ho!

§2

Pearson, H. In his The last actor-managers, 1950.

WYSTAN HUGH AUDEN
b. 1907

See cols 207–20, above.

ENID BAGNOLD
b. 1889

Collections

Two plays: Lottie Dundass and Poor Judas. 1951, New York 1951 (as Theatre: two plays).

The girl's journey, containing The happy foreigner and The squire. Foreword by A. Calder-Marshall 1954.

Four plays. 1970. The chalk garden; The last joke; The Chinese prime minister; Call me Jacky.

§1

A diary without dates. 1918, New York 1935. Experience as a VAD.

The sailing ships and other poems. 1918.

The happy foreigner. 1920, New York 1920. Novel.

Serena Blandish: or the difficulty of getting married. By a lady of quality. 1924, New York 1925. Novel. Anon. Adapted as a play with title Serena Blandish by S. N. Behrman (Morosco, New York 23 Jan 1929, Gate 13 Sept 1938), New York 1925 (in his Three plays).

Alice and Thomas and Jane. 1930, New York 1931. Adapted as children's play with same title by V. Beringer (Westminster 20 Dec 1933), [1934].

Alexander of Asia. 1935. Tr of Alexandre asiatique by M. L. Bibescu.

'National Velvet'. 1935, New York 1935. Novel. As play (Embassy 20 April 1946), [1946] (in Embassy successes, 2), New York 1961 Dramatists' Play Service. Filmed MGM 1944.

The door of life. New York 1938. Novel. Pts pbd serially under title, Birth.

The squire. 1938. Novel.

Lottie Dundass: a play in three acts. (Wimbledon 5 Oct 1942, Vaudeville 21 July 1943). 1941, [1944] French (rev, in two acts).

Poor Judas. (Bradford Civic Theatre Nov 1946, Arts 18 July 1951). In Two plays, 1951, Collections above.

The loved and envied. 1951, New York 1951. Novel.

The chalk garden. (Ethel Barrymore Theatre, New York 26 Oct 1955, Haymarket 11 April 1956). 1956, New York [1956] French, London [1959] (rev). Filmed 1964.

The last joke. (Phoenix 28 Sept 1960). In Four plays, 1970, Collections above.

The Chinese prime minister: a comedy in three acts. (Royale, New York 2 Jan 1964; Arts, Cambridge 26 April 1965 [rev], Globe 20 May 1965). New York 1964 French.

Call me Jacky. (Playhouse, Oxford 27 Feb 1968). In Plays of the year, vol 34, 1968.

Enid Bagnold's autobiography. 1969.

The following play was not pbd: Gertie (*Plymouth, New York 30 Jan 1952, Q 10 Nov 1953* [as Little idiot]).

§2

'Katherine Mansfield'. In her Novels and novelists, 1930.

Ede, H. S. In his Savage messiah, New York 1931.

Behrman, S. N. Foreword to his Three plays, New York [1934].

Nathan, G. J. In his The theatre in the fifties, New York 1953.

Tynan, K. In his Curtains, 1961.

For further criticism of E. Bagnold's plays in jnls and newspapers see H. H. Palmer and A. J. Dyson, European drama criticism, Hamden Conn 1968.

ELIZABETH BAKER
1876–1962
§1

Chains: a play in four acts. (Court 18 April 1909; Duke of York's 17 May 1910). 1911.

Miss Tassey: a play in one act. (Court 20 March 1910). 1913.

Edith: a comedy in one act. (Prince's 9 Feb 1912). 1927. Produced by Women Writers' Suffrage League.

The price of Thomas Scott: a play in three acts. (Gaiety, Manchester 22 Sept 1913). 1913.

Partnership: a comedy in three acts. (Birmingham Repertory 2 June 1917). [1921] French.

Miss Robinson: a play in three acts. (Birmingham Repertory 9 Nov 1918). 1920.

Bert's girl: a comedy in four acts. (Court 30 March 1927). 1927.

Umbrellas: a fantastic comedy in one act. 1927.

One of the Spicers: a play in one act. (Shaftesbury 14 Feb 1932). 1933.

The following plays were unpbd: Cupid in Clapham (*Court 20 March 1910*); Over a garden wall (*Birmingham Repertory 20 Nov 1915*).

§2

Archer, W. In his Playmaking, 1912.

Cunliffe, J. W. In his Modern English playwrights, New York 1927.

K.J.W.

CLIFFORD BAX
1886–1963
Selections

Twelve short plays, serious and comic. 1932. Prelude and fugue; The summit; The cloak; The rose and the cross; Aucassin and Nicolette; The wandering scholar; The unknown hand; The volcanic island; Square pegs; The apricot tree; Silly Willy; The poetasters of Ispahan.

§1

Twenty Chinese poems paraphrased. 1910, [1916] (rev and enlarged, as Twenty-five Chinese poems).

Poems dramatic and lyrical. 1911.

The poetasters of Ispahan: a comedy in verse. (Little 28 April 1912). In Antique pageantry, 1921 below. Pbd separately Boston 1929.

The masque of the planets. In Orpheus no 17, 1912. Play.

Friendship. 1913, New York 1913. Essay.

The summit. In Orpheus no 21, 1913; rptd 1921 in Antique pageantry, below.

The game of death. In Orpheus no 23, 1913. Play.

Aucassin and Nicolette: a verse play. In Orpheus no 26, 1914; rptd 1921 (in Antique pageantry, below), Boston [1930].

Japanese impromptus. Speen 1914. Verse. With D. Bax.

Square pegs: a rhymed fantasy for two girls. (Edwards Sq, Kensington, 9 Jan 1920). 1920, [1927] French.

A house of words. Oxford 1920. Poems.

Antique pageantry: a book of verse plays. 1921. The poetasters of Ispahan; The apricot tree; The summit; Aucassin and Nicolette.

Old King Cole. 1921, Boston 1922, [1935] French (subtitled: a play for children in three acts).

Shakespeare: a play in five episodes. 1921, [1933] French. With H. F. Rubinstein.

The traveller's tale. Oxford 1921. Poem.

The apricot tree: a play in one act. (Deansgate, Manchester 23 Oct 1922). In Orpheus no 25, 1914; rptd 1921 in Antique pageantry, above.

Prelude & fugue: a play in one act. (Studio plays 1). (Etlinger Theatre School 7 Dec 1922). [1924].

Polite satires. 1922. The unknown hand; The volcanic island; Square pegs.

Midsummer madness: a play for music. (Lyric, Hammersmith 3 July 1924). 1923.

Nocturne in Palermo. 1924. Play.

The rose and the cross: a play in one act. (Studio plays, 2). [1924].

The cloak: a play in one act. (Studio plays 3). [1924], [1954] French.

Up stream: a drama in three acts. (Duke of York's 20 Dec 1925). Oxford 1922, New York 1923.

Inland far: a book of thoughts and impressions. 1925.

Mr Pepys: a ballad-opera. (Everyman 11 Feb 1926; Royalty 9 March 1926). 1926, [1927] French.

Bianca Capello. 1927, New York 1928. Biography.

Many a green isle. 1927. Story.

Socrates: a play in six scenes. (Prince of Wales 23 March 1930). 1930.

The Venetian. (Little 28 Feb 1931). In Valiant ladies, 1931 below. Pbd separately [1934] French.

The immortal lady. (Royalty 9 Oct 1931). In Valiant ladies, 1931 below. Pbd separately 1932 French.

The chronicles of Cupid: being a masque of love throughout the ages. [1931] French. With G. Dearmer.

Valiant ladies: three new plays. 1931, New York 1931. The Venetian, The rose without a thorn, The immortal lady.

The rose without a thorn: a play in three acts. (Duchess 10 Feb 1932). In Valiant ladies, 1931 above. Pbd separately [1933] French.

Farewell, my muse. 1932, New York 1932. Poems.

Leonardo da Vinci. 1932, New York 1932. Biography.

Pretty witty Nell: an account of Nell Gwynn and her environment. 1932, New York 1933 (with subtitle: the story of Nell Gwynn and her times).

Silly Willy. In Twelve short plays, 1932, Selections above.

That immortal sea: a meditation upon the future of religion and sexual morality. 1933.

April in August: a play in three acts. (Comedy 13 May 1934). [1934] French.

The quaker's cello: a play in one act. [1934] French.

Tragic Nesta: a play in one act. [1934] French.

Ideas and people. 1936. Sketches and articles.

Battles long ago. In Eight one-act plays of 1936, ed W. Armstrong 1937.

The life of the white devil [Vittoria Orsini, Duchess of Bracciano]. 1940.

Evenings in Albany. 1942. Reminiscences.

Hemlock: a radio play. (BBC 30 May 1943). 1946. With L. M. Lion.

Time with a gift of tears: a modern romance. 1943. Novel.

Whither the theatre—? a letter to a young playwright. 1945.

Golden eagle: a drama. (Whitehall 29 Jan 1946). 1946.

The beauty of women. 1946.

The Buddha: a radio version of his life and ideas. (BBC 16 March 1947). 1947.

The play of St Lawrence: a pageant play for production in a church. [1947] French.

Circe: a play in three acts (Q 19 Oct 1948 as A day, a night and a morrow). 1949.

Rosemary for remembrance. 1948. Reminiscences.

Some I knew well. 1951, New York 1952. Biographical sketches.

Who's who in Heaven: a sketch. Meldreth 1954 (limited edn).

The following were not pbd: The marriage of the soul (*Little 3 July 1913*), The sneezing charm (*Court 9 June 1918*) *and* The house of Borgia (*Embassy 9 Sept 1935*), Mr Williams of Hamburg (*BBC Home Service 14 Feb 1943*), Out of his senses (*BBC 6 May 1943*), The shrouded candle (*BBC 11 July 1948*) *and* The life that I gave him, *by Pirandello, tr Bax* (*BBC Third Programme 18 Nov 1951*). *Bax also wrote a life of W. G. Grace and a travel guide to Essex. Among the numerous works which he edited were*: Orpheus: a quarterly magazine of mystical art [*the organ of the Art-movement of the* Theosophical Soc] *1909–14*; The Orpheus Series [*of works by AE, D. O'Byrne, Bax et al*] *1909–17*; *Ruskin*, Crown of wild olive *and* The cestus of Aglaia, *1908*; *Delville*, The new mission of art, *1910*; *Boehme*, The signature of all things, *1912*; *Florence Farr, Bernard Shaw, W. B. Yeats*, Letters, *1941, Dublin 1942*; The silver casket: being love letters and love poems attributed to Mary Stuart, *1946*; an anthology of the poetry of the Brownings, *1947*; *and various verse anthologies. He tr R. Steiner*, Initiation and its results, *1909, and Tasso*, The age of gold, *1944*; *and adapted John Gay*, Polly, *four comedies by Goldoni, A. N. Tolstoy*, Rasputin, *and the brothers Capek*, Insect play. A.P.H.

ENOCH ARNOLD BENNETT
1867–1931

See cols 429–36, above.

REGINALD CHEYNE BERKELEY
1890–1935

The oilskin packet: a tale of the southern seas. 1917, New York 1918. With J. Dixon.

French leave: a light comedy in three acts. (Devonshire Park, Eastbourne 7 June 1920, Globe 15 July 1920). [1921] French.

Eight o'clock. (Little 15 Dec 1920). In The world's end, 1926 below.

Decorations and absurdities. [1923]. With J. G. B. Lynch. Caricatures and satires.

Unparliamentary papers and other diversions. 1924. Introd by J. C. Squire, illustr J. G. B. Lynch. Includes parodies of contemporary dramatic styles.

Mango Island. (Prince's 14 June 1925). In The world's end, 1926 below.

The world's end. (Aldwych 8 Nov 1925). In The world's end, 1926 below.

The white château. (BBC 11 Nov 1925, Everyman 29 March 1927, St Martin's 28 April 1927). 1925.

The quest of Elizabeth. (Playhouse 1 March 1926). In The world's end, 1926 below.

The world's end, The quest of Elizabeth and other plays [Eight o'clock, Mango Island]. 1926.

The history of the Rifle Brigade in the war of 1914–18. Vol 1, 1927. Vol 2 by W. W. Seymour.

Dawn: a biographical novel of Edith Cavell. [1928], New York 1928, London [1940] (as Nurse Edith Cavell).

The lady with a lamp. (Arts 5 Jan 1929, Garrick 24 Jan 1929). 1929, [1930] French (includes alternative final scene).

Machines: a symphony of modern life. (Arts 6 Nov 1930). 1927. Includes a correspondence with the BBC about its rejection for broadcasting and a preface by Berkeley on writing for radio, with an account of the circumstances leading to the broadcast performance of The white château, above.

Cassandra. 1931. Novel.

England's opportunity: a reply to an argument and an outline of policy. 1931.

The queen of Moturea. [1931] Deane.

The dweller in the darkness: a play of the unknown in one act. (BBC 3 Aug 1932). [1931] Deane.

Berkeley wrote the unpbd plays, Mr Abdulla (*Playhouse 10 Feb 1926*) *and* OHMS (*Arts 4 March 1931, New 11 March 1931*). *He wrote a number of unpbd screen plays, including* French leave (*1930*), Dreyfus (*1931*), Broken lullaby (*1932*), Cavalcade (*1933*), The world moves on, Carolina, Marie Galante (*1934*).

RUDOLF BESIER
1878–1942

§I

The virgin goddess: a tragedy. (Adelphi 23 Oct 1906). 1907.

Don: a comedy in three acts. (Haymarket 12 Oct 1909). [1910].

Lady Patricia: a comedy in three acts. (Haymarket 22 March 1911). [1911], New York 1911.

Secrets: a play in a prologue, three acts and an epilogue. (Comedy 7 Sept 1922). [1929] French. With M. Edginton. A version with same title made by R. Batchelder, [1924].

The Barretts of Wimpole Street: a comedy in five acts. (Malvern Festival 20 Aug 1930, Queen's 23 Sept 1930). 1930, Boston 1930. Tr French, 1934 (as Miss Ba).

Besier wrote the unpbd plays, Olive Latimer's husband (*Vaudeville 19 Jan 1909*) *and* The crisis (*Pier Pavilion, Hastings 22 Aug 1910, New 31 Aug 1910*). *He collaborated with H. G. Wells on an adaptation of* Kipps (*Vaudeville 6 March 1912*), *with Hugh Walpole on* Robin's father, *with May Edginton on* The ninth earl *and* The prude's fall. *An account of the American production of* The Barretts of Wimpole Street *is given by Katharine Cornell*, New York Times 16 June 1942.

§2

Nathan, G. J. In The Theatre book of the year 1944–5, New York 1945.
Brown, J. M. Overseas edition of the Brownings. In his Seeing things, New York [1946].
For further criticism of Besier's plays in jnls and newspapers, see H. H. Palmer and A. J. Dyson, European drama criticism, Hamden Conn 1968.

BRIDGET BOLAND
b. 1913

The wild geese. 1938. Novel.
Portrait of a lady in love. 1942. Novel.
Cockpit: a play in two acts. (Playhouse 19 Feb 1948). In Plays of the year vol 1, 1949. Film version, The lost people, 1949.
The return: a play in three acts. (Duchess 9 Nov 1953). [1954] French. An earlier version, Journey to earth, was broadcast (BBC 14 Jan 1953).
The prisoner: a play in three acts. (Globe 14 April 1954). In Plays of the year, vol 10 [1954]. Pbd separately, New York [1955] Dramatists Play Service. Film version 1955.
Temple folly: a comedy in three acts. (Marlow Players, Canterbury in Repertory Festival 14 May to 8 June 1957). 1958 Evans.
Gordon. (Playhouse, Derby 18 Sept 1961). In Plays of the year, vol 25 1963.
The zodiac in the establishment. (Nottingham Playhouse 23 April 1963). 1963 Evans.
Bridget Boland wrote numerous unpbd screen plays from 1937 onwards, the unpbd radio plays, Damascus blade (BBC 7 Jan 1952) and Sheba (BBC 6 Dec 1954), and adaptations, including The Arabian nights (Playhouse, Nottingham 20 Dec 1948).

GORDON BOTTOMLEY
1874–1948

See cols 238–40, above.

'JOHN BRANDANE',
JOHN MACINTYRE
1869–1947

§1

Glenforsa: a play in one act. (Scottish National Players at Royal Institute, Glasgow 13 Jan 1921). 1921, Boston 1921. With A. W. Yuill.
The change-house. (Scottish National Players at Athenaeum Theatre, Glasgow 1 Nov 1921). 1921, Boston 1921.
The Spanish galleon: a play in one act. (Scottish National Players in Argyllshire Gathering Hall, Oban 25 Sept 1922). 1932. With A. W. Yuill.
The glen is mine: a comedy in two acts. (Scottish National Theatre Soc at Athenaeum Theatre, Glasgow 25 Jan 1923). In The glen is mine, 1925, below.
The treasure ship: a comedy in four acts. (Scottish National Theatre Soc at Athenaeum Theatre, Glasgow 11 March 1924). In The treasure ship, 1928, below.
The lifting: a play in three acts. (Scottish National Theatre Soc at Athenaeum Theatre, Glasgow 3 Feb 1925). In The glen is mine, 1925, below.
The inn of adventure. (Scottish National Theatre Soc at Athenaeum Theatre, Glasgow 13 Oct 1925). In The inn of adventure, 1933, below.
The glen is mine, and The lifting: two plays of the Hebrides. 1925.

Rory aforesaid: a comedy in one act. (Scottish National Theatre Soc at Lyric, Glasgow 21 Oct 1926). In The treasure ship, 1928, below.
Heather gentry. (Scottish National Theatre Soc at Lyric, Glasgow 24 Dec 1927). In The inn of adventure, 1933, below.
The treasure ship; Rory aforesaid; The happy war: three plays. 1928.
The inn of adventure; Heather gentry: two comedies. 1933.
Man of Uz. 1938. One-act play.
Brandane also pbd the novels, My lady of Aros (*1910*), The Captain More (*1923*), Straw-feet (*1932*).

§2

Bannister, W. In her Bridie and his theatre, [1955].

'JAMES BRIDIE',
OSBORNE HENRY MAVOR
1888–1951

Bibliographies

In The year's work in the theatre, 1950–1, 1951.
Gerber, U. In her James Bridies Dramen, Berne [1961], §2 below.

Selections

A sleeping clergyman and other plays. 1934. A sleeping clergyman; Tobias and the angel; Jonah and the whale; The anatomist; The amazed evangelist.
Moral plays. 1936. Marriage is no joke [with alternative version of Act II, scene 1]; Mary Read; The black eye. With a preface, The anatomy of failure.

§1

Some talk of Alexander: a revue with interludes in the antique mode. 1926. Wartime reminiscences.
The sunlight sonata: or, To meet the seven deadly sins. (Lyric, Glasgow 20 March 1928). In The switchback [etc], 1930, below.
The switchback (Birmingham Repertory 9 March 1929; rev version Malvern Festival 8 Aug 1931). In The switchback [etc], 1930, below.
What it is to be young. (Birmingham Repertory 2 Nov 1929, Q 26 April 1937). In Colonel Wotherspoon and other plays, 1934, below.
The anatomist: a lamentable comedy of Knox, Burke and Hare and the West Port murders. (Lyceum, Edinburgh 6 July 1930, Westminster 7 Oct 1931). In The anatomist and other plays, 1931, below.
The girl who did not want to go to Kuala Lumpur. (Lyric, Glasgow Nov 1930). In Colonel Wotherspoon and other plays, 1934, below.
Tobias and the angel: a comedy. (Festival Theatre, Cambridge 20 Nov 1930; Westminster 9 March 1932). In The anatomist and other plays, 1931, below.
The switchback; The pardoner's tale; The sunlight sonata: a comedy; a morality; a farce-morality. 1930.
The dancing bear: a comedy in three acts. (Lyric, Glasgow 24 Feb 1931). In Colonel Wotherspoon and other plays, 1934, below.
The anatomist and other plays: The anatomist; Tobias and the angel; The amazed evangelist. 1931.
The perilous adventure of Sir Bingo Walker of Alpaca Square. 1931. Children's story.
The amazed evangelist: a comedy in one act. (Westminster 12 Dec 1932). In The anatomist and other plays, 1931, above. Pbd separately 1932 (as The amazed evangelist: a nightmare).
Jonah and the whale: a morality in three acts and a prologue. (Westminster 12 Dec 1932; preceded by The

amazed evangelist). 1932. A 2nd version broadcast (BBC 22 Feb 1942) as The sign of the prophet Jonah: a play for broadcasting, and pbd, with another version, Jonah 3, in Plays for plain people, 1944, below.

A sleeping clergyman: a play in two acts. (Malvern Festival 29 July 1933, Piccadilly 19 Sept 1933). 1933, New York 1934.

Marriage is no joke: a melodrama. (Globe 6 Feb 1934). 1934.

Colonel Wotherspoon: or The fourth way of greatness: a comedy in three acts. (Lyric, Glasgow 23 March 1934; Arts 24 June 1934). In Colonel Wotherspoon and other plays, 1934, below.

Mary Read: a play in three acts. (His Majesty's 21 Nov 1934). 1935. With C. Gurney.

Colonel Wotherspoon and other plays, with a preface. 1934. Colonel Wotherspoon; What it is to be young; The dancing bear; The girl who did not want to go to Kuala Lumpur.

Mr Bridie's alphabet for little Glasgow highbrows. 1934. Satirical essays rptd from Glasgow Herald.

The black eye: a comedy. (Shaftesbury 11 Oct 1935). 1935. With author's note to J. Agate.

Mrs Waterbury's millennium: a play in one act. [1935] French.

The tragic muse: a farce in one act. In Scottish one-act plays, ed J. M. Reid, Edinburgh 1935.

Storm in a teacup: an Anglo-Scottish version of Sturm im Wasserglas by Bruno Frank. (Edinburgh 20 Jan 1936; Royalty 5 Feb 1936). 1936.

Susannah and the elders. (Duke of York's 31 Oct 1937). In Susannah and the elders and other plays, 1940, below.

Roger—not so jolly: a drama in one act. By Ronald Mavor and Bridie. [1937] (French's plays for boys).

The Scottish character as it was viewed by Scottish authors from Galt to Barrie: being the John Galt lecture for 1937. Greenock 1937; rptd in Tedious and brief, 1944, below.

The king of nowhere: a play in three acts. (Old Vic 15 March 1938). In The king of nowhere and other plays, 1938, below.

Babes in the wood: a quiet farce. (Embassy 14 June 1938). In The king of nowhere and other plays, 1938, below.

The last trump. (Malvern Festival 5 Aug 1938, Duke of York's 13 Sept 1938). In The king of nowhere and other plays, 1938, below.

The kitchen comedy: a play for broadcasting. (BBC Glasgow Regional 18 Nov 1938). In Susannah and the elders and other plays, 1940, below.

The king of nowhere and other plays. 1938. The king of nowhere; Babes in the wood; The last trump.

The letter-box rattles: a sentimental comedy. [1938]. Specially written for the News Chronicle Amateur Dramatic Contest 1938–9.

The golden legend of Shults: a play in three acts. (Perth 24 July 1939). In Susannah and the elders and other plays, 1940, below.

What say they?: a play in two acts. (Malvern Festival 7 Aug 1939). 1939.

One way of living. 1939. Autobiography.

The theatre: a paper read to The Thirteen. [Glasgow 1939]; rptd in Tedious and brief, 1944, below.

Susannah and the elders and other plays, with a preface. 1940. Susannah and the elders; What say they?; The golden legend of Shults; The kitchen comedy.

The niece of the hermit Abraham. (Lyric, Glasgow Aug 1942). Re-titled The dragon and the dove: or How the hermit Abraham fought the devil for his niece: a play in two acts. (Arts 9 March 1943, in double bill with A change for the worse.) In Plays for plain people, 1944, below.

Jonah 3: a new version of Jonah and the whale. (Unnamed Society, Manchester Nov 1942). In Plays for plain people, 1944, below.

Holy Isle: a play in three acts. (Arts 11 Dec 1942). In Plays for plain people, 1944, below.

A change for the worse. (Arts 9 March 1943). In Tedious and brief, 1944, below.

Mr Bolfry: a play in four scenes. (Westminster 3 Aug 1943). In Plays for plain people, 1944, below.

It depends what you mean: an improvisation for the Glockenspiel: a play in three acts. (Westminster 12 Oct 1944). 1948.

The Forrigan reel. (Glasgow Citizens' at Athenaeum, Glasgow 25 Dec 1944). The rev version, The Forrigan reel: a ballad opera (Sadler's Wells 24 Oct 1945) pbd 1949 in John Knox and other plays, 1949, below.

Plays for plain people: Lancelot, Holy Isle, Mr Bolfry, Jonah 3, The sign of the prophet Jonah, The dragon and the dove. 1944.

Tedious and brief. 1944. Essays, lectures, dramatic fragments, including radio dialogue on J. M. Barrie.

Lancelot: a play in two acts. (Glasgow Citizens' 30 Oct 1945). In Plays for plain people, 1944, above.

The British drama. Glasgow 1945.

Dr Angelus: a play in three acts. (Edinburgh, 23 June 1947, Phoenix 30 July 1947). In John Knox and other plays, 1949, below.

John Knox: a play in three acts. (Glasgow Citizens' 18 Aug 1947). In John Knox and other plays, 1949, below.

Gog and Magog. (Arts 1 Dec 1948). Unpbd. Ms in Br Drama League Library.

Daphne Laureola: a play in four acts. (Wyndham's 23 March 1949). 1949.

A small stir: letters on the English. 1949. With M. McLaren.

The Christmas card. [1949]. Story.

John Knox and other plays. 1949. John Knox; Dr Angelus; It depends what you mean; The Forrigan reel.

The queen's comedy: a Homeric fragment. (Lyceum, Edinburgh Festival 21 Aug 1950). 1950.

Mr Gillie: a play. (Glasgow Citizens' 13 Feb 1950; Garrick 9 March 1950). 1950.

The Baikie Charivari: or The seven prophets—a miracle play. (Glasgow Citizens' 6 Oct 1952). 1953. Preface by W. Elliott.

Meeting at night. (Glasgow Citizens' 17 May 1954). 1956 (rev A. Batty). Introd by J. B. Priestley.

For details of Bridie's other unpbd plays, including adaptations of Ibsen, Molière and Chekhov, pantomime-reviews and screenplays, see Brown and Bannister, §2, below.

Bridie used the pseudonym 'Mary Henderson' (e.g. for The sunlight sonata) *and 'Archibald P. Kellock' (e.g. for* The pyrate's den [unpbd]). *From 1945 the Glasgow Citizens' Theatre performed at the Royal Princess's, Glasgow. The Lyric, Glasgow was commonly used by the Scottish National Players.*

§2

Brown, I. J. C. In Specimens of English dramatic criticism, ed A. C. Ward 1945.
— In The year's work in the theatre 1950–1, 1951 (Br Council).

Linklater, E. In his Art of adventure, 1947.

Birch, L. Bridie—wybitny dramaturg. Glos Anglii no 30 1948.

Crawford, I. Auld Nick and Mr Bridie. Theatre Arts Monthly 34 1950.

Renwick, W. L. Bridie the playwright. College Courant 3 1951.

Robson, F. A tribute to Bridie. Drama Summer 1951.

Bax, C. Bridie. Drama Autumn 1952.

Bannister, W. James Bridie and his theatre: a study of Bridie's personality, his stage plays and his work for the foundation of a Scottish National Theatre. [1955].

Priestley, J. B. Bridie and the theatre. Listener 27 Sept 1956.

Marcel, G. Le théâtre de Bridie. Etudes Anglaises 10 1957.

Walter, M. The grateful dead: an old tale newly told. Southern Folklore Quart 23 1959.
— The grateful dead as good theater. Midwest Folklore 9 1959.
Gerber, U. James Bridies Dramen: Versuch einer Analyse. Berne [1961].
Weales, G. In his Religion in modern English drama, Philadelphia 1961.
Luyben, H. L. The dramatic method of Bridie. Educational Theatre Jnl 15 1963.
— Bridie's last play. Modern Drama 5 1963.
— Bridie and the prodigal son story. Modern Drama 7 1964.
— Bridie: clown and philosopher. Philadelphia 1965.
Greene, A. Bridie's concept of the master experimenter. Stud in Scottish Lit 2 1964. Includes discussion of newspaper and periodical criticism of Bridie.
Leary, D. J. Bridie. Independent Shavian 7 1968.
Michie, J. A question of success. English 17 1968.
— Educating the prophets. Modern Drama 11 1969.
K. J. W.

HAROLD BRIGHOUSE
1882–1958

§I

Brighouse wrote a number of plays with J. Walton under the pseudonym 'Olive Conway'.

The doorway: a play in one act. (Gaiety, Manchester 10 April 1909). [1913].
Dealing in futures: a play in three acts. (Royalty, Glasgow 7 Oct 1909). [1913] French. Televised (1960) under title Vitriol, q.v.
The price of coal. (Scottish Repertory, Glasgow 15 Nov 1909; Playhouse 28 Nov 1911). 1911.
Graft: a comedy in four acts. (Court 5 Feb 1911, as The polygon). [1913] French. Televised (1960) under the title Fiddlers four, q.v.
Lonesome-like: a play in one act. (Royalty, Glasgow 6 Feb 1911). 1914, [1955] French. Tr Welsh [1932].
Spring in Bloomsbury: a play in one act. (Gaiety, Manchester 3 April 1911). [1913], 1924.
The oak settle: a one-act comedy. (Dalston 7 April 1911). [1911] French.
The scaring off of Teddy Dawson: a comedy in one act. (Dalston 7 April 1911). [1911] French.
The odd man out: a comedy in three acts. (Royalty, Glasgow 16 April 1912). [1912] French.
Little red shoes: a play in one act. (Prince of Wales 20 May 1912). Boston 1925.
Garside's career: a comedy in four acts. (Gaiety, Manchester 2 Feb 1913). 1914, Boston 1915.
The game: a football comedy in a prologue and three acts. (Playhouse, Liverpool 19 Nov 1913; King's, Hammersmith 29 Aug 1921). In Three Lancashire plays, 1920 below.
The northerners. (Gaiety, Manchester 27 Aug 1914). In Three Lancashire plays, 1920 below.
Followers: a 'Cranford' sketch. (Prince's, Manchester 12 April 1915; Criterion 6 June 1915). 1922.
Converts: a comedy in one act. (Gaiety, Manchester 23 Aug 1915; Duke of York's 16 Sept 1915). 1920, Boston 1920.
Hobson's choice: a three act comedy. (Princess, New York 2 Nov 1915; Apollo 22 June 1916). 1916 (with introd by B. I. Payne), New York 1916; ed E. R. Wood 1964. Tr Welsh [1932]. Filmed 1920 and 1954.
Zack: character comedy in three acts. (Syracuse, New York 30 Oct 1916; Comedy 23 April 1922). In Three Lancashire plays, 1920 below.
Maid of France: a play in one act. (Metropolitan 16 July 1917). 1917, Boston 1917.

Fossie for short. 1917. Novel. (As comedy in one act, 1927 (French)).
Hobson's: the novel of Hobson's choice. 1917. With C. Forrest.
The silver lining. 1918. Novel.
'The bantam VC': a farce in three acts. (St Martin's 16 July 1920). Boston 1920.
The Marbeck Inn. [1920], Boston 1920. Novel.
The starlight widow: a comedy in three acts. New York 1920, 1929 French. By 'Olive Conway'.
Three Lancashire plays: The game; The northerners; Zack. [1920] French.
Plays for the meadow and plays for the lawn. [1921] French. Maypole morning; The Paris doctor; The prince who was a piper (reissued separately 1953 [French]); The man about the place.
Once a hero: a comedy in one act. (Ambassadors, Southend 26 June 1922). 1922.
Hepplestall's. 1922, New York 1922. Novel.
The apple-tree: or, why misery never dies: a play in one act. 1923, Boston 1923.
Captain Shapely. 1923, New York 1924. Novel based on Vanbrugh's Relapse.
The wrong shadow: a romantic comedy. 1923, New York 1923. Novel.
A marrying man. (Playhouse, Liverpool 5 May 1924). [1924] French.
Mary's John: a comedy in three acts. (Playhouse, Liverpool 30 Sept 1924). [1925] French.
Becky Sharp: a play in one act, by 'Olive Conway'. Boston [1924].
The happy hangman: a grotesque in one act. (Court 15 June 1925). 1922, Boston 1922.
Costume plays, by 'Olive Conway'. [1926] French. Becky Sharp; Mimi; Prudence corner; The king's waistcoat.
What's bred in the bone: a comedy in three acts. (Playhouse, Liverpool 4 April 1927). [1927] French.
Hindle wakes. 1927. Novel, from S. Houghton's play.
The little liberty: a comedy in one act. [1927] French.
The night of 'Mr H': a Charles Lamb pastiche. 1927 French.
Open air plays. [1927] French. The laughing wind; The oracles of Apollo; The rational princess; The ghosts of Windsor Park; How the weather is made.
When did they meet again? a play in one act. [1927] French.
The witch's daughter. In One-act plays for stage and study, ser 4, New York 1928.
Safe among the pigs: a comedy in three acts. (Birmingham Repertory 27 April 1929). [1930] French.
Behind the throne: a comedy in three acts. Evanston Ill 1929.
Coincidence: a comedy in three acts. New York [1929] French.
The sort-of-a-prince: a comedy in three acts. New York [1929] French.
The stoker: a play in one act. [1929] French.
Four fantasies for the open air. [1931] French. The exiled princess; The ghost in the garden; The romany road; Cupid and Psyche. Also as Six fantasies 1931 French (with the addition of The ghosts of Windsor Park and The oracles of Apollo).
The wish shop: a fantasy in one act. In Four new plays for women and girls, ed J. Hampden 1932, 1936 French.
A bit of war: a play in one act. [1933] French.
Exhibit C. In Best one-act plays of 1933, ed J. W. Marriott 1934.
Smoke-screens: a comedy in one act. [1933] French.
Under the pylon. In Oct-act plays for stage and study no 9, 1933.
The dye-hard. In One-act plays of today ser 6, ed J. W. Marriott 1934.
The great dark: a play in one act by D. Totheroh, revised by Brighouse. [1934] French.

Back to Adam: a glimpse of three periods. [1935] French, Boston 1937.

The boy: what will he become? In Best onn-act plays of 1934, ed J. W. Marriott 1935.

The friendly king: a fantasy. [1935].

Below ground. In Eight new one-act plays of 1936, ed W. Armstrong 1937.

New leisure. In Best one-act plays of 1936, ed J. W. Marriott 1937.

Passport to romance: a play. [1937] French, Boston 1938.

The funk-hole: a farce of the crisis. [1938] French.

Air-raid refugees: a farce of the crisis. New York [1939] French.

British passport: a play in one act. [1939] French.

The man who ignored the war: a war-time comedy. [1940] French.

Golden ray: an idealistic melodrama in one act. New York [1941] French.

London front: a little picture of war-conditions in one act. New York [1941] French.

Hallowed ground. In Best one-act plays of 1941, ed J. W. Marriott 1942.

Sporting rights: a one-act comedy. [1943] French.

Modern plays in one act, by 'Olive Conway'. 1937 French. One of those letters; Dux; When the bells rang; The bureaucrats; The desperationist; Wireless can't lie; Women do things like that.

Albert Gates: a comedy in one act. [1945] French.

The inner man: a comedy in one act. [1945] French.

One of those letters: a play in one act by 'Olive Conway'. [1945] French.

Let's live in England. In Best one-act plays of 1944–5, ed J. W. Marriott 1946.

Alison's island. In Best one-act plays of 1946–7, ed J. W. Marriott 1948.

Above rubies. In Best one-act plays of 1952–3, ed H. Miller 1954.

What I have had: chapters in autobiography. 1953.

Fiddlers four. (Granada Television, Manchester 26 Feb 1960). Adaptation for television by G. Savory of Graft (1912). In Granada's Manchester plays, Manchester 1962.

Vitriol. (Granada Television, Manchester 30 Aug 1960). Adaptation for television by G. Savory of Dealing in futures (1909). Ibid.

The following plays were not pbd: The road to Raebury (*Prince's, Manchester 12 April 1915*), The clock goes round (*Globe 4 Oct 1916*), Other times (*Little 6 April 1920*), Once a year (*Playhouse, Liverpool 5 June 1923*). *Brighouse collaborated with S. Houghton in* The Hillarys (*Kelly's, Liverpool 30 April 1915*) *and edited Houghton's* Works, *3 vols 1914*.

§2

Bagshaw, W. The work of Brighouse. Manchester Literary Club Papers 58 1932.

A.P.H.

WYNYARD BARRY BROWNE
1911–64

Dark summer: a play in three acts. (Lyric, Hammersmith 14 Oct 1947; St Martin's 15 Dec 1947). [1950] Evans.

The holly and the ivy: a play in three acts. (Lyric, Hammersmith 28 March 1950; Duchess 10 May 1950). [1950] Evans, 1967 Evans (rev).

A question of fact: a play in three acts. (Piccadilly 10 Dec 1953). 1955 Evans.

The ring of truth: a comedy. (Savoy 16 July 1959). 1960 Evans.

Browne wrote 3 novels, Queenie Molson, *1934*, Sheldon's way, *1935*, and The fire and the fiddle, *1937*.

K.J.W.

GEORGE LESLIE CALDERON
1868–1915

Collections

Eight one-act plays. Ed K. Calderon 1922.

Three plays and a pantomime. Ed K. Calderon 1922.

§1

The adventures of Downy V. Green, Rhodes scholar at Oxford. 1902.

Dwala: a romance. 1904.

The fountain: a comedy in three acts. (Aldwych 28 March 1909; Royalty, Glasgow Oct 1909, rev). 1911.

The little stone house: a play in one act. (Stage Society, at the Aldwych 29 Jan 1911). In Eight one-act plays, 1922, above.

Revolt: a play in four acts. (Gaiety, Manchester 11 Nov 1912). In Three plays and a pantomime, 1922 above.

Thompson: a comedy in three acts. (Royalty 22 April 1913). [1913], 1924 French. Completed from St John Hankin's ms.

Geminae: a farce. (Devonshire Park, Eastbourne 3 Nov 1913; Little 7 Nov 1913). In Eight one-act plays, 1922, above.

Tahiti. Ed K. Calderon 1921.

Peace: a farce. In Eight one-act plays, 1922, above.

Derelicts. In Eight one-act plays, 1922, above.

Parkin Bros: a comedy. In Eight one-act plays, 1922 above.

The two talismans: a comedy. In Eight one-act plays, 1922, above.

The lamp. In Eight one-act plays, 1922, above.

Longing: a subjective drama in two scenes. In Eight one-act plays, 1922, above.

Cromwell: Mall o' monks: a historical play in five acts. In Three plays and a pantomime, 1922, above.

Cinderella: an Ibsen pantomime in three acts. In Three plays and a pantomime, 1922, above.

Calderon translated Tolstoy, Reminiscences, *and Chekhov*, Seagull *and* Cherry orchard. *He left in ms comedies, farces, operettas and a five-act blank verse historical drama (see Lubbock, below). The brave little tailor, which he wrote with W. Caine, was never performed or pbd, but adapted as a story by W. Caine (1923). The Maharani of Arakán (Coliseum 19 June 1916), an adaptation of a story of Tagore's, was never pbd.*

§2

Lubbock, P. Calderon: a sketch from memory. 1921.

A.P.H.

'DENIS CANNAN',
DENNIS PULLEIN-THOMPSON
b. 1919

Captain Carvallo. (St James's 9 Aug 1950). [1951] French.

Colombe. (New 13 Dec 1951). 1952. Adapted from the play by Anouilh.

Misery me: a comedy of woe. (Duchess 16 March 1955). [1956] French.

You and your wife. (Bristol Old Vic 28 June 1955). [1956] French.

The power and the glory: a drama in three acts. (Phoenix 5 April 1956). New York [1959] French. Adapted from the novel by Graham Greene. With P. Bost.

Who's your father? a comedy in three acts. (Cambridge 16 Dec 1958). [1959] French.

Cannan's first play, Max (*People's Palace, Playgoers Club 10 April 1949*) *was unpbd. He wrote several unpbd screen plays and radio scripts, including* Headlong Hall, *adapted from the novel by T. L. Peacock* (*BBC 30 July 1950*), The moth and the star, *adapted from* Liber amoris *by W. Hazlitt* (*BBC 7 Nov 1950*) *and* The greeting, *adapted from the work by O. Sitwell* (*BBC 16 Nov 1964*).

GILBERT CANNAN
1884-1955
See cols 547-8, above.

PAUL VINCENT CARROLL
1900-68
Selections

Three plays: The white steed; Things that are Caesar's; The strings, my lord, are false. 1944.
Two plays: The wise have not spoken; Shadow and substance. 1948.
Irish stories and plays. New York 1958. Includes Beauty is fled; The conspirators [Coggerers]; Interlude; The devil came from Dublin.

§1

Things that are Caesar's: a tragedy in three acts. (Abbey, Dublin 15 Aug 1932; Arts 11 Jan 1933). [1934]. First called The bed of Procrustes.
Shadow & substance: a play in four acts. (Abbey, Dublin 25 Jan 1937; Duke of York's 25 May 1943). New York 1937, London 1938, [1944] French, New York 1948 (rev).
Coggerers. (Abbey, Dublin 22 Nov 1937). In The white steed and Coggerers, 1939, below. Pbd separately [1947] French (as The conspirators: a play in one act).
The white steed: a play in three acts. (Cort, New York 10 Jan 1939; Embassy 3 March 1947). In The white steed and Coggerers, 1939, below. Pbd separately [1943] French.
Plays for my children. New York 1939. The king who could not laugh: a play for children of all ages; 'His excellency the governor': adapted from an incident in Don Quixote; St Francis and the wolf; Beauty is fled; Death closes all: based on the love of Sara Curran for Robert Emmet; Maker of roads: based on the martyrdom of St Alban. Each play pbd separately [1947] in French's Plays for juvenile performers.
The white steed and Coggerers. [New York 1939].
The old foolishness: a play in three acts. (Windsor, New York 20 Dec 1940; Arts 7 May 1943). [1944] French.
The strings, my lord, are false. (Olympia, Dublin 16 March, 1942). In Three plays, 1944, Selections above.
The wise have not spoken: a drama in three acts. (Abbey, Dublin 7 Feb 1944; King's, Hammersmith 19 March 1946). [1947] French, New York [1954] Dramatists' Play Service.
Interlude: a play in one act. 1947 French.
Green cars go east: a play in two acts. (Glasgow Citizens', Ayr 10 Nov 1952; Glasgow Citizens' 17 Nov 1952). [1947] French.
The devil came from Dublin (Embassy 21 Jan 1953). In Irish stories and plays, 1958, Selections above. Earlier versions were performed under titles, The chuckey-head story (Bournemouth 9 Oct 1950), and The border be damned (Olney Theatre, Olney 25 June 1951).
The wayward saint: a satirical comedy in three acts. (Cort, New York 17 Feb 1955). New York [1955] Dramatists' Play Service.

Farewell to greatness! (BBC Television 13 Oct 1957). Dixon, California 1966. Ed R. Hogan.

For account of Carroll's unpbd plays, including The watched pot (*Abbey* [*Peacock*], *Dublin 17 Nov 1930*), Kindred (*Abbey, Dublin 25 Sept 1939*), Weep for tomorrow (*Glasgow Citizens' 1947-8*), *see Bannister, 1955, and Hogan, 1967, below. Carroll also wrote unpbd plays for television in USA.*

§2

Brown, J. M. Cathleen ni Houlihan and Shadow and substance. In his Two on the aisle: ten years of the American theatre in performance, New York 1938.
—— Ireland and The white steed. In his Broadway in review, New York 1940.
MacLiammoir, M. Problem plays. In L. Robinson (ed), Irish theatre, New York 1939.
Gassner, J. W. In his Masters of the drama, New York 1940.
Kavanagh, P. In his The story of the Abbey Theatre, New York 1950.
Bannister, W. In her James Bridie and his theatre, 1955.
Coleman, Sr. A. G. Carroll's view of Irish life. Catholic World 192 1960.
Pallette, D. B. Carroll: since The white steed. Modern Drama 7 1965.
Hogan, R. In his After the Irish renaissance, Minneapolis 1967.
For further criticism of Carroll's plays in jnls and newspapers, see H. H. Palmer and A. J. Dyson, European drama criticism, *Hamden Conn 1968.*

HAROLD CHAPIN
1886-1915
Collections

The comedies of Chapin. Introd by J. M. Barrie 1921. The new morality; Art and opportunity; Elaine; The marriage of Columbine.
Three one act plays. [1921] French. It's the poor that 'elps the poor; The autocrat of the coffee stall; Innocent and Annabel.

§1

Augustus in search of a father. (Court 30 Jan 1910). 1911.
The marriage of Columbine: a comedy in four acts. (Court 20 Feb 1910). In The comedies of Chapin, 1921, above; pbd separately 1924 French.
Muddle-Annie: a play in one act. (Royalty, Glasgow 13 March 1911; Court 19 May 1912). 1921.
The autocrat of the coffee stall. (Royalty, Glasgow 27 April 1911; Court 19 May 1912). In Three one act plays, 1921, above.
The dumb and the blind: a play in one act. (Royalty, Glasgow 20 Nov 1911; Court 19 May 1912). 1914. First called God and Mrs Henderson. Diffidence, a version in Scots by F. Fair, pbd [1936] French.
Elaine: a comedy in three acts. (Gaiety, Manchester 1912; Court 26 May 1913). In The comedies of Chapin, 1921, above; pbd separately 1924 French.
Art and opportunity: a comedy in three acts. (Prince of Wales's 5 Sept 1912). In The comedies of Chapin, 1921, above; pbd separately 1924 French.
It's the poor that 'elps the poor. (Court 19 May 1913). In Three one act plays, 1921, above. The quality of mercy, a version in Scots, by F. Fair, pbd [1935] French.
Dropping the baby: a fable in one act. (Playhouse 12 Feb 1914). 1927.
Innocent and Annabel. (Queens 14 Dec 1915). In Three one act plays, 1921, above.

'The philosopher of Butterbiggins': a comedy in one act. (Queen's 14 Dec 1915). 1921, [1921] French. Welsh version, by J. E. Williams, pbd [1929] French.

The new morality: a comedy in three acts. (Comedy 28 Nov 1920). In The comedies of Chapin, 1921, above; pbd separately 1924 French.

The threshold: a play in one act. [1921] French.

The following plays were not pbd: Wonderful Grandmama and the wand of youth: a children's play (*Gaiety, Manchester 26 Dec 1912*), Every man for his own: a comedy in one act (*Court 14 June 1914*) *and* The well made dress coat.

Letters

Soldier and dramatist: being the letters of Chapin. 1916, New York 1916. Includes a list of plays, a memoir by S. Dark, a critical note by W. Archer and a programme of the Harold Chapin Memorial Performance at the Queen's Theatre, 14 Dec 1915. K.J.W.

DAME AGATHA MARY CLARISSA CHRISTIE
(afterwards MALLOWAN)
b. 1890

See cols 552–4, above.

AUSTIN CLARKE
b. 1896

See cols 248–9, above.

DANIEL CORKERY
1878–1964

§1

King and hermit: a play in one act. (Dûn, Cork 2 Dec 1909). In The yellow bittern and other plays, 1920, below.

The yellow bittern. (Dûn, Cork 10 May 1917). In The yellow bittern and other plays, 1920, below.

A Munster twilight. Dublin 1917, New York 1917, Cork 1963. Stories.

The threshold of quiet. Dublin 1917, London 1917. Gaelic trn 1933. Novel.

Clan Falvey. (Dûn, Cork 4 April 1919). In The yellow bittern and other plays, 1920, below.

The Labour leader: a play in three acts. (Abbey, Dublin 30 Sept 1919). 1920.

The yellow bittern and other plays. Dublin 1920, London 1920.

The hounds of Banba. Dublin 1921. Stories.

I Bhreasail: a book of lyrics. 1921.

The hidden Ireland: a study of Gaelic Munster in the eighteenth century. Dublin 1925.

The stormy hills. 1929. Stories.

Synge and Anglo-Irish literature: a study. [Cork] 1931, New York 1965.

Earth out of earth. Dublin 1939. Stories.

Resurrection. Dublin [1942]. Play.

The wager and other stories. New York 1950.

The fortunes of the Irish language. Dublin 1954.

Three plays, Fohnam the sculptor (*Abbey, Dublin 28 Aug 1939*), Israel's incense, *and* The onus of ownership *were not pbd. Corkery also wrote some Gaelic League pamphlets.*

§2

Furlong, A. Welcome, Daniel Corkery! Irish Monthly 46 1918.

O'Faolain, S. Corkery. Dublin Mag 11 1936.

Saul, G. B. The short stories of Corkery. Poet Lore 58 1963.

SIR NOËL PIERCE COWARD
b. 1899

Bibliographies

Mander, R. and J. Mitchenson. In their Theatrical companion to Coward: a pictorial record of the first performances of the theatrical works, [1957], §2 below. Includes films, songs and records.

Morley, S. In his A talent to amuse: a biography of Noel Coward. 1969, §2 below.

Collections and Selections

Three plays: The rat trap; The vortex; Fallen angels; with The author's reply to his critics. 1925.

Home chat; Sirocco; 'This was a man': three plays with a preface. 1928.

The plays: first series. New York 1928. Sirocco; Home chat; The queen was in the parlour.

Bitter sweet and other plays [Easy virtue; Hay fever], with a few comments on the younger dramatists by W. S. Maugham. Garden City NY 1929.

Collected sketches and lyrics. [1931], New York 1932.

Play parade. (The collected plays of Noël Coward). With introds by the author.

Vol 1. Cavalcade; Bitter sweet; The vortex; Hay fever; Design for living; Private lives; Post-mortem. 1934. Previously pbd Garden City NY 1933, with plays in different order.

Vol 2. This year of grace; Words and music; Operette; Conversation piece. 1939, 1950 (with addn of Fallen angels and Easy virtue).

Vol 3. The queen was in the parlour; I'll leave it to you; The young idea; Sirocco; The rat trap; 'This was a man'; Home chat; The marquise. 1950.

Vol 4. Tonight at 8.30; Present laughter; This happy breed. 1954.

Vol 5. Pacific 1860; Peace in our time; Relative values; Quadrille; Blithe spirit. 1958.

Vol 6. Point Valaine; South Sea bubble; Ace of clubs; Nude with violin; Waiting in the wings. [1962].

Curtain calls. New York 1940. Tonight at 8.30; Conversation piece; Easy virtue; Point Valaine; 'This was a man'.

The Noël Coward song book. 1953, New York 1953.

Short stories, short plays and songs. Ed G. Millstein, New York 1955.

Collected short stories. [1962]. Selected from To step aside and Star quality.

The lyrics. 1965, New York 1967.

Three plays: Blithe spirit; Hay fever; Private lives. With an introd by E. Albee, New York 1965.

The wit of Coward. Ed D. Richards 1968.

§1

'I'll leave it to you': a light comedy in three acts. (Gaiety, Manchester 3 May 1920; New 21 July 1920). [1920] French.

The young idea: a comedy in three acts. (Prince's Bristol 25 Sept 1922, Savoy 1 Feb 1923). [1924] French, New York 1924.

A withered nosegay. 1922, New York 1922 (as Terribly intimate portraits). Sketches.

Poems by Hernia Whittlebot [Noël Coward], with an appreciation by Coward. [1923]. Parody of Edith Sitwell's poetry.

The vortex: a play in three acts. (Everyman 25 Nov 1924). 1925, New York 1925. Silent film version 1927.

Fallen angels: a comedy in three acts. (Globe 21 April 1925). 1925, 1958 French (rev).

Hay fever: a light comedy in three acts. (Ambassadors 8 June 1925). 1925, New York 1925, London 1927 (rev) French.

Easy virtue: a play in three acts. (Empire, New York, Winter 1925; Opera House, Manchester 31 May 1926; Duke of York's 9 June 1926). 1926, New York 1926. Silent film version 1927.

Chelsea buns, by Hernia Whittlebot. Ed [i.e. written by] N. Coward [1925]. Parody of Edith Sitwell's poetry.

The queen was in the parlour: a romance in three acts. (St Martin's 24 Aug 1926). 1926. Film versions 1927 (silent), 1928 (talking).

The rat trap: a play in four acts. (Everyman 18 Oct 1926). 1924.

'This was a man': a comedy in three acts. (Klaw Theatre, New York 23 Nov 1926). New York 1926, London 1928 (in Home chat; Sirocco; 'This was a man': three plays). Not performed in England.

The marquise: a comedy in three acts. (Criterion 16 Feb 1927). 1927.

Home chat. (Duke of York's 25 Oct 1927). 1927.

Sirocco. (Daly's 24 Nov 1927). 1927.

This year of Grace. [C. B. Cochran's 1928 revue]. (Palace, Manchester 28 Feb 1928; Pavilion 22 March 1928). In Play parade vol 2, 1939, see Collections, above. Lyrics pbd 1928.

Bitter sweet. (Palace, Manchester 2 July 1929; His Majesty's 18 July 1929). 1929, New York 1929. Film versions 1933, 1941.

Private lives: an intimate comedy in three acts. (King's, Edinburgh 18 Aug 1930; Phoenix 24 Sept 1930). 1930, New York 1931, London [1947] French. Film version 1931.

Cavalcade. (Drury Lane 13 Oct 1931). 1932, New York 1933. Film version 1932.

Words and music: a revue. (Opera House, Manchester 25 Aug 1932; Adelphi 16 Sept 1932). In Play parade vol 2, 1939, see Collections, above.

Spangled unicorn: a selection from the works of Albrecht Drausler [et al]. [1932], New York 1933. Parodies.

Design for living: a comedy in three acts. (Hanna Theatre, Cleveland, Ohio 2 Jan 1933; Ethel Barrymore, New York 24 Jan 1933; Theatre Royal, Brighton 16 Jan 1939; Haymarket 25 Jan 1939). 1933, New York 1933. Film version 1933.

Conversation piece: a romantic comedy (His Majesty's, 16 Feb 1934). 1934, New York 1934.

Point Valaine: a play in three acts. (Colonial, Boston 25 Dec 1934; Ethel Barrymore, New York 16 Jan 1935; Playhouse, Liverpool 18 Oct 1944; Embassy 3 Sept 1947). 1935, New York 1935.

To-night at 8.30: plays. 3 vols 1936, New York 1936. Pbd separately (French) 1938.

1. We were dancing; The astonished heart; Red peppers (all at Opera House, Manchester 15 Oct 1935; Phoenix 29 Jan 1936). Played in Manchester as To-night at 7.30.

2. Hands across the sea; Fumed oak; Shadow play (all at Opera House, Manchester 18 Oct 1935, Phoenix 13 Jan 1936). Played in Manchester as To-night at 7.30.

3. Ways and means (Phoenix 5 May 1936); Still life (Phoenix 22 May 1936); Family album (Theatre Royal, Birmingham 9 Dec 1935; Phoenix 9 Jan 1936). Film versions: The astonished heart 1950, Red peppers, Fumed oak and Ways and means (as Meet me tonight) 1952; Still life (as Brief encounter) 1945 (screen play pbd 1950 in Three British screenplays, ed R. Manvell); We were dancing 1942.

Present indicative. 1937, New York 1937. Autobiography.

Operette. (Opera House, Manchester 17 Feb 1938; His Majesty's 16 March 1938). 1938.

To step aside: seven short stories. 1939, New York 1939.

Blithe spirit: an improbable farce in three acts. (Opera House, Manchester 16 June 1941; Piccadilly 2 July 1941). New York 1941, London 1942, [1942] French, New York 1966 (television adaptation by R. Hartung). Film version 1944.

Australia visited, 1940. 1941. Broadcasts.

Present laughter: a light comedy in three acts. (Grand, Blackpool 20 Sept 1942; Haymarket 29 April 1943). 1943, New York 1947, London [1949] French, New York [1949].

This happy breed: a play in three acts. (Grand, Blackpool 21 Sept 1942; Haymarket 30 April 1943). 1943, [1945] French, New York 1947. Film version 1943.

Middle East diary: July to October 1943. 1944, New York 1944.

Pacific 1860; a musical romance. (Drury Lane 19 Dec 1946). In Play parade vol 5, 1958, see Collections, above.

'Peace in our time': a play in two acts and eight scenes. (Theatre Royal, Brighton 15 July 1947; Lyric 22 July 1947). 1947, New York 1948, London [1949] French.

The ace of clubs: a musical play in 2 acts. (Palace, Manchester 16 May 1950; Cambridge 7 July 1950). In Play parade vol 6, 1962, see Collections, above.

Relative values: a light comedy in three acts. (Theatre Royal, Newcastle 15 Oct 1951; Savoy 28 Nov 1951). 1952, [1954] French.

Star quality. 1951, New York 1951. Stories.

Quadrille: a romantic comedy in three acts. (Opera House, Manchester 15 July 1952; Phoenix 12 Sept 1952). 1952, [1954] French, New York 1955.

After the ball: an operette based on Lady Windermere's fan. (Royal Court, Liverpool 1 March 1954; Globe 10 June 1954). Book of lyrics [1954].

Future indefinite. 1954, New York 1954. Autobiography 1939-45.

South Sea bubble: a comedy in three acts. (Opera House, Manchester 19 March 1956; Lyric 25 April 1956). 1956, [1958] French.

Nude with violin: a light comedy in three acts. (Olympia, Dublin 24 Sept 1956; Globe 7 Nov 1956). 1957, [1958] French.

Waiting in the wings: a play in three acts. (Olympia, Dublin 8 Aug 1960; Duke of York's 7 Sept 1960). 1960, [1960] French.

Pomp and circumstance. 1960. New York 1960. Novel.

Seven stories. Garden City NY 1963.

Pretty Polly Barlow and other stories. 1964, New York 1965 (as Pretty Polly and other stories).

Suite in three keys: A song at twilight; Shadows of the evening; Come into the garden, Maud (all at Queen's 14–25 April 1966). 1966, Garden City NY 1967. Pbd separately 1967 French.

Pretty Polly. (ABC Television 23 July 1966). In Pretty Polly Barlow and other stories, 1964, above. Filmed 1967.

Bon voyage and other stories. 1967, New York 1968 (as Bon Voyage).

Not yet the dodo and other verses. 1967, New York 1968.

Post-mortem: a play in eight scenes. (BBC 2 Television 17 Sept 1968). 1931, New York 1931.

Coward also composed the following unpbd plays, revues and musical plays: The last chapter (later Ida collaborates) (Theatre Royal, Aldershot 20 Aug 1917) and Woman and whisky (Wimbledon 21 Jan 1918) [both with E. Wynne], Bottles and bones (Drury Lane 16 May 1921), The better half: comedy in one act (Little 31 May 1922), London calling (Duke of York's 4 Sept 1923), with Ronald Jeans, On with the dance (Palace, Manchester 17 March 1925; Pavilion 30 April 1925), Set to music (Haymarket 4 July 1939), Star chamber (BBC Home Service 18 May 1940), Sigh no more (Piccadilly 28 Aug 1945), The kindness of Mrs Redcliffe (BBC Home Service 2 June 1951), Sail away (Broadhurst, New York 3 Oct 1961; Hippodrome, Bristol 31 May 1962; Savoy 21 June 1962), Mr and Mrs [based on Fumed oak and Brief encounter] (*Manchester Repertory 10 Nov 1968*; *Palace 11 Dec 1968*). *He adapted G. Feydeau*, Occupe-toi d'Amélie *as* Look after Lulu (*Royal, Newcastle 20 July 1959*; *Court 29 July 1959*). *The script of the film,* In which we serve (*1942*) *is unpbd. Mander and Mitchenson,* Theatrical companion to Coward, *1957, below, lists plays unproduced as well as unpbd.*

§2

Canfield, M. C. In her Grotesques and other reflections, New York 1927.
Cunliffe, J. W. In his Modern English playwrights, 1927.
Beerbohm, M. Heroes and heroines of Bitter sweet. 1931. Caricatures.
Macdonnell, A. G. The plays of Coward. London Mercury 25 1931.
Braybrooke, P. The amazing Mr Coward. 1933.
Carmer, C. The work of Coward. Theatre Arts Monthly 17 1933.
Furnas, J. C. The art of Coward. Fortnightly Rev 140 1933.
Hamilton, C. In his People worth talking about, New York 1933.
Swinnerton, F. In his The Georgian scene, New York 1934, London 1935 (as The Georgian literary scene).
Ervine, St J. The plays of Coward. Essays by Divers Hands 14 1935.
Nathan, G. J. In his Passing judgments, New York 1935.
Snider, R. Satire in the comedies of Congreve, Sheridan, Wilde and Coward. Orono, Maine 1937.
Brown, J. M. Somerset Maugham and Coward compared [and] Farewell to Design for living. In his Two on the aisle, New York 1938.
Woodbridge, H. E. South Atlantic Quart 37 1938.
Stokes, S. Theatre Arts Monthly 27 1944.
Beaton, C. Theatre Arts 33 1949.
Greacen, R. The art of Coward. Aldington Kent [1953].
MacCarthy, D. Maugham and Coward. In his Humanities, 1953.
— Coward. In his Theatre, 1954.
Trewin, J. C. In his Dramatists of today, 1953.
Mander, R. and J. Mitchenson. Theatrical companion to Coward: a pictorial record of the first performances of the theatrical works, with an appreciation of Coward's work in the theatre by T. Rattigan. [1957]. Includes extracts from selected first night notices.
Gehman, R. Impeccable skipper of Sail away. Theatre Arts 45 1961.
Levin, M. Noel Coward. New York 1968.
Morley, S. A talent to amuse: a biography of Noël Coward. 1969.

For further criticism of Coward's plays in journals and newspapers, see H. H. Palmer and A. J. Dyson, European drama criticism, Hamden Conn 1968.

'CLEMENCE DANE',
WINIFRED ASHTON
1887?–1965

Collections

Recapture: a Clemence Dane omnibus. 1932.
Collected plays. 1961–.

§1

Regiment of women. 1917, New York 1917. Novel.
First the blade: a comedy of growth. 1918, New York 1918. Novel.
Legend. 1919, New York 1920. Novel.
A bill of divorcement: a play in three acts. (St Martin's 14 March 1921). 1921, New York 1921.

Will Shakespeare: an invention in four acts. (Shaftesbury 17 Nov 1921). 1921, [1951] French.
The way things happen: a story in three acts. (Broad Street, Newark NJ 24 Dec 1923; Ambassadors 2 Feb 1924). 1924. Based on Legend, 1919 above.
Shivering shocks: or the hiding place—a play for boys. [1923] French.
Wandering stars, together with The lover. 1924, New York 1924. Stories.
Naboth's vineyard: a stage piece. 1925.
Granite: a tragedy. (Ambassadors 15 June 1926). 1926, [1949] French.
The woman's side. 1926. New York 1927. Feminist essays.
Mariners. (Plymouth, New York 4 March 1927; Wyndham's 29 April 1929). 1927, New York 1927.
The dearly beloved of Benjamin Cobb: a tale. 1927.
Mr Fox: a play for boys. [1927] French.
A traveller returns: a play in one act. [1927] French.
A Scots version, The wraith, by F. Fair, [1937] French.
Adam's opera: the text of a play, set to music by R. Addinsell. (Old Vic 3 Dec 1928). 1928, New York 1929.
The Babyons: a family chronicle. 1928. 4 vols New York 1928.
The king waits: a tale. 1929.
Tradition and Hugh Walpole. New York 1929, London 1930.
Broome stages. 1931, New York 1931. Novel.
Wild Decembers: a play in three acts. (Apollo 26 May 1933), 1932, New York 1933, [1934] French. A Brontë play.
Come of age: a play in music [by R. Addinsell] and verse. (Maxine Elliott, New York Jan 1934). 1933, New York 1934. About Thomas Chatterton.
Moonlight is silver: a play in three acts. (Queen's 19 Sept 1934). 1934.
Fate cries out: nine tales. 1935, New York 1935.
The moon is feminine. 1938, New York 1938. Novel.
The arrogant history of White Ben. 1939, New York 1939. Novel.
Cousin Muriel: a play in three acts. (Globe 7 March 1940). 1940.
The saviours: seven [radio] plays on one theme. (BBC Home Service 24 Nov 1940 to 11 Nov 1941). 1942, New York 1942. Merlin; The hope of Britain; England's darling; The May king; The light of Britain; Remember Nelson; The unknown soldier.
Trafalgar Day 1940. 1940, New York 1941. Poem.
The golden reign of Queen Elizabeth. (Theatre Royal, York 21 Jan 1941). [1941] French.
Alice's adventures in wonderland and through the looking-glass dramatised, with music by R. Addinsell. (Scala 24 Dec 1943). [1948] French; 1951.
The lion and the unicorn: a play in three acts. 1943.
He brings great news: a story. 1944, New York 1945.
Call home the heart: a play. (St James's 10 April 1947). 1947.
The flower girls. 1954, New York 1955. Novel.
Scandal at Coventry. (BBC 17 March 1958). In Collected plays vol 1, 1961, above.
Eighty in the shade: a play in three acts. (Royal, Newcastle 24 Nov 1958; Globe 8 Jan 1959). 1959, [1960] French.
Till time shall end: a play in two acts. (BBC Television 30 Nov 1958). In Collected plays vol 1, 1961, above.
Approaches to drama. 1961. Address.
The godson: a [Shakespearean] fantasy. 1964.
London has a garden. 1964. On Covent Garden.
Three plays were not pbd: The terror (*Playhouse, Liverpool 10 Sept 1921*), Gooseberry fool (*Players 1 Nov 1929*), *and* The happy hypocrite [*based on Max Beerbohm's story*] (*His Majesty's 8 April 1936*). *Clemence Dane adapted E. Rostand,* L'Aiglon (*1934*), *C. F. Hebbel*, Herodes und Mariamne (*1938*), *Shakespeare*, Henry VIII (*BBC 14 June 1954*) *and Schiller*, Don Carlos (*BBC 18 July 1955*),

and wrote scripts for 7 films: Anna Karenina (*1935*), The amateur gentleman (*1936*), Farewell again (*1937*), Fire over England (*1937*), St Martin's Lane (*1938*). *She wrote 3 detective novels with H. Simpson and edited* One hundred enchanted tales (*1937*), The shelter book (*1940*) *and* The Nelson touch: an anthology of Nelson's letters (*1942*).

§2

Johnson, R. B. In his Some contemporary novelists: women, 1920.

Mais, S. P. B. In his Books and their writers, 1920.

— In his Some modern authors, 1923.

Ervine, St J. G. A bill of divorcement. Observer 20 March 1921; rptd in Specimens of English dramatic criticism, ed A. C. Ward 1945.

— On C. Dane's Will Shakespeare. Observer 26 March 1922; rptd in The English dramatic critics, ed J. Agate [*1932*].

Sutton, G. In his Some contemporary dramatists, 1924.

Dottin, P. Clemence Dane: romancière et dramaturge. Revue de France 15 March 1934.

Lawrence, M. In her School of femininity, New York 1936.

WILLIAM AUBREY CECIL DARLINGTON
b. 1890

§1

Alf's button. 1919, New York 1920. Novel, first pbd in the weekly Passing Show (1917). Filmed 1920.

Through the fourth wall. 1922. Dramatic essays rptd from Daily Telegraph.

Alf's button: an extravaganza in three acts. (Royal, Portsmouth 22 Sept 1924; Prince's 24 Dec 1924). 1925, [*1934*] French. Based on his novel of that name.

Literature in the theatre, and other essays. 1925. Rptd from Fortnightly Rev and Daily Telegraph.

Alf's carpet. 1928. Novel, dramatized as Magic slippers (Golders Green 29 July 1929), filmed 1929.

Carpet slippers: a play in three acts. (Embassy 24 Dec 1930). [*1937*] Year Book Press series.

Sheridan. 1933, New York 1933.

J. M. Barrie. 1938.

I do what I like. 1947. Autobiography.

The key of the house: a comedy in three acts. (County, Hereford 11 April 1949). [*1950*] Deane.

The actor and his audience. 1949, New York 1949.

The world of Gilbert and Sullivan. New York [*1950*], London 1951.

Sheridan 1751–1816. 1951 (Br Council pamphlet).

Six thousand and one nights: forty years a critic. 1960.

Laurence Olivier. 1969.

Darlington wrote 4 other novels. He adapted 3 plays by J. Fabricius, A knight passed by (*Ambassadors 6 June 1931*), Night of the masquerade (*Q 29 April 1952*); *and* The village doctor; *and he revised D. Boucicault,* The streets of London (*Ambassadors 20 Dec 1932*). Marcia gets her own back (*Aldwych 27 March 1938*) *was not pbd. He contributed dramatic criticism to Daily Telegraph regularly from 1920 to 1968, and to New York Times 1939–60.*

HUBERT HENRY DAVIES
1869–1917

Collections

Plays. Introd by H. Walpole. 2 vols 1921 New York 1922.

§1

Cousin Kate: a comedy in three acts. (Royal, Newcastle 26 Aug 1889; Haymarket 18 June 1903). 1910, Boston 1910.

Mrs Gorringe's necklace: a new comedy in four acts. (Wyndham's 12 May 1903). 1910, Boston 1910.

Captain Drew on leave: a comedy in four acts. (New 24 Oct 1905). Boston 1924.

The mollusc: a new comedy in three acts. (Criterion 15 Oct 1907). 1914, Boston 1914.

Lady Epping's lawsuit: a satirical comedy in three acts. (Criterion 12 Oct 1908). 1914, Boston 1914.

A single man: a new comedy in four acts. (Playhouse 8 Nov 1910). 1914, Boston 1914.

Doormats: a comedy in three acts. (Wyndham's 3 Oct 1912). 1920 French.

Outcast: a play in four acts. (Wyndham's 1 Sept 1914). In Plays vol 2, 1921, above.

The following plays were not pbd: The Weldons (*Empire, New York 6 April 1899*), Fifty years ago (*1900*), Cynthia (*Madison Sq, New York 16 March 1903*), Bevis (*Comedy 1 April 1909*).

§2

Walpole, H. In his Introduction to The Plays, 2 vols 1921, above.

Darlington, W. A. In his Through the fourth wall, 1922.

Beerbohm, M. In his Around theatres, 1924.

'GORDON DAVIOT', ELIZABETH MACKINTOSH
1896–1952

Collections

Plays. 3 vols 1953–4.

§1

Richard of Bordeaux: a play in two acts. (Arts 10 June 1932). 1933, Boston 1933, [*1935*] French; tr German, [*1959*].

The laughing woman: a play. (New 7 April 1934). 1934.

Queen of Scots: a play in three acts. (New 8 June 1934). 1935, [*1935*] French.

The stars bow down: a play in three acts. (Malvern 10 Aug 1939). 1939.

Leith sands. (BBC Home Service 13 Nov 1941). This and the following 3 pbd in Leith Sands and other short plays, 1946, below.

The three Mrs Madderleys. (BBC Home Service 14 June 1944).

Mrs Fry has a visitor. (BBC Home Service 6 Dec 1944).

Remember Caesar. (BBC 4 Jan 1946).

Leith Sands and other short plays. 1946. Rahab; The mother of Masé; Sara (the first act of The little dry thorn, below); Mrs Fry has a visitor; The three Mrs Madderleys; Clarion call; Remember Caesar.

The little dry thorn. (Lyric, Hammersmith 11 Nov 1947). In Plays vol 1, 1953, above.

Valerius. (Saville 1948: single performance; BBC Home Service 29 April 1961). In Plays vol 1, 1953.

The pen of my aunt. (BBC Home Service 15 Feb 1950). In Plays vol 2, 1954.

Patria. In Plays vol 2, 1954.

The Balwhinnie bomb. In Plays vol 2, 1954.

The princess who liked cherry pie. In Plays vol 2, 1954.

The pomp of Mr Pomfret. (BBC Scottish Service 23 Oct 1954). In Plays vol 2, 1954.

Lady Charing is cross. In Plays vol 3, 1954.

Reckoning. In Plays vol 3, 1954.

Barnharrow. In Plays vol 3, 1954.

The staff-room. In Plays vol 3, 1954.

Cornelia. (BBC Home Service 22 Jan 1955). In Plays vol 2, 1954.

Dickon. (Playhouse, Salisbury 9 May 1955). In Plays vol 1, 1953.

Sweet coz. (Castle, Farnham 19 Nov 1956). In Plays vol 3, 1954.

Elizabeth Mackintosh wrote 11 novels (including 8 detective novels) under the pseudonyms of Gordon Daviot and Josephine Tey, as well as a biography of Claverhouse.

§2

Gielgud, J. Foreword to vol 1 of Plays, 1953, above.

BASIL DEAN
b. 1888

The repertory theatre. Liverpool 1911. Lecture.

Fifinella: a fairy frolic. (Repertory, Liverpool 26 Dec 1912; Scala 20 Dec 1919). [1912]. With Barry Jackson.

Hassan: the story of Hassan and how he came to make the Golden Journey to Samarkand: a play in five acts by J. E. Flecker, arranged for production on the stage by B. Dean. (His Majesty's 20 Sept 1923). 1951, 1966 (rev). With introd by Dean. The first performance was in the Hessische Landestheater, Darmstadt, 1 June 1923 in the German trn by Freisler.

The constant nymph. (New 23 Sept 1926). 1926, New York 1926, 1930 French. French adaptation by J. Giraudoux, Paris 1934. Film versions: silent, 1928; talking 1934 (produced by Dean), 1943. With M. M. Kennedy, from her novel of that name.

Come with me. (New 26 April 1928). 1928. With M. M. Kennedy.

Diary of a nobody. (Arts, Cambridge 23 Aug 1955; Arts 1 Sept 1955). [1955] French. Adaptation, by Dean and R. Blake, of G. & W. Grossmith's novel.

The theatre at war. 1956. History of the Entertainments National Service Association.

The following plays were not pbd: Marriages are made in Heaven (His Majesty's 2 June 1909), Mother-to-be (Gaiety, Manchester 7 Feb 1910), Effie (Gaiety, Manchester 29 Aug 1910), Love cheats (Coronet 1 June 1914), an adaptation of P. C. Wren's Beau Geste (His Majesty's 30 Jan 1929). Dean was a leading theatrical producer 1919–61 and film director and producer 1928–40. Among his films were: The water gypsies (1931), Lorna Doone (1934), and Twenty one days together [based on Galsworthy's play, The first and the last] (1940).

TERESA DEEVY
1900–63

§1

The King of Spain's daughter: a play in one act. (Abbey, Dublin 29 April 1935). In Three plays, 1939, below; Dublin 1948 (in The King of Spain's daughter and other one act plays).

Katie Roche: a play in three acts. (Abbey, Dublin 16 March 1936; Torch 25 Nov 1938). In Famous plays of 1935–6 (1936), and in Three plays (1939) below.

The wild goose: a play in three acts. (Abbey, Dublin 9 Nov 1936). In Three plays, 1939, below.

The enthusiast: a one-act play. One Act Play Mag 1 1938.

Three plays: Katie Roche; The King of Spain's daughter; The wild goose. 1939.

Strange birth: a one act play. (BBC N Ireland Service 28 Feb 1947). Irish Writing no 1 1946, 1948 (in The King of Spain's daughter and other one act plays).

The King of Spain's daughter and other one act plays [In search of valour; Strange birth]. Dublin 1948.

Going beyond Alma's glory: a radio play in one act. (BBC N Ireland Service 16 Feb 1949). Irish Writing no 17 1951.

The following plays were not pbd: The reapers: a play in three acts (Abbey, Dublin 18 March 1930), A disciple: a comedy in one act (Abbey, Dublin 24 Aug 1931), Temporal powers: a play in three acts (Abbey, Dublin 12 Sept 1932), Dignity (BBC 7 June 1939), Polinka (adapted from Tchekov) (BBC N Ireland Service 10 July 1946), Light falling (BBC N Ireland Service 18 Feb 1948; Abbey, Dublin 25 Oct 1948; Lyric Hammersmith 14 Jan 1950); Wife to James Whelan (BBC N Ireland Service 23 Feb 1956; Mme Cogley's Studio Theatre Club 4 Oct 1956), and Supreme dominion [also called Luke Wadding] (Radio Eireann 1957).

Miss Deevy pbd a study of Patricia Lynch in Irish Writing no 5 1948 and a child's tale, Strange people, in Lisheen at the Valley farm and other stories, Dublin 1945.

§2

Riley, J. D. On Teresa Deevy's plays. Irish Writing no 32 1955.

Hogan, R. In his After the Irish renaissance, Minneapolis 1967.

RONALD FREDERICK DELDERFIELD
b. 1912

This is my life: a comedy in three acts. (Grand, Wolverhampton 13 July 1942, as Matron). [1944]. With B. Thomas.

Worm's eye view: a comedy. (King's, Hammersmith 23 April 1945; Embassy 4 Dec 1945; Whitehall 5 May 1947). 1946, [1948] French.

Peace comes to Peckham: a comedy in three acts. (Embassy 2 Oct 1946; Prince's 17 March 1947). [1948] French.

All over the town. 1947. Novel. Dramatized (Playhouse 21 Oct 1947), [1948] French. Filmed 1948.

The queen came by: a play in three acts. (Embassy 14 Sept 1948; Duke of York's 30 March 1949). [1949].

Spark in Judaea: a play in three acts. (Playhouse, Oxford 6 Feb 1950). [1953].

Sailors beware: an Elizabethan improbability in one act. [1950].

Waggonload o' monkeys—further adventures of Porter and Taffy: a farcical comedy in three acts. (Savoy 9 Oct 1951). [1952].

Nobody shouted author. [1951]. Reminiscences.

Golden rain: a comedy. (Theatre Royal, Windsor 24 Nov 1952). [1953].

Miaow! Miaow! a comedy in one act. [1952] French.

The old lady of Cheadle: a comedy in one act. 1952.

Made to measure: a play in one act. (BBC Home Service 14 Jan 1953). [1952] French.

The testimonial: a play in one act. (BBC Home Service 27 May 1953). [1953] French.

The offending hand: a play in three acts. (Northampton Repertory 7 Sept 1953; BBC Home Service 20 June 1964). [1955].

The orchard walls: a play in three acts. (Hippodrome, Aldershot 26 Oct 1953; St Martin's 30 Nov 1953). [1954] French.

Absent lover: a Plantagenet improbability in one act. [1953] French.

Smoke in the valley: a play in one act. (BBC Home Service 3 March 1954). [1953] French.

The bride wore an opal ring: a comedy in one act. (BBC Home Service 15 Sept 1954). [1952] French.

Bird's eye view: an autobiography. [1954].

The guinea-pigs: a one-act comedy for women. [1954].

Home is the hunted: a Cockney comedy in one act. [1954] French.

Musical switch: a comedy in one act. [1954].

The Rounderlay tradition: an all-woman comedy. [1954].

Ten till five: a comedy in one act. [1954].

Where there's a will...: a comedy in three acts. [1954] French.

And then there were none: a comedy in one act. (BBC Home Service 9 March 1955). [1954] French.

Uncle's little lapse: a comedy in three acts. [1955].

The adventures of Ben Gunn. 1956, Indianapolis [1957]. A story based on Stevenson's Treasure Island.

The Mayerling affair: a play in three acts. (Pitlochry Festival 4 May 1957). [1958] French.

Flashpoint: a play in three acts. [1958] French.

Once aboard the lugger: a comedy in three acts. [1962] French.

Wild mink: a play in one act. [1962] French.

Under an English sky. 1964. Travel sketches.

For my own amusement. 1968. Reminiscences.

The following plays have not been pbd: The Cocklemouth cornet (*BBC Empire Service 22 July 1938*), The comet covers a wedding (*BBC Empire Service 18 Feb 1939*), Printer's devil (*Q 10 July 1939*), The spinster of South Street (*King's, Hammersmith 27 Aug 1945*), The elephant's graveyard (*Civic, Chesterfield 8 Oct 1951*), Follow the plough (*Leatherhead 23 March 1953; Q 1 Dec 1953*), This happy brood (*BBC Home Service 7 Nov 1956*), Duty and the beast (*Connaught, Worthing 27 May 1957*) [*adapted from H. Keuls*], Midas beach (*BBC Home Service 15 Oct 1960*), My dearest angel (*Pitlochry Festival 13 April 1963*), and The day of the sputnick (*BBC Home Service 21 Sept 1963*).

Delderfield has also written three Napoleonic studies and the following novels: Seven men of Gascony (*1949*), Farewell the tranquil mind (*1950*), The Avenue goes to war (*1958*) (serialized *BBC Home Service 1961*), The dreaming suburb (*1958*), There was a fair maid dwelling (*1960*), Stop at a winner (*1961*), The unjust skies (*1962*), The Spring madness of Mr Sermon (*1963*), Too few for drums (*1964*), A horseman riding by (*1966*) (serialized *BBC Home Service 1967*), Cheap day return (*1967*), The green gauntlet (*1968*) *and* Come home, Charlie, and face them (*1969*).

NIGEL FORBES DENNIS
b. 1912
See col 562, above.

PATRIC THOMAS DICKINSON
b. 1914
See col 262, above.

WILLIAM DOUGLAS-HOME
b. 1912

Selections

The plays of William Douglas Home. 1958. 'Now Barabbas...'; The Chiltern Hundreds; The thistle and the rose; The bad Samaritan; The reluctant debutante.

§I

Home truths. 1939. Verse.

'Now Barabbas...' (Bolton's 11 Feb 1947; Vaudeville 7 March 1947). 1947. Screenplay: Warner Brothers 1949.

The Chiltern Hundreds: a comedy in three acts. (Vaudeville 26 Aug 1947). [1949] French. Screen play: Two Cities 1949.

Master of Arts: a farcical comedy in three acts. (Royal, Brighton 20 June 1949; Strand 1 Sept 1949). [1950] French.

The thistle and the rose. (Bolton's 6 Sept 1949; Vaudeville 15 May 1951). In The plays of W. D. Home, 1958, above.

The bad Samaritan. (New, Bromley 2 Sept 1952; Criterion 24 June 1953, with Prologue and Epilogue omitted). 1954 Evans. Original version pbd in The plays of W. D. Home, 1958, above.

The manor of Northstead: a comedy in three acts. (Duchess 28 April 1954). [1956] French.

Half-term report: an autobiography. 1954.

The reluctant debutante: a play in three acts. (Cambridge 24 May 1955; Henry Miller, New York 10 Oct 1956). 1956 Evans, [1957] French. Screen play: MGM 1958.

The iron duchess: a play in two acts. (Royal, Brighton 25 Feb 1957; Cambridge 14 March 1957). 1958 Evans.

Aunt Edwina: a comedy. (Devonshire Park, Eastbourne 14 Sept 1959; Fortune 3 Nov 1959). [1960] French.

The bad soldier Smith. (Westminster 14 June 1961). 1962.

The reluctant peer: a comedy in three acts. (Duchess 15 Jan 1964). [1965] Evans.

A friend indeed: a comedy. (Windsor Repertory 8 Sept 1965; Cambridge 27 April 1966). [1966] French.

The secretary bird: a comedy. (Opera House, Manchester 9 Sept 1968; Savoy 16 Oct 1968). [1969] French.

The bishop and the actress. [1969] French.

The following plays have not been pbd: Great possessions (*Q 8 Feb 1937*); Passing by (*Q 29 April 1940*); Ambassador extraordinary (*Aldwych 30 June 1948*); Caro William (*Embassy 22 Oct 1952*); Up a gum tree (*Ipswich 13 June 1960*; The cigarette girl (*Duke of York's 19 June 1962*); The drawing tragedy (*1963*); Two accounts rendered: The Home Secretary and Lady's P.2. (*Comedy, 15 Sept 1964*); Betzi (*Playhouse, Salisbury 23 March 1965*); The queen's highland servant (*Playhouse, Salisbury 14 Nov 1967*; Windsor Repertory 8 Apr 1968*; Savoy 2 May 1968*); and The grouse moor image (*Athenaeum, Plymouth 8 July 1968*).

For reviews and articles on Douglas-Home see H. H. Palmer and A. J. Dyson's European drama criticism, Hamden Conn 1968.

JOHN DRINKWATER
1882–1937
See cols 263–6, above.

ASHLEY DUKES
1885–1959

Selections

Five plays of other times. 1931. The man with a load of mischief; Ulenspiegel; The fountain-head; The dumb wife of Cheapside; Matchmaker's arms.

§I

Civil war: a comedy in four acts. (Aldwych 5 June 1910). 1911.

Modern dramatists. [1911].

The youngest drama: studies of fifty dramatists. 1923, New York 1923.

The man with a load of mischief: a comedy in three acts. (New 7 Dec 1924). 1924, New York 1924, London 1926 French.

Drama. 1926, New York 1927, London 1936 (rev).

The song of drums: a heroic comedy in a prologue and three acts. 1926. First pbd serially in Theatre Arts Monthly 10, 1926 as Tyl Ulenspiegel or the song of drums. Rev version in Five plays of other times, 1931, above.

One more river: a modern comedy in three acts. (Stage Society 16 Feb 1927). 1927, New York 1927.

The fountain-head: a play in three acts. (Arts 17 Oct 1928). 1928.

The world to play with. 1928, New York 1928. Essays on the drama.

The dumb wife of Cheapside: a comedy [after Rabelais] in a prologue and two acts. (Broadcast BBC 17 April 1929; Arts 16 July 1930). [1929] French.

Matchmaker's arms: a comedy in three acts. (Grand, Croydon 12 Feb 1931). 1931, [1933] French.

The players' dressing room: a tragic comedy in one act. [1936] French.

The scene is changed. 1942. Autobiography.

Return to Danes Hill: a tragic comedy in three acts. [1958] French.

The following plays were unpbd: Pride of life (*Aldwych 29 Jan 1911*), Vintage wine [*with Seymour Hicks*] (*Daly's 2 June 1934*), Charlotte's progress (*Mercury 11 July 1934*), Vauxhall Gardens (*Mercury 18 Oct 1934*), In such a world (*Grafton 3 Oct 1935*), House of assignation (*Mercury 4 Nov 1937*), A glass of water [*adapted from E. Scribe*] (*Mercury 11 Dec 1950*), Celestina (*Embassy 9 Jan 1951*), The trap [*from F. Bruckner's play*] (*Grand, Blackpool 12 May 1952, Duke of York's 1 July 1952*).

Dukes pbd the following adaptations of the work of foreign authors: The comedy of the man who married a dumb wife, *and* One can but try [*A. France*] (*Haymarket 15 Feb 1914*), 1925; From morn to midnight [*G. Kaiser*] (*Lyric, Hammersmith 28 March 1920; Regent 9 March 1926*), 1920; The machine-wreckers [*E. Toller*] (*Stage Society 10 May 1923*), 1923, 1926; The mask of virtue [*C. Sternheim*] (*Ambassadors 15 May 1935*), 1935; The swallow book [*E. Toller: verse*], 1924; Such men are dangerous [*from A. Neumann's The patriot*] (*King's, Edinburgh 6 Feb 1928; Duke of York's 19 Sept 1928*), 1928, New York 1928 (as The patriot); Jew Süss [*L. Feuchtwanger*] (*Opera House, Blackpool 29 July 1929; Duke of York's 19 Sept 1929*), 1929, New York 1930; Elizabeth of England [*F. Bruckner*] (*Cambridge 30 Sept 1931*), A woman of this world [*H. Becque*] (*Mercury 29 Jan 1934*), [*1943*]; In theatre street [*H. R. Lenormand*] (*Mercury 28 April 1937*), 1937; Mandragola [*N. Machiavelli*] (*Mercury 19 Dec 1939*), 1940; Midsummer fire [*H. Sudermann*] (*BBC Third Programme 11 March 1951*).

Dukes contributed regularly to Theatre Arts Monthly *1926-45.*

§2

Carmer, C. Dukes. Theatre Arts Monthly 16 1932.

RONALD FREDERICK HENRY DUNCAN
b. 1914

§1

The dull ass's hoof: three plays. [1940], New York 1940. The unburied dead (first serialised in Townsman 1938-9); Ora pro nobis: a miracle play; Pimp, skunk and profiteer: a lampoon.

Postcards to Pulcinella. [1941]. Verse.

This way to the tomb: a masque and anti-masque. (Mercury 11 Oct 1945). 1946, New York 1967.

The rape of Lucretia: a libretto [for Britten's opera from Obey's play, Le viol de Lucrèce]. (Glyndebourne 12 July 1946). [1946]; 1948 (with other material, as The rape of Lucretia: a symposium by B. Britten, R. Duncan and others); 1953 (introd Earl of Harewood).

Stratton: a play in two acts and five scenes. (Theatre Royal, Brighton 31 Oct 1949; Mercury 30 May 1950). 1950.

Our Lady's tumbler. (Salisbury Cathedral 5 June 1950; St Thomas, Regent St 25 April 1955). 1951.

The mongrel and other poems. 1950.

The last Adam: a story. 1952.

Don Juan: a play in verse. (Palace, Bideford 13 July 1953; BBC Home Service 13 Feb 1956; Court 15 May 1956). 1954.

The death of Satan: a comedy. (Palace, Bideford 5 Aug 1954; Court 15 May 1956). 1955.

The catalyst: a comedy in two acts. (Arts 25 March 1958). 1964.

Abélard & Héloise: a correspondence for the stage in two acts. (Arts Theatre Club 24 Oct 1960). 1961.

Judas. 1960. Poems.

The solitudes: poems. 1960.

Saint Spiv. 1961. Novel.

All men are islands: an autobiography. 1964.

O-B-A-F-G [etc]: a play in one act for stereophonic sound. 1964.

How to make enemies. 1969. Autobiography

The perfect mistress and other stories. 1969.

Unpopular poems. 1969.

The following plays remain unpbd: Nothing up my sleeve (*Watergate 5 Dec 1950*), Christopher Sly: libretto for the chamber opera by T. Eastwood (*Court 24 Jan 1960*), Ménage à trois (*1963*), The seven deadly virtues (*1964*) *and* The rebel (*BBC Television 4 April 1969*).

Jan's Journal, *1949;* The blue fox, *1951, New York 1952;* Jan at The blue fox, *1952, were articles and stories on country themes rptd from the* Evening Standard. *Also on country subjects were* The journal of a husbandman, *1944;* Home-made home, *1947;* Tobacco cultivation in England, *1951;* Where I live [*Devonshire*], *1953; and* A guide to Devon and Cornwall, *1966.*

Duncan edited and contributed to Townsman, *1938-45, and edited selections from Pope's letters, the poems of Ben Jonson and the Earl of Rochester, and from the writings of Mahatma Gandhi.*

*He translated and adapted the following works of foreign dramatists :*The eagle has two heads [*Cocteau*] (*Lyric, Hammersmith 4 Sept 1946; Haymarket 12 Feb 1947*), 1948, New York 1948; The typewriter [*Cocteau*], (*Watergate 14 Nov 1950*); The diary of a film—La belle et la bête [*Cocteau*], *1950;* A man named Judas [*P. Bost and C. A. Puget*], (*Devon Festival 7 Aug 1956*); The cardinal [*H. Bratt*], (*Arts, Cambridge 18 Feb 1957*); The Apollo de Bellac [*Giraudoux*], *1958;* The rabbit race [*M. Walser*], (*Edinburgh Festival 19 Aug 1963*); and The Trojan women [*Sartre*], *1967.*

§2

Eliot, T. S. A commentary [on Duncan's Townsman and The dull ass's hoof]. New Eng Weekly 5 Dec 1940.

Spender, S. Duncan's Death of Satan and Nicholson's Match for the devil. London Mag 2 1955.

Blondel, J. La thème de la découverte de soi dans le théâtre de Duncan. Etudes Anglaises 10 1957.

Weales, G. In his Religion in modern English drama, Philadelphia 1961.

Spanos, W. V. In his The Christian tradition in modern British verse drama, New Brunswick NJ 1967.

Haueter, M. W. Ronald Duncan: the metaphysical content of his plays. 1969.

THOMAS STEARNS ELIOT
1888-1965

See cols 157-201, above.

JAMES BERNARD FAGAN
1873-1933

The prayer of the sword: a play in five acts. (Adelphi 19 Sept 1904). 1904.

The earth: a modern play in four acts. (Kingsway 14 April 1909). [1910], New York 1910, London 1913 (rev).

Doctor O'Toole: a farcical comedy. (Coliseum 5 March 1917). [1938] French. Welsh trn [1938].

Hawthorne of the USA: a play in four acts. New York [1917] French.

The wheel: a play in three acts. (Apollo 1 Feb 1922; Stamford Conn 10 Nov 1922 as The wheel of life). 1922, New York 1923 (as The wheel of life).

Treasure Island: a play in four acts, based on R. L. Stevenson's story. (Strand 23 Dec 1922). 1936.

'And so to bed'—an adventure with Pepys: a comedy in three acts. (Opera House, Manchester 30 Aug 1926, Queen's 6 Sept 1926). 1927, 1929 (rev), [1930] French.

The improper duchess: a modern comedy in three acts. (Empire, Southampton 12 Jan 1931; Globe 22 June 1931). 1931, [1933] French.

The following plays were not pbd: The rebels (*1899*), Under which king (*1905*), The dressing room (*1910*), Bella Donna [*from R. Hichens' novel*] (*St James's 9 Dec 1911*), The happy island [*from the Hungarian of M. Lengyel*] (*His Majesty's 24 March 1913*), The fourth of August (*Coliseum 3 July 1916*), The flame [*adapted from C. Méré*] (*Opera House, Leicester 10 Sept 1923; Wyndham's 7 Jan 1924*) *and* The greater love (*Prince's 23 Feb 1927*). With E. Palmstierna Fagan translated Strindberg, Spook sonata, Intoxication, Easter *and* Thunderstorm *which he produced during his management of the Oxford Playhouse (1923–9). See N. Marshall, Fagan and the Oxford Playhouse, in his The other theatre, 1947.*

HERBERT FARJEON
1887–1945

Friends: a play in one act. (Abbey, Dublin 20 Nov 1917). [1923] French. Welsh trn [1936].

Advertising April: or the girl who made the sunshine jealous: a comedy in three acts. (Birmingham Repertory 9 Dec 1922; Criterion 25 Jan 1923). Oxford 1922, 1923 French (rev), New York 1923. With H. Horsnell.

Happy new year: a hard-hearted revue sketch in one act; and Your kind indulgence: a sketch in one act. [1929] French.

Kings and queens. 1932, New York 1933, London 1953 (rev), Philadelphia 1953. With E. Farjeon. Verse.

Heroes and heroines. 1933, New York 1933. With E. Farjeon. Verse.

Spread it abroad: revue. (Saville 1 April 1936). Sketches from Spread it abroad pbd [1936] French.

The two bouquets: a Victorian comedy with music. (Ambassadors 13 Aug 1936). 1936, [1938] French. With E. Farjeon. As novel by E. Farjeon 1948.

Nine sharp. (Little 26 Jan 1938). Sketches from Nine sharp pbd [1938] French. With E. Farjeon et al.

A room at the inn: a Christmas masque. (BBC Regional Service 18 Dec 1938). [1957] French. With E. Farjeon.

Nine sharp & earlier. 1938. Verse.

The Little revue. (Little 21 April 1939). More sketches from Farjeon's Little revue, 1939: a companion to Sketches from Nine sharp pbd 1938 French.

Diversions. (Wyndham's No 1, 28 Oct 1940; No 2, 2 Jan 1941). [1942] French.

Herbert Farjeon omnibus. 1942. Sketches rptd from magazines and lyrics from his revues.

The glass slipper: a fairy tale with music [by C. Parker]. (St James's 22 Dec 1944). 1946, [1948] French. With E. Farjeon. As novel by E. Farjeon 1955, New York 1956.

Herbert Farjeon's cricket bag. 1946.

The Shakespeare scene: dramatic criticisms. [1949] New York 1949.

The following were not pbd: Picnic revue (*Arts Theatre Club 20 April 1927*), Many happy returns (*Duke of York's 4 June 1928*), A masque of Neptune (*BBC Regional 13 Aug 1932*), The pursuit of Adonis (*Cambridge Festival 1932*), Why not tonight?: revue (*Palace 24 April 1934*),

London calling 1600 (*BBC National Service 18 Aug 1938*), An elephant in Arcady (*Kingsway 5 Oct 1938*), In town again: a triple Farjeon revue (*Criterion 6 Sept 1940*), Big top (*His Majesty's 8 May 1942*), Light and shade (*Ambassadors 29 July 1942*) *and* The Farjeon revue (*Royal, Windsor 6 April 1965*).

Farjeon was dramatic critic on a great number of jnls, notably Sunday Pictorial, *1917–38;* Daily Herald *1919–23;* Vogue, *1921–3 and 1927–35;* Sphere *1924–7;* Graphic *1927–32; and* Bystander *1936–42.*

He edited the Shakespeare League Journal, 1922–5; a number of edns of Shakespeare for the Nonesuch Press and the Limited Editions Club and produced a series of arrangements of Shakespeare for BBC 1943–5. His trn of Goldoni's The fan *was pbd in* Four comedies by Goldoni, *ed C. Bax 1922, and in* Goldoni: Three comedies *1961.*

JAMES ELROY FLECKER
(b. HERMAN ELROY FLECKER)
1884–1915

See cols 274–6, above.

CHRISTOPHER FRY
b. 1907

Bibliographies
Schear, B. L. and E. G. Prater. A bibliography on Fry. Tulane Drama Rev 4 1960.

Selections
Three plays: The firstborn; Thor, with angels; A sleep of prisoners. 1960, New York [1961]. The text of The firstborn is revised.

Plays. A phoenix too frequent; Thor, with angels; The lady's not for burning. 1969.

§1

The boy with a cart—Cuthman, Saint of Sussex: a play. (Colman's Hatch, Sussex 1937; BBC Third Programme 15 March 1948; Lyric, Hammersmith 19 Jan 1950). 1939, Boston 1939, London 1945 (rev), New York 1951.

A phoenix too frequent: a comedy. (Mercury 25 April 1946). 1946, New York 1950, 1953 Dramatists' Play Service, London 1959.

The firstborn: a play in three acts. (BBC Third Programme 3 Sept 1947; Gateway, Edinburgh 6 Sept 1948; Winter Garden 29 Jan 1952). Cambridge 1946, New York 1947, London 1952 (rev), New York [1958] Dramatists' Play Service.

The lady's not for burning: a comedy in verse in three acts. (Arts 10 March 1948; Globe 11 May 1949). 1949, 1950 (rev), New York 1950, 1953 Dramatists' Play Service, London 1958 (rev), New York [1960].

Thor, with angels: a play. (Chapter House, Canterbury 19 June 1948; Lyric, Hammersmith 27 Sept 1951). Canterbury 1948 (acting edn), London 1949, New York [1953] Dramatists' Play Service.

Ring round the moon: a charade with music. (Royal, Brighton 9 Jan 1950; Globe 26 Jan 1950). 1950, New York [1952] Dramatists' Play Service. Trn of J. Anouilh, L'invitation au château.

Venus observed: a play. (St James's 18 Jan 1950). 1950, New York 1953 Dramatists' Play Service.

A sleep of prisoners: a play. (University Church, Oxford 23 April 1951; St Thomas's, Regent Street 15 May 1951). 1951, New York [1953] Dramatists' Play Service.

An experience of critics; and The approach to dramatic criticism by W. A. Darlington et al. Ed K. Webb 1952, New York 1952.

The dark is light enough: a winter comedy. (Lyceum, Edinburgh 22 Feb 1954; Aldwych 30 April 1954). 1954, New York [1957] Dramatists' Play Service.

The lark. (Lyric, Hammersmith 11 May 1955). 1955. [1965] French, New York [1956], [1957] Dramatists' Play Service. Trn of J. Anouilh, L'alouette.

Tiger at the gates. (Apollo 2 June 1955). 1955, New York [1956] French. Trn of J. Giraudoux, La guerre de Troie n'aura pas licu.

Duel of angels. (Theatre Royal, Newcastle 3 March 1958; BBC Third Programme 14 Aug 1964). 1958, New York [1961] Dramatists' Play Service. Trn of J. Giraudoux, Pour Lucrèce.

Judith: a tragedy in three acts. (Her Majesty's 20 June 1962). In J. Giraudoux, Plays vol 1, tr Fry, 1963.

Curtmantle: a play. (Lyceum, Edinburgh 4 Sept 1962; Aldwych 9 Oct 1962). 1961, New York 1961, London 1965 (rev).

The programme of the revue, To sea in a sieve *by C. Harris [i.e. C. Fry] was pbd Reading 1935. The following plays have not been pbd*: Youth and the Peregrines (*Pump Room, Tunbridge Wells 1 May 1934*); Thursday's child (*Albert Hall 1 June 1939*); Siege (*Tewkesbury Festival 22 June 1939*); The tall hill (*BBC Home Service 22 Oct 1939*); The open door [*a dramatized life of Dr Barnardo*]; Rhineland journey (*BBC Home Service 14 Nov 1948*) *and* She shall have music (*Savoy 1951*). *He wrote extra lyrics for the film of* The Beggar's opera (*1953*) *and script for the film of* Ben Hur.

§2

Arrowsmith, W. Notes on English verse drama. Hudson Rev 3 1950.

Feist, H. Fry: ein metaphysischer Dramatiker. Neue Rundschau 61 1950.

Sanvic, R. Fry: dramaturge anglais. Revue Générale Belge Sept 1950.

Scott-James, R. A. Fry's poetic drama. New Statesman 7 Oct 1950.

Trewin, J. C. The plays of Fry. Adelphi 27 1950.

Astre, G. A. Fry et la résurrection du poème dramatique. Critique 7 1951.

Bewley, M. The verse of Fry. Scrutiny 18 1951.

Braybrooke, N. English poetic drama: Eliot and Fry, their recent work. Irish Monthly 79 1951.

— Modern religious drama: Fry's Sleep of prisoners. Irish Monthly 80 1952.

Morgenstern, C. Fantastical banquet. Theatre Arts Monthly 35 1951.

Nathan, G. J. In his Theatre book of the year 1950–1, 1951.

— The young man named Fry. American Mercury 72 1951.

— In his Theatre in the fifties, 1953.

Short, E. Expressionism and the expressionists: T. S. Eliot and Fry. In his Sixty years of theatre, 1951.

Spears, M. K. Fry and the redemption of joy. Poetry 78 1951.

Stanford, D. Christopher Fry: an appreciation. 1951.

— A Christopher Fry album. 1952.

— Christopher Fry. 1954, 1962 (rev) (Br Council pamphlet).

— Contemporary Rev 188 1955.

— Comedy and tragedy in Fry. Modern Drama 2 1959.

Vallette, J. Fry: dramatiste ou poète? Mercure de France 313 1951.

Behl, C. F. W. Fry. Deutsche Rundschau 78 1952.

Davis, E. Fry: the twentieth-century Shakespeare? Kansas Mag 1 1952.

Findlater, R. In his The unholy trade, 1952.

Fitzgerald, D. and P. M. Fitzgerald. The verse plays of Fry. World Rev no 38 1952. Reply by R. Gittings no 39 1952.

Leasor, J. In his Author by profession, 1952.

Corrigan, R. W. Fry and religious drama. Ivory Tower 5 1953.

Redman, B. R. Fry: poet–dramatist. College Eng 14 1953.

Ferguson, J. A sleep of prisoners. English 10 1954.

— 'The boy with a cart'. Modern Drama 8 1965.

Hagopian, J. V. Fry: poet of the theater. Folio (Indiana) 19 1954.

Lambert, J. W. Verse drama. In Theatre programme, ed J. C. Trewin, 1954

Stamm, R. Fry and the revolt against realism in modern English drama. Anglia 72 1954.

— Fry. Scholastic Rev 56 1956.

Dupont, V. L'oeuvre dramatique de Fry. Annales (Toulouse) 1955.

Koziol, H. Die Dramen Frys. Die Neueren Sprachen 4 1955.

Lemarchant, J. Fry: Le prince d'Egypte. Nouvelle Revue Française 35 1955.

MacArthur, R. The dark is light enough. Theatre Arts Monthly 39 1955.

Marcel, G. Le prince d'Egypte—The firstborn—de Fry. Les Nouvelles Littéraires 13 1955.

Merchant, W. M. The verse-drama of Eliot and Fry. Die Neueren Sprachen 4 1955.

— Reconquérir la joie. Cahiers de la Compagnie Renaud-Barrault 39 1962.

— In his Creed and drama: an essay in religious drama, 1965.

Palette, D. B. Eliot, Fry and Broadway. Arizona Quart 11 1955.

Alexander, J. Fry and religious comedy. Meanjin 15 1956.

Becker, W. Some French plays in translation. Hudson Rev 9 1956.

Dotzenrath, T. 'A phoenix too frequent': Versuch einer Deutung des Titels. Die Neueren Sprachen 5 1956.

Lokhorst, E. van. Toneelkroniek: teleurstelling en voldoening. Gids 119 1956.

Maura, S. Fry: an angle of experience. Renascence 8 1956.

Osten-Sacken, M. L. von der. Frys theatralische Sendung. Hochland 49 1956.

Woodbury, J. The witch and the nun: a study of 'The lady's not for burning'. Manitoba Arts Rev 10 1956.

Mandel, O. Theme in the drama of Fry. Etudes Anglaises 10 1957.

— Les thèmes dans l'oeuvre de Fry. Cahiers de la Compagnie Renaud-Barrault 39 1962.

Subrahmanyam, N. S. Fry and the comic spirit in modern poetic drama. Modern Rev June 1957.

Fox, R. C. Venus observed. Explicator 16 1958.

Knepler, H. W. The lark. Modern Drama 1 1958.

Spael, K. Wandlungen der Wirklichkeit im Traumspiel A sleep of prisoners. Die Neueren Sprachen 7 1958.

Adler, J. H. Shakespeare and Fry. Educational Theatre Jnl 12 1959.

Donoghue, D. Fry's theatre of words. In his Third voice, Princeton 1959.

Hooker, W. Giraudoux's last play. Hudson Rev 12 1959.

Lecky, E. Mystery in the plays of Fry. Tulane Drama Rev 4 1960.

Metwally, A. A. Fry as poet dramatist. In Cairo Stud in Eng 1960.

Otten, K. Die Überwindung des Realismus im modernen Englischen Drama. Die Neueren Sprachen 9 1960.

Dobrée, B. Fry. Literary Half-Yearly (Bangalore) 2 1961.

Erzgräber, W. Zur Liebesthematik in Frys Komödie Venus Observed. Die Neueren Sprachen 10 1961.

Pons, C. De Shakespeare à Fry. Cahiers du Sud 51 1961.

Roy, E. The imagery in the religious plays of Fry. Drama Critique 4 1961.

— The imagery in the comedies of Fry. Modern Drama 7 1964.

— The Becket plays: Eliot, Fry and Anouilh. Modern Drama 8 1965.

— Archetypal patterns in Fry. Comparative Drama 1 1967.

— Fry as tragic comedian. Modern Drama 11 1968.

—— Christopher Fry. Carbondale 1968.

Selz, J. Fry et le théâtre confidentiel. Lettres Nouvelles 9 1961.

Stemmler, T. Fry als Übersetzer. Die Neueren Sprachen 10 1961.

—— Bukolische Elemente in Frys A phoenix too frequent. Germanisch-Romanische Monatsschrift 44 1963.

—— Zur Deutung der Eigennamen in den Komödien Frys. Archiv für das Studium der Neueren Sprachen 200 1963.

Weales, G. T. S. Eliot and Christopher Fry. In his Religion in modern English drama, Philadelphia 1961.

Browne, E. M. Henry II as hero: Fry's new play, Curtmantle. Drama Survey 2 1962.

Diericks, J. King and Archbishop: Henry II and Becket from Tennyson to Fry. Revue des Langues Vivantes 28 1962.

Greene, A. Fry's cosmic vision. Modern Drama 4 1962.

Lutyens, D. B. The dilemma of the Christian dramatist: Claudel and Fry. Tulane Drama Rev 6 1962.

Urang, G. The climate is the comedy: a study of Fry's The lady's not for burning. Christian Scholar 45 1962.

Barnes, L. W. Fry: the Chestertonian concept of comedy. Xavier Univ Stud 2 1963.

Bullough, G. Fry and the 'revolt' against Eliot. In W. A. Armstrong (ed), Experimental drama, 1963.

Carnell, C. S. Creation's lonely flesh: T. S. Eliot and Fry on the life of the senses. Modern Drama 6 1963.

Parker, G. A study of Fry's Curtmantle. Dalhousie Rev 43 1963.

Itschert, H. Studien zur Dramaturgie des 'religious festival play' bei Fry. Tübingen 1964.

Louis, D. G. Tragedy in Fry and Shakespeare: a companion of Curtmantle and Richard II. College Languages Assoc Jnl 9 1965.

Prater, E. G. Fry reconsidered. Ball State Univ Forum 6 1965.

Pryce-Jones, D. Fry and verse drama. London Mag 5 1965.

Sion, G. Fry. Revue Générale Belge 160 1965.

Vos, N. The comedy of faith: the drama of Fry. Gordon Rev 8 1965.

Wiersma, S. M. A phoenix too frequent: a study in source and symbol. Modern Drama 8 1965.

Spanos, W. V. A sleep of prisoners: the choreography of comedy. Ibid.

—— In his The Christian tradition in modern British verse drama, New Brunswick NJ 1967.

Becker, S. Fry: Curtmantle. Die Neueren Sprachen 16 1967.

JOHN GALSWORTHY
1867–1933

See cols 579–86, above.

WILFRID WILSON GIBSON
1878–1962

See cols 281–2, above.

VAL HENRY GIELGUD
b. 1900

Chinese white. (Arts 13 Nov 1929). In Five three-act plays, ed W. G. Fay 1933.

How to write broadcast plays, with three examples: Friday morning (BBC 4 Feb 1932), Red tabs (1 Oct 1930), Exiles (27 Feb 1930). [1932].

Radio theatre: plays especially written for broadcasting. 1946. Includes Gielgud's Mr Pratt's Waterloo [with P. Wade] (BBC 19 Dec 1937) and Music at dusk (17 May 1939).

Away from it all: a play in two acts. (Embassy 22 Oct 1946; BBC Home Service 23 Feb 1948, as South sea bubble).

Years of the locust. 1947. Autobiography.

The right way to radio playwriting. Kingswood [1948].

Party manners: a comedy in three acts. (Buxton Opera House 22 Aug 1949; Embassy 17 Jan 1950). 1950, with introd by the author.

One year of grace: a fragment of autobiography. 1950.

British radio drama, 1922–56: a survey. 1957.

Years in a mirror. 1965. Reminiscences.

Cats: a personal anthology. 1966.

The following plays were not pbd: Self: a play in three acts (*Scala 11 July 1926*), Exiles (*BBC 27 Feb 1928*), The job (*Strand 25 March 1928*), The double man [*with E. Maschwitz*] (*1930*), Man's company (*York Repertory 1932*), I may be old-fashioned (*Piccadilly 7 Jan 1932*), Red triangle [*based on the novel* Special providence *by M. A. Hamilton*] (*Savoy 10 April 1932*), Waterloo (*BBC National 18 June 1932*), Fours into seven won't go (*BBC 16 Oct 1934*), Gallipoli (*BBC 25 April 1935*), Death at Broadcasting House: screen drama, *1935*, The sergeant major (*BBC Regional 31 Aug 1936*), Punch and Judy (*Vaudeville 22 Oct 1937*), Ending it (*BBC Regional 7 Oct 1938*), Africa flight (*Richmond 27 Feb 1939*; *broadcast BBC 4 Jan 1940*), Scott in the Antarctic (*12 July 1940*) *with* P. Cresswell, Valiant-for-truth (*BBC 11 Nov 1940*) *with* I. Vinogradoff, Life is like that (*BBC Home Service 3 May 1941*), Man's company (*BBC Home Service 5 April 1943*), Roman holiday (*BBC Home Service 28 June 1949*), Iron curtain (*Playhouse, Buxton 21 Aug 1950*; *Embassy 6 Feb 1951*), Poison in jest (*Playhouse, Buxton 3 Sept 1951*), Unhurrying chase (*BBC Light Programme 28 Feb 1954*) *with* M. G. Browne, The bombshell (*Grand, Croydon 22 March 1954*; *Westminster 11 May 1954*), In memoriam (*BBC Home Service 10 Nov 1954*) *with* E. A. Harding, By misadventure (*BBC Home Service 7 May 1955*), Mediterranean blue (*Northampton Repertory 28 May 1956*; *Richmond 15 July 1957*), Not enough tragedy (*Colchester Repertory 16 Feb 1959*; *BBC Home Service 26 Sept 1959*), The female of the species (*BBC Home Service 30 March 1959*), Fog (*BBC Light Programme 9 Jan 1964*), The goggle box affair (*serialized BBC Home Service 1964*), Over the wall (*serialized BBC Light Programme 1965*), The bad Samaritan (*BBC Home Service 20 June 1966*), Wild justice (*serialized BBC 1967–8*), Too clever by half (*BBC Home Service 23 August 1967*), Conduct of a member (*BBC Radio 4, 11 May 1968*).

Gielgud produced radio adaptations of the following: H. Belloc, Marie Antoinette (as Death of a queen) (*CBS 12 Sept 1937*), T. Maulnier, The field of kings (*BBC 12 Nov 1947*) *with* C. Pughe, S. Dagerman, Shadow of death (*BBC Third Programme 11 Jan 1950*), H. Waddell, Lyrics from the Chinese (*BBC Home Service 8 April 1956*), G. F. Bradby, The Lancaster tradition (*BBC Home Service 3 Dec 1956*), E. W. Hornung, Mr Justice Raffles (*BBC Home Service 8 Feb 1964*), A. Hope, The crimson star (*BBC Home Service 19 Dec 1964*), H. S. Merriman, The tents of Kedar (*BBC Radio 14 Oct 1967*), C. S. Forester, The Hornblower story (*serialized BBC Radio 4 1968*), W. S. Maugham, The fall of Edward Barnard (*BBC Radio 4, 21 Dec 1968*) *and* Flotsam and jetsam (*BBC Radio 4, 12 Feb 1969*).

Gielgud has also written many novels of crime and adventure.

NORMAN GINSBURY
b. 1903

Viceroy Sarah: a play in three acts. (Arts 27 May 1934). 1935, 1938 French. Adapted by M. C. Canfield and E. Borden as Anne of England in Theatre Arts 25 1941.

The first gentleman: a play in two acts. (Opera House, Manchester 2 April 1945; New 18 July 1945). 1940,

1946 (rev), 1948 French, New York 1957. Screen play 1948.

The following plays have not been pbd: Walk in the sun (*Q 23 Jan 1939*), Neighbourhood (*Q 20 Aug 1940*), The firstcomers (*Civic Playhouse, Bradford 25 July 1944*), The happy man (*New 27 June 1948*), Portrait by Lawrence (*Theatre Royal, Stratford 2 July 1949*), School for rivals (*Old Vic, Bristol 3 Oct 1949*), My dear Isabella (*BBC Home Service 17 Feb 1951*), Ladies, for you (*BBC 20 July 1952*), The recording angel (*BBC Home Service 7 Aug 1954*), The man in the next carriage (*BBC Home Service 14 July 1956*), The fabulous moneylender (*BBC Television 1959*), The plantation (*BBC Home Service 23 June 1962*), The voyage to Guiana (*BBC Home Service 18 Sept 1965*).

Ginsbury revised and completed Winifred Holtby, Take back your freedom (*ed T. Guthrie 1939*) *and adapted the following: Charles Reade*, There's many a slip (*BBC Home Service 8 March 1961*), *Ayn Rand*, Night of January 16th (*BBC Home Service 4 Aug 1962*), *Henry James*, Beltrafio (*BBC Home Service 28 Aug 1963*), *S. O. Jewett*, The only rose (*BBC Home Service 11 Aug 1964*), *W. Pett Ridge*, Old Lags' league (*in* Best one-act plays of 1960–1, *1962*).

He tr and adapted the following: H. Ibsen, Ghosts (*Buxton Festival 31 Aug 1937*; *Vaudeville 10 Nov 1937*), *1938 French*; An enemy of the people (*Old Vic 21 Feb 1939*), *1939 French*; Peer Gynt (*BBC Home Service 10 Aug 1943*; *New 31 Aug 1944*), *1946*; A doll's house (*Devonshire Park, Eastbourne 29 Oct 1945*; *Winter Garden 3 March 1946*), *1950*; Rosmersholm (*Playhouse, Sheffield 29 Feb 1960*), *1961 French*; Pillars of society (*BBC Home Service 30 May 1960*), *1962 French*; John Gabriel Borkman (*Mermaid 10 Feb 1961*), *1960 French*; *F. Dostoevsky*, The gambler (*Embassy 7 Nov 1945*), *A. Dumas, fils* The lady of the camellias (*BBC Light Programme 11 Oct 1950*) *with J. Sarch and* The queen's necklace (*BBC Home Service 29 May 1954*); *V. Sardou*, Madame Sans-gêne (*BBC Home Service 31 Aug 1957*), The story of La Tosca (*BBC Home Service 6 Sept 1958*), Poison for the king (*BBC Home Service 24 Jan 1959*), The patriots (*BBC Home Service 22 Oct 1960*); *T. Bernard*, Le petit café (*BBC Home Service 28 July 1962*); *and Strindberg*, Dance of death (*Guthrie, Minneapolis 1965*, *Arnaud, Guildford 1966*) (*in* Plays of the year, *ed J. C. Trewin, vol 32, 1966*).

RONALD GOW
b. 1897

Breakfast at eight: a play in one act. [1921] French.
The sausage: a play for three boys. [1924] (French's Plays for boys).
Under the skull and bones: a piratical play with songs in three scenes. 1929.
Higgins, the highwayman of Cranford: a play for boys. 1930.
Henry, or the house on the moor: a melodrama in one act. 1931.
Five Robin Hood plays. [1932]. The king's warrant; The sheriff's kitchen; All on a summer's day; Robin goes to sea; The affair at Kirklees.
The golden west: a farce on the instalment plan. 1932.
OHMS: a comedy in one act. (Garrick Playhouse, Altrincham, 19 Jan 1933). [1933], 1935 (Welsh trn).
Gallows glorious: a play in three acts. (Garrick Playhouse, Altrincham 13 March 1933; Shaftesbury 23 May 1933). 1933, [1937] French.
Plays for the classroom. 1933.
The vengeance of the gang: a play for boys in six scenes. 1933.
Love on the dole: a play adapted from W. Greenwood's novel. (Manchester Repertory 26 Feb 1934; Garrick

30 Jan 1935). 1935, New York [1936] French, London [1938]. Screen play 1941. With W. Greenwood.
My lady wears a white cockade: a play in three acts. (Embassy 17 July 1934). [1935], [1939] French.
Compromise: a comedy in one act. [1935].
The marrying sort: a farce in one act. [1935].
The miracle on Watling Street: a play for the open air. [1935].
Ma's bit o' brass: a comedy in three acts. (Q 31 Oct 1938). [1938].
Scuttleboom's treasure: a play for boys. [1938] (French's Plays for boys).
Grannie's a hundred: a comedy for women in one act. [1939].
Ann Veronica: made into a comedy in two acts. (Opera House, Manchester 4 May 1949; Piccadilly 20 May 1949). [1951] French. From the novel by H. G. Wells.
The lawyer of Springfield: a play in one act. (BBC Home Service July 1940). [1949], Boston 1949.
The Edwardians, from the novel by V. Sackville-West. (Royal, Windsor 14 Sept 1959; Saville 15 Oct 1959). [1960] French.
A Boston story: a comedy in three acts based on a novel, Watch and ward, by Henry James. (Royal, Windsor 14 Sept 1964 as Watch and ward; Birmingham Repertory 31 May 1966, Duchess 19 Sept 1968). 1969.
The following plays were not pbd: Lovejoy's millions (*Streatham Hill 14 Nov 1938*); Enter, Fanny Kemble (*BBC Home Service 6 May 1940*); Mr Darwin comes ashore (*BBC Home Service 14 March 1942*); Jenny Jones: musical play, adapted from stories by Rhys Davies (*Hippodrome 2 Oct 1944*); Patience on a monument (*BBC Home Service 14 Oct 1944*); Tess of the D'Urbervilles: a tragedy adapted from Hardy's novel (*New 26 Nov 1946*); Jassy, adapted from the novel by N. Lofts (*Wimbledon 20 Oct 1947*); The full treatment (*with R. Morley*) (*Q 3 Feb 1953*); Westward ho!, from C. Kingsley (*serialized BBC 1953*); Lorna Doone, from R. D. Blackmore (*serialized BBC 1953*); Mr Rhodes (*Royal, Windsor 30 Oct 1961*).

HARLEY GRANVILLE-BARKER
1877–1946

A number of typescripts and mss are held at the BM and elsewhere. See May and Morgan, Bibliographies, below.

Bibliographies

Davis, M. L. Reading list on Barker. Bull of Bibliography 7 1913.
May, F. and M. M. Morgan. A list of writings. In C. B. Purdom, Harley Granville Barker, 1955, below.

Collections

Collected plays. 1967–. (Watergate edn). Foreword by J. B. Priestley; introd by I. Brown.

§1

The marrying of Ann Leete: a comedy in four acts. (Royalty 26 Jan 1902). 1909, Boston 1916.
Prunella: or Love in a Dutch garden. (Court 23 Dec 1904). 1906, New York 1906, London 1930 (rev). With L. Housman.
Scheme and estimates for a National Theatre. 1904 (priv ptd), 1907 (as A National Theatre: schemes & estimates), New York 1908. With W. Archer. Completely rewritten by Barker alone as A National Theatre, 1930.
The Voysey inheritance: a play in five acts. (Court 7 Nov 1905). 1909, 1913 (rev), Boston 1916, London 1938 (rev), 1967 (with introd by E. R. Wood).

Waste: a tragedy in four acts. (Imperial 24 Nov 1907). 1909, Boston 1916, London 1927 (rev).

Three plays: The marrying of Ann Leete; The Voysey inheritance; Waste. 1909, New York 1909, London 1913 (with rev text of The Voysey Inheritance).

The Madras House: a comedy in four acts. (Duke of York's 9 March 1910). 1911, New York 1911, London 1925 (rev).

Rococo: a farce in one act. (Little 3 Oct 1911; Glasgow Repertory 20 Nov 1911). In Rococo, 1917 below; pbd separately 1925.

The harlequinade: an excursion. (St James's 25 Oct 1913). 1918, Boston 1918. With D. C. Calthrop.

Souls on Fifth. Boston 1916. Short story.

Vote by ballot. (Court 16 Dec 1917). In Rococo, 1917 below; pbd separately 1925.

Farewell to the theatre. In Rococo 1917 below; pbd separately 1925.

Rococo; Vote by ballot; Farewell to the theatre. 1917, Boston 1917 (as Three short plays).

The exemplary theatre. 1922, Boston 1922.

Prefaces to the Players' Shakespeare. 7 vols 1923-7 (limited edn). Pbd separately as follows: Macbeth 1923, Merchant of Venice 1923, Cymbeline 1923, Midsummer nights dream 1924, Loves labours lost 1924, Julius Caesar 1926, King Lear 1927.

The secret life: a play in three acts. 1923, Boston 1923.

From Henry V to Hamlet. [1925]. Br Acad Annual Shakespeare Lecture. Rptd (rev) in Aspects of Shakespeare, ed J. W. Mackail, Oxford 1933.

Prefaces to Shakespeare. 5 ser 1927-47, 2 vols Princeton 1946-7 (rev), London 1958, 4 vols 1963 (with foreword and notes by M. St C. Byrne). Based on Barker's prefaces to the plays included in The players' Shakespeare, 7 vols 1923-7, with the addition of prefaces to Romeo and Juliet, Antony and Cleopatra, Hamlet, Othello and Coriolanus.

His Majesty: a play in four acts. 1928, Boston 1929.

A National Theatre. 1930. See Schemes and estimates for a National Theatre, 1904, above.

On dramatic method. 1931, New York 1956. Clark lectures 1930.

Associating with Shakespeare. 1932. Address to Shakespeare Association.

The study of drama. Cambridge 1934. Lecture.

On poetry in drama: the Romanes lecture. 1937.

The perennial Shakespeare. 1937. Broadcast lecture.

Quality. 1938. Eng Assoc presidential address.

The use of drama. Princeton 1945, London 1946 (rev). Based on the Trask lectures, Princeton 1944.

According to May and Morgan, Bibliographies, above, Barker wrote the following unpbd plays: The family of the Oldroyds; The weather-hen (Terry's 29 June 1899); and Our visitor to 'work-a-day' (all 3 in collaboration with B. Thomas); Agnes Colander; A miracle (Terry's 23 March 1907); The wicked man (a fragment) (all by Barker alone); Schnitzler's Das Märchen (adapted with C. E. Wheeler; Adelphi Play Soc 28 Jan 1912); and The pied piper (with L. Housman). He adapted plays by A. Schnitzler, S. Guitry and J. Romains, and with his wife, Helen Granville-Barker, he adapted 5 plays of G. Martinez Sierra and 8 by S. and J. Álvarez Quintero. (For details of production and pbn see May and Morgan). Barker wrote an account of the Red Cross in France, 1916, and edited The eighteen-seventies: essays by Fellows of the Royal Society of Literature, 1929, A companion to Shakespeare studies, 1934 (with G. B. Harrison), and The locked book: an anthology, 1936. He contributed a number of introds and short prefaces to various works, including acting edns of The winter's tale (1912), Twelfth night (1912) and A midsummer night's dream (1914).

§2

Symons, A. In his Plays, acting and music, 1903.

Archer, W. The Vedrenne-Barker season 1904-5: a record and a commentary. [1905].

— In his The old drama and the new, 1923.

Lytton, E. B. et al. The complimentary dinner to Vedrenne and Barker: a transcript of the proceedings. 1907.

MacCarthy, D. The Court Theatre 1904-7: a commentary and criticism. 1907. With reprint of programmes.

— In his Theatre, 1954.

Walkley, A. B. In his Drama and life, 1907.

Dukes, A. In his Modern dramatists, 1911.

Henderson, A. In his European dramatists, 1914, New York 1926.

Howe, P. P. The plays of Barker. Fortnightly 94 1913.

Scott, W. Barker and an alibi. In his Men of letters, 1916.

Williams, H. In his Modern English writers, 1918.

Pearson, H. In his Modern men and mummers, 1921.

— In his The last actor-managers, 1950.

Beerbohm, M. In his Around theatres, 1924.

Morgan, A. E. In his Tendencies of modern English drama, 1924.

Sutton, G. H. In his Some contemporary dramatists, 1924.

Vernon, F. In his The twentieth century theatre, 1924.

Darlington, W. A. In his Literature in the theatre, 1925.

Murray, D. L. In his Scenes and silhouettes, 1926.

Cunliffe, J. W. In his Modern English playwrights, 1927.

Aas, L. Tre engelske Dramatikere. Tilskueren 46 1929. Barker, Ervine, Drinkwater.

Shaw, G. B. Barker: some particulars. Drama new ser 3 1946; rptd in Shaw on theatre, ed E. J. West, New York 1958.

— Letters to Barker. Ed C. B. Purdom 1956.

Downer, A. S. Sewanee Rev 55 1947.

Whitworth, G. Barker 1877-1946: reprint of a broadcast. 1948.

Bridges-Adams, W. The lost leader. 1954. With Beerbohm's portrait of Barker.

— Barker and the Savoy. Drama new ser 16 1959.

Purdom, C. B. Harley Granville Barker: man of the theatre, dramatist and scholar. 1955. Includes list of Barker's acting roles, productions and writings.

Thomas, N. K. Barker and the Greek drama. Educational Theatre Jnl 7 1955.

Morgan, M. M. and F. May. The early plays of Barker. MLR 51 1956.

Farmer, A. J. Barker. Etudes Anglaises 10 1957.

Evans, T. F. Barker: Shavian disciple. Shaw Bulletin 2 1958.

Wilson, J. D. Memories of Barker and two of his friends. In Elizabethan and Jacobean studies presented to F. P. Wilson, 1959.

Weales, G. The Edwardian theater and the shadow of Shaw. In Edwardians and late Victorians, ed R. Ellmann, New York 1960 (Eng Institute Essays 1959).

Morgan, M. M. A drama of political man: a study in the plays of Barker. 1961.

— Bernard Shaw on the tight-rope. Modern Drama 4 1962. Compares Misalliance with Barker's The Madras house.

— Two varieties of political drama: The apple cart and Barker's His Majesty. Shavian 2 1962.

Motta, S. L'esperienza drammatica di Barker. Acme 15 1962. With a list of Barker's acting roles and productions.

Norton, R. C. Hugo von Hofmannsthal's Der Schwierige and Barker's Waste. Comparative Lit 14 1962.

Winandy, D. Barker's Shakespearean theory and practice. Drama Critique 8 1966.

Aylmer, F. The one that got away. Drama Autumn 1967.

Stier, T. Barker and Shaw at the Court Theatre. Shaw Review 10 1967.

Hunt, H. Barker's Shakespearean productions. Theatre Research 10 1969.

GRAHAM GREENE
b. 1904

See cols 503–12, above.

WALTER GREENWOOD
b. 1903

Love on the dole: a tale of the two cities. 1933, New York 1934. Novel. Dramatized (with R. Gow) (Manchester Repertory 26 Feb 1934, Garrick 30 Jan 1935). 1935, New York [1936] French, London [1948]. Screen play 1941.

His worship the mayor: or 'It's only human nature after all'. 1934, New York 1935 (as The time is ripe). Novel. Dramatized as Give us this day (Torch 30 April 1940).

Standing room only: or 'A laugh in every line'. 1936, New York 1936. Novel.

The cleft stick: or 'It's the same the whole world over'. 1937, New York 1938. Stories.

Only mugs work: a Soho melodrama. [1938]. Novel.

The secret kingdom. 1938. Novel. Serialized BBC television 1960.

Something in my heart. 1944, Leeds 1969. Novel.

The cure for love: a Lancashire comedy in three acts. (Westminster 12 July 1945). [1947] French. Screen play 1949.

So brief the spring: a Cornish comedy. (Wimbledon 18 Feb 1946). 1952 (as novel).

Too clever for love: a comedy in three acts. (St George's, Kendal 8 Jan 1951). [1952] French. First produced as Never a dull moment (Coliseum, Oldham 5 July 1948).

Saturday night at the Crown: a comedy in three acts. (Royalty, Morecambe 7 June 1954; BBC Home Service 31 Dec 1955; Garrick 9 Sept 1957). [1958] French. 1959 (as novel).

What everybody wants. 1954. Novel.

Down by the sea. 1956. Novel.

There was a time. 1967. Autobiography to 1932.

Unpbd work includes the following plays: The practised hand: one act play (*1936*); My son's my son [*completed from a ms by D. H. Lawrence*] (*Playhouse 26 May 1936*); Happy birthday: one act play (*1954*), Happy days (*Coliseum, Oldham 17 Nov 1958*), Fun and games (*Victoria, Salford 28 Jan 1963*; *Alhambra, Bradford as* This is your wife); There was a time (*Dundee Repertory 23 Oct 1967*) *and the following screen plays*: No limit (*1935*), Six men of Dorset (*1944*), *Kipling's* The village that voted the earth was flat (*1945*), Eureka stockade (*1947*) *and* Chance of a lifetime (*1949*).

SIR WILLIAM TYRONE GUTHRIE
1900–71

Bibliographies

Jones, D. E. & A. Rossi. The writings of Guthrie: a selective bibliography. Drama Survey 3 1963. Includes articles.

§1

Squirrel's cage (BBC 4 March 1929) and two other microphone plays [Matrimonial views (BBC 4 June 1928) and The flowers are not for you to pick (BBC 10 April 1930)]. 1931.

Theatre prospect. 1932, Edinburgh 1933.

Top of the ladder: a play. (Glasgow Citizens' 3 April 1950; St James's 11 Oct 1950). [1952] French.

Birthday message. 1952. One-act play.

A life in the theatre. New York 1959, London 1960.

The theatre and God. Drama Survey 1 1961. A slightly revised version of a BBC television programme, 16 April 1961.

A new theatre. Toronto 1964.

Theatre at Minneapolis. In Actor and architect, by Guthrie et al, ed S. Joseph, Manchester [1964].

In various directions: a view of the theatre. [1965].

The following plays remain unpbd: Victorian nights: charade in one act (*Lyric, Glasgow 8 Nov 1927*), Gala (*BBC Scotland 6 Oct 1928*), Follow me (*Westminster 11 Nov 1932*), Haste to the wedding (*Toronto 4 May 1954*), Mitchenor's dog (*BBC Third Programme 10 May 1959*), Idols of wood and stone (*BBC Third Programme 23 Jan 1960*), Mother complex (*BBC Third Programme 30 April 1964*). *Guthrie has collaborated in 3 books on the Stratford (Ontario) Shakespeare Festival*: Renown at Stratford, Toronto 1953; Twice have the trumpets sounded, Toronto 1954; Thrice the brinded cat hath mew'd, Toronto 1955. *He adapted the following*: Lyndsay, Satire of the Three estates; Congreve, Love for love; Dumas, The three musketeers (*BBC Home Service, 14 Nov 1932*); Ibsen, Peer Gynt (*BBC Home Service 10 Aug 1943*); Maeterlinck, Interior (*BBC Home Service 9 Jan 1945*); Tennyson, Queen Mary (*BBC Home Service 8 Jan 1947*); Marlowe, Tamburlane (*BBC Home Service 14 May 1952*); Chekhov, Three sisters, *and* K. Simonov, The Russians (tr G. Shelley). *He wrote a general introd and commentaries for* The New Stratford Shakespeare (*5 plays*) *1954 and* Shakespeare: ten great plays [*1963*].

§2

Stokes, S. Guthrie. Theatre Arts 27 1943.

Findlater, R. The producer. In Theatre programme, ed J. C. Trewin 1954.

Jones, D. E. A note on the Tyrone Guthrie theatre [with photographs and plans]. Drama Survey 1 1961.

Jones, D. E. (ed). A symposium to mark the opening of the Tyrone Guthrie Repertory Theatre, Minneapolis 7 May 1963. Drama Survey 3 1963. Articles by A. Miller, F. M. Whiting, M. Saint-Denis, P. Chayefsky, N. Houghton, R. Davies, N. Marshall, D. Campbell and T. Moiseiwitsch, with selective bibliography by D. E. Jones and A. Rossi.

Hatch, R. Guthrie the artist as man of the theatre. Horizon (New York) 5 1963.

Newquist, R. Guthrie. In his Counterpoint, 1964.

WALTER HACKETT
1876–1944

The white sister: drama. (Daly's New York 2 Oct 1909). New York 1937. With F. M. Crawford.

Overnight guests: a one act comedy. (Duke of York's 1 Oct 1912). Boston 1944.

'Don't weaken': a comedy in three acts. (Maxine Elliott's, New York 15 Jan 1914). [1914] French.

It pays to advertise: a farcical fact in three acts. (Cohan Theatre, New York 2 Oct 1914; Aldwych 1 Feb 1924). 1917 French, 1928 French (rev). With R. C. Megrue.

The Barton mystery: a play in four acts. (Savoy 22 March 1916). [1930] French.

The freedom of the seas: a play in three acts. (Haymarket 1 Aug 1918). [1929] French.

Ambrose Applejohn's adventure: an Arabian Nights entertainment in three acts. (Royal, Brighton 11 July 1921, Criterion 19 July 1921). [1928] French. For US edn, *see* next.

Captain Applejack: an Arabian Nights adventure in three acts. (Cort, New York 30 Dec 1921). [1925] French.

Other men's wives: a play in three acts. (St Martin's 9 April 1928). [1929] French.

77 Park Lane: an adventure in three acts. (St Martin's 25 Oct 1928). [1929] French.

Sorry you've been troubled: a play in three acts. (St Martin's 24 Sept 1929). [1931] French; 1930 (as novel).

The way to treat a woman: a play in three acts. (Duke of York's 11 June 1930). [1931] French.

Good losers. (Whitehall 16 Feb 1931). [1933] French. With M. Arlen.

Take a chance: a comedy in three acts. (Whitehall 28 July 1931). [1933] French.

The gay adventure: a play in three acts. (Whitehall 23 Dec 1931). [1933] French.

Road house: a play in three acts. (Whitehall 6 Oct 1932). [1933] French.

Afterwards: a play in three acts. (Whitehall 7 Nov 1933). [1934] French.

Hyde Park Corner: a play in three acts. (Apollo 5 Oct 1934). [1935] French.

Intrigue: a play in three acts. [1935] French.

The fugitives: a play in a prologue and three acts. (Apollo 28 May 1936). [1937] French.

The following plays have not been pbd: The prince of dreams. (*1908*); The invaders (*1908*); Paying the price (*1908*); The regeneration (*1908*); Get busy with Emily [*from the French of G. Feydeau*] (1910); In the mountains (*1911*); Our world (*1911*); Fine feathers [*with E. Walter*] (*1912*); Honest Jim Blunt (*1912*); From 9 to 11 (*Wyndham's 14 July 1914*); He didn't want to do it: (*Prince of Wales 6 March 1915*) [*with G. Broadhurst*]; Mr & Mrs Ponsonby (*Comedy 14 June 1915*); Mr Jubilee Drax (*Haymarket 30 Sept 1916*) [with H. A. Vachell]; The profiteers [*adaptation of P. Veber's Gonzague*] (*Ambassadors 16 March 1917*); £150: war economy revue [*lyrics by D. Furber*] (*Ambassadors 30 April 1917*); The invisible foe (*Savoy 23 Aug 1917*); Mr Todd's experiment (*Queen's 30 Jan 1920*); Pansy's Arabian night (*Queen's 16 Aug 1924*); The wicked earl (*His Majesty's 22 Feb 1927*); Espionage (*Apollo 15 Oct 1935*); London after dark (*Apollo 7 April 1937*); Toss of a coin (*Vaudeville 17 March 1938*); *and* Motive for murder (*Harrow Coliseum 12 Dec 1955*).

ANTHONY WALTER PATRICK HAMILTON
1904–62

§1

Monday morning. 1925, Boston, New York 1925. Novel.

Craven House. 1926, Boston 1927, London 1943 (rev, with preface). Novel.

Twopence coloured. 1928, Boston 1928. Novel.

Rope: a play with a preface on thrillers. (Strand 3 March 1929). 1929, New York 1930 (as Rope's end). Radio play (BBC 18 Jan 1932). Filmed 1948.

The midnight bell: a love story. 1929, Boston 1930. Novel.

The siege of pleasure. 1932, Boston 1932. Novel.

The plains of cement. 1934, Boston 1935. Novel.

Twenty thousand streets under the sky: a London trilogy. Introd J. B. Priestley 1935. The midnight bell; The siege of pleasure; The plains of cement. Filmed 1962.

Money with menaces (BBC 4 Jan 1937); and To the public danger (BBC 25 Feb 1939): two radio plays. 1939.

Gas light: a Victorian thriller in three acts. (Richmond 5 Dec 1938; Apollo 31 Jan 1939). 1939, New York [1942] French (as Angel Street).

Impromptu in Moribundia. 1939. Satirical fantasy.

This is impossible: a play in one act. (BBC 27 Dec 1941). 1942 French.

Hangover Square: or, the man with two minds—a story of darkest Earl's Court in the year 1939. 1941, New York 1942. Novel. Filmed 1945.

The duke in darkness: a play in three acts. (Lyceum, Edinburgh 7 Sept 1942; St James's 8 Oct 1942). 1943.

The slaves of solitude. 1947, New York 1947 (as Riverside). Novel.

The West pier. 1951, New York 1952. Novel.

The man upstairs: a play in three acts. (Grand, Blackpool 19 Jan 1953). 1954.

Mr Stimpson and Mr Gorse. 1953. Novel.

Unknown assailant. 1955. Novel.

The following plays were not pbd: The Procurator of Judea [*adapted from Anatole France*] (*Arts 2 July 1930*), John Brown's body (*Phoenix 11 Jan 1931*), The governess (*Embassy 26 March 1946*), Caller anonymous (*BBC Home Service 7 March 1952*), Miss Roach (*adapted from* Slaves of solitude) (*BBC Home Service 4 Jan 1958*) *and* Hangover Square (*adapted from the novel*) (*BBC Home Service 8 Feb 1965*).

§2

Taylor, J. R. Patrick Hamilton. London Mag 6 1966. Study of his novels.

ST JOHN EMILE CLAVERING HANKIN
1869–1909

Bibliographies

Engel, G. In her St John Hankin als Dramatiker, Giessen 1931, below.

Collections

The dramatic works. 3 vols 1912, New York 1913. Introd by J. Drinkwater.

The plays. 2 vols 1923. New edn of the above, omitting the essays but adding Thompson.

§1

Mr Punch's Dramatic sequels. 1901, 1925 (as Dramatic sequels), New York 1926. The new wing at Elsinore [a sequel to Hamlet] was rptd in Ten modern plays, ed J. Hampden 1928.

The two Mr Wetherbys: a middle-class comedy in three acts. (Imperial 15 March 1903). [1921] French.

Lost masterpieces and other verses. 1904. Rptd from Punch.

The return of the prodigal: a comedy for fathers. (Court 26 Sept 1905). In Three plays with happy endings, 1908, below; pbd separately 1949 (introd St John Ervine).

The charity that began at home: a comedy for philanthropists. (Court 23 Oct 1906). In Three plays with happy endings, 1908, below.

The Cassilis engagement: a comedy for mothers. (Imperial 10 Feb 1907). In Three plays with happy endings, 1908, below.

The burglar who failed. (Criterion 27 Oct 1908). In Dramatic works vol 3, 1912, above.

The last of the De Mullins: a play without a preface. (Haymarket 6 Dec 1908). 1909.

Three plays with happy endings. [1908] French. The return of the prodigal; The charity that began at home; The Cassilis engagement.

The constant lover: a comedy of youth in one act. (Royalty 30 Jan 1912). [1912] French.

Thompson: a comedy in three acts. (Royalty 22 April 1913). [1913], [1924] French. Completed by G. Calderon.

Andrew Patterson (*Bijou 22 June 1893*), *written in collaboration with N. Vynne, was never pbd. His trn of E. Brieux,* The three daughters of M. Dupont *was pbd in* Three plays by Brieux, *ed Bernard Shaw 1911.*

§2

Drinkwater, J. Hankin. Forum 48 1912; rptd, slightly enlarged, as Introduction to the Dramatic works, 1912, above.

Hankin's plays. TLS 9 Jan 1913.

Howe, P. P. Hankin and his comedy of recognition. Fortnightly 93 1913.

Palmer, J. In his Future of the theatre, 1913.

Storer, E. The work of Hankin. Br Rev 5 1914.

Williams, H. In his Modern English writers, 1918.

Morgan, A. E. In his Tendencies of modern English drama, 1924.

Nicoll, A. In his British drama, 1925.

Cunliffe, J. W. In his Modern English playwrights, 1927.

Engel, G. St John Hankin als Dramatiker: Dissertation. Giessen 1931.

Ervine, St J. Introd to The return of the prodigal, 1949, above.

HAROLD MARSH HARWOOD
1874–1959

Honour thy father. (Little 15 Dec 1912). In Three one-act plays, 1926, below.

The supplanters: a play in four acts. (Royalty 15 Sept 1913, as Interlopers). 1926.

The pelican. (Playhouse 27 Jan 1916; Lyceum, New York 14 Aug 1916). 1926. With F. T. Jesse.

Please help Emily: a flirtation in three acts. (Playhouse 27 Jan 1916). 1926.

Billeted: a comedy. (Royalty 22 Aug 1917, as Lonely soldiers). [1920] French. With F. T. Jesse.

The grain of mustard seed: a play in three acts and four scenes. (Ambassadors 20 April 1920). 1926.

A social convenience: in four acts. (Royalty 22 Feb 1921). 1926.

Three one-act plays: The mask (adapted, with F. T. Jesse, from her story); Honour thy father; Confederates. 1926. The mask pbd separately 1951 [French].

The transit of Venus: a play in four acts. (Ambassadors 26 April 1927). 1927.

A girl's best friend: a play in three acts. (Ambassadors 22 Oct 1929). 1929.

The man in possession: a play in three acts and an epilogue. (Ambassadors 22 Jan 1930). 1930. Screenplay MGM 1937 as Personal property.

Confederates. (Ambassadors 24 Feb 1930). With G. Enthoven. Pbd as by Harwood alone in Three one-act plays, 1926, above.

How to be healthy though married: a play in three acts. (Strand 25 May 1930). 1930. With F. T. Jesse.

Cynara: a play in a prologue, three acts and an epilogue. (Playhouse 26 June 1930; Moresco, New York 2 Nov 1931). 1930. Adapted with R. Gore-Browne from Browne's novel An imperfect lover. Screenplay United Artists 1932.

So far and no father: a play in four scenes. (Ambassadors 16 Feb 1932). 1932.

King, queen, knave: a play in three acts. (Playhouse 17 Feb 1932). 1932. With R. Gore-Browne.

The old folks at home: a play in three acts. (Queen's 21 Dec 1933). 1934.

These mortals: a scrapbook of history from notes by H. and R. F. Gore-Browne. (Aldwych 8 Dec 1935). 1937.

Married life behind the 'scenes'. 1936. Episodes pbd in Daily Mail. With H. Dearden.

The following plays remain unpbd: The golden calf (*Globe 14 Sept 1927*), A pinch hitter (*Henry Miller, New York 6 May 1929*), A pin to see the peepshow (*New Boltons 8 May 1951*), *with F. T. Jesse, adapted from the latter's novel*, The thin line (*Whitehall 8 March 1953*) *adapted from the novel by E. Atiyah, and* The innocent party (*St James's 30 Jan 1958*) *with L. Kirk.*

Harwood translated and adapted the following: Eileen (*Globe 27 May 1922*) *by P. Armont and J. Bosquet*; Excelsior (*1928*) *by P. Armont and M. Gerbidon, and* Promise (*Shaftesbury 26 Feb 1936*) *by H. Bernstein*; *also the libretto for Beecham's production of* Figaro (*Drury Lane 11 July 1917*).

He wrote the following screen plays: Looking forward (*1933*) *adapted from C. L. Anthony's play*, Service; Queen Christina (*1934*) *with S. Viertel, founded on a story by S. Viertel and M. B. Leving*; *and* The iron duke (*1934*).

With G. Grossmith he wrote the book for Novello and Kern's Theodore & Co. (*Gaiety* 19 Sept 1916).

CHRISTOPHER VERNON HASSALL
1912–63

§1

Glamorous night: a romantic play with music by I. Novello, lyrics by Hassall. (Drury Lane 2 May 1935). 1938 (vocal score), [1939] French.

Poems of two years. 1935.

Careless rapture: a musical play by I. Novello, lyrics by Hassall. (Drury Lane 11 Sept 1936). 1936 (vocal score).

Devil's dyke, with Compliment and satire. 1936. Verse. Devil's dyke produced at the Oxford Festival 1937.

Christ's comet—the story of a thirty years' journey that began and ended on the same day: a play in three acts. (Canterbury Cathedral 25 June 1938; BBC Third Programme 25 Dec 1946). 1937, New York [1938], London 1958 (rev, in 2 acts with preface).

Penthesperon. [1938]. Verse.

The dancing years: a musical play by I. Novello, lyrics by Hassall. (Drury Lane 23 March 1939). 1939 (vocal score), [1953] French.

Crisis. 1939. Verse.

S.O.S.... 'Ludlow'. 1940. Verse.

Notes on the verse drama. 1948. (The Masque no 6).

The timeless quest: Stephen Haggard. 1948.

King's rhapsody: a musical romance by I. Novello, with lyrics by Hassall. (Palace 15 Sept 1949). 1949 (vocal score), [1955] French.

The slow night and other poems, 1940–48. 1949.

The rainbow: a tale of Dunkirk, set to music by T. Wood. [1951] (vocal score).

Voices of night: a cantata by F. Reizenstein, text composed and arranged by Hassall. (BBC Third Programme 21 June 1952). [1952] (vocal score).

The player king. (Royal Court, Liverpool 18 Aug 1952, Edinburgh Festival 26 Aug 1952; BBC Home Service 22 Nov 1954). 1953.

Words by request: a selection of occasional pieces in verse and prose. 1952.

Out of the whirlwind: a play for Westminster Abbey. (10 June 1953). 1953.

Eddie Marsh: sketches for a composite literary portrait. 1953. With D. Mathews.

Salutation, by E. Rubbra, words by Hassall. 1953 (vocal score).

Troilus and Cressida: opera in three acts by W. Walton, libretto by Hassall. (Covent Garden 3 Dec 1954). 1954.

The red leaf: poems. 1957.

Genesis: an oratorio by F. Reizenstein, text by Hassall [1958] (vocal score).

Edward Marsh, patron of the arts: a biography. 1959, New York 1959 (as A biography of Edward Marsh).

Tobias and the angel: an opera in two acts, libretto by Hassall, music by A. Bliss. (BBC Television 19 May 1960). 1962.

Bell Harry and other poems. 1963, New York 1964.

Mary of Magdala: a cantata by A. Bliss, text by Hassall. 1963 (vocal score).

Poems for children, with drawings by D. A. H. Morgan. 1963.

Valley of Song: a musical romance in three acts by I. Novello, lyrics by Hassall, book by P. Park. (Grand, Blackpool 2 March 1964; Toynbee Hall 4 March 1965). [1964] (acting edn).

Ambrosia and small beer: the record of a correspondence [with E. Marsh]. 1964, New York 1965.

Rupert Brooke: a biography. 1964, New York 1964.

The following were unpbd: The great endeavour (*Drury Lane Nov 1948*); The story of G. F. Handel (*BBC, 5 pts March–April 1949*); Dear Miss Phoebe: a musical play, *based on Barrie's* Quality Street, *music by H. P. Davies* (*Royal, Birmingham 31 July 1950*; *Phoenix 13 Oct 1950*); Tomorrow, Mr Tompion, and about time too (*BBC Home Service 19 Jan 1956*) *with C. Brahms*; *the dramatisation of Beddoes'* Death's jest book (*BBC Third Programme 4 June 1957*); *and* The song of Simeon, a nativity play, *with music by M. Arnold* (*Drury Lane 5 Jan 1960*). *Hassall also wrote the lyrics for Novello's unpbd* Crest of the wave (*Drury Lane 1 Sept 1937*) *and* Arc de triomphe (*Phoenix 9 Nov 1943*), *and the words for A. Hopkins'* The man from Tuscany (*Canterbury Cathedral 20 July 1951*), *T. Wood's cantata* Yggdrasil (*Bryanston Summer School 1951*) *and F. Reizenstein's radio opera* Anna Kraus (*BBC Sept 1952*).

He produced English versions of Dvorak's Rusalka *and Rimsky-Korsakov's* Kitesh (*both probably unpbd*) *and of C. Zuckmayer's* The devil's general (*Lyceum 17 Aug 1953*; *Savoy 23 Sept 1953*) *with R. Gore-Booth*; The merry widow (*Sadler's Wells 20 Jan 1958*); Die Fledermaus (*Coliseum 15 Apr 1959*); The land of smiles (*Coliseum 9 July 1959*); *Donizetti's* Il Campanello (*New York 1960*; *Bartok's* Bluebeard's castle, *1963*; *and Prokofieff's* The fiery angel, *1965*.

He edited The unpublished poems of Stephen Haggard, *1945, the P.E.N. anthology* New Poems (*with R. Warner and L. Lee*) *1954, and* The prose of Rupert Brooke, *1956.*

§2

Leasor, L. In his Author by profession, 1952.
Weales, G. In his Religion in modern English drama, Philadelphia 1961.
Spanos, W. V. In his The Christian tradition in modern British verse drama, New Brunswick NJ 1967.

'IAN HAY',
JOHN HAY BEITH
1876–1952

See cols 598–600, above.

SIR ALAN PATRICK HERBERT
1890–1971

See cols 288–90, above.

MERTON HODGE
(HORACE EMERTON HODGE)
1904–58

The wind and the rain: a play in three acts. (Opera House, Manchester 9 Oct 1933; St Martin's 18 Oct 1933). 1934, [1938] French. 1936 as novel. The original version of this play, As it was in the beginning, was produced at the Arts 4 June 1932.
Grief goes over: a play in three acts. (Opera House, Manchester 20 May 1935; Globe 6 June 1935). 1935, [1936] French.
The island: a play in three acts. (Q 26 July 1937; Comedy 10 Feb 1938). 1938, [1939] French.
Story of an African farm: a play in three acts. (New 30 Nov 1938). 1939. Based on O. Schreiner's novel.
The following plays were not pbd: Men in white (*Lyric 4 June 1934*), *an adaptation of the play by S. S. Kingsley*; The orchard walls (*St James's 3 Feb 1937*), *adapted from the Hungarian of L. Fodor*; To whom we belong (*Q 11 Dec 1939*); *and* Once there was music (*Q 10 March 1942*).

WILLIAM STANLEY HOUGHTON
1881–1913

Collections

Five one act plays: The dear departed; Fancy free; The master of the house; Phipps; The fifth commandment. 1913.
The works of Stanley Houghton, ed H. Brighouse 3 vols 1914. Vol 1, Independent means; Marriages in the making; The younger generation. Vol 2, Partners; Hindle wakes; The perfect cure. Vol 3, One-act plays—The old testament and the new; The dear departed; The master of the house; The fifth commandment; Fancy free; Phipps. Dramatic criticism; Essays and sketches; Short stories; Life—an unfinished novel.

§1

The dear departed: a comedy in one act. (Gaiety, Manchester 2 Nov 1908; Coronet 7 June 1909). [1910] French. Scots version by F. Fair as Twixt cup and lip, pbd [1937] French.
Independent means: a comedy in four acts. (Gaiety, Manchester 30 Aug 1909). [1911] French.
The master of the house. (Gaiety, Manchester 26 Sept 1910; Coronet 8 May 1912). In Five one-act plays, 1913, above. A Scots version by F. Fair as A tartar caught pbd [1937] French.
The younger generation: a comedy for parents in three acts. (Gaiety, Manchester 21 Nov 1910; Coronet 8 May 1912; Haymarket 4 Nov 1912). [1910] French, New York 1918.
Fancy free: a fantastic comedy in one act. (Gaiety, Manchester 6 Nov 1911; Tivoli 17 June 1912). [1912] French.
Hindle wakes: a play in three acts. (Aldwych 16 June 1912). 1912, New York 1913 French. Screen plays: Gaumont British 1932, Monogram 1952.
Phipps. (Garrick 19 Nov 1912). In Five one-act plays, 1913, above.
The perfect cure: a comedy in three acts. (Apollo 17 June 1913). In The works of Stanley Houghton, vol 2, 1914, above.
The fifth commandment. (Gaiety, Manchester 14 July 1914). In Five one-act plays, 1913, above.
The old testament and the new. (Gaiety, Manchester 22 June 1914). In The works of Stanley Houghton, vol 3, 1914, above.
The following plays remain unpbd: The intriguers (*1906*) *with F. Nasmith*; The day of reckoning (*Crown, Eccles 4 Sept 1912*); Pearls (*Coliseum 6 Jan 1913*); Trust the people (*Garrick 6 Feb 1913*); *and* Ginger (*Royal, Halifax 26 Sept 1913*).
The dramatic criticism, stories, etc were mostly contributed to Manchester Guardian, *1907–12.*

§2

Archer, W. In his Old drama and the new, 1923.
Morgan, A. E. In his Tendencies of modern English drama, 1924.
Cunliffe, J. W. In his Modern English playwrights, New York 1927.
Pogson, R. In his Miss Horniman and the Gaiety Theatre, Manchester 1952.

RICHARD ARTHUR WARREN
HUGHES
b. 1900

See col 607, above.

NORMAN CHARLES HUNTER
1908–71

Let's fight till six, by 'Noel Nicholson' [i.e. N. C. Hunter]. [1933].

Marriage with Nina. New York 1934.

The servitors. 1934. Novel.

All rights reserved: a comedy in three acts. (Criterion 30 April 1935). [1935] French.

Riot. [1935] Novel.

Ladies and gentlemen (Strand 18 May 1937). 1937.

A party for Christmas: a comedy in three acts. (Haymarket 26 Oct 1938). [1938] French.

Grouse in June: a farcical comedy in three acts. (Richmond 24 April 1939, as Galleon Gold; Criterion 6 May 1939). 1939, 1943 French.

The ascension of Mr Judson. 1949. Novel.

The losing hazard. 1950. Novel.

The Romsea Romeo. [1950] Novel.

Waters of the moon: a comedy in three acts. (Royal, Brighton 26 March 1951; Haymarket 19 April 1951). [1951] Guild.

Adam's apple: a Victorian fairy tale in three acts. (Royal, Brighton 14 April 1951; Leas Pavilion, Folkestone 16 July 1951, as Now the serpent...; Golders Green Hippodrome 28 April 1952, as Adam's apple). [1953] Guild.

A day by the sea: a play in three acts. (Royal Court, Liverpool 26 Oct 1953; Haymarket 26 Nov 1953). [1954] Guild.

A picture of autumn: a comedy in three acts. (BBC Home Service 25 Feb 1956). [1957] Guild.

A touch of the sun: a play in three acts. (Grand, Blackpool 6 Jan 1958; Saville 31 Jan 1958). [1958] Guild.

The tulip tree: a play in three acts. (Haymarket 29 Nov 1962). [1964] Guild.

The excursion: a comedy in three acts. (Ashcroft, Croydon 10 Feb 1964). [1964] Guild.

The following plays remain unpbd: The merciless lady (*1934*) *with J. Ferguson; Hunter's English version of* Little Stranger *by K. Hilliker and H. H. Caldwell* (*Royalty 10 Aug 1938*); The Cooneen ghost (*BBC Radio Belfast 19 June 1939*); The phantom island (*BBC Home Service 13 Aug 1941*); Smith in Arcady (*Embassy 2 Feb 1947*); The affair at Assino (*Royal, Windsor 13 Nov 1950*); The clerk's story (*BBC Home Service 6 Jan 1958*); A piece of silver (*Everyman, Cheltenham 2 May 1960*); Henry of Navarre (*BBC Home Service 24 Oct 1966*) *adapted from the biography by H. Pearson; and* The adventures of Tom Random (*Yvonne Arnaud, Guildford 19 Sept 1967*).

ALDOUS LEONARD HUXLEY
1894–1963

See cols 609–17, above.

CHRISTOPHER WILLIAM BRADSHAW ISHERWOOD
b. 1904

See cols 619–20, above.

WILLIAM WYMARK JACOBS
1863–1943

See cols 620–1, above.

GERTRUDE ELEANOR JENNINGS
1877–1958

§1

Between the soup and the savoury. (Albert Hall 31 May 1910; Playhouse 19 Oct 1910; Lyceum, New York 2 Jan 1916). In Four one-act plays, 1914, below.

A woman's influence: a play in one act. [1913].

Acid drops: a play. (Royalty 28 Feb 1914). [1914] French.

The rest cure: a playlet. (Vaudeville 10 March 1914). In Four one-act plays, 1914, below.

Four one-act plays: The rest cure; Between the soup and the savoury; The pros and the cons; Acid drops. 1914. French.

Poached eggs and pearls: a canteen comedy in two scenes. (Apollo 21 Nov 1915). [1917] French.

Five birds in a cage: a play in one act. [1915] French. Also pbd in J. W. Marriott's One-act plays of today, 4th ser, 1928.

The bathroom door: a farce in one act. (Victoria Palace 10 Jan 1916). [1916] French.

The pros and the cons. (Lyceum, New York 31 Jan 1916). In Four one-act plays, 1914, above.

Elegant Edward: a comedy in one act. (Haymarket 30 May 1916). [1919] French. With C. Boulton.

No servants: a comedy in one act. (Prince's 17 April 1917). [1919] French.

Waiting for the 'bus: a one-act play. (Haymarket 26 June 1917). [1919] French.

Allotments. [1918]. French.

At the ribbon counter: a play in one act. [1919] French.

The young person in pink: a play. (Prince of Wales's 10 Feb 1920 [one matinee only]; Haymarket 29 March 1920). [1921] French.

Bobbie settles down: a comedy. (Coliseum 15 March 1920). [1920] French.

'I'm sorry—it's out!': a comedy in one act. (A.D.A. 30 March 1920). [1920] French.

In the cellar: a play in one act. [1920] French.

The new poor: a farce in one act. [1920] French.

Love among the paint pots: a comedy in three acts. (Aldwych 2 May 1921). [1922] French.

Mother-of-pearl: a play in one act. (Winter Garden 30 May 1921). [1921] French.

'Me and my diary': a comedy in one act. (Strand 19 Jan 1922). 1921 French.

Money doesn't matter: a comedy. (Aldwych 31 Jan 1922). [1922] French.

Calais to Dover: a farce in one act. (Academy 23 July 1922). [1922] French.

Hearts to sell. [1922] French.

The secret of the castle. [1922] French.

Isabel, Edward and Anne: a comedy in three acts. (Haymarket 31 March 1923). [1923] French.

Cat's claws: a comedy in one act. (New 20 Jan 1925). [1923] French.

Oh, these authors!: a comedy in two scenes. (New 3 April 1925). [1925] French.

Fireworks: a comedy in one act. [1927] French.

Have you anything to declare?: a farce. [1927] French.

'Spot': a comedy for two people. [1927] French.

These pretty things: a farcical comedy in three acts. (Garrick 14 Dec 1928). [1930] French.

Scraps: a comedy in one act. [1928] French.

The helping hands: a farce in one act. [1930] French.

The bride: a comedy in one act. [1931] French.

Pearly gates: a comedy in one act. [1931] French.

Family affairs: a comedy in three acts. (Ambassadors 22 Aug 1934). 1934, [1935] French.

Our own lives: a comedy. (Ambassadors 27 Nov 1935). 1935.

The christening: a comedy in one act. In The one-act theatre: new comedies and dramas, 1936. Pbd separately [1937] French.
How now, brown cow!: a comedy in one act. [1937] French.
Knit one, purl one: a comedy in one act. [1938] French.
Good neighbours: a one-act comedy for three women. [1942] French.
In the black out: a farce in one act. [1942] French.
Whiskers and Co: a Cinderella pantomime in three scenes. [1943] French.
A sleeping beauty pantomime in two acts. [1944] French.
Too much Bluebeard: a farce in three scenes. [1944] French.
Puss in the corner: a play in one act. [1946] French.
Aladdin's cave: a pantomime in two acts. [1947] French.
Happy as a king: a comedy in one act. [1947] French.
In the fog: a farce in one act. [1947] French.
Bubble and squeak in three acts. [1948] French.
I'll pay your fare: a comedy in one act. [1951] French.
The Olympian: a comedy in three acts. (Pavilion, Folkestone 18 Oct 1954). [1955] French.
Happy memories. (Northampton Repertory 25 April 1955). [1955] French.
The following plays were not pbd: Uncle Robert's airship (Albert Hall 31 May 1910); Our nervous system (Playhouse 15 April 1911); The 'mind the gates' girl: a futurist cubist harlequinade (His Majesty's 21 May 1912) with H. Graham, D. C. Calthrop and N. Playfair; The girl behind the bar (Finsbury Park Empire 17 June 1912); The lady in red (Coliseum 23 July 1917); After the war (Playhouse, Liverpool 27 Sept 1917); and Richmond Park (Coliseum 12 Dec 1927).
Gertrude Jennings also adapted the musical comedy, Riquette, by R. Schanzer and E. Welisch (Kings, Glasgow 21 Dec 1925).

§2

Sutton, G. In his Some contemporary dramatists, 1924.

DENIS WILLIAM JOHNSTON
b. 1901

Collections

Collected plays. 2 vols 1960, 1 vol Boston 1960 (as The old lady says 'No!' and other plays). With introds by Johnston.

§1

The old lady says 'No!': a romantic play with choral interludes in two parts. (Gate, Dublin 3 July 1929). In The moon in the yellow river, 1932 below.
The moon in the yellow river: a play in three acts by 'E. W. Tocher' [i.e. D. Johnston]. (Abbey, Dublin 27 April 1931; Guild, New York 29 Feb 1932; Westminster 24 Sept 1934). In The moon in the yellow river 1932, below. Pbd separately New York 1933 (French), London 1934, 1949 (rev).
The moon in the yellow river and The old lady says 'No!': two plays. 1932.
A bride for the unicorn: an imaginary adventure in play form. (Gate, Dublin 9 May 1933; Westminster 3 July 1933). In Storm Song 1935, below.
Storm song: a play in three acts. (Gate, Dublin 30 Jan 1934; Embassy 6 July 1936). In Storm song, 1935 below.
Storm song and a bride for the unicorn: two plays. 1935.
Blind man's buff: a play in three acts. (Abbey, Dublin 26 Dec 1936; BBC Home Service 22 Aug 1949; St Martin's 14 Oct 1953). 1948. With E. Toller, adapted from Toller's Die blinde Göttin.
The golden cuckoo. (Duchess 2 Jan 1940). In The golden cuckoo and other plays, 1954, below.

The dreaming dust. (Gate, Dublin 25 March 1940; BBC Television 21 Aug 1947, as Weep for the Cyclops). In The golden cuckoo and other plays, 1954, below.
A fourth for bridge: a war play in one act. In The golden cuckoo and other plays, 1954, below.
The golden cuckoo and other plays. 1954.
'Strange occurrence on Ireland's eye': a play about a murder trial. (Abbey, Dublin 20 Aug 1956). In Collected plays, vol 2, 1960, above. Rev version of Blind man's buff.
The scythe and the sunset: a play in three acts. (Poets' Theatre, Cambridge, Mass, 14 March 1958; Abbey, Dublin 19 May 1958; Questor's, Ealing 14 June 1958). In Collected plays, vol 1, 1960, above.
In search of Swift. Dublin 1959. Biography.
John Millington Synge. New York 1965. (Columbia essays on modern writers).
Johnston wrote the following unpbd radio and television plays: Death at Newtonstewart (BBC Regional 7 Oct 1937; BBC Television 4 Jan 1948) Multiple studio blues (BBC Regional 24 Nov 1938); Nansen of the 'Fram' (BBC Home Service 23 Feb 1940); The gorgeous Lady Blessington (BBC Home Service 21 Aug 1941); Weep for Polyphemus (BBC Home Service 19 Oct 1945) (about Swift); Not one returns to tell (BBC N. Ireland 14 Feb 1946); The unthinking lobster (BBC Television 18 Aug 1948); and The call to arms (BBC Television 10 June 1949).
Johnston was director of the Gate Theatre, Dublin 1931–6, BBC feature-programme writer and producer, 1937–42, BBC Television programme director, 1946–7. He pbd 2 books on his experiences as BBC war correspondent, Dionysia (1949) and Nine rivers from Jordan (1953). Since 1948 he has been writing and producing for American radio and Radio Eireann.

§2

MacLiammoir, M. Problem plays. In The Irish theatre, ed L. Robinson, 1939.
Spinner, K. Die alte Dame sagt Nein! Drei irische Dramatiker: L. Robinson, O'Casey, Johnston. Berne [1961] (Schweizer Anglistische Arbeiten 52).
Hogan, R. The adult theatre of Johnston. In his After the Irish renaissance, Minneapolis 1967.

JAMES AUGUSTINE ALOYSIUS JOYCE
1882–1941

See cols 444–72, above.

MARGARET MOORE KENNEDY
1896–1967

See cols 626–7, above.

WILLIAM STEPHEN RICHARD KING-HALL, BARON KING-HALL
1893–1966

Verses from the Grand Fleet. By 'Etienne (Lt. R.N.)' [i.e. S. King-Hall]. 1917.
Strange tales from the Fleet. By 'Etienne'. 1919.
The romantic adventure. 1926. Novel.
The uncharted sea. 1926. Novel.
The middle watch: a romance of the Navy in three acts. (Shaftesbury 12 Aug 1929). [1931] French. With 'Ian Hay' (J. H. Beith). Screen plays: British International 1930, Associated British 1940.

B. J. One: a play in one act. (Globe 9 April 1930). [1930] French (3rd act only). Full text in Three plays and a plaything, 1933, below.

The midshipmaid: a naval manoeuvre in three acts. (Shaftesbury 10 Aug 1931). [1932] French. With 'Ian Hay' (J. H. Beith). Screen play: Gaumont British 1937.

Post-war pirate. 1931. Novel.

Bunga-Bunga. 1932, New York [1933]. Novel.

Three plays and a plaything: 1, The Republican-princess: a satirical farce in three acts; 2, The second generation; 3, B. J. One; 4, Posterity. 1933.

Admirals all: an amphibious adventure in three acts. (Shaftesbury 6 Aug 1934). [1935] French. With 'Ian Hay' (J. H. Beith).

Off the record: a naval comedy in three acts. (King's, Edinburgh 17 March 1947; Apollo 3 June 1947). [1949] French. With 'Ian Hay' (J. H. Beith). Screen play: Renown Pictures, 1957, as Carry on Admiral.

Number 10 Downing Street: a political play in two acts and five scenes. (Bolton's 10 May 1949). [1948].

The Trumpeter (*BBC Home Service 22 Dec 1956*), *a dramatization by C. Pughe of the short story by King-Hall, has not been pbd. King-Hall was a prolific writer on political and naval affairs, broadcaster and founder of the King-Hall News Letter Service (1936) and the Hansard Society (1944).*

EDWARD KNOBLOCK
(KNOBLAUCH)
1874–1945

Selections

Kismet and other plays. Introd by J. Vere, 1957. Kismet; The faun; Milestones: My Lady's dress.

§1

The faun: a comedy in three acts. (Daly's, New York 15 Jan 1911; Prince of Wales's 10 June 1911). In Kismet and other plays, 1957, *see* Selections above.

Kismet: an 'Arabian night' in three acts. (Garrick 19 April 1911). New York, Toronto 1911, London 1912. Screen plays: International Motion Pictures 1931; MGM 1935. Adapted as musical comedy by C. Lederer and L. Davis, 1953.

Milestones: a play in three acts. (Royalty 5 March 1912; Liberty, New York 12 Sept 1912). 1912, New York [1912]. With A. Bennett.

The headmaster: a domestic comedy in four acts. (Playhouse 22 Jan 1913). New York [1913] French, London [1916] French. With Wilfred T. Coleby (T. Pellatt).

My lady's dress: a play in three acts. (Royalty 23 April 1914). Ottawa 1914, New York 1916 (with introd by F. C. Brown).

'Marie-Odile': a play in three acts. (Belasco, New York 26 Jan 1915; His Majesty's 8 June 1915). New York [1915]; rptd in The lullaby and other plays, 1924, below.

A war committee and The little silver ring. 1915 French.

'Paganini': a play in three acts. (Criterion, New York 11 Sept 1916). New York [1915].

Cot 5. 1917 (anon), 1918 (adds one poem).

Tiger! Tiger! a play in four acts. (Belasco, New York 12 Nov 1918; Strand 30 May 1920). In The lullaby and other plays, 1924, below.

Our Peg: a musical play in three acts, founded upon Masks and faces [by Tom Taylor and C. Reade], lyrics by H. Graham. (Prince's, Manchester 24 Dec 1919). [1929] French.

Three plays: Mumsee (Little 20 Feb 1920); One (Belasco, New York 5 Sept 1920); Cherry: musical play by M. Gideon, book by Knoblock (Apollo 22 July 1920). 1920.

The lullaby (Knickerbocker, New York 17 Sept 1923; Globe 6 Nov 1925) and other plays: 'Marie-Odile' and Tiger! Tiger! 1924. Introd by G. P. Baker. The screen play of The lullaby (MGM 1931) was entitled The sin of Madelon Claudet.

London life: a play in three acts and nine scenes. (Drury Lane 3 June 1924). 1924, New York 1924. With A. Bennett.

The mulberry bush: a comedy. (Republic, New York 26 Oct 1927; Criterion 29 April 1930). 1930.

Mr Prohack: a comedy in three acts. (Court 16 Nov 1927). 1927. With A. Bennett, adapted from Bennett's novel.

The ant heap. 1929, New York 1930. Novel.

Grand Hotel: a play. (National, New York 18 Nov 1930; Adelphi 5 Sept 1931). 1931. Adapted from the novel by V. Baum.

The good companions: a play in two acts. (His Majesty's 14 May 1931). [1935] French. With J. B. Priestley, adapted from Priestley's novel.

The man with the two mirrors. 1931. Novel.

Evensong: a play in three acts. (Queen's 30 June 1932). [1933] French. With B. Nichols, adapted from Nichols' novel.

The love lady. 1933. Novel.

A charity committee: a comedy for nine women. (Haymarket 20 June 1938). [1939] French.

The ladies of Cranford: a play in two scenes. [1938] French. Dramatized from Mrs Gaskell's Cranford.

Round the room: an autobiography. 1939.

Inexperience. 1941. Novel.

Bird of passage. 1943. Novel.

The following plays were not pbd: The Shulamite (*Savoy 12 May 1906*) *with C. Askew, adapted from a novel by A. and C. Askew*; The cottage in the air (*New, New York 30 Oct 1909*); Sister Beatrice (*1910*) (*adaptation of Maeterlinck's play*); Discovering America (*Daly's, New York 1 Sept 1912*); England expects (*Drury Lane 30 Sept 1914*) *with S. Hicks*; Hajj (*Palace 22 Feb 1915*); The way to win (*Coliseum 14 June 1915*); How to get on (*Victoria Palace 12 July 1915*); Long live England (*Botanical Gardens, Regents Park 20 July 1915*); Mouse (*Royalty 5 Dec 1915*); The hawk (*Royalty 20 Sept 1916*) *adapted from the play by F. de Croisset*; Home on leave (*Royalty 18 Oct 1916*); Simon, called Peter (*Klaw Theatre, New York 10 Jan 1922*) *with J. E. Goodman, adapted from the novel by R. Keable*; Conchita (*Queen's 19 March 1924*); Speakeasy (*Mansfield, New York 26 Sept 1927*) *with G. Rosener*; Hatter's castle (*1932*) (*adapted from the novel by A. J. Cronin*); If a body (*1935*) (*adaptation from the French*) *with G. Rosener*; The Edwardians (*Richmond 19 April 1937*) (*from the novel by V. Sackville-West*); *and* Rolling stone (*Richmond 26 June 1939*).

Knoblock wrote several filmscripts, including The three musketeers (*1921*) (*with D. Fairbanks*); Rosita (*1923*); The thief of Baghdad; Red wagon; Evensong; Chu-chin-chow (*1934*); *and* Moonlight sonata (*1937*) (*based on a story by H. Rameau*).

DAVID HERBERT LAWRENCE
1885–1930

See cols 481–503 above.

BENN WOLFE LEVY
b. 1900

This woman business: a play in three acts. (Royalty 18 Oct 1925; Ritz, New York 7 Dec 1926). 1925, Boston 1927.

A man with red hair. (Little 27 Feb 1928; Garrick, New York 8 Nov 1928). 1928. From the novel by H. Walpole.

Mud & treacle—or the course of true love: a shameless tract in three acts, and a post-dated prologue. (Globe 9 May 1928). 1928.

Mrs Moonlight: a piece of pastiche in three acts. (Kingsway 5 Dec 1928). 1929, New York 1931 (with Art and Mrs Bottle, below).

Art and Mrs Bottle—or the return of the Puritan: a comedy in three acts. (Empire, Southampton 21 Oct 1929; Criterion 12 Nov 1929; Maxine Elliott's, New York 18 Nov 1930). 1929, New York 1931 (with Mrs Moonlight, above).

The devil: a religious comedy in three acts and a prologue. (Arts 12 Jan 1930; Selwyn, New York 4 Jan 1932 as The devil passes). 1930, New York 1932 French.

Hollywood holiday: an extravagant comedy in three episodes. (New 15 Oct 1931). 1931. With J. Van Druten.

Springtime for Henry: a farce in three acts. (Bijou, New York 9 Dec 1931; King's, Southsea 1 Nov 1932; Apollo 8 Nov 1932). 1932, New York [1932].

The jealous god: a play in four acts. (King's, Edinburgh 30 Jan 1939; Lyric 1 March 1939). 1939.

Clutterbuck: an artificial comedy. (New, Hull 2 June 1946; Wyndham's 14 Aug 1946; Biltmore, New York 3 Dec 1949). 1947, New York [1950] Dramatists' Play Service, London [1951] French.

Return to Tyassi. (Royal, Brighton 20 Nov 1950; Duke of York's 29 Nov 1950). 1951.

Cupid and Psyche. (King's, Edinburgh 31 March 1952). 1952.

The great healer: a play in one act. (BBC Television 14 Sept 1952). [1954] French.

The island of Cipango: a play in one act. (BBC Television 14 Sept 1952). [1954] French.

The rape of the belt: a comedy. (Grand, Leeds 12 Nov 1957; Piccadilly 12 Dec 1957; Martin Beck, New York 5 Nov 1960). 1957, [1957] French.

Public and confidential. (Malvern Festival 26 July 1966; Duke of York's 17 Aug 1966). 1968 Evans (as The member for Gaza).

The following plays have not been pbd: Topaze (*New 1 Oct 1930*) (*adapted from the play by M. Pagnol*); Evergreen (*Adelphi 3 Dec 1930*) (*screenplay 1935*); The church mouse (*Playhouse 16 April 1931*) (*adapted from the play by L. Fodor and S. Geyer*); Young Madame Conti (*Savoy 13 Nov 1936*) (*from the play by B. Frank*); and Madame Bovary (*Broadhurst, New York 15 Nov 1937*) (*screen play 1937*).

Levy wrote several film scripts, including The old, dark house (*1932*) (*founded on the novel,* Benighted, *by J. B. Priestley*); The dictator (*1935*); Farewell to love (*1935*).

ERIC ROBERT RUSSELL
LINKLATER
b. 1899

See cols 636–8, above.

'FREDERICK LONSDALE',
LIONEL FREDERICK LEONARD
1881–1954

§1

Aren't we all?: a comedy in three acts. (Globe, New York 10 April 1923). New York [1924], London [1925], French [1935]. Screen plays: 1925 (as A kiss in the dark) and 1932.

Spring cleaning: a comedy in three acts. (Adelphi, Chicago 9 Sept 1923; Eltinge, New York 9 Nov 1923; St Martin's 29 Jan 1925). [1925], [1930] French. Screen play 1924 (as The fast set).

The fake: a play in three acts. (Apollo 13 March 1924). [1927] French.

The street singer: a musical play in three acts. (Lyric 27 June 1924). [1929] French. Lyrics by P. Greenbank, music by H. Fraser-Simson.

The last of Mrs Cheyney: a comedy in three acts. (St James's 22 Sept 1925). [1925], [1929] French. Novelized by D. G. Herriot 1930. Screen plays: 1929, 1937, 1951 (as The law and the lady).

On approval: a comedy in three acts. (Gaiety, New York 18 Oct 1926; Fortune 19 April 1927). [1927], [1928] French (rev). Screen play 1945.

The high road: a comedy in three acts. (Shaftesbury 7 Sept 1927). [1927], [1928] French. Screen play 1930 (as The lady of scandal).

Canaries sometimes sing: a comedy in three acts. (Globe 21 Oct 1929). [1930], New York 1930, London [1931] French.

Once is enough: a comedy in three acts. (Henry Miller, New York 15 Feb 1938). New York [1938] French. Revived as Half a loaf (Royal, Windsor 4 July 1948) and as Let them eat cake (Cambridge 6 May 1959). Pbd as Let them eat cake in Plays of the year 1958–59 [1961] Evans.

Another love story: a play in two acts. (Fulton, New York 12 Oct 1943; BBC Home 23 April 1944; Phoenix 13 Dec 1944). [1948] Guild.

The way things go: a comedy in two acts. (Phoenix 2 Mar 1950). [1951] French.

Much of Lonsdale's work remained unpbd, including the following plays: The early worm (*Wyndham's 7 Sept 1908*); The best people (*Wyndham's 5 Aug 1909*); The woman of it (*Thirty Ninth Theatre, New York 10 Jan 1913*); Waiting at the church (*Coliseum 25 Sept 1916*); Never come back (*Phoenix 20 Oct 1932*) (*screen play as* Just Smith, *1933*); *and* But for the grace of God (*St James's 3 Sept 1946*); *also several musical plays:* The king of Cadonia (*Prince of Wales's 3 Sept 1908*); The Balkan princess (*Prince of Wales's 19 Feb 1910*) *with F. Curzon*; Betty (*Daly's 24 April 1915*) *with G. Unger*; The patriot (*Grand, Clapham 14 May 1915*); High jinks (*Adelphi 24 Aug 1916*) *adapted from the farce by P. Bilhaud and M. Hennequin*; The maid of the mountains (*Daly's 10 Feb 1917*) *with H. Graham*; Monsieur Beaucaire (*Prince's 19 April 1919*) *adapted from the novel by B. Tarkington*; The lady of the rose (*Daly's 21 Feb 1922*) *adapted from the book by R. Schanzer and E. Welisch*; Madame Pompadour (*Daly's 20 Dec 1923*) *with H. Graham*; The street singer (*Lyric 27 June 1924*); Katja the dancer (*Gaiety 21 Feb 1925*) *with H. Graham from the play by L. Jacobsohn and R. Osterreicher*; Lady Mary (*Daly's 23 Feb 1928*) *with J. H. Turner*; Foreigners (*Belasco, New York 5 Dec 1939*); *and the following screen plays:* The devil to pay (*1931*); The city of song (*1931*); Lovers courageous (*1932*); The maid of the mountains (*1933*); *and* The private life of Don Juan (*1934*) *with L. Biro from the story by H. Bataille.*

§2

Donaldson, F. Freddy Lonsdale. 1957, Philadelphia 1957 (as Freddy).

ESTHER HELEN McCRACKEN
1902–71

The willing spirit: a play in two scenes. [1936] (Amateur Theatre Series), [1938] French.

Behind the lace curtains: a play in one act. [1937] (Amateur Theatre Series).

Quiet wedding: a play in three acts. (Wyndham's 14 Oct 1938). 1938, [1940] French.

Quiet week-end: a comedy. (Wyndham's 22 July 1941). [1946] French.

Living room: a comedy in three acts. (Garrick 9 June 1943). [1944].

No medals: a play in three acts. (Vaudeville 4 Oct 1944). [1947] French.

Esther McCracken also wrote Counter attractions: a farcical comedy (*Richmond Theatre 27 June 1938*), White elephants (*Richmond Theatre 26 Feb 1940*), *and* Cry liberty: a comedy (*Vaudeville 21 April 1950*).

DONAGH MACDONAGH
1912–68

§1

Twenty poems. Dublin 1934.

Veterans and other poems. Dublin 1941.

Happy as Larry: a play in four scenes (Mercury 18 Sept 1947; Criterion 16 Dec 1947; BBC Television 9 May 1948; Coronet, New York 6 Jan 1950). 1946, 1957 (in Four modern verse plays, ed E. M. Browne), Dublin 1967.

The hungry grass: poems. 1947.

Step-in-the-hollow. (Gaiety, Dublin 11 March 1957). In Three Irish plays, ed E. M. Browne 1959.

A warning to conquerors. Dublin 1968. Verse.

Some of his short stories were pbd in The Faber Book of Irish Short Stories *and in* New Writing.

Macdonagh's unpublished plays include: Lady Spider; Fading mansion (*Duchess 31 Aug 1949*) *adapted from Anouilh's Roméo et Jeannette*; God's gentry (*Arts, Belfast 15 Aug 1951*; *BBC Home Service 2 March 1953*) *adapted by M. Greenhalgh and R. Raikes*; The last hero (*BBC Home Service 22 Dec 1952*); *and* The law and the prophets (*BBC Light Programme 14 March 1954*). *He also wrote stories and short plays for Radio Eiréann and collaborated with A. J. Potter in a ballet*, Careless Love, *and an opera*, Patrick. *He edited* Poems from Ireland, *and, with L. Robinson*, The Oxford book of Irish verse 1958.

§2

Colum, P. Macdonagh of Dublin. Saturday Rev of Lit 19 March 1948.

Hogan, R. In his After the Irish Renaissance, Minneapolis 1967.

ROGER MACDOUGALL
b. 1910

Macadam and Eve: a play in three acts. (Q 7 Feb 1950; Aldwych 12 March 1951). [1951] French.

The gentle gunman. (Arts, Cambridge 24 July 1950; Arts, London 2 Aug 1950). In Plays of the year 1950–1. Screen play 1952.

To Dorothy, a son: farcical comedy in two acts. (Savoy 23 Nov 1950; John Golden, New York 19 Nov 1951). [1952] French. Screen play 1954.

Escapade: a play in three acts. (St James's 20 Jan 1953; 48th Street Theatre, New York 18 Nov 1953). 1952, [1953] French. Screen play 1955.

The facts of life: a comedy. (Grand, Blackpool 5 April 1954; Duke of York's 4 May 1954). 1955 French.

Double image: a play in three acts. (Royal, Nottingham 16 Oct 1956; Savoy 14 Nov 1956). [1957] French. With T. Allan, based on a story by R. Vickers. Screen play 1959.

The following plays have not been pbd: This man is news (*BBC Home Service 16 Dec 1940*), *adapted by Macdougall and A. Mackinnon from their film*; The man in the white suit (*Pitlochry Festival 8 May 1954*); The delegate (*Opera House, Manchester 11 July 1955*); Hide

and seek (*1957*) *with S. Mann*; Close relations (*BBC Home Service 23 Jan 1958*); *and* Trouble with father (*Northampton Repertory 3 Nov 1964*).

CHARLES ALFRED McEVOY
1879–1929

David Ballard: a play in three acts. (Imperial 9 June 1907). 1907, Boston [1925].

His helpmate: a play in one act. (Midland, Manchester 23 Sept 1907). 1907.

Lucifer: a play in one act. (Midland, Manchester 9 Nov 1907). 1907.

When the devil was ill: a play in four acts. (His Majesty's, Carlisle 29 Aug 1908; Coronet 14 June 1909). 1908.

The three barrows: a play in four acts. (Gaiety, Manchester 22 March 1909; Coronet 10 June 1909). 1924.

Gentlemen of the road: a play in one act. (Haymarket 12 Oct 1909). 1907.

All that matters: a play in four acts. (Haymarket 8 Feb 1911). 1911 (priv ptd).

Brass faces. [1912], Boston 1913. Novel.

Private affairs. [1914], Boston 1914. Novel.

The paper wedding. 1921. Short stories.

The likes of 'er: a play in three acts. (Town Hall, Battersea 30 Jan 1922; St Martin's 15 Aug 1923). [1923] French. Screen play 1932 (as Sally in our alley).

The dew necklace: a little play for Brownies. 1922 French.

The following plays were unpbd: The village wedding (*Coronet 25 May 1910*); *and* The situation at Newbury (*Liverpool Repertory 18 March 1912*; *Croydon Repertory 28 April 1912*).

RONALD MACKENZIE
1903–32

Musical chairs: a play in three acts. (Arts 15 Nov 1931). 1932, [1940] French.

Unhampered: a play for boys in three scenes. 1933.

The Maitlands: a play in three acts. (Wyndham's 4 July 1934). 1934, [1950] French.

MICHÉAL MACLIAMMÓIR
b. 1899

§1

Fairy nights. Dublin 1922. Short stories: text in English and Irish.

Diarmuid and Grainne. (Gaelic, Galway 27 Aug 1928, Irish version; Peacock, Dublin 10 Sept 1928, English version). Galway 1935.

Lá agus oidhche. Dublin 1929. Short stories and sketches in Irish.

Where stars walk: a fantasy. (Gaiety, Dublin 19 Feb 1940; Embassy 16 Dec 1947). Dublin 1962.

Ill met by moonlight: a play in three acts. (Gaiety, Dublin 5 Apr 1946; Vaudeville 5 Feb 1947). Dublin 1954.

All for Hecuba: an Irish theatrical autobiography. 1946, Dublin 1961 (rev), 1967 (rev).

Oidhche Bhealtaine. (Abbey 22 March 1949). Dublin 1932. In Irish.

Theatre in Ireland. Dublin 1950, 1964 (rev).

Put money in thy purse: the diary of the film [by Orson Welles] of 'Othello'. 1952.

The importance of being Oscar. (Dublin Festival 18 Sept 1960; Apollo 31 Oct 1960). Dublin 1963. A dramatic recital on the life and work of Oscar Wilde.

Two lights on actors. 1960.

Each actor on his ass. 1961. Diary of German and Egyptian tours.

Bláth agus Taibhse (Flower and ghost). 1965. Verse. In Irish.

An Oscar of no importance: being an account of the author's adventures with his one-man show about Wilde, The importance of being Oscar. 1968.

The following have not been pbd: Ford of the hurdles (*1928*); Easter, 1916; Dancing shadows (*1941*); Portrait of Miriam (*1947*); The mountains look different (*Gaiety, Dublin 25 Oct 1948*); Home for Christmas: or the grand tour (*Gate, Dublin 26 Dec 1950*) *with music by P. Murray*; A slipper for the moon (*1954*); Saint Patrick (*1955*); Gateway to Gaiety (*Gaiety, Dublin 20 Aug 1956*); *and* I must be talking to my friends (*Queen's 4 Jan 1965*), *a one-man entertainment.*

MacLiammóir also wrote dramatic adaptations, as yet unpbd, of the following novels: Jane Eyre, Trilby, The picture of Dorian Gray, A tale of two cities, Juliet in the rain (*from Lenormand*), An apple a day (*from J. Romains' Dr Knock*) *and* The informer (*Olympic, Dublin 10 Nov 1958*) (*from O'Flaherty's novel*).

§2

Hogan, R. In his After the Irish renaissance, Minneapolis 1967.

'BRINSLEY MACNAMARA', JOHN WELDON
1891–1963

§1

The valley of the squinting windows: a novel. Dublin 1918, New York 1919, London [1928].

The clanking of chains: a story of Sinn Fein. New York [1919], Dublin and London 1920.

In clay and bronze: a study in personality. New York [1920].

The mirror in the dusk. Dublin 1921, London 1928. Novel.

The glorious uncertainty: a comedy in three acts. (Abbey, Dublin 27 Nov 1923). Dublin 1929, 1944 (in Irish).

Look at the Heffernans! a comedy in three acts. (Abbey, Dublin 12 April 1926). Dublin 1929, 1944 (in Irish).

The smiling faces and other stories. 1929.

The various lives of Marcus Igoe. 1929. Novel.

Return to Ebontheever. 1930. Novel.

Margaret Gillan: a play in three acts. (Abbey, Dublin 17 July 1933). 1934, Dublin 1953 (in Irish).

Othello's daughter. [1942]. Novel.

Marks and Mabel. (Abbey, Dublin 6 Aug 1945). Dublin 1945. A sequel to Look at the Heffernans!

Some curious people: short stories. Dublin 1945.

Michael Caravan. Dublin 1946. Novel.

The whole story of XYZ. Belfast 1951. Short story.

Macnamara edited Abbey plays 1899–1948, *Dublin 1949. His unpbd plays include* The rebellion in Ballycullen (*Abbey, Dublin 11 March 1919*); The land for the people (*Abbey, Dublin 30 Nov 1920*); The master (*Abbey, Dublin 6 March 1928*); The grand house in the city (*Abbey, Dublin 3 Feb 1936*); The three thimbles (*Abbey, Dublin 24 Nov 1941*); The three mad schoolmasters (*BBC Home Service 28 Jan 1951*), *a short story by Macnamara dramatized by P. Rooney*; *and* The Wildes of Merrion Square (*BBC Third Programme 15 Jan 1951*), *a conversation between Macnamara and O. St John Gogarty about Oscar Wilde.*

§2

Murray, T. C. George Shiels [and] Macnamara. In Irish theatre, ed Lennox Robinson, 1939.

Hogan, R. In his After the Irish renaissance, Minneapolis 1967.

FREDERICK LOUIS MACNEICE
1907–63

See cols 303–5, above.

WILLIAM MILES MALLESON
1888–1969

A man of ideas: a play in one act. (Court 16 Nov 1913). In Young heaven & three other plays, 1918, below.

The little white thought inside the mind of a bank clerk: a fantastic scrap. (Wyndham's 30 March 1915). 1916.

Youth: a play in three acts. (Court 26 March 1916; Comedy, New York 20 Feb 1918). 1918.

Paddly pools: a little fairy play. (New 11 April 1916). 1916, [1934] (French's plays for juvenile performers).

Michael: Leo Tolstoy's What men live by, adapted for the stage. (St James's 3 April 1917). In Young heaven & three other plays, 1918, below. Pbd separately 1949 French.

Maurice's own idea: a little dream play. (Wyndham's 26 March 1918). [1924].

Young heaven [one act play with J. Cavendish] & three other plays. 1918. A man of ideas; Michael; The artist.

Conflict: a comedy in three acts. (Q 30 Nov 1925). 1925.

'D' Company, and Black 'ell: two plays. (Gate 21 June 1926). 1916 (copies seized by the War Office); rptd 1925.

Merrileon Wise: a play in three acts. (Strand 28 Nov 1926). 1926, [1927] French.

The fanatics: a comedy in three acts. (Ambassadors 15 March 1927; Forty Ninth Street Theatre, New York 7 Nov 1927). 1924.

The artist. (Playgoers 13 June 1927). In Young heaven & three other plays, 1918, above.

Love at second sight: a light comedy in three acts. (Royalty 22 Aug 1927). 1929 French. From the novel, Safety first, by M. Neville.

Four people: a comedy in three acts. (St Martin's 10 May 1928). 1928.

Yours unfaithfully: a comedy in three acts. 1933.

Six men of Dorset: a play in two acts and an epilogue. (Grand, Wolverhampton 8 Feb 1937). 1934, 1952 (without the epilogue). With H. Brooks.

April clouds: a comedy in three acts. (Royalty 20 April 1938). [1938] French. With P. Barwell, based on a play by P. Jacobi.

Tartuffe. (BBC 11 Dec 1947; Bristol Theatre Royal 21 Feb 1950; Lyric 27 June 1950). [1950] French, 1960. Adapted from Molière's play.

A provincial lady. (BBC Television 24 July 1949). [1950] French. Based on Turgenev's story.

The miser. (New 17 Jan 1950). [1950] French. Adapted from Molière's L'avare.

The prodigious snob. (BBC Television 13 Feb 1950) [1952] French. Adapted from Molière's Le Bourgeois gentilhomme.

The bachelor. (BBC Television 19 Aug 1951). [1953]. Adapted from Turgenev's story.

The bet: a play in one act. (Associated Rediffusion 30 Aug 1956; BBC Radio 4 Dec 1956, rev). 1957 French (rev stage version). Adapted from a story by Chekhov.

The great Boko [a play in one act]. [1956] French. From the story by M. Ewer.

The school for wives. (Royal, Stratford 20 March 1957). [1954] French, 1960. Adapted from Molière's L'école des femmes.

Sganarelle. (Birmingham Repertory 16 April 1957; Old Vic 20 May 1959). [1955]. Adapted from Molière's play.

The slave of truth. (Birmingham Repertory 16 April 1957). [1957] French. Adapted from Molière's Le misanthrope.

The imaginary invalid. 1959. Adapted from Molière's Le malade imaginaire.

Last appearance: a play in one act. [1959] French. Based on a story by Malleson.

The following were not pbd: The threshold (*Royalty, Glasgow 9 March 1914*); Hide and seek (*Criterion 12 May 1914*); The bargain (*Pier, Eastbourne 14 June 1926*) *adapted from Mrs B. Reynolds' novel* The daughter pays; A night in Montmartre (*Q 20 Dec 1926*) *with W. Peacock*; The ace (*Lyric 20 Aug 1933*) *adapted from the play by H. Rossmann*; Before sunset (*Shaftesbury 20 Sept 1933*) *adapted from the play by G. J. R. Hauptmann; and* The mother (*Garrick 27 Feb 1939*) *from the play by K. Čapek. Malleson wrote 2 pacifist pamphlets, and the scenarios for the following screen plays*; Nell Gwynn (*1934*) *with E. German and P. Braham*; Victoria the Great (*1937*) *with C. de Grandcourt*; The thief of Baghdad (*1940*) *with L. Biro*; Wings and the woman (*1942*); *and* Spitfire (*1943*) *with A. de Grunwald*.

JOHN EDWARD MASEFIELD
1878–1967

See cols 306–13, above.

WILLIAM SOMERSET MAUGHAM
1874–1965

See cols 661–8, above.

RONALD MILLAR
b. 1919

Collections

The affair; The new men; The masters: three plays based on the novels [of C. P. Snow] and with a preface by Snow. 1964.

§1

Frieda: a new play in three acts. (Westminster 2 May 1946). [1947] Guild.

Waiting for Gillian: a play in three acts, from A way through the wood, by N. Balchin. (St James's 21 April 1954). In Plays of the year vol 10, [1954]; rptd 1955 (French).

The bride and the bachelor: a farcical comedy in three acts. (Duchess 19 Dec 1956). [1958] French.

A ticklish business: a light comedy in three acts. (Royal, Brighton 7 April 1958; as The big tickle, Duke of York 23 May 1958). [1959] French.

The more the merrier: a comedy in three acts. (Strand 2 Feb 1960). [1960] French.

The bride comes back: a comedy in three acts. (Vaudeville 25 Nov 1960). [1961] French.

The affair: a play in three acts from the novel by C. P. Snow. (Strand 21 Sept 1961). New York 1962, London [1963] French.

The new men. (Strand 6 Sept 1962). In The affair; The new men; The masters, 1964. *See* Collections, above.

The masters: a play based on the novel by C. P. Snow. (Savoy 29 May 1963). [1964] French.

Robert and Elizabeth: a new musical based on The Barretts of Wimpole Street by R. Besier. (Lyric 20 Oct 1964). [1967] French.

Number 10: a play based on the novel by W. Clark. (King's, Glasgow 29 Aug 1967). 1967.

ALAN ALEXANDER MILNE
1882–1956

See cols 671–3, above.

ALAN NOBLE MONKHOUSE
1858–1936

§1

Books and plays. 1894. Essays, some rptd from Manchester Guardian.

A deliverance. 1898. Novel.

The Manchester stage 1880–1900: criticisms reprinted from The Manchester Guardian. (1900). Includes 2 pieces by Monkhouse.

Love in a life. 1903. Novel.

Reaping the whirlwind: a play in one act. (Gaiety, Manchester 28 Sept 1908). In Four tragedies, 1913, below.

Mary Broome: a comedy in four acts. (Gaiety, Manchester 9 Oct 1911; Coronet 24 May 1912). 1913.

Resentment: a play in one act. (Temperance Hall, Sheffield 8 Oct 1912). In Four tragedies, 1913, below.

The education of Mr Surrage: a comedy in four acts. (Liverpool Repertory 4 Nov 1912; BBC Home Service 22 July 1950). 1913.

Dying fires. 1912, New York 1913. Novel.

Nothing like leather: an indiscretion in one act. (Gaiety, Manchester 29 Sept 1913). 1930.

Four tragedies. 1913. The Hayling family; The Stricklands; Resentment; Reaping the whirlwind.

War plays. 1916. The shamed life: a play in one act; Night watches: a comedy in one act; The choice: a play in one act (Gaiety, Manchester 6 June 1916). The choice and Night watches both rptd Boston [1930].

The Grand Cham's diamond: a play in one act. (Birmingham Repertory 21 Sept 1918; BBC 28 Dec 1927). 1924, Boston [1924], London [1956] French.

Men and ghosts. 1919. Novel.

True love. 1919, New York 1920. Novel.

The Stricklands: a play in three acts. (Lyceum, New York 5 Feb 1920). In Four tragedies, 1913, above.

My daughter Helen. 1922, New York [1924]. Novel.

The conquering hero: a play in four acts. (Albert Hall, Leeds 23 Feb 1924; Queens 3 April 1924). 1923.

The Hayling family: a play in three acts. (Aldwych 26 Oct 1924). In Four tragedies, 1913, above.

Marmaduke. 1924. Novel; sequel to My daughter Helen.

Suburb. 1924. Short stories.

First blood: a play in four acts. (Little, Leeds 11 Jan 1926; Gate 6 Dec 1926). 1924.

Sons & fathers: a play in four acts. (St Martin's 24 Jan 1926). 1925.

Alan Monkhouse (Essays of Today and Yesterday). 1926. Selection of essays, rptd from Manchester Guardian.

O death, where is thy sting? a play in one act. 1926.

Alfred the great. 1927. Novel.

The king of Barvender: a melodrama in one act. 1927.

The rag: an incident in three acts. 1928.

The wily one. In One-act plays for stage and study, New York 1928.

Paul Felice: a play in four acts. (Liverpool Repertory 15 Sept 1930). 1930.

Farewell, Manchester. 1931. Novel.

Cecilia: a play in four acts. (Liverpool Repertory 14 Nov 1932; Arts Theatre Club 10 March 1933). 1932.

§2

Sutton, G. In his Some contemporary dramatists, 1924.

Darlington, W. A. In his Literature in the theatre, 1925.

Cunliffe, J. W. In his Modern English playwrights, New York 1927.

Swinnerton, F. In his Georgian scene, New York 1934, London 1935 (as The Georgian literary scene).

Pogson, R. In his Miss Horniman and the Gaiety Theatre, Manchester 1952.

THOMAS STURGE MOORE
1870–1944
See cols 315–16, above.

CHARLES LANGBRIDGE MORGAN
1894–1958
See cols 676–7, above.

'C. K. MUNRO',
CHARLES KIRKPATRICK
MACMULLAN
b. 1889

Selections
Three plays: The rumour; At Mrs Beam's; The birth, death and life of Mr Eno. 1932.

§1

At Mrs Beam's: a comedy. (Kingsway 27 Feb 1921; Guild, New York 26 April 1926). [1923], New York 1923, London [1925] French.
The rumour: a play in two parts. (Globe 3 Dec 1922). [1923], New York 1924.
Progress: a play in two parts. (New 20 Jan 1924). [1924].
Storm, or the battle of Tinderley Down: a comedy. (Ambassadors 13 Aug 1924). [1924].
The mountain, or the story of Captain Yevan: a symbolic drama. (Shaftesbury 30 May 1926). [1926].
The birth, death and life of Mr Eno. (Arts 22 Oct 1930 as Mr Eno: his birth, death and life). In Three plays, 1932; *see* Selections above.
Bluestone quarry. (Duchess 8 Nov 1931). 1931.
The true woman: a handbook for husbands and others. [1932]. Essays.
Watching a play. [1933]. Shute Lectures, Liverpool Univ, 1930–1.
The fountains in Trafalgar Square: some reflections on the Civil Service. 1952.
The following remain unpbd: Wanderers (*Queens 21 March 1915*); Beau strings (*1926*); Cocks and hens (*Royalty 3 March 1927*); Veronica (*Arts 14 Sept 1929*); Bletheroe (*Duchess 17 Nov 1931*); Ding and Co (*Embassy 20 Nov 1934*); The new vicar (*BBC Home Service 21 Aug 1962*); *and* Jonsen (*BBC Home Service 13 Jan 1965*).

§2

Sutton, G. In his Some contemporary dramatists, 1924.
Malone, A. E. The strange case of Munro. Dublin Rev 185 1929.
Cunliffe, J. W. In his Modern English playwrights, New York 1927.

GEORGE GILBERT AIMÉ MURRAY
1866–1957
See cols 1089–92, below.

NORMAN CORNTHWAITE
NICHOLSON
b. 1914
See cols 320–1, above.

IVOR NOVELLO
(formerly DAVID IVOR DAVIES)
1893–1951

§1

The truth game: a light comedy in three acts. (Globe 5 Oct 1928; Ethel Barrymore, New York 29 Dec 1930). [1929] French. Screen play 1932 (as But the flesh is weak).
Symphony in two flats: a play in three acts. (New 14 Oct 1929; Shubert, New York 16 Sept 1930; screen play 1931). In I lived with you [etc], 1932, below.
I lived with you: a comedy in three acts. (Prince of Wales's 23 March 1932; screen play 1935). In I lived with you [etc], 1932, below.
Party. (Arts 19 May 1932). In I lived with you [etc], 1932, below.
I lived with you; Party; Symphony in two flats. Introd by E. Marsh 1932.
Fresh fields: a comedy in three acts. (Criterion 5 Jan 1933). [1934] French, New York 1936.
Proscenium: a play in three acts. (Globe 14 June 1933). [1934] French.
Glamorous night: a romantic play with music. (Drury Lane 2 May 1935). Lyrics by C. Hassall. [1938] (vocal score), [1939] French.
Full house: a light comedy in three acts. (Haymarket 21 Aug 1935). [1936] French.
Careless rapture: a musical play. (Drury Lane 11 Sept 1936). Lyrics by C. Hassall. 1936 (vocal score).
Comedienne: a comedy in three acts. (Haymarket 16 June 1938). [1938] French.
The dancing years: a musical play. (Drury Lane 23 March 1939). Lyrics by C. Hassall. [1939] (vocal score), [1953] French.
Perchance to dream: a musical play. (Hippodrome 21 April 1945). 1945 (vocal score), [1953] French.
We proudly present: a comedy in two acts and a prologue. (Duke of York's 2 May 1947). [1947] French.
King's rhapsody: a musical romance. (Palace, Manchester 25 Aug 1949; Palace, London 15 Sept 1949). Lyrics by C. Hassall. 1949 (vocal score), [1955] French.
The following plays have not been pbd: The rat *by 'David L'Estrange' [i.e. Novello] (Prince of Wales's 9 June 1924; Colony, New York 10 Feb 1925) with C. Collier, screen play 1927*; Down Hill *by 'David L'Estrange' (Palace, Manchester 2 Dec 1925; Queen's 16 June 1926) with C. Collier, screen play 1928*; Flies in the sun (*Playhouse 18 Jan 1933*); Sunshine sisters (*Queen's 8 Nov 1933*); Murder in Mayfair (*Globe 5 Sept 1934*); Crest of the wave (*Drury Lane 1 Sept 1937*) lyrics by C. Hassall; Second helping (*Streatham Hill 4 Dec 1939*; Lyric 8 April 1940, *as* Ladies into action); Breakaway (*Royal, Windsor 4 June 1941*); Arc de triomphe (*Phoenix 9 Nov 1943*); *and* Gay's the word (*Saville 16 Feb 1951*) lyrics by A. Melville.
Novello wrote the music, alone or in collaboration, and an occasional lyric, for twelve other musical comedies between 1916 and 1929, and set to music many songs including a few of his own, viz Spring of the year (1910), Not really (1913), Carnival time (1914), Laddie in khaki (1915) and The radiance in your eyes (1915)

§2

Bottome, P. In her From the life, 1944.
Hassall, C. Novello: an appreciation. Spectator 9 March 1951.
Macqueen-Pope, W. J. Ivor: the story of an achievement. 1951, 1954 (rev).
Noble, P. Ivor Novello; man of the theatre. 1951.
Short, E. In his Sixty years of theatre, 1951.

A.P.H.

SEUMAS O'KELLY
1881–1918

See cols 687–8, above.

LOUIS NAPOLEON PARKER
1852–1944

§1

The bracelet: a tragi-comedy. Sherborne 1881.

A buried talent: an original play in three acts. (Digby Hotel, Sherborne 3 Dec 1886; Vaudeville 5 June 1890). Sherborne [?1890].

Madame Rebelle: a play. [1887]. From story by 'Rowland Grey' (L. K. R. Brown).

Rosmersholm. [1889]. Trn of Ibsen's play.

In Taunton Vale: an original play in three acts. (Manchester 12 June 1890, as Taunton Vale). Sherborne 1890.

Brother Matteo: a poem for recitation; Dawn: a dramatic fancy. Sherborne [c. 1890].

Prologue. [c. 1890]. Verses.

St George and the dragon: a farcical comedy in two acts. Sherborne 1890.

The love knot: a play in four acts. (York 7 Oct 1892). Sherborne 1889.

The man in the street: an original play in one act. (Avenue 14 May 1894). [1894] (Lynn's acting edn), [1899] (Lacy's acting edn).

Rosemary—that's for remembrance: a comedy in four acts. (Criterion 16 May 1896). [1924] French (rev from acted version). With S. M. Carson.

The happy life. (Duke of York's 6 Dec 1897). [1897] (priv ptd).

The termagant. (Her Majesty's 1 Sept 1898). 1899 (priv ptd). With S. M. Carson.

Richard Wagner and the ring of the Nibelungs. (Souvenir of 3 Wagner cycles at the Royal Opera House, Covent Garden). [1898].

The Mayflower. (Metro 6 March 1899). [1897?] (priv ptd).

The cardinal: a play in four acts. (Montreal 21 Nov 1901; St James's 31 Aug 1903). [1923] French.

The monkey's paw: a story in three scenes. (Haymarket 6 Oct 1903). [1910] (Lacy's acting edn), [1910] French. From story by W. W. Jacobs.

Beauty and the barge: a farce in three acts. (New 30 Aug 1904). [1910] French. With W. W. Jacobs.

The Sherborne pageant: in celebration of the twelve-hundredth anniversary of the founding of the town of Sherborne, the Bishopric of Sherborne and Sherborne School, by St Ealdhelm, A.D. 705. (Sherborne 12 June 1905). Sherborne 1905.

The Warwick pageant: in celebration of the thousandth anniversary of the conquest of Mercia by Queen Ethelfleda. (Warwick 12 July 1906). Warwick [1906].

The Bury St Edmund's pageant. (Bury 8 July 1907). Bury [1907].

The Dover pageant. (Dover 27 July 1908). Dover [1908].

Souvenir and book of words of the Colchester pageant. (Colchester 21 June 1909). Norwich [1909].

Pomander walk: a comedy in three acts. (Montreal 12 Dec 1910; Wallack's, New York 20 Dec 1910; Playhouse 29 June 1911). 1915 [French].

Disraeli: a play in three acts. (Princess's, Montreal 23 Jan 1911; Royalty 4 April 1916). New York 1911, London 1916. *See also* Parker's Disraeli: the story of the play, [1930].

Drake: a pageant play in three acts. (His Majesty's 3 Sept 1912). 1912, New York 1912.

Joseph and his brethren: a pageant play. (Century, New York 11 Jan 1913; His Majesty's 2 Sept 1913). 1913, New York 1913.

How to write a play, by Parker, wanderer to ye Sette of Odd Volumes: read before ye Sette on May 27, 1913. [1913] (priv ptd, 133 copies).

Parsifal and Tristan und Isolde. 1914. With R. Fynes. Stories of Wagner's operas told in verse.

Some of my first nights, by Parker, wanderer to ye Sette of Odd Volumes: read before ye Sette on May 26, 1914. [1914] (priv ptd, 133 copies).

The masque of war and peace. (Drury Lane 27 April 1915, as The masque of peace and war). 1915.

Mavourneen: a comedy in three acts. (His Majesty's 23 Oct 1915). New York 1916.

The aristocrat: a play in three acts. (St James's 25 Jan 1917). New York 1917.

The pageant of Drury Lane Theatre 1663–1918. (Drury Lane 27 Sept 1918). 1918.

L'aiglon. (Globe 19 Nov 1918). 1900. From Rostand's play.

Summer is a-comin' in: a light comedy in three acts. (Royalty 30 Oct 1919, as Summertime). [1922] French.

A minuet: a little play in verse. [1922] French.

The lord of death. 1923. Trn of play by M. Allotte de la Fuije.

The quest: a pageant of the Girls' Friendly Society. (Royal Albert Hall 4 July 1925). 1925.

Several of my lives. 1928. Autobiography.

Their business in great waters: a play in one act. 1928. Royal National Life-Boat Institution.

On board the 'Golden Hind': a play. In Seven modern plays for younger players, ed J. Hampden, [1932].

Lourdes: a play in three acts. Boston [1935].

See J. Rhoades, Collected poems, 1925, *for a collection of songs and choruses from Parker's pageants. Parker wrote about 60 unpbd plays and pageants, 24 of which are listed in A Nicoll,* A history of late nineteenth-century drama, *1850–1900, 1946. There is no comparable record of unpbd plays after 1900; the following is a provisional list:* Magda (*Lyceum 3 June 1896*), *from H. Sudermann's* Heimath; The swashbuckler (*Duke of York's 17 Nov 1900*), *from L. Fulda's* Zwillingsschwester; The heel of Achilles (*Globe 6 Feb 1902*), *with B. Lawrence;* The house of Burnside (*Terry's 28 April 1904*), *from G. Mitchell's* La maison; Everybody's secret (*Haymarket 14 March 1905*), *from P. Wolff's* Sécret de Polichinelle; The creole (*Haymarket 6 May 1905*), *in one act;* Harlequin King (*Imperial 3 Jan 1906*), *from R. Lothar's play;* Jemmy: a play in one act (*Vaudeville 25 April 1907*); Mr George: a comedy in three acts (*Vaudeville 25 April 1907*); A masque of life (*Claremont 9 July 1907*); Pete (*Lyceum 29 Aug 1908*), *from Hall Caine's* Manxman; Beethoven (*His Majesty's 25 Nov 1909*), *from R. Fauchois' play;* The lady of Coventry (*New York, 21 Nov 1911*); La princesse lointaine (*1912*), *from Rostand's play;* Bluff King Hal (*Garrick 4 Sept 1914*); David Copperfield (*New York 26 Oct 1914; His Majesty's 24 Dec 1914*); Through toil to victory: a pageant in three scenes (*Drury Lane 14 April 1916*) (*Women munition workers' matinee*); The womens' tribute: an extraordinary general meeting (*Covent Garden 8 July 1916*); An English nosegay (*Alhambra 19 Oct 1916*); Wonderful James (*Royal, Manchester 26 Feb 1917; Garrick 26 March 1917*), (*New title of* Gudgeons; *see A. Nicoll, op cit*); The pageant of freedom (*1918*); The great day: a drama in five acts (*Drury Lane 12 Sept 1919*), *with G. R. Sims.*

§2

In Theatre and stage, ed B. Downs, vol 2, 1954.

K. J. W.

LAWRENCE DU GARDE PEACH
b. 1890

Collections

Collected plays. 4 vols Manchester 1955.

§I

Many of du Garde Peach's plays were written for, and first produced by, the Great Hucklow Village Players. For details of production dates etc see The Village Players, Great Hucklow, present, *1952, below.*

Wind o' the moors: a Derbyshire play in one act. In Three one act plays, Oxford 1925 (British Drama League Library of Modern British Drama 12).

Ever ready plays. [1926] French.

Five country plays. [1926] French.

More ever-ready plays. [1926] French.

Numbered chickens: a cockney intrigue in one scene. [1926] French.

Sale by auction: a comedy in one act. [1926] French, Boston 1926.

Broadcast sketches. [1927] French.

Unknown Devon. 1927. Travel.

The proposals of Peggy: five duologues for a man and a woman. [1928] French.

Motoring without tears: a sketch for a revue. [1929] French.

The charcoal burner's son: a dramatic story for children. 1930. Music by C. V. H. Hutchinson.

Crooks' Christmas: a play in one act. [1931] (Year Book Press ser).

The dumb wife of Tideswell. Derby [1931?] (Plays of Derbyshire Life).

History repeats itself: a revue for boys by S. Blow from a scenario by du Garde Peach entitled Heterodyned history. [1931] French.

Radio plays. [1931].

Love one another: a satirical comedy. (BBC Regional 5 Jan 1932). In Collected plays vol 3, 1955, above.

The mystery of the Mary Celeste: a drama of the sea. (BBC National 7 May 1932). In Collected plays vol 2, 1955, above.

The path of glory: a comedy in a prologue and three acts. (BBC National 15 Dec 1933), [1934] (Year Book Press ser).

Meet Mrs Beeton: a culinary comedy in one act. (BBC National 4 Jan 1934). [1934] (Year Book Press ser).

Practical plays for stage and classroom. 1935; 2nd ser 1936.

Mrs Grundy comes to tea: a comedy of morals in one act. (BBC National 15 Oct 1937). [1938] (Year Book Press ser).

The cohort marches. In Eight new one act plays of 1937, ed W. Armstrong 1937.

Five plays for boys. 1937.

The new mayor. In Fourteen sketches, ed F. S. Box 1937.

Patriotism Ltd: a satirical farce. (1937). In Collected plays vol 3, 1955, above.

Plays for young players. 1937.

Scenario: a comedy in one act. [1937] (Year Book Press ser).

Shells: a play in one act. [1937] (Amateur Theatre ser).

The castles of England: plays for stage and classroom. 2 vols 1938.

Famous men of Britain: five plays. [1938].

Famous women of Britain. 1938.

A dramatic history of England A.D. 900–1901. 1939.

Loser takes all. In Nelson's theatrecraft plays bk 2, 1939.

Plays of the family Goodman: 1485–1666 (1720–1914). 2 vols 1939.

Smuggler Jack: a play in one act. 1939.

Knights of the round table: five plays from the Arthurian legend. [1940].

Music makers: four short plays of great musicians. 1940.

The story of Sigurd: five plays from the Nordic sagas. 1940.

Story-tellers of Britain: plays for schools. 3 vols 1941.

Biographical plays. [Glasgow] 1942.

According to plan: a comedy of the Home Guard in three acts. [1943] French.

The sage of Chelsea. In Ten selected one act plays, ed M. H. Fuller 1943.

Co-operative century: a pageant of the people. (Handbook to the centenary pageant). 2 vols Manchester [1944].

Decline and fall. In Recent one act plays, ed A. E. M. Bayliss 1944.

Phoebe in love. In Theatrecraft annual, 1944.

The story of David—David and Goliath and David in exile: two Bible plays. 1944.

The story of David—King over Israel and The last days of David: two Bible plays. 1944.

Plays for youth groups. 21 nos [1945–8] French.

Tomorrow: a pageant of youth. 1945.

A criminal introduction: a play in one act. [1946] French.

A first social and dramatic history by E. H. Carter and G. H. Holroyd, vols 1 and 2 with additional plays and dialogue by du G. Peach. 1946.

Mate in three: a matrimonial comedy in four acts. (As Three blind mice, Hippodrome, Margate 31 Oct 1949; Intimate, Palmer's Green 10 June 1951). [1950] French.

The white sheep of the family: a felonious comedy. (Royal Court, Liverpool 3 Sept 1951; Piccadilly 11 Oct 1951). 1953 French, New York 1959. With Ian Hay (J. H. Beith).

Queen's pawn: a play in one act. [1951] French.

Roots go deep: a play in one act. [1951] French.

The spinsters of Lavender Lane: a play in one act. [1951] French.

The surprising story of Alfred, warder of the Tower. In Plays for puppets, ed J. Bussell, 1951.

The town that would have a pageant: a delirium in two acts. 1952 French.

The Village Players, Great Hucklow, present: Twenty-five years of play producing, 1927–52, a record compiled by du Garde Peach. 1952.

Women are like that. (LAMDA 1 Dec 1953). 1954 (priv ptd).

A horse! A horse!: a comedy. [1953] French.

John Smedley of Matlock and his hydro. [1954].

Fire burn and cauldron bubble: an episode in one act for women. [1956] French.

For those in peril: a play in one act for six women. [1956] French.

A ghost of a chance: a play in one act. [1956] French.

Six wives in favour: a play in one act for eight women. [1956] French.

Jam for Mrs Hooper: a play in one act for eight women. [1958] French.

Landed gentry: a comedy in one act. 1958 French.

Rough diamond: a comedy in one act. [1958] French.

Alice, where art thou?: a play in one act. 1959.

Danger on the right: a play in one act. [1960] French.

The Saxon wives of Ellandune: a comedy in one act. 1960 Evans.

Welcome home: a comedy in one act. 1960 French.

A wife for the captain: a comedy in one act. 1960 French.

Christmas and Mrs Hooper: a comedy in one act. [1961] French.

Just a princess: a comedy in one act for five women. [1961] French.

Mrs Hooper in the round: a comedy in one act. [1961] French.

If you please, ladies: a comedy for women in one act. [1963] French.

The Lopotkin inheritance. [1963] French. Adapted from V. G. Smirnov.

For details of unpbd plays, adaptations etc written for, and produced by, the Great Hucklow Village Players, see The

Village Players, Great Hucklow, present, *1952, above.*
Du Garde Peach wrote a number of booklets for children in
the Ladybird *ser on historical figures.*

ROLAND PERTWEE
1885–1963

Falling upstairs: a play in one act. (Court 26 June 1914). [1946].

Early birds: a sketch in one act. (Savoy 30 May 1916). [1927] French.

Postal orders: a farce. (Haymarket 15 Nov 1916). [1919]. French.

The creaking chair. (Comedy 22 July 1924). [1926], [1927] (rev). Adapted from the play by A. T. Wilkes.

Evening dress indispensable: a playlet in one act. [1925] French. Also pbd in Ladies Home Journal one act plays, Garden City NY 1925, London 1925.

The loveliest thing: a comedy in one act. In Ladies Home Journal one act plays, Garden City NY 1925, London 1925; pbd separately [1927] French.

Interference: a play in three acts. (St James's 29 Jan 1927). [1929] French. With H. Dearden, from Pertwee's mystery story, 1927.

A voice said 'Good night': a play in one act. [1928] French.

Heat wave. (St James's 15 Oct 1929). 1933. In Five three-act plays, 1933, New York 1939.

A few essentials. 1930 French.

To kill a cat: a play in three acts. (Aldwych 7 June 1939). 1939. With H. Dearden. Previously produced as Independence at Q Theatre 1 May 1939.

Master of none. 1940. Autobiography.

Home guard: a comedy. [1942] Guild One-Act Library.

Pink string and sealing wax. (Duke of York's 1 Sept 1943). [1945] Guild.

Bridge of sighs: a play in one act. [1946] Guild.

Expert evidence: a play in one act. [1946] Guild.

Fly away birdie: a comedy in one act. [1946] Guild.

Speaking terms: a play in one act. [1946] Guild.

'Test me!' [1946] Guild.

School for spinsters: a comedy in three acts. (Criterion 11 Sept 1947). [1948] Guild.

The paragon: a play in two acts. (Fortune 10 May 1948). [1949] Guild. Also pbd in Plays of the year 1948–9, 1949. With M. Pertwee.

Many happy returns: a comedy in two acts. (Royal, Windsor 24 April 1950). [1953] Guild. With N. Streatfeild.

Food for thought. [1950]. Guild One-Act Library.

Happy the bride: a play in one act. [1950] Guild.

Dirty work: a comedy-thriller. [1954] Guild.

The baby-sitters: a play in one act. [1955] French. With M. Pertwee.

Deadly poison. [1955] French. With M. Pertwee.

Don't talk to strangers. [1955] French. With M. Pertwee.

Dramatic licenses: an incident in the life of the Grove family. [1955] French. With M. Pertwee.

A fair cow: an incident in the life of the Grove family. [1955] French. With M. Pertwee.

A good turn-out. [1955] French. With M. Pertwee.

Looking her best. [1955] French. With M. Pertwee.

Pardon my French: a play in one act. [1955] French. With M. Pertwee.

A pound of flesh: a play in one act. [1955] French. With M. Pertwee.

Royal welcome. [1955] French. With M. Pertwee.

A place in the shade: an adventure in two acts. (Leas Pavilion, Folkestone 6 Jan 1958). [1958] Guild.

What heaven'll send you: a comedy in one act. [1958] Guild.

Pertwee wrote more than twenty unpbd plays; and also pbd verse, short stories and novels.

EDEN PHILLPOTTS
1862–1960

See cols 699–704, above.

JOHN BOYNTON PRIESTLEY
b. 1894

See cols 712–17, above.

SIR TERENCE MERVYN RATTIGAN
b. 1911

Collections

The Winslow boy, with two other plays: French without tears; Flare path. 1950.

The collected plays of Terence Rattigan. 1953–. With preface to each vol by the author.

The deep blue sea, with three other plays: Harlequinade; Adventure story; The Browning version. 1955.

§I

First episode. (Q 11 Sept 1933). With P. Heimann.

French without tears: a play in three acts. (Criterion 6 Nov 1936). 1937, [1937] French, New York 1938.

After the dance: a play in three acts. (St James's 21 June 1939). 1939.

Follow my leader. (Apollo 16 June 1940). With A. Maurice.

Grey farm. (1940). Unpbd. With H. Bolitho.

Flare path: a play in three acts. (Apollo 13 Aug 1942). 1942, [1943] French.

While the sun shines: a comedy. (Globe 24 Dec 1943). 1944, New York [1945] French, London [1946] French.

Love in idleness. (Lyric 20 Dec 1944). 1945, [1947] French, New York [1949] French (as O mistress mine: a comedy in three acts).

The Winslow boy. (Lyric 23 May 1946). 1946, New York 1946 Dramatists' Play Service, London [1948] French.

Playbill: comprising The Browning version and Harlequinade. (Royal Court, Liverpool 26 July 1948; Phoenix 8 Sept 1948). [1949]. Also pbd separately in French edns 1949.

Adventure story: a play in three acts. (Royal, Brighton 11 Jan 1949; St James's 17 March 1949). 1950, [1950] French.

Who is Sylvia? A light comedy. (Arts, Cambridge 9 Oct 1950; Criterion 24 Oct 1950). 1951, [1951] Evans.

A tale of two cities. (BBC Home Service 28 Oct 1950). From C. Dickens. Unpbd.

The deep blue sea. (Royal, Brighton 4 Feb 1952; Duchess 6 March 1952). 1952, New York 1953, London [1954] French.

The sleeping prince. (Opera, Manchester 28 Sept 1953; Phoenix 5 Nov 1953). 1954, [1956] French, New York 1957.

Separate tables—two plays: Table by the window; Table number seven. (Royal Court, Liverpool 23 Aug 1954; St James's 22 Sept 1954). 1955, [1957] French, New York 1957.

The final test. (BBC Light Programme 14 Nov 1956). Unpbd.

The prince and the showgirl: the script for the film. New York 1957.

Variation on a theme. (Opera, Manchester 31 March 1958; Globe 8 May 1958). 1958.

Ross: a dramatic portrait. (Royal Court, Liverpool 29 April 1960; Haymarket 12 May 1960). 1960, New York 1962, London [1962] French.

Heart to heart: a play for television. (BBC 6 Dec 1962). Unpbd.

Man and boy. (Royal, Brighton 19 Aug 1963; Queens
4 Sept 1963). New York [1963] French, London
1964.
A bequest to the nation. (Haymarket 23 Sept 1970).
Unpbd.
*Rattigan has also written a musical and a number of film
scripts.*

§2

Trewin, J. C. The plays of Rattigan. Adelphi 27 1951.
Bax, C. Contemporary British dramatists: Rattigan.
Drama new ser 30 1953.
Hyams, B. A chat with Rattigan. Theatre Arts 40 1956.
Simon, J. Rattigan talks. Theatre Arts 46 1962.
Bryden, R. Rattigan and his tycoons. New Statesman 20
Sept 1963.
Deter, E. Einführung in die Schichtung des Englischen
bei der Lektüre von T. Rattigan The Winslow boy. Die
Neueren Sprachen new ser 13 1964.
Worsley, T. C. Rattigan and his critics. London Mag new
ser 4 1964.

ANNE BARBARA RIDLER,
née BRADBY
b. 1912
See cols 331–2, above.

HAROLD FREDERICK RUBINSTEIN
b. 1891

Old boyhood: a comedy in one act. (Lyric, Hammersmith
14 Dec 1919). 1924.
Shakespeare: a play in five episodes. 1921, [1933] French.
With C. Bax.
What's wrong with the drama?: five one act plays—The
theatre; A specimen; Repertory; Arms and the drama;
Grand Guignol. 1923, New York 1923.
Peter & Paul: a play in three acts. (Scala 1 Feb 1925).
1924.
Exodus—a dramatic sequence in five episodes: The
dreamer; The ark of bullrushes; Moses the Egyptian;
The passover; Prophecy. (Circus, Glasgow 30 March
1925). 1923. With H. Glover.
Revanche: a mystery. In New Coterie 1 1925.
Churchill: a chronicle-comedy in eight scenes. (Little,
Leeds 8 Nov 1926). 1925. With A. J. Talbot.
Insomnia: a modern morality play. (Etlinger Sch, Padding-
ton 31 March 1927). [1927] French.
The house: a play in three acts. (Blackfriars 13 June 1927).
1926.
Isabel's eleven: a comedy in four acts. 1927.
What isn't wrong with the drama? An address. 1927.
Great English plays. Ed Rubinstein 1928, New York 1928.
Plays out of time: Hippodrome hill—a play of conscience
in five prospects; Britannia calling—an adventure in four
acts; Stephen into Dickens—a comedy of three pieces in
parenthesis. 1930.
The theatre: a play in one act. [1930] French. First pbd
in What's wrong with the drama? 1923, above.
The Dickens of Gray's Inn and On the Portsmouth road:
two one act plays. [1931] French, Boston 1931.
Posterity: a comedy in one act. 1931, New York 1931.
On the father's side: Jew Dyte and They went forth.
[1933] French. Two one-act plays.
Dramatic endeavour: a display in one act. [1934] French.
The deacon and the Jewess. [1935] French. Also pbd in
The best one-act plays of 1935, ed J. W. Marriott 1936.
All things are possible: a play in one act. 1936. (The
Amateur Theatre series of plays).
Israel set free—five one-act plays: The deacon and the
Jewess; Whitehall, 1656; Jew Dyte; They went forth;
To the poets of Australia. 1936.

To the poets of Australia. (Players 21 May 1937). Pbd
separately In Israel set free, 1936, above. 1937 French.
After-glow: a play in one act. [1937] (The Amateur
Theatre series of plays), Boston 1937.
Whitehall, 1656: a play in one act. 1937, [1937] French.
First Corinthians: a play in one act. [1938].
Johnson was no gentleman: a comedy. 1938.
Prelude to a tragedy. [1938].
London stone. [1939] (Nelson's plays for amateurs).
Moneys from Shylock. [1940] (Nelson's plays for
amateurs).
Ohad's woman. In The best one-act plays of 1941, ed
J. W. Marriott 1942.
Hated servants—eight one act plays: Rahab of Jericho;
Helen of Alexandria; Ohad's woman; Chosen people;
First Corinthians; Holyest Erth; All things are possible;
Farewell Jerusalem. 1944.
The fifth gospel: a play in a prologue and three acts. 1946.
Four Jewish plays. Ed Rubinstein 1948.
Six London plays: Hamlet in Aldwych; Poets and peasants;
Incident in a fire; Blake's comforter; Words by Mr
Gilbert; Post War. 1950. With V. I. Arlett.
Bernard Shaw in heaven. (Court 26 July 1952). 1954.
Night of errors: a play about Shakespeare in one act. 1964.
Unearthly gentleman—a trilogy of one act plays about
Shakespeare: Night of errors; One afternoon in Henley
Street; Gentleman of Stratford. 1965.
Rubinstein has also written a number of unpbd plays.

GERALD SAVORY
b. 1909

George and Margaret: a comedy in three acts. (Strand
17 Jan 1937). [1937], New York [1937], [1938] French's
Standard Lib Edn, London [1940] French.
A likely tale: a play in three acts. (Grand, Blackpool 16
Jan 1956; Globe 22 March 1956). [1957] French.
A month of Sundays: a comedy in three acts. (Royal,
Nottingham 25 March 1957; Cambridge 28 May 1957).
[1957] French.
Come rain, come shine: a play in three acts [later entitled
So many children]. (Lyceum, Sheffield 10 March 1958).
[1959] French.
Fiddlers four. (Granada Television, Manchester 26 Feb
1960). Adaptation for television by Savory of H. Brig-
house's Graft. In Granada's Manchester plays, Man-
chester 1962.
Vitriol. (Granada Television, Manchester 30 Aug 1960).
Adaptation for television by Savory of Brighouse's
Dealing in futures. Ibid.
Cup and saucer: a play in two acts. (Queen's, Hornchurch
18 July 1961). [1963] French.
The twinkling of an eye: a comedy. (Royal, Windsor 8
March 1965). [1965] French.
*Savory has also written a number of unpbd plays and has pbd
several novels.*

DOROTHY LEIGH SAYERS
1893–1957
See cols 730–1, above.

ALEXANDER MORDAUNT SHAIRP
1887–1939

The offence: a play in three acts. (Wyndham's 26 Aug
1925). 1925.
The crime at Blossoms: a play in three acts. (Little, Hull
11 Feb 1929; Embassy 21 April 1931). 1932.
The phoby. In Modern plays in one act, ed A. Shairp
1929.
The green bay tree: a play in three acts. (St Martin's 25
Jan 1933). 1933.
Shairp also wrote an unpbd play and a filmscript.

ROBERT CEDRIC SHERRIFF
b. 1896

Profit and loss. (Gables, Surbiton 10 Jan 1923). Unpbd.

Cornlow-in-the-downs. (Gables, Surbiton 10 Dec 1923). Unpbd.

Mr Birdie's finger. (Assembly Rooms, Surbiton 26 Feb 1926). Unpbd.

Journey's end: a play in three acts. (Apollo 10 Dec 1928). 1929, New York 1929, London [1931] French. As novel 1930, with V. Bartlett.

Badger's green: a play in three acts. (Prince of Wales's 12 June 1930). 1930, [1934] French, 1962 (rev).

The fortnight in September: a novel. 1931, New York 1932.

Windfall. (Embassy 26 Feb 1934). Unpbd.

Two hearts doubled: a playlet. [1935] French.

St Helena: a play in twelve scenes. (Old Vic 4 Feb 1936). 1934, New York 1935, London [1937] French. With J. de Casalis.

Greengates. 1936, New York 1936. Novel.

The Hopkins manuscript. 1939, New York 1939, London 1958 (rev, as The cataclysm). Novel.

Chedworth: a novel. New York 1944.

Miss Mabel: a play in three acts. (Royal, Brighton 21 Sept 1948; Duchess 23 Nov 1948). 1949, [1949] French.

Another year: a novel. 1948, New York 1948.

Quartet: stories by W. S. Maugham, screen plays by Sherriff. 1948, Garden City N Y 1949.

The Hopkins manuscript. (BBC Light Programme 5, 6 Oct 1949). With E. J. King-Bull.

Home at seven: a play in three acts. (Royal, Brighton 6 Feb 1950; Wyndham's 7 March 1950). 1950, New York 1950, London [1951] French.

Odd man out: a screen play. In Three British screen plays, ed R. Manvell 1950. With F. L. Green.

Trio: stories by W. S. Maugham, screen adaptation by Maugham, Sherriff and N. Langley. 1950, Garden City N Y 1950.

The white carnation: a play in two acts. (Royal, Brighton 5 Jan 1953; Globe 20 March 1953). 1953, [1954] French.

King John's treasure: an adventure story. 1954, New York 1954. For children.

The long sunset: a play in three acts. (BBC Home Service 23 April 1955; Repertory, Birmingham 30 Aug 1955; Mermaid 7 Nov 1961). In Plays of the year vol 12, 1955. Pbd separately 1956, 1958 French.

The night my number came up: film screen play. (BBC Home Service 28 April 1956). Unpbd.

The telescope. (BBC Light programme 31 Oct 1956; Guildford 13 May 1957). [1957] French; [1958].

The colonel's lady: screenplay from a story by W. S. Maugham. In A college treasury, ed P. A. Jorgensen and F. P. Schroyer, New York [1956].

A shred of evidence. (Royal, Brighton 28 March 1960; Duchess 27 April 1960). [1961] French. Also pbd in Plays of the year 1960, 1961.

The wells of St Mary's. 1962. Novel.

No leading lady: an autobiography. 1968.

Sherriff also wrote other unpbd plays for stage, radio and television, and screenplays based on other writers' works.

GEORGE SHIELS
1886–1949

Selections

Three plays: Professor Tim; Paul Twyning; The new gossoon. 1945.

§1

Bedmates: a play in one act. (Abbey, Dublin 6 Jan 1921). Dublin 1922.

Insurance money. (Abbey, Dublin 13 Dec 1921). Unpbd.

Professor Tim & Paul Twyning: comedies in three acts. (Abbey, Dublin 3 Oct 1922; Shilling, Fulham 4 Dec 1933; Little, 14 Feb 1934). 1927.

First aid. (Abbey, Dublin 26 Dec 1923). Unpbd.

The retrievers. (Abbey, Dublin 12 May 1924). Unpbd.

Two Irish plays: Mountain dew, a play in three acts & Cartney and Kevney, a comedy in three acts. (Abbey, Dublin 5 March 1929; 29 Nov 1929). 1930.

The new gossoon: a comedy in three acts. (Abbey, Dublin 19 April 1930; Apollo 7 April 1931, as The girl on the pillion). 1936.

Grogan and the ferret. (Abbey, Dublin 13 Nov 1933). Dublin 1947.

The passing day: a play in six scenes. (Abbey, Dublin 13 April 1936; Lyric, Hammersmith 20 March 1951; Ambassadors 3 July 1951), & The jailbird: a comedy in three acts (BBC Northern Ireland Radio 11 Feb 1936; Abbey, Dublin 12 Oct 1936). 1937.

Quin's secret. (Abbey, Dublin 29 March 1937). Dublin, 1947.

Neal Maquade. (Abbey, Dublin 17 Jan 1938). Unpbd.

Give him a house. (Abbey, Dublin 30 Oct 1939). Dublin 1947.

The rugged path (Abbey, Dublin 5 Aug 1940; Chepstow 13 Nov 1953) & The summit (Abbey, Dublin 10 Feb 1941): plays in three acts. 1942.

The fort field. (Abbey, Dublin 13 April 1942). Dublin 1947.

The new regime. (Abbey, Dublin 6 March 1944). Unpbd.

Tenants at will. (Abbey, Dublin 10 Sept 1945). Dublin 1947.

The old broom. (Abbey, Dublin 25 March 1946). Dublin 1947.

Macook's corner. (BBC Northern Ireland Home Service 7 Oct 1947). Unpbd.

The caretakers. (Abbey, Dublin 16 Feb 1948). Dublin 1948.

Tolly's experts. (BBC Northern Ireland Home Service 13 Dec 1951). Unpbd.

§2

Murray, T. C. In Irish theatre, ed L. Robinson 1939.

DODIE SMITH
(DOROTHY GLADYS SMITH)
b. 1896

Selections

Autumn crocus; Service; Touch wood: three plays. 1939.

§1

Autumn crocus: a play in three acts. (Lyric 6 April 1931). 1931, [1933] French. As by 'C. L. Anthony'.

Service: a play in three acts. (Wyndham's 12 Oct 1932). 1932, [1937] French. As by 'C. L. Anthony'.

Touch wood: a play in three acts. (Haymarket 16 May 1934). 1934, [1935] French. As by 'C. L. Anthony'.

Call it a day: a comedy in three acts. (Globe 30 Oct 1935). 1936, [1937] French.

Bonnet over the windmill: a play in three acts. (New 8 Sept 1937). 1937.

Dear Octopus: a comedy in three acts. (Queen's 14 Sept 1938). 1938, [1939] French.

Lovers and friends: a play in three acts. (Plymouth, New York 29 Nov 1943). New York [1947].

Letter from Paris: a comedy. (Royal, Brighton 10 Aug 1952; Aldwych 10 Oct 1952). 1954. Adapted from The reverberator by H. James.

I capture the castle: a romantic comedy. (Grand, Blackpool 19 Jan 1954; Aldwych 4 March 1954). [1954] French. Adapted from her novel.

Amateur means lover. (Playhouse, Liverpool 12 Sept 1961). [1962] French.
Dodie Smith also wrote an unpbd play and pbd several novels and books for children.

FRANCIS SLADEN SMITH
b. 1886

St Simeon Stylites. In Four one-act plays, 1923, Oxford 1926.
Edward about to marry: an extravaganza in one act. 1926.
The invisible duke: a gothic farce in one act. 1927.
The saint's comedy. 1927.
The crown of St Felice: a play in one act. 1928.
The sacred cat: a diversion in one act. 1928.
The man who wouldn't go to heaven: a play in one act. 1929.
Wonderful zoo: a play. (Unnamed Society, Manchester 24 March 1930). 1930.
The resurrection of Joseph: a play in one act. 1931.
Spring on Wyn Hill: a play in two parts. (Unnamed Society, Little, Manchester 16 Jan 1932). [1933] (Year Book Press ser).
The golden fisherman. In Modern short plays 3, 1932.
A guilty passion: a play in one act. 1932.
The herald: a play in one act. 1932.
Mrs Noah gives the sign: a play in one act. [1932] French.
The afflictions of St Thomas: a play in one act. 1933.
The amateur producer's handbook. 1933, 1948 (rev).
An Assyrian afternoon. 1933.
The confutation of wisdom: a Chinese episode in one act. 1933.
The destiny of Paolo: a play in one act. 1933.
In an art gallery: a comedy in one act. [1933] French.
The long gallery: a play in one act. [1933] French.
Love in the ape-house: a comedy in one act. [1933] French.
The poison party: a burlesque comedy in one act. [1933] French.
Surprise in the portico: a comedy in one act. [1933] (Year Book Press ser).
Happy Death, Ltd: a one act play. [1935].
The insuperable obstacle: a comedy in one act. 1935.
Skyscraper. In Eight new one act plays of 1935, ed J. Bourne 1935.
Sunset at Baghdad: an Arabian interlude. [1935]. (Amateur Theatre series of plays).
The wonderful tourist: a play in one act. [1935].
Presentation. In Putting on a play, by E. M. Browne, F. Sladen Smith et al, 1936.
Five plays and a pantomime: Paradise perplexed; The perfect hero; Pongo; Stephen; Henbury; Wherry knows. 1937.
The pretty toys: a play in one act. [1938] French.
Time's visitors. In Eight new one act plays of 1938, ed W. Armstrong 1938.
Westbury fair. In Best one act plays of 1939, ed J. W. Marriott 1940.
Diminutive comedies for women. 1942.
Polonaise. In Best one act plays of 1941, ed J. W. Marriott 1942.
All change for Peterborough: a play in three acts. (Unnamed Society, Queen's Hall, Manchester 5 Nov 1943). 1945.
The harlequin bridge. In Best one act plays of 1942–3, ed J. W. Marriott 1944.
The mixture as before. In Seagull plays: first collection, [1946].
Mary Frobisher. In North light: ten one-act plays from the North, ed W. Bannister 1947.
The waters of Lethe. In Best one act plays of 1950–51, ed J. W. Marriott 1952.
Sweet master William: a play in one act. [1953] French.

GITHA KATHERINE SOWERBY
18?–1970

Little plays for little people. [1910].
Rutherford and son: a play in three acts. (Court 31 Jan 1912). 1912.
Before breakfast: a comedy in one act. (Playhouse 2 May 1912). [1912] Lacy.
Githa Sowerby has also written a number of unpbd plays, as well as books of verse and stories for children.

STEPHEN HAROLD SPENDER
b. 1909

See cols 355–7, above.

'LESLEY STORM',
Mrs MABEL MARGARET CLARK
b. 1903

Tony draws a horse: a light comedy in three acts. (Criterion 26 Jan 1939). [1939] French.
Heart of a city: a play in three acts. (Henry Miller, New York 12 Feb 1942). New York [1942].
Great day: a play in three acts. (Playhouse 14 March 1945). [1946].
Black chiffon. (Westminster 3 May 1949). 1950, New York 1951.
The day's mischief: a play in two acts. (Grand, Blackpool 22 Oct 1951; Duke of York's 11 Dec 1951). [1952] French.
The long echo: a play in three acts. (Connaught, Worthing 23 Jan 1956; St James's 1 Aug 1956). [1957] French.
Favonia: a play in two acts. (Playhouse, Liverpool 12 Feb 1957). [1958] French.
Roar like a dove: a comedy in three acts. (Grand, Leeds 2 Sept 1957; Phoenix 26 Sept 1957). 1958, [1961] French.
The paper hat. (Globe 22 April 1965). [1966] French.
Lesley Storm has written unpbd plays and pbd short stories and novels.

WARREN CHETHAM STRODE
b. 1897

Selections
Three plays and a prologue. 1960. A play for Ronnie; The guinea-pig; Background.

§ I
Sometimes even now: a play in three acts. (Embassy 18 May 1933). 1933.
Man proposes: a play in a prologue and three acts. (Wyndham's 29 Nov 1933). [1934] French.
Heart's content: a play in three acts. (Golders Green 30 Nov 1936; Shaftesbury 23 Dec 1936). [1937] (Year Book Press ser).
The day is gone: a play in three acts. (Embassy 13 Sept 1937). [1938] (Embassy ser).
Stranger's road: a play in three acts. [1943] (Year Book Press ser).
Young Mrs Barrington: a play in three acts. (Winter Garden 5 Sept 1945). [1947] French.
The guinea-pig: a play in three acts. (Criterion 19 Feb 1946). [1946], [1949] French.
The gleam: a play in three acts. (Globe 4 Dec 1946). [1947], [1949] French.
A play for Ronnie: a play in three acts. [1947] Deane.
Background: a play in three acts. (Theatre Royal, Brighton 8 May 1950; Westminster 17 May 1950). [1951].

The pet shop: a play in three acts. (Playhouse, Liverpool 17 Feb 1953; St Martin's 7 Sept 1954). [1955] French.

The stepmother: a play in three acts. (St Martin's 5 Nov 1958). [1959] French. Adapted from the novel by R. C. Hutchinson.

Chetham Strode has also written unpbd plays and pbd a children's story and several novels.

ALFRED SUTRO
1863–1933

§1

Aglavaine and Selysette. 1897. From the French of Maeterlinck.

Carrots. (Theatre Royal, Dublin 18 Oct 1900; Prince of Wales, Kensington 21 Nov 1900; Garrick 22 April 1902). 1904 Lacy. Adapted from Poil de carotte by J. Renard.

The cave of illusion: a play in four acts. 1900.

A marriage has been arranged—a duologue: a comedy in one act. (Haymarket 6 May 1902). 1904 Lacy, New York 1904.

Monna Vanna. (Bijou, Bayswater 19 June 1902; Queen's 21 July 1914). 1904. From the French of Maeterlinck.

Alladine and Palomides; The death of Tintagiles. (St George's Hall 22 July 1902). 1899. From the French of Maeterlinck.

Women in love: eight studies in sentiment. 1902. The correct thing; The gutter of time; Ella's apology; A game of chess; The salt of life; Mr Steinmann's corner; Maggie: a monologue; A maker of men.

The walls of Jericho: a play in four acts. (Garrick 31 Oct 1904). [1906].

A maker of men: a duologue. (St James's 27 Jan 1905). In Women in love, 1902 above. Also pbd separately 1905 (Lacy).

Mollentrave on women: a comedy in three acts. (St James's 13 Feb 1905). 1905.

The correct thing. (Drury Lane 27 June 1905). In Women in love, 1902 above. Also pbd separately 1905 (Lacy).

The perfect lover: a play in four acts. (Imperial 14 Oct 1905). New York [1921].

A game of chess: a duologue. In Women in love, 1902, above. Also pbd separately 1905 (Lacy).

The salt of life. In Women in love, 1902 above. Also pbd separately 1905 (Lacy).

The fascinating Mr Vanderveldt: a comedy in four acts. (Garrick 26 April 1906). [1906].

Ella's apology: a duologue. (Bloomsbury Hall 8 Nov 1906). In Women in love, 1902 above. Also pbd separately 1905 (Lacy).

The open door: a duologue. [1906] Lacy, New York 1912.

The price of money. New York 1906.

John Glayde's honour: a new and original play in four acts. (St James's 8 March 1907). [1907].

Mr Steinmann's corner. (His Majesty's 4 June 1907). In Women in love, 1902 above. Also pbd separately 1905 (Lacy).

The barrier: a new and original play in four acts. (Comedy 10 Oct 1907). 1907 (priv ptd), [1921].

The man on the kerb: a duologue. (Aldwych 24 March 1908). [1908] Lacy.

The gutter of time: a duologue. (Eastbourne pier 3 Aug 1908). In Women in love, 1902, above. Also pbd separately 1905 (Lacy).

The builder of bridges: a play in four acts. (St James's 11 Nov 1908). 1909.

The bracelet: a play in one act. (Lyceum New York 15 March 1910; Repertory, Liverpool 26 Feb 1912). [1912] Lacy, New York [1912] French.

The perplexed husband: a comedy in four acts. (Wyndham's 12 Sept 1911). 1913.

The man in the stalls. (Palace 6 Oct 1911). [1911] Lacy, New York [1911] French.

The firescreen: a comedy in four acts. (Garrick 7 Feb 1912). [1912].

Five little plays: The man in the stalls; A marriage has been arranged; The man on the kerb; The open door; The bracelet. 1912, New York 1913.

The two virtues: a comedy in four acts. (St James's 5 March 1914). 1914.

Freedom: a play in three acts. 1914.

Rude Min and Christine: a comedy in three acts. (As The two Miss Farndons, Gaiety, Manchester 21 May 1917; as Uncle Anyhow, Haymarket 1 May 1918). 1915, [1919] French.

The marriage...will not take place: a play in one act. (Coliseum 13 Aug 1917). [1917] French.

The egoist. 1919. From Meredith's novel.

The choice: a play in four acts. (Wyndham's 8 Sept 1919). [1920].

The laughing lady: a comedy in three acts. (Globe 17 Nov 1922). 1922.

The great well: a play in four acts. (New 19 Dec 1922). [1922].

Far above rubies: a comedy in three acts. (Comedy 27 March 1924). 1924.

A man with a heart: a play in four acts. (Wyndham's 14 March 1925). 1925.

The desperate lovers: a frivolous comedy in three acts. (Comedy 28 Jan 1927). 1927.

Living together: a play in four acts. (Wyndham's 29 Jan 1929). 1929.

The blackmailing lady: a play in one act. [1929] French.

Celebrities and simple souls. 1933. Autobiographical reminiscences.

Sutro also wrote the following unpbd plays: The Chili widow (Royalty 7 Sept 1895), with A. Bourchier, from Monsieur le directeur by A. Busson; The desperate duke: or The culpable countess (Chelsea Hospital 5 July 1907), with R Marshall; The lonely life (Queen's, Manchester 22 July 1907); The romantic barber (Theatre Royal, Dublin 2 March 1908; Grand, Fulham 23 March 1908); Making a gentleman (Garrick 11 Sept 1909); The clever ones (Wyndham's 23 April 1914) (typescript in Library of Congress); The great Redding Street burglary (Coliseum 31 July 1916); The trap (Coliseum 11 March 1918).

He also pbd short-stories, and trns from the prose works of Maeterlinck.

§2

Sutton, G. Some plays of Sutro. Bookman (London) 63 1923.

VERNON SYLVAINE
1897–1957

The road of poplars: a one act play. (Coliseum 18 Aug 1930). [1930], [1954] French.

The actress: a comedy in one act. [1931] (Year Book Press ser).

A bite of the apple: a comedy in one act. (Repertory Birmingham 1932). [1932] (Year Book Press ser).

Not what they seem: a farce in one act. [1932] (Year Book Press ser).

Everything's just the same! a possibility in one act. (Embassy 15 Jan 1934). Birmingham 1934.

Cards on the table: a comedy in one act. [1934] (Year Book Press ser).

Legionnaire: a play in one act. [1934] (Year Book Press ser).

Wisdom: an incident in one act. Birmingham 1934.

A woman passed by: a play in three acts. (Duke of York's 9 April 1935). [1945].

Aren't men beasts! a farce in three acts. (Strand 13 May 1936). [1938] French.

A spot of bother: a farce in three acts. (Streatham Hill 28 June 1937; Strand 6 July 1937). [1938] French.

Women aren't angels: a farce in three acts. (Streatham Hill 1 July 1940; Strand 18 July 1940). [1943] French.

Warn that man!: a play in three acts. (Garrick 23 Dec 1941). [1943] French.

Madame Louise: a farce in three acts. (Garrick 22 Feb 1945). [1946].

The anonymous lover: a comedy in three acts. (Duke of York's 13 March 1947). [1948] French.

Quiet in the forest. (Q 15 April 1947). [1945].

One wild oat: a farce in three acts. (Garrick 8 Dec 1948). [1951] French.

Will any gentleman? a farce in three acts. (Strand 6 Sept 1950). [1952] French.

As long as they're happy: a farcical comedy in three acts. (Garrick 8 July 1953). In Plays of the year 1953, 1954; pbd separately [1954] French.

Vernon Sylvaine also wrote a number of unpbd plays and a novel.

JOAN TEMPLE
?–1965

The widow's cruise: a comedy in three acts. (Ambassadors 3 March 1926). 1926.

Charles and Mary: a play on the life of Charles Lamb. (Everyman 4 Feb 1930). 1930.

No room at the inn. (Embassy 10 July 1945). [1946].

Deliver my darling. (Embassy 11 Oct 1947). 1948.

Joan Temple wrote about 8 unpbd plays and pbd several novels.

DYLAN MARLAIS THOMAS
1914–53

See cols 220–30, above.

BEN TRAVERS
b. 1886

A cuckoo in the nest: a play in three acts. (Court, Liverpool 13 July 1925; Aldwych 25 July 1925). [1938]. From his own novel pbd 1922.

Rookery nook: a farce in three acts. (Aldwych 30 June 1926). [1930]. From his own novel pbd 1923.

Thark: a farce in three acts. (King's, Southsea 27 June 1927; Aldwych 4 July 1927). [1932].

Plunder: a farce in three acts. (Aldwych 26 June 1928). [1931].

A cup of kindness: a farce in three acts. (Aldwych 7 May 1929). [1934].

Turkey time: a farce in three acts. (Aldwych 26 May 1931). [1934].

Dirty work. (Aldwych 7 March 1932). 1932.

O mistress mine. (St James's 11 Dec 1936). [1956] French (rev, as Nun's veiling).

Banana ridge: a comedy in three acts. (Strand 27 April 1938). [1939].

She follows me about: a comedy in three acts. (Royal, Birmingham 14 June 1943; Garrick 15 Oct 1943). [1945] French.

Outrageous fortune: a farce in three acts. (Winter Garden 13 Nov 1947). [1948] French.

Wild horses: a farcical comedy in three acts. (Opera, Manchester 18 Aug 1952; Aldwych 6 Nov 1952). [1953] French.

Vale of laughter: an autobiography. 1957.

Travers has written the following unpbd plays: The dippers (*Royal Court, Liverpool 10 April 1922; Criterion 22 Aug*

1922), *from his own novel of 1920*; The three graces (*Empire 26 Jan 1924*), *a musical in three acts, adapted from the libretto by Carl Lombardi and Dr A. M. Willner*; Mischief (*Fortune 17 July 1928*), *from his own novel of 1925*; A night like this (*Aldwych 18 Feb 1930*); The chance of a night time (*1931*); Just my luck (*1932*); A bit of a test (*Aldwych 30 Jan 1933*); Lady in danger (*1934*); Up to the neck (*1934*); Fighting stock (*1935*); Foreign affairs (*1935*); Stormy weather (*1935*); Certain of the brethren (*later entitled* Chastity, my brother) (*Embassy, Swiss Cottage 1936*); Dishonour bright (*1936*); Pot luck (*1936*); For valour (*1937*); Second best bed (*1937*); Old iron (*1938*); Spotted Dick (*Strand 23 Aug 1939*); Runaway Victory (*Theatre Royal, Brighton 23 May 1949*).

Travers has also pbd short stories and selections of humorous writing.

PETER ALEXANDER USTINOV
b. 1921

Selections

Five plays. 1965, Boston 1965. Romanoff and Juliet; The moment of truth; Beyond; The love of four colonels; No sign of the dove.

§1

House of regrets: a tragi-comedy in three acts. (Arts 6 Oct 1942). 1943.

Beyond: a play in one act. (Arts 17 March 1943). [1944] Guild.

Blow your own trumpet. (Playhouse, Liverpool 26 July 1943; Playhouse 11 Aug 1943). In Plays about people, 1950, below.

The Banbury nose: a play in four acts. (Wyndham's 6 Sept 1944). 1945.

The tragedy of good intentions. (Playhouse, Liverpool 5 Oct 1945). In Plays about people, 1950 below.

The indifferent shepherd. (Criterion 5 Feb 1948). Ibid.

Plays about people. 1950. The tragedy of good intentions; Blow your own trumpet; The indifferent shepherd. With a preface on the nature of acting and its effect on the playwright.

The love of four colonels: a play in three acts. (Alexandra, Birmingham 26 March 1951; Wyndham's 23 May 1951). [1951] Guild, New York 1953 Dramatists Play Service.

The moment of truth: a play in four acts. (Royal, Nottingham 15 Oct 1951; Adelphi 21 Nov 1951). [1953] Guild.

No sign of the dove. (Grand, Leeds 19 Oct 1953; Savoy 3 Dec 1953). In Five plays, 1965, above.

Romanoff and Juliet: a comedy in three acts. (Opera, Manchester 2 April 1956; Piccadilly 11 May 1956). [1957] Guild, New York 1958.

Photo-finish: an adventure in biography in three acts. (Gaiety, Dublin 26 March 1962; Saville 25 April 1962). 1962, [1963] Guild, Boston 1963.

The unknown soldier and his wife. (Chichester Festival 22 May 1968). New York 1967, London 1968.

Ustinov has also written more than ten unpbd plays and several filmscripts and has pbd novels, short stories and cartoons.

§2

Williams, G. Peter Ustinov. 1957.

JOHN WILLIAM VAN DRUTEN
1901–57

§1

Young Woodley: a play in three acts. (Belmont, New York 2 Oct 1925; Hollis St, Boston 5 Oct 1925). New

York 1926, London 1928, [1930] French (rev), New York 1930.

Diversion: a play in three acts. (Lyceum, Rochester NY Aug 1927; Forty-ninth Street, New York 11 Jan 1928; Arts 26 Sept 1928). 1928, [1933] French.

The return of the soldier: a play in three acts. (Playhouse 12 June 1928). 1928. Adapted from novel by Rebecca West.

After all: a play in three acts. (Apollo 5 May 1929). 1929, New York 1931, London [1933] French.

Young Woodley. 1929, New York 1929. Novel based on his play.

A woman on her way. 1930, New York 1931. Novel.

London wall: a comedy in three acts. (Duke of York's 1 May 1931). 1931, [1932] French.

There's always Juliet: a comedy in three acts. (Apollo 12 Oct 1931). 1931, [1932] French.

Hollywood holiday: an extravagant comedy in three episodes. (New 15 Oct 1931). 1931. With B. Levy.

Somebody knows. (St Martin's 12 May 1932). 1932, [1935] French.

Behold we live. (St James's 16 Aug 1932). 1932, [1935] French.

The distaff side: a play in three acts. (Apollo 5 Sept 1933). 1933, New York 1934, London [1934] French.

Flowers of the forest: a play in three acts. (Whitehall 20 Nov 1934). 1934, New York 1936.

Most of the game: a light comedy in three acts. (Cort, New York 1 Oct 1935). New York 1936.

And then you wish. 1936, Boston 1937. Novel.

Gertie Maude: a play in three acts. (St Martin's 17 Aug 1937). 1937.

The way to the present: a personal record. 1938.

Leave her to heaven: a play in three acts. (Longacre, New York Feb 1940). New York 1941.

Old acquaintance: a comedy in three acts. (Morosco, New York 23 Dec 1940; Apollo 18 Dec 1941). New York 1941, London 1943, [1946] French.

The damask cheek: a comedy in three acts. (Playhouse, New York Oct 1942; Repertory, Birmingham 17 Feb 1948; Lyric, Hammersmith 2 Feb 1949). New York 1943, London [1949] French. With L. Morris.

The voice of the turtle: a comedy in three acts. (Shubert, New Haven Conn 4 Dec 1943; Morosco, New York 8 Dec 1943; Piccadilly 9 July 1947). New York [1944] Dramatists Play Service.

I remember mama: a play in two acts. (Music Box, New York 19 Oct 1944; Aldwych 2 March 1948). New York 1945, London [1948] French, New York 1952 (rev) Dramatists Play Service. Adapted from Mama's bank account by K. Forbes.

The mermaids singing: play in three acts. (Shubert, New Haven Conn 8 Nov 1945; Empire, New York 28 Nov 1945). New York [1946] Dramatists Play Service.

The druid circle: a play in three acts. (Morosco New York 22 Oct 1947). New York [1948] Dramatists Play Service.

Make way for Lucia: comedy in three acts. (Cort, New York 22 Dec 1948). New York [1949] Dramatists Play Service. Based on the novels of E. F. Benson.

Bell, book and candle: a comedy. (Shubert, New Haven Conn 25 Oct 1950; Ethel Barrymore, New York 14 Nov 1950; Royal Court, Liverpool 13 Sept 1954; Phoenix 5 Oct 1954). New York 1951, London [1956] French.

I am a camera: a play in three acts. (Empire, New York 28 Nov 1951; Theatre Royal, Brighton 1 March 1954; New 12 March 1954). New York [1952], London 1954. Adapted from the Berlin stories of Christopher Isherwood.

I've got sixpence: a play in two acts. (Ethel Barrymore, New York 2 Dec 1952). New York [1953] Dramatists Play Service. With a preface by the author.

Playwright at work. New York 1953, London 1953. Record of Van Druten's methods as a dramatist.

The vicarious years. 1955, New York 1957. Novel.

Widening circle. 1957, New York 1957. An autobiography.

John Van Druten also wrote the following unpbd plays: The return half (*RADA 5 Oct 1924*); Chance acquaintance (*Strand 11 Sept 1927*); Sea fever (*New 30 June 1931*) (*with Auriol Lee from the play* Marius by M. *Pagnol*); Solitaire (*Plymouth, New York 27 Jan 1942*) (*from the novel by E. Corle*); The king and I (*St James, New York 29 March 1951; Drury Lane 8 Oct 1953*) (*lyrics for musical*); Dancing in the chequered shade (*McCarter, Princeton 20 Dec 1955*).

He pbd poems, numerous short stories and articles including criticisms of contemporary dramatists and productions.

§2

Hewes, H. John Van Druten's wholesome sinners. Theatre Arts 37 1953.

VANE HUNT SUTTON VANE
1888–1963

Outward bound. (Everyman 17 Sept 1923). 1924, New York [1924] French. As novel 1929.

Falling leaves. (Pleasure Gardens, Folkestone 2 June 1924; Little 25 Nov 1924). 1924.

Overture: a play in three acts. (Everyman, Hampstead 11 April 1925). 1925.

Sutton Vane also wrote several unpbd plays.

FRANK VOSPER
1899–1937

Surmise. (Apollo, Atlantic City 17 Oct 1927; Lyric 21 June 1929 as Murder on the second floor). 1929, [1930] French.

Spellbound. (Earl Carroll, New York 14 Nov 1927; Strand 3 Nov 1929, as People like us; Wyndham's 6 July 1948). 1929, [1951] French.

Lucky dip: a comedy in three acts. (Comedy 23 Oct 1930). [1931] French.

All is not gold: a play in one act. [1931] (Year Book Press ser).

Marry at leisure: a comedy in three acts. (Haymarket 4 June 1931). [1931] French.

Love from a stranger: a play in three acts. (Wyndham's 2 Feb 1936). [1936], [1937] French. From a story by Agatha Christie.

Vosper also wrote the following unpbd plays: The combined maze (*Strand 13 March 1927*) (*adapted from the novel by M. Sinclair*); Debonair (*Lyric 23 April 1930*) (*with G. B. Stern*); Something strange (*Phoenix 22 Feb 1931*) (*based on the story by H G. Wells*).

RICHARD HORATIO EDGAR WALLACE
1875–1932

See cols 754–8, above.

CHARLES WALTER STANSBY WILLIAMS
1886–1945

See cols 772–4, above.

GEORGE EMLYN WILLIAMS
b. 1905

Collections

The corn is green, with two other plays: The wind of heaven; The druid's rest. 1950.

The collected plays. 1961–, New York 1961–. With introd by Williams.

§1

Vigil. (O.U.D.S., Oxford Nov 1925). In The second book of one-act plays, 1954.

Full moon. (Playhouse, Oxford 28 Feb 1927; Arts 30 Jan 1929). Unpbd.

Glamour. (Embassy 10 Dec 1928). Unpbd.

A murder has been arranged: a ghost story in three acts. (Strand 9 Nov 1930). 1930.

Port Said. (Wyndham's 1 Nov 1931). Unpbd.

The late Christopher Bean: a comedy. (St James's 16 May 1933). 1933. Adapted from S. Howard's version of Prenez garde à la peinture! by R. Fauchois.

Vessels departing. (Embassy 3 July 1933). Unpbd.

Spring 1600: a comedy in three acts. (Shaftesbury 21 Jan 1934; rev version Lyric, Hammersmith 6 Dec 1945). 1946.

Josephine. (His Majesty's 25 Sept 1934). Adapted from H. Bahr. Unpbd.

Night must fall: a play in three acts. (Duchess 31 May 1935). 1935.

He was born gay: a romance in three acts. (Queen's 26 May 1937). 1937.

The corn is green: a comedy in three acts. (Duchess 20 Sept 1938). [1938], New York 1941, 1945 (rev) Dramatists Play Service.

The light of heart: a play in three acts. (Apollo 21 Feb 1940). 1940.

The morning star: a play in three acts. (Globe 10 Dec 1941). 1942.

A month in the country: a comedy. (St James's 11 Feb 1943). 1943. Adapted from Turgenev.

Pen Don. (Grand, Blackpool Dec 1943). Unpbd.

The druid's rest: a comedy in three acts. (St Martin's 26 Jan 1944). 1944.

The wind of heaven: a play in six scenes. (St James's 12 April 1945). 1945.

Thinking aloud: a dramatic sketch. (Stage Door Canteen July 1945). [1946] French.

Pepper and sand: a duologue. (BBC 14 July 1947). [1948].

Trespass: a ghost story in six scenes. (Globe 16 July 1947). Unpbd.

Accolade: a play in six scenes. (Aldwych 6 Sept 1950). 1951 Deane.

Someone waiting: a play in three acts. (Royal Court, Liverpool 14 Sept 1953; Globe 25 Nov 1953). 1954, New York 1956 Dramatists Play Service.

Readings from Dickens. [1953]. Adaptations.

Beth: a play in four scenes. (Royal, Brighton 10 Feb 1958; Apollo 20 March 1958). 1959.

George: an early autobiography. 1961, New York 1962.

The master builder. (Old Vic 9 June 1964). Adapted from Ibsen. Unpbd.

Beyond belief: a chronicle of murder and its detection. 1967.

Williams has also written a number of filmscripts.

§2

Stokes, S. Emlyn Williams. Theatre Arts 26 1942.

Hope-Wallace, P. Emlyn Williams. Theatre Arts 32 1948.

Trewin, J. C. The plays of Williams. Adelphi 28 1951.

'Findlater, Richard' (K. B. F. Bain). Emlyn Williams: an illustrated study of his work, with a list of his appearances on stage and screen [and of his plays]. 1957.

HUGH ROSS WILLIAMSON
b. 1901

In a glass darkly. (Cambridge Festival 1932). In The seven deadly virtues [etc], 1936, below.

'After the event': a play in one act. (Welwyn Dramatic Festival 20 May 1933; Playhouse, Liverpool 1 Nov 1933). [1935].

Rose and glove. (Westminster 8 Sept 1934). 1934.

The seven deadly virtues. (Gate 13 Feb 1935). In The seven deadly virtues [etc], 1936, below.

Various heavens. (Gate 12 Feb 1936). Ibid.

Cinderella's grandchild: a play in one act. (Rodney Dramatic Club, Cambridge 25 Oct 1936). [1936].

The seven deadly virtues; In a glass darkly; Various heavens: a play sequence. 3 pt 1936.

Mr Gladstone: a play in three acts. (Gate 30 Sep 1937). 1937.

Stories from history—ten plays for schools: A king of Egypt founds a new city; An Indian prince becomes Buddha; The Greeks win a victory; Alexander tries to conquer the world; Mohammed founds a new religion; Bernard builds a monastery; Louis of France goes on a crusade; A knight of the Middle Ages; Leonardo da Vinci invents an aeroplane; Christopher Columbus discovers a new world. 1938.

Paul, a bond slave: a radio play. (BBC Home Service 24 Sept–26 Nov 1944). 1945.

Conversation with a ghost. (BBC Home Service 1 Aug 1945). In The best one-act plays of 1950–1, ed J. W. Marriott 1952.

The story without an end: dramatized meditations on the life, death and resurrection of Jesus. 1947. Radio plays.

Queen Elizabeth: a play in three acts. (Arts, Ipswich 6 Sept 1948; Arts 10 Oct 1950). 1947.

Fool's paradise. (Arts, Ipswich 21 March 1949). 1954 Evans.

The cardinal's learning. (BBC Home Service 26 Nov 1949). In The best one-act plays of 1948–9, ed J. W. Marriott 1950.

Gunpowder, treason and plot. (Arts, Ipswich 28 May 1951). In Plays of the year 1951, [1952].

His Eminence of England: a play in two acts. (Canterbury Cathedral 14 July 1953). 1953.

Diamond cut diamond. (Library, Manchester 31 Aug 1954). In Plays of the year 1951–2, [1953].

King Claudius. In The best one-act plays of 1954–55, ed H. Miller 1956.

The walled garden. 1956, New York 1957. Autobiography.

The mime of Bernadette. [1958].

Heart of Bruce. (Lauriston Hall, Edinburgh 24 Aug 1959). In Plays of the year 1959, [1960].

Teresa of Avila. (Dublin Festival 11 Sept 1961; Vaudeville 20 Oct 1961). In Plays of the year, 1961. [1962].

Ross Williamson has also written a number of unpbd plays and pbd books on historical, theological and critical subjects.

JOHN KEITH WINTER
b. 1906

The rats of Norway: a play in three acts. (Playhouse 6 April 1933). 1933.

The shining hour: a play in three acts. (Booth, New York 13 Feb 1934; St James's 4 Sept 1934). 1934, New York 1934, London [1935] French.

Ringmaster: a play in three acts. (Shaftesbury 11 March 1935). 1937.

Worse things happen at sea!: a comedy in three acts. (St James's 26 March 1935). 1935.

Old music: a play in a prologue, epilogue and three acts. (St James's 18 Aug 1937). 1938.

Air raid. In 8 new one act plays of 1937, ed W. Armstrong 1937.

Keith Winter has also written a number of unpbd plays, and has pbd short stories and novels.

PELHAM GRENVILLE WODEHOUSE
b. 1881

See cols 778–81, above.

HUMBERT WOLFE
1885–1940

See cols 377–9, above.

EDWARD WOOLL
1878–1970

Libel! a play in three acts. (Playhouse 2 April 1934). 1934, [1936] French.

Edward Wooll has also written a number of unpbd plays, and has pbd novels and books on legal topics.

PETER YATES
b. 1914

The assassin: a drama in two acts. 1945.
The burning mask. (Manchester Green Room 18 March 1955). 1948.

Yates has also pbd a mystery story and books of verse.

L.O.

5. PROSE

There is no history or bibliography of the non-fictional prose of the period as a whole. For surveys of comparatively small parts of the period, see J. Hayward, Prose literature since 1939, 1947, and A. Pryce-Jones, Prose literature 1945-50, 1951 (both Br Council pamphlets). For an essay on some general features of the expository prose of the period, see E. W. F. Tomlin, The prose of thought, in the Pelican guide to English literature vol 7, The modern age, ed B. Ford 1961. For bibliographies, reference books, literary histories and surveys which include treatment of the prose of the period, e.g. BM Subject Catalogue, Annual Register etc, see Introduction, cols 1–14, above.

Since this section is concerned with writers whose work is of some literary standing, it excludes purely technical scholars and scientists, however distinguished (e.g. Rutherford). For the same reason, the general studies listed deal with writers and their setting; discussions which are only technical or theoretical have been omitted. The general studies do not, except in a few cases, include anthologies or periodical articles as these are far too numerous to list and, so far as anthologies are concerned, are generally popular or elementary.

Single lectures by a writer are normally excluded, as are subtitles which indicate that the text of a book was originally given in the form of a lecture series, and periodical articles discussing technical aspects of a scientist's or a scholar's work.

I. CRITICS AND LITERARY SCHOLARS, ESSAYISTS AND HUMOURISTS

GENERAL STUDIES

For bibliographies relevant to the period, see the following: A selected bibliography of modern criticism, *in* Critiques and essays in criticism 1920-48, ed R. W. Stallman, New York 1949; Bibliography 1920-50, *in* The critic's notebook, ed R. W. Stallman, Minneapolis 1950 (more specific to the nature and function of criticism than the previous title); A supplementary list of essays in criticism 1900-50 *and* A note on contemporary English criticism, *in* Literary opinion in America vol 2, ed M. D. Zabel, New York 1962 (3rd rev edn); Literary criticism in English, *in* A guide to English literature, ed F. W. Bateson 1965; *and the section on literary criticism in the annual bibliography of* PMLA.

Williams, O. C. Contemporary criticism of literature. 1924.
O'Leary, J. G. English literary history and bibliography. 1928.
Dobrée, B. Modern prose style. Oxford 1934, 1964 (rev and enlarged).
Potter, S. The muse in chains. 1937. Critical examination of the growth of English literature as a field of study and scholarship.
West, A. Crisis and criticism. 1937.
Ransom, J. C. The new criticism. Norfolk Conn 1941.
Ong, W. J. The meaning of the new criticism. In Twentieth-century English, ed W. S. Knickerbocker, New York 1946.
— The vernacular matrix of the new criticism. In his Barbarian within, New York 1962.
Bentley, E. Introduction. In The importance of Scrutiny, ed Bentley, New York 1948.
Hyman, S. E. The armed vision: a study in the methods of modern literary criticism. New York 1948.
Dingle, H. Science and literary criticism. 1949.
Elton, W. A glossary of the new criticism. Chicago 1949, 1951 (rev and enlarged, as A guide to the new criticism).
Wellek, R. and A. Warren. Theory of literature. New York 1949, 1956 (rev), London 1963 (rev) (Peregrine).
O'Connor, W. V. An age of criticism, 1900-50. Chicago 1952.
— Some notes on modern literary criticism. In his The grotesque: an American genre, Carbondale 1962.
Crane, R. S. The languages of contemporary criticism. In his Languages of criticism and the structure of poetry, Toronto 1953.

Bloomfield, P. The Bloomsbury tradition in English literary criticism. In The craft of letters in England, ed J. Lehmann 1956.
Cranston, M. The literature of ideas. Ibid.
Daiches, D. Critical approaches to literature. Englewood Cliffs NJ 1956.
— Critical and general prose. In his The present age after 1920, 1958.
Krieger, M. The new apologists for poetry. Minneapolis 1956.
— Recent criticism, thematics and the existential dilemma. In his Tragic vision, New York [1960].
Lerner, L. D. The new criticism. In The craft of letters in England, ed J. Lehmann 1956.
Wimsatt, W. K. and C. Brooks. Literary criticism: a short history. New York 1957.
Leary, L. G. (ed). Contemporary literary scholarship: a critical review. New York [1958].
Pulos, C. E. The new critics and the language of poetry. Lincoln Nebraska 1958.
Tillyard, E. M. W. The muse unchained: an intimate account of the revolution in English studies at Cambridge. [1958].
Holloway, J. The critical intimidation; The new and the newer critics; The new establishment in criticism. In his Charted mirror, 1960.
Gomme, A. Criticism and the reading public. In The Pelican guide to English literature vol 7, The modern age, ed B. Ford 1961.
Stallman, R. W. The new critics. In his Houses that James built, [East Lansing] 1961.
Foster, R. J. The new romantics: a reappraisal of the new criticism. Bloomington 1962.
Goldberg, G. J and N. M. (ed). The modern critical spectrum: the major schools of modern literary criticism explained and illustrated. Englewood Cliffs NJ 1962.
Watson, G. The early twentieth century; The mid-century scene. In his Literary critics, 1962 (Pelican), 1964 (rev).
Weimann, R. 'New criticism' und die Entwicklung bürgerlicher Literaturwissenschaft: Geschichte und Kritik neuer Interpretationsmethoden. Halle 1962.
Leavis, F. R. Scrutiny: a retrospect. Scrutiny 20 1963.
— (ed). A selection from Scrutiny. 2 vols Cambridge 1968.
Righter, W. Logic and criticism. 1963.
Wellek, R. Concepts of criticism. New Haven 1963.

Palmer, D. J. The rise of English studies: an account of the study of English language and literature from its origin to the making of the Oxford English school. Hull 1965.

Rogerson, B. and L. D. Lerner. Criticism. In Encyclopedia of poetry and poetics, ed A. Preminger, Princeton 1965.

Weitz, M. Hamlet and the philosophy of literary criticism. Chicago 1965.

Wimsatt, W. K. Horses of wrath: recent critical lessons. In his Hateful contraries, [Lexington Kentucky] 1965.

Bush, D. Literary history and literary criticism. In his Engaged and disengaged, Cambridge Mass 1966.

Casey, J. P. The language of criticism. 1966.

Lee, B. The new criticism and the language of poetry. In Essays on style and language, ed R. Fowler 1966.

Morrison, C. C. Freud and the critic: the early use of depth psychology in literary criticism. Chapel Hill [1968].

Gross, J. The rise and fall of the man of letters: aspects of English life since 1800. 1969.

M. S.

LASCELLES ABERCROMBIE
1881–1938

An extensive collection of mss is held in the Brotherton Library, Univ of Leeds; one of the mss of The sale of St Thomas, Act 1, *and those of* The staircase, The Olympians *and the first act of an unfinished, untitled play are held in Bodley.*

Bibliographies

'John Gawsworth' (T. I. F. Armstrong). In his Ten contemporaries: notes towards their definitive bibliography, ser 1, 1932. Prefaced by 'A personal note' by Abercrombie.

Elton, O. In his Lascelles Abercrombie, [1939]. *See §2, below.*

Cooper, J. A bibliography and notes on the works of Abercrombie. 1969.

§1
Prose

Thomas Hardy: a critical study. 1912, New York 1927.

Speculative dialogues. 1913.

Poetry and contemporary speech. 1914 (Eng Assoc pamphlet).

The epic. [1914] (Art and Craft of Letters).

An essay towards a theory of art. 1922.

Principles of English prosody, pt 1: the elements. 1923. A 'systematic conspectus of versification' was projected as a sequel but not pbd.

Stratford-upon-Avon: a report on future development. 1923. With L. P. Abercrombie.

The theory of poetry. 1924, New York [1926] (with different preface).

The idea of great poetry. 1925.

Romanticism. 1926, New York 1963. Contains 186 lines of verse tr from Empedocles with original lines by Abercrombie not rptd in Poems, 1930, below.

Progress in literature: the Leslie Stephen lecture. Cambridge 1929.

Colloquial language in literature. [Oxford] 1931 (Soc for Pure Eng Tract 36). With other essays by O. Jespersen, C. T. Onions, H. W. Fowler.

Tennyson. In Revaluations: studies in biography, by L. Abercrombie [et al], 1931.

Principles of literary criticism. In An outline of modern knowledge, ed W. Rose 1931; rptd separately (without synopsis) 1932 (Outline Ser), New York 1961.

Poetry: its music and meaning. 1932.

The art of Wordsworth. 1952, New York 1952. Lectures, ed with preface by R. Abercrombie.

A number of Abercrombie's other academic lectures were pbd separately. See Cooper, Bibliographies, above.

Poetry, Verse Plays

Interludes and poems. 1908, New York 1908, London 1928 (2 poems slightly rev).

Mary and the bramble. Much Marcle 1910 (priv ptd). Poem.

The sale of Saint Thomas. Dymock 1911 (priv ptd). One act, rptd in The sale of Saint Thomas in six acts, 1930, below. Included in Georgian poetry, 1911–12, 1912.

Emblems of love, designed in several discourses. 1912, New York 1912.

Deborah: a play in three acts. (Josca's Little Theatre, Oxford 27 April 1964; first act only). 1913, New York 1913, London 1923 (slightly rev).

The adder. (Liverpool Repertory 3 March 1913; Birmingham Repertory 17 May 1913). In Four short plays, 1922, below.

New numbers. Vol 1, nos 1–4. Dymock 1914. By W. W. Gibson, Brooke, Drinkwater and Abercrombie; no further nos pbd. Abercrombie contributed The Olympians (no 1, Feb) and The innocents (no 3, Aug), both rptd (largely rewritten) in Twelve idylls, 1928; The end of the world (no 2, April, performed Birmingham Repertory 12 Sept 1914 and Theatre Royal, Bristol 26 Oct 1914) and The staircase (no 4, Dec, performed Playhouse, Liverpool 4 March 1920), both rptd in Four short plays, 1922, below.

Four short plays. 1922. The adder, The staircase, The end of the world, The deserter.

Phoenix: tragicomedy in three acts. (St Martin's 20 Jan 1924). 1923.

Twelve idylls and other poems. 1928.

The poems of Lascelles Abercrombie. 1930. In the Oxford Poets Ser; contains all previously pbd poems and plays save the lines in Romanticism, 1926, above, Prose.

The sale of Saint Thomas in six acts. 1930. Act 1 first pbd 1911.

To Sir Walford Davies at Gregynog June, 1934. [Newtown 1934]. Broadsheet; rptd in next.

Lyrics and unfinished poems. [Newtown] 1940 (175 copies). Note on Abercrombie's poetry by W. Gibson.

Vision and love. [1966] (priv ptd, 28 copies). 9 previously unpbd poems.

Abercrombie contributed to Georgian Poetry *1911–12, 1913–15, 1918–19 and 1920–2, and he compiled (with a preface and note)* New English poems: a miscellany, *1931; he contributed a number of prefaces and introds to other works. He held a staff post on the* Liverpool Daily Courier *1908–9, contributing leading articles and reviews till 1912; he also contributed reviews to* Manchester Guardian *1910–14 and contributed to many other periodicals and jnls.*

§2

Sturgeon, M. C. In her Studies of contemporary poets, 1916.

Maynard, T. Abercrombie: an egoistic sceptic. In his Our best poets, 1922.

Jones, L. Abercrombie: poet and critic. In his First impressions, New York 1925.

Lucas, F. L. Greatness in poetry. In his Authors dead and living, 1926. Essay-review of The idea of great poetry, 1925.

Stenberg, T. Abercrombie's view of poetry. Sewanee Rev 37 1929.

Williams, C. In his Poetry at present, Oxford 1930.

Thouless, P. In her Modern poetic drama, Oxford 1934.

Elton, O. Dr Lascelles Abercrombie. Oxford Mag 10 Nov 1938.

— Lascelles Abercrombie. [1939]. Rptd from Proc Br Acad 25 1939.

Vallette, J. En relisant les poèmes d'Abercrombie. Etudes Anglaises 3 1939.

Abercrombie: the homage of friends. English 4 1943.
Poems, with an article by P. Withers, Abercrombie as
I knew him.
Ross, R. H. In his The Georgian revolt: rise and fall of
a poetic ideal 1910–22, Carbondale 1965.

JAMES EVERSHED AGATE
1877–1947

Selections

[Selected essays]. 1926 (Essays of Today and Yesterday).
Here's richness: an anthology of and by Agate. 1942.
Foreword by O. Sitwell.
Agate: an anthology. Ed H. Van Thal 1961, New York
1961. Introd by A. Dent.

§1

L. of C. (Lines of communication): being the letters of
a temporary officer in the Army Service Corps. 1917.
First pbd (in part) in Manchester Guardian.
Buzz, buzz!: essays of the theatre. [1918]. First pbd in
Manchester Guardian, Manchester Playgoer.
Responsibility. 1919, New York [1920], London 1943
(rev). Novel.
Alarums and excursions. 1922, New York 1922. Essays on
the contemporary theatre.
At half-past eight: essays of the theatre, 1921–2. 1923,
New York 1924. First pbd in Saturday Rev.
Fantasies and impromptus. [1923]. Essays.
Blessed are the rich: episodes in the life of Oliver Sheldon.
1924, 1944 (rev). Novel.
The contemporary theatre, 1923–6. 4 vols 1924–7. Introd
to vol 2 by N. Coward; to vol 3 by C. E. Montague; to
vol 4, by A. Bennett. Dramatic criticisms mainly first
pbd in Saturday Rev, Sunday Times.
On an English screen. 1924. Essays.
White horse and red lion: essays in gusto. [1924].
Agate's folly: a pleasaunce. 1925. Essays.
The common touch. 1926. Essays.
A short view of the English stage, 1900–26. 1926 (Today
Lib).
Playgoing. 1927, New York 1927.
Gemel in London. 1928, 1945 (rev). Novel.
Rachel [Elisabeth Rachel Félix]. 1928, New York 1928.
(Representative Women ser).
Their hour upon the stage. Cambridge 1930. Essays on
the London stage, 1925–9.
The English dramatic critics: an anthology, 1660–1932.
Ed Agate 1932, New York 1958.
My theatre talks. 1933. Broadcasts 1925–32.
First nights. 1934. Dramatic criticisms first pbd in
Sunday Times 1930–4.
Ego (Ego 2–9): the autobiography of Agate. 9 pts 1935–48,
3 vols 1945–9 (abridged, as A shorter ego). Ego 8 and 9
pbd with introd and notes by J. Barzun (as The later ego)
New York 1951.
Kingdoms for horses. 1936. Essays.
More first nights. 1937. Dramatic criticisms first pbd in
Sunday Times 1934–7.
Bad manners. 1938. Essays.
The amazing theatre. 1939. Dramatic criticisms first pbd
in Sunday Times, 1937–9.
Speak for England: an anthology of prose and poetry for
the forces. Ed Agate [1939].
Express and admirable: the breakfast table talk of Agate.
[1941]. First pbd in Daily Express.
Thursdays and Fridays. [1941], New York 1941. Book
reviews first pbd in Daily Express and dramatic criti-
cisms first pbd in John O'London's Weekly.
Brief chronicles: a survey of the plays of Shakespeare and
the Elizabethans in actual performance. 1943. Rptd

from The contemporary theatre, 1924–7; More first
nights, 1937; The amazing theatre, 1939.
These were actors: extracts from a newspaper cutting
book, 1811–33. [Compiled by J. Saint Aubyn]. [1943],
New York [1943]. Selected and annotated by Agate.
Lewis, D. B Wyndham. Take it to bed, selected, with
a preface, by Agate. [1944]. Articles first pbd in Tatler,
Tatler-Bystander.
Noblesse oblige: another letter to another son. 1944.
Reply to O. Sitwell's Letter to my son, 1944.
Red letter nights: a survey of the post-Elizabethan drama
in actual performance on the London stage, 1921–43.
1944. Rptd from The contemporary theatre, 1924–7;
More first nights, 1937; The amazing theatre, 1939.
Immoment toys: a survey of light entertainment on the
London stage, 1920–43. 1945.
Around cinemas. 1946; ser 2, 1948.
The contemporary theatre, 1944 and 1945. 1946. Drama-
tic criticisms first pbd in Sunday Times.
Oscar Wilde and the theatre. [1947] (The masque 3).
Those were the nights. Ed Agate [1947], New York [1947].
Extracts from 2 collections of newspaper cuttings of
dramatic criticisms, 1887–1906.
Thus to revisit. 1947. Essays, 1917–42.
Words I have lived with: a personal choice. Ed Agate
[1949], New York [1949]. Anthology of prose and verse.
Agate was dramatic critic in succession to Daily Dispatch,
Manchester Guardian, Saturday Rev, Sunday Times,
BBC.

§2

Sutton, G. Agate and dramatic criticism. Bookman
(London) Feb 1923.
Stokes, S. James Agate. Theatre Arts 29 1945.
Barzun, J. Agate and his nine Egos. Saturday Rev of Lit
24 Feb 1951; rptd (rev) as introd to The later ego, New
York 1951. *See* Ego, 1935, above.
Laver, J. Critics who have influenced taste: 28, Agate.
Times 14 Nov 1963.   M. P.

PETER ALEXANDER
1893–1969

§1

Shakespeare's Henry VI and Richard III. Cambridge
1929.
Shakespeare's life and art. 1939, New York 1961.
A Shakespeare primer. 1951 (for 1952).
Complete works of William Shakespeare. Ed P. Alexander
1951, New York 1952, 4 vols London [1954]–8, 3 vols
New York 1958–9 (as The Heritage Shakespeare).
Hamlet, father and son. Oxford 1955.
Alexander's Introductions to Shakespeare. 1964, New
York 1964.
Shakespeare. 1964 (Home Univ Lib).
Studies in Shakespeare: British Academy lectures. Ed
P. Alexander 1964.
The poems of William Shakespeare. Ed P. Alexander,
Cambridge 1967 (priv ptd).

                                                      N. J. S.

WALTER ERNEST ALLEN
b. 1911

See col 514, above.

KENNETH ALLOTT
b. 1912

See col 230, above.

'ANTHONY ARMSTRONG', GEORGE ANTHONY ARMSTRONG WILLIS
b. 1897

See cols 906–8, above.

WYSTAN HUGH AUDEN
b. 1907

See cols 207–20, above.

ARTHUR OWEN BARFIELD
b. 1898

§1

The silver trumpet. 1925, Grand Rapids [1968]. Children's story.

History in English words. 1926, 1933 (rev), 1954 (rev, adds Afterword, omits bibliography), Grand Rapids 1967.

Poetic diction: a study in meaning. 1928, 1952 (rev), New York 1964 (introd H. Nemerov).

Law, association and the Trade Union Movement. [1938]. Pamphlet.

Romanticism comes of age. 1944, 1966 (rev), Middletown Conn [1967].

Poetic diction and legal fiction. In Essays presented to Charles Williams, by Barfield [et al], 1947.

This ever diverse pair, by 'G. A. L Burgeon' [i.e. Barfield], with introd by W. de la Mare. 1950. Legal anecdotes.

Saving the appearances: a study in idolatry. 1957, New York [1965].

Worlds apart: a dialogue of the 1960's. 1963, Middletown Conn [1963].

Unancestral voice. 1965, Middletown Conn 1965. Imaginary philosophical discussions.

Gibb, J. (ed). Light on C. S. Lewis, by O. Barfield [et al]. Introd by Barfield 1965, New York 1965.

Speaker's meaning. Middletown Conn 1967.

Barfield has also tr or edited a number of the works of Rudolf Steiner and Hermann Poppelbaum for the Anthroposophical Soc.

Letters

Mark vs Tristram: correspondence between C. S. Lewis and Barfield. Ed W. Hooper, Cambridge Mass 1967 (126 copies).

§2

Norwood, W. D. C. S. Lewis, Barfield and the modern myth. Midwest Quart 8 1967.

FREDERICK NOEL WILSE BATESON
b. 1901

§1

English comic drama 1700–50. Oxford 1929, New York 1963.

English poetry and the English language: an experiment in literary history. Oxford 1934, New York 1961 (rev).

The Cambridge bibliography of English literature. Ed Bateson 4 vols Cambridge 1940, New York 1941. Vol 5, suppl, ed G. Watson 1957.

Mixed farming and muddled thinking: an analysis of current agricultural policy; a report of an inquiry organised by Viscount Astor and B. S. Rowntree. [1946]. Anon.

Towards a Socialist agriculture: studies by a group of Fabians. Ed Bateson 1946.

English poetry: a critical introduction. 1950, 1966 (rev), New York 1966.

Pope, A. Epistles to several persons; Moral essays. Ed Bateson 1951, 1961 (rev) (Twickenham edn of the poems of Pope vol 3 pt 2).

Wordsworth: a re-interpretation. 1954, 1956 (rev).

Selected poems of William Blake. Ed Bateson 1957, New York 1957 (Poetry Bookshelf).

A guide to English literature. New York 1965, London 1965 (rev), 1967 (rev). General essays and critical bibliographies.

Brill: a short history. [Oxford] 1966.

Bateson was agricultural correspondent of Observer, New Statesman *1944–8; he is general editor of the series* Longman's annotated English poets *1965–; he was the founder of and is editor and frequent contributor to* EC *1951–.*

§2

Leavis, F. R. Criticism and literary history. Scrutiny 4 1935. Essay-review of English poetry and the English language; reply by Bateson, rejoinder by Leavis, ibid.

— The responsible critic: or the function of criticism at any time. Scrutiny 19 1953. In reply to Bateson, The function of criticism at the present time, EC 3 1953; editorial commentary Oct 1953; correspondence Scrutiny Oct 1953.

SIR HENRY MAXIMILIAN BEERBOHM
1872–1956

Details of Beerbohm's surviving mss and unpbd caricatures are contained in Catalogue of the library and literary ms of Sir Max Beerbohm, *sold by Messrs Sotheby & Co, 12 Dec 1960, and in the bibliographies by Gallatin, Gallatin and Oliver, and Riewald, below.*

Bibliographies

Danielson, H. Bibliography of Beerbohm first editions. Bookman's Jnl 2 Jan 1920; rptd with addns in his Bibliographies of modern authors, 1921.

Gallatin, A. E. Beerbohm: bibliographical notes. Cambridge Mass 1944. Includes notes on unpbd writings and caricatures, catalogues of exhibitions, Maxiana and books and articles on Beerbohm.

— Beerbohm: notes on an exhibition of books, caricatures, mss, portraits and other memorabilia at the Grolier Club, New York 1944. [1944]. First pbd in Gazette of the Grolier Club.

— and L. M. Oliver. A bibliography of the works of Beerbohm. 1952 (Soho Bibliographies); rptd with revisions from Harvard Lib Bull 5 1951. Describes collected and separately pbd works only.

Riewald, J. G. Beerbohm, man and writer: a critical analysis with a brief life and a bibliography. The Hague 1953. Notes original pbn of individual essays, changes of title, degree of revision in their appearance in book form, and lists uncollected writings and Beerbohmiana.

Collections and Selections

Works. 10 vols 1922–8. Sometimes known as 'Harlequin' edn. Texts of 1st edns with minor revisions. Beerbohm contributed a general preface to vol 1, notes to vols 5–7 and 10 and an Epistle dedicatory to E. G. Craig to vol 8. Vols 8–10 are first edns (*see* Around theatres, 1924, and A variety of things, 1928, below).

Selected essays. Ed N. L. Clay 1958 (Twentieth-Century Ser).

The incomparable Max: a selection, introduced by S. C. Roberts. 1962, New York 1962.

Max in verse: rhymes and parodies, collected and annotated by J. G. Riewald. Foreword by S. N. Behrman, Brattleboro Vermont 1963, London 1964 (omits foreword and text of poem in note 8, p. 159).

§1

Carmen becceriense, cum prolegomenis et commentario critico edidit HMB. [Godalming 1890?]; rptd in Carthusian, April 1912. Copy with autograph ms in Charterhouse School Library. See C. Evans, A note on Carmen becceriense, Book Collector 1 1952 (includes facs).

Works of Max Beerbohm. New York 1896, London 1896 (adds Bibliography by J. Lane). Essays; rptd 1930 with More, 1899, below, as Works and More.

The happy hypocrite: a fairy tale for tired men. New York 1897, London 1897 (Bodley Booklets 1), 1918 (with note by Beerbohm); rptd in A variety of things, 1928, below. For possible trial copy with undated title page and colophon dated 1896 see Gallatin and Oliver's Bibliography, above, p. 7. Dramatized by Beerbohm (unpbd) as one-act play (Royalty, Dec 1890) and as a 3 act play (His Majesty's, April 1936) with words by C. Dane (unpbd).

More. 1899, New York 1899. Essays. Rptd 1930 with Works, 1896, above, as Works and More.

Yet again. 1909, New York 1910. Essays.

Zuleika Dobson: or an Oxford love story. [1911], New York 1911, London 1947 (adds frontispiece and note by Beerbohm).

Ballade tragique à double refrain. [1912?] (priv ptd). Signed: Max.

A Christmas garland, woven by Beerbohm. 1912, New York 1912, London 1950 (adds Postscript and All roads, a hitherto unpbd parody on Maurice Baring). Parodies.

Seven men. 1919, New York 1920 (adds Appendix and 5 plates with letterpress by Beerbohm), London 1950 (enlarged as Seven men and two others), 1966 (WC) (with introd by Lord D. Cecil). Stories. First pbd in Century and Eng Rev.

A note on 'Patience' [by W. S. Gilbert]. [1919]. Given away at the performances of Patience, Princess Th 24–29 Nov 1919.

And even now. 1920, New York 1921. Essays. Mainly first pbd in Harper's Monthly Mag, Saturday Rev, Harper's Weekly, Fortnightly Rev, TLS, Land and Water, Living Age, Cornhill Mag, Athenaeum, Eng Rev, Century.

Herbert Beerbohm Tree: some memories of him and his art, collected by Beerbohm. [1920] Contains From a brother's standpoint by Beerbohm.

A defence of cosmetics. New York 1922. First pbd in Yellow book and rptd in the Works of Max Beerbohm, 1896, above, (as The pervasion of rouge).

A peep into the past. [New York] 1923 (priv ptd, unauthorized, 300 copies). Satire on Wilde.

Around theatres. 2 vols 1924 (Collected works viii, ix), New York 1930 (with note by Beerbohm), 1 vol London 1953, New York 1954. 153 slightly rev items of dramatic criticism first pbd in Saturday Rev 1898–1910. For the other items here excluded, see More theatres, 1969, and Last theatres, 1970, below.

The guerdon. New York 1925 (priv ptd, unauthorized). Parody of Henry James; rptd in A variety of things, 1928, below. 110 copies.

Leaves from the garland. New York 1926 (priv ptd, unauthorized, 72 copies). Parodies.

Max Beerbohm: a self-caricature. [Green Bay Wis] 1926 (priv ptd). Facs of a letter to E. E. Fisk containing the caricature, with a note by Fisk.

A variety of things. 1928 (Collected works x), New York 1928 (expands Note and omits A note on the Einstein theory and The happy hypocrite). Miscellany. Mainly first pbd in London Mercury, Pall Mall Mag, Idler, The parade: an illustrated gift book, The pageant and Yellow book.

The dreadful dragon of Hay Hill. 1928. Also pbd in A variety of things, 1928, above.

The fetish of speed. [1936] (Pedestrians' Assoc pamphlet). Portion of a broadcast 19 April 1936; rptd in full in Mainly on the air, 1946, below.

Lytton Strachey: the Rede lecture. Cambridge 1943, New York 1943; rptd in 1957 edn of Mainly on the air.

William Rothenstein: an address delivered at the memorial service held at St Martin-in-the-Fields, 6 March 1945. 1945 (priv ptd, 100 copies).

Mainly on the air. 1946, New York 1947 (for 1946), London 1957 (enlarged). Broadcast talks and other pieces, mainly first pbd in Listener.

A luncheon. [Ewelme] 1946 (priv ptd, 25 copies). A poem on the visit by the Prince of Wales to Thomas Hardy, 1923.

The mote in the middle distance: a parody of Henry James. [Berkeley 1946] (priv ptd, unauthorized, 100 copies). First pbd in A Christmas garland, 1912.

Sherlockiana: a reminiscence of Sherlock Holmes. Tempe 1948 (priv ptd, unauthorized, 36 copies).

More theatres 1898–1903. 1969. Ed R. Hart-Davis. This and the next reprint the dramatic criticism in Saturday Rev excluded from Around theatres, 1924, above.

Last theatres 1904–1910. 1970.

Caricatures

Caricatures of twenty-five gentlemen. 1896. Introd by L. Raven-Hill; title-page vignette by Beardsley.

The poets' corner. 1904, New York 1904, London 1943 (King Penguin) (introd by J. Rothenstein; adds 4 plates from Rossetti and his circle). 20 caricatures.

A book of caricatures. 1907. 48 caricatures.

Cartoons: 'The second childhood of John Bull'. [1911]. 15 cartoons.

Fifty caricatures. 1913, New York 1913.

A survey. 1921, New York 1922 (for 1921). 51 caricatures (limited edn has 52).

Rossetti and his circle. 1922, New York 1922. 22 caricatures.

Things new and old. 1923, New York 1923. 49 caricatures (limited edn has 50).

Observations. 1925, New York 1925. 51 caricatures (limited edn has 52).

Heroes and heroines of Bitter Sweet. [1931]. 5 drawings of members of cast of Noel Coward's Bitter sweet, 1929, with introductory note by Beerbohm in facsimile.

Max's nineties: drawings, 1892–9. 1958, Philadelphia 1958. Introd by O. Lancaster.

Caricatures by Max from the collection of the Ashmolean Museum. [Oxford 1958].

Letters

Letters to Reggie Turner. Ed R. Hart-Davis 1964, Philadelphia 1965 (for 1964).

Details of further pbd and unpbd letters and of Beerbohm's contributions and introds to other books are contained in the bibliographies by Gallatin and Oliver, and Riewald, above.

§2

Jackson, H. In his All manner of folk, 1912.

Hillebrand, H. N. Max Beerbohm. JEGP 24 1920.

Lynch, B. Max Beerbohm. London Mercury 2 1920; enlarged as Beerbohm in perspective, 1921.

— Max's caricatures. Saturday Rev 18 April 1925.

— Mr Beerbohm's caricatures. Fortnightly Rev new ser 117 1925.

— In his History of caricature, 1926.

Lynd, R. In his Books and authors, 1922; rptd in his Essays on life and literature, 1951 (EL).

Cross, W. The humor of Beerbohm. Yale Rev new ser 14 1924.

Woolf, V. The common reader ser 1, 1925. Notes on Beerbohm in ch, The modern essay.

'E. T. Raymond' (E. R. Thompson). Henry James and Beerbohm. In his Portraits of the new century (the first ten years), 1928.

Rothenstein, J. In his Artists of the 1890's, 1928.

'Rebecca West' (C. I. Andrews). A London letter: Mr Beerbohm and the literary ladies. Bookman (New York) June 1929; rptd (rev) in her Ending in earnest: a literary log, New York 1931.

Rothenstein, W. Beardsley and Max; The Beerbohms and Gordon Craig. In his Men and memories, 1872–1900, 1931.

Tuell, A. K. The prose of Beerbohm. South Atlantic Quart 31 1931; rptd in her Victorian at bay, Boston 1932.

Bottome, P. In her From the life, 1944.

Kronenberger, L. The perfect trifler. Saturday Rev of Lit 21 June 1947.

Wilson, E. Analysis of Beerbohm. New Yorker 1 May 1948; rptd in his Classics and commercials, New York 1950.

— Meetings with Beerbohm. Encounter 21 1963; rptd in his Bit between my teeth, 1965 (as A miscellany of Beerbohm).

Riewald, J. G. Beerbohm, man and writer. The Hague 1953.

Roberts, S. C. In his Dr Johnson and others, Cambridge 1958.

— Max Beerbohm. Essays by Divers Hands 30 1960.

Behrmann, S. N. Conversation with Max. 1960, New York 1960 (as Portrait of Max).

Cecil, D. The man who never stopped playing. Horizon (New York) 3 1961.

— Max: a biography. 1964.

Huss, R. Max the 'incomparable' and GBS the 'irrepressible'. Shaw Rev 5 1962.

— Beerbohm's drawings of theatrical figures. Theatre Notebook 21 1967.

Pearson, H. In his Lives of the wits, 1962.

Schöne, A. Beerbohm: ein Meister der literarischen Kurzform. Die Neueren Sprachen 11 1962.

Mix, K. L. Max on Shaw. Shaw Rev 6 1963.

Gollin, R. M. Beerbohm, Wilde, Shaw and 'The good-natured critic': some new letters. BNYPL 68 1964.

Langbaum, R. Max and dandyism. Victorian Poetry 4 1966.

Felstiner, J. Beerbohm and the wrongs of Henry James. Kenyon Rev 29 1967.

McElderry, B. R., Jr. Beerbohm: essayist, caricaturist, novelist. In On stage and off: eight essays in English literature, ed J. W. Ehrstine et al, Pullman 1968.

ARTHUR CLIVE HEWARD BELL
1881–1964

§1

Art. 1914, New York 1914.

Peace at once. Manchester [1915]. Pamphlet.

Ad familiares. 1917 (priv ptd). Verse.

Pot-boilers. 1918. Rptd reviews.

Poems. Richmond Surrey 1921.

Since Cézanne. 1922, New York 1922. Essays.

The legend of Monte della Sibilla; or, le paradis de la Reine Sibille. Richmond Surrey 1923. Verse.

On British freedom. 1923, New York 1923.

Landmarks in nineteenth-century painting. 1927, New York 1927.

Civilization: an essay. 1928, New York 1928.

Proust. 1928, New York 1929.

An account of French painting. 1931, New York 1932.

Enjoying pictures: meditations in the National Gallery and elsewhere. 1934, New York 1934.

Modern French painting: the Cone Collection. Baltimore 1951. Address.

Old friends: personal recollections. 1956, New York 1957 (for 1956).

Bell contributed introds to a number of books of reproductions. He also contributed frequently to New Statesman, *and other jnls.*

§2

Weitz, M. Aesthetic formalism. In his Philosophy of the arts, Cambridge Mass 1950.

Lake, B. Bell's theory about works of art. In Aesthetics and language: essays, ed W. Elton, Oxford 1954.

Fishman, S. In his The interpretation of art: essays on the art criticism of Ruskin [et al], Berkeley 1963.

Russell, J. Notes and topics: Bell. Encounter 23 1964.

Read, H. Clive Bell. Br Jnl of Aesthetics 5 1965.

Elliott, R. K. Bell's aesthetic theory and his critical practice. Ibid.

Meager, R. Bell and aesthetic emotion. Ibid.

Osborne, H. Alison and Bell on appreciation. Ibid.

Casey, J. P. In his Language of criticism, 1966.

JOSEPH HILAIRE PIERRE RENÉ BELLOC
1870–1953

Bibliographies

Nicholls, N. The first editions of Belloc. Bookman (London) 81 1931.

Cahill, P. The English first editions of Belloc: a chronological catalogue. 1953.

Collections and Selections

The Hilaire Belloc calendar. 1913.

A picked company. 1915. Prose and light verse selected by E. V. Lucas.

The bad child's book of beasts: together with More beasts for worse children and Cautionary tales. [1923], New York 1930.

Hilaire Belloc. 1926 (Essays of Today and Tomorrow).

[Selected works]. 9 vols [1927] (Minerva Edns of Modern Authors).

Hilaire Belloc. 1935 (Methuen's Lib of Humour). Prose and verse selected by E. V. Knox.

Selected essays, compiled by J. E. Dineen. Philadelphia 1936.

Stories, essays and poems. 1938 (introd by A. G. Macdonnell), 1957 (enlarged, introd by J. B. Morton) (EL).

Cautionary verses: the collected humorous poems. 1939, 1940 (Album edn, with original pictures; omits The modern traveller), New York 1941.

On sailing the sea: a collection of the seagoing writings of Belloc, selected by W. N. Roughead. 1939, 1951 (enlarged).

Selected essays. Introd by J. B. Morton 1948.

Selected cautionary verses. 1950, 1964 (rev). Selected from Album edn, above.

Hilaire Belloc: an anthology of his prose and verse, selected by W. N. Roughead. 1951.

Songs of the south country. 1951.

The verse of Belloc. Ed W. N. Roughead, 1954, 1970 (slightly rev) (as Complete verse). Includes verse from prose works and some previously unpbd verse.

Belloc essays. Ed A. Forster 1955. With introd by R. Knox.

Selected essays. Ed with introd by J. B. Morton 1958, Baltimore 1959. A different selection from that pbd in 1948, above.

The bad child's book of beasts, and More beasts for worse children and A moral alphabet. New York 1961.

Belloc: a biographical anthology. Ed H. Van Thal [and Jane Soames Nickerson], 1970.

§1

Much of Belloc's work, especially his essays, was first pbd in various journals. See R. W. Speaight, The life of Belloc, 1957.

Miscellaneous Prose

CTS = Catholic Truth Soc pamphlets and leaflets.

Lambkin's remains, by H.B. Oxford 1900, London 1920 (with The aftermath, below). Undergraduate satire.

The aftermath: or gleanings from a busy life, called upon the outer cover, for purposes of sale, Caliban's guide to letters, by H. B. 1903, New York 1903, London 1920 (with Lambkin's remains, above). Humorous sketches.

The great inquiry—only authorised version—faithfully reported by H.B. [1903]. Political satire, illustr G. K. Chesterton.

Avril: being essays on the poetry of the French Renaissance. 1904, New York 1904.

An open letter on the decay of faith. [1906].

Hills and the sea. 1906, New York 1906. Essays.

The Catholic Church and historical truth. Preston 1908 (Catholic Evidence Lectures 3).

On nothing and kindred subjects. 1908. Essays.

An examination of socialism. [1908] (CTS). According to P. Cahill, Bibliography, above, rev as The alternative in 1940s.

On everything. 1909, New York 1910.

The Church and socialism. [1909] (CTS).

The Ferrer case. [1910] (CTS). On the trial and execution of Francesco Ferrer y Guardia.

On anything. 1910, New York 1910. Essays.

On something. 1910. Essays.

The party system. 1911. With C. Chesterton.

Socialism and the servile state: a debate between Belloc and J. Ramsay Macdonald. 1911.

First and last. 1911. Essays.

The servile state. 1912, 1913 (with new preface), 1927 (with new preface), New York [1946] (introd by C. Gauss).

This and that and the other. 1912, New York 1912. Essays.

Anti-Catholic history: how it is written. 1914 (CTS). An examination of J. B. Bury, A history of freedom of thought, 1913.

Three essays. Portland Maine 1914. Contains On sacramental things, On rest, On coming to an end.

At the sign of the lion and other essays from the books of Belloc. Portland Maine 1916. Adds title essay and The autumn and the fall of leaves to contents of preceding vol.

The free press. 1918.

Religion and civil liberty. 1918 (CTS). On an article by Hypatia Bradlaugh entitled Christianity versus liberty.

The Catholic Church and the principle of private property. 1920 (CTS).

The House of Commons and monarchy. 1920.

Pascal's Provincial letters. 1921 (CTS).

Catholic social reform versus socialism. 1922 (CTS).

The Jews. 1922, Boston 1937 (with new introductory ch). See W. R. Inge, The Jews, [1922].

On. 1923, New York [1923]. Essays.

The contrast. 1923, New York 1924. On Europeans and Americans.

Economics for Helen. 1924, New York 1924, 1925 (as Economics for young people).

The political effort. [1924]. True Temperance Assoc pamphlet.

Advice to the rich. [1925] (50 copies). Aphorisms. Anon, attributed to Belloc [BM Catalogue].

England and the Faith. [1925] (CTS).

Short talks with the dead and others. 1926. Essays.

Mrs Markham's new history of England. 1926. Satire on contemporary institutions.

A companion to Mr Wells's Outline of history. 1926, [1929] (rev). See H. G. Wells, Mr Belloc objects to the Outline of history, 1926.

Mr Belloc still objects to Mr Wells's Outline of history. 1926, San Francisco 1927. See V. Brome, Belloc versus H. G. Wells, in his Six studies in quarrelling, 1958, §2 below.

A conversation with an angel and other essays. 1928, New York 1929.

Survivals and new arrivals. 1929, New York 1929. Apologetics.

World conflict. Horsham 1930 (priv ptd) (anon), London 1951 (CTS) (as by Belloc).

A conversation with a cat and others. 1931, New York 1931. Essays.

On translation: the Taylorian lecture. Oxford 1931.

Essays of a Catholic layman in England. 1931, New York 1931 (as Essays of a Catholic).

Nine nines: or novenas from a Chinese litany of odd numbers. Oxford 1931. Rptd from Short talks with the dead and others, above.

Usury. [1931]. Pamphlet rptd (rev) from Essays of a Catholic layman, above.

The question and the answer. New York [1932], London 1938. Apologetics.

Milton. 1935, Philadelphia 1935.

An essay on the restoration of property. 1936, New York 1936 (as The restoration of property). Distributist League pamphlet.

An essay on the nature of contemporary England. 1937, New York 1937.

The issue. [1937], New York [1937]. Apologetics. Pamphlet.

The case of Dr Coulton. 1938. Reply to G. G. Coulton, Divorce, Mr Belloc and the Daily Telegraph, 1937. See also V. Brome, Dr Coulton versus Belloc, in his Six studies in quarrelling, 1958, §2 below.

The Catholic and the war. 1940. Pamphlet.

On the place of Chesterton in English letters. 1940, New York 1940.

The silence of the sea and other essays. New York 1940, London 1941.

Places. New York 1941, London 1942. Essays.

The alternative. [1940s]. See An examination of socialism, above.

One thing and another: a miscellany from his uncollected essays. Ed P. Cahill 1955.

Advice. 1960. Introd by E. Waugh. Advice to Bridget Grant on wine and food.

Conversation with a cat. Wolverhampton 1962 (priv ptd). Rptd from A conversation with a cat and others, above.

History and Biography

Danton: a study. 1899, New York 1899, London 1928 (rev with new preface), New York 1928.

Robespierre: a study. 1901, New York 1901, London 1927 (with new introd), New York 1928.

The eye-witness. 1908. Sketches of 'incidents and periods in history as from the testimony of a person present at each'.

Marie Antoinette. 1909, New York 1909.

The French Revolution. [1911], New York [1911].

British battles. 6 vols 1911–13, 1 vol Bristol 1931 (rev, as Six British battles). Contains Blenheim; Malplaquet; Waterloo (rev, 1915); Tourcoing; Crécy; Poitiers.

The history of England from the first invasion by the Romans to the accession of King George the Fifth. 11 vols New York 1912–15, London 1915. Vols 1–10 by J. Lingard, vol 11 (1689–1910) by Belloc.

Warfare in England. [1912], New York [1912].

The book of the Bayeux Tapestry, presenting the complete work in a series of colour facsimiles. 1914, New York 1914. Introd and narrative by Belloc.

Land and water map of the war and how to use it, drawn under the direction of Belloc. 1915. With explanatory article by Belloc.

A general sketch of the European war. 2 vols 1915 (subtitled The first phase) and 1916 (subtitled The second phase), New York 1915–16 (as The elements of the Great War).

High lights of the French Revolution. New York 1915.

The two maps of Europe and some other aspects of the Great War. 1915.

The last days of the French monarchy. 1916.

The second year of the war. 1916.

Europe and the Faith. 1920, New York 1920, London 1962 (introd by D. Woodruff). See G. G. Coulton, Medieval studies 19, Belloc as historian, 1930.

The campaign of 1812 and the Retreat from Moscow. [1924], New York 1926 (as Napoleon's campaign of 1812 and the Retreat from Moscow).

A history of England. 4 vols [B.C. 55–A.D. 1612] 1925–31, New York 1925–32, vol 1 [to 1066] (corrected, with new preface) London 1926. 3 further vols not pbd.

Miniatures of French history. [1925], New York 1926.

The Catholic Church and history. 1926, New York 1926 (Calvert ser).

Oliver Cromwell. 1927.

James the Second. 1928, Philadelphia 1928.

How the Reformation happened. 1928, New York 1928.

Joan of Arc. 1929, New York 1949.

Richelieu: a study. Philadelphia 1929, London 1930.

Wolsey. 1930, Philadelphia 1930.

Cranmer. 1931, Philadelphia 1931.

Six British battles. 1931. See British battles 1911–13, above.

How we got the Bible. 1932 (CTS). Extracts from Cranmer, above.

Napoleon. 1932, Philadelphia 1932.

The tactics and strategy of the great Duke of Marlborough. Bristol 1933.

William the Conqueror. 1933, New York 1934.

Beckett. 1933 (CTS).

Charles the First, King of England. 1933, Philadelphia 1933.

Cromwell. 1934, Philadelphia 1934.

A shorter history of England. 1934, New York 1934.

The battle ground. 1936, Philadelphia 1936. History of Syria to 1187.

Characters of the Reformation. 1936, New York 1936.

The Crusade: the world's debate. 1937, Milwaukee [1937] (as The Crusades: the world's debate). On the military aspect of the Crusades.

The crisis of our civilization. 1937, New York [1937] (as The crisis of civilization).

The great heresies. 1938, New York 1938.

Monarchy: a study of Louis XIV. 1938, New York 1938 (as Louis XIV).

Charles II: the last rally. New York 1939, London 1940 (as The last rally: a story of Charles II).

Elizabethan commentary. 1942, New York 1942 (as Elizabeth, creature of circumstance).

Travel and Topography

Paris. 1900.

The path to Rome. 1902, New York 1902. Illustr Belloc.

The old road [the Pilgrim's Way]. 1904, New York 1923.

Esto perpetua: Algerian studies and impressions. 1906.

Sussex, painted by William Ball. 1906 (anon), 1936 (as The county of Sussex, 'virtually rewritten').

The historic Thames. 1907.

The Pyrenees. 1909, 1923 (rev), 1928 (with new preface). Sketches and maps by Belloc.

The four men: a farrago. [1912]. Illustr Belloc. On Sussex.

The river of London. 1912.

The Stane Street: a monograph. 1913. See W. A. Grant, The topography of Stane Street: a critical review of The Stane Street, 1922.

The road. Manchester 1923, New York 1925.

The cruise of the Nona. 1925, Boston 1925, London 1955 (introd by Lord Stanley of Alderley), Westminster Md 1955.

The highway and its vehicles. 1926. Studio special no. Mainly illustrations.

Towns of destiny. New York 1927, London 1928 (as Many cities).

The county of Sussex. 1936. See Sussex, above.

Return to the Baltic. 1938.

Poetry and Verse

Verses and sonnets. 1896. Withdrawn from circulation by Belloc.

The bad child's book of beasts: verses by H.B., pictures by B.T.B. [Basil Blackwood]. Oxford [1896], New York 1923.

More beasts—for worse children, by H.B.; pictures by B.T.B. [1897], New York 1923.

The modern traveller, by H.B. and [with illustrations by] B.T.B. 1898.

A moral alphabet, by H.B., with illustrations by B.B. 1899.

Cautionary tales for children: designed for the admonition of children between the ages of eight and fourteen years; pictures by B.T.B. [1908].

Verses. 1910, New York 1916 (introd by J. Kilmer).

More peers; pictures by B.T.B. [1911], New York 1924.

You wear the morning like your dress: song, the words and music by Belloc. [1913]. Text from Verses, above.

Sonnets and verse. 1923, 1938 (enlarged), New York 1939 (enlarged with biographical introd by R. Jebb), London 1954, 1958 (as Collected verse, with introd by R. Knox).

Hilaire Belloc. [1925] (Augustan Books of Modern Poetry). Nineteen poems.

The chanty of the Nona: poem and drawings by Belloc. [1928] (Ariel Poem). Rptd (rev) from Sonnets and verse, above.

New cautionary tales; pictures by N. Bentley. 1930, New York 1931.

Tarantella: song, words and music by Belloc. 1930. Text from Sonnets and verse, above.

The praise of wine: an heroic poem. 1931 (priv ptd), 1932 (as An heroic poem in praise of wine) (100 copies), [Long Crendon] 1933 (priv ptd) (as In praise of wine). Rptd in Sonnets and verse, above, 1938 edn.

Ladies and gentlemen: for adults only and mature at that; pictures by N. Bentley. 1932.

Ballade of illegal ornaments. Shipley [1934]. Rptd from Sonnets and verse, above, 1938 edn.

Collected verse. 1958. See Sonnets and verse, above.

The frog. Northampton Mass 1960. Rptd from The bad child's book of beasts, above.

Fiction

Emmanuel Burden, merchant. [1904], New York 1904. Illustr G. K. Chesterton.

Mr Clutterbuck's election. 1908.

A change in the Cabinet. 1909.

Pongo and the bull. 1910.

The Girondin. 1911.

The green overcoat. Bristol 1912, New York 1912. Illustr G. K. Chesterton.

[Rehmatt-Allah, in Arabic script]: that is, The mercy of Allah. 1922, New York 1922.

Mr Petre: a novel. 1925, New York 1925. Illustr G. K. Chesterton.

The emerald of Catherine the Great. 1926, New York 1926. Illustr G. K. Chesterton.

The haunted house. 1927, New York 1928. Illustr G. K. Chesterton.

But soft—we are observed! 1928, New York 1929 (as Shadowed!). Illustr G. K. Chesterton.

Belinda: a tale of affection in youth and age. 1928, New York 1929.

The missing masterpiece. 1929, New York 1929. Illustr G. K. Chesterton.

The man who made gold. 1930, New York [1931]. Illustr G. K. Chesterton.

The postmaster-general. 1932, Philadelphia 1932. Illustr G. K. Chesterton.

The hedge and the horse. 1936. Illustr G. K. Chesterton.

Principal Works Edited or with Contributions by Belloc

The Liberal tradition. In Essays in Liberalism by six Oxford men, 1897.

Extracts from the diaries and letters of Hubert Howard, with a recollection by a friend [Belloc]. Ed Belloc, Oxford 1899.

Froude, J. A. Essays in literature and history. 2 vols [1906] (EL). Introd by Belloc.

Carlyle, T. The French Revolution. 2 vols [1906] (EL). Introd.

Lowell, J. R. Poems. 1908. Introd.

Coburn, A. L. London. [1909]. Introd.

The footpath way: an anthology for walkers. Ed with introd by Belloc 1911.

Vassall-Phillips, O. R. The mustard tree. 1912. Epilogue by Belloc.

Jørgensen, J. Lourdes. 1914. Preface.

Chesterton, C. E. The perils of peace. 1916. Introd.

Nickerson, H. The Inquisition. 1923. Preface.

Shaw, G. P. An old story of a highland parish. 1926. Preface.

Pitter, R. First and second poems, 1912–25. 1927. Preface.

The witness to abstract truth. In The fame of the Blessed Thomas More: being addresses delivered in his honour in Chelsea, July 1929, 1929.

Leighton, C. Woodcuts. 1930. Introd.

Allison, J. M. Travel notes on a holiday tour in France. Ed with introd and commentary by Belloc 1931 (priv ptd).

If Drouet's cart had stuck. In If it had happened otherwise: lapses into imaginary history, by H. Belloc [et al]. Ed J. C. Squire 1931.

Man and the machine. In Science and the changing world, by T. Holland, Belloc [et al]. Ed M. Adams, New York 1933. Broadcast talk.

St Thomas of Canterbury. In The English way: studies in English sanctity from St Bede to Newman, by H. Belloc [et al], ed M. Ward 1933.

William Cecil, Lord Burghley. In The great Tudors, ed K. Garvin 1935.

Magee, B. The English recusants. 1938. Introd.

Letters

Letters from Hilaire Belloc. Selected and edited by R. Speaight [1958], New York 1958.

Belloc tr 2 books by Marshal Foch and a version of The Romance of Tristan and Iseult *from the French; he was general editor of the* Calvert ser *13 vols 1926–30. With A. H. Pollen he founded and edited* Paternoster Rev *(6 nos 1890–1); he was literary editor of* Morning Post *1906–9; with M. Baring he founded and edited* North Street Gazette *(1 no, 1910); with C. Chesterton he founded* Eye-Witness *in 1911 and edited it till 1912, and also edited its successor,* G.K.'s Weekly, *for a short period 1936–8. He edited* Illustrated Rev *(1923?). During the First World War he wrote a weekly article on the military situation for* Land and Water. *He contributed regularly to the Distributist* Weekly Rev; *and for* Sunday Times *wrote regularly* A wanderer's notebook *from 1938, and a weekly commentary on military affairs 1939–40. See* Speaight, Life of Belloc, *below.*

§2

Mandell, C. C. and E. B. Shanks. Hilaire Belloc: the man and his work. 1916. Introd by G. K. Chesterton.

Thomas, P. E. In his Literary pilgrim in England, 1917.

Lynd, R. Chesterton and Belloc. In his Old and new masters, 1919.

Adcock, A. St J. In his Gods of modern Grub street, 1923.

Braybrooke, P. Some thoughts on Belloc. [1923].

— Belloc as a novelist. In his Some Catholic novelists: their art and outlook, 1931.

Shanks, E. B. Belloc: some characteristics. In his First essays on literature, 1923.

Poynter, J. W. Belloc keeps the bridge: an examination of his defence of Roman Catholicism. 1929.

Link, H. Bellocs Weltanschauung. Erlangen 1930.

Burdett, O. Hilaire Belloc. London Mercury 30 1934.

Longaker, J. M. Bias and brilliance: Belloc. In his Contemporary biography, Philadelphia 1934.

Hollis, C. Belloc's interpretation of history. Dublin Rev 197 1935. Essay-review of A shorter history of England, above.

MacCarthy, D. Borrow and Belloc. In his Experience, 1935.

— Most various of living authors. Listener 27 July 1950.

Chesterton, G. K. Portrait of a friend. American Rev 7 1936.

Las Vergnas, R. Portraits anglais: Chesterton, Belloc, Baring. Paris 1937; tr 1938.

Woelwer, W. Belloc und sein Eintreten für den Katholizismus in England. Bonn 1937.

Woodruff, J. D. (ed). For Belloc: essays in honour of his 72nd birthday. 1942. Contains: D. Jerrold, On the influence of Belloc.

Phillips, A. Why Belloc will live. Poetry Rev 35 1944.

Hamilton, R. Hilaire Belloc: an introduction to his spirit and work. 1945.

Crichton, J. D. Belloc, historian. Blackfriars 30 1949.

Haynes, R. Hilaire Belloc. 1953, 1958 (rev) (Br Council pamphlet).

Mackintosh, H. S. Memories of Belloc. Listener 8 Oct 1953.

Speaight, R. W. Hilaire Belloc. Month new ser 10 1953.

— The life of Belloc. 1957.

Reckitt, M. B. Belloc and Chesterton: the study of an impact. In his The world and the faith, 1954.

TLS 21 May 1954. The European mind: Belloc's thought and writings. Essay-review of The verse of Belloc, 1954.

Wilhelmsen, F. Belloc, no alienated man: a study in Christian integration. 1954.

Morton, J. B. Belloc: a memoir. 1955.

Jebb, E. and R. Testimony to Belloc. 1956.

Koschmieder, I. Belloc als Essayist und Erzähler. Freiburg 1956.

Lowndes, M. A. B. The young Belloc. New York 1956.

Pearson, H. Chesterton and Belloc. Listener 28 June 1956.

— Belloc. In his Lives of the wits, 1962.

Pryce-Jones, A. A French Romantic in England. Listener 21 March 1957.

Wyndham Lewis, D. B. Breathing marble. Month 17 1957. Essay-review of R. W. Speaight, Life of Belloc, 1957.

Bordeaux, A. La personnalité de Belloc et sa réputation d'écrivain. Etudes Anglaises 11 1958.

Brome, V. Dr Coulton versus Belloc; Belloc versus Wells. In his Six studies in quarrelling, 1958.

Knox, R. A. Belloc's verse. In his Literary distractions, 1958.

Bergonzi, B. Chesterton and/or Belloc. CQ 1 1959.

Bodelsen, C. A. Belloc. In his Essays and papers, Copenhagen [1964].

Kantra, R. A. Irony in Belloc. Renascence 17 1965.

Mason, M. Chesterbelloc. Twentieth Century 177 1968–9.

M.P.

ENOCH ARNOLD BENNETT
1867–1931

See cols 429–36, above.

HENRY STANLEY BENNETT
1889–1972

Bibliographies

Brewer, D. A list of his writings presented to H. S. Bennett on his eightieth birthday. Cambridge 1969. Includes a short biographical sketch.

§1

The Pastons and their England: studies in an age of transition. Cambridge 1922 (Cambridge Stud in Medieval Life and Thought), 1932 (rev).

England from Chaucer to Caxton. 1928.

Life on the English manor: a study in peasant conditions, 1150–1400. Cambridge 1937 (Cambridge Stud in Medieval Life and Thought), New York 1937.

Chaucer and the fifteenth century. Oxford 1947 (OHEL 2 pt 1); rptd with corrections 1948, 1954, 1958.

English books and readers, 1475 to 1557: being a study in the history of the book trade from Caxton to the incorporation of the Stationers' Company. Cambridge 1952; 2nd ed 1969.

Six medieval men and women. Cambridge 1955, New York 1962.

English books and readers, 1558 to 1603: being a study in the history of the book trade in the reign of Elizabeth I. Cambridge 1965.

Bennett also pbd papers on bibliographical and antiquarian subjects, and edited a number of English classics.

P.G.B.

EDMUND CHARLES BLUNDEN
b. 1896

See cols 234–8, above.

MAUD BODKIN
1875–1967

§1

Archetypal patterns in poetry: psychological studies of imagination. 1934, New York 1958, London 1963 (with additional preface).

The quest for salvation in an ancient and a modern play [Aeschylus: The Eumenides; T. S. Eliot: The family reunion]. 1941, New York 1941.

Studies of type-images in poetry, religion and philosophy. 1951, New York 1951.

§2

Hyman, S. E. Maud Bodkin and psychological criticism. In his Armed vision, New York 1948.

SIR CECIL MAURICE BOWRA
1898–1971

Pindar. Pythian odes, translated by H. T. Wade-Gery and C. M. Bowra. 1928; rptd, with corrections, in The odes of Pindar, 1969, below.

Tradition and design in the Iliad. Oxford 1930.

Ancient Greek literature. 1933, New York 1959, London 1967 (rev).

Pindari carmina, cum fragmentis. Oxford 1935, 1947 (corrected) (Oxford Classical Texts). Ed Bowra.

Greek lyric poetry from Alcman to Simonides. Oxford 1936, 1961 (rev).

Sappho. Dichtung. Berlin 1936. Ed Bowra.

Early Greek elegists. 1938, Cambridge Mass 1938.

The Oxford book of Greek verse in translation. Oxford 1938, 1943 (as From the Greek, abridged). Ed Bowra, with T. F. Higham.

A book of Russian verse, translated into English by various hands. 1943. Ed, with trns, by Bowra.

The heritage of symbolism. 1943, New York 1961.

Sophoclean tragedy. Oxford 1944, 1945 (corrected).

From Virgil to Milton. 1945.

Edith Sitwell. Monaco 1947.

A second book of Russian verse, translated into English by various hands. 1948. Ed, with trns, by Bowra.

The creative experiment. 1949, New York 1958. On certain aspects of European poetry since 1910.

The Romantic imagination. Cambridge Mass 1949, London 1950.

Some Oxford compositions. Oxford 1949. Trns into Greek and Latin prose and verse by Bowra et al.

Athens: the Periclean age. In Golden ages of the great cities, by Bowra et al, 1952.

Heroic poetry. 1952.

Problems in Greek poetry. Oxford 1953.

Inspiration and poetry. 1955, Folcroft Pa 1969. Essays, including single lectures previously pbd separately.

The Greek experience. 1957, New York [1957].

Primitive song. [1962], Cleveland 1962.

In general and particular. 1964, Cleveland 1964. Essays, including single lectures previously pbd separately.

Pindar. Oxford 1964.

Classical Greece, by C. M. Bowra and the editors of Time–Life books. New York 1965.

Landmarks in Greek literature. [1966], Cleveland 1966.

Memories 1898–1939. [1966], Cambridge Mass 1967.

Poetry and politics 1900–60. Cambridge 1966.

The odes of Pindar, translated with an introduction by Bowra. 1969 (Penguin), Baltimore 1969.

MURIEL CLARA BRADBROOK
b. 1909

Elizabethan stage conditions: a study of their place in the interpretation of Shakespeare's plays. Cambridge 1932, Hamden Conn 1962 (with additional preface).

Themes and conventions of Elizabethan tragedy. Cambridge 1935.

The school of night: a study in the literary relationships of Sir Walter Ralegh. Cambridge 1936, New York 1965.

Andrew Marvell. Cambridge 1940. With M. G. Lloyd Thomas.

Joseph Conrad: Poland's English genius. Cambridge 1941, New York 1965.

Ibsen the Norwegian: a revaluation. 1946, 1966 (rev), Hamden Conn 1966.

T. S. Eliot. 1950, New York 1950, London 1951 (rev), 1955 (rev), 1958 (rev), 1960 (rev), 1963 (rev), 1968 (rev) (Br Council pamphlet).

Shakespeare and Elizabethan poetry: a study of his earlier work in relation to the poetry of the time. 1951, New York 1952, London 1964 (for 1965) (with new preface).

The Queen's garland: verses made by her subjects for Elizabeth I, Queen of England, now collected in honour of Queen Elizabeth II. Compiled by M. C. Bradbrook 1953, New York 1953.

The growth and structure of Elizabethan comedy. 1955, Berkeley 1956.

Sir Thomas Malory. 1958, New York 1958 London 1965 (rev) (Br Council pamphlet).

The rise of the common player: a study of actor and society in Shakespeare's England. 1962, Cambridge Mass 1962.
English dramatic form: a history of its development. 1965, New York 1965.
Shakespeare the craftsman. 1969, New York 1969.
'That infidel place': a short history of Girton College 1869–1969, with an essay on the collegiate university in the modern world. 1969.

ANDREW CECIL BRADLEY
1851–1935
Some mss of juvenilia are held by Bodley.

Bibliographies
In M. Blish, Bradley: a summary account, PBSA 62 1968. Includes contributions to books and journals.

§1
A commentary on Tennyson's In memoriam. 1901, 1902 (rev), 1910 (rev), 1930 (rev), Hamden Conn 1966.
Shakespearean tragedy: lectures on Hamlet, Othello, King Lear, Macbeth. 1904, Cleveland 1961.
Oxford lectures on poetry. 1909, 1909 (corrected), New York 1959, London 1965 (introd by M. R. Ridley). Includes single lectures previously pbd separately.
International morality: the United States of Europe. In The international crisis in its ethical and psychological aspects: lectures at Bedford College by A. C. Bradley [et al], 1915.
A miscellany. 1929, Freeport NY 1969. Includes single lectures previously pbd separately.
Ideals of religion: Gifford lectures 1907. 1940.
Bradley edited T. H. Green's Prolegomena to ethics, Oxford 1883, and (with G. R. Benson) R. L. Nettleship's Philosophical lectures and remains 2 vols 1897.

§2
Walkley, A. B. Bradley's Hamlet. In his Drama and life, 1907.
Knights, L. C. In his How many children had Lady Macbeth?: an essay in the theory and practice of Shakespeare criticism, Cambridge 1933. *See* J. Britton, Bradley and those children of Lady Macbeth, Shakespearean Quart 12 1961.
Mackail, J. W. Bradley. Proc Br Acad 21 1935.
Bradley: the surrender to poetry. TLS 23 May 1936.
Campbell, L. B. Bradley revisited: forty years after. SP 44 1947.
—— Concerning Bradley's Shakespearean tragedy. HLQ 13 1949. Both essays rptd in her Shakespeare's tragic heroes, New York 1959.
Siegel, P. N. In defence of Bradley. College Eng 9 1948.
Murry, J. M. In his Katherine Mansfield and other literary portraits, 1949.
Joseph, B. The problem of Bradley. Use of English 5 1953.
Weisinger, H. The study of Shakespearian tragedy since Bradley. Shakespeare Quart 6 1955.
Alexander, P. Critics who have influenced taste: 15. Bradley. Times 11 July 1963.
Palmer, D. J. Bradley. Critical Survey 2 1964.
Paolucci, A. Bradley and Hegel on Shakespeare. Comparative Lit 16 1964.
Weitz, M. In his Hamlet and the philosophy of literary criticism, Chicago 1964.
Spikes, J. T. Bradleyism at mid-century: the death of King Lear, Southern Quart 5 1967.
Hunter, G. K. Bradley's Shakespearian tragedy. E & S 21 1968.

M.P.

GERALD BRENAN
(EDWARD FITZGERALD BRENAN)
b. 1894

Jack Robinson: a picaresque novel. By 'George Beaton' [i.e. Brenan]. 1933.
Doctor Partridge's almanack for 1935 collected and set forth by 'George Beaton'. 1934. Fiction.
The Spanish labyrinth: an account of the social and political background of the Civil War. Cambridge 1943, 1950 (corrected).
Spanish scene. 1946 (Current Affairs pamphlet).
The face of Spain. 1950, New York 1951.
The literature of the Spanish people. Cambridge 1951, 1953 (rev), New York 1957.
South from Granada. 1957, New York 1957.
A holiday by the sea. 1961, New York 1961. Fiction.
A life of one's own: childhood and youth. 1962, New York 1962.
The lighthouse always says yes. 1966. Fiction.

M.S.

IVOR JOHN CARNEGIE BROWN
b. 1891

§1
Years of plenty. 1915, New York 1916. Fiction.
Security. 1916. Fiction.
English political theory. 1920, 1929 (rev).
Lighting-up time. 1920. Fiction.
The meaning of democracy. [1920], 1926 (rev), 1950 (rev).
H. G. Wells. 1923.
Masques and phases. 1926. Essays.
First player: the origin of drama. 1927.
Parties of the play. 1928. Stage history.
Now on view. 1929. Essays.
[Selected essays]. 1929 (Essays of Today and Yesterday).
Brown studies. 1930. Essays.
Puck, our peke. 1931.
Marine parade. 1932. Fiction.
Journalism in our time. [1933]. Lecture.
I commit to the flames. 1934. Essays.
Master Sanguine, who always believed what he was told. 1934, New York 1935. Fiction.
The heart of England. 1935, New York 1935.
The great and the goods. 1937. Fiction.
Amazing monument: a short history of the Shakespeare industry. 1939, New York 1939 (as This Shakespeare industry). With G. Fearon.
Life within reason. 1939. Politics.
The Shakespeares and the birthplace. [1939]. With G. Fearon.
A word in your ear. 1942, 1944 (with Just another word, as Ivor Brown's book of words), New York 1945 (as A word in your ear and Just another word, with foreword by J. D. Adams). 'An anthology of words'; first of a series.
Just another word. 1943, 1944 (with A word in your ear, as Ivor Brown's book of words), New York 1945 (as A word in your ear and Just another word, with foreword by J. D. Adams).
I give you my word. 1945, New York 1948 (with Say the word, introd by J. D. Adams).
Say the word. 1947, New York 1948 (with I give you my word, introd by J. D. Adams).
No idle words. 1948, New York 1951 (with Having the last word, introd by J. D. Adams).
Shakespeare. 1949, Garden City NY 1949.
Having the last word. 1950, New York 1951 (with No idle words, introd by J. D. Adams).
I break my word. 1951.

Winter in London. 1951, Garden City NY 1952. Topography.
Summer in Scotland. 1952. Topography.
The complete works of William Shakespeare: the Nonesuch text established 1929 by H. Farjeon, with new introd by Brown. 4 vols 1953.
A word in edgeways. 1953.
The way of my world. 1954. Autobiography.
Balmoral: the history of a home. 1955.
Chosen words. 1955.
Theatre 1954–5, (1955–6). 2 vols 1955, 56. Theatre reviews.
Dark ladies. 1957. Biographies.
J. B. Priestley. 1957, 1964 (rev) (Br Council pamphlet).
Royal homes in colour: a collection of colour photographs by A. F. Kersting and others, with introductory text and notes on the illustrations by Brown. 1958, 1961 (as part of Stately homes in colour).
Words in our time. 1958.
London. 1960, New York 1961 (Cities of enchantment).
Shakespeare in his time. Edinburgh [1960].
Words in season. 1961.
Mind your language! 1962, Chester Springs Pa 1964.
Dickens in his time. [1963].
How Shakespeare spent the day. 1963, New York 1964.
What is a play? 1964.
London: an illustrated history. 1965.
Shaw in his time. 1965.
Dr Johnson and his world. 1966, New York 1966.
Jane Austen and her world. 1966, New York 1966.
A ring of words. 1967.
William Shakespeare. 1968 (International Profiles ser).
The women in Shakespeare's life. 1968, New York 1969.
A rhapsody of words. 1969.
Brown wrote a number of one act plays; critical introds to Shakespeare Memorial Theatre: a photographic record; *and a few books for children on Shakespeare and the theatre. He also compiled several anthologies. He was editor of* Observer *1942–8, and dramatic critic 1929–54. He was dramatic critic and leader writer for* Manchester Guardian *1919–35.*

J.G.

EDWARD BULLOUGH
1880–1934

Bibliographies
In Æsthetics: lectures and essays, 1957, §1, below.

§1

The modern conception of æsthetics. 1907 (priv ptd). Rptd in Æsthetics: lectures and essays, 1957, below.
The philosophy of St Thomas Aquinas, by E. Gilson. Tr Bullough, Cambridge 1924, 1929 (rev and enlarged).
Two essays by Karl Adam: Christ and the western mind; Love and belief. Tr Bullough 1930.
Essays in history written between the years 1896–1912, by Pope Pius XI. [Tr Bullough] 1934.
The voyage of Captain Bellingshausen to the Antarctic seas 1819–1821. [Tr Bullough et al] 2 vols 1945 (Hakluyt Soc ser 2, 91–2).
Æsthetics: lectures and essays. Ed E. M. Wilkinson 1957, Stanford Calif 1957.
Bullough also jointly edited an edn of Tolstoy's Sevastopol *(1916) and edited* Cambridge readings in Italian literature *(1920).*

§2

Bennett, E. K. Cambridge Rev 56 1934.
Chandler, A. R. In his Beauty and human nature: elements of psychological æsthetics, New York 1934.
[Oakeshott, M.] Caian 43 1934.
Evennett, H. O. Dublin Rev 196 1935.

C.H.E.P.

OSBERT HENRY BURDETT
1885–1936

§1

The last ten years of English literature. 1907.
The idea of Coventry Patmore: an attempt to present the substance of Patmore's poetry. 1921.
The Beardsley period: an essay in perspective. 1925.
Critical essays. 1925.
William Blake. 1925, New York 1926 (EML).
W. E. Gladstone. 1927.
The Brownings. 1928, New York 1929, London 1933 (rev).
The two Carlyles. 1930, New York 1931.
The art of living. 1933. Essays.
The Rev Smith, Sydney. 1934.
A little book of cheese. 1935.
Memory and imagination. 1935. Reminiscences.
Edward Perry Warren: the biography of a connoisseur. 1941. With E. H. Goddard.
Burdett edited Makers of the modern age, *4 vols 1930–2, and wrote* The silent heavens (mystery play), 1914, Songs of exuberance, 1915, *and* The resurrection of Rheims: a poem, 1920, The very end (stories) 1929.

§2

Warren, D. Introduction to Osbert Burdett. South Atlantic Quart 33 1934.

H.M.R.

SIR NEVILLE CARDUS
b. 1889
See col 1313, below.

'CHRISTOPHER CAUDWELL', CHRISTOPHER ST JOHN SPRIGG
1907–37

Selections
The concept of freedom. Introd by G. Thomson, 1965. Selections from Studies in a dying culture, Further studies and The crisis in physics.

§1

The airship: its design, history, operation and future, by C. St J. Sprigg. [1931].
Fly with me: an elementary textbook on the art of piloting, by H. D. Davis and C. St J. Sprigg. 1932.
British airways, by C. St J. Sprigg. [1934], New York 1934 (Discovery Books 1). For boys.
Great flights, by C. St J. Sprigg. 1935, New York 1935 (Nelsonian Lib 35). For boys.
This my hand. 1936. Novel.
Illusion and reality: a study of the sources of poetry. 1937, 1946 (with biographical note by G.T. [i.e. G. Thomson], and index), New York 1947.
'Let's learn to fly!', by C. St J. Sprigg. 1937 (Nelsonian Lib 43).
Studies in a dying culture. Introd by J. Strachey, 1938, New York 1938, 1958 (with Further studies, 1959), 1963 (with biographical note by G. Thomson).
The crisis in physics. Ed H. Levy 1939, New York 1951.
Poems. 1939. With biographical note.
Further studies in a dying culture. Ed with preface by E. Rickword 1949, New York 1949, 1958 (with Studies, 1938).
Caudwell also wrote 7 detective novels as C. St J. Sprigg and a number of unpbd short stories; he founded an aeronautical

publishing house; he was the founder and editor of Technical Engineering; *he edited the jnl* Br Malaya, *and, with an introd, an anthology* Uncanny stories, *1936; he contributed to several newspapers including* Yorkshire Observer.

§2

Forster, E. M. The long run. New Statesman 10 Dec 1938. Essay-review of Studies in a dying culture, 1938.
Harap, L. Caudwell, critic. New Masses 20 Nov 1945.
— Caudwell; Marxist critic, poet and soldier. Worker 24 Nov 1946.
Frankel, H. Christopher Caudwell. World News and Views 15 Feb 1947.
Spender, S. Horatio hits back. New Statesman 12 April 1947. Review of Illusion and reality (reissue) 1946.
Hyman, S. E. Caudwell and Marxist criticism. In his Armed vision, New York 1948.
Comfort, A. The illusion of the thirties. World Rev new ser no 14 1950.
Modern Quart new ser 6 1950–1. No 1, 1950, M. Cornforth, Caudwell and Marxism; no 2, 1951, reply by G. Thomson, In defence of poetry; no 3, 1951, The Caudwell discussion: A. Bush, M. Slater, A. West; no 4, 1951, The Caudwell discussion: M. Heinemann, E. York, W. Thierry, O. Robb, J. D. Bernal, E. S. Smith, M. Cornforth.
Cumming, J. Caudwell and Marxist aesthetics. Slant 18 1967.
Hawley, A. R. Art for man's sake: Caudwell as communist aesthetician. College Eng 30 1968.
Margolies, D. N. The function of literature: a study of Caudwell's aesthetics. 1969.
Ray, P. C. The anti-surrealism of Caudwell. Comparative Lit Stud 6 1969.

LORD EDWARD CHRISTIAN DAVID GASCOYNE CECIL
b. 1902

Cans and can'ts. [1927]. A game. With C. Asquith.
The stricken deer: or the life of Cowper. 1929, Indianapolis [1930].
William Cowper. 1932 (English Assoc pamphlet).
Selections from Cowper: poetry and prose. 1933. Ed Cecil.
Sir Walter Scott. 1933 (Raven Miscellany).
Early Victorian novelists: essays in revaluation. 1934, Indianapolis [1935], Chicago 1958 (as Victorian novelists: essays in revaluation, with a new foreword), London 1964.
The new book of English verse. Ed C. Williams, associate editors D. Cecil [et al]. 1935, New York 1936.
An anthology of modern biography 1936. Ed Cecil.
The young Melbourne and the story of his marriage with Caroline Lamb. 1939, Indianapolis [1939], New York 1943 (foreword by C. Van Doren).
The Oxford book of Christian verse. Oxford 1940. Ed Cecil.
The English poets. 1941 (Britain in Pictures).
A layman's glimpse. In W. Rothenstein, Men of the R.A.F., 1942.
Hardy the novelist: an essay in criticism. 1943, Indianapolis 1946.
Two quiet lives: Dorothy Osborne, Thomas Gray. 1948, Indianapolis [1948].
Poets and story-tellers: a book of critical essays. 1949, New York 1949. Includes lectures previously pbd separately.
Hatfield House: an illustrated survey of the Hertfordshire home of the Cecil family. Derby [1951]. Booklet. History written by D. Cecil.
Lord M.: or the later life of Lord Melbourne. 1954. Includes a brief selection from The young Melbourne, 1939.

Melbourne. Indianapolis 1954, London 1965. Contains The young Melbourne, 1939 and Lord M, 1954, above.
The fine art of reading and other literary studies. 1957, Indianapolis 1957. Includes lectures previously pbd separately.
Modern verse in English. 1958, New York 1958. Ed Cecil, with A. Tate.
Max: a biography. 1964, Boston 1965.
Visionary and dreamer: two poetic painters, Samuel Palmer and Edward Burne-Jones. 1969, Princeton NJ 1970.

M.P.

HECTOR MUNRO CHADWICK
1870–1947
Bibliographies

National Library of Scotland. A list of the published writings of Hector Munro Chadwick and of Nora Kershaw Chadwick. Edinburgh 1971. Includes appreciation by D. Whitelock.

§1

The cult of Othin: an essay in the ancient religion of the North. 1899.
Studies on Anglo-Saxon institutions. Cambridge 1905.
The origin of the English nation. Cambridge 1907.
Early national poetry. In CHEL vol 1, Cambridge 1907.
The heroic age. Cambridge 1912.
The growth of literature: vol 1, The ancient literatures of Europe; vol 2, Russian, Yugoslav, early Indian, early Hebrew; vol 3, The Tatars, Polynesia, Sea Dyaks, African peoples, General survey. Cambridge 1932–40. With N. K. Chadwick.
The study of Anglo-Saxon. Cambridge 1941, 1955 (rev N. K. Chadwick).
The nationalities of Europe and the growth of national ideologies. Cambridge 1945.
Early Scotland: the Picts, the Scots and the Welsh of southern Scotland. Cambridge 1949. Prepared for the press by N. K. Chadwick.
Chadwick contributed to the Encyclopaedia Britannica *(11th edn), to the* Encyclopaedia of Religion and Ethics, *and to a number of collaborative volumes.*

§2

Leavis, F. R. For whom do universities exist? Scrutiny 14 1946.
Navarro, J. M. de. Hector Munro Chadwick. Proc Br Acad 33 1947.
Professor Chadwick and English studies. Scrutiny 14 1947. Comments by J. C. Maxwell and 'Redbrick', ibid.
Telfer, W. Hector Munro Chadwick. Cambridge Rev 68 1947.
Fox, C. and Dickins, B. (ed). The early cultures of north-west Europe: H. M. Chadwick memorial studies. Cambridge 1950. Includes biographical note and list of publications.
Tillyard, E. M. W. In his Muse unchained: an intimate account of the revolution in English studies at Cambridge, 1958.
Whitelock, D. In her Changing currents in Anglo-Saxon studies, Cambridge 1958.

P.G.B.

SIR EDMUND KERCHEVER CHAMBERS
1866–1954

§1

The history and motives of literary forgeries: being the Chancellor's English essay for 1891. Oxford 1891.
English pastorals, selected by Chambers. 1895, 1924 (with different introd) (Warwick Lib), Freeport NY 1969.
The poems of Donne. Ed Chambers 2 vols 1896 (ML).
The poems of Vaughan. Ed Chambers 2 vols 1896 (ML).
The mediæval stage. 2 vols Oxford 1903.
Notes on the history of the Revels office under the Tudors. 1906, New York 1967.
Early English lyrics amorous, divine, moral and trivial. Ed Chambers and F. Sidgwick 1907, New York 1967.
Aurelian Townshend's Poems and masks. Ed Chambers, Oxford 1912 (Tudor and Stuart Lib).
Carmina argentea. Oxford 1918 (priv ptd). Verse.
The Elizabethan stage. 4 vols Oxford 1923, 1961 (rev).
Shakespeare: a survey. 1925. 34 essays, first pbd as introds to plays in the Red Letter Shakespeare. *See* footnote, below.
Arthur of Britain. 1927, Cambridge 1964 (with supplementary bibliography by B. F. Roberts), New York 1967.
William Shakespeare: a study of facts and problems. 2 vols Oxford 1930.
The Oxford book of sixteenth-century verse. Ed Chambers, Oxford 1932, 1961 (corrected).
The English folk-play. Oxford 1933, New York 1964.
Sir Thomas Wyatt and some collected studies. 1933, New York 1965.
Eynsham under the monks. Oxford 1936 (Oxfordshire Record ser).
Sir Henry Lee: an Elizabethan portrait. Oxford 1936.
Samuel Taylor Coleridge: a biographical study. Oxford 1938, 1963 (corrected).
A sheaf of studies. 1942, Freeport NY 1969. Includes single lectures previously pbd separately.
Shakespearean gleanings. 1944, Folcroft Pa 1969.
English literature at the close of the Middle Ages. Oxford 1945, 1947 (corrected) (OHEL 2 pt 2).
Sources for a biography of Shakespeare. Oxford 1946.
Matthew Arnold: a study. Oxford 1947, New York 1964.
Chambers edited the Red Letter Shakespeare *1904–8 and, with C. H. Herford, A. D. Innes et al, the* Warwick Shakespeare *1893 onwards; he was the first President of the Malone Soc and edited, sometimes with W. W. Greg et al, a number of dramatic records for the Malone Soc collections. He also pbd a number of school edns of various English authors.*

§2

Wilson, F. P. and J. D. Wilson. E. K. Chambers. Proc Br Acad 42 1956.

RAYMOND WILSON CHAMBERS
1874–1942

Bibliographies
Husbands, H. W. In C. J. Sisson, R. W. Chambers, 1944 §2, below.

§1

The chronicle of Froissart, tr by Lord Berners; introd by W. P. Ker. 6 vols 1901–3 (Tudor Translations 27–32). Chambers edited vols 2–6 and compiled index in vol 6. *See* letter by Chambers in TLS 8 Dec 1927.
Widsith: a study in Old English heroic legend. Cambridge 1912, New York 1965. Text ed with commentary by Chambers.

Beowulf, with the Finnsburg fragment. Ed A. J. Wyatt, rev by R. W. Chambers, Cambridge 1914, 1920 (rptd with 3 pages of additional notes), 1932 (rev), 1959 (with a suppl by C. L. Wrenn).
Beowulf: an introduction to the study of the poem, with a discussion of the stories of Offa and Finn. Cambridge 1921, 1932 (rev and enlarged), 1959 (suppl by C. L. Wrenn).
The teaching of English in the universities of England. Oxford 1922 (Eng Assoc pamphlet 53).
The expression of ideas, particularly political ideas, in the three pages [believed to be in Shakespeare's handwriting] and in Shakespeare. In Shakespeare's hand in the play of Sir Thomas More, by A. W. Pollard [et al], Cambridge 1923.
On the continuity of English prose from Alfred to More and his school: an extract from the introduction to N. Harpsfield's Life and death of Sr Thomas More. Ed E. V. Hitchcock and Chambers 1932.
The Exeter book of Old English poetry. 1933. With M. Förster and R. Flower.
Thomas More. 1935, New York 1935.
The place of Sir Thomas More in English literature and history: being a revision of a lecture delivered to the Thomas More Society. 1937, New York 1964.
The chronicles of Scotland, compiled by Hector Boece, translated by John Bellenden. 1531. Ed in continuation of the work of W. Seton by R. W. Chambers and E. C. Batho, Edinburgh 1938 (Scottish Text Soc 3rd ser 10).
Man's unconquerable mind: studies of English writers from Bede to A. E. Housman and W. P. Ker. 1939.
See Husbands' bibliography, above, for Chambers' articles on Piers Plowman *and for his writings on University College London and its library. Chambers also edited, with F. Norman and A. H. Smith,* London mediaeval studies, *monographs nos 1 and 2 1938–9. In 1928 he edited* Form and style in poetry: lectures and notes by W. P. Ker.

§2

Sisson, C. J. R. W. Chambers. Proc Br Acad 30 1944.
—— R. W. Chambers: a portrait of a professor. 1951 (Chambers Memorial Lecture 1 1950).
Wilks, J. The influence of Chambers on the development of university libraries. 1953 (Chambers Memorial Lecture 2 1953).

ROBERT WILLIAM CHAPMAN
1881–1960

§1

The portrait of a scholar and other essays written in Macedonia 1916–18. 1920, Freeport NY 1968.
Some account of the Oxford University Press 1468–1921. Oxford 1922. Anon.
—— 1468–1926. Oxford 1926. Anon.
Boswell's revises of the Life of Johnson. In Johnson and Boswell revised by themselves and others: three essays by D. Nichol Smith, R. W. Chapman and L. F. Powell, Oxford 1928.
Cancels. 1930 (Bibliographia ser).
Jane Austen: facts and problems. Oxford 1948, 1961 (corrected).
The sense of the past. In Book collecting: four broadcast talks by R. W. Chapman [et al], Cambridge 1951.
Jane Austen: a critical bibliography. Oxford 1953, 1955 (corrected).
Johnsonian and other essays and reviews. Oxford 1953.
Chapman also wrote a number of tracts for the Society for Pure English.

Principal Editions

Selections from Boswell's Life of Johnson. Oxford 1919.

Johnson: prose and poetry. Oxford 1922.

Austen, J. The novels: the text based on collation of the early editions. 5 vols 1923, 1926 (corrected), 1933 (corrected). For vol 6, Minor works, see 1954, below. Chapman's text has been used in a number of subsequent edns of the individual novels.

Johnson's Journey to the Western Islands of Scotland and Boswell's Journal of a tour to the Hebrides. 1924.

Austen, J. Fragment of a novel [Sanditon], now first printed from the manuscript. Oxford 1925. Text rptd in Minor works, 1954, below.

Johnson, S. The history of Rasselas. Oxford 1927.

Austen, J. Letters to her sister Cassandra and others. 2 vols Oxford 1932, 1 vol London 1952 (rev).

—— Volume the first [of 3 notebooks of juvenilia] now first printed from the manuscript in the Bodleian Library. Oxford 1933. Text rptd in Minor works, 1954, below.

—— Volume the third [of 3 notebooks of juvenilia] now first printed from the manuscript. Oxford 1951. Text rptd in Minor works, 1954, below.

The letters of Samuel Johnson with Mrs Thrale's genuine letters to him. 3 vols Oxford 1952.

The works of Jane Austen vol 6: Minor works, now first collected and edited from the manuscripts. 1954. Vols 1–5 see 1923, above.

Selections from Johnson 1709–84. 1955.

From 1920–42 Chapman was Secretary to the Delegates of the Oxford Univ Press and sponsored and contributed to a number of scholarly works, notably the Supplement to the Oxford English Dictionary 1933.

§2

Lane, M. Dr R. W. Chapman. TLS 6 Aug 1954. Essay-review of Johnsonian and other essays 1953. Rptd in her Purely for pleasure, 1966.

Lascelles, M. R. W. Chapman. Proc Br Acad 47 1961.

Roberts, S. C. R. W. Chapman. E & S new ser 14 1961.

GILBERT KEITH CHESTERTON
1874–1936

An extensive collection of mss, letters, notebooks and other Chesterton material is held by Dorothy Collins, Chesterton's literary executrix; other collections include the Robert John Bayer Chesterton Collection, John Carroll Univ, Cleveland, Ohio, and that of J. B. Shaw, Tulsa, Oklahoma; some mss of juvenilia are held in the library of St Paul's School.

Bibliographies

Sullivan, J. J. Chesterton: a bibliography. 1958. Includes trns.

—— The trials of bibliography. Manchester Rev 8 1959. Mainly on Chesterton's books.

—— Chesterton continued: a bibliographical supplement together with some uncollected prose and verse. 1968.

Sprug, J. W. (ed). An index to Chesterton. Washington 1966. Subject-index to all the writings in book form.

Collections and Selections

A Chesterton calendar. 1911, New York 1911 (as Wit and wisdom of Chesterton; omits The moveable feasts). Some items first pbd here in book form.

A defence of nonsense and other essays. New York 1911.

Thoughts from Chesterton, selected by E. E. Morton. [1913].

The Chesterton calendar, selected by H. C. Palmer. 1916.

A shilling for my thoughts. 1916. Prose, selected by E. V. Lucas.

G. K. Chesterton. 1925. Poems, selected by J. C. Squire (Augustan Books of Modern Poetry).

A gleaming cohort. 1926. Prose and verse, selected by E. V. Lucas.

[Selected works]. 9 vols [1926] (Minerva Edns of Modern Authors).

Collected poems. 1927, New York 1932, London 1933 (rev).

G. K. Chesterton. 1928 (Essays of Today and Yesterday).

G. K. Chesterton. 1928 (Short Stories of Today and Yesterday).

Christmas poems. [1928]. Selected from Poems, 1915.

A Chesterton Catholic anthology. Ed P. Braybrooke 1928.

G.K.C. as M.C.: being a collection of thirty-seven introductions. 1929, Freeport NY 1967. Selected by J. P. de Fonseka.

The Father Brown stories. 1929, New York [1935] (as The Father Brown omnibus), London 1947 (adds The scandal of Father Brown), New York 1951 (as The Father Brown omnibus; adds The vampire of the village).

G. K. Chesterton. 1933 (Methuen's Lib of Humour), New York 1933 (as On running after one's hat and other whimsies). Ed E. V. Knox.

Stories, essays and poems. 1935, 1957 (introd by M. Ward) (EL).

A G. K. Chesterton omnibus. 1936. The Napoleon of Notting Hill; The man who was Thursday; The flying inn.

The man who was Chesterton. New York 1937, 1960 (abridged). Prose and verse, selected by R. T. Bond.

Essays, selected with a preface by J. Guest. [1939], 1953 (as Selected essays).

Pocket book of Father Brown. Philadelphia 1943.

Selected essays, chosen by D. Collins. Introd by E. C. Bentley 1949.

The amazing adventures of Father Brown. New York [1954]. Selection.

Father Brown: selected stories. With introd by R. Knox 1955 (WC).

New World Chesterton. 8 vols. New York 1955–6.

Chesterton: an anthology, selected with an introduction by D. B. Wyndham Lewis. 1957 (WC).

Essays and poems. Ed W. Sheed 1958, Baltimore 1958.

Father Brown stories. 1959 (Folio Soc). Selection.

Chesterton reprint series. 11 vols 1960–4 (vols 9–11 pbd Beaconsfield), Philadelphia 1962–. Fiction, excluding The flying inn and the Father Brown stories.

Father Brown mystery stories. Selected with introd by R. T. Bond, New York 1962.

The man who was orthodox: a selection from the uncollected writings. Ed A. L. Maycock 1963.

Chesterton: a selection from his non-fictional prose, selected by W. H. Auden. 1970.

§1

Most of Chesterton's writings were first pbd in journals. See J. J. Sullivan, Bibliography, above. According to M. Ward's biography of Chesterton, 1943, p. 145, all his essays were revised for pbn in book form.

The defendant. 1901, New York 1902, London 1903 (adds In defence of a new edition). Essays.

Twelve types. 1902, New York 1903 (as Varied types; adds 7 further essays).

Thomas Carlyle. 1902. With J. E. H. Williams. Booklet.

Robert Louis Stevenson. 1902. With W. R. Nicoll. Booklet.

Leo Tolstoy. 1903. With G. H. Perris and E. Garnett. Booklet.

Charles Dickens. 1903. With F. G. Kitton. Booklet. A different work from that pbd 1906.

Robert Browning. 1903 (EML), New York 1903.

Tennyson. 1903, 1906 (with minor changes). With R. Garnett. Booklet.

Thackeray. 1903. With L. Melville. Booklet.

G. F. Watts. [1904].

Heretics. 1905, New York 1905. Essays.

Charles Dickens. 1906, New York, 1906 (as Charles Dickens: a critical study), 1942 (as Charles Dickens, the last of the great men; enlarged, foreword by A. Woollcott), 1965 (introd by S. Marcus).

All things considered. 1908, New York 1908. Essays.

Orthodoxy. 1909 (for 1908), New York 1908 (with preface by Chesterton). *See* 'Alan Handsacre', Authordoxy: being a discursive examination of Chesterton's Orthodoxy, 1921.

George Bernard Shaw. 1910 (for 1909), New York 1909, London 1935 (with new ch), New York 1950.

Tremendous trifles. 1909, New York 1909. Essays.

Five types. 1910, New York 1911. Five essays rptd from Twelve types, 1902, above.

What's wrong with the world. 1910, New York 1910.

The glory of grey. [1910] (priv ptd). Essay, rptd in Alarms and discursions, below.

Alarms and discursions. 1910, New York 1911 (adds The fading fireworks). Essays.

William Blake. [1910].

The ultimate lie. Riverside Conn 1910 (priv ptd). Essay.

Appreciations and criticisms of the works of Dickens. 1911, 1933 (as Criticisms and appreciations of the works of Dickens), New York 1966 (with original title). First pbd as introds to Dickens' works in EL.

The future of religion. [Cambridge 1911]. Reply to Shaw's The religion of the future. Pamphlet.

Simplicity and Tolstoy. 1912. 3 essays rptd from Twelve types, 1902, above.

A miscellany of men. 1912, New York 1912 (adds Preface and The suffragist). Essays.

The Victorian age in literature. [1913], New York [1913], Notre Dame 1962 (foreword by A. Ryan).

The barbarism of Berlin. 1914.

London, with ten photographs by A. L. Coburn. 1914, Minneapolis 1914. Priv ptd.

Prussian versus Belgian culture. [1914]. Pamphlet.

Letters to an old Garibaldian. 1915.

The appetite of tyranny. New York 1915. Contains The barbarism of Berlin and Letters to an old Garibaldian, above.

The so-called Belgian bargain. [1915]. Pamphlet.

The crimes of England. 1915, New York 1916.

Divorce versus democracy. 1916. Pamphlet.

Temperance and the great alliance. [1916]. Pamphlet.

Lord Kitchener. 1917. Booklet.

A short history of England. 1917, New York 1917, London 1924 (with new foreword).

Utopia of usurers and other essays. New York 1917.

How to help annexation. 1918. Pamphlet.

Irish impressions. [1919], New York 1920.

The superstition of divorce. 1920, New York 1920.

Charles Dickens fifty years after. 1920 (priv ptd, 25 copies). Pamphlet.

The uses of diversity. 1920, New York 1921. Essays.

The new Jerusalem. [1920], New York [1921]. Travel.

Eugenics and other evils. 1922. Essays.

What I saw in America. 1922, New York 1922, 1968 (introd by G. H. Knoles).

Fancies versus fads. 1923, New York 1923. Essays.

St Francis of Assisi. [1923], New York [1924].

The end of the Roman road: a pageant of wayfarers. 1924.

The superstition of the sceptic; with a correspondence between the author and G. G. Coulton. Cambridge 1925. The discussion was continued by Chesterton in Dublin Rev 176 1925 and by Coulton in Rev of the Churches new ser 2 1925.

The everlasting man. [1925], New York 1925 (slightly different, text of Appendix 1).

William Cobbett. [1925].

The outline of sanity. 1926, New York 1927. Essays on Distributism.

The Catholic Church and conversion. New York 1926, London 1926 (for 1927) (Calvert ser), 1960 (adds 2 essays).

Social reform versus birth control. [1927]. Pamphlet.

Culture and the coming peril. 1927. 7th Centenary address, University College London.

Robert Louis Stevenson. [1927], New York 1928.

Generally speaking. 1928, New York 1929. Essays.

The thing. 1929, New York 1930 (adds Why I am a Catholic). Essays.

The resurrection of Rome. [1930], New York 1930 (omits 2 appendices).

Come to think of it. 1930, New York 1931. Essays.

At the sign of the world's end. [Palo Alto] 1930 (priv ptd, 25 copies). Essay.

Is there a return to religion? Debate—Yes: Chesterton; No: E. Haldemann Julius. Girard Kansas 1931.

All is grist. 1931, New York 1932. Essays.

Chaucer. 1932, New York [1932].

Sidelights on new London and Newer York and other essays. 1932, New York 1932.

Christendom in Dublin. 1932, New York 1933. On the Eucharistic Congress, 1932.

All I survey. 1933, New York 1933. Essays.

St Thomas Aquinas. 1933, New York 1933.

Avowals and denials. 1934, New York 1935. Essays.

The well and the shadows. 1935, New York 1935. Essays.

The way of the Cross: an interpretation by F. Brangwyn [plates], with a commentary by Chesterton. [1935].

Chesterton explains the English. [1935] (Br Council pamphlet).

As I was saying. 1936, New York 1936. Essays.

Autobiography. 1936, New York 1936, London 1969 (introd A. Burgess).

The legend of the sword. [Dublin] 1936 (priv ptd). Rptd in The coloured lands, below. Parable.

The coloured lands, illustrated by the author. 1938, New York 1938. Introd by M. Ward. Prose, verse and drawings, much hitherto unpbd, including juvenilia.

The end of the armistice. 1940, New York 1940. Essays, ed F. J. Sheed.

'I say a democracy means...'. New York [1941] (priv ptd). Pt of a letter to Nation 26 Jan 1911; full text with other relevant letters ptd in M. Ward, Gilbert Keith Chesterton, 1943, §2, below. 125 copies.

The common man. 1950, New York 1950. Essays, articles and introds first pbd 1901–36.

A handful of authors. Ed D. Collins 1953, New York 1953. Essays first pbd 1901–35.

The glass walking-stick and other essays from Illustrated London News 1905–36. Ed D. Collins 1955. Preface by A. Bryant.

Lunacy and letters. Ed D. Collins 1958, New York 1958. Essays from Daily News 1901–11.

The spice of life and other essays. Ed D. Collins, Beaconsfield 1964, Philadelphia 1966. Essays contributed to various books and jnls.

Fiction

The Napoleon of Notting Hill. 1904, New York 1904.

The club of queer trades. 1905 (illustr Chesterton), New York 1905 (illustr W. E. Mears). Stories.

The man who was Thursday: a nightmare. 1908, New York 1908. Dramatized version by Mrs Cecil Chesterton and R. Neale with foreword by Chesterton, pbd 1926.

The ball and the cross. New York 1909, London 1910 (rev).

The innocence of Father Brown. 1911, New York 1911. Stories.

Manalive. 1912, New York 1912.

The flying inn. 1914, New York 1914. Songs rptd (with 1 addn) as Wine, water and song, 1915.

The wisdom of Father Brown. 1914, New York 1915. Stories.

The man who knew too much and other stories. 1922, New York 1922 (omits last 3 stories).

Tales of the long bow. 1925, New York 1925.

The incredulity of Father Brown. 1926, New York 1926. Stories.

The return of Don Quixote. 1927, New York 1927.

The secret of Father Brown. 1927, New York 1927. Stories.

The sword of wood: a story. 1928.

The poet and the lunatics: episodes in the life of Gabriel Gale. 1929, New York [1929].

Four faultless felons. 1930, New York 1930. Stories.

The scandal of Father Brown. 1935, New York 1935. Stories.

The paradoxes of Mr Pond. [1937], New York 1937. Stories.

Verse and Plays

Greybeards at play—literature and art for old gentlemen: rhymes and sketches. 1900.

The wild knight and other poems. 1900, 1905 (adds Prefatory note), 1914 (adds 3 poems).

The ballad of the white horse. 1911, New York 1911.

Magic: a fantastic comedy. (Little Theatre 7 Nov 1913). [1913], York 1913.

Poems. 1915, New York 1915.

Wine, water and song. 1915. Verses first pbd in The flying inn, 1914, with one addition.

Old King Cole. [1920]. Text of the rhyme with versions parodying Tennyson, Yeats, Whitman, Browning.

The ballad of St Barbara and other verses. 1922, New York 1923.

The queen of seven swords. 1926. Poems.

Gloria in profundis. [1927] (Ariel Poem).

The judgement of Dr Johnson: a comedy. (Arts Theatre Club 20 Jan 1932). 1927, New York 1928.

Ubi ecclesia. 1929 (Ariel Poem).

Lepanto. New York 1929. Rptd from Poems, 1915, above.

The grave of Arthur. 1930 (Ariel Poem).

The turkey and the Turk. Ditchling 1930 (St Dominic's Press, 100 copies). Dramatic poem.

A Beaconsfield ballad. [c. 1935].

The surprise. (Hull Univ Dramatic Soc 5 June 1953). 1952, New York 1953. Preface by D. L. Sayers.

Principal Contributions to Books

The religious doubts of democracy. Ed G. Haw 1904. Pamphlet, reprinting the controversy between Chesterton, R. Blatchford et al in Clarion.

The patriotic idea. In England, a nation: being the papers of the Patriots' Club, 1904.

Mr Crowley and the creeds and The creed of Mr Chesterton. [1904] (priv ptd). Rptd review of A. Crowley, The sword of song, with reply and post-script by Crowley.

Vox populi, vox Dei; The citizen, the gentleman and the savage. In Preachers from the pew, ed W. H. Hunt 1906. Christian Social Union lectures.

Do miracles happen? [1914]. Report of a discussion between Chesterton, J. McCabe, Belloc et al.

Trial of John Jasper for the murder of Edwin Drood, heard by Mr Justice Gilbert Keith Chesterton. [1914]. Verbatim report. Shaw and C. Chesterton also took part.

The false motive of the movement. In Liberty, by J. Crichton-Browne, Chesterton [et al], 1917. Against prohibition.

The return of Christendom, by a group of churchmen, with an epilogue by Chesterton. 1922.

The dragon at hide and seek. In Number two, Joy street: a medley of prose and verse, Oxford [1924]. A story for children.

Why I am a Catholic. In Twelve modern apostles and their creeds by Chesterton [et al], New York 1926. Rptd as The reason why, in The Catholic Church and conversion, 1960.

The purpose of the [Distributist] League. In Leaflets for Leaguers, 1, [1926].

Do we agree? a debate between Chesterton and Shaw with Belloc in the chair. 1928, Hartford Conn 1928.

A turning-point in history. In The fame of Blessed Thomas More: being addresses delivered in his honour by R. Knox, Chesterton [et al], 1929.

The end of wisdom. In The Fothergill omnibus, 1931. Short story.

Mary Queen of Scots. In Revaluations: studies in biography by L. Abercrombie, Chesterton [et al], 1931.

Alfred the Great; Thomas More. In The English way: studies in English sanctity from St Bede to Newman, by Chesterton [et al], ed M. Ward 1933, Freeport New York 1968.

G.K.'s: a miscellany of the first 500 issues of G.K.'s Weekly. 1934. Introd, many contributions in prose and verse and illustrations.

Freedom, by E. Benn, Chesterton [et al]: based on a series of broadcast talks. 1935. *See* Sullivan, Bibliography, above, for details of the resulting Coulton-Chesterton controversy in Listener 1935–6.

Many of Chesterton's letters and much unpbd prose, verse and some drawings are contained in M. Ward, Gilbert Keith Chesterton, New York 1943, and Return to Chesterton, 1952. Further uncollected prose and verse is contained in Sullivan, Chesterton continued, Bibliographies, above. His many other contributions, illustrations, prefaces, introds, pamphlets etc are listed in Sullivan, Bibliography, above. He edited Essays by divers hands vol 6, 1926, and, with H. Jackson and R. B. Johnson, the Readers' Classics ser, 1922. Many of his numerous contributions to journals have not yet been collected. He contributed regularly to the Belloc-Chesterton journal which started as Eye Witness (June 1911–Oct 1912), became New Witness (Nov 1912–May 1923) and was revived as G.K.'s Weekly (1925–38), and from 1916 to 1923 and 1925–36 he was editor. He contributed a weekly article and occasional reviews to Daily News 6 Jan 1901 to 1 Feb 1913, and a weekly essay, Our notebook, to Illustrated London News from 1905 until his death. Sullivan's Bibliography, above, lists only those contributions to journals rptd in book form, with the following additions: Debater (St Paul's School) 1891–3; Listener, 1932–6 (complete list of rptd broadcast talks); and reports of speeches, debates and controversies (including details of the Blatchford controversy, in Daily News, Commonwealth and Clarion, 1903–4; the Chesterton-Belloc-Wells-Shaw and the Chesterton-Bax-Shaw controversies in New Age, 1907–9; the Chesterton-Belloc-Coulton controversy in Daily Telegraph, 1929; and the Chesterton-Coulton controversy in Listener, 1935–6).

§2

For replies to Chesterton's religious writings, see J. J. Sullivan, Bibliography, above.

Books

[Chesterton, C.] Chesterton: a criticism. 1908.

Scott, W. T. Chesterton and other essays. Cincinnati 1912.

Bridges, H. J. Chesterton as theologian. Philadelphia 1913.

West, J. Chesterton: a critical study. 1915.

Tonquédec, J. de. Chesterton: ses idées et son caractère. Paris 1920.

Anderson, K. H. Chesterton. Copenhagen 1922, 1945 (enlarged as Chesterton: den muntre strid).

Braybrooke, P. Gilbert Keith Chesterton. 1922, 1926 (enlarged).

—— The wisdom of Chesterton. 1929.

—— I remember Chesterton. [1938].

Bullett, G. W. The innocence of Chesterton. 1923.

Arns, K. Gilbert Keith Chesterton. Dortmund-Würzburg 1925.

Borowy, W. Gilbert Keith Chesterton. Cracow 1929. In Polish.

Stegmeyer, F. C. Chesterton. Cologne 1934.

Titterton, W. R. Chesterton: a portrait. 1936.

Cammaerts, E. The laughing prophet. 1937.

Hoffmann, G. Chesterton als Propagandist. Dresden 1937.

Las Vergnas, R. Portraits anglais: Chesterton, Belloc, Baring. Paris 1937; tr 1938.

O'Connor, J. Father Brown on Chesterton. 1937.

Evans, M. G. K. Chesterton. Cambridge 1938.

Clemens, C. Chesterton as seen by his contemporaries. Webster Groves Mo 1939. Introd by E. C. Bentley.

Kuhn, H. Der Gemeinschaftsgedanke bei Chesterton. Bochum 1939.

Menrad, A. Der Fortschrittsgedanke bei Chesterton. Freiburg i B. 1939.

Belloc, H. On the place of Chesterton in English letters. 1940.

Bogaerts, A. M. A. Chesterton and the Victorian age. Hilversum 1940.

Chesterton, Mrs C. The Chestertons. 1941.

Ward, M. Gilbert Keith Chesterton. New York 1943.
— Return to Chesterton. 1952.

Lea, F. A. The Wild Knight of Battersea. [1945].

Chisholm, F. Chesterton and his biographers. Webster Groves Mo 1945.

Kenner, H. Paradox in Chesterton. 1948.

Hollis, C. G. K. Chesterton. 1950, 1954 (rev bibliography), 1964 (rev bibliography) (Br Council pamphlet).
— The mind of Chesterton. 1970.

Reckitt, M. B. Chesterton: a Christian prophet for England today. 1950. Rptd in his The world and the faith, 1954.

Wills, G. Chesterton: man and mask. New York 1961.

Fabritius, R. M. Das Komische im Erzählwerk Chestertons. Tübingen 1964.

Chapters in Books and Periodical Articles

Ward, W. Chesterton among the prophets. In his Men and matters, 1914.

Wells, H. G. About Chesterton and Belloc. In his An Englishman looks at the world, 1914. First pbd in New Age 11 Jan 1908 as pt of the Chesterton-Belloc-Wells-Shaw controversy. See footnote to §1, above.

Meynell, A. G. K. Chesterton. Dublin Rev 172 1923.

Freeman, J. A Canterbury pilgrim. In his English portraits and essays, 1924.

Bliss, W. H. G. K. Chesterton, poet. Month 152 1928.

Edwards, D. In Scrutinies, ed E. Rickword, vol 1, 1928.

Williams, C. In his Poetry at present, Oxford 1930.

Braybrooke, P. The peculiar novels of Chesterton. In his Some Catholic novelists, 1931.
— Chesterton and Dickens. Dickensian 41 1945.

Hardie, W. F. R. The philosophy of Chesterton. Hibbert Jnl 30 1931.

Shaw, G. B. The Chesterbelloc; Chesterton on Shaw; The case against Chesterton; Something like a History of England; How free is the press?; Chesterton on eugenics and Shaw on Chesterton. In his Pen portraits and reviews, 1932.

Titterton, W. R. In his A candle to the stars, 1932.

Maurois, A. In his Magiciens et logiciens, Paris 1935. Tr 1935 as Prophets and poets; 1968 as Points of view.

Knox, R. A. Chesterton in his early romances. Dublin Rev 199 1936.
— G. K. Chesterton. In Great Catholics, ed C. Williamson 1938. Rptd, with an essay on Father Brown, in his Literary distractions, 1958.

McLuhan, M. Chesterton: a practical mystic. Dalhousie Rev 15 1936.

Mark Twain Quart 1 1937. Chesterton memorial number.

Palmer, H. Chesterton and his school. In his Post-Victorian poetry, 1938.

Bentley, E. C. At school with GKC. In his Those days, 1940.

Murray, J. Chesterton: a new appreciation. Studies 33 1944. Review-article of M. Ward, Gilbert Keith Chesterton, 1943.

O'Connor, J. Chesterton: recognita decennalia. Nineteenth Century and After 139 1946. Signed 'Father Brown'.

Stephens, J. The 'period talent' of Chesterton. Listener 17 Oct 1946. Reply by C. S. Lewis, Time & Tide 9 Nov 1946.

Irvine, W. Shaw and Chesterton. Virginia Quart Rev 23 1947.

Jones, W. S. H. Chesterton and the discovery of Christianity. London Quart & Holborn Rev Oct 1948, rptd in his The priest and the siren, 1953.

Robbins, H. The last of the realists: Chesterton and his work. The Cross and the Plough 15 1948. Chesterton and Distributism.

Hamilton, K. Chesterton and George Orwell: a contrast in prophecy. Dalhousie Rev 31 1951.

Noyes, A. The centrality of Chesterton. Quart Rev 291 1953.

Reckitt, M. B. Belloc and Chesterton: the study of an impact. In his The world and the faith, 1954.

Belloc, H. Gilbert Chesterton. In his One thing and another, 1955.

Clarke, M. Chesterton the classicist. Dublin Rev 229 1955.

Sewell, E. Chesterton: the giant upside-down. Thought 30 1955.

Raymond, J. Jeekaycee. New Statesman 23 March 1957. Rptd in his England's on the anvil! 1958.

Brome, V. Chesterton versus Bernard Shaw. In his Six studies in quarrelling, 1958.

Bergonzi, B. Chesterton and/or Belloc. CQ 1 1959.

Eaker, J. G. Chesterton among the moderns. Georgia Rev 13 1959.

Mason, M. In his The centre of hilarity, 1959.
— Chesterbelloc. Twentieth Century 177 1968-9.

Bradbrook, B. R. The literary relationship between Chesterton and Karel Capek. Slavonic & East European Rev 39 1961.

Versfeld, M. Chesterton and St Thomas. Eng Stud in Africa 4 1961.

Pearson, H. In his Lives of the wits, 1962.

Hart, J. In praise of Chesterton. Yale Rev 53 1963.

Maycock, A. L. Introduction to his The man who was orthodox: a selection from the uncollected writings of Chesterton, 1963.

Thibault, A. A. Chesterton et la langue française. Univ of Windsor Rev (Ontario) 1 1966.

Shaw Rev 10 1967. Contains: H. J. Donaghy, Chesterton on Shaw's views of Catholicism; W. B. Furlong, Shaw and Chesterton: the link was magic.

Almeida, M. d'. O gênio de Chesterton. Brotéria 87 1968.

Dhar, B. Chesterton as a journalist. Modern Rev 62 1968.

Albérès, R. M. Chesterton contre le pessimisme. Revue de Paris 76 1969.

Robson, W. W. Chesterton's Father Brown stories. Southern Rev new ser 5 1969.

RICHARD THOMAS CHURCH
1893-1972

See cols 246-8, above.

KENNETH MACKENZIE CLARK, BARON CLARK
b. 1903

Bibliographies

Sir Kenneth Clark. Bournemouth [1968]. (Guides to the published work of art historians, 1).

§1

The gothic revival: an essay in the history of taste. 1928, 1950 (rev and enlarged), 1962 (rev), New York 1962.

A commemorative catalogue of the Exhibition of Italian art held in the Royal Academy 1930. Ed Lord Balniel and Clark 2 vols 1931.

A catalogue of the drawings of Leonardo da Vinci in the collection of His Majesty the King at Windsor Castle. 2 vols Cambridge 1935, New York 1935, 3 vols London 1968–9 (rev, with C. Pedretti).

One hundred details from pictures in the National Gallery. 1938. Plates with introd and notes.

Fry, R. E. Last lectures. Ed Clark, Cambridge 1939.

Leonardo da Vinci: an account of his development as an artist. Cambridge 1939, New York 1939, Cambridge 1952 (rev), London 1958 (rev).

Constable, J. The hay wain, in the National Gallery. [1944] (Gallery Books 5). Essay, with plates.

Landscape into art. 1949, New York 1950 (as Landscape painting); London 1956 (corrected), Boston 1961.

Piero della Francesca. 1951, New York 1951, London 1969 (rev). Monograph with plates.

The nude: a study of ideal art. 1956, New York 1956.

Looking at pictures. [1960], New York 1960. With plates.

Pater, W. H. The Renaissance: studies in art and poetry, to which is added the essay on Raphael from Miscellaneous studies. Ed Clark 1961 (Fontana Lib).

Ruskin today: chosen and annotated by Clark. [1964], New York 1965.

Rembrandt and the Italian Renaissance. 1966, New York 1966.

A failure of nerve: Italian painting 1520–35. Oxford 1967.

Civilisation: a personal view. 1969, New York 1969.

Clark has also written introds to other books of reproductions and writings on art by various artists and authors, and is the editor of the series Penguin modern painters, 1943–.

ARTHUR CLUTTON-BROCK
1868–1924

§1

The cathedral church of York. 1899, 1931 (rev and enlarged by F. Harrison) (Bell's Cathedral ser).

Eton. 1900 (Handbooks to the Great Public Schools).

Shelley: the man and the poet. 1910 (for 1909), 1923 (rev).

Thoughts on the War. 1914. From TLS.

William Morris: his work and influence. 1914, New York [1914].

Are we to punish Germany, if we can? 1915, 1931 (rev and enlarged by F. Harrison). Pamphlet.

More thoughts on the War. 1915. From TLS.

Simpson's choice: an essay on the future life. 1915. Verse pamphlet.

Socialism and the arts of use. 1915 (Fabian Tract).

The philosophy of socialism. 1916 (Fabian Tract).

Studies in gardening. New York 1916. Preface and notes by F. King; rptd letters to Times.

The ultimate belief. 1916, New York [1916].

A dream of heaven; Presuppositions and prejudgments. In Immortality, by B. H. Streeter, Clutton-Brock et al, 1917, New York 1917.

A modern creed of work. 1917. Pamphlet.

Studies in Christianity. 1918, New York [1918].

Spirit and matter; Spiritual experience. In The spirit, ed B. H. Streeter 1919, New York 1919.

What is the Kingdom of Heaven? 1919, 1929 (abridged by C. Grant and F. House). *See* J. G. Jameson, The good news: what is it?, Edinburgh 1921.

Essays on art. 1919, New York 1920.

Essays on books. 1920, Freeport NY 1968.

More essays on books. 1921, New York 1921.

Dead metaphors. In Metaphor, by E. B. and H. W. Fowler and Clutton-Brock, Oxford 1922 (SPE Tract).

Shakespeare's Hamlet. 1922.

Art and the escape from banality. In: The necessity of art, by Clutton-Brock et al, 1924, Freeport NY 1969.

Essays on life. Introd by J. L. Hammond 1925.

Essays on literature and life. 1926.

Essays on religion. 1926, Freeport NY 1969. Introd by B. H. Streeter.

The miracles of love and other poems. Introd by E. Clutton-Brock 1926.

More essays on religion. Introd by B. H. Streeter 1927.

With F. S. Marvin, Clutton-Brock edited and arranged the essays in the Unity series, 8 vols Oxford 1915–28, and contributed to vol 8, Art and civilization, 1928. He was literary editor of Speaker 1904–6 and was on the staff of The Times from 1908 until his death, contributing frequently to TLS.

§2

Lynd, R. In his Books and authors, [1922].

Dearmer, G. Arthur Clutton-Brock. Saturday Rev 19 Jan 1924.

Murray, D. L. Arthur Clutton-Brock. London Mercury 9 1924; rptd in his Scenes and silhouettes, 1926.

Willson, C. H. S. The influence of Clutton-Brock on religious thought. London Quart Rev 152 1929.

Smith, N. The religious philosophy of Clutton-Brock. Hibbert Jnl 29 1931.

CYRIL VERNON CONNOLLY
b. 1903

§1

The rock pool. Paris 1936 (Obelisk Press), New York 1936, London 1947 (adds Postscript). Novel.

Enemies of promise. 1938, Boston 1939, New York 1948 (rev with introd), Garden City NY 1960 (as Enemies of promise and other essays: an autobiography of ideas). With an autobiographical section, A Georgian boyhood.

Horizon stories. Ed Connolly 1943, New York [1946]. 18 stories (American edn 20 stories) rptd from Horizon.

The unquiet grave: a word cycle, by 'Palinurus' [i.e. C. Connolly]. 1944, 1945 (rev), New York 1945, London 1951 (rev with introd), 1967 (rev with new introd).

'Vercors' (Jean Bruller). Put out the light: a translation of Le silence de la mer. 1944, New York 1944 (as The silence of the sea). Tr Connolly.

The condemned playground: essays 1927–44. 1945, New York 1946.

The missing diplomats. 1952 (for 1953). On Burgess and Maclean.

The golden Horizon. Ed Connolly 1953, New York [1955]. Miscellany rptd from Horizon.

Great English short novels. Ed Connolly, New York 1953.

Ideas and places. 1953, New York 1953. Selection of editorial comments from Horizon.

Les pavillons: French pavilions of the eighteenth century. New York 1962, London 1962. With J. Zerbe.

[James] Bond strikes camp. 1963 (priv ptd, 50 copies). Story, rptd in next.

Previous convictions. 1963, New York 1963. Articles mainly rptd from Sunday Times.

The modern movement: one hundred key books from England, France and America 1880–1950, 1965, New York 1966.

Jarry, A. The Ubu plays. Tr Connolly and S. W. Taylor 1968.

Connolly founded and edited Horizon 1940–50; he was literary editor of Observer 1942–3 and has contributed weekly to Sunday Times.

§2

Lienhardt, R. G. From Playground to Grave. Scrutiny 13 1945. Essay-review of The unquiet grave, 1944, and The condemned playground, 1945.

Wilson, E. A cry from the unquiet grave. In his Classics and commercials, New York 1950.

Bradbury, M. 'Horizon' and the English nineteen-forties. Gemini 2 1959.

Wain, J. Lost Horizons? Encounter 1961; rptd, as Four contemporary critics, IV, Connolly. In his Essays on Literature and ideas, 1963.

Ewart, G. Cyril Connolly. London Mag 3 1963.

M.P.

FRANCIS MACDONALD CORNFORD
1874-1943

Bibliographies

Guthrie, W. K. C. In The unwritten philosophy and other essays, 1950, below.

§1

The Cambridge classical course: an essay in anticipation of further reform. Cambridge 1903.

Thucydides mythistoricus. 1907.

Microcosmographia academica: being a guide for the young academic politician. Cambridge 1908 (anon), Chicago 1945.

From religion to philosophy: a study in the origins of western speculation. 1912, New York 1912.

The origin of Attic comedy. 1914; ed T. H. Gaster New York 1961.

Before and after Socrates. Cambridge 1932.

The unwritten philosophy and other essays. Ed W. K. C. Guthrie, Cambridge 1950.

Principium sapientiae: the origins of Greek philosophical thought. Ed W. K. C. Guthrie, Cambridge 1952.

Among his best known work is the series of trns with running commentaries of the following: Aristotle's Physics (with P. H. Wicksteed) 1929, Plato's Theaetetus and Sophist 1935, his Timaeus 1937, his Parmenides 1939 and his Republic 1941. Cornford contributed chs to vols 4 and 6 of Cambridge Ancient History and to Jane Harrison's Themis and was general editor with D. S. Robertson et al of Cambridge Classical Studies. He pbd an anthology Greek religious thought, 1923.

§2

Murray, G. G. A. Cornford. Proc Br Acad 29 1943.

Guthrie, W. K. C. Memoir [prefixed to] Cornford's The unwritten philosophy, 1950, above.

Barker, E. Note on Cornford prefixed to the 1950 reissue of Greek religious thought, ed Cornford.

A.P.H.

EDWARD HENRY GORDON CRAIG
1872-1966

The Gordon Craig Collection, Bibliothèque de l'Arsenal, Paris, includes unpbd mss; books and documents relating to Craig are held by the Br Institute Library, Florence.

Bibliographies etc

In E. Rose, Gordon Craig and the theatre, [1931], §2 below. Includes writings on Craig.

Fletcher, I. K. Checklist of books and periodicals written, designed and edited by Craig. Theatre Notebook 10 1956.

—— and A. Rood. Craig: a bibliography. 1967.

Craig: 90th birthday celebration: a Mermaid Theatre exhibition. [Westerham 1962]. Catalogue by Craig.

Gordon Craig et le renouvellement du théâtre. Paris 1962. Catalogue of an exhibition at the Bibliothèque Nationale.

Nash, G. Edward Gordon Craig, 1872-1966. 1967. Exhibition catalogue.

Oenslager, D. and A. Rood. Craig, artist of the theatre 1872-1966: introduction and catalogue. BNYPL 71 1967.

§1

Gordon Craig's Book of penny toys. Hackbridge 1899 (priv ptd 550 copies). Woodcuts facing verses.

Henry Irving, Ellen Terry, etc: a book of portraits. Chicago [1899]. Plates.

Bookplates. 2 vols Hackbridge 1900-2 (priv ptd). 65 plates.

Bookplates, designed and cut on wood. Hackbridge 1900 (priv ptd 350 copies). Booklet, 11 plates.

The London school of theatrical art. 1903. Booklet.

The art of the theatre, together with an introduction, 1905. Preface by R. G. Robertson, A dialogue, illustr Craig, rptd in next.

On the art of the theatre. 1911, Chicago 1911, London 1912 (with new notes), Chicago 1912, London 1924 (with new preface), Boston 1924, London 1957 (with new illustrations).

School for the art of the theatre. [1911] Booklet.

A living theatre—the Gordon Craig School—The Arena Goldoni—The Mask: setting forth the aims and objects of the movement and showing by many illustrations the city of Florence, the Arena. Florence 1913.

Towards a new theatre: forty designs for stage scenes, with critical notes by the inventor, E. G. Craig. 1913.

The theatre—advancing. Boston 1919, London 1921 (adds foreword).

Puppets and poets. 1921 (Monthly Chapbook no 20).

Scene, with a foreword and an introductory poem by J. Masefield, 1923. Stage designs.

Nothing: or, the bookplate, with a handlist (of bookplates designed by Craig) by E. Carrick. 1924 (280 copies), 1925.

Woodcuts and some words. Introd by C. Dodgson 1924, Boston 1925.

Books and theatres. 1925.

Henry Irving. 1930, New York 1930.

A production: being thirty-two collotype plates of designs projected or realised for The pretenders of Henrik Ibsen and produced at the Royal Theatre, Copenhagen, 1926. 1930 (605 copies).

Ellen Terry and her secret self. 1931, New York [1932]. With Annex: a plea for G.B.S. on the publication of the correspondence of Ellen Terry and Shaw and on Shaws' preface to that publication.

On eight pages from The story of the theatre, by Glenn Hughes, with some fourteen notes by E. G. Craig. Seattle 1931 (Univ of Washington Quartos no 2). Booklet.

Index to the story of my days: some memoirs, 1872-1907. 1957, New York 1957.

Extracts from a diary: woodcuts. [1962]. With a record of Craig's radio talks, 1951-7; pbd on his 90th birthday.

Craig also pbd a number of other pamphlets containing designs for the theatre, portfolios of etchings, models and reprints of items first ptd in the periodicals he edited. Details of these, together with his contributions to books and periodicals, the plays he produced, the programmes he designed and exhibitions of his graphic work, are listed in the bibliography by I. K. Fletcher and A. Rood, above. He founded, pbd, edited and contributed extensively to Page, 1898-1901; Mask, Florence 1908-15, 1918, 1923-9 and Marionette, 12 nos, Florence 1918-19.

§2

Macfall, H. Some thoughts on the art of Craig, with particular reference to stage craft. Studio 23 1901.

B[ulloch], J. M. Craig: contributions towards his biography. [1906].

Duncan, I. E. G. Craig. Die Schaubühne 2 1906.

Terry, E. A. In her Story of my life, 1908, 1933 (rev).

Symons, A. Craig and the painters in tempera. In his Studies on modern painters, New York 1925.

Cheney, S. Gordon Craig. Theatre Arts Monthly 11 1927.

Shaw, M. In his Up to now, 1929. Reminiscences.

Rose, E. Craig and the theatre: a record and an interpretation. [1931].

Simonson, L. Day-dreams: the case of Craig. In his The stage is set, New York [1932].

—— In his Art of scenic design, New York [1950].

Housman, L. In his Unexpected years, 1937.

Jackson, H. In his Printing of books, 1938.

Hewitt, B. Craig and Post-Impressionism. Quart Jnl of Speech 30 1944.

Leeper, J. Craig: designs for the theatre. 1948 (King Penguin). With chronology by Craig.

Valogne, C. Gordon Craig. Paris 1953.

Brook, P. The influence of Craig in theory and practice. Drama no 37 1955.

Eliot, T. S. Craig's Socratic dialogues. Drama no 36 1955.

Swan, M. In his A small part of time, 1957.

Bablet, D. Edward Gordon Craig. Paris 1962; tr 1966.

Marotti, F. Profilo di Craig. Veltro 6 1962.

—— Amleto o dell'assoluto: saggi e note su Craig. In his Amleto o dell'oxymoron, Rome 1966.

Laver, J. Shakespeare and Craig. Apollo 79 1964.

Lyons, C. R. Craig's concept of the actor. Educational Theatre Jnl 16 1964.

Herstand, T. Craig on the nature of the artist. Educational Theatre Jnl 18 1966.

Talley, P. M. Architecture as Craig's interim symbol: Ruskin and other influences. Educational Theatre Jnl 19 1967.

Craig, E. A. Gordon Craig: the story of his life. 1968.
M.P.

SIR WILLIAM ALEXANDER CRAIGIE
1867-1957

Bibliographies
A memoir and a list of the published writings of Craigie. Oxford 1952.

§1

A new English dictionary on historical principles, founded mainly on the materials collected by the Philological Society, edited by J. A. H. Murray, H. Bradley, W. A. Craigie, C. T. Onions 11 vols Oxford 1884–1933, 13 vols Oxford 1933 (corrected re-issue, with introd, suppl and bibliography, as The Oxford English Dictionary).

A primer of Burns. 1896.

Scandinavian folk-lore: selected and translated by W. A. Craigie. Paisley and London 1896.

The poems (The songs) of Robert Burns. Ed Craigie 2 vols 1898 (Temple Classics).

The religion of ancient Scandinavia. 1906.

Skotlands Rímur. Icelandic ballads on the Gowrie conspiracy, edited by W. A. Craigie, Oxford 1908.

The Icelandic sagas. Cambridge 1913, New York 1913.

The Oxford book of Scandinavian verse, xviith century-xxth century, chosen by E. Gosse and W. A. Craigie, Oxford 1925.

A dictionary of the older Scottish tongue, from the twelfth century to the end of the seventeenth. Ed Craigie,

Chicago, London 1931 onwards. From pt 17 onwards ed A. J. Aitken.

The northern element in English literature. Toronto [1933].

A dictionary of American English, on historical principles, edited by Sir William Craigie, with the collaboration of J. R. Hulbert, G. Watson [et al]. 4 vols Chicago 1936–44, London 1938–44.

Sýnisbók íslenzkra rímna (Specimens of the Icelandic metrical romances). 3 vols Edinburgh and Reykjavík 1952 [1953].

Craigie also edited a number of works for the STS. He wrote tracts for the Soc for Pure English, and compiled a number of Anglo-Saxon, Modern English, Scandinavian and Icelandic readers, and textbooks on English spelling and phonetics.

§2

A memoir and a list of the published writings of Craigie. Oxford 1952.

J. M. Wyllie. Sir William Craigie. Reykjavík 1953.

—— Craigie. Proc Br Acad vol 47 1961.
J.M.P.

ALEISTER CROWLEY
(EDWARD ALEXANDER CROWLEY)
1875-1947

The G. J. Yorke Collection of Crowley mss is in the Warburg Institute, Univ of London. Other Crowley mss are in the Univ of Texas Humanities Research Center.

Bibliographies
Yorke, G. J. Bibliography of the Works of Crowley. In J. Symonds, The great beast: the life of Crowley, 1951, below.

Collections and Selections
The works of Aleister Crowley. 3 vols Foyers 1905–7.

Ambergris: a selection from the poems of Crowley. 1910.

§1

Crowley's works were issued under a large number of pseudonyms, many of which appear in the entries below; a number of works were issued by the Society for the Propagation of Religious Truth and by the 'OTO' ('Ordo Templi Orientis').

Aceldama, a place to bury strangers in: a philosophical poem, by a gentleman of the University of Cambridge. 1898 (priv ptd).

Jephthah: a tragedy, by a gentleman of the University of Cambridge (Aleister Crowley). 1898 (priv ptd, 25 copies). Verse.

Jezebel and other tragic poems, by Count Vladimir Svareff [i.e. Crowley]. Ed with introd and epilogue by Crowley. 1898 (priv ptd).

The poem: a little drama in four scenes. 1898 (priv ptd, 10 copies). An advance edn of pt of Jephthah and other mysteries, 1899, below.

Songs of the spirit. 1898.

The tale of Archais: a romance in verse, by a gentleman of the University of Cambridge. 1898.

White stains: the literary remains of George Archibald Bishop, a neuropath of the Second Empire. [Amsterdam] 1898 (100 copies only; many destroyed by HM Customs in 1924). Erotic verse.

An appeal to the American Republic. 1899. Verse.

The honourable adulterers: a tragedy by A.E.C. 1899 (priv ptd, 5 copies). An advance edn of pt of Jephthah and other mysteries, below. Verse.

Jephthah and other mysteries, lyrical and dramatic. 1899.

Carmen saeculare, by St E. A. of M. and S. 1901 (priv ptd, 50 copies), 1901 (trade edn).

The mother's tragedy and other poems. 1901 (priv ptd, 500 copies), Foyers 1907.

The soul of Osiris: a history. 1901. Verse.

Tannhäuser: a story of all times. 1902.

Ahab and other poems, with an introduction and epilogue by Count Vladimir Svareff. 1903 (priv ptd).

Alice: an adultery [and other poems]. 1903 (priv ptd) (with essay by G. F. Kelly), Foyers 1905 (without essay).

[Berashith, in Hebrew characters]: an essay in ontology with some remarks on ceremonial magic, by Abhavananda. [Paris 1903] (priv ptd).

The god-eater: a tragedy of satire. 1903. Verse.

The star and the garter. 1903. Verse.

Summa spes. 1903. Poem.

The Argonauts. Foyers 1904. Verse drama.

The book of the Goetia of Solomon the King, translated into the English tongue by a dead hand [i.e. S. L. Macgregor Mathers] and adorned with divers other matters germane, delightful to the wise; the whole edited, verified, introduced and commented by Aleister Crowley. Foyers 1904. Undated pirated edn, The Goetia, by order of the secret chief of the Rosicrucian Order, pbd Chicago. Magical.

In residence: the don's guide to Cambridge. Cambridge 1904. Verse.

Snowdrops from a curate's garden, 1881 AD. Paris [c. 1904] (100 copies; many destroyed by HM Customs in 1924). Erotic verse.

The sword of song, called by Christians The book of the beast. Benares 1904. Verse. See G. K. Chesterton, Mr Crowley and the creeds and the creed of Mr Chesterton, [1904]. Reprint of Chesterton's review of the above with Crowley's reply.

Why Jesus wept: a study of society and of the grace of God. 1904 (priv ptd), Foyers 1904.

Oracles: the biography of an art, unpublished fragments of the work of Crowley with explanatory notes by R. P. Lester and the author. Foyers 1905. Verse.

Orpheus: a lyrical legend. 2 vols Foyers 1905. Verse.

Rosa mundi: a poem by H. D. Carr, with an original composition by Auguste Rodin. 1905.

Gargoyles: being strangely wrought images of life and death. Foyers 1906. Verse.

Konx om pax: essays in light. Foyers 1907, New York 1907. Magical.

Rodin in rime: seven lithographs by Clot from the watercolours of Auguste Rodin, with a chaplet of verse by Aleister Crowley. 1907 (priv ptd).

Rosa coeli: a poem, by H. D. Carr, with an original composition by Auguste Rodin. 1907.

Rosa inferni: a poem, by H. D. Carr, with an original composition by Auguste Rodin. 1907.

Amphora. 1908 (anon, priv ptd), 1909 (anon, withdrawn), 1912 (as Hail Mary; without the Epilogue). Verse.

Alexandra. [Paris 1909]. Poem. The whole stock is said to have been destroyed by HM Customs on the grounds of obscenity and lèse-majesty.

Clouds without water. Edited from a private ms by the Rev C. Verey. 1909 (priv ptd). Verse.

777: vel prolegomena symbolica ad systemam scepticomysticae viae explicandae, fundamentum hieroglyphicum sanctissimorum scientiae summae. 1909, [1956] (rev and enlarged). Magical.

Bagh-I-Muattar, translated from a rare Indian ms by the late Major Lutiy and another. The scented garden of Abdullah the satirist of Shiraz. 1910 (priv ptd, 200 copies; the bulk of the edn was destroyed by HM Customs in 1924 on the ground of obscenity). Erotica.

Rosa decidua. [1910] (priv ptd, 20 copies). Verse.

[The Holy Book] vol 1, Liber LXI vel causae—Liber cordis cincti serpente vel LXV sub figura ADNI; vol 2, Liber liberi vel lapis lazuli; vol 3, Liber L vel legis. 3 vols [n.p., c. 1909]. Magical. Vol 3 reissued Tunis 1926 as AL, liber legis, London 1938 (as The book of the law).

The winged beetle. 1910 (priv ptd). Verse.

The world's tragedy. Paris 1910 (priv ptd). Verse.

Hail Mary. 1911. See Amphora, 1908, above.

The high history of good Sir Palamedes, the Saracen knight, and of his following of the Questing Beast, by Aleister Crowley. 1912. Verse.

Household gods: a comedy. Pallanza 1912 (priv ptd). Verse.

Mortadello, or the angel of Venice: a comedy. 1912. Verse drama.

Baudelaire, C. Little poems in prose. Tr Aleister Crowley 1913, Paris 1928. ('With several added versions of the Epilogue by various hands [i.e. Crowley]').

Book Four, by Frater Perdurabo [Crowley] and Soror Virakam [Mary d'Este Sturges]. 2 vols 1913 Magical.

Liber CCCXXXIII: the book of lies which is also falsely called Breaks, the wanderings or falsifications of the one thought of Frater Perdurabo, which thought is itself untrue. 1913, Ilfracombe 1962 (as The book of lies [etc], with an additional commentary to each chapter). Magical.

The writing on the ground, by E.G.O. [1913] (priv ptd). Poem, A slim gilt soul, and a paper on Lord Alfred Douglas.

Chicago May: a love poem. [New York] 1914 (priv ptd).

The giant's thumb. New York 1915. Verse; never issued; only a set of page proofs survives.

The diary of a drug fiend. [1922], New York 1923.

Songs for Italy: No 1, Tyrol. [Tunis] 1923 (single sheet), [London] 1923.

Magick in theory and practice, by the Master Therion. Paris 1929, London 1929.

Moonchild: a prologue. 1929. Novel.

The spirit of solitude: an autohagiography, subsequently re-antichristened The confessions of Aleister Crowley. Vols 1–2, 1929 (vols 3–6 not pbd), 1 vol 1969 (as The confessions of Aleister Crowley: an autobiography, ed J. Symonds and K. Grant; 'this is the text of all six volumes, after some redundancies have been removed').

The stratagem and other stories. 1930.

The heart of the master, by Khaled Khan. 1938 (priv ptd). Magical.

Little essays toward truth. 1938 (priv ptd). Magical.

Liber XXI [inscription in Chinese] Khing Kang King: the classic of purity first written down by me [Chinese characters] in the Episode of the Dynasty of Wu and now made into a rime by me, Aleister Crowley. [1939]. 100 copies.

Temperance: a tract for the times. 1939 (priv ptd, 100 copies). Verse.

Thumbs up!: a pentagram—a pantacle to win the war. [1941] (priv ptd, 100 copies), New York 1942 (as Thumbs up!: five poems).

The fun of the fair—Nijni Novgorod, 1913 e.v. Barstow Calif and London 1942. Verse.

The city of God: a rhapsody. 1943.

Olla: an anthology of sixty years of song. 1946.

Magick without tears. Hampton NJ 1954. Magical.

'Eliphas Levi' (A. L. Constant). The key of the mysteries, translated from the French with an introduction and notes by Aleister Crowley. 1959. Trn originally pbd in Equinox.

Crowley also wrote a number of other pamphlets and broadsheets in verse and prose, the majority priv ptd (for details see Yorke, Bibliography, above). He edited and largely wrote The Equinox: the official organ of the A∴A∴— *the review of scientific illuminism, vol 1–vol 3, no 5, 1909–44; vol 2 and vol 3, no 2, were not pbd.*

§2

Fuller, J. F. C. The star in the west: a critical essay upon the works of Crowley. 1907.

Stephenson, P. R. The legend of Crowley. 1930.

Cammell, C. R. Aleister Crowley: the man, the mage, the poet. 1951.

Symonds, J. The great beast: the life of Crowley. New York 1951.
— The magic of Crowley. 1958.
'Louis Marlow' (L. U. Wilkinson). In his Seven friends, 1953.
Dickie, F. Aleister 'black magic' Crowley. Amer Book Collector 11 1961.

M.P.

DAVID DAICHES
b. 1912

§I

The place of meaning in poetry. Edinburgh 1935.
New literary values: studies in modern literature. Edinburgh 1936, Freeport NY 1968.
Literature and society. 1938. Unauthorized edn Folcroft, Pennsylvania 1969.
The novel and the modern world. Chicago 1939, 1960 (rev with new chs on Lawrence and Conrad), Cambridge 1960.
Poetry and the modern world: a study of poetry in England between 1900 and 1939. Chicago 1940.
The King James version of the English Bible: an account of the development and sources of the English Bible of 1611 with special reference to the Hebrew tradition. Chicago 1941, Hamden Conn 1968.
Virginia Woolf. Norfolk Conn 1942, London 1945, New York 1963 (rev).
Robert Louis Stevenson. Norfolk Conn 1947, Glasgow 1947.
A study of literature for readers and critics. Ithaca NY 1948, London 1968 (with textual changes).
Poems in English 1530–1940. Ed Daiches and W. Charvat, New York 1950.
Robert Burns. New York 1950, London 1952, New York 1966 (with textual changes), London 1966.
A century of the essay. Ed Daiches, New York 1951.
Willa Cather: a critical introduction. Ithaca NY [1951].
Two worlds: an Edinburgh Jewish childhood. New York 1956, London 1957.
Critical approaches to literature. Englewood Cliffs NJ 1956, London 1956.
Literary essays. 1956, Chicago 1957 (with additional preface).
Milton. 1957, 1959 (rev), New York 1966.
Robert Burns. 1957 (Br Council pamphlet).
The present age: after 1920. 1958 (Introductions to English Literature, 5). Rptd as The present age in British literature, Bloomington Indiana 1958.
Two studies: the poetry of Dylan Thomas; Walt Whitman, impressionist poet. 1958 (priv ptd, 70 copies).
A critical history of English literature. 2 vols New York 1960, London 1960, New York 1970 (with new concluding chs), London 1970.
D. H. Lawrence. Brighton 1963 (priv ptd, 70 copies). Text of a broadcast.
George Eliot: Middlemarch. 1963, Great Neck NY 1964.
English literature. Englewood Cliffs NJ 1964 (Princeton Stud in Humanistic Scholarship in America).
The idea of a new university: an experiment in Sussex. Ed Daiches 1964, 1970 (with new concluding ch).
The paradox of Scottish culture: the eighteenth-century experience. 1964.
More literary essays. Edinburgh 1968, Chicago 1968.
Scotch whisky: its past and present. 1969. New York 1969.
Some late Victorian attitudes. 1969.

§2

Alter, R. Criticism as performance. Commentary 47 1969.

P. G. B.

ERNEST DE SÉLINCOURT
1870–1943

§I

English poets and the national ideal: four lectures. 1915.
The study of poetry. 1918. Pamphlet.
Dorothy Wordsworth: a biography. Oxford 1933.
Oxford lectures on poetry. Oxford 1934, Freeport NY 1967.
Wordsworthian and other studies. Oxford 1947, New York 1964. Includes individual lectures previously pbd separately.

Editions

Hyperion: a facsimile of Keats's autograph ms, with transliteration of the ms of The fall of Hyperion: a dream. Oxford 1905.
The poems of Keats. 1905, 1907 (rev), 1920 (rev), 1926 (rev).
Wordsworth's Guide to the Lakes, fifth edition 1835. 1906.
Spenser's minor poems. Oxford 1910. Vol 1 of The poetical works of Spenser, 3 vols Oxford 1909, 1910.
The poetical works of Spenser. 1912. With J. C. Smith.
Landor, W. S. Imaginary conversations: a selection. 1915 (WC).
Whitman, W. Leaves of grass. 1920 (WC). A selection.
Wordsworth, W. The Prelude. Oxford 1926, 1959 (rev H. Darbishire). 1805 and 1850 parallel texts.
Wordsworth, W. The Prelude: text of 1805. 1933. Editorial matter based on relevant sections of 1926 parallel texts edn.
The letters of William and Dorothy Wordsworth. 6 vols Oxford 1935–9, 1967– (rev C. L. Shaver, M. Moorman, A. G. Hill). Vol 1 of first edn entitled The early letters [etc].
Wordsworth D. George and Sarah Green: a narrative. Oxford 1936.
The poetical works of Wordsworth. 5 vols (vols 3–5 with H. Darbishire) Oxford 1940–49, vols 1–3 1952–4 ('corrected' H. Darbishire, with new appendix to vol 2).
Journals of Dorothy Wordsworth. 2 vols 1941.
De Sélincourt also edited the school series The way of literature, *6 vols* [*1924*].

§2

Darbishire, H. Proc Br Acad 29 1943.

J. G.

GOLDSWORTHY LOWES DICKINSON
1862–1932

See cols 1158–9, below.

BONAMY DOBRÉE
b. 1891

Bibliographies

Britton, M. C. A selected list of the published writings of Dobrée. In Of books and humankind: essays and poems presented to Dobrée, ed J. Butt [et al] 1964. Includes all books and important essays and periodical articles pbd between 1919 and 1962.

§I

Restoration comedy 1660–1720. Oxford 1924, New York 1924.
Histriophone: a dialogue on dramatic diction. 1925.

Essays in biography 1680–1726. 1925, New York 1925. Contains: Vanbrugh, Addison, Etherege.

Timotheus: the future of the theatre. 1925, New York 1925.

Rochester: a conversation between Sir George Etherege and Mr Fitzjames. 1926; rptd (rev) in As their friends saw them, 1933, below.

The complete works of Sir John Vanbrugh. 4 vols 1927–8. Plays ed Dobrée; letters ed G. Webb.

Sarah Churchill, Duchess of Marlborough. 1927 (Representative Women); rptd in Three eighteenth-century figures, 1962, below.

Sir John Denham: a conversation between Henry King and Edmund Waller at the Palace, Chichester, March 1669. 1927 (Cayme Press Pamphlets 8); rptd (rev) in As their friends saw them, 1933, below.

The lamp and the lute: studies in six modern authors. Oxford 1929, New York 1929, London 1964 (rev) (as The lamp and the lute: studies in seven authors), New York 1964. Contains: Ibsen, Hardy, Kipling, E. M. Forster, D. H. Lawrence and T. S. Eliot. The 1964 edn adds On two plays by T. S. Eliot, and Lawrence Durrell: the Alexandrian series; the Kipling essay is expanded by: The breaking strain, healing and compassion.

Restoration tragedy, 1660–1720. Oxford 1929, New York 1929, Oxford 1950 (corrected), 1959 (corrected). Contains material first pbd, in different form, as introd to Five Restoration tragedies, 1928 (WC).

William Congreve: a conversation between Swift and Gay. Seattle 1929; rptd in As their friends saw them, 1933, below.

The London book of English prose, selected and ordered by H. Read and Dobrée. 1931, New York 1931 (as The anthology of English prose), London 1949 (rev) (as The London book of English prose).

The letters of Philip Dormer Stanhope, 4th Earl of Chesterfield. 6 vols 1932. Ed Dobrée.

St Martin's summer. 1932. A novel.

Variety of ways: discussions on six authors. Oxford 1932, New York 1932. Contains: Dryden, Savile, Marquis of Halifax, Steele, Bunyan, Congreve and Mandeville's The fable of the bees.

William Penn, Quaker and pioneer. 1932, Boston 1932.

Giacomo Casanova, Chevalier de Seingalt. 1933, New York 1933; rptd in Three eighteenth-century figures, 1962, below.

John Wesley. 1933, New York 1933; rptd in Three eighteenth-century figures, 1962, below.

As their friends saw them: biographical conversations. 1933, Freeport NY 1967.

Modern prose style. Oxford 1934, New York 1934, London 1964 (rev).

The floating republic: an account of the mutinies at Spithead and the Nore in 1797. 1935, New York 1935. With G. E. Manwaring.

An open letter to a professional man. 1935. (Pamphlets on the New Economics 14).

English revolts. 1937.

The Victorians and after 1830–1914. 1938, New York 1938, London 1950 [1951] (rev), [1962] (rev) (Introductions to English Lit 4). With E. C. Batho.

The unacknowledged legislator: conversation on literature and politics in a warden's post, 1941. 1942 (PEN books).

English essayists. 1946. (Britain in Pictures).

The amateur and the theatre. 1947. (The Hogarth Essays 3rd ser 1).

The London book of English verse, selected by H. Read and Dobrée. 1949, New York 1949, London 1952 (rev).

Alexander Pope. 1951, New York 1952.

Rudyard Kipling. 1951, 1965 (for 1966) (rev) (Br Council pamphlet). Rev version of essay in The lamp and the lute, 1929, above.

The broken cistern: the Clark lectures, 1952–3. 1954, Bloomington Ind 1955. On public themes in English poetry.

John Dryden. 1956, 1961 (rev) (Br Council pamphlet).

English literature in the early eighteenth century, 1700–40. Oxford 1959, 1964 (corrected) (OHEL 7).

Three eighteenth-century figures: Sarah Churchill, John Wesley, Giacomo Casanova. 1962.

William Congreve. 1963 (Br Council pamphlet).

Radcliffe, A. The mysteries of Udolpho. 1966 (Oxford English novels). Ed Dobrée.

Rudyard Kipling: realist and fabulist. 1967.

Dobrée also pbd edns of a number of Restoration and early eighteenth-century authors in WC, EL and other series, and a selection of the letters of George III. He was editor of the series Introductions to English literature *5 vols 1938–40, 1950–8 (rev); he took over the editorship of the series* Writers and their work *(Br Council pamphlets) in 1954; he is one of the general editors of OHEL.*

§2

Young, G. M. Prose old and new. In his Daylight and champaign: essays. 1937. On Modern prose style.

Hoggart, R. Dobrée: teacher and patron of young men. In Of books and humankind: essays and poems presented to Dobrée, ed J. Butt, assisted by J. M. Cameron, D. W. Jefferson and R. Skelton 1964.

Read, H. The art of collaboration. Ibid.

JOHN DRINKWATER
1882–1937
See cols 263–6, above.

THOMAS STEARNS ELIOT
1888–1965
See col 157–201, above.

UNA MARY ELLIS-FERMOR
1894–1958

Bibliographies

Muir, K. A select list of the published writings of U. Ellis-Fermor. In Shakespeare the dramatist and other papers, 1961, below.

§1

Christopher Marlowe. 1927, Hamden Conn 1967.

Marlowe, C. Tamburlaine the Great. Ed U. M. Ellis-Fermor 1930, New York 1930, London 1951 (rev). (The works and life of Marlowe, ed R. H. Case, vol 2).

Greville, F. Cælica. Ed U. Ellis-Fermor, Newtown 1936 (225 copies).

The Jacobean drama: an interpretation. 1936, 1947 (rev), 1953 (rev), 1958 (rev), 1961 (with addns to the biographical and bibliographical notes by M. Cardwell), New York [1964], London 1965 (corrected).

Twenty-two poems. Oxford [1938]. By 'Christopher Turnley'.

The Irish dramatic movement. 1939, 1954 (rev).

Sharpness of death. Cambridge 1939. Poems. By 'Christopher Turnley'.

Masters of reality. 1942. On 'certain of the functions of the imagination in daily life'.

The frontiers of drama. 1945, 1946 (corrected), 1964 (introd by A. Nicoll, bibliography by H. Brooks).

Ibsen, H. Three plays: The pillars of the community; The wild duck; Hedda Gabler. Tr U. Ellis-Fermor 1950.

Ibsen, H. The master builder and other plays (Rosmersholm; Little Eyolf, John Gabriel Borkman). Tr U. Ellis-Fermor 1958, Baltimore 1959.

Shakespeare the dramatist and other papers. Ed K. Muir
1961, New York 1961.
Una Ellis-Fermor was general editor of The Arden Shakespeare *1946-58.*

OLIVER ELTON
1861-1945

§1

Einarr, Haflið̆ason. The life of Laurence, Bishop of Hólar.
Tr Elton 1890.
The first nine books of the Danish history of Saxo Gram-
maticus. Tr Elton 1894.
An introduction to Michael Drayton. Manchester 1895,
London 1905 (rev and enlarged with a new biblio-
graphy) (as Michael Drayton: a critical study), New York
1966.
The Augustan ages. Edinburgh 1899 (Periods of European
Literature 8), New York 1899.
The Manchester stage 1880-1900. [1900]. Criticisms,
with introd, rptd from Manchester Guardian. With
W. T. Arnold, A. N. Monkhouse, C. E. Montague.
Johnstone, A. G. W. Musical criticisms, with a memoir of
the author. Ed H. Reece and Elton, Manchester 1905.
Frederick York Powell: a life and a selection from his
letters and occasional writings. 2 vols Oxford 1906.
Modern studies. 1907, Freeport NY [1967]. Includes
lectures previously pbd separately.
A survey of English literature 1780-1830. 2 vols 1912;
1830-80, 2 vols 1920, New York 1920. The chs on
Scott, Wordsworth, Shelley, Tennyson and Matthew
Arnold, The Brownings, Dickens and Thackeray were
pbd separately (rev) 1924.
Saxo's Amleth. Tr Elton 1913 (10 copies).
A miscellany presented to J. M. Mackay. Ed Elton,
Liverpool 1914.
A sheaf of papers. Liverpool 1922. Includes lectures
previously pbd separately.
Sixteen poems. Liverpool [1922?] (priv ptd).
A survey of English literature 1730-80. 2 vols 1928, New
York 1928.
C. E. Montague: a memoir. 1929, Garden City NY 1929.
The English muse: a sketch. 1933.
Saintsbury, G. E. B. Prefaces and essays. Ed Elton 1933.
Verse from Pushkin and others. Tr Elton 1935.
Pushkin, A. S. Evgeny Onegin. Tr Elton 1937.
Essays and addresses. 1939, Freeport NY 1969.
*Elton also pbd a number of class-room edns of Shakespeare's
plays and Milton's early poems 1889-1903.*

§2

Martin, L. C. Oliver Elton. Proc Br Acad 31 1945.
M.P.

WILLIAM EMPSON
b. 1906

See cols 272-4, below.

FORD MADOX FORD
formerly
JOSEPH LEOPOLD FORD
HERMANN MADOX HUEFFER
1873-1939

See cols 569-75, above.

EDWARD MORGAN FORSTER
1879-1970

See cols 437-44, above.

HENRY WATSON FOWLER
1858-1933

§1

More popular fallacies. 1904. By 'Quillet'.
The works of Lucian of Samosata. Tr H. W. Fowler and
F. G. Fowler 4 vols Oxford 1905.
The King's English. Oxford 1906, 1906 (with new ex-
amples), 1930 (rev). With F. G. Fowler.
Si mihi—! 1907 (by 'Egomet'), 1929 (as If wishes were
horses, by H. W. Fowler). Essays.
Between boy and man: being lectures to sixth-form boys.
1908. By 'Quilibet'.
The concise Oxford dictionary of current English. Oxford
1911, 1929 (rev), 1934 (rev, with H. G. Le Mesurier),
1951 (rev E. McIntosh), 1964 (rev E. McIntosh, ety-
mologies rev G. W. S. Friedrichsen). First edn with
F. G. Fowler.
The pocket Oxford dictionary of current English. Oxford
1924, 1934 (rev, with H. G. Le Mesurier), 1939 (rev
H. G. Le Mesurier), 1942 (rev H. G. Le Mesurier and
E. McIntosh), 1969 (rev E. McIntosh, etymologies rev
G. W. S. Friedrichsen). First edn with F. G. Fowler.
A dictionary of modern English usage. Oxford 1926, 1965
(rev E. Gowers), New York 1965.
—— Find it in Fowler: an alphabetical index to the rev edn
of Modern English usage, by J. A. Greenwood, Prince-
ton NJ 1969.
Some comparative values. Oxford 1929. Essays.
Rhymes of Darby to Joan. 1931.
*Fowler also wrote several Soc for Pure English Tracts and
he contributed to the Shorter Oxford English dictionary,
2 vols 1933. Fowler's correspondence with H. G. Hart of
Sedbergh School and his war letters of 1915-16 are preserved complete in the library of St John's College, Cambridge.*

§2

Coulton, G. G. H. W. Fowler. [Oxford] 1934. Pamphlet.
Highet, G. A. Fowler: Modern English usage. In his
People, places and books, New York 1953.
Gowers, E. A. H. W. Fowler: the man and his teaching.
1957. Pamphlet.
Quirk, R. Fowler's toils [as a lexicographer]. Listener
13 March 1958.
Partridge, E. H. Fowler. In his A charm of words, 1960.
J.G.

GEORGE SUTHERLAND FRASER
b. 1915

See cols 276-7, above.

ROGER ELIOT FRY
1866-1934

*Fry's papers are in the possession of Mrs Pamela Diamond,
his daughter. See Smart, Fry and early Italian art, Apollo 83
1966, §2, below.*

Selections

French, Flemish and British art. 1951, New York 1951.
Contains Characteristics of French art, 1932; Flemish
art, 1927; Reflections on British painting, 1934.

§1

Giovanni Bellini. 1899.
Trevelyan, R. C. Polyphemus and other poems. Designs
by Fry 1901.
Reynolds, J. Discourses. Introds and notes by Fry 1905.

Exhibition of Venetian painting of the eighteenth century. Introd, Venice in the eighteenth century, by Fry 1911.

Dürer, A. Records of journeys to Venice and the Low Countries. Ed Fry, Boston 1913.

The new movement in art: exhibition of representative works selected and arranged by Fry. Birmingham [1917]. Catalogue.

Catalogue of an exhibition of Florentine painting before 1500. 1919. Preface, The art of Florence, by Fry.

Vision and design. 1920, New York 1924, London 1925 (rev).

Twelve original woodcuts. Richmond Surrey 1921.

J. H. d'A. de Tizac. Animals in Chinese art. Introd by Fry 1923.

A sampler of Castile. Richmond Surrey 1923. Impressions of Spain.

The artist and psycho-analysis. 1924 (Hogarth Essays).

The significance of Chinese art. In Chinese art: an introductory review by Fry [et al], 1925 (Burlington Mag monographs), 1935 (rev), 1946 (rev), New York [1946-7].

Art and commerce. 1926 (Hogarth Essays).

English handwriting by R[obert] B[ridges], with facsimile plates and artistic and palaeographical criticisms by Fry and E. A. Lowe. Oxford 1926-7 (SPE Tracts).

Transformations: critical and speculative essays on art. 1926, Garden City NY 1956.

Cézanne: a study of his development. 1927, New York 1952.

Flemish art: a critical survey. 1927, New York 1927.

Mauron, C. The nature of beauty in art and literature. Trn and preface by Fry 1927 (Hogarth Essays).

Painting. In Georgian art, 1760-1820: an introductory review by Fry [et al], 1929 (Burlington Mag monographs).

Henri-Matisse. Paris 1930, London [1930], 1935 (with different plates).

Russian icon painting from a Western-European point of view. In Masterpieces of Russian painting, ed M. Farbman 1930. Text by Fry [et al].

The arts of painting and sculpture. 1932.

Characteristics of French art. 1932.

Art-history as an academic study. Cambridge 1933, Folcroft Pa 1969. Lecture.

Reflections on British painting. 1934, Freeport NY 1969.

Mauron, C. Aesthetics and psychology. Tr Fry and K. John 1935.

Mallarmé, S. Poems. Tr by Fry 1936, New York [1951] (with commentaries by C. Mauron).

Last lectures. Cambridge 1939, New York 1939. Introd by K. Clark; includes one previously pbd lecture.

§ 2

MacColl, D. S. A note on Fry. Burlington Mag 65 1934.

Borenius, T. Fry as art historian. Ibid.

Price-Jones, G. Fry and aesthetic criticism. Criterion 14 1935.

Woolf, V. The Roger Fry Memorial Exhibition: an address. 1935; rptd in her The moment and other essays, 1947, and in Collected essays, vol 4, 1967.

— Roger Fry: a biography. 1940.

Hannay, H. Fry's theory of art. In his Roger Fry and other essays, 1937.

Read, H. Fry as an art critic. Listener 12 Oct 1939.

Pevsner, N. Ω. Architectural Rev 90 1941.

Gaunt, W. Threshold of a new age. In his Aesthetic adventure, 1945.

— How well have they worn? 16, Vision and design. Times 21 April 1966.

Hough, G. Ruskin and Fry: two aesthetic theories. Cambridge Jnl 1 1947.

Weitz, M. Aesthetic formalism. In his Philosophy of the arts, Cambridge Mass 1950.

Fry's art criticism. TLS 12 Oct 1951.

Nicolson, B. Post-impressionism and Fry. Burlington Mag 93 1951.

Bell, C. Roger Fry. Cornhill Mag 166 1952.

MacCarthy, D. In his Memories, 1953.

Johnstone, J. K. Bloomsbury aesthetics. In his Bloomsbury group, 1954.

Fishman, S. The interpretation of art: essays on the art criticism of Ruskin, Pater, Bell, Fry and Read. Berkeley 1963.

Bell, Q. Roger Fry. Leeds 1964. Lecture.

Smart, A. Fry and early Italian art. Apollo 83 1966.

Vision and design: the life, work and influence of Fry: an exhibition arranged by the Arts Council and the University of Nottingham. [1966]. Catalogue.

JOHN GALSWORTHY
1867–1933
See cols 579-86, above.

HEATHCOTE WILLIAM GARROD
1878–1960

Bibliographies

List of the writings of Garrod. [Oxford 1948?]. By Garrod.

§ I

Erasmus on the renascence of learning: Gaisford Greek prose prize. Oxford 1900.

Galileo: the Newdigate prize poem. Oxford 1901.

The religion of all good men and other studies in Christian ethics. 1906, New York 1906 (replacing fifth essay with a new one).

The Oxford book of Latin verse. Ed Garrod, Oxford 1912.

Oxford poems. 1912.

A book of Latin verse. Oxford 1915. Based on The Oxford book of Latin verse, above.

Worms and epitaphs. Oxford 1919. Poems.

Wordsworth: lectures and essays. Oxford 1923, 1927 (enlarged).

Coleridge: poetry and prose. Ed Garrod, Oxford 1925.

Keats. Oxford 1926, 1939 (corrected).

Latin anthology, translated from the Latin [by various authors, including Garrod]. Ed Garrod [1927] (Augustan Books of English Poetry).

Collins. Oxford 1928, Folcroft Pa 1969.

Merton muniments. Ed with P. S. Allen, Oxford 1928.

Poems from the French. Tr Garrod [1928] (Augustan Books of English Poetry).

The profession of poetry and other lectures. Oxford 1929, Freeport NY 1967. Mainly lectures given as Professor of Poetry, Oxford, 1923-8.

Ancient painted glass in Merton College, Oxford. 1931.

Poetry and the criticism of life. Cambridge Mass 1931, London 1931.

The study of poetry. Oxford 1936.

The poetical works of John Keats. Ed Garrod, Oxford 1939, 1958 (rev) (Oxford English Texts). Text also used in OSA edn 1956.

Epigrams. Oxford 1946.

John Donne: poetry and prose. Ed Garrod, Oxford 1946.

Scholarship: its meaning and value. Cambridge 1946.

Genius loci and other essays. Oxford 1950.

The study of good letters. Ed J. Jones, Oxford 1963. Essays, including single lectures previously pbd separately.

Garrod also contributed the section on Merton College to the Victoria County History of Oxfordshire *vol 3 1954*. He *pbd edns of Statius and Horace* (Oxford Classical Texts); Manili Astronomicon liber II; *Einhard's Life of Charlemagne: the Latin text (with R. B. Mowat); and* Opus epistolarum Des. Erasmi Roterodami, *tom 9–11 (with H. M. Allen); he was editor of* Jnl of Philology *1914–20*.

§2

Jones, J. Heathcote William Garrod 1878–1960. Proc Br Acad 48 [1963].

ARTHUR ERIC ROWTON GILL
1882–1940

The Eric Gill Collection at the William Andrews Clark Memorial Library, Univ of California, Los Angeles, contains a substantial amount of ms material, including diaries and Gill's autobiography. See L. C. Powell, William Andrews Clark Memorial Library, Report of the third decade 1956–66, *Los Angeles, 1966*.

Bibliographies

In Engravings by Eric Gill: a selection representative of his work to the end of 1927 with a chronological list of engravings and a preface by the artist, 1929. Lists D1–241 (engraved at Ditchling) and nos 1–214.
In Engravings 1928–33 by Eric Gill, 1934, below. Lists nos 215–543.
Gill, E. R. Bibliography of Eric Gill. 1953. Foreword by W. Shewring; appendix lists wood engravings 1934–40 (nos 544–679). Trns are not included.
— The inscriptional work of Eric Gill: an inventory. 1964.
Stanford University Library. Catalogue of an exhibition of Eric Gill from the collections of A. Sperisen and others, compiled by J. T. Bender. Introd by E. R. Gill, Stanford 1954.
Elizabeth Marie, Sr. Gill: twentieth-century book designer. New York 1962. Bibliography lists primary and secondary sources for Gill's work as a book designer.
Physick, J. F. The engraved work of Gill. 1963. Catalogue of the collection presented to Victoria and Albert Museum by Gill's widow, with addns. Companion vol pbd in same year consists of plates with catalogue.
Smith, R. Gill: a catalogue of manuscripts, books, engravings, drawings and sculpture in the collection of Mr and Mrs S. Samuels. Liverpool 1963.

§1

Serving at Mass: being instructions and directions for laymen as to the manner of serving at Low Mass. Ditchling 1916 (S. Dominic's Press). Compiled chiefly from J. Baldeschi's Ceremonial according to the Roman rite.
Welch, G. S. The ship painters' handbook. 3rd edn, rev, Portsmouth 1916. Rev by Gill.
Essential perfection. [Ditchling 1917] (S. Dominic's Press); rptd (rev) in Art-nonsense, 1929, below.
Slavery and freedom. [Ditchling 1917] (S. Dominic's Press) (Penny Tracts 1); rptd in Art-nonsense, 1929, below.
The restoration of the monarchy. Ditchling 1917 (S. Dominic's Press) (Penny Tracts 3). With D. Pepler.
Sculpture: an essay. Ditchling 1918 (S. Dominic's Press); rptd (rev, as Stone-carving) in Sculpture: an essay on stone-cutting, 1924, and (further rev) in Art-nonsense, 1929, below. 400 copies.
Birth control. Ditchling 1919 (S. Dominic's Press) (Welfare Handbook 5).
Dress: being an essay in masculine vanity and an exposure of the un-Christian apparel favoured by females.

Ditchling 1921 (S. Dominic's Press) (Welfare Handbook 7); rptd (rev) in Art-nonsense, 1929, below.
Songs without clothes: being a dissertation on the Song of Solomon and such-like songs. Ditchling 1921 (S. Dominic's Press); rptd (rev) in Art-nonsense, 1929, below. 240 copies.
War memorial. Ditchling 1923 (S. Dominic's Press) (Welfare Handbook 10); rptd (rev) in Art-nonsense, 1929, below.
Sculpture: an essay on stone-cutting, with a preface about God. Ditchling 1924 (S. Dominic's Press); both pieces rptd (rev) in Art-nonsense, 1929, below.
Wood-engravings: a selection. Ditchling 1924 (S. Dominic's Press), New York 1924. Unauthorized.
Id quod visum placet: a practical test of the beautiful. Waltham St Lawrence 1926 (Golden Cockerel Press); rptd (rev) in Art-nonsense, 1929, below. 150 copies.
Architecture and sculpture. Manchester [1927]; rptd (rev) in Art-nonsense, 1929, below.
Art and love. Bristol 1927 (for 1928) (Golden Cockerel Press); rptd in Art-nonsense, 1929, below. 260 copies.
Christianity and art. Capel-y-ffin 1927 (for 1928) (Shakespeare Head Press); rptd (rev) in Art-nonsense, 1929, below. 200 copies.
Art and prudence: an essay. Waltham St Lawrence 1928 (Golden Cockerel Press); rptd (rev) in Beauty looks after herself, 1933, below.
The future of sculpture. 1928 (priv ptd); rptd in Art-nonsense, 1929, below. 55 copies.
Art and manufacture. [1929] (Handworkers' Pamphlets 4) (Fanfare Press); rptd (rev, as Art and industrialism) in Beauty looks after herself, 1933, below.
Art-nonsense and other essays. 1929.
Engravings by Eric Gill: a selection representative of his work to the end of 1927 with a chronological list of engravings and a preface by the artist. Bristol 1929 (Fanfare Press).
Specimen booklet showing the new sans-serif capitals designed by Eric Gill from matrices cut by the Lanston Monotype Corporation. [Birmingham] 1929 (Birmingham School of Printing, Booklet no 7).
Clothes: an essay upon the nature and significance of the natural and artificial integuments worn by men and women. 1931.
Clothing without cloth: an essay on the nude. Waltham St Lawrence [1931] (Golden Cockerel Press); rptd in In a strange land, 1944, below.
An essay on typography. 1931, 1936 (rev, adds But why lettering?) (Hague and Gill).
Sculpture and the living model. 1932 (Hague and Gill); rptd in Beauty looks after herself, 1933, below.
Beauty looks after herself: essays. 1933.
Unemployment. 1933 (Hague and Gill).
Art and a changing civilization. 1934, 1946 (as Art), New York 1950 (Twentieth-Century Lib).
Engravings, 1928–33. 1934 (Hague and Gill). 133 wood-engravings. 400 copies.
John Ruskin. In To the memory of John Ruskin, Cambridge 1934; rptd in In a strange land, 1944, below.
The Lord's song: a sermon. 1934 (Golden Cockerel Press); rptd in In a strange land, 1944, below.
Money and morals. 1934, 1937 (adds Unemployment, first pbd 1933). Illustr D. Tegetmeier.
A specimen of three book types designed by Gill: Joanna, Joanna italic, Perpetua. High Wycombe 1934 (priv ptd) (Hague and Gill).
Work and leisure. 1935. Lectures.
The necessity of belief: an enquiry into the nature of human certainty, the causes of scepticism and the grounds of morality, and a justification of the doctrine that the end is the beginning. 1936.
Sculpture on machine-made buildings. [Birmingham] 1937. Lecture; rptd in In a strange land, 1944, below.
Trousers and the most precious ornament. High Wycombe 1937 (Hague and Gill).

Work and property. 1937 (Hague and Gill). Illustr D. Tegetmeier.

And who wants peace? 1938 (Hague and Gill) (Pax pamphlets 1); rptd in It all goes together, 1944, below.

Twenty-five nudes, engraved by Gill with an introduction. 1938 (Hague and Gill).

Unholy Trinity. 1938. Illustr D. Tegetmeier. 11 essays.

Work and culture. Newport RI 1938 (John Stevens pamphlets). Lecture. 400 copies.

Sacred and secular in art and industry. 1939, Newport RI 1939 (John Stevens pamphlets). Lecture; rptd in Sacred & secular &c, 1940, and in Last essays, 1942, below. 400 copies.

Social justice and the stations of the Cross. 1939 (Hague and Gill), Wilkes-Barre Pa [1940?], Union Village NJ 1944 (as The stations of the Cross).

Social principles and directions, extracted from the three Papal Encyclicals: Rerum novarum, Quadragesimo anno, Divini redemptoris, arranged according to subject matter. Compiled E. Gill, High Wycombe 1939, 1940 (rev).

All that England stands for. [1940]. Pamphlet.

Autobiography. 1940, New York 1941.

Christianity and the machine age. 1940, New York 1940 (Christian News-letter Books 6).

Drawings from life. 1940 (Hague and Gill). 36 drawings with introd by Gill.

The human person and society. 1940 (Bond of Peace 1) (Hague, Gill and Davey); rptd in In a strange land, 1944, below.

On social equality. [Manchester 1940]. Single sheet pamphlet specially written for Activist Group.

Sacred & secular &c. 1940 (Hague, Gill and Davey). Illustr D. Tegetmeier.

Last essays. Introd by M. Gill 1942. Rptd with next as Essays by Eric Gill, 1947. The earlier New York edn, 1944, is entitled It all goes together, and substitutes Who wants peace? (1938) for A diary in Ireland (from In a strange land, 1944, below).

In a strange land: essays. 1944.

Not by such means. In A Catholic approach to the problem of war: a symposium, ed H. G. Scarfe, High Wycombe [1944].

First nudes. Introd by J. Rothenstein 1954. Plates.

The Procrustean bed. Philadelphia 1957 (Pickering Press). Discussion of spacing in typography.

Caelum et terra transibunt. [San Francisco 1958] (Black Vine Press). English poem first pbd in Game 5 1922.

An alphabet stone cut by Eric Gill. Introd by J. W. Wells [Chicago? 1963].

Letters and Diaries

Letters. Ed W. Shewring 1947, New York 1948.

From the Palestine diary of Gill. 1949 (Hague and Gill), 1953 (as From the Jerusalem diary of Gill). Extracts selected by M. E. Gill, covering period 10 March–13 May 1934.

Gill's prefaces and introds to books, his many contributions to periodicals (including a full list of those to Game, *pbd* S. Dominic's Press) *and his many illustrations to books and other pbns are listed in E. R. Gill,* Bibliography, *above.*

§2

E. R. Gill, Bibliography, *above, lists early reviews of Gill's works.*

R[othenstein], J. K. M. Eric Gill. 1927 (Contemporary Br Artists).

Thorp, J. Eric Gill, with a critical monograph by C. Marriott. 1929.

'Beaujon, Paul' (B. Warde). Gill: sculptor of letters. Fleuron 7 1930.

Bennigsen, G. The art of Gill. Blackfriars 11 1930.

Chesterton, G. K. Gill and no nonsense. Studio 99 1930. Review-article of Art-nonsense and other essays.

Lawrence, D. H. Gill's 'Art nonsense'. Book-Collector's Quart 12 1933; rptd in his Phoenix, New York 1936. Lawrence died before finishing this review-article.

Jackson, H. Views and reviews: Gill epitomized; The testament of an artist. New Eng Weekly 31 Dec 1936, 7 Jan 1937. Review-articles of The necessity of belief and An essay on typography.

Blackfriars 22 1941. Eric Gill: memorial number. Appreciations: F. Lockyer, J. M. Murry, M. C. D'Arcy, N. Gorton, B. Delany, H. Pepler, D. Attwater, A. Foster. Articles: D. Jones, K. Foster, B. Kelly, W. Shewring, R. Hague.

Gray, N. William Morris, Gill and Catholicism. Architectural Rev 89 1941.

Pax Bulletin 20 1941. Eric Gill: memorial number. Appreciations: C. Gill, G. Vann, T. B. Richards, H. Robbins, and extracts from others.

Read, H. Gill—anarchist. War Commentary 2 1941; rptd (as Eric Gill) in his Coat of many colours, 1945.

Shebbeare, A. The autobiography of Gill. Downside Rev 69 1941. Review-article.

Shewring, W. Considerations on Gill. Dublin Rev 18 1944; rptd in his Making and thinking, 1954.

Attwater, D. Gill: workman. 1945. (Modern Christian revolutionaries.)

Pepler, C. A study in integrity. Blackfriars 28 1947.

Chute, D. Gill: a retrospect. Blackfriars 31 1950, 32 1951.

Greene, G. In his Lost childhood and other essays, 1951. First pbd Spectator 10 Jan 1941.

Heppenstall, R. Four absentees. 1960. Reminiscences of Gill, Orwell, Dylan Thomas and J. M. Murry.

Speaight, R. The life of Gill. 1966.

William Andrews Clark Memorial Library. The life and works of Gill: papers by C. Gill, B. Warde and D. Kindersley. Los Angeles 1968.

ROBERT WILLIAM VICTOR GITTINGS
b. 1911

See cols 282–3, above.

GERALD GOULD
1885–1936

See cols 284–5, above.

HARLEY GRANVILLE-BARKER
1877–1946

See cols 944–6, above.

ROBERT VON RANKE GRAVES
b. 1895

See cols 201–7, above.

GRAHAM GREENE
b. 1904

See cols 503–12, above.

SIR WALTER WILSON GREG
1875–1959

Bibliographies

Francis, F. C. A list of Greg's writings. 1945. Rptd from Library 4th ser 26 1945. Suppl 1945–59, by D. F. McKenzie, Library 5th ser 15 1960.

Collections

Collected papers. Ed J. C. Maxwell, Oxford 1966.

§ 1

A list of English plays written before 1643 and printed before 1700. 1900.

Notes and elucidations to Henley's Lyra heroica. 1900. With L. C. Cornford.

Verses. By 'W.W.G.' Cambridge 1900 (for 1901).

A list of masques, pageants &c, supplementary to A list of English plays. 1902.

Catalogue of the books presented by Edward Capell to the library of Trinity College in Cambridge. Cambridge 1903. Suppl of 14 plates was issued in 12 sets for priv distribution.

Pastoral poetry and pastoral drama: a literary inquiry with special reference to the pre-Restoration stage in England. 1906, New York 1959.

A descriptive catalogue of the early editions of the works of Shakespeare preserved in the library of Eton College. Oxford 1909.

John Phillip: notes for a bibliography. 1911. 'Further notes' in Library 4 1913.

Bibliographical and textual problems of the English Miracle cycles. 1914. Lectures.

Two Elizabethan stage abridgements: The battle of Alcazar and Orlando furioso: an essay in critical bibliography. Oxford 1923 (another issue as Malone Soc extra vol 1923).

Shakespeare's hand in the play of Sir Thomas More. Cambridge 1923. Papers by W. W. Greg et al.

1623–1923: studies in the First Folio, written for the Shakespeare Assoc by W. W. Greg [et al]. 1924.

The calculus of variants: an essay on textual criticism. Oxford 1927.

Dramatic documents from the Elizabethan playhouses: stage plots, actors' parts, prompt books. 2 vols Oxford 1931. Commentary, reproductions and transcripts.

A bibliography of the English printed drama to the Restoration. 4 vols 1939 (for 1940)–59 (Bibl Soc Illustrated Monographs 24).

The variants in the first quarto of King Lear: a bibliographical and critical inquiry. 1940 (Suppl to Trans Bibl Soc 15).

The editorial problem in Shakespeare: a survey of the foundations of the text. Oxford 1942, 1951 (with new preface and additional notes), 1954 (for 1955) (slightly rev). Lectures.

The Shakespeare first folio: its bibliographical and textual history. Oxford 1955.

Some aspects and problems of London publishing between 1550 and 1650. Oxford 1956. Lectures.

Biographical notes, 1877–1947. Oxford 1960 (priv ptd, 100 copies).

Licensers for the press &c to 1640: a biographical index based mainly on Arber's Transcript of the registers of the Company of Stationers. Oxford 1962 (Oxford Bibl Soc Pbns, new ser 10).

A companion to Arber: being a calendar of documents in Edward Arber's Transcript of the registers of the Company of Stationers of London, 1554–1640, with text and calendar of supplementary documents. Oxford 1967.

Editions

Henslowe, P. Diary. 2 vols 1904–08.

The elder brother. In The works of Francis Beaumont and John Fletcher, Variorum edition vol 2, 1905.

Henslowe, P. Papers: being documents supplementary to Henslowe's Diary. 1907.

Lodge, T. Rosalynde: being the original of Shakespeare's As you like it. 1907, 1931 (corrected) (Shakespeare Lib).

The faithful shepherdess. In The works of Beaumont and Fletcher, Variorum edition vol 3, 1908.

Shakespeare, W. Merry wives of Windsor, 1602. Oxford 1910 (Tudor and Stuart Lib).

Peele, G. The old wife's tale new vamp't and adorned with figures. 1911. The 'figures' by E. E. Greg.

Facsimiles of twelve early English manuscripts in the library of Trinity College, Cambridge. Oxford 1913.

The assumption of the Virgin: a miracle play from the N-town cycle. Oxford 1915 (Studies in the Religious Drama 1).

English literary autographs, 1550–1650, selected for reproduction and edited by W. W. Greg et al. 4 pts Oxford 1925–32.

Beaumont, J. The theatre of Apollo: an entertainment. 1926 (250 copies).

Records of the Court of the Stationers' Company 1576 to 1602 from Register B. 1930. With E. Boswell.

The play of Antichrist from the Chester cycle. Oxford 1935.

Marlowe, C. Doctor Faustus, 1604–16: parallel texts. Oxford 1950.

—— The tragical history of the life and death of Dr Faustus: a conjectural reconstruction. Oxford 1950.

Jonson, B. Masque of gipsies, in the Burley, Belvoir and Windsor versions: an attempt at reconstruction. 1952.

Respublica: an interlude for Christmas, 1553, attributed to Nicholas Udall. Re-edited by W. W. Greg 1952 (for 1953) (EETS original ser 226).

Greg also edited MLQ 6–7 1903–4 and assisted in the founding of MLR; he edited (sometimes with W. Bang) a number of plays in the ser Materialien zur Kunde des älteren englischen Dramas; *at A. W. Pollard's suggestion he founded the Malone Soc, was General Editor of the Malone Soc reprints 1906–39 and* Collections *1907–31 and was President of the Soc 1939–59; he edited or assisted in the editing of most of the Soc's pbns; he was editor of the Shakespeare Assoc's* Shakespeare Quarto Facsimiles 1–12, *1939–59; he was President of the Bibl Soc 1930–2; he contributed the articles on R. B. McKerrow and A. W. Pollard to* DNB.

§ 2

Tannenbaum, S. A. Shakespeare and 'Sir Thomas More'. New York 1929. Answer to Greg's review of his 2 books, The booke of Sir Thomas Moore, 1927, and Problems in Shakespeare's penmanship, 1927.

Shepard, W. P. Recent theories of textual criticism. MP 28 1931. On The calculus of variants, 1927.

Grierson, H. J. C. A review of Pastoral poetry and pastoral drama. In his Essays and addresses, 1940.

Wilson, F. P. Shakespeare and the 'new bibliography'. In The Bibliographical Society 1892–1942: studies in retrospect, 1945. Rev H. Gardner 1970.

—— Sir W. W. Greg. Proc Br Acad 45 1960.

Mackie, J. Scientific treatment in textual criticism. Australian Jnl of Philosophy 25 1947.

Walter Wilson Greg, 9 July 1875–4 March 1959. Library 5th ser 14 1959. Tributes by J. D. Wilson, A. Walker, M. St Clare Byrne, F. Bowers, F. C. Francis.

SIR HERBERT JOHN CLIFFORD GRIERSON
1866–1960

Bibliographies

A list of Grierson's publications 1906–37. In Seventeenth-century studies presented to Sir Herbert Grierson, Oxford 1938.

§ 1

The first half of the seventeenth century. Edinburgh 1906, New York 1906 (Periods of European Literature 7).

Poems of Tennyson. Edinburgh [1907] (Golden Poets). Selection, ed Grierson.

The English Parnassus: an anthology of longer poems. Ed with M. Dixon, Oxford 1909.

The poems of John Donne. 2 vols Oxford 1912 (with commentary), 1 vol London 1929 (without commentary) (OSA). Grierson's text has been used in a number of subsequent edns of the poems.

Macbeth. Ed Grierson, Oxford 1914 (Select plays of Shakespeare ed J. C. Smith).

Metaphysical lyrics & poems of the seventeenth century: Donne to Butler. Ed with an essay by Grierson, Oxford 1921.

Poems of Byron. 1923 (260 copies). Selection, ed Grierson.

The background of English literature and other collected essays & addresses. 1925, New York 1960 (for 1961).

The poems of Milton: English, Latin, Greek and Italian. Ed Grierson 2 vols 1925.

Lyrical poetry from Blake to Hardy. 1928, New York 1929 (as Lyrical poetry of the nineteenth century).

Cross currents in English literature of the XVIIth century: or the world, the flesh and the spirit, their actions and reactions. 1929, New York 1958 (with additional preface) (as Cross-currents in 17th-century English literature, etc).

The flute, with other translations and a poem [Shakespeare and Scotland]. Warlingham 1931 (120 copies), Edinburgh 1949.

The letters of Scott. Ed Grierson 12 vols 1932–7 (Centenary edn).

Sir Walter Scott: broadcast lectures to the young. Edinburgh 1932.

Sir Walter Scott today: some retrospective essays and studies. Ed with a preface by Grierson 1932.

The Oxford book of seventeenth-century verse. Ed with G. Bullough, Oxford 1934.

Two Dutch poets [P. C. Hooft, P. C. Boutens]. Oxford 1936 (Taylorian lecture). Grierson also pbd trns of Boutens' Christ child and Three poems (1938), and Hooft's Montaigne (1949).

Milton and Wordsworth, poets and prophets: a study of their reactions to political events. Cambridge 1937, New York 1937.

Sir Walter Scott, Bart: a new life, supplementary to, and corrective of, Lockhart's biography. 1938, New York 1938.

Essays and addresses. 1940.

Songs and lyrics of Scott. Edinburgh 1942 (Saltire Classics). Selection, ed Grierson.

The English Bible. 1943 (Britain in Pictures).

A critical history of English poetry. 1944, New York 1946, London 1947 (rev). With J. C. Smith.

Rhetoric and English composition. Edinburgh 1944, 1945 (rev).

The personal note: or first and last words from prefaces, introductions, dedications, epilogues. Ed with S. Wason 1946.

And the third day: a record of hope and fulfilment. 1948, New York 1948. Anthology of religious verse and prose, ed Grierson.

With A. M. Clark, Grierson contributed the section The Elizabethan period: poetry and prose *to* The years work in English studies *2–11 1920–30.*

§2

Williamson, G. Textual difficulties in Donne's poetry. In his Seventeenth-century contexts, 1960. Essay-review of Grierson's edn 1912.

Daiches, D. Sir Herbert Grierson. Proc Br Acad 46 [1961]; rptd in his More literary essays, 1968.

GEOFFREY EDWARD HARVEY GRIGSON
b. 1905

The arts today. 1935. Ed with ch, Painting and sculpture, by Grigson.

Essays by Francis Bacon. Introd by Grigson 1937 (WC).

The year's poetry, 1937(–1938), compiled by D. K. Roberts, G. Grigson. 2 vols 1937–8.

New verse: an anthology. 1939. Poems which appeared in the first 30 nos of New verse, ed Grigson 1933–9.

Several observations: thirty five poems. [1939].

The journals of George Sturt, 'George Bourne', 1890–1902. Ed Grigson 1941.

The Romantics: an anthology, chosen by G. Grigson. 1942, Cleveland 1962. Prose and poetry.

Henry Moore. 1943 (Penguin Modern Painters). Plates, with introd by Grigson; introd rptd in The harp of Aeolus, 1947, below.

Under the cliff and other poems. 1943.

Visionary poems and passages: or the poet's eye, chosen by G. Grigson. 1944. With original lithographs by J. Craxton.

Wild flowers in Britain. 1944.

Before the Romantics: an anthology of the Enlightenment, chosen by G. Grigson. 1946. Prose and verse.

The Isles of Scilly and other poems. 1946.

The mint: a miscellany of literature, art and criticism. Ed G. Grigson 2 vols 1946–8.

English Romantic art. 1947. Arts Council exhibition selected and catalogue prepared by Grigson.

The harp of Aeolus and other essays on art, literature and nature. 1947.

Samuel Palmer: the visionary years. 1947.

An English farmhouse and its neighbourhood. 1948.

The Scilly Isles. 1948. Drawings and watercolours by F. Uhlman.

Places of the mind. 1949. Topography.

Poems of John Clare's madness. Ed Grigson 1949.

Poetry of the present: an anthology of the thirties and after, compiled and introduced by G. Grigson. 1949.

Clare, J. Selected poems. Ed Grigson 1950 (ML).

The crest on the silver: an autobiography. 1950.

Flowers of the meadow. 1950.

Horse and rider: eight centuries of equestrian paintings. 1950. Plates chosen with introd by G. Grigson.

Selected poems of William Barnes, 1800–66. Ed Grigson 1950 (ML).

The Victorians: an anthology chosen by G. Grigson. 1950. Prose and poetry.

Essays from the air. 1951. Broadcast talks.

A master of our time: a study of Wyndham Lewis. 1951.

Thornton's Temple of Flora, with plates reproduced from the original engravings and the work described by G. Grigson. 1951.

English country: a series of illustrations, with an introduction by G. Grigson. 1952.

Gardenage: or, the plants of Ninhursaga. 1952.

The female form in painting. 1953, New York 1953. With J. Cassou.

Legenda Suecana: twenty-odd poems. 1953. Anon; 25 copies.

Freedom of the parish. 1954. On Pelynt, East Cornwall, Grigson's birth place.

People, places and things. General editors: G. Grigson and C. H. Gibbs-Smith, 4 vols 1954, New York 1957. Each vol separately pbd New York 1955–7.

English drawing from Samuel Cooper to Gwen John, introduced and chosen by G. Grigson. 1955.

The Englishman's flora, illustrated with woodcuts from sixteenth-century herbals. 1955.

Gerard Manley Hopkins. 1955, New York 1955, London 1958 (rev bibliography) (Br Council pamphlet); rptd in Poems and poets, 1969, below.

The Shell guide to flowers of the countryside, painted by
E. and R. Hilder, chosen and described by G. Grigson.
[1955] (Shell Nature Studies); rptd in the Shell nature
book, 1964, below.
Art treasures of the British Museum, chosen and intro-
duced by G. Grigson. [1957], New York [1957?].
Célébonovic, S. Old Stone Age. 1957. New York 1957.
Photographs, with commentary by Grigson.
— The living rocks. [1957], New York 1957. Photo-
graphs, with commentary by Grigson.
England, photographed by E. Smith; text by Grigson.
[1957], New York 1958 [1957].
Fossils, insects and reptiles. Edited and written by G.
Grigson and painted by T. Hillier. 1957 (Shell Nature
Studies); rptd in the Shell nature book, 1964, below.
Painted caves. 1957. On the cave art of France and Spain.
The Wiltshire book. 1957.
English villages in colour: a collection of colour photo-
graphs, with an introductory text and notes on illustra-
tions by G. Grigson. 1958.
Looking and finding and collecting and reading and investi-
gating and much else. 1958. Drawings by C. Chamber-
lain. For children.
The Shell guide to trees and shrubs, painted by S. R.
Badman; text by G. Grigson. 1958 (Shell Nature
Studies); rptd in the Shell nature book, 1964, below.
The Three Kings: a Christmas book of carols, poems and
pieces, chosen with an account of the legend by G.
Grigson. Bedford 1958.
The cherry-tree: a collection of poems chosen by G. Grig-
son. 1959, New York [1959]. For children.
Country poems, selected by G. Grigson. 1959 (Pocket
Poets).
A herbal of all sorts. 1959, New York 1959.
The Shell guide to wild life, painted by J. Leigh-Pemberton;
text by G. Grigson. 1959 (Shell Nature Studies); rptd
in the Shell nature book, 1964, below.
English excursions. 1960.
Samuel Palmer's Valley of vision. 1960. Plates with
a selection of Palmer's writings, introd and notes by
Grigson.
Christopher Smart. 1961 (Br Council pamphlet); rptd in
Poems and poets, 1969, below.
Poets in their pride. 1962, New York 1964. Essays on
10 English poets with selections and portraits.
The Shell country book. 1962.
The collected poems of Geoffrey Grigson, 1924–62.
1963.
The concise encyclopedia of modern world literature. Ed
Grigson New York 1963, London 1963.
O rare mankind!: a short collection of great prose chosen
by G. Grigson. 1963.
Landor, W. S. Poems. Ed Grigson 1964, Carbondale
(1965) (Centaur Classics).
Shapes and stories: a book about pictures. 1964, New
York 1965 (for 1964). With J. Grigson. For children.
The Shell book of roads, painted by D. Gentleman; line
drawings by P. Branfield. [1964].
The Shell nature book. 1964. New edn of 4 vols pbd
1955–9 as Shell nature studies, with 'Birds and beasts'
by J. Fisher.
The Shell country alphabet. 1966.
The English year: from diaries and letters, compiled by
G. Grigson. 1967.
Shapes and adventures. 1967. With J. Grigson. For
children.
A skull in Salop and other poems. 1967, Chester Springs
[1967].
Ingestion of ice-cream, and other poems. 1969.
Poems and poets. 1969, Chester Springs 1969. Essays.
Grigson was also general editor of the About Britain *guides,
13 vols 1951, and wrote the text of nos 1 and 2,* West
country *and* Wessex; *he compiled selections from the poems
of Coleridge, Crabbe and Dryden in the ser* Crown Classics
and other selections of Hardy and William Morris.

JAMES THOMAS FRANK
HARRIS
1856–1931

§1

Elder Conklin and other stories. New York 1894, London
1895 (for 1894).
How to beat the Boer: a conversation in Hades. 1900.
Pamphlet.
Montes the matador, and other stories. 1900, New York
1910.
The bomb. 1908, New York 1909, Chicago 1963 (introd
by J. Dos Passos). Novel.
The man Shakespeare and his tragic life story. 1909, New
York 1909.
Shakespeare and his love: a play in four acts and an epi-
logue. 1910.
The women of Shakespeare. 1911. Mainly on theory that
Mary Fitton was 'Dark Lady' of the Sonnets.
Unpath'd waters. 1913, New York 1913. Stories.
Great days. 1914 (for 1913), New York 1914. Novel.
The yellow ticket, and other stories. 1914.
Contemporary portraits. Ser 1–4, 4 vols New York 1915–
23, London 1915–24.
England or Germany? New York 1915.
The veils of Isis, and other stories. New York [1915].
Love in youth. New York [1916]. Novel.
Oscar Wilde: his life and confessions. 2 vols New York
1916, 1918 (with Memories of Oscar Wilde by Bernard
Shaw), 1 vol 1930 (including hitherto unpbd confession
by Lord Alfred Douglas and Memories by Shaw), Lon-
don 1938 (as Oscar Wilde, preface by Shaw), [East
Lansing] 1959 (with Memories by Shaw and introductory note by L. Blair), [New York] 1960 (with note by
L. Blair, Memories by Shaw and Oscar's last drop,
a letter from R. Ross).
A mad love: the strange story of a musician. New York 1920.
My life and loves. Vols 1–4 only, Paris 1922–7 (priv ptd)
(vols 2–4 are entitled My life; vol 2 has imprint Nice, the
author, Imprimerie niçoise, vols 3–4 Comiez, Nice, the
author; vols 3–4 have several chs inserted after original
printing), 5 vols ed J. F. Gallagher, New York 1963,
London 1964 (vol 5 based on Harris' final typescript in
Humanities Research Center, Univ of Texas). According to Gallagher the 5th vol pbd Paris 1958 is not
authentic. (See also A. Trocchi, The fifth volume of
Frank Harris' My life and loves: an irreverent treatment,
1966). A number of partial, expurgated, unexpurgated
etc edns of the work pbd after the first edn. An abridge-
ment, introd by G. Richards, pbd 1947 (as Frank Harris:
his life and adventures).
Undream'd of shores. 1924, New York [1924]. Stories.
New preface to The life and confessions of Oscar Wilde, by
F. Harris and Lord Alfred Douglas. 1925; rptd in New
York 1930 edn of Wilde, above.
Joan la Romée: a drama. Nice [1926] (priv ptd), New York
1926, London [1926]. Introd consists of a letter from
Shaw criticizing the play and a reply by Harris.
Latest contemporary portraits. New York [1927].
Confessional: a volume of intimate portraits, sketches and
studies. New York [1930].
My reminiscences as a cowboy. New York 1930, London
1930 (as On the trail: my reminiscences as a cowboy;
with slight textual changes and omission of last ch).
Largely written by F. Scully. See Scully, Rogue's
gallery, 1943, §2 below.
Pantopia. New York [1930] (priv ptd, Panurge Press).
Novel based on his short story, Temple to the forgotten
dead.
Frank Harris on Bernard Shaw: an unauthorized biography based on first hand information, with a postscript
by Mr Shaw. 1931, Garden City NY [1931] (as Bernard
Shaw: an unauthorized biography).

Mr and Mrs Daventry: a play in four acts based on the scenario by Oscar Wilde. (Royalty Theatre 25 Oct 1900). Introd by H. M. Hyde 1956.

Letters

Moore versus Harris: an intimate correspondence between George Moore and Harris. Chicago 1925 (priv ptd). Ed G. Bruno, with caricatures by Beerbohm et al and a letter from Shaw.

Frank Harris to Bennett: fifty-eight letters, 1908-10. Merion Station 1936 (priv ptd, 99 copies).

Harris edited Evening News, *1882-6*; Fortnightly Rev, *1886-94*; Saturday Rev, *1894-8*; Candid Friend, *1901-2*; Vanity Fair, *1907-10*; Hearth & Home, *1911-12*; Modern Society, *1913-14*; Pearson's Mag, *1916-22*; View of Truth, *1927-8*.

§2

Carrel, F. The adventures of John Johns. 1897. Fictional account of Harris's pre-Fortnightly career in London.

Pearson, H. In his Modern men and mummers, 1921.

—— H. G. Wells and Harris. Listener 5 July 1956.

Mencken, H. L. In his Prejudices: ser 3, New York [1922].

Burdett, O. The writings of Harris. In his Critical essays, 1925.

'Hugh Kingsmill' (H. K. Lunn). In his After puritanism, 1850-1900, 1929. With special reference to Butler, Harris and W. T. Stead.

—— Frank Harris. 1932.

Smith, G. and M. C. (ed). Lies and libels of Harris [selections from his correspondence and My life, relating to Byron Caldwell Smith]: arguments by K. Stephens. New York 1929.

Roth, S. The private life of Harris. New York 1931.

Tobin, A. I. and E. Gertz. Harris—a study in black and white: an authorized biography. Chicago 1931.

Murry, J. M. In his Between two worlds: an autobiography, 1935. Reminiscences.

Baumann, A. A. In his Personalities, 1936.

Sherard, R. H. Shaw, Harris and Wilde, with a preface by Lord Alfred Douglas and an additional chapter by H. Kingsmill. 1937.

Cargill, O. Intelligentsia. In his Intellectual America, 1941.

Scully, F. J. X. In his Rogue's gallery, Hollywood 1943.

Woollcott, A. The last of Harris. In his Portable Woollcott, New York 1946.

Root, E. M. Frank Harris: a biography. New York 1947.

Mordell, A. Harris and Haldeman-Julius: the record of a series of quarrels, without equal in the annals of American letters. Girard Kansas [1950].

'Louis Marlow' (L. U. Wilkinson). In his Seven friends, 1953.

Ross, J. M. A visit to the Villa Edouard Sept. London Mag 2 1955. Reminiscences.

Stokes, S. Portraits of Harris in exile. Listener 5 Dec 1957.

Brome, V. The five faces of Harris. Saturday Book 19 1959.

—— Frank Harris. 1959.

GEORGE BAGSHAWE HARRISON
b. 1894

§1

Shakespeare: the man and his stage. 1923. With E. A. G. Lamborn.

Shakespeare's fellows: being a brief chronicle of the Shakespearean age. 1923.

The story of the Elizabethan drama. Cambridge 1924.

Shakespeare. [1927].

The genius of Shakespeare. New York 1927.

An Elizabethan journal: being a record of those things most talked of during the years 1591-4. 1928, New York 1929.

England in Shakespeare's day. 1928.

John Bunyan: a study in personality. 1928, Garden City NY 1928.

Elizabethan England. 1930.

A second Elizabethan journal: being a record of those things most talked of during the years 1595-8. 1931.

A last Elizabethan journal: being a record of those things most talked of during the years 1599-1603. 1933.

Shakespeare under Elizabeth. New York [1933], London 1933 (as Shakespeare at work, 1592-1603), Ann Arbor 1958 (with a new preface).

A companion to Shakespeare studies. Cambridge 1934, New York 1934. With H. Granville-Barker.

Queen Elizabeth and her subjects. 1935. With A. L. Rowse.

Digging for history. 1937. For children.

The life and death of Robert Devereux, Earl of Essex. 1937, New York [1937].

The day before yesterday: being a journal of the year 1936. 1938.

The Elizabethan journals: being a record of those things most talked of during the years 1591-1603. 1938, Ann Arbor 1955, Garden City NY 1965 (abridged). A reissue in one vol of 3 Journals pbd separately, above.

Introducing Shakespeare. 1939, New York 1947 (rev), London 1948 (rev), 1954 (rev), 1966 (rev and enlarged) (Pelican).

Elizabethan plays and players. 1940, Ann Arbor 1956.

A Jacobean journal: being a record of those things most talked of during the years 1603-6. 1941.

Shakespeare's tragedies. 1951, New York 1952 (for 1951).

A second Jacobean journal: being a record of those things most talked of during the years 1607-10. 1958, Ann Arbor 1958.

Profession of English. New York [1962].

The fires of Arcadia. New York 1965, London 1966. Novel.

Harrison also pbd a number of re-tellings of stories from the Bible, Shakespeare etc for children.

Editions

Bunyan, J. The pilgrim's progress and The life and death of Mr Badman. 1928.

The church book of Bunyan Meeting, 1650-1820: being a reproduction in facsimile of the original folio. 1928.

Breton, N. Melancholike humours. 1929. With essay on Elizabethan melancholy by Harrison.

Potts, T. The trial of the Lancaster witches AD MDCXII. 1929.

Advice to his son, by Henry Percy, ninth Earl of Northumberland. 1930.

Hurault, A. De Maisse: a journal of all that was accomplished by Monsieur de Maisse, Ambassador in England from King Henry IV to Queen Elizabeth, Anno Domini 1597. 1931. Tr by Harrison, with R. A. Jones.

The letters of Queen Elizabeth. 1935.

A book of English poetry: Chaucer to Rossetti. 1937 (Pelican), 1958 (enlarged, Penguin Poets).

Major British writers, under the general editorship of G. B. Harrison. 2 vols New York 1954, [1959] (enlarged).

Harrison also edited The Bodley Head Quartos *1922-6*, Fortune Play Books *1926-7 and* Shakespeare Association Facsimiles *1931-8; he has edited a number of edns of Shakespeare's works for the general reader, including* New Readers' Shakespeare *19 vols 1925-8*, Works 6 vols *1934*, Penguin Shakespeare *1937-8*, New Stratford Shakespeare *1954-*, Harbinger Shakespeare *New York 1962-, and an edn for the* Shakespeare Recording Soc *New York 1962-; he has edited a number of 'casebooks' of Shakespearean criticism; and has also edited Marston's*

Malcontent, *Webster's* White devil, *and Tourneur's* Revenger's tragedy *for the Temple Dramatists ser 1933–4.*

JANE ELLEN HARRISON
1850–1928

Bibliographies

Stewart, J. G. In her Jane Ellen Harrison, 1959, §2, below. Includes contributions to books and periodicals, unpbd lectures, reviews of her work and obituary notices.

§1

Myths of the Odyssey in art and literature. 1882 (for 1881).
Introductory studies in Greek art. 1885.
Collignon, M. Manual of mythology in relation to Greek art. Tr and enlarged by J. E. Harrison 1890.
Paris, P. Manual of ancient sculpture. Ed and augmented by J. E. Harrison 1890.
Pausanias. Mythology and monuments of ancient Athens: being a translation of a portion of the Attica of Pausanias by M. de G. Verrall. 1890. Introd and archaeological commentary by J. E. Harrison.
Peticus, A. H. The gods of Olympus. 1892. Introd by J. E. Harrison.
Greek vase paintings: a selection of examples. 1894. Preface, introd and descriptions by J. E. Harrison and D. S. MacColl.
Prolegomena to the study of Greek religion. Cambridge 1903, 1908 (corrected), New York 1960. With critical appendix on the Orphic tablets by G. Murray.
The religion of ancient Greece. 1905.
Primitive Athens as described by Thucydides. Cambridge 1906.
Heresy and humanity. Cambridge 1911. Lecture. Reply by E. G. Selwyn, Tradition and reason, Cambridge 1911.
Themis: a study of the social origins of Greek religion, with an excursus on the ritual forms preserved in Greek tragedy by G. Murray and a chapter on the origin of the Olympic games by F. M. Cornford. Cambridge 1912, 1927 (rev and enlarged), Cleveland 1962.
'Homo sum': being a letter to an Anti-suffragist from an anthropologist. [1913]; rptd in Alpha and omega, 1915.
Unanimism: a study in conversion and some contemporary French poets. Cambridge 1913; rptd in Alpha and omega, 1915.
Ancient art and ritual. [1914], New York [1914].
Peace with patriotism. Cambridge 1915. Pamphlet; rptd in Alpha and omega, 1915, below.
Alpha and omega. 1915. Essays, including single lectures and pamphlets previously pbd separately.
Russia and the Russian verb: a contribution to the psychology of the Russian people. Cambridge 1915. Pamphlet.
Aspects, aorists and the Classical Tripos. Cambridge 1919.
Epilegomena to the study of Greek religion. Cambridge 1921, New Hyde Park NY 1962.
The life of the Archpriest Avvakum by himself. Tr by J. Harrison and H. Mirrlees, 1924. Preface by D. S. Mirsky.
Mythology. Boston [1924], London [1925] (Our Debt to Greece and Rome).
Reminiscences of a student's life. 1925.
The book of the bear: being twenty-one tales newly tr from the Russian. 1926. With H. Mirrlees.
Myths of Greece and Rome. 1927, Garden City NY 1928 (Benn's Sixpenny Lib).

Letters

See J. G. Stewart, Jane Ellen Harrison, 1959, §2 below.

§2

Murray, G. Jane Ellen Harrison: an address. Cambridge 1928.
Svyatopolk-Mirsky, D. P. Jane Ellen Harrison and Russia. Cambridge 1930.
Stewart, J. G. Jane Ellen Harrison: a portrait from letters. [1959].
Hyman, S. E. Leaping for goodly Themis. In his Standards: a chronicle of books for our time, New York [1966].

M.P.

JOHN DAVY HAYWARD
1905–65

§1

Collected works of John Wilmot, Earl of Rochester. Ed J. Hayward 1926.
Donne, J. Complete poetry and selected prose. Ed J. Hayward 1929.
The letters of Saint Evremond. Ed J. Hayward 1930.
Nineteenth century poetry: an anthology chosen by J. Hayward. 1932.
Charles II. 1933.
Swift, J. Gulliver's travels and selected writings in prose and verse. Ed J. Hayward 1934.
Silver tongues: famous speeches from Burke to Baldwin, compiled and ed by J. Hayward. 1937.
Love's Helicon: or the progress of love described in English verse, arranged and edited by J. Hayward. 1940.
A catalogue of printed books and manuscripts by Jonathan Swift DD exhibited in the Old Schools in the University of Cambridge to commemorate the 200th anniversary of his death. Cambridge 1945.
English poetry: a catalogue of first and early editions of works of the English poets from Chaucer to the present day exhibited by the National Book League, compiled by J. Hayward. 1947, 1950 (illustrated edn).
Prose literature since 1939. 1947 (Br Council pamphlet).
Dr Johnson: some observations and judgements upon life and letters, chosen by J. Hayward. 1948.
Seventeenth century poetry: an anthology, chosen by J. Hayward. 1948.
Selected prose works of Jonathan Swift. Ed J. Hayward 1949.
John Donne: a selection of his poetry. Ed J. Hayward 1950.
Book collecting: four broadcast talks. Cambridge 1950 (for 1951). By J. Hayward et al.
Eliot, T. S. Selected prose. Ed J. Hayward 1953.
The Sterling Library: a catalogue. Cambridge 1954 (priv ptd). Compiled by M. B. C. Canney and ed J. Hayward.
Swift, J. Gulliver's travels. Ed J. Hayward 1955.
The Penguin book of English verse. Ed J. Hayward 1956, 1958 (enlarged as The Faber book of English verse).
Herrick, R. Poems from Hesperides and Noble numbers. Ed J. Hayward 1961, Baltimore 1962 (Penguin Poets).
The Oxford book of nineteenth-century English verse. Ed J. Hayward, Oxford 1964.
Hayward was editorial director of Book Collector *1952–65, editor of* Soho Bibliographies *and editorial adviser to the Cresset Press, editing the* Cresset Library.

§2

John Hayward 1904[sic]–1965: some memories. Book Collector 14 1965.

N.J.S.

JOHN FRANCIS ALEXANDER HEATH-STUBBS
b. 1918
See col 287, above.

SIR ALAN PATRICK HERBERT
1890–1971
See cols 288–90, above.

ARTHUR HUMPHRY HOUSE
1908–55

The Dickens world. 1941, 1942 (rev).
Coleridge. 1953, Philadelphia 1965.
All in due time: the collected essays and broadcast talks of Humphry House. 1955.
Aristotle's Poetics: a course of eight lectures. Rev by C. Hardie 1956.
House also edited The note-books and papers of Gerard Manley Hopkins (*1937*). *His projected edn of Dickens's letters has been continued by M. House and G. Storey.*
C.H.E.P.

THOMAS ERNEST HULME
1883–1917

A number of mss are held at the Universities of Keele, Hull and Texas.

Bibliographies
In T. E. Hulme. Further speculations, ed S. Hynes [1955], below.
In A. R. Jones. The life and opinions of Hulme, 1960, below.
Martin, W. Hulme: a bibliographical note. N & Q 9 1962. Addenda to both the above.

Collections
The poetical works of Hulme. In A. R. Jones, bibliographies, above. Gives textual variants. Contains several unpbd poems.

§1
A city sunset; Autumn. In For Christmas MDCCCCVIII, The Poets' Club [1909].
A conversion; The embankment. In The book of The Poets' Club, 1909.
The complete poetical works of T. E. Hulme. New Age 23 Jan 1912. Rptd as an appendix to Ezra Pound, Ripostes, 1912 etc, with a prefatory note by Pound. Also rptd in Hulme, Speculations, 1924, below. Contains Mana Aboda and Above the dock, as well as Autumn, Conversion [sic] and The embankment.
Bergson, H. L. An introduction to metaphysics. Authorised trn by Hulme. New York 1912, London 1913.
Sorel, G. Reflections on violence. Authorized trn by Hulme. New York 1914, London 1916 (with introd and bibliography by Hulme), 1925 (omitting introd), Glencoe Ill [1950] (trn corrected by J. Roth, introd by E. A. Shils). Hulme's introd rptd in Speculations, 1924, below.
Poem, abbreviated [?by Ezra Pound] from the conversation of Mr T.E.H.: trenches—St Eloi. In Catholic anthology 1914–15 [ed Pound], 1915. Rptd in Pound, Umbra, 1920.
Fragments, from the note-book of T. E. Hulme who was killed in the war. New Age 6 Oct 1921. Rptd in Further speculations, 1955, below. Verse fragments.
Speculations: essays on humanism and the philosophy of art. Ed H. Read [with some assistance from A. R.

Orage] 1924 [1923], New York 1924, London 1936 (corrected).
Notes on language and style. Ed H. Read, Seattle 1929 (Univ of Washington Chapbooks no 25). First pbd in Criterion 3 1925; a larger selection from Hulme's mss ptd in next.
Three poems; A lecture on modern poetry; Notes on language and style. In 'Michael Roberts', T. E. Hulme, 1938, below. Rptd in next. Includes ms version of A city sunset, first pbd in For Christmas MDCCCCVIII, [1909], above.
Further speculations. Ed S. Hynes, Minneapolis [1955]. Mainly rptd from New Age and Cambridge Mag. Diary from the trenches first pbd here.
Jones, The life and opinions of Hulme, *1960, below, rpts* A Tory philosophy, *first pbd pseudonymously (by 'Thomas Gratton') in* Commentator 4 *1912, and* A personal impression of Bergson, *first pbd pseudonymously ('by T. K. White') in* Saturday Westminster Gazette (*weekly edn*) *no 5771 1911.*

§2
Flint, F. S. The history of Imagism. Egoist 2 1915.
C., R. H. [A. R. Orage]. Readers and writers. New Age 26 Aug 1920. Contains quotations from Hulme's mss not rptd elsewhere.
Tate, J. O. A. Poetry and the absolute. Sewanee Rev 35 1927.
Riding, L. Hulme, the new barbarism & Gertrude Stein. In her Contemporaries and snobs, 1928.
Collin, W. E. Beyond humanism: some notes on Hulme. Sewanee Rev 38 1930.
Hughes, G. In his Imagism and the Imagists, Stanford 1931.
Daniels, J. R. T. S. Eliot and his relation to Hulme. UTQ 2 1933.
Lewis, P. W. 'Hulme of original sin'. In his Blasting & bombardiering, 1937.
'Michael Roberts' (W. E. Roberts). T. E. Hulme. 1938.
Mason, H. A. The T. E. Hulme myth. Scrutiny 7 1938. Essay-review of the above.
Pound, E. This Hulme business. Townsman 2 1939; rptd in Kenner, H., The poetry of Pound, 1951.
Wecter, D. Hulme and the tragic view. Southern Rev 5 1939. Essay-review of Roberts' T. E. Hulme, above.
Daiches, D. Hulme and T. S. Eliot. In his Poetry and the modern world, Chicago 1940.
Epstein, J. Hulme and his friends. In his Let there be sculpture, 1940, 1955 (rev as Epstein: an autobiography).
Hendry, J. F. Hulme as Horatio. Life & Letters Today 35 1942.
Browning, W. R. F. Hulme. Church Quart Rev 145 1947.
Ward, A. Speculations on Eliot's time-world: an analysis of The family reunion in relation to Hulme and Bergson. Amer Lit 21 1949.
Nelson, F. W. Valet to the absolute: a study of the philosophy of Hulme. Univ of Wichita Bull 25 1950.
Coffman, S. K. In his Imagism: a chapter for the history of modern poetry, Norman Oklahoma [1951].
Krieger, M. The ambiguous anti-romanticism of Hulme. ELH 20 1953.
—— Hulme: classicism and the imagination. In his New apologists for poetry, Minneapolis 1956.
Nott, K. Mr Hulme's sloppy dregs. In her The emperor's clothes, 1953.
Read, H. E. The isolation of the image: T. E. Hulme. In his The true voice of feeling, 1953.
Davie, D. Syntax as unpoetical: T. E. Hulme. In his Articulate energy: an inquiry into the syntax of English poetry, 1955.
Bayley, J. Romantic or classic? In his Romantic survival, 1957.
Kermode, J. F. Hulme. In his Romantic image, 1957.

Viebrock, H. Englischer Klassizismus und europäische Kunstrevolution: T. E. Hulme. Akzente 4 1957.

Pulos, C. E. Hulme. In his The new critics and the language of poetry, Lincoln Nebraska 1958.

Williams, R. Interregnum: T. E. Hulme. In his Culture and society 1780–1950, 1958.

Jones, A. R. Hulme, Wilhelm Worringer and the urge to abstraction. Br Jnl of Aesthetics 1 1960.
— The life and opinions of Hulme. 1960.
— Notes towards a history of Imagism: an examination of literary sources. South Atlantic Quart 60 1961; reply 61 1962 by F. MacShane, To establish the facts: a communication on Mr A. R. Jones and Ford Madox Ford. Ford not Hulme was centre of Imagist movement.

Bianchi, R. Fenellosa, Hulme e gli imagisti. Eng Miscellany (Rome) 12 1961.
— Il problema dell' espressione nella filosofia di Hulme. Rivista di Estetica 7 1962.
— Hulme. In his La poetica dell imagismo, Milan 1965.

Fairchild, H. N. Hulme and the Imagists. In his Religious trends in English poetry vol 5 1880–1920: Gods of a changing poetry, New York 1962.

Toppen, W. H. Enkele achtergronden van het werk van T. S. Eliot, vooral in verband met de ideeën van I. Babbitt en Hulme. Groningen 1964.

Ceserani, R. T. E. Hulme. Belfagor 20 1965.

Martin, W. In his The New Age under Orage, Manchester [1967].

Paliwal, B. B. Hulme's poetics. Lit Criterion (Mysore) 8 1967.

Kamerbeek, J. Hulme and German philosophy: Dilthey and Scheler. Jnl of Comparative Lit 21 1969.

Pondrom, C. N. Hulme's A lecture on modern poetry, and the birth of Imagism. Papers on Lang and Lit 5 1969.

ALDOUS LEONARD HUXLEY
1894–1963

See cols 609–17, above.

WILLIAM RALPH INGE
1860–1954

See cols 1261–2, below.

HOLBROOK JACKSON
1874–1948

Selections

Holbrook Jackson. 1927 (Essays of Today and Yesterday).

§1

Edward Fitzgerald and Omar Khayyám: an essay and a bibliography. 1899.

The eternal now: a quatrain sequence and other verses. 1900.

Everychild: a book of verses for children, compiled by Jackson. Leeds [1905]. Includes poems by Jackson.

Bernard Shaw. 1907, Philadelphia 1907, London 1909 (with new preface).

Great English novelists. [1908], Freeport NY 1967.

William Morris: craftsman-socialist. 1908 (Social Reformers Ser), 1926 (rev and enlarged).

The Caradoc Press. Edinburgh 1909. Rptd from Booklover's Mag 8 1909.

Platitudes in the making: precepts and advices for gentlefolk. New York 1910, London 1911.

Great soldiers. By 'George Henry Hart' [i.e. Jackson]. [1911].

Romance and reality: essays and studies. 1911, New York 1912.

All manner of folk: interpretations and studies. 1912.

The eighteen nineties: a review of art and ideas at the close of the nineteenth century. 1913, New York 1914.

Town: an essay. 1913 (priv ptd) (Flying Fame Chapbook 2).

Southward ho! and other essays. [1914] (Wayfarer's Lib), Freeport NY 1968. Selected from Romance and reality and All manner of folk, above, (rev) with 4 new essays.

Brown, F. S. Contingent ditties and other soldier songs of the Great War. Ed Jackson 1915.

Occasions: a volume of essays. 1922, Freeport NY 1969.

A brief survey of printing history and practice. 1923. With S. Morison.

End papers: adventures among ideas and personalities. By 'Bernard Lintot' [i.e. Jackson]. 1923.

The anatomy of bibliomania. 2 vols 1930–1 (48 copies), New York 1931, 1 vol London 1932 (rev).

Burton, R. The anatomy of melancholy. Ed Jackson 3 vols 1932 (EL).

A catalogue for typophiles, preceded by an essay on typophily by H. Jackson. [1932]. Essay rptd as a separate booklet [1945].

The fear of books. 1932, New York 1932.

William Caxton: an essay. 1933 (100 copies, nos 1–68 accompanied by an original Caxton leaf).

Maxims of books and reading. 1934 (400 copies). Booklet; rptd in The reading of books, below.

William Morris and the arts & crafts. Berkeley Heights 1934 (160 copies). Rptd from Book Collectors' Quart no 14 1934.

A cross-section of English printing: the Curwen Press 1918–34. 1935 (75 copies).

The Double Crown Club—early history: fifteenth dinner address delivered by the President, Holbrook Jackson. Edinburgh 1935 (100 copies).

The First Edition Club. Opening speech at an exhibition of Percy Smith's typographical work, 1935. 1936 (priv ptd, 500 copies).

On the printing of books. New York [1937?] (150 copies).

On the use of books. New York [1937?].

The printing of books. 1938, New York 1939. Essays, some previously pbd separately.

The story of Don Vincente. 1939 (Corvinus Press, 60 copies).

The aesthetics of printing: an essay. [1940?].

Bookman's holiday: a recreation for booklovers, designed by H. Jackson. 1945, New York 1947 (as Bookman's pleasure: a recreation for booklovers). Anthology.

Typophily. [1945]. Rptd from A catalogue for typophiles, 1932, above.

The reading of books. 1946, New York 1947.

The complete nonsense of Edward Lear. Ed Jackson 1947.

Morris, W. On art and socialism: essays and lectures. Ed Jackson 1947.

Dreamers of dreams: the rise and fall of 19th-century idealism. 1948, New York [1949?].

Pleasures of reading. 1948 (National Book League Reader's Guide).

William Caxton, the first English printer. Berkeley Heights 1959 (priv ptd, 220 copies).

Ulysses à la Joyce. Berkeley Heights 1961 (priv ptd, 150 copies).

The eighteen-nineties, prelude to the nineteen-hundreds: the recapture of something of a remarkable era. Berkeley Heights 1964 (priv ptd, 60 copies). Rptd from Radio Times 25 Dec 1936.

Letters

XX unpublished letters to Joseph Ishill, with an appreciation by J. Brophy. Berkeley Heights 1960 (priv ptd, 50 copies).

Jackson also pbd a number of pamphlets on printing processes and on the fashion trade and export; and with others some

booklets of prose and verse issued by Flying Fame, *1913.
He also edited* New Age *May–Dec 1907 (jointly with
A. R. Orage) and* The Beau, *1910; he was acting editor of*
T.P.'s Mag *1911–12 and* T.P.'s Weekly *1911–14 and
edited the latter 1914–16; he founded* Today *and edited it
1917–23; with G. K. Chesterton and R. B. Johnson he
edited the* Readers' Classics ser *from 1922.*

§2

More, P. E. Decadent wit. In his With the wits: Shelburne
essays ser 10, Boston 1919.
The Holbrook Jackson library: a memorial catalogue, with
an appreciation by F. Meynell. Bishop's Stortford 1951.

DAVID GWILYM JAMES
1905–68

Scepticism and poetry: an essay on the poetic imagination.
1937, New York 1960.
The Romantic comedy. 1948. On the English Romantic
movement.
The life of reason: Hobbes, Locke, Bolingbroke. 1949,
New York 1949. Vol 1 of a series entitled The English
Augustans. No more pbd.
The dream of learning: an essay on The advancement of
learning, Hamlet and King Lear. Oxford 1951.
The universities and the theatre. Ed James 1952 (Colston
papers vol 4).
Matthew Arnold and the decline of English Romanticism.
Oxford 1961.
The dream of Prospero. Oxford 1967. On The tempest.

MONTAGUE RHODES JAMES
1862–1936

See cols 621–2, above.

REGINALD BRIMLEY JOHNSON
1867–1932

Verse essays. 1890.
Christ's Hospital: recollections of Lamb, Coleridge and
Leigh Hunt, edited by R. B. Johnson, with some account
of its foundation. 1896.
Leigh Hunt. 1896.
The Cambridge colleges. [1909]. Pamphlet.
Towards religion. [1912].
Tennyson and his poetry. 1913.
The women novelists. 1918, Freeport NY 1967.
Some contemporary novelists—women (men). 2 vols
1920–2, Freeport NY 1967–70.
Moral poison in modern fiction. [1922] (Blue Booklets
no 3).
Out of my keeping [sonnets] and A character [essay].
1922.
New study of Jane Austen. In L. Villard, Jane Austen,
1924 (for 1923).
Story lives of xixth-century authors. [1925].
Jane Austen. 1927.
Poems. 1927 (priv ptd, 100 copies).
Jane Austen: her life, her work, her family and her critics.
1930.
Little biographies of Tennyson, Arnold, Butler, Stevenson.
[1931]. This and next item extracted from Story lives of
xixth-century authors, 1925, above.
Little biographies of Thackeray, Eliot, Browning. [1933].
R. B. Johnson founded and edited The Gownsman *(Cam-
bridge Univ), 1912–13; he edited* The English Literature
Library: *a series of group selection; 1928–9; and, with
G. K. Chesterton and H. Jackson, the* Readers' Classics
ser, *1922. He also edited selections from the letters of many*

*English writers, chiefly of the nineteenth century, and also
works of English literature, including a number of school
texts.*

M.P.

SIR GEOFFREY LANGDON KEYNES
b. 1887

Bibliographies

In Geoffrey Keynes: tributes on the occasion of his
seventieth birthday, 1961 (Osler Club). Bibliography by
W. R. Le Fanu from Keynes' own register.

§1

Bibliography of the works of Dr John Donne, Dean of St
Paul's. Cambridge 1914, 1932 (rev), 1958 (rev).
A handlist of the works of John Evelyn. Cambridge 1916
(priv ptd).
A bibliography of William Blake. New York 1921.
A bibliography of Sir Thomas Browne. Cambridge 1924,
Oxford 1968 (rev).
William Pickering, publisher: a memoir and a handlist of
his editions. 1924.
A bibliography of the writings of William Harvey, 1628–
1928. Cambridge 1928, 1953 (rev, as A bibliography of
the writings of Dr William Harvey, 1578–1657).
Jane Austen: a bibliography. 1929.
Bibliography of William Hazlitt. 1931.
The Honourable Robert Boyle: a handlist of his works.
1932 (priv ptd).
John Evelyn: a study in bibliophily and a bibliography of
his writings. Cambridge 1937, New York 1937 (Grolier
Club), Oxford 1968 (rev).
The library of Edward Gibbon: a catalogue of his books.
1940.
John Ray, FRS: a handlist of his works. Cambridge 1944
(priv ptd).
Blake studies: notes on his life and works in seventeen
chapters. 1949.
John Ray: a bibliography. 1951.
William Blake's illuminated books: a census. New York
1953. With E. Wolf. Rev edn of section of Keynes'
bibliography of Blake, 1921.
A bibliography of Rupert Brooke. 1954, 1959 (rev) (Soho
Bibliographies).
Engravings by William Blake—the separate plates: a cata-
logue raisonnée. Dublin 1956.
William Blake's illustrations to the Bible. [Clairvaux]
1957 (506 copies). A catalogue compiled by Keynes.
A bibliography of Dr Robert Hooke. Oxford 1960.
A bibliography of Siegfried Sassoon. 1962 (Soho Biblio-
graphies).
Dr Timothie Bright, 1550–1615: a survey of his life with
a bibliography of his writings. 1962.
Bibliotheca bibliographici: a catalogue of the library formed
by Geoffrey Keynes. 1964.
A study of the illuminated books of William Blake, poet,
printer, prophet. Paris 1964 (525 copies), New York
1964, London 1965.
The life of William Harvey. Oxford 1966.
Henry James in Cambridge. Cambridge 1967.

Editions

The commonplace book of Elizabeth Lyttelton, daughter
of Sir Thomas Browne. Cambridge 1919 (54 copies).
Letters of Hugh Stanley Wilson to his family and friends.
Cambridge 1919 (priv ptd). With Cosmo Gordon.
Donne, J. Paradoxes and problemes. 1923.
—— X sermons. 1923. Selected by Keynes.
The writings of William Blake. 3 vols 1925.
Evelyn, J. Memoires for my grand-son. 1926.
Milton's poems in English with illustrations by William
Blake. 2 vols 1926.

Poetry and prose of William Blake. 1927, 1927 (rev), 1932 (rev).

The anatomical exercises of Dr William Harvey: De motu cordis, 1628; De circulatione sanguinis, 1649. [1928]. The English text of 1653.

The works of Sir Thomas Browne. 6 vols 1928–31, 4 vols 1964, Chicago 1964. Vol 5, Miscellaneous writings, and vol 6, The letters, reissued separately 1946.

Walton, I. The compleat angler [and other works]. 1929. The compleat angler rptd New York 1947.

Selected essays of William Hazlitt 1778–1830. 1930.

Evelyn, J. Directions for the gardiner at Says-Court but which may be of use for other gardens. 1932.

Letters between Samuel Butler and Miss E. M. A. Savage, 1871–85. 1935. With B. Hill.

The notebook of William Blake called the Rossetti Manuscript. 1935.

Browne, T. Religio Medici. Eugene Oregon 1939.

—— Religio Medici and Christian morals. 1940.

Brooke, R. Democracy and the arts. 1946.

—— The poetical works. 1946, 1947 (rev).

The apologie and treatise of Ambroise Paré containing the voyages made into divers places with many of his writings upon surgery. 1951.

Keynes, J. M. Essays in biography. 1951. (2nd edn, with 3 additional essays).

Samuel Butler's notebooks. 1951. Selections, with B. Hill.

The letters of William Blake. 1956.

The complete writings of William Blake with all the variant readings. 1957, New York 1957, London 1966 (with addns and corrections).

The letters of Rupert Brooke. 1968.

Selected writings by Sir Thomas Browne. 1968.

Keynes edited much of Blake's graphic work, provided introds or bibliographical notes to Blakes facs, including the Trianon Press ser, and to reprints or facs of works by Donne, Evelyn, Thomas Fuller, Herbert, Osler and Samuel Palmer. He also pbd a number of medical works.

§2

Geoffrey Keynes: tributes on the occasion of his seventieth birthday. 1961.

Oates, J. C. T. Sir Geoffrey Keynes. (Contemporary Collectors XXXIX). Book Collector 13 1964.

N.J.S.

'HUGH KINGSMILL', HUGH KINGSMILL LUNN
1889–1949

§1

The will to love by H. K. Lunn. 1919. Fiction.

The dawn's delay. 1924. 3 short novels.

Blondel. 1927. Fiction.

Matthew Arnold. 1928, New York 1928.

After Puritanism 1850–1900. 1929. On F. W. Farrar, Samuel Butler, Frank Harris, W. T. Stead.

The return of William Shakespeare. [1929], Indianapolis [1929]. Fiction.

Behind both lines. 1930. War-time reminiscences.

Frank Harris. 1932, New York [1932].

Samuel Johnson. [1933], New York 1934.

The Casanova fable: a satirical revaluation. 1934. With W. A. Gerhardie.

The sentimental journey: a life of Charles Dickens. 1934, New York 1935.

Skye high: the record of a tour through Scotland in the wake of Johnson and Boswell. 1937, New York 1938. With H. Pearson.

D. H. Lawrence. 1938, New York [1938] (as The life of D. H. Lawrence).

The fall. 1940. Fiction.

This blessed plot. 1942. Travel in England and Ireland. With H. Pearson.

The poisoned crown. 1944. Studies of Queen Elizabeth, Cromwell, Napoleon, Lincoln.

Talking of Dick Whittington. 1947. Travel in Southern England. With H. Pearson.

The progress of a biographer. 1949. Collected literary criticism.

Kingsmill edited the following anthologies: Invective and abuse; The worst of love; The English genius; Parents & children; Courage; Made on earth: a panorama of marriage; What they said at the time; The high hill of the muses. *He edited* Johnson without Boswell: a contemporary portrait of Johnson, *and pbd 3 books of parodies (one with M. Muggeridge). He was literary editor of* Punch *1939–45 and of* New Eng Rev *1945–9.*

§2

Pearson, H. and M. Muggeridge. About Kingsmill. 1951.

Holroyd, M. Kingsmill: a critical biography. Introd by M. Muggeridge 1964.

A.P.H

GEORGE WILSON KNIGHT
b. 1897

Some unpbd works on Shakespeare are held in the Shakespeare Memorial Library. See preface to The sovereign flower, *1958, below.*

Bibliographies

Van Domelen, J. E. A select list of the published writings of Knight. In The morality of art: essays presented to Knight, ed D. W. Jefferson, 1969.

§1

Myth and miracle: an essay on the mystic symbolism of Shakespeare. [1929], Folcroft Pa 1969. Rptd with additional notes in The crown of life, 1947, below.

The wheel of fire: essays in interpretation of Shakespeare's sombre tragedies. 1930, 1949 (rev with 3 new essays), New York 1949, London 1954 (corrected). Introd by T. S. Eliot.

The imperial theme: further interpretations of Shakespeare's tragedies, including the Roman plays. 1931, 1951 (with new preface), 1954 [1955] (corrected), New York 1961.

The Shakespearian tempest. 1932, 1953 (with new preface and a chart of Shakespeare's dramatic universe).

The Christian renaissance, with interpretations of Dante, Shakespeare and Goethe and a note on T. S. Eliot. Toronto 1933, London 1962 (rev with 'new discussions of Oscar Wilde and the Gospel of Thomas', and omitting note on T. S. Eliot), New York 1962.

Shakespeare and Tolstoy. 1934 (English Assoc pamphlet). Rptd as Tolstoy's attack on Shakespeare in the Wheel of fire, 1949 edn, above.

Atlantic crossing: an autobiographical design. 1936.

Principles of Shakespearian production, with especial reference to the tragedies. 1936, 1949 (with new preface), 1964 (rev, with addns, as Shakespearian production, with especial reference to the tragedies), Evanston Ill 1964.

The burning oracle: studies in the poetry of action. 1939.

This sceptred isle: Shakespeare's message for England at war. Oxford 1940, Folcroft Pa 1969. Booklet.

The starlit dome: studies in the poetry of vision. 1941, 1959 (corrected, with an introd by W. F. J. Knight and an appendix on spiritualism and poetry), New York 1960.

Chariot of wrath: the message of John Milton to democracy at war. 1942. Rptd (abridged) in Poets of action, 1968, below.

The olive and the sword: a study of England's Shakespeare. 1944, Rptd (abridged) as This sceptred isle in The sovereign flower, 1958, below.

The dynasty of Stowe. 1945. On Stowe and Stowe School, in part autobiographical.

Hiroshima: on prophecy and the sun-bomb. 1946.

The crown of life: essays in interpretation of Shakespeare's final plays. 1947, 1952 (corrected), 1958 (corrected), New York 1964.

Christ and Nietzsche: an essay in poetic wisdom. 1948.

Lord Byron: Christian virtues. 1952, New York 1953.

The last of the Incas: a play on the conquest of Peru. Leeds 1954.

Laureate of peace: on the genius of Alexander Pope. 1954, New York 1955, 1965 (corrected, as The poetry of Pope, laureate of peace).

The mutual flame: on Shakespeare's Sonnets and The phoenix and the turtle. 1955.

Lord Byron's marriage: the evidence of asterisks. 1957, New York 1957.

The sovereign flower: on Shakespeare as the poet of royalism, together with related essays and indexes to earlier volumes [on Shakespeare]. 1958, New York 1958.

The golden labyrinth: a study of British drama. 1962, New York 1962.

Ibsen. Edinburgh 1962, New York 1963 (as Henrik Ibsen) (Writers and Critics).

The saturnian quest: a chart of the prose works of John Cowper Powys. 1964 (for 1965), New York 1964.

Byron and Shakespeare. 1966, New York 1966.

Shakespeare and religion: essays of forty years. 1967, New York 1967.

Gold dust, with other poetry. 1968, New York [1968].

Poets of action: incorporating essays from The burning oracle. 1968.

§2

Babcock, R. W. The White Knight as critic: Mr G. Wilson Knight's criticism of Shakespeare. Sewanee Rev 42 1934.

Fausset, H. I'A. Post-Renaissance man. In his Poets and pundits, 1947. Essay-review of the Burning oracle, 1939.

Jones, J. Shakespeare and Knight. Listener 9 Dec 1954.

Rodway, A. E. and G. Salgado. The school of Knight. EC 4 1954. Reply, G. W. Knight; comment, F. W. Bateson, ibid.

Schoff, F. C. Hamlet and his critics: III, The 'New critics'. Discourse 5 1962. On the Wheel of fire, 1930.

Kaufmann, R. J. Remembering Dionysus: the achievement of Knight. Educational Theatre Jnl 15 1963.

Weitz, M. In his Hamlet and the philosophy of literary criticism, Chicago 1964.

Palmer, D. J. G. W. Knight. Critical Survey 2 1965.

Sale, R. G. W. Knight. MLQ 29 1968.

Berry, F. Knight: stage and study. In The morality of art: essays presented to Knight, ed D. W. Jefferson, 1969.

LIONEL CHARLES KNIGHTS
b. 1906

§1

How many children had Lady Macbeth?: an essay in the theory and practice of Shakespeare criticism. Cambridge 1933. Rptd (rev) in Explorations, 1946, below.

Drama and society in the age of Jonson. 1937, New York 1951.

Explorations: essays in criticism, mainly on the literature of the seventeenth century. 1946, New York 1947.

Some Shakespearean themes. 1959, Stanford 1960.

An approach to Hamlet. 1960, Stanford 1961.

Metaphor and symbol. Ed L. C. Knights, B. Cottle 1960 (Colston papers vol 12). Knights' paper Idea and symbol: some hints from Coleridge rptd in Further explorations, 1965, below.

William Shakespeare: the historics, Richard III, King John, Richard II, Henry V. 1962, 1965 (rev) (Br Council pamphlet).

Further explorations. 1965, Stanford 1965.

Knights was on the editorial board of Scrutiny *1932–53 and a frequent contributor.*

§2

Bateson, F. W. Second thoughts II: L. C. Knights and Restoration comedy. EC 7 1957. On Restoration comedy: the reality and the myth, in Explorations, 1946.

Everett, B. The figure in Professor Knights' carpet. CQ 2 1960. Essay-review of Some Shakespearean themes, 1959.

Bailey, J. The critic as explorer. Spectator 30 April 1965. Essay-review of Further explorations, 1965.

M.P.

EDMUND GEORGE VALPY KNOX
1881–1971
See col 295, above.

RONALD ARBUTHNOTT KNOX
1888–1957
See cols 1268–71, below.

OSBERT LANCASTER
b. 1908

Except for Our sovereigns, *all Lancaster's books are illustr by the author.*

Our sovereigns: from Alfred to Edward VIII. 1936, 1937 (to George VI).

Progress at Pelvis Bay. 1936. Satirical essay in architectural history.

Pillar to post: the pocket lamp of architecture. 1938, New York 1939, London 1956 (enlarged). *See also* Here, of all places, 1958, *and* A cartoon history of architecture, 1964, below.

Homes sweet homes. 1939, 1953 (enlarged, as Home sweet homes). Interior decoration. *See also* Here, of all places, 1958, and A cartoon history of architecture, 1964, below.

Classical landscape with figures. 1947, Boston 1949. Travel in Greece.

The Saracen's head: or the reluctant crusader. 1948, Boston 1949. Children's tale.

Drayneflete revealed. 1949, Boston 1950 (as There'll always be a Drayneflete). Satirical essay in architectural history.

Façades and faces. 1950.

All done from memory. 1953, Boston 1953. Autobiography.

Here, of all places. Boston 1958, London [1959] (as Here, of all places: the pocket lamp of architecture, incorporating Homes sweet homes and Pillar to post, and homes across the Atlantic). Architecture and interior decoration in England and the US.

A cartoon history of architecture. Introd by J. Coolidge, Boston 1964. Parts of this book originally pbd in Pillar to post, Homes sweet homes, and Here, of all places, above.

With an eye to the future. 1967, Boston 1967. Autobiography.

Sailing to Byzantium: an architectural companion. 1969, Boston 1969.

Lancaster has been cartoonist with Daily Express *since 1939, publishing selections of the cartoons beginning with* Pocket cartoons, *1940.*

JAMES LAVER
b. 1899

Selections

Ladies' mistakes. 1933, New York 1934. Contains Cupid's changeling; A stitch in time; Love's progress. Poems.

§1

Cervantes: the Newdigate Prize poem, 1921. Oxford [1921].

His last Sebastian, and other poems. 1922.

Portraits in oil and vinegar: studies of contemporary English artists. 1925.

The young man dances, and other poems. 1925.

A stitch in time: or pride prevents a fall. 1927. Poem.

English costume of the nineteenth century. 1929.

A history of British and American etching. 1929.

Love's progress: or the education of Araminta. 1929. Poem.

Macrocosmos: a poem. 1929.

Vera Willoughby, illustrator of books: an appreciation. 1929. Pamphlet.

A complete catalogue of the etchings and dry-points of Arthur Briscoe. 1930.

Whistler. 1930, New York 1930.

English costume of the eighteenth century. 1931, New York 1958.

Nymph errant. 1932, New York 1932. Fiction.

Wesley. 1932, New York 1933.

Background for Venus. 1934, New York 1935. Fiction.

Winter wedding: a decoration. [1934]. Poem.

The laburnum tree and other stories. 1935. Rptd in 24 short stories by Graham Greene, Laver and S. T. Warner, [1939].

Panic among Puritans. 1936, New York [1936]. Fiction.

'Vulgar society': the romantic career of James Tissot 1836–1902. 1936.

French painting and the nineteenth century. 1937.

Taste and fashion from the French Revolution until to-day. 1937, 1945 (rev, with ch on fashion and the Second World War).

Nostradamus: or the future foretold. 1942 [1941]. Biography.

A letter to a girl on the future of clothes. 1946. Pamphlet.

Hatchards of Piccadilly 1797–1947. 1947.

Style in costume. 1949.

Dress: how and why fashions in men's and women's clothes have changed during the past two hundred years. 1950.

Drama: its costume and décor. 1951.

Clothes. 1952, New York 1953.

The first decadent: being the strange life of J. K. Huysmans. 1954, New York 1955.

Oscar Wilde. 1954 (Br Council pamphlet).

Costume. 1963, New York 1964.

Museum piece: or the education of an iconographer. 1963, Boston 1964. Autobiography.

Costume in the theatre. 1964, New York 1965.

Women's dress in the Jazz Age. 1964.

The age of optimism: manners and morals 1848–1914. [1966], New York [1966] (as Manners and morals in the age of optimism 1848–1914).

Victoriana. [1966], New York 1967. Art history.

Dandies. 1968.

A concise history of costume. 1969, New York 1969.

Modesty in dress: an inquiry into the fundamentals of fashion. 1969, Boston 1969.

Laver also wrote a number of plays, monographs on country houses and a few children's books. He compiled several illustrated books on costume and fashion, stage design, posters etc; vols of reproductions of individual artists; and various art and period anthologies. He edited Baudelaire, Charles Churchill, the series Pleiades art books (*1946–*) *and* Costume of the western world (*1951–*).

J.G.

DAVID HERBERT LAWRENCE
1885–1930

See cols 481–503, above.

FRANK RAYMOND LEAVIS
b. 1895

Bibliographies

McKenzie, D. F. and M-P. Allum. F. R. Leavis: a checklist, 1924–64. 1966. Includes indications of textual changes and a selection of secondary material.

Selections

The importance of Scrutiny: selections from Scrutiny, a quarterly review, 1932–48. Ed E. Bentley, New York 1948.

A selection from Scrutiny, compiled by Leavis. 2 vols Cambridge 1968.

§1

Mass civilization and minority culture. Cambridge 1930 (Minority pamphlet 1); rptd in For continuity, 1933, and in Education and the university, 1948 edn, below.

D. H. Lawrence. Cambridge 1930 (Minority pamphlet 6); rptd in For continuity, 1933, below.

New bearings in English poetry: a study of the contemporary situation. 1932, 1950 (adds Retrospect 1950), New York 1950, London 1954 (with textual changes).

How to teach reading: a primer for Ezra Pound. Cambridge 1932; rptd in Education and the university, 1943, below.

For continuity. Cambridge 1933, Freeport NY 1968. Essays, mainly first pbd in Scrutiny or as Minority pamphlets.

Culture and environment: the training of critical awareness. 1933, 1934 (with textual changes). With D. Thompson.

Towards standards of criticism: selections from The calendar of modern letters, 1925–7, chosen and with an introduction by Leavis. 1933.

Determinations: critical essays. Ed with introd by Leavis. 1934. Includes The irony of Swift first pbd in Scrutiny.

Revaluation: tradition and development in English poetry. 1936, New York 1947, London 1964 (with textual changes). All chs, except that on Pope, first pbd, without the Notes, in Scrutiny.

Education and the university: a sketch for an 'English school'. 1943, 1948 (adds Mass civilization and minority culture), New York 1948. Most chs first pbd in Scrutiny. Includes How to teach reading.

The great tradition: George Eliot, Henry James, Joseph Conrad. 1948, New York 1948, London 1960 (with textual changes). Apart from title essay and appendix, first pbd in Scrutiny.

Mill on Bentham and Coleridge. 1950, New York 1951. With introd by Leavis. First pbd in Scrutiny 16 1949 (as Mill, Beatrice Webb and the 'English school').

The common pursuit. 1952, New York 1952, London 1962 (with textual changes). Essays, mainly first pbd in Scrutiny.

D. H. Lawrence, novelist. 1955, New York 1956 (ptd from uncorrected proof sheets of the English edn), London 1957 (with textual changes), 1962 (with textual changes). Most of the chs first pbd in Scrutiny.

Two cultures?: the significance of C. P. Snow. Richmond lecture 1962, with an essay on Snow's Rede lecture by M. Yudkin. 1962, New York 1963 (with a new preface for the American reader). First pbd in Spectator 9 March 1962; a letter by Leavis to Spectator 16 March corrects misprints in this text.

Scrutiny: a retrospect. Cambridge 1963; also ptd in Scrutiny (reissue) 20 1963.

Anna Karenina and other essays. 1967, New York [1967]. Includes previously pbd introds to works by others.

English literature in our time and the university. 1969 (Clark lectures).

Lectures in America. 1969, New York 1969. With Q.D. Leavis.

A list of Leavis's contributions to books and journals (including letters) is contained in McKenzie and Allum's check list. He was the principal editor of Scrutiny *1932–53. A letter by Leavis to* TLS *2 Sept 1955 disclaims authorship of any part of* C. Gilliard's *History of Switzerland: with concluding pages by F. R. Leavis, 1955.*

§2

Sitwell, E. In her Aspects of modern poetry, 1934.

Wellek, R. Literary criticism and philosophy. Scrutiny 5 1937. Criticism of Revaluation.

— The literary criticism of Leavis. In Literary views: critical and historical, ed C. Camden, Chicago 1964.

McLuhan, H. M. Poetic v. rhetorical exegesis: the case for Leavis against Richards and Empson. Sewanee Rev 52 1944.

Mason, H. A. Leavis and Scrutiny. Critic 1 1947.

Greenberg, M. The influence of Mr Leavis. Partisan Rev 16 1949.

Trilling, L. The moral tradition. New Yorker 24 Sept 1949; rptd in his Gathering of fugitives, Boston 1956 (as Leavis and the moral tradition).

— Science, literature and culture: a comment on the Leavis–Snow controversy. Commentary 33 1962; rptd in his Beyond culture: essays on life and literature, New York 1965 (as The Leavis–Snow controversy). Reply by M. B. Green, Lionel Trilling and the two cultures, in his Science and the shabby curate of poetry: essays about the two cultures, 1964.

Gregor, I. The criticism of Leavis. Dublin Rev 457 1952.

Jarrett-Kerr, M. The literary criticism of Leavis. EC 2 1952.

Stein, W. F. R. Leavis. Northern Miscellany of Literary Criticism 1 1953.

Heyl, B. C. The absolutism of Leavis. Jnl of Aesthetics & Art Criticism 13 1954.

Liddell, R. Lawrence and Leavis: the case of St Mawr. EC 4 1954.

Lerner, L. D. The life and death of Scrutiny. London Mag 2 1955.

Cronin, A. A massacre of authors: Leavis and recent criticism. Encounter 6 1956.

Holloway, J. The new 'establishment' in criticism. Listener 20, 27 Sept 1956; rptd with addns in his Charted mirror, 1960.

Nury, D. Scrutiny: a quarterly review, 1932–53. Etudes Anglaises 20 1956.

Robson, W. W. Literary studies. Univ Quart 10 1956; reply by Leavis, Univ Quart 11 1957; reply by Robson, Mr Leavis on literary studies, ibid (rptd in his Critical essays, 1966).

Traversi, D. Leavis and the case of D. H. Lawrence. Month 15 1956.

Davie, D. Leavis' How to teach reading. EC 7 1957.

Priestley, J. B. Leavis. In his Thoughts in the wilderness, 1957.

Vivas, E. Leavis on D. H. Lawrence. Sewanee Rev 65 1957.

Williams, R. Leavis. In his Culture and society, 1780–1950, 1958.

—, R. J. Kaufmann and A. Jones. Our debt to Leavis (symposium). CQ 1 1959.

Buckley, V. Poetry and morality: studies on the criticism of Arnold, Eliot and Leavis. 1959.

— Leavis and his 'line'. Critical Rev 8 1965.

Fraser, J. A tribute to Leavis. Western Rev 23 1959.

Green, M. B. British decency: 1, Leavis. Kenyon Rev 21 1959.

— In his A mirror for Anglo-Saxons, 1961. Includes previous item.

— A literary defence of the two cultures. CQ 4 1962; rptd in his Science and the shabby curate of poetry: essays about the two cultures, 1964.

Grigson, G. Leavis against Eliot. Encounter 12 1959.

Dyson, A. E. The new puritanism: Leavis and the universities. Times Educational Suppl 19 Aug 1960.

Putt, S. G. Technique and culture: three Cambridge portraits. ES 14 1961.

— The Snow–Leavis rumpus. Antioch Rev 23 1963.

Steiner, G. Men and ideas: Leavis. Encounter 10 1962; rptd in his Language and silence, 1967.

Watson, G. In his Literary critics, 1962, 1964 (rev).

Betsky, S. Scrutiny rescrutinized. Univ Quart 18 1963.

Coulson, P. The attack on Leavis. EC 13 1963; reply by F. Kermode, rejoinder by P. Coulson, ibid.

Enright, D. J. Thirty years on: reflections on the reprinting of Scrutiny, 1963. Rptd in his Conspirators and poets, 1966.

Leavis: some aspects of his work. Ed C. D. Narasimhaiah, [Mysore 1963]. Contains: C. D. Narasimhaiah, Better literary history and better literary criticism: the work of Leavis and how it strikes an Indian; S. Betsky, Integrity in criticism: Leavis and Scrutiny in perspective; W. Walsh, Critical practice and educational ideals: the work of Leavis; J. C. F. Littlewood, Leavis, Lawrence and the state of criticism; Appendix F. R. Leavis, A note on the critical function.

Strickland, G. The question of tone: reflections on the Leavis–Snow controversy. Delta 30 1963.

Black, M. The third realm: an expository essay on Scrutiny. Use of English 16 1964.

EC 14 1964. Contains: S. A. Dawson, Scrutiny and the Idea of a university; F. W. Bateson, The alternative to Scrutiny; K. Trodd, Report from the younger generation; G. W. Knight, Scrutiny and criticism; J. Vaizey, Scrutiny and education.

Kenner, H. A monument to a great critic. Virginia Quart Rev 40 1964.

Mills, A. R. The Portrait of a lady and Leavis. EC 14 1964.

Trodd, K. Scrutiny in the thirties. Review (Oxford) 11–12 1964; reply by G. R. Jackson, Mr Trodd and Scrutiny, EC 14 1964.

Walsh, W. A sharp, unaccommodating voice: the criticism of Leavis. In his Human idiom: literature and humanity, 1964.

De Ville, D. Leavis: the apotheosis of the critic. Hexagon 1 1965.

F. R. Leavis: the modern mind. Current Affairs Bull 21 June 1965.

Singh, G. S. Better history and better criticism: the significance of Leavis. Eng Miscellany (Rome) 16 1965.

Casey, J. Object, feeling and judgment: Leavis. In his The language of criticism, 1966.

Gomme, A. The limits of relevance. In his Attitudes to criticism, Carbondale 1966.

Hand, H. E. The paper curtain: the divided world of Snow and Leavis revisited. Jnl of Human Relations (Wilberforce Ohio) 14 1966.

Levin, H. In his Refractions, New Year 1966.

Deurbergue, J. Leavis: esquisse d'un portrait critique. Recherches Anglaises et Américaines 1 1967.

Gersh, G. The moral imperatives of Leavis. Antioch Rev 28 1968. Essay-review.

Gross, J. In his Rise and fall of the man of letters, 1969.

QUEENIE DOROTHY LEAVIS
née ROTH

Selections

A selection from Scrutiny, compiled by F. R. Leavis. 2 vols Cambridge 1968.

§1

Fiction and the reading public. 1932, New York 1965.
Lectures in America. 1969, New York 1969. With F. R. Leavis. Q. D. Leavis, A fresh approach to Wuthering Heights.
Mrs Leavis was a frequent contributor to Scrutiny *and has written a number of introds to novels by Jane Austen and others.*

§2

Eliot, T. S. A commentary. Criterion 11 1932. On Fiction and the reading public, 1932.
Southam, B. C. Mrs Leavis and Miss Austen: the 'critical theory' reconsidered. Nineteenth-Century Fiction 17 1962.
Ricks, C. Fiction and the reading public. Listener 2 June 1966.

M.P.

RUDOLPH JOHN FREDERICK LEHMANN
b. 1907

See col 297, above.

JAMES BLAIR LEISHMAN
1902–63

§1

The metaphysical poets: Donne, Herbert, Vaughan, Traherne. Oxford 1934, New York 1963.
The monarch of wit: an analytical and comparative study of the poetry of John Donne. 1951.
Themes and variations in Shakespeare's sonnets. 1961.
The art of Marvell's poetry. 1966, New York 1968.
Milton's minor poems. Ed G. Tillotson 1969.
Leishman was a translator, especially of Rilke (the Duino elegies, *with S. Spender), also of Hölderlin and Horace. He edited the* Three Parnassus plays, 1598–1601, *1949.*

§2

Butt, J. J. B. Leishman. Proc Br Acad 49 1963; rptd in Milton's minor poems, 1969 above.

H.M.R.

CECIL DAY-LEWIS
1904–72

See cols 253–6, above.

CLIVE STAPLES LEWIS
1898–1963

The ms of The Screwtape letters, 1942, is held in the Berg Collection, New York Public Library.

Bibliographies

Hooper, W. In Light on Lewis, ed J. Gibb 1965. Includes some verse not collected in Poems, 1964.

Selections

Kilby, C. S. (ed). A mind awake: an anthology of Lewis. 1968.
Selected literary essays. Ed W. Hooper, Cambridge 1969.

§1

Spirits in bondage: a cycle of lyrics, by 'Clive Hamilton' [i.e. C. S. Lewis]. 1919.
Dymer. By 'Clive Hamilton'. 1926, New York 1926, London 1950 (as by C. S. Lewis, with a preface), New York 1950; rptd in Narrative poems, 1969, below.
The pilgrim's regress: an allegorical apology for Christianity, reason and Romanticism. 1933, 1943 (rev with a preface on Romanticism), New York 1944. The poems rptd in Poems, 1964, below.
The allegory of love: a study in medieval tradition. 1936, New York 1936, London 1938 (corrected).
Out of the silent planet. 1938, New York 1949. Vol 1 of trilogy.
Rehabilitations and other essays. 1939, New York 1939.
The personal heresy: a controversy [between] E. M. W. Tillyard and Lewis. 1939, New York 1939. On the relation between poetry and the personality of the poet.
The problem of pain. 1940 (Christian Challenge ser), New York 1944.
The Screwtape letters. 1942, New York 1944, London 1961 (enlarged, with a new preface) (as The Screwtape letters and Screwtape proposes a toast), New York 1962. Preface and Screwtape proposes a toast rptd in Screwtape proposes a toast and other pieces, 1965, below.
A preface to Paradise lost. 1942, New York 1942. Lectures.
Broadcast talks: reprinted with some alterations from two series of broadcast talks (Right and wrong: a clue to the meaning of the universe and What Christians believe) given in 1941 and 1942. 1942, New York 1943 (as The case for Christianity); rptd (rev) in Mere Christianity, 1952, below.
The weight of glory. 1942 (Little Books on Religion). First pbd in Theology 23 1941 and rptd in Transposition and other addresses, 1949, and in They asked for a paper, 1962, below.
Christian behaviour: a further series of broadcast talks. 1943, New York 1943. Rev versions of broadcast talks with 4 additional essays; rptd (rev) in Mere Christianity, 1952, below.
Perelandra. 1943, New York 1944, London 1953 (as Voyage to Venus). Vol 2 of trilogy.
The abolition of man: or reflections on education with special reference to the teaching of English in the upper forms of schools. 1943, New York 1947. Lectures.
Beyond personality: the Christian idea of God. 1944, New York 1945. Rev versions of broadcast talks; rptd (rev) in Mere Christianity, 1952, below.
That hideous strength: a modern fairy-tale for grown-ups. 1945, New York 1946, London 1955 (abridged by Lewis, with a new preface). Vol 3 of trilogy.
George Macdonald: an anthology. Ed Lewis 1946. Preface rptd (abridged) in G. Macdonald, Phantastes and Lilith, 1962.
The great divorce: a dream. 1945 (for 1946), New York 1946 (as The great divorce).
Miracles: a preliminary study. 1947, New York 1947, 1958 (abridged), London 1960 (ch 3 rev).
Vivisection. Boston [1947] (foreword by G. R. Farnum), London [1948] (foreword by R. Fielding-Ould).
Arthurian torso: The figure of Arthur by Charles Williams and a commentary on the Arthurian poems of Charles Williams by C. S. Lewis. 1948, New York 1948.
Transposition and other addresses. 1949, New York 1949 (as The weight of glory and other addresses).
The lion, the witch and the wardrobe: a story for children. 1950, New York 1950.

Prince Caspian: the return to Narnia. 1951, New York
1951. Sequel to above.
Mere Christianity: a revised and amplified edition, with
a new introduction, of the three books Broadcast talks,
Christian behaviour and Beyond personality. 1952,
New York 1952.
The voyage of the Dawn Treader. 1952, New York 1952.
For children.
The silver chair. 1953, New York 1953. For children.
The horse and his boy. 1954, New York 1954. For
children.
English literature in the sixteenth century, excluding
drama: the completion of the Clark lectures, 1944.
Oxford 1954 (OHEL 3).
The magician's nephew. 1955, New York 1955. For
children.
Surprised by joy: the shape of my early life. 1955, New
York 1956.
The last battle: a story for children. 1956, New York
1956.
Till we have faces: a myth retold. 1956, New York 1957.
Reflections on the Psalms. 1958, New York 1958.
Shall we lose God in outer space? 1959; rptd in The
world's last night and other essays, 1960, below, as
Religion and rocketry.
The four loves. 1960, New York 1960.
Studies in words. Cambridge 1960, 1967 (enlarged).
Based on lectures.
The world's last night and other essays. New York [1960].
A grief observed. By 'N. W. Clerk' [i.e. C. S. Lewis].
1961, Greenwich Conn 1963, London 1964 (as by C. S.
Lewis).
An experiment in criticism. Cambridge 1961.
They asked for a paper: papers and addresses. 1962.
Letters to Malcolm, chiefly on prayer. 1964, New York
1964. Chs 15–17 first priv ptd New York [1963] (as
Beyond the bright blur).
The discarded image: an introduction to medieval and
renaissance literature. Cambridge 1964. Based on
lectures.
Poems. Ed W. Hooper 1964, New York 1965. Includes
poems in The pilgrim's regress, 1933, but not Spirits in
bondage, 1919, or Dymer, 1926. Appendix lists previous
pbn of poems already ptd.
Screwtape proposes a toast and other pieces. 1965. A slip
of the tongue first pbd in book form here.
Of other worlds: essays and stories. Ed W. Hooper 1966.
Includes essays on fiction, especially children's and
science fiction, 2 short stories rptd from the Magazine of
Fantasy & Science Fiction, and a fragment of an unfinished novel.
Studies in medieval and renaissance literature, collected by
W. Hooper. Cambridge 1966.
Christian reflections. Ed W. Hooper 1967. Contains,
apart from Christianity and literature, essays not pre-
viously pbd in book form.
Spenser's images of life. Ed A. D. S. Fowler. Cambridge
1967.
Narrative poems. Ed W. Hooper 1969. Dymer; Launce-
lot; The nameless isle; The queen of the drum.

Letters

Letters of Lewis. Ed W. H. Lewis 1966, New York 1966.
With memoir.
Letters to an American lady. Ed C. S. Kilby, Grand
Rapids 1967.
Mark vs. Tristram: correspondence between Lewis and
O. Barfield. Ed W. Hooper, Cambridge Mass 1967
(126 copies).
C. S. Lewis's many contributions in verse and prose to
periodicals, jnls and newspapers are listed in W. Hooper's
bibliography, above. With D. Nichol Smith Lewis was
general editor of Oxford English Monographs from 1940
and he was general editor of Nelson's Medieval and
Renaissance Lib from 1959.

§ 2

A history of romantic love: Provençal sentiment in
English poetry. TLS 6 June 1936. Essay-review of The
allegory of love, 1936. For other essay-reviews see
O. Elton, MÆ 6 1937; V. S. M. Fraser, Criterion 16
1937; K. Tillotson, RES 13 1937; G. M. Young, Love-
in-the-mist, in his Daylight and champaign, 1937.
Knights, L. C. Lewis and the status quo. Scrutiny 8 1939.
Essay-review of Rehabilitations, 1939.
Theology 39–41 1939–40. Controversy between Lewis,
S. L. Bethell, E. F. Carritt and G. Every on Christian-
ity and culture. Lewis' contribution rptd in his Christian
reflections, 1967, above.
Garrod, H. W. Lewis on Paradise lost. Oxford Mag 19
Nov 1942. Essay-review of A preface to Paradise lost,
1942. For other essay-reviews see H. J. C. Grierson,
MLR 38 1943; L. C. Knights, Milton again, Scrutiny 11
1942; E. E. Stoll, Give the Devil his due: a reply to
Lewis, RES 20 1944.
Brady, C. A. Introduction to Lewis. America 27 May,
10 June 1944.
— Finding God in Narnia. America 27 Oct 1956.
Hartshorne, C. Philosophy and orthodoxy. Ethics 54
1944. Essay-review of The problem of pain, 1940 and
Broadcast talks, 1942.
Lee, E. G. Lewis and some modern theologians. 1944
(Religion in a Changing World 2).
Meyers, E. O. The religious works of Lewis. Theology
Today 1 1944.
Allen, E. L. The theology of Lewis. Modern Churchman
34 1945.
Hamm, V. M. Lewis in Perelandra. Thought 20 1945.
Johnson, M. E. Dialogues of devils. Congregational Quart
23 1945. Comparison between The Screwtape letters,
1942, and J. Macgowan's Infernal conference, 1862.
Churchill, R. C. Lewis as an evangelist. Modern Church-
man 35 1946.
Dock, E. K. T. Lewis's theology. Scrutiny 14 1946.
Essay-review of The great divorce, 1945.
Haldane, J. B. S. Auld Hornie, FRS. Modern Quart 1
1946. On the science-fiction trilogy; rptd in Hillegas,
1969, below. See A reply to Professor Haldane, in
Lewis's Of other worlds, 1966, above.
— God and Lewis. Rationalist Annual for the Year 1948.
Essay-review of Broadcast talks, 1942.
Gilbert, A. H. Critics of Lewis on Milton's Satan. South
Atlantic Quart 47 1948.
Socratic Digest no 4 1948. Controversy between Lewis,
H. H. Price and G. E. M. Anscombe on argument in
ch 3 of Lewis' Miracles, 1947, The self-contradiction of
the naturalist.
Brooke, N. S. Lewis and Spenser: nature, art and the
Bower of Bliss. Cambridge Jnl 2 1949. On passage in
The allegory of love, 1936.
Walsh, C. Lewis: apostle to the skeptics. New York 1949.
Joad, C. E. M. The pains of animals: a problem in theo-
logy. Month 3 1950. Reply by Lewis in the same
issue. On argument in ch 9 of The problem of pain,
1940.
Hilton-Young, W. The contented Christian. Cambridge
Jnl 5 1952. Mainly on the science-fiction trilogy.
Milne, M. Dymer: myth or poem? Month 8 1952.
Nott, K. The emperor's clothes. 1953. Attack on dog-
matic orthodoxy of Lewis et al.
Res Judicatae 6 1953–4. Controversy between Lewis,
N. Morris, D. Buckle and J. J. C. Smart on 'The
humanitarian theory of punishment'.
Wain, J. Pleasure, controversy, scholarship. Spectator 1
Oct 1954. Essay-review of OHEL vol. For other essay-
reviews see D. Davie, Entering into the sixteenth century,
EC 5 1955; C. I. Harrison, The Renaissance epitomized,
Sewanee Rev 63 1955; Y. Winters, English literature in
the sixteenth century, Hudson Rev 8 1955.

—— Notes and topics: Lewis. Encounter 22 1964.

Hough, G. Old Western Man. Twentieth Century 157 1955. On De descriptione temporum, 1955 (Lewis' inaugural lecture at Cambridge).

—— How well have they worn? 6, The Screwtape letters. Times 10 Feb 1966.

Masterman, M. Lewis: the author and the hero. Twentieth Century 158 1955. Essay-review of Surprised by joy, 1955. For another essay-review, see T. Corbishley, C. S. Lewis, Month 15 1956.

Maud, R. Lewis' Inaugural. EC 5 1955.

Shumaker, W. The cosmic trilogy of Lewis. Hudson Rev 8 1955.

Tillyard, E. M. W. Lilies or dandelions? Cambridge Rev 12 Nov 1955; rptd in his Essays: literary and educational, 1962. Reply to Lewis's article, Lilies that fester, Twentieth Century 157 1955.

Thompson, C. H. The unmaking of an atheist. Emory Univ Quart 12 1956.

Zandvoort, R. W. In E Studies 37 1956. Essay-review of OHEL vol and Cambridge Inaugural.

Deasy, P. God, space and Lewis. Commonweal 25 July 1958.

Pittenger, W. N. Apologist versus apologist: a critique of Lewis as 'defender of the faith'. Christian Century 1 Oct 1958. Reply by Lewis 26 Nov 1958.

Sharrock, R. Second thoughts: Lewis on Chaucer's Troilus. EC 8 1958. On ch in The allegory of love, 1936.

Approach: a literary quart no 32 1959. Lewis special no. A. Fowler, The lost relevance of religion; H. Fowler, Lewis: sputnik or dinosaur?

Spacks, P. M. The myth-maker's dilemma: three novels by Lewis. Discourse 2 1959.

Moorman, C. Arthurian triptych: mythic materials in C. Williams, Lewis and T. S. Eliot. Berkeley and Los Angeles 1960.

—— In his The precincts of felicity: the Augustinian city of the Oxford Christians, Gainesville 1966.

Del Zama, L. La nostalgia dell' Eden in Lewis. Letture 16 1961.

Irwin, W. R. There and back again: the romances of Williams, Lewis and Tolkien. Sewanee Rev 69 1961.

Davies, H. Lewis and B. L. Manning: lay champions of Christianity. Religion in Life 31 1962.

Fuller, E. The Christian spaceman: Lewis. In his Books with men behind them, New York 1962.

Goldberg, S. L. Lewis and the study of English. Melbourne Critical Rev 5 1962.

Kelly, J. C. Lewis' good reader. Studies 51 1962. Essay-review of An experiment in criticism, 1961.

Bateson, F. N. W. C. S. Lewis. New Statesman 6 Dec 1963.

Green, R. L. C. S. Lewis. 1963 (Bodley Head Monographs).

Kilby, C. S. The Christian world of Lewis. Grand Rapids 1964. Bibliography summarizes recent American dissertations on Lewis.

Sale, R. England's Parnassus: Lewis, C. Williams and J. R. R. Tolkien. Hudson Rev 17 1964.

Barrington-Ward, S. The uncontemporary apologist. Theology 68 1965.

Bennett, J. A. W. The humane medievalist. [1965]. Lecture.

Gardner, H. L. C. S. Lewis. Proc Br Acad 61 1965.

Gibb, J. (ed). Light on Lewis. 1965. By O. Barfield, A. Farrer, J. A. W. Bennett, N. Coghill, J. Lawlor, S. Gibbons, K. Raine, C. Walsh, W. Hooper.

Kruener, H. H. Tribute to Lewis. Religion in Life 34 1965.

Loomis, R. S. Literary history and literary criticism: a critique of Lewis. MLR 60 1965.

The scholar's tale. TLS 7 Jan 1965. Essay-review of Poems, 1964.

Griffith, B. Light on Lewis. Month 35 1966. Essay-review of J. Gibb, above.

Patterns of love and courtesy: essays in memory of Lewis. Ed J. Lawlor 1966.

Robson, W. W. The romanticism of Lewis. In his Critical essays, 1966.

Samaan, A. B. Lewis, the utopist, and his critics. Cairo Stud in Eng 1963-6. 1966.

Cunningham, R. B. Lewis: defender of the faith. Philadelphia 1967.

Norwood, W. D. Lewis, Owen Barfield and the modern myth. Midwest Quart 8 1967.

—— Unifying themes in Lewis' trilogy. Criticism 9 1967.

Utley, F. L. Anglicanism and anthropology: Lewis and John Spiers. Southern Folklore Quart 31 1967.

Aymard, E. On Lewis and the Narnian chronicles. Caliban 5 1968.

Glasson, T. F. Lewis on St John's Gospel. Theology 71 1968.

Hillegas, M. R. (ed). Shadows of imagination: the fantasies of Lewis, J. R. R. Tolkien and C. Williams. Carbondale [1969].

Kreeft, P. Lewis: a critical essay. Grand Rapids 1969 (Contemporary Writers in Christian Perspective).

Sundaram, P. S. Lewis: literary critic. Quest (Bombay) 60 1969.

White, W. L. The image of man in Lewis. Nashville 1969.

M.P.

DOMINIC BEVAN WYNDHAM LEWIS
1894–1969

A London farrago. 1922.

At the Green Goose. [1923]. Mostly rptd from Daily Express.

At the sign of the Blue Moon. 1924. Rptd from Daily Mail.

At the Blue Moon again. New York 1924, London 1925. Rptd from Daily Mail.

On straw, and other conceits. 1927, New York 1929. Rptd from Daily Mail.

François Villon: a documented survey. 1928, New York [1928].

King Spider: some aspects of Louis XI of France and his companions. New York 1929, London 1930.

The stuffed owl: an anthology of bad verse. 1930, 1930 (enlarged), 1930 (further enlarged). With C. Lee.

Emperor of the West: a study of the Emperor Charles the fifth. New York 1931, London 1932. Pbd in America as Charles of Europe.

Welcome to all this. 1931. Rptd from Daily Mail.

The London spectacle, 1935, by F. Topolski. 1935. Introd and notes by Lewis.

The nonsensibus, driven by D. B. Wyndham Lewis. 1936. Anthology.

Ronsard. 1944, New York 1944.

Take it to bed. [1944]. Selected, with a preface by J. Agate. From the Tatler and the Tatler-Bystander.

The hooded hawk: or, the case of Mr Boswell. 1946, New York 1947, London 1952 (as James Boswell: a short life), New York 1952.

Four favourites. 1948, New York 1949. Mme de Pompadour, Melbourne, Godoy, Potemkin.

The soul of Marshal Gilles de Raiz, with some account of his life and times, his abominable crimes and his expiation. 1952.

Doctor Rabelais. 1957, New York 1957.

A Florentine portrait: Saint Philip Benizi 1233-85. 1959, New York 1959.

Molière: the comic mask. 1959, New York [1959].

The shadow of Cervantes. [1962], New York 1962.

The world of Goya. 1968, New York 1968.

Lewis was a columnist for Daily Express, Daily Mail and, as 'Timothy Shy', for News Chronicle. He translated B.

d'Aurevilly, The anatomy of dandyism, *1928 and co-edited, with G. C. Heseltine*, A Christmas book, *from 1928*.
H.M.R.

PERCY WYNDHAM LEWIS
1882–1957

See cols 631–4, above.

JACK LINDSAY
b. 1900

See cols 635–6, above.

PERCY LUBBOCK
1879–1965

Selections
Percy Lubbock reader. Ed M. G. Harkness, Freeport Maine 1957.

§1
Elizabeth Barrett Browning in her letters. 1906.
Samuel Pepys. 1909.
James, H. The middle years. [1917], New York 1917. Ed Lubbock.
—— The letters of Henry James. 2 vols 1920, New York 1920. Ed Lubbock.
The craft of fiction. 1921, New York 1929.
George Calderon: a sketch from memory. 1921.
Earlham. 1922, New York 1922. Childhood reminiscences.
Roman pictures. 1923, New York 1923. Novel.
The region cloud. 1925, New York 1925. Novel.
The diary of A. C. Benson. [1926], New York 1926. Ed Lubbock.
Mary Cholmondeley: a sketch from memory. 1928.
Shades of Eton. 1929. Reminiscences.
Portrait of Edith Wharton. 1947, New York 1947.
Lubbock also edited a book of English prose for schools, 1913.

§2
Gosse, E. W. Earlham. In his More books on the table, 1923. Essay-review.
—— Roman pictures. In his Silhouettes, 1925. Essay-review.
MacCarthy, D. Eton. In his Experience, 1935. Essay-review.
Graham, W. H. Percy Lubbock—his craft. National Rev 121 1943.
Woolf, V. On re-reading novels. In her The moment and other essays, 1947. On The craft of fiction.
Wilson, E. Edith Wharton: a memoir by an English friend. In his Classics and commercials, New York 1950. Essay-review.
Stanford, D. Percy Lubbock, OM. Month 8 1952.
Liddell, R. Percy Lubbock. Kenyon Rev 29 1967.
M.P.

EDWARD VERRALL LUCAS
1868–1938

Collections and Selections
The Minerva edition. 9 vols [1926].
A little of everything. 1912, New York 1912.
Harvest home. 1913, New York 1913.
Selected essays. Ed E. A. Wodehouse 1926.
Three hundred and sixty-five days and one more: being selections for every morning of the year. 1926.
As the bee sucks: essays. 1934.
E. V. Lucas. 1934 (Methuen's Library of Humour).
Cricket all his life: cricket writings in prose and verse. Ed R. Hart-Davis 1950.
Selected essays of E. V. Lucas. Ed H. N. Wethered 1954.

§1
Bernard Barton and his friends: a record of quiet lives. 1893.
Domesticities: a little book of household impressions. 1900. Essays.
The works of Charles and Mary Lamb. 7 vols 1903–5. Ed Lucas.
Highways and byways in Sussex. 1904, 1935 (rev). Re-issued 1937 in 3 vols: West Sussex; Mid-Sussex; East Sussex.
The life of Charles Lamb. 2 vols 1905, New York 1905, 1 vol London 1907 (rev and corrected), 2 vols 1921 (rev and corrected).
A wanderer in Holland. 1905, New York 1905, London 1923 (rev), New York 1924, London 1929 (rev).
Fireside and sunshine. 1906. Essays.
Listener's lure: an oblique narration. 1906, New York 1906 (as Listener's lure: a Kensington comedy).
A wanderer in London. 1906, 1913 (rev), New York 1918, London 1923 (rev), New York 1924, London 1926 (rev), 1931 (rev); rptd in E. V. Lucas' London, 1926, below.
Character and comedy. 1907, New York 1907. Essays.
A swan and her friends. 1907. An account of the life and times of Anna Seward, the 'Swan of Lichfield'.
Over Bemerton's: an easy-going chronicle. 1908, New York 1908.
One day and another. 1909, New York 1909. Essays.
A wanderer in Paris. 1909, New York 1909, London 1911 (rev), 1922 (rev), New York 1924, London 1928 (rev), 1952 (rev by A. Lucas).
Mr Ingleside. 1910, New York 1910. Fiction.
Old lamps for new. 1911, New York 1911. Essays.
London lavender. 1912, New York 1912. Fiction.
A wanderer in Florence. 1912, New York 1912, London 1923 (rev), New York 1924, London 1928 (rev).
The British school: an anecdotal guide to the British painters and paintings in the National Gallery. 1913, New York 1913.
Loiterer's harvest: a book of essays. 1913, New York 1913.
Landmarks. 1914, New York 1914. Fiction.
A wanderer in Venice. 1914, New York 1914, London 1923 (rev), New York 1924.
Cloud and silver. 1916, New York 1916. Essays and sketches.
London revisited. 1916, New York [1916] (as More wanderings in London), London 1926 (rev); rptd in E. V. Lucas' London, 1926, below.
Variety Lane. 1916. Essays and sketches.
The vermilion box. 1916, New York [1916]. Fiction.
A Boswell of Baghdad with diversions. 1917, New York 1917. Essays.
Outposts of mercy: the record of a visit to various units of the British Red Cross in Italy. 1917.
'Twixt eagle and dove. 1918. Essays.
Mixed vintages: a blend of essays old and new. 1919.
The phantom journal and other essays and diversions. 1919.
David Williams: founder of the Royal Literary Fund. 1920.
Specially selected: a choice of essays. 1920.
Verena in the midst: a kind of a story. 1920, New York [1920].
Edwin Austen Abbey: the record on his life and work. 2 vols 1921.
Rose and rose. 1921, New York 1921. Fiction.
Roving east and roving west. 1921, New York [1921].
Urbanities: essays new and old. 1921.
Genevra's money. 1922, New York 1923. Fiction.
Giving and receiving: essays and fantasies. 1922, New York 1922.
Vermeer of Delft. 1922.
You know what people are. 1922 Sketches.
Advisory Ben: a story. 1923, New York 1924, London 1932 (rev and enlarged).

Luck of the year: essays, fantasies and stories. 1923, New York [1923].

Encounters and diversions. 1924. Essays.

John Constable the painter. 1924.

Little books on great masters [of painting]. 8 vols 1924-6, New York 1924-6.

The same star: a comedy in three acts. 1924.

A wanderer among pictures: a companion to the galleries of Europe. 1924, New York [1924].

Introducing London. 1925.

Zigzags in France and various essays. 1925.

Events and embroideries. 1926, New York 1927. Essays.

E. V. Lucas's London: being A wanderer in London and London revisited in one volume, rearranged with new matter. 1926.

A wanderer in Rome. 1926, New York [1926], London 1930 (rev), Philadelphia 1932, London 1951 (rev).

A fronded isle and other essays. 1927.

The more I see of men: stray essays on dogs. 1927.

The Colvins and their friends. 1928.

Introducing Paris. 1928.

Out of a clear sky: essays and fantasies about birds. 1928; rptd in Animals all, 1934, below.

A rover I would be: essays and fantasies. 1928.

If dogs could write: a second canine miscellany. 1929, Philadelphia 1930.

Turning things over: essays and fantasies. 1929, New York 1929.

Vermeer the magical. 1929. Based on a lecture.

Windfall's eve: an entertainment. 1929, Philadelphia 1930. Fiction.

'—And such small deer'. 1930, Philadelphia 1931; rptd in Animals all, 1934, below.

Down the sky: an entertainment. 1930, Philadelphia 1930.

Traveller's luck: essays and fantasies. 1930.

The barber's clock: a conversation piece. 1931, Philadelphia 1932.

French leaves. 1931. Short essays on French subjects.

Visibility good: essays and excursions. 1931, Philadelphia 1931.

At the sign of the dove. 1932. Essays.

Lemon Verbena and other essays. 1932, Philadelphia 1932.

Reading, writing and remembering: a literary record. 1932, New York 1932.

English leaves. 1933, Philadelphia 1933. Essays.

Saunterer's rewards. 1933. Philadelphia 1934.

Animals all: being '—And such small deer' and Out of a clear sky. 1934.

At the shrine of St Charles: stray papers on Lamb brought together for the centenary of his death in 1834. 1934, New York 1934.

The letters of Charles Lamb to which are added those of his sister, Mary Lamb. 3 vols 1935, 2 vols 1945 (rev and abridged by G. Pocock). Ed Lucas.

The old contemporaries. 1935. Reminiscences.

Pleasure trove. 1935, Philadelphia 1935. Essays and sketches.

London afresh. 1936, Philadelphia [1937].

Only the other day: a volume of essays. 1936.

All of a piece: new essays. 1937, New York 1937.

Adventures and misgivings. 1938.

Lucas also pbd vols of stories and verse for children as well as light verse. He collaborated with other writers, particularly C. L. Graves, in a number of humorous books. He compiled various anthologies of prose and verse and edited popular edns of Lamb and other writers. He contributed to Punch for many years and was a member of its staff.

§2

Overton, G. M. That literary wanderer, Lucas. In his Cargoes for Crusoes, New York 1924.

Adcock, A. St J. In his Glory that was Grub Street, [1928].

Lucas, A. E. V. Lucas: a portrait. 1939.

Swinnerton, F. A. In his Figures in the foreground, 1963.

P.C.

FRANK LAURENCE LUCAS
1894-1967

§1

Seneca and Elizabethan tragedy. Cambridge 1922, New York 1966.

Euripides and his influence. Boston Mass [1923], London [1924]. (Our Debt to Greece and Rome).

Authors dead and living. 1926, New York 1926. Essays.

The river flows. 1926, New York 1926. Novel.

The complete works of John Webster. Ed Lucas 4 vols 1927, New York 1937. The texts of The white devil and The Duchess of Malfi (rev) rptd separately 1958, New York 1959.

Tragedy in relation to Aristotle's Poetics. 1927, New York [1928], London 1957 (rev and enlarged, as Tragedy: serious drama in relation to Aristotle's Poetics), New York 1958.

Time and memory. 1929 (Hogarth Living Poets).

The art of dying: an anthology. Ed F. Birrell and Lucas 1930.

Cécile. 1930, New York [1930]. Novel.

Eight Victorian poets. Cambridge 1930, 1940 (enlarged, as Ten Victorian poets), Hamden Conn 1966. On Tennyson, Browning, Arnold, Clough, D. G. Rosseti, Morris, Swinburne, Hardy; 1940 edn adds Patmore, Christina Rossetti.

Marionettes. Cambridge 1930, New York 1930. Verse.

Ariadne. Cambridge 1932 (500 copies). Verse.

Poets in brief. 4 vols Cambridge 1932-3. Anthologies of Tennyson, Beddoes, D. G. Rossetti, Crabbe.

The wild tulip. 1932. Novel.

The bear dances. 1933. Play.

From Olympus to the Styx. 1934. With P. D. Lucas. Travel book on Greece.

Mauron, M. Mount Peacock: or progress in Provence. Cambridge 1934, New York 1935. Tr Lucas.

Studies French and English. 1934, Freeport NY 1969. Essays.

The awakening of Balthazar. 1935. Verse.

Four plays. Cambridge 1935, New York 1935. Land's end, Surrender to discretion, The loves of Gudrun, Death of a ghost.

Poems, 1935. Cambridge 1935, New York 1935.

The decline and fall of the Romantic ideal. Cambridge 1936, New York 1936.

The Golden Cockerel Greek anthology: a selection, edited with English verse translations by Lucas. [1937] (206 copies). 100 poems rptd in A Greek garland, 1939, below.

The woman clothed with the sun and other stories. 1937, New York 1938.

The delights of dictatorship. Cambridge 1938. Pamphlet.

Doctor Dido. 1938. Novel.

Journal under the terror, 1938. 1938.

A Greek garland: a selection from the Palatine anthology, with translations into English verse by Lucas. 1939.

Messene redeemed. 1940, New York 1940. Verse play.

Ten Victorian poets. Cambridge 1940. See Eight Victorian poets, 1930, above.

Critical thoughts in critical days. 1942 (PEN books). See G. Cetrangolo, L'universo dantesco e la terra di Shakespeare, incontro con F. Lucas, Rome 1952 [1953]. Contests opinions in this book.

Tennyson: poetry and prose. 1947. Selected by Lucas.

Gilgamesh, King of Erech. 1948 (500 copies). Poems.

Greek poetry for everyman. 1951, New York 1951, London 1966 (as Greek poetry) (EL). Chosen and tr by Lucas.

Literature and psychology. 1951, New York 1957 (rev).
From many times and lands. 1953. Verse.
Greek drama for everyman. 1954, New York 1954, London 1967 (corrected), (as Greek drama for the common reader), New York [1967] (as Greek tragedy and comedy). Chosen and tr by Lucas.
Style. New York 1955.
Tennyson. 1957, New York 1957, London 1961 (rev) (Br Council pamphlet).
The search for good sense: four eighteenth-century characters: Johnson, Chesterfield, Boswell, Goldsmith. 1958, New York 1958.
The art of living; four eighteenth-century minds: Hume, Horace Walpole, Burke, Benjamin Franklin. 1959, New York 1959.
The greatest problem, and other essays. 1960, New York 1961.
The drama of Ibsen and Strindberg. 1962, New York 1962.
The drama of Chekhov, Synge, Yeats and Pirandello. 1963.
The English agent: a tale of the Peninsular War. 1969.
Lucas pbd a number of other trns from the classics: Euripides (*Medea, 1923*); Pervigilium Veneris (*1939*), Catullus (*three poems, 1942*), Homer (The Homeric Hymn to Aphrodite, *1948*, *selections from* The Odyssey, *1948*, *and from* The Iliad, *1950*), Musaeus (Hero and Leander, *1949*).

§2

Rickword, E. Criticism as 'a charming parasite'. Calendar of Modern Letters 3 1926. Essay-review of Authors dead and living, 1926.

ROBERT WILSON LYND
1879–1949
Selections

Selected essays. [1923] (King's Treasuries of Literature).
Dr Johnson and company. [1927], Garden City NY 1928 (People's Lib).
The goldfish. 1927. Essays.
'Y.Y.': an anthology of essays, selected with an introduction by E. Squire. 1933.
Essays on life and literature. Introd by D. MacCarthy 1951 (EL), New York 1951.
Books and writers. 1952. Foreword by R. Church.

§1

The mantle of the emperor: being the adventures and observations of Richard Blennerhasset in the following of the third Napoleon. 1906. With L. L. D. Black. Novel.
The Orangemen and the nation. Belfast 1907. Pamphlet.
Irish and English: portraits and impressions. 1908.
Home life in Ireland. 1909.
The ethics of Sinn Fein. Limerick 1910. Pamphlet.
Rambles in Ireland. 1912, Boston 1912. Illustr J. B. Yeats.
The book of this and that. 1915. Essays.
If the Germans conquered England and other essays. Dublin 1917.
Ireland a nation. 1919, New York 1920.
Old and new masters. 1919. Literary essays.
The art of letters. 1920, New York 1921. Literary essays.
The murders in Ireland: who began it. 1920. Pamphlet.
The passion of labour. 1920, Freeport NY 1969. Essays on socialism mainly rptd from New Statesman.
The pleasures of ignorance. 1921. Essays.
Books and authors. [1922], New York 1923. Essays.
Solomon in all his glory. 1922, New York 1923. Essays.
The sporting life and other trifles. 1922, New York 1922. Essays.

The blue lion and other essays. 1923, New York 1923.
The peal of bells. 1924, New York 1925. Essays.
The money box. 1925, New York 1926. Essays.
The little angel: a book of essays. 1926.
The orange tree: a volume of essays. 1926.
The silver book of English sonnets: a selection of less-known sonnets with an introduction by Lynd. 1927 (priv ptd, 550 copies).
The green man. 1928. Essays.
It's a fine world. 1930. Essays.
Rain, rain, go to Spain. 1931. Essays.
Great love stories of all nations. Ed Lynd 1932, New York 1932 (as Love throughout the ages: love stories of all nations).
The cockleshell. 1933. Essays.
Both sides of the road. 1934. Essays.
I tremble to think. 1936. Essays.
In defence of pink. 1937. Essays.
Modern poetry: chosen by Lynd. 1939, New York 1939.
Searchlights and nightingales. 1939. Essays.
Life's little oddities. 1941. Essays.
Things one hears. 1945. Essays.
Lynd contributed regularly to Daily News (*afterwards* News Chronicle) *from 1908 until he retired, as literary editor, in 1947 and to* New Statesman, *first anonymously, then under his own name and finally for many years under the pseudonym 'Y.Y.'; for a number of years he was 'John O'London' of* John O'London's Weekly.

§2

Priestley, J. B. Robert Lynd. London Mercury 7 1923; rptd in his Figures in modern literature, 1924.
Adcock, A. St J. In his Glory that was Grub Street, 1928.
Hodgson, S. In his Portraits and reflections, 1929.
MacCarthy, D. 'Y.Y.' New Statesman 15 Oct 1949.
Sastri, C. L. R. Lynd passes away: greatest English essayist of modern times. Modern Rev (Calcutta) 85–6 1949.
Sen, M. K. Robert Lynd. Calcutta Rev 106–7 1950.
— The life and art of Lynd. Modern Rev (Calcutta) 101–2 1957.
Swinnerton, F. A. In his Figures in the foreground, 1963.

SIR DESMOND MACCARTHY
1878–1952

§1

The Court Theatre, 1904–7: a commentary and criticism, with an appendix containing reprinted programmes of the 'Vedrenne-Barker performances'. 1907, Coral Gables Florida [1966] (ed with additional material by S. Weintraub).
Lady John Russell: a memoir, with a selection from her diaries and correspondence. Ed MacCarthy and Agatha Russell 1910, New York 1911.
Romains, J. The death of a nobody. Tr MacCarthy and S. Waterlow 1914.
Remnants. 1918. Miscellaneous essays rptd from New Statesman, New Witness, Eye Witness, Speaker.
Ellen Melicent Cobden: a portrait. 1920 (priv ptd, 50 copies).
Ben Kedim: a record of Eastern travel, by Aubrey Herbert. Ed MacCarthy 1924.
Portraits. 1, 1931, New York 1931. No more pbd. Essays on literary and other personalities, past and present.
Criticism. 1932, New York [1932]. Essays.
H.H.A.: letters of the Earl of Oxford and Asquith to a friend. Ed MacCarthy 2 vols 1933–4.
William Somerset Maugham, 'the English Maupassant': an appreciation, with a bibliography. 1934; rptd in Memories, 1953.

Experience. 1935 (100 copies), Freeport NY 1968. Miscellaneous essays mainly rptd from New Statesman.

The European tradition in literature from 1600 onwards. In European civilization, its origin and development, vol 6, ed E. Eyre 1937.

Leslie Stephen. Cambridge 1937. Lecture; rptd in Memories, 1953.

Drama. 1940, New York 1940. Dramatic criticism. Some essays rptd in Theatre, 1954.

Shaw. 1951, New York 1951 (as Shaw's plays in review).

Humanities. Preface by D. Cecil, 1953, New York 1954. Essays on literature and the theatre ed T. R. Fyvel, mainly rptd from Sunday Times and New Statesman, with 2 short stories rptd from Life & Letters.

Memories. 1953, New York 1953. Forewords by R. Mortimer and C. Connolly. Essays on Writers and People mainly rptd from Sunday Times, selected by R. Kee.

The story of a nutcracker: a free version by D. MacCarthy and B. Guinness from the tale by Hoffmann. 1953.

Theatre. 1954, New York 1955. Essays, mainly rptd from New Statesman, and broadcast talks.

MacCarthy also edited and contributed to New Quart, Eye Witness (*later* New Witness) *and* Life & Letters; *he was literary editor and later dramatic critic of* New Statesman, *and from 1928 until his death contributed weekly to* Sunday Times.

§ 2

Forster, E. M. Desmond MacCarthy. Stanford Dingley 1952 (72 copies).

Listener 26 June 1952. Tributes to Sir Desmond MacCarthy. 1, Max Beerbohm; 2, E. M. Forster; 3, V. S. Pritchett; 4, P. Hope-Wallace; 5, C. V. Wedgwood.

Mortimer, R. Critics who have influenced taste: xix, MacCarthy. Times 12 Sept 1963.

'HUGH MACDIARMID',
CHRISTOPHER MURRAY GRIEVE
b. 1892

See cols 299–302, above.

ARTHUR LLEWELYN JONES
MACHEN
1863–1947

See cols 644–8, above.

JOHN WILLIAM MACKAIL
1859–1945

§ 1

Mensae secundae: verses written in Balliol College. Oxford 1879. With H. C. Beeching and J. B. B. Nichols.

The masque of B-ll-l. Oxford 1881 (broadsheet, 25 copies); ed W. G. Hiscock, 1939 (as The Balliol rhymes, enlarged). Verse caricatures by Mackail, Beeching, Nichols et al; *see* Mackail, The masque of Balliol, Times 11 March 1939.

Love in idleness. 1883. Verse. With Beeching and Nichols.

The Aeneid of Virgil. 1885, 1908 (rev). Tr Mackail.

The Eclogues and Georgics of Virgil. 1889, New York 1915. Tr by Mackail.

Select epigrams from the Greek Anthology. 1890, 1906 (rev), 1911 (rev). Ed and tr Mackail.

Love's looking glass. 1891. Verse. With Beeching and Nichols.

Biblia innocentium: being the story of God's chosen people, written anew for children. 2 pts 1892–1901.

The sayings of the Lord Jesus Christ as recorded by his Four Evangelists. 1894. Based on the Authorised Version with some modernization.

Latin literature. 1895, New York 1895, 1962 (ed with introd by H. C. Schnur).

Homer. Odysseus in Phaeacia. 1896, Portland Me 1897. Verse trn of the Odyssey bk 6.

The life of William Morris. 2 vols 1899, 1 vol 1950 (introd by S. Cockerell) (WC), 2 vols New York 1968.

Cornelii Taciti De vita et moribus Iulii Agricolae liber. 1900 (230 copies). Ed Mackail.

Homer. The Odyssey. 3 vols 1903–10, 1 vol Oxford 1932. Verse trn by Mackail.

The hundred best poems—lyrical—in the Latin language, selected by J. W. Mackail. 1905, 1906 (corrected).

The springs of Helicon: a study of the progress of English poetry from Chaucer to Milton. 1909, New York 1909.

Lectures on Greek poetry. 1910, 1926 (rev), New York 1966.

Lectures on poetry. 1911, Freeport NY 1967.

Pervigilium Veneris—The eve of St Venus. In Catullus, Tibullus and Pervigilium Veneris, 1912. Tr Mackail (Loeb Classical Lib). Latin text, ed Mackail, first pbd 1910 (162 copies).

Russia's gift to the world. 1915, 1917 (rev).

The case for Latin in secondary schools. 1922. Pamphlet.

Virgil and his meaning to the world of today. Boston Mass [1922], London 1923.

Literature. In The legacy of Rome, ed C. Bailey, Oxford 1923.

Classical studies. 1925, Freeport NY 1968. Includes single lectures, addresses previously pbd separately.

James Leigh Strachan-Davidson, Master of Balliol: a memoir. Oxford 1925.

Life and letters of George Wyndham. 2 vols [1925]. With Guy Wyndham.

Studies of English poets. 1926, Freeport NY 1968. Includes single lectures, addresses previously pbd separately.

The approach to Shakespeare. Oxford 1930.

Virgil. The Aeneid. Oxford 1930. Ed Mackail.

Studies in humanism. 1938, Freeport NY 1969. Includes single lectures, addresses previously pbd separately.

Mackail also pbd some political tracts on William Morris, socialism etc through the Doves Press and the Hammersmith Publishing Soc 1901–5. He pbd an edn of J. B. B. Nichols' poems in 1943. He assisted in the editing of the Westminster Shakespeare 5 vols 1915.

§ 2

Bailey, C. John William Mackail, OM, 1859–1945. [1947] (Proc Br Acad 31).

Macleod, R. D. Morris without Mackail—as seen by his contemporaries. Glasgow 1954.

RONALD BRUNLEES MCKERROW
1872–1940

Bibliographies

Francis, F. C. A list of the writings of McKerrow. Rptd from Library 4th ser 21 1940–1.

§ 1

Joan of Arc: a poem which obtained the Chancellor's medal at the Cambridge Commencement. [1895].

Richard Grafton. In Hand-lists of English printers 1501–56, Part III, by McKerrow [et al], 1905.

The story of Asseneth. 1908. A Christmas-card booklet: the French text from L. E. D. Moland and C. D. D'Héricault, Nouvelles françoises en prose du xive siècle, Paris 1858, with an English version by McKerrow.

Printers and publishers' devices in England and Scotland, 1485–1640. 1913 (Illustrated Monographs of the Bibl Soc).

Notes on bibliographical evidence for literary students and editors of English works of the sixteenth and seventeenth centuries. 1914. Pamphlet rptd from Trans Bibl Soc 12 1893; subsequently the basis of An introduction to bibliography for literary students, 1927, below.

Booksellers, printers and the stationers' trade. In Shakespeare's England vol 2, Oxford 1916.

A note on the teaching of English language and literature, with some suggestions. 1921 (Eng Assoc pamphlet).

A dictionary of the printers and booksellers who were at work in England, Scotland and Ireland from 1668 to 1725, by H. R. Plomer, with the help of McKerrow [et al]. Ed A. Esdaile 1922.

Information for students. 1925. Pamphlet rptd from notes ptd on wrappers of first 8 nos of RES 1 1925.

An introduction to bibliography for literary students. Oxford 1927, 1928 (corrected).

Title-page borders used in England and Scotland, 1485–1640. 1932 (Illustrated Monographs of the Bibl Soc). With F. S. Ferguson, who pbd a list of addns in 1936.

The treatment of Shakespeare's text by his earlier editors, 1709–68. Proc Br Acad 19 1933. Lecture.

Prolegomena for the Oxford Shakespeare: a study in editorial method. Oxford 1939.

The typescript of McKerrow's unpbd Sandars Lectures, The relationship of English printed books to authors' manuscripts, *is held by Cambridge Univ Library.*

Editions

Barnes, B. The Devil's charter, edited from the quarto of 1607. Louvain 1904 (Materialen zur Kunde des älteren englischen Dramas).

Dekker, T. The gull's horn-book. 1904.

The works of Thomas Nashe, edited from the original texts. 5 vols 1904–10, Oxford 1958 (with corrections and supplementary notes by F. P. Wilson).

The Enterlude of Youth nebst Fragmenten des Playe of Lucres und von Nature. Louvain 1905 (Materialen zur Kunde des älteren englischen Dramas). With W. Bang.

The Spanish curate; Wit without money. In The works of Francis Beaumont and John Fletcher: Variorum edn vol 2, 1905.

A dictionary of printers and booksellers in England, Scotland and Ireland, and of foreign printers of English books, 1557–1640, by H. G. Aldis [et al]. 1910. Ed McKerrow.

B.R.-R.B. Greenes newes both from heaven and hell, 1593, and Greenes funeralls, 1594, reprinted from the original editions with notes etc. 1911.

A newe interlude of impacyente pouerte, from the quarto of 1560. Louvain 1911 (Materialen zur Kunde des älteren englischen Dramas).

Weever, J. Epigrammes in the oldest cut and newest fashion, 1599. Reprinted from the original edition with notes, &c, 1911.

Greg, W. W. English literary autographs, 1550–1650, selected and edited by W. W. Greg in collaboration with McKerrow [et al]. 4 pts Oxford 1925–32.

McKerrow also wrote A book on English phonetics, *in collaboration with H. Katayama, pbd only in a Japanese version, 1901; he helped to found the Malone Soc in 1906 and edited or assisted in editing 5 plays for* Malone Soc Reprints, *1907–11; he edited* Library *1934–7 (in 1937 with F. C. Francis); he founded* RES *in 1925 and edited it 1925–39.*

§2

Greg, W. W. R. B. McKerrow. Proc Br Acad 26 1940.
—— McKerrow's Prolegomena reconsidered. RES 17 1941.
—— Prolegomena: on editing Shakespeare, a criticism and expansion of the principles laid down in McKerrow's

Prolegomena for the Oxford Shakespeare. In his Editorial problem in Shakespeare, Oxford 1942, 1951 (corrected).

Harrison, G. B. R. B. McKerrow. RES 16 1940.
Williams, H. H. R. B. McKerrow. Library 4th ser 20 1940.
Bowers, F. T. McKerrow's editorial principles for Shakespeare reconsidered. Shakespeare Quart 6 1955.

M.P.

'KATHERINE MANSFIELD', KATHLEEN MANSFIELD BEAUCHAMP
1888–1923
See cols 653–9, above.

JOHN EDWARD MASEFIELD
1878–1967
See cols 306–13, above.

WILLIAM SOMERSET MAUGHAM
1874–1965
See also cols 661–8, above.

CHARLES EDWARD MONTAGUE
1867–1928
See cols 675–6, above.

JOHN BINGHAM MORTON
b. 1893

Selections

The best of Beachcomber. Ed M. Frayn 1963.

§1

The barber of Putney. 1919. Fiction.
Enchanter's nightshade. 1921.
Penny royal. 1921.
The cow jumped over the moon: a story. [1923].
Old man's beard. 1923. Essays.
Drink up, gentlemen. 1930. Fiction.
By the way. 1931.
Maladetta. 1932. Fiction.
1933 and still going wrong! 1932.
Sobieski, King of Poland. 1932.
Hag's harvest. 1933. Fiction.
Morton's folly. 1933.
The death of the dragon: new fairy tales. 1934.
Sky lighters. 1934. Fiction.
Vagabond. [1934]. Containing Enchanter's nightshade, Penny royal, and Old man's beard.
Mr Thrale and the ladies. 1935.
Stuff and nonsense. 1935.
The Bastille falls, and other studies of the French Revolution. 1936.
Gallimaufry. 1936.
The Dauphin. 1937. Louis XVII.
Sideways through Borneo: an unconventional journey. 1937.
The new Ireland. 1938.
Pyrenean: being the adventures of Miles Walker on his journey from the Mediterranean to the Atlantic. 1938.
A bonfire of weeds. 1939.
Saint-Just. 1939.
Bridge over the rainbow: a survey of humorous sketches by J. B. Morton, N. Gubbins [et al]. 1940.
I do not think so. 1940.
Fool's paradise. 1941.

Captain Foulenough and company. 1944. Selection from By the way in Daily Express.

The Gascon: a story of the French Revolution. 1946.

Here and now. 1947.

Brumaire—the rise of Bonaparte: a study of French history from the death of Robespierre to the establishment of the Consulate. 1948.

The misadventures of Dr Strabismus. 1949.

Camille Desmoulins and other studies of the French Revolution. 1950.

The Tibetan Venus. 1951. Selection from By the way.

St Thérèse of Lisieux: the making of a saint. 1954.

Hilaire Belloc: a memoir. 1955, New York 1955.

Springtime: tales of the Café Rieu. 1956.

Marshall Ney. 1958.

Merry-go-round. [1959].

Morton also pbd vols of verse. Many of his books consist of reprints of humourous pieces first contributed to Daily Express *under the pseudonym 'Beachcomber'.*

H.M.R.

EDWIN MUIR
1887–1959
See cols 316–19, above.

GEORGE GILBERT AIMÉ MURRAY
1866–1957
After his death Murray's papers were deposited in Bodley.

Collections and Selections

The plays of Euripides, translated into rhyming verse with explanatory notes. 2 vols 1911, Newtown 1931 (Gregynog Press, 500 copies), New York 1931, 1 vol London 1954 (as Collected plays of Euripides).

Gilbert Murray. [1926] (Augustan Books of Modern Poetry). 21 poems from the trns and from original plays.

Aeschylus. The Oresteia, translated into English rhyming verse. 1928, 1946 (rev). With introd and notes.

Complete plays of Aeschylus, translated into English rhyming verse with commentaries and notes. 1952.

Humanist essays. 1964, New York 1964. Chosen from Essays and addresses, 1921, and Stoic, Christian and humanist, 1940.

§1

Greek comic verse. (Gaisford Prize). Oxford 1886. Tr from Shakespeare's Henry IV, pt 2, act III. 2.

Olympia: carmen latinum Cancellarii praemio donatum. Oxford 1886.

'Mesolonghi capta'. (Gaisford Prose). Oxford 1887. In Greek.

Gobi or Shamo: a story of three songs. 1889, New York 1889.

A history of ancient Greek literature. 1897, New York 1897, Chicago 1956 (as The literature of ancient Greece).

Andromache: a play in three acts. 1900, Portland Maine 1913 (450 copies), London 1914 (corrected).

Carlyon Sahib: a drama in four acts. 1900.

Euripides [The Hippolytus and Bacchae together with The frogs of Aristophanes], translated into English rhyming verse by Murray. 1902 (Athenian Drama 3). With introductory essay (partly rptd in Essays and addresses, 1921, below), notes and appendix on the lost plays. The Hippolytus separately pbd 1904, The Bacchae 1904, New York 1920, The frogs, 1908 (and in the same year 'adapted for the performance by the OUDS').

Euripidis Fabulae: recognovit brevique adnotatione critica instruxit Gilbertus Murray. 3 vols Oxford 1902–9 (Scriptorum Classicorum Bibliotheca Oxoniensis).

The Electra of Euripides, translated into English rhyming verse with explanatory notes. 1905, New York 1915 (with The Trojan women and The Medea).

The Trojan women of Euripides, translated into English

rhyming verse with explanatory notes. 1905, New York 1915 (with The Medea and The Electra).

The Medea of Euripides, translated into English rhyming verse with explanatory notes. 1906, New York 1906, 1915 (with The Trojan women and The Electra).

The rise of the Greek epic: being a course of lectures delivered at Harvard University. Oxford 1907, 1911 (rev and enlarged), 1924 (rev and enlarged), New York 1961.

Anthropology in the Greek epic tradition outside Homer. In Anthropology and the classics: six lectures by Murray [et al], ed R. R. Marett, Oxford 1908.

Wilamowitz-Moellendorff, U. von. Greek historical writing and Apollo. Oxford 1908. Tr Murray.

The Iphigenia in Tauris of Euripides, translated into English rhyming verse with explanatory notes. 1910, New York 1910.

Oedipus King of Thebes, by Sophocles, translated into English rhyming verse with explanatory notes. 1910, New York 1910.

The story of Nefrekepta from a demotic papyrus, put into verse by Murray. Oxford 1911.

Four stages of Greek religion: studies based on a course of lectures delivered at Columbia University. New York 1912, London 1912, Oxford 1925 (enlarged as Five stages of Greek religion).

Greek and English tragedy: a contrast. In English literature and the classics, by Murray [et al], ed G. S. Gordon, Oxford 1912.

Harrison, J. E. Themis: a study of the social origins of Greek religion, with an excursus on the ritual forms preserved in Greek tragedy by Murray. Cambridge 1912, 1927 (rev and enlarged), Cleveland 1962.

Euripides and his age. [1913], New York 1913, London 1946 (rev), New York 1946, London 1965 (introd by H. D. F. Kitto), New York 1965.

The Rhesus of Euripides, translated into English rhyming verse with explanatory notes. 1913, New York 1913.

The Alcestis of Euripides, translated into English rhyming verse with explanatory notes. 1915, New York 1915.

The foreign policy of Sir Edward Grey, 1906–15. Oxford 1915. *See* B. Russell, The policy of the Entente, 1904–14: a reply to Professor Gilbert Murray, Manchester [1916].

Faith, war and policy: lectures and essays. Boston 1917, London 1918 (with new preface).

Aeschylus' Agamemnon, translated into English rhyming verse with explanatory notes. 1920, New York 1920.

Essays and addresses. 1921, Boston 1922 (as Tradition and progress).

The problem of foreign policy: a consideration of present dangers and the best methods for meeting them. 1921, Boston 1921.

The value of Greece to the future of the world. In The legacy of Greece: essays by Murray [et al], ed R. W. Livingstone, Oxford 1921.

The Choëphoroe—Libation bearers—of Aeschylus, translated into English rhyming verse. 1923, New York 1923. With preface and notes.

Toynbee, A. J. (ed). Greek historical thought from Homer to the age of Heraclitus, with two pieces [from the Iliad and from Antigone] newly translated by Gilbert Murray. 1924, Boston 1950.

The Eumenides—The furies—of Aeschylus, translated into English rhyming verse. 1925, New York 1925. With introd and notes.

Five stages of Greek religion. Oxford 1925. *See* above, Four stages of Greek religion, 1912.

The classical tradition in poetry: the Charles Eliot Norton lectures, 1926. 1927, Cambridge Mass 1927.

The ordeal of this generation: the war, the League and the future. 1929, New York 1929.

Aeschylus' Suppliant women: Supplices, translated into English rhyming verse with introduction and notes. 1930, New York 1930.

The Oxford book of Greek verse, chosen by Murray [et al]. Oxford 1930. Murray also contributed 25 poems to the Oxford book of Greek verse in translation, ed T. F. Higham and C. M. Bowra, Oxford 1938.

Aeschylus' Prometheus bound, translated into English rhyming verse with introduction and notes. 1931, New York 1931.

Aristophanes: a study. Oxford 1933, New York 1933.

Aeschylus' Seven against Thebes, translated into English rhyming verse with introduction and notes. 1935, New York 1935.

Aeschyli Septem quae supersunt tragoediae, recensuit Gilbertus Murray. Oxford 1937, 1955 (rev) (Scriptorum Classicorum Bibliotheca Oxoniensis).

Liberality and civilization. 1938, New York 1938.

Aeschylus' The Persians—Persae—translated into English rhyming verse with preface and notes. 1939, New York 1939.

Aeschylus: the creator of tragedy. Oxford 1940.

Stoic, Christian and humanist. 1940, Boston 1950 (with a new preface), London 1950. Essays.

Sophocles' Antigone, translated into English rhyming verse with introduction and notes. 1941, New York 1941.

The rape of the locks: the Perikeiromenê of Menander, the fragments translated and the gaps conjecturally filled in by Murray. 1942, New York 1945 (with The arbitration).

Classical humanism. In Humanism (three BBC talks), by Murray [et al]. [1944]. Rptd from Listener.

The arbitration: the Epitrepontes of Menander, the fragments translated and the gaps conjecturally filled in by Murray. 1945, New York 1945 (with The rape of the locks).

Greek studies. Oxford 1946.

The wife of Heracles: being Sophocles' play The Trachinian women, translated into English verse with explanatory notes. 1947, New York 1948.

From the League to UN. 1948. Includes addresses etc previously pbd separately.

Sophocles' Oedipus at Colonus, translated into English rhyming verse with introduction and notes. 1948, New York 1948.

Aristophanes' The birds, translated into English verse with introduction and notes. 1950, New York 1950.

Croce as a European. In Benedetto Croce: a commemoration, by Murray [et al]. 1953 (Pubblicazioni dell' Istituto Italiano di Cultura di Londra 2).

Hellenism and the modern world: six talks on the Radio-Diffusion Française and the BBC. 1953, Boston 1954.

Euripides. Ion, translated into English rhyming verse with explanatory notes. 1954, New York 1954.

Aristophanes. The knights, translated into English rhyming verse with introduction and notes. 1956.

The literature of ancient Greece. Chicago 1956. See above, A history of ancient Greek literature, 1897.

Gilbert Murray: an unfinished autobiography, with contributions by his friends. Ed J. Smith and A. Toynbee 1960. Contains Two Greek versions from modern English by Murray.

Murray also wrote many booklets and pamphlets on the Great War, Liberalism and the League of Nations. With H. A. L. Fisher he was editor of Home Univ Lib; he contributed many prefaces and introds to other works.

§2

Chapman, J. J. Euripides and the Greek genius. In his Greek genius and other essays, New York 1915.

Eliot, T. S. Euripides and Gilbert Murray: a performance at the Holborn Empire. Art & Letters 3 1920; rptd in his Sacred wood, 1920 (as Euripides and Professor Murray).

Clutton-Brock, A. The scholar's religion. In his More essays on books, 1921. Essay-review of Religio grammatici (an address), 1918; rptd from TLS.

Thomson, J. A. K. and A. J. Toynbee (ed). Essays in honour of Murray. 1936. 18 essays by H. A. L. Fisher, J. Masefield, H. Granville-Barker et al.

Thomson, J. A. K. Gilbert Murray. Proc Br Acad 43 1958.

Sarton, G. Tribute to Murray and a plea for Greek studics. Isis 38 1947.

Price, L. Murray at ninety. Atlantic Monthly 197 1956.

Austin, M. N. Gilbert Murray, OM, 1866–1957. Educand 3 1957.

Curgenven, A. Murray at home. Contemporary Rev 192 1957.

— Murray: some memories. Meanjin 17 1958.

Stanford, D. Gilbert Murray. Aryan Path 28 1957.

Toynbee, A. J. Reminiscences of Murray. Listener 22 Aug 1957.

Bowra, M. Gilbert Murray. Atlantic Monthly 201 1958.

— In his Memories, 1898–1939, 1966.

Langdale, I. S. R. Murray: a personal tribute. Hibbert Jnl 56 1958.

Gilbert Murray: an unfinished autobiography, with contributions by his friends. Ed J. Smith and A. Toynbee 1960. Includes essays by E. R. Dodds, J. Smith, I. Henderson, S. Thorndike and L. Casson, S. de Mandariaga, B. Russell and A. Toynbee.

West, P. Murray: 'civic monk'. Dalhousie Rev 41 1961.

Ward, D. Eliot, Murray, Homer and the idea of tradition. EC 18 1968.

JOHN MIDDLETON MURRY
1889–1957
Selections

Selected criticism 1916–57, chosen and introduced by R. Rees. 1960, New York 1960.

Poets, critics, mystics: a selection of criticism written between 1919 and 1955, ed R. Rees. Carbondale Ill 1970.

§1

Chekhov, A. P. The bet and other stories. Dublin 1915 (Modern Russian Library), Boston 1915. Tr with S. S. Koteliansky.

Dostoevsky, F. M. Pages from the journal of an author. Dublin 1916 (introd Murry) (Modern Russian Library), Boston 1917, London 1960 (without introd, as The dream of a queer fellow and The Pushkin speech), New York 1961. Tr with S. S. Koteliansky; introd rptd (abridged) as The dream of a queer fellow in The evolution of an intellectual, 1920.

Fyodor Dostoevsky: a critical study. 1916, New York 1916.

Kuprin, A. I. The river of life and other stories. Dublin 1916 (Modern Russian Library), Boston 1916. Tr with S. S. Koteliansky.

Shestov, L. I. Anton Tchekhov and other essays. Dublin 1916 (Modern Russian Library), Boston 1917 (as Penultimate words and other essays). Tr with S. S. Koteliansky; Murry's introd rptd as The honesty of Russia in The evolution of an intellectual, 1920.

Still life. 1916, New York 1922. Novel.

Poems: 1917–18. Hampstead 1918 (120 copies).

The critic in judgment: or, Belshazzar of Baronscourt. Richmond Surrey [1919]. Verse.

Aspects of literature. 1920, New York 1921. Essays, all but 3 first pbd in Athenaeum.

Cinnamon and Angelica: a play. 1920, [1941] (rev), New York 1941. Verse.

The evolution of an intellectual. 1920, New York 1920, London 1927 (one essay replaced by 2 others) (Travellers' Library). Essays mainly first pbd in TLS, Nation, Athenaeum.

Poems: 1916–20. [1921]. Some poems first pbd in Nation, Athenaeum.

Countries of the mind: essays in literary criticism. [1922]. New York 1922, London 1931 (rev, with 2 additional essays, as Countries of the mind [etc] first ser), 1937 (rev, with 2nd ser, 1931 below) (Oxford Bookshelf ser). Mainly first pbd in TLS.

The problem of style. 1922, New York 1922. Lectures given at Oxford.

The things we are. 1922, New York 1922, [1930] (introd by D. B. Leary). Novel.

Dostoevsky, F. M. Letters and reminiscences. 1923, New York 1923. Tr with S. S. Koteliansky.

Pencillings: little essays on literature. [1923], New York 1925. Mainly first pbd in Times.

Discoveries: essays in literary criticism. [1924], 1930 (3 essays replaced by 4 others) (Travellers' Library). Some essays first pbd in TLS, Quart Rev, Yale Rev.

The necessity of art, by Murry [et al]. 1924, New York 1924. Murry's essay, Literature and religion, rptd in his To the unknown God, 1924.

To the unknown God: essays towards a religion. 1924, New York 1930. With appendix, Religion and Christianity: a reply by W. E. Orchard. Apart from Literature and religion, first pbd in Adelphi.

The voyage. 1924. Novel.

Wrap me up in my Aubusson carpet. New York 1924 (500 copies). On George Moore's criticism of Hardy in his Conversations in Ebury Street, 1924; first pbd in Adelphi 1 1924.

Keats and Shakespeare: a study of Keats' poetic life from 1816 to 1820. 1925, New York 1925. Based on the Clark Lectures for 1924.

The life of Jesus. 1926, New York 1926 (as Jesus: man of genius). First pbd in Adelphi 4 1926.

Godwin, W. Memoirs of Mary Wollstonecraft. 1928. Ed Murry.

Poems by Anne, Countess of Winchester, 1661–1720, selected with an introductory essay by Murry. 1928.

Things to come: essays. 1928, New York 1928, London 1938 (with new ch On love: human and divine). Mainly first pbd in Adelphi.

God: being an introduction to the science of metabiology. 1929, New York 1929.

D. H. Lawrence: two essays. Cambridge 1930 (Minority pamphlets 4). First pbd in New Adelphi, rptd in Reminiscences of D. H. Lawrence, 1933.

The poems and verses of John Keats, edited and arranged in chronological order by Murry. 2 vols 1930 (765 copies), New York 1930, 1 vol London 1949 (rev), New York 1949.

Studies in Keats. 1930, New York 1930, London 1939, New York 1939 (with 3 additional essays, as Studies in Keats, new and old), 1949 (extensively rev, as The mystery of Keats), New York 1949, London 1955 (rev with 3 additional essays, as Keats), New York 1955.

Countries of the mind: essays in literary criticism, 2nd ser. 1931, 1937 (with first ser, rev, 1931, above) (Oxford Bookshelf ser), Freeport NY 1968. All but 3 first pbd in TLS.

Son of woman: the story of D. H. Lawrence. 1931, New York [1931], London 1954 (with new introd, as D. H. Lawrence, son of woman).

Blake, W. Visions of the daughters of Albion; reproduced in facsimile, with a note by Murry. 1932, New York 1932.

The fallacy of economics. 1932 (Criterion miscellany 37).

The necessity of Communism. 1932, New York 1933.

The life of Katherine Mansfield, by Ruth E. Mantz. 1933, Toronto 1933. Introd, rev and last ch by Murry.

Reminiscences of D. H. Lawrence. 1933, New York [1933]. Reprinting of Adelphi and other articles and other early criticism by Murry of Lawrence, with reply to Catherine Carswell's The savage pilgrimage, 1932.

William Blake. 1933, Toronto 1933, New York 1964.

Between two worlds: an autobiography. 1935, New York [1936] (as The autobiography of Murry: between two worlds).

Marxism, by J. M. Murry [et al]. 1935, New York 1935. Contains: Marxism in general, Marxism and the individual, The new man, The political problem in Britain by Murry.

Shakespeare. 1936, New York [1936], London 1954 [1955] (with new preface).

God or the nation? [1937?]. Pacifist pamphlet.

The necessity of pacifism. 1937, Toronto 1937.

Heaven—and earth. 1938, New York [1938] (adds To the American reader) (as Heroes of thought). Literary and biographical essays.

Peace at Christmas. [Birmingham] 1938. Pamphlet rptd from TLS.

The pledge of peace. 1938. Pacifist articles first pbd in Peace News, Adelphi.

The defence of democracy. 1939, Toronto 1939.

The price of leadership. 1939, New York [1939].

Studies in Keats, new and old. New York 1939. See Studies in Keats, 1930, above.

The betrayal of Christ by the Churches. [1940], Toronto 1940.

The brotherhood of peace. 1940 (The Bond of Peace 4). Pamphlet.

Democracy and war. 1940. Pamphlet.

Europe in travail. 1940, New York 1940. Christian Newsletter books 2). 6 broadcast talks 1939–40.

Christocracy. 1942, Toronto 1942.

The dilemma of Christianity. [1942] (New Foundations 3). Pamphlet.

The economics of peace. [1943]. Pamphlet.

Adam and Eve: an essay towards a new and better society. 1944.

The third challenge. [1945] (Peace Aims pamphlet 33).

Trust or perish. [Edinburgh 1946?]. Pacifist pamphlet.

The challenge of Schweitzer. 1948. See G. F. Seaver, Albert Schweitzer: a vindication, being a reply to The challenge of Schweitzer by Murry, 1950.

The free society. 1948. See E. L. Allen, Pacifism and the free society: a reply to Murry. 1948.

Looking before and after: a collection of essays. 1948. Collected by F. A. Lea mainly from Adelphi; Richard Hillary rptd (rev) in Katherine Mansfield and other literary portraits, 1949, below.

Poems of John Keats edited with introduction by Murry. 1948.

Katherine Mansfield and other literary portraits. 1949.

The mystery of Keats. 1949. See Studies in Keats, 1930, above.

John Clare and other studies. 1950, New York 1950. Rev versions of various essays first pbd in the 1920's.

The conquest of death. 1951, New York 1951. Trn and analysis of B. H. Constant de Rebecque, Adolphe.

Community farm. 1952, New York 1952. Account of a co-operative farm in Suffolk founded by Murry in 1942; illustr R. Murry.

Jonathan Swift: a critical biography. 1954, New York 1955.

Hindus, M. (ed). Leaves of grass: one hundred years after. New essays by Murry [et al]. Stanford 1955. Whitman: the prophet of democracy, rptd in Unprofessional essays, 1956, below.

Keats. 1955. See Studies in Keats, 1930, above.

Swift. 1955, New York 1955, London 1961 (rev) (Br Council pamphlet).

Unprofessional essays. 1956, Fairlawn NJ 1956. Ed M. M. Murry. Contains: In defence of Fielding; Clare revisited; Whitman: poet-prophet of democracy; The plays of T. S. Eliot.

Love, freedom and society. 1957, Toronto 1957. On the religious beliefs of Lawrence and Schweitzer.

Katherine Mansfield and other literary studies, with a foreword by T. S. Eliot. 1959, Chester Springs Pa 1959. Contains: George Gissing; Katherine Mansfield; The novels of Henry Williamson.

Not as the scribes: lay sermons, ed with introd by A. R. Vidler. 1959, New York 1960.

Murry also contributed many chs, prefaces etc to books by other authors, some of which are included in Selections, *ed R. Rees, above. For the various works of Katherine Mansfield edited by Murry see Katherine Mansfield, cols 653–4, above. Murry founded* Adelphi *(became* New Adelphi*) in 1923 and edited and contributed to it 1923–48; he also edited and contributed to* Rhythm *(became* Blue Rev*) 1911–13;* Signature *(3 nos) 1915;* Daily Rev of the Foreign Press *(War Office);* Athenaeum *1919–21;* Wanderer *1933–4;* Peace News *1940–6; he contributed regularly to* Westminster Gazette, TLS, Nation, Aryan Path *and* London Mag.

§2

Dalglish, D. N. Portrait of a critic. Friends' Quart Examiner 61 1927.

Woolf, L. S. Look up there, with me. In his Essays on literature, history and politics etc. 1927. Murry's style in To the unknown God, 1924, compared with conversation of Pecksniff in Martin Chuzzlewit.

Carswell, C. The savage pilgrimage: a narrative of D. H. Lawrence. 1932. Contains fictitious account of Murry's relationship with Lawrence; reply by Murry ptd in his Reminiscences of D. H. Lawrence, 1933, above.

Heppenstall, R. Murry: a study in excellent normality. 1934.

—— Four absentees. 1960. Reminiscences of Murry, Dylan Thomas, Orwell and Eric Gill.

Glicksberg, C. I. Murry: Christ among the critics. South Atlantic Quart 38 1939.

Heath, W. M. The literary criticism of Murry. PMLA 70 1955.

Swinnerton, F. A. Rhythm. In his Background with chorus, 1956. On the beginnings of Murry's periodical.

—— Athenaeum and Adelphi. In his Figures in the foreground, 1963.

Seymour-Smith, M. Zero and the impossible: Roy Campbell, Wyndham Lewis, Joyce Cary, Murry. Encounter 9 1957.

Stanford, D. The religious approach of Murry. Aryan Path 28 1957.

—— Murry as a literary critic. EC 8 1958; rev and enlarged, South Atlantic Quart 58 1959.

Mairet, P. John Middleton Murry. 1958 (Br Council pamphlet).

Girard, D. Murry, D. H. Lawrence et Albert Schweitzer. Etudes Anglaises 12 1959.

Jones, J. Murry revaluated. New Statesman 12 Dec 1959. Review article.

Lea, F. A. The life of Murry. 1959.

—— Murry and marriage. D. H. Lawrence Rev 2 1969.

Murry, M. M. To keep faith. 1959. Memoir of his last years.

Watson, J. H. A good workman and his friends: recollections of Murry. London Mag 6 1959.

Kaufman, R. J. On using an obsessed critic: Murry. Graduate Student of English 3 1960.

Read, H. In London Mag 7 1960. Review-article of Mairet, above, and other works.

Beer, J. B. John Middleton Murry. CQ 3 1961. Essay-review of Selected criticism, 1916–57, 1961.

Crépin, A. Murry et le sens allégorique de la vie. Etudes Anglaises 14 1961.

Rees, R. L. E. M. A theory of my time: an essay in didactic reminiscence. 1963. Contains sketch of Murry.

Glenavy, B. M. Today we will only gossip. 1964. Reminiscences of Murry.

Knight, G. W. J. M. Murry. In J. Butt (ed), Of books and humankind: essays and poems presented to Bonamy Dobrée, 1964.

Casey, J. Style and feeling: Murry. In his The language of criticism, 1966.

D. H. Lawrence Rev 2 1969. Includes: J. R. Bennett, The problem of style [on Murry's book, 1922]; P. M. Griffith, Murry on Swift: 'the nec plus ultra of objectivity'; C. G. Thayer, Murry's Shakespeare; R. H. Fogle, Beauty and truth: Murry on Keats.

Griffin, E. G. The circular and the linear: the Murry–D. H. Lawrence affair. D. H. Lawrence Rev 2 1969.

—— John Middleton Murry. New York 1969.

M.P.

ERNEST NEWMAN
1868–1959

§1

Gluck and the opera: a study in musical history. 1895.

A study of Wagner. 1899, New York 1899.

Wagner. [1904].

Musical studies. 1905.

Elgar. 1906, New York 1906.

Hugo Wolf. 1907, New York 1966 (introd by W. Legge).

Richard Strauss: with a personal note by A. Kalisch. 1908.

Wagner as man and artist. 1914, New York 1914.

A musical motley. 1919, New York 1919, 1925 (rev). Essays.

The piano-player and its music. 1920.

A musical critic's holiday. 1925, New York 1925.

The stories of the great operas. 15 pts [1927], 3 vols New York 1928–30, 1935 (in 1 vol, as Stories of the great operas and their composers).

The unconscious Beethoven: an essay in musical psychology. 1927, New York 1927.

Fact and fiction about Wagner. 1931, New York 1931. Critique of P. Hurn and W. Root, The truth about Wagner.

The life of Richard Wagner. 4 vols 1933–47, New York 1933–46.

The man Liszt: a study of the tragi-comedy of a soul divided against itself. 1934, New York 1935.

More stories of famous operas. New York 1943.

Opera nights. 1943.

Wagner nights. 1949, New York 1949 (as The Wagner operas).

More opera nights. 1954, New York 1955 (for 1954) (as Seventeen famous operas).

From the world of music: essays from the Sunday Times. 1956, New York 1957. Selected by F. Aprahamian.

Great operas, the definitive treatment of their histories, stories and music. New York 1958. Rptd from More stories of famous operas, and Seventeen famous operas, above.

More essays from the world of music: essays from the Sunday Times. 1958, New York 1958. Selected by F. Aprahamian.

Testament of music: essays and papers by E. Newman. Ed H. van Thal 1962, New York 1963.

Formerly William Roberts; also used the pseudonym Hugh M. Cecil. Newman was a prolific translator; he edited Handbooks for Musicians *1914–22 and was general editor of the* New Library of Music *from 1907. In 1905 he was music critic of* Manchester Guardian; *from 1906–19 of* Birmingham Post, *from 1920–58 of* Sunday Times, *and for a short time of* Observer.

§2

Grew, E. In The Sackbut. Nov 1928.

—— Newman: twenty-five years of reading his writings. Br Musician & Musical News July–Nov 1931, July 1932.

—— His [Newman's] life and opinions. Br Musician & Musical News Jan–Dec 1934.

Cooper, M. Music—pure and impure. London Mercury 31 1935.

Fanfare for Ernest Newman. Ed H. van Thal 1955. Collection of articles; includes a list of his works.

Blissett, W. Newman and English Wagnerism. Music & Letters 40 1959. Reply by H. G. Farmer 41 1960.

Hollinrake, R. Nietzsche, Wagner and Newman. Music & Letters 41 1960.

Kivy, P. Herbert Spencer and a musical dispute. Musical Rev 23 1962.

Newman, V. Ernest Newman: a memoir. 1963.

Westrup, J. Editorial. Music & Letters 44 1963. On Newman's criticism.

H.M.R.

JOHN RAMSAY ALLARDYCE NICOLL
b. 1894

William Blake and his poetry. 1922.

Dryden and his poetry. 1923, New York 1967.

A history of Restoration drama 1660-1700. Cambridge 1923, 1928 (rev), 1940 (rev), 1952 (rev, with supplementary notes, as vol 1 of A history of English drama, 1952-9, below).

An introduction to dramatic theory. 1923, 1931 (rev and enlarged as The theory of drama), New York 1931.

British drama: an historical survey from the beginnings to the present time. 1925, New York [1925], London 1932 (rev), 1947 (rev), New York [195-?], London 1962 (rev), New York [1963].

A history of early eighteenth-century drama 1700-1750. Cambridge 1925, 1927 (with addns), 1952 (rev, with supplementary notes, as vol 2 of A history of English drama, 1952-9, below).

The development of the theatre: a study of theatrical art from the beginnings to the present day. 1927, New York 1927, London 1937 (rev), New York 1937, 1946 (rev and enlarged), London 1948, 1958 (rev), New York 1958, London 1966 (rev), New York 1967.

A history of late eighteenth-century drama 1750-1800. Cambridge 1927, 1952 (with supplementary notes, as vol 3 of A history of English drama, 1952-9, below).

Studies in Shakespeare. 1927, New York [1928].

The English stage. 1928.

A history of early nineteenth-century drama 1800-1850. 2 vols Cambridge 1930, 1 vol 1955 (rev, with supplementary notes, as vol 4 of A history of English drama, 1952-9, below).

Masks, mimes and miracles: studies in the popular theatre. 1931, New York 1931.

The English theatre: a short history. 1936.

Film and theatre. New York [1936], London [1936].

Stuart masques and the Renaissance stage. 1937, New York 1938.

A history of late nineteenth-century drama 1850-1900. 2 vols Cambridge 1946, 1 vol 1959 (with supplementary notes, as vol 5 of A history of English drama, 1952-9, below).

World drama from Æschylus to Anouilh. 1949, New York [1950?].

A history of English drama 1660-1900. 6 vols Cambridge 1952-9. For earlier edns of vols 1-5, see above. Vol 6, A short-title alphabetical catalogue of plays produced or printed in England from 1660 to 1900.

Shakespeare. 1952, New York 1952 (as Shakespeare: an introduction).

The theatre and dramatic theory. 1962, New York 1962.

The world of Harlequin: a critical study of the commedia dell'arte. Cambridge 1963.

English drama: a modern viewpoint. 1968, New York 1968.

Nicoll has also edited Holinshed's Chronicle (1927), the works of Tourneur [1929], Chapman's Homer (1957), plays by Sharpham (1926) and Boucicault (1940), and several anthologies. Nicoll is also general editor of the

London Series of English Texts [1925-] *and was editor of Shakespeare Survey (1948-65).*

C.H.E.P.

SIR HAROLD GEORGE NICOLSON
1886-1968
See cols 1198-9, below.

'FRANK O'CONNOR', MICHAEL FRANCIS O'DONOVAN
1903-66
See cols 684-5, above.

CHARLES KAY OGDEN
1889-1957

The history and theory of vitalism, by H. Dreisch. Tr Ogden 1914.

The problem of the continuation school. 1914. With R. H. Best.

The schools and the nation, by A. G. Kerschensteiner. Tr Ogden 1914.

Militarism versus feminism: an enquiry and a policy demonstrating that militarism involves the subjection of women. 1915. Anon.

Above the battle, by R. Rolland. Tr Ogden 1916.

The foundations of aesthetics. 1922, New York 1948. With I. A. Richards and J. Wood.

The meaning of meaning: a study of the influence of language upon thought and of the science of symbolism. 1923, 1927 (rev), 1930 (rev), 1936 (rev), 1944 (rev), New York 1956. With I. A. Richards.

Eyeless sight, by J. Romains. Tr Ogden 1924.

The philosophy of As if, by H. Vaihinger. Tr Ogden 1924.

The meaning of psychology. New York 1926.

The origin of instinct, by E. Bugnion. Tr Ogden 1927.

Thought and the brain, by H. Piéron. Tr Ogden 1927.

The social world of the ants compared with that of man, by A. H. Forel. Tr Ogden. 2 vols 1928.

The ABC of psychology. 1929.

Basic English: a general introduction with rules and grammar. 1930.

The Basic vocabulary: a statistical analysis, with special reference to substitution and translation. 1930.

The laws of feeling, by F. Paulhan. Tr Ogden 1930.

Basic English applied-science. 1931.

Brighter Basic: examples of Basic English for young persons of taste and feeling. 1931.

Debabelization, with a survey of contemporary opinion on the problem of a universal language. 1931.

The theory of legislation, by J. Bentham. Ed Ogden 1931.

The ABC of Basic English, in Basic. 1932.

The Basic dictionary: being the 7,500 most useful words with their equivalent in Basic English. 1932.

The Basic words: a detailed account of their uses. 1932, 1964 (rev).

Bentham's Theory of fictions. Ed Ogden 1932.

International talks in Basic English, by H. W. Steed. 1932. Put into Basic by Ogden.

Jeremy Bentham, 1832-2032. 1932.

Opposition: a linguistic and psychological analysis. 1932, Bloomington 1967.

Basic by examples. 1933.

The system of Basic English. New York 1934, New York 1968 (rev E. C. Graham as Basic English: international second language).

Basic English versus the artificial languages. 1935.

Basic step by step. 1935.

The three signs and other American stories put into Basic English. Ed Ogden 1935.

Times of India guide to Basic English. Ed A. Myers, Bombay 1938. With I. A. Richards.

The general Basic English dictionary: giving more than 40,000 senses of over 20,000 words in Basic English. Ed Ogden 1940, New York 1942.

Basic for science. 1942.

Ogden also pbd Basic English textbooks for foreign students and prepared Basic English edns of certain works, e.g. stories from the Bible. He founded and edited Cambridge Mag 1912–22, contributed to Basic News, and was general editor of the International Library of Psychology, Philosophy and Scientific Method, and other ser.

N. J. S.

ALFRED RICHARD ORAGE
1873–1934
Selections

Selected essays and critical writings. Ed H. Read and D. Saurat 1935, Freeport NY 1967.

§1

Friedrich Nietzsche: the Dionysian spirit of the age. Edinburgh 1906 (Spirit of the age ser), Chicago 1911.

Consciousness: animal, human and superhuman. 1907.

Nietzsche in outline and aphorism. Edinburgh 1907, Chicago 1910. Selection ed Orage.

Hobson, S. G. National Guilds: an enquiry into the wage system and the way out. Ed Orage 1914, New York 1914. Anon. Mainly first pbd in New Age 1912–13.

An alphabet of economics. 1917.

An Englishman talks it out with an Irishman. Dublin 1918, London 1918. Pamphlet.

Douglas, C. H. Credit-power and democracy, with a commentary on the included scheme by A. R. Orage. 1920, 1934 (rev and enlarged).

Readers and writers 1917–21, by 'R.H.C.'—A. R. Orage. 1922, New York 1922. Essays first pbd in New Age.

The art of reading. New York [1930]. Essays mostly first pbd under the initials R.H.C. in New Age.

Psychological exercises. Ed Orage New York 1930. Pamphlet.

On love, freely adapted from the Tibetan. 1932. Pamphlet. Rptd 1957 with Essays and aphorisms (1954, below) as On love, with some aphorisms and other essays.

Politicians and the public service: being a reprint of a series of articles appearing in New English Weekly on the British Dreyfus case [the case of the Hon Violet Douglas-Pennant]. Ed Orage 1934.

Social credit: broadcast, 1934; and The fear of leisure: an address, 1935. 1935 (Pamphlets on the New Economics 5).

Political and economic writings from New English Weekly 1932–4, with a preliminary section from New Age 1912. Arranged by M. Butchart. 1936, Freeport NY 1967.

The active mind: adventures in awareness. 1954, New York 1954.

Essays and aphorisms. 1954. With biographical note by S. C. Nott; rptd 1957 with On love, 1932, above (as On love, with some aphorisms and other essays).

Gurdjieff, G. I. Meetings with remarkable men. 1963. A revision of a trn by Orage.

Orage contributed introds and prefaces to other works. He edited New Age 1907–22 (jointly with Holbrook Jackson May–Dec 1907). He founded New English Weekly and edited it 1932–4.

§2

Gould, F. J. Labour's unrest and Labour's future: brief notes on Orage [et al]. 1919. Orage and National Guilds.

Murry, J. M. Transcendental criticism. Nation & Athenaeum 11 Feb 1922. Essay-review of Readers and writers, 1922.

New English Weekly 15 Nov 1934. Orage memorial number. Contributions by Chesterton, Shaw, T. S. Eliot, Ezra Pound et al. Chesterton's contribution rptd as introd to P. Mairet, A. R. Orage, 1936, below.

Eliot, T. S. A commentary [on the death of Orage]. Criterion 14 1935.

Pound, E. In the wounds—memoriam A. R. Orage. Criterion 14 1935. Rptd (condensed) in his Impact: essays on ignorance and the decline of American civilization, 1960.

Hastings, B. The old 'New Age': Orage and others. 1936.

Mairet, P. A. R. Orage: a memoir. 1936 (introd by G. K. Chesterton), New Hyde Park NY 1966 (with a Re-introduction, omits Chesterton's introd).

Hobson, S. G. In his Pilgrim to the Left: memoirs of a modern revolutionist, 1938.

Jackson, H. Orage: personal recollections. Windmill [no 11] 1948.

King, C. D. The Oragean version. New York [1951]. Orage's version of the teaching of Gurdjieff.

Selver, P. Orage and the 'New Age' circle: reminiscences and reflections. 1959.

Nott, C. S. Teachings of Gurdjieff—the journal of a pupil: and account of some years of Gurdjieff and Orage in New York and at Fontainebleau-Avon. 1961.

'Oliver Edwards'. Orage and others. Times 11 Aug 1966.

Martin, W. The New Age under Orage: chapters in English cultural history. Manchester [1967].

TLS 25 April 1968. The little magazine IX: The New Age.

M. P.

'GEORGE ORWELL',
ERIC ARTHUR BLAIR
1903–50

See cols 690–6, above.

ERIC HONEYWOOD PARTRIDGE
b. 1894
Selections

A covey of Partridge: an anthology. 1937.

§1

The French romantics' knowledge of English literature 1820–48. Paris 1924.

A critical medley: essays, studies and notes in English, French and comparative literature. Paris 1926.

Robert Eyres Landor: a biographical and critical sketch. 1927.

Songs and slang of the British soldier 1914–18. 1930, 1930 (rev and enlarged), 1931 (rev and enlarged). With J. Brophy; further revision, by Brophy, pbd 1965 (as The long trail: what the British soldier sang and said in the Great War of 1914–18).

Slang today and yesterday: with a short historical sketch and vocabularies of English, American and Australian slang. 1933, New York 1934, London 1935 (rev), 1950 (rev), New York 1950, London [1960] (rev), New York 1960.

Words, words, words! 1933. Essays.

Name this child: a dictionary of English and American Christian names. 1936, 1938 (rev and enlarged), 1951 (rev and enlarged), 1959 (abridged).

A dictionary of slang and unconventional English. 1937, New York 1937; suppl 1938. Frequently rev and enlarged.

For these few minutes: almost an anthology. Ed Partridge 1938.

The world of words: an introduction to language in general and to English and American in particular. 1938, New York 1939, London 1948 (rev).

A dictionary of clichés with an introductory essay. 1940, New York 1940, London 1950 (rev).

A New Testament word book: a glossary. 1940.

Précis writing: passages judiciously selected with an introduction on the art of précis. London 1940.

A dictionary of abbreviations: with especial attention to wartime abbreviations. 1942, 1949 (rev and enlarged).

Usage and abusage: a guide to good English. New York and London 1942, London 1947 (rev), New York 1949 (as A dictionary of effective speech), London 1957 (rev and enlarged), 1965 (rev and enlarged). A shortened and simplified version pbd 1954 (as The concise usage and abusage: a modern guide to good English).

A dictionary of RAF slang: with an introductory essay. 1945.

Shakespeare's bawdy: a literary and psychological essay and a comprehensive glossary. 1947, New York 1948, London 1955 (rev), New York 1955, London 1968 (rev and enlarged).

A dictionary of Forces' slang 1939-45. Ed Partridge et al 1948.

Words at war, words at peace: essays on language in general and particular words. 1948.

A dictionary of the underworld, British and American. 1949, New York 1950, London 1961 (with addenda), New York 1961, London 1968 (much enlarged).

English: a course for human beings. 1949.

Name into word: proper nouns that have become common property—a discursive dictionary. 1949, New York 1950 (rev and enlarged).

Here, there and everywhere: essays upon language. 1950.

British and American English since 1900. 1951, New York 1951, London 1951 (corrected). With J. W. Clark.

Chamber of horrors: a glossary of official jargon both English and American, by 'Vigilans' [i.e. Partridge]. 1952. With introd by Partridge.

From Sanskrit to Brazil: vignettes and essays upon languages. 1952.

You have a point there: a guide to punctuation and its allies. 1953.

What's the meaning?: a book for younger people. 1956.

A first book of quotations. Ed Partridge 1958, 1964 (rev, as A book of essential quotations).

Origins: a short etymological dictionary of modern English. 1958, New York 1958, London 1959 (rev and enlarged), New York 1959, London 1961 (rev), London 1966 (rev), New York 1966.

A charm of words: essays and papers on language. 1960, New York 1961.

Comic alphabets: their origin, development, nature. 1961, New York 1967.

Smaller slang dictionary. 1961, New York 1961, London 1964 (corrections and addns).

The gentle art of lexicography, as pursued and experienced by an addict. 1963, New York 1963.

Partridge also contributed to or helped to edit various dictionaries and philological works. He pbd several vols of essays and a number of textbooks, manuals, essays and introds on language and literature. He edited various anthologies of prose and verse. With B. Ratcliffe he edited Window *Jan–Oct 1930. He is editor, too, of the* Language Library *1952–.*

P.C.

SIR NIKOLAUS BERNHARD LEON PEVSNER
b. 1902

Bibliographies

Barr, J. A select bibliography of the publications of Pevsner. In Conerning architecture: essays on architectural writers and writing presented to Nikolaus Pevsner, ed J. Summerson 1968. Includes trns.

§ 1

Barockmalerei in den romanischen Ländern. Potsdam [1928]. With O. Grautoff. Pt 1, on Italian rococo, by Pevsner.

Leipziger Barock: die Baukunst der Barockzeit in Leipzig. Dresden [1928].

Pioneers of the modern movement from William Morris to Walter Gropius. 1936, New York 1949 (rev, as Pioneers of modern design), London 1960 (rev and partly rewritten) (Penguin), 1964 (corrected).

An enquiry into industrial art in England. Cambridge 1937.

Academies of art past and present. Cambridge 1940, New York 1940.

An outline of European architecture. 1942 (Pelican), New York 1948. With frequent subsequent revisions.

The leaves of Southwell. 1945 (King Penguin). Photographs by F. L. Attenborough.

Charles R. Mackintosh. Milan 1950. In Italian, tr by C. Tamborini; English trn by A. Hartcup in Studies in art, architecture and design, 1968, below.

High Victorian design: a study of the exhibits of 1851. 1951.

The buildings of England. 1951 onwards (Penguin). Some vols with collaborators.

The Englishness of English art. 1955, 1956 (rev and enlarged), New York 1956.

Christopher Wren 1632–1723. Milan 1958, New York 1960. In Italian, tr E. Labò.

The Penguin dictionary of architecture. 1966. With J. Fleming and H. Honour.

The sources of modern architecture and design. [1968], New York 1968.

Studies in art, architecture and design: vol 1, From mannerism to romanticism; vol 2, Victorian and after. 2 vols 1968. Includes items previously pbd separately.

Pevsner has edited Pelican history of art *1953 onwards and is art editor of* Penguin Books.

J.M.P.

VIVIAN de SOLA PINTO
b. 1895

Sir Charles Sedley, 1639–1701: a study in the life and literature of the Restoration. 1927.

Peter Sterry, Platonist and Puritan, 1613–72: a biographical and critical study. Cambridge 1934.

Rochester: portrait of a Restoration poet. 1935, 1962 (rev, as Enthusiast in wit: a portrait of John Wilmot, Earl of Rochester 1647–80), Lincoln Nebraska 1962.

The English Renaissance, 1510–1688. 1938, 1951 (rev), 1966 (rev).

Crisis in English poetry, 1880–1940. 1951, New York 1951.

Restoration carnival: five courtier poets—Rochester, Dorset, Sedley, Etherege and Sheffield. 1954. Short biographies and selections.

The city that shone: an autobiography. 1969.

Pinto has edited the works of Lord Berners, Sedley, Rochester, Blake, Byron, Hardy etc. He edited The common muse: an anthology of popular British ballad poetry *(with A. E. Rodway), and is editor of both the* Life, literature and thought library *and* A series of English texts. *He has also written 5 vols of poetry:* Spindrift *(1918),* Duality *(1922),* Twelve poems *(1927),* The invisible sun *(1934) and* This is my England *(1941).*

H.M.R.

ALFRED WILLIAM POLLARD
1859–1944
Bibliographies
Murphy, G. A select bibliography of the writings of Pollard. Oxford 1938 (priv ptd).

§1
Athletic training: prize essays by R. V. S. Smith, Pollard [et al] 1882.
Last words on the history of the title-page, with notes on some colophons and twenty seven fac-similes of title-pages. 1891 (250 copies).
Chaucer. 1893, 1926 (corrected), 1931 (rewritten and enlarged), New York 1969.
Early illustrated books: a history of the decoration and illustration of books in the 15th and 16th centuries. 1893 (Books About Books), New York 1968.
Italian book illustrations, chiefly of the fifteenth century. 1894 (Portfolio Artistic Monographs).
The illustrations in French Books of Hours, 1486–1500. [1897]. Rptd from Bibliographica.
Old picture books, with other essays on bookish subjects. 1902.
Books in the house: an essay on private libraries and collections for young and old. Indianapolis 1904 (510 copies), London 1907.
An essay on colophons, with specimens and translations. Chicago 1905 (255 copies). Introd by R. Garnett.
Shakespeare folios and quartos: a study in the bibliography of Shakespeare's plays, 1594–1685. 1909.
Fine books. 1912 (Connoisseur's Lib), New York 1964.
A census of Shakespeare's plays in quarto, 1594–1709. New Haven 1916, London 1916. With H. C. Bartlett.
Modern fine printing in England and Mr Bruce Rogers, with a list of books and other pieces of printing designed by Mr Rogers. Newark NJ 1916. Pamphlet.
Two brothers [G. B. and R. T. Pollard]: accounts rendered. 1916 (priv ptd), 1917 (enlarged). On his sons killed in the 1914–18 war.
Shakespeare's fight with the pirates and the problems of the transmission of his text. 1917, Cambridge 1920 (rev with an introd) (Shakespeare Problems). Lectures.
St Catherine of Siena. 1919.
The foundations of Shakespeare's text. [1923]. Lecture.
Shakespeare's hand in the play of Sir Thomas More: papers by Pollard [et al], ed Pollard, Cambridge 1923 (Shakespeare Problems).
A short-title catalogue of books printed in England, Scotland and Ireland and of English books printed abroad, 1475–1640. 1926. With G. R. Redgrave and the help of others.
Cobden-Sanderson and the Doves Press. 1929 (priv ptd).
The trained printer and the amateur and the pleasure of small books. 1929. Pamphlet.
Shakespeare's text. In A companion to Shakespeare studies, ed H. G. Barker and G. B. Harrison, Cambridge 1934.
William Shakespeare. In The great Tudors, ed K. Garvin 1935. With J. D. Wilson.
My first fifty years. In G. Murphy, A select bibliography of the works of Pollard, Oxford 1938, above.
Pollard also assisted in the preparation of a number of library, sale and exhibition catalogues; from 1915–25 he wrote a number of pamphlets on religious matters, mainly in connection with the Anglican Fellowship; he also tr works by Aristotle, Sallust and Émile Laveleye.

Editions
Chaucer's Canterbury tales. 2 vols 1886–7. 12 tales.
Iohannis Wycliffe Dialogus sive Speculum ecclesie militantis. 1886 (Wyclif Soc).
Sir Philip Sidney's Astrophel and Stella. 1888 (50 copies).

Iohannis Wyclif Tractatus de officio regis. 1887 (for 1889), New York 1966. (Wyclif Soc). With C. Sayle.
English miracle plays, moralities and interludes: specimens of the pre-Elizabethan drama. Oxford 1890, with many subsequent revisions.
Odes from the Greek dramatists, translated into lyric metres by English poets and scholars. 1890.
Herrick, R. The Hesperides and Noble numbers. 2 vols 1891, 1898 (rev), New York 1898 (ML).
Chaucer's Canterbury tales. 2 vols 1894.
Reed, T. B. A list of books and papers on printers and printing. [1895]. Rptd from Trans Bibl Soc.
The Towneley Plays. 1897 (EETS extra ser 71).
The works of Geoffrey Chaucer. Ed Pollard et al 1898 (Globe edn).
Arber, E. An English garner (Fifteenth-century prose and verse). Westminster 1903, New York 1964.
Heywood, J. The play of the wether, and A mery play betwene Johan Johan, the husbande, Tyb, his wife. New York 1903, London 1903 (Representative English Comedies 1).
The Queen's Majesty's entertainment at Woodstock, 1575, from the unique fragment of the edition of 1585, including the Tale of Hemetes the hermit, and a comedy in verse, probably by George Gascoigne. Oxford 1903–10 (115 copies).
The Macro plays. 1904 (EETS extra ser 91).
Proctor, R. G. C. Bibliographical essays. 1905 (200 copies). With memoir.
Records of the English Bible: the documents relating to the translation and publication of the Bible in English, 1525–1611. 1911.
On active service: letters of G. B. Pollard. 1915 (priv ptd).
The romance of King Arthur abridged from Malory's Morte d'Arthur. 1917.
Messages of the saints. 3 vols 1918–19.
English literary autographs 1550–1650. Selected and ed W. W. Greg in collaboration with Pollard [et al]. 4 pts Oxford 1925–32.
A world list of scientific periodicals published in the years 1900–21. 2 vols 1925.
Earliest printing in England: an Indulgence of 1476. Ed and tr Pollard 1929.
Le Morte Darthur, now modernised as to spelling and punctuation by Pollard. 3 vols New York 1936.
Pollard also edited Bibl Soc News Sheet, 1894–1920 (largely written by him); Library, 1903–34 (1903–19 with J. Y. W. MacAllister); Books about books 6 vols 1893–4; Bibliographica 3 vols 1895–7; The English Bookman's Lib 3 vols 1899; Lib of Eng Classics 30 vols 1900–4 (with bibliographical notes); Shakespeare Problems Ser, 1920–44 (with J. D. Wilson) and a number of school edns of Chaucer's Canterbury tales.

§2
Thomas, H. From fifty to seventy-five. In G. Murphy, A select bibliography of the writings of Pollard, Oxford, 1938, above. Continuation of Pollard's My first fifty years.
Francis, F. C. A. W. Pollard. Library ser 4 25 1945.
—— The Bibliographical Society: a sketch of the first fifty years. In The Bibliographical Society: studies in retrospect, 1945.
Wilson, J. D. A. W. Pollard. Proc Br Acad 31 1945.
M.P.

STEPHEN MEREDITH POTTER
1900–69
Selections
Three-upmanship. New York 1962. The theory and practice of gamesmanship; Some notes on lifemanship; One-upmanship.

§1

The young man. 1929. Novel.

D. H. Lawrence: a first study. 1930.

Coleridge and S.T.C. 1935, New York 1965.

The muse in chains: a study in education. 1937.

The theory and practice of gamesmanship: or the art of winning games without actually cheating. 1947, New York 1948.

Some notes on lifemanship: with a summary of recent researches in gamesmanship. 1950, New York 1951.

One-upmanship: being some account of the activities and teaching of the Lifemanship Correspondence College of one-upness and gameslifemastery. 1952, New York 1952.

Sense of humour. 1954, New York 1954. Anthology.

Potter on America. 1956, New York 1957.

Supermanship: or how to continue to stay top without actually falling apart. 1958, New York 1959.

The magic number: the story of '57'. 1959. History of H. J. Heinz & Co Ltd.

Steps to immaturity. 1959. Autobiography.

Squawky: the adventures of a clasperchoice. New York 1964, London [1965]. For children.

Anti-woo: the lifeman's improved primer for non-lovers (the first lifemanship guide). 1965, New York 1965.

The complete golf gamesmanship. 1968, New York 1968 (as Golfmanship).

Potter also edited selections from Coleridge; and a volume of Sara Coleridge's letters to Thomas Poole, pbd as Minnow among tritons, *1934.*

J.G.

JOHN COWPER POWYS
1872–1963

See cols 706–10, above.

LLEWELYN POWYS
1884–1939

A catalogue of Powys mss by G. F. Sims (Rare Books), Hurst, Berks (1953) lists over 200 items, some unpbd, and includes Powys' own collection of offprints of his reviews and articles; a collection of 185 items is held by Univ of California Library.

Bibliographies

Siberell, L. E. A check list of the books of Powys. In 'Louis Marlow' (L. U. Wilkinson), Welsh ambassadors, 1936, §2 below.

Hopkins, K. A check list of books by [and on] Powys. In Llewelyn Powys, a selection, 1952, Selections below.

Selections

The book of days of Powys: thoughts from his philosophy selected by J. Wallis. 1937 (Golden Cockerell Press, 300 copies). Etchings by E. Corsellis, with introd by Powys.

Llewelyn Powys: a selection from his writings made by K. Hopkins. 1952, New York 1961. Includes 20 unpbd letters and 3 essays not previously collected in bk form.

Somerset and Dorset essays. Foreword by J. C. Powys, 1957. Selections from the 2 collections pbd in 1935 and 1937.

§1

Confessions of two brothers, J. C. Powys, Llewellyn [sic] Powys. Rochester NY 1916. Includes extracts from Powys' diaries with commentary by J. C. Powys.

Ebony and ivory. New York 1923 (preface by T. Dreiser), London 1923 (preface by E. Shanks), 1939 (rev) (Penguin), 1960 (introd by L. Wilkinson). Stories and sketches of life in East Africa.

Thirteen worthies. New York 1923 (preface by V. W. Brooks), London 1924. Essays, mainly on English literature.

Black laughter. New York [1924], London 1925, 1953 (foreword by N. Farson). Sketches of life in East Africa; some chs are rev versions of articles first pbd in New York Evening Post, Freeman.

Honey and gall. Girard, Kansas [1924] (Little Blue Book). Essays.

Cup-bearers of wine and hellebore. Girard, Kansas [1924] (Little Blue Book). Essays on writers.

Skin for skin. New York [1925], London 1926 (900 copies), 1948 (with The verdict of Bridlegoose, 1926). Autobiography.

The verdict of Bridlegoose. New York [1926], London 1927 (900 copies), 1948 (with Skin for skin, 1925). Autobiography.

Henry Hudson. 1927, New York 1928. Biography.

Out of the past. Pasadena [1928] (25 copies); rptd in Earth memories, 1934, below.

The cradle of God. New York [1929], London 1929, 1949 (introd by E. Carr). Jewish development in Biblical times.

Apples be ripe. New York [1930], London 1930. Novel.

The pathetic fallacy: a study of Christianity. 1930, Philadelphia [1930] (as An hour on Christianity).

Impassioned clay. New York 1931, London 1931. Philosophical essay.

A pagan's pilgrimage. New York [1931], London 1931. A journey to Palestine.

The life and times of Anthony à Wood, abridged from A. Clark's edition and with an introduction by L. Powys, 1932.

Now that the gods are dead. New York 1932 (400 copies), London 1949 (with Glory of life, 1934). Philosophical essay.

Glory of life. 1934 (277 copies; Golden Cockerel press, wood engravings by R. Gibbings), 1949 (with Now that the gods are dead, 1932). Philosophical essay.

Earth memories. 1934. Essays on country life; rptd in Earth memories, New York 1938, below. Woodcuts by G. M. Powys.

Damnable opinions. 1935.

Dorset essays. 1935. Photographs by W. Goodden. 18 essays rptd in Earth memories, New York 1938.

The twelve months. 1936. Wood engravings by R. Gibbings. Essays.

Somerset essays. 1937. Photographs by W. Goodden.

Rats in the sacristy. 1937. Preface by J. C. Powys, wood engravings by G. M. Powys. Essays on writers.

Earth memories. New York (1938). Introd by V. W. Brooks. A reprint of Earth memories, London 1935 with a selection from Dorset essays, 1935.

Love and death: an imaginary autobiography. 1939, New York [1941]. Introd by A. Gregory (Powys).

A baker's dozen. Herrin, Ill [1939] (493 copies, introd by L. E. Siberell, illustr M. Noheimer), London 1941 (introd by J. C. Powys, decorations by G. M. Powys). Essays.

Old English Yuletide. Introd by G. and H. H. Trovillion, Herrin Ill 1940 (202 copies). A Somerset Christmas, and The New Year, rptd from A Baker's dozen.

Swiss essays. 1947.

A voyage to the West Indies. In The pleasure ground: a miscellany of English writing, ed M. Elwin, 1947.

Thomas Bewick, 1753–1828: an essay, to which is now added a letter from England from Alyse Powys. Lexington 1951. Essay rptd from Thirteen worthies, 1923, above.

Letters

The letter of Powys, selected and ed by L. Wilkinson 1943. Introd by A. Gregory [Powys]. Excludes letters. ptd in L. Marlow's Welsh ambassadors, 1936, §2, below.

Advice to a young poet. 1949, ed R. L. Blackmore, Rutherford NJ 1969. Letters to K. Hopkins.

See also Llewelyn Powys: a selection, *1952, Selections, above.*

Llewelyn Powys contributed to a large number of jnls and newspapers; many essays have not been collected and some remain unpbd.

§2

'Louis Marlow' (L. U. Wilkinson). A chaste man. New York 1917. As Wilkinson. The character Cyprian Strange is a caricature of Powys.

— In his Swan's milk, 1934. Reminiscences.

— Welsh ambassadors: Powys lives and letters. 1936. Contains a selection of L. Powys' letters (not rptd in Letters, 1943) with reminiscences.

— In his Forth, beast!, 1946. A continuation of Swan's milk, 1934.

— The brothers Powys [Cincinnati] 1946 (for 1947). Rptd in Essays by Divers Hands 24 1948. As Wilkinson.

— In his Seven friends, 1953.

Sherman, S. P. Llewelyn Powys: a sick man's vision or the naked truth? In his Critical woodcuts, New York 1926.

— Llewelyn Powys: five years with the American intelligentsia. In his main stream, New York 1927. Essayreview of The verdict of Bridlegoose, 1926.

Powys, J. C. In his Autobiography, 1934.

Arns, K. Die Geschwister Powys. E Studien 69 1935.

Ward, R. H. In his Powys brothers, 1935.

Powys, L. C. In his The joy of it, 1937. Reminiscences.

— The Powys family. Welsh Rev 7 1948; rptd separately, West Pennard 1952.

— In his Still the joy of it, 1956.

Govan, G. E. The Powys family. Sewanee Rev 46 1938.

Peters, E. C. A poet who wrote no verse. Poetry Rev 32 1941.

Elwin, M. The life of Llewelyn Powys. 1946.

Martin, E. W. In The new spirit, ed E. W. Martin 1946.

Brooks, V. W. In his Chilmark miscellany, New York 1948.

Allen, W. G. Llewelyn Powys: a village radical. Wind & the Rain 6 1949.

Gregory, A. A famous family. London Mag 5 1958.

Churchill, R. C. The Powys brothers 1962 (Br Council pamphlet).

— Not least Llewelyn. REL 4 1963.

Philobiblon (Colgate Univ Lib) no 8 1966. J. C. Powys special issue. Includes: L. Wilkinson, The brothers Powys; T. Davies, The Powys family.

Hopkins, K. The Powys brothers: a biographical appreciation. 1967.

M.P.

JOHN BOYNTON PRIESTLEY
b. 1894

See cols 712–17, above.

VICTOR SAWDON PRITCHETT
b. 1900

See col 717, above.

PETER COURTNEY QUENNELL
b. 1905

§1

Masques and poems. Waltham St Lawrence 1922.

Poems. 1926, New York 1930 (adds Inscription on a fountain-head; Calligraphy).

Baudelaire and the Symbolists. 1929, 1954 (rev). Essays. Inscription on a fountain-head. 1929 (Ariel Poem).

The phoenix-kind: a novel. 1931, New York 1931.

A letter to Mrs Virginia Woolf. 1932 (Hogarth Letters no 12). Reply to A letter to a young poet.

A superficial journey through Tokyo and Peking. 1932.

Aspects of seventeenth-century verse [an anthology]. Ed Quennell 1933, 1947 (rev).

Sympathy, and other stories. 1933.

Byron. 1934.

Byron: the years of fame. 1935, New York 1935, London 1967 (rev), Hamden Conn 1967.

Victorian panorama: a survey of life and fashion from contemporary photographs. 1937, New York 1937. With commentary by Quennell.

Caroline of England: an Augustan portrait. [1939], New York 1940.

'To Lord Byron': feminine profiles, based upon unpbd letters 1807–24. 1939. With 'George Paston' (E. M. Symonds).

Byron in Italy. 1941, New York 1941.

Time exposure, by Cecil Beaton. [Photographs of period 1923–40]. 1941, 1946 (rev). With commentary and captions by Quennell.

Four portraits: studies of the eighteenth century (Boswell, Gibbon, Sterne, Wilkes). 1945, New York 1945 (as The profane virtues: four studies of the eighteenth century), London 1965 (rev, original title), Hamden Conn 1965.

John Ruskin: the portrait of a prophet. 1949, New York 1949.

The singular preference: portraits and essays. 1952, New York 1953.

Spring in Sicily. 1952. Travel.

Hogarth's progress. 1955, New York 1955. Biography.

John Ruskin. 1956 (Br Council pamphlet).

The past we share: an illustrated history of the British and American peoples. Ed Quennell and A. Hodge 1960, New York 1960.

The sign of the fish. 1960, New York 1960. Essays.

Shakespeare: the poet and his background. [1963], Cleveland Ohio [1963]. Biography.

Alexander Pope: the education of genius 1688–1728. [1968], New York 1968.

Quennell also edited a number of English authors, principally Byron; some French authors; and made trns from the French, notably Memoirs of the Comte de Gramont, 1930, and The private letters of Princess Lieven to Prince Metternich 1820–6, 1937. He edited Cornhill Mag 1944–51, History Today from its foundation in 1951, and English Life series (pbd by Batsford) 1960–6.

§2

Prince, F. T. The poetry of Peter Quennell. Art & Literature 9 1966.

J.G.

KATHLEEN JESSIE RAINE
b. 1908

See col 329, above.

SIR HERBERT EDWARD READ
1893–1968

For details of mss in the Herbert Read Archive at the McPherson Lib of the Univ of Victoria, see Gerwing, Bibliographies, below.

Bibliographies

In Read, Selected writings, 1963, below. Checklist of books only.

Gerwing, H. A checklist of the Herbert Read Archive in the McPherson Library of the University of Victoria. In Herbert Read: a memorial symposium. 1970, §2, below.

Collections

Selected writings: poetry and criticism, with foreword by Allan Tate. 1963, New York 1964. With some new material.

Collected poems. 1966, New York 1966. With minor revisions and with notes. For Collected poems 1946 etc see Verse, below.

§1
Prose

Most of the pieces in Read's books of essays first appeared, often in an earlier version and occasionally under a different title, in various jnls or as pamphlets (the latter are listed below). They were often further rptd, again with revisions and changes of title, in later books of essays.

English pottery: its development from early times to the end of the eighteenth century. 1924 (75 copies). With B. Rackham.

In retreat. 1925 (Hogarth essays). Experiences of the British Fifth Army, March 1918; rptd in Annals of innocence and experience, 1946 edn, below.

English stained glass. 1926, New York 1926.

Reason and Romanticism: essays in literary criticism. 1926, New York 1963.

English prose style. 1928, New York [1928], London 1952 (rev), New York [1952].

Phases of English poetry. 1928 (Hogarth lectures on literature ser), New York [1929], London 1950 (rev and enlarged), Norfolk Conn 1950.

The sense of glory: essays in criticism. Cambridge 1929, New York 1967.

Staffordshire pottery figures. 1929.

Ambush. 1930 (Criterion Miscellany no 16). Autobiographical sketches and a poem, partly rptd in Annals of innocence and experience, 1940, below.

Julien Benda and the New Humanism. Seattle 1930 (Univ of Washington Chapbooks no 37).

Wordsworth: the Clark lectures. 1930, New York [1931], London 1949 (rev).

The place of art in a university: an inaugural lecture. Edinburgh 1931; rptd in The meaning of art, below.

The meaning of art. 1931, New York 1932 (as The anatomy of art: an introduction to the problems of art and aesthetics; adds The place of art in a university, above), London 1936 (rev and enlarged), 1949 (rev and enlarged) (Pelican), 1951 (rev and enlarged), New York 1951, London 1968 (rev).

Form in modern poetry. 1932 (Essays in Order no 11).

Art now: an introduction to the theory of modern painting and sculpture. 1933, 1936 (rev), New York 1937, London 1948 (rev and enlarged), New York [1948?], London 1960 [1961] (rev and enlarged), New York 1960 [1961].

The innocent eye. 1933. Recollections of childhood; rptd in Annals of innocence and experience, 1940, and in The contrary experience, 1963, below.

Art and industry: the principles of industrial design. 1934, 1944 (rev and enlarged), 1953 (rev), New York 1954, London 1956 [1957] (rev), Bloomington Indiana 1961, London 1966 (with rev introd).

Essential communism. 1935 (Pamphlets on the New Economics no 12); rptd in Poetry and anarchism, 1938, and in Anarchy and order, 1954, below.

In defence of Shelley and other essays. 1936, Freeport NY 1968.

Art and society. 1937, New York 1937, London 1945 (rev with new appendix: William Hogarth), 1956 [1957] (corrected), New York 1966, London 1967 (with new preface).

Collected essays in literary criticism. 1938, 1951 (corrected), New York 1956 (as The nature of literature).

Poetry and anarchism. 1938; rptd in Anarchy and order, 1954, below.

Annals of innocence and experience. 1940, 1946 (rev and enlarged to include In retreat, 1925, above), New York 1947 (as The innocent eye). A substantial part rptd in The contrary experience, 1963, below.

The philosophy of anarchism. 1940. Pamphlet; rptd in Anarchy and order, 1954, below.

To hell with culture: democratic values are new values. 1941 (The Democratic Order no 4). Pamphlet rptd in The politics of the unpolitical, 1943, and in To hell with culture and other essays, 1963, below.

The weathering of art. [Stoke-on-Trent 1942]. Address given to the Society of Staffordshire Artists, partly rptd in The politics of the unpolitical, 1943, below.

Education through art. 1943, New York [1945], London 1958 (rev), New York [1958].

The future of industrial design. In Four lectures on design delivered at meetings of the Design and Industries Association, [1943]. Rptd separately as a Design and Industries Association leaflet [1946] and in The grass roots of art, 1946, below, as The future of art in an industrial civilisation.

The politics of the unpolitical. 1943. Essays, mostly rptd in To hell with culture, and other essays, 1963, below.

The education of free men. 1944. Pamphlet; rptd in Education for peace, 1949, below.

A coat of many colours: occasional essays. 1945, 1956 (rev), New York 1956. On literature and art.

The grass roots of art: four lectures on social aspects of art in an industrial age. New York 1947 [1946], London 1947 (without subtitle, adds The future of art in an industrial civilisation [1943]), 1955 (with subtitle, rev and enlarged), New York 1955.

The innocent eye. New York 1947. See Annals of innocence and experience, 1940, above.

Culture and education in world order. New York 1948. Address; rptd in Education for peace, 1949, below.

Coleridge as critic. 1949, New York 1964. Essay: rptd in The true voice of feeling, 1953, below.

Education for peace. New York 1949, London 1950. Papers.

Existentialism, Marxism and anarchism: chains of freedom. 1949. Pamphlet, rptd in Anarchy and order, 1954, below.

Art and the evolution of man. 1951. Lecture.

Byron. 1951 (Br Council pamphlet). Rptd in The true voice of feeling, 1953, below.

Contemporary British art. 1951 (Pelican), 1964 (for 1965) (rev), Baltimore 1964.

The philosophy of modern art: collected essays. 1952, New York 1953.

The true voice of feeling: studies in English Romantic poetry. 1953, New York 1953.

Anarchy and order: essays in politics. 1954.

Icon and idea: the function of art in the development of human consciousness. Cambridge Mass 1955, London 1955 (Charles Eliot Norton lectures).

The psychopathology of reaction in the arts. [1955?]. Pamphlet for the Institute of Contemporary Arts.

The art of sculpture: the A. W. Mellon lectures in the fine arts, 1954. New York 1956, London 1956.

The significance of children's art; Art as a symbolic language. Vancouver 1957. 2 lectures, the 2nd rptd in The forms of things unknown, 1960, below.

The tenth muse: essays in criticism. 1957, New York 1958. On literature, philosophy and art.

A concise history of modern painting. 1959, New York 1959, London 1968 (rev), New York [1968].

Eric Craven Gregory (Peter Gregory), 1887–1959. [1959]. Tributes by Read and C. E. Morris.

The forms of things unknown: essays towards an aesthetic philosophy. 1960, New York 1960.

Zum 85. Geburtstag von Professor Dr C. G. Jung, 26 Juli 1960. Zurich 1960. Address.

Truth is more sacred: a critical exchange on modern literature between Edward Dahlberg and Herbert Read. 1961, New York [1961?].

Design and tradition: the Design Oration 1961 of the Society of Industrial Artists. Hemingford Grey 1962 (150 copies).

A letter to a young painter [and other essays]. [1962], New York 1962.

The contrary experience: autobiographics. 1963, New York 1963. Includes previously unpbd material.

Eric Gill: an essay. Berkeley Heights NJ 1963 (100 copies); rptd from A coat of many colours, 1945, above.

To hell with culture, and other essays on art and society. 1963, New York 1963.

Art and education. Melbourne 1964. Essays.

A concise history of modern sculpture. [1964], New York 1964.

Henry Moore: a study of his life and work. [1965], New York 1966.

High noon and darkest night. [Middletown Conn] 1965. Pamphlet, on José Ortega y Gasset; rptd in The origins of form in art, 1965, below.

The origins of form in art. [1965], New York 1965. Essays.

The modern art book. [1966?] (50 copies). Lecture before the Columbiad Club, 1965.

The redemption of the robot: my encounter with education through art. New York 1966.

T. S. E[liot]: a memoir. [Middletown Conn] 1966.

Art and alienation: the role of the artist in society. [1967], New York 1967. Essays.

Poetry and experience. 1967, New York 1967. Essays.

The cult of sincerity. 1968, New York 1968. Essays.

Essays in literary criticism: particular studies. 1969. Originally pbd as pt 2 of the 1951 edn of Collected essays in literary criticism, 1938, above.

Read frequently contributed introds, notes etc to books of reproductions, exhibition catalogues etc of work by contemporary artists; he also contributed, chs, introds etc to symposia and to surveys of art and literature. Many of these pieces were rptd, often rev, in the various books of essays listed above. With M. Ludwig, Read tr R. Arnheim, Radio, 1936.

Verse, Novel and Plays

Songs of chaos. 1915.

Auguries of life and death. 1919 (priv ptd). Poem in memory of Charles Read, killed in action 1918.

Eclogues: a book of poems. 1919.

Naked warriors. 1919. Poems, and a sketch rptd in Ambush, 1930, above (§1, Prose).

Mutations of the Phœnix. Richmond Surrey 1923. Poems.

Collected poems 1913-25. 1926 (56 copies).

The end of a war. 1933. Poem.

The green child: a romance. 1935, 1947 (introd by Graham Greene), New York 1948 (introd by K. Rexroth).

Poems 1914-34. 1935, New York 1935. Poems 1913-25 with omissions and some 30 new poems; some revisions.

Thirty-five poems. 1940. Selected from the previous, with addns.

A world within a war. 1943 (50 copies). Poem, rptd in next.

A world within a war: poems. 1944, New York 1945.

Collected poems. 1946, Norfolk Conn 1951, London 1953 (corrected). Omits some early poems; with slight revisions.

Aristotle's mother: an argument in Athens; Thieves of mercy. In Imaginary conversations: eight radio scripts by Read [et al]. Ed R. Heppenstall 1948. Aristotle's mother rptd separately, North Harrow [1960] (Herbert Read Reprints 1); broadcast 24 Nov 1946, 20 April 1947 respectively.

Moon's farm, and poems mostly elegiac. 1955, New York 1956. Title piece a dramatic dialogue for radio broadcast 21 Jan 1951.

The parliament of women: a drama in three acts. Hemingford Grey 1960 [1961] (100 copies). In prose and verse.

Lord Byron at the opera: a play for broadcasting. North Harrow 1963 (Herbert Read Reprints 2); broadcast 11 March 1953.

Principal Works Edited by Read

Hulme, T. E. Speculations: essays on humanism and the philosophy of art. 1924 [1923], New York 1924, London 1936 (corrected). Ed with assistance of A. R. Orage.

Worringer, W. R. Form in Gothic: authorized translation. 1927, New York 1964.

Hulme, T. E. Notes on language and style. Seattle 1929 (Univ of Washington Chapbooks).

The London book of English prose. 1931, New York 1931 (as The anthology of English prose), London 1949 (rev, as The London book of English prose). With B. Dobrée.

The English vision (the English ideal as expressed by representative Englishmen): an anthology. 1933.

Unit I: the modern movement in English architecture, painting and sculpture. 1934.

Orage, A. R. Selected essays and critical writings. 1935. With D. Saurat.

Surrealism. 1936. Essays by various authors.

The knapsack: a pocket-book of prose and verse. 1939.

Kropotkin: selections from his writings. 1942.

The practice of design. 1946. Essays by various authors.

The London book of English verse. 1949, New York 1949, London 1952 (rev). With B. Dobrée.

Nash, P. Outline: an autobiography, and other writings, 1949.

The collected works of C. J. Jung. New York 1953-, London 1953-. With M. Fordham, G. Adler.

This way delight: a book of poetry for the young. New York 1956, London 1957.

Read also edited Burlington Mag 1933-9, E & S vol 21 1936, the English master painter series 1940-, and the Acanthus history of sculpture 1960-.

Letters

Correspondence of Herbert Read with James Hanley 1936-8. [1938?]. Vol of 11 letters prepared by and in possession of Picton Library, Liverpool.

§2

Monro, H. E. In his Some contemporary poets, 1920.

Murry, J. M. Reason and criticism. TLS 8 Jul 1926; rptd in his Countries of the mind 2nd ser 1931. Essay-review of Reason and Romanticism 1926.

—— The anarchism of Read. Adelphi 11 1941.

Blackmur, R. The criticism of Read. Larus 1 1928. Mainly on Reason and Romanticism, 1926.

Richards, I. A. In Criterion 8 1928. Essay-review of English prose style 1928.

Porteus, H. G. In Criterion 15 1936. Essay-review of In defence of Shelley and other essays, 1936.

Ramsay, A. A. W. Psychology and literary criticism. Criterion 15 1936. Largely on Read.

Emerson, D. Read's war poetry. Scholastic 31 1937.

Burke, K. The calling of the tune. Kenyon Rev 1 1939. Largely an essay-review of Poetry and anarchism, 1938; rptd in his The philosophy of literary form, [Baton Rouge] 1941.

Greene, G. Read. Horizon 3 1941; rptd in his Lost childhood, 1951 and Collected essays, 1969. On Annals of innocence and experience, 1940.

Moore, G. Portrait of the artist as an anarchist. Poetry Rev 35 1944. See also Read's poems, Poetry Rev 37 1946; and correspondence with T. Astore, ibid.

Treece, H. (ed). Read: an introduction to his work by various hands. 1944.

'George Orwell' (E. A. Blair). [Review of A coat of many colours]. Poetry Quart Winter 1945; rptd in his Collected essays, vol 4 1968.

Glicksberg, C. I. Read: Reason and Romanticism. UTQ 16 1946.

Grattan, C. H. Gentlemen, I give you Herbert Read. Harper's Mag 194 1947.

Stanford, D. Read: the poet as stoic. Poetry Quart 12 1950.

Hodin, J. P. Read's philosophy of art. Norseman 9 1951.

Tschumi, R. The philosophical poetry of Read. In his Thought in twentieth-century English poetry, 1951.

Berry, F. Herbert Read. 1953, 1961 (rev) (Br Council pamphlet).

Davie, D. Read's Romanticism. Twentieth Century 153 1953.

Fishman, S. Read: poetics vs. criticism. Jnl of Aesthetics & Art Criticism 13 1954; reply by Read ibid.

—— The interpretation of art: essays on the art criticism of Ruskin, Pater, Bell, Fry and Read. Berkeley 1963.

Wasson, R. The green child: Read's ironic fantasy. PMLA 77 1962.

Bosshard, H. Mythisches und utopisches Dasein in Reads Erzählung The green child. Zurich 1964.

Dahlberg, E. Read. Texas Quart 7 1964.

Haüsermann, H. W. Read's surrealist poetry. In English studies presented to R. W. Zandvoort, Amsterdam 1964.

Locke, F. W. The interpretation of Read's The green child in the light of its sources and their transformation. In Linguistic and literary studies in honor of Helmut A. Hatzfeld, ed A. S. Crisafulli, Washington 1964.

Ray, P. C. Read and English surrealism. Jnl of Aesthetics & Art Criticism 24 1966.

Fraser, G. S. The last English imagist: on Sir Herbert Read. Encounter 28 1967. Essay-review of Collected poems 1966.

Tate, A. In his Essays of four decades, Chicago [1968].

Bunting, B. What about Read? Agenda 7 1969.

Raine, K. Read as a literary critic. Sewanee Rev 77 1969.

Herbert Read: a memorial symposium. Ed R. Skelton 1970. Originally pbd as the Jan 1969 number of Malahat Rev.

IVOR ARMSTRONG RICHARDS
b. 1893

§1

The foundations of aesthetics. 1922, New York 1948. With C. K. Ogden and J. Wood.

The meaning of meaning: a study of the influence of language upon thought and of the science of symbolism. 1923, 1927 (rev), 1930 (rev), 1936 (rev), 1944 (rev), New York 1956. With C. K. Ogden.

Principles of literary criticism. 1924, New York 1925 (1924), London 1926 (with 2 new appendices).

Science and poetry. 1926, 1935 (rev and enlarged) (Psyche Miniatures).

Practical criticism: a study of literary judgment. 1929, 1930 (corrected), New York 1950.

Mencius on the mind: experiments in multiple definition. 1932, New York 1932. With passages from Mencius in Chinese and English.

Basic rules of reason. 1933 (Psyche Miniatures). Basic English.

Coleridge on imagination. 1934, New York 1950, London 1962 (with a new foreword).

Basic in teaching: East and West. 1935 (Psyche Miniatures). Basic English.

The philosophy of rhetoric. New York 1936, London 1936.

Interpretation in teaching. [1938], New York [1938].

Times of India guide to Basic English. Ed A. Myers, Bombay 1938. With C. K. Ogden.

How to read a page: a course in effective reading, with an introduction to a hundred great words. New York 1942, London 1943.

The interactions of words. In The language of poetry, by Richards (et al), ed A. Tate, Princeton [1942].

Basic English and its uses. 1943, New York 1943.

Words on paper: first steps in reading. Cambridge Mass 1943 (with C. M. Gibson; reproduced from typescript), New York 1955 (with collaboration of D. Weinstein adapted as Hebrew reader).

A world language: an address. New York 1944. Basic English.

Learning Basic English: a practical handbook for English-speaking people. New York 1945. With C. M. Gibson.

The pocket book of Basic English: a self-teaching way into English with directions in Spanish, French, Italian, Portuguese and German. New York 1945, 1946 (rev), 1952 (with C. M. Gibson as English through pictures). The following adaptations have been made. French self-taught with pictures, New York 1950 (with M. H. Ilsley); Spanish self-taught through pictures, New York 1950 (with R. C. Metcalf); German through pictures, New York 1953 (with W. F. Mackey and I. S. Mackey); Hebrew through pictures, New York 1954 (with D. Weinstein); Italian through pictures, New York 1955 (with I. Evangelista); Russian through pictures, New York 1961 (with E. Jasiulko). Work books for use with the English and French courses pbd 1960.

Nations and peace. New York 1947. Basic English.

The Republic of Plato: a version in simplified English. 1948.

The portable Coleridge. Ed Richards, New York 1950.

The wrath of Achilles: The Iliad of Homer shortened and in a new translation by I. A. Richards. New York 1950, London 1951.

Hebrew reader. New York 1955. See Words on paper, 1943, above.

Speculative instruments. 1955, Chicago 1955. Essays on interpretation and language.

First steps in reading English: a first book for readers to be. New York 1957. With C. M. Gibson.

Goodbye earth, and other poems. New York 1958, London 1958 [1959].

Coleridge's minor poems: a lecture. [Missoula Mont 1960].

The screens, and other poems. New York 1960, London 1960 [1961]. Includes an essay, the Future of poetry, rptd in So much nearer, 1968, below.

Tomorrow morning, Faustus!: an infernal comedy. New York 1962, London 1962.

Why so, Socrates?: a dramatic version of Plato's dialogues, Euthyphro, Apology, Crito, Phaedo. Cambridge 1964.

Development of experimental audio-visual devices and materials for beginning readers. Cambridge Mass [1965?]. With C. M. Gibson.

Plato's Republic. Ed and tr by I. A. Richards, Cambridge 1966.

So much nearer: essays towards a world English. New York 1968.

§2

Russell, B. The meaning of meaning. Dial 81 1926.

Murry, J. M. Poetry and reality. Adelphi 3 1926; rptd in his Things to come, 1928.

Eliot, T. S. Literature, science and dogma. Dial 82 1927. On Science and poetry, 1926.

—— The modern mind. In his Use of poetry and the use of criticism, 1933.

Belgion, M. What is criticism? Criterion 10 1931. On Richards; reply, ibid.

Harding, D. W. Evaluations 1. Richards. Scrutiny 1 1933; rptd in Determinations: critical essays, with an introduction by F. R. Leavis, 1934.

Bethell, S. L. Suggestions towards a theory of value. Criterion 14 1935.

Hara, I. Poetry and belief: Richards versus Eliot. Stud in Eng Lit (Tokyo) 15 1935.

Leavis, F. R. Richards, Bentham and Coleridge. Scrutiny 3 1935; reply by W. Empson, 4 1935; essay-review of Coleridge on imagination, 1934.
— Advanced verbal education. Scrutiny 6 1937. Essay-review of The philosophy of rhetoric, 1936.

Ransom, J. C. The psychologist looks at poetry. Virginia Quart Rev 11 1935; rptd in his World's body, New York 1938.
— In his New criticism, Norfolk Conn [1941].

Vivas, E. Four notes on Richards' aesthetic theory. Philosophical Rev 44 1935; rptd in his Creation and discovery, New York 1955.

James, D. G. A denial of the 'prime agent' and its consequences. In his Scepticism and poetry, 1937.

Glicksberg, C. I. Richards and the science of criticism. Sewanee Rev 46 1938.

Tomlin, E. W. F. Richards and belief. Twentieth-Century Verse 2 1938.

Eastman, M. Richards' psychology of poetry. In his Enjoyment of poetry, New York 1939 (enlarged edn).

Tate, A. Literature as knowledge: comment and comparison. In his Reason in madness, New York 1941.

Black, M. Some objections to Ogden and Richards' theory of interpretation. Jnl of Philosophy 39 1942.
— Some questions about emotive meaning. Philosophical Rev 57 1948; both rptd in his Language and philosophy, Ithaca 1949.

A theory of meaning analyzed: a critique of Richards' theory of language and literature, by T. C. Pollock; Elementalism: the effect of an implicit postulate of identity on I. A. Richards' theory of poetic value. Proc 2nd American Congress on General Semantics, Chicago 1942.

Bentley, E. R. Examination of modern critics; the early Richards, an autopsy. Rocky Mountain Rev 8 1944.

Blissett, W. I. A. Richards. UTQ 14 1944.

Gilbert, K. The intent and tone of Richards. Jnl of Aesthetics & Art Criticism 3 1944.

McLuhan, H. M. Poetic vs rhetorical exegesis: the case for Leavis against Richards and Empson. Sewanee Rev 52 1944.

Garard, A. Quelques aspects de la poétique du XXe siècle: 5, Richards et le moralisme littéraire. Revue des Langues Vivantes 11 1945.

Hyman, S. E. Richards and the criticism of interpretation. In his Armed vision, New York 1948.

Crane, R. S. Richards on the art of interpretation. Ethics 59 1949; rptd in Critics and criticism, ed R. S. Crane, Chicago 1952.

Bilsky, M. Richards on belief. Philosophy & Phenomenological Research 12 1951.
— Richards' theory of metaphor. MP 50 1952.
— Richards' theory of value. Philosophy & Phenonenological Research 14 1954.

Empson, W. In his Structure of complex words, 1951.

Richards: the critical view of 1929; Reflections on the tactics of response. TLS 28 Aug 1953.

Viswanathan, K. Richards and significs. Eng Stud Andhra Univ (Waltair) 35 1954.

Krieger, M. Richards: neurological and poetic; Richards: some tools for an organic criticism; The transformation of Richards. In his New apologists for poetry, Minneapolis 1956.
— The critical legacy of Matthew Arnold: or, the strange brotherhood of T. S. Eliot, Richards and Northrop Frye. Southern Rev 5 1969.

Rudolph, G. A. The aesthetic field of Richards. Jnl of Aesthetics & Art Criticism 14 1956.

Wimsatt, W. K. and C. Brooks. Richards: a poetics of tension; The semantic principle. In their Literary criticism: a short history, New York 1957.

Cruttwell, P. Second thoughts IV: Richards' Practical criticism. EC 8 1958.

Hochmuth, M. Richards and the New Rhetoric. Quart Jnl of Speech 44 1958.

Williams, R. In his Culture and society, 1780–1950, 1958.

Fogarty, D. J. Richards' theory. In his Grass roots for a new rhetoric, New York 1959.

Foster, R. J. The romanticism of Richards. ELH 26 1959; rptd in his New Romantics, Bloomington 1962.

Watson, G. In his Literary critics, 1962, 1964 (rev).

Hotopf, W. H. N. Language, thought and comprehension: a case study of the writings of Richards. Bloomington 1965.

Karnani, C. The scientism of Richards. In Essays presented to Amy G. Stock, ed R. K. Kaul, Jaipur 1965.
— Criticism and Gestalt: a study of Richards' poetics. Banasthali Patrika 9 1967.
— The aesthetics of Richards: illusion and reality. Literary Criterion (Mysore) Winter 1968.

Campbell, H. M. Aesthetics as religion in the works of Richards. Annali Sezione Germanica, Istituto Orientale di Napoli, 1966.

Graff, G. E. The later Richards and the new criticism. Criticism 9 1967.

Wellek, R. On rereading Richards. Southern Rev 3 1967.

Bermabei, F. Attualità dell' estetica di Richards. Rivista di Estetica (Univ of Padua) 13 1968.

Schiller, J. P. Richards' theory of literature. New Haven 1969. Includes a bibliography.

MICHAEL SADLEIR
(MICHAEL THOMAS HARVEY SADLER)
1888–1957

Sadleir signed his work M. T. H. Sadler up to 1919 in which year he adopted the name Sadleir to avoid confusion with his father.

Bibliographies

Nowell-Smith, S. Sadleir Sadleirized. New Colophon 2 1949. Details of the publishing history of Sadleir's works.
— Sadleir: a handlist. Library 5th ser 13 1958. Includes selected contributions to books and periodicals.

§1

Lappalien. M.T.H.S. to E.G. [Weybridge 1907] (100 copies, nearly all later destroyed by author). Poems.

The political career of Richard Brinsley Sheridan, followed by some hitherto unpublished letters of Mrs Sheridan. Oxford 1912 (Stanhope Prize Essay).

Hyssop: a novel. 1915.

[The romantic woman]. 1916. Pamphlet; appreciation of 'Bridget Maclagen' (i.e. Mary Borden), The romantic woman.

The anchor: a love story. 1918.

New paths: verse, prose, pictures, 1917–18. Ed C. W. Beaumont and M. T. H. Sadler 1918. With contributions by Sadler.

Privilege: a novel of the transition. 1921, New York [1921].

Excursions in Victorian bibliography. 1922. On first edns.

Desolate splendour. 1923, New York 1923, London 1945 (with new author's note), 1948 (rewritten). Novel.

Trollope, A. The noble jilt: a comedy. Ed Sadleir 1923 (500 copies).

Daumier: the man and the artist. 1924.

Henry Kingsley: a portrait. New York 1924 (12 copies). Text also pbd in Edinburgh Rev 145 1924.

The noblest frailty. 1925, Boston 1925 (as Obedience: a tale).

Servants of books: a lecture delivered to the London branch of the Associated Booksellers. 1925.

The Northanger novels: a footnote to Jane Austen. Oxford 1927 (Eng Assoc pamphlet). On the novels mentioned in ch 6 of Northanger Abbey; rptd in Things past, 1944, below.

Trollope: a commentary. 1927, Boston 1927, London 1945 (rev), New York 1947.

The Dunciad of to-day: a satire [here attributed to Disraeli] and, The modern Aesop. Ed Sadleir 1928.

Trollope—a bibliography: an analysis of the history and structure of the works of Trollope and a general survey of the effect of original publishing conditions on a book's subsequent rarity. 1928; Addenda and corrigenda 1934 (leaflet).

The Shakespeare Head edition of the novels of Trollope. Ed Sadleir 14 vols Oxford 1929–30. The Barsetshire novels and the Autobiography.

The evolution of publishers' binding styles, 1770–1900. 1930 (500 copies), New York 1930 (Bibliographia ser).

Publishers' advertising: being the reactions of a practising publisher-advertiser to the exhortations of non-publisher theorists. 1930. Based on anon articles ptd in Constable's Monthly List, 1924–9. Anon.

Bulwer—a panorama: Edward and Rosina, 1803–36. 1931, Boston 1931, London 1933 (as Bulwer and his wife: a panorama, 1803–36).

Authors and publishers: a study in mutual esteem. 1932, 1933 (enlarged).

Bentley's Standard Novel Series: its history and achievement. Edinburgh 1932 (50 copies). Pre-print of contribution to Colophon 3 1932.

In memoriam Dorothy Wynne Wilson, 1909–32. 1932 (100 copies priv ptd). Pamphlet, rptd from Constable's Quart.

Blessington-D'Orsay: a masquerade. 1933, 1933 (corrected), Boston 1933 (as The strange life of Lady Blessington), New York 1947 (rev and enlarged), London 1947. Biography of Marguerite, Countess Blessington, and Alfred, Count d'Orsay.

Yellow backs. In New paths in book collecting, ed J. Carter 1934.

Studs Lonigan, by J. T. Farrell: an appreciation. 1936. Pamphlet.

Archdeacon Francis Wrangham, 1769–1842. [London] 1937 (Trans Bibl Soc suppl); rptd in Things past, 1944, below.

These foolish things: a story. 1937, New York 1937, London 1944 (rev and enlarged).

Dublin University Magazine: its history, contents and bibliography. Dublin 1938 (300 copies) (Bibl Soc of Ireland Pbns). A paper.

Carter, J. More binding variants, with contributions by Sadleir. 1938.

Fanny by gaslight. 1940, New York [1940]. Novel.

Tommy, 1916–42. Oxford 1943 (105 copies, priv ptd). Biographical sketches of his son by Sadleir et al.

Things past. 1944. Essays.

Thyrza, 1887–1944. [Ewelme 1944] (17 copies, priv ptd). Poem.

The development during the last 50 years of bibliographical study of books of the xixth century. In The Bibliographical Society, 1892–1942: studies in retrospect, 1945.

Forlorn sunset. New York 1946, London 1947. Novel.

Book collecting. 1947 (National Book League Reader's Guide).

Penelope's suitors, by the author of the Odyssey. [Througham] 1947 (for 1946) (10 copies, priv ptd). Poems, anon.

The Oxford Trollope: Crown edition. General editors, M. Sadleir and F. Page 1948–54.

Michael Ernest Sadler (Sir Michael Sadler, KCSI), 1861–1943: a memoir by his son. 1949.

Bookshop and auction room. In Book-collecting: four broadcast talks, by M. Sadleir [et al], ed J. Carter, Cambridge 1950.

XIX century fiction: a bibliographical record based on his own collection by M. Sadleir. 2 vols 1951.

Rumpal Stilts Kin, by B[enjamin] D[israeli] and W[illiam] G[eorge] M[eredith]. Ed Sadleir, Glasgow 1952 (66 copies, priv ptd) (Roxburghe Club).

Fred Bason's 3rd diary. Ed Sadleir 1955.

Sadleir also pbd a number of trns from the French and German, including Kandinsky's Art of spiritual harmony, Verhaeren's Belgium's agony, and the private journal of Jeanne-Aurélie Grivolin. Copies of the typescript of Sadleir's 1937 Sandars lectures, Bibliographical aspects of the Victorian novel, are in BM and Cambridge Univ Library. Sadleir founded Rhythm with J. M. Murry and with him edited nos 1–4, 1911–12; he was the editor or assistant editor of Blue Book (Oxford) no 1, 1912, Blue Rev nos 1–3, 1913 (all pbd), New Europe, 1919–20, New Decameron vols 1–3 (vol 1 with D. L. Sayers), Oxford 1919–? (contributing to vol 1). He also founded, edited and for the most part wrote (anon) Constable's Monthly List 1–111, 1921–31, Constable's Quart, 1–5, 1931–2; he edited the series Bibliographia: studies in book history and book structure, 1750–1900, from 1930.

§ 2

Carter, J. Michael Sadleir. TLS 13 April 1951; rptd in his Books and book-collectors, 1956. Essay-review of XIX century fiction, 1951.

— Sadleir: a valediction. Book Collector 7 1958.

— Sadleir rides again. TLS 30 Oct 1970. On Sadleir's influence.

O'Hegarty, P. S. Notes and comments on Sadleir's Nineteenth-century fiction. Bibl Soc of Ireland Pbns 6 1954.

Pollard, G. Michael Sadleir. Library 5th ser 13 1958.

M.P.

GEOFFREY SCOTT
1885–1929

§ 1

The death of Shelley: the Newdigate poem 1906. Oxford 1906.

The national character of English architecture: the Chancellor's Essay MCMVIII. Oxford 1908.

The architecture of humanism: a study in the history of taste. 1914, 1924 (rev), Garden City NY 1954.

A box of paints. 1923. Poems.

The portrait of Zélide (Isabelle de Charrière). 1925, New York 1925, 1927 (with postscript on Benjamin Constant), 1959 (introd by G. Dangerfield).

Private papers of James Boswell from Malahide Castle. Ed G. Scott 18 vols [New York] [1928]–34 (priv ptd). Vols 7–18 completed by F. A. Pottle.

Poems. 1931.

§ 2

Swan, M. Promise and achievement: Scott. In his A small part of time, 1957.

J.G.

WALTER DIXON SCOTT
1881–1915

§ 1

Liverpool: painted by J. H. Hay, described by D. Scott. 1907.

Colour photography. 1908 (Studio special number).

Stratford-on-Avon with Leamington and Warwick. 1911 (Beautiful Britain).

The first Morris. In Primitiae: essays by students of the University of Liverpool, Liverpool 1912.

Men of letters. 1916.

A number of things. Edinburgh 1917. Essays.

Bhartrihari says. 1940. Selections from Bhartrihari, tr Scott.

Letters

The letters of W. Dixon Scott. Ed M. McCrossan 1932.

§2

Waugh, A. Dixon Scott's criticism. In his Tradition and change, 1919.

N.J.S.

DAME EDITH LOUISA SITWELL
1887–1964
See also cols 342–6, above.

SIR SACHEVERELL SITWELL BART
b. 1897
See cols 349–51, above.

DAVID NICHOL SMITH
1875–1962

Bibliographies

In Essays on the eighteenth century, presented to David Nichol Smith, Oxford 1945. Compiled by F. P. Wilson.

§1

Some observations on eighteenth-century poetry. 1937, Toronto 1937.
John Dryden. Cambridge 1950.

Editions

Boileau-Despréaux, N. L'art poétique. Cambridge 1898.
Eighteenth century essays on Shakespeare. Glasgow 1903, Oxford 1963 (rev).
Jeffrey's literary criticism. 1910.
The letters of Thomas Burnet to George Duckett 1712–22. 1914.
Characters from the histories and memoirs of the seventeenth century. Oxford 1918. With essay on the characters and historical notes.
Swift, J. A tale of a tub. Oxford 1920. With A. C. Guthkelch.
The Oxford book of eighteenth-century verse. Oxford 1926.
The letters of Jonathan Swift to Charles Ford. Oxford 1935.
Chapman, G. A humorous day's mirth. Oxford 1938 (Malone Soc reprints).
The poems of Samuel Johnson. Oxford 1941. With E. L. McAdam.
Smith also edited selections from Brunetière, Byron, Dryden and Wordsworth, assisted in edns of Arden of Feversham, The Spanish tragedy and Mother Bombie; and was joint general editor with C. Brooks of The Percy letters 1944–.

§2

Sutherland, J. D. Nichol Smith. Proc Br Acad 48 1962.

H.M.R.

LLOYD LOGAN PEARSALL SMITH
1865–1946

Bibliographies

Muir, P. H. In his Points, ser 2 1934.
The Logan Pearsall Smith papers: a catalogue. Serif 2 1965. 53 items, chiefly letters and notebooks.

Collections

All trivia. New York [1933], London 1933, New York 1945 (rev). Contains Trivia, More trivia, Afterthoughts, Last words.

§1

The youth of Parnassus and other stories. 1895, New York [1895], Oxford 1909 (as The youth of Parnassus and other stories of Oxford life).
Trivia: printed from the papers of Anthony Woodhouse esq by [i.e. written by] Pearsall Smith. 1902 (priv ptd, 300 copies), Garden City NY 1917 (rev), London 1918.
The life and letters of Sir Henry Wotton. 2 vols Oxford 1907.
Sonnets. [1908?] (priv ptd, 50? copies). Most rpt in next.
Songs and sonnets. 1909.
The English language. [1912], New York [1912], London 1952 (for 1953) (with epilogue by R. W. Chapman).
Donne's sermons: selected passages with essay by Pearsall Smith. Oxford 1919.
Stories from the Old Testament, retold by Pearsall Smith. Richmond 1920, Boston 1921 (pirated).
More trivia. New York 1921, London 1922.
Words and idioms: studies in the English language. 1925.
The prospects of literature. 1927.
Afterthoughts. 1931, New York [1931]. Aphorisms.
On reading Shakespeare. 1933, New York [1933].
R. P. Smith. How little Logan was brought to Jesus. Ed Pearsall Smith, Stanford Dingley 1934 (65 copies).
Reperusals and re-collections. 1936, Freeport NY 1968. Essays.
Unforgotten years. 1938, Boston 1939. Reminiscences.
Milton and his modern critics. 1940, Boston 1941.
A religious rebel: the letters of 'H.W.S.', Mrs Pearsall Smith. Ed by her son Logan Pearsall Smith, 1949 (for 1952).

Letters, Diaries, etc.

A portrait of Logan Pearsall Smith, drawn from his letters and diaries and introduced by J. Russell. 1950.
Pearsall Smith assisted Robert Bridges and others to found the Society for Pure English 1913, and he contributed several of the Society's Tracts. With Bernard Berenson he edited Golden Urn 3 issues Fiesole 1897–8 (priv ptd). He compiled a number of anthologies, including A treasury of English aphorisms, 1928.

§2

Morley, C. D. Trivia. In his Shandygaff, Garden City NY 1918; rptd in his Essays, Garden City NY 1928.
— Reperusal. In his Letters of askance, Philadelphia [1939]; rptd in Carrousel for bibliophiles, ed W. Targ, New York 1947.
Mackenzie, C. Quod scribebis? In his Literature in my time, 1933.
Whitall, J. In his English years, 1936.
Hall, J. N. Mr Smith's umbrella. In his Under a thatched roof, Boston 1942.
Gathorne-Hardy, R. Recollections of Pearsall Smith. 1949.
Lynd, R. Pearsall Smith. In his Books and writers, 1952.
Connolly, C. V. Pearsall Smith. In his Ideas and places, 1953.
MacCarthy, D. Pearsall Smith. In his Memories, 1953.
Parker, R. A. In his A family of friends: the story of the transatlantic Smiths, 1960.
Wilson, E. Pearsall Smith. In his The bit between my teeth, New York 1965.

J.G.

STEPHEN HAROLD SPENDER
b. 1909
See cols 355–7, above.

CAROLINE FRANCES ELEANOR SPURGEON
1869–1942

§ 1

The works of Dr Samuel Johnson. 1898 (Quain essay).
Chaucer devant la critique en Angleterre et en France depuis son temps jusqu'à nos jours. Paris 1911.
Mysticism in English literature. Cambridge 1913, New York 1913.
Five hundred years of Chaucer criticism and allusion 1357–1900. 3 vols Cambridge 1925. First pbd in pts by the Chaucer Soc 1914–25. New York 1960.
Keats's Shakespeare: a descriptive study based on new material. 1928, 1929 (with addns).
Shakespeare's imagery and what it tells us. Cambridge 1935, New York 1935.

§ 2

Hyman, S. E. Caroline Spurgeon and scholarship in criticism. In his The armed vision, New York 1948.
J.M.P.

SIR JOHN COLLINGS SQUIRE
1884–1958
See cols 357–9, above.

ENID MARY STARKIE
1897–1970

§ 1

Les sources du lyrisme dans la poésie d'Émile Verhaeren. Paris 1927.
Baudelaire. [1933], New York 1933, London 1957 (re-written), Norfolk Conn 1958. Biography.
Arthur Rimbaud in Abyssinia. Oxford 1937, Paris 1938 (as Rimbaud en Abyssinie, with new unpbd material).
Arthur Rimbaud. 1938, 1947 (rev), New York 1947, London 1961 (rev), New York 1962.
A lady's child. 1941. Autobiography.
Pétrus Borel en Algérie: sa carrière comme inspecteur de la colonisation. Oxford 1950.
André Gide. Cambridge 1953 (for 1954), New Haven Conn 1954.
Petrus Borel, the lycanthrope: his life and times. 1954, Norfolk Conn 1954.
From Gautier to Eliot: the influence of France on English literature 1851–1939. 1960.
Flaubert: the making of the master. [1967], New York 1967.
Enid Starkie also edited Baudelaire, Les fleurs du mal, 1942.
J.G.

WALTER FITZWILLIAM STARKIE
b. 1894
See col 1325, below.

ADRIAN DURHAM STOKES
b. 1902

§ 1

The thread of Ariadne. 1925.
Sunrise in the West: a modern interpretation of past and present. [1926].
The Quattro Cento—a different conception of the Italian renaissance: part 1, Florence and Verona. 1932.

Stones of Rimini. 1934.
To-night the ballet. 1934, New York [1935].
Russian ballets. 1935, New York [1936].
Colour and form. 1937.
Venice: an aspect of art. 1945.
Inside out: an essay in the psychology and aesthetic appeal of space. 1947. Autobiographical.
Art and science: a study of Alberti, Piero della Francesca and Giorgione. 1949.
Smooth and rough. 1951. Autobiographical.
Michelangelo: a study in the nature of art. 1955, New York 1956.
Greek culture and the ego: a psycho-analytic survey of an aspect of Greek civilization and of art. 1958.
Three essays on the painting of our time. 1961.
Painting and the inner world. 1963.
The invitation in art. 1965.
Venice. 1965.
Reflections on the nude. 1967.
Stokes was ballet critic for Spectator in the mid-30's.

§ 2

Davie, D. Stokes and Pound's Cantos. Twentieth Century 160 1956.
Rhode, E. Impact on art. Listener 28 Jan 1965.
H.M.R.

GILES LYTTON STRACHEY
1880–1932
See cols 1215–18, below.

ALPHONSUS JOSEPH-MARY AUGUSTUS MONTAGUE SUMMERS
1880–1948

Bibliographies

Smith, T. d'A. A bibliography of the works of Summers. With a foreword by B. Sewell. 1964. Includes contributions to books and periodicals, and details of untraced, unpbd and projected works.
—— Bibliographical check-list. In J. Jerome, Montague Summers: a memoir, 1965. Based on the above.

§ 1

Antinous, and other poems. [1907].
The Marquis de Sade: a study in algolagnia. [1920]. Pamphlet; rptd in Essays in petto, 1928, below.
The history of witchcraft and demonology. 1926, New York 1956 (foreword by F. Morrow).
The geography of witchcraft. 1927, Evanston Ill 1958.
Sinistrari de Ameno, L. M. Demoniality. [1927]. Tr from Latin with introd and notes by Summers; ordered to be destroyed in 1934 under the Obscene Publications Act, 1857.
The discovery of witches: a study of Master Matthew Hopkins, commonly call'd Witch Finder Generall; together with a reprint of The discovery of witches, from the rare original of 1647. 1928 (Cayme Press pamphlet).
Essays in petto. [1928].
Sprenger, J. and H. Institoris. Malleus maleficarum. 1928, 1948 (with new introd). Tr with introd, bibliography and notes by Summers.
The vampire: his kith and kin. 1928, New York 1929, New Hyde Park NY [1960] (foreword by F. Morrow, The quest for Montague Summers).
The vampire in Europe. 1929, New York 1929, New Hyde Park NY [1962] (foreword by B. Sewell).

The confessions of Madeleine Bavent. [1933]. Tr from the French with introd, notes and bibliography by Summers; ordered to be destroyed in 1934 under the Obscene Publications Act, 1857.

Taillepied, N. A treatise of ghosts. [1933]. Tr with introd and commentary by Summers.

The werewolf. 1933, New York 1934.

The Restoration theatre. 1934, New York 1934.

A bibliography of the Restoration drama. [1935] (limited and trade edns), [1943] (enlarged).

The playhouse of Pepys. 1935, New York 1964. Intended as 2nd pt of the Restoration theatre, 1934.

A popular history of witchcraft. 1937. Incorporates sections from The geography of witchcraft, 1927.

The Gothic quest: a history of the Gothic novel. [1938], New York 1964.

The glories of Mary: a work designed both for devout readers and for preachers. Tr from the Italian of S. Alfonso Maria De'Liguori. Ed and tr [anon] by Summers 2 vols 1938–43.

A Gothic bibliography. [1940], New York 1964.

Witchcraft and black magic. [1946], New Hyde Park NY [1962] (foreword by B. Sewell). Incorporates sections from The geography of witchcraft, 1927.

The physical phenomena of mysticism, with especial reference to the stigmata, divine and diabolical. [1950], New York [1950].

Editions

Villiers, G. The rehearsal. Stratford-upon-Avon 1914.

The works of Aphra Behn. 6 vols 1915.

Restoration comedies: The parson's wedding; The London cuckolds; & Sir Courtly Nice, or it cannot be. 1921.

Shakespeare adaptations: The tempest (Davenant and Dryden), The mock tempest (T. Duffett) and King Lear (Tate). 1922.

The complete works of William Congreve. 4 vols 1923, New York 1964.

Walpole, H. Constable's edition of The castle of Otranto and The mysterious mother. 1924.

The complete works of William Wycherley. 4 vols 1924, New York 1964.

The complete works of Thomas Otway. 3 vols 1926 [1927].

B., A. Covent Garden drollery. 1927.

'Flammenberg, Lorenz'. The necromancer: or, a tale of the Black Forest. Tr by P. Teuthold, introd by Summers 1927. With next, all pbd of projected reprints of 7 novels mentioned in Jane Austen's Northanger Abbey.

Grosse, K. F. A. Horrid mysteries: a story from the German. Tr by P. Will, introd by Summers 1927.

The complete works of Thomas Shadwell. 5 vols 1927.

Tuke, S. The adventures of five hours. Ed B. Van Thal, introd by Summers [1927].

Byrne, C. Zofloya: or, the Moor. Introd by Summers [1928].

Downes, J. Roscius Anglicanus. [1928].

Boguet, H. An examen of witches. Tr by E. A. Ashwin 1929.

Scot, R. The discoverie of witchcraft. Introd by Summers 1929.

Guazzo, F. M. Compendium maleficarum. Tr by E. A. Ashwin 1930.

Remy, N. Demonolatry. Tr by E. A. Ashwin 1930.

Dryden: the dramatic works. 6 vols 1931–2.

The supernatural omnibus: being a collection of stories. 1931, Garden City NY 1932 (omits 8 and adds 6 stories).

Victorian ghost stories. [1933].

The Grimoire, and other supernatural stories. [1936]. Includes 2 stories and a trn by Summers.

The poems of Richard Barnfield. [1936] (500 copies).

Bovet, R. Pandæmonium, 1684. Aldington 1951.

Summers was one of the founders of The Phoenix, a society for the production of old plays, in 1919, and wrote theatre programmes for this society 1919–24 and for the Renaissance Theatre and other societies: details are given in T. d'A Smith, Bibliography above.

§2

Mencken, H. L. In his Prejudices, ser 6, [1927]. Essay-review of History of witchcraft and demonology, 1926.

Thurston, H. Diabolism. 1927. Contains essay-reviews of The geography of witchcraft, 1927, and The history of witchcraft and demonology, 1926.

Graham, W. One of the most extraordinary men of his age. In her Observations, casual and intimate: being the second volume of That reminds me, [1947].

Cammell, C. R. In his Aleister Crowley: the man, the mage, the poet, 1951.

— The Reverend Montague Summers. Insight 5 1968.

Bromage, B. Montague Summers. Light 79 1959.

'Joseph Jerome' (M. B. Sewell). Montague Summers: a memoir. 1965. Quotes extensively from Summers' unpbd Galanty show: an autobiography, and from J. R. Anderson's unpbd Recollections of Montague Summers.

M.P.

JAMES RUNCIEMAN SUTHERLAND
b. 1900

Leucocholy. Oxford 1926. Verse.

The narrative of Jasper Weeple. 1930. Novel.

The medium of poetry. 1934.

Defoe. 1937, Philadelphia 1938.

Background for Queen Anne. 1939. Essays.

Alexander Pope. The Dunciad. Ed Sutherland 1943, 1953 (rev), 1963 (rev) (Twickenham edn of the Poems of Pope, vol 5).

A preface to eighteenth-century poetry. Oxford 1948.

The Oxford book of English talk. Ed Sutherland, Oxford 1953.

Defoe. 1954 (Br Council pamphlet).

On English prose. Toronto 1957, London 1966.

English satire. Cambridge 1958.

English literature of the late seventeenth century. Oxford 1969 (OHEL).

Sutherland also edited Dekker's Shoemaker's holiday (1928), Three plays by Nicholas Rowe, Dryden's Marriage à la mode (1934), The Tempest (1938), W. P. Ker's On modern literature (1955), Savage's An author to be lett (1960), Defoe's Captain Singleton (EL 1963); the anthologies Early eighteenth-century poetry (1965) and One crowded hour: selections from the Waverley novels (1963); and, with J. Hurstfield, the lecture series Shakespeare's world (1964). From 1940–7 he edited RES.

A.P.H.

FRANK ARTHUR SWINNERTON
b. 1884

See cols 746–7, above.

PHILIP EDWARD THOMAS
1878–1917

See cols 364–7, above.

GEORGE DERWENT THOMSON
b. 1903

Bibliographies

ΓΕΡΑΣ: studies presented to Thomson. Ed L. Varcl and R. F. Willetts, Prague 1963. Contains a short biographical note as well as the bibliography.

§1

Greek lyric metre. Cambridge 1929, 1961 (rev).
Aeschylus and Athens: a study in the social origins of drama. 1941.
Marxism and poetry. 1945, New York 1946, Bombay 1953 (rev).
An essay on religion. 1949.
Studies in ancient Greek society. Vol 1, The prehistoric Aegean, 1949, 1954 (rev); vol 2, The first philosophers, 1955.
The Greek language. Cambridge 1960.
Thomson translated The Prometheus bound *and* The Oresteia *of Aeschylus and also, with M. L. Davies,* Twenty years a-growing, *by Maurice O'Sullivan.*

§2

Pickard-Cambridge, A. W. Aeschylus and Athens. Classical Rev 56 1942.
Winspear, A. D. Aeschylus and Athens. Science & Society 6 1942.
Cornford, F. M. Marxist view of ancient philosophy. In his Unwritten philosophy and other essays, Cambridge 1950.

H. M. R.

GEOFFREY TILLOTSON
1905–69

On the poetry of Pope. Oxford 1938.
Alexander Pope. The rape of the lock and other poems. 1940, 1954 (rev), 1962 (rev) (Twickenham edn of the Poems of Pope, vol 2). Ed Tillotson.
Essays in criticism and research. Cambridge 1942, Hamden Conn 1967 (with new preface).
Criticism and the nineteenth century. 1951, Hamden Conn 1967. Essays.
Thackeray the novelist. Cambridge 1954, London 1963 (corrected).
Pope and human nature. Oxford 1958.
Augustan studies. 1961. Chs 1–4 rptd (corrected) as Augustan poetic diction, 1964.
Vanity Fair: a novel without a hero, by William Makepeace Thackeray. Ed Tillotson, with K. Tillotson 1963.
Mid-Victorian studies. With K. Tillotson 1965.
Milton's minor poems, by J. B. Leishman. Ed with a preface by G. Tillotson 1969.
Tillotson also edited The larke: a seventeenth century poem ascribed to Dr Arthur Duke, *1934 (priv ptd); a selection of Newman's prose and poetry for* The Reynard Library, *1957; with D. Hawes, a selection of Thackeray criticism for* The Critical Heritage ser *1968; and, with others, an anthology of eighteenth-century English literature (New York 1969). He was also joint-editor of the series* Anglistica, *Copenhagen 1953 onwards.*

J. M. P.

EUSTACE MANDEVILLE WETENHALL TILLYARD
1889–1962

§1

The Athenian empire and the Great Illusion [N. Angell, The great illusion]. Cambridge 1914. Garton Prize Essay.
The Hope vases. Cambridge 1923. A catalogue and a discussion of the Hope collection of Greek vases.
Lamb's criticism: a selection. Ed Tillyard, Cambridge 1923.

The poetry of Sir Thomas Wyatt: a selection and a study by Tillyard. 1929.
Milton. 1930, 1966 (rev, with preface by P. B. Tillyard), New York 1967.
Milton: L'allegro and Il penseroso. 1932. Pamphlet.
Milton: private correspondence and academic exercises. Cambridge 1932. Tr by P. B. Tillyard, with introd and commentary by E. M. W. Tillyard.
Poetry direct and oblique. 1934, 1945 (rev).
The Miltonic setting past and present. Cambridge 1938, New York 1949.
Shakespeare's last plays. 1938, New York 1964.
The personal heresy: a controversy. 1939. On poetry and the poet; with C. S. Lewis.
The Elizabethan world picture. 1943, New York 1944.
Shakespeare's history plays. 1944, New York 1946.
Orchestra: or a poem of dancing, by Sir John Davies. Ed Tillyard 1945.
Five poems 1470–1870: an elementary essay on the background of English literature. 1948, 1955 (as Poetry and its background: illustrated by five poems 1470–1870).
Shakespeare's problem plays. Toronto 1949, London 1950.
Studies in Milton. 1951.
The English Renaissance: fact or fiction? 1952, Baltimore 1952.
Milton. 1952, 1959 (rev) (Br Council pamphlet).
The English epic and its background. 1954, New York 1954.
Poetry and its background. 1955. *See* Five poems, 1948, above.
The Metaphysicals and Milton. 1956.
The epic strain in the English novel. 1958, Fair Lawn NJ 1958.
The muse unchained: an intimate account of the revolution in English studies at Cambridge. [1958].
Some mythical elements in English literature. 1961, New York 1962 (as Myth and the English mind).
Essays: literary and educational. 1962, New York 1962.
Shakespeare's early comedies. Ed S. Tillyard 1965, New York 1965.
Tillyard also edited some of Milton's works for Harrap's English Classics *series.*

§2

Willey, B. Proc Br Acad 49 1963.

J. G.

JOHN RONALD REUEL TOLKIEN
b. 1892

See cols 748–9, above.

SIR DONALD FRANCIS TOVEY
1875–1940

§1

Essays in musical analysis. 3 pts [1902].
A companion to Beethoven's pianoforte sonatas: complete analyses. 1931.
A companion to The art of fugue—Die Kunst der Fuge— J. S. Bach. 1931.
Essays in musical analysis. 6 vols 1935–9. Some English symphonists: a selection from Essays in musical analysis pbd 1941.
A musician talks. 2 vols 1941.
Walter Parratt: Master of the Music. 1941. With G. Parratt.
Beethoven. Ed H. Foss 1944.
Essays in musical analysis: chamber music. Ed H. Foss 1944.

Musical articles from the Encyclopaedia Britannica. Ed H. Foss 1944.

Essays and lectures on music. Ed H. Foss 1949, New York 1949.

The forms of music. New York 1956, London 1957. Essays, mostly from Encyclopaedia Britannica.

§ 2

Wells-Harrison, W. Donald Francis Tovey. Musical Standard 45 1916. About his songs.

Wilson, S. D.F.T. Monthly Musical Record 60 1930.

Strangeways, A. H. F. Donald Francis Tovey. Music & Letters 21 1940.

Wordsworth, W. B. Tovey's teaching. Music & Letters 22 1941. With 3 letters from Tovey.

Dent, E. J. Donald Tovey. Music Rev 3 1942.

Fishman, S. The aesthetics of Tovey. Jnl of Aesthetics & Art Criticism 6 1947.

Haggin, B. H. Music in the Nation. New York 1949. Commentaries on Tovey from 1940, 1941, and 1945.

Grierson, M. Donald Francis Tovey: a biography based on letters. 1952. Contains a bibliography.

Dickson, J. H. D. Dr Grierson's life of Tovey. Music & Letters 33 1952.

Highet, G. Enigma with variation: Donald Tovey. In his People, places and books, New York 1953.

H.M.R.

WALTER JAMES REDFERN TURNER
1889–1946

See cols 371–2, above.

HELEN JANE WADDELL
1889–1965

Lyrics from the Chinese. 1913, New York 1935. Verse, based on J. Legge's prose trn of the Shih Ching.

The spoiled Buddha: a play in two acts. Dublin and London 1919.

The fairy ring (ten books of fairy tales for standards I–III) 10 pts 1921. Anon; texts simplified by another hand. Selection (with some additional unpbd tales), ed E. Colwell, restoring the original texts, pbd 1969 as The princess Splendour and other stories.

The wandering scholars. 1927, 1932 (rev and enlarged), 1934 (rev), New York 1934.

Mediaeval Latin lyrics. 1929, 1933 (rev), New York [1949]. Anthology, with trns and biographical notes.

The Abbé Prévost: a play in a prologue and three acts. Bungay [1931] (priv ptd), 1933 (Raven Miscellany).

The history of Chevalier des Grieux and of Manon Lescaut by the Abbé Prévost d'Exiles. Translated by H. Waddell, with an introduction by G. Saintsbury. 1931, New York 1931.

Peter Abelard: a novel. 1933, New York [1933].

Beasts and saints: translations by H. Waddell. 1934, New York [1934]. Extracts from mediaeval lives of saints.

New York City. [Newtown] 1935 (350 copies). Gregynog Press Christmas greeting.

The desert fathers: translations from the Latin with an introduction by H. Waddell. 1936, Ann Arbor 1957.

Lament for Damon: translated from the Epitaphium Damonis of John Milton by H. Waddell. 1943 (priv ptd).

Poetry in the Dark Ages. Glasgow 1948, New York [1958]. W. P. Ker Memorial Lecture.

Stories from Holy Writ. 1949, New York 1950. For children.

Helen Waddell also translated The hollow field, by M. Aymé, 1933, and A French soldier speaks, by 'Jacques', 1941. She edited A book of medieval Latin for schools, 1931.

P.G.B.

ARTHUR DAVID WALEY
1889–1966

See cols 372–4, above.

ERNEST WEEKLEY
1865–1954

The romance of words. 1912, 1913 (rev and enlarged), 1961 (introd by I. Brown), New York 1961.

The romance of names. 1914, 1922 (rev).

Surnames. 1916, New York 1927.

An etymological dictionary of modern English. 1921.

A concise etymological dictionary of modern English. 1924, New York 1924, London 1952 (rev), New York 1952. An abridgement of An etymological dictionary of modern English, 1921, above.

Words ancient and modern. 1926, New York 1926. See also Words ancient and modern, 1946, below.

More words ancient and modern. 1927. See also Words ancient and modern, 1946, below.

The English language. 1928, New York 1929, London 1952 (rev and enlarged with a ch on the history of American English by J. W. Clark).

Collins' essential English dictionary. [1929], [1934] (as The new essential English dictionary), [1939], (rev, as The modern English dictionary).

Adjectives—and other words. 1930.

Saxo Grammaticus: or first aid for the best seller. 1930, New York [1931] (as Cruelty to words: or first aid for the best seller).

Words and names. 1932.

Jack and Jill: a study in our Christian names. 1934, New York 1940.

Something about words. 1935.

Words ancient and modern. 1946, New York 1965. Selections, rev and extended, from Words ancient and modern, 1926, and More words ancient and modern, 1927, above.

Weekley also pbd many French text-books for schools, edited various dictionaries pbd by Collins, and collaborated in writing elementary text-books with C. Gilli, B. J. Hayes, E. Paget and A. J. Wyatt.

P.C.

DAME 'REBECCA WEST', CICILY ISABEL ANDREWS
b. 1892

See cols 770–1, above.

REGINALD HOWARD WILENSKI
b. 1887

Draughtsmen: E. Clarke Hall, H. Rushbury, R. Schwabe, L. Underwood. 1924 (Contemporary British Artists). Text signed R.H.W.

Stanley Spencer. 1924 (Contemporary British Artists). Text signed R.H.W.

The modern movement in art. 1927, 1935 (rev), New York 1935, London 1945 (rev), 1957 (rev), New York 1957.

An introduction to Dutch art. 1929, 1945 (rev, as Dutch painting), 1955 (rev and enlarged), New York 1955.

Italian painting. [1929]. With P. G. Konody.

A miniature history of European art. 1930, New York 1930 (as A miniature history of art, with ch on American art by E. A. Jewell).

French painting. 1931, Boston 1931, London 1949 (rev), Boston 1949.

The meaning of modern sculpture. 1932, Boston 1961 (with new preface).

An outline of French painting. 1932.

English painting. 1933, Boston 1934 (as Masters of English painting), 1937 (original title), London 1954 (rev), 1964 (rev).

John Ruskin: an introduction to the further study of his life and work. 1933, New York 1967.

An outline of English painting from the middle ages to the period of the Pre-Raphaelites. 1933, 1946 (as An outline of English painting, rev and extended to 1945), 1969 (rev and further extended).

The study of art. 1934.

Modern French painters. 1940, New York 1940.

Sickert. [Reproductions]. With essay on his art by Wilenski, 1943.

Dutch painting. 1945. *See* An introduction to Dutch art, 1929, above.

Flemish painters 1430–1830. 2 vols 1960, New York 1960.

Wilenski edited the series The Faber gallery, *1945– and wrote many of the individual monographs.*

BASIL WILLEY
b. 1897

§ 1

Tendencies in Renaissance literary theory. Cambridge 1922. Le Bas Prize Essay.

The seventeenth-century background: studies in the thought of the age in relation to poetry and religion. 1934, New York 1950.

The eighteenth-century background: studies on the idea of nature in the thought of the period. 1940, New York 1941.

Nineteenth-century studies: Coleridge to Matthew Arnold. 1949, New York 1949.

Christianity past and present. Cambridge 1952.

More nineteenth-century studies: a group of honest doubters. 1956, New York 1956.

Darwin and Butler: two versions of evolution. 1960, New York 1960.

The English moralists. 1964, New York 1964.

Spots of time: a retrospect of the years 1897–1920. 1965, New York 1965.

Cambridge and other memories 1920–53. 1968, New York 1969.

Religion to-day. 1969.

§ 2

Nott, K. Mr Willey's lunar spots, and Old Puritan writ large. In her The emperor's clothes, 1953.

Butterfield, H. Basil Willey: a tribute. In The English mind: studies in the English moralists presented to Basil Willey, ed H. S. Davies and G. Watson, Cambridge 1964.

J.G.

JOHN DOVER WILSON
1881–1969

Bibliographies

A list of his published writings presented to John Dover Wilson on his eightieth birthday. Cambridge 1961; rptd (with addns by Dover Wilson) in Milestones on the Dover Road, 1969, below.

§ 1

John Lyly. Cambridge 1905. Harness Prize essay.

The Marprelate controversy. In CHEL vol 3, Cambridge 1909.

The puritan attack upon the stage. In CHEL vol 6, Cambridge 1910.

Martin Marprelate and Shakespeare's Fluellen: a new theory of the authorship of the Marprelate tracts. 1912.

The copy for Hamlet 1603, and the Hamlet transcript 1593. 1918.

Bibliographical links between the three pages [believed to be in Shakespeare's handwriting] and the Good Quartos. In Shakespeare's hand in the play of Sir Thomas More, ed A. W. Pollard, Cambridge 1923 (Shakespeare Problems ser).

The task of Heminge and Condell. In Studies in the First Folio, written for the Shakespeare Association, 1924.

Six tragedies of Shakespeare: an introduction for the plain man. 1929 (Workers' Educational Assoc Outlines).

The essential Shakespeare: a biographical adventure. Cambridge 1932.

The manuscript of Shakespeare's Hamlet and the problem of its transmission: an essay in critical bibliography. 2 vols Cambridge 1934, New York 1934 (Shakespeare Problems ser).

What happens in Hamlet. Cambridge 1935, New York 1935.

The fortunes of Falstaff. Cambridge 1943, New York 1944.

Shakespeare histories at Stratford 1951. 1952, New York 1952. With T. C. Worsley.

Shakespeare's happy comedies. 1962, Evanston Ill 1962.

An introduction to the sonnets of Shakespeare for historians and others. Cambridge 1963.

Milestones on the Dover Road. 1969. Autobiography.

Editions

Lodge, T. The wounds of civil war 1594. 1910 (Malone Soc reprint).

Life in Shakespeare's England: a book of Elizabethan prose. Cambridge 1911 (Cambridge Anthologies ser), 1944 (rev) (Pelican). Abridged for children 1939 (as Through Elizabethan eyes).

The Resurrection of Our Lord. 1912 (Malone Soc reprint). With B. Dobell.

The war and democracy. 1914. With A. E. Zimmern. Dover Wilson wrote The national idea in Europe 1789–1914, and Russia.

The new Shakespeare. 39 vols Cambridge 1921–66. Ed with A. Quiller-Couch (to 1931), and (later) with G. I. Duthie, J. C. Maxwell and A. Walker. Wilson edited most of the plays. Known as 'New Cambridge' edn.

The schools of England: a study in renaissance. 1928, Chapel Hill 1928. Ed Dover Wilson, who wrote The schools and the nation.

Lavater, L. Of ghostes and spirites walking by nyght 1572. 1929. With M. Yardley.

Shakespeare, W. The tragedie of Hamlet. Weimar 1930 (priv ptd, Cranach press, 322 copies; illustr G. Craig).

Arnold, M. Culture and anarchy. Cambridge 1932, 1935 (corrected) (Landmarks in the History of Education ser).

Silver, G. Paradoxes of defence 1599. 1933 (facs, Shakespeare Assoc).

Dover Wilson pbd much on education, largely wrote the Board of Education report, The teaching of English in England, *1921, and pbd some Workers' Educational Assoc pamphlets. He edited* Cambridge anthologies, *1910–32 (with W. T. Young),* Shakespeare problems, *1920–53 (to 1944 with A. W. Pollard), and* Landmarks in the history of education, *1931–5. He also edited school texts of Shakespeare, facs edns of plays from the First Folio, and the* Cambridge Pocket Shakespeare, *based on* New Shakespeare, *above. Before 1914 he wrote on Finland in* Manchester Guardian.

§2

Wietz, M. In his Hamlet and the philosophy of literary criticism, Chicago 1964.

THOMAS JAMES WISE
1859–1937

Wise's unpbd correspondence with Gosse is held in the Brotherton Library, Univ of Leeds; a virtually complete collection of his forged pamphlets, with other material relating to him, is held by the Wrenn Library, Univ of Texas (listed in Wise, Letters to J. H. Wrenn, below; addenda in W. B. Todd's Handlist); among private collections is that of M. P. Pariser (see Wise after the event, below).

Bibliographies

In W. Partington, Forging ahead, New York [1939], §2, below.
Certain nineteenth-century forgeries: an exhibition of books and letters at the Univ of Texas, 1946, described by F. E. Ratchford. [Austin 1946].
Todd, W. B. A handlist of Wise. In T. J. Wise: centenary studies, ed Todd, Austin [1959], §2 below.
Guildhall Miscellany 2 1962. A handlist of books in Guildhall Library associated with Wise; additional items, 2 1965.
Wise after the event: a catalogue of books, pamphlets, manuscripts and letters relating to Wise, displayed in an exhibition in Manchester Central Library, September 1964. Ed G. E. Haslam, Manchester 1964 (500 copies). Foreword by J. Carter; largely from the collection of M. P. Pariser.

§1

The material in Wise's bibliographies and library catalogues of the same author is to a certain extent duplicated; the number of copies ptd was probably in excess of the number given in the works themselves and reproduced below.

Verses. 1882 (priv ptd, 35 copies).
A complete bibliography of the writings in prose and verse of John Ruskin, with a list of the more important Ruskiniana. Ed Wise 2 vols 1893 (for 1889–93). With J. P. Smart.
The Ashley Library: a list of books printed for private circulation by T. J. Wise. 1893 (priv ptd). Other lists ptd in 1895 and 1897.
A reference catalogue of British and foreign autographs and manuscripts. 1893–8. Pts 1–7 ed Wise.
Spenser's Faerie Queene. Ed Wise 6 vols 1894–7.
Literary anecdotes of the nineteenth century. Ed Wise 2 vols 1895–6. With W. R. Nicoll. Materials for a bibliography of the writings of Robert Browning, by Wise, in vol 1; A bibliographical list of the scarcer works and uncollected writings of Swinburne, in vol 2; last rptd, rev, separately 1897 (priv ptd, 50 copies).
Browning, R. Bells and pomegranates. Ser 1–2, ed Wise 2 vols 1896–7 (XIXth Century Classics).
A complete bibliography of the writings in prose and verse of Robert Browning. 1897 (priv ptd, 50 copies).
The Ashley Library: a catalogue of books, manuscripts and autograph letters, collected by T. J. Wise. 1901 (priv ptd, 20 copies).
The Ashley Library: a catalogue of printed books, manuscripts and autograph letters, collected by T. J. Wise. 2 vols 1905–8 (priv ptd, 12 sets).
A bibliography of the writings of Alfred, Lord Tennyson. 2 vols 1908 (priv ptd, 110 copies).
A bibliography of the writings in prose and verse of Samuel Taylor Coleridge. (Coleridgeiana: a supplement). 2 vols 1913–19 (500 sets).

A bibliography of the writings in prose and verse of George Henry Borrow. 1914 (priv ptd, 100 copies).
A bibliography of the writings in prose and verse of William Wordsworth. 1916 (priv ptd, 100 copies).
A bibliography of the writings in prose and verse of the members of the Brontë family. 1917 (priv ptd, 100 copies).
Swinburne, A. C. The posthumous poems. Ed Wise 1917. With E. Gosse.
A bibliography of the writings in prose and verse of Elizabeth Barrett Browning. 1918 (priv ptd, 100 copies).
The letters of Swinburne. Ed Wise 2 vols 1918. With E. Gosse.
A bibliography of the writings in prose and verse of Algernon Charles Swinburne 2 vols 1919–20 (priv ptd, 125 sets). A rev version was pbd in Wise's edn of The complete works of Swinburne, 1925–7, below.
A bibliography of the writings in prose and verse of Walter Savage Landor. 1919. With S. Wheeler.
Selections from Swinburne. Ed Wise 1919 (525 copies). With E. Gosse.
A bibliography of the writings of Joseph Conrad, 1895–1920. 1920 (priv ptd, 150 copies), 1921 (rev and enlarged) (priv ptd, 170 copies).
A catalogue of the library of the late J. H. Wrenn, compiled by H. B. Wrenn. Ed Wise 5 vols Austin 1920 (120 sets).
A bibliography of the writings of John Keats. In The John Keats memorial volume, ed G. C. Williamson 1921.
The Ashley Library: a catalogue of printed books, manuscripts and autograph letters, collected by T. J. Wise. 11 vols 1922–36 (priv ptd, 200 sets).
A Shelley library: a catalogue of printed books, manuscripts and autograph letters by Shelley, Harriet Shelley and Mary Wollstonecraft Shelley. 1924 (priv ptd, 180 copies).
A Swinburne library: a catalogue of printed books, manuscripts and autograph letters collected by Wise. 1925 (priv ptd, 200 copies).
The complete works of Swinburne. Ed Wise 20 vols 1925–7 (Bonchurch edn). With E. Gosse.
Two Lake Poets: a catalogue of printed books, manuscripts and autograph letters by Wordsworth and Coleridge collected by Wise. 1927 (priv ptd, 160 copies).
A Byron library: a catalogue of printed books, manuscripts and autograph letters collected by Wise. 1928 (priv ptd, 230 copies).
A Conrad library: a catalogue of printed books, manuscripts and autograph letters collected by Wise. 1928 (priv ptd, 205 copies).
A Landor library: a catalogue of printed books, manuscripts and autograph letters collected by Wise. 1928 (priv ptd, 195 copies). Introd by S. Wheeler.
A Brontë library: a catalogue of printed books, manuscripts and autograph letters by the members of the Brontë family, collected by Wise. 1929 (priv ptd, 150 copies).
A Browning library: a catalogue of printed books, manuscripts and autograph letters by Robert and Elizabeth Barrett Browning, collected by Wise. 1929 (priv ptd, 190 copies).
A Dryden library: a catalogue of printed books, manuscripts and autograph letters collected by Wise. 1930 (priv ptd, 160 copies). Title corrected by erratum slip to A catalogue of the plays, poems and prose-writings of John Dryden.
A Pope library: a catalogue of plays, poems and prose writings, collected by Wise. 1931 (priv ptd, 160 copies).
The Shakespeare Head Brontë. Ed Wise 19 vols Oxford 1931–8. With J. A. Symington.
A bibliography of the writings in verse and prose of George Gordon Noel, Baron Byron with letters illustrating his life and work and particularly his attitude towards Keats. 2 vols 1932–3 (priv ptd, 180 sets).
Letters of Robert Browning collected by Wise, edited with an introduction and notes by T. L. Hood. New Haven 1933, London 1933.

Wise also edited and issued a large number of priv ptd type-facs and reprints, in limited edns, of individual works by many 19th-century authors, in particular Borrow, Charlotte Brontë, the Brownings, Conrad, Ruskin, Shelley, Stevenson, Swinburne and Tennyson. (Details of these, and of Wise's known and suspected counterfeit or 'binary' edns, forgeries and piracies, are listed in W. B. Todd, Handlist, above.) Wise was involved with the Shelley Soc and Browning Soc and supervised the making for them of facs reprints of Shelley's and Browning's works.

Letters

Letters of Thomas J. Wise to John Henry Wrenn: a further inquiry into the guilt of certain nineteenth-century forgers. Ed F. E. Ratchford, New York 1944.

Between the lines: letters and memoranda interchanged by H. B. Forman and Wise, with a foreword by C. H. Pforzheimer and an introductory essay and notes by F. E. Ratchford. Austin 1945. Implicating Forman in the Wise forgeries.

§2

Carter, J. and G. Pollard. An enquiry into the nature of certain 19th-century pamphlets. 1934.
— Wise and H. B. Forman: further light on the 19th-century pamphlets. TLS 1 June 1946; rptd in Carter's Books and book-collectors, 1956.
— The firm of Charles Ottley, Landon & Co: footnote to An enquiry. 1948.
— Working papers for a second edition of An enquiry into the nature of certain nineteenth century pamphlets. Oxford 1967–.
Carter, J. T. J. Wise. Spectator 21 May 1937; rptd (corrected) in his Books and book-collectors, 1956.
— Wise and his forgeries. Atlantic Monthly 175 1945; rptd, ibid.
— Wise after the event. Bookseller 5 Sept 1964; rptd, ibid.
Baughman, R. Some Victorian forged rarities. Huntington Lib Bull 9 1936.
Partington, W. Forging ahead: the true story of the upward progress of Wise. New York [1939], London [1946] (enlarged, as T. J. Wise in the original cloth, with an appendix by G. B. Shaw).
Ratchford, F. E. Wise forgeries in the Wrenn Library. Southwest Rev 25 1940.
— Idylls of the hearth: Wise's forgery of Enoch Arden. [1941].
— Wise to J. H. Wrenn on nineteenth-century bibliography. PBSA 36 1942.
— A review of reviews. Part 1, An enquiry [by Carter and Pollard, above]; part 2, Wise's letters [to J. H. Wrenn]. [Austin 1946].
Raymond, W. O. The forgeries of Wise and their aftermath. JEGP 44 1945; rptd (rev) in his Infinite moment and other essays in Robert Browning, Toronto 1950.
Draper, J. W. Wise and the Wrenn catalogue. MLN 63 1948. With text of a letter by Wise and comment by F. E. Ratchford.
Foxon, D. F. T. J. Wise and the pre-Restoration drama: a study in theft and sophistication. 1959 (Trans Bibl Soc, suppl 19).
Pariser, M. P. Bibliographer, vandal and thief. Manchester Guardian 25 April 1959.

Todd, W. B. (ed). T. J. Wise centenary studies: essays by J. Carter, G. Pollard, W. B. Todd. Austin [1959]. Includes letters by Wise.
— Some Wiseian ascriptions in the Wrenn catalogue. Library 5th ser 23 1968.
Trevanion, M. Wise's descriptive formula. Book Collector 13 1964.
Paden, W. D. Tennyson's Lover's tale, R. H. Shepherd and Wise. SB 18 1965.
Kendall, L. H., jr. The not-so-gentle art of puffing: W. G. Kingland and Wise. PBSA 62 1968.

M.P.

ADELINE VIRGINIA WOOLF, née STEPHEN
1882–1941

See cols 472–81, above.

HENRY CECIL KENNEDY WYLD
1870–1945

Contributions to the history of the guttural sounds in English. 1899.
The neglect of the study of the English language in the training of teachers: criticisms and suggestions. Liverpool 1904. Pamphlet.
The historical study of the mother tongue: an introduction to philological method. 1906, New York 1906.
The place of the mother tongue in national education. 1906. Pamphlet.
The growth of English: an elementary account of the present form of our language and its development. 1907, New York 1907.
The teaching of reading in training colleges. 1908.
Elementary lessons in English grammar. Oxford 1909.
A booke in Englysh metre, of the great marchaunt man called Dives pragmaticus. Manchester 1910. Facs of 1563 edn with notes and glossary by H. C. Wyld.
The place names of Lancashire: their origin and history. 1911. With T. O. Hirst.
Collected papers of Henry Sweet, Ed H. C. Wyld, Oxford 1913.
A short history of English. 1914, 1927 (rev), New York 1927.
A history of modern colloquial English. 1920, 1921 (rev), Oxford 1936 (with addns), New York 1937.
Studies in English rhymes from Surrey to Pope: a chapter in the history of English. 1923, New York 1965.
The universal dictionary of the English language. Ed H. C. Wyld. [1931–2], New York 1932.
Some aspects of the diction of English poetry. Oxford 1933.
The best English: a claim for the superiority of Received Standard English. Oxford 1934. SPE tract.
Little and Ives complete standard universal dictionary, Ed H. C. Wyld and E. Partridge, New York 1957 (also as Little and Ives Webster dictionary).
Wyld edited the New world literary ser (selections from English authors) 1920.

N.J.S.

II. HISTORIANS, AUTOBIOGRAPHERS, WRITERS ON POLITICS, SOCIETY, ECONOMICS ETC.

GENERAL STUDIES

Nicolson, H. The present age. In his Development of English biography, 1927.

Longaker, M. Contemporary biography. Philadelphia 1934.

Barnes, H. E. A history of historical writing. Norman Oklahoma 1937, New York 1962 (rev and enlarged).

—— et al. English sociologists since Herbert Spencer. In An introduction to the history of sociology, ed H. E. Barnes, Chicago 1948.

Johnson, E. One mighty torrent: the drama of biography. New York 1937.

West, H. F. The literature of war. In his Mind on the wing, New York 1947. World Wars I and II.

Matthews, W. British diaries: an annotated bibliography of British diaries written between 1442 and 1942. Berkeley 1950.

—— British autobiographies: an annotated bibliography [to 1951]. Berkeley 1955.

Some modern historians of Britain: essays in honour of R. L. Schuyler, ed H. Ausubel [et al], New York 1951.

House, H. The present art of biography. In his All in due time, 1955.

Powicke, F. M. Modern historians and the study of history. 1955.

Stewart, J. I. M. Biography. In The craft of letters in England, ed J. Lehmann 1956.

Wedgwood, C. V. Historical writing. Ibid.

Edel, L. Literary biography. Toronto 1957.

Halperin, S. W. (ed). Some 20th-century historians: essays on eminent Europeans. Chicago 1961.

Clifford, J. L. (ed). Biography as an art: selected criticism, 1560–1960. 1962.

Davenport, W. H. and B. Siegel (ed). Biography past and present: selections and critical essays. New York 1965.

Kendall, P. M. The art of biography. 1965.

Altick, R. D. Lives and letters: a history of literary biography in England and America. New York 1966.

M.S.

HAROLD MARIO MITCHELL ACTON
b. 1904

See col 229, above.

JAMES EVERSHED AGATE
1877–1947

See cols 997–8, above.

RICHARD ALDINGTON
1892–1962

See cols 511–14, above.

SIR CARLETON KEMP ALLEN
1887–1966

§1

The judgement of Paris. 1924, New York 1925. Novel.

Oh, Mr Leacock! 1925, New York 1925. Humorous essay on Stephen Leacock.

Law in the making. Oxford 1927. Rev and enlarged successively in 1930, 1939, 1946, 1951, 1958, 1964.

The law of contracts and torts. 1928 (Stephen's Commentaries on the Laws of England, vol 3). With G. S. Cheshire and C. H. S. Fifoot.

Bureaucracy triumphant. 1931. Collected articles.

Legal duties and other essays in jurisprudence. Oxford 1931.

Democracy and the individual. 1943.

Law and orders: an enquiry into the nature and scope of delegated legislation and executive powers in England. 1945, 1956 (rev).

The queen's peace. 1953.

Law and disorders: legal indiscretions. 1954. Collected 'trifles'.

Administrative jurisdiction. 1956.

Aspects of justice. 1958.

§2

Allen, Dorothy F. Sunlight and shadow: an autobiography. With preface by Allen 1960.

Goodhart, A. L. Proc Br Acad 53 1967.

C.H.E.P.

SIR RALPH NORMAN ANGELL
formerly
RALPH NORMAN ANGELL LANE
1874–1967

§1

Patriotism under three flags: a plea for rationalism in politics. 1903. As Ralph Lane.

Europe's optical illusion. [1909].

The great illusion: a study of the relation of military power in nations to their economic and social advantage. 1910, 1911 (rev and enlarged), 1933 (summarized, rearranged, as The great illusion, 1933), 1938 (as The great illusion—now [extracts plus 2 new introductory chs] (Penguin Special). *See* 'Rifleman', The struggle for bread: a reply to The great illusion, 1912; A. W. Alderson, Causes and cures of armaments and war, 1914 (includes a refutation); 'R.J.L.', The great illusion: a summary, [1914]; E. M. W. Tillyard, The Athenian empire and the great illusion, 1914; J. H. Jones, The economics of war and conquest: an examination of Angell's economic doctrines, 1915.

Peace theories and the Balkan war. 1912.

The foundations of international polity. [1914].

Prussianism and its destruction, with which is reprinted part 2 of The great illusion. 1914.

The world's highway: some notes on America's relation to sea power. New York 1915.

The dangers of half-preparedness: a plea for a declaration of American policy. New York 1916.

War aims: the need for a Parliament of the Allies. [1917].

Why freedom matters. [1917].

The political conditions of allied success: a plea for the protective union of the democracies. New York 1918.

The peace treaty and the economic chaos of Europe. 1919.

The fruits of victory: a sequel to The great illusion. [1921].

The press and the organization of society. 1922, Cambridge 1933 (rev).

If Britain is to live. 1923.

Foreign policy and our daily bread. [1925]. Chs from The
fruits of victory, above, with addns.
Human nature and the peace problem. [1925]. Chs from
The fruits of victory, above, with addns.
Must Britain travel the Moscow road?, with special reference
to Leon Trotsky's book, Where is Britain going? [1926].
The public mind: its disorders, its exploitation. 1926,
New York [1927].
The money game—how to play it: a new instrument of
economic education. 1929.
The story of money. New York 1929, London 1930.
Can governments cure unemployment? 1931. With
H. Wright.
The unseen assassins. 1932.
From chaos to control. 1933.
The menace to our national defence. 1934.
Preface to peace: a guide for the plain man. 1935, New
York 1935 (as Peace and the plain man).
The money mystery: an explanation for beginners. 1936.
This have and have-not business: political fantasy and
economic fact. 1936. Pt pbd Boston 1936 (as Raw
material, population pressure and war).
The defence of the Empire. 1937, New York 1938.
Peace with the dictators?: a symposium and some conclu-
sions. 1938.
For what do we fight? 1939.
Must it be war? [1939].
You and the refugee: the morals and economics of the
problem. 1939 (Penguin Special). With D. F. Buxton.
America's dilemma. 1940.
Why freedom matters. 1940 (Penguin Special). A differ-
ent work from that pbd 1917.
What kind of peace? 1941.
Let the people know. New York 1942. On the Second
World War.
The steep places: an examination of political tendencies.
1947.
After all: the autobiography of Norman Angell. 1951.
Contains a list of his works.
Defence and the English-speaking role. 1958.
*Angell edited Foreign Affairs 1928–31 and was a busy
pamphleteer.*

§2

Bennett, J. B. S. Norman Angellism. 1914.
Benson, G. Thirty points for Angellism. [1914].
Roberts, G. What about Norman Angell now? [1915].
Coulton, G. G. The main illusions of pacifism: a criticism
of Angell. 1916.

H. M. R.

'W. N. P. BARBELLION',
BRUCE FREDERICK CUMMINGS
1889–1919

§1

The louse and its relation to disease: its life-history and
how to deal with it. 1915 (BM Natural History, Economic Ser 2). By B. F. Cummings.
The bed-bug: its habits and life-history and how to deal
with it. 1917 (by B. F. Cummings), 1932 (rev, enlarged
and partly rewritten by E. E. Austen) (BM Natural
History, Economic Ser 5).
The journal of a disappointed man, with introduction by
H. G. Wells. 1919, New York [1919], London 1948
(Penguin) (with the substance of The life and character
of Barbellion, by A. J. Cummings. *See* A last diary, 1920,
below).
Enjoying life, and other literary remains. 1919, New York
[1920?]. Preface by H. R. Cummings. Essays and 2
short stories.
A last diary. Ed A. J. and H. R. Cummings 1920, New
York 1920. Preface, The life and character of Barbel-

lion, by A. J. Cummings. Extracts first pbd in London
Mercury May, June 1920. *See* A. F. Pollard, An essay
in historical method: the Barbellion diaries, History
new ser 6 1921; reply by H. R. Cummings, ibid (with
further note by Pollard).

§2

Shanks, E. W. N. P. Barbellion. London Mercury 1 1920;
rptd (rev) in his First essays on literature, 1923.
Krutch, J. W. Whom the gods love. Sewanee Rev 29 1921.
Tomlinson, H. M. In his Waiting for daylight, 1922.
Collins, J. Psychology of the diarist: W. N. P. Barbellion.
In his The doctor looks at literature, [1923].
Hellyar, R. H. W. N. P. Barbellion. 1926.
Murry, J. M. A disappointed man. In his Evolution of an
intellectual, 1927 (rev). Essay-review of The Journal,
1919.
Martin, E. W. W. N. P. Barbellion, 1889–1919. English 6
1947.
Braybrooke, N. Savage wars: a comparative study of
Barbellion and Denton Welch. Contemporary Rev 205
1964; rptd in Queen's Quart 75 1968.
Cummings, H. R. New light on Barbellion. Contempor-
ary Rev 208 1966.

M. P.

SIR ERNEST BARKER
1874–1960

§1

The political thought of Plato and Aristotle. 1906, New
York 1906.
A direct reply to each of Mr Chiozza Money's Free Trade
points. [1909].
Italy and the west 410–476. In Cambridge medieval his-
tory vol 1, Cambridge 1911.
The Dominican order and Convocation: a study of the
growth of representation in the church during the thir-
teenth century. Oxford 1913.
Nietzsche and Treitschke: the worship of power in
modern Germany. Oxford 1914.
Why we are at war: Great Britain's case, by members of
the Oxford Faculty of Modern History [Barker et al].
Oxford 1914, 1914 (rev and enlarged).
Great Britain's reasons for going to war. 1915. Pamphlet.
Mothers and sons in war time, and other pieces. 1915,
1917 (rev and enlarged), 1918 (enlarged). Rptd from
The Times.
Political thought in England from Herbert Spencer to the
present day. [1915], 1928 (rev as Political thought in
England 1848 to 1914).
The relations of England and Holland. [1915?]. Pamphlet.
The submerged nationalities of the German empire.
Oxford 1915.
Ireland in the last fifty years 1866–1916. Oxford 1917,
1919 (enlarged).
A confederation of the nations: its powers and constitution.
Oxford 1918. Pamphlet.
Greek political theory: Plato and his predecessors. 1918,
New York [1960]. Rev and enlarged edn of The political
thought of Plato and Aristotle 1906, above.
Linguistic oppression in the German empire. 1918, New
York 1918.
The future government of India and the Indian civil
service. Ed Barker 1919.
The crusades. 1923.
Greek political thought and theory in the fourth century.
In Cambridge ancient history vol 6, Cambridge 1927.
National character and the factors in its formation. 1927,
1948 (rev).
Church, state and study: essays. 1930, Michigan 1957
(as Church, state and education; with a new preface).

Burke and Bristol: a study of the relations between Burke and his constituency during the years 1774–80. Bristol 1931. Lectures.

Universities in Great Britain: their position and their problems. 1931. Pamphlet.

Natural Law and the theory of society 1500–1800 by O. F. von Gierke. With introd by Barker. 2 vols Cambridge 1934.

The citizen's choice. Cambridge 1937. Essays.

The development of administration, conscription, taxation, social services and education. In European civilization vol 5, ed E. Eyre 1937.

Oliver Cromwell and the English people. Cambridge 1937 (Cambridge Miscellany no 18).

The values of life: essays on the circles and centres of duty. 1939.

British statesmen. 1941 (Britain in Pictures).

The ideas and ideals of the British Empire. Cambridge 1941, New York 1969.

Britain and the British people. 1942, 1955 (rev).

Reflections on government. 1942. New York 1958.

The development of public services in Western Europe 1660–1930. 1944, Hamden Conn 1966.

British constitutional monarchy [1945], 1950 (rev), New York 1950 (Br Information ser), London 1952 (rev), 1955 (rev). Pamphlet.

Essays on government. Oxford 1945, 1951 (rev and enlarged).

British universities. 1946, 1949 (rev). Pamphlet.

The politics of Aristotle. Tr with introd, notes and appendix by Barker, Oxford 1946, New York 1958. A shortened form of the trn pbd 1948.

The character of England. Ed Barker, Oxford 1947.

Reflections on leisure: adapted from broadcast talks originally composed for Persia. [1947].

Father of the man: memories of Cheshire, Lancashire and Oxford 1874–98. [1948].

Traditions of civility: eight essays. Cambridge 1948, Hamden Conn 1967.

Principles of social and political theory. Oxford 1951.

Age and youth: memories of three universities; and Father of the Man. 1953.

W. P. Ker, a scholar. By E. B. [i.e. Barker]. Cambridge 1953. Rptd from The Times.

The European inheritance. Ed Barker et al 3 vols Oxford 1954.

From Alexander to Constantine: passages and documents illustrating the history of social and political ideas, 336 BC–AD 337. Tr with introd, notes and essays by Barker, Oxford 1956.

Social and political thought in Byzantium, from Justinian I to the last Palaeologus; Passages from Byzantine writers and documents. Tr with introd and notes by Barker, Oxford 1957.

Barker edited The library of Greek thought *from 1923,* Current problems ser, *from 1940 and* World History ser *1925–7. He wrote a number of introds to works on political theory and to an edn of Shakespeare.*

§2

Catlin, G. E. G. Ernest Barker. Proc Br Acad 46 1960.
J.M.P.

JOSEPH HILAIRE PIERRE RENÉ BELLOC
1870–1953

See cols 1004–10, above.

ENOCH ARNOLD BENNETT
1867–1931

See cols 429–36, above.

SIR ISAIAH BERLIN
b. 1909

Karl Marx: his life and environment. 1939, 1948 (bibliography rev), New York 1959, London 1960 (corrected), 1963 (rev), New York [1963] (with new introd by R. Heilbroner).

The hedgehog and the fox: an essay on Tolstoy's view of history. 1953, New York 1953.

A marvellous decade [Russian literature 1838–48]. In Encounter nos 21 26 27 32 1955–6. Delivered as the Northcliffe Lectures 1954.

The age of enlightenment: the 18th century philosophers. Selected with introd and commentary by Berlin, Boston 1956.

Mr Churchill in 1940. [1964], Boston 1964. Rptd essay-review of Churchill, Gathering storm.

Four essays on liberty. 1969.

Berlin tr Turgenev, First love *1950. With S. Hampshire and R. Wollheim he edited* Library of Ideas *series 1954–.*
J.G.

WILLIAM HENRY BEVERIDGE, 1ST BARON BEVERIDGE
1879–1963

§1

Unemployment: a problem of industry. 1909, 1912 (with additional appendices), 1930 (with substantial new section, as Unemployment: a problem of industry 1909 and 1930).

The public service in war and peace. 1920. Lecture at London School of Economics.

Insurance for all and everything. [1924]. Rptd from Daily News.

British food control. 1928, New Haven 1928 (Economic and social history of the war: British ser).

Causes and cures of unemployment. 1931. 6 wireless talks.

Tariffs: the case examined. 1931. By a committee of economists with Beveridge as chairman.

Changes in family life. 1932. 7 wireless talks by Beveridge et al.

Planning under Socialism, and other addresses. 1936. Mainly wireless talks, Herbert Spencer lecture 1936, and 'My Utopia', 1934.

Prices and wages in England, from the twelfth to the nineteenth century. Vol 1, 1939. By Beveridge et al; International Scientific Committee on Price History.

Social insurance and allied services. 2 pts 1942. Report presented to Parliament Nov 1942 ('Beveridge Report'). Abridged as Social insurance and allied services: the Beveridge report in brief, 1942. *See* G. D. H. Cole, Beveridge explained, 1942; J. W. Nisbet et al, The Beveridge plan: a symposium, R. C. Davison, Insurance for all and everything, and Social security, C. C. Saxton, Beveridge report criticised, H. W. Singer, Can we afford 'Beveridge'?, L. Watt, A Catholic view of the Beveridge plan, [all 1943]; J. S. Clarke, Social security guide, H. C. Palmer, The debit side of the Beveridge Report, B. Wootton, Social security and the Beveridge Plan, [all 1944]; A. Seldon, Beveridge 20 years after, New Society 14 Feb 1963; B. A. Smith, Beveridge II: another viewpoint, New Society 28 Feb 1963. *See also* Subject Index to Periodicals, *and* International Index to Periodicals, *for the appropriate periods for other articles on The Beveridge Report.*

The pillars of security and other war-time essays and addresses. 1943, New York 1943.

Full employment in a free society: a report. 1944, New York 1945, London 1953 (with new preface).

The price of peace. 1945, New York 1945.
Why I am a Liberal. [1945].
India called them. 1947. Biography of his parents.
Voluntary action: a report on methods of social advance. 1948, New York 1948.
Antipodes notebook. 1949. With J. Beveridge.
The evidence for voluntary action. 1949. Ed Beveridge with A. F. Wells.
The London School of Economics and the University of London. In The Webbs and their work, ed M. Cole 1949.
On and off the platform: under the Southern Cross. Wellington, New Zealand 1949. With J. Beveridge.
Power and influence. 1953, New York 1955. Autobiography; with bibliography.
A defence of free learning. 1959.
The London School of Economics and its problems, 1919–37. 1960.
Beveridge was, with A. J. Sargent, editor of Studies in commerce, *5 vols 1922–[9], and also wrote many official reports (see* Power and influence, *above, pp. 417–18).*

§2

Gordon, M. William Beveridge. In his How to tell progress from reaction, New York 1944.
Orton, W. A. Liberalism in crisis. In his Liberal tradition, New Haven 1945.
Simons, H. C. Beveridge program: an unsympathetic interpretation. In his Economic policy for a free society, Chicago 1948.
Beveridge, J. Beveridge and his Plan. 1954.
Hertz, F. What the world owes to William Beveridge. Contemporary Rev 203 1963.
Moos, S. A pioneer of social advance: Beveridge. Durham Univ Jnl 55 1963.
Salter, Lord. Lord Beveridge. Proc Br Acad 49 1963.

H. M. R.

EDMUND CHARLES BLUNDEN
b. 1896

See cols 234–8, above.

HENRY NOEL BRAILSFORD
1873–1958

§1

The broom of the war-god: a novel. 1898, New York 1898.
Macedonia: its races and their future. 1906.
Adventures in prose: a book of essays. 1911.
Shelley, Godwin and their circle. [1913], New York 1913, London 1951 (rev bibliography).
The war of steel and gold: a study of the armed peace. 1914, 1915 (with additional ch), New York 1915.
A league of nations. 1917, New York 1917, London 1917 (rev).
A share in your motherland and other articles. [1918].
Across the blockade: a record of travels in enemy Europe. 1919, New York 1919.
After the peace. 1920, New York 1922 (rev).
The Russian workers' republic. 1921.
Socialism for today. 1925.
How the Soviets work. 1927, New York 1928.
Olives of endless age: being a study of this distracted world and its need for unity. 1928.
Rebel India. 1931, New York 1931.
Property or peace? 1934, New York 1934.
Voltaire. 1935, New York [1935].
Why capitalism means war. 1938.
America our ally. 1940.

From England to America: a message. New York [1940].
Subject India. 1943, New York 1943, Bombay 1946.
Our settlement with Germany. 1944, New York 1944.
The levellers and the English revolution. Ed C. Hill 1961, Stanford 1961.
Brailsford was leader writer successively on Manchester Guardian, Tribune, Daily News *and* Nation, *and editor of* New Leader *1922–6. He collaborated in a work on Gandhi and edited Trelawny's* Adventures *of a younger son and a selection of the writings of H. W. Nevinson. He wrote many pamphlets and articles on international affairs, socialism and women's suffrage.*

A. P. H.

GERALD BRENAN
(EDWARD FITZGERALD BRENAN)
b. 1894

See col 1014, above.

SIR DENIS WILLIAM BROGAN
b. 1900

The American political system. 1933, New York 1933 (as Government of the people), London 1943 (new preface), New York 1944 (new preface), London 1947 (rev preface).
Proudhon. 1934.
Abraham Lincoln. 1935, New York 1963.
The development of modern France 1870–1939. 1940, New York 1940 (as France under the Republic), London 1967 (rev).
Is innocence enough?: some reflections on foreign affairs. 1941.
Politics and law in the United States. Cambridge 1941.
USA: an outline of the country, its people and institutions. Oxford 1941.
The English people: impressions and observations. 1943, New York 1943.
The American problem. 1944.
The free state: some considerations on its practical value. 1945, New York 1945.
French personalities and problems. 1946, New York 1947.
American themes. 1948, New York 1949. Articles from periodicals.
The era of Franklin D. Roosevelt: a chronicle of the New Deal and global war. New Haven 1950, London 1952 (as Roosevelt and the New Deal).
The price of revolution. 1951, New York [1951].
An introduction to American politics. 1954, New York 1954 (as Politics in America).
The American character. New York 1956.
The French nation from Napoleon to Pétain 1814–1940. 1957, New York 1957.
America in the modern world. New Brunswick NJ 1960, London 1960 (for 1961).
Political patterns in today's world. 1963, New York 1963. With D. V. Verney.
American aspects. 1964, New York 1964.
Worlds in conflict. 1967, New York 1967.
Also a novel, Stop on the green light, *1950 (under the pseudonym Maurice Barrington).*

H. M. R.

IVOR JOHN CARNEGIE BROWN
b. 1891

See cols 1014–15, above.

SIR ARTHUR WYNNE MORGAN BRYANT
b. 1899

§1

The spirit of conservatism. 1929.
King Charles II. 1931, 1955 (rev).
Macaulay. 1932, New York 1933.
Samuel Pepys: the man in the making. Cambridge 1933.
The England of Charles II. 1934, 1960 (as Restoration England).
The national character. 1934. Broadcast talks.
Samuel Pepys: the years of peril. Cambridge 1935.
The American ideal. 1936. Biographical essays.
George V. 1936.
Stanley Baldwin: a tribute. [1937], New York [1937].
Humanity in politics. [1938]. Essays.
Samuel Pepys: the saviour of the navy. Cambridge 1938.
English saga 1840–1940. 1940, New York [1941] (as Pageant of England 1840–1940).
Unfinished victory. 1940. On Germany 1918–33.
The years of endurance 1793–1812. 1942, New York 1942.
Years of victory 1802–12. 1944, New York 1945.
Historian's holiday. 1946, 1951 (enlarged). Essays.
The age of elegance 1812–22. 1950, New York 1951.
The story of England: [vol 1] makers of the realm. 1953, Boston 1954, London 1961 (illustrated edn), New York 1962 (as Makers of England: vol 1 of an historical trilogy entitled Atlantic saga).
The turn of the tide 1939–43: a study based on the diaries and autobiographical notes of Viscount Alanbrooke. 1957, New York 1957.
Triumph in the West 1943–6: based on the diaries and autobiographical notes of Viscount Alanbrooke. 1959, New York 1959.
The story of England: [vol 2] the age of chivalry. 1963, New York 1964.
The fire and the rose. 1965, New York 1966. Narrative of 9 decisive events in English history.
The medieval foundation. 1966, New York 1967 (as The medieval foundation of England).
Protestant island. 1967, New York 1967.
Bryant edited Letters and speeches of Charles II, Memoirs of James II *and* Speeches of Neville Chamberlain, *as well as* The man and the hour (*biographical essays by various authors*) *and* Postman's horn (*an anthology of 17th-century letters*). *He was a frequent contributor to* Illustrated London News.

§2

Parkinson, C. N. A master of pageantry. Fortnightly 158 1945.
—— In his A law unto themselves. 1966.

A.P.H.

JOHN BUCHAN, 1st BARON TWEEDSMUIR
1875–1940
See cols 540–4, above.

JOHN BAGNELL BURY
1861–1927

Bibliographies

Baynes, N. H. A bibliography of the works of Bury, with a memoir. Cambridge 1929.

§1

The Hippolytus of Euripides. Ed J. P. Mahaffy and Bury 1881.
A history of the later Roman Empire from Arcadius to Irene, 395 AD to 800 AD. 2 vols 1889.
The Nemean odes of Pindar. Ed Bury 1890.
The Isthmian odes of Pindar. Ed Bury 1892.
The students' Roman Empire: a history of the Roman Empire from its foundation to the death of Marcus Aurelius, 27 BC to 180 AD. 1893, New York [190?].
The history of the decline and fall of the Roman Empire by E. Gibbon. Ed Bury. 7 vols 1896–1900, 1909–14 (rev), 3 vols New York 1946.
A history of Greece to the death of Alexander the Great. 1900, 2 vols 1902 (rev), 1 vol 1913 (rev), New York 1937, London 1951 (rev by R. Meiggs). An abridgment, History of Greece for beginners, was pbd 1903, New York 1907 (as A student's history of Greece).
The Ottoman conquest. In The Cambridge modern history vol 1, Cambridge 1902.
The life of Saint Patrick and his place in history. 1905.
Russia 1462–1682. In The Cambridge modern history vol 5, Cambridge 1908.
The ancient Greek historians. 1909, New York 1909.
The imperial administrative system in the ninth century, with a revised text of the Kletorologion of Philotheos. 1911 (Br Acad Supplemental Papers 1), New York [1958].
A history of the Eastern Roman Empire from the fall of Irene to the accession of Basil I, AD 802–67. 1912, Ann Arbor 1958.
A history of freedom of thought. [1913], New York [1913], London 1952 (epilogue by H. J. Blackham). *See also* H. Belloc, Anti-Catholic history: how it is written, 1914; J. G. Vance, Freedom of thought and Christianity: a criticism of Bury's History of freedom of thought, 1914.
The early history of the Slavonic settlements in Dalmatia, Croatia & Serbia (Constantine Porphyrogennetos, De administrando imperio, chs 29–36). Ed Bury 1920.
The idea of progress: an inquiry into its origin and growth. 1920, New York 1932 (introd by C. A. Beard). *See also* H. Ellis, Stepping heavenward, Nation 22 May 1920; rptd in his Views and reviews 2nd ser, 1932 (as The idea of progress).
The Hellenistic age and the history of civilization. In The Hellenistic age: aspects of Hellenistic civilization treated by Bury et al, Cambridge 1923.
History of the later Roman Empire from the death of Theodosius I to the death of Justinian, AD 395 to AD 565. 2 vols 1923, New York 1958.
The Achaeans and the Trojan war; Homer; Greek literature from the eighth century to the Persian wars; The age of illumination; Dionysius of Syracuse. In Cambridge ancient history vols 2, 4–6, ed Bury et al, Cambridge 1924, 1926–7.
The invasion of Europe by the barbarians. 1928, New York 1963.
History of the Papacy in the 19th century 1864–78. Ed with a memoir by R. H. Murray 1930, New York 1964 (augmented edn by F. C. Grant).
Selected essays. Ed H. Temperley, Cambridge 1930. Includes lectures previously pbd separately.
Bury edited E. A. Freeman, History of federal government in Greece and Italy, *1893, and* The historical geography of Europe, *3rd edn 1903. The* Cambridge medieval history, *8 vols Cambridge 1911–36, was planned as a whole, and the scheme of each vol drawn up, by him. He was general editor of the series* Foreign statesmen, *11 vols 1896–1903, and* Byzantine texts, *5 vols 1898–1904. He was a prolific contributor to journals, especially* Classical Rev, EHR, Hermathena *and* Kottabos, *which he edited 1888–91, contributing also many Greek trns of Latin verse.*

§2

Baynes, N. H. Memoir. In his A bibliography of the works of Bury, 1929, above. With list of obituary notices.

D.K.

SIR HERBERT BUTTERFIELD
b. 1900

Bibliographies
Hinton, R. W. K. In The diversity of history: essays in honour of Butterfield, ed J. H. Elliott and H. G. Koenigsberger, 1970. With notes of trns.

§1

The historical novel: an essay. Cambridge 1924.
The peace tactics of Napoleon 1806–8. Cambridge 1929.
Select documents of European history, general editor R. G. D. Laffan: vol 3, 1715–1920, ed Butterfield 1931.
The Whig interpretation of history. 1931, New York 1951.
Napoleon. 1939, 1940 (rev), New York 1956.
The statecraft of Machiavelli. 1940, New York 1956.
The Englishman and his history. Cambridge 1944.
Lord Acton. 1948 (Historical Assoc pamphlet).
Christianity and history. 1949, New York 1950.
George III, Lord North and the people 1779–80. 1949, New York 1968.
The origins of modern science 1300–1800. 1949, New York 1951, London 1957 (rev), New York 1957.
Christianity in European history. 1951.
History and human relations. 1951, New York 1952.
Liberty in the modern world. Toronto 1952.
Christianity, diplomacy and war. 1953, New York 1953.
Man on his past: the study of the history of historical scholarship. Cambridge 1955, Boston 1960 (with new preface).
George III and the historians. 1957, New York 1959 (rev).
From Revolution to Second Empire. In A short history of France from early times to 1958, ed J. H. Jackson, Cambridge 1959.
International conflict in the twentieth century: a Christian view. 1960, New York 1960.
The universities and education today. 1962.
Diplomatic investigations: essays in the theory of international politics. 1966, Cambridge Mass 1966. Ed Butterfield, with M. Wight; contributions by Butterfield.
Butterfield also edited Cambridge Historical Jnl 1938–52.

§2

Parker, H. T. In Some 20th-century historians, ed S. W. Halperin, Chicago 1961.
Brogan, D. Butterfield as a historian: an appreciation. In The diversity of history: essays in honour of Butterfield, ed J. H. Elliott and H. G. Koenigsberger, 1970.

M.P.

EDWARD HALLETT CARR
b. 1892

§1

Dostoevsky. 1931, Boston 1931. Biography.
The romantic exiles. 1933, New York 1933. Portraits of nineteenth-century political exiles from Russia.
Karl Marx: a study in fanaticism. 1934.
International relations since the peace treaties. 1937, 1940 (enlarged), 1947 (as International relations between the two world wars 1919–39), New York 1966.
Michael Bakunin. 1937, New York 1961. Biography.

Britain: a study of foreign policy from the Versailles Treaty to the outbreak of war. 1939.
Propaganda in international politics. Oxford 1939, New York 1939. Pamphlet.
The twenty years' crisis 1919–39: an introduction to the study of international relations. 1939, New York 1964.
The future of international government. 1941. Pamphlet; with S. de Madariaga.
The future of nations: independence or interdependence? 1941.
Conditions of peace. 1942, New York 1942.
Nationalism and after. 1945, New York 1945.
The Soviet impact on the western world. 1946, New York 1947.
International relations between the two world wars 1919–39. 1947. See International relations since the peace treaties, 1937, above.
A history of Soviet Russia. 1950–, New York 1951–. Pt 4 vol 1 with R. W. Davies.
Studies in revolution. 1950, 1962 (with corrections), New York 1964.
German–Soviet relations between the two world wars 1919–39. Baltimore 1951, London 1952.
The new society. 1951, Boston 1957 (with new preface).
What is history? 1961, New York 1962.
1917: before and after. 1969, New York 1969 (as The October Revolution: before and after).
Carr edited the series Ambassadors at large: studies in the foreign policies of the leading powers. He was assistant editor of The Times 1941–6.

§2

Deutscher, I. Carr as historian of the Bolshevik régime. In his Heretics and renegades, 1955, New York 1957 (as Russia in transition); rptd in Soviet Studies 6 1955 (as Carr as historian of Soviet Russia).
Crossman, R. H. S. Illusions of power: Carr. In his The charm of politics, 1958.
Morgenthau, H. J. The surrender to the immanence of power: Carr. In his Dilemmas of politics, Chicago 1958; rptd in his The restoration of American politics, Chicago 1962.

J.G.

CATHERINE ROXBURGH
CARSWELL, née MACFARLANE
1879–1946

See col 548, above.

'CHRISTOPHER CAUDWELL',
CHRISTOPHER ST JOHN SPRIGG
1907–37

See cols 1016–17, above.

LORD EDWARD CHRISTIAN
DAVID GASCOYNE CECIL
b. 1902

See cols 1017–18, above.

RAYMOND WILSON CHAMBERS
1874–1942

See cols 1019–20, above.

GILBERT KEITH CHESTERTON
1874–1936

See cols 1021–28, above.

VERE GORDON CHILDE
1892–1957

Bibliographies

Smith, I. F. Bibliography of the publications of Childe. Prehistoric Soc Proc 21 1956.

§1

How labour governs: a study of workers' representation in Australia. 1923, Melbourne 1964.

The dawn of European civilization. 1925, 1939 (rev), 1947 (rev), 1950 (rev), New York 1951, London 1957 (rev), New York 1958, 1964 (rev).

Delaporte, L. J. Mesopotamia. 1925. Tr Childe.

The Aryans: a study of Indo-European origins. 1926.

Moret, A. and G. Davy. From tribe to empire. 1926. Tr Childe.

Homo, L. Primitive Italy. 1927, New York 1927. Tr Childe.

Borovka, G. I. Scythian art. 1928. Tr Childe.

The most ancient East: the oriental prelude to European prehistory. 1928, 1934 (rewritten, as New light on the most ancient East), New York 1953.

The Danube in prehistory. Oxford 1929.

The bronze age. Cambridge 1930, New York 1930.

Skara Brae: a Pictish village in Orkney. 1931.

The prehistory of Scotland. 1935.

Man makes himself. 1936, 1941 (rev), New York 1951, 1961 (rev), London 1965 (preface by G. Daniel).

Prehistoric communities of the British Isles. 1940.

Prehistoric Scotland. 1940 (Historical Assoc pamphlet).

What happened in history. 1942, New York 1946, London 1954 (rev), 1960 (rev), Baltimore 1960, London 1964 (new foreword by G. Clark and footnotes), Baltimore 1964. (Pelican).

Progress and archaeology. 1944.

The story of tools. 1944.

Scotland before the Scots. 1946.

History. 1947, New York 1953 (as What is history?).

Prehistoric migrations in Europe. Oslo 1950.

Social evolution. 1951, New York 1951, ed M. Wheeler, London 1963.

Piecing together the past: the interpretation of archaeological discovery. 1956, New York 1956.

A short introduction to archaeology. 1956, New York 1958.

Society and knowledge. New York [1956], London 1956.

The prehistory of European society. 1958 (Pelican), Baltimore [1958].

Childe also compiled several official guidebooks to archaeological sites in Scotland.

§2

Piggott, S. Childe. Proc Br Acad 44 1958.

N.J.S.

RICHARD THOMAS CHURCH
1893–1972

See cols 246–8, above.

SIR WINSTON LEONARD SPENCER CHURCHILL
1874–1965

The Chartwell Trust Archives are now housed in Bodley.

Bibliographies

Farmer, B. J. Bibliography of the works of Churchill. 1958. Duplicated.

Woods, F. A bibliography of the works of Churchill. 1963, 1967 (rev). Includes trns, and books on Churchill.

§1

There have been a number of popular anthologies from Churchill's writings and speeches; see Woods, Bibliographies, above. Churchill often serialized his books before pbn and issued unrevised as well as rev reprints. For details, see Woods, and for a brief summary, see The Churchill industry, *in the* Historical appendix *to* M. Wolff, Winston Churchill, *1970, below.*

The story of the Malakand Field Force: an episode of the frontier war. 1898, 1899 (rev, with new preface).

The river war: an historical account of the reconquest of the Soudan. Ed F. Rhodes 2 vols 1899, 1 vol 1902 (rev, with new preface and additional ch), 1933 (with new introd).

Savrola: a tale of the revolution in Laurania. New York 1900, London 1900, New York 1956 (with new foreword).

London to Ladysmith via Pretoria. 1900.

Ian Hamilton's march: together with extracts from the diary of Lieutenant H. Frankland, a prisoner of war at Pretoria. 1900. Continuation of above. These, and the Story of the Malakand Field Force and the River war, reissued, abridged, 1962 (as Frontiers and wars).

Mr Brodrick's army. 1903. Speeches on the Army Scheme of 1901.

Lord Randolph Churchill. 2 vols 1906, 1 vol 1907, [1952] (enlarged with new introd).

For free trade: a collection of speeches delivered at Manchester or in the House of Commons during the fiscal controversy preceding the late general election. 1906.

For Liberalism and free trade: principal speeches of Churchill during the campaign in Dundee, May 1908. Dundee 1908. Pamphlet.

My African journey. 1908, New York 1909.

Liberalism and the social problem. 1909, New York 1910. Speeches; introd by H. W. Massingham.

The people's rights, selected from his Lancashire and other recent speeches. [1910].

The world crisis. 5 vols in 6, 1923–31, New York 1923–31, 1 vol London 1931 (abridged and rev with additional ch on The battle of the Marne), New York 1931, 3 vols London [1933–4] (as The Great War, abridged edn pbd in parts with new foreword dated 1933), 1 vol 1933 (priv ptd) (as Sandhurst edition of The world crisis, abridged and rev), 2 vols 1939 (enlarged with new foreword dated 1938).

Parliamentary government and the economic problem: the Romanes lecture. Oxford 1930; rptd in Thoughts and adventures, 1932, below.

My early life: a roving commission. 1930, New York 1930 (as A roving commission: my early life; preface enlarged for American readers), 1939 (introd by D. Thompson).

India: speeches and an introduction. 1931.

Thoughts and adventures. 1932, New York 1932 (as Amid these storms: thoughts and adventures). Preface by E. Marsh.

Marlborough: his life and times. 4 vols 1933–8 (vol 1 rev 1934), 6 vols New York 1933–8, 2 vols London 1947, 1 vol New York [1968] (abridged with introd by H. S. Commager). An excerpt, Blenheim: from Marlborough vol II, pbd 1941.

Charles, IXth Duke of Marlborough, K.G. Tributes by Churchill and C. C. Martindale. 1934.

Great contemporaries. 1937, New York 1937, London 1938 (rev and enlarged), 1943 (omitting chs on Trotsky and Roosevelt).

Arms and the covenant: speeches, compiled by R. S. Churchill. [1938], New York 1938 (as While England slept: a survey of world affairs, 1932–8).

Step by step, 1936–9. 1939, New York [1939]. Collected newspaper articles.

Addresses delivered in the year nineteen hundred and forty to the people of Great Britain, of France and to the members of the English House of Commons. San Francisco 1940 (250 copies).

The war speeches of Churchill, ser 1 (–2). [Bombay 1940–1].

Blenheim. 1941. *See* above, Marlborough, 1933–8.

Broadcast addresses to the people of Great Britain, Italy, Poland, Russia and the United States. San Francisco 1941 (250 copies).

Into battle: speeches, compiled by R. S. Churchill. 1941, New York [1941] (as Blood, sweat and tears).

The unrelenting struggle: war speeches, compiled by C. Eade. 1942, Boston 1942.

The end of the beginning: war speeches, 1942, compiled by C. Eade. 1943, Boston 1943.

Onwards to victory: war speeches, 1943, compiled by C. Eade. 1944, Boston 1944.

The dawn of liberation: war speeches, 1944, compiled by C. Eade. 1945, Boston 1945.

Victory: war speeches, 1945, compiled by C. Eade. 1946, Boston 1946.

Secret session speeches, compiled by C. Eade. 1946, New York 1946.

The Second World War. 6 vols Boston 1948–53, London 1948–54, [1955] ('Chartwell' rev edn), 1 vol 1959 (as Memoirs of the Second World War: an abridgement [by D. Kelly] with an epilogue by the author on the post war years), Boston 1959, 2 vols New York 1959 (as The Second World War: extracts from Kelly's abridgement), 12 vols London 1964 (illustr). *See* The Second World War: printing and publishing history; the status of the galleys, in Woods, Bibliographies, above.

The sinews of peace: post-war speeches. Ed R. S. Churchill 1948, Boston 1949.

Painting as a pastime. 1948, New York 1950. Reproductions of paintings by Churchill, with text rptd from Hobbies and Painting as a pastime in Thoughts and adventures, 1932, above.

Europe unite: speeches 1947 and 1948. Ed R. S. Churchill 1950, Boston 1950.

In the balance: speeches 1949 and 1950. Ed R. S. Churchill 1951, Boston 1952.

The war speeches, compiled by C. Eade. 3 vols 1952, Boston 1953. Contains addns to and omissions from the 7 vols pbd 1941–6.

Stemming the tide: speeches 1951 and 1952. Ed R. S. Churchill 1953, Boston 1954 (for 1953).

A history of the English-speaking peoples. 4 vols 1956–8, New York 1956–8, London 1958 ('Chartwell' edn, illustr), 1 vol 1964 (as The island race, abridged by T. Baker), New York 1964, 1965 (abridged by H. S. Commager). An excerpt, The American Civil War, pbd 1961.

The unwritten alliance: speeches 1953 to 1959. Ed R. S. Churchill 1961.

Frontiers and wars. 1962. *See* Ian Hamilton's march, 1900, above.

Many of Churchill's speeches, addresses, broadcasts etc were first pbd separately. For details of these, of Churchill's many forewords to works by others, and uncollected pieces of journalism, see Woods, Bibliographies, above. Churchill edited Br Gazette, 8 nos 5–13 May 1926. The risings on the North-West Frontier, Allahabad 1898 is not by him. See Woods, op cit, and his letter to TLS 20 June 1958.

§2

For the many books and pamphlets of popular biography, polemics, and for books studying various aspects of Churchill's public life, as distinct from his career as a writer, see Woods Bibliographies, above.

Freeman, J. Churchill as a prose-writer. London Mercury 15 1927. Essay-review of The world crisis.

Johnston, J. A puckish Burke: Churchill. In his Westminster voices: studies in parliamentary speech, [1928].

Keynes, J. M. Churchill on the war; Churchill on the peace. In his Essays in biography, 1933. Essay-reviews of The world crisis.

Hay, M. V. Winston Churchill and James II of England. 1934.

Marsh, E. H. In his A number of people: a book of reminiscences, 1939.

Moir, P. I was Churchill's private secretary. New York 1941.

Norwood, G. The eloquence of Churchill. UTQ 12 1943.

Major, J. C. Churchill's figures of speech. Word Study 20 1944.

Rowse, A. L. Churchill and English history. In his English spirit, 1944.

— The later Churchills. 1958.

— Churchill as historian. HLQ 25 1962.

Berlin, I. Churchill and F. D. Roosevelt. Cornhill Mag 164 1949; Atlantic Monthly 184 1949. Pbd separately 1964 (as Mr Churchill in 1940). Essay-review of The Second World War vol 1.

Treneer, A. Churchills Prosa. Die Brücke (Essen) 136 1949.

Hamilton, W. B. Churchill: actor as historian. South Atlantic Quart 50 1951.

Hurwitz, S. J. In Some modern historians of Britain: essays in honor of R. L. Schuyler, ed H. Ausubel et al, New York 1951.

Cairns, J. E. Clio and the Queen's First Minister. South Atlantic Quart 52 1953.

Churchill, by his contemporaries. Ed C. Eade 1953.

Cowles, V. Winston Churchill: the era and the man. 1953

Stewart, H. L. Winged words: Churchill as writer and speaker. Toronto 1953, London 1954 (as Sir Winston Churchill as writer and speaker).

Whittemore, R. Churchill and the limitations of myth. Yale Rev 44 1954.

'Connell, John' (J. H. Robertson). Winston Churchill. 1956, 1965 (rev) (Br Council pamphlet).

Lomas, C. W. Churchill's concept of his audience. Western Speech Spring 1958.

— Churchill: orator-historian. Quart Jnl of Speech 44 1958.

Hassall, C. In his Edward Marsh, patron of the arts: a biography, 1959. Marsh was Churchill's literary executor.

Mendelssohn, P. The age of Churchill: [vol 1] heritage and adventure 1874–1911. 1961.

Norwood, W. D. Churchill as novelist. BNYPL 66 1962.

Bullock, A. Churchill's characteristics as an historian. Listener 4 Feb 1965.

Magee, B. Churchill's novel [Savrola]. Encounter 25 1965.

Plumb, J. H. The literary Churchill. Saturday Rev of Lit 6 Feb 1965.

— Churchill as historian: a brontosaurus among minnows. Spectator 1 July 1966.

— The historian. In A. J. P. Taylor [et al], Churchill revised, New York 1969, London 1969 (as Churchill: four faces and the man).

Ashley, M. P. Churchill and history. International Affairs 42 1966.

— Churchill as historian. 1968.

Churchill, R. S. Winston S. Churchill. 1966 onwards.

Gilbert, M. Winston Churchill. 1966 (Clarendon Biographies).

Jones, R. V. Winston Leonard Spencer Churchill, 1874–1965. In Biographical memoirs of Fellows of the Royal Soc 12 1966.

Deakin, F. W. D. Churchill the historian. Schweizer Monatshefte Sonderbeilage 49 1969.

Wolff, M. Winston Churchill. [1970] (Great Nobel Prizes ser).

M. P.

SIR JOHN HAROLD CLAPHAM
1873–1946

Bibliographies

Bibliography of Clapham. Cambridge Historical Jnl 8 1946.

§1

The causes of the war of 1792. Cambridge 1899 (Prince Consort Dissertation 1898).

Economic change. In Cambridge modern history vol 10, Cambridge 1907.

The woollen and worsted industries. 1907.

Christianity and the problem of poverty. In Social ideals: papers by W. Crooks, Clapham [et al], [1909].

Great Britain and free trade 1841–52. In Cambridge modern history vol 11, Cambridge 1909.

The Abbé Sieyès: an essay in the politics of the French Revolution. 1912.

The economic development of France and Germany 1815–1914. Cambridge 1921.

Pitt's first decade 1782–92. In Cambridge history of British foreign policy vol 1, Cambridge 1922.

Zollverein negotiations. In Cambridge history of British foreign policy vol 2, Cambridge 1923.

An economic history of modern Britain. 3 vols Cambridge 1926–38, vol 1 1930 (rev), 3 vols 1950–2 (vol 1 with corrections).

Commerce and industry in the Middle Ages. In Cambridge medieval history vol 6, Cambridge 1929.

The study of economic history. Cambridge 1929. Inaugural lecture.

The Bank of England: a history. 2 vols Cambridge 1944.

A concise economic history of Britain from the earliest times to 1750. Ed J. Saltmarsh, Cambridge 1949.

Clapham was chairman of the Committee on the provision for social and economic research (Report 1946). He contributed often to Alpine Jnl. He was the first editor of Cambridge Studies in Economic History, *and with Eileen Power was editor of the* Cambridge economic history of Europe.

§2

Clark, G. N. Sir John Clapham. Proc Br Acad 32 1947.

John Harold Clapham 1873–1946: a memoir, prepared by direction of the Council of King's College, Cambridge. Cambridge 1949.

H. M. R.

SIR GEORGE NORMAN CLARK
b. 1890

Unifying the world. London and New York 1920. (Swarthmore International Handbooks 7). The role of communications in international affairs.

The Dutch alliance and the war against French trade 1688–1697. Manchester 1923.

The seventeenth century. Oxford 1929, 1947 (rev and enlarged), New York 1961.

The later Stuarts 1660–1714. Oxford 1934. Frequently rptd with corrections. (Oxford History of England 10).

Science and social welfare in the age of Newton. Oxford 1937, 1949 (rev).

Guide to English commercial statistics 1696–1782, with a catalogue of materials by B. M. Franks. 1938 (Royal Historical Soc Handbooks 1).

The wealth of England from 1496 to 1760. 1946.

The colonial conferences between England and the Netherlands in 1613 and 1615: vol 2, An outline of the historical setting. Leiden 1951.

The early modern period. In The European inheritance, ed E. Barker, Clark, P. Vaucher, Oxford 1954. Rptd

separately with corrections as Early modern Europe from about 1450 to about 1720, 1957, New York 1960.

War and society in the seventeenth century. Cambridge 1958.

The Campden wonder. Ed [with contributions by] Clark 1959. The Harrison-Perry mystery 1660–62.

Three aspects of Stuart England. 1960.

A history of the Royal College of Physicians of London. 2 vols Oxford 1964–66.

Clark was sometime editor of the EHR and has since assisted as editor, joint editor, or adviser, in the preparation of a number of historical series, including the Oxford History of England, *the* Oxford Historical Series, *the* Home University Library of Modern Knowledge *and the* New Cambridge Modern History. *He has also edited H. W. C. Davis,* Europe from 800 to 1789 *(1930) and jointly edited a collection of Oxfordshire records (1925).*

C. H. E. P.

KENNETH MACKENZIE CLARK, BARON CLARK
b. 1903

See cols 1028–9, above.

GEORGE DOUGLAS HOWARD COLE
1889–1959

Bibliographies

Owen, G. Cole's historical writings, with a bibliography. International Rev of Social History 11 1966.

§1

The world of labour: a discussion of the present and future of trade unionism. 1913, 1915 (rev), 1919 (new introd).

Labour in war time. 1915.

Self-government in industry. 1917, 1920 (rev). Rptd in pt from New Age and other periodicals.

Trade unionism on the railways: its history and problems. 1917. With R. Page Arnot.

Labour in the Commonwealth: a book for the younger generation. [1918], New York 1920.

The payment of wages: a study in payment by results under the wage-system. [1918], 1928 (rev).

Chaos and order in industry. 1920.

Guild socialism re-stated. 1920.

Social theory. 1920, New York 1920, London 1921 (rev).

The future of local government. 1921.

Guild socialism: a plan for economic democracy. New York 1921.

Labour in the coal-mining industry 1914–21. Oxford 1923 (Economic and social history of the World War, British ser).

Out of work: an introduction to the study of unemployment. 1923, New York 1923.

Trade unionism and munitions. Oxford 1923 (Economic and social history of the World War, British ser).

Workshop organisation. Oxford 1923 (Economic and social history of the World War, British ser).

The life of William Cobbett. [1924], 1947 (rev).

Organised labour: an introduction to trade unionism. 1924.

Robert Owen. 1925, 1930 (as The life of Robert Owen).

A short history of the British working class movement 1789–1925(–7). 3 vols 1925–7, 1932 (new foreword), 1937 (with supplementary ch to 1937), 1948 (rev and continued to 1947).

The next ten years in British social and economic policy. 1929.

Politics and literature. 1929, New York 1929 (Hogarth lectures on literature 11).

Gold, credit and employment: four essays for laymen. 1930, New York 1931.

British trade and industry, past and future. 1932.

Economic tracts for the times. 1932.

The intelligent man's guide through world chaos. 1932, New York 1932 (as A guide through world chaos).

Modern theories and forms of industrial organisation. 1932.

Theories and forms of political organisation. 1932.

The intelligent man's review of Europe today. 1933, New York 1933. With M. Cole.

What everybody wants to know about money: a planned outline of monetary problems, by nine economists from Oxford. 1933, New York 1933. Planned and edited by Cole.

What is this socialism?: letters to a young inquirer. 1933.

A guide to modern politics. 1934, New York 1934. With M. Cole.

Some relations between political and economic theory. 1934.

Studies in world economics. 1934, Freeport, New York 1967.

What Marx really meant. 1934, New York 1934.

Principles of economic planning. 1935, New York 1935 (as Economic planning).

The simple case for socialism. 1935.

The condition of Britain. 1937. With M. Cole.

The People's Front. 1937.

Practical economics: or studies in economic planning. 1937 (Pelican).

The common people 1746–1938. 1938, 1946 (enlarged, brought up to date), 1956 (corrected) (Pelican); New York 1939 (as The British common people 1746–1938), 1947 (as The British people 1746–1946). With R. W. Postgate.

The machinery of socialist planning. 1938.

Persons and periods: studies. 1938, 1945 (shorter version) (Pelican), New York 1967. Articles etc from the 30's.

Socialism in evolution. 1938 (Pelican).

British trade-unionism to-day: a survey, with the collaboration of thirty trade union leaders and other experts. 1939, 1953 (rev, as An introduction to trade unionism), New York 1955.

Plan for democratic Britain. [1939].

War aims. 1939.

British working class politics 1832–1914. 1941.

Chartist portraits. 1941, 1965 (for 1964) (introd by A. Briggs), New York 1964.

Europe, Russia and the future. 1941, New York 1942.

Great Britain in the post-war world. 1942.

Fabian socialism. 1943.

The means to full employment. 1943.

A century of co-operation. 1944. History of the Co-operative Movement.

Money: its present and future. 1944, 1947 (rev), 1954 (rev, as Money, trade and investment).

Building and planning. 1945.

The intelligent man's guide to the post-war world. 1947.

Local and regional government. 1947.

Samuel Butler and The way of all flesh. 1947, Denver 1948 (as Samuel Butler).

A history of the Labour Party from 1914. 1948.

The meaning of Marxism. 1948, Ann Arbor 1964. Largely based on What Marx really meant, 1934, above.

World in transition: a guide to the shifting political and economic forces of our time. New York 1949. Based on The intelligent man's guide to the post-war world, 1947, above.

Essays in social theory. 1950. Articles from the 40's.

Socialist economics. 1950.

The British Co-operative movement in a socialist society: a report written for the Fabian Society. 1951.

Introduction to economic history 1750–1950. 1952.

A history of socialist thought. 5 vols 1953–60, New York 1953–60.

Attempts at General Union: a study in British trade union history 1818–34. 1953.

An introduction to trade unionism. 1953. See British trade-unionism today, 1939, above.

Studies in class structure. 1955.

The post-war condition of Britain. 1956, New York 1957 (for 1956).

The case for industrial partnership. 1957.

Cole also pbd a large number of pamphlets, Fabian tracts, study outlines etc. He edited Cobbett, Hutchinson's University Library, Library of Social Studies, Oxford Studies in Economics, Nuffield College Social Reconstruction Survey (with A. D. Lindsay) etc. He also edited Guildsman Sept 1919–Aug 1923 (it became Guild Socialist in July 1921), and New Standards Oct 1923–Oct 1924. He has also written 2 vols of poetry, New beginnings and The record, 1914, and The crooked world, 1933; a novel, The Brooklyn murder, 1923, and further numerous detective stories with Margaret Postgate, afterwards Cole.

§2

Cole, M. Growing up into revolution. 1949. Autobiography.

Heffer, E. S. Cole: an appraisal of his life and work. Social Rev Feb 1959.

Briggs, A. and J. Saville. Essays in labour history: in memory of Cole with recollections. 1960. By I. Brown, H. Gaitskell, S. Bailey, G. D. N. Worswick.

Briggs, A. The intellectuals and the Labour movement: Cole. Listener 20 Oct 1960.

Glass, S. The responsible society. 1966. On Cole's involvement in Guild Socialism.

Owen, G. Cole's historical writings. International Rev of Social History 11 1966.

H.M.R.

ROBIN GEORGE COLLINGWOOD
1889–1943

See cols 1247–8, below.

MAURICE STEWART COLLIS
b. 1889

See col 1314, below.

ALEXANDER COMFORT
b. 1920

See cols 249–50, above.

ALFRED DUFF COOPER,
1ST VISCOUNT NORWICH
1890–1954

§1

The Conservative point of view: an address. [1926].

House of Lords or Senate? 1932. With C. M. Headlam.

Talleyrand. 1932, New York 1932.

Haig. 2 vols 1935–6, Garden City NY 1936.

The Second World War: first phase. 1939, New York 1939. Speeches and articles, with connecting narrative.

David. 1943, New York 1943. Biography of David, King of Israel.

Sergeant Shakespeare. 1949, New York 1950. Biography.

Translations and verses. 1949.

Operation heartbreak: a story. 1950, New York 1951.

Vilmorin, L. de. Madame de. Tr Duff Cooper 1952.

Old men forget: the autobiography of Duff Cooper. 1953, New York 1954.

§2

'Audax'. Duff Cooper. In his Men in our time, New York [1940].

Cooper, D. The rainbow comes and goes. 1958. Reminiscences.

— The light of common day. 1959. Reminiscences.

— Trumpets from the steep. 1960. Reminiscences.

J. G.

GEORGE GORDON COULTON
1858–1947

Bibliographies

Langstadt, E. Select list of the historical writings of Coulton. Cambridge Historical Jnl 9 1947. Excludes all purely religious or theological writings and all the more controversial works.

§1

Father Rhine. [1899]. An account of a summer tour, illustr by the author.

Public Schools and the public needs: suggestions for the reform of our teaching methods in the light of modern requirements. 1901.

Medieval studies. 20 nos separately pbd 1905–31. (Nos 1, 3–7 rptd, rev, with A revivalist of six centuries ago, as Medieval studies: first series 1915; again rptd, with nos 8, 9, 13, as Ten medieval studies, Cambridge 1930, Gloucester Mass 1967). Among others are no 1, The monastic legend: a criticism of Abbot Gasquet's Henry VIII and the English monasteries, 1905. (See also Popular Romanist church history, 1905, below); no 17, Roman Catholic truth: an open discussion between Coulton and L. J. Walker, 1924 (see also L. J. Walker, A protestant controversialist's methods, Dublin Rev 175 1924); no 19, Mr Hilaire Belloc as historian, 1930 [a review of Belloc's Europe and the faith]. No 2, Guelf and Ghebelline was rptd in the rev edn of From St Francis to Dante, 1907, below.

Popular Romanist Church history. [1905]. Pamphlet containing correspondence between Coulton and W. Lescher relative to Medieval studies no 1.

Friar's lantern. 1906. A novel.

From St Francis to Dante: a translation of all that is of primary interest in the Chronicle of the Franciscan Salimbene, 1221–1288. 1906, 1907 (rev and enlarged), New York [1968].

Chaucer and his England. 1908, 1910 (corrected, with 2nd preface in reply to review by G. K. Chesterton in Daily News 16 Oct 1908), 1921 (corrected with note), 1927 (with new preface), 1963 (with new bibliography by T. W. Craik).

A medieval garner: human documents from the four centuries preceding the Reformation. Ed Coulton 1910, 4 vols Cambridge 1928–30 (rev, as Life in the Middle Ages), 1 vol 1930.

Medieval studies: first series. 1915. See Medieval studies, above.

Social life in Britain from the Conquest to the Reformation. Cambridge 1918, New York 1918, Cambridge 1919 (with index). Extracts and trns from medieval authorities.

Christ, St Francis and to-day. Cambridge 1919.

Five centuries of religion. 4 vols Cambridge 1923–50. Vol 1 rptd 1929 (corrected).

A Victorian schoolmaster: Henry Hart of Sedburgh. 1923.

The medieval village. Cambridge 1925. See H. Thurston, Some inexactitudes of Coulton: a sheaf of criticism of The medieval village, 1927.

Chesterton, G. K. The superstition of the sceptic. With a correspondence between the author and Coulton. Cambridge 1925. The discussion was continued by

Chesterton in Dublin Rev 176 1925 and by Coulton in Rev of the Churches new ser 2 1925.

Art and the Reformation. Oxford 1928, Hamden Conn 1969.

Life in the Middle Ages. 1928–30. See A medieval garner, above.

The Black Death. 1929 (for 1928), New York 1929 (for 1930).

The Inquisition. 1929, New York 1929.

Crusades, commerce and adventure. 1930.

The chronicler of European chivalry [Froissart]. 1930 ('Studio' special winter no 1930).

The medieval scene: an informal introduction to the Middle Ages. Cambridge 1930.

Reservation and catholicity: a discussion between A. H. Villiers and Coulton on the Bishop of Gloucester's text: Reservation is, in every sense of the word, a Catholic custom. Oxford 1930.

Ten medieval studies. 1930. See Medieval studies, above.

Romanism and truth. 2 vols 1930–1, Milwaukee 1930–1.

In defence of the Reformation: three lectures, with discussions. 1931. Infallibility; Persecution; The Reformation.

Papal infallibility. 1932, Milwaukee 1932.

Two saints: St Bernard & St Francis. Cambridge 1932. Chs from vols 1–2 of Five centuries of religion, above.

Scottish abbeys and social life. Cambridge 1933.

H. W. Fowler. Oxford 1934 (SPE tract 43).

Divorce, Mr Belloc and the Daily Telegraph. Taunton 1937, 1937 (rev). See H. Belloc, The case of Dr Coulton, 1938. See also V. Brome, Coulton versus Belloc, in his Six studies in quarrelling, 1958, §2, below.

Sectarian history. Taunton 1937. A defence of H. C. Lea against the attacks of Roman Catholic historians. See H. Thurston, How history is miswritten: a text applied to the work of H. C. Lea at the instance of Dr Coulton, 1938. See also Coulton, The scandal of Cardinal Gasquet: a sequel to Sectarian history, Taunton 1937; Sectarian history: a fresh development, Taunton 1938; A premium upon falsehood: a postscript to The scandal of Cardinal Gasquet, Taunton 1939.

Inquisition and liberty. 1938, Gloucester Mass 1969.

Medieval panorama: the English scene from Conquest to Reformation. Cambridge 1938, New York 1938.

Europe's apprenticeship: a survey of medieval Latin, with examples. 1940.

Studies in medieval thought. 1940, New York 1965 (for 1966).

Fourscore years: an autobiography. Cambridge 1943, 1944 (corrected), New York 1944.

Is the Catholic Church anti-social?: a debate between Coulton and A. Lunn. 1946.

Early drawings and etchings. Cambridge [1948]. 22 drawings etc.

Coulton wrote a number of other controversial pamphlets and also a large number of pamphlets advocating compulsory military service. He edited a number of school text books; the series Cambridge Studies in Medieval Life and Thought, 18 vols Cambridge 1920–50; and, with Eileen Power, the series Broadway Medieval Library, 10 vols 1928–31.

§2

Bennett, H. S. G. G. Coulton. Proc Br Acad 33 1947.

Powicke, F. M. Three Cambridge scholars: C. W. Previté-Orton, Z. N. Brooke and Coulton. Cambridge Historical Jnl 9 1947; rptd in his Modern historians and the study of history, 1955.

'Sarah Campion' (M. R. Coulton). Father: a portrait of Coulton at home. 1948.

Brome, V. Coulton versus Belloc. In his Six studies in quarrelling, 1958.

M. P.

WILLIAM HENRY DAVIES
1871–1940
See cols 251–3, above.

CHRISTOPHER HENRY DAWSON
1889–1970

Bibliographies
O'Connor, D. A. Bibliography. In his The relation between religion and culture according to Dawson, 1952, below. Works by Dawson to 1950 and works about him to 1945.

Selections
The dynamics of world history. 1957, New York 1957 (for 1956). Selected writings, ed J. J. Mulloy.

§ 1
The age of the gods: a study in the origins of culture in prehistoric Europe and the ancient East. 1928.
Progress and religion: an historical enquiry. 1929.
Christianity and sex. 1930 (Criterion Miscellany 13).
Christianity and the new age. 1931 (Essays in Order 3).
The making of Europe: an introduction to the history of European unity. 1932, New York 1934.
The modern dilemma: the problem of European unity. 1932 (Essays in Order 8).
Enquiries into religion and culture. 1933, New York 1933.
The spirit of the Oxford Movement. 1933, New York 1944.
Medieval religion—the Forwood lectures 1934—and other essays. 1934, New York 1934.
Religion and the modern state. 1935.
Beyond politics. 1939, New York 1939.
The judgment of the nations. New York 1942, London 1943.
Religion and culture. 1948, New York 1948.
Religion and the rise of western culture. 1950, New York 1950.
Understanding Europe. 1952, New York 1952.
Medieval essays. 1953, New York 1954.
The Mongol mission: narratives and letters of the Franciscan missionaries in Mongolia and China in the thirteenth and fourteenth centuries. 1955, New York 1955 (Makers of Modern Christendom). Ed Dawson.
The movement of world revolution. 1959, New York 1959.
The historical reality of Christian culture: a way to the renewal of human life. New York 1960, London 1960.
The crisis of western education. 1961, New York 1961.
The dividing of Christendom. New York 1965.
Dawson edited Essays in Order *14 vols 1931–4 with T. F. Burns, and 2 vols 1936 with B. Wall. He also edited* Dublin Rev *1940–4 and* Makers of Christendom *ser 1954 onwards. He has written pamphlets for the Catholic Truth Soc, Sword of the Spirit and National Peace Council.*

§ 2
The age of the gods. Dublin Rev 182 1928.
Taylor, R. A. Progress and religion. Sociological Rev 22 1930.
Alexander, C. In his The Catholic literary revival. Milwaukee [1936].
Huxley, A. Historical generalizations. In his The olive tree, 1936.
Corbishley, T. Our present discontents. Month 173 1939.
Demant, V. A. Importance of Dawson. Nineteenth Century & After 129 1941.
Sheed, F. J. In his Sidelights on the Catholic revival, 1941.
Davey, W. P. The judgment of the nations. Thomist 8 1945.

Donahue, C. Dawson: a note on experience. Thought 25 1950.
Foster, K. Dawson and Christendom. Blackfriars 31 1950.
Toynbee, A. Religion and the rise of western culture. Hibbert Jnl 49 1950.
O'Connor, D. A. The relation between religion and culture according to Dawson. Montreal 1952.
Mulloy, J. J. Continuity and development in Dawson's thought. In C. Dawson, The dynamics of world history, 1957. *See Selections above.*

H. M. R.

GOLDSWORTHY LOWES DICKINSON
1862–1932

Bibliographies
Balfour, R. E. In E. M. Forster, Goldsworthy Lowes Dickinson, 1934, below. Includes contributions to books, periodicals and newspapers, and obituaries.

Collections
Letters from John Chinaman and other essays. Introd by E. M. Forster 1946.

§ 1
Savonarola: a poem. In Prolusiones academicae, Cambridge 1884.
Jacob's ladder. 1887 (priv ptd). Poem.
From king to king: the tragedy of the puritan revolution. 1891, New York 1907 (rev). Dialogues on historical figures, 1632–62.
Revolution and reaction in modern France. 1892, 1927 (rev with new preface and conclusion).
The development of parliament during the nineteenth century. 1895.
The Greek view of life. 1896, 1909 (rev with new preface), 1957 (with preface by E. M. Forster), Ann Arbor 1958.
Poems. 1896 (priv ptd). Anon.
Letters from John Chinaman. 1901 (anon), New York 1903 (as Letters from a Chinese official: being an Eastern view of Western civilization, with a new introduction; anon), London 1907 (as by Dickinson), New York 1932 (as Hands off China!: the letters of a Chinese official; anon), London 1946 (introd by E. M. Forster). Reply by W. J. Bryan in Letters to a Chinese official: being a Western view of Eastern civilization, 1906.
The meaning of good: a dialogue. Glasgow 1901, New York 1906.
A modern symposium. 1905, New York 1905, London 1962 (introd by E. M. Forster), New York 1962, 1963 (introd, The uses of Dickinson, by L. Filler).
Religion: a criticism and a forecast. 1905, New York 1905.
Justice and liberty: a political dialogue. 1908, New York 1908.
A wild rose and other poems. 1910 (priv ptd).
Religion and immortality. 1911, Boston 1911. Essays, with one previously pbd lecture.
Appearances: being notes of travel. 1914, Garden City NY 1914.
An essay on the civilizations of India, China and Japan. 1914.
De profundis. 1916. Anon. Poem, rptd from Cambridge Mag 10 June 1916.
The European anarchy. 1916, New York 1916.
The choice before us. 1917, New York 1917.
Causes of international war. 1920, New York 1920 (Swarthmore International Handbooks).
The Magic Flute: a fantasia. 1920.
War: its nature, cause and cure. 1923.
The international anarchy, 1904–14. 1926, New York [1926], London 1937 (foreword by A. Salter).
Goethe and Faust: an interpretation, with passages newly translated into English verse. 1928. With F. M. Stawell, and largely by her.

After two thousand years: a dialogue between Plato and a modern young man. 1930, New York [1931].

Points of view: a series of broadcast addresses. 1930, Freeport NY [1969]. By Dickinson et al; introd and summing-up by Dickinson.

John McT. E. McTaggart. Cambridge 1931. With chs by B. Williams and S. V. Keeling.

Plato and his dialogues. 1931, New York [1932].

Dickinson also wrote a number of pamphlets on the First World War and the League of Nations and wrote introds to similar pamphlets by others; he edited The Swarthmore International Handbooks, *8 vols 1920–1 and, with H. O. Meredith,* The Temple Greek and Latin Classics, *6 vols 1906–7. He also edited works by Carlyle and Browning for* Temple Classics *and by Shelley for* Temple Dramatists.

§2

Chesterton, G. K. Paganism and Dickinson. In his Heretics, 1905.

More, P. E. The socialism of Dickinson. In his Shelburne essays ser 7, New York 1910.

Laski, H. J. Dickinson and Graham Wallas. Political Quart 3 1932.

Tomlinson, H. M. In New Clarion 27 Aug 1932.

Goldsworthy Lowes Dickinson, 6 August 1862–3 August 1932. Cambridge 1933. Contains memoir by Roger Fry; obituary by J. T. Sheppard rptd from Cambridge Rev 14 Oct 1932, a poem by Dickinson and a short list of his books.

Wedd, N. Goldie Dickinson: the latest Cambridge Platonist. Criterion 12 1933.

Forster, E. M. Goldsworthy Lowes Dickinson. 1934.

—— A great humanist. Listener 11 Oct 1956.

M.P.

KEITH CASTELLAIN DOUGLAS
1920–44

See cols 262–3, above.

JOHN DRINKWATER
1882–1937

See cols 263–6, above.

CLIFFORD DYMENT
b. 1914

See cols 271–2, above.

THOMAS STEARNS ELIOT
1888–1965

See cols 157–201, above.

SIR ROBERT CHARLES
KIRKWOOD ENSOR
1877–1958

Arminius. Oxford 1899. Chancellor's prize poem.

Modern poems. 1903.

Modern socialism: as set forth by socialists in their speeches, writings and programmes. Ed with introd by Ensor 1904, 1907 (rev and enlarged), 1910 (rev and enlarged).

Belgium. [1915], New York 1915.

Odes, and other poems. 1917.

Catherine: a romantic poem; with a preface on narrative poetry. 1921.

Columbus: a historical poem. 1925.

Courts & judges in France, Germany and England. 1933.

England 1870–1914. Oxford 1936 (Oxford History of England 14).

Herr Hitler's self-disclosure in Mein Kampf. Oxford 1939, New York 1939. Pamphlet.

Who Hitler is. 1939, New York 1939. Pamphlet.

Hedge leaves. 1942. Verse.

A miniature history of the war, down to the liberation of Paris. 1944, New York 1945, London 1945 (enlarged, to the end of the war in Europe).

The uphill war, Sept 1939–Nov 1942. 1944. Pamphlet.

Ensor was leader-writer for Manchester Guardian *1902–4,* Daily News *1909–11, and chief leader-writer for* Daily Chron *1912–30. He contributed weekly articles on foreign affairs to* Sunday Times *under pen-name Scrutator 1940–53.*

J.G.

EDWARD EVAN
EVANS-PRITCHARD
b. 1902

Witchcraft, oracles and magic among the Azande. Oxford 1937.

The Nuer: a description of the modes of livelihood and political institutions of a Nilotic people. Oxford 1940.

The political system of the Anuak of the Anglo-Egyptian Sudan. 1940.

Some aspects of marriage and the family among the Nuer. Livingstone, Northern Rhodesia 1945.

The Sanusi of Cyrenaica. Oxford 1949.

Kinship and marriage among the Nuer. Oxford 1951.

Social anthropology. 1951, Glencoe Ill 1952. Broadcast lectures.

Nuer religion. Oxford 1956.

Essays in social anthropology. 1962, New York 1963. Includes single lectures and essays previously pbd separately.

The position of women in primitive societies and other essays in social anthropology. 1965, New York 1965. Includes single lectures and essays previously pbd separately.

Theories of primitive religion. Oxford 1965.

Evans-Pritchard is a general editor of Oxford Monographs on Social Anthropology *(1963–) and also the* Oxford Library of African Literature *(1964–) for which he edited a collection of folk-tales,* The Zande trickster *(1967). He has also jointly edited and contributed to* Essays presented to C. G. Seligman *(1934) and* African political systems *(1940).*

C.H.E.P.

SIR KEITH GRAHAME FEILING
b. 1884

Bibliographies

In Essays in British history presented to Sir Keith Feiling, ed H. R. Trevor-Roper 1964.

§1

Toryism: a political dialogue. 1913.

Italian policy since 1870. 1914 (Oxford pamphlets 10).

A history of the Tory party 1640–1714. Oxford 1924, 1959 (corrected).

England under the Tudors and Stuarts. [1927], New York [1927] (HUL).

British foreign policy 1660–1672. 1930.

Sketches in nineteenth-century biography. 1930.

What is conservatism? 1930 (Criterion miscellany).

The second Tory party 1714–1832. 1938.

The life of Neville Chamberlain. 1946.

A history of England from the coming of the English to 1918. 1950, New York 1951.

Warren Hastings. 1954, Hamden Conn 1967.
In Christ Church hall. 1960, New York 1960. Essays.
N.J.S.

SIR CHARLES HARDING FIRTH
1857–1936

Bibliographies
A bibliography of the writings of Firth. [Compiled by himself]. Oxford 1928.

§1

Firth's extensive collection of books, mainly on 17th-century history and literature, bequeathed after his death to the Bodleian, is briefly described in Notes and news: Lady Firth's donation, Bodleian Quart Record *8 1936.*

The Marquis Wellesley. Oxford 1877. Stanhope Prize Essay.
Oliver Cromwell and the rule of the Puritans in England. 1900, New York 1900, London 1953 (introd by G. M. Young) (WC), 1962 (introd P. H. Hardacre).
Cromwell's army. 1902, 1912 (illustr, corrected, with new preface), 1921 (corrected, new preface).
A plea for the historical teaching of history: an inaugural lecture. Oxford 1904.
The last years of the Protectorate 1656–8. 2 vols 1909, New York 1964.
The House of Lords during the Civil War. 1910.
The Oxford School of Geography. Oxford 1918.
Historical novels. 1922 (Historical Assoc leaflet).
Modern languages at Oxford 1724–1929. Oxford 1929.
A commentary on Macaulay's History of England. Ed G. Davies 1938, New York [1965].
Essays, historical & literary. Ed G. Davies, Oxford 1938. Includes single lectures previously pbd separately.
The regimental history of Cromwell's army. 2 vols Oxford 1940. By Firth, assisted by G. Davies.

Principal Works Edited by Firth
Hutchinson, Mrs L. Memoirs of the life of Colonel Hutchinson. 2 vols 1885, 1906 (rev).
Cavendish, M. The life of William Cavendish, Duke of Newcastle. 1886, 1906 (rev).
The Clarke papers: selections from the papers of William Clarke, secretary to the Council of the Army 1647–9, and to General Monck and the commanders of the army in Scotland 1651–60. 4 vols 1891–1901 (Camden Soc new ser 49, 54, 61–2), New York 1965.
The memoirs of Edward Ludlow 1625–72. 2 vols Oxford 1894.
Scotland and the Commonwealth: letters and papers relating to the military government of Scotland 1651–3. Edinburgh 1895 (Scottish History Soc Pbns 18).
The journal of Joachim Hane 1653–4. Oxford 1896.
Scotland and the Protectorate: letters and papers relating to the military government of Scotland 1654–9. Edinburgh 1899 (Scottish Historical Soc Pbns 31).
The narrative of General Venables, with an appendix of papers relating to the expedition to the West Indies and the conquest of Jamaica 1654–5. 1900.
Naval songs and ballads. 1908 (Navy Records Soc Pbns 33). Selection.
Acts and ordinances of the Interregnum 1642–60. 3 vols 1911. With R. S. Rait.
Macaulay, T. B. The history of England. 6 vols 1913–15, New York 1968.
An American garland: being a collection of ballads relating to America 1563–1759. Oxford 1915, Detroit 1969.
Firth also wrote a number of pamphlets and leaflets (some priv ptd) on questions connected with the study of history, English, foreign languages and geography, with research degrees and advanced studies at Oxford (see Bibliography, *above). He was on the editorial board of* DNB *1885–1901*

and contributed over 200 biographies, mainly of 17th-century figures. With W. A. Raleigh he edited the series Oxford historical and literary studies *12 vols 1913–21. He was active in connection with the* Eng Historical Rev, *the Historical Mss Commission and other historical societies; from 1910–19 he was a member of the Royal Commission on Public Records and contributed 15 memoranda.*

§2

Beer, E. S. de. Charles Firth. History new ser 21 1936.
Clark, G. N. Charles Firth. Eng Historical Rev 51 1936.
Powicke, F. M. Charles Firth. Oxford Mag 12 March 1936; rptd in his Modern historians and the study of history, 1955.
Davies, G. Charles Harding Firth. Proc Br Acad 22 1936.
Godfrey, E. S. Charles Firth. In Some historians of modern Europe, ed B. E. Schmitt, Chicago 1942.
Rex, M. B. Charles H. Firth. In Some modern historians of Britain: essays in honor of R. L. Schuyler, New York 1951.
Ashley, M. Charles Firth: a tribute and a re-assessment. History Today 7 1957.
M.P.

HERBERT ALBERT LAURENS FISHER
1865–1940

§1

The medieval empire. 2 vols 1898, New York 1898.
Studies in Napoleonic statesmanship: Germany. Oxford 1903, New York 1968.
Brumaire; The Codes; The French dependencies, 1800–14; The first Restoration, 1814–15; St Helena. In The Cambridge Modern History, vols 8, 9, Cambridge 1904–6.
The history of England from the accession of Henry VII to the death of Henry VIII, 1485–1547. 1906, New York 1969.
Bonapartism. Oxford 1908.
Frederick William Maitland: a biographical sketch. Cambridge 1910.
The republican tradition in Europe. 1911, New York 1911.
Napoleon. [1913], New York [1913].
Educational reform: speeches. Oxford 1918.
Studies in history and politics. Oxford 1920, New York 1967.
The common weal. Oxford 1924, New York 1968.
James Bryce. 2 vols 1927, New York 1927.
Paul Vinogradoff: a memoir. Oxford 1927; rptd in Collected papers of Vinogradoff vol 1, Oxford 1928.
Our new religion. 1929, New York 1930. On Christian Science.
If Napoleon had escaped to America. In If it had happened otherwise, ed J. C. Squire 1931.
A history of Europe. 3 vols 1935, Boston 1935, 1936, 1 vol London 1936, 3 vols 1938 (rev and enlarged), Boston 1939, 2 vols London 1943, 1952 (as A history of Europe from the earliest times to 1713; A history of Europe from the beginning of the 18th century to 1937).
Pages from the past. 1939, New York 1969.
The background and issues of the war, by H. A. L. Fisher [et al]. Oxford 1940.
An unfinished autobiography. 1940.
Fisher also pbd pamphlets on the war in 1914, 1915. He edited F. W. Maitland, Constitutional history, *1908 and* Collected papers, *1911. He also edited the series* The modern world: a survey of historical forces, *1924–35; and he was joint editor of the* Home Univ Lib *1911–39.*

§2

M[urray], G. Fisher. Proc Br Acad 26 1940.
Ogg, D. Herbert Fisher: a short biography. 1947.

J.M.P.

FORD MADOX FORD
formerly
JOSEPH LEOPOLD FORD HERMANN MADOX HUEFFER
1873–1939

See cols 569–75, above.

EDWARD MORGAN FORSTER
1879–1970

See cols 437–44, above.

ALFRED GEORGE GARDINER
1865–1946

Selections

A. G. Gardiner. 1926 (Essays of Today and Yesterday). Selected essays.

§1

Prophets, priests and kings. 1908. Rptd from Daily News.
Pillars of society. 1913, New York 1914. Rptd from Daily News.
The war lords. 1915, 1915 (rev, enlarged).
Pebbles on the shore, by 'Alpha of the plough' [i.e. Gardiner]. [1916]. Rptd from Star.
Leaves in the wind, by 'Alpha of the plough'. 1918, New York [1919]. Rptd from Star.
'Alpha of the plough': selected essays from Pebbles on the shore and Leaves in the wind. [1920]. Epilogue by S. E. Maltby.
The Anglo-American future. 1920, New York 1921.
What I saw in Germany: letters from Germany and Austria. [1920]. Rptd from Daily News.
Windfalls, by 'Alpha of the plough'. 1920.
Life of George Cadbury. 1923.
The life of Sir William Harcourt. 2 vols 1923.
Many furrows, by 'Alpha of the plough'. 1924.
John Benn and the progressive movement. 1925.
Certain people of importance. 1926, New York 1926 (as Portraits and portents).
Alpha of the plough: second series, chosen by the author. [1927].
Alpha of the plough: third series, chosen by the author. 1932.
Gardiner edited Daily News *1902–20; he wrote for* Nation (London) *1920–4.*

§2

'E. T. Raymond' (E. R. Thompson). Five editors. In his Portraits of the new century, 1928.
Hodgson, S. In his Portraits and reflections, 1929.
Orage, A. R. On essay writing. In his Selected essays and critical writings, ed H. Read and D. Saurat, 1935.
Burnet, R. G. Gardiner: a great editor. London Quart Rev 171 1946.

H.M.R.

DAVID GARNETT
b. 1892

See col 586, above.

SIR PHILIP HAMILTON GIBBS
1877–1962

Collections

The novels of Philip Gibbs: uniform edition. 16 vols 1929–34.

§1

Founders of the empire. 1899. Ch 1 rptd separately 1900 (as Alfred: the model of English kings).
The troubadour. 1900. Selections from English verse, ed Gibbs.
Australasia: the Britains of the south. 1903.
India: our eastern empire. 1903.
Knowledge is power: a guide to personal culture. 1903.
Facts and ideas: short studies of life and literature. 1905.
Men and women of the French Revolution. 1906.
The romance of empire. 1906, [1924] (rev and enlarged).
The romance of George Villiers, first Duke of Buckingham, and some men and women of the Stuart court. 1908, New York 1931 (as The reckless Duke: the romantic story of the first Duke of Buckingham and the Stuart court).
King's favourite: the love story of Robert Carr and Lady Essex. 1909.
Adventures of war with Cross and Crescent. 1912, Boston Mass [1913] (as The Balkan war). With B. Grant.
The eighth year: a vital problem of married life. 1913, New York [1913].
The new man: a portrait study of the latest type. 1913.
The tragedy of Portugal. 1914.
The pilgrim's progress to culture. Ed H. Cramp, Philadelphia 1915.
The soul of the war. 1915, [1929] (rev).
The battles of the Somme. 1917, New York [1917].
From Bapaume to Passchendaele, 1917. 1918, New York [1918], New York [1919] (as The struggle in Flanders).
Open warfare: the way to victory. 1919, 2 vols New York [1919] (as The way to victory).
People of destiny. 1920, New York 1920 (subtitled Americans as I saw them at home and abroad).
Realities of war. 1920, New York 1920 (as Now it can be told), London [1929] (rev).
The hope of Europe. 1921, New York [1921] (as More that must be told).
Adventures in journalism. 1923, New York [1923].
Ten years after: a reminder. 1924, New York [1925].
The day after to-morrow: what is going to happen to the world? [1928], Garden City NY [1928].
The unknown future. In If I could preach just once, by B. Russell [et al], New York 1929.
Since then. 1930, New York 1930. On post-war conditions in various countries.
World production at a crossroads. In A philosophy of production: a symposium, ed J. G. Frederick, New York 1930.
Ways of escape. 1933, New York 1933 (as The way of escape). On the economic crisis.
European journey: being the narrative of a journey in France, Switzerland, Italy, Austria, Hungary, Germany and the Saar in the spring and summer of 1934. 1934, Garden City NY 1934.
The book of the King's jubilee: the life and times of our King and Queen and their people, 1865–1935. Ed Gibbs [1935], [1936] (enlarged as George the faithful), Philadelphia [1936] (as The life and times of King George V).
England speaks: being talks with all manner of folk of humble and exalted rank, with a panorama of the English scene in 1935. 1935, Garden City NY 1935.
Ordeal in England: England speaks again. 1937, Garden City NY 1937, London 1938 (rev and enlarged).
Across the frontiers. 1938, New York 1938, London 1939 (rev).
America speaks. 1942, Garden City NY 1942.

War correspondents past and present. In The English spirit, ed A. Weymouth 1942.

Bridging the Atlantic: Anglo-American fellowship as the way to world peace. Ed Gibbs [1943], Garden City NY 1944.

The pageant of the years: an autobiography. 1946.

Crowded company. 1949, New York [1949]. Autobiographical reminiscences.

The journalist's London. 1952.

The new Elizabethans. 1953.

Life's adventure. [1957].

How now, England? 1958.

The riddle of the changing world. 1960.

The war dispatches. [Ed C. Prigg] [1964]. Rptd from Daily Telegraph and Daily Chron.

Novels and Stories

The individualist. 1908, New York [1925].

The spirit of revolt. 1908, New York 1926.

The street of adventure. 1909, New York 1919.

Intellectual Mansions, S.W. 1910.

Oliver's kind women. 1911, Boston 1912.

Helen of Lancaster Gate. 1912.

A master of life. 1913.

The custody of the child. 1914, New York [1914] (as Beauty and Nick).

Back to life. 1920, New York [1920] (as Wounded souls).

Venetian lovers, and other stories. [1921].

The middle of the road. [1922], New York [1923].

Heirs apparent. [1923], New York [1924].

Little novels of nowadays. [1924], New York [1924].

The reckless lady. [1924], New York [1925].

Unchanging quest. [1925], New York [1926].

Young anarchy. [1926], New York [1926].

Out of the ruins, and other little novels. [1927], Garden City NY 1928.

The age of reason. [1928], Garden City NY 1928.

Darkened rooms. [1929], Garden City NY 1929.

The hidden city. [1929], Garden City NY 1930.

The wings of adventure and other stories. [1930], Garden City NY 1930.

The golden years. 1931, Garden City NY 1932.

The winding lane. [1931], Garden City NY 1931.

The anxious days. [1932], Garden City NY 1932.

The cross of peace. [1933], Garden City NY 1934.

Paradise for sale, and other little novels. [1934].

Blood relations. [1935], Garden City NY 1935.

Cities of refuge. [1936], Garden City NY 1937.

Great argument. [1938], Garden City NY 1938.

Broken pledges. [1939], New York 1940.

This nettle, danger. [1939], New York 1939.

Sons of the others. [1940], New York 1941.

The amazing summer. [1941], Garden City NY 1941.

The long alert. [1941], Garden City NY 1942.

The interpreter. [1943], Garden City NY 1943.

The battle within. [1944], Garden City NY 1945.

Through the storm. [1945], Garden City NY 1946.

The hopeful heart. [1947], Chicago 1948.

Behind the curtain. [1948].

The key of life. [1948].

Both your houses. [1949].

Thine enemy. [1950], New York [1950].

The spoils of time. 1951.

The cloud above the green. 1952, New York 1953.

Called back. 1953, New York 1953.

Lady of the Yellow River. 1953, New York [1955?].

No price for freedom. 1955.

The ambassador's wife. 1956.

The healing touch. 1957.

The curtains of yesterday. 1958.

One of the crowd. 1959.

The wheel of fortune. 1960.

His Lordship. 1961.

Oil lamps and candlelight. 1962.

The law-breakers. 1963.

From 1902–8 Gibbs was successively literary editor of Daily Mail, Daily Chron *and* Tribune. *He contributed to many papers, and in particular his war correspondence appeared in* Daily Telegraph *and* Daily Chron. (*See* The war despatches, *1964, above*). *From 1921–2 he edited* Rev of Reviews.

§2

Hind, C. L. In his More authors and I, 1922.

Overton, G. M. The knightliness of Gibbs. In Cargoes for Crusoes, New York 1924.

Marble, A. R. In her Study of the modern novel, New York 1928.

Braybrooke, P. The fascinating novels of Gibbs. In Some Catholic novelists, 1931.

Hamilton, C. In his People worth talking about, New York 1933.

Swinnerton, F. Four journalists. In his Figures in the foreground, 1963.

D.K.

ARTHUR ERIC ROWTON GILL
1882–1940
See cols 1045–8, above.

OLIVER ST JOHN GOGARTY
1878–1957
See cols 283–4, above.

GEORGE PEABODY GOOCH
1873–1968

Bibliographies

Hirsch, F. E. Published works of Gooch. In Studies in diplomatic history and historiography in honour of Gooch, ed A. O. Sarkissian 1961. Includes trns.

§1

History of English democratic ideas in the seventeenth century. Cambridge 1898, New York 1912, Cambridge 1927 (as English democratic ideas in the seventeenth century, with notes and appendices by H. J. Laski), New York [1959].

Europe and the French Revolution; Great Britain and Ireland 1792–1815 (1832–41); The growth of historical science. In The Cambridge Modern History, vols 8, 9, 10, 12, Cambridge 1904–10.

History of our time 1885–1911. [1911], New York [1911], London 1946 (as History of our time 1885–1914).

History and historians in the nineteenth century. 1913, New York 1949, London 1952 (rev), Boston 1959.

Political thought in England from Bacon to Halifax. 1915.

Germany and the French revolution. 1920, New York 1966.

Life of Lord Courtney. 1920.

History of modern Europe 1878–1919. 1923, New York 1923.

Germany. 1925.

Recent revelations of European diplomacy. 1927; enlarged successively 1928, 1930, 1940.

Studies in modern history. 1931. Collected articles and addresses.

Before the war: studies in diplomacy. 2 vols 1936, 1938.

Studies in diplomacy and statecraft. 1942.

Courts and cabinets. 1944, New York 1946. Biographical studies.

Frederick the Great: the ruler, the writer, the man. 1947, New York 1947.

Studies in German history. 1948.

Maria Theresa, and other studies. 1951, Hamden Conn 1965.

Catherine the Great, and other studies. 1954, Hamden
Conn 1966.
Louis XV: the monarchy in decline. 1956.
Under six reigns. 1958. Autobiography.
The Second Empire. 1960.
French profiles: prophets and pioneers. 1961.
Historical surveys and portraits. 1966, New York 1966.
Collected articles and addresses.
Gooch rev and completed Life of Charles 3rd Earl Stanhope
by Ghita Stanhope and edited Memoirs of Catherine the
Great *and* Later correspondence of Lord John Russell.
He compiled Annals of politics and culture 1492–1899,
contributed to and edited (with A. W. Ward) Cambridge
History of British foreign policy *and (with H. Temper-
ley)* British documents on the origin of the War. *He
edited* Contemporary Rev *1911–60 and pbd many pamphlets on current affairs 1911 onwards.*

§2

Hirsch, F. E. Gooch. Jnl of Modern History 26 1954.
Hadsel, F. L. Gooch. In Some 20th-century historians,
ed S. W. Halperin, Chicago 1961.
Butterfield, H. Gooch. Proc Br Acad 55 1969.

A.P.H.

GEOFFREY EDGAR SOLOMON
GORER
b. 1905

§1

The revolutionary ideas of the Marquis de Sade. 1934,
New York 1934 (as The Marquis de Sade: a short
account of his life and work), London 1953 (rev, as The
life and ideas of the Marquis de Sade), New York 1963,
London 1964 (rev).
Africa dances: a book about West African negroes. 1935,
New York 1935, London 1949 (rev).
Bali and Angkor: or looking at life and death. 1936,
Boston Mass 1936.
Nobody talks politics: a satire, with an appendix on Our
political intelligentsia. 1936.
Hot strip tease, and other notes on American culture. 1937.
Himalayan village: an account of the Lepchas of Sikkim.
1938, New York 1967 (with new foreword).
The Americans: a study in national character. 1948, New
York 1948 (as The American people: a study in national
character), 1964 (rev).
The people of Great Russia: a psychological study. 1949,
New York 1950. With J. Rickman.
Exploring English character. 1955, New York 1955.
Modern types [of people]. 1955. With R. Searle.
Death, grief and mourning in contemporary Britain. 1965,
Garden City NY 1965 (as Death, grief and mourning).
The danger of equality, and other essays. 1966.
Psychoanalysis observed. Ed C. Rycroft 1966, New York
1967. By G. Gorer et al.

N.J.S.

ROBERT VON RANKE GRAVES
b. 1895
See cols 201–7, above.

PHILIP GUEDALLA
1889–1944

Collections and Selections
Collected essays. 4 vols [1927].
Uniform edition of the works. 5 vols 1937–8.

Philip Guedalla. 1926 (Essays of Today and Yesterday).
Selection.
Rag-time and tango. 1938. Conquistador; Argentine
tango; together with rev versions of some uncollected
articles.

§1

The partition of Europe: a text-book of European history
1715–1815. Oxford 1914.
Supers and supermen: studies in politics, history and
letters. 1920, New York 1924.
The second Empire: Bonapartism, the Prince, the Presi-
dent, the Emperor. 1922, New York 1922, London 1932
(rev).
Masters and men: essays. 1923, New York 1923.
A gallery. 1924, New York 1924. Studies mainly of con-
temporary authors and politicians.
Independence day: a sketch book. 1926, New York 1926
(as Fathers of the Revolution).
Palmerston. 1926, New York 1927.
Conquistador: American fantasia. 1927, New York 1928.
Bonnet and shawl: an album. [1928], New York 1930.
Biographical sketches of six women of the 19th century.
The Duke [of Wellington]. 1931, New York 1931 (as
Wellington).
Argentine tango. 1932, New York 1933.
The Hundred Days. 1934, New York [1934].
The hundred years [1837–1936]. 1936, New York 1937.
The hundredth year [1930]. 1939, New York 1939.
Mr Churchill: a portrait. 1941, New York [1942].
The two marshals: Bazaine, Pétain. 1943, New York
[1943].
Middle East 1940–2: a study in air power. 1944.
*Guedalla edited works by the Marquis of Lansdowne and
Sir J. Fortescue, Macaulay's* Two essays on Pitt, *the*
Palmerston papers (Gladstone & Palmerston) *and selec-
tions from the correspondence of Queen Victoria and Glad-
stone. He also edited* Curiosities in politics: a series of
monographs on remarkable personalities of the XVIIIth
and XIXth centuries. *He pbd 2 vols of light verse at
Oxford and several lectures and broadcast talks on Zionist
and other topics.*

§2

Murray, D. L. Guedalla. London Mercury 14 1926.
Ritchie, C. Strachey and Guedalla: an essay in compari-
son. Dalhousie Rev 12 1933.
Longaker, J. M. Erudition and epigram: Guedalla. In his
Contemporary biography, Philadelphia 1934.

A.P.H.

JOHN LAWRENCE LE BRETON
HAMMOND
1872–1949

§1

Liberalism and the Empire. 1900. With F. Hirst and
G. Murray.
Charles James Fox: a political study. 1903.
Lord Hobhouse: a memoir. 1905. With L. T. Hobhouse.
Past and future. 1918. Under pseudonym Jason.
Britain and the modern world order: a synopsis of talks
broadcast April–June 1932. 1932. With A. J. Toynbee.
C. P. Scott of the Manchester Guardian. 1934.
Gladstone and the Irish nation. 1938, 1964 (introd by
M. R. D. Foot).
Gladstone and Liberalism. 1952. With M. R. D. Foot.
Hammond was editor of Speaker *1899–1907 and also wrote
for* Manchester Guardian.

§2

Tawney, R. H. J. L. Hammond. Proc Br Acad 46 1960.

LUCY BARBARA HAMMOND
1873–1961
and
JOHN LAWRENCE LE BRETON HAMMOND
1872–1949

§1

The village labourer 1760–1832: a study in the government of England before the Reform Bill. 1911.
The town labourer 1760–1832: the new civilization. 1917.
The skilled labourer 1760–1832. 1919.
Lord Shaftesbury. 1923, New York 1924.
The rise of modern industry. 1925, New York 1926, London 1937 (rev and enlarged).
The age of the Chartists 1832–54: a study of discontent. 1930, Hamden Conn 1962.
James Stansfeld: a Victorian champion of sex equality. 1932.
The bleak age: based on The age of the Chartists. 1934, 1947 (rev) (Pelican).

§2

Fraser, J. Theories and practices: the Hammonds' Village labourer. REL 8 1967.
Toynbee, A. J. The Hammonds. In his Acquaintances, 1967.

H.M.R.

JAMES THOMAS FRANK HARRIS
1856–1931
See cols 1054–5, above.

FRIEDRICH AUGUST VON HAYEK
b. 1899
Bibliographies
In Roads to freedom: essays in honour of Hayek, ed Erich Streissler 1969, §2, below.

§1

Prices and production. 1931, 1935 (rev and enlarged), New York 1967.
Collectivist economic planning: critical studies on the possibilities of socialism by N. G. Pierson [et al]. Ed with contributions by Hayek 1935, New York 1967.
Monetary nationalism and international stability. 1937, New York 1964.
Profits, interest and investment, and other essays on the theory of industrial fluctuations. 1939.
The pure theory of capital. 1941.
The road to serfdom. 1944, Chicago 1944, 1956 (with foreword by Hayek). *See also* H. Finer, Road to reaction, Boston 1945, London 1946 (corrected); B. Wootton, Freedom under planning, 1945.
Individualism and economic order. 1949, Chicago 1957.
John Stuart Mill and Harriet Taylor: their correspondence and subsequent marriage. Ed Hayek 1951, Chicago 1951.
The counter-revolution of science: studies on the abuse of reason. Glencoe Ill [1952].
The sensory order: an inquiry into the foundations of theoretical psychology. 1952, Chicago 1952.
The political ideal of the rule of law. Cairo 1955.
The constitution of liberty. Chicago 1960, London 1960.
Studies in philosophy, politics and economics. 1967, Chicago 1967.

Hayek pbd a number of works in German and also edited, with introductory essays, H. Thornton, An enquiry into the nature and effects of the paper credit of Great Britain [1802], (1939), and Capitalism and the historians: essays, (1954).

§2

Cole, G. D. H. Hayek's triangle. In his Studies in world economics, 1934.
Frank, L. K. Apology for irresponsibility. In his Society as the patient: essays on culture and personality, New Brunswick NJ 1948.
Grattan, C. H. Hayek's hayride. In Opinions and attitudes of the twentieth century, ed S. S. Morgan, New York 1948.
Harrod, R. F. Hayek on individualism. In his Economic essays, 1952.
Sweezy, P. M. Hayek's Road to serfdom. In his Present as history: essays and reviews on capitalism and socialism, New York 1053.
Gilbert, J. C. Hayek's contribution to trade cycle theory. In Economic essays in commemoration of the Dundee School of Economics, ed J. K. Eastham, [Dundee] 1955.
Seldon, A. (ed). Agenda for a free society: essays on Hayek's The constitution of liberty. 1961.
Streissler, E. Hayek on growth: a reconsideration of his early theoretical work. In Roads to freedom: essays in honour of Hayek, ed Streissler 1969.

C.H.E.P.

HERBERT HENSLEY HENSON
1863–1947
See cols 1257–8, below.

RICHARD HOPE HILLARY
1919–43

§1

The last enemy. 1942, New York 1942 (as Falling through space), London 1943 (foreword by E. Linklater).

§2

Koestler, A. The birth of a myth. Horizon 1943. *See* correspondence, ibid, June 1943. Rptd in his Yogi and the commissar, 1945 (as In memory of Richard Hillary).
Murry, J. M. Richard Hillary. Adelphi 20 1944. *See* M. Bodkin, Richard Hillary again, 21 1945. Rptd rev, in his Katherine Mansfield and other literary portraits, 1949.
Linklater, E. In The art of adventure, 1947. Includes foreword to 1943 edn of The last enemy, above.
Dickson, L. Richard Hillary. 1950.

P.C.

LEONARD TRELAWNY HOBHOUSE
1864–1929
Bibliographies
In H. S. Carter, The social theories of Hobhouse, Chapel Hill 1927, below. Includes important periodical articles, and reviews and articles on Hobhouse.

Collections and Selections
Selected articles and essays. In J. A. Hobson and M. Ginsberg, L. T. Hobhouse: his life and work, 1931, §2, below. Mainly rptd from Manchester Guardian.
Sociology and philosophy: a centenary collection of essays and articles. 1966, Cambridge Mass 1966. Introd by M. Ginsberg.

§1

The Labour movement. 1893, New York 1912 (rev), London 1913. Preface by R. B. Haldane.

The theory of knowledge: a contribution to some problems of logic and metaphysics. 1896, [1921] (with new preface).

Mind in evolution. 1901, 1915 (rev), 1926 (with 2 new appendices).

Democracy and reaction. 1904.

Lord Hobhouse: a memoir. 1905. With J. L. Le B. Hammond.

Morals in evolution: a study in comparative ethics. 2 vols 1906, 1 vol 1915 (rev), New York 1915, London 1951 (introd by M. Ginsberg).

Bridges, J. H. Essays and addresses. Ed Hobhouse 1907.

Government by the people. [1910] (People's Suffrage Federation pamphlet).

Liberalism. [1911], New York 1911, 1964 (introd by A. P. Grimes).

Social evolution and political theory. New York 1911. Lectures.

J. G. Gibbon. Unemployment insurance. Introd by Hobhouse 1911.

Development and purpose: an essay towards a philosophy of evolution. 1913, 1927 (rev and partly rewritten).

The historical evolution of property in fact and in idea. In Property—its duties and rights: essays by various writers, 1913, New York 1922.

The material culture and social institutions of the simpler peoples: an essay in correlation. 1915 (Univ of London Monographs on Sociology). With G. C. Wheeler and M. Ginsberg.

The world in conflict. 1915. Articles rptd from Manchester Guardian with addns.

Questions of war and peace. 1916.

Principles of sociology. 4 vols 1918–24, vols 1–3 New York 1918–22.

The philosophy of development. In Contemporary British philosophy: personal statements ser 1, ed J. H. Muirhead 1924, New York 1924. By Hobhouse et al.

Hobhouse was closely associated with Manchester Guardian *from 1897 until the end of his life, contributing frequently 1915–25; he edited* Sociological Rev *1903–5, and was political editor of* Tribune *1906–7; with E. A. Westermarck he edited* Univ of London Monographs on Sociology, *from 1913.*

§2

Nicholson, J. A. Some aspects of the philosophy of Hobhouse: logic and social theory. Urbana 1926.

Carter, H. S. The social theories of Hobhouse. Chapel Hill 1927.

Barker, E. L. T. Hobhouse. Proc Br Acad 14 1929.

Ginsberg, M. The contribution of Hobhouse to philosophy and sociology. Economica 9 1929; rptd in his Reason and unreason in society, 1947.

Hobson, J. A. and M. Ginsberg. L. T. Hobhouse: his life and work. 1931.

Barnes, H. E. Hobhouse: evolutionary philosophy in the service of democracy and social reform. In Introduction to the history of sociology, ed H. E. Barnes, Chicago 1948.

JOHN ATKINSON HOBSON
1858–1940

§1

The physiology of industry: being an exposure of certain fallacies in existing theories of economics. 1889 New York 1956. With A. F. Mummery.

Problems of poverty: an inquiry into the industrial condition of the poor. 1891.

The evolution of modern capitalism: a study of machine production. 1894, 1906 (rev), 1917 (rev), 1926 (rev), New York 1926.

Co-operative labour upon the land and other papers: the report of a conference. Ed Hobson 1895.

The problem of the unemployed: an enquiry and an economic policy. 1896.

John Ruskin: social reformer. 1898, Boston 1898.

The economics of distribution. 1900.

The ethics of industrialism. In Ethical democracy: essays in social dynamics by Hobson [et al], ed S. Coit 1900.

The war in South Africa: its causes and effects. 1900, New York 1969.

The psychology of jingoism. 1901.

The social problem: life and work. 1901.

Imperialism: a study. 1902, New York 1902, London 1905 (rev), 1938 (rev), Ann Arbor 1965 (introd by P. Siegelman).

International trade: an application of economic theory. 1904, New York 1966.

Canada today. 1906.

Science and industry. In Science in public affairs [essays by Hobson et al], ed J. E. Hand 1906.

The fruits of American protection: the effects of the Dingley Tariff upon the industries of the country and especially upon the well being of the people. 1907.

Lloyd, H. D. A sovereign people: a study of Swiss democracy. Ed Hobson 1907.

Ruskin, J. Unto this last. Ed Hobson 1907.

William Clarke: a collection of his writings. Ed Hobson and H. Burrows 1908.

The crisis of Liberalism: new issues of democracy. 1909.

The industrial system: an inquiry into earned and unearned income. 1909, 1910 (rev), New York 1969 (introd by A. L. Bekenstein).

A modern outlook: studies of English and American tendencies. 1910. Rptd from Nation.

An economic interpretation of investment. [1911].

The science of wealth. [1911], New York [1911], London 1934 (rev), 1950 (rev by R. F. Harrod).

Character and society. In Character and life: a symposium, by Hobson [et al], ed P. L. Parker 1912.

Industrial unrest. [1912]. Pamphlet.

The German panic. 1913. Pamphlet. Introd by Earl Loreburn.

Gold, prices and wages, with an examination of the quantity theory. 1913.

Traffic in treason: a study of political parties. 1914.

Work and wealth: a human valuation. 1914, New York 1914, London 1933 (rev).

A league of nations. 1915 (Union of Democratic Control pamphlet).

Towards international government. 1915.

Labour and the costs of war. 1916 (Union of Democratic Control pamphlet).

The new protectionism. 1916, New York 1916.

Democracy after the war. 1917.

Forced labour. 1917 (National Council for Civil Liberties pamphlet).

Die 'offene Tür': Vortrag auf dem internationalen Kongress zum Studium der Grundlagen für einen dauernden Frieden im Haag 1916. Tr W. Borgius, Berlin 1918. Pamphlet. See E. Zimmerman, Völkerbund und Kolonialpolitik: zwei Erwiderungen auf Heft 5: J. A. Hobson, Die offene Tür, Brandenburg 1919.

Richard Cobden: the international man. 1918, New York 1919, London 1968 (introd by N. Masterman).

Taxation in the new state. 1919.

The morals of economic internationalism. Boston 1920.

The obstacles to economic recovery in Europe. 1920. Pamphlet.

The economics of reparation. 1921. Pamphlet.

Problems of a new world. 1921.

The economics of unemployment. 1922, 1931 (rev).

Incentives in the new industrial order. 1922.

Britain's economic outlook in Europe. In Some aspects of recent British economics: [papers by] Hobson [et al], Chicago 1923.

Free-thought in the social sciences. 1926.

The living wage: a report. 1926. With H. N. Brailsford, A. C. Jones.

Notes on law and order. 1926 (Hogarth Essays).

The conditions of industrial peace. 1927.

Wealth and life: a study in values. 1929, Boston [1929] (as Economics and ethics: a study in social values).

Rationalization and unemployment: an economic dilemma. 1930.

God and mammon: the relations of religion and economics. 1931, New York 1931.

L. T. Hobhouse: his life and work. 1931. With M. Ginsberg.

The modern state. [1931]. Pamphlet.

Poverty in plenty: the ethics of income. 1931, New York 1931.

Towards social equality. 1931. Lecture.

From capitalism to socialism. 1932. Pamphlet.

The recording angel: a report from earth. 1932.

The moral challenge to the economic system. 1933. Lecture.

Rationalism and humanism. 1933. Lecture.

Democracy and a changing civilization. 1934.

Veblen. 1936, New York 1937.

Property and improperty. 1937.

Confessions of an economic heretic. 1938.

The sense of responsibility. In Le sens de la responsabilité dans la vie sociale: contributions de J. A. Hobson [et al], Paris [1938].

§2

Douglas, C. H. The Douglas theory: a reply to Hobson. [1922].

Homan, P. T. In his Contemporary economic thought, New York 1928.

Gottschalk, H. Die Kaufkraftlehre: eine Kritik der Unterverbrauchslehren von J. A. Hobson [et al]. Jena 1932.

Grether, E. J. John Ruskin—J. A. Hobson. In Essays in social economics in honor of Jessica Blanche Peixotto, Berkeley 1935.

Cole, G. D. H. J. A. Hobson. Economic Jnl 50 1940.

Brailsford, H. N. The life-work of Hobson. 1948. Lecture.

Nemmers, E. E. Hobson and underconsumption. Amsterdam 1956.

Davis, H. B. Hobson and human welfare. Science and Society 21 1957.

Mitchell, H. Hobson revisited. JHI 26 1965.

M.P.

SIR WILLIAM
SEARLE HOLDSWORTH
1871–1944

§1

The law of succession, testamentary and intestate. Oxford 1899. With C. W. Vickers.

A history of English law. 16 vols 1903–66. Vols 13–16 ed A. L. Goodhart and H. G. Hanbury. Rev edns commencing 1922, 1927, 1931, 1938, 1956. Tables and index to vols 1–9 by E. Potton, 1932.

A digest of English civil law, ed E. Jenks. 1905–17, 1921 (rev), 1938 (rev). Bk 5, Succession, by Holdsworth.

Sources and literature of English law. Oxford 1925.

An historical introduction to the land law. Oxford 1927.

Charles Dickens as a legal historian. New Haven 1928.

The historians of Anglo-American law. New York 1928.

Some lessons from our legal history. New York 1928.

Some makers of English law. Cambridge 1938.

Essays in law and history, ed A. L. Goodhart and H. G. Hanbury, Oxford 1946. Includes single lectures previously pbd separately.

Holdsworth contributed extensively to Law Quart Rev *etc and edited several volumes of the* Year Books of Edward II *for the Selden Soc.*

§2

Law Quart Rev 60 1944. Containing memorial articles on W. S. Holdsworth by A. L. Goodhart, H. G. Hanbury, J. A. Simon, W. T. S. Stallybrass and R. A. Wright.

W. S. Holdsworth. Proc Br Acad 30 1944. Biographical note by R.W.L., and memoir by P.H.W. [P. H. Winfield].

Wagner, D. O. William Holdsworth. In Some modern historians of Britain: essays in honor of R. L. Schuyler, ed H. Ausubel, J. B. Brebner and E. M. Hunt, New York 1951.

Goodhart, A. L. W. S. Holdsworth: a memorial address. 1954.

Frankfurter, F. William Holdsworth. In his Of law and men, ed P. Elman, New York 1956.

N.J.S.

CHRISTOPHER WILLIAM
BRADSHAW ISHERWOOD
b. 1904

See cols 619–20, above.

DOUGLAS FRANCIS JERROLD
1893–1964

The Royal Naval Division. 1923.

The Hawke battalion: some personal records 1914–18. 1925.

The truth about Quex. [1927], New York 1928 (as Quex). Novel.

The war on land 1914–18. 1928.

The lie about the war: a note on some contemporary war books. 1930.

Soldier's testament: selected maxims of René Quinton. Tr with critical introd by Jerrold 1930.

Storm over Europe. 1930. Novel.

The Spanish Republic: a survey of two years of progress. 1933. Anon. With L. Bolín [et al].

England. 1935.

They that take the sword: the future of the League of Nations. 1936.

Georgian adventure. 1937, New York 1938. Autobiography.

The necessity of freedom: notes on Christianity and politics. 1938, New York 1938 (as The future of freedom [etc]).

Britain and Europe 1900–40. 1941.

World order or world ruin? The menace of international 'planning'. 1942. Pamphlet.

An introduction to the history of England: from the earliest times to 1204. 1949, Boston 1952.

England: past, present and future. 1950.

The lie about the west: a response to Professor Toynbee's challenge. 1954, New York 1954. A reply to The world and the west by A. J. Toynbee, 1953.

Jerrold edited English Rev *1930–6, and* New English Rev *1945–50.*

J.G.

JOHN MAYNARD KEYNES, 1ST BARON KEYNES
1883–1946

Bibliographies

Harris, S. E. and M. Willfort. Bibliography of Keynes's writings. In The new economics, ed S. E. Harris, New York 1947, §2, below. Includes contributions to books, official reports, periodicals and newspapers.

§ 1

Indian currency and finance. 1913.

The economic consequences of the peace. 1919, New York 1920. *See* W. Walsh, The economic consequences of the peace: or, the doom according to Keynes, [1920].

Mr Lloyd George's general election. 1920. Pamphlet, extracted from preceding.

A treatise on probability. 1921.

Manchester Guardian. Reconstruction in Europe—section 10: the United States and Europe emigration. Ed Keynes, Manchester 1922.

A revision of the treaty: being a sequel to The economic consequences of the peace. 1922, New York 1922.

Stocks of staple commodities, by Keynes [et al]. 1923–30.

A tract on monetary reform. 1923, New York 1924 (as Monetary reform).

Alfred Marshall, 1842–1924: a memoir. [1924]; rptd in Essays in biography, 1933, below.

The economic consequences of Mr Churchill. 1925, New York [1925] (as The economic consequences of sterling parity); rptd, in part, in Essays in persuasion, 1931, below.

A short view of Russia. 1925 (Hogarth Essays); rptd in Essays in persuasion, 1931, below.

The end of laissez-faire. 1926. Pamphlet, based on lectures; rptd, in part, in Essays in persuasion, 1931, below.

Laissez-faire and Communism. New York 1926. Contains The end of laissez-faire, 1926, and A short view of Russia, 1925.

Official papers by Alfred Marshall. Ed Keynes 1926.

Réflexions sur le franc. [Paris?] 1928; rptd, in part, in Essays in persuasion, 1931, below.

Can Lloyd George do it?: an examination of the Liberal pledge [to reduce unemployment]. 1929. Pamphlet, with H. D. Henderson.

A treatise on money. 2 vols 1930, New York 1930.

An economic analysis of unemployment. In Unemployment as a world-problem, ed P. Q. Wright, Chicago 1931. By Keynes [et al]; lectures.

Essays in persuasion. 1931, New York 1932.

The world's economic crisis and the way of escape. 1932. By Keynes [et al].

Essays in biography. 1933, New York 1933, London 1951 (with 3 new essays, ed G. Keynes), New York 1951.

The means to prosperity. 1933, New York [1933], Buffalo 1959 (bibliography by S. E. Harris). Pamphlet.

The general theory of employment, interest and money. 1936, New York 1936.

Herbert Somerton Foxwell, 1849–1936. Proc Br Acad 33 1937.

The theory of the rate of interest. In The lessons of monetary reform: essays in honor of Irving Fisher, ed A. D. Gayer, New York 1937. By Keynes [et al].

Hume, D. An abstract of A treatise of human nature, 1740: a pamphlet hitherto unknown. Ed with introd by Keynes and P. Sraffa, Cambridge 1938.

How to pay for the war: a radical plan for the Chancellor of the Exchequer. 1940, New York [1940]. Pamphlet. *See* E. Burns, Mr Keynes answered: an examination of the Keynes plan, 1940.

The balance of payments of the United States. [1946]. Rptd from Economic Jnl; pamphlet.

GBS and Isaac Newton. In GBS 90: aspects of Shaw's life and works, ed S. Winsten 1946.

Two memoirs: Dr Melchior, a defeated enemy; and My early beliefs. 1949, New York 1949. Introd by D. Garnett.

The Arts Council: its policy and hopes. [1951]. Rptd from Listener.

Essays and sketches in biography: including the complete text of Essays in biography and Two memoirs. New York 1956.

Keynes edited Economic Jnl *1912–45, and, with others,* Cambridge Economic Handbooks *from 1922.*

§2

Gardiner, A. G. In his Certain people of importance, 1926, New York 1926 (as Portraits and portents).

Hodgson, S. In his Portraits and reflections, 1929.

Rowse, A. L. Socialism and Mr Keynes. Nineteenth Century 119 1932; rptd in his End of an epoch, 1947.

—— Mr Keynes and the Labour movement. 1936.

Blondot, G. Les théories monétaires de Keynes. Paris 1933.

Greidanus, T. The development of Keynes's economic theory. 1939.

Timlin, M. F. Keynesian economics. Toronto 1942, 1948 (corrected).

Mantoux, E. La paix calomniée, ou les conséquences économiques de Keynes. [Paris] 1946; tr 1946.

Munby, A. N. L. Keynes and his books. TLS 19 Oct 1946.

Pigou, A. C. J. M. Keynes. Proc Br Acad 32 1946.

—— Keynes's 'General theory': a retrospective view. 1950.

Harris, S. E. (ed). The new economics: Keynes's influence on theory and public policy. New York 1947.

—— Keynes: economist and policy maker. New York 1955.

Klein, L. R. The Keynesian revolution. New York 1947, [1966] (rev).

Plumptre, A. F. W. Keynes in Cambridge. Canadian Jnl of Economics & Political Science 13 1947.

Robinson, E. A. G. J. M. Keynes. Economic Jnl 57 1947.

Dillard, D. The economics of Keynes: the theory of a monetary economy. New York 1948.

John Maynard Keynes, 1883–1946: a memoir prepared by direction of the Council of King's College. Cambridge 1949.

Leavis, F. R. Keynes, Lawrence and Cambridge. Scrutiny 16 1949; rptd in his Common pursuit, 1952. Essay-review of Two memoirs, 1949.

—— Keynes, Spender and currency-values. Scrutiny 18 1951. Essay-review of Harrod, below, and S. Spender, World within a world, 1951.

Evans, B. I. Keynes and the arts. Yale Rev 40 1950.

Keynes, F. A. In her Gathering up the threads: a study in family biography, Cambridge 1950.

Meek, R. L. The place of Keynes in the history of economic thought. Modern Quart 6 1950; rptd (rev) in his Economics and ideology, 1967.

Grisewood, H. Keynes and the Cambridge outlook. Month 3 1951.

Harrod, R. F. The life of Keynes. 1951.

Russell, B. Portraits from memory II: Keynes and Strachey. Listener 17 July 1952.

Hansen, A. H. A guide to Keynes. New York 1953 (Economics Handbook ser).

Garnett, D. Keynes, Strachey and Virginia Woolf in 1917. London Mag 2 1955.

Gillman, J. M. Evaluation of Keynes. Science & Society 19 1955.

Bell, C. In his Old friends: personal recollections, 1956. *See* R. F. Harrod, Bell on Keynes. Economic Jnl 67 1957.

Hazlitt, H. (ed). The critics of Keynesian economics. Princeton 1960.

Lambert, P. L'œuvre de Keynes: exposé, analyse critique, prolongements. Liège 1963–.

Lekachman, R. Men and ideas: Keynes. Encounter 21 1963. Reply by R. F. Harrod, Are we all Keynesians now?, 22 1964.

—— (ed). Keynes and the classics. Boston Mass [1964].

—— (ed). Keynes' General theory: reports of three decades. New York [1964].

—— The age of Keynes. New York 1966.

Martin, B. K. Arguing with Keynes: a memoir. Encounter 24 1965.

Hutton, D. G. How well have they worn? 3, The consequences of Mr Keynes. The Times 20 Jan 1966.

Stewart, M. Keynes and after. 1967.

M.P.

'HUGH KINGSMILL', HUGH KINGSMILL LUNN
1889–1949
See cols 1065–6, above.

DAVID KNOWLES (MICHAEL CLIVE KNOWLES)
b. 1896

Bibliographies
In his The historian and character and other essays, ed C. N. L. Brooke and G. Constable, 1963, below.

§1
The American Civil War: a brief sketch. Oxford 1926.

The English mystics. 1927.

The Benedictines. 1929, New York 1930 (with introd by J. H. Diman), Saint Leo Fla 1962 (with introd by M. R. Bowman).

The monastic order in England: a history from the times of St Dunstan to the Fourth Lateran Council. Cambridge 1940, 1963 (with additional bibliography and notes).

The religious houses of medieval England. 1940. A catalogue; see also Medieval religious houses 1953, below.

Collected papers, by R. A. L. Smith. 1947. With memoir by Knowles.

The religious orders in England. 3 vols Cambridge 1948–59.

The episcopal colleagues of Archbishop Thomas Becket. Cambridge 1951.

The monastic constitutions of Lanfranc. Tr with introd and notes by Knowles 1951.

Monastic sites from the air. Cambridge 1952 (Cambridge Air Surveys 1). With J. K. S. St Joseph.

Medieval religious houses: England and Wales. 1953. Additions and corrections in EHR 72 1957. With R. N. Hadcock. An expanded version of The religious houses of medieval England, 1940, above.

Charterhouse: the medieval foundation in the light of recent discoveries. 1954. With W. F. Grimes.

The English mystical tradition. [1960], New York 1961.

The evolution of medieval thought. 1962, Baltimore 1962.

Saints and scholars: twenty-five medieval portraits. Cambridge 1962.

Great historical enterprises [and] Problems in monastic history. [1963].

The historian and character and other essays. Cambridge 1963. Ed C. N. L. Brooke and G. Constable; includes single lectures previously pbd separately.

From Pachomius to Ignatius: a study in the constitutional history of the religious orders. Oxford 1966.

The nature of mysticism. New York 1966 (Twentieth-Century Encyclopedia of Catholicism 38 section 4), London 1967 (as What is mysticism?).

The Middle Ages. New York [1968] (The Christian Centuries 2), London 1969. With D. Obolensky.

Christian monasticism. 1969, New York 1969.

Knowles edited Downside Rev *1930–4; the new series of* Cambridge studies in medieval life and thought *1951–; and was one of the general editors of* Cambridge air surveys *1952–.*

J.G.

ARTHUR KOESTLER
b. 1905
See cols 628–9, above.

HAROLD JOSEPH LASKI
1893–1950

Bibliographies
In H. A. Deane, The political ideas of Laski, New York 1955, §2, below. This and the following include contributions to books and periodicals and literature on Laski.

In B. Zylstra, From pluralism to collectivism, Assen 1968, §2, below.

§1
On the correlation of fertility with social value: a cooperative study. By Laski [et al] 1913.

Studies in the problem of sovereignty. 1917, New Haven 1917.

The problem of administrative areas: an essay in reconstruction. Northampton Mass 1918; rptd in The foundations of sovereignty, 1921, below.

Authority in the modern state. New Haven 1919.

Duguit, L. Law in the modern state. New York 1919, London 1921. Tr by F. and H. J. Laski.

Holmes, O. W. Collected legal papers. Ed Laski, New York 1920.

Political thought in England from Locke to Bentham. [1920], New York [1920].

The foundations of sovereignty and other essays. New York 1921, London [1922].

Burke, E. Letters: a selection. Ed Laski 1922 (WC).

Karl Marx: an essay. [1922] (Fabian pamphlet), New York 1933 (as Karl Marx: an essay, with the Communist Manifesto; introd by N. Thomas).

The state in the new social order. 1922 (Fabian tract); rptd in Studies in law and politics, 1932.

Mill, J. S. Autobiography. Ed Laski 1924 (WC).

The position of parties and the right of dissolution. 1924 (Fabian tract).

A grammar of politics. 1925, 1930 (with additional notes), New Haven 1931, London 1934 (with new preface), 1937 (with a new ch), New Haven 1938.

The problem of a Second Chamber. 1925 (Fabian tract); rptd in Studies in law and politics, 1932, below.

Socialism and freedom. 1925 (Fabian tract).

On the study of politics. 1926. Lecture; rptd in The danger of being a gentleman, 1939, below.

Communism. 1927, New York [1927]. See R. W. Fox, A defence of Communism, in reply to H. J. Laski, 1927.

Gooch, G. P. English democratic ideas in the seventeenth century. Second edn with supplementary notes and appendices by Laski, Cambridge 1927.

The Trades Disputes and Trade Unions Bill. [1927]. With E. J. P. Benn. Pamphlet.

The British cabinet: a study of its personnel, 1801–1924. 1928 (Fabian tract); rptd in Studies in law and politics, 1932, below.

The present evolution of the parliamentary system. In The development of the representative system in our times: five answers to an inquiry instituted by the Inter-Parliamentary Union. By Laski [et al], Lausanne 1928.

The recovery of citizenship. 1928. Pamphlet; rptd in The dangers of obedience, 1930, below.

The dangers of obedience and other essays. 1930, New York 1930.

Liberty in the modern state. 1930, New York 1930, London 1937 (with new introd), 1948 (rev), New York 1949.

The socialist tradition in the French Revolution. 1930. Fabian lecture; rptd in Studies in law and politics, 1932, below.

Justice and the law. 1930. Lecture rptd in Studies in law and politics, 1932, below.

The decline of parliamentary government, discussed by Laski [and] J. Redlich. New York 1931. Pamphlet.

The limitations of the expert. 1931 (Fabian tract).

Politics. Philadelphia 1931, London 1931 (as An introduction to politics), 1951 (for 1952) (ed M. Wight).

The crisis and the Constitution: 1931 and after. 1932 (Fabian pamphlet).

Nationalism and the future of civilization. 1932. Lecture; rptd in The danger of being a gentleman, 1939, below.

Studies in law and politics. 1932, New Haven 1932.

The theory of an international society. In Problems of peace, ser 6: lectures delivered at the Geneva Institute of International Relations, 1931, by Laski [et al]. 1932.

Democracy in crisis. 1933, Chapel Hill 1933. Lectures.

England confronts a new world. In Recovery through revolution, by Laski [et al], ed S. D. Schmalhausen, New York 1933.

The Labour Party and the constitution. 1933. Pamphlet.

The present position of representative democracy. In Where stands Socialism today? 1933 (Fabian lectures, by Laski et al).

The Roosevelt experiment. 1933. Pamphlet.

The social philosophy of William Morris. In Speeches in commemoration of Morris, by Laski [et al], Walthamstow 1934.

Brinton, H. (ed). Does capitalism cause war? 1935. Discussed by Laski [et al].

The committee system in local government. In A century of municipal progress 1835-1935, ed Laski [et al] 1935; rptd in The danger of being a gentleman, 1939, below.

Law and justice in Soviet Russia. 1935. Pamphlet; rptd in The danger of being a gentleman, 1939, below.

The state in theory and practice. 1935, New York 1935.

Political theory in the later Middle Ages. In Cambridge Medieval History vol 8, ed J. B. Bury, Cambridge 1936.

The rise of European liberalism: an essay in interpretation. 1936, New York 1936 (as The rise of liberalism: the philosophy of a business civilization).

The spirit of co-operation. Manchester [1936]. Lecture.

China and democracy. In China, body and soul, by Laski [et al], ed E. R. Hughes 1938.

The outlook for civil liberties. In Dare we look ahead, by Laski [et al], 1938.

Parliamentary government in England: a commentary. 1938, New York 1938.

The danger of being a gentleman and other essays. 1939, New York 1940.

Introduction to contemporary politics: selected lectures given at the University of Washington. Ed F. G. Wilson, Seattle 1939.

The Labour Party, the war and the future. 1939. Pamphlet.

The prospects of democratic government. Williamsburg Virginia 1939. Lecture.

The American Presidency: an interpretation. 1940, New York [1940].

The decline of liberalism. 1940. Lecture.

Government in wartime. In Where stands democracy?: a collection of essays by members of the Fabian Society, by Laski [et al], 1940.

Is this an imperialist war? 1940. Pamphlet.

Political offences and the death penalty. 1940. Lecture.

The rights of man. 1940. Pamphlet.

Where do we go from here?: an essay in interpretation. 1940, New York 1940.

The economic revolution. [1941]. Pamphlet. By Laski et al.

The freedom of the press in wartime. 1941. Pamphlet.

The Germans—are they human?: a reply to Sir Robert Vansittart [i.e. to his Black record, 1941]. 1941. Pamphlet.

The need for a European revolution. In Programme for victory: a collection of essays prepared for the Fabian Society, by Laski [et al], 1941.

The strategy of freedom: an open letter to American youth. New York 1941, London 1942 (as The strategy of freedom: an open letter to students, especially American).

London, Washington, Moscow: partners in peace? [1943]. Pamphlet.

Marx and today. [1943]. Fabian pamphlet.

Reflections on the revolution of our time. 1943, New York 1943.

Faith, reason and civilization: an essay in historical analysis. 1944, New York 1944.

Will planning restrict freedom? Cheam [1944]. Pamphlet.

Will the peace last? [1944]. Pamphlet.

The place of the scientist in post-war administration. 1945. Speech.

The secret battalion: an examination of the Communist attitude to the Labour Party. [1946]. Pamphlet.

What is democracy? [1946]. Pamphlet. By Laski et al.

Edmund Burke: an address delivered on the occasion of the bi-centenary of the foundation of Burke's Club. Dublin 1947.

Russia and the West: policy for Britain. [1947]. Pamphlet.

The Webbs and Soviet Communism. 1947. Lecture.

The American democracy: a commentary and an interpretation. New York 1948, London 1949.

Communist Manifesto—socialist landmark: a new appreciation written for the Labour Party, together with the original texts and prefaces. 1948.

Efficiency in government. In The road to recovery: Fabian lectures, 1947, by Laski [et al], ed D. P. T. Jay 1948.

Socialism as internationalism. 1949. Fabian lecture.

State, worker and technician. In Industrialisation et technocratie: exposés de Laski [et al], ed G. Gurvitch, Paris 1949.

Trade unions in the new society. New York 1949, London 1950.

Reflections on the Constitution: the House of Commons, the Cabinet, the Civil Service. Manchester 1951.

The dilemma of our times: an historical essay. 1952. Ed R. T. Clark; unfinished supplement to Faith, reason and civilization, 1944.

For Laski's many other contributions to books and pamphlets where his name does not appear on the title-page, see the bibliographies by Deane and Zylstra, above. Laski edited the Library of European political thought *5 vols 1926-8, and, with M. Ginsberg,* Studies in science and sociology, *1931-.*

Letters

Holmes–Laski letters: the correspondence of Mr Justice Holmes and Laski, 1916–35. Ed M. De W. Howe 2 vols Cambridge Mass 1953, London 1953.

§2

Elliott, W. Y. The pragmatic politics of Laski. Amer Political Science Rev 18 1924; rptd in his Pragmatic revolt in politics, New York 1928.

Hoog, A. Les théories d'Harold Laski et le pluralisme démocratique. Archives de Philosophie et de Droit et de Sociologie Juridique 7 1937.

Catlin, G. E. G. Laski and Strachey. In his Story of the political philosophers, New York [1939].

Fourest, M. Les théories du professeur Laski: le déclin de l'état moniste et l'avènement de l'état pluraliste. Paris 1943.

Zerby, L. Normative, descriptive and ideological elements in the writings of Laski. Philosophy of Science 12 1945.

Kampelman, M. M. Laski: a current analysis. Jnl of Politics 10 1948.

Watkins, J. W. N. Laski on conscience and counter-revolution. Nineteenth Century & After 145 1949.

Beloff, M. The age of Laski. Fortnightly 167 1950.

Hawkins, C. Laski: a preliminary analysis. Political Science Quart 65 1950.

Ray, N. C. B. Laski the sociologist. Indian Jnl of Political Science 11 1950.

Sarma, G. N. Laski. Ibid.

Soltau, R. H. Laski and political science. Political Quart 21 1950.

Martin, K. Harold Laski, 1893-1950: a biographical memoir. 1953.

— Intellectuals and the Labour movement: Laski. Listener 27 Oct 1960.

Deane, H. A. The political ideas of Laski. New York 1955.

Spitz, D. Labor and liberty: the discourse of Laski. In his Essays in the liberal ideal of freedom, Tucson 1964.

Gupta, R. C. Laski: a critical analysis of his political ideas. Agra [1966].

Peretz, M. Laski redivivus. Jnl of Contemporary History 1 1966.

Zylstra, B. From pluralism to collectivism: the development of Laski's political thought. Assen 1968.

THOMAS EDWARD LAWRENCE
1888-1935

A most important collection of papers relating to Lawrence has been placed in Bodley by his executors, under embargo until A.D. 2000. Bodley also holds a ms of Seven pillars of wisdom. *The BM holds the ms of Lawrence's trn of the* Odyssey, *an early draft of* The mint, *and several minor mss. The Public Record office holds important wartime reports, and documents related to his later service. The Kilgour Collection in the Houghton Library, Harvard Univ, contains a ms of* The mint, *the unpbd draft abridgement of* Seven pillars of wisdom *made by Lawrence and Edward Garnett in 1922, and minor mss. The T. E. Lawrence Collection, Univ of Texas, contains an early ms abridgement of* Seven Pillars of wisdom *and minor mss (see A. Bowden, Texas Quart 5 1962). Jesus College, Oxford holds the examiners' copy of Lawrence's BA thesis (pbd as* Crusader castles*).*

Bibliographies

German-Reed, T. Bibliographical notes on Lawrence's Seven pillars of wisdom and Revolt in the desert. 1928 (375 copies).

'John Gawsworth' (T. I. F. Armstrong). Annotations on some minor writings of T. E. Lawrence by G. [i.e. John Gawsworth]. 1935 (500 copies).

Duval, E. W. T. E. Lawrence: a bibliography. New York 1938 (500 copies).

A list of references by and on Lawrence in the Imperial War Museum Library. [1966]. Revised periodically. Duplicated.

Houston, G. B. T. E. Lawrence (1888-1935): a checklist of Lawrenciana, 1915-65, Oklahoma 1967; suppl 1970. Duplicated.

Baxter, F. C. An annotated checklist of a collection of writings by and about Lawrence—Lawrence of Arabia—with many other things collateral to the story of his military, literary and personal life and to the history of the Arab Revolt and the Palestine Campaign of World War I. Los Angeles 1968 (60 copies, duplicated).

Wilson, J. M. Lawrence: a bibliographical check-list. 1972. Includes biographical references.

Selections

The essential Lawrence. Ed D. Garnett 1951, New York 1951.

§1

As an RAF recruit in 1922 Lawrence used the name J. H. Ross; he changed it in 1923 to T. E. Shaw, and legalized this by deed poll in 1927. All posthumous edns use the name T. E. Lawrence. Articles known to have been written by him appeared over the initials CJG, CD and JC.

Carchemish: report on the excavations at Djerabis conducted by C. L. Woolley, Lawrence [et al]. 3 pts 1914-52. Pts 1 and 2 rptd with note by R. D. Barnett, 1969. Lawrence contributed directly to pt 1 and his notes and photographs were used in pts 2 and 3.

The wilderness of Zin: archaeological report. [1915]. (Annual for 1914-15 of Palestine Exploration Fund), 1936 (introd by F. Kenyon), New York 1936. With C. L. Woolley.

Sherifian co-operation in September; Story of the Arab movement; From the fall of Damascus to the armistice. In A brief record of the advance of the Egyptian Expeditionary Force July 1917 to October 1918, compiled from official sources and published by the Palestine News, Cairo 1919, London 1919. Anon. Other sections probably contain material drawn from Lawrence's official reports.

Catalogue of an exhibition of Arab portraits by Eric H. Kennington with a prefatory note by T. E. Lawrence. 1921; rptd, abridged, in Catalogue of an exhibition of paintings, pastels, drawings and woodcuts illustrating Col T. E. Lawrence's book Seven pillars of wisdom, 1927 (with preface by Bernard Shaw), rptd in Oriental assembly, 1939, below.

Doughty, C. M. Travels in Arabia Deserta. 2 vols 1921 (500 copies, with private issue of 6 large paper copies), New York 1923, 1 vol London 1926. Introd by Lawrence.

Seven pillars of wisdom: a triumph. Oxford 1922 (8 copies priv ptd from ms now in Bodley by Oxford Times, 5 of which with holograph corrections and addns circulated; complete set of sheets later used for the unpbd Garnett-Lawrence abridgement held by Harvard Univ (see headnote above); remaining 2 copies distributed as single leaves or destroyed), London 1924 (anon; small priv printing of rev Introduction, i.e. chs 1-8 of the book, which includes 1st ch later suppressed), 1925 (Introduction, i.e. chs 1-7 of the book, further rev with G. B. Shaw, together with prefatory letter signed T. E. Shaw; 100 copies, priv ptd), 1926 (1922 text completely rev and abridged, with new prefatory note signed TES; 202 copies, priv ptd; holograph signed note on collation distinguishes 170 complete copies from 32 lacking some illustrations), New York 1926 (22 [= 24] copies), London 1935 (trade edn; 5 passages omitted; preface by A. W. Lawrence which includes Some notes on the writing of the Seven pillars of wisdom by T. E. Shaw, 1927, below), 1935 (by T. E. Lawrence; limited edn of 750 copies with additional facs and coloured plates not included in trade edn), 1935 (priv ptd, 60 copies as above, but in trade binding and lacking one facs); New York 1935 (trade and limited edns, as London edns), London 1940 (this and all subsequent UK edns include original 1st ch, suppressed 1944, as 'introductory chapter', and addn to the preface by A. W. Lawrence). The 'suppressed introductory chapter' also pbd in Oriental assembly, 1939, below.

Garnett, R. The twilight of the Gods and other tales. 1924 (illustrated), New York 1926. Introd by Lawrence.

Le Corbeau, A. The forest giant. Tr from the French [Le Gigantesque] by J. H. Ross. 1924, New York 1924, London 1935 (with trn by Lawrence of Le Corbeau's dedication, and publisher's note), Garden City NY 1936.

Revolt in the desert, by T. E. Lawrence. 1927 (limited edn, 315 copies, and trade edn), New York 1927 (limited edn, 250 copies, and trade edn; with anon introd). Abridgement by Lawrence of Seven pillars of wisdom.

Some notes on the writing of the Seven pillars of wisdom by T. E. Shaw. 1927 (priv ptd, 200 copies); rptd in Seven pillars of wisdom, 1935 edn, above).

Notes on handling the RAF 200 class seaplane tender. [Hythe 1932.] Anon. Duplicated. An extract rptd in The essential Lawrence, 1951, Selections, above.

The Odyssey of Homer. 1932 (530 copies; anon trn, but some presentation copies signed 'T. E. Shaw'), New York 1932 (limited edn, 34 copies, and trade edns; signed 'T. E. Shaw'), 1934 (introd by J. Finley), London 1935 (without Finley introd, which reappears in later issues of this edn), New York 1940 (limited edn, 2500 copies, without Finley introd), London 1955 (introd by M. Bowra) (WC).

Thomas, B. S. Arabia felix: across the empty quarter of Arabia. 1932, New York 1932. Introd by Lawrence.

Crusader castles: vol 1, The thesis. 1936 (1000 copies, Golden Cockerel Press; foreword by A. W. Lawrence. Also 75 copies 'not part of the first edition' (see Chanticleer: a bibliography of the Golden Cockerel Press, 1936). For vol 2, The letters, see Letters, below.

The mint: notes made in the RAF Depot between August and December 1922, and at Cadet College in 1925 by 352087 A/C Ross, regrouped and copied in 1927 and 1928 at Aircraft Depot, Karachi. Garden City NY 1936 (50 copies ptd from text of ms now held by Harvard), London 1955 (rev; limited edn of 2000 copies unexpurgated; trade edn expurgated; as The mint: a day-book of the RAF Depot between August and December 1922, with later notes, prefatory note by A. W. Lawrence), Garden City NY 1955 (limited edn of 1000 copies, and trade edn), both unexpurgated and retaining the 1936 form of the title).

The diary of T. E. Lawrence, MCMXI. 1937 (203 copies, Corvinus Press), Garden City NY 1937 (small printing for copyright purposes only). With notes by A. W. Lawrence, poem by W. G. Lawrence, and 3 letters from T. E. Lawrence to his mother. The diary rptd in Oriental Assembly, below; the poem and letters rptd in The home letters, below.

An essay on Flecker. 1937 (32 copies, Corvinus Press), Garden City NY 1937 (small printing for copyright purposes only). The ms text rptd in facs in Men in print, below (30 copies only); the text, rev by A. W. Lawrence, rptd in Men in print, below (all copies).

Two Arabic folk tales, tr by T. E. Lawrence. 1937 (31 copies, Corvinus Press).

Oriental assembly. Ed A. W. Lawrence, with photographs by the author, 1939, New York 1940, 1947 (corrected). Miscellaneous writings.

Secret despatches from Arabia. Foreword by A. W. Lawrence. [1939] (Golden Cockerel Press). Mainly rptd from Arab Bull (Cairo) 1916–18. 30 copies include facs of 3 chs in Bodleian ms of Seven pillars of wisdom (ptd in the Oxford 1922 edn).

Men in print: essays in literary criticism. 1940 (500 copies, Golden Cockerel Press). Introd by A. W. Lawrence; 30 copies include facs of ms of An essay on Flecker, above.

Evolution of a revolt: early postwar writings of T. E. Lawrence. Ed S. and R. Weintraub, University Park Pa 1968. Reprints a selection of articles in periodicals.

Letters

Letters from T. E. Shaw to Bruce Rogers. New York 1933 (priv ptd, 200 copies). Concerning Lawrence's trn of Homer's Odyssey.

More letters from T. E. Shaw to Bruce Rogers. New York 1936 (priv ptd, 300 copies).

A letter from T. E. Lawrence to his mother. 1936 ('24' [= 30] copies, Corvinus Press); rptd in The home letters, below.

Letters from T. E. Shaw to Viscount Carlow. 1936 (17 copies, Corvinus Press); 2 letters rptd in The letters, 1938, below.

Crusader castles: vol 2, The letters. 1936 (1,000 copies and 35 copies 'not part of the first edn'; see Chanticleer: a bibliography of the Golden Cockerel Press, 1936); Garden City NY 1937 (small printing for copyright purposes). Preface by Mrs Lawrence.

The letters of T. E. Lawrence. Ed D. Garnett 1938, Garden City NY 1939, London 1964 (corrected, foreword by B. H. Liddell Hart). Includes some contributions to newspapers and other minor writings. For abridged edn, see Selected letters, 1941, below. French trn 1948 contains first printing of 4 additional letters.

T. E. Lawrence to his biographer Robert Graves: information about himself in the form of letters, notes and answers to questions, edited with a critical commentary [by Graves]; T. E. Lawrence to his biographer Liddell Hart: information about himself in the form of letters, notes, answers to questions and conversations. [Ed Liddell Hart]. 2 vols New York 1938 (1000 sets, of which 500 distributed in London 1938 with different binding and title-page), 1 vol London 1963, New York 1963.

Eight letters from TEL [to Harley Granville Barker]. 1939 (priv ptd, 50 copies). One letter also ptd in The letters, 1938, above.

Meynell, V. (ed). Friends of a lifetime: letters to S. C Cockerell. 1940. Includes 7 letters from Lawrence not ptd elsewhere.

Smith, C. S. The golden reign: the story of my friendship with Lawrence of Arabia. 1940. Foreword by Mrs Lawrence. Includes 50 letters to Sidney Smith and his wife not ptd elsewhere.

Williamson, H. Genius of friendship: Lawrence. 1941. Passages from letters with a commentary by Williamson.

Shaw-Ede: Lawrence's letters to H. S. Ede, 1927–35. Foreword and running commentary by H. S. Ede, 1942 (500 copies, Golden Cockerel Press; 30 copies contain facs of some of the letters).

Selected letters of Lawrence. Ed D. Garnett 1941 (Reprint Soc). Includes some letters not in The letters, 1938, above.

The home letters of Lawrence and his brothers. Oxford 1954 (introd by Winston Churchill), New York 1954. Transcribed and ed M. R. Lawrence.

T. E. Lawrence: 50 letters. Austin Texas 1962 (2000 copies). Exhibition catalogue.

Some unpublished letters from Lawrence to Frederic Manning. Ed L. T. Hergenhan, Southerly 23 1963.

§2

For a more complete list of articles and other biographical sources see checklists by F. C. Baxter and G. B. Houston in Bibliographies, above. Valuable references appear in works by or about people who knew Lawrence, and these also often contain letters. For names of many of these see Letters, ed Garnett 1938, above, or T. E. Lawrence by his friends, 1937, below.

Thomas, L. J. With Lawrence in Arabia. New York [1924], London [1927]. The source book for many of the legends about Lawrence.

Graves, R. Lawrence and the Arabs. 1927, New York 1928 (as Lawrence and the Arabian adventure), London 1934 (Concise edn). Authorized by Lawrence. For Lawrence's contributions see T. E. Lawrence to his biographer, Robert Graves, in Letters, above.

Liddell Hart, B. H. T. E. Lawrence in Arabia and after. 1934, New York 1934 (as Colonel Lawrence: the man behind the legend), London 1935 (enlarged). Authorized by Lawrence. For Lawrence's contributions *see* T. E. Lawrence to his biographer, Liddell Hart, above.

Richards, V. Portrait of T. E. Lawrence. 1936.
— T. E. Lawrence. 1939.

Lawrence, A. W. (ed). T. E. Lawrence by his friends. 1937, 1954 (abridged), New York 1963 (with article by W. H. Auden).
— Letters to T. E. Lawrence. 1962, 1962 (corrected).

'Christopher Caudwell' (C. St J. Sprigg). Lawrence: a study in heroism. In his Studies in a dying culture, 1938.

Blackmur, R. P. The everlasting effort: a citation of Lawrence. In his Expense of greatness, New York [1940].

Ocampo, V. 338171 T.E. Buenos Aires 1942; tr (rev) 1963.

Lönnroth, N. E. M. Lawrence av Arabien. Stockholm 1943; tr 1958.

Malraux, A. N'était-ce donc que cela? Saisons Winter 1946–7.
— Lawrence and the demon of the absolute. Hudson Rev 8 1955.
— *See* also D. Boak, Malraux and Lawrence, MLR 61 1966.

Aldington, R. Lawrence l'imposteur. Paris 1954; tr (rev) London 1955, 1969 (introd by C. Sykes). *See* also B. H. Liddell Hart, T. E. Lawrence, Aldington and the truth, London Mag 2 1955, and Aldington's reply, with further comment by Liddell Hart, in following issue.

Béraud Villars, J. Le Colonel Lawrence ou la recherche de l'absolu. Paris 1955; tr 1958.

Armitage, F. The desert and the stars: a biography of Lawrence of Arabia. New York 1955.

Benoist Méchin, J. Lawrence d'Arabie ou la rêve fracassée. Lausanne 1961.

Nutting, H. A. Lawrence of Arabia: the man and the motive. 1961.

Howe, I. Lawrence: the problem of heroism. Hudson Rev 15 1962; rptd in his A world more attractive, New York [1963].

Texas Quart 5 1962. Contains a group of articles on Lawrence and the Texas collection.

Payne, R. Lawrence of Arabia: a triumph. New York 1962, London 1965 (rev).

Weintraub, S. Private Shaw and Public Shaw: a dual portrait of Lawrence of Arabia and GBS. 1963.

Notopoulos, J. A. The tragic and the epic in Lawrence. Yale Rev 54 1965.

Stéphane, R. Portrait de l'aventurier: Lawrence, Malraux, von Salomon, précédé d'une étude de J.-P. Sartre. Paris 1965.

Mousa, S. T. E. Lawrence: an Arab view. 1966. Tr from the Arabic.

Knightley, P. and C. Simpson. The secret life of Lawrence of Arabia. Sunday Times 9–30 June 1968.
— The secret lives of Lawrence of Arabia. 1969. A substantial revision and enlargement of the 4 articles in Sunday Times. *See* also letter from A. W. Lawrence to Times 22 Nov 1969 referring to this and to articles by J. Bruce in Scottish Field Aug 1938 and Helensburgh Advertiser 15 Feb 1963.

M.P.

FRANK RAYMOND LEAVIS
b. 1895

See cols 1070–2, above.

LAURIE LEE
b. 1914

See col 296, above.

RUDOLPH JOHN FREDERICK LEHMANN
b. 1907

See col 297, above.

SIR JOHN RANDOLPH SHANE LESLIE
1885–1971

§1

The landlords of Ireland at the cross-roads: a letter. Dublin 1908. Pamphlet.

Songs of Oriel. Dublin 1908.

Lough Derg in Ulster: the story of St Patrick's purgatory. Dublin 1909, St Louis Miss 1917 (as The story of St Patrick's purgatory), [Dublin 1961] (greatly abridged, as Saint Patrick's purgatory).

A sketch of the Oxford movement. Dublin 1909. Pamphlet.

Isle of Columbcille: a pilgrimage and a sketch. 1910.

Memorials of Robert Hugh Benson, pt 2. 1915.

The end of a chapter. 1916, New York 1916, London 1917 (rev), 1929 (rev).

Verses in peace and war. 1916.

The Celt and the world. New York 1917.

The Irish issue in its American aspect: a contribution to the settlement of Anglo-American relations during and after the Great War. New York 1917, London 1918.

Henry Edward Manning: his life and labours. 1921, Dublin 1953 (shortened, with new material), New York 1954.

The oppidan. 1922, New York 1922. Fiction.

Doomsland. 1923. Fiction.

Mark Sykes: his life and letters. 1923.

Memories of many years, 1839–1922, by R. Seton. Ed Leslie 1923.

Masquerades: studies in the morbid. 1924. Fiction.

Memoirs of Brigadier-General Gordon Shephard. Ed Leslie 1924 (priv ptd).

Plato's symposium or supper. [1924]. Tr F. Birrell and Leslie.

An anthology of Catholic poets. Ed Leslie 1925, 1952 (rev), Westminster Md 1953.

The Cantab. 1926, 1926 (rev). Fiction.

George the Fourth. 1926.

The delightful, diverting and devotional play of Mrs Fitzherbert. 1928.

The poems of Shane Leslie. 1928.

The skull of Swift. Indianapolis [1928], London 1928. Biography.

The unknown quantity [Fonction d'X], by 'G. Mauge' [i.e. E. de La Rochefoucauld]. [1928]. Tr Leslie.

The Anglo-Catholic: a sequel to The Cantab. 1929. Fiction.

A ghost in the Isle of Wight. 1929. Story.

The Greek anthology. 1929. Selected and translated by Leslie.

The Hyde Park pageant. 1930. Verse.

Jutland: a fragment of epic. 1930.

Memoir of John Edward Courtenay Bodley. 1930.

St Patrick's purgatory: a record from history and literature. 1932. Compiled by Leslie.

Studies in sublime failure. 1932. Cardinal Newman et al.

The Oxford movement, 1833–1933. 1933, Milwaukee [1933].

Poems and ballads. 1933.

The passing chapter. 1934, New York 1934. Satire on post-war English life.

Fifteen odd stories. [1935].

The script of Jonathan Swift, and other essays. Philadelphia 1935, London 1935.

American wonderland: memories of four tours in the United States of America, 1911–35. 1936.

Men were different: five studies in late Victorian biography—Randolph Churchill, Augustus Hare, Arthur Dunn, George Wyndham, Wilfred Blunt. 1937, Freeport NY 1967.

The film of memory. 1938. Autobiography.

Sir Evelyn Ruggles-Brise: a memoir of the founder of Borstal. 1938.

Mrs Fitzherbert: a life [and The letters]. 2 vols 1939-40.

Letters of Herbert Cardinal Vaughan to Lady Herbert of Lea, 1867 to 1903. Ed Leslie 1942.

Poems of the north: a handful. Dublin 1945.

The Irish tangle for English readers. [1946].

Salutation to five. 1951. Mrs Fitzherbert et al.

Cardinal Gasquet: a memoir. 1953, New York [1953].

Lord Mulroy's ghost. Dublin [1954]. Play.

Shane Leslie's ghost book. 1955, New York 1956.

Edward Tennyson Reed 1860–1933: a memoir. 1957.

Twenty-five poems. Dublin 1959.

Long shadows: a book of reminiscences. 1966, Wilkes-Barre Pa 1967.

§2

Monrc, H. E. In his Some contemporary poets, 1920.
N.J.S.

DOMINIC BEVAN
WYNDHAM LEWIS
1894–1969

See cols 1078–9, above.

PERCY WYNDHAM LEWIS
1882–1957

See cols 631–4, above.

SIR BASIL HENRY
LIDDELL HART
1895–1970

§1

The framework of a science of infantry tactics. [1921], 1923 (rev and enlarged, as A science of infantry tactics simplified), 1926 (rev and enlarged).

Paris: or, the future of war. 1925, New York [1925].

A greater than Napoleon: Scipio Africanus. Edinburgh 1926.

The lawn tennis masters unveiled. 1926.

Great captains unveiled. Edinburgh 1927, Freeport NY 1967.

The remaking of modern armies. 1927.

Reputations. 1928, Boston 1928 (as Reputations, ten years after). Sketches of military commanders in the European war.

The decisive wars of history: a study in strategy. 1929, Boston 1929, London 1941 (as The strategy of indirect approach), [1943] (as The way to win wars), 1946 (enlarged, as The strategy of indirect approach), 1954 (rev and further enlarged, as Strategy: the indirect approach), New York 1954 (as Strategy), London 1967 (rev and further enlarged, as Strategy: the indirect approach), New York 1967 (as Strategy).

Sherman: soldier, realist, American. New York 1929, London 1930 (as Sherman: the genius of the Civil War), [1959] (original title).

The real war 1914–18. 1930, Boston 1930, London 1934 (enlarged, as A history of the world war 1914–18), Boston 1935, London 1970 (as History of the First World War).

Foch: the man of Orleans. 1931, Boston 1932, 2 vols London 1937.

The British way in warfare. 1932, 1935 (rev and enlarged, as When Britain goes to war: adaptability and mobility).

The future of infantry. 1933, Harrisburg Pa [1936].

The ghost of Napoleon. 1933. A history of military thought from the 18th to the 20th century.

'T. E. Lawrence', in Arabia and after. 1934, New York 1934 (as Colonel Lawrence: the man behind the legend), London 1935 (enlarged, original title), New York 1935 (as Colonel Lawrence: etc), 1937 (enlarged, as The man behind the legend: Colonel Lawrence).

The war in outline 1914–18. 1936, New York [1936].

Europe in arms. 1937, New York [1937].

T. E. Lawrence to his biographer Liddell Hart. 1938, New York 1938, London [1963] (with T. E. Lawrence to his biographer R. Graves), Garden City NY 1963. Ed B. H. L. Hart. Information about Lawrence in the form of correspondence and conversations.

Through the fog of war. 1938, New York [1938]. On military aspects of the European war 1914–18.

The defence of Britain. 1939, New York 1939.

Dynamic defence. 1940.

The current of war. [1941].

The strategy of indirect approach. 1941. *See* The decisive wars of history, 1929, above.

This expanding war. 1942.

The way to win wars. [1943]. *See* The decisive wars of history, 1929, above.

Thoughts on war. 1944.

Why don't we learn from history? 1944. Enlarged version of a lecture, We learn from history that we do not learn from history, pbd 1938.

The revolution in warfare. 1946, New Haven 1947.

The other side of the hill: Germany's generals, their rise and fall, with their own account of military events 1939–45. 1948, New York 1948 (as The German generals talk).

Defence of the west. 1950, New York 1950.

The letters of Private Wheeler 1809–28. Ed with a foreword by B. H. L. Hart 1951.

The Rommel papers. Ed B. H. L. Hart 1953, New York 1953.

Strategy: the indirect approach. 1954. *See* The decisive wars of history, 1929, above.

The Soviet army. Ed B. H. L. Hart 1956, New York 1956 (as The Red Army).

The tanks: the history of the Royal Tank regiment and its predecessors. 2 vols 1959, New York 1959.

Deterrent or defence: a fresh look at the West's military position. 1960, New York 1960.

Sherman, W. T. From Atlanta to the sea. Ed with an introd by Hart 1961.

Memoirs. 2 vols 1965, New York 1965–66 (as The Liddell Hart memoirs).

[Churchill]: the military strategist. In Churchill revised, by A. J. P. Taylor [and others], New York 1969, London 1969 (as Churchill: four faces and the man).

History of the First World War. 1970. *See* The real war 1914–18, 1930, above.

History of the Second World War. 1970.

Liddell Hart was military correspondent of Daily Telegraph *1925–35, and of* Times *1935–9. He was military editor of* Encyclopaedia Britannica *14th edn 1929. He compiled various infantry training manuals. He edited* Small arms training *1924, and the series* The next war, *6 vols 1938.*

§2

Crossman, R. H. S. Strange case of Liddell Hart. In his The charm of politics, 1958.

Luvaas, J. The captain who teaches generals. In his The education of an army: British military thought 1815–1940, Chicago 1964.

Howard, M. E. (ed). The theory and practice of war: essays presented to B. H. L. Hart on his seventieth birthday. [1965].

J.G.

ERIC ROBERT RUSSELL LINKLATER
b. 1899
See cols 636–8, above.

SIR RICHARD WINN LIVINGSTONE
1880–1960

§1

The Greek genius and its meaning to us. Oxford 1912.
A defence of classical education. 1916.
Greek ideals and modern life. Oxford 1935, Cambridge
  Mass 1935.
The future in education. Cambridge 1941. Rptd with
  next, 1954, as On education.
Education for a world adrift. Cambridge 1943.
Some tasks for education. 1946.
Education and the spirit of the age. Oxford 1952.
The rainbow bridge and other essays in education. 1959,
  Toronto 1961.
Livingstone edited The legacy of Greece: essays, *Oxford
  1921*; The mission of Greece: some Greek views of life
  in the Roman world, *Oxford 1928*; The Clarendon Latin
  and Greek ser, *and, with J. T. Shepherd*, Classical Rev
  *1920–2. He also translated and edited Plato and Thucy-
  dides.*

§2

Richards, H. E. Contemporary education and Livingstone.
  Religion in Life 18 1949.
Grassi, G. Richard Livingstone. Florence 1967. Con-
  tains a bibliography.

H. M. R.

SIR ROBERT HAMILTON BRUCE LOCKHART
1887–1970

Memoirs of a British agent: being an account of the
  author's early life in many lands and of his official
  mission to Moscow in 1918. 1932, New York 1933 (as
  British agent).
Retreat from glory. 1934, New York 1934. Reminiscences.
Return to Malaya. 1936, New York 1936.
My Scottish youth. 1937, New York 1938 (as A son of
  Scotland).
Guns or butter: war countries and peace countries of
  Europe revisited. 1938, Boston 1938.
Comes the reckoning. 1947. Wartime experiences, 1938–
  46.
My rod my comfort. 1949. Angling in Europe.
The marines were there: the story of the Royal Marines in
  the Second World War. 1950.
Britain and Europe. Copenhagen 1951. Lecture.
Jan Masaryk: a personal memoir. 1951, 1956 (with
  preface).
Scotch: the whisky of Scotland in fact and story. 1951,
  1959 (rev with preface).
My Europe. 1952.
What happened to the Czechs? 1953. Pamphlet.
Your England. 1955, New York 1955. Reminiscences.
Friends, foes and foreigners. 1957. Biographical
  sketches.
The two revolutions: an eye-witness study of Russia 1917.
  1957, 1967 (with foreword and postscript), Chester
  Springs Pa 1967.
Giants cast long shadows. 1960. Biographical sketches.

C. H. E. P.

PERCY LUBBOCK
1879–1965
See col 1079, above.

SIR EDWARD MONTAGUE COMPTON MACKENZIE
b. 1883
See cols 650–2, above.

CHARLES HENRY MADGE
b. 1912
See cols 305–6, above.

BRONISŁAW KASPAR MALINOWSKI
1884–1942

Bibliographies

In Man and culture, ed R. W. Firth, 1957, below.

§1

The family among the Australian Aborigines: a socio-
  logical study. 1913, New York 1963.
Wierzenia pierwotne i formy ustroju społecznego. Kra-
  kóv 1915. Primitive religion and social differentiation.
Argonauts of the Western Pacific: an account of native
  enterprise and adventure in the archipelagoes of Melanesian New Guinea. 1922, New York 1953.
Crime and custom in savage society. 1926, New York
  1926.
Myth in primitive psychology. 1926 (Psyche Miniatures),
  New York [1926] (New Science ser).
The father in primitive psychology. 1927 (Psyche Minia-
  tures), New York [1927] (New Science ser).
Sex and repression in savage society. 1927, New York
  1955.
The sexual life of savages in North-Western Melanesia.
  1929, New York [1929], London 1932 (with special
  foreword).
Essays presented to C. G. Seligman. Ed B. Malinowski
  [et al] 1934.
Coral gardens and their magic: a study of the methods of
  tilling the soil and of agricultural rites in the Trobriand
  Islands. 2 vols 1935, Bloomington 1965.
Freedom and civilisation. New York [1944]. Ed A. V.
  Malinowska.
A scientific theory of culture, and other essays, with
  preface by H. Cairns. Chapel Hill 1944.
The dynamics of culture change: an inquiry into race
  relations in Africa. Ed P. M. Kaberry, New Haven
  1945.
Magic, science and religion, and other essays. Ed R.
  Redfield, Boston Mass 1948.
Marriage, past and present: a debate between Robert
  Briffault and Malinowski. Ed M. F. Ashley Montagu,
  Boston Mass 1956. Appeared originally in Listener
  Jan 7–Feb 11 1931.
Sex, culture and myth. New York 1962, London 1963.
A diary in the strictest sense of the term. 1967, New York
  1967. Tr N. Guterman.

§2

Homans, G. C. Anxiety and ritual: the theories of Malinowski and Radcliffe-Brown. Amer Anthropologist 43
  1941.
Bronislaw Malinowski: an account of the memorial meeting
  held at the Royal Institution in London on July 13th
  1942. 1943.

Firth, R. W. (ed). Man and culture: an evaluation of the work of Malinowski. 1957. The bibliography contains a select list of obituary notices and discussions of specific aspects of Malinowski's work.

Kardiner, A. and E. Preble. Malinowski, the man of songs. In their They studied man, Cleveland 1961.

N. J. S.

KARL MANNHEIM
1893–1947

§1

Ideology and Utopia: an introduction to the sociology of knowledge. 1936, New York 1936. Trn by L. Wirth and E. Shils of Ideologie und Utopie, Bonn 1929, with 2 additional essays.

Man and society in an age of reconstruction: studies in modern social structure, with a bibliographical guide to the study of modern society. 1940. Based on Mensch und Gesellschaft im Zeitalter des Umbaus, Leiden 1935, rev and enlarged by Mannheim, tr by E. Shils.

Diagnosis of our time: wartime essays of a sociologist. 1943, New York 1944.

Freedom, power and democratic planning. Ed H. Gerth and E. K. Bramstedt, New York 1950, London 1951.

Essays on the sociology of knowledge. Ed (and tr) by P. Kecskemeti. 1952, New York 1952. This and the following include trns of papers originally pbd by Mannheim before Ideologie und Utopie, 1929, above.

Essays on sociology and social psychology. Ed (and tr) by P. Kecskemeti. 1953, New York 1953.

Essays on the sociology of culture. Ed (and tr) by E. Mannheim in co-operation with P. Kecskemeti. 1956, New York 1956.

Systematic sociology: an introduction to the study of society. Ed J. S. Erös and W. A. C. Stewart 1957, New York 1958.

An introduction to the sociology of education. 1962. With W. A. C. Stewart.

Mannheim, with W. J. H. Sprott, edited the series International Lib of Sociology and Social Reconstruction from 1942.

§2

Adams, J. L. Freud, Mannheim and the liberal doctrine of war. Jnl of Liberal Religion Winter 1941.

Merton, R. K. Mannheim and the sociology of knowledge. Ibid. Rptd in his Social theory and Social Structure, 1949.

Salomon, A. Karl Mannheim, 1893–1947. Social Research 14 1947.

Robinson, D. S. Karl Mannheim's sociological philosophy. Personalist 29 1948.

Maquet, J. J. P. Sociologie de la connaissance: sa structure et ses rapports avec la philosophie de la connaissance: étude critique des systèmes de K. Mannheim et de P. A. Sorokin. Louvain 1949, tr Boston 1951.

Murry, J. M. In his Katherine Mansfield, and other literary portraits, 1949.

Floud, J. In The function of teaching: seven approaches to purpose, tradition and environment, ed A. G. Judges 1959.

— Karl Mannheim. New Society 29 Dec 1966.

Remmling, G. W. Karl Mannheim: revision of an intellectual portrait. Social Forces 40 1961.

Corradini, D. Karl Mannheim. Milan 1967.

M. P.

'KATHERINE MANSFIELD', KATHLEEN MANSFIELD BEAUCHAMP
1888–1923

See cols 653–9, above.

ROBERT RANULPH MARETT
1866–1943

Bibliographies

In Custom is king: essays presented to Marett, ed L. H. D. Buxton 1936.

§1

Origin and validity in ethics. In Personal idealism: philosophical essays by eight members of the University of Oxford, ed H. Sturt 1902.

The threshold of religion. 1909, 1914 (rev and enlarged). Essays.

Anthropology. [1912], 1914 (rev).

Psychology and folk-lore. 1920. Addresses, essays and reviews.

Man in the making: an introduction to anthropology. 1927, New York 1928, London 1937 (rev and enlarged).

Faith, hope and charity in primitive religion. Oxford 1932, New York 1932.

Sacraments of simple folk. Oxford 1933.

Head, heart and hands in human evolution. 1935.

Tylor. 1936, New York 1936.

A Jerseyman at Oxford. 1941. Autobiography.

Marett jointly edited W. B. Spencer's journal of his expedition to Tierra del Fuego (1931) and Spencer's scientific correspondence with J. G. Frazer (1932). He also edited a collection of papers by E. im Thurn (1934).

§2

Rose, H. J. Marett. Proc Br Acad 29 1943.

C. H. E. P.

SIR JOHN ARTHUR RANSOME MARRIOTT
1859–1945

The makers of modern Italy: Mazzini, Cavour, Garibaldi. 1889, Oxford 1931 (enlarged, as The makers of modern Italy: Napoleon—Mussolini).

George Canning and his times: a political study. 1903.

The life and times of Lucius Cary, Viscount Falkland. 1907, New York 1907.

The remaking of Modern Europe, from the outbreak of the French Revolution to the Treaty of Berlin, 1789–1878. 1909, 1933 (rev).

English political institutions: an introductory study. Oxford 1910, 1913 (corrected), 1925 (enlarged, with introductory ch on the constitution 1910–24 [issued separately as The English constitution in transition 1910–24]), 1938 (enlarged, with introductory chs on the constitution 1910–38).

Second chambers: an inductive study in political science. Oxford 1910, 1927 (rev).

England since Waterloo. 1913, 1954 (with new bibliography by M. R. D. Foot), New York 1957. (A history of England, ed C. Oman, vol 7).

The French revolution of 1848 in its economic aspect: vol 1, Louis Blanc's Organisation du travail; vol 2, Emile Thomas's Histoire des ateliers nationaux. 2 vols Oxford 1913. With introd critical and historical by Marriott. Introd rptd separately 1919 as The right to work: an essay introductory to the economic history of the French revolution of 1848.

The English land system: a sketch of its historical evolution in its bearing upon national wealth and national welfare. 1914.

The evolution of Prussia: the making of an empire. Oxford 1915, 1937 (enlarged), 1946 (rev). With C. G. Robertson.

The Eastern question: an historical study in European diplomacy. Oxford 1917, 1918 (rev), 1924 (rev), 1940 (rev).

English history in Shakespeare. 1918.
The European commonwealth: problems historical and diplomatic. Oxford 1918.
Syndicalism: economic and political. 1920.
Europe and beyond: a preliminary survey of world-politics in the last half century, 1870-1920. 1921, 1925 (corrected), 1933 (rev), 1943 (rev, and enlarged to 1939).
Economics and ethics: a treatise on wealth and life. 1923.
Empire settlement. 1927.
The mechanism of the modern state: a treatise on the science and art of government. 2 vols Oxford 1927.
How we are governed. 1928 (also issued as How England is governed), 1934 (rev).
The crisis of English liberty: a history of the Stuart monarchy and the Puritan revolution. Oxford 1930.
How we live. 1930, New York 1930 (as How England lives), London 1938 (rev).
A history of Europe from 1815 to 1923. 1931, New York 1931, London 1933 (corrected and rev), 1938 (rev and enlarged), 1945 (rev and enlarged), New York 1952. (Methuen's History of medieval and modern Europe, 8).
The English in India: a problem of politics. Oxford 1932.
The evolution of modern Europe, 1453-1932. 1933, New York 1933.
The life of John Colet. 1933.
Oxford: its place in national history. Oxford 1933.
Queen Victoria and her ministers. 1933, New York 1934.
Modern England, 1885-1932: a history of my own times. 1934, 1941 (rev and enlarged), 1946 (rev and enlarged), New York 1960. (A history of England, ed C. Oman vol 8).
Dictatorship and democracy. Oxford 1935.
Twenty-five years of the reign of King George V: a silver jubilee memorial. 1935.
Castlereagh: the political life of Robert, second Marquess of Londonderry. 1936.
Commonwealth or anarchy?: a survey of projects of peace from the sixteenth to the twentieth century. 1937, 1939 (rev), New York 1939.
Robert Forman Horton. 1937. With A. Peel.
This realm of England: monarchy, aristocracy, democracy. 1938.
The evolution of the British Empire and Commonwealth. 1939.
English history in English fiction. 1940.
The tragedy of Europe. 1941. A history, 1918-39.
A short history of France. 1942, New York 1944, London 1944 (corrected and enlarged), 1947 (rev).
Federalism and the problem of the small state. 1943.
Anglo-Russian relations, 1689-1943. 1944.
Memories of four score years. 1946. Autobiography.
Marriott edited Univ Extension Jnl *1895-1920, contributing many articles and reviews. From 1900 onwards he was a prolific contributor to* Nineteenth Century, Fortnightly Rev, Quart Rev *and similar jnls.*

D.K.

CHARLES FREDERICK GURNEY MASTERMAN
1874-1927

§ 1

Tennyson as a religious teacher (Burney Prize Essay 1899). 1900.
The heart of the Empire: discussions of problems of modern city life in England, with an essay on imperialism. 1901. Ed Masterman, with ch, Realities at home, by him.
From the abyss: of its inhabitants. By one of them. 1902 (anon), 1911 (cover: By C. F. G. Masterman).
In peril of change: essays written in the time of tranquillity. 1905, New York 1905.

Frederick Denison Maurice. 1907 (Leaders of the Church, 1800-1900).
To colonise England: a plea for a policy, by C. F. G. Masterman, W. B. Hodgson and others. 1907.
The condition of England. 1909, 1911 (with additional preface), ed J. T. Boulton 1960.
The new liberalism. 1920.
How England is governed. 1921, New York 1922, London 1924 (abridged), rev D. Foot 1937.
England after the war: a study. [1922], New York [1923].
Masterman also contributed to other symposia, and pbd some wartime pamphlets and an abridgement of Morley's Life of Gladstone. *He became editor of* Commonwealth: a Christian social magazine *in 1901 and literary editor of* Daily News *in 1903.*

§ 2

Masterman, L. Masterman: a biography. 1939.
Hynes, S. Undecided prophets [Masterman and Galsworthy]. In his The Edwardian turn of mind, Princeton 1968.

M.S.

NANCY FREEMAN MITFORD
b. 1904
See col 674, above.

ALAN McCRAE MOOREHEAD
b. 1910

Mediterranean front. 1941, New York 1942. The campaigns in the Middle East 1940-1.
A year of battle. 1943, New York 1943 (as Don't blame the generals).
The end in Africa. 1943, New York 1943.
African trilogy. (Mediterranean front; A year of battle; The end in Africa). 1944, 1965 (with additional preface and new foreword by Viscount Montgomery), 1965 (abridged as The desert war: the north African campaign 1940/43), London 1967 (abridged by L. Moorehead), New York 1967 (as The march to Tunis: the North African war 1940-3).
Eclipse. 1945, New York 1945, London 1967 (abridged by L. Moorehead). Campaigns in Europe 1943-45.
Montgomery: a biography. 1946, New York 1946, London 1967 (introd by A. Clark).
The rage of the vulture. 1948, New York 1948. Fiction.
The Villa Diana. 1951, New York 1951. Articles from periodicals.
The traitors: the double life of Fuchs, Pontecorvo and Nunn May. 1952, New York 1952 (as The traitors), 1963 (rev with new preface), 1965 (rev).
Rum Jungle. 1953, New York 1954. A journey in Australia.
A summer night. 1954, New York 1954. Fiction.
Winston Churchill in trial and triumph. Boston 1955.
Gallipoli. 1956, New York 1956, 1967 (rev).
The Russian revolution. 1958, New York 1958.
No room in the ark. 1959, New York 1960, London 1965 (abridged for children), New York [1966]. Author's experiences in Africa.
Churchill: a pictorial biography. [1960], New York 1960, London 1965 (rev, as Churchill and his world: a pictorial biography, with a postscript by D. Sutherland).
The White Nile. 1960, New York 1960, London 1966 (abridged for children by L. Moorehead), New York 1967 (as The story of the White Nile).
The Blue Nile. 1962, New York 1962, London 1965 (abridged for children), New York 1966.
Cooper's creek. 1963, New York [1963], London 1968 (abridged for children by L. Moorehead).

The fatal impact: an account of the invasion of the South Pacific 1767–1840. 1966, New York 1966, London 1969 (abridged for children by L. Moorehead).
Darwin and the 'Beagle'. 1969, New York 1969.

P.C.

ROBERT BALMAIN MOWAT
1883–1941

The Wars of the Roses, 1377–1471. 1914.
Einhard's Life of Charlemagne: the Latin text. Ed with introd and notes by H. W. Garrod and Mowat, Oxford 1915.
Select treaties and documents, to illustrate the development of the modern European states-system. Ed Mowat, [1915], Oxford 1916 (enlarged).
The later middle ages: a history of western Europe 1254–1494. Oxford 1917.
The great European treaties of the nineteenth century. Ed A. Oakes and Mowat, Oxford 1918.
Henry V. 1919.
A new history of Great Britain. 3 vols 1920–2, 1 vol 1926 (enlarged); abridged and shortened edns 1927, 28.
A history of European diplomacy 1815–1914. 1922.
The European states system: a study of international relations. 1923, 1929 (enlarged).
A hundred and sixty years of British history, 1763–1922. 1923, [1934] (reissued as The making of modern Britain, 1763–1922).
The Near East and France, 1829–47. In The Cambridge history of British foreign policy, ed A. W. Ward and G. P. Gooch, vol 2, Cambridge 1923.
The diplomacy of Napoleon. 1924, New York 1924.
The diplomatic relations of Great Britain and the United States. 1925, New York 1925.
Makers of British history. 3 vols [1926].
Europe in the age of Napoleon. 1927, New York 1931.
A history of Europe and the modern world, 1492–1914. Oxford 1927, 1929 (enlarged to 1928). Also issued 1927 with Europe in the middle ages, by I. L. Plunket, as A history of Europe.
A history of European diplomacy, 1914–25. 1927, New York 1927.
A history of Europe, 476–1925. 1928.
A history of European diplomacy, 1451–1789. 1928, New York 1928.
Europe, 1715–1815. 1929, New York 1929.
The life of Lord Pauncefote, first ambassador to the United States. 1929.
The concert of Europe. 1930. International relations 1871–1914.
Contemporary Europe and overseas, 1898–1920. 1931 (Periods of European history, ed A. Hassall, vol 9).
International relations. 1931, New York 1931.
England in the eighteenth century. 1932.
The states of Europe, 1815–71: a study of their domestic development. 1932, New York 1932.
Problems of the nations. Bristol 1933.
Public and private morality. Bristol 1933.
A short history of the British Empire. 1933.
The age of reason: the continent of Europe in the eighteenth century. 1934, Boston 1934.
Revolution and recovery. Bristol 1934.
Americans in England. Cambridge Mass 1935, London [1935].
Diplomacy and peace. 1935, New York 1936.
Europe in crisis: the political drama in Western Europe. Bristol 1936.
Gibbon. 1936.
A chronicle of kingship, 1066–1937. [1937]. With J. D. G. Davies.
The fight for peace. 1937. Diplomatic history of Europe 1936–7.

The romantic age: Europe in the early nineteenth century. 1937.
Jean-Jacques Rousseau. 1938.
Peace in sight?: a chronicle and commentary on the war crisis. Bristol 1938.
The United States of America. Bristol 1938.
The American entente. 1939.
The Victorian age: the age of comfort and culture. 1939.
The American venture. 1942.
History of the English-speaking peoples. New York 1943. With P. W. Slosson.
Mowat edited, with a brief memoir, Letters to the Times 1884–1922, by T. Case, Oxford 1927, and was general editor of the Bristol Record Soc's Pbns vols 1–10, 1930–9, and Modern States ser 1933–8. He wrote several school history text-books.

D.K.

EDWIN MUIR
1887–1959

See cols 316–19, above.

SIR LEWIS BERNSTEIN NAMIER
1888–1960

Bibliographies
Brooke, J. List of books by Namier. In Charles Townshend, 1964, below.

Collections
Collected essays. 2 vols (vol 1, Vanished supremacies; vol 2, Crossroads of power) 1958, New York 1958, London 1962, New York 1963. Vol 2 includes the first 3 Ford lectures, 1934, hitherto unpbd.

§ 1
Germany and Eastern Europe. Ed with introd by H. A. L. Fisher 1915.
The structure of politics at the accession of George III. 2 vols 1929, 1957 (rev).
England in the age of the American revolution. 1930, 1961 (rev Lady Namier and J. Brooke).
Skyscrapers and other essays. 1931.
Additions and corrections to Sir John Fortescue's edition of the Correspondence of King George the Third, vol 1. Manchester 1937.
In the margin of history. 1939. Essays.
Conflicts: studies in contemporary history. 1942.
1848: the revolution of the intellectuals. 1946. Expanded version of the Raleigh lecture 1944.
Facing East. 1947, New York 1948. Essays, mainly on East European history.
Diplomatic prelude 1938–9. 1948.
Europe in decay: a study in disintegration 1936–40. 1950, Gloucester Mass 1963. Essays.
Avenues of history. 1952. Essays.
In the Nazi era. 1952. Essays.
Personalities and powers. 1955. Includes single lectures previously pbd separately.
Vanished supremacies: essays on European history 1812–1918 (Collected essays 1). 1958, New York 1958.
Crossroads of power: essays on eighteenth-century England (Collected essays 2). 1962, New York 1963. Includes single lectures, some previously unpbd.
Charles Townshend. 1964. Completed by J. Brooke.
The history of Parliament: the House of Commons 1754–90. 3 vols 1964. Completed by J. Brooke.
Namier wrote pamphlets for the Czech National Alliance (1917) and several letters to the press on Zionist subjects were rptd. He was general editor of the series Studies in modern history, and England in the age of the American revolution.

§2

Sims, C. S. In Some modern historians of Britain: essays in honor of R. L. Schuyler, ed H. Ausubel [et al], New York 1951.

Kearney, H. F. Historical achievement [of Namier]. Studies 45 1956.

Butterfield, H. George III and the Namier school. In his George III and the historians, 1957.

Sutherland, L. S. Namier. Proc Br Acad 48 1962.

Phillips, N. C. Namier and his method. Political Science 14 1962.

Brooke, J. Namier and Namierism. History & Theory 3 1964.

Berlin, I. Namier: a personal impression. In A century of conflict 1850–1950: essays for A. J. P. Taylor, ed M. Gilbert, 1966.

Plumb, J. H. Atomic historian. New Statesman 1 Aug 1969.

A.P.H.

SIR JOHN ERNEST NEALE
b. 1890

Bibliographies

The historical writings of Neale. In Elizabethan government and society: essays presented to Neale, ed S. T. Bindoff [et al] 1961.

§1

Queen Elizabeth 1934, New York [1934], London 1952 (corrected, as Queen Elizabeth I), New York 1957.

The age of Catherine de Medici. 1943, New York 1959.

The Elizabethan House of Commons. 1949, New Haven 1950, London 1963 (rev, Penguin).

Elizabeth I and her parliaments 1559–1581. 1953, New York 1966.

Elizabeth I and her parliaments 1584–1601. 1957.

Essays in Elizabethan history. 1958, New York 1959. Includes some single lectures previously pbd separately.

The age of Catherine de Medici and [a selection from] Essays in Elizabethan History. 1963.

Neale is a member of the editorial board of the official History of parliament *1964–.*

J.M.P.

HENRY WOODD NEVINSON
1856–1941

Bibliographies

Sharp, E. Books by Nevinson. In Visions and memories, 1944, below.

Selections

Henry W. Nevinson. 1926 (Augustan Books of Modern Poetry). Selected poems.

Fire of life. 1935. An abridgment by E. Roberts of Changes and chances, More changes, more chances and Last changes, last chances.

Essays, poems and tales. Ed H. N. Brailsford 1948.

§1

A sketch of Herder and his times. 1884.

Life of Friedrich Schiller. 1889.

Neighbours of ours. Bristol [1895], New York 1895. Fiction.

In the valley of Tophet. 1896, New York 1896. Stories.

Scenes in the thirty days war between Greece and Turkey, 1897. 1898.

Ladysmith: the diary of a siege. 1900, New York 1900. Rptd from Daily Chron.

The plea of Pan. 1901. Essays.

Between the acts. 1904. Autobiographical and other sketches.

Books and personalities. 1905.

A modern slavery (travels in Angola). 1906, Castle Hedingham 1963 (introd by B. Davidson), New York 1968. Travels in Angola, Sâo Tomé, Principe.

The dawn in Russia: or, scenes in the Russian revolution. 1906.

The new spirit in India. 1908.

Essays in freedom. 1909, New Haven 1921 (with Essays in rebellion).

The growth of freedom. 1912.

Essays in rebellion. 1913, New Haven 1921 (with Essays in freedom).

The Dardanelles campaign. 1918.

Lines of life. 1920. Verse.

Original sinners. 1920, New York 1921. Stories.

The English. 1920 (Routledge Introductions to Modern Knowledge).

Changes and chances. 1923, New York [1923]. Autobiography.

More changes, more chances. 1925. Sequel to preceding.

Last changes, last chances. 1928. Sequel to More changes, more chances.

Rough islanders: or the natives of England. 1930, New York 1931 (as The natives of England).

Goethe: man and poet. 1931, New York [1932].

In the dark backward. 1934, New York [1934]. Historical sketches.

Running accompaniments. 1936. Autobiographical reminiscences.

Between the wars. 1936. Essays.

Films of time: twelve fantasies. 1939.

Thomas Hardy. 1941 (PEN books).

Words and deeds. 1942 (Pelican). Essays.

Visions and memories. Ed E. Sharp, introd G. Murray 1944. Selection of articles not previously collected and some hitherto unpbd.

Nevinson wrote regularly, frequently as war reporter, for Daily Chron *1897–1902 (being the literary editor 1899– 1903), for* Nation *1907–23 (in both cases under H. W. Massingham's editorship); for* Daily News *1908–9, for* Manchester Guardian *under C. P. Scott 1912 onwards and for* New Leader *1922–6.*

He supplied the preface and the French chs to A. H. H. Murray, Sketches on the old road through France to Florence, *the text for J. Fulleylove,* Pictures of classic Greek landscape and architecture, *and edited R. Burton,* First footsteps in East Africa *for EL. He edited* England's voice of freedom: an anthology of liberty, *pbd pamphlets and rptd letters and articles on women's suffrage and other political subjects.*

§2

Whitehouse, J. H. Nevinson. Contemporary Rev 161 1942.

A.P.H.

SIR HAROLD GEORGE NICOLSON
1886–1968

§1

Paul Verlaine. [1921], Boston 1921.

Sweet waters: a novel. 1921.

Tennyson: aspects of his life, character and poetry. 1923, Boston 1925.

Byron: the last journey, April 1923–April 1824. 1924, Boston 1934, London 1940 (with supplementary ch), 1948 (with new preface).

Swinburne. 1926 (EML), New York 1926.

The development of English biography. 1927, New York [1928].

Some people. 1927, Boston 1927, New York 1957 (with introd).

Sir Arthur Nicolson, Bart, first Lord Carnock: a study in the old diplomacy. 1930, Boston 1930 (as Portrait of a diplomatist: being the life of Sir Arthur Nicolson, first Lord Carnock, and a study of the origins of the Great War), New York 1939 (as Portrait of a diplomatist, Sir Arthur Nicolson, Bart, first Lord Carnock: a study in the old diplomacy).

People and things: wireless talks. 1931.

Public faces: a novel. 1932, Boston 1933.

Peacemaking 1919. 1933, Boston 1933, London 1944 (with new introd).

Curzon: the last phase 1919–25, a study in post-war diplomacy. 1934, Boston 1934.

Dwight Morrow. 1935, New York [1935].

In search of the past: vol 1, Helen's tower [a biography of the Marquis of Dufferin]; vol 2, The desire to please: a story of Hamilton Rowan and the United Irishmen. 2 vols 1937–43, New York [1938–43].

Small talk. 1937, New York [1937].

Diplomacy. 1939, New York [1939], London 1950 (rev), 1963 (rev).

Marginal comment: January 6–August 4 1939. 1939. Articles rptd from Spectator.

Why Britain is at war. 1939 (Penguin Special).

Friday mornings 1941–4. 1944. Articles rptd from Spectator.

The congress of Vienna: a study in allied unity 1812–1822. 1946, New York 1946.

The English sense of humour. 1946 (Dropmore essays 1) (550 copies); rptd in The English sense of humour and other essays, 1956, below.

Comments 1944–8. 1948. Articles rptd from Spectator.

Benjamin Constant. 1949, New York 1949.

King George the Fifth: his life and reign. 1952, New York 1953.

The evolution of diplomatic method. 1954, New York 1962 (as The evolution of diplomacy) (Chichele lectures).

Good behaviour: being a study of certain types of civility. 1955, New York 1956, Boston 1960 (with new introd).

The English sense of humour and other essays. 1956, New York 1968. Includes lectures etc previously pbd separately.

Journey to Java. 1957, New York 1958.

Sainte-Beuve. 1957, New York 1957. Biography.

The age of reason 1700–89. 1960, New York 1961 (as The age of reason: the eighteenth century).

Monarchy. [1962], New York 1962 (as Kings, courts and monarchy).

Letters and Diaries

Diaries and letters. Ed N. Nicolson 3 vols 1966–8, New York 1966–8.

Nicolson also pbd addresses and pamphlets on political, international and current affairs. With V. M. Sackville-West (afterwards Nicolson) he edited an anthology, Another world than this, 1945, and wrote introds to a number of books including a biographical introd to Fox by C. B. Hobhouse.

P.C.

SEAN O'CASEY
1880–1964

See cols 879–85, above.

'FRANK O'CONNOR',
MICHAEL FRANCIS O'DONOVAN
1903–66

See cols 684–5, above.

CAROLA MARY ANIMA OMAN
(LADY LENANTON)
b. 1897

See cols 688–9, above.

SIR CHARLES WILLIAM
CHADWICK OMAN
1860–1946

§ I

The art of war in the Middle Ages. Oxford 1885, Ithaca 1953 (rev and ed J. H. Beeler). Lothian prize essay.

The Anglo-Norman and Angevin administrative system, 1100–1265. In Essays introductory to the study of English constitutional history, ed H. O. Wakeman and A. Hassall 1887 (for 1886).

A history of Greece from the earliest times to the Macedonian conquest. 1890, 1891 (rev).

All Souls' College. In The colleges of Oxford, ed A. Clark 1891.

Warwick the Kingmaker. 1891.

Aids to study in Oxford. In Oxford and Oxford life, ed J. Wells 1892.

The Byzantine empire. 1892, New York 1892.

Europe, 476–918. 1893, 1898 (as The dark ages, 476–918). The Oxford manuals of English history. Ed C. W. C. Oman 7 vols 1894–1910.

A history of England. [1895], 1919 (rev), New York 1955.

England and the Hundred Years' War. 1898, New York 1898. Vol 3 of Oxford manuals, above.

A history of the art of war: the Middle Ages, from the fourth to the fourteenth century. 1898, 2 vols 1924 (rev, as A history of the art of war in the Middle Ages), Boston 1924, New York 1959 (rev).

Alfred as warrior. In Alfred the great, by A. Bowker, 1899.

An elementary history of Greece. 1899.

England in the nineteenth century. 1899, New York 1899, London 1902 (rev), 1920 (rev).

The reign of George VI, 1900–25: a forecast written in the year 1763. Ed C. W. C. Oman 1899.

Adventures with the Connaught Rangers, 1809–14, by W. Grattan. Ed C. Oman 1902.

A history of the Peninsular war. 7 vols Oxford 1902–30.

My adventures during the late war, 1804–14, by D. H. O'Brien. Ed C. Oman 1902.

Seven Roman statesmen of the later Republic. 1902.

A history of England. Ed C. W. C. Oman 8 vols 1904–34.

A junior history of England. 1904. With M. Oman.

War. In L. Whibley, A companion to Greek studies, Cambridge 1905, 1916 (rev).

The great revolt of 1381. Oxford 1906, 1969 (new introd and notes by E. B. Fryde).

The history of England from the accession of Richard II to the death of Richard III, 1377–1485. 1906.

The Peninsular war, 1808–14; The hundred days, 1815; In Cambridge modern history vol 9, Cambridge 1907.

England before the Norman conquest. 1910, New York 1910, London 1929 (rev), 1938 (rev). Vol 1 of A history of England, 1904–34, above.

The text of the old betting book of All Souls' College, 1815–73. Ed C. Oman, Oxford 1912 (priv ptd).

Wellington's army, 1809–14. 1912, New York 1912.

The outbreak of the war of 1914–18: a narrative based mainly on British official documents. 1919.

The unfortunate Colonel Despard and other studies. 1922.

The art of war. In Medieval England, ed H. W. C. Davis, Oxford 1924.

The pageant of empire: an historical survey. 1924. Pamphlet.

Castles. 1926.

The German losses on the Somme, July–December 1916. In The world crisis by Winston Churchill: a criticism, by Colonel the Lord Sydenham of Combe [et al], [1927].

Studies in the Napoleonic wars. 1929, New York 1930.
The coinage of England. Oxford 1931.
Things I have seen. 1933.
The art of war in the fifteenth century. In Cambridge medieval history vol 8, Cambridge 1936.
The sixteenth century. 1936. Essays.
A history of the art of war in the sixteenth century. 1937, New York 1937.
The text of the second betting book of All Souls' College, 1873–1919, ed C. Oman, Oxford 1938 (priv ptd).
On the writing of history. 1939, New York 1939.
Memories of Victorian Oxford and of some early years. 1941.
The Lyons mail: being an account of the crime of April 27, 1796. 1945.

§2

Robertson, C. G. Sir Charles Oman. Proc Br Acad 32 1946.

N.J.S.

'GEORGE ORWELL', ERIC ARTHUR BLAIR
1903–50

See cols 690–6, above.

EDWARD HESKETH GIBBONS PEARSON
1887–1964

Modern men and mummers. 1921, New York [1922].
A Persian critic. 1923. Essays.
The whispering gallery: being leaves from the diary of an ex-diplomat. 1926, New York 1926. Anon.
Iron rations. 1928. Tales and essays.
Doctor Darwin [i.e. Erasmus Darwin]. 1930, New York 1964.
Ventilations: being biographical asides. Philadelphia 1930.
Common misquotations. Collected by Pearson [1934].
The fool of love: a life of Hazlitt. 1934.
The Smith of Smiths. 1934, New York 1934. Life of Sydney Smith.
Gilbert and Sullivan. 1935, New York 1935.
Labby. 1936, New York 1937. Life of H. Labouchere.
The Swan of Lichfield: being a selection from the correspondence of Anna Seward. Ed with short biography by Pearson 1936.
Skye high: the record of a tour through Scotland in the wake of Johnson and Boswell. 1937, New York 1938. With H. Kingsmill.
Tom Paine. 1937, New York 1937.
Thinking it over: the reminiscences of Hesketh Pearson. 1938, New York 1938.
The hero of Delhi: the life of John Nicholson. [1939].
Bernard Shaw: his life and personality. 1942, New York 1942 (as G.B.S.: a full length portrait), 1952 (with A postscript [pt of G.B.S.: a postscript, 1950, below]), London 1961 (original title), New York 1963 (as George Bernard Shaw: his life and personality).
A life of Shakespeare. 1942, 1949 (with an anthology of Shakespeare's poetry), New York 1961.
This blessed plot. 1942. Travel in England and Ireland. With H. Kingsmill.
Conan Doyle. 1943, New York 1961.
The life of Oscar Wilde. 1946, New York 1946 (as Oscar Wilde: his life and wit).
Talking of Dick Whittington. 1947. Travel in Southern England. With H. Kingsmill.
Dickens. 1949, New York 1949.
G.B.S.: a postscript. New York 1950, London 1951. *See* Bernard Shaw, above.
The last actor-managers. 1950, New York [1950].

About Kingsmill. 1951. With M. Muggeridge.
Dizzy: the life and nature of Benjamin Disraeli. 1951, New York 1951.
The man Whistler. 1952, New York 1953.
Walter Scott. 1954, New York 1954.
Beerbohm Tree. 1956, New York [1956].
Gilbert. 1957, New York 1957. Life of W. S. Gilbert.
Johnson and Boswell. 1958, New York 1959.
Charles II. 1960, New York 1960 (as Merry monarch).
The pilgrim daughters. 1961, New York 1961 (as The marrying Americans). Anglo-American marriages 1786–1937.
Lives of the wits. 1962, New York 1962.
Henry of Navarre. [1963], New York [1963].
Extraordinary people. 1965, New York 1965.
Hesketh Pearson, by himself. 1965, New York 1966.
Pearson also pbd edns of works by Oscar Wilde.

J.G.

SIR CHARLES ALEXANDER PETRIE
b. 1895

The white rose: historical drama in three acts. 1923.
The history of government. 1929, Boston 1929 (as The story of government).
George Canning. 1930, 1946 (rev).
Mussolini. 1931.
The Jacobite movement. 1932, Boston 1933 (as The Stuart pretenders: a history of the Jacobite movement), London 2 vols 1948–50 (rev), 1 vol 1959 (rewritten).
Monarchy. 1933.
The British problem. 1934.
Spain. 1934.
The four Georges: a revaluation of the period 1714–1830. 1935, Boston 1936.
William Pitt. 1935.
Walter Long and his times. 1936.
Bolingbroke. 1937.
Lords of the inland sea: a study of the Mediterranean powers. 1937.
The Stuarts. 1937.
The Chamberlain tradition. 1938, New York 1938, London 1968 (continued down to 1968).
Louis XIV. 1938.
Life and letters of Austen Chamberlain. 2 vols 1939, 1940.
Joseph Chamberlain. 1940.
Twenty years' armistice—and after: British foreign policy since 1918. 1940.
When Britain saved Europe: the tale and the moral. 1941. On the Napoleonic war.
Diplomatic history 1713–1933. 1946, New York 1949.
Earlier diplomatic history 1492–1713. 1949, New York 1949.
Chapters of life. 1950. Autobiography.
Monarchy in the twentieth century. 1952.
The Marshal Duke of Berwick: the picture of an age. 1953.
Lord Liverpool and his times. 1954.
The Carlton Club. 1955.
Wellington: a reassessment. 1956.
The powers behind the prime ministers. 1958.
The Spanish royal house. [1958].
The Victorians. 1960, New York 1961.
The modern British monarchy. 1961.
King Alfonso XIII and his age. 1963.
Philip II of Spain. 1963, New York 1963.
Scenes of Edwardian life. 1965, New York 1965 (as The Edwardians).
Don John of Austria. 1967, New York 1967.
Great beginnings in the age of Queen Victoria. 1967.
The drift to world war 1900–14. 1968, New York 1969.
Petrie edited The Duke of Berwick and his son: some unpbd papers, The letters and speeches of Charles I *and J. Pla,* Gibraltar. *He tr Paul Baudouin's diaries, adapted and expanded L. M. E. Bertrand,* History of Spain, *wrote an*

introd for T. Beamish, Battle royal *and pbd various single lectures and essays.*

He was assistant editor of the weekly Outlook *1925–8 and of* Saturday Rev *1928–30, foreign editor of* Eng Rev *1931–7, editor of* Empire Rev *1940–3, managing editor of* New Eng Rev *1945–50. He contributed to* Quart Rev *and reviewed for the* Illustrated London News *1965–6.*

A.P.H.

ALBERT FREDERICK POLLARD
1869–1948

§1

The Jesuits in Poland: Lothian essay 1892. Oxford 1892.

Political pamphlets. 1897 (Pamphlet Lib). Selected with introd and notes by Pollard.

England under Protector Somerset: an essay. 1900, New York 1966.

Henry VIII. 1902, 1905 (rev and enlarged), New York 1966 (introd A. G. Dickens), London 1970 (introd J. E. Neale).

Tudor tracts 1532–1588. 1903. Ed Pollard (English Garner ser).

Thomas Cranmer and the English Reformation 1489–1556. 1904, New York [1905].

The conflict of creeds and parties in Germany; National opposition to Rome in Germany; The reformation under Edward VI; Religious war in Germany; Social revolution and Catholic reaction in Germany. In Cambridge modern history vol 2, Cambridge 1903.

Factors in modern history. 1907, 1926 (enlarged and corrected), 1932 (enlarged), Boston 1960.

The Germanic federation 1815–40. In Cambridge modern history vol 10, Cambridge 1907.

The British empire: its past, its present and its future. Ed Pollard 1909 (League of the Empire Text-books ser).

The history of England from the accession of Edward VI to the death of Elizabeth 1547–1603. 1915, New York 1969. (Political History of England, ed W. Hunt and R. L. Poole vol 6).

On the educational value of the study of history. 1911 (Historical Assoc pamphlet).

The history of England: a study in political evolution [1912], New York [1912].

The reign of Henry VII from contemporary sources. Ed Pollard 3 pts 1913–14, New York 1967.

The war—its history and its morals: a lecture. 1915.

The Commonwealth at war. 1917. Essays.

The League of Nations: an historical argument. Oxford 1918.

The League of Nations in history. 1918. Pamphlet.

The evolution of Parliament. 1920, 1926 (rev), New York 1964.

A short history of the Great War. 1920.

Factors in American history. Cambridge 1925, New York 1925.

Wolsey. 1929, 1953 (corrected, with additional notes), 1965 (introd by G. R. Elton), New York 1966 (as Wolsey: church and state in sixteenth century England; introd by A. G. Dickens).

Pollard was an assistant editor of DNB *1893–1901, and contributed to it. He edited* History *1916–22,* Bull Historical Research *1923–9, and* League of the Empire Text-books ser *1909.*

§2

Neale, J. E. In EHR 64 1949.

Williams, C. H. In Bull Inst Historical Research 22 1949.

Galbraith, V. H. A. F. Pollard. Proc Br Acad 35 1949.

Hexter, J. H. Factors in modern history. In his Reappraisals in history, 1961.

J.M.P.

SIR KARL RAIMUND POPPER
b. 1902

Bibliographies

Writings of Popper [to 1964]. In The critical approach to science and philosophy, ed M. Bunge, New York 1964. *See* §2, below.

§1

The open society and its enemies. 2 vols 1945, 1 vol Princeton 1950 (rev, enlarged), 2 vols London 1952 (rev, enlarged), 1957 (rev with addendum), 1962 (rev and new addenda), 1966 (rev).

The poverty of historicism. 1957, Boston 1957, London 1960 (rev).

The logic of scientific discovery. 1959, New York 1959, London 1960 (rev), New York 1961 (rev), London 1968 (rev). Originally pbd as Logik der Forschung, Vienna 1935 (for 1934).

Conjectures and refutations: the growth of scientific knowledge. 1963, New York 1963, London 1969 (rev). Essays and lectures.

§2

Aiken, H. D. The open society and its enemies. Jnl of Philosophy 44 1947.

Rhees, R. The open society and its enemies. Mind 56 1947.

Ryle, G. The open society and its enemies. Ibid.

Kaufmann, W. A. The Hegel myth and its method. Philosophical Rev 60 1951.

Robinson, R. Popper's defense of democracy. Ibid.

Vries, G. J. de. Antisthenes redivivus: Popper's attack on Plato. 1952.

Jordan, R. Revolt against philosophy: the spell of Popper. In Return to reason: essays in realistic philosophy, ed J. D. Wild, New York 1953.

Cobban, A. Open society: a reconsideration. Political Science Quart 69 1954.

Marcuse, H. Poverty of historicism. Partisan Rev 26 1959.

Cohen, F. S. The open society and its enemies. In The legal conscience, ed L. K. Cohen, New Haven 1960.

Kirk, G. S. Popper on science and Pre-Socratics. Mind 69 1960.

Ayer, A. J. Popper's work in progress. New Statesman 1 Feb 1963.

Boyle, E. C. G. The importance of Popper. New Society 2 1963.

Olssen, E. A. On re-reading Plato and Popper. Political Science 14 1963.

The critical approach to science and philosophy: in honor of Popper. Ed M. Bunge, New York 1964. Contains a number of articles on Popper.

Bambrough, R. (ed). Plato, Popper and politics: some contributions to modern controversy. Cambridge 1967.

Cornforth, M. The open philosophy and the open society: a reply to Popper's refutations of Marxism. 1968.

H.M.R.

RAYMOND WILLIAM POSTGATE
1896–1971

§1

The International (Socialist Bureau) during the War. 1918.

The Bolshevik theory. 1920.

The Workers' International. 1920.

Out of the past: some revolutionary sketches. [1922], Madras 1922 (as Revolutionary biographies), New York 1926.

The builders' [i.e. building trade unions'] history. [1923].

A short history of the British workers. 1926.

A workers' history of the Great Strike. 1927. With E. Wilkinson and J. F. Horrabin.

'That devil Wilkes'. New York [1929], London 1930, 1956 (rev).

Robert Emmet. 1931, New York [1932] (as Dear Robert Emmet).

No epitaph. [1932], New York 1933 (as Felix and Anne). Fiction.

Karl Marx. 1933.

How to make a revolution. 1934, New York 1934.

A pocket history of the British workers to 1919. 1937.

The common people 1746–1938. 1938, 1946 (brought down to 1946), 1956 (corrected) (Pelican); New York 1939 (as The British common people 1746–1938), 1947 (as The British people 1746–1946). With G. D. H. Cole.

Verdict of twelve. 1940, New York 1940. Fiction.

A pocket history of the British working class. Tillicoultry [1943]. Incorporates portions of A short history of the British workers, 1926, and A pocket history of the British workers to 1919, 1937.

Somebody at the door. 1943, New York 1943. Fiction.

Life of George Lansbury. 1951.

The ledger is kept. 1953. Fiction.

Story of a year: 1848. 1955, New York 1956.

Every man is God. 1959, New York 1960. Fiction.

Postgate edited several Socialist journals, rev and continued Wells' Outline of History to the end of the second World War, rev and continued his Short history of the world to date. He edited Boswell's Conversations of Johnson and tr the Pervigilium Veneris and Colette's Mitsou. He edited a collection of revolutionary documents 1789–1906, and Those foreigners: the English people's opinion on foreign affairs since Waterloo, also anthologies of detective stories and notable trials. He has written extensively on food and wine.

A.P.H.

EILEEN EDNA POWER
1889–1940

§I

The Paycockes of Coggeshall. 1920.

Albert Kahn Travelling Fellowships: report to the trustees, 1920–1. [1922].

Medieval English nunneries, c. 1275–1535. Cambridge 1922, New York 1964.

Medieval people. 1924, Boston 1935, London 1939 (rev), New York 1950.

Tudor economic documents. Ed E. Power and R. H. Tawney 3 vols 1924, New York 1963.

Boys and girls of history. Cambridge 1926, New York 1927. With R. D. le P. Power.

The Broadway travellers. Ed E. D. Ross and E. Power 26 vols 1926–37.

Twenty centuries of travel: a simple survey of British history. 1926. With R. D. le P. Power.

Cities and their stories: an introduction to the study of European history. 1927. With R. D. le P. Power.

Life and work in medieval Europe, by P. Boissonnade. 1927. Tr E. Power.

Poems from the Irish. Ed E. Power [1927].

Broadway medieval library. Ed G. G. Coulton and E. Power 10 vols 1928–31.

The goodman of Paris. 1928. Tr E. Power.

More boys and girls of history. Cambridge 1928. With R. D. le P. Power.

Broadway diaries, memoirs and letters. Ed E. Power and E. Drew 7 vols 1929–31.

Europe throughout the ages (ancient and medieval). 1929. With N. H. Baynes.

Richard the Lionheart and the third crusade, by R. D. le P. Power. Ed E. Power 1931.

Peasant life and rural conditions. In Cambridge medieval history vol 7, Cambridge 1932.

Studies in English trade in the fifteenth century. Ed E. Power and M. M. Postan 1933.

The Cambridge economic history vol 1. Ed J. H. Clapham and E. Power, Cambridge 1941.

The wool trade in English medieval history. 1941.

Eileen Power edited other historical series, and helped with the founding of Economic History Rev, 1927.

§2

Robinton, M. R. In Some modern historians of Britain, ed H. Ausubel [et al], New York 1951.

N.J.S.

SIR FREDERICK MAURICE POWICKE
1879–1963

Bibliographies

Tyson, M. In Studies in medieval history presented to Powicke, ed R. W. Hunt et al, Oxford 1948. Continued in R. W. Southern, Proc Br Acad 50 1964: see §2 below.

§I

The loss of Normandy 1189–1204: studies in the history of the Angevin empire. Manchester 1913, 1961 (rev).

Bismark and the origin of the German empire. 1914.

Ailred of Rievaulx and his biographer Walter Daniel. Manchester [1922]. Rptd from Bull of the John Rylands Lib 1922, and rptd (rev and enlarged) as introd to W. Daniel, Life of Ailred, 1950, below.

Essays in medieval history presented to T. F. Tout. Ed A. G. Little and Powicke, Manchester 1925, New York 1967.

Stephen Langton. Oxford 1928, New York 1965.

England: Richard I and John; The reigns of Philip Augustus and Louis VIII of France. In Cambridge medieval history vol 6, Cambridge 1929.

The medieval books of Merton College. Oxford 1931.

Medieval England 1066–1485. 1931.

The collected papers of Thomas Frederick Tout, vol 1. Manchester 1932. Ed with a memoir by Powicke; memoir rptd in Modern historians, 1955, below.

The Christian life in the middle ages and other essays. Oxford 1935.

Rashdall, H. The universities of Europe in the middle ages. 3 vols Oxford 1936. A new edn by Powicke and A. B. Emden.

The Reformation in England. In European civilisation: its origin and development vol 4, ed E. Eyre 1936. Pbd separately, with minor corrections, 1941 (as The reformation in England).

History, freedom and religion. 1938.

Handbook of British chronology. Ed Powicke, with the assistance of C. Johnson and W. J. Harte, 1939, 1961 (rev Powicke with E. B. Fryde).

The muniments of the Dean and Chapter of Durham: a report to the Pilgrim Trustees 1939 (priv ptd). With W. A. Pantin.

King Henry III and the Lord Edward: the community of the realm in the thirteenth century. 2 vols Oxford 1947.

Three lectures given in the hall of Balliol College. Oxford 1947.

Ways of medieval life and thought: essays and addresses. [1950], New York 1964.

The life of Ailred of Rievaulx, by Walter Daniel. 1950. Tr with introd by Powicke.

The thirteenth century 1216–1307. Oxford 1953, 1954 (corrected), 1962 (rev) (Oxford History of England 4).

Modern historians and the study of history: essays and papers. 1955. Includes items previously pbd separately.

Councils and synods with other documents relating to the English church 1205–1313. Ed Powicke and C. R. Cheney 2 vols 1964.

Powicke edited Oxford Historical ser *1932–50 (with G. N. Clark and C. R. Cruttwell).*

§2

Southern, R. W. Sir Maurice Powicke. Proc Br Acad 50 1964.

J.M.P.

PETER COURTNEY QUENNELL
b. 1905

See cols 1107–8, above.

ALFRED REGINALD RADCLIFFE-BROWN
1881–1955

Bibliographies

Pardoe, R. In Social structure: studies presented to Radcliffe-Brown, ed M. Fortes, Oxford 1949. Suppl in Fortes, 1956, below.

§1

The Andaman islanders: a study in social anthropology. Cambridge 1922, 1933 (addns), Glencoe Ill 1948.

The social organization of Australian tribes. 1931 ('Oceania' Monographs 1).

African systems of kinship and marriage. Ed A. H. Radcliffe-Brown and D. Forde 1950.

Structure and function in primitive society: essays and addresses. 1952, Glencoe Ill 1952.

A natural science of society. Glencoe Ill 1957.

Method in social anthropology: selected essays. Ed M. N. Srinivas, Chicago 1958.

Radcliffe-Brown edited Oceania *from 1931.*

§2

Frazer, J. G. Andaman islanders. In his Garnered sheaves, 1931.

Lowie, R. H. In his History of ethnological theory, New York 1937.

Redfield, R. In Social anthropology of North American tribes: essays presented to Radcliffe-Brown, ed F. Eggan, Chicago 1937.

Homans, G. C. Anxiety and ritual: the theories of Malinowski and Radcliffe-Brown. Amer Anthropology 43 1941.

Wilson, E. L. G. In his But to what purpose, 1946.

Fortes, M. Radcliffe-Brown's contributions to the study of social organization. Br Jnl of Sociology 6 1955.

—— Radcliffe-Brown. Man 56 1956.

Eggan, F. and W. L. Warner. Radcliffe-Brown. Amer Anthropologist 58 1956. With selected bibliography.

Firth, R. Radcliffe-Brown. Proc Br Acad 42 1956.

Beattie, J. H. M. Founders of social science: Radcliffe-Brown. New Society 17 Dec 1965.

H.M.R.

HASTINGS RASHDALL
1858–1924

§1

John Huss. Oxford 1879 (Stanhope Historical Essay 1879).

The friar preachers v. the University [of Oxford] AD 1311–1313. Oxford 1890 (Oxford Historical Society, Collectanea ser 2 pt 3).

The universities of Europe in the Middle Ages. 2 vols [in 3] Oxford 1895, 3 vols 1936 (ed F. M. Powicke and A. B. Emden).

Doctrine and development: university sermons. 1898.

New College. 1901 (University of Oxford: College Histories). With R. S. Rait.

Personality, human and divine. In Personal idealism: philosophical essays by eight members of the University of Oxford, ed H. Sturt 1902.

Christus in ecclesia: sermons on the Church and its institutions. Edinburgh 1904.

The theory of good and evil: a treatise on moral philosophy. 2 vols Oxford 1907, London 1924 (corrected).

Philosophy and religion: six lectures delivered at Cambridge. 1909, New York 1910.

Bacon, R. Fratris Rogeri Bacon Compendium studii theologiae. Ed Rashdall, Aberdeen 1911. (British Soc of Franciscan Studies vol 3).

Ethics. 1913, New York 1913 (The People's Books).

Is conscience an emotion? Three lectures on recent ethical theories. 1914, Boston 1914.

Conscience and Christ: six lectures on Christian ethics. 1916.

The idea of atonement in Christian theology. 1919.

Jesus human and divine: three sermons together with a theological essay. 1922.

Principles and precepts. Ed H. D. A. Major and F. L. Cross, Oxford 1927. Addresses and sermons.

Ideas and ideals. Ed Major and Cross, Oxford 1928. Papers, articles and essays in theology, ethics and metaphysics.

The medieval universities. In Cambridge medieval history vol 6, ed J. B. Bury, Cambridge 1929.

God and man. Ed Major and Cross, Oxford 1930. Essays and articles.

Much of Rashdall's correspondence is printed in P. E. Matheson, The life of Rashdall, *1928. See* §2, *below.*

§2

Matheson, P. E. The life of Rashdall. 1928.

C.H.E.P.

SIR HERBERT EDWARD READ
1893–1968

See cols 1108–13, above.

LIONEL CHARLES ROBBINS, BARON ROBINS
b. 1898

§1

Wages: an introductory analysis of the wage system under modern capitalism. [1926].

An essay on the nature and significance of economic science. 1932, 1935 (rev, extended).

The Great Depression. 1934.

Economic planning and international order. 1937.

The economic basis of class conflict, and other essays in political economy. 1939.

The economic causes of war. 1939, New York 1968.
The economic problem in peace and war: some reflections
on objectives and mechanisms. 1947.
The theory of economic policy in English classical political
economy. 1952.
The economist in the twentieth century, and other lectures
in political economy. 1954, New York 1954.
Robert Torrens and the evolution of classical economics.
1958, New York 1958.
Politics and economics: papers on political economy. 1963,
New York 1963.
The university in the modern world, and other papers on
higher education. 1966, New York 1966.
The theory of economic development in the history of
economic thought. 1968.
Robbins was chairman of the Committee on Higher Education,
1963 (the 'Robbins Report'). With A. Plant he edited
Studies in economics and commerce *from 1933.*

§ 2

Fraser, L. M. Nature and significance of economic science.
Economic Jnl 42 1932.
Lerner, M. Do free markets make free men? In his Ideas
are weapons, 1939.
Checkland, S. G. Theory of economic policy in English
classical political economy. Economica 20 1953.
Knight, F. H. Theory of economic policy in English classi-
cal political economy. Ethics 63 1953.
Hutchinson, T. W. Robert Torrens and the evolution of
classical economics. Economic History Rev 11 1958.
H. M. R.

JOAN VIOLET ROBINSON
b. 1903

The economics of imperfect competition. 1933.
Essays in the theory of employment. 1937, New York
1937, Oxford 1947 (rev).
Introduction to the theory of employment. 1937.
An essay on Marxian economics. 1942, 1947 (rev), New
York 1967.
Collected economic papers. Oxford 1951–.
Conference sketch book: Moscow, April 1952. Cambridge
[1952].
The rate of interest and other essays. 1952.
On re-reading Marx. Cambridge 1953.
Letters from a visitor to China. Cambridge 1954.
The accumulation of capital. 1956, Homewood Ill 1956.
Exercises in economic analysis. 1960.
Economic philosophy. 1962, Chicago 1962.
Essays in the theory of economic growth. 1962, New
York 1962.
Economics: an awkward corner. 1966, New York 1967
(introd by R. Lekachman).
The cultural revolution in China. 1969, New York 1969
(Pelican).
Joan Robinson also pbd several pamphlets on economic and
political topics, including a Workers' Educational Assoc
study outline, The problem of full employment, *1943.*
She collaborated in the preparation of Can planning be
democratic?, *1944 (Fabian Soc).*
P. C.

BENJAMIN SEEBOHM ROWNTREE
1871–1954
Bibliographies
In A. Briggs, Social thought and social action: a study of
the work of Rowntree, 1961. *See* §2, below.

§ 1

Poverty: a study in town life. 1901, 1902 (enlarged), 1922
(new preface).
Betting and gaming: a national evil. Ed Rowntree 1905.
By Rowntree et al.
Land and labour: lessons from Belgium. 1910.
Unemployment: a social study. 1911. With B. Lasker.
How the labourer lives: a study of the rural labour problem.
[1913]. With M. Kendall.
Lectures on housing. Manchester 1914. With A. C. Pigou.
The way to industrial peace and the problem of unemploy-
ment. 1914.
The human needs of labour. [1919], 1937 (rewritten).
The human factor in business. 1921, 1925 (rev), 1938
(largely rewritten).
Poverty and progress: a second social survey of York. 1941.
Portrait of a city's housing: being the results of a detailed
survey in the city of York 1935–9. Ed R. L. Reiss 1945.
English life and leisure: a social study. 1951. With G. R.
Lavers.
Poverty and the welfare state: a third social survey of York
dealing only with economic questions. 1951. With
G. R. Lavers.
Rowntree also wrote or collaborated in a number of booklets
and pamphlets on social and labour problems. With Lord
Astor he organised enquiries into agricultural problems of
which reports were pbd. See A. Briggs, Bibliographies,
above.

§ 2

Briggs, A. Social thought and social action: a study of the
work of Rowntree. 1961.
P. C.

ALFRED LESLIE ROWSE
b. 1903

§ 1

On history: a study of present tendencies. 1927, New York
[1928] (as Science and history: a new view of history).
Politics and the younger generation. 1931.
Industry in the transition to socialism. In Where stands
socialism today?, 1933. Fabian lecture.
The question of the House of Lords. 1934. Pamphlet.
Henderson, C. G. Essays in Cornish history. Ed Rowse
and M. I. Henderson, Oxford 1935.
Queen Elizabeth and her subjects. 1935. With G. B.
Harrison.
Mr Keynes and the Labour Movement. 1936.
Sir Richard Grenville of the Revenge: an Elizabethan hero.
1937, Boston, 1937.
Poems of a decade 1931–41. 1941.
Tudor Cornwall: portrait of a society. 1941, 1969 (cor-
rected, with new preface), New York 1969.
A Cornish childhood. 1942, New York 1947. Autobio-
graphy.
The spirit of English history. 1943, New York 1945.
The English spirit: essays in history and literature. 1944,
1966 (rev), New York 1967.
Poems chiefly Cornish. 1944.
West-country stories. 1945.
Poems of deliverance. 1946.
The use of history. 1946, New York 1948, London 1963
(rev), New York 1963 (Teach Yourself History Lib).
The end of an epoch: reflections on contemporary history.
1947.
The west in English history. 1949.
The Elizabethan age: vol 1, The England of Elizabeth: the
structure of society; 1950, New York 1951; vol 2, The
expansion of Elizabethan England, 1955, New York
1955.

The English past: evocations of persons and places. 1951, New York 1952, London 1965 (as Times, persons, places: essays in literature).

An Elizabethan garland. 1953, New York 1953. Essays.

Romier, L. A history of France. 1953, New York 1953. Tr and completed by Rowse.

The early Churchills: an English family. 1956, New York 1956.

The later Churchills. 1958, New York 1958 (as The Churchills from the death of Marlborough to the present).

The Elizabethans and America. 1959, New York 1959.

Poems partly American. 1959.

St Austell: church, town, parish. St Austell 1960.

All Souls and appeasement: a contribution to contemporary history. 1961, New York 1961 (as Appeasement: a study in political decline 1933–9).

Ralegh and the Throckmortons. 1962, New York 1962 (as Sir Walter Ralegh, his family and private life).

William Shakespeare: a biography. 1963, New York 1963, London 1967 (rev).

Christopher Marlowe: a biography. 1964, New York 1965 (as Christopher Marlowe: his life and work).

Shakespeare's sonnets. Ed Rowse, 1964, New York 1964.

A Cornishman at Oxford. 1965. Autobiography.

Shakespeare's Southampton, patron of Virginia. 1965, New York 1965.

Bosworth Field and the wars of the Roses. 1966, New York 1966 (as Bosworth Field: from medieval to Tudor England).

The Churchills: the story of a family. 1966, New York [1966]. Abridged edn of The early Churchills, 1956, and The later Churchills, 1958, above.

Cornish stories. 1967.

Poems of Cornwall and America. 1967.

A Cornish anthology, chosen by A. L. Rowse, 1968.

The Cornish in America. 1969, New York 1969 (as The cousin Jacks: the Cornish in America).

The two chiefs of Dunboy: a story of 18th-century Ireland by J. A. Froude. Ed with a foreword by A. L. Rowse 1969.

Rowse edited the Teach Yourself History Lib *from 1946.*

J.M.P.

SIR JAMES COCHRAN STEVENSON RUNCIMAN
b. 1903

§1

The emperor Romanus Lecapenus and his reign. Cambridge 1929.

A history of the first Bulgarian empire. 1930.

Byzantine civilisation. 1933, New York 1956 (abridged), 1959 (complete).

The medieval Manichee: a study of the Christian Dualist heresy. Cambridge 1947, New York 1961.

A history of the crusades. 3 vols Cambridge 1951–4, New York 1964–.

Byzantine trade and industry. In The Cambridge economic history of Europe vol 2, Cambridge 1952.

The eastern schism: a study of the papacy and the eastern churches during the XIth and XIIth centuries. Oxford 1955.

The fall of Constantinople. By Runciman [et al] 1955. A symposium.

The Sicilian Vespers: a history of the Mediterranean world in the later thirteenth century. Cambridge 1958, Baltimore 1960.

The white rajahs: a history of Sarawak from 1841 to 1946. Cambridge 1960.

The fall of Constantinople 1453. Cambridge 1965.

The Great Church in captivity: a study of the Patriarchate of Constantinople from the eve of the Turkish conquest to the Greek War of Independence. 1968.

§2

Rexroth, K. Notes on historians. In his Assays, Norfolk Conn [1961].

J.G.

BERTRAND ARTHUR WILLIAM RUSSELL, 3RD EARL RUSSELL
1872–1970
See cols 1283–91, below.

SIEGFRIED LORAINE SASSOON
1886–1967
See cols 337–40, above.

SIR FRANCIS OSBERT SACHEVERELL SITWELL BART
1892–1969
See cols 346–9, above.

JOHN ALFRED SPENDER
1862–1942

§1

The state and pensions in old age. 1892, New York 1900.

A modern journal: being the diary of Greville minor for the year of agitation 1903–1904. Ed [or rather written by?] Spender. 1904.

The comments of Bagshot. 2 ser 1907–11, 1 vol [1914]. First ser pbd New York 1908.

The foundations of British policy. [1912]. Pamphlet.

The Indian scene. 1912. Articles.

The life of the Right Hon Sir Henry Campbell-Bannerman, GCB. 2 vols [1923].

The public life. 2 vols 1925.

The changing East. 1926, New York 1926, London 1935 (rev).

Life, journalism and politics. 2 vols 1927. Autobiography.

The America of to-day. 1928, New York 1928 (as Through English eyes).

Sir Robert Hudson: a memoir. 1930.

Weetman Pearson, first Viscount Cowdray, 1856–1927. 1930.

Life of Herbert Henry Asquith, Lord Oxford and Asquith. 2 vols 1932. With C. Asquith.

Fifty years of Europe: a study in pre-war documents. 1933, 1936 (rev).

A short history of our times. 1934.

These times. 1934. Essays and notes.

Great Britain, Empire and Commonwealth 1886–1935. [1936].

Men and things. 1937. Essays.

The government of mankind. 1938.

New lamps and ancient lights. 1940. Essays.

Between two wars. 1943.

Last essays. 1944.

The majority of Spender's early works were rptd from his many articles in Westminster Gazette, *of which he was assistant editor (1893–6) and editor (1896–1922). Spender also pbd an edn of the poems of William Watson (1905) and contributed to a biography of Joseph Chamberlain [1912].*

§2

'E. T. Raymond' (E. R. Thompson). Five editors. In his Portraits of the new century: the first ten years, 1928.

Harris, H. W. J. A. Spender. 1946.

C.H.E.P.

STEPHEN HAROLD SPENDER
b. 1909

See cols 355–7, above.

SIR LAURENCE DUDLEY STAMP
1898–1966

An introduction to stratigraphy, British Isles. 1923, 1934 (rev), 1957 (rev).
The vegetation of Burma from an ecological standpoint. Rangoon 1924.
Handbook of commercial geography, by G. G. Chisholm: eleventh edition, revised and edited by L. D. Stamp. 1928, 1937 (rewritten by Stamp).
Asia: an economic and regional geography. 1929. Frequently rev.
The British Isles. 1933. Frequently rev. With S. H. Beaver.
Slovene studies. Ed L. D. Stamp 1933.
The Land Utilization Survey of Britain: an outline description of the first twelve one-inch maps. 1934, 1935 (rev), Ramsgate 1961 (in Land use survey handbooks, by A. Coleman). With E. C. Willatts.
A commercial geography. 1936.
The face of Britain. 1940, 1944 (rev), 1956 (rev).
Fertility, productivity and classification of land in Britain: an explanatory bulletin to the land fertility map of Britain. 1941.
Britain's structure and scenery. 1946 (New Naturalist 1).
The land of Britain and how it is used. 1946.
The land of Britain: its use and misuse. 1948.
London essays in geography: Rodwell Jones memorial volume. Ed L. D. Stamp 1951, Cambridge Mass 1951.
Land for tomorrow: the underdeveloped world. Bloomington 1952, London 1953 (as Our undeveloped world), 1960 (as Our developing world).
Africa: a study in tropical development. New York and London [1953].
Man and the land. 1955, 1964 (rev) (New Naturalist).
Natural resources, food and population in inter-tropical Africa: a report. Ed L. D. Stamp 1956. Pbd by the International Geographical Union.
Applied geography. 1960 (Pelican), Baltimore [1963].
A glossary of geographical terms. Ed L. D. Stamp 1961, New York 1961. Pbd by Assoc for the Advancement of Science.
A history of land use in arid regions. Ed L. D. Stamp, Paris 1961.
The common lands of England and Wales. 1963. With W. G. Hoskins.
The geography of life and death. 1964, Ithaca 1965.
Some aspects of medical geography. 1964.
Land use statistics of the countries of Europe. Bude 1965. Pamphlet.
A dictionary of geography. Ed L. D. Stamp 1966, New York 1966.
Stamp also pbd a large number of geography text books apart from those listed here, and several atlases. He edited the University Geographical ser, and, with James Fisher, New Naturalist, and also the report of the Land Utilization Survey of Great Britain, contributing in whole or in part many counties to the Land of Britain ser.

N.J.S.

ENID MARY STARKIE
1897–1970

See col 1121, above.

SIR RONALD HENRY AMHERST STORRS
1881–1955

A chronology of Cyprus. Nicosia 1930.
Orientations. 1937, New York 1937 (as The memoirs of Sir Ronald Storrs). Pt rptd 1940 as Lawrence of Arabia, Zionism and Palestine (Penguin).
A record of the war: the first quarter, September–November 1939; the second quarter, December 1939–February 1940. 2 vols 1940. Remaining 22 vols of this work by P. Graves.
Dunlop in war and peace. [1946].
Kennington, E. Drawing the RAF. 1942. Introd by Storrs.
Ad Pyrrham: a polyglot collection of translations of Horace's Ode to Pyrrha. 1950. Introd by Storrs.
Storrs also pbd articles on the arts in Near East from 1926 into the 30's; he was special correspondent for Sunday Times from Portugal and Persia 1942–3.

H.M.R.

EVELYN JOHN SAINT LOE STRACHEY
1901–63

§1

Revolution by reason: an account of the financial proposals submitted to the Labour movement by Mr Oswald Mosley. 1925.
After-dinner philosophy. 1926. With C. E. M. Joad.
Workers' control in the Russian mining industry. [1928]. Pamphlet.
A national policy, drafted by A. Young, J. Strachey [et al]. 1931.
What we saw in Russia. 1931. With A. Bevan and G. Strauss. Pamphlet.
The coming struggle for power. 1932, New York 1933, 1933 (rev).
The menace of fascism. 1933, New York 1933.
Literature and dialectical materialism. New York [1934].
The nature of capitalist crisis. 1935, New York [1935].
Social credit: an economic analysis. 1936. Pamphlet.
The theory and practice of socialism. 1936, New York [1936].
Capital, by K. Marx, abridged by Strachey. [1937].
Communism or distributism?: a debate between Fr V. McNabb and Strachey. [1937]. Pamphlet.
Hope in America. New York [1938].
What are we to do? (a study of the Labour movement). 1938, New York [1938].
Why you should be a socialist. 1938, 1944 (rev).
How socialism works. New York [1939].
The banks for the people. 1940.
Federalism or socialism? 1940.
A programme for progress. 1940, New York [1940].
The betrayal of the left, by V. Gollancz, Strachey, G. Orwell and a labour candidate. 1941.
A faith to fight for. 1941, New York [1941].
Post D: some experiences of an air raid warden. 1941, New York [1941] (as Digging for Mrs Miller).
Socialism looks forward. New York 1945.
Bread rationing. 1946. Speech in Parliament.
The just society: a re-affirmation of faith in socialism. [1951]. Pamphlet.
Labour's task. 1951. Pamphlet.
The frontiers. 1952, New York 1952. Fiction.
Contemporary capitalism. 1956, New York 1956.
Scrap all the H-bombs. [1958]. Pamphlet.
The end of empire. 1959, New York 1960.
The pursuit of peace: the defence debate. 1960. Pamphlet.

The great awakening: or, from imperialism to freedom. 1961.
On the prevention of war. 1962, New York 1963.
The strangled cry and other unparliamentary papers. 1962, New York 1962.

§2

Catlin, G. E. G. Laski and Strachey. In his Story of the political philosophers, New York 1939.
Crossman, R. H. S. John Strachey and the Left Book Club. In his Charm of politics and other essays, 1958.
N. J. S.

GILES LYTTON STRACHEY
1880–1932

Mss of Eminent Victorians, Queen Victoria *and* Elizabeth and Essex *are in the* BM, *Univ of Texas and Duke Univ respectively. See J. Stratford,* Eminent Victorians, *BM Quart 32 1968.*

Bibliographies

Muir, P. H. Strachey: bibliographical check-list. In his Points: 2nd ser, 1934. Books only, with some details of limited edns and numbers of copies.
Sanders, C. R. A chronological check list of Strachey's writings. In his Strachey: his mind and art, 1957, below. Expanded from MP 44 1947. Includes some unpbd writings.
Kallich, M. Strachey: an annotated bibliography of writings about him. Eng Lit in Transition 5 1962.

Collections

The collected works. 6 vols 1948. Ed J. Strachey. Contents of Books and characters, Portraits in miniature and Characters and commentaries (omitting 6 essays) included as Biographical essays and Literary essays. Biographical essays adds Charles Grenville, not previously collected. These two vols also pbd New York 1949. Excludes Strachey's poetry.

§1

Prolusiones academicae. Cambridge 1902. Contains Ely, an ode: a poem which obtained the Chancellor's Medal 1902.
Euphrosyne: a collection of verse. Cambridge 1905. Includes Ningamus sarta rosarum, The cat, and other unidentified poems by Strachey.
Inchbald, E. A simple story. 1908. With introd by Strachey, rptd in Characters and commentaries, 1933 below.
Landmarks in French literature. 1912, New York 1912. For a note on the variant issues see P. H. Muir's Points, 1st ser 1931.
Eminent Victorians: Cardinal Manning; Florence Nightingale; Dr Arnold; General Gordon. 1918, New York 1918. Rptd with Queen Victoria, below, as Five Victorians 1942. Florence Nightingale rptd separately 1938.
Queen Victoria. 1921, New York 1921. Rptd with Eminent Victorians, above as Five Victorians, 1942.
Books and characters, French and English. 1922, New York 1922.
Pope: the Leslie Stephen lecture for 1925. Cambridge 1925. Rptd in Characters and commentaries, 1933.
The son of heaven. A play, performed at the Scala Theatre July 12, 13, 1925; revived at the New Lindsey Theatre May 1949. Unpbd.
Elizabeth and Essex: a tragic history. 1928, New York 1928.
Rylands, G. W. H. Words and poetry. 1928. With introd by Strachey, rptd in Characters and commentaries, 1933 below.

Portraits in miniature and other essays. 1931, New York 1931.
Characters and commentaries. 1933, New York 1933. Ed with preface by J. Strachey.
Florence Nightingale. 1938. First pbd in Eminent Victorians 1918.
Greville, C. C. F. The Greville memoirs. Ed Strachey and R. Fulford, 8 vols 1938.
Five Victorians. 1942. *See* Eminent Victorians, 1918.
Spectatorial essays: [ed] with a preface by J. Strachey. 1964, New York 1965. Selected book and theatre reviews appearing in Spectator 1904–14.

Letters

Virginia Woolf and Lytton Strachey: letters. Ed L. Woolf and J. Strachey 1956, New York 1956.

§2

Gosse, E. The agony of the Victorian age. Edinburgh Rev 228 1918; rptd in his Some diversions of a man of letters, 1919. Review of Eminent Victorians.
— Queen Victoria. In his More books on the table, 1923. Review; rptd from Sunday Times.
— Pope and Mr Strachey. In his Leaves and fruit, 1927. Review; rptd from Sunday Times.
Pearson, H. Lytton Strachey. In his Modern men and mummers, 1921.
— A biographer. In his Thinking it over, 1938.
Harrison, F. My Victorian memories. Fortnightly Rev new ser no 654, 1921; rptd in his De senectute, 1923. Supports the historical accuracy of Strachey's Queen Victoria.
Huxley, A. The author of Eminent Victorians. Vanity Fair 19 Sept 1922; rptd in his On the margin, 1923.
Mirsky, D. S. Strachey. London Mercury 7 1923.
Bell, C. Strachey. New Statesman 4 Aug 1923; rptd (enlarged) as Recollections of Strachey, Cornhill 165 1950, and as Strachey in his Old Friends, 1956.
Muir, E. Contemporary writers 1: Strachey. Nation and Athenaeum 25 April 1925; rptd in his Transition, 1926.
Nicolson, H. Strachey and Queen Victoria. In his Development of English biography, 1927.
'André Maurois' (E. S. W. Herzog). The modern biographer. Yale Rev 17 1928.
— Strachey. In his Magiciens et logiciens, Paris 1935; tr 1935 as Prophets and poets.
Nash, R. Florence Nightingale according to Strachey. Nineteenth Century 103 1928.
Johnston, G. A. The new biography: Ludwig, Maurois and Strachey. Atlantic Monthly 143 1929.
Smyth, C. A note on historical biography and Strachey. Criterion 8 1929.
Lehmann, B. H. The art of Strachey. Essays in Criticism (Berkeley) 1 1929.
Mortimer, R. Mrs Woolf and Strachey. Bookman (New York) 68 1929; rptd as Lytton Strachey, in his Channel Packet, 1943.
Gelber, L. M. History and the new biography. Queen's Quart 37 1930.
Hollis, C. Elizabeth and Strachey. Dublin Rev 186 1930.
Kronenberger, L. Strachey. Bookman (New York) 71 1930.
Saltmarshe, C. Strachey. In Scrutinies, collected by E. Rickword, vol 2, 1931.
Woolf, L. Strachey. New Statesman 30 Jan 1932. Obituary.
— Cambridge. In his Sowing: an autobiography of the years 1880–1904, 1960. Strachey, J. M. Keynes and their circle at the university. The subsequent vols of the autobiography also contain references to Strachey.
Sheean, V. Strachey: Cambridge and Bloomsbury. New Republic 17 Feb 1932.
MacCarthy, D. Strachey as a biographer. Life & Letters 7 1932.

— Strachey and the art of biography. Sunday Times 5 Nov 1933; rptd in his Memories, 1953.

Gordon, G. S. The art and ethics of modern biography. Listener 23 March 1932; rptd (rev) in his The lives of authors, 1950.

Birrell, F. Souvenirs et réflexions sur Strachey. Revue Hebdomadaire 23 July 1932.

Wilson, E. Strachey. New Republic 2 Sept 1932; rptd in his The shores of light, New York 1952.

Hartwell, R. M. Strachey. Univ of California Chron 34 1932.

Bower-Shore, C. Strachey: an essay. Introd R. L. Mégroz 1933.

Dobrée, B. Strachey. In The post-Victorians, with an introd by W. R. Inge, 1933.

Ritchie, C. Strachey and Guedalla: an essay in comparison. Dalhousie Rev 12 1933.

Longaker, J. M. The art of Strachey. In his Contemporary biography, Philadelphia 1934.

Boas, G. Lytton Strachey. 1935 (English Assoc pamphlet).

— Strachey—dramatic critic. English 8 1950.

— Strachey—reviewer. Spectator 7 April 1950.

O'Neill, E. H. The new biography. In his A history of American biography, Philadelphia 1935. Influence of Strachey on American biography.

Johnson, E. Art and irony. In his One mighty torrent: the drama of biography, New York 1937.

Köntges, G. Die Sprache in der Biographie Stracheys. Marburg 1938.

Srinivasa Iyengar, K. R. Lytton Strachey: a critical study. 1938.

Dangerfield, G. Strachey. Sat Rev of Lit 23 July 1938.

Woolf, V. The art of biography. Atlantic Monthly 163 1939; rptd in her Death of the moth, 1942, and Collected essays, vol 4 1968.

Clemens, C. Strachey. Dalhousie Rev 20 1940; rptd separately with addns Webster Groves Mo 1942.

Bacon, L. An eminent post-Victorian. Yale Rev 30 1940.

Beerbohm, M. Lytton Strachey. Cambridge 1943 (The Rede Lecture 1943).

Simpson, F. A. Methods of history. Spectator 7 Jan 1944. An attack on Strachey's treatment of Manning in Eminent Victorians.

Sanders, C. R. Strachey's revisions in Books and characters. MLN 60 1945. Primarily a list.

— Strachey improves his style, 1904–1922. College Eng 7 1948. Discussion of the revisions in Books and characters.

— The Strachey family, 1588–1932: their writings and literary associations. Durham NC 1953.

— Strachey: his mind and art. New Haven 1957.

Russell, J. Strachey. Horizon 15 1947.

Trevor-Roper, H. Books in general—the Collected works of Strachey. New Statesman 12 Feb 1949; rptd as Strachey as historian, in his Historical essays, 1957.

Harrod, R. F. In his The life of John Maynard Keynes, 1951. On Keynes' friendship with Strachey.

Russell, B. Portraits from memory—II: Maynard Keynes and Strachey. Listener 17 July 1952.

Elton, G. Anatomy of a slander. In his Gordon of Khartoum, 1954. On the treatment of Gordon in Eminent Victorians.

Johnstone, J. K. The Bloomsbury Group: a study of E. M. Forster, Strachey, Virginia Woolf and their circle. 1954.

Garnett, D. Keynes, Strachey and Virginia Woolf in 1917. London Mag 2 1955.

Scott-James, R. A. Lytton Strachey. 1955 (Br Council pamphlet).

Dyson, A. E. The technique of debunking. Twentieth Century 157 1955; rptd (rev) in his The crazy fabric: essays in irony, 1965.

Raymond, J. Strachey's Eminent Victorians. New Statesman 16 April 1955; rptd in his England's on the anvil, 1958.

Kallich, M. Psychoanalysis, sexuality, and Strachey's theory of biography. American Imago 15 1958.

— The psychological milieu of Strachey. New York 1961.

Clive, J. More or less eminent Victorians: some trends in recent Victorian biography. Victorian Studies 2 1958.

Partin, R. Eminent Victorians and Robert E. Lee [by D. S. Freeman]: a cast study. Jnl of the Central Mississippi Valley American Stud Assoc 2 1961.

Merle, G. Strachey au Spectator. Etudes Anglaises 18 1965.

— Eléments pour une étude biographique de Strachey. Etudes Anglaises 19 1966.

— Eminent Victorians de Strachey. Langues Modernes 1 1968.

Holroyd, M. Lytton Strachey: a critical biography. 2 vols 1967–68.

Rees, G. A case for treatment: the world of Strachey. Encounter 20 1968.

M.P.

JOHN SAINT LOE STRACHEY
1860–1927

§1

The great bread riots: or what came of fair trade, by S.L.S. 1885, 1903 (as by Strachey).

The best plays of the old dramatists Beaumont and Fletcher. Ed Strachey 2 vols 1887 (5 plays), [1904] (10 plays) (Mermaid ser).

How England became a republic: a romance. Bristol [1891].

National workshops. In A policy of free exchange, ed T. Mackay 1894.

Industrial and social life and the empire. 1895. Pt 2 of The citizen and the state, by E. J. Mathew.

From grave to gay: being essays and studies. 1897.

The ethics of journalism. 1908. Pamphlet.

The practical wisdom of the Bible. Ed Strachey 1908.

The problems and perils of socialism: letters to a working man. 1908.

A new way of life. 1909. Papers on national defence rptd from Spectator.

The adventure of living: a subjective autobiography. 1922, New York 1922.

Economics of the hour. [1923], New York 1923.

The referendum. 1924.

The river of life: a diary. [1924], New York 1924.

John Dryden, [selected poems]. Ed Strachey [1925].

The madonna of the barricades: being the memoirs of George Lord Chertsey 1847, '48, '49. 1925, New York [1925]. Fiction.

American soundings. [1926], New York 1926.

Strachey edited Cornhill Mag 1896–7, edited and was proprietor of Spectator 1898–1925, contributing until 1927, and edited, with C. L. Graves, Liberal Unionist 1887–92. He also contributed to Saturday Rev, Pall Mall Gazette, Manchester Guardian etc.

§2

Collins, J. In his The doctor looks at literature, 1923.

'E. T. Raymond' (E. R. Thompson). Five editors. In his Portraits of the new century, 1928.

Strachey, A. St Loe Strachey: his life and his paper. 1930.

N.J.S

ALPHONSE JAMES ALBERT SYMONS
1900–41

§1

A bibliography of the first editions of books by W. B. Yeats. 1924 (First Editions Club).

Bierce, A. Ten tales. Introd by Symons 1925.

H. D. Lowry, 1864–1906. [1925]. Memoir and bibliography.

An anthology of 'Nineties' verse. Ed Symons 1928.

Emin, the governor of Equatoria. 1928, 1950 (as Emin, governor of Equatoria).

An episode in the life of the queen of Sheba. 1929 (priv ptd, 150 copies).

H. M. Stanley. 1933, New York 1933.

Rolfe, F. ('Baron Corvo'). The desire and the pursuit of the whole: a romance of modern Venice. Ed Symons 1934.

The quest for Corvo: an experiment in biography. 1934, New York 1934, London 1952 (introds by N. Birkett and S. Leslie), 1955 (introd by J. Symons), East Lansing 1955.

Rolfe, F. ('Baron Corvo') and C. Gordon. Hubert's Arthur: being certain curious documents found among the literary remains of Mr. N. C. Ed with introd by Symons, 1935.

The epicure and the epicurean. In The epicure's anthology, ed N. Quennell 1936.

The Nonesuch century: an appraisal, a personal note and a bibliography of the first hundred books issued by the press, 1923–34. 1936. By Symons et al.

Symons edited Book-Collector's Quart *1930–4 (with D. Flower)*.

§2

Symons, J. A. J. A. Symons: his life and speculations. 1950.

P. C.

RICHARD HENRY TAWNEY
1880–1962

§1

The agrarian problem in the sixteenth century. 1912, New York 1961.

Poverty as an industrial problem. 1913 (London School of Economics Memoranda on Problems of Poverty).

English economic history: select documents. Ed A. E. Bland and P. A. Brown, and Tawney 1914.

The establishment of minimum rates in the chain-making industry under the Trade Boards Act of 1909. 1914 (London School of Economics Stud in the Minimum Wage).

The establishment of minimum rates in the tailoring industry under the Trade Boards Act of 1909. 1915 (London School of Economics Stud in the Minimum Wage).

The acquisitive society. New York 1920, London 1921.

Life and struggles of William Lovett, with an introduction by R. H. Tawney. 2 vols 1920, New York 1920.

Secondary education for all: a policy for Labour, edited for the Education Advisory Committee of the Labour Party by R. H. Tawney. [1922].

Tudor economic documents. 3 vols 1924, New York 1963. Ed Tawney, with E. Power.

The British Labor Movement. New Haven 1925.

Wilson, T. A discourse upon usury, with an historical introduction by R. H. Tawney. 1925, New York 1963.

Religion and the rise of capitalism. 1926, New York [1926].

Studies in economic history: the collected papers of George Unwin. 1927. Ed with memoir by Tawney.

Equality. 1931, [1931] (rev), New York [1931], London 1952 (rev with new ch), New York 1961, London 1964 (introd by R. M. Titmuss), New York 1965.

Land and labour in China. 1932, New York 1964.

The reorganisation of education in China. 1932. With C. H. Becker.

The attack and other papers. 1953, New York 1953.

Business and politics under James I: Lionel Cranfield as merchant and minister. Cambridge 1958.

The radical tradition: twelve essays on politics, education and literature. 1964, New York 1964. Ed R. Hinden; includes a selection of pamphlets, lectures, etc previously pbd separately.

Tawney edited Stud in Economic and Social History *from 1934 (with E. Power), and was joint editor with E. Lipson of* Economic History Rev, *1926–33*.

§2

Nelson, W. H. In Some modern historians of Britain: essays in honor of R. L. Schuyler, ed H. Ausubel [et al], New York 1951.

Williams, R. In his Culture and society 1780–1950, 1958.

Ashton, T. S. Tawney. Proc Br Acad 48 1962.

Toynbee, A. J. The Tawneys. In his Acquaintances, 1967.

J. M. P.

ALAN JOHN PERCIVALE TAYLOR
b. 1906

Selections

Europe: grandeur and decline. 1967 (Pelican). Selected from From Napoleon to Stalin, Rumours of wars and Englishmen and others.

§1

The Italian problem in European diplomacy 1847–49. Manchester 1934.

Germany's first bid for colonies 1884–5: a move in Bismarck's European policy. 1938, New York 1967.

The Habsburg monarchy 1815–1918: a history of the Austrian empire and Austria-Hungary. 1941, 1948 (rewritten), New York 1965.

The course of German history: a survey of the development of Germany since 1815. 1945, New York 1946.

From Napoleon to Stalin: comments on European history. 1950.

Rumours of wars. 1952. Essays.

The struggle for mastery in Europe 1848–1918. Oxford 1954.

Bismarck: the man and the statesman. 1955, New York 1955.

Englishmen and others. 1956. Essays.

The trouble makers: dissent over foreign policy 1792–1939. 1957, Bloomington 1958.

Origins of the second world war. 1961, New York 1962.

The first world war: an illustrated history. 1963, New York 1964.

Politics in wartime and other essays. 1964, New York 1965. Includes single lectures previously pbd separately.

English history 1914–45. Oxford 1965 (Oxford History of England 15).

From Sarajevo to Potsdam. 1966, New York 1967.

War by time-table: how the first World War began. 1969.

Taylor compiled A select list of books on European history 1815–1914 *(with A. Bullock). He edited the* Communist Manifesto, *Lord Beaverbrooks's* Abdication of King Edward VIII, *a* History of the twentieth century *(with J. M. Roberts),* Essays presented to Sir Lewis Namier *(with R. Pares) and (with others)* Churchill's History of the English speaking peoples. *He tr and edited various foreign historical works and reviewed for* New Statesman *1965–6 and* Listener *1966.*

§2

Namier, L. B. The course of German history. In his Facing East, 1947. Essay review.
Segel, E. B. Taylor and history. Review of Politics 26 1964.
Briggs, A. Taylor's own times. Encounter 26 1966.
Littlewood, J. C. F. 'The rise of the people'. Cambridge Quart 1 1966. Essay-review of English history 1914–45.
A.P.H.

SIR HAROLD WILLIAM VAZEILLE TEMPERLEY
1879–1939

§1

Life of Canning. 1905.
Great Britain: 1815–32. In Cambridge modern history vol 10, Cambridge 1907.
The revolution and the revolution settlement in Great Britain: 1, England 1687–1702; Party government under Queen Anne. In Cambridge modern history vol 5, Cambridge 1908.
The age of Walpole and the Pelhams. In Cambridge modern history vol 6, Cambridge 1909.
Great Britain and her colonies: 1, the new colonial policy 1840–70. In Cambridge modern history vol 11, Cambridge 1909.
Senates and upper chambers: their use and functions in the modern state, with a chapter on the reform of the House of Lords. 1910.
Frederic the Great and Kaiser Joseph: an episode of war and diplomacy in the eighteenth century. 1915, 1968 (introd by H. Butterfield).
History of Serbia. 1917.
The second year of the League: a study of the second assembly of the League of Nations. [1922].
The foreign policy of Canning 1820–7. In Cambridge history of British foreign policy vol 2, Cambridge 1923.
The foreign policy of Canning 1822–7: England, the Neo-Holy Alliance and the New World. 1925, 1966 (introd by H. Butterfield), Hamden Conn 1966.
Europe in the nineteenth century 1784–1914. 1927, 1929 (rev and corrected), 1932 (rev and enlarged as Europe in the nineteenth and twentieth centuries 1789–1932), 1934 (extended to 1938), 1940 (with supplementary section on 1938–9 by L. M. Penson), 1952 (rev and ed L. M. Penson). With A. J. Grant.
The peace of Paris. In Cambridge history of the British empire vol 1, Cambridge 1929.
Europe: the revolutionary and Napoleonic eras. 1935. Rptd with addns from Europe in the nineteenth and twentieth centuries 1789–1932, 1932, above. With A. J. Grant.
England and the near east: the Crimea. 1936, Hamden Conn 1964. 3 vols planned; only one pbd.
Temperley also wrote an introd to H. Marczali, Hungary in the eighteenth century, *Cambridge 1910. He also wrote a number of pamphlets for the Historical Assoc.*

Works Edited by Temperley

A history of the peace conference of Paris. 6 vols 1920–4. Temperley contributed chs to these vols.
The unpublished diary and political sketches of Princess Lieven, together with some of her letters. 1925.
British documents on the origins of the war 1898–1914, 11 vols 1926–38. With G. P. Gooch.
Bury, J. B. Selected essays. Cambridge 1930.
Scenes from modern history by great imaginative writers. 1931.

Studies in Anglo-French history during the eighteenth, nineteenth and twentieth centuries. Cambridge 1935, Freeport NY 1967. With A. A. Coville.
A century of diplomatic blue books 1814–1914. Cambridge 1938, New York 1966. With L. M. Penson. Lists with historical introds.
Foundations of British foreign policy, from Pitt 1792 to Salisbury 1902: or documents old and new. Cambridge 1938, New York 1966. With L. M. Penson.
Temperley also edited Annual Bull of Historical Lit *1922–8 and* Cambridge Historical Jnl *1923–38.*

§2

Gooch, G. P. Harold Temperley. Proc Br Acad 25 1940; rptd (rev) in Maria Theresa and other studies, 1951.
Faissler, M. In Some historians of modern Europe: essays in historiography by former students of the department of history of the university of Chicago, ed B. E. Schmitt. Chicago 1942.

THOMAS FREDERICK TOUT
1855–1929

Bibliographies

Tout, M. In Essays in medieval history presented to Tout, ed A. G. Little and F. M. Powicke, Manchester 1925. Suppl in A. G. Little's memoir of Tout, History new ser 14 1930.
A select bibliography of the historical writings of Tout. In Collected papers of Tout vol 1, Manchester 1932. *See* §1, below.

§1

Edward the first. 1893 (Twelve English Statesmen ser).
The empire and the papacy 918–1273. 1898 (Periods of European history vol 2, ed A. Hassall).
Germany and the empire. In Cambridge modern history vol 1, Cambridge 1902.
The history of England from the accession of Henry III to the death of Edward III, 1216–1377. 1905, 1920 (with corrections and addns). (Political history of England, ed W. Hurst and R. L. Poole).
The place of the reign of Edward II in English history. Manchester 1914, 1936 (rev H. Johnstone).
Chapters in the administrative history of medieval England: the wardrobe, the chamber and the small seals. 6 vols Manchester 1920–33; 1937 (vols 1 and 2 only, corrected).
France and England: their relations in the middle ages and now. Manchester 1922.
The collected papers of T. F. Tout: with a memoir by F. M. Powicke and bibliography. 3 vols Manchester 1932–34.
Tout also pbd several school text-books, including Longmans' historical series for schools, *1902 etc.*; A short analysis of English history, *1891 (in* History Primers, *ed J. R. Green); and parts 2 and 3 of* History of England *by F. Y. Powell and Tout, 1898, 1890. With H. Johnstone he edited* State trials of the reign of Edward the first 1289–93, *1906. He also edited* Historical essays by members of Owens College, *1902, and edited and completed* The Chartist movement *by M. Howell, 1925. He wrote an introd for* The register of John de Hatton, Bishop of Carlisle 1292–1324, *transcribed by W. N. Thompson, 2 vols 1906, 1913. He pbd many lectures ptd from* Bull of the John Rylands Lib *(most further ptd in his collected papers above), and made contributions to* Encyclopaedia Britannica, Dictionary of English history, *ed S. Low and F. S. Pulling, and* DNB.

§2

Powicke, F. M. Tout. Proc Br Acad 15 1932; rptd in The collected papers of Tout vol 1, 1932 above, and in Powicke's Modern historians and the study of history, 1955.

P.C.

ARNOLD JOSEPH TOYNBEE
b. 1889

Bibliographies

Sattler, R-J. Zur Diskussion um Toynbee: Würdigung und Kritik seines Werkes in deutschen Zeitschriften. Internationales Jahrbuch für Geschichtsunterricht 3 1954.

Popper, M. A bibliography of the works in English of Toynbee, 1910–54. 1955. Foreword by Toynbee; includes contributions to books and periodicals.

Greenslade, R. Toynbee: a checklist. Twentieth-Century Lit 2 1956. Includes contributions to books and periodicals.

O'Callaghan, P. A selective bibliography of A study of history. Historical Bull 34 1956.

Anderle, D. F. Die Toynbee-Kritik: das universalhistorische System Toynbees im Urteil der Wissenschaft. Saeculum 9 1958. Reprint of M. Popper's bibliography above (abridged), with a survey of literature on Toynbee.

Rule, J. C. and B. S. Crosby. Bibliography of works on Toynbee, 1946–60. History & Theory 4 1965.

§1

Greek policy since 1882. 1914. Pamphlet.

Armenian atrocities: the murder of a nation, with a speech delivered by Lord Bryce in the House of Lords. 1915, 1915 (rev and enlarged).

Nationality and the war. 1915.

The new Europe: some essays in reconstruction. 1915.

The Belgian deportations, with statement by Viscount Bryce. [1916].

The destruction of Poland: a study in German efficiency. [1916]. Pamphlet.

The German terror in Belgium. 1917, New York 1917.

The German terror in France. 1917, New York 1917. Continuation of the above.

'The murderous tyranny of the Turks'. 1917, New York 1917. Pamphlet. Preface by Viscount Bryce.

Turkey: a past and a future. 1917, New York 1917.

The League in the East. 1920. Pamphlet.

The Western question in Greece and Turkey: a study in the contact of civilizations. 1922, 1923 (rev with new preface). See G. M. Mélas, The Turk as he is: an answer to a libel, Hove [1922].

Greek civilization and character: the self-revelation of ancient Greek society. 1924. Anthology; introd and trn by Toynbee.

Greek historical thought from Homer to the age of Heraclius. 1924, Boston 1950. Anthology; introd and trn by Toynbee with 2 pieces newly tr by G. Murray.

The world after the Peace Conference: being an epilogue to the History of the Peace Conference of Paris [ed H. W. V. Temperley] and a prologue to the Survey of international affairs, 1920–3. 1925, New York 1965.

Turkey. 1926, New York 1927. With K. P. Kirkwood.

The conduct of British Empire foreign relations since the Peace Settlement. 1928.

World order or downfall?: six broadcast talks. [1930].

A journey to China: or things which are seen. 1931.

Britain and the modern world order: a synopsis of talks broadcast April–June 1932. 1932. With J. L. Hammond.

A study of history. 12 vols 1934–61. Vols 1–3, 1935 (corrected); vols 1–10 (abridged by D. C. Somervell, preface by Toynbee) 1946–57, New York 1947–57.

—— War and civilization. New York 1950, London 1951. Selected by A. V. Fowler from above, preface by Toynbee.

—— Marxism, socialism and Christianity. Bromdon, Bridgnorth [1959?]. Rptd from vol 5 of above.

Civilization on trial. New York 1948, London 1948, New York 1960 (with The world and the West, 1953, below).

The prospects of Western civilization. New York 1949 (400 copies). Bampton lectures, on subjects to be treated in vol 12 of A study of history, 1961.

War and civilization. 1950. See A study of history, 1934–61, above.

Twelve men of action in Graeco-Roman history. Boston [1952]. Anthology; tr with an introd by Toynbee.

The world and the West: the BBC Reith lectures, 1952. 1953, New York 1953, 1960 (with Civilization on trial, 1948, above).

A study of history: what the book is for, how the book took shape. [1954?]. Pamphlet.

An historian's approach to religion, based on Gifford lectures. 1956, New York 1956.

Christianity among the religions of the world. New York 1957, London 1958. Lectures.

Democracy in the atomic age. Melbourne 1957. Lectures.

East to west: a journey round the world. 1958, New York 1958.

Hellenism: the history of a civilization. 1959, New York 1959.

One world and India. [New Delhi] 1960. Azad Memorial Lectures.

Between Oxus and Jumna. 1961, New York 1961. Travel.

The Toynbee debate. [Cairo] 1961. Pamphlet. On the Arabs in Palestine.

America and the world revolution: public lectures, University of Pennsylvania, 1961. 1962, New York 1962.

The economy of the Western hemisphere. 1962. Lectures.

Importance of the Arab world. [Cairo] 1962. Lectures.

The present-day experiment in Western civilization. 1962. Lectures.

The Toynbee lectures on the Middle East and problems of underdeveloped countries. [Cairo] 1962.

Comparing notes: a dialogue across a generation. [1963]. With P. Toynbee.

Janus at seventy-five. New York 1964. Autobiography.

Between Niger and Nile. 1965. Travel.

Hannibal's legacy: the Hannibalic wars' effect on Roman life. 2 vols 1965.

Change and habit: the challenge of our time. 1966, New York 1966.

Acquaintances. 1967. Reminiscences.

Between Maule and Amazon. 1967. Travel.

Cities of destiny. Ed Toynbee [1967].

The crucible of Christianity: Judaism, Hellenism and the historical background to the Christian faith. Ed Toynbee 1969.

Experiences. 1969. Sequel to Acquaintances, 1967, above.

Some problems of Greek history. 1969.

Toynbee edited and contributed to a number of collections of papers on foreign affairs. He also edited, for the Royal Inst of International Affairs, the Survey of International Affairs, 1920/3–1925, vol 1, 1926–7 and (with others) 1928–38, vol 1, 1939–46, and Documents on International Affairs, 1939–46, vol 1.

§2

Feibleman, J. K. Toynbee's theory of history. In his Revival of realism, Chapel Hill 1946 (for 1947).

Chase, R. Toynbee: the historian as artist. Amer Scholar 16 1947.

Lean, T. A study of Toynbee. Horizon 15 1947; rptd in Montague, 1956, below.

Macdonald, F. Toynbee as an artist. Approach Fall 1947.

Neilson, F. Toynbee's Study of history. In his Modern man and the liberal arts, New York 1947.

Barnes, H. E. Toynbee: Orosius and Augustine in modern dress. In his Introduction to the history of sociology, Chicago 1948.

Geyl, P., A. J. Toynbee and P. A. Sorokin. The pattern of the past: can we determine it? Boston 1949.

Geyl, P. From Ranke to Toynbee: five lectures on histories and historiographical problems. Northampton Mass 1952.

— Toynbee the prophet. JHI 16 1955; rptd (with other essays on Toynbee) in his Debates with historians, Groningen 1955, and in Montague, 1956, below.

— Toynbee's answer. Amsterdam 1961. (Mededelingen der Koninklijke Nederlandse Akademie van Wetenschappen, Afd. Letterkunde new ser 24). On A study of history vol 12, Reconsiderations.

Lattimore, O. Spengler and Toynbee. Atlantic Monthly 181 1948.

Watkins, L. H. Toynbee and the anthropologists. Contour 3 1948.

Wolfe, B. D. Dissenting opinion on Toynbee. Amer Mercury 64 1947.

Sorokin, P. A. In his Social philosophies of an age of crisis, Boston 1950.

Erdmann, K. D. Toynbee – eine Zwischenbilanz. Archiv für Kulturgeschichte 33 1951.

Francovich, G. Toynbee, Heidegger y Whitehead. Preface by Toynbee, Buenos Aires 1951.

Drees, L. Die Botschaft Toynbees an die abendländische Welt. Stuttgart 1952.

Rossi, P. Indagine storica e visione della storia in Toynbee. Turin 1952.

Kirkwood, K. P. Arnold J. Toynbee, philosopher of history. Karachi 1953. Address.

Sweezy, P. M. Toynbee's universal history. In his Present as history, New York 1953.

Hudson, G. F. Toynbee versus Gibbon. Twentieth Century 156 1954.

Jerrold, D. The lie about the West: a response to Toynbee's challenge. 1954. On The world and the West, 1953. See 'Counsels of hope'—the Toynbee–Jerrold controversy: letters to the editor of TLS with leading articles, 1954.

Zahn, E. F. M. Toynbee und das Problem der Geschichte: eine Auseinandersetzung mit dem Evolutionismus. Cologne 1954.

Anderle, O. F. Das universalhistorische System Toynbees. Frankfurt 1955.

— Die Toynbee-Kritik: das universalhistorische System Toynbees im Urteil der Wissenschaft. Saeculum 9 1958.

Blackmur, R. P. Reflections of Toynbee. Kenyon Rev 17 1955; rptd in his A primer of ignorance, New York 1967.

Eban, E. The Toynbee heresy. New York [1956?] Address; rptd in Montague, 1956, below.

Fiess, E. Toynbee as poet. JHI 16 1955; rptd in Montague, 1956, below.

Kaufmann, W. Toynbee and super-history. Partisan Rev 22 1955; rptd in Montague, 1956, below.

Kremp, H. Die Überwindung der Kulturzyklentheorie Spenglers durch die Weltalterlehre der Heidelberger Schule und die Toynbee'sche Lehre von der Filiation der Kulturen. Frankfurt 1955.

Martin, P. W. Experiment in depth: a study in the work of Jung, Eliot and Toynbee. 1955.

Woolf, L. What is history? Political Quart 26 1955. Essay-review of A study of history, 1934–61 and other works.

Diogenes no 13 1956. Special no: The contribution of Toynbee.

Hourani, A. Toynbee's vision of history. Dublin Rev 229 1956.

Montagu, A. (ed). Toynbee and history: critical essays and reviews. Boston 1956. Includes items listed separately, above. With contributions and comment by Toynbee.

Samuel, M. The Professor and the fossil: some observations on Toynbee's Study of history. New York 1956. On Toynbee's view of the Jews.

Crubellier, M. Sens de l'histoire et religion: Comte, Northrop, Sorokin, Toynbee. [Paris] 1957.

Herberg, W. Toynbee—historian or religious prophet? Queens Quart 64 1957.

Trevor-Roper, H. Toynbee's millenium. Encounter 8 1957; rptd in his Historical essays, 1957.

White, H. V. Collingwood and Toynbee: transitions in English historical thought. Eng Miscellany (Rome) 8 1957; reply by L. Dondoli (in Italian) ibid 15 1964.

Mason, H. L. Toynbee's approach to world politics. New Orleans 1958.

Bierstedt, R. Toynbee and sociology. Br Jnl of Sociology 10 1959.

Sullivan, R. E. Toynbee's debtors. South Atlantic Quart 58 1959.

Dray, W. H. Toynbee's search for historical laws. History & Theory 1 1960.

Fox, E. W. History and Mr Toynbee. Vancouver Quart Rev 36 1960.

— Divine dilemma of Toynbee. Vancouver Quart Rev 39 1963.

Centre Culturel International de Cerisy-la-Salle 10–19 juillet 1958. L'histoire et ses interprétations: entretiens autour de Toynbee. Paris 1961.

Gargan, E. T. (ed). The intent of Toynbee's history: a co-operative appraisal. Chicago 1961. Papers presented at a conference at Loyola Univ, Chicago, 1955; preface by Toynbee.

Fàbrega, V. Toynbee i el problema del pluralisme religiós de la història. Barcelona 1962.

Walsh, W. H. Toynbee reconsidered. Philosophy 38 1963. Essay-review of A study of history vol 12, Reconsiderations, 1961.

Mazlish, B. In his Riddle of history: the great speculators from Vico to Freud, New York 1966.

Kaupp, P. Toynbee and the Jews. Wiener Lib Bull 21 1967.

— Toynbee und die Juden: eine kritische Untersuchung der Darstellung des Judentums im Gesamtwerk Toynbees, mit einer ausgewählten Bibliographie und zwei Beiträge von Toynbee. Meisenheim am Glan 1967.

M.P.

GEORGE MACAULAY TREVELYAN
1876–1962

Bibliographies

Plumb, J. H. Trevelyan: a select bibliography. In his G. M. Trevelyan, 1951, §2, below.

§1

England in the age of Wycliffe. 1899, 1904 (rev), New York 1963.

The Peasants' Rising and the Lollards: a collection of unpublished documents forming an appendix to England in the age of Wycliffe. 1899. Ed Trevelyan, with E. Powell.

The past and the future. In The heart of the empire: discussions of problems of modern city life in England. 1901. By various authors. Ed C. F. G. Masterman.

England under the Stuarts. 1904, 1925 (rev and corrected), 1946 (rev), New York 1949, London 1960 (with new bibliography) (Pelican). First 2 chs ed J. Turral 1908 for schools (as English life three hundred years ago).

The poetry and philosophy of George Meredith. 1906, New York 1966.

Garibaldi's defence of the Roman republic, 1848–9. 1907. See also Garibaldi, 1933, below.

Garibaldi and the thousand: Naples and Sicily 1859–60. 1909. See also Garibaldi, 1933, below.

English songs of Italian freedom, selected with an introduction by Trevelyan 1911.

Garibaldi and the making of Italy. 1911. *See also* Garibaldi, 1933, below.

King, H. E. H. Letters and recollections of Mazzini. Ed Trevelyan 1912.

Clio, a muse, and other essays literary and pedestrian. 1913, 1919 (enlarged, as The recreations of an historian), 1930 (enlarged, as Clio, a muse and other essays).

The life of John Bright. 1913, Boston 1913.

Scenes from Italy's war. London 1919, Boston 1919.

Lord Grey of the Reform Bill: being the life of Charles, second Earl Grey. 1920.

British history in the nineteenth century 1782–1901. 1922, 1937 (enlarged as British history in the nineteenth century and after 1782–1919), New York 1962.

Manin and the Venetian revolution of 1848. 1923.

History of England. 1926, 1937 (rev and enlarged), 1952 (corrected), Garden City NY 1953, London 1956 (with illustrations, as Illustrated history of England), 1959 (abridged, as A shortened history of England) (Pelican).

Must England's beauty perish? a plea on behalf of the National Trust for Places of Historic Interest or Natural Beauty. 1929.

Select documents of Queen Anne's reign down to the union with Scotland 1702–7. Ed Trevelyan, Cambridge 1929.

England under Queen Anne. 3 vols 1930–4. Vol 1, Blenheim; vol 2, Ramillies and the Union with Scotland; vol 3, The peace and the protestant succession. Chs 1–4 of Blenheim rptd 1932 (as The England of Queen Anne).

Sir George Otto Trevelyan: a memoir. 1932.

Garibaldi: being Garibaldi's defence of the Roman republic, Garibaldi and the thousand, Garibaldi and the making of Italy. 3 pts 1933.

Grey of Fallodon: being the life of Sir Edward Grey, afterwards Viscount Grey of Fallodon. 1937, Boston 1937.

The English revolution 1688–9. 1938, New York [1939].

English social history: a survey of six centuries, Chaucer to Queen Victoria. 1942, 4 vols 1949–52 (with illustrations, as Illustrated English social history).

Trinity College: an historical sketch. Cambridge 1943.

An autobiography and other essays. 1949. Includes single lectures previously pbd separately.

A layman's love of letters. 1954 (Clark lectures 1953).

Trevelyan pbd an edn of The poetical works of George Meredith, *1912,* Selected poetical works of George Meredith, *1955, and pbd* The Meredith pocket book, *1906. He also pbd an edn of Macaulay's* Lays of ancient Rome and other historical poems, *1928, and compiled* Carlyle: an anthology, *1953.*

§2

Plumb, J. H. G. M. Trevelyan. 1951 (Br Council pamphlet).

Winkler, H. R. In Some 20th century historians, ed S. W. Halperin, Chicago 1961.

Clark, G. N. Trevelyan. Proc Br Acad 49 1963.

J. M. P.

HUGH REDWALD TREVOR-ROPER
b. 1914

§1

Archbishop Laud, 1573–1645. 1940, 1962 (corrected, with new preface), Hamden Conn. 1962.

The last days of Hitler. 1947, New York 1947, London 1950 (new introd), 1952 (omitting some footnotes and appendices), 1965 (with new introd and footnotes), 1962 (rev), New York 1962 (with new preface).

The gentry, 1540–1640. [1953] (Economic History Rev suppl 1).

Hitler's table talk 1941–4. 1953. Introd, The mind of Adolf Hitler, by Trevor-Roper.

The Bormann letters. 1954. Ed Trevor-Roper.

Historical essays. 1957, New York 1957 (as Men and events: historical essays), 1966 (as Historical essays).

The testament of Adolf Hitler. 1961. Selections with introd by Trevor-Roper.

Hitler's war directives 1939–45. 1964, New York 1965 (as Blitzkrieg to defeat: Hitler's war directives 1939–45). Ed Trevor-Roper from Hitler's Weisungen für die Kriegführung 1939–45 by W. Hubatsch.

The rise of Christian Europe. [1965], New York 1965.

Religion, the Reformation and social change, and other essays. 1967, New York 1968 (as The crisis of the seventeenth century: religion, the Reformation and social change). Includes contributions to previously pbd Festschriften.

The Philby affair: espionage, treason and secret services. 1968.

Trevor-Roper also edited Essays in British history presented to K. Feiling, *1964;* The poems of Richard Corbett, Oxford *1965 (with J. A. W. Bennet);* The age of expansion: Europe and the world 1559–1660, *and selections from Gibbon and Macaulay.*

P. C.

WILFRED BATTEN LEWIS TROTTER
1872–1939

§1

Instincts of the herd in peace and war. 1916, 1919 (enlarged and corrected), New York 1947, London 1953 (ed with index and notes R. W. Chapman).

Collected papers. Ed W. R. Trotter 1941.

§2

Elliott, T. R. In Obituary Notices of Fellows of the Royal Soc 3 1941. Includes bibliography.

J. M. P.

SIR PAUL GAVRILOVICH VINOGRADOFF
1854–1925

Bibliographies

In The collected papers of P. Vinogradoff vol 2, 1928, below.

§1

Villainage in England: essays in English mediaeval history. Oxford 1892 (for 1891).

The growth of the manor. 1905, 1911 (rev).

English society in the eleventh century: essays in English mediaeval history. Oxford 1908.

Roman law in mediaeval Europe. New York 1909, Oxford 1929 (preface by F. De Zulueta).

Social and economic conditions of the Roman empire in the fourth century. In The Cambridge medieval history vol 1, Cambridge 1911.

Essays in legal history read before the International Congress of Historical Studies held in London in 1913. 1913. Ed Vinogradoff.

Foundations of society—origins of feudalism. In The Cambridge medieval history vol 2, Cambridge 1913.

Commonsense in law. [1914], 1946 (rev H. G. Hanbury).

Russia: the psychology of a nation. 1914. Rptd from The Times.

The Russian problem. 1914, New York [1915].

Survey of the Honour of Denbigh, 1334. 1914. Ed Vino-
gradoff and F. Morgan.
Self-government in Russia. 1915.
The reconstruction of Russia: essays edited by Sir P.
Vinogradoff. 1919.
Outlines of historical jurisprudence. 2 vols 1920–2. Introd
reissued 1923 (as Historical jurisprudence).
Feudalism. In The Cambridge medieval history vol 3,
Cambridge 1922.
Historical types of international law. Leyden 1923.
Custom and right. Oslo and Cambridge Mass 1925.
The collected papers of Paul Vinogradoff, with a memoir by
H. A. L. Fisher. Ed L. Vinogradoff 2 vols Oxford 1928.
*Vinogradoff also pbd several works in Russian (for details see
bibliography in his Collected papers, above). He edited
Oxford studies in social and legal history, and the Selden
Soc edn of the Yearbooks of Edward II.*

§2

Holdsworth, W. S. Sir Paul Vinogradoff 1854–1925. Proc
Br Acad 11 1925.
Fisher, H. A. L. Paul Vinogradoff: a memoir. Oxford
1927. Rptd in The collected papers, 1928, above.
N. J. S.

GRAHAM WALLAS
1858–1932

§1

The life of Francis Place 1771–1854. 1898, 1918 (rev),
New York 1919.
Human nature in politics. 1908, New York 1921.
The great society: a psychological analysis. 1914, New
York 1914.
Our social heritage. 1921, New Haven 1921.
The art of thought. 1926, 1945 (abridged by M. Wallas);
New York [1926].
Social judgment. 1934, New York [1935]. Ed M. Wallas.
Men and ideas: essays. 1940. Ed M. Wallas. Contains
a biographical note.

§2

Dickinson, T. H. Dramatic art and The great society.
Forum 53 1915.
Laski, H. J. Life of Francis Place. Dial 68 1920.
— Lowes Dickinson and Wallas. Political Quart 3 1932.
Barnes, H. E. Wallas and the attempt to provide a synthetic
interpretation of political psychology. Amer Jnl of
Sociology 28 1922.
— Wallas and the socio-psychological basis of politics
and social reconstruction. In Introduction to the history
of sociology, ed H. E. Barnes, Chicago 1948.
Birrell, A. Radical tailor of Charing Cross. In his More
obiter dicta, 1924. About Wallas's Life of Place.
Economica 12 1932. Obituary appreciations by J. Stamp,
H. J. Laski, W. Beveridge, S. Webb.
Ratcliffe, S. K. Early Fabians. In Great democrats, ed
E. B. Brown 1934.
Lerner, M. Wallas: the Fabian or the tiger? In his Ideas
are weapons, New York 1939.
Waldo, D. Wallas: reason and emotion in social change. Jnl
of Social Philosophy & Jurisprudence 7 1942.
Beardsley, M. C. Rationality in conduct: Wallas and
Pareto. Ethics 54 1944.
Chapman, D. Wallas and the study of social problems in
industry. Occupational Psychology 24 1950.
Bowle, J. Modern sociologists: Durkheim on environ-
ment; Wallas and social psychology. In his Politics and
Opinion in the Nineteenth Century, 1954.
Namier, L. B. Human nature in politics. In his Person-
alities and powers, 1955.

Mack, M. P. Wallas' new individualism. Western Political
Quart 11 1958.
Qualter, T. H. Manipulations of popular impulse: Wallas
revisited. Canadian Jnl of Economics 25 1959.
H. M. R.

EVELYN ARTHUR
ST JOHN WAUGH
1903–66
See cols 764–8, above.

BEATRICE WEBB, née POTTER
1858–1943
For location of mss see under Sidney Webb, col 1231, below.

Bibliographies
Tawney, R. H. Proc Br Acad 29 1943.

§1

*For works written in collaboration with Sidney Webb see
under Sidney Webb, below.*

The docks; The tailoring trade; The Jewish community.
In Life and labour of the people in London, by C. Booth
assisted by various contributors, 2 vols 1889–91, 10 vols
1892–97, 17 vols 1902–3.
The Co-operative Movement in Great Britain. 1891, New
York 1899, London 1930 (with additional preface).
The economics of factory legislation. In The case for the
Factory Acts [by various authors], ed B. Webb 1901;
rptd 1909 in Socialism and national minimum, by
B. Webb, B. L. Hutchins and the Fabian Soc.
The case for the national minimum [by various authors].
Ed with preface by B. Webb 1913.
The wages of men and women: should they be equal?
[1919].
My apprenticeship. 1926, New York 1926. Autobio-
graphy.
Reminiscences. St Martin's Rev Nov 1928, March 1929.
On the Consumers' Co-operative Movement and science,
religion and politics.
[Credo]. In Living philosophies, by Albert Einstein [et al],
New York 1931; rptd (with postscript, An interposition)
in I believe, [by] W. H. Auden [et al], London 1940.
Diseases of organized society. In The modern state, ed
M. G. A. Adams 1933.
Our partnership. Ed B. Drake, M. I. Cole 1948, New
York 1948. Autobiography.

Diaries
Beatrice Webb's diaries 1912–24, 1924–32. Ed M. I. Cole
2 vols 1952–56.
Visit to New Zealand in 1898: B. Webb's diary, with
entries by S. Webb. Wellington 1959.
American diary 1898. Ed D. A. Shannon, Madison 1963.
The Webbs' Australian diary 1898. Ed A. G. Austin,
Melbourne 1965.
*B. Webb also pbd a number of pamphlets chiefly in connection
with the crusade for the prevention of destitution, factory
legislation, and the Co-operative Movement. For information about joint ventures in journalism with S. Webb see
footnote under S. Webb.*

§2

For works dealing with both the Webbs see under S. Webb.

Cole, M. I. In her Women of today, 1938.
— Beatrice Webb. 1945.
Cole, G. D. H. Beatrice Webb as an economist. Economic
Jnl 53 1943; rptd in The Webbs and their work, ed
M. I. Cole 1949.

Tawney, R. H. Beatrice Webb. Proc Br Acad 29 1943; rptd in his Attack, and other papers 1953.

Leavis, F. R. Mill, Beatrice Webb and the 'English school'. Scrutiny 16 1949; rptd as introd to his edn of Mill on Bentham and Coleridge, 1950.

Letwin, S. B. The pursuit of certainty: Hume, Bentham, Mill, Beatrice Webb. Cambridge 1965.

Muggeridge, K. and R. Adam. Beatrice Webb: a life. 1967.

Hynes, S. L. The Fabians: Mrs Webb and Mr Wells. In his Edwardian turn of mind, Princeton 1968.

SIDNEY JAMES WEBB,
1ST BARON PASSFIELD
1859–1947

The British Library of Political and Economic Science has the Webbs' research collections on trade unionism and local government on which their History of trade unionism, Industrial democracy *and* English local government *were based. It also has their private papers: the Passfield Papers. For a description of these and other Webb collections in the Library, see* Manuscript collections in the British Library of Political and Economic Science, *by C. G. Allen, in* Jnl of the Soc of Archivists 2 1960.

Bibliographies

Tawney, R. H. In Beatrice Webb, Proc Br Acad 29 1943.

§ 1

Works by S. Webb alone, or with authors other than Beatrice Webb.

The basis of socialism: historic. In Fabian essays in socialism, ed G. B. Shaw 1889, ed H. G. Wilshire New York 1891, ed Shaw London 1908 (with new preface), 1920 (with introd by S. Webb), 1931 (with new preface by Shaw), 1948 (with postscript by Shaw entitled Sixty years of Fabianism).

Socialism in England. [Baltimore] 1889, London 1890 (rev), 1908 (with introductory ch).

The eight hours day. [1891]. With H. Cox.

The London programme [of reforms in the administration of the metropolis]. 1891, 1895 (as Vestry and guardian elections, parish councils: the London programme. With new introductory ch).

The reform of London. 1892. An 'Eighty' Club pamphlet.

Labour in the longest reign 1837–97. 1897. Rptd, with alterations, from the Wholesale Co-operative Soc's Annual for 1893.

London education. 1904.

The basis & policy of socialism. 1908. With the L.C.C. and the Fabian Soc. Rptd (rev) from Fabian Tracts.

Secondary education. 1908. Appendix to A century of education, by H. B. Binns.

Social movements. In Cambridge Modern History vol 12, Cambridge 1910; London [1916] (pbd separately with appendix as Towards social democracy? A study of social evolution during the past three-quarters of a century).

Grants in aid: a criticism and a proposal. 1911, 1920 (rev and enlarged).

Great Britain after the war. 1916. With A. Freeman.

How to pay for the war: being ideas offered to the Chancellor of the Exchequer by the Fabian Research Department. Ed S. Webb 1916.

The restoration of trade union conditions. 1917, New York 1917.

The works manager today. 1917.

The story of the Durham miners 1662–1921. 1921.

Reminiscences. St Martin's Rev Oct, Dec 1928, Jan, Feb 1929. On trade unionism, the London County Council, the London School of Economics, the birth of the Labour party.

The future of Soviet communism. In What is ahead of us? by G. D. H. Cole [et al], [1937].

The evolution of local government. 1951. Lectures, rptd from Municipal Jnl 1899.

Works written in collaboration with Beatrice Webb.

The history of trade unionism. 1894, 1920 (rev and extended to 1920), New York 1920.

Industrial democracy. 2 vols 1897, 1 vol 1902 (with new introd), 1920 (with new introd).

Problems of modern industry. 1898, 1902 (with new introd). Essays, each previously pbd separately.

The history of liquor licensing in England, principally from 1700 to 1830. 1903, 1963 (as vol 11 of reissue of English local government, below), Hamden Conn 1963.

Bibliography of road making and maintenance in Great Britain. 1906.

English local government from the Revolution to the Municipal Corporations Act. 9 vols 1906–29:
The parish and the county. 1906.
The manor and the borough. 2 pts 1908.
The story of the King's Highway. 1913.
English prisons under local government. 1922.
Statutory authorities for special purposes. 1922.
English poor law history. 2 pts in 3 vols 1927–29.
11 vols 1963 (with new introds by various authors. The 2 additional vols, English poor law policy and The history of liquor licensing in England, originally pbd separately, 1910 and 1903, respectively), Hamden Conn 1963.

The break-up of the poor law: being part one of the Minority Report of the Poor Law Commission. Ed with introd by S. and B. Webb 1909.

The public organisation of the labour market: being part two of the Minority Report of the Poor Law Commission. Ed with introd by S. and B. Webb 1909.

English poor law policy. 1910, 1963 (as vol 10 of reissue of English local government, above), Hamden Conn 1963.

The state and the doctor. 1910.

The prevention of destitution. 1911.

A constitution for the socialist commonwealth of Great Britain. 1920.

The Consumers' Co-operative Movement. 1921.

The decay of capitalist civilisation. 1923, New York [1923].

Methods of social study. 1932, New York 1968.

Soviet communism: a new civilisation? 2 vols 1935, New York 1936, London 1937 (title without question mark; with postscript), 1941 (new introd by B. Webb. See The truth about Soviet Russia, below).

Is Soviet communism a new civilisation? 1936. Pamphlet. Reprint of epilogue to Soviet communism, above.

Soviet communism: dictatorship or democracy? 1936. Pamphlet.

The truth about Soviet Russia. With a preface on the Webbs by B. Shaw. 1942. Consists mainly of B. Webb's introd to the 1941 reissue of their Soviet communism: a new civilisation, above.

The development of English local government 1689–1835. With introd by G. Clark, 1963. Originally appeared as chs 5 and 6 of their Statutory authorities for special purposes, above.

Diaries

Visit to New Zealand in 1898: Beatrice Webb's diary, with entries by S. Webb. Wellington 1959.

The Webbs' Australian diary 1898. Ed A. G. Austin, Melbourne 1965.

Webb wrote many tracts pbd by the Fabian Soc (see appendix 4 of E. R. Pease: The history of the Fabian Soc, *below, for list of Fabian tracts and other Fabian pbns); lectures and pamphlets on the work of the London County Council; papers for the War Emergency Workers' National Committee (1914–); etc. Many of these were pbd anon.*

With Beatrice Webb he founded the monthly Crusade against destitution, *3 vols 1910–13. Both wrote for it, e.g. their* What syndicalism means (*suppl to vol 3*). New Statesman, *founded by the Webbs in 1913, developed out of* Crusade. *Both wrote for it in its early days. Notable joint contributions were the series of 22 articles* What is socialism? *in vol 1, and the special suppls on co-operation and methods of organisation in the skilled professions (1914–15) and on professional associations (1917) arising out of the Fabian Research Department's enquiry into the control of industry.*

§2

Including works that deal with the Webbs together.

Taylor, G. R. S. Sidney Webb. In his Leaders of socialism, 1908.

Pease, E. R. The history of the Fabian Society. 1916, 1925 (with supplementary ch), 1963 (new introd by M. I. Cole).

'E. T. Raymond' (E. R. Thompson). Mr and Mrs Webb. In his Uncensored celebrities, 1918.

Riddell, G. A. The socialist plan for a new world. In his More things that matter, 1925. On A constitution for the socialist commonwealth of Great Britain.

Hamilton, M. A. Sidney and Beatrice Webb: a study in contemporary biography. [1933].

—— In her Remembering my good friends, 1944. Explanation of the Webbs' conversion to Soviet communism.

Ratcliffe, S. K. The early Fabians. In Great democrats, ed A. B. Brown 1934.

Vannier, W. The problem of social investigation: the method of S. and B. Webb. In Essays in social economics in honor of J. B. Peixotto, Berkeley 1935.

Cole, G. D. H. The Webbs: prophets of the new order. In his Persons & periods, 1938.

Fichter, J. H. Social philosophy of the Webbs. In his Roots of change, New York 1939.

Tawney, R. H. The Webbs and their work. 1945 (pamphlet); rptd in The development of economic thought: great economists in perspective, ed H. W. Spiegel, New York [1952] and in Tawney's Attack and other papers, London 1953.

—— The Webbs in perspective. 1953. Pamphlet.

Cole, M. I. Social services and the Webb tradition. 1946. Pamphlet.

—— (ed). The Webbs and their work. 1949. Essays by various authors.

—— Beatrice and Sidney Webb. 1955. Pamphlet.

—— The story of Fabian socialism. 1961.

—— The Webbs and social theory. Br Jnl of Sociology 12 1961.

Laski, H. J. The Webbs and Soviet communism. 1947. Lecture.

Webb, B. Our partnership. Ed B. Drake, M. I. Cole 1948. On the earlier years of the marriage of S. and B. Webb.

—— Diaries, 1912–24, 1924–32. Ed M. I. Cole 2 vols 1952–56.

Oxnam, G. B. The scholar as social reformer: S. and B. Webb. In his Personalities in social reform, New York 1950.

Russell, B. S. and B. Webb. In his Portraits from memory, 1956.

Lancaster, L. W. The Fabians: S. and B. Webb. In his Hegel to Dewey, 1959.

Fremantle, A. M. H. This little band of prophets: the story of the gentle Fabians. 1960.

Macrae, D. G. The Webbs and their work. In his Ideology and society, 1961.

Simey, T. S. The contribution of S. and B. Webb to sociology. Br Jnl of Sociology 12 1961.

Gregory, R. G. Sidney Webb and East Africa: Labour's experiment with the doctrine of native paramountcy. Berkeley 1962.

Society for the Study of Labour History. Fourth conference, 27 Jan 1962: the Webbs as historians of trade-unionism. Abstracts of papers by V. L. Allen, A. E.

Musson, H. Clegg. Soc for the Study of Labour History Bull 4 1962.

Strachey, E. J. St L. The Webbs. In his Strangled cry and other unparliamentary papers, 1962.

Stigler, G. J. Shaw, Webb and the theory of Fabian socialism. In his Essays in the history of economics, Chicago 1965.

J. G.

SIR CHARLES KINGSLEY WEBSTER
1886–1961

§1

The Congress of Vienna, 1814–15. [1919], 1934 (enlarged), 1963 (with introd by P. A. Reynolds), New York 1963.

British diplomacy, 1813–15. 1921. Select documents, ed Webster.

The pacification of Europe, 1813–15; The American war and the Treaty of Ghent, 1812–14. In The Cambridge history of British foreign policy, ed A. W. Ward and G. P. Gooch, vol 1, Cambridge 1922.

The foreign policy of Castlereagh, 1815–22. 1925, 1934 (with new appendix).

The European alliance, 1815–25. Calcutta 1929.

The foreign policy of Castlereagh, 1812–15. 1931.

The League of Nations in theory and practice. 1933. With some chs by S. Herbert.

British diplomatic representatives, 1789–1852. Ed S. T. Bindoff, E. F. M. Smith and Webster 1934 (Camden third ser 50).

Britain and the independence of Latin America, 1812–30: select documents from the Foreign Office archives. Ed Webster 2 vols 1938.

British foreign policy since the Second World War. In United Kingdom policy (Royal Institute of International Affairs), 1950.

The foreign policy of Palmerston, 1830–41. 2 vols 1951.

The art and practice of diplomacy. 1961, New York 1962.

The strategic air offensive against Germany, 1939–45. 4 vols 1961 (History of the Second World War). With N. Frankland.

C. K. Webster was a contributor to A history of the peace conference of Paris, ed H. W. V. Temperley, *vols 1 and 2, 1920 and also frequently contributed to* Nation and Athenaeum *1923–5.*

§2

Fagg, J. E. Sir Charles Webster. In Some 20th-century historians, ed W. S. Halperin, Chicago 1961.

Bindoff, S. T. Charles Kingsley Webster 1886–1961. Proc Br Acad 48 1962. With note on Webster and Br Acad by G. N. Clark.

D. K.

DAME CICELY VERONICA WEDGWOOD
b. 1910

Bibliographies

Curle, R. H. P. The Richard Curle collection of the works of C. V. Wedgwood. Beaminster 1961. Annotated check-list.

§1

Strafford 1593–1641. 1935, 1961 (extensively rev) (as Thomas Wentworth, first earl of Strafford, 1593–1641: a revaluation), New York 1962.

The Thirty Years War. 1938, New Haven 1939, London 1957 (Penguin) (slightly corrected, with new introd).

Brandi, K. The emperor Charles V: the growth and destiny of a man and of a world empire. Tr C. V. Wedgwood 1939.

Oliver Cromwell. 1939, New York 1956, London 1962 (with rev bibliographical note). Also pbd New York 1966 (as The life of Cromwell).

Battlefields in Britain. 1944 (Britain in pictures).

William the Silent: William of Nassau Prince of Orange 1533-84. 1944, New Haven 1944.

Canetti, E. Auto da fé. Tr C. V. Wedgwood 1946.

Velvet studies. 1946. Historical essays rptd with slight corrections from various jnls.

Leith Hill Place. [1947] (priv ptd). Descriptive pamphlet.

Richelieu and the French monarchy. 1949, New York 1950, 1962 (rev).

Reading history. 1950 (Reader's guides).

Seventeenth-century English literature. 1950.

The last of the Radicals: Josiah Wedgwood MP. 1951.

Montrose. 1952, Hamden Conn 1966.

Edward Gibbon. 1955 (Br Council pamphlet).

The great rebellion: 1, The King's peace 1637-41. 1955, New York 1955. 2, The King's war 1641-7. 1958, New York 1959.

Poetry and politics under the Stuarts. Cambridge 1960, Ann Arbor 1964.

Truth and opinion: historical essays. 1960, New York 1960, 1967 (as The sense of the past). Includes single lectures previously pbd separately.

Thomas Wentworth, first Earl of Strafford. 1961. *See* Strafford, 1935, above.

The trial of Charles I. 1964, New York 1964 (as A coffin for King Charles: the trial and execution of Charles I).

New poems: a P.E.N. anthology. 1965. Ed C. V. Wedgwood.

The world of Rubens 1577-1640 by C. V. Wedgwood and the editors of Time-Life books. New York 1967.

Milton and his world. 1969, New York 1969. For children.

§2

Johnson, E. C. V. Wedgwood and her historiography. Contemporary Rev 201 1962.

MAURICE DENTON WELCH
1914-48

See cols 769-70, above.

HERBERT GEORGE WELLS
1866-1946

See cols 417-28, above.

EDWARD ALEXANDER WESTERMARCK
1862-1939

§1

The history of human marriage. Pt 1, Helsingfors 1889, London 1891 (enlarged), 3 vols London 1921 (rewritten), New York 1922, 1 vol London 1929 (for 1928) (abridged as Marriage) (Benn's Sixpenny Lib), New York 1929.

On the position of women in early civilization. 1905 (Sociological Soc Sociological Papers vol 1).

The influence of magic on social relationships. 1906 (Sociological Soc Sociological Papers vol 2).

The origin and development of the moral ideas. 2 vols. 1906-8, 1912-17 (corrected).

Christianity and war. In H. Bradlaugh, Essays towards peace, 1913.

Marriage ceremonies in Morocco. 1914.

The belief in spirits in Morocco. Åbo 1920. (Acta Academiae Aboensiae. Humaniora vol 1 no 1).

The origin of sexual modesty. 1921. Pamphlet.

The goodness of gods. 1926 (Forum Ser).

Ritual and belief in Morocco. 2 vols 1926.

A short history of marriage. 1926, New York 1926.

Memories of my life. 1929. Tr by A. Barwell from Minnen ur mitt liv, Helsingfors 1927.

Wit and wisdom in Morocco: a study of native proverbs. 1930. With the assistance of Shereef 'Abd-es-Salam el-Baqqali.

Early beliefs and their social influence. 1932.

Ethical relativity. 1932, New York [1932].

Pagan survivals in Mohammedan civilisation. 1933.

Three essays on sex and marriage. 1934.

The future of marriage in western civilisation. 1936, New York 1936.

Christianity and morals. 1939.

Westermarck also wrote a number of works on marriage, religion and morals, in Swedish. With L. T. Hobhouse, he edited Univ of London Monographs on Sociology, from 1913.

§2

Ginsberg, M. The life and work of Westermarck. Sociological Rev 32 1940; rptd in his Reason and unreason in society, 1947.

Letters from E. B. Tylor and A. R. Wallace to Westermarck, edited, with introductory remarks concerning the publication of The history of human marriage, by K. R. V. Wikman. Åbo 1940.

Hirn, Y. Westermarck and his English friends. Trans Westermarck Soc 1 1947.

Mills, C. W. Westermarck and the application of ethnographic methods to marriage and morals. In Introduction to the history of sociology, ed H. E. Barnes, Chicago 1948.

Lagerborg, R. H. H. Westermarck och verken från hans verkstad under hans tolv sista år 1927-39. Helsingfors 1951.

Wikman, K. R. V. Westermarck as anthropologist and sociologist. Trans Westermarck Soc 9 1962.

M. P.

PHILIP HENRY WICKSTEED
1844-1927

Bibliographies

In C. H. Herford, P. H. Wicksteed, 1931, §2, below.

§1

The ecclesiastical institutions of Holland, treated with special reference to the position and prospects of the modern school of theology: a report presented to the Hibbert Trustees. 1875.

Dante: six sermons. 1879, 1890 (corrected).

Christianity and the personal life; Christianity and social life; Christianity and trade; Christianity and politics; Elimination or redemption?: being an attempt to answer the question, Is Christianity practical? [1885], 1920 (as Is Christianity practical?). Sermons.

Our prayers and our politics. 1885. 3 sermons.

The alphabet of economic science. 1888, New York 1955.

Four lectures on Henrik Ibsen, dealing chiefly with his metrical works. 1892.

An essay on the co-ordination of the laws of distribution. 1894, Cleveland [1965?].

The religion of time and the religion of eternity: being a study of certain relations between mediaeval and modern thought. 1899; rptd, rev, in next.

Studies in theology. 1903. With J. E. Carpenter.

Brooke Herford: a biographical sketch. In Anchors of the soul: sermons by the Rev B. Herford, 1904.

Dante and Aquinas. 1913, New York 1913.

The reactions between dogma and philosophy, illustrated from the works of S. Thomas Aquinas. 1920.

From Vita Nuova to Paradiso: two essays on the vital relations between Dante's successive works. Manchester 1922.

Das Kapital: a criticism; The Jevonian criticism of Marx: a rejoinder [to G. B. Shaw]. In Bernard Shaw and Karl Marx: a symposium, ed R. W. Ellis, New York 1930; rptd in 1933 edn of The common sense of political economy, below.

The common sense of political economy, including a study of the human basis of economic law. 1910, 2 vols 1933 (ed with introd by L. Robbins), New York 1950. 1933 edn includes reprints of Selected papers and reviews by Wicksteed on economic theory.

Wicksteed also pbd a number of separate sermons, addresses, etc, some priv. For details, see Herford, Bibliographies, above.

Editions and Translations

The Bible for young people, by H. Oort and I. Hooykaas. 6 vols 1873–9, 3 vols Boston 1878–9 (as The Bible for learners). Authorized trn from Dutch.

National religions and universal religions, by A. Kuenen. 1882. Tr from Dutch.

Lectures on the origin and growth of religion as illustrated by the native religions of Mexico and Peru, by A. Réville. Tr Wicksteed 1884.

An historico-critical inquiry into the origin and composition of the Hexateuch (Pentateuch and Book of Joshua) by A. Kuenen. 1886. Tr from Dutch.

Memorials of the Rev C. Wicksteed. Ed Wicksteed 1886.

Controversial lectures by the Rev C. Wicksteed. Ed Wicksteed 1887.

Lectures on the origin and growth of the conception of God as illustrated by anthropology and history, by Count Goblet d'Alviella. 1892. Tr Wicksteed.

Our Lady's tumbler: a twelfth century legend. 1894. Tr from French.

Dante. The De Monarchia, books i–iii, translated into English and annotated by Wicksteed. Hull 1896 (priv ptd); rptd (rev) in A translation of the Latin works, 1904, below.

Selections from the first nine books of the Croniche Fiorentine of Giovanni Villani, translated for the use of students of Dante and others by R. E. Selfe. Ed Wicksteed 1896, 1906 (rev, as Villani's Chronicle).

Essays on Dante by Dr Karl Witte (being selections from the two volumes of 'Dante-Forschungen'), selected, translated and edited with introductions, notes and appendices by Wicksteed. 1898. With C. M. Lawrence.

A provisional translation of Dante's political letters, by P. H. Wicksteed; to which is added the section of the Convivio that concerns the Roman Empire. Hull 1898 (priv ptd); rptd (rev) in The Convivio 1903 and in A translation of the Latin works 1904, below.

A provisional translation of the early lives of Dante, and of his poetical correspondence with Giovanni del Virgilio. Hull 1898 (priv ptd); rptd (rev) in Dante and del Virgilio, 1902 and in The early lives of Dante, 1904, below.

The Paradiso of Dante Alighieri. 1899 (Temple Classics), New York 1950 (in The Divine Comedy: the Carlyle-Wicksteed translation). Ed and tr, with arguments and notes, by Wicksteed. With H. Oelsner.

The Purgatorio of Dante Alighieri. 1901 (Temple Classics), New York 1950 (in The Divine Comedy: the Carlyle-Wicksteed translation). Ed with notes and arguments by Wicksteed. With H. Oelsner and T. Okey.

Dante and Giovanni del Virgilio, including a critical edition of the text of Dante's "Eclogae Latinae" and the poetic remains of Giovanni del Virgilio. 1902. With E. G. Gardner.

The Convivio of Dante Alighieri. 1903 (Temple Classics). Tr, with notes, by Wicksteed.

The early lives of Dante [by G. Boccaccio and L. Bruni]. Tr Wicksteed 1904 (King's Classics).

Life of Dante, written by G. Boccaccio. Tr Wicksteed, Boston 1904.

A translation of the Latin works of Dante Alighieri. 1904 (Temple Classics).

Agnosticism and theism in the nineteenth century: an historical study of religious thought. 1905. 6 lectures by R. A. Armstrong, ed with introd by Wicksteed.

The Vita Nuova and Canzoniere of Dante Alighieri. 1906 (Temple Classics). The Canzoniere, tr Wicksteed.

A voice from the trees, and other poems, by C. H. Frogley. Ed with introd by Wicksteed 1915.

Aristotle. The Physics. 2 vols 1929–34 (Loeb Classical Library), Cambridge Mass 1952–7 (rev). Tr Wicksteed, with F. M. Cornford.

Wicksteed was a prolific contributor to Inquirer 1872–1923 (see Herford, Bibliographies, above, for an attempt at a complete list); with J. Reynolds he edited Sunday School teachers' manual, Manchester 1872–4, and he contributed to Palgrave's Dictionary of political economy, 3 vols 1894.

§2

Herford, C. H. Wicksteed: his life and work. 1931.

Knight, F. H. The common sense of political economy (Wicksteed reprinted). Jnl of Political Economy 42 1934; rptd in his On the history and method of economics, Chicago 1956.

Stigler, G. J. In Production and distribution theories: the formative period, New York 1941.

Hutchison, T. W. In his Review of economic doctrines 1870–1929, Oxford 1953.

SIR ERNEST LLEWELLYN WOODWARD
1890–1971

§1

Christianity and nationalism in the later Roman Empire. 1916.

The Congress of Berlin 1878. 1920 (Foreign Office handbook).

Three studies in European conservatism: Metternich; Guizot; the Catholic Church in the nineteenth century. 1929, Hamden Conn 1963.

The twelve-winded sky. 1930. Essays.

War and peace in Europe 1815–70, and other essays. 1931, Hamden Conn 1963.

France. In H. Brown, Woodward [et al], Our neighbours to-day and yesterday, 1933. Broadcast talks.

French revolutions. Oxford 1934.

Great Britain and the German navy. Oxford 1935, Hamden Conn 1964. Anglo-German relations 1898–1914.

The age of reform 1815–70. Oxford 1938, 1962 (rev) (Oxford History of England 13).

Short journey. 1942, New York 1946. Autobiography.

British historians. 1943 (Britain in Pictures).

Documents on British foreign policy 1919–39. Ed Woodward and R. Butler 1946–. Woodward retired from the editorship in 1955.

History of England. 1947, 1962 (rev), New York 1962.

British foreign policy in the Second World War. 1962 (History of the Second World War).

Great Britain and the war of 1914–18. 1967.

D. K.

ADELINE VIRGINIA WOOLF, née STEPHEN
1882–1941

See cols 472–81, above.

LEONARD SIDNEY WOOLF
1880–1969

§1

The village in the jungle. 1913, New York 1926. Novel.
The wise virgins: a story of words, opinions and a few emotions. 1914. Novel.
International government: two reports. 1916, New York 1916. For the Fabian Soc.
The framework of a lasting peace. Ed L. Woolf 1917. Anthology of various schemes for international organization.
The future of Constantinople. 1917.
Co-operation and the future of industry. 1918.
International economic policy. [1919?]. Pamphlet.
Economic imperialism. 1920, New York 1920.
Empire and commerce in Africa: a study in economic imperialism. [1920] (Labour Research Department).
'Gor'ky, Maksim' (Aleksyei Maksimovich Pyeshkov). Reminiscences of Leo Nicolayevitch Tolstoi. 1920. Tr by S. S. Koteliansky and Woolf.
Mandates and Empire. 1920. Pamphlet.
The note-books of Anton Tchekov. Richmond 1921. Tr by S. S. Koteliansky and Woolf.
Socialism and co-operation. 1921.
Stories of the East. Richmond 1921; rptd in Diaries in Ceylon, 1908–11, 1962, below.
The autobiography of Countess Sophie Tolstoi. Richmond 1922, New York 1922. Tr with preface and notes by V. Spiridonov, S. S. Koteliansky and Woolf.
Bunin, I. A. The gentleman from San Francisco, and other stories. Richmond 1922, New York 1923. Tr by Woolf, D. H. Lawrence and S. S. Koteliansky.
International co-operative trade. 1922 (Fabian tract).
Fabian essays on co-operation. Ed Woolf 1923.
Fear and politics: a debate at the Zoo. 1925 (Hogarth Essays).
Essays on literature, history, politics etc. 1927.
Hunting the highbrow. 1927 (Hogarth Essays).
Imperialism and civilization. 1928, New York [1928].
The way of peace. 1928. Booklet.
After the deluge: a study of communal psychology. 2 vols 1931–9, New York 1931–9. *See also Principia politica, 1953, below.*
The intelligent man's way to prevent war. 1933. By various authors, ed Woolf.
The modern state. By Woolf [et al], ed M. Adams. 1933, New York 1933.
'Gor'ky, Maksim' (Aleksyei Maksimovich Pyeshkov). Reminiscences of Tolstoy, Chekhov and Andreev. Authorized translation by K. Mansfield, S. S. Koteliansky and Woolf. 1934.
Quack, quack! 1935, New York [1935]. Essays on unreason and superstition in politics, belief and thought.
The League and Abyssinia. 1936. Pamphlet.
Barbarians at the gate. 1939, New York [1939] (as Barbarians within and without).
The hotel. 1939, New York 1963 (with new introd). Play.
The war for peace. 1940.
The international post-war settlement. [1944] (Fabian pamphlet).
Foreign policy: the Labour Party's dilemma. 1947 (Fabian pamphlet).
The early Fabians and British socialism. In Shaw and society: an anthology and a symposium, with contributions by Woolf [et al]. Ed C. E. M. Joad 1953.

Principia politica: a study of communal psychology. 1953, New York 1953. Intended as vol 3 of After the deluge, 1931–9, above.
Sowing: an autobiography of the years 1880–1904. 1960, New York 1960.
Growing: an autobiography of the years 1904–11. 1961, New York 1962.
Diaries in Ceylon, 1908–11: records of a colonial administrator; and Stories from the East: three short stories on Ceylon. Dehiwala 1962, London 1963.
Beginning again: an autobiography of the years 1911–18. 1964, New York 1964.
A calendar of consolation: a comforting thought for every day in the year. 1967, New York 1968.
Downhill all the way: an autobiography of the years 1919–39. 1967, New York 1967.
The journey not the arrival matters: an autobiography of the years 1939–69. 1969, New York 1970.
For the various works of Virginia Woolf edited by Woolf see Virginia Woolf, cols 472–4, above. Woolf edited International Rev 1919 and Nation 1922. He helped to found Political Quart in 1930 and, with W. A. Robson, was joint editor 1931–59. With Virginia Woolf he founded the Hogarth Press in 1917 and, with G. H. W. Rylands, edited Hogarth Lectures on Literature from 1927; he contributed regularly to New Statesman.

§2

Elkin, P. Woolf's masterpiece [The village in the jungle]. Jnl of Australasian Univ Lang & Lit Assoc no 13 1960.
M.P.

SIR CHARLES LEONARD WOOLLEY
1880–1960

Bibliographies
Mallowan, M. E. L. Bibliography of the principal publications on Ur. In his Memories of Ur, Iraq 22 1960.

§1

Dead towns and living men: pages from an antiquary's notebook. 1920, 1954 (rev and enlarged), New York 1956.
The Sumerians. Oxford 1928, New York 1965.
The excavations at Ur and the Hebrew records. 1929.
Ur of the Chaldees: a record of seven years of excavation. 1929, 1950 (rev), New York 1965.
Digging up the past. 1930, New York 1931, London 1954 (rev), New York 1954.
The development of Sumerian art. 1935.
Abraham: recent discoveries and Hebrew origins. 1936, New York 1936.
A forgotten kingdom: a record of the results obtained from the excavation of two mounds in the Turkish Hatay. 1953, Baltimore 1953, London 1959 (rev).
Spadework: adventures in archaeology. 1953, New York 1953 (as Spadework in archaeology).
Excavations at Ur: a record of twelve years' work. 1954, New York [1954], London 1955 (corrected).
Alalakh: an account of the excavations at Tell Atchana in the Hatay 1937–49. 1955. With C. J. Gadd and R. D. Barnett.
History unearthed: a survey of eighteen archaeological sites throughout the world. 1958, New York 1962.
Mesopotamia and the Middle East. 1961, New York 1961 (as The art of the Middle East including Persia, Mesopotamia and Palestine) (Art of the World ser).
The young archaeologist. Edinburgh [1961]. Illustr A. Sorrell.
As I seem to remember. 1962. Illustr Sprod.
Prehistory and the beginnings of civilisation. 1963, New York 1963 (History of Mankind—Cultural and Scientific

Development). With J. J. Hawkes. Pt 2, The beginnings of civilization, by Woolley.

Woolley collaborated in the composition of reports of many archaeological expeditions including those to Nubia (1907–12), Carchemish (1912–14, 1919), Al-'Ubaid (1919, 1922–3), El-'Amarneh (1921, 1922), Ur (8 vols 1927–65), Tell Atchana (1937–49).

§2

Mallowan, M. E. L. and D. J. Wiseman (ed). Ur in retrospect: [essays] in memory of Woolley. Iraq 22 1960.

A.P.H.

GEORGE MALCOLM YOUNG
1882–1959

Selections
Victorian essays. Ed W. D. Handcock 1962.

§1

Gibbon. 1932, New York 1933, London 1948 (with new introd).

Early Victorian England 1830–65. 2 vols 1934, New York 1951. Ed Young, who wrote the introd, Portrait of an age, later pbd separately (rev) as Victorian England: portrait of an age, 1936, 1953 (with new introd), New York 1953.

Charles I and Cromwell: an essay. 1935.

Daylight and champaign: essays. 1937.

The government of Britain. 1941 (Britain in Pictures ser).

Ourselves. 1944 (Signpost Booklet 1; no more pbd).

Today and yesterday: collected essays and addresses. 1948.

Last essays. 1950. Includes addresses previously pbd separately.

Stanley Baldwin. 1952. *See* D. C. Somervell, Stanley Baldwin: an examination of some features of Young's biography, 1953.

Young edited selections from Hardy, Meredith and Macaulay; he edited, in its early stages, English historical documents 1833–74, 1956 (with W. D. Handcock); and edited and wrote the introd for Country and town: a summary of the Scott and Uthwatt reports, *1943 (Penguin Special).*

P.C.

III. PHILOSOPHERS, THEOLOGIANS, WRITERS ON NATURAL SCIENCE AND ON PSYCHOLOGY

General Studies

Blanshard, B. On philosophical style. Manchester 1954.

Savory, T. H. The language of science: its growth, character and usage. 1953, 1967 (rev).

Passmore, J. A hundred years of philosophy. 1957, 1966 (rev and enlarged).

Warnock, G. J. English philosophy since 1900. 1958.

Henn, T. R. Science in writing: a selection of passages from the writings of scientific authors, with notes and a section on the writing of scientific prose. 1960.

Davies, H. Varieties of English preaching 1900–60. 1963.

—— The early development of theology 1900–33; The later development of theology 1933–65; Trends and types of preaching. In his Worship and theology in England vol 5: The ecumenical century 1900–65, Princeton 1965.

Macquarrie, J. Twentieth-century religious thought: the frontiers of philosophy and theology, 1900–60. 1963.

Quinton, A. Thought. In Edwardian England 1901–14, ed S. Nowell-Smith, Oxford 1964.

M.S.

SAMUEL ALEXANDER
1859–1938

Bibliographies
In Philosophical and literary pieces, 1939, below. Includes contributions to books, periodicals and newspapers.

§1

Moral order and progress: an analysis of ethical conceptions. 1889.

Locke. 1908.

Space, time and deity: the Gifford lectures, 1916–18. 2 vols 1920, 1927 (with a new preface), 1966 (foreword by D. Emmet), New York 1966.

Beauty and other forms of value. 1933, New York [1968] (introd by R. Ross).

Philosophical and literary pieces, edited, with a memoir, by his literary executor (John Laird). 1939. Includes lectures and essays previously pbd separately.

§2

Devaux, P. Le système d'Alexander: exposé critique d'une théorie néo-réaliste du changement. Paris and Liège 1929.

Wickham, H. Colossus: Professor Alexander. In his Unrealists, New York 1930.

Van Hall, G. The theory of knowledge of Alexander. Roosendaal [1936].

[Laird, J.]. Samuel Alexander. Proc Br Acad 24 1938; rptd, enlarged, in Alexander's Philosophical and literary pieces, 1939, above, §1.

Ritchie, A. D. Samuel Alexander. Memoirs of Manchester Literary & Philosophical Soc 84 1939–41.

Stout, G. F. The philosophy of Alexander. Mind 49 1940.

Konvitz, M. R. On the nature of value: the philosophy of Alexander. New York 1946.

McCarthy, J. W. The naturalism of Alexander. New York 1948.

Lowe, V. The influence of Bergson, James and Alexander on Whitehead. JHI 10 1949; rptd in his Understanding Whitehead, Baltimore 1962.

Stiernotte, A. P. God and space-time: deity in the philosophy of Alexander. New York [1954].

Passmore, J. A. The new realists. In his A hundred years of philosophy, 1957, 1966 (rev).

Emmet, D. The philosophy of Alexander. Listener 8 Jan 1959.

Brettschneider, B. D. Philosophy of Alexander. New York 1964.

Maurer, A. A. The philosophy of evolution. In Recent philosophy: Hegel to the present, ed E. H. Gilson 1966.

SIR ALFRED JULES AYER
b. 1910

§1

Language, truth and logic. 1936, 1946 (rev), New York 1952.
The foundations of empirical knowledge. 1940.
The British empirical philosophers: Locke, Berkeley, Hume, Reid and J. S. Mill. 1952, New York 1968. Anthology ed Ayer and R. Winch.
Philosophical essays. 1954.
What is communication? In Studies in communication contributed to the Communication Research Centre, University College, London, by A. J. Ayer [et al], 1955.
The problem of knowledge. 1956.
The Vienna Circle. In The revolution in philosophy, by A. J. Ayer [et al], 1956.
Logical positivism. 1959, Glencoe Ill 1959. Anthology, ed with introd by Ayer.
The concept of a person and other essays. 1963. Includes several lectures previously pbd separately.
The humanist outlook. 1968. Anthology, ed with introd by Ayer.
The origins of pragmatism: studies in the philosophy of Charles Sanders Peirce and William James. 1968, San Francisco 1968.
Metaphysics and common sense. 1969. Collection of previously pbd essays.
A. J. Ayer is editor of the Pelican Philosophy Ser, *1951– and the* International Lib of Philosophy and Scientific Method, *1961–.*

§2

Technical discussions of Ayer's work are listed in the bibliography appended to Logical positivism, *1959, above.*

Toynbee, P. Sense and nonsense. Encounter 3 1954. Essay-review of Language, truth and logic 1946 (rev).
Dubois, P. Querelles autour d'un petit livre: Language, truth and logic. Revue Philosophique de la France et de l'Etranger 152 1962.
Maurer, A. A. Language and metaphysics. In Recent philosophy: Hegel to the present, ed E. H. Gilson 1966.
M.P.

JOHN BAILLIE
1886–1960

The roots of religion in the human soul. 1926.
The interpretation of religion: an introductory study of theological principles. New York 1928, Edinburgh 1929.
The place of Jesus Christ in modern Christianity. Edinburgh 1929, New York 1929.
And the life everlasting. New York 1933, London 1934.
A diary of private prayer. 1936, New York 1949, 1958 (rev).
Revelation. Ed Baillie and H. Martin 1937. Theological essays by various authors.
Our knowledge of God. 1939, New York 1939.
Invitation to pilgrimage. 1942, New York 1942.
What is Christian civilization? 1945, New York 1945, London 1947 (enlarged).
The belief in progress. 1950, New York 1951.
A diary of readings: being an anthology of pages suited to engage serious thought. Ed Baillie 1955, New York 1955.
The idea of revelation in recent thought. New York 1956, London 1956.
The theology of the sacraments and other papers [by] D. M. Baillie. [Ed] with a biographical essay by J. Baillie 1957.

Christian devotion: addresses. 1962. With biographical essay by I. M. Forrester.
The sense of the presence of God. 1962, New York 1962.
Baptism and conversion. New York 1963, London 1964.
A reasoned faith: collected addresses. 1963.
Baillie was a co-editor of the Library of Christian Classics *from 1953.*
C. H. E. P.

JOHN DESMOND BERNAL
1901–71

Bernal's literary papers have been deposited in the library of Birkbeck College.

Bibliographies

In J. C. Poggendorf, Biographisch-literarisches Handwörterbuch der exacten Naturwissenschaften vols 6, 7, Berlin 1936, 1967.

§1

The world, the flesh and the devil: an enquiry into the future of the three enemies of the rational soul. 1929.
The social function of science. 1939, New York 1939, Cambridge Mass 1967 (rev).
Comenius' visit to England and the rise of scientific societies in the seventeenth century. In The teacher of nations, ed N. J. T. M. Needham, Cambridge 1942.
The freedom of necessity. 1949. Essays.
Science against war. In Science for peace and socialism, by J. D. Bernal and M. Cornforth, [1949].
The physical basis of life. 1951.
The way to peace. [1951]. Pamphlet.
Disarmament. Vienna 1952, London 1952. Pamphlet.
Marx and science. 1952, New York 1952.
Science and industry in the nineteenth century. 1953.
Science and society. Moscow 1953. In Russian.
Science in history. 1954, 1965 (rev), New York 1965, 4 vols London 1969 (rev).
World without war. 1958, New York 1958, London 1961 (rev).
A prospect of peace. 1960. Based on World without war, above.
Science for a developing world: a symposium. Ed J. D. Bernal 1962.
Need there be need? Harrow Weald [1963]. Pamphlet.
The origin of life. 1967.

Bernal contributed numerous papers to various scientific periodicals (see Poggendorf, above), and also to the proceedings of several peace conferences.

§2

Lucas, C. E. Bernal's Social function of science. Scrutiny 8 1939.
Rozhansky, I. D. J. D. Bernal. Uspekhi Fizicheskikh Nauk 45 1951. In Russian.
Snow, C. P. Bernal: a personal portrait. In The science of science, ed M. Goldsmith and A. Mackay 1964. Containing contributions by Bernal and others orientated towards his work.

SIR WILLIAM HENRY BRAGG
1862–1942

§1

Studies in radioactivity. 1912.
X-rays and crystal structure. 1915, 1924 (rev). With W. L. Bragg.
The world of sound. 1920. Christmas Lectures at the Royal Institution.

Concerning the nature of things. 1925, New York 1925. Christmas Lectures at the Royal Institution.

Old trades and new knowledge. 1926, New York 1927 (as Creative knowledge: old trades and new science). Christmas Lectures at the Royal Institution.

An introduction to crystal analysis. 1928.

The universe of light. 1933, New York 1933. Christmas Lectures at the Royal Institution.

The need of the day. In Moral rearmament, by W. H. Bragg [et al], 1938.

The story of electromagnetism. 1941.

Bragg wrote and edited other works on crystallography, some with W. L. Bragg.

§2

Andrade, E. N. da C. William Henry Bragg. In Obituary notices of Fellows of the Royal Soc 4 1943. With bibliography.

Grant, K. The life and work of Bragg. Brisbane 1952.

Heathcote, N. H. de V. W. H. Bragg; W. L. Bragg. In his Nobel prize winners in physics 1901-50, New York 1953.

N.J.S.

CHARLIE DUNBAR BROAD
1887-1971

§1

Perception, physics and reality: an enquiry into the information that physical science can supply about the real. Cambridge 1914.

Scientific thought. 1923, New York 1923.

Critical and speculative philosophy. In Contemporary British philosophy: personal statements, series 1, ed J. H. Muirhead 1924.

The mind and its place in nature. 1925, New York 1925.

Five types of ethical theory (Spinoza, Butler, Hume, Kant, Sidgwick). 1930, New York 1930.

Examination of McTaggart's philosophy. 2 vols Cambridge 1933-8.

Ethics and the history of philosophy: selected essays. 1952.

Religion, philosophy and psychical research: selected essays. 1953.

Autobiography. In The philosophy of Broad, ed P. A. Schilpp, New York 1959 (for 1960).

A reply to my critics. In The philosophy of Broad, ed P. A. Schilpp, New York 1959 (for 1960).

Lectures on psychical research. 1962, New York 1962.

Induction, probability and causation: selected papers. Dordrecht 1968.

Broad edited McTaggart's Nature of existence, 1927, and wrote the introd to McTaggart's Some dogmas of religion, 1930.

§2

Martineau, R. Trinity Mag 8 1927. Biography of Broad; also contains an interview with Broad.

Lean, M. Sense-perception and matter: a critical analysis of Broad's theory of perception. 1953.

The philosophy of Broad. Ed P. A. Schilpp, New York 1959 (for 1960). This is the major consideration of Broad's works, comprising several articles and a bibliography compiled by C. Lewy.

H.M.R.

SIR CYRIL LODOWIC BURT
1883-1971

Bibliographies

List of Burt's publications. In Stephanos, ed C. Banks and P. L. Broadhurst, 1965.

§1

The sub-normal school-child. vol 1, The young delinquent, 1925, New York 1925, London 1938 (rev) Bickley 1944 (rev), London 1957 (rev); vol 2, The backward child, 1937, New York 1937, London 1946 (rev).

The measurement of mental capacities: a review of the psychology of individual differences. Edinburgh 1927.

How the mind works. 1933, New York 1934. Ed Burt. Essays by Burt et al.

The subnormal mind. 1935. Lectures.

The factors of the mind: an introduction to factor analysis in psychology. 1940, New York 1941.

The causes and treatment of backwardness. 1953, 1953 (rev and enlarged), New York 1953. Lecture.

A psychological study of typography. Cambridge 1959. Pamphlet.

Burt also pbd research for the London County Council Education Committee and the Eugenics Soc and he edited Northumberland Standardised Tests, 1925. He was co-founder and editor of Br Jnl of Statistical Psychology from 1947.

§2

Valentine, C. Burt: a biographical sketch and appreciation. In Stephanos: studies in psychology presented to Burt, ed C. Banks and P. L. Broadhurst, 1965.

J.M.P.

EDGAR FREDERICK CARRITT
1876-1964

§1

The theory of beauty. 1914, New York 1914, London 1923 (enlarged), 1928 (rev), 1949 (rev), 1962 (rev).

The theory of morals. 1928.

Philosophies of beauty from Socrates to Robert Bridges: being the sources of aesthetic theory. Oxford 1931. Selected and ed by Carritt.

What is beauty? a first introduction to the subject and to modern theories. Oxford 1932.

Morals and politics: theories of their relation from Hobbes and Spinoza to Marx and Bosanquet. Oxford 1935.

Ethical and political thinking. Oxford 1947.

A calendar of British taste from 1600 to 1900: being a museum of specimens and landmarks chronologically arranged. [1949].

An introduction to aesthetics. [1949].

Fifty years a don. 1960. Memoirs. Mimeographed.

Carritt also translated Croce, The defence of poetry, 1933, My philosophy and other essays, 1949.

§2

Saw, R. L. Carritt. Br Jnl of Aesthetics 4 1964.

Raphael, P. D. Carritt. Proc Br Acad 51 1965.

H.M.R.

GILBERT KEITH CHESTERTON
1874-1936
See cols 1021-8, above.

ARTHUR CLUTTON-BROCK
1868-1924
See cols 1029-30, above.

ROBIN GEORGE COLLINGWOOD
1889–1943

Bibliographies

In R. B. McCallum [et al], Robin George Collingwood, [1944], §2 below.
In Essays in the philosophy of history, 1965, §1 below. Includes literature on Collingwood, including reviews.

§1

Croce, B. The philosophy of Giambattista Vico. Tr Collingwood, 1913, New York 1913.
The devil. In Concerning prayer, its nature, its difficulties and its value, by Collingwood [et al], ed B. H. Streeter 1916.
Religion and philosophy. 1916.
Ruggiero, G. de. Modern philosophy. Tr A. H. Hannay and Collingwood, 1921.
Roman Britain. 1923, Oxford 1932 (corrected), 1934 (corrected), 1942 (corrected).
Speculum mentis: or, the map of knowledge. Oxford 1924.
Outlines of a philosophy of art. 1925.
Croce, B. An autobiography. Tr Collingwood, Oxford 1927.
Ruggiero, G. de. The history of European Liberalism. Tr Collingwood, 1927.
Faith and reason: a study of the relations between religion and science. 1928.
The archaeology of Roman Britain. 1930. New edn, 1969, thoroughly rev and enlarged by I. Richmond.
Bruce, J. C. The handbook to the Roman Wall. 9th edn ed [and largely rewritten by] R. G. Collingwood, Newcastle-upon-Tyne 1933.
An essay on philosophical method. (Philosophical essays vol 1). Oxford 1933.
Roman Britain and the English settlements. Oxford 1936, 1937 (corrected) (Oxford History of England 1). With J. N. L. Myres.
Roman Britain. In T. Frank, An economic survey of ancient Rome, vol 3, Baltimore 1937.
The principles of art. Oxford 1938, New York 1958.
An autobiography. 1939.
The first mate's log of a journey to Greece in the schooner yacht Fleur de Lys in 1939. 1940.
An essay on metaphysics. (Philosophical Essays vol 2). Oxford 1940.
The new Leviathan: or, man, society, civilization and barbarism. Oxford 1942, 1944 (corrected).
The idea of nature. Ed T. M. Knox, Oxford 1945, New York 1960.
The idea of history. Ed with preface by T. M. Knox, Oxford 1946, New York 1956.
Essays in the philosophy of art. Ed A. Donagan, Bloomington Ind [1964].
Essays in the philosophy of history. Ed W. Debbins, Austin Texas 1965.
The Roman inscriptions of Britain, vol 1: Inscriptions on stone. Oxford 1965. With R. P. Wright.
Faith and reason: essays in the philosophy of religion. Ed by L. Rubinoff, Chicago 1968.
Collingwood also phd guide books to various Roman antiquities in the North of England. He contributed the sections on Roman Britain to Cambridge Ancient History vols 10–12. He assisted in the editing of Trans of the Cumberland & Westmorland Antiquarian & Archaeological Soc new ser vols 21–34.

§2

McCallum, R. B. R. G. Collingwood 1889–1943; T. M. Knox, Notes on Collingwood's philosophical works; I. A. Richmond, Appreciation of Collingwood as an archaeologist. Proc of the British Acad 29 1943.

Schneider, F. D. C. Collingwood and The idea of history. UTQ 22 1952–3.
Tomlin, E. W. F. R. G. Collingwood. 1953, 1961 (rev) (Br Council pamphlet).
Grant, C. K. Collingwood's theory of historical knowledge. Renaissance & Modern Studies 1 1957.
White, H. V. Collingwood and Toynbee: transitions in English historical thought. Eng Miscellany (Rome) 8 1957; reply by L. Dondoli (in Italian) ibid 15 1964.
Donagan, A. The later philosophy of Collingwood. Oxford 1962. Appendix III contains letters from Collingwood to Croce. See D. Rynin, Donagan on Collingwood: absolute presuppositions, truth and metaphysics. Rev of Metaphysics 18 1964.
Walpole, H. Collingwood and the idea of language. Univ of Wichita Bull 38 1963.
Brown, M. E. Neo-idealist aesthetics: Croce, Gentile, Collingwood. Detroit 1966.
Johnston, W. M. The formative years of Collingwood. The Hague 1967.
Shalom, A. R. G. Collingwood: philosophe et historien. Paris 1967.
Mink, L. O. Collingwood's dialectic of history. History & Theory 7 1968.
—— Mind, history and dialectic: the philosophy of Collingwood. Bloomington 1969.

M.P.

FRANCIS MACDONALD CORNFORD
1874–1943

See col 1031, above.

MARTIN CYRIL D'ARCY
b. 1888

Bibliographies

In Bibliography of the English province of the Society of Jesus, 1773–1953, compiled by E. F. Sutcliffe, 1957. Includes trns.

§1

The problem of evil. 1922, 1926 (expanded) (Catholic Truth Soc pamphlet).
The Mass and the Redemption. 1926.
Catholicism. 1927, Garden City NY 1928, Dublin 1954 (with new introd).
Christ, Priest and Redeemer. 1928, New York 1928.
The spirit of charity. 1929.
Thomas Aquinas. 1930, Westminster Maryland 1944, Dublin 1953 (as St Thomas Aquinas, with new introd and rev bibliography).
The philosophy of St Augustine. In A monument to St Augustine: essays on some aspects of his thought, by M. C. D'Arcy [et al], 1930, New York 1957.
Christianity and the modern mind. In God and the universe: the Christian position, ed J. L. May 1931.
The nature of belief. 1931, New York 1945, Dublin 1953 (enlarged, with new introd).
The life of the Church. [By M. C. D'Arcy et al]. 1932. Ed D'Arcy, with foreword and contributions to ch on Catholicism in the nineteenth century and at the beginning of the twentieth.
Cardinal Newman. In The English way: studies in English sanctity from St Bede to Newman by D'Arcy [et al], ed M. Ward, 1933, Freeport NY 1968.
Mirage and truth. 1935, New York 1935.
The pain of this world and the providence of God. 1935, Milwaukee [1935] (as Pain and the providence of God).
Christian morals. 1937.
Thomas Aquinas: selected writings. Ed D'Arcy 1939, 1964 (rev) (EL).

Death and life. 1942.
Belief and reason. 1944. Six broadcast talks with 3 additional essays.
The mind and heart of love—lion and unicorn: a study in Eros and Agape. 1945, New York 1947, London 1954 (rev), New York 1956.
Communism and Christianity. 1956, New York 1957.
The meeting of love and knowledge: perennial wisdom. New York 1957, London 1958.
The sense of history, secular and sacred. 1959, New York 1959 (as The meaning and matter of history).
No absent God: the relations between God and the self. New York 1962, London 1962 (for 1963).
Of God and man: thoughts on faith and morals. 1964, Dublin 1964, Wilkes-Barre Pa 1964.
Dialogue with myself. New York 1966, London 1966 (expanded, as Facing God).
Facing the people. Wilkes-Barre Pa 1968.
Facing the truth. Denville NJ 1969, London 1969.
Humanism and Christianity. New York [1969].

M.P.

SIR FRANK FRASER DARLING
b. 1903

A herd of red deer: a study in animal behaviour. 1937, 1941 (corrected), 1956 (corrected), New York 1964 (with additional preface).
Bird flocks and the breeding cycle: a contribution to the study of avian sociality. Cambridge 1938.
Wild country: a Highland naturalist's notes and pictures. Cambridge 1938.
A naturalist on Rona: essays of a biologist in isolation. Oxford 1939.
The seasons and the farmer: a book for children. Cambridge 1939.
Island years. 1940.
The seasons and the fisherman: a book for children. Cambridge 1941.
The story of Scotland. 1942 (Britain in Pictures).
Island farm. 1943.
Wild life of Britain. 1943 (Britain in Pictures).
Crofting agriculture: its practice in the West Highlands and Islands. Edinburgh 1945.
Natural history in the Highlands and Islands. 1947, 1964 (rev, as The Highlands and Islands; with J. M. Boyd), 1969 (rev).
The cattle of St Mochua: a paraphrase of the Irish tale. Edinburgh 1950.
Sandy the red deer. 1949 [1950]. Children's story.
Wildlife in Alaska: an ecological reconnaissance. New York 1953. With A. S. Leopold.
West Highland survey: an essay in human ecology. 1955. By Darling et al. Ed Darling.
Pelican in the wilderness: a naturalist's odyssey in North America. 1956, New York 1956.
An ecological reconnaissance of the Mara plains in Kenya Colony. 1960 (Wildlife Soc, Wildlife Monographs 5).
Wildlife in an African territory: a study made for the Game and Tsetse Control Department of Northern Rhodesia. 1960.
Darling has also written works for the Commonwealth Bureau of Agricultural Breeding and Genetics, the National Federation of Young Farmers' Clubs, and the Conservation Foundation (Washington D.C.).

M.S.

CHARLES HAROLD DODD
b. 1884
Bibliographies
In The background of the New Testament and its eschatology, edited by W. D. Davies and D. Daube, in honour of C. H. Dodd, Cambridge 1956.

§1
The gospel of the Cross. 1918. By Dodd et al.
The meaning of Paul for today. [1920], New York 1957, London 1958 (rev).
The gospel in the New Testament. [1926].
The authority of the Bible. 1928, New York 1929, London 1960 (rev).
The Bible and its background. 1931.
The epistle of Paul to the Romans. 1932, New York 1932 (Moffatt New Testament commentary).
There and back again: tales. 1932.
The Bible and the Greeks. 1935.
The parables of the kingdom. 1935, 1936 (rev), New York 1958, London [1961] (rev), New York 1961.
The apostolic preaching and its developments: three lectures with an appendix on eschatology and history. 1936, Chicago 1937.
History and the gospel. 1938, New York 1938, London 1964 (rev).
The Bible today. Cambridge 1946, New York 1947.
The Johannine epistles. 1946, New York 1946 (Moffatt New Testament commentary).
About the Gospels. Cambridge 1950. 4 broadcast addresses; reissued with The coming of Christ, 1958.
The coming of Christ: four broadcast addresses for the season of Advent. Cambridge 1951.
Gospel and law: the relation of faith and ethics in early Christianity. Cambridge 1951.
According to the scriptures: the sub-structure of New Testament theology. 1952, New York 1953.
The interpretation of the Fourth Gospel. Cambridge 1953.
New Testament studies. Manchester 1953, New York 1954, London 1967 (corrected).
The Jews and the beginning of the Christian church. In The European inheritance vol 1, ed E. Barker et al, Oxford 1954.
Historical tradition in the Fourth Gospel. Cambridge 1963.
More New Testament studies. Manchester [1968].
Dodd also pbd many other addresses, sermons, pamphlets and talks and contributed a number of essays to Bull John Rylands Lib *(for details see* The background of the New Testament *and its eschatology, Bibliographies, above). He is editor of the new ser* Texts and studies: contributions to Biblical and patristic literature, *Cambridge 1954 onwards. He was General Director, later Joint Director, of the* New English Bible.

§2
Hamilton, N. Q. Dodd's realized eschatology. In his The Holy Spirit and eschatology in Paul, Edinburgh 1957.
Bruce, F. F. In Creative minds in contemporary theology, ed P. E. Hughes, Grand Rapids 1966, 1969 (rev).
Robinson, J. A. T. Theologians of our time, xii: Dodd. Expository Times 75 1963–4; rptd in Theologians of our time, ed A. W. Hastings and E. Hastings, Edinburgh 1966.

P.C.

JOHN WILLIAM DUNNE
1875–1949

§1
Sunshine and the dry fly. 1924.
An experiment with time. 1927, New York 1927, London 1938 (rev).
The serial universe. 1934, New York 1938.
The league of North-West Europe: a solution to the present European crisis. [1936].
The jumping lions of Borneo. 1937, New York [1938]. Children's story.

The new immortality. 1938.

An experiment with St George. 1939, New York [1939] (as St George and the witches). Children's story.

Nothing dies. 1940, 1951 (rev).

Intrusions? 1955.

§2

Broad, C. D. Dunne's theory of time. In his Religion, philosophy and psychical research, 1953.

Smith, G. Time alive: Dunne and J. B. Priestley. South Atlantic Quart 56 1957.

Borges, J. L. Time and J. W. Dunne. In his Other inquisitions, 1937–52, Austin 1964.

N.J.S.

SIR ARTHUR STANLEY EDDINGTON
1882–1944

§1

Stellar movements and the structure of the universe. 1914.

Report [to the Physical Soc] on the relativity theory of gravitation. 1918.

Space, time and gravitation: an outline of the general relativity theory. Cambridge 1920, New York 1959.

The mathematical theory of relativity. Cambridge 1923, 1924 (enlarged).

The domain of physical science. In Science, religion and reality, ed J. Needham 1925, New York 1925.

The internal constitution of the stars. Cambridge 1926, New York 1959.

Stars and atoms. Oxford 1927, New Haven 1927.

The nature of the physical world. Cambridge 1928, New York 1928.

Science and the unseen world. 1929, New York 1929.

The expanding universe. Cambridge 1933, New York 1933.

New pathways in science. Cambridge 1935, New York 1935.

Relativity theory of protons and electrons. Cambridge 1936, New York 1936.

The philosophy of physical science. Cambridge 1939, New York 1939, Cambridge 1949 (corrected).

Fundamental theory. Ed E. T. Whittaker, Cambridge 1946.

§2

Joad, C. E. M. The idealism of Eddington. In his Philosophical aspects of modern science, 1932.

Russell, J. L. The Scientific best seller. Scrutiny 2 1934; rptd in Determinations, ed F. R. Leavis 1934.

Stebbing, L. S. In her Philosophy and the physicists, 1937.

Plummer, H. C. Arthur Stanley Eddington. Obituary notice of Fellows of Royal Soc 5 1945.

Whittaker, E. T. From Euclid to Eddington: a study of conceptions of the external world. Cambridge 1949.

Crowther, J. G. In his British scientists of the twentieth century, 1952.

Douglas, A. V. Life of Eddington. 1956.

Slater, N. B. The development and meaning of Eddington's Fundamental theory, including a compilation from Eddington's unpublished mss. Cambridge 1957.

Witt-Hansen, J. Exposition and critique of the conceptions of Eddington concerning the philosophy of physical science. Copenhagen 1958.

Yolton, J. W. The philosophy of science of Eddington. Hague 1960.

Kilmister, C. W. and B. O. J. Tupper. Eddington's statistical theory. Oxford 1962.

Merleau-Ponty, J. Philosophie et théorie physique chez Eddington. Paris 1965.

Kilmister, C. W. Men of physics: Eddington. Oxford 1966. Includes selection of Eddington's technical prose.

Many of the Eddington Memorial Lectures, Cambridge 1948– deal with Eddington.

J.M.P.

CHARLES GORE
1853–1932

Bibliographies

In J. Carpenter, Gore, 1960. See §2, below. Includes works about Gore.

§1

Leo the Great. [1880].

The church and the ministry: a review of the Rev E. Hatch's Bampton lectures. 1882, 1882 (with new preface).

The Roman Catholic claims. [1886] (anon), 1889 (for 1888) (enlarged, as The Roman Catholic claims by C. Gore). See L. Rivington, Dust: a letter to Gore on his book, Roman Catholic claims, 1888; and Gore's reply, Some remarks on Dust, Oxford 1888.

The clergy and the creeds. 1887. Sermon.

The Holy Spirit and inspiration. In Lux mundi: a series of studies in the religion of the Incarnation. Ed Gore 1889, 1890 (with new preface and appendix), New York [1890?]. For the many replies to Lux mundi and to Gore's essay, see Carpenter, Bibliographies, above.

The ministry of the Christian church. 1889, 1893 (rev), 1899 (rev, as The church and the ministry), 1919 (rev by C. H. Turner), 1936 (rev with appendix), New York 1936.

The Incarnation of the Son of God. 1891, New York 1891, London 1904 (shortened for popular use by T. C. Fry, as Why we Christians believe in Christ).

The mission of the church. 1892.

The creed of the Christian. 1895.

Dissertations on subjects connected with the Incarnation. 1895, New York 1895.

The Sermon on the Mount: a practical exposition. 1896, 1910 (with new preface).

Essays in aid of the reform of the Church. Ed Gore 1898; ed D. Eyre 1915 (rev, as Reform in the Church of England).

Prayer, and the Lord's Prayer. 1898, New York [1947] (introd by A. Dunn).

St Paul's Epistle to the Ephesians: a practical exposition. 1898.

St Paul's Epistle to the Romans: a practical exposition. 2 vols 1899–1900, New York 1899.

The body of Christ: an enquiry into the institution and doctrine of Holy Communion. 1901, 1901 (with new preface and expanded notes), 1907 (with new preface).

Spiritual efficiency. 1904. Primary charge, as Bishop of Worcester.

The new theology and the old religion. 1907. Lectures and sermons.

Orders and unity. 1909, New York 1909.

The question of divorce. 1911, New York 1911.

The basis of Anglican fellowship in faith and organization: an open letter to the clergy of the diocese of Oxford. 1914.

The war and the church, and other addresses. 1914, Milwaukee 1914.

Crisis in church and nation. [1915].

The religion of the church as presented in the Church of England: a manual of membership. 1916, 1917 (rev), Milwaukee 1917.

Dominant ideas and corrective principles. 1918.

Christianity applied to the life of men and of nations. 1920, 1940 (introd by R. H. Tawney). Lecture.

The Epistles of St John. 1920.

Belief in God. 1921, New York 1923. Vol 1 of The reconstruction of belief.

Christian moral principles. 1921.

Belief in Christ. 1922, New York 1922. Vol 2 of The reconstruction of belief.

The deity of Christ. Oxford 1922.

Catholicism and Roman Catholicism. 1923.

The doctrine of the infallible book. 1924, New York [1925]. With a section by H. R. Mackintosh.

The Holy Spirit and the church. 1924. Vol 3 of The reconstruction of belief. This and the previous 2 vols reissued 1926 in one vol as The reconstruction of belief.

The Anglo-Catholic movement to-day. 1925.

Can we then believe? Summary of volumes on Reconstruction of belief, and reply to criticisms. 1926.

Christ and society. 1928, New York 1928.

The Holy Communion; together with a sermon on The church in the world. 1928.

A new commentary on Holy Scripture, including the Apocrypha. Ed Gore, H. L. Goudge, A. Guillaume 1928, New York 1928.

Jesus of Nazareth. 1929, New York [1929].

The philosophy of the good life. 1930.

Reflections on the Litany. 1932.

Gore also pbd numerous smaller pamphlets, sermons etc, for which see Carpenter, Bibliographies, above. He also edited (with J. O. Nash) W. Law's Defense of church principles, 1893, and G. J. Romanes' Thoughts on religion, 1895.

§2

For the many contemporary replies etc to Gore's books, see Carpenter, Bibliographies, above.

Inge, W. R. Gore and the Church of England. Edinburgh Rev 207 1908; rptd in his Outspoken essays, 1919.

Shears, H. Christ or Bentham? A criticism of Gore's work on the Sermon on the Mount. 1927.

Crosse, G. Gore: a biographical sketch. 1932.

Gore, J. F. Charles Gore, father and son: a background to the early years and family life of Gore. 1932.

Mansbridge, A. Edward Stuart Talbot and Gore: witnesses to and interpreters of the Christian faith in church and state. 1935.

Prestige, G. L. The life of Gore. 1935.

Ekström, R. The theology of Gore. Lund 1944.

Ramsey, A. M. Gore and Anglican theology. 1955. Lecture.

—— In his From Gore to Temple: the development of Anglican theology between Lux mundi and the Second World War, 1960.

Vidler, A. R. Gore and Liberal Catholicism. In his Essays in liberality, 1957.

Carpenter, J. Gore: a study in Liberal Catholic thought. 1960.

Rice, H. A. L. Post-tractarian prophet: Gore. In his The bridge builders, 1961.

Brown, C. In Creative minds in contemporary theology, ed P. E. Hughes, Grand Rapids 1966, 1969 (rev).

D.K.

JOHN BURDON SANDERSON HALDANE
1892–1964

Bibliographies

Pirie, N. W. In Biographical memoirs of Fellows of the Royal Soc 12 1966. Rptd in R. Clark, J.B.S., 1968, below.

Collections

La science en marche. Paris 1952. Collection of Haldane's periodical articles, tr G. Gratiant.

§1

Daedalus: or science and the future. 1924 (for 1923), New York [1924].

Callinicus: a defence of chemical warfare. 1925, New York [1925].

Animal biology. Oxford 1927. With J. S. Huxley.

The last judgment: a scientist's vision of the future of man. New York 1927.

Possible worlds, and other essays. 1927, New York 1928.

Enzymes. 1930, Cambridge Mass 1965.

The causes of evolution. 1932, New York 1932.

The inequality of man, and other essays. 1932, New York 1933 (as Science and human life).

Biology in everyday life. 1933. With J. R. Baker.

Fact and faith. 1934.

Science and the supernatural: a correspondence between A. Lunn and J. B. S. Haldane. 1935, New York 1935.

My friend Mr Leakey. 1937, New York 1938. For children.

ARP. [Air Raid Precautions]. 1938. *See* 'Martian', ARP: a reply to Haldane, 1938.

Heredity and politics. 1938, New York [1938].

How to be safe from air raids. 1938.

The Marxist philosophy and the sciences. 1938, New York [1939].

Science and everyday life. 1939, New York 1940.

Science and you. [1939].

You and heredity, by A. Scheinfeld. Ed J. B. S. Haldane 1939.

Dialectics of nature, by F. Engels. 1940. Preface and notes by J. B. S. Haldane.

Keeping cool, and other essays. 1940, New York [1940] (as Adventures of a biologist).

Science in peace and war. 1940.

New paths in genetics. 1941, New York 1942.

Dialectical materialism and modern science. [1942]. Pamphlet.

A banned broadcast, and other essays. 1946.

Science advances. 1947, New York 1947.

What is life? New York 1947, London 1949.

Is evolution a myth?: a debate. 1949. With D. Dewar and C. M. Davies.

Everything has a history. 1951. Essays.

The biochemistry of genetics. 1954, New York 1954.

Karl Pearson 1857–1957: the centenary celebrations at University College London, 13 May 1957: the address by J. B. S. Haldane. 1958 (priv ptd).

The unity and diversity of life. Delhi 1958.

Science and Indian culture. Calcutta 1965.

Haldane was a regular contributor to Daily Worker *and* Reynold's News.

§2

Watkin, E. I. Haldane and religion. Dublin Rev 183 1928. Rptd in his Men and tendencies, 1937.

Belloc, H. An article of Mr Haldane's. In his Essays of a Catholic layman in England, 1931, New York 1931 (as Essays of a Catholic).

Belgion, M. Men like ants. Eng Rev 56 1933. On Haldane, Huxley et al.

Phillips, P. J. B. S. Haldane. [1944]. Pamphlet.

Clark, R. E. D. Scientific rationalism and Christian faith, with particular reference to the writings of Haldane and Huxley. 1945.

Moore, R. E. Haldane: two camps in one. In her Man, time and fossils, New York 1953.

Pirie, N. W. J. B. S. Haldane. In Biographical Memoirs of Fellows of the Royal Soc 12 1966.

Clark, R. W. J.B.S.: the life and work of Haldane. [1968].

JOHN SCOTT HALDANE
1860–1936

Bibliographies

In J. S. Haldane centenary symposium: the regulation of human respiration, Oxford 1961. Ed D. J. C. Cunningham and B. B. Lloyd, Oxford 1963, Philadelphia 1963.

§1

Mechanism, life and personality: an examination of the mechanistic theory of life and mind. 1913, 1921 (rev), New York 1923.

Organism and environment as illustrated by the physiology of breathing. New Haven 1917, London 1917 [1918]. Pbd in full in 1922 as Respiration.

Are physical, biological and psychological categories irreducible? 1918. By J. S. Haldane et al.

The new physiology, and other addresses. 1919.

Respiration. New Haven 1922, Oxford 1935 (new edn with J. G. Priestley), New Haven 1935.

Gases and liquids: a contribution to molecular physics. Edinburgh 1928.

The sciences and philosophy. [1929], Garden City NY 1929.

The theory of heat-engines, including the action of muscles. Edinburgh 1930.

The philosophical basis of biology. 1931, Garden City NY 1931.

Materialism. [1932].

The philosophy of a biologist. Oxford 1935, 1936 (rev).

Science and religion. [1936]. Pamphlet.

§2

Douglas, C. G. J. S. Haldane. In Obituary Notices of Fellows of the Royal Soc 2 1936.

Routh, H. V. Review of our conclusions. In his Towards the twentieth century, Cambridge 1937.

Sampson, A. H. The philosophy of J. S. Haldane with special reference to education. Philadelphia 1938.

Needham, J. Thoughts of a young scientist on the testament of an elder one [J. S. Haldane]. In his Time: the refreshing river, 1943.

N.J.S.

DONALD WILLIAM ALERS HANKEY
1884–1916

§1

The Lord of all good life: a study of the greatness of Jesus and the weakness of his Church. 1914.

A passing in June 1915. 1915. Rptd from Spectator.

The church and the man. In Faith or fear?: an appeal to the Church of England. Ed C. H. S. Matthews 1916; rptd separately New York 1917.

A student in arms. Introd by J. St Loe Strachey. 2 ser 1916, 1917, New York 1917. Rptd from Spectator. Ser 2 contains Something about A student in arms, signed H.M.A.H. [Hilda Hankey]. Selections and extracts pbd 1917 (as The beloved captain), 1923 (as The wisdom of A student in arms); ed R. S. Wright 1956 (as The beloved captain).

Religion and common sense. 1917, New York 1918.

The Cross. 1919, New York [1919]. Foreword signed E.M.

Letters

Letters. Ed E. Miller 1919, New York [1920].

§2

Budd, K. G. The story of Donald Hankey: A student in arms. 1931.

J.M.P.

GODFREY HAROLD HARDY
1877–1947

Bibliographies

Titchmarsh, E. C. Works by Hardy. In Proc London Mathematical Soc 25 1950.

Collections

Collected papers of G. H. Hardy. Vol 1, Oxford 1966–. With a bibliography of his mathematical papers.

§1

Orders of infinity: the 'Infinitärcalcül' of Paul Du Bois-Reymond. Cambridge 1910, 1924 (rev).

Collected papers of Srinivasa Ramanujan. Ed G. H. Hardy [et al], Cambridge 1927, New York 1962.

A mathematician's apology. Cambridge 1940, 1967 (foreword by C. P. Snow).

Ramanujan: twelve lectures on subjects suggested by his life and work. Cambridge 1940, New York [1959?].

Bertrand Russell and Trinity: a college controversy of the last war. Cambridge 1942 (priv ptd), 1970 (with introd by C. D. Broad).

Hardy edited and wrote a number of mathematical treatises, alone and with others, and contributed several hundred papers to mathematical journals.

§2

Snow, C. P. A mathematician and cricket. In The Saturday book, 1948.

—— G. H. Hardy. In his Variety of men, 1967. Same as the foreword to A mathematician's apology, above.

Titchmarsh, E. C. G. H. Hardy. In Obituary notices of Fellows of the Royal Soc 6 1949. *See* also Proc London Mathematical Soc 25 1950 (with a number of specialist appreciations of his work).

N.J.S.

GERALD HEARD
(HENRY FITZGERALD HEARD)
b. 1889

§1

Narcissus: an anatomy of clothes. 1924, New York 1924.

The ascent of humanity: an essay on the evolution of civilization. 1929, New York [1929].

The emergence of man. 1931, New York [1932].

Social substance of religion: an essay on the evolution of religion. 1931, New York 1931.

This surprising world: a journalist looks at science. 1932.

These hurrying years: an historical outline 1900–33. 1934. New York 1934.

Science in the making. 1935.

The source of civilization. 1935.

Exploring the stratosphere. 1936.

Science front 1936. 1937.

The third morality. 1937, New York [1937].

Pain, sex and time: a new hypothesis of evolution. 1939.

The creed of Christ: an interpretation of the Lord's Prayer. New York [1940], London 1941.

The code of Christ: an interpretation of the Beatitudes. New York [1941], London 1943.

A taste for honey. New York [1941], London 1942. Fiction.

Training for the life of the spirit. 2 pts 1941, 1944.

A dialogue in the desert. 1942.

Man the master. 1942.

Murder by reflection. New York 1942, London 1945.

Reply paid: a mystery. New York 1942.

The great frog and other weird tales. New York 1944, London 1947.

A preface to prayer. New York 1944, London 1945.

The gospel according to Gamaliel. New York 1945, London 1946.

The eternal gospel. New York 1946, London 1948.

Doppelgangers: an episode of the fourth, the psychological revolution 1997. New York 1947, London 1948.

Is God evident? an essay toward a natural theology. New York 1948, London 1950.

The lost cavern and other tales of the fantastic. New York 1948, London 1949.

The notched hairpin: a Mycroft mystery. New York 1949, London 1951.

Prayers and meditations. New York 1949.

The black fox: a novel of the seventies. 1950, New York 1951.

Is God in history? an inquiry into human and pre-human history in terms of the doctrine of creation, fall and redemption. New York 1950, London 1951.

Morals since 1900. 1950, New York 1950.

The riddle of the flying saucers. 1950, New York 1951 (as Is another world watching? the riddle of the flying saucers).

Gabriel and the creatures. New York 1952, London 1953 (as Wishing well: an outline of the evolution of the mammals told as a series of stories).

The human venture. New York 1955.

Training for a life of growth. Santa Monica, Calif 1959.

The five ages of man: the psychology of human history. New York 1964.

Heard was literary editor of Realist in 1929. From 1941 on he often used the initials 'H.F.' instead of the 'Gerald' for his fiction.

§2

Ellis, H. H. The future of religion. In his Views and reviews, ser 2 1932. Review of Heard's Social substance of religion.

Mackworth, M. H. Between the unseen and the seen. In her Notes on the way, 1937. Review of Heard's Third morality.

Forster, E. M. Heard. In his Two cheers for democracy, 1951.

A.P.H.

HERBERT HENSLEY HENSON
1863–1947

§1

Light and heaven: historical and social sermons to general congregations. 1897.

Apostolic Christianity: notes and inferences mainly based on S. Paul's Epistles to the Corinthians. 1898.

Ad rem: thoughts for critical times in the church. [1899].

Church problems: a view of modern Anglicanism by various authors. 1900. Ed Hensley Henson who also wrote the first 2 articles.

Cross-bench views of current church questions. 1902.

Godly union and concord: sermons preached mainly in Westminster Abbey in the interest of Christian fraternity. 1902, New York 1902.

Preaching to the time in St Margaret's Westminster during the Coronation year. 1902.

Studies in English religion in the seventeenth century. 1903.

Notes on popular rationalism. 1904.

The value of the Bible and other sermons, 1902–4. 1904.

Moral discipline in the Christian church, being lectures delivered during Lent 1904 in Westminster Abbey. 1905.

Religion in the schools: addresses on fundamental Christianity. 1906.

Christian marriage. 1907.

Christ and the nation: Westminster and other sermons. 1908.

The national church: essays on its history and constitution and criticisms of its present administration. 1908.

The liberty of prophesying, with its just limits and temper considered with reference to the circumstances of the modern church. 1909.

Westminster sermons. 1910.

The road to unity: an address delivered to the National Council of the Evangelical Free Churches together with and introduction and two sermons. [1911].

The creed in the pulpit. [1912]. Sermons.

Puritanism in England. 1912.

Notes of my ministry. 1913.

War-time sermons. 1915.

Robertson of Brighton 1816–53. 1916.

Christian liberty, and other sermons 1916–17. 1918.

Anglicanism. 1921.

In defence of the English church. [1923].

Quo tendimus? [1924]. Primary charge.

Notes on spiritual healing. 1925.

Church and parson in England. 1927. Ordination addresses and sermons.

The Book and the vote. 1928. On the revision of the Book of Common Prayer.

Disestablishment. 1929. Diocesan charge.

The Oxford groups. 1933, New York 1934 (as The Oxford group movement). Diocesan charge.

Christian morality: natural, developing, final. Oxford 1936.

Ad clerum. 1937. Ordination charges and addresses to the clergy.

The Church of England. Cambridge 1939.

Last words in Westminster Abbey. 1941.

Retrospect of an unimportant life. 3 vols 1942–50. Autobiography.

Bishoprick papers. 1946.

Theology and life. 1957, New York 1957. Sermons.

Letters

Letters. Ed E. F. Braley 2 vols 1950–4.

§2

Richardson, L. de C. An important life and important issues. Modern Churchman 32 1942.

Bezzant, J. S. A great and generous episcopate. Modern Churchman 33 1944.

Sykes, N. Good or great bishops. Theology 47 1944.

Jones, E. D. Henson: the royalty of the pulpit. New York [1951].

Walker, D. H. H. Henson 1863–1947. Durham Univ Jnl 52 1960.

GEORGE DAWES HICKS
1862–1941

§1

Berkeley. 1932.

The philosophical basis of theism. 1937.

Critical realism: studies in the philosophy of mind and nature. 1938.

Hicks was subeditor of Hibbert Jnl from 1902 and editor of the Cambridge Psychological Library; he also edited J. Ward, Psychology applied to education, 1926.

§2

Price, H. H. Critical realism. Mind 47 1938.
de Burgh, W. G. George Hicks. Proc Br Acad 27 1942.

H. M. R.

LANCELOT THOMAS HOGBEN
b. 1895

§1

Alfred Russel Wallace: the story of a great discoverer.
1918 (Pioneers of Progress).
Exiles of the snow, and other poems. 1918.
An introduction to recent advances in comparative physio-
logy. [1924]. With F. R. Winton.
The pigmentary effector system. Edinburgh 1924.
Comparative physiology. 1926, New York 1926.
The comparative physiology of internal secretion. Cam-
bridge 1927.
Principles of evolutionary biology. Cape Town [1927].
The nature of living matter. 1930.
Principles of animal biology. 1930, 1940 (rev), New York
1940.
Genetic principles in medicine and social science. 1931.
A journey to Nineveh, and other verses. 1932. By 'Ken-
neth Calvin Page' [i.e. Hogben].
Nature and nurture. 1933, New York 1933, London 1939
(rev).
Mathematics for the million: a popular self-educator.
1936, New York [1937], London 1937 (rev) (Primers for
the Age of Plenty 1), New York 1940 (rev), 1943 (rev),
London 1951 (rev), New York 1951, London 1953
(rev), 1967 (rev).
The retreat from reason. 1936, New York [1937].
What is ahead of us? 1937. By G. D. H. Cole, L. Hogben
et al.
Political arithmetic: a symposium of population studies.
1938. Ed Hogben.
Science for the citizen: a self-educator based on the social
background of scientific discovery. 1938, New York
1938, London 1943 (rev) (Primers for the Age of Plenty
2), 1951 (rev), New York 1951 London 1956 (rev), New
York [1956?].
Dangerous thoughts. 1939, New York 1940.
Author in transit. New York [1940].
Race, reason and rubbish, by G. Dahlberg. 1942. Tr
Hogben.
Interglossa: a draft of an auxiliary for a democratic world
order, being an attempt to apply semantic principles to
language design. 1943 (Pelican).
The loom of language: a guide to foreign languages for the
home student, by F. Bodmer. Ed and arranged by
Hogben 1943 (Primers for the Age of Plenty 3).
An introduction to mathematical genetics. 1946.
From cave painting to comic strip: a kaleidoscope of
human communication. 1949, New York 1949.
Chance and choice by cardpack and chessboard: an introduction to probability in practice by visual aids. 2 vols
1950-5, vol 1 New York 1950.
Statistical theory—the relationship of probability, credi-
bility and error: an examination of the contemporary
crisis in statistical theory from a behaviour standpoint.
1957, New York [1957?].
Design of documents: a study of mechanical aids to field
enquiries. 1960. With K. W. Cross.
Mathematics in the making. 1960, Garden City NY 1961
(for 1960).
Essential world English. 1963, New York 1963.
Science in authority: essays. 1963, New York 1963.
The mother tongue. 1964, New York 1965 (for 1964).
Whales for the Welsh: a tale of war and peace, with notes
for those who teach or preach. 1967.

*Hogben also produced or assisted with a number of educational
books, and edited several series, including Primers for the
Age of Plenty.*

§2

Van Gelder, R. Hogben: an 'author in flight'. In his
Writers and writing, New York 1946.

N. J. S.

SIR JULIAN SORELL HUXLEY
b. 1887

§1

Holyrood: the Newdigate poem. Oxford 1908.
The individual in the animal kingdom. Cambridge
1912.
Essays of a biologist. 1923, New York 1923.
Essays in popular science. 1926, New York 1927.
Religion without revelation. 1927, New York 1927, Lon-
don 1941 (abridged), 1957 (rev), New York 1957.
Ants. 1930, New York 1930, London 1935 (enlarged).
Bird-watching and bird behaviour. 1930. Broadcast talks.
Africa view. 1931, New York 1931.
What dare I think? the challenge of modern science to
human action and belief. 1931, New York 1931.
The captive shrew and other poems of a biologist. Oxford
1932, New York 1933.
Problems of relative growth. 1932, New York 1932.
A scientist among the Soviets. 1932, New York 1932.
The elements of experimental embryology. Cambridge
1934, New York 1963. With G. A. De Beer.
If I were dictator. 1934, New York 1934.
Scientific research and social needs. 1934.
We Europeans: a survey of 'racial' problems. 1935, New
York 1936. With A. C. Haddon.
The uniqueness of man. 1941, New York 1941 (as Man
stands alone).
Evolution: the modern synthesis. 1942, New York 1943,
London 1963 (rev).
On living in a revolution. 1944, New York 1944. Essays.
Evolution and ethics 1893-1943. 1947. By T. H. Huxley
and J. Huxley; includes J. Huxley, Evolutionary ethics,
1943 (Romanes lecture).
Man in the modern world. 1947, New York 1948. Essays
selected from the Uniqueness of man and On living in
a revolution.
Soviet genetics and world science: Lysenko and the mean-
ing of heredity. 1949, New York 1949 (as Heredity,
East and West: Lysenko and world science).
Evolution in action. 1953, New York 1953.
From an antique land: ancient and modern in the Middle
East. 1954, New York 1954.
New bottles for new wine: essays. 1957, New York 1960
(as Knowledge, morality and destiny: essays).
Biological aspects of cancer. 1958, New York 1958.
The story of evolution. 1958, 1969 (as The wonderful
world of evolution).
Essays of a humanist. 1964.
Charles Darwin and his world. 1965. With H. B. D.
Kettlewell.
*Huxley edited T. H. Huxley's Diary of the voyage of HMS
Rattlesnake, 1935; The science of life, 1925 (with H. G.
and G. P. Wells); the collections of essays, The new syst-
ematics, 1940 and The humanist frame, 1961; and
wrote or edited numerous popular scientific books in col-
laboration with E. N. da C. Andrade, J. B. S. Haldane
(Animal biology, 1927), A. C. Hardy et al. A number of
pamphlets and broadcast talks on political and sociological
subjects, including speeches given as Director-General of
UNESCO, were pbd separately.*

§2

Belgion, M. Men like ants. Eng Rev 56 1933. On Huxley, Haldane et al.

Russell, J. L. The religion of progress. Scrutiny 3 1934.

Clark, R. E. D. Scientific rationalism and Christian faith, with particular reference to the writings of Haldane and Huxley. 1945.

Clark, R. W. Sir J. Huxley, FRS. 1960.

— The Huxleys. 1968.

A.P.H.

WILLIAM RALPH INGE
1860–1954

Selections

Wit and wisdom of Dean Inge. Ed J. Marchant 1927, New York 1968.

§1

Society in Rome under the Caesars. 1888, New York 1888.

Christian mysticism. 1899, 1933 (new preface), New York 1956.

The person of Christ; The sacraments. In Contentio veritatis: essays in constructive theology, by six Oxford tutors, 1902.

Faith and knowledge: sermons. Edinburgh 1904.

Light, life and love: selections from the German mystics of the Middle Ages. 1904. Tr and ed W. R. Inge.

Ignatius. In The New Testament in the apostolic fathers, by a committee of the Oxford Society of Historical Theology, Oxford 1905.

Studies of English mystics. 1906, Freeport NY 1969.

Truth and falsehood in religion. 1906, New York 1907.

All Saints' sermons, 1905–7. 1907.

Personal idealism and mysticism. 1907, New York 1907.

Faith. 1909, New York 1910 (as Faith and its psychology).

Speculum animae: four devotional addresses. 1911.

The church and the age. 1912.

Causes of the decline in church-going. In Lay views of six clergy, ed H. B. Colchester 1914.

Types of Christian saintliness. 1915.

The philosophy of Plotinus. 2 vols 1918, New York 1968.

Outspoken essays. 2 ser 1919, 1922, New York 1968, 1969.

Ruskin and Plato. In Ruskin the prophet, ed J. H. Whitehouse 1920.

Christian mysticism. [1924]. Pamphlet. Different from that pbd 1899.

Liberalism in religion. 1924. Pamphlet.

Personal religion and the life of devotion. 1924, New York 1924.

England. 1926, New York 1926, London 1933 (rev), 1953 (rev), New York 1953.

The future of Christianity. In Twelve modern apostles and their creeds, by G. K. Chesterton [et al], New York 1926.

Lay thoughts of a dean. New York 1926.

The Platonic tradition in English religious thought. 1926, New York 1926.

Hebrews. In The study Bible, ed J. F. Stirling 1926.

The church in the world: collected essays. 1927, Freeport Ny 1969.

Protestantism. 1927, Garden City NY 1928, London 1935 (rev).

Assessments and anticipations. 1929, New York 1929 (as Labels and libels).

Christian ethics and modern problems. 1930, New York 1930.

The social teaching of the church. 1930, New York [1930].

What we mean by hell. In What is the real hell?, by W. R. Inge [et al], 1930.

More lay thoughts of a dean. 1931.

God and the astronomers. 1933.

Things new and old: sermons and addresses. 1933.

Vale. 1934. Autobiography.

The Bible and how to read it. 1935. Introd to Every man's Bible: an anthology, ed W. R. Inge 1931.

The causes of war, by W. R. Inge [et al]. Ed H. J. Stenning 1935.

The gate of life. 1935. Sermons.

Freedom, love and truth: an anthology of the Christian life. 1936.

A rustic moralist. 1937.

Dean Inge indicts the Red Government of Spain. [1938]. Pamphlet.

Our English Bible, by W. R. Inge [et al]. 1938.

Our present discontents. 1938. Essays.

A pacifist in trouble. 1939. Articles.

The fall of the idols. 1940.

Possible recovery? [1941]. Pamphlet.

Talks in a free country. 1942. Imaginary dialogues.

Ultimate values. [1946]. Pamphlet.

God, King and Empire: a trilogy, by W. R. Inge [et al]. 1947.

Mysticism in religion. [1947], Chicago 1948.

The end of an age and other essays. 1948, New York 1949.

The twilight of freedom. [1948]. Pamphlet.

Diary of a Dean: St Paul's 1911–34. [1949], New York 1950.

Radhakrishnan. Festschrift ed W. R. Inge [et al], 1951.

Goodness and truth, ed A. F. Judd. 1958, New York 1958 (as The things that remain). Sermons.

The awakening of the soul: an introduction to Christian mysticism. Ed A. F. Judd 1959.

Inge was a regular contributor to a number of newspapers, especially Evening Standard.

§2

Chesterton, G. K. New theologian. In his Miscellany of men, 1912.

— Inge versus Barnes, and Protestant superstitions. In his The thing, 1929.

Newton, J. F. In his Some living masters of the pulpit, New York [1923].

Dark, S. In his Five deans, 1928.

MacCarthy, D. In his Criticism, 1932.

Frauchiger, S. Der englische Modernismus in seinen neuzeitlichen Auswirkungen nach den Werken von Inge. Zurich [1936]. Bibliography.

Matthews, W. R. W. R. Inge. Proc Br Acad 40 1954.

Fox, A. Dean Inge. 1960.

Helm, R. M. Gloomy Dean: the thought of Inge. Winston-Salem NC 1962.

N.J.S.

EDWIN OLIVER JAMES
b. 1888

Bibliographies

A list of the principal published writings of James. In The saviour God: comparative studies in the concept of salvation, presented to James. Ed S. G. F. Brandon, Manchester [1963].

§1

God's eight days of creation. 1909.

Primitive ritual and belief: an anthropological essay. 1917.

An introduction to anthropology: a general survey of the early history of the human race. 1919.

The stone age. 1927, New York 1927.

The beginnings of man. [1928], New York 1929.

The Christian faith in the modern world: a study in scientific theology. 1930, Milwaukee 1930.

Origins of sacrifice: a study in comparative religion. 1933.

Christian myths and ritual: a historical study. 1933, Cleveland 1965.

In the fullness of time. 1935, New York 1935. Lectures on the historical background of Christianity.
The Old Testament in the light of anthropology. 1935, New York 1935.
The origins of religion. 1937.
Comparative religion: an introductory and historical study. 1938, 1961 (rev).
The social function of religion: a comparative study. 1940.
The beginnings of religion: an introductory and scientific study [1948], 1958 (new preface).
A history of Christianity in England. [1949].
The concept of deity: a comparative and historical study. 1950.
Marriage and society. 1952, New York 1955, 1965 (as Marriage customs through the ages).
The nature and function of priesthood: a comparative and anthropological study. [1955], New York 1961.
History of religions. 1956 (for 1957), New York 1958.
Prehistoric religion: a study in prehistoric archaeology. [1957], New York 1957.
Myth and ritual in the ancient Near East: an archaeological and documentary study. [1958], New York 1958.
The cult of the mother-goddess: an archaeological and documentary study. [1959], New York 1959.
The ancient gods: the history and diffusion of religion in the ancient Near East and the eastern Mediterranean. [1960], New York 1960.
Seasonal feasts and festivals. 1961, New York 1961.
Sacrifice and sacrament. [1962], New York 1962.
The worship of the sky-god: a comparative study in Semitic and Indo-European religion. 1963.
From cave to cathedral: temples and shrines of prehistoric, classical and early Christian times. [1965], New York 1965.
The tree of life: an archaeological study. Leyden 1966.
Christianity and other religions. 1968.
James also pbd a number of pamphlets, essays and lectures. For details see Bibliographies, above. He was editor of Folklore *1932–57, of* History of religion *ser 1960– and of* World religions *in Hutchinson's Univ Lib ser.*

P.C.

SIR JAMES HOPWOOD JEANS
1877–1946

Bibliographies
In E. A. Milne, Sir James Jeans, 1952, below.

§1

The dynamical theory of gases. Cambridge 1904, 1916 (rev and enlarged), 1921 (rev and enlarged), 1925 (rev), New York 1954.
An elementary treatise on theoretical mechanics. Boston Mass [1907].
The mathematical theory of electricity and magnetism. Cambridge 1908, 1911 (rev), 1920 (rev), 1925 (rev).
Report on radiation and the quantum-theory. 1914.
Problems of cosmogony and stellar dynamics. Cambridge 1919.
Astronomy and cosmogony. Cambridge 1928, 1929 (rev), New York 1961.
Eos: or the wider aspects of cosmogony. 1928, New York [1929], 1931 (as Man and the stars).
The universe around us. Cambridge 1929, New York [1929], Cambridge 1930 (rev), New York 1931, Cambridge 1933 (rev), 1944 (rev), New York 1944.
The mysterious universe. Cambridge 1930, 1930 (corrected), New York 1930, Cambridge 1931 (rev), New York [1932].
The stars in their courses. Cambridge 1931, New York 1931.

The new background of science. Cambridge 1933, New York 1933, Cambridge 1934 (rev), New York 1934.
Through space and time. Cambridge 1934, New York 1934.
Man and the universe. In Scientific progress, by Jeans [et al], 1936. Lectures.
Science and music. Cambridge 1937, New York 1937.
An introduction to the kinetic theory of gases. Cambridge 1940, New York 1940.
Physics and philosophy. Cambridge 1942, New York 1943.
The growth of physical science. Cambridge 1947, New York 1948; ed P. J. Grant, Cambridge 1951.

§2

Russell, J. L. The scientific best seller. Scrutiny 2 1934; rptd in Determinations, ed F. R. Leavis 1934.
Chesterton, G. K. About Jeans. In his As I was saying, 1936.
Stebbing, L. S. In her Philosophy and the physicists, 1937.
Crowther, J. G. In his British scientists of the twentieth century, 1952.
Milne, E. A. Sir James Jeans: a biography. Cambridge 1952.
Graves, R. Lucretius and Jeans. In his Crowning privilege, 1955.

J.M.P.

HAROLD HENRY JOACHIM
1869–1938

§1

A study of the ethics of Spinoza—Ethica ordine geometrico demonstrata. Oxford 1901.
The nature of truth. Oxford 1906.
Spinoza's Tractatus de intellectus emendatione: a commentary. Ed W. D. Ross, Oxford 1940.
Logical studies. Oxford 1948.
Aristotle: the Nichomachean ethics: a commentary. Ed D. A. Rees, Oxford 1951.
Descartes's rules for the direction of mind. Ed E. E. Harris 1957.
Joachim contributed trns of De lineis insecabilibus, *1908, and* De generatione et corruptione (*based on his own edn, pbd 1922*) to The works of Aristotle *translated into English. He also assisted in the editing of 2 vols of the work of F. H. Bradley*: Ethical studies, *1927, and* Collected essays, *1935.*

§2

Russell, B. The monistic theory of truth. In his Philosophical essays, 1910.
Joseph, H. W. B. Harold Henry Joachim. Proc Br Acad 24 1938. Contains a bibliography.
Bidney, D. Spinoza's Tractatus de intellectus emendatione. Philosophical Rev 51 1942.

H.M.R.

CYRIL EDWIN MITCHINSON JOAD
1891–1953

§1

Robert Owen, idealist 1917. Fabian tract.
Essays in common sense philosophy. 1919, 1933 (rev).
Common-sense ethics. 1921.
Common-sense theology [1922]. Extracts rptd as Unorthodox dialogues on education and art, 1930.

The highbrows: a modern novel. 1922.
Introduction to modern philosophy. 1924.
Introduction to modern political theory. Oxford 1924.
Priscilla and Charybdis and other stories. 1924. Fiction.
Samuel Butler 1835–1902. 1924, Boston 1924.
Mind and matter: the philosophical introduction to modern science. [1925], New York 1925.
Thrasymachus: or, the future of morals, 1925, New York 1925, London 1936 (rev, as The future of morals).
After-dinner philosophy. 1926. By Joad and J. Strachey.
The Babbitt Warren. 1926, New York 1927. A satire on the United States.
The bookmark, 1926. Essays.
The mind and its workings. 1927, New York 1928.
Diogenes: or, the future of leisure. [1928], New York 1928.
The future of life: a theory of vitalism. 1928, New York 1928.
Great philosophies of the world. 1928, New York 1930, London 1937 (rev).
The meaning of life, as shown in the process of evolution. 1928.
Matter, life and value. 1929.
The present and future of religion. 1930, New York 1930.
The horrors of the countryside. 1931. Pamphlet.
The story of civilization. 1931.
Philosophical aspects of modern science. 1932, New York 1964.
Under the fifth rib: a belligerent autobiography. 1932, New York 1933, London 1935 (as The book of Joad: a belligerent autobiography).
Counter attack from the East: the philosophy of Radhakrishnan. 1933.
Guide to modern thought. 1933, New York 1933, London 1948 (Pan books; rev and enlarged).
Is Christianity true? a correspondence between A. Lunn and Joad. 1933, 1943 (with new introd by Joad).
A charter for ramblers: or the future of the countryside [1934].
Liberty to-day. 1934, New York [1935], London 1938 (rev).
Manifesto: being the book of the Federation of Progressive Societies and Individuals. Ed Joad 1934.
Return to philosophy: being a defence of reason, an affirmation of values and a plea for philosophy. 1935, New York 1936.
The dictator resigns. 1936.
Guide to philosophy. 1936, New York 1936.
The story of Indian civilization. 1936.
The testament of Joad. 1937.
Guide to the philosophy of morals and politics. 1938, New York 1938.
Guide to modern wickedness. 1939.
How to write, think and speak correctly. Ed Joad [1939].
Why war? 1939 (Penguin Special).
For civilization. 1940. Pamphlet.
Journey through the war mind. 1940.
Philosophy for our times. 1940.
What is at stake, and why not say so? 1940.
The philosophy of federal union, 1941. Pamphlet.
The Brains Trust book: answers to 'Any questions?'. Ed H. Thomas. [1942]. With A. B. Campbell, J. S. Huxley et al.
God and evil. 1942, New York 1943.
An old countryside for new people. London [1942]. Pamphlet.
Pieces of mind. 1942. Selections from his works, by Joad.
The adventures of the young soldier in search of the better world. 1943, New York 1944.
Culture and the community. In Can planning be democratic?, 1944. Fabian tract.
Philosophy. 1944, Greenwich Conn 1962 (Teach Yourself books).
About education, 1945.
Conditions of survival. [1946]. Pamphlet.

How our minds work. 1946, New York 1947.
Spiritualism: S. Desmond for, and C. E. M. Joad against [1946].
The untutored townsman's invasion of the country. 1946.
More opinions. 1947.
The rational approach to conscription. 1947. Pamphlet.
Decadence: a philosophical inquiry. 1948, New York 1949.
The English counties. 1948, [1957] (rev by B. Webster Smith), New York 1959. Ed Joad.
A year more or less. 1948. Autobiographical essays.
The principles of parliamentary democracy. 1949.
Shaw. 1949.
A critique of logical positivism. 1950, Chicago 1950.
An introduction to contemporary knowledge. Leeds [1950].
The pleasure of being oneself. 1951, New York 1951.
A first encounter with philosophy: an introduction especially designed for young men and women. [1952].
Philosophy and ethics. Nottingham [1952]. Introd to vol 8 of International Univ Soc reading course.
The recovery of belief: a restatement of Christian philosophy. 1952.
Shaw and society: an anthology and a symposium. Ed Joad 1953.
Folly farm. 1954. Fiction.

§2

Demaray, J. G. Bernard Shaw and Joad: the adventures of two Puritans in their search for God. PMLA 78 1963.

J.M.P.

WILLIAM ERNEST JOHNSON
1858–1931

§1

Logic. 3 vols Cambridge 1921–4, New York 1964. The first 3 chs of the projected 4th vol pbd Mind 41 1932.
Johnson also pbd Treatise on trigonometry (*1889*).

§2

Broad, C. D. Proc Br Acad 17 1931.

C.H.E.P.

ERNEST JONES
1879–1958

§1

Papers on psychoanalysis. 1913, 1918 (rev and enlarged), New York 1961.
Treatment of the neuroses. 1920, New York 1963.
Essays in applied psycho-analysis. 1923, 2 vols 1951 (enlarged). First ch rptd (rev) as Hamlet and Oedipus, below.
Psycho-analysis. 1928, New York 1929, 1948 (rev and enlarged, as What is psychoanalysis?), London 1949.
The elements of figure skating. 1931, 1952 (rev and enlarged).
On the nightmare. 1931, New York 1931 (as Nightmare, witches and devils).
Hamlet and Oedipus. 1949, New York [1949].
Sigmund Freud: life and work. 3 vols 1953–7, New York 1953–7 (as The life and work of Sigmund Freud); 1 vol edn (abridged by L. Trilling and S. Marcus) New York 1961, London 1961.
Sigmund Freud: four centenary addresses. New York 1956.
Free associations: memories of a psycho-analyst. 1959, New York 1959. Autobiography.
Jones also edited Social aspects of psycho-analysis (*1924*) *and a* Glossary for the use of translators of psycho-

analytical works (*1928*); *he was founder and editor of the* International Jnl of Psychoanalysis *1920–39, and editor of the* International psycho-analytical library.

§2

Rieff, P. Life and work of Sigmund Freud. World Politics 7 1955.

Glover, E. Ernest Jones. Br Jnl of Psychology 49 1958.

Kenner, H. Tales of the Vienna Woods. In his Gnomon: essays on contemporary literature, New York 1958. On Jones' life of Freud.

Fraiberg, L. B. Ernest Jones and the psychoanalytical interpretation of Hamlet. In his Psychoanalysis and American literary criticism, Detroit 1960.

Evans, R. I. Conversations with Carl Jung and reactions from Jones. 1964.

Veszy-Wagner, L. In Psychoanalytic pioneers, ed F. Alexander [et al], New York 1966.

Morrison, C. C. Jones, Hamlet and the Oedipus complex. In her Freud and the critic: the early use of depth psychology in literary criticism, Chapel Hill [1968].

HORACE WILLIAM BRINDLEY JOSEPH
1867–1943

§1

An introduction to logic. Oxford 1906, 1916 (rev).
The labour theory of value in Karl Marx. 1923.
Some problems in ethics. Oxford 1931.
Essays in ancient and modern philosophy. Oxford 1935.
Knowledge and the good in Plato's Republic. 1948.
Lectures on the philosophy of Leibniz. Ed J. L. Austin, Oxford 1949.

§2

Smith, A. H. H. W. B. Joseph. Proc Br Acad 31 1945. With bibliography compiled by R. L. Rickard.

H.M.R.

SIR ARTHUR KEITH
1866–1955

Bibliographies

Keith, A. List of contributions made by the author to racial problems. In his The place of prejudice in modern civilization, 1931, §1 below.

Clark, W. E. Le G. Selected bibliography. In Biographical memoirs of Fellows of the Royal Soc 1 1955, §2 below.

§1

An introduction to the study of anthropoid apes. 1897.
Human embryology and morphology. 1902; successively rev and enlarged 1904, 1913, 1921, 1933 and 1948.
Illustrated guide to the Museum of the Royal College of Surgeons, England. 1910.
Ancient types of man. 1911.
The human body. [1912], New York 1912 (as Man: a history of the human body).
The antiquity of man. 1915, Philadelphia 1915, 2 vols London 1925 (rev).
The engines of the human body. 1919, Philadelphia 1920, London 1925 (rev).
Menders of the maimed: the principles underlying the treatment of injuries to muscles, nerves, bones and joints. 1919, Philadelphia 1952.
New discoveries relating to the antiquity of man. 1931, New York 1931.

Ethnos: or the problems of race considered from a new point of view. 1931.

The place of prejudice in modern civilization. 1931 (Rectorial address, Aberdeen University).

See M.M., The benefits moral and secular of assassination: an essay to correct Keith's eugenical speculations on the merits of war and peace, 1932.

The stone age of Mount Carmel: the fossil human remains from the Levalloiso-Mousterian. Oxford 1939. With T. D. McCown. Vol 2 of the report on the Mount Carmel excavations.

Essays on human evolution. 1946, New York 1947 (as Evolution & ethics, pref by E. A. Hooton).

A new theory of human evolution. 1948, New York 1949.

An autobiography. 1950, New York 1950.

Darwin revalued. 1955. Biographical study.

Keith pbd several lectures and booklets on Darwinian evolutionary theory and edited Darwin, Origin of species, *Hughes,* Manual of practical anatomy *and F. Treves,* Surgical applied anatomy. *He contributed to a report on human and other remains found at Newport, Monmouthshire (1911), to T. Wrightson,* Analytical mechanism of the inner ear (*1918*), *to vol 2 of the* Ur excavation reports (*1927*), *to F. T. Petre,* Researches in prehistoric Galilee (*1927*) *and to B. S. Thomas,* Arabia felix (*1932*).

§2

Chesterton, G. K. The mask of the agnostic. In his The thing, 1929.

Clark, W. E. Le G. Keith. Biographical Memoirs of Fellows of the Royal Soc 1 1955.

A.P.H.

JOHN MAYNARD KEYNES, BARON KEYNES
1883–1946

See cols 1175–7, above.

RONALD ARBUTHNOTT KNOX
1888–1957

Collections and Selections

A selection from the occasional sermons. Ed E. Waugh 1949.

In three tongues. Ed L. E. Eyres 1959. Anthology of Knox's Greek, Latin and English verses with some English prose pieces.

Occasional sermons; The pastoral sermons; University and Anglican sermons. Ed P. Caraman 3 vols 1960–3, New York 1960–4.

§1

Signa severa. Eton 1906. Verses.

Juxta salices. Oxford 1910. Verse and prose.

Remigium alarum. Oxford 1910. Chancellor's prize for Latin verse.

A still more sporting adventure! humbly dedicated to the authoresses of 'An adventure' and transcribed by the Misses Lavinia and Priscilla Daisyfield. Oxford 1911. Pp. 44–76 are Knox's work. A skit on the book by C. A. E. Moberley and E. F. Jourdain.

Naboth's vineyard in pawn: three sermons on the Church of England in the past, in the present and in the future. 1913; rptd in The Church in bondage, 1914, below.

Some loose stones: being a consideration of certain tendencies in modern theology illustrated by reference to the book called 'Foundations' [ed B. H. Streeter]. 1913, New York 1913, 1915 (with new preface and additional note).

The Church in bondage. 1914. Sermons preached 1911–14.

An hour at the front. 1914, 1916 (abridged, as Ten minutes at the front). Prayers.

Reunion all round: or, Jael's hammer laid aside: being a plea for the inclusion within the Church of England of all Mahometans, Jews, Buddhists, Brahmins, Papists and Atheists, by the author of Absolute and Abitofhell. 1914; rptd in Essays in satire, 1928, below.

Absolute and Abitofhel: being a satire in the manner of Dryden on a newly-issued work entitl'd Foundations [ed B. H. Streeter], by RAK. 1915 (Fulham Books 4). First pbd Oxford Mag 28 Nov 1912 and 27 Feb 1913 [not Oct 1913 as stated on title-page]; rptd in Essays in satire, 1928 below.

Bread or stone: four conferences on impetrative prayer. 1915.

An apologia. 1917 (priv ptd). For distribution to members of the Society of SS. Peter and Paul after Knox's conversion.

The essentials of spiritual unity. 1918.

A spiritual Aeneid. 1918, New York 1918, London 1950 (corrected, adds 'After 33 years'), 1958 (introd by E. Waugh).

Meditations on the Psalms. 1919.

Patrick Shaw-Stewart. 1920.

Q. Horati Flacci Carminum librum quintum, a R. Kipling and C. Graves anglice redditum, edidit A. Godley, Oxford. 1920. Parody.

Memories of the future: being memories of the years 1915–72, written in 1988 by Opal, Lady Porstock. Ed [or rather written by] Knox 1923.

The miracles of King Henry VI. Cambridge 1923. Introd and trn by Knox.

A book of acrostics. 1924.

Sanctions: a frivolity. 1924. Novel.

Virgil. Aeneid Books vii to ix, partly in the original and partly in English verse translation. Ed [and tr] Knox, Oxford 1924.

Londinium defensum: a play in three acts, produced by G. E. Headlam. [Ware 1925]. Pbd as suppl to Edmundian, Oct 1925. In Latin.

Thesauropolemopompus: a play in two acts. [Ware 1925]. With A. B. Purdie. Pbd as suppl to Edmundian, May 1925. In Latin.

The viaduct murder. 1925, New York 1926. Detective novel.

An open-air pulpit. 1926. Essays, mainly first pbd in Evening Standard.

Other eyes than ours. 1926. Novel.

The belief of Catholics. 1927, New York 1927, London 1939 (with a new preface and slight corrections) ('What I Believe' ser).

The three taps: a detective story without a moral. 1927, New York 1927.

Anglican cobwebs. [1928]. Substance of course of sermons.

Essays in satire. 1928, New York 1930.

The footsteps at the lock. 1928. Detective novel.

The mystery of the kingdom and other sermons. 1928.

The rich young man: a fantasy. [1928]. On the Crucifixion.

The best detective stories of the year 1928. Ed Knox and H. Harrington, with introd by Knox [1929]. Introd largely rptd in Literary distractions, 1958, below.

The Church on earth. 1929, New York 1929.

On getting there. 1929. Essays first pbd in Universe and Evening Standard.

Caliban in Grub Street. 1930, New York 1930. On current attitudes towards religion.

Broadcast minds. 1932. A criticism of the works of scientific publicists such as H. G. Wells, J. Huxley, B. Russell, H. L. Mencken, G. Heard, J. Langdon-Davies.

Difficulties: being a correspondence about the Catholic religion between Knox and Arnold Lunn. 1932, 1952 (adds 1 letter).

The body in the silo. [1933], New York 1934 (as Settled out of court). Detective novel.

Still dead. 1934, New York 1934. Detective novel.

Barchester pilgrimage. 1935, New York 1936. Tales in continuation of Trollope's novels, in his style.

Heaven and Charing Cross: sermons on the Holy Eucharist. 1935, New York 1936. 3 sermons rptd in The window in the wall, 1956, below.

The Holy Bible: an abridgement and rearrangement. 1936, New York 1936.

Double cross purposes. 1937. Detective novel.

Let dons delight: being variations on a theme in an Oxford common-room. 1939, New York 1939. Imaginary dialogues.

Captive flames: a collection of panegyrics. 1940, New York 1941.

Nazi and Nazarene. 1940 (Macmillan War Pamphlets 5).

In soft garments: a collection of Oxford conferences. 1942.

I believe: the religion of the Apostles' creed. Reading 1944. Abridged revisions of sermons pbd as The Creed in slow motion, 1949, below.

God and the atom. 1945, New York 1945.

A retreat for priests. 1946, New York 1946.

The Mass in slow motion. 1948, New York 1948. Sermons.

The Creed in slow motion. 1949, New York 1949. Sermons.

The trials of a translator. New York 1949, London 1949 (as On Englishing the Bible; adds 1 essay). Mainly first pbd in Clergy Rev.

Enthusiasm: a chapter in the history of religion, with special reference to the xvii and xviii centuries. Oxford 1950, New York 1950.

The Gospel in slow motion. New York 1950, London 1950. Sermons.

St Paul's gospel. 1950, New York 1950 (for 1951). Lenten Conferences, Westminster Cathedral 1950.

Stimuli. 1951, New York 1951. Sermons first pbd in Sunday Times.

The hidden stream: a further collection of Oxford conferences. 1952, New York 1953.

A New Testament commentary for English readers. 3 vols New York 1952–6, London 1953–6.

Off the record. 1953, New York 1954. Selected letters on religious matters.

A retreat for lay people. 1955, New York 1955.

The window in the wall and other sermons on the Holy Eucharist. 1956, New York 1957 (for 1956).

Bridegroom and bride. 1957, New York 1957. Essays on marriage.

On English translation: the Romanes lecture. Oxford 1957; rptd in next.

Literary distractions. 1958, New York 1958.

The priestly life: a retreat. New York 1958, London 1959.

Lightning meditations. New York [1959], London 1959. First pbd in Sunday Times.

Proving God: a new apologetic. [1959]. Preface by E. Waugh. 4 chs from an unfinished work.

Retreat for beginners. New York [1960], London 1961 (as Retreat in slow motion).

The layman and his conscience: a retreat. New York 1961, London 1962 (without subtitle).

A number of Knox's sermons, addresses etc were first pbd separately. Many were rptd by him in the collections listed and most have been rptd by Caraman (see Collections, above). He also contributed many introds, chs etc to books, a few of which were rptd in Literary distractions, *1958, above.*

Translations of the Bible, the Liturgy and other Devotional Works

The Holy Gospel of Jesus Christ according to Matthew. [1941] (priv ptd).

The New Testament of our Lord and Saviour Jesus Christ, newly tr from the Vulgate. 1944 (priv ptd), 1945 (first authorized edn with slight changes), New York 1946 (Chanticleer edn, illustrated). The 4 Gospels and Acts were each separately issued in 1949.

The Epistles and Gospels for Sundays and holidays. Tr with notes 1946.

The Book of Psalms in Latin and English with the Canticles used in the Divine Office. 1947, 1964 (ed II. Richards, The Golden Lib). English tr and notes by Knox.

The Old Testament, newly translated from the Vulgate: vol 1, Genesis to Esther, New York 1948, London 1949; vol 2, Job-Machabees. 1949, New York 1950; 1 vol 1958 (as The shorter Knox Bible: Old Testament). An abridgement, ed L. Johnson.

Holy Week: the text of the Holy Week Offices with a new translation. 1951, New York 1951.

Day, M. All my life love: a commentary on St Thérèse's poem 'Vivre d'amour'. Harrow [1953]. Trn of poem by Knox.

The Holy Bible: a translation from the Latin Vulgate. 1955, New York 1956. First 1 vol edn.

Autobiography of a saint: Thérèse of Lisieux. [1958].

The imitation of Christ, by Thomas à Kempis. Tr Knox and M. Oakley [1959]. Completed by Oakley after Knox's death.

Knox also contributed trns to the revision of The Westminster hymnal, 1940, and the revision of The manual of prayers, 1942, (withdrawn 1943).

§2

[Begbie, E. H.]. In his Painted windows: a study in religious personality, 1922.

Lunn, A. H. M. In his Roman converts, 1924.
—— Knox: some memories. Month new ser 18 1957.

Waugh, E. Mgr Ronald Knox. Horizon 17 1948.
—— The life of Knox. 1959.

Meehan, D. Knox 1950. Irish Ecclesiastical Record 5 ser 76 1951.

Ham, E. B. Knox on Jansenist enthusiasm. JHI 19 1958.

Rich, E. C. Knox's conversion. Month new ser 19 1958.

Speaight, R. A modern Virgilian: a memorial lecture to R. Knox delivered to the Virgil Soc, 1958. [1959].
—— Ronald Knox the writer. 1966.

Corbishley, T. Ronald Knox the priest. 1964.

M.P.

CLIVE STAPLES LEWIS
1898–1963
See cols 1073–8, above.

WILLIAM MCDOUGALL
1871–1938

Bibliographies
Robinson, A. L. William McDougall: a bibliography, together with a brief outline of his life. Durham, North Carolina 1943.

Selections
William McDougall, explorer of the mind: studies in psychical research. Ed R. Van Over et al, [New York 1967].

§1

Physiological psychology. 1905, New York 1905 (Temple Primers).

An introduction to social psychology. 1908, Boston 1909. Rev and enlarged successively in 1909, 1910, 1912, 1914, 1919, 1926, 1928, 1931, 1936.

Body and mind: a history and a defense of animism. 1911, New York 1911.

The pagan tribes of Borneo: a description of their physical, moral and intellectual condition, with some discussion of their ethnic relations. 2 vols 1912, New York 1912. With C. Hose.

Psychology: the study of behaviour. 1912, New York [1912], London 1914 (rev), 1937 (with new preface).

The group mind: a sketch of the principles of collective psychology with some attempt to apply them to the interpretation of national life and character. Cambridge 1920, New York 1920, Cambridge 1927 (with new preface).

Is America safe for democracy? New York 1921, London 1921 (as National welfare and national decay). Essay on eugenics.

An outline of psychology. 1923, New York [1923], London 1928 (rev with new preface).

Ethics and some modern world problems. 1924, New York 1924.

The indestructible union: rudiments of political science for the American citizen. Boston 1925, London [1926] (as The American nation: its problems and psychology).

Outline of abnormal psychology. New York [1926], London 1933.

Character and the conduct of life: practical psychology for everyman. 1927, New York 1927.

Janus—the conquest of war: a psychological enquiry. [1927], New York [1927].

The battle of behaviorism: an exposition and an exposure. 1928, New York 1929. With J. B. Watson.

Modern materialism and emergent evolution. 1929, New York 1929.

[Reminiscences]. In A history of psychology in autobiography vol 1, ed C. Murchison, Worcester Mass 1930.

World chaos: the responsibility of science. 1931, New York [1932].

The energies of men: a study of the fundamentals of dynamic psychology. 1932, New York 1933, London 1933 (rev with new preface).

The frontiers of psychology. London and Cambridge 1934, New York 1935.

Religion and the sciences of life, with other essays on allied topics. 1934, Durham North Carolina 1935.

Psycho-analysis and social psychology. 1936.

The riddle of life: a survey of theories. 1938.

McDougall was joint or associate editor of the Br Jnl of Psychology, *the* Jnl of General Psychology *and the* Jnl of Parapsychology.

§2

Robinson, Bibliography, *above, lists reviews, discussions of technical aspects of McDougall's work, and other obituary notices.*

Flugel, J. C. In his A hundred years of psychology. 1933, 1951 (rev), 1964 (rev D. J. West).

Spearman, C. The life and work of McDougall. Character & Personality 7 1939.

Greenwood, M. and M. Smith. In Obituary Notices of Fellows of the Royal Soc 3 1940–1.

Roback, A. A. McDougall and hormic psychology. In his A history of American psychology, New York 1952.

Evans, J. W. Biographical introduction. In William McDougall, explorer of the mind: studies in psychical research, ed R. Van Over et al, [New York 1967].

C.H.E.P.

JOHN McTAGGART ELLIS
McTAGGART
1866–1925

§1

Studies in the Hegelian dialectic. Cambridge 1896, New York 1964.

Studies in Hegelian cosmology. Cambridge 1901.

Some dogmas of religion. 1906, 1930 (with memoir by C. D. Broad), New York 1968 (1906 edn rptd).

A commentary on Hegel's logic. Cambridge 1910, New York 1964.

Dare to be wise: an address delivered before the Heretics Society in Cambridge. 1910. Rptd in Philosophical studies, 1934, below.

Human immortality and pre-existence. 1915, New York 1915. First pbd as chs 2 and 4 of Some dogmas of religion, 1906, above.

The nature of existence. 2 vols (vol 2 ed C. D. Broad) Cambridge 1921, 1927, Grosse Pointe Mich 1968.

Philosophical studies. Ed S. V. Keeling, Cambridge 1934, New York 1934. Includes addresses previously pbd separately.

§2

Broad, C. D. McTaggart. Proc Br Acad 13 1927; rptd in Some dogmas of religion, 1930, above, and in Broad's Ethics and the history of philosophy, 1952.

— Examination of McTaggart's philosophy. 2 vols Cambridge 1933–8. See also R. L. Patterson, A critical account of Broad's estimate of McTaggart, in The philosophy of Broad, ed P. A. Schilpp, New York [1959].

Dickinson, G. L. J. McT. E. McTaggart; with chs by B. Williams and S. V. Keeling. Cambridge 1931.

J.G.

CYRIL CHARLIE MARTINDALE
1879–1963

Bibliographies

In Bibliography of the English province of the Society of Jesus, 1773–1953, compiled by E. F. Sutcliffe 1957. Includes trns.

§1

Saint Christopher, breaker of men, and other stories. 1908.

In God's nursery. 1913. Stories.

Theosophy. 1913, 1928 (rev).

Old Testament stories. [1913].

New Testament stories. [1914].

The waters of twilight. 1914.

The goddess of ghosts. 1915. Stories.

In God's army. Vol 1, Commanders-in-chief: St Ignatius Loyola, St Francis Xavier; vol 2, Captains of Christ: St Francis Borgia, St John Francis Regis, St Peter Claver; vol 3, Christ's cadets: St Aloysius Gonzaga, St Stanislaus Kostka, St John Berchmans. 3 vols 1915–17. Vol 3 originally pbd in Stella Maris ser 1913.

The life of Monsignor Robert Hugh Benson. 2 vols 1916.

Upon God's holy hills. 1, The guides: St Anthony of Egypt, St Bruno of Cologne, St John of the Cross. 1919.

Catholic thought and thinkers: introductory. 1920.

Princes of his people. 1, St John the Evangelist; 2, Saint Paul. 3 vols 1920–4. Pt 1 in 2 vols. Vol 2, The Apocalypse of St John, rptd separately as St John and the Apocalypse, 1958.

Jock, Jack, and the corporal. 1921, 1960 (abridged), New York 1961. Fiction.

Marie Thérèse Couderc, foundress of the Congregation of Our Lady of the Cenacle. 1921.

Marie Thérèse de Soubiran, 1834–89, foundress of the Society of Marie Auxiliatrice, and Marie Elisabeth de Luppé, 1841–1903. 1921. Reissued with the preceding, 1921, with cover title King's daughters, 1.

Mr Francis Newnes. 1921. Fiction; a continuation of Jock, 1921, above.

Richard Philip Garrold, SJ. 1921.

St Justin the Martyr. 1921.

Charles Dominic Plater, SJ. 1922.

Bernard Vaughan, SJ. 1923.

Albert Alfred, PC. 1925. Stories.

The difficult Commandment. 1925.

Christ is king: a course of sermons. 1927.

The faith of the Roman Church. 1927, New York 1951.

The religions of the world. 1927.

The sacramental system. 1927, New York 1928.

The vocation of Aloysius Gonzaga. 1927, New York 1945.

The Kingdom and the world: a course of sermons. [1928].

Man and his destiny. 1928, New York 1928.

The creative words of Christ. 1929. A course of sermons.

The mind of the Missal. [1929], New York 1929.

The risen sun: impressions in New Zealand and Australia. 1929.

The wounded world: a course of sermons. 1929.

The cup of Christ. 1930. A course of sermons; this and the previous 4 courses of sermons reissued as Christianity is Christ, 1935, below.

Bill. 1931. Religious essays in the form of letters.

Mother Francesca Saverio Cabrini, foundress of the Missionary Sisters of the Sacred Heart. 1931.

What think ye of Christ? 1931.

African angelus: episodes and impressions. 1932.

What are saints?: fifteen chapters in sanctity. 1932, New York 1933.

The words of the Missal. 1932, New York 1932.

The holy year, 1933–4. 1933.

Some broadcast sermons. 1934.

Athens, Argentine, Australia. 1935. Travel reminiscences.

Christianity is Christ: five courses of sermons. 1935, New York 1936. Collected sermons.

From bye-ways and hedges: Hermann the cripple, B. Martin de Porres and St Benedict Joseph Labre. 1935.

The foundress of the Sisters of the Assumption—Mother Marie-Eugénie Milleret de Brou. 1936.

The gates of the church: sermons. 1936.

Does God matter for me? 1937, New York 1937.

Our Blessed Lady: sermons. 1938, New York 1938.

Letters from their aunts. [1939]. Fictitious letters on Christianity.

Poplar leaves and seaweed. 1940. Poems.

The sweet singer of Israel. 1940, New York 1940 (as Towards loving the Psalms). Meditations on verses from the Psalms.

The fountain of life: six readings written for broadcasting in the BBC Home Service during Holy Week 1946. 1946.

Life of Saint Camillus. 1946.

The manifold mass, and The invisible child. 1947, New York 1947.

Portuguese pilgrimage, July 1st—September 4th, 1947. 1949, New York 1949.

Can Christ help me? [1950], Westminster Maryland 1950.

The message of Fatima. 1950, New York [1950] (as The meaning of Fatima).

The spirit of God. 1950.

The Queen's daughters: a study of women-saints. 1951, New York 1951.

The two voices: spiritual conferences of R. H. J. Steuart SJ: edited, with a memoir, by C. C. Martindale, SJ. 1952.

The life of Mère Anne-Marie Javouhey. 1953.

The castle and the ring. New York 1955, London [1959]. Fiction.

Jesus Christ and his gospel. 1958.

Martindale also edited parts of the Catholic liturgy, with trns and explanatory notes, and the Gospels and Acts of the Apostles in the Stonyhurst Scripture manuals ser, with introds and commentaries. He produced many small pamphlets, especially for the Catholic Truth Soc, including 6 in their ser, Lectures on the history of religions, 1908–11, which he also edited, and 6 in their Studies in comparative religion 1934–5. He was also responsible for edns and trns of the works of several other authors, and, with W. B. O'Dowd, edited the ser Catholic thought and thinkers, from 1920.

§2

Martindale: a symposium. Month new ser 30 1963.
Caraman, P. C. C. Martindale: a biography. 1967.

D.K.

ERIC LIONEL MASCALL
b. 1905

Death or dogma? Christian faith and social theory. [1937].
A guide to Mount Carmel: being a summary and an analysis of The ascent of Mount Carmel by St John of the Cross, with some introductory notes. 1939.
The God-man. 1940.
Man: his origin and destiny. 1940.
He who is: a study in traditional theism. 1943.
Christ, the Christian and the Church: a study of the Incarnation and its consequences. 1946.
Existence and analogy: a sequel to He who is. 1949, Hamden Conn 1967.
Corpus Christi: essays on the Church and the Eucharist. 1953, 1965 (rev and enlarged).
Christian theology and natural science: some questions on their relations. 1956, New York 1956.
Via media: an essay in theological synthesis. 1956, Greenwich Conn 1957.
Words and images: a study in theological discourse. 1957, New York 1957.
The importance of being human: some aspects of the Christian doctrine of man. New York 1958, London 1959.
The recovery of unity: a theological approach. 1958.
Pi in the High. 1959. Verse.
Grace and glory. 1961, New York 1961.
Theology and images. 1963.
Up and down in Adria: some considerations of the volume entitled Soundings [ed A. R. Vidler]. 1963.
The secularization of Christianity: an analysis and a critique. 1965, New York 1966.
The Christian universe. 1966, New York 1966.
Theology and the future. 1968, New York 1968.
Mascall edited The Church of God: an Anglo-Russian symposium, The Mother of God, *and other devotional works for the Fellowship of St Alban and St Sergius. He edited* (with H. S. Box) The Blessed Virgin Mary *and* (with J. V. L. Casserley) Signposts *12 vols 1940–1, and pbd pamphlets on ecumenical and other theological subjects.*

WALTER ROBERT MATTHEWS
b. 1881

§1

Studies in Christian philosophy. 1921, 1928 (rev).
The idea of revelation. 1923.
The gospel and the modern mind. [1925], New York [1925].
The psychological approach to religion. 1925.
God and evolution. 1926.
Some modern problems of faith. 1928.
God in Christian thought and experience. 1930.
The adventures of Gabriel in his search for Mr Shaw: a modest companion for Mr Shaw's Black girl. 1933.
Essays in construction. 1933, New York [1934] (as God and this troubled world: essays in spiritual construction).
Seven words [the Seven Words from the Cross]. 1933.
The purpose of God. 1935.
The hope of immortality. 1936, 1966 (rev).
Our faith in God. 1936.
Christ. 1939. (What did they teach?)

Following Christ. 1940.
The moral issues of the war. 1940.
The foundations of peace. 1942.
Strangers and pilgrims. 1945. Sermons.
St Paul's Cathedral in wartime 1939–45. 1946.
The problem of Christ in the twentieth century: an essay on the Incarnation. 1950.
Week by week: a year's reflections. First ser 1952. Rptd articles.
Some Christian words. 1956.
The search for perfection. 1957, New York 1957. Rptd articles.
The Lord's prayer: an exposition for today. [1958], New York 1960.
The Thirty-nine Articles. 1961.
Memories and meanings. 1969.
Matthews also pbd a number of collections of broadcast addresses. He edited a number of Joseph Butler's sermons; a symposium, Dogma in history and thought; the King's College lectures on immortality; and A history of St Paul's Cathedral and the men associated with it (with W. M. Atkins). He also edited the series The library of constructive theology (with J. Marchant et al), The new library of devotion, Problems of worship (with F. W. Dwelly), and The Colet library of modern Christian thought. He contributed to various collections of essays on theological subjects, pbd several single lectures and pamphlets on religious and social topics, and has contributed a regular weekly article to Daily Telegraph since 9 April 1949.

A.P.H.

JAMES MOFFATT
1870–1944

§1
Translations of the Bible

The historical New Testament: being the literature of the New Testament arranged in the order of its literary growth and according to the dates of the documents— a new translation edited with prolegomena, historical tables, critical notes and an appendix. Edinburgh 1901, 1901 (rev).
The New Testament: a new translation. 1913, 1914 (rev), 1922 (parallel edn with the Authorized version), New York [1922].
The Old Testament: a new translation. 2 vols [1924], New York [1924–5]. *See also* O. T. Allis, Dr Moffat[t]'s 'New translation' of the Old Testament. Princeton Theological Rev 23 1925.
The Bible: a new translation, containing the Old and New Testaments. 1926, New York [1926] (as The Holy Bible, containing the Old and New Testaments: a new translation), London 1935 (rev, as A new translation of the Bible, containing the Old and New Testaments), New York [1935]. A reissue of the two preceding.

Other Works

Harnack, C. G. A. von. The expansion of Christianity in the first three centuries. Tr and ed Moffatt. 2 vols 1904–5, 1908 (rev and enlarged as The mission and expansion of Christianity in the first three centuries), New York 1962.
George Meredith: a primer to the novels. 1909, New York 1909 (as George Meredith: introduction to his novels).
Paul and Paulinism. 1910, Boston 1910.
The second things of life. [1910].
An introduction to the literature of the New Testament. Edinburgh 1911, New York 1911, Edinburgh 1912 (rev), 1918 (rev). *See also* W. M. Ramsay, The first Christian century: notes on Dr Moffatt's Introduction to the literature of the New Testament, 1911.
The life of John Owen. [1911].

Reasons and reasons. 1911. Sermons.

The theology of the Gospels. 1912, New York 1913. Studies.

The approach to the New Testament. 1921.

The Bible in Scots literature. [1924].

A critical and exegetical commentary on the Epistle to the Hebrews. Edinburgh 1924. (International Critical Commentary on the Holy Scriptures 39).

Handbook to The Church hymnary [of 1927]. Ed Moffatt 1927, 1935 (with supplement by M. Patrick).

The General Epistles: James, Peter and Judas. 1928, Garden City NY 1928. (Moffatt New Testament Commentary).

The Presbyterian churches. 1928, Garden City NY 1928.

Love in the New Testament. 1929, New York 1930.

A tangled web. [1929]. Detective fiction.

The day before yesterday. 1930, Nashville Tenn 1930. A survey of late nineteenth-century literature with special reference to religion.

Grace in the New Testament. 1931, New York 1932.

His gifts and promises: being twenty-five reflections and directions on phases of our Christian discipline, from the inside. Edinburgh 1934, New York 1934.

The First Epistle of Paul to the Corinthians. 1938. (Moffatt New Testament Commentary).

The first five centuries of the Church. 1938, Nashville Tenn 1938.

Jesus Christ the same. New York and Nashville Tenn [1940], London 1942.

The thrill of tradition. 1944, New York 1944.

Moffatt also pbd a number of devotional works, other surveys of theological literature, anthologies and collections of religious and literary quotations, and selections from his translations of the Bible. He also edited the letters of J. Denney [1922], selections from the writings of J. Owen (1904) and J. Tillotson (1926), The expositor's year book (1926, 1927) and the Moffatt New Testament Commentary (18 vols 1928–50). He was executive secretary, 1930–44, to the American Standard Bible Committee responsible for the Revised Standard Version of the Bible (pbd 1946–52).

C.H.E.P.

GEORGE EDWARD MOORE
1873–1958

Bibliographies

Buchanan, E. and G. E. Moore. Bibliography of the writings of Moore. In The philosophy of Moore, ed P. A. Schilpp, Evanston Ill 1942, New York 1952 (rev), §2 below.

In Klemke, E. D. (ed). Studies in the philosophy of Moore, 1969, §2 below. Includes works on Moore.

§1

Principia ethica. Cambridge 1903.

Ethics. [1912], New York 1912.

Philosophical studies. 1922, New York 1922.

A defence of common sense. In Contemporary British philosophy: personal statements 2nd ser, by G. E. Moore et al, ed J. H. Muirhead 1925; rptd in Philosophical papers, 1959, below.

Proof of an external world. Proc Br Acad 25 1939; rptd in Philosophical papers, 1959, below.

An autobiography; A reply to my critics. In The philosophy of Moore, ed P. A. Schilpp, Evanston Ill 1942, New York 1952 (adds Addendum to my reply).

Russell's Theory of descriptions. In The philosophy of Russell, ed P. A. Schilpp, Evanston Ill 1942.

Some main problems of philosophy. 1953, New York 1953. Lectures given 1910–11, with appendix and notes.

Visual sense-data. In British philosophy in the mid-century: a Cambridge symposium, ed C. A. Mace 1957, New York 1957.

Philosophical papers. 1959, New York 1959.

Common-place book, 1919–53. Ed C. Lewy 1962 (for 1963).

Lectures on philosophy. Ed C. Lewy [1966]. Lectures given 1925–34.

Moore edited Mind 1921–47.

§2

Schilpp, P. A. (ed). The philosophy of Moore. Evanston Ill 1942, New York 1952 (rev).

Keynes, J. M. In his Two memoirs, 1949. The effect of Principia ethica on Bloomsbury.

In W. B. Yeats and T. Sturge Moore: their correspondence, 1901–37, ed U. Bridge 1953. Moore's philosophy discussed at length by his brother and Yeats.

Johnstone, J. K. Bloomsbury philosophy. In his Bloomsbury group, 1954.

Paul, G. A. Moore: analysis, common usage and common sense. In The revolution in philosophy, by A. J. Ayer [et al], 1956.

Passmore, J. Moore and Russell. In his A hundred years of philosophy, 1957.

Warnock, G. J. In his English philosophy since 1900, 1958.

White, A. R. Moore: a critical exposition. Oxford 1958.

Ewing, A. C. The work of Moore. Indian Jnl of Philosophy 1 1959.

Listener 30 April 1959. Influence and thought of Moore: symposium of reminiscences by four of his friends, B. Russell, L. Woolf, M. White and J. Wisdom.

Jacques, J. H. The appeal to common sense: the philosophers T. Reid and Moore. Listener 21 April 1960.

Jnl of Philosophy 57 1960. Contains: M. White, Memoirs of G. E. Moore; E. Nagel, The debt we owe to Moore; A. Ambrose, Three aspects of Moore's philosophy, rptd in Ambrose and Lazerowitz, 1970, below.

Warnock, M. In her Ethics since 1900, 1960.

Woolf, L. In his Sowing: an autobiography of the years 1880–1904, 1960.

Braithwaite, R. B. G. E. Moore, Proc Br Acad 47 1961; rptd in Ambrose and Lazerowitz, 1970, below.

Malcolm, N. In his Knowledge and certainty, Englewood Cliffs NJ 1963; rptd in Ambrose and Lazerowitz, 1970, below.

Brunius, T. G. E. Moore's analysis of beauty: an impasse and a way out. Upsala 1964.

Lewy, C. Moore on the naturalistic fallacy. Proc Br Acad 50 1964; rptd in Ambrose and Lazerowitz, 1970, below.

Addis, L. C. and D. Lewis. Moore and Ryle: two ontologists. Iowa 1965.

Dickie, G. T. Clive Bell and the method of Principia ethica. Br Jnl of Aesthetics 5 1965.

Loring, L. M. The ethical values of Moore. In her Two kinds of values, 1966.

Klemke, E. D. The epistemology of Moore. Evanston Ill 1969.

— (ed). Studies in the philosophy of Moore. Chicago 1969.

M.P.

JOHN MIDDLETON MURRY
1889–1957

See cols 1092–6, above.

NOEL JOSEPH TERENCE MONTGOMERY NEEDHAM
b. 1900

§1

Mechanistic biology and the religious consciousness. In Science, religion and reality, [by various authors]. Ed Needham 1925, New York 1925, 1955 (with introductory essay by G. Sarton).

Man a machine: in answer to a romantical and unscientific treatise written by E. Rignano & entitled Man not a machine. 1927, New York [1928].

Materialism and religion. 1929. Pamphlet.

The sceptical biologist: ten essays. 1929, New York [1930].

Chemical embryology. 3 vols Cambridge 1931, New York 1963.

The great amphibium: four lectures on the position of religion in a world dominated by science. 1931. All except the third lecture previously pbd separately.

A history of embryology. Cambridge 1934, London 1959 (rev, with A. Hughes), New York 1959. First appeared as pt 2 of Chemical embryology, above.

Adventures before birth, by Jean Rostand. Tr Needham 1936.

Order and life. New Haven 1936, Cambridge 1936.

The Nazi attack on international science. 1941.

Biochemistry and morphogenesis. Cambridge 1942.

Time: the refreshing river. Essays and addresses 1932–42. 1943, New York 1943.

Chinese science. 1945.

History is on our side: a contribution to political religion and scientific faith. 1946, New York 1947.

Science and civilisation in China. Cambridge 1954–.

Chinese astronomy and the Jesuit mission: an encounter of cultures. 1958. Pamphlet.

Heavenly clockwork: the great astronomical clocks of medieval China. Cambridge 1960. With W. Ling and D. J. de Solla Price.

Science and China's influence on the world. In The legacy of China, ed R. S. Dawson, Oxford 1964.

The grand titration: science and society in East and West. 1969.

Within the four seas: the dialogue of East and West. 1969. Includes single lectures previously pbd separately.

Needham edited and contributed to a number of other collections of papers and symposia on scientific and related subjects.

J. G.

JOHN WOOD OMAN
1860–1939

§1

On religion: speeches by F. D. E. Schleiermacher. 1893, New York 1958 (introd by R. Otto). Tr Oman.

Vision and authority: or the throne of St Peter. 1902, 1928 (rev).

The problem of faith and freedom in the last two centuries. 1906.

The church and the divine order. [1911].

The war and its issues: an attempt at a Christian judgement. Cambridge 1915.

Grace and personality. Cambridge 1917, 1919 (rev), 1925 (rev), New York 1961.

The paradox of the world: sermons. Cambridge 1921.

The Book of Revelation: theory of the text. Cambridge 1923.

The office of the ministry. 1928.

The text of Revelation: a revised theory. Cambridge 1928.

The natural and the supernatural. Cambridge 1931, New York 1931.

Concerning the ministry. 1936, New York 1937.

Honest religion. Cambridge 1941, New York 1941. With a memoir of the author by G. Alexander and H. H. Farmer.

A dialogue with God, and other sermons and addresses. [1951].

§2

Tennant, F. R. John Wood Oman. Proc Br Acad 25 1939.

Healey, F. G. Religion and reality: the theology of Oman. Edinburgh 1965.

N. J. S.

MICHAEL POLANYI
b. 1891

Bibliographies

Polanyi, J. An index to Polanyi's contributions to science. In The logic of personal knowledge: essays presented to Polanyi, 1961.

Bibliography [of Polanyi's work to 1960]. Ibid.

§1

Atomic reactions. 1932.

The contempt of freedom: the Russian experiment and after. 1940.

Full employment and free trade. Cambridge 1945.

Science, faith and society. Oxford 1946, Chicago 1964.

The logic of liberty: reflections and rejoinders. 1951, Chicago 1958.

Personal knowledge: towards a post-critical philosophy. 1958, Chicago 1958.

The study of man. 1959, Chicago 1959.

Beyond nihilism. Cambridge 1960.

The tacit dimension. 1967.

Knowing and being. 1969, Chicago 1969. Essays, ed M. Grene.

§2

Knight, F. H. Foundations of academic freedom. Ethics 59 1949.

— Science, faith and society. Ibid.

Hamilton, B. Morality and social progress. Blackfriars 41 1960. On Beyond nihilism.

Ignotus, P. The Hungary of Polanyi. In The logic of personal knowledge: essays presented to Polanyi, 1961.

Aron, R. Max Weber and Polyani. Ibid.

Hook, S. Enlightenment and radicalism. In History and hope: tradition, ideology and change in modern society, ed K. A. Jelenski, New York 1962. On Beyond nihilism.

Gelwick, R. L. Polanyi: modern reformer. Religion in Life 34 1965.

Langford, T. A. Polanyi and the task of theology. Jnl of Religion 46 1966.

Buchanan, J. M. Politics and science: reflections on Knight's critique of Polanyi. Ethics 77 1967.

SIR KARL RAIMUND POPPER
b. 1902

See col 1204, above.

HENRY HABBERLEY PRICE
b. 1889

Perception. 1932, 1950 (rev), 1961 (new preface).

Hume's theory of the external world. Oxford 1940.

Thinking and experience. 1953, Cambridge Mass 1953.

Belief. 1969, New York 1969.

H. M. R.

HAROLD ARTHUR PRICHARD
1871–1947

§1

Kant's theory of knowledge. Oxford 1909.
Moral obligation: essays and lectures. Oxford 1949,
London 1968 (adds Duty and interest: an inaugural
lecture; introd by J. O. Urmson).
Knowledge and perception: essays and lectures. Oxford
1950.

§2

Price, H. H. Prichard. Proc Br Acad 33 1947.

D. K.

CHARLES EARLE RAVEN
1885–1964

Selections

In praise of birds. 1950. Selections from In praise of
birds, The ramblings of a bird lover, Bird haunts and
bird behaviour, Musings and memories.

§1

What think ye of Christ? being lectures on the Incarnation
and its interpretation in terms of modern thought. 1916.
Christian socialism 1848–54. 1920.
Apollinarianism: an essay on the Christology of the early
church. Cambridge 1923.
In praise of birds. 1925.
Our salvation: a course of addresses on the Atonement.
1925.
The eternal spirit: an account of the Church Congress.
1926. [1926].
The creator spirit: a survey of Christian doctrine in the
light of biology, psychology and mysticism, with appen-
dix on Biochemistry and mental phenomena by J.
Needham. 1927.
The ramblings of a bird lover. 1927.
Christ and modern education. 1928.
The quest of religion. 1928, New York 1928.
A wanderer's way. 1928, New York 1929. Autobiography.
Women and holy orders: a plea to the Church of England.
[1928], New York 1929 (as Women and the ministry).
Bird haunts and bird behaviour. 1929.
Jesus and the gospel of love. 1931, New York [1931].
Looking forward—towards 1940. [1931]. On the 1930
Lambeth Conference.
Musings and memories. 1931. Collected essays.
The New Testament. 1931.
The life and teaching of Jesus Christ. Cambridge 1933.
With E. Raven.
Is War obsolete? a study of the conflicting claims of reli-
gion and citizenship. 1935.
One called Help! the life and work of Beatrice Hankey.
1937. With R. F. Heath.
War and the Christian. 1938, New York 1938.
The Cross and the crisis. 1940.
The Gospel and the Church: a study of distortion and its
remedy. 1940.
John Ray, naturalist. Cambridge 1942.
Lessons of the Prince of Peace. 1942.
Good news of God: being eight letters dealing with
present problems and based on Romans I–VIII. 1943.
Science, religion and the future. Cambridge 1943.
English naturalists from Neckam to Ray: a study of the
making of the modern world. Cambridge 1947.
The theological basis of Christian pacifism. New York
1951, London 1952.
Science and the Christian man. 1952. Broadcast talks.

Natural religion and Christian theology. 2 ser Cambridge
1953.
Christianity and science. 1955, New York 1955.
Christ and the modern opportunity. 1956, Greenwich
Conn 1956.
Science, medicine and morals: a survey and a suggestion.
[1959], New York 1959.
St Paul and the Gospel of Jesus: a study of the basis of
Christian ethics. 1961.
Teilhard de Chardin: scientist and seer. 1962, New York
1962.
*Raven also pbd a report of the mission to Cambridge Univer-
sity in 1920. He contributed to the symposia* The Church
of today *and* Anglican essays, *and pbd numerous single
lectures and addresses on theological and social subjects.*

§2

Hildebrandt, F. This is the message: a continental reply
to Raven, 1944.
Ramsey, I. T. Raven. Proc Br Acad 51 1965.

A. P. H.

WILLIAM HALSE RIVERS RIVERS
1864–1922

§1

The Todas. 1906.
The influence of alcohol and other drugs on fatigue. 1908.
The history of Melanesian society. 2 vols Cambridge 1914.
Kinship and social organization. 1914.
Instinct and the unconscious: a contribution to a biological
theory of the psycho-neuroses. Cambridge 1920.
Conflict and dream. 1923, New York 1923.
Psychology and politics, and other essays. 1923. With an
appreciation by C. S. Myers.
Medicine, magic and religion. [Ed] with a preface by
G. Elliot Smith 1924, New York 1924.
Social organization. Ed W. J. Perry 1924.
Psychology and ethnology. Ed G. Elliot Smith 1926,
New York 1926.
With J. H. Ward Rivers edited Br Jnl of Psychology *from
1904 and was one of the supervisors of the* Cambridge
archaeological and ethnological ser *from 1906. He con-
tributed* Report on anthropological research outside
America *to* Reports upon the present condition and
future needs of the science of anthropology, *Washington
DC 1902, and edited* Essays on the depopulation of
Melanesia, *Cambridge 1922.*

§2

Myers, C. S. Influence of Rivers on the development of
psychology in Great Britain. Nature 110 1922.
Bennett, A. Rivers: some recollections. In his Things
that have interested me ser 2, 1923.
Lowie, R. H. In his History of ethnological theory, New
York 1937.

SIR WILLIAM DAVID ROSS
1877–1971

§1

Aristotle. 1923, 1930 (rev), 1937 (rev), 1949 (rev).
The right and the good. Oxford 1930.
Foundations of ethics. Oxford 1939.
Plato's theory of ideas. Oxford 1951.
Kant's ethical theory: a commentary on the Grundlegung
zur Metaphysik der Sitten. Oxford 1954.

Ross was first joint (with J. A. Smith), then sole editor of The
works of Aristotle translated into English *1908-52
(some vols of which he undertook himself), and pbd standard
edns of a number of Aristotle's works.*

§2

Ewing, A. C. Recent developments in British ethical
thought. In British philosophy in the mid-century, ed
C. A. Mace 1957.

H. M. R.

BERTRAND ARTHUR WILLIAM
RUSSELL, 3RD EARL RUSSELL
1872–1970

A detailed catalogue of the archives of Bertrand Russell:
archive administrator and editor, B. Feinberg, *1967 (300
copies) contains lists of the Amberley papers, mss of books,
articles and speeches, personal and public correspondence; the
archives are held by McMaster Univ, Hamilton, Ontario.*

Bibliographies

Jacob, G. Russell: an essay toward a bibliography. Bull of
Bibliography 13–14 1929–30.

Denoun, L. E. Bibliography of the writings of Russell. In
The philosophy of Russell, ed P. A. Schilpp, Evanston Ill
1944, 1946 (rev), New York 1951 (rev), 2 vols 1963 (rev).
Includes contributions to books and periodicals.

Ruja, H. Russell: a classified bibliography 1929–67. Bull
of Bibliography 25–6 1968–9.

Selections

Selected papers of Bertrand Russell, selected with a special
introduction by Russell. New York 1927.

Let the people think: a selection of essays. 1941.

The wit and wisdom of Russell. Ed L. E. Denoun, Boston
1951. Aphorisms.

Russell: dictionary of mind, matter and morals. Ed L. E.
Denoun, New York 1952, 1968 (as The wisdom of
Russell; abridged).

Why I am not a Christian and other essays on religion and
related subjects. Ed P. Edwards 1957 (omits A free
man's worship), New York 1957 (omits The existence of
God). With appendix on the Russell case.

Russell's best: silhouettes in satire, selected and introduced
by R. E. Egner. 1958, New York 1961.

The basic writings of Russell 1903–59. Ed R. E. Egner
and L. E. Denoun 1961, New York [1961].

On the philosophy of science. Ed C. A. Fritz, Indianapolis
1965. Mainly selected chs from Russell's books.

§1

German social democracy: six lectures, with an appendix
on social democracy and the women question in Germany by A. Russell. 1896, 1965 (with new preface and
without appendix), New York [1965].

An essay on the foundations of geometry. Cambridge
1897, New York 1956 (foreword by M. Kline). French
trn (Paris 1901) has revisions and annotations which
have never appeared in English.

A critical exposition of the philosophy of Leibniz; with an
appendix of leading passages. Cambridge 1900, London
1937 (with new introd). French trn (Paris 1908) has
new preface.

The principles of mathematics. Vol 1, Cambridge 1903,
London 1937 (with new introd), New York 1938. All
pbd.

To the electors of the Wimbledon division of Surrey.
1907. Election manifesto.

Anti-Suffragist anxieties. [1910]. People's Suffrage Federation pamphlet.

Philosophical essays. 1910, 1966 (rev), New York 1967.
For '2nd edn' *see* Mysticism and logic, 1918, below.

Principia mathematica. 3 vols Cambridge 1910–13, 1925–
7 (rev); abridged edn of vol 1 pbd 1962 (as Principia
mathematica to *56). With A. N. Whitehead; Russell
was responsible for all new material in 1925–7 edn.

The problems of philosophy. [1912], New York [1912].

Our knowledge of the external world as a field for scientific
method in philosophy. Chicago 1914, London 1914,
1926 (rev), New York 1929 (with new preface). Lowell
Lectures.

The philosophy of Bergson, with a reply by H. W. Carr
and a rejoinder by Mr Russell. Cambridge 1914; rptd in
A history of western philosophy, 1945, below.

Scientific method in philosophy: the Herbert Spencer
lecture. Oxford 1914; rptd in Mysticism and logic,
1918, below.

War—the offspring of fear. [1914]. Union of Democratic
Control pamphlet.

Justice in war-time. Manchester 1915, Chicago 1916
(includes The policy of the Entente, below), London
1916, Chicago 1917 (rev), London 1917.

The philosophy of pacifism. [1915]. Pamphlet. Also ptd
in Towards ultimate harmony: report of Conference on
Pacifist Philosophy of Life, pbd for the League of Peace
and Freedom 1916.

The policy of the Entente, 1904–14: a reply to Professor
Gilbert Murray [i.e. to his pamphlet, The foreign policy
of Sir Edward Grey, 1906–15, Oxford 1915]. Manchester [1915]; rptd in Justice in war-time (1916 edn),
above.

Bertrand Russell and the War Office. [1916]. Pamphlet;
rptd in Justice in war-time, (1917 edn), above.

The case of Ernest F. Everett. [1916]. No-Conscription
Fellowship leaflet; discussion of the case of a conscien-
tious objector which led to Russell's prosecution; rptd in
the Autobiography of Russell, 1914–44, 1967, below.

Principles of social reconstruction. 1916, New York 1917
(as Why men fight: a method of abolishing the international duel).

Rex vs. Russell: report of the proceedings before the Lord
Mayor. 1916. No-Conscription Fellowship pamphlet;
a speech in his own defence.

Political ideals. [1916]. Pamphlet; rptd in Political ideals,
New York 1917, below.

What are we fighting for? [1916]. No-Conscription Fellowship leaflet.

Why not peace negotiations? [1916]. No-Conscription
Fellowship leaflet.

Political ideals. New York 1917, London 1963 (with new
foreword), New York 1964. Lecture ser.

Mysticism and logic and other essays. 1918, New York
1929 (with new preface). Includes 2nd and 3rd essays of
Philosophical essays, above.

Roads to freedom: socialism, anarchism and syndicalism.
1918, 1919 (rev), New York 1919 (as Proposed roads to
freedom), 1949 (rev).

Introduction to mathematical philosophy. 1919, New
York 1919.

The practice and theory of Bolshevism. 1920, New York
1920 (as Bolshevism: practice and theory), London 1949
(rev), New York 1964.

The analysis of mind. 1921, New York 1921.

Free thought and official propaganda. 1922, New York
1922. Lecture; rptd in Sceptical essays 1928, below.

The problem of China. 1922, New York 1922, London
[1926] (with postscript), 1966 (with new foreword).

The ABC of atoms. 1923, New York 1923, London 1924
(rev).

A free man's worship, with a special preface. Portland
Maine 1923, Girard Kansas 1927 (as What can a free
man worship?). Rptd from Philsophical essays, 1910.

The prospects of industrial civilization. 1923, New York
1923, 1959 (with new preface by Dora Russell). With
Dora Russell.

Bolshevism and the West: a debate on the resolution 'that the Soviet form of government is applicable to Western civilization'; S. Nearing, affirmative; B. Russell, negative. 1924, New York 1924 (as Debate: resolved that the Soviet form of government is applicable to Western civilization).

How to be free and happy. New York 1924. Lecture.

Icarus: or, the future of science. 1924, New York 1924; rptd in The future of science, 1959, below.

The ABC of relativity. 1925, New York 1925, London 1958 (rev, ed F. Pirani), Fair Lawn NJ 1958, London 1969 (rev).

What I believe. 1925, New York 1925; rptd in Why I am not a Christian, 1927, below.

On education, especially in early childhood. 1926, New York 1926 (as Education and the good life). Pt 2 rptd as Education of character, New York 1961.

The analysis of matter. 1927, New York 1927, New York 1954 (introd by L. E. Denoun), London 1954.

An outline of philosophy. 1927, New York [1927] (as Philosophy).

Why I am not a Christian. 1927, [New York] 1927.

Sceptical essays. 1928, New York 1928.

A liberal view of divorce. Girard Kansas [1929]. Pamphlet.

Marriage and morals. 1929, New York 1929. *See* L. Dewar, Marriage without morals [1931]. A reply.

The conquest of happiness. 1930, New York 1930.

Debate! Is modern marriage a failure? Resolved: that the present relaxing of family ties is in the interest of the good life; B. Russell, affirmative; J. C. Powys, negative. New York 1930.

Has religion made useful contributions to civilization?: an examination and a criticism. 1930, Girard Kansas 1930. Pamphlet.

The scientific outlook. 1931, New York 1931, 1949 (rev).

Education and the social order. 1932, New York 1932 (as Education and the modern world).

Freedom and organization, 1814–1914. 1934, New York 1934 (as Freedom versus organization). Rptd 1965, pts 1, 2 as Legitimacy versus industralism 1814–48; pts 3, 4 as Freedom versus organization 1774–1914.

In praise of idleness, and other essays. 1935, New York 1935.

Religion and science. 1935, New York [1935].

Determinism and physics: being the 18th Earl Grey Memorial Lecture. Newcastle-upon-Tyne 1936.

Which way to peace? 1936.

The Amberley papers: the letters and diaries of Lord and Lady Amberley [Bertrand Russell's parents]. Ed Bertrand and Patricia Russell 2 vols 1937, New York 1937. Selection; a complete list of the Amberley Papers is given in A detailed catalogue of the archives of Bertrand Russell, above.

Education for democracy: an address. 1937.

Power: a new social analysis. 1938, New York 1938.

An inquiry into meaning and truth. 1940, New York 1940. William James Lectures, Harvard Univ.

How to become a philosopher: the art of rational conjecture; How to become a logician: the art of drawing inferences; How to become a mathematician: the art of reckoning. Girard Kansas 1942, New York 1968 (as The art of philosophizing).

How to read and understand history: the past as the key to the future. Girard Kansas 1943. Pamphlet; rptd in Understanding history, 1957, below.

An outline of intellectual rubbish: a hilarious catalogue of organized and individual stupidity. Girard Kansas 1943. Pamphlet; rptd in Unpopular essays, 1950, below.

The value of free thought: how to become a truth-seeker and break the chains of mental slavery. Girard Kansas 1944. Pamphlet; rptd in Understanding history, 1957, below.

A history of Western philosophy and its connection with political and social circumstances from the earliest times to the present day. New York 1945, London 1946, 1961 (rev).

Ideas that have helped mankind. Girard Kansas 1946. Pamphlet.

Is materialism bankrupt?: mind and matter in modern science. Girard Kansas 1946. Pamphlet; rptd in Understanding history, 1957, below.

Physics and experience: the Henry Sidgwick lecture. Cambridge 1946.

The faith of a rationalist. [1947], Girard Kansas 1947. Pamphlet.

Philosophy and politics. 1947. National Book League Lecture; rptd in Unpopular essays, 1950, below.

Human knowledge: its scope and limits. 1948, New York 1948.

Towards world government. [1948]. New Commonwealth pamphlet.

Am I an atheist or an agnostic?: a plea for tolerance in the face of new dogmas. Girard Kansas 1949.

Authority and the individual: the Reith lectures, 1948–9. 1949, New York [1949], Boston 1960 (adds Terminal essay, Philosophy and politics).

The philosophy of logical atomism: lectures delivered in 1918 and published as a series of articles by the Monist, 1918 and 1919. [Minneapolis 1949]. Unauthorized reprint. Text again rptd in Logic and knowledge, 1956, below.

Unpopular essays. 1950, New York [1951?].

The impact of science on society. New York 1951, London 1952 (enlarged), New York 1953.

New hopes for a changing world. 1951, New York [1952?].

How near is war? 1952. Pamphlet.

What is freedom? 1952. Pamphlet; rptd (rev) in Fact and fiction, 1961, below.

The good citizen's alphabet. 1953, New York 1958, London 1970 (adds History of the world in epitome, 1962). Drawings by F. Themerson, captions by Russell.

Satan in the suburbs, and other stories. 1953, New York 1953.

What is democracy? 1953. Pamphlet; rptd in Fact and fiction, 1961, below.

History as an art: the Herman Ould Memorial Lecture. Aldington Kent 1954; rptd in Portraits from memory, 1956, below.

Human society in ethics and politics. 1954, New York 1955.

Nightmares of eminent persons, and other stories. 1954, New York 1955.

Man's duel from the hydrogen bomb. 1955. Pamphlet; rptd in Portraits from memory, 1956, below.

Logic and knowledge: essays 1901–50. Ed R. C. Marsh 1956, New York 1956.

Portraits from memory, and other essays. 1956, New York 1956.

Understanding history, and other essays. New York 1957.

The will to doubt. New York 1958.

Common sense and nuclear warfare. 1959, New York 1959.

The future of science, with a 'self-portrait' of the author. New York 1959.

My philosophical development. 1959, New York 1959. With appendix, Russell's philosophy, by A. Wood.

Wisdom of the West: a historical survey of Western philosophy in its social and political setting. Ed P. Foulkes 1959, New York 1959.

Act or perish. [1960]. By Rev Michael Scott and Russell (but written by Russell). The statement that launched the Committee of 100.

Russell speaks his mind. Cleveland 1960, London [1960]. Text of a ser of television interviews by W. Wyatt in 1959.

Civil disobedience. Birmingham 1961. Speech.

Education of character. New York 1961. Pt 2 of On education, especially in early childhood, 1926, above.

Fact and fiction. 1961, New York 1962. Essays and stories.

Has man a future? 1961, New York 1962.

Win we must. Birmingham 1961. Speech; rptd in the Autobiography of Russell vol 3, 1969, below.

Essays in skepticism. New York 1962.

History of the world in epitome: for use in Martian infant schools. 1962. Drawings by F. Themerson; rptd in The good citizen's alphabet (1970 edn), above.

You are to die. [1962]. Leaflet issued at the time of the Cuban crisis.

Unarmed victory. 1963, New York 1963.

Legitimacy versus industrialism, 1814–48. 1965. Pts 1, 2 of Freedom and organization, 1934, above.

Freedom versus organization 1776–1914. 1965. Pts 3, 4 of Freedom and organization, 1934, above.

Danger in South-East Asia. [1965]. Leaflet.

The Labour party's foreign policy. 1965. Speech.

Appeal to the American conscience. [1966]. Russell Peace Foundation pamphlet on Vietnam; rptd in War crimes in Vietnam, 1967, below.

The autobiography of Russell (1872–1914; 1914–44; 1944–67). 3 vols 1967–9; vols 1, 2 Boston [1967–8], vol 3 (subtitled 1944–69) New York [1969?].

War crimes in Vietnam. 1967, New York [1967].

Principal Contributions to Books

L'idée d'ordre et la position absolue dans l'espace et le temps. In Bibliothèque du Congrès international de philosophie vol 3, Paris 1901.

What happened at Leeds: report published by the Council of Workers' and Soldiers' Delegates. 1917. Speech praising Clifford Allen.

Collected speeches of Russell and Dora Black. Peking 1921. In Chinese.

Lectures of John Dewey and Russell. Ed C. L. Cheung, Shanghai 1921.

Wittgenstein, L. Tractatus logico-philosophicus. 1922, New York 1922. Introd by Russell.

Government by propaganda. In These eventful years: the twentieth century in the making as told by many of its makers, 1924, New York 1924.

Logical atomism. In Contemporary British philosophy: personal statements ser 1, by B. Russell [et al], ed J. H. Muirhead 1924; rptd in Logic and knowledge, 1956, above.

Styles in ethics. In Our changing morality: a symposium, ed F. Kirchwey, New York 1924.

Marchant, J. (ed). The ethics of birth control. 1925. Russell contributes a long statement on behalf of the Workers' Birth Control League.

Science. In Whither mankind: a panorama of modern civilization, ed C. A. Beard, New York 1928.

On the evils due to fear. In If I had only one sermon to preach, 1929, New York 1929 (as If I could preach just once).

Divorce by mutual consent. In Divorce as I see it, by B. Russell [et al]. 1930, New York [1930?] (as Divorce).

Living philosophies. New York 1931, London 1940 (as I believe). Contribution.

Scientific society. In Science in the changing world, by B. Russell [et al], ed M. G. A. Adams 1933.

Why I am not a communist. In The meaning of Marx: a symposium, New York 1934.

Some psychological difficulties of pacifism in war time. In We did not fight: 1914–18 experiences of war resisters, ed J. Bell 1935.

Science and social institutions. In Dare we look ahead?, by B. Russell [et al], 1938, New York 1938.

Democracy and economics. In 'Calling America': a special number of Survey Graphic on the challenge to democracy, ed P. Kellogg, New York 1939.

Dewey's new logic. In The philosophy of Dewey, ed P. A. Schilpp, Evanston Ill 1939.

Freedom and government. In Freedom: its meaning, by B. Russell [et al], ed R. N. Anshen, New York 1940, London 1942.

The philosophy of Santayana. In The philosophy of Santayana, ed P. A. Schilpp, Evanston Ill 1940.

My mental development: reply to criticisms. In The philosophy of Russell, ed P. A. Schilpp, Evanston Ill 1944, 1946 (rev), New York 1951 (rev), 2 vols 1963 (rev).

Marchant, J. (ed). What life has taught me. 1948. Contribution.

Ideas and beliefs of the Victorians: Toleration. In Ideas and beliefs of the Victorians, 1949.

Nature and origin of scientific method: Scepticism and intolerance. In The western tradition: a series of talks given in the BBC European programme, 1949, Boston 1951.

Values in the atomic age. In The atomic age, [1949].

The political and cultural influence. In The impact of America on European culture, by B. Russell [et al], Boston 1951.

Why Communism must fail, by B. Russell [et al]. 1951.

Science and human life. In What is science?, ed J. Newman, New York 1955, London 1956.

The road to peace. In The bomb: challenge and answer, by B. Russell [et al], ed G. McAllister 1955.

Why I oppose Communism: a symposium, by B. Russell [et al]. 1956.

Can scientific man survive? In The challenge of sputniks, ed R. Witkin, New York 1958.

Lady Carlisle's ancestry. In D. Henley, Rosalind Howard, Countess of Carlisle, 1958.

In search of peace. In A study of Nehru, ed R. Zakaria, Bombay 1959.

A fifty-six year friendship. In Gilbert Murray: an unfinished autobiography, ed J. Smith and A. Toynbee 1960.

The expanding mental universe. In Adventures of mind, ed R. Thruelsen and J. Kobler, 1960, New York 1960.

Neutralism: a debate with Hugh Gaitskell. In Background and foreground: an anthology of articles from the New York Times, ed L. Markel, Great Neck NY 1961. For Russell's rejoinder see New York Times Mag 14 Aug 1960.

Bertrand Russell in the lions' den. In G. McKnight, The compleat after-dinner speaker, 1962. A speech to Foyle's literary luncheon soon after his release from prison in 1961.

The early history of the Pugwash movement. In Disarmament: its politics and economics, ed S. Melmann, Boston 1962.

On civil disobedience. In Instead of violence, ed A. and L. Weinberg, New York 1963.

On the committee of 100. In A matter of life, ed C. Urquhart 1963, Boston 1963.

A plea for neutral action. In Disarmament: a world view, ed J. Davis, New York 1964.

Three statements. In Seeds of liberation, ed P. Goodman, New York 1964. Statements on entering prison in 1961.

Napalm och massmord. In Napalm, ed J. Takman, Stockholm 1967. In Swedish.

Rotblat, J. Pugwash—the first ten years. 1967. Contains the Russell–Einstein manifesto.

Whitrow, G. J. Einstein, the man and his achievement. 1967. Broadcast discussions.

Mr Wilson speaks 'frankly and fearlessly' on Vietnam to Bertrand Russell. 1968. Pamphlet containing Russell's correspondence with Wilson.

Appeal to the Stockholm conference on Czechoslovakia. In Czechoslovakia and socialism, Nottingham 1969.

Russell edited Tribune (*organ of the No-Conscription Fellowship*) *1916–17.*

Letters

Other dimensions: a selection from the later correspondence of Victoria Lady Welby, ed Mrs Henry Cust 1931. Letters to Lady Welby.

Malleson, Constance. In the north: autobiographical fragments in Norway, Sweden, Finland: 1936–46. 1946. Letters to Lady Constance Malleson.

Rolland, R. Journal des années de guerre. 1914–19. Paris 1952. Letters to Rolland.

The vital letters of Russell, Krushchev, Dulles. 1958. Introd by K. Martin. Rptd from New Statesman.

Sinclair, U. My lifetime in letters. Columbia Montana 1960. Letters to Sinclair.

Gathorne-Hardy, R. (ed). Ottoline: the early memoirs of Lady Ottoline Morrell. 1963. Letters to Lady Ottoline.

Hart, H. Dr Barnes of Merion. New York 1963. Letters to Dr Barnes.

Gilbert, M. Plough my own furrow: the story of Lord Allen of Hurtwood as told through his writings and correspondence. 1965. Letters to Allen.

Kindinger, R. (ed). Philosophenbriefe aus der wissenschaftlichen Korrespondenz von Alexius Meinong. Graz 1965. Letters to Meinong.

van Heijenoort, J. (ed). From Frege to Gödel: a source book in mathematical logic, 1879–1931. Cambridge Mass 1967. Letters to Frege and van Heijenoort.

Feinberg, B. and R. Kasrils (ed). Dear Bertrand Russell …a selection of his correspondence with the general public, 1950–68. 1969.

Utley, F. Odyssey of a liberal. Washington 1969. Letters to Utley and Bernard Shaw.

Many additional letters are contained in the Autobiography of Bertrand Russell, *1967–9, above. Facs of letters are to be found in* A detailed catalogue of the archives of Bertrand Russell, *1967, Bibliographies, above.*

§2

Santayana, G. The philosophy of Russell. In his Winds of doctrine, 1913, New York 1925.

Bradley, F. H. In his Essays on truth and reality, Oxford 1914.

Jourdain, P. E. B. The philosophy of Mr B*rtr*nd R*ss*l. 1918. A humorous account.

Scott, J. W. Syndicalism and philosophical realism. London 1919. Criticism of Russell's political philosophy and his views on Bergson.

Bosanquet, B. The Russell mind. In his Three chapters on the nature of mind, 1923.

Russell, J. F. S., 2nd Earl Russell. My life and adventures. 1923. Autobiography of Russell's brother.

Watkin, E. I. Religion without dogma: Russell's purely subjective religion. Dublin Rev 180 1927; rptd in his Men and tendencies, 1937.

Wood, H. G. Why Russell is not a Christian. 1928. Reply to Why I am not a Christian, 1927. For Russell's counter-reply, *see* Literary Guide March 1929.

Belgion, M. Our present philosophy of life, pt 5: according to Russell. 1929.

Lovejoy, A. O. Russell and the unification of mind and matter. In his Revolt against dualism: an inquiry concerning the existence of ideas, New York [1930].

Mannin, Ethel. In her Confessions and impressions, [1930].

Malleson, Constance. In her After ten years: a personal record, 1931.

Wickham, H. In his Unrealists, 1931.

Jørgensen, J. J. F. T. Russell: en praktisk idealist og hans filosofi. Copenhagen 1935.

Mirsky, D. In his Intelligentsia of Great Britain, 1935.

Bremond, A. Russell's religion without God. In his Religions of unbelief, Milwaukee, 1939.

Dewey, J. and H. M. Kallen (ed). The Russell case. New York 1941. Essays by various authors on the revocation of Russell's appointment to the chair of philosophy in the College of the City of New York.

Hardy, G. H. Russell and Trinity: a college controversy of the last war. Cambridge 1942 (priv ptd), 1970 (with introd by C. D. Broad).

Schilpp, P. A. (ed). The philosophy of Russell. Evanston 1944, 1946 (rev), New York 1951 (rev), 2 vols 1963 (rev).

Lawrence, D. H. Letters to Russell. Ed H. T. Moore, New York 1948. Russell's letters have not survived.

Webb, B. Our partnership. Ed B. Drake and M. I. Cole 1948. Contains early character sketches of Russell.

Darbon, A. La philosophie des mathématiques: étude sur la logistique de Russell. Paris 1949.

Keynes, J. M. My early beliefs. In his Two memoirs, 1949.

Dorward, A. J. Russell: a short guide to his philosophy. 1951 (Br Council pamphlet).

Fritz, C. A. Russell's construction of the external world. 1952.

Götlind, E. J. A. Russell's theories of causation. Uppsala 1952.

Rivista Critica di Storia della Filosofia 8 1953. No 2 contains several articles on Russell's philosophy.

Pears, D. F. Logical atomism: Russell and Wittgenstein. In The revolution in philosophy, by A. J. Ayer [et al], 1956.

— Russell and the British tradition in philosophy. 1967.

Urmson, J. O. In his Philosophical analysis—its development between two world wars, Oxford 1956.

Horowitz, I. L. Russell: man against man. In his Idea of war and peace in contemporary philosophy, New York 1957.

Wood, A. Russell: the passionate sceptic. 1957.

Clark, C. H. D. Christianity and Russell: a critique of the essay Why I am not a Christian. 1958.

Feibleman, J. K. Inside the great mirror: a critical examination of the philosophy of Russell, Wittgenstein and their followers. The Hague 1958.

Warnock, G. J. In his English philosophy since 1900, 1958.

Riveroso, E. Il pensiero di Russell. Naples 1958.

Jarrett, J. L. D. H. Lawrence and Russell. In A D. H. Lawrence miscellany, ed H. T. Moore, Carbondale 1959.

Parker, R. A. Alys and Bertie, 1894–1921. In his Transatlantic Smiths, New York 1959, London 1960 (as A family of friends: the story of the transatlantic Smiths).

Chow, Tse-tsung. In his May fourth movement: intellectual revolution in modern China, Cambridge Mass 1960.

Philosophy 35 1960. Contains A. R. Quinton, Russell's philosophical development (essay review of My philosophical development, 1959); D. H. Monroe, Russell's moral theories; and Russell's reply.

Woolf, L. Sowing: an autobiography of the years 1880–1904. 1960. Russell's effect on Cambridge at the turn of the century is discussed.

Aomi, J. Bertrand Russell. Tokyo 1961. In Japanese.

Gottschalk, H. Russell: eine Biographie. Berlin 1962; tr 1965.

Aiken, L. W. Russell's philosophy of morals. New York 1963.

Park, J. Russell on education. Columbus Ohio 1963.

Driver, C. In his Disarmers: a study in protest, 1964.

Greer, H. In his Mud pie: the CND story. 1964.

Bowne, G. D. In his Philosophy of logic 1880–1908, 1966.

Trent, C. The Russells. 1966.

Boulton, D. Objection overruled. 1967. Details of Russell's work in the No-Conscription Fellowship during World War I.

Devaux, P. Russell ou la paix dans la vérité. Paris 1967. Biography.

Schoenman, R. (ed). Russell—philosopher of the century: essays in his honour. 1967.

Eames, E. R. Contemporary British criticism of Russell. Jnl of Southern Philosophy 6 1968.

— Russell's theory of knowledge. 1969.

Lewis, J. Russell: philosopher and humanist. 1968.

Perez, D. Bertrand Russell. Barcelona 1968. Biography and an exposition of Russell's thought.

Vuillemin, J. Leçons sur la première philosophie de Russell. Paris 1968.
Clark, R. J. Russell's theory of language. The Hague 1969.
Hampshire, S. The autobiography of Russell. In his Modern writers and other essays, 1969.
Ready, W. Necessary Russell. Toronto 1969. Short biography quoting from previously unpbd letters.

GILBERT RYLE
b. 1900

§1

Proceedings of the Seventh International Congress of Philosophy, Oxford 1930. Ed Ryle 1931.
John Locke on the human understanding. In John Locke: tercentenary addresses at Christ Church 1932, by J. L. Stocks and Ryle, 1933.
Bibliography for the Honours School of Philosophy, Politics and Economics. Oxford 1935 (compiled by E. L. Hargreaves, J. P. R. Maud and Ryle), 1937 (rev by J. E. Meade, K. C. Wheare and Ryle).
Philosophical arguments. Oxford 1945. Lecture.
The concept of mind. 1949, New York 1959.
Systematically misleading expressions. In Essays on logic and language, ed A. Flew, Oxford 1951, New York 1951. By Ryle et al.
Dilemmas. Cambridge 1954. Lectures.
Feelings. In Aesthetics and language: essays, ed W. Elton, Oxford 1954. By Ryle et al.
The theory of meaning. In British philosophy in the mid-century: a Cambridge symposium, ed C. A. Mace 1957, New York 1957.
A puzzling element in the notion of thinking. [1958]. Lecture.
A rational animal. 1962. Lecture.
Plato's progress. Cambridge 1966.
Thinking and reflecting. In The human agent: Royal Institute of Philosophy lectures vol 1, 1966-7, 1968.
The thinking of thoughts. Saskatoon 1968. Lecture.
Ryle has edited Mind *since 1947.*

§2

Mandelbaum, M. Professor Ryle and psychology. Philosophical Rev 67 1958.
Addis, L. C. and D. Lewis. Moore and Ryle: two ontologists. Iowa 1965.
Jha, G. D. A study of Ryle's theory of mind. Santiniketan 1967.

DOROTHY LEIGH SAYERS
1893-1957
See cols 730-1, above.

FERDINAND CANNING SCOTT SCHILLER
1864-1937
Bibliographies
In R. Abel, The pragmatic humanism of F. C. S. Schiller, New York 1955, §2 below. Includes contributions to books and periodicals, and literature on Schiller.

Selections
Humanistic pragmatism: the philosophy of Schiller. Ed with an introd by R. Abel, New York 1966. Selected from Humanism, 1903; Studies in humanism, 1907.

§1

Riddles of the Sphinx: a study in the philosophy of evolution, by 'A troglodyte' [i.e. Schiller]. 1891, 1910 (rev, as Riddles of the Sphinx: a study in the philosophy of humanism; as by Schiller), New York 1910.
Axioms as postulates. In Personal idealism: philosophical essays by eight members of the University of Oxford, ed H. Sturt 1902.
Humanism: philosophical essays. 1903, New York 1903, London 1912 (enlarged).
Studies in humanism. 1907, New York 1907, London 1912 (with new preface).
Plato or Protagoras?: being a critical examination of the Protagoras speech in Theætetus, with some remarks upon error. Oxford 1908. Pamphlet.
Science and religion. 1908. Pamphlet.
Formal logic: a scientific and social problem. 1912, 1931 (with new preface).
Scientific discovery and logical proof; Hypothesis. In Studies in the history and method of science, ed C. J. Singer 2 vols Oxford 1917-21.
Problems of belief. [1924], New York 1924.
Psychology and logic. In Psychology and the sciences, with contributions by Schiller [et al], ed W. Brown 1924.
Tantalus: or the future of man. 1924, New York [1924], London 1931 (rev).
Why humanism? In Contemporary British philosophy: personal statements, by Schiller [et al], ed J. H. Muirhead, first ser 1924, New York 1924.
Cassandra: or the future of the British Empire. [1926], New York 1926, London 1936 (enlarged, as The future of the British Empire after ten years).
Eugenics and politics: essays. 1926.
Some logical aspects of psychical research. In The case for and against psychical belief, ed C. Murchison, Worcester Mass 1927.
Logic for use: an introduction to the voluntarist theory of knowledge. 1929.
Social decay and eugenical reform. 1932, New York 1932.
Must philosophers disagree?—and other essays in popular philosophy. 1934.
Our human truths. New York 1939. Essays; foreword by Louise F. Schiller.

§2

James, W. Nation 3 March 1904. Essay-review of Humanism, 1903; rptd in his Collected essays and reviews, ed R. B. Perry, New York 1920.
Bloch, W. Der Pragmatism von James und Schiller, nebst Exkursen über Weltanschauungen und über die Hypothese. Leipzig 1913.
Slosson, E. E. Schiller: a British pragmatist. In his Six major prophets, Boston 1917.
Perry, R. B. James and Schiller. In his Thought and character of William James vol 2, Boston 1935. Correspondence, with a commentary.
Marett, R. R. F. C. S. Schiller. Proc Br Acad 23 1937.
Abel, R. The pragmatic humanism of Schiller. New York 1955.
Raphael, D. D. Schiller: puns, parodies and pragmatism. Listener 26 May 1955.
Winetrout, K. Schiller and the dimensions of pragmatism. [Columbus Ohio 1967].

M. P.

SIR CHARLES SCOTT SHERRINGTON
1857-1952

Bibliographies

In U. S. National Institute of Neurological Diseases and Blindness, Public Health bibliography ser 17, Bethesda Md 1957.
Cohen, H. In his Sherrington, 1958, §2 below.

Selections

Selected writings of Sherrington. Ed D. Denny-Brown 1939.

§1

The integrative action of the nervous system. 1906, New York 1906, Cambridge 1947 (with a new foreword by the author and a bibliography of his writings), New Haven 1947.
The assaying of Brabantius and other verse. 1925.
Man on his nature. Cambridge 1940, New York 1941. Chs 3–5 rptd 1943 (as Life's unfolding).
Goethe on nature and on science. Cambridge 1942, 1949 (rev and extended).
The endeavour of Jean Fernel. Cambridge 1946.
Sherrington wrote wholly or in pt several important textbooks on neurology and physiology.

§2

Ekehorn, G. Sherrington's Endeavour of Jean Fernal and Man on his nature. Stockholm 1947–.
Liddell, E. G. T. Sherrington. Obituary Notices of Fellows of the Royal Soc 8 1952.
Stevenson, L. G. C. S. Sherrington; E. D. Adrian. In his Nobel prize winners in medicine and physiology 1901–1951, New York 1953.
Sherrington, C. E. R. Charles Scott Sherrington: memories. 1957.
Cohen, H. Sherrington: physiologist, philosopher and poet. Liverpool 1958 (Sherrington Lectures 4, with bibliography).
Granit, R. Charles Scott Sherrington: an appraisal. [1966].

CHARLES JOSEPH SINGER
1876-1960

§1

The development of the doctrine of contagium vivum, 1500–1750: a preliminary sketch. 1913 (priv ptd). Pamphlet.
The cure of the diseased, by G. Wateson, London 1598, Oxford 1915 (facs, with notes by C. Singer).
Studies in the history and method of science. Ed C. Singer 2 vols Oxford 1917–21.
The discovery of the circulation of the blood. 1922, 1956 (rev bibliography).
Greek biology and Greek medicine. Oxford 1922 (Chapters in the history of science 1).
Essays on the history of medicine presented to K. Sudhoff. Ed C. Singer and H. E. Sigerist 1924.
The evolution of anatomy: a short history of anatomical and physiological discovery to Harvey. 1925, New York 1925, 1957 (as A short history of anatomy).
The legacy of Israel. Ed E. R. Bevan and C. Singer, Oxford 1927.
From magic to science: essays on the scientific twilight. 1928, New York 1928.
Religion and science considered in their historical relations. 1928, New York nd.
A short history of medicine. Oxford 1928, New York 1928, Oxford 1962 (rev, with E. A. Underwood), New York 1962.

A short history of biology. Oxford 1931, New York 1931 (as The story of living things), London 1950 (rev, as A history of biology: a general introduction to the study of living things), New York 1950, London 1959 (rev).
The Christian approach to the Jews. 1937. Pamphlet.
A short history of science to the nineteenth century. Oxford 1941.
The Christian failure. 1943.
A prelude to modern science: being a discussion of the history, sources and circumstances of the Tabulae anatomicae sex of A. Vesalius. Cambridge 1946. With C. Rabin.
The earliest chemical industry: an essay in the historical relations of economics and technology illustrated from the alum trade. 1948.
New worlds and old: essays. 1951.
Anglo-Saxon magic and medicine. 1952. With J. H. G. Grattan.
Vesalius on the human brain. 1952, New York 1952. Tr Singer.
A history of technology, ed C. Singer, E. J. Holmyard and A. R. Hall. 5 vols Oxford 1954–8.
Galen on anatomical procedures. 1956. Tr Singer.
A short history of scientific ideas to 1900. Oxford 1959. Based on A short history of science, 1941, above.
Singer was also general editor of Classics of medicine, *from 1920, and* Chapters in the history of science, *from 1922.*

§2

Science, medicine and history: essays in honour of Singer. Ed E. A. Underwood 2 vols 1953. Includes bibliography.

N. J. S.

NORMAN KEMP SMITH
1872-1958

§1

Studies in the Cartesian philosophy. 1902, New York 1962.
A commentary to Kant's Critique of pure reason. 1918, 1923 (rev and enlarged), New York 1962.
Prolegomena to an idealist theory of knowledge. 1924.
The philosophy of David Hume: a critical study of its origins and central doctrines. 1941.
New studies in the philosophy of Descartes: Descartes as pioneer. 1952.
The credibility of divine existence: the collected papers of N. Kemp Smith. Ed A. J. D. Porteous, R. D. Maclennan and G. E. Davie, 1967.
Kemp Smith edited Hume's Dialogues concerning natural religion *and A. A. Bowman's* Studies in the philosophy of religion. *He tr Descartes'* Philosophical writings *and Kant's* Critique of pure reason.

§2

Wright, J. N. Kemp Smith's Descartes. Philosophical Quart 5 1955.
Ewing, A. C. Kemp Smith. Proc Br Acad 45 1959.
Davie, G. E. The significance of the philosophical papers [of Kemp Smith]. In The credibility of divine existence, 1967, above.
Maclennan, R. D. Divine existence: a personal recollection [of Kemp Smith]. Ibid.
Porteous, A. J. D. Biographical sketch. Ibid.

A. P. H.

CHARLES EDWARD SPEARMAN
1863–1945

§1

Die Normaltäuschungen in der Lagewahrnehmung. Leipzig 1906.
The nature of 'intelligence' and the principles of cognition. 1923.
A measure of 'intelligence' for use in schools. 1925. Pamphlet.
The abilities of man: their nature and measurement. 1927, New York 1927.
Creative mind. 1930, New York [1931].
Psychology down the ages. 2 vols 1937.
Human ability: a continuation of The abilities of man. 1950. With L. W. Jones.

§2

Spearman, C. In A history of psychology in autobiography, ed C. Murchison vol 1, Worcester Mass 1930.
Thomson, G. Obituary Notices of Fellows of the Royal Society 5 1945–8. Includes a check-list of Spearman's writings.
Ballard, P. B. Br Jnl of Educational Psychology 16 1946.
Burt, C. and C. S. Myers. Psychological Rev 53 1946.
Flugel, J. C. Spearman and the 'factor' school. In his A hundred years of psychology, 1951.

D.K.

WILLIAM OLAF STAPLEDON
1886–1950
See cols 741–2, above.

LIZZIE SUSAN STEBBING
1885–1943

Bibliographies
In J. Wisdom, Philosophical studies: essays in memory of Susan Stebbing, 1948. *See §2, below.*

§1

Pragmatism and French voluntarism: with especial reference to the notion of truth in the development of French philosophy from Maine de Biran to Professor Bergson. Cambridge 1914 (Girton College Stud).
A modern introduction to logic. 1930, 1933 (rev), New York 1961.
Logic in practice. 1934, 1954 (rev C. W. K. Mundle).
Imagination and thinking. 1936. With C. Day Lewis; 2 addresses.
Philosophy and the physicists. 1937, New York 1958. A discussion of the views of Eddington and Jeans.
Thinking to some purpose. 1939 (Pelican).
Ideals and illusions. 1941.
A modern elementary logic. 1943, 1952 (rev C. W. K. Mundle).

§2

Wisdom, J. In Philosophical studies: essays in memory of L. Susan Stebbing, 1948 (Aristotelian Soc).

N.J.S.

BURNETT HILLMAN STREETER
1874–1937

§1

Foundations: a statement of Christian belief in terms of modern thought by seven Oxford men, B. H. Streeter [et al]. 1912.
Restatement and reunion: a study in first principles. 1914.
Concerning prayer, its nature, its difficulties and its value. 1916. With L. Dougall et al.
Immortality: an essay in discovery, co-ordinating scientific, psychical and biblical research. 1917, New York 1917. With A. Clutton-Brock et al.
Woman and the Church. 1917. With E. Picton-Turbervill.
God and the struggle for existence. 1919. With C. F. D'Arcy and L. Dougall.
The spirit: God in his relation to man considered from the standpoint of philosophy, psychology and art. 1919, New York 1919. With A. S. Pringle-Pattison et al.
The Sadhu [Sundar Singh]: a study in mysticism and practical religion. 1921, New York 1921 (as The message of Sadhu Sundar Singh). With A. J. Appasami.
The four gospels: a study of origins. 1924, New York 1925. Rptd (rev) 1926, 1927, 1936.
Reality: a new correlation of science and religion. 1926, New York 1926.
Adventure: the faith of science and the science of faith. 1927, New York 1928. With C. N. Chilcott et al. One of Streeter's chs, Moral adventure, rptd 1928.
The primitive Church: studied with specific reference to the origins of the Christian ministry. 1929.
The chained library: a survey of four centuries in the evolution of the English library. 1931.
The Buddha and the Christ: an exploration of the meaning of the universe and of the purpose of human life. 1932, New York 1933.
The God who speaks. 1936, New York 1936.
Streeter also contributed to Sanday's Studies in the synoptic problem, 1911; and pbd numerous single lectures and addresses on theological subjects.

§2

Knox, R. A. Some loose stones: being a consideration of certain tendencies in modern theology illustrated by reference to the book called Foundations. 1913. See also Knox's satire, Absolute and Abitofhell, 1915.
'Ignotus'. The new theology and its teachings, with some remarks on the book Foundations. 1915.
Nash, J. O. S. S. Ignatius of Antioch: a comment on Streeter's Primitive Church. [1930].
Thornhill, A. One fight more. 1943. Streeter and the Oxford Group.

JOHN WILLIAM NAVIN SULLIVAN
1886–1937

§1

An attempt at life. 1917. Fiction.
Aspects of science. 2 ser [1923], [1926]; New York 1924, 1926. Collected essays.
Atoms and electrons. [1923] (Hodder and Stoughton's People's Lib).
The history of mathematics in Europe from the fall of Greek science to the rise of the conception of mathematical rigour. 1925.
Three men discuss relativity. [1925]. Galileo, Newton, Einstein.
Beethoven: his spiritual development. 1927, New York 1949.

Gallio: or the tyranny of science. [1927] (Today and Tomorrow).

The bases of modern science: an account of physical ideas from Newton to the present day. 1928.

Present-day astronomy. [1930] (Outline Lib).

But for the grace of God. 1932. Fiction.

How things behave: a child's introduction to physics. 1932.

The physical nature of the universe. 1932 (Outline Ser).

The limitations of science. 1933, New York 1956.

Contemporary mind: some modern answers to questions put to various thinkers by Sullivan. 1934.

Science: a new outline. 1935.

A holiday task. 1936. Fiction.

Isaac Newton 1642–1727, with memoir of the author by C. Singer. 1938.

Living things. 1938.

Sullivan edited (with W. Grierson) Outline of modern belief: modern science, modern thought, religious thought, *and contributed regularly to* Athenaeum, Nature *and* TLS, *1917 onwards.*

§2

Singer, C. [Sullivan]. In Isaac Newton 1642–1727, 1938, above.

A.P.H.

ALFRED EDWARD TAYLOR
1869–1945
Bibliographies

In W. D. Ross, below, §2. Includes contributions to books and periodicals.

§1

The problem of conduct: a study in the phenomenology of ethics. 1901, New York 1901.

Elements of metaphysics. 1903, 1924 (with a new preface).

Aristotle on his predecessors: being the first book of his Metaphysics, tr from the text edition of W. Christ, with introduction and notes by Taylor. Chicago 1907.

Plato. 1908, Ann Arbor 1960 (as The mind of Plato).

Thomas Hobbes. 1908.

Epicurus. 1911, Freeport NY 1969.

Varia Socratica. Ser 1, Oxford 1911. Reply by G. C. Field, Socrates and Plato, Oxford 1913.

Aristotle. [1912], 1919 (rev), 1943 (corrected), New York 1955 (with index by G. M. Smith).

Human mind and will. 1924.

Platonism and its influence. Boston [1924], London [1925].

The freedom of man. In Contemporary British philosophy, ed J. H. Muirhead 2nd ser, 1925, New York 1925.

De Morgan, A. Formal logic. Ed Taylor 1926.

Plato: the man and his work. 1926, New York 1927, London 1929 (rev and enlarged).

A commentary on Plato's Timaeus. Oxford 1928.

Plato. Timaeus and Critias. Tr with introds and notes on the text by Taylor 1929.

The problem of evil. 1929. Pamphlet.

The faith of a moralist. 2 vols 1930. Reply by S. P. Lamprecht, Morality and religion, International Jnl of Ethics 41 1931.

Socrates. 1932, New York 1933.

The laws of Plato. Tr by Taylor 1934.

The Parmenides of Plato. Tr with introd and appendixes by Taylor, Oxford 1934.

Philosophical studies. 1934. Includes single lectures previously pbd separately.

Ancient and medieval philosophy. 1935 (European Civilization, ed E. Eyre, vol 3).

Modern philosophy. 1937 (European Civilization, ed E. Eyre, vol 6).

The Christian hope of immortality. 1938.

Does God exist? 1945, New York 1947.

Plato. Philebus and Epinomis. Tr and introd by Taylor, ed R. Klibansky with G. Calogero and A. C. Lloyd. 1956, New York 1956.

Plato. The sophist and The Statesman. Tr and introd by Taylor, ed R. Klibansky and E. Anscombe. 1961, New York 1961.

§2

Ross, W. D. A. E. Taylor. Proc Br Acad 31 1945.

Lofthouse, W. F. A. E. Taylor. London Quart Rev 171 1946.

M.P.

WILLIAM TEMPLE
1881–1944
Bibliographies

Fletcher, J. F. In his William Temple, 1963. *See* §2, below.

Selections

William Temple and his message. Ed A. E. Baker 1946. With memoir by G. K. A. Bell.

Daily readings from William Temple. Ed H. C. Warner 1948, New York 1950.

William Temple's teaching. Ed A. E. Baker [1949], Philadelphia 1951.

The wisdom of William Temple. Ed F. H. C. Tatham 1949.

Religious experience and other essays and addresses, collected and edited with introduction by A. E. Baker. 1958. Includes lectures, sermons and articles.

Lent with William Temple. Ed G. P. M. Belshaw 1966, New York 1966.

§1

The faith and modern thought. 1910.

Principles of social progress. Melbourne 1910.

The nature of personality. 1911.

Foundations: a statement of Christian belief in terms of modern thought by seven Oxford men. Ed B. H. Streeter 1912. By Temple et al.

The kingdom of God. 1912.

Repton school sermons: studies in the religion of the Incarnation. 1913.

Studies in the spirit and truth of Christianity. 1914. University and school sermons, some previously pbd in Repton school sermons, above.

Church and nation. 1915.

Plato and Christianity. 1916.

A challenge to the church. 1917. On the National mission 1916.

Competition: a study in human motive. 1917. By Temple et al.

Issues of faith. 1917.

Mens creatrix: an essay. 1917.

Fellowship with God. 1920. Sermons.

Life of Bishop Percival. 1921.

The universality of Christ. 1921, New York [1922], London 1962 (as About Christ; with Christ's revelation of God, 1925 below).

Christus veritas: an essay. 1924, New York 1924 (as Christ the truth). Sequel to Mens creatrix, above.

Christ in his church: a charge delivered at his primary visitation [of the Manchester diocese] 1924. 1925.

Christ's revelation of God. 1925. See The universality of Christ, above.

Personal religion and the life of fellowship. 1926.

Essays in Christian politics and kindred subjects. 1927. Includes articles and addresses previously pbd separately.

Christianity and the state. 1928.

Christian faith and life. 1931, New York 1931, London 1963 (with foreword by F. R. Barry).

Thoughts on some problems of the day: a charge delivered at his primary visitation [of the York diocese]. 1931.
Nature, man and God. 1934, New York 1949.
Basic convictions. New York 1936, London 1937.
Christianity in thought and practice. 1936, New York 1936.
The church and its teaching today. New York 1936.
The preacher's theme today. 1936, New York 1936 (as The centrality of Christ).
Readings in St John's gospel, 2 ser 1939, 1940, 1 vol 1945.
The hope of a new world. 1940. Broadcast talks and other addresses and sermons.
Thoughts in war-time. 1940. Includes addresses, articles and letters previously pbd separately.
Citizen and churchman. 1941.
Christianity and social order. 1942, New York 1942 (Penguin Special).
Palm Sunday to Easter. 1942, New York 1942. Addresses broadcast during Holy Week 1942.
The church looks forward. 1944, New York 1944. Sermons and addresses, including some previously pbd separately.
Religious experience and other essays and addresses. Ed with introd by A. E. Baker 1958.
About Christ. 1962. *See* The universality of Christ, above.

Letters

Some Lambeth letters. Ed F. S. Temple 1963.
For Temple's many other sermons, addresses, speeches, broadcasts, pamphlets, booklets and contributions to books, see J. F. Fletcher, William Temple, 1963, above. Temple edited Papers for wartime 1914, 1915, The challenge 1915–18 and The pilgrim 1920–7. He also edited Frederick Temple, Thoughts on the divine love, 1910, and wrote a biographical introd for E. G. Sandford, Frederick Temple: an appreciation, 1907.

§2

Dark, S. The people's archbishop. [1942]. With an appendix, Temple as a diocesan, by A. E. Baker.
Matthews, W. R. [et al]. William Temple: an estimate and an appreciation. 1946.
Reckitt, M. B. Maurice to Temple: a century of the social movement in the Church of England. 1947.
Iremonger, F. A. William Temple Archbishop of Canterbury: his life and letters. 1948.
Ramsey, A. M. From Gore to Temple: the development of Anglican theology between Lux mundi and the Second World War. 1960.
Thomas, O. C. William Temple's philosophy of religion. 1961.
Carmichael, J. D. and H. S. Goodwin. William Temple's political legacy: a critical assessment. 1963.
Craig, R. Social concern in the thought of William Temple. 1963.
Davies, D. H. M. Apologetical and theological preaching: Temple and Farmer. In his Varieties of English preaching 1900–60. 1963.
Fletcher, J. F. William Temple, twentieth-century Christian. New York 1963.
Rinne, W. R. The kingdom of God in the thought of William Temple. Åbo 1966.

P.C.

FREDERICK ROBERT TENNANT
1866–1957
Bibliographies

Scudder, D. L. In his Tennant's Philosophical theology, 1940, §2 below. Includes reviews of Philosophical theology and major references to Tennant.

§1

The origin and propagation of sin. Cambridge 1902, 1906 (rev).
The sources of the doctrines of the Fall and Original Sin. Cambridge 1903.
The concept of sin. Cambridge 1912.
The aim and scope of philosophy of religion. 1913.
Miracle & its philosophical presuppositions. Cambridge 1925.
Philosophical theology. 2 vols Cambridge 1928, 1930.
Philosophy of the sciences: or the relations between the departments of knowledge. Cambridge 1932.
The nature of belief. 1943.
Tennant contributed to various collections of theological essays.

§2

Bertocci, P. A. Tennant's teleological argument for God. In his Empirical argument for God in late British thought, Cambridge Mass 1938.
Scudder, D. L. Tennant's Philosophical theology. New Haven 1940.
Broad, C. D. Tennant. Proc Br Acad 44 1958.

SIR D'ARCY WENTWORTH THOMPSON
1860–1948
Bibliographies

Bushnell, G. H. List of the published writings of Thompson. In Essays on growth and form presented to Thompson, ed W. E. Le Gros Clark and P. B. Medawar, Oxford 1945.
Dobell, C. Short list of publications [of Thompson]. In his obituary of Thompson in Obituary notices of Fellows of the Royal Society, 1949, §2 below.
Thompson, R. D'A. List of principal publications of Thompson. In her Thompson: the scholar-naturalist, 1958, §2 below.

§1

A bibliography of protozoa, sponges, cœlenterata and worms, including also the polyzoa, brachiopoda and tunicata, for the years 1861–83. Cambridge 1885.
A glossary of Greek birds. Oxford 1895, London 1936 (illustr).
On growth and form. Cambridge 1917, 1942 (rev), 1961 (abridged J. T. Bonner).
Science and the classics. 1940. Collected articles and addresses.
A glossary of Greek fishes. 1947.
Thompson wrote many official papers and reports on fishery statistics and oceanography, and translated Aristotle's Historia animalium and H. Müller's Fertilisation of flowers, 1883. He contributed to The legacy of Greece and The companion to Greek studies.

§2

Dobell, C. In Obituary notices of Fellows of the Royal Society, 1949.
Hutchinson, G. E. In memoriam D'A. W. Thompson. In his Itinerant ivory tower, 1953.
Read, H. E. In his Tenth muse, 1957.
Thompson, R. D.'A. Thompson: the scholar-naturalist. 1958. Includes P. B. Medawar, Postscript: Thompson and Growth and form.
Bonner, J. T. Introduction to his abridged edn of On growth and form, Cambridge 1961, above.

A.P.H.

EVELYN UNDERHILL
1875–1941

Collections and Selections

Evelyn Underhill. 1932 (Augustan Books of Poetry).
Collected papers. Ed L. Menzies 1946, New York 1946. Introd by L. Barkway.
The wisdom of Evelyn Underhill: an anthology from her writings, compiled by J. Stobbart. 1951. Booklet.
An anthology of the love of God from the writings of E. Underhill. Ed L. Barkway and L. Menzies 1953, New York 1954.
The Evelyn Underhill reader, compiled by T. S. Kepler. New York [1962].
Lent with Evelyn Underhill: selections from her writings. Ed G. P. M. Belshaw 1964, New York 1964.

§1

The miracles of Our Lady Saint Mary, brought out of divers tongues and newly set forth in English by E. Underhill. 1905, New York 1906.
Mysticism: a study in the nature and development of man's spiritual consciousness. 1911, 1912 (rev), 1930 (rev), New York 1930.
The path of the eternal wisdom: a mystical commentary on the Way of the Cross, by 'John Cordelier' [i.e. E. Underhill]. 1911.
A book of contemplation, the which is called The cloud of unknowing, in which a soul is oned with God. BM ms Harl 674, ed E. Underhill 1912.
The spiral way: being meditations upon the fifteen mysteries of the soul's ascent, by 'John Cordelier'. 1912, 1922 (rev).
The mystic way: a psychological study in Christian origins. 1913.
One hundred poems of Kabir. Tr R. Tagore, assisted by E. Underhill 1914. Introd by E. Underhill.
Practical mysticism: a little book for normal people. 1914, New York [1915].
Mysticism and war. 1915. Rptd from Quest, rev and enlarged. Pamphlet.
Ruysbroeck. 1915.
Ruysbroeck, J. van. The adornment of the spiritual marriage; The sparkling stone; The book of supreme truth. Ed E. Underhill 1916. Tr from the Flemish by C. A. W. Dom.
Jacopone da Todi, poet and mystic, 1228–1306: a spiritual biography. 1919.
The essentials of mysticism and other essays. 1920, New York 1960.
The life of the spirit and the life of to-day. 1922, New York [1922].
Hylton, W. The scale of perfection, newly edited from manuscript sources by E. Underhill. 1923.
The mystics of the Church. [1925], New York 1926.
Concerning the inner life. 1926, New York [1926] (introd by C. L. Slattery).
Man and the supernatural. 1927, New York [1928].
Life as prayer. Edinburgh [1928]. Pamphlet.
The house of the soul. 1929, New York [1930].
Worship. [1929]. Pamphlet.
The golden sequence: a fourfold study of the spiritual life. 1932, New York [1933].
The inside of life. [1932]. Pamphlet.
Medieval mysticism. In The Cambridge medieval history vol 7, Cambridge 1932.
Mixed pasture: twelve essays and addresses. 1933, New York 1933. On the spiritual life.
The school of charity: meditations on the Christian creed. 1934.
What is mysticism? [1936]. Pamphlet.
Worship. 1936, New York 1937. A different work from the pamphlet pbd in 1929.

The parish priest and the life of prayer. 1937. 2 addresses.
The spiritual life: four broadcast talks. 1937, New York 1937.
The mystery of sacrifice: a meditation on the Liturgy. 1938.
Eucharistic prayers from the ancient liturgies. Ed E. Underhill 1939.
A meditation on peace. [1939?]. Fellowship of Reconciliation pamphlet.
A service of prayer for use in war-time, arranged by E. Underhill. [1939]. Pamphlet.
Abba: meditations based on the Lord's Prayer. 1940.
The Church and war. [1940?]. Anglican Pacifist Fellowship pamphlet.
The fruits of the spirit. 1942, 1949 (enlarged).
Light of Christ: addresses given at the house of retreat, Pleshey, 1932. 1944, New York 1945. With memoir by L. Menzies.
Meditations and prayers. 1949. Booklet.
Shrines and cities of France and Italy. 1949. Ed L. Menzies from an early diary, 1901–7. Written and illustr E. Underhill.

Poetry and Fiction

A bar-lamb's ballad book. 1902. Humorous verse on the law.
The grey world. 1904, New York 1904. Novel.
The lost word. 1907. Novel.
The column of dust. 1909. Novel.
Immanence: a book of verses. [1913], New York [1913].
Theophanies: a book of verses. 1916.

Letters

The letters of Evelyn Underhill. Ed C. Williams 1943.

§2

Kepler, T. S. A journey with the saints. Cleveland 1951.
Cropper, M. B. Evelyn Underhill. 1958. With memoir of Lucy Menzies by L. Barker. See E. I. Watkin, in Month 208 1959.
Fairchild, H. N. Mystics. In his Religious trends in English poetry vol 5, 1880–1920. New York 1962.
Wyon, O. Teachings toward Christian perfection: introducing three spiritual classics. New York 1963, London 1966 (as Desire for God: a study of three spiritual classics). Fénelon, Christian perfection; Wesley, Christian perfection; E. Underhill, The spiritual life.
Noon, W. T. In his Poetry and prayer, New Brunswick NJ [1967].

M.P.

CONRAD HAL WADDINGTON
b. 1905

§1

How animals develop. 1935, New York 1936.
An introduction to modern genetics. 1939, New York 1939.
Organisers and genes. Cambridge 1940 (Cambridge Biological Stud).
The scientific attitude. 1941 (Pelican), 1948 (rev), 1968 (with new foreword by Waddington and introd by S. A. Barnett) (Nucleus Books).
Science and ethics: an essay, together with a discussion between the author and the Right Rev E. W. Barnes [et al]. 1942.
The epigenetics of birds. Cambridge 1952 (Cambridge Biological Stud).
Quantitative inheritance: papers read at a colloquium held at the Institute of Animal Genetics, Edinburgh University. Ed E. C. R. Reeve and Waddington, 1952.

Principles of embryology. 1956, New York 1956.
The strategy of the genes: a discussion of some aspects of theoretical biology. 1957, New York [1957].
Biological organization, cellular and sub-cellular: proceedings of a symposium organised on behalf of UNESCO by Waddington, held at the University of Edinburgh 1957. 1959.
The ethical animal. 1960, New York 1961.
The nature of life. 1961, New York 1962.
Biology for the modern world. 1962, New York, 1962.
New patterns in genetics and development. New York 1962.
Principles of development and differentiation. New York [1966].
Towards a theoretical biology. Ed Waddington, Edinburgh 1968 onwards. A series of symposia arranged for the International Union of Biological Sciences by Waddington.
Behind appearance: a study of the relations between painting and the natural sciences in this century. Edinburgh 1969.
Waddington was general editor of Cambridge Biological Stud 1938–52 and is chairman of the editorial board of Genetical Research.

§2
Genetics at Edinburgh: Waddington. Nature 159 1947.

D.K.

HERBERT GEORGE WELLS
1866–1946
See cols 417–28, above.

ALFRED NORTH WHITEHEAD
1861–1947

At his own request all Whitehead's unpbd MSS were destroyed after his death; they probably represented in the main work done from 10 to 50 years earlier. See The Philosophy of Whitehead, *ed P. A. Schilpp 1941, p. 749, §2 below.*

Bibliographies
In The Philosophy of Whitehead, ed P. A. Schilpp, 1941, §2 below. Includes contributions to books and periodicals and selected reviews of his works.
Johnson, A. H. In his Whitehead's philosophy of civilization, 1958, §2 below.
Parker, F. Whitehead (1861–1947): a partial bibliography. Bull of Bibliography 23 1961; rptd in Lib World 62 1960–1.
Ruybinx, J. Whitehead: une bibliographie. Rev Internationale de Philosophie 15 1961.
Stokes, W. E. A select and annotated bibliography of Whitehead. Modern Schoolman 39 1962.
Kline, G. L. In Process and divinity, ed W. L. Reese and E. Freeman, 1964, §2 below. Writings by and about Whitehead in languages other than English.
Parmentier, A. In his La philosophie de Whitehead et le problème de Dieu, 1968, §2 below.

Selections
The wit and wisdom of Whitehead. Ed A. H. Johnson, Boston 1947.
Whitehead: an anthology. Ed F. S. C. Northrop and M. W. Gross. Cambridge 1953 (for 1954), New York 1953 (for 1954).
American essays in social philosophy. Ed with introd by A. H. Johnson, New York 1959. Texts of uncollected articles.
The interpretation of science: selected essays. Ed A. H. Johnson, New York 1961.

Whitehead: his reflections on man and nature. Ed R. N. Anshen, New York [1961].
A philosopher looks at science. New York 1965.

§1
A treatise on universal algebra, with applications. Vol 1, Cambridge 1898, New York 1960. No more vols pbd.
The axioms of projective geometry. Cambridge 1906, New York [1960?].
The axioms of descriptive geometry. Cambridge 1907, New York 1960.
Principia mathematica. 3 vols Cambridge 1910–13, 1925–7 (rev); abridged edn of vol 1 pbd 1962 (as Principia mathematica to *56). With B. Russell, who was responsible for all the new matter in the rev edn.
An introduction to mathematics. 1911, New York 1911, London 1927 (rev), 1942 (rev under the direction of J. H. C. Whitehead), New York 1948.
The organisation of thought: educational and scientific. 1917, Philadelphia 1917. The larger pt rptd (rev) in The aims of education and other essays, below.
An enquiry concerning the principles of natural knowledge. Cambridge 1919, 1925 (rev).
The concept of nature. Cambridge 1920, Ann Arbor 1957. Companion vol to An enquiry concerning the principles of natural knowledge, above.
The principle of relativity, with applications to physical science. Cambridge 1922.
Science and the modern world. New York 1925, Cambridge 1926.
Religion in the making. New York 1926, Cambridge 1926; rptd in Essays in science and philosophy, below.
Symbolism: its meaning and effect. New York 1927, Cambridge 1928.
Process and reality: an essay in cosmology. Cambridge 1929, New York 1929.
The function of reason. Princeton 1929, London 1929.
The aims of education and other essays. New York 1929, London 1959 (foreword by Lord Lindsay).
Adventures of ideas. New York 1933, Cambridge 1933.
Nature and life. Chicago [1934], Cambridge 1934. 2 lectures rptd in next and (without corrigenda) in Essays in science and philosophy, below.
Modes of thought. New York 1938, Cambridge 1938.
Essays in science and philosophy. New York 1947, London 1948, New York 1957 (as Science and philosophy). Previously uncollected articles and contributions to books, with some personal reminiscences.
Dialogues of Whitehead as recorded by L. Price. 1954, Boston 1954.
Whitehead's juvenilia were ptd in Shirburnian Mag; *his many contributions to periodicals and books are listed in the bibliography in* The philosophy of Whitehead, *ed P. A. Schilpp, Evanston Ill 1941, above.*

§2
Lovejoy, A. O. In his Revolt against dualism, Chicago 1930.
Emmet, D. M. Whitehead's philosophy of organism. 1932, 1966 (corrected).
— In her Nature of metaphysical thinking, 1945.
— A. N. Whitehead. Proc Br Acad 33 1947.
Smith, J. Evaluations III: Whitehead. Scrutiny 3 1934–5.
Stallknecht, N. P. Studies in the philosophy of creation, with especial reference to Bergson and Whitehead, Princeton 1934.
Das, R. The philosophy of Whitehead. 1938.
Miller, D. L. and G. V. Gentry. The philosophy of Whitehead. Minneapolis 1938.
Bowman, A. A. In his A sacramental universe, Princeton 1939.
Sarkar, A. K. An outline of Whitehead's philosophy. 1940.

Blyth, J. W. Whitehead's theory of knowledge. Providence 1941.

Hartshorne, C. In his Man's vision of God, and the logic of theism, Chicago 1941.

— In his Divine relativity, New Haven 1948.

— In his Reality as social process, Glencoe Ill 1953.

Schilpp, P. A. (ed). The philosophy of Whitehead. Evanston Ill 1941, New York 1951 (rev).

Ely, S. L. The religious availability of Whitehead's God. Madison 1942.

Bodkin, M. Physical agencies and the Divine persuasion. Philosophy 20 1945. On Whitehead's system.

Mack, R. D. The appeal to immediate experience in Bradley, Whitehead and Dewey. New York 1945.

Hammerschmidt, W. W. Whitehead's philosophy of time. New York 1947.

Bera, M. A. Whitehead: un philosophe de l'expérience. Paris 1948.

Whittaker, E. T. Whitehead. Obituary Notices of Fellows of the Royal Soc 6 1948–9.

Cesselin, F. La philosophie organique de Whitehead. Paris 1950.

Lowe, V. A., C. Hartshorne and A. H. Johnson. Whitehead and the modern world. Boston 1950.

Lowe, V. A. Understanding Whitehead. Baltimore 1962.

Shahan, E. P. Whitehead's theory of experience. New York 1950.

Wells, H. K. Process and reality: a criticism of method in Whitehead's philosophy. New York 1950.

Dwight, C. A. S. Whitehead the inscrutable. Personalist 32 1951.

Francovich, G. Toynbee, Heidegger y Whitehead. Buenos Aires 1951.

Synge, J. L. The relativity theory of Whitehead. [Westminster Maryland] 1951.

Hoffman, C. G. Whitehead's philosophy of nature and Romantic poetry. Jnl of Aesthetics & Art Criticism 10 1952.

Johnson, A. H. Whitehead's theory of reality. Boston 1952.

— Whitehead's philosophy of civilization. Boston 1958.

Russell, B. Portraits from memory: I, Whitehead. Listener 10 July 1952.

— In his Autobiography vol 1 1967.

Smith, R. Whitehead's concept of logic. Westminster Maryland 1953.

Lawrence, N. Whitehead's philosophical development: a critical history of the background of Process and reality. Berkeley 1956.

Wyman, M. A. Whitehead's philosophy of science in the light of Wordsworth's poetry. Philosophy of Science 23 1956; rptd in her Lure of feeling, New York 1960.

Bense, M. Kosmologie und Literatur: über Whitehead und Gertrude Stein. Texte und Zeichen 3 1957.

Mohanby, S. J. N. Nicolai Hartmann and Whitehead: a study in recent Platonism. Calcutta 1957.

Bright, L. Whitehead's philosophy of physics. 1958.

Leclerc, I. Whitehead's metaphysics: an introductory exposition. 1958.

— (ed). The relevance of Whitehead: philosophical essays. 1961.

Buehrer, E. T. Mysticism and Whitehead. In Mysticism and the modern mind, ed A. P. Stiernotte, New York 1959.

Christian, W. A. An interpretation of Whitehead's metaphysics. New Haven 1959.

Clarke, B. L. Whitehead's cosmology and the Christian drama. Jnl of Religion 39 1959.

Harrah, D. The influence of logic and mathematics on Whitehead. JHI 20 1959.

Mays, W. The philosophy of Whitehead. 1959.

Campbell, H. M. Emerson and Whitehead. PMLA 75 1960.

Meland, B. E. From Darwin to Whitehead: a study in the shift in ethos and perspective underlying religious thought. Jnl of Religion 40 1960.

Palter, R. M. Whitehead's philosophy of science. Chicago 1960.

Britton, K. Portrait of a philosopher. Listener 9 March 1961.

Jnl of Philosophy 58 1961. Whitehead centennial issue, ed G. L. Kline; rptd as Whitehead: essays on his philosophy, ed G. L. Kline. Englewood Cliffs NJ 1963.

Sherburne, D. W. A. A Whiteheadian aesthetic. New Haven 1961.

— (ed). A key to Whitehead's Process and reality. New York 1966.

Tulane Stud in Philosophy 10 1961. Studies in Whitehead's philosophy.

Studies in Whiteheadian philosophy. In Process and divinity: philosophical essays presented to Charles Hartshorne, ed W. L. Reese and E. Freeman, Lasalle 1964.

Dunkel, H. B. Whitehead on education. Columbus [1965].

Sini, C. Whitehead e la funzione della filosofia. [Padua] 1965.

Wendler, H. W. Whitehead: a shift of emphasis. Texas Quart 8 1965.

Laszlo, E. Beyond scepticism and realism: a constructive exploration of Husserlian and Whiteheadian methods of enquiry. The Hague 1966.

Rajagopal, L. V. The philosophy of Whitehead: the concept of reality and organism. Mysore 1966.

Pols, E. Whitehead's metaphysics: a critical examination of Process and reality. Carbondale 1967.

Schmidt, P. P. Perception and cosmology in Whitehead's philosophy. New Brunswick NJ 1967.

Jordan, M. New shapes of reality: aspects of Whitehead's philosophy. 1968.

Parmentier, A. La philosophie de Whitehead et la problème de Dieu. Paris [1968].

Pittenger, W. N. Alfred North Whitehead. 1969.

M.P.

CHARLES WALTER STANSBY WILLIAMS
1886–1945

See cols 772–3, above.

JOHN COOK WILSON
1849–1915

Bibliographies

See Statement and inference, 1926, §1, below. List of pbd works and contributions to reviews.

§1

Aristotelian studies 1: on the structure of the seventh book of the Nicomachean ethics chapters 1–x. Oxford 1879, 1912 (with postscript).

On the interpretation of Plato's Timaeus: critical studies with special reference to a recent edition [by R. D. Archer-Hind]. 1889.

Statement and inference, with other philosophical papers. Ed A. S. L. Farquharson 2 vols Oxford 1926, 1969 (corrected). With memoir and selected correspondence.

Cook Wilson also pbd On the traversing of geometrical figures (1905), *and several short works on military cycling.*

§2

Joseph, H. W. B. In Proc Br Acad 7 1915–16.

Prichard, H. A. In Mind 28 1919.

Farquharson, A. S. L. Memoir. In Statement and inference, 1926. *See* §1, above.

Robinson, R. G. F. The province of logic: an interpretation of certain parts of Cook Wilson's Statement and inference. 1931.

Passmore, J. A. Cook Wilson and Oxford philosophy. In his A hundred years of philosophy, 1957.

C.H.E.P.

ARTHUR JOHN TERENCE DIBBEN WISDOM
b. 1904

Interpretation and analysis, in relation to Bentham's theory of definition. 1931.
Problems of mind and matter. Cambridge 1934.
Other minds. Oxford 1952, New York 1952.
Philosophy and psycho-analysis. Oxford 1953 (for 1952), New York 1953.
Paradox and discovery. Oxford 1965 (for 1966).

LUDWIG JOSEF JOHANN WITTGENSTEIN
1889–1951

Most of Wittgenstein's notebooks, containing his preliminary work, were destroyed by his orders in 1950. See preface to Notebooks, 1914–16, 1961, §1 below.

Bibliographies
Fann, K. T. In his Wittgenstein's conception of philosophy, Oxford 1969, §2 below. Rptd, with addenda, from International Philosophical Quart 7 1967. Includes trns.

Collections
Schriften. Frankfurt 1960. In progress.

§1
Logisch-philosophische Abhandlung. Annalen der Naturphilosophie 14 1921; London 1922 (as Tractatus logico-philosophicus, German text with Eng trn by C. K. Ogden, introd by B. Russell), New York 1922, London 1933 (corrected), 1955 (with index), 1961 (German text with a new trn by D. F. Pears and B. F. McGuinness, introd by Russell), New York 1961, London 1963 (corrected).
Some remarks on logical form. Aristotelian Soc Suppl Vol 9 1929; rptd in Essays on Wittgenstein's Tractatus, ed I. M. Copi and R. W. Beard 1966. See §2, below.
Philosophical investigations. Ed G. E. M. Anscombe, R. Rhees and G. H. von Wright, Oxford 1953, New York 1953, Oxford 1958 (rev), 1967 (with index); tr Anscombe; German and English texts.
Moore, G. E. Wittgenstein's lectures in 1930–3. Mind 63 1954, 64 1955; rptd in Moore's Philosophical papers, 1959.
Remarks on the foundations of mathematics. Ed G. H. von Wright, R. Rhees, G. E. M. Anscombe, Oxford 1956, New York 1956. Tr Anscombe; German and English texts.
Preliminary studies for the Philosophical investigations, generally known as the Blue and Brown books. Oxford 1958, New York 1958, Oxford 1960 (corrected), 1969 (with index). Dictated to students, Cambridge 1933–5.
Notebooks, 1914–16. Ed G. H. von Wright and G. E. M. Anscombe, Oxford 1961, New York 1961. Tr Anscombe. 3 notebooks not destroyed used in the preparation of the Tractatus, 1922.
Philosophische Bemerkungen. Oxford 1964 (aus dem Nachlass herausgegeben von R. Rhees).
A lecture on ethics. Philosophical Rev 74 1965. Transcript of shorthand notes by F. Waismann of a paper given at Cambridge 1929 or 1930.
Lectures and conversations on aesthetics, psychology and religious belief compiled from notes taken by Y.

Smithies, R. Rhees and J. Taylor. Ed C. Barrett, Oxford 1966, Berkeley 1966.
Waismann, F. Wittgenstein und der Wiener Kreis. Aus dem Nachlass herausgegeben von B. F. McGuinness. Oxford 1967. Discussion between Wittgenstein, Waismann and M. Schlick transcribed from Waismann's shorthand notes.
Zettel. Ed G. E. M. Anscombe and G. H. von Wright. Oxford 1967. Tr Anscombe. Unpbd fragments, German and English texts.
On certainty. (Über Gewissheit). Ed G. E. M. Anscombe and G. H. von Wright. Oxford 1969. Tr D. Paul and Anscombe; German and English texts.
Wittgenstein. Prototractatus: an early version of Tractatus logico-philosophicus. Ed B. F. McGuinness, T. Nyberg and G. H. von Wright, with a trn by D. F. Pears and B. F. McGuinness 1971.
See Fann, Bibliography, above, for other notes of lectures etc taken by his associates and pupils and pbd in jnls or circulated privately. Wittgenstein also pbd a Wörterbuch für Volksschulen, Vienna 1926.

Letters
Englemann, P. Letters from Ludwig Wittgenstein, with a memoir. Oxford 1967. Tr L. Furtmüller, ed B. F. McGuinness; the letters in parallel German and English texts.

§2
Ramsey, F. P. In Mind 32 1923. Essay-review of Tractatus, 1922; rptd in his The foundations of mathematics and other essays, 1931, and in Copi and Beard, 1966, below.
Black, M. Some problems connected with language. Proc Aristotelian Soc 39 1938; rptd as Wittgenstein's Tractatus, in his Language and philosophy, Ithaca 1949, and in Copi and Beard, 1966, below.
— A companion to Wittgenstein's Tractatus. Cambridge 1964.
G[asking], D. A. T. and A. C. J[ackson]. Ludwig Wittgenstein. Australasian Jnl of Philosophy 29 1951; rptd in Fann, 1967, below.
Ryle, G. Ludwig Wittgenstein. Analysis 12 1951; rptd in Copi and Beard, 1966 and in Fann, 1967, below.
Daitz, E. The picture theory of meaning. Mind 62 1953; rptd in Essays in conceptual analysis, ed A. G. N. Flew, 1956.
Kraft, V. In his Vienna circle, tr A. Pap, New York 1953.
Bilsky, M. and J. L. Cobitz. Wittgenstein: philosophy in extremis. Chicago Rev 2 1954.
Britton, K. Recollections of Wittgenstein. Cambridge Jnl 7 1954.
— Portrait of a philosopher. Listener 10 June 1955; rptd in Fann, 1967, below.
Moore, G. E. Wittgenstein's lectures in 1930–3. Mind 63 1954, 64 1955; rptd in his Philosophical papers, 1959.
Paul, G. A. Wittgenstein. In The revolution in philosophy, by A. J. Ayer [et al], 1956.
Pears, D. F. Logical atomism: Russell and Wittgenstein. Ibid.
Russell, B. The philosophy of logical atomism. In his Logic and knowledge, ed R. C. Marsh 1956.
— In his My philosophical development, 1959.
Hawkins, D. J. B. Wittgenstein and the cult of language. 1957 (Aquinas Papers 27); rptd in his Crucial problems of modern philosophy, 1957.
Feibleman, J. K. Inside the great mirror: a critical examination of the philosophy of Russell, Wittgenstein and their followers. The Hague 1958.
Malcolm, N. Wittgenstein: a memoir, with a biographical sketch by G. H. von Wright. 1958, 1966 (rev).
Pole, D. The later philosophy of Wittgenstein: a short introduction with an epilogue on J. Wisdom. 1958.
Anscombe, G. E. M. An introduction to Wittgenstein's Tractatus. 1959, 1963 (rev), 1967 (rev).

Heller, E. Wittgenstein: unphilosophical notes. Encounter 13 1959; rptd in his An artist's journey into the interior and other essays, New York 1965, and in Fann, 1967, below.

Schlick, M. The turning point in philosophy. In Logical positivism, ed A. J. Ayer, Glencoe Ill 1959.

Hartnack, J. Wittgenstein og den moderne filosofi. Copenhagen 1960; tr New York 1965.

Listener 28 Jan 1960. Assessments by E. Heller and M. O'C. Drury; 4 Feb 1960, by N. Malcolm and R. Rhees.

Stenius, E. Wittgenstein's Tractatus: a critical exposition of its main lines of thought. Oxford 1960.

Maslow, A. A study in Wittgenstein's Tractatus. Berkeley 1961.

Plochmann, G. K. and J. B. Lawson. Terms in their propositional context in Wittgenstein's Tractatus: an index. [Carbondale Ill 1962].

Specht, E. K. Die sprachphilosophischen und ontologischen Grundlagen im Spätwerk Ludwig Wittgensteins. Cologne 1963. Eng trn by D. E. Walford as The foundations of Wittgenstein's late philosophy, Manchester 1969.

Farvholdt, D. An interpretation and critique of Wittgenstein's Tractatus. Copenhagen 1964.

Griffin, J. Wittgenstein's logical atomism. Oxford 1964.

Pitcher, G. The philosophy of Wittgenstein. Englewood Cliffs NJ [1964].

— Wittgenstein, nonsense and Lewis Carroll. Massachusetts Rev 6 1965; rptd in Fann, 1967, below.

— (ed). Wittgenstein: the Philosophical investigations. New York 1966. An anthology.

Riverso, E. Il pensiero di Ludovico Wittgenstein. Naples 1964, 1970 (rev).

Naess, A. Moderne filosofer: Carnap, Wittgenstein, Heidegger, Sartre. Stockholm 1965; tr Chicago 1967.

Peursen, C. A. von. Ludwig Wittgenstein. Baarn, Holland 1965. Eng trn by R. Ambler 1969.

Ambrose, A. and M. Lazerowitz. Wittgenstein: philosophy, experiment and proof. In British philosophy in the mid-century: a Cambridge symposium, ed C. A. Mace, 2nd edn 1966.

Casey, J. Wittgenstein and the philosophy of criticism. In his Language of criticism, 1966.

Copi, I. M. and R. W. Beard (ed). Essays on Wittgenstein's Tractatus. 1966. An anthology.

Gargani, A. G. Linguaggio ed esperienza in Ludwig Wittgenstein. Florence 1966.

Peterson, R. G. A picture is a fact: Wittgenstein and The naked lunch [by William Burroughs]. Twentieth-Century Lit 12 1966.

Fann, K. T. (ed). Wittgenstein—the man and his philosophy: an anthology. New York 1967.

— Wittgenstein's conception of philosophy. Oxford 1969.

Hester, M. B. The meaning of poetic metaphor: an analysis in the light of Wittgenstein's claim that meaning is use. The Hague 1967.

High, D. M. Language, person and belief: studies in Wittgenstein's Philosophical investigations and religious uses of language. New York 1967.

Mauro, T. de. Wittgenstein: his place in the development of semantics. Dordrecht 1967.

Micheletti, M. Lo Schopenhauerismo di Wittgenstein. Bologna 1967.

Morick, H. (ed). Wittgenstein and the problem of other minds. New York 1967. An anthology.

Schulz, W. Wittgenstein: die Negation der Philosophie. Pfullingen 1967.

Falck, C. Poetry and Wittgenstein. Review (Oxford) no 18 1968.

Hudson, W. D. Wittgenstein: the bearing of his philosophy upon religious belief. 1968.

Shibles, W. A. Wittgenstein: language and philosophy. Dubuque 1969.

Toulmin, S. Ludwig Wittgenstein. Encounter 32 1969.

Winch, P. (ed). Studies in the philosophy of Wittgenstein. 1969.

M.P.

JOSEPH HENRY WOODGER
b. 1894

§1

Biological principles: a critical study. 1929, New York 1929.

The axiomatic method in biology. 1937.

The technique of theory construction. Chicago 1939 (International Encyclopedia of Unified Science vol 2 no 5).

Biology and language: an introduction to the methodology of the biological sciences including medicine. Cambridge 1952.

Physics, psychology and medicine: a methodological essay. Cambridge 1956.

Woodger translated and adapted L. von Bertalanffy, Modern theories of development (Kritische Theorie der Formbildung) 1933, and translated A. Tarski, Logic, semantics, mathematics, 1956.

§2

Smart, J. J. C. Theory construction. In Logic and language, ed A. G. N. Flew, Oxford 1953.

Martin, R. H. On Woodger's analysis of biological language. Rev of Metaphysics 8 1954.

Robinson, A. Formalization in biology: critique. Jnl Symbolic Logic 25 1960.

Gregg, J. R. and F. T. C. Harris (ed). Form and strategy in science: studies dedicated to Woodger on the occasion of his seventieth birthday. Dordrecht 1964. Some biographical information and a bibliography.

H.M.R.

IV. WRITERS ON TRAVEL, THE COUNTRYSIDE AND SPORT

For bibliographies which include books on 20th-century sport, see The sportsman's library: being a descriptive list of the most important books on sport, *ed E. R. Gee, New York 1940; and A. H. Higginson,* British and American sporting authors: their writings and biographies, *with a bibliography by S. R. Smith, 1951. For chs on the literature of mountaineering, nature writers and books on travel and exploration, see H. F. West,* The mind on the wing, *New York 1947.*

ADRIAN HANBURY BELL
b. 1901

See cols 522–3, above.

GERTRUDE MARGARET LOWTHIAN BELL
1868–1926

§1

Safar Nameh—Persian pictures: a book of travel. 1895 (anon), 1928 (as Persian pictures, with preface by E. D. Ross), New York 1928, London 1937 (introd by V. Sackville-West), 1947 (preface by A. J. Arberry).
Poems from the Divan of Hafiz. Tr G. Bell 1897, 1928 (preface by E. D. Ross).
The desert and the sown. 1907, New York 1907 (as Syria: the desert and the sown), London 1928.
The thousand and one churches. 1909. With W. M. Ramsay.
Amurath to Amurath. 1911. Travels in Asia Minor and Persia.
Palace and mosque at Ukhaiḍir: a study in early Mohammadan architecture. Oxford 1914.
The Arab War—confidential information for general headquarters from G. Bell: being despatches reprinted from the secret Arab Bulletin. [1940].
Gertrude Bell also prepared an official report Review of the civil administration of Mesopotamia, *1920. Her private library is now at the University of Newcastle (see W. C. Donkin,* Catalogue of the Gertrude Bell Collection, *Newcastle-upon-Tyne 1960).*

Letters

The letters of Gertrude Bell. Ed Lady Bell 2 vols 1927, New York 1927.
The earlier letters of Gertrude Bell. Ed E. Richmond 1937, New York [1937].

§2

Ross, E. D. Gertrude Bell. In The post Victorians, 1933.
Ridley, M. R. Gertrude Bell. 1941.
Bonsal, S. Arabs plead for freedom: Emir Faisal, Colonel Lawrence and Gertrude Bell—the desert queen. In his Suitors and suppliants, New York 1946.
Swan, M. The Emma of the desert. In his A small part of time, 1957.
Burgoyne, E. Gertrude Bell from her personal papers 1889–1914. 2 vols 1958.
Edmonds, C. J. Gertrude Bell in the Near and Middle East. Royal Central Asian Jnl 56 1969.
Dearden, S. Gertrude Bell: a journey of the heart. Cornhill no 1062 1969/70.

JOSEPH HILAIRE PIERRE RENÉ BELLOC
1870–1953

See cols 1004–10, above.

SIR JOHN BETJEMAN
b. 1906

See cols 233–4, above.

'GEORGE BOURNE', GEORGE STURT
1890–1927

The ms of Sturt's Journal *is in the BM, with other miscellaneous mss.*

§1

A year's exile. 1898. A tale.
The Bettesworth book: talks with a Surrey peasant. 1901, 1911 (with author's note).
Memoirs of a Surrey labourer: a record of the last years of Frederick Bettesworth. 1907.
The ascending effort. 1910.
Change in the village. 1912, New York 1912.
Lucy Bettesworth. 1913.
William Smith, potter and farmer, 1790–1858. 1920.
A farmer's life, with a memoir of the farmer's sister. 1922.
The wheelwright's shop, by G. Sturt. Cambridge 1923.
A small boy in the sixties. Cambridge 1927. By G. Sturt.
The journals of George Sturt, 'George Bourne', 1890–1902. Ed with introd by G. Grigson 1941.
The journals of George Sturt, 1890–1927: a selection, edited and introduced by E. D. Mackerness. 2 vols Cambridge 1967.

§2

Thompson, D. A cure for amnesia. Scrutiny 2 1933.
Esdaile, A. J. K. George Sturt of Farnham. In his Autolycus' pack, 1940.
Mackerness, E. D. The early career of Sturt. N & Q 206 1961.
Fraser, J. Sturt's apprenticeship. REL 5 1964.

P.C.

GERALD BRENAN (EDWARD FITZGERALD BRENAN)
b. 1894

See col 1014, above.

ROBERT BYRON
1905–41

§1

Europe in the looking-glass: reflections of a motor drive from Grimsby to Athens. 1926.
The station: Athos, treasures and men. 1928, New York 1928, London 1949 (introd by C. Sykes), New York 1949.
The Byzantine achievement: an historical perspective. 1929, New York 1929.

The birth of western painting. 1930, New York 1931.
With D. T. Rice.
An essay on India. 1931.
The appreciation of architecture. 1932.
First Russia, then Tibet. 1933.
Innocence & design, by Richard Waughburton [Byron and
C. Sykes]. 1935. Fiction.
The road to Oxiana. 1937, 1950 (introd by D. T. Rice).
*Byron was special correspondent in India for Daily Express
1929. He pbd a travel guide to Wiltshire and contributed
to U. Pope, Survey of Persian art, 1938.*

§2

Young, G. M. Cities and harvests. In his Daylight and
champaign, 1937.
—— Robert Byron. In his Today and yesterday, 1948.
Sykes, C. Robert Byron. In his Four studies in loyalty,
1946.
Acton, H. In his Memoirs of an aesthete, 1948.

A.P.H.

SIR NEVILLE CARDUS
b. 1889

Selections

The essential Neville Cardus, selected with an introduction by R. Hart-Davis. 1949.
The Playfair Cardus: essays. 1963.

§1

A cricketer's book. 1922.
Days in the sun: a cricketer's journal. 1924.
Langford, S. Musical criticisms. Ed Cardus 1929.
The summer game: a cricketer's journal. [1929].
Cricket. 1930 (English Heritage ser).
Good days: a book of cricket. 1934.
Bat and ball: a new book of cricket, ed T. Moult 1935.
With contributions by N. Cardus [et al].
Die schöne Müllerin: Schubert. 1935. The text of the
song-cycle, pbd by Die schöne Müllerin Soc. Introd
and notes by Cardus.
Australian summer. [1937]. The test matches in Australia
1936–7.
Music for pleasure. Sydney 1942.
English cricket. 1945 (Britain in Pictures).
Ten composers. 1945, 1958 (rev as A composers eleven,
with additional ch on Bruckner), New York 1959.
Autobiography. 1947.
The Ashes: with background of the Tests and pen pictures
of the 1948 Australian team. [1948].
Second innings. 1950. Autobiographical reminiscences.
Cricket all the year. 1952.
Kathleen Ferrier: a memoir, ed Cardus 1954, New York
1955. With contributions by Cardus [et al].
Close of play. 1956. Essays on cricket.
Talking of music. 1957, New York 1957. Mainly rptd
from Manchester Guardian.
A composers eleven. 1958. *See* Ten composers, 1945,
above.
Cricket heroes, ed J. Kay 1959. By members of the
Cricket Writers Club: N. Cardus et al.
Sir Thomas Beecham: a memoir. 1961.
Gustav Mahler: his mind and his music. 1965–, New
York [1965–].
The delights of music: a critic's choice. 1966.
*Since 1917 Cardus has contributed regularly to Manchester
Guardian (Guardian), mainly on cricket and music. He
also contributed to Sydney Morning Herald 1941–7.*

M.P.

RICHARD THOMAS CHURCH
b. 1893

See cols 246–8, above.

MAURICE STEWART COLLIS
b. 1889

§1

Siamese White. 1936, New York 1940.
She was a Queen. 1937, New York 1962. Biography of
Ma Saw, Queen of Burma.
Lords of the sunset: a tour in the Shan states. 1938.
Trials in Burma. 1938, New York 1945. Autobiographical.
The great within. 1941. On interaction between China
and Europe since 17th century.
The Burmese scene: political, historical, pictorial. [1943].
The land of the great image: being experiences of Friar
Manrique in Arakan. 1943, New York 1943.
Foreign mud: being an account of the opium imbroglio at
Canton in the 1830's and the Anglo-Chinese war that
followed. 1946, New York 1947 (for 1946).
Quest for Sita. 1946.
The first holy one. 1948, New York 1948. On Confucius.
The grand peregrination: the life and adventures of Fernão
Mendes Pinto. 1949.
Marco Polo. 1950, New York 1961 (for 1960).
The discovery of L. S. Lowry: a critical and biographical
essay. 1951.
The journey outward: an autobiography. 1952.
Into hidden Burma: an autobiography. 1953.
Cortés and Montezuma. 1954, New York 1955 (for 1954).
Last and first in Burma 1941–8. 1956, New York 1956.
The hurling time. 1958. History of England 1346–81.
Nancy Astor: an informal biography. 1960, New York
1960.
Stanley Spencer: a biography. 1962.
Wayfoong: the Hongkong and Shanghai Banking Corpora-
tion: a study of East Asia's transformation, political,
financial and economic, during the last hundred years.
1965.
Raffles. 1966.
Somerville and Ross: a biography. 1968.
*Collis also pbd poetry, novels, plays and 2 vols of paintings
and drawings under the pseudonym 'Alva'. He was art
critic on Sunday Observer Jan 1942–Aug 1947 and on
Time & Tide from about 1937.*

§2

Whittingham-Jones, B. Works of Collis. Asiatic Rev new
ser 41 1945. On his historical writing in an Asiatic
setting.
Leasor, J. Collis: author by profession. 1952.

BERNARD RICHARD MEIRION
DARWIN
1876–1961

§1

The golf courses of the British Isles. 1910, 1925 (rev, as
The golf courses of Great Britain).
Tee shots, and others. 1911. Essays.
A friendly round. 1922. Essays from the Times.
A round of golf on the LNER. York [1924].
Eton v. Harrow at Lords. 1926.
Green memories. [1928].
The English public school. 1929.
Second shots: casual talks about golf. 1930.

Out of the rough. [1932]. Essays on golf.
Dickens. 1933, New York 1933.
Playing the like. 1934. Essays on golf.
W. G. Grace. 1934.
John Gully and his times. 1935, New York 1935.
Rubs of the green. 1936. Essays on golf.
A round of golf. [1937].
Life is sweet, brother. 1940. Autobiographical reminiscence.
Pack clouds away. 1941. Autobiographical reminiscence.
Golf between two wars. 1944.
Golfing by-paths. 1946. Essays from Country Life.
War on the line: the story of the Southern Railway in wartime. 1946.
Every idle dream. 1948. Essays.
A history of golf in Britain. 1952. By Darwin et al.
James Braid. 1952.
Golf. 1954.
The world that Fred made: an autobiography. 1955.
Darwin also pbd tales and verses for children, mostly with his wife E. M. Darwin (see col 792, above). He contributed to Country Life from 1908 and was on the staff of the Times 1919–53, after which he wrote leaders for the same paper.

§2

Darwin, F. The story of a childhood. Edinburgh 1920 (priv ptd).
Ward-Thomas, P. A. The incomparable Bernard Darwin. Country Life 26 Oct 1961.

H.M.R.

GEORGE NORMAN DOUGLAS [DOUGLASS]
1868–1952

See cols 563–5, above.

LAWRENCE GEORGE DURRELL
b. 1912

See cols 266–71, above.

ROBERT PETER FLEMING
1907–71

Brazilian adventure. 1933, New York 1934, [1942] (with foreword by C. Fadiman).
Spectator's gallery. Ed Fleming and D. Verschoyle 1933. Selections from Spectator 1932.
Variety: essays, sketches and stories. 1933.
One's company: a journey to China. 1934, New York 1934, London 1948 (with News from Tartary, below, as Travels in Tartary).
News from Tartary: a journey from Peking to Kashmir. 1936, New York 1936, London 1948 (as Travels in Tartary, with One's company, above). See also E. K. Maillart, Oasis interdites, de Pékin au Cachemire. Paris 1937, London 1937 (as Forbidden journey, from Peking to Kashmir).
The flying visit. 1940, New York 1940. Fiction.
A story to tell, and other tales. 1942, New York 1942.
Travels in Tartary. 1948. See One's company, 1934, and News from Tartary, 1936, above.
The sixth column: a singular tale of our times. 1951, New York 1951.
A forgotten journey. 1952. Diary of a journey through Russia, Manchuria and Northern China in 1934.
Migot, A. Tibetan marches. Tr Fleming 1955.
Spical operations. Ed P. J. F. Howarth 1955. By Fleming [et al]; accounts by British agents of underground movements during the Second World War.

My aunt's rhinoceros and other reflections. 1956, New York 1958. Essays.
Invasion 1940: an account of the German preparations and the British counter-measures. 1957, New York 1957 (as Operation Sea lion: the projected invasion of England in 1940).
With the Guards to Mexico! and other excursions. 1957.
The Gower Street poltergeist. 1958. Rptd from Spectator.
The siege at Peking. 1959, New York 1959.
Bayonets to Lhasa: the first full account of the British invasion of Tibet in 1904. 1961, New York 1961.
Goodbye to the Bombay bowler. 1961. Rptd from Spectator.
The fate of Admiral Kolchak. 1963, New York 1963.
Fleming contributed to Spectator *from 1931 and to* Times *from 1932.*

J.G.

JOAN ROSITA FORBES,
1893–1967

§1

Unconducted wanderers. 1919.
The secret of the Sahara: Kufara. 1921, New York [1921] (introd by H. Johnston).
The jewel in the lotus: a novel. 1922.
Quest: the story of Anne, three men and some Arabs. 1922. Fiction.
A fool's hell. 1923, New York 1924. Fiction.
El Raisuni, the Sultan of the mountains: his life story. 1924, New York 1924 (as The Sultan of the mountains: the life story of Raisuli).
From Red Sea to Blue Nile: Abyssinian adventures. 1925, New York [1925], [1935] (introd by Viscount Allenby), London [1939].
If the gods laugh. 1925, New York [1926]. Fiction.
Sirocco. 1927, New York [1928] (as Pursuit). Fiction.
Account rendered, and King's mate. 1928. Fiction.
Adventure, being a gypsy salad: some incidents, excitements and impressions of twelve highly-seasoned years. 1928.
The cavaliers of death. 1930. Fiction.
One flesh. 1930, New York 1930. Fiction.
Conflict: Angora to Afghanistan. 1931, New York 1931.
Ordinary people. 1931, New York 1932 (as Promise you won't marry me). Fiction.
Eight republics in search of a future: evolution and revolution in South America. 1933.
The extraordinary house. 1934. Fiction.
Women called wild. 1935, New York 1937. On the position of women.
The golden vagabond. 1936. Fiction.
Forbidden road: Kabul to Samarkand. 1937, New York 1937, London 1940 (as Russian road to India: by Kabul and Samarkand).
These are real people. 1937, New York [1939]. Travel sketches.
India of the princes. 1939, New York 1941.
A unicorn in the Bahamas. 1939, New York 1940.
The prodigious Caribbean: Columbus to Roosevelt. 1940.
These men I knew. [1940], New York 1940. Interviews with various statesmen.
Gypsy in the sun. 1944, New York 1944. Memoirs.
Appointment with destiny. 1946, New York 1946. Sequel to Gypsy in the sun. Both abridged as Appointment in the sun, 1949.
Henry Morgan, pirate. New York 1946, London 1948 (as Sir Henry Morgan, pirate & pioneer).
Islands in the sun. 1949. On the West Indies.
Rosita Forbes edited Women of All Lands [*weekly magazine*] *1938–9.*

§2

Cole, M. I. In her Women of today, 1938.

A.P.H.

EDWARD MORGAN FORSTER
1879-1970

See cols 437-44, above.

ROBERT JOHN GIBBINGS
1889-1958
Bibliographies

Kirkus, A. M. Robert Gibbings: a bibliography. Ed P. Empson and J. Harris 1962.

§1

The 7th man: a true cannibal tale. Waltham Saint Lawrence 1930. For children.
Iorana! a Tahitian journal. Boston 1932, London 1932.
A true tale of love in Tonga. 1935, 1954 (enlarged). For children.
Coconut island: or the adventures of two children in the south seas. 1936, Letchworth 1949 (rev). For children.
John Graham, convict, 1824: an historical narrative. 1937, New York 1957.
Blue angels and whales: a record of personal experiences below and above water. [1938], 1946 (rev and enlarged), New York 1946.
Sweet Thames run softly. 1940, New York 1941.
Coming down the Wye. 1942, New York 1943.
Lovely is the Lee. 1945 (for 1944), New York 1945.
Over the reefs. 1948, New York 1949. Account of a tour of the Polynesian islands.
The wood-engravings of Robert Gibbings. 1949. Introd by T. Balston.
Sweet Cork of thee. 1951, New York 1951.
Coming down the Seine. 1953, New York 1953.
The perfect wife: a fable from France, transmogrified into the Anglo-Irish idiom and illustrated by Gibbings. Glenageary 1955.
Trumpets from Montparnasse. 1955, New York 1955.
Till I end my song. 1957, New York 1957.
The wood engravings of R. Gibbings, with some recollections by the artist. Ed P. Empson, introd by T. Balston, 1959, Chicago 1959.
Gibbings illustrated all his own books and approximately 50 books by other authors. He also pbd vols of wood engravings. About half the books in these two latter categories were pbd by the Golden Cockerel Press of which Gibbings was Director 1924-33.

§2

Balston, T. The river books of Gibbings. Alphabet & Image 8 1948.

J.G.

LOUIS GOLDING
1895-1958

See cols 591-2, above.

ROBERT BONTINE CUNNINGHAME GRAHAM
1852-1936
Bibliographies

Chaundy, L. A bibliography of the first editions of the works of Graham. 1924.
West, H. F. The H. F. West Collection of Graham. Hanover NH 1938 (priv ptd).

Selections

Thirty tales and sketches. Ed E. Garnett 1929, New York 1929.
Rodeo: a collection of tales and sketches. Ed A. F. Tschiffely 1936, New York 1936.
The essential Graham. Ed P. Bloomfield 1952.

§1

Notes on the district of Menteith for tourists and others. 1895.
Father Archangel of Scotland and other essays. 1896. With his wife Gabriela.
Mogreb-el-Acksa: a journey in Morocco. 1898, 1921 (rev); ed E. Garnett, New York 1930.
The Ipané. 1899, New York 1925. Stories and sketches.
Thirteen stories. 1900, New York 1942.
A vanished Arcadia: being some account of the Jesuits in Paraguay 1607 to 1767. 1901, New York 1924.
Success. 1902. Stories and sketches.
Hernando de Soto, together with an account of one of his captains, Gonçalo Silvestre. 1903, New York 1924.
Progress and other sketches. 1905.
His people. 1907. Stories and sketches.
Faith. 1909. Stories and sketches.
Hope. 1910. Stories and sketches.
Charity. 1912. Stories and sketches.
A hatchment. 1913. Stories and sketches.
Scottish stories. 1914.
Bernal Diaz del Castillo: being some account of him taken from his True history of the conquest of New Spain. 1915.
Brought forward. 1916. Stories and sketches.
A Brazilian mystic: being the life and miracles of Antonio Conselheiro. 1920, New York 1920.
Cartagena and the banks of the Sinú. 1920, New York 1921.
The conquest of New Granada: being the life of Gonzalo Jimenez de Quesada. 1922.
The conquest of the River Plate. 1924, New York 1924.
Doughty deeds: an account of the life of Robert Graham of Gartmore, poet and politician 1735-97. 1925.
Pedro de Valdivia, conqueror of Chile. 1926.
Redeemed and other sketches. 1927.
José Antonio Páez. 1929.
The horses of the Conquest. 1930; ed R. M. Denhardt, Norman Oklahoma 1949.
Writ in sand. 1932. Stories and sketches.
Portrait of a dictator: Francisco Solano Lopez, Paraguay 1865-70. 1933.
Mirages. 1936. Essays and sketches.
Three fugitive pieces, foreword by H. F. West. Hanover NH 1960. A fragment on Garibaldi; Report on the cattle resources of the Republic of Colombia, March 1917; Prologue to W. H. Hudson's The purple land.
Graham wrote and priv ptd various pamphlets and short sketches and contributed prefaces to a variety of English and foreign literary works and books of travel.

§2

Parker, W. M. A modern Elizabethan. In his Modern Scottish writers, Edinburgh 1917.
Harris, F. Graham. In his Contemporary portraits, 3rd ser, 1920.

Graham, S. Laird and caballero: Graham. In his Death of yesterday, 1930.

West, H. F. A modern conquistador: Graham, his life and works. 1932.

— Don Roberto. Hanover NH 1936 (priv ptd).

Garnett, E. Graham: man and writer. London Mercury 33 1936.

Tschiffely, A. F. Don Roberto: being an account of the life and works of Graham. 1937, 1955 (abridged as Tornado cavalier: a biography of Graham).

Hudson, W. H. Letters to Graham. Ed R. Curle 1941.

Stallman, R. W. Graham's South American sketches. Hispania 28 1945.

Price, H. T. Graham. Quarto no 17 1948.

Espinoza, E. El 'singularísimo' Cunninghame Graham. In his Tres clásicos ingleses de la Pampa, Santiago de Chile 1951.

'Hugh MacDiarmid' (C. M. Grieve). Cunninghame Graham: a centenary study. Glasgow [1952].

Macaulay, R. Stranger, tread lightly. Kenyon Rev 17 1955.

Hay, E. K. Political use and abuse: Conrad's letters to Graham. Dartmouth College Lib Bull. 6 1964.

Haymaker, R. E. Prince-errant and evocator of horizons: a reading of Cunninghame Graham. Kingsport Tenn 1967.

Conrad, J. Letters to Cunninghame Graham. Ed C. T. Watts 1969.

MacShane, F. Cunninghame Graham. South Atlantic Quarterly 68 1969.

Smith, J. S. Cunninghame Graham as a writer of short fiction. Eng Lit in Transition 12 1969.

A.P.H.

STEPHEN GRAHAM
b. 1884

§ I

A vagabond in the Caucasus, with some notes on his experiences among the Russians. 1911.

A tramp's sketches. 1912.

Undiscovered Russia. 1912.

Changing Russia. 1913.

With the Russian pilgrims to Jerusalem. 1913.

With poor immigrants to America. 1914, New York 1914.

Russia and the world: a study of the war and a statement of the world-problems that now confront Russia and Great Britain. 1915, New York 1915, London 1917 (rev and enlarged).

The way of Martha and the way of Mary. 1915, New York 1915. On eastern Christianity.

Through Russian central Asia. 1916, New York 1916.

Russia in 1916. 1917, New York 1917.

The quest of the face [of Christ]. 1918, New York 1918.

A private in the guards. 1919, New York 1919.

Children of the slaves. 1920, New York 1920 (as The soul of John Brown).

The challenge of the dead: a vision of the war and the life of a common soldier in France, seen two years afterwards between August and November 1920. 1921.

Europe—whither bound?: being letters of travel from the capitals of Europe. 1921, New York 1922.

Tramping with a poet [Vachel Lindsay] in the Rockies. 1922, New York 1922.

In quest of El Dorado. New York 1923, London 1924.

Life and last words of Wilfrid Ewart. 1924.

London nights: a series of studies and sketches of London at night. [1925].

Russia in division. 1925, New York 1925 (as The dividing line of Europe).

The gentle art of tramping. New York 1926, London 1927.

New York nights. New York [1927], London 1928.

The tramp's anthology. Ed Graham 1928.

Great Russian short stories. Ed Graham 1929, New York 1960.

Peter the Great: a life of Peter I of Russia called the Great. 1929, New York 1929.

The death of yesterday. 1930. Literary essays.

Great American short stories. Ed Graham 1931.

Stalin: an impartial study of the life and work of Joseph Stalin. 1931, 1939 (rev).

Ivan the terrible. 1932, New Haven 1933.

Boris Godunof. 1933, New Haven 1933.

One of the ten thousand. 1933.

Twice round the London clock and More London nights. 1933.

A life of Alexander II, Tsar of Russia. 1935, New Haven 1935 (as Tsar of freedom).

Characteristics. 1936. Travel notes.

Alexander of Jugoslavia: strong man of the Balkans. 1938, New Haven 1939.

The moving tent: adventures with a tent and fishing-rod in Southern Jugoslavia. 1939.

From war to war: a date-book of the years between. [1940].

Liquid victory. [1940]. On the importance of oil supplies in war.

Thinking of living? 1949.

Summing-up on Russia. 1951.

100 best poems in the English language, chosen with an introduction by S. Graham. 1952.

Part of the wonderful scene: an autobiography. 1964.

Novels

Priest of the ideal. 1917, New York 1917.

Under-London. 1923.

Midsummer music. [1926], New York [1927].

The lay confessor. 1928, New York 1929.

St Vitus Day. 1930, New York 1931.

A modern Vanity Fair. 1931.

Everybody pays. 1932.

Lost battle. 1934.

The padre of St Jacob's. 1934.

Balkan monastery. 1935, New York 1936.

African tragedy. 1937.

Pay as you run. 1955.

Graham edited Stephen Graham's news letter about the Orthodox churches in war time, *March 1940 to November 1943, for the Anglican and Eastern Churches Assoc, and was general editor of Constable's Russian Library, 6 vols 1915–18. He has also selected and edited or tr several other Russian works, particularly novels. As well as writing for various reviews, he contributed signed articles to the* Times *1914–16, 1924 and 1926.*

D.K.

GRAHAM GREENE
b. 1904

See cols 503–12, above.

GEOFFREY EDWARD HARVEY GRIGSON
b. 1905

See cols 1052–3, above.

ALDOUS LEONARD HUXLEY
1894–1963

See cols 609–17, above.

CHRISTOPHER WILLIAM BRADSHAW ISHERWOOD
b. 1904

See cols 619–20, above.

JAMES FALCONER KIRKUP
b. 1918

See cols 294–5, above.

DAVID HERBERT LAWRENCE
1885–1930

See cols 481–503, above.

THOMAS EDWARD LAWRENCE
1888–1935

See cols 1181–5, above.

DAME EMILIE ROSE MACAULAY
1881–1958

See cols 642–3, above.

HAROLD JOHN MASSINGHAM
1888–1952

St Francis of Assisi, by J. A. Péladan. 1913. Tr Massingham.

Letters to X. 1919, Freeport NY 1967. Essays in English literature.

People and things: an attempt to connect art and humanity. 1919.

A treasury of seventeenth-century English verse, 1616–1660. Ed H. J. Massingham 1919, 1920 (rev).

Dogs, birds and others: natural history letters from The Spectator. Ed H. J. Massingham 1921.

Some birds of the countryside: the art of nature. 1921.

Poems about birds from the middle ages to the present day. Ed H. J. Massingham 1922, New York [1922?].

Untrodden ways: adventures on English coasts, heaths and marshes and also among the works of Hudson, Crabbe and other country writers. 1923.

In praise of England. 1924.

Sanctuaries for birds and how to make them. 1924.

A selection of the writings of H. W. Massingham. Ed H. J. Massingham 1925.

Downland man. 1926.

Fee, fi, fo, fum: or the giants in England. 1926.

The golden age: the story of human nature. 1927.

Pre-Roman Britain. 1927.

The heritage of man. 1929. Essays.

The friend of Shelley: a memoir of Edward John Trelawny. 1930, New York 1930.

Birds of the seashore. 1931.

The great Victorians. Ed H. J. and H. Massingham 1932, Garden City NY 1932.

Wold without end. 1932.

London scene. 1933.

Country. 1934.

English country: fifteen essays. Ed H. J. Massingham 1934.

Through the wilderness. 1935.

English downland. 1936, 1949 (rev).

Cotswold country: a survey of limestone England from the Dorset coast to Lincolnshire. 1937, New York 1938, London 1942 (rev), New York 1942, London [1947] (rev).

Genius of England. 1937.

Shepherd's country: a record of the crafts and people of the hills. 1938.

The writings of Gilbert White. Ed H. J. Massingham 1938.

Country relics: an account of some old tools and properties once belonging to English craftsmen and husbandmen. Cambridge 1939.

A countryman's journal. 1939.

The English countryside. Ed H. J. Massingham 1939, New York 1939 (as Rural England).

The sweet of the year: March, April, May, June. 1939.

Chiltern country. 1940, New York 1940.

England and the farmer: a symposium. Ed H. J. Massingham 1941.

The fall of the year. 1941.

The English countryman: a study of the English tradition. 1942.

Field fellowship. 1942. Essays.

Home. 1942, [1947] (rev, as England, home and beauty). Pamphlet.

Remembrance: an autobiography. [1942].

Men of earth. 1943.

The tree of life. 1943.

This plot of earth: a gardener's chronicle. 1944.

The natural order: essays in the return to husbandry by E. Blunden, H. J. Massingham et alia. Ed H. J. Massingham 1945.

The wisdom of the fields. 1945.

Where man belongs. 1946.

The small farmer: a survey by various hands. Ed H. J. Massingham 1947.

An Englishman's year. 1948.

The curious traveller. 1950.

The faith of a fieldsman. 1951.

The Southern Marches. 1952.

Prophecy of famine: a warning and the remedy. 1953. With E. Hyams.

Massingham was literary editor of Athenaeum.

WILLIAM SOMERSET MAUGHAM
1874–1965

See cols 661–8, above.

HENRY CANOVA VOLLAM MORTON
b. 1892

Selections

H. V. Morton's London. 1940, New York 1941. The heart of London, The spell of London and The nights of London.

H. V. Morton's Britain. Ed G. Carter, New York 1969.

§1

The heart of London. 1925.

London. 1926, New York 1926, London 1937 (rev).

The London year. 1926, New York 1927 (as When you go to London), London 1933 (rev).

The nights of London. 1926.

The spell of London. 1926.

In search of England. 1927, New York 1928, London 1929 (rev), New York 1935 (rev), London 1936 (rev), New York 1960 (rev).

The call of England. 1928, New York 1928, London 1936 (rev), New York 1936.

The land of the Vikings: from Thames to Humber. Bungay [1928].

In search of Scotland. 1929, New York 1930.

In search of Ireland. 1930, New York 1931.

Blue days at sea and other essays. 1932, New York 1933.

In search of Wales. 1932, New York 1932.

In Scotland again. 1933, New York 1933.

What I saw in the slums. [1933]. Pamphlet.

In the steps of the Master. 1934, New York 1934, London 1962 (with rev introd).

In the steps of St Paul. 1936, New York 1936.

Our fellow men. 1936.

Through the lands of the Bible. 1938, New York 1938.
Ghosts of London. 1939, New York 1940.
Women of the Bible. 1940, New York 1941.
Middle East: a record of travel in the countries of Egypt, Palestine, Iraq, Turkey and Greece. 1941, New York 1941.
I, James Blunt. 1942, New York 1942. Imaginary diary describing England under German occupation.
I saw two Englands: the record of a journey before the war, and after the outbreak of war, in the year 1939. 1942, New York 1943.
Atlantic meeting. 1943, New York 1943. Churchill and Roosevelt in August 1941.
In search of South Africa. 1948, New York 1948.
In search of London. 1951, New York 1951.
A stranger in Spain. 1955, New York 1955.
A traveller in Rome. 1957, New York 1957.
This is Rome: a pilgrimage in words and pictures [by Karsh]. Kingswood 1960, New York 1960.
This is the Holy Land. Kingswood 1961, New York 1961.
A traveller in Italy. 1964, New York 1964.
The waters of Rome. 1966, New York 1966 (as The fountains of Rome).
A traveller in southern Italy. 1969.
Morton was assistant editor of Birmingham Gazette & Express *and sub-editor of* Daily Mail.

N.J.S.

ARTHUR MICHELL RANSOME
1884–1967

See cols 718–19, above.

ALAN ROSS
b. 1922

See cols 334–5, above.

VICTORIA MARY SACKVILLE-WEST
1892–1962

See cols 335–7, above.

CLARE CONSUELO SHERIDAN
1885–1970

§1

Russian portraits. 1921, New York [1921] (as Mayfair to Moscow: Clare Sheridan's diary).
My American diary. New York [1922].
In many places. 1923, New York [1923] (as West and East).
Stella defiant. 1924, New York 1925. Fiction.
Across Europe with Satanella. 1925, New York 1925.
The thirteenth. [1925]. Fiction.
Make believe. 1926. Fiction.
A Turkish kaleidoscope. 1926.
Nude veritas. 1927, New York 1928 (as Naked truth). Reminiscences.
Green amber. 1930. Fiction.
El Caïd. 1931, New York 1931 (as The substitute bride). Fiction.
Genetrix. 1935. Fiction.
Arab interlude. 1936.
Redskin interlude. 1938.
Without end. 1939. On R. B. Sheridan, the writer's son.
The mask. [1942]. Fiction.
My crowded sanctuary. 1945. Reminiscences.
To the four winds. 1957. Autobiography.

§2

Cole, M. I. In her Women of today, 1938.

FRANCIS SYDNEY SMYTHE
1900–49

§1

Climbs and ski runs: mountaineering and ski-ing in the Alps, Great Britain and Corsica. 1929.
The Kangchenjunga adventure. 1930.
Kamet conquered. 1932.
An Alpine journey. 1934.
The spirit of the hills. 1935.
Over Tyrolese hills. 1936.
Camp six: an account of the 1933 Mount Everest expedition. 1937.
The mountain scene. 1937.
Peaks and valleys. 1938.
The valley of flowers. 1938, New York 1949.
A camera in the hills. 1939.
The adventures of a mountaineer. 1940.
Edward Whymper. 1940.
Mountaineering holiday. 1940.
My Alpine album. 1940.
The mountain vision. 1941.
Over Welsh hills. 1941.
Alpine ways. 1942.
British mountaineers. 1942 (The British People in Pictures ser).
Snow on the hills. 1946.
Again Switzerland. 1947.
The mountain top: an illustrated anthology from the prose and pictures of F. S. Smythe. 1947.
Rocky mountains. 1948.
Swiss winter. 1948.
Mountains in colour. 1949, New York 1949 (as Behold the mountains).
Climbs in the Canadian Rockies. 1950, New York 1951.
Smythe was a frequent contributor to the Times *on mountaineering from 1930; he also pbd a novel,* Secret mission, *in 1942.*

§2

Lunn, A. The religion of a mountaineer. London Mercury 21 1930.
Francis Sydney Smythe 1900–49. Alpine Jnl 57 1949.

H.M.R.

DAME FREYA MADELINE STARK
b. 1893

Selections

The Freya Stark story. New York 1953. Condensation of Traveller's prelude, Beyond Euphrates and The coast of incense.
The journey's echo: selections from Freya Stark. [1963], New York 1964.

§1

Baghdad sketches. Baghdad 1932, London 1937 (enlarged), New York [1938].
The valleys of the Assassins and other Persian travels. 1934.
The southern gates of Arabia: a journey in the Hadhramaut. 1936, New York [1936].
Seen in the Hadhramaut. 1938, New York 1939. A collection of photographs with a preface.
A winter in Arabia. 1940, New York 1940.
Letters from Syria. 1942.
East is West. 1945, New York 1945 (as The Arab island: the Middle East 1939–43).
Perseus in the wind. 1948, Boston 1956. Essays.
Traveller's prelude. 1950, Baltimore 1962. Autobiography.

Beyond Euphrates: autobiography 1928–33. 1951.
The coast of incense: autobiography 1933–9. 1953.
Ionia: a quest. 1954, New York [1954].
The Lycian shore. 1956, New York 1956.
Alexander's path from Caria to Cilicia. [1958], New York 1958.
Riding to the Tigris. [1959], New York 1960.
Dust in the lion's paw: autobiography 1939–46. [1961], New York 1962.
Rome on the Euphrates: the story of a frontier. [1966], New York 1967.
The zodiac arch. 1968, New York 1969. Essays and stories.
Space, time & movement in landscape. [1969].
Freya Stark contributed articles to Times *and to various jnls on Arab problems both during and after World War II. She also wrote poems and short stories, mostly for* Cornhill Mag.

J.G.

WALTER FITZWILLIAM STARKIE
b. 1894

§1

Jacinto Benavente. 1924.
Luigi Pirandello. 1926, 1937 (rev and enlarged), New York 1937, Berkeley 1965 (rev and enlarged).
Modern Spain and its literature. Houston 1929.
Raggle-taggle: adventures with a fiddle in Hungary and Roumania. 1933, New York [1933].
Spanish raggle-taggle: adventures with a fiddle in North Spain. 1934, New York 1935, London 1961 (abridged by the author).
Don Gypsy: adventures with a fiddle in Barbary, Andalusia and La Mancha. 1936, New York [1937].
The waveless plain: an Italian autobiography. 1938, New York [1938].
Grand Inquisitor: being an account of Cardinal Ximenez de Cisneros and his times. 1940.
Eternal travellers. In Traveller's quest: original contributions towards a philosophy of travel, ed M. A. Michael 1950.
In Sara's tents. 1953, New York [1954]. On gypsies.
The road to Santiago: pilgrims of St James. 1957, New York 1957.
St James the Apostle. In Saints and ourselves, third series: personal studies by W. Starkie [et al], ed P. Caraman 1958.
Spain: a musician's journey through time and space. 3 vols Geneva 1958.
Scholars and gypsies: an autobiography. [1963], Berkeley 1963.

Editions and Translations

Tiger Juan, by R. Pérez de Ayala. Tr with an introductory essay by Starkie, 1933.
The Spaniards in their history, by R. Menéndez Pidal. Tr with a prefatory essay on the author's work by Starkie, 1950, New York [1950].
Don Quixote of La Mancha by M. Cervantes Saavedra: an abridged version translated and edited with a biographical prelude by Starkie. 1954, New York 1957; New York 1964 (complete version).
This is Spain, by I. Olagüe. Tr with introd by Starkie, 1954.
Tower of ivory, by Rodolfo L. Fonseca. Tr Starkie, 1954.
Eight Spanish plays of the golden age. Tr and ed with introd by Starkie, New York 1964.

§2

Ensayos Hispano-Ingleses: homenaje a Walter Starkie. Barcelona [1948].

D.K.

ARTHUR GEORGE STREET
1892–1966

§1

Farmer's glory. 1932.
Strawberry roan. 1932. Fiction.
Country days. 1933. Broadcast talks.
Hedge-trimmings. 1933. Essays.
The endless furrow. 1934. Fiction.
Land everlasting. 1934.
Thinking aloud. 1934. Broadcast talks on country life.
Country calendar. 1935.
To be a farmer's boy. 1935, [1939] (as Farming: how to begin).
The gentleman of the party. 1936. Fiction.
Moonraking. 1936.
Farming in England. 1937.
Already walks tomorrow. 1938. Fiction.
A year of my life. 1939.
A crook in the furrow. 1940. Fiction.
Harvest by lamplight. 1941. Selection.
Round the year on the farm. [1941].
Wessex wins. 1941.
From dusk till dawn. 1942, [1947] (rev). On the Home Guard.
Hitler's whistle. 1943. Diary 1939–42.
Ditchampton farm. 1946.
Holdfast. 1946. Fiction.
Landmarks. 1949. Reminiscences.
In his own country. 1950. Selection.
Wheat and chaff. 1950. Selection.
Shameful harvest. 1952. Fiction.
Feather-bedding. 1954.
Kittle cattle. 1954. Fiction.
Master of none. 1956. Essays.
Sweetacres. 1956. Fiction.
Bobby Bocker. 1957. Fiction.
Cooper's crossing. 1962. Fiction.
Fish and chips. 1964. Fiction.
Johnny Cowslip. 1964. Fiction.
From 1932–5 Street contributed Countryman's diary *for* Eng Rev.

§2

Burrell, M. Redolent of the soil. In his Crumbs are also bread, Toronto 1934.
Street, P. My father, A. G. Street. 1969.

H.M.R.

PHILIP EDWARD THOMAS
1878–1917

See cols 364–7, above.

FLORA THOMPSON
1877–1947

§1

Bog-myrtle and peat. 1921. Verse.
Lark Rise. 1939, New York 1939.
Over to Candleford. 1941, New York 1941.
Candleford Green. 1943, New York 1943.
Lark Rise to Candleford: a trilogy. 1945, New York 1945. Contains the 3 previous novels. Introd by H. J. Massingham.
Still glides the stream. 1948, New York 1948.

§2

Lane, M. Flora Thompson. Cornhill Mag 169 1957; rptd in her Purely for pleasure, 1966.

C.P.C.

HENRY MAJOR TOMLINSON
1873–1958

See cols 749–50, above.

EVELYN ARTHUR ST JOHN WAUGH
1903–66

See cols 764–8, above.

DAME 'REBECCA WEST', CICILY ISABEL ANDREWS
b. 1892

See cols 770–1, above.

TERENCE HANBURY WHITE
1906–64

See cols 771–2, above.

HENRY WILLIAMSON
b. 1895

See cols 774–6, above.

6. NEWSPAPERS AND MAGAZINES

A. *Historical and general studies: Histories and studies of the press; Newspapers and their contents; Magazines, general studies; Little magazines; University magazines; Reminiscences and biographies.*

B. *Journalism: Bibliographies; General works; The profession of journalism (Training of journalists; Manuals and guides for journalists; Journalists' associations; Periodicals); News agencies; Advertising (General works; Periodicals); Periodicals relating to newspaper and magazine publishing.*

C. *Accounts and studies of individual newspapers and magazines: newspapers; magazines.*

D. *Lists, indexes and directories.*

E. *Individual newspapers and magazines: Literary papers and magazines; Amateur journals; Romance, detective, thriller, western and science fiction magazines (as indictated by their titles); University and college magazines; Newspapers and magazines not primarily devoted to literature.*

All the following lists are confined to titles thought to be of use to students of literature. For a more exhaustive coverage of the subject, see the bibliographies and the reference works cited in W. C. Price, The literature of journalism, *Minneapolis 1969* (*Suppl 1958–68 by Price and C. M. Pickett, Minneapolis 1970*). For house journals see D. Weiss, La communication dans les organisations industrielles, *Paris 1971*.

For theatrical periodicals and children's periodicals, see cols 823–80 and 819–20 above.

A. HISTORICAL AND GENERAL STUDIES

Studies concerned with newspapers and magazines in America have been included where it is thought that these complement English studies or suggest approaches to the study of English newspapers and magazines. See also Journalism, below.

(1) HISTORIES AND STUDIES OF THE PRESS

Courtney, L. H. The making and reading of newspapers. 1901.
Dafoe, J. W. The Imperial Press Conference: a retrospect with comment. Winnipeg 1909.
Imperial [later, Commonwealth] Press Conference. [Official reports compiled by the Empire, later Commonwealth, Press Union]. 1909 onwards.
Hemphill, J. C. Some present-day problems for the press. 1910.
Dibblee, G. B. The newspaper. 1912.
Le Musée International de la Presse. Brussels. 1912.
Given, J. L. Making a newspaper. 1913.
Scott-James, R. A. The influence of the press. 1913.
Lucas, E. V. and C. L. Graves. All the papers: a journalistic review. 1914.
Symon, J. D. The press and its story: an account of the birth and development of journalism up to the present day, with the history of all the leading newspapers. 1914.
Thorpe, M. The coming newspaper. New York 1915.
Hayward, F. H. and B. N. L. Davies. Democracy and the press. Manchester 1919.
Cook, E. T. The press in war-time with some account of the Official Press Bureau: an essay. 1920.
Angell, N. The press and the organization of society. 1922, Cambridge 1933 (rev).
Harmsworth, A. C. W. Newspapers and their millionaires. 1922.
Salmon, L. M. The newspaper and the historian. New York 1923.
Independent Labour Party. The capitalist press: who owns it and why. [?1925].
Aitken, W. M. (Lord Beaverbrook). Politicians and the press. 1926.
Lundberg, G. A. The newspaper and public opinion. Social Forces 4 1926.
Herd, H. The making of modern journalism. [1927].
— The march of journalism: the story of the British press from 1622 to the present day. 1952.
Robbins, A. The press. [1928].
Hicks, J. C. Newspaper finance. 1929.
Seldes, G. You can't print that! The truth behind the news 1918–28. Garden City NY 1929.

Blake, G. The press and the public. 1930 (Criterion Miscellany no 21).
Morison, S. The English newspaper: some account of the physical development of journals printed in London between 1622 and the present day. Cambridge 1932. Sandars Lectures 1931–2.
'Phayre, Ignatius'. The British press and the United States. Quart Rev 259 1932.
Blumenfeld, R. D. The press in my time. 1933.
Ervine, St J. G. The future of the press. 1933.
Stutterheim, K. von. Die englische Presse. Berlin 1933; tr 1934.
The people and the press. Spectator 30 March 1934.
Siebert, F. S. The rights and privileges of the press. New York [1934].
Weil, G. Le journal. Paris 1934.
Cummings, A. J. The press and a changing civilization. 1936.
— Political journalism: a British view. Journalism Quart 15 1938.
Hawke, E. G. A brief history of the British newspaper press. Paris 1936.
Milton, G. F. The newspaper of tomorrow. Amer Scholar 5 1936.
Brown, S. T. M. The press in Ireland. Dublin 1937.
Desmond, R. W. The press and world affairs. New York 1937. Introd by H. J. Laski.
Mansfield, F. J. Royal interest in the press. Newspaper World 8 May 1937.
Maitland, F. H. One hundred years of headlines 1837–1937. 1938.
Political and Economic Planning. Report on the British press. 1938.
— The work of newspaper trusts. 1959.
Steed, H. W. The press. [1938].
Hood, P. Ourselves and the press: a social study on news, advertising and propaganda. 1939.
Mason, H. A. The press. Scrutiny 7 1939. Replies, ibid.
Harrisson, T. The popular press? Horizon 2 1940.
Hughes, H. M. News and the human interest story. Chicago 1940.

Park, R. E. News as a form of knowledge: a chapter in the sociology of knowledge. Amer Jnl of Sociology 45 1940; rptd in Mass media and communication, ed C. S. Steinberg, New York 1966.

Ickes, H. Le C. (ed). Freedom of the press today. New York 1941.

Bird, G. L. and F. E. Merwin (ed). The newspaper and society: a book of readings. New York 1942.

Kimble, P. Newspaper reading in the third year of the war. 1942.

Harris, H. W. The daily press. Cambridge 1943 (Current Problems no 18).

Moss, L. and K. Box. Newspapers and the public. 1943. Central Office of Information.

Hudson, D. British journalists and newspapers. 1945 (Britain in Pictures).

Berry, W. E. (Viscount Camrose). British newspapers and their controllers. 1947.

Hocking, W. E. Freedom of the press. Chicago 1947. Includes Summary of principle: a statement of the commission on freedom of the press.

Lea, T. Privacy and the press. Ed H. M. Hyde 1947.

UNESCO. Report of the commission on technical needs in press, radio, film. Paris 1947.

— Press, film and radio in the world today. Paris 1949 onwards.

Gerald, J. E. The press and the constitution. 1948.

— The British press under government economic controls. Minneapolis 1956.

— The British Press Council. Journalism Quart 36 1959.

— The social responsibility of the press. Minneapolis 1963.

The press 1898–1948. Pbd for golden jubilee of Newspaper World. 1948.

Royal Commission on the Press. Reports. 1949, 1962.

Innis, H. A. The press: a neglected factor in the economic history of the twentieth century. 1949.

Curtis, M. The press. 1951. Pbd by News Chron.

Pool, I. de S. The prestige papers. Stanford 1952.

The press and the people: annual report of the General Council of the Press. No 1, 1954 onwards.

Wadsworth, A. P. Newspaper circulations 1800–1954. Trans Manchester Statistical Soc 1955.

Peterson, T. et al. Four theories of the press. Urbana Ill 1956.

Churchill, R. S. What I said about the press. 1957.

UNESCO. The daily press. Paris 1957.

Williams, F. Dangerous estate: the anatomy of newspapers. 1957.

— The right to know: the rise of the world press. 1969.

Benenson, P. A free press. 1961.

International Press Institute. Press councils and press codes. Zurich 1961.

Labour Party Research Department. Who owns the press? 1961.

Rourke, F. E. Secrecy and publicity: dilemmas of democracy. Baltimore 1961.

Bagdikian, B. H. Why dailies die. New Republic 16 April 1962; rptd in People, society and mass communications, ed L. A. Dexter and D. M. White, New York 1964.

Terrou, F. L'information. Paris 1962.

Christoph, J. B. The press and politics in Britain and America. Political Quart 34 1963.

Buzek, A. How the communist press works. 1964.

Martin, G. The press. In Discrimination and popular culture, ed D. Thompson 1964 (Pelican).

Bradley, D. The newspaper: its place in a democracy. 1965.

Hornby, R. The press in modern society. 1965.

Economist Intelligence Unit. The national newspaper industry: a survey. 1966.

Hildick, E. W. A close look at newspapers. 1966.

King, C. The future of the press. 1967. Granada lectures.

Levy, H. P. The Press Council: history, procedure, cases. 1967.

National Board for Prices and Incomes. Costs and revenues of national daily newspapers. 1967. Report 43.

Robbins, J. C. The paradox of press freedom: a study of British experience. Journalism Quart 44 1967.

Merrill, J. C. The elite press: great newspapers of the world. New York 1968.

Ure, C. S. The press, politics and the public. 1968.

(2) NEWSPAPERS AND THEIR CONTENTS

Flint, L. N. The conscience of the newspaper. New York 1925.

Willey, M. M. The country newspaper: a study of socialization and newspaper content. Chapel Hill 1926.

Follett, W. The printed word: the economy of editors. Amer Bookman 69 1929.

Bastian, G. G. and L. D. Case. Editing the day's news. New York 1932.

Mortlock, C. B. The church and the press. Green Quart 2 1936.

Harding, D. W. General conceptions in the study of the press and public opinion. Sociological Rev 29 1937.

Kingsbury, S. et al. Newspapers and the news: an objective measurement of ethical and unethical behaviour by representative newspapers. New York 1937.

Madge, C. The press and social consciousness. Left Rev 3 1937.

Mansfield, F. J. Social and personal. Journalist 20 1937. On gossip columns etc.

Postgate, R. and A. Vallance. Those foreigners: the English people's opinions on foreign affairs as reflected in their newspapers since Waterloo. 1937, Indianapolis [1937] (as England goes to press).

Rosten, L. C. The Washington correspondents. New York 1937. Selection of news: 'the gatekeeper'.

Morgan, W. T. The British general election of 1935: public opinion as expressed in ten daily newspapers. South Atlantic Quart 37 1938.

Reid, L. The morality of the newspaper. South Bend 1938.

Hughes, H. M. News and the human interest story. Chicago 1940.

Thompson, D. Between the lines: or how to read a newspaper. 1940.

Spender, J. A. The press in wartime. In his Last essays, 1944.

Bird, C. The influence of the press upon the accuracy of report. Jnl of Abnormal Social Psychology 22 1947.

White, D. W. The 'gatekeeper': a case study in the selection of news. Journalism Quart 27 1950; rptd in People, Society and mass communication, ed L. A. Dexter and D. M. White, New York 1964.

Martin, R. G. Condensation: a check list of current techniques. Journalism Quart 28 1951.

International Press Institute. The flow of news. Zurich 1953.

Kayser, J. et al. One week's news: comparative study of seventeen major dailies for a seven-day period. Paris 1953 (UNESCO pbn).

Tannenbaum, P. H. The effect of headlines on the interpretation of news stories. Journalism Quart 30 1953.

Tannenbaum, P. H. and J. E. Noah. Sportuguese: a study in sports page communication. Journalism Quart 36 1959.

British Council Staff Association. The Beaverbrook press and the British Council. 1954.

Breed, W. Social control in the newsroom: a functional analysis. Social Forces 33 1955; rptd in Mass communications, ed W. Schramm, rev edn, Urbana, 1960.

Political and Economic Planning. Performance of the press. 1956.

Swanson, G. E. Agitation through the press: a study of the personalities of publicists. Public Opinion Quart 20 1956.

Pool, I. de S. and I. Shulman. Newsmen's fantasies, audiences and newswriting. Public Opinion Quart 23 1959; rptd in People, society and mass communications, ed L. A. Dexter and D. M. White, New York 1964.

Hutt, A. Newspaper design. 1960, 1967 (rev).

Murphy, D. R. A record of experiments with readership, 1938–1961. Ames Iowa 1962.

Wicker, B. An analysis of Newspeak. Blackfriars 42 1962.

Glenton, G. and W. Patterson. The last chronicle of Bouverie Street, 1963.

Chalmers, D. The social and political ideas of the muckrakers. New York 1964.

Gieber, W. News is what newspapermen make it. In People, society and mass communications, ed L. A. Dexter and D. M. White, New York 1964.

Sharf, A. The British press and Jews under Nazi rule. 1964.

Shibutani, T. Improvised news: a sociological study of rumor. Indianapolis 1966.

Donohew, L. Newspaper gatekeepers and forces in the news channel. Public Opinion Quart 31 1967.

Friendly, A. and R. Goldfarb. Crime and publicity: the impact of news on the administration of justice. New York 1967.

Hoggart, R. (ed). Your Sunday paper. 1967.

Marland, L. Following the news: a course in the effective reading of newspapers. 1967.

Smith, A. C. H. Gossip columns. New Society 27 Dec 1967.

Butler, D. and D. Stokes. The flow of political information. In their Political change in Britain, 1969; rptd in part in Media sociology, ed J. Tunstall, 1970.

Jackson, I. The provincial press and the community. 1971.

(3) MAGAZINES, GENERAL STUDIES

Canby, H. S. The family magazine. North Amer Rev 214 1921.

The romance of the Amalgamated Press. 1925.

Read, H. Periodical reviews. Criterion 5 1927.

Follett, W. The printed word: 'Altogether feminine'. Amer Bookman 70 1929. Linguistic and stylistic peculiarities of women's magazines.

Graham, W. English literary periodicals. New York 1930.

Bakeless, J. Magazine making. New York 1931.

Morgan, W. L. and A. M. Leahy. The cultural content of general interest magazines. Jnl of Educational Psychology 25 1934.

Slater, M. The purpose of a left review. Left Rev 1 1935.

Thompson, D. A hundred years of the higher journalism. Scrutiny 4 1935.

Kerr, W. A. and H. H. Remmers. Cultural values of 100 representative magazines. School & Society 54 1941.

Lowenthal, L. Biographies in popular magazines. In Radio research 1942–3, ed P. F. Lazarsfeld and F. K. Stanton, New York 1943; rptd in part in Reader in public opinion, and communication, ed B. Berelson and M. Janowitz, Glencoe Ill 1950.

Berelson, B. and P. J. Salter. Majority and minority Americans: an analysis of magazine fiction. Public Opinion Quart 10 1946.

Cox, R. G. The critical view today: 1, prolegomena to an historical inquiry; 2, the ideas of a literary periodical. Scrutiny 14 1947.

Wain, J. Scrutiny and the bomb. Mandrake no 11 1947.

Leavis, F. R. The progress of poesy. Scrutiny 15 1948. Standards of criticism, with particular reference to T.L.S. and Horizon.

Johns-Heine, P. and H. H. Gerth. Values in mass periodical fiction 1921–1940. Public Opinion Quart 13 1949; rptd in Mass culture: the popular arts in America, ed B. Rosenberg and D. M. White, New York 1957.

Pryce-Jones, A. Literary periodicals. In The year's work in literature 1950, ed J. Lehmann 1951.

Wolseley, R. E. The magazine world. New York 1951.

Hopkinson, T. The periodical press: the big fourpennies. Author 65 1954. Everybody's etc.

Laski, M. The periodical press: the women's magazines. Author 65 1954.

Noel, M. Villains galore: the heyday of the popular story weekly. New York 1954.

Rice, P. B. The intellectual quarterly in a non-intellectual society. Kenyon Rev 16 1954.

Williams, R. Editorial commentary. EC 4 (no 3) 1954. On literary periodicals.

Amis, K. The periodical press: the cheesecake periodicals. Author 66 1955.

Snow, C. P. The periodical press: monthlies and the less frequent. Author 66 1955.

Brams, L. and E. Morin. Caractéristiques de la presse hebdomadaire féminine. Ecole des Parents, no 6 1956.

Peterson, T. Magazines in the twentieth century. Urbana 1956, 1957 (rev), 1964 (rev). Chiefly American.

Singleton, F. The periodical press: the weeklies. Author 65 1956.

Hargreaves, J. The plight of the magazines. Author 67 1957. Effect of television.

Bagdikian, B. H. The newsmagazines. Providence Jnl-Bull 5–17 Oct 1958.

Gerbner, G. The social role of the confession magazine. Social Problems 6 1958.

Men's magazines. Writer 71 1958.

Bradbury, M. Will there always be an English periodical? Saturday Rev of Lit 18 July 1959.

McCarthy, M. Up the road from Charm to Vogue. In her On the contrary, New York 1961.

Stowell, G. et al. Producing and selling the church magazine. 1961.

Welch, H. M. and M. F. Tauber (eds). Current trends in US periodical publishing. Lib Trends 10 1962. Includes H. M. Welch, The economics of periodical publishing; L. Ash, Subsidized periodical publishing; F. J. Kirschenbaum, Periodicals in the humanities.

Friedan, B. The happy housewife heroine. In her The feminine mystique, New York 1963.

Iversen, W. The pious pornographers. New York 1963. Women's magazines.

Holbrook, D. Magazines. In Discrimination and popular culture, ed D. Thompson 1964 (Pelican).

McClelland, W. D. Women's weeklies. New Society 31 Dec 1964.

Martel, M. V. and G. J. McCall. Reality-orientation and the pleasure principle; a study of the American mass-periodical fiction 1890–1955. In People, society and mass communications, ed L. A. Dexter and D. M. White, New York 1964.

Hildick, E. W. A close look at magazines and comics. 1966.

Gerson, W. M. and S. H. Lund. Playboy magazine: sophisticated smut or social revolution? Jnl of Popular Culture 1 1967. General implications.

Alderson, C. Magazines teenagers read. 1968.

Ford, J. L. C. Magazines for the millions: the story of specialized publications. Carbondale 1969.

McLean, R. Magazine design. 1969.

Hoggart, R. H. A sense of occasion. In his Speaking to each other, 1970. On magazine content.

White, C. L. Women's magazines, 1693–1968. 1970.

(4) LITTLE MAGAZINES

Eliot, T. S. The function of a literary review. Criterion 1 1923.
— The idea of a literary review. Criterion 4 1926.
Pound, E. Small magazines. English Jnl 19 1930.
Troy, W. The story of the little magazines. Amer Bookman 70 1930.
Tate, A. The function of the critical quarterly. Southern Rev 1 1936.
Munson, G. How to run a little magazine. Saturday Rev of Lit 27 March 1937.
Baker, D. V. Little reviews 1914–43. 1943.
— The little reviews. Author 58 1947.
Hoffman, F. J. The research value of the little magazine. College & Research Libraries 6 1945.
— et al. The little magazine: a history and a bibliography. Princeton 1946, 1947 (enlarged).
Trilling, L. The function of the little magazine. Introd to Partisan reader, ed W. Phillips and P. Rahv, New York 1946; rptd in his Liberal imagination, New York 1951.
Muller, H. J. The function of a critical review. Arizona Quart 4 1948.
O'Connor, W. V. The direction of the little magazine. Poetry 71 1948.
— The little magazine as a cultural journal. Poetry 72 1948.
Swallow, A. Postwar little magazines. Prairie Schooner 23 1949.
Lehmann, J. The case for the literary magazine. Listener 15 Feb 1951.

Vivas, E. Criticism and the little magazines. Western Rev 16 1951.
Symposium on the little magazines. Golden Goose 3 1951. Includes M. Moore, W Frank.
Running a literary review. TLS 29 Aug 1952. Correspondence 19 Sept.
Wagner, G. The minority writer in England. Author 64 1953. Writing for little magazines.
May, J. B. Twigs as varied bent. New York 1954.
Barrett, W. Declining fortunes of the literary review: 1945–55. Anchor Rev 2 1957.
Ferguson, R. Editing the small magazine. New York 1958.
Spears, M. The present function of the literary quarterlies. Texas Quart 3 1960.
Symons, J. The little magazines. In his The thirties, 1960.
Pollak, F. Landing in little magazines: capturing (?) a trend. Arizona Quart 19 1963.
Whittemore, R. Little magazines. Minneapolis 1963. Pamphlet.
Ross, R. H. In his The Georgian revolt 1910–22, 1965.
Library of Congress. The little magazines and contemporary literature: a symposium, 2–3 April 1965. Washington 1966. Pbd for Modern Lang Assoc.
Janssens, G. A. M. The tradition of the literary review. In his The American literary review, The Hague 1968.
The little review. TLS 25 April 1968. Issue devoted to little magazines.

(5) UNIVERSITY MAGAZINES

Marillier, H. C. University magazines and their makers. 1899, 1902 (enlarged).
Seccombe, T. and H. S. Scott. In praise of Oxford: an anthology of prose and verse. 2 vols 1910, 1912.
Godley, A. D. The casual ward: academic and other oddments. 1912.
Leask, W. K. The story of the University magazine 1836–1914. Aberdeen Univ Rev 4 1914.
Rice, F. A. The Granta and its contributors 1889–1914. 1924.

Hawgood, J. A. University College [London] and its magazines. Univ College Mag 4 1927.
Sadleir, M. The Dublin University Magazine: its history, contents and bibliography. Pbns of Bibl Soc of Ireland 5 1938.
Edinger, G. Oxford in Fleet street. Cherwell 17 Jan 1942.
MacKenzie, C. Oxford magazines. Harlequin no 2 1950.
Clay, R. The college newspaper. New York 1965.
Philip, J. et al. The best of Granta 1889–1966. 1967.

(6) REMINISCENCES AND BIOGRAPHIES

Anderson, M. My thirty years' war: beginning and battles to 1930. New York 1930.
Barron, E. M. (ed). A highland editor: selected writings of James Barron of the Inverness courier. Inverness 1928.
Bartlett, V. And now tommorrow. 1960.
Driberg, T. E. N. Beaverbrook: a study in power and frustration. 1956.
Bennett-England, R. Inside journalism. 1967.
Nethercott, A. H. The first five lives of Annie Besant. 1961.
— The last four lives of Annie Besant. 1963.
Bishop, G. W. My betters. 1957.
Blatchford, R. My eighty years. 1931.
Thompson, L. Robert Blatchford: portrait of an Englishman. 1951.
Blumenfeld, R. D. R.D.B.'s diary 1887–1914. 1930.
— The press in my time. 1933.
Boon, J. Victorians, Edwardians and Georgians: the impressions of a veteran journalist extending over forty years. 2 vols 1928.
Symons, J. Horatio Bottomley. 1955.
Sir Emsley Carr: fifty years an editor. World's Press News 1 May 1941.
Catling, T. My life's pilgrimage. 1911.
Christiansen, A. Headlines all my life. 1961.

Colles, R. In castle and courthouse: being the reminiscences of thirty years in Ireland. 1911.
Connolly, C. Previous convictions. 1963.
Cook, E. T. Literary recreations. 1918.
Mills, J. S. Sir Edward Cook: a biography. 1921.
Gooch, G. P. The life of Courtney. 1920.
Courtney, W. L. The making of an editor 1850–1928. 1930.
Cox, A. B. Jugged journalism. 1925.
Cudlipp, H. Publish and be damned. 1953.
— At your peril. 1961.
Wrench, J. E. L. Geoffrey Dawson and our times. 1955.
Dunlop, A. Fifty years of Irish journalism. 1911.
Minney, R. J. Viscount Southwood [J. S. Elias]: a biography. 1954.
Escott, T. H. S. Masters of English journalism. 1911.
Felbermann, H. The memoirs of a cosmopolitan. 1936.
Foster, E. An editor's chair. 1909.
Fyfe, H. H. My seven selves. 1935.
— Sixty years of Fleet street. 1949.
Garvin, K. J. L. Garvin: a memoir. 1948.
Gibbs, P. Adventures in journalism. 1923.
Greenwall, H. I hate tommorrow. 1940.
Grieve, M. Millions made my story. 1964.
Hammerton, J. A. Books and myself: memoirs of an editor. [1944].

Tobin, A. I. and E. Gertz. Frank Harris: an study in black and white. Chicago 1931.
'Hugh Kingsmill' (H. K. Lunn). Frank Harris. 1932.
Richards, G. (ed). Frank Harris: his life and adventures. 1947.
Hunt, C. There's fun in Fleet street. 1938.
— Ink in my veins. 1948.
Hutcheon, W. Gentlemen of the press: memories and friendships of forty years. 1933.
Jeffs, H. Press, preachers and politicians: reminiscences 1874–1932. 1933.
Low, S. Samuel Henry Jeyes: a sketch of his personality and work. Ed W. P. Ker 1915.
Jennings, H. J. Chestnuts and small beer. 1920.
Jones, K. Fleet street and Downing street. [1920].
Thorold, A. L. The life of Labouchere. 1913.
Pearson, H. Labby. 1936.
Lehmann, J. The whispering gallery; I am my brother; The ample proposition. 3 vols 1955–66. Autobiography.
Chapman-Huston, D. The lost historian: a memoir of Sir Sidney Low. 1936.
Lucy, H. W. Sixty years in the wilderness. 1909.
— Sixty years in the wilderness: a second series. 1912.
— Nearing Jordan: being the third and last volume of sixty years. 1916.
— The diary of a journalist. 1920.
— The diary of a journalist: later entries. 1922.
MacDonagh, M. The reporters' gallery. 1913.
[Mackay, W.] Bohemian days in Fleet street, by a journalist. 1913.
Mackintosh, A. Fifty-seven years in the Press Gallery. World's Press News 7 April 1938.
Maclaren-Ross, J. Memoirs of the forties. 1965.
Hassall, C. Edward Marsh, patron of the arts: a biography. 1959, New York 1959 (as A biography of Edward Marsh).
Martin, K. Editor. 1968.
Massingham, H. J. (ed). H.W.M.: a selection from the writing of H. W. Massingham. 1925.
Hammerton, J. A. Child of wonder. 1947. Arthur Mee.
Monroe, H. A poet's life: seventy years in a changing world. New York 1938. Poetry, Chicago.
Elton, O. C. E. Montague: a memoir. 1929.
Morley, J. Recollections. 2 vols 1917.
Knickerbocker, F. W. Free minds: Morley and his friends. Cambridge Mass 1943.
Staebler, W. The liberal mind of Morley. Princeton 1943.
Morris, C. I bought a newspaper. 1963.
Moseley, S. A. The truth about a journalist. 1935.

— The private diaries. 1960.
Lea, F. A. The life of John Middleton Murry. 1959.
Nevinson, H. W. Changes and chances. 1923.
Nicoll, W. R. A bookman's letters. 1913.
Parker, W. M. A great Scots journalist. Scots Mag 56 1951. W. R. Nicoll.
Pemberton, M. Lord Northcliffe: a memoir. 1922.
Swaffer, H. Northcliffe's return. 1925.
Wilson, R. M. Lord Northcliffe. 1927.
Fyfe, H. H. Northcliffe: an intimate biography. 1930.
Owen, L. Northcliffe: the facts. 1931.
Ryan, A. P. Lord Northcliffe. 1953.
Greenwall, H. J. Northcliffe: Napoleon of Fleet street. 1957.
Pound, R. and G. Harmsworth. Northcliffe. 1959.
O'Connor, T. P. Memoirs of an old parliamentarian. 2 vols 1929.
Fyfe, H. H. T. P. O'Connor. 1934.
Dark, S. The life of Sir Arthur Pearson. 1922.
Robertson-Scott, J. W. We and me. 1956.
Hammond, J. L. C. P. Scott of the Manchester Guardian. 1934.
C. P. Scott 1846–1932: the making of the Manchester Guardian. 1946.
Scott, J. W. R. Faith and works in Fleet street. 1947.
— The day before yesterday: memories of an uneducated man. 1951.
Sewell, B. My dear time's waste. Aylesford 1966. Aylesford Review.
Simonis, H. The street of ink: an intimate history of journalism. 1917.
Smith, E. Fields of adventure. 1923.
Spender, J. A. Life, journalism and politics. 2 vols 1927.
Harris, W. J. A. Spender. 1946.
Stark, M. The pulse of the world: Fleet street memories. 1915.
Whyte, F. The life of W. T. Stead. 2 vols 1927.
Steed, H. W. Through thirty years 1892–1922. 2 vols 1924.
Strachey, J. St L. The adventure of living. 1922.
Strachey, A. St Loe Strachey: his life and his paper. 1930.
Taylor, H. A. Through fifty years. Inst of Journalist' Jnl 28 1940.
Singleton, F. Tillotsons 1850–1950: a centenary of a family business. 1951. Bolton Evening News.
Braddon, R. Roy Thomson of Fleet street. 1965.
Watson, A. A newspaper man's memories. 1925.
Colquhoun, A. H. U. Press, politics and people: the life and letters of John Willison, journalist and correspondent of the Times. Toronto 1936.

B. JOURNALISM

Studies concerned with journalism in America have been included where it is thought that these complement English studies or suggest approaches to the study of English journalism. See also Historical and General Studies, above.

(1) BIBLIOGRAPHIES

Peel, H. W. A bibliography of journalism. 1915. Originally issued as part of introd to Sell's world press guide, 1915.
Cannon, C. L. Journalism: a bibliography. New York 1924.
Journalism Quarterly. 1924 onwards (as Journalism Bull 1924–7). Index vols 1–40, 1924–63, 1964.

Nafziger, R. International news and the press: an annotated bibliography. New York 1940.
Price, W. C. The literature of journalism: an annotated bibliography. Minneapolis 1959.
— and C. M. Pickett. An annotated journalism bibliography 1958–1968. Minneapolis 1970.
Wolseley, R. E. The journalist's bookshelf. Philadelphia 1961 (7th edn).

(2) GENERAL WORKS

The economic position of women in journalism. Humanitarian 18 1900.
Baynton, H. W. Journalism and literature. Boston 1904.
Wellcome, H. S. The evolution of journalism. 1909.
Dunlop, A. Fifty years of Irish journalism. Dublin 1911.

Eastman, M. Journalism versus art. New York 1916.
Crawford, N. A. The ethics of journalism. New York 1924.
Brown, I. Journalism and literature. Fortnightly Rev 137 1932.

Desmond, R. W. Newspaper reference methods. Minneapolis 1933.

Leavis, Q. D. Fleet street and Pierian roses. Scrutiny 2 1934.

Mansfield, F. J. Who started the new journalism? World's Press News 3 March 1938. On W. T. Stead.

Marshall, A. C. The journalist in our midst. Author 54 1944. The journalist as author.

Heilman, R. The professor as journalist and vice versa. Sewanee Rev 53 1945.

Sinclair, R. The British press: the journalist and his conscience. 1949.

Soule, G. Liberal journalism, a diagnosis. Yale Rev 39 1949.

Herd, H. The march of journalism: the story of the British press from 1622 to the present day. 1952.

Fisher, J. (ed). Eye-witness: an anthology of British reporting. 1960.

Ryan, A. P. The art of the editor. Listener 13 Oct 1960.

Hohenberg, J. The professional journalist. New York 1960.

Gross, G. (ed). Editors on editing. New York 1962.

International Press Institute. Professional secrecy and the journalist. Zurich 1962.

Samuelson, M. A standardized test to measure job satisfaction in the newsroom. Journalism Quart 39 1962.

Rivers, W. L. The mass media: reporting, writing, editing. New York 1964.

Baylen, J. O. W. T. Stead and the new journalism. Emory Univ Quart 21 1965.

Collision course? Free press and the courts. Toronto [1966]. A symposium of journalists and lawyers on free trials and a free press.

Matejko, A. Newspaper staff as a social system. Polish Sociological Bull 1 1967; rptd in Media sociology ed J. Tunstall 1970.

(3) THE PROFESSION OF JOURNALISM

Training of Journalists

Peaker, F. The training of the journalist. 1927.

Knapp, V. Training for journalism at the University of London. Journalism Quart 7 1930.

Barlow, R. P. The French and British schools of journalism: a comparative analysis. Journalism Quart 13 1936.

Desmond, R. W. Professional training of journalists. Paris 1949, 1958. Pbd by UNESCO.

Boyd-Barrett, O. Journalism recruitment and training: problems in professionalization. In Media sociology, ed. J. Tunstall 1970.

Manuals and Guides for Journalists

Kingston, A. Pitman's guide to journalism. [1898], [1904] (rev).

How to write for the press: a practical handbook for beginners in journalism. By an editor. 1899, 1904 (rev).

Tozer, B. Free-lance journalism: how to embark upon it and make it pay. 1901.

Lawrence, A. Journalism as a profession. 1903.

Modern journalism: a guide for beginners. By a London editor. 1909. With introd by G. R. Sims.

Goodyer, R. A. H. The writers' brain book: an album of inspiration for journalists. Scarborough 1911.

Bull, E. A. How to write for the papers. 1912.

Magazines and their contributors. Author 23 1913. Terms of contract.

Bleyer, W. G. Newspaper writing and editing. 1914.

Davies, B. J. How to succeed as a writer: or lessons in journalism. 1914.

Baker, A. Pitman's practical journalism. 1915.

Cunliffe, J. W. and G. R. Lomer (ed). Writing of today: models of journalistic prose. New York 1915.

Hyde, G. M. Newspaper editing. New York 1915.

— A course in journalistic writing. New York 1922, 1946 (as Journalistic writing: textbook for classes and handbook for staffs of student newspapers, magazines and year-books).

Joseph, M. Journalism for profit. 1924.

Blumenfeld, R. D. What is a journalist? Do's and don'ts. [1930] (2nd edn) (World's Press News Library no 1).

Robertson, S. An introduction to modern journalism. New York 1930.

The writer's market guide to 100 provincial newspapers. Cambridge [1931].

Mansfield, F. J. Sub-editing. 1932, 1946 (4th edn).

— The complete journalist. 1935.

Journalism. By some masters of the craft. 1932.

Russell, L. Writing for the press. 1935 (Black's Writers' and Artists' Library no 4).

Peacocke, E. H. Writing for women. 1936 (Black's Writers' and Artists' Library no 7).

Thornhill, M. B. Commercial opportunities for the free-lance journalist. 1937 (Black's Writers' and Artists' Library no 9).

Charnley, M. V. and B. Converse. Magazine writing and editing. New York 1938.

Hunt, C. You want to be a journalist? 1938.

Harrison, R. and W. A. Bagley. The free-lance journalist 1945, 1946 (rev).

Reddick, D. W. C. Modern feature writing. New York 1949.

Viscount Kemsley et al. The Kemsley manual of journalism. 1950.

D'Ewes, D. Pen money: a course on how to write for the press. 1951.

Wolseley, R. E. The magazine world: an introduction to magazine journalism. Englewood Cliffs NJ 1951. Includes comment on social effects of magazines.

White, D. M. and S. Levine. Elementary statistics for journalists. New York 1954.

Charnley, M. V. Reporting. 1959, 1966 (rev).

Wilcox, W. Liberal education and professional journalism education. Iowa City, 1959.

Boland, B. J. Free-lance journalism. 1960 (New Writers' Guide ser).

Copple, N. Depth reporting: an approach to journalism. Englewood Cliffs NJ 1964.

Revill, L. and C. Roderick (ed). The journalist's craft: a guide to modern practice. Sydney 1965.

Goulden, J. Newspaper management. 1967. Council for the Training of Journalists.

Writing for periodicals. Author 78 1967.

Hall, B. J. Basic training in journalism. 1968.

Hilton, P. Writing saleable press articles. [1968].

Journalists' Associations

Society of Women Journalists. Annual Report. 1911–?

Murasken, E. Newswriters' unions in English-speaking countries. New York 1938.

Fifty years of institute leadership. Institute of Journalists' Jnl 27 1939.

Mansfield, F. J. Gentlemen, the press! Chronicles of a crusade: official history of the National Union of Journalists. [1943].

Periodicals

London, provincial and colonial press news. 15 Jan 1866–Dec 1912.

The journalist. 15 Oct 1886–May 1909.

The Institute of Journalists. Proceedings. 1892–1912. Quarterly.

Quill: the journal of the Quill club. 1902–?

The Fleet Street gleaner. Vols 1–3 no 7, March 1910–July/Sept 1912.

The woman journalist. 1910–?

Institute of journalists' journal. 23 Nov 1912 onwards.

The once only. 1922. Issued to commemorate 40th anniversary of the Press Club.

The reading lamp. 1946–?

(4) NEWS AGENCIES

Jones, R. International telegraphic news: a lecture at the University of London 23 May 1921. 1921.
—— News agencies and their work: address to the International Congress of the Press 6 July 1927. 1927.
Collins, M. H. From pigeon post to wireless. 1925. History of Reuters'.
Pillars of the press. World's Press News June–July 1929. 4 articles on press agencies.

Central News Agency. Diamond jubilee souvenir. 1931.
D[avies], E. W. The Newspaper Society 1836–1936. 1936.
Cooper, K. Barriers down: the story of the news agency epoch. New York 1942.
Storey, G. Reuters' century 1851–1951. 1951. See World's Press News 6–13 July 1951.
UNESCO. News agencies: their structure and operation. Paris 1953.

(5) ADVERTISING

General works

Street, E. and L. Jackson. Advertising. Jnl of the Royal Soc of Arts 24 Jan 1913.
Praigg, N. T. Advertising and selling. 1923. See D. Thompson, Scrutiny 1 1932.
Jones, S. R. Art and publicity: fine printing and design. The Studio. Special Autumn no 1925.
Meynell, F. The typography of newspaper advertisements. 1929.
The romance of advertising. 1931. Rptd from Morning Post.
Report on questionnaire on advertising. Week-End Rev 9 July 1932.
Pearce, T. M. Advertising with machine made words. New Mexico Quart 3 1933.
Crawford, W. et al. Advertising and the man in the street. [c. 1935].
Link, H. C. Psychology of advertising, prepared especially for home study. Scranton Pa, 1937.
Riding, L., R. Graves et al. Advertising. Epilogue no 3 1937.
Thompson, D. Voice of civilization: an enquiry into advertising. 1943. See R. C. Churchill, Scrutiny 12 1943.
Watkins, J. L. The 100 best advertisements: who wrote them and what they did. New York 1949, 1959 (rev).
McLuhan, M. The mechanical bride: folklore of industrial man. New York 1951.
Harris, R. and A. Seldon. Advertising in a free society. 1952.
Turner, E. S. The shocking history of advertising! 1952.
Crosland, A., M. Abrams and D. Bell. Three broadcasts about advertising. Listener 13, 20, 27 Dec 1956.
Packard, V. The hidden persuaders. New York 1957.
Institute of Practitioners in Advertising. Subliminal communication. 1958.
Gloag, J. Advertising in modern life. 1959.
Taplin, W. Advertising: a new approach. 1960.
Williams, R. The magic system. New Left Rev 4 1960.
Baker, S. Visual persuaders. New York 1961.
Cox, D. F. Clues for advertising strategists. Harvard Business Rev 39 1961; rptd in People, society and mass communications, ed L. A. Dexter and D. M. White, New York 1964.
Macrae, D. G. Advertising and sociology. In his Ideology and society, 1961.
Pear, T. H. Advertising and publicity. In his Moulding of modern man, 1961.
Birch, L. The advertising we deserve? An assessment. 1962.
Elliott, B. B. A history of English advertising. 1962.
Harris, R. and A. Seldon. Advertising and the public. 1962.
Tunstall, J. The advertising man in London advertising agencies. 1964.
Whitehead, F. Advertising. In Discrimination and popular culture, ed D. Thompson 1964 (Pelican).
Aspects of advertising. TLS 21 May 1964.
The changing pattern of British publicity. TLS 4 June 1964.

Labour Party. Report of a commission of enquiry into advertising. [1965?].
Krugman, H. E. The measurement of advertising involvement. Public Opinion Quart 30 1967.
Thomas, D. The visible persuaders. 1967.
Buzzi, G. Advertising: its cultural and political effects. Minneapolis 1968.

Periodicals

Smith's Advertising Agency. Successful advertising. By T. Smith. 1878–? Annual.
The advertiser's guardian. 1885–1891, 1900–2. Ed L. Collins 1885–91, Thomas Dixon 1900–2.
The advertisers' ABC of official scales and charges (Advertising ABC and advertisement press directory). Title varies. Nos 1–45, 1887–1931/2. Annual.
Advertising. Vols 1–23 no 1, Oct 1891–Jan 1914.
Mather and Crowther. Practical advertising. 1895–1923. Annual.
Profitable advertising (formerly Advertising notes vols 1–4 no 5, Jan 1897–Dec 1898), vols 5–17 no 6, Jan 1899–Dec 1904.
The poster. Vols 1–6, June 1898–April/May 1901. As Poster and art collector 1900–01. Monthly.
The advertiser's review. Vols 1–6 no 298, 8 April 1899–24 Dec 1904. Incorporated in Advertising news, 5 Feb 1904–Nov/Dec 1905. Then incorporated in Progressive advertising and outdoor publicity, 25 Oct 1901–Aug 1909. Also incorporated Newspaper and poster advertising (nos 1–70, 28 July 1900–21 Dec 1901).
Modern advertising. June 1900–April 1901.
The advertising world. Oct 1901 (registration issue); Vols 1–72 no 6, Dec 1901–July/Aug 1940. As suppl to World's press news, April 1941. Suppl, Advertising news No 1–64, June 1928–Nov 1932. Incorporated Twentieth-century advertising.
Advertising news. Vols 1–2 no 66, 5 Feb 1904–Nov/Dec 1905. Incorporated Advertisers' review. Incorporated in Progressive advertising and outdoor publicity.
Advertisers' weekly. 19 April 1913 onwards.
Circulations: specially prepared for advertisers in the press. Nos 1–4, Jan 1915–Jan 1916.
The advertiser's annual (and convention year book). Title varies. 1915–?
Publicity world. Nos 1–803, 15 March 1919–28 Dec 1935.
The advertiser's aid. Vols 1–5 no 4, 1 Oct 1919–16 July 1923; July 1927–July 1933; 1936/37–?
The metro: an advertising journal. Nos 1–6, Oct 1921–March 1922. An amateur journal (see col 1384, below).
Commercial art. Vols 1–5 no 6. Oct 1922–June 1926; new ser vols 1–11 no 66, July 1926–Dec 1931. Continued as Commercial art and industry, vol 12 no 67–vol 20 no 120, Jan 1932–June 1936; Continued as Art and industry, vol 21 no 121–vol 65 no 390, July 1936–Dec 1958. Continued as Design for industry, vol 66 no 391–401, Jan–Dec 1959.
Twentieth-century advertising. Vols 1–2 no 4, Oct 1923–July 1924. Incorporated in Advertising world.
Who's who in British advertising? 1924–?
The advertising year book. London 1925; ptd USA.

Advertising display (and press publicity). Title varies. Vols 1–21 (unnumbered), July 1927–May 1937; nos 1–2 as suppls to Advertisers' weekly. Continued as Advertising monthly, June 1937–Dec 1939, Feb–May 1940. Suppls: Artists in advertising and their work, nos 1–7, 1935–7; Continued as Artists and photographers in advertising, no 8, 1938.

Posters and publicity: fine printing and design (Commercial art annual). Title varies. 1927–9. Continued as Modern publicity, 1930–? Earlier vols, Posters and their designers, Art and publicity, Posters and publicity, issued as special nos of Studio.

Advertising news. Nos 1–58, June 1928–May 1932. Suppl to Advertising world.

Advertising. April 1931. Registration issue only.

Who's who in the press, publicity and printing [etc] 1932.

Advertising review. 4 Jan 1936–?

Portfolio of 450 advertising illustrations. 1936. Suppl to Advertising display.

Printed advertising (direct mail). Title varies. June 1939–Dec 1948. Continued as Advertising, marketing, packaging, print, Jan 1949–?

The advertising manager. Nos 1–4, Sept 1937–May 1938.

Print and publicity. Coventry. Sept 1938–? Quarterly.

Persuasion, advertising, public relations and propaganda. Vols 1–2 no 2, Sept 1939–summer 1944; spring 1946–autumn 1951. Not pbd March 1940–March 1944, nor in 1945.

The advertising art annual and art buyers' guide. 1 only. 1939.

Press advertising and trade under war conditions 1939/40. 1940.

The announcer. Jan 1945–? Organ of the Publicity Club, occasional.

(6) PERIODICALS RELATING TO NEWSPAPER AND MAGAZINE PUBLISHING

See also Lists, Indexes and Directories, below.

The newspaper press directory. 1846 onwards. Irregular at first.

The newspaper owner and modern printer (formerly Newspaper owner and manager, 5 Jan 1898–11 Oct 1899) 18 Oct 1899–May 1903. Continued as Master printer and newspaper owner, 27 May 1903–1 April 1905. Continued as The newspaper owner. 8 April 1905–28 June 1913. Continued as The newspaper world, 5 July 1913–28 Dec 1935. Continued as Newspaper world and advertising review, 4 Jan 1936–12 March 1953.

Monthly guide to periodical literature. Nos 1–5 1900.

The press world. Nos 1–4 Dec 1905–April/May 1906.

The editor's magazine. Nos 1–6 Sept 1910–Feb 1911.

A list of the principal newspapers published in the UK 1912–?

Weekly Newspaper and Periodical Proprietors' Association

Authorised list of weekly and monthly publications. 1919–?

International press review. Nos 1–2, 1924. International press cutting bureau.

The news-letter of the LXIVMOS. Nos 1–21, Nov 1927–Nov 1929. Ed J. D. Henderson and ptd in 16 cities. Re-issued 1969 ed R. E. Adomeit, Cleveland, introd and index by R. E. Massmann.

World's press news. 7 March 1929 onwards. Printing supplements vols 1–7 no 81, 1932–Aug 1939. World's press news library, 1930–? Ed T. Korda.

Who's who in press, publicity and printing [etc] 1932.

Investigated press circulations and markets. 1933–?

UNESCO. Press, film and radio in the world today. Paris 1949 onwards.

The press and the people: annual report of the Press Council. 1954 onwards.

C. ACCOUNTS AND STUDIES OF INDIVIDUAL NEWSPAPERS AND MAGAZINES

See also Reminiscences and biographies, cols 1335–8 above.

(1) NEWSPAPERS

Only the principal studies which are given in vol 3 are repeated here, together with additional accounts; reference should be made to cols 1827–38 of vol 3 for further titles and for centenary numbers.

Daily Mail
  Harmsworth, A. C. (Viscount Northcliffe). The romance of the Daily Mail. 1903.
  Gardiner, A. G. The Daily Mail and the liberal press. 1914.
  McKenzie, F. A. The mystery of the Daily Mail 1896–1921. 1921.
  News in our time 1896–1946: Golden jubilee book of the Daily Mail. 1946.
Daily Mirror
  Cudlipp, H. Publish and be damned. 1953.
  — At your peril. 1961. Account of Mirror-Pictorial merger.
  Matthews, T. S. The sugar pill. 1957. Daily Mirror and Guardian.
  Edelman, M. The Mirror: a political history. 1966.
  Hoggart, R. The Daily Mirror and its readers. In his Speaking to each other, 1970.
Daily Sketch
  Daily Sketch blue book. 1933. Analysis of circulation with maps.

Daily Telegraph
  Schüssler, W. Die Daily-Telegraph-Affaire: Fürst Bülow, Kaiser Wilhelm und die Krise des Zweiten Reiches, 1908. Göttingen 1952.
  Lawson, E. F. (Baron Burnham). Peterborough court: the story of the Daily Telegraph. 1955.
Guardian
  Mills, W. H. The Manchester guardian: a century of history. 1921.
  Wallace, A. S. et al. C. P. Scott 1846–1932: the making of the Manchester Guardian. 1946.
  Matthews, T. S. The sugar pill. 1957. Guardian and Daily Mirror.
  How good is the Guardian?: Symposium. Delta nos 31–2 1963–4.
Morning Post
  Douglas, A. Fashionable intelligence about the Morning Post. 1918.
  — A touching ceremony. 1918. Morning Post and its editor.
  Ferguson, M. T. The Morning Post 1772–1921. National Rev 78 1922.

Hindle, W. H. The Morning Post 1772–1937. 1937.
Colgate, W. Death at 164: the portrait of a newspaper. Queen's Quart 45 1938.

Observer

The Observer 1791–1921. [1922].
Gollin, A. M. The Observer and J. L. Garvin 1908–14. 1960.

The Times

Palmer's index to the Times newspaper (1790–1941). 1868–1943.
Publishers' Association. 'The Times' and the publishers. 1906.
The annual index to the Times 1906(–1913), [1907–14]. Continued as The official index to the Times, 1914 onwards.
The Times: past—present—future. 1932.
The Times: a newspaper history 1785–1935. 1935.
The history of the Times. Vol 3, The twentieth-century test 1884–1912, 1947; vol 4, The 150th anniversary and beyond, 2 pts 1952.
Printing the Times since 1785. 1953.
Monopolies Commission. Report on The Times newspaper and The Sunday Times newspaper. 1966.

Other London newspapers (in alphabetical order)

Cruikshank, R. J. The roaring century 1846–1946. 1946. Daily News.
Daily Worker Defence League. The Daily Worker and war. 1941.
Rust, W. and A. Hutt. Story of the Daily Worker. 1948.
Handover, P. M. A history of the London Gazette 1665–1965. 1965.
Berrey, R. P. The romance of a great newspaper. [c. 1938]. News of the World.
The story of the Star 1888–1938. 1938.
Sunday Times. A hundred years of history. 1920.
Gibbs, P. The street of adventure. 1909. A novel concerned with the Liberal newspaper Tribune.

Berry, W. E. (Baron Camrose). London newspapers: their owners and controllers. 1939.

Scottish and provincial newspapers (in alphabetical order)

Mitchell, W. A. Or was it yesterday? Aberdeen 1947. Aberdeen Journal.
Whates, H. R. G. The Birmingham post 1857–1957. Birmingham 1957.
Wells, C. History of the Bristol Times and Mirror 1713–1913. 1913.
Fenton, W. A. Cambridge periodicals 1750–1931. Cambridge Public Lib Record & Book List March 1931.
Edinburgh Evening News. Fifty years 1873–1923. Edinburgh 1923.
Stewart, W. The Glasgow Herald: the story of a great newspaper from 1783–1911. Glasgow 1911.
Chance, H. G. The bicentenary of the Gloucester Journal. Gloucester 1922.
Newton, D. Mercury story: a brief record of the Lincoln, Rutland and Stamford Mercury. Stamford 1962.
Hadley, W. W. The bicentenary record of the North ampton Record. Northampton 1920.
The Norwich Post: its contemporaries and successors. Norwich 1951.
Sheffield Daily Telegraph: a record of seventy years, 8 June 1855–8 June 1925. 1925.
Sewell, G. Echoes of a century: the centenary history of Southern Newspapers Ltd 1864–1964. Southampton 1964.
Griffiths, I. Berrow's Worcester Journal. Worcester 1941.
Gibbs, M. A. and F. Beckwith. The Yorkshire Post: two centuries. [Leeds] 1954.
Producing a newspaper: the story of the Yorkshire Post. [nd].
Laughton, G. E. and L. R. Stephen. Yorkshire newspapers: a bibliography with locations. 1960.

(2) MAGAZINES

See the headnote cols 1343–4 above. For little magazines, see also F. J. Hoffman et al., The little magazine: a history and a bibliography, Princeton 1946, 1947 (enlarged).

Blackwood's Magazine

Tredrey, F. D. The house of Blackwood 1804–1954. Edinburgh 1954.

The Blue Review

Bradbury, M. Rhythm and the Blue Review. TLS 25 April 1968.

The Calendar of Modern Letters

Leavis, F. R. Introduction to Towards standards of criticism, 1933.
Bradbury, M. The Calendar of Modern Letters. London Mag new ser 1 1961.

Contemporary Poetry and Prose

Contemporary Poetry and Prose. TLS 25 April 1968.

Country Life

Darwin, B. Fifty years of Country Life. 1947.

The Criterion

Schwartz, D. The Criterion 1922–39. Kenyon Rev 1 1939.
Bradbury, M. The Criterion: a literary review in retrospect. London Mag 5 1958.
Howarth, H. In his Notes on some figures behind T. S. Eliot, 1965.
The Criterion. TLS 25 April 1968.

The Dial

Wasserstrom, W. T. S. Eliot and the Dial. Sewanee Rev 70 1962.

The Edinburgh Review

Karminski, A. The Edinburgh Review after 150 years. Listener 30 Oct 1952.

The Enemy

The Enemy. TLS 25 April 1968.

The English Review

Goldring, D. South lodge: reminiscences of Violet Hunt, Ford Madox Ford and the English Review circle 1943.
Bradbury, M. The English Review. London Mag 5 1958.
MacShane, F. The English Review. South Atlantic Quart 60 1961; rptd in his Life and works of Ford Madox Ford, 1965.

The Field

Rose, R. N. The Field 1853–1953: a centenary volume. 1953.

Fortnightly Review

Waugh, A. A hundred years of publishing. 1930.

Horizon

Spender, S. In his World within world, 1951.
Connolly, C. In his Previous convictions, 1963.

The Jewish Chronicle

The Jewish Chronicle 1841–1941: a century of newspaper history. 1949.
Gross, J. The Jewish Chronicle and others. Commentary 36 1963.

John Bull

Symons, J. John Bull. In his Horatio Bottomley, 1955.
Holles, R. Death of a magazine: the end of John Bull. Encounter 15 1960.

The London Aphrodite

Lindsay, J. In his Fanfrolico and after, 1962.

London Magazine

Roberts, M. Organs of critical opinion 3: reviewing in the London Magazine and some other monthlies. EC 7 1957.

The New Age
  Mairet, P. A. R. Orage: a memoir. 1936.
  Selver, P. Orage and the New Age circle. 1959.
  Martin, W. The New Age under Orage. Manchester 1967.
  The New Age. TLS 25 April 1968.
The New Statesman
  Hayman, R. Organs of critical opinion 2: reviewing in the New Statesman and the Spectator. EC 6 1956.
  New statesmanship. 1956. Survey of readership.
  Mander, J. The New Statesman and the English left. Commentary 37 1964.
New Verse
  Grigson, G. Recollections of New Verse. TLS 25 April 1968.
Pall Mall Gazette
  Stead, E. W. My father: personal and spiritual reminiscences. 1913.
  Harper, E. K. Stead: the man. 1914.
  Scott, J. W. R. The story of the Pall Mall Gazette. 1950.
  — The life and death of a newspaper. 1952.
Picture Post
  Hopkinson, T. (ed). Picture Post 1938–1950. 1970.
Poetry London
  Dickins, A. Tambimuttu and Poetry London. London Mag 5 1965.
  Ewart, G. Tambi the great. London Mag 5 1965.
The Poetry Review
  Grant, J. Harold Monro and the Poetry Bookshop. 1967.
Publishers' Weekly
  The publishers' voice. TLS 30 Aug 1947.
Punch
  Punch: an interesting talk about himself and his renowned contributors. 1910.
  James, M. R. Punch and the flood. TLS 30 March 1933.
  Anstey, F. A long retrospect. 1936.
  Köhler, W. Punch und Deutschland. Neuphilologische Monatsschrift 8 1937.
  Clark, P. O. Punch's apotheosis. PQ 31 1952.
  Loomis, C. G. Jonathanisms in Punch. Western Folklore 14 1955.
  Williams, R. E. A century of Punch. 1956.
  Price, R. G. G. A history of Punch. 1957.

Adburgham, A. A Punch history of manners and modes 1841–1940. 1961.
Pulling, C. Mr Punch and the police. 1964.
The Review of English Studies
  Bateson, F. W. Organs of critical opinion 1: The Review of English Studies. EC 6 1956.
Rhythm
  Bradbury, M. Rhythm and the Blue Review. TLS 25 April 1968.
The Scots Magazine
  Imrie, D. S. M. The story of the Scots Magazine. Scots Mag 30–31 1939.
Scrutiny
  Leavis, F. R. The Kenyon Review and Scrutiny. Scrutiny 14 1946.
  — Valedictory. Scrutiny 19 1953.
  — A retrospect. Scrutiny 20 1963.
  The importance of Scrutiny, ed E. Bentley, New York 1948.
  Lerner, L. D. The life and death of Scrutiny. London Mag 2 1955.
The Spectator
  Thomas, W. B. The story of the Spectator 1828–1928. 1928.
  Hayman, R. Organs of critical opinion 2: reviewing in the New Statesman and the Spectator. EC 6 1956.
The Strand Magazine
  Pound, R. The Strand Magazine 1891–1950. 1966.
Times Literary Supplement
  Bateson, F. W. Organs of critical opinion 4: the Times Literary Supplement. EC 7 1957.
Transatlantic Review
  MacShane, F. The Transatlantic Review. London Mag 7 1960; rptd in his The life and work of Ford Madox Ford, 1965.
  Poli, B. J. Ford Madox Ford and the Transatlantic Review. Syracuse 1967.
transition
  In Plastique, no 3 1938.
Wales Magazine
  Jenkins, D. C. Dylan Thomas and Wales Magazine. Trace no 30 1959.
The Week
  Cockburn, P. The year of the Week. 1968.

D. LISTS, INDEXES AND DIRECTORIES

Reference should also be made to the British Museum Newspaper Library Catalogue at Colindale (unpbd) and to the appropriate sections of vol 3, cols 1783–88.

Willing's British and Irish press guide (formerly May's British and Irish press guide and advertiser's handbook and dictionary, 1874–88). 1899–1905, ?1907–9, 1911 onwards. Annual.
Sell, Henry. Sell's dictionary of the world's press. 1883/4, 1885, 1887–1905. Continued as Sell's world's press, 1906–21. Annual, but none issued in 1911, 1913, 1916–18, 1920.
Browne, T. B. (from 1888). Advertising ABC and the advertisement press directory 1887–1931/2. Annual.
Poole, W. F. Index to periodical literature, 1802–91. Boston 1891 (rev edn); suppl 1882–1907; 6 vols in 7, 1969 (rev). See also M. V. Bell and J. C. Bacon, Poole's index: date and volume key, Chicago 1957.
Mather and Crowther. Practical advertising. 1895–1923. Annual.
Vickers's newspaper gazetteer: an annual reference book of the press for the United Kingdom, the Colonies etc 1900–16. Annual.
Cotgreave, A. A contents-subject index to general and periodical literature. 1900.
Readers' guide to periodical literature (1900). Minneapolis, then New York 1901 onwards.

Faxon, F. W. The magazine subject index (1907–49). Boston 1908–52. Cumulated in 2 vols Boston 1964.
Athenaeum subject index to periodicals. Nos 1–2, 1915–16 and 1915–18. Continued as Subject index to periodicals to 1961. Continued as British humanities index 1962 onwards. Annual to 1953, thereafter quarterly.
Stephens, E. American popular magazines: a bibliography. Bull of Bibliography 9 1916. Also pbd separately as Bull of Bibliography pamphlet no 23, Boston 1916.
International index to periodicals (1907–1965). New York 1916–65. Continued as Social sciences and humanities index, 1965 onwards.
Clark, A. W. (ed). Checklist of indexed periodicals. New York 1917.
[Muddiman, J. G.]. Tercentenary handlist of English and Welsh newspapers, magazines and reviews 1620–1920. 1920. Based on British Museum holdings and with some misinformation. See N & Q 1921–2 for amendments.
Firkins, I. T. E. Index to short stories 1923; suppls 1929, 1936. Superseded by Short story index, New York, 1953 onwards.
Gregory, W. Union list of serials in libraries of the

United States and Canada. 3 vols New York 1927–33, 1 vol 1943 (rev) 5 vols 1965 (rev).

Ulrich's periodicals directory 1932. New York 1932. Frequent revisions. From 1965 as Ulrich's international periodicals directory.

Haskell, D. A checklist of cumulated indexes to individual periodicals in the New York Public Library. New York 1942.

Bibliographic index: a cumulative bibliography of bibliographies. New York. Vol 1. 1937–1942, 1945; onwards. Includes periodical articles.

Lewis, J. Newspaper libraries. 1952 (Lib Assoc pamphlet no 11).

Library of Congress. Newspapers on microfilm. Washington 1953, 1963 (5th edn).

British union catalogue of periodicals. 4 vols 1955–8; with suppls. Merged with World list of scientific periodicals as BUCOP new periodical titles, March 1964, quarterly. Cumulative annuals, 1965 onwards.

Gerstenberger, D. L. and G. Hendrick. Directory of periodicals publishing articles in English and American literature and language. Denver 1959. With suppls.

Koltay, E. Irregular serials and annuals: an international directory. New York 1967.

Wilcox, D. L. English language dailies abroad. Detroit 1967. 202 papers in 56 non-English speaking countries.

Wall, C. E. Periodical title abbreviations. Detroit 1969.

Little Magazines

The University of Wisconsin holds Dr Marvin Sukov's collection of 10,621 issues of 716 little mags (purchased Dec 1958). The Benjamin Franklin Memorial Library, Philadelphia, holds the Edwin Hadley Smith Collection of some 40,000 amateur jnls of which 1,976 are from England and Wales.

Hoffman, F. J. et al. The little magazine: a history and a bibliography. Princeton 1946, 1947 (enlarged).

Ulrich, C. F. and E. Patterson. Little magazines. BNYPL 51 1947.

Index to little magazines. Denver, New York 1949, onwards. Ed Alan Swallow, Stephen Goode.

Trace. London, Hollywood. June 1952–1971. Ed J. B. May. Includes bibliographies; titles from 1940.

Midwest Inter-Library Center. Union list of little magazines in six Midwestern universities. Chicago 1956.

International guide to literary and art periodicals, 1960. London. Suppls in Trace, above.

LOC-sheets. Leeds, Blackburn. 1964 onwards, irregular, as suppl to Tlaloc (irregular). Ed C. McCarthy.

Nagel, A. and B. Brückner (ed). Almanach: zweite literarische Pfingstmesse Frankfurt am Main. Frankfurt 1964.

Directory of little magazines (and small presses). Title varies. El Cerrito Calif 1965 onwards. Ed L. V. Fulton in collaboration with C. McCarthy (England) to 4th edn 1968, thereafter M. Zeki.

Small press review. El Cerrito Calif. Vol 1 no 1 spring 1967 onwards. Quarterly Ed L. V. Fulton. Bibliographies and reviews.

Catalogue of small press publications. San Francisco 1969. Introd by F. Pollak. Reviews early attempts to produce bibliographies of little magazines.

E. INDIVIDUAL NEWSPAPERS AND MAGAZINES

An asterisk before an entry indicates that no copy of the paper or magazine has been located. For further details of the earlier history of papers and magazines starting before 1900, see vols 2 and 3.

(1) LITERARY PAPERS AND MAGAZINES

Academic journals are excluded as in the main are foreign journals which occasionally published work of English authors. For theatrical periodicals and children's periodicals, see cols 823–80 and 819–20 above.

The gentleman's magazine. Jan 1731–Sept (?) 1907. Token registration nos (covers only) Oct 1907–Sept 1922. Annuals 1871–1901. The gentleman's magazine library (selections of the chief contents 1731–1868), 30 vols 1883–1905. Monthly.

The Edinburgh review: or critical journal. Vols 1–250, Oct 1802–Oct 1929.

The quarterly review. Feb 1809 onwards.

Blackwood's Edinburgh magazine. (Started as Edinburgh monthly magazine, April 1817.) Oct 1817–Dec 1905. Continued as Blackwood's magazine, Jan 1906 onwards. Monthly.

The Westminster review. Vols 1–181, Jan 1824–Jan 1914. Ed Mrs John Chapman 1894–1914.

The athenaeum. Nos 1–4737, 2 Jan 1828–11 Feb 1921. Editors in 20th century include N. MacColl, Vernon Randall, Arthur Greenwood, John Middleton Murry. Incorporated in Nation.

The spectator. 5 July 1828 onwards. Selection: Spectator's gallery, ed P. Fleming and D. Verschoyle 1933.

Chambers's journal. (Started as Chambers's Edinburgh journal, 4 Feb 1832.) 6th series, vols 1–13, 4 Dec 1897–26 Nov 1910. 7th series, vols 1–21, 3 Dec 1910–28 Nov 1931. Continued monthly, 8th series, vols 1–15, Jan 1932–Dec 1946. 9th series, vols 1–10, Jan 1947–Dec 1956.

The Dublin review. May 1836 onwards. Index: complete list of articles pbd May 1836– April 1936. 1936. Centenary article vol 198 1936.

The art-journal. (Started as The art-union, Feb 1839.) Jan 1849–Feb 1912.

Punch: or the London Charivari. 17 July 1841 onwards. Selections from Punch are given in chronological order in this section, but listed with main entry in Section (5), col 1400, below.

The family herald. 17 Dec 1842–22 June 1940. Supplement, nos 1–3208, 1877–1940; Family herald monthly, pts 1029–1166, Feb 1929–July 1940; both subsequently incorporated in Christian novels. Complete story-teller (another monthly supplement; title varies slightly) nos 1–196, June 1912–1928, incorporated in Magazine of fiction and the complete story-teller. 'I'll tell you' book (another supplement) nos 1–25, 1917.

The London journal and weekly record of literature, science and art. 1 March 1845–28 April 1906. Continued as New London journal, 5 May 1906–8 May 1909. Continued as London journal, 15 May 1909–27 June 1912. Incorporated in Spare moments; absorbed Weekly novelist.

The family friend. (Started 1849.) New series, with illustrations. Vols 1–52, 1870–Sept 1921. New series, nos 1–8, 4 Feb–25 March 1929. Incorporated in Girls' mirror.

The appeal: a magazine for the people. Vols 1–82 no 1, 1848–1918. Religious but with much poetry.

The leisure hour: a family journal of instruction and recreation. Jan 1852–Oct 1905.

The London quarterly review. Nos 1–313, Sept 1853–Jan 1932. Continued as London quarterly and Holborn review, April 1932 onwards.

Cassell's magazine. (Started as Cassell's illustrated family paper, 31 Dec 1853.) Dec 1897–March 1912. Continued as Cassell's magazine of fiction (and popular literature), April 1912–June 1919. Continued as Cassell's (magazine), July 1919–Dec 1932. Incorporated in Story-teller.

The Saturday review of politics, literature, science and art. Vols 1–166 no 4320, 3 Nov 1855–23 July 1938. Weekly. Ed Harold Hodge 1898–1913, G. A. B. Dewar 1913–17, A. A. Baumann 1917–21, Sydney Brooks 1921, Filson Young 1921–4, George Pinckard 1930–2, J. W. Day 1933–4, Lady Houston 1934–6, George Freeman 1936–8. Selection of articles rptd in Recreations and reflections, 1902.

Macmillan's magazine. Vols 1–59, Nov 1859–Oct 1907.

The Cornhill magazine. Jan 1860 onwards. Editors since 1900 include Reginald J. Smith Jan 1898–1916, Leonard Huxley Feb 1925–June 1933, Lord Gorell July 1933–Dec 1939, Peter Quennell Jan 1944–spring 1951. Not pbd Jan 1940–Dec 1943. Monthly till suspension, then quarterly. Sheaves from The Cornhill, ed L. Huxley 1926.

Temple Bar: a London magazine for town and country readers. London and New York. Vols 1–132, Dec 1860–Dec 1905. New series, vols 1–2, Jan–Dec 1906.

Fun. 21 Sept 1861–Aug 1901. Incorporated in Sketchy bits.

The London reader of literature, science, art and general information. Vols 1–80, 1863–May 1903.

The month: a Catholic magazine. (Started as Month: an illustrated magazine of literature, science, and art, July 1864.) 1890–1913. Continued as Month July–Dec 1948. New series, Jan 1949 onwards. Index from 1864–1908, 1909. From 1909 to 1921, 1922. Editors include Sydney F. Smith, Joseph Keating and Philip Caraman. Jubilee issue Jan, June 1914; 75th anniversary issue, July 1939.

The sporting times [= The pink 'un]: a chronicle of racing literature, art and the drama. Nos 1–3559, 11 Feb 1865–5 Dec 1931. Weekly. The Pink 'un holiday annual. 1908–?

The fortnightly review. 15 May 1865–Dec 1954 (as Fortnightly from July 1934). Incorporated in Contemporary review. Monthly from 15 Oct 1866.

Wayside words (Started as Gilead, July 1865). Vols 8–35, Jan 1877–Dec 1904.

The argosy: a magazine of tales, travels, essays and poems. Vols 1–75, Dec 1865–Sept 1901.

Contemporary review. Jan 1866 onwards.

Judy: or the London serio-comic journal. 1 May 1867–23 Oct 1907.

Literary world. Vols 1–2, 1868–9 (as supplements to Christian world). New series, vols 1–85, 5 Nov 1869–Nov 1919. Absorbed by Christian world. Weekly to 1905, then monthly.

The academy. 9 Oct 1869–11 Jan 1902. Monthly to 1874, then weekly from 1874. As Academy till 11 Jan 1902. Amalgamated with Literature and continued as Academy and literature, 18 Jan 1902–4 March 1905. Continued as Academy 11 March 1905–10 Dec 1910. Continued as Academy and literature 17 Dec 1910–24 Jan 1914. Continued as Academy 31 Jan–11 Sept 1915. Copyright registration issues 24 Aug 1918–24 May 1920. Continued as Plain English, vols 1–4, 10 July 1920–18 March 1922.

Portfolio: monographs on artistic subjects. Nos 1–48, 1894–1907. (Started as Portfolio, Jan 1870). Ed Philip Gilbert Hamerton.

The century. New York (and London to 1913). (Started as Scribner's monthly, vols 1–22, 1870–81). Vols 23–120, 1881–1930. Subtitles vary.

Central literary magazine: conducted by the Birmingham Literary Association. Jan 1873 onwards.

The Irish monthly. (Started as Irish monthly magazine, July 1873.) Vols 3–83, Dec 1874–Sept 1954.

Lloyd's magazine. (Started as Poet's magazine, 1876.) 1895–June 1900. Ed Leonard Lloyd.

Truth. 4 Jan 1877–27 Dec 1957. Weekly.

The nineteenth century. Vols 1–48, March 1877–Dec 1900. Continued as Nineteenth century and after, Jan 1901–Dec 1950. Continued as Twentieth century, Jan 1951 onwards. 75th anniversary no, March 1952. Extracts in Nineteenth-century opinion, 1877–1901, ed Michael Goodwin, 1951. Index to vols 1–50.

The magazine of art, illustrated. Vols 1–26, May 1878–Oct 1902. New series, vols 1–2 (= vols 27, 28), Nov 1902–July 1904.

The family novelist. (Started as Illustrated family novelist, 1878.) Nos 1008–1326, 1897–1903.

Moonshine. Vols 1–45 no 1, July 1879–Aug 1902. Ed Arthur Clements and C. Harrison (who also illustrated).

The theosophist. Madras Oct 1879 onwards. Ed H. S. Olcott Oct 1887–Feb 1907, Annie Besant March 1907–1932, A. P. Warrington Oct 1933–July 1934; then editors include G. S. Arundel, C. Jinarajadasa, N. Sri Ram. Absorbed Theosophical review March 1909. Absorbed The Adyar bulletin Jan 1930. Called Adyar theosophist for vols 51 and 52, 1930, whilst Annie Besant published The theosophist in an American edition from Hollywood.

The dial. Chicago. Vols 1–86 no 7, May 1880–July 1929.

The Downside review. July 1880 onwards. Index to vols 1–25, vol 25 1906.

Tit-bits. No 1, 22 Oct 1881 onwards. Fifty prize stories from Tit-bits, 1908.

The Manchester quarterly: a journal of literature and art. Vols 1–55, Oct 1882–1940. Organ of the Manchester Literary Club.

Longman's magazine. Vols 1–46, Nov 1882–Oct 1905.

The Scottish review. London, Paisley, Edinburgh. Vols 1–36, Nov 1882–Oct 1900. New series, vols 37–43 no 1, 1914–20. Ed W. M. Metcalfe, 1882–1900; then R. Erskine.

The English illustrated magazine. Vols 1–49, Oct 1883–Aug 1913.

Great thoughts from master minds. Vols 1–107, 5 Jan 1884–Sept 1937. Continued as Great thoughts and great reading, Jan–Oct 1939. Incorporated in Sunday at home and overseas.

Ally Sloper's half holiday. 3 May 1884–9 Sept 1916. Incorporated in London Society.

Good housekeeping. New York. 1 May 1885 onwards.

The literary guide and rationalist review. (Started as Watts's literary guide, 1885.) Nos 1–546, Oct 1894–March 1954. Continued as Literary guide, vol 69 no 4–vol 71 no 8, April 1954–Sept 1956 (Rationalist review being pbd separately, April 1954–Jan 1956). Continued as Humanist, vol 71 no 9, Oct 1956 onwards.

The monthly magazine of fiction. Nos 1–504, 1885–1927. Continued as Magazine of fiction, nos 505–22, 1927–8. Continued as Magazine of fiction and complete story teller, nos 523–60, 1928–31. Continued as Magazine of fiction: the complete story teller monthly, nos 561–79, 1931–3. Continued as Complete story-teller etc, nos 580–673, 1933–41.

The princess's novelettes. Nos 1–955, 1886–1904. Continued as Princess novels, nos 1–118(?), 1904–6. Ed E. J. Brett.

Melia's magazine: a journal of entertaining and instructive reading. Manchester. Vols 1–18 no 9, Feb 1887–Sept 1903. Issued by the store of that name.

The theosophical review. (Started as Lucifer: a theosophical monthly, 1887.) Sept 1897–Feb 1909. Ed Annie Besant, G. R. S. Mead. Incorporated in Theosophist.

Answers. (Started as Answers to correspondents 2 June 1888.) 28 Dec 1889–18 Feb 1956. Annual, 1926–? Summer fun book, 1937.

The expository times. Oct 1889 onwards. Index to vols 1–20. By James Donald. [1910]. Ed James Hastings.

Short stories. (Started as Magazine of short stories, 1899.) Nos 237–807, 15 July 1893–18 June 1904.

The speaker. 4 Jan 1890–23 Feb 1907. Continued as Nation, vols 1–28 no 20, 2 March 1907–12 Feb 1921. Absorbed Athenaeum and continued as Nation and

Athenaeum, vol 28 no 21–vol 48 no 21, 19 Feb 1921–21 Feb 1931. Incorporated in New statesman. Weekly.

The review of reviews. Vols 1–87, Jan 1890–Feb 1936. Continued as World review of reviews, 1 vol, March–Aug 1936. Continued as World review, Sept 1936–May 1953. Ed W. T. Stead 1890–1912.

The author. Vols 1–36, May 1890–July 1926. Continued as Author, playwright and composer, vols 37–59, Oct 1926–winter 1948. Continued as Author vol 60, spring 1949 onwards. Organ of Society of Authors, Playwrights and Composers.

The gipsy novelette. Vols 1–8, 1890–1900. New series, vols 1–3 no 66, 5 July 1900–30 Sept 1901. Incorporated in Something to read.

Folklore. 1890 onwards.

T'Pogmoor olmenack an Bairnsla foak yearly jottins. Barnsley. 1890–1909. 'Be Tom Treddlehayle'.

The Strand magazine: an illustrated monthly. Jan 1891–March 1950. Incorporated in Men only. The 'Strand' best stories, 1915.

Hearth and home. May 1891–Jan 1914. Incorporated in Vanity fair.

The Ludgate. (Started as Ludgate monthly, May 1891.) New series, vols 1–11, Nov 1895–Feb 1901. Incorporated in Universal magazine.

Tales from town topics. New York and London. Vols. 1–38, Sept 1891–Sept 1906; then as Transatlantic tales to March 1908.

The bookman: a monthly journal for book readers. Vols 1–87, Oct 1891–Dec 1934. Incorporated in London mercury, Jan 1935–April 1939, and in Life and letters, May 1939–Feb 1946.

The idler. (Started as Idler magazine, Feb 1892.) Vols 9–39, Feb 1896–Oct 1911. Ed Jerome K. Jerome and Robert Barr, to vol 14; vols 15–21 ed Arthur Lawrence and Sidney H. Sime; vols 22–38, ed Robert Barr.

The Celtic monthly: a magazine for highlanders. Glasgow. Vols 1–25, Oct 1892–1917.

Encore. Nos 1–1972, 11 Nov 1892–9 Oct 1930.

Sketchy bits. 25 April 1893–9 May 1910. Incorporated in Fun.

The studio. April 1893 onwards. Index to vols 1–21, 1893–1901, 1911. An American edn made up from part of Studio and, with American material, issued as International studio, 1897–1921. Relationship of art and literature.

The butterfly: a humorous and artistic magazine. May 1893–Feb 1894. New series, nos 1–12, March 1899–Feb 1900. Ed L. Raven-Hill and Arnold Golsworthy.

The Pall Mall magazine. Vols 1–53, May 1893–Sept 1914. New series, vols 1–5, May 1927–Sept 1929. From Oct 1914 to April 1927, and again from Oct 1929 to Sept 1937, amalgamated with Nash's magazine as Nash's and Pall Mall magazine, nos 437–532. Incorporated in Good housekeeping. See Nash's magazine, col 1359, below.

Today. 11 Nov 1893–19 July 1905. Superseded by London opinion. Revived as Today, 6 May 1916–Dec 1923 in three series: 6 May–28 Oct 1916 (superseding T.P.'s weekly); 4 Nov 1916–6 Jan 1917, weekly; vols 1–10 no 58 March 1917–Dec 1923, ed Holbrook Jackson. Monthly to Sept 1920, then quarterly. Incorporated in Life and letters, March 1924 (see col 1366) (title to be distinguished from Life and letters 1928). The third series (March 1917–Dec 1923) is significant as a literary journal.

The Aldine half-holiday library. Nos 1–904, 1893–1910.

Phil May's illustrated annual. 1893–1905. Ed Grant Richards and then Harry Thompson.

New Ireland review. Dublin. March 1894–Feb 1911.

The duchess novelette. Nos 1–416, 17 Sept 1894–15 Sept 1902. Continued as Smart novels, no 417–?, 22 Sept 1902–?

The new age. Vols 1–19 no 659, new series, vols 1–62 no 22, 4 Oct 1894–7 April 1938. Becomes significant with the new series, ed A. R. Orage, 2 May 1907–27 April or Oct? 1922. Orage assisted by Holbrook Jackson, 2 May–28 Dec 1907, W. R. Titterton, Clifford Sharp (?), St John Ervine and Ashley Dukes. From 5 Oct 1922, ed Arthur Moore. From 5 July 1923 ed Arthur Benson and becomes organ of New Age Social Credit Society. Weekly, then irregular in later stages. Amalgamated with New English weekly and continued as New English weekly and the new age (see cols 1369–70, below).

The Windsor magazine. Vols 1–90, Jan 1895–Sept 1939.

The Irish homestead. Dublin. Vols 1–30 no 36, 9 March 1895–8 Sept 1923. Ed H. F. Norman and George W. Russell. Incorporated in Irish statesman.

The prize reciter, reader and speaker. Vols 1–10, Dec 1895–Nov 1905.

Crampton's magazine. (Started as Chapman's magazine of fiction, 1895.) May 1899–Nov 1902. Ed Oswald Crawfurd.

Pearson's magazine. Vols 1–88, Jan 1896–Nov 1939.

The border magazine. Glasgow etc. Vols 1–44 no 528, Feb 1896–Dec 1939.

Home stories. 14 March 1896–10 Oct 1900. New series, no 261–?, 17 Oct 1900–?

The lady's realm. Vols 1–37, Nov 1896–May 1915.

'My queen' library. Nos 1–717, 1896–1909. Continued as My queen novels, nos 718–977, 1909–14.

The Temple magazine for home and sundry reading. (Started as Temple magazine, 1896–9.) Vol 4, Oct 1899–Sept 1900.

The new century review: a monthly international journal of literature, politics. Vols 1–8, Jan 1897–Dec 1900. Succeeded by Twentieth century.

The dome: a quarterly containing examples of all the arts. Nos 1–5, March 1897–May 1898. New series (monthly), vols 1–7, Oct 1898–May/July 1900. Ed Ernest J. Oldmeadow.

Literature. Vols 1–10 no 1, 23 Oct 1897–11 Jan 1902. Weekly. Ed H. D. Traill. Incorporated in The Academy. Published by The Times; precursor of Times literary supplement.

Country life. 1897 onwards. Illustrated. Anthology of verse, ed P. Anderson Graham, 1915; Anniversary issue 12 Jan 1967.

The empress novelette. Nos 1–223, 1897–1901. Continued as Empress dainty novels, nos 1–25, 1901–2. Continued as Dainty novels, nos 27–1214, 1902–24; then incorporated in Smart novels.

The heartsease library of high class fiction. Vols 1–27, new series, vols 1–2 no 30, 1897–1905. Nos 1–461, 11 July 1908–5 May 1917.

The favourite magazine. (Started as Eureka, 1897.) Vols 3–9, 1898–1903.

The literary year-book. 1897–1917. Not pbd 1918, 1919. Continued as Literary who's who, 1920. Continued as Literary year-book, 1921–3.

The page. Carshalton. Vols 1–4 no 2, Jan 1898–1901. Ed Edward Gordon Craig. Monthly to 1898, then quarterly.

Saint George: the journal of the Ruskin society of Birmingham—the Society of the Rose. Vols 1–14 no 53, Jan 1898–May 1911.

The outlook. 5 Feb 1898–30 June 1928. Editors include Filson Young. Weekly.

The eagle and the serpent: a journal of egoistic philosophy and sociology. Nos 1–19, 15 Feb 1898–Sept 1903. Irregular. Ed John Erwin McCall.

The black cat: a monthly magazine of short stories. Nos 1–25, Feb 1898–Feb 1900. Ed G. C. Dusart.

The wide world magazine. Vols 1–135, April 1898–Dec 1965. Incorporated in Geographical magazine.

Golden stories. Nos 1–769, 18 June 1898–8 March 1913. Continued as Golden hours, vol 1–4 no 103, 15 March 1913–27 Feb 1915.

The Harmsworth monthly pictorial magazine. Vols 1–4, July 1898–July 1900. Continued as Harmsworth magazine, vols 5–6, Aug 1900–July 1901. Continued as

Harmsworth London magazine vols 7–10, Aug 1901–July 1903. Continued as London magazine vols 11–65, Aug 1903–Oct 1930. Continued as New London magazine, new series, vols 1–6, Nov 1930–May 1933. Incorporated in Story-teller.

The windmill. Nos 1–6 Oct 1898–winter 1900.

The royal magazine. Vols 1–44 nos 1–385, Nov 1898–Nov 1930. Continued as New royal magazine, vol 1 no 1–vol 2 no 18, Dec 1930–May 1932. Continued as Royal pictorial, vol 2 no 19–vol 4 no 24, June 1932–Dec 1934. Continued as Royal screen pictorial, Jan–June 1935. Continued as Screen pictorial, July 1935–Sept 1939.

The X: an unknown quantity. Cambridge. Vols 1–3 no 51, 10 Nov 1898–6 Dec 1900.

The lady's world. Vols 1–28, Dec 1898–Sept 1926.

Woman. Dec 1898–June 1907.

The bull's eye: novels founded mainly on the annals of Scotland Yard. Vols 1–4 no 94, 1898–1900.

The home magazine. Vols 1–6 no 141, 1898–1900. Incorporated in Sunday Strand. Ed George Clarke from vol 3 no 63.

The new penny magazine. Vols 1–17, 1898–1903. Continued as The penny magazine (The P.M.), nos 222–1,372, 1903–25. Continued as Cassell's popular magazine, new series, vols 1–2 no 26, Feb–Aug 1925.

An occasional magazine. Reading and London. Vols 1–4, Feb 1899–Dec 1903.

Beltaine: the organ of the Irish Literary Theatre. No 1, May 1899; no 2, Feb 1900; no 3, April 1900. Ed W. B. Yeats.

The Anglo-Saxon review. Vols 1–10, June 1899–Sept 1901. Ed Lady Randolph Churchill.

The elf: a little book. Ingrave. Nos 1–4, 1899–1900. Continued as The elf: a sequence of the seasons, nos 1–4, spring and summer 1902, autumn 1903, winter 1904. Continued as The elf: a magazine of drawings and writings, autumn 1903, winter 1904. Continued as The elf: a magazine of drawings and writings, new series, nos 1–3, 1905–12. By James Guthrie.

Poet's corner. Vols 1–36, 1899–1907.

All Ireland review. Dublin. 6 Jan 1900–Jan 1907 (as All Ireland review and Irish manufacturers' and traders' gazette, 20 Sept 1902–Jan 1903). Ed Standish O'Grady. Weekly but irregular, especially in later years; vol 7 no 1, twice (28 April 1906 and Aug 1906).

The spear. 24 Jan–2 May 1900. Amalgamated with Sketch.

The universal magazine. Vols 1–4 no 1, Feb 1900–Dec 1901 (March–Nov 1901 as Universal and Ludgate magazine).

The monthly review. Vols 1–27 no 3, Oct 1900–June 1907. Ed Charles Hanbury-Williams and H. Newbolt.

The new century review: a monthly review of politics, literature, the fine arts and social questions of the day. 1 only. Nov 1900.

The tulip: a little book of music, poetry and woodcuts. Shortlands. Nos 1–2, summer, winter 1900. Ed Martin Klingender.

The leader. Dublin 1900 onwards.

The thrush: a periodical for the publication of original poetry. Vols 1–2 no 14, 1 Jan 1901–Feb 1902. Ed T. Mullet Ellis.

The yellow dwarf. Liverpool. Nos 1–4, 12 Jan–2 Feb 1901.

The herb o' grace. Wrotham, 1901; London 1902. Nos 1–18, Jan 1901–June 1902. Ed Laurence Alma-Tadema.

The lady's magazine. Vols 1–7 no 40, Jan 1901–April 1904. Continued as Lady's home magazine (of fiction), vol 7 no 41–vol 9 no 49, May 1904–Jan 1905. Continued as Home magazine of fiction, vol 9 nos 50 and 51, Feb and March 1905.

Mine host. 1 only. Jan 1901 (BM copy marked 'published Oct 1908'). Ed W. Calvert.

The twentieth century. Jan 1901–Nov 1901 (?) Superseded New century review 1897–1900.

The Kensington: a magazine of art, literature and the drama. Nos 1–7, March–Sept 1901. Oct issue promised, but not issued? Ed Mrs Steuart Erskine and R. J. Richardson.

Newnes' family stories. Nos 1–67. April 1901–July 1902.

The candid friend. Vols 1–3 no 67, May 1901–Aug 1902. Incorporates Traveller from no 50 on. Ed Frank Harris.

The rambler. 29 June 1901–26 June 1902. Numbering and pagination continue from Dr Johnson's Rambler (see vol 2 col 1129; thus first issue is no 209, beginning page 246). Weekly. Incorporated in Sunrise.

The jester. Nos 1–6, July–Christmas 1901. Ed S. Gluckstein and S. Joseph. Issued by Salmon and Gluckstein Ltd?

Samhain: an occasional review. Dublin. Nos 1–7, Oct 1901–Nov 1908. Irregular, not pbd Dec 1905–Nov 1906. Ed for Irish Literary Theatre by W. B. Yeats.

Scottish art and letters. Glasgow. Vols 1–3 no 1, Nov 1901–Feb 1904. Antiquarian supplement, 2 pts, 1903. Ed A. Fraser-Lovat.

Sunrise. Nos 1–36, 9 Nov 1901–July 1902. Absorbed Rambler and continued as Sunrise and rambler, nos 37–48, 26 July–11 Oct 1902.

Am Bàrd (a monthly bilingual magazine). Edinburgh. 1901.

A broadsheet. Nos 1–24, Jan 1902–Dec 1903. Ed Pamela Colman Smith?

The tiger. Nos 1–2, 15 March, 15 April, 1902. Ed T. W. H. Crosland.

The biographist and (British) review. Gillingham, Dorset. April, July, Oct 1902. Continued as British review and journal of biography, Dec 1902, Feb, May, June, 1903. Ed N. B. Martin.

The shrine. Stratford-on-Avon. Nos 1–4, 1 May 1902–April 1903. Ed R. H. Fitzpatrick.

The sheaf: a perhaps quarterly magazine. Oxford. Nos 1–4, 20 May 1902–10 June 1904.

Gossip: the home series magazine. Vols 1–4 no 81, Aug 1902–Feb 1904.

The protest: a journal for Philistines. Edenbridge. Nos 1–4, Sept–Dec 1902.

The treasury. Vols 1–35, Oct 1902–Sept 1920. Ed Anthony Deane.

T.P.'s weekly. Vols 1–27, 14 Nov 1902–29 April 1916. Ed T. P. O'Connor, later Holbrook Jackson. Superseded by Today (see col 1353) 6 May 1916–Dec 1923. Revived 27 Oct 1923–29 Nov 1929, vols 1–12, ed T. P. O'Connor. From 31 Oct 1923–17 Sept 1927 incorporated Cassell's weekly as T.P's and Cassell's weekly.

The trawl: an occasional miscellany. Birmingham. Nos 1–3, Midsummer 1902–May 1903. Amateur (?).

The 'music and poetry' 'art and language' society: an instructive monthly for the English-speaking world. Nos 1–12, 1902.

*Recreative reading. Nos 1–2, 1902.

The Holborn monthly magazine. April 1903–April 1904. Running title of first 5 numbers: Our magazine.

The notion. Paisley. Nos 1–3, May–July 1903. Ed Henry James Reade.

The Avon booklet: a monthly reprint for booklovers of famous contributions to English literature. Vols 1–3 (22 nos in 19 issues nos 3–6 as one), July 1903–March 1905.

Choice stories for quiet hours (Gee's weekly). July 1903–March 1905. Monthly.

The Irish packet. Dublin. Vols 1–13 no 326, 3 Oct 1903–24 Dec 1909.

The armadillo. Edinburgh. Oct 1903–June 1904.

The independent review. Vols 1–12 no 42, Oct 1903–March 1907. Ed Edward Jenks. Continued as Albany review, vols 1–3 no 17, April 1907–Aug 1908. Ed Charles Roden Buxton.

*The interval. 1 only(?) Nov 1903. Ed H. C. Shelley.

London opinion. No 1, 26 Dec 1903 (registration issue). Vol 1–109 no 1421, 24 March 1904–April 1954. Absorbed Easy chair and Today. Incorporated in Men only.

Art and humour: or the sketch. 1903–? Includes Phil May.

Fiction. Nos 1–15, 1903.

Germinal. Nos 1–3, 1903.

The green sheaf. Nos 1–13, 1903–4, With supplements (e.g. to nos 7, 9, 13). Ed Pamela Colman Smith.

The ideal. 1 only, 1903. Ed A. G. Temple. Mainly art.

The Jewish literary annual. 1903–8. Organ of the Union of Jewish Literary Societies.

Nat Gould's annual. 1903–?

Printers' pie. 1903–25. (Christmas nos entitled Winter's pie, 1912–24.) Continued as Sketch book and printers' pie, 1926–8 (winter nos 1925–8/9). Continued as Printers' pie, 1934–40. New series no 1 onwards, 1950 onwards.

The venture: an annual of art and literature. No 1 is known as either 1903 or 1904; no 2, 1905. Ed Laurence Housman and W. Somerset Maugham.

The crank (and open road): an unconventional magazine. Vols 1–5 no 6, Jan 1904–June 1907. Ed F. E. Worland. Continued as The open road, vols 1–12 no 1, July 1907–May 1913. Ed Florence and C. W. Daniel.

The five o'clock: a magazine of these days. Vols 1–2 no 2, April–Sept 1904. New series, vol 1 no 1, Oct 1904.

Occasional papers. Bournemouth, Oxford. Vols 1–3 no 22, April 1904–Feb 1906. Ed T. Beechey Newman.

Dana: a magazine of independent thought. Dublin. Nos 1–12, May 1904–April 1905. Ed 'John Eglinton' [W. K. Magee] and Frederick Ryan.

London record: a weekly illustrated journal of London life, literature, the drama, science, politics and religion. Nos 1–5, 29 June–27 July 1904.

The Celtic review. Edinburgh, London, Dublin. Vols 1–10 no 40, 15 July 1904–June 1916. Consulting editor July 1904–Dec 1914, Donald MacKinnon; acting editor 1904–15, editor 1915–16, Miss E. C. Carmichael (Mrs W. J. Watson).

Discovery: a monthly illustrated magazine of popular science, literature and art. Nos 1–2, Sept–Oct 1904. Ed G. McKenzie.

Fortune: a family paper for cheery folks. 25 Oct 1904–?

The easy chair. No 4, 1 Oct 1904–nos 20, 21, Jan 1905. Merged in London opinion.

The Albany magazine. 1 only, Christmas 1904. Ed E. H. Lacon Watson.

Banba. Dublin. Vols 1–3, 1904–6. Chiefly Erse. Distinguish from journal of same name 1921, see col 1365.

The Edinburgh magazine. Edinburgh. Vols 1–10, 1904–Jan 1909.

Horlick's magazine and home journal for Australia, India and the colonies. Vols 1–3, 1904–5. Ed A. E. Waite. Includes Arthur Machen et al.

Inisfáil, a magazine for the Irish in London. Nos 1–67, 1904–10.

Queer stories from Truth. Tenth [etc] series, 1904–?

*The realm. Nos 1–6. 1904.

The cosy corner novels. Nos 1–53, 11 Feb 1905–10 Feb 1906. Continued as Cosy corner and girls' home paper, nos 54–70, 17 Feb–9 June 1906. Continued as Cosy corner and the ladies' home paper, nos 71–138, 16 June 1906–28 Sept 1907. Continued as Ladies' home paper, cosy corner, nos 139–209, 5 Oct 1907–6 Feb 1909.

The novel magazine. Nos 1–393, April 1905–Dec 1937. Incorporated in Grand magazine.

The acorn: an illustrated quarterly magazine devoted to literature and art. London and Philadelphia. Vols 1–2, Oct 1905–Feb 1906.

The Millgate monthly: a popular magazine devoted to association, education, literature & general advancement. Manchester. Vols 1–40, Oct 1905–May/June 1944. Continued as Millgate and playgoer, July/Aug 1944–May/June 1945. Organ of the People's Entertainment Society. Continued as Playgoer and Millgate, July/Aug 1945–March 1949. Continued as Playgoer, April 1949–Feb 1951. Continued as Millgate and playgoer, new series, April 1951–spring 1953. Replaced by Agenda.

The magazine of fine arts. Vols 1–2, Nov 1905–Aug 1906.

Christian novels. 1905 onwards. Weekly.

The circle: a monthly periodical of art, music and drama. Nos 1–3, [1905–6]. Ed R. Percy and Rose d'Evelyn.

Fannie Eden's penny stories. Nos 1–252, 1905–13.

Smith's magazine. New York. Vols 1–34, 1905–22.

The arrow. Dublin. Nos 1–5, 20 Oct 1906–25 Aug 1909. Commemoration issue, summer 1939. Irregular. First four ed W. B. Yeats.

The laresol review: a quarterly journal to proclaim the unity of religion, science and art in the knowledge and love of God. 1 only, Nov 1906.

The '05 Club magazine. Nos 1–2(?), Nov–Dec 1906. Ed W. Herbert Cox and H. Dallas.

The Shanachie. Dublin. Vols 1–2 nos 1–6, summer 1906–winter 1907.

John Bull. 12 May 1906–Feb 1960. Incorporated Illustrated Oct 1958.

Punch library of humour. 1st ser, vols 1–25, 1906 onwards; 2nd ser, The 'new' Punch library, vols 1–20.

Bibby's annual. Nos 1–13, 1906(?)–1918. Ed Joseph Bibby.

Hermes. Dublin. Nos 1–4, Feb 1907–Feb 1908.

My journal: a monthly journal dealing with all matters of general interest, literature and the drama. Nos 1–20, July 1907–June 1910. Ed Dr Dabbs.

The favourite: sport, satire and the drama. Nos 1–12, 12 Oct–28 Dec 1907. Weekly. Ed Charles Villiers-Chapman.

The busy bee. Birmingham. Nos 1–16, Oct 1907–Jan 1909. Issued by department store, The Bee-Hive.

Good luck magazine: organ of social literature, art handicrafts and home industries. Nos 1–2, Oct, Dec 1907. Continued as Lady workers' magazine, good luck, etc, nos 3–6, March 1908–Dec 1909.

Leisure: to instruct, amuse and interest. 1 only. Oct 1907. Ed G. W. Forth. Sometimes classed as an amateur magazine.

The future. Nos 1–6(?), Nov–Dec 1907. Ed T. W. H. Crosland.

The neolith. Nos 1–4, Nov 1907–Aug 1908. 'Directed' by Mrs E. Nesbit Bland, Grailey Hewitt, F. E. Jackson, and Spencer Pryse.

The new quarterly: a review of science and literature. Vols 1–3 no 10, Nov 1907–May 1910. Ed Desmond MacCarthy.

The 'Rex' review, devoted to commerce, art and literature. 1 only, Dec 1907. Ed Ernest A. Watts.

Transactions of the Theosophical Art-Circle. Nos 1–3, 24 Dec 1907–26 June 1908. Continued as Orpheus: the transactions of the Theosophical Art-Circle, nos 4–5, 1 Oct 1908–Jan 1909. Continued as Orpheus: a quarterly magazine of mystical (of imaginative) art, nos 6–26, April 1909–April 1914. Quarterly. Ed Clifford Bax from no 6.

Daily mail sixpenny novels. Nos 1–153, 1907–12.

The imp. Nos 1–8(?), 1907–?

The story-teller. 1907–? Ed Arthur Spurgeon.

The stormy petrel. 29 Feb–30 May 1908. Ed John Shaw.

The readers' review: a monthly guide to books and reading. Vols 1–3 no 26, Feb 1908–March 1910.

Woman's realm. Nos 1–49, Feb 1908–Jan 1909.

The bibliophile, a magazine and review for the collector, student and general reader. Vols 1–4 no 1 (= nos 1–19), March 1908–Sept 1909.

A broadside. Dundrum, 1908–15; thereafter Dublin. Nos 1–7, 'published' by E. C. Yeats, June 1908–May 1915. New series, nos 1–12, Jan–Dec 1935, ed W. B. Yeats and F. R. Higgins, with Walter Duff as musical editor. New series, nos 1–12, Jan–Dec 1937, ed W. B. Yeats and Dorothy Wellesley.

Red rose novels. Nos 1–23, 31 Oct 1908–3 April 1909. Continued as Red rose magazine, nos 1–11, 10 April–19 June 1909. New series, ser 1–ser 8 no 43, 19 June 1909–21 Dec 1912. Continued as Home weekly, 28 Dec 1912–24 Nov 1923.

The English review. Vols 1–64 no 7, Dec 1908–July 1937. Ed Ford Madox Ford 1908–10; Austin Harrison, March 1910–June 1923; Ernest Remnant, 1923–30; Douglas Jerrold, 1930–6; Derek Walker-Smith, 1936–July 1937. Absorbed Oxford fortnightly, Theatre-craft. Merged in National review. *See* also New English review, 1945, col 1376 below.

The mask. Florence. Vols 1–15, 1908–29. Not pbd May 1915–25 March 1918, 1919–22. Quarterly. Ed E. Gordon Craig.

*The London 'Owl'. Nos 1–25, 1908.

The odd volume: literary and artistic. Nos 1–8, 1908–15; no 9 not pbd?; no 10, 1917. Annual. Ed John G. Wilson and B. W. Matz for National Book Trade Provident Society.

The red magazine (a complete story every month). 2 only. 1908.

The red magazine: stories for all. Vols 1–101, 1908–Sept 1939.

The city: a quarterly magazine written and produced in the first garden city. Letchworth. Vols 1–2 no 4, Jan 1909–Jan 1911. Ed Henry Bryan Binns.

The Sunday (story) journal. Nos 1–27, 8 March–6 Sept 1909. Continued as Story journal, nos 28–287, 13 Sept 1909–31 Aug 1914.

The modern magazine. Liverpool. Nos 1–3? March–May 1909.

The equinox: the official organ of the A∴ A∴—the review of scientific illuminism. London and Detroit. Vol 1 nos 1–10, March 1909–Sept 1913; vol 2 unpublished; vol 3 no 1, March 1919 (Detroit); vol 3 no 2 unpbd; vol 3 nos 3–5, Sept 1936–44. Ed Aleister Crowley; vol 1 no 6 and 7 list Victor Neuberg as subeditor; no 8 announces Crowley's retirement and Mary d'Este Sturgis as editor; no 10 lists Soror Virakam as editor, Lampada Tradam as sub-editor and adds 'there is no such person as Aleister Crowley'.

Nash's magazine. Vols 1–10, April 1909–Sept 1914. Continued as Nash's and Pall Mall magazine, Oct 1914–April 1927. Continued as Nash's magazine, 1927–9. Continued as Nash's–Pall Mall magazine, nos 437–532, Oct 1929–Sept 1937. Incorporated in Good Housekeeping. *See* also Pall Mall magazine, col 1353, above.

The new magazine. Vols 1–44 no 260, April 1909–Dec 1930.

The family journal. Nos 1–1036, 8 May 1909–29. Absorbed The weekly friend.

The weekly tale-teller. Nos 1–356, 8 May 1909–29 April 1916.

The journal of the Poetry Recital Society. No 1, June 1909. Continued as The poetical, vol 1 no 1, Oct 1909. Continued as The poetical gazette, vol 1 nos 2–15, 1910–Dec 1911. Continued as The poetry review, no 1 Jan 1912 onwards. Vol 1 nos 4–7, 15 Oct–31 Dec 1910, pbd as supplements to Academy. Editors include Harold Monro (Jan–Dec 1912), Stephen Phillips (1913–Jan/Feb 1916), Galloway Kyle (1916–?1948), 'John Gawsworth' (T. I. F. Armstrong), Muriel Spark and John Smith. During 1920s sometimes incorporated Poetry of today which was otherwise pbd as a supplement. Monthly, 1912–Dec 1914; bimonthly Jan/Feb 1915–Dec 1954; thereafter quarterly.

Ouseley's magazine for lovers of good literature. Vol 1 nos 1–3, July, Oct, Nov, 1909. New series, vol 1 nos 1–3, Feb–April 1910. Ed W. Burton Baldry.

The serial magazine. Nos 1–6, Aug 1909–Jan 1910.

Everybody's story magazine. Nos 1–26, Nov 1909–Dec 1911. Continued as Everyone's story magazine, nos 27–48, Jan 1912–Oct 1913. Continued as Everyone's, vol 1 nos 1–6, Nov 1913–April 1914. Ed Flora Klickmann (Mrs Henderson-Smith).

The literary and musical review. Vols 1–3 no 1, Nov 1909–summer 1914.

The national monthly: a magazine for everybody. No 1, Nov 1909. Continued as The national magazine, nos 2–6, Dec 1909–May 1910.

The thrush. Vols 1–2 no 2, Dec 1909–May 1910. Ed Noel H. Wills?

The book [second book; third book] of the Poet's Club. 1909, 1911, 1913.

The Englishwoman. Vols 1–49 no 1, 1909–21. Ed Elisina Grant Richards. Includes Galsworthy.

Garnered grain: the poetical annual for 1909 [–?], containing the representative work of contemporary poets, known and unknown.

*Masters of literature. 1909–?

One-story magazine. Nos 1–116?, ?1909–23.

*Parts I have played. Westminster. 1909–20. Dramatic?

Later poems from Punch. 1887–1908. 1909.

The short-story timetable. Eastbourne. 1909–? Ed Bob Stubbs.

Stories for all. Nos 1–29, 1909.

The white magazine. 1909–?

The London library. Nos 1–8, 5 Feb–10 Sept 1910.

*Laughter grim and gay. Manchester. Nos 1–24, 26 Feb–6 Aug 1910.

The literary post. 15 March–Sept 1910.

The tramp: an open air magazine. Vols 1–2 no 6, March 1910–March 1911. Ed Douglas Goldring.

Answers' library. Nos 1–539, March 1910–Sept 1920. New series, nos 1–167, Sept 1920–Dec 1923. Continued as Home stories, nos 1–80, Dec 1923–June 1925. Continued as Women's home stories, nos 81–91, June–Aug 1925. Continued as Women's stories, 92–167, Sept 1925–Feb 1927.

The open window. Vols 1–2 no 12, Oct 1910–Sept 1911.

The vineyard. Vols 1–8 no 6, Oct 1910–Sept 1914. Monthly. New series, nos 1–8, Christmas 1918–Sept 1920. Continued as The country heart: a quarterly magazine, nos 1–8, Jan 1921–Dec 1922. Organ of the Peasant Arts Guild. Ed Maud Egerton King April 1911–Sept 1920.

The family magazine. 1–2, 1910.

Good stories library. 1910–?

My weekly. 1910 onwards.

Tales well told. 1910–?

The scallop-shell: the Pilgrim review. Birmingham. Nos 1–2, Feb, April 1911. Organ of the Pilgrim Players. Ed John Drinkwater.

The Irish review. Dublin. Vols 1–4 no 42, March 1911–Sept/Nov 1914. Monthly, then irregular. Ed Padraic Colum, March 1912–July 1913; Joseph Plunkett Aug 1913–Sept/Nov 1914.

The trifle. Nos 1–8, March 1911–Dec 1912.

The W.K. [West Kensington] magazine. Vols 1–2 no 4, March 1911–April 1912. Ed G. E. Slocombe for the Post Office Savings Bank junior staff. Includes fiction.

Jeannie Maitland's stories and pansy stories. Vols 1–3 no 67, 15 July 1911–19 Oct 1912. Continued as Jeannie Maitland's weekly, vol 4, nos 78–94, 4 Jan–26 April 1913.

The magpie: stories for men and women. Vols 1–5 no 25, Aug 1911–Dec 1914.

Fun and fiction. Vols 1–5, nos 124, 14 Oct 1911–21 Feb 1914. Replaced by The firefly.

Fact and fiction. Nos 1–5, Nov 1911–March 1912.

Rhythm: art, music, literature. Vols 1–2 no 1–14, summer 1911–March 1913. Quarterly to June 1912, then monthly. Superseded by Blue review. Ed John Middleton Murry; assistant editors Katherine Mansfield and M. T. H. Sadler; art editor J. D. Fergusson.

The gateway: a journal of life and literature. Cottingham etc. Vols 1–30 no 361, July 1912–Jan/Aug 1945. Ed James Leatham.

Weekly friend and family stories. Nos 1–126, 12 Oct 1912–6 March 1915. Continued as a newspaper.

Everyman: his life, his work, his books. Nos 1–195, 18 Oct 1912–7 July 1916. Ed Charles Sarolea, pbd by Dent. Title sold and becomes Everyman: a weekly journal of literature and international politics, nos 196–412, 14 July 1916–4 Sept 1920. Belgian supplement Oct 1914–

March 1917. Incorporated Foreign opinion nos 1–16, 24 March–7 July 1915. Registration nos issues 413–657, 11 Sept 1920–2 May 1925 (text changes with each issue). Title reverts to Dent, thus, Everyman: books, drama, music, travel, vols 1–11, nos 1–243, 31 Jan 1929–23 Sept 1933 (first number referring to original Everyman). Ed C. B. Purdom? Title again sold, thus, Everyman: world news weekly, new series, vol 1–2, nos 1–54 (1–20 also numbered 244–63), 29 Sept 1933–5 Oct 1934. Ed Viscountess Dunedin from no 20. New series, nos 1–32, 12 Oct 1934–17 May 1935. Weekly. Title reverts once again to Dent and is incorporated in Bookmark, nos 41–46, as Bookmark and everyman, to cessation of that quarterly in spring 1938. Continued as Everyman: Britain views the world, vol 12, no 244 (also numbered New series 1)–vol 13 no 251/2 [new series, 7/8], August 1946–March/April 1947. First issue states it is a continuation of Dent's pbn which concluded with no 243, 23 Sept 1933. Ed Peter Ratazzi, new series 1–4; Philip Paneth 5–7/8. Monthly. Continued as Everyman, new series, vols 1–3 no 12, March 1952–Christmas 1961. Pbd Dent. References in other bibliographies to a separate Everyman of 1924 seem to be ghost entries.

The antidote. Nos 1–4, 21 Dec 1912–12 June 1915. Irregular. Nos 1–3 ed T. W. H. Crosland; no 4, Lord Alfred Douglas.

Root and branch: a seasonal of the arts. Flansham, Bognor. Vols 1–3 no 3/4, spring 1912–1926? Ed James Guthrie.

Georgian poetry 1911–1912 [–1920–2]. 1912–22. 5 vols. Ed E. M. [Edward Marsh]. Supplementary vol, Recent poetry 1923–33, ed A. Monro, 1933.

Spare moments. 1912–15. Absorbed London journal.

Studies: an Irish quarterly review (of letters, philosophy and science). Dublin. 1912 onwards.

The venture: a magazine of literary interest for civil servants. Bristol. 1912–? Ed E. A. Smith and W. H. Hodges.

The British review. Vols 1–14 no 3, Jan 1913–Aug 1915. Ed R. J. Walker. Supersedes Oxford and Cambridge review.

Dial monthly: a magazine for church women and others. Vols 1–2 no 19, Jan 1913–July 1914. Includes K. Tynan and T. Moult.

Poetry and drama. Vols 1–2 no 8, March 1913–Dec 1914. Ed Harold Monro. Superseded by The monthly chapbook. July 1919.

The new statesman. 12 April 1913 onwards. Absorbed Nation and Athenaeum, and Week-end review of politics, books, the theatre, art and music. Turnstile one: a literary miscellany from the New statesman and nation, ed V. S. Pritchett, 1948.

The blue review: literature, drama, art, music. Nos 1–3, May–July 1913. Ed John Middleton Murry with Katherine Mansfield, M. Sadler. Supersedes Rhythm.

The new freewoman: an individualist review. Nos 1–13, 15 June–15 Dec 1913. Ed Dora Marsden. Superseded by Egoist.

The Scottish nation. Edinburgh. Nos 1–33, Nov 1913–Sept 1917.

Woman's stories. Vols 1–4 no 2, Nov 1913–Nov 1914. Continued as Live stories, vol 4 no 3–?, Dec 1914–?

The cerebralist. 1 only? Dec 1913. Ed E. H. Preston; founded by E. C. Grey.

Bill-o'-Jack's summer annual. Rochdale. 1913, 1914; Christmas annual, 1913, 1914. Ed William Baron.

The 'Golden Hynde'. 1913–? Ed Beatrice Oliver and Marjorie Napier.

Mascot novels. Nos 1–220, 1913?–24?

The penny story-teller and popular magazine. 1913–20.

Smart fiction. Nos 1–614, 1913–24. Incorporated in Smart novels.

Woman's world library. Nos 1–393, 1913–25. New series, nos 1–748, 1925–41. New series, no 1–?, 1941–?

The egoist. Vols 1–6 no 5, 1 Jan 1914–Dec 1919; vol 1 bimonthly, then monthly. Ed Dora Marsden Jan–June 1914, Harriet Weaver 1914–19; assistant editors Richard

Aldington, with Leonard A. Compton-Rickett, 1914–May 1917, with Hilda Doolittle June 1916–May 1917; T. S. Eliot, June 1917–19.

The critic. 1 only? Jan 1914.

Best books [of the year]. Issue for Jan/June 1914, 1915. New series, issue for 1929 [etc], 1931 onwards.

The weekly companion. Vols 1–8 no 44, 14 Feb 1914–29 Oct 1921.

The firefly. Nos 1–51, 28 Feb 1914–13 Feb 1915. See also Fun and fiction, col 1360.

The candid: quarterly review of public affairs—political, scientific, social and literary. Nos 1–6 [= 1–12], Feb 1914–Nov 1916. Conducted by Thomas Gibson Bowles.

New numbers. Ryton. Nos 1–4, Feb–Dec 1914. Solely work of Rupert Brooke, Lascelles Abercrombie, John Drinkwater and W. W. Gibson.

The little review. Chicago, New York, Paris. March 1914–May 1929. Irregular. Ed Margaret C. Anderson (with Jane Heap from 1922–9). Ezra Pound acted as foreign editor, then collaborator, April 1917–Spring 1924.

Short stories: illustrated. Vol 1 nos 1–19. 30 May–3 Oct 1914.

The premier magazine. May 1914–March 1931.

Blast: review of the great English vortex. Nos 1–2, June 1914, July 1915. Ed P. Wyndham Lewis.

My queen magazine. Nos 1–12, 21 July–17 Nov 1914.

Land and water. 22 Aug 1914–23 Sept 1920, when incorporated in The field. Literary editor J. C. Squire. The original of this journal was The sporting gazette, 1 Nov 1862; became Country gentleman 3 Jan 1880 with which the original Land and water (vols 1–79, 27 June 1866–27 May 1905) merged, 3 June 1905. The journal was bought by Neville Foster in 1914 and though full title continued to be The country gentleman and land and water, Land and water was set in prominent type.

The patch-box. 1 only? 1914.

The woman's home magazine. 1914–?

Bruno chap books. New York. Vols 1–3 no 5, Jan 1915–May 1916? Ed Guido Bruno. Special issue on Richard Aldington and the Imagists, 1915.

The cartoon. Nos 1–14, 4 Feb–6 May 1915.

The weekly friend. 13 March 1915–28 April 1917. Merged in The family journal.

The lantern. San Francisco. Vols 1–3, March 1915–March 1918. Monthly. Ed Theodore Bonnet and Edward F. O'Day. Includes much British writing.

*Man. No 1, March 1915. Continued as Superman, April 1915–Oct 1916.

The gypsy. Nos 1–2, May 1915, May 1916.

New Ireland [Irish title: Áf n-Éire]. Dublin. 15 May 1915–1 July 1922. Suspended 18 Oct 1919–3 Dec 1921 (when Old Ireland pbd, see col 1364, below). Weekly.

The trifle: a monthly magazine. Nos 1–2, July–Aug 1915.

New days. Vols 1–2 no 3, Sept 1915–1 April 1916. Ed Louis Vincent.

Signature. Nos 1–3, 4 Oct–1 Nov 1915. Ed John Middleton Murry, D. H. Lawrence, Katherine Mansfield. All contributions by the editors, Katherine Mansfield's being signed Matilda Berry.

The microcosm. Leeds. Vols 1–10, 1915–26. Ed Dorothy Una Ratcliffe. With supplements and anthologies.

* 'Khaki': a monthly magazine. 1915–18.

Poems of today: an anthology. 1915–63. Annual. Pbd by Eng Assoc.

*Tip-top semi-monthly. 1915–?

The palatine review. Oxford. Nos 1–5, Jan/Feb 1916–March 1917. Ed T. W. Earp (?).

The Wipers times. Ypres etc. Vols 1–2 no 4, 12 Feb–20 March 1916. Continued as The 'new church' times, vol 1 nos 1–4, 17 April–29 May 1916. Continued as The Kemmel times, no 1, 3 July 1916. Continued as The Somme-times, no 1, 31 July 1916. Continued as The B.E.F. times, vols 1–2 no 6, 1 Dec 1916–26 Feb 1918. Continued as The 'better times', vol 1 nos 1–2, Nov–

Dec 1918. Facsimile reprints in whole or part, 1918 (2), 1930. The best-known of the many trench journals.

Form: a quarterly of the arts. Vol 1 nos 1–2, April 1916–April 1917. Ed Austin O. Spare with Francis Marsden. Then nominally as monthly, new series vol 1 nos 1–3, Oct 1921–Jan 1922. Ed Austin O. Spare with W. H. Davies.

Future. Nov 1916–Sept 1919. Monthly. Ed Axel Gerfalk and Alfred Hayes. From June 1919 became organ of English Language Union. Superseded by Tomorrow.

The game: an occasional magazine. Ditchling. Vols 1–6 1916–22. Printed and pbd by Douglas Pepler.

The link: an intermediary for literary men. Upton St Leonard. Vols 1–2, 1916–17. Continued as The linkman, Gloucester, vol 3–?, 1918–?

Wheels: an anthology of verse. Oxford, London 1st–6th cycles, 1916–21. Annual. Ed Edith Sitwell.

Art and letters, an illustrated quarterly. Vols 1–3 no 2 (new series), July 1917–Spring 1920. Ed Frank Rutter (with Charles Ginner and Harold Gilman), July–Oct 1917; with Osbert Sitwell, summer 1919–spring 1920.

Poetry: a magazine of verse, comment and criticism. Ventnor?; Alvechurch; from 1920 Birmingham; from 1922 Birmingham and London. Vols 1–8 no 74, 1917(?)–April/May(?) 1925. Continued as Poetry and the play, vols 8 no 75 to 13 no 90, July/Aug 1925–31 (?). Monthly, then bimonthly, then from July/Sept 1926, quarterly and taken over by Empire Poetry League.

An annual of new poetry. 1917–?

The vine: a volume from the Symbolists' press. Birmingham. 1917.

The marionette. Florence. Nos 1–12. April 1918–Aug 1919? Cover title: The marionette to-night...at 12.30. Ed Edward Gordon Craig. Suppl to no 11, Three men of Gotham.

New paths: verse, prose, pictures. 1 only, May 1918. Ed C. W. Beaumont and M. T. H. Sadler.

The bookmark: yesterday, today and tomorrow. 1–6, Aug 1918–July 1920. House journal of Morgan and Scott.

Reveille: devoted to the disabled sailor and soldier. Nos 1–3, Aug 1918–Nov 1919. Ed John Galsworthy; assistant editor C. S. Evans. Continuation of non-literary journal, Recalled to life, June 1917–April 1918.

The Britannia quarterly. Jan 1919 onwards. Organ of the Bank of England Printing Department, St Luke's.

Change: the beginning of a chapter in twelve volumes. Vol 1, Jan 1919, vol 2 Feb 1919–? Ed John Hilton and Joseph Thorp.

The landmark: the monthly magazine of the English-Speaking Union. Vols 1–20 no 5, Jan 1919–May 1938. Continued as The English-speaking world, vol 20 no 6, June 1938 onwards.

Playboy. New York. Jan 1919–July 1924. Not pbd June 1921–Feb 1923. Irregular. Includes D. H. Lawrence and James Joyce.

Arts gazette: drama, music, art, literature. Nos 1–62, 1 Feb 1919–May 1920? New series, nos 1–41, 18 March 1922–24 Feb 1923.

Pan: a journal for saints and cynics. 3 registration issues, Feb 1919. Vols 1–5 no 3, Nov 1919–June 1921. Continued as Pan: the fiction magazine, vols 6 no 1–11 no 35, July 1921–May 1924.

English: for all the lovers of the English language. Vols 1–3, no 32, March 1919–Dec 1921. New series, vol 4, nos 1–5, Jan–May 1922.

The Irish commonwealth. Dublin. Nos 1–3, March–May 1919.

The new world: monthly allied and international review. Vols 1–5 no 27, April 1919–Sept 1921. Continued as Looking forward: a monthly review of world movements. Nos 1–2, Oct–Nov 1921. Incorporated in Beacon.

Coterie. Oxford. Nos 1–7, May-day 1919 to winter 1920/21. Nos 1–6 ed Chaman Lall. No 7 ed Russell Green. Superseded by New Coterie.

Peg's paper. Nos 1–1108, 15 May 1919–10 Aug 1940.

Good luck: the new paper for men and women, incorporating Home companion and Good luck. Nos 1–28, May–Nov 1919.

The owl. Nos 1–3, May, Oct 1919; Nov 1923 (as The winter owl). Ed Robert Graves.

Picture show. 3 May 1919–31 Dec 1960. Stories from film-plays.

Vision: a magazine and review of mysticism. Vols 1–2 no 7, May 1919–July 1920. Ed Dorothy Grenside and Galloway Kyle.

Irish statesman. Vols 1–2 no 52, 28 June 1919–19 June 1920. Then began again as The Irish statesman with which is incorporated Irish homestead, vols 1–14 no 6 15 Sept 1923–12 April 1930. Includes Joyce.

The monthly chapbook. Nos 1–40, July–Dec 1919. Continued as The chapbook, Jan 1920–5. Not pbd July 1921–Jan 1922. 1924 and 1925 complete in single nos for each year. Ed Harold Monro. Superseded Poetry and drama.

Bow bells: the home story paper. Vols 1–12 no 288, Sept 1919–March 1925.

Old Ireland. Glasgow (for Dublin). Vols 1–3 no 49, 18 Oct 1919–3 Dec 1921 (whilst New Ireland suspended, see col 1362, above).

The home mirror (Home mirror novels). Nos 1–207, new series nos 1–133; Oct 1919–April 1926.

The venturer. New series, vols 1–2 no 2, Oct 1919–Nov 1920. Ed Gilbert Thomas.

Week-end novels. Vols 1–33, Oct 1919–Dec 1935.

The London mercury. Vols 1–39 nos 1–234, Nov 1919–April 1939. Monthly. Absorbed The bookman, Jan 1935. Incorporated in Life and letters and today, May 1939. Ed J. C. Squire to Sept 1934, thereafter R. A. Scott-James. See col 1368.

The sovereign magazine. Vols 1–13 no 88, Nov 1919–April 1927. Incorporated in The jolly magazine.

Aengus: an all poetry journal. Dublin. 1 only?, Midsummer 1919. Ed D. L. Kelleher.

Hutchinson's story magazine. 1919–?

John o'London's weekly. Vols 1–63 no 10, 1919–54. New ser 1959–.

Poetry of to-day: the Poetry review new verse supplement. Vols 1–2, 1919–20. Then incorporated in Poetry review. Continued as Poetry of to-day: a quarterly 'extra' of the Poetry review, vols 1–77, June 1924–47.

Theatre-craft. 1–5, 1919–21, undated. Ed Norman Macdermott, Herman Ould, Horace Shipp. Absorbed by English review.

The violet novels. Nos 1–340, 1919(?)–33(?).

Voices. Vols 1–5 no 4. 1919–21. Irregular. Ed Thomas Moult.

Ye Pepys journal: on the fine arts, anecdotes, literature. 1919–?

Short stories. March 1920–Jan 1955.

Poesia. Milan. Nos 1–7/9, 15 April 1920–Dec 1920? Ed Mario Dessy. Includes James Joyce.

Hillmn [sic]. Nos 1–5, July 1920–July 1921. Ed Ernest Collings and Vera Millar.

Outward bound: an illustrated monthly magazine. Vols 1–4 no 42, Oct 1920–March 1924. Includes Drinkwater.

The apple—of beauty and discord. Vols 1–2 no 2 (6 issues). 1920–2. Quarterly. Ed Herbert Furst.

Green and gold: a magazine of fiction. Waterford. 1920–?

The Liverpool chapbook. Liverpool. 1 only 1920.

The magazine of the Buxton Literary Society. Nos 1–4, 1920/1–4.

Music and letters. Taunton. 1920–51 (?). Editors include Eric Blom. Index vols 1–15, 1920–34.

A book [second book, third book] of poems by the Poet's fellowship. Bristol. 1920–2.

The quorum. 1 only. ?1920.

Reader's forum. Liverpool. 1920–?

The country heart: a quarterly magazine. Nos 1–8, Jan/March 1921–Oct/Dec 1922. Superseded The vineyard.

The old lady [of Threadneedle street]. March 1921

onwards. Bank of England house journal with much creative writing.

Banba. Dublin. Vols 1–3 no 3, May 1921–Aug 1922.

Now and then. Nos 1–76 [64–76 = wartime issues 1–13], Sept 1921–autumn 1944. New series, 1–?, Sept 1948–? Selections from first fifty issues in Then and now [sic], 1935.

Fanfare: a musical causerie. Nos 1–7, 1 Oct 1921–1 Jan 1922. Ed Leigh Henry. Resuscitated by Musical mirror, Dec 1930. Fortnightly.

The beacon. Oxford, Tunbridge Wells etc. Vols 1–3, no 32, Oct 1921–June 1924. New series, nos 1–2, Feb– March 1925. Ed E. R. Appleton. Incorporated New world, 1919–21.

Broom: an international magazine of the arts. Rome, Berlin, New York, London. Vols 1–6 no 1, Nov 1921– Jan 1924. Monthly. Ed Harold Loeb with Alfred Kreymborg, Nov 1921–Feb 1922, with Slater Brown, Matthew Josephson and Malcolm Cowley, Jan 1924. American editor Lola Ridge; London editor Cecil Palmer.

The forum. Nos 1–9/10, Nov 1921–Aug 1922. Ed C. F. Holland and W. R. Marshall.

Peg's companion. Nos 1–572, Nov 1921–Oct 1932.

Gaiety: a magazine of humour. Vols 1–11 no 5, 1921–7. Annual for 1924.

Lloyd's Saturday stories. Nos 1–44, 1921–2.

The tyro: a review of the arts of painting, sculpture and design. Nos 1–2, 1921–2. Ed P. Wyndham Lewis.

The yellow magazine 1921–?

Youth: the authors' magazine. Nos 1–3, 15 Feb–June 1922. Distinguish from journal of same title, 1920–34, Cambridge University.

Good housekeeping. London. Vols 1–15, March 1922–Aug 1929. Distinguish from New York jnl, col 1352. Twelve best stories, selected Alice M. Head, 1932.

The adelphi magazine. 1 only, June 1922. Ed Henry Danielson; decorations by C. Lovat Fraser. Distinguish from The adelphi, June 1923.

The violet magazine. Nos 1–309, July 1922–Nov 1939. Merged in Girls' friend library.

The pocket magazine. 26 Aug 1922–?

The Scottish chap book. Aug 1922–Oct 1923. Ed 'Hugh MacDiarmid'.

Letters: a journal of correspondence and debate. 1 only?, 20 Sept 1922. Conducted by J. L. Hornibrook.

The criterion. Vols 1–18 no 71, Oct 1922–Jan 1939 (Jan 1926–Jan 1927 as The new criterion; May 1927–March 1928 as The monthly criterion). Ed T. S. Eliot. Quarterly, with irregularities. Criterion miscellany, 1929–? Index compiled E. A. Baker 1967.

The golden hind: a magazine of art and literature. Vols 1–2 no 8, Oct 1922–July 1924. Ed Clifford Bax and Austin O. Spare.

The hamyarde. Vol 1 no 1, Oct 1922; vol 2 no 1 [sic] Nov 1922. Ed Anthony Praga with Charles Beard and George Hill.

The green magazine. Vols 1–5 no 30, Nov 1922–Dec 1933.

The maskerpiece: an educational magazine profusely illustrated, showing the link of literature and drama of all ages in the mask and the mime. Nos 1–2, Nov 1922, Feb 1923. (Three issues a year proposed.) Ed Sivori Levi.

The best of the year: speeches, stories, essays, poems etc. 1922–?

The best poems of 1922 [–43]. Vols 1–22, 1923–44. Ed Thomas Moult.

The best short stories of 1923[–1933]: I, English, 1924–33. Then amalgamated with The best short stories of 1922 [–1933]: II, American as The best short stories 1934 [–1939]: English and American, 1934–9. Ed Edward J. O'Brien.

The corner magazine. Nos 1–81, 1922–9.

Dublin opinion: the national humorous journal of Ireland. 1922–?

Georgian stories 1922[–1927]. 1922–7. No vol for 1923.

Poems from Punch 1909–20. 1922.

Reader's digest. Pleasantville, NY; London. Nos 1–8 [9–16 omitted in numbering], no 17 [= New series, no 1] onwards, 1922 onwards.

True story magazine. 1922–?

The twenty story magazine. 1922–?

Cassell's weekly, concerning men, women and books. Nos 1–23, 21 March 1923–24 Oct 1923. Ed Newman Flower. Incorporated in T.P.s weekly as T.P's and Cassell's weekly, 31 Oct 1923–17 Sept 1927.

The Scottish nation. Montrose. Vols 1–2 no 8, 8 May– 25 Dec 1923. Ed 'Hugh MacDiarmid'.

Orpheus: the magazine of distinction. Paisley. May 1923– 4th year, no 6 [= March/April 1927]. Ed Godfrey Wengenroth. Began as amateur journal; increases in size from May 1924.

The adelphi. Vols 1–4, June 1923–June 1927. Continued as New adelphi, vols 1–3 no 4, Sept 1927–June/Aug 1930. Continued as Adelphi, new series, Oct 1930–55. Ed John Middleton Murry, June 1923–June/Aug 1930; July (?) 1931–Sept 1938; July 1941–8 Max Plowman, Oct 1930–June 1931; Oct 1938–May 1941; Richard Rees, Oct 1930–June 1931.

Germinal. Nos 1–2, July 1923 and 1924.

Stories: a magazine devoted to fiction. Nos 1–2, July, Aug 1923.

The Dublin magazine. Dublin. Vols 1–3 no 1, Aug 1923– Aug 1925. Not pbd Sept–Dec 1925. New series, vols 1– 33, Jan 1926–58. Monthly. Ed S. O'Sullivan.

Eve's own stories (Eve's own). Nos 1–831, Oct 1923–Sept 1939. Incorporated in Woman's illustrated.

The flying horse. Vol 1 nos 1–2, Oct 1923–March 1924. New series, nos 1–2, 1927. Ed T. W. H. Crosland.

Life and letters. Nos 1–10, Nov 1923–Aug 1924.

The Bermondsey book. Vols 1–7 no 2, Dec 1923–March/ May 1930. Quarterly. Ed Frederick Heath.

Pam's paper. Nos 1–179, 1 Dec 1923–14 May 1927. Continued as Up-to-date, vol 1 nos 1–8, 21 May–9 July 1927.

The choice story magazine. Nos 1–171, 1923–6.

Down west: being the year book of the West Country Essay Club. 1923–4.

Joy street poems. Oxford. 1–12 (?), 1923–34. Includes Rose Fyleman, Marian Allen, Edith Sitwell.

Sport and fiction: monthly magazine. 1923–?

Vision: a literary quarterly. Sydney. Nos 1–4, 1923. Ed John (= Jack) Lindsay, Frank C. Johnson and K. Slessor.

The green quarterly: an Anglo-Catholic magazine. Vols 1– 11 no 4, Jan 1924–Oct 1934. Continued as New green quarterly, vols 1–3 no 2, Jan 1935–spring 1937.

The transatlantic review. Paris. Vols 1–2 no 6, Jan 1924– Jan 1925. Ed Ford Madox Ford.

The decachord. March/April 1924–? Not pbd 1926–Jan 1927 and March–June 1931. Ed to Jan/Feb 1931, Charles John Arnell; thereafter Philippa Hole. Bi-monthly. Ran at least to 1947.

The voyager. Bristol. Nos 1–4, March–June 1924. Ed S. W. Smith.

The Scots magazine. Glasgow. April 1924 onwards.

Woman. Vols 1–11 no 4, April 1924–July 1929.

The merry mag. Nos 1–68, July 1924–Feb 1930.

To-morrow. Dublin. Nos 1–2, Aug–Sept 1924.

New leader reprints. Nos 1–2, 1924; New leader book, nos 1–2, 1925–6.

Weekly liar. Birmingham. Nos 1–8 (?), 1924–5. A 'spoof' journal.

The calendar of modern letters. Vols 1–4 no 2, March 1925–July 1927 (April 1926–July 1927 as The calendar). Monthly. Ed Edgell Rickword, Douglas Garman and Bertram Higgins. Selections in Towards standards of criticism, ed F. R. Leavis, 1933.

Contemporary poetry. Dublin. Nos 1–8, March 1925–7 (from spring 1926 as Contemporary poetry and song). Ed G. Edmund Lobo.

The Parnassian. March 1925 onwards. Organ of the Calder Valley Poets' Society.

Le navire d'argent. Paris. Nos 1–12, June 1925–May 1926. Ed Adrienne Monsieur and Sylvia Beach. Much English writing, including T. S. Eliot.

The outpost: a monthly magazine of literature, art & national life. Nos 1–5, June–Dec 1925.

Standard stories: incorporating The smart set, nos 1–11, July 1925–May 1926.

The sunny mag. Vols 1–16 no 94, July 1925–April 1933.

Voice and verse. Nos 1–4, Aug 1925–Oct 1926.

Two worlds: literary quarterly devoted to the increase of the gaiety of nations. New York. Vols 1–2 no 8, Sept 1925–June 1927. Ed Samuel Roth; contributing editors: Arthur Symons, Ezra Pound, Ford Madox Ford, Paul Morand.

Argus: political, financial, satirical and theatrical. Nos 1–15, Oct 1925–Dec 1926.

The complete novel weekly. Nos 1–763, 7 Nov 1925–15 June 1940.

The new coterie: a quarterly of literature and art. 1–6, Nov 1925–summer/autumn 1927. Supersedes Coterie.

This quarter. Paris, Milan, Monte Carlo. Vols 1–5 no 2; spring 1925–Oct/Dec 1932. Ed Ernest Walsh 1925–6; Ethel Moorhead 1925–7; Edward W. Titus 1929–32.

The bookmark nos 1–46, spring 1925–spring 1938. Incorporates Everyman from no 41, summer 1935. Quarterly. See col 1360; see same title, col 1363.

Bristol Poets Fellowship quarterly. Nos 1–4, 1925–6.

*First flights. Paisley. 1 only, 1925. Amateur journal?

G.K.C. [G. K. Chesterton]: a rectorial newspaper. Nos 1–10, 1925.

*The modern literary course. 1925(?)–?

The new decameron. Oxford . Vol 4 = 1925.

Two worlds monthly: devoted to the increase of the gaiety of nations. New York. Vols 1–3 no 4, 1925–Sept 1927. Ed Samuel Roth.

*Casual letters. Jan 1926–July 1930.

The argosy: the world's best stories. June 1926–Jan 1940. Continued as Argosy of complete stories, Feb 1940 onwards.

All-story magazine. Nos 1–16, Oct 1926–Jan 1928.

Hutchinson's best story magazine. 1926–?

The enemy: a review of art and literature. 1–3, Jan 1927–first quarter 1929. Not pbd Oct 1927–Dec 1928. Ed P. Wyndham Lewis.

The Panton magazine: literature, art, music, drama. Nos 1–4, Jan/March–Oct/Dec 1927. Organ of the Panton arts club.

transition. Hague and Paris. Nos 1–27, April 1927–spring 1938; 1948–50(?). Suspended summer 1930–March 1932. Irregular. Ed Eugene Jolas and Elliot Paul; and, in contributory capacities, Robert Sage and from summer 1928 Matthew Josephson, Harry Crosby.

The happy magazine. Vols 1–36 no 214. New series 1–?, June 1927–?

The Heaton review: a northern miscellany of art and literature. Vols 1–7, June 1927–34.

The complete storyteller. Nos 1–26, 23 July 1927–14 Jan 1928.

Close-up. Territet, Switzerland. Vols 1–10 no 4, July 1927–Dec 1933. Ed Kenneth Macpherson and Bryher, later assisted by Oswell Blakeston. Articles on influence of cinema on literature. Also title of magazine for film-goers, 1947–?

The Merseyside home journal. Liverpool. Nos 1–4, Aug–Nov 1927. Continued as The home journal, no 5–? 1927–?

My story weekly. Nos 1–31, 15 Oct 1927–12 May 1928.

The outline: books, popular science, and things of to-day. Vols 1–4 no 85, Nov 1927–29 June 1929. Weekly. Incorporated in John o' London's weekly.

The exile. Dijon. Spring 1927–autumn 1928. Semi-annual. Ed Ezra Pound. Includes Yeats.

The countryman. 1927 onwards. Ed J. W. Robertson Scott. The countryman anthology, ed John Cripps, 1962.

The golden book magazine. New York. Nos 1–10, 1927–8. Includes English writing.

The jongleur, a quarterly sheaf of verse. Bradford. Nos 1–59, spring 1927–autumn/winter 1955 [1956]. Ed Alberta Vickridge.

Emotionism. 1 only Feb 1928. Includes Peggy Ashcroft.

*The Chelsea review. Nos 1–2, March–April 1928.

The free critic. Vol 1 nos 1–12, March 1928–Feb 1929. Continued as The critic, vol 2 nos 1–2, March–April 1929.

The speaking of poetry: the bulletin of the Verse-speaking Fellowship. Vols 1–10, April 1928–Jan 1931. Continued as Good speech, vols 11–49, April 1931–July/Aug 1940. Continued as News-letter to members, vol 1–41, Jan 1941–July 1948. Continued as Speech news, vol 91 (resumption of numbering from 1928), Sept 1948 onwards.

Life and letters. Vols 1–12 no 64, June 1928–April 1935. Ed Desmond MacCarthy, June 1928–Dec 1933/Feb 1934; Hamish Miles, March–Aug 1934; R. Ellis Roberts, Oct 1934–April 1935. Continued as Life and letters to-day, vols 13–45 no 94, Sept 1935–June 1945 and as Life and letters vols 46–65 no 154, July 1945–June 1950. Ed Robert Herring 1934–50, with Petrie Townshend 1935–spring 1937. Absorbed London Mercury and Bookman May 1939 (see also Today, col 1353, and compare same title, col 1366).

Prize story magazine. Dunellen NJ. July 1928–? American, also issued in Britain.

The London Aphrodite. Nos 1–6, Aug 1928–July 1929. Ed Jack Lindsay and P. R. Stephensen.

Onward. Nos 1–2, Sept, Oct 1928.

The venture. Cambridge. Nos 1–6, Oct 1928–June 1930. Ed Anthony Blunt to June 1929, H. Romilly Fedden and Michael Redgrave Nov 1928–June 1930.

Experiment. Cambridge. Nos 1–7, Nov 1928–spring 1931. Irregular. Ed William Empson to May 1929, J. Bronowski and Hugh Sykes Davies Nov 1929–spring 1931.

The literary review. Bedford. 1928–?

London novels. 1928–?

Soldiers' tales. 1928–?

Verse and song. Nos 1–6, 1928. Incorporated in Writer's own magazine.

World stories. 1928?

Tambour. Paris. Nos 1–8, Feb 1929–Jan 1930. Irregular. In English and French.

The echo: a quarterly review of American and British college literature. Hamilton NY. Ed Arthur B. Berthold March 1929–Sept 1930, George Scott Gleason autumn 1930–autumn 1932. Superseded by Connecticut echo, spring 1933.

The realist: a journal of scientific humanism. Vols 1–2 no 4, April 1929–Jan 1930(?). Ed Archibald Church and Gerald Heard. Includes Arnold Bennett, Rebecca West, John Galsworthy.

*The quaint quarterly. 1–25, Easter 1929–Nov 1938. Supplement: Occasional news sheet, Aug 1937.

*The English magazine. Vols 1–3 no 25, May 1929–Jan 1932.

Novelty: a Leeds monthly magazine. Leeds. Vols 1–2 no 4, Sept 1929–June 1930.

The bookworm. Nos 1–5, Sept/Oct 1929–May/June 1930. Incorporates Onward.

Bifur. Paris. Nos 1–8, 1929–30. Includes Joyce.

The Capuchin annual. Dublin. 1929 onwards.

The new forget-me-not. 1929. Supersedes The annual. Superseded by New keepsake 1931.

The plain dealer...the smallest critical journal in the world. East Grinstead. 1929–?

Poetry: past and present. Vol 1 no 1, 1928–9.

The poets on the poets. 1929–?

Purpose: a quarterly magazine. Vols 1–11, 1929–40 (?). Ed John Marlow 1929, W. T. Symons 1930–40 (with Philip Mairet 1930–5, and A. Desmond Hawkins 1936–40).

Songs for sixpence: a series of single new poems by young Cambridge poets. Nos 1–6, 1929.

Songs from the dramatists. Norwich. 1929–?

Treasuries of modern prose. 1929–?

The window: a quarterly magazine. Nos 1–4, Jan–Oct 1930. Ed Eric Partridge and Bertram Ratcliffe. Similarly titled journal, ed J. Sankey, nos 1–8, 1951–5.

Experimental cinema. Philadelphia. Nos 1–5, Feb 1930–June 1934(?). Irregular. Ed David Platt, Lewis Jacobs, Seymour Stern, Alexander Brailovsky, and Barnet Braver-Mann. Influence of film on literature.

*Cullen's home magazine. Vols 1–3 no 5, Feb 1930–May 1932? Issued by the store of that name.

The week-end review of politics, books, the theatre, art and music. Vols 1–8 no 200, 15 March 1930–6 Jan 1934. Incorporated in New statesman.

The magazine of today: an illustrated review of modern life and literature. Nos 1–5, May–Sept 1930. Incorporated in Today and tomorrow.

Carmina. Westcliff-on-Sea. Nos 1–12, Aug 1930–2. Irregular. Ed Maurice Leahy.

The black hat: an unusual review. Nos 1–8, Sept 1930–Oct 1932. Ed D. Thompson and H. Kelly.

The modern Scot (the organ of the Scottish renaissance). Dundee. Vols 1–6 no 4, spring 1930–Jan 1936. Ed J. H. Whyte. Amalgamated with Scottish standard to form The outlook, Edinburgh, vol 1 nos 1–10, April 1936–Jan 1937. Selections: Towards a new Scotland, ed J. H. Whyte, London 1935.

Awake! 1930. Organ of the Writers' International, British section.

The Clarion: politics, books, drama. 1930–?

*Contributor's journal. Cambridge. 1930–?

The gate. 1–10, 1930–3.

*Hush. Vols 1–3 no 13, 1930–1.

*Motley. Oxford. 1930.

Songs from the ship and castle. Bristol. 1930. Continued as More songs from the ship and castle, 1931–? Annual.

Wideawake magazine. 1930–?

The penny-farthing. Vols 1–3, Jan 1931–Dec 1933.

The twentieth century. Vols 1–6 no 36, March 1931–4. Organ of The Promethean society. Ed John Randell Evans. See also Nineteenth century, col 1351.

The island: a quarterly. Nos 1–4, June–Dec 1931. [Nos 2 and 3 as one, Sept 1931). Ed Josef Bard.

Soma. Nos 1–5, June 1931–4. Pbd by K. S. Bhat.

London forum. 1 only, July 1931. Ed Harold Kelly and Bonar Thompson.

Nan's novels. Vols 1–3 no 65. 17 Oct 1931–7 Jan 1933.

Home novels. Nos 1–40, Nov 1931–Aug 1932.

*The critic. Bournemouth. 1931.

Literature of the world revolution. Nos 1–3, 1931. Continued as International literature, 3 issues in 1932, 6 in each of 1933 and 1934; thereafter 12 annually to 1945 no 19. 150 issues in all. (From 1946 as Soviet literature and restricted thereto.) Organ of the International Union of Revolutionary Writers. British contributors include Sean O'Casey, Jack Lindsay, Richard Aldington, James Hanley, John Lehmann.

The melody. Cambridge. Vols 1–2 no 2, 1931(?)–33. Organ of the National Poetry Circle. Incorporated in Rejection.

Mutt's mutterings. 1931–? Organ of the Maidenhead Mutts. Includes de la Mare, G. K. Chesterton.

The new keepsake. 1 only. 1931. Decorations by Rex Whistler.

New melody. Culmstock etc. 1931 onwards. Ed Arthur L. Woolf.

Poet's Guild quarterly. Buckhurst Hill. 1931–? Ed Ruth Elliott?

*Static. Nos 1–2 [or 3?], 1931(?). Ed Richard Kersey, with T. J. B. Spencer.

The new English weekly: a review of public affairs, literature and the arts. Vols 1–14 no 11, 21 April 1932–22 Dec 1938. Amalgamated with New age and continued as New English weekly and the new age, vol 14 no 12/

13–vol 35 no 24, 5 Jan 1939–22 Sept 1949. Ed A. R. Orage (and Philip Mairet?).

Scrutiny. Cambridge. Vols 1–19, May 1932–Oct 1953. Quarterly. Eds May–Sept 1932, L. C. Knights and Donald Culver; Dec 1932–June 1933, L. C. Knights, Donald Culver, F. R. Leavis and Denys Thompson; Sept 1933–June 1939, D. W. Harding, L. C. Knights, F. R. Leavis, and Denys Thompson; Sept 1939–Oct 1941, D. W. Harding, L. C. Knights, and F. R. Leavis; Jan 1942–spring 1947, D. W. Harding, L. C. Knights, F. R. Leavis, and W. H. Mellers; Sept 1947–summer 1948, L. C. Knights, F. R. Leavis, H. A. Mason, and W. H. Mellers; Dec 1948–Oct 1953, L. C. Knights, H. A. Mason, and F. R. Leavis; 1963 (vol 20). Retrospect by F. R. Leavis and indexes by M. Hussey pbd as vol 20, 1963. (Journal of same name with subtitle 'digest of controversy' pbd Jan and Feb 1948.)

'Cheerio!': a magazine produced and published by the unemployed clerical workers in the Occupational Centres of Birkenhead. Birkenhead. Vols 1–2 no 5, Dec 1932–March 1934.

Service in life and work: a quarterly review. Vols 1–8 no 32, spring 1932–winter 1939. Organ of the Rotary International Assoc for Great Britain and Ireland. Ed W. W. Blair-Fish. Includes John Masefield, J. B. Priestley, Hilaire Belloc.

Cinema quarterly. Edinburgh. Vols 1–3 no 4, autumn 1932–summer 1935; vol 3 no 2, winter 1934 as winter 1935. Continued as World film news and television progress, vols 1–3 no 4, April 1936–Aug 1938. Continued as See, world film news, vol 3 nos 5–7, Sept–Nov 1938. Ed Norman Wilson. Articles on relation of film to literature.

The bare aspect: a magazine for some who think differently. Nos 1–18, 1932–5. Ed Alex R. Zoccola.

Dope. Nos 1–2, 1932. Ed Bernard Causton.

The Jewish review; a quarterly of Jewish life and literature. Vols 1–8, 1932–4.

Mascot novelettes. Nos 1–62, 1932–3.

Poets in brief. Cambridge. 1932–?

A Punch anthology. 1932. Compiled Guy Boas.

Rejection: a magazine of literary and general interest. Vols 1–2 no 11, 1932–4. Absorbed Melody.

New verse. Nos 1–32. New series, vol 1 nos 1 and 2, Jan 1933–May 1939. Ed Geoffrey Grigson et al. 34 numbers in 32?

The poetry quarterly: devoted to British and American poetry and drama. Nos 1–6, Jan 1933–spring 1934. Last issue as Poetry quarterly and dramatic review. Ed William Kingston Fudge, Jan–July 1933; George Whybrow autumn 1933–spring 1934.

Seed. Nos 1–2? Jan–April/July 1933. Ed Herbert Jones and Oswell Blakeston.

David: an international review of politics and literature. Nos 1–3, March–May 1933. Ed A. J. Henderson, Allan N. Taylor and Erik Warman.

Grangewood magazine. March 1933. 1 only?

New Britain, a weekly organ of national renaissance. Vols 1–3 no 64, 24 May 1933–8 Aug 1934. Ed C. B. Purdom.

Lovat Dickson's magazine: new short stories. Vols 1–4, Nov 1933–June 1935. Ed P. Gilchrist Thompson, Nov 1933–Sept 1934, Lovat Dickson Oct 1934–March 1935, L. A. G. Strong, April–June 1935. Monthly.

The survey. Nos 1–3, Nov 1933–Jan 1934. Monthly.

The wanderer. Larling. Nos 1–11/12, Dec 1933–Nov 1934. Ed John Middleton Murry.

Contemporaries and makers. Cambridge. Spring 1933. Continued as Contemporaries, summer 1933–spring 1934. Ed John Kaestlin. Quarterly.

Poetry studies. Vols 1–6 no 22, spring 1933–?1939. Replaced by Poetry quarterly, Dawlish, 1939–53. Ed Katherine Hunter Coe and E. M. Channing-Renton.

The Evening Standard book of best short stories. 1933–?

The masquerade. Eton college. 1 only? 1933.

Nursery rhymes: Daily Express living models series. 16 vols, 1933.

The oracle: a story paper for women. 1933 onwards. Incorporated Poppy's paper. Described in Writers' and artists' year book, 1945, as aimed at 'women readers of the working class'.

Storm: stories of the struggle (A magazine of socialist fiction). Nos 1–3, Feb–(?) 1933.

Chanticleer. New York. Jan 1934–? Ed Jacob Hauser.

*The fight against superstition, clericalism and cultural revolution. Nos 1–4, Jan(?)–Dec 1934.

Medley: a magazine for odd moments. Vols 1–6, Jan 1934–9.

Rejected mss. Oxford. No 1, Jan 1934. Continued as Rejected mss and other, no 2, Dec 1934. Ed N. F. Hidden, H. D. Willcock, N. R. Cohn.

The monologue. Nos 1–24, Feb 1934–Feb 1935. Ed Lyn Irvine.

New stories. Oxford. Feb/March 1934–April/May 1936. Bimonthly. Editorial board: Edward J. O'Brien, Arthur Calder-Marshall, Hamish Miles, I. A. Pavey and Geoffrey West.

The Colosseum. Vols 1–5 no 22, March 1934–July/Sept 1939. Quarterly. Ed Bernard Wall.

Out of bounds: against reaction in the public schools. Nos 1–4, March/April 1934–June 1935. Subtitle varies. Ed Esmond Romilly.

Viewpoint: a critical review. Croydon. 12 April–Sept 1934. Ed D. A. Willis? Absorbed by The left review.

The European quarterly. May 1934–Feb 1935. Ed Edwin Muir and Janko Lavrin.

The left review. Vols 1–3 no 16, Oct 1934–May 1938. Organ of the Writers' International, British Section. Ed Montagu Slater, Amabel Williams-Ellis, T. H. Wintringham et al Oct 1934–5, Edgell Rickword 1936–June 1937, Randall Swingler July 1937–May 1938. Absorbed Viewpoint. New left review, 1960 onwards.

Satire and burlesque. Vols 1–2 no 5, Oct 1934–July/Aug 1935.

Caravel: an American quarterly. Majorca. Summer 1934–March 1936? Ed Sydney Salt and Jean Rivers (with Charles Henri Ford, March 1936); English editor Oswell Blakeston. Includes Dylan Thomas, Edith Sitwell.

The chap book: the magazine of the Glasgow Literary Club. Nos 1–4, 1934–5.

Fact and fiction: a magazine of short stories. 1934–?

Mr Punch's limerick book. 1934.

The year's poetry. 1934–8. Ed Denys Kilham Roberts, Geoffrey Grigson, John Lehmann, Gerald Gould.

Woman's hour. Nos 1–22, Jan–June 1935.

The Scottish standard. Glasgow. Vol 1 nos 1–13, Feb 1935–Feb 1936. Amalgamated with The modern Scot to form Outlook (see also cols 1369 and 1372).

Eye: the Martin Lawrence gazette (gazette of Socialist literature). Nos 1–9(?), Sept 1935–spring 1938 (?). Pbd by Lawrence and Wishart.

New Scotland (Alba nuadh). Glasgow. Nos 1–9, 12 Oct–7 Dec 1935.

*The rocket. Bath. 26 Oct 1935–22 Oct 1938. Then united with Target.

Comment. Vols 1–3 no 58, 7 Dec 1935–30 Jan 1937. Weekly. Selections: The first comment treasury, ed Sheila Macleod and Victor B. Neuburg, 1937. Incorporates Poet's corner.

Axis: a quarterly review of contemporary 'abstract' painting and sculpture. Nos 1–8, 1935–winter 1937. Ed Myfanwy Evans.

Epilogue: a critical summary. Deyá Majorca. 1–4, 1935–8(?). Annual. Ed Laura Riding and Robert Graves. (No 4 is a monograph, The world and ourselves, by Laura Riding, pbd in London.)

Men only. 1935 onwards. Additional series: Men only at sea, 1940; in sport, 1943; in the army, 1942; in the navy, 1942; A stag party with men only, 1955. Absorbed Strand magazine 1950 and London opinion 1954.

The present age: a monthly journal. Vols 1–4, 1935–9.

Programme. Oxford. Nos 1–23, 1935–6. Irregular. Ed George Sayer, Venonica Ward, Alan Hodge, Kenneth Allott et al.

The wayfarer. Birmingham. 1935–? Ed C. W. Hervey.

Woman's sphere. 1935–?

Young authors and artists of 1935 [1936–?] 1935–? Ed Stephen King-Hall.

Janus. Nos 1–2, Jan, May 1936. Ed Reginald Hutchings, John Royston Morley and John Mair.

Fords and bridges: an Oxford and Cambridge magazine. Oxford. Vols 1–5 no 2, 4 Feb 1936–May 1939.

Outlook: incorporating The modern Scot and The Scottish standard. Nos 1–10, April 1936–Jan 1937.

Contemporary poetry and prose. Nos 1–10, May 1936–autumn 1937. Ed Roger Roughton. Also *Contemporary poetry and prose editions, 1936–?

The fig tree: a Douglas social credit quarterly review. Nos 1–12, June 1936–? Includes Ezra Pound, Eric Gill.

The poet. Balerno. July/Aug 1936 onwards. Bimonthly. Ed H. C. 'Harry Crouch' [G. L. R. Wilson].

Prose. Nos 1–4, Aug–Nov 1936.

New writing. Nos 1–5, spring 1936–spring 1938. New series, nos 1–3, autumn 1938–Christmas 1939. Continued as Folios of new writing, nos 1–4, spring 1940–autumn 1941. Amalgamated with Daylight and continued as New writing and daylight, nos 1–7, 1942–6. Associated with Penguin new writing from 1940. Selections: English stories from new writing, 1951; Poems from new writing, 1936–46, 1946; Pleasures of new writing, 1952. Ed John Lehmann.

Daily Express fiction library. 1936–?

Daily Express library of famous books. 1936–?

English: the magazine of the English Assoc. 1936 onwards. Three a year. Includes literature and criticism.

*Leisure: the quality magazine for women. 1936–?

The literary review. Nos 1–10? March–Dec 1936.

Loquela mirabilis. Langford (Bristol). Vols 1–2 no 1, 1936–7.

The right review. Nos 1–16, Oct 1936–May 1946. Ed Count Potocki of Montalk. With special supplement, 1 copy only, on vellum, for the BM.

The west-country magazine. Dawlish. Vols 1–4 no 13, Winter 1935/6–9.

Twentieth-century verse. Nos 1–18, Jan 1937–June/July 1939. Ed Julian Symons.

Arena: a quarterly review. Nos 1–4 April 1937–Jan/March 1938. Ed Martin Turnell. Distinguish from journal of same name edited by Randall Swingler, col 1379.

The high hatter. Vols 1–3, May–June 1937.

Lilliput. Vols 1–46 no 7, July 1937–July 1960. Incorporated in Men only. Nos 1–6 reissued, 1938; nos 3–6 reissued as The Lilliput pocket omnibus, 1938. Selections: The bedside Lilliput 1950; Good to read (For good reading): stories out of Lilliput magazine. 4 pts, 1937.

Night and day. Nos 1–26, 1 July–23 Dec 1937.

The booster: a monthly magazine in French and English. Paris. As a little magazine from Sept 1937–Easter 1939 (from April 1938 as Delta). Ed Alfred Perlès, Lawrence Durrell, Henry Miller, William Saroyan et al; assisted by Anais Nin, Hilaire Hiler, Patrick Evans et al.

The quiet hour. Birmingham. Nos 1–12, Nov 1937–Oct 1938. Ed James Bailey.

Verve: an artistic and literary quarterly. Paris. Vols 1–2, Dec 1937–Sept/Nov 1940; 1943–? In English and French.

Poet anthology. 1937–?; Poet supplement, 1939–48.

Plastique. Paris, New York. Nos 1–5, spring 1937–9(?). In English, French and German.

Wales (a literary journal). Llangadock. Nos 1–11, summer 1937–winter 1939/40. Wartime broadsheet, Lalnybri, 1 only?, 1940 (?). New series, as Wales, the national magazine, vols 1–9 no 31, July 1943–Oct 1949. Ed Keidrych Rhys summer 1937–March 1939 (with Dylan

Thomas, March 1939). Ed Nigel Heseltine Aug 1939–winter 1939/40. Ed Rhys 1943–? Revived as Wales, the national monthly magazine of literature, the arts, and Welsh affairs [32]–47?, Sept 1958–Dec 1959.

Courier: picturing to-day—fact, fiction, art, satire. Vols 1–45 no 6, May 1937–Dec 1965. Quarterly at first; then monthly. Not pbd for a time during war.

Bonaventure: the Father Mathew record. Dublin. 1937–? Quarterly. Partly in Irish.

*Eve's journal. 1937–?

New universe—'try': a review devoted to the defence of Madame Blavatsky. Worthing. 1937–9(?). Ed Beatrice Hastings.

Northern magazine: incorporating Garvin's gazette. Isleworth, 1937–? Largely Scandinavian.

Parade: the British digest of good reading. Vols 1–4 no 12, Oct 1937–Sept 1941.

The poetry journal. 1937–?

Volontés. Paris. Nos 1–21, 1937?–March 1940. Includes English writing. Title used by Resistance pbn 1944–5.

The candle. Nos 1–3, Holmbury St Mary; 4, College of William and Mary, Virginia. Jan 1938–June 1940. Ed Oliver W. F. Lodge.

Townsman: a quarterly review. London and Cambridge (?) Vols 1–5 no 20, Jan 1938–Feb 1944. Continued as Scythe, new series, nos 21–8, summer 1944–April 1946. Ed Ronald Duncan to June 1945, L. C. Powell from autumn 1945. Scythe described as technical farming journal in 1945. No 9, Jan 1940, is separate pamphlet, Our strategy in war, by Maj Gen Sir Geoffrey Maitland.

Synopsis: a magazine of literary plunder. Feb–Nov 1938; Feb 1939–March 1940; summer 1944–June 1949.

The plough: towards the coming order. Vols 1–3 no 2, March 1938–?1940. Ed C. H. Arnold for Cotswold Bruderhof. New ser vols 1–8, 1953–60.

London Gallery bulletin. No 1, April 1938. Continued as London bulletin, nos 2–20(?), May 1938–June (?) 1940. Monthly. Ed E. L. T. Mesens, for Surrealist group in England.

The voice of Scotland: a quarterly magazine of Scottish arts and affairs. Dunfermline. June 1938–49; 1955–8. Ed 'Hugh MacDiarmid'.

Poetry and the people. Nos 1–20, July 1938–40. Absorbed by Our time, 1941.

Forum. Walthamstow. Nov/Dec 1938–? Organ of the Academy of Poetry.

Phoenix. Eastbourne. Nos 1–2, Dec 1938, July 1939. Edited at Eastbourne College in aid of distressed areas.

The phoenix. Woodstock, NY. Spring 1938–autumn 1940. Quarterly. Ed James Peter Cooney. Includes D. H. Lawrence.

Seven: the new magazine. Taunton, London, Cambridge. Vols 1–7 no 2, summer 1938–47. Ed John Goodland summer–winter 1938, Nicholas Moore summer 1938–spring 1940, Sydney D. Tremayne, 1943.

Albannach. 1 only 1938. Ed C. J. Russell and J. F. Hendry.

The British annual of literature. 1938–9; 1946–49.

*Idea and form. Kidderminster. 1938–?

Penguin parade. Nos 1–11, 1938–45. Ed Denys Kilham Roberts. New series 1–3 1947–8. Ed J. E. Morpurgo.

The pick of Punch: an annual selection. 1938 onwards.

The little revue. Edinburgh. Nos 1–3, Feb–April 1939.

Poetry London. Nos 1–6 no 23, Feb 1939–winter 1951. Bimonthly. Ed Tambimuttu and later Richard Marsh and Nicholas Moore. Also PL pamphlets 1–?, 1948–?

The Welsh review. Cardiff. Vols 1–7 no 4, Feb 1939–winter 1948. Not pbd Dec 1939–Feb 1944. Ed Gwyn Jones. 30 issues (vol 1 has 6 numbers).

Golden star. Nos 1–76, 4 March 1939–17 Aug 1940.

Lucky charm. Nos 1–64, 4 March 1939–18 May 1940.

The literary herald. Liverpool. Vols 1–2 no 9, April 1939–April/July 1940.

Yellow jacket. Oxford. Nos 1–2, March, May 1939. Ed

Constantine Fitzgibbon, with Margaret Aye Moung and John Orbach.

Cross channel: a monthly journal of books, travel and the arts. Vols 1–2 no 1, June 1939–June 1940.

This week. Vol 1 nos 1–6?, 28 July–1 Sept 1939? Eds include Graham Greene?

The English digest. July 1939 onwards. Founder editor 'John Gawsworth' [T. I. F. Armstrong].

Causerie: the intimate magazine. Nos 1–4, Nov 1939–Feb 1940. Ed Horace Shipp.

Kingdom come: the magazine of war-time Oxford. Vols 1–3 no 12, Nov 1939–autumn 1943. Irregular. Ed John Waller, Nov 1939–?, Kenneth Harris, Nov 1939–summer 1940; Miles Vaughan Williams, summer 1940–?, Mildred Clinkard, summer 1940; Alan Rook, Stefan K. Schimanski, Henry Treece, Nov/Dec 1941–? Incorporated Bolero and Light and dark.

Free expression. Nos 1–9?, Dec 1939–Aug 1941 (?) Includes Ethel Mannin.

The Abinger chronicle. Dorking. Vols 1–5 no 1, Christmas 1939–Sept 1944. 1 supplement, The Abinger garland, 1945. Ed Sylvia Sprigge.

I spy. Hastings. By Donald B. Cameron. Spring 1939 [1 only, or summer also?].

*Northern lights. Milnthorpe. Nos 1–2, 1939–? Ed Alan Hadfield.

Poetry quarterly. Dawlish, Billericay. Vols 1–15 no 5, spring 1939–spring/summer 1953. Nos 1–2 ed E. M. Channing-Renton with Katherine Hunter Coe, America, and Wrey Gardiner, assistant editor. Wrey Gardiner as editor thereafter and sole editor from spring 1941. Supersedes Poetry studies.

The new alliance: printing chiefly the work of Scottish and Irish writers and artists. Edinburgh. Autumn 1939. New series, vols 1–6, March 1940–Dec 1945/Jan 1946. Irregular. Continued as New alliance and Scots review, April 1946–?

British songwriter and poet. 1939–? Ed N. S. Armstrong and W. Aida Reubens. Quarterly.

Letter-mag: a magazine especially designed for enclosing in letters. 1939–? Associated with Medley.

Opus. Tring. Nos 1–14, 1939 (?)–spring 1943. Ed Denys Val Baker?

Phoenix: a magazine for young writers. Ayton. 1–41 (?), 1939–? Ed Cynthia Crashaw et al.

Poets of tomorrow: first (-third) selection. 1939–42. No 2 also as Cambridge poetry 1940.

Poet's parade. Wakefield. 1939–?

Sky raiders. 1939–?

*Terence White's verse-reel. 1939–?

Horizon: a review of literature and art. Nos 1–121, Jan 1940–Jan 1950. Ed Cyril Connolly. Selection: The golden horizon, ed Cyril Connolly, 1953. Index to nos 1–108, 1949.

La France libre. Vols 1 no 1–13 no 73 (in 75 issues), Nov 1940–Nov 1946. Ed André Labarthe. Many English contributors.

Oasis: an anthology to divert an idle hour. From 1940–? Ed John Bate, with Conan Nicholas, summer 1944–last issue? Produced by group of bomb-disposal men. Superseded by Leaven, Easter 1946. Title also used in 1951 for journal pbd in Cambridge.

The bell: a survey of Irish life. Dublin 1940 onwards. Ed Séan O'Fáolain; later P. O' Donnell. Not pbd May 1948–Oct 1950.

The bond of peace. Pamphlets 1–4, 1940. Peace Pledge Union. Includes Eric Gill and J. Middleton Murry.

C.E.M.A. [Council for the Encouragement of Music and the Arts] bulletin. Nos 1–62, 1940–4. Continued as Arts Council bulletin July 1945–March 1946.

Crux: controversial—constructive—critical. Glasgow 1940–?

Indian writing: a quarterly. Nos 1–5, 1940–2.

Now. Cookham Dean, Cambridge, London. Nos 1–7, 1940–1. New series, 1–9, 1943–July/Aug 1947. Irregular. Ed George Woodcock.

Penguin new writing. Nos 1–40, 1940–50. Ed John Lehmann. Associated with New writing.

'Resurgam' younger poets: broadsheets written under the impact of war. Nos 1–8(?), 1940–spring 1943 (?). Irregular. Anthology: Today's new poets, [1944].

Our time: incorporating Poetry and the people. Vols 1–8 no 7, Feb 1941–July/Aug 1949. Ed Beatrix Lehmann, John Banting, Birkin Howard, Ben Frankel, Randall Swingler et al; in 1945 Edgell Rickword: from 1949 (?) Frank Jellinek.

Commentary—the magazine of the Picture Hire Club: a causerie for artists, actors, picture lovers, playgoers and writers. Dublin, etc. Ed Sean Dorman. Vol 1 no 1, Nov 1941. Continued as Commentary, art drama, literature: the magazine of the Picture Hire Club, vol 1 no 2 Dec 1941. Continued as Commentary, art, drama, literature: vol 1 no 3–vol 5 no 3 Jan 1942–March 1946 (subtitle continues to change). Continued as Irish commentary, vol 5 no 4–vol 6 no 2, April 1946–Feb 1947. Continued as Irish cinema, vol 6 nos 3–4, March–April 1947.

The wind and the rain. Vols 1–7 no 3, summer 1941–1951. Ed Michael Allmand, Neville Braybrooke, Terence Marks. Quarterly. Yearbook, ed Neville Braybrooke, 1, 1941–?; an Easter book, 1962.

Adam: international review. No 152 onwards, 1941 onwards. Numeration continues from that of a journal formerly pbd in Bucharest. Ed Miron Grindea. Monthly. Partly in English and partly in French. Cumulative index every five years. Not pbd 1942–5.

Daylight. 1 vol 1941. Amalgamated with Folios of new writing and continued as New writing and daylight, nos 1–7, 1942–6. Ed John Lehmann. Distinguish from later literary journal of the same name, 1952–4.

English story. Series 1–10, 1941–50. Irregular. Ed Woodrow Wyatt with Susan Wyatt.

Here and now. Nos 1–5, 1941–9. Occasional. Ed Peter Albery and Sylvia Read.

Manuscript: a bimonthly. Southampton. Nos 1–3, June, Aug/Sept, Nov/Dec 1941.

Modern reading. 1–22, 1941–spring 1952. Ed Reginald Moore.

Salamander. Egypt, then Southsea about 1947. 1941–? Occasional. Ed John Cromer and John Gawsworth.

The Saturday book, 1941–2 [etc]: a new miscellany. Nos 1–12, 1941–52. Annual. Ed Leonard Russell; thereafter John Hadfield.

Selected writing. Nos 1–5, 1941–6. Occasional. Ed Reginald Moore.

Ulster parade. Belfast. Nos 1–10, 1941–45. Occasional.

Zenith. Manchester. 1941–.

Arson: an ardent review—part one of a surrealist manifestation. 1 only, 1942. Ed Toni del Renzio.

Broadsheet. ?–1942(?)–?

Ink. No 29 [= April] 1942; Oct 1949 onwards. Not pbd 1942–9. No issue Sept 1950. Ed Oct 1949–Feb 1952 Peter Davison.

*Personal landscape. Cairo. Vols 1–2 pt 4, 1942(?)–1945. Ed Lawrence Durrell, Bernard Spencer, Robin Felden. Anthology: Personal landscape, an anthology of exile, London 1945.

Poetry folios. Barnet. Nos 1–10, 1942–6. New series, no 1–? summer 1951–? Irregular. Ed Alex Comfort and Peter Wells.

Poets now in the services. Nos 1–2(?) 1942–3 (?). Ed A. E. Lowry.

Tempest. Oct 1943–? Irregular. Ed John Leatham and Neville Braybrooke.

Ulster voices. Belfast. Spring 1943–? Quarterly. Ed Roy McFadden and Robert Greacen.

Review –43[–46]: a review of literature, art and science. Winter 1943/4–summer 1946. Quarterly. Ed Walter Berger and Pavel Tigrid.

Bugle blast: an anthology from the services. 4 series, 1943–7. Annual. Ed Jack Aistrop and Reginald Moore.

Christmas [spring, summer, autumn] pie: a pocket miscellany. 1943–?

Little reviews anthology. Vols 1–5, 1943, 1945, 1946, 1947–8, 1949. Ed Denys Val Baker.

Million: (new left writing) (the people's review). Glasgow. Nos 1–3 1943(?)–5(?). Occasional. Early issues undated. Ed John Singer.

New road: new directions in European art and letters. Billericay. Nos 1–5, 1943–9. Annual. Ed Alex Comfort and John Bayliss nos 1 and 2, Fred Marnau nos 3 and 4, Wrey Gardiner no 5.

The norseman: an independent literary and political review. Vols 1–16, 1943–58.

Outposts. Blackpool. 1943 onwards. No 79 = winter 1968. Occasional. Ed Howard Sergeant.

Phoenix: a literary journal. Manchester, then Lewes. 1943(?)–? Ed Norman Swallow to spring 1946(?), Nigel Storm, autumn 1946–? Quarterly.

Poetry-Scotland. Glasgow. Nos 1–3, 1943–6. Occasional. Ed Maurice Lindsay.

Scots writing. Glasgow. 1943(?)–? Occasional. Ed P. McCrory and Alec Donaldson.

Staples digest: mirror of English life and letters. 1943–? Issue for Sept 1944 titled Staples commonplace book.

Transformation. Nos 1–4, 1943–7. Annual. Ed Stefan Schimanski and Henry Treece.

Voices: an anthology of individualist writings. Wigginton and Port Isaac. 1943–? New series, nos 1–2, autumn 1946; winter 1946. Ed Denys Val Baker.

Writing today. Tring. Nos 1–4, Oct 1943–Dec 1946. Ed Denys Val Baker.

Convoy. Nos 1–6, Feb 1944–7. No 6 titled Christmas convoy. Ed Robin Maugham.

The new Saxon pamphlets. Edenbridge, Oswestry. Nos 1–5, March 1944–7 (nos 4–5 as The new Saxon review). Irregular. Continued as Albion, vol 4 no 6. Ed John Atkins.

Air force poetry. 1944. Ed John Pudney and Henry Treece.

The arts in war time: a report on the work of C.E.M.A. [Council for the Encouragement of Music and the Arts] 1942/3 [etc]. 1944–?

Here today. Reading. Nos 1–4, 1944–5. Ed Pierre Edmunds and Roland Mathias.

International short stories. Tring, Hayle. 1944–? Ed Denys Val Baker.

New short stories. Glasgow. Vols 1–2, 1944, 1945–6. Ed John Singer.

Scottish art and letters. Glasgow. Nos 1–5, 1944–50. Quarterly. Ed R. Crombie Saunders with J. D. Fergusson, art editor.

The windmill. Nos 1–12, 1944–8. Ed Reginald Moore and Edward Lane. At first annually, then more frequently.

Gangrel. Nos 1–4, Jan 1945–6. Ed J. B. Pick and Charles Neill.

Mandrake. Oxford, London. Nos 1–11, May 1945–autumn/winter 1955/6. Occasional. Ed Arthur Boyars and John Wain.

The new English review. Started as Home and empire 1930–9. Vol 11 no 1–vol 17 no 2, May 1945–Aug 1948. Continued as New English review magazine, new series vol 1 no 1–vol 3 no 2 Sept 1948–Aug 1949. Continued as English review magazine, vol 3 no 3–vol 4 no 5, Sept 1949–May 1950. Ed D. Jerrold. Merged in National review as National and English review; ed Lord Altrincham.

New poetry. 1945. Ed Nicholas Moore. 1 only.

The plow: magazine of Malvern Piers Plowman Club. 1 only? Sept 1945.

Polemic: a magazine of philosophy, psychology and aesthetics. Nos 1–8, Sept 1945–7. Occasional. Ed Humphrey Slater.

Equator (Mombasa Arts Club). Nos 1–2(?), Dec 1945–? Ed Edward Lowbury. Includes Roy Campbell, Roy Fuller and first poems by John Press.

The modern quarterly. New series, vols 1–8 no 4, Dec 1945–autumn 1953. Ed John Lewis.

Compass: current reading. 1945–?

Focus one [–five]. 1945–50. Ed B. Rajan and Andrew Pearse. No 6 advertised but not published.

Hutchinson's Punch anthologies. 1945 onwards.

Khaki and blue. 1945. Occasional. Ed Peter Ratazzi. Merged in Civvy street.

Lagan: a miscellany of Ulster writing. Lisburne. 1945–? Quarterly. Ed John Boyd.

Modern poets. Malvern. 1945–?

Orion: a miscellany. Vols 1–4, 1945–7. Ed Rosamond Lehmann, Edwin Muir, Denys Kilham Roberts and Cecil Day Lewis.

Ploy. Glasgow. 1945. Ed R. Crombie Saunders.

Prospect: the voice of the younger generation of poets. Little Chalfont, Birmingham, Worcester. Nos 1–12, 1945–Christmas 1949. Quarterly. Ed Edward Toeman, F. S. Round and Barry Keegan; then by Edward Toeman, Gladys Keighley, Harold F. Bradley and David West.

Soldier: the British army magazine. 1945 onwards.

Translation. 2 issues, 1945, 1947. Ed Neville Braybrooke and Elizabeth King.

Writers of tomorrow. Bristol. 1945–? Occasional. Ed Peter Ratazzi.

English life and language. Vols 1–2 no 24, Jan 1946–Dec 1947.

Northern review: the magazine of the North. Pontefract, Clapham etc. Vols 1–2 no 3, June 1946–Jan/March 1948. New series, 1–9, May 1948–50. Quarterly.

Free unions. 1 only, July 1946. Ed Simon Watson Taylor for Surrealist Group in England.

The reading lamp. Nos 1–9, Aug 1946–Aug 1947.

Behind the scenes: a monthly review for all tastes—stage, screen, radio, sport, literature, music. Nos 1–11, Dec 1946–Dec 1947. Aug and Sept combined as no 8.

Echo: digest of the world's wit, wisdom and humour. Birmingham. 1 only? Dec 1946.

Nash's annual. Dec 1946–winter 1949/50.

London forum: a quarterly review of literature, art and current affairs. No 1, winter 1946, ed Peter Baker and Roland Gant; no 2, spring 1947, ed Warwick Charlton.

The arts. Nos 1–2, 1946–7. Ed Desmond Shaw-Taylor.

The arts in Britain. 1946 onwards. Pbd by Br Council.

The Baker street journal: a quarterly of Sherlockiana. New York. Vols 1–4, 1946–49; new ser 1951 onwards. Irregular.

The book for the train. Hunstanton. 1 only? 1946.

Carnaval. Nos 1–6, 1946–7.

Celtic story. 1946–?

Contact. Nos 1–17 [1946–9]. Continued as Contact: the magazine of pleasure, vol 1 nos 1–4, May–Dec 1950. Ed George Weidenfeld.

Counterpoint. Oxford 1946–? Occasional. Ed Conrad Senat.

Days off: the new quarterly magazine. 1946–?

Encore. Dublin. 1946–? Short stories.

Facet: arts magazine of the west. Vols 1–3 no 4, Oct 1946–autumn 1949. Ed P. Britten Austen to vol 2 no 2; then Ergo Jones and J. Knapman.

Future books. Nos 1–4, 1946. Ed Marjorie Bruce Milne. Then Magazine of the future. Numbering confused.

Irish writing: the magazine of contemporary Irish literature. Cork. 1946–? Quarterly. Ed David Marcus and Terence Smith.

Jazz forum: a quarterly review of jazz and literature. Fordingbridge. Nos 1–5, 1946–7. Ed Albert J. McCarthy.

Leaven. Croydon. 1 only, Easter 1946. Ed John Bate. Supersedes Oasis.

The literary digest: a monthly magazine of popular literary interest. 1946–?

Mid-day. Oxford. Winter 1946. 1 only? Ed Antoinette Pratt Barlow. Cover by B. Wolpe.

The mint: a miscellany of literature, art and criticism. No 1 1946, no 2 1948. Ed Geoffrey Grigson.

Modern story magazine: a Winter brothers midget magazine. Birmingham. 1 only? Winter 1946.

New era. 1946–?

New generation. Nos 1–2?, spring/summer 1946–winter 1947. Ed Peter Ratazzi. Quarterly.

New poets series. Woodford Green. Nos 1–3, 1946–7.

Phoenix quarterly: a journal devoted towards the recovery of unity in religion, politics and art. 1–3 1946–8(?). Ed Maurice Cranston.

Poems for Christmas and the New Year. Ilfracombe 1946–62(?). Some variations in title. Annual.

Poetry in Nottingham. West Bridgford. 1946–?

Resistance: a social-literary magazine. 1 only. Oct 1946. Ed Derek Stanford and David West.

Seascape: the coast quarterly. Summer 1946–autumn 1948(?) Ed A. William Ellis.

The signpost. 1946–?

Story: a magazine of new stories. Woodford Green. 1946–?

The storyteller: Britain's miniature modern fiction digest. 1946–?

Tattoo. Glasgow. Nos 1–4, 1946–7. Ed Patrick McCrory.

Triad. Vols 1–2, 1946–7. Ed Jack Aistrop. A miscellany.

The verist. Bristol and Cardiff. 1–2, 1946–spring 1947.

Vistas: a literary and philosophical review. Taunton. 1946–1949(?) Quarterly. Ed Donald Mullins.

The west country magazine. Denham. Vols 1–7 no 3, 1946–52. Ed Malcolm Elwin; J. C. Trewin.

Writers of the midlands. Birmingham. 1–2, 1946–7. Occasional. Ed Stanley Derricourt.

Wit: the magazine of humour and comment. Dublin. Nos 1–2(?), Jan, Feb 1947.

The new Shetlander. Lerwick. March 1947 onwards. Ed Peter Jamieson.

The new Athenian broadsheet. Edinburgh. Nos 1–16, Aug 1947–Christmas 1951.

The critic: a quarterly review of criticism. Mistley. Ed Wolf Mankowitz, Clifford Collins and Raymond Williams. Vol 1 nos 1–2, spring, autumn 1947. Incorporated in Politics and letters.

Now-days: book reviews, theatre, music, poetry, art. Brighton. Vol 1 nos 1–5, spring 1947–spring 1948. Ed Cyril Stone.

Changing world. Nos 1–7, summer 1947–Feb/April 1949.

Politics and letters. Nos 1–4 in 3 issues, summer 1947–summer 1948. Ed Clifford Collins, Raymond Williams, and Wolf Mankowitz. Incorporated Critic.

Scottish periodical. Edinburgh. Nos 1–2, summer 1947, summer 1948. Ed Ronald Gregor Smith.

Verse. Winter 1947–? Ed Dannie Abse.

Anvil: life and the arts—a miscellany. 1947–?

*Chelsea. 1947–? Monthly.

Collected poems [and prose]. Ilfracombe. 1947–54. Continued as Poems, 1955–7. Annual.

Folio: the magazine of the Folio Society. 1947 onwards.

Future: the magazine of industry, government, science, arts. Nos 1–4, ?1947; also an overseas number.

Informed reading. Nos 1–4(?), 1947(?)–?

Irish harvest. Dublin. 1947(?)–? Occasional. Ed Robert Greacen.

Life line. Nos 1–13(?), 1947–? Ed Noel Wynyard.

Male mag. Vol 1 nos 1–4, 1947–9.

The new man: a bimonthly publication devoted to Socialist culture and world outlook. 1947–9(?). Ed P. N. Harker.

The new meridian magazine. 1947–? Bimonthly. Ed Robert Muller, David Hack and Harry Klopper.

New Savoy. 1947(?)–? Occasional. Ed M. Meulen and Francis Wyndham.

Poetry folio. Horsmonden. 1947–? Organ of the Kent and Sussex Poetry Society.

West-countryman. 1947–? Bimonthly. Market Lavington. Ed Hugh Brandon-Cox.

Enquiry: a journal of modern thought. Feb 1948 (registration issue). Vols 1–3 no 7, April 1948–June 1950. Ed Alfred Ridgway and Nigel Cox. Includes Roy Campbell and 'Hugh MacDiarmid' (C. M. Grieve).

Poetry Ireland. Cork. Nos 1–19, April 1948–Oct 1952.

Alba: a Scottish miscellany in Gaelic and English. Glasgow. 1948.

Contemporary issues. 1948–?

The glass: magazine of fantasy and journals. Lowestoft. Nos 1–11? 1948–54? Ed Antony Borrow.

Harlequin. Oxford. Nos 1–2, 1949–50. Ed Oliver Carson and Anthony Blond. Then amalgamated with Panorama, Cambridge.

Nature stories. Edinburgh. 1948–?

Orpheus: a symposium of the arts. Vols 1–2, 1948–9. Ed John Lehmann.

Poetry commonwealth. Dulwich Village. 1–8, summer 1948–spring 1951. Ed Lionel Monteith.

Rann: quarterly of Ulster poetry. Belfast. Nos 1–17, 1948–52?

World review: incorporating Review of reviews, and World. New series, nos 1–50, March(?) 1949–April/May 1953. Ed Edward Hulton.

The catacomb. Nos 1–14, April 1949–May 1950, monthly. New series, vols 1–2 no 4, summer 1950–winter 1951/2, quarterly. Ed Robert Lyle and Roy Campbell.

The 'lisp of leaves': a magazine for discerning people. Lancaster. Vol 1 nos 1–9, April–Dec 1949. Continued as The north-west monthly: incorporating The 'lisp of leaves', vol 1 no 10–vol 2 no 1, Jan–May/June 1950.

Gemini: a pamphlet magazine of new poetry. Derby. 1–5 May 1949–Sept 1950. Ed Frederic Vanson. Anglo-American poetry review.

Verse lover. 1–3, spring–autumn 1949. Ed Neville Armstrong.

Forum stories and poems. Nos 1–2, summer 1949–50. Ed Muriel Spark.

Delphic review: an anarchistic quarterly. Vol 1 nos 1–2, winter 1949–spring 1950. Ed Albert J. McCarthy.

Dock leaves. Milford Haven. Vols 1–8 no 22, 1949–57. Ed R. Mathias. Continued as Anglo-Welsh review. Vol 9 no 23, 1958 onwards. Ed R. Garlick.

Arena: a literary magazine. Nos 1–4, 1949–51; ed John Davenport, Jack Lindsay and Randall Swingler; nos 5–9, Sept/Oct 1950–2, bimonthly, ed Jack Lindsay.

Botteghe oscure: an international review of new literature. Rome. Nos 1–25, 1949–60. Ed Marguerite Caetani. Contributions in language of origin.

The Cornish review. Hayle. Nos 1–8(?), 1949–51(?) Quarterly. Ed Denys Val Baker.

Country town. Par. 1949(?)–? Quarterly. Ed H. J. Willmott.

Envoy: an Irish review of literature and art. Dublin. Vols 1–5, April 1949–51. Quarterly. Ed John Ryan.

New acorn. (Selected short stories by contemporary authors). Harrow. 1949–?

Nine: (a magazine of poetry and criticism) (a magazine of literature and the arts). Tunbridge Wells. Nos 1–11, 1949–56. Ed Peter Russell.

Poetry. Liverpool. 1949–? Ed Hardiman Scott.

Poetry awards 1949[–52]: a compilation of original poetry published in magazines of the English-speaking world in 1948[–51]. Philadelphia, 1949–52. Continued as Borestone Mountain poetry awards, 1953–5. Continued as Best poems of 1955 [etc], Stanford, 1956 onwards.

Points. Paris. Nos 1–19?, 1949–54?

The year's work in literature 1949[–1950]. 1950–1. Ed John Lehmann. Pbd by Br Council.

The arts and philosophy. Nos 1–2, summer 1950–autumn 1951. New series, no 1–?, spring 1962. Ed Sidney Arnold.

Books and authors: a review of modern literature. 1950–?

Border forum: an independent miscellany of writing presenting Wales to the non-Welsh. Llandudno. 1950–?

Circus: the pocket review of our time. Nos 1–3, April–June 1950. Ed Randall Swingler, with John Davenport and Paul Hogarth.

English miscellany: a symposium of history, literature and the arts. Rome. 1950 onwards. Pbd by Br Council. Ed Mario Praz.

Key poets. Nos 1–10. 1950.

Nightwatchman. Leicester. Nos 1–6, winter 1950/1–53.

Poetry Manchester. Leigh. 1950(?). Ed Doreen Taylor and B. Wright; 4, 5 ed P. Robins and H. Webster, 1952.

Review fifty: poetry and prose. Stockport, Thelnetham, Botesdale. Nos 1–3(?), winter 1950, spring 1951, summer–autumn 1951. Ed E. Cooper.

The window. No 1, [1950]–? Nos 1–6 ed John Sankey, assistant editor Jean Anderson; no 7, Feb 1954, ed Philip Inman; no 9 (larger format) undated.

(2) AMATEUR JOURNALS

The amateur literary movement was well established by the beginning of the twentieth century. Its productions are particularly difficult to trace as their circulation is restricted and their life often, though by no means always, very brief. The BM was rarely favoured with copies and some of those sent were destroyed by bombing in the Second World War. It has been possible to examine only a small proportion of all amateur jnls and the convention of marking with an asterisk those not found has been dispensed with in this section. It is difficult to draw a sharp line between what is and what is not an amateur, or free-lance, or aspirant, jnl, and the productions of some editors seem to hover between the professional and the amateur (see, for example, The tulip, 1900; and compare Orpheus 1923–7 in its first and later stages). Examples of all kinds of jnls are given in this list, but most hobby magazines, magazines for boys, and some ms magazines have been omitted, as well as what seem to be facetiae.

Bibliographical details have been obtained by examining copies of amateur jnls in the BM, which often refer to other jnls, but chiefly from Almon Horton, Amateur journalism survey, Manchester, pts 1–10, 1946–53; see also his The hobby of amateur journalism, Manchester 1955 (chs after 32 pbd as supplements to British amateur journalist); and a certain amount of inconsistency and incompleteness of detail has been inevitable.

The Benjamin Franklin Memorial Library, Philadelphia, holds the Edwin Hadley Smith Collection of some 40,000 amateur jnls of which 1,976 are from England and Wales.

Herdman's miscellany. Berwick. Vol 1, nos 1–121; vol 2, ?; vol 3, ?–36; nos 37–45; vol 4, no 46–?; 1886–92; 1897–? Ed E. F. Herdman.

Amateur litterateur. Leeds. Vols 1–4 no 17, Sept 1899–Sept 1905 (formerly Amateur journalist: organ of the British Amateur Press Literary Association, vols 1–8, 1890–9). Continued as British amateur: organ of the British Amateur Press Association, Bishop Auckland etc. Vols 1–4 no 16, Sept 1910–Dec 1914. Continued as British amateur journalist, Shanklin, etc, vol 4 no 17 [= no 100]–vol 7 no 26, Feb 1915–Nov 1921. Continued as British amateur journalist, new series, no 1 onwards, 15 April 1926. Ed R. A. Breed; in 1948 Arthur Harris

(see Interesting items, below, no 646, Nov 1940 and no 658, Nov 1941).

Craftsman. Egham. [no 5 = July 1900]. Ed E. James.

The trawl: an occasional miscellany. Birmingham. Nos 1–3, midsummer 1902–May 1903.

Llandudno's weekly. 5 March 1904–Dec 1907. Continued as Interesting items, 21 Dec 1907 onwards. [No 700 = May 1945, pbd Oct 1953]. Ed Arthur Harris, with Irene Harris from no 600, Jan 1934 onwards.

The literary aspirant. Leicester. Vols 1–4 no 16, 1904–7. Ed Atkinson Ward.

Northern glim. Darwen. 1–27, ?1904–Dec 1906. Ed J. Davison.

Llandudno and Croxton mail. Jan 1905–Jan 1906, weekly. Continued as Friday fun, 1 July 1906–Jan 1909. Nos 1–239 in all. Ed Arthur Harris.

Laughable comic. Llandudno. Nos 1–175, 1905–Jan 1909. Ed A. Harris.

Laughmixture. Llandudno. Nos 1–158, 27 Jan 1906–Jan 1909. Ed A. Harris.

My garden. Llandudno. Nos 1–43, 16 June 1906–April/May 1907. Ed A. Harris.

People's paper. Llandudno. Nos 1–130, 6 Oct 1906–March 1909. Ed H. Jones.

Comic bits. Llandudno. 1 only. 27 Oct 1906. Ed A. Harris.

The cat. Bishop Auckland. Nos 1–91, Dec 1906–Oct 1926 [nos 73–6, 78, 79, not pbd]. From no 92, March 1928, as Hobby world. No 4, April 1907, 'April fool number'—page 1 ptd normally; remaining pages one line only per page. Ed E. and R. Herdman.

Bright sparks. Llandudno. Nos 1–4, 19 Oct–9 Nov 1907. New series, 1 only?, Nov 1912.

Coloured journal. Llandudno. Nos 1–69, Oct 1907–Jan 1909. Ed H. Jones.

Miniature news journal. Llandudno. Nos 1–100, Oct 1907–Sept 1909. Ed A. Harris.

Coloured fun. Llandudno. Nos 1–52, 6 Nov 1907–Nov 1908. Ed A. Harris.

McEwan's amateur journalist and literary aspirant. Nos 1–12, 1907. Continued as Modern journalist and literary aspirant, new series, nos 1–12, 1908. Ed Oliver McEwan.

Weekly news. Llandudno. Nos 1–2, 1907. Ed H. Jones.

Young gardener. Llandudno. Nos 1–57, 1 Feb 1908–27 Feb 1909.

Laughmaker. Llandudno. Nos 1–44, 14 March 1908–Jan 1909. Ed H. Jones.

Junior. Darwen. Nos 1–4? April–July 1908. Ed J. Davison.

Comical circle. Llandudno. Nos 1–14, 17 Oct 1908–Jan 1909. Ed A. Harris.

Scraplets. Llandudno. Nos 1–2, 9 Jan 1909–?16 Jan 1909. Ed E. Atkinson.

Free notes. Llandudno. 1 only 20 Feb 1909. Ed H. Jones.

Amateur. Walsall. Nos 1–5, March 1909–? New series, Jan 1915. Ed F. R. Day.

Amateurs' review. May 1909–?

Recorder. May 1909–?

Juvenile chatter. Llandudno. Nos 1–22, 12 June–6 Nov 1909. Ed A. Harris.

Surrey amateur. Nos 1–3, Nov 1909–?1910. Ed S. A. Hickox.

Amateur's weekly. Nos 1–8, ?1909–Sept 1910. Ed E. A. Dench.

Explorer. Nos 1–4, 1909–? Ed L. G. Dryden.

Monthly midget. Liverpool. Nos 1–4, 1909–March 1910. Ed B. Holloway.

The bee. Liverpool. Nos 1–21, ?Feb 1910–14; nos 22–3, 1926. Ed B. Holloway.

O.P. record. Nos 1–4, April 1910–March 1911. Ed E. D. Odam.

Spider. Nos 1–13, April 1910–15. Ed L. G. Dryden (later as Wheeler). No 11, Jan 1914, India; no 13, 1915, Hong Kong. Issued in association with a travelling theatre group. From 1915 Dryden issued The China amateur journalist.

The owl. May 1910–?

White rosebud. Nos 1–2, Aug 1910, 1912. Ed V. King.

Amateur siftings. Margate. 1 only? Oct 1910. Ed H. J. Winterbone.

Amateurs' own monthly. Bishop Auckland. Oct 1910–? Ed E. and R. Herdman.

Leek. Griffithstown. Oct 1910–? Ed C. E. Nicholls.

Youth's advertiser. Bishop Auckland. Oct 1910–? Ed E. and R. Herdman.

Emerald. Dec 1910–?

The raven. Dec 1910–19? Ed Albert E. Amos.

Amateur advertiser. Nos 1–3? 1910. Ed J. A. Laker.

Amateur editor. Nos 1–2, 1910. Ed J. A. Laker and E. and R. Herdman.

Amateur's help. Peckham. 1910. Ed E. A. Dench.

Cobweb. Nos 1–4, 1910–Feb 1911. Ed G. Varley.

Comedian. Brighton. 1910.

Comet. Saltburn. Nos 1–2 1910. Joseph Parks.

Echo. 1910–11? Ed H. E. Blankart.

Gossip. Newcastle upon Tyne. 1910? Ed R. Tetlow.

Jester. Newcastle upon Tyne. c. 1910. Ed F. C. Thornborough.

Monthly advertiser. 1910. Ed V. King.

Novice. Dorset. Nos 1–13, 1910–? Ed E. M. Ventura.

Ruby. Nos 1–5, 1910. Ed J. A. Laker.

Weekly report. Nos 1–10, 1910–12. Ed V. King.

Little yellow dog. Bishop Auckland. Jan 1911. Ed E. Herdman.

Pastimes. Llandudno. 11 March 1911–? Ed H. Jones.

Rosemary. Folkestone and Manchester. Nos 1–4, March 1911–? New series, 5–?, July 1917. Ed B. Winskill and J. Goss.

Lilliputian. Folkestone. Nos 1–2?, March 1911–? Ed R. Matthews.

Fairy. Nos 1–?, March 1911–? [no 9 = 1919]. Ed Lottie Winskill.

Competitor. April 1911–?

Li-ver. Liverpool. Nos 1–6?, April 1911–12? Ed A. O. Hooker (with J. W. Hoare for no 6).

The wee nipper. Bishop Auckland. Nos 1–12, April 1911–Feb 1914.

Young Welshman. Griffithstown. April 1911. Ed L. Cornfield.

Alarum. May 1911–? Ed J. L. Goss.

Hawk. London, Shipley, Mitcham. May 1911–?; New series, 1919; new series, vol 2 no 1–21?, April 1946–Aug 1950? Ed F. S. Gorrell.

Dwarf. Berlin? June 1911–13? Ed H. D. Cowen-Hoven.

Amateur scribe. Folkestone. Aug 1911. Ed R. Matthews.

Amateur times. Sept 1911? Ed V. King.

Echo. Sept 1911–? Ed H. Bankart.

Items of news. Dec 1911. Ed E. A. Dench.

Amateur's daily report. Colchester. Nos 1–7, 1911. Daily. Ed A. E. Amos.

Amateur's monthly. 1 only?, 1911. Ed F. Pontet.

Firefly. London and Shipley. 1911? Ed F. S. Gorrell.

For the cause. Sandown. 1911? Ed R. D. Roosmale-Cocq.

International amateur. Folkestone. 1911; 1 no, Jan 1916. New series 1917–? Ed B. Winskill.

Jolly Roger. Folkestone. 1911? Ed B. Winskill.

Northern pencraft. Newcastle upon Tyne. 1911. Ed G. W. Stokes.

Northern searchlight. Bishop Auckland. 1911? Ed E. Herdman.

Official news. 1911?

Phonetic record. Colchester. 1911? Ed A. E. Amos.

Recorder. Bradford. Nos 1–8, ?1911–Jan 1912. Ed N. E. Scott.

Reflector. Nos 1–6?, 1911–Jan 1915. No 6 pbd in America. Ed E. A. Dench.

Scroll. 1911? Ed J. L. Goss.

Trident. Colchester. ?1911. Ed A. E. Amos.

Wheel. Cambridge. 1911. Ed F. Mason.

King's amateur newspaper. Nos 1–5, Feb 1912. Ed V. King.

Junior review. Faversham. Nos 1–2? April 1912. Ed A. F. Court.

Octopus. Manchester. 1 only, June 1912. Ed R. Hyndman.

Excelsior. Aug 1912. Ed R. A. Breed.

London amateur. Nos 1–12, Sept 1912–26. Ed A. Lewis (except no 12, ed R. A. Breed).

Mintoft magazine. York. Sept 1912.

The south eastern amateur. Nos 1–18, Sept 1912–19; Jan 1920–July 1928. New series, 1–25?, Nov 1946–Nov 1950? Ed R. A. Breed.

Amateur journal. Dorset. 1912 (several issues). Ed G. M. Ventura.

Bull's eye. Nos 1–3, 1912. Ed A. C. Lewis (no 3 with D. R. Betts).

Diamond. Dec 1912. Ed Jessie Wood.

Midget magazine. Newcastle upon Tyne. 1912. Ed E. L. McKeag.

Northern star. 1912?

Sun. Liverpool. Nos 1–4?, 1912? Incorporated Amateur review. Ed A. E. Mitchell.

Triumvirate. Folkestone. 1912?

Venture. Nos 1–2, 1912. Ed V. King and H. W. Spiers.

Western star. Bath. 1912. Ed D. R. Betts.

Wilbert magazine. 1912. Ed T. A. Scruby.

The amateur atom: a magazine published in the interests of British amateur journalism. Sandown. Nos 1–6, April 1913–May 1914. Ed R. Roosmale and R. le Cocq. Compare editor's name, For the cause, 1911 (see col 1382).

Humber amateur. April 1913.

Folkestone breeze. July 1913? Ed B. Winskill.

Graph herald. July 1913–? Ed A. A. Bishop.

Amateur gazette. Nos 1–6, 1913; then becomes Sentinel.

Crooked billet. Newcastle upon Tyne. Jan 1914. Ed G. W. Stokes.

Hour glass. Bishop Auckland. 1 only? 1914. Ed E. Herdman. 120 pp in first issue.

Record. Margate. Nos 1–26? 1914–15? Ed H. J. Winterbone.

The patriot. Bishop Auckland. June 1915–? Ed E. Herdman.

Red-white-blue. Sandown. 1 only. June 1915. Ed R. D. Roosmale-Cocq.

Poesy. Bishop Auckland. Vols 1–2 no 15, July 1915–Nov 1917. Ed E. Herdman. Vol 1 bound up as Gathered leaves.

The Scot. Dundee. Nos 1–69? Sept 1915–Feb 1923. Ed G. T. McColl.

Cobweb nest. Newcastle upon Tyne. 1 only. 1915. Issue 2 destroyed when H.M.S. India sunk.

Merry minutes. Vols 1–3 no 12, ?1915–March 1917. Ed Margaret Trafford.

Outward bound. Newcastle upon Tyne. 1915. Ed G. W. Stokes.

Haermai [sic]: a little magazine. Leytonstone. Nos 1–2?, April, Dec 1916. Ed G. Dolden.

Blue bell magazine. Nos 1–14, 1916–37. Ed Baroness de Laci.

Conservative. ?1916. Ed — Lovecraft.

Coyote. ?1916. Ed — Harrington.

Enterprise. ?1916. Ed — Chaplin.

Northward Ho! 1916? Ed W. Hall.

Oratava observer. ?1916. Ed E. L. McKeag.

Southern Cross. Saltburn. ?1916. Ed J. Parks.

Tryout. ?1916. Ed — Smith.

Postscript. Sandown. Feb 1917. Ed R. D. Roosmale-Cocq.

Vanity fair: an amateur magazine. Saltburn. Vols 1–3 no 31, June 1917–May/June 1927. Continued as Collector's monthly, nos 1–18, April 1928–Sept 1932. 3rd new series, nos 1–24, Nov 1932–June 1939. 4th new series, nos 1–7, spring 1941–3. 5th new series, nos 1–20, Oct 1945–Sept 1951. Ed J. Parks. As Collector's monthly devoted to variety of subjects but especially collecting boys' magazines.

The little budget of knowledge and nonsense. Vol 1 nos 1–11/12; vol 2 in one issue complete. April 1917–18? Ed Margaret Trafford.

Mesopotamia amateur. 1917. Ed W. Yaldren.

Silver star. [No 2 = 1917].

Spindrift. Nos 1–3, 1917. Ed (aboard warship?) E. L. McKeag.

Just a line. Sandown. 1 only. July 1918. Ed R. D. Roosmale-Cocq.

Veritas. 1 only. Aug 1918.

Amateur's gazette. Ashton-under-Lyne. Nos 1–12, 1918–June 1920. Ed J. W. Mayer, W. Bowker, and later F. H. McCarthy.

The literary club magazine. [Vol 1 no 6; vol 2 no 1 = 1918].

T.B. no 31 telegraph. 1918.

The castlean. Rastrick. June 1919. Ed J. A. Binns.

Amateur advertiser. Saltburn. 1–2, 1919. Ed Joseph Parks.

On patrol. [Nos 15–16 = 1919].

Pastime. 1919. Ed J. Hetherington.

Quill. [Nos 11–12 = 1919].

Bazaar. Easington colliery. 1920? Ed J. A. Birkbeck.

Forum. Bishop Auckland. 1920. Ed A. E. Dalkin.

Pals. Paisley. 1920–1? Ed G. C. Wegenroth.

Mouse. Easington Colliery. 1920. Ed J. A. Birkbeck.

Nulli secundus. 1920–?, alternate months. New series, 1926–? Ed S. G. Kitchell.

Le Cocq's comment. Sandown. 1921. Ed R. D. Roosmale-Cocq.

Mag-pie. Dover. Nos 1–2, 1921. Ed — Waters and F. C. Bissenden.

Northern amateur. Belfast. 1921? Ed F. Gamble.

Sphinx. 1921. Ed F. Warren.

Will o' the wisp. Uckfield. 1921. Ed E. W. Chatfield.

The metro: an advertising journal. Nos 1–6; [nos 2–6 subtitled: an amateur free-lance] Oct 1921–March 1922. A slip in no 6 records the circulation of earlier issues: no 1–59; no 2–84; no 3–143; no 4–241; no 5–138.

Forum. Bishop Auckland. 1921.

Under cover. Bishop Auckland. 1921. Ed A. Humble.

The literary amateur: official organ of the British Amateur Literary Association. Rochdale, Wigan, Derby etc. Vols 1–11 no 1, March 1922–Oct 1931. Ed R. le Cocq, Lillian Crawford, C. Hoare etc. Continued as Literary aspirant, vols 11 no 2–12 no 6, Nov 1931–Oct 1933. Continued as Twelve pages, vol 13 nos 1–4, Nov/Dec 1933–July/Oct 1934. Continued as Literary adventurer, vol 14 onwards, Jan/Feb 1935. See The cat vol 8 no 83 Oct 1925, and Literary amateur Sept/Oct 1925.

Vinovia. Bishop Auckland. Nov 1922. Ed A. E. Dalkin.

Orpheus. Paisley. [Vol 1, nos 1–6, May 1923–March 1924; year 4 no 6 = March/April 1927] alternate months. Ed G. C. Wegenroth. According to The cat, Christmas 1925, 'to our mind, ceased to be an amateur affair'.

Stories. Nos 1–2, July, Aug, 1923. Ed E. C. Ford.

The pen! an amateur magazine. Nos 1–3, Oct–Dec 1923. Ed E. C. Ford and A. St. John.

The 'lit' magazine. Salford. No 1, 1924. Continued as Unit, Manchester, nos 2–3, 1926–7.

A query. Nos 1–2, 1924.

Report. Ringwood. Nos 1–38?, 1924–Sept 1929. Ed H. G. Dell.

Companion. Dublin. Nos 1–31?, ?1925–7. Ed J. W. Carpenter, then W. A. Downes (also ed of The collector, 1925).

News circular. Stillorgan. 1925. Ed W. A. Downes.

Shrapnel. Aberdeen and Bexhill. ?1925. Ed T. L. Lamond and B. G. Stoner.

Stray thoughts. 1925? Ed S. G. Kitchell.

Waverley. Aberdeen. 1925? Ed T. C. Lamond.

A fragment. Dover. No 1, July 1926; no 2, Sept 1926. New series, nos 1–11?, Feb 1948–Jan 1957 [no 10 ptd in USA]. Ed F. G. Bissenden.

Erdington amateur. Birmingham. (Began as The boys' chronicle, 26 Dec 1926.) April 1928–Jan 1931; 1937; 1938; Dec 1945 [= no 26].

Amateur's advertiser. 1926. Ed E. E. Geer.

Amateur annual. 1926.

British amateur journalism in ye olden tyme. 1 only. 1926. By E. Herdman.

Caledonia. Greenock. 1926? Ed A. M. McNeill.

Co-optimists. Nos 1–10. 1926?

Inkdrops. Nos 1–15, 1926–June 1934. Ed B. Winskill.

Irish amateur journalist: official organ of Irish Amateur Press Association. Dublin. Jan 1926–? Ed W. A. Downes.

Modern gladiator. 1926? Ed F. E. Hope.

Owl of Kent (Owl). Dover, Preston. 1926–? Ed Julia Binfield; Nina Jamieson.

Parnassus. Glasgow. 1926? Monthly. Ed A. S. Muir.

Torch. Dublin. 1926? Ed J. W. Carpenter.

Twentieth-century amateur magazine. Leicester. 1926? Ed E. S. Holthan-Hobson.

Twilight. Dublin. 1926. Ed W. A. Downes.

Amateur mart. Surrey, Dorset. Vols 1–9 no 54, Feb 1927–March 1936. Ed J. O. Ventura.

The amateur magazine. Dover. Nos 1–3, 1927; nos 4–?14, April 1947–Feb 1950. Ed F. G. Bissenden.

Novice. Dublin. 1927. Ed F. Hoban.

Screen. Dublin. Aug 1927. Ed W. A. Downes.

Amateur bulletin. Middlesborough. 1928? Ed A. Bradley. New series, nos 1–5, 1931, ed A. Bradley and E. Drywood. Replaced by Excelsior, 1 only?, March/April 1932.

Gleam. Belturbet. Nos 1–3?, 1928. Ed T. Clarke.

Glow worm. Hove. 1928. Ed R. Webb.

Lilliputian. Edgbaston. 1928?

Modern magazine. Nos 1–16, 1928–? Ed A. Horton.

New idea. Dublin. 1928. Ed W. A. Downes.

Onward. 1928–? Incorporated in Bookworm, 1929. Ed J. R. Procter. In part to advertise books for sale.

Punchbowle. West Bromwich. 1928–36. Ed H. G. Moore. An Annual in 1946.

Valhalla. 1928? New series, nos 1–30? March/April 1937–June 1953. Ed A. C. Kennington.

Ace magazine. Mansfield Woodhouse. 1 only? Sept 1929. Ed F. G. Barnes.

Bookworm. 1929. Ed J. R. Procter. Incorporates Onward.

Free lance. Jersey. 1929. Ed A. C. Voisin.

Golden bowl. Guildford. 1929? Ed J. S. Dunn.

Meanderer. Edgbaston. 1929.

Newcomer. Bocking. 1929. Ed F. S. Wiffen.

Leisure moments. Nos 1–3, Christmas 1930–summer 1931. Organ of the British Amateur Literary Assoc, Birmingham. Ed J. Tovey. Pbd by Lawrence Warner.

Esmerica. 1930? Ed W. Titchell.

Poets' Guild quarterly. Berkhamsted. 1930? Ed Ruth Elliott.

Sea-gull. Dover. ?1930–34? Ed Julia Binfield; from 1934, B. Ridgwell.

Silver spray. Wolverhampton. 1930. Ed Marjorie Higgs and E. A. Drywood. Continued as Silver standard magazine, ed Marjorie Higgs.

Midget mail. Nos 1–11, Feb–27 April 1931.

The amateur scribe. Hayes and Reading. Nos 1–19, 1931–46. Ed R. K. Southey. No 20 incorporates Raconteur (1 issue, May 1945, also ed R. K. Southey); jnl then becomes Raconteur with no 21 and title The amateur scribe then adopted by C. W. Russell who begins new series.

The amateur journalist's annual. 1931.

Aphro. Jan 1932. Bimonthly. Ed A. F. Arnold.

Our own mag. Halifax and Bristol. July 1932. Ed Olive Rhodes and Margaret Bull. Continued as International amateur, Brighouse. New series, spring 1943 onwards. Ed Olive Teugels (formerly Rhodes). Pbd Lawrence Warner at first. Annual: Who's who (in amateur journalism) 1945–?

The outlet: the literary live wire. Nos 1–3, 1932.

White heather. Inverness. ?1932–45. Ed Lena Budge.

Harbinger. Chatham. 1 only. March 1933. Ed E. A. Drywood.

The free-lance's own. Wolverhampton. Nos 1–12. Nov 1933–Aug 1935. Ed Marjorie Higgs.

Amateur writers' annual guide. Nos 1–3, 1933–5. Ed A. Horton.

The writers' medley. 1 only? 1933. Ed T. Loring.

The amateur recorder. Bishop Auckland. Nos 1–2, June 1934–? Ed E. Herdman.

Amateur press world. Bromley. Nos 1–55, July 1934–Sept 1946? Ed C. W. Russell. Organ of the British Amateur Literary Assoc.

Air news. Nos 1–17? Sept 1934–? Ed H. M. Stephens.

Pass-round review. Hayes Middlesex Oct 1934. Ed C. W. Russell. Intended to improve standard of single-copy jnls.

Amateur writers' journal. Glasgow. 1 only, Dec 1934. Ed T. C. Cowan.

Scrap book. Herne Bay. Nos 1–109? 1934–47? Ed C. W. Russell.

Splinters. Aberdeen and Chatham. 1934. Ed T. L. Lamond and E. A. Drywood.

Wanderer. Hayes Middlesex. Nos 1–18? April 1935–52 [continued longer?]. Ed C. W. Russell.

Silver jubilee book. Herne Bay. May 1935.

The golden magazine. Parkston. 1935–47? Ed Marguerite Bull.

Omnibus book. West Bromwich. 1935–? Ed H. G. Moore.

Thalia. West Bromwich. 1935. Ed L. G. Moore.

The wayfarer. 1935. Pbd Lawrence Warner.

Inky ways. Ringwood. Jan 1936. Ed E. M. Haines.

International favourite. Burley. 1936? Ed J. P. Grant.

The truth about writing. Hinckley. 1936–? Pbd Lawrence Warner?

Darker side. Hayes Middlesex. 1 Feb 1937. Ed R. K. Southey. With a companion issue, Lighter side.

Amateur writer's circular. Glasgow. [No 2 March 1937]. Ed T. C. Cowan.

March (Easter) annual. Sacriston. 1937–44. Ed Stella Hunter; with E. E. Beacham for 1940; 1945–6, ed E. E. Beecham.

April (Spring) annual. (Also as Avril.) 1937–9; 1944–5; 1947.

May annual. 1937; 1938; 1944; 1945–6 [as Debate]; 1947. Various editors.

June (Summer) annual. 1937–9, ed F. F. Eliot; 1944–7, Grimsby, ed C. and E. Stamper.

July (Leisure) annual. Mortimer. 1937 (as Boomerang?); 1945–7/8; 1951; 1952.

The chaplet. Dover. Aug 1937. Ed Julia Binfield.

August annual (Bank holiday budget). 1937; 1944–5; 1947; 1951.

Melody. Nos 1–2, Aug 1937–? Ed Julia Binfield.

September (Autumn) annual. West Wickham. 1937–44, ed Amelia Chapman; 1945, Glasgow, T. C. Cowen; 1946–7, London, J. Williams.

Amateur science stories. Leeds. Nos 1–3, Oct, Dec 1937; March 1938. Ed W. F. Mayer.

October (Owl) annual. 1937; 1944–7. Various editors.

The quiet hour. Nov 1937. Pbd Lawrence Warner.

December (Christmas) annual. 1937–41; 1944; 1946–7; 1952. Ed C. W. Russell.

Poet's parade. Wakefield. 1 only? [c. 1937]. Ed A. Chapple. Pbd Lawrence Warner.

Romantic stories. 1937? Ed K. Hoskin and W. Attard.

Selections. Preston. Nos 1–3, 1937. Ed Nina Jamieson.

Underneath the arches. 1937. Ed H. M. Stephens.

Electioneer. Hayes Middlesex. 1 Jan 1938; 2–3 Nov, Dec 1951. Ed C. W. Russell.

Good cheer. April 1938. Ed S. A. Andrews and W. F. Gibbons. Pbd Lawrence Warner.

Bronx: a literary cocktail. Preston. 1 only? 1938. Ed A. J. F. Thornley.

The aristocrat. Leicester. Nos 1–4, Jan–Sept 1939. Ed E. Rogers. Pbd Lawrence Warner.

Midnight oil: the literary magazine of the British Amateur Press association. Hinckley, Hayes Middlesex, Erdington. Nos 1–12? March 1939–51. Pbd Lawrence Warner (at first only?). Ed R. D. Chamberlin.

Spare moments. Morecambe. Nos 1–3, April–June 1939. Ed L. France. Pbd Lawrence Warner.

The Blackcountryman. West Bromwich. 1 only, 1939. Ed H. G. and L. G. Moore.

Gas alert. Glasgow. 1 only? 1939. Pbd Lawrence Warner.

Pleasure. Llandudno. 1939. Ed Irene Harris.

Warner's world-wide writers' weekly. Hinckley. 1939–? Pbd Lawrence Warner.

Intimate. Leicester. Nos 1–2, Oct 1939–Jan 1940. Ed E. Rogers. Pbd Lawrence Warner.

Independent. Preston. Winter 1939. New series, Nov 1944. Ed G. Bamber.

The nose: the organ of the unwashed Bolshie. Nos 1–7?, ?Oct 1940–April/May 1941. Ed G. Smith and S. D. Francis with A. R. Maddoks.

Variete [sic]. Hayes Middlesex and London. Nos 1–14? Dec 1940-March 1953. Ed C. W. Russell and A. C. Kennington.

B.A.P.A. [British Amateur Press Assoc] war-time bulletin. Nos 1–30, 1940–June 1945. Continued as B.A.P.A. monthly news bulletin. Ed C. W. Russell.

England calling. Hayes Middlesex. 1940. Ed C. W. Russell.

Your own magazine. Hayes Middlesex. 1940. Ed C. W. Russell.

Phoenix: a magazine for young writers. Ayton. Ramsbottom. [Vol 3 no 1 = Oct/Nov 1941].

Harbinger. West Bromwich. June 1941. Ed H. G. Moore.

Bring out your dead. 1 only. Aug 1941. Ed H. M. Stephens.

Blitz blotz. (R.K.'s wartime A.J. chronicle.) Bromley. Nos 1–2? 1941–Aug 1942. Ed R. K. Southey.

Blitz budget. Smethwick. Nos 1–5, 1941–April 1948. Ed Mildred Mayer et al.

Erimus. Northallerton. Nos 1–17? 1941–51? Ed Mary Whitelock.

Dozens. Nos 1–20? Sept 1942–April 1947. Ed Amelia Chapman.

Silver lining. Wolverhampton. 1–2, 1942. Ed Marjorie Higgs.

Romany. Yeovil. Nos 1–13? Oct 1943–April 1947. Ed Monica Hutchings.

Gemini. Manchester. Nos 1–2? 1943? Ed R. Lane.

Bric-a-brac. Rochdale. Nos 1–4, May 1944–? Ed C. Steele.

Interim. Smethwick. Nos 1–4, July 1944–? Ed Mildred Mayer.

November (Novan) annual. Bargoed. [1944–7; no 8 = May 1953.] Ed Molly Wright.

The lit. news. Withington. Vols 1–2 no 3. 1944–6.

Manxmaid. Douglas. 1944–7. Ed Joyce Corlett.

Gay cornet. Coleshill. 1 only? Jan/March 1945. Ed A. C. C. Sculthorpe.

Manuscript magazine monthly. Northallerton, Accrington. Nos 1–63?, Jan 1945–Dec 1952. Ed S. and M. Whitelock; L. Lowe.

Caribbean corners. Dartford. March 1945. Ed F. Exeter.

Raconteur. 1 only, May 1945. Ed R. K. Southey. Incorporated in Amateur scribe, no 20, Aug 1946; that jnl then renamed Raconteur from no 21.

Iota. Hayes Middlesex. Nos 1–2. Sept 1945 and April 1947. Ed H. Ludlam.

Creep shadow. Nos 1–2, Nov 1945–? Ed E. J. Carnell.

Free Lance Literary and Book Club news letter. Dec 1945. Ed R. Day.

Bullring. Worthing. 1945–? Also associated are the titles Papuri and Parley.

Fantasia. West Worthing. Nos 1–2, Sept 1946–Jan 1947. Continued as Fantasma, nos 3–22, March/May 1947–autumn/winter 1952.

The scrap book. Brighouse. Nov 1946. Ed Olive Teugels.

The London amateur recorder. Dec 1946 onwards, monthly. Organ of the London Amateur Journalists' Club. Ed R. Coomber, B. Davies.

The voyager. Manchester. Nos 1–3?, spring 1946–spring 1947. Ed Kathleen Banks.

Amateur journalism survey. Manchester. Pts 1–10, 1946–53. Continued as Hobby press guide. Ed A. Horton.

Chats with writers. St Helens. 1946? Ed W. C. Hayes.

Green leaf. 1946? Ed D. P. Faux.

Apple pie. Birmingham. Nos 1–3? April 1947–51? Ed R. C. Mason.

Writers news. Hayes Middlesex. May–Nov 1947; Feb 1948. Ed H. Ludlam.

Reflections. Nos 1–3, June, Sept, 1947; March 1948. Ed W. H. Ordish.

The Battersea amateur magazine. Nos 2–11? Dec 1947–51. Ed J. W. Worth.

Critic. Nos 1–2? Dec 1947–Jan 1948. Ed L. Gaunt.

The free lancer. Vol 1 no 1–? Dec 1947–? Ed R. Day.

Log. Bideford. Dec 1947. Ed W. Stanbury.

Topix. 1947? Ed Zena Blau.

Wright and wrong. Cottingham and Bargoed. 1947 Ed E. and M. Wright.

The writer's gazette. Knowle. 1947?

Motley. Birkenhead. June 1948. Ed A. Brack.

Crier of London. 1 only? July 1948. Ed H. E. Rose.

Metropolis. July 1948. Organ of the London Amateur Press Club. Ed Constance Stamper.

Minerva. Dagenham. July 1948. Ed A. G. Cremlin.

The West Middlesex amateur. Aug 1948. Ed L. Gaunt.

Circles' choice: quarterly competitive magazine of British writers' circles. Nottingham. 1948–?

Taurus. Chelmsford. Nos 1–5, 1948–? Ed Rose Lamont.

Ushas. Worthing. No 1, 1948–9. Ptd by Lawrence Warner. Fiction only. No 2 as Fantasma story collection; Tamarind tales.

Samples. Worthing. 1 only? [c. 1949]. Poetry only.

Fantasma Readers' and Writers' Club journal. West Worthing. No 1. March 1949. Continued as Suppose pig walk [sic], no 2, autumn 1949?; no 3, 1950?

The seagull. Worthing. 1949–? Ptd by Lawrence Warner, pbd by Fantasma.

Yours. Cottingham. 1949? Ed E. M. Wright.

The market place. Nos 1–19? March 1950–July 1952. Ed M. Bannister.

The library chronicle and historical recorder. Manchester and London. Nos 1–13?, June 1950–June 1953? Becomes The historical recorder c. 1952. Ed A. Horton and C. A. Toase.

Type talk. June 1950. Ed F. G. Bissenden.

Tabloid. Sutton Coldfield. Nos 1–2, Sept–Dec 1950. Succeeded by Amateur press miscellany. 1951. Ed R. Hollins.

Plays. Worthing. 1 only? 1950.

Press. Southport. 1950–? Title on cover: Press & free lance writer & photographer.

Collecting juvenile literature. Hollywood USA and Edgware Middlesex. Nos 1–2? 1951. Ed W. Dryden.

(3) ROMANCE, DETECTIVE, THRILLER, WESTERN, AND SCIENCE-FICTION MAGAZINES

(as indicated by their titles)

This selection has been made from the BM General Catalogue of Printed Books. It is based on what is available (war losses apart) at Bloomsbury and does no more than indicate the nature of the field. Most of the pbns derive ostensibly from Britain, though some are reprints of magazines originally issued in America. A small number of American magazines distributed in Britain have been included (e.g. those pbd in Dunellen NJ) to indicate the existence of such imports, most of which are not to be found in the Union List of Serials (which includes Library of Congress). Many more periodicals of the kind noted here are available at the BM Newspaper Library, Colindale.

A number of periodicals listed in section A above (the main creative writing list) are hardly to be distinguished in terms of content from those given here, especially those concerned with romantic writing of a popular kind. Such periodicals were particularly numerous in the first two decades of the century. Some of those pbns also included writing by authors selected for individual treatment in CBEL and, except by the convention of distinction by title, it is difficult to separate the kinds of periodical at a particular point, however obvious the difference between periodicals at the extremes.

A useful anthology of detective fiction is: The hard-boiled dicks: an anthology of detective fiction from the pulp magazines 1932–41, ed R. Goulart, New York 1965. See also Index to the science-fiction magazines 1926–1950, ed D. B. Day, Portland, Oregon 1952 (mainly American). See also cols 123–30, above, for bibliographies in this field.

Romance—illustrated: a complete weekly novelette (companion novelette to My queen). 1897–?

Lloyd's News war novels nos 1, 2. 1916. Continued as Lloyd's News home novels nos 3–226, 1916–23.

Hutchinson's adventure-story magazine. 1922–?

The detective magazine. Vols 1–5, 24 Nov 1922–8 May 1925.

Romance: everywoman's story magazine. Vols 1–7, Feb 1923–July 1927.

Tip top stories of adventure and mystery. Dec 1923–March 1924. Continued as The regent magazine, June 1924–Jan 1925. Incorporated in the Jolly magazine, 1927.

Hutchinson's mystery-story magazine. 1923.

Action stories. April 1923–Jan 1928.

True love stories. Vols 1–7, Aug 1924–Dec 1927.

The frontier. Garden City NY Oct 1924–May 1927. Continued as Frontier stories, June 1927–July 1929. Continued as Empire frontier, Aug 1929–Nov 1930. English edn May 1925–?

West. Vols 1–32 no 8, Aug 1926–early Oct 1939; Nov 1939–Feb 1954. Incorporated in Short stories (1920), section 1, col 1364, above.

Hutchinson's adventure and mystery story magazine. Nos 1–21, Oct 1927–June 1929. Incorporated in Hutchinson's story magazine, section 1, col 1364, above.

Red blooded stories. Dunellen. Vol 1 nos 1–5, Oct 1928–Feb 1929. Continued as Tales of danger and daring, vol 1 no 6, March 1929–?

Flying stories. Dunellen. 1928–?

The master detective. Dunellen. Vols 1–24 no 6, Sept 1929–Aug 1941.

True strange stories. Dunellen. 1929–?

The world's greatest stories. Dunellen. Nos 1–8, Feb–Sept 1929.

Love stories. Vols 1–4 no 102, 2 Nov 1929–3 Oct 1931. Incorporated in Nan's novels, section 1, col 1369, above.

Best detective stories of the year. Nos 1–2, 1929. Ed R. A. Knox and M. Harrington.

The thriller. Nos 1–578, 9 Feb 1929–9 March 1940. Continued as War thriller nos 579–89, 9 March–10 May 1940.

The crime club bulletin. 1930–?

All star. Kingswood. Vol 1 nos 1–8, April–Nov 1931. Continued as All star western story magazine, new series, vol 1 nos 1–7, Dec 1931–June 1932. Continued as All star western and frontier magazine, new series, vols 1–2 no 5, July 1932–June 1933. Continued as All star detective stories, new series, vol 1 nos 1–3, July–Sept 1933. Continued as All detective magazine, new series, vol 1 no 4–, Oct 1933–? From July 1933 on consists of a reissue of All detective magazine, New York vol 2 nos 5 and 6, vol 3 no 7 onwards.

Secrets. Nos 1–6, 24 Sept–29 Oct 1932; nos 1–402, 5 Nov 1932–13 July 1940. Continued as Secrets and flame, nos 403–?, 20 July 1940–?

Detective weekly…incorporating Union Jack. Nos 1–379, 25 Feb 1933–25 May 1940. Same title used for the successor to Daring detective, below.

The Evening Standard book of strange stories. 1934; second book, 1937.

Mystery and detection. 1934–?

Romance. 1934–?

True romances. 1934–?

Air stories. 1935–?

Famous detective cases. Dunellen. March 1935–Dec 1936.

Flame. Nos 1–256, 24 Aug 1935–13 July 1940; then, with Secrets, above, to form Secrets and flame.

War stories. 1935–?

Inside detective. Dunellen. Vol 3 no 3–? Sept 1936–?

Western adventures. 1936–?

Scientifiction: the British fantasy review. Ilford. Vols 1–2 no 7, Jan 1937–March 1938. Ed W. H. Gillings.

Amateur science stories. Leeds. Nos 1–3, Oct 1937–March 1938. Pbd by the Science-fiction Association.

Bulletin of the Leeds Science Fiction League. Leeds. 1937. Merged in Futurian, 1938.

The futurian: the independent British science-fiction magazine. Leeds. Vols 1–3 no 2, 1937–Sept 1940. Continued as Futurian war digest, vols 1–3 no 3?, 1940–5?. Continued as New futurian, spring 1954–? Ed J. M. Rosenblum.

The new at ninepence illustrated thrillers. 1937–?

Wild west weekly. Nos 1–50, 12 March 1938–18 Feb 1939. Incorporated in Thriller, above.

Confession: the paper of human secrets. Nos 1–53, 1938–9. Incorporated in Lucky charm.

Fantasy: a magazine of thrilling science-fiction. Nos 1–3, 1938–9.

Lucky charm. Nos 1–64, 4 March 1939–18 May 1940.

Street & Smith's western story magazine. British edn, Sept 1939–Jan 1953. Continued as Western story magazine, British edn, March 1953–? Consists of selections from the New York edns.

True gangster stories. London (ptd USA). Vol 2 no 4–? Oct 1939–?

Western action. London (ptd USA). Vol 5 no 5–? Oct 1939–?

Double-action detective. Nov 1939–?

The lone eagle, fighting ace. British edn. Vol 19 no 3–? Dec 1939–?

Detective and murder mysteries. 1939–?

Detective yarns. London (ptd USA). 1939–?

Double-action western. [? 1939]–?

Greater western action novels magazine. Vols 1–2 no 3?, 1939–41.

New worlds. Leeds. 1939–? Pbd by the Science-fiction Association.

Science fiction. London (ptd USA). 1939–?

Smashing western. 1939–?

Texas rangers. [?1939]–?
Thrilling detective. British edn. Vol 32 no 2–?Jan 1941–?
  New series, 1945–54.
International detective cases. 1941–?
Love: romantic magazine. 1941–?
New western magazine. 1941–?
Strange detective mysteries. 1941–?
Western yarns. 1942–5.
G-men detective. British edn. [?1944]–1952.
Daring detective. 1944–7? New series, 1950–4. Incorporated in Detective weekly.
Romances album 1944 [–7]. 1943–6. Annual.
Startling detective. 1944–9. New series, 1950–4. Incorporated in Detective weekly.
Thrilling ranch stories. British edn. Vol 7 no 4–? 1944–?
Thrilling western. British edn. ?1944–?
Detective album 1946 [etc]. 1945–?
Front page detective. Dunellen. Vol 9 no 7–? Nov 1945–?
Affinity love stories. 1946–?
Confession! 1946–?

Fantasy: the magazine of science fiction. 1946–?
New worlds: a fiction magazine of the future. 1946–?
Western album. 1946 and 1947.
Weird story magazine. 1947–?
Wit: modern mirth and mystery. 1947–?
Love and romance: the new magazine of romantic fiction. May/June 1948. One only.
Romances (formerly Yankee romance shorts). New series, nos 1–19, June–Sept 1948; not pbd 1949; 4 March–5 Aug 1950.
Crime book magazine: the journal of the Crime Book Society. New series, July/Aug 1949 [–?May/June 1950].
The London mystery magazine. 1949–?
Thrilling wonder stories. Nos 1–3, 1949–50.
Exciting western. Vols 1–5 no 5, Oct 1950–June 1956.
The Evening Standard detective book. 1950; 2nd series 1951.
Master detective. 1950–?
Science-fantasy. 1950–?
True detective. 1950–?

(4) UNIVERSITY AND COLLEGE MAGAZINES

The very large number of school pbns which began to appear in the twentieth century makes their inclusion in this volume impracticable. They require (like parish magazines, omitted from this and earlier edns of CBEL) special study. School pbns of longer standing are given in vol 3, col 1870–1.

Most universities issue official gazettes, handbooks and similar pbns. These are not listed nor are more than a small selection of 'rag' pbns. The entries are based on BM holdings.

Jnls pbd from individual colleges within a university are listed in the same chronological sequence as the university's own jnls. Jnls devoted wholly to drama are not included here but in the lists of dramatic jnls—see cols 823–80 above.

General or involving more than one University or College

The university magazine and free review (formerly Free review) 1893–7, vols 8–12, 1897–1900, Ed 'Democritus'.
The student: a monthly journal for students and teachers. Bristol. Vols 1–2 no 7, Sept 1903–April 1904. Ed J. W. Knipe and S. H. Hooke.
The university review. Vols 1–7 no 43, May 1905–April 1909. Incorporated Pipe (Oxford).
Oxford and Cambridge illustrated. Nos 1–12 20 Feb–15 June 1907 (Oxford edn); 21 Feb–14 June 1907 (Cambridge edn).
The Oxford and Cambridge review. Nos 1–26, June 1907–Dec 1912. Ed Oswald R. Dawson; then R. J. Walker, 1911–12. At first one issue each term; then quarterly; then monthly. Incorporated in British review, Jan 1913.
The Oxford and Cambridge miscellany. Oxford. June 1920. Ed Herbert Baxter and Alan Porter (Oxford), L. de G. Sieveking and Alec Macdonald (Cambridge).
The basilisk: the inter-varsity magazine. Cambridge. Nos 1–2, March, May 1925.
The beacon: the magazine of adult education classes in Hull, East Yorks, and North Lincs. Hull. March 1932–?
Oxford and Cambridge. Vols 1–10 no 297, 10 June–May 1934.
The student front. Nov 1934–summer 1936. Continued as Student forum, vols 1–3 no 9, Nov 1936–7 June 1939.
Fords and bridges: an Oxford and Cambridge magazine. Oxford. Vols 1–5 no 2, 4 Feb 1936–May 1939.
Student news: organ of the National Union of Students. 1–31, 19 Oct 1939–summer 1947.
Universities quarterly. 1946 onwards.
Student chronicle. 10 March 1948–? National Union of Students.
The university: a journal of enquiry. Oxford 9 Nov 1950–?

Individual Universities and Colleges

Aberdeen
  Alma mater. 28 Nov 1883 onwards.
  Aberdeen university studies. 1900–?
  The premier. Nos 1–4, 1908.

The suffragette. 1 only, 1908.
  The Aberdeen university review. Nov 1913–?
Belfast
  The northman. Vols 1–3 no 6, 1927–summer 1932; continued as New northman.
Birmingham
  Mermaid. Vols 1–20 no 6, Oct 1904–Jan 1924. Continued as The university gazette, vols 1–6 no 7, Dec 1924–July 1930. Continued as (The) mermaid new series 1, Oct 1930 onwards.
  The coxcomb. Nos 1–2, Dec 1905, Feb 1906.
  The open book. Nos 1–3, Dec 1922–March 1923.
  The woolsack. Nos 1–3, March 1927–May 1929.
  Guild news. Nos. 1–616, 5 Feb 1936–20 June 1962. Continued as Redbrick, 617, 28 Sept 1962 onwards.
Bristol
  The magnet. Vol 1 no 1–?, 1898–? Continued as Bristol University College gazette, vol 1, nos 1–6, Feb 1908–Oct 1909. Continued as University of Bristol gazette, vol 2 no 7, July 1910. Continued as Bristol nonesuch, vols 1–3 no 8, 1911–13. Continued as The nonesuch, vol 3 no 9 1914 onwards. Literary supplement, vol 1 no 1, Dec 1925. Special supplement, Jan 1919.
  The student. Vols 1–2 no 7, Sept 1903–April 1904.
  University of Bristol studies. 1–6, 1932–7.
Cambridge
  The eagle (St John's). Lent term 1858 onwards.
  The Cambridge university reporter. No 1, 19 Oct 1870 onwards.
  The Cambridge review. No 1, 15 Oct 1879 onwards. Weekly in term to 30 May 1969, then twice termly.
  The university pulpit. Nos 2–661, 1879–1905. No 1 as pt of The Cambridge review, to which the whole is a supplement.
  The Girton review. No 1 1882 onwards. Jubilee no, 1920.
  Chanticlere (Jesus) (formerly The chanticleer, 1885–92), no 22, 1892 onwards.
  The Christ's College magazine. No 1, Easter term 1886 onwards.
  The Granta. No 1, 18 Jan 1889 onwards. In term time. Suspended from June 1914 to May 1919 and from June 1939 to March 1946. Various parodies thereof, e.g. Follower magazine, March 1950.

Emmanuel College magazine. May 1889 onwards.

The silver crescent (Trinity Hall). Nos 1–136, Nov 1890–March 1953.

The Caian (Gonville and Caius). 1891 onwards.

The Pem (Pembroke). Nos 1–13, May 1893–March 1896. New series, no 1 March 1897 onwards.

The Pheon (Sidney Sussex). Vols 1–5, 1896–1902. New series, vols 1–21 no 2, Lent 1922–June 1950.

The Sex (Peterhouse). 1897 onwards.

The Cambridge gazette. No 1, 15 Oct 1898–6 Oct 1900.

The Benedict (Corpus Christi). Nos 1–59, 1898–1928.

Lady Clare magazine. vol 1 nos 1–2 1898–9. New series, vols 1–22 no 3, 1902–28. Continued as Lady Clare, vol 23 onwards, Michaelmas term 1928.

The alma mater: a journal of literature and art. Nos 1–5, 1899–1900.

Basileona (King's College). No 1, June 1900–March 1903. Continued as Basileon, 1907–14, 1919–25, 1928–9, 1931, 1934–5, 1937, 1940 onwards.

The Jack-daw (St John's). Nos 1–5, 1900.

The griffin (Downing). 1903 onwards.

The Cam. Vols 1–2 no 12, ?Feb–6 June 1906.

The May bee and other [bees]. 1906.

Queens' courier. Vol 1 nos 1–2, 1906. Continued as The dial, vol 1 no 3, 1907–?

The Cam (St John's). Nos 1–6, 1907.

*Agenda. Vols 1–3 no 2, 1907–9.

Fitzwilliam Hall magazine. 1908 onwards. Title varies.

The sell (Selwyn). Vols 1–18 no 46, Nov 1909–Lent 1946. Continued as The cell, vol 19 no 47, Easter 1947. Continued as Seldom, vol 19 no 48, Lent 1948 onwards.

Magdalene College magazine. 1909 onwards.

The eaglet (St John's) 1 only. June 1910.

The Cambridge magazine. Vols 1–12, 20 Jan 1912–spring 1923. Weekly to 12 June 1920 then irregular. Reprints vols 1–5, 1916–17. The Cambridge calendar: a weekly supplement, nos 1–34, 31 Jan–4 June 1921 (but The Cambridge magazine not then being issued).

The tripod. Nos 1–7, April 1912–Feb 1913.

Elysium (Selwyn). Nos 1–7, Aug 1913–March 1915.

Mandragora. May week, 1913, 1914.

St Catharine's College magazine. No 1–? (unnumbered), 1913–Lent 1934. Continued as The spokesman, Lent 1935–May 1937; purported to incorporate Woodlark in 1937. Continued as The woodlark, Michaelmas 1937; 1938; purported to incorporate Spokesman in 1937.

The Trinity magazine. Vols 1–10 no 2 (unnumbered), 25 Feb 1914–Easter 1939. Continued as Magpie, May 1940–Easter 1941. Continued as Trinity magazine, June 1947 onwards.

*Buzz. Feb 1916–May 1918.

The blunderbuss: being the book of the 5th Officer Cadet Battalion, Trinity College. Nos 1–7, 1916–1918. Includes A. E. Housman.

Youth: an expression of progressive, university thought (St John's). Nos 1–15, May 1920–autumn/winter 1924. Supplement Dec 1923: German youth. Incorporated The cocoon. Ed W. A. Harris, nos 1–2; nos 3–6 not named; J. W. F. Hill, no 7; S. D. Coldwell, no 8; P. P. Ross Nichols (with Rolf Gardiner), no 9; Rolf Gardiner, nos 10–13? Distinguish from Youth, the authors' magazine, col 1365.

The cocoon. Nos 1–4, 1920–1. Incorporated in Youth.

*Adrift and astern. May–Aug 1921.

The query magazine. 1 only? March 1922.

The raven (Girton). 1 only, 1 May 1922. Issued on behalf of Russian famine relief.

Cambridge review 'new blue' series. Nos 1–10, 1922–5.

The Cambridge mercury: an illustrated review. Vols 1–3 no 16, 27 April 1923–1 Dec 1924.

Cambridge gownsman. Vols 1–30 no 8, 20 Oct 1923–

June 1933. Continued as Gownsman, vol 30 no 1–vol 49 no 8, 14 Oct 1933–10 June 1939. Incorporated in Cambridge University journal.

The K.P. magazine. Nos 1–8, 21 April–2 June 1923.

Cambridge University times. Nos 1–2, 16 Feb, 1 March 1924.

Fanfreluche: a miscellany. Nos 1–2, 1924–5.

St Catharine's Society magazine. 1927 onwards.

Experiment. Nos 1–7, Nov 1928–spring 1931, irregular. Ed William Empson, Nov 1928–May 1929; J. Bronowski and Hugh Sykes Davies, Nov 1929–spring 1931.

The venture. Nos 1–6, Nov 1928–June 1930. In term time. Ed Anthony Blunt (June 1929), H. Romilly Fedden and Michael Redgrave.

The portico. Downing. 1929.

Songs for sixpence: a series of single new poems by young Cambridge poets. Nos 1–6, 1929.

Varsity. Vols 1–3 no 24, 17 Jan–28 Nov 1931. Continued as Varsity weekly, vol 3 no 25–vol 20 no 129, 16 Jan 1932–11 June 1938.

The outpost. Nos 1–3, Feb–June 1932.

The May card (Pembroke). June 1932.

Contemporaries and makers (St John's). Spring 1933. Continued as Contemporaries, summer 1933–summer 1935. Ed John Kaestlin.

Cambridge left (Queen's). Vols 1–2 no 1, summer 1933–autumn 1934. 3 issues a year.

The tea phytologist (Botany School, Downing). Vol 10 no 1 23 Jan 1934 (first to be pbd); 27 Nov 1939; Dec 1950; March 1954.

Apes and angels. Nos 1–4, 25 Jan–8 March 1935.

The Cam: a Cambridge town magazine. Nos 1–6, Jan–June 1937.

Cambridge varsity post. Vol 1 nos 1–8, 15 Oct–2 Dec 1938. Continued as Varsity vol 2 no 1–vol 3 no 8, 21 Jan–10 June 1939. Incorporated in Cambridge University journal (but distinguish from next entry).

Cambridge University journal. Vols 1–4 no 5, 21 Oct 1939–7 Dec 1940. Temporarily absorbed Varsity.

Babel: a multi-lingual critical review. Nos 1–3, Jan, March, summer 1940. Ed Peter G. Lucas, John Fleming, G. Gordon Mosely.

Cambridge front. 1 only, summer 1940. Ed George Scurfield in association with Nicholas Moore and Mark Holloway.

The bridge (Emmanuel). 1 only? April 1946. Ed Geoffrey Moore.

Varsity 19 April 1947 onwards. Supplement nos 1–10, 6 Nov 1948–May 1950. Continued as Cambridge today nos 11–18, Oct 1950–Lent term 1952.

The Cambridge journal. Vols 1–7 no 12, Oct 1947–spring 1954.

Sheaf. 1 only, 1947? Ed B. Rajan and W. Mankowitz.

Cambridge writing. Nos 1–8, 1948–52.

Panorama. Nos 1–4, May 1949–winter 1950–1. Amalgamated with Harlequin (Oxford) as Panorama and harlequin, nos 5–6, spring 1951, summer 1952.

Brobdigranta. 1949.

Imprint (Caius). Nos 1–5, Oct 1949–summer 1950.

Follower magazine: a Granta parody. March 1950. Ed Anthony Shaffer.

Dublin

Hermathena: a series of papers on literature, science and philosophy by members of Trinity College. 1873 onwards. Index of contributors 1873–1943 by J. G. Smyly 1944. Annual.

St Stephen's (University College). Nos 1–7, June 1901–June 1902? Ed Hugh Kennedy in 1902; then Constantine Curran?

Dana: a magazine of independent thought. Nos 1–12, May 1904–April 1905. Ed 'John Eglinton' [W. K. Magee] and Frederick Ryan.

Hermes: an illustrated university literary quarterly. Nos 1–4, Feb 1907–Feb 1908.

Studies: an Irish quarterly review (of letters, philosophy and science), 1912 onwards.
Icarus (Trinity College). 1950–? 3 times a year.

Dundee

The college. 1921–?

Durham

The Durham university journal. 1876–? [No 32 = new series no 1].
Ushaw magazine (St Catherine's). March 1891–?
St Cuthbert's magazine. 1948–?

Edinburgh

The student: a casual. Nos 1–12, 8 Nov 1887–27 June 1888. Continued as The student: Edinburgh university magazine, new series nos 1–17; new series no 1–; 10 May 1889–?
The gambolier: a light journal. Vols 1–17, Oct 1908–25.
Jabberwock: Edinburgh university review, 1945.

Exeter

The ram. Summer 1922–summer 1940.
The south westerner. 193?–?
Exe. 1947–50? Quarterly. Ed John Hocknell.

Glasgow

The Glasgow University magazine. 1889 onwards.
The literary student. Nos 1–2?, 1909–10.
*The Glaswegian.

Hull

The torch. 1928–?

Lampeter

St David's College and School gazette (magazine). Vols 1–10; new series, 1–13 no 4 (13 misnumbered as 12), 1885–1933. Continued as The wasp, vol 14 no 1, 1935. Continued as The lamp, vol 15 nos 1–2, 1936–7. Continued as The Lampeter magazine, vol 16 nos 1–4, 1938–41. Continued as Gateway, new series 1, March 1947 onwards. Not published 1927, 1929, 1934.

Leeds

Leeds University poetry, 1949 [etc]. Leeds etc. 1949–?
The gryphon. April 1950–summer 1952.

Leicester

The Luciad. Dec 1924–?

Liverpool

The sphinx. 1893–?
Otia merseiana. Vols 1–4, 1899–1904.
Pantosfinx. 1932; 1934–5; 1937–9/40; 1947–.
The university digest. 1945–? Occasional.

London

St John's magazine (London School of Divinity). 1–?, July 1885–1907. Continued as The Johnian, new series 1–31, April 1907–April 1921. Continued as St John's magazine, new series, vols 1–3 no 9, 1921–summer 1930. Continued as The Johnian, vol 4, Michaelmas 1930–? Absorbed The lion.
The Working Men's College journal. Vols 1–22, Feb 1890–1932. Continued as The journal, vol 23, 1933 onwards.
Ἑρμῆς (Westfield). 1892–?
The University College gazette. Vols 1–3 no 53, Nov 1895–June 1904. Continued as UCL Union magazine, vols 1–9 no 3, Christmas 1904–June 1919. Continued as University College magazine, 1–16, 1919–39. Merged in Phineas.
The King's College magazine (ladies' dept). Nos 1–52, Michaelmas term 1896–1914.
The King's College review (Lucifer). 1899–?
Bedford College magazine. 1–100, 18??–July 1921. Continued as Bedford College union magazine, 1–5?, Dec 1920–40? Continued as Bedford writing, ?5–8, ?1944–5. Continued as The unicorn, Dec 1946–?
The Londinian (City of London College). 1913–?
The undergraduate: university of London magazine. 1 only, 1913.
The lion: special war issue. 1–4, 1916–21. Merged in St John's magazine.
Vincula (University of London Union). Vols 1–2 no 7, Nov 1922–18 Feb 1925. Continued as New Troy, vol 2 no 8–vol 11 no 2; new series 1, 4 March 1926–?

London University magazine. 1922–24.
London University Journalism Society gazette. Nos 1–36, 1927–35.
The walrus (King's college hospital). 1929–?
The chain (Connaught Hall). Vols 1–3 no 3, 1935–summer 1938.
Phineas (University College). 1–7, 1937–9. Continued as New phineas 1, 1939 onwards. Absorbed University College gazette (as early as 1920s?).
Erinna (Royal Holloway). 1941–?
Pi (University College) 21 Feb 1946 onwards.
Cub (Queen Mary's). [no 11 = 1948].
The beaver (L.S.E.) 5 May 1949–? Not pbd 1951–2.
Ark (Royal College of Art). 1950 onwards.
Leopardess (Queen Mary's). [date?].

Loughborough Technical College

The limit. Vols 1–24 no 3, Dec 1918–July 1942; new series 1, March 1947–?

Manchester

The circle. 1921–? Organ of the Literary Circle of the University.
Solem. 1925–? Three a year.
Humanitas. Vols 1–2 no 3/4, 1946–autumn 1948. Ed O. G. Dodge, J. I. McCabe, Roy Shaw, Walter Stein.

Newcastle

The northerner (Armstrong College). ? Dec 1914–?
King's courier (King's College). Vols 1–11 no 13, 18 Nov 1948–12 March 1959. Continued as Courier, vol 12 no 1, 7 May 1959 onwards.

Nottingham

The gong. Vols 1–18; new series, vols 1–37 no 3; new series vol 1, 1884–?
The gongster. 1 only?, 8 May 1939.

Oxford

The Oxford review: a weekly record of university life. Formerly The Oxford undergraduate's journal [and subsequent variations in title], 1866–84. Nos 1–4342, Jan 1885–19 June 1914.
The Oxford magazine. 1883–1971. Weekly.
The pelican record (Corpus Christi). 1891 onwards.
Isis. 27 April 1892–13 June 1914, 30 April 1919–36; 29 Nov 1945 onwards. Weekly in term. Incorporated in Varsity, 13 June 1914–30 April 1919.
Fritillary: a magazine of Oxford women's colleges. 1–37, 1893–June 1931.
The Wadham College gazette. 1897–1903?
Bump. 1898–1909? Annual.
The X: an unknown quantity. Vols 1–3 no 51, 10 Nov 1898–6 Dec 1900.
Young Oxford: a monthly magazine devoted to the Ruskin Hall movement. 1899–1903?
The barge. 1900, 1904, 1905.
The vacuum. May 1900.
The May bee: an 8-day buzzer. Buzz 1, 22 May 1900.
The quad: a terminal magazine. 1–4, 1900–1. Ed C. Scott-Moncrieff.
The pipe. Nos 1–4, Oct 1900–March 1901. Incorporated in University review.
The Broad. Nos 1–3, 1901.
Varsity (Varsity life). Vols 1–15, new ser vols 1–2, 1901–29.
The jester. 6 Feb 1902.
Oxford point of view. Nos 1–10, May 1902–Nov 1904. Twice a term, then quarterly. Ed Compton Mackenzie and Clinton Pirie-Gordon.
The sheaf: a perhaps quarterly magazine. Nos 1–4, May 1902–June 1904.
Παν: the eights' week piper [sic]. 1 only, 21 May 1903.
The Ox. 23 June 1903.
The Stapledon magazine (Exeter college). 1904–?
The parasol. 25 May 1905.
The protean. Nos 1–5, 1905–6.
The brown book (Lady Margaret Hall). 1906–14?
Oxford herald: a literary guide for social reformers. 1 only ?Jan 1907. Ed H. V. Storey.
The pageant post. 1907.

The usher. 1907.

The round robin. May 1908.

The squirt. May 1908.

The brazen nose (Brasenose). 1909.

Oriel record. Vols 1–8 no 7, 1909–?; new series 1–2, April 1946, April 1947.

The chaperon: or, the Oxford cheri-vari. Nos 1–8, 15 Oct–3 Dec 1910.

The Magdalen College record. 1910–?

The Ruskin Collegian. Vols 1–5 no 8, Jan 1911–18.

The budget. 1911.

The clock tower (Keble). 1912–?

Jesus College magazine. Vols 1–7 no 98, 1912–52. Continued as Dragon, vol 7 no 99–?, 1952–?

The twit. 1912.

The blue book: conducted by Oxford undergraduates. Continued as The undergraduate review. Nos 1–6, May 1912–June 1913.

The Oxford fortnightly. Vols 1–3 no 7, 24 Jan 1913–5 May 1914. Continued as The new Oxford review, with which is incorporated the Oxford fortnightly, vol 4 nos 1–5, Jan–May 1914. Fortnightly then monthly. Merged in The English review.

Oxford poetry. 1910–13 (1 vol) ed G. D. H. Cole, G. P. Dennis, Sherard Vines; 1914, G. D. H. Cole, Sherard Vines; 1915, G. D. H. Cole, T. W. Earp; 1916, W. R. Childe, T. W. Earp, A. L. Huxley; 1917, W. R. Childe, T. W. Earp, Dorothy L. Sayers; 1918, T. W. Earp, Dorothy L. Sayers, E. F. A. Geach; 1919, T. W. Earp, Dorothy L. Sayers, 'S.S.'; 1920, Vera M. Brittain, C. H. B. Kitchin, Alan Porter; 1921, Alan Porter, Richard Hughes, Robert Graves; 1922, not named; 1923, F. W. Bateson, D. C. Thompson; 1924, Harold Acton, Peter Quennell; 1925, Patrick Monkhouse, Charles Plumb; 1926, Charles Plumb, W. H. Auden; 1927, W. H. Auden, C. Day Lewis; 1928, Clere Parsons, 'B.B.'; 1929, Louis MacNeice, Stephen Spender; 1930, Stephen Spender, Bernard Spencer; 1931, Bernard Spencer, Richard Goodman; 1933–5 not issued; 1936 (titled New Oxford poetry), A. W. Sandford; 1937 (titled New Oxford Poetry) Nevil Coghill, A. W. Sandford; 1938–41 suspended; 1942–43, Ian Davie; 1944–46 suspended; 1947 Martin Starkie, Roy MacNab; 1948, Arthur Boyars, Barry Harmer; 1949, Kingsley Amis, James Michie; 1950, J. B. Donne, Donald Watt; 1951, J. B. Donne; 1952, Derwent May, James Price; 1953, Donald Hall, Geoffrey Hill; 1954, Jonathan Price, Anthony Thwaite; 1955, Adrian Mitchell, Richard Selig; 1956, Bernard Donaghue, Gabriel Pearson; 1957, Peter Ferguson, Dennis Keene. Annual (with omissions as noted).

The new weekly. 1–2, 21 March–22 Aug 1914.

The palatine review. Nos 1–4, Jan–Oct 1916.

The rattler: a literary magazine (Somerville Hospital). 1 only?, 1917?

The Oxford outlook. Vols 5–12 no 48, May 1919–May 1932. Irregular. Ed N. A. Beechman, Beverley Nichols et al. Superseded by New Oxford outlook, May 1933–?

The Oxford review (Oxford fortnightly review): a political, social and literary journal for undergraduates. Vols 1–4 no 38, Oct 1919–Dec 1922.

The cardinal's hat (Christ church). 1919–?

The topaz of Ethiopia. 1919–?

The Cherwell. 9 Nov 1920–?

Bumps. 1920–1.

The Lincoln imp. 1920–?

The periodical. 1–35? ?1920–63/64?

A Queen's College miscellany. 1920–?

The beacon. Vols 1–3 no 22, Oct 1921–June 1924.

The free Oxford: an independent socialist review of politics and literature. Nos 1–6, 1921–2.

St Edmund's Hall magazine. Nos 1–5, 1920–4.

The Oxford University review. Vols 1–5 no 3, 1926–8?

The University news. 1928–?

Farrago. Nos 1–6, Feb 1930–June 1931. Quarterly. Ed Peter Burra.

New Oxford outlook. May 1933–Nov 1935. Twice a year. Ed Richard Crossman and Gilbert Highet, with Derek Kahn, May 1933–Feb 1934; Jack Winocour, May 1934–Jan 1935, and with Paul Engle, Nov 1935. Supersedes The Oxford outlook.

*This unrest. [1930s].

First words (St Edmund's Hall). 1935–49/50. Irregular. Suspended during war.

Light and dark. Vols 1–2 no 3, Jan 1937–Feb 1938. Incorporated in Kingdom come.

Bolero. Nos 1–3, summer 1938–spring 1939. Ed John Waller. Incorporated in Kingdom come, Nov 1939.

Kingdom come. Vols 1–3 no 12, Nov 1939–autumn 1943. Irregular. Ed John Waller, Nov 1939–?; Kenneth Harris, Nov 1939–summer 1940; Miles Vaughan Williams, summer 1940–?; Mildred Clinkard, summer 1940; Alan Rook, Stefan K. Schimanski, Henry Treece, Nov/Dec 1941–? Incorporates Light and dark and Bolero.

Mandrake: a miscellany of prose and verse. 1945–55.

Crux. 1946–? Vol 8 no 3 not pbd.

Mid-day. 1946–?

New epoch (Ruskin College). 1946–?

The gate (also Das Tor). Vols 1–3 no 1, 1947–8. In English and German.

The Oxford viewpoint. 1947–50. Ed G. E. Scott.

Siesta. 1 only, spring 1947.

Harlequin. Nos 1–2, 1949–50. Ed Oliver Carson and Anthony Blond. Then amalgamated with Panorama, Cambridge.

The fantasy poets (Oxford University Poetry Society). Nos 1–35, 1950–7.

Trio. 1 only 1950? Ed E. Greenwood, K. Lund, G. MacBeth.

Reading

The Reading University College review. Vols 1–9 no 25, 1908–16.

Rattler. 1950–?

St Andrew's

College echoes. Nov–March 1889; 20 Oct 1905–?

Sheffield

Floreamus! 1–13, Oct 1897–June 1928.

Arrows. 1935–? 3 a year.

Sheffield University magazine. 1937–?

Darts. 1946–?

Oakholme (Crewe Hall). New series 1–?, 1949–?

Southampton

Clarion. 1946–?

Goblio. 1949–?

Wales

The dragon (Aberystwyth). ?1877–?

Magazine (Cardiff). 1–3, 1885–7; new series 1–13, 1888–1901. Continued as Cap and gown, 1903–?

The magazine of the University College of North Wales (Bangor). Vols 1–22 no 3, 1891–1913. Continued as The mascot, vol 23 nos 1–3, 1913–14. Continued as The magazine etc, vol 24 no 1–vol 36 no 1, 1915–27. Continued as Omnibus vol 36 no 2–?, 1928–?

Aberystwyth studies. 1–14, 1912–36.

Y wawr (Aberystwyth). Vols 1–5 no 1, 1913–17.

The undergrad (Swansea). 1–3, 1920–5. Continued as Dawn, 1925–?

Eastern wail (Cardiff). No 1, 1926. Continued as Wail, vol 1 no 2–?, 1926–?

The alpha (Bangor). 1927–?

Undertaker redivivus (University of Wales, Wrexham). 1933–?

College clarion (Aberystwyth). 193?–?

Welsh anvil (also Yr einion) (University of Wales, Llandebie). 1949–?

(5) NEWSPAPERS AND MAGAZINES NOT PRIMARILY DEVOTED TO LITERATURE

Between 1900 and 1950 there have been one or more journals associated with every city and large town in Britain, and with a very large number of smaller places and areas. These range from parish magazines to journals of international standing. The list given here is a selection of those which might be of use to the literary scholar, either because of the interest in literature itself (if only intermittently) or because of the part they have played in forming and expressing opinion, nationally and locally.

Although some minority interests are represented, and some periodicals are included because of their social implications, this list represents only a small number of the periodicals published in this period which are not primarily devoted to literature. It is based chiefly (though not entirely) on the British Museum catalogues of holdings at Colindale and Bloomsbury and it is to these catalogues that reference should be made for a more nearly comprehensive collection of such publications.

The Birmingham daily gazette. (Started as Aris's Birmingham gazette, 16 Nov 1741.) 12 May 1862–30 Jan 1904. Amalgamated with Midland express and continued as Birmingham gazette and express, 1 Feb 1904–16 Nov 1912. Continued as Birmingham gazette, 18 Nov 1912–2 Nov 1956. Incorporated in Birmingham post.

The Newcastle weekly chronicle. (Started as Newcastle chronicle, 24 March 1764.) 18 June 1864–21 Dec 1940. Continued as Weekly chronicle 20 July 1946–5 April 1953.

The morning post. 2 Nov 1772–30 Sept 1937. Incorporated in Daily telegraph.

The times. (Started as Daily universal register, 1 Jan 1785.) No 940, 1 Jan 1788 onwards.
Supplements and reprints (a selection):
The Times and the publishers. 1906.
The history of the book war: fair book prices versus publishers' trust prices. 1907.
Articles on commercial advertising, 1911.
Printing. 1912; 1927; 1940; 1955.
Fourth leaders from the Times. Vols 1–11, 1915–59. Irregular (except annually 1949–55).
Modern essays. Ed J. W. Mackail 1915. From leading articles.
War poems. 1919.
The spirit of man: being essays from the Times. Ed Sir James Marchant 1924.
Vision and strength. Ed Marchant 1925.
Strike nights in Printing House Square, 1926.
Third leaders. 1928.
A book of broadsheets. Ed G. Dawson, 1928; A second book, 1929. Passages from English literature.
Light and leading. 1929. Light leading articles.
Memorandum on a proposal to revise the typography of the Times. 1930. By S. Morison.
Printing in the twentieth century. 1930.
Fifty years: memories and contrasts. 1932.
Printing the Times. 1932.
The Times: past-present-future. 1932.
'The Times': an anthology. 1933.
Follow my leader: commentaries from the Times. 1934.
A newspaper history 1785–1935. 1935.
Dear sir: a selection of letters to the editor. Ed D. Woodruff 1936.
Through the eyes of the Times. 1937. Selected articles.
Old and true. [1940]. Quotations ptd in the Times.
Old and true 1939–41. 1942; 1939–45, 1945.
Book production. 10 Feb 1950.
Printing the Times since 1785. 1953.

The mail. (Started as Evening mail, 1789.) 30 June 1868–11 Oct 1922. Incorporated in the Times weekly edition.

The observer. 4 Dec 1791 onwards.

The Bristol mercury and daily post. (Started as Bristol mercury, 15 Sept 1806.) Jan 1878–19 Dec 1901. Continued as Bristol daily mercury, 21 Dec 1901–30 Nov 1909. Supplement: Bristol weekly mercury, 26 Jan 1878–12 June 1909 (at first bound with parent paper then issued separately).

The Liverpool courier. (Started as Liverpool courier and commercial advertiser, 6 Jan 1808.) 3 Oct 1882–2 Sept 1922. Continued as Daily courier 9 Oct 1922–31 Dec 1929.

The Scotsman (Edinburgh). 25 Jan 1817 onwards.

The Durham county advertiser. [Pre-1818] onwards.

The Sunday times. (Started as New observer 18 Feb 1821.) 20 Oct 1822 onwards.

The Manchester guardian. 5 May 1821–22 Aug 1959. Continued as Guardian, 24 Aug 1959 onwards.

The Dublin evening mail. 3 Feb 1823–1 Feb 1928. Continued as Evening mail, 2 Feb 1928–19 July 1962.

The (evening) standard. 21 May 1827–13 March 1905. Continued as Evening Standard and St James gazette, 14 March 1905–23 Oct 1916. Continued as Evening Standard, 24 Oct 1916 onwards. Issue 35941, 17 Feb 1940, is fictitious; issued by German government. The standard [as morning paper] 29 June 1857–16 March 1916.

The spectator. 5 July 1828 onwards. Selection: Spectator's gallery. Ed P. Fleming and D. Verschoyle 1933.

The Newcastle daily journal. (Started as Newcastle journal, 13 May 1832.) 2 Jan 1861–29 March 1930. Continued as Newcastle journal, 31 March 1930–5 July 1958. Continued as Journal, 7 July 1958 onwards.

Sussex county herald (Eastbourne). (Started as Sussex agricultural express, 4 Feb 1837.) 3 June 1876–30 Sept 1938. Incorporated in Sussex express.

The tablet. 16 May 1840 onwards.

Punch: or the London charivari. 17 July 1841 onwards. Ed F. C. Burnand 1880–1906, O. Seaman 1906–32, E. V. Knox 1932–49; K. Bird 1949–52. Selections include: Later poems from Punch 1887–1908, 1909; Poems from Punch 1909–20, 1922; A Punch anthology, ed G. Boas 1932; Mr Punch's limerick book, 1934; Punch library of humour vols 1–25, 1906, 1907 onwards; The pick of Punch: an annual selection, 1938 onwards; Hutchinson's Punch anthologies, [1944] onwards.

The Jewish chronicle. 12 Nov 1841 onwards.

Evening citizen. (Started as Glasgow citizen in 1842.) 8 Aug 1864–7 Aug 1914. Continued as Glasgow citizen 8 Aug 1914–27 Oct 1923. Continued as Evening citizen 29 Oct 1923 onwards.

The illustrated London news. 14 May 1842 onwards.

Lloyd's weekly newspaper. (Started as Lloyd's illustrated London newspaper, 27 Nov 1842.) 15 Jan 1843–26 May 1918. Continued as Lloyd's Sunday news, 2 June 1918–30 Sept 1923. Continued as Sunday news, 7 Oct 1923–9 Aug 1931. Incorporated in The Sunday graphic.

The Economist. 2 Sept 1843 onwards. Supplement: Records and statistics, 4 Jan 1947–.

The news of the world. 1 Oct 1843 onwards.

Clarion. 1844–1934. Incorporated in Weekly illustrated.

The daily news. 21 Jan 1846–11 May 1912. Continued as Daily news and leader, 13 May 1912–31 May 1930. Amalgamated with Daily chronicle and continued as News chronicle, 2 June 1930–17 Oct 1960.

The weekly times and echo. (Started as Weekly times, 1847.) 4 Oct 1885–29 Dec 1912. Amalgamated with Reynold's newspaper.

Reynold's newspaper. (Started as Reynold's weekly newspaper, 5 May 1850.) 16 Feb 1851–25 Feb 1923. Continued as Reynold's news, 4 March 1923–14 Sept 1924. Continued as Reynold's illustrated news, 21 Sept 1924–23 Feb 1936. Continued as Reynold's news, 1 March 1936–13 Aug 1944. Continued as Reynold's news and Sunday citizen, 20 Aug 1944–16 Sept 1962. Continued as Sunday citizen, 23 Sept 1962–18 June 1967.

The daily express (Dublin). 3 Feb 1851–10 Feb 1917. Continued as Daily express and Irish daily mail 12 Feb 1917–18 June 1921.

The daily chronicle. (Started as Clerkenwell news and general advertiser, 1855.) 25 Nov 1872–31 May 1930. Amalgamated with Daily news and continued as News chronicle, 2 June 1930–17 Oct 1960.

Dundee weekly news. 2 June 1855 onwards. Also appearing in Edinburgh, Fifeshire and Kinross-shire, Forfarshire, Glasgow, Perthshire, Stirling, and English editions for various periods between then and 28 June 1941. *See* BM Newspaper Catalogue for full details.

The Sheffield daily telegraph. 8 June 1855–14 July 1934. Continued as Sheffield telegraph, 16 July 1934–29 Oct 1938. Continued as Sheffield telegraph and daily independent, 31 Oct 1938–13 May 1939. Continued as Telegraph and independent, 15 May 1939–12 June 1942. Continued as Sheffield telegraph and independent, 13 June–14 July 1942. Continued as Sheffield telegraph 15 July 1942 onwards.

The Liverpool daily post. (Started as Daily post, 11 June 1855.) 29 Oct 1879–12 Nov 1904. Continued as Liverpool daily post & Liverpool mercury, 14 Nov 1904–5 June 1916. Continued as Liverpool post & mercury 6 June 1916–24 Jan 1935. Continued as Liverpool daily post onwards.

The daily telegraph. (Started as Daily telegraph and courier 20 June 1855.) 28 Oct 1856–30 Sept 1937. Continued as Daily telegraph and morning post, 1 Oct 1937 onwards.

Swansea journal. 27 Oct 1855 onwards.

Local government chronicle. 18 May 1872 onwards. (Started as Knight's official advertiser for local management in England and Wales, 1 Nov 1855.)

The Saturday review of politics, literature, science and art (Saturday review). Nos 1–4320, 3 Nov 1855–23 July 1938.

Cardiff times and south Wales weekly news. Oct 1857–1 Sept 1928. Incorporated with Weekly mail (Cardiff).

The Birmingham daily post. 4 Dec 1857–20 May 1918. Continued as Birmingham post 21 May 1918 onwards (as Birmingham post and Birmingham gazette 3 Nov 1956–23 Sept 1964).

The Newcastle daily chronicle and northern counties advertiser. (Started as Daily chronicle and nothern counties advertiser 1 May 1858.) 1 Jan 1862–16 March 1923. Continued as North mail and Newcastle daily chronicle, 19 March 1923–18 Sept 1939. Incorporated in Newcastle journal.

The Western morning news (Plymouth). 3 Jan 1860–31 Jan 1921. Continued as Western morning news and mercury 1 Feb 1921 onwards.

The universe. 8 Dec 1860–17 Sept 1909. Continued as Universe and Catholic weekly, 24 Sept 1909–14 June 1912. Continued as Universe, 14 June 1912–1 June 1962. Continued as Universe and Catholic times, 8 June 1962 onwards.

Penrith observer. 31 Dec 1860 onwards.

The Methodist recorder. 4 April 1861 onwards.

The queen. 7 Sept 1861 onwards.

Public opinion. 5 Oct 1861–22 June 1951.

The penny illustrated paper. 12 Oct 1861–24 May 1913 (title as P.I.P. 4 June 1908–3 March 1917). Continued as London society, 10 March–18 Aug 1917. Continued as London life and modern society, 25 Aug 1917–25 May 1918. Continued as London life, 1 June 1918–July 1960.

Glasgow weekly mail. 1 March 1862–15 May 1915. Continued as Weekly mail and record, 22 May 1915–17 Jan 1920. Continued as Weekly record, 24 Jan 1920–9 May 1931.

The Church times. 7 Feb 1863 onwards.

Stratford-upon-Avon herald [1865]–no 311, 15 June 1866 onwards.

The Yorkshire post (Leeds). (Begun as a weekly 2 July 1754). 2 July 1866 onwards.

The Glasgow evening news. (Started as Glasgow evening post, 9 July 1866.) 11 Feb 1888–23 Sept 1905. Continued as Glasgow news, 23 Sept 1905–3 Oct 1915. Continued as Evening news, 4 Oct 1915–17 Jan 1957.

Oban times. [1867]–no 39, 30 March 1867 onwards.

The Oxford times. Sept 1867 onwards.

The Bradford daily telegraph. 16 July 1868–15 Dec 1926. Amalgamated with Yorkshire evening argus and continued as Bradford telegraph and argus, 16 Dec 1926–3 Nov 1956. Continued as Telegraph and argus and Yorkshire observer, and eventually as Telegraph and argus, 5 Nov 1956 onwards.

The Manchester evening news. 10 Oct 1868–26 July 1963. Continued as Manchester evening news and chronicle, 29 July 1963 onwards.

Vanity fair. 7 Nov 1868–June 1929.

The Western mail (Cardiff). 1 May 1869 onwards.

The graphic. 4 Dec 1869–23 April 1932. Continued as National graphic, 28 April–14 July 1932. Incorporated in Sphere.

Weekly mail (Cardiff). 12 Feb 1870–1 Sept 1928. Continued as Weekly mail and Cardiff times, 8 Sept 1928 onwards.

The Birmingham daily mail. [1870]–16 May 1918. Continued as Birmingham mail, 17 May 1918–8 April 1963. Continued as Birmingham evening mail and despatch, 9 April 1963 onwards.

The Belfast evening telegraph. [Sept 1870]–18 April 1918. Continued as Belfast telegraph, 19 April 1918 onwards.

The evening express (Liverpool). [1870]–13 Oct 1958.

The evening telegraph (Dublin). 1 July 1871–19 Dec 1929. Not pbd 5 Nov 1873–Aug 1875 and 29 May 1916–Jan 1919.

The Leeds daily news. [1872]–29 May 1905. Continued as Yorkshire evening news, 1 June 1905–3 Dec 1963. Amalgamated with Yorkshire evening post.

Edinburgh evening news. 27 May 1873 onwards.

The illustrated sporting and dramatic news. 28 Feb 1874–22 Jan 1943. Continued as Sport and country, 5 Feb 1943–16 Oct 1957. Continued as Farm and country, 30 Oct 1957 onwards.

The Manchester evening mail. 4 May 1874–10 July 1915. Not pbd 16 Aug 1902–29 Aug 1914.

The world. 8 July 1874–25 March 1922.

The Yorkshireman (Bradford). Jan 1875–23 Feb 1923.

The Whitehall review. 20 May 1876–25 Oct 1912.

The Bristol evening news. 29 May 1877–30 Jan 1932.

The referee. 19 Aug 1877–9 Sept 1928. Continued as Sunday referee, 16 Sept 1928–4 June 1932. Incorporated in Sunday chronicle.

The Cornishman (Penzance). 18 July 1878 onwards. Various local edns.

The owl. (Birmingham.) ?30 Jan 1879–1 Sept 1911.

Life. 12 July 1879–15 Dec 1906.

The Derby daily telegraph. (Started as Derby daily telegraph and reporter, 28 July 1879.) 14 Oct 1881–29 Jan 1932. Continued as Derby daily express, 30 Jan–12 March 1932. Continued as Derby evening telegraph and Derby daily express, 14 March 1932–14 Aug 1933. Continued as Derby evening telegraph, 15 Aug 1933 onwards.

The St James's gazette. 31 May 1880–13 March 1905. Amalgamated with Evening standard.

The lady's pictorial. 5 March 1881–26 Feb 1921. Incorporated in Eve.

The evening news. 26 July 1881–24 Aug 1901 (as Evening news and post, 13 May 1889–15 Sept 1894). Incorporated Evening mail (1 April 1896–9 Oct 1901) and continued as Evening news and evening mail, 26 Aug 1901–13 March 1905. Continued as Evening news, 14 March 1905–17 Oct 1960. Incorporated Star and continued as Evening news and star, 18 Oct 1960 onwards.

The people. 16 Oct 1881 onwards.

Tit-bits. 22 Oct 1881 onwards. Fifty prize stories from Tit-bits, 1908.

The eastern evening news (Norwich). 13 Feb 1882 onwards.

Scottish nights (Glasgow). 1883–no 906, 25 May 1901 (as Good times, 503–28, 1 Oct 1892–25 March 1893). Not pbd 16 June 1900–25 May 1901.

The national review. Vols 1–134, March 1883–May 1950. Continued as National and English review, vols 135–54 June 1950–June 1960. Absorbed The English review and The popular review.

Cassell's Saturday journal. 6 Oct 1883–19 Feb 1921.

Ally Sloper's half holiday. Nos 1–1788, 3 May 1884–9 Sept 1916. Incorporated in London society. New series, nos 1–23, Guy Fawkes day 1922–14 April 1923. Continued as Half-holiday, nos 24–47, 21 April–29 Sept 1923. Amalgamated with London life.

The umpire (Manchester). 4 May 1884–25 March 1917. Continued as Empire, 1 April–15 July 1917. Continued as Empire news, 22 July 1917–26 Nov 1944. Continued as Sunday empire news, 3 Dec 1944–1 Oct 1950. Continued as Empire news and the umpire (Empire news incorporating Umpire), 8 Oct 1950–15 Nov 1953. Continued as Empire news 22 Feb 1953–6 Nov 1955. Continued as Empire news and Sunday chronicle, 13 Nov 1955–16 Oct 1960. Incorporated in News of the world.

The Derby express. 22 Oct 1884–27 Feb 1909. Continued as Derby daily express, 1 March 1909–29 Jan 1932. Incorporated in Derby daily telegraph.

The lady. 19 Feb 1885 onwards.

The Sunday chronicle (Manchester). 23 Aug 1885–4 June 1939. Continued as Sunday chronicle and Sunday referee, 11 June 1939–26 Dec 1943. Continued as Sunday chronicle, 2 Jan 1944–6 Nov 1955. Incorporated in Empire news. A London edn, Sunday chronicle and Sunday referee, ran from 11 June 1939–9 March 1952.

The Edinburgh evening despatch. 4 Jan 1886–10 Dec 1921. Continued as Evening despatch, 12 Dec 1921–18 Nov 1963. Incorporated in Edinburgh Evening News. Run in conjunction with Scotsman.

The northern daily telegraph (Blackburn). No 1, 26 Oct 1886–13 Oct 1956. Continued as Northern evening telegraph, 15 Oct–11 Dec 1956. Continued as Evening telegraph, 12 Dec 1956–31 Aug 1963. Continued as Lancashire evening telegraph, 2 Sept 1963 onwards.

Evening express (Cardiff). April 1887–27 Oct 1917. Continued as South Wales evening express and evening mail, 29 Oct 1917–30 May 1930. Incorporated with South Wales echo.

The Yorkshire telegraph and star (Sheffield). 18 Jan 1898–7 Oct 1937. (Started as Sheffield evening telegraph, 4 June 1887.) Continued as Telegraph and star, 8 Oct 1937–12 Nov 1938. Continued as Star, 14 Nov 1938 onwards.

The Star. 17 Jan 1888–17 Oct 1960. Incorporated in Evening news.

Answers. (Started as Answers to correspondents 1888–9.) 28 Dec 1889–18 Feb 1956. Annual, 1928–? Summer fun book 1937.

The financial times. 13 Feb 1888 onwards.

South Wales echo (Cardiff). 1 July 1889 onwards.

The daily graphic. 4 Jan 1890–16 Oct 1926. Incorporated in Daily Sketch.

Pearson's weekly. 26 July 1890–10 Sept 1938. Continued as New Pearson's and today, 17 Sept–19 Nov 1938. Continued as New Pearson's weekly, 26 Nov 1938–1 April 1939. Amalgamated with Tit-bits.

Black and white. 6 Feb 1891–13 Jan 1912. Incorporated in Sphere.

The Sunday sun. 10 May 1891–3 Jan 1909. Style changed to Weekly sun, and back again.

The daily argus (Birmingham). 9 Nov 1891–31 Jan 1902. Incorporated in Birmingham evening despatch.

The Bradford daily argus. 16 June 1892–14 July 1923. Continued as Yorkshire evening argus, 16 July 1923–31 Dec 1925. Amalgamated with Bradford daily telegraph, above, as Bradford telegraph and argus.

The Westminster gazette. 31 Jan 1893–31 Jan 1928. Incorporated in Daily news. Saturday Westminster gazette, no 3383 9 Feb 1904–11 Feb 1922. Continued as Weekly Westminster gazette, nos 1–89, 18 Feb 1922–27 Oct 1933. Continued as Weekly Westminster, vols 1–5 no 13, 3 Nov 1923–30 Jan 1926. Ed J. A. Spender 1896–1922.

The sketch. 1 Feb 1893–17 June 1959. Weekly to May 1941 then fortnightly.

The South Wales daily post (Swansea). 13 Feb 1893–12 March 1932. Continued as South Wales evening post, 14 March 1932 onwards.

The Sunday graphic. Vols 1–3 no 26, 30 July 1893–31 March 1901.

To-day. Nos 1–611, 11 Nov 1893–19 July 1905. For later series, see col 1353.

The troubadour (Bournemouth). (Started as 'Jo, Feb 1894.) 23–257, June 1896–Dec 1915.

The councils' journal. (Started as Parish councils' journal, Jan 1895.) Vol 5 pt 1–vol 15 pt 126, April 1899–Sept 1909. Incorporated in Local government review.

Western evening herald (Plymouth). [1895]–no 3, 24 April 1895 onwards.

The daily record (Glasgow). 28 Oct 1895–8 June 1901. Continued as Daily record and daily mail, 10 June 1901–29 March 1902. Continued as Daily record and mail, 31 March 1902–12 March 1954. Continued as Record, 13 March 1954 onwards.

Woman's life. 14 Dec 1895–22 Sept 1934. Incorporated in Woman's own.

Britannia. Vols 1–14 no 5, Jan 1896–Jan 1911.

The daily mail. Nos 1–65, 15 Feb–2 May 1896 (registration copies); no 1, 4 May 1896 onwards.

The Sunday mail. 17 May 1896–27 Dec 1914.

The lady's realm. Vols 1–22, Nov 1896–Oct 1907.

Country life. 8 Jan 1897 onwards.

The Manchester evening chronicle. 10 May 1897–31 March 1914. Continued as Evening chronicle, 1 April 1914–26 July 1963. Incorporated in Manchester Evening News.

The magpie (Belfast). 10 Sept 1898–25 Aug 1900. Continued as Belfast critic, 1 Sept 1900–11 June 1902.

Critique. Nos 1–40, Oct 1898–July 1902.

The Birmingham Sunday mail. [1899]–28 May 1916.

The illustrated mail. 17 June 1899–1 June 1907. Continued as Weekly illustrated.

Tribune. Nos 1–4, 6–27 Jan 1900 (registration issues). Continued as Pilot: ecclesiastical and general politics, literature and learning, nos 1–218, 3 March 1900–21 May 1904.

The sphere. 27 Jan 1900–27 Jan 1964.

The daily express. 24 April 1900 onwards.

The tatler. Vols 1–158 no 2,053, 3 July 1901–30 Oct 1940. Amalgamated with The bystander and continued as The tatler and bystander, vol 159 no 2,054, Nov 1940 onwards.

The Midland express (Birmingham). Nos 1–713, 22 Oct 1901–30 Jan 1904. Amalgamated with Birmingham daily gazette.

The Birmingham evening despatch. 9 Jan 1902–13 May 1907. Continued as Evening despatch, 14 May 1907–8 April 1963.

Dawn (Ilkeston). Nos 1–35, Jan 1902–Feb 1905.

The bystander. Nos 1–1924, 9 Dec 1903–30 Oct 1940. Amalgamated with The tatler as The tatler and bystander. Annual, 1919–?

Tribune: devoted to the cause of progress and nationalism. Vol 1 nos 1–3, 16 Jan–6 Feb 1904. New (registration?) issue, vol 1 no 2, 19 March 1904; new series vol 1 nos 2–7, 19 March–23 April 1904 (issue of 19 March repeated); ?–vol 4 nos 1–2, 15 Jan–12 Feb 1906. Ed S. and L. Henniker.

The Times literary supplement. 17 Jan 1902 onwards. Ed K. R. Thursfield 1902–3, Bruce Richmond 1903–37, D. L. Murray 1938–45, Stanley Morison 1945–7, A. Pryce-Jones 1947–59. Contemporary essays: a selection from the Literary and Educational Supplements to the Times. Ed N. C. Lindsay, Bombay, 1930.

T.P.'s weekly. Vols 1–27 14 Nov 1902–29 April 1916. Ed T. P. O'Connor, then Holbrook Jackson. Superseded by Today. Revived 27 Oct 1923–29 Nov 1929, vols 1–12 (Title as T.P.'s and Cassell's weekly, 31 Oct 1923–17 Sept 1927). Ed T. P. O'Connor. See col 1353.

The Irish peasant (Dublin). [1903]–no 109, 11 Feb 1905–15 Dec 1906. Continued as The peasant, nos 1–99, 9 Feb 1907–26 Dec 1908. Continued as The Irish nation and the peasant, nos 1–100, 2 Jan 1909–3 Dec 1910. Pbd in Navan, 1905–06.

The weekly critical review. 22 Jan 1903–25 March 1904.

The daily mirror. Nos 1–95, 16 July–31 Oct 1903 (registration issues); no 1, 2 Nov 1903 onwards. (Nos 72–150 as Daily illustrated mirror).

Woman's world. 7 Nov 1903.

Germinal. 1903.

The daily paper. Nos 1–32, 4 Jan–9 Feb 1904.

Broad views. Vols 1–8 no 44, Jan 1904–Aug 1907. Ed A. P. Sinnett.

The Bristol evening times. 3 Oct 1904–30 Nov 1909. Continued as Evening times and echo (incorporating Bristol echo, 26 Oct 1901–30 Nov 1909), 1 Dec 1909–29 Jan 1932; incorporated in Evening world.

The leprecaun: cartoon monthly (Dublin). 1–123, May 1905–Feb 1915. (Not pbd Jan 1915.)

The eastern evening mail (Norwich). 2 Oct 1905 onwards. Incorporates Norfolk daily standard.

Tribune. Nos 1–647, 15 Jan 1906–7 Feb 1908; (registration issues nos 648–721, to 4 May 1908).

John Bull. 12 May 1906–Feb 1960. Founder and first editor Horatio Bottomley. Incorporated Illustrated Oct 1958.

*Forward (Glasgow). 13 Oct 1906–?

The daily liar. 1906–39. Intermittent. A 'spoof' journal.

The romance journal: a Jewish illustrated literary weekly. Nos 1–15, 27 Nov 1908–5 March 1909. In Yiddish.

The highway: a monthly journal of education for the people. Pbd by the Workers' Educational Assoc 1908 onwards.

The daily sketch. 23 Dec 1908–1 June 1946. Continued as Daily sketch and daily graphic, 3 June 1946 onwards (as Daily graphic and daily sketch, 1 July 1946–3 Jan 1953). Unnumbered from 9 July 1946.

The native: a magazine for Irish homes (Belfast). Nos 1–40, 10 July 1909–9 April 1910.

The London library. Nos 1–8, 5 Feb–10 Sept 1910.

Mrs Bull. 24 June 1910–22 Feb 1913. Continued as Mary Bull, to March 1915. Continued as Everywoman's weekly, 27 March 1915–5 Feb 1916. Continued as Everywoman's, 12 Feb 1916–20 Jan 1923. Incorporated in Romance. (Registration issues: Mrs Bull, 14 Sept 1910; Mrs Bull's magazine, Oct 1910; Mrs Bull's monthly, Oct 1910; Mrs John Bull, 14 Sept 1910.)

The Times educational supplement. 6 Sept 1910 onwards.

The herald of revolt: an organ of the coming socialist revolution. Vols 1–4 no 5, Dec 1910–May 1914. (Final issue announces pbn of The spur.) Ed Guy Aldred.

The daily herald. Nos 1–66, 25 Jan–26 April 1911. New series 15 April 1912–19 Sept 1914. Continued as Herald 3 Oct 1914–29 March 1919. Continued as Daily herald 31 March 1919–14 Sept 1964.

Everywoman. ? June 1911–July 1914.

Woman's weekly. 4 Nov 1911 onwards.

Fact and fiction. Nos 1–5, Nov 1911–March 1912.

The Sunday mirror. 21 Jan 1912–17 Feb 1918.

Woman. 1 only, 8 Feb 1912.

Everyman: his life, his work, his books. Nos 1–195, 18 Oct 1912–7 July 1916. Ed C. Sarolea; pbd by Dent. Title sold and becomes Everyman: a weekly journal of literature and international politics, nos 196–412, 14 July 1916–4 Sept 1920. Incorporated Foreign opinion (1–16, 24 March–7 July 1915). Registration issues nos 413–657, 11 Sept 1920–2 May 1925 (text changes with each issue). For details of re-emergence as literary journal, see section A col 1361 above.

Woman's own. 3 May 1913–9 June 1917. Amalgamated with Horner's penny stories.

Scottish country life (Glasgow). Vols 1–24 no 10, Feb 1914–Oct 1935. Incorporated with S. M. T. Magazine.

The spur: because the workers need a spur to the communist republic. Vols 1–7 no 8, June 1914–April 1921. Ed Guy Aldred; then Rose Witcop. Vol 7 no 8 also ed Guy Aldred and pbd in Glasgow after his arrest.

The daily financial mail. 21 Sept 1914–22 March 1919.

Britannia abroad. Nos 1–8, Oct 1914–May 1915.

The Sunday pictorial. 14 March 1915 onwards.

Passing show. New series, 1–362, 20 March 1915–25 Feb 1939. Incorporated in Illustrated.

Parade. 1915 onwards.

Blighty. Nos 1–193, 31 May 1916–3 April 1920. New series, 1–?, 21 Oct 1939–?

Satire. Vols 1–2 no 17, Dec 1916–April 1918.

The Sunday express. [1918]–no 2 5 Jan 1919 onwards.

Woman. Nos 1–23, March 1919–Jan 1921.

Nash's weekly. 1–? New series, 1–18, 14 June 1919–4 Sept 1920.

The Irish statesman. Dublin. Vols 1–2, no 52, 28 June 1919–19 June 1920.

The Sunday sun (Newcastle). 31 Aug 1919 onwards.

The family pictorial. Nos 1–52, 20 Sept 1919–11 Sept 1920. Continued as Woman's pictorial, 18 Sept 1920–11 Feb 1956.

Eve. No 1, Sept 1919, advance copy. Nos 1–476, Nov 1919–24 April 1929. Incorporated in Britannia.

The Sunday graphic. Nos 1–347, 8 Feb 1920–10 Oct 1926.

Leisure and sport (Glasgow). Feb 1920–Dec 1921.

Time and tide. 14 May 1920 onwards.

Out of work. Nos 1–60, 19 March 1921–8 June 1923. Continued as New charter, nos 1–4, 22 June–3 Aug 1923.

Sunday illustrated. Nos 1–126, 3 July 1921–25 Nov 1923. Incorporated in Sunday pictorial.

Labour monthly (a magazine of international labour) (a magazine of labour unity). 1921 onwards.

The leader. 1922–50. Incorporated in Picture Post.

G.K.'s weekly (and the weekly review). Registration issue, 8 Nov 1924; vols 1–26 no 678, 21 March 1925–10 March 1938. Continued as The weekly review (incorporating G.K.'s weekly) vol 27 [= new series 1]–?; 17 March 1938–? Founded by G. K. Chesterton and ed by him until his death (14 June 1936) then by H. Belloc. Selection—G.K.'s: a miscellany of the first 500 issues. Ed E. J. Macdonald, 1934.

Sunday worker. 15 March 1925–1 Dec 1929.

The Midlander (Birmingham). Vols 1–5 no 10, Oct 1925–Nov 1930.

The British gazette. Nos 1–8, 5 May–13 May 1926. Government news-sheet published during the general strike. Ed Winston Churchill.

The British worker. Nos 1–10, 5 May–15 May 1926. TUC's response to preceding.

Woman and home. Nov 1926 onwards.

Woman's companion. 5 Nov 1927 onwards.

Woman's journal. Nov 1927 onwards.

The countryman. 1927 onwards. Ed J. W. Robertson Scott. The countryman anthology. Ed John Cripps 1962.

Everybody's. 1927 onwards.

Britannia. Nos 1–10, 20 July–21 Sept 1928 (registration issues). Vols 1–2 no 31, 28 Sept 1928–26 April 1929. Incorporated Eve and continued as Britannia and Eve, vol 1 no 1 May 1929 onwards.

The listener. 16 Jan 1929 onwards. Literary editor 1935–59 J. R. Ackerley.

The evening world (Bristol). (Title varies between this and Bristol evening world). 1 Oct 1929–27 Jan 1962.

The daily worker. 1 Jan 1930–23 April 1966. Incorporated in Morning star, 25 April 1966 onwards. Suppressed 22 Jan 1941–6 Sept 1942 by government order.

Woman and beauty. April 1930 onwards.

Today and tomorrow. Vols 1–4 no 2 Oct 1930–New Year 1934. Ed H. Herd. Incorporates Magazine of today.

Woman's own. 15 Oct 1932 onwards.

The week. Nos 1–400, 29 March 1933–15 Jan 1941. Then suppressed by government order. New series, 1–211, 23 Oct 1942–18 Dec 1946.

The listener's pictorial. Nos 1–2, 1–8 Dec 1933.

The new spur: because the workers need a spur more than ever. Nos 1–5, Dec 1933?–April 1934. Printed in Nimes.

Everywoman's. Vols 1–6 no 12, March 1934–Feb 1940. Continued as Everywoman, new series, vol 1 no 1, March 1940 onwards.

The quarterly journal of the New Fabian research bureau. Nos 1–10, March 1934–June 1936. Continued as N.F.R.B. quarterly, nos 11–20 autumn 1936–winter 1938/39. Continued as Fabian quarterly nos 21–58, spring 1939–summer 1948.

Weekly illustrated. Vols 1–5 no 35, 7 July 1934–25 Feb 1939. Continued as Illustrated. 4 March 1939–Sept 1958. Incorporated in John Bull.

London critic. Nos 1–5, Oct 1934–March 1935.

Woman's mirror. Nos 1–30, 3 Nov 1934–25 May 1935. Incorporated in Woman's world.

The Sunday critic. Nos 1–47, 12 Jan 1936–7 Feb 1937.

The K-H news-letter service (K-H news-letter). Nos 1–269, 1936–41. With supplements. Continued as National newsletter nos 270–1,066, 1941–56. With supplements. Continued as King-Hall news-letter, no 1,067, 1957 onwards. Also News-letter news: a supplement, nos 1–2, March–July 1948. National news letter reports, 1946–? Personal letter. Nos 1–117, 30 May 1946–24 Nov 1950. New series, nos 1–93, 8 Dec 1950–18 June 1954. By Stephen King-Hall.

Tribune. 1 Jan 1937 onwards.

Fact: a monograph a month. Nos 1–27, April 1937–June 1939.

Courier: picturing today—fact, fiction, art, satire. Vols 1–45 no 6, May 1937–Dec 1965. Quarterly, then monthly. Suspended for a time during war.

Woman. 5 June 1937 onwards.

[Living newspaper (e.g. 1: Busmen). Theatrical production, Unity Theatre, London; not a printed publication. See Left review, April 1938].

To-day. Nos 1–16, 28 May–10 Sept 1938. Incorporated in Pearson's weekly.

Woman's national newspaper. Nos 1–6, 22 Sept–3 Nov 1938.

The English digest (London, Dublin). 1938–?

Picture post: Hulton's national weekly. Vols 1–75 no 9, 1 Oct 1938–1 June 1957.

Woman's daily newspaper. 1 only? 7 Nov 1938.

The woman's newspaper. Nos 1–21, 16 June–15 Nov 1939.

The Berlin liar (London). 1 only? Oct 1939. Fiction?

Us: Mass-Observation weekly intelligence service. Nos 1–17 in 16 issues, 3 Feb–17 May 1940. Ed Charles Madge and Tom Harrisson. Records effect of war on British people.

World review, incorporating Review of reviews. Nos 1–103; new ser, 1–50; Aug 1940–April/May 1953. Ed Edward Hulton.

Pilot papers: social essays and documents. No 1, April 1945; then vols 1–2 no 4, Dec 1947. Ed Charles Madge. 9 issues in all.

Far and wide. 1946 onwards.

The front page review. 1947–? Ed M. Rosenbaum.

Humphreys: a monthly review of Parliamentary and local government. 1947 onwards.

Scotland. 1947 onwards.

The British editorial. New series, 1–6, 3/9 June–8/14 July 1948.

Spiv's gazette (Exeter). Nos 1–7? 1948–July 1949.

The arts news and review. 12 Feb 1949–11/25 March 1961. Continued as Arts review, 25 March/8 April onwards.

Britannia. 1950 onwards. Monthly except July, Aug, Sept.

P.D.

INDEX

*To volume 4, containing the names of primary authors together with certain headings.
Numerals refer to columns.*

'A.A.' ('Anthony Armstrong'), 906–8
Abercrombie, Lascelles, 995–7
Ackerley, J. R., 905
Ackland, Rodney, 905–6
Acton, H. M. M., 229
actors and acting, 863–8
adventure stories, 129–30
advertising, 1341–4
Agate, J. E., 997–8
Ainsworth, Ruth G., 810
Aldington, Richard, 511–14
Alexander, Peter, 998
Alexander, Samuel, 1241–2
Allan, Mabel E., 813
Allen, Carleton K., 1135–6
Allen, W. E., 514
Allott, Kenneth, 230
amateur journals, 1379–88
American literature, relations with, 29–32
Angell, Ralph N., 1136–7
anthologies: poetry, 149–58; children's books, 815–16; drama, 827–30
Ardizzone, E. J. I., 806
Arlen, Michael, 514–15
'Armstrong, Anthony', 906–8
Armstrong, M. D., 796
Armstrong, Richard, 808
'Asche, Oscar', 908
Ashford, Daisy, 794
Atkinson, Mary E., 805
Auden, W. H., 207–20
Ault, Norman, 793
autobiographers, 1135–1242 *passim*
Avery, C. H., 790
Awdrey, Wilbert Vere, 811–12
Ayer, A. J., 1243

Bagnold, Enid, 799, 908–9
Bailey, H. C., 515–16
Baillie, John, 1243–4
Baker, Elizabeth, 909
Baker, Margaret, 799
Baker, Margaret J., 814
Balchin, Nigel, 516–17
Balfour, Margaret M., 811
'Barbellion, W. N. P.', 1137–8
Barclay, Vera C., 800
Barfield, A. O., 999
Baring, Maurice, 517–19
Barker, Cicely M., 801
Barker, Ernest, 1138–9
Barker, George, 231
'Barne, Kitty', 796
Baron, J. A., 519
Batchelor, Margaret, 798
Bates, H. E., 520–1
Bates, Ralph, 521–2
Bateson, F. N. W., 999–1000
Bax, Clifford, 910–11
'B.B.' (D. J. Watkins-Pitchford), 808
'Beachcomber' (J. B. Morton), 1088–9
Beachcroft, T. O., 522
Beaman, S. G. H., 807

Beckett, Samuel B., 885–906
Beerbohm, Henry M., 1000–3
Bell, A. C. H., 1003–4
Bell, A. H., 522–3
Bell, Gertrude M. L., 1311
Bell, J. H., 231–2
'Bell, Neil', 523–4
Belloc, Hilaire, 1004–10
Bennett, Arnold, 429–36
Bennett, H. S., 1011
Benson, E. F., 790
Benson, Eleanor T. R., 524
Benson, Stella, 524–5
Bentley, E. C., 525
Bentley, Phyllis E., 525–6
Beresford, J. D., 526–8
'Berkeley, Anthony', 528
Berkeley, R. C., 911–12
Berlin, Isaiah, 1140
Bernal, J. D., 1244
Berners, Lord, 529
Berry, Francis, 232
Besier, Rudolf, 912–13
Best, O. H., 801
best-sellers, 123–4
Betjeman, John, 233–4
'Bettina', 808
Beveridge, W. H., 1140–1
binding, 79
Binyon, Helen, 811
'Bird, Richard', 794
'Birmingham, George A.', 529–30
Blackwood, A. H., 530–1, 791
Blake, George, 531–2
Blunden, Edmund, 234–8
Blyton, Enid M., 805
Bodkin, Maud, 1011
Boland, Bridget, 913
Bone, David W., 532
Bone, Stephen, 808
book collecting, 107–10
book design, 83–90
book jackets, 90
book plates and stamps, 108
book production and distribution, 33–130
booksellers' organizations, 106
bookselling, 103–8
bookshops and auctions, 105–6
Borer, Mary I. C., 809
Bottome, Phyllis, 532–3
Bottomley, Gordon, 238–40
Bottrall, F. J. R., 240–1
Boumphrey, Esther, 802
Boumphrey, G. M., 801
'Bourne, George', 1312
Bowen, Elizabeth D. C., 534–5
'Bowen, Marjorie', 535–8, 799
Bowes-Lyon, Lilian H., 241
Bowra, Cecil M., 1011–12
Bradbrook, Muriel C., 1012–13
Bradley, A. C., 1013
Bragg, William H., 1244–5
Brailsford, H. N., 1141–2
'Bramah, Ernest', 538–9
'Brandane, John', 913–14

Brazil, Angela, 790
Brenan, Gerald, 1014
Brent-Dyer, Elinor, 801
Brereton, F. S., 791
'Bridie, James', 914–17
Brighouse, Harold, 917–19
Brisley, Joyce L., 802–3
Broad, C. D., 1245
broadcasting, 58–60; writing for, 68
Brogan, Denis W., 1142
Brooke, L. L., 789
Brooke, Rupert, 241–3
Brophy, John, 539–40
Brown, I. J. C., 1014–15
Brown, Pamela, 814
Browne, W. B., 919–20
Bruce, Dorita F., 799–800
Bryant, Arthur W. M., 1143
Buchan, John, 540–4
Buckeridge, A. M., 812
Budden, John, 797
Bullett, G. W., 544–5, 801
Bullough, Edward, 1015
Bunting, Basil, 243–4
Burdett, O. H., 1016
Burke, Thomas, 545–6
Burt, Cyril L., 1245–6
Bury, J. B., 1143–5
Butterfield, Herbert, 1145
Butts, Mary F., 546–7
Byron, Robert, 1312–13

Calder-Marshall, Arthur, 546–7
Calderon, G. L., 920
'Cam', 814
Cameron, J. N., 244
Campbell, I. R. D., 244–6
'Cannan, Denis', 920–1
Cannan, Gilbert, 547–8
Cannan, Joanna M., 804
Cardus, Neville, 1313
Carr, E. H., 1145–6
Carritt, E. F., 1246
Carroll, P. V., 921–2
Carswell, Catherine R., 548
Cary, A. J. L., 548–51
Castellain, Lois, 809
'Caudwell, Christopher', 1016–17
Cecil, Lord Edward C. D. G., 1017–18
censorship, 101–2; theatre, 875–6
Chadwick, H. M., 1018
Chambers, Edmund K., 1019
Chambers, R. W., 1019–20
Chapin, Harold, 922–3
Chapman, R. W., 1020–1
Charles, R. H., 796
Charlton, Yvonne M. G., 814
Chaundler, Christine, 798
Chesterman, Hugh, 797
Chesterton, G. K., 1021–8
Childe, V. G., 1147
Childe, Wilfred Rowland Mary, 246
Childers, R. E., 551
children's books, 783–820
China, literary relations with, 33

Christie, Agatha M. C., 552–4
Church, R. T., 246–8, 800
Churchill, Winston L. S., 1147–50
Clapham, J. H., 1151
Clark, Audrey, 814
Clark, George N., 1151–2
Clark, K. M., 1028–9
Clarke, Austin, 248–9
Cleaver, H. R., 800
Clutton-Brock, Arthur, 1029–30
Coats, Alice M., 808
Coke, D. F. T., 793
Cole, G. D. H., 1152–4
Collas, Clare, 813
college magazines, 1391–8
Collier, J. H. N., 554–5
Collingwood, R. G., 1247–8
Collins, N. R., 809
Collis, M. S., 1314
Comfort, Alexander, 249–50
comics, 123–5, 819–20
Compton-Burnett, Ivy, 555–6
Connolly, C. V., 1030–1
Conrad, Joseph, 395–417
Cooper, Alfred Duff, 1154–5
Coppard, A. E., 556–7, 793
Copyright, 100–1
Corbett, J. E., 792
Corkery, Daniel, 923–4
Cornford, F. C., 251
Cornford, F. M., 1031
Cornford, R. J., 251
'Corvo, Baron' (Frederick Rolfe),
    724–5
Coulton, G. G., 1155–6
countryside, writers on, 1311–28
    passim
Coward, Noël P., 924–7
Cradock, Mrs Henry C., 794
Craig, E. H. G., 1031–3
Craigie, Dorothy, 814
Craigie, William A., 1033–4
Creswell, H. B., 791
crime and detective fiction, 125–6
critics and literary scholars, 993–
    1134 passim
Crompton, Richmal, 799
Cronin, A. J., 557
Cross, J. K., 813
Crowley, Aleister, 1034–7

Daiches, David, 1037
'Dane, Clemence', 927–9
D'Arcy, M. C., 1248–9
Darling, Frank F., 1249
Darlington, W. A. C., 929
Darwin, B. R. M., 792, 1314–15
Davies, H. H., 929–30
Davies, Rhys, 558
Davies, W. H., 251–3
'Daviot, Gordon', 930–1
'Dawlish, Peter', 805
Dawson, A. J., 791
Dawson, C. H., 1157–8
Day-Lewis, Cecil, 253–6, 808
Dean, Basil, 931
Deeping, G. W., 559–60
Deevy, Teresa, 931–2
Dehn, Olive, 813
'Delafield, E. M.', 560–1
de la Mare, Walter, 256–62, 791–2
Delderfield, R. F., 932–3
de Morgan, W. F., 561–2
Dennis, N. F., 562
de Sélincourt, Aubrey, 801

de Sélincourt, Ernest, 1038
de Sélincourt, Hugh, 562–3
designers and typographers, 87–8
detective magazines, 1389–92
detective and mystery fiction,
    manuals on, 66
Dickinson, G. L., 1158–9
Dickinson, P. T., 262
Dickinson, W. C., 803
Diver, Katherine H. M. M., 563
Dobrée, Bonamy, 1038–40
Dodd, C. H., 1249–50
Doorly, Victoria E. L., 793
Douglas, G. N., 563–5
Douglas, K. C., 262–3
Douglas-Home, William, 933–4
drama, 821–992
Drinkwater, John, 263–6
Drummond, Violet H., 812
Dukes, Ashley, 934–5
du Maurier, Daphne, 565–6
Duncan, R. F. H., 935–6
Dunne, J. W., 792, 1250–1
Durrell, L. G., 266–71
Dyment, Clifford, 271–2

economics, writers on, 1135–1242
    passim
Eddington, Arthur S., 1251–2
Edwards, Monica le Doux, 812
Elder, Josephine, 807
Eliot, T. S., 157–201, 799
Ellis-Fermor, Una M., 1040–1
Elton, Oliver, 1041
Emett, Mary, 809
Empson, William, 272–4
Englefield, Cicely, 800
Ensor, Robert C. K., 1159–60
essayists, 993–1134 passim
Evans, Caradoc, 566
Evans, E. R. G. R., 794
'Evans, Margiad', 567
Evans-Pritchard, E. E., 1160
Evens, G. B., 797
'Evoe' (E. V. Knox), 295

Fagan, J. B., 936–7
Farjeon, Eleanor, 794–5
Farjeon, Herbert, 937–8
Feiling, Keith G., 1160–1
fiction writing, manuals on, 66
film, 54–6; periodicals, 56–8; writing
    for, 67–8
Firbank, A. A. R., 567–9
Firth, Charles H., 1161–2
'Fidler, Kathleen', 813
Finnemore, John, 789
Fisher, H. A. L., 1162–3
Fitzpatrick, James P., 789
Flecker, J. E., 274–6
Fleming, R. P., 1315–16
Flint, F. S., 276
Forbes, Joan R., 1316–17
Ford, Ford Madox (formerly
    J. L. F. H. M. Hueffer), 569–75
Forest, Antonia, 813
Forester, C. S., 576–7, 805
forgeries, 109–10
Forster, E. M., 437–44
Fowler, Ellen T., 577
Fowler, H. W., 1042
Fox-Smith, Cicely, 811
France, literary relations with, 25–6
Frankau, Gilbert, 577–8
Fraser, G. S., 276–7

Fraser, Ronald, 579
Freeman, John, 277–8
Fry, Christopher, 938–41
Fry, R. E., 1042–4
Fuller, R. B., 278, 812
Fyleman, Rose, 793

Galsworthy, John, 579–86
Gardiner, A. G., 1163
'Garioch, Robert', 278
Garnett, David, 586
Garnett, Eve, 811
Garrod, H. W., 1044–5
Gascoyne, D. E., 279
'Gawsworth, John', 279–81
George, W. L., 586–7
Gerhardie, W. A., 587–8
Germany, literary relations with, 26–7
ghost stories, 129–30
ghosting, 68
Gibbings, R. J., 799, 1317
'Gibbon, Lewis Grassic', 588–9
Gibbons, Stella D., 589, 807
Gibbs, Philip H., 1164–6
Gibson, W. W., 281–2
Gielgud, Val, 941–2
Gill, A. E. R., 1045–8
Ginsbury, Norman, 942–3
Gittings, R. W. V., 282–3
Glyn, Elinor S., 589–90
Godden, Margaret R., 590–1, 809
Gogarty, Oliver St John, 283–4
'Golden Gorse', 807
Golding, Louis, 591–2
Gooch, G. P., 1166–7
Goodyear, R. A. H., 793
Gore, Charles, 1252–3
Gorer, G. E. S., 1167
Goudge, Elizabeth, 806
Gould, Gerald, 284–5
Gow, Ronald, 943–4
Graham, Eleanor, 803
Graham, Harry, 792
Graham, R. B. C., 1318–19
Graham, Stephen, 1319–20
Graham, W. S., 285
Grahame, Kenneth, 593
gramophone, 53–4
Grant, Joan M., 810
Granville-Barker, Harley, 944–6
Graves, Robert, 201–7, 801–2
Green, F. L., 593–4
'Green, Henry', 594–5
Greene, Graham, 503–12, 808
Greenwood, Walter, 947
Greg, Walter W., 1048–50
Grenfell, J. H. F., 285
Grierson, H. J. C., 1050–1
Grigson, G. E. H., 1052–3
Guedalla, Philip, 1167–8
Gunn, N. M., 595
Guthrie, William T., 947–8

Hackett, Walter, 948–9
Hadath, J. E. G., 794
Haldane, J. B. S., 800, 1253–4
Haldane, J. S., 1255
Hale, Kathleen, 804
Hall, Alice, 802
Hall, Marguerite R., 596
Hamilton, A. W. P., 949–50
Hamilton, George R., 286
Hammond, J. L. le B., 1168–9
Hammond, Lucy B., 1169
'Hammond, Ralph', 812

'Hampson, John', 596
Hankey, D. W. A., 1255–6
Hankin, St John E. C., 950–1
Hanley, James, 596–7
Hann, Dorothy, 800
Hardy, G. H., 1256
Harnett, Cynthia M., 800–1
Harris, J. T. F., 1054–5
Harris, Mary K., 808–9
Harrison, G. B., 1055–7
Harrison, Jane E., 1057–8
Hartley, L. P., 597–8
Harwood, H. M., 951–2
Haskell, A. L. D., 808
Hassall, C. V., 952–3
Hatch, R. W., 804
Hatt, Ella M., 810
'Hay, Ian', 598–600
Hayek, F. A. von, 1169–70
Hayward, J. D., 1058
Heard, Gerald, 1256–7
Heath-Stubbs, J. F. A., 287
Hendry, J. F., 287–8
Henson, H. H., 1257–8
Herald, Kathleen W., 816
Herbert, A. P., 288–90
Heward, Constance, 797
Hewlett, M. H., 600–2
Hichens, R. S., 602–3
Hickey, Theodosia F. W., 811
Hicks, G. D., 1258–9
Higgins, F. R., 290
Hillary, R. H., 1170
Hilton, James, 604
historians, 1135–1242 passim
Hobhouse, L. T., 1170–1
Hobson, J. A., 1171–3
Hodge, Merton, 953
Hodges, C. W., 810
Hodgson, Ralph, 291
Hogben, L. T., 1259–60
Hogg, G. L., 807
Holdsworth, William S., 1173–4
Holme, Constance, 604
Holtby, Winifred, 605
Houghton, W. S., 954
Hoult, Norah, 605–6
House, A. H., 1059
Household, G. E. W., 606, 806
'Hudson, Stephen', 606–7
Hudson, W. H., 789
Hueffer, J. L. F. H. M. (afterwards
    Ford Madox Ford), 569–75
Hughes, G. F., 814
Hughes, R. A. W., 607, 806
Hull, Katharine, 814
Hulme, T. E., 1059–61
humour writing, 66
humourists, 993–1134 passim
Hunt, Isobel V., 607–8
Hunter, Norman, 805–6
Hunter, N. C., 955
Hutchinson, A. S. M., 608
Hutchinson, R. C., 609
Hutton, Clarke, 804
Huxley, A. L., 609–17, 801
Huxley, J. S., 1260–1

'Iles, Francis', 528
illustration and graphic processes,
    88–90; illustration of children's
    books, 789
India, literary relations with, 34
Inge, W. R., 1261–2
ink, 78

'Innes, Michael', 617–18
Irwin, Margaret E. F., 618–19
Isherwood, C. W. B., 619–20
Italy, literary relations with, 27
Jacobs, W. W., 620–1
Jackson, Holbrook, 1061–3
James, D. G., 1063
James, E. O., 1262–3
James, Grace, 798
James, M. R., 621–2, 789
Jameson, Margaret S., 622–3
Japan, literary relations with, 33–4
Jeans, James H., 1263–4
Jennings, Gertrude E., 956–7
Jerrold, D. F., 1174
Jesse, Fryniwyd M. T., 623–4
Joachim, H. H., 1264
Joad, C. E. M., 1264–6
'John O' London' (R. W. Lynd),
    1083–4
Johns, W. E., 801
Johnson, Pamela H., 624–5
Johnson, R. B., 1063–4
Johnson, W. E., 1266
Johnston, Arnrid, 802
Johnston, D. W., 957–8
Jones, D. M., 292
Jones, Ernest, 1266–7
Jones, Harold, 808
Joseph, H. W. B., 1267
journalism, 1337–44
Joyce, James, 444–72, 796

Kaye-Smith, Sheila, 625–6
Kavanagh, Patrick, 292–3
Keith, Arthur, 1267–8
Kendon, F. S. H., 293
Kennedy, Margaret M., 626–7
Keyes, S. A. K., 294
Keynes, Geoffrey L., 1064–5
Keynes, J. M., 1175–7
Kiddell-Monroe, Joan, 810
King-Hall, Magdalen, 808
King-Hall, William S. R., 958–9
'Kingsmill, Hugh', 1065–6
Kirkup, J. F., 294–5
Kitchin, C. H. B., 627
Knight, G. W., 1066–7
Knights, L. C., 1067–8
Knoblock, Edward, 959–60
Knowles, David, 1177–8
Knox, E. G. V., 295
Knox, R. A., 1268–71
Koestler, Arthur, 628–9
'Kyle, Elizabeth', 811

Lancaster, Osbert, 1068–9
Langley, Noel, 812
Laski, H. J., 1178–81
Laver, James, 1069–70
law and publishing, the, 100–2
Lawrence, D. H., 481–503
Lawrence, T. E., 1181–5
Leavis, F. R., 1070–2
Leavis, Queenie D., 1073
Ledwidge, Francis, 295–6
Lee, Laurie, 296
Lehmann, R. J. F., 297
Lehmann, Rosamond N., 630
Leighton, Clare V. H., 806
Leishman, J. B., 1073
Leslie, John R. S., 1186–7
lettering and type design, 83–7
Leverson, Ada, 630
Levy, B. W., 960–1

Lewis, Alun, 298
Lewis, C. S., 804, 1073–8
Lewis, D. B. Wyndham, 1078–9
Lewis, Hilda, 803
Lewis, Lorna, 811
Lewis, P. Wyndham, 631–4
Lewitt, Jan, 810
librarianship, 109–18
libraries: circulating, 114; national,
    111–12; public, 112–14; school,
    114; special, 114; university and
    college, 112
Liddell Hart, Basil H., 1187–8
Lindsay, David, 634–5
Lindsay, Jack, 635–6, 806
Linklater, E. R. R., 636–8, 806
literary agents, 69–70
literary conferences and festivals, 71–2
literary histories, 3–14
literary memoirs, 15–26
literary prizes, 123–4
literary scholars, 993–1134 passim
literature, society and communication,
    35–60
little magazines, 1335–6, 1345–8
Livingstone, Richard W., 1189
'Llewellyn, Richard', 638
Locke, W. J., 638–9
Lockhart, Robert H. B., 1189
Lofting, Hugh, 798–9
'Lonsdale, Frederick', 961–2
Lovell, Dorothy A., 809
Lowndes, Joan S., 813
Lowndes, Marie A. B., 639–40
Lowry, C. M., 640–2
Lubbock, Percy, 1079
Lucas, E. V., 1079–82
Lucas, F. L., 1082–3
Lynch, Patricia N., 804–5
Lynd, R. W., 1083–4

Macaulay, Emilie R., 642–3
MacCaig, Norman, 298–9
MacCarthy, Desmond, 1084–5
McCracken, Esther H., 962–3
'MacDiarmid, Hugh', 299–302
MacDonagh, Donagh, 963
MacDonagh, Thomas, 302–3
Macdonell, A. G., 643
MacDougall, Roger, 963–4
McDougall, William, 1271–2
McEvoy, C. A., 964
McFee, W. M. P., 643–4
McGregor, R. J., 807
Machen, A. L. J., 644–8
Mackail, D. G., 648–9
Mackail, J. W., 1085–6
McKay, Herbert, 795
McKenna, Stephen, 649–50
Mackenzie, Edward M. Compton,
    650–2, 796–7
Mackenzie, Ronald, 964
McKerrow, R. B., 1086–8
MacLiammóir, Mícheál, 964–5
'Macnamara, Brinsley', 965
MacNeice, F. L., 303–5
McTaggart, J. McT. E., 1272–3
Madge, C. H., 305–6
magazines, 1329–1408
Malinowski, B. K., 1190–1
Malleson, W. M., 966–7
Mannheim, Karl, 1191
Manning, Frederic, 652
Manning, Olivia, 653
Manning-Sanders, Ruth, 802

'Mansfield, Katherine', 653–9
manuscript preparation, 66
Marett, R. R., 1192
'Marlow, Louis', 659
Marriott, John A. R., 1192–3
Marshall, Archibald, 789–90
Martindale, C. C., 1273–5
Marx, Enid, 807
Mascall, E. L., 1275
Masefield, J. E., 306–13, 793
Mason, A. E. W., 660–1
Massingham, H. J., 1321–2
Masterman, C. F. G., 1193–4
Matthews, W. R., 1275–6
Maugham, W. Somerset, 661–8
Maxwell, W. B., 668–9
Mayne, Ethel C., 669
Mew, Charlotte M., 313
Meynell, Viola, 669–70
Middleton, R. B., 670
Millar, Ronald, 967
Mills, Clifford, 800
Milne, A. A., 671–3, 796
Mitchell, J. L. ('Lewis Grassic
    Gibbon'), 588–9
Mitchison, Naomi M. M., 673–4, 803
Mitford, Nancy F., 674
Moffatt, James, 1276–7
Moncrieff, A. Scott, 811
Monkhouse, A. N., 968
Monro, H. E., 313–4
Monsarrat, N. J. T., 674–5
Montague, C. E., 675–6
Moore, G. E., 1277–8
Moore, Nicholas, 314–15
Moore, Sturge, 315–16
Moorehead, A. McCrae, 1194–5
Morgan, C. L., 676–7
Morrison, Nancy A. B., 677–8
Morton, H. C. V., 1322–3
Morton, J. B., 801, 1088–9
Mottram, R. H., 678–9
Mowat, R. B., 1195–6
Muir, Edwin, 316–19
Muir, Willa, 679–80
'Munro, C. K.', 969
Munro, Elsie S., 802
Murray, G. G. A., 1089–92
Murry, J. M., 1092–6
music hall, 853–62
musical comedy, 853–8
Myers, L. H., 680
'Myles na gCopaleen' ('Flann
    O'Brien'), 683

Namier, L. B., 1196–7
National Book League, 99
natural science, writers on, 1241–1310
    passim
nature, writers on, 1311–28 passim
Neale, John E., 1197
Needham, N. J. T. M., 1279
Needham, Violet, 811
Net Book Agreement, 106
Nevinson, H. W., 1197–8
Newby, P. H., 680–1, 814
Newman, Ernest, 1096–7
news agencies, 1341–2
newspapers, 1329–1408
Nichols, J. B., 681–2, 806
Nichols, R. M. B., 319–20
Nicholson, N. C., 320–1
Nicholson, William, 791
Nicoll, J. R. A., 1097–8
Nicolson, Harold G., 1198–9

Norris, W. E., 682–3
Norton, Mary, 808
novel, 381–784
Novello, Ivor, 970
Noyes, Alfred, 321–3, 793

'O'Brien, Flann', 683
O'Brien, Kate, 683–4
obscenity, 101–2
O'Casey, Sean, 879–85
'O'Connor, Frank', 684–5
O'Faoláin, Seán, 685–6
O'Flaherty, Liam, 686–7
Ogden, C. K., 1098–9
'Oke, Richard', 687
O'Kelly, Seumas, 687–8
Olivier, Edith M., 688
Oman, Carola M. A., 688–9, 803
Oman, Charles W. C., 1200–1
Oman, J. W., 1279–80
Onions, G. O., 689–90
Orage, A. R., 1099–1100
Oriental literatures, relations with,
    32–4
'Orwell, George', 690–6
'O'Sullivan, Seumas', 323–4
Owen, W. E. S., 324–6
Oxenham, Elsie, 798
'Oxenham, John', 696–7

Pain, B. E. O., 697–9
Palmer, H. E., 326–7
pantomime, 853–62
paper, 76–7
paperback editions, 98–9
Pardoe, Margot M., 807
Parker, L. N., 971–2
Parsons, C. T. J. H., 327
Partridge, E. H., 1100–1
Peach, L. du G., 973–5
Peake, M. L., 699, 812
Pearson, E. H. G., 1201–2
periodicals: advertising, 1342–4;
    authorship, 71–4; book collecting,
    110; book plates and book stamps,
    108; bookselling, 106–8; broad-
    casting, 60; children's, 819–20;
    current books, 117–20; drama,
    823–8, 848–52, 854, 858–62, 864,
    866–8, 873–4, 877–8, 879–80;
    film, 56–8; gramophone, 54;
    journalism, 1340; librarian-
    ship, 116–18; newspaper and
    magazine, 1343–4; printing trade,
    81–4; publishing, 100; relating to
    printing paper, 77–8; song-
    writing, 74
Pertwee, Roland, 975
Petrie, Charles A., 1202–3
Pevsner, Nikolaus B. L., 1101–2
Phillpotts, Eden, 699–704
philosophers, 1241–1310 passim
Pinto, V. de Sola, 1102
Pitter, Ruth, 327–8
plays, collections of, 827–30
Plomer, W. C. F., 704–5
poetry, 131–380
Polanyi, Michael, 1280
politics and the author, 71–2
politics, writers on, 1135–1242 passim
Pollard, A. F., 1203
Pollard, A. W., 1103–4
Popper, Karl R., 1204
pornography, 101–2
Porter, Alan, 328

postcards, picture, 126
Postgate, R. W., 1204–5
Potter, S. M., 1104–5
Powell, A. D., 705–6
Power, Eileen E., 1205–6
Power, Rhoda D. le P., 802
Powicke, Frederick M., 1206–7
Powys, J. C., 706–10
Powys, Llewelyn, 1105–7
Powys, T. F., 710–12
'Preedy, George R.', 535–8
Price, H. H., 1280
Prichard, H. A., 1281
Priestley, J. B., 712–17
Prince, F. T., 328–9
printers and printing houses, 80–1
printing, 73–84
printing and allied trade organizations,
    79–80
Pritchett, V. S., 717
private presses, 96–8
private publishing, 96
psychology, writers on, 1241–1310
    passim
publishers and editors, authors'
    relations with, 69–72
publishers, individual, 93–5
publishers' memoirs, 93–5
publishing, 89–102
publishing and the law, 100–2
publishing, private, 96
publishing, specialized methods in,
    99–100
Pugh, E. W., 717–18
Pullein-Thompson, Christine, 814–15
pulp novels, 127
Pye, Virginia, 807
Pym, Barbara M. C., 718

Quennell, P. C., 1107–8

Radcliffe-Brown, A. R., 1207
radio drama, 861–4
Rae, Gwynedd, 800
Raine, Kathleen J., 329
Ransome, A. M., 718–19, 797
Rashdall, Hastings, 1208
Rattigan, T. M., 976–7
Raven, C. E., 1281–2
Read, H. E., 1108–13
reading, 119–30
Redlich, Monica, 810
Reed, Henry, 330
Reed, Langford, 807
'Reeves, James', 330–1, 810
Reid, Forrest, 719–20
reprints, 98
reviewing, 103–4
Reynolds, S. S., 720
Rhys, Grace, 789
Rhys, Jean, 720
Rhys, 'Mimpsy', 811
'Richards, Frank', 792
Richards, I. A., 1113–16
Richardson, Dorothy M., 721–2
Ridge, Antonia Florence, 813
Ridge, W. P., 722–3
Ridler, Anne B., 331–2
Rieu, E. V., 799
Rivers, W. H. R., 1282
Robbins, L. C., 1208–9
Roberts, C. E. M., 723–4
'Roberts, Michael', 332–3
Robinson, Joan V., 1209
Robinson, W. H., 791

Rochester, G. E., 809
Rodgers, W. R., 333
Rolfe, Frederick ('Baron Corvo'), 724–5
romance and confession (fiction), 127–8
romance magazines, 1389–92
romantic novel writing, 66
Rosenberg, Isaac, 333–4
Ross, Alan, 334–5
'Ross, Diana', 810–11
'Ross, Martin', 739–40
Ross, William D., 1282–3
Rouse, W. H. D., 789
Rowntree, B. S., 1209–10
Rowse, A. L., 1210–11
Royde-Smith, Naomi G., 725–6
Rubinstein, H. F., 977–8
Ruddock, Margot, 335
Runciman, James C. S., 1211–12
Russell, Bertrand, 1283–91
Ryle, Gilbert, 1291

Sackville-West, E. C., 726
Sackville-West, Victoria M., 335–7
Sadleir, Michael, 1116–18
'Saki' (H. H. Munro), 727–8
Sansom, William, 728–9
'Sapper' (H. C. McNeile), 729–30
Sassoon, S. L., 337–40
Saville, L. M., 807
Savory, Gerald, 978
Sayers, Dorothy L., 730–1
Scales, Catherine, 811
Scandinavia, literary relations with, 27
Schiller, F. C. S., 1291–2
science fiction, 128–9; magazines, 1389–92
Scott, Geoffrey, 1118
Scott, J. D., 732
Scott, W. D., 1118–19
Scovell, Edith J., 340
Seaman, Owen, 340
Serraillier, Ian, 812
'Severn, David', 814
Seymour, Beatrice K., 732
Shairp, A. M., 978
Shakespeare Memorial Theatre, 847
Shanks, E. B., 341
'Shearing, Joseph', 535–8
Sheridan, C. C., 1323
Sherriff, R. C., 979
Sherrington, Charles S., 1293
Shiels, George, 979–80
short story and article writing, 67
Shove, Fredegond, 342
'Shute, Nevil', 734
'Shy, Timothy' (D. B. Wyndham Lewis), 1078–9
Sidgwick, Ethel, 734–5
Sinclair, May, 735–6
Singer, C. J., 1293–4
Sitwell, Edith L., 342–6
Sitwell, Francis O. S., 346–9
Sitwell, Sacheverell, 349–51
Skipper, Mervyn, 802
Slavonic and East European literatures, relations with, 28
Smith, D. N., 1119
Smith, Dodie, 980–1
Smith, E. A. W., 791
Smith, Francis S., 981
Smith, Sidney Goodsir, 351–2
Smith, L. L. P., 1119–20

Smith, N. K., 1294
Smythe, F. S., 1324
Snaith, J. C., 736–7
Snaith, Stanley, 352
Snow, C. P., 737–9
society, writers on, 1135–1242 passim
Somerville, Edith Œnone, 739–40
song and ballad, popular, 127
Sorley, C. H., 353
Soutar, William, 353–4
Sowerby, Githa K., 982
Spearman, C. E., 1295
Spencer, C. B., 354
Spender, J. A., 1212
Spender, S. H., 355–7
sport, writers on, 1311–28 passim
Sprigg, C. St J. ('Christopher Caudwell'), 1016–17
Spring, R. H., 741, 799
Spurgeon, Caroline F. E., 1121
Squire, John C., 357–9
Stamp, Laurence D., 1213
Stapledon, W. O., 741–2
Stark, Freya M., 1324–5
Starkie, Enid M., 1121
Starkie, W. F., 1325
Stead, Christina E., 742
Stebbing, Hilary, 814
Stebbing, Lizzie S., 1295
Stephens, James, 360–2
Stern, Gladys B., 742–3
Stewart, J. I. M. ('Michael Innes'), 617–18
Stokes, A. D., 1121–2
'Storm, Lesley', 982
Storrs, Ronald H. A., 1214
Strachey, Evelyn John St L., 1214–15
Strachey, Giles L., 1215–18
Strachey, John St L., 1218
Strachey, R. P. F., 807
'Strang, Herbert', 794
Streatfeild, Noel, 803–4
Street, A. G., 1326
Streeter, B. H., 1296
Strode, W. C., 982–3
Strong, L. A. G., 744–6, 803
Sturt, George ('George Bourne'), 1312
Suddaby, W. D., 806
Sullivan, J. W. N., 1296–7
Summers, A. J-M. A. M., 1122–4
Sutherland, J. R., 1124
Sutro, Alfred, 983–4
Swingler, R. C., 362
Swinnerton, F. A., 746–7
Sylvaine, Vernon, 984–5
Symons, A. J. A., 1219
Symons, J. G., 362–3

Tarn, William W., 791
Tawney, R. H., 1219–20
Taylor, A. E., 1297–8
Taylor, A. J. P., 1220–1
Taylor, Rachel A., 363
technical and educational writing, 67
television drama, 861–4
Temperley, Harold W. V., 1221–2
Temple, Joan, 985
Temple, William, 1298–9
Tennant, F. R., 1299–1300
Tessimond, A. S. J., 364
theatre: amateur, 875–80; censorship, 875–6; economics of, 871–4; in

Ireland, 853–4; outside London, 845–52; producers, 867–8; stage and theatre design, 869–72
theologians, 1241–1310 passim
Thirkell, Angela M., 747–8
Thomas, Dylan, 220–30
Thomas, P. E., 364–7, 793
Thomas, R. S., 368
Thompson, D'Arcy W., 1300
Thompson, Flora, 1326–7
Thomson, G. D., 1124–5
Thornton, A. G., 748
thrillers, 129–30; magazines, 1389–92
Tiller, Terence, 368
Tillotson, Geoffrey, 1125
Tillyard, E. M. W., 1125–6
Todd, Barbara E., 802
Todd, Ruthven, 368–9
Tolkien, J. R. R., 748–9, 800
Tomlinson, H. M., 749–50
Tourtel, Mary, 792
Tout, T. F., 1222–3
Tovey, Donald F., 1126–7
Townend, Jack, 813
Toynbee, A. J., 1223–6
Toynbee, T. P., 750–1
Tozer, Katharine, 809
travel, writers on, 1311–28 passim
Travers, Ben, 985–6
Travers, Pamela L., 809
Treadgold, Mary, 811
Trease, R. G., 810
Treece, Henry, 369–70
'Tressell, Robert', 751
Trevelyan, G. M., 1226–7
Trevelyan, R. C., 370–1
Trevor-Roper, H. R., 1227–8
'Tring, A. Stephen', 806
Trotter, W. B. L., 1228
Turner, W. J. R., 371–2
type design, 83–7
Tyrwhitt-Wilson, G. H., 529

Underhill, Evelyn, 1301–2
University and college magazines, 1335–6, 1391–8
University presses, 95
University publishing, 95
Upward, E. F., 751–2
Ustinov, P. A., 986
Uttley, Alison, 797–8

Vachell, H. A., 752–4
Van Druten, J. W., 986–8
Vane, V. H. S., 988
Vinogradoff, Pavel P. G., 1228–9
'Vipont, Elfrida', 808
'Visiak, E. H.', 799
Vosper, Frank, 988

Waddell, Helen J., 799, 1127–8
Waddington, C. H., 1302–3
Waley, A. D., 372–4
Walker, K. M., 796
Wallace, Edgar, 754–8
Wallas, Graham, 1229–30
Walmsley, Leo, 800
Walpole, Hugh S., 758–61, 798
war stories, 129–30
Warner, Rex, 761–2, 809
Warner, Sylvia T., 762–3
Watkins, V. P., 374–5
Waugh, Alec, 763–4
Waugh, Evelyn, 764–8
Webb, Beatrice, 1230–4

Webb, Clifford, 802
Webb, Gladys M., 768–9
Webb, Marion St John, 794
Webb, S. J., 1231–4
Webster, Charles K., 1234
Wedgwood, Cicely V., 1234–5
Weekley, Ernest, 1128
Welch, M. D., 769–70
Wellesley, Dorothy V., 375–6
Wells, H. G., 417–28, 790
West, A. P., 770
'West, Rebecca', 770–1
Westerman, P. F., 792
Westermarck, E. A., 1235–6
westerns, 130; magazines, 1389–92
Whistler, A. C. L., 376
White, T. H., 771–2, 809
Whitehead, A. N., 1303–6
'Wickham, Anna', 377
Wicksteed, P. H., 1236–8
Wilenski, R. H., 1128–9

Wilkins, W. V., 799
Wilkinson, L. U. ('Louis Marlow'), 659
Willey, Basil, 1129
Williams, C. W. S., 772–4
Williams, E. G. Harcourt, 793
Williams, G. E., 989
Williams-Ellis, Mary A. N., 801
Williams, Margery W., 793–4
Williams, Ursula M., 812
Williamson, Henry, 774–6
Williamson, H. R., 990
Wilson, A. E. C., 813–14
Wilson, A. F. J., 776–7
Wilson, Dover, 1129–31
Wilson, J. C., 1306–7
'Wilson, Romer', 777
Wingfield, Sheila C., 377
Winter, J. K., 990–1
Wisdom, A. J. T. D., 1307
Wise, T. J., 1131–4

Wittgenstein, L. J. J., 1307–10
Wodehouse, P. G., 778–81, 795–6
Wolfe, Humbert, 377–9, 798
Woodger, J. H., 1310
'Woodruff, Philip', 809
Woodward, Ernest Ll., 1238
Woolf, L. S., 1239–40
Woolf, Virginia, 472–81, 796
Wooll, Edward, 992
Woolley, Sir Charles L., 1240–1
words for songs, 67
Wyld, H. C. K., 1134

'Yates, Dornford', 781
Yates, Peter, 992
Young, A. J., 379–80
Young, Emily H., 781–2, 794
Young, F. B., 782–4
Young, G. M., 1241–2
'Y.Y.' (R. W. Lynd), 1083–4